July 11–15, 2015
Madrid, Spain

Association for Computing Machinery

Advancing Computing as a Science & Profession

GECCO'15

Proceedings of the 2015 Genetic and Evolutionary Computation Conference

Sponsored by:

ACM SIGEVO

Association for
Computing Machinery

Advancing Computing as a Science & Profession

The Association for Computing Machinery
2 Penn Plaza, Suite 701
New York, New York 10121-0701

Notice to Past Authors of ACM-Published Articles
ACM intends to create a complete electronic archive of all articles and/or other material previously published by ACM. If you have written a work that has been previously published by ACM in any journal or conference proceedings prior to 1978, or any SIG Newsletter at any time, and you do NOT want this work to appear in the ACM Digital Library, please inform permissions@acm.org, stating the title of the work, the author(s), and where and when published.

ISBN: 978-1-4503-3472-3 (Digital)

ISBN: 978-1-4503-3883-7 (Print)

Additional copies may be ordered prepaid from:

ACM Order Department
PO Box 30777
New York, NY 10087-0777, USA

Phone: 1-800-342-6626 (USA and Canada)
+1-212-626-0500 (Global)
Fax: +1-212-944-1318
E-mail: acmhelp@acm.org
Hours of Operation: 8:30 am – 4:30 pm ET

Printed in the USA

Welcome from the General Chair

It is my pleasure to welcome you to Madrid for the 2015 Genetic and Evolutionary Computation Conference—GECCO 2015. This is a special year for several reasons. Firstly, sixteen years ago, in 1999, GECCO was born and held for the first time in Orlando, Florida, USA. So happy birthday sweet sixteen, GECCO! We are now in our teenage years, and still growing stronger. Second, thirty years ago the first ICGA, the International Conference on Genetic Algorithms, was held in 1985. Several people who attended that event are still with us today to bear witness to the strength of the (r)evolutionary ideas that were presented there. And last but not least, this year witnesses the highest ever proportion of women in the Organizing Committee, following the spirit of Women@GECCO.

This year's GECCO is comprised of 18 regular tracks, plus, for the second year, the Hot Off the Press (HOP) track, which offers authors of outstanding research recently published in journals and other conferences the opportunity to present their work to the GECCO community. Under the guidance of Editor-in-Chief Sara Silva, the Track Chairs and Program Committee have selected 182 out of the 505 submissions received in all tracks (excluding HOP) for oral presentation as full papers, resulting in an acceptance rate of 36%. Close to 100 short papers will be presented in the regular poster session. This year we also include an additional poster session, where late-breaking abstracts will be presented together with student papers.

A highlight of the conference is the keynote talks given by salient figures in the GECCO fields of interest. This year we wanted to enhance the experience by going back to our origins and have included a third talk from the Natural Sciences field. Our speakers and their subjects are

- Ricard Solé, "Re-designing nature with synthetic biology: from artificial ants and tissues to a new biosphere",
- Kate Smith-Miles, "Visualising the diversity of benchmark instances and generating new test instances to elicit insights into algorithm performance",
- Manuel Martín-Loeches, "Origins and evolution of human language: saltation or gradualism?".

Altogether 32 tutorials cover topics ranging from broad and introductory to specialized and at the frontier of current research. GECCO also hosts fifteen workshops, including several new ones as well as at least one that predates GECCO itself. Further high points include the 12th Annual "Humies" Awards for Human-Competitive Results, which are again generously supported by John Koza, and a record number of nine competitions, ranging from Art to Industry. Finally, Evolutionary Computation in Practice continues to be an important and integral part of GECCO, aiming at getting us in touch with the "real world".

All this would not have been possible without the hard work and dedication of the Organizing Committee over the past year. First of all a special mention is due to Sara Silva, who did a superb job of maintaining the high quality of the conference. Anabela Simões and Gisele Pappa ensured an interesting mixture of Tutorials and Workshops respectively, while Mike Preuss was in charge of finding challenging Competitions. Katia Rodríguez-Vázquez's efforts were devoted to that key component which ensures the conference's future development: the students. Şima Etaner Uyar and Pablo García-Sánchez made us reach the public via publicity and social media, and Juan Luis Jiménez-Laredo compiled all the useful information as Proceedings Chair. Thanks also go to the Track Chairs and the Program Committee for their careful reviewing of the large number of submissions received, and to the workshop chairs and tutorial presenters.

Good advice is worth more than gold and here my sincerest acknowledgement goes to the SIGEVO Business Committee, Pier Luca Lanzi and Jürgen Branke, to SIGEVO Officers Wolfgang Banzhaf, Una-May O'Reilly, Marc Schoenauer and Franz Rothlauf and to former GECCO chairs Dirk Arnold (2014) and Enrique Alba (2013). Thanks are also due to Roxane Rose and Cara Candler from ExecutivEvents, who have been in charge of logistical aspects and registration. Finally, a big hand to Iñaki Hidalgo and his team at the Universidad Complutense, who have ensured we all get the fullest Madrid experience.

Of course, all this effort would not make any sense without you, who are reading this right now, and all GECCO's attendees. So thanks to you too and I wish you all a productive and enjoyable conference!

Anna I Esparcia Alcázar
General Chair
Universitat Politècnica de València, Spain

A Word from the Chair of SIGEVO

Welcome to the Proceedings of GECCO 2015, the seventeenth GECCO, the "recombination" of the 24th International Conference on Genetic Algorithms (ICGA) and the 20th Genetic Programming Conference (GP). Our team this year are: Anna Esparcia-Alcazar serving as General Chair of GECCO 2015 and Sara Silva serving as Editor-in-Chief of the proceedings. Both have worked diligently since many months to prepare a high-quality event in Madrid and a lasting legacy in the form of these proceedings. The results of their and their team's effort can be seen in these pages.

We at SIGEVO are proud that GECCO is the *premiere* venue for presenting work in the area of Genetic and Evolutionary Computation world-wide. The quality of papers submitted to GECCO is very high, and GECCO has a rigorous paper selection process. Over the years we have steadily increased the selection pressure and improved the quality of selected papers. This means that only the best and most important work in Evolutionary Computation and related topics is presented at GECCO. Our conference is consistently ranked at the top of Evolutionary Computation conferences, exceeding in citation counts other venues and even well known journals.

If you were not able to attend GECCO 2015 in person, the Proceedings are in the ACM Digital Library; they are globally accessible and readily found, which benefits both readers and authors.

ACM SIGEVO

Members of ACM SIGEVO, the main sponsor of GECCO, continue to draw major benefits from joining ACM. First is a discount at SIGEVO sponsored conferences, at GECCO, for instance, as much as $100 per registrant. Members have, for a fee, access to the ACM Digital Library, a large and continuously growing resource for research in computing. Another key benefit is the outstanding newsletter SIGEVOlution produced by Pier Luca Lanzi and his excellent editorial board. If you want to access these proceedings and are not a member of SIGEVO, please consider joining (for the low price of $25/year for non-students, and $10/year for student members). This will help us a lot in promoting our community.

Involvement in ACM SIGEVO

SIGEVO became a Special Interest Group (SIG) of the ACM in 2005. ACM is the largest professional organization for Computer Science and considers its SIGs the lifeblood of its organization. We are governed by bylaws available on the SIGEVO web pages. There, you also find a list of members of the 18-member Executive Committee. I have served as chair of SIGEVO since 2011, together with a team of officers: Una-May O'Reilly (Vice-Chair), Marc Schoenauer (Secretary), and Franz Rothlauf (Treasurer). Our term ends this year and a new team (which might partially overlap with the current one) will be elected at our annual meeting in July. For me, however, it is time to say farewell as this will be the last GECCO as Chair. From the vintage point of 2015, I wish future GECCOs and ACM SIGEVO all the best.

Wolfgang Banzhaf
SIGEVO Chair
Department of Computer Science
Memorial University of Newfoundland

Table of Contents

TRACK: Artificial Immune Systems and Artificial Chemistries

TRACK: Artificial Life/Robotics/Evolvable Hardware

TRACK: Biological and Biomedical Applications

TRACK: Continuous Optimization

TRACK: Digital Entertainment Technologies and Arts

TRACK: Evolutionary Combinatorial Optimization and Metaheuristics

TRACK: Estimation of Distribution Algorithms

TRACK: Evolutionary Machine Learning

TRACK: Evolutionary Multiobjective Optimization

TRACK: Genetic Algorithms

TRACK: Generative and Developmental Systems

TRACK: Genetic Programming

TRACK: Integrative Genetic and Evolutionary Computation

TRACK: Parallel Evolutionary Systems

TRACK: Real World Applications

TRACK: Search-Based Software Engineering and Self-* Search

TRACK: Theory

GECCO'15 Organization

General Chair:	Anna I Esparcia-Alcázar *(Universitat Politècnica de València, Spain)*
Editor in Chief:	Sara Silva *(Universidade de Lisboa, Portugal)*
Proceedings Chair	Juan Luis Jiménez-Laredo *(Université du Havre, France)*
Local Chair	José Ignacio (Iñaki) Hidalgo *(Universidad Complutense de Madrid, Spain)*
Tutorials Chair:	Anabela Simões *(Instituto Politécnico de Coimbra, Portugal)*
Workshops Chair:	Gisele Pappa *(Universidade Federal de Minas Gerais, Brazil)*
Publicity Chair	A. Şima Etaner-Uyar *(Istanbul Technical University, Turkey)*
Competitions Chair:	Mike Preuss *(University of Münster, Germany)*
Students Chair:	Katya Rodríguez-Vázquez *(Universidad Nacional Autónoma de México)*
Social Media Chair	Pablo García-Sánchez *(Universidad de Granada, Spain)*
Late-breaking Abstracts Chair	Dirk Sudholt *(University of Sheffield, UK)*
Evolutionary Computation in Practice	Thomas Bartz-Beielstein *(FH Köln - Cologne University of Applied Sciences, Germany)* Jörn Mehnen *(University of Cranfield, UK)*
Local arrangements	Luis Hernández-Yáñez *(Universidad Complutense de Madrid, Spain)*
Business Committee	Jürgen Branke *(University of Warwick, UK)* Pier-Luca Lanzi *(Politecnico di Milano, Italy)*
SIGEVO Officers	Wolfgang Banzhaf, *Chair (Memorial University of Newfoundland, Canada)* Una-May O'Reilly, *Vice-chair (MIT, USA)* Marc Schoenauer, *Secretary (INRIA-Saclay, France)* Franz Rothlauf, *Treasurer (University of Mainz, Germany)*

GECCO 2015 Program Committee

Hussein Abbass *(UNSW@ADFA)*
Ashraf Abdelbar *(Brandon University)*
Ajith Abraham *(Machine Intelligence Research Labs)*
Giovanni Acampora *(Nottingham Trent University)*
Adnan Acan *(Eastern Mediterranean University)*
Andrew Adamatzky *(University of the West of England)*
Michael Affenzeller *(FH Hagenberg)*
Hernan Aguirre *(Shinshu University)*
Chang Wook Ahn *(Sungkyunkwan University)*
Barry Ahrens *(Nova Southeastern University)*
Enrique Alba *(University of Málaga)*
Kieran Alden *(University of York)*
Ricardo Aler *(Universidad Carlos III de Madrid)*
Eva Alfaro-Cid *(Instituto Tecnologico de Informatica)*
Shaukat Ali *(Simula Research Laboratory)*
Richard Allmendinger *(University College London)*
Nadia Alshahwan *(UCL)*
Sergio Jesus Alvarado Garcia *(CINVESTAV-IPN)*
Maria Joao Alves *(Faculty of Economics of University of Coimbra)*
Jhon Edgar Amaya *(UNET)*
Michele Amoretti *(University of Parma)*
Ng Amos *(University of Skövde)*
Sinha Ankur *(Aalto University School of Economics)*
Giuliano Antoniol *(Ecole Polytechnique de Montreal)*
Carlos Antunes *(DEEC-UC)*
Andrea Arcuri *(Simula Research Laboratory)*
Alfredo Arias Montaño *(IPN-ESIME)*
Takaya Arita *(Nagoya University)*
Ignacio Arnaldo *(MIT)*
Dirk V. Arnold *(Dalhousie University)*
Farshad Arvin *(University of Lincoln)*
Joshua E. Auerbach *(École Polytechnique Fédérale de Lausanne)*
Anne Auger *(INRIA)*
Mehmet Emin Aydin *(University of the West of England)*
Nizamettin Aydin *(Yildiz Technical University)*
Dogan Aydın *(Dumlupınar University)*
Raja Muhammad Atif Azad *(University of Limerick)*
Jaume Bacardit *(Newcastle University)*
Mohamed Bader-El-Den *(University of Essex)*
Golnaz Badkobeh *(University of Sheffield)*
Pedro J. Ballester *(Cancer Research Centre of Marseille)*
Wolfgang Banzhaf *(Memorial University of Newfoundland)*
Tiago Baptista *(CISUC, University of Coimbra)*
Helio J.C. Barbosa *(LNCC)*
Marcio Barros *(UNIRIO)*
Thomas Bartz-Beielstein *(Cologne University of Applied Sciences)*
Jeffrey K. Bassett *(Smithsonian Institute National Museum of Natural History)*
Matthieu Basseur *(Université d'Angers)*
Jacob Beal *(BBN Technologies)*
Slim Bechikh *(University of Michigan-Dearborn)*
Nacim Belkhir *(Thales Research&Technology)*
Peter J. Bentley *(University College London)*
James Bergstra *(University of Waterloo)*
Heder Bernardino *(DCC/UFJF)*
Matthias Bernt *(University Leipzig)*
Tom Bersano *(Google)*
Vincent Berthier *(Inria Tao)*
Eva Besada-Portas *(Universidad Compluntense de Madrid)*
Hans-Georg Beyer *(Vorarlberg University of Applied Sciences)*
Leonardo Bezerra *(IRIDIA, CoDE, ULB)*
Bir Bhanu *(University of California at Riverside, USA)*
Marco Biazzini *(INRIA - Bretagne Atlantique)*
Concha Bielza *(Technical University of Madrid)*
Benjamin Biesinger *(Vienna University of Technology)*
Mauro Birattari *(Université Libre de Bruxelles)*
Bernd Bischl *(TU Dortmund)*
Tim Blackwell *(Goldsmiths, University of London)*
Konstantinos Blekas *(University of Ioannina)*
Maria J. Blesa *(Universitat Politècnica de Catalunya - BarcelonaTech)*
Christian Blum *(University of the Basque Country)*
Josh Bongard *(University of Vermont)*
Mohammadreza Bonyadi *(The University of Adelaide)*
Lashon Booker *(The MITRE Corporation)*
Peter A.N. Bosman *(Centre for Mathematics and Computer Science)*
Alexandre Botazzo Delbem *(University of São Paulo)*

lydia boudjeloud *(LITA)*
Amine Boumaza *(Université de Lorraine / LORIA)*
Pascal Bouvry *(University of Luxembourg)*
Ollie Bown *(University of Sydney)*
Anthony Brabazon *(University College Dublin)*
Juergen Branke *(University of Warwick)*
Nicolas Bredeche *(ISIR, Université Pierre et Marie Curie)*
David E. Breen *(Drexel University)*
Karl Bringmann *(ETH Zurich)*
Dimo Brockhoff *(INRIA Lille - Nord Europe)*
Will Neil Browne *(Victoria University of Wellington)*
Alexander Brownlee *(University of Stirling)*
Lam Thu Bui *(Le Quy Don Technical University)*
Thang Bui *(Penn State Harrisburg, USA)*
Zdenek Buk *(Czech Technical University in Prague)*
Larry Bull *(University of the West of England)*
John A. Bullinaria *(University of Birmingham, UK)*
Paolo Burelli *(Aalborg University Copenhagen)*
Keki Mehernosh Burjorjee *(Brandeis University)*
Martin V. Butz *(University of Tübingen)*
Maxim Buzdalov *(ITMO University)*
Arina Buzdalova *(ITMO University)*
Aleksander Byrski *(AGH University of Science and Technology)*
Leticia Cagnina *(Universidad Nacional de San Luis)*
Xinye Cai *(Nanjing University of Aeronautics and Astronautics)*
David Cairns *(University of Stirling)*
Alexandre Campo *(Université Libre de Bruxelles)*
Angelo Cangelosi *(University of Plymouth)*
Nicola Capodieci *(University of Modena and Reggio Emilia)*
Bastos Filho Carmelo J A *(University of Pernambuco, Politechnic School of Pernambuco)*
Andre Carvalho *(USP)*
Mauro Castelli *(NOVA IMS, Universidade Nova de Lisboa)*
Alberto Castellini *(University of Verona, Italy)*
Pedro Castillo *(UGR)*
Nohe Ramon Cazarez-Castro *(Instituto Tecnologico de Tijuana)*
Sara Ceschia *(University of Udine)*
Uday Chakraborty *(University of Missouri)*
Pei-Chann Chang *(Yuan Ze University)*
Zeineb Chelly *(LARODEC, University of Tunis, Higher Institute of Management of Tunis)*
Tianshi Chen *(ICT, CAS)*
Ying-ping Chen *(National Chiao Tung University, TAIWAN)*
Yu-wang Chen *(Manchester Business School)*
Nick Cheney *(Cornell University)*
Marco Chiarandini *(University of Southern Denmark)*
Raymond Chiong *(The University of Newcastle)*
Siang Yew Chong *(University of Nottingham)*
Alexandre Adrien Chotard *(INRIA)*
Anders Christensen *(Instituto de Telecomunicações / ISCTE-IUL)*
Dominique Chu *(University of Kent, UK)*
Chung-Yao Chuang *(The Robotics Institute, Carnegie Mellon University)*
John Clark *(University of York)*
Maurice Clerc *(Independent Consultant)*
Jeff Clune *(University of Wyoming)*
Leandro Coelho *(Pontifical Catholic University of Parana)*
Carlos A. Coello Coello *(CINVESTAV-IPN)*
Mitch K. Colby *(Oregon State University)*
J. Manuel Colmenar *(Rey Juan Carlos University)*
Simon Colton *(Goldsmiths College)*
Brian Connelly *(University of Washington)*
Michael Cook *(Goldsmiths College, University of London)*
Oscar Cordon *(University of Granada)*
Ernesto Costa *(University of Coimbra)*
Lino António Costa *(University of Minho)*
M. Fernanda P. Costa *(University of Minho)*
Bart G.W. Craenen *(University of Edinburgh)*
Antoine CULLY *(ISIR)*
Ronan Cummins *(University of Cambridge)*
Sylvain Cussat-Blanc *(University of Toulouse)*
Steve Dahlskog *(Malmö University)*
Palle Dahlstedt *(University of Gothenburg / Chalmers University of Technology)*
David B. D'Ambrosio *(University of Central Florida)*
Duc-Cuong Dang *(University of Nottingham)*
Christian Darabos *(Dartmouth College)*
Angan Das *(Intel)*
Sanjoy Das *(Kansas State University)*
Dilip Datta *(Tezpur University)*
Rituparna Datta *(IIT Kanpur)*

Cornforth David *(UNSW@ADFA)*
Patrick De Causmaecker *(KU Leuven)*
Kenneth De Jong *(George Mason University)*
Luis Gerardo de la Fraga *(CINVESTAV)*
Luis de la Ossa *(Universidad de Castilla-La Mancha)*
Anthony Deakin *(University of Liverpool)*
Antonio Della Cioppa *(Natural Computation Lab - DIEM, University of Salerno)*
Aydin Demircioglu *(Ruhr-Universität Bochum)*
Bilel DERBEL *(INRIA USTL LIFL)*
Andre Deutz *(Leiden University)*
Clarisse Dhaenens *(LIFL / CNRS / INRIA)*
Gianni Di Caro *(IDSIA)*
Luca Di Gaspero *(University of Udine)*
Massimiliano Di Penta *(RCOST - University of Sannio)*
Victor Diaz Ramirez *(CITEDI-IPN)*
Yongsheng Ding *(Donghua University)*
Huy Dinh *(University of Tokyo)*
Michael J. Dinneen *(University of Auckland)*
Federico Divina *(Pablo de Olavide University)*
Benjamin Doerr *(Ecole Polytechnique)*
Christian Dominguez-Medina *(CIC-IPN)*
Stéphane Doncieux *(ISIR/UPMC)*
Alan Dorin *(Monash University)*
Bernabe Dorronsoro *(University of Cadiz)*
Rene Doursat *(Institut des Systemes Complexes, CNRS)*
León Dozal *(CICESE)*
Jan Drchal *(Department of Computer Science and Engineering, Faculty of Electrical Engineering, Czech Technical University)*
Martin Drozdik *(Shinshu University)*
Madalina Drugan *(AI-lab VUB)*
Jérémie Dubois-Lacoste *(IRIDIA, Université Libre de Bruxelles)*
Enrique Dunn *(University of North Carolina)*
Marc Ebner *(Ernst-Moritz-Universit\"at Greifswald, Germany)*
Aniko Ekart *(Aston University)*
Mohammed El-Abd *(American University of Kuwait)*
Emanuel Emil-Savan *(University of Manchester)*
Michael T. M. Emmerich *(LIACS)*
Andries P. Engelbrecht *(University of Pretoria)*
Anton V. Eremeev *(Omsk Branch of Sobolev Institute of Mathematics)*
Isabel Espirito Santo *(University of Minho)*
Fernando Esponda *(ITAM)*
Richard Everson *(University of Exeter)*
Muddassar Farooq *(Institute of Space Technology)*
Robert Feldt *(Dept of Computer Science and Engineering, Chalmers University of Technology)*
Serge Fenet *(Universite Lyon 1)*
Lavinia Ferariu *(Gheorghe Asachi Technical University of Iasi)*
Jose David Fernandez *(Université de Mons)*
Antonio J. Fernández Leiva *(University of Málaga)*
Juan Luis Fernandez Martinez *(Universidad de Oviedo)*
Paola Festa *(Universitá degli Studi di Napoli)*
Álvaro Fialho *(GE Global Research)*
Stefka Fidanova *(Institute of Information and Communication Technologies)*
Jonathan Edward Fieldsend *(University of Exeter)*
Grazziela Figueredo *(The University of Nottingham)*
Bogdan Filipic *(Jozef Stefan Institute)*
Steffen Finck *(Vorarlberg University of Applied Sciences)*
Andreas Fink *(Helmut-Schmidt-University)*
Asja Fischer *(Ruhr-University Bochum)*
Peter Fleming *(University of Sheffield)*
Gianluigi Folino *(ICAR-CNR)*
Carlos M. Fonseca *(University of Coimbra)*
James A. Foster *(University of Idaho)*
Alberto Franzin *(Université Libre de Bruxelles)*
Gordon Fraser *(University of Sheffield)*
Bernd Freisleben *(Universität Marburg)*
Alex A. Freitas *(University of Kent)*
Tobias Friedrich *(University of Jena)*
Charlie Frowd *(University of Winchester)*
Marcus R. Gallagher *(University of Queensland)*
Jose Enrique Gallardo *(Universidad de Málaga)*
Edgar Galvan *(Trinity College Dublin)*
Leo Galway *(University of Ulster)*
Luca Maria Gambardella *(IDSIA)*
Jose A. Gamez *(Universidad de Castilla-La Mancha)*
Xavier Gandibleux *(Université de Nantes)*
Pablo García Sánchez *(University of Granada)*
Carlos García-Martínez *(Univ. of Córdoba)*
Jose Garcia-Nieto *(University of Malaga)*
Alvaro Garcia-Piquer *(Institute of Space Sciences (IEEC-CSIC))*
Mario Garcia-Valdez *(Instituto Tecnologico de Tijuana)*
Simon Garnier *(New Jersey Institute of Technology)*

Deon Garrett *(Icelandic Institute for Intelligent Machines)*
Jason Gauci *(University of Central Florida)*
Shahin Gelareh *(University of Artois/ LGI2A)*
Arka Ghosh *(Indian Statistical Institute)*
Ioannis Giagkiozis *(The University of Sheffield)*
Raffaele Giancarlo *(University of Palermo)*
Jean-Louis Giavitto *(CNRS - IRCAM, UPMC, Inria)*
Christian Gießen *(DTU Compute, Technical University of Denmark)*
Rosalba Giugno *(University of Catania)*
Orazio Giustolisi *(Technical University of Bari)*
Adrien Goeffon *(LERIA, University of Angers)*
Chi-Keong Goh *(Rolls-Royce Singapore)*
Marco César Goldbarg *(Universidade Federal do Rio Grande do Norte)*
Brian W. Goldman *(Michigan State University)*
Juan A. Gomez-Pulido *(University of Extremadura)*
Ivo Gonçalves *(University of Coimbra)*
Wenyin Gong *(China University of Geosciences)*
Mario Graff *(Universidad Michoacana de San Nicolas de Hidalgo)*
Gary Greenfield *(University of Richmond)*
Julie Greensmith *(University of Nottingham)*
David Greiner *(Universidad de Las Palmas de Gran Canaria)*
Christian Grimme *(Münster University)*
Roderich Gross *(The University of Sheffield)*
Paul Grouchy *(University of Toronto Institute for Aerospace Studies)*
Feng Gu *(Kingston University, London)*
Andreia P. Guerreiro *(University of Coimbra)*
Frederic Guinand *(Université Le Havre)*
Walter J. Gutjahr *(University of Vienna)*
Evert Haasdijk *(VU University Amsterdam)*
Heiko Hamann *(University of Paderborn)*
Lutz Hamel *(University of Rhode Island)*
Ali Hamzeh *(Shiraz University)*
Said Hanafi *(university of Valenciennes)*
Hisashi Handa *(Kindai University)*
Jin-Kao Hao *(University of Angers - LERIA)*
Mark Harman *(UCL)*
Inman Harvey *(University of Sussex)*
Geir Hasle *(SINTEF)*
Erin Hastings *(University of Central Florida)*
Sabine Hauert *(MIT)*
Mark W. Hauschild *(University of Missouri-St. Louis)*
Shinpei Hayashi *(Tokyo Institute of Technology)*
Jun He *(University of Wales, Aberystwyth)*
Verena Heidrich-Meisner *(CAU Kiel)*
Tim Hendtlass *(Swinburne University of Technology)*
James Hereford *(Murray State University)*
Daniel Eduardo Hernandez *(CICESE)*
Carlos Hernández *(CINVESTAV-IPN)*
Arturo Hernández-Aguirre *(Centre for Research in Mathematics)*
Alfredo G. Hernández-Díaz *(Pablo de Olavide University)*
Malcolm Heywood *(Dalhousie University)*
Simon John Hickinbotham *(University of York, UK)*
Philip Hingston *(Edith Cowan University)*
Martin Holena *(Institute of Computer Science)*
John H. Holmes *(University of Pennsylvania)*
Gerard Howard *(CSIRO)*
Michael Hsiao *(Virginia Tech)*
Bin Hu *(Technische Universität Wien)*
Jianjun Hu *(University of South Carolina)*
Ting Hu *(Memorial University)*
Joost Huizinga *(University of Wyoming)*
Phil Husbands *(Sussex University)*
Frank Hutter *(UBC)*
David Andrei Iclănzan *(Sapientia Hungaryan University of Transylvania)*
Christian Igel *(Department of Computer Science, University of Copenhagen)*
Fumiya Iida *(ETH Zurich)*
Takashi Ikegami *(University of Tokyo)*
Manuel Iori *(University of Modena and Reggio Emilia)*
Hisao Ishibuchi *(Osaka Prefecture University)*
Juhos Istvan *(University of Szeged)*
David Jackson *(University of Liverpool)*
Cezary Z. Janikow *(UMSL)*
Thomas Jansen *(Aberystwyth University)*
Yue Jia *(UCL)*
Juan Luis Jimenez Laredo *(University of Le Havre)*
Yaochu Jin *(University of Surrey)*
Daniel Johannsen *(SAP Innovation Center)*
Ulf Johansson *(University of Borås)*
Colin Graeme Johnson *(University of Kent)*
Mark Johnston *(Victoria University of Wellington)*
Ayush Joshi *(University of Birmingham)*
Laetitia Jourdan *(INRIA Lille Nord Europe)*

Bryant Arthur Julstrom *(St. Cloud State University)*
Ata Kaban *(University of Birmingham)*
Michael Kampouridis *(University of Kent)*
Sindhya Karthik *(University of Jyväskylä)*
Ahmed Kattan *(UQU)*
Pascal Kerschke *(University of Münster)*
Gul Muhammad Khan *(NWFP University of Engineering and Technology)*
Vineet Khare *(Amazon Development Centre (India) Pvt ltd)*
Shuhei Kimura *(Tottori Universit)*
Timoleon Kipouros *(University of Cambridge)*
Michael Kirley *(University of Melbourne)*
Evan Kirshenbaum *(HP Labs)*
Joshua D. Knowles *(University of Manchester)*
Patrick Koch *(Cologne University of Applied Sciences, Institute of Computer Science)*
Mario Koeppen *(Kyushu Institute of Technology)*
Joanna Kolodziej *(Cracow University of Technology)*
Maciej Komosinski *(Poznan University of Technology, Institute of Computing Science)*
Wolfgang Konen *(Cologne University of Applied Sciences)*
Lysimachos Kontis *(University of Ioannina)*
Oliver Korb *(Cambridge Crystallographic Data Centre)*
Ilias Kotsireas *(WLU)*
Timo Kötzing *(MPI-INF)*
Miha Kovacic *(University Of Nova Gorica)*
Oliver Kramer *(University of Oldenburg)*
Jozef Kratica *(Mathematical Institute, Serbian Academy of Sciences and Arts)*
Oswin Krause *(University of Copenhagen)*
Gabriel Kronberger *(Unversity of Applied Sciences Upper Austria)*
Jiri Kubalik *(CTU Prague)*
Marvin Künnemann *(Max-Planck-Institut für Informatik)*
Gary Byron Lamont *(AF Institute of Technology)*
Jouni Lampinen *(University of Vaasa)*
Ricardo Landa *(Cinvestav Tamaulipas)*
Dario Landa-Silva *(University of Nottingham)*
William B. Langdon *(University College London)*
Pier Luca Lanzi *(Politecnico di Milano)*
Adriana Lara *(CINVESTAV-IPN)*
Raul Lara-Cabrera *(University of Malaga)*
Antonio LaTorre *(Universidad Politécnica de Madrid)*
Henry Lau *(The University of Hong Kong)*
Hoong-Chuin Lau *(Singapore Management University)*
Claire Le Goues *(Carnegie Mellon University)*
Pierrick Legrand *(Université de Bordeaux)*
Guillermo Leguizamon *(Universidad Nacional de San Luis)*
Joel Lehman *(The University of Texas at Austin)*
Per Kristian Lehre *(University of Nottingham)*
Kenji Leibnitz *(National Institute of Information and Communications Technology)*
Johannes Lengler *(ETH Zurich)*
Cazenille Leo *(Université Paris 7 Diderot - LIED Team)*
Coromoto Leon *(Universidad de La Laguna)*
Dan Lessin *(The University of Texas at Austin)*
Kwong Sak Leung *(The Chinese University of Hong Kong)*
Matthew Lewis *(The Ohio State University)*
Peter R. Lewis *(Aston University)*
Juan Carlos Leyva López *(Universidad de Occidente)*
Ke Li *(Michigan State University)*
Xianneng Li *(Waseda University, Japan)*
Xiaoou Li *(CINVESTAV-IPN)*
Feng Liang *(Nanyang Technological University)*
Yiwen Liang *(Wuhan University)*
Tianjun Liao *(IRIDIA)*
Antonios Liapis *(Center for Computer Games Research, IT University of Copenhagen)*
Peter Lichodzijewski *(Dalhousie University)*
Arnaud Liefooghe *(Université Lille 1)*
Steffen Limmer *(University Erlangen)*
Ping Ling *(Jiangsu Normal University)*
Piotr Lipinski *(Institute of Computer Science, University of Wroclaw, Poland)*
Andrei Lissovoi *(Technical University of Denmark)*
Bo Liu *(Academy of Mathematics and Systems Science, Chinese Academy of Sciences)*
Jialin Liu *(TAO, INRIA)*
Daniel Lobo *(Tufts University)*
Fernando G. Lobo *(University of Algarve)*
Daniele Loiacono *(Politecnico di Milano)*
Michael Lones *(Heriot-Watt University)*
Rui Lopes *(University of Coimbra)*
Antonio López-Jaimes *(Centro de Investigación y de Estudios Avanzados (CINVESTAV))*
Ilya Loshchilov *(INRIA, University Paris-Sud)*

Sushil Louis *(UNR)*
Nuno Lourenço *(Universidade de Coimbra)*
Jose A. Lozano *(University of the Basque Country)*
Manuel Lozano *(University of Granada (SPAIN))*
Emiao Lu *(Manchester Business School)*
Simon Lucas *(University of Essex)*
Simone A. Ludwig *(North Dakota State University)*
Francisco Luna *(University of Extremadura)*
J. M. Luna *(University of Cordoba, Spain)*
Wenjian Luo *(University of Science and Technology of China)*
Thibaut Lust *(UPMC)*
Robert J. Lygoe *(Ford Motor Co Ltd)*
Robert Lyon *(University of Manchester)*
Shingo Mabu *(Yamaguchi University)*
Penousal Machado *(University of Coimbra)*
Ana Maria Madureira *(Institute of Engineering - Polytechnic Institute of Porto)*
Domenico Maisto *(Institute for High Performance Computing and Networking, National Research Council of Italy (ICAR–CNR))*
Stephen Majercik *(Bowdoin College)*
Luigi Malago *(Shinshu University)*
Yazmin Maldonado *(Instituto Tecnologico de Tijuana)*
Pekka Malo *(Aalto University School of Business)*
Andrea Mambrini *(University of Birmingham)*
Bernard Manderick *(VUB)*
Jacek Mandziuk *(Faculty of Mathematics and Information Science, Warsaw University of Technology)*
Maszatul M. Mansor *(University of Sheffield)*
Luca Manzoni *(Università degli Studi di Milano-Bicocca)*
Elena Marchiori *(Radboud University)*
Ana Maria, Rocha *(University of Minho)*
Yannis Marinakis *(Technical University of Crete)*
Dietmar Maringer *(University of Basel)*
Luis Martí *(Pontificia Universidade Católica do Rio de Janeiro)*
Andrew Martin *(Dept Biochem & Mol Biol, UCL)*
Simon Martin *(University of Stirling)*
Hector P. Martinez *(IT-Universitetet i København)*
Ivette C. Martinez *(Universidad Simon Bolivar)*
Franco Mascia *(Université Libre de Bruxelles)*
Antonio D. Masegosa *(University of Deusto)*
Igor V. Maslov *(EvoCo Inc)*
Shouichi Matsui *(SERL, CRIEPI)*
Giancarlo Mauri *(University Milano-Bicocca)*
Michalis Mavrovouniotis *(De Montfort University)*
Helmut A. Mayer *(University of Salzburg)*
James McDermott *(University College Dublin)*
Phil McMinn *(University of Sheffield)*
Nicholas Freitag McPhee *(University of Minnesota, Morris)*
Jorn Mehnen *(Cranfield University)*
David Meignan *(University of Osnabrück)*
Stephan Meisel *(Münster University)*
Nouredine Melab *(Université Lille 1)*
Alexander Melkozerov *(Tomsk State University of Control Systems and Radioelectronics)*
Rui Mendes *(CCTC/UM)*
Alexander Mendiburu *(University of the Basque Country UPV/EHU)*
Stefan Menzel *(Honda Research Institute Europe)*
Tim Menzies *(ComSci / NcState University)*
Jose M. Merigo Lindahl *(University of Barcelona)*
Olaf Mersmann *(TU Dortmund)*
Pablo Mesejo Santiago *(INRIA)*
Bernd, Meyer, *(Monash University)*
Silja Meyer-Nieberg *(Universitaet der Bundeswehr Muenchen)*
Efren Mezura-Montes *(University of Veracruz)*
Thomas Miconi *(The Neurosciences Institute)*
Martin Middendorf *(University of Leipzig)*
Risto Miikkulainen *(The University of Texas at Austin)*
Damjan Miklic *(University of Zagreb)*
Rob Mills *(University of Lisbon)*
Leandro Minku *(The Centre of Excellence for Research in Computational Intelligence and Applications, School of Computer Science, The University of Birmingham)*
Luis Miramontes Hercog *(Self-Organizing Solutions)*
Eduardo Reck Miranda *(University of Plymouth)*
Mustafa MISIR *(University of Freiburg)*
George Mitchell *(CCKF Ltd)*
Hans Jonas Fossum Moen *(Norwegian Defence Research Estblishment)*
Chilukuri K. mohan *(Syracuse University)*
Julian Molina *(University of Malaga)*
Jean-Marc Montanier *(BSC)*
Roberto Montemanni *(Dalle Molle Institute for Artificial Intelligence)*
Marco A. Montes de Oca *(University of Delaware)*

Antonio Mora *(Dpto. Arquitectura y Tecnología de Computadores)*
Melanie Moses *(University of New Mexico)*
Alison Motsinger *(North Carolina State University)*
Santiago Muelas *(DATSI - Facultad de Informática - Universidad Politécnica de Madrid)*
Nysret Musliu *(Vienna University of Technology)*
Amir Nakib *(Laboratoire LISSI)*
Kaname Narukawa *(Honda Research Institute Europe GmbH)*
Boris Naujoks *(Cologne University of Applied Sciences)*
Antonio Nebro *(University of Málaga)*
Roman Neruda *(Institute of Computer Science of ASCR)*
Frank Neumann *(The University of Adelaide)*
Hoai Nguyen Xuan *(Hanoi University, Vietnam)*
Miguel Nicolau *(University College Dublin)*
Julio Cesar Nievola *(PUCPR)*
Geoff Nitschke *(University of Cape Town)*
Marco Nobile *(Università degli Studi di Milano-Bicocca, Dipartimento di Informatica, Sistemistica e Comunicazione)*
Yusuke Nojima *(Osaka Prefecture University)*
Nasimul Noman *(University of Newcastle)*
Mel Ó Cinnéide *(National University of Ireland, Dublin)*
Charles Ofria *(Michigan State University)*
Choong Kun Oh *(U.S. Naval Research Laboratory)*
Tatsuya Okabe *(Honda Research Institute Japan)*
Markus Olhofer *(Honda Research Institute Europe GmbH)*
Pedro Oliveira *(University of Porto)*
Pietro S. Oliveto *(The University of Sheffield)*
Tomasz Oliwa *(The University of Georgia)*
Juan Luis Olmo *(University of Cordoba)*
Mohammed Omran *(Gulf University for Science & Technology)*
Michael O'Neill *(University College Dublin)*
Isao Ono *(Tokyo Institute of Technology)*
Colm O'Riordan *(NUI, Galway)*
Carlotta Orsenigo *(Politecnico di Milano)*
Julio Ortega *(Universidad de Granada)*
Eneko Osaba *(Deusto University)*
Fernando Otero *(University of Kent)*
Ali Ouni *(University of Montreal)*
Ben Paechter *(Edinburgh Napier University)*
Federico Pagnozzi *(Université Libre de Bruxelles)*
Leon Palafox *(The University of Arizona)*
Michael E. Palmer *(Stanford University)*
Wei Pang *(University of Aberdeen)*
Luis Paquete *(University of Coimbra)*
Victor Parque *(Toyota Technological Institute)*
Konstantinos Parsopoulos *(University of Ioannina)*
Philippe Pasquier *(SIAT - Simon Fraser University)*
Castillo Pedro *(UGR)*
Paola Pellegrini *(IRIDIA-CoDE ULB)*
Jose-Maria Peña *(Universidad Politécnica de Madrid)*
Kalin Penev *(Southampton Solent University)*
Leslie Perez Caceres *(Iridia - ULB)*
Steve Phelps *(University of Essex)*
Andrew Philippides *(University of Sussex)*
Martin Pilát *(Faculty of Mathematics And Physics, Charles University in Prague)*
Nelishia Pillay *(University of KwaZulu-Natal)*
Clara Pizzuti *(Institute for High Performance Computing and Networking - ICAR National Research Council of Italy - CNR)*
Daniel Polani *(University of Hertfordshire)*
Silvia Poles *(EnginSoft)*
Petrica Pop *(North University of Baia Mare, Romania)*
Elena Popovici *(Icosystem Corp)*
Daniel Porumbel *(CEDRIC, CNAM (Conservatoire National des Arts et Métiers))*
Petr Pošík *(Czech Technical University in Prague)*
Walter Potter *(University of Georgia)*
Simon Poulding *(Blekinge Institute of Technology)*
Matthias Prandtstetter *(AIT Austrian Institute of Technology GmbH)*
Steve Prestwich *(University College Cork)*
Jakob Puchinger *(AIT - Austrian Institute of Technology)*
Cesar Puente *(Universidad Autónoma de San Luis Potosi)*
Jose Miguel Puerta *(UCLM)*
William F. Punch *(Michigan State University)*
Robin Purshouse *(University of Sheffield)*
Jianlong Qi *(Ancestry.com)*
A. K. Qin *(RMIT University)*
Günther R. Raidl *(Vienna University of Technology)*
Marcus Christian Randall *(School of Information Technology, Bond University)*
Ranji S. Ranjithan *(North Carolina State Univ)*

Khaled Rasheed *(University of Georgia)*
Tapabrata Ray *(School of Aerospace, Civil and Mechanical Engineering)*
Tom Ray *(University of Oklahoma)*
Michael Raymer *(Wright State University)*
Mark Read *(University of Sydney)*
Patrick M. Reed *(Cornell University)*
Lewis Rhyd *(Cardiff University)*
Hendrik Richter *(HTWK Leipzig University of Applied Sciences)*
John Rieffel *(Union College)*
Maria Cristina Riff *(UTFSM)*
Wille Robert *(University of Bremen)*
Denis Robilliard *(LISIC, ULCO, Univ Lille-Nord de France)*
Peter Rockett *(Dept of Electronic & Electrical Engineering)*
Eduardo Rodriguez-Tello *(CINVESTAV,Tamaulipas)*
Philipp Rohlfshagen *(Schneider-Electric)*
Andrea Roli *(Alma Mater Studiorum Universita' di Bologna)*
Simona E. Rombo *(Dep. of Mathematics and Computer Science, University of Palermo)*
Carlos Romero *(Technical University of Madrid)*
Marc Roper *(University of Strathclyde)*
Brian J. Ross *(Brock University)*
Peter Ross *(Napier University)*
Franz Rothlauf *(University of Mainz)*
Jonathan Rowe *(University of Birmingham)*
Guenter Rudolph *(TU Dortmund University)*
Guenther Ruhe *(University of Calgary)*
Ruben Ruiz *(Polytechnic University of Valencia)*
Thomas Runkler *(Siemens AG)*
Conor Ryan *(University of Limerick)*
Ramon Sagarna *(University of the Basque Country)*
Erol Sahin *(Middle East Technical University)*
Houari Sahraoui *(DIRO, Univ. de Montreal)*
Jun Sakuma *(University of Tsukuba)*
Ziad Salem *(Graz University)*
Luciano Sanchez *(Universidad de Oviedo)*
Roberto Santana *(University of the Basque Country (UPV/EHU))*
Iván Santibáñez Koref *(Technical Univ. Berlin)*
Federica Sarro *(University College London)*
Hiroyuki Sato *(The University of Electro-Communications)*
Yuji Sato *(Hosei University)*
Fredéric Saubion *(University of Angers, France)*
Hideyuki Sawada *(Kagawa University, Japan)*
Robert Schaefer *(AGH University of Science and Technology)*
Massimiliano Schillaci *(STMicroelectronics)*
Manuel Schmitt *(University of Erlangen-Nuremberg)*
Marc Schoenauer *(INRIA)*
Peter Scully *(Aberystwyth University)*
Michele Sebag *(Université Paris-Sud)*
Carlos Segura *(Universidad de La Laguna)*
Lukas Sekanina *(Brno University of Technology, Czech Republic)*
Yann Semet *(Thales)*
Sandip Sen *(University of Tulsa)*
Kevin Seppi *(Brigham Young University)*
Martin Serpell *(University of the West of England)*
Marc Sevaux *(Université de Bretagne-Sud - Lab-STICC)*
Ugur Sezerman *(Sabancı University)*
Fatima Shaheen *(Loughborough University)*
Noor Shaker *(IT University of Copenhagen)*
Siddhartha Shakya *(Business Modelling & Operational Transformation Practice, BT)*
Jonathan Lee Shapiro *(University of Manchester)*
Yang Shengxiang *(De Montfort Unviersity)*
Pradyumn Kumar Shukla *(KIT)*
Patrick Siarry *(University of Paris-Est Créteil)*
Arlindo Silva *(Polytechnic Institute of Castelo Branco)*
Fernando Silva *(Instituto de Telecomunicações; BioISI, University of Lisbon)*
Kevin Sim *(Edinburgh Napier University)*
Moshe Sipper *(Ben-Gurion University)*
Alexei N. Skurikhin *(Los Alamos National Laboratory)*
Alice Smith *(Auburn University)*
Jim Smith *(University of the West of England)*
Tamara Smyth *(University of Califronia San Diego)*
Christine Solnon *(LIRIS, INSA de Lyon)*
Eduardo J. Solteiro Pires *(UTAD University)*
Andrea Soltoggio *(Loughborough University)*
Andy Song *(RMIT University)*
Victor Adrian Sosa Hernandez *(CINVESTAV-IPN)*
Humberto Sossa *(Instituto Politécnico Nacional)*
Jerffeson Souza *(State University of Ceara)*
Lee Spector *(Hampshire College)*
Giovanni Squillero *(Politecnico di Torino)*

Russell Standish *(High Performance Coders)*
Susan Stepney *(University of York)*
Sebastian Stich *(Université catholique de Louvain)*
Forrest Stonedahl *(Northwestern University)*
Umberto Straccia *(ISTI-CNR, Italy)*
Giovanni Stracquadanio *(University of Oxford)*
Thomas Stützle *(Université Libre de Bruxelles)*
Dirk Sudholt *(University of Sheffield)*
Ponnuthurai Suganthan *(NTU)*
Chaoli Sun *(Taiyuan University of Science and Technology)*
Yi Sun *(Google Inc)*
Andrew Michael Sutton *(Friedrich-Schiller-Universität Jena)*
Reiji Suzuki *(Nagoya University)*
Keiki Takadama *(UEC)*
Ricardo Takahashi *(Universidade Federal de Minas Gerais)*
El-Ghazali Talbi *(INRIA)*
Ying Tan *(Peking University)*
Kiyoshi Tanaka *(Shinshu University)*
Ivan Tanev *(Faculty of Engineering, Doshisha University)*
Ernesto Tarantino *(ICAR - CNR)*
Daniel R. Tauritz *(Missouri University of Science and Technology)*
Jorge Tavares *(Microsoft)*
Roberto Tavares *(UFSCAR)*
Tim Taylor *(University of London International Academy)*
Jürgen Teich *(University of Erlangen-Nuremberg)*
Hugo Terashima Marín *(ITESM - CSI)*
Andrea G. B. Tettamanzi *(Université de Nice Sophia Antipolis)*
Christof Teuscher *(Portland State University)*
Johannes Textor *(University of Utrecht)*
Fabien Teytaud *(University of Lille Nord de France)*
Ruck Thawonmas *(Ritsumeikan University)*
Lothar Thiele *(ETH Zurich)*
Dirk Thierens *(Utrecht University)*
Tommy Thompson *(University of Derby)*
Chuan-Kang Ting *(Department of Computer Science and Information Engineering, National Chung Cheng University)*
Peter Tino *(University of Birmingham)*
Renato Tinos *(University of São Paulo)*
Ashutosh Tiwari *(Cranfield University)*
Santosh Tiwari *(General Motors Company)*
Julian Togelius *(IT University of Copenhagen)*
Marco Tomassini *(University of Lausanne)*
Alberto Paolo Tonda *(INRA)*
Martin Trefzer *(University of York)*
Vito Trianni *(ISTC-CNR)*
Krzysztof Trojanowski *(Institute of Computer Science, Polish Academy of Sciences)*
Giuseppe A. Trunfio *(University of Sassari)*
Alexis Tsoukias *(Université Paris Dauphine)*
Elio Tuci *(Aberystwyth University)*
Matthias Tuma *(Ruhr-Universität Bochum)*
Tea Tusar *(Jozef Stefan Institute)*
Cem Celal Tutum *(Michigan State University)*
Jamie Twycross *(University of Nottingham)*
Man Chon U *(Las Vegas Sands Corporate)*
Roberto Ugolotti *(University of Parma)*
Paulo Urbano *(University of Lisbon)*
Neil Urquhart *(Edinburgh Napier University)*
Guillermo Valencia-Palomo *(Instituto Tecnologico de Hermosillo)*
H. Jaap Van den Herik *(Tilburg University)*
Leonardo Vanneschi *(NOVA IMS, Universidade Nova de Lisboa)*
Zdeněk Vašíček *(Brno University Of Technology)*
Igor Vatolkin *(TU Dortmund)*
Nadarajen Veerapen *(University of Stirling)*
Nubia Velasco *(Universidad de los Andes)*
Sebastian Ventura *(Universidad de Cordoba)*
Phillip Verbancsics *(Space and Naval Warfare Systems Center - Pacific)*
Sebastien Verel *(Université du Littoral Côte d'Opale)*
Silvia Vergilio *(Federal University of Paraná)*
Ana Viana *(INESC TEC, Polytechnic of Porto)*
Petra Vidnerova *(Institute of Computer Science of ASCR)*
Fernando J. Von Zuben *(Unicamp)*
Michael N. Vrahatis *(University of Patras)*
Tobias Wagner *(Institute of Machining Technology, TU Dortmund University)*
Rolf Wanka *(University of Erlangen-Nuremberg)*
Westley Weimer *(University of Virginia)*
Simon Wessing *(Technische Universität Dortmund)*
Peter Alexander Whigham *(University of Otago)*
David White *(University of Glasgow)*
Bartosz Wieloch *(Poznan University of Technology)*

Josh Wilkerson *(NAVAIR)*
Garnett Wilson *(Afinin Labs Inc)*
Stewart W. Wilson *(Prediction Dynamics)*
Manuel Wimmer *(Vienna University of Technology)*
Mark Wineberg *(University of Guelph)*
Stephan Winkler *(University Of Applied Sciences Upper Austria)*
Carsten Witt *(Technical University Of Denmark)*
M. L. Dennis Wong *(Swinburne University of Technology)*
John R. Woodward *(S T I R L I N G U N I)*
Alden H. Wright *(University of Montana)*
Borys Wrobel *(Adam Mickiewicz University)*
Annie S. Wu *(University of Central Florida)*
Huayang Xie *(Oracle New Zealand)*
Takeshi Yamada *(NTT Communication Science Labs)*
Lidia Yamamoto *(University of Strasbourg)*
Georgios Yannakakis *(IT University of Copenhagen)*
Wei-Chang Yeh *(National Tsing Hua University)*
Gary G. Yen *(Oklahoma State University)*
Shin Yoo *(University College London)*
Jason Yosinski *(Cornell University)*
Tian-Li Yu *(Taiwan Evolutionary Intelligence Lab)*
Tina Yu *(Memorial University)*
Yang Yu *(Nanjing University)*
Martin Zaefferer *(Cologne University of Applied Sciences)*
Amelia Zafra *(University of Cordoba)*
Payam Zahadat *(Artificial Life Lab, University of Graz)*
Daniela Zaharie *(West University of Timisoara)*
Fabio Zambetta *(RMIT University)*
Saúl Zapotecas Martínez *(CINVESTAV-IPN)*
Andreas Zell *(University of Tübingen)*
Zhu Zexuan *(Shenzhen University)*
Fu Zhang *(Mathworks)*
Mengjie Zhang *(Victoria University of Wellington)*
Yuanyuan Zhang *(University College London)*
Yanfei Zhong *(Wuhan university)*
Aimin Zhou *(Department of Computer Science, East China Normal University)*
Jayadeva *(Indian Institute of Technology, Delhi)*

GECCO 2015 Track Chairs

Ant Colony Optimization and Swarm Intelligence (ACO-SI):	Manuel López-Ibáñez *(Université Libre de Bruxelles)* Sanaz Mostaghim *(Otto von Guericke University of Magdeburg)*
Artificial Immune Systems and Artificial Chemistries (AIS-AChem):	Jon Timmis *(University of York)* Christine Zarges *(University of Birmingham)*
Artificial Life / Robotics / Evolvable Hardware (ALIFE):	Luis Correia *(University of Lisbon)* Terrence Soule *(University of Idaho)*
Biological & Biomedical Applications (BIO):	Mario Giacobini *(University of Torino)* Ryan Urbanowicz *(Dartmouth College)*
Continuous Optimization - Evolution Strategies & Evolutionary Programming (CO):	Youhei Akimoto *(Shinshu University)* Tobias Glasmachers *(Ruhr-University Bochum)*
Digital Entertainment Technologies & Arts (DETA):	Francisco Fernandez de Vega *(University of Extremadura)* Amy Hoover *(University of Malta)*
Estimation of Distribution Algorithms (EDA):	Pedro Larrañaga *(Technical University of Madrid)* Marta Soto *(Institute of Cybernetics, Mathematics & Physics)*
Evolutionary Combinatorial Optimization & Metaheuristics (ECOM):	Carlos Cotta *(University of Málaga)* Francisco B. Pereira *(Polytechnic Institute of Coimbra)*
Evolutionary Machine Learning (EML):	Julia Handl *(University of Manchester)* Jan Koutnik *(IDSIA)*
Evolutionary Multiobjective Optimization (EMO):	Antonio Gaspar-Cunha *(University of Minho)* Heike Trautmann *(University of Münster)*
Generative and Developmental Systems (GDS):	Jean-Baptiste Mouret *(University Pierre and Marie Curie)* Sebastian Risi *(IT University of Copenhagen)*
Genetic Algorithms (GA):	Ernesto Costa *(University of Coimbra)* Oliver Schuetze *(Cinvestav-IPN)*
Genetic Programming (GP):	Krzysztof Krawiec *(Poznan University of Technology)* Alberto Moraglio *(University of Exeter)*
Integrative Genetic & Evolutionary Computation (IGEC):	Julian F. Miller *(University of York)* Pawel Widera *(Newcastle University)*
Parallel Evolutionary Systems (PES):	Stefano Cagnoni *(University of Parma)* JJ Merelo *(University of Granada)*
Real World Applications (RWA):	Emma Hart *(Edinburgh Napier University)* Leonardo Trujillo *(Edinburgh Napier University)*
Search-Based Software Engineering & Self-* Search (SBSE-SS):	Marouane Keswsentini *(University of Michigan)* Gabriela Ochoa *(University of Stirling)*
Theory (THEORY):	Francisco Chicano *(University of Málaga)* Carola Doerr *(University Pierre and Marie Curie)*

A Tensor Analysis Improved Genetic Algorithm for Online Bin Packing

Shahriar Asta, Ender Özcan
ASAP Research Group
School of Computer Science
University of Nottingham
Nottingham, NG8 1BB, U.K.
{sba,exo}@cs.nott.ac.uk

ABSTRACT

Mutation in a Genetic Algorithm is the key variation operator adjusting the genetic diversity in a population throughout the evolutionary process. Often, a fixed mutation probability is used to perturb the value of a gene. In this study, we describe a novel data science approach to adaptively generate the mutation probability for each locus. The trail of high quality candidate solutions obtained during the search process is represented as a 3rd order tensor. Factorizing that tensor captures the common pattern between those solutions, identifying the degree of mutation which is likely to yield improvement at each locus. An online bin packing problem is used as an initial case study to investigate the proposed approach for generating locus dependent mutation probabilities. The empirical results show that the tensor approach improves the performance of a standard Genetic Algorithm on almost all classes of instances, significantly.

Keywords

packing, data science, tensor, mutation

1. INTRODUCTION

There is a wide variety of population based approaches, solving computationally hard problems, which are referred to as 'knowledge-based' evolutionary computation methods. Knowledge can be extracted and used in many ways in various stages of the evolutionary process. For instance, Knowledge Based Genetic Algorithm (KBGA) [26] used problem domain knowledge to produce an initial population and guide the operators of a Genetic Algorithm (GA) using that knowledge at all the stages of the evolution. In [11] problem specific 'knowledge' was represented in form of ground facts and training examples of Horn clauses. This knowledge is exploited in a GA for inductive concept learning and is used in mutation and crossover operators to evolve populations of if-then rules. [23] employed prior problem specific 'knowledge' to generate locus level bias probabilities when selecting allele for crossover, resulting in a Knowledge Based Nonuniform Crossover (KNUX). In [9], a mutation operator was designed based on knowledge capturing the distribution of candidate solutions in Extremal Optimization context. This method was successfully applied to PID tuning. The approach proposed in [35] utilized rough set theory to explore hidden knowledge during the evolutionary process of a GA. The extracted knowledge is then used to partition the solution space into subspaces. Each subspace is searched using a separate GA.

In this study, we use tensor analysis to generate mutation probabilities for each locus of a chromosome, also referred to as individual, representing a candidate solution. Tensorial techniques are powerful analysis methods for high dimensional data and are nowadays widely used in data mining and machine learning applications. In our approach, within a GA, the trail of high quality solutions, where each solution has a matrix form, is represented as a 3rd order tensor. Factorizing such a tensor reveals the latent relationship between various chromosome locations through identifying common subspaces of the solutions where mutation is more likely to succeed in producing better offspring. In addition to subspace learning, one would expect a powerful data mining approach to discover the related genes. Possession of such information should naturally result in having similar probability values for closely related genes. Our experiments show that tensor factorization achieves this objective and identifies genes which should have similar mutation likelihoods due to their close relationship.

An online bin-packing problem is used as a case study to analyse the performance of the proposed approach. The approach in [24] represents candidate solutions to a given packing problem as index policies (e.g., [14]). These policies have a matrix form in which an entry scores each potential packing option separately and the highest value option is selected. Due to this implicit two dimensional encoding of policies as candidate solutions, their trail during the evolutionary search process takes the form of a 3rd order tensor. Hence, online bin packing forms a good playground for testing the proposed approach. The first results (reported in [24] and later in [4] and [36]) indicates that the GA approach finds high quality policies for the specific packing problems that perform significantly better than the generic 'human designed' heuristics, such as, first fit and best fit [27, 10]. In

GECCO '15, July 11 - 16, 2015, Madrid, Spain
© 2015 ACM. ISBN 978-1-4503-3472-3/15/07... $15.00
DOI: http://dx.doi.org/10.1145/2739480.2754787

this paper, we show that by modifying mutation probabilities using tensor analysis, the performance of this framework can be improved significantly (when compared to the results achieved for our implementation of the GA approach in [24] as well as standard heuristics) on almost all instances.

The structure of the paper is as follows: Section 2 gives basic definitions of the bin-packing problem, the instances that we use, and the existing standard heuristics. In Section 3, index policies (policy matrices) are introduced and the original GA framework which evolves these policies is presented. Subsequently, Section 4 gives an introduction to tensorial representation and the factorization method used in this study. Section 5 describes the proposed approach which integrates tensor analysis into the GA approach. The setting used during the experiments as well as the experimental results are given in Section 6. Finally, Section 7 concludes the study and discusses future research directions.

2. ONLINE BIN PACKING PROBLEM

An online bin packing problem deals with the packing of items having various sizes which arrive one at a time. Each item has to be immediately packed into one of the open bins before the next item arrives and its size is revealed. This decision process is extremely difficult, since the future impact of the decisions made is extremely difficult to predict. Each bin has a fixed capacity of $C > 1$. The size of each item is chosen from a given range $[s_{min}, s_{max}]$ where $s_{min} > 0$ and $s_{max} < C$. If an item is placed into an empty bin, a new bin is opened immediately, guaranteeing that there always exists a new empty bin. A bin is closed whenever its remaining capacity is too small to take in any new item.

A parameterized stochastic generator is used to produce uniform bin packing instances. Such a generator is represented by the formalism UBP (C, s_{min}, s_{max}, N) (adopted from [24]). In this formalism C is the bin capacity, s_{min} and s_{max} are minimum and maximum item sizes and N is the number of total items. As an example, $UBP(30, 4, 25, 10^5)$ is a random instance generator, producing a class of problem instances where each one is a sequence of 10^5 integer values. Each value represents the size of items and is randomly drawn from the range $[4, 25]$. It should be remembered that UBP's are instances of distributions. The actual sequence representing an instance varies depending on the seed given to the random number generator. That is, the generator is seeded with different seed values to generate a different sequence of items at each time used. This is indeed the case when our approach is tested as it will be seen in the coming sections.

Note that there are various instances available in the literature ([30] and [13]), however, these instances are devised for offline bin packing algorithms and usually consist of a small number of instances. That is the reason why we generate our own random instances. In this study, we always deal with instances for which the number of items is 10^5. Therefore, throughout the remainder of the paper, we use a shortened notation for UBP's, omitting the last term. For example the UBP in the above example is simply denoted by $UBP(30, 4, 25)$

There are well known 'human-designed' heuristics for online bin packing such as First Fit (FF), Best Fit (BF) and Worst Fit (WF) [17, 27, 10]. The FF heuristic assigns the item to the first open bin where an assignment is feasible. The BF heuristic places the current item into the bin with the least remaining space among all open bins whereas the WF heuristic assigns the item to the bin with the largest remaining space. Another well known heuristic for online bin packing is the harmonic based approach [22, 28]. Compared to other heuristics, harmonic based algorithms provide a better worst case performance ratio. However, the assumption is the items sizes are chosen from the range $(0, 1]$. The harmonic algorithm partitions the range into sub-intervals and each arriving item is assigned to its category depending on its size.

The performance of a bin packing solution can be evaluated based on various criteria. For example, one could use the number of bins used B for this purpose. B increases as larger number of items (N) are considered. Another performance evaluation criteria is the average generic fullness F_{gf} which provides an insight into the variation of resulting fullness between bins. Consider that the fullness of bin t is equal to f_t, $t \in \{1, \ldots, B\}$ then the average generic bin fullness is calculated as: $F_{gf} = 1/B \sum_t f_t^2$. In our study however, average fullness is considered as the fitness value of function evaluations. Average fullness, denoted by F_{af} is the value of the occupied space, averaged over the number of used bins and is calculated according to Eq.1 below.

$$F_{af} = 1/B \sum_t f_t \tag{1}$$

3. POLICY MATRIX REPRESENTATION

A packing policy/heuristic can be represented as a matrix, referred to as 'policy matrix'. In a policy matrix, each entry at the rth row and s^{th} column, denoted as $W_{r,s}$ is a score. $W_{r,s}$ determines the priority of placing an item of size s in a bin with remaining capacity r. The values for scores $W_{r,s}$ are integer values and chosen from a range $[w_{min}, w_{max}]$. Given a policy matrix, one could simply scan the remaining bin capacity of existing (and feasible) open bins, assign each bin a score from the policy matrix, and then choose the bin with the highest score. The placement of an item in an open bin is *feasible* when the bin has sufficient free space to accommodate that item ($r \geq s$). During the packing process, an open empty bin is always considered as an option.

Some elements of the policy matrix do not require a placement strategy. For instance, cases were $s > r$ can never occur, i.e , a policy matrix always has a lower triangular structure. Thus, not all the elements in the policy matrix correspond to real cases and therefore no policy is required to handle such cases. The elements for which a handling policy is required are referred to as active entries whereas the rest of elements are called inactive entries. In other words, inactive entries correspond to pairs of item size and bin remaining capacity which either can never occur or are irrelevant. The active entries along columns of the policy matrix contain score values and represent a policy for a specific item size. Since the policy for a certain item size can be very different than that of other item size, the scores in each column are considered to be independent from each other.

In order to further clarify how a policy matrix functions, an example is given here. The policy matrix in Figure 1 is evolved to solve packing instances generated by $UBP(15,5,10)$. Assume that, during the packing process, an item of size 5 arrives. This item size corresponds to the fifth column in the given policy matrix. The entries of this column represent the set of scores which are associated to each possible remaining bin capacity for the current item size. Assume that, currently, only bins with remaining capacities of 9 and 10 are open. As always, the empty bin is also available for item placement. The scores associated with remaining bin capacities 9 and 10 are 4 and 1 respectively. The empty bin has a score of 2. Since the bin with the remaining capacity 9 has the highest score, the item is placed in this bin.

In all policy matrices, the last row represents the scores assigned to the empty bin for different item sizes. Suppose that, in the previous example, the score associated to the empty bin is 7 (instead of 2 in Figure 1). In this case, the item would be no longer put in bin with remaining capacity 9. Instead it would be placed in the empty bin (bin with remaining capacity 15) and a new empty bin would be opened immediately.

Ties can occur and the tie breaking strategy employed here is first fit. As an example, assume that the arriving item has a size 8. Therefore, in order to determine which bin to choose for item placement, the scores in column 8 will be investigated. Assume that currently there are open bins with all possible remaining bin capacities as well as the always available empty bin. Scanning the scores, bins with remaining capacities 8 and 10 emerge as top scoring ones because they both have the highest score which is 7. However, due to the first fit tie breaking strategy, the first bin from the top is chosen and the item is put in the bin with remaining capacity 8.

r\s	1	2	3	4	5	6	7	8	9	10	11	12	13	14	15
1:	.	.	.	.	.	.	.	.	.	.	.	.	.	.	.
2:	.	.	.	.	.	.	.	.	.	.	.	.	.	.	.
3:	.	.	.	.	.	.	.	.	.	.	.	.	.	.	.
4:	.	.	.	.	.	.	.	.	.	.	.	.	.	.	.
5:	.	.	.	.	6	.	.	.	.	.	.	.	.	.	.
6:	.	.	.	.	3	7	.	.	.	.	.	.	.	.	.
7:	.	.	.	.	7	4	2	.	.	.	.	.	.	.	.
8:	.	.	.	.	1	2	2	7	.	.	.	.	.	.	.
9:	.	.	.	.	4	3	6	4	5	.	.	.	.	.	.
10:	.	.	.	.	1	7	3	7	2	4	.	.	.	.	.
11:	.	.	.	.	.	.	.	.	.	.	.	.	.	.	.
12:	.	.	.	.	.	.	.	.	.	.	.	.	.	.	.
13:	.	.	.	.	.	.	.	.	.	.	.	.	.	.	.
14:	.	.	.	.	.	.	.	.	.	.	.	.	.	.	.
15:	.	.	.	.	2	5	6	5	3	4	.	.	.	.	.

Figure 1: An example of a policy matrix for $UBP(15, 5, 10)$

There is a growing interest on automating the design of heuristics (e.g. for some recent work see [29, 7]). In [24], a GA framework was proposed in which policy matrices as described above were evolved, resulting in automatic generation of heuristics in form of index policies. In addition to this original study, there has been a number of studies related to this topic. For example, in [25], an approach based on policy matrices was proposed for analysing the effect of the mutation operator in Genetic Programming (GP) in a regular run using online bin packing. In [4] dimensionality reduction was considered for policy matrices in that they were derived from one dimensional vectors (say, policy vectors). Evolving policy vectors in a fashion similar to the evolution of policy matrices was shown to produce high quality solutions. In [5] an Apprenticeship Learning approach was proposed where an agent observes and learns the actions of high quality policy matrices during packing and generalizes its knowledge to unseen instances of various sizes exhibiting high performance particularly for larger instances. In [36], policy matrices are seen as heuristics with many parameters and are approached from a parameter tuning perspective. The Irace package was used to tune policies during training. Trained policies were then tested on unseen instances with performances close to that of the GA framework and significantly better than the man-made heuristics. In this study, we use the same GA with the same settings as described in [24], however, we present a tensor-based approach for improving its performance via an adaptive locus based mutation operator, instead of using a generic one.

4. TENSOR ANALYSIS

There is a plethora of applications and research areas benefiting from tensorial representation and tensor analytic approaches. Tensor tools have a great record of contribution to many research fields, such as, computer vision [33], video processing [20], data compression [34], web mining [1] and etc. Generally speaking, many problems produce data which are high dimensional in nature. For instance, video streams constitute a data which is three dimensional (pixel coordinates and time) or higher (when information such as audio, text, change of environment and etc are also considered). The traditional approach in data mining has been to collapse this data into a two dimensional dataset in order to apply machine learning techniques and perform tasks such as classification and prediction. However, recent research ([33],[2] and [1]) shows that preserving the natural dimensionality of the data is useful in that it keeps the information regarding latent relationship between variables along different dimensions. Tensor representation fulfils this requirement as tensors are multidimensional arrays and can represent data with high dimensions. The *order* of a tensor indicates its dimensionality where each dimension of a tensor is referred to as a *mode*. The interested readers can refer to a comprehensive survey on tensors and their applications in [19] for further information. The method widely used to extract the latent relationship between various modes of data involves in factorising (decomposing) the tensor into its *basic factors*. Basic factors are then used in different ways depending on the objective of the algorithm. The tensor decomposition methods are mainly generalizations of the Singular Value Decomposition (SVD) to higher dimensions. Higher Order SVD (HOSVD) [21], Tucker decomposition [32], Parallel Factor (a.k.a PARAFAC or CANDECOMP or CP) [16] and Non-negative Tensor Factorization (NTF) [31] are among numerous factorization methods proposed by researchers. In this paper, we use CP factorization ([3]) as described in the following subsection with the goal of enabling an adaptive locus based mutation operator within a GA for online bin packing.

4.1 CP Factorization

We use, boldface Euler script letters, boldface capital letters and boldface lower-case letters to denote tensors (e.g., $\mathcal{T}$), matrices (e.g., $\mathbf{M}$) and vectors (e.g., $\mathbf{v}$), respectively. Scalar values (e.g., tensor, matrix and vector entries) are indexed by lower-case letters. For instance, t_{pqr} is the (p, q, r) entry of a $3^{rd}-$order (three dimensional) tensor $\mathcal{T}$.

CP decomposition uses the Alternating Least Square (ALS) algorithm ([8],[15]) to factorize (decompose) a tensor. Fac-

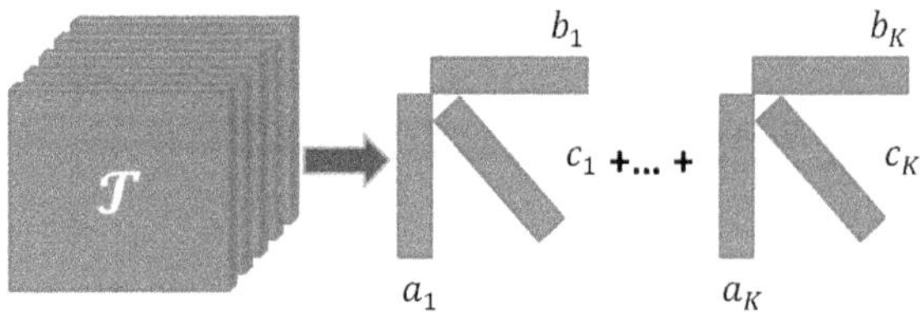

Figure 2: Factorizing a tensor to K components.

torizing a 3rd order tensor[1] $\mathcal{T}$ of size $P \times Q \times R$ using the CP factorization results in another tensor $\hat{\mathcal{T}}$ which approximates $\mathcal{T}$ as in Equation 2. This process is also illustrated in Figure 2.

$$\hat{\mathcal{T}} = \sum_{k=1}^{K} \lambda_k \ \mathbf{a}_k \circ \mathbf{b}_k \circ \mathbf{c}_k \tag{2}$$

In Eq.2, $\lambda_k \in \mathbb{R}_+$, $\mathbf{a}_k \in \mathbb{R}^P$, $\mathbf{b}_k \in \mathbb{R}^Q$ and $\mathbf{c}_k \in \mathbb{R}^R$ for $k = 1 \cdots K$, where K is the number of desired components. A component is expressed as ($\lambda_k \ \mathbf{a}_k \circ \mathbf{b}_k \circ \mathbf{c}_k$) and the resulting vectors (e.g., $\mathbf{a}_k$, $\mathbf{b}_k$ and $\mathbf{c}_k$) are called basic factors. λ_k is the weight of the kth component. Note that "$\circ$" is the outer product operator. The outer product of three vectors produces a 3rd-order tensor. For instance, the product $\lambda \ \mathbf{a}_1 \circ \mathbf{b}_1 \circ \mathbf{c}_1$ results in a 3rd-order tensor where each tensor entry, indexed as pqr is computed through a simple multiplication like $a_p b_q c_r$. In a special case, the outer product of two vectors $\mathbf{a}_k$ and $\mathbf{b}_k$ produces a matrix $\mathbf{B}_k$ of size $P \times Q$ for each component k

$$\mathbf{B}_k = \mathbf{a}_k \circ \mathbf{b}_k \tag{3}$$

The matrix $\mathbf{B}_k$ will be referred to as the *Basic Frame* throughout the paper. The basic frame $\mathbf{B}_k$ quantifies the relationship between the object pairs across the first two dimensions in each component. In other words, this quantity indicates the "level of interaction" between pairs of object, each from a separate tensor dimension, in component k [19].

The ALS algorithm approximates the original tensor $\mathcal{T}$ by minimizing the error difference between $\mathcal{T}$ and the estimation ($\hat{\mathcal{T}}$). This error is denoted as ε and calculated as in Eq.4 (the subscript F refers to the Frobenious norm as in Eq.5).

$$\varepsilon = \frac{1}{2} ||\mathcal{T} - \hat{\mathcal{T}}||_F^2 \tag{4}$$

$$||\mathcal{T} - \hat{\mathcal{T}}||_F^2 = \sum_{p=1}^{P} \sum_{q=1}^{Q} \sum_{r=1}^{R} \left(t_{pqr} - \hat{t}_{pqr}\right)^2 \tag{5}$$

The approximated tensor is, to some extent, a generalized representation of the original tensor and immune to data anomalies, such as, missing data. Basic factors produced by the factorization method can be used to represent the high dimensional data in a compressed manner. The tensor factorization exhibit other interesting characteristics. It enables the detection of more comprehensible sub-space from the original data. This can be very useful in many applications. In computer vision, for instance, [18] and [20] separately showed that factorization of a 3rd-order tensor of a video sequence results in basic frames which reveal the location and functionality of synchronously moving human body parts. Evolutionary algorithms are among many approaches which produce high dimensional data. This possibility was first acknowledged in [3] where the trail of a hyper-heuristic search algorithm was represented as a tensor. The space of heuristics where the hyper-heuristic conducts the search was then partitioned using the basic factors obtained from factorizing the tensor. The proposed tensor based approach achieves impressive results despite its simplicity. The search history formed by GA can be turned into multi-dimensional data in a similar fashion to the search history of a hyper-heuristic as described in [3]. For example, collecting high quality individuals (candidate solutions) from the populations in several successive generations while GA operates, naturally, yields a 3rd-order tensor, representing the changing individuals in time.

[1]In this study we only focus on 3rd order tensors.

5. PROPOSED APPROACH

In the original framework [24], policy matrices are produced using GA in a train and test fashion. The evolutionary cycle is performed for a given stochastic sequence generator (UBP) resulting in a policy matrix for that UBP. At the beginning, a random population of policy matrices is generated. At each generation, mutation and crossover are applied to the individuals (policy matrices). Each individual representing a packing policy/heuristic is then handed over to a separate evaluator (bin packer) which applies the policy to a stream of items, returning the fitness (Eq.1) as feedback. The cycle of evolution continues until the stopping criterion is met. Our method modifies the training procedure as illustrated in Figure 3. During every 5 generations, a tensor ($\mathcal{T}$) containing the top 20% individuals (policy matrices) is constructed and factorized into its basic factor, producing a basic frame. The elements of the basic frame is used as mutation probabilities for the next 5 generations from which a new tensor is constructed. Subsequent to training, the best individual is then tested on several unseen instances for evaluation.

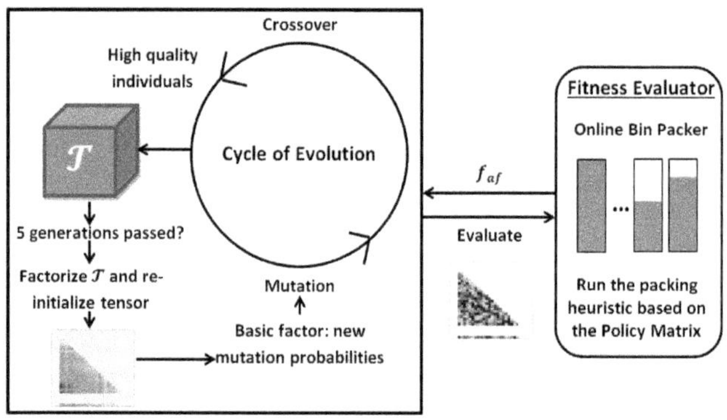

Figure 3: The GA+TA framework

The tensor $\mathcal{T}$ has the size $C \times C \times R$ where R is the number of the top 20% individuals and C is the bin capacity as described in Section 2. The order according to which the policy matrices are put into the tensor is precisely the order in which they are generated by the GA framework. This tensor is then factorized where K in Eq.2 is set to 1. That is, the original tensor $\mathcal{T}$ is approximated by $\hat{\mathcal{T}}$ as the following

$$\hat{\mathcal{T}} = \lambda\, \mathbf{a} \circ \mathbf{b} \circ \mathbf{c} \quad (6)$$

where the length of the vectors **a**, **b** and **c** are C, C and R respectively. As depicted in Figure 4, the outer product of vectors **a** and **b** results in a basic frame **B** which is exactly the shape of a policy matrix with the size $C \times C$ (Eq.3 is used with $k = 1$ to produce **B**). The difference between **B** and a policy matrix is that instead of containing integer score values in the range of $[w_{min}, w_{max}]$, it contains real values between 0 and 1. These values point towards regions in policy matrices where change of score values has been a common pattern among good quality matrices.

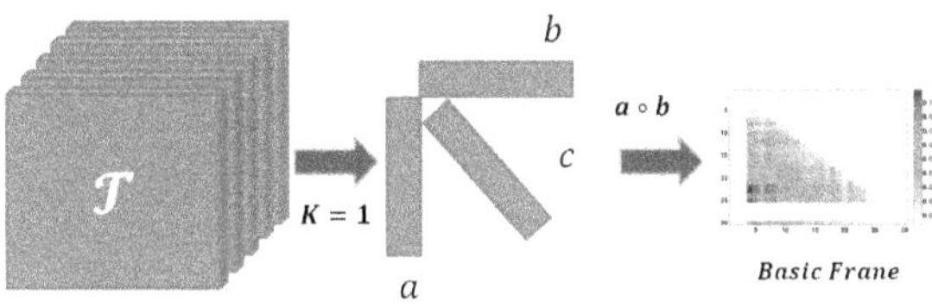

Figure 4: Extracting the basic frame for $K = 1$ in Eq.2.

Thus, the values in **B** are perceived as mutation probability of each locus for the next 5 generations. That is, during the next 5 generations, a gene indexed (i, j) is mutated with a probability $\mathbf{B}(i, j)$. The initial mutation probabilities are fixed as $\frac{1}{chromosomeLength}$ for the first 5 generations. Data collection for tensor construction occurs at the same time when the generated basic frame **B** has been applied.

6. EXPERIMENTS

In this section, after providing the details of our experimental setting, we discuss the results. In order to to gain a better understanding of our approach, the basic frames achieved from our experiments are investigated first. Subsequently, we compare our approach to the original framework by conducting a comparative study between the performance of the two algorithms on ten different classes of instances.

6.1 Experimental Setting

The setting used for the GA framework is adopted from [24]. That is, for each training phase, the number of generations is set to 200 while the population size is $\lceil C/2 \rceil$. Tournament selection is the strategy of choice for parent selection and the tour size is 2. Crossover and mutation operators are uniform and traditional respectively and the crossover probability is equal to 1.0. As discussed in Section 3, the scores in policy matrices are chosen from the range $[w_{min}, w_{max}]$. In our experiments $w_{min} = 1$ and w_{max} is equal to the maximum number of active entries along the columns of the policy matrix (i.e. for the policy matrix in Figure 1, $w_{max} = 7$). For tensor operations, Matlab Tensor Toolbox [6] has been used. The GA framework is implemented in the C language. In order to use the toolbox, the Matlab DeployTool has been used to generate an executable of the Matlab code. This executable is then called when necessary from the C code without a need to load the Matlab environment. The approach proposed in this paper is compared to the original GA framework. Throughout the experiments, our approach is referred to by the GA+TA whereas the original work in [24] is referred to by GA. The experiments regarding the original GA framework have been repeated here (instead of using the results reported elsewhere) and the train-test conditions (seeding etc.) for both GA and GA+TA are the same.

6.2 Basic Frames: An Analysis

As discussed in Section 5, the GA+TA algorithm frequently constructs and factorizes a tensor of high quality candidate solutions. The factorization process results in the basic frame which is used as a mutation probability. This section is dedicated to the analysis of these basic frames and the manner with which they evolve along side the main cycle of evolution.

Figure 5 illustrates the gradual change in probabilities produced by tensor analysis throughout the generations. The instance generator on which the policies were trained in Figure 5 is $UBP(30, 4, 25)$. The basic frame generated after the first factorization (Figure 5(a)) is notably less detailed compared to the ones generated in later generations. However, during the time, a common pattern seems to emerge. This pattern reveals that, for this UBP, good quality matrices tend to frequently change the score values corresponding to small item sizes and large remaining bin capacities. Thus, subjecting these locus to mutation more frequently would probably result in better packing performance.

Different UBP's indicate different patterns though. For instance, Figure 6 shows one of the basic frames produced for the instance generator $UBP(40, 10, 20)$. Using this basic frame, the best policy matrix was found during training. The pattern here is certainly different from those in Figure 5 indicating a whole different group of items sizes and remaining bin capacities as the most frequently changing genes. It also is less focused and more disconnected compared to the basic frames in Figure 5(d).

A closer look at Figure 5 shows another interesting aspect of the generated basic frame. It seems that in addition to finding common changing locus in the chromosome, the basic frame also identifies groups of different genes with similar (if not equal) probabilities. In other words, basic frames seems to partition genes into groups (with no clear border) where genes within each group are related. This is no surprise and it is one of the achievements of the ALS algorithm. In Eq.6, the factor **a** captures the gene patterns corresponding to bin remaining capacity while **b** does the same for gene patterns concerning the item size. The factor **c** captures the temporal profile of the patterns in the first two factors. Hence, our approach is able to detect recurring gene patterns along each dimension (remaining capacity and item size). Moreover, when constructing the tensor, only *good* quality solutions were allowed in the tensor. Thus, any pattern detected along each dimension is equally promising. The basic frame is calculated from the outer product of **a** and **b**, combining the gene patterns related to each dimension of the tensor. It has been observed in many studies (such as [12] and [20]) that the basic frame quantifies the relationship between the elements of the two factors. Hence, the relationship between any gene pattern detected along the first and the second dimensions is scored in the basic frame. Thus, if there are

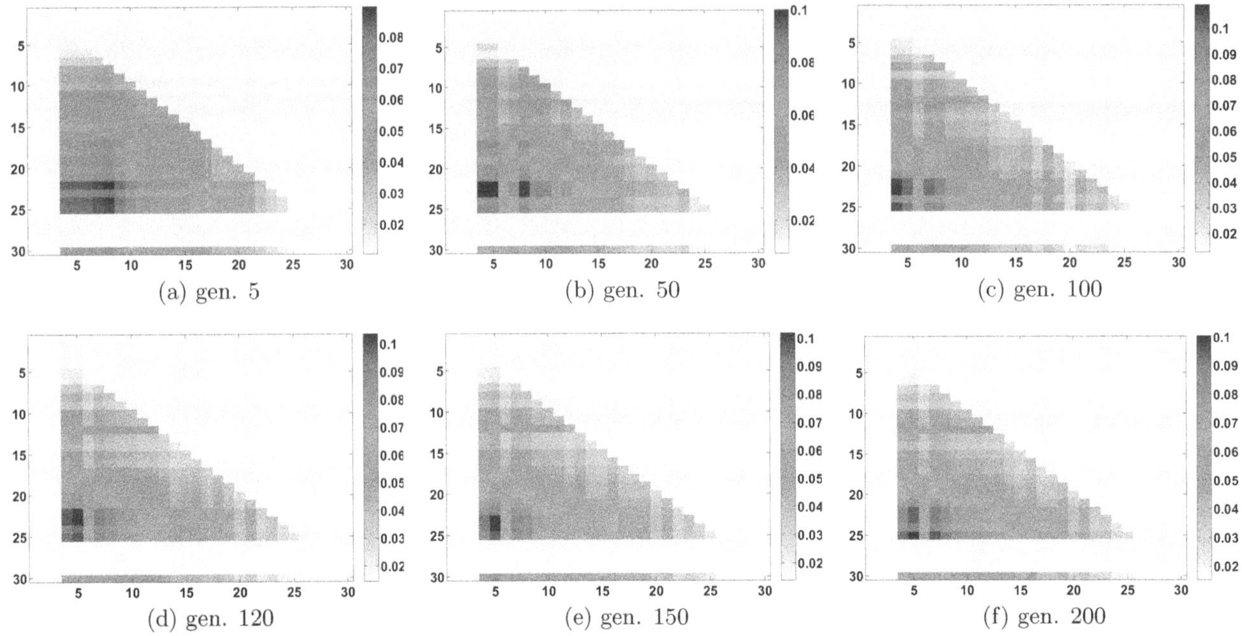
(a) gen. 5 (b) gen. 50 (c) gen. 100

(d) gen. 120 (e) gen. 150 (f) gen. 200

Figure 5: Various basic frames achieved in different stages of the search for an instance generated by $UBP(30, 4, 25)$. The basic frame in 5(d) is the probability matrix using which the best policy is achieved (gen 121)

regions with similar score values [2] in the basic frame (as it is visible in both figures 5 and 6), the genes are considered to be *related*.

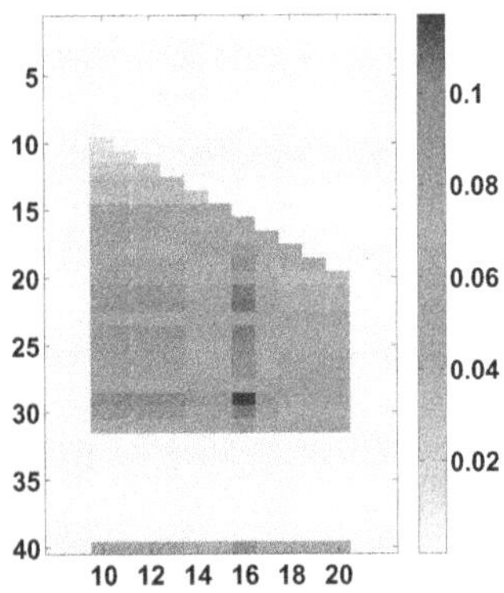

Figure 6: The basic frame for $UBP(40, 10, 20)$ using which the best policy matrix was found.

It is important to stress the fact that the produced basic frames are in no way representing the index scores generated by the GA framework. That is, we are not trying to infer score values in the policy matrix from the corresponding elements of a basic frame. The policy matrix in Figure 7 is generated using the probabilities in Figure 5(d) and solves instances generated by $UBP(30, 4, 25)$ instance generator. It is evident from the figures that although the two matrices are similar in dimensions, they are not similar at all when it comes to the contents. The rough structure of the policy matrix itself compared to the smooth structure of the basic frame confirms that there is little correlation between scores and mutation probabilities.

[2]Not to be confused with the scores in the policy matrix. The score here refers to the quantity achieved from the factorization procedure.

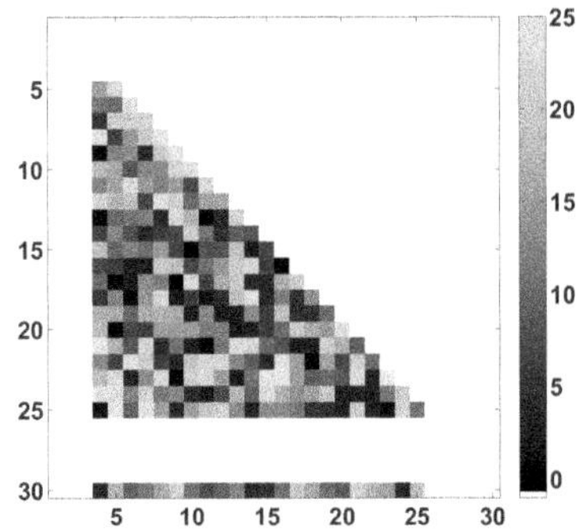

Figure 7: The best policy matrix obtained by GA+TA for $UBP(30, 4, 25)$ using the basic frame entries (see Figure 5(d)) as mutation probabilities.

6.3 Experimental Results

The experimental results show that our algorithm (GA+TA) outperforms the original GA framework on almost all instances significantly. A Wilcoxon sign rank test is performed to confirm this. Table 1 summarizes the results. The only instance generator on which GA+TA seems to be under-performing is UBP(60, 15, 25). On all other instances, GA+TA outperforms the GA framework.

Our studies show that it is very hard to increase the performance of the GA algorithm even slightly. Nevertheless, the GA+TA algorithm has improved the performance substantially. One major reason that contributes to the success of the GA+TA algorithm is the representation. Tensor factorization algorithms are designed for high dimensional data where it is expected that various dimensions of data are correlated. Perhaps the study in [20] is a very good example confirming this argument. Thus, matrix representation of packing policies prepares a suitable ground for analytic algorithms with an expectation of existing relations between various dimensions of data. The fact that the first dimension of a policy matrix is dedicated to remaining bin capacities and the second to item sizes fits very well to the factorization algorithm. This is something which couldn't be achieved if the policies were vectorized (as in [4]). Therefore, the representation matters and it has a great contribution to the performance of GA+TA. However, apart from representation, the strength of tensor analytic approaches has also a great impact on the performance. In previous study [3] introduced the use of these approaches in heuristic research for the first time. The impressive results achieved in this study confirms this and is encouragement for further research in transferring tensor analytic approaches to the field of (meta)heuristic optimization.

7. CONCLUSION

In this study, a powerful data mining tool, namely, tensor analysis is integrated into a GA framework [24] for solving an online bin packing problem. Online bin packing policies with matrix representation enables construction of a 3rd-order tensor as the high quality candidate solutions vary from one generation to another under the genetic operators in GA. This construction process is repeated periodically throughout the evolutionary process. At the end of each period, the obtained tensor is factorized into its basic factors. Then those basic factors are used to identify recurring gene patterns identifying the frequency with which genes are modified in high quality solutions. This information is directly used to set the mutation probability for each gene, accordingly. The empirical results show that the proposed tensor analysis approach is capable of adaptation at the gene level during the evolutionary process yielding a successful locus based mutation operator. The tensor analysis embedded into GA significantly improves the performance of the generic GA with standard mutation on almost all online bin packing instance classes used during the experiments.

8. REFERENCES

[1] E. Acar, D. Dunlavy, and T. Kolda. Link prediction on evolving data using matrix and tensor factorizations. In *IEEE International Conference on Data Mining Workshops, 2009. ICDMW '09.*, pages 262–269, Dec 2009.

[2] A. Anandkumar, R. Ge, D. Hsu, S. M. Kakade, and M. Telgarsky. Tensor decompositions for learning latent variable models. *CoRR*, abs/1210.7559, 2012.

[3] S. Asta and E. Özcan. A tensor-based selection hyper-heuristic for cross-domain heuristic search. *Information Sciences*, 299(0):412 – 432, 2015.

[4] S. Asta, E. Özcan, and A. J. Parkes. Dimension reduction in the search for online bin packing policies. In *Proceedings of the 15th Annual Conference Companion on Genetic and Evolutionary Computation*, GECCO '13 Companion, pages 65–66, New York, NY, USA, 2013. ACM.

[5] S. Asta, E. Özcan, A. J. Parkes, and A. S. Etaner-Uyar. Generalizing hyper-heuristics via apprenticeship learning. In M. Middendorf and C. Blum, editors, *Evolutionary Computation in Combinatorial Optimization*, volume 7832 of *Lecture Notes in Computer Science*, pages 169–178. Springer Berlin Heidelberg, 2013.

[6] B. W. Bader, T. G. Kolda, et al. Matlab tensor toolbox version 2.5. Available online, January 2012.

[7] E. K. Burke, M. R. Hyde, G. Kendall, G. Ochoa, E. Özcan, and J. R. Woodward. Exploring hyper-heuristic methodologies with genetic programming. In J. Kacprzyk, L. C. Jain, C. L. Mumford, and L. C. Jain, editors, *Computational Intelligence*, volume 1 of *Intelligent Systems Reference Library*, pages 177–201. Springer Berlin Heidelberg, 2009.

[8] J. Carroll and J.-J. Chang. Analysis of individual differences in multidimensional scaling via an n-way generalization of âĂIJeckart-youngâĂİ decomposition. *Psychometrika*, 35(3):283–319, 1970.

[9] J. Chen, Y. Xie, and H. Chen. A population-based extremal optimization algorithm with knowledge-based mutation. In Y. Tan, Y. Shi, and C. Coello, editors, *Advances in Swarm Intelligence*, volume 8794 of *Lecture Notes in Computer Science*, pages 95–102. Springer International Publishing, 2014.

[10] E. G. Coffman Jr, G. Galambos, S. Martello, and D. Vigo. Bin packing approximation algorithms: Combinatorial analysis. In D.-Z. Du and P. Pardalos, editors, *Handbook of Combinatorial Optimization*, volume 1 of *Intelligent Systems Reference Library*, pages 151–207. Kluwer Academic Publishers, 1999.

[11] F. Divina and E. Marchiori. Knowledge-based evolutionary search for inductive concept learning. In Y. Jin, editor, *Knowledge Incorporation in Evolutionary Computation*, volume 167 of *Studies in Fuzziness and Soft Computing*, pages 237–253. Springer Berlin Heidelberg, 2005.

[12] D. M. Dunlavy, T. G. Kolda, and E. Acar. Temporal link prediction using matrix and tensor factorizations. *ACM Trans. Knowl. Discov. Data*, 5(2):10:1–10:27, Feb. 2011.

[13] E. Falkenauer. A hybrid grouping genetic algorithm for bin packing. *Journal of Heuristics*, 2:5–30, 1996.

[14] J. C. Gittins. Bandit processes and dynamic allocation indices. *Journal of the Royal Statistical Society. Series B (Methodological)*, 41(2):pp. 148–177, 1979.

[15] R. A. Harshman. Foundations of the PARAFAC procedure: Models and conditions for an" explanatory" multi-modal factor analysis. *UCLA Working Papers in Phonetics*, 16(1):84, 1970.

[16] R. A. Harshman. *PARAFAC: Methods of three-way factor analysis and multidimensional scaling according to the principle of proportional profiles.* PhD thesis, University of California, Los Angeles, CA, 1976.

[17] D. S. Johnson, A. Demers, J. D. Ullman, M. R. Garey, and R. L. Graham. Worst-case performance bounds

Table 1: **Performance comparison of the GA+TA, GA and BF algorithms for each UBP over 100 trials. The values *avg*, *min* and *max* indicate the mean, minimum and maximum bin fullness in persentages, respectively. The 'vs' column in middle highlights the results of the Wilcoxon sign rank test where > (<) means that GA+TA is significantly better (worse) than GA within a confidence interval of 95%. Similarly, ≥ shows that GA+TA performs slightly better than GA (with no statistical significance). The sign = refers to equal performance.**

Instance	GA+TA				GA			BF		
	avg	min	max	vs	avg	min	max	avg	min	max
UBP(6, 2, 3)	**99.99**	99.99	100	=	99.99	99.99	100	92.29	92.26	92.31
UBP(15, 5, 10)	**99.62**	99.28	99.88	≥	99.58	99.16	99.86	99.62	99.15	99.89
UBP(20, 5, 10)	**98.28**	98.19	98.34	>	97.89	97.68	98	91.55	91.45	91.62
UBP(30, 4, 20)	**99.53**	99.41	99.61	>	99.09	98.95	99.23	96.84	96.80	96.90
UBP(30, 4, 25)	**99.53**	99.23	99.7	>	98.39	98.06	98.57	98.38	98.31	98.46
UBP(40, 10, 20)	**96.27**	95.99	96.39	>	96.08	95.86	96.35	90.23	90.12	90.31
UBP(60, 15, 25)	99.47	99.14	99.77	<	**99.68**	99.1	99.91	92.55	92.43	92.66
UBP(75, 10, 50)	**98.53**	98.4	98.6	>	98.27	98.12	98.36	96.08	96.04	96.13
UBP(80, 10, 50)	**98.66**	98.58	98.72	>	98.07	97.98	98.13	96.39	96.32	96.44
UBP(150, 20, 100)	**98.22**	98.12	98.32	>	97.78	97.68	97.86	95.82	95.77	95.87

for simple one-dimensional packing algorithms. *SIAM Journal on Computing*, 3(4):299–325, 1974.

[18] T.-K. Kim and R. Cipolla. Canonical correlation analysis of video volume tensors for action categorization and detection. *IEEE Trans. Pattern Anal. Mach. Intell.*, 31(8):1415–1428, Aug. 2009.

[19] T. G. Kolda and B. W. Bader. Tensor decompositions and applications. *SIAM Rev.*, 51(3):455–500, Aug. 2009.

[20] B. Krausz and C. Bauckhage. Action recognition in videos using nonnegative tensor factorization. In *ICPR*, pages 1763–1766. IEEE, 2010.

[21] L. D. Lathauwer, B. D. Moor, and J. Vandewalle. A multilinear singular value decomposition. *SIAM J. Matrix Anal. Appl.*, 21(4):1253–1278, Mar. 2000.

[22] C. C. Lee and D. T. Lee. A simple on-line bin-packing algorithm. *Journal of the ACM*, 32(3):562–572, 1985.

[23] H. Maini, K. Mehrotra, C. K. Mohan, and S. Ranka. Knowledge-based nonuniform crossover. In *IEEE World Congress on Computational Intelligence*, volume 8-4, pages 22–27, Jun 1994.

[24] E. Özcan and A. J. Parkes. Policy matrix evolution for generation of heuristics. In *Proceedings of the 13th annual conference on Genetic and evolutionary computation*, GECCO '11, pages 2011–2018, New York, NY, USA, 2011. ACM.

[25] A. J. Parkes, E. Özcan, and M. R. Hyde. Matrix analysis of genetic programming mutation. In *Proceedings of the 15th European Conference on Genetic Programming*, EuroGP'12, pages 158–169, Berlin, Heidelberg, 2012. Springer-Verlag.

[26] A. Prakash, F. T. Chan, and S. Deshmukh. Fms scheduling with knowledge based genetic algorithm approach. *Expert Systems with Applications*, 38(4):3161 – 3171, 2011.

[27] W. T. Rhee and M. Talagrand. On line bin packing with items of random size. *Mathematics of Operations Research*, 18(2):pp. 438–445, 1993.

[28] M. B. Richey. Improved bounds for harmonic-based bin packing algorithms. *Discrete Applied Mathematics*, 34(1-3):203 – 227, 1991.

[29] P. Ross. Hyper-heuristics. In E. K. Burke and G. Kendall, editors, *Search Methodologies: Introductory Tutorials in Optimization and Decision Support Techniques*, chapter 17, pages 529–556. Springer, 2005.

[30] A. Scholl, R. Klein, and C. Jürgens. Bison: A fast hybrid procedure for exactly solving the one-dimensional bin packing problem. *Computers & Operations Research*, 24(7):627 – 645, 1997.

[31] A. Shashua and T. Hazan. Non-negative tensor factorization with applications to statistics and computer vision. In *ICML*, pages 792–799, 2005.

[32] L. R. Tucker. Some mathematical notes on three-mode factor analysis. *Psychometrika*, 31:279–311, 1966c.

[33] M. A. O. Vasilescu and D. Terzopoulos. Multilinear analysis of image ensembles: Tensorfaces. In A. Heyden, G. Sparr, M. Nielsen, and P. Johansen, editors, *ECCV (1)*, volume 2350 of *Lecture Notes in Computer Science*, pages 447–460. Springer, 2002.

[34] D. Wang, J. Zhou, K. He, C. Liu, and J. Xia. Using tucker decomposition to compress color images. In *2nd International Congress on Image and Signal Processing, 2009. CISP '09.*, pages 1–5, Oct 2009.

[35] G. Yan, G. Xie, Z. Chen, and K. Xie. Knowledge-based genetic algorithms. In G. Wang, T. Li, J. Grzymala-Busse, D. Miao, A. Skowron, and Y. Yao, editors, *Rough Sets and Knowledge Technology*, volume 5009 of *Lecture Notes in Computer Science*, pages 148–155. Springer Berlin Heidelberg, 2008.

[36] A. Yarimcam, S. Asta, E. Özcan, and A. J. Parkes. Heuristic generation via parameter tuning for online bin packing. In *Evolving and Autonomous Learning Systems (EALS), 2014 IEEE Symposium on*, pages 102–108, Dec 2014.

A Genetic Algorithm to Solve a Real 2-D Cutting Stock Problem with Setup Cost in the Paper Industry

Stéphane Bonnevay
ERIC, Université de Lyon
5 av. Pierre Mendès France
69676 Bron Cedex, France

Philippe Aubertin
AXOPEN
149 bd Stalingrad
69100 Villeurbanne, France

Gérald Gavin
ERIC, Université de Lyon
5 av. Pierre Mendès France
69676 Bron Cedex, France

stephane.bonnevay@univ-lyon1.fr

ABSTRACT

This paper deals with the Two-Dimensional Cutting Stock Problem with Setup Cost (2CSP-S). This problem is composed of three optimization sub-problems: a 2-D Bin Packing (2BP) problem (to place images on patterns), a Linear Programming (LP) problem (to find for each pattern the number of stock sheets to be printed) and a combinatorial problem (to find the number of each image on each pattern). In this article, we solve the 2CSP-S focusing on this third sub-problem. A genetic algorithm was developed to automatically find the proper number of each image on patterns. It is important to notice that our approach is not a new packing technique. This work was conducted for a paper industry company and experiments were realized on real and artificial datasets.

Keywords

Two-dimensional cutting stock problem, Setup cost, Combinatorial optimization, Genetic algorithms, Paper industry.

1. INTRODUCTION

The classical Cutting Stock Problem (CSP) deals with the problem of cutting stock materials (paper, steel, glass, etc.) in order to satisfy the customer demand while minimizing the trim loss [13, 4, 2, 19, 12]. The Bin Packing Problem, where a set of items must be grouped into bins, and the CSP belong to the same family of problems. In literature, several methods were developed in order to solve this couple of problems, including linear programming, heuristics, and meta-heuristics [2, 4, 5, 9, 13, 19, 12]. In CSP, a sufficient number of setups/patterns are used to solve the problem. In some real-world applications, optimizing the number of patterns is important because the manufacturing cost of one pattern can be expensive in regard to the cost of one stock sheet. The Pattern Minimization Problem (PMP) tries to minimize the number of different cutting patterns while satisfying the demand [1, 14]. The Cutting Stock Problem with Setup Cost (CSP-S) takes into account the cost of the setup and the cost of the stock sheet printed in order to minimize the total production cost [10, 15, 18]. Most of existing papers deal with one dimensional problems [8, 3, 6].

In this paper, we give a solution to the Two-Dimensional Cutting Stock Problem with Setup Cost (2CSP-S). In this problem, customer demands are the number of prints of several rectangular images. The goal consists of satisfying customer demands while minimizing the total production cost (stock sheet cost and setup cost) by automatically fixing: the number of patterns, the number of stock sheets to be printed for each pattern, the number and the position of each rectangular image on patterns. Here, we do not solve a 2-D bin cutting (or packing) problem (where the number of objects to be placed is known); in this work the number of objects (rectangular images) to be set on each pattern is unknown (only the demands are known). Our objective is to find the best number of each image on each pattern (and to find the optimal number of patterns). For this purpose, we developed a genetic algorithm combined with different other techniques and heuristics. 2BP and LP sub-problems of the 2CSP-S are solved by well-known algorithms. In our case, images could be rotated by 90°. This positioning consists in placing images without overlap. Positions of images have to satisfy the guillotine cut constraint meaning that the cutting must be a sequence of edge-to-edge cuts parallel to the edges of the pattern.

Section 2 presents the mathematical formulation of the 2CSP-S and sets out an example case as way of explanation. Our algorithm with all specific methods are detailed in Section 3. Results are presented in Section 4. This work was conducted for the Seripress[1] company, which is a paper industry company.

2. PROBLEM DEFINITION

2.1 Mathematical formulations

Let I be the set of n rectangular images. An image i is defined by its width w_i, its height h_i and its demand d_i (the number of prints of image i). Let J be the set of m patterns with the same size $H \times W$. The number m is unknown. Let p_{ji} be the number of image i in the pattern j. We note $p_j = (p_{j1}, \ldots, p_{jn})$. Let π_j be a placement (rectangle packing) of all the images of the pattern j (π_j includes

[1] http://www.seripress.com/

GECCO '15, July 11 - 16, 2015, Madrid, Spain

DOI: http://dx.doi.org/10.1145/2739480.2754660

exact position and rotation information). The set of possible positions is limited by the algorithm (see Section 3.2). Thereby, a pattern j could be defined as the couple (p_j, π_j). In the following of this paper, we shall only consider feasible couples (p_j, π_j) (i.e. with feasible placement). Let x_j be the number of stock sheets to be printed for the pattern j. The decision variables are: m, p_j, x_j and π_j $\forall j \in J$.

The main objective (fitness) is to minimize the total cost:

$$f(m, x_1, \ldots, x_m) = mC_{su} + C_{ss} \sum_{j \in J} x_j \qquad (1)$$

where C_{su} is the manufacturing cost of one setup, and C_{ss} is the printing cost of one stock sheet.

To satisfy the demand d_i requested for each image i, there are n constraints:

$$\sum_{j \in J} p_{ji} x_j \geq d_i \ \forall i \in I \qquad (2)$$

These n constraints and the objective function f (defined by Equation 1) define an integer linear program (where the decision variables are $x_{j \in J}$).

A solution of 2CSP-S is composed of a tuple $((p_1, \pi_1), \ldots, (p_m, \pi_m))$ and a tuple $(x_1, \ldots, x_m)$ which is the solution of the integer linear program defined above. Let S be the set of all possible solutions.

In order to take into account the overproduction in our model, we define r_i as the quantity of images i overproduced and $Over$P the total overproduction:

$$r_i = \sum_{j \in J} p_{ij} x_j - d_i \ \forall i \in I \text{ and } Over\mathsf{P} = \sum_{i \in I} r_i \qquad (3)$$

In our model, the main objective is the minimization of the fitness f (see Equation 1). But if two solutions s and s' of S have the same fitness f then the one which minimize $Over$P is chosen. Thereby, a method called *BestSolution*(s,s') is used to return the best solution between s and s'. This method combines f and $Over$P.

2.2 Example

In order to illustrate the 2CSP-S problem, a simple example is displayed with 4 customers demands given in Table 1. The pattern size is equal to 60×40.

Table 1: Width, height and demand of the 4 images.

Image	Height	Width	Demand
1	30	24	246
2	56	13	562
3	22	14	1000
4	23	9	3498
pattern	60	40	

The objective is to reduce the total material cost depending exclusively on C_{su} and C_{ss} (see Equation 1). Here, $C_{su} = 20\$$ and $C_{ss} = 1\$$. As an example, calculations have been performed with one pattern ($m = 1$) and with two patterns ($m = 2$). Results are displayed in Figures 1 and 2. In all the figures of this paper, a star (*) next to the image number indicates that the corresponding image was rotated 90°. As shown in Table 2, the best solution is got with two patterns (see Figure 2) even if the manufacturing cost of one setup is 20 times greater than the printing cost of one stock sheet.

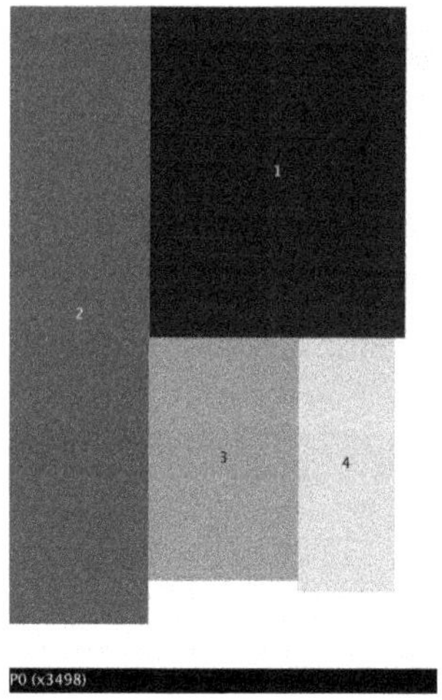

Figure 1: Solution with 1 pattern (3498 prints).

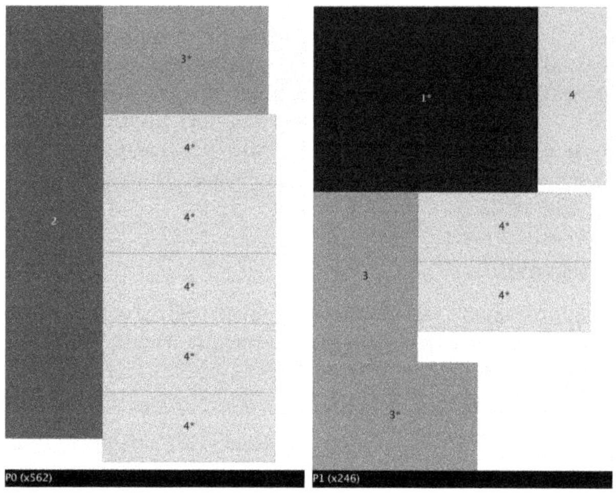

Figure 2: Solution with 2 patterns (246 + 562 = 808 prints).

Table 2: Costs of solutions of Figures 1 and 2

Nb patterns	Total cost
1	$1 \times 20\$ + 3498 \times 1\$ = 3518\$$
2	$2 \times 20\$ + 808 \times 1\$ = 848\$$

It is important to understand that the best result is not achieved by fully completing all the patterns. This means that we cannot use the blank area rate to define the quality of a solution or the quality of a pattern (unlike what is done in [5] to select parts of solutions in their genetic algorithm). According to the overproduction, with one pattern, the overproduction is very large: 3498 copies of the images 1, 2 and 3 are printed, instead of respectively, 246, 562 and 1000 copies. With two patterns, only 54 copies of the image 3 and 50 copies of the image 4 are overly printed.

2.3 Bounds

We first calculate a lower bound L_0 of the number of patterns:

$$L_0 = \left\lceil \frac{\sum_{i \in I} h_i w_i}{H \times W} \right\rceil \quad (4)$$

L_0 corresponds to the minimum number of patterns when positioning only one copy of every image with no unoccupied areas on the patterns. Thus, $m \geq L_0$.

We define the upper bound $L_{\max}(i)$ of the number of images i which can be placed on one pattern as:

$$L_{max}(i) = \left\lfloor \frac{H \times W}{h_i w_i} \right\rfloor \quad (5)$$

$L_{max}(i)$ is the theoretical maximum number of image i in one pattern. It is used to limit the process of adding an image in a pattern when building the neighborhood of a solution.

3. OUR ALGORITHM

2CSP-S is a combination of three optimization sub-problems:

i) a 2-D Bin Packing (2BP) problem which consists of finding the placement $(\pi_1, \ldots, \pi_m)$ of all images on the m patterns,

ii) a Linear Programming (LP) problem which consists of finding the number $(x_1, \ldots, x_m)$ of stock sheets to be printed for each pattern,

iii) a combinatorial problem which consists of finding the proper tuple $(p_1, \ldots, p_m)$ where $p_j = (p_{j1}, \ldots, p_{jn})$ and p_{ji} is the number of image i in the pattern j (and find the number of patterns m).

In this paper, we present our genetic algorithm used to solve the sub-problem iii): find the proper number of each image on each pattern. A well-known algorithm (see Section 3.2) and a classical linear programming solver were used to solve the sub-problems i) and ii). The following subsections detail each part of our genetic algorithm to solve the sub-problem iii).

One important constraint of this work is the limitation of the computation time. Indeed, this work was developed in order to be applied to a real-world problem in the paper industry. Therefore, in the following we always took into account this time constraint in our choices. By construction, our algorithm has a very small memory footprint.

3.1 Stock sheets prints

The fitness, $f(s)$, of a solution $s \in S$ is a combination of the total cost given by Equation 1 and overproduction quantities. In order to compute this fitness, the number of stock sheets to be printed $(x_1, \ldots, x_m)$ have to be computed. As explained in Section 2.1, $f(s)$ is the result of an integer programming problem. Indeed, given a tuple $(p_1, \ldots, p_m)$ which represents the numbers of all images in the m patterns (this tuple will be found by our genetic algorithm), the aim is to find $(x_1, \ldots, x_m)$ minimizing Equation 1 under constraints given by Equation 2.

As we must evaluate the fitness of each solution during our algorithm, it is crucial to optimize this phase. Thereby, the corresponding relaxation problem (real-LP) is solved and the solution $(x_1^*, \ldots, x_m^*)$ rounded to upper whole numbers $(\lceil x_1^* \rceil, \ldots, \lceil x_m^* \rceil)$ is returned. Thus, the number of stock sheets to be printed $x_j = \lceil x_j^* \rceil \; \forall j \in J$.

The method which calculates the number of stock sheets to be printed and the fitness of the solution s is called *ComputePrintsAndFitness*(s). The time complexity of this method is denoted by $cpaf(n, m)$.

3.2 2-D bin packing algorithm

In order to deal with only feasible solutions, a 2-D Bin Packing (2BP) algorithm has to be used to build the placement $(\pi_1, \ldots, \pi_k)$ on k patterns according to a list of images $(q_1, \ldots, q_n)$, where q_i is equal to the number of image i. There are several methods to make a 2BP from a list of images [11, 13]. In our case, we slightly adapted an existing algorithm, named *maximal rectangles best short side fit*, which satisfies the guillotine cut constraint and which is one of the best constructive algorithms of [11].

In the following, this method is called *2DBinPacking*(q), where $q = (q_1, \ldots, q_n)$ is a n-tuple of the total number q_i of each image i. The output is a list $(\pi_1, \ldots, \pi_k)$ of placements on k patterns. As, this algorithm is deterministic, a tuple $(q_1, \ldots, q_n)$ always corresponds to the same placement (and then, on the same number of patterns).

According to [11], the time complexity of this method is $O(n_q^2)$ (where $n_q = \sum_{i \in I} q_i$).

3.3 Neighborhood of a solution

To create some random initial solutions, to build the mutation operator or to improve a solution with an hill-climbing process, we define a neighborhood of any solution s by modifying the tuple $(p_1, \ldots, p_m)$.

Let $s \in S$ be a solution composed of a vector $(\pi_1, \ldots, \pi_m)$ according to a tuple $(p_1, \ldots, p_m)$, and a vector $(x_1, \ldots, x_m)$ which is the solution of the relaxed linear program (see Section 3.1). A neighbor of s is built from one of these four elementary operators: *add*, *remove*, *move* and *swap*. The operator *add* adds one image i in the pattern j involves incrementing p_{ij} if p_{ij} is less than $L_{max}(i)$. The operator *remove* consists of removing one image i from the pattern j involves decrementing p_{ij} if the total number of image i in the whole solution s remains strictly positive. The operator *move* moves one image from a pattern to another one, and the operator *swap* swaps two images from two different patterns.

A neighbor of a solution is generated by randomly selecting one elementary operator, and then by randomly selecting one (*add* and *remove*) or two (*move* and *swap*) patterns, and one (*add*, *remove* and *move*) or two (*swap*) images in these patterns. Of course, these elementary operators can lead to an unfeasible solution (unfeasible placement). So, the method *2DBinPacking*(p_j) (see Section 3.2) is applied on each modified pattern j in order to check the placement feasibility and to build π_j (if feasible).

Thereby, the method *ChooseNeighbor*(s) chooses a neighbor of s, checks the feasibility on each modified pattern and returns either the solution corresponding to this neighbor, or *null* if there is no feasible packing.

The time complexity of this method only depends on the *2DBinPacking* complexity.

3.4 Initial solution generator

To create the initial population, some feasible solutions have to be generated. The first step of our process is inspired by [10]. The objective is to place only one copy of each image i on k patterns. Thus, the method *2DBinPacking*$(q_1, \ldots, q_n)$ is run with $q_i = 1\ \forall i \in I$. The objective is to place only one copy of each image i in the solution. The method returns a feasible placement $(\pi_1, \ldots, \pi_k)$. An initial feasible solution s_0 is created from this placement. Then, from s_0, a random walk, *RandomWalk*(s_0), is performed: a solution s_1 is chosen in the neighborhood of s_0, a solution s_2 is chosen in the neighborhood of s_1, and so on, until a fixed iterations number `NbWalk`.

A method *CreateInitialPopulation*() returns a list of *NbPop* random initial solutions. The time complexity is $O(\texttt{NbPop} \times (\texttt{NbWalk} \times n_{max}^2 + cpaf(n, m)))$, where n_{max} is the total number of images in q during the random walk.

3.5 Main algorithm

Our algorithm, *GA-2CSP-S* (see Algorithm 1), combines all the previous methods: the *Crossover* and the *Mutation* operators (see Sections 3.6 and 3.7) in a classical genetic algorithm.

There are **NbGen** generations (loop line 5). The population at the kth generation is denoted by P_k. Each generation is composed of **NbPop** solutions.

Line 6, the *RouletteWheelReproduction*(P_{k-1}) method reproduces a population composed of **NbPop** solutions according to the classical fitness proportionate selection (roulette-wheel selection). Thus, it returns an intermediate population $P^\star_{k-1}$ selected from P_{k-1}. In order to create a new generation P_k, the **NbBest** best solutions of P_{k-1} are first reproduced (elitist strategy) in P_k (line 7). Then P_k is filled up to the full size by generating solutions either through our crossover method *Crossover*$(P^\star_{k-1})$ (line 10) or our mutation method *Mutation*$(P^\star_{k-1})$ (line 12). *Crossover* and *Mutation* operators are detailed in Sections 3.6 and 3.7. At each step, the best found solution is updated from the set of all generated solutions (line 15).

Algorithm 1 GA-2CSP-S

1: **function** GA-2CSP-S
2: BestKnown ← new Solution()
3: P_0 ← *CreateInitialPopulation*()
4: BestKnown ← *UpdateBestSolution*(P_0)
5: **for** $k \leftarrow 1$ **to** `NbGen` **do**
6: $P^\star_{k-1} \leftarrow$ *RouletteWheelReproduction*(P_{k-1})
7: $P_k \leftarrow$ *BestSolutionsReproduction*(**NbBest**,P_{k-1})
8: **for** $i \leftarrow$ `NbBest`+1 **to** `NbPop` **do**
9: **if** *Random*$(0,1) <$ `ProbaCross` **then**
10: **add** *Crossover*$(P^\star_{k-1})$ **to** P_k
11: **else**
12: **add** *Mutation*$(P^\star_{k-1})$ **to** P_k
13: **end if**
14: **end for**
15: BestKnown ← *UpdateBestSolution*(P_k)
16: **end for**
17: *HillClimbing*(BestKnown)
18: *DeleteOverproduction*(BestKnown)
19: **return** BestKnown
20: **end function**

At the end of this algorithm, a local improvement is applied on the best found solution with a hill-climbing process followed by an overproduction removal (line 18) from the population $P^\star_{k-1}$.

This *HillClimbing*(s) method locally improves a solution s. This algorithm searches the best neighbor s' of s; if s' is better than s, it repeats this search from s' and so on, until no further improvements can be found. Instead of building all the neighbors of the curent solution, we randomly generate a given number of neighbors in the neighborhood of the current solution and select the best one. This method is used in Algorithm 1 line 17 and in our crossover and mutation operators.

The *DeleteOverproduction*(s) method was developed in order to delete some overproduced images i of s (where $r_i > 0$, see Equation 3) which do not affect the computation of stock sheet prints (see Section 3.1). An image i can be deleted on a pattern j if $r_i \geq x_j$.

According to the complexities of *Crossover* and *Mutation* operators (see Sections 3.6 and 3.7), the time complexity of our main algorithm is equal to $O(\texttt{NbGen} \times \texttt{NbPop} \times (n_{max}^2 + cpaf(n, m)))$.

3.6 Crossover operator

The crossover method, *Crossover*(P) (described by Algorithm 2), builds a new offspring from two different parent solutions (lines 3-4). At first the offspring is initialized to empty (0 pattern). A subset of patterns is randomly selected in the first parent and another one in the second parent (lines 5-6). The number of patterns selected in each parent is a random number, it is a percentage of the parents' patterns numbers, taken in $[25\%, 50\%]$. These patterns are transferred in the offspring (line 7). As explained in Section 2.2, the choice of patterns in parents was realized as in [5] because the blank area rate can not be used as a quality of a pattern. Then, the offspring is completed with the help of the *2DBinPacking*(q) with $q_i = 1$ for all missing items i (line 8).

The total offspring's patterns number could be different from its parents, then a larger part of space solutions could be explored.

Algorithm 2 Crossover process

1: **function** CROSSOVER(P)
2: OffSpring ← new Solution()
3: Parent1 ← **choose** a solution $\in P$
4: Parent2 ← **choose** a different solution $\in P$
5: SetPattern1 ← **choose** some patterns $\in$ Parent1
6: SetPattern2 ← **choose** some patterns $\in$ Parent2
7: **add** SetPattern1 ∪ SetPattern2 **to** OffSpring
8: **complete** OffSpring **with** *2DBinPacking*(q)
▷ with $q_i = 1$ for all missing item i in OffSpring
9: *HillClimbing*(OffSpring)
10: **return** OffSpring
11: **end function**

The complexity of *Crossover*(P) is $O(n_q m + cpaf(n, m))$ (where $n_q = \sum_{i \in I} q_i$).

3.7 Mutation operator

The method *Mutation*(P) (see Algorithm 3) selects a parent at random in the population P (line 3) and applies a random walk from this parent (line 4) as done in Section 3.4 when generating initial solutions.

The complexity of *Mutation*(P) is $O(\texttt{NbWalk} \times n_{max}^2 + cpaf(n, m))$.

Algorithm 3 Mutation process

```
function MUTATION(P)
    Offspring ← new Solution()
    Parent ← choose a solution ∈ P
    Offspring ← RandomWalk(Parent)
    HillClimbing(Offspring)
    return Offspring
end function
```

4. EXPERIMENTS

A *Java* application was developed, using a Java Simplex Solver package to compute the number of stock sheets (x_1, $\dots, x_m$). Thereby, the complexity $O(cpaf(n, m))$ depends on this Simplex Solver package; this complexity is not in $O(n^2)$. Thus, the global time complexity depends primarily on $O(cpaf(n, m))$ and it is equal to $O(\texttt{NbGen} \times \texttt{NbPop} \times cpaf(n, m))$. Computations were run on a MacBook Pro 2.2GHz Intel Quad Core i7 16Go.

There are several existing modeling approaches to manipulate a solution like the graph-theoretical characterization [7], the binary tree [17] or the sequence pair [16]. Here, the *2DBinPacking(q)* method stores only the coordinates and the orientation of each image on each pattern.

4.1 Real-world datasets

The objective of this work was to deal with a real-world application. Every day the company gets a dataset composed of 40 to 50 images. The size of patterns is always equal to $88 \times 59\ cm^2$. The spacing between two side by side images must be equal to 1.6 cm. Thus, we added 0.8 cm to height and width of each image. The costs are $C_{su} = 20\$$ and $C_{ss} = 1\$$. An example of this kind of data, composed of 40 images, is displayed in Table 3.

Table 3: Example of a daily dataset of the company.

i	h_i	w_i	d_i	i	h_i	w_i	d_i
1	13.2	8.9	62	21	13.2	8.9	530
2	13.2	8.9	31	22	19.4	13.2	100
3	18.5	14.9	500	23	40.4	28.1	80
4	40.4	28.1	10	24	28.1	19.4	25
5	21.9	17.2	250	25	40.4	28.1	31
6	4.9	2.0	250	26	31.0	22.0	400
7	13.2	8.9	200	27	40.4	28.1	10
8	40.4	28.1	45	28	40.4	28.1	10
9	20.0	18.2	500	29	40.4	28.1	10
10	28.1	19.4	10	30	19.4	13.2	110
11	28.1	19.4	45	31	40.4	28.1	25
12	19.4	13.2	160	32	40.4	28.1	50
13	22.7	22.0	100	33	40.4	28.1	20
14	9.0	5.0	10	34	33.0	22.0	74
15	13.2	8.9	25	35	20.0	4.7	510
16	13.2	8.9	25	36	28.1	19.4	300
17	13.2	8.9	25	37	13.2	8.9	120
18	13.2	8.9	25	38	28.1	19.4	15
19	13.2	8.9	25	39	13.2	8.9	35
20	13.2	8.9	50	40	40.4	28.1	100
				pattern	88.0	59.0	

In the company, creation of patterns (choice and placement of images) is done daily by an employee by hand taking more than one hour. From the dataset of Table 3, the solution found by the company was composed of 5 patterns and required 815 stock sheets printed. The total cost is equal to 915$. From the same dataset, our algorithm took 505 seconds to automatically find a solution with 6 patterns but with only 493 stock sheets printed. In our case, the total cost is equal to 613$, which is a gain of 33.0% (see Figure 3).

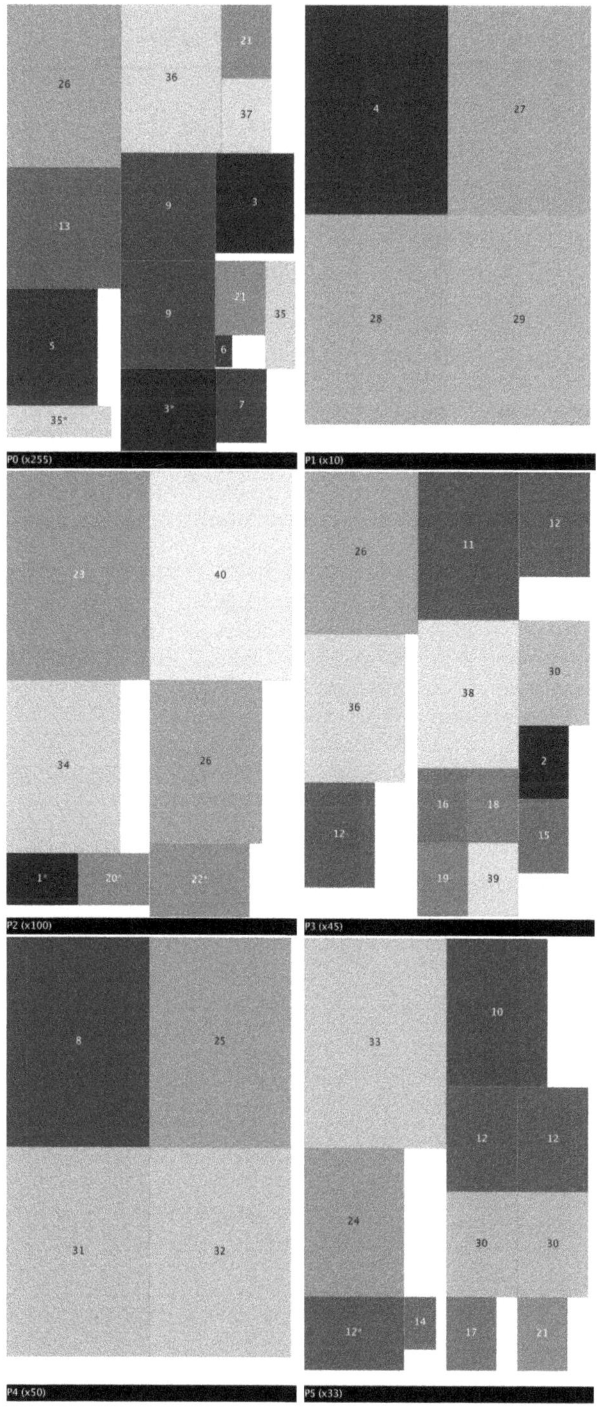

Figure 3: Best solution found by our algorithm from the dataset displayed in Table 3: 6 patterns and a total of 493 stock sheets printed (total cost: 613$).

Parameters for this calculation are: NbGen $= 30$, NbPop $=$ 60, NbBest $= 10$, ProbaCross $= 0.75$ and NbWalk $= 10000$. These parameters were obtained from some experimental tests. For example, these tests showed that a large population was better than a higher number of generations.

We tested our algorithm on 20 datasets of the company and our results were consistently better (in terms of costs) than those from its currently used method. In 100% of cases, these better results are obtained by reducing the number of stock sheets printed, and in 20% of cases by modifying the number of patterns. The mean gain of stock sheets printed was equal to 26.1%, and the mean percentage of cost improvement was equal to 22.2%.

Overall, the three main advantages are: the automatization of the process, the reduction of the manufacturing time and the global cost reduction.

4.2 Artificial datasets

The best evaluation of our algorithm was presented in the previous section on some real datasets of the Seripress company. However, it would be interesting to compare our algorithm to those already published in the literature. The difficulty is to perform a real comparison because most of other studies deal with some slightly different problems (in one-dimension, with a fixed orientation, with no guillotine constraint...). Moreover, papers dealing with a similar problem to ours do not compare their results to other algorithms. Indeed, in these papers, a kind of "best" solution is either a lower bound, which is not relevant in 2CSP-S problem, or a solution calculated by their own algorithm during a very long time (2, 3 or 4 hours of calculations). According to this "best" solution, authors calculate the gap between this solution and solutions given by their algorithm. Thus, no comparison could be performed.

However, we uploaded some datasets created by [10] and we tested our algorithm on these datasets. These datasets are composed of four different numbers of images (20, 30, 40 and 50 images), three different types of demands (type S randomly taken from $[1, 25]$, type L taken from $[100, 200]$ and type V taken from either $[1, 25]$ or $[100, 200]$) and two different pattern size (α for 1400×700 and δ for 2800×1400).

Table 4: Dataset 30Sα created by [10].

i	h_i	w_i	d_i	i	h_i	w_i	d_i
1	894	417	25	16	344	318	7
2	763	433	13	17	385	263	8
3	624	430	19	18	260	380	17
4	949	262	2	19	778	118	3
5	778	318	22	20	663	126	5
6	593	415	23	21	158	489	1
7	960	256	7	22	810	83	20
8	907	248	17	23	248	229	5
9	462	468	4	24	259	179	6
10	873	234	15	25	233	177	1
11	595	333	16	26	143	281	10
12	673	246	23	27	384	87	15
13	844	185	12	28	165	173	11
14	894	174	23	29	162	175	24
15	422	323	24	30	208	98	24
				pattern	1400	700	

Figure 4 displays a solution given by our algorithm from the dataset named 30Sα (see Table 4), with the same parameters as the previous ones.

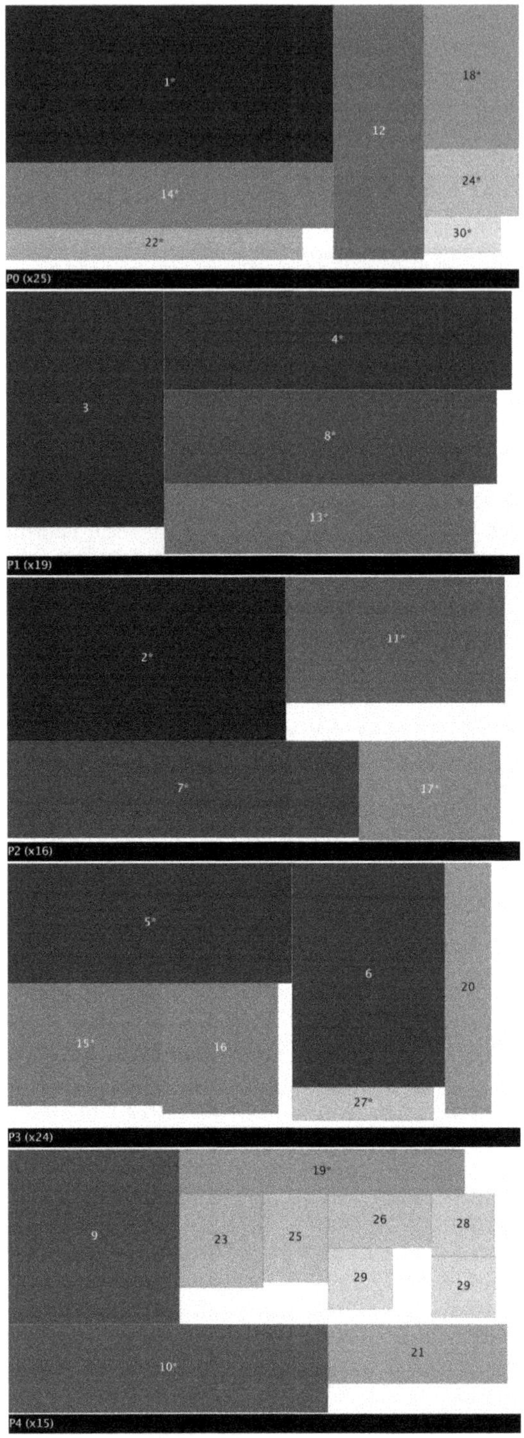

Figure 4: Best solution found by our algorithm from the dataset 30Sα: 5 patterns and a total of 99 stock sheets printed (total cost: 199$).

The averages of running time are summarized in the left side of Table 5. We applied our algorithm 10 times to each dataset. For each dataset, the theoretical lower bound L_0, the average number of patterns (column m), the average number of stock sheets printed (column prints), the average total cost (column cost) and the average CPU time in seconds (column time) are displayed. As in the previous subsection, the manufacturing cost of one setup C_{ss} is equal to 1$ and the printing cost of one stock sheet C_{su} is equal to 20$. The best solutions found from these 10 runs on each dataset are displayed in right side of Table 5.

We can logically observe that as the number of images increases (from 20 to 50), m becomes larger and the computational time increases.

For datasets with small demands (type S) the total numbers of stock sheets printed are small in regard to the setup cost of one pattern ($C_{su} = 20\$$), thus adding a pattern penalizes the total cost of solutions. That is the reason why solutions are composed of a small number of patterns. The gap between the setup cost of one pattern ($C_{su} = 20\$$) increases with the total demand of datasets of type V and L. The more demands there are, the more the addition of a pattern influences the best solution (see Figure 2). For datasets with a large pattern size (type δ) the number of patterns is logically smaller than for datasets with a smaller pattern size (type α). Even if the number of patterns is lower, the running time is greater because the number of images on patterns of type δ is much larger than the number of images in the small patterns (type α).

The average values (m, prints, cost and time) are always close to those of the best solution; thus, even if it is a non-deterministic process, our algorithm is fairly stable.

As explained at the begin of this section, it is difficult to compare our results to existing ones. It is all the more so difficult as the results depend on the prices of the manufacturing cost of one setup C_{ss} and the printing cost of one stock sheet C_{su}. Figure 5 displays the influence of prices on the average number of patterns computes from 10 runs on the dataset 30Vα (the price of the printing cost of one stock sheet C_{su} is constant and equal to 1$). It shows that the number of patterns of the best found solution decreases (from 9.2 to 7.2) when the price of the manufacturing cost of one setup increases (from 1$ to 25$). A decrease of m is observed with all the datasets of this study.

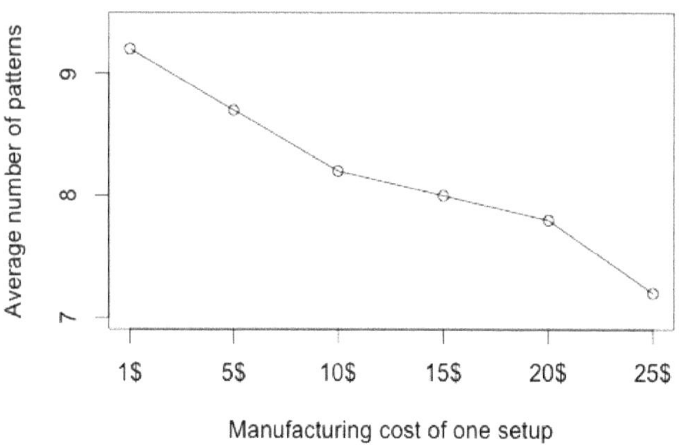

Figure 5: The influence of the manufacturing cost of one setup (C_{ss}) on the average number of patterns. These average numbers are obtained from 10 runs on the dataset 30Vα (C_{ss} is constant and equal to 1$).

5. CONCLUSION

We developed a genetic algorithm, combined with several other techniques and heuristics, especially designed to deal with the Two-Dimensional Cutting Stock Problem with Setup Cost. Our algorithm was applied to real-world applications in paper industry. The obtained results are very significant and very useful for the company. They improve the manufacturing time (solutions are automatically built in few minutes) and the global cost. Moreover, it is an algorithm which is able to return a feasible solution at any time of the process.

Some additional work is currently in progress. These works attempt to improve the computation time and the quality of solutions. The use of some better 2-D Bin Packing algorithms should improve the placement process and thus improve the quality of the final solution, but it should increase the computation time too.

In the crossover process developed in [5], patterns (layers) are selected according to the filling rate. As the filling rate makes no sense in 2CSP-S, patterns are randomly selected in our *Crossover* operator. To overcome this, a new quality definition of a pattern or of a subset of patterns should be defined to improve our algorithm.

The Seripress company has some new colorimetric constraints: images with same color must be set side by side. We are going to adapt our algorithm to take into account these new constraints.

Finally, some parallelization processes could be added in the main algorithm. For example, initial solutions and offsprings could be generated in parallel in order to decrease the running time.

6. ACKNOWLEDGMENTS

We would like to acknowledge the Seripress company for this collaboration.

7. REFERENCES

[1] A. Aloisio, C. Arbib, and F. Marinelli. On lp relaxations for the pattern minimization problem. *Networks*, 57(3):247–253, 2011.

[2] G. Belov and G. Scheithauer. A branch-and-cut-and-price algorithm for one-dimensional stock cutting and two-dimensional two-stage cutting. *EJOR*, 171(1):85–106, 2006.

[3] G. Belov and G. Scheithauer. Setup and open-stacks minimization in one-dimensional stock cutting. *INFORMS Journal on Computing*, 19(1):27–35, 2007.

[4] H. Ben Amor and J. Valerio de Carvalho. Cutting stock problems. In G. Desaulniers, J. Desrosiers, and M. Solomon, editors, *Column Generation*, pages 131–161. Springer US, 2005.

[5] A. Bortfeldt. A genetic algorithm for the two-dimensional strip packing problem with rectangular pieces. *EJOR*, 172:814–837, 2006.

[6] Y. Cui, X. Zhao, Y. Yang, and P. Yu. A heuristic for the one-dimensional cutting stock problem with pattern reduction. *Proc. of the Institution of Mechanical Engineers*, 222(6):677–685, 2008.

[7] S. Fekete and J. Schepers. On more-dimensional packing i: Modeling, 2000.

[8] R. Haessler. One-dimensional cutting stock problems

Table 5: Results from artificial datasets given by [10].

Data	L_0	Average				Best		
		m	prints	cost	time	m	prints	cost
20Sα	4	4.0	63.0	143.0 $	53.4	4	63	143 $
30Sα	5	5.0	98.4	198.4 $	144.3	5	97	197 $
40Sα	7	7.4	117.6	265.6 $	216.6	7	116	256 $
50Sα	8	9.0	146.4	326.4 $	374.7	9	143	323 $
20Vα	4	5.4	402.0	510.0 $	132.2	5	405	505 $
30Vα	6	7.8	601.4	757.4 $	253.6	8	591	751 $
40Vα	8	10.0	495.0	695.0 $	504.3	10	491	691 $
50Vα	10	11.8	1110.4	1346.4 $	582.9	11	1081	1301 $
20Lα	3	4.2	541.6	625.6 $	161.7	4	528	608 $
30Lα	6	8.0	1252.0	1412.0 $	239.2	8	1252	1412 $
40Lα	7	8.4	1292.8	1460.8 $	221.6	9	1268	1448 $
50Lα	8	9.6	1536.0	1728.0 $	349.0	10	1514	1714 $
20Sδ	1	1.0	22.0	42.0 $	24.1	1	22	42 $
30Sδ	2	2.1	26.8	65.8 $	299.1	2	24	64 $
40Sδ	2	2.3	34.6	74.2 $	311.4	2	33	73 $
50Sδ	2	3.0	38.8	98.4 $	541.2	3	38	98 $
20Vδ	1	1.0	197.0	217.0 $	32.2	1	197	217 $
30Vδ	2	2.0	192.6	232.2 $	286.6	2	191	231 $
40Vδ	2	3.0	132.9	192.9 $	568.4	3	132	192 $
50Vδ	3	3.8	291.2	362.8 $	1046.6	4	284	364 $
20Lδ	1	1.0	179.0	199.0 $	37.7	1	179	199 $
30Lδ	2	2.4	264.0	314.2 $	407.9	3	257	317 $
40Lδ	2	2.5	342.0	382.2 $	399.3	3	322	382 $
50Lδ	2	3.0	396.7	456.0 $	789.1	3	395	455 $

and solution procedures. *Mathematical and Computer Modeling*, 16(1):1–8, 1992.

[9] E. Hopper and T. B.C.H. An empirical investigation of meta-heuristic and heuristic algorithms for a 2d packing problem. *EJOR*, 128:34–57, 2001.

[10] S. Imahori, M. Yagiura, S. Umetani, S. Adachi, and T. Ibaraki. Local search algorithms for the two-dimensional cutting stock problem with a given number of different patterns. In *Metaheuristics International Conference, Lyon (France)*, volume 35, pages 1–6, september 2003.

[11] J. Jylanki. A thousand ways to pack the bin - a practical approach to two-dimensional rectangle bin packing. research report, 2010.

[12] J. Kallrath, S. Rebennack, J. Kallrath, and R. Kusche. Solving real-world cutting stock-problems in the paper industry: Mathematical approaches, experience and challenges. *European Journal of Operational Research*, 238(1):374–389, 2014.

[13] A. Lodi, S. Martello, and D. Vigo. Heuristic and metaheuristic approaches for a class of two-dimensional bin packing problems. *INFORMS Journal on Computing*, 11(4):345–357, 1999.

[14] C. McDiarmid. Pattern minimisation in cutting stock problems. *Discrete Appl. Math.*, 98(1-2):121–130, 1999.

[15] A. Mobasher and A. Ekici. Solution approaches for the cutting stock problem with setup cost. *Computers and OR*, 40(1):225–235, 2013.

[16] H. Murata, K. Fujiyoshi, S. Nakatake, and Y. Kajitani. Vlsi module placement based on rectangle-packing by the sequence pair. *IEEE TRANS. ON CAD*, 15(12):1518–1524, 1996.

[17] B. Preas and W. van Cleemput. Placement algorithms for arbitrarily shaped blocks. In D. Hightower, editor, *DAC*, pages 474–480. ACM, 1979.

[18] F. Vanderbeck. Exact algorithm for minimizing the number of setups in the one-dimensional cutting stock problem. *Operations Research*, 45(5):915–926, 2000.

[19] G. Wäscher, H. Haussner, and H. Schumann. An improved typology of cutting and packing problems. *European Journal of Operational Research*, 183(3):1109–1130, 2007.

Money for Nothing: Speeding Up Evolutionary Algorithms Through Better Initialization

Axel de Perthuis de Laillevault
École Polytechnique
Univ. Paris-Saclay, France

Benjamin Doerr
École Polytechnique
Univ. Paris-Saclay, France

Carola Doerr
CNRS & Univ. Pierre et Marie Curie
Paris, France

ABSTRACT

That the initialization can have a significant impact on the performance of evolutionary algorithms (EAs) is a well known fact in the empirical evolutionary computation literature. Surprisingly, it has nevertheless received only little attention from the theoretical community.

We bridge this gap by providing a thorough runtime analysis for a simple *iterated random sampling* initialization. In the latter, instead of starting an EA with a random sample, it is started in the best of k search points that are taken from the search space uniformly at random. Implementing this strategy comes at almost no cost, neither in the actual coding work nor in terms of wall-clock time.

Taking the best of two random samples already decreases the $\Theta(n \log n)$ expected runtime of the (1+1) EA and Randomized Local Search on OneMax by an additive term of order $\sqrt{n}$. The optimal gain that one can achieve with iterated random sampling is an additive term of order $\sqrt{n \log n}$. This also determines the best possible mutation-based EA for OneMax, a question left open in [Sudholt, IEEE TEC 2013].

At the heart of our analysis is a very precise bound for the maximum of k independent Binomially distributed variables with success probability $1/2$.

Categories and Subject Descriptors

F.2.2 [**Theory of Computation**]: Analysis of Algorithms and Problem Complexity—*Nonnumerical Algorithms and Problems*

Keywords

Theory; Runtime Analysis; Random Restarts; Initialization

1. INTRODUCTION

A widely applied initialization technique in evolutionary computation is *random initialization.* An evolutionary algorithm (EA) using this method samples its first search point uniformly at random from the search space. Clearly, this method is useful only if no a priori or just little knowledge about the fitness landscape is available. Otherwise, one would start the search close to the known areas of attraction.

For many practical applications it has proven beneficial to generate not only one random search point at the beginning but to sample instead some k random search points and to take the best one of these as starting point of the main optimization routine. The simplest such approach takes the random samples independently and uniformly at random from the search space, an approach that we call *iterated random sampling* in the following. Iterated random sampling is a very easy to implement initialization that can reduce the runtime of an EA significantly.

Interestingly, for discrete search spaces the initialization phase of EAs has not been thoroughly looked at from a theoretical perspective. With this work we contribute such a mathematical investigation for iterated random sampling. More precisely, we analyze for the well-known OneMax function the expected number of function evaluations that one can save by equipping the random hill climber Randomized Local Search (RLS) or the (1+1) EA with this initialization technique. Our results show that one can gain an additive number of $\Theta(\sqrt{n \log n})$ function evaluations by investing $k = \sqrt{n}/\log n$ initial samples.

We recall that OneMax is defined by $\text{Om}(x) := \sum_{i=1}^{n} x_i$, $x \in \{0,1\}^n$, thus counting the number of ones in the bit string x. This function is easily optimized by the all-ones string. However, the optimization behavior of RLS is identical on all strictly monotone functions, our result for OneMax naturally extends to that class of functions, which has a rather complex structure that is not well understood to date (e.g., for the (1+1) EA, an algorithm which is very well studied for a large range of problems, its expected runtime on the class of strictly monotone functions is not known [5]). However, for the (1+1) EA, too, the result naturally extends to a more complex class of functions. Indeed, the (1+1) EA does not distinguish between the so-called generalized OneMax functions $\text{Om}_z(\cdot) : x \mapsto |\{i \in \{1,\ldots,n\} \mid x_i = z_i\}|$ (cf. Section 2 for a brief discussion of these functions) and the result for OneMax therefore applies to any function from that class.

From a technical perspective, we believe that our result is interesting for the evolutionary computation community for the following three reasons.

1. Our result determines the best possible mutation-based EA for OneMax, a question that has been repeatedly ad-

GECCO '15, July 11 - 15, 2015, Madrid, Spain

ISBN 978-1-4503-3472-3/15/07...$15.00

DOI: http://dx.doi.org/10.1145/2739480.2754760

dressed in the runtime analysis literature [3, 12, 14]. Sudholt [12, Theorem 12] proves that the best such EA is a version of the $(1+1)$ EA with standard bit mutation $1/n$ and k iterated random samples, for some k that he does not determine further than noting that it is of order at most $\sqrt{n}\log n$. Our analysis shows that the optimal k is between $\sqrt{n}/\log n$ and $\sqrt{n/\log n}$.

2. Our bound for RLS with iterated random sampling improves the best known upper bound for the unary unbiased black-box complexity of OneMax, a problem that is studied in the black-box complexity literature, which itself has recently attracted substantial attention in the theory of evolutionary computation. While we know by a result of Lehre and Witt [10] that this complexity is of order $\Theta(n\log n)$, we do not know to date the best unary unbiased algorithm for this function. Based on the results from this paper, we strongly suspect that this algorithm is a variant of RLS with iterated random sampling and fitness-dependent mutation steps, but proving that this is indeed the best one can do remains an open problem. Still our result reduces the size of the interval in which this unary unbiased black-box complexity of OneMax is located. For the reader who is unfamiliar with black-box complexity we briefly recall that, intuitively, the unary unbiased black-box complexity of a function f is the expected number of function evaluations that a best possible purely mutation-based black-box algorithm can exhibit on f. This algorithm does not necessarily have to be "evolutionary". We refer the interested reader to [10] for a more extensive description.

3. We give a very precise estimate for the maximum of k independently sampled binomially distributed variables with success probability $1/2$ (Theorem 3). We believe that the techniques used here, albeit not new (but not or at least not intensively used in the runtime analysis community) are very useful for a precise runtime analysis of other functions, a problem that is gaining importance in the recent literature [4, 7, 9, 12, 14].

In his work [12] Sudholt claims that "As a word of caution, we remark that it is clearly not worth optimizing for k in practice as the differences in the expected running time only concern additive terms of small orders." Naturally, we disagree with this view. In practical applications, saving runtime can be very important, even if it concerns only lower order terms. In particular when this comes at almost no extra cost there is no reason not to use iterated random sampling. Note that for optimizing OneMax with RLS or the $(1+1)$ EA sampling just two random initial search points instead of one saves already $\Theta(\sqrt{n})$ function evaluations in expectation at the negligible cost of sampling and evaluating one more random search point.

We recall that our main result shows that we can reduce the expected runtime of RLS and the $(1+1)$ EA by starting them in the best of k independently sampled search points. One may wonder if we cannot do even better if we smartly design the initial search points instead of just sampling them independently and uniformly at random. We address this question in Section 6. Interestingly, we can show that this is not the case. More precisely, regardless of how we choose the $k=\omega(1)$ initial search points, the best one of them has OneMax value at most $n/2+O(\sqrt{n\log k})$ with high probability. Here, of course, we regard the OneMax value with respect to an arbitrary OneMax function OM_z and not with respect to the classic OneMax function $\mathrm{OM}_{(1,\ldots,1)}$ (which is a trivial problem anyway). The claimed bound is much more precise in the actual statement (cf. Theorem 8) and shows that for $k=\omega(1)\cap o(\sqrt{n})$ random initial search points are essentially best possible.

While the technical details of our analysis as well as the statements of the main results (Theorems 1 and 2) are rather tedious, we illustrate the expected gain from iterated random sampling in a series of figures, cf. Section 4. We also provide in that section, for n varying between 2^5 and 2^{20}, the optimal values k^* of random initial samples and the resulting expected gain in terms of function evaluations.

2. ALGORITHMS WITH ITERATED RANDOM SAMPLING

We regard in this work RLS (Algorithm 1) and the $(1+1)$ EA (Algorithm 2) with iterated random sampling. Our presentation focuses on the maximization of pseudo-Boolean functions $f:\{0,1\}^n\to\mathbb{R}$, though the concept of iterated random resampling is easily extensible to other search spaces.

The initialization phase **BestOf**(k) (cf. Algorithm 3) for both algorithms is identical. In the version with k random initial samples, k bit strings are taken from the search space independently and uniformly at random. The best one of these (ties broken uniformly at random) serves as the parent for the next generation. Both algorithms maintain a population size of one always. While RLS creates in each iteration a new search point y from the parent x by flipping in x a random bit, the $(1+1)$ EA applies to x so-called standard bit mutation, i.e., it creates y by flipping each bit in x independently with probability $1/n$. In the selection step of both algorithms the parent x is replaced by its offspring y if and only if $f(y)\geq f(x)$.

For convenience we abbreviate in the following by RLS_k ($(1+1)$ EA_k) the RLS ($(1+1)$ EA) variant with a **BestOf**(k) initialization.

As a side note we remark that these algorithms differ from a $(k+1)$ EA in that they can only store one search point at a time (i.e., they follow a $(1+1)$ scheme). This, together with the typically employed uniform or fitness-proportional selection for reproduction, can make a crucial difference. Indeed, the performance of a $(k+1)$ EA can substantially differ from that of a $(1+1)$ EA_k, see [13, Section 6] for an example function that the $(1+1)$ EA fails to optimize efficiently but that, for large enough k, is efficiently optimized by a $(k+1)$ EA.

We use the standard notation $[n]:=\{i\mid i\in\mathbb{N}, i\leq n\}$. All logarithms in this work are natural logarithms, i.e., logarithms to base $e:=\exp(1)$.

Algorithm 1: Randomized Local Search with iterated random sampling for maximizing $f:\{0,1\}^n\to\mathbb{R}$.

```
Initialization:
x ← BestOf(k);
Optimization:
for t = 1, 2, 3, ... do
    Choose j ∈ [n] uniformly at random;
    Set y ← x ⊕ e_j^n ; //mutation step
    if f(y) ≥ f(x) then x ← y ; //selection step
```

Algorithm 2: The (1+1) EA with iterated random sampling for maximizing $f\colon \{0,1\}^n \to \mathbb{R}$.

$x \leftarrow$ **BestOf**(k);
Optimization: for $t = 1, 2, 3, \ldots$ **do**
  Sample $y \in \{0,1\}^n$ by flipping each bit in x with probability $1/n$ and query $f(y)$; //mutation step
  if $f(y) \geq f(x)$ **then** $x \leftarrow y$; //selection step

Algorithm 3: The **BestOf**(k) initialization operator.

for $i = 1, 2, \ldots, k$ **do** Sample $x^{(i)} \in \{0,1\}^n$ uniformly at random;
Select $j \in [k]$ with $f(x^{(j)}) = \max\{f(x^{(i)}) \mid i \in [k]\}$ uniformly at random;
$x \leftarrow x^{(j)}$;

2.1 Known Runtime Bounds

As commented in the introduction RLS behaves identical on all strictly monotonic functions, i.e., on all functions f for which $f(y) > f(x)$ whenever $y_i \geq x_i$ for all $i \in [n]$ and $y_j > x_j$ for at least one index j. This is due to the fact that in every iteration RLS flips exactly one bit. It is well known that the runtime of RLS on any such strictly monotonic function is $\Theta(n \log n)$. This follows from the coupon collector's problem, a classic problem in the analysis of algorithms community, cf. [1]. Tight bounds for the runtime of RLS on such functions (up to a $\pm o(1)$ term) have recently been proven in [7]. More precisely, it is shown there that the runtime is $nH_{n/2} - 1/2 \pm o(1)$, where $H_{n/2}$ denotes the $(n/2)$th harmonic number when n is even, and $H_{n/2} := (1/2)H_{\lfloor n/2 \rfloor} + (1/2)H_{\lceil n/2 \rceil}$ when n is odd.

Note that the $(1+1)$ EA may flip more than one bit per iteration. Its optimization behavior therefore crucially depends on the exact combination of bits flipped (and, typically, on the state of all other bits as well). Results for OneMax do therefore not extend to the class of monotonic functions. In fact, it is not even known to date whether or not the asymptotic runtimes are of the same order, see [5] for a discussion. Multiple bit flips make analyzing the runtime of the $(1+1)$ EA much more difficult than analyzing local search algorithms such as RLS.

Still, results that hold for the (1+1) EA on OneMax hold also for every generalized OneMax function

$$\mathrm{OM}_z : \{0,1\}^n \to \{0,1,\ldots,n\}, x \mapsto \sum_{i=1}^{n} 1(x_i = z_i), \quad (1)$$

where $z \in \{0,1\}^n$ is the *target string* of OM_z and the binary indicator function $1(x_i = z_i)$ is one if and only if x_i equals z_i. Function OM_z therefore counts the number of positions in which x and z agree. The traditional OneMax function counting the number of ones is $\mathrm{OM}_{(1,\ldots,1)}$. It is easy to see that for all z the fitness landscape of OM_z is isomorphic to that of $\mathrm{OM}_{(1,\ldots,1)}$. This also explains that the optimization behavior of the (1+1) EA is identical on all generalized OneMax functions. Furthermore, the unique global optimum of OM_z is z, hence the name *target string.* For simplicity, we regard in the following mainly the classic OneMax function counting the ones in a bit string. All results extend to any other OM_z function in a trivial way.

For the $(1+1)$ EA, too, it is well known that its expected runtime on OneMax is of order $n \log n$. This result has first been proven in [11]. The known upper and lower bounds have been improved in a sequence of papers. The currently best known, and actually very tight, bound can be found in the preprint [9]. It states that the expected runtime of the $(1+1)$ EA on OneMax is $en \log n + c_1 n + \frac{1}{2} e \log(n) + c_2 + O(\log(n)/n)$ for some explicitly computable constants c_1 and c_2.

While the above mentioned bounds hold for the RLS and the $(1+1)$ EA without iterated random sampling, not much can be found in the evolutionary computation literature about the versions that we are interested in. Only Sudholt [12, Section 7] observes that the performance of the $(1+1)$ EA can be improved through iterated random sampling. He shows that for $k = \Theta(\log n)$ the $(1+1)$ EA with a **BestOf**(k) initialization is faster than the standard $(1+1)$ EA by an additive term of order $\sqrt{n}$. He also observes that the best trade-off between random initial samples and saved runtime bounds is achieved for some $1 < k = O(\sqrt{n} \log n)$.

3. OVERVIEW OVER MAIN RESULT

We aim at analyzing the trade-off between the number k of iterated random samples that **BestOf**(k) evaluates and the expected gain that this gives for the running times of RLS and the $(1+1)$ EA, respectively. Let $\Delta_{k,\mathrm{RLS}}$ ($\Delta_{k,(1+1)\ \mathrm{EA}}$) be total expected time that we save if we start RLS (the (1+1) EA) with the **BestOf**(k) search point. Then the **BestOf**(k) initialization saves in expectation $\Delta_{k,\mathrm{RLS}}$ ($\Delta_{k,(1+1)\ \mathrm{EA}}$) iterations at the cost of $k-1$ additional random samples. We therefore aim at maximizing the quantities $\Delta_{k,\mathrm{RLS}} - k + 1$ and $\Delta_{k,(1+1)\ \mathrm{EA}} - k + 1$, respectively. We state below the theorems for both algorithms. For reasons of space, however, we cannot describe the full proof details for both RLS and the $(1+1)$ EA. We therefore provide in this extended abstract the proof for the expected savings on RLS (see Section 5.2), while we defer the analysis for the (1+1) EA to the journal version. We will remark, however, where and how the analysis for the $(1+1)$ EA differs from that of RLS. Furthermore, we would like to note that the statement below is rather technical. We will explain all the details in the subsequent sections, and perhaps more importantly for those less interested in the mathematical details, we will illustrate our findings with the help of several numeric examples in Section 4.

Theorem 1. *Let $k = O(\sqrt{n})$ and let $\phi : \mathbb{R} \to \mathbb{R}, x \mapsto \frac{1}{\sqrt{\pi}} \int_{-\infty}^{x} e^{-t^2} \mathrm{d}t$ denote the cumulative distribution function (CDF) of the Normal distribution with mean zero and variance $1/2$. Then*

$$\Delta_{k,\mathrm{RLS}} = 2\sqrt{\frac{n}{2}} \int_{-\infty}^{+\infty} \phi(t) \left(1 - \phi(t)^{k-1}\right) \mathrm{d}t + O\left(k\sqrt{\log n}\right).$$

In particular, $\Delta_{k,\mathrm{RLS}}$ equals

$$2\sqrt{\frac{n}{2}\left(\log k - \frac{1}{2}\log\log k\right)} + O\left(k\sqrt{\log n} + \sqrt{\frac{n}{\log k}}\right).$$

Numerical approximations of the term $\int_{-\infty}^{+\infty} \phi(t) \left(1 - \phi(t)^{k-1}\right) \mathrm{d}t$ for $k = 2^i$, $i = 1, \ldots, 33$, are provided in Table 1. The claimed approximation of this integral can be found in Theorem 7.

The second statement of the theorem is in general less accurate than the first, but much easier to compute. For $k \in \Omega\left(\frac{\sqrt{n}}{\log n}\right)$, both statements are equally accurate. The term $2\sqrt{\frac{n}{2}}$ was not simplified to respect the analogy with Theorem 2.

THEOREM 2. *For k and ϕ as in Theorem 1*

$$\Delta_{k,(1+1)\text{ EA}} = \eta\sqrt{\frac{n}{2}}\int_{-\infty}^{+\infty}\phi(t)\left(1-\phi(t)^{k-1}\right)\mathrm{d}t + O\left(k\sqrt{\log n}\right),$$

where $\eta \approx 2.969$ is an absolute constant.

In particular, $\Delta_{k,(1+1)\text{ EA}}$ equals

$$\eta\sqrt{\frac{n}{2}\left(\log k - \frac{1}{2}\log\log k\right)} + O\left(k\sqrt{\log n} + \sqrt{\frac{n}{\log k}}\right).$$

From Theorems 1 and 2 we see that the respective bounds on Δ_k differ only in the leading constant. In fact, this constant corresponds to the time that it takes on average to gain one fitness level, provided that the algorithms start in a search point of fitness $n/2$. That this value is two for RLS is easily seen, since the probability that a one-bit flip changes a zero into a one equals $1/2$ when the number of ones equals the number of zeros. For the (1 + 1) EA, one can show that the expected progress of one iteration starting in a search point of OneMax-value $n/2$ is approximately $0.337 = 1/2.969$.

3.1 Discussion of the Main Result For RLS

We will show in Theorem 3 that the expected fitness value of the search point returned by **BestOf**(k) is by an additive term of $\sqrt{\frac{n}{2}\left(\log k - \frac{1}{2}\log\log k + O(1)\right)}$ better than the expected fitness $n/2$ of a random search point. Intuitively, it is logical that the gain $\Delta_{k,\text{RLS}}$ should be the product of this expected fitness gain and the expected cost of going from one fitness level to the next. This is what the second statement in Theorem 1 shows.

From this second expression in Theorem 1 one can see that choosing $k = \sqrt{n}/\log n$ guarantees that $\Delta_k - k + 1$ is

$$\tfrac{c}{2}\sqrt{n(\log n - 3\log\log n)} + O(\sqrt{n}/\log n)$$
$$= \tfrac{c}{2}\sqrt{n\log n} + O\left(\frac{\sqrt{n}\log\log n}{\sqrt{\log n}}\right).$$

Unfortunately, we see that the error term in Theorem 1 is quite large. Indeed, it is larger than the cost of sampling k random bitstrings. This makes it difficult to estimate precisely the optimal value of k, i.e., the value which maximizes $\Delta_{k,\text{RLS}} - k + 1$. Still it is interesting to compute the optimal value of k assuming that there is no error term, i.e. assuming that $\Delta_k = c\sqrt{\frac{n}{2}\left(\log k - \frac{1}{2}\log\log k + \lambda\right)}$ exactly for some constant λ.[1] Using this equality we can differentiate $\Delta_k - k$ to find the optimal value of k, which we denote by k^*. This yields

$$k^* = \frac{c}{2}\sqrt{\frac{n}{\log n}}\left(1 + \frac{\log\log n + O(1)}{\log n}\right), \quad (2)$$

where the $O(1)$ term is a function of λ and c. For $c = 2$ (i.e., in particular, for RLS), this $O(1)$ term is experimentally between -0.3 and $+0.3$. For this k^* we get an expected gain in runtime of size

$$\Delta_{k^*} - k^* + 1 = \frac{c}{2}\sqrt{n\log n} + O(\sqrt{n}). \quad (3)$$

See Figures 2 and 3 for Graphs illustrating the accuracy of this estimation.

[1]Here again we replace the 2 preceding the $\sqrt{\frac{n}{2}\left(\log k - \frac{1}{2}\log\log k + O(1)\right)}$ term by c to get a result that is applicable also to other search heuristics, in particular the $(1+1)$ EA.

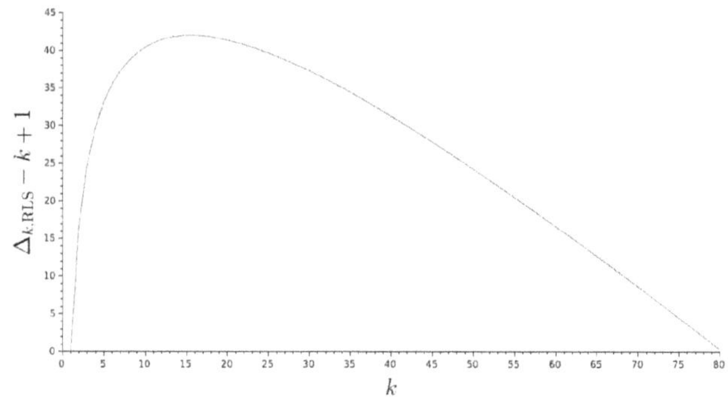

Figure 1: The expected gain of RLS_k over RLS_1 (in number of function evaluations) for $n = 1000$ and different values of k.

4. NUMERIC EXAMPLES

While for the runtime analysis community the analysis of Theorems 1 and 2 may be of independent interest, the practitioner certainly cares more about the absolute gains that can be achieved with iterated random sampling. We therefore provide in this section a few numeric examples helping us understand the rather complex terms of the main theorems.

We start with Figure 1 which plots for different values of k the expected runtime gain of the RLS_k on a strictly monotonic function of length $n = 1,000$. The graph nicely illustrates that the diminishing rate of return. More precisely, while for $k = 10$ we gain an expected number of approximately 40 function evaluations, this expected gain is only approximately 24 for $k = 50$. For $k > 80$ the expected gain is negative, that is, each additional random sample saves in expectation less than one fitness value.

We see from Figure 1 that for $n = 1,000$ the optimal number of random initial samples is around 16. After that number, the expected gain decreases. We use Table 2 to displays the optimal number $k*$ of initial random samples for RLS on OneMax with varying solution length. Table 2 also lists the resulting gains in the expected runtime of the RLS_k over the standard RLS. Figures 2 and 3 show that the estimations (2) and (3) from Section 3.1 are quite accurate.

Finally, we present one typical run of the **BestOf**(k) routine for $n = 100$. That is, we plot in Figure 4 the outcome of 100 independently sampled binomially distributed variables with success probability $1/2$ (these are the dots in

k	2^1	2^2	2^3	2^4	2^5	2^6	2^7	2^8	2^9	2^{10}	2^{11}
	0.3967507	0.7276378	1.0066125	1.2487419	1.4634766	1.6572698	1.8346574	1.9988942	2.1523646	2.2968522	2.4337195
k	2^{12}	2^{13}	2^{14}	2^{15}	2^{16}	2^{17}	2^{18}	2^{19}	2^{20}	2^{21}	2^{22}
	2.5640273	2.6886174	2.8081689	2.9232380	3.0342866	3.1417030	3.2458170	3.3469117	3.4452321	3.5409920	3.6343791
k	2^{23}	2^{24}	2^{25}	2^{26}	2^{27}	2^{28}	2^{29}	2^{30}	2^{31}	2^{32}	2^{33}
	3.7255593	3.8146802	3.9018738	3.9872584	4.0709409	4.1530181	4.2335780	4.3127008	4.3904599	4.4669230	4.5421517

Table 1: Numerical approximations of $\int_{-\infty}^{+\infty} \phi(t)\left(1-\phi(t)^{k-1}\right) dt$ for k varying from 2^1 to 2^{33}.

n	2^5	2^6	2^7	2^8	2^9	2^{10}	2^{11}	2^{12}	2^{13}	2^{14}	2^{15}	2^{16}	2^{17}	2^{18}	2^{19}	2^{20}
$k*$	4	5	7	9	12	16	21	28	38	51	69	93	127	173	237	325
$\Delta_{k^*} - k^* + 1$	3.0	5.7	9.9	16.5	26.9	42.7	66.9	104	159	241	364	546	815	1212	1796	2653

Table 2: Optimal value of $\Delta_k - k + 1$ for n varying from 2^5 to 2^{20}.

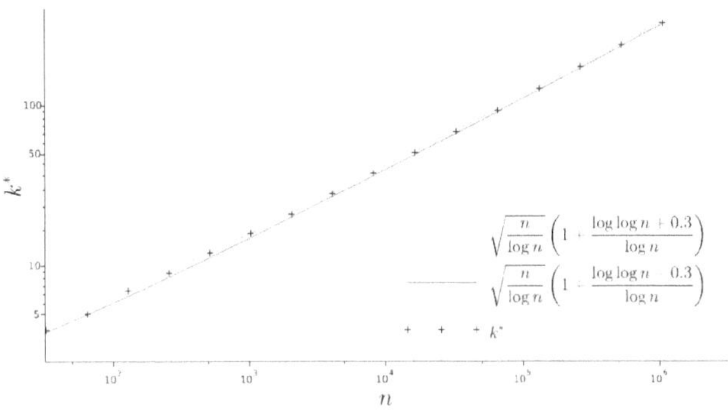

Figure 2: Comparison of k^* with the bounds from our estimation (2) for different sizes of n.

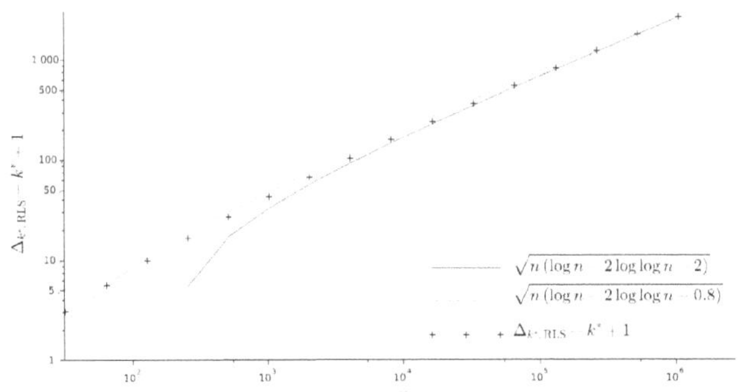

Figure 3: Comparison of $\Delta_{k^*,\mathrm{RLS}} - k^* + 1$ with the bounds from estimation (3) for different sizes of n. The upper line plots $\sqrt{n(\log n - 2\log\log n - 0.8)}$, while the lower line plots $\sqrt{n(\log n - 2\log\log n - 2)}$.

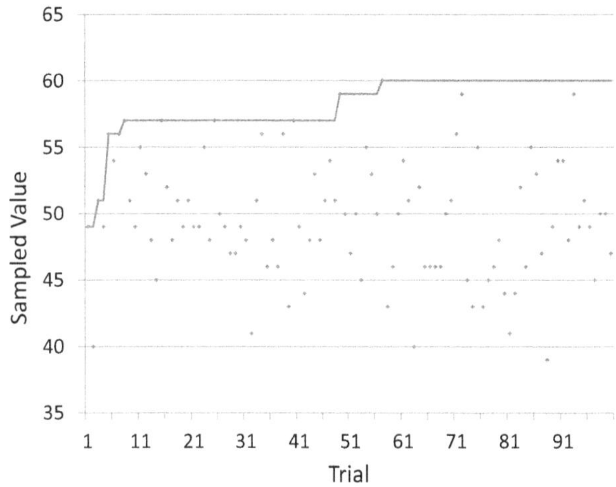

Figure 4: The dots represent the values of 100 independent Binomially distributed variables with 100 trials and success probability 1/2 each. The solid line at value k displays the maximum of the first k values.

Figure 4). The line represents the maximum of the sampled values, and thus the ONEMAX-value of the individual that the **BestOf(k)** initialization would return if it had sampled search points according to the plotted points in that graph. E.g., for $k = 20$ it would have returned a value of 57. This figure illustrates that in the beginning we typically gain quite a bit from resampling while we have to wait the longer the more samples we already have.

5. PROOF OF THEOREM 1

As mentioned above we present the proof of Theorem 1 and point out differences to the proof of Theorem 2. As a preliminary step, we analyze the maximum of k independent binomially distributed variables.

5.1 Bounding the Starting Fitness

Intuitively, to bound the runtime of RLS_k on ONEMAX we need to know the fitness value of the starting point returned by the **BestOf**(k) initialization routine. Since the k samples of the **BestOf**(k) routine are sampled independently, and since the OneMax fitness value of a random search point follows a binomial distribution with n trials (corresponding to the n positions) and success probability $1/2$ (corresponding to the fact that in a uniform search point each bit position is one with probability exactly $1/2$), analyzing the fitness of the starting point corresponds to analyzing the maximum of k independent binomially distributed variables. Our analysis presented below hence addresses also a classic problem in the theory of computation literature.

We provide in this section an analysis of the expected fitness value of the starting search point. This will give us insights needed in the later runtime analysis of RLS_k. However, as a word of caution, we recall that the expected runtime $\text{E}[T(\text{RLS}_k)]$ of RLS_k on OneMax is

$$\sum_{i=0}^{n} \text{E}[T(\text{RLS}_k) \mid f_k = i] \Pr[f_k = i], \tag{4}$$

where f_k denotes the fitness of the starting point returned by the **BestOf**(k) routine. Hence, to bound this runtime, we need not only analyze the *expected* value f_k of the starting point, but also its distribution. Still we will gain from this section a first intuition of how to analyze the distribution f_k and we can also describe the main intuition for the proof of Theorem 1. Furthermore, the rate with which RLS progresses in the range where most random samples are found is more or less constant. Therefore if we manage to calculate the difference between the fitness of a random sample, f_1 and that of the best of k samples, f_k, the gain obtained by starting in the output of the **BestOf**(k) is approximately $c(f_k - f_1)$ for some suitably chosen constant c.

The main result of this section is the following.

Theorem 3. *Let $n \in \mathbb{N}$, $k \in \omega(1) \cap o(\sqrt{n})$. Let $X_1, \dots, X_k$ be independently sampled from the Binomial distribution $\text{Bin}(n, 1/2)$ with n trials and success probability $1/2$. Let X be the maximum of $X_1, \dots, X_k$.*

With high probability (i.e., with probability $1 - o(1)$), X is between

$$i_- = \frac{n-1}{2} + \sqrt{\frac{n}{2}}\sqrt{\log k - \frac{1}{2}\log\log k - c_k}$$

and

$$i_+ = \frac{n-1}{2} + \sqrt{\frac{n}{2}}\sqrt{\log k - \frac{1}{2}\log\log k + c_k},$$

where c_k is an arbitrary sequence that tends to infinity.

To prove Theorem 3 we make use of the well-known approximation of Binomially distributed variables by the Normal distribution, which is often called *Gaussian* distribution. The Berry-Essen theorem bounds the difference of these two distributions. We recall from Theorem 1 that ϕ denotes the CDF of the Normal distribution with mean zero and variance $1/2$. An important theorem bounding the error of this approximation is the following theorem, which was proven independently by Berry [2] and Esseen [8] in 1941 and 1942, respectively. Note here that a binomially distributed variable $X = \text{Bin}(n, p)$ can be decomposed into the sum of n independent Bernoulli variables $\text{Ber}(p)$.

Theorem 4. *[2, 8] Let $n \in \mathbb{N}$. Let $X_1, \dots, X_n$ be n independently identically distributed (i.i.d.) random variables of mean $E(X_1) = \mu$, variance $E(|X_1 - \mu|^2) = \sigma^2$ and third centralized moment $E(|X_1 - \mu|^3) = \rho^3$.*

Let

$$Y_n = \frac{1}{\sigma\sqrt{2n}}(X_1 + \ldots + X_n - n\mu)$$

and let F_n be the cumulative distribution function (CDF) of Y_n.

Then there exists a constant C such that for all $x \in \mathbb{R}$

$$|F_n(x) - \phi(x)| \le \frac{C\rho^3}{\sigma^3\sqrt{n}}.$$

The constant C has been refined over the years. For the sum of Bernoulli variables of parameter $1/2$—this is the case we are interested in in our applications—it is known that $\frac{C\rho^3}{\sigma^3} \le 1$.

We recall that the cumulative distribution function of the Binomial distribution $\text{Bin}(n,p)$ is given by $F(i) = \sum_{t=0}^{\lfloor i \rfloor}\binom{n}{t}/2^n$. Clearly we have $\Pr[\max(X_1, \dots, X_k) \le i] = \Pr[X_1, \dots, X_k \le i] = \Pr[X_1 \le i]^k = F(i)^k$. Though this is a nice-looking formula, it is not straightforward to bound the individual terms precisely. In the proof of Theorem 3 we shall estimate these expressions using Theorem 4 for values i that are close to the mean, and using Theorem 5 below for values that are far from the mean value. Here, by "close" and "far" we mean within, respectively outside, of an $\sqrt{n \log n}$ interval around the mean $n/2$. As for the Berry-Esseen theorem, the important fact is that it allows us to write

$$F(i) = (\phi(x_i) + \varepsilon(x_i))^k,$$

for some function ε satisfying $\sup_{x\in\mathbb{R}} |\varepsilon(x)| = O(1/\sqrt{n})$ and $x_i := \sqrt{\frac{2}{n}}\left(i + \frac{1}{2} - \frac{n}{2}\right)$. This is the approximation that we use in the proofs of Theorems 3, 1, and 2.

Theorem 5. *Let $n \in \mathbb{N}, k \in \mathbb{N}$. Let F be the CDF of $\text{Bin}(n, 1/2)$, the Binomial distribution with n trials and success probability $1/2$. Then,*

$$F(i) \le \exp\left(-\frac{2}{n}\left(i - \frac{n}{2}\right)^2\right),$$

and

$$1 - F(i)^k \le k \exp\left(-\frac{2}{n}\left(i - \frac{n}{2}\right)^2\right).$$

Furthermore, for $\alpha > 0$, $n_+ := \frac{n}{2} + \alpha\sqrt{\frac{n}{2}}$, and $n_- := \frac{n}{2} - \alpha\sqrt{\frac{n}{2}}$, it holds that

$$0 \le \sum_{i=n_+ + 1}^{n-1} 1 - F(i)^k \le k\sqrt{\frac{n}{2}}\frac{e^{-\alpha^2}}{2\alpha}$$

and

$$0 \le \sum_{i=0}^{n_- - 1} F(i) \le \sqrt{\frac{n}{2}}\frac{e^{-\alpha^2}}{2\alpha}.$$

This theorem can be proven by Hoeffding's inequality, which is sometimes called the additive version of Chernoff's bound, cf. [6].

Using the two approximations from Theorems 4 and 5 one can show Theorem 3. However, the proof remains quite technical, for which reason we do not give the full proof details here.

We remark that experimental results suggest that the bounds provided by Theorem 3 are, unfortunately, not as accurate as they could be. This possible inaccuracy causes us to choose $k = O(\sqrt{n})$ throughout this paper, though we strongly suspect that the statements in Theorem 1 and 2 hold for much more general (that is, larger) values of k as well.

5.2 Proof Details

To prove Theorem 1, we need to bound the terms in equation (4). As indicated above, this will be done by approximating the cumulative distribution function of the Binomial distribution by a Normal distribution. Useful tools in this analysis are Theorems 6 and 7 below.

Theorem 6 gives an approximation of the weighted sum $\sum_{i=0}^{n-1} F(i)\left(1 - F(i)^{k-1}\right) c_i$. In our applications of this theorem in the proofs of Theorem 1 and 2 the weights c_i correspond to the time that it takes to advance one fitness level, provided that you start in a search point of fitness i, while $F(i)\left(1 - F(i)^{k-1}\right)$ measures the difference of the probabilities that level i is visited, where the difference is with respect to the standard RLS vs. RLS_k with a **BestOf**(k) initialization.

THEOREM 6. *Let $n \in \mathbb{N}$, $k \in O(\sqrt{n})$, and let F be the CDF of* $\text{Bin}(n, 1/2)$. *Furthermore, let $(c_i)_{i=0}^{n-1}$ be a sequence of positive numbers satisfying the following conditions. (i) There exist positive constants p and K such that, for all $i \in [n]$, $c_i \le Kn^p$ and (ii) there exists a constant c such that, for $i = n/2 \pm \sqrt{\frac{p+1}{2} n \log n}$, $c_i = c\left(1 + O(\sqrt{\log(n)/n})\right)$.*

Then

$$\sum_{i=0}^{n-1} F(i)\left(1 - F(i)^{k-1}\right) c_i$$

$$= c\sqrt{\frac{n}{2}} \int_{-\infty}^{+\infty} \phi(t)\left(1 - \phi(t)^{k-1}\right) \mathrm{d}t + O\left(k\sqrt{\log n}\right).$$

The next theorem gives an evaluation of the integral of the first statement in Theorem 1.

THEOREM 7. *For $k \in \mathbb{N}$ the integral $\int_{-\infty}^{+\infty} \phi(t)\left(1 - \phi(t)^{k-1}\right) \mathrm{d}t$ equals*

$$\sqrt{\log k - \frac{1}{2} \log\log k + O\left(\frac{1}{\sqrt{\log k}}\right)}.$$

Note that the equality from Theorem 7 can be rewritten as

$$\int_{-\infty}^{+\infty} \phi(t)\left(1 - \phi(t)^{k-1}\right) \mathrm{d}t = \sqrt{\log k - \frac{1}{2} \log\log k + O(1)}.$$

Figure 5 shows that this $O(1)$-term is between -0.6 and -0.8 for k between two and 2^{33}.

PROOF OF THEOREM 1. We recall that RLS needs $\frac{n}{n-i}$ function evaluations on average to increase the fitness by one, provided that it is started in a search point of fitness i, $0 \le i \le n-1$. We can thus rewrite expression (4) to

$$\mathrm{E}[T(\text{RLS}_k)] = \mathrm{E}\left(\sum_{i=0}^{n-1} 1_{\{X \le i\}} \frac{n}{n-i}\right),$$

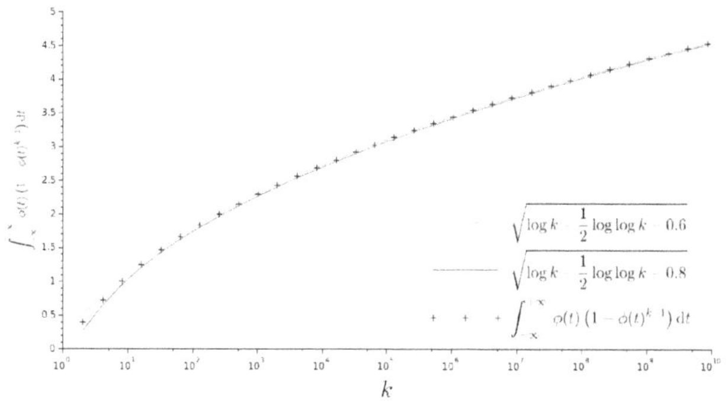

Figure 5: $\int_{-\infty}^{+\infty} \phi(t)\left(1 - \phi(t)^{k-1}\right) \mathrm{d}t$ for $k \in [2, 2^{33}]$.

where X is the number of ones of the search point returned by **BestOf**(k). By the linearity of expectation this can be written as

$$\sum_{i=0}^{n-1} \mathrm{E}\left(1_{\{X \le i\}}\right) \frac{n}{n-i} = \sum_{i=0}^{n-1} \Pr[X \le i] \frac{n}{n-i}.$$

As we have noted above, $\Pr[X \le i] = \Pr[X_1, \ldots, X_k \le i] = F(i)^k$, for F being the CDF of the binomial distribution with parameters n and $1/2$. Clearly, $F(i) = \sum_{t=0}^{\lfloor i \rfloor} \binom{n}{t}/2^n$.

This shows that we can write

$$\begin{aligned}\Delta_{k,\text{RLS}} &= \mathrm{E}[T(\text{RLS}_1)] - \mathrm{E}[T(\text{RLS}_k)] \\ &= \sum_{i=0}^{n-1} F(i) \frac{n}{n-i} - \sum_{i=0}^{n-1} F(i)^k \frac{n}{n-i} \\ &= \sum_{i=0}^{n-1} F(i)\left(1 - F(i)^{k-1}\right) \frac{n}{n-i}.\end{aligned}$$

Clearly we have $\frac{n}{n-i} \le n$ for all $0 \le i \le n-1$, while for $i = n/2 \pm \sqrt{n \log n}$ we also have $\frac{n}{n-i} = 2(1 \pm O(\sqrt{\log(n)/n}))$, so that, according to Theorem 6,

$$\Delta_{k,\text{RLS}} = 2\sqrt{\frac{n}{2}} \int_{-\infty}^{+\infty} \phi(t)\left(1 - \phi(t)^{k-1}\right) \mathrm{d}t + O\left(k\sqrt{\log n}\right).$$

Finally, Theorem 7 yields that $\Delta_{k,\text{RLS}}$ equals

$$2\sqrt{\frac{n}{2}}\sqrt{\log k - \frac{1}{2}\log\log k} + O\left(\sqrt{\frac{n}{\log k}}\right) + O\left(k\sqrt{\log n}\right).$$

□

6. OPTIMALITY OF RANDOM RESAMPLING

Now that we have seen that we can gain an additive number of $\Theta(\sqrt{n \log n})$ function evaluations by repeated random initialization, we may ask ourselves if a more clever way of choosing the initial search points cannot do even better. Interestingly, this is not possible, as we will show in this section.

We shall use here an assumption implicitly made in most analyses regarding the ONEMAX test function, namely that we are not interested in solely optimizing the particular function ONEMAX, but in algorithms that perform well on any generalized OneMax function (as defined in equation (1)). Otherwise, of course, there would be better initializations, including taking as first (and last) search point the all-ones string.

Theorem 8. *Let $k \in \mathbb{N}$. Let $x^{(1)}, \ldots, x^{(k)} \in \{0,1\}^n$ and $C > 0$. Then the ratio of $z \in \{0,1\}^n$ such that*

$$\max\{\mathrm{OM}_z(x^{(1)}), \ldots, \mathrm{OM}_z(x^{(k)})\} \geq \frac{n}{2} + C\sqrt{n \log k} \quad (5)$$

is at most k^{-2C^2+1}.

The theorem, for example, implies the following special case: Let $k = \omega(1)$ and $C = \frac{1+\varepsilon}{\sqrt{2}}$ for any $\varepsilon > 0$. Then any choice of $x^{(1)}, \ldots, x^{(k)} \in \{0,1\}^n$ as set of initial search points will for a $1 - o(1)$ fraction of the generalized OneMax functions not give a better initial fitness than $\frac{n}{2} + \sqrt{(1+\varepsilon)(n/2)\log k}$. Recall from Theorem 3 that $k \in \omega(1) \cap o(\sqrt{n})$ random initial search points for a $1 - o(1)$ fraction of the generalized OneMax functions do give an initial fitness of at least $\frac{n}{2} + \sqrt{(1-\varepsilon)(n/2)\log k}$, $\varepsilon > 0$ any constant. Hence in this range of k, essentially random initial search points give the best possible initial fitness.

Although Theorem 8 may come as a surprise, it is actually not difficult to prove. We replace the counting implicit in talking about the ratio by a probabilistic view and then a simple Chernoff and union bound give the answer.

Proof of Theorem 8. Let us call a $z \in \{0,1\}^n$ satisfying (5) *good*. Let $Z \subseteq \{0,1\}^n$ be the set of all good $z \in \{0,1\}^n$. Now the ratio $|Z|/|\{0,1\}^n| = 2^{-n}|Z|$ of good z is nothing more than the probability that a random $z \in \{0,1\}^n$ is good. We compute this probability and thus prove the theorem.

Let $z \in \{0,1\}^n$ be chosen uniform at random. This is equivalent to saying that each z_i is chosen independently and uniformly at random from $\{0,1\}$. For each $i \in [k]$, regardless of how $x^{(i)}$ is chosen, the additive Chernoff bound (see, e.g., [6, Theorem 1.11]) yields

$$\Pr[\mathrm{OM}_z(x^{(i)}) > \tfrac{n}{2} + C\sqrt{n \log k}] \leq \exp\left(-2C^2 \log k\right) = k^{-2C^2}.$$

Therefore, by a simple union bound, we have

$$\begin{aligned}
&\Pr[\max\{\mathrm{OM}_z(x^{(1)}), \ldots, \mathrm{OM}_z(x^{(k)})\} \geq \tfrac{n}{2} + C\sqrt{n \log k}] \\
&= \Pr[\exists i \in [k] : \mathrm{OM}_z(x^{(i)})\} \geq \tfrac{n}{2} + C\sqrt{n \log k}] \\
&\leq k \Pr[\mathrm{OM}_z(x^{(1)})\} \geq \tfrac{n}{2} + C\sqrt{n \log k}] \leq k^{-2C^2+1}.
\end{aligned}$$

□

7. CONCLUSIONS

We have shown that the expected optimization time of search heuristics can be reduced by a simple initialization routine which, instead of sampling just one search point, returns the best of k points that are sampled from the search space independently and uniformly at random. We have shown that for RLS and the $(1+1)$ EA on the generalized OneMax problem we gain an expected number of $\Theta(\sqrt{n}\log n)$ fitness evaluations for $k = O(\sqrt{n}/\log n)$. We have also seen that we can not do substantially better than this; not even if we allow ourselves to specifically design k search points for the OneMax problem.

Our result answers a problem left open in [12]. In addition, it is a first step towards a tight bound for the unary unbiased black-box complexity of OneMax.

While it would be interesting to study the resampling initialization for other, more complex, optimization problems, we remark that even for the simple OneMax function our analysis can possibly be tightened. In fact, as commented in the main part, we believe that the condition $k = O(\sqrt{n})$ is not needed. Removing this, however, seems to require an improved version of the Berry-Esseen theorem (Theorem 4).

8. REFERENCES

[1] A. Auger and B. Doerr. *Theory of Randomized Search Heuristics*. World Scientific, 2011.

[2] A. C. Berry. The accuracy of the gaussian approximation to the sum of independent variates. *Transactions of the American Mathematical Society*, 49:122–136, 1941.

[3] P. A. Borisovsky and A. V. Eremeev. Comparing evolutionary algorithms to the (1+1)-EA. *Theoretical Computer Science*, 403:33–41, 2008.

[4] S. Böttcher, B. Doerr, and F. Neumann. Optimal fixed and adaptive mutation rates for the LeadingOnes problem. In *Proc. PPSN'10*, pages 1–10. Springer, 2010.

[5] S. Colin, B. Doerr, and G. Férey. Monotonic functions in EC: anything but monotone! In *Proc. GECCO'14*, pages 753–760. ACM, 2014.

[6] B. Doerr. Analyzing randomized search heuristics: Tools from probability theory. In A. Auger and B. Doerr, editors, *Theory of Randomized Search Heuristics*, pages 1–20. World Scientific Publishing, 2011.

[7] B. Doerr and C. Doerr. The impact of random initialization on the runtime of randomized search heuristics. In *Proc. GECCO'14*, pages 1375–1382. ACM, 2014.

[8] C.-G. Esseen. On the liapunoff limit of error in the theory of probability. *Arkiv för matematik, astronomi och fysik*, A28:1–19, 1942.

[9] H. Hwang, A. Panholzer, N. Rolin, T. Tsai, and W. Chen. Probabilistic analysis of the (1+1)-evolutionary algorithm. *CoRR*, abs/1409.4955, 2014. Available online from http://arxiv.org/abs/1409.4955.

[10] P. K. Lehre and C. Witt. Black-box search by unbiased variation. *Algorithmica*, 64:623–642, 2012.

[11] H. Mühlenbein. How genetic algorithms really work: Mutation and hillclimbing. In *Proc. PPSN'92*, pages 15–26. Elsevier, 1992.

[12] D. Sudholt. A new method for lower bounds on the running time of evolutionary algorithms. *IEEE Transactions on Evolutionary Computation*, 17:418–435, 2013.

[13] C. Witt. Runtime analysis of the (mu + 1) EA on simple pseudo-boolean functions. *Evolutionary Computation*, 14:65–86, 2006.

[14] C. Witt. Tight bounds on the optimization time of a randomized search heuristic on linear functions. *Combinatorics, Probability & Computing*, 22:294–318, 2013.

A Genetic Algorithm for Searching the Shortest Lattice Vector of SVP Challenge*

[Extended Abstract]

Dan Ding
Dept. of Computer Sciences,
Tsinghua University
Beijing, China P. R.
dingd09@mails.tsinghua.edu.cn

Guizhen Zhu†
Communication Science and Technology Research Institute
Beijing, China P. R.
zhugz08@gmail.com

Xiaoyun Wang
Inst. for Advanced Study,
Tsinghua University
Beijing, China P. R.
xiaoyunwang@mail.tsinghua.edu.cn

ABSTRACT

In this paper, we propose a genetic algorithm for solving the shortest vector problem (SVP) based on sparse representation of short lattice vectors, which, we prove, can guarantee finding the shortest lattice vector under a Markov analysis. With some heuristic improvements (local search and heuristic pruning), the SVP genetic algorithm, by experimental results, outperforms other SVP algorithms, like the famous Kannan-Helfrich algorithm under SVP challenge benchmarks. In summary, we, for the first time, adopt the genetic algorithm in solving the shortest vector problem, based on which lattice-based cryptosystem is as a promising candidate for post-quantum cryptography.

Categories and Subject Descriptors

I.2.8 [**Artificial Intelligence**]: [Problem Solving, Control Methods, and Search]

Keywords

Shortest Vector Problem (SVP), Genetic Algorithms, Chromosome, Local Search, and Lattice-Based Cryptography

1. INTRODUCTION

A lattice $\mathcal{L}$ is a discrete additive subgroup of $\mathbb{R}^m$. It can be generated by integral combinations of n linear independent vectors $\mathbf{b}_1, \ldots, \mathbf{b}_n$ in $\mathbb{R}^m$, and the n vectors constitute the basis of the generated lattice. The discreteness of lattices implies that there exists a nonzero vector with the smallest non-zero Euclidean norm in each lattice, denoted as λ_1, and a lattice vector closest to a given target vector $\mathbf{t}$ in $\mathbb{R}^m$. Finding the two special lattice vectors leads to the two famous computational problems regarding lattices:

- Shortest Vector Problem (SVP): Given a lattice basis, find the shortest nonzero vector in the lattice;
- Closest Vector Problem (CVP): Given a lattice basis and a target vector, find the lattice vector closest to the target.

The CVP has been proved to be NP-complete by van Emde Boas [17] under Karp/Cook reduction in 1981 and refined by Micciancio and Goldwasser [9] in 2002. However, it was unknown whether the SVP is NP-hard until 1998 when Ajtai [1] proved the NP-hardness of SVP through randomized reduction. Although the hardness of factorization and discrete logarithm problems, on which most current public-key cryptosystems are based, collapses under the attacks of quantum computers[15], yet SVP and CVP are still hard against the quantum counterparts to classical computers. Since, as a promising candidate for post-quantum cryptography,, a variety of cryptosystems[10] based on SVP and CVP are proposed in the past two decades, the two problems SVP and CVP have been of prime importance to modern cryptography in recent years. Therefore, research into algorithms solving SVP and CVP becomes a hotspot for cryptology community nowadays.

During the last three decades, a number of algorithms aiming at solving the shortest (short) lattice vectors problems (SVP or SVP-variants) have been proposed, all of which are of the following two sorts in terms of the space complexity: algorithms with polynomial space complexity and those with exponential space complexity. The former includes basis reduction algorithms: the celebrated **LLL** algorithm [8] which can find a vector as short as $2^{O(n)}\lambda_1$ within time polynomial in the rank n, and Kannan-Helfrich's enumeration algorithm [6] which can find exactly the shortest vector within

*Supported by 973 Program (Grant No.2013CB834205) and National Natural Science Foundation of China (Grant No.61133013).

†Supported by the National Development Foundation for Cryptological Research (No.MMJJ201401003).

GECCO'15, July 11–15, 2015, Madrid, Spain.
© 2015 ACM. ISBN 978-1-4503-3472-3/15/07..
DOI: http://dx.doi.org/10.1145/2739480.2754639

$n^{O(n)}$ time complexity, and the blockwise Korkin-Zolotarev basis reduction[14] which can find a short vector subexponential to the shortest vector, within subexponential time complexity[5]. The second type of the algorithms include various sieve algorithms [2][12][18] which can find the shortest vector with high probability in $2^{O(n)}$ time complexity and $2^{O(n)}$ space complexity. Another SVP algorithm based on Voronoi cell computation [11] is able to find the shortest vector deterministically with exponential time $2^{2n+o(n)}$ and the space complexity $2^{n+o(n)}$.

In this paper, we devote to developing a new type of search algorithm based on the genetic algorithm, which works on the polynomial space complexity.

Our contributions in this paper are twofold. First, we discover sparse integer representations of the short vectors in lattices, which might be of independent interest to the existing SVP algorithms, and an appropriate way to encode lattice vectors into bit strings. Second, we propose a genetic algorithm for the shortest lattice vector problem based on the sparse representation of short vectors. A Markov chain analysis of the genetic algorithm assures that it converges to, precisely, the shortest vector with a negligible probability of failure. Furthermore, we also present some improvements of our algorithm by adopting some heuristic techniques: local search and heuristic pruning. Experimental results show that the improved algorithm behaves fairly well on the benchmarks of the SVP challenge[13], generating short vectors, most of which are better than the previous challenge results, of lattices of dimensions up to 118, and a comparison of running times implies that the genetic algorithm outperforms present-day enumeration algorithms, like the Kannan-Helfrich enumeration and the enumeration with conservative pruning. We have posted 25 results on the SVP challenge since Feb. 2013. In summary, for the first time, we propose an SVP genetic algorithm, and its heuristically-revised version gains advantages over previous challenges in quality of generated vectors, and over other practical algorithms in their running times.

2. PRELIMINARIES

The closed sphere in $\mathbb{R}^n$ is denoted as $\mathcal{B}_n(\mathbf{O}, r)$ with $\mathbf{O}$ as its origin and r its radius. We denote $\lfloor \cdot \rceil$ as the closest integer to a real number, and $\vdash$ as the concatenation of two bit string, and we denote $\|\cdot\|$ and $|\cdot|$ as the Euclidean norm of a vector and length of a bit string, respectively.

A *lattice* $\mathcal{L}$ is defined as the set of all integral combinations of n linear independent vectors $\mathbf{b}_1, \mathbf{b}_2, \ldots, \mathbf{b}_n \in \mathbb{R}^m (m \geq n)$, where the vectors are referred to as the *basis* of the lattice, and n as its *rank*. If $m = n$, the lattice is called *full-rank.* All the lattices we discuss throughout this paper are full-rank lattices unless specified otherwise.

Conveniently, if given a matrix $\mathbf{B} = [\mathbf{b}_1, \ldots, \mathbf{b}_n] \in \mathbb{R}^{n \times n}$ with the n linear independent vectors as its columns, the lattice $\mathcal{L}$ generated by the basis $\mathbf{B}$ is defined as

$$\mathcal{L}(\mathbf{B}) = \{\mathbf{Bx} | \mathbf{x} \in \mathbb{Z}^n\} = \{\mathbf{v} \in \mathbb{R}^n \; | \mathbf{v} = \sum_{i=1}^{n} \mathbf{b}_i x_i, x_i \in \mathbb{Z}\}.$$

A single lattice can be generated by a series of the basis, or, in other words, the basis of one lattice is not unique. The ith *successive minimum* $\lambda_i(\mathcal{L})$ (for $i = 1, \ldots, n$) of a lattice $\mathcal{L}$ implies the smallest radius of a sphere within which there are i linearly independent lattice points, i.e.,

$$\lambda_i(\mathcal{L}) = \inf\{r \in \mathbb{R}^n | \dim\{\text{span}(\mathcal{L} \cap \mathcal{B}_n(\mathbf{O}, r))\} = i\}.$$

For a basis $\mathbf{B} = [\mathbf{b}_1, \ldots, \mathbf{b}_n]$ of a lattice $\mathcal{L}(\mathbf{B}) \in \mathbb{R}^{n \times n}$, its *Gram-Schmidt Orthogonalization* $\mathbf{B}^* = [\mathbf{b}_1^*, \ldots, \mathbf{b}_n^*]$ is defined as,

$$\mathbf{b}_i^* = \mathbf{b}_i - \sum_{j=1}^{i-1} \mu_{ij} \mathbf{b}_j^*,$$

where

$$\mu_{ij} = \frac{\langle \mathbf{b}_i, \mathbf{b}_j^* \rangle}{\langle \mathbf{b}_j^*, \mathbf{b}_j^* \rangle}, \text{ for } 1 \leq j \leq i \leq n.$$

In other words, the Gram-Schmidt procedure projects $\mathbf{b}_i$ to the space orthogonal to the space spanned by $\mathbf{b}_1, \ldots, \mathbf{b}_{i-1}$, and keeps the determinant unchanged, i.e., $\det(\mathbf{B}) = \prod_{i=1}^n \|\mathbf{b}_i^*\|$. For more details about lattices, you can refer to [9].

If we fix all $\mu_{ij} = 0$ for $i > j$ (and it is clear that $\mu_{ii} = 1$ for $1 \leq i \leq n$), we can obtain its upper-triangular *factor matrix* $\mu = \{\mu_{ij}\}_{1 \leq i,j \leq n}$ by putting the factors μ_{ij} together.

Let $\mathbf{B} = [\mathbf{b}_1, \ldots, \mathbf{b}_n]$ be a basis of a lattice $\mathcal{L} \subset \mathbb{R}^n$. We define $\pi_i : \mathbb{R}^n \mapsto \text{span}(\mathbf{b}_1, \ldots, \mathbf{b}_{i-1})^\perp$ as the projection on the orthogonal complement of the span of the first $i-1$ bases of $\mathbf{B}$, for all $i \in \{1, 2, \ldots, n\}$. $\pi_i(\mathbf{b}_j)$ is expressed as

$$\pi_i(\mathbf{b}_j) = \mathbf{b}_j^* + \sum_{k=i}^{j-1} \mu_{jk} \mathbf{b}_k^*, \quad \text{if} \quad i < j.$$

In particular, $\pi_i(\mathbf{b}_i) = \mathbf{b}_i^*$ and $\pi_i(\mathbf{b}_j) = 0$ for $j < i$.

$\mathcal{L}_i^{(k)}$ is the lattice of rank k generated by the basis $[\pi_i(\mathbf{b}_i), \ldots, \pi_i(\mathbf{b}_{i+k-1})]$ in which $i+k \leq n+1$. Clearly, it is true that $\mathcal{L}_i^{(n-i+1)} = \pi_i(\mathcal{L})$, which implies the lattice of rank $n-i+1$ generated by basis $[\pi_i(\mathbf{b}_i), \ldots, \pi_i(\mathbf{b}_n)]$.

A basis $\mathbf{B} = [\mathbf{b}_1, \ldots, \mathbf{b}_n]$ is defined as a *β-blockwise Korkin-Zolotarev basis*, or ***BKZ**-reduced basis*, if the following conditions hold:

1. Its $|\mu_{ij}| \leq 1/2$, for $1 \leq j < i \leq n$;

2. and $\pi_i(\mathbf{b}_i)$ is the shortest vector of the lattice $\mathcal{L}_i^{(\min(\beta, n-i+1))}$ under the Euclidean norm, for $1 \leq i \leq n$.

For details of the Blockwise-Korkin-Zolotarev (**BKZ**) algorithm (the algorithm to obtain **BKZ** basis), you can refer to [14].

3. SPARSE REPRESENTATIONS OF LATTICE VECTORS: THE LATTICE VECTORS FROM ANOTHER POINT OF VIEW

Before devoting to the genetic algorithm, we should encode a lattice vector into a bit string, or, namely, a *chromosome* in genetic algoithms, since genetic algorithms can only operate on bit sequences.

3.1 An Equivalent Integer Representations of Lattice Vectors Relating to Gram-Schmidt Orthorgonalization

In this subsection, we lay no assumptions on the lattice basis $[\mathbf{b}_1, \ldots, \mathbf{b}_n]$, or, in other words, the basis is arbitrary. Given a lattice $\mathcal{L}(\mathbf{B})$, any vector $\mathbf{v}$ in this lattice can be represented as:

$$\mathbf{v} = \mathbf{Bx} = \sum_{i=1}^{n} x_i \mathbf{b}_i,$$

in which $\mathbf{x} = (x_1, \ldots, x_n) \in \mathbb{Z}^n$. Putting it in another way, we can represent the vector $\mathbf{v}$ in terms of the Gram-Schmidt orthorgonalization $\mathbf{B}^*$ in place of $\mathbf{B}$ as described in the following.

Definition 1. Given a lattice basis $\mathbf{B} = [\mathbf{b}_1, \ldots, \mathbf{b}_n]$ and its Gram-Schimdt orthogonalization $\mathbf{B}^* = [\mathbf{b}_1^*, \ldots, \mathbf{b}_n^*]$ with the matrix $\mathbf{R} = [\mu_{ij}]_{1 \le i,j \le n} \in \mathbb{R}^{n \times n}$ such that $\mathbf{B} = \mathbf{B}^*\mathbf{R}$, any vector $\mathbf{v} \in \mathcal{L}(\mathbf{B})$, and $\mathbf{v} = \mathbf{Bx}$, in which $\mathbf{x} = (x_1, x_2, \ldots, x_n)$, we define a vector $\mathbf{t} = (t_1, \ldots, t_n) \in \mathbb{R}^n$ as

$$t_i = \begin{cases} 0 & \text{for } i = n, \\ \sum_{j=i+1}^{n} \mu_{ji} x_j & \text{for } i < n. \end{cases}$$

and another vector $\mathbf{y} = (y_1, y_2, \ldots, y_n) \in \mathbb{Z}^n$ such that,

$$y_i = \lfloor x_i + t_i \rceil$$

Since $x_i \in \mathbb{Z}$, we have

$$y_i = x_i + \lfloor t_i \rceil (1 \le i \le n),$$

and thus,

$$x_i = y_i - \lfloor t_i \rceil (1 \le i \le n).$$

Thereby we establish a one-to-one correspondence between $\mathbf{x}$ and $\mathbf{y}$, and, also, a one-to-one correspondence between $\mathbf{v}$ and $\mathbf{y}$ as described below:

$$\mathbf{y} \xleftrightarrow{\mathbf{y}=\mathbf{x}+\lfloor \mathbf{t} \rceil} \mathbf{x} \xleftrightarrow{\mathbf{v}=\mathbf{Bx}} \mathbf{v},$$

where $\lfloor \mathbf{t} \rceil = (\lfloor t_1 \rceil, \ldots, \lfloor t_n \rceil) \in \mathbb{Z}^n$. Therefore, we call the $\mathbf{y}$ corresponding to a lattice vector $\mathbf{v}$ as $\mathbf{y} \sim \mathbf{v}$.

This is quite important to represent a lattice vector as a chromosome in the genetic algorithm to be described in the next section.

For any vector $\mathbf{v}$ in the lattice $\mathcal{L}(\mathbf{B})$, the new integer vector $\mathbf{y} = (y_1, \ldots, y_n) \in \mathbb{Z}^n$ described above satisfies that:

$$\mathbf{v} = \sum_{i=1}^{n} (y_i + \epsilon_i) \mathbf{b}_i^*,$$

in which $0 \le |\epsilon_i| \le 1/2$.

Then,

$$\sum_{y_i \ne 0} \left(|y_i| - \frac{1}{2}\right)^2 \|\mathbf{b}_i^*\|^2 \le \|\mathbf{v}\|^2 \le \sum_{i=1}^{n} \left(|y_i| + \frac{1}{2}\right)^2 \|\mathbf{b}_i^*\|^2. \tag{1}$$

Provided that $\mathbf{y}$ is the integer vector relating to the shortest vector $\mathbf{v}(\|\mathbf{v}\| = \lambda_1(\mathcal{L}))$, it satisfies:

$$\sum_{y_i \ne 0} \left(|y_i| - \frac{1}{2}\right)^2 \|\mathbf{b}_i^*\|^2 \le \|\mathbf{v}\|^2.$$

Since $\|\mathbf{v}\| = \lambda_1(\mathcal{L})$ and $y_i \in \mathbb{Z}$ for $1 \le i \le n$, we have

$$\sum_{i=1}^{n} \left(\frac{1}{2}|y_i|\right)^2 \|b_i^*\|^2 \le \sum_{y_i \ne 0} \left(|y_i| - \frac{1}{2}\right)^2 \|\mathbf{b}_i^*\|^2 \le \|\mathbf{v}\|^2 = \lambda_1^2(\mathcal{L}).$$

That is to say,

$$\sum_{i=1}^{n} |y_i|^2 \|b_i^*\|^2 \le 4\lambda_1^2(\mathcal{L}). \tag{2}$$

This means that we can bound the bit-length of $\mathbf{y}$ by a heuristic λ_1. It remains to find an appropriate Gram-Schmidt orthogonalization (like a BKZ-reduced basis), and decrease the length of y as much as possible.

3.2 The Estimate of y under β-Blockwise Korkin-Zolotarev Basis

Rewriting Proposition 4.2 in [7] gives the following lemma.

Lemma 1. Let $\mathbf{B} = [\mathbf{b}_1, \ldots, \mathbf{b}_n]$ be a Korkin-Zolotarev basis of a lattice $\mathcal{L}(\mathbf{B})$, with Gram-Schmidt orthogonalization $[\mathbf{b}_1^*, \ldots, \mathbf{b}_n^*]$. Then we have

$$\frac{\lambda_1(\mathcal{L})}{\|\mathbf{b}_i^*\|} \le i^{\frac{1+\log i}{2}}. \tag{3}$$

With this lemma in consideration, we can prove the theorem that follows.

Theorem 1. Let $1 < \beta < n$. For a β-blockwise Korkin-Zolotarev basis $\mathbf{B} = [\mathbf{b}_1, \ldots, \mathbf{b}_n]$ and its Gram-Schmidt orthogonalization $[\mathbf{b}_1^*, \ldots, \mathbf{b}_n^*]$, we have, for $1 \le i \le \beta$,

$$\frac{\|\mathbf{b}_1^*\|}{\|\mathbf{b}_i^*\|} < i^{\frac{1+\log i}{2}}, \tag{4}$$

and, for $\beta < i \le n$,

$$\frac{\|\mathbf{b}_1^*\|}{\|\mathbf{b}_i^*\|} \le \beta^{\frac{1+\log \beta}{2}\left(\frac{i-1}{\beta-1}+1\right)}. \tag{5}$$

PROOF. Since $\mathbf{B} = [\mathbf{b}_1, \ldots, \mathbf{b}_n]$ is a β-Blockwise Korkin-Zolotarev basis, the sequence of its first β vectors $[\mathbf{b}_1, \ldots, \mathbf{b}_\beta]$ constitutes a Korkin-Zolotarev basis. Then, Lemma 1 yields that, for any such sequence, we have, for $1 \le i \le \beta$,

$$\frac{\|\mathbf{b}_1^*\|}{\|\mathbf{b}_i^*\|} \le i^{\frac{1+\log i}{2}},$$

which proves the Inequality (4).

Likewise, for every $1 \le i \le n$, $[\pi_i(\mathbf{b}_i), \ldots, \pi_i(\mathbf{b}_{\min(n,i+\beta-1)})]$ constitutes a Korkin-Zolotarev basis. Then, Lemma 1 yields that,

$$\frac{\|\mathbf{b}_i^*\|}{\left\|\mathbf{b}_{\min(n,i+\beta-1)}^*\right\|} \le \beta^{\frac{1+\log \beta}{2}}.$$

So, for $\beta < i \le n$,

$$\frac{\|\mathbf{b}_1^*\|}{\|\mathbf{b}_i^*\|} \le \frac{\|\mathbf{b}_1^*\|}{\|\mathbf{b}_\beta^*\|} \times \frac{\|\mathbf{b}_\beta^*\|}{\|\mathbf{b}_{2\beta-1}^*\|} \times \cdots \times \frac{\left\|\mathbf{b}_{\lfloor \frac{i-1}{\beta-1} \rfloor (\beta-1)+1}^*\right\|}{\|\mathbf{b}_i^*\|}$$
$$\le \beta^{\frac{1+\log \beta}{2}\lceil \frac{i-1}{\beta-1} \rceil} \le \beta^{\frac{1+\log \beta}{2}\left(\frac{i-1}{\beta-1}+1\right)}.$$

This completes the proof. □

3.3 y-Sparse Representations of the Short Lattice Vectors

Equation (2) shows that, for $\mathbf{y} \sim \mathbf{v}$ that is the shortest vector in the lattice $\mathcal{L}(\mathbf{B})$, $\sum_{i=1}^{n} |y_i|^2 \|b_i^*\|^2$ is bounded by four times the squared first minima λ_1. If the lattice basis $\mathbf{B}$ is **LLL** or β-**BKZ** reduced, the absolute values of elements in $\mathbf{y}$ corresponding to a short vector are even smaller, as Theorem 1 shows, and, for example, fixing $\beta = \sqrt{n}$ yields

$$|y_i| \leq 2^{o(n)}. \quad (6)$$

However, the $\mathbf{y}$ corresponding to the short vectors behaves much better than described above. For example, after performing only **LLL**-reduction on basis of random lattice of dimension 50 (seed = 0) in the SVP challenge [13], its $\mathbf{y}$ corresponding to the shortest vector $\mathbf{v}$, whose norm $\|\mathbf{v}\|$ is 1893 as posted on the website, has got only 7 nonzero elements and all the absolute value of the non-zero $|y_i| = 1$, as shown below: the shortest vector $\mathbf{v}$ = [-13 -124 -146 277 -107 -180 673 -311 -167 47 200 395 167 -25 -136 -392 117 -165 147 -515 185 637 343 8 247 44 -220 -146 52 135 -347 -369 -332 -102 469 -285 1 167 397 84 -97 -138 -135 218 567 141 72 21 312 -41], and its corresponding $\mathbf{y}$ under the **LLL**-reduced basis is $\mathbf{y}$ = [0 0 0 0 0 0 0 0 0 0 0 0 0 0 0 0 0 0 0 0 0 0 0 0 0 0 0 0 1 0 0 -1 0 0 -1 1 0 0 0 0 0 1 0 0 0 0 0 -1 0 0 0 -1]. After computing $\mathbf{y}$ corresponding to the short vectors in the random lattices with dimension 50-120 under **LLL**-reduced or β-**BKZ** basis (β is as small as $\sqrt{n}$), we find that $\mathbf{y}$ representations of the short vectors in random lattices with larger dimensions are similarly well-behaved: $\mathbf{y}$s are quite *sparse* for short vectors, i.e. most of the elements in $\mathbf{y}$ are zero and the non-zero elements are of small absolute values, at most 3, for all the random lattices with dimensions less than 120.

We call the sparse $\mathbf{y} = (y_1, \ldots, y_n)$ corresponding to the short lattice vectors as *the y-sparse representations* of the short lattice vectors under a BKZ-reduced basis. The genetic algorithm to be described in details in the next section will be based on the y-sparse representation. In addition, the y-sparse representation is of independent importance to the algorithms for Shortest Vector Problem (SVP).

4. A GENETIC ALGORITHM FOR SVP

4.1 Encoding a Lattice Vector as a Chromosome

Definition 2. Given a signed integer x, we define the bit string $(x)_2 = \mathbf{sgn}(x) \vdash (|x|)_2$ as x's binary representation with a sign at the leftmost bit. And its length is

$$|(x)_2| = 1 + (1 + \lfloor \log |x| \rfloor) = 2 + \lfloor \log |x| \rfloor.$$

Still, we can also represent a signed integer into a bit string of a fixed length ℓ as $(x)_2^\ell = \mathbf{sgn}(x) \vdash (|x|)_2^{\ell-1}$.

Definition 3. Given an integer vector $\mathbf{x} = (x_1, x_2, \ldots, x_n)$ including n signed integers, we define the chromosome $\mathbf{ch}(\mathbf{x}) \in \{0,1\}^\ell$ with regards to $\mathbf{x}$ as a bit string $(x_1)_2 \vdash (x_2)_2 \vdash \ldots \vdash (x_n)_2 = \mathbf{sgn}(x_1) \vdash (|x_1|)_2 \vdash \mathbf{sgn}(x_2) \vdash (|x_2|)_2 \vdash \ldots \vdash \mathbf{sgn}(x_n) \vdash (|x_n|)_2$. Then, the length ℓ of the chromosome is

$$\ell = \sum_{i=1}^{n} (1 + |(|x_i|)_2|).$$

We can also represent the integer vector $\mathbf{x}$ as a chromosome of a fixed length as

$$\begin{aligned} \mathbf{ch}_{\ell_1,\ell_2,\ldots,\ell_n}(\mathbf{x}) &= (x_1)_2^{\ell_1} \vdash (x_2)_2^{\ell_2} \vdash \ldots \vdash (x_n)_2^{\ell_n} \\ &= \mathbf{sgn}(x_1) \vdash (|x_1|)_2^{\ell_1-1} \vdash \mathbf{sgn}(x_2) \vdash (|x_2|)_2^{\ell_2-1} \\ &\quad \vdash \ldots \vdash \mathbf{sgn}(x_n) \vdash (|x_n|)_2^{\ell_n-1}, \end{aligned} \quad (7)$$

whose length is, clearly, $\ell_1 + \ell_2 + \ldots + \ell_n$.

Finally, we define the reverse transformation from a chromosome $\mathbf{a} \in \{0,1\}^{\ell_1+\ell_2+\ldots+\ell_n}$ back into the integer vector as $\mathbf{ch}^{-1}_{\ell_1,\ell_2,\ldots,\ell_n}(\mathbf{a}) = \mathbf{x}$ if and only if

$$\mathbf{ch}_{\ell_1,\ell_2,\ldots,\ell_n}(\mathbf{x}) = \mathbf{a}.$$

As we will see in the following sections, genetic algorithms can only operate on chromosomes, therefore, we must represent each lattice vector as a sequence of 0 and 1. Given a lattice vector $\mathbf{v} = \mathbf{Bx}$, we can compute $\mathbf{t} = (t_1, \ldots, t_n)$ as

$$t_i = \sum_{j=i+1}^{n} \mu_{ji} \cdot x_j,$$

and $\mathbf{y} = \mathbf{x} + \lfloor \mathbf{t} \rceil$, we encode the chromosome regarding to the lattice point $\mathbf{v}$ using the integer vector $\mathbf{y}$ instead of $\mathbf{x}$. Then, the chromosome of $\mathbf{v}$ is represented as

$$\mathbf{ch}_{\ell_1,\ldots,\ell_n}(\mathbf{y}) = (y_1)_2^{\ell_1} \vdash (y_2)_2^{\ell_2} \vdash \ldots \vdash (y_n)_2^{\ell_n},$$

and the length ℓ of the whole chromosome for lattice vector $\mathbf{v}$ is

$$\ell = \sum_{i=1}^{n} \ell_i.$$

4.2 Description of the Genetic Algorithm with an Elitist Strategy

In this subsection, we describe our genetic algorithm for the shortest vector problem, and we prove the correctness of the algorithm in the following two subsections.

A classical genetic algorithm operates on a number of binary strings $[\mathbf{c}_1, \mathbf{c}_2, \ldots, \mathbf{c}_p]$ of a certain length ℓ, called a *population*, and the number of the population p is called the *population size*, in which each individual ℓ-length bit string is called a *chromosome* (recall what we defined above). With each chromosome the algorithm endows a real-valued fitness function $f : \{0,1\}^\ell \to \mathbb{R}$ to signify how good a chromosome is. The genetic algorithm randomly generates an initial population of p chromosomes, and performs iterations of genetic operations, like `selection`, `crossover` and `mutation`, to generate a new population as long as the algorithm has not found the chromosome with the maximum fitness among all chromosomes, i.e., the optimum solution.

As described in Table 1, after an initialization as in Table 2, the algorithm reproduces new population of new vectors

Table 1: The Genetic Algorithm for Searching the Shortest Vector

Input: A lattice basis $\mathbf{B} \in \mathbb{R}^{n\times n}$, the block size β, the mutation rate p_m, and the population size p.
Output: A lattice vector $\mathbf{v}_0$, such that $\|\mathbf{v}_0\| = \lambda_1(\mathcal{L})$.

1. Preprocess the original basis $\mathbf{B}$ with β-**BKZ** procedure, generating $\mathbf{B}'$;
2. Compute $\mathbf{B}'$ Gram-Schmidt orthogonalization sequence $\mathbf{B}^* = [\mathbf{b}_1^*, \cdots, \mathbf{b}_n^*]$ and $[\mu_{ij}]_{1\le i,j\le n}$;
3. Perform **initialization**($\mathbf{B}^*, p$) and get p tuples and bit length $\ell_1, \ldots, \ell_n$;// get p lattice vectors randomly;
4. Exchange the p tuples in a non-descending order as $[(\mathbf{x}_1, \mathbf{y}_1), (\mathbf{x}_2, \mathbf{y}_2), \ldots, (\mathbf{x}_p, \mathbf{y}_p)]$ according to $\|\mathbf{Bx}_i\|$.
5. Let $\mathbf{v}_0 \leftarrow \mathbf{Bx}_1$. **While** $\|\mathbf{v}_0\| > \lambda_1(\mathcal{L})$ **dočž**//$\lambda_1(\mathcal{L})$ can be its Gaussian Heuristic
   (a) Let $k \leftarrow 1$;
   (b) Select i, j from $[1, \ldots, p]$ using proportional selection;
   (c) $\mathbf{b} = \textbf{mutation}(\textbf{crossover}(\mathbf{ch}_{\ell_1,\ldots,\ell_n}(\mathbf{y}_i), \mathbf{ch}_{\ell_1,\ldots,\ell_n}(\mathbf{y}_j)))$;
   (d) Compute $\mathbf{y}'_k = \mathbf{ch}^{-1}_{\ell_1,\ldots,\ell_n}(\mathbf{b})$ and $\mathbf{x}'_k = \mathbf{y}'_k - \lfloor \mathbf{t}'_k \rceil$ and store the tuple $(\mathbf{x}'_k, \mathbf{y}'_k)$;
   If $\mathbf{x}'_k$ is a zero vector, remove $(\mathbf{x}'_k, \mathbf{y}'_k)$ and go to (c);// zero vector is not in consideration.
   (e) Let $k \leftarrow k+1$, and if $k < p-1$, go to (b);
   (f) Let $(\mathbf{x}'_p, \mathbf{y}'_p) \leftarrow (\mathbf{x}_1, \mathbf{y}_1)$ and get new p tuples $[(\mathbf{x}'_1, \mathbf{y}'_1), (\mathbf{x}'_2, \mathbf{y}'_2), \ldots, (\mathbf{x}'_p, \mathbf{y}'_p)]$;
   // reserve the best vector in the last generation of population as the elitism strategy
   (g) Exchange them in a non-descending order and store again as $[(\mathbf{x}_1, \mathbf{y}_1), (\mathbf{x}_2, \mathbf{y}_2), \ldots, (\mathbf{x}_p, \mathbf{y}_p)]$ according to $\|\mathbf{Bx}_i\|$;
   (h) **If** $\|\mathbf{v}_0\| \ge \|\mathbf{Bx}_1\|$, let $\mathbf{v}_0 \leftarrow \mathbf{Bx}_1$;
6. **Return** $\mathbf{v}_0$.

Table 2: Initialization

Input: $\mathbf{B}^*$, and the population size p.
Output: p tuples $(\mathbf{x}_1, \mathbf{y}_1), \ldots, (\mathbf{x}_p, \mathbf{y}_p)$ and $\ell_1, \ldots, \ell_n$.

1. Compute $\alpha_i = \frac{\|\mathbf{b}_1^*\|}{\|\mathbf{b}_i^*\|}$
   and $\ell_i = 2 + \lfloor \log \alpha_i \rfloor$ for all $1 \le i \le n$;
2. **For** $k \leftarrow 1$ to p **do**
   (a) Choose uniformly at random n integers $|y_i| \le \alpha_i$ in which $1 \le i \le n$;
   (b) Let $x_i = y_i - \lceil t_i \rfloor$ in which $t_i = \sum_{j=i+1}^{n} \mu_{ji} x_j$ for each i;
   (c) Let $\mathbf{x}_k = (x_1, \ldots, x_n)$, and $\mathbf{y}_k = (y_1, \ldots, y_n)$;
   (d) Store the kth tuple $(\mathbf{x}_k, \mathbf{y}_k)$;
3. **Return** the p tuples $(\mathbf{x}_1, \mathbf{y}_1), (\mathbf{x}_2, \mathbf{y}_2), \ldots, (\mathbf{x}_p, \mathbf{y}_p)$ and $\ell_1, \ldots, \ell_n$.

Table 3: Crossover

Input: Two bit strings $\mathbf{a} = (a_1, \ldots, a_\ell)$
$\mathbf{b} = (b_1, \ldots, b_\ell)$ of length ℓ bits.
Output: A bit string $\mathbf{c}$ of length ℓ

1. **For** $i \leftarrow 1$ to ℓ **do**
   (a) Choose a number $r \in [0, 1)$ uniformly at random;
   (b) **If** $r < 0.5$, let $c_i \leftarrow a_i$, and, otherwise, $c_i \leftarrow b_i$;
2. **Return** $\mathbf{c} = (c_1, \ldots, c_\ell)$.

from the current population in each iteration, until we find a shortest vector in the new generation. We call each population produced in an iteration a *generation* of population. In the iteration, we generate $p-1$ new vectors by using the following scheme. First, we choose two vectors in the current population $(\mathbf{x}_i, \mathbf{y}_i)$ and $(\mathbf{x}_j, \mathbf{y}_j)$ $(1 \le i, j \le n)$ by the proportional selection based on the fitness function. Second, we perform $\mathbf{ch}_{\ell_1,\ldots,\ell_n}(\mathbf{y}_i)$ (as in Table 5) and $\mathbf{ch}_{\ell_1,\ldots,\ell_n}(\mathbf{y}_j)$ (as in Table 6) to obtain two chromosomes for the two vectors.

Table 4: Mutation

Input: One bit string $\mathbf{a} = (a_1, \ldots, a_\ell)$ of length ℓ bits, and the mutation probability $p_m = 1/\ell$.
Output: A bit string $\mathbf{c}$ of length ℓ bits.

1. **For** $i \leftarrow 1$ to ℓ **do**
   (a) Choose a number $r \in [0, 1)$ uniformly at random;
   (b) **If** $r < 1/\ell$, let $c_i \leftarrow \bar{a}_i$, and, otherwise, $c_i \leftarrow a_i$;
2. **Return** $\mathbf{c} = (c_1, \ldots, c_\ell)$.

Table 5: $\mathbf{Ch}_{\ell_1,\ldots,\ell_n}$

Input: An integer vector $\mathbf{y} = (y_1, \ldots, y_n)$ and $\ell_1, \ldots, \ell_n$;
Output: A bit string $\mathbf{a}$ of length $\ell = \sum_{i=1}^{n} \ell_i$ bits.

1. $\mathbf{a} = \mathbf{sgn}(y_1) \vdash (|y_1|)_2^{\ell_1 - 1} \vdash \ldots \vdash \mathbf{sgn}(y_n) \vdash (|y_n|)_2^{\ell_n - 1}$;
   //$(|\cdot|)_2^{\ell}$ means transforming an integer into its binary representation of length exactly ℓ;
2. **Return** $\mathbf{a}$.

Table 6: $\mathbf{Ch}^{-1}_{\ell_1,\ldots,\ell_n}$

Input: A bit string $\mathbf{a} = (a_1, \ldots, a_\ell)$ of length $\ell = \sum_{i=1}^{n} \ell_i$;
Output: An integer vector $\mathbf{y} = (y_1, \ldots, y_n)$.

1. Let $\ell \leftarrow 1$; **For** $i \leftarrow 1$ to n **do**
   (a) $y_i = \sum_{i=1}^{\ell_i - 1} a_{\ell+i} \cdot 2^i$;
   // transform a bit string back into a decimal integer
   (b) If a_ℓ is 1, $y_i \leftarrow -y_i$; // add the sign
   (c) $\ell \leftarrow \ell + \ell_i$;
2. **Return** $\mathbf{y} = (y_1, \ldots, y_n)$.

Thirdly, perform the subroutine `crossover` (as in Table 4.2) and `mutation` (as in Table 4.2) on the two chromosomes to gain a new bit string $\mathbf{b} \in \{0,1\}^{\ell_1+\ell_2+\ldots+\ell_n}$. Finally, we recover the $\mathbf{y} = ch_{\ell_1,\ldots,\ell_n}(\mathbf{b})$ and $\mathbf{x} = \mathbf{y} - \lfloor \mathbf{t} \rceil$ to reconstruct a tuple $(\mathbf{x}, \mathbf{y})$. Thereby, we yield a new vector from two vectors in the current population, if $\mathbf{x}$ is not a zero vector for the reason that the shortest vector problem means to find the nonzero shortest vector in a lattice. Similarly, we can generate independently $p-1$ such tuples (vectors) to constitute a new population. Besides, we reserve the vector with the shortest Euclidean norm in the current population as the pth vector in the new population, which is called *an Elitist Strategy*. The elitist strategy assures the convergence in the finite generations to the optimum population as we will prove in the next section.

In our genetic algorithm, we use the *proportional selection* to select a chromosome from a population based on its fitness as:

$$\Pr[\mathbf{c}_i \text{ is selected}] = \frac{f(\mathbf{c}_i)}{\sum_{j=1}^{p} f(\mathbf{c}_j)}.$$

As far as the shortest lattice vector problem (**SVP**) is concerned, we regard the lattice vectors $\mathbf{v} = \mathbf{Bx}$ as the individuals and, as defined in Section 4.1, we encode the vectors into chromosomes using the **ch** operation based on the vectors $\mathbf{y} = \mathbf{x} + \lfloor \mathbf{t} \rceil$. We define the fitness function f as the inverse of the Euclidean norm of the vector as:

$$f(\mathbf{v}) = \frac{1}{\|\mathbf{v}\|^2} = \frac{1}{\|\mathbf{Bx}\|^2}.$$

Thereby, the shortest vector obtains the maximum fitness, and enjoys the largest probability that it is selected in the procedure of proportional selection. We choose the square of the Euclidean norm as the fitness function to avoid computing the square root, which is time-assuming in the program implementation.

The optimum of the mutation probability in genetic algorithms is proved to be $1/\ell$ by Bäck [3]. Therefore, the probability that mutation generates the solution a' from individual a is given by,

$$\Pr(a \xrightarrow{\text{mutation}} a') = p_m^{\text{Ham}(a,a')}(1-p_m)^{(\ell-\text{Ham}(a,a'))} > 0,$$

which is very important to ensure the convergence of the algorithm, and here $\text{Ham}(a, a')$ denotes the hamming distance of two chromosomes a and a'.

The SVP genetic algorithm adopting the elitist strategy is proved to converge to the shortest lattice vector with only negligible failure probability after enough iterations, as in the full version of this paper[4].

5. FURTHER IMPROVEMENTS ON OUR GENETIC ALGORITHM

In this section, we adopt some heuristic techniques to the genetic algorithm to improve its efficiency: the local search and heuristic pruning, which we will discuss in details.

5.1 Local Search

Local search is a kind of hill-climbing algorithm which is capable of finding the locally optimal point nearby a given point. As shown in Table 7, given an integer vector $\mathbf{y}$ which represents a specific vector $\mathbf{v}$ in lattice $\mathcal{L}(\mathbf{B})$, we first choose the lattice vector $\mathbf{v} \sim \mathbf{y}$ as the critical vector which serves as

Table 7: Local Search

Input: $\mathbf{B}$, and an integer vector $\mathbf{y} = (y_1, \ldots, y_n)$;
Output: An integer vector $\mathbf{y}'' = (y_1'', \ldots, y_n'')$.

1. Let $\mathbf{y}'' \leftarrow \mathbf{y}$, and compute $\mathbf{v}''$ such that $\mathbf{y}'' \sim \mathbf{v}''$;
2. $p \leftarrow 1$;
3. **While** $p = 1$ **do** // if $\mathbf{y}'$ has been updated
   (a) Compute $\mathbf{v}$ such that $\mathbf{y} \sim \mathbf{v}$;
   (b) Let $p \leftarrow 0$. **For** all $\mathbf{y}'$ such that $\|\mathbf{y}' - \mathbf{y}\| = 1$ **do**
      (i) Compute $\mathbf{v}'$ such that $\mathbf{y}' \sim \mathbf{v}'$;
      (ii) **If** $0 < \|\mathbf{v}'\| < \|\mathbf{v}''\|$,
      then let $\mathbf{y}'' \leftarrow \mathbf{y}'$, $\mathbf{v}'' \leftarrow \mathbf{v}'$ and $p \leftarrow 1$;
   (c) Let $\mathbf{y} \leftarrow \mathbf{y}''$; //Choose the best $\mathbf{y}''$ nearby $\mathbf{y}$;
4. **Return** $\mathbf{y}'' = (y_1'', \ldots, y_n'')$.

the starting point from which we search all the nearby vectors. Starting from Step (b), the algorithm searches all the vectors $\mathbf{y}'$ in $2n$ directions with distance 1, i.e. $\|\mathbf{y}' - \mathbf{y}\| = 1$, and finds the best nearby vector $\mathbf{y}''$ whose corresponding lattice vector $\mathbf{v}'' \sim \mathbf{y}''$ is shorter than the critical vector $\mathbf{v}$. Then the algorithm chooses $\mathbf{v}''$ as the new critical vector, and repeats the steps above until all the $2n$ nearby vectors are no better than the critical vector. For short, local search always takes the steepest direction. Note that local search can always find a vector which is at least as short as the given vector, and that is a locally optimal vector near the given one. Local search may sometimes not find the globally optimal vector, i.e. the shortest vector, in the sense of "greedy" algorithm, but it can never miss it if the given vector is near the shortest vector. So it enhances the probability that it succeeds in finding the shortest vector for a random search algorithm.

In the genetic algorithm, we perform local search on all the newly-generated vectors after performing `crossover` and `mutation`, and we can find a locally optimal vector nearby. Experiments in the next section show that local search helps reduce the running time greatly.

5.2 Optimizations: Heuristic Pruning

As in the y-sparse representation of the shortest vector of the random lattice with dimension 50 under a **LLL**-reduced basis, $\mathbf{y}$ =[0 0 0 0 0 0 0 0 0 0 0 0 0 0 0 0 0 0 0 0 0 0 0 0 0 0 0 1 0 0 -1 0 0 -1 1 0 0 0 0 0 1 0 0 0 0 0 -1 0 0 0 -1], we can observe that: first, the first half of the elements of $\mathbf{y}$ are all zeros; second, all the nonzero elements are quite small. Experiments show that the two observations hold in the y-sparse representation of the random lattice with dimensions 50-120 under a **LLL**- or **BKZ**-reduced basis. Therefore, in order to obtain short vectors, we can adopt the two heuristic techniques below.

Technique 1: We fix the first half of the elements y_i, for $1 \le i \le \lfloor n/2 \rfloor$, of $\mathbf{y}$ as 0 beforehand.

Technique 2: We bound the rest elements y_i, for $\lfloor n/2 \rfloor \le i \le n$, of $\mathbf{y}$ as $\alpha_i = \sqrt{\frac{\|\mathbf{b}_1^*\|}{\|\mathbf{b}_i^*\|}}$ instead of $\alpha_i = \frac{\|\mathbf{b}_1^*\|}{\|\mathbf{b}_i^*\|}$.

The two techniques help narrow the search space dramatically, like the pruning techniques in the enumerations. So we call the two techniques as *Heuristic Pruning*. Albeit heuristically, the two techniques never miss any shortest vectors in dimensions 50-120 as the experiments show below. Adopting the two heuristic techniques, we modify the **initialization** procedure as heuristic initialization shown in Table 8 as in Step (1) and Step (2). In fact, we can try much smaller α_i than the suggested in Table 8.

Table 8: Heuristic Initialization

Input: $\mathbf{B}^*$, and the population size p.
Output: p tuples $(\mathbf{x}_1, \mathbf{y}_1), \ldots, (\mathbf{x}_p, \mathbf{y}_p)$

1. Let $\ell_i \leftarrow 0$ for $1 \le i \le \lfloor n/2 \rfloor$;
2. Compute $\alpha_i = \sqrt{\frac{\|\mathbf{b}_1^*\|}{\|\mathbf{b}_i^*\|}}$ and $\ell_i = 2 + \lfloor \log \alpha_i \rfloor$ for all $\lfloor n/2 \rfloor < i \le n$;
3. **For** $k \leftarrow 1$ to p **do**
   (a) Choose uniformly at random n integers $|y_i| \le \alpha_i$ in which $1 \le i \le n$;
   (b) Let $x_i = y_i - \lceil t_i \rfloor$ in which $t_i = \sum_{j=i+1}^{n} \mu_{ji} x_j$ for each i;
   (c) Let $\mathbf{x}_k = (x_1, \ldots, x_n)$, and $\mathbf{y}_k = (y_1, \ldots, y_n)$;
   (d) Store the kth tuple $(\mathbf{x}_k, \mathbf{y}_k)$;
4. **Return** The p tuples $(\mathbf{x}_1, \mathbf{y}_1), (\mathbf{x}_2, \mathbf{y}_2), \ldots, (\mathbf{x}_p, \mathbf{y}_p)$ and $\ell_1, \ldots, \ell_n$.

6. EXPERIMENTAL RESULTS

Experiments are performed on a workstation with 16 Intel Xeon 2.4Ghz CPUs and 16G RAM under a Red Hat Linux Server release 5.4. Our genetic algorithm is implemented in C++ using Victor Shoup's Number Theory Library version 6.0.0 [16]. The genetic algorithm chooses the mutation rate $p_m = 1/\ell$, and the population size as twice the rank of the lattice, i.e., $p = 2n$. All the genetic algorithms start on a basis which is $\sqrt{n}$-BKZ reduced, and the basis and its negative vectors serve as the initial population. All the experiments are performed on the random lattices in the SVP challenge [13], which are of extremely large volume (determinant).

The first experiment means to justify our local search and heuristic techniques, the experiment runs on a random lattice of dimension 40 generated using seed 0. As shown in Table 9, the genetic algorithm without heuristic techniques finds the shortest vector of norm 1702 using 255.5810 seconds, and the genetic algorithm with local search finds the solution within only 21.8347 seconds. Adopting the two heuristic techniques, the algorithm runs even faster, only

Running Time	Heuristic Techniques Adopted
255.5810s	Genetic Algorithm
21.8347s	GA with Local Search
11.8442s	GA with Local Search and Techniques 1 and 2

Table 9: Running Times (Dimension 40) with and without Heuristic Techniques

Dimension	Seed	Previous Challenge	Our Results
40	0	1702	1702
50	0	1893	1893
51	0	1885	1885
66	3	2099	2036
67	0	n/a	2187
69	0	2226	2212
73	0	2220	2190
79	0	n/a	2346
81	0	n/a	2276
83	0	n/a	2433
85	0	n/a	2412
86	0	2456	2387
87	0	n/a	2497
91	0	n/a	2468

Table 10: Comparison of Results (Euclidean Norm) on SVP challenge

11.8442 seconds. Therefore, we conclude that local search and the heuristic pruning do make sense. All the following experiments are performed using the genetic algorithms with both local search and heuristic pruning.

Second, we perform experiments using the improved genetic algorithm on the random lattices of dimensions 40-118 generated using mostly seed 0 except for seed 3 of dimension 66. As shown in Table 10, it shows that our genetic algorithm can always find vectors at least as good as previous challenges in the same lattice, some of them even shorter. For example, the previous challenge of lattice of dimension 66 seed 3 is of norm 2099, while we obtain a vector of norm 2036. The previous challenge for dimension 69 is 2226, and our result is 2212, and for dimension 73 our result is 2190 compared to 2220 of previous challenge, and for dimension 86 ours is 2387 as for previous 2456. We also make some records without any previous challenge results as in the table 11, like the dimension 91, 87, 85, and so on. So far, we have posted 25 challenge results (with the largest dimension 91, most in Feb. 2013) on the SVP challenge website (See link [13]), and we have performed experiments on lattices up to dimension 118. We are still performing more experiments using our genetic algorithm on random lattices with even larger dimensions in SVP challenge. Moreover, we have attempted 200-dimensional q-ary lattices of lattice challenge[13].

Finally, we compare our improved genetic algorithm with Kannan-Helftich enumeration and Enumeration with Pruning, which are of polynomial space complexity as the genetic algorithm is. Both algorithms are implemented using the same NTL library as our genetic algorithm, and both run on the same 16-CPU workstation. In order to obtain a fair comparison, we preprocess the three algorithms with a $\sqrt{n}$-**BKZ** reduction. The running times of the three algorithms are compared in the Fig. 1. The experiments are performed on random lattices from dimension 20 to 118 generated with seed 0. As shown in the Table, the genetic algorithm out-

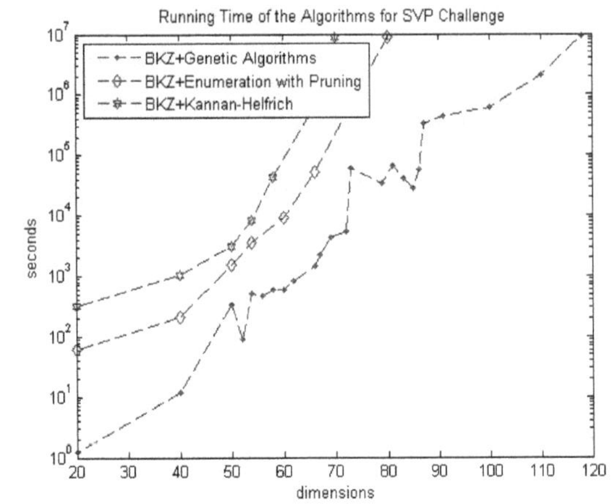

Figure 1: Comparison of the Logarithms of the Running Times of Main SVP Algorithms

performs the other two algorithms in running times over all the dimensions. The Kannan-Helfrich enumeration runs the slowest among the three, and it succeeds in finding the shortest vector only up to dimension 70. The enumeration with pruning, which we implement only the conservative pruning to make sure the shortest vector can always be found, runs faster than Kannan-Helfrich enumeration and can only find the shortest vector at most dimension 80. As for the genetic algorithm, its performance is much better than the other two greatly. The genetic algorithm manages to find the shortest vectors for random lattices of up to dimension 118.

7. CONCLUSION

In this paper, we are the first to propose a genetic algorithm aiming at searching the shortest vector of the random lattices from the SVP challenge [13], which has attracted numerous attention from cryptography community. Our algorithm can converge to the shortest vector at a probability close to 1, and experimental results show that it is efficient and gains some advantages over other SVP algorithms.

8. REFERENCES

[1] M. Ajtai. The shortest vector problem in ℓ_2 is np-hard for randomized reductions. *Proceeding of the 30th Symposium on the Theory of Computing (STOC 1998)*, (284-406), 1998.

[2] M. Ajtai, R. Kumar, and D. Sivaumar. A sieve algorithm for the shortest lattice vector problem. *Proceedings of the 33th annual ACM symposium on Theory of computing (STOC'01)*, 33(601-610), 2001.

[3] T. Bäck. Optimal mutation rates in genetic search. *Proceedings of the fifth International Conference on Genetic Algorithms*, 5(2-8), 1993.

[4] D. Ding, G. Zhu, and X. Wang. A genetic algorithm for searching shortest lattice vector of svp challenge. Cryptology ePrint Archive, Report 2014/489, 2014.

[5] G. Hanrot and D. Stehlé. Analyzing blockwise lattice algorithms using dynamical systems. *Advances in Cryptology-CRYPTO*, 4622(170-186), 2007.

[6] R. Kannan. Improved algorithms for integer programming and related lattice problems. *Proc. of the 15th Symposium on the Theory of Computing (STOC1983)*, 15(99-108), 1983.

[7] J. C. Lagrias, H. W. Lenstra, and C. P. Schnorr. Korkin-zolotarev basis and successive minima of a lattice and its reciprocal lattice. *Combinatorica*, 10(4)(333-348), 1990.

[8] A. K. Lenstra, H. W. Lenstra, and L. Lovász. Factoring polynomials with rational coefficients. *Mathematische Annalen*, 261(513-534), 1982.

[9] D. Micciancio and S. Goldwasser. *Complexity of Lattice Problems: A Cryptographic Perspective.* Kluwer Academic Publishers, 2002.

[10] D. Micciancio and O. Regev. Lattice-based cryptography. *Proceeding of the Post-Quantum Cryptography (PQC'09)*, (147-191), 2009.

[11] D. Micciancio and P. Voulgaris. A deterministic single exponential time algorithm for most lattice problems based on voronoi cell computations. *Proceedings of the 42th annual ACM symposium on Theory of computing (STOC'10)*, 42(351-358), 2010.

[12] P. Q. Nguyen and T. Vidick. Sieve algorithms for the shortest vector problem are practical. *Journal of Mathematical Cryptography*, 2(2(181ÍC207)), 2008.

[13] M. Schneider and N. Gamma. http://www.latticechallenge.org/svp-challenge/.

[14] C. P. Schnorr. A hierarchy of polynomial lattice basis reduction algorithms. *Theoretical Computer Sciences*, 53(201-224), 1987.

[15] P. W. Shor. Algorithms for quantum computation: discrete logarithms and factoring. In *Foundations of Computer Science, 1994 Proceedings., 35th Annual Symposium on*, pages 124–134. IEEE, 1994.

[16] V. Shoup. Number theory c++ library (ntl) version 6.0.0, available at http://www.shoup.net/ntl/.

[17] P. van Emde Boas. Another np-complete partition problem and the complexity of computing short vectors in a lattice. *Technical Report, Mathematisch Instituut, Universiteit van Amsterdam*, 81-04, 1981.

[18] X. Wang, M. Liu, C. Tian, and J. Bi. Improved nguyen-vidick heuristic sieve algorithm for shortest vector problem. In *Proceedings of the 6th ACM Symposium on Information, Computer and Communications Security*, pages 1–9. ACM, 2011.

Solving Problems with Unknown Solution Length at (Almost) No Extra Cost

Benjamin Doerr
École Polytechnique,
Univ. Paris-Saclay, France

Carola Doerr
CNRS & Univ. Pierre et Marie Curie
Paris, France

Timo Kötzing
Friedrich-Schiller-Universität
Jena, Germany

ABSTRACT

Most research in the theory of evolutionary computation assumes that the problem at hand has a fixed problem size. This assumption does not always apply to real-world optimization challenges, where the length of an optimal solution may be unknown a priori.

Following up on previous work of Cathabard, Lehre, and Yao [FOGA 2011] we analyze variants of the (1+1) evolutionary algorithm for problems with unknown solution length. For their setting, in which the solution length is sampled from a geometric distribution, we provide mutation rates that yield an expected optimization time that is of the same order as that of the (1+1) EA knowing the solution length.

We then show that almost the same run times can be achieved even if *no* a priori information on the solution length is available.

Finally, we provide mutation rates suitable for settings in which neither the solution length nor the positions of the relevant bits are known. Again we obtain almost optimal run times for the OneMax and LeadingOnes test functions, thus solving an open problem from Cathabard et al.

Categories and Subject Descriptors

F.2.2 [**Theory of Computation**]: Analysis of Algorithms and Problem Complexity—*Nonnumerical Algorithms and Problems*

Keywords

Theory; Run Time Analysis; Evolutionary Computation; Unknown Solution Length; Non-Uniform Mutation Probability

1. INTRODUCTION

While the theory for evolutionary algorithms (EAs) in static problem settings is well developed [1, 6, 9], a topic that is not so well studied in the theory of EA literature is the performance of EAs in uncertain environments. Uncertainty can have many faces, for example with respect to function evaluations, the variation operators, or the dynamics of the fitness function. Understanding how evolutionary search algorithms can tackle such uncertain environments is an emerging research topic; see [2] for a survey on examples in combinatorial optimization, but also [7] for an excellent survey also discussing different sources of uncertainty.

In this work we study what evolutionary algorithms can achieve in the presence of uncertainty with respect to the solution length. Quite surprisingly, we show that already some variants of the simplest evolutionary algorithm, the $(1+1)$ EA, can be very efficient for such problems.

1.1 Previous Work

Our work builds on previous work of Cathabard, Lehre, and Yao [4], who were the first to consider, from a theoretical point of view, evolutionary algorithms in environments with unknown solution lengths. Cathabard et al. assume that the solution length is sampled from a fixed and known distribution D with finite support. More precisely, they assume that the solution length n is sampled from a truncated version of the geometric distribution, in which the probability mass for values greater than some threshold N is shifted to the event that $n = N$. In this situation, the algorithm designer has access to both the upper bound N for the solution length and the success probability q of the distribution.

Cathabard et al. analyze a variant of the $(1+1)$ EA in which each bit is flipped with probability $1/N$ and they also study a variant with non-uniform bit-flip probabilities. In the latter, the i-th bit is flipped independently of all other bits with probability $1/(i+1)$. They show that these variants have polynomial expected run times on OneMax and LeadingOnes function, where the expectation is taken with respect to the solution length and the random decisions of the algorithm. An overview of the precise bounds obtained in [4] is given in Table 2.

1.2 Our Results

We extend the work of Cathabard et al. in several ways. In a first step (Section 3) we show that the regarded mutation probabilities are sub-optimal. Making use of the concentration of the (truncated) geometric distribution, we design bit flip probabilities that yield significantly smaller expected run times (for both the OneMax and the LeadingOnes function). We complement this finding by a lower bound that shows the optimality of our result. This proves that no mu-

GECCO '15, July 11 - 16, 2015, Madrid, Spain

ISBN 978-1-4503-3472-3/15/07...$15.00
DOI: http://dx.doi.org/10.1145/2739480.2754681

tation probabilities can yield a performance that is better by more than a constant factor than our suggested ones.

While in the setting of Cathabard et al. we are in the convenient situation that we have full knowledge of the distribution D from which the solution length is sampled, one is sometimes faced with problems for which this knowledge is not readily available. We therefore study in Section 4 what can be done without any a priori knowledge about the solution length. In this situation we require that the algorithm designer chooses bit flip probabilities $(p_i)_{i\in\mathbb{N}}$ such that, regardless of the solution length n, the expected performance of the $(1+1)$ EA with bit flip probabilities $(p_1,\ldots,p_n)$ is as small as possible. It is not obvious that this can be done in polynomial time. In fact, for both algorithms studied by Cathabard et al. as well as for any uniform choice of the bit flip probabilities, the expected run time on this problem is exponential in n (cf. Theorems 12 and 13).

We show (Theorems 14 and 15) that not only can we tackle this problem with non-uniform bit flip probabilities, but, quite surprisingly, this can be even done in a way that yields almost optimal run times. Indeed, our results are only a $\log^{1+\varepsilon} n$ factor worse than the best possible choice of mutation probabilities leading to $\Theta(n \log n)$ and $\Theta(n^2)$ run time bounds for OneMax and LeadingOnes, respectively. This factor can be made even smaller as we shall comment at the end of Section 4.2.

Finally, we provide in Section 4.3 a second way to deal with unknown solution lengths. We provide an alternative variant of the (1+1) EA in which the bit flip probabilities are chosen according to some (fixed) distribution at the beginning of each iteration. For suitably chosen distributions Q, the expected run times of the respective (1+1) EA_Q on OneMax and LeadingOnes are of the same asymptotic order as those of the previously suggested solution with non-uniform bit flip probabilities. In particular, they are, simultaneously for all possible solution lengths n, almost of the same order as the expected run time of a best possible choice of bit flip probabilities knowing the solution length.

This second approach has an advantage over the non-uniform bit flip probabilities in that it effectively ignores bits that do not contribute anything to the fitness function (*irrelevant bits*). Thus, even if only n bits at unknown positions have an influence on the fitness function, the same run time bounds apply. In contrast, all previously suggested solutions require that the n relevant bits are the leftmost ones. This also answers a question posed by Cathabard et al. [4, Section 6].

Our run time results are summarized in Tables 1 and 2.

2. ALGORITHMS AND PROBLEMS

In this section we define the algorithms and problems considered in this paper. For any problem size n, fitness function $f:\{0,1\}^n \to \mathbb{R}$, and vector $\vec{p}=(p_1,\ldots,p_n)$ of bit flip probabilities $0 \le p_i \le 1$, we consider the $(1+1)$ $\text{EA}_{\vec{p}}$, as given by Algorithm 1.

The $(1+1)$ $\text{EA}_{\vec{p}}$ samples an initial search point from $\{0,1\}^n$ uniformly at random. It then proceeds in rounds, each of which consists of a mutation and a selection step. Throughout the whole optimization process the $(1+1)$ $\text{EA}_{\vec{p}}$ maintains a population size of one, and the individual in this population is always a best-so-far solution. In the *mutation step* of the $(1+1)$ $\text{EA}_{\vec{p}}$ the current-best solution x is *mutated* by flipping the bit in position i with probability p_i, $1 \le i \le n$. The fitness of the resulting search point y is evaluated and in the *selection step* the parent x is replaced by its offspring y if and only if the fitness of y is at least as good as the one of x. Since we consider maximization problems here, this is the case if $f(y) \ge f(x)$. We are interested in expected *run times*, i.e., the expected number of rounds it takes until the $(1+1)$ $\text{EA}_{\vec{p}}$ evaluates for the first time a solution of maximal fitness and we therefore do not specify a termination criterion. It is not difficult to see that the $(1+1)$ $\text{EA}_{\vec{p}}$ indeed generalized the standard $(1+1)$ EA. In fact, we obtain the $(1+1)$ EA from the $(1+1)$ $\text{EA}_{\vec{p}}$ if we set $p_i = 1/n$ for all $i \in [n] := \{1,\ldots,n\}$. We call such mutation vectors with $p_i = p_j$ for all i,j *uniform* mutation rates, while we speak of *non-uniform* mutation rates if $p_i \ne p_j$ for at least one pair (i,j).

Algorithm 1: The $(1+1)$ $\text{EA}_{\vec{p}}$ for $\vec{p}=(p_1,\ldots,p_n)$ optimizing a pseudo-Boolean function $f:\{0,1\}^n \to \mathbb{R}$.

```
Initialization: Sample x ∈ {0,1}^n uniformly at random and query f(x);
Optimization: for t = 1,2,3,... do
    for i = 1,...,n do
        With probability p_i set y_i ← 1 − x_i and set y_i ← x_i otherwise;
    Query f(y);
    if f(y) ≥ f(x) then x ← y;
```

The two test functions we consider in this work are OneMax and LeadingOnes. For a given problem size n, they are defined as

$$\text{Om}_n := \text{OneMax}_n(x) = \sum_{i=1}^{n} x_i, \text{ and}$$

$$\text{Lo}_n := \text{LeadingOnes}_n(x) = \max\{i \in [0..n] \mid \forall j \le i : x_j = 1\},$$

where $[0..n] := \{0\} \cup [n]$. That is, the OneMax function counts the number of ones in a bit string, while the LeadingOnes function counts the number of initial ones. While these two functions are certainly easy to optimize without evolutionary algorithms, the $(1+1)$ $\text{EA}_{\vec{p}}$ performs exactly the same on all generalized OneMax and LeadingOnes functions, which are obtained from the functions above through an XOR of an arbitrary and unknown bit string $z \in \{0,1\}^n$. Understanding how an evolutionary algorithm behaves on these two functions is an important indicator for how it manages to cope with the easier parts of more complex optimization problems. OneMax and LeadingOnes functions are for this reason the two best-studied problems in the theory of evolutionary computation literature.

If a distribution D is known from which the solution length is sampled we consider the expected run time of the $(1+1)$ $\text{EA}_{\vec{p}}$ on OneMax_D and LeadingOnes_D, respectively, which are the problems Om_n resp. Lo_n with random solution length $n \sim D$. Note here that the expectation is thus taken both with respect to the random solution length and with respect to the random samples of the algorithm.

3. RANDOM SOLUTION LENGTH

We first consider the setting that has been introduced by Cathabard, Lehre, and Yao [4]. After a short presentation

setting	bit flip probability	OneMax		LeadingOnes	
Random Length $\sim$ Geo(q)	uniform and fixed	$O(q^{-1}\log q^{-1})$	Theorem 7	$O(q^{-2})$	Theorem 10
Adversarial Length	uniform and fixed	$2^{\Omega(n)}$	Theorem 12	$2^{\Omega(n)}$	Theorem 13
	fixed	$O(n\log^{2+\varepsilon} n)$	Thm. 14, Cor. 16	$O(n^2\log^{1+\varepsilon} n)$	Thm. 15, Cor. 16
	uniform and random	$O(n\log^{2+\varepsilon} n)$	Thm. 17, Cor. 19	$O(n^2\log^{1+\varepsilon} n)$	Thm. 18, Cor. 19

Table 1: Overview of Results for $1/N < q < 1/2$ and $\varepsilon > 0$.

of the model in Section 3.1, a general lower bound for this problem (Section 3.2), and the results of [4] in Section 3.3, we show that the bounds in [4] can be improved by using different (uniform) mutation rates (Section 3.4).

Table 2 summarizes the previously known bounds and our contributions for the setting regarded in this section.

3.1 The Model

Cathabard et al. [4] consider the following model. The algorithm designer knows the distribution D from which the unknown solution length is drawn; only distributions with finite support are considered, so the algorithm designer knows an upper bound N on the actual solution length n. He also knows the class of functions from which the optimization problem is taken (for example OneMax or LeadingOnes).

Based on this knowledge, the algorithm designer chooses a vector $(p_1,\dots,p_N)$ of bit flip probabilities indicating with which probability a bit is flipped in each round. In this work we also regard a slightly more general model in which the distributions over $\mathbb{N}$ may possibly have infinite support; the algorithm designer then chooses an infinite sequence of bit flip probabilities $(p_1,p_2,\dots) = (p_i)_{i\in\mathbb{N}}$. After this choice of bit flip probabilities, the actual solution length n is sampled from the given distribution D. Then the (1+1) EA$_{\vec{p}}$ (Algorithm 1) is run with mutation probabilities $\vec{p} = (p_1,\dots,p_n)$ on the given problem with the given problem length.

Cathabard et al. [4] consider as distribution D the following *truncated geometric distribution*, based on a geometric distribution where the probability mass for values greater than n are moved to n.

Definition 1 ([4]). *The* truncated geometric distribution TrunkGeo(N,q) *with truncation parameter N and success probability $q \geq 1/N$ satisfies, for all $n\in\mathbb{N}$, that the probability of* TrunkGeo$(N,q) = n$ *is*

$$\begin{cases} q(1-q)^{n-1} & \text{if } 1\le n\le N-1,\\ (1-q)^{n-1} & \text{if } n = N,\\ 0 & \text{otherwise.}\end{cases}$$

Note that the truncated geometric distribution recovers the geometric distribution Geo(q) for $N=\infty$.

It is well known, respectively can be found in [4, Proposition 1], that for $X = \text{Geo}(q)$ and $Y = \text{TrunkGeo}(N,q)$ with $q \geq 1/N$

$$E[X] = q^{-1} \text{ and } E[Y] = \Theta(q^{-1}). \tag{1}$$

Note that we trivially have $E[Y] \leq E[X]$.

3.2 A General Lower Bound

What is a good lower bound for the expected run time of *any* (1+1) EA$_{\vec{p}}$ on OneMax or LeadingOnes when the length is sampled from some given distribution D on $\mathbb{N}$? If the algorithm designer would know the true length n before he has to decide upon the mutation probabilities $(p_1,\dots,p_n)$, then the optimal bit flip probability for this solution length could be chosen. For OneMax, the best choice is to set $\vec{p} = (1/n,\dots,1/n)$ as has been proven in [10, 11] (note here that for fixed problem sizes, due to the symmetry of OneMax, non-uniform mutation rates cannot be advantageous over uniform ones). This results in an expected run time of $\Theta(n\log n)$.

For LeadingOnes, if the true length n is known, any setting of the bit-flip probabilities leads to an expected run time of $\Omega(n^2)$ regardless of the choice of $\vec{p}$, as the next lemma shows.

Lemma 2. *For any fixed solution length n and any vector $\vec{p} = (p_1,\dots,p_n)$ of mutation probabilities, the expected run time of the* (1+1) *EA$_{\vec{p}}$ on* LeadingOnes$_n$ *is $\Omega(n^2)$.*

Using these lower bounds for fixed solution lengths, Jensen's Inequality and the convexity of $n\mapsto n\log n$ and $n\mapsto n^2$, respectively, we get the following general lower bound.

Theorem 3. *Let D be any distribution on $\mathbb{N}$ with a finite expectation of m. Then the expected run time of any* (1+1) *EA$_{\vec{p}}$ on* OneMax$_D$ *is $\Omega(m\log m)$ and the expected run time of any* (1+1) *EA$_{\vec{p}}$ on* LeadingOnes$_D$ *is $\Omega(m^2)$. Both bounds apply also to the setting in which the algorithm designer can choose the mutation probabilities $\vec{p} = (p_1,\dots,p_n)$* after *the solution length $n \sim D$ has been drawn.*

Using Equation (1), we get the following corollary.

Corollary 4. *Let $N\in\mathbb{N}$ and $q\geq 1/N$. Let $D =$* TrunkGeo(N,q) *or $D =$* Geo(q). *The expected run time of any* (1+1) *EA$_{\vec{p}}$ on* OneMax$_D$ *is $\Omega(q^{-1}\log q^{-1})$ and the expected run time of any* (1+1) *EA$_{\vec{p}}$ on* LeadingOnes$_D$ *is $\Omega(q^{-2})$. Both bounds apply also to the setting in which the algorithm designer can choose the mutation probabilities $\vec{p} = (p_1,\dots,p_n)$* after *the solution length $n \sim D$ has been drawn.*

3.3 Known Upper Bounds

Cathabard et al. [4] analyze the run time of the (1+1) EA$_{\vec{p}}$ with uniform mutation probabilities $p_1 = \ldots = p_N = 1/N$ and of the (1+1) EA$_i$ with $p_i = 1/(i+1)$, $1\leq i\leq N$.

For OneMax they obtain the following results.

Theorem 5 (Results for OneMax from [4]). *Let $N\in\mathbb{N}$, $\varepsilon\in(0,1)$, and $q = N^{-\varepsilon}$. For $D =$* TrunkGeo(N,q) *the expected run time of the* (1+1) *EA$_{\vec{p}}$ with*

problem	lower bound Corollary 4	Results from [4] $p_i = 1/N$	$p_i = 1/(i+1)$	Theorems 7 (OM) resp. 10 (LO) $p_i = q/2$	$p_i = q$
ONEMAX_D	$\Omega\left(q^{-1} \log q^{-1}\right)$	$\Theta\left(N \log q^{-1}\right)$	$O\left(q^{-2} \log N\right)$	$\Theta\left(q^{-1} \log q^{-1}\right)$	$\Theta\left(N \log N\right)$
LEADINGONES_D	$\Omega\left(q^{-2}\right)$	$\Theta\left(Nq^{-1}\right)$	$\Theta\left(q^{-3}\right)$	$\Theta\left(q^{-2}\right)$	$\Theta\left(Nq^{-1}\right)$

Table 2: Expected run times of the $(1+1)$ EA$_{\vec{p}}$ with $\vec{p} = (p_i)_{i=1}^N$ for $D = \text{TrunkGeo}(N, q)$ and $1/N \le q \le 1/2$

$\vec{p} = (1/N, \ldots, 1/N)$ on ONEMAX$_D$ *is* $\Theta(N \log q^{-1})$*, while the expected run time of the* $(1+1)$ *EA$_i$ on* ONEMAX$_D$ *is* $O(q^{-2} \log N)$.

This result shows that the $(1+1)$ EA$_{\vec{p}}$ with $\vec{p} = (1/N, \ldots, 1/N)$ outperforms the $(1+1)$ EA$_i$ for $q < 1/\sqrt{N}$, while the latter algorithm is preferable for larger q. As we shall see in the following section one should not conclude from this result that non-uniform bit flip probabilities are the better choice for this problem.

Remark: By using a slightly more careful analysis than presented in [4], the bound for the $(1+1)$ EA$_i$ on ONEMAX$_D$ can be improved to $O(q^{-2} \log q^{-1})$. In fact, an analysis similar to the one in Section 3.4, that is disregarding outcomes that are much larger than the expectation, will give that result. It can also be shown that the requirement $q = N^{-\varepsilon}$ is not needed as the $O(q^{-2} \log q^{-1})$ holds for all $q > 1/N$. It also holds for the (non-truncated) geometric distribution $D = \text{Geo}(q)$.

For LEADINGONES, Cathabard et al. show the following results.

THEOREM 6 (RESULTS FOR LEADINGONES FROM [4]). *For N, ε, q, and D as in Theorem 5, the expected run time of the* $(1+1)$ *EA$_{\vec{p}}$ with $\vec{p} = (1/N, \ldots, 1/N)$ on* LEADINGONES$_D$ *is* $\Theta(Nq^{-1})$*, while the expected run time of the* $(1+1)$ *EA$_i$ on* LEADINGONES$_D$ *is* $\Theta(q^{-3})$.

Thus also for LEADINGONES the $(1+1)$ EA$_i$ performs better than the $(1+1)$ EA$_{\vec{p}}$ with $\vec{p} = (1/N, \ldots, 1/N)$ when $q > 1/\sqrt{N}$ while the uniform $(1+1)$ EA$_{\vec{p}}$ should be preferred for smaller q.

Remark: As in the ONEMAX case the $\Theta(q^{-3})$ bound for the $(1+1)$ EA$_i$ holds more generally for all geometric distributions Geo(q) with parameter $q > 1/N$.

From Theorems 5 and 6 we can see that for both ONEMAX$_D$ and LEADINGONES$_D$ the $(1+1)$ EA$_i$ looses a factor of $1/q$ with respect to the lower bound given by Corollary 4. This will be improved in the following section.

3.4 Optimal Upper Bounds With Uniform Mutation Probabilities

We show that for D being the (truncated or non-truncated) geometric distribution there exist bit flip probabilities $\vec{p} = (p_1, \ldots, p_N)$ and $\vec{p} = (p_i)_{i \in \mathbb{N}}$, respectively, such that the expected run time of the $(1+1)$ EA$_{\vec{p}}$ on ONEMAX$_D$ and LEADINGONES$_D$ is significantly lower than those of the two algorithms studied by Cathabard et al. The expected run times of our algorithm match the lower bounds given in Corollary 4 and are thus optimal in asymptotic terms.

In both cases, i.e., both for ONEMAX$_D$ and for LEADINGONES$_D$, the mutation rates yielding the improvement over the results in [4] are uniform. Our results therefore imply that for these two problems, unlike conjectured in [4], one cannot gain more than constant factors from using non-uniform mutation probabilities.

The key observation determining our choice of the mutation probability is the fact that the (truncated) geometric distribution is highly concentrated. Hence, if we know the parameters of the distribution, we can choose the mutation probability such that it is (almost) reciprocal in each position to the expected length of the solution. Thus, in the setting of [4], i.e., for the truncated geometric distribution with parameters N and q, we set $p_i := q/2$ for all $i \in [N]$ (recall equation (1)). Our approach naturally also works for the (non-truncated) geometric distribution Geo(q), which is also highly concentrated around its mean $1/q$.

We remark without proof that similar results hold for other distributions that are highly concentrated around the mean, e.g., binomial distributions, and also highly concentrated unbounded distributions, such as Poisson distributions.

THEOREM 7. *For $N \in \mathbb{N}$ let $1/N \le q < 1/2$, q possibly depending on N. For $D = \text{Geo}(q)$ and $D = \text{TrunkGeo}(N, q)$ the expected run time of the* $(1+1)$ *EA$_{\vec{p}}$ with $\vec{p} = (q/2, \ldots, q/2)$ on* ONEMAX$_D$ *is* $\Theta(q^{-1} \log q^{-1})$.

For the proof we will use the following upper bound for the expected run time of the $(1+1)$ EA on ONEMAX. A similar upper bound can be found in [11, Theorem 4.1].

LEMMA 8 ([10, THEOREM 8]). *For a fixed length n and a uniform mutation vector $\vec{p} = (p, \ldots, p)$ with $0 < p < 1$, the expected run time of the* $(1+1)$ *EA$_{\vec{p}}$ on* ONEMAX$_n$ *is at most* $(\ln(n) + 1)/(p(1-p)^n)$.

PROOF OF THEOREM 7. We first consider $D = \text{TrunkGeo}(N, q)$. We do not worry about constant factors in this analysis and thus bound some expressions generously.

Using Lemma 8 we can bound the expected run time of the $(1+1)$ EA$_{\vec{p}}$ on ONEMAX$_D$ from above by

$$\sum_{n=1}^{N-1} \frac{q(1-q)^{n-1}(\ln(n)+1)}{q/2(1-q/2)^n} + \frac{(1-q)^{N-1}(\ln(N)+1)}{q/2(1-q/2)^N}. \quad (2)$$

To bound the last summand in this expression, we first observe that, for all positive n,

$$(1 - \tfrac{q}{2})^n = (1 - q + \tfrac{q^2}{4})^{n/2} > (1-q)^{n/2}. \quad (3)$$

This shows that the last summand in (2) is at most

$$2(1-q)^{N/2-1}(\ln(N)+1)/q,$$

which is $O(q^{-1} \log q^{-1})$. This can be seen as follows. For $q \ge 2 \ln \ln(N)/N$ it holds (using the inequality $1 - q \le \exp(-q)$) that $(1-q)^{N/2-1} \le \exp(-qN/2) \le 1/\ln(N)$ and thus $2(1-q)^{N/2-1}(\ln(N)+1)/q = O(1/q)$, while for $1/N \le q \le 2\ln\ln(N)/N$ we have (for some suitably chosen constant C) $(1-q)^{N/2}\ln(N) \le (1-1/N)^{N/2}\ln(N) \le C(\ln(N) - \ln(2\ln\ln N)) = C\ln(N/(2\ln\ln N)) \le C\ln(1/q)$.

Using again (3) we bound the first part of the sum (2) by

$$\begin{aligned} &\frac{2}{1-q}\sum_{n=1}^{N-1}\frac{(1-q)^n(\ln(n)+1)}{(1-q/2)^n} \\ &\le \frac{2}{1-q}\sum_{n=1}^{N-1}(\ln(n)+1)(1-q)^{n/2} \\ &= 2\sum_{n=1}^{N-1}(\ln(n)+1)(1-q)^{n/2-1}. \end{aligned}$$

To show that this expression is $O(q^{-1}\log q^{-1})$ we split the sum into blocks of length $k := \lceil 1/q \rceil$ and use again the inequality $1-q \le \exp(-q)$. This shows that the last expression is at most

$$\begin{aligned} &2\sum_{j=0}^{\lceil N/k\rceil-1}\sum_{\ell=1}^{k}\exp(-q(\tfrac{jk+\ell}{2}-1))(\ln(jk+\ell)+1) \\ &\le 2k\sum_{j=0}^{\lceil N/k\rceil-1}\exp(-\tfrac{1}{k}(\tfrac{jk}{2}-1))(\ln(j+1)+\ln(k)+1) \\ &= O(k\ln k), \end{aligned}$$

where the last equality can be best seen by first considering that $\sum_{j=0}^{\lceil N/k\rceil-1}\exp(-\frac{1}{k}(\frac{jk}{2}-1))(\ln(k)+1) = \Theta(\log k)$, while $\sum_{j=0}^{\lceil N/k\rceil-1}\exp(-\frac{1}{k}(\frac{jk}{2}-1))(\ln(j+1)) = O(1)$. Summarizing the computations above we see that (2) is of order at most $q^{-1}\log q^{-1}$.

For $D = \mathrm{Geo}(q)$ the computations are almost identical. By Lemma 8 and (3) the expected run time of the (1+1) $\mathrm{EA}_{\vec{p}}$ on ONEMAX_D is at most

$$\begin{aligned} &\frac{2}{1-q}\sum_{n=1}^{\infty}\frac{(1-q)^n(\ln(n)+1)}{(1-q/2)^n} \\ &\le 2\sum_{n=1}^{\infty}(1-q)^{n/2-1}(\ln(n)+1) = O(q^{-1}\log q^{-1}), \end{aligned}$$

which can be seen in a similar way as above by splitting the sum into blocks of size $k := \lceil 1/q \rceil$ and using $1-q \le \exp(-q)$. □

It is interesting to note that the expected run time increases to between $\Omega(N)$ and $O(N\log N)$ when the mutation probability is chosen to be $\vec{p} = (q,\dots,q)$. This can easily be seen as follows. For the upper bound we use Lemma 8 (ignoring the "+1" terms which are easily seen to play an insignificant role) to obtain that the expected run time of the (1+1) $\mathrm{EA}_{\vec{p}}$ with $\vec{p} = (q,\dots,q)$ on $\mathrm{ONEMAX}_{\mathrm{TrunkGeo}(N,q)}$ is at most $\sum_{n=1}^{N-1}\frac{q(1-q)^{n-1}\ln n}{q(1-q)^n} + \frac{(1-q)^{N-1}\ln N}{q(1-q)^N} = \sum_{n=1}^{N-1}\frac{\ln n}{1-q} + O(\log(N)/q) = \frac{\ln((N-1)!)}{1-q} + O(N\log N) = O(N\log N)$.

We can derive a strong lower bound of $\Omega(N\log N)$ in the case of $2^{-N/3} \le q \le 1/N$ from the following one for static solution lengths.

Lemma 9 ([10, Theorem 9], [11, Theorem 4.1]). *For a fixed length n and a uniform mutation vector $\vec{p} = (p,\dots,p)$, the expected run time of the (1+1) $EA_{\vec{p}}$ on ONEMAX_n is at least $(\ln(n) - \ln\ln n - 3)/(p(1-p)^n)$ for $2^{-n/3} \le p \le 1/n$ and at least $(\ln(1/(p^2 n)) - \ln\ln n - 3)/(p(1-p)^n)$ for $1/n \le p \le 1/(\sqrt{n}\log n)$.*

Thus, the expected run time of the (1+1) $\mathrm{EA}_{\vec{p}}$ with $\vec{p} = (q,\dots,q)$ and $2^{-N/3} \le q \le 1/N$ on $\mathrm{ONEMAX}_{\mathrm{TrunkGeo}(N,q)}$ is at least $\sum_{n=1}^{N-1}q(1-q)^{n-1}\frac{(\ln(n)-\ln\ln n-3)}{q(1-q)^n} \ge \sum_{n=1}^{N-1}\frac{1}{2}\frac{\ln n}{1-q} = \frac{1}{2}\frac{\ln((N-1)!)}{1-q} = \Omega(N\log N)$. Similarly we can get a lower bound of $\Omega(N)$ in case of $1/N \le q \le 1/(\sqrt{N}\log N)$ by using the lower bound of $1/(q(1-q)^n)$ for any fixed solution length n.

We now turn our attention to the LeadingOnes problems, where a similar approach as above yields the following result.

Theorem 10. *Let $N \in \mathbb{N}$ and $1/N \le q \le 1/2$. For $D = \mathrm{TrunkGeo}(N,q)$ and $D = \mathrm{Geo}(q)$ the expected run time of the (1+1) $EA_{\vec{p}}$ with $\vec{p} = (q/2,\dots,q/2)$ on $\mathrm{LEADINGONES}_D$ is $\Theta(q^{-2})$.*

We will derive this result from the following lemma, which was independently proven in [3, Theorem 3], [10, Corollary 2], and in a slightly weaker form in [8, Theorem 1.2].

Lemma 11 ([3], [10], and [8]). *For a fixed length n and a mutation vector $\vec{p} = (p,\dots,p)$ with $0 < p < 1/2$, the expected run time of the (1+1) $EA_{\vec{p}}$ on $\mathrm{LEADINGONES}_n$ is exactly $1/(2p^2)\left((1-p)^{-n+1} - (1-p)\right)$.*

Proof of Theorem 10. We first consider the case that the solution length is sampled from the truncated geometric distribution $\mathrm{TrunkGeo}(N,q)$. Using Lemma 11 and (3) (in the third and in the last step) the expected run time of the (1+1) $\mathrm{EA}_{\vec{p}}$ on $\mathrm{LEADINGONES}_D$ is

$$\begin{aligned} &\sum_{n=1}^{N-1}q(1-q)^{n-1}\frac{2}{q^2}\left((1-q/2)^{-n+1} - (1-q/2)\right) + A \\ &\le \frac{2}{q}\sum_{n=1}^{N-1}\left(\frac{(1-q)^{n-1}}{(1-q/2)^{n-1}}\right) + A \\ &\le \frac{2}{q}\sum_{n=0}^{\infty}(1-q)^{n/2} + A \\ &= \frac{2}{q}\frac{1}{1-(1-q)^{1/2}} + A = O(q^{-2}) + A, \end{aligned}$$

where A is the summand that accounts for the event that the solution length is N, i.e.,

$$A = (1-q)^{N-1}\frac{1}{2q^2}\Big((1-q)^{-N+1} - (1-q)\Big) = O\left(q^{-2}\right).$$

Similarly for $D = \mathrm{Geo}(q)$ the expected run time of the (1+1) $\mathrm{EA}_{\vec{p}}$ on $\mathrm{LEADINGONES}_D$ is bounded from above by

$$\begin{aligned} &\frac{2}{q}\sum_{n=1}^{\infty}\frac{(1-q)^{n-1}}{(1-q/2)^{n-1}} \le \frac{2}{q}\sum_{n=0}^{\infty}(1-q)^{n/2} \\ &= \frac{2}{q}\frac{1}{1-(1-q)^{1/2}} \le \frac{4}{q^2}, \end{aligned}$$

where we recall that the last step follows from (3) for $n = 1$, which provides $(1-q)^{1/2} \le 1 - q/2$. □

Just as for ONEMAX_D (with $D = \mathrm{TrunkGeo}(N,q)$) we see that also on $\mathrm{LEADINGONES}_D$ the expected run time increases (in this case to $\Theta(N/q)$) when the mutation probability is chosen to be $\vec{p} = (q, \ldots, q)$. By Lemma 11 this run time equals $\sum_{n=1}^{N-1} q(1-q)^{n-1} \frac{1}{2q^2}\left((1-q)^{-n+1} - (1-q)\right) + A = \frac{1}{2q}\sum_{n=1}^{N-1}(1-(1-q)^n) + A = \frac{1}{2q}\left(N - 1 - \frac{1-(1-q)^N}{q} + 1\right) + A = \Theta(N/q) + A$, where A is the summand that accounts for the event that the solution length is N, i.e.,

$$A = (1-q)^{N-1} \frac{1}{2q^2}\left((1-q)^{-N+1} - (1-q)\right) = \Theta\left(q^{-2}\right).$$

4. ARBITRARY SOLUTION LENGTHS

In the setting described in Section 3 it is assumed that the algorithm designer has quite a good knowledge about the solution length. Not only does he know an upper bound N on the solution length, but he may also crucially exploit its distribution. Indeed, we make quite heavy use in Theorems 7 and 10 of the fact that the (truncated) geometric distribution is highly concentrated around its expected value. That so much information is available to the algorithm designer can be a questionable assumption in certain applications. We therefore regard in this section a more general setting in which *no* a priori information is given about the possible solution length n. That is, we regard a setting in which the solution length can be an arbitrary positive integer. In this setting neither do we have any upper bounds on n nor any information about its distribution.

As before, our task is to decide upon on a sequence $(p_i)_{i\in\mathbb{N}}$ of mutation probabilities $0 \le p_i \le 1$. An adversary may then choose the solution length n and we run the (1+1) $\text{EA}_{\vec{p}}$ with $\vec{p} = (p_1, \ldots, p_n)$. In practical applications, this can be implemented with a (possibly generous) upper bound on the problem size.

We first show that uniform fixed bit flip probabilities necessarily lead to exponential run times (see Section 4.1). We then show two ways out of this problem. In Section 4.2 we consider non-uniform bit flip probabilities and in Section 4.3 we show that we can have an efficient algorithm with uniform bit flip probabilities if we choose the bit flip probability randomly in each iteration.

4.1 Uniform Bit Flip Probabilities

It seems quite intuitive that if nothing is known about the solution length there is not much we can achieve with uniform bit flip probabilities. In fact, for any fixed mutation probability $p \in [0,1]$, we just need to choose a large enough solution length n to see that the $(1+1)$ $\text{EA}_{\vec{p}}$ with uniform mutation probability p is very inefficient. More precisely, using [11, Theorem 6.5] we get the following theorem regarding optimizing OneMax with uniform bit flip probabilities.

Theorem 12. *Let $p \in [0,1]$ be a constant. Then there exists a positive integer $n_0 \in \mathbb{N}$ such that for all $n \ge n_0$ the expected run time of the $(1+1)$ $EA_{\vec{p}}$ with $\vec{p} = (p, \ldots, p)$ on OneMax_n is $2^{\Omega(n)}$.*

It is quite intuitive that for large p the expected optimization time of the (1+1) $\text{EA}_{\vec{p}}$ with $\vec{p} = (p, \ldots, p)$ is very large also for small problem sizes, as in this case typically too many bits are flipped in each iteration. This has been made precise by Witt, who showed that for p, n with $p = \Omega(n^{\varepsilon-1})$, the expected run time of the (1+1) $\text{EA}_{\vec{p}}$ is $2^{\Omega(n^\varepsilon)}$ with probability at least $1 - 2^{-\Omega(n^\varepsilon)}$ [11, Theorem 6.3].

For LeadingOnes we get a similar lower bound from Lemma 11.

Theorem 13. *Let $p \in (0, 1/2)$. Then the expected run time of the $(1+1)$ $EA_{\vec{p}}$ with $\vec{p} = (p, \ldots, p)$ on LeadingOnes_n is $2^{\Omega(n)}$.*

Proof. From Lemma 11 we have that the expected run time of the $(1+1)$ $\text{EA}_{\vec{p}}$ is, for n large enough,

$$\frac{1}{2p^2}\left((1-p)^{-n+1} - (1-p)\right) \ge \frac{1}{2}\left(e^{pn-p} - 1\right) = 2^{\Omega(n)}.$$

□

4.2 Non-Uniform Bit Flip Probabilities

One way to achieve efficient optimization with unknown solution length is by using non-uniform mutation rates, that is, different bit positions have different probabilities associated for being flipped during a mutation operation.

To state our results we need the concept of *summable sequences*. Such sequences will be the basis for the sequence of bit flip probabilities. In short, a sequence $(p_i)_{i\in\mathbb{N}}$ is *summable* if its series $(\sum_{k=1}^{n} p_k)_{n\in\mathbb{N}}$ converges (that is, if it is bounded). The advantage of using summable sequences is that the probability of flipping only one single bit is *always* constant, regardless of the total number of bits considered, i.e., regardless of the problem length n. This is in contrast to the sequence $(1/(i+1))_{i\in\mathbb{N}}$ considered in [4], which is not summable, and which has a chance of $(1/2)\prod_{i=2}^{n}(1 - 1/(i+1)) = 1/n$ of flipping only the first bit and a chance of $(1/n)\prod_{i=1}^{n-1}(1 - 1/(i+1)) = 1/n^2$ of flipping only the nth bit. For this reason the $(1+1)$ EA_i is very inefficient for the setting in which the solution length can be arbitrary.

Theorems 14 and 15 show that not knowing the solution length n does not harm the run time more than by a factor of order $\log^{1+\varepsilon} n$ with respect to the optimal bound when the problem length is known a priori, cf. also Corollary 16 for an explicit sequence yielding this bound. In fact, we prove that the additional cost caused by not knowing the solution length in advance is even a bit smaller, cf. the comments after Corollary 16.

We start with the theorem regarding OneMax.

Theorem 14. *Let $(p_i)_{i\in\mathbb{N}}$ be a monotonically decreasing summable sequence with $\Sigma := \sum_{i=1}^{\infty} p_i < 1$. Then, for any $n \in \mathbb{N}$, the expected run time of the $(1+1)$ $EA_{\vec{p}}$ with $\vec{p} = (p_1, \ldots, p_n)$ on OneMax_n is at most $\log n/(p_n(1-\Sigma)) = O(\log n/p_n)$.*

Proof. We make use of the multiplicative drift theorem [5, Theorem 3] and show that for every n and every search point x with $n-k$ ones, the probability to create in one iteration of the (1+1) $\text{EA}_{\vec{p}}$ with $\vec{p} = (p_1, \ldots, p_n)$ a search point y with $\text{OneMax}_n(y) > \text{OneMax}_n(x)$ is at least of order k/p_n. This can in fact be seen quite easily by observing that the probability to increase the OneMax-value of x by exactly one is at least

$$kp_n \prod_{j=1}^{n}(1-p_j) \ge kp_n\left(1 - \sum_{j=1}^{n} p_j\right) \ge kp_n\left(1 - \sum_{j=1}^{\infty} p_j\right)$$
$$= kp_n(1-\Sigma).$$

From this an upper bound of $\log n/(p_n(1-\Sigma))$ for the run time of the $(1+1)$ $\text{EA}_{\vec{p}}$ follows immediately from the multiplicative drift theorem. □

Next we consider LEADINGONES. The proof follows along similar lines as the one for ONEMAX and uses a fitness level argument instead of multiplicative drift (using additive drift would also be possible).

THEOREM 15. *Let $(p_i)_{i\in\mathbb{N}}$ be a monotonically decreasing summable sequence with $\Sigma := \sum_{i=1}^{\infty} p_i < 1$. Then, for any $n \in \mathbb{N}$, the expected run time of the $(1+1)$ $EA_{\vec{p}}$ with $\vec{p} = (p_1, \ldots, p_n)$ on LEADINGONES$_n$ is at most $n/(p_n(1-\Sigma)) = O(n/p_n)$.*

PROOF. Let $n, k \in \mathbb{N}$ with $k < n$ and let $x \in \{0,1\}^n$ with $\text{Lo}(x) = k-1$. The probability to get in one iteration of the $(1+1)$ EA$_{\vec{p}}$ with $\vec{p} = (p_1, \ldots, p_n)$ a search point y with $\text{Lo}(y) > \text{Lo}(x)$ is at least

$$p_k \prod_{j=1}^{k-1}(1-p_j) \geq p_k(1 - \sum_{j=1}^{k-1} p_j) \geq p_k(1-\Sigma) \geq p_n(1-\Sigma).$$

By a simple fitness level argument (see, e.g., the work by Sudholt [10] for background and examples of this method), the expected run time of the $(1+1)$ EA$_{\vec{p}}$ on LEADINGONES$_n$ is thus at most $n/(p_n(1-\Sigma))$. □

It is well known that for every constant $\varepsilon > 0$ the sequence $(1/(i \log^{1+\varepsilon} i))_{i\in\mathbb{N}}$ is summable (this can be proven via Cauchy's condensation test). It is obviously also monotonically decreasing in i. Theorems 14 and 15, together with the sequence $(p_i)_{i\in\mathbb{N}} := (1/(2Si\log^{1+\varepsilon} i))_{i\in\mathbb{N}}$ for $S := \sum_{i=1}^{\infty} 1/(i\log^{1+\varepsilon} i)$, therefore imply the following corollary.

COROLLARY 16. *For every positive constant ε there exists a sequence of mutation probabilities $(p_i)_{i\in\mathbb{N}}$ such that for any n the expected run time of the $(1+1)$ $EA_{\vec{p}}$ with $\vec{p} = (p_1, \ldots, p_n)$ on ONEMAX$_n$ is $O(n\log^{2+\varepsilon} n)$ and is of order $n^2\log^{1+\varepsilon} n$ for LEADINGONES$_n$.*

The bound from Corollary 16 can be improved by regarding the following summable sequences.

For any $r \in \mathbb{R}$ and any $i \in \mathbb{N}_{\geq 2}$ let

$$\log^{(i)} r := \begin{cases} \log_2(\log^{(i-1)} r), & \text{if } \log^{(i-1)}(r) \geq 2; \\ 1, & \text{otherwise;} \end{cases}$$

where $\log^{(1)} r := \log_2 r$ if $r \geq 2$ and $\log^{(1)} r := 1$ otherwise. For every constant $\varepsilon > 0$ and all positive integers s, i let

$$p_i^{s,\varepsilon} := 1/\left(i(\log^{(s)}(i))^{1+\varepsilon}\prod_{j=1}^{s-1}\log^{(j)}(i)\right). \qquad (4)$$

For every $\varepsilon > 0$ and every $s \geq 1$ the sequence $(p_i^{s,\varepsilon})_{i\in\mathbb{N}}$ is summable. Furthermore, this sequence clearly is monotonically decreasing. Choosing larger and larger s therefore gives better and better asymptotic run time bounds in Theorems 14 and 15.

4.3 Randomized Bit Flip Probability

In the conclusions of [4] the authors ask the following: how can we optimize efficiently when an upper bound N on the problem length is known, but only n bits *at unknown positions* are relevant for the fitness? It is not difficult to see that our previous solutions with non-uniform bit flip probabilities will not be able to assign appropriate bit flip probabilities to the *relevant* bit positions. However, any uniform choice of bit flip probabilities will effectively ignore irrelevant bit positions. In this section we consider a variation of the $(1+1)$ EA where the bit flip probability p is chosen randomly from a distribution Q on $(0,1)$ in each iteration (the distribution Q does not change over time). This mutation probability is then applied independently to each bit, i.e., each bit of the current best solution is independently flipped with probability p. See Algorithm 2 for the detailed description of the $(1+1)$ EA$_Q$.

Algorithm 2: The $(1+1)$ EA$_Q$ for a distribution Q on $(0,1)$ optimizing a pseudo-Boolean function $f : \{0,1\}^n \to \mathbb{R}$.

```
Initialization: Sample x ∈ {0,1}^n uniformly at
  random and query f(x);
Optimization: for t = 1,2,3,... do
    Sample bit flip probability p_t from Q;
    for i = 1,...,n do
        With probability p_t set y_i ← 1 − x_i and set
        y_i ← x_i otherwise;
    Query f(y);
    if f(y) ≥ f(x) then x ← y;
```

To make the problem more explicit, we are asked to find a distribution Q on $(0,1)$ such that the $(1+1)$ EA$_Q$ efficiently optimizes for any $n \in \mathbb{N}$ and any pairwise different $b_1, \ldots, b_n \in \mathbb{N}$ the functions

$$\text{ONEMAX}_{b_1,\ldots,b_n}(x) := \sum_{i=1}^{n} x_{b_i}, \text{ respectively}$$

$$\text{LEADINGONES}_{b_1,\ldots,b_n}(x) := \max\{i \in [0..n] \mid \forall j \leq i : x_{b_j} = 1\}.$$

In Theorems 17 and 18 we show that such a distribution Q exist. That is, there is a distribution Q such that the corresponding $(1+1)$ EA$_Q$ efficiently optimizes any ONEMAX$_{b_1,\ldots,b_n}$ and any LEADINGONES$_{b_1,\ldots,b_n}$ function, regardless of the number of relevant bits and regardless of their positions.

We start with our main result regarding ONEMAX.

THEOREM 17. *Let $(p_i)_{i\in\mathbb{N}} \in (0,1)^{\mathbb{N}}$ be a monotonically decreasing summable sequence. Set $\Sigma := \sum_{j=1}^{\infty} p_j$. Let Q be the distribution which assigns the mutation probability $1/i$ a probability of p_i/Σ.*

For any $n \in \mathbb{N}$ and any pairwise different positive integers $b_1, \ldots, b_n$ the expected run time of the $(1+1)$ EA_Q on ONEMAX$_{b_1,\ldots,b_n}$ is $O(\log(n)/p_{2n})$.

PROOF. The probability to sample a mutation probability between $1/(2n)$ and $1/n$ is

$$\sum_{j=n}^{2n} p_j \geq np_{2n}.$$

We disregard all iterations in which we do not sample a mutation probability between $1/(2n)$ and n (they can only be beneficial). Thus, on average, we consider at least one iteration out of $1/(np_{2n})$.

Assuming that x is a search point with $n-\ell$ ones (in the relevant positions) and that the sampled bit flip probability p satisfies $1/(2n) \leq p \leq 1/n$, the probability to make a progress of exactly one is at least

$$\ell p(1-p)^{n-1} \geq \ell/(2n)(1-1/n)^{n-1} \geq \ell/(2en).$$

Thus, we have an expected progress in each iteration of at least $\frac{\ell}{2en} n p_{2n} = O(\ell p_{2n})$. Therefore, by the multiplicative drift theorem [5, Theorem 3], we need in expectation $O(\log(n)/p_{2n})$ iterations to optimize function $\text{ONEMAX}_{b_1,\dots,b_n}$. □

For LEADINGONES we obtain the following.

THEOREM 18. *Let $(p_i)_{i\in\mathbb{N}}$ and Q as in Theorem 17.*
For any $n \in \mathbb{N}$ and any pairwise different $b_1, \dots, b_n \in \mathbb{N}$ the expected run time of the $(1+1)$ EA_Q on $\text{LEADINGONES}_{b_1,\dots,b_n}$ is $O(n/p_{2n})$.

PROOF. This proof follows along similar lines as the one for ONEMAX. We have again that the probability to have a bit flip probability between $1/(2n)$ and $1/n$ in an iteration is at least np_{2n}.

Let x be a search point with $\text{LEADINGONES}_{b_1,\dots,b_n}(x) = \ell$. Given a mutation probability p between $1/(2n)$ and $1/n$, the probability to create in one iteration of the $(1+1)$ EA_Q a search point y of fitness greater than ℓ is at least

$$p(1-p)^{\ell-1} \geq 1/(2n)(1-1/n)^{n-1} \geq 1/(2en).$$

Thus, we have an expected progress in each iteration of at least $\frac{1}{2en} n p_{2n} = O(p_{2n})$. Therefore, by the fitness level method (see again [10] for a discussion of this method), we need in expectation $O(n/p_{2n})$ iterations to optimize $\text{LEADINGONES}_{b_1,\dots,b_n}$. □

By choosing the summable sequence with entries as in (4) and $s = 1$, the two theorems above immediately yield the following result.

COROLLARY 19. *The expected run time of the described $(1+1)$ EA_Q with Q using the summable sequence (4) with $s = 1$ on $\text{ONEMAX}_{b_1,\dots,b_n}$ is $O(n \log^{2+\varepsilon} n)$ and on $\text{LEADINGONES}_{b_1,\dots,b_n}$ it is $O(n^2 \log^{1+\varepsilon} n)$.*

Note that, just as discussed after Corollary 16, choosing larger and larger s gives asymptotically better and better bounds.

5. SUMMARY AND OUTLOOK

We have analyzed the performance of variants of the $(1+1)$ EA in the presence of unknown solution lengths. While for highly concentrated solution length non-uniform mutation probabilities are not advantageous (or at least not to a significant degree), they are crucial in a setting in which we do not have any knowledge about the solution length. Surprisingly, even in the latter situation, a sequence of (non-uniform) mutation probabilities exists such that the corresponding $(1+1)$ EA is almost optimal, simultaneously for all possible solution lengths.

We have also investigated a setting in which the relevant bit positions can be arbitrary in number and position. Possibly even more surprisingly, even this can be handled quite efficiently by a $(1+1)$ EA variant for the two test functions ONEMAX and LEADINGONES.

We believe the setting of unknown solution length to be relevant for numerous real-world applications. As a next step toward a better understanding of how this uncertainty can be tackled efficiently with evolutionary algorithms, we suggest to investigate more challenging function classes, e.g., starting with the class of all linear functions. It is not clear a priori if bounds similar to the ones presented in Section 4 can be achieved for such problems.

From a mathematical point of view it would also interesting to investigate the tightness of our bounds in Section 4. We do not know whether some choice of mutation probabilities gives an upper bound of $O(n \log n)$ for ONEMAX or $O(n^2)$ for LEADINGONES. We recall that the sequences $(1/(n\log(n)))_{n\in\mathbb{N}}$ as well as $(1/p_i^{\infty,\varepsilon})_{i\in\mathbb{N}}$ with $p_i^{\infty,\varepsilon} := \lim_{s\to\infty} p_i^{s,\varepsilon}$ are not summable. Removing the gap entirely is therefore likely to require a substantially different approach.

Acknowledgments

This research benefited from the support of the "FMJH Program Gaspard Monge in optimization and operation research", and from the support to this program from EDF.

Parts of this work have been done while Timo Kötzing was visiting the Université Pierre et Marie Curie (Paris 6).

6. REFERENCES

[1] A. Auger and B. Doerr. *Theory of Randomized Search Heuristics.* World Scientific, 2011.

[2] L. Bianchi, M. Dorigo, L. Gambardella, and W. Gutjahr. A Survey on Metaheuristics for Stochastic Combinatorial optimization. *Natural Computing*, 8:239–287, 2009.

[3] S. Böttcher, B. Doerr, and F. Neumann. Optimal fixed and adaptive mutation rates for the LeadingOnes problem. In *Proc. of the 11th International Conference on Parallel Problem Solving from Nature (PPSN'10)*, pages 1–10. Springer, 2010.

[4] S. Cathabard, P. K. Lehre, and X. Yao. Non-uniform mutation rates for problems with unknown solution lengths. In *Proc. of the 11th ACM Workshop on Foundations of Genetic Algorithms (FOGA'11)*, pages 173–180. ACM, 2011.

[5] B. Doerr, D. Johannsen, and C. Winzen. Multiplicative drift analysis. *Algorithmica*, 64:673–697, 2012.

[6] T. Jansen. *Analyzing Evolutionary Algorithms—The Computer Science Perspective.* Springer, 2013.

[7] Y. Jin and J. Branke. Evolutionary Optimization in Uncertain Environments—A Survey. *IEEE Transactions on Evolutionary Computation*, 9:303–317, 2005.

[8] V. Ladret. Asymptotic hitting time for a simple evolutionary model of protein folding. *Journal of Applied Probability*, 42:39–51, 2005.

[9] F. Neumann and C. Witt. *Bioinspired Computation in Combinatorial Optimization – Algorithms and Their Computational Complexity.* Springer, 2010.

[10] D. Sudholt. A new method for lower bounds on the running time of evolutionary algorithms. *IEEE Transactions on Evolutionary Computation*, 17:418–435, 2013.

[11] C. Witt. Tight bounds on the optimization time of a randomized search heuristic on linear functions. *Combinatorics, Probability & Computing*, 22:294–318, 2013.

Elitist Black-Box Models: Analyzing the Impact of Elitist Selection on the Performance of Evolutionary Algorithms

Carola Doerr
CNRS & Univ. Pierre et Marie Curie
Paris, France

Johannes Lengler
ETH Zürich
Zürich, Switzerland

ABSTRACT

Black-box complexity theory provides lower bounds for the runtime of black-box optimizers like evolutionary algorithms and serves as an inspiration for the design of new genetic algorithms. Several black-box models covering different classes of algorithms exist, each highlighting a different aspect of the algorithms under considerations. In this work we add to the existing black-box notions a new *elitist black-box model*, in which algorithms are required to base all decisions solely on (a fixed number of) the best search points sampled so far. Our model combines features of the ranking-based and the memory-restricted black-box models with elitist selection.

We provide several examples for which the elitist black-box complexity is exponentially larger than that the respective complexities in all previous black-box models, thus showing that the elitist black-box complexity can be much closer to the runtime of typical evolutionary algorithms.

We also introduce the concept of p-Monte Carlo black-box complexity, which measures the time it takes to optimize a problem with failure probability at most p. Even for small p, the p-Monte Carlo black-box complexity of a function class $\mathcal{F}$ can be smaller by an exponential factor than its typically regarded Las Vegas complexity (which measures the *expected* time it takes to optimize $\mathcal{F}$).

Categories and Subject Descriptors

F.2.2 [**Theory of Computation**]: Analysis of Algorithms and Problem Complexity—*Nonnumerical Algorithms and Problems*

Keywords

Black-Box Complexity; Elitist Selection; Comparison-Based Algorithms; Evolutionary Computation

1. INTRODUCTION

Black-box models are classes of algorithms that are designed to help us understand how efficient commonly used search strategies like evolutionary algorithms (EAs) and other randomized search heuristics (RSHs) are. Several models exist, each designed to analyze a different aspect of search heuristics. For example, the memory-restricted model [10, 16] helps us to understand the influence of the population size on the efficiency of the search strategy, while the ranking-based black-box model [11, 17, 27] analyzes how much a heuristic loses by not using absolute but merely relative fitness values.

Having been introduced to the evolutionary computation community in [14, 16], black-box complexity is a young but highly active area of current research efforts [1, 3, 4, 6–8, 10–12, 17, 21, 22, 26, 27]. The insights from black-box complexity studies can be used to design more efficient genetic algorithms, as the recent $(1 + (\lambda, \lambda))$ GA from [5] shows.

We contribute to the existing literature a new model, which we call the *elitist black-box model*. As the name suggests, our model is designed to analyze the effect of elitist selection rules on the performance of search heuristics. In evolutionary computation, elitist selection is very common as it can be seen as a literate interpretation of the "survival of the fittest" principle in an optimization context. We remark already here that the usage of "elitist selection" is not standardized in the EA literature. Some subcommunities would therefore rather call our elitist black-box model a *black-box model with truncation selection*. Thus, to be precise, the algorithms in our $(\mu + \lambda)$ elitist model are required to select from the offspring and the parent population some μ search points of largest fitness values.

1.1 Previous Work

In contrast to classical complexity notions discussed in the computer science literature, black-box complexity focuses on so-called black-box optimizers, i.e., algorithms that do not have access to the function at hand other than by evaluating possible solutions, which are referred to as *search points*. If $\mathcal{C}$ is a class of black-box optimizers, then the $\mathcal{C}$-black-box complexity of a class $\mathcal{F}$ of functions is measured by the expected number of function evaluations that are needed by a best possible algorithm in $\mathcal{C}$ to optimize any instance $f \in \mathcal{F}$ (formal definitions will be given in Section 2). This number is a lower bound for the efficiency of any algorithm $\mathcal{A} \in \mathcal{C}$ and thus helps us understand how adequate an algorithmic choice is for the given problem class $\mathcal{F}$.

Among the most important algorithmic choices in the design of evolutionary algorithms are the population size, the sampling strategies (often called variation operators), and the selection rules. Existing black-box models cover these aspects in the following way. While the *memory-restricted*

GECCO '15, July 11 - 16, 2015, Madrid, Spain

ISBN 978-1-4503-3472-3/15/07...$15.00
DOI: http://dx.doi.org/10.1145/2739480.2754654

model [10,16] and the *parallel* black-box model [3,4] analyze the influence of the population-size, the *unbiased* model [8, 22,26] considers the efficiency of search strategies using only so-called unbiased variation operators. The influence of the selection rules have been analyzed in the *comparison-based* and *ranking-based* black-box model [11,17,27], with a focus on not revealing full fitness information to the algorithm but rather the comparison or the ranking of search points. The idea behind these models is that, in contrast to other search strategies like the physics-inspired simulated annealing, many evolutionary algorithms base their selection solely on *relative* and not on *absolute* fitness values.

While the comparison-based and the ranking-based models provide only relative fitness values, they do not require the algorithms to always select the better ones. Search strategies that adhere to this selection rule are called *elitist* algorithms in the evolutionary computation literature. Many common and widely applied black-box optimization strategies like $(\mu + \lambda)$ and (μ, λ) EAs as well as local hill climbers such as Randomized Local Search (RLS) are of this type. On the other hand, many practical algorithms intentionally keep suboptimal solutions to enhance population diversity, or to better explore the search space [28, 29]. It has been shown that in some situations, specific elitist algorithms like RLS or the $(\mu + 1)$ EA are inferior to non-elitist algorithms [18, 20, 25]. In this paper, we go one step further and investigate the performance of *all* elitist algorithms simultaneously.

As mentioned before, algorithms in the ranking-based and comparison-based models do not need to be elitist. (Ab-)Using this, algorithms can be designed in both models that have much smaller runtimes than typical EAs [10, 11]. As we shall see in Section 3 this even remains true if we regard (1+1) memory-restricted unary unbiased comparison-based algorithms, which constitutes the most restrictive combination of the restrictions from existing black-box models. We will see that such algorithms can crucially profit from eventually giving preference to search points of fitness inferior to that of the current best search points.

1.2 Our Model, New Complexity Measures, and Results

We provide in this work a model to analyze the impact of elitist selection on the runtime of black-box optimizers. In this *elitist black-box model* the population of the algorithms may contain only search points of best-so-far fitness values. That is, if the population size is μ, then at any point in time only the μ best-so-far search points (of possibly different fitness values) are allowed to be kept in the population (ties broken arbitrarily). All other previously sampled search points are not allowed to influence the behavior of the algorithm any more. We show (Section 3) that already for quite simple function classes there can be an exponential gap between the efficiency of elitist and non-elitist black-box algorithms. We also show (Section 4) that some shortcomings of previous models can be eliminated when they are combined with an elitist selection requirement. More precisely we show that the elitist unary unbiased black-box complexity of JUMP_k is of order $\Omega(n^k)$ and thus non-polynomial for $k = \omega(1)$. In contrast, the unary unbiased black-box complexity of JUMP_k is known to be polynomial even for extreme values of k [6].

In previous models, the black-box complexity has been defined in a *Las Vegas* manner, i.e, it measures the expected number of function evaluations until the algorithm hits the optimum. On the other hand, many proofs actually show that with high (or constant) probability the optimum is found after a certain number of steps, and then *random restarts* are used to bound the expected runtime. In (the strict version of) the elitist model the algorithms are not allowed to do random restarts, since new search points can be kept in the population only if they are among the μ best ones sampled so far. Since this is a rather artificial problem (many real-world optimization routines make use of restarts), we introduce in this work the concept of *Monte Carlo black-box complexities*. Roughly speaking, the p-Monte Carlo black-box runtime of a black-box algorithm A on a function f is the minimal number of queries A needs in order to find the optimum of f with probability at least $1 - p$. The complexity class is then derived in the usual way, cf. Section 2.1. We regard in our work both Monte Carlo complexities and standard (i.e., *Las Vegas*) complexities. For elitist black-box algorithms these two notions can differ substantially as we shall see in Section 3.1.

In the following we consider only discrete search spaces, and even more restrictively, only pseudo-Boolean functions $f : \{0,1\}^n \to \mathbb{R}$. Generalizations to non-finite or continuous search spaces are straightforward.

2. THE ELITIST BLACK-BOX MODEL

The *elitist black-box model* covers all algorithms that follow the pseudo-code in Algorithm 1. That is, a $(\mu + \lambda)$ *elitist black-box algorithm* is initialized by sampling μ search points. In each subsequent round it samples λ new search points from distributions that depend only on the current population X and the ranking of X with respect to the fitness function f.[1] When all λ search points have been evaluated, the algorithm proceeds to the selection step. A newly created search point replaces a point in X if its fitness is at least as good as one of the search points in X; it is discarded otherwise. In case of ties we allow the algorithm to select the search points it prefers.

The elitist black-box model covers many common EAs such as $(\mu + \lambda)$ EAs, Randomized Local Search (RLS), and other hill climbers. It does not cover algorithms with non-elitist selection rules like tournament or fitness-proportional selection.

Several extensions and variants of the model are possible, including in particular one in which the μ first search points cannot be sampled adaptively, where the selection has to be unbiased among search points of the same rank, where only offsprings can be selected (comma strategies), or a non-ranking-based one where absolute instead of relative fitness information is provided. Note that the latter would allow for fitness-dependent mutation rates, which are excluded by the variant analyzed here. The lower bounds presented in Sections 3 and 4 actually hold for this non-ranking-based model (and are thus even more powerful than such only applicable to the model described in Algorithm 1). The model can certainly also be extended to an unbiased elitist one, in which the distribution $p^{(t)}$ in line 7 of Algorithm 1 has to be

[1]Two search points have the same rank if and only if they have the same fitness. The search points of X with maximal f-values are rank one, the ones with second largest f-values are rank two etc.

Algorithm 1: The $(\mu + \lambda)$ elitist black-box algorithm for maximizing an unknown function $f : \{0,1\}^n \to \mathbb{R}$

1 **Initialization:**
2 $X \leftarrow \emptyset$;
3 **for** $i = 1, \ldots, \mu$ **do**
4 Depending only on the multiset X and the ranking $\rho(X, f)$ of X induced by f, choose a probability distribution $p^{(i)}$ over $\{0,1\}^n$ and sample $x^{(i)}$ according to $p^{(i)}$;
5 $X \leftarrow X \cup \{x^{(i)}\}$;
6 **Optimization: for** $t = 1, 2, 3, \ldots$ **do**
7 Depending only on the multiset X and the ranking $\rho(X, f)$ of X induced by f choose a probability distribution $p^{(t)}$ on $(\{0,1\}^n)_{i=1}^{\lambda}$ and sample $(y^{(1)}, \ldots, y^{(\lambda)})$ according to $p^{(t)}$;
8 Set $X \leftarrow X \cup \{y^{(1)}, \ldots, y^{(\lambda)}\}$;
9 **for** $i = 1, \ldots, \lambda$ **do** Select $x \in \arg\min X$ and update $X \leftarrow X \setminus \{x\}$;

unbiased in the sense of Lehre and Witt [22]. See Section 4 for results on the unbiased elitist model.

Note that elitist black-box algorithms covered by Algorithm 1 are *memory-restricted* in the sense of [10, 16], that is, they cannot store any other information than the current population and its ranking. All information about previous search points (e.g., their number) has to be discarded. The (1+1) version of the elitist model is *comparison-based* (that is, a query reveals only if an offspring has worse, equal, or better fitness than its parent), while the $(\mu+\lambda)$ versions are *ranking-based* in the sense of [11]. This means that the algorithm has no information about absolute fitness values, but only knows how the fitnesses of the $(\mu + \lambda)$ search points compare to each other. For memory-restricted algorithms these two notions coincide, while for non-memory-restricted models the ranking-based complexity can be smaller by a logarithmic factor than the comparison-based complexity, since in the ranking-based model the algorithm always gets a full ranking of the previously sampled search points while in the comparison-based model it has to specify two search points whose fitness is compared with each other.[2]

2.1 Monte Carlo vs. Las Vegas Black-Box Complexities

As discussed in Section 1.2, usually the black-box complexity of a function class $\mathcal{F}$ is defined in a *Las Vegas* manner (measuring the *expected number* of function evaluations), while in the case of elitist black-box complexity we also introduce a *p-Monte Carlo black-box complexity*, where we allow some failure probability p (see below for formal definitions). If we make a statement about the Monte Carlo complexity without specifying p, then we mean that for *every constant* $p > 0$ the statement holds for the p-Monte Carlo complexity. However, we sometimes also regard p-Monte Carlo complexities for non-constant $p = p(n) = o(1)$, thus yielding high probability statements.

For most black-box complexities, the Las Vegas and the Monte Carlo notions are closely related: every Las Vegas algorithm is also (up to a factor of $1/p$ in the runtime) a p-Monte Carlo algorithm by Markov's inequality, and a Monte Carlo algorithm can be turned into a Las Vegas algorithm by restarting the algorithm until the optimum is found. In particular, if restarts are allowed then Las Vegas and Monte Carlo complexities differ by at most a constant factor. This has been made explicit in [7, Remark 2] and is heavily used there as well as in a number of other results on black-box complexity. It is not difficult to see that such a reasoning fails for elitist black-box algorithms, as they are not allowed to do arbitrary restarts: if the sampled solution intended for a restart is not as good as the ones currently in the memory, it has to be discarded (line 9 of Algorithm 1). Las Vegas and Monte Carlo elitist black-box complexities may therefore differ significantly from each other, see Section 3.1 for an example with exponentially large gap.

We come to the formal definition. Let $\mathcal{F}$ be a class of pseudo-Boolean functions, and let $p \in [0, 1)$. The *Las Vegas complexity* of an algorithm A for $\mathcal{F}$ is the maximum expected number of function evaluations of f before A evaluates an optimal search point for the first time, where the maximum is taken over all $f \in \mathcal{F}$. The Las Vegas complexity of $\mathcal{F}$ with respect to a class $\mathcal{A}$ of algorithms is the minimum ("best") Las Vegas complexity among all $A \in \mathcal{A}$ for $\mathcal{F}$. The p-Monte Carlo complexity of $\mathcal{F}$ with respect to $\mathcal{A}$ is the minimum number T such that there is an algorithm in $\mathcal{A}$ which has for all $f \in \mathcal{F}$ a probability of at least $1-p$ to find an optimum with T function evaluations. The $(\mu + \lambda)$ *elitist Las Vegas (elitist p-Monte Carlo) black-box complexity* of $\mathcal{F}$ is the Las Vegas (p-Monte Carlo) complexity of $\mathcal{F}$ with respect to the class of all $(\mu + \lambda)$ elitist black-box algorithms.

To ease terminology, we will say that an algorithm *spends time t* on a function f if it uses at most t function evaluations on f. Moreover, we call the *runtime* of an algorithm A on a function f to be the expected number of function evaluations of A until it evaluates an optimal search point. In this way, the Las Vegas complexity of $\mathcal{A}$ on $\mathcal{F}$ is the worst-case (over all $f \in F$) runtime of the best algorithm $A \in \mathcal{A}$.

If we are interested in the asymptotic p-Monte Carlo complexity of an algorithm A on a function class $\mathcal{F}$ then we will frequently make use of the following observation, which follows from Markov's inequality and the law of total expectation. We omit the proof.

REMARK 1. *Let $p \in (0,1)$. Assume that there is an event $\mathcal{E}$ of probability $p_{\mathcal{E}} < p$ such that conditioned on $\neg\mathcal{E}$ the algorithm A finds the optimum after* expected *time at most T. Then the p-Monte Carlo complexity of A on f is at most $(1 - p_{\mathcal{E}})(p - p_{\mathcal{E}})^{-1}T$. In particular, if $p - p_{\mathcal{E}} = \Omega(1)$ then the p-Monte Carlo complexity is $O(T)$.*

2.2 (Non-)Applicability of Yao's Principle

A convenient tool in black-box complexity theory is Yao's Principle. In simple words, Yao's Principle allows to restrict one's attention to the runtime T of a best-possible *deterministic* algorithms on a *random* input instead of regarding the best-possible performance of a *random* algorithm on an *arbitrary* input. Analyzing the former is often considerably easier than directly bounding the performance of any possible randomized algorithm. Yao's Principle states that T is a

[2]Binary search shows that the gap between the two notions cannot be larger than a logarithmic factor, but on the other hand this logarithmic gap occurs already for the simple ONEMAX problem. While it's ranking-based black-box complexity is only $\Theta(n/\log n)$ [11], its comparison-based complexity is $\Theta(n)$ by a straightforward application of Yao's Principle.

lower bound for the expected performance of a best possible randomized algorithm for the regarded problem. Formally, Yao's Principle is the following.

LEMMA 2 (YAO'S PRINCIPLE [30]). *Let Π be a problem with a finite set $\mathcal{I}$ of input instances (of a fixed size) permitting a finite set $\mathcal{A}$ of deterministic algorithms. Let p be a probability distribution over $\mathcal{I}$ and q be a probability distribution over $\mathcal{A}$. Then,*

$$\min_{A \in \mathcal{A}} \mathrm{E}[T(I_p, A)] \leq \max_{I \in \mathcal{I}} \mathrm{E}[T(I, A_q)], \quad (1)$$

where I_p denotes a random input chosen from $\mathcal{I}$ according to p, A_q a random algorithm chosen from $\mathcal{C}$ according to q and $T(I, A)$ denotes the runtime of algorithm A on input I.

It is interesting to note that the informal interpretation of Yao's Principle given above does not apply to elitist algorithms. To illustrate this phenomenon, let us consider the (1+1) elitist model, though the argument can be easily extended to population-based elitist algorithms. Let p be the uniform distribution over the instances

$$\mathrm{OM}_z : \{0,1\}^n \to \mathbb{R}, x \mapsto n - \sum_{i=1}^{n} (x_i \oplus z_i), \quad (2)$$

$z \in \{0,1\}^n$, of the well-known ONEMAX problem (see Section 3 for some background on this problem). Let A be any deterministic algorithm. Then A has a positive (in fact, fairly large) probability during the optimization of I_p of getting stuck in some search point x: As a deterministic (1+1) elitist algorithm there exists a search point $y = y(x)$ such that whenever the algorithm sees x in the memory it samples y next. If the OM_z-fitness of y is strictly smaller than that of x, offspring y has to be discarded immediately, in which case the algorithm is in exactly the same situation as before. It can thus never escape from x, and the expected runtime of the algorithm on OM_z is infinite. This situation happens frequently and indeed it is not difficult to show that every deterministic (1+1) elitist algorithm has an infinite expected runtime on a uniformly chosen ONEMAX instance. The lower bound in (1) is thus infinite, too, suggesting that the elitist black-box complexity of this problem is infinite as well. However, there are simple elitist randomized search strategies that have finite expected runtime on ONEMAX, for example, RLS and the $(1+1)$ EA.

Why does this example not contradict Yao's Principle? Reading Lemma 2 carefully, we see that it makes a statement only about such randomized algorithms that are a convex combination of deterministic ones. In other words, the randomized algorithms (on a fixed input size) are given by making one random choice at the beginning, determining which of the finitely many deterministic algorithms we apply. For typical classes of algorithms *every* randomized algorithm is such a convex combination of deterministic algorithms (and randomized algorithms are, in fact, often defined this way). In this case Yao's Principle can be summarized in the way we described before Lemma 2, i.e., as a statement that links the worst-case expected runtime of randomized algorithms with the best expected runtime of deterministic algorithms on random input. The previous paragraph, however, explains that in the elitist black-box model there are randomized algorithms which cannot be expressed as a convex combination of deterministic ones. For this reason, we can never apply Yao's Principle directly to the class of elitist black-box algorithms. Similar considerations hold for other classes of memory-restricted black-box algorithms, but have not been mentioned explicitly in the literature. We are not aware of any other class of evolutionary algorithm where such an anomaly occurs and find the putative non-applicability of Yao's Principle quite noteworthy.

Due to the problems outlined above, we will often consider in our lower bound proofs a superset $\mathcal{A}'$ of algorithms which contains all elitist ones and which has the property that every randomized algorithm in $\mathcal{A}'$ can be expressed as a convex combination of deterministic ones. A lower bound shown for this broader class trivially applies to all elitist black-box algorithms. Observe in particular that in a class of black-box algorithms where every algorithm knows the number of previous steps, every randomized strategy is a convex combination of deterministic strategies: the algorithm can just flip all coins in advance, and essentially use the i-th random bit (or bit string) in the i-th step. Hence, such classes may be used to apply Yao's Principle. Note that still we obtain lower bounds that are much stronger than those of any of the previous black-box models.

3. EXPONENTIAL GAPS TO PREVIOUS MODELS

We provide some function classes for which the elitist black-box complexity is exponentially larger than their black-box complexities in any of the previously regarded models. The basis for these functions is ONEMAX, one of the best studied example functions in the theory of evolutionary computation. The original ONEMAX function simply counts the number of ones in a bitstring. Maximizing ONEMAX thus corresponds to finding the all-ones string.

Search heuristics are typically invariant with respect to problem encoding, and as such they have the same runtime for any function from the generalized ONEMAX function class ONEMAX $:= \{\mathrm{OM}_z \mid z \in \{0,1\}^n\}$, where OM_z is defined by (2). We call z, the unique global optimum of function OM_z, the *target string* of OM_z.

A very simple heuristic optimizing ONEMAX in $\Theta(n \log n)$ steps is *Randomized Local Search* (RLS). Since a variant of RLS will be used in both our upper bounds, we briefly recall that this algorithm is initialized with a uniform sample x. In each iteration one bit position $j \in [n]$ is chosen uniformly at random. The j-th bit of x is flipped and the fitness of the resulting search point y is evaluated. The better of the two search points x and y is kept for future iterations (favoring the newly created individual in case of ties). As is easily verified, RLS is a unary unbiased (1+1) elitist black-box algorithm.

3.1 The Double OneMax Problem

Our first example is a class of functions with two local optima that are far apart from each other, but both of which can be found efficiently by standard heuristics. As mentioned we will show that for such problems there can be an exponential gap between the elitist black-box complexity and the black-box complexity in a model in which all algorithms have to be unbiased, memory-restricted with size bound one, and purely comparison-based. This shows that our model strengthens the existing landscape of black-box models considerably. The example also shows that the Las

Vegas complexity of a problem can be exponentially larger than its Monte Carlo complexity.

The example is surprisingly simple and can easily be extended to similar functions with two local optima that are sufficiently far apart. To keep things simple we consider the following concrete class of functions. For a string $z^1 \in \{0,1\}^n$ and a set $S \subseteq [n]$ let $z^2 := z^2(z^1, S)$ be the string whose entries in $[n] \setminus S$ equal those of z^1 while the other entries are inverted. That is, $z^2 = z^1 \oplus e_S$, where here and in the following e_S is the binary vector whose entries in positions $i \in S$ are one and all other entries are zero. Let

$$\text{OM}_{z^1,S} := \begin{cases} \max\{\text{OM}_{z^1}(x), \text{OM}_{z^2}(x)\}, & \text{if } x \neq z^2, \\ n+1, & \text{otherwise.} \end{cases}$$

The unique global optimum of this function is z^2, while the search point z^1 is a local optimum whenever $|S| > 1$. For all $x \notin \{z^1, z^2\}$ the fitness $\text{OM}_{z^1,S}(x)$ equals $\text{OM}_{z^2,S}(x)$. Unless the algorithm queries either z^1 or z^2 it can therefore not distinguish between the two functions.

We consider the class of functions $\mathcal{F} := \{\text{OM}_{z^1,S} \mid z^1 \in \{0,1\}^n, S \subseteq [n] \text{ with } |S| = n/2\}$ and show the following.

THEOREM 3. *Let $\varepsilon > 0$. The (1+1) elitist $(1/2+\varepsilon)$-Monte Carlo black-box complexity of $\mathcal{F}$ and its unary unbiased, (1+1)-memory restricted, comparison-based black-box complexity is $O(n \log n)$, while the (1+1) elitist Las Vegas black-box complexity of $\mathcal{F}$ is exponential in n even if the algorithm has access to the absolute fitness values.*

The key idea beyond Theorem 3 is the fact that in all previous models an algorithm that gets trapped by the wrong local optimum z^1 can simply do a restart and with constant probability it will climb up a path leading to z^2 in the next trial. Indeed, a simple version of Randomized Local Search with random restarts will achieve the $O(n \log n)$ upper bound. On the other hand, an elitist black-box algorithm needs to test either z^1 or z^2, and may be trapped there with (almost) no more information than that the true optimum is at distance $n/2$. Since it cannot do a simple restart, it (roughly speaking) has to sample points at distance $n/2$ until it eventually finds the optimum.

The example in Theorem 3 also shows that there can be an exponential gap between the Monte Carlo and the Las Vegas complexity of a class $\mathcal{F}$ of functions. Indeed, it is easy to see that the probability of RLS to have found the optimum of the functions within some $O(n \ln n)$ iterations is $(1-o(1))1/2$.

PROOF OF THEOREM 3. For the upper bound, consider the following random local search algorithm (RLS) with random restarts. We start with a uniform sample x. In each iteration, with probability $1/(10n \log n)$ the algorithm restarts, i.e., replaces x by a a new uniform sample. Otherwise, one bit position $j \in \{1, 2, \ldots, n\}$ is chosen uniformly at random. The j-th bit of x is flipped and the fitness of the resulting search point y is evaluated. The better of the two search points x and y replaces x for future iterations (favoring y in case of ties). We show that this algorithm has expected optimization time $O(n \log n)$.

Whenever $x \notin \{z^1, z^2\}$ then the one-bit flip has probability at least $n - f(x)$ to increase the fitness of x (this can be proven by an easy case distinction whether or not $\text{OM}_{z^1}(x) \geq \text{OM}_{z^2}(x)$). This is at least as large as the progress probability for ONEMAX. Therefore, if no restart happens in, say, $5n \log n$ steps (which is true with constant probability) then with high probability RLS finds a local optimum of $\text{OM}_{z^1,S}$ in this time. In this case, the local optimum will be the global one with probability $1/2$. Summarizing, after each restart, the algorithm has at least a constant probability to find the global optimum in the next $5n \log n$ steps. This proves the first claim in Theorem 3.

For the lower bound, we essentially show that every algorithm (that terminates) ends up in z^1 with probability $1/2$, at which point an elitist algorithm only knows that the true optimum z^2 is (roughly) randomly distributed among the search points at distance $n/2$ of z^1. Since it can never "escape" from z^1 (unless it eventually samples z^2), the expected time after having reached z^1 is exponential in n.

To turn this intuition into a formal proof, we employ Yao's Principle (Lemma 2). As described in Section 2.2, we need to consider a larger class $\mathcal{A}$ of algorithms defined as follows. We call the time until the algorithm queries for the first time z^1 or z^2 "first phase", and the remaining time "second phase". Since we are not too much interested in the time that an algorithm spends in the first phase, we simply give away to the algorithm the two local optima z^1 and z^2. That is, during the first phase the algorithm may access the set $\{z^1, z^2\}$. We also allow the algorithm to store all search points that it samples throughout this phase. During this phase every randomized algorithm is a convex combination of deterministic ones, so we may use Yao's Principle and restrict ourselves to an algorithm A that is deterministic in the first phase. We assume that the problem instance $\text{OM}_{z^1,S}$ is taken from $\mathcal{F}$ uniformly at random.

Note that in the first phase the algorithm does not gain any additional information by querying any search point $x \notin \{z^1, z^2\}$ since it can predict the fitness value of x without actually querying it. We may thus assume that the first query of A is either z^1 or z^2. Let $\mathcal{C}$ be the set of all sets $\{z^1, z^2\}$, where $z^1, z^2 \in \{0,1\}^n$ have Hamming distance $n/2$. In the first phase the algorithm A essentially assigns to each set $\{z^1, z^2\} \in \mathcal{C}$ either z^1 or z^2. Let us denote the corresponding function by $h_A : \mathcal{C} \to \{0,1\}^n$. With probability $1/2$, $h_A(z^1, z^2)$ is the global optimum, and with probability $1/2$ it is not.

With probability $1/2$ the algorithm enters the second phase, in which we no longer allow it to access $\{z^1, z^2\}$. The algorithm A can be randomized in this phase. Recall that the instance is taken uniformly at random, and that A samples z^1 whenever $z^2 \in \mathcal{C}_{z^1} := h_A^{-1}(z^1)$. Therefore, conditioned on seeing z^1, the global optimum is uniformly distributed in $\mathcal{C}_{z^1}$. The algorithm therefore needs an expected number of $\Omega(\mathcal{C}_{z^1})$ additional queries to find z^2, and the probability to find the optimum with $\alpha|\mathcal{C}_{z^1}|$ additional queries is at most α.

It remains to show that $\mathcal{C}_{z^1}$ is large with high probability. Let $p > 0$. Note that the average size over all z^1 (not the expectation over all instances!) of $\mathcal{C}_{z^1}$ is $E := |\mathcal{C}|/2^n = \binom{n}{n/2}/2 \sim 2^n/\sqrt{2\pi n}$. Let $D := \{z^1 \in \{0,1\}^n \mid |\mathcal{C}_{z^1}| \leq pE\}$. Then $|h_A^{-1}(D)| \leq 2^n pE \leq p|\mathcal{C}|$. Since the random instance is chosen uniformly at random from $\mathcal{F}$, the set $\{z^1, z^2\} \in \mathcal{C}$ is also uniformly at random, and with probability at least $1-p$ an instance from $\mathcal{C} \setminus h_A^{-1}(D)$ is chosen, and thus $|\mathcal{C}_{z^1}| > pE$. Thus for every $p > 0$, conditioned on entering the second phase $|\mathcal{C}_{z^1}| > pE = \Omega(p2^n/\sqrt{n})$ with probability at least $1-p$. Choosing somewhat arbitrarily $\alpha = p = n^{-1/4}$ shows that with probability at least $1/2 - o(1)$ the algorithm needs at least $\Omega(2^n/n)$ steps. This concludes the proof. □

3.2 Hidden Paths

We provide another example with an exponential gap between elitist and non-elitist black-box complexities, which gives some more insight into the disadvantage of elitist algorithms. We use essentially the OneMax function, patched with a path of low fitness that leads to the global optimum. In this example, every elitist algorithm fails with high probability to find the optimum in polynomial time, since it is blind to all search points of small fitness value. Both the Monte Carlo and the Las Vegas elitist black box complexity of the problem are exponential in n, so that (unlike the example from Section 3.1) the problem cannot be easily mended by allowing restarts. On the other hand, there are memory-restricted, unary unbiased (but not elitist) algorithms that solve the problem efficiently.

For $z \in \{0,1\}^n$, let $\bar{z}$ be the bitwise complement of z, i.e., $\bar{z}_i = 1 - z_i$ for all $i \in [n]$. Let further $\mathcal{I}_\ell = \{\vec{i} = (i_1, \ldots, i_\ell) \in [n]^\ell \mid i_1, \ldots, i_\ell \text{ pairwise distinct}\}$. To each $\vec{i} \in \mathcal{I}_\ell$ and each $z^0 \in \{0,1\}^n$, we associate a path $P(z^0, \vec{i}) = (z^0, \ldots, z^\ell)$ of length ℓ as follows. For $j \in [\ell]$, let $z^j \in \{0,1\}^n$ be the search point obtained from z^{j-1} by flipping the i_j-th bit. Note that z^j differs from z^0 in exactly j bits.

Now we regard the set of all OneMax functions OM_z padded with a path of length $n/4$ starting at the minimum $z^0 := z^0(z) = \bar{z}$ and leading to the unique global maximum $z^{n/4}$. Formally, let $\mathcal{F} := \{\text{OM}_{z,\vec{i}} \mid z \in \{0,1\}^n, \vec{i} \in \mathcal{I}_{n/4}\}$, where for $\vec{i} \in \mathcal{I}_\ell$ and $P(z^0, \vec{i}) = (z^0, \ldots, z^\ell)$,

$$\text{OM}_{z,\vec{i}}(x) := \begin{cases} n + \text{OM}_z(x), & \text{if } x \notin P(z^0, \vec{i}), \\ j, & \text{if } x = z^j \text{ for } 0 \le j < \ell, \\ 2n+1, & \text{if } x = z^\ell. \end{cases}$$

Theorem 4. *The unary unbiased (1+1) memory-restricted black-box complexity of $\mathcal{F}$ is $O(n^2)$, while its (1+1) Monte Carlo (and thus, also Las Vegas) elitist black-box complexity is $2^{\Omega(n)}$, also for the non-ranking-based version of the elitist model in which full (absolute) fitness information is revealed to the algorithm.*

Proof. For the upper bound, we need to describe a memory-restricted unary unbiased black-box algorithm A that optimizes $f \in F$ in quadratic time. The algorithm proceeds as follows. While its current search point has fitness at least n, it finds the local optimum z using Randomized Local Search (RLS). This takes expected time $O(n \log n)$. From z it jumps to the starting point $z^0 = \bar{z}$ of the path $P(z, \vec{i})$. The algorithm now follows the path by using again RLS but accepting an offspring if and only if it increases the parent's fitness by exactly 1 or if the offspring's fitness is $2n+1$. In particular, in this phase the algorithm rejects any search point with fitness between n and $2n$. Since this algorithm needs time $O(n)$ to advance one step on the path, and the path has length $O(n)$, it has expected runtime $O(n^2)$.

For the lower bound we again extend the class of elitist black-box algorithms to a larger class $\mathcal{A}$ that allows to apply Yao's Principle. After an algorithm in $\mathcal{A}$ has sampled its first search point, we distinguish two cases. If the search point has fitness at most $n + n/4$, then the algorithm may access the position of the global optimum (and thus, terminate in one more step). If the first search point has fitness larger than $n + n/4$, then the algorithm may access the position of the local optimum z. Moreover, it may access a counter that tells it how many steps it has performed so far. Apart from that, it may only access (one of) the best search point(s) it has found so far, and its fitness. Then $\mathcal{A}$ is the set of all algorithms that can be implemented with this additional information. In this way, every randomized algorithm in $\mathcal{A}$ is a convex combination of deterministic ones, so that we can apply Yao's Principle. So let $A \in \mathcal{A}$ be a deterministic algorithm, and consider the uniform distribution on $\mathcal{F}$.

If the first search point has fitness $2n+1$ or at most $n+n/4$, then A is done after one query or it can terminate in at most one additional step, respectively. However, by the Chernoff bound these two events happen only with probability $e^{-\Omega(n)}$, so from now on we assume that the first search point has fitness larger than $n + n/4$. Observe that by the accessible information the algorithm can determine the OneMax value $\text{OM}_z(x)$ for all $x \in \{0,1\}^n$. In particular, for every search point of larger fitness except for z^ℓ the algorithm can predict the fitness value without querying it. On the other hand, if it queries a search point of lower fitness, then it is not allowed to keep its fitness value. Thus A cannot obtain additional information about f except by querying the optimum z^ℓ. Since $\mathcal{F}$ was chosen uniformly at random, all search points in distance $\ell = n/4$ from $z^0 = \bar{z}$ have the same probability to be the global optimum. Hence, A needs in expectation at least $\binom{n}{n/4}/2 = 2^{\Omega(n)}$ queries to find the optimum. □

Remark 5. *A similar statement as the one in Theorem 4 holds also for ranking-based algorithms if we slightly increase the memory of the algorithms regarded. Indeed, there exists a unary unbiased (2+1) memory-restricted ranking-based algorithm optimizing $\mathcal{F}$ in expected $O(n^2)$ function evaluations. Regard, e.g., the algorithm that maintains throughout the second phase a search point x^1 of fitness $n+1$ and that accepts an offspring y of z^j if and only if the fitness of y is larger than that of z^j but smaller than that of x^1 (in which case $y = z^{j+1}$). Then z^ℓ is sampled (but not accepted into the population, see Remark 6) after $O(n^2)$ steps.*

On the other hand, the (2+1) elitist black-box complexity is still exponential, since with high probability the first two search points the algorithm samples have fitness $n/2 + o(n)$.

Remark 6. *As indicated in Remark 5 it can make a difference for black-box algorithms if we only require them to* sample *an optimum or whether we require the algorithm to* accept *it into the population. The algorithm described in Remark 5 does not accept the optimum when finding it. In order to achieve the same (asymptotic) black-box complexity with an algorithm that accepts the optimum, it has to be modified (and thus becomes more complicated).*

4. COMBINING UNBIASED AND ELITIST BLACK-BOX MODELS

In this section we demonstrate that apart from providing more realistic lower bounds for some function classes, the elitist black-box model is also an interesting counterpart to existing black-box models. Indeed, we show that some of the unrealistically low black-box complexities of the unbiased black-box model proposed in [22] disappear when elitist selection is required.

More specifically, we regard the unary unbiased (1+1) elitist black-box complexity[3] of JUMP functions, which (in line with [6]) we define in the following way. For a parameter k the function JUMP_k assigns to each bit string x the function value $\text{JUMP}_k(x) = \text{ONEMAX}(x)$ if $\text{ONEMAX}(x) \in \{0\} \cup \{k+1, \dots, n-k-1\} \cup \{n\}$ and $\text{JUMP}_k(x) = 0$ otherwise. Despite the fact that all common search heuristics need $\Omega(n^{k+1})$ fitness evaluations to optimize this function, the unary unbiased black-box complexity of these functions are surprisingly low, see Table 1 for a summary of results presented in [6] ([9] for $k = 1$). Interestingly, even for extreme jump functions in which only the fitness value $n/2$ is visible and all other ONEMAX values are replaced by zero, polynomial-time unary unbiased black-box algorithms exist. It is thus interesting to see that the situation changes dramatically when the algorithms are required to be elitist, as the following theorem shows.

THEOREM 7. *For $k = 0$ the (Las Vegas and Monte Carlo) unary unbiased (1+1) elitist black-box complexity of the jump function JUMP_k is $\Theta(n \log n)$. For all $1 \le k \le n/2 - 1$ it is $\Theta(\binom{n}{k+1})$. In particular, for $k = \omega(1)$ the runtime is superpolynomial in n and for $k = \Omega(n)$ it is exponential.*

PROOF OF THE UPPER BOUND IN THEOREM 7. For any constant k the upper bound is achieved by the simple (1 + 1) EA [15]. For general k, consider the algorithm A that produces an offspring as follows. With probability 1/3 the offspring is a search point uniformly at random from $\{0,1\}^n$, with probability 1/3 the algorithm flips exactly one bit (uniformly at random), and with probability 1/3 it flips exactly $k+1$ bits (also uniformly at random). The offspring is accepted if its fitness is at least the fitness of the current search point. This algorithm finds a point of positive fitness in expected time $O(\sqrt{n})$ since it produces random search points with probability 1/3 and each such uniform sample has ONEMAX value $n/2$ with probability $\Theta(1/\sqrt{n})$. Then with high probability it increases the fitness to $n - k - 1$ in at most $O(n \log n)$ steps by one-bit flips (and possibly $(k+1)$-bit flips). Afterwards, since there are $\binom{n}{k+1}$ search points in distance $k + 1$, the algorithm needs in expectation at most $3\binom{n}{k+1}$ steps to find the optimum. This proves the upper bound for the Las Vegas complexity, which in turn implies the upper bound for the Monte Carlo complexity. □

It remains to prove the lower bound. For $k = 0$ it follows from [22, Theorem 6]. For general k, as an intermediate step, we show the following general result.

THEOREM 8. *Assume that f is a function with a unique global maximum x_{opt}, and assume further that a unary unbiased (1+1) elitist black-box algorithm A is currently at a search point $x \neq x_{opt}$. Let $0 < d \le n/2$, and let* dist *denote the Hamming distance. Let*

$$S := \{x' \neq x_{opt} \mid \text{dist}\{x', x_{opt}\} \le d \text{ or } \text{dist}\{x', x_{opt}\} \ge n-d\}$$

be the distance-d neighborhood of x_{opt} and of its bitwise complement $\overline{x_{opt}}$. If all search point in S have fitness less than $f(x)$, then A needs in expectation at least $\binom{n}{d+1}$ additional queries to find the optimum. Moreover, for every $\alpha \ge 0$, the probability that it needs at most $\alpha\binom{n}{d+1}$ additional queries is at most α.

[3]That is, the complexity with respect to all (1+1) elitist black-box algorithms for which the sampling distributions in line 7 of Algorithm 1 are unbiased in the sense of Lehre and Witt [22].

PROOF. Since A is elitist, it can never accept a point in S. Therefore, in every subsequent step before finding the optimum, it will be in some search point y with distance $d' \in [d+1, n-d-1]$ from the optimum. If an unbiased mutation has some probability p to produce x_{opt} from y, then every other search point in distance d' has also probability p to be the offspring. In particular, since there are $\binom{n}{d'}$ such points, $p\binom{n}{d'}$ equals the probability that the offspring has distance d' of y, which is at most 1. Hence, at any point the probability to sample the optimum in the next step is at most $1/\binom{n}{d'} \le 1/\binom{n}{d+1}$. Therefore, A needs in expectation at least $\binom{n}{d+1}$ steps to find the optimum. Moreover, by the union bound the probability that A needs less than $\alpha\binom{n}{d+1}$ steps is at most α. □

PROOF SKETCH FOR THE LOWER BOUND IN THEOREM 7. Assume for simplicity that n is a power of 2. In order to apply Yao's Principle (Lemma 2), we allow the algorithm to remember its complete search history. We then regard a deterministic algorithm A on a uniformly chosen JUMP_k function. That is, the target string z of the ONEMAX function underlying the JUMP_k function is chosen from $\{0,1\}^n$ uniformly at random.

It is known that we can partition the hypercube $\{0,1\}^n$ into $2^n/n$ sets $S_1, \dots, S_{2^n/n}$ of size n each such that for each $i \in [2^n/n]$ the pairwise distance between any two points in S_i is exactly $n/2$ (e.g., the cosets of the Hadamard code [2]).

Let i be the index of the set containing the target string z, i.e., $z \in S_i := \{s^1, \dots, s^n\}$. Regardless of the jump-size k, each search point in S_i has positive fitness. Indeed, for each j either we have $s^j = z$ (in which case the fitness of s^j equals n) or the distance and thus the fitness of s^j to z equals $n/2$. Since z is chosen uniformly at random, the probability that the first search point of set S_i that the algorithm A queries is the target string z equals $1/n$. This shows that with probability at least $1 - 1/n$ the first search point with positive fitness that A queries is not the optimum. But then Theorem 8 tells us that the algorithm needs at least $\binom{n}{k+1}$ additional steps in expectation, and at least $\alpha\binom{n}{k+1}$ with probability at least α. This proves the claim. □

5. CONCLUSIONS

We have introduced elitist black-box complexity as a tool to analyze the performance of search heuristics with elitist selection rules. Several examples provide evidence that the elitist black-box complexities can give a much more realistic estimation of the runtime of typical search heuristics. We have also seen that some unrealistically low black-box complexities in the unbiased model disappear when elitist selection is enforced.

We have also introduced the concept of Monte Carlo black-box complexities and have brought to the attention of the community the fact that these can be significantly lower than the previously regarded Las Vegas complexities. In addition, it can also be significantly easier to derive bounds for the Monte Carlo black-box complexities, see [13]. Both complexity notions correspond to runtime analysis statements often seen in the evolutionary computation literature and should thus co-exist in black-box complexity research.

While we regard in this work toy-problems, it would be interesting to analyze the influence of elitist selection on the performance of algorithms in more challenging optimization problems. Our findings enliven the question for which

Model	Constant Jump $1 \le k = \Theta(1)$	Short Jump $k = O(n^{1/2-\varepsilon})$	Long Jump $k = (1/2-\varepsilon)n$	Extreme Jump $k = n/2 - 1$
unary unbiased	$\Theta(n \log n)$	$\Theta(n \log n)$	$O(n^2)$	$O(n^{9/2})$
elitist unary unbiased	$\Theta(n^{k+1})$	$\Theta(\binom{n}{k+1}) = \Omega\left((n/k)^k\right)$	$\Theta(\binom{n}{k+1}) = 2^{\Theta(n)}$	$\Theta(2^n/\sqrt{n})$

Table 1: Comparison of the unary unbiased black-box complexities of Jump_k with the respective (Las Vegas and Monte Carlo) elitist ones for different regimes of k.

problems non-elitist selection like tournament or so-called fitness-dependent selection can be beneficial, initial findings for which can be found in [18, 25]. Negative examples are presented in [19, 23, 24].

Acknowledgments

This research benefited from the support of the "FMJH Program Gaspard Monge in optimization and operation research", and from the support to this program from EDF.

6. REFERENCES

[1] G. Anil and R. P. Wiegand. Black-box search by elimination of fitness functions. In *FOGA'09*, pages 67–78. ACM, 2009.

[2] S. Arora and B. Barak. *Computational Complexity: A Modern Approach.* Cambridge University Press, 2009.

[3] G. Badkobeh, P. K. Lehre, and D. Sudholt. Unbiased black-box complexity of parallel search. In *PPSN'14*, volume 8672 of *LNCS*, pages 892–901. Springer, 2014.

[4] G. Badkobeh, P. K. Lehre, and D. Sudholt. Black-box complexity of parallel search with distributed populations. In *FOGA'15*. ACM, 2015. To appear.

[5] B. Doerr, C. Doerr, and F. Ebel. From black-box complexity to designing new genetic algorithms. *Theoretical Computer Science*, 567:87–104, 2015.

[6] B. Doerr, C. Doerr, and T. Kötzing. Unbiased black-box complexities of jump functions: how to cross large plateaus. In *GECCO'14*, pages 769–776. ACM, 2014.

[7] B. Doerr, C. Doerr, and T. Kötzing. The unbiased black-box complexity of partition is polynomial. *Artificial Intelligence*, 216:275–286, 2014.

[8] B. Doerr, T. Kötzing, J. Lengler, and C. Winzen. Black-box complexities of combinatorial problems. *Theoretical Computer Science*, 471:84–106, 2013.

[9] B. Doerr, T. Kötzing, and C. Winzen. Too fast unbiased black-box algorithms. In *GECCO'11*, pages 2043–2050. ACM, 2011.

[10] B. Doerr and C. Winzen. Playing Mastermind with constant-size memory. *Theory of Computing Systems*, 55:658–684, 2014.

[11] B. Doerr and C. Winzen. Ranking-based black-box complexity. *Algorithmica*, 68:571–609, 2014.

[12] B. Doerr and C. Winzen. Reducing the arity in unbiased black-box complexity. *Theoretical Computer Science*, 545:108–121, 2014.

[13] C. Doerr and J. Lengler. Onemax in black-box models with several restrictions. In *GECCO'15*. ACM, 2015. Full version: http://arxiv.org/abs/1504.02644.

[14] S. Droste, T. Jansen, K. Tinnefeld, and I. Wegener. A new framework for the valuation of algorithms for black-box optimization. In *FOGA'03*, pages 253–270. Morgan Kaufmann, 2003.

[15] S. Droste, T. Jansen, and I. Wegener. On the analysis of the (1+1) evolutionary algorithm. *Theoretical Computer Science*, 276:51–81, 2002.

[16] S. Droste, T. Jansen, and I. Wegener. Upper and lower bounds for randomized search heuristics in black-box optimization. *Theory of Computing Systems*, 39:525–544, 2006.

[17] H. Fournier and O. Teytaud. Lower bounds for comparison based evolution strategies using vc-dimension and sign patterns. *Algorithmica*, 59:387–408, 2011.

[18] T. Friedrich, P. S. Oliveto, D. Sudholt, and C. Witt. Analysis of diversity-preserving mechanisms for global exploration. *Evolutionary Computation*, 17(4):455–476, 2009.

[19] E. Happ, D. Johannsen, C. Klein, and F. Neumann. Rigorous analyses of fitness-proportional selection for optimizing linear functions. In *GECCO'08*, pages 953–960. ACM, 2008.

[20] J. Jägersküpper and T. Storch. When the plus strategy outperforms the comma strategy and when not. In *FOCI'07*, pages 25–32. IEEE, 2007.

[21] T. Jansen. On the black-box complexity of example functions: The real jump function. In *FOGA'15*. ACM, 2015. To appear.

[22] P. K. Lehre and C. Witt. Black-box search by unbiased variation. *Algorithmica*, 64:623–642, 2012.

[23] F. Neumann, P. S. Oliveto, and C. Witt. Theoretical analysis of fitness-proportional selection: landscapes and efficiency. In *GECCO'09*, pages 835–842. ACM, 2009.

[24] P. S. Oliveto and C. Witt. On the runtime analysis of the simple genetic algorithm. *Theoretical Computer Science*, 545:2–19, 2014.

[25] P. S. Oliveto and C. Zarges. Analysis of diversity mechanisms for optimisation in dynamic environments with low frequencies of change. *Theoretical Computer Science*, 561, Part A:37 – 56, 2015.

[26] J. Rowe and M. Vose. Unbiased black box search algorithms. In *GECCO'11*, pages 2035–2042. ACM, 2011.

[27] O. Teytaud and S. Gelly. General lower bounds for evolutionary algorithms. In *PPSN'06*, volume 4193 of *LNCS*, pages 21–31. Springer, 2006.

[28] R. K. Ursem. Diversity-guided evolutionary algorithms. In *PPSN'02*, volume 2439 of *LNCS*, pages 462–471. Springer, 2002.

[29] M. Črepinšek, S.-H. Liu, and M. Mernik. Exploration and exploitation in evolutionary algorithms: A survey. *ACM Computing Surveys*, 45(3):35:1–35:33, 2013.

[30] A. C.-C. Yao. Probabilistic computations: Toward a unified measure of complexity. In *FOCS'77*, pages 222–227. IEEE, 1977.

Reconstructing Cross-Cut Shredded Text Documents: A Genetic Algorithm with Splicing-Driven Reproduction

Yong-Feng Ge[a,b], Yue-Jiao Gong[a,b,*], Wei-Jie Yu[b,c], Xiao-Min Hu[b,d] and Jun Zhang[a,b]
[a] School of Advanced Computing, Sun Yat-sen University
[b] Key Laboratory of Machine Intelligence and Advanced Computing, Ministry of Education
[c] School of Information Management, Sun Yat-sen University
[d] School of Public Health, Sun Yat-sen University, P.R. China
*(Corresponding author) gongyuejiao@gmail.com

ABSTRACT
In this work we focus on reconstruction of cross-cut shredded text documents (RCCSTD), which is of high interest in the fields of forensics and archeology. A novel genetic algorithm, with splicing-driven crossover, four mutation operators, and a row-oriented elitism strategy, is proposed to improve the capability of solving RCCSTD in complex space. We also design a novel and comprehensive objective function based on both edge and empty vector-based splicing error to guarantee that the correct reconstruction always has the lowest cost value. Experiments are conducted on six RCCSTD scenarios, with experimental results showing that the proposed algorithm significantly outperforms the previous best-known algorithms for this problem.

Categories and Subject Descriptors
I.2.8 [**Artificial Intelligence**]: Problem Solving, Control Methods, and Search; I.7.m [**Document and Text Processing**]: Miscellaneous.

General Terms
Algorithms, Performance, Experimentation.

Keywords
Document reconstruction; genetic algorithm; row-oriented elitism strategy.

1. INTRODUCTION
Although electronic documents are now commonly used in most fields, the printed documents are still necessary due to the long-time storage requirements and some legal reasons. In this case, document shredding is a frequently used method to obfuscate sensitive documents, which happens either by purpose or by accident. The former is related to forensic science whereas the latter attracts the interest of archeology. Specifically, paper can be destroyed by hands or, more professionally, by shredders. Within this work, we focus on the reconstruction of cross-cut shredded text documents (RCCSTD) problem [1], in which documents are cut into rectangular shreds of equal size and shape by shredders.

GECCO'15, July 11-16, 2015, Madrid, Spain.
© 2015 ACM. ISBN 978-1-4503-3472-3/15/07…$15.00
http://dx.doi.org/10.1145/2739480.2754677

In previous literature, some approaches have been developed to solve the RCCSTD problem. Clustering method is used by Sleit *et al.* [2], as part of the reconstruction process instead of a preprocessing step. Variable neighborhood search [3] is embedded in evolutionary algorithms in [4]-[5] and it works as a global improvement procedure.

Two problems related to RCCSTD problem in the field of document reconstruction are restoration of hand torn paper documents and reconstruction of strip shredded text documents (RSSTD). On one hand, different from the shredder cut problem, each piece of the hand torn problem has a unique shape. In this case, geometric information could be utilized efficiently during the reconstruction process. Justino *et al.* [6] applied a polygonal approximation to reduce the complexity of construction. On the other hand, Prandtstetter and Raidl [7] proposed some effective approaches to solve the RSSTD problem, which contain a variable neighborhood search approach with a semi-automatic system in the optimization process. Moreover, they proved that the reconstruction of strip shredded documents is NP-complete. Since RSSTD problem could be regarded as a special case of RCCSTD problem, we conclude that RCCSTD problem is also NP-complete. Possibility of using MPEG-7 descriptors for the strip content description is showed in [8].

Genetic algorithm [9] has gained successes in various fields [10]-[11]. In the area of reconstruction, an enhanced genetic algorithm with solution archive is applied in [12]. Solution archive helps avoid the duplicate solutions. Accordingly, diversity of population is maintained. Moreover, the genetic algorithm is extended to a memetic algorithm by embedding the variable neighborhood search in [4].

Different from the previous genetic algorithms for document reconstruction, the process of our proposed algorithm has a tighter connection with reconstruction. In this algorithm, a novel splicing-driven crossover is defined to emphasize the adjacency information in the sequences. Most correctly positioned links are extracted and appear in the offspring. Several mutation operators are designed according to common misleading situations in the reconstruction. In addition to introducing diverse genetic materials, these mutation operators are also efficient in removing incorrect links. Additionally, a row-oriented elitism strategy is proposed based on the fact that the performance of traditional genetic algorithm often deteriorates rapidly as the dimensionality of the problem increases [13]. Similar to the effective decomposition strategy applied in large scale optimization problem, this elitism strategy focuses on the rows which are more likely to be correctly positioned.

The remainder of this paper is organized as follows. Section 2 is a definition of RCCSTD problem. In Section 3, the cost function is defined in detail. A genetic algorithm with splicing-driven reproduction is proposed in Section 4. Experimental results are showed in Section 5, followed by conclusions drawn in Section 6.

2. PROBLEM DEFINITION

Based on [1], the formal definition of RCCSTD problem is expressed as follows. A set of rectangular shreds $S = \{1,\ldots,n\}$ with identified numbers containing text of original document is given firstly. These shreds must appear exactly once in the solution. To simplify this process, the correct orientation of each shred is assumed to be known, whose related pattern recognition technique is proposed in [14]. Standard solution of RCCSTD problem could be expressed as a matrix, whose elements represent the shreds in set *S*. The aim of RCCSTD problem is to find an assignment of shreds with the lowest cost. The cost functions in two directions are defined in the next section. The horizontal function $H_{i,j}$ shows the cost made by positioning shred *i* left to shred *j*. Analogously, the vertical function $B_{i,j}$ returns the cost value when shred *i* is on the top of *j*.

3. COST FUNCTION DEFINITION

One crucial issue in solving RCCSTD problem is the definition of an appropriate cost function, which will be utilized to evaluate the individuals of GA afterwards. It is remained to be a challenging task to define a perfect cost function for RCCSTD. If the function is not sophisticatedly defined, in some scenarios, there always exists a situation that an incorrect solution has a lower cost value than a correct one does. Such situations would result in selection error and hence bad performance of GA. To avoid such situations, a new cost function is defined in this section.

Since the majority of text documents are black text on the white background, we take the gray-scale (which ranges from 0 to 255) information as input. The edges of shreds are represented as vectors. Suppose $\mathbf{A}_i$ represents the edge of shred *i* and $\mathbf{B}_j$ represents the edge of shred *j*. Then we have

$$\begin{aligned} \mathbf{A}_i &= \left[a_1^i, a_2^i, a_3^i \ldots a_h^i\right], a_n^i \in [0,255] \\ \mathbf{B}_j &= \left[b_1^j, b_2^j, b_3^j \ldots b_h^j\right], b_n^j \in [0,255] \end{aligned} \quad (1)$$

where *h* is the length of the edge.

3.1 Edge Splicing Cost

The edge splicing cost function makes use of the pixel information on each edge of two shreds. The function can either contain the "non-blank edge cost" when neither of these two edges is blank, or the "blank edge cost" otherwise. The two situations are illustrated in Figure 1 and the corresponding functions are defined as follows.

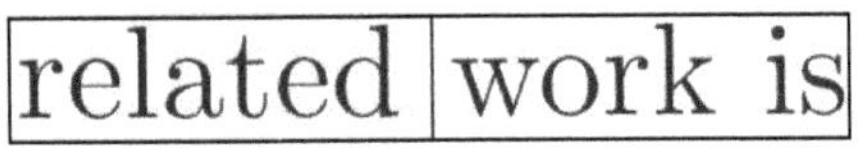

(a) Two shreds are linked with two blank edges.

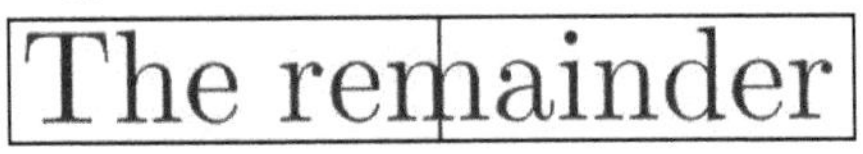

(b) Two shreds are linked without blank edge.

Figure 1. Two situations to consider.

"Non-blank edge cost function" adopts the idea in [7]. When considering the difference of current two pixels on each edge, information of two pixels above and two pixels below to each current pixel is included. It is proved that the application of continuous pixels information helps reflect the consistency of text indeed. The cost $d_{i,j}$ when shred *j* is positioned next to shred *i* is defined as:

$$d_{i,j} = \sum_{k=3}^{h-2} p_{i,j}^k \quad (2)$$

$$p_{i,j}^k = \begin{cases} 1, if\ p_{i,j}'^k \geq \tau \\ 0, otherwise \end{cases} \quad (3)$$

$$p_{i,j}'^k = \left| \begin{matrix} 0.7(a_k^i - b_k^j) + 0.1(a_{k+1}^i - b_{k+1}^j) + 0.1(a_{k-1}^i - b_{k-1}^j) + \\ 0.05(a_{k+2}^i - b_{k+2}^j) + 0.05(a_{k-2}^i - b_{k-2}^j) \end{matrix} \right| \quad (4)$$

where $p_{i,j}'^k$, $p_{i,j}^k$ refer to the actual and boolean differences of shred *i* and shred *j* at the point *k* respectively. The threshold value τ should be carefully defined, which has a great influence on computing results.

On the other hand, the "blank edge cost function" utilizes the length of blank space generated by connecting two shreds. In general, the blank spaces in a routine text document have a standard range, which could help detect the possibility of two shreds with blank edges positioned correctly. Either a larger one or a smaller one indicates a wrong connection. The cost $b_{i,j}$ when shred *j* is positioned next to shred *i* is defined as:

$$b_{i,j} = \begin{cases} 0, if (c^i + d^j) \in standard\_blank\_range \\ length, otherwise \end{cases} \quad (5)$$

where c^i is the length of shred *i*'s margin. Accordingly, d^j represents the length of margin on shred *j*. To unify the costs here with results of "non-blank edge cost function", the minimum and maximum values are set to 0 and length of edge.

3.2 Empty Vector-Based Splicing Cost

Although the edge splicing cost function returns logical results in most cases, we need another cost function named "empty vector-based splicing cost function", especially when considering whether two shreds are from different rows in the document (see Figure 2). "Empty vector" is a vector has the same height as shreds, whose value in *k*th row represents whether the *k*th row in the shred is blank. In most cases, shreds on different lines in the correct solution have clear differences in empty vectors. The cost between shreds *i* and *j* is defined as:

$$f_{i,j} = \sum_{k=1}^{h} (e_k^i \oplus e_k^j) \quad (6)$$

$$e_k^i = \begin{cases} 1, if\ row_k\ is\ blank \\ 0, otherwise \end{cases} \quad (7)$$

where e_k^i represents the truth value of whether the *k*th row of shred *i* is blank.

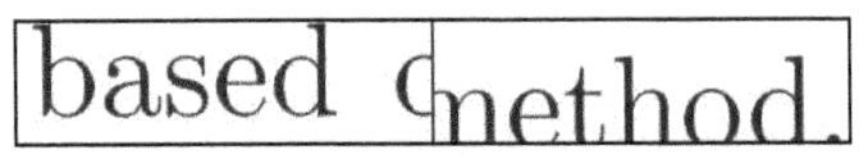

Figure 2. Two shreds from different rows are linked by mistake.

3.3 Overall Cost Function

In the horizontal direction, to utilize the results of two functions efficiently, they are combined as follows. "non-blank edge cost function" and "blank edge cost function" are used based on the defined situations. The horizontal cost when positioning shred i left to shred j is defined as:

$$H_{i,j} = \begin{cases} d_{i,j} + f_{i,j}, if\, c^i + d^j = 0 \\ b_{i,j} + f_{i,j}, otherwise \end{cases} \quad (8)$$

where c^i and d^j represent the same meanings in Eqs. (5). Since the text on the columns is not aligned on the same lines, "empty vector-based splicing cost function" is not appropriate on the vertical direction. In this occasion, vertical cost is simpler and defined as:

$$B_{i,j} = \begin{cases} d_{i,j}, if\, c^i + d^j = 0 \\ b_{i,j}, otherwise \end{cases} \quad (9)$$

An example of overall cost is defined as:

$$Cost = H_{a,b} + H_{b,c} + B_{a,d} + H_{d,e} + B_{b,e} + H_{e,f} + B_{c,f} \quad (10)$$

where shreds *a-f* form a 2×3 solution for reconstruction in turn.

4. The PROPOSED ALGORITHM

4.1 Initial Population

A solution with n shreds is represented by an $x \times y$ matrix, whose elements stand for the shreds in RCCSTD problem and labeled with letters. This form is used in the following process. Besides the traditional random building method (RBM), greedy building heuristic (GBH) is proposed to create initial solutions. A good initial heuristic could help supply more effective genetic materials. Accordingly, it helps increase the efficiency of the whole algorithm. In this algorithm, 40% of the individuals in initial population are created by GBH while the other 60% are generated by RBM.

4.1.1 RBM

Lesson from the original genetic algorithm, random initial method could help increase the diversity of initial individuals. In this case, the shreds in initial solutions built by this method are completely randomly chosen.

4.1.2 GBH

In general, text documents are laid out such that there is a blank margin on the left of every page. In this way, it is very likely that those shreds with blank left margins are on the left edge in the final solution. The GBH firstly chooses a shred with the left blank margin. Subsequently, the initial solution is built row by row selecting shreds by greedy strategy. This greedy strategy is with respect to the evaluation of cost function, which is the sum of cost values generated by already processed left and top shreds, if exist. Additionally, the shreds on first row of solution just focus on their left neighbors, while shreds on leftmost edge only concern their top neighbors.

4.2 Recombination

Although it is very unlikely that the optimal solution is one of the initial individuals, it is common that some of those initial solutions have perfectly arranged parts. Those members turn out to be more competitive in the evolving population and be more likely to be chosen as parents in the following crossover operators, respecting the nature selection. As an ideal result of recombining individuals with the perfect parts, an offspring with more shreds on correct positions should be generated.

Different genetic sequencing operators emphasize different factors during the recombination. Some focus on the order, such as order crossover [15] and position-based crossover, while others highlight the position information just like partially mapped crossover (PMX) [16] and cycle crossover [17].

Respect to the fact that a solution with more correct links is likely to provide more available information from the text document, we here adopt the idea of enhanced edge recombination (EER) proposed in [19], which emphasizes the adjacency information in the sequence. However, although EER is an efficient recombination operator in solving TSP problem, it is useless to be directly applied in RCCSTD problem due to the differences in dimension and direction. A new crossover operator based on EER is proposed here named "EER-2D".

4.2.1 EER

In this operator, "edge table" is a list structure which storages the adjacency information extracted from parents. Take a sequence [*b d e a c*] as an example, it contains the connections [*bd*, *de*, *ea*, *ac*, *cb*]. Based on this structure, the generation of offspring proceeds as following steps: (1) Select the initial member from one of the parents. (2) Choose a subsequent member according to the edge table and already processed members. (3) Repeat step 2 until a valid solution is complete. The word "enhanced" in EER operator refers to the strategy that the links appear in both parents are labeled with minus and have higher priority to get emersion in the offspring.

Figure 3 shows an example of parents and their corresponding edge table with offspring. Suppose element a is selected randomly to start the offspring. Element a has links to b, c and e. Since link "*a-b*" appears in both parents and is labeled with minus in the edge table, it is chosen to get emersion in offspring. Element d is then chosen because it has lower quantity of remaining links. This process continues until offspring is complete.

Parent 1: a b c d e **Parent 2**: d b a c e

Offspring: a b d e c

Edge table

a: -b, c, e **b**: -a, c, d **c**: a, b, d, e

d: b, c, -e **e**: a, c, -d

Figure 3. Elements of EER operator.

4.2.2 EER-2D

According to the differences between RCCSTD problem and traditional TSP problem, some ideas are proposed in this new recombination method named EER-2D.

On one hand, recombination of RCCSTD problem is associated with both horizontal direction and vertical direction. In this way, there should be two edge tables in EER-2D operator, namely, "horizontal edge table" and "vertical edge table". Links on these two directions are added to respective edge tables. As a result of using two edge tables, two results would be generated during the process of recombination. If two results are not the same, a selection priority is important and defined as: the result from horizontal table has higher priority on the first row while vertical result has higher priority on the first column; they two have the same priority in other positions with being chosen in random fashion.

On the other hand, the graph in TSP problem is directed while it is undirected in RCCSTD problem. Specifically, link "*a-b*" and link "*b-a*" both means "the road between these two cities" in TSP problem. However, these two links indicate opposite meanings in RCCSTD problem: the former link indicates that shred *a* is left to shred *b*; the latter link means shred *a* is right to shred *b*. In this case, successive information in the two edge tables of EER-2D is not sufficient as the adjacency information in original EER's single edge table. For instance, link "*a-b*" is in the list of shred *a*, but it is not in the list of shred *b*.

To ensure there is enough successive information to generate the offspring, the third genetic individual besides traditional two parents is necessary. In the genetic process in natural world, environment plays the role of the third factor impacting on the generation of offspring. Based on this theory, the third individual is named "environment". The rule in EER operator is still adopted, successive links with two or more appearances are labeled with minus and have higher priority to be chosen.

To sum up, edge tables in two directions and the third genetic parent named "environment" are incorporated into EER-2D to improve the performance of recombination in two-dimensional structure. Figure 4 shows an example of parents with their corresponding edge tables and offspring. Firstly, element *a* is selected randomly to start the offspring. Secondly, element *d* is inserted based on the links in horizontal edge table. The left positions on the first row are filled with the help of horizontal edge table. Element *e* is chosen due to the link "*a-e*" in vertical edge table. Next, element *f* is chosen by two directions. This process continues until offspring is complete.

Parent1: a b c
d e f

Parent2: b a d
c e f

Environment: e d c
b f a

Offspring: a d c
e f b

Horizontal edge table

a: b, d	**b**: c, a, f	**c**: e
d: c, e	**e**: -f, d	**f**: a

Vertical edge table

a: e, d	**b**: c, e	**c**: a, f
d: -f	**e**: b	**f**: /

Figure 4. Elements of EER-2D operator.

4.3 Mutation

Mutation is an operator of innovation, which helps introduce new genetic materials to prevent the algorithm from converging too fast. The appropriate mutation operators could additionally help remove the incorrect and misleading links. The following mutation operators are proposed based on this thought.

4.3.1 Slide on Line (SOL)

Generally, a small difference in two costs is caused by the sliding of small sets of genetic sequences. In the SOL operator, mutation makes the selected gene segment slide to a random position on its current line. The length and position of the segment are chosen by random. An example of SOL operator is showed in Figure 5, where shred *i*, *j* slide to the head of the second row.

$$\begin{bmatrix} a & b & c & d & e \\ f & g & h & \boldsymbol{i} & \boldsymbol{j} \\ k & l & m & n & o \end{bmatrix} \Rightarrow \begin{bmatrix} a & b & c & d & e \\ \boldsymbol{i} & \boldsymbol{j} & f & g & h \\ k & l & m & n & o \end{bmatrix}$$

Figure 5. SOL operator.

4.3.2 Swap within Line (SWL)

The basic idea of SWL operator is to amend the reverse pairs within the same row. During a SWL operator, two shreds on the same are chosen by random and exchanged.

Moreover, since some rows of the individual are more likely to be misled than others, the possibility p_n that *n*th row is chosen for mutation is defined to be variable. Since adaptive strategy is proved to be efficient in most evolutionary algorithms [19]-[21] in recent years, a simple self-adaptive strategy is designed to change its value:

$$p_n = \frac{k_n}{k_{sum}} \tag{11}$$

$$k_{sum} = \sum_{n=1}^{row} k_n \tag{12}$$

$$k_n = \begin{cases} k_n + 1, \text{if generate a better result and } p_n < 2/row \\ k_n - 1, \text{if generate a worse result and } p_n > 1/row \\ k_n, \text{otherwise} \end{cases} \tag{13}$$

where parameter k_n is adjusted to keep p_n in the range defined above. k_{sum} is the total value of k_n in the solution. The same strategy is also used in SOL operator.

4.3.3 Slide through Line (STL)

Distinct from horizontal SOL operator, STL operator is carried out vertically. It is designed to focus on the rows with blank edges, which is more likely to appear in the wrong position. In the STL operator, a randomly chosen row slides to a random position and the other rows in the solution move accordingly.

4.3.4 Swap between Line (SBL)

SBL is the simplest but also most flexible in these four operators. The swap of random two shreds from different rows could help improve the diversity of genetic population.

4.4 Row-Oriented Elitism Strategy (ROES)

In the genetic process, finding a correct solution needs cooperation of a large amount of genetic individuals during hundreds of generations. To shorten this time-consuming genetic process as well as improve the possibility of finding correct solution, a decomposition strategy is proposed, which is named "row-oriented elitism strategy".

It is obvious that the correctly positioned rows are not difficult to find as the correct solution. Since these correct rows are necessary elements of final solution, they are named "final rows". Furthermore, considering that the judgment of whether the current rows are final rows is impossible, the rows with lowest costs are put into use, which are more likely to be the final rows. These rows are named "elitism-rows" and identified by the first elements of the rows.

The ROES operator contains the following two steps. Firstly, a construction rule is defined to select appropriate elitism-rows and assemble these rows. The approach used here is to follow the leading shreds on the rows of best individual in current generation. Then elitism-rows beginning with these shreds are chosen and stitched together according to the order in the best individual. An original "elitism-individual" is generated through the first step.

Secondly, there might be several shreds appearing more than once in the original elitism individual. To make the solution available and logical, these redundant shreds are randomly replaced by the unused shreds. A logical elitism-individual is generated through the second step.

The ROES operator proceeds as the following steps: (1) Elitism-rows are selected and stored during every genetic generation. (2) Elitism-individual is generated through the two steps mentioned above. (3) Elitism-individual is inserted into population of next generation.

Figure 6 shows an example of step (2) in the ROES operator. Shreds *a* and *d* are leading two rows in the best individual. The first and fourth elitism-rows which begin with the leading shreds are chosen and stitched together. However, there are two shreds *c* in original elitism-individual. To make this individual available, one of shreds *c* is replaced by shred *f* in the logical elitism-individual.

Elitism-rows:		**Best individual**: a b c
[1]	a b c	d e f
[2]	b a c	
[3]	c e f	**Original "elitism-individual"**: a b c
[4]	d e c	d e c
[5]	e f a	**Logical "elitism-individual"**: a b f
[6]	f a c	d e c

Figure 6. Elements of ROES operator.

```
Procedure Proposed Algorithm
Begin
    t←0;
    initialize (P(t));
    evaluate (P(t));
    Do
        P(t) ← selection (P(t));
        P(t) ← crossover (P(t));
        P(t) ← mutation(P(t));
        P(t) ← ROES operator(P(t));
        t ← t+1;
        P(t) ← P(t-1);
    While (Reach process not converged and allowed generation not reached)
    Return best individual
End Procedure
```

Figure 7. Pseudo code of the combing algorithm.

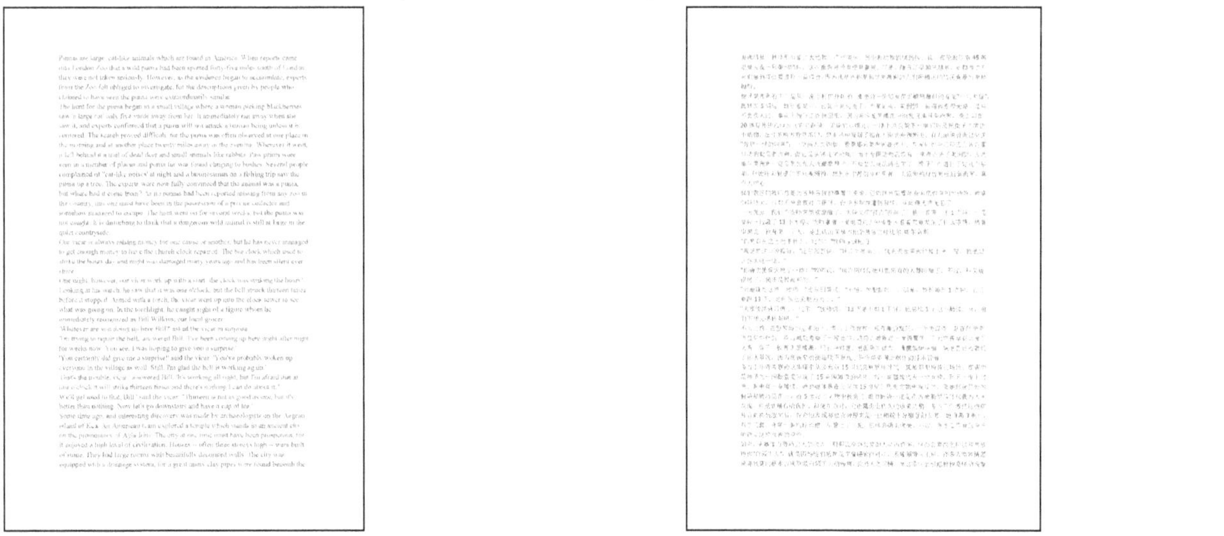

(a) e1 (b) c1

Figure 8. Pages e1 and c1.

4.5 Overall Process

In this section, a genetic algorithm with splicing-driven reproduction is proposed, whose whole procedure is showed in Figure 7. ROES operator is inserted into the process of genetic algorithm and cooperates with other operators.

5. EXPERIMENTAL RESULTS

5.1 Experimental Setup

Within this section, three methods are presented to compare. Besides the proposed algorithm, a method named "EER-2D" is involved to show the effect of genetic operations in the paper, which represents the proposed method without ROES operator. The genetic part of HV^2 method proposed in [4] is also used. To unify the cost values for comparison, all three methods use the same cost functions and initial methods in this paper. In the proposed algorithm, the rates of mutation operators are set to 0.02-0.08, and the rates of crossover operator and ROES operator are both set to 0.8.

All the methods were implemented in C and performed on a Core i3-3240 CPU with 4GB RAM. The test instances were generated by shredding text documents using three different cutting patterns, which involve 36 to 81 shreds. Pages e1 and c1 are composed of continuous text only and showed in Figure 8. Furthermore, e2 and c2 contain tables with horizontal and vertical lines while e3 and c3 show listings. Respectively, pages begin with "e" are English text documents while the others are in Chinese.

5.2 Solution Measurement

To find out the effect of introduced methods, two standards are defined to help reflect the quality of solutions. Firstly, the quality of a single solution is described by the proportion of correct links and shreds appearing in total links and shreds. A link is defined to be correct if it also appears in the correct solution. A shred is correct if it has the same position as the same shred in correct solution. In general, a solution with higher proportion of correct links and shreds could help extract more useful information from documents. It is worth noting that the percentage gap with respect to the objective value of original document page is more likely to be useless in this quality measure. This is motivated by the fact that the percentage gap is directly affected by the definition of cost functions. Secondly, the quality of a set of solutions is described by the standard deviation of the proportion, which could help reflect the stability of the method. Since the experimental results are based on 20 tests, the mean and stand deviation of the defined proportion are applied.

Table 1. Results and comparisons of the three algorithms

Methods		Proposed Algorithm		EER 2D		HV^2	
Page	Patterns	Mean %	Std %	Mean %	Std %	Mean %	Std %
e1	6×6	**100**	**0**	**100**	**0**	**100**	**0**
	6×9	**100**	**0**	**100**	**0**	**100**	**0**
	9×9	**81.67**	14.01	49.56	2.15	47.39	**1.69**
e2	6×6	**100**	**0**	**100**	**0**	**100**	**0**
	6×9	**98.16**	**3.85**	81.73	11.44	75.61	11.57
	9×9	**82.67**	11.50	45.17	1.37	46.11	**1.11**
e3	6×6	**100**	**0**	**100**	**0**	**100**	**0**
	6×9	**100**	**0**	**100**	**0**	**100**	**0**
	9×9	**89.78**	8.72	48.22	**2.32**	47.94	2.52
c1	6×6	**100**	**0**	**100**	**0**	97.81	9.54
	6×9	**100**	**0**	**100**	**0**	**100**	**0**
	9×9	**83.28**	10.87	64.44	**4.41**	67.61	7.67
c2	6×6	**100**	**0**	**100**	**0**	**100**	**0**
	6×9	**100**	**0**	92.82	5.23	70.54	4.75
	9×9	**87.5**	11.2	65.28	8.62	62.06	**7.69**
c3	6×6	**94.38**	**6.06**	84.90	14.83	80.52	13.12
	6×9	**100**	**0**	**100**	**0**	**100**	**0**
	9×9	**95.61**	8.35	61.78	6.86	53.28	**4.39**

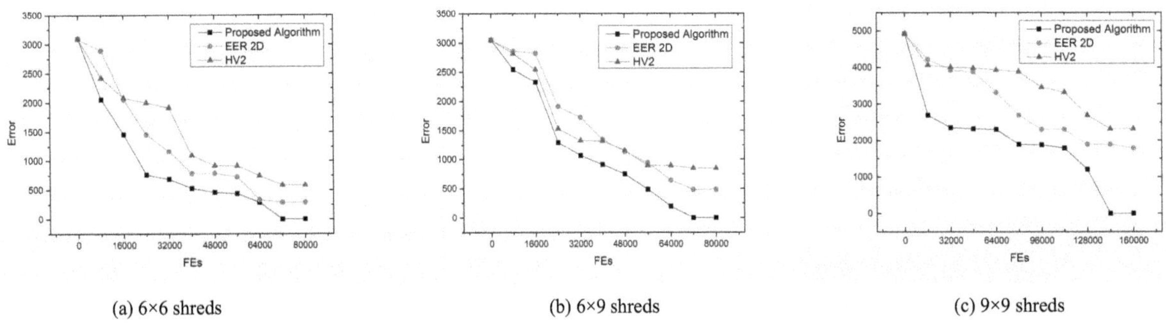

(a) 6×6 shreds (b) 6×9 shreds (c) 9×9 shreds

Figure 9. Convergence curves of the three algorithms.

Table 2. Average computation time of the three algorithms (ms).

Patterns	Proposed Algorithm	EER 2D	HV^2
6×6	6104.71	6008.25	5811.79
6×9	8866	8478.39	7991.25
9×9	28381.09	27486.83	26867.61

5.3 Comparison of Results

Table 1 shows the results obtained by applying proposed algorithm; EER-2D and HV^2 in the instances mentioned above and the best results are marked in bolt. It can be observed that: the proposed algorithm clearly outperforms other two algorithms. On one hand, for instances of 36 and 54 shreds, the proposed algorithm exhibits higher degree of stability. On the other hand, for instances of 81 shreds, the proposed algorithm could achieve higher accuracy rates during the same generation. Comparing the proposed algorithm with EER-2D algorithm, we can see that the ROES operator helps improve the search efficiency of proposed algorithm. Furthermore, the results of EER-2D algorithm show that the proposed mutation and crossover operators are efficient for this problem.

In addition, the convergence curves of the three algorithms are plotted in Figure 9. The figure clearly shows that the proposed algorithm converges fastest to achieve the correct solution. Moreover, the figure also shows the strong search ability of proposed algorithm at the beginning of reconstruction. The data of average computation time in table 2 shows that the efficiency of proposed algorithm is enhanced without costing too much computation time. To summarize, the proposed algorithm is a very competitive algorithm in solving RCCSTD problem.

6. CONCLUSION

In this work we propose a genetic algorithm with splicing-driven reproduction for the reconstruction of cross-cut shredded text documents. To improve the capability of solving this problem, a splicing-driven crossover, four mutation operators, and a row-oriented elitism strategy is designed. Additionally, a new cost function based on both edge and empty vector-based splicing error is defined. To test the performance of the algorithm, shreds from six documents in two languages are used. Based on the experimental results, this proposed algorithm clearly outperforms the previous best-known algorithms.

7. ACKNOWLEDGMENTS

This work was supported in part by the High-Technology Research and Development Program (863 Program) of China No. 2013AA01A212, in part by the NSFC for Distinguished Young Scholars 61125205, in part by the NSFC Joint Fund with Guangdong under Key Projects U1201258 and U1135005.

8. REFERENCES

[1] Prandtstetter M. 2009. Hybrid optimization methods for warehouse logistics and the reconstruction of destroyed paper documents. Ph.D. thesis, Vienna University of Technology.

[2] Sleit A, Massad Y, Musaddaq M. 2013. An alternative clustering approach for reconstructing cross cut shredded text documents. *Telecommunication Systems*, *52*(3), 1491-1501.

[3] Mladenović N, Hansen P. 1997. Variable neighborhood search. *Computers & Operations Research*, *24*(11), 1097-1100.

[4] Schauer C, Prandtstetter M, Raidl G R. 2010. A memetic algorithm for reconstructing cross-cut shredded text documents. In *Hybrid Metaheuristics*, 103-117.

[5] Prandtstetter M, Raidl G R. 2009. Meta-heuristics for reconstructing cross cut shredded text documents. In *Genetic and Evolutionary Computation Conference*, 349-356.

[6] Justino E, Oliveira L S, Freitas C. 2006. Reconstructing shredded documents through feature matching. *Forensic science international*, *160*(2), 140-147.

[7] Prandtstetter M, Raidl G R. 2008. Combining forces to reconstruct strip shredded text documents. In *Hybrid Metaheuristics*, 175-189.

[8] Ukovich A, Ramponi G, Doulaverakis H, et al. 2004. Shredded document reconstruction using MPEG-7 standard descriptors. In *International Symposium on Signal Processing and Its Applications*, 334-337

[9] Holland J H. 1975. Adaptation in natural and artificial systems: an introductory analysis with applications to biology, control, and artificial intelligence. University of Michigan Press.

[10] Leardi R. 2000. Application of genetic algorithm–PLS for feature selection in spectral data sets. *Journal of Chemometrics*, *14*(5-6), 643-655.

[11] Rahmat-Samii Y, Michielssen E. 1999. Electromagnetic optimization by genetic algorithms. John Wiley & Sons Inc.

[12] Raidl G R, Hu B. 2010. Enhancing genetic algorithms by a trie-based complete solution archive. In *Evolutionary Computation in Combinatorial Optimization*, 239-251.

[13] Li X, Yao X. 2012. Cooperatively coevolving particle swarms for large scale optimization. *IEEE Transactions on Evolutionary Computation*, *16*(2), 210-224.

[14] Lu S, Tan C L. 2007. Automatic detection of document script and orientation. In *International Conference on Document Analysis and Recognition*, 237-241.

[15] Davis L. 1985. Applying adaptive algorithms to epistatic domains. In *International Joint Conference on Artificial Intelligence*, 162-164.

[16] Goldberg D E, Lingle R. 1985. Alleles, loci, and the traveling salesman problem. In *International conference on Genetic Algorithms and Their Applications*, 154-159.

[17] I. Oliver, D. Smith, and J. Holland. 1987. A Study of permutation crossover operators on the traveling salesman problem. In *International Conference on Genetic Algorithms*, 224-230.

[18] Starkweather T, McDaniel S, Mathias K E, et al. 1991. A comparison of genetic sequencing operators. In *International Conference on Genetic Algorithms*, 69-76.

[19] Zhan Z H, Zhang J, Li Y, et al. 2009. Adaptive Particle Swarm Optimization. *IEEE Transactions on Systems, Man, and Cybernetics, Part B*, *39*(6), 1362-1381.

[20] Yu W J, Shen M, Chen W N, et al. 2014. Differential evolution with two-level parameter adaptation. *IEEE Transactions on Cybernetics*, *44*(7), 1080-1099.

[21] Gong Y J, Zhang J. 2013. Small-world particle swarm optimization with topology adaptation. In *Genetic and Evolutionary Computation Conference*, 25-32.

Gray-Box Optimization using the Parameter-less Population Pyramid

Brian W. Goldman
BEACON Center for the Study of Evolution in Action
Michigan State University, U.S.A.
brianwgoldman@acm.org

William F. Punch
BEACON Center for the Study of Evolution in Action
Michigan State University, U.S.A.
punch@msu.edu

ABSTRACT

Unlike black-box optimization problems, gray-box optimization problems have known, limited, non-linear relationships between variables. Though more restrictive, gray-box problems include many real-world applications in network security, computational biology, VLSI design, and statistical physics. Leveraging these restrictions, the Hamming-Ball Hill Climber (HBHC) can efficiently find high quality local optima. We show how 1) a simple memetic algorithm in conjunction with HBHC can find *global* optima for some gray-box problems and 2) a gray-box version of the Parameter-less Population Pyramid (P3), utilizing both the HBHC and the known information about variable relationships, outperforms all of the examined algorithms. While HBHC's inclusion into P3 adds a parameter, we show experimentally it can be fixed to 1 without adversely effecting search.

We provide experimental evidence on NKq-Landscapes and Ising Spin Glasses that Gray-Box P3 is effective at finding the global optima even for problems with thousands of variables. This capability is complemented by its efficiency, with running time and memory usage decreased by up to a linear factor from Black-Box P3. On NKq this results in a 375x speedup for problems with at least 1,000 variables.

Categories and Subject Descriptors

I.2.8 [**Artificial Intelligence**]: Problem Solving, Control Methods, and Search

Keywords

Local Search; Global Search; Parameter-less

GECCO '15, July 11 - 16, 2015, Madrid, Spain

DOI: http://dx.doi.org/10.1145/2739480.2754775

1. INTRODUCTION

Recent work [10, 2] has shown that providing local search with more problem specific information than just an evaluation function can greatly improve search power and efficiency. These improvements require information easily derived for a broad range of interesting NP-Hard problems.

Here we extend those benefits to global optimization on binary problems by integrating this local search with additional heuristics [1]. We introduce a novel algorithm designed to combine local and global search as simply as possible. To test the true power of this process we also extend the Parameter-less Population Pyramid (P3) [4], the current state-of-the-art in black-box optimization [5]. This "Gray-Box P3" utilizes both efficient local search and the additional problem information to drastically improve performance and reduce memory usage.

2. GRAY-BOX DOMAIN

In black-box optimization, the only information available is a specification for what constitutes a valid solution and a function which returns the quality of a given solution. While these very simple requirements allow almost any optimization task to fit into this domain, many problems have additional knowledge which could be used by search algorithms. At the other end of the spectrum is white-box optimization, in which everything about the problem is known. Search techniques in this domain specialize at the cost of generality. Gray-box optimization exists between these two extremes, exposing additional information which is available for a variety of problems to be exploited by search.

Here we shall consider the gray-box optimization domain with the following characteristics [2]: The function which evaluates the quality of a solution is determined by the summation of subfunctions. Each subfunction uses at most k variables in the given solution, such that k remains constant as the number of problem variables N increases. Each subfunction is independently evaluable and the variables each subfunction uses are known.

While more restrictive than black-box optimization, this domain is still very general. MAX-SAT, and by extension all NP-hard problems, can be represented as a summation of subfunctions which evaluate each clause [10]. Previous approximation studies of Vertex Cover [6], Set Cover [12], MAX-CUT [3], and Ising Spin Glasses [7] all work with problems which fit in the gray-box domain. These relate back to problems of real world interest such as network security, computational biology, VLSI design, and statistical physics.

In order to obtain efficiency bounds for optimization algorithms, the following assertions are also included [2]: The total number of subfunctions grows no more than linearly with N, which holds true for randomized MAX-SAT, mesh spin glasses, and NK Landscapes. Furthermore, each variable participates in at most c subfunctions, which holds true for mesh spin glasses and Nearest Neighbor NK. If violated, these assertions do not necessarily prevent the gray-box optimization algorithms from solving the problem, but may result in slower than predicted performance.

3. HAMMING-BALL HILL CLIMBING

The first algorithm to rigorously exploit the features of the gray-box domain described in Section 2 was [10]. In this study a hill climber was developed that found the approximate next-best move in $\mathcal{O}(1)$ time given $\mathcal{O}(N)$ setup. This is achieved by first determining the fitness effect of making each move, and then updating only effected moves each time a change to the solution is made. Due to the requirements of the domain, at most $\mathcal{O}(ck)$ moves can be effected, with each requiring at most $\mathcal{O}(1)$ subfunction calls to update their fitness effects. Combined with move binning, this technique is able to perform both first improvement and next-best hill climbing in $\mathcal{O}(I+N)$, where I is the number of improving moves required to reach a local optimum. In comparison, the black-box approach for these searches can require $\mathcal{O}(IN^2)$.

By again leveraging the properties of this domain, the Hamming-Ball Hill Climber (HBHC) [2] extends this method to find solutions that cannot be improved by flipping r or fewer bits called r-bit local optima. While naïvely this would require testing $\mathcal{O}(N^r)$ moves, in the gray-box domain only $\mathcal{O}((3ck)^r N)$ must be checked. This is due to the bounded relationships between variables. If i and j do not share a subfunction, the effect of flipping both variables must be equal to the sum of flipping both separately. Therefore, only variables that share a subfunction must be flipped together when checking $r = 2$. The problem of determining which variables must be flipped together is equivalent to finding the connected induced subgraphs of G with r or fewer vertices, such that each vertex in G is a variable and an edge exists between two vertices if and only if those variables share a subfunction. In [2] an upper bound is derived for how many moves this could create, but no algorithm was given to efficiently discover these moves. This process was not included in their timing calculations as it only has to be performed once per problem instance.

Under the assertion that $r \ll N$ and that r does not increase with N, the Hamming-Ball Hill Climber requires only $\mathcal{O}(I+N)$ time to find r-bit local optima starting from a random solution. As I is likely in $\mathcal{O}(N)$ this means finding random r-bit local optima is no more than a constant amount slower than generating random solutions.

While these techniques make it possible to choose the best move just as efficiently as choosing any random improving move, the findings of [10] suggest that, especially when paired with subsequent search heuristics, using random improving moves is more effective. In [2] this decision was amended slightly to include the requirement that smaller distance moves are chosen before larger distance moves.

3.1 Novel r-order Subgraphs Algorithm

In order to determine which moves in the hamming-ball must be evaluated, we developed C I B-

```
procedure C I B
    closed ← ∅
    found ← [ ]
    for all v ∈ V do
        closed ← closed ∪ {v}
        found ← found+CI G(v, ∅, closed, ∅)
    return found
procedure CI G(v, subset, closed, open)
    subset' ← subset ∪ {v}
    found ← [subset']
    if |subset'| ≥ r then return found
    closed_here ← ∅
    open' ← open ∪ adjacent(v)
    for all v' ∈ open' such that v' ∉ closed do
        closed_here ← closed_here ∪ {v'}
        closed ← closed ∪ {v'}
        recurse ←CI G(v', subset', closed, open')
        found ← found + recurse
    closed ← closed − closed_here
    return found
```

Figure 1: Algorithm to recursively find all connected induced subgraphs of size r or fewer.

given in Figure 1. CI G is a recursive helper function which finds all subgraphs which contain a given *subset* and a given vertex v, while excluding any other vertices added to *closed*. To find all subgraphs, CI G is called once for each vertex in the graph, such that *closed* contains all previously searched vertices, and *subset* = *open* = $\emptyset$. In the initial call all desired subgraphs which contain v are found, which is why v remains in *closed* to prevent duplicate subgraphs from being returned.

At each recursive level CI G expands *open* to include any vertices adjacent to v in the graph. By construction this means that *open'* contains all possible ways of adding a single vertex to the current *subset'*. As each v' is tested it is temporarily added to *closed* to prevent recursive calls from adding it again to *subset'*.

When applied to the sparse graphs inherent in the gray-box domain, this algorithm requires $\mathcal{O}(r!(ck)^r N)$ time, which reduces to $\mathcal{O}(N)$. The time spent in each call is dominated by the loop over *open'*. In the worst case, *open'* increases in size by the full adjacency of v, which is bounded by ck. This creates a worse case complexity for a single top level call of $\prod_i^r ick = r!(ck)^r$. This must be called once for each of the N variables resulting in $\mathcal{O}(r!(ck)^r N)$.

4. TOURNAMENT UNIFORM CROSSOVER: TUX

Hamming-Ball Hill Climbing is not sufficient to efficiently find the global optima on problems with even moderate epistasis [2]. This is because, like all random restart hill climbers, it relies on random initialization to fall inside the global optima's basin of attraction.

To remedy this limitation, we set out to develop a minimally complex memetic algorithm to help increase this probability. Figure 2 presents the Tournament Uniform Crossover (TUX) algorithm, which combines simplistic selection with equal probability uniform crossover, the most basic unbiased

procedure I - X
Create random *solution*
Hamming-Ball Hill Climb *solution*
for all $T_i \in T$ **do**
  if T_i is empty **then**
    $T_i \leftarrow solution$
    return
  Cross *solution* with T_i to create 2^{i+1} offspring
  Hamming-Ball Hill Climb each offspring
  $solution \leftarrow$ best of offspring, *solution*, and T_i
  $T_i \leftarrow$ empty
Add *solution* to end of T

Figure 2: One iteration of TUX optimization. T **is an ordered list of solutions, each position of which could be empty, awaiting a crossover partner.**

procedure I -P3
Create random *solution*
Apply hill climber
if $solution \notin hashset$ **then**
  Add *solution* to P_0
  Add *solution* to *hashset*
for all $P_i \in pyramid$ **do**
  Mix *solution* with P_i
  if *solution*'s fitness has improved **then**
    if $solution \notin hashset$ **then**
      Add *solution* to P_{i+1}
      Add *solution* to *hashset*

Figure 3: One iteration of P3 optimization. *pyramid* **is an ordered set of populations and** *hashset* **is a set of all solutions in** *pyramid*.

crossover, to generate starting solutions likely to be in the global optima's basin of attraction.

Conceptually TUX iteratively builds a structure similar to a single elimination bracket for solutions. Each "match" in the tournament takes in two candidate solutions, produces offspring via uniform crossover, applies hill climbing to each offspring, with the "winner" being the best of all those solutions. The tournament "bracket" is constructed iteratively, storing an initially empty list of solutions T, such that $|T|$ is equal to the height of the tournament. Iterative construction is possible because when a sub-bracket is complete only a single solution emerges and solutions only need to be stored until their partner is found. TUX is fully elitist but does not prematurely converge. This is because search continuously integrates new randomly generated solutions through other parts of the bracket. Whenever the top of the current bracket is reached, TUX doubles the size of the virtual tournament.

When crossing solutions at T_i, TUX produces 2^{i+1} offspring. This relationship ensures that in total all levels of the tournament, including random initialization, perform the same number of hill climbing steps. It also shifts the focus of search toward areas expected to be of higher fitness. The expectation is also that it becomes progressively harder to improve solutions the higher up the tournament you advance, so more attempts are necessary to create new useful solutions.

The primary advantages of TUX are that it does not introduce any new parameters (though it still requires an r for the hill climber) and is relatively simple to implement. Even so it allows for learning from previous local optima and as Section 6 will show it is quite effective at optimization.

5. PARAMETER-LESS POPULATION PYRAMID: P3

5.1 Origins

The Parameter-less Population Pyramid (P3) is a recently introduced black-box optimization method which requires no problem specific configuration [4, 5]. Unlike previous parameter-less methods it was shown to be more efficient than competing state-of-the-art algorithms across a number of problem classes.

P3 combines hill climbing and model building using a novel, iteratively constructed, pyramid of populations. Figure 3 provides the high level description of how the algorithm works. To exploit information from multiple solutions, P3 performs global optimal mixing [9]. Each time a solution is added to a level of the pyramid P_i, linkage learning is performed to create a collection of variable clusters. These clusters, collectively referred to as a linkage tree, are learned from the pairwise variable entropy of P_i. When a solution is mixed with P_i each cluster is used to donate variable values from a random donor in P_i into the solution. After each donation the modified solution is evaluated, with the change being reverted if solution quality decreased. In this way P3 performs multiple evaluations per mixing event. This also means that unlike TUX, which uses information from only two solutions to perform crossover, P3 uses information from an entire population. Due to this model building, P3 requires $\mathcal{O}(N)$ amortized time per evaluation and $\mathcal{O}(N^2)$ memory usage.

5.2 Gray-Box Specialization

P3 represents a natural method for integrating the HBHC into a global optimization algorithm as P3 already utilizes local search. While HBHC's inclusion adds a parameter, Section 6.1 and Section 6.2 provide evidence that r can be fixed to 1, preserving the parameter-less nature of P3. Beyond using HBHC, there are also a number of ways in which P3 can be made more efficient by leveraging the additional information available in the gray-box domain.

First and foremost, linkage learning is no longer necessary. By definition the direct non-linear relationships between variables are known. As a result P3 no longer needs to store the pairwise frequency information which leads the black-box version to require $\mathcal{O}(N^2)$ memory. Instead, we have developed a method for creating a linkage tree which learns clusters from the same dependency graph defined in Section 3. The goal is for each cluster to be a connected induced subgraph, with the size of clusters mirroring those produced by the agglomerative linkage learning process normally used with P3. To form a single cluster, a random graph search is performed from a random starting vertex until a desired number of unique vertices have been explored. Cluster sizes are set recursively. For each cluster of size $l > 1$ a cluster of size a and a cluster of size $l - a$ are also created, with a chosen uniformly from the range $[1..l-1]$. This recursive process begins by initializing $l = N$ and splitting to form the first two clusters.

This linking algorithm has a number of useful properties. First, it creates exactly $2N - 2$ clusters, distributed in size similarly to the black-box clustering algorithm. Performing a random graph search to find l unique vertices requires $\mathcal{O}(lck)$ time, meaning cluster creation is optimally efficient. The cluster splitting process has identical properties as random pivot quicksort, meaning the sum of cluster sizes is $\mathcal{O}(N \log N)$ in the average case. This efficiency allows new clusters to be created before every mixing event, unlike Black-Box P3 where they are created only when new solutions are added to the population. For simplicity the clusters are shuffled after they are created, not sorted on size like in Black-Box P3.

Beyond efficiency, there are good reasons to believe these clusters will be useful for search. The closer two variables are in the dependency graph, the more likely they are to appear in the same cluster. All variables on average are expected to appear in at least one cluster, but variables which are central in the graph will appear in more clusters than those on the periphery. The more paths of a given length between two variables, the higher the probability of them being in the same cluster. Unlike Black-Box P3, this linkage tree does not require clusters to be nested, allowing more diversity in the types of clusters appearing in a single tree.

In effect the clusters are sampling moves which the HBHC would make if $r \geq l$. For any solution in the search space which is not globally optimal, there must exist some move which will improve its quality. However, this move may be arbitrarily large and it is intractable to test all possible moves of even moderate size. By sampling from all possible large moves, we can maintain tractability while gaining a potentially non-zero probability of improvement. As clusters are used to donate values between solutions, these moves are always in the direction of previously found high quality solutions. This assumes that the density of high quality solutions is higher than average between good solutions.

Another efficiency gain possible due to the gray-box domain is that each time a donation is made, only the effected part of the solution's fitness needs to be recalculated. As a result the number of subfunction evaluations required to determine the change in fitness is only $\mathcal{O}(l)$. This also allows for Gray-Box P3 to efficiently reapply hill climbing after each donation as only effected moves need to be rechecked. As a result, a donation and its resulting modifications from hill climbing are kept only if the new local optima is at least as fit as the solution before the donation occurred. All combined a single donation plus returning to a local optimum requires $\mathcal{O}(l + I)$ time, while just the donation in Black-Box P3 requires $\mathcal{O}(N)$.

6. EXPERIMENTS

To compare these gray-box optimization techniques we have chosen NKq-Landscapes [2] and Ising Spin Glasses [8]. NKq-Landscapes create a collection of randomly generated problem instances given a higher level problem class description. Each instance is described by a series of N subfunctions, each corresponding to a variable in the solution. This subfunction uses its variable and K other variables in the solution to calculate a fitness value. Fitness values are represented as a randomly generated lookup table, such that table entries are integers in the range $[0..q-1]$. As each subfunction reads $K + 1$ variables, the table's size and q are set to 2^{K+1}. The quality of a solution is equal to the sum of the values returned by these subfunctions.

In this work we shall consider two methods for choosing the K variables each subfunction depends on: Nearest Neighbor NKq and Unrestricted NKq. In Nearest Neighbor NKq each variable depends on the K variables which sequentially follow it in the solution, with dependencies wrapping around the end of the solution. Landscapes of this form can be solved in polynomial time [11], allowing comparisons of how quickly each optimization algorithm can find the global optima. Nearest Neighbor NKq also ensures that $c = k = K + 1$ and that both c and k do not increase as N increases, meaning the efficiency conclusions made in Section 3 are applicable.

Unrestricted NKq landscapes draw the K dependencies at random without replacement. For $K > 1$ it is NP-Hard to find the global optimum of these landscapes. This also means that while k remains fixed, the maximum number of subfunctions a variable appears in (c) can increase as N increases. As a result some of the efficiency claims in Section 3 may not be applicable.

Ising Spin Glasses are a type of MAX-CUT problem relevant in statistical physics. Each spin glass encodes spins (vertices) and their relationships (edges) with the goal of assigning each spin a direction which minimizes relationship energy. Just as with NKq-Landscapes, Ising Spin Glasses as a whole are NP-Hard, but the $2D\pm J$ subset is polynomially solvable [8][1]. In this subset the graph is a 2D toroidal grid, with edge weights of ± 1. In gray-box terms, problems of this subset have $k = 2$ and $c = 4$ regardless of N.

For each problem class tested, we generated 50 instances. Extreme problem sizes were chosen to stress each algorithm. Each method was run once on each instance, and limited to 3 hours of computation and 4 GB of memory. Runs were performed on 2.5GHz Intel Xeon E5-2670v2 processors using the C++11 code available from our website.[2] Each time the run achieved a new best fitness we recorded the current amount of processing time used. Timing includes the discovery of subgraphs to allow for comparison between different radius values. When reporting the "best" fitness for an instance we mean the best fitness found by any method before the time limit is reached. On all Nearest Neighbor NKq instances the "best" fitness is also the global optimum, verified using dynamic programming. For Ising Spin Glass the "best" fitness was the global optimum 44 out of 50 times.

All figures report the median, upper and lower quartiles for either percentage error or seconds to reach the best. A run's percentage error is equal to the difference between its fitness and the best, divided by the best. When reporting seconds to reach the best fitness, any run which did not find the best fitness is treated as slower than any run that did. If the median run was unsuccessful, no data point is drawn.

6.1 The Effect of Radius

The only algorithm parameter in the HBHC, TUX, and Gray-Box P3 is the radius of the hamming-ball. Therefore our first experiments are designed to determine the effect of this parameter on solution quality.

Figure 4 shows the effect on final solution fitness as r increases. As expected from [2] the HBHC obtains higher qual-

[1]http://www.informatik.uni-koeln.de/spinglass/

[2]https://github.com/brianwgoldman/GrayBoxOptimization/releases

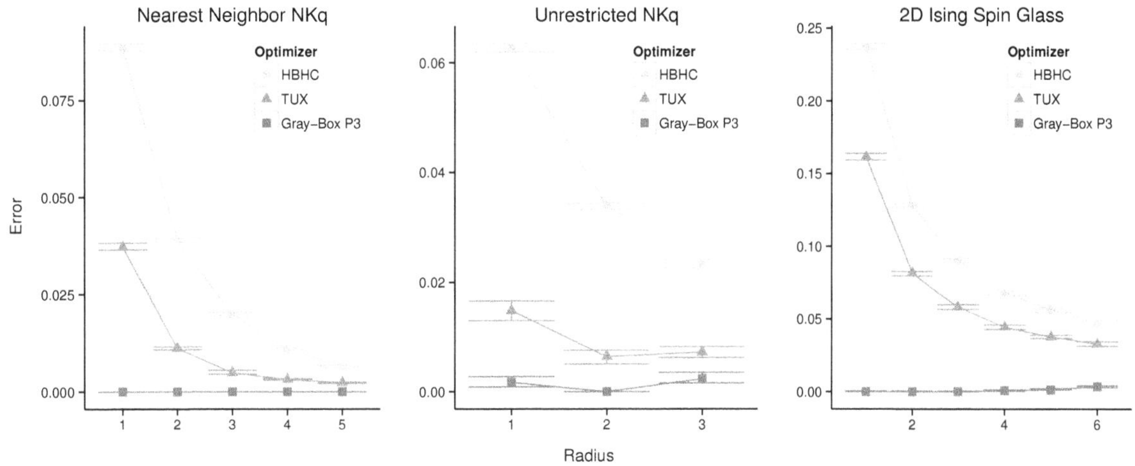

Figure 4: Comparison of how radius effects solution quality at termination. For NKq-Landscapes $N = 6,000$ and $K = 4$ and for Ising Spin Glasses $N = 6,084$. Range of radius values limited by memory constraints.

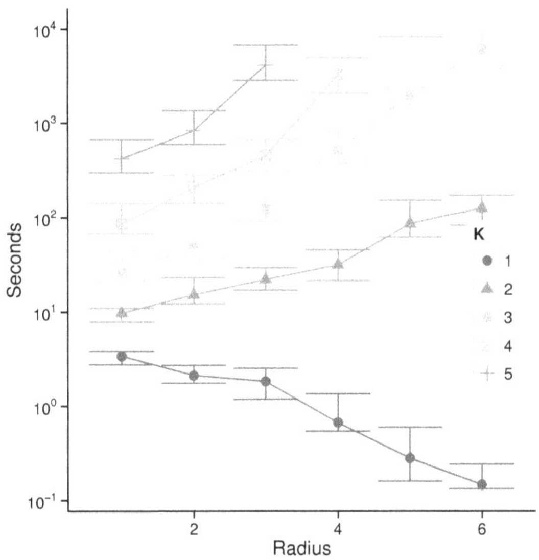

Figure 5: Time required for Gray-Box P3 to reach the global optimum of Nearest Neighbor NKq instances with $N = 6,000$.

ity as r increases, with the magnitude of the improvement decreasing. TUX has a similar relationship and outperforms HBHC on all three problems for all r values. Regardless of r, Gray-Box P3 outperforms both, with almost all r values reaching the same best fitness. For Nearest Neighbor NKq, Gray-Box P3 finds the global optimum in every run for $r < 4$, with only a single unsuccessful run at $r = 4$.

To further examine the effect of r on Gray-Box-P3, Figure 5 shows the number of seconds required to reach the global optimum. Setting $r = 1$ was the most efficient configuration for all $K > 1$, supporting the trend that Gray-Box P3 works best with small r values. With $K = 1$, the landscape is smooth enough that with a sufficiently high r the HBHC is able to find the global optimum.

6.2 Fitness Over Time

Reaching high quality solutions quickly can sometimes be more important than reaching the global optimum eventually. Figure 6 shows how solution quality progresses during search for each algorithm. HBHC and TUX have significant early delays caused by their high r values. Larger r's require a large amount of initial partial evaluation before performing hill climbing. After one full iteration HBHC effectively stalls, with TUX continuing to improve. Both are eclipsed by Gray-Box P3, which quickly descends to the global optimum, outperforming HBHC and TUX at every time point.

Figure 7 further illustrates the effect of r on Gray-Box P3. On Nearest Neighbor NKq and Ising Spin Glasses, increasing r does not change the shape of the curve. Instead the quality reached is simply time shifted, such that given more time higher r values will reach the same quality. As a result, for these problems we conclude that higher r values simply add more expense for no overall gain. On Unrestricted NKq this relationship is less certain, with $r = 1$ potentially having a different, and worse, shape than $r > 1$. However, due to memory and time restrictions it is difficult to know if this trend continues.

6.3 Scalability

Perhaps the most critical test of an optimization algorithm's quality is how it scales as problem difficulty increases. To test this behavior, we ran all three algorithms using the optimal r values determined experimentally in Section 6.1, varying N from 200 to 10,000 for NKq and 196 to 6,084 for Ising Spin Glass. In these plots we also include the black-box version of P3 to show the efficiency gains available for using gray-box information.

Figure 8 and Figure 9 show how long each algorithm required to reach the best overall quality found on Nearest Neighbor NKq and Ising Spin Glasses, respectively. For Nearest Neighbor NKq the best found is the global optimum for all runs of all lengths, while for Ising Spin Glasses the best quality found by any method was worse than the global optimum in 7 runs of $N = 4,096$ and 21 runs of $N = 6,084$. The median run of the HBHC was unable to

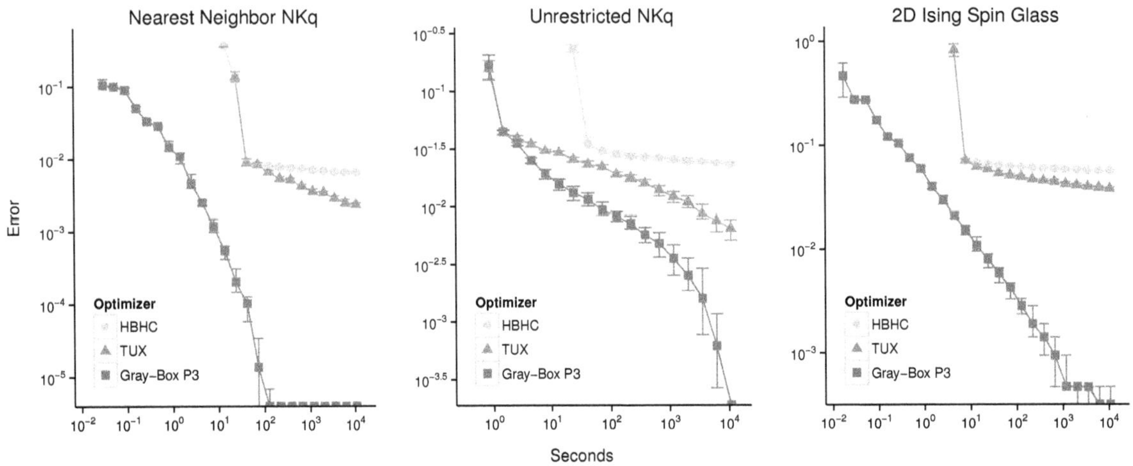

Figure 6: Comparison of solution quality during optimization on a log-log scale for different algorithms. For NKq-Landscapes $N = 6,000$ and $K = 4$ and for Ising Spin Glasses $N = 6,084$. Each algorithm uses its best found r value.

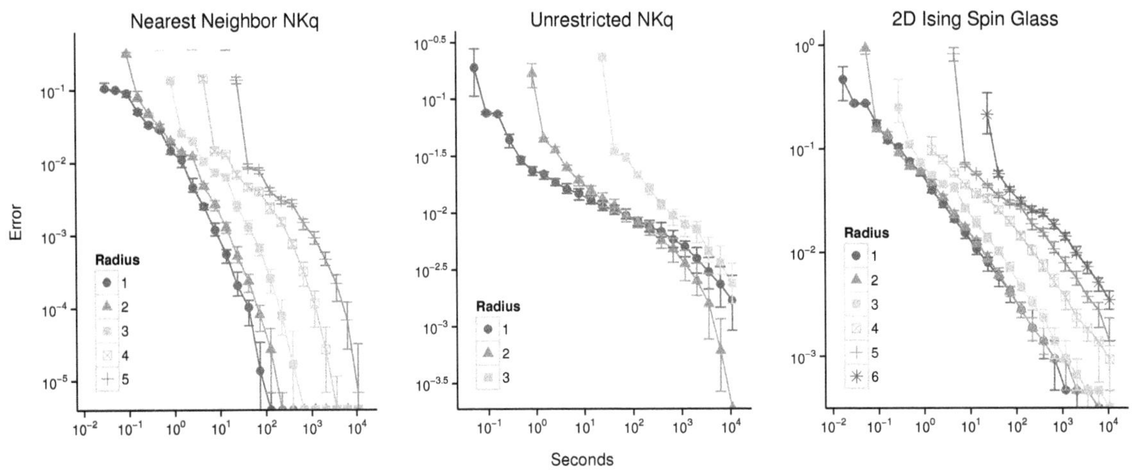

Figure 7: Comparison of Gray-Box P3's solution quality during optimization on a log-log scale for different r values. For NKq-Landscapes $N = 6,000$ and $K = 4$ and for Ising Spin Glasses $N = 6,084$.

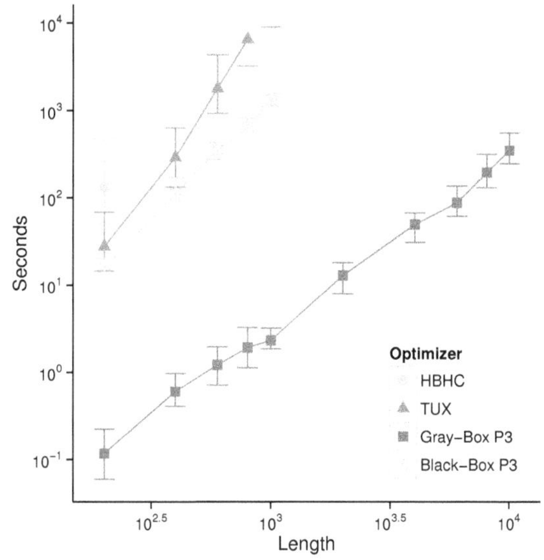

Figure 8: Comparison of how each algorithm's time required to reach the best fitness found scales with problem size on Nearest Neighbor NKq with $K = 4$. With $N = 1000$ Gray-Box P3 is 375x faster than Black-Box P3.

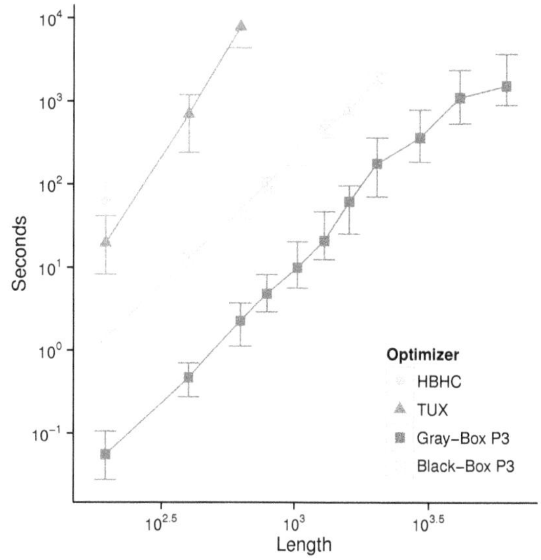

Figure 9: Comparison of how each algorithm's time required to find the best fitness found scales with problem size on Ising Spin Glass. With $N = 2025$ Gray-Box P3 is 4.6x faster than Black-Box P3.

reach the best fitness for any problems tested using more than 200 bits. TUX performed somewhat better, reaching the best fitness more than half of the time on problem sizes up to $N = 800$ and $N = 625$ for Nearest Neighbor NKq and Ising Spin Glass, respectively. Black-Box P3, which does not utilize partial reevaluation or the HBHC, was able to consistently reach the best fitness until it it hit the memory limit on $N = 2,000$ for NKq and $N = 2,916$ for Ising Spin Glass. This limitation is due to Black-Box P3's $\mathcal{O}(N^2)$ memory requirements.

For all sizes of both problems, Gray-Box P3 was the fastest to reach the best fitness. On Nearest Neighbor NKq the improvement is very significant, with no alternative finishing within two orders of magnitude. On its largest successful problem size, the mean time to completion for Black-Box P3 was 375 times slower than Gray-Box P3. Using the Mann-Whitney test to compare their run times results in $p < 10^{-16}$. This is especially impressive considering previous work has shown Black-Box P3 is faster to reach the global optimum than other leading black-box methods [5]. Applying regression, we estimate that Black-Box P3's time to global optimum on Nearest Neighbor NKq is $\mathcal{O}(N^{2.75})$ while Gray-Box P3's is $\mathcal{O}(N^{1.98})$.

The results on Ising Spin Glass are similar, with a less extreme difference between Black-Box P3 and Gray-Box P3. In general Gray-Box is the fastest technique to find the global optimum by an order of magnitude, with Black-Box P3's mean run finishing 4.6 times slower than Gray-Box on $N = 2,025$. Using the Mann-Whitney test to compare their run times results in $p < 10^{-14}$. The regression line suggests that while Gray-Box P3 scales at $\mathcal{O}(N^{3.35})$, Black-Box P3 scales at $\mathcal{O}(N^{3.05})$.

As Unrestricted NKq does not have a known global optimum, and the different algorithms rarely found the same best fitness, Figure 10 compares the error for each technique at termination. Gray-Box P3 in general finds the best fitness, with TUX occasionally performing better. When $N > 2,000$, Gray-Box P3 finds better quality solutions that all other methods for every instance. Using the Mann-Whitney test to compare the fitness of Gray-Box P3 and TUX when $N = 10,000$ results in $p < 10^{-16}$. HBHC and Black-Box P3 only reach similar qualities as TUX and Gray-Box P3 when $N = 200$, doing so in 4 and 7 runs, respectively. As the problem size increase TUX begins to fall behind Gray-Box P3, with the HBHC stabilizing at about 2.5% worse than the best found. Here Black-Box P3 performs worse than the other techniques, falling further behind as the problem size increases.

7. DISCUSSION AND CONCLUSIONS

In line with previous work, we have found that HBHC cannot effectively find global optima on problems with even moderate epistasis. In general it also obtains almost no improvement in fitness after only a few restarts. We designed TUX as a simplistic way of choosing restart locations based on previously found local optima. Unlike HBHC alone, TUX was able to continue improving given more time, finding global optima on problems three times as large.

TUX's effectiveness is likely due to the HBHC acting as a super repair operator for uniform crossover. Given a sufficiently large r the HBHC can return sections of the crossover offspring to either parents' original version of a given subfunction. The HBHC is elitist meaning there is a bias toward returning to the better of the two parent's versions. Furthermore, by being so disruptive, uniform crossover potentially allows for the HBHC to also find unrelated improvements.

While TUX improves over plain HBHC, Gray-Box P3 is required to perform truly successful global optimization. Gray-Box P3 replaces naïve local search with the HBHC and utilizes known non-linear relationships instead of statis-

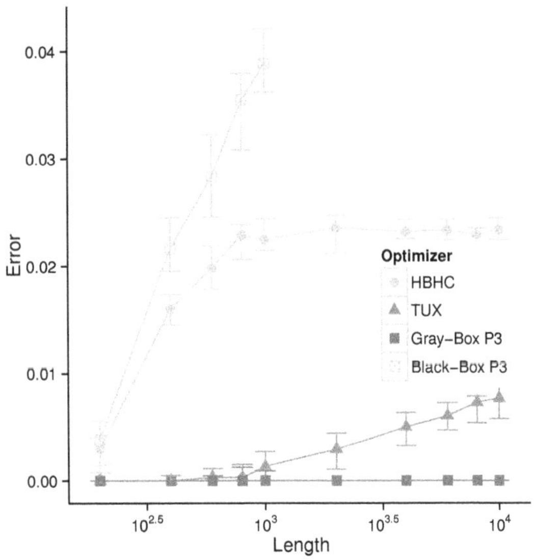

Figure 10: Relative qualities of each method as problem size increases on Unrestricted NKq with $K = 4$.

tical linkage learning. On NKq-Landscapes this drastically improves search effectiveness. A major source of this improvement is likely how difficult it is for Black-Box P3 to learn linkage relationships on these landscapes. Furthermore, Gray-Box P3 can perform partial reevaluation and efficient hill climbing during the mixing phase.

Gray-Box P3's success is less dramatic on Ising Spin Glasses. While it still outperformed all competitors, Black-Box P3 may actually scale better to larger problems. One explanation for this deviation is that Ising Spin Glasses require more exploration of equal fitness plateaus. For instance in Figure 6 and Figure 7 there is a significant pause in improvement when Gray-Box P3 reaches the second best fitness in the landscape. Nothing in its design suggests that Gray-Box P3 should be more effective at neutral drift. Another potential issue is that on these landscapes the importance of each non-linear relationship may be detectably unequal. As a result Black-Box linkage learning may better cluster variables which having meaningful impact on fitness while Gray-Box assumes all are equally important. A useful direction for future work would be to explore methods of performing efficient learning on top of the known variable interactions.

Somewhat surprising is the difference in behavior between the polynomially solvable problems and Unrestricted NKq. While Black-Box P3 performed very well in the former, it was the least successful in the latter. The optimal radius for Gray-Box P3 also shifted from 1 to 2. A potential explanation is that in both Ising Spin Glass and Nearest Neighbor NKq the number of unique variables r or fewer steps away from a given variable is significantly lower than the worst case. This explains why on Unrestricted NKq even moderately high r values hit our memory limit. For Black-Box P3 this may also be causing increased difficulty in linkage learning as variables become indirectly dependent on much larger sets. Furthermore, Black-Box P3 may be benefiting from an increased rate of duplicate dependencies on Nearest Neighbor NKq not present in Unrestricted NKq.

While the inclusion of HBHC into Gray-Box P3 introduces a parameter, it requires trivial configuration. In the worst case there may be a handful of r values to test. Furthermore, our evidence suggests setting $r = 1$ is quite powerful, with higher values likely to be only a time shift in quality. This is in contrast to r's role in HBHC, where low r values are never expected to reach the same quality has higher r values. Therefore we conclude that Gray-Box P3 maintains the out-of-the-box quality of Black-Box P3, while drastically improving efficiency for this new domain of problems.

8. REFERENCES

[1] X. Chen, Y.-S. Ong, M.-H. Lim, and K. C. Tan. A multi-facet survey on memetic computation. *IEEE Transactions on Evolutionary Computation*, 15(5):591–607, 2011.

[2] F. Chicano, D. Whitley, and A. M. Sutton. Efficient identification of improving moves in a ball for pseudo-boolean problems. In *GECCO '14: Proceedings of the 2014 conference on Genetic and evolutionary computation*, pages 437–444, Vancouver, BC, Canada, 12-16 July 2014. ACM.

[3] P. Festa, P. M. Pardalos, M. G. Resende, and C. C. Ribeiro. Randomized heuristics for the max-cut problem. *Optimization methods and software*, 17(6):1033–1058, 2002.

[4] B. W. Goldman and W. F. Punch. Parameter-less population pyramid. In *GECCO '14: Proceedings of the 2014 conference on Genetic and evolutionary computation*, pages 785–792, Vancouver, BC, Canada, 12-16 July 2014. ACM.

[5] B. W. Goldman and W. F. Punch. Fast and efficient black box optimization using the parameter-less population pyramid. *Evolutionary computation*, 2015.

[6] P. S. Oliveto, J. He, and X. Yao. Analysis of the (1+1)-ea for finding approximate solutions to vertex cover problems. *Evolutionary Computation, IEEE Transactions on*, 13(5):1006–1029, 2009.

[7] M. Pelikan and D. E. Goldberg. Hierarchical BOA solves ising spin glasses and MAXSAT. In *Genetic and Evolutionary Computation - GECCO-2003*, volume 2724 of *LNCS*, pages 1271–1282, Chicago, 12-16 July 2003. Springer-Verlag.

[8] L. Saul and M. Kardar. The 2d±j ising spin glass: exact partition functions in polynomial time. *Nuclear Physics B*, 432(3):641–667, 1994.

[9] D. Thierens and P. A. N. Bosman. Optimal mixing evolutionary algorithms. In *GECCO '11: Proceedings of the 13th annual conference on Genetic and evolutionary computation*, pages 617–624, Dublin, Ireland, 12-16 July 2011. ACM.

[10] D. Whitley, A. E. Howe, and D. Hains. Greedy or not? best improving versus first improving stochastic local search for maxsat. In *AAAI*, 2013.

[11] A. H. Wright, R. K. Thompson, and J. Zhang. The computational complexity of N-K fitness functions. *IEEE Transactions on Evolutionary Computation*, 4(4):373–379, Nov. 2000.

[12] Y. Yu, X. Yao, and Z.-H. Zhou. On the approximation ability of evolutionary optimization with application to minimum set cover. *Artificial Intelligence*, 180–181:20–33, 2010.

Adaptive Control of Parameter-less Population Pyramid on the Local Distribution of Inferior Individuals

Kazuyuki Inoue, Taku Hasegawa, Yuta Araki, Naoki Mori and Keinosuke Matsumoto
Graduate School of Engineering Osaka Prefecture University
1-1 Gakuencho, Sakai City, Osaka, 599-8531, Japan
{inoue@ss, hasegawa@ss, araki@ss, mori@, matsu@}.cs.osakafu-u.ac.jp

ABSTRACT

Many evolutionary techniques such as genetic algorithms (GAs) employ parameters that facilitate user control of search dynamics. However, these parameters require time-consuming tuning processes to avoid problems such as premature convergence. Unlike many GAs, the Parameter-less Population Pyramid (P3) is an optimization model that avoids premature convergence due to the pyramid-like structure of populations, and thus P3 can be applied to a wide range of problems without parameter tuning. P3 approaches to search would be useful for constructing a novel theory for optimal search using GAs. In this study, we propose a novel technique "analysis based on the Distribution of Inferior Individuals in the local neighborhood" (DII analysis). DII analysis can be applied to local search techniques, including P3. The computational complexity of applied problems can be estimated based on a number of local optima according to the results obtained using DII. We also propose combining P3 with DII analysis (P3-DII), which controls the maximum number of fitness evaluations performed by genetic operators. The computational experiments were carried out taking several combinational problems as examples. According to our experimental results, we demonstrated that P3-DII found several optimal solutions that P3 failed to find.

Categories and Subject Descriptors

I.2.8 [Artificial Intelligence]: Problem Solving—Control Methods, and Search

Keywords

Genetic Algorithm; Local Search; Fitness Landscape; Adaptation; Parameter-less

GECCO '15, July 11–15, 2015, Madrid, Spain
 ISBN 978-1-4503-3472-3/15/07...$15.00
DOI: http://dx.doi.org/10.1145/2739480.2754818

1. INTRODUCTION

Many evolutionary techniques such as genetic algorithms (GAs) employ parameters that provide user control of search dynamics. Therefore, reducing the number of these parameters or building a theory for tuning parameters adaptively are fundamental goals in the area of GAs. One approach is to learn the fitness landscape to develop a surrogate model [1]. GAs utilize the surrogate model to guide genetic operators during the irreversible search process [2], and then sometimes cause several problems including premature convergence due to a failure of prediction at one step.

By contrast, the Parameter-less Population Pyramid (P3) [3] can avoid premature convergence due to the pyramid-like structure of the populations employed. P3 performs additional search according to P3 iterators, and thus P3 is a robust optimization model to the accuracy of the prediction obtained at each step. In the present study, we propose a technique "analysis based on the Distribution of Inferior Individuals in the local neighborhood" (DII analysis), which facilitates adaptive search using P3. While no optimizer can solve all problems equally well [4], we focus on getting optimizers based on DII analysis for the problems which are structured as partial fitness functions.

DII analysis predicts the computational complexity of the problem based on the features of a simple model by comparing the quality of the solutions in the local neighborhood. In this study, we introduce DII analysis with Hamming distance of 1 (DII-1 analysis). DII-1 analysis provides the maximum number of fitness evaluations used in genetic operators according to the estimated complexity of the problem. We also propose combining P3 with DII-1 analysis (P3-DII) and we demonstrate that P3-DII can find several optimal solutions that P3 fails to find.

2. PARAMETER-LESS POPULATION PYRAMID

P3 is an optimization algorithm that requires no user parameters. P3 employs a pyramid-like population structure rather than a single population of solutions. Each level of the pyramid comprises a population of solutions, which behaves as different generations during evolution. P3 utilizes these populations to improve the solutions by hill climbing and crossover operations.

2.1 Algorithm

As mentioned above, P3 maintains a pyramid-like population structure where each level of the pyramid comprises a population of solutions. More optimized solutions are found

Algorithm 1 ITERATE-P3

Create random solution
Apply hill climber
if solution $\notin$ *hashset* then
  Add solution to P_0
  Add solution to *hashset*
for all $P_i \in$ *pyramid* do
  Mix solution with P_i
  if the solution's fitness has improved then
    if solution $\notin$ *hashset* then
      Add solution to P_{i+1}
      Add solution to *hashset*

Figure 1: One iteration of P3 optimization. *pyramid* is an ordered set of populations and *hashset* is a set of all solutions in *pyramid*, referred to [3].

at the higher levels. The different levels comprise unique solutions such that $\forall_{i,j \in P, i \neq j} P_i \cap P_j = \phi$ where i and j are the levels of the pyramid. If new solutions do not exist in any levels of the pyramid, they can only be added to a level.

Figure 1 provides a high level summary of P3. Figure 1 shows how P3 constructs populations iteratively and utilizes them to improve the randomly generated solutions using hill climbing and crossover.

2.2 Local Search

P3 uses the First Improvement Hill Climber (FIHC). In FIHC, we consider all gene loci and select the gene s_i as the focus. If the fitness value improves when the solution is evaluated using all possible values, the original value of s_i is replaced with the improved value. The process is iterated until it reaches the local optimum [5].

2.3 Crossover

P3 uses a crossover method derived from Linkage Tree Genetic Algorithm (LTGA) [6]. P3 calculates the gene value entropy to construct clusters of genes and the value is considered during crossover. Crossover comprises two processes: *clustercreation* and *clusterusage*.

2.3.1 Cluster creation

During cluster creation, P3 creates a binary tree of clusters. The leaves of the tree represent the gene loci of individuals and each internal node represents the subset of loci created by joining the subsets encoded by its children. Each level also has a table of pairwise gene value frequencies. Equation 1 calculates the linkage "distance" between clusters of loci using the average pairwise entropy values in the table. The average pairwise entropy is given by Equation 2. Figure 3 shows the cluster creation process.

$$D(C_i, C_j) = \frac{1}{\|C_i\| \cdot \|C_j\|} \sum_{c_i \in C_i} \sum_{c_j \in C_j} 2 - \frac{H(c_i) + H(c_j)}{H(c_i \cup c_j)} \quad (1)$$

$$H(C) = -\sum_{r \in R} p_c(r) \log(p_c(r)) \quad (2)$$

Algorithm 2 CLUSTER CREATION

unmerged $\leftarrow \{\{0\}, \{1\}, \{2\}, \cdots, \{N-1\}\}$
useful $\leftarrow$ *unmerged*
while $\|unmerged\| > 1$ do
  $C_i, C_j \leftarrow min_{C_i, C_j \in unmerged} D(C_i, C_j)$
  $unmerged \leftarrow unmerged - \{C_i, C_j\} + \{C_i \cup C_j\}$
  $useful \leftarrow useful + \{C_i \cup C_j\}$
  if $D(C_i, C_j) = 0$ then
    $useful \leftarrow useful - \{C_i, C_j\}$
Order *useful* based on cluster size, with the smallest first, and remove the largest cluster from *useful* return useful

Figure 2: Algorithm describing how clusters are created using Equation 1 for each P_i. *unmerged* and *useful* are ordered sets of gene loci, referred to [3].

Algorithm 3 CLUSTER USAGE

for all $C_i \in useful$ do
  for all $d \in shuffled(P_i)$ do
    Copy d's gene values for C_i into the solution
    if solution changes then
      if solution's fitness decreases then
        Revert changes
      break

Figure 3: Algorithm describing how clusters are used to perform crossover, referred to [3].

2.3.2 Cluster usage

A candidate solution is recombined with individuals at each level of the pyramid based on the linkage tree shown in Section 2.3.1. A donor is selected randomly and if a new solution is created using a cluster, P3 performs crossover with the next cluster. If the donor cannot obtain a new solution with higher fitness than the candidate solution using the cluster, the method reverts to the candidate's original gene values; otherwise, the candidate changes are kept. Figure 2 shows the cluster usage process.

New solutions are created according to the following criteria.

- Clusters with a size of one are utilized in crossover.
- All of the clusters are tested in order with the smallest first, where clusters of equal size are tested in random order.
- The donor used for clustering is selected randomly from the current level of the pyramid.
- P3 ensures that at least one gene value differs between the donor and the candidate solution.
- P3 does not allow donations that do not change any gene values.
- P3 does not use clusters that are fully contained within their direct superset during crossover ($D(C_i, C_j) = 0 \Rightarrow C_i, C_j$ are not used).

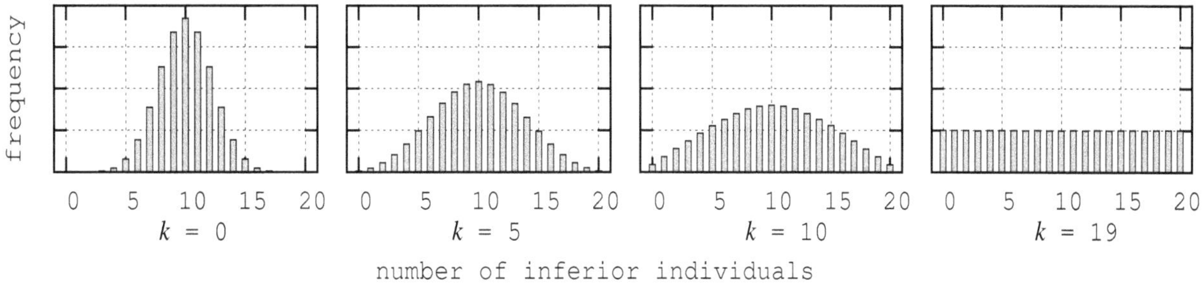

Figure 4: Frequency with respect to the number of inferior individuals in the neighborhood with Hamming distance of 1.

3. DII ANALYSIS

We propose a novel approach to estimate complexity of problems based on DII which is the distribution of the number of inferior individuals in the local neighborhood. In this paper, we focus on DII with a Hamming distance of 1, named DII-1. For simplification, we define the complexity analysis based on DII(DII-1) as just "DII(DII-1) analysis".

In DII-1 analysis, the procedure is divided into two parts, where the first estimates the distribution of inferior individuals with local search techniques and the second uses the features derived from the distribution based on a simple model, Nt landscape problem.

DII-1 analysis can be applied to any problem with a discrete representation, but we focus on problems with a binary domain for simplicity. In this section, we explain DII analysis with examples of the Nk landscape problem and the deceptive trap problem, which are described in Section 5, and the Nt landscape problem described in the next subsection.

The main symbols used in this section are as follows.
F: fitness function
f_i: partial fitness function
t: random functional size
N: chromosome length
s: individual
s_i: gene of individual s at locus i

3.1 Nt landscape problem

We define the Nt landscape problem as follows.

1. The fitness function F is given by sum of the partial functions f.
2. All of the partial functions are given by genes in t loci. The number of partial functions is N/t, where N is the chromosome length. N/t is not a need to be an integer in our theory.
3. All of the partial functions are given by random variables based on the positions of the genes. The function values in partial functions are different from each other.

Nt landscape problem is a type of simplified Nk landscape with no overlapping genes of partial functions. In this study, we focus on the computational complexity derived from the value of t in Nt landscape problem. We refer to the value t as the "random functional size". Let f_i be the partial function given by the set of loci $L = \{i, i+1, \cdots, i+t-1\}$. We define the genes $S = \{s_i, s_{i+1}, \cdots, s_{i+t-1}\}$ in loci I with higher values of f_i than any combinations of genes at a Hamming distance of 1 in loci I as the partial local optima in the Nt landscape problem. DII-1 analysis predicts the computational complexity based on the partial local optima in the Nt landscape problem.

3.2 Inferior individuals

The individuals inferior to individual s are defined as the individuals with not greater fitness than the fitness value of s. In this study, we focus on the number of individuals inferior to individual s in the neighborhood, which number is represented by I_s, and we define a local optimum as the genotype of individual s with $I_s = N$.

The distribution of inferior individuals represents many features related to the problem's complexity in GAs based on the rank of individuals, but we mainly consider an increase in the local optima according to an increase in the size of a partial function given by random variables. In the first example, we specify problems with a linear function and no fitness plateaus, i.e., the One Max problem and Nk landscape problem with $k = 0$. In these problems, the distribution of inferior individuals is a binomial distribution $\mathrm{B}(N, \frac{1}{2})$ because a partial function on a locus is independent of another locus. As another example, we specify a problem with a completely random fitness function such as the Nk landscape problem with $k = N - 1$. In this case, the probability that the number of individuals inferior to s equals $I_s (I_s = 0, 1, \cdots, N)$ is $\frac{1}{N+1}$, and the number of inferior individuals is given by the discrete uniform distribution $\mathrm{U_d}(0, N)$. Figure 4 shows the frequency distribution of the number of inferior individuals in the Nk landscape problem with $N = 20$. In this figure, the distribution of the number of inferior individuals in the neighborhood is affected by problem features, such as the value of k.

3.3 DII-1 analysis

DII-1 analysis is divided into two steps. In the first step, DII-1 analysis estimates the distribution of inferior individuals with a beta-binomial distribution [7]. In the second step, DII-1 analysis estimates a random functional value t for applied problem, and estimates the maximum number of fitness evaluations in local search and crossover based on t.

3.3.1 *Beta-binomial distribution*

A random variable X is given by the beta-binomial distribution $\mathrm{BB}(n, \alpha, \beta)$, where a random variable X is given by the binomial distribution $\mathrm{B}(n, Y)$ and a random variable Y is given by the beta distribution $\mathrm{Be}(\alpha, \beta)$. The beta distribution $\mathrm{Be}(j, n - j + 1)$ gives the jth order statistic with

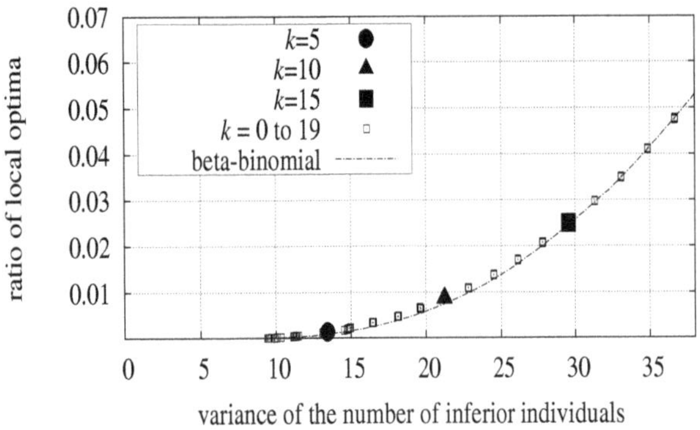

Figure 5: Ratio of local optima with respect to the variance in the number of inferior individuals.

a uniform distribution U(0, 1) in n trials, and the beta distribution is related to the order statistic of many distributions, which can be converted into a uniform distribution. If we select numbers from a set of integers $\{1, 2, \cdots, N'\}$ in n' trials, $X_j - j$ is given by the beta-binomial distribution $\mathrm{BB}(N' - n', j, n' - j + 1)$, where X_j denotes the jth order statistics.

Let f_i be a partial function affected by loci $I = \{i, i+1, \cdots, i+t-1\}$ in the Nt landscape problem. The rank of the partial function value of the genes $S_i = \{s_i, s_{i+1}, \cdots, s_{i+t-1}\}$ in the neighborhood of the genes S_i, which is represented by X_{S_i}, is given by the discrete uniform distribution $\mathrm{U_d}(0, t)$. Therefore, the distribution of the number of genes with a lower value of f_i in the neighborhood of S_i is given by $\mathrm{B}(t, 1 - \frac{X_{S_i - 1}}{2^t})$. The beta-binomial distribution predicts the distribution of the number of inferior individuals with high accuracy in problems with a structure similar to the Nt problem.

The probability function $P(X = x)$ for the beta-binomial distribution $\mathrm{BB}(n, \alpha, \beta)$ is:

$$P(X = x) =_n C_k \frac{B(x + \alpha, n - x + \beta)}{B(\alpha, \beta)} \quad (3)$$

where $B(\alpha, \beta)$ is the beta function.

In this study, we simply estimate the parameters α, β for the beta-binomial distribution with an average μ and variance σ^2.

$$\alpha = \frac{-\mu^3 - \mu\sigma^2 + \mu^2 n}{\mu^2 - \mu n + \sigma^2 n} \quad (4)$$

$$\beta = \frac{\mu^3 + \mu\sigma^2 - 2\mu^2 n - \sigma^2 n + \mu n^2}{\mu^2 - \mu n + \sigma^2 n} \quad (5)$$

Where the beta-binomial distribution is used for the estimation of the distribution of inferior individuals, the probability $P(X = N)$ in the beta-binomial distribution represents the estimated ratio of the local optima relative to the solutions in the search space. Figure 5 shows the ratio of the local optima relative to the variance σ^2 in the inferior individuals in the Nk landscape problem with $N = 20$ and $k = 0, 1, \cdots, 19$. The line in this figure shows the probability $P(X = N)$ in the beta-binomial distribution, where the average $\mu = \frac{N}{2}$. Based on this figure, we can estimate the proportion of the local optima in the problem that have a similar structure to the Nk landscape problem.

3.3.2 Random functional size

Next, we estimate the random functional size t. The probability that a set of genes S_i is a partial local optimum is $1/(t+1)$. Then, the expected value of the number of local optima is $(2^t/(t+1))^{\frac{N}{t}}$. The random functional size t is obtained from the solutions to the following equations if we have found the number of local optima N_{local}.

$$N_{\mathrm{local}} = (\frac{2^t}{t+1})^{\frac{N}{t}} \quad (6)$$

We estimate N_{local} at $2^t P(X = N)$, where $P(X = x)$ is the probability function of the beta-binomial distribution obtained in the previous section. The right-hand side member in Equation 6 is monotone increasing where $t > 0$, and thus we use Newton's method to obtain the solution to this equation.

t will be a smaller value than the deceptive trap function size when we estimate the random functional size t for the deceptive trap problem. The result is affected mainly by a few partial local optima in the deceptive trap function. In many problems similar to this example, the partial function with random variables has more local optima than the regular partial function, so the random functional size is smaller than the average size of many regular partial functions. However, this feature is not considered in this study because our main aim is to estimate the number of local optima or partial local optima.

After the estimation of t, we can set upper limits to the number of fitness evaluations in local search techniques and crossover.

3.3.3 Maximum number of evaluations in local search techniques

FIHC determines the local optima in $N + 1$ evaluations of problems with linear functions, but we cannot find the solutions to local optima until the number of fitness evaluation reaches almost $2N$. However, if $t = 1$ is given in the Nt landscape problem, FIHC can reduce the number of wasteful fitness evaluations. In particular, the distribution of fitness evaluations among operators should be efficient to obtain good performance for Genetic Local Search (GLS)[8]. Therefore, we use the following criteria to determine the number of fitness evaluations in local search techniques for an individual E_{LS} based on the value of t:

$$E_{\mathrm{LS}} = \frac{N}{t}(2^t - 1) \quad (7)$$

where E_{LS} represents the minimum number of fitness evaluations where all of partial function values are observed. The same partial function is observed several times in the Nt landscape problem if there are over E_{LS} evaluations.

3.3.4 Number of partial local optima for crossover

$2^t/(t+1)$ represents the expected number of partial local optima for a partial function in the Nt landscape problem. Local search techniques can obtain a partial local optimum in $2^t/(t+1)$ types. Therefore, the crossover performed after local search is expected to recombine these partial local optima.

The random functional size t is much smaller than the deceptive trap function size in the deceptive trap problem, as described in Section 3.3.2. A deceptive trap function has only two partial local optima, and thus crossover only needs

Algorithm 4 Local search technique in P3-DII

```
Create random solution s
number n_count ← 0
for all s' ∈ neighborhood of s do
    calculate fitness of s'
    if fitness of s' > fitness of s then
        n_count ← n_count + 1
add n_count to data set G_data
estimate random functional size t from G_data
calculate E_LS
number n_eval ← 0
while n_eval < E_LS and not finding local optima do
    apply FIHC to s with an evaluation
    n_eval ← n_eval + 1
```

Figure 6: Algorithm describing the local search technique in P3-DII. G_{data} represents the data set of the number of inferior individuals.

Algorithm 5 CLUSTER USAGE in P3-DII

```
Order useful based on cluster size, with the nearest t first.
for all C_i ∈ useful do
    for all d ∈ shuffled(P_i) do
        Copy d's gene values for C_i into the solution
        estimate random functional size t from G_data
        calculate E_C
        n_eval ← 0
        if solution changes then
            n_eval ← n_eval + 1
            if solution's fitness decreases then
                Revert changes
            else
                break
            if n_eval ≥ E_C then
                break
```

Figure 7: Algorithm describing how clusters are used to perform crossover in P3-DII.

to recombine two types of partial local optima. Therefore, t depends on the types of partial local optima that should be recombined during crossover.

4. P3-DII

The P3-DII algorithm employs different algorithms compared with P3, as follows:

- Control the number of fitness evaluations employed in the local search technique.
- Control the number of fitness evaluations and the order of clusters during crossover.

4.1 Local Search in P3-DII

The number of inferior individuals I_s is observed based on N evaluations before applying FIHC. DII-1 analysis estimates the distribution of the number of inferior individuals based on the data during this procedure. For many problem, the search performance will be better if we apply the best improvement to individuals in this procedure, especially for deceptive trap problem, but we did not applied any improvements in this procedure before applying FIHC to find the potential of DII analysis here.

In P3, FIHC continues the fitness evaluations until the local optima are obtained, whereas P3-DII continues to apply FIHC until the local optima are obtained, or until E_{LC} fitness evaluations, obtained in Equation 7, are performed in FIHC. Figure 6 shows the local search technique employed in P3-DII.

At least two data points are necessary for DII-1 analysis to estimate α and β in Equations (4) and (5) . Therefore, we add two data points $I_s = 0.5N \pm \sqrt{0.25N}$ to the sampling data for DII-1 analysis in advance.

4.2 Crossover in P3-DII

In P3-DII, the crossover process differs at two points compared with P3: the order of the clusters and the number of fitness evaluations. During crossover, the clusters are tested in order with the nearest random functional size t first. The smallest first order employed by P3 helps preserve diversity, but the diversity in the population is on a rising trend with an increase in t. The order that employs the nearest random functional size t first helps primarily to build several blocks in a random function, which are usually the most difficult structures to optimize with local search techniques.

The maximum number of fitness evaluations for crossover E_{C} is obtained as follows:

$$\begin{aligned} t' &= \min(t, t_{\text{cluster}}) \\ E_{\text{C}} &= \max([\frac{2^{t'}}{t'+1} - 1 + \delta_{\text{U}}], 1) \end{aligned} \quad (8)$$

where t_{cluster} denotes the cluster size in cluster usage and δ_{U} is a random variable given by the uniform distribution $\text{U}(0, 1)$. P3-DII continues to perform crossover in a cluster until it reaches E_{C}, no candidate can be recombined in the cluster or the solutions are improved. $2^{t'}/(t'+1)$ represents the estimated number of partial local optima in a partial function, described in Section 3.3.4, where this procedure helps to avoid building blocks being generated rarely when the population size is larger.

4.3 Advantages of P3 for DII analysis

DII-1 analysis can be applied to many applications that employ local search techniques, but we do not know applications more suited to DII-1 analysis than P3. In many GAs that employ techniques based on learning fitness landscape, the accuracy when estimating the fitness landscapes depends on the irreversible search state. The accuracy in one step greatly affects the search performance and it can sometimes cause premature convergence. However, the use of more data to obtain stable high accuracy can reduce the usage of computational resource in other operators. This trade-off [9] has complex effects on the quality of techniques that learn fitness landscape. However, P3 is a suitable optimization model for avoiding premature convergence and it requires no parameters. Thus, the experimental results are affected directly by the quality of the techniques employed.

Moreover, P3 creates a random solution at every iteration.

DII-1 analysis requires randomized solutions to estimate the distribution of inferior individuals, which means that P3 can help DII-1 analysis to obtain high accuracy results depending on the number to P3 iterations.

5. TEST PROBLEMS

In this section, we explain the test benchmark problems used to demonstrate the effectiveness of our proposed method. Let F be a fitness function and f_i and g are partial functions. We mainly consider the problem where $F = \sum_i f_i$, $F = \sum_{i,j}(f_i \cdot f_j)$ and $F = g \cdot \sum_i f_i$.

5.1 Deceptive trap and hierarchical if and only if problem (HIFF)

In the deceptive trap problem, the fitness function combines the sub-functions into separate traps with lengths of k bits where each trap is given by Equation 3:

$$trap(n_{\text{trap}}) = \begin{cases} k - 1 - n_{\text{trap}} & (n_{\text{trap}} < k) \\ k & (n_{\text{trap}} = k) \end{cases} \quad (9)$$

where n_{trap} represents the number of genes with a value of 1 in the trap. Each partial function has one local optimum (all bits are 0) and one global optimum (all bits are 1). In this study, we set a trap size of $k = 7$.

The HIFF [10] is a hierarchical building-block test problem. In this problem, the genome is broken up hierarchically into a complete binary tree, with each gene represents a leaf and each internal node represents the union between all the genes in that node's subtree. A node in the tree contributes to the fitness only if all of the genes in its subset have the same value.

It is easy for P3 to obtain optimal solutions to these two problems because FIHC can optimize the sub-functions and crossover can optimize the combination of sub-functions based on few evaluations.

5.2 Discretized Rosenbrock and discretized Rastrigin

The discretized Rastrigin problem and the discretized Rosenbrock problem convert the standard Rastrigin and Rosenbrock problems into gray-coded problems.

The standard Rastrigin evaluation function is as follows.

$$10n + \sum_{i=1}^{n}(x_i^2 - 10\cos 2\pi x_i) \qquad \forall x \in [-5.12, 5.12] \quad (10)$$

The Rastrigin problem has a highly multimodal landscape.

The standard Rosenbrock evaluation function is as follows.

$$\sum_{i=1}^{n-1}(100(x_{i+1} - x_i^2)^2 + (1 - x_i)^2) \qquad \forall x \in [-2.048, 2.048] \quad (11)$$

The Rosenbrock has a unimodal landscape and the global optimum lies in a narrow parabolic valley.

In these two problems, depending on the gray code size, the number of fitness evaluations increases until the local optimum is reached by local search [11]. We set the gray code size $g = 10$ or 20.

Table 1: Comparison of the average evaluations in successful runs.

	Average (successful runs)	Standard Deviation
Deceptive Trap, $N = 805$, Speedup $= 0.9521$		
P3	656518 (100/100)	145708.87
P3-DII	689558 (100/100)	182440.42
HIFF, $N = 2048$, Speedup $= 1.0011$		
P3	590334 (100/100)	58346.46
P3-DII	589705 (100/100)	61403.82
Nk ($k = 5$), $N = 600$, Speedup $= 1.1458$		
P3	7384160 (100/100)	1833219.16
P3-DII	6444105 (100/100)	2154310.22
Nk ($k = 7$), $N = 63$, Speedup $= 1.6324$		
P3	3960321 (98/100)	4418552.20
P3-DII	2426127 (100/100)	2827449.64
Nkp ($k = 5, p = 0.85$), $N = 400$, Speedup $= 1.1561$		
P3	2386852 (100/100)	1033718.89
P3-DII	2064617 (100/100)	1080500.07
Knapsack, $N = 200$, Speedup $= 1.4523$		
P3	2356600 (100/100)	1563299.89
P3-DII	1622658 (100/100)	986737.24
Rastrigin ($g = 10$), $N = 800$, Speedup $= 1.2041$		
P3	134984 (100/100)	31370.79
P3-DII	112106 (100/100)	28254.47
Rastrigin ($g = 20$), $N = 800$, Speedup $= 1.2853$		
P3	245104 (100/100)	49367.82
P3-DII	190693 (100/100)	35525.86
Rosenbrock ($g = 10$), $N = 400$, Speedup $= 1.6438$		
P3	689007 (100/100)	499553.85
P3-DII	419160 (100/100)	312958.53
Rosenbrock ($g = 20$), $N = 200$, Speedup $=$ NaN		
P3	NaN (0/100)	NaN
P3-DII	493096 (100/100)	557567.85

5.3 Nk landscape and Nkp landscape

The function of the Nk landscape problem comprises evaluation tables. Each locus has an evaluation table and the partial function value depends on the linked k of other loci. The Nk landscape problem has a multimodal landscape and we can control the amount of epistasis in the landscape by changing k. A dynamic programming algorithm is polynomial in N and exponential in k to optimize Nk landscape problem[12]. We chose to set $k = 5$ or 7.

The Nkp landscape problem[13] has similar functions to the Nk landscape problem, except the partial function value $= 0$ with a given probability p. The neutrality in the fitness landscape depends on p[14]. We chose to set $k = 5$ and $p = 0.85$.

5.4 Knapsack problem

This problem requires the maximization of knapsack items where the item weight < weight limit of the knapsack. In this study, the fitness of solutions that exceed the weight limit is set as zero as a penalty. The knapsack problem has a complex landscape around optimal solutions because many solutions that exceed the weight limit are present around the optimal solutions.

6. EXPERIMENTS

We analyzed the performance of P3 and P3-DII for 100 trials, where each run was limited to 30 million evaluations for seven kinds of benchmark problems. The experimental results comprise the average number of successful evalua-

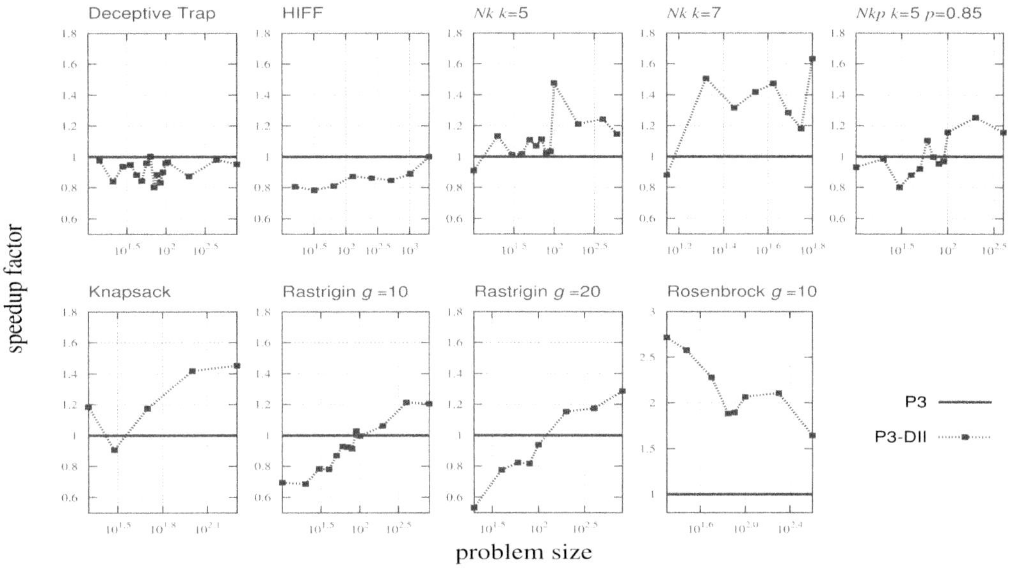

Figure 8: Speedup factor for P3-DII compared with P3. Abscissa given on a log scale.

Table 2: p-value obtained using the Mann-Whitney U-test.

problem name	p-value
Deceptive Trap, $N = 805$	0.274747473312
HIFF, $N = 2048$	0.968815255782
$Nk(k = 5)$, $N = 600$	$4.78093039091 \times 10^{-11}$
$Nk(k = 7)$, $N = 63$	$5.15069608997 \times 10^{-4}$
$Nkp(k = 5, p = 0.85)$, $N = 400$	$5.31409206993 \times 10^{-5}$
Knapsack, $N = 200$	$1.98214506757 \times 10^{-4}$
Rastrigin($g = 10$), $N = 800$	$9.22435265463 \times 10^{-9}$
Rastrigin($g = 20$), $N = 800$	$2.5546650876 \times 10^{-9}$
Rosenbrock($g = 10$), $N = 400$	$6.74326053768 \times 10^{-5}$

tions required for each algorithm and the speedup factor represented by $E_{\text{P3-DII}}/E_{\text{P3}}$ where $E_{\text{P3-DII}}$ and E_{P3} are the average number evaluations in P3-DII and P3, respectively. We performed a pairwise Mann-Whitney U-test for each problem with the maximum problem size except for the discretized Rosenbrock problem where $g = 20$.

6.1 Results and Discussion

Figure 8 shows the speedup factor for P3-DII compared with P3. Table 1 shows the average evaluation results and standard deviations in successful runs. Table 2 shows the p-values obtained using the Mann-Whitney U-test.

P3 performed almost no wasteful evaluations in the deceptive trap problem and HIFF, as specified in [3], and the performance of P3-DII was similar to that of P3. For these problems, P3-DII performed more wasteful evaluations than P3 due to the error when estimating DII-1 with a specific probability. However, in our experiments, the Mann-Whitney U-test did not detect any significant difference between the performance of P3 and P3-DII (p-value = 0.05) in the deceptive trap problem ($N = 805$) and HIFF ($N = 2048$).

The speedup factor increased with the problem size in the discretized Rastrigin problem. By contrast, the speedup factor appeared to decrease with the problem size in the Rosenbrock problem with $g = 10$, according to the results shown in Figure 8. These results represent that P3 has several possibilities to outperform P3-DII in the discretized Rosenbrock problem with a larger problem size. However, P3 failed to obtain optimal solutions in all trials for the discretized Rosenbrock function with $g = 20$, even when the problem size was $N = 40$ which was the minimum size in our experiments. By contrast, P3-DII successfully obtained optimal solutions in all of our experiments. Many evaluations tended to be required by FIHC with the discretized Rosenbrock problem. In particular, the number of evaluations until FIHC determined the local optima was about 20000 where $N = 100$, which was $20 \sim 100$ times that for the other problems. These results suggest that controlling the number of evaluations in local search techniques is important for the discretized Rosenbrock problem.

In the Nk landscape, Nkp landscape, knapsack, and Rastrigin problems, the speedup factor increased with the problem size. P3 outperformed P3-DII in most of the problems with a small size, which may have been caused by differences in the number of evaluations between crossover operations. In P3, the fitness evaluations were performed in a cluster during crossover. By contrast, P3-DII performed several fitness evaluations during crossover according to Equation 8. Equation 8 is based on the estimated partial local optima, but it does not yield the optimal distribution of the fitness evaluations. In P3-DII, crossover recombines x times at most, where x is the estimated number of the partial local optima based on DII analysis, although some wasteful evaluations were performed when the problem size was small. However, P3 could obtain high quality solutions in an efficient manner when the problem size was small, and thus P3 might pass over the building blocks that are generated rarely, depending on the increase in the problem size and the population size in the pyramid. While the probability that a crossover operation in P3 will recombine a unique alternative is $O(E_i)$ where E_i is the number of P3 iterations, the probability of that in P3-DII is $O(N_{\mathrm{p}})$, where N_{p} is the number of partial local optima, if DII-1 analysis completely estimates partial local optima. This agreed with the results of our experiments, except the discretized Rosenbrock problem.

7. CONCLUSION

In this study, we proposed DII-1 analysis to estimate partial local optima based on the distribution of inferior individuals. DII-1 analysis gives the novel view point of the problem difficulty and search efficiency. We applied DII-1 analysis to control the number of fitness evaluations in crossover operations and local search techniques. We also proposed P3-DII, which combines DII-1 analysis with P3 in order to control the fitness evaluations required for operators in P3.

To summarize this research:

- P3 has a helpful model for techniques to learn fitness landscape, including DII analysis, because P3 avoids premature convergence and it requires no parameters.
- We can observe a change of the value of k in the Nk landscape problem from the distribution of inferior individuals.
- DII-1 estimates the maximum number of fitness evaluations required in crossover operations and local search techniques based on the Nt landscape model.
- P3-DII obtained optimal solutions that P3 failed to find. The performance of P3-DII was almost the same as that of P3 in the deceptive trap problem and HIFF with a large size, where P3 performed almost no wasteful evaluations.
- P3-DII outperformed P3 in large size problems without the deceptive trap problem and HIFF.

In our future research, we plan to extend the control of fitness evaluations according to the population size. If the partial local optima are given, the necessary number of individuals required in a population can be estimated. The estimated number allows us to control the fitness evaluations according to the search state. Obtaining estimates for other models and building the theory for DII within an arbitrary Hamming distance are also fundamental issues.

This work was supported by JSPS KAKENHI Grant, Grant-in-Aid for Scientific Research(C), 26330282 and by Program for Leading Graduate Schools of Ministry of Education, Culture, Sports, Science and Technology in Japan.

8. REFERENCES

[1] Y. Jin. A comprehensive survey of fitness approximation in evolutionary computation. Soft Comput., Vol. 9, No. 1, pp. 3–12, January 2005.

[2] K. Rasheed and H. Hirsh. Informed operators: Speeding up genetic-algorithm-based design optimization using reduced models. In In Proceedings of the Genetic and Evolutionary Computation Conference, pp. 628–635. Morgan Kaufmann, 2000.

[3] B. W. Goldman and W. F. Punch. Parameter-less population pyramid. In Proceedings of the 2014 Conference on Genetic and Evolutionary Computation, GECCO '14, pp. 785–792, New York, NY, USA, 2014. ACM.

[4] D.H. Wolpert and W.G. Macready. No free lunch theorems for optimization. Evolutionary Computation, IEEE Transactions on, Vol. 1, No. 1, pp. 67–82, Apr 1997.

[5] H. Hoos and T. Stützle. Stochastic Local Search: Foundations & Applications. Morgan Kaufmann Publishers Inc., San Francisco, CA, USA, 2004.

[6] B. W. Goldman and D. R. Tauritz. Linkage tree genetic algorithms: Variants and analysis. In Proceedings of the 14th Annual Conference on Genetic and Evolutionary Computation, GECCO '12, pp. 625–632, New York, NY, USA, 2012. ACM.

[7] M. Shakil. Using Beta-binomial Distribution in Analyzing Some Multiple-Choice Questions of the Final Exam of a Math Course, and its Application in Predicting the Performance of Future Students. 2009.

[8] P. A. N. Bosman and D. Thierens. The roles of local search, model building and optimal mixing in evolutionary algorithms from a bbo perspective. In Proceedings of the 13th Annual Conference Companion on Genetic and Evolutionary Computation, GECCO '11, pp. 663–670, New York, NY, USA, 2011. ACM.

[9] J. Chen, B. Xin, Z. Peng, L. Dou, and J. Zhang. Optimal contraction theorem for exploration-exploitation tradeoff in search and optimization. IEEE Transactions on Systems, Man, and Cybernetics, Part A, Vol. 39, No. 3, pp. 680–691, 2009.

[10] D. Thierens and P. A. N. Bosman. Hierarchical problem solving with the linkage tree genetic algorithm. In Proceedings of the 15th annual conference on Genetic and evolutionary computation, 2013.

[11] J. E. Rowe and D. Hidovic. An evolution strategy using a continuous version of the gray-code neighbourhood distribution. In Proceedings of the annual conference on Genetic and Evolutionary Computation - GECCO 2004, 2004.

[12] A. H. Wright, R. K. Thompson, and J. Zhang. The computational complexity of n-k fitness functions. IEEE Trans. on Evolutionary Computation, Vol. 4, pp. 373–379, 1999.

[13] L. Barnett. Tangled webs – evolutionary dynamics on fitness landscapes with neutrality, 1997.

[14] Y. Katada, K. Ohkura, and K. Ueda. Measuring neutrality of fitness landscapes based on the nei ' s standard genetic distance. In Proceedings of 2003 Asia Pacific Symposium on Intelligent and Evolutionary Systems: Technology and Applications, pp. 107–114, 2003.

Evolutionary Bilevel Optimization for Complex Control Tasks

Jason Liang and Risto Miikkulainen
Dept. of Computer Science, University of Texas at Austin
Austin, Texas, United States
jasonzliang@utexas.edu, risto@cs.utexas.edu

ABSTRACT

Most optimization algorithms must undergo time consuming parameter adaptation in order to optimally solve complex, real-world control tasks. Parameter adaptation is inherently a bilevel optimization problem where the lower level objective function is the performance of the control parameters discovered by an optimization algorithm and the upper level objective function is the performance of the algorithm given its parametrization. In this paper, a novel method called *MetaEvolutionary Algorithm* (MEA) is presented and shown to be capable of efficiently discovering optimal parameters for neuroevolution to solve control problems. In two challenging examples, double pole balancing and helicopter hovering, MEA discovers optimized parameters that result in better performance than hand tuning and other automatic methods. Bilevel optimization in general and MEA in particular, is thus a promising approach for solving difficult control tasks.

Categories and Subject Descriptors

I.2.11 [**Artificial Intelligence**]: Control methods

Keywords

Genetic Algorithms;Metaheuristics;Neural Networks;Fitness Approximation;Parameter Tuning

1. INTRODUCTION

For many traditional control tasks that involve few state variables, classical approaches such as PID controllers are sufficient [1]. However, many modern control problems involve a large number of state of variables that interact in a nonlinear manner, making it difficult to apply classical methods to them [2]. A common way to solve such problems is to pose the control task as a reinforcement learning (RL) problems where the goal is find an optimal policy function that maps states to actions [3]. Given the state of the system as input, an optimal policy outputs a control action that maximizes the performance of the system with respect to some reward criteria.

Unfortunately, traditional RL methods are based on tabular representations and dynamic programming, making it difficult to extend these methods to large, partially observable continuous state spaces in many modern control problems. Recently, much progress has been made in using policy search methods to solve such control tasks [4, 5, 6]. Instead of trying to compute a Q-value for each possible combination of state and action, the policy function is parametrized as a fixed set of parameters p and optimization algorithms are used to find $\text{argmax}_p E(\pi(p))$, where $E(\pi)$ is the expected reward obtained by following the policy π. For many control problems, the fitness landscape described by $E(\pi)$ is non-convex and sometimes even non-differentiable, which means gradient descent is intractable and heuristic based approaches such as evolutionary algorithms (EA) must be used instead [7, 8]. This paper builds on a particular approach called neuroevolution (NE) [9, 10, 11] that combines EAs and neural networks to search for an optimal policy. In NE, the policy is encoded by a neural network where the input is the state vector and the output is an action vector. A population of potential weight vectors for the neural network is then formed and operators such as selection, mutation, and crossover are used to improve the overall fitness of the population over time. EAs have been demonstrated to perform well in many complex control problems, such as finless rocket stabilization, race-car driving, bipedal walking, and helicopter hovering [12, 13, 14, 15].

One major issue with EAs is that their performance is highly sensitive to the parameters used. Even more so than gradient based optimization algorithms, incorrectly set parameters not only make EAs run slowly but make it difficult for them to converge onto the optimal solution. A commonly used and yet vastly inefficient parameter adaptation method is grid search [16], where the parameter space is discretized and all possible combinations of parameters are exhaustively evaluated. Unfortunately, the computational complexity of grid search increases exponentially with the dimensionality of the parameters and is intractable once the number of parameters exceed three or four.

In this paper, the issues with grid search are avoided by framing parameter adaptation as a bilevel optimization problem [17]. Formally, a bilevel problem has two levels: an upper level optimization task with parameters p_u and objective function F_u, and a lower level optimization task with parameters p_l and objective function F_l. The goal is find a p_u that allows p_l to be optimally solved:

GECCO '15, July 11–15, 2015, Madrid, Spain
© 2015 ACM. ISBN 978-1-4503-3472-3/15/07...$15.00
DOI: http://dx.doi.org/10.1145/2739480.2754732

$$
\begin{aligned}
&\underset{p_u}{\text{maximize}}\ F_u(p_u) = E[F_l(p_l)|p_u] \\
&\text{subject to } p_l = O_l(p_u),
\end{aligned}
\tag{1}
$$

where $E[F_l(p_l)|p_u]$ is the expected performance of the lower level solution p_l obtained by lower level optimization algorithm O_l with p_u as its parameters. The maximization is done by a separate upper level optimization algorithm O_u. In this paper, O_u is the proposed MEA, p_u are the parameters for NE, O_l is NE, p_l are the weights of the neural network, and F_l measures performance in two simulated and separate control tasks: double pole balancing and helicopter hovering. As will be shown, the right heuristics for O_u allow optimal parameters for O_l to be found much faster than with grid search. Specifically, MEA makes use of fitness approximation to reduce the number of F_u evaluations by O_u. Thus the key contributions of this paper are:

1. Casting parameter adaptation for neuroevolution as a blievel optimization problem.
2. Presenting an efficient upper level algorithm O_u that achieves best results to date on two real-world control tasks.
3. Showing that a more complex parametrization of O_l can increase its potential performance.

The rest of the paper is organized as follows: Related work on parameter adaptation is first summarized and then the MEA algorithm is described in detail. MEA is evaluated in the double pole balancing and helicopter hovering tasks, comparing its performance to other hand-designed and automatic parameter adaptation methods.

2. RELATED WORK

Automatic parameter adaptation is a widely studied problem with extensive previous research done in the area. A survey and systematic categorization of current existing techniques is provided by Eiben and Smit [18]. Many conventional methods for parameter adaptation are fundamentally based on the grid search approach (evaluating all possible parameter configurations) with additional heuristics to reduce computational complexity by a constant factor [16, 19]. These include racing algorithms that try to aggressively prune out bad parameters [20]. However, such approaches quickly become intractable as the number of parameters to be tuned increases beyond three or four.

Modern algorithms for parameter adaptation focus on intelligently searching through the space of parameter configurations. One such example is ParamILS [21], which combines hill climbing with restart heuristics. Recently, metaevolutionary algorithms have been developed for solving the parameter adaptation problem [22, 23, 24, 25]. In metaevolution, the upper level algorithm O_u is an EA and the objective function of O_u is the performance of O_l, another EA that solves the target problem. Although more efficient than brute-force search, metaevolution is inherently a nested procedure and still computationally complex. To address this issue, GGA [25] divided the upper level population into two genders and only evaluated a subset of the population every generation. Furthermore, because EA's are stochastic, it is only possible to estimate the performance

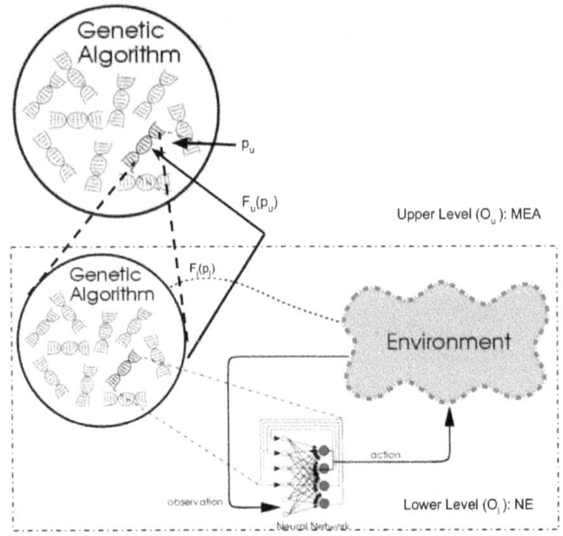

Figure 1: Overview of MEA (O_u) and how it is used for parameter adaptation of NE (O_l). The population in O_u consists of individuals that represent various possible p_u for O_l. To determine $F_u(p_u)$, i.e. the fitness of an upper level individual, $O_l(p_u)$ is run repeatedly q times. During each run, O_l terminates once a fixed number of evaluations $f_{\max}$ is reached. $F_u(p_u)$ is then set as the average fitness of the best solutions returned by all the runs of O_l. The individuals in O_l consists of weights for a neural network and the network is used as the policy for the control task. The network takes as input the state vector of the system being controlled and outputs an action vector that updates the state of the system for the next time step. This process repeats until a termination criterion of the control simulation is met and a fitness value $F_l(p_l)$, measuring performance in the control task, is then assigned to the lower level individual p_l.

of O_l by averaging results from multiple runs. Diosan and Oltean attempted to alleviate this problem by not optimizing p_u but instead optimizing the order in which genetic operators such as mutation and crossover are applied to the population [23].

Metaevolutionary algorithms are closely related to but distinct from self-adaptive EAs [26]. The main difference is that metaevolution attempt to find optimal parameters in an offline environment whereas self-adaptive EAs do so online. Self-adaptive EAs thus can change their parameters dynamically based on the state of the population [26]. On the other hand, they run slower than EAs with static, adapted parameters.

Most current research into metaevolutionary algorithms focuses on fitness function approximation to reduce computational complexity [24, 17]. $F_u(p_u)$ is not always determined by running $O_l(p_u)$, but is sometimes estimated using a regression model. Numerous models have been proposed, including both parametric and nonparametric ones [27, 28, 29, 30]. BAPT, the most recent such algorithm [17], uses a localized quadratic approximation model and achieves good results on classic test problems. However, BAPT has not been tested on real-world problems and in problems with more than three parameters in p_u. Such more challenging problems are the focus of this paper.

Algorithm 1: MEA

1. Randomly initialize a population of K individuals. Set $F_u(p_u)$ of individuals to actual fitness from evaluating $O_l(p_u)$. Add them to archive Z, and fit regression model R to Z.
2. Create X new individuals via tournament selection, uniform crossover, and uniform Gaussian mutation.
3. Sort population by fitness, and replace X worst individuals in population with the new individuals.
4. Set $F_u(p_u)$ of new individuals to approximate fitness predicted by R.
5. Sort population by fitness again. Set $F_u(p_u)$ of top Y individuals to actual fitness from evaluating $O_l(p_u)$. Add them to Z, and fit R to Z.
6. Repeat from Step 2 until the total number of lower level evaluations by O_l exceeds $t_{\max}$. Return best individual in population.

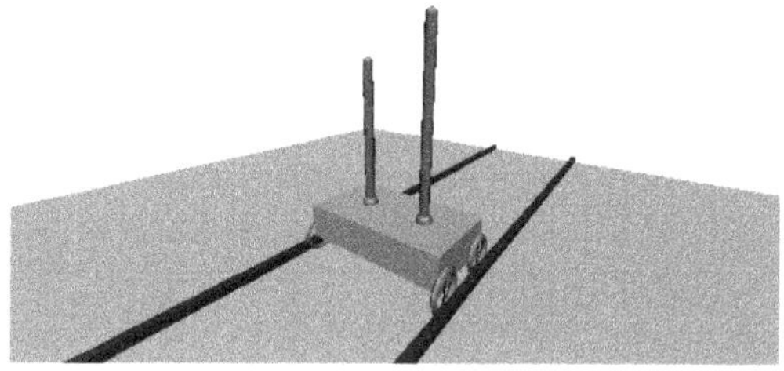

Figure 2: The double pole balancing task. The system consists of two vertical poles with different lengths that are attached to a movable cart with one degree of freedom. The goal is to apply a force to the cart at regular time intervals to ensure that both poles remain upright and that the cart remains within fixed distance of its starting position. The six state variables of the system are the angular position and velocities of the poles, as well as the position and velocity of the cart. The fitness of the controller (F_l) is t_s, the number of time steps it can prevent either pole from falling over or the cart from straying too far away. A pole balancing episode/evaluation is terminated when $t_s = 100,000$ or when failure occurs.

3. ALGORITHM DESCRIPTION

MetaEvolutionary Algorithm (MEA) is fundamentally a real valued genetic algorithm [31], a type of EA that uses genetic operators such as selection, mutation, crossover, and replacement to improve the overall fitness of a population of solutions, represented by vectors of real numbers, iteratively over generations. NE is another real-valued GA that evolves weights for a neural network with a fixed topology. MEA serves as the upper level algorithm O_u while NE serves as the lower level algorithm O_l. The roles of both MEA and NE within the bilevel optimization framework are described in detail by Fig. 1. A step by step summary of MEA is given by Algorithm 1.

In BAPT [17], $F_u(p_u)$ is sometimes approximated using a regression model in order to reduce the number of times $O_l(p_u)$ is called. However, BAPT's model assumes that the fitness landscape can be described by a quadratic function and requires a large number of data points to avoid overfitting. In contrary, MEA uses a regression model based on randomized decision trees, also known as Random Forests [32]. Random Forests are used for two main reasons: (1) They are nonparametric and make no prior assumptions regarding the shape of $F_u(p_u)$. (2) Random Forests are robust to overfitting [33]. Furthermore, in preliminary experiments, Random Forests gave more accurate approximations, especially when the number of data points is small.

There are two undesirable side effects of fitness approximation: (1) The approximate fitness estimated by the regression model is noisy and (2) as the dimensionality of p_u increases, the archive Z and population K must increase to avoid overfitting. For example in BAPT, which uses R to fit p_u directly, K must increase quadratically with the dimension of p_u [17], which makes it difficult to scale up the approach.

To deal with (1), Step 5 is included in MEA to ensure that the actual fitness of promising but approximately evaluated individuals is always known. In addition, MEA deals with issue (2) by replacing p_u with performance metrics that remain fixed in dimensionality. $O_l(p_u)$ is run for roughly $f_{\max}/\alpha$ ($\alpha > 1$) evaluations and the following six metrics m_u regarding the population of O_l are collected: (1) best fitness, (2) average fitness, (3) fitness standard deviation, (4) population diversity, (5) increase in average fitness over last 10 generations and (6) exact number of function evaluations, which can vary depending on K. Finally, R is fitted using the m_u and actual fitness of individuals in Z, averaged over q runs. The metrics m_u can be used to predict the performance of $O_l(p_u)$ since there is usually strong correlation between an algorithm's initial and final performance. Because the size of m_u is independent of p_u, MEA has no problems dealing with high-dimensional p_u.

As an additional way of smoothing noise, if an upper level individual remains in the population for multiple generations, its fitness is averaged over multiple evaluations. Constraints for p_u are enforced by clipping them to the desired minimum and maximum values after mutation is performed. The archive Z has a maximum size to limit the computational costs of fitting R and when it is full, the newly added individuals replace the oldest ones. MEA terminates automatically when the total number of lower level fitness evaluations by O_l exceeds $t_{\max}$ and returns the p_u with highest fitness. If there is a tie, the individual that remained longest in the population is returned.

4. EXPERIMENTAL RESULTS

In order to judge the performance of MEA better, it is compared against two other EAs designed for parameter adaptation on two real-world control tasks. The first one is SMEA, a simplified version of MEA that does not perform any fitness function approximation. Instead of performing Steps 4 and 5, the actual fitness of every individual in the population is evaluated before proceeding to the next generation. The second EA is a version of BAPT designed for comparison with MEA and thus named BAPTM; it has the same localized quadratic approximation scheme as BAPT

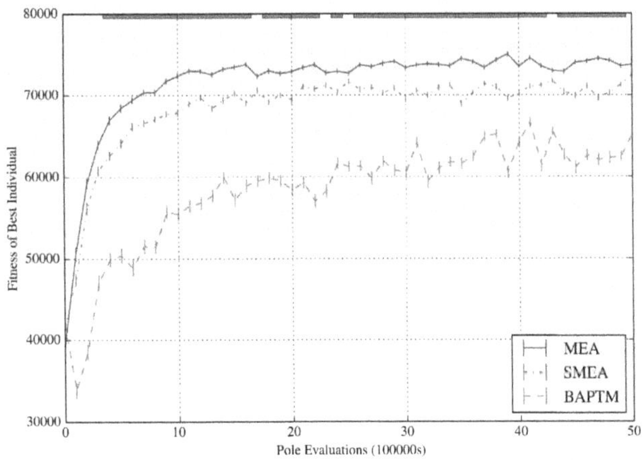

Figure 3: The fitness of the best upper level individual p_u over the number of lower level evaluations F_l. Each plot is an average over 150 O_u runs, where the best individual in the population each generation is retested with another independent set of 30 evaluations. Vertical bars show standard error while black lines at top of plot indicate regions where differences between MEA and SMEA are statistically significant (p-value < 0.05). MEA overtakes SMEA in performance after 500,000 evaluations.

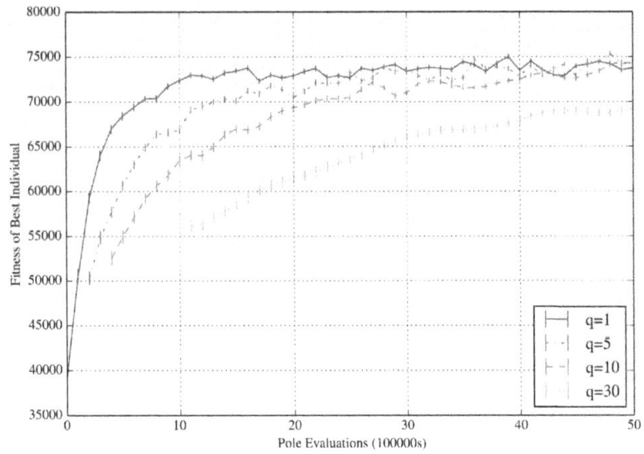

Figure 4: The fitness of the best p_u over the number of evaluations of F_l for different values of q with MEA. The data is gathered in the same manner as Fig. 3. Lower values of q result in better performance, suggesting that MEA is surprisingly robust against evaluation noise.

but uses MEA's uniform crossover in place of PCX crossover [34]. Uniform crossover is a commonly used operator that is shown to be effective in many domains [35, 36], including preliminary experiments in double pole balancing and helicopter hovering. For all experiments except where indicated, the maximum size of Z is set to $100K$, $K = 20$, $X = K/2$, $Y = K/2$ and $\alpha = 4$. Because of an elitist replacement scheme and constraints on p_u, a high mutation rate of 0.5 can be utilized, along with a crossover rate of 0.5. As mentioned in the introduction, NE is utilized as the lower level O_l since it is well suited for finding robust, efficient solutions to difficult control problems [12, 13, 14, 15].

4.1 Double Pole Balancing

Pole balancing, or inverted pendulum, has long been a standard benchmark for control algorithms [37, 38, 3, 7]. It is easy to describe and is a surrogate for other real-world control problems such as finless rocket stabilization. While the original version with a single pole is too easy for modern methods, the double-pole version can be made arbitrarily hard, and thus serves as a good first benchmark for bilevel optimization. A detailed description of the double pole balancing task is given by Fig. 2.

For O_l, a conventional NE algorithm common in the literature [39] is used and the label PNE refers to this NE with hand-designed parameters. The evolved genotype is a concatenation of real-valued weights of a feedforward neural network (with five hidden units) and PNE performs 1-point crossover and uniform mutation. In the first experiment (PNE_5), p_u adapts five of its parameters; in the second (PNE_{15}), 15. The details of these parameters are given in the Appendix.

For PNE_5, the following parameters are set for each O_u: $q = 1$, $f_{\max} = 2{,}000$, and $t_{\max} = 5{,}000{,}000$. $K = 26$ is used for BAPTM as the minimum population size required for optimizing the five parameters of p_u [17]. In Fig. 3, the performances of all three O_u with PNE_5 as O_l are compared. MEA achieves statistically significant higher fitness than SMEA after approximately 500,000 lower level evaluations; both are significantly better than BAPTM in both metrics. Fig. 4 shows how the performance of MEA is affected by different values of q, the number of times $O_l(p_u)$ is evaluated. Interestingly, lower values of q result in faster learning with no difference in peak fitness achieved.

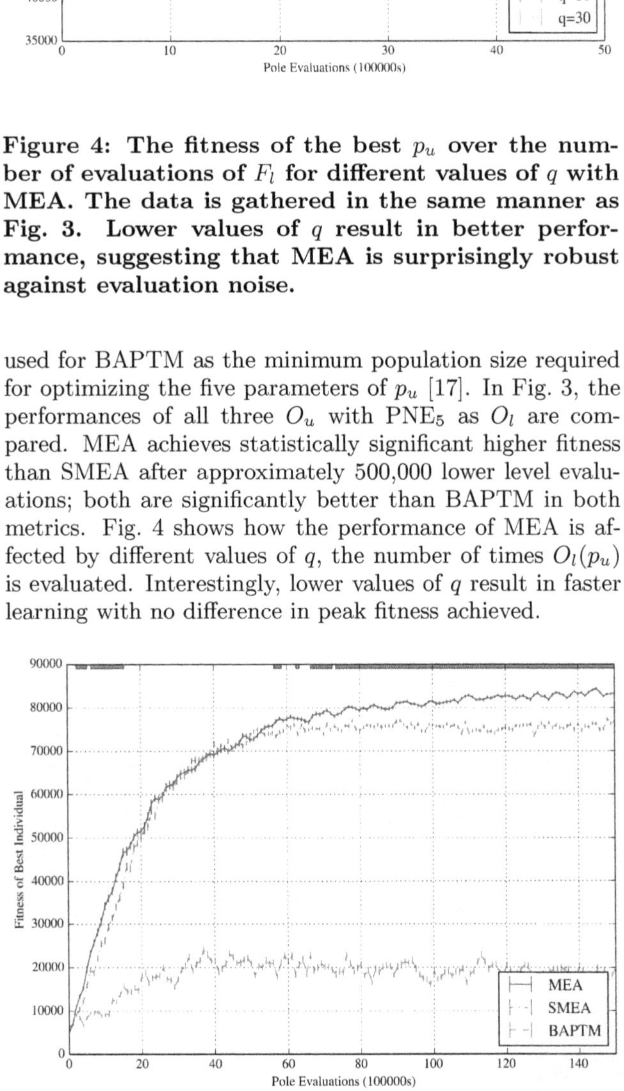

Figure 5: Similar plot as Fig. 3, but with PNE_{15} as O_l. Both MEA and SMEA perform better than BAPTM by a wide margin. MEA begins to overtake SMEA in performance after roughly six million lower level evaluations.

PNE_{15} is a generalization of PNE_5, with 10 of the hand selected parameters of PNE_5 replaced by adaptable parameters. These 10 additional parameters allow the EA to choose what selection and crossover operators to use. The follow-

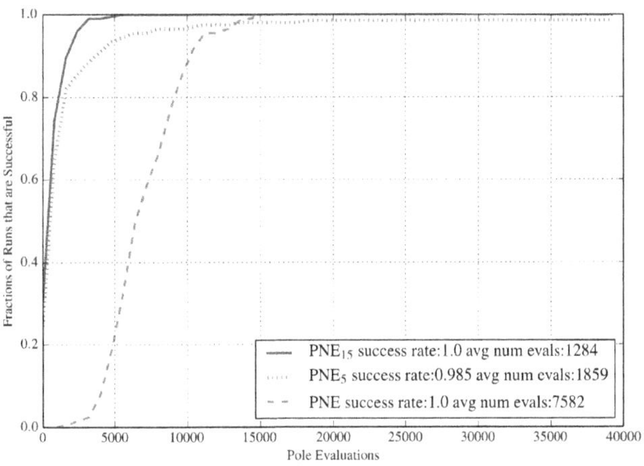

Figure 6: Cumulative histogram of success rate of PNE, PNE_5, and PNE_{15} over the number of evaluations of F_l, with success defined as balancing the poles for t_s time steps. Results are from 200 independent runs of each O_l. All runs solved the task in significantly less time than $f_{\max} = 40,000$ evaluations. PNE_{15} is 1.5 times faster than PNE_5, and five times faster than PNE.

ing parameters are set for each O_u : $K = 30$, $q = 1$, $f_{\max} = 2,000$, and $t_{\max} = 15,000,000$. For BAPTM, $K = 151$ as the minimum required size for 15 parameters. The performance of all three O_u are compared in Fig. 5. While MEA and SMEA learn equally fast initially, the difference between the two become statistically significant after six million lower level evaluations and MEA terminates with a higher peak fitness. BAPTM only achieves a fraction of the peak fitness of MEA and SMEA.

So far, the results of PNE_5 and PNE_{15} only show their performance when evaluated up to $f_{\max}$. It remains to be shown that they can consistently and successfully evolve networks that balance poles for $t_s = 100,000$ time steps. Thus, $f_{\max}$ is increased to 40,000 evaluations and O_l is run 200 times with the parameters p_u of the median performing individual returned by MEA from its 150 runs. As Fig. 6 shows, PNE_{15} performs better than PNE_5 and both PNE_{15} and PNE_5 perform much better than hand-designed PNE, verifying that the optimal p_u are indeed discovered in the full double pole balancing task.

4.2 Helicopter Hovering

The goal in the helicopter hovering task [15] is to keep a simulated helicopter in a fixed position in the air subject to a constant wind velocity. Compared to double pole balancing, helicopter hovering is a significantly more difficult task due to the larger state and action space, sensor noise, complex dynamics, and a fitness function that punishes any deviation from the optimal control policy (Fig. 7).

For O_l, a specialized NE algorithm that has additional mutation replacement and crossover averaging operators [15] is used. The original version with hand-designed parameters is referred to as HNE and the version of this algorithm that adapts eight parameters (specified in the Appendix), is referred to as HNE_8. The network evolved by HNE has a hand-designed topology and consists of 11 linear and sig-

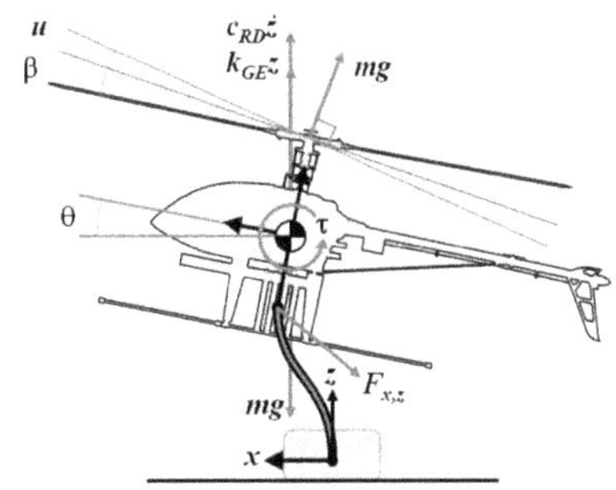

Figure 7: The helicopter hovering task. The goal is to steer a simulated helicopter to remain as close as possible to a fixed point in 3D space. There are 12 state variables that describe the helicopter's position, rotation, linear/angular velocities and four continuous action variables which determine the pitch of the aileron, elevator, rudder, and main rotor. The system takes into account a constant wind velocity (chosen from 10 preset velocities) and sensor noise. The simulation lasts for 60,000 time steps and $F_l(p_l) = 1/\log(X)$ where X is the sum of (1) the cumulative deviation error of the helicopter from its starting position and (2) a additional large penalty if the helicopter exceeds certain bounds on its position and crashes.

moid hidden units [15]. The following parameters are set for each O_u: $q = 1$, $f_{\max} = 5,000$, and $t_{\max} = 15,000,000$; for BAPTM, $K = 51$. As seen in Fig. 8, the performance improvement of MEA over SMEA becomes statistically significant after roughly four million evaluations and both are significantly better than BAPTM. Fig. 9 compares the performance of representative examples (median performing individual for each wind velocity) of HNE_8 and HNE when the task is solved fully with $f_{\max} = 25,000$. In comparison to HNE, HNE_8 learns faster and achieves higher peak fitness, demonstrating the value of bilevel optimization over hand-design.

5. DISCUSSION AND FUTURE WORK

The results from the experiments show that MEA performs better than SMEA and that both are much better than BAPTM. The main cause of BAPTM's poor performance are the inaccurate approximations given by its regression model. The relatively few number of individuals in Z during the first generations and noise in evaluating $O_l(p_u)$ cause the quadratic model to overfit initially. Furthermore, the fitness landscape of F_u is irregular and not well described by a quadratic approximation. For example, preliminary experiments show that doubling the population size of PNE_5 can result in $F_u(p_u)$ decreasing by an order of magnitude.

Surprisingly, running MEA with lower values of q results in better performance and faster convergence to the optimal fitness value. This result is counter-intuitive because there is more evaluation noise with smaller values of q and some averaging of evaluations should be useful. One explanation is that as the number of generations increase, both the fitness averaging and approximation mechanisms of MEA become more accurate. They eventually help smooth out the evaluation noise, retaining individuals with good fitness, and elim-

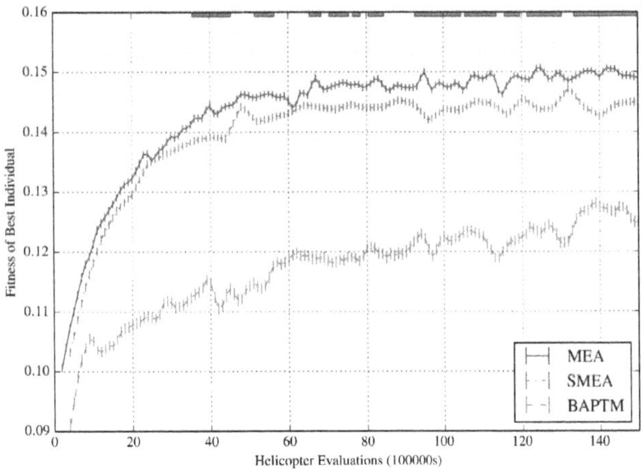

Figure 8: Similar plot as Fig. 3, but with HNE$_8$ as O_l. O_u is run with each of the 10 wind velocities 15 times, for a total of 150 runs. Because the helicopter simulation is more computationally complex, data is only collected after every fourth generation. Both MEA and SMEA perform better than BAPTM by a wide margin. MEA begins to overtake SMEA in performance after roughly four million lower level evaluations.

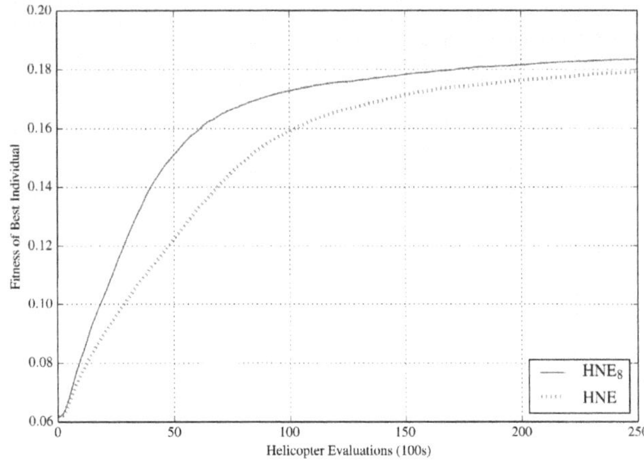

Figure 9: The fitness of the best individual over the number of evaluations of F_l by HNE and HNE$_8$. Results are averaged over 500 runs, with 50 runs for each of the 10 wind velocities. HNE$_8$ both learns faster and achieves higher peak fitness than HNE.

inating those with bad fitness. This conclusion is supported by observations that the performance of MEA steadily becomes less noisy and more consistent over the generations. As seen in Figs. 3, 5, and 8, MEA's fitness approximation mechanism also explains why its performance continues to increase even SMEA, which does not use fitness approximation, is flattening out.

Interestingly, although PNE$_{15}$ has three times as many p_u as PNE$_5$, the performance of PNE$_{15}$ is noticeably better. A more complex parametrization of an optimization algorithm allows it to adapt better to a problem, especially if it is using parameters discovered through bilevel optimization. With MEA, it might thus be possible to discover specialized optimization algorithms that excel in solving particular problem domains.

There are several interesting directions of future work: (1) Evolving a policy for an EA that, based on the current state of the population, adaptively changes parameters such as population size, mutation, and crossover rate. Preliminary results on multimodal objective functions such as Shekel's foxholes show that an effective policy (parametrized as weights of a neural network) can be discovered through metaevolution. (2) Optimizing not only the parameters of NE at the upper level, but also the topology of the neural network. (3) Combining various heuristics from existing EAs, such as differential evolution and particle swarm optimization, to create a general purpose lower level parametrization that performs well on a wide variety of optimization problems.

6. CONCLUSION

In this paper, parameter adaptation for NE is cast as a bilevel optimization problem. A novel upper level optimization algorithm, MEA, is proposed and shown to be capable of achieving better results in optimizing parameters for NE. The optimized parameters discovered by MEA result in significantly better performance over hand-designed ones in two difficult real-world control tasks. Remarkably, evolving a more complex parametrization of the lower level optimization algorithm results in better performance, even though such a parametrization would be very difficult to manage by hand. Bilevel optimization is thus a promising approach for solving complex control tasks.

7. APPENDIX

For the double pole balancing task, the length and mass of the longer pole is set to 0.5 meters and 0.1 kilogram. The length and mass of the shorter pole is set to 0.05 meters and 0.01 kilogram. The mass of the cart itself is 1.0 kilogram. The shorter pole is initialized in a vertical position while the longer pole is initialized with one degree offset from the shorter pole. Both poles and the cart have zero initial velocity. For the helicopter hovering task, the physical dynamics of the helicopter simulator is described in more detail in [15].

The table below lists the parameter names, constraints, and default values for the p_u of PNE$_5$, PNE$_{15}$, and HNE$_8$. At the beginning of every generation in PNE$_{15}$, the probability a particular selection or crossover operator is chosen to help generate next generation's population is proportional to the probability parameter assigned to that operator. In HNE$_8$, mutation replacement rate is the probability that a randomly generated value replaces a particular gene instead of being added to it. Crossover averaging rate is the probability that corresponding genes in two individuals are averaged together instead of being swapped. The meaning of the other parameters should be clear from their names.

PNE_5 Parameters	Constraints	Default
Mutation Rate	[0,1]	0.40
Mutation Amount	[0,1]	0.30
Replacement Fraction	[0,1]	0.50
Initial Weight Range	[0,12]	6.00
Population Size	[0,400]	400
Extra PNE_{15} Parameters	**Constraints**	**Default**
Mutation Probability	[0,1]	1.00
Crossover Probability	[0,1]	1.00
Uniform Crossover Rate	[0,1]	0.00
Tournament/Truncation Fraction	[0,1]	0.25
Tournament Selection Probability	[0,1]	0.00
Truncation Selection Probability	[0,1]	1.00
Roulette Selection Probability	[0,1]	0.00
1-pt Crossover Probability	[0,1]	1.00
2-pt Crossover Probability	[0,1]	0.00
Uniform Crossover Probability	[0,1]	0.00
HNE_8 Parameters	**Constraints**	**Default**
Mutation Probability	[0,1]	0.75
Mutation Rate	[0,1]	0.10
Mutation Amount	[0,1]	0.80
Mutation Replacement Rate	[0,1]	0.25
Replacement Fraction	[0,1]	0.02
Population Size	[0,200]	50
Crossover Probability	[0,1]	0.50
Crossover Averaging Rate	[0,1]	0.50

To illustrate how evolution improves upon the default values, the table below lists the final parameters evolved by the median performing run of MEA.

PNE_5 Parameters	Values Found by MEA
Mutation Rate	0.46
Mutation Amount	0.59
Replacement Fraction	0.87
Initial Weight Range	6.53
Population Size	17
PNE_{15} Parameters	**Values Found by MEA**
Mutation Rate	0.65
Mutation Amount	1.00
Replacement Fraction	1.00
Initial Weight Range	2.67
Population Size	32
Mutation Probability	1.00
Crossover Probability	0.85
Uniform Crossover Rate	0.18
Tournament/Truncation Fraction	0.57
Tournament Selection Probability	0.96
Truncation Selection Probability	0.01
Roulette Selection Probability	0.03
1-pt Crossover Probability	0.00
2-pt Crossover Probability	0.42
Uniform Crossover Probability	0.58
HNE_8 Parameters	**Values Found by MEA**
Mutation Probability	1.00
Mutation Rate	0.03
Mutation Amount	0.77
Mutation Replacement Rate	0.21
Replacement Fraction	0.04
Population Size	28
Crossover Probability	0.94
Crossover Averaging Rate	0.03

8. ACKNOWLEDGMENTS

This research was supported in part by NSF grants DBI-0939454, IIS-0915038, and SBE-0914796, and by NIH grant R01-GM105042.

9. REFERENCES

[1] Karl Johan Åström and Tore Hägglund. *Advanced PID control.* ISA-The Instrumentation, Systems, and Automation Society; Research Triangle Park, NC 27709, 2006.

[2] Faustino John Gomez and Risto Miikkulainen. *Robust non-linear control through neuroevolution.* Computer Science Department, University of Texas at Austin, 2003.

[3] Andrew G Barto. *Reinforcement learning: An introduction.* MIT press, 1998.

[4] Leemon Baird and Andrew W Moore. Gradient descent for general reinforcement learning. *Advances in neural information processing systems*, pages 968–974, 1999.

[5] J Andrew Bagnell and Jeff G Schneider. Autonomous helicopter control using reinforcement learning policy search methods. In *Robotics and Automation, 2001. Proceedings 2001 ICRA. IEEE International Conference on*, volume 2, pages 1615–1620. IEEE, 2001.

[6] Nate Kohl and Peter Stone. Policy gradient reinforcement learning for fast quadrupedal locomotion. In *Robotics and Automation, 2004. Proceedings. ICRA'04. 2004 IEEE International Conference on*, volume 3, pages 2619–2624. IEEE, 2004.

[7] Faustino Gomez, Jürgen Schmidhuber, and Risto Miikkulainen. Accelerated neural evolution through cooperatively coevolved synapses. *The Journal of Machine Learning Research*, 9:937–965, 2008.

[8] John J Grefenstette, David E Moriarty, and Alan C Schultz. Evolutionary algorithms for reinforcement learning. *arXiv preprint arXiv:1106.0221*, 2011.

[9] Xin Yao. Evolving artificial neural networks. *Proceedings of the IEEE*, 87(9):1423–1447, 1999.

[10] Dario Floreano, Peter Dürr, and Claudio Mattiussi. Neuroevolution: from architectures to learning. *Evolutionary Intelligence*, 1(1):47–62, 2008.

[11] Joel Lehman and Risto Miikkulainen. Neuroevolution. *Scholarpedia*, 8(6):30977, 2013.

[12] Faustino J Gomez and Risto Miikkulainen. Active guidance for a finless rocket using neuroevolution. In *Genetic and Evolutionary Computation-GECCO 2003*, pages 2084–2095. Springer, 2003.

[13] Julian Togelius and Simon M Lucas. Evolving controllers for simulated car racing. In *Evolutionary Computation, 2005. The 2005 IEEE Congress on*, volume 2, pages 1906–1913. IEEE, 2005.

[14] Brian F Allen and Petros Faloutsos. Evolved controllers for simulated locomotion. In *Motion in Games*, pages 219–230. Springer, 2009.

[15] Rogier Koppejan and Shimon Whiteson. Neuroevolutionary reinforcement learning for generalized control of simulated helicopters. *Evolutionary intelligence*, 4(4):219–241, 2011.

[16] Richard Myers and Edwin R Hancock. Empirical modelling of genetic algorithms. *Evolutionary computation*, 9(4):461–493, 2001.

[17] Ankur Sinha, Pekka Malo, Peng Xu, and Kalyanmoy Deb. A bilevel optimization approach to automated parameter tuning. 2014.

[18] Agoston E Eiben and Selmar K Smit. Parameter tuning for configuring and analyzing evolutionary algorithms. *Swarm and Evolutionary Computation*, 1(1):19–31, 2011.

[19] Belarmino Adenso-Diaz and Manuel Laguna. Fine-tuning of algorithms using fractional experimental designs and local search. *Operations Research*, 54(1):99–114, 2006.

[20] Mauro Birattari, Zhi Yuan, Prasanna Balaprakash, and Thomas Stützle. F-race and iterated f-race: An overview. In *Experimental methods for the analysis of optimization algorithms*, pages 311–336. Springer, 2010.

[21] Frank Hutter, Holger H Hoos, Kevin Leyton-Brown, and Thomas Stützle. Paramils: an automatic algorithm configuration framework. *Journal of Artificial Intelligence Research*, 36(1):267–306, 2009.

[22] John J Grefenstette. Optimization of control parameters for genetic algorithms. *Systems, Man and Cybernetics, IEEE Transactions on*, 16(1):122–128, 1986.

[23] Laura Silvia Diosan and Mihai Oltean. Evolving evolutionary algorithms using evolutionary algorithms. In *Proceedings of the 2007 GECCO conference companion on Genetic and evolutionary computation*, pages 2442–2449. ACM, 2007.

[24] Volker Nannen and Agoston E Eiben. Relevance estimation and value calibration of evolutionary algorithm parameters. In *IJCAI*, volume 7, pages 975–980, 2007.

[25] Carlos Ansótegui, Meinolf Sellmann, and Kevin Tierney. A gender-based genetic algorithm for the automatic configuration of algorithms. In *Principles and Practice of Constraint Programming-CP 2009*, pages 142–157. Springer, 2009.

[26] Oliver Kramer. Evolutionary self-adaptation: a survey of operators and strategy parameters. *Evolutionary Intelligence*, 3(2):51–65, 2010.

[27] Alain Ratle. Accelerating the convergence of evolutionary algorithms by fitness landscape approximation. In *Parallel Problem Solving from Nature-PPSN V*, pages 87–96. Springer, 1998.

[28] Iloneide CO Ramos, Marco César Goldbarg, Elizabeth G Goldbarg, and Adrião Duarte Dória Neto. Logistic regression for parameter tuning on an evolutionary algorithm. In *Evolutionary Computation, 2005. The 2005 IEEE Congress on*, volume 2, pages 1061–1068. IEEE, 2005.

[29] Yaochu Jin. A comprehensive survey of fitness approximation in evolutionary computation. *Soft computing*, 9(1):3–12, 2005.

[30] Frank Hutter, Holger H Hoos, and Kevin Leyton-Brown. Sequential model-based optimization for general algorithm configuration. In *Learning and Intelligent Optimization*, pages 507–523. Springer, 2011.

[31] Lawrence Davis et al. *Handbook of genetic algorithms*, volume 115. Van Nostrand Reinhold New York, 1991.

[32] Leo Breiman. Random forests. *Machine learning*, 45(1):5–32, 2001.

[33] Marko Robnik-Šikonja. Improving random forests. In *Machine Learning: ECML 2004*, pages 359–370. Springer, 2004.

[34] Ankur Sinha, Aravind Srinivasan, and Kalyanmoy Deb. A population-based, parent centric procedure for constrained real-parameter optimization. In *Evolutionary Computation, 2006. CEC 2006. IEEE Congress on*, pages 239–245. IEEE, 2006.

[35] Gilbert Syswerda. Uniform crossover in genetic algorithms. 1989.

[36] William M Spears and Kenneth D De Jong. On the virtues of parameterized uniform crossover. Technical report, DTIC Document, 1995.

[37] Alexis P Wieland. Evolving neural network controllers for unstable systems. In *Neural Networks, 1991., IJCNN-91-Seattle International Joint Conference on*, volume 2, pages 667–673. IEEE, 1991.

[38] Hamid R Berenji and Pratap Khedkar. Learning and tuning fuzzy logic controllers through reinforcements. *Neural Networks, IEEE Transactions on*, 3(5):724–740, 1992.

[39] Faustino Gomez, Jürgen Schmidhuber, and Risto Miikkulainen. Efficient non-linear control through neuroevolution. In *Machine Learning: ECML 2006*, pages 654–662. Springer, 2006.

A New Perspective on Channel Allocation in WLAN: Considering the Total Marginal Utility of the Connections for the Users

Thiago A. Luiz
Departament of Computer Science
Federal University of Ouro Preto
Morro do Cruzeiro, 35400-000, Ouro Preto, MG, Brazil
thiagoalcantaraluiz@yahoo.com.br

Alan R. R. Freitas
Departament of Computer Science
Federal University of Ouro Preto
Morro do Cruzeiro, 35400-000, Ouro Preto, MG, Brazil
alandefreitas@iceb.ufop.br

Frederico G. Guimarães
Department of Electrical Engineering
Federal University of Minas Gerais
Av. Antônio Carlos 6627, 31270-901, Belo Horizonte, MG, Brazil
fredericoguimaraes@ufmg.br

ABSTRACT

The channel allocation problem consists in defining the frequency used by Access Points (APs) in Wireless Local Area Networks (WLAN). An overlap of channels in a WLAN is the major factor of performance reduction for the users in a network. For this reason, we propose a new model for channel allocation that aims to maximize the total quality of the connection of the user by considering their marginal utility. The results show that an allocation model that does not take into account the total utility of each connection tends to prioritize the quality of connection of a few users and lead to a large unbalance in the distribution of connection speed between users. Thus, the new model can handle the importance of degradation caused by the levels of interference in the user connection separately.

CCS Concepts

•**Networks** → **Wireless local area networks;** •**Mathematics of computing** → Evolutionary algorithms;

Keywords

Channel Allocation, Wireless Local Area Network, Marginal Utility, Genetic Algorithms

1. INTRODUCTION

In recent years, there has been a rapid growth of the utilization of wireless networks following the standard IEEE 802.11, given their easy installation and use, reduced costs, and high data transfer rates. With these factors combined, Wireless Local Area Networks (WLAN) have become attractive to companies, institutions, residences and even in public environments. A set of Access Points (AP) can be densely installed and interconnected on a single local network, leading to a WLAN whose topology is referred to as Extended Service Set (ESS).

The increasing demand of users and APs inserted in the network, the proximity of different WLANs, the intensity of the signal transmitted by APs and the intensity of the signal perceived by the users are some examples of the characteristics that make the design of an efficient WLAN a very complex task. The channel allocation problem for the APs in the WLAN (Section 2) is very important, specially if the network is of a larger scale. Most projects are oriented only towards the minimization of signal interference in the network. Nevertheless, solutions oriented towards the global reduction of interference usually neglect the quality of the connection for the users individually. This allows that users with low connection speeds are deliberately overlooked, which is compensated by an increase in the quality of the connection for users already well served.

Channel allocation models that focus only on the summation of connection speed do not contribute effectively to the balance of quality for the users in the network. Usually, those designs do not consider estimates of the utility of establishing a new connection between a user and an AP in a given channel. As a consequence, users tend to connect to the closest AP instead of an AP that maximizes the quality of their connection.

In this context, we present in this work: (i) A channel allocation model that maximizes the total utility of the connection for each user (Section 3); and (ii) an Evolutionary Algorithm [6] and related genetic operators for the proposed channel allocation model (Section 4).

This work is structured as follows. The problem of utility to the users in IEEE 802.11 networks is first discussed in Section 2. In Section 3, we propose a channel allocation model in WLANs using the total marginal utility of the connection for the users. Details on the Evolutionary Algorithm developed for the experiments are presented in Section 4. In Section 5, we compare the solutions found by using the proposed model with the results obtained by using a channel allocation model that does not consider the total utility of the connections. The solutions obtained with the pro-

GECCO '15, July 11 - 15, 2015, Madrid, Spain
© 2015 ACM. ISBN 978-1-4503-3472-3/15/07...$15.00
DOI: http://dx.doi.org/10.1145/2739480.2754663

posed model generate a greater balance in the distribution of connection speeds in the whole network and the quality of service perceived by all the users. In Section 6, we present the conclusions and ideas for follow-up studies.

2. THE UTILITY OF CONNECTIONS

The quality of the connection offered to the user by an AP is highly influenced by the number of users connected to this AP and by the interference in the network. Attending a user involves establishing a connection that favours the utilization of the network capacity. For this reason, channel allocation mechanisms should consider the utility of that connection for the users with the goal of balancing the distribution of the capacity of the network. A balanced distribution of connection speeds is an important factor affecting the perceived quality of the network, since it is directly related to the satisfaction of users.

Networks IEEE 802.11a, 802.11b, 802.11g and 802.11n operate in ISM (Industrial, Scientific and Medical Band) with 2,4 GHz bandwidth, making a total of 11 channels of 22 MHz bandwidth. However, only three channels do not interfere with each other (channels 1, 6 and 11). These channels are termed non overlapping channels since there is a separation of 3 MHz between them.

In environments with many users, the network requires dozens of APs and finding solutions that maximize the connection utility for the users becomes a non trivial task. In large wireless networks, it is virtually impossible to find a channel allocation in such a way that no user will experience some interference, given the severe restriction of non overlapping channels and the overload of the AP attending on it. Therefore, the mapping of channels in a WLAN requires additional strategies to maximize the quality of connections.

2.1 Related work

Akl and Arepally [1] proposed a method in which each AP periodically runs the allocation mechanism. Each AP determines the maximum interference that it can suffer. If the current allocation causes an interference greater than this threshold, the proposed method allows that each AP defines its channel trying to minimize the interference from neighbouring APs by using an attenuation loss model. In the channel allocation model proposed, there are not any users in the environment, i.e., interference is calculated only between APs. Sometimes users are far from the APs and moving towards the coverage area of another APs. The impact of these on the connection of the user is not considered. These characteristics can be noticed in other works, such as in Hills [10], Hills and Schlegel [11], Mahonen, Riihijarvi and Petrova [15], and Vanhatupa, Hännikäinen and Hämäläinen [20].

Drieburg et al. [5] proposed some modifications to the distributed and dynamic channel allocation method proposed by Luo and Shankaranarayanan [13], with the goal of making it simpler, more efficient and with lower computational cost. In their new method, each AP calculates the best channel to be used in the next time slot in order to maximize the network throughput, along predefined time slots. The simulation results showed that the proposed modifications improve the network throughput in dynamic environments when opposed to the original version. However, the interference level affecting users and disconnections caused by the movement of users is neglected.

Lima, Carrano and Takahashi [12] addressed location and coverage problems of the APs, load balance and channel allocation. The channel allocation problem was treated separately by using a greedy heuristic consisting in a weighted variation of a sequential algorithm, commonly used in channel allocation and proposed by Brélaz [4], known as Degree of Saturation (DSATUR). The algorithm developed considers the demand of the APs and the interference level generated by those operating in the same channel. However, they adopted a channel allocation model that estimates the interference as the percentage of users affected by APs sharing the same operating channel. The model could become more realistic if it had used another estimation of interference, for instance, the intensity of conflicting signals received by a user at a region of overlapping spectra. Additionally, the absence of a mechanism for ensuring the quality of connections for the users is another critical point.

Handrizal et al. [9] proposed a graph coloring algorithm known as Vertex Merge to perform the channel allocation. The algorithm is designed to minimize the number of colors needed to color a graph such that adjacent nodes use different colors. This characteristic makes the algorithm incapable of solving some instances. Another important factor is that, in the channel allocation problem in a WLAN, minimizing the number of colors does not lead necessarily to a scenario with low interference, due to the proximity of some neighbouring APs. The frequency allocation involves the reuse of some channels in an efficient way, with as low as possible interference or greater balance in the connections of the users.

A tool capable of optimizing critical problems related to the design of WLANs was proposed in Yao et al. [21]. Among these problems, the channel allocation problem is discussed using a strategy based on adjusting the transmission power. The goal is to reduce the overlapping region between neighbouring AP operating in the same channel. According to this strategy, if two APs use the same channel, both should adjust their transmission power as recommended in Bae, Choi and Chae [2]. Moreover, it is suggested that this strategy can become more efficient if a mechanism to force disconnection is adopted. In this case, after an adjustment, a user is disconnected and then reconnects with the AP having the strongest signal, according to Park, Bea and Kwon [18]. However, this method focusses on decreasing the probability of collisions given the reduction of the overlapping region. Users can have their signal intensity reduced and be located at an overlapping region at the same time. There is no relationship between the signal intensity offered to a user and the effective loss of quality with the subjected interference level.

The distributed method with the presence of heterogeneous users, proposed by Gong, Zhao and Yang [8], considers the crucial points mentioned before. However, it was not established a relationship between the signal intensity received by a user, caused by the AP to which it is connected, and its submitted interference level. For this reason, there is no mechanism for reallocating this user to another AP capable of attending it with better connection quality. In the same way, did not adopt any mechanism to verify if all the users have quality in their connections, only the global index is considered. In this approach, users can be subjected to high levels of interference and with connection failures.

In this paper, we introduce a new channel allocation model that maximizes the total utility of the connection for each user. In this approach, solutions related to a better balance in the distribution of connection speeds can be found and the quality of the connections for users individually is not disregarded. The proposed model is outlined in the next section.

3. CHANNEL ALLOCATION MODEL

3.1 Marginal Utility

The concept of Utility is related to the satisfaction of an individual after acquiring a unit of a good or service. Utility cannot be directly observed or measured but we know the utility that an item or service generates to an individual is greater or smaller according to the action taken (acquiring it or not). Whereas the individual alone is responsible for defining his/her satisfaction according to the goods or services he/she has. If an individual understands that his/her satisfaction increased, then the utility of the goods or services acquired also increased. For this reason, the utility is a relative measure employed to inform if something is preferable compared to another (ordinal utility) instead of determining an absolute measure of how much it is preferable (cardinal utility).

The utility that acquiring an extra unit of a good or service provides to the individual is known as marginal utility. Due to the scarcity of resources, one cannot obtain an unlimited amount of a good or service, thus one should save the use of the means in order to achieve one's goals. First, one's means should be allocated to serve the most desired goal. The next mean will serve the second most desired goals and so forth. This is to say that each additional unit of a good or service will satisfy relatively less of a goal and hence, provide us with less marginal utility. This behaviour defines the Law of Decreasing Marginal Utility [7]. More details can be found in Mankiw [17].

3.2 Allocation model based on utility

The channel allocation model proposed in this paper considers criteria that favor the utilization of the network by all users, without any priority due to its location in the environment and the current traffic. The model consists of the following variables:

- n: number of users.
- m: number of APs.
- $c_i \in$ C: client i.
- $p_j \in$ P: access point j.
- e_{ij}: quality of the connection offered by AP p_j when connected to c_i.
- l_{ij}: percentage loss in the quality of the connection for the client c_i if p_j is using the same channel of its AP.
- $u(v)$: decreasing function that returns the utility of having a connection at speed v.

The utility is related to the law of decreasing marginal utility discussed before. The utility is used in the model to allow that a user being served with slow connection speed is not damaged even more because of the interference level.

The decision variables are:

- g_j: operating channel of the AP p_j.
- d_{ij}: 1, if c_i is being attended on by p_j, and 0 otherwise.

The decision variable d_{ij} is used to inform if the user i is connected to the AP j and, to guarantee that every user is connected to an AP, we should have: $\sum_{j=1}^{m} d_{ij} = 1; \forall i \in$ C.

Let μ_i be the index of the AP attending client c_i. μ_i can be formally defined by (1).

$$\mu_i = \{j | d_{ij} = 1\} \tag{1}$$

We can now refer to the AP attending client c_i as simply p_{μ_i}. From this definition, the function $h(c_i, p_j)$ in (2) can be defined as:

$$h(c_i, p_j) = \begin{cases} 0, & \text{if } d_{ij} = 1 \\ 0, & \text{if } d_{ij} = 0 \wedge g_j \neq g_{\mu_i} \\ l_{ij}, & \text{if } d_{ij} = 0 \wedge g_j = g_{\mu_i} \end{cases} \tag{2}$$

This function $h(c_i, p_j)$ indicates if client c_i is subject to some level of interference from AP p_j.

Equation (2) refers to the effective loss that AP p_j causes to the connection of client c_i. This function gives $h(c_i, p_j) = 0$ if the AP p_j is attending on client c_i. In the same way, $h(c_i, p_j) = 0$ if p_j is not operating on the same channel that p_{μ_i} is.

If the AP p_j does not attend client c_i and, at the same time, operates in the frequency of the AP p_{μ_i} to which c_i is connected, then there is interference, which is given by $h(c_i, p_j) = l_{ij}$.

Equation (3) corresponds to the multiplying factor of the final quality of connection for client c_i due to the interference from other APs, that is, it is the total percentage loss that the user will experience in its connection for the given channel mapping.

$$q(c_i, P) = \prod_{j=1}^{m} (1 - h(c_i, p_j)) \tag{3}$$

Finally, Equation (4) represents the overall problem statement, which corresponds to maximizing the utility of having a connection at speed v, considering the given channel allocation, the quality of connection between a client i and the AP p_{μ_i}, and the possible losses caused by connections of users to the APs in the network.

$$\max f(x) = \sum_{i=1}^{n} \sum_{j=1}^{m} d_{ij} u(e_{ij} q(c_i, P)) \tag{4}$$

4. EVOLUTIONARY ALGORITHM AND GENETIC OPERATORS

4.1 Representation of solutions

In the Genetic Algorithm (GA) developed for the problem, a candidate solution (individual) is represented by the vectors a and b, which correspond to the decision variables g_j and d_{ij}, respectively. To obtain the value of g_j (channel used by the AP p_j), one can simply access the position j in the vector a and check the stored value. Supposing the

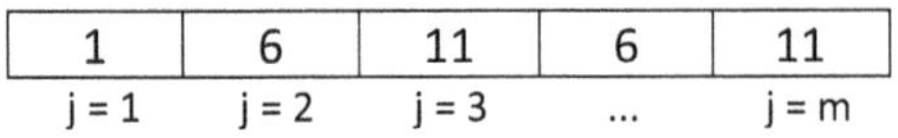

Figure 1: Representation of the variable g_j, $j = 1, \ldots, m$.

utilization of non overlapping channels {1, 6 and 11}, a possible mapping could be such as the one in Figure 1 for m APs.

On the other hand, in the representation of d_{ij}, each position i of the vector b corresponds to a client c_i and the index j stored in each position represents an AP p_j. Figure 2 illustrates the representation of d_{ij} for n users.

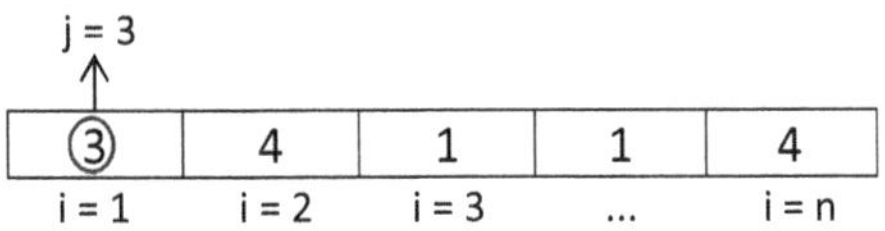

Figure 2: Representation of the variable d_{ij}.

With these two vectors, it is possible to obtain the channel mapping that an individual represents and which AP is attending on each user. There are many ways of creating the initial population in this case, for instance, vectors a and b can be generated at random, through heuristics or extracted from a database, among others.

4.2 Genetic Operators

In the Evolutionary Algorithm developed, we adopt uniform crossover. In this operator, a binary random vector of the same size of vectors a and b is generated. Figure 3 illustrates two candidate vectors a, showing how the crossover between them is performed. The crossover for the vector b is analogous. The values on those positions in the binary vector corresponding to 1 are exchanged between the parents.

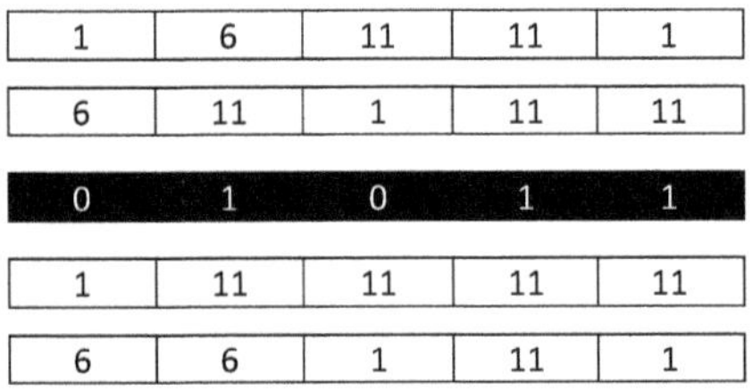

Figure 3: Example of a uniform crossover.

In addition to the crossover operator, each child is subject to mutation. Each position j of the vector a has a probability $1/m$ of being changed. Assuming a mutation at the position j, this change consists in exchanging the channel of the AP p_j for any other channel available. If the APs utilize only non overlapping channels, a modification in the position j corresponds to exchanging the channel 1 by either channel 6 or 11. Figure 4 presents the mutation operator with the available channels.

Still considering the individual under mutation, each position of the vector b has a probability $1/n$ of being modified. The modification in the position i of the vector b consists of assigning another AP to attend on user c_i. The AP is chosen according to a Gaussian distribution in such a way that closer APs have a higher probability of being selected for the new assignment. Figure 5 illustrates the possibilities for each position j of the vector b under mutation.

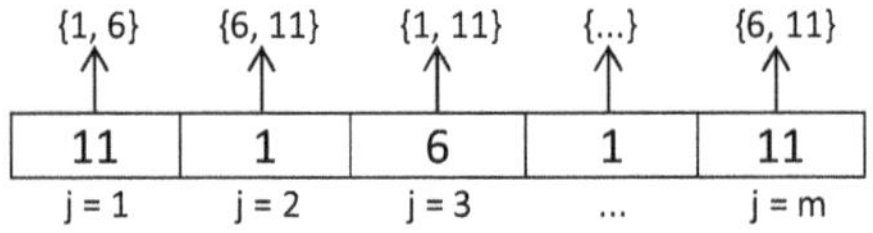

Figure 4: Example of a mutation in the vector a.

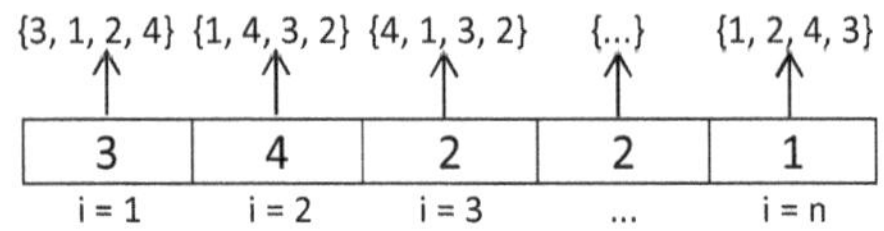

Figure 5: Example of a mutation in the vector b.

4.3 Configuration and parameters

The values for the control parameters of the Genetic Algorithm are presented in Table 1.

Table 1: Parameters of the GA

Parameter	Value
Execution time	90 seconds
Population size	50 individuals
Crossover rate	0.9
Mutation rate per gene (a_j)	$1/m$
Mutation rate per gene (b_j)	$1/n$
Selection method	Binary tournament

5. EXPERIMENTS

5.1 Instances

The scenario initially used for the experiments has real characteristics of a WLAN, with 400 users in an environment of 160,000 m^2. The scenario was created with two Gaussian clusters of 100 users each. Other 200 users are distributed randomly with a uniform distribution. All these characteristics follow guidelines given in Lima, Carrano and Takahashi [12]. A multi-objective algorithm minimizes the quantity of APs and the load imbalance of the APs. In this way, the method proposed by Lima, Carrano and Takahashi [12] was used to determine the number and location of the APs in our scenario. Therefore the network is created with 18 APs. The communication range of each AP is 100m.

Apart from this most representative scenario, we also analyse 300 other instances with slightly different planning features that were generated ad-hoc for our experiments. In this set of instances, each scenario has a different number of clusters (between 1 and 5) and a proportion of users per cluster (between 75 and 125 users). The users were randomly distributed around clusters with a Gaussian distribution, as it was done for the first test scenario we presented. The centers of the clusters were chosen randomly and the standard deviation of the users is 30. The number of users randomly distributed was set between 200 and 300 users. On the other hand, the scenarios have between 15 and 30 APs and the position of the APs was determined by a k-means clustering algorithm [14].

We define the quality of the connection e_{ij} provided to the user c_i by the AP p_j as the bandwidth of the AP, in Mbps (Megabits per second), divided between the number of users connected to it. However, due to the distance between a user and the AP, the decrease in the quality of the connection follows the decrease of the signal intensity received by the user. The loss in signal intensity is estimated with the log-distance path loss model. More details on the path loss model can be found in Gong, Zhao and Yang [8].

The loss l_{ij}, with $0 \leq l_{ij} \leq 1$, is zero for the conditions presented before. It is also zero if the distance between the user c_i and the AP p_j is greater or equal to 100 m. It is one if the distance is inferior to 1 m. Otherwise, the loss l_{ij} in the connection of the user c_i caused by the AP p_j is given by the Log-distance path loss model.

The bandwidth of the AP range from 54 Mbps (protocol 802.11g) to 600 Mbps in the best case. Nevertheless, we define the bandwidth of the AP as 54 Mbps.

5.1.1 Utility function

As discussed in the previous section, we use the concept of Marginal Utility to determine the quality of the connection for a user. As a strict measure of ordinal utility would not allow interpersonal comparisons of value, we define a function that gives the cardinal marginal utility of a solution, see (5). This is a possible quantification of the marginal utility with respect to the connection speed. In this equation, $m(v)$ represents the marginal utility, u_0 is the initial utility, d is the utility loss in the next Mbps and v is the connection speed.

$$m(v) = u_0 \times (1 - d)^v \tag{5}$$

The initial utility u_0 represents the utility of a connection to the user when he/she does not have any. Changing the constant u_0 would simply linearly transform the objective function and we would have an equivalent problem. The utility loss $0 < d < 1$ is a parameter that indicates how much the marginal utility decreases as the user increase 1 Mbps in the speed. When the parameter $d = 0$, this model corresponds to the summation of conection speed. When d approaches 1, the model focuses on equity in the distribution of connection speed. The loss of utility is associated with the connection speed v, because the higher the speed of the connection, the smaller is the impact in its connection and the smaller is the marginal utility. For this reason, users with low connection speed should be protected from a high interference level. Figure 6 illustrates the marginal utility of a connection using $u_0 = 100$ and $d = 0.1$.

The total utility is the area from speed zero up to the speed v, and it is shown in Figure 6. After some point, there is no significant increase in the total utility, i.e., allocating a user with high connection speed to an AP that provides even more speed does not cause a significant increase in the total utility. On the other hand, allocating a user with low connection speed to an AP that provides better service causes a more noticeable increase in the total utility. The total utility $u(v)$ is given by the integral of the marginal utility, see (6).

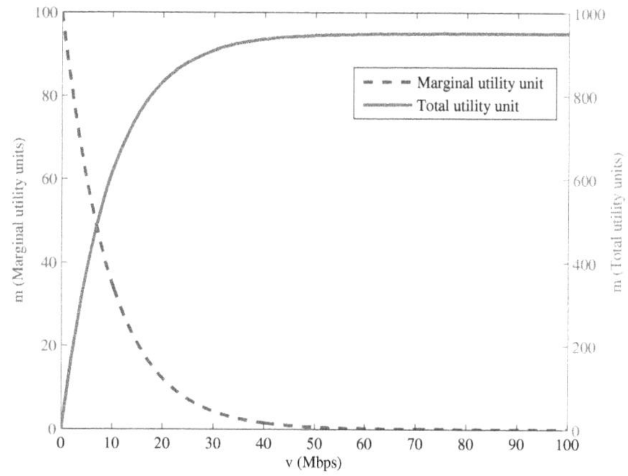

Figure 6: Marginal utility and total utility of a connection.

$$u(v) = \int_0^v m(v) = \left[\frac{u_0}{\ln(1-d)}\right] \times [(1-d)^v - 1] \tag{6}$$

5.1.2 Channels

Using just the three non overlapping channels is a solution often adopted by network designers and administrators, given the difficulty in considering a systematic approach to deal with the interference between overlapping channels. For this reason, we consider the channels {1, 6, 11} in the channel allocation problem as in Bae, Choi and Chae [2], Balbi et al. [3], Lima, Carrano and Takahashi [12], Manitpornsut, Landfeldt and Boukerche [16] and Park, Bea and Kwon [18].

5.2 Model used for comparison

The channel allocation model proposed in Section 3 has the goal of maximizing the total utility of the connection for the users. Removing the decreasing function $u(v)$ from (4) in Section 3, we have a model that maximizes the global quality of connection, similarly to the models usually found in the literature. Solutions found by using the proposed channel allocation model are compared with solutions obtained by using the model as in (7).

$$\max f(x) = \sum_{i=1}^{n} \sum_{j=1}^{m} d_{ij} e_{ij} q(c_i, P) \tag{7}$$

The Genetic Algorithm developed for the problem was executed 33 times on each model. From these executions, we extract the best, worst and average results. In the figures illustrating the solutions found, the blue, green and red colors correspond to the channels 1, 6, and 11, respectively. Squares and dots represent the APs and the users in the network respectively. The line joining a dot to a square indicates the connection between a user and an AP.

5.3 Results

Figure 7(a) and Figure 7(b) illustrate, respectively, the best solution found by the GA when maximizing the global quality of the network and when maximizing the total utility of the connection for the users. One can see from Figure 7(a) that most APs are overloaded, while five APs provide service to only one user. These users are getting a quality of connection close to 54 Mbps, while the other users have to share this speed with another 40 users in addition to suffering from the effects of interference. This is the classic behaviour obtained by adopting the channel allocation models that disregard the satisfaction of the user in the formulation of the optimization problem.

Users under low connection speeds are also subject to some level of interference, damaging even more the utilization of the network and causing a large scale imbalance in the distribution of the quality of service. The same is not observed in Figure 7(b). By using the proposed channel allocation model, the satisfaction of all the users is taken into consideration. Some users who are inevitably subjected to high levels of interference should receive more bandwidth. In this way, the negative impact provoked by the interference in these users is compensated. Figure 8 presents the evolution of the best solution in the GA until converging to the solutions shown in Figure 7.

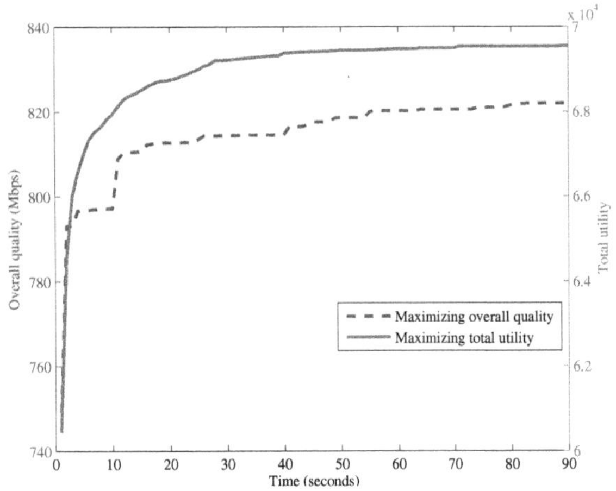

Figure 8: Evolution of the best solution in two Genetic Algorithms. The first GA considers the total utility as fitness function and the second GA uses the total quality of connection to the users.

Table 2 details the solutions found by the GA for the test scenario when adopting the model for the maximization of the global quality. Considering that 18 APs were set up in the environment and each one of them provides 54 Mbps, we have an available speed equivalent to 972 Mbps. That means that about 15% of the available capacity was lost due to interference.

Table 2: Solutions found by maximizing the global quality.

	Quality (Mbps)	% of users with interference	Total utility
Best	821.93	27.25%	56977.49
Average	818.85	30.11%	56083.65
Worst	814.33	33.00%	53731.78

In the worst case, there was a loss of 16% of the total capacity, affecting one third of the users. However, channel allocation models with this global perspective of the problem do not provide useful information about the quality of each user individually, not even if there are users without connection. Even for those solutions with small losses in the available global quality, there is no guarantee of satisfaction of the users. The percentage of users with interference means in practice the quantity of users subject to some damage, but no conclusion about the impact on the connection speed of this user.

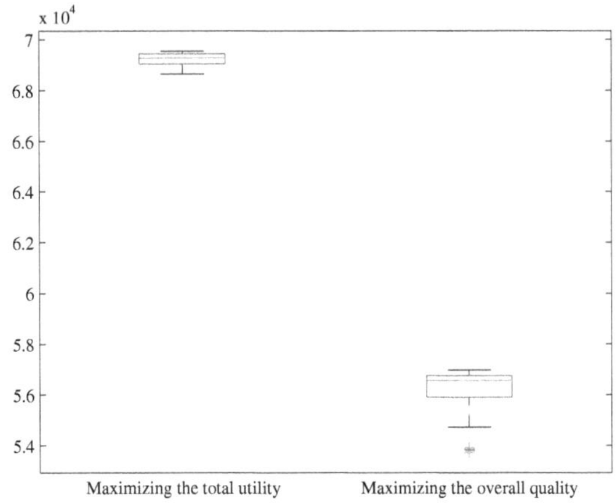

Figure 9: Distribution of the solutions in terms of total utility.

Table 3 details the solutions found by the GA when adopting the proposed model. When the objective is to maximize the total utility of the network, one can notice that the global quality is decreased, compare with Table 2.

Table 3: Solutions found by maximizing the total utility.

	Quality (Mbps)	% of users with interference	Total utility
Best	785.78	25.75%	69539.76
Average	781.84	29.17%	69217.51
Worst	773.79	34.25%	68238.19

Figure 9 shows the distribution of the solutions in terms of total utility. One can conclude that, despite the fact that the used capacity of the network is greater when maximizing the global quality, the users are more unsatisfied with their connections. The satisfaction of a user is not related to the global quality of the network, instead, it is more related to the quality of the connection provided to the user. Given that most of the capacity is concentrated on few users, the majority of the users are not satisfied.

In order to demonstrate the variability in the distribution of the network capacity, we calculate the quality of the connection, in Mbps, of each user in the network according to the best solution found by the GA on each model. Figure 10 presents the number of users with up to a certain connection speed. The disadvantage of maximizing the global quality is apparent when compared with the maximization of the total utility.

It is possible to see in Figure 10 that about 250 users have a connection speed inferior to 1 Mbps when the total quality is considered. In other words, few users receive high connection speeds and most users get low quality service. On the other hand, with the proposed model, the distribution of the

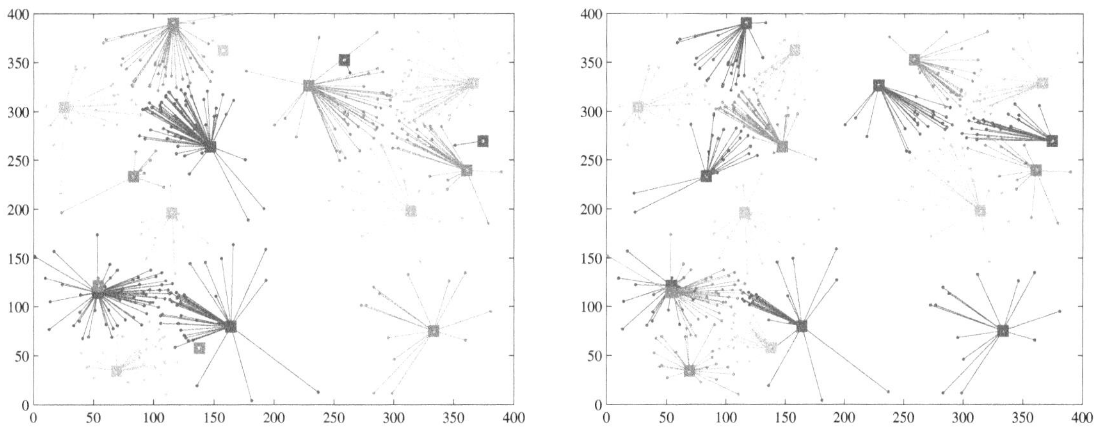

(a) Maximizing the global quality.

(b) Maximizing the total utility.

Figure 7: Best solutions found by the Genetic Algorithm.

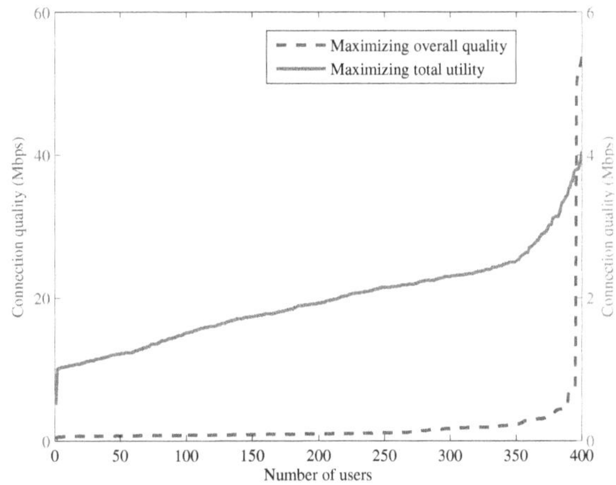

Figure 10: Quality of the connections for the users.

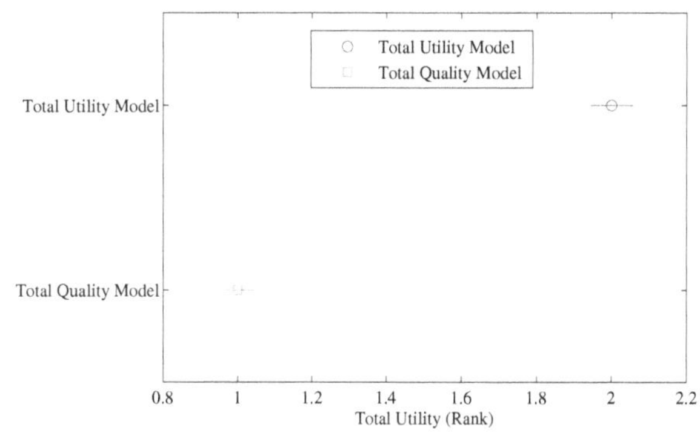

Figure 11: Multiple comparison of mean column ranks.

quality of service to the users is more homogeneous. There are no users deliberately damaged in order to compensate for the satisfaction of already well served users. Only two users experience connections inferior to 1 Mbps while other users are served with connection speeds between 1 and 4 Mbps.

For each scenario in our set of 300 instances, we executed the GA for each model of channel allocation. The average total utility obtained for these test instances was approximately 7% higher when using the GA with the allocation model that maximizes the total utility. As in the first test scenario, user satisfaction was higher in the proposed allocation model. Similarly, the global average speed of the connection was smaller in our proposed model only by approximately 1% when compared with the usual model that maximizes global speed.

In order to investigate the statistical difference between the allocation models, we used a Friedman test [19]. The test had a p-value= 0, indicating that the difference between the two models is statistically significant, as presented in Figure 11.

The satisfaction of the users is directly related to the quality of the connection experienced by each user. For this reason, the higher the number of satisfied users, the higher is the total satisfaction of the network. This characteristic justifies the overall satisfaction of the users when the total utility is considered in the optimization problem, as proposed in this paper.

6. CONCLUSIONS

Channel allocation models in WLANs usually do not consider the quality of the connection for each user individually. Motivated by this, we proposed a new channel allocation model that incorporates the total utility of the connection for a user. The model has the goal of maximizing the satisfaction of all the users in the network.

The proposed channel allocation model estimates the utility of establishing a connection between a user and an AP given the channel mapping. Therefore, the goal is to find the AP that best serves the user in addition to determining the operating frequencies of the APs. This characteristic is an essential contribution of this work to the balance of quality of service in the network, as illustrated in the experiments.

The scenario tested in the simulation has real characteristics of a WLAN but in the future we plan to consider obstacles in the environment such as walls and floors. Experiments performed with the Genetic Algorithm showed that models that consider a global objective generate imbalance in the distribution of the quality of the connections, favoring some users in detriment of a majority. As future work, we mention the comparison of the proposed model with additional channel allocation models in the literature and the study of conflict between users in terms of connection quality. Moreover, only non overlapping channels were considered in this paper. It would be interesting to evaluate the utilization of the additional available frequencies and the effect of this arrangement on the performance.

Acknowledgements

This research has been supported by the following Brazilian agencies: FAPEMIG (APQ-00040-14), CAPES, and CNPq.

7. REFERENCES

[1] R. Akl and A. Arepally. Dynamic channel assignment in ieee 802.11 networks. *IEEE International Conference on Portable Information Devices*, pages 1–5, 2007.

[2] S. J. Bae, B. G. Choi, and H. S. Chae. Self-configuration scheme to alleviate interference among aps in ieee 802.11 wlan. *The 23rd IEEE International Symposium on Personal Indoor and Mobile Radio Communications (PIMRC)*, pages 1025–1030, 2012.

[3] H. Balbi, N. Fernandes, F. Souza, R. Carrano, C. Albuquerque, D. Muchaluat-Saade, and L. Magalhaes. Centralized channel allocation algorithm for ieee 802.11 networks. *Global Information Infrastructure and Networking Symposium (GIIS)*, pages 1–7, 2012.

[4] D. Brélaz. New methods to color the vertices of a graph. *Communications of the ACM*, 22:251–256, 1979.

[5] M. Drieburg, F.-C. Zheng, R. Ahmad, and S. Olafsson. An improved distributed dynamic channel assignment scheme for dense wlans. *Proc. of the 6th International Conference on Information, Communications and Signal Processing (ICICS)*, pages 1–5, 2007.

[6] A. E. Eiben and J. E. Smith. *Introduction to Evolutionary Computing.* Natural Computing. Springer, 2010.

[7] R. Frank and B. Bernanke. *Principles of Economics.* McGraw-Hill Irwin, 4 edition, 2009.

[8] D. Gong, M. Zhao, and Y. Yang. Distributed channel assignment algorithms for 802.11n wlans with heterogeneous clients. *In Journal of Parallel and Distributed Computing*, 74:2365–2379, 2014.

[9] Handrizal, M. Zarlis, A. Noraziah, and A. N. Abdalla. An improved of channel allocation for wlan using vertex merge algorithm. *International Conference on Computational Science and Information Management (ICoCSIM)*, 1:205–213, 2012.

[10] A. Hills. Large-scale wireless lan design. *IEEE Communications Magazine*, 39:98–107, 2001.

[11] A. Hills and J. Schlegel. Rollabout: A wireless design tool. *IEEE Communications Magazine*, 42:132–138, 2004.

[12] M. P. Lima, E. G. Carrano, and R. H. C. Takahashi. Multiobjective planning networks wlan using genetic algorithms. *WCCI IEEE Congress on Computational Intelligence*, 2012.

[13] H. Luo and N. K. Shankaranarayanan. A distributed dynamic channel allocation technique for throughput improvement in a dense wlan environment. *IEEE International Conference on Acoustics, Speech, and Signal Processing (ICASSP)*, 5:345–348, 2004.

[14] J. MacQueen. Some methods of classification and analysis of multivariate observations. *Proc. of the Fifth Berkeley Symposium on Mathematical Statistics and Probability*, 1:281–297, 1967.

[15] P. Mahonen, J. Riihijarvi, and M. Petrova. Frequency allocation for wlans using graph colouring techniques. *Proc. WONS'05*, 2005.

[16] S. Manitpornsut, B. Landfeldt, and A. Boukerche. Efficient channel assignment algorithms for infrastructure wlans under dense deployment. *Proc. of the 12th ACM International Conference on Modeling, Analysis and Simulation of Wireless and Mobile Systems*, pages 329–337, 2009.

[17] N. G. Mankiw. *Principles of Economics.* Cengage Learning, 6 edition, 2011.

[18] B. H. Park, S. J. Bea, and Y. M. Kwon. Connection management of mobile nodes for transmission power control in wlan aps. *International Conference on ICT Convergence*, pages 770–771, 2012.

[19] K. M. Ramachandran and C. P. Tsokos. *Mathematical Statistics with Applications in R.* 2 edition, 2014.

[20] T. Vanhatupa, M. Hännikäinen, and T. D. Hämäläinen. Evaluation of throughput estimation models and algorithms for wlan frequency planning. *Computer Networks*, 51:3110–3124, 2007.

[21] T. Yao, X. Guo, Y. Qiu, and L. Ge. An integral optimization framework for wlan design. *International Conference on Communication Technology (ICCT)*, pages 360–365, 2013.

Parasite Diversity in Symbiogenetic Multiset Genetic Algorithm - Optimization of Large Binary Problems

António Manso[1,2]
1 - Instituto Politécnico de Tomar
Quinta do Contador - Estrada da Serra
2300-313 Tomar - Portugal
manso@ipt.pt

Luís Correia[2]
2 - BioISI – Biosystems and Integrative Sciences Institute
Faculdade de Ciências da Universidade de Lisboa
Campo Grande, 1749-016 Lisboa – Portugal
Luis.Correia@ciencias.ulisboa.pt

ABSTRACT
Symbiogenetic MuGA (SMuGA) is a co-evolutionary model exploiting the concept of symbiosis over the Multiset Genetic Algorithm (MuGA). It evolves two species: hosts that represent a solution to the problem, and parasites that represent part-solutions. SMuGA has been proved valuable in the optimization of a variety of deceptive functions. However its performance decreased in large scale difficult problems.

This paper presents a new version of SMuGA with improvements centered on the evolution process of the parasites. The most significant advance is provided by using a diversity measure to modulate the evolution of parasites. The algorithm is tested with very good results in deceptive functions with up to 1024 bits. The paper is concluded with an analysis of the advantages and limitations of the approach, and with perspectives for future developments.

Categories and Subject Descriptors
I.2.8 [**Artificial Intelligence**]: Problem Solving, Control, Methods and Search.
D.2.2 [**Design Tools and Techniques**]: Evolutionary prototyping.

General Terms
Algorithms, Performance, Experimentation.

Keywords
Multiset; Symbiosis; Genetic diversity; Genetic operators; Deceptive problems.

1. INTRODUCTION
Symbiogenesis is the generation of a new species through genetic integration of different organisms, the symbionts. This is a form of cooperative coevolution that takes advantage of independent evolution of the symbionts. It has been shown that symbiogenetic evolutionary algorithms are useful to solve problems in which some decomposition is possible [1, 2].

GECCO '15 July 11 - 15, 2015, Madrid, Spain.

ACM. ISBN 978-1-4503-3472-3/15/07. . . $15.00.
DOI: http://dx.doi.org/10.1145/2739480.2754780

Another model of evolutionary algorithm that has been successful uses the mathematical concept of multiset [3] to represent the population and is designated Multiset Genetic Algorithm (MuGA). This algorithm has obtained competitive results in difficult optimization problems coded by binary strings and vectors of real numbers [4].

A recent development proposed the integration of a symbiogenetic model with MuGA, named SMuGA [5]. SMuGA brings together the multiset concept from MuGA and the symbogenic representation from Wallin et al.[2] in which one of the symbionts is a host and the other is a parasite. Both populations evolve separately and in SMuGA they form symbiotic combinations, every predefined number of generations. Results obtained in difficult binary problems were promising. However the evolutionary model used with parasites had intricacies that left room for improvement, and had a limited robustness that did not allow it to scale well in large difficult problems.

In this paper we focus on streamlining and improving the robustness of SMuGA. This has been accomplished by modifications in the evolution of parasites. Namely crossover is significantly simplified, a new mutation variant is introduced and a bit diversity evaluation is used in parasite evolution. Both fitness evaluation and mutation of parasites are modulated by diversity.

In the next section we present the context of symbiogenetic algorithms. Following that, in section 3 we provide a brief description of SMuGA and in the next section we detail the modifications made to this algorithm, as the original part of this work. The section 5 describes experiments performed and their results. The paper ends with a section dedicated to highlight the main conclusions and suggest future developments.

2. SYMBIOGENETIC ALGORITHMS
Evolutionary algorithms using symbiogenesis were first proposed by Nils Barricelli, the pioneer of evolutionary algorithms (see [6] for example). However the concept only re-emerged in the 90s with the work of Ikegami and Kaneko [7] and later models of Dumeur [8] and Moriarty and Miikkulainen [9]. While the former is focused on studying the effects of symbiogenesis as a model of the biological phenomena, the latter applies the model to simple optimization problems, sinusoidal function and neural network respectively. In both these two models, organisms may be composed by several symbionts. These may be from a population,

different in nature from the symbiosis, as neurons form a neural network [9], or using the concept of host and parasite, with the host being a recursive composition of symbionts, with some measure of compatibility to the existing symbiosis [8].

In more recent work the combination uses symbionts with coding and non-coding regions [10]. This allows exploitation of linkage between distant coding bits, although with symbionts that need to have the same length as the combination. Further development of this line of work led to the exploitation of a synergy measure of combining a pair of symbionts [11]. This model produced good results in shuffled composed functions that typically needed some form of linkage learning.

SMuGA [5] uses a symbiogenesis model based on the Symbiogenetic Coevolutionary Algorithm (SCA), proposed by Wallin et all [2], in which two populations, of hosts and smaller parasites, combine. In SCA only one parasite combines with one host and the parasite genome length is constant. SMuGA relaxes this, allowing multiple parasites to form a combination with a single host, and varying the length of parasite genomes along evolution. Results obtained with this model were good in large deceptive problems, but we wanted to exploit the scaling capabilities of the algorithm further, and therefore we introduced some modifications to the symbiogenetic model, in order to simplify it and increase its robustness.

3. Symbiogenetic Evolution Model

SMuGA is an algorithm that uses two cooperative species, hosts and parasites, which evolve together in a mutualistic relationship. The host population contains solutions of the problem and the parasite population evolves part-solutions. The parasite population evolves to achieve good genes and then integrate hosts through the incorporation of those genes, a step named *infection* for clarity, although the effect is not necessarily negative for the host. The interaction between hosts and parasites produces a new population using symbiosis that mimics what occurs in the natural world. We call collaboration the result of a host infected by one or more parasites, using symbiosis.

Parasites are composed of a tuple *<position, genome>*. *Position* represents the location in the host genome where the parasite genome starts to be applied and *genome* represents the genetic material of the parasite. The host genome is replaced by the genome of the parasite in the location defined by the position attribute (**Fig. 1**). The parasite considers the host genome as a ring, which means that when applying the parasite genome to the host if we reach the end of the host genome, the copy continues in the beginning of that genome. In **Fig. 1**, parasite ***p1*** is applied in host genome alleles 4 and 5 and parasite ***p2*** is applied in the host genome alleles 8, 9, 0 and 1. The collaboration in this case (**Fig. 1**) is the combination of host genes and the genes introduced by parasites p1 and p2.

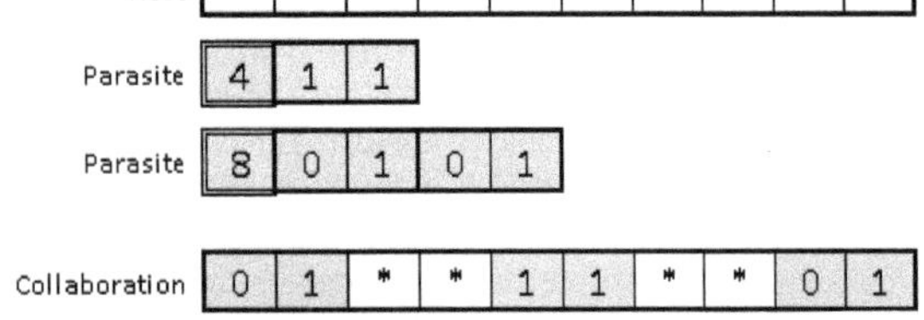

Fig. 1. Collaboration formed by the symbiosis of a host and two parasites.

3.1 Cooperative Coevolutionary Evolution

Algorithm 1 describes the global evolutionary process of SMuGA. It starts by generating and evaluating a host population, ***hPop***, with ***h*** hosts of ***problem***, and a parasite population, ***pPop***, with ***p*** parasites. The only information about the problem needed by parasites is the size of the host. The evolutionary iterative process starts with the collaboration phase followed by the evolution phase until a stop criteria is reached.

```
SMuGA (h, p, problem, iterations)
hPop = generate h MultiIndividuals from problem
Evaluate hPop
pPop = generate p MultiParasites from problem
Repeat
   /* Collaboration phase */
     sPop = collaboration(pPop, hPop)
     hPop = Select h hosts from sPop and hPop
   /* Evolution phase */
      Repeat iterations times
        Evolve hPop
        Evolve pPop
      End repat
Until stop criteria is done
End Function.
```

Algorithm 1- SMuGA – Symbiogenetic Multiset Genetic Algorithm

Collaboration phase is performed by Algorithm 2 (analyzed in the next section) and uses the population of parasites and the host population to produce a population of collaborations that contains host clones infected by the parasites. Given that, one host may be infected by many parasites and the algorithm saves clones when a host is infected by one parasite, the number of symbiosis is huge when compared to the number of parasites and number of hosts. This phase is computationally expensive. Therefore hosts and parasites evolve independently for a number (***iterations***) of generations before each collaboration episode (see **Fig. 2**). The collaboration phase ends with the selection of ***h*** hosts from the union of host population, ***hPop*** and symbiosis population, ***sPop***.

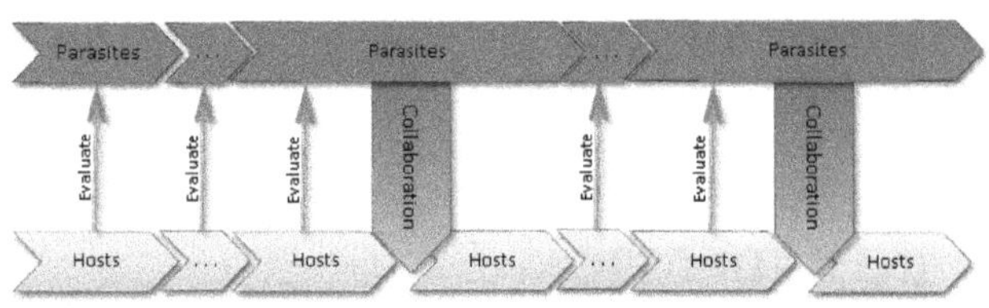

Fig. 2. Interaction between populations in SMuGA algorithm: evolution and collaboration.

The evolution phase starts with the evolution of the host population ***hPop*** using MuGA algorithm [4, 12] and the evolution of the parasite population ***pPop*** using **Algorithm 3** (explained in sec. 4.1 Evolution of Parasites). Host population evolves on its own, however, parasite population still uses hosts, since parasites are evaluated using the genes of host population as a proxy for fitness evaluation. When hosts evolve and change their genes, the fitness value of parasites may change too.

3.2 Collaboration detailed

As mentioned, collaboration is obtained by copying the alleles of the parasite into the host, replacing the alleles of the host. For efficiency reasons the collaboration of a parasite with a host is only performed if the host does not have the alleles of the parasite in corresponding locus. This means that a parasite can infect a host only once. This detail allows the elimination of collaborations that do not add anything new, giving place to collaborations that modify something in the host.

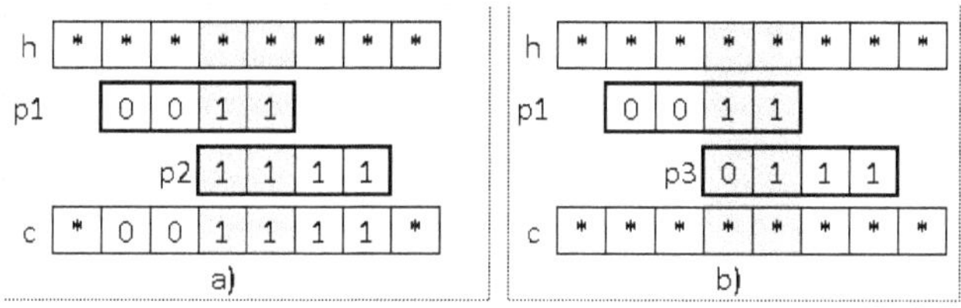

Fig. 3. Infection of a host by two parasites: a) compatible overlapping parasites c) incompatible overlapping parasites

We restrict application of multiple parasites to cases where parasites do not have incompatible bits (**Fig. 3**). This means that the parasites may overlap, provided that the overlapping segment does not contain different bits.

```
Collaboration (parPop, sortedHostsPop)
  symPop = empty Population
  for index = 1 to sortedHostsPop.size
    host = sortedHostsPop.get(index)
    probInfection = index / parPop.size
    ind = host.genotype
    randomize parasites in parPop
    foreach par in parPop
      if compatible(par, ind) and
            uniformRandom(0,1)<probInfection
        ind = ind + par
        add ind.clone to symbPop
      end if
    next parasite
  next index
  return symbPop
End Function.
```

Algorithm 2 - Collaboration between Hosts and Parasites

Algorithm 2 controls the formation of collaborations among a population of hosts and a population of parasites. Algorithm 2 takes parameters a host population as input, ***sortedHostPop***, sorted in descending order of fitness, and a parasite population, ***parasitePop***. Descend ordering of host population is important because the rank of each host divided by the size of parasite population determines the ratio of it receiving parasites. The algorithm continues with the definition of the population ***symbPop*** resulting from the collaboration among populations that are passed as parameters.

After selecting a host and calculating the probability of infection the algorithm continues with the application of parasites to each of its copies (in a multiset population each element is a multi-individual, meaning that a chromosome may have multiple copies, see [12] for further details). The parasites are randomly arranged within the population of parasites ensuring no preference in their application. In the next step the algorithm tries to apply each parasite to the selected host using the compatibility rules previously explained (see also **Fig. 3**). In order to preserve good individuals of the population from generalized infection, and hence the sudden change of their genomes, parasites are applied in a probabilistic manner. A host has a higher probability of being infected by parasites when its rank in the population is lower. This allows fitter individuals to receive fewer parasites, thereby preserving their genes, while lower-ranked individuals are subject to a generalized infection accommodating several parasites promoting exploration of other regions of the search space. On average, each host receives a number of parasites equal to its rank.

4. Improved Symbiogenetic Muga

From now on we describe the new version of Symbiogenetic MuGA although we maintain the name, SmuGA. The new version presented here shares the same methodology of the previous one [5], with improvements in the parasite evolutionary process. The improvements not only simplify the model, but also increase performance of the algorithm and its robustness. In sections 4.1 and 4.2 we describe in detail the evolution of parasites and the diversity modulation of parasite evolution, which are the new features in the improved version of SMuGA.

4.1 Evolution of Parasites

In order to avoid having a human choice interfering significantly in performance, we eliminate the need to specify the size of the parasites. The work of Wallin et al. [2] showed that there was a very strong dependence of performance on the size of the parasite. In our approach the user does not have to know the size of the problem building blocks (BB), in case they exist, because the algorithm adapts parasites' genome length as necessary. This system is important to solve problems in which the size of BB is not known or the BB has a variable size. The length of the parasites can be changed by genetic operators of recombination and mutation.

4.1.1 Recombination

We define the recombination of the parasites as an opportunity for parasites to change their length in addition to combine genetic material of the parents. The recombination of two parasites occurs only if the parasites, by virtue of their defining tuples, are adjacent or overlap in the host genome.

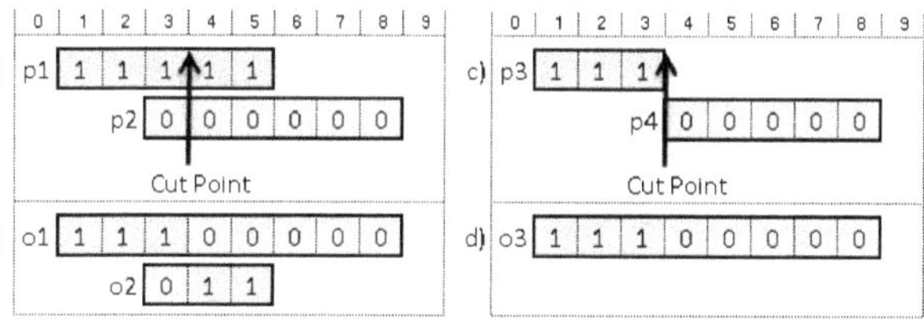

Fig. 4. Parasite recombination.

When the parasites share some allele positions in the host genome, **Fig. 4 a**, the offspring is constructed selecting a cut point from the overlapping region and swapping the alleles on each side of the cut, **Fig. 4 b**. If the parasites are adjacent in the host genome, **Fig. 4 c**, the offspring is the concatenation of the parents' genomes and the position is taken from the parent that has the smallest value **Fig. 4 d**. This model is significantly simpler than the previous one [5] without compromising the capability to recombine genetic material.

Notice that this operator may decrease, as well as increase parasites' lengths. In fact, this is the only transformation in the algorithm that may increase parasite genome length.

4.1.2 Mutation

The mutation operator randomly changes features of a parasite. We use three types of parasite mutation:

1. Change in anchoring position;
2. Change of the alleles;
3. Change in the size of genome.

Examples of these variants can be observed in **Fig. 5.** In the first situation, **Fig. 5 b**, the parasite, **Fig. 5 a**, changes the position where it is applied in the host. In this way a parasite may bring to a new position genetic material that has generally proved valuable at the current position.

In the second case, **Fig. 5 c**, two alleles are changed. This mutation type enables the appearance of new alleles in the parasites' population.

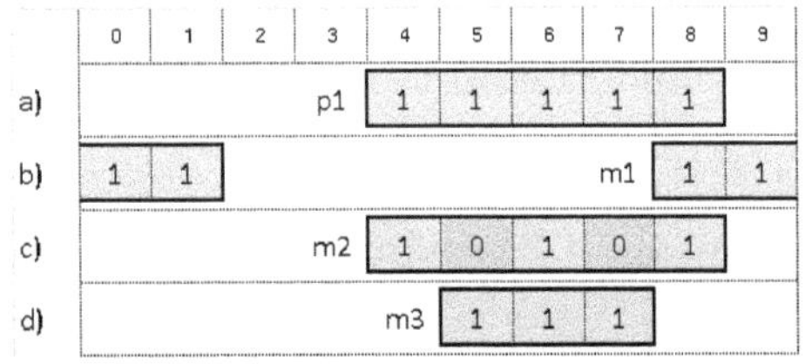

Fig. 5. Parasite Mutations: a) Parasite; b) Mutation of position; c) Mutation of genetic material; d) Mutation by genome break

In the latter situation, **Fig. 5 d**, the parasite genome loses genetic material at its extremities. This is the result of recursively applying a uniformly random cut operation on the genome, in each step retaining the longest segment. Recursion is performed until the probability of cut, done by equation (1), fails.

The probability p to cut a segment is computed by an adapted sigmoid logistic function, equation (1),

$$p = \frac{1}{1+e^{-(x*s+t)}} \quad (1)$$

where x is the *ratio* between size of parasite and the size of host, s is the *scale factor* and t the *translation*.

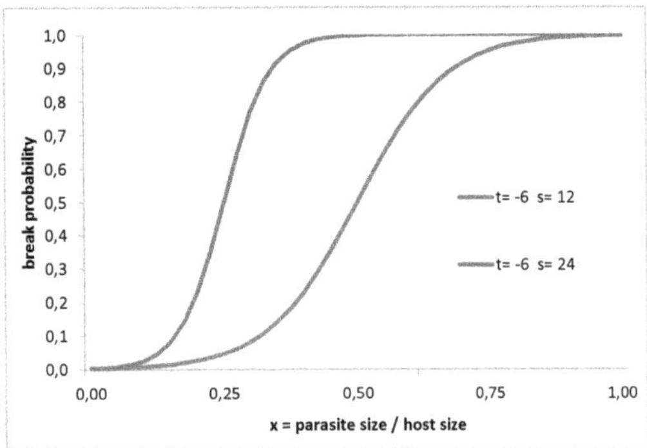

Fig. 6. Probability to genome break with t= -6 and s = 12 and s=24

The standard logistic sigmoid function (s=1, t=0) is massively concentrated among the values -6 and 6. In order to approach a probability distribution function we need to bring this concentration to the interval [0,1]. Thus t= -6 and s=12. However since we want to limit excessive growth of parasite genomes we solved it by increasing sharpness, s=24. **Fig. 6** shows the quasi-probability distribution with these values, for visual comparison.

When applying this type of mutation, if the second part of the genome is retained, the anchoring position of the parasite is updated. This procedure is repeated recursively, until the probability fails, and enables the parasite to loose alleles in both extremities.

This type of mutation inhibits excessive growth of parasites' length, thereby preventing overtfit. Long parasites are hard to relocate and therefore they will impair propagation of useful genetic material to other host locations, which is why we consider them to produce overfit.

4.1.3 Parasite fitness evaluation

The evaluation of parasites is obtained indirectly through the genomes present in the population of hosts. This feature allows parasites to be evaluated without the need of applying them to the hosts and the subsequent need of calling the fitness function to evaluate the collaboration. In this way we replace fitness function calls for a proxy consisting on simply checking if the parasite genome is present in host genome and using the host fitness rank. To accomplish this, hosts are sorted in a descending rank according to their fitness. With n hosts, the host rank is defined in the interval [1, n], where the rank of fittest host is n and the rank of the worst host is 1.

Parasites use those ranks to compute their own evaluation. The parasite evaluation algorithm sums the ranks of the hosts that have the parasite in their genome. This means that a parasite showing in the entire host population has maximum fitness value. However its contribution to the diversity of the population is zero. To circumvent this inconvenience we shifted the rank of the hosts to the interval [-n/2-1, n/2]. This shift provides a number of significant advantages. First of all, the fitness of parasites that infect the entire population is zero; parasites present only in the best individuals have positive fitness; and by opposition, parasites that are present only in worst individuals have negative fitness.

When evolution produces a new parasite, whose genotype does not exist in the population, the evaluation function should reward its discovery with a fitness that allows it to survive and reproduce if it is a good parasite. On the other hand the length of a new parasite should decrease its fitness to prevent the emergence of large parasites with random genomes that contrast with large parasites evolved from good BB. Supported by preliminary experimental results, we decided to assign each new parasite a fitness value equal to the host population size subtracted by the new parasite's length in bits, as a reward for the discovery of new parasite genomes. The evaluation function allows small parasites with new genotypes to appear in the population and to recombine themselves with existing ones thereby promoting their growth if they contain genetic material useful for solving the problem.

We try different approaches to reward the appearance of new genomes in the parasite population and the one described above produces good results.

4.1.4 Parasite Evolution algorithm

Evolution of parasites is performed by Algorithm 3 that is a variant of (μ + λ) evolutionary strategies. The algorithm receives as parameters the population of parasites to evolve, ***pPop***, the population of hosts to perform the evaluation of the parasites, ***hPop***, and the number of parasites that will be selected to evolve, ***k***. The algorithm starts by selecting ***k*** parasites from ***pPop***. It continues with the recombination of the selected population, giving rise to the population ***offspringPop***. This step recombines genetic material of selected parasites with the rules described above. The population ***offspringPop*** is constructed by removing a pair of individuals from the selected parasite population, applying the recombination algorithm to the parents, and inserting the offspring in ***offspringPop***, if the recombination was performed, otherwise inserting the parents. Once the selected population is exhausted, the algorithm continues increasing ***offsringPop*** through successive mutations of clones of randomly selected individuals in ***offsringPop***, until it reaches ***pPoP*** size. One of the three types of mutation described above is randomly applied with uniform probability. This way of completing a population allows a parasite to undergo several mutations in a single generation, because a mutant parasite can be selected and cloned several times.

Population ***offspringPop*** is evaluated through the individuals of population ***hPop***, as explained above, and then becomes the new ***pPop*** replacing the previous one.

```
ParasiteEvolution (pPop, hPop, k)
  selectPop = select k parasites from pPop
  offspringPop = recombine selectPop
  while offspringPop.size < pPop.size
       Select random parasite from offspringPop
       Mutate a clone of parasite
       Insert mutated clone in offspringPop
  End while
  Evaluate offspringPop in hPop
  pPop = offspringPop
End Function.
```

Algorithm 3 - Parasite Evolution Algorithm

4.2 Parasite diversity

Success of SMuGA is much dependent on the quality of parasites. Previous results [5] showed that deceptive multimodal functions were difficult to optimize, the main reason being attributed to the low genetic diversity of the parasite population. Parasites tend to concentrate on local maxima, and the fact that the function is deceptive, prevents them from reaching new regions of the search space. Moreover, they tend to grow in length, successively propagating the local maxima solutions and further preventing escape and the possibility of reaching the optimum. We notice that parasite population diversity quickly tends to low values.

To circumvent this difficulty, the current version of SMuGA uses a set of metrics to assess the coverage of the genome space. These metrics are then used to help genetic operators producing and maintaining a diversified parasite population along evolution.

4.2.1 Diversity in changing anchoring position

The inoccupation rate of each host gene is computed dividing the number of empty slots that gene has in the parasite population by the total number of empty slots in that population (**Fig. 7**).

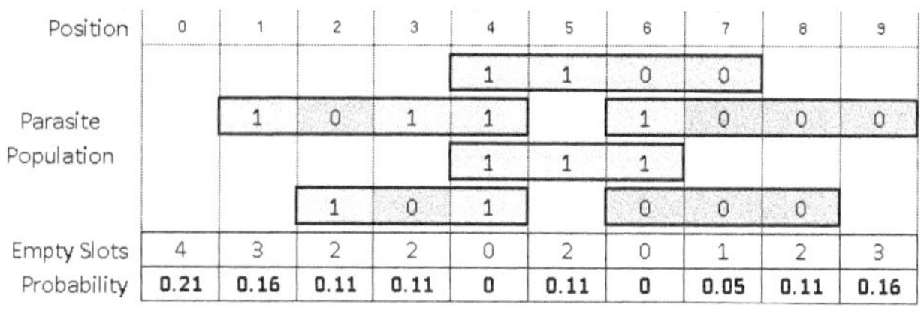

Fig. 7. Diversity of locus occupation by parasites.

This information is used in the *"change anchoring position"* variant of the mutation operator, to draw probabilities of starting a parasite in a given gene position. Therefore the mutation of parasite positions tends to move parasites to less occupied regions of the parasite space.

4.2.2 Diversity in gene mutation

Another metric that is computed over the parasite population is the diversity of alleles in each host locus. To that effect we compute the ratios of 0 and 1 alleles over the total number of parasites (**Fig. 8**). We then use these ratios to modulate the bit mutation probability of each gene according their value (**Fig. 8** prob. of bit "0" and **Fig. 8** prob. of bit "1"). The higher the ratio the higher the probability to mutate the allele by flipping the bit value.

With this modified mutation, whenever an allele probability is low, mutation will tend to reestablish the balance of alleles in that gene over the parasite population.

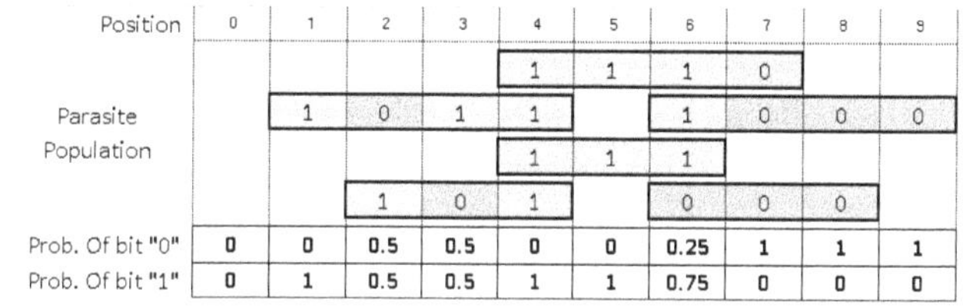

Fig. 8. Probability of parasite alleles in each locus.

4.2.3 Diversity in parasite evaluation

In order to further avoid parasites to concentrate on small regions, we also modify their fitness taking into account diversity. In this case first we define a parasite's diversity as the average diversity of all its alleles, with allele diversity defined as the complement of the allele ratio as described in the previous section.

For each parasite, its diversity value is used to scale the fitness evaluation described above. The end result is that the fitness of parasites crowding some region of the search space will be demoted by comparison to isolated parasites.

5. EXPERIMENTAL RESULTS

To evaluate the influence of the improvements in solving hard problems we conducted a set of experiments with the new version of SMuGA algorithm and compared the results with the previous version and with the state of the art. In order to assess the scalability capabilities, we applied the algorithm to big deceptive problems.

5.1 Experimental Setup

SMuGA is configured with 64 Multi-individuals (MI) in the host population and 128 MI in the parasite Populations. The number of iterations of the evolution phase in Algorithm 1 is set to 32.

The size of the population of parasites is higher than that of the host because they represent only partial solutions and are subjected to a more aggressive evolutionary dynamics. The combination of stable solutions produced by the evolutionary process of the hosts with greater dynamics of parasites produces positive effects on the symbiogenetic process.

The evolution of hosts uses tournament selection with tournament size 3 and selects 64 individuals. Recombination is done by uniform crossover with probability 0.6 and mutation, replacement and rescaling are performed by the operator Multiset Wave Mutation (MWM) [4] with roughness set to 2 and thinness set to

3. Replacement is done by Multiset Decimation Replacement (MDR) [4] with tournaments of size 2. We use the Adaptive Decimation operator with population factor set to 2 to control the number of copies of the MI.

The evolution of parasites uses Algorithm 1 and the number of selected parasites to reproduction (**k**) is set to 64. The parameter **s** of equation (1) is set to 24 and the **t** parameter is set to -6. These parameters were chosen in order to produce probability values greater than zero and do not allow the parasites to become too large. The resulting probability distribution of breaking genomes is shown in red line of **Fig. 6**. All the parameters values of SMuGA are tuned by preliminary experimental results.

To obtain statistical confidence we performed 32 independent runs for each experiment. In each run, random initial populations were generated for hosts and parasites. For each experiment we compute the average number of evaluations to find the optimum. We also compute what we consider a more revealing result, which is the success rate, meaning the percentage of runs that reach the optimum.

The three fitness functions used are described next. They are all deceptive, multimodal and are formed by a set of concatenated patterns with non-trivial bit configurations.

5.1.1 Trap pattern function

The key to the success of Evolutionary Algorithms (EA) is their combination of low-order building blocks (BB) to form higher-order BB, which eventually leads to the optimum. When the solution cannot be built through this incremental combination of BB, we are in the presence of deceptive problems and we need to improve the artificial evolutionary process in order to solve those problems. The concept of deceptive functions was first introduced by Goldberg [13].

Binary deceptive functions, also referred to as trap functions, are defined in the unitation space. In this space, only the number of ones in the genome counts, regardless of the order. Equation 2 presents the formula of a trap function where **x** is the number of ones in the chromosome and **l** represents the length of chromosome. **Fig. 9** presents a trap function with eight bits in the unitation space.

$$trap(x) = \begin{cases} l - x - 1 & if\ x < l \\ l & if\ x = l \end{cases} \qquad (2)$$

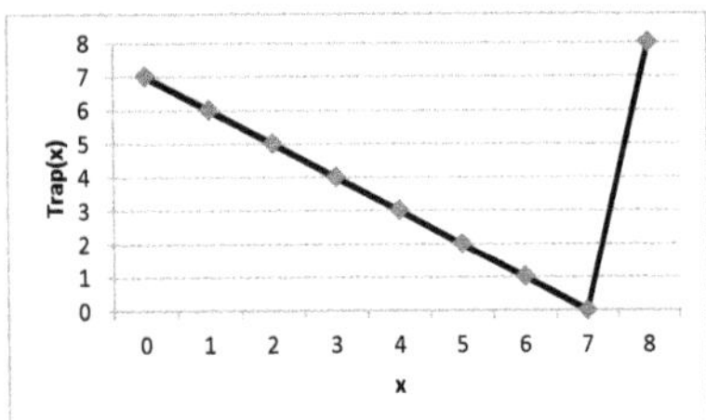

Fig. 9. Trap function with 8 bits

In the results presented in [4] SMuGA showed to be able to find BBs in the chromosome and to translocate them to other positions, by action of parasites. When base MuGA algorithm working on the hosts finds BBs, parasites tend to mimic them (due to the parasite evaluation function) and them being translocated replicate the BBs in other regions of the chromosome.

The trap function (2) has the optimum with the bits all 1s. This results in a particularly favorable situation to SMuGA, producing artificially good results. In fact, patterns of all 1s tend to be very useful in parasites. In order to convert the function into one that is not specially tailored to SMuGA, we replace the unitation function by another that computes de Hamming distance between the chromosome and a given bit pattern. Trap pattern function uses the pattern "01001101" to that effect.

5.1.2 Intertwined Trap function

The Pair-Intertwined function, Trap01, proposed by Wallin et al. [2] is defined as two deceptive functions where the bits are intertwined in the same function. The Trap01 function was many local optima introduced by the combination of the pair of deceptive functions. In this experiment, we use as building block two deceptive functions of four bits each, composing a deceptive intertwine function with eight bits. One function is evaluated by equation (2) using the number of ones and the other is evaluated by its binary dual using the number of zeros. **Fig. 10** presents the values of the two intertwined functions.

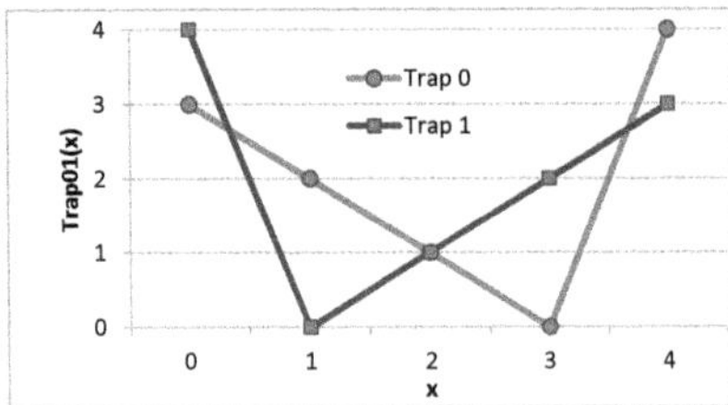

Fig. 10. Intertwined Trap functions

5.1.3 Massivevely Multimodal Deceptive Problem

Massively Multimodal Deceptive Problem (MMDP), introduced by [14], is a bipolar function with two optima and a deceptive attractor in the middle of the unitation space. Placing the deceptive attractor in that place implies that there are massively more local optima in the genotype space (any four bit pattern is a local optimum). **Fig. 11** presents the MMDP function with eight bits.

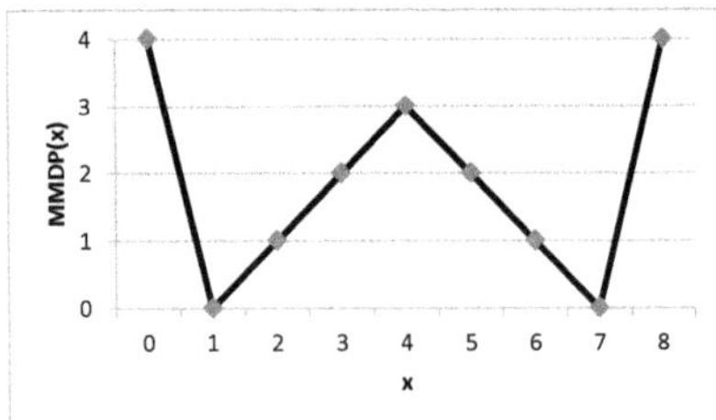

Fig. 11. Massively Multimodal Deceptive Problem with 8 bits

5.2 Experimental Results

We experiment these functions with different chromosome lengths. For each function we use 8, 16, 32, 64, and 128 concatenated blocks, which results in chromosomes of 64, 128, 256, 512, and 1024 bits.

Table 1 shows the average and standard deviation of the number of necessary evaluations to find the optimum. Table 2 shows the success rate of the 32 simulations made for each function. The three pictures that follow (**Fig. 12**, **Fig. 13**, and **Fig. 14**) somehow condense this information. They show the progression of the success rate after launching 32 runs in parallel. We can observe the point (number of evaluations) where a given success was attained.

Table 1. Number of evaluations to reach the optimum

Chromossome length (bits)	Trap pattern		Trap01		MMDP	
	Mean	Std	Mean	Std	Mean	Std
64	5,125.38	3,199.28	18,894.75	8,592.47	24,533.69	15,983.06
128	11,199.84	4,241.10	28,027.75	14,818.14	66,049.19	33,877.22
256	27,353.88	7,118.75	56,726.10	20,140.50	242,783.31	104,416.92
512	70,989.09	18,760.75	114,742.30	53,445.19	657,490.13	217,403.41
1024	130,180.94	23,790.68	213,681.50	60,069.77	1,577,875.25	427,051.77

Table 2. Success rate

Chromossome length (bits)	Trap pattern		Trap01		MMDP	
	Mean	Std	Mean	Std	Mean	Std
64	1.00	0.00	1.00	0.00	1.00	0.00
128	1.00	0.00	1.00	0.00	1.00	0.00
256	1.00	0.00	1.00	0.00	1.00	0.00
512	1.00	0.00	1.00	0.00	1.00	0.00
1024	1.00	0.00	1.00	0.00	0.97	0.18

Notice that only in MMDP with 128 blocks of 8 bits SMuGA is not able to attain a success rate of 100% within the maximum number of evaluations that we defined as 2.5M (**Fig. 14**). In this case, the corresponding entry in Table 1 is computed over the successful runs. By inspecting the yellow curve of **Fig. 14** we observe that SMuGA revealed no signal of stagnation and we may speculate that with more evaluations it would soon attain 100% success rate also in this difficult problem configuration.

The TrapPattern function was optimized seamlessly and the results are comparable with the previous version for similar problems [5]. A different picture appears in the Intertwined trap function where results have much improved, nearly one order of magnitude.

In the MMDP function results are comparable with the most recent known ones [15]. Notice that for this comparison we are interpolating, since Laredo et al. [15] have used blocks of 6 bits. However we have shown that SMuGA optimizes 31/32 runs of MMDP with 1024 bits while the aforementioned work maximum length optimized is with 768 bit chromosome.

Comparing SMuGA results, Table 1, and the results produced by the ASF procedure proposed by M. J. Streeter [16], SMuGA only wins in the TrapPattern function. ASF procedure is strongly dependent of the size of deceptive pattern, and uses brute force to discover the bit pattern. The brute force of pattern discovery uses an exponential number of function evaluations. MMDP and Trap01 functions have two deceptive patterns with 4 bits each and TrapPattern function has deceptive patterns with 8 bits. The length of deceptive pattern in TrapPattern function explains the difficulty of ASF procedure to solve that function.

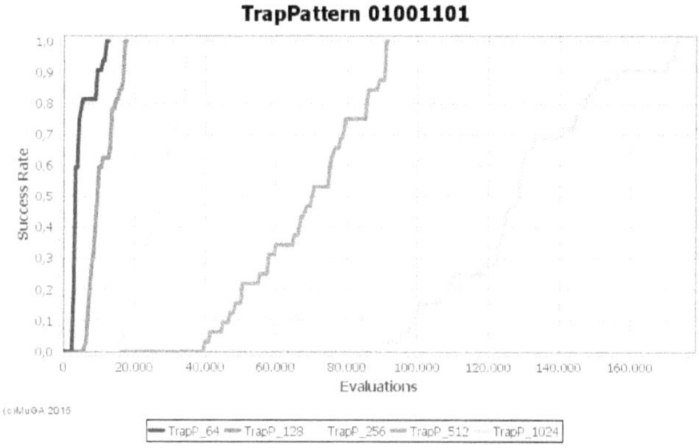

Fig. 12. TrapPattern function with 8 bit blocks – evolution of the success rate of 32 parallel runs

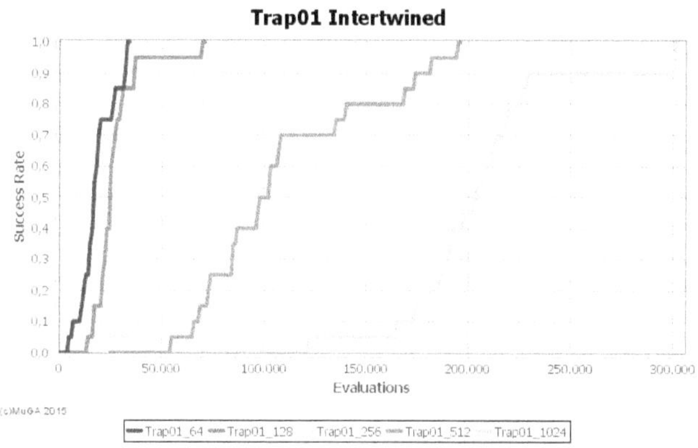

Fig. 13. Intertwined Trap function with 8 bit blocks – evolution of the success rate of 32 parallel runs

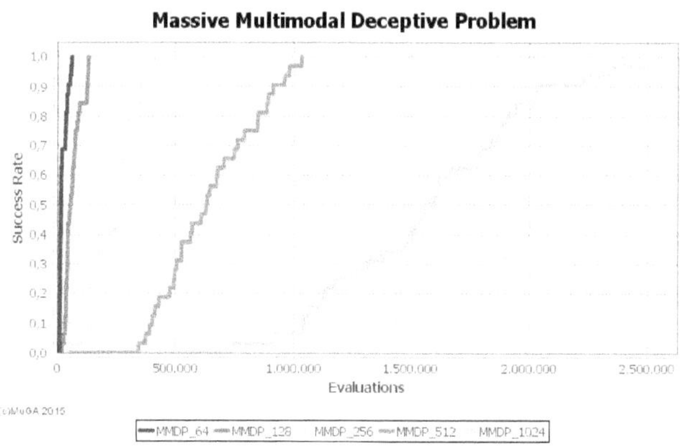

Fig. 14. Massive Multimodal Deceptive Problem with 8 bit blocks – evolution of the success rate of 32 parallel runs

6. CONCLUSIONS

The results show that the improved SMuGA is able to handle very large deceptive optimization problems with competitive results better, or at least matching the state of the art. The significant improvement of this version can be attributed to the diversity modulation used in parasite mutation and evaluation.

The improved version of SMuGA showed being able to escape local optima in fitness landscapes crowded with them, in very large problems. This is especially evident in the MMDP function. Such capability can be attributed to the diversity modulation introduced in the evolution of the parasite population. In this way regions of the search space with low concentration of parasites are preferred by newly formed ones, promoting a homogeneous space occupation.

Hosts explore the search space as usual in an evolutionary algorithm, although the underlying multiset population provided by MuGA is a significant advantage. Complementarily, parasites perform a much more dynamical exploration of the space, guided by a diversity homogenization evolutionary process. This combination of a stable and dynamic exploration is possible by using symbiogenesis and has high robustness by exploiting diversity informed search in the more dynamic component, the parasites.

A current limitation of SMuGA is the optimization of shuffled bit functions. In these problems small building blocks are not too useful in general. Future work will concentrate on balancing short and long parasites so that long distance linkages between genes can be solved by SMuGA, which we expect to produce efficacy in shuffled functions.

7. ACKNOWLEDGMENTS

The authors thank Rob Mills and Guida Manso for the precious revisions that made this text more clear and readable. This work was partially supported by centre grant of BioISI, Centre Reference: UID/MULTI/04046/2013, from FCT/MCTES/PIDDAC, Portugal.

8. REFERENCES

[1] M. I. Heywood and P. Lichodzijewski, Symbiogenesis as a Mechanism for Building Complex Adaptive Systems: A Review, in *Applications of Evolutionary Computation*, C. D. Chio, S. Cagnoni, C. Cotta, M. Ebner, A. Ekárt, A. I. Esparcia-Alcazar, C.-K. Goh, J. J. Merelo, F. Neri, M. Preuß, J. Togelius, e G. N. Yannakakis, Eds. Springer Berlin Heidelberg, pp. 51–60, 2010.

[2] D. Wallin, C. Ryan, and R. M. A. Azad, Symbiogenetic coevolution, in *Proceedings of the 2005 IEEE Congress on Evolutionary Computation, 2005*, vol. 2, pp. 1613–1620, 2005.

[3] J.L. Hickman, A note on the concept of multiset, *Bulletin of the Australian Mathematical Society* (22), pp. 211-217, 1980.

[4] A. M. R. Manso and L. M. P. Correia, A multiset genetic algorithm for the optimization of deceptive problems, in *Proceeding of the fifteenth annual conference on Genetic and evolutionary computation conference*, New York, NY, USA, pp. 813–820, 2013.

[5] L. M. P. Correia and A. M. R. Manso, A multiset model of multi-species evolution to solve big deceptive problems, in *eprint arXiv:1502.00839v1* [cs.NE], 2015.

[6] D. B. Fogel and Nils Barricelli, Artificial life, coevolution, self-adaptation, in *IEEE Computational Intelligence Magazine*, pp. 41–45, 2006.

[7] T. Ikegami and K. Kaneko, Computer symbiosis - emergence of symbiotic behavior through evolution, in *Physica D: Nonlinear Phenomena*, 42(1), pp. 235-243, 1990.

[8] R. Dumeur, Evolution through cooperation: The symbiotic algorithm, *in Proceedings of the International Conference on Artificial Evolution*, pp 145–158. Springer, 1995.

[9] D. E. Moriarty and R. Miikkulainen, Efficient reinforcement learning through symbiotic evolution, *Machine learning*, 22.1-3 (1996): 11-32.

[10] R. A. Watson and J. B. Pollack, How symbiosis can guide evolution, in *European Conference on Artificial Life*, pages 29–38, Springer, 1999.

[11] R. Mills and R. A. Watson, Symbiosis, synergy and modularity: Introducing the reciprocal synergy symbiosis algorithm, in *Proceedings of the European Conference on Artificial Life*, pages 1191–1201, Springer, 2007.

[12] A. M. R. Manso and L. M. P. Correia, MuGA: multiset genetic algorithm, in *Proceedings of the 13th annual conference companion on Genetic and evolutionary computation, GECCO '11*, pages 791–794, New York, NY, USA, 2011. ACM

[13] D.E Goldberg, Simple Genetic Algorithms and the Minimal, Deceptive Problem. Genet. Algorithms Simulated Annealing, L. Davis, editor, San Mateo, CA: Morgan Kaufmann, 74–88, 1987.

[14] D.E. Goldberg, K. Deb, and J. Horn Massive Multimodality, Deception, and Genetic Algorithms, in *Parallel Problem Solving from Nature* – PPSN II, Elsevier, Brussels, Belgium, pp. 37–48, 1992.

[15] J. Laredo, A. Eiben, M. Steen, P. Castillo, A. Mora, J. Merelo, P2P evolutionary algorithms: a suitable approach for tackling large instances in hard optimization problems, in *Proceedings of the 14th International EuroPar Conference on Parallel Processing, Euro-Par '08*, Springer-Verlag, Berlin, Heidelberg, pp. 622–631, 2008.

[16] M. J. Streeter, Upper bounds on the time and space complexity of optimizing additively separable functions, In *Genetic and Evolutionary Computation - GECCO2004 Part 2*, Lecture Notes in Computer Science 3103, pp. 186–197. Springer-Verlag, 2004.

An Empirical Analysis on Dimensionality in Cellular Genetic Algorithms

Alicia Morales-Reyes, Hugo Jair Escalante, Martin Letras, Rene Cumplido
Instituto Nacional de Astrofisica, Optica y Electronica
Luis Enrique Erro No. 1
Tonantzintla, Puebla, Mexico
[a.morales, hugojair, mletras, rcumplido]@inaoep.mx

ABSTRACT

Cellular or fine grained Genetic Algorithms (GAs) are a massively parallel algorithmic approach to GAs. Decentralizing their population allows alternative ways to explore and to exploit the solutions landscape. Individuals interact locally through nearby neighbours while the entire population is globally exploring the search space throughout a predefined population's topology. Having a decentralized population requires the definition of other algorithmic configuration parameters; such as shape and number of individuals within the local neighbourhood, population's topology shape and dimension, local instead of global selection criteria, among others. In this article, attention is paid to the population's topology dimension in cGAs. Several benchmark problems are assessed for 1, 2, and 3 dimensions while combining a local selection criterion that significantly affect overall selective pressure. On the other hand, currently available high performance processing platforms such as Field Programmable Gate Arrays (FPGAs) and Graphics Processing Units (GPUs) offer massively parallel fabrics. Therefore, having a strong empirical base to understand structural properties in cellular GAs would allow to combine physical properties of these platforms when designing hardware architectures to tackle difficult optimization problems where timing constraints are mandatory.

General Terms

Cellular Genetic Algorithms, Topology's Dimension, Selective Pressure.

1. INTRODUCTION

A general taxonomy for parallel Genetic Algorithms (PGAs) classifies them in coarse or distributed and fined or cellular GAs [5]. Dealing with coarse or fine grained populations or sub-populations also helps defining suitable processing platforms. Among the most used massively parallel processing platforms are Field Reconfigurable Gate Arrays (FPGAs) and Graphics Processing Units (GPUs). Both provide processing resources that can be interconnected in such a way that massively parallel algorithmic techniques could replicate their internal processing structure. In this regard, fine grained or cellular GAs (cGAs) are particularly appropriate to adapt to these fabrics while taking advantage of their implicit massive parallelism when the population is decentralized. Moreover, additional structural characteristics in cellular GAs affect the searching process and in particular these parameters can directly modify the induced selective pressure [2, 7]. This article presents an empirical analysis of a specific structural characteristic in cellular GAs, the topology's dimension. It includes an extended experimental benchmarking and an initial overview of the implication of changing dimension on the fly during the search.

This study is carried out at an algorithmic level with the purpose of leaving a strong empirical base to exploit structural characteristics in cGAs when designing hardware architectures using FPGAs or parallel programming models when using GPUs as processing platforms. Several authors have proposed different approaches to design hardware architectures to implement GAs in order to accelerate their searching process. Most of these proposals are based on centralized or panmictic GAs.

In [9] a GA based hardware architecture is proposed with variable configuration parameters for population size and selection criteria, it also offers interchangeable objective function module. Connecting several FPGA devices is optional in case computing resources are not enough. This architectural design does not exploit implicit parallelism in GAs. Zhu et. al. proposed an architecture that only evolves one individual at a time reducing memory storage; although resources usage is significantly reduced, also GAs searching capabilities are affected [20]. In [6], a centralized GA based IP core (Intellectual Property core) module is proposed. Having an independent module implementing a GA allows its integration within embedded systems that requires an optimization module for specific problem domains. Having problem independent GA based optimization engines is investigated in [15], where authors proposed to use Neural Networks (NN) as fitness function evaluators, every time a different problem is tackled the design needs to be resynthesized. On the other hand, several studies have been made targeting cellular GAs in order to take advantage of their implicit parallelism at an algorithmic level from an architectural perspective. Dos Santos et. al. proposed a toroidal array of Processor Elements (PEs) which deal with small sub-populations each; however, toroidal connection is

GECCO'15, July 11-15, 2015, Madrid, Spain.

DOI: http://dx.doi.org/10.1145/2739480.2754699 .

lost among individuals and therefore the canonical algorithmic structure of a cellular GA is significantly modified [8, 19].

Cellular GAs are massively parallel GAs which ideally can evolve one generation in few clock cycles. Normally, they imply simpler PEs which deal with one individual each. Having decentralized populations requires defining a structure to allocate individuals and from a structural perspective to limit the interaction of individuals. Therefore, structural characteristics like topology's shape and size, neighbourhood's shape and size and topology's dimension are defined. These structural properties not only affect the processing structure of the search but also the search itself. Several authors have studied structural properties in cGAs [2]. In [3], a study on the relationship between topology and neighbourhood in cGAs is carried out. Authors show the influence of these structural parameters in the searching process, specifically in the applied selective pressure. Alba et. al. also proposed to dynamically change the population's shape in order to affect the selective pressure, algorithmic performance metrics were improved [1].

Comparing the effect of local selection versus topology modification as well as studying the internal dynamic change of the topology configuration has been approached [13, 12]. Both studies show how effective is to modify structural configuration in cGAs in order to improve their performance. A double structural level criterion to affect the search locally and globally is presented [14]. Although adaptive criteria to modify structural parameters are proposed, their computational cost is high and applying constant changes result in very similar performances. Previously, an initial study on dimension was presented in [11]; however, few test problems were evaluated and therefore the empirical assessment was limited. In this article, authors continue studying cGAs structural properties, specifically dimension, in order to improve their algorithmic performance and to have a robust experimental base over a widen benchmark.

This article is organized as follows, in Section 2 cGAs structural properties are described as well as their effect in the searching process. Section 3 presents this study's experimental framework as well as algorithmic performance metrics and applied statistical tests. In Section 4, results obtained over several difficult optimization problems are presented and analysed. Finally, Section 5 draws conclusions and future research directions.

2. ALGORITHMIC STRUCTURE

Cellular GAs are massively parallel GAs with decentralized populations that are normally placed on a toroidal grid-like structure where each crossing point holds an individual or solution. Having a structure requires defining other parameters, such as the shape and size of the population's topology and the local neighbourhood, as well as their dimension. This study focuses on the effect topology's dimension has over the searching process. In Figure 1, cGAs topologies for 1, 2, and 3 dimensions are shown. Local neighbourhoods are also visible in every configuration, these are composed by individuals located to East and West in 1-D arrays; to North, East, South and West of every individual in a 2-D array and in a 3-D grid, individuals at front and back of the central one are also within the local neighbourhood.

In Algorithm 1, steps for a canonical cGAs on a 2-D topology are described. A population is randomly initialized considering one individual per crossing point. According to the targeted problem the fitness function is evaluated for every individual. Evolution starts for all individuals with a selection process. Common selection methods are tournament and roulette-wheel which are also normally applied in cGAs. However, other selection techniques have been proposed specifically for cGAs; in this study a method called anisotropic selection is applied [16, 17]. Current individuals are assumed as one of the parents, and a second one is selected from the neighbourhood. Once both parents are selected, genetic operators are applied, recombination followed by mutation. These operators are defined according to individuals representation. In this study single point crossover is applied with probability equals to 1.0 and mutation is applied with probability $\frac{1}{n}$ where n is the chromosomes length which varies according to each benchmark problem.

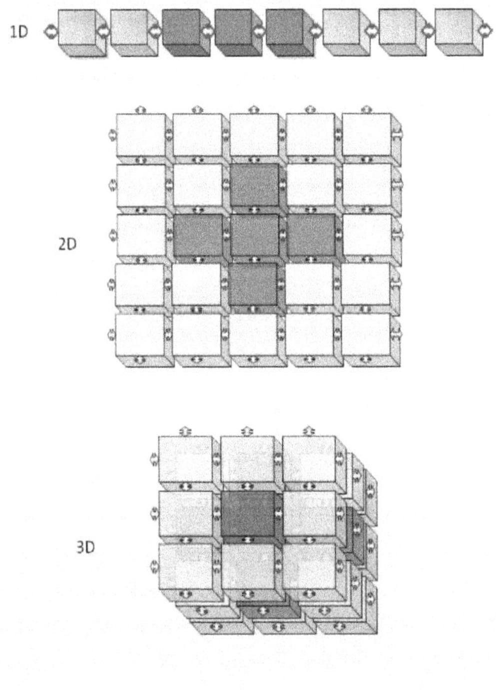

Figure 1: Different dimensions arrays in cGAs

Because cGAs carry out exploitation locally and exploration globally throughout population's topology; replacement or updating criterion normally exchange central individuals only if one of the evolved children is better or more fitted than its parent. Neighbourhoods are overlapped, thus updating criterion can be synchronous or asynchronous; in this study synchronous updating is always applied. One generation corresponds to an execution of this operations set. A number of generations is executed until the stop condition is fulfilled either after a certain number of generations or evaluations (number of fitness function evaluations) or when an error threshold is reached.

2.1 Local selection

Anisotropic selection consist in applying different selection probabilities to individuals within the local neighbour-

Algorithm 1 Canonical cGA

```
procedure GA
    random(x)                                   ▷ Initialize population
    f = calulateFit(x)                          ▷ Calculate individuals fitness
    for i ← 1, generations do
        for j ← 1, population do
            x_0, f_0                            ▷ Current individual
            (x_n, x_e, x_s, x_w) ← getNeigh(x_0)
            (f_n, f_e, f_s, f_w) ← getFit(x_n, x_e, x_s, x_w)
            (x') ← localSel(x_n, x_e, x_s, x_w)
            (x_1, x_2) ← recombine(x_0, x')
            (x'_1, x'_2) ← mutate(x_1, x_2)
            (f'_1, f'_2) ← calculateFit(x'_1, x'_2)
            (f'_0) ← selBest(f_0, f'_1, f'_2)
            (x_temp(i, j), f_temp(i, j)) ←
                    replace(x'_0, f'_0, [ifBetter])
        end for
        x = x_temp, f = f_temp                  ▷ Synchronous updating
        if f̄ <= threshold then
            stop
        else
            next
        end if
    end for
end procedure
```

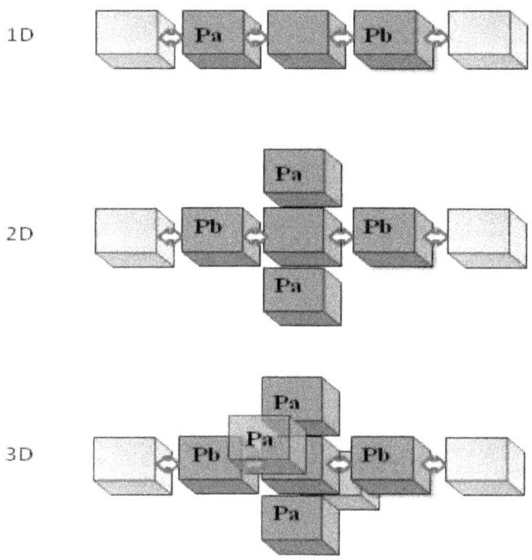

Figure 2: Local anisotropic selection

hood according to their position. Figure 2 shows population topologies for 1, 2, and 3 dimensions. For example, in a 2-D topology, higher probabilities could be assigned to individuals located to the North and the South and lower ones to the East and the West of the central individual. Similarly, in a 3-D grid, neighbours located at North, South and front of the central individual could have higher or lower probability for selection, opposite to individuals located at East, West and back of the current individual. In a 1-D array, neighbours are located to left and right of the central individual, thus probabilities can be higher or lower depending on their direction. In all cases larger Manhattan distances from central individuals can be implemented affecting selective pressure accordingly. In anisotropic selection, an α parameter is required in order to assign selection probabilities for individuals within the neighbourhood. For example, in a 2-D array, selection probability for individuals located at North and South of central one is $P_{NS} = (1 + \alpha) \times P_{uni}$, where P_{uni} is the uniform probability for all neighbours; and $P_{EW} = (1+\alpha) \times P_{uni}$ is the selection probability for individuals located at East and West positions of central individual. Similar equations are applied to 1 and 3 dimensions while modifying uniform probability accordingly.

A concept known as take over times allows to draw applied selective pressure on specific topologies when applying a local selection method. Take over time refers to the number of generations the fittest individual of an initial population needs to conquer all positions within the grid. Figure 3 shows take over times for 1, 2, and 3 dimensions considering local neighbourhoods configurations in Figure 2. Curves in Figure 3 are calculated over a 100 experimental samples per case with very similar population size distributed on different dimensional grids. Weaker selective pressure is applied through a 1-D array while strongest selective pressure is applied on a 3-D grid. A 2-D array's selective pressure is in the middle of both cases. For $\alpha = 0.1$ (strong selective pressure), it takes approximately 210, 25 and 15 generations in a 1, 2, and 3 dimension array respectively for the best individual of an initial population to conquer the grid. In contrast, for $\alpha = 0.9$ (weaker selective pressure), it takes approximately 325, 60 and 25 generations in a 1, 2, and 3 dimension array to conquer the grid. These ranges in terms of number of generations show how exploitative or explorative a cGA would be from a structural perspective. This study focuses on dimension both of topologies and of neighbourhoods. Anisotropic selection implies structural properties when defining internal selection probabilities by individuals' location within neighbourhoods. Assessing a combination of both structures would provide a better understanding of the internal working in a cGA.

2.2 Constant dimensional change

In this study, an empirical comparison among dimensions and their effect in the algorithmic performance of cGAs is carried out. Moreover, an additional empirical set-up is also included. It consists in applying a constant change among 1, 2, and 3 dimensions. A constant population size is used and solutions are re-allocated when dimension is changed. All experimental samples start evolving on a 1-D array and after a certain number of generations, individuals are re-arranged following a 2-D square array; after another number of generations, solutions are mapped to a 3-D cubical array closing a cycle of constant dimension change. Different sizes of generations blocks are assessed. A short block of 15 generations, a medium block of 30 generations and a large block of 60 generations for most problems are specified. For the Minimum Tardy Task Problem (MTTP) blocks of 5, 10, and 15 generations are defined and for the System of Linear Equations (SLE) problem blocks of 20, 40 and 80 generations are set.

The mechanism to re-allocate individuals within a different grid dimension is straight forward. It consists in taking a number of individuals of a 1-D array and filling every row of a 2-D square grid until all individuals are allocated. Once

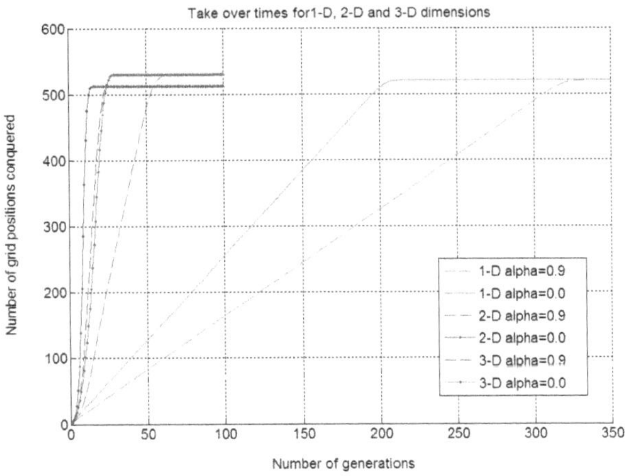

Figure 3: Take over times for 1, 2, and 3 dimensions

in a 2-D square topology, tiles of individuals are moved to a 3-D cubical topology until the whole population is migrated. Considerations about population size are needed, normally few individuals positions remain available when dimension is modified and therefore some extra-criterion to generate new or to replicate current individuals is required. In the experimental set-up, population size fits 1, 2, and 3 dimensions in order to avoid new or to replicate previous solutions. The experimental framework is detailed in the the next section.

3. EXPERIMENTAL FRAMEWORK

In order to assess the effect dimension has in cGAs algorithmic performance several test problems have been tackled. Experimental constraints are provided in this section as well as results validation using statistical tests.

3.1 Benchmark problems

Several optimization problems considered difficult for GAs have been tackled. In total, nine problems from combinatorial and continuous domains are evaluated. Continuous domain problems (Rastrigin, Langerman, Griewank and a System of Linear Equations) have been discretized. Authors acknowledge GAs' drawbacks when dealing with continuous problems in their discrete domain. However one of the aims in this study is to assess GAs' ability to solve difficult optimization problems when binary representation of solutions is used; this kind of representation would be mostly used when designing hardware architectures in order to avoid using specialized processing units within the device. On the other hand, a group of five combinatorial problems are also tackled: Error Code Correction design problem (ECC) problem, Frequency Modulation Sound (FMS) problem, Massively Multi-modal Deceptive Problem (MMDP), Minimum Tardy Task Problem (MTTP) and P-Peaks problem. Objective functions of these problems are presented in Table 1 as well as significant configuration details are included for each problem, if more details are needed, readers are referred to provided references.

3.2 Experimental constraints

The following experimental contrainst are common to all cGAs configurations for their empirical assessment.

- Solutions representation: binary
- Population size: 729 individuals
- Topology shape: square
- Topology dimension: 1-D, 2-D, 3-D
- Selection: anisotropic, $\alpha = 0.1||0.9$
- Recombination: single point, $P_c = 1.0$
- Mutation: bit flip, $P_m = \frac{1}{n}$ where n is chromosome's length
- Local replacement (within neigbhourhoods): only if better
- Global replacement (whole grid): synchronous
- Convergence condition: error threshold or maximum of 1500 generations (2000 generations for SLE)

Individuals are represented as binary strings in both continuous and combinatorial problems. A population size of 729 individuals is implemented. This number of individuals allow for having a 1-D array of 729 solutions, a 2-D square array of 27×27 and a 3-D square array of 9×9×9. Anisotropic selection (see Subsection 2.1) is configured for border values where $\alpha = 0.1$ implies strong exploitation and $\alpha = 0.9$ means promoting exploration of solutions. Genetic operations, recombination and mutation, are single point and bit flip with specific probabilities to affect solutions. Recombination is always carried out with probability ($P_c = 1.0$). Because of cGAs massive parallelism, solutions replacement require local and global criteria. Locally, current individuals are replaced only if any of their offspring is a better solution. Globally synchronous replacement is implemented, this means that individuals in one generation evolve into the next generation.

Algorithmic performance is measured in terms of efficiency and efficacy. Efficiency consists of the number of generations cGAs require to converge to a problem's solution together with the solutions quality which in this case is given by specific problems' error threshold. On the other hand, efficacy is given by the number of success experimental samples out of the total number of experiments carried out. A total of 100 experimental samples per case per problem are performed.

3.3 Statistical analysis

Results are statistically supported by an initial normality test performed on each set of experimental results regarding the convergence time. First, normality is determined by the Kolmorov-Smirnov test or the lilliefors test, both at 5% of significance. Lilliefors test is suitable when a fully-specified null distribution is unknown, contrary to the Kolmorov-Smirnov test. Once the normality of results has been established, an Analysis of Variance (ANOVA) is applied to results with normal distribution whereas Kruskal-Wallis is applied in any other case. In the next section, experimental results and their analysis are drawn.

A total of 100 experimental samples per algorithmic case per problem are carried out. In order to assess algorithmic efficacy for statistical significance, every experiment is considered as a Bernoulli trial which output is to converge or not to a problem's solution according to a stopping condition

Table 1: Benchmark problems

Problem	Fitness function	Properties
Rastrigin fn. [4]	$f(\vec{x}) = 10q + \sum_{i=1}^{q} \left(x^2 - cos\left(2\pi x_i\right)\right)$	$q = 15$, $f_T \leq 0.0005$, multi-modal, non epistatic, regular
Griewank fn. [4]	$f(\vec{x}) = 1 + \sum_{i=1}^{q} \frac{x_i^2}{4000} - \prod cos\left(\frac{x_i}{\sqrt{i}}\right)$	$q = 15$, $f_T \leq 0.0001$ Multi-modal, epistatic, regular
Langerman fn. [4]	$f(\vec{x}) = -\sum_{i=1}^{q} c_i e^{-\frac{1}{\pi}\sum_{j=1}^{D}\left(x_j - a_{ij}^2\right)} cos\left(\pi \sum_{j=1}^{D}\left(x_j - a_{ij}\right)^2\right)$	$q = 15$, $f_T \geq -1.4990$ Multi-modal, epistatic, non-regular
FMS [2]	$f(t) = a_1 \cdot sin(w_1 \cdot t \cdot \theta + a_2 \cdot sin\left(w_2 \cdot t \cdot \theta + a_3 \cdot sin\left(w_3 \cdot t \cdot \theta\right)\right))$	$q = 6$, $f_T \leq 0.0005$ Multi-modal, epistatic, non-regular
SLE[2]	$Ax = b$	$q = 10$, $f_T \leq 0.04$ Epistatic
ECC[2]	$f(n, M, d) = \frac{1}{\sum_{i=1}^{M} \sum_{j=1, i \neq j}^{M} \frac{1}{d_{ij}^2}}$	$M = 24, n = 12$, $f_T \leq 0.0674$ Multi-modal, epistatic, non-regular
MMDP[2]	$f_{MDDP}(q) = \sum_{i=1}^{k} fitness_{q_i}$	$q = 25$, k sub-problems, $f_T \geq 0.99$ Multi-modal, combinatorial
MTTP[10, 2]	$f_{MTTP}(\vec{x}) = \sum_{i=1}^{q} weight_{x_i}$	$q = 100$, $f_T \leq 0.0051$ NP-combinatorial, epistatic
P-Peaks Problem [2]	$f_{P-Peaks}(\vec{x}) = \frac{1}{Q} max_{i=1}^{P}\left(Q - Hamming\left(\vec{x}, P_i\right)\right)$	$P = 100$, $\bar{f}_T = 1.0$, non-manually tunable, multi-modal, non-regular

[18]. In a series of Bernoulli trials, successful experimental samples follow a binomial distribution with a maximum likelihood estimator calculated as the number of successful experiments divided by the total of experimental samples.

4. EXPERIMENTAL RESULTS

The main objective in this study is to compare cGAs algorithmic performances when populations evolve on 1, 2, and 3 topology dimensions. Difficult optimization problems are tackled in both continuous and combinatorial domains. Locally, anisotropic selection is applied (see Subsection 2.1). Two border values for anisotropic selection are assessed: $\alpha = 0.1$ and $\alpha = 0.9$. Having a small α value implies that strong selective pressure is induced locally; while a large α value means selective pressure is weak, therefore exploration is promoted within neighborhoods.

In Tables 2 and 3, efficiency in terms of convergence time (number of generations) and efficacy in terms of percentages of successful experimental samples are drawn. In both tables, implicit selective pressure strength induced by different dimensions in all test problems is clearly observed. A 1-D array promotes exploration and therefore takes a large number of generations to find solutions, in contrast to a 3-D cubical array where strong selective pressure modifies the search and successful experiments converge faster. At a local level through anisotropic selection, induced selective pressure also influences convergence times. However, for discretized continuous problems (Rastrigin, Griewank and Langerman functions, and SLE and FMS problems) a weak selection pressure induced by a 1-D linear array overcomes the locally induced selective pressure either strong or weak ($\alpha = 0.1$ or $\alpha = 0.9$); results do not show significant difference between convergence times and percentages of successful experiments are low. In contrast, for combinatorial problems (ECC, MMDP, MTTP and P-Peaks problems), significant difference is observed when weak or strong local selective pressure is induced.

In terms of efficacy, Table 2 shows statistically higher percentages of successful experiments for Rastrigin, Griewank, SLE and FMS problems when evolving on a 2-D topology with strong induced local selective pressure ($\alpha = 0.1$). In these cases, using a 3-D cubical array negatively affects cGAs algorithmic efficacy. On the other hand, combinatorial problems: ECC, MMDP, MTTP and P-Peaks problems achieve 100% efficacy; in this regard using a 3-D array positively affects convergence times with a significant reduction in the number of generations required to converge. A 3-D array improves both convergence time and efficacy when tackling the Langerman problem; this problem has a difficult landscape not only for its multi-modality and solutions epistasis but also for its non-regular search space. Similar results are achieved when anisotropic local selection induces weak selective pressure ($\alpha = 0.9$), see Table 3. However, efficacy is significantly improved for Rastrigin and Griewank problems when cGAs are evolving on a 2-D square topology; for Langerman, SLE and FMS problems, efficacy percentages are very similar when using a 3-D cubical grid. Combinatorial problems present highest efficacy while lower convergence times are achieved when cGAs run on a 3-D topology. For these problems applying a strong local (anisotropic $\alpha = 0.1$) and global (3-D topology) selective pressure results in shortest convergence times without affecting cGAs efficacy.

Modifying the induced selective pressure by changing structural cGAs properties like topology's shape and dimension adds certain flexibility to their searching capacity. Modifying topology's shape has been studied before by Alba et. al. in [1] with successful results. This study also presents, in

Table 2: Convergence time[1] and hit rate[2] for test problems in 1-D, 2-D and 3-D cGAs, anisotropic $\alpha = 0.1$

Problem	**1-D**	**2-D**	**3-D**	**1-2-3-D** Small gens block	**1-2-3-D** Large gens block	Statistical [3] Test
Rastrigin	1387.6 ± 74.06 27%, 4.43	262.11 ± 25.49 63%, 4.82	**175.15 ± 15.87** 13%, 3.36	**224.73 ± 26.80** **66%**, 4.73	286.76 ± 26.52 25%, 4.33	*(+)*
Griewank	1255.3 ± 146.67 41%, 4.91	318.81 ± 29.64 **76%**, 4.27	**225.68 ± 21.90** 16%, 3.66	**240.30 ± 27.56** 67%, 4.70	293.17 ± 22.89 26%, 4.38	*(+)*
Langerman	$--\pm--$ $--$%,	550.12 ± 224.48 39%, 4.87	336.35 ± 157.20 59%, 4.91	**245.80 ± 59.86** 65%, 4.76	431.90 ± 266.22 **67%**, 4.70	(+)
SLE	$--\pm--$ $--$%,	631.53 ± 161.31 32%, 4.66	**378.76 ± 192.54** 26%, 4.38	**391.00 ± 157.87** 69%, 4.62	516.64 ± 342.55 **75%**, 4.33	*(+)*
FMS	1371.0 ± 77.5 4%, 1.95	296.93 ± 69.15 **95%**, 2.17	**269.13 ± 133.53** 65%, 4.76	**250.10 ± 86.71** 50%, 5.0	364.71 ± 165.33 62%, 4.85	*(+)*
ECC	455.3 ± 88.42 100%, 0.0	207.78 ± 29.41 100%, 0.0	**163.27 ± 29.45** 100%, 0.0	190.44 ± 37.79 100%, 0.0	229.28 ± 44.16 100%, 0.0	(+)
MMDP	519.19 ± 48.45 100%, 0.0	134.77 ± 5.46 100%, 0.0	106.9 ± 23.57 100%, 0.0	**105.86 ± 6.29** 99%, 0.99	144.41 ± 4.73 100%, 0.0	(+)
MTTP	723.93 ± 74.97 100%, 0.0	268.50 ± 19.18 100%, 0.0	**189.5 ± 9.35** 100%, 0.0	**196.23 ± 13.08** 100%, 0.0	239.42 ± 19.54 100%, 0.0	*(+)*
P-Peaks	171.48 ± 4.35 100%, 0.0	116.19 ± 2.96 100%, 0.0	**95.21 ± 2.92** 100%, 0.0	**96.6 ± 3.56** 100%, 0.0	105.48 ± 3.19 100%, 0.0	*(+)*

1 average number of generations and standard deviation are included.
2 standard deviation for the success search rate is included next to the percentage.
3 ANOVA/K-W based statistical difference: *(+)* is proved between 3-D or 1-2-3-D small block and 1-D, 2-D or 1-2-3-D large block / (+) statistical difference is proved between 1-2-3-D small block and 1-D, 2-D, 3-D or 1-2-3-D large block / (•) is not proved.

addition to directly compare cGAs performance on different topology's dimensions, an experimental base to constantly change grid's dimension. Three size blocks of generations are assessed, see Subsection 2.2. In Tables 2 and 3, results for dimension's change every small and large generations block sizes are shown; in terms of efficiency, statistical difference is proved between using a small or a large generations block when changing among 1, 2, and 3 dimensions in most cases except for SLE problem when weak selection pressure is locally applied ($\alpha = 0.9$). Another significant observation from the statistical analysis is that there is no significant difference in efficiency when applying a constant change among dimensions when using a small generations block and evolving on a 3-D topology for strong selective pressure ($\alpha = 0.1$) in most problems. In contrast, when weak selective pressure ($\alpha = 0.9$) is locally induced only three benchmark problems (Rastrigin, FMS and ECC) show this behavior. In general, it is observed that significant statistical difference exist between evolving on a 3-D topology or changing constantly among dimensions considering a small generations block and evolving on a 1-D, 2-D and constantly change among dimensions considering a large generations block.

Promoting locally solutions exploitation ($\alpha = 0.1$) shows in general no significant improvement in efficacy. It is worth mentioned, results for SLE problem where the number of successful experimental samples increases from 26% to 75%; authors acknowledge GAs limitations when tackling this problem but recognize their ability of improvement when taking advantage of cGAs structural properties. Similarly occurs when exploration is promoted locally ($\alpha = 0.9$) not only for SLE but for Langerman problem too, in both cases not only efficacy is significantly improved but also efficiency.

Overall, best efficiency results are concentrated when a 3-D topology or a constant change of dimensions with a small generations block are used. However, best efficacy is not always achieved by these two configuration cases except for combinatorial problems (ECC, MMDP, MTTP and P-Peaks) where 100% efficacy is always achieved. These results widen cGAs empirical base to show how their algorithmic ability is significantly modified and in several cases improved when taking advantage of their structural properties. From an architectural design perspective, demonstrating that in all combinatorial problems, cGAs achieve better convergence times on a 3-D topology and on constantly changing topology dimensions show at an algorithmic level a strong basis to implement cGAs on FPGAs or GPUs while taking advantage of their massively parallel fabrics.

5. CONCLUSIONS

This article presented an empirical study on the effect dimension has in algorithmic cGAs performance when it is

Table 3: **Convergence time[1] and hit rate[2] for test problems in 1-D, 2-D and 3-D cGAs, anisotropic** $\alpha = 0.9$

Problem	1-D	2-D	3-D	1-2-3-D Small gens block	1-2-3-D Large gens block	Statistical [3] Test
Rastrigin	1391.2 ± 93.46 29%, 4.53	471.59 ± 63.45 **83%**, 3.75	$\mathbf{249.87 \pm 17.99}$ 58%, 4.93	$\mathbf{220.45 \pm 24.53}$ 60%, 4.89	288.27 ± 27.42 23%, 4.20	*(+)*
Griewank	1351.8 ± 94.93 8%, 2.71	551.43 ± 80.23 **87%**, 3.36	298.61 ± 38.13 52%, 4.99	$\mathbf{266.23 \pm 28.45}$ 66%, 4.73	295.10 ± 25.47 35%, 4.76	(+)
Langerman	$- - \pm - -$ $- -$ %,	924.85 ± 230.19 35%, 4.76	507.35 ± 182.92 34%, 4.73	$\mathbf{278.12 \pm 85.83}$ **68%**, 4.66	396.82 ± 156.26 54%, 4.98	(+)
SLE	$- - \pm - -$ $- -$ %,	1310.4 ± 316.56 31%, 4.62	1299.5 ± 350.50 30%, 4.58	$\mathbf{455.26 \pm 171.91}$ 62%, 4.85	$\mathbf{573.75 \pm 156.91}$ **64%**, 4.8	**(+)**
FMS	$- - \pm - -$ $- -$ %,	720.93 ± 217.27 **62%**, 4.85	$\mathbf{344.05 \pm 120.74}$ 57%, 4.95	$\mathbf{273.50 \pm 120.56}$ 50%, 5.0	463.28 ± 125.54 **62%**, 4.85	*(+)*
ECC	600.98 ± 101.73 99%, 0.99	323.21 ± 37.90 100%, 0.0	$\mathbf{214.88 \pm 33.16}$ 100%, 0.0	$\mathbf{198.14 \pm 41.04}$ 100%, 0.0	265.25 ± 40.03 100%, 0.0	*(+)*
MMDP	757.87 ± 55.01 100%, 0.0	225.88 ± 14.6 100%, 0.0	126.59 ± 6.68 100%, 0.0	$\mathbf{117.4 \pm 5.9}$ 100%, 0.0	165.16 ± 5.6 100%, 0.0	(+)
MTTP	1040.6 ± 104.49 100%, 0.0	445.03 ± 36.75 100%, 0.0	244.45 ± 18.92 100%, 0.0	$\mathbf{215.32 \pm 14.64}$ 100%, 0.0	287.14 ± 22.39 100%, 0.0	(+)
P-Peaks	205.7 ± 6.23 100%, 0.0	155.51 ± 3.75 100%, 0.0	109.73 ± 2.66 100%, 0.0	$\mathbf{101.05 \pm 2.73}$ 100%, 0.0	117.64 ± 2.96 100%, 0.0	(+)

1 average number of generations and standard deviation are included.
2 standard deviation for the success search rate is included next to the percentage.
3 ANOVA/K-W based statistical difference: *(+)* is proved between 3-D or 1-2-3-D small block and 1-D, 2-D or 1-2-3-D large block / (+) statistical difference is proved between 1-2-3-D small block and 1-D, 2-D, 3-D or 1-2-3-D large block / (+) statistical difference is proved between 1-2-3-D small and large blocks and 1-D, 2-D, 3-D / (•) is not proved.

modified. Structural properties in cGAs directly affects the induced selective pressure at a local level via the selection criterion and at a global level via the topology's dimension.

Several benchmark problems considered difficult for GAs were tackled and results showed better results when a 3-D topology or a constant change among dimensions every certain number of generations (1-2-3-D small generations block) is used. Overall, efficiency when inducing a locally strong selective pressure results in no statistical significant difference between these topologies configuration; behavior that is not repeated when weak selective pressure is applied locally. In terms of efficacy for combinatorial problems highest success search rate is achieved by different topology dimensions and after a constant dimension's change. For continuous domain, efficacy improvement is noticed for two difficult problems (Langerman and SLE) in which efficacy is improved when dimension is constantly changed.

Having a strong experimental base regarding cGAs structural properties and their searching ability makes them a suitable algorithmic optimization technique for acceleration from a processing perspective. Specifically, FPGAs have been targeted as a platform to accelerate GAs but to the best of the Authors knowledge, there is not research reported yet to approach cellular GAs structural properties as an alternative for acceleration. Another platform that offers massive parallelism are GPUs; as a future direction of this research both platforms will be targeted as processing platforms.

6. REFERENCES

[1] E. Alba and B. Dorronsoro. The exploration/exploitation tradeoff in dynamic cellular genetic algorithms. In *IEEE Transactions on Evolutionary Computation*. IEEE, 2005.

[2] E. Alba and B. Dorronsoro. Cellular genetic algorithms. In *Operations Research / Computer Science Interfaces*. Springer, 2008.

[3] E. Alba and J. Troya. Cellular evolutionary algorithms: Evaluating the influence of ratio. In *Proceeding of the 6th International Conference on Parallel Problem Solving from Nature*, pages 29–38. LNCS Springer, 2000.

[4] T. Bäck. *Evolutionary Algorithms in Theory and Practice*. Oxford University Press, 1996.

[5] E. Cantu-Paz. *Efficient and Accurate Parallel Genetic Algorithms*. Genetic Algorithms and Evolutionary Computation. Kluwer Academic Publishers, 2000.

[6] P.-Y. Chen, R.-D. Chen, Y.-P. Chang, L. san Shieh, and H. Malki. Hardware implementation for a genetic algorithm. *Instrumentation and Measurement, IEEE Transactions on*, 57(4):699–705, April 2008.

[7] B. Dorronsoro and E. Alba. A simple cellular genetic algorithm for continous optimization. In *Proceedings of 2006 IEEE Congress on Evolutionary Computation*. IEEE, 2006.

[8] P. dos Santos, J. Alves, and J. Ferreira. A scalable array for cellular genetic algorithms: Tsp as case study. In *Reconfigurable Computing and FPGAs (ReConFig), 2012 International Conference on*, pages 1–6, Dec 2012.

[9] P. Fernando, S. Katkoori, D. Keymeulen, R. Zebulum, and A. Stoica. Customizable fpga ip core implementation of a general-purpose genetic algorithm engine. *Evolutionary Computation, IEEE Transactions on*, 14(1):133–149, Feb 2010.

[10] S. Khuri, T. Bäck, and J. Heitkötter. An evolutionary approach to combinatorial optimization problems. In *Proceedings of the 1994 Computer Science Conference (CSC'94)*, page (to appear). ACM Press, 1994.

[11] A. Morales-Reyes, A. Al-Naqi, A. Erdogan, and T. Arslan. Towards 3d architectures: A comparative study on cellular gas dimensionality. In *Proceedings of IEEE NASA/ESA Conference on Adaptive Hardware and Systems (AHS'09)*, page (to appear). IEEE, 2009.

[12] A. Morales-Reyes and A. Erdogan. Internal lattice reconfiguration for diversity tuning in cellular genetic algorithms. In *PLoS ONE*, page 7(7): e41279. PloS ONE, 2012.

[13] A. Morales-Reyes, A. Erdogan, and T. Arslan. Lattice reconfiguration vs. local selection criteria for diversity tuning in cellular gas. In *Proceedings of the 2010 IEEE Congress on Evolutionary Computation (CEC 2010)*, pages 1 – 8. IEEE, 2010.

[14] A. Morales-reyes and A. T. Erdogan. A structure-based coarse-fine approach for diversity tuning in cellular gas. *Advances in Electrical and Computer Engineering*, 12(3):39–46, 2012.

[15] N. Nedjah and L. de Macedo Mourelle. An efficient problem-independent hardware implementation of genetic algorithms. *Neurocomput.*, 71(1-3):88–94, Dec. 2007.

[16] D. Simoncini, P. Collard, S. Verel, and M. Clergue. From cells to islands: An unified model of cellular parallel genetic algorithms. In *2006 International Conference on Cellular Automata*, page 248Öš57. Springer-Verlag, 2006.

[17] D. Simoncini, P. Collard, S. Verel, and M. Clergue. On the influence of selection operators on performances in cellular genetic algorithms. In *Proceeding of IEEE Congress on Evolutionary Computation (CEC'07)*, page 4706Öt'713. IEEE, 2007.

[18] M. Tomassini. *Spatially Structured Evolutionary Algorithms, Artificial Evolution in Space and Time*. Springer. Series: Natural Computing Series, 2005.

[19] P. Vieira dos Santos, J. Alves, and J. Canas Ferreira. A framework for hardware cellular genetic algorithms: An application to spectrum allocation in cognitive radio. In *Field Programmable Logic and Applications (FPL), 2013 23rd International Conference on*, pages 1–4, Sept 2013.

[20] Z. Zhu, D. Mulvaney, and V. Chouliaras. Hardware implementation of a novel genetic algorithm. *Neurocomputing*, 71(1Öş):95 – 106, 2007. Dedicated Hardware Architectures for Intelligent Systems Advances on Neural Networks for Speech and Audio Processing.

Maintaining 2-Approximations for the Dynamic Vertex Cover Problem Using Evolutionary Algorithms

Mojgan Pourhassan
Optimisation and Logistics
School of Computer Science
The University of Adelaide
Adelaide, SA 5005, Australia
mojgan.pourhassan@adelaide.edu.au

Wanru Gao
Optimisation and Logistics
School of Computer Science
The University of Adelaide
Adelaide, SA 5005, Australia
wanru.gao@adelaide.edu.au

Frank Neumann
Optimisation and Logistics
School of Computer Science
The University of Adelaide
Adelaide, SA 5005, Australia
frank.neumann@adelaide.edu.au

ABSTRACT

Evolutionary algorithms have been frequently used to deal with dynamic optimization problems, but their success is hard to understand from a theoretical perspective. With this paper, we contribute to the theoretical understanding of evolutionary algorithms for dynamic combinatorial optimization problems. We examine a dynamic version of the classical vertex cover problem and analyse evolutionary algorithms with respect to their ability to maintain a 2-approximation. Analysing the different evolutionary algorithms studied by Jansen et al. [7], we point out where two previously studied approaches are not able to maintain a 2-approximation even if they start with a solution of that quality. Furthermore, we point out that the third approach is very effective in maintaining 2-approximations for the dynamic vertex cover problem.

Categories and Subject Descriptors

F.2 [**Theory of Computation**]: Analysis of Algorithms and Problem Complexity

Keywords

Dynamic Vertex Cover Problem; Local Search; (1+1) EA; Combinatorial Optimisation.

1. INTRODUCTION

Evolutionary algorithms have been frequently applied to dynamic optimization problems. With this paper, we contribute to the theoretical understanding of evolutionary algorithms for one of the most classical combinatorial optimization problems, namely the vertex cover problem. The vertex cover problem is a well-known NP-hard combinatorial optimisation problem with various applications in scheduling, networking, bioinformatics, etc [1, 5, 10]. Several algorithms are known that achieve a 2-approximation for this problem. The goal of our investigations is to contribute to the understanding of how evolutionary algorithms can maintain a 2-approximation when dynamic changes such as edge addition and deletion are applied to the current graph. We study different variants of the classical Randomised Local Search (RLS) and (1+1) EA that have already been investigated for the static vertex cover problem in the context of approximations. This includes a node-based representation examined in [3, 9, 8] as well as different edge-based representations analyzed in [7].

For both of the representations there are hard instances introduced [3, 7] in which with high probability a 2-approximation solution can not be found in less than exponential time by means of (1+1) EA. Nevertheless, inspired by the approximation algorithms for the vertex cover problem using maximal matchings, Jansen et al. [7] have suggested that evolutionary algorithms using edge-based representation instead of the node-based representation can solve the problem faster. They have shown that with edge-based representation and a fitness function that penalizes edges sharing nodes, the algorithm can find a 2-approximation solution in $O(m \log m)$ where m denotes the number of edges in the given graph.

We adapt the three approaches of Jansen et al. [7] to the dynamic vertex cover problem [6] where edges may be added or deleted from the graph. For the first two approaches, we point out where they are not able to maintain 2-approximations for the dynamic vertex cover problem. In contrast to this, we show that the third approach maintains solutions of that quality very efficiently.

The rest of the paper is structured as follows. In Section 2 the problem definition is given and the algorithms are introduced. Section 3 and 4 include hard instances of the dynamic vertex cover problem for the node-based and edge-based approaches respectively. Run time behaviour of the edge-based approach with the complex fitness function is analysed in Section 5 and the conclusion is presented in the last section.

GECCO '15, July 11 - 15, 2015, Madrid, Spain

DOI: http://dx.doi.org/10.1145/2739480.2754700

2. ALGORITHMS AND THE DYNAMIC VERTEX COVER PROBLEM

The vertex cover problem can be defined as follows. Given a graph $G = (V, E)$ with vertex set $V = \{v_1, \dots, v_n\}$ and edge set $E = \{e_1, \dots, e_m\}$, the goal is to find the minimum subset of nodes, $V_C \subseteq V$, that covers all edges, i.e. $\forall e \in E, e \cap V_C \neq \emptyset$.

Algorithm 1 Node-Based RLS (RLS_{NB})

1: The initial solution, s, is given: a bit-string of size n which used to be a 2-approximation solution before changing the graph.
2: Set $s' = s$
3: Select $i \in \{1, \ldots, n\}$ uniformly at random and flip ith bit of s'
4: If $f(s') \leq f(s)$ then $s := s'$
5: If stopping criteria not met continue at line 2

Algorithm 2 Node-Based (1+1) EA ((1+1) EA_{NB})

1: The initial solution, s, is given: a bit-string of size n which used to be a 2-approximation solution before changing the graph.
2: Set $s' = s$
3: Flip each bit of s' with probability $\frac{1}{n}$
4: If $f(s') \leq f(s)$ then $s := s'$
5: If stopping criteria not met continue at line 2

Algorithm 3 Edge-Based RLS (RLS_{EB})

1: The initial solution, s, is given: a bit-string of size m which used to be a 2-approximation solution before changing the graph.
2: Set $s' = s$
3: Select $i \in \{1, \ldots, m\}$ uniformly at random and flip ith bit of s'
4: If $f(s') \leq f(s)$ then $s := s'$
5: If stopping criteria not met continue at line 2

Algorithm 4 Edge-Based (1+1) EA ((1+1) EA_{EB})

1: The initial solution, s, is given: a bit-string of size m which used to be a 2-approximation solution before changing the graph.
2: Set $s' = s$
3: Flip each bit of s' with probability $\frac{1}{m}$
4: If $f(s') \leq f(s)$ then $s := s'$
5: If stopping criteria not met continue at line 2

In dynamic version of vertex cover problem, the given instance is subject to the addition and deletion of edges. We assume that these changes happen one by one each τ iterations where $\tau \in poly(n)$ and $poly(n)$ is a polynomial function in n.

In most of the work on the vertex cover problem using evolutionary algorithms, the natural node-based representation is used [3, 9, 8]. In this representation the search space is $\{0,1\}^n$ where n is the number of nodes in the graph. A potential solution is a search point $s \in \{0,1\}^n$ describing a selection of nodes, i.e. the 1-bits identify the nodes that are in the cover-set for that solution:

$$V_C(s) = \{v_i \in V \mid s_i = 1\}.$$

In the work of Jansen et al. [7] the edge-based representation is introduced for this problem. In this representation the search space is $\{0,1\}^m$ where m is the number of edges in the graph, and a search point $s \in \{0,1\}^m$ describes a selection of edges $E(s) = \{e_i \in E \mid s_i = 1\}$. The cover set then is the subset of all vertices that are on either side of the selected edges:

$$V_C(s) = \{v \in V \mid \exists e \in E(s) : v \in e\}.$$

Note that in the dynamic version of the problem, the size of the bit-string corresponding to a search point increases and decreases when edges are added or removed respectively. In our analysis, m is the largest number of edges in the graph at all stages.

Jansen et al. [7] have suggested that this representation can help evolutionary algorithms solve the problem faster. They first investigated the fitness function

$$f(s) = |V_C(s)| + (|V|+1) \cdot |\{e \in E \mid e \cap V_C(s) = \emptyset\}|. \quad (1)$$

The first part of this fitness function is the cardinality of the cover set which needs to be minimised. The second part is a penalty for the edges that this set does not cover.

For $f(s)$ of Equation 1, they have managed to show that a (1+1) EA performs equally poor in worst cases for both defined representations. Furthermore, Jansen et al. [7] have shown that with adding a penalty for adjacent edges to the fitness function, the (1+1) EA with edge-based representation can solve the vertex cover problem in $O(m \log m)$. The fitness function with an extra penalty that they have used is defined as

$$\begin{aligned} f_e(s) &= f(s) + (|V|+1) \cdot (m+1) \\ &\cdot |\{(e,e') \in E(s) \times E(s) \mid e \neq e', e \cap e' \neq \emptyset\}| \quad (2) \end{aligned}$$

The fitness function $f_e(s)$ is inspired by the well-known approximation algorithm that finds a 2-approximation for the vertex cover problem based on a maximal matching [2].

In this paper, we analyse the behaviour of RLS and the (1+1) EA on the dynamic vertex cover problem with similar approaches that were studied in [7] on vertex cover problem. These algorithms are supposed to modify the given solution if needed to make it keep its quality of 2-approximation, after an edge has been added to or deleted from the graph. In our runtime analysis, we measure runtime by the number of fitness evaluations to reach a certain goal. The expected runtime refers to the expected number of fitness evaluations to reach the desired goal. In our case, the goal is to recompute a 2-approximation after one or more sequentially applied dynamic changes have occurred.

The Node-Based RLS (RLS_{NB}) and Node-Based (1+1) EA ((1+1) EA_{NB}) are defined in Algorithm 1 and Algorithm 2, respectively. Similarly, Edge-Based RLS (RLS_{EB}) and Edge-Based (1+1) EA ((1+1) EA_{EB}) using the fitness function $f(s)$ are presented in Algorithm 3 and 4, respectively. The definition of the algorithms for the third approach is quite similar to the second approach except that for comparing two solutions in line 4, where instead the fitness function with the extra penalty of Formula 2 is used. In the following sections, we denote the RLS and (1+1) EA variants of the third approach by RLS_e and (1+1) EA_e, respectively.

3. HARD INSTANCE FOR NODE-BASED APPROACH

In this section, we introduce a bipartite graph for which it is hard to maintain a 2-approximation solution by means of RLS_{NB} and (1+1) EA_{NB}. We go even further by showing that for our instance and a sequence of dynamic changes, only a very bad approximation will be found by these two algorithms. In our instance, both of the algorithms stick to a local optimum with a bad approximation ratio of $\Omega(n^{1-\epsilon})$,

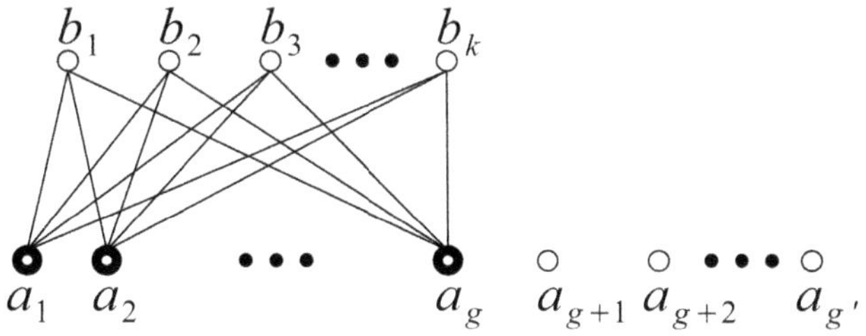

Figure 1: G_1, a hard instance for node-based approach

$\epsilon > 0$ a small constant, if the graph is subject to a polynomial number of changes. In this section, we assume that $\tau \geq n^{(3+\delta)}$, $\delta > 0$ a small constant. An Illustration of our instance, G_1, is given in Figure 1.

$G_1 = (V, E)$ is a bipartite graph and the set of nodes, V, is partitioned into two sets $W = \{a_1, \ldots, a_{g'}\}$ and $U = \{b_1, \ldots, b_k\}$. If n denotes the total number of nodes, then we assume that $k = \frac{1}{3}n^\epsilon$ and $g' = n - \frac{1}{3}n^\epsilon$. Initially, $g = 2k$ nodes from part W are connected to all the nodes of part U, i.e. the sub-graph consisting of nodes $U \cup \{a_1, \ldots, a_g\}$ and all edges between them, which we denote by ${G_1}'$, is a complete bipartite graph. The other nodes, $\{a_i \mid g+1 \leq i \leq g'\}$, are initially not adjacent to any edge, but will be connected to the nodes of part U one by one. In other words, the dynamic changes that the graph is subject to, are adding edges $\{\{a_i, b_j\} \mid g+1 \leq i \leq g', 1 \leq j \leq k\}$. Among these, edges $\{e \mid a_i \in e\}$ are added prior to edges $\{e \mid a_{i+1} \in e\}$; and edge $\{a_i, b_j\}$, is added prior to edge $\{a_i, b_{j+1}\}$. The number of these edges is $(g' - g) \cdot k = (n - n^\epsilon) \cdot (\frac{1}{3}n^\epsilon) = O(n^{1+\epsilon})$.

PROPERTY 1. *The optimal solution for G_1 at all stages of dynamic changes, is the set U of size k.*

PROOF. At all stages, the sub-graph G_1' is a complete bipartite graph; and a vertex cover for a complete bipartite graph, contains at least all of the nodes of one of the parts. Therefore, either all the nodes of U need to be in the solution or all the nodes $\{a_i \mid 1 \leq i \leq g\}$. Since $g = 2k$, any cover set containing $\{a_i \mid 1 \leq i \leq g\}$, has a size of at least $2k$; whereas any cover set containing U has a size of at least k. Therefore, the optimal solution has a size of at least k.

On the other hand, the set U is a complete cover for G_1 at all the stages because it is one of the partite sets of G_1. Therefore, the optimal cover set at all the stages of the graph is U with a size of k. □

The initial 2-approximation solution that is given consists of $\{a_i \mid 1 \leq i \leq g\}$. This is a 2-approximation solution because $g = 2k$ and the optimal solution has a size of k as we saw in Property 1. In Sections 3.1 and 3.2 we show that algorithms RLS$_{NB}$ and (1+1) EA$_{NB}$ find a locally optimal solution consisting of all nodes of W when the dynamic changes are done and G_1 is a complete bipartite graph.

Based on the fitness function $f(s)$ that is used in the node-based approach, we bring 6 lemmata here that hold for both RLS$_{NB}$ and (1+1) EA$_{NB}$, and help us with the proofs in Section 3.1, and 3.2.

LEMMA 2. *If the number of uncovered edges by the current solution s is A, then any solution s' with B uncovered edges is rejected by RLS$_{NB}$ and (1+1) EA$_{NB}$ if $B > A$.*

PROOF. Recalling Equation 1, $f(s) = |V_C(s)| + (n+1) \cdot A$. Since $B > A$, $f(s') \geq |V_C(s')| + (n+1) \cdot (A+1)$. Moreover, the maximum and minimum value of $|V_C(s)|$ and $|V_C(s')|$ are n and 0 respectively. As a result $f(s) \leq n + (n+1) \cdot A$ and $f(s') \geq 0 + (n+1) \cdot (A+1)$. Since $(n+1) \cdot (A+1) > (n+1) \cdot A$, this upper and lower bounds on $f(s)$ and $f(s')$ imply that $f(s') > f(s)$ and s' will be rejected by RLS$_{NB}$ and (1+1) EA$_{NB}$. □

LEMMA 3. *If the current solution s, is a cover, any solution s' where $|V_C(s')| > |V_C(s)|$, is rejected by RLS$_{NB}$ and (1+1) EA$_{NB}$.*

PROOF. For any solution s' the following inequality holds:

$$f(s') \geq |V_C(s')|$$

Since solution s is a cover, we have $f(s) = |V_C(s)|$. Therefore, $|V_C(s')| > |V_C(s)|$ implies that $f(s') > f(s)$, which results in rejecting s' by RLS$_{NB}$ and (1+1) EA$_{NB}$. □

LEMMA 4. *If the solution s is a cover, with probability $1 - e^{-\Omega(n^\epsilon)}$, RLS$_{NB}$ and (1+1) EA$_{NB}$ find a solution s' which is a minimal cover, in time $O(n^{1+\epsilon} \log n)$.*

PROOF. According to Lemma 2, any solution that is accepted by RLS$_{NB}$ or (1+1) EA$_{NB}$ after solution s, is a cover. Assume s' to be a cover with $|V_C(s')| < |V_C(s)|$. According to Lemma 3, s' is better in terms of fitness and will replace solution s. Since s is not a minimal cover, there are some extra nodes in it, removing which does not uncover any edges while reduces the size of the cover set. The process of removing extra nodes from the solution is similar to optimizing OneMax [7] and is expected to be done in time $O(n \log n)$ by RLS and (1+1) EA since $|V_C(s)| \leq n$.

If the expected time until all of extra nodes are removed is $Cn \log n$, where C is a constant, and if X is the first time that they are removed from the solution, then by Markov's inequality

$$Prob(X \geq 2Cn \log n) \leq \frac{1}{2}$$

Considering n^ϵ phases of $2Cn \log n$ steps, then

$$Prob(X \geq 2Cn^{1+\epsilon} \log n) \leq \left(\frac{1}{2}\right)^{n^\epsilon}$$

As a result, with a probability in $1 - e^{-\Omega(n^\epsilon)}$ a minimal cover will be found in time $O(n^{1+\epsilon} \log n)$. □

LEMMA 5. *If the solution s is a cover before the new edge e is added, then with probability $1 - e^{-\Omega(n^\epsilon)}$ starting with s, (1+1) EA$_{NB}$ and RLS$_{NB}$ find a solution s' which is also a cover after e is added, in time $O(n^{1+\epsilon})$.*

PROOF. Since s had been a cover before e was added, the only edge that might not be covered by s is e. Therefore, the number of uncovered edges is at most 1. This number does not increase according to Lemma 2 during the process of RLS$_{NB}$ and (1+1) EA$_{NB}$. On the other hand, there are always two nodes (included in the uncovered edge itself) that adding at least one of them to the solution s, results in a cover. This move is accepted according to Lemma 2 and has the probability of $\Omega(n^{-1})$ for both RLS$_{NB}$ and (1+1) EA$_{NB}$. Therefore, the expected time until this improvement is found is Cn, C a positive constant, and using Markov's inequality and n^ϵ phases of $2 \cdot Cn$ steps (similar to proof of Lemma 4), with probability $1 - e^{-\Omega(n^\epsilon)}$, a cover will be found in time $O(n^{1+\epsilon})$. □

LEMMA 6. *Consider the given solution s, a cover which does not include $b_{j'}$; $3 \leq j' \leq k$, before new edge $e = \{a_i, b_j\}$ is added to the graph. With probability $1 - e^{-\Omega(n^{\epsilon})}$, the resulting solution of (1+1) EA$_{NB}$ and RLS$_{NB}$ after e is added, includes at least all nodes $a_{i'}$; $1 \leq i' \leq i-1$.*

PROOF. As s does not include $b_{j'}$; $3 \leq j' \leq k$, it must contain all $a_{i'}$; $1 \leq i' \leq i-1$; otherwise, it is not a cover before $e = \{a_i, b_j\}$ is added. Therefore, the only edge that might not be covered after e is added, is e itself. The number of uncovered edges does not increase during the process of (1+1) EA$_{NB}$ and RLS$_{NB}$ (Lemma 2); therefore, none of a-nodes can be removed from the solution unless all b-nodes are added at the same step. This move is not possible with RLS$_{NB}$ because only single-bit flips can be done in that algorithm. (1+1) EA$_{NB}$ also needs to flip at least $k-2$ bits at one step which has the probability of at most $e^{-\Omega(k)} = e^{-\Omega(n^{\epsilon})}$. As a result, starting from s, with probability $1 - e^{-\Omega(n^{\epsilon})}$, any solution accepted by (1+1) EA$_{NB}$ and RLS$_{NB}$ after e is added, includes at least all nodes $a_{i'}$; $1 \leq i' \leq i-1$. □

LEMMA 7. *Consider $g < i \leq g'$ and two stages of the graph G_1: stage X at which $\{a_i, b_2\}$ is added, and stage Y which is before $\{a_{i+1}, b_1\}$ is added. At all stages from X to Y, a solution consisting of $\{a_1, \dots, a_i\}$ is a locally optimal solution for RLS$_{NB}$. Moreover, with probability of $1 - e^{-\Omega(n^{\epsilon})}$, (1+1) EA$_{NB}$ can not improve this solution in a polynomial number of steps.*

PROOF. Since edges connected to $a_{i'}$; $i' > i$ have not been added to the graph yet, s, consisting of $\{a_1, \dots, a_i\}$, is a cover. Therefore, any solution that has at least one uncovered edge (Lemma 2) or has a larger number of nodes in the cover set(Lemma 3) is rejected by RLS$_{NB}$ and (1+1) EA$_{NB}$.

Since the sub-graph consisting of the nodes $\{a_1, \dots, a_i\} \cup U$ and all edges between them, is a complete bipartite graph, any solution which is a cover, must contain either U or $\{a_1, \dots, a_i\}$. Similar to Lemma 6, jumping to any solution which contains U, in one step by RLS$_{NB}$ is not possible and by (1+1) EA$_{NB}$ has a probability of $e^{-\Omega(n^{\epsilon})}$. Moreover, among solutions containing the set $\{a_1, \dots, a_i\}$, s has the minimum number of nodes in the cover set. Therefore, s is a local optimum for RLS$_{NB}$ and with probability $e^{-\Omega(n^{\epsilon})}$, (1+1) EA$_{NB}$ can not improve it in a polynomial number of steps. □

3.1 Analysis of RLS$_{NB}$ on G$_1$

In this section, we first bring two lemmata that help us identify local optimums. Using them, we analyse the behaviour of RLS$_{NB}$ on G_1.

LEMMA 8. *Any solution s which is a minimal cover, is a locally optimal solution for RLS$_{NB}$.*

PROOF. Only single-bit flips can be preformed by RLS$_{NB}$ which can be either adding a new node to s or removing one from it. Since s is a cover, adding new nodes to it is rejected according to Lemma 3 because it increases $|V_C(s)|$. Moreover, any move that removes a node, uncovers at least one edge as s is a minimal cover. Therefore, according to Lemma 2 deleting nodes from s also is rejected; hence, s is a local optimum. □

LEMMA 9. *Consider $g < i \leq g'$ and two stages of the graph G_1: stage X at which $\{a_i, b_1\}$ is added, and stage Y which is before $\{a_{i+1}, b_1\}$ is added. If the given solution of RLS$_{NB}$ at stage X is $\{a_1, \dots, a_{i-1}\}$, then with probability $1 - e^{-\Omega(n^{\epsilon})}$, the resulting solution of the algorithm at stage Y is $\{a_1, \dots, a_i\}$.*

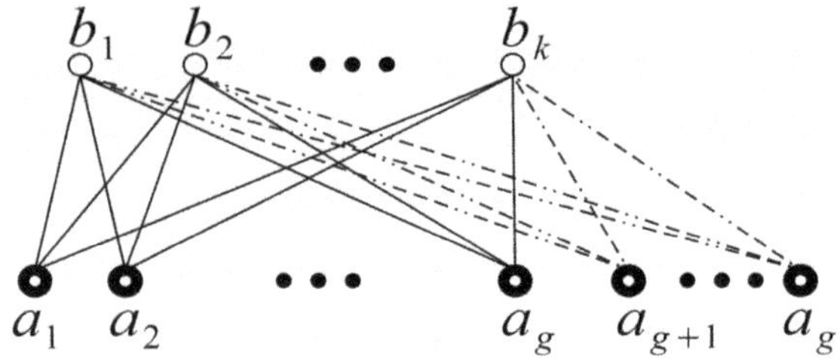

Figure 2: A solution consisting of set W

PROOF. After stage X, when the edge $\{a_i, b_1\}$ is added to the graph, the current solution, $\{a_1, a_2, \dots, a_{i-1}\}$, is not a cover any more.

The RLS$_{NB}$ flips bits of search point s, one bit at a time, to achieve an improvement on the fitness $f(s)$. Flipping a 1 to 0 indicates removing a node from the solution; which uncovers k edges and according to Lemma 2, is rejected. Flipping a 0 to 1 increases $|V_C(s)|$, but if the corresponding node covers the new edge; then the fitness is improved by n. If not, the fitness is increased by 1. Therefore, the only flips that are accepted by RLS$_{NB}$ are the ones that add a node that covers the new edge. The only such nodes are a_i and b_1. Note that in both cases the resulting solution is worse than a 2-approximation, because it contains $i \geq 2k+1$ nodes.

At each step, the probability of selecting one of these two nodes is $\frac{2}{n}$. Therefore, the expected time until one of them is selected is $\frac{n}{2}$. Let X be the first time that one of them is selected. Using Markov's inequality and n^{ϵ} phases of n steps (similar to proof of Lemma 4) with probability $1 - e^{-\Omega(n^{\epsilon})}$, the solution is improved in $n^{1+\epsilon}$ steps.

If a_i is added, then according to Lemma 7 the solution is a local optimum until edge $\{a_{i+1}, b_1\}$ is added. Here we consider adding b_1 to the cover set.

At this stage, i.e. before the next edge is added to the graph, the solution $\{a_1, a_2, \dots, a_{i-1}, b_1\}$, is a minimal cover and a local optimum according to Lemma 8.

Similar to the first one, when the edge $\{b_2, a_i\}$ is added to the graph, the current solution is no more a complete cover. Either b_2 or a_i need to be added to the cover set. The situation is similar to what we had for the first change and will be repeated in the next stages while the b-node is selected.

For each of the k edges $\{a_i, b_j\}; 1 \leq j \leq k$, the probability that the b-node is added to the cover set instead of a_i is $\frac{1}{2}$. Therefore, with probability $1 - (\frac{1}{2})^k = 1 - e^{-\Omega(n^{\epsilon})}$, at least one of these changes results in adding a_i to the selected set of nodes. Let us assume that the $\{a_i, b_j\}$ is the first edge for which a_i is added to the cover set. The new solution $\{a_1, \dots, a_i, b_1, \dots, b_{j-1}\}$ is a cover, but not a minimal cover, because removing b-nodes from the set does not uncover any edges. According to Lemma 4, they will be removed from the solution and with a probability in $1 - e^{-\Omega(n^{\epsilon})}$ the locally optimal solution of $\{a_1, \dots, a_i\}$ (Lemma 7) will be found in time $O(n^{1+\epsilon} \log n)$. □

THEOREM 10. *For G_1, with probability $1 - e^{-\Omega(n^{\epsilon})}$, the eventual resulting solution of RLS$_{NB}$ is the set W. The approximation ratio of this solution is in $\Omega(n^{1-\epsilon})$.*

PROOF. Since the initial solution is $\{a_1, \ldots, a_g\}$, according to Lemma 9, the resulting solution of RLS$_{NB}$ before edge $\{a_{g+2}, b_1\}$ is added is $\{a_1, \ldots, a_{g+1}\}$, with probability $1 - e^{-\Omega(n^{\epsilon})}$. This satisfies the requirement for Lemma 9 again, and the algorithm repeats the whole process for each of $(n - n^{\epsilon})$ a-nodes. As a result, after node is added, the algorithm finds a solution consisting of W with probability $1 - (n - n^{\epsilon})e^{-\Omega(n^{\epsilon})} = 1 - e^{-\Omega(n^{\epsilon})}$ (Figure 2).

There are $g = n - \frac{1}{3}n^{\epsilon}$ nodes in this solution, which gives the approximation ratio of:

$$\frac{g}{k} = \frac{n - \frac{1}{3}n^{\epsilon}}{\frac{1}{3}n^{\epsilon}} = \Omega(n^{1-\epsilon})$$

□

3.2 Analysis of (1+1) EA on G_1

We here introduce a lemma using which the main theorem of this section about the behaviour of (1+1) EA$_{NB}$ on G_1 is proved.

LEMMA 11. *Consider $g < i \le g'$ and two stages of the graph G_1: stage X at which $\{a_i, b_1\}$ is added, and stage Y which is before $\{a_{i+1}, b_1\}$ is added. If the given solution of (1+1) EA$_{NB}$ at stage X is $s = \{a_1, \ldots, a_{i-1}\}$, then with probability $1-e^{-\Omega(n^{\delta})}$, the resulting solution of the algorithm at stage Y is $s' = \{a_1, \ldots, a_i\}$.*

PROOF. The given solution $\{a_1, \ldots, a_{i-1}\}$ is a cover for the graph before stage X. According to Lemma 5, after $\{a_i, b_1\}$ is added, the algorithm finds s_1 which is a cover, in polynomial time. Similarly, after $\{a_i, b_2\}$ is added, a solution s_2 that is also a cover is found in polynomial time.

On the other hand, according to Lemma 6, s_1 contains all nodes $a_{i'}$; $1 \le i' \le i - 1$. And according to Lemma 4, it is a minimal cover because $\tau > O(n^{1+\epsilon} \log n)$, meaning that in addition to $\{a_1, \ldots, a_{i-1}\}$, it only includes one other node to cover $\{a_i, b_1\}$ i.e. either a_i or b_1. Therefore, s_1 does not include $b_{j'}$; $3 \le j' \le k$; which satisfies the condition of Lemma 6 for the next stage. In other words, s_2 also includes all nodes $a_{i'}$; $1 \le i' \le i - 1$. According to Lemma 4 it is also a minimal cover. Any minimal solution including all nodes $a_{i'}$; $1 \le i' \le i - 1$ which also covers $\{a_i, b_1\}$ and $\{a_i, b_2\}$, contains either a_i or b_1 and b_2. So far, we have proved that (1+1) EA$_{NB}$ finds s_2 which consists of either $V_1 = \{a_1, \ldots, a_i\}$ or $V_2 = \{a_1, \ldots, a_{i-1}, b_1, b_2\}$. We here show that (1+1) EA$_{NB}$ finds the solution which includes V_1.

Since both V_1 and V_2 are covers and $|V_1| < |V_2|$, the solution consisting of V_1 is less costly. Therefore, (1+1) EA$_{NB}$ does not accept a change from V_1 to V_2 but accepts the opposite move. The probability of flipping only the bits corresponding to a_i, b_1 and b_2 is

$$\left(\frac{1}{n}\right)^3 \left(1 - \frac{1}{n}\right)^{n-3} \ge \frac{1}{en^3}$$

As a result, a move from V_2 to V_1 can be performed at expected time of at most $E(T) = en^3$, where T is the first step that this move happens. Using Markov's inequality,

$$Prob(T \ge 2 \cdot en^3) \le \frac{1}{2}$$

Considering $\frac{n^{(3+\delta)}}{2en^3}$ phases of $2en^3$ steps,

$$Prob(T \ge n^{3+\delta}) \le \left(\frac{1}{2}\right)^{\frac{n^{(3+\delta)}}{2en^3}}$$

This implies that with probability $1-e^{-\Omega(n^{\delta})}$ the (1+1) EA$_{NB}$ finds s_2 consisting of V_1 in a phase of τ steps.

From this point according to Lemma 7, s_2 is a local optimum until $\{a_{i+1}, b_1\}$ is added. □

THEOREM 12. *For G_1, with probability $1 - e^{-\Omega(n^{\delta})}$, the eventual resulting solution of (1+1) EA$_{NB}$ is the set W. The approximation ratio of this solution is in $\Omega(n^{1-\epsilon})$.*

PROOF. Since the initial solution is $\{a_1, \ldots, a_g\}$, according to Lemma 11, the resulting solution of (1+1) EA$_{NB}$ before edge $\{a_{g+2}, b_1\}$ is added is $\{a_1, \ldots, a_{g+1}\}$, with probability $1-e^{-\Omega(n^{\delta})}$. This satisfies the requirement for Lemma 11 again, and the algorithm repeats the whole process for each node a_i, $g < i \le g'$. As a result, after the last change of the graph, the algorithm finds a solution consisting of all nodes of W with a probability of at least $1 - (n - n^{\epsilon})e^{-\Omega(n^{\delta})} = 1 - e^{-\Omega(n^{\delta})}$.

Similar to Theorem 10 the approximation ratio of this solution is $\Omega(n^{1-\epsilon})$. □

4. HARD INSTANCE FOR STANDARD EDGE-BASED APPROACH

In this section, we assume that $\tau \ge m^{(4+\delta)}$, where $\delta > 0$ is a small constant. The graph of instance G_2 that we introduce in this section as a hard instance for edge-based approach is exactly the same as G_1 with one slight difference. The difference is that $g = 2k - 1$ instead of $2k$.

PROPERTY 13. *The optimal solution for G_2 at all stages of dynamic changes, is the set U of size k.*

PROOF. The proof is similar to the proof of Property 1 on G_1. □

Since we are using the edge-based representation in this section, the initial solution needs to be a search point in $\{0, 1\}^m$, representing the set of selected edges. We assume that $\{\{a_i, b_1\} \mid 1 \le i \le g\}$ is the given initial set of selected edges. The cover set induced from this set is $\{b_1\} \cup \{a_i \mid 1 \le i \le g\}$ which has a size of $2k$; therefore, is a 2-approximation because according to Property 13 the size of the optimal solution is k. In what follows, we analyse the behaviour of RLS$_{EB}$ and (1+1) EA$_{EB}$ on G_2 with the given initial solution.

Note that Lemma 2 and Lemma 3 of Section 3 are also valid in this section, because they are based on the fitness function $f(s)$ and not the representation. We bring three other lemmata here which hold for both RLS$_{EB}$ and (1+1) EA$_{EB}$.

LEMMA 14. *Starting with the given solution s which is a cover before edge e is added, with probability $1 - e^{-\Omega(m^{\epsilon})}$, RLS$_{EB}$ and (1+1) EA$_{EB}$ find a solution s' which is also a cover in $O(n^{1+\epsilon})$ after e is added.*

PROOF. The proof of this lemma is similar to the proof of Lemma 5 except that we are using the edge-based approach and we should use the probability of finding the proper edge instead of the probability of finding the proper node.

There always exists an edge (the uncovered edge itself) adding which to s results in a cover. This move has the probability of $\Omega(m^{-1})$ for both RLS$_{EB}$ and (1+1) EA$_{EB}$. Therefore, similar to Lemma 5, with probability $1-e^{-\Omega(m^{\epsilon})}$, a cover will be found in $O(m^{1+\epsilon})$. □

LEMMA 15. *For the instance G_2 starting with the given initial solution, with probability $1 - e^{-\Omega(m^{\epsilon})}$, RLS$_{EB}$ and (1+1) EA$_{EB}$ result in a solution which is a cover at all stages.*

PROOF. Using Lemma 14 as inductive steps and the initial solution as the base of induction, we can conclude that with probability $1-e^{-\Omega(m^{\epsilon})}$, RLS$_{EB}$ and (1+1) EA$_{EB}$ result in a solution which is a cover at all stages. □

LEMMA 16. *Before new edge $e = \{a_i, b_j\}$ is added to the graph, consider the given solution s, a cover which does not include $b_{j'}$; $4 \le j' \le k$. With probability $1-e^{-\Omega(m^{\epsilon})}$, the resulting solution of (1+1) EA$_{EB}$ and RLS$_{EB}$ after e is added, includes at least all nodes $a_{i'}$; $1 \le i' \le i-1$.*

PROOF. The proof is similar to proof of Lemma 6. However, notice that with edge-based representation, adding and removing nodes from the cover set of solution s can be done by adding and removing edges from s. Since G_2 is a bipartite graph, adding all nodes $b_{j'}$; $4 \le j' \le k$ at one step, requires at least $k = 3$ flips. □

4.1 Analysis of RLS$_{EB}$ on G$_2$

In this section, we analyse the behaviour of RLS$_{EB}$ on G_2 and show that there is a stage at which this algorithm fails to find a solution with a better approximation ratio than $\frac{3k-1}{k}$. We first bring a lemma that helps us with the proof.

LEMMA 17. *With probability $1-e^{-\Omega(m^{\epsilon})}$, the node b_k can only be added to the solution by RLS$_{EB}$, at a stage in which $\{a_i, b_k\}$ has been added to the graph, where $g+1 \le i \le g'$.*

PROOF. Consider stage X in which node b_k is added to the solution. If adding an edge $e = \{a_{i'}, b_k\}; 1 \le i' \le g'$ is accepted, it must cover an uncovered edge; otherwise, this move will be rejected because it increases the cardinality of the cover set. On the other hand, according to Lemma 15, the solution obtained by the algorithm before stage X, is a cover; therefore the only uncovered edge is the one that is added in stage X which we denote by e_n. As a result, e is covering e_n; i.e. $e_n = \{a_i, b_k\}$; $g+1 \le i \le g'$ which is what the lemma claims, or, $e_n = \{a_{i'}, b_{k'}\}$; $1 \le k' \le k$. In this case, $k' = k$ because otherwise, the edge $\{a_{i'}, b_k\}$ has not been added to the graph yet. This completes the proof. □

THEOREM 18. *Before edge $\{a_{3k}, b_1\}$ is added to G_2, with probability $1-e^{-\Omega(m^{\epsilon})}$, there is a stage at which RLS$_{EB}$ does not find any solution better than $\frac{3k-1}{k}$-approximation.*

PROOF. Before $\{a_{3k}, b_1\}$ is added to the graph, all edges connected to nodes a_i; $2k \le i < 3k$, are added. We partition these stages into k phases so that in phase i $(2k \le i < 3k)$, edges $\{a_i, b_j \mid 1 \le j \le k\}$ are added.

We analyse the situation based on containing or not containing the node b_k in the obtained solution of at least one stage.

- If an edge containing nodes b_k is added to the solution, according to Lemma 17, it must have been added after edge $e_n = \{a_i, b_k\}$; $2k \le i < 3k$ is added to G_2. Furthermore, adding b_k to a solution s increases $|V_C(s)|$. If s was a cover, according to Lemma 3 this move was rejected. Therefore, b_k must have covered a new edge. According to Lemma 15, before e_n is added; the algorithm has managed to find a cover; therefore, the only edge that may not be covered after adding e_n, is e_n itself. Therefore, the edge containing b_k, that is added to the solution, must cover $e_n = \{a_i, b_k\}$, to be accepted. This implies that the node a_i has not been previously added to the solution. Otherwise, e_n was already covered.

  Consider stage X, at which $\{a_i, b_{k-1}\}$ has been added. According to the above explanation, the solution obtained at this stage (before e_n is added) must not contain a_i. Moreover, according to Lemma15, this solution is a cover. Since a_i has been connected to all other b-nodes in the past stages, all the nodes b_j; $1 \le j \le k-1$, must be included in that solution as it does not contain a_i. Similarly, all the nodes a_l; $1 \le l \le i-1$ must be included in that solution because b_k is connected to all of them and is not included in the cover set yet.

  As a result, the achieved solution by the end of stage X, contains nodes a_l; $1 \le l \le i-1$ and b_j; $1 \le j \le k-1$. Since $i \ge 2k$, the total number of nodes in the cover set is at least $3k-1$.

- If b_k is not included in the solution of any stage; then the cover set must include all of the nodes that are connected to b_k. At the last stage of phase $3k-1$, all nodes $a_l, 1 \le l \le 3k-1$ are connected to b_k; therefore, the cover set that the algorithm finds at that stage contains at least $3k-1$ edges.

In both cases, we proved that there is a stage at which the achieved cover set contains at least $3k-1$ nodes; while the size of the optimal cover set is k at all stages. Therefore, the approximation ratio of the mentioned solutions is $\frac{3k-1}{k}$. □

4.2 Analysis of EA on G$_2$

Here we introduce two lemmata that helps us with the proof of the main theorem about the behaviour of (1+1) EA$_{EB}$ on G_2. Lemma 19 is obtained similar to Lemma 7.

LEMMA 19. *Consider $g < i \le g'$ and two stages of the graph G_1: stage X at which $\{a_i, b_3\}$ is added, and stage Y which is before $\{a_{i+1}, b_1\}$ is added. At all stages from X to Y, a solution s, consisting of $\{a_1, \ldots, a_i, b_j\}$; $1 \le j \le k$ is a locally optimal solution for (1+1) EA$_{EB}$.*

LEMMA 20. *Consider $g < i \le g'$ and two stages of the graph G_1: stage X at which $\{a_i, b_1\}$ is added, and stage Y which is before $\{a_{i+1}, b_1\}$ is added. If the given solution of (1+1) EA$_{EB}$ at stage X, s, includes the nodes $\{a_1, \ldots, a_{i-1}\}$, then with probability $1 - e^{-\Omega(m^{\delta})}$, the resulting solution of the algorithm at stage Y also includes $\{a_1, \ldots, a_i\}$.*

PROOF. The given solution s is a cover for the graph before stage X. According to Lemma 14, after $\{a_i, b_1\}$, $\{a_i, b_2\}$ and $\{a_i, b_3\}$ are added, the algorithm finds s_1, s_2 and s_3 which are also covering solutions, in polynomial time.

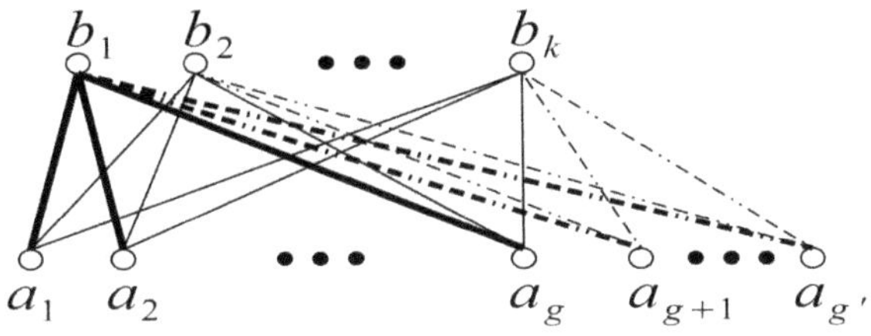

Figure 3: A solution including the set W

On the other hand, according to Lemma 16, s_1, s_2 and s_3 contain all nodes $a_{i'}$; $1 \leq i' \leq i-1$. A covering solution that contains the three new edges, must contain either a_i or b_1, b_2 and b_3. Among solutions with these properties, $s_3 = \{\{a_l, b_j\} \mid 1 \leq l \leq i\}$ has the minimum cost and is achievable from others at each step with a probability of at least $(\frac{1}{m})^4(1-\frac{1}{m})^{(m-4)}$ because at most 4 bits of s need to be flipped. Similar to proof of Lemma 11, we can conclude that with probability $1 - e^{-\Omega(m^\delta)}$ the (1+1) EA$_{EB}$ finds $s_3 = \{\{a_l, b_1\} \mid 1 \leq l \leq i\}$ in a phase of τ steps which is due to Lemma 19, a local optimum until $\{a_{i+1}, b_1\}$ is added. □

Similar to Theorem 12 we obtain the following result.

THEOREM 21. *For G_2, with probability $1 - e^{-\Omega(m^\delta)}$, the (1+1) EA$_{EB}$ finds a locally optimal solution containing the set W (Figure 3). The approximation ratio of this solution is in $\Omega(n^{1-\epsilon})$.*

5. EDGE-BASED APPROACH WITH EXTRA PENALTY

In this section, we analyse the impact of using the fitness function $f_e(s)$, defined in Equation 2, on the behaviour of RLS$_e$ and (1+1) EA$_e$. It is already proved [7] that starting from any initial solution, both of these algorithms find a maximal matching in time $O(m \log m)$, which induces a 2-approximation solution for the vertex cover problem. As a result, considering $\tau \geq m^{(1+\delta)}$, both algorithms find a 2-approximation solution for the dynamic vertex cover problem with probability $1 - e^{-\Omega(\frac{m^\delta}{\log m})}$. We aim to analyse the behaviour of the two algorithms when an initial solution with that quality is given. Both kind of dynamic changes on the graph, *add* and *delete*, are analysed in this section. The following two lemmata are proved based on the fitness function $f_e(s)$ that RLS$_e$ and (1+1) EA$_e$ use.

LEMMA 22. *Consider a search point $s \in \{0,1\}^m$ which is a matching. Any move that results in search point s' is rejected by RLS$_e$ and (1+1) EA$_e$ if s' is not a matching.*

PROOF. We here show that for any s which is a matching and any s' which is not a matching, $f_e(s') > f_e(s)$; therefore, both algorithms reject s'.

If s' is not a matching, $f_e(s') \geq (|V|+1)\cdot(m+1) = (n+1)\cdot(m+1)$. Moreover, if s is a matching $f_e(s) = f(s) \leq n + (n+1)(m)$ because the maximum number of uncovered edges is m. On the other hand, $(n+1)\cdot(m+1) > n + (n+1)(m)$ which implies that $f_e(s') > f_e(s)$ □

LEMMA 23. *Consider a search point $s \in \{0,1\}^m$ which is a matching. Any move that results in search point s' is rejected by RLS$_e$ and (1+1) EA$_e$ if $|\{e \in E \mid e \cap V_C(s) = \emptyset\}| > |\{e \in E \mid e \cap V_C(s') = \emptyset\}|$.*

PROOF. For any search point s', $f_e(s') \geq f(s')$ holds. Since solution s is a matching, $f_e(s) = f(s)$. Therefore, if $f(s') > f(s)$, $f_e(s') > f_e(s)$ also holds. Moreover, according to Lemma 2, if the number of uncovered edges of solution s' is larger than that of solution s, $f(s') > f(s)$ holds which completes the proof. □

5.1 Analysis of RLS

In this section, using the following lemma, we prove that RLS$_e$ maintains a 2-approximation solution in $O(m)$ on expectation. This gives the probability of $1-e^{-\Omega(m^\delta)}$ for maintaining the quality of the problem with $\tau = m^{(1+\epsilon)}$.

LEMMA 24. *Any search point $s \in \{0,1\}^m$ which is a maximal matching, is a locally optimal solution for RLS$_e$.*

PROOF. By RLS$_e$ only single-bit flips can be performed: adding one edge to s, or deleting one edge from it. We show that both kinds are rejected; hence s is a local optimum.

Since s is a matching, removing an edge from it uncovers at least one edge, and according to Lemma 23, is rejected. And since it is a maximal matching, adding any edge to it will result in a solution which is not a matching, and according to Lemma 22, is rejected. □

THEOREM 25. *Starting with a 2-approximation solution s, which is also a maximal matching for an instance of the problem, RLS$_e$ maintains the quality of the solution for dynamic changes of adding or deleting an edge on the graph in expected time of $O(m)$.*

PROOF. We investigate the situation for adding an edge or deleting an edge separately.

When an edge is added to the graph, s is still a matching, but it might be or not be a maximal matching. If s is still a maximal matching then it is a local optimum (Lemma 24) and a 2-approximation, because all maximal matchings induce a 2-approximation cover set.

If s is not a maximal matching, then only the new edge, e, might not be covered. According to Lemma 22 and Lemma 23, s remains matching during the process of the algorithm and the number of uncovered edges does not increase. Moreover, while there is an uncovered edge, there is a probability of at least $\frac{1}{m}$ to make an improvement, because adding the uncovered edge to s reduces the number of uncovered edges to 0. This means that in expectation, it takes m steps for RLS$_e$ to find this improvement.

When an edge, $e = \{v_1, v_2\}$, is deleted from the graph, if $e \notin E(s)$ then s is still a maximal matching and corresponds to a 2-approximation solution. If $e \in E(s)$, then it is deleted from the solution as well. The new s is still a matching but might be or not be a maximal matching. If s is still a maximal matching then it is already a 2-approximation and we are done.

We examine the case where s does not constitute a maximal matching anymore. If s is not a maximal matching, then there is a non-empty set E' such that:

$$E' = \{e_1 \mid e_1 \in E \wedge (\forall e_2 \in E(s) \Rightarrow e_1 \cap e_2 = \emptyset)\}.$$

Consider the set E'':

$$E'' = \{e_1 \mid e_1 \in E \wedge (\forall e_2 \in E(s), e_1 \cap e_2 = \emptyset) \wedge e_1 \cap e \neq \emptyset\}$$

The definition implies that $E'' \subseteq E'$. Here we show that $E' = E''$. If not, $\exists e'' \in E' \setminus E''$ which means that $e'' \cap e = \emptyset$

and s was not covering e'' before removing e, and therefore was not a maximal matching which is in contrast to the given assumption on s.

Now we can define $U_1 = \{e_1 \mid e_1 \in E'' \wedge v_1 \in e_1\}$ and $U_2 = \{e_1 \mid e_1 \in E'' \wedge v_2 \in e_1\}$. We know that $U_1 \cap U_2 = \emptyset$ because the edge containing both v_1 and v_2 was e which is deleted from the graph. Therefore, U_1 and U_2 define a partition over E'' and in order to cover edges in E'', edges from both of these sets need to be covered. All edges in U_1 include the node v_1 which implies that selecting any edge from U_1 covers all other edges from this set. Similarly selecting any edge from U_2 covers all edges from this set. Therefore, using RLS$_e$, at each step there is a probability of $\frac{|U_1|}{m}$ to cover all edges of U_1 and a probability of $\frac{|U_2|}{m}$ to cover all edges of U_2.

Note that any other move is rejected: No edge can be deleted from s, because s is a matching and deleting any edge from it increases the number of uncovered edges; therefore is rejected (Lemma 23). Furthermore, all edges other than $e'' \in E''$ are covered by s and adding them to s results in a solution which is not a matching; hence, is rejected (Lemma 22).

With the mentioned probabilities of covering U_1 and U_2 in one step, each of them will be covered in expected time of Cm, where C is a constant. Using Markov's inequality and m^ϵ phases of Cm, with probability $1 - e^{-\Omega(m^\epsilon)}$ all the uncovered edges will be covered in $O(m^{1+\epsilon})$. The new solution is a maximal matching which induces a 2-approximation solution. □

5.2 Analysis of (1+1) EA

In this section, we consider the (1+1) EA$_e$ and analyse maintaining a 2-approximation solution for the dynamic vertex cover problem for that. We have obtained new results for the dynamic change of adding an edge; but deleting an edge is more complicated to analyse. The reason is that the number of uncovered edges can be as large as $O(m)$ and when more than one flip can happen at each step, some uncovered edges can get covered but a smaller number of covered edges get uncovered. The best expected optimization time for this situation known so far is $O(m \log m)$ which is the same as the expected time of (1+1) EA$_e$ starting from scratch.

The following theorem, gives the result of our analysis for (1+1) EA$_e$ when edges are dynamically added to the graph.

THEOREM 26. *Starting with a 2-approximation solution s, which is also a maximal matching for an instance of the problem, (1+1) EA$_e$ maintains the quality of the solution when one new edge is dynamically added to the graph in expected time of $O(m)$.*

PROOF. The proof is similar to the proof of the first part of Theorem 25, except that the probability of flipping the bit of uncovered edge in (1+1) EA$_e$ is $\frac{1}{m}(1-\frac{1}{m})^{(m-1)}$. However, this probability also gives the expected time of $O(m)$ to make the improvement. □

6. CONCLUSION

In this paper, we have carried out rigorous runtime analyses on how the different evolutionary approaches already examined by Jansen et al. [7] (for the static vertex cover problem) can deal with the dynamic vertex cover problem. For the first two examined approaches, we have presented classes of instances of bipartite graphs where adding edges lead to bad approximation behaviours even if the algorithms started with a 2-approximation. For the third approach, we have shown that 2-approximations are maintained easily by recomputing maximal matchings of the dynamically changing graph.

Acknowledgements

The research leading to these results has received funding from the Australian Research Council (ARC) under grant agreements DP130104395 and DP140103400.

7. REFERENCES

[1] N. Bansal and S. Khot. Inapproximability of hypergraph vertex cover and applications to scheduling problems. In S. Abramsky, C. Gavoille, C. Kirchner, F. Meyer auf der Heide, and P. Spirakis, editors, *Automata, Languages and Programming*, volume 6198 of *Lecture Notes in Computer Science*, pages 250–261. Springer Berlin Heidelberg, 2010.

[2] T. H. Cormen, C. Stein, R. L. Rivest, and C. E. Leiserson. *Introduction to Algorithms*. McGraw-Hill Higher Education, 2nd edition, 2001.

[3] T. Friedrich, J. He, N. Hebbinghaus, F. Neumann, and C. Witt. Approximating covering problems by randomized search heuristics using multi-objective models. *Evolutionary Computation*, 18(4):617–633, 2010.

[4] T. Friedrich, N. Hebbinghaus, F. Neumann, J. He, and C. Witt. Approximating covering problems by randomized search heuristics using multi-objective models. In *Proceedings of the 9th Annual Conference on Genetic and Evolutionary Computation*, GECCO '07, pages 797–804, New York, NY, USA, 2007. ACM.

[5] S. Guha, R. Hassin, S. Khuller, and E. Or. Capacitated vertex covering. *JOURNAL OF ALGORITHMS*, 48:257–270, 2003.

[6] Z. Ivković and E. Lloyd. Fully dynamic maintenance of vertex cover. In J. van Leeuwen, editor, *Graph-Theoretic Concepts in Computer Science*, volume 790 of *Lecture Notes in Computer Science*, pages 99–111. Springer Berlin Heidelberg, 1994.

[7] T. Jansen, P. S. Oliveto, and C. Zarges. Approximating vertex cover using edge-based representations. In *Proceedings of the Twelfth Workshop on Foundations of Genetic Algorithms XII*, FOGA XII '13, pages 87–96, New York, NY, USA, 2013. ACM.

[8] S. Kratsch and F. Neumann. Fixed-parameter evolutionary algorithms and the vertex cover problem. *Algorithmica*, 65(4):754–771, 2013.

[9] P. S. Oliveto, J. He, and X. Yao. Analysis of the (1+1) -ea for finding approximate solutions to vertex cover problems. *IEEE Trans. Evolutionary Computation*, 13(5):1006–1029, 2009.

[10] S. Pirzada and A. Dharwadker. Applications of graph theory. *Journal of Korean society for Inductrial and applied mathematics*, 11(4):19–38, 2007.

A Clustering-Based Model-Building EA for Optimization Problems with Binary and Real-Valued Variables

Krzysztof L. Sadowski
Department of Computer Science
Utrecht University
P.O. Box 80089
3508 TB Utrecht
The Netherlands
k.l.sadowski@uu.nl

Peter A.N. Bosman
Centrum Wiskunde & Informatica (CWI)
P.O. Box 94079
1090 GB Amsterdam
The Netherlands
peter.bosman@cwi.nl

Dirk Thierens
Department of Computer Science
Utrecht University
P.O. Box 80089
3508 TB Utrecht
The Netherlands
d.thierens@uu.nl

ABSTRACT

We propose a novel clustering-based model-building evolutionary algorithm to tackle optimization problems that have both binary and real-valued variables. The search space is clustered every generation using a distance metric that considers binary and real-valued variables jointly in order to capture and exploit dependencies between variables of different types. After clustering, linkage learning takes place within each cluster to capture and exploit dependencies between variables of the same type. We compare this with a model-building approach that only considers dependencies between variables of the same type. Additionally, since many real-world problems have constraints, we examine the use of different well-known approaches to handling constraints: constraint domination, dynamic penalty and global competitive ranking. We experimentally analyze the performance of the proposed algorithms on various unconstrained problems as well as a selection of well-known MINLP benchmark problems that all have constraints, and compare our results with the Mixed-Integer Evolution Strategy (MIES). We find that our approach to clustering that is aimed at the processing of dependencies between binary and real-valued variables can significantly improve performance in terms of required population size and function evaluations when solving problems that exhibit properties such as multiple optima, strong mixed dependencies and constraints.

CCS Concepts

•**Mathematics of computing → Evolutionary algorithms; Mixed discrete-continuous optimization;**

Keywords

Genetic algorithms, Multiple solutions/ Niching, Empirical study

GECCO '15, July 11–15, 2015, Madrid, Spain

© 2015 ACM. ISBN 978-1-4503-3472-3/15/07...$15.00

DOI: http://dx.doi.org/10.1145/2739480.2754740

1. INTRODUCTION

Research in Evolutionary Computation often focuses on either discrete or continuous optimization. However, many academic and industrial problems are known where discrete and continuous variables are present simultaneously. Additionally, many such problems, especially in the real-world, are accompanied by a set of constraints, which limit the feasibility of the solutions in the search space.

In a black-box setting little is known about the problem landscape. The presence of both discrete and continuous variables in this setting introduces many challenges. Variable dependencies may exist within the discrete and continuous sub-domains, as well as across both domains. Constraints limit the feasibility of the solution space, and multimodality of a landscape may create deceptive attractors towards local optima.

Model-based Evolutionary Algorithms (EAs) have been successful in solving black-box optimization problems for both discrete and continuous domains. EAs can build models by either learning linkage between variables in the discrete domain, or estimating probability distributions in the continuous domain, which leads to identifying search space regions with high quality solutions. The Linkage Tree Genetic Algorithm (LTGA) and Incremental Adapted Maximum Likelihood Gaussian Model Iterated Density Estimation Evolutionary Algorithm (iAMaLGaM)[1] are state-of-the-art model-building EAs for discrete and continuous problems respectively [9] [1]. A recently introduced approach extends the use of these model-based EAs from the individual respective domains to the mixed discrete-continuous domains, by combining and interleaving their model-building mechanisms. Results indicate that integrating those two algorithms can produce an efficient optimization algorithm for various unconstrained mixed discrete-continuous problems [8]. This promising approach is still limited however, as it only considers the continuous and discrete domains independently. By doing so, possible dependencies between discrete and continuous variables are ignored. We aim to improve this approach by adjusting the variable sampling mechanism and by integrating a clustering mechanism to process mixed dependencies.

Clustering the solution space provides the means for focusing the optimization process on multiple important regions

[1]LTGA and iAMaLGaM code is available at http://homepages.cwi.nl/~bosman/

of the search space simultaneously. This ability has the potential to explore problems with multiple optima efficiently, as well as model and exploit dependencies present in a problem due to existing constraints or inter-variable interactions. We consider different ways of clustering the search space by treating the discrete and continuous variables jointly or independently. Our goal is examining our novel clustering mechanism's ability to improve performance on problems that exhibit dependencies, constraints or consist of multiple optima.

Recent work on Mixed-Integer optimization include Evolution Strategies [6] as well as Bayesian Optimization approaches [5]. We consider different types of constraint-handling mechanisms and compare the results of our clustering based EA with the Mixed-Integer Evolution Strategy (MIES) on constrained problem benchmarks provided in [6].

2. BACKGROUND

The clustering-based model-building EA we introduce in this paper is based on two known model-building Evolutionary Algorithms: LTGA and iAMaLGaM, whose models are carefully interleaved to sample discrete and continuous variables respectively. The performance of the algorithm is tested on unconstrained benchmarks which are designed based on existing discrete and continuous problems, as well as a Mixed-Integer Nonlinear Programming (MINLP) set of constrained problems [4].

2.1 Model-Building EAs

The Linkage Tree Genetic Algorithm (LTGA) is a state-of-the-art model building GA designed for solving discrete problems [9] [10]. Variable dependences are learned in every generation with a hierarchical clustering algorithm and represented in a linkage tree. Every node of this linkage tree is a subset containing between one and $l_d - 1$ problem variables. These nodes represent linkage subsets which are important for the solution. LTGA iterates over all solutions in the population and attempts to improve them: for each solution, the linkage tree is traversed and each subset of the tree is used as a crossover mask between a donor and the parent solution. A random donor from the population is selected for every subset mask. A result of each such crossover is immediately evaluated. If the resulting offspring solution is better or equal than its parent, it replaces the parent. Otherwise, the offspring is discarded.

The Incremental Adapted Maximum-Likelihood Gaussian Model Iterated Density Estimation Evolutionary Algorithm (iAMaLGaM) is a state-of-the-art EDA for real-valued black-box optimization (BBO) [3]. Following the general EDA paradigm, iAMaLGaM estimates a Gaussian distribution every generation from the selected solutions and generates new solutions by sampling the estimated distribution. The mean vector and covariance matrix are estimated incrementally using intergenerational memory decay on maximum-likelihood estimates. A mechanism which scales up the covariance matrix when needed is used to counteract the risk of premature convergence. Finally, the intergenerational Anticipated Mean Shift procedure improves the behavior of iAMaLGaM in slope-like regions of the search space.

2.2 GAMBIT: Integrated LTGA-iAMaLGaM

A novel mechanism for solving unconstrained mixed-integer problems which relies on interleaving the model-building capabilities of LTGA and iAMaLGaM is introduced in [8]. This integrated approach builds models in the discrete and continuous space independently. An important aspect of this mechanism is maintaining a proper balance between sampling the discrete and continuous models. Sampling or updating one of the models too often can lead to premature convergence, or unnecessary exploration of the search space. In standalone iAMaLGaM, each solution is sampled once within a single generation. Standalone LTGA updates each solution up to $2l_d - 1$ times, once for every mask in the linkage tree within a generation. Because of this difference, the individual models cannot be updated at the same time in the integrated version of the two algorithms. To achieve effective sampling rates, every mask evaluation of LTGA for a given solution is followed by sampling the continuous space for the same solution from the iAMaLGaM model. Once all solutions have been sampled the continuous model is updated. The discrete model is only updated after all the masks have been tried on all solutions. This way, the continuous and discrete variables of a given solution are sampled consecutively, however the rebuilding of discrete and continuous models takes place at different times, following the specifications of the individual algorithms.

Sampling of discrete and continuous variables to create new solutions follows mechanisms of LTGA and iAMaLGaM. The continuous model is learned from the top $\tau = 0.35$ fraction of the population, following iAMaLGaM. When continuous variables are sampled, they are accepted without any restrictions. The discrete model is built from the entire population. To generate selection pressure, when a mask is applied, the resulting solution is only accepted if it improves, or is equal to the solution following LTGA.

This integrated LTGA-iAMaLGaM algorithm has not yet been referenced under a specific name. From now on, we will refer to it as the Genetic Algorithm for Model-Based mixed-Integer opTimization, or GAMBIT.

2.3 MIES

In addition to analyzing the performance of our novel clustering-based EA, we take a closer look at results acquired with the Mixed-Integer Evolution Strategy (MIES). MIES extends $(\mu + \lambda)$-ES for continuous problems to mixed-integer search spaces. After a uniformly distributed initial population is created, new solutions are generated by the following procedure. Two solutions are randomly chosen from the current population $P(t)$ to act as parent solutions. A recombination operator is applied to parent solutions, followed by a mutation operator. Those operators are defined differently for continuous, nominal discrete and integer problem variables. This procedure repeats until λ offspring solutions are created. The best μ solutions from the union of the μ parent solutions and the λ offspring are selected and carried over into the population $P(t+1)$ [6].

3. BENCHMARK PROBLEMS

To study the behavior of our algorithm we first consider a set of unconstrained problems. In these problems constraint-handling mechanisms are not needed, which helps in acquiring better insight and understanding of the algorithm behavior. We designed mixed-integer benchmarks based on well-known discrete and continuous problems, which exhibit different problem characteristics. A specification of the individual functions can be found in Table 1. Table 2 summarizes how these functions are used together to create unconstrained mixed discrete-continuous benchmarks. Initialization range for all the unconstrained problems is [-5,5].

The first mixed benchmark F_1 is the Onemax-Sphere function. It is a concatenation of two problems where all the variables are completely independent. DT5-R.Ellipse, or F_2, is a problem where discrete variables are strongly dependent on each other because of the Deceptive Trap Function behavior, while the continuous variables are strongly dependent on each other due to parameter rotation of 45 degrees. However, no dependence between the discrete and continuous domains exist. Cross-Dependent function F_3 includes dependencies between both domains as well as mixed dependencies between the variables. It is a specific combination of the previously defined F_{DT5} function with the rotated ellipsoid. It is additively decomposable and consists of subfunctions pertaining to blocks of k discrete and k continuous variables. For a trap function with $k = 5$, there are $2^k = 32$ different binary combinations per block. A differently translated and rotated ellipsoid function corresponds with each of those combinations. The continuous function which is being optimized depends on the binary counterpart, introducing dependencies between the discrete and continuous variables that pertain to the same subset. In the function definition, D_i^{block} is a block of five discrete variables. C^{block} are the corresponding five real-valued variables. The D block variables determine which of the 2^k different rotated ellipsoid functions are being optimized, while C block provides the values of the ellipsoid function variables. In this benchmark the number of discrete variables is the same as the continuous variables: $l_d = l_c = l/2$. Finally, Twomax-Cos, or F_4, is a symmetry-breaking problem with three local optima and one global optimum. This function is a combination of the $cosine(\boldsymbol{x_c})$ function with the $Twomax(\boldsymbol{x_d})$ function. There are four symmetric optima - two from the cosine function and two from Twomax, however only one is the global optimum.

Table 1: Continuous and Discrete functions used to define our unconstrained mixed benchmarks

Functions
$F_{Sphere}(\boldsymbol{x_c}) = \sum_{i=0}^{l_c-1} c_i^2$
$F_{R.Ellip.}(\boldsymbol{x_c}) = F_{Ellip.}(\mathbf{R} * \boldsymbol{x_c})$, where $F_{Ellip.}(\boldsymbol{x_c}) = \sum_{i=0}^{l_c-1} 10^{6*i/(l_c-1)} * c_i^2$
$F_{Onemax}(\boldsymbol{x_d}) = \sum_{i=0}^{l_d-1} d_i$
$F_{DT5}(\boldsymbol{x_d}) = \sum_{i=0}^{l_d/k-1} f_{Trap-k}^{sub}(\sum_{j=ki}^{ki+k-1} d_j)$, where $f_{Trap-k}^{sub}(u) = \begin{cases} 0 & : if\ u = k \\ 1-(k-1-u)/k & : otherwise \end{cases}$
$F_{Twomax}(\boldsymbol{x_d}) = max(F_{Onemax}, F_{Zeromax})$

Table 2: Unconstrained Problems

ID	Definition
F_1	$F_1(\boldsymbol{x_d}, \boldsymbol{x_c}) = F_{Onemax}(\boldsymbol{x_d}) + F_{Sphere}(\boldsymbol{x_c})$
F_2	$F_2(\boldsymbol{x_d}, \boldsymbol{x_c}) = F_{DT5}(\boldsymbol{x_d}) + F_{R.Ellip.}(\boldsymbol{x_c})$
F_3	$F_3(\boldsymbol{x_d}, \boldsymbol{x_c}) = \sum_{i=0}^{0.5l/k-1}(1 + 10^a f_{sub}^{trap}(\sum_{j=ki}^{ki+k-1} d_j)) *(1 + f_{Ellipse}^{sub}(D_i^{block}, C_i^{block}))$
F_4	$F_4(\boldsymbol{x_d}, \boldsymbol{x_c}) = F_{Twomax}(\boldsymbol{x_d}) + F_{COS}(\boldsymbol{x_c})$

Many industrial mixed continuous-discrete problems include constraints. Very often, it is the constraints, not the function itself that makes the problem much more difficult to solve. We consider a set of Mixed-Integer problems from the MINLP Benchmark Library [4]. Specification of the objective function, constraints and parameters ranges can be found in Table 3. Minimization is assumed for both unconstrained and constrained problems.

4. CLUSTERING-BASED MIXED DEPENDENCY MODELING

4.1 Motivation

Understanding the underlying problem structure can be key in effectively optimizing a black-box mixed-integer problem. GAMBIT is a promising recent approach which joins the model building capabilities of LTGA and iAMaLGaM. Variable dependencies are thereby still independently modeled for each domain, while the frequency of sampling solutions and model updates is carefully balanced [8]. Considering dependencies between different types of variables (i.e. discrete and continuous) could be a very important step in solving difficult problems more efficiently. We study if integrating a clustering-based approach with GAMBIT improves performance on problems that exhibit variable dependencies, constraints or contain multiple optima.

Similar to LTGA, one could arguably consider explicitly modeling mixed dependencies on a variable level by means of calculating mutual information between discrete and continuous variables. This information could then be used to learn important mixed linkage subsets in a similar fashion to how LTGA generates and samples from a linkage tree of discrete subsets. To process dependencies for such mixed masks, clustering could be used, for instance to model the distribution in the continuous space conditionally on a clustering of the discrete space. However, mixed mask configurations acquired this way may differ in subsequent generations, resulting in intrinsically different ways of clustering the search space and learning the parameters of the Gaussian distributions in iAMaLGaM. This invalidates the use of the intergenerational mechanisms of iAMaLGaM as they are currently defined. It is not straightforward to change these mechanisms accordingly.

This does not completely invalidate the use of clustering, however. Clustering on the solution level allows the preservation of these crucial intergenerational mechanism, as models created in the previous generation can be mapped to models resulting from the clustering in the current generation. Furthermore, clustering has the capacity to partition the search space into regions representing different optima if they exist within a problem space. This feature is likely to also improve performance of GAMBIT and further motivates the use of a cluster-based mechanism.

4.2 Implementation

The overview of this clustering-based mechanism is as follows. A constant number k of clusters is predetermined. A population is generated randomly with n solutions that are evaluated. From this population k equally-sized (n/k) clusters which exert some level of similarity in accordance with the chosen distance metric are selected. Details on how the clusters are determined is explained later in this section. It is possible for the same solution to exist in multiple

Table 3: Specifications of the MINLP selected constrained benchmark problems

Name	Function	Constrains	Range
F_5	$2r_1 + d_1$	$-r_1^2 - d_1^2 \leq -1.5, r_1 + d_1 \leq 1.6$	$r_1 \in [0, 1.6]$ $d_1 \in \{0, 1\}$
F_6	$2r_1 + 3r_2 + 1.5d_1 + 2d_2 - 0.5d_3$	$r_1^2 + d_1 = 1.25, r_2^{1.5} + 1.5d_2 = 3$ $r_1 + d_1 \leq 1.6, 1.333r_2 + d_2 \leq 3$ $-d_1 - d_2 + d_3 \leq 0$	$r_{1,2} \in [0, 10]$ $d_{1,2,3} \in \{0, 1\}$
F_7	$0.8 + 5(r_1 - 0.5)^2 - 0.7d_1$	$-exp(r_1 - 0.2) - r_2 \leq 0$ $r_2 + 1.1d_1 \leq -1, r_1 - 1.2d_1 \leq 0$	$r_1 \in [0.2, 1]$ $r_2 \in [0.22554, -1]$ $d_1 \in \{0, 1\}$
F_8	$6 + (r_1 - 1)^2 + (r_2 - 2)^2$ $+(r_3 - 3)^2 - d_1 - 3d_2 - d_3$ $-0.693147180559945d_4$	$r_1 + r_2 + r_3 + d_1 + d_2 + d_3 \leq 5$ $r_1^2 + r_2^2 + r_3^2 + d_3 \leq 5.5$ $r_1 + d_1 \leq 1.2, r_2 + d_2 \leq 1.8$ $r_3 + d_3 \leq 2.5, r_1 + d_4 \leq 1.2$ $r_2^2 + d_2 \leq 1.64, r_3^2 + d_3 \leq 4.25$ $r_3^2 + d_2 \leq 4.64$	$r_{1,2,3} \in [0, 10]$ $d_{1,2,3,4} \in \{0, 1\}$
F_9	$-5r_1 + 3r_2$	$8r_1 - 2r_1^{0.5}r_2 + 11r_2 + 2r_2^2 - 2r_2^{0.5} \leq 39$ $r_1 - r_2 \leq 3, 3r_1 + 2r_2 \leq 24$ $r_2 - d_1 - 2d_2 - 4d_3 = 1, d_2 + d_3 \leq 1$	$r_1 \in [1, 10]$ $r_1 \in [1, 6]$ $d_{1,2,3} \in \{0, 1\}$
F_{10}	$(r_4 - 1)^2 + (r_5 - 2)^2 + (r_6 - 1)^2$ $-log(1 + r_7) + (r_1 - 1)^2$ $+(r_2 - 2)^2 + (r_3 - 3)^2$	$r_1 + r_2 + r_3 + d_1 + d_2 + d_3 \leq 5$ $r_6^2 + r_1^2 + r_2^2 + r_3^2 \leq 5.5, r_1 + d_1 \leq 1.2$ $r_2 + d_2 \leq 1.8, r_3 + d_3 \leq 2.5, r_1 + d_4 \leq 1.2$ $r_5^2 + r_2^2 \leq 1.64, r_6^2 + r_3^2 \leq 4.25$ $r_5^2 + r_3^2 \leq 4.64$ $r_4 - d_1 = 0, r_5 - d_2 = 0$ $r_6 - d_3 = 0, r_7 - d_4 = 0$	$r_{1,2,3} \in [1, 10]$ $r_{4,5,6,7} \in [0, 1]$ $d_{1,2,3,4} \in \{0, 1\}$

clusters. A separate continuous-discrete model is associated with one cluster of solutions. Within each cluster, the variable linkages and Gaussian parameters for the discrete and continuous variables are learned respectively. Based on the learned information, each model instance generates n/k new solutions, which are added into the main population. The clustering process begins anew for every generation. After clustering takes place, the model instances from previous generation are matched with the newly created clusters using a well-known distance-minimizing Hungarian method, where the cluster distance is the sum of all pairwise distances between solutions. The distance between individual solutions is the same as the one used for clustering. By doing so, the intergenerational mechanisms needed by iAMaLGaM are preserved. The clustering process is shown in Figure 1.

The clustering process itself takes place at the beginning of every generation. Depending on the number of clusters k, cluster leaders are selected. The best solution available in the population is always selected as a cluster center. Other centers are solutions with the furthest distance from all already chosen centers. Once the centers are determined, n/k solutions closest to the chosen centers are added to the clusters in accordance with the chosen distance metric. This cluster selection process is based on a similar approach used for Multi-Objective optimization in [2].

```
Clustering-Based Model-Building EA
for i ∈ {0, 1, ..., n − 1} do
    P_i ← CreateRandomSolution()
    EvaluateFitness(P_i)

while ¬TerminationCriterionSatisfied do
    C ← PopulateClusters(P)
    for j ∈ {0, 1, ..., C} do
        P_i ← IntegratedAlgorithm(C_i)
    C ← MatchClusters
```

Figure 1: Pseudo-Code overview of the Clustering-based mechanism

4.3 Distance Measures

By clustering the current solution space we attempt to identify groups of solutions within the entire population that represent common properties or dependencies. In order to perform such clustering, a distance measure is required. We want to compare the performance of our algorithm when the clustering process takes into account discrete and continuous variables together and when only one sub-domain is used. To accomplish this we consider four different distance measures. Two of them perform clustering using a distance measure which considers the discrete and continuous domains independently, while the remaining two attempt to process the discrete and real-valued domains jointly.

Independent distance measures consider either the discrete or continuous domain only. For the discrete measure, clustering is done only on the discrete variables with the use of the Hamming distance between two solutions. In the continuous variant, Euclidean distance is calculated.

In order to consider both discrete and continuous variables together, a joint distance metric is required. One option is to consider all variables as discrete. For this, the continuous domain is discretized. Each continuous variable is converted into a binary one, depending on if it lies above or below the median value of the current population for this variable. This is a very crude discretization, as each continuous variable is represented only by one bit. Once all variables are processed, the distance between different solutions is calculated using the Hamming distance which considers the

```
Integrated Model Sampling
for i ∈ {0,1,...,n−1} do
  P_i ← CreateRandomSolution()
  EvaluateFitness(P_i)

while ¬TerminationCriterionSatisfied do
  LearnDiscreteModel(P)
  for i ∈ {0,1,...,(2l_d − 1 + 2l_c − 1)} do
    if sampleType(i) = continuous then
      S ← TruncationSelection(P, τ)
      LearnContinuousModel(S)
      for j ∈ {0,1,...,n−1} do
        X_i ← GenerateContinuousPart(P_i)
    else
      for j ∈ {0,1,...,n−1} do
        X_i ← GenerateDiscretePart(j, X_i, P)
  P ← X

GenerateContinuousPart(P_i)
  X_c ← SampleContinuousModel()
  X ← X_c ∪ P_{i_d}
  EvaluateFitness(X)
  return X

GenerateDiscretePart(j, X_i, P)
  X_prev ← X_i
  donor ← GetRandomSol(P)
  X_d ← CopySubset(j, donor, X_i)
  X ← X_{i_c} ∪ X_d
  EvaluateFitness(X)
  if fitness(X) ≥ fitness(X_prev) then
    return X
  else
    return X_prev
```

Figure 2: Pseudo-code for generating solutions with GAMBITs Learning Models.

discretized continuous variables and the discrete variables together. Encoding continuous variables with more than one bit would unbalance calculating the Hamming distance, giving the continuous variables more weight.

Another way of modeling mixed similarities is to consider discrete and continuous variables together in the continuous domain. The continuous variables are normalized and scaled down to a 0-1 range where the current largest value in the population takes on the value of one, and the smallest zero. Binary variables are then treated as real values. This way Euclidean distances can be computed between two solutions using discrete and continuous variables together.

4.4 Generating Offspring

In the first generation k continuous-discrete models are created. Each cluster of solutions is assigned to one model. In this phase, each model uses solutions provided by the clustering mechanism to learn variable dependencies and update the discrete and continuous models. With this new information, new solutions are generated from every model. We make a significant change to the sampling mechanism of the continuous-discrete model. The algorithm proposed in [8] achieves a good balance between sampling the discrete and continuous models by sampling the entire continuous space every time a discrete mask is sampled. The downside of this approach is that the rate of sampling the continuous space relies on the number of discrete masks only. This means that continuous evaluations will happen every time discrete ones do. This is not necessarily desired behavior, as we might want to increase the number of times continuous domain is sampled when the ratio of continuous to discrete variables is large, and lower it when this ratio is small. We remedy this by including the number of continuous variables as a factor in determining how many continuous evaluations will take place every generation. More specifically, the number of sampled discrete masks is $2l_d - 1$, as specified by LTGA. Instead of basing the continuous sampling on this number as well, we now sample the continuous space $2l_c - 1$ times. Additionally, instead of a discrete sampling always preceding a continuous one, sampling happens in a randomized order. These changes allow GAMBIT to allocate additional processing to continuous variables when they make up a large portion of the total problem size, and saves on unnecessary evaluations in the continuous space when real-valued variables make up a small part of the problem. Integrated model building and solution generation done by GAMBIT is summarized in Figure 2.

In experiments on constrained problems we consider different constraint-handling techniques with our clustering-based algorithm. Constraint violation checking takes place every time a new solution is introduced to the population.

5. CONSTRAINT HANDLING

A constrained mixed discrete-continuous problems can be defined as follows:

$$min\ f(\boldsymbol{x_d}, \boldsymbol{x_c})$$

$$\text{s.t. } \mathbf{h}(\boldsymbol{x_d}, \boldsymbol{x_c}) = 0, \quad \mathbf{g}(\boldsymbol{x_d}, \boldsymbol{x_c}) \leq 0$$

Where x represents the solution

$$x = \boldsymbol{x_d}\boldsymbol{x_c} = d_0...d_{l_d-1}\ c_0...c_{l_c-1}$$

where $d_i \in \{0,1\}, c_i \in \mathbb{R}$ and $\boldsymbol{x_d}$, $\boldsymbol{x_c}$ are the sets of all discrete and continuous variables, respectively. f is the objective function. $\mathbf{h}$ and $\mathbf{g}$ are the sets of equality and inequality constraint functions respectively.

Mixed discrete-continuous problems are often accompanied by constraints. No matter how good the objective function value of a certain solution is, if any of the constraints is violated, the solution is considered infeasible. A set of equality and inequality constraints may exist simultaneously within a problem. Within a black-box setting, we cannot make assumptions about the number or type of constraints that may be present. The only feedback we may hope to have is an indication of how much the constraints are violated. We obtain this indicator by computing a squared sum of all constraint violations for a given solution. This constraint violation value indicates the relative strength of constraint violation. A constraint violation value of 0 indicates a feasible solution. Because of precision issues, in our experiments a solution with a constraint value less than 10^{-10} is considered feasible.

We consider three prominent constraint handling techniques: Constraint Domination, Global Competitive Ranking and the Dynamic Penalty Function [7]. Constraint domination strongly favors feasible solutions. A feasible solutions is always better than an infeasible one. A better function value determines which solutions are better when solutions are feasible. Infeasible solutions are ranked by their constraint violation value. Constraint Domination can quickly converge on high function value solutions in the feasible space, but avoids exploration of infeasible regions when possible.

Global competitive ranking maintains two independent rankings. All solutions (feasible and unfeasible) are ordered by their objective function as well as their constraint violation values independently. The final ranking is generated based on a combination of the objective function and constraint violation rankings. This approach finds a balance between solutions in the feasible and infeasible space. Infeasible solutions of high objective function values are kept in the population, which could potentially allow for good feasible regions nearby them to be explored.

We also consider the Dynamic Penalty Method for constraint handling. In this method the fitness value of a solution is diminished by a penalty factor if the solution is not feasible. The penalty factor is proportional to the constraint violation value. Additionally, this penalty factor is proportional to the number of generations which already passed. If a solution cannot reach feasible values, over time the penalty factor becomes stronger. With this method promising infeasible regions can be explored, however as time passes, feasible solutions become increasingly favorable. In our implementation the penalty function value is the square of the total constraint violation value multiplied by the number of generations which had already passed.

6. RESULTS

Experiments are performed on a set of unconstrained as well as constrained benchmarks. Bisection was performed for all problems to determine the population size for which the number of evaluations is minimal, while the optimum is reached at least 19 out of 20 runs. The maximum population size used was 2500.

6.1 Unconstrained Problems

As specified in the previous section we consider two approaches that cluster the population using only information from one domain (either discrete or continuous domain) or from both domains jointly. Figure 3 shows representative results of our experiments with different clustering distance measures. "Discrete" and "Continuous" labels refer to the distance measures considering only the discrete and real-valued domains independently. "Mixed (D)" and "Mixed (C)" refer to the clustering mechanism using joint information, by discretization of the continuous variables, or by treating discrete variables as continuous respectively. The results are presented on the F_4 benchmark that exhibits symmetries or large, prominent multi-modalities with a cluster setting $k = 2$. The presented results are representative of the behavior with larger cluster sizes.

From 3 we can see that the "Mixed" configurations perform significantly better in terms of minimally required population size to solve the problem, as well the number of evaluations. This indicates that by clustering on the solution level when considering both discrete and continuous variables together, the clustering mechanism is capable of capturing some mixed dependencies, which allow GAMBIT to exploit the search space more efficiently.

Out of the two configurations which consider mixed variable dependencies, "Mixed (C)" performs slightly better. This could be attributed to the fact that discretizing continuous variables with "Mixed (D)" may result in significant loss

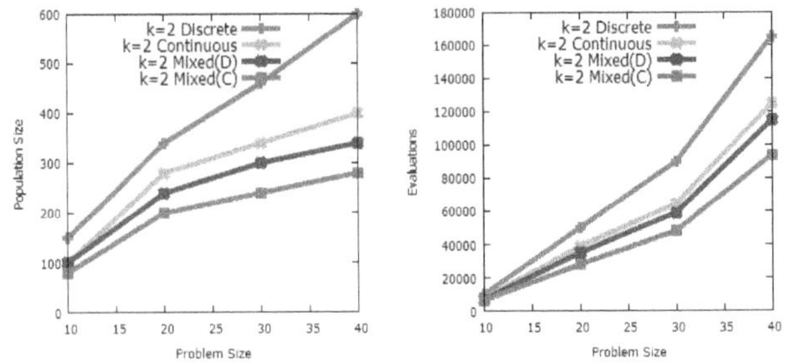

Figure 3: Effects of clustering on Discrete and Continuous variables independently vs. jointly on F_4

of information in comparison with the "Mixed (C) " configuration. This loss of information effect is not as strong with "Mixed (C)" where the continuous variables are normalized instead.

Further experiments on the unconstrained benchmarks are conducted with different cluster sizes k and summarized in Figure 4. In all graphs in this figure the mixed distance measure is used. "NoCluster" refers to the original integrated algorithms as presented in [8]. "$k = 1$" represents our new implementation of the algorithm with cluster size of 1. The results show that our new implementation with k=1 is always more efficient than the old approach. The results presented show problem instances with the same number of continuous and discrete variables. The "k=1" configuration was also tested on functions with $f = 0.25$ and $f = 0.75$ fraction of continuous variables and still always outperformed the "NoCluster" configuration.

When k is increased, the behavior changes depending on the type of the benchmark. F_1 is the simplest benchmark in the set. All variables are completely independent, and the search space is not deceptive. A single cluster has no difficulty solving this problem efficiently. F_2 contains strong dependencies in the continuous and discrete domains, but no cross-dependencies. Here a single cluster configuration is also favorable, as the underlying models of GAMBIT are very efficient in dealing with dependencies contained within each domain, without any need to partition the space and process mixed dependencies. Because of this, larger clusters also solve these problems, but are less efficient. The results change when the benchmarks become more difficult. F_3 consists of cross-dependencies in addition to discrete and continuous dependencies. Allowing the clustering mechanism to process the mixed dependencies results in significantly better performance in terms of population size and evaluations needed with $k = 2$ than with $k = 1$. F_4 is a symmetry-breaking problem with multiple optima. Thanks to the processing and clustering the solution space $k = 2$ and $k = 4$ perform much better than a non-clustering approach.

6.2 Constrained Problems

We have tested a selection of MINLP Benchmarks with the Clustering-based Model-Building EA corresponding with the benchmarks used in [6]. Results are presented for two settings of the clustering size: $k = 1$ and $k = 10$. Similarly to the unconstrained problem analysis, we consider different approaches to clustering : "Discrete" and "Continuous" cluster the population based on the continuous and discrete variables respectively only. "Mixed (D)" and "Mixed (C)"

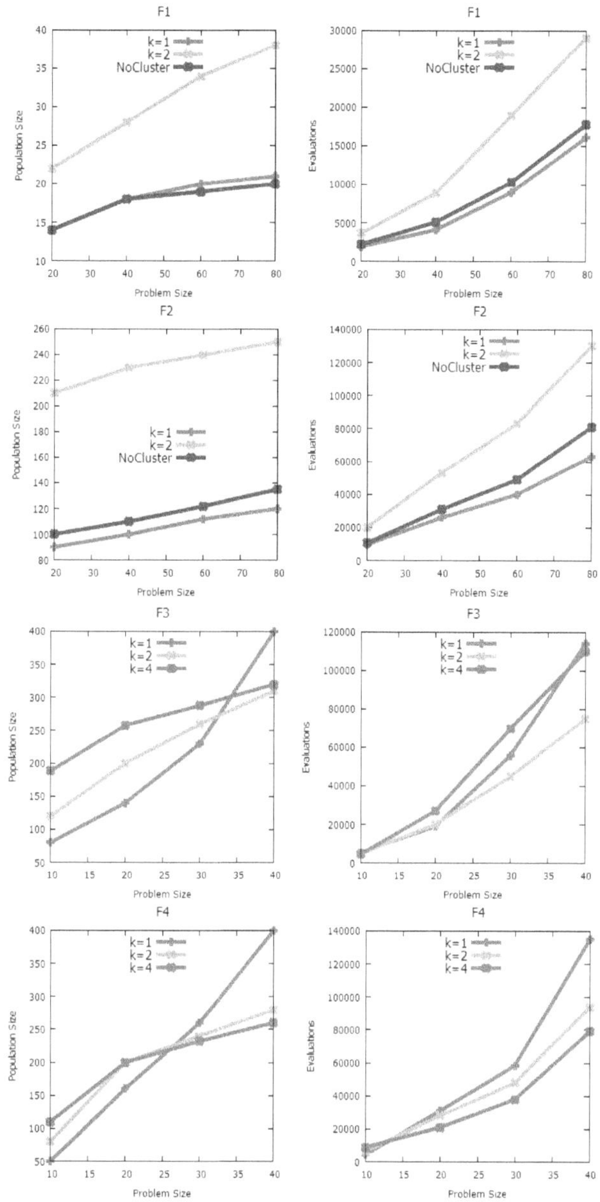

Figure 4: Performance of the clustering mechanism with changing cluster sizes on unconstrained functions

use the discrete and continuous variables together (either in Discrete space or Continuous space). In order to handle constraints, we test each algorithm configuration with different constraint handling techniques: constraint domination (CD), global competitive ranking (GCR) and dynamic penalty function (DPF). Success criteria is defined as reaching the optimal value to a precision of 10^{-5}.

Table 4 summarizes the experiments. It shows that the only consistently successful configurations are Mixed with k=10. This confirms our previous observations and further implies that the clustering algorithm which uses both discrete and continuous variables on which the clustering is performed, is able to successfully process certain dependencies and features of the constrained landscape. For simpler problems, such as F_6, additional clustering is not needed, and a configuration with $k = 1$ can successfully find the optimum. However, in many problems with stronger dependencies and constraints $k = 1$ is not sufficient. Similarly to results from the previous section, "Mixed (C)" outperforms the "Mixed (D)" configuration.

Additionally we observe that constraint-handling techniques have a strong effect on the performance of any configuration of the clustering algorithm. While constraint domination and global competitive ranking perform similarly, the dynamic penalty method is more successful. Performance of MIES on the same benchmarks set is presented in [7] and summarized here in Table 5 which shows the median evaluations needed to reach near-optimal values, as well as the standard deviation of the results. Direct comparison is difficult, as the reported MIES performance does not indicate the success rate. Additionally, our implementation considers different population sizes while MIES does not. MIES however allows for parameterization of its constraint handling method, while we do not. Despite these differences, the results indicate that the clustering algorithm is competitive with MIES in terms of evaluations needed to reach the optimum on most of the tested benchmarks.

Table 5: Median number of evaluations and S.Dev. of MIES

Function	Evals	SD
F_5	7000	$1.9870 * 10^{-13}$
F_6	21700	$3.5616 * 10^{-15}$
F_7	22400	$3.6293 * 10^{-15}$
F_8	23800	$1.5132 * 10^{-13}$
F_9	20300	$2.3570 * 10^{-1}$
F_{10}	131600	$6.0510 * 10^{-1}$

7. CONCLUSIONS AND SUMMARY

In this paper we studied the added value of clustering in a previously introduced model-building EA named the Genetic Algorithm for Model-Based mixed-Integer opTimization (GAMBIT). Using a distance metric that considers discrete and continuous variables jointly, this clustering mechanism partitions the search space based on mixed continuous-discrete variables on the solution level, and learns discrete variable linkage and continuous covariance independently within each cluster. Our results showed that through integration of the clustering mechanism and a more balanced integration of sampling discrete and contentious variables, we significantly improve the performance of GAMBIT for problems exhibiting features such as variable dependencies or multiple optima in a black-box environment. Analysis of performance on unconstrained benchmarks showed that if such features exist in the problem, generating clusters with the consideration of both variable types together performs significantly better than considering the continuous and discrete domains only independently, or not clustering in the solution space at all.

Some drawbacks still exist. This clustering procedure is sensitive to the number of clusters k. If the problem does not exert strong mixed dependencies or multi modality, a high setting for k may lead to unnecessary overhead in terms of minimal required population sizes and number of evaluations.

Table 4: Performance of different variants of the clustering-based algorithms with different constraint handling techniques. Best results are bold. Equal statistical significance (T-test) is annotated with *.

			CD			GCR			DPF		
Problem	k	Clustering	Pop	Evals	Success	Pop	Evals	Success	Pop	Evals	Success
F_5	1	-	40	1104	1	40	1104	1	**40**	**897***	**1**
F_5	10	Discrete	100	1271	1	100	1271	1	200	970	1
F_5	10	Real	100	1473	1	100	1473	1	100	1402	1
F_5	10	Mixed (D)	100	1350	1	100	1350	1	100	1101	1
f_5	10	Mixed (C)	100	1112	1	100	1112	1	100	910*	1
F_6	1	-	2500	-	0	2500	-	0	2500	0	0
F_6	10	Discrete	480	19014	1	240	19014	1	240	6308	1
F_6	10	Real	2500	39014	0.1	2500	-	0	2500	45665	0.3
F_6	10	Mixed (D)	160	7402	1	180	7812	1	140	6304	1
F_6	10	Mixed (C)	160	6867	1	180	7114	1	**120**	**4001**	**1**
F_7	1	-	70	11627	0.95	70	11104	1	300	30886	1
F_7	10	Discrete	**100**	**3551**	**1**	100	4211	1	400	20422	1
F_7	10	Real	100	6788	1	100	6537	1	500	28995	1
F_7	10	Mixed (D)	100	5330	1	100	6151	1	400	18664	1
F_7	10	Mixed (C)	100	7133	1	100	7715	1	400	19910	1
F_8	1	-	2500	-	0	2500	-	0	2500	-	0
F_8	10	Discrete	1000	146332	0.95	1100	167554	1	900	50885	0.95
F_8	10	Real	2500	-	0	2500	-	0	2500	-	0
F_8	10	Mixed (D)	900	79664	0.95	900	85244	1	600	56744	1
F_8	10	Mixed (C)	800	49774	1	800	52274	1	**400**	**20155**	**1**
F_9	1	-	60	4919	1	70	5067	1	**40**	**2996***	**1**
F_9	10	Discrete	100	6446	1	100	6223	1	100	4359	1
F_9	10	Real	100	6674	1	100	6530	1	100	4102	1
F_9	10	Mixed (D)	100	7350	1	100	7004	1	100	6412	1
F_9	10	Mixed (C)	100	4789	1	100	4951	1	100	3084*	1
F_{10}	1	-	2500	-	0	2500	-	0	2500	-	0
F_{10}	10	Discrete	2500	545633	0.35	2500	545633	0.35	2500	454855	0.35
F_{10}	10	Real	2500	-	0	2500	-	0	2500	-	0
F_{10}	10	Mixed (D)	2500	534428	0.4	2500	534428	0.4	2500	387765	0.5
F_{10}	10	Mixed (C)	2500	527754	0.6	2500	527754	0.6	**2000**	**232445**	**0.95**

Our results extend to constrained MINLP problems. Comparison with MIES on selected benchmark problems shows that the clustering-based EA approach can be competitive, and often outperforms MIES in terms of evaluations needed. Different types of constraint-handling methods show a strong impact on optimization efficiency. In the benchmarks tested the dynamic penalty method generated best results in most of the cases, while the constraint domination and global competitive ranking method performed similarly to each other.

8. REFERENCES

[1] P. Bosman, J. Grahl, and D. Thierens. Benchmarking Parameter-Free AMaLGaM on Functions With and Without Noise. *Evolutionary Computation*, 21(3):445–469, Sept 2013.

[2] P. A. N. Bosman. The Anticipated Mean Shift and Cluster Registration in Mixture-based EDAs for Multi-Objective Optimization. In *Proceedings of the Genetic and Evolutionary Computation Conference*, GECCO-2010, pages 351–358, New York, NY, USA, 2010. ACM.

[3] P. A. N. Bosman, J. Grahl, and D. Thierens. Enhancing the Performance of Maximum-Likelihood Gaussian EDAs Using Anticipated Mean Shift. In *Parallel Problem Solving from Nature - PPSN X*, LNCS, pages 133–143, 2008.

[4] M. Bussieck and A. Pruessner. Mixed-integer Nonlinear Programming. *SIAG/OPT Viewsand-News*, 14(1):19–22, 2003.

[5] M. T. Emmerich, R. Li, A. Zhang, I. Flesch, and P. Lucas. Mixed-Integer Bayesian Optimization Utilizing A-Priori Knowledge on Parameter Dependences. In *Proceedings of the 20th Belgium-Netherlands Conference on Artificial Intelligence (BNAIC)*, pages 65–72, 2008.

[6] R. Li, M. T. M. Emmerich, J. Eggermont, T. Bäck, M. Schütz, J. Dijkstra, and J. H. C. Reiber. Mixed Integer Evolution Strategies for Parameter Optimization. *Evolutionary Computation*, 21(1):29–64, 2013.

[7] T. Runarsson and X. Yao. Constrained evolutionary optimization. In *Evolutionary Optimization*, volume 48 of *International Series in Operations Research and Management Science*, pages 87–113. Springer US, 2002.

[8] K. L. Sadowski, D. Thierens, and P. A. N. Bosman. Combining Model-Based EAs for Mixed-Integer Problems. In *Parallel Problem Solving from Nature — PPSN XIII*, LNCS, pages 342–351. Springer, 2014.

[9] D. Thierens. The linkage tree genetic algorithm. In *Parallel Problem Solving from Nature — PPSN XI*, LNCS, pages 264–273, Berlin, 2010. Springer–Verlag.

[10] D. Thierens and P. A. N. Bosman. Optimal mixing evolutionary algorithms. In *Proceedings of the Genetic and Evolutionary Computation Conference*, GECCO '11, pages 617–624, New York, NY, USA, 2011. ACM.

A Biased Random-key Genetic Algorithm for Placement of Virtual Machines across Geo-Separated Data Centers

Fernando Stefanello
Instituto de Informática
Universidade Federal do Rio Grande do Sul
Porto Alegre, Brazil
fstefanello@inf.ufrgs.br

Vaneet Aggarwal
School of Industrial Engineering
Purdue University
West Lafayette, IN 47907 USA
vaneet@purdue.edu

Luciana S. Buriol
Instituto de Informática
Universidade Federal do Rio Grande do Sul
Porto Alegre, Brazil
buriol@inf.ufrgs.br

José F. Gonçalves
Faculdade de Economia
Universidade do Porto
Porto, Portugal, 4200-464
jfgoncal@fep.up.pt

Mauricio G. C. Resende
Mathematical Optimization and Planning (MOP)
Amazon.com
Seattle, WA 98109 USA
resendem@amazon.com

ABSTRACT

Cloud computing has recently emerged as a new technology for hosting and supplying services over the Internet. This technology has brought many benefits, such as eliminating the need for maintaining expensive computing hardware and allowing business owners to start from small and increase resources only when there is a rise in service demand. With an increasing demand for cloud computing, providing performance guarantees for applications that run over cloud become important. Applications can be abstracted into a set of virtual machines with certain guarantees depicting the quality of service of the application. In this paper, we consider the placement of these virtual machines across multiple data centers, meeting the quality of service requirements while minimizing the bandwidth cost of the data centers. This problem is a generalization of the NP-hard Generalized Quadratic Assignment Problem (GQAP). We formalize the problem and propose a novel algorithm based on a biased random-key genetic algorithm (BRKGA) to find near-optimal solutions for the problem. The experimental results show that the proposed algorithm is effective in quickly finding feasible solutions and it produces better results than a baseline aproach provided by a commercial solver and a multi-start algorithm.

Categories and Subject Descriptors

I.2.8 [Artificial Intelligence] [**Problem Solving, Control Methods,and Search**]: [Heuristic methods]

GECCO'15, July 11-15, 2015, Madrid, Spain.
Copyright 2015 ACM. ISBN 978-1-4503-2662-9/14/07 ...$15.00.
http://dx.doi.org/10.1145/2739480.2754768.

Keywords

Combinatorial optimization; Cloud computing; Biased Random-Key Genetic Algorithm.

1. INTRODUCTION

Virtualization of physical servers have gained prominence in enterprise data centers. This is because virtualization offers virtually unlimited resources without any upfront capital investment and a simple pay-as-you-go charging model. Long term viability of virtualization depends, among other factors, on cost and performance. In order to attain performance guarantees, application providers can offer requirements for a number of virtual machines, bandwidth/latency requirements between virtual machines, and latency requirements between users of the service and virtual machines. Having all these performance guarantees for the application can help give an optimized service to the users. However, the service provider has to match the requirements of different applications to the placement of virtual machines with the limited bandwidth links between geographically separated data centers while minimizing its cost. This paper considers this placement problem, and gives novel solutions using a class of genetic algorithms.

Unfortunately, today's public cloud platforms such as Amazon EC2 [2] do not provide any performance guarantee, which in turn affects tenant cost. Specifically, the resource reservation model in today's clouds only provisions CPU and memory resources but ignores networking completely. Because of the largely oversubscribed nature of today's data center networks (e.g., [6]), network bandwidth is a scarce resource shared across many tenants. In order to meet the reliability and the demand requirements, the data centers have to be placed all across the world. For instance, a teleconference call connects people from all over the world, and a data center within a reasonable distance to the end users is needed. For distributed data centers, networking cost is the major cost, which has not been accounted in the prior works on virtual machine placement to the best of our knowledge. With the limited bandwidth links between the data centers, networking intensive phases of applications collide and compete for the scarce network resources, which leads to their running times become unpredictable. The uncertainty in execution time further translates into unpredictable cost as tenants need to pay for the reserved virtual machines (VMs) for the entire duration of their jobs.

Placement of virtual machines within a data center have been widely explored [7, 3, 16]. These papers account for the networking needs in addition to the CPU and memory needs within a data center. For example, [7] proposes bandwidth reservation between every pair of VMs. [3] proposes a simpler virtual cluster (VC) model where all virtual machines are connected to a virtual switch with links of bandwidth B. [16] extends these approaches to consider time-varying network requirement. However, all these works account for a single data center where the bandwidths are much larger as compared to the bandwidths across data centers. Instead, this paper deals with the placement of virtual machines across geo-separated data centers

In this paper, we consider multiple data centers that are connected with limited bandwidth links. The latency between every pair of data centers is known. In order to meet the application's quality of service guarantees, there is a required minimum bandwidth and maximum latency between each pair of virtual machines. We assume that there are multiple users who would use these services, and users are connected to some data center. In order to meet the overall application performance, there is an additional requirement of maximum latency between users and the virtual machines. Intuitively, if there is a set of VMs needed by a user and the set does not have any requirement with any other user or VM, it can be placed in a single data center. However, a VM interacts with multiple VMs which may be needed by other users, thus increasing the set of options for placement. There is a cost of transferring data between data-centers and the placement minimizes this cost thus preferring placement of all VMs in a single data center which may not be feasible due to the quality of service requirements for the application.

This problem is a generalization of the NP-hard Generalized Quadratic Placement Problem given in [11]. Solving this problem optimally is possible only in very small instances, which may not represent the size found in real-world applications. Thus, we propose a Biased Random-key Genetic Algorithm (BRKGA) for solving the Virtual Machine Placement Problem. We test the performance of the proposed algorithm in a dataset comprised of instances with sizes ranging from small to large. We show that the algorithm is able to quickly find feasible solutions, producing better results than a classic multi-start algorithm and an exact approach using CPLEX [10].

The paper brings several contributions: i) We model a multi-data center virtual machine placement problem with quality of service guarantees for the application; ii) The quadratic problem with integer constraints is reduced to a mixed integer linear program for placement of virtual machines; iii) Novel algorithms based on BRKGA are proposed to place virtual machines across multiple data centers; iv) A generator of instances which contain at least one feasible solution is provided; v) We provide experimental results for CPLEX and the BRKGA applied on the proposed instances.

The rest of the paper is organized as follows. In Section 2, we present mathematical models for the Virtual Machine Placement Problem in multiple data centers. The biased random-key genetic algorithm with local search is presented in Section 3. Computational results are presented in Section 4. Finally, conclusions are drawn in Section 5.

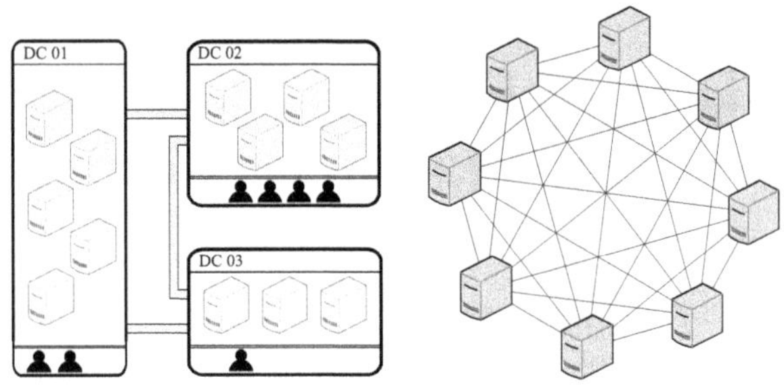

(a) Data centers. (b) Virtual machines.

Figure 1: Input data representation.

2. VIRTUAL MACHINE PLACEMENT PROBLEM

In the Virtual Machine Placement Problem (VMPlacement), the objective is to place a set K of virtual machines (VM) in a set N of data centers (DC) in order to minimize the communication cost among virtual machines.

In this problem, each data center has a capacity a_i, which represents the number of virtual machines that can be placed in DC i. Also, between two data centers i and j, there are a bandwidth capacity (B_{ij}), a latency (L_{ij}), and a cost C_{ij} to transfer a data unit between the pair of data centers.

In order to meet the reliability and demand requirements of the applications, certain bandwidth and latency requirements can be imposed on the different VMs that are placed on the data centers. Each pair of virtual machines v and w has a required bandwidth (b_{vw}) whose sum overall VMs placed between DCs i and j cannot exceed B_{ij}. Furthermore, there is a required latency (l_{vw}), such that VMs v and w cannot be placed in data centers i and j if the required latency is greater than the respective data center latency.

Finally, there is a set U of users who access the system. Each user u is located at a data center $d(u)$ and has a required latency t_{uv} for each VM v.

Figure 1 shows a representation of the input data components: the data centers (Figure 1a), and the virtual machines (Figure 1b). The first component is composed by three data centers (rounded rectangles). Each data center has a number of users and a capacity (represented as a number of spots where VMs can be placed). The connection between each pair of DCs represents the bandwidth capacity, latency, and cost. The second component is composed by eight virtual machines, where each link represents the bandwidth and required latency.

The performance of mixed integer linear programming solvers has improved considerably over the last few years. IBM ILOG CPLEX Optimizer [10] is a general-purposed black-box solver based on the state-of-the-art exact algorithms for integer programming and has been successfully applied in many combinatorial optimization problems. In order to investigate the CPLEX performance and provide baseline results for comparison of heuristic methods, we present a quadratic and a linear mathematical model for the VMPlacement problem. Results are provided in Section 4.

Next we present the quadratic mathematical model for the VMPlacement (QMMVMP).

Parameters:

N : set of data centers;
K : set of virtual machines;
U : set of users;
a_i : capacity in number of VMs DC i can host;
B_{ij} : bandwidth between DCs i and j;
L_{ij} : latency between DCs i and j;
Cij : cost of transferring a data unit between DCs i and j;
b_{vw} : required bandwidth between VMs v and w;
l_{vw} : required latency between VMs v and w;
$d(u)$: DC which hosts user u;
t_{vu} : required latency between user u and VM v.

The binary decision variable x_{iv} is set to one when VM v is located into DC i, and zero otherwise.

$$\min \sum_{i \in N} \sum_{j \in N} \sum_{v \in K} \sum_{w \in K} C_{ij} b_{vw} x_{iv} x_{jw} \quad \text{(1a)}$$

subject to:

$$\sum_{v \in K} x_{iv} \leq a_i \quad \forall\, i \in N, \quad \text{(1b)}$$

$$\sum_{i \in N} x_{iv} = 1 \quad \forall\, v \in K, \quad \text{(1c)}$$

$$\sum_{v \in K} \sum_{w \in K} x_{iv} x_{jw} b_{vw} \leq B_{ij} \quad \forall\, i, j \in N, \quad \text{(1d)}$$

$$\sum_{i \in N} \sum_{j \in N} x_{iv} x_{jw} L_{ij} \leq l_{vw} \quad \forall\, v, w \in K, \quad \text{(1e)}$$

$$\sum_{i \in N} x_{iv} L_{i,d(u)} \leq t_{vu} \quad \forall\, u \in U,\ \forall\, v \in K, \quad \text{(1f)}$$

$$x_{iv} \in \{0, 1\} \quad \forall\, i \in N,\ \forall\, v \in K. \quad \text{(1g)}$$

Objective function (1a) minimizes the cost of placing each pair of virtual machines v and w to DCs i and j. Constraints (1b) require that the number of VMs in each DC must not exceed the DC capacity. Constraints (1c) require that each VM must be assigned to exactly one DC. Constraints (1d) require that the given bandwidth between each pair i and j of DCs should not be surpassed by the total sum of bandwidth required among the virtual machines placed in these DCs. Constraints (1e) require that the latency required between each pair of VMs should be respected, i.e, if VMs v and w are placed respectively to DCs i and j, then the latency between DCs i and j should not exceed the required latency between VMs v and w. Constraints (1f) require that the latency between a VM v and the DC where the user u is located be respected, i.e, a VM v can be only placed on a DC i if the latency between i and $d(u)$ is less than or equal to a given latency between the VM v and the user u. Finally, constraints (1g) define the variables domain.

The VMPlacement is an generalization of the NP-hard Generalized Quadratic Assignment Problem (GQAP), formulated in [11]. Thus, based on model $L3$ from [11], we present a mixed-integer linear model for the VMPlacement. Let $y_{ivjw} = x_{iv} x_{jw},\ \forall\, i, j = \{1, \ldots, N\}$ and $v, w = \{1, \ldots, K\}$, the mixed-integer linear mathematical model for VMPlacement named as LMMVMP, can be formulated as the following:

$$\min \sum_{i \in N} \sum_{j \in N} \sum_{v \in K} \sum_{w \in K} C_{ij} b_{vw} y_{ivjw} \quad \text{(2a)}$$

subject to:

$$\sum_{v \in K} x_{iv} \leq a_i \quad \forall\, i \in N, \quad \text{(2b)}$$

$$\sum_{i \in N} x_{iv} = 1 \quad \forall\, v \in K, \quad \text{(2c)}$$

$$\sum_{i \in N} y_{ivjw} = x_{jw} \quad \forall\, v, w \in K,\ \forall\, j \in N, \quad \text{(2d)}$$

$$y_{ivjw} = y_{jwiv} \quad \forall\, v, w \in K,\ \forall\, i, j \in N, \quad \text{(2e)}$$

$$\sum_{v \in K} \sum_{w \in K} y_{ivjw} b_{vw} \leq B_{ij} \quad \forall\, i, j \in N, \quad \text{(2f)}$$

$$\sum_{i \in N} \sum_{j \in N} y_{ivjw} L_{ij} \leq l_{vw} \quad \forall\, v, w \in K, \quad \text{(2g)}$$

$$\sum_{i \in N} x_{iv} L_{i,d(u)} \leq t_{vu} \quad \forall\, u \in U,\ \forall\, v \in K, \quad \text{(2h)}$$

$$x_{iv} \in \{0, 1\} \quad \forall\, i \in N,\ \forall\, v \in K, \quad \text{(2i)}$$

$$0 \leq y_{ivjw} \leq 1 \quad \forall\, i, j \in N,\ \forall\, v, w \in K. \quad \text{(2j)}$$

The LMMVMP is obtained by replacing the product $x_{iv} x_{jw}$ by y_{ivjw} from QMMVMP. In addition four sets of constraints are added. Constraints (2d) and (2e) define the relation between variables x and y. Constraints (2e) also impose the symmetry relation to variables y. Finally, constraints (2j) define the domain of variables y.

We note that the model QMMVMP has quadratic constraints, while LMMVMP not. The objective function also changes from a quadratic function in QMMVMP to a linear function in LMMVMP. However, the mixed-integer linear problem LMMVMP has a considerable higher number of variables, having variables y_{ivjw} in addition to the previous variables x_{iv}. Thus, the number of variables change from $O(NK)$ in QMMVMP to $O(N^2K^2)$ in LMMVMP. We note that if the optimal solution of LMMVMP is (x^*_{iv}, y^*_{ivjw}), then (x^*_{iv}) is the optimal solution for QMMVP. The proof that both models are equivalent can be easily obtained by extending the proof for QAP provided in [11].

3. A BIASED RANDOM-KEY GENETIC ALGORITHM

A biased random-key genetic algorithm (BRKGA) is a metaheuristic for finding optimal or near-optimal solutions for hard combinatorial optimization problems [5]. A BRKGA is a class of genetic algorithms based on random keys, where solutions are encoded as a vectors of random keys, i.e. randomly generated real numbers from uniform distribution in the interval $[0, 1)$. A vector of random keys is translated into a solution of the optimization problem by *decoders*. A decoder is a deterministic algorithm that takes as input a vector of random keys and returns a solution of the optimization problem as well as its cost (or *fitness*).

Figure 2 [5] shows a flowchart of a general scheme of a BRKGA, that starts with a set of p random vectors of size n (*population*). Parameter n depends on the encoding while parameter p is user-defined. Starting from the initial population, the algorithm generates a series of populations. Each

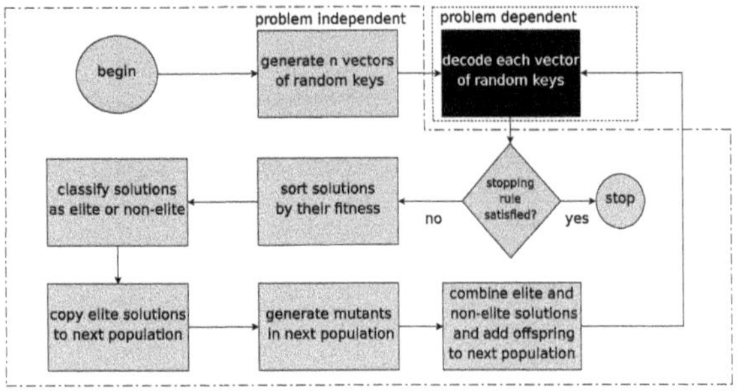

Figure 2: Flowchart of a BRKGA.

iteration of the algorithm is called a *generation*. The algorithm evolves the population over the generations by combining pairs of solutions from one generation to produce offspring solutions to the following generation.

At each generation g, the decoder is applied to all newly created random keys, and the population is partitioned into a smaller set of p_e elite solutions, i.e., the best fittest p_e solutions in the population, and another larger set of $p - p_e > p_e$ non-elite solutions. Population $g+1$ is generated as follows. All p_e elite solutions of population g are copied without changing to population $g+1$. This elitist strategy maintains the best solutions on hand. To ensure that mutation is present in the evolution, p_m *mutants* are added to population $g+1$. A mutant is simply a vector of random keys, generated in the same fashion than an initial solution.

With $p_e + p_m$ solutions accounted for population $g+1$, $p - p_e - p_m$ additional solutions must be generated to complete the p solutions that make up population $g+1$. This is done through *mating* or *crossover*. A parent-A is selected randomly from the elite solutions, and the parent-B parent is selected randomly between the set of non-elite solutions. A child C is produced by combining the parents using parameterized uniform crossover. Let $\rho_A > 1/2$ be the probability that the offspring solution inherits the key of parent-A and $\rho_B = 1 - \rho_A$ be the probability that it inherits the key of parent-B, i.e. $c_i = a_i$ with probability ρ_A or $c_i = b_i$ with probability $\rho_B = 1 - \rho_A$, where a_i and b_i are, respectively, the i-th key of parent-A and parent-B, for $i = 1, \ldots, n$.

Figure 2 from [5] shows the *problem-independent* and *problem-dependent* components of a BRKGA. The independent components are applied without any acknowledgement of the problem. The problem-dependent components are the only connection with the problem. Thus, to describe a BRKGA, one needs only to show how solutions are encoded and decoded, what choice of parameters p, p_e, p_m, and ρ_A were made, and how the algorithm stops. We next describe the encoding and decoding procedures for the proposed algorithm, and give values for parameters and stopping criterion in Section 4.

3.1 Decoders

Solutions of the optimization problem are encoded as a vector $\mathcal{X}$ with $n = |K|$ random keys. To translate this vector into the solution of the VMPlacement problem, we propose two decoders, as described next.

Greedy Ordered Decoder - D1: In this decoder, the keys provide the order of placement. Following this order, a greedy strategy is used, placing each VM to the DC which produces the least increase in the objective function.

The decoder starts with a list whose each element is composed of the random key and the index of the virtual machine. The list is sorted by the keys. Now, the sorted list of index of virtual machines is used as an order in which virtual machines should be placed. Following this order, the next step is to place each virtual machine v to a DC. This is done by placing virtual machine v in DC i which produces the least increase in the objective function. Note that the cost to insert the VM v in each DC considers the previous virtual machines placed. When all VMs are placed, the decoder returns the fitness value for the respective vector $\mathcal{X}$ of random keys.

Location Decoder - D2: In this decoder, each key is decoded as the data center in which the virtual machine should be placed. Let k_i be the key corresponding to the VM of index i in $\mathcal{X}$, then this decoder simply places the VM of index i to DC $\lfloor k_i * N \rfloor$.

Place a virtual machine to a data center can violate some of the constraints. In order to alleviate this problem, we use a penalization strategy to minimize the number of violated constraints. Thus, the cost of placing a VM v in DC i is calculated by the regular placement cost added by a sufficiently large number M for each violated constraint. This penalization strategy is applied whenever a solution is evaluated, including in both decoders, and in both local search strategy describe in the next subsection. In our experiments we use $M = 10^{10}$.

3.2 Local search

Local search is a general approach for finding and improving solutions to hard combinatorial optimization problems. The most basic strategy of local search algorithms is to start from an initial solution and iteratively try to replace the current solution by a better neighbor solution, until no improvement can be reached. A neighbor solution can be obtained by applying moves defined by a neighborhood structure. Two classical neighborhood structures are used to obtain neighbor solution, namely *shift* and *swap*.

A shift operation moves a virtual machine from the current data center to a different data center. In a *shift search*, we test all shift moves selecting virtual machines in a circular order of their indexes (starting from index zero), and calculating the cost to remove and insert the virtual machine in all others data centers, also chosen in a circular order of index. Once an improvement is reached, the virtual machine is shifted to the new data center and the search continues considering the next data center. The procedure stops when no shift move can improve the solution.

A swap operation interchanges the positions of two virtual machines. In a *swap search*, we evaluate the cost of all swap moves between two virtual machines i and j in a circular order of their indexes (starting from index zero). When an improvement is reached, the virtual machines positions are interchanged and the search continues by selecting a next virtual machine. Moves where $j \leq i$ and i and j are in the same data center are not evaluated. The procedure ends when no swap move can improve the solution.

The local search is applied after each decoder. In our experiments, we evaluated the performance of two local search strategies. The first, called *LSS*, considers only the shift search. The second, called *LSW*, considers shift search and swap search applied sequentially, until no improvement is reached in both searches. Note that using a penalization strategy described in the previous subsection, the local search is also applied to infeasible solutions.

4. COMPUTATIONAL RESULTS

The experiments were conducted on a cluster with quad-core Intel Xeon E5530 2.4 GHz CPUs, with at least 48 GB of RAM running GNU/Linux. BRKGA was implemented in C++, using the API described in [15] and a commercial solver IBM ILOG CPLEX Optimizer version 12.6.0.0 (C++ API) was used to evaluate the mathematical model. All experiments used a single thread but multiple experiments were run in parallel.

Experiments were conducted with two main objectives. The first was to investigate the CPLEX performance in order to obtain a lower bound, analyze which size of instance the solver can handle, and obtain baseline results for comparison of heuristic methods. The second was to evaluate the performance of the proposed BRKGA, comparing two decoders, the impact of the local improvement procedures when embedded in the decoders, and comparing it with a simple multi-start algorithm [13]. We next describe the method to generate the dataset used in the experiments.

4.1 Data set

In this subsection we present an instance generator that we proposed and implemented to generate the data set used to evaluate CPLEX and BRKGA for VMPlacement. For generating each instance the generator receives as input four parameters: $|N|$, $|K|$, $|U|$, and P (the latter represents the percentage of the overall data center occupation).

To ensure the generator creates instances that admit feasible solutions, we generate the data for each instance based on n sets of pre-placed virtual machines to data centers (by default $n = 3$). Given a capacity of each data center, each set of pre-placed $s \in \mathcal{S}$ is generated by randomly placing each virtual machine to a data center, with probability proportional to the data center capacity, ensuring the capacity is not violated. Biased on these pre-placements, we generate the remaining data respecting the constraints of the problem, ensuring at least n feasible solutions for each instance.

Let a random numbers generator by uniform distribution, and M' be a sufficiently large number, we generate the parameter data for each instance using the following steps.

Data center capacity: The total number of available virtual machines is given by $n' = \max\left(|N|, \left\lceil \frac{|K|}{|P|} \right\rceil\right)$. Thus, to define the values of a_i for each DC i, we start with all $a_i = 0$ and select n' times a random data center i, and increase a_i by one. We also ensure that each data center has a capacity a_i greater or equal to one. At this step, the n pre-placements described before are generated.

Required virtual machine bandwidth: For each pair of virtual machine $v \in K$ and $w \in K$ the bandwidth b_{vw} is a random number in the interval $[0 : 9]$. This matrix is symmetric, i.e, $b_{vw} = b_{wv}$, and $b_{vv} = 0$.

Data center bandwidth: Having defined the bandwidth between each pair of virtual machines in the previous step, we generate the values of data center bandwidth based in the pre-placements $\mathcal{S}$. Let b^s_{ij} be the sum of bandwidth between all virtual machines pre-placed to i and j in $s \in \mathcal{S}$. For each pair of data centers ij, we associate a bandwidth $B_{ij} = \max\{b^s_{ij}\}$, $\forall s \in S$. This matrix also is symmetric, i.e $B_{ij} = B_{ji}$, with $B_{ii} = M'$.

Data center latency: For each pair of data center ij, the latency L_{ij} is a random number selected the interval $[5 : 20]$. This matrix is symmetric, i.e, $L_{ij} = L_{ji}$, with $L_{ii} = 0$.

Required virtual machine latency: Let l^s_{vm} be the latency L_{ij} between the data centers ij where v is placed in i and w is placed in j in the pre-placement $s \in \mathcal{S}$. We randomly select $n = |K| * 2$ distinct pairs vw to associate a required latency $l_{vw} = \max\{l^s_{vm}\}$, $\forall s \in \mathcal{S}$. The remaining latency l_{vw} is defined as M', indicating that no latency is required. We also ensure that $l_{vw} = l_{wv}$, and $l_{vv} = 0$.

Users in data centers: Users are allocated at random to data centers chosen with probability proportional to their capacity. More than one user can be located at the same data center.

Required user latency: For each user, we randomly select a virtual machine v to define a required latency. Let $i(s)$ be the data center where v is placed in $s \in \mathcal{S}$, thus the required latency between u and v is given by $t_{vu} = \max\{L_{d(u),i(s)}\}, \forall s \in \mathcal{S}$. The remaining user required latency t is set to M'.

Transferring data center cost: For each pair of data center ij, the cost C_{ij} is a random number in the interval $[10.00 : 100.00]$. This matrix is symmetric, i.e $C_{ij} = C_{ji}$, and $C_{ii} = 0$.

The parameters $|N|$ and $|K|$ can be used to define the instances sizes, while parameters $|U|$ and P can be used to adjust how the problem should be restricted. Finally, we generate 36 instances by combining values from $N = \{10, 25\}$, $K = \{25, 50, 100, 150, 200\}$, $U = \{K_i * 0.5, K_i, K_i * 1.5\}$, and $P = \{70, 90\}$. Table 2 contains all instances we generated, and the values of $|N|$, $|K|$, $|U|$ and P are encoded in the name of instance in this respective order. All instances and their best known solutions are available at `www.inf.ufsm.br/~stefanello/instances/`.

4.2 CPLEX results

In the first experiment we evaluate the performance of CPLEX with the mathematical models described in Section 2. We used the standard CPLEX solvers for models QMMVMP and LMMVMP. The running time limit was set to one day (86,400 seconds) and the number of threads was set to one. The remaining parameters were maintained on the default values. The CPLEX performance with LMMVMP was considerably better than with QMMVMP model, and for this reason we report only results for the mixed-integer linear model.

Table 1 shows CPLEX results. The first column shows the name of instances. The second column (BKS) shows the objective function of best known solution value for each instance. The next three columns show respectively the values of lower bound, best integer solution and the percentage gap returned by CPLEX. Finally the last column shows the percentage gap between the best integer solution and BKS.

We can draw three main observations from this experiment. First, we omitted the results for instances with 25 data centers because CPLEX spent the whole time in the presolve phase without solving the root relaxation node. This shows that CPLEX cannot be applied with this mathematical model to large instances. Second, CPLEX gaps are still high after 24h of computation. We think this is due to the low relaxation quality of this model. Finally, for the set of instances with 10 data centers, CPLEX was able to find at least one feasible solution (column Integer Solution), in many cases, even before starting a node exploration of the branch-and-bound. However, the solver still has a high gap from BKS.

Table 1: CPLEX detailed results.

Instance	BKS	Lower Bound	Integer Solution	CPLEX GAP	BKS GAP
10_025_012_70	114,582.50	67,006.63	116,264.44	42.37	1.47
10_025_012_90	84,461.30	40,592.25	88,087.12	53.92	4.29
10_025_025_70	90,997.90	65,997.32	93,729.48	29.59	3.00
10_025_025_90	124,763.66	86,281.96	125,365.26	31.18	0.48
10_025_037_70	100,801.80	79,139.70	104,350.38	24.16	3.52
10_025_037_90	106,617.94	81,678.77	107,558.00	24.06	0.88
10_050_025_70	414,689.30	74,248.43	442,548.40	83.22	6.72
10_050_025_90	460,414.96	117,147.62	480,146.00	75.60	4.29
10_050_050_70	360,102.12	116,523.45	374,071.02	68.85	3.88
10_050_050_90	403,272.24	113,953.64	420,173.88	72.88	4.19
10_050_075_70	349,135.78	166,802.77	362,853.92	54.03	3.93
10_050_075_90	500,668.88	233,743.38	513,161.02	54.45	2.50
10_100_050_70	1,677,015.90	159,285.07	1,884,262.62	91.55	12.36
10_100_050_90	1,804,385.34	200,022.30	1,916,126.76	89.56	6.19
10_100_100_70	1,465,034.60	213,163.82	1,546,897.78	86.22	5.59
10_100_100_90	2,145,917.62	389,652.74	2,256,408.46	82.73	5.15
10_100_150_70	1,572,976.60	367,091.18	1,702,573.74	78.44	8.24
10_100_150_90	1,858,242.74	575,983.27	1,968,341.96	70.74	5.92
Average				61.86	4.59

In summary, CPLEX was not able to prove the optimality of any instance and presented on average a high percentage gap of 4.59 %. Thus, these results motivated us to propose heuristic solutions to solve the problem.

4.3 Multi-start and feasibility results

This section presents results and analysis of a greedy constructive heuristic combined with a local search in a multi-start algorithm (MS). The main goals of the following experiments are two-fold: to show the difficulty of finding feasible solutions using a constructive heuristic, and to explore the effect of embedding a local search procedure in order to obtain a feasible solution.

In order to support our analysis, we evaluate the performance of a greedy constructive heuristic embedded in a multi-start algorithm. The greedy constructive heuristic starts from a random order of virtual machines and uses the same idea of decoder D1 to generate greedy solutions, i.e, VMs are placed in the DC that produces the least increase in the objective function. The multi-start algorithm repeats the constructive heuristic until the stop criteria is reached. Once a solution is obtained by the constructive algorithm, the local search is applied until reaching a local minimum.

We run three algorithms on each instance. The stopping criteria of each run was a time limit of $|K| * |N| * \theta$ seconds, where $\theta = 0.8$. The algorithms are the multi-start algorithm without applying local search (NoLS), by applying the local search with only shift moves (LSS), and by applying both moves (LSW). The values in Table 2 refer to the percentage of solutions evaluated that were feasible. Results represent an average over 10 runs.

The first observation is that the probability of finding a feasible solution using only a greedy constructive heuristic without local search is low. In most instances, the percentage of feasible solutions was less than 0.2%, and the average over all instances was slightly more than 1%. In five cases, no feasible solution was found, as for example in instance 25_200_300_90, even haven evaluated 529,769 solutions.

With LSS the percentage of feasible solutions increased considerable in comparison with NoLS. The number of evaluated solutions decreased around 42%, but the percentage of feasible solutions increased to more than 21%. When applying the local search LSW, the percentage of feasible solutions increased even more, and on average, more than three in four evaluated solutions are feasible. However, the number of solution evaluated decreased to around 2% of the number of solutions evaluated by LSS. This results show

Table 2: Percentage of feasible solutions found by the multi-start algorithm with the greedy constructive heuristic.

Instance	NoLS	LSS	LSW	Instance	NoLS	LSS	LSW
10_025_012_70	7.95	54.26	91.99	25_100_050_70	3.70	58.54	95.41
10_025_012_90	1.49	22.43	93.03	25_100_050_90	0.00	8.49	79.85
10_025_025_70	14.88	84.55	99.65	25_100_100_70	0.24	25.29	83.61
10_025_025_90	0.03	4.13	51.59	25_100_100_90	0.00	1.37	61.83
10_025_037_70	3.23	57.01	78.97	25_100_150_70	0.41	27.45	90.82
10_025_037_90	0.02	3.64	47.14	25_100_150_90	0.00	0.98	60.82
10_050_025_70	1.48	33.85	95.35	25_150_075_70	0.90	40.04	91.46
10_050_025_90	0.05	15.32	90.57	25_150_075_90	0.00	3.25	84.98
10_050_050_70	0.03	15.62	63.60	25_150_150_70	0.08	17.25	78.37
10_050_050_90	0.02	10.55	60.16	25_150_150_90	0.00	2.10	58.95
10_050_075_70	0.41	53.26	77.68	25_150_225_70	0.12	20.19	80.31
10_050_075_90	0.01	6.15	66.07	25_150_225_90	0.00	0.67	47.80
10_100_050_70	0.17	40.90	98.71	25_200_100_70	0.01	11.69	80.63
10_100_050_90	0.00	4.09	82.51	25_200_100_90	0.00	15.82	95.59
10_100_100_70	1.40	58.51	00.48	25_200_200_70	0.02	12.90	76.35
10_100_100_90	0.00	5.46	87.55	25_200_200_90	0.00	8.73	92.86
10_100_150_70	0.07	34.88	83.72	25_200_300_70	0.00	7.81	61.87
10_100_150_90	0.00	0.43	64.05	25_200_300_90	0.00	1.72	85.64
Average	1.74	28.06	79.05		0.30	14.68	78.18

that a large neighborhood helps to improve the feasibility, even if the local search procedure is applied few times.

Even with a large increase in the percentage of feasible solutions found when the local search is applied, some instances still have a low percentage of feasible solutions. This shows that the instance generator produces instances not trivial to solve.

4.4 BRKGA results

This subsection presents results for the biased random-key genetic algorithm. First we describe experiments for tuning the parameters, and finally we present the main results obtained by the proposed BRKGA. We also compare results with the multi-start algorithm described in the previous subsection.

We used the *iterated racing* procedure [4] to tune the BRKGA parameters. This method consists of sampling configurations from a particular distribution, evaluating them using either the Friedman test or the t-test, and refining the sampling distribution with repeated applications of F-Race. We uses the irace package [12], implemented in R [14].

For each heuristic, we used a budget of 2,000 experiments in the tuning procedure, and two digits for real number parameters. Twelve instances were selected from the original set in order to include the most different values. The stopping criteria for all runs was a time set to $|K| * |N| * \theta$ seconds (where $\theta = 0.8$). The following ranges are used in the tuning: p - population size $\in \{25, 50, 75\}$; p_e - elite percentage $\in [0.10, 0.30]$; p_m - percentage of mutants introduced at each generation $\in [0.05, 0.30]$; and ρ_A - probability of inheriting each key from elite parent $\in [0.5, 0.8]$. Finally, a restart parameter $r \in [50, 800]$ was used to restart the population after r generations without improvement in the incumbent solution.

The tuning was applied to four algorithm configurations, that include both decoders and both local search strategies. In all results returned by irace, values p_e, p_m, and ρ_A were similar and we adopted the elite size $p_e = 0.24p$, the set of mutants $p_m = 0.12p$, and the probability of inheriting $\rho_A = 0.6$. For the restart parameter, we decided to disable it when the local search LSW is used. This choice is supported by the fact that most of the processing time is spent in the local search procedure and the total number of generations tends to be small. For the case of LSS, the restart parameter was set to $r = 350$ for D1, and $r = 650$ for D2. Finally, for the population size parameter, irace suggested four sets of parameter setting, and the three populations

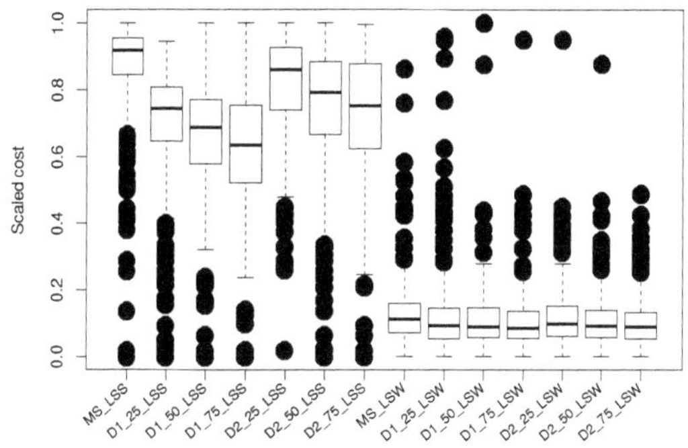

Figure 3: Dispersion of scaled cost for each algorithm.

sizes appear in the suggested values. For this reason, we decided to run a large experiment to analyse the best population size, comparing both local searches procedures and both decoders, and also to provide a comparison between the results of BRKGA and the results of MS obtained in the previous subsection. The experiment consists in evaluating the BRKGA in all instances running all combinations of decoders, local searches and population size. We made ten independent runs for each instance with the time limit set to $|K| * |N| * \theta$ seconds, where $\theta = 0.8$.

To compare the results with respect the cost, we first scale the results to the range $[0, 1]$ since each instance can have very different values. The scale is a simple transformation where for each instance, the largest cost over all analysed algorithms is scaled to 1 and the lowest is scaled to 0. Figure 3 shows the distribution of the scaled cost for each algorithm. The box plots show the location of the minimum value, lower quartile, median, upper quartile, and maximum value of each algorithm. The dots are the outliers. Algorithms are represented on the horizontal axis. BRKGA algorithms are encoded by the decoder, population size, and local search. Multi-start algorithms are encoded by MS plus type of local search.

Figure 3 shows that the results with local search LSW clearly overcome the results obtained with LSS. The results with $p = 75$ and decoder D1 tend to be better than the other approaches. Regarding the comparison of algorithms, BRKGA produces better results than MS.

To confirm the results presented in Figure 3, we use the R package to test the normality of these distributions using the Shapiro-Wilk test and apply the Mann-Whitney-Wilcoxon U test. For all tests, we assume a confidence interval of 99%. Shapiro-Wilk tests indicate that no cost distribution fits a normal distribution since the p-values for all tests are less than 0.01. Therefore, we applied the U test which assumes as null hypothesis that the location statistics are equal in both distributions. We also use a p-value correction procedure based on false discovery rate (FDR) to minimize the number of false positives.

Table 3 shows U test results for each pair of algorithms. The structure of this table is as follows: Each row and column is indexed by one algorithm. Each element in the diagonal (bold) is the median of the scaled cost of the corresponding algorithm. The upper-right diagonal elements are the differences in location statistics for each pair of algorithms. A negative difference indicates that the "row algorithm" has its location statistics lower (better) than the "column algorithm", and the positive difference is the opposite. The bottom-left diagonal elements are the p-values of each test. Math signals indicate when p<0.01 for a U test between "row algorithm" and "column algorithm" for the respective signal alternative hypothesis. The case "less" indicates that the "row algorithm" overcome the "column algorithm", or the opposite in the case "greater".

Table 3 shows tests only with local search LSW since all test between LSS and LSW indicate that both strategies are statistically significant. This corroborate the analysis from Figure 3 showing that use LSW produce better results than use LSS.

Table 3: Values of medians, p-values, and difference in median location for cost distributions using a confidence interval of 99%.

	MS	D1_25	D1_50	D1_75	D2_25	D2_50	D2_75
MS	**0.112**	0.013	0.016	0.023	0.008	0.016	0.021
D1_25	<	**0.092**	0.003	0.006	-0.003	0.005	0.009
D1_50	<	0.427	**0.089**	0.006	-0.007	0.002	0.006
D1_75	<	0.087	0.065	**0.084**	-0.013	-0.003	0.001
D2_25	0.025	0.486	0.036	>	**0.098**	0.010	0.012
D2_50	<	0.181	0.484	0.366	<	**0.091**	0.003
D2_75	<	0.034	0.120	0.727	<	0.424	**0.088**

Table 3 shows that the difference between BRKGA and MS is statistically significant and BRKGA produces better results than MS, except for D2_25 where the test is inconclusive for a confidence interval of 99%. Tests between BRKGA algorithms indicate that the differences are not statistically significant, except in some cases where D2_25 performed worst. However, the medians and the difference in median location indicate that the best results are obtained with D1_75.

A set of statistical tests was also performed with results for instances with 10 data centers, considering the BRKGA with the default stopping criteria (maximum 800 seconds for the larger instance) and CPLEX running per 24h (Subsection 4.2). The tests confirm that any BRKGA approach produces better results than CPLEX.

In summary, BRKGA with the parameters $p = 75$, $p_e = 0.24p$, $p_m = 0.12p$, $\rho_A = 0.6$, using local search LSW, and decoder D1 produced the better results for the instances evaluated in comparison with MS and CPLEX.

Finally, the last experiment uses the Time-To-Target (TTT) plots to display the running time distribution for the algorithm to find a solution at least as good as a given target value. TTT plots were used by [1] and have been advocated by Hoos and Stützle [9, 8] as a way to characterize the running times of stochastic algorithms for combinatorial optimization. The experiment consists in performing 200 runs of BRKGA and MS algorithm for two instances until a timelimit is reached. The instances chosen was one at random from each group of data centers, and the target value was set as the higher result from all runs and both algorithms. Defined the target, we extract on each run the time to rearch a solution at least as good as the target, i.e 467,305 for `010_050_025_090` and 4,426,014 for `025_150_225_070`.

Figures 4a and 4b illustrate the cumulative probability plot obtained by using BRKGA and MS for two instances. For the instance `010_050_025_090`, we observe that the probability that the BRKGA finds a solution that is at least as good as the target value in less than 20 seconds is 50%, in less than 60 seconds is 80%, and in less than 120 seconds in 95%. For the instance `025_150_225_070`, the probability that the BRKGA finds a solution that is at least as good as the target value in less than 230 seconds in 50%, in less

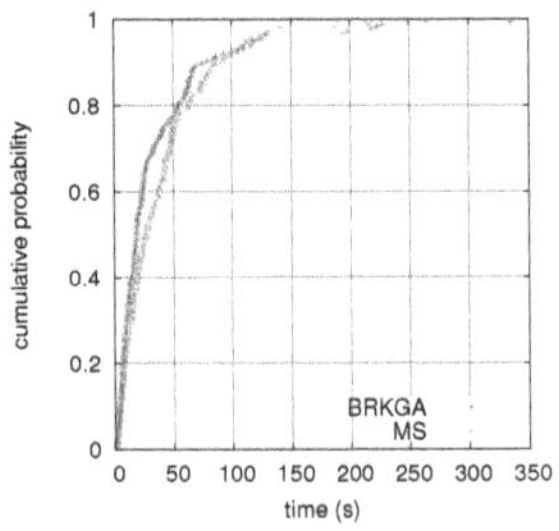

(a) TTT plot for the instance 010_050_025_090.

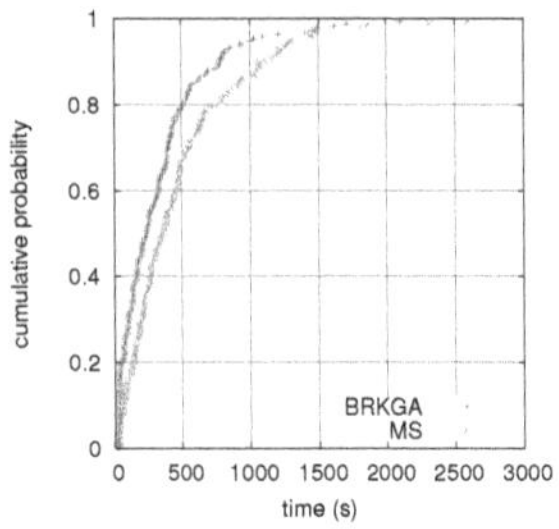

(b) TTT plot for the instance 025_150_225_070.

Figure 4: Cumulative probability distribution.

than 500 second in 80%, and in less than 1020 seconds is 95%. In both instances, BRKGA overcomes MS obtaining higher probability in the same running time.

A final observation about running times of BRKGA is that results are reported using single-thread in order to provide a fair comparison with the MS and CPLEX results. However, the BRKGA API provides an efficient multi-thread decoding [15], that could be used to reduce substantially the running time when multiple processors are available.

5. CONCLUDING REMARKS

In this paper we presented the problem of minimizing the cost of virtual machines placement across geo-separated data centers. A quadratic and a linear mathematical formulation were presented. Moreover, a biased random-key genetic algorithm was proposed in order to find near-optimal solutions for the problem. Computational tests were conducted in a set of synthetic instances to evaluate the performance of CPLEX using the proposed mathematical formulations. Furthermore, the BRKGA was applied on the same set of instances. A set of experiments shows that BRKGA outperforms CPLEX significantly in terms of running times, achieving significantly better solutions in less time, and also produces better results than a simple multi-start algorithm. Thus, the proposed algorithm is a competitive algorithm which reduces costs while maintaining the reliability and the demand requirements of data centers.

6. ACKNOWLEDGMENTS

The authors would like to thank Kaustubh Joshi, Moo-Ryong Ra, and Alexander Varshavsky from AT&T Labs-Research, Bedminster NJ for helpful discussions.

This work has been partially supported by CAPES, CNPq project 462425/2014-2, PRH PB-217 Petrobras S.A. from Brazil; AT&T Labs Research from USA; and projects PTDC/EGE-GES/117692/2010 and NORTE-07-0124-FEDER-000057 funded by NPROP (ON.2 - O Novo Norte), under NSRF Framework, through ERDF and the Programme COMPETE, and by national funds through FCT from Portugal. The research of Mauricio G. C. Resende and Vaneet Aggarwal was done while they were employed at AT&T Labs Research.

7. REFERENCES

[1] R. M. Aiex, M. G. C. Resende, and C. C. Ribeiro. TTT plots: A perl program to create time-to-target plots. *Optimization Letters*, 1(4):355–366, 2007.

[2] Amazon Elastic Compute Cloud. http://aws.amazon.com/ec2/. Last accessed: February, 2015.

[3] H. Ballani, P. Costa, T. Karagiannis, and A. Rowstron. Towards predictable datacenter networks. In *ACM SIGCOMM Computer Communication Review*, volume 41, pages 242–253, New York, NY, USA, 2011. ACM Press.

[4] M. Birattari, Z. Yuan, P. Balaprakash, and T. Stützle. F-race and iterated F-race: An overview. In T. Bartz-Beielstein, M. Chiarandini, L. Paquete, and M. Preuss, editors, *Experimental Methods for the Analysis of Optimization Algorithms*, pages 311–336. Springer Berlin Heidelberg, 2010.

[5] J. F. Gonçalves and M. G. C. Resende. Biased random-key genetic algorithms for combinatorial optimization. *J. of Heuristics*, 17(5):487–525, 2011.

[6] A. Greenberg, J. R. Hamilton, N. Jain, S. Kandula, C. Kim, P. Lahiri, D. a. Maltz, P. Patel, and S. Sengupta. VL2: A Scalable and Flexible Data Center Network. *ACM SIGCOMM Computer Communication Review*, 39(4):51, 2009.

[7] C. Guo, G. Lu, H. J. Wang, S. Yang, C. Kong, P. Sun, W. Wu, and Y. Zhang. SecondNet: A Data Center Network Virtualization Architecture with Bandwidth Guarantees. In *Proceedings of the 6th International COnference on - Co-NEXT '10*, Co-NEXT '10, page 1, New York, NY, USA, 2010. ACM.

[8] H. H. Hoos and T. Stützle. Evaluating Las Vegas Algorithms: Pitfalls and Remedies. In *Proceedings of the Fourteenth Conference on Uncertainty in Artificial Intelligence*, UAI'98, pages 238–245, San Francisco, CA, USA, 1998. Morgan Kaufmann Publishers Inc.

[9] H. H. Hoos and T. Stutzle. On the empirical evaluation of Las Vegas algorithms. Technical report, CS Department, University of British Columbia, 1998.

[10] IBM ILOG CPLEX Optimizer. www.cplex.com. Last accessed: February, 2015.

[11] C. G. Lee and Z. Ma. The generalized quadratic assignment problem. Technical report, Department of Mechanical and Industrial Engineering at the University of Toronto, Toronto, Canada, 2004.

[12] M. Loopez-Ibanez, J. Dubois-Lacoste, T. Stützle, and M. Birattari. The irace Package: Iterated Race for Automatic Algorithm Configuration. Technical report, IRIDIA, Université Libre de Bruxelles, Belgium, 2011.

[13] R. Martí, M. G. C. Resende, and C. C. Ribeiro. Multi-start methods for combinatorial optimization. *European J. of Operational Research*, 226(1):1–8, 2013.

[14] R Core Team. *R: A Language and Environment for Statistical Computing.* R Foundation for Statistical Computing, Vienna, Austria, 2013.

[15] R. Toso and M. Resende. A C++ application programming interface for biased random-key genetic algorithms. *Optimization Methods and Software*, 30(1):1–15, 2014.

[16] D. Xie and Y. C. Hu. The Only Constant is Change: Incorporating Time-Varying Network Reservations in Data Centers. In *Sigcomm*, SIGCOMM '12, pages 199–210, New York, NY, USA, 2012. ACM.

Mk Landscapes, NK Landscapes, MAX-kSAT: A Proof that the Only Challenging Problems are Deceptive

Darrell Whitley
Computer Science Department
Colorado State University
Fort Collins, Colorado, USA
whitley@cs.colostate.edu

ABSTRACT

This paper investigates *Gray Box Optimization* for pseudo-Boolean optimization problems composed of M subfunctions, where each subfunction accepts at most k variables. We will refer to these as Mk Landscapes. In Gray Box optimization, the optimizer is given access to the set of M subfunctions. If the set of subfunctions is k-bounded and separable, the Gray Box optimizer is guaranteed to return the global optimum with 1 evaluation. A problem is said to be *order k deceptive* if the average values of hyperplanes over combinations of k variables cannot be used to infer a globally optimal solution. Hyperplane averages are always efficiently computable for Mk Landscapes. If a problem is not deceptive, the Gray Box optimizer also returns the global optimum after 1 evaluation. Finally, these concepts are used to understand the nonlinearity of problems in the complexity class P, such as Adjacent NK Landscapes. These ideas are also used to understand the problem structure of NP Hard problems such as MAX-kSAT and general Mk Landscapes. In general, NP Hard problems are profoundly deceptive.

Categories and Subject Descriptors

I.2.8 [**Artificial Intelligence**]: Problem Solving, Control Methods, and Search

Keywords

Pseudo Boolean Functions; Walsh Analysis; NK-landscapes; MAX-kSAT

GECCO '15, July 11 - 15, 2015, Madrid, Spain

© 2015 ACM. ISBN 978-1-4503-3472-3/15/07...$15.00

DOI: http://dx.doi.org/10.1145/2739480.2754809

1. INTRODUCTION

The class of pseudo-Boolean optimization problems corresponds to a class of functions, $f : \mathbb{B}^n \rightarrow \mathbb{R}$ that use bit strings as the natural representation, and which can output any real value. The class of k-bounded pseudo-Boolean optimization problems refers to problems that restrict the nonlinearity of the function to at most order k interactions. Let X denote the set of binary strings of length n which constitutes the search space. These k-bounded pseudo-Boolean functions can be expressed in the following form:

$$f(x) = \sum_{i=1}^{M} f_i(x, mask_i), \quad (1)$$

where $mask_i$ selects the k bits that are extracted from the bit string x; these k bits are then used to evaluate the subfunction f_i. In practice, the mask can be dropped in as much as the mask is inherent in the definition of subfunction f_i. This class of problems include MAX-kSAT problems, NK Landscapes (from theoretical biology) and spin glass problems (from physics). Thus, this represents an important and widely studied class of optimization problems. Furthermore, just as every SAT problem can be expressed as a MAX-kSAT problem, every pseudo-Boolean function with an algebraic evaluation function can be expressed as a quadratic pseudo-Boolean function [1]. This means that virtually all problems that can be found in the optimization literature that use a bit representation can be expressed as a k-bounded optimization problem.

This paper will use the term "Mk Landscape" to refer to any problem that is expressed as a k-bounded pseudo-Boolean optimization problem. M refers to the number of subfunctions in equation 1. Given n variables, M $= O(n)$. And k is an upper bound on the number of variables that can be passed as input to any one subfunction. In some ways, this is a new term for an old concept. The concept of spin glass problems is also general enough to refer to any k-bounded pseudo-Boolean optimization problem [23]. Furthermore, Heckendorn [9] has already used the label *embedded landscapes* for the same class of problems.

So why introduce a new label? One good reason is that **NK Landscapes** have become popular as test functions. And there are interesting theoretical results for NK Landscapes. But NK Landscapes impose unnecessary restrictions on the structure of the functions. In an NK Landscape, $M = N$ and $k = K + 1$ (which is confusing) and variable x_i must appear in subfunction f_i. None of these requirements turn out to be important to most fundamental theoretical properties of NK Landscapes. Furthermore, the Mk notation is much closer in form to the range of problems seem in MAX-kSAT problems. For example, random MAX-3SAT problems are characterized by a phase transition at $M = 4.27n$; below this phase transition, most random MAX-3SAT problems are satisfiable and above this phase transition, most problems are unsatisfiable. Furthermore, there is a general notion that as K increases in an NK Landscapes, the problems become more difficult. This may be generally true, but it is not always true. Furthermore, every NK landscape can be converted into an Mk Landscape where k=2 (K=1), but the resulting landscape does not always meet the definition of an NK Landscape.

By transferring what we know about NK Landscapes to Mk Landscapes, we remove unnecessary restrictions and create new connections to problems such as MAX-kSAT.

This paper makes several fundamental contributions.

First, we will generalize and extend the concept that certain types of Mk Landscapes fall into the complexity class P. "Adjacent NK Landscapes" localize variable interactions to the point that a classic optimization method, dynamic programming, can be used to guarantee a globally optimal solution in polynomial time. Adjacent NK Landscapes are still being used to test the effectiveness of optimization methods such as Estimation of Distribution Algorithms (EDAs). "Localized Mk Landscapes" can be constructed that are not adjacent, but which also can be solved in polynomial time. Furthermore, *separable functions* that use bit representations also fall in the class of Mk Landscapes, and are a special class of "Localized Mk Landscapes." Mk Landscapes that are also *separable functions* also fall into the complexity class P. Separable Mk Landscape include toy problems like ONEMAX, as well as the "trap functions" introduced to test simple genetic algorithms.

Second, a preprocessing algorithm is introduced that solves all separable Mk Landscapes problems in one evaluation in $O(n)$ time. This preprocessor is used before a general optimizer is called. The result is general, and it means that both trap functions as well as ONEMAX are easily solved in one evaluation. This is not Black Box Optimization. Instead it is a form of *Gray Box Optimization*. The optimizer does not need to know the specific application. The application could be an encryption problem, or an AI Planning problem: all that the Gray Box Optimizer needs to know is that the problem is a k bounded pseudo-Boolean optimization problem (i.e., an Mk Landscape) and the optimizer must have access to the M subfunctions. Unlike in Black Box Optimization (where exponential work can be hidden because only function evaluations are counted) this preprocessor will return a global optimum in polynomial time if the problem is separable, if the problem is not deceptive, or if variable interaction is sufficiently localized (e.g., as is the case for Adjacent NK Landscapes).

Third, we show that the concept of *deception* is not just relevant to the search behavior of a simple genetic algorithm [20]. It is also a provable requirement for the class of Mk Landscape problems (and the class of MAX-kSAT problems) to be NP Hard. Hyperplane averages can be computed in $O(n)$ time for all Mk Landscapes where $M = O(n)$. The concept of *deception* is closely relate to hyperplane statistics; basic statistics about hyperplanes for every Mk Landscape can be computed in polynomial time. Therefore *deception* is not related to any specific algorithm. In fact, statistical summaries over the order 1 hyperplanes have long been used in the SAT community as a heuristic to guide search.

Finally, some observations are offered about variable localization and reoccurring structure that can found in real applications for Mk Landscapes.

2. PSEUDO-BOOLEAN FUNCTIONS

Let n denote a positive integer, and let $V = \{1, 2, ..., n\}$ denote a set of variables, where $v_i \in V$. We denote a subset $S \subset V$. All pseudo-Boolean functions can be uniquely represented as multi-linear polynomials:

$$f(x_1, ..., x_n) = \sum_{S \subset V} c_S \prod_{j \in S} v_j$$

where c_S is a constant weight associated with subset S.

Every pseudo-Boolean function minimization problem with an algebraic form can be converted into a quadratic pseudo-Boolean function. This can be seen my making the following observations (from Boros and Hammer [1]). Assume x, y, z are Boolean variables.

$$xy = z \;\; \textit{iff} \;\; xy - 2xz - 2yz + 3z = 0,$$

$$xy \neq z \;\; \textit{iff} \;\; yx - 2xz - 2yz + 3z > 0.$$

The variable z acts as a new auxiliary variable. This means pairs of nonlinearly interacting variables can be replaced by a single auxiliary variable and additional quadratic expressions (subfunctions) that act as constraints to guarantee the new problem has the same global optima as the original problem.

Clearly, we could also reduce any pseudo-Boolean function to an Mk Landscape where k=3 instead of assuming that the function is reduced to a quadratic form. For example, a function such as $f(v1, v2, v3, v4)$ might be split into two functions $f_1(z, v_1, v_2)$ and $f_2(z, v_3, v_4)$ where all of the new constraints are found in f_1 and the auxiliary variable z replaces v_1 and v_2 in the original function to yield f_2. It should be stressed that the exact nature of the decomposition will depend on the nonlinearity found in the original function.

The reduction is computed in polynomial time [1]. Again, this is analogous to the fact that every SAT instance can be reduced to a MAX-kSAT problem [3].

It should be noted that while the new k bounded optimization problem is guaranteed to have the same global optima as the original problem, is not guaranteed to induce exactly the same search space.

3. MK LANDSCAPES & LOCAL SEARCH

Figure 1 presents a general model of a k-bounded pseudo-Boolean optimization problem. This is an Mk Landscape where k=3. Each subfunction takes k bits as input. Let X represent the set of bit strings of length n. In general, the k bits referenced by any one subfunction can have any arbitrary position in the input string $x \in X$.

The evolutionary computation community has long used pseudo Boolean optimization problems as test functions. There was a bias toward using bit representations in the genetic algorithm community starting in the 1970s and continuing until the turn of the century [7] [10]. Of course, random mutation and/or recombination are considered to be key elements of almost any evolutionary algorithm.

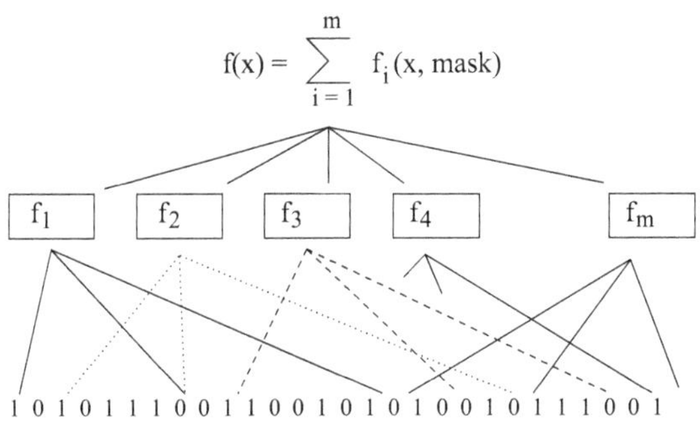

Figure 1: Models of a pseudo-Boolean function.

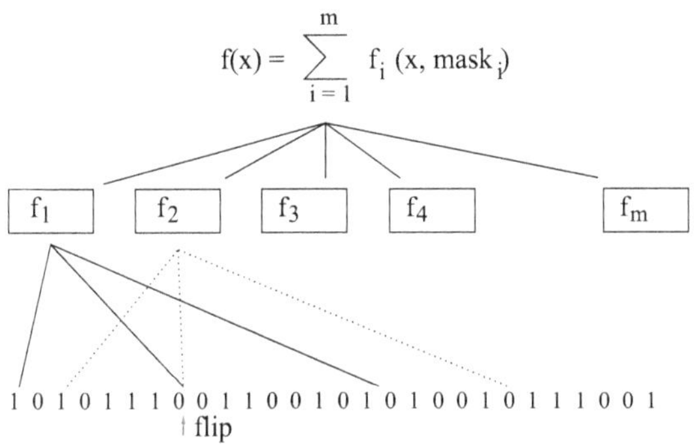

Figure 2: The location of potential new improves is known deterministically. When one bit is flipped, it affects only a subset of subfunctions. The only *new* improving moves must be among the bits that feed into the affected subfunctions.

However, random mutation is completely unnecessary for any Mk Landscape problem. All improving moves can be found deterministically, and usually this can be done in constant time per move [19] [2] [21].

In general, we will consider the search space to be a hypercube. A local search neighborhood can be defined over the Hamming distance 1 "bit flip" neighborhood. When a bit flips it only changes the evaluation of those subfunctions in which that bit appears. Furthermore, new improving moves can only occur among those bits that feed into the affected subfunctions. This is illustrated in Figure 2. By clever bookkeeping (using either derivative calculations, or tracking the contribution of Walsh coefficients), the location of improving moves can be tracked in constant $\Theta(1)$ time [19] [2]. This means that we *never* need to use "mutation operators" to locate improving moves in the Hamming distance 1 neighborhood.

The MAX-kSAT community have long exploited a specialized fast form of local search that exploits this idea. For example, the GSAT algorithm exploits this insight [14] [12]. However, it can be shown that a generalization of this fast form of update holds for all Mk Landscapes [19].

To determine the location of improving moves, we first note that if the most recent bit flip was applied to bit x_i, then the creation of a *new* improving move at location x_j is only possible if there is a nonlinear interaction between bit x_i and x_j. Two variables can have a nonlinear interaction only if they appear together in some subfunction in an MK Landscape.

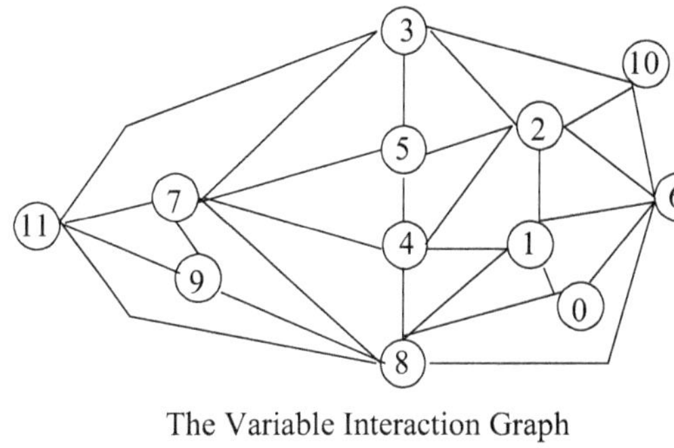

Figure 3: The Variable Interaction Graph (VIG) tracks sources of nonlinearity.

The nonlinear interaction of variables in an Mk Landscapes can be captured by the *Variable Interaction Graph* [2]. A vertex in the Variable Interaction Graph corresponds to a variable. We will assume that every pair of variables that appears together in some subfunction are connected by an edge in the Variable Interaction Graph (VIG). (It is possible for two variables to appear together in a subfunction and still not to have a nonlinear interaction.)

We will use the following subfunctions to illustrate the VIG. In this case, $n = 10$ and $k = 3$. The subfunctions are as follows:

$$\begin{array}{lll} f_0(x_0, x_1, x_6) & f_1(x_1, x_4, x_8) & f_2(x_2, x_3, x_5) \\ f_3(x_3, x_2, x_{10}) & f_4(x_4, x_2, x_1) & f_5(x_5, x_7, x_4) \\ f_6(x_6, x_8, x_1) & f_7(x_7, x_3, x_5) & f_8(x_8, x_9, x_{11}) \\ f_9(x_9, x_7, x_8) & f_{10}(x_{10}, x_6, x_2) & f_{11}(x_{11}, x_7, x_3) \end{array}$$

This set of subfunctions results in the Variable Interaction Graph shown in Figure 3. Thus, if the most recent variable to flip was variable x_5, the VIG tells us that the only possible new improving moves will be at bits x_4, x_7, x_3 or x_2. Furthermore, if there already exists improving moves at one of these bits locations, it is also possible that an improving move may have been destroyed; both the creation and destruction of improving moves must be tracked. But, on average, tracking improving moves can be done on average in constant time per move for the Hamming distance 1 neighborhood [19].

Recently, Chicano et al. [2] have shown that under relatively general conditions, improving moves can also be identified in constant $\Theta(1)$ time in a Hamming radius r neighborhood; they present results for 10,000 variable NK-landscape problems using radius $r = 7$. This idea can also be explained using the Variable Interaction Graph. Note that there are no edges between variables x_4, x_9 and x_6 in Figure 3. Also assume there are no improving moves in the Hamming distance 1 neighbor. Then flipping the bits x_4, x_9 and x_6 together simultaneously can *never* yield an improving move. Assuming improving moves less than r have already been exploited, all Hamming distance r improving moves must utilize bit flips using combinations of variables that are linked in the Variable Interaction Graph.

This also means that for most Mk Landscape problems, evolutionary algorithms using mutation operators that randomly change a small number of bits are unnecessary. Rather than randomly searching for improving moves, we can rapidly compute the location of improving moves.

4. TRIVIAL PROBLEMS (THAT ARE NOT VERY DECEPTIVE)

We next consider Mk Landscapes that result in problems that are trivial to solve using a Gray Box Optimizer.

4.1 Separable Functions

Consider again the general form of Mk Landscapes as a summation of subfunctions.

$$f(x) = \sum_{i=1}^{M} f_i(x), \tag{2}$$

Definition: An Mk Landscape is *order k separable* if it can be written as a sum of subfunctions, and every variable is restricted so that it appears in one and only one subfunction.

Theorem: *A global optimum of an order k separable Mk Landscape is found in one evaluation in $O(n)$ time by a Gray Box Optimizer.*

Proof: Since each subfunction is independent from every other subfunction each of the M $= O(n)$ subfunctions is optimized in $O(2^k)$ time by brute force enumeration. The full evaluation function is executed only once. □

Trap functions are a form of order k separable Mk Landscape. What makes these problems "challenging" is that an order k subfunction is constructed so that the order $k-1$ nonlinear interactions lead away from the order k solution that optimizes that particular subfunction. (Deceptive constructions exist where both the hyperplane statistics and the local search moves lead away from the order k solution.) In addition, when used in Black Box optimization, the optimizer does not automatically know which bits belong to a particular subfunction. However, for a Gray Box optimizer that has access to the definitions of the subfunctions, these problems become trivial. This means that the global optimum is found for trivial toy problems such as ONEMAX as well as trap functions using one evaluation of the combined evaluation $f(x)$. Since k is a constant and $M = O(n)$, separable problems are solved in $O(n)$ time.

It should also be pointed out that separable Mk Landscapes are just a special form of "Localized Mk Landscapes." This topic will appear again in section 4.3.

4.2 Walsh Analysis & Hyperplanes

The evaluation function for any Mk Landscape can be expressed as follows:

$$f(x) = \sum_{i}^{M} f_i(x)$$

We can transform the evaluation function into a polynomial form by applying a discrete Fourier transform, which is also known as a Walsh transform. Let W denote the Walsh matrix.

$$W(f(x)) = \sum_{i}^{M} W(f_i(x))$$

When all subfunctions have exactly k variables, W can be used unnormalized. Assuming $M = O(n)$, there are at most 2^k coefficients per subfunction and at most $2^k M = O(n)$ coefficients in the Walsh polynomial. Thus, the resulting Walsh polynomial has only $O(n)$ nonlinear coefficients.

The Walsh coefficients can be used to efficiently compute the average evaluation of solutions contained in any $(n-j)$-dimensional hyperplane [16, 6]. Let h denote a $(n-j)$ dimensional hyperplane where j variables have preassigned bit values and $\alpha(h)$ be a mask with 1 bits marking the locations where the j variables appear in the problem encoding and 0 bits elsewhere. Let solution x assign values to the j variables. Let $\beta(h) = \alpha(h) \wedge x$. This means $\beta(h)$ has value 0 in all of the positions where the j bits do not appear and has the assigned values of the relevant j bits in the appropriate bit locations. Then the mean fitness of hyperplane h is

$$Avg(h) = w_0 + \sum_{\forall b, b \subseteq \alpha(h)} w_b(-1^{b^T \beta(h)})$$

Clearly, for all Mk Landscapes where k is a constant and $M = O(n)$, there are at most $O(n)$ Walsh coefficients, and thus is it always possible to compute any hyperplane mean in $O(n)$ time. The mean for a single order k hyperplane can be computed in constant $\Theta(1)$ time.

Assume all of the means for all hyperplanes of some order j been computed. Let $MAX(x, \alpha(h))$ return the hyperplane with the best mean over all of the 2^j order j hyperplanes that can be defined using the $\alpha(h)$ mask. The j bit values returned y $MAX(x, \alpha(h))$ represent the bits that match those in the hyperplane with the maximal mean over the order j set encapsulated by $\alpha(h)$.

Definition: Order j Deceptive. If the j bit values returned by $MAX(x, \alpha(h))$ for all hyperplanes of order j are *not* the same as the bit values found in a string which is a global optimum, then a problem is **order j deceptive**.

Theorem: *Given a fixed constant j, every Mk Landscape that is less than order j deceptive can be exactly solved in polynomial time by a Gray Box Optimizer.*

Proof: If an Mk Landscape is less than order j deceptive, then by definition the order j hyperplanes that optimize the hyperplane means also identify the variable assignments which yield a globally optimal solution. The order j hyperplane means are obtained from the Walsh decomposition of the evaluation function f in polynomial time. □.

We can, of course, also reverse engineer problems that are not deceptive. One easy way to construct a problem that is not deceptive is to pick a global optimum (e.g., a string of 1 bits of length n) and then construct an Mk-Landscape such that each subfunction is optimal using a bit pattern that matches the global optimum (e.g., a string of 1 bits of length k). Finally, by construction, we can build each subfunction by selecting Walsh coefficients such the bits returned by $MAX(x, \alpha(h))$ match the bits found in a target pattern corresponding to a global optimum.

Assume we construct an Mk Landscape where all of the subfunctions are identical. The subfunction could be a variant of a simple "royal road" like function [15]:

$$f_i(x, y, z) = x + y + z + 2xy + 2xz + 2yz + 4xyz$$

In this case, we can analyze the subfunctions, calculate the Walsh coefficients, and then use this information to infer a global optimum. This can be done even if the subfunctions are not separable and share random variables because the hyperplane statistics will still point to the global optimum. There can even be "low level deception" as long as higher order hyperplane statistics point to the correct solution.

And even for Mk Landscapes that are not separable, variants of "royal road" like problems can be constructed such that all roads and all order k information lead in the right direction. Holland [11] has similarly suggested how to construct "Hyperplane Defined Functions." But, Hyperplane Defined Functions are also easy to solve if they are Mk Landscapes and we explicitly know they are not deceptive above some order j.

There are also simple problems that are not separable, but nevertheless, are still not deceptive. The "Leading Ones" problem is an example [13]. It is easy to prove mathematically that $MAX(x, \alpha(h))$ will always return a 1 bit for all of the order 1 hyperplanes for the maximization Leading Ones problem. A simple proof that "Leading Ones" is not deceptive is given in the appendix. This should not be surprising: trivial problems are trivial to solve.

It would seem intuitive that most difficult problems are deceptive. Obviously, this must be true for NP-Hard problems. Since classic decision problems such as MAX-3SAT are a form of Mk Landscapes, hyperplane statistics that can be computed in polynomial time cannot provide a reliable tool for locating globally optimal solutions unless P=NP.

Håstad [8] has shown that in the worst case one cannot guarantee even an above average solution to a MAXSAT instance unless P=NP. By extension, in the worst case, hyperplane statistics cannot be used to guarantee even an above average solution to any arbitrary Mk Landscape. Thus, while order k hyperplane statistics are relatively inexpensive to compute, they cannot be used to reliably guide search in the worst case. This is of course bad news (but now new news [16] [17]) for theories from before 1999 about genetic algorithms as hyperplane sampling algorithms.

On the other hand, there are many exact SAT solvers that regularly find solutions to large real world applications with millions of variables. It can be argued that this is only possible because good SAT solvers exploit problem structure.

4.3 Localized Mk Landscapes

There can be various kinds of problem structure in Mk Landscapes. One way in which problems can be structured is by restricting variable interactions.

Separable NK Landscapes are one way that Mk Landscapes can have localized variable interactions. "Adjacent NK Landscapes" are another way to localize interactions. In an Adjacent NK Landscape, each subfunction f_i takes as input the variables x_i, x_{i+1}, x_{i+2} where index i wraps around.

This idea can also be generalized to create "Localized Mk Landscapes" that are loosely adjacent.

Consider the following subfunctions:

$$f(x) = f_1(x_1, x_3, x_4) + f_2(x_5, x_4) + f3(x_5, x_6)$$

These subfunctions are not part of an "Adjacent NK Landscapes." However an adjacent relationship can be created between subfunctions by adding additional dummy variables:

$$f(x) = f_1(x_1, x_2, x_3, x_4) + f_2(x_2, x_3, x_4, x_5) + f_3(x_3, x_4, x_5, x_6)$$

Definition: A Localized Mk Landscape is an Mk Landscape where each subfunction f_i is defined over a window of variables from x_i to $x_{((i+K) \ mod \ M)}$, however, the actual number of variables used in each subfunction is $\leq K+1$.

function	Local Optima				codomain vector
$f_1(x_1, x_2, x_3)$	000	001	100	111	<1,1,0,0,1,0,0,1>
$f_2(x_2, x_3, x_4)$	011	001	100	111	<0,1,0,1,1,0,0,1>
$f_3(x_3, x_4, x_5)$	001	010	101	111	<0,1,1,0,0,1,0,1>
$f_4(x_4, x_5, x_6)$	110	100	011	111	<0,0,0,1,1,0,1,1>
$f_5(x_5, x_6, x_7)$	001	100	110	111	<0,1,0,0, 1,0,1,1>
$f_6(x_6, x_7, x_8)$	000	100	010	111	<1,0,1,0,1,0,0,1>
$f_7(x_7, x_8, x_9)$	001	010	101	111	<0,1,1,0,0,1,0,1>
$f_8(x_8, x_9, x_0)$	000	001	100	111	<1,1,0,0,1,0,0,1>
$f_9(x_9, x_0, x_1)$	000	010	011	111	<1,0,1,1,0,0,0,1>
$f_0f(x_0, x_1, x_2)$	000	101	110	111	<1,0,0,0,0,1,1,1>

Table 1: This is a simple Adjacent Mk Landscape. Each subfunction has four local optima with evaluation 1; all other points have evaluation 0. The global optimum is the string of all 1 bits, and each subfunction has 111 as a local optimum.

Theorem: *A Localized Mk Landscape can be globally optimized in polynomial time.*

Proof: By definition, a Localized Mk Landscape can be transformed into an Adjacent NK Landscape in polynomial time and then solved using the dynamic programming algorithm of Wright et al. [22].

The definition could perhaps be made even more general, but this definition guarantees that any Localized Mk Landscape can be solved in polynomial time.

Are Adjacent NK Landscapes therefore inherently easy? Are they deceptive? Table 1 presents an Mk Landscape with 10 variables. It is an Adjacent NK Landscape. It is also an "NKq" landscape [5] [18], because the evaluation of each subfunction returns only 0 or 1; the "q" in the "NKq" label refers to the fact that the codomain values are discrete and can take on only 1 of q values. Thus, $q = 2$ in this case. This yields a search space with plateaus containing neighboring moves with the same evaluation.

The problem in Table 1 has a very simple solution. Every subfunction has a local optimum at the substring 111. And indeed the global optimum is the string 1111111111. So, this is not a difficult problem.

The "Adjacent NK Landscape" falls into the complexity class P since there is an exact dynamic programming algorithm that is guaranteed to return a globally optimal solution in polynomial time for all string lengths as long as k is bounded [22]. Do simple "Adjacent Mk Landscapes" display deception, or are hyperplane statistics useful for inferring solutions to these problems?

One might expect that computing order 3 statistics that match up with the 3 variables that appear in each subfunction might be useful. However, this does not appear to be the case. Computing the order 3 hyperplane averages for the problem in Table 1 revealed no pattern that might suggest that the global optimum is the string of all 1 bits.

What about high order hyperplanes? Statistics about 5th order hyperplanes were also computed. For each subfunction $f_i = (x_i, x_{i+1}, x_{i+2})$ all of the hyperplanes for the bit combinations of $x_{i-1}, x_i, x_{i+1}, x_{i+2}, x_{i+3}$ were considered. This span of variables captures all of the nonlinear Walsh coefficients that touch the middle variable x_{i+1}. This is sufficient to capture the nonlinearity of a subfunction f_i as well as the nonlinearity of the two subfunctions that are adjacent: f_{i-1} and f_{i+1}. When the hyperplane statistics were computed over these sets of variables, a general pattern emerged that displayed a bias for 1 bits, but the pattern was imperfect and still too weak to guide search. The hyperplanes with the highest averages are shown in the following table.

$MAX(x, \alpha(h))$ for $(x_0, x_1, x_2, x_3, x_4) = 11001$
$MAX(x, \alpha(h))$ for $(x_1, x_2, x_3, x_4, x_5) = 11111$
$MAX(x, \alpha(h))$ for $(x_2, x_3, x_4, x_5, x_6) = 11111$
$MAX(x, \alpha(h))$ for $(x_3, x_4, x_5, x_6, x_7) = 11100$
$MAX(x, \alpha(h))$ for $(x_4, x_5, x_6, x_7, x_8) = 11000$
$MAX(x, \alpha(h))$ for $(x_5, x_6, x_7, x_8, x_9) = 11111$
$MAX(x, \alpha(h))$ for $(x_6, x_7, x_8, x_9, x_0) = 01001$ & 00001 *(tie)*
$MAX(x, \alpha(h))$ for $(x_7, x_5, x_6, x_7, x_8) = 11111$
$MAX(x, \alpha(h))$ for $(x_8, x_9, x_0, x_1, x_2) = 00000$
$MAX(x, \alpha(h))$ for $(x_9, x_0, x_1, x_2, x_3) = 11001$

Despite the fact that this is a simple Adjacent NK Landscape (with localized variable interactions and localized nonlinearity) the order 5 hyperplane statistics do not provide any recognizable mechanism for identifying the global optimum. This simple function is still deceptive at order 5.

One of the things that makes this simple function a difficult optimization problem are the plateaus. Locally, for any reasonably good solution almost all Hamming distance 1 neighbors might look equally good.

The problem in Table 1 is, in fact, also a MAXSAT problem. The evaluation has been simplified to be only 1 or 0 (true or false). The "local optima" are also Disjunctive Normal Form (DNF) clauses: one of the DNF clauses must be true for all of the subfunctions to be satisfied.

We next turn to the issue of finding problem structure in variants of MAXSAT problems, and look at new ways of representing MAXSAT problems as Mk Landscapes.

5. MAX-KSAT AS MK LANDSCAPES

All nontrivial MAX-kSAT problems are deceptive. The "clause count" counts the number of times that a variable appears as a positive variable compared to the number of time it appears as a negated variable across all CNF clauses. Modern exact solvers, such as MiniSat, use a "polarity vector" that guides the initial assignment of variables [4]. One way the polarity vector can be set is using the clause count. Observations from Rana et al. [16] can be used to compute order 1 Walsh coefficients from the clause counts. If a MAX-kSAT problem with fixed k is not deceptive, then initializing the polarity vector using the clause count will guarantee an optimal solution in polynomial time because the clause count is a proxy for the best order 1 hyperplane. Obviously, both real world and random CNF SAT problems are not solved so easily.

By definition, MAX-kSAT problems that are in Conjunctive Normal Form (CNF) are also MK-Landscapes. In this case, each CNF clause is a subfunction in an Mk Landscape, and the evaluation function f sums over the (0 or 1) evaluation of each individual clause. However, there are other compact representations for SAT that are also Mk Landscapes that might more concisely capture variable interactions.

When unrestricted SAT expressions are converted into CNF-SAT, the SAT formula is broken into groups of k or fewer variables where each group of variables is represented in an intermediate form such as the following expression:

$$\phi = (x_{18} \leftrightarrow (x_{38} \vee x_{14}))$$

This intermediate form can be directly converted into CNF SAT. Following the DIMACS format, we will represent variables by their integer index, and a negative variable (e.g. -38) indicates a negated variable. The CNF3SAT expression for $(x_{18} \leftrightarrow (x_{38} \vee x_{14}))$ is as follows:

$$\phi = (-38 \vee 14 \vee 18) \wedge (-38 \vee -14 \vee 18) \wedge (38 \vee 14 \vee -18) \wedge (38 \vee -14 \vee 18)$$

However, we can also directly convert the intermediate form into a Disjunctive Normal Form (DNF) formula:

$$\phi = (-38 \wedge -14 \wedge -18) \vee (-38 \wedge 14 \wedge 18) \vee (38 \wedge -14 \wedge 18) \vee (38 \wedge 14 \wedge 18)$$

Disjunctive Normal Form formulas are awkward, however, because one cannot use logical "and" to sum over and combine DNF formulas. Still there are distinct advantages to DNF formulas: the formulas indicate exactly which combinations of variables must be satisfied in order to achieve an overall satisfying assignment. As a compromise, we will introduce "DNF Functions."

Definition: A DNF function is a Boolean function over k variables, $B^k \to B$, which evaluates a DNF formula ϕ for the same k variables. For any given assignment of variables, the DNF function returns true if and only if ϕ is true.

In effect, the DNF function is just a truth table. We will represent the output of a DNF function as a binary vector of the evaluation of the truth table. For example

$$\phi = \quad F(38, 14, 18) = < 1, 0, 0, 1, 0, 1, 0, 1 >$$

where the binary vector $< 1, 0, 0, 1, 0, 0, 1, 1 >$ indicates exactly which variable assignments will satisfy the DNF function. To improve readability, we will represent a DNF function and the codomain vector in the following form

$$F(38, 14, 18) = 1001\ 0101$$

where the codomain vector is a binary string broken into blocks of four bits.

To evaluate the DNF function, assignments to the variables are converted into an integer from 0 to $2^k - 1$ and the integer then indexes the corresponding truth value from the codomain vector. Thus, if $x_{38} = 0, x_{14} = 1, x_{18} = 1$ then F(0,1,1) = F(3) = 1. The positions 0, 3, 5, 7 in the codomain vector 1001 0101 directly correspond to the DNF clauses in the DNF formula.

Every DNF function must be true for the overall SAT instance to evaluate to true. Thus, a constraint that must hold for one DNF function is also a constraint over the entire SAT instance. We can easily "and" over DNF functions, or we can sum DNF functions to create a form of MAXSAT.

5.1 Structure in Real World Problems

By examining many large CNF-SAT applications from recent SAT Competitions, we have discovered that these problems display "natural blocks." A"natural block" is a set of clauses that are generated consecutively (by algorithms that convert SAT into CNF) and which utilize the same variables.

$F1(2,3,4,5) := F1(7,8,9,10) :=$ 0111 1111 1111 1111

$F2(42,16,20,41,43) := F2(44,17,21,43,45) :=$
$F2(50,25,29,49,51) := F2(52,26,30,51,53) :=$
$F2(54,27,31,53,55) := F2(60,46,34,59,61) :=$
$F2(62,47,35,61,63) := F2(70,42,48,69,71) :=$
$F2(72,58,50,71,73) := F2(74,60,52,73,75) :=$
$F2(76,62,54,75,77) := F2(78,64,56,77,79) :=$
$F2(80,66,57,79,81) := F2(40,15,19,39,41) :=$
1000 0001 0001 0100 0010 1000 1000 0001

$F3(46,22,45,47) := F3(48,24,28,49) := F3(56,32,55,57) :=$
$F3(58,44,33,59) := F3(66,37,65,67) := F3(68,40,23,69) :=$
$F3(82,67,81,83) := F3(64,36,63,65) := F3(38,14,18,39) :=$
1000 0001 0010 1000

$F4(13,1,6,18,7) := F4(23,1,8,28,9) :=$
$F4(14,2,6,19,7) := F4(24,2,8,29,9) :=$
$F4(15,3,6,20,7) := F4(25,3,8,30,9) :=$
$F4(16,4,6,21,7) := F4(26,4,8,31,9) :=$
$F4(17,5,6,22,7) := F4(27,5,8,32,9) :=$
1100 1100 1001 0000 0000 0000 0000 1001

$F5(33,1,10) := F5(34,2,10) := F5(35,3,10) := F5(36,4,10) :=$
$F5(37,5,10) :=$ 1110 0001

$V := \{13, -38, -68, -70, 72, -74, -76, -78, 80, -82, -83\}$

Table 2: The prime factoring SAT problem after converting into DNF functions. The vector V holds variables where the truth assignment is already constrained after exactly one step of unit propagation.

The following is an example of a "natural block" of CNF clauses in the DIMACS format. Each line denotes one clause, and integers denote variables. A positive number is a positive variable, and a negative number is a negated variable and the final 0 is an end of line marker. These are in the same order in which they were generated.

```
-38 14 18 0
-38 -14 -18 0
38 14 -18 0
38 -14 18 0
-14 -18 39 0
14 18 -39 0
14 -39 0
18 -39 0
```

This "natural block" can be converted into the following DNF function with $k = 5$ variables:

$$F3(38,14,18,39) := 1000\ 0001\ 0010\ 1000$$

Table 2 is the DNF function representation of an actual CNF-SAT problem. (As with standard DIMACS notation for clauses, we don't really need to name different functions, e.g., F1, F2, but the labels in Table 2 will aid the reader.) This SAT problem is a prime factorization problem from the Tough SAT Project website (https://toughsat.appspot.com). The generator asks for two prime numbers as input. When two primes are multiplied together it results in a number that is a *semiprime*. Large semiprimes result in some of the most difficult factorization problems. Many encryption methods rely on the fact that factoring large composite integers is difficult. For example, the RSA public-key crytosystem uses a large semiprime as part of the encryption.

The prime factoring problem in Table 2 used the factors 13 and 21. This resulted in a CNF-SAT instance with 83 variables and 369 clauses. We have done nothing to simplify this problem at this point. Only one step of unit propagation was applied. By combining the "natural blocks" of adjacent clauses, the 83 variables and 369 clauses can be compressed into 36 DNF functions, which is a 10 fold compression of the representation. All of the DNF functions have either 4 or 5 variables. What is even more surprising is that all of the functions are one of only 5 types, which means that all of the codomain vectors are of just 5 types. Most of these are of just 3 types: F2, F3 and F4.

These same DNF functions reoccur across other prime factoring problems of different sizes. For the problem with factors 15485863 and 15485867 the corresponding CNF-SAT instance generated by Tough Sat has 1824 variables with 9673 clauses after one step of unit propagation. When converted into DNF functions, there are 526 of type F2 (accounting for 7364 clauses), 68 of type F3 (accounting for 544 clauses) and 288 of type F4 (accounting for 1728). This means that over 99 percent of all clauses (9636/9673) can be assigned to DNF functions of type F2, F3 or F4.

Our preliminary findings also indicate this kind of symmetry and repetition is extremely common in very large real world applications with millions of variables. There is a very powerful take home message here: Real problems are not trivial, but they are also not random. There is structure, and usually that structure has modularity and repetition. Some variable interactions are very localized interactions; other variable interactions are more global. If we really want to solve real problems more effectively, we need to break open the Black Box and examine problem structure.

6. CONCLUSIONS

This paper has introduced Mk Landscapes as a way of unifying what we know about NK Landscapes and other k bounded pseudo Boolean problems such as MAX-kSAT. The concept of "Localized Mk Landscapes" was introduced. These problems are not Adjacent NK Landscapes, but can be converted into an Adjacent Mk Landscape, and thus are solvable in polynomial time using dynamic programming. Separable Mk Landscape instances are also trivial to solve. The paper has also shown that if any Mk Landscape is not deceptive, that problem can also be solved in polynomial time.

Insights about trivial problems probably tell us nothing about solving difficult Mk Landscape problems that are NP Hard. However, studying random NK Landscape and random MAXSAT problems may be equally misleading. Random problems do not have the kind of structure and repetition that is found in real world applications.

An overarching theme that emerges from this work is that exploiting problem structure is critical to solving real world problems. The concept of *Gray Box Optimization* is introduced to replace the concept of *Black Box Optimization.* If we know that a problem is an Mk Landscape, we can use a number of tools to efficiently solve trivial problems that are not NP Hard. Trivial problems such as ONEMAX and "Leading Ones" can be solved in 1 evaluation in $O(n)$ time. For Mk Landscapes, there is no need to use a random mutation operator; the location of improving moves can be efficiently computed. In general, an algorithm with access to more information about problem structure has major advantages over a blind Black Box Optimizer. The best way to make real progress on real applications is to focus on exploiting problem structure.

7. ACKNOWLEDGMENTS

This research was sponsored by the Air Force Office of Scientific Research, Air Force Materiel Command, USAF, under grant number FA9550-11-1-0088. The U.S. Government is authorized to reproduce and distribute reprints for Governmental purposes notwithstanding any copyright notation thereon.

8. REFERENCES

[1] E. Boros and P. Hammer. Pseudo-boolean optimization. *Discrete applied mathematics*, 123(1):155–225, 2002.

[2] F. Chicano, D. Whitley, and A. Sutton. Efficient identification of improving moves in a ball for pseudo-boolean problems. In *Genetic and Evolutionary Computation Conference*, 2014.

[3] T. Cormen, C. Leiserson, R. Rivesti, and C. Stein. *Introduction to Algorithms, 2nd Edition.* McGraw Hill, New York, 1990.

[4] N. Een and N. Sorensson. The MiniSat page. http://www.minisat.se, 2015.

[5] N. Geard, J. Wiles, J. Hallinan, B. Tonkes, and B. Skellett. A comparison of neutral landscapes: Nk, nkp and nkq. In *The IEEE Congress on Evolutionary Computation (CEC 2002)*, 2002.

[6] D. Goldberg. Genetic Algorithms and Walsh Functions: Part I, A Gentle Introduction. *Complex Systems*, 3:129–152, 1989.

[7] D. Goldberg. *Genetic Algorithms in Search, Optimization and Machine Learning.* Addison-Wesley, Reading, MA, 1989.

[8] J. Håstad. Some optimal inapproximability results. In *Proc. 29th ACM Symposium on Theory of Computation*, pages 1–10, 1997.

[9] R. B. Heckendorn. Embedded landscapes. *Evolutionary Computation*, 10(4):345–369, 2002.

[10] J. Holland. *Adaptation in Natural and Artificial Systems.* University of Michigan Press, 1975.

[11] J. Holland. Building Blocks, Cohort Genetic Algorithms and Hyperplane Defined Functions. *Evolutionary Computation*, 8(4):373–391, 2000.

[12] H. H. Hoos and T. Stützle. *Stochastic Local Search: Foundations and Applications.* Morgan Kaufman, 2004.

[13] T. Jansen. *Analyzing Evolutionary Algorithms.* Springer, 2013.

[14] D. Mitchell, B. Selman, and H. Levesque. Hard and easy distributions of SAT problems. In *Proceedings of the 10th National Conference on Artificial Intelligence*, 1992.

[15] M. Mitchell and S. Forrest. Fitness landscapes: Royal road functions. In Bäck, Fogel, and Michalewicz, editors, *Handbook of Evolutionary Computation*, volume B2.7, pages 1–25. Institute of Physics Publishing, 1997.

[16] S. Rana, R. B. Heckendorn, and L. D. Whitley. A tractable Walsh analysis of SAT and its implications for genetic algorithms. In *Proceedings of the Fifteenth National Conference on Artificial Intelligence (AAAI'98)*, pages 392–397, 1998.

[17] S. Rana and D. Whitley. Genetic algorithm behavior in the MAXSAT domain. In *Proceedings of Parallel Problem Solving from Nature V*, pages 785–794. Springer, 1998.

[18] S. Verel, G. Ochoa, and M. Tomassini. Local optima networks of nk landscapes with neutrality. *IEEE Trans Evolutionary Computation*, 15(6), 2011.

[19] D. Whitley and W. Chen. Constant time steepest descent local search with lookahead for nk-landscapes and max-ksat. In *Genetic and Evolutionary Computation Conference GECCO-2012*, 2012.

[20] D. Whitley and R. Das. The Only Challenging Problems are Deceptive: Global Search by Order-1 Hyperplane Sampling. In *Intern. Conf. on Genetic Algorithms*, pages 166–173. Morgan Kaufmann, 1991.

[21] D. Whitley, A. Howe, and D. Hains. Greedy or not? best improving versus first improving stochastic local search for maxsat. In *Proc.of AAAI-2013*, 2013.

[22] A. H. Wright, R. K. Thompson, and J. Zhang. The computational complexity of N-K fitness functions. *IEEE Transactions on Evolutionary Computation*, 4(4):373–379, 2000.

[23] A. Young. Spin Glasses. *J. of Statistical Physics*, 34:871–881, 1984.

9. APPENDIX: LEADING ONES IS NOT DECEPTIVE

The "Leading Ones" problem is a maximization problem. All strings on a level set with the same evaluation can be characterized as a hyperplane with l leading ones followed by a 0, followed by an arbitrary substring of bits. For a string of length n, the hyperplane this level set can be denoted by 1^l0*^{n-l-1} where the $*$ symbol represents a wildcard matching either 0 or 1. The case of all one bits (where no zero appears) can be dealt with as a special case. From this observation, we can sum over all the points in the search space.

$$\sum_{x \in X} f(x) = n + \sum_{i=0}^{n-2} 2^i(n-i-1)$$

Let $*0*^r$ and $*1*^r$ denote order 1 hyperplanes with a bit in the rth position, where $r = 0$ to $n-1$.

If the evaluation of a string is less than $n-r-1$ then there must a zero to the left of the fixed bit in the hyperplane. Thus, for every string with evaluation less than $n-r-1$ that contributes to $*0*r$, there is exactly one string with the same evaluation that contributes to $*1*r$. Thus, to select the hyperplane with the higher average, we only need to sum the evaluation of strings of the form $1^{n-r-1}0*^r$ which contribute to $*0*^r$ and strings of the form $1^{n-r-1}1*^r$ which contribute to $*1*^r$.

Thus, the sum of all of the strings in hyperplane $*1*^r$ is greater than the sum of all the strings in hyperplane $*0*^r$ if and only if

$$n + \sum_{i=0}^{r-1} 2^i(n-i-1) > 2^r(n-r-1)$$

The result holds by simple induction.

Evolving Soft Robots in Tight Spaces

Nick Cheney
Creative Machines Lab
Cornell University
Ithaca, NY, USA
nac93@cornell.edu

Josh C. Bongard
Morphology, Evolution &
Cognition Lab.
University of Vermont
Burlington, VT, USA
jbongard@uvm.edu

Hod Lipson
Creative Machines Lab
Cornell University
Ithaca, NY, USA
hod.lipson@cornell.edu

ABSTRACT

Soft robots have become increasingly popular in recent years – and justifiably so. Their compliant structures and (theoretically) infinite degrees of freedom allow them to undertake tasks which would be impossible for their rigid body counterparts, such as conforming to uneven surfaces, efficiently distributing stress, and passing through small apertures. Previous work in the automated deign of soft robots has shown examples of these squishy creatures performing traditional robotic task like locomoting over flat ground. However, designing soft robots for traditional robotic tasks fails to fully utilize their unique advantages. In this work, we present the first example of a soft robot evolutionarily designed for reaching or squeezing through a small aperture – a task naturally suited to its type of morphology. We optimize these creatures with the CPPN-NEAT evolutionary algorithm, introducing a novel implementation of the algorithm which includes multi-objective optimization while retaining its speciation feature for diversity maintenance. We show that more compliant and deformable soft robots perform more effectively at this task than their less flexible counterparts. This work serves mainly as a proof of concept, but we hope that it helps to open the door for the better matching of tasks with appropriate morphologies in robotic design in the future.

Categories and Subject Descriptors: [**Distributed Artificial Intelligence**]:Intelligent Agents, Mobile Agents

General Terms: Algorithms, Design

Keywords: Soft Robot, Generative Encoding, Artificial Life, CPPN-NEAT, HyperNEAT, Multi-Objective, Morphology, Material

GECCO '15, July 11 - 15, 2015, Madrid, Spain

ISBN 978-1-4503-3472-3/15/07 . . . $15.00
DOI: http://dx.doi.org/10.1145/2739480.2754662

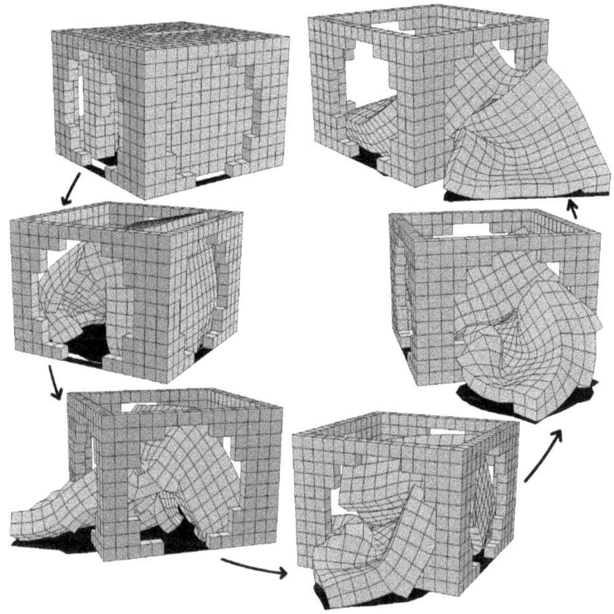

Figure 1: ***(counter-clockwise rotating-viewpoint time series starting from top left).*** **An evolved soft robot reaches through a hole in the side of a cage surrounding it. The width of this aperture is smaller than any of the dimensions of this creature – thus a robot of the same size without a soft body would not be able to squeeze through it.**

1. INTRODUCTION

Recent interest and developments in the study of soft robotics [2, 5, 10, 15, 18, 19, 20] have pointed towards a number of potential benefits of using soft material in the design of artificial creatures.

Recent work has also demonstrated the use of evolutionary computation to design effective soft robot bodies [4, 6, 11, 12]. Such an approach holds the potential for significant impact, since the extreme nonlinearities and degrees of freedom apparent in soft robots make their design unintuitive, compared to traditional rigid body robots. The design automation inherent in evolutionary computation removes the prerequisite of an intuitive understanding of these systems for their effective design.

In reviewing the "lessons from biology" that soft robots should inherit, Kim et al. note that "Soft materials are essential to the mechanical design of animals... These soft components provide numerous advantages, helping animals negotiate and adapt to changing, complex environments. They conform to surfaces, distribute stress over a larger volume, and increase contact time, thereby lowering the maximum impact force. Soft materials also lend themselves to highly flexible and deformable structures, providing additional functional advantages to animals, such as enabling entrance into small apertures for shelter or hunting... all of them can squeeze through gaps smaller than their unconstrained body. These are important lessons for building soft robots" [8].

However, up to this point, there has been no attempt to demonstrate the ability of these artificially evolved robots to perform the tasks which their biological counterparts have been evolved for. This is especially important, as Kim et al. make explicit the intuitive notion that "Ultimately it is probably the ecological niche that determines the evolutionary tendency to be stiff or soft" [8].

This work attempts to provide the first demonstration of an evolved creature for an explicitly "soft-body-oriented" task, by evolving creatures for the task of "entrance into small apertures." In this work, a soft robot bounded by a $11 \times 11 \times 11$ maximum size is placed within a cage of a 15×15 footprint, with height 11. The cage has holes in each side of its sides with a diameter of 10. This aperture may be more restrictive than it first appears, as a square of side length 11 has an area of 121, while a circle of diameter 10 has an area of 78.5 (just 65% of the maximum potential face area of the robot). We evolve soft robots to reach or squeeze through this aperture using the CPPN-NEAT evolutionary algorithm, and demonstrate a variety of effective, creative, and entertaining behaviors (such as Fig. 1).

We hypothesize that softer, more deformable, robots will have an easier time accomplishing these tasks. At either extreme, one could imagine that a (maximum size of 11^3) robot that is a rigid solid would be physically unable to fit through a hole of diameter 10, while a creature composed of that volume of extremely soft material (liquid at the pure extreme) would easily flow through the aperture. Of course, neither of these robots are likely to take on the structure of a lattice of voxels, as our soft robots do (a rigid robot would be likely to include joints, while a flowing liquid would require the free movement of particles), nor would our soft body physics simulator be equipped to handle either of these cases. Thus, we approach this investigation by comparing the ability of more or less compliant soft robots to move through this aperture, and leave the reader to extrapolate to these extreme cases.

Secondarily, this work also demonstrates an example of multi-objective NEAT with speciation. While this is not the focus of the paper, and thus we do not provide comparisons to other examples of multi-objective NEAT without speciation, it is a novel implementation and may be of interest to those hoping to explore added diversity maintenance within multi-objective optimization.

2. BACKGROUND

The notion of soft robots being good at squeezing though small openings has been approached previously by hand designed robots. Sheperd et al. created a molded silicon robot which was able to squeeze under a barrier with a $2cm$ clearance (the maximum dimensions of the robot were $13.6cm \times 5.9cm \times 0.6cm$) [15]. However, the design of the robot's morphology was created by hand, and the robot was controlled manually via tethered pneumatic actuation.

Various examples of evolved soft robots have also been demonstrated [4, 6, 11, 12], however they all focused on the task of locomotion over flat ground. While not to say that soft robots do not hold any advantages for locomotion over a smooth planar surface, the advantages of such an approach are not as inherently apparent as a task in which rigid body robots are unable to perform – such as navigating through an aperture smaller than the robot's body.

3. METHODS

The source code (including a configuration file with parameter values) can be found at: http://git.io/vfSLV

3.1 SIMULATED TASK ENVIRONMENT

In this work (and consistent with [4, 6, 11]), these soft robots are simulated in the soft-body physics simulator VoxCad [7]. Approximating an array of soft voxels as lattice of points connected by simulated beams, this physics engine is capable of efficiently modeling soft bodies, while maintaining physical and quantitative realism. VoxCad creates actuation within these soft robots by employing a sinusoidally varying global temperature. All passive cells (such as the blue support tissue or gold cage voxels) are unaffected by this temperature and remain a constant volume. Active muscle cells (two types: green and red) vary in size as this temperature changes. They do so out of phase to one another, with the green cells contracting then expanding, and the red cells expanding then contracting. The variation in size due to these temperature changes results in a 14% linear contraction/expansion from their baseline size, which results in approximately a 48% volumetric change. Each individual's evaluation period lasted for 20 of these actuation cycles.

New to this study, each soft robot is placed within a cage at the beginning of each simulation for fitness evaluation. The cage has dimensions $15 \times 15 \times 11$, leaving a one voxel gap between in the x and y directions between the edge of the cage and the $11 \times 11 \times 11$ maximum size of the evolved creature. The top is left open for ease of viewing – and no evolved creatures manage to fully escape out of the top of the cage. The cage is simulated to be perfectly rigid and immobile, as well as indestructible – forcing the robot to contort itself and travel through one of the openings in the side of the cage. Each side has an opening which is approximately (rounded to the nearest voxel) a circle of diameter 10 – thus in the 15×11 side face of the cage, there is one voxel above the opening, two voxels to one side of it, and three voxels to the other. This produces a circular opening of area 78.5 (before being discretized to the nearest voxel), which represents about 65% of the area of a full 11×11 face of a soft robot (it's maximum, but not guaranteed size).

A modification to the default operation of VoxCad was necessary to ensure that collisions detection between the cage and the robot ensured the robot was never able to accidentally pass through a part of the cage other than the opening. This modification caused collisions to be calculated between every voxel at every time step (as opposed to just surface voxels in VoxCad's default settings). The expense of this technique varies with the surface area to volume ratio of the evolved creatures, but it could result in as much as a six-fold slow down in simulation speed.

3.2 FITNESS METRICS

At the end of an individual's 20 action cycle evaluation period, one of two metrics were taken to summarize its behavioral outcome. In one configuration, the single farthest voxel from the center of the cage was recorded, and that voxel's position was returned to give the creature's "maximum reach" score. This fitness criteria incentivized the robots to stretch as far out of the cage as possible – and while leaving the cage entirely is one way to maximize this score, it was not necessary to successfully attain a successful reach (e.g. for object manipulation) outside of the cage boundaries.

To incentivize creatures to entirely leave the cage (important for locomotion rather than object manipulation), trials of an alternative configuration were conducted where the behavioral fitness score of an individual was total number of voxels the robot was able to move outside of the cage by the end of the trial. The total number of voxels (rather than the proportion of the creature's mass) was used at a method or further incentivize evolution to create large creatures (as robots small enough to walk out of the cage without having to contort and squeeze themselves through the aperture are less interesting for thus study).

In both cases, creatures were also incentivized along a second objective – to maximize their size (Sec. 3.4. This metric was defined simply as the number of voxels from which a creature was composed. However, one could certainly imagine alternative size metrics (such as the diameter or maximal inter-voxel distance of the creature).

3.3 CPPN-NEAT

Consistent with [4, 11], we allow the soft robots to optimize their topology using the CPPN-NEAT evolutionary algorithm [1, 16].

The CPPN encoding represents the voxel phenotype as a network. This network takes a voxel's relative coordinates as inputs, and transforms this information into a material selection for that particular voxel. This transformation takes place by querying each potential voxel (discretized cell in the $11 \times 11 \times 11$ grid of the design space) with the same genotype network.

To query a voxel, the input layer of this network consists of four nodes, encoding the relative (-1 to 1) Cartesian coordinates (x, y, z) and polar radius (r) of that voxel. The network is updated through a series of hidden nodes, and produces real valued numbers for the three output nodes. Then a threshold (all thresholds occur at zero) on the first output node determines whether that potential voxel space contains a solid voxel or is empty space. If there is a voxel, a threshold on the second output determines whether the voxel is a passive support tissue or an active muscle. If the voxel is a muscle cell, the final output node determines which of the two out-of-phase muscle types the cell belongs to.

Thus, similarities in coordinate values for nearby voxels produce gradual changes in the expression of output values (i.e. morphogens) that determine cell fate. This produces global structure in the resulting creatures. Further regularities are produced through the varying activation functions at each hidden node. For example, a node which contains a Gaussian activation function would create a symmetric pattern along the gradient of that node's input values. Similarly, a node with a sinusoidal activation function would create repetition along its input gradient. As these transformations are applied one on top of another, complex shapes quickly emerge [14].

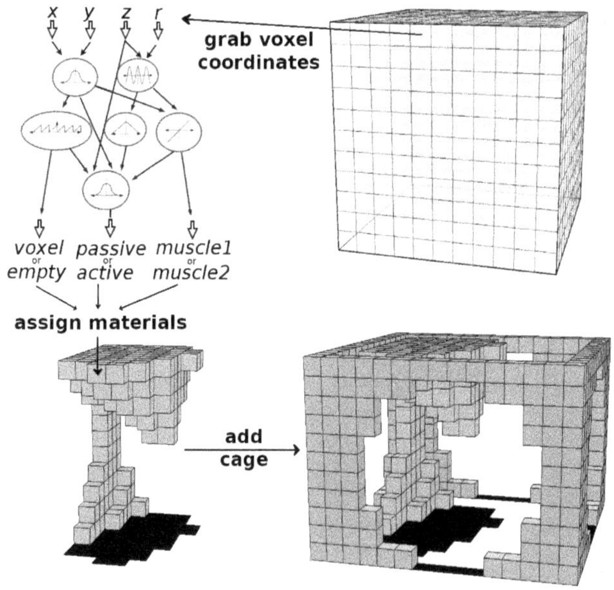

Figure 2: A sketch of the genotype to phenotype decoding. For each voxel in the potential design space, the relative coordinates values are taken and input into the network genotype. The material of each voxel is assigned based on the output of the network for that location. After each voxel has been individually queried for its material properties, the external environment (a cage surrounding the creature – Sec. 3.1) is put in place for the fitness evaluation.

A sketch of this genotype to phenotype decoding is provided in Fig. 2. The authors also note that this study is not directly in regards to the encoding employed, and will not explore the comparison of CPPN-NEAT to alternative encodings.

3.4 MULTI-OBJECTIVE NEAT

While the design flexibility afforded to the CPPN encoding creates a variety of complex forms, it also allows for the evolved creatures to simply produce topologies which would be smaller than the existing aperture, meaning that there would be no need for them to squeeze through a tight opening, and the resulting behavior would not be as interesting. To incentivize large forms which still squeeze through the smaller aperture, we created a multi-objective implementation of the NEAT algorithm. With this implementation, we are able to reward creatures for being large and also for squeezing though the aperture.

While various implementations of multi-objective NEAT have appeared recently [9, 21, 13], we believe that our implantation happens to be the only one which does not require the removal of the NEAT speciation (noted as one of the key features of the NEAT algorithm [17]). Instead of removing speciation and replacing it with a different diversity metric, or considering the added diversity inherent in multi-objective search to be sufficient on its own, our implementation performs a Pareto ranking of individuals within each species. We then perform the traditional tournament selection based on this ranking.

It is also noteworthy to mention that other implementation decisions were made to provide a bias towards the behavioral objective (squeezing through the narrow aperture) above the static objective (being larger in size). This implementation decision was made following the assumption that producing new individuals who were able to move farther (but were smaller) was a more difficult task than producing new individuals who were larger (but not able to move as effectively). This stems from the observation that any individual who adds one or more additional voxel to an existing fit phenotype would fulfill the later category, while not all individuals who were smaller (and likely a very small subset of them, who happened to be coordinated enough to improve their movement and behavior) would prove to be Pareto optimal in the former scenario. This intentional bias was instantiated by favoring locomotion behavior over size when comparing two individuals on the same Pareto front, and also by using the behavioral objective as the single objective required for NEAT's fitness sharing between species.

We should make explicit that this implementation of mulit-objective NEAT is not the focus of this paper. Thus no claims or comparisons relative to other implementations are presented, nor will the results section of this paper provide any quantitative support for any of the implementation decisions made above. Future work is needed to investigate multi-objective speciation in a variety of task scenarios, in order to make claims of its suitability and potential advantages or disadvantages within them.

3.5 RUN CHAMPIONS

Since this work relies on multi-objective optimization, the best resulting creatures from each of the 30 independent runs will fall along a Pareto front (on behavioral performance and size). While this variety is generally beneficial, it makes comparison between trials and treatments more difficult. In order to simplify the comparison, we provide a more specific definition of the optimal robot we seek to create.

Consistent with our preference for behavioral outcomes over size outcomes (Sec. 3.4), we seek to optimize along the single objective of behavioral performance (reaching or moving). However, moving through an aperture becomes trivial if the size of the robot is less than that of the aperture, so we place a strict size constraint on the robots we consider for run champions. This constraint relates not to the volume of the evolved robots, but deals explicitly with a 2D slice of the robot – which must fit through the 2D aperture of the cage.

In an effort to ensure that the evolved morphologies actually do have a full 11×11 face (and thus have to deform or compress themselves to "squeeze" through the aperture on the side of the cage. In all comparisons below, we consider only robots who have at least one 2D slice that spans the maximum 11 voxel width (at some point along the face) in both directions. Those robots who do not have at least one slice (along the Cartesian coordinate axes) that meets this criteria are thrown out and not considered in the analysis below. While we realize that this is only a proxy, and not an exact match, for the criteria of needing to constrict oneself to squeeze through the cage aperture, we believe it to be a good first pass approximation – and informal visual inspection of evolved topologies supports this belief.

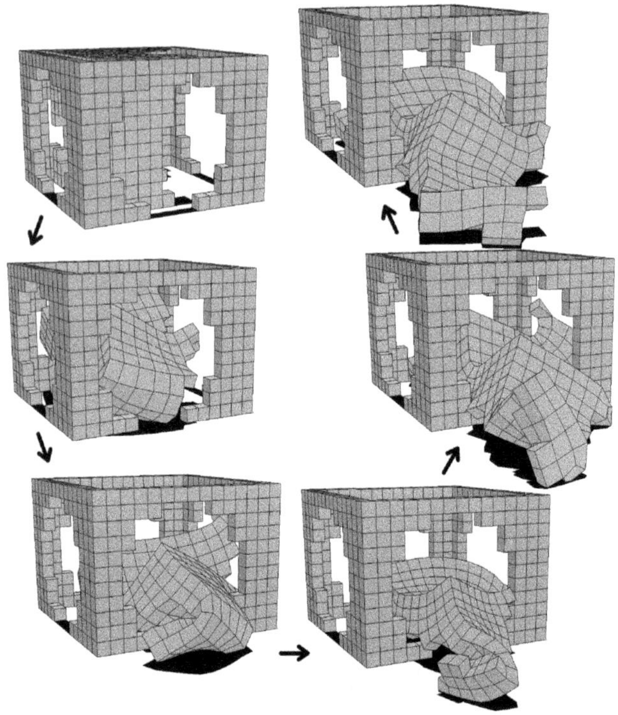

Figure 3: ***(counter-clockwise side-view time series starting from top left)*** **This creature, evolved for reaching, writhes back and forth in an effort to unroll itself and produce a long "arm" which reaches out from its cage.**

At the end of each run, the evolved robot which meets this size criteria threshold and demonstrates the farthest movement (or reaching) performance, is considered to be the best individual (the "champion") of that run. It is worth noting that this thresholding process does not take place during the actual optimization, but simply performed in post hoc analysis.

3.6 STATISTICAL ANALYSIS

Any statistical values reported below come from the Mann-Whitney U test, since normality of the distributions cannot be assumed. Since the distributions are unknown (and in an effort to help inform the skew of the distributions) both mean and median values are reported.

4. RESULTS

Since this work serves only as a first-pass proof of concept and demonstration of soft robots evolved to reach or squeeze through a small aperture, we primarily seek to demonstrate that is possible to successfully evolve soft robots for this task. For the case of reaching as far as possible outside of the cage, the best evolved robots of each run are able to reach an average length of 15.69 voxels (1.43 times their original body length of 11) outside of the cage (standard deviation: 3.21 voxels, median: 15.18). The fact that their farthest point is more than one original body length form the outside edge of the cage should not be an indication that these creatures frequently were able to completely exit the cage in the allotted time, as often they would unfold and spread out (e.g. Fig 3) to reach a significant distance while still remaining partially inside the cage.

In response to selection for the total number of voxels outside of the cage, the best of each run in the baseline conditions were able to move a mean of 140.30 voxels outside of their enclosure (median: 120.50). These results showed a great deal of variation (standard deviation: 98.77 voxels), with the most fit creature (on the movement objective) able to move 611 (of its 1130 voxels) out of the cage in the allotted time. The most fit creature of the run champions on the size objective was able to fill all 1331 of its voxels, but only move 60 of them out of the cage.

Perhaps a more compelling case for the ability to design squishy creatures who are able to navigate through their enclosures is the visual inspection of the resulting evolved soft robots. We believe that the diversity of forms and strategies, the effectiveness of these creatures towards their behavioral goals, as well as the clear necessity and use of physical deformation presented in the following examples, more strongly supports the existence of effective and successful evolutionary design than the values cited above. Here are a couple more examples of this:

The top of each cage is intentionally left open – not for creatures to climb out of, but for viewing purposes. Fig. 4 shows how this view of a reaching robot clearly demonstrates an example of a creature which spans the entire frame of the cage, yet is able to deform itself and fold its body in upon itself to provide additional reaching opportunities. While this creatures would be able to fit through the aperture in its deformed state, it was simply incentivized for reaching distance – and one of its "supports" in the upright starting position provides an excellent "arm" for effortlessly reaching out through the aperture.

The case of a robot squeezing its entire body through the aperture is demonstrated in Fig. 5, as this creature comes from a trial in which the entire mass of the robot had to be moved (instead of simply considering its farthest reaching voxel). This example clearly demonstrates a creature squeezing itself and using its pliability to fit through an aperture smaller than the width of its body. The frames of the time series in which the robot is moving through the aperture clearly show the sides of the robot curled and folded back in upon themselves, creating a narrow enough girth to fit through the opening. This would not be possible without the deformability of the soft materials. To our knowledge, this creature represents the first evolved robot to fit though an opening smaller than the width of its body.

4.1 SOFT/STIFFNESS COMPARISON

We find it intuitive, and take for granted, that rigid body robots of equal size and shape would be not able to navigate through the openings of the cages presented here. This conjecture may not be more clearly demonstrated than in the case of Fig. 1. This creature fills up nearly the entire potential voxel space (leaving just a thin strip of empty voxels separating its front and back segments) and spans the full 11 voxels wide on each face. However one may attempt to turn or twist this robot, it would not be physically possible to fit it through one of the apertures without deforming the creature. Despite this, the time series of this creature clearly and simply demonstrates how it is able to deform itself, folding and twisting the flat face of its front half to squeeze it through the tight aperture and reach out of its cage.

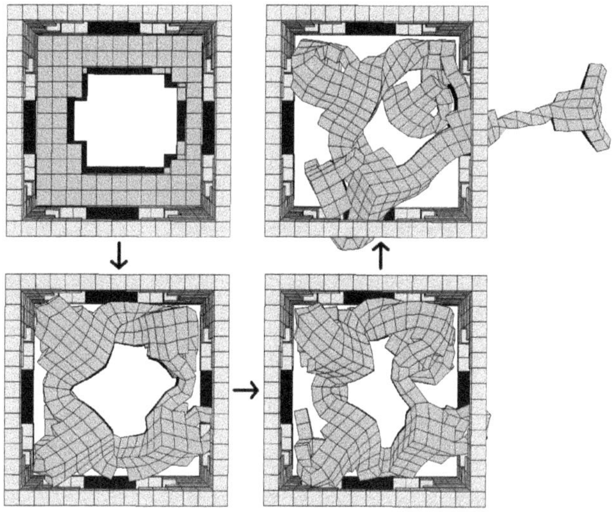

Figure 4: ***(counter-clockwise top-view time series starting from top left)*** **This evolved soft robot demonstrates a pure reaching behavior, where the majority of its body stays within the cage, but a dedicated arm reaches out through the aperture. This robot also exemplifies a highly deformable structure. In its starting configuration, its thin frame spans the entire inside of the cage, yet once it is given the chance to deform, it folds in upon itself to produce an entangled and complex morphology. Unlike its initial configuration (which a rigid body robot would have to stay in), the deformed morphology allows enough flexibility to position itself next a hole in the cage and reach out through it.**

However, the implementation of a completely rigid robot in this context (a voxel array with no explicit joints) makes little sense. Thus a fair comparison cannot be made between fully rigid and soft – so our comparison will be between two soft robots of varying stiffness. The above result provides the stiff(er) creatures, which have a Young's modulus (measuring tensile elasticity) of 10 megapascals (MPa). We also test a treatment which employs muscle and tissues that are an order of magnitude more elastic (Young's modulus of 1 MPa). For contextual grounding, this is approximately the range of values corresponding to the least elastic and the most elastic silicone rubbers. The more elastic (i.e. softer) robots are able to move, on average, 174.43 voxels outside of the cage (standard deviation: 69.18, median: 155.50). According to the Mann Whitney U test, this is a significant increase from the stiffer treatment (with mean of 140.30, standard deviation: 98.77, median: 120.50), with a one-sided p-value of 0.0002.

Additionally, the softer treatment also scores better on the second objective for total voxel size. The softer robots (mean: 905.08, standard deviation: 266.20, median: 971.63 voxels) were significantly larger than the stiffer robots (mean: 718.74, standard deviation: 306.13, median: 612.26 voxels), with a one-sided p-value of 0.0107. Presumably this made it more difficult for them to fit through the opening (though both treatments were subjected to the post hoc size thresholding noted above, so neither one should be able to do so effortlessly).

This suggests that, at least for intermediate stiffnesses, softer robots are more effective at squeezing through a small aperture.

4.2 NUMBER OF MATERIALS

A surprising result from Figs. 1, 3, and 4 is that the creatures commonly appear to be made out of only a single material. This is unlike previously published results [4], where a figure is presented to demonstrate the variety and consistency of the material compositions for locomotion over flat ground.

Fig. 5, which shows a creature rewarded for moving its entire body through the aperture, does exemplify multiple materials. Perhaps one might assume that this task is more closely related to locomotion over flat ground, and thus more likely to match the previous result of mult-material evolved soft robots noted previously for that task.

However, the statistical data does not support this assumption. Run champions on the reaching task have, on average, 1.23 different materials (the median number of materials is 1 for all tasks). In comparison, run champions from the movement task tended to have even less material diversity, with an average value of 1.20 materials per individual. Not surprisingly, there is no statistically significant difference between material composition of robots evolved for the two different tasks ($p = 0.76$).

An analysis of the the entire population (not just run champions) shows average number of different materials per individual of 1.36 and 1.37 (of reaching and movement, respectively). While the difference is not statistically significant ($p = 0.19, 0.09$), the fact that the run champions have a mean towards a lower level of material diversity – compared to a randomly drawn individual during the optimization process – may suggest that this task actually incentivizes creatures to be of a single material to effectively and efficiently solve both the reaching and traveling tasks.

4.3 VOXEL PENALTY

Also in slight disagreement with previously work in this area [4], is the notion that larger creatures with more voxels are less able to move around. Cheney et al. show a weak tie between robots composed of more voxels and more distance traveled across flat ground. However in this scenario, more voxels lead to worse performance metrics. This relationship is true of the reaching task ($slope = -11.99, r^2 = 0.70$) as well as the movement task ($slope = -5.26, r^2 = 0.51$). This relationship is not surprising, as larger creatures have the obvious disadvantage of struggling to fit through the narrow aperture. It is interesting to note that the movement task in this work is more closely related to the task of locomotion over flat ground (than is reaching), perhaps helping to explain why larger sized robots correlate less strongly with negative behavioral outcomes in the movement task.

5. DISCUSSION

The results presented above clearly exemplify soft robots evolved to reach or squeeze through apertures smaller than their own body, and are the first of their kind to do so. We find the pictorial representations of these behaviors to

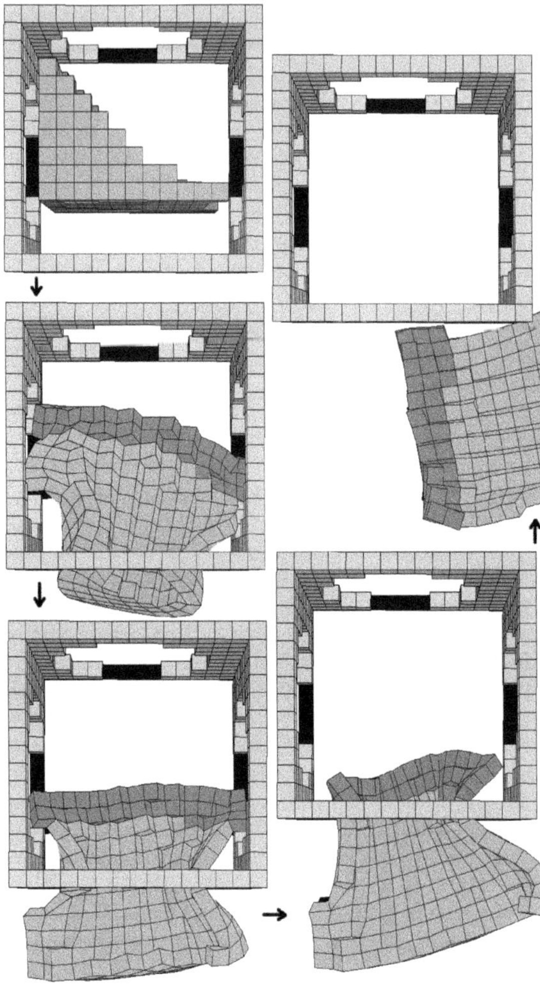

Figure 5: ***(counter-clockwise top-view time series starting from top left)*** **This example of a multi-material soft robot squeezes entirely through the aperture to escape the cage – as it is rewarded for the movements of all its voxels. Notice in the lower three frames how the creature's body is clearly wider than the opening of the aperture, yet it is able to squeeze and roll/fold itself up to fit through the tight opening. This is a prime example of the abilities afforded by the deformable bodies of soft robots. (Note: To fully escape the enclosure, this creature required more than the allotted 20 actuation cycles, and was thus only able to do so in post hoc analysis.)**

be more clarifying and convincing than the accompanying statistics, and are amazed at the power of this evolutionary process to design creatures which achieve these tasks in such creative and unintuitive ways.

The case of primarily single material creatures is slightly puzzling if one approaches the results expecting similar robots to those which tend to be evolved for locomotion on flat ground. But a couple potential causes for the single material beasts may be suggested. For the case of the reaching task, only the farthest (and not the average) distance was incentivized. A long arm which contains muscles of both types would have a part of the arm contract as the rest of it extended (and vise versa) – potentially leading to hindered reaching abilities. Since the two muscle types contract with opposite sinusoidal actuations, and only the reach at the last time step was recorded for fitness purposes, the material composition of the robot was originally assumed not to affect its behavior – as the simulations stopping point was chosen to come at the end of a temperature cycle, where both muscle groups were supposed to be their original size (and the same size as the support tissue). However, due to non-zero simulation time steps, it is unlikely that this stopping point occurred when the voxels were all exactly the same volume.

The case of single materials in creatures incentivized for movement follows a similar logic of opposing muscle groups. These creatures were implicitly rewarded for contracting as tightly as possible in order to squeeze their entire body through one of the apertures. Once part way through the aperture, expanding again is not a significant problem, since the soft body will simply deform around the edge of the opening. Thus, creatures with a continuous muscle type are afforded the advantage of being able to constrict themselves more compactly, with relatively little penalty for ballooning to a much larger size afterward.

The opposing selection pressures towards single material creatures in this work and towards multi-material composition in previous results [4] suggest that squeezing through an aperture and locomotion over flat ground require different muscle contraction patterns. Additionally, the fact that these creatures require more than 20 actuation cycles to produce a behavior which has them entirely exit their cage suggests that there is room for significant gains in efficiency. We believe that this points towards the potential (and perhaps necessity) of a closed loop controller for this task. The feedback of sensory information (regarding position in or out of the enclosure, as well as normal force applied against/from the structure) certainly hold the potential to encourage specific pulling/pushing motions, which would effectively and efficiently squeeze the soft robot through the opening. Furthermore, once the creature escaped the enclosure, and the tactile feedback from the cage is no longer apparent, it would be free to employ a movement pattern specifically tailored towards locomotion over flat ground.

It is also unclear to what extent these traditional locomotion behaviors are incentivized in the results above. One may imagine that a creature (once it has unfolded to lay on the ground, as in Fig. 3) would benefit from the ability to move along the surface, as doing so would push its farthest voxel further away from the cage and also pull its back end further out of the cage (the selected behaviors in both the treatments). However, one may also imagine that such a significant amount of selection pressure involves navigating around the cage, that any morphology alteration which benefits locomotion at the cost of additional interference with the structure would results in poor fitness. This is especially true when one considers the relatively short evaluation time of 20 actuation cycles (relative in comparison to the time it must take for a creature to fully escape the cage, given by the fact that creatures here do not tend to do so). In such a short period, the robots may not be on the ground (and at the edge of the an opening) long enough to make significant gains by crawling out of it – even if they happen to evolve the ability to do so. Extended trials of 100 actuation cycles were performed for some of the run champions to explore this idea, but no significant improvements were noted. This is not especially surprising, given that these creatures had little (or no) selection pressure to evolve behaviors which would continue to be effective past the end of their evaluation periods. To ensure that this is the case, the creatures would need to be evolved with 100 actuation cycle lifetimes for the entire optimization process (a treatment not possible with our current implementation and the limitations imposed by our Advanced Supercomputing Division).

6. FUTURE WORK

As this serves primarily as a demonstration and proof of concept, there is much future work left to be done.

This work included a number of implementation decisions which should be explored in a rigorous manner. The size of the cage, size of the aperture, shape of the aperture, shape of the cage, size of the contractions/expansions, rate of contractions, number of materials, stiffness of materials, length of evaluations, and many additional parameters of the evolutionary algorithm itself were all set arbitrarily or based on previously published parameter values [4]. A rigorous exploration into this parameter space would likely lead to greater information and understanding of the system.

Another improvement to this system would be the implementation of a more sophisticated controller than VoxCad's global temperature. This could take the form of a high-level neural network controller, as is common in the field, or the form of low level morphological computation, as was previously implemented in this system [3]. While the deformability of soft robots plays a crucial part in the ability of biological creatures to fit through small openings, so too does their control – an aspect currently missing from the initial implementation of this system.

Additionally, the implementation of multi-objective NEAT with speciation was not compared to prior multi-objective implementations of NEAT without it. Such a comparison would need to be made if one desired to make any claim of efficiency or desirability for this implementation.

A natural next step for future work, and perhaps the most exciting and open-ended avenue of future work, is to investigate the evolution of other behaviors which soft robots are particularly well suited for. These could include the aforementioned conformation to surfaces or shock absorption, or could take the form of higher-level behaviors relating to the brain-body interactions rather than the body-environment interactions in these brain-body-environment systems. The intersection of body shape, material, control, and environment are rarely studied in conjunction – yet each of these aspects plays a significant role in the behavior of an embodied system, and are desired in future work.

7. CONCLUSION

This work presents the first case of a soft robot evolved to perform a task specifically suited for soft robots. Specifically, this entailed designing creatures to reach or squeeze through a small opening – a task explicitly noted in the literature as one which soft robots are advantageous for. The interpretation of a "small" opening was one in which an equally sized and fully rigid robot would be unable to pass though, further supporting the claim that this task is one for which soft robots are better suited than rigid robots – and thus represents a task for which soft robots should be explicitly designed for. It was found that softer robots were better suited for this task than their (slightly) more rigid counterparts. In optimizing these robots, we also demonstrate a novel implementation of multi-objective NEAT, which relaxes the previous requirement of the removal of diversity maintenance through speciation. While this work serves primarily as an existence proof for evolved squishy robots squeezing through tight spaces, we believe this work also serves as a statement that soft robots should be designed for the tasks in which they excel, and thus we hope that this work opens up a host of questions and future possibilities along this avenue.

8. ACKNOWLEDGMENTS

This work was funded by NASA Space Technology Research Fellowship #NNX13AL37H. Nick would also like to thank the Santa Fe Institute and Ken Stanley for resources, discussions, and feedback during the time of this writing.

9. REFERENCES

[1] J. E. Auerbach and J. C. Bongard. Evolving cppns to grow three-dimensional physical structures. In *Proceedings of the 12th annual conference on Genetic and evolutionary computation*, pages 627–634. ACM, 2010.

[2] M. Calisti, M. Giorelli, G. Levy, B. Mazzolai, B. Hochner, C. Laschi, and P. Dario. An octopus-bioinspired solution to movement and manipulation for soft robots. *Bioinspiration & biomimetics*, 6(3):036002, 2011.

[3] N. Cheney, J. Clune, and H. Lipson. Evolved electrophysiological soft robots. In *ALIFE 14: The Fourteenth Conference on the Synthesis and Simulation of Living Systems*, volume 14, pages 222–229, 2014.

[4] N. Cheney, R. MacCurdy, J. Clune, and H. Lipson. Unshackling evolution: evolving soft robots with multiple materials and a powerful generative encoding. In *Proceedings of the 15th annual conference on Genetic and evolutionary computation*, pages 167–174. ACM, 2013.

[5] K.-J. Cho, J.-S. Koh, S. Kim, W.-S. Chu, Y. Hong, and S.-H. Ahn. Review of manufacturing processes for soft biomimetic robots. *International Journal of Precision Engineering and Manufacturing*, 10(3):171–181, 2009.

[6] J. Hiller and H. Lipson. Automatic design and manufacture of soft robots. *Robotics, IEEE Transactions on*, 28(2):457–466, 2012.

[7] J. Hiller and H. Lipson. Dynamic simulation of soft multimaterial 3d-printed objects. *Soft Robotics*, 1(1):88–101, 2014.

[8] S. Kim, C. Laschi, and B. Trimmer. Soft robotics: a bioinspired evolution in robotics. *Trends in biotechnology*, 31(5):287–294, 2013.

[9] J. Lehman, K. O. Stanley, and R. Miikkulainen. Effective diversity maintenance in deceptive domains. In *Proceedings of the 15th annual conference on Genetic and evolutionary computation*, pages 215–222. ACM, 2013.

[10] C. Majidi. Soft robotics: a perspectiveâĂŤcurrent trends and prospects for the future. *Soft Robotics*, 1(1):5–11, 2014.

[11] G. Methenitis. Evolution of soft robots by novelty search. 2014.

[12] J. Rieffel, D. Knox, S. Smith, and B. Trimmer. Growing and evolving soft robots. *Artificial life*, 20(1):143–162, 2014.

[13] J. Schrum and R. Miikkulainen. Evolving multimodal behavior with modular neural networks in ms. pac-man. In *Proceedings of the 2014 conference on Genetic and evolutionary computation*, pages 325–332. ACM, 2014.

[14] J. Secretan, N. Beato, D. B. D'Ambrosio, A. Rodriguez, A. Campbell, and K. O. Stanley. Picbreeder: evolving pictures collaboratively online. In *Proc. of the 26th SIGCHI Conf. on Human Factors in Computing Systems*, pages 1759–1768. ACM, 2008.

[15] R. F. Shepherd, F. Ilievski, W. Choi, S. A. Morin, A. A. Stokes, A. D. Mazzeo, X. Chen, M. Wang, and G. M. Whitesides. Multigait soft robot. *Proceedings of the National Academy of Sciences*, 108(51):20400–20403, 2011.

[16] K. O. Stanley. Compositional pattern producing networks: A novel abstraction of development. *Genetic programming and evolvable machines*, 8(2):131–162, 2007.

[17] K. O. Stanley and R. Miikkulainen. Evolving neural networks through augmenting topologies. *Evolutionary computation*, 10(2):99–127, 2002.

[18] A. Stilli, H. A. Wurdemann, and K. Althoefer. Shrinkable, stiffness-controllable soft manipulator based on a bio-inspired antagonistic actuation principle. In *Intelligent Robots and Systems (IROS 2014), 2014 IEEE/RSJ International Conference on*, pages 2476–2481. IEEE, 2014.

[19] Y. Sugiyama and S. Hirai. Crawling and jumping by a deformable robot. *The International journal of robotics research*, 25(5-6):603–620, 2006.

[20] B. A. Trimmer, A. E. Takesian, B. M. Sweet, C. B. Rogers, D. C. Hake, and D. J. Rogers. Caterpillar locomotion: a new model for soft-bodied climbing and burrowing robots. In *7th International Symposium on Technology and the Mine Problem*, volume 1, pages 1–10. Mine Warfare Association Monterey, CA, 2006.

[21] W. van Willigen, E. Haasdijk, and L. Kester. Evolving intelligent vehicle control using multi-objective neat. In *Computational Intelligence in Vehicles and Transportation Systems (CIVTS), 2013 IEEE Symposium on*, pages 9–15. IEEE, 2013.

Devising Effective Novelty Search Algorithms: A Comprehensive Empirical Study

Jorge Gomes
BioMachines Lab &
Instituto de Telecomunicações
& Faculdade de Ciências,
Universidade de Lisboa, BioISI
Lisbon, Portugal
jgomes@di.fc.ul.pt

Pedro Mariano
Faculdade de Ciências,
Universidade de Lisboa, BioISI
Lisbon, Portugal
plmariano@fc.ul.pt

Anders Lyhne Christensen
BioMachines Lab &
Instituto de Telecomunicações
& Instituto Universitário de
Lisboa (ISCTE-IUL)
Lisbon, Portugal
anders.christensen@iscte.pt

ABSTRACT

Novelty search is a state-of-the-art evolutionary approach that promotes behavioural novelty instead of pursuing a static objective. Along with a large number of successful applications, many different variants of novelty search have been proposed. It is still unclear, however, how some key parameters and algorithmic components influence the evolutionary dynamics and performance of novelty search. In this paper, we conduct a comprehensive empirical study focused on novelty search's algorithmic components. We study the k parameter — the number of nearest neighbours used in the computation of novelty scores; the use and function of an archive; how to combine novelty search with fitness-based evolution; and how to configure the mutation rate of the underlying evolutionary algorithm. Our study is conducted in a simulated maze navigation task. Our results show that the configuration of novelty search can have a significant impact on performance and behaviour space exploration. We conclude with a number of guidelines for the implementation and configuration of novelty search, which should help future practitioners to apply novelty search more effectively.

Categories and Subject Descriptors

I.2.8 [**Artificial Intelligence**]: Problem Solving, Control Methods, and Search

Keywords

Novelty search, evolutionary robotics, neuroevolution, premature convergence, empirical study

1. INTRODUCTION

Novelty search [15, 18] is an evolutionary technique that guides evolution towards behavioural novelty, in contrast with traditional evolutionary approaches where a static objective is pursued. In novelty search, individuals are rewarded for being behaviourally different from the other individuals in the population, and optionally, from past individuals stored in an archive. The behavioural difference is given by a behaviour similarity measure provided by the experimenter for the specific task. The main rationale behind novelty search is to avoid deception and premature convergence [36]. By having a dynamic objective based on behavioural novelty, the evolutionary process avoids convergence to a single region of the search space.

Since its introduction in 2008 by Lehman and Stanley [15], novelty search has been applied to a wide range of problems in different domains with considerable success. Novelty search has, however, been predominantly studied in the evolutionary robotics domain, including the evolution of: (i) single-robot controllers [18, 26], (ii) controllers for homogeneous [11] and heterogeneous [7] multirobot systems, (iii) robot morphologies [19], and (iv) plastic neural networks [30]. A few applications outside robotics can also be found in, for instance, machine learning [27, 28] and game content generation [23]. Previous works have shown that novelty search can find good solutions faster and more consistently than fitness-based evolution in many different applications, especially in deceptive domains. It has also been shown that novelty search can discover a diverse set of solutions, as opposed to fitness-based evolution that typically converges to a single region in the solution space [11, 19].

Alongside the large number of applications of novelty search, a wide range of algorithmic variants have been proposed. Most previous works that study novelty search's evolutionary dynamics focus on the most crucial aspect of novelty search: the definition of a behavioural similarity measure [13, 26]. The remaining algorithmic components and parameters have not received much attention, and it is still unclear how some of them affect the novelty search process. For instance, there is no consensus on whether an archive of individuals from previous generations should be used in the computation of novelty scores, or how this archive should be composed. It is also unclear how many individuals should be used to obtain the novelty score of a new individual (the number k of nearest neighbours). Additionally, a number of techniques have been proposed to combine novelty search with fitness-driven evolution, but many of these techniques have not yet been compared.

Since novelty search only influences the scoring of individuals, another open question is how the underlying evolutionary algorithm and its genetic operators should be configured

GECCO '15, July 11 - 15, 2015, Madrid, Spain

DOI: http://dx.doi.org/10.1145/2739480.2754736

to facilitate an effective exploration of the behaviour space. The relation between the exploration of the genotype space and the exploration of the behaviour space should be further investigated: how the amount of genetic diversity generated by the evolutionary algorithm affects novelty search's performance.

In this paper, we analyse the impact of the aforementioned algorithmic components. We conduct a comprehensive empirical study that encompasses the typical novelty search parameters, and most of the variants found in previous works. Our experiments are based on the maze navigation task, commonly used in novelty search works [18,26]. The performance of the different novelty search variants is compared along two dimensions: we focus not only on the capacity of reaching a solution to the task, but also on the capacity to explore the behaviour space thoroughly and uniformly.

Our work sheds light on how the key algorithmic components influence novelty search's performance. We do, however, acknowledge that some of these choices might be tied to the domain or task where novelty search is applied. We therefore do not seek to find universally optimal values for each parameter, but rather to gain insight into how changing certain parameters affects the evolutionary dynamics of novelty search. Based on our findings, we conclude with a list of guidelines that will aid experimenters in applying novelty search effectively.

2. RELATED WORK

2.1 Novelty Search

Implementing novelty search requires little change to any evolutionary algorithm aside from replacing the fitness function with a domain-dependent novelty metric. The metric measures how far an individual is from other individuals in behaviour space. The novelty of an individual is given by the mean behaviour distance to other individuals, including the individuals from the current population, and optionally, an archive of past individuals. The novelty metric thereby rewards individuals that appear in previously unexplored regions of the behaviour space, continuously guiding the evolutionary process towards behavioural novelty and diversity.

In order to apply novelty search, the experimenter has to provide an adequate behavioural similarity measure. To this end, the behaviour of each individual is typically characterised by a real-valued vector, and the behaviour distance between two individuals is then given by the distance between the corresponding vectors. The design of a behaviour characterisation has direct implications on the effectiveness of novelty search [13]. This topic has received considerable attention in previous works [4,9,13,18,26], and is beyond the scope of this paper. Originally, it was argued that the characterisation should be designed with task-specific knowledge [18]. Later works, however, have shown that it is possible to devise task-independent characterisations. Some of the possibilities include automatically extracting characterisations from the sensor-effector states of the agents [3,6,26], systematically crafting a characterisation based on a formal description of the task [7], and combining multiple different characterisations [4].

2.2 Novelty Search Variations

In this section, we review the different variants of novelty search that have been used in previous works. We consider three key aspects in the algorithm's configuration: (i) the novelty score computation; (ii) the archive storing individuals from previous generations; and (iii) the method used to combine novelty and fitness scores. The variants studied in previous works are summarised in Table 1.

Table 1: Summary of the novelty search variants found in the current literature.

Studies	Archive			k			Comb.				Underlying EA			
	N	R	∅	15	∅	...	∅	M	S	C	NEAT	FT	DNN	...
[13–15, 18, 20, 30, 35]	•			•			•				•			
[27, 28]	•			•			•							GP
[21]	•			•			•	•			•			
[1]	•			•			•		•			•		
[10]	•			•			•		•	•	•			
[17]	•			•			•			•	•			
[12]	•			•			•	*other*			•			
[23]	•					20	•			•				GA
[16]		•		•			•							GP
[19]		•		•			•	•						ERO
[9]		•		•				•				•		
[7]		•		•					•			•		
[6]		•		•					•		•			
[11]		•		•			•		•	•	•			
[8]		•		•			•			•		•		
[29]	•		•	•	•		•	•				•	•	
[24]	•		•	•	•		•	•					•	
[26]			•		•			•				•	•	
[22]			•		•			•				•		
[3, 4, 25]			•		•			•					•	
[33, 34]			•			3–10	•							GE

From the left to the right: *Archive*: N – Novelty-based archive; R – Randomly composed archive; ∅: No archive. *k number of nearest neighbours*: k=15; ∅ – the entire population is used. *Technique to combine novelty and fitness*: ∅ – pure novelty search; M – Pareto-based multi-objectivisation; S – Linear scalarisation of novelty and fitness scores; C – Combination based on minimal criteria. *Underlying evolutionary algorithm*: NEAT [31]; FT – Fixed-topology neuroevolution; DNN – Direct Encoding of Neural Networks [26]. More than one dot in each column means that multiple variants were used/compared.

2.2.1 Novelty score computation

In the original novelty search algorithm, the novelty score of each individual is computed as the mean distance to the k nearest neighbours in behaviour space:

$$\rho(x) = \frac{1}{k}\sum_{i=1}^{k} dist(x, \mu_i) \ , \tag{1}$$

where μ_i is the ith-nearest neighbour of x with respect to the behaviour distance metric $dist$.

The parameter k must be provided by the experimenter, but its effect on performance has not been studied in detail in previous works. In [15], a value of k=15 was proposed, and it was stated that the value is robust to moderate variation although no concrete results were provided. The vast majority of subsequent works used this value without further study (see Table 1). Slightly different values have been used in a few works [23,33,34], with the authors stating that the parameter was tuned for performance. A different approach was taken in [3,4,25,26], which was named *behavioural diversity* instead of novelty search. In this approach, the novelty score of an individual is given by the mean behaviour distance to *all* other individuals in the current population, but without considering individuals from past generations.

In Section 4.1, we evaluate the influence of the k parameter in novelty search's performance.

2.2.2 Archive

The purpose of the archive in novelty search is to encourage exploration of new behaviour regions, besides maintaining diversity in the population. Without the memory effect provided by the archive, it is argued [18] that evolution may cycle between behaviour regions, due to the lack of evolutionary pressure towards novel regions of the search space.

Originally, it was proposed [15] that the archive should be composed of individuals that have high novelty scores when they first appear. All individuals that receive a novelty score higher than ρ_{min} are added to the archive. This threshold is dynamic to achieve a constant flow of individuals into the archive: ρ_{min} is increased by a fixed percentage if more than n individuals were added to the archive in the previous g generations, and decreased if no individuals were added in that interval. This configuration has been used in the majority of previous works (see Table 1). A simpler version, with fewer parameters, was used in [23], where the n most novel individuals of each generation are added to the archive.

In [16], the authors argue that it might be preferable to abandon the novelty criterion for composing the archive, and instead rely on a purely stochastic criterion. Every generation, each individual has a fixed (small) probability of being added to the archive. Although no results were provided, it was argued that adding only highly novel individuals to the archive has the disadvantage of potentially penalising areas of the behaviour space that may merit further exploration.

The necessity of using an archive at all has also been disputed [24, 29]. A typical argument against the use of an archive is the increased complexity of the nearest neighbours computation. This increase can, however, be significantly reduced if space-partitioning data structures are used, such as KD-trees. As mentioned before, in the *behavioural diversity* approach [25], no archive is used. This approach is combined with fitness-based evolution, and compared with novelty search in [24, 29]. The results show that novelty search can reach higher fitness scores in fewer generations, but *behavioural diversity* still manages to achieve good solutions for the given tasks. In [33, 34], no archive is used, and the novelty score is computed based only on k nearest neighbours. Although no results are provided, the authors state that the archive was not used since it did not lead to any performance gains.

In Section 4.1, we study how the type of archive used influences novelty search. We evaluate performance when a randomly-composed archive is used, when a novelty-based archive is used, and when there is no archive.

2.2.3 Combination of novelty and fitness

It has been shown that novelty search can struggle to find good solutions when the behaviour space is vast [1, 17], as a great effort might be spent exploring regions that are irrelevant for the task objective. This problem is typically overcome by combining the exploratory pressure of novelty search with the exploitative character of fitness-based evolution. Such combination can lead to a more effective evolutionary process [21], where solutions can be reached faster and more consistently, with a relatively low impact on the diversity of behaviours explored.

A number of techniques have been proposed to accomplish this combination. The first class of techniques relies on a minimal criterion that the individuals must meet in order to be considered viable for selection. This minimal criterion can either be static and provided by the experimenter (*MCNS* – Minimal Criteria Novelty Search) [17], or dynamic and calculated based on the fitness scores of the current population (*PMCNS* – Progressive MCNS) [10]. In [23], two populations are used: one contains feasible individuals, which are scored based on novelty, and the other contains infeasible individuals, which are scored based on their proximity to the feasibility threshold.

The second class of techniques base their selection process on novelty and fitness scores simultaneously. In [24], the task objective (fitness function) is combined with the novelty objective in a Pareto-based multi-objectivisation. A simpler multi-objectivisation is proposed in [1], where the score of each individual is based on a *linear scalarisation* of its novelty and fitness scores, allowing the experimenter to control the relative weight of the novelty and fitness scores. In [12], half of the population is subject to novelty-based selection, while the other half is subject to fitness-based selection.

Comparisons between different combination techniques can be found in [10, 11]. The authors compare PMCNS with a linear scalarisation of novelty and fitness scores, using two different behaviour spaces. The reported results show that the performance of the two techniques is very similar, with PMCNS pushing exploration slightly more towards high-fitness regions. In Section 4.2, we compare the techniques most commonly found in previous works: multi-objectivisation, linear scalarisation, and PMCNS.

2.2.4 Underlying evolutionary algorithm

Novelty search only influences the scoring of the individuals. The underlying evolutionary algorithm (including genetic operators, chromosome representation, etc.) is therefore independent from the novelty search algorithm itself. When implementing novelty search, there are thus additional choices to make: which evolutionary algorithm to use, and how to configure its parameters. Most previous novelty search studies rely on neuroevolution algorithms (see Table 1). While it was argued that the NEAT algorithm [31] was especially suited for novelty search in early studies (e.g. [18]), later works have shown that simpler direct-encoding genetic algorithms can yield equally good results [26].

A relatively unexplored dimension is how the parameters of the underlying evolutionary algorithm influence novelty search. Previous studies in evolutionary robotics have shown that the genotype distance between two individuals can be uncorrelated with their behavioural distance [32]: very different genotypes can result in similar behaviours, and very different behaviours can originate from similar genotypes. An open question is therefore how the degree of genetic diversity influences the behavioural diversity and novelty generated in the novelty search process. In Section 4.3, we focus on the most ubiquitous evolutionary parameter: the mutation rate, which is closely associated with the degree of genetic diversity. We study the mutation rate in NEAT and in a direct-encoding genetic algorithm.

3. EXPERIMENTAL SETUP

3.1 Maze Navigation Task

For our experiments, we use a maze navigation task, in which a simulated robot controlled by an artificial neural network must navigate from a starting-point to an end-point within a fixed time limit. Such tasks have been commonly used in novelty search studies [12, 13, 15–18, 20–22, 24, 26, 34, 35], as they facilitate the design of experimental setups with different levels of deception. The fitness function rewards the candidate solutions according to the distance between the final position of the robot and the end-point of the maze, which can potentially deceive evolution towards dead-ends. Maze navigation can be seen as an abstraction for more complex domains, as dead-ends in the path towards the end-point represent local optima in the search space.

In our experimental setup, the robot is equipped with six rangefinders that read the distance to the nearest obstacle, and four pie-slice radar sensors that detect when the goal is within the pie-slice (see Figure 1). The readings of these sensors are the input to the neural network, and the two outputs control respectively the linear speed (mapped to $[-2, 2]$ units/step) and the turning speed of the robot (mapped to $[-\pi/4, \pi/4]$ rad/step). The simulation terminates when the end-point is reached, or when 500 time steps elapse. The task was simulated in MASON[1].

The fitness function and behaviour characterisation are the same as used in previous works (e.g. [18]). The fitness function is given by the distance between the final position of the robot (p) and the end-point of the maze (e), according to: $F = 1500 - dist(p, e)$ (a constant is added to keep fitness scores positive). The behaviour characterisation of a robot is given by its final position: $\beta = (p_x, p_y)$.

We experiment with a set of mazes that explores different levels of deceptiveness and behaviour space difficulty. A behaviour space is difficult to explore when most of the behaviour space is *irrelevant*[2] for solving the task, which is frequent in more complex tasks [1, 7, 11, 26]. This difficulty can be further increased if the *relevant* behaviour regions are harder to explore than the irrelevant ones. The mazes are depicted in Figure 2 and described below:

Hard Deceptive maze with an easy behaviour space: discovering new regions is often a step towards the goal (only ~30% of the space is irrelevant).

Zigzag Non-deceptive maze with a harder behaviour space: ~60% of the space is irrelevant.

Star A maze where the fitness gradient is roughly correct, but there are multiple small deceptive regions along the path.

Subset Very hard behaviour space: ~85% of the space is irrelevant to reach the objective. The relevant space is furthermore hard to explore due to narrow corridors.

Multi A maze with four different paths to reach the goal, all of them with some degree of deceptiveness.

Open Unbounded behaviour space. The exploration of the behaviour space can lead to regions that are very far away from the objective. 99.5% of the reachable behaviour space is irrelevant.

[1] http://cs.gmu.edu/~eclab/projects/mason/

[2] We consider as irrelevant the portions of the maze that do not need to be traversed in order to reach the goal.

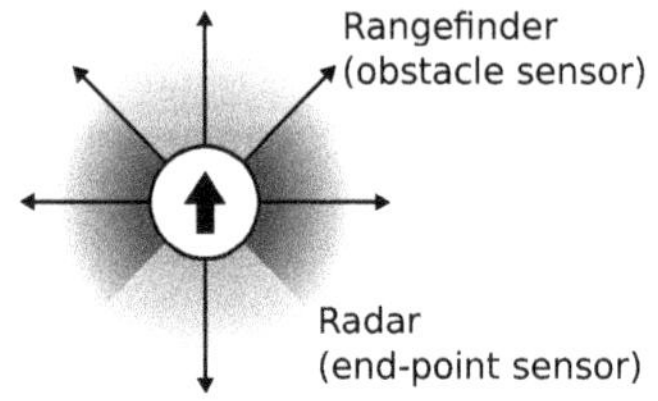

Figure 1: Maze navigating robot. The robot has a diameter of 8 units, the six rangefinder sensors have a range of 50 units, and the four radar sensors have unlimited range.

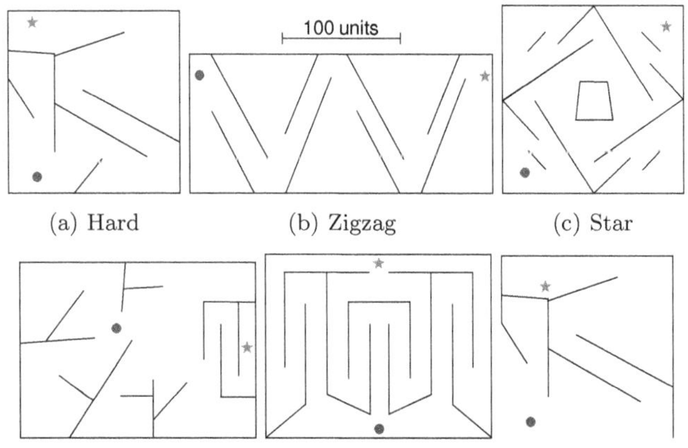

(a) Hard (b) Zigzag (c) Star

(d) Subset (e) Multi (f) Open

Figure 2: Mazes used in the experiments. The circle represents the initial position of the robot, scaled to match its size. The star marks the end-point.

3.2 Evolutionary Setup

The neural networks are evolved with NEAT [31], which evolves both the topology and the connection weights of the networks. The evolutionary algorithms are implemented on ECJ[3] and using NEAT4J[4]. The NEAT parameter values are the default values of NEAT4J implementation: mutation probability is 0.25 (except when indicated otherwise), crossover probability is 0.2, and the probability of adding new connections and nodes is 0.05 and 0.03. Population size is 200 and the target number of NEAT species is 5.

Besides studying the quality of the solutions achieved, another important aspect is the degree of behaviour space exploration. Since novelty search's objective is to explore the behaviour space, the degree of exploration uniformity is a measure of novelty search's effectiveness, regardless of the task objective. To analyse exploration uniformity, we first divide the reachable behaviour space of each maze into 100 equal-sized regions. Based on this set of regions R, we compute the exploration uniformity $U(\varphi)$ in each evolutionary run. Let φ be the set of all individuals evolved in a run. $U(\varphi)$ is given by the distance between the distribution of φ over R, $\mathbf{P}_\varphi$, and the uniform distribution $\mathbf{Q}$. The distance metric is the *Jensen-Shannon distance* (JSD), a popular metric to measure distances between probability distributions [5]. Exploration uniformity is thus given by:

$$U(\varphi) = 1 - JSD(\mathbf{P}_\varphi, \mathbf{Q}) \text{ , where:} \tag{2}$$

$$\mathbf{P}_\varphi = \left(\frac{|I_1|}{|\varphi|}, \cdots, \frac{|I_{|R|}|}{|\varphi|}\right) \text{ , } I_r = \{i \in \varphi \,|\, region(i) = r\}$$

$$\mathbf{Q} = \left(\frac{1}{|R|}, \overset{\times |R|}{\cdots\cdots}\right)$$

[3] http://cs.gmu.edu/~eclab/projects/ecj/

[4] http://neat4j.sourceforge.net/

4. RESULTS

4.1 Novelty Search Parameters

We begin by studying the parameters that directly influence the computation of the novelty score. In these experiments, we use pure novelty search — the fitness function is not used at all. To understand how the archive configuration affects the optimal value for k, and vice-versa, we test multiple combinations of k values and archive types. Six values for k are used, ranging from 1 to 199. With k=1, only the distance to the closest individual is considered, and the maximum value of 199 was chosen as the population size is 200. We consider three types of archive, based on the configurations used in previous works:

None No archive is used, only the current population.

Novel Every generation the most novel λ individuals are added to the archive.

Random Every generation, λ randomly chosen individuals are added to the archive.

The archive (when used) has no size limit, to avoid additional parameters. The search for nearest neighbours was implemented with KD-trees, which allowed the use of large archives with an almost negligible computational cost.

Figure 3 shows the success ratio of each treatment (the proportion of evolutionary runs that evolved an effective solution), and the mean behaviour exploration uniformity, as defined in Section 3.2.[5] Our results show that performance varies smoothly with the value of k, across all archive types and in both metrics. This result is consistent with previous works that argued for the robustness of this parameter [15, 18]. The results also show that the optimal value for k depends on the configuration of the archive. For all archive types, however, a value of k=15 yields either the best success ratio, or one that is not significantly different from it (Mann-Whitney test, $p > 0.25$).

When an archive is used, low to medium values of k yield the best performance. Regarding the novelty-based archive approach, the k values that yield the highest success ratio are in the interval [15, 100] ($p < 0.05$). The random-based archive approach is less sensitive to the k parameter, and the k values that yield the highest performance are in the interval [5, 100] ($p < 0.05$). When no archive is used, however, very low values of k are preferred, with the optimal values being in the interval [5, 15] ($p < 0.05$). When no archive is used, performance drops significantly as k increases.

Regarding archive types, our results show that a random-based archive is generally preferable: it yields the highest success ratios, it causes a more uniform exploration of the behaviour space, and it reduces the sensitivity to the parameter k. For all values of k, the random-based archive approach yields a significantly higher behaviour exploration uniformity than the novelty-based archive approach ($p <$ 0.001). This result is consistent with [16], but in contrast to most previous works in which a novelty-based archive was used without justification (see Table 1). The use of no archive at all, however, should not be disregarded. When a low value of k is used (5), the success ratio achieved by this treatment is not significantly different to the ratio achieved by the best treatment with a novelty-based archive (k=50, p=0.91), or a random-based archive (k=15, p=0.09). This result is in line with [33, 34], where the authors use low values of k (3, 5, and 10) and state that the introduction of an archive did not bring performance improvements.

The use of the entire population and no archive to compute novelty scores, as done in the *behavioural diversity* approach [25], does not seem advantageous. This treatment (k=199 and no archive) actually yielded a significantly lower performance than all other evolutionary treatments. While the use of no archive does not seem deterrent, the use of the entire population to compute the novelty score consistently yielded significantly inferior results. It should be noted, however, that in previous works *behavioural diversity* was always used in combination with fitness-based evolution.

Finally, we analyse the influence of the archive growth rate λ. Figure 4 shows how performance varies with different growth rates, for different combinations of archive types and values of k. In all considered treatments (combinations of archive type and k), the growth rate has no significant impact on the success ratio (Kruskal-Wallis test, $p > 0.28$). The impact on exploration uniformity is also negligible. These results support previous works [18] in which it is argued that limiting the archive size has no significant performance impact when reasonable limits are used.

[5]Due to space restrictions, we do not show the results obtained in each maze separately. Each data point was obtained with 30 runs for each of the six mazes, yielding a total of 180 runs for each treatment. As these distributions are not normal, error bars are not shown in any of the plots.

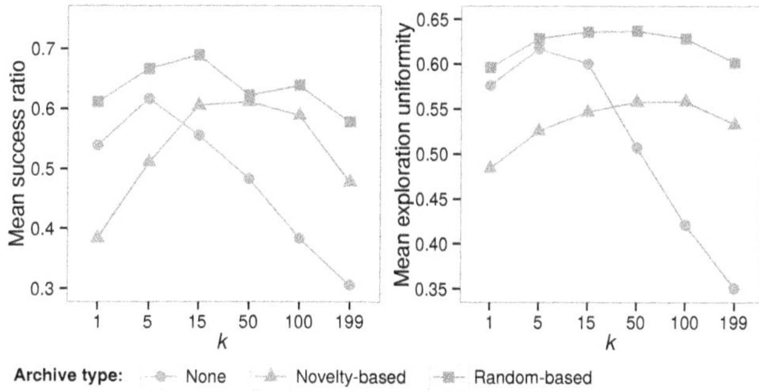

Figure 3: Performance of novelty search with multiple archive types, different values of k, and λ=6. Each point was obtained with 180 evolutionary runs (6 mazes $\times$ 30 runs).

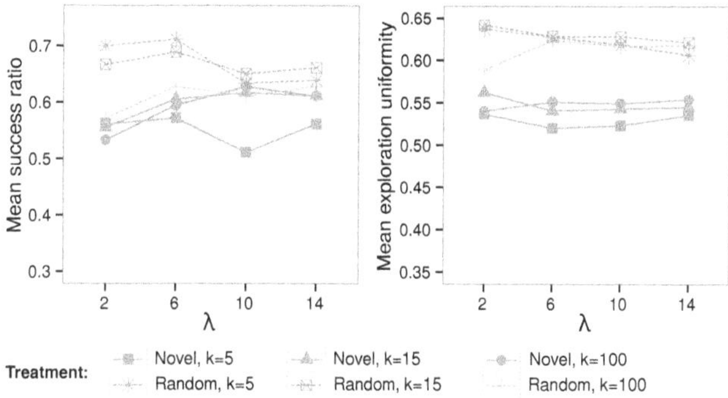

Figure 4: Performance impact of the archive growth rate λ on different novelty search treatments. Each point was obtained with 180 evolutionary runs (6 mazes $\times$ 30 runs).

4.2 Combination of Novelty and Fitness

A significant point of divergence in the configuration of novelty-based search is if and how novelty scores should be combined with fitness scores. A number of techniques have been proposed in previous works (see Section 2.2.3), but comparisons between them are scarce. In our study, we compare the techniques commonly used in previous works:

Fit Only the fitness scores are used.

LS-50 The score of an individual is given by the weighted sum of the normalised novelty and fitness scores [1]. Fitness and novelty have the same weight (50%).

LS-75 As the above, but novelty contributes to 75% of the score and fitness 25%.

NS Only the novelty scores are used.

NSGA Multiobjectivisation of novelty and fitness scores [24], using the NSGA-II algorithm [2]. As in previous works [21], the speciation mechanism of NEAT was disabled for compatibility with NSGA-II.

PMCNS Progressive minimal criteria novelty search [10]. The minimal criterion is given by the value of the 50th percentile of the fitness scores found in the current generation. Individuals above the criterion receive their normal novelty score, while individuals below receive a score of zero.

The results are shown in Figure 5. The computation of novelty scores is done with the parameters found in the previous section: k=15, and a randomly-composed archive with λ=6. Besides the metrics used in the previous section, we also measured the proportion of high-fitness individuals evolved: considering all individuals evolved in a given run, which percentage of them are solutions for the task.

The results show that *LS-50* and *NSGA* are the approaches with the highest success ratios (proportion of runs that evolved a solution for the task). No significant difference was found between these two ($p = 0.75$), and they are significantly superior to all other approaches ($p < 0.01$). *NSGA* yielded a significantly higher exploration uniformity than *LS-50* ($p < 0.001$). It is noteworthy that *NSGA*, when compared to pure novelty search, was considerably more biased towards high-fitness individuals, and reached solutions faster and more consistently. Nevertheless, the exploration uniformity in *NSGA* is just slightly inferior to that of pure novelty search, meaning that *NSGA* appears to balance exploration and exploitation exceptionally well. Linear scalarisation is considerably simpler to implement, and it is compatible with virtually any underlying evolutionary algorithm, but it should be used with caution in complex tasks or when the behaviour space is vast.

Previous works have shown that in linear scalarisation, a medium-high novelty weight (50–80%) yields the best results [1,6,7,10,11], hence the choice of 50% and 75% for this study. Our results confirm the importance of choosing an adequate novelty weight. In the maze navigation tasks used in study, a higher novelty weight (*LS-75*) offered little benefit over pure novelty search, and performed significantly worse than *LS-50* ($p < 0.01$). It should be noted, however, that the optimal novelty-fitness weight could be task-dependent.

PMCNS was generally ineffective, and did not offer significant advantages over pure novelty search, except in the amount of high-fitness individuals evolved ($p < 0.01$). This lack of effectiveness contrasts with previous works where PMCNS was successfully used [8, 10, 11]. Our results suggest that PMCNS's low performance is due to the high degree of deception in most mazes. PMCNS performed better than pure novelty search in less deceptive mazes (*star* and *zigzag*), but worse in highly deceptive ones (*hard* and *multi*).

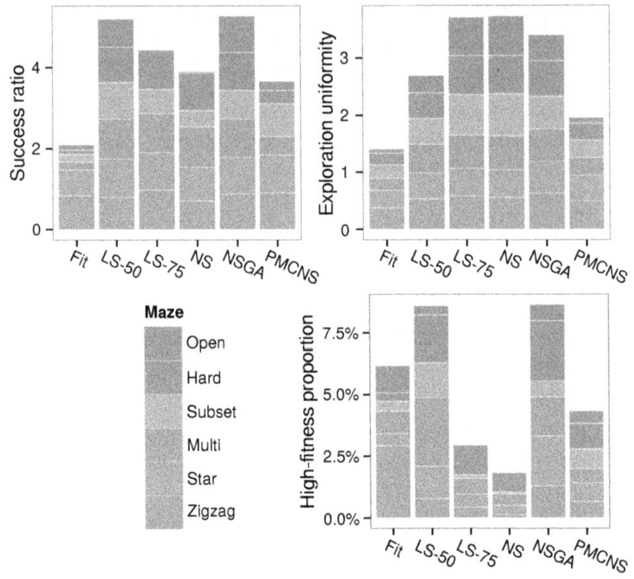

Figure 5: Comparison of multiple techniques for combining novelty search with fitness-based evolution. The high-fitness proportion is the proportion of evolved individuals that were able to solve the task.

4.3 Underlying Evolutionary Algorithm

While the underlying evolutionary algorithm typically has a large number of parameters, we only focus on the mutation rate in this study due to space restrictions. Mutation is a genetic operator present in all evolutionary algorithms, and the mutation rate directly influences the amount of genetic diversity in the population.

We study the mutation rate in two different neuroevolution algorithms, to cover most of the setups used in previous works (see Table 1): (i) the NEAT algorithm used in the previous sections, and (ii) a canonical genetic algorithm that evolves fixed-topology neural networks. For all mazes, the fixed-topology is a recurrent Elman network with 10 hidden neurons, resulting in a chromosome comprised of 232 weights. This topology was used in previous works [26] and was found to yield a good performance in preliminary experiments. The genetic algorithm uses tournament selection, an elite of size 5, per-gene Gaussian mutation, no crossover, and the population size is set to 200 (the same as in NEAT). The configuration of the NEAT algorithm is described in Section 3.2.

Novelty search is implemented over these two algorithms using the parameters found in Section 4.1: k=15 and a randomly-composed archive with λ=6. Fitness-based evolution is presented as a baseline in both cases. The results are depicted in Figure 6.

Overall, our results show that novelty search does not benefit from higher mutation rates, when compared to a traditional fitness-based algorithm. In the NEAT algorithm, the best mutation rates (with respect to the success ratio) were in the interval $[0.25, 0.8]$ for fitness-based evolution and in the interval $[0.1, 0.6]$ for novelty search ($p < 0.05$). In the genetic algorithm, the mutation rates that yielded the best results were in the interval $[0.025, 0.1]$ ($p < 0.05$) for both novelty search and fitness-based evolution.

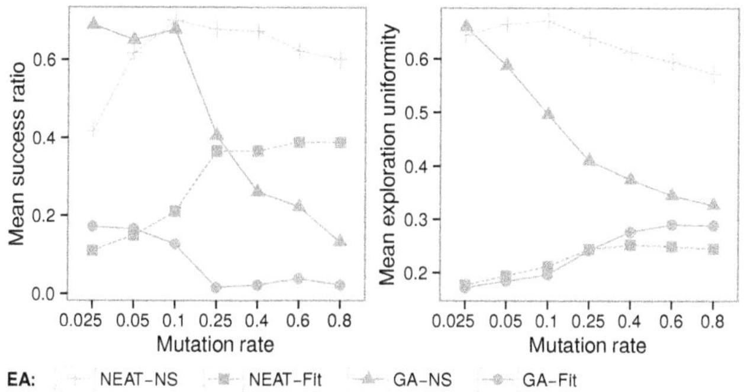

Figure 6: Success ratio and mean exploration uniformity of different techniques using different mutation rates. *GA-Fit*: Fitness-based evolution with a canonical genetic algorithm (no crossover); *GA-NS*: Pure novelty search with the same genetic algorithm; *NEAT-Fit*: Fitness-based evolution with NEAT; *NEAT-NS*: Novelty search with NEAT.

Regarding the behaviour exploration uniformity, the results show that novelty search does not benefit from higher mutation rates. In both NEAT and the genetic algorithm, the exploration uniformity of novelty search has a strong negative correlation with the mutation rate (Pearson's correlation coefficient, r=−0.96 and r=−0.88 respectively).

These results highlight the substantial difference between genetic and behavioural diversity, and suggest that novelty search actually works better with lower mutation rates. Although additional experiments would be needed to fully understand this effect, our hypothesis is that low mutation rates do not lead to premature convergence due to the dynamic nature of the novelty objective, while they contribute to fine tuning the behaviours in the current population.

It is also noteworthy that the best *NEAT-NS* treatment (mutation rate = 0.1) was not significantly different from the best *GA-NS* treatment (mutation rate = 0.025), both in terms of the success ratio and exploration uniformity ($p < 0.01$). This confirms results from previous works [26] that show that NEAT is not a requirement for novelty search. The simpler genetic algorithm, however, has to be fine-tuned to use an adequate neural network topology.

5. CONCLUSION

We conducted a comprehensive empirical study on the parameters and configuration choices of novelty search, including: (i) the number k of nearest neighbours used in computation of novelty scores; (ii) the use of the archive, and how it should function; (iii) how novelty search can be combined with fitness-based evolution; and (iv) how the mutation rate of the underlying evolutionary algorithm affects the novelty search process. Our study is based on the simulated maze navigation task. We used a set of mazes that confront novelty search with different levels of deception and behaviour space difficulty. We analysed our results in two dimensions: (i) whether an evolutionary run is able to produce an effective solution or not; and (ii) whether novelty search is able to explore the behaviour space thoroughly and uniformly, regardless of the objective.

In summary, our findings can be distilled into the following guidelines:

- The parameter k is robust to moderate variation, but the optimal value depends on the type of archive used.
- Low to medium values of k are generally preferable. A value of k=15 yielded relatively good performance across all the tested archive types.
- A randomly composed archive is preferable over a novelty-based one, yielding better results across all the considered metrics.
- Novelty search is robust to moderate variations of the archive growth rate.
- The use of no archive at all should not be discarded: when used together with low values of k, it yielded satisfactory results.
- The highest performing methods for combining novelty and fitness were the multi-objectivisation of novelty and fitness scores, and the linear scalarisation with an equal weight for novelty and fitness. There were no major differences between these two.
- High mutation rates did not cause better exploration of the behaviour space. Novelty search actually benefited from lower mutation rates, when compared to fitness-based evolution.

Maze navigation tasks have been used in a large number of previous novelty search works, and it has been shown that most conclusions drawn in this domain generally transfer to more complex and realistic domains [11, 18, 26]. Nevertheless, in future work, we will extend our study and assess how the reported results generalise to other domains. In this work, we vary the behaviour space by varying the task environment. Another possibility would be to vary the behaviour characterisation. We intend to assess if certain features of the characterisation, such as its length, should influence the choice of novelty search parameters.

Acknowledgements This research is supported by Fundação para a Ciência e Tecnologia (FCT), with grant SFRH/BD/89095/2012 and projects UID/EEA/50008/2013, UID/Multi/04046/2013, and EXPL/EEI-AUT/0329/2013.

6. REFERENCES

[1] G. Cuccu and F. J. Gomez. When novelty is not enough. In *European Conference on the Applications of Evolutionary Computation (EvoApplications)*, volume 6624 of *LNCS*, pages 234–243. Springer, 2011.

[2] K. Deb, A. Pratap, S. Agarwal, and T. Meyarivan. A fast and elitist multiobjective genetic algorithm: NSGA-II. *IEEE Transactions on Evolutionary Computation*, 6(2):182–197, 2002.

[3] S. Doncieux and J.-B. Mouret. Behavioral diversity measures for evolutionary robotics. In *IEEE Congress on Evolutionary Computation (CEC)*, pages 1–8. IEEE Press, 2010.

[4] S. Doncieux and J.-B. Mouret. Behavioral diversity with multiple behavioral distances. In *IEEE Congress on Evolutionary Computation (CEC)*, pages 1427–1434. IEEE Press, 2013.

[5] D. M. Endres and J. E. Schindelin. A new metric for probability distributions. *IEEE Transactions on Information Theory*, 49(7):1858–1860, 2003.

[6] J. Gomes and A. L. Christensen. Generic behaviour similarity measures for evolutionary swarm robotics.

In *Genetic and Evolutionary Computation Conference (GECCO)*, pages 199–206. ACM Press, 2013.

[7] J. Gomes, P. Mariano, and A. L. Christensen. Avoiding convergence in cooperative coevolution with novelty search. In *International Conference on Autonomous Agents & Multiagent Systems (AAMAS)*, pages 1149–1156. IFAAMAS, 2014.

[8] J. Gomes, P. Mariano, and A. L. Christensen. Novelty search in competitive coevolution. In *Parallel Problem Solving from Nature (PPSN)*, volume 8672 of *LNCS*, pages 233–242. Springer, 2014.

[9] J. Gomes, P. Mariano, and A. L. Christensen. Systematic derivation of behaviour characterisations in evolutionary robotics. In *International Conference on the Synthesis and Simulation of Living Systems (ALIFE)*, pages 212–219. MIT Press, 2014.

[10] J. Gomes, P. Urbano, and A. L. Christensen. Progressive minimal criteria novelty search. In *Ibero-American Conference on Artificial Intelligence (IBERAMIA)*, volume 7637 of *LNAI*, pages 281–290. Springer, 2012.

[11] J. Gomes, P. Urbano, and A. L. Christensen. Evolution of swarm robotics systems with novelty search. *Swarm Intelligence*, 7(2–3):115–144, 2013.

[12] B. Inden, Y. Jin, R. Haschke, H. Ritter, and B. Sendhoff. An examination of different fitness and novelty based selection methods for the evolution of neural networks. *Soft Computing*, 17(5):753–767, 2013.

[13] S. Kistemaker and S. Whiteson. Critical factors in the performance of novelty search. In *Genetic and Evolutionary Computation Conference (GECCO)*, pages 965–972. ACM Press, 2011.

[14] P. Krcah. Solving deceptive tasks in robot body-brain co-evolution by searching for behavioral novelty. In *Advances in Robotics and Virtual Reality*, volume 26 of *Intelligent Systems Reference Library*, pages 167–186. Springer, 2012.

[15] J. Lehman and K. O. Stanley. Exploiting open-endedness to solve problems through the search for novelty. In *International Conference on Artificial Life (ALIFE XI)*, pages 329–336. MIT Press, 2008.

[16] J. Lehman and K. O. Stanley. Efficiently evolving programs through the search for novelty. In *Genetic and Evolutionary Computation Conference (GECCO)*, pages 837–844. ACM Press, 2010.

[17] J. Lehman and K. O. Stanley. Revising the evolutionary computation abstraction: minimal criteria novelty search. In *Genetic and Evolutionary Computation Conference (GECCO)*, pages 103–110. ACM Press, 2010.

[18] J. Lehman and K. O. Stanley. Abandoning objectives: Evolution through the search for novelty alone. *Evolutionary Computation*, 19(2):189–223, 2011.

[19] J. Lehman and K. O. Stanley. Evolving a diversity of virtual creatures through novelty search and local competition. In *Genetic and Evolutionary Computation Conference (GECCO)*, pages 211–218. ACM Press, 2011.

[20] J. Lehman and K. O. Stanley. Improving evolvability through novelty search and self-adaptation. In *IEEE Congress on Evolutionary Computation (CEC)*, pages 2693–2700. IEEE Press, 2011.

[21] J. Lehman, K. O. Stanley, and R. Miikkulainen. Effective diversity maintenance in deceptive domains. In *Genetic and Evolutionary Computation Conference (GECCO)*, pages 215–222. ACM Press, 2013.

[22] J. Li, J. Storie, and J. Clune. Encouraging creative thinking in robots improves their ability to solve challenging problems. In *Genetic and Evolutionary Computation Conference (GECCO)*, pages 193–200. ACM Press, 2014.

[23] A. Liapis, G. N. Yannakakis, and J. Togelius. Constrained novelty search: A study on game content generation. *Evolutionary Computation*, 2014. *In press.*

[24] J.-B. Mouret. Novelty-based multiobjectivization. In *New Horizons in Evolutionary Robotics*, volume 341 of *Studies in Computation Intelligence*, pages 139–154. Springer, 2011.

[25] J.-B. Mouret and S. Doncieux. Overcoming the bootstrap problem in evolutionary robotics using behavioral diversity. In *IEEE Congress on Evolutionary Computation (CEC)*, pages 1161–1168. IEEE Press, 2009.

[26] J.-B. Mouret and S. Doncieux. Encouraging behavioral diversity in evolutionary robotics: An empirical study. *Evolutionary Computation*, 20(1):91–133, 2012.

[27] E. Naredo and L. Trujillo. Searching for novel clustering programs. In *Genetic and Evolutionary Computation Conference (GECCO)*, pages 1093–1100. ACM Press, 2013.

[28] E. Naredo, L. Trujillo, and Y. Martínez. Searching for novel classifiers. In *Genetic Programming (EuroGP)*, volume 7831 of *LNCS*, pages 145–156. Springer, 2013.

[29] C. Ollion and S. Doncieux. Why and how to measure exploration in behavioral space. In *Genetic and Evolutionary Computation Conference (GECCO)*, pages 267–274. ACM Press, 2011.

[30] S. Risi, C. E. Hughes, and K. O. Stanley. Evolving plastic neural networks with novelty search. *Adaptive Behavior*, 18(6):470–491, 2010.

[31] K. Stanley and R. Miikkulainen. Evolving neural networks through augmenting topologies. *Evolutionary Computation*, 10(2):99–127, 2002.

[32] L. Trujillo, G. Olague, E. Lutton, F. F. De Vega, L. Dozal, and E. Clemente. Speciation in behavioral space for evolutionary robotics. *Journal of Intelligent & Robotic Systems*, 64(3-4):323–351, 2011.

[33] P. Urbano and L. Georgiou. Improving grammatical evolution in Santa Fé trail using novelty search. In *European Conference on Artificial Life (ECAL)*, pages 917–924. MIT Press, 2013.

[34] P. Urbano, E. Naredo, and L. Trujillo. Generalization in maze navigation using grammatical evolution and novelty search. In *Theory and Practice of Natural Computing*, volume 8890 of *LNCS*, pages 35–46. Springer, 2014.

[35] R. Velez and J. Clune. Novelty search creates robots with general skills for exploration. In *Genetic and Evolutionary Computation Conference (GECCO)*, pages 737–744. ACM Press, 2014.

[36] L. D. Whitley. Fundamental principles of deception in genetic search. In *Foundations of Genetic Algorithms*, pages 221–241. Morgan Kaufmann, 1991.

Enhancing Divergent Search through Extinction Events

Joel Lehman
University of Texas at Austin
joel@cs.utexas.edu

Risto Miikkulainen
University of Texas at Austin
risto@cs.utexas.edu

ABSTRACT

A challenge in evolutionary computation is to create representations as evolvable as those in natural evolution. This paper hypothesizes that extinction events, i.e. mass extinctions, can significantly increase evolvability, but only when combined with a *divergent* search algorithm, i.e. a search driven towards diversity (instead of optimality). Extinctions amplify diversity-generation by creating unpredictable evolutionary bottlenecks. Persisting through multiple such bottlenecks is more likely for lineages that diversify across many niches, resulting in indirect selection pressure for the capacity to evolve. This hypothesis is tested through experiments in two evolutionary robotics domains. The results show that combining extinction events with divergent search increases evolvability, while combining them with convergent search offers no similar benefit. The conclusion is that extinction events may provide a simple and effective mechanism to enhance performance of divergent search algorithms.

Categories and Subject Descriptors

I.2.6 [**Artificial Intelligence**]: Learning—*connectionism and neural nets, concept learning*

Keywords

Extinction events; evolvability; divergent search

1. INTRODUCTION

Biological organisms are evolvable, i.e. they have significant capacity to evolve further [6, 30]. In contrast, evolvability remains an ambitious challenge in evolutionary computation (EC) [4, 18, 30], hinting that some important mechanisms of natural evolution may be missing. Confounding the issue, some such mechanisms may be synergistic and provide little benefit in isolation. In such cases, the usual methodology of introducing and testing mechanisms individually may fail to identify promising modifications to evolutionary algorithms (EAs).

GECCO '15, July 11 - 15, 2015, Madrid, Spain
© 2015 ACM. ISBN 978-1-4503-3472-3/15/07...$15.00
DOI: http://dx.doi.org/10.1145/2739480.2754668

This paper hypothesizes that *extinction events*, i.e. mass extinctions, are such a mechanism. Extinctions can increase evolvability, but only when coupled with a divergent reward scheme, which is another non-canonical EA mechanism. That is, most EAs aim to optimize towards an underlying fixed objective, which leads to *convergence* to a single phenotype. In contrast, natural evolution inherently *diverges*, accumulating a growing diversity of novel solutions to the problems of surviving and reproducing [27]. Extinction events may enhance the effectiveness only of EAs that similarly diverge.

Although well-studied in evolutionary biology, extinction events are rarely included in EAs [8, 14]. One reason is that in the short term they are often idiosyncratic and destructive, selecting individuals arbitrarily or for reasons uncharacteristic of its evolutionary history as a whole. In this view, extinction events may act merely as upheavals or impediments to the evolutionary process. Thus beyond increased biological accuracy, there is little reason to model them.

However, although extinction events exterminate stochastically a large proportion of ways of life, they may still produce beneficial evolutionary regularities. In particular, extinction events can create unpredictable evolutionary bottlenecks by filtering out most pre-existing phenotypic niches. Lineages that are able to diversify more quickly than others, i.e. those that are more evolvable, may have a greater chance of persisting across multiple such bottlenecks. By radiating through multiple niches, such evolvable lineages in effect have multiple tickets in the lottery of extinction. Thus extinction events indirectly select for evolvability.

Interestingly, diversity-driven EAs also select for evolvability, but through a different mechanism. For instance, if selection rewards novelty, those lineages that *consistently* produce diversity over time will be selected. In this way, adaptations enabling evolvability hitchhike through the immediate advantage they provide in selection.

Because extinction events and divergent EAs encourage evolvability in a different manner, there may be an additive benefit when they are combined. In contrast, convergent search, such as a traditional objective-seeking EA, does not necessarily encourage evolvability [18]. Thus the hypothesis of this paper is that combining extinction events with divergent EAs can increase evolvability, whereas no such benefit may arise when extinctions are combined with a traditional convergent EA.

To test this hypothesis, representative divergent and convergent search methods are augmented with extinction events and compared to unaugmented ones in two evolutionary robotics (ER) domains. The results demonstrate that when divergent EAs are combined with extinction events, the result is more evolvable populations and more effective solutions. In contrast, the tested convergent EA shows no similar benefit. In this way, extinction events may provide a simple and powerful mechanism to enhance divergent EAs.

2. BACKGROUND

This section first reviews the neuroevolution technique and the measure of evolvability applied in the experiments. Extinction in EC and divergent search are then described.

2.1 NeuroEvolution of Augmenting Topologies (NEAT)

In experiments in this paper, behaviors are evolved that are controlled by artificial neural networks (ANNs). Thus a neuroevolution (NE; [32]) method is needed to implement these experiments. The NEAT method is appropriate because it is widely applied [1, 2, 28, 29] and well understood.

The NEAT method was originally developed to evolve ANNs to solve difficult control and sequential decision tasks [28, 29]. Evolved ANNs control agents that select actions based on their sensory inputs. Like the SAGA method [12] introduced before it, NEAT begins evolution with a population of small, simple networks and *complexifies* them. The population expands into diverse with diverse ANN topologies over generations, leading to increasingly sophisticated behavior. A similar process of gradually adding new genes is seen in natural evolution [21]. This section briefly reviews the NEAT method; for comprehensive introductions see Stanley and Miikkulainen [28, 29].

To keep track of which gene is which while new genes are added, a historical marking is assigned uniquely to each new structural component. During crossover, genes with the same historical markings are aligned, producing meaningful offspring efficiently. Speciation in NEAT protects new structural innovations by reducing competition among differing structures and network complexities, thereby giving newer, more complex structures room to adjust. Networks are assigned to species based on the extent to which they share historical markings. Complexification, which resembles how genes are added over the course of natural evolution [21], is thus supported by both historical markings and speciation, allowing NEAT to establish high-level features early in evolution and then later to elaborate on them.

Note that speciation and crossover in NEAT are disabled in this paper's experiments to simplify the EA. This simplification facilitates integration of NEAT with the behavioral grid search algorithm described later, which allows uniform comparison between all implemented search algorithms. Additionally, NEAT is augmented in all experiments with self-adaptive mutation rates, as supported by Lehman and Stanley [18]. Such self-adaptation was found to enhance performance in initial experiments.

To implement self-adaption, each genome is augmented with a list of three pairs of mutation settings, and each connection is augmented with an integer parameter that indexes within the list. Typically, when an individual is mutated, every one of its connections are altered by adding to its weight a random number chosen from the same uniform distribution. In contrast, with self-adaptation, each connection can be *exempted* from mutation with probability determined by a floating point parameter in its associated mutation settings. If it is not exempted from mutation, the uniform distribution from which the weight is perturbed is scaled by a separate floating point parameter in its associated mutation settings. In this way, an individual can encode an architecture of mutation that potentially complements its evolved representation, thus making it more evolvable.

2.2 Measuring Evolvability

Natural evolution has produced flexible, highly evolvable representations that facilitate its prolific discovery of diverse organisms. An important question that could inform EC is: What properties of natural evolution led to such evolvability? Investigating this question is aided by quantitative measures of evolvability. Such measures enable empirical studies of how different evolutionary features affect evolvability.

While there is no overall consensus on evolvability's definition or its measurement [26], one common conception is to consider evolvability as an organism's phenotypic variability [3, 7, 13, 30]; that is, the capacity of an organism's lineage to generate novel phenotypic traits captures some significant part of what enables some lineages to adapt more quickly than others, although there exist alternative definitions that focus on different or overlapping aspects of evolvability [26]. This conception (of evolvability as phenotypic variability) is adopted in this paper, as in previous related studies [18, 19].

The evolvability measure used in this paper was originally proposed by Lehman and Stanley [18]. At regular intervals during evolution, a sample of individuals is taken from the population and their evolvability is estimated in the following way: First, the mutational neighborhood of that individual is approximated through creating $1,000$ clones and mutating each clone independently once. Second, each clone is evaluated in the experimental domain and its behavior is quantified. Third, a regular grid is superimposed over the entire space of such quantified behaviors, and each of the mutated clones is mapped into the grid square that contains its behavior. The original individual's evolvability is then the number of populated grid squares, i.e. a quantification of the propensity of the genotype's offspring to realize diverse behaviors.

This measure is applied in this paper's experiments to test whether evolvability is enhanced by algorithmic extinction, which is described in the next section.

2.3 Extinction in Evolutionary Computation

Because on their surface extinction events appear simply destructive, they are not often integrated into EAs. When extinction-like mechanisms are included in EAs, they often serve to *focus* search [9, 11, 14, 31] and remove seemingly unpromising classes of solutions [8, 28]. As a result, extinctions are often initiated when the search for higher performance stagnates [11, 28]. Overall, typical incarnations of algorithmic extinctions implicitly or explicitly protect the overall best-performing individual [8, 11, 14, 20].

In contrast, the implementation of extinction events in this paper does not inherently favor any particular behavior in the population over any other and is not triggered by stagnating performance. Instead, extinctions wipe out particular classes of behaviors irrespective of performance. The idea is to shift the focus from particular high-performing individuals to the overall evolvability of the population as a whole. Giving credence to this idea, Palmer and Feldman [25] demonstrated in an abstract model that indiscriminate extinctions acting upon spatially-divided populations can lead to increasing evolvability, which is similar to the approach in this paper.

A more typical example of extinction-like strategies in EC is *burst mutation* [9, 11]. Burst mutation (which is similar to delta-coding [31]), is initiated when performance stagnates for a fixed number of generations, and extinguishes all but the highest performing solution. Evolution then focuses on the neighborhood in the search space centered on this solution. Weight mutations are applied from the Cauchy distribution, which result in mainly small tweaks, with occasional large changes. The overall idea is that sometimes greater *precision* is needed to solve some tasks, which is facilitated by corresponding greater *focus* on promising individuals.

Another relevant approach is random restarts [10], which can be seen as total extinction. The entire population is re-initialized if the task is not solved within a fixed number of evaluations. The hope is that a random restart may allow evolution to uncover a different (and more promising) attractor. The approach in this paper is somewhat similar to random restarts in that nearly all individuals are extinguished; however, a critical difference is that a small diverse set of individuals persists extinction.

Importantly, the effect of adding extinctions to an EA may depend on characteristics of the underlying EA. In particular, while most EAs converge as they seek to optimize towards a fixed objective, other EAs are instead driven to explore many divergent possibilities simultaneously. The next section reviews such divergent EAs.

2.4 Divergent Evolutionary Algorithms

A signature characteristic of natural evolution is its tendency to accumulate diversity over time [27], expanding through niches and discovering a wide range of solutions to the problems of life. In this way, natural evolution is *divergent*, i.e. it is inherently driven to explore many divergent possibilities in parallel. In contrast, optimization algorithms are most often *convergent*, i.e. they are driven to seek the singular highest value of a provided objective function. Similarly, most EAs apply an abstraction of natural evolution as an optimizer, i.e. the concept of biological fitness is often abstracted as a static fitness function that the EA optimizes. Thus, in a striking contrast to their natural inspiration, EAs themselves are often convergent [15, 16].

However, while dominant in EC, abstracting evolution as an optimizer is only one out of many possible foundations for creating an EA. By focusing on different aspects of natural evolution, other abstractions may produce EAs with different characteristics, e.g. those that agree with natural evolution's tendency towards divergence. For example, EAs that abstract nature as an accumulator of novelty [16, 19, 24] diverge as they continually uncover novel forms. Because these kinds of algorithms are not inherently driven towards optimization, they are less susceptible to deception (often outperforming objective-based search on such problems [16]), and are more likely to increase evolvability [18]. Interestingly, even when objective-based search is as efficient, representations provided by divergent search are often more evolvable [15].

3. APPROACH

Just as there are many ways to perform convergent search, there are also many ways to create an EA with a drive towards diversity [5, 16, 19, 24]. Two representative methods, novelty search and behavioral grid search, will be used in this paper. They are each reviewed in this section, followed by a description of how extinction events are implemented.

3.1 Novelty Search

Novelty search is inspired by natural evolution's drive towards novelty, and rewards novel behavior directly *instead* of progress towards a fixed objective [16]. Tracking novelty requires little change to any evolutionary algorithm aside from replacing the objective-based fitness function with a *novelty metric*. Such a metric measures how different an individual is from other individuals, thereby creating a constant pressure to produce something new. The key idea is that instead of rewarding performance on an objective, novelty search rewards diverging from prior behaviors. Therefore, novelty in behavior needs to be *measured*.

The novelty metric characterizes how far away the new individual is from the rest of the population and its predecessors in *behavior space*, i.e. the space of unique behaviors. A good metric should thus compute the *sparseness* at any point in the behavior space. Areas with denser clusters of visited points are less novel and therefore rewarded less.

A simple measure of sparseness at a point is the average distance to the k-nearest neighbors of that point. Intuitively, if the average distance to a given point's nearest neighbors is large then it is in a sparse area; if the average distance is small, it is in a dense region. The sparseness ρ at point x is given by

$$\rho(x) = \frac{1}{k}\sum_{i=0}^{k} \mathrm{dist}(x, \mu_i), \qquad (1)$$

where μ_i is the ith-nearest neighbor of x with respect to the distance metric dist, which is a domain-dependent measure of behavioral difference between two individuals in the search space. Candidates from more sparse regions of the behavior space thus receive higher novelty scores.

With fixed probability an individual is entered into the permanent archive that characterizes the distribution of prior solutions in behavior space. The current generation plus the archive constitute a comprehensive sample of where the search has been and where it currently is; that way, by attempting to maximize the novelty metric, the gradient of search is simply towards what is *new*, with no other explicit objective. However, even without an explicit objective, novelty search is still driven by meaningful information; that is, behaving in a novel way often requires learning the structure of the domain.

Once objective-based fitness is replaced with novelty, the underlying EA operates as usual, selecting the most novel individuals to reproduce. Over generations, the population spreads out across the space of possible behaviors.

Another divergent search algorithm used in this paper is behavioral grid search, described next.

3.2 Behavioral Grid Search

Behavioral grid search represents grid-based divergent search algorithms such as those described in Lehman and Stanley [19] and Cully et al. [5], and is tested in the experiments to demonstrate that the results are not specific to one particular divergent search algorithm.

Similar to novelty search, behavioral grid search is inspired by natural evolution's tendency to explore many niches in parallel. One simple way to facilitate diversity is to divide search resources explicitly across a variety of behavioral niches. Instead of encouraging behavioral diversity directly as in novelty search, a regular grid can be superimposed over the space of behaviors, wherein each grid square acts as a discrete niche. That is, each new individual is mapped to the grid square that contains the behavior it demonstrates. If each grid square only supports a limited capacity of organisms then the search as a whole will not converge, but will be driven to expand through the space of niches [19]. Note that this algorithm is in effect a steady-state version of the limited capacity niche model explored by Lehman and Stanley [19]; it is also similar to the MAP-ELITES algorithm of Cully et al. [5, 23].

While each such niche could impose competitive selection pressure among organisms with similar behavior (as in MAP-ELITES [5, 23] or novelty search with local competition [17]), for simplicity both divergent search algorithms in this paper are driven *only* by diversity. In particular, behavioral grid search applies steady-state replacement that is biased towards less-populated niches. Selection chooses an individual to reproduce asexually by picking one at random from a populated niche that is also chosen at random. To replace this new offspring, a randomly-chosen individual is removed from the most populous niche. Thus individuals in less-populated niches are more likely to be chosen to reproduce and will not be replaced. The overall effect is that the EA is driven to colonize unoccupied niches through evolving diverse behaviors, resulting in divergent search.

3.3 Extinction Events

The approach in this paper is to augment EAs with extinction events. The idea is that mass extinctions may indirectly select for the ability to diversify quickly. That is, if extinctions vacate a large proportion of occupied niches stochastically, then lineages that radiate through many niches are more likely to survive repeated such extinctions.

Thus, while there are many ways to implement extinction events [8, 14, 20], the one in this paper is motivated by extinction events as probabilistic filters biased towards evolvable lineages. In particular, the approach is at regular intervals to extinct a large proportion of evolved behaviors, without any consideration for their performance. That is, even the current champion is not immune from extinction.

From this general idea, the concrete implementation of extinctions is separately fitted to the three search methods applied in the experiments: behavioral grid search, novelty search, and traditional objective-based search. The idea is to implement extinctions to respect the distinct features of each search method.

Behavioral grid search defines explicit discrete niches. Thus in that model, an extinction event acts to vacate all but a fixed number of randomly-chosen niches; one individual from each selected niche is randomly-chosen to survive. Because each niche supports a different set of similar phenotypic behaviors, evolvable lineages (with higher phenotypic variability) that colonize many such niches are more likely to persist. Individuals from these few surviving niches are amplified as they repopulate vacated niches.

In contrast, there are no discrete niches in the novelty search and objective-based fitness EAs. To establish a similar effect, a greedy algorithm chooses a few surviving individuals spread across the space of behaviors. First, a set of accumulated survivors is initialized with a random member of the population. Then, the set is augmented incrementally until it is of the desired size. To decide which individual to add to the set, the population is sorted by each individual's minimum behavioral distance to an existing member of the set; an individual is then chosen at random from the top 20% of the sorted list. In this way, a small but diverse set of behaviors will survive each extinction. The stochasticity of the greedy algorithm ensures that extreme behaviors that are ranked highest will not always persist multiple extinctions; otherwise, because the underlying EA is a steady-state one, the same extreme behavior might always survive extinctions regardless of its evolvability or ability to diversify.

In all search methods, after the population is decimated, replacement is disabled temporarily until the population is replenished to its previous size. The experiments utilizing these techniques will be described next.

4. EXPERIMENTS

To explore whether EAs augmented with extinction events produce more evolvable populations, experiments were conducted in two representative ER domains: maze navigation [18] and biped locomotion [16]. These domains will be described first, followed by experimental setup and results.

4.1 Maze Navigation Domain

In the maze navigation domain, a simulated wheeled robot (figure 1) is embedded in a two-dimensional maze (figure 2). The objective for the robot is to traverse the maze and arrive at a fixed goal point. Thus, the fitness f of an individual for objective-based search is $f = b_f - d_g$, where b_f is a constant bias and d_g is the distance of the robot to the goal at the end of the evaluation. For novelty search and behavioral grid search, evolution instead requires a characterization of behavior. Because ending location is a critical factor in navigating mazes, the behavior of a robot is defined as its location in the maze at the end of the evaluation [16, 22]. For behavioral grid search, each grid square within a regular grid superimposed over all ending locations acts a discrete niche. Individuals are mapped into the niche that contains the behavior they exhibit when evaluated.

The particular instantiation of the domain is the fragile hard maze of Lehman and Stanley [18]. It was chosen because it is one of the well-studied hard maze domains [16, 18, 19, 24] that offer significant capacity for increased evolvability relative to random initial populations [18, 19].

In the hard maze's original conception [16], a robot is not penalized when it collides with a wall. However, in the fragile version, a robot's evaluation is immediately terminated in such a case. For objective-based search, a colliding robot receives a fitness value f_{low} which is a minuscule value that is lower than otherwise possible. For novelty search, such a robot receives a minimal novelty score, n_{low}. For behavioral grid search, a colliding robot is mapped to a special niche that fills up quickly and renders colliding behavior inviable after the first few evaluations. The motivation for such penalties is to make the domain more *fragile*, i.e. more sensitive to mutation. That way the domain accentuates the challenge of discovering evolvable representations [18].

4.2 Biped Locomotion Domain

As the second domain, the biped domain of Lehman and Stanley [16] is adapted for these experiments (figure 3). In

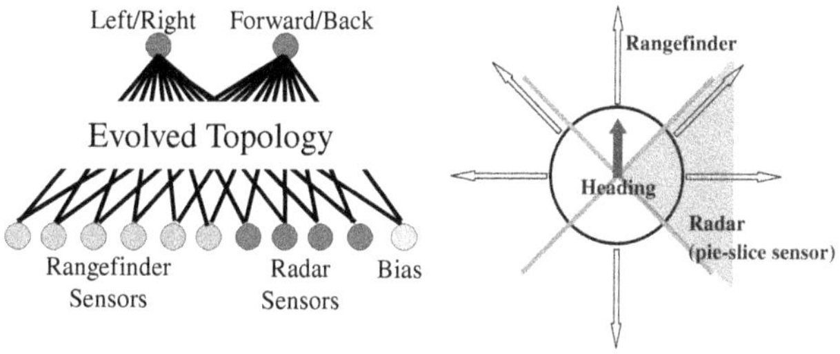

(a) Neural Network (b) Sensors

Figure 1: **A Maze-Navigating Robot.** The artificial neural network that controls the maze navigating robot is shown in (a). The layout of the sensors is shown in (b). Each arrow outside of the robot's body in (b) is a rangefinder sensor that indicates the distance to the closest obstacle in that direction. The robot has four pie-slice sensors that act as a compass towards the goal, activating when the goal falls within the infinite projection of that pie-slice. The solid arrow indicates the robot's heading.

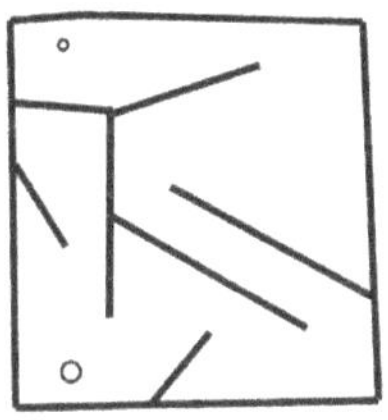

Figure 2: **Maze Navigation Map.** In this map, the larger circle represents the starting position of the robot and the smaller circle represents the goal. To solve the task, the robot must navigate a circuitous path, which requires the evolution of non-trivial behavior. Further complicating the task, colliding with any wall immediately terminates the evaluation and renders the individual inviable. In this way, the domain presents a significant challenge for discovering evolvable representations.

this domain, the goal is to evolve a controller for a simulated biped robot that results in a stable walking gait. The problem is challenging because both balance and oscillation are needed. Like the maze domain it is also fragile: Most mutations to controllers are fatal and cause the robot to fall over quickly [18]. Thus biped locomotion provides a natural challenge domain for exploring how to increase evolvability and performance of EAs.

The domain works as follows (for more details see [16]). A biped robot in a physically realistic three-dimensional simulation is controlled by an ANN for a fixed duration (15 seconds). The evaluation is terminated if the robot falls or after the allocated time expires. The objective is for the robot to travel the greatest possible distance from the starting location.

The fitness of a biped controller for objective-based search is evaluated as the squared distance the robot walks before it falls. Its behavior for calculating novelty is derived from sampling its center of gravity each second it walks. The additional information provided by temporal sampling allows novelty search to differentiate two gaits that end up at the same location by different means.

For behavioral grid search, behavior is characterized simply by the robot's center of gravity at the simulation's completion. Such simplification is applied because the size of the grid of niches grows exponentially with increasing dimensionality. As in the maze domain, a regular two-dimensional

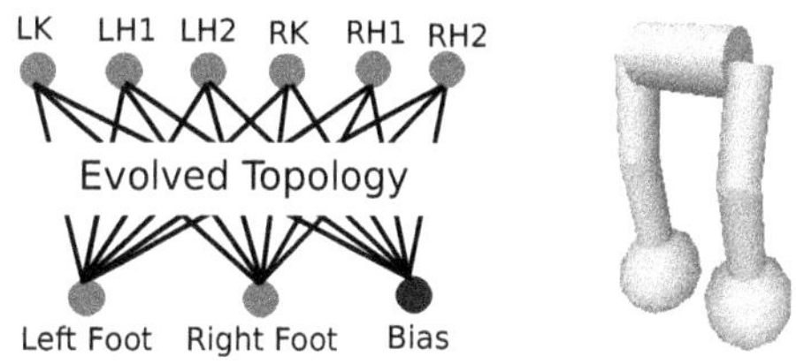

(a) Neural Network (b) Visualization

Figure 3: **Biped Robot.** In the biped locomotion domain, the ANN in (a) controls the biped robot that is visualized in (b). The robot has motors that apply forces to achieve the joint angles that are output by the ANN. In particular, there are motors for each of the six degrees of freedom: One in its left and right knees (LK and RK), and two in each hip (LH1, LH2, RH1, and RH2). Additionally, the robot's ANN receives input from sensors in its feet that activate when they touch the ground. The challenge for the robot is to locomote as far as possible.

grid is superimposed over this behavior space, where each grid square defines a discrete niche shared by robots demonstrating behaviors encompassed by that square.

4.3 Experimental Setups

Across these two domains, three representative search algorithms are applied. Divergent search is represented by behavioral grid search and novelty search, while convergent search is represented by a traditional objective-based EA. While behavioral grid search is based on a geometric space of niches, novelty search and objective-based search share the same underlying steady-state EA and differ only in their underlying incentive scheme. All three search algorithms evolve ANNs represented by NEAT.

For each search method, four experimental setups are considered. In the *Control* setup there are no extinction events, i.e. the underlying EA operates as usual. In the *Extinction 100k*, *Extinction 200k* and *Extinction 400k* setups, extinction events occur every 100,000, 200,000, and 400,000 evaluations, respectively. The idea is to explore the effect of varying the inclusion and frequency of extinctions on the resulting evolvability of the different EAs.

In the maze domain, the population size was 250, while in the biped domain it was 500. Novelty search and objective-based search both used the same underlying steady-state EA with tournament selection and tournament size of five. Over both search algorithms and both domains, evolution ran for 3,000,000 evaluations and extinction events spare only 10 individuals; 40 independent runs were conducted for each combination of domain, setup, and algorithm.

For behavioral grid search, the resolution of the grid that was superimposed over the space of behaviors in the maze domain was 20×20. The resolution was 40×40 in the biped domain over possible ending positions between $[-8.0, 8.0]$ meters for both planar coordinates. In both domains these same grids served to calculate evolvability, i.e. for all methods the evolvability of an individual was measured by the amount of unique grid squares exhibited by mutants of that individual. In particular, the evolvability of the population was estimated every 250,000 evaluations by applying the evolvability measure to 200 individuals chosen at random from the population.

4.4 Results

Figure 6 shows how the evolvability of final populations is distributed in all setups. Supporting this paper's hypothesis, the main result is that extinction events result in increased evolvability only when combined with divergent search algorithms. A representative comparison of the temporal dynamics of evolvability increase between convergent and divergent search is shown in figure 4. Additionally, figure 5 visualizes how increasing evolvability allows evolution to rebound more quickly. (Corresponding figures for the maze domain and behavioral grid search are shown in the supplemental website http://nn.cs.utexas.edu/downloads/papers/lehman.gecco2015-supplement.html). Reflecting its label, in all experimenter observations across domains and setups the convergent objective-based search algorithm consistently converged to a single champion behavior.

Beyond evolvability, extinction events also affect the *performance* of search methods. Figure 7 highlights differences in evolutionary success, showing that extinction events lead to more effective adaptation when combined with divergent search. Independently of setup, objective-based search never solved the maze. This result is likely due to the deceptive nature of this domain [16]. Additionally, with objective-based search in the biped domain no significant differences in performance result from introducing extinction events. In contrast, extinctions increase performance of divergent search: In nearly all combinations of domains and divergent search algorithms, performance is highest with the Extinction 100k setup, suggesting that more frequent extinction events are the most effective. In the maze domain, differences between the divergent algorithms are not significant, while in the biped domain, each novelty search setup significantly outperforms its corresponding behavioral grid search setup (Mann-Whitney U-test; $p < 0.05$). The likely reason is that biped behaviors are differentiated better by the high-dimensional behavior characterization used in novelty search than with the simplified behavior characterization necessary for behavioral grid search.

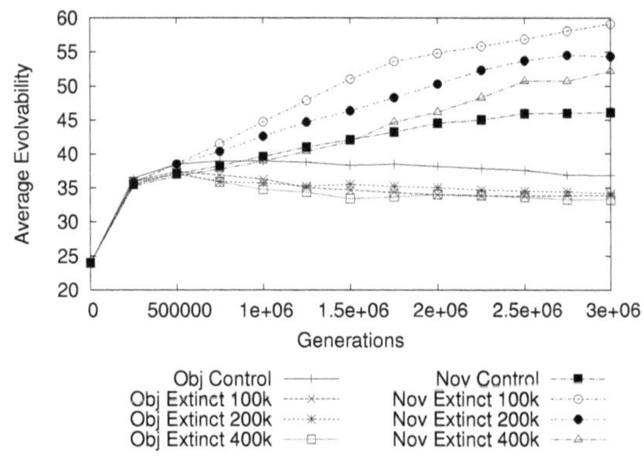

Figure 4: **The Change in Evolvability over Evolution.** The average (mean) evolvability of individuals in the population is shown for objective-based search (labeled Obj) and novelty search (labeled Nov) in the biped domain. Extinction setups combined with novelty search result in increased evolvability and an overall increasing trend. Extinction setups combined with objective-based search result in decreased evolvability and an overall stagnating trend. The conclusion is that there is a qualitative difference in how evolvability changes over time between the two search methods.

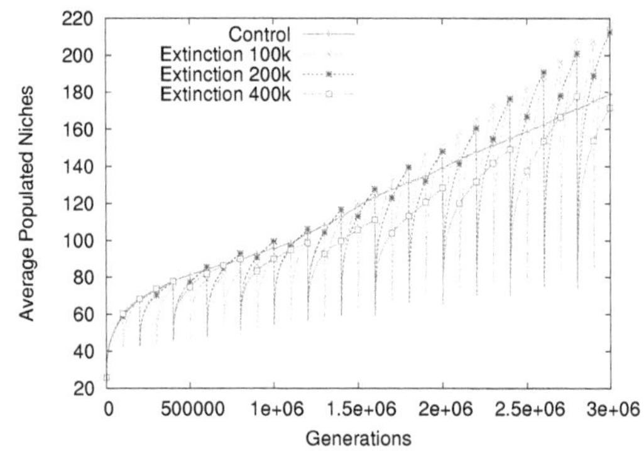

Figure 5: **Dynamics of Niche Occupation.** The average (mean) number of niches occupied over evolution is shown for behavioral grid search in the biped domain. The Control setup accumulates niches monotonically, whereas the Extinction setups are decimated at regular intervals. Because each extinction event spares only 10 niches, increasingly quick repopulation in the Extinction setups suggest that the representations are more evolvable in these setups than in the others. Note that each extinction always brings the model to exactly 10 niches, although this is not visible due to sampling error.

5. DISCUSSION

This paper provides evidence for the counter-intuitive insight that repeated short-term destruction may enhance the long-term potential of an evolutionary process. Such robustness through upheaval is reminiscent of creative destruction in business and wildfires in ecosystems. Thus such events can serve as simple and effective enhancements to EAs.

However, echoing previous results with self-adaptation [18], the results also demonstrate that extinction events accelerate evolution only when combined with divergent search. In this way, powerful mechanisms of natural evolution may often be interdependent, and some such mechanisms may provide little benefit in isolation. In particular, a search reward scheme facilitating divergence (e.g. as in behavioral grid search or novelty search) may prove a critical ingredient enabling many mechanisms seen in natural evolution. Furthermore, differential benefit of this kind suggests that best practices learned for convergent search may not apply to divergent search. Thus, the conclusions forged in the context of the more dominant convergent search paradigm may need to be re-evaluated for divergent search.

6. CONCLUSION

This paper forwards the hypothesis that extinction events can accelerate evolution in divergent search algorithms. The hypothesis is supported by results from two evolutionary robotics domains, in which extinction events benefit divergent search but not a more traditional convergent objective-based search. Thus extinction events may provide a simple and effective mechanism for improving the long-term performance of divergent EAs.

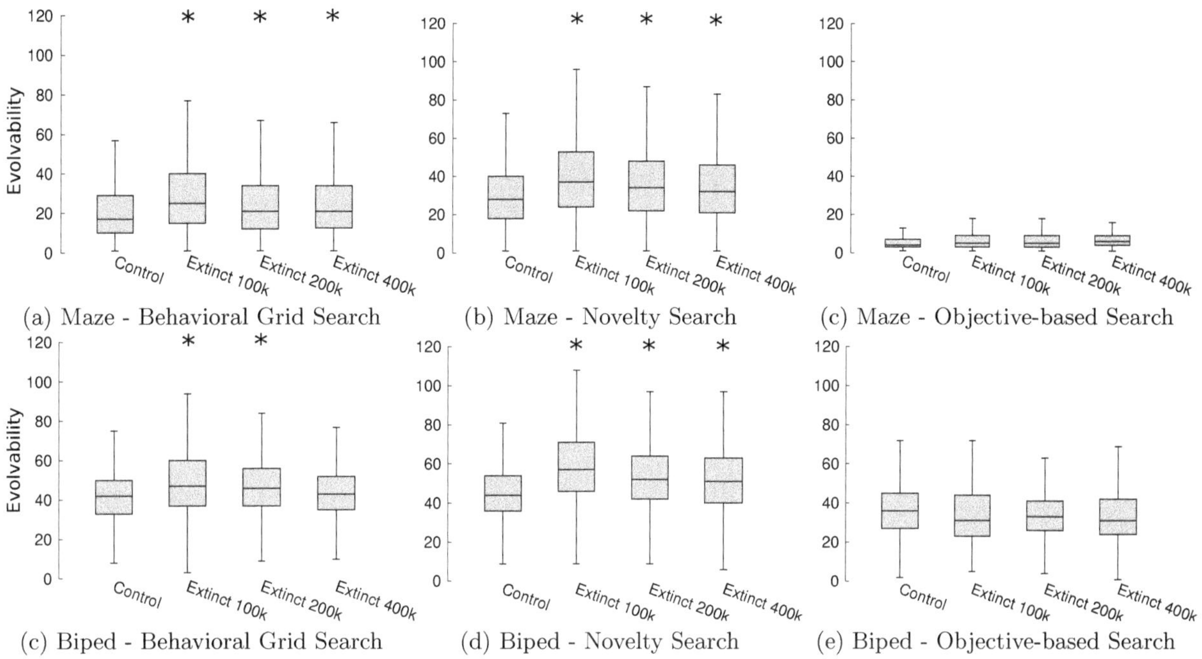

(a) Maze - Behavioral Grid Search (b) Maze - Novelty Search (c) Maze - Objective-based Search

(c) Biped - Behavioral Grid Search (d) Biped - Novelty Search (e) Biped - Objective-based Search

Figure 6: **Distribution of Evolvability in Final Populations.** The box plots show the evolvability of individuals in final populations for the four setups of the three search methods in the maze and biped domains. First, protective one-way ANOVA tests showed that there were significant differences between the extinction setups and the control with divergent search methods (i.e. behavioral grid search and novelty search; $p < 0.05$), but not with objective-based search. Second, pairwise Mann-Whitney U tests showed that with the divergent search algorithms, the average final evolvability in the extinction setups was significantly higher than in the control in 11 of the 12 pair-wise comparisons (those indicated with "*"; $p < 0.05$). The conclusion is that extinction events enhance evolvability only when paired with divergent search.

7. ACKNOWLEDGMENTS

This research was supported in part by NSF grants DBI-0939454, IIS-0915038, and SBE-0914796, and by NIH grant R01-GM105042.

References

[1] T. Aaltonen et al., Measurement of the top quark mass with dilepton events selected using neuroevolution at CDF, *Physical Review Letters* (2009).

[2] B. Allen and P. Faloutsos, Complex networks of simple neurons for bipedal locomotion, in: *IEEE/RSJ International Conference on Intelligent Robots and Systems (IROS)* (2009).

[3] J. Brookfield, Evolution: The evolvability enigma, *Current Biology*, 11(3):R106 – R108 (2001).

[4] J. Clune, J.-B. Mouret, and H. Lipson, The evolutionary origins of modularity, *Proceedings of the Royal Society of London B: Biological Sciences*, 280(1755):20122863 (2013).

[5] A. Cully, J. Clune, D. Tarapore, and J.-B. Mouret, Robots that can adapt like natural animals, *arXiv preprint arXiv:1407.3501* (2014).

[6] R. Dawkins, The evolution of evolvability, *On Growth, Form and Computers*, 239–255 (2003).

[7] M. Dichtel-Danjoy and M. Félix, Phenotypic neighborhood and micro-evolvability, *Trends in Genetics*, 20(5):268–276 (2004).

[8] G. B. Fogel, G. W. Greenwood, and K. Chellapilla, Evolutionary computation with extinction: experiments and analysis, in: *Evolutionary Computation, 2000. Proceedings of the 2000 Congress on*, volume 2, 1415–1420, IEEE (2000).

[9] F. Gomez and R. Miikkulainen, Incremental evolution of complex general behavior, *Adaptive Behavior*, 5:317–342 (1997).

[10] F. J. Gomez and R. Miikkulainen, Solving non-markovian control tasks with neuroevolution, in: *IJCAI*, volume 99, 1356–1361 (1999).

[11] F. J. Gomez and R. Miikkulainen, Active guidance for a finless rocket using neuroevolution, in: *Proceedings of the Genetic and Evolutionary Computation (GECCO 2003)*, 2084–2095, Springer (2003).

[12] I. Harvey, *The Artificial Evolution of Adaptive Behavior*, Ph.D. thesis, School of Cognitive and Computing Sciences, University of Sussex, Sussex (1993).

[13] M. Kirschner and J. Gerhart, Evolvability, *Proceedings of the National Academy of Sciences of the United States of America*, 95(15):8420 (1998).

[14] T. Krink and R. Thomsen, Self-organized criticality and mass extinction in evolutionary algorithms, in: *Evolutionary Computation, 2001. Proceedings of the 2001 Congress on*, volume 2, 1155–1161, IEEE (2001).

[15] J. Lehman, S. Risi, and K. O. Stanley, On the benefits of divergent search for evolved representations, in: *Proceedings of the EvoNet 2012 Workshop at ALIFE XIII* (2012).

[16] J. Lehman and K. O. Stanley, Abandoning objectives: Evolution through the search for novelty alone, *Evol. Comp.*, 19(2):189–223 (2011).

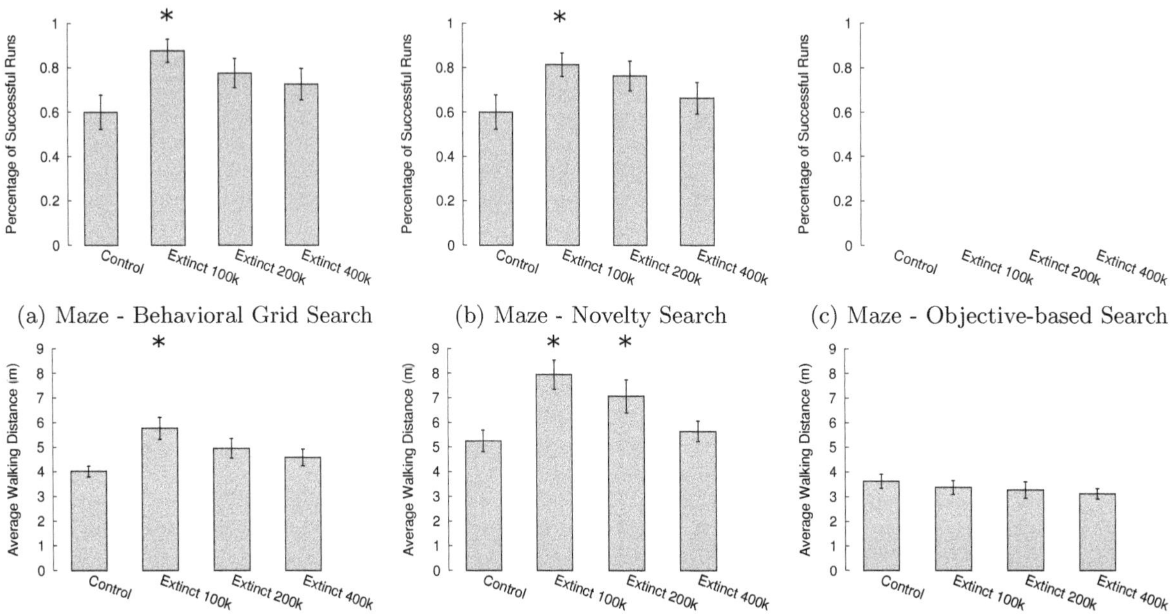

(a) Maze - Behavioral Grid Search (b) Maze - Novelty Search (c) Maze - Objective-based Search

(c) Biped - Behavioral Grid Search (d) Biped - Novelty Search (e) Biped - Objective-based Search

Figure 7: **Performance of Evolved Solutions.** The ability of evolution to generate well-adapted solutions is shown for the four setups of the three search methods in the maze and biped domains. In the maze navigation domain, a successful robot can navigate the full extent of the maze. In the biped domain, better solutions walk a longer distance. First, protective one-way ANOVA tests showed that there were significant differences between the extinction setups and the control with divergent search methods (i.e. behavioral grid search and novelty search; $p < 0.05$), but not with objective-based search. Second, pairwise Mann-Whitney U tests showed that with each divergent search method in each domain, the Extinction 100k setup significantly outperformed the control (those indicated with "*"; $p < 0.05$; the lines indicate standard error), and no extinction setups significantly underperformed the control. The conclusion is that extinction events enhance divergent search's ability to uncover well-adapted solutions, but provide no comparable enhancement for convergent search.

[17] J. Lehman and K. O. Stanley, Evolving a diversity of virtual creatures through novelty search and local competition, in: *Proceedings of the Genetic and Evolutionary Computation Conference (GECCO-2011)*, ACM (2011).

[18] J. Lehman and K. O. Stanley, Improving evolvability through novelty search and self-adaptation, in: *Evolutionary Computation (CEC), 2011 IEEE Congress on*, 2693–2700, IEEE (2011).

[19] J. Lehman and K. O. Stanley, Evolvability is inevitable: Increasing evolvability without the pressure to adapt, *PloS one*, 8(4):e62186 (2013).

[20] J. Marin and R. V. Sole, Macroevolutionary algorithms: a new optimization method on fitness landscapes, *Evolutionary Computation, IEEE Transactions on*, 3(4):272–286 (1999).

[21] A. P. Martin, Increasing genomic complexity by gene duplication and the origin of vertebrates, *The American Naturalist*, 154(2):111–128 (1999).

[22] J.-B. Mouret, Novelty-based multiobjectivization, in: *Proceedings of the Workshop on Exploring New Horizons in Evolutionary Design of Robots,2009 IEEE/RSJ International Conference on Intelligent Robots and Systems* (2009).

[23] J.-B. Mouret and J. Clune, Illuminating search spaces by mapping elites., *arXiv preprint arXiv:1504.04909* (2015).

[24] J.-B. Mouret and S. Doncieux, Encouraging behavioral diversity in evolutionary robotics: an empirical study, *Evolutionary Computation*, 20(1):91–133 (2012).

[25] M. E. Palmer and M. W. Feldman, Spatial environmental variation can select for evolvability, *Evolution*, 65(8):2345–2356 (2011).

[26] M. Pigliucci, Is evolvability evolvable?, *Nature Reviews Genetics*, 9(1):75–82 (2008).

[27] R. Standish, Open-ended artificial evolution, *International Journal of Computational Intelligence and Applications*, 3(167) (2003).

[28] K. O. Stanley and R. Miikkulainen, Evolving neural networks through augmenting topologies, *Evolutionary Computation*, 10:99–127 (2002).

[29] K. O. Stanley and R. Miikkulainen, Competitive coevolution through evolutionary complexification, 21:63–100 (2004).

[30] G. Wagner and L. Altenberg, Complex adaptations and the evolution of evolvability, *Evolution*, 50(3):967–976 (1996).

[31] D. Whitley, K. Mathias, and P. Fitzhorn, Delta coding: An iterative search strategy for genetic algorithms, in: *ICGA*, volume 91, 77–84 (1991).

[32] X. Yao, Evolving artificial neural networks, *Proceedings of the IEEE*, 87(9):1423–1447 (1999).

Innovation Engines: Automated Creativity and Improved Stochastic Optimization via Deep Learning

Anh Nguyen
University of Wyoming
anguyen8@uwyo.edu

Jason Yosinski
Cornell University
yosinski@cs.cornell.edu

Jeff Clune
University of Wyoming
jeffclune@uwyo.edu

ABSTRACT

The Achilles Heel of stochastic optimization algorithms is getting trapped on local optima. Novelty Search avoids this problem by encouraging a search in all interesting directions. That occurs by replacing a performance objective with a reward for novel behaviors, as defined by a human-crafted, and often simple, behavioral distance function. While Novelty Search is a major conceptual breakthrough and outperforms traditional stochastic optimization on certain problems, it is not clear how to apply it to challenging, high-dimensional problems where specifying a useful behavioral distance function is difficult. For example, in the space of images, how do you encourage novelty to produce hawks and heroes instead of endless pixel static? Here we propose a new algorithm, the Innovation Engine, that builds on Novelty Search by replacing the human-crafted behavioral distance with a Deep Neural Network (DNN) that can recognize *interesting* differences between phenotypes. The key insight is that DNNs can recognize similarities and differences between phenotypes at an abstract level, wherein novelty means *interesting* novelty. For example, a novelty pressure in image space does not explore in the low-level pixel space, but instead creates a pressure to create new *types* of images (e.g. churches, mosques, obelisks, etc.). Here we describe the long-term vision for the Innovation Engine algorithm, which involves many technical challenges that remain to be solved. We then implement a simplified version of the algorithm that enables us to explore some of the algorithm's key motivations. Our initial results, in the domain of images, suggest that Innovation Engines could ultimately automate the production of endless streams of interesting solutions in any domain: e.g. producing intelligent software, robot controllers, optimized physical components, and art.

Categories and Subject Descriptors

I.2.6 [**AI**]: Learning—*Connectionism and neural nets*

Keywords

Deep Neural Networks; Deep Learning; MAP-Elites

GECCO '15, July 11 - 15, 2015, Madrid, Spain
© 2015 ACM. ISBN 978-1-4503-3472-3/15/07...$15.00
DOI: http://dx.doi.org/10.1145/2739480.2754703

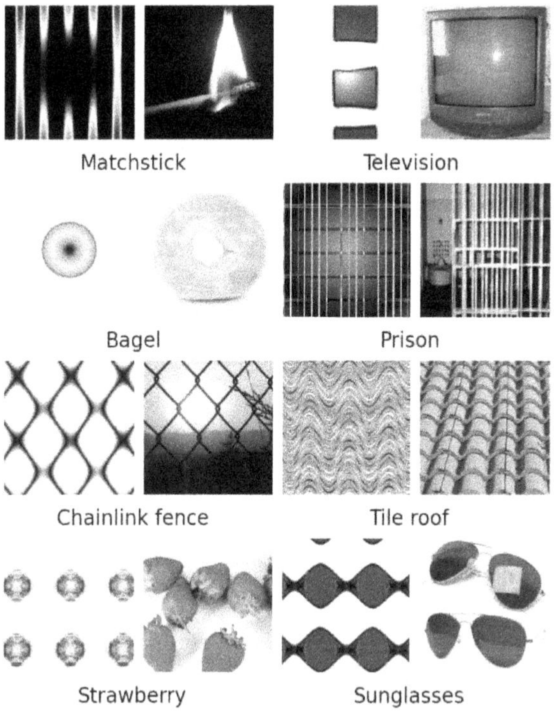

Figure 1: Images produced by an Innovation Engine that look like example target classes. In each pair, an evolved image (left) is shown with a real image (right) from the training set used to train the deep neural network that evaluates evolving images.

1. INTRODUCTION

Stochastic optimization and search algorithms, such as simulated annealing and evolutionary algorithms (EAs), often outperform human engineers in several domains [11]. However, there are other domains in which these algorithms cannot produce effective solutions yet. Their Achilles Heel is the trap of local optima [29], where the objective given to an algorithm (e.g. a fitness function) prevents the search from leaving sub-optimal solutions and reaching better ones. Novelty Search [13, 14] addresses this problem by collecting the stepping stones needed to ultimately lead to an objective instead of directly optimizing towards it. The algorithm encourages searching in all directions by replacing a performance objective with a reward for novel behaviors, the novelty of which is measured with a distance function in the behavior space [16]. This recent conceptual breakthrough has been shown to outperform traditional stochastic optimization on problems where specifying distances between desired behaviors is easy [13, 14]. Reducing a high-dimensional search space to a low-dimensional one is essential to the success of Novelty Search, because in high-dimensional search spaces there are too many ways to be novel without being interesting [5]. For example, if novelty is measured directly in the high-dimensional space of pixels in a 60,000 pixel image, being different can mean different static patterns, which are not *interestingly different types* of images.

Here we propose a novel algorithm called an *Innovation Engine* that enables searching in high-dimensional spaces for which it is difficult for humans to define what constitutes *interestingly different behaviors.* The key insight is to use a deep neural network (DNN) [2] as the evaluation function to reduce a high-dimensional search space to a low-dimensional search space where novelty means *interesting* novelty. State-of-the-art DNNs have demonstrated impressive and sometimes human-competitive results on many pattern recognition tasks [12, 2]. They see past the myriad pixel differences, such as lighting changes, rotations, zooms, and occlusions, to recognize abstract concepts in images, such as tigers, tables, and turnips. Here we suggest harnessing the power of DNNs to recognize different types of things in the abstract, high-level spaces they can make distinctions in.

A second reason for choosing DNNs is that they work by hierarchically recognizing features. In images, for example, they recognize faces by combining edges into corners, then corners into eyes or noses, and then they combine these features into even higher-level features such as faces [2]. Such a hierarchy of features is beneficial because those features can be produced in different combinations to produce new types of ideas/solutions.

We first describe our long-term, ultimate vision for Innovation Engines that require no labeled data to endlessly innovate in any domain. Because there are many technical hurdles to overcome to reach that vision, we also describe a simpler, version 1.0 Innovation Engine that harnesses labeled data to simulate how the ultimate Innovation Engine might function. While Innovation Engines should work in any domain, we test one in the image generating domain that originally inspired the Novelty Search algorithm and show that it can automatically produce a diversity of interesting images (Fig. 1). We also confirm some expectations regarding why Innovation Engines are expected to work.

2. INNOVATION ENGINES

The Innovation Engine algorithm seeks to abstract the process of curiosity and habituation that occurs in humans. Historically, humans create ideas based on combinations of, or changes to, previous ideas, evaluate whether these ideas are interesting, and retain the interesting ideas to create more advanced ideas (Fig. 2). We propose to automate the entire process by having stochastic optimization (e.g. an evolutionary algorithm) generate new behaviors and a DNN evaluate whether the behaviors are interestingly new. The DNN will then be re-trained to learn all behaviors generated so far and evolution will be asked to produce new behaviors that the network has not seen before. This algorithm should be able to automatically create an endless stream of interesting solutions in any domain, e.g. producing robot controllers, optimized electrical circuits, and even art.

Creating an Innovation Engine requires generating and retaining "stepping stones to everywhere." The stepping stones on the path to any particular innovation are not known ahead of time [14]. From the stone age, for example, the path to create a telephone did not involve inventing only things that improved long-distance communication, but instead involved accumulating all interesting innovations (Fig. 2). In fact, had human culture been restricted to only producing inventions that improve long-distance communication, it is likely that the telephone would never have been developed. That is because many of the fundamental telephone-enabling inventions were not invented because they contributed to long-distance communication (e.g. wires, electricity, electromagnets, etc) but to completely different goals. The same is true for nearly every significant invention in human history: many of the key enabling technologies were originally invented for other purposes [15]. In art, just as in science, there is a similar accumulation of interesting ideas over time and a pressure to "make something new", which leads to a steady discovery of new artistic ideas over time [15]. Human culture, therefore, can be seen as an "Innovation Engine" that steadily produces new inventions in many different domains, from math and science to art and engineering.

2.1 The ultimate goal

Our long-term vision is to create an Innovation Engine that does not require labeled data, or perhaps is not even shown data from the natural or man-made world. It would learn to classify the types of things it has produced so far and seeks to produce new types of things. Technically, one way to implement this algorithm is by training generative deep neural network models with unsupervised learning algorithms: these generative models can learn to compress the types of data they have seen before [2, 8]. One could thus measure if a newly generated thing is a new type of thing by how well the generative DNN model can compress it. Evolution will be rewarded for producing things that the DNN cannot compress well, which should endlessly produce novel types of things. If certain types of data (e.g. static) cannot be compressed, those can be deemed uninteresting (unfit).

Imagine such an Innovation Engine in the image domain. A network trained on all images produced so far will attempt to compress each newly generated image, and it will fail more on new types of images. We hypothesize that the DNN will continuously become "bored" with (i.e. highly compress) easily produced classes of images (initially static and solid colors, but soon more complex patterns), which will encourage evolution to generate increasingly complex images in order to produce new types of images. The process thus becomes a coevolutionary *innovation arms race.*

This version of the Innovation Engine is motivated by Schmidhuber's curiosity work [23] – which emphasizes the production of things that are not compressed yet, but are most easily compressed next – but our work involves modern compressors (state-of-the-art DNNs) and our algorithm does not require the seemingly impossible task of *predicting* which classes of artifacts are highly compressible. Our proposal is similar to [17], but prevents cycling by attempting to produce things different than everything produced so far, not just the current population. If it works, this Innovation Engine could produce innovations in the multitude of fields

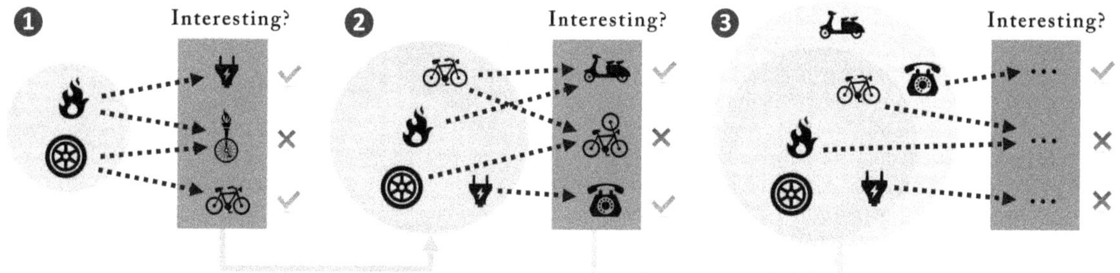

Figure 2: The Innovation Engine: Human culture creates amazing inventions, such as the telephone, by accumulating a multitude of interesting innovations in all directions. These stepping stones are collected, improved and then combined to create new innovations, which in turn, serve as the stepping stones for innovations in later generations. We propose to automate this process by having stochastic optimization (e.g. evolutionary algorithms) generate candidate solutions from the current archive of stepping stones and Deep Neural Networks evaluate whether they are *interestingly new* and should thus be archived.

and problem domains that currently benefit from stochastic optimization.

2.2 Version 1.0

Unsupervised learning algorithms for generative models do not yet scale to high dimensional data [3]; for example, they can handle 28×28 pixel MNIST images [8] but not 256×256 pixel ImageNet images [7]. In this section we describe a simpler Innovation Engine version that can be implemented with currently available algorithms. A key piece of the ultimate Innovation Engine is automatically recognizing new types of classes, which function as newly created niches for evolution to specialize on. We can emulate that endless process of niche creation by simply starting with a lot of niches and letting evolution exploit them all. To do that, we can take advantage of two recent developments in machine learning: (1) the availability of large, supervised datasets, and (2) the ability of modern supervised Deep Learning algorithms to train DNNs to reach near-human-competitive levels in classifying the things in these datasets [8, 12, 2]. We can thus challenge optimization algorithms (e.g. evolution) to produce things that the DNN recognizes as belonging to each class.

Innovation Engines require two key components: (1) a diversity-promoting EA that generates and collects novel behaviors, and (2) a DNN capable of evaluating the behaviors to determine if they are interesting and should be retained. The first criterion could be fulfilled either by Novelty Search or the multi-dimensional archive of phenotypic elites (MAP-Elites) algorithm [19, 6]. We show below that both can work.

3. TEST DOMAIN: GENERATING IMAGES

The test domain for the paper is generating a diverse set of interesting, recognizable images. We chose this domain for four reasons. The first is because an experiment in image generation served as the inspiration for Novelty Search [25]. That experiment occurred on Picbreeder.org, a website that allowed visitors to interactively evolve images [24], resulting in a crowd of humans that evolved a diverse, recognizable set of images. Key enablers of this diversity were [24, 25]: the fact that collectively there was no goal; that individuals periodically had a target image type in mind, creating a local pressure for high-performing (recognizable) images; users were open to the possibility of switching to a new goal if the opportunity presented itself (e.g. if the eyes of a face started to look like the wheels of a car); that users saved any image that they found interesting (usually a new type of image, or an improvement upon a previous type of image) and future users could branch off of any saved stepping stone to create a new image. Critically, all of these elements should also occur in Innovation Engine 1.0; thus one test of that hypothesis is whether Innovation Engine 1.0 can automatically produce a diverse set of images like those generated by humans on Picbreeder. One attempt was made to automatically recreate the diversity of recognizable images produced on Picbreeder, but it produced only abstract patterns [1].

The second motivation for the image-generating domain is that DNNs are nearly human-competitive at recognizing images [12, 10, 28]. The third reason is that DNNs can recognize and sensibly classify the type of images from Picbreeder (Fig. 3), specifically images encoded by compositional pattern producing networks (CPPNs) [27]. We also encode images with CPPNs in our experiments (described below). The fourth reason is because humans are natural pattern recognizers, making us quickly and intuitively able to evaluate the diversity, interestingness, and recognizability of evolved solutions. Additionally, while much of what we learn from this domain comes from subjective results, there is also a quantitative aspect regarding the confidence a DNN ascribes to the generated images. In future work we will test whether the conclusions reached in this mostly subjective domain translate into more exclusively quantitative domains.

To experiment in this domain, we use a modern off-the-shelf DNN trained with 1.3 million images to recognize 1000 different types of objects from the natural world. We then challenge evolution to produce images that the DNN confidently labels as members of each of the 1000 classes. Evolution is therefore challenged to make increasingly recognizable images for all 1000 classes. Generating CPPN-encoded images that are recognizable is challenging [29], making recognizability a notion of performance in this domain. Being recognizable is also related to being interesting, as Picbreeder images that are recognizable are often the most highly rated [24].

4. METHODS

4.1 Deep neural network models

The DNN in our experiments is the well-known convolutional "AlexNet" architecture from [12]. It is trained on the

1.3-million-image 2012 ImageNet dataset [7, 22], and available for download via the Caffe software package [9]. The Caffe-provided AlexNet has small architectural differences from Krizhevsky 2012 [12], but it performs similarly (42.6% top-1 error rate vs. the original 40.7% [12]). For each image, the DNN outputs a post-softmax, 1000-dimensional vector reporting the probability that the image belongs to each ImageNet class. The softmax means that to produce a high confidence value for one class, all the others must be low.

4.2 Generating images with evolution

To simultaneously evolve images that match all 1000 ImageNet classes, we use the new multi-dimensional archive of phenotypic elites (MAP-Elites) algorithm [19, 6]. MAP-Elites keeps a map (archive) of the best individuals found so far for each class. Each iteration, an individual is randomly chosen from the map, mutated, and then it replaces the current champion for any class if it has a higher fitness for that class. Fitness is the DNN's confidence that an image is a member of that class.

We also test another implementation of the Innovation Engine, but with Novelty Search instead of MAP-Elites. Novelty Search encourages organisms to be different from the current population and an archive of previously novel individuals. The behavioral distance between two images is defined as the Euclidean distance between the two 1000-dimensional vectors output by the DNN for each image. Because all of our experiments were performed with the Sferes evolutionary computation framework [20], we set all Novelty Search parameters to those in [18], which was also conducted in Sferes, but followed closely the parameters in [13].

Images are encoded with compositional pattern producing networks (CPPNs) [27], which abstract the expressive power of developmental biology to produce regular patterns (e.g. those with symmetry or repetition). CPPNs encode the complex, regular, recognizable images on Picbreeder.org (e.g. Fig. 3) and the 3D objects on EndlessForms.com [4]. The details of how CPPNs encode images and are evolved have been repeatedly described elsewhere [24, 27]. Briefly, a CPPN is like a neural network, but each node's activation function is one of a set (here: sine, sigmoid, Gaussian and linear). The Cartesian coordinates of each pixel are input into the network and the network's outputs determine the color of that pixel. Importantly, evolved CPPN images can be recognized by the DNN (Fig. 3), showing that evolution can produce CPPN images that both humans and DNNs can recognize.

As is customary [24, 27, 4] we evolve CPPNs with the principles of the NeuroEvolution of Augmenting Topologies (NEAT) algorithm [26], a version of which is provided in Sferes. CPPNs start with no hidden nodes, and add nodes and connections over time, forcing evolution to first search for simple, regular images before increasing complexity [26]. All of our code and parameters are available at http://EvolvingAI.org. Because each run required 128 CPU cores running continuously for ~4 days, our run number is limited.

5. RESULTS

5.1 Evolving images to match ImageNet

If the Innovation Engine is a promising idea, then Innovation Engine 1.0 in the image domain should produce the

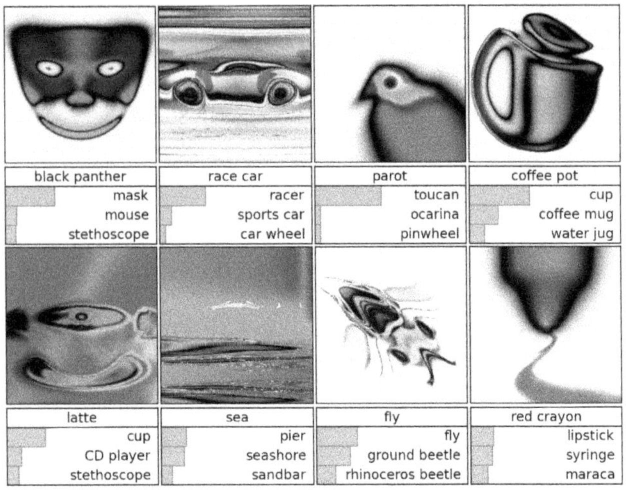

Figure 3: CPPN-encoded images evolved and named (centered text) by Picbreeder.org users. The DNN's top three classifications and associated confidence (size of the pink bar) are shown. The DNN's classifications often relate to the human breeder's label, showing that DNNs can recognize CPPN-encoded, evolved images. Adapted from [21].

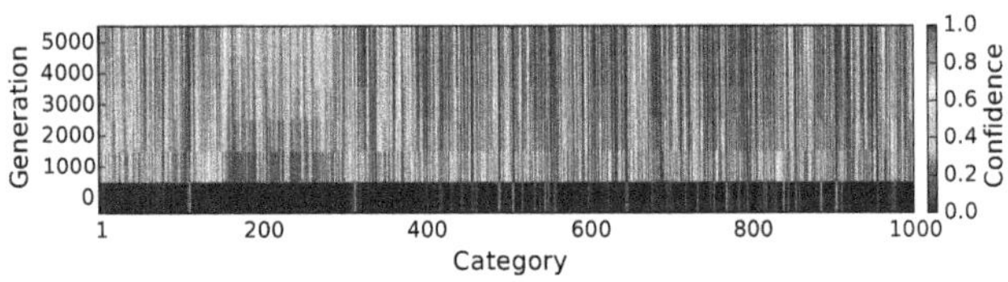

Figure 4: The MAP-Elites evolutionary algorithm produces images that the DNN declares with high confidence to belong to most ImageNet classes. Colors represent median confidence scores from 10 runs.

following: (1) images that the DNN is confident are class members and (2) a diverse set of interesting images that are (3) recognizable as members of the target class.

In 10 independent MAP-Elites runs, evolution produced high-confidence images in most categories (Fig. 4). It struggles most in classes 156-286, which represent subtly different species of dogs and cats, where it is hard to look like one type without also looking like other types. While the reader must draw their own conclusions, in our opinion the images exhibit a tremendous amount of interesting diversity. Selected examples are in Figs. 5, 1, 7: all 10,000 evolved images are shown at http://EvolvingAI.org. The diversity is especially noteworthy because many images are phylogenetically related, which should curtail diversity.

In many cases the evolved images are recognizable as members of the target class (Fig. 7). This result is remarkable given that it has been shown with the same encoding (CPPN) and evolutionary algorithm (NEAT), that it is impossible to evolve an image to resemble a complex, target image [29]. The lesson from that paper is that if evolution is given a specific objective, such as to evolve a butterfly or skull, that it will not succeed because objective-driven evolution only rewards images that increasingly look like butterflies or skulls, and that CPPN lineages that lead

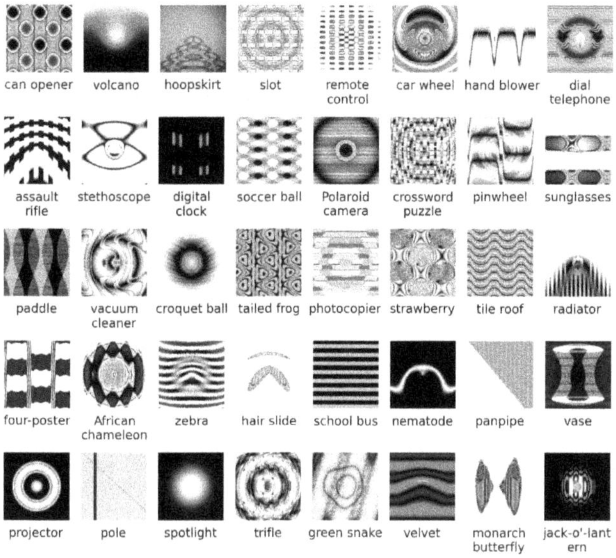

Figure 5: Innovation Engines in the image domain generate a tremendous diversity of interesting images. Shown are images selected to showcase diversity from 10 evolutionary runs. The diversity results from the pressure to match 1000 different ImageNet classes. In this and subsequent figures, the DNN's top label for each evolved image is shown below it.

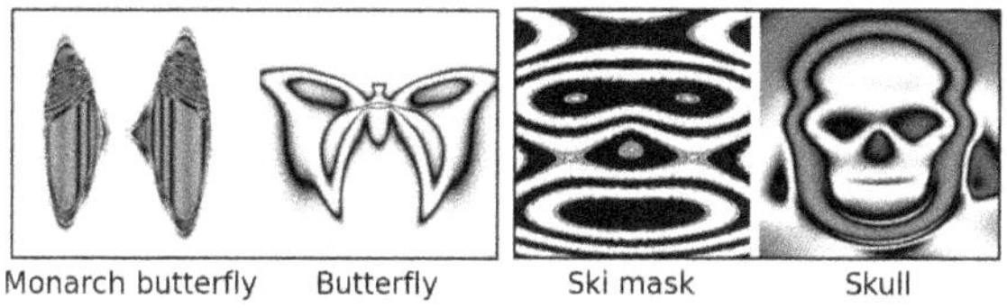

Figure 6: The Innovation Engine 1.0 evolved images that resemble those originally evolved on Picbreeder, but that a previous paper [29] showed were impossible to re-evolve with single-objective, target evolution. ImageNet has a "Monarch butterfly" class; it does not have a "skull" class, but its "Ski mask" class contains the key eyes, nose and mouth features. Shown are images evolved with Innovation Engine 1.0 (*left*) and Picbreeder (*right*).

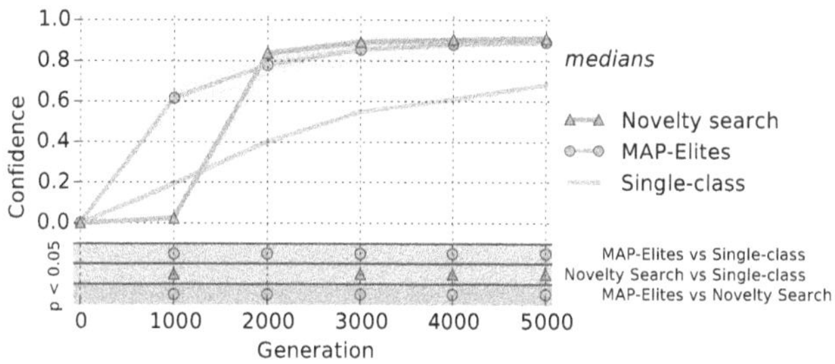

Figure 8: Innovation Engines built with MAP-Elites or Novelty Search perform similarly to each other, and both significantly outperform a single-class evolutionary algorithm. Solid lines show median performance and shaded areas indicate the 95% bootstrapped confidence interval of the median. The bottom three rows show statistical significance.

to butterflies or skulls tend to pass through images that look nothing like either. Innovation Engines, like crowds on Picbreeder, simultaneously collect improvements in a large number of objectives. That allows evolutionary lineages to be rewarded for steps that do not resemble butterflies or skulls (provided they resemble something else) and then to be rewarded as butterflies or skulls if they resemble either. Thus, a main result of this paper is that the problem is not being objective-driven, but instead being driven by only a few objectives. The key is to collect "stepping stones in all interesting directions", which can be approximated by simultaneously selecting for a vast number of objectives. Supporting this argument, our algorithm was able to produce many complex structures (Figs. 5, 1, 7) , including some that are similar to butterflies and skulls (Fig. 6). Confirming that these images can be considered art, they were accepted to a selective art competition (35% acceptance rate) and displayed at the University of Wyoming Art Museum.

Some evolved images are not recognizable, but often do contain recognizable features of the target class. For example, in Fig. 5, the *remote control* has a grid of buttons and the *zebra* has black-and-white stripes.

As was recently reported in [21], this algorithm also produces many images that DNNs assign high confidence scores to, but that are totally unrecognizable, even when knowing their class labels (e.g. Fig. 5, *tailed frog* & *soccer ball*). That study emphasized that the existence of such "fooling images" is problematic for anything that relies on DNNs to accurately classify objects, because DNNs sometimes make mistakes. This paper emphasizes the opposite, but not mutually exclusive, perspective: while using DNN as evaluators sometime produces fooling examples, it also sometimes works really well, and can thus automatically drive the evolution of a diverse set of complex, interesting, and sometimes recognizable images. In future work we investigate increasing the percent of evolved images that are recognizable.

5.2 Evolving towards multiple objectives

As discussed in the previous section, a key hypothesis underpinning Innovation Engines is that evolving toward a vast number of objectives simultaneously is more effective than evolving toward each objective separately. In this section, we probe that hypothesis directly by comparing how MAP-Elites performs on all objectives vs. how evolution fares when evolving to each single-class objective separately. Because we did not have the computational resources to perform 1000 single-class runs, we randomly selected 100 categories and performed two single-class MAP-Elites runs per category. We compare that data to how the 10 runs of 1000-class MAP-Elites performed on the same 100-class subset.

1000-class MAP-Elites produced images with significantly higher median DNN confidence scores (Fig. 8, 90.3% vs. 68.3%, $p < 0.05$ via Mann-Whitney U test). The theory behind why more objectives helps is because a lineage that is currently the champion in class X may be trapped on a local optima, such that mutations to it will not improve its fitness on that objective (a phenomenon we observe in the single-class case: Fig. 9 inset). With many objectives, however, a lineage that has been selected for other objectives can mutate to perform better on class X, which occurs fre-

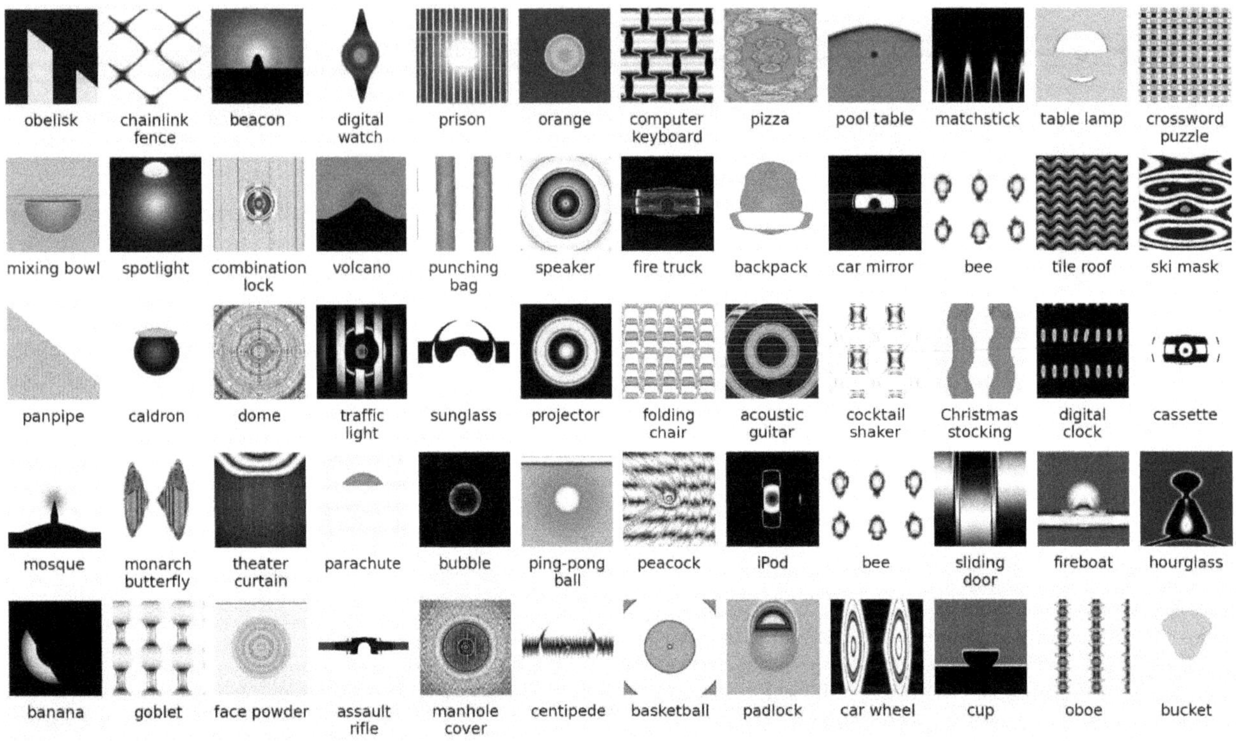

Figure 7: Innovation Engines are capable of producing images that are not only given high confidence scores by a deep neural network, but are also qualitatively interesting and recognizable. To show the most interesting images we observed evolve, we selected images from both the 10 main experiment runs and 10 preliminary experiments with slightly different parameters.

quently with MAP-Elites. For example, on the *water tower* class (Fig. 9 inset), the lineage of images that produce a large, top-lit sphere do not improve for 250 generations, but at generation 1750 a descendant of an organism that was the champion for the *cocker spaniel dog* class (Fig. 9) became a recognizable water tower and was then further refined.

Inspecting the phylogenetic tree of the 1000 images produced by MAP-Elites in one run, we found that the evolutionary path to a final image often went through other classes, a phenomenon we call *goal switching*. For example, the path to a beacon involved stepping stones that were rewarded because they were at one point champions for the *tench*, *abaya*, *megalith*, *clock*, and *cocker spaniel dog* classes (Fig. 9). A different descendent of *abaya* traversed the *stingray* and *boathouse* classes en route to a recognizable *planetarium* (Fig. 9). A related phenomenon occurs on Picbreeder, where the evolutionary path to a target image often involves images that do not resemble the target [24].

We quantitatively measured the number of goal switches per class (the number of times during a run that a new class champion was the offspring of a champion of another class). The code to track this statistic was only available for the last 3 MAP-Elites runs. Each class had a *mean* of 12.5 goal switches, which was 21.7% of the 57.6 mean new champions per class. Thus, a large percentage of improvements in a class came not from refining the current class champion, but from a mutation to a different class champion, helping to explain why Innovation Engines work.

Another expectation, which we indeed observed, is that the evolved images for many semantically related categories are also phylogenetically related. For example, according to WordNet hierarchy [7], *planetarium*, *mosque*, *church*, *obelisk*, *yurt* and *beacon* are subclasses of the *structure* class. The evolved images for these classes often are closely related phylogenetically, which also entails visual similarity (Fig. 9).

If two CPPN genomes produce equivalent behaviors (here, images), it is taken as a sign of increased evolvability if one has fewer nodes and connections [29]. It has been shown that objectives "corrupt" genomes by adding piecewise hacks that lead to small fitness gains, and thus do not find the simple, elegant solutions produced by divergent searches (e.g. novelty search or Picbreeder crowds). If Innovation Engines behave like traditional single- or multi-objective algorithms, one might expect them to produce large CPPN genomes. On the other hand, if Innovation Engines, which are *many*-objective algorithms, are more divergent in nature, they should produce smaller genomes like those reported for Picbreeder [29]. While the comparison is not apples to apples for many reasons, Innovation Engine genomes are actually more compact than those for Picbreeder. The 10,000 MAP-Elites CPPN genomes contain a median of 27 nodes (SD = 5.9) and 37.5 connections (SD= 8.6) vs. the ~7,500 Picbreeder image genomes analyzed in [24], which have 50.3 nodes and 146.7 connections (SD not reported).

5.3 Innovation Engine with Novelty Search

To support the case that Innovation Engines should work with any diversity-promoting EA combined with a DNN-provided *deep distance function*, we implemented Innovation Engine 1.0 with Novelty Search instead of MAP-Elites.

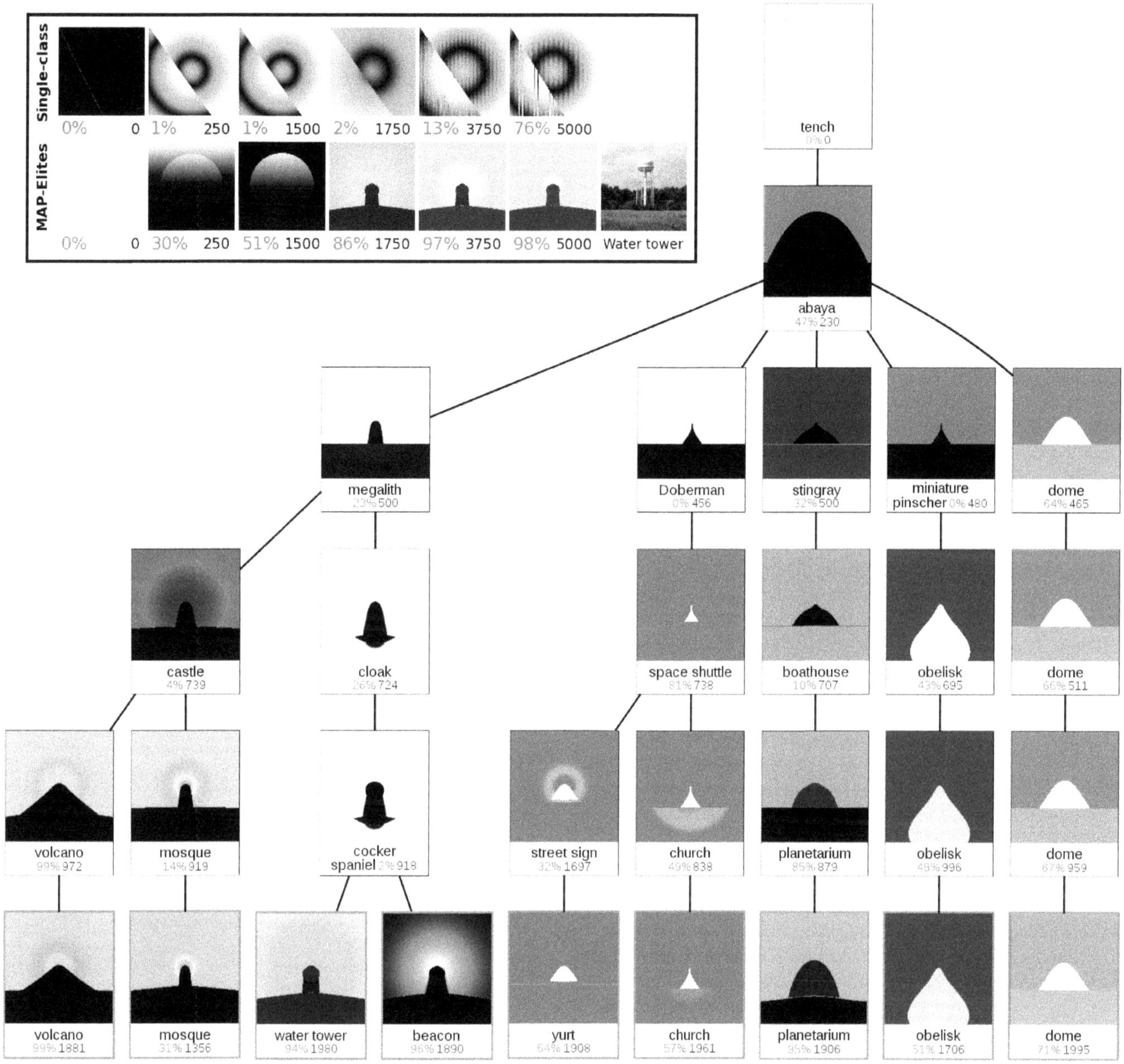

Figure 9: *Inset Panel:* The champions for the water tower class over evolutionary time for a single-class evolutionary algorithm (*top*) and the MAP-Elites variant of the Innovation Engine (*bottom*). Under each evolved image is the percent confidence the DNN has that the image is a water tower (left) and the generation in which the image was created (right). The single-class EA gets trapped on a local optima and refines the same basic idea, resulting in an unrecognizable image with mediocre performance. However, because MAP-Elites simultaneously evolves towards many objectives, often a lineage that is a champion of one class will produce an offspring that becomes a champion of a different class, a phenomenon we call *goal switching*. That occurs here at the 1750th generation, when the offspring of a champion of the cocker spaniel (dog) class (see main panel in this figure) becomes the best water tower produced so far. Its descendants are refined to produce a high-confidence, recognizable image. A water tower image from the training set is provided for reference. *Main Figure:* A phylogenetic tree depicting how lineages evolve and *goal switch* from one class to another in an Innovation Engine (here, version 1.0 with MAP-Elites). Each image is displayed with the class the DNN placed it in, the associated DNN confidence score (*red*), and the generation in which it was created. Connections indicate ancestor-child relationships. One reason Innovation Engines work is because similar types of things (e.g. various building structures) can be produced by phylogenetically related genomes, meaning that the solution to one problem can be repurposed for a similar type of problem. Note the visual similarity between the related solutions. Another reason they work is because the path to a solution often involves a series of things that do not increasingly resemble the final solution (at least, not without the benefit of hindsight). For example, note the many unrelated classes that served as stepping stones to recognizable objects (e.g. the path through cloaks and cocker spaniels to arrive at a beacon).

After Novelty Search was afforded the same number of image evaluations, we found the best image it produced for each class according to the DNN. We performed 9 independent runs of Novelty Search. To facilitate comparison to the single-class control, we compare performance on the 100 classes randomly selected for the single-class control (Sec. 5.2). The MAP-Elites vs. Novelty Search comparison on 100 classes is qualitatively the same on all 1000 classes.

As expected, Novelty Search also produced high-confidence images in most classes (Fig. 8). Its median confidence of 91.2% significantly outperforms the 68.3% for the single-class control ($p < 0.05$ via Mann-Whitney U test). While it significantly underperforms MAP-Elites at the 1000th generation, for the 2000th generation and beyond Novelty Search slightly, but significantly outperforms MAP-Elites ($p < 0.05$ via Mann-Whitney U test), although MAP-Elites has a higher final mean (79.5% vs. 74.0%). The images produced by two treatments are qualitatively similar (data not shown). This result confirms that on this domain either MAP-Elites or Novelty Search can serve as the diversity promoting EA.

6. DISCUSSION AND CONCLUSION

This paper provides a first, rough sketch of the Innovation Engine idea. Much work remains to investigate the simple version of it we presented and push toward more ambitious versions. In the short term, we will investigate improving the frequency of recognizable images produced. We will also create Innovation Engines in more quantitative domains. For example, we will pair DNNs trained to recognize different actions in videos (e.g. cartwheels, backflips, handshakes) with evolutionary algorithms to attempt to automatically create robot controllers for thousands of different behaviors.

Our preliminary results have shown that the Innovation Engine concept is worth exploring further. Specifically, we have supported some of its key assumptions: that evolving toward many objectives simultaneously approximates divergent search; that DNNs can provide informative, abstract distance functions in high-dimensional spaces; and that Innovation Engines can generate a large, diverse, interesting set of solutions in a given domain (here images). Innovation Engines will only get better as DNNs are improved, especially when generative DNN models can scale to higher dimensions. Ultimately, Innovation Engines could potentially be applied to the countless number of domains where stochastic optimization is applied. Like human culture, they could eventually enable endless innovation in any domain, from software and science to arithmetic proofs and art.

Acknowledgments: We thank Joost Huizinga, Chris Stanton, Tyler Hughes, Jessica Erickson, & Jean-Baptiste Mouret.

7. REFERENCES

[1] J. E. Auerbach. Automated evolution of interesting images. In *Artificial Life 13*. MIT Press, 2012.

[2] Y. Bengio. Learning deep architectures for AI. *Foundations and Trends in Machine Learning*, 2009.

[3] Y. Bengio, É. Thibodeau-Laufer, G. Alain, and J. Yosinski. Deep generative stochastic networks trainable by backprop. In *Proc. of the ICML*, 2014.

[4] J. Clune and H. Lipson. Evolving three-dimensional objects with a generative encoding inspired by developmental biology. In *Proc. of the European Conference on Artificial Life*, pages 144–148, 2011.

[5] G. Cuccu and F. Gomez. When novelty is not enough. In *Applications of Evolutionary Computation*. 2011.

[6] A. Cully, J. Clune, and J.-B. Mouret. Robots that can adapt like natural animals. *arXiv preprint arXiv:1407.3501*, 2014.

[7] J. Deng et al. Imagenet: A large-scale hierarchical image database. In *Conference on Computer Vision and Pattern Recognition*, pages 248–255. IEEE, 2009.

[8] G. E. Hinton and R. R. Salakhutdinov. Reducing the dimensionality of data with neural networks. *Science*, 2006.

[9] Y. Jia et al. Caffe: Convolutional architecture for fast feature embedding. In *Proc. of the International Conference on Multimedia*, pages 675–678, 2014.

[10] A. Karpathy. What I learned from competing against a convnet on ImageNet. http://goo.gl/iqCbC0, 2014.

[11] M. Keane et al. *Genetic programming IV: Routine human-competitive machine intelligence.* 2006.

[12] A. Krizhevsky, I. Sutskever, and G. E. Hinton. Imagenet classification with deep convolutional neural networks. In *Advances in neural information processing systems*, pages 1097–1105, 2012.

[13] J. Lehman and K. O. Stanley. Exploiting open-endedness to solve problems through the search for novelty. In *ALIFE*, pages 329–336, 2008.

[14] J. Lehman and K. O. Stanley. Abandoning objectives: Evolution through the search for novelty alone. *Evolutionary computation*, 19(2):189–223, 2011.

[15] J. Lehman and K. O. Stanley. Novelty search and the problem with objectives. In *Genetic Programming Theory and Practice IX*, pages 37–56. Springer, 2011.

[16] J. Li, J. Storie, and J. Clune. Encouraging creative thinking in robots improves their ability to solve challenging problems. *Algorithms*, 13:14.

[17] A. Liapis, H. P. Martınez, J. Togelius, and G. N. Yannakakis. Transforming exploratory creativity with delenox. In *Proc. of the Fourth International Conference on Computational Creativity*, 2013.

[18] J.-B. Mouret. Novelty-based multiobjectivization. In *New Horizons in Evolutionary Robotics*. Springer, 2011.

[19] J.-B. Mouret and J. Clune. Illuminating search spaces by mapping elites. *arXiv preprint*, 2015.

[20] J.-B. Mouret and S. Doncieux. Sferes v2: Evolvin'in the multi-core world. In *Congress on Evolutionary Computation*, pages 1–8, 2010.

[21] A. Nguyen, J. Yosinski, and J. Clune. Deep neural networks are easily fooled: High confidence predictions for unrecognizable images. In *Proc. of the Conference on Computer Vision and Pattern Recognition*, 2015.

[22] O. Russakovsky et al. Imagenet large scale visual recognition challenge. *arXiv:1409.0575*, 2014.

[23] J. Schmidhuber. Developmental robotics, optimal artificial curiosity, creativity, music, and the fine arts. *Connection Science*, 18(2):173–187, 2006.

[24] J. Secretan et al. Picbreeder: A case study in collaborative evolutionary exploration of design space. *Evolutionary Computation*, 19(3):373–403, 2011.

[25] K. Stanley and J. Lehman. *Why Greatness Cannot Be Planned: The Myth of the Objective.* Springer, 2015.

[26] K. Stanley and R. Miikkulainen. Evolving neural networks through augmenting topologies. *Evolutionary computation*, 10(2):99–127, 2002.

[27] K. O. Stanley. Compositional pattern producing networks: A novel abstraction of development. *Genetic programming and evolvable machines*, 2007.

[28] C. Szegedy et al. Going deeper with convolutions. *arXiv preprint arXiv:1409.4842*, 2014.

[29] B. G. Woolley and K. O. Stanley. On the deleterious effects of a priori objectives on evolution and representation. In *Proc. Genetic & Evolutionary Computation Conf.*, 2011.

Confronting the Challenge of Quality Diversity

Justin K. Pugh, L. B. Soros, Paul A. Szerlip, and Kenneth O. Stanley
Department of EECS, Computer Science Division
University of Central Florida
Orlando, FL 32816 USA
{ jpugh, lsoros, pszerlip, kstanley } @eecs.ucf.edu

ABSTRACT

In contrast to the conventional role of evolution in evolutionary computation (EC) as an optimization algorithm, a new class of evolutionary algorithms has emerged in recent years that instead aim to accumulate as diverse a collection of discoveries as possible, yet where each variant in the collection is as fit as it can be. Often applied in both neuroevolution and morphological evolution, these new *quality diversity* (QD) algorithms are particularly well-suited to evolution's inherent strengths, thereby offering a promising niche for EC within the broader field of machine learning. However, because QD algorithms are so new, until now no comprehensive study has yet attempted to systematically elucidate their relative strengths and weaknesses under different conditions. Taking a first step in this direction, this paper introduces a new benchmark domain designed specifically to compare and contrast QD algorithms. It then shows how the degree of alignment between the measure of quality and the behavior characterization (which is an essential component of all QD algorithms to date) impacts the ultimate performance of different such algorithms. The hope is that this initial study will help to stimulate interest in QD and begin to unify the disparate ideas in the area.

Categories and Subject Descriptors:
I.2.6 [**Artificial Intelligence**]: Learning;
I.2.6 [**Software Engineering**]: Metrics—*complexity measures, performance measures*

General Terms: Algorithms

Keywords: novelty search; non-objective search; quality diversity; neuroevolution

1. INTRODUCTION

In evolutionary computation (EC), evolution has conventionally played the role of an optimization algorithm, wherein the performance of the algorithm is judged by how quickly and how close it comes to reaching an objective [6]. The idea that evolution can act as an efficient objective optimizer is inspired by the feats of evolution in nature, where it appears to have optimized a myriad of complex yet highly functional forms. While some niche areas of EC deviate from this objective-driven paradigm (such as open-ended evolution in artificial life [2, 21, 23]), it has nevertheless broadly encompassed even newer research areas such as generative and developmental systems (GDS [25]) and neuroevolution [8].

One potential downside of this emphasis on objective optimization is that it has pitted EC as a direct competitor to virtually the entire field of machine learning, which similarly focuses largely on the problem of efficient optimization [1, 16]. While one consequence of this similar emphasis is a view among some in machine learning that EC is an inferior optimization algorithm, even if that view is arguably uninformed, it still leaves evolution in the position of seemingly "just another optimization algorithm."

Yet evolution in nature is clearly not only about optimization. It is notable not for solving one particular problem, but *many* problems, and in uncountably diverse ways. In this sense, evolution is not a mere alternative to (for example) backpropagation [22] or support vector machines [3], which are not designed to generate a vast diversity of high-quality solutions. (As explained later, this kind of evolutionary diversity is also not the same conceptually as a multi-objective Pareto front [7] either.) This incongruity between EC in practice and its natural inspiration suggests a misalignment between the conventional application of EC and its full potential as a genuinely unique paradigm for search that can separate it from much of machine learning.

Hints of this broader interpretation of evolution within EC have begun to emerge with non-objective algorithms like novelty search (NS) [12, 14], which searches for novelty without an explicit objective. NS has in turn inspired a succession of variant algorithms that elaborate on the idea of a search through novelty alone [9, 13, 18, 19]. Yet even while this new generation of evolutionary algorithms begins to deviate from the traditional objective paradigm, such algorithms are still predominantly *evaluated* based on their ability to reach a particular objective [14, 19]. That is, while they may not function internally through the compass of the objective, *externally* they are often still treated merely as alternatives to objective-driven optimization algorithms.

However, some researchers have begun to take non-objective search in a different direction. They have instead embraced the potential for evolution to collect *quality diversity* (QD) [4, 5, 11, 17, 27], which means searching for as many possible variations (with respect to a chosen characterization)

GECCO '15, July 11–15, 2015, Madrid, Spain
 ISBN 978-1-4503-3472-3/15/07...$15.00
DOI: http://dx.doi.org/10.1145/2739480.2754664

as possible, but where each such variation is as good as it can possibly be (with respect to a separate measure of quality). QD is particularly intriguing as an application of EC because it is explicitly *not* what most algorithms in machine learning are suited to achieving, yet nevertheless well-aligned with the achievements of evolution in nature. In this way QD is an opportunity for EC to shine as an essential option for the kinds of problems that require accumulating a multitude of diverse yet high-quality alternatives.

In this spirit, the aim of this paper is to begin to introduce a framework for understanding and relating QD algorithms. While the literature analyzing the nuances of algorithms in EC and elsewhere for the purpose of optimization is vast, almost no studies to date investigate the tradeoffs among different approaches to QD. This paper begins such an enterprise by introducing a domain designed explicitly to analyze approaches to QD in the context of neuroevolution, and then compares several leading algorithms in that new framework, including one new variant algorithm called *MAP-Elites+Novelty*, elaborated from the original MAP-Elites algorithm [5, 17]. The result is fresh insight into the consequences for different approaches to QD of varying the degree of alignment of the behavior characterization (which is essential to all such algorithms so far) with the notion of *quality* in the domain: some algorithms perform best when such alignment is high, while others excel without it. Because QD is such a promising new direction for EC with many possible future applications (as discussed in the next section), this initial investigation of algorithms in this area helps to lay the groundwork for an emerging new field.

2. BACKGROUND

Early hints of a science of QD within EC first appeared in the 1990s with work on multimodal function optimization (MMFO); a good review is provided by Mahfoud [15]. MMFO aims to discover as many high-scoring (though not necessarily global) optima within a fitness landscape as possible. While MMFO spawned a number of important diversity-preservation mechanisms (mainly focusing on genetic diversity), a shift more than ten years later towards methods focused on *behavioral diversity* [12, 14, 18, 19] revived interest in the potential for diversity to transform the application of EC. This new wave of algorithms, starting with novelty search [12], differed from the older work on MMFO in particular in its focus on discovering the full spectrum of possible behaviors within a particular domain, often represented by evolved neural networks. While much work in this area centered on the possibility that a side effect of seeking behavioral diversity is sometimes the discovery of very high performers, another view that emerged is that the diversity of discoveries *itself* is a desirable byproduct.

Unlike in multi-objective optimization [7], where the aim is to collect a Pareto front of performance trade-offs, these diversity-collecting algorithms focus instead on sampling the full behavior space as comprehensively as possible without concern for objective performance. In some cases a collection of diverse behaviors on its own offers direct practical value; for example the recent divergent discriminative feature accumulation (DDFA) algorithm [28] accumulates a vast collection of diverse feature detectors that are then aggregated into a neural network for later training in classification problems.

However, for many applications a collection of diverse behaviors on its own is not enough because the ideal outcome would be that each variant is not only unique but also as high-performing as it can be. For example, merely discovering that self-ambulating pogo sticks exist in the morphology and behavior space of virtual creatures is not as good as discovering the *best possible* self-ambulating pogo sticks, in addition to the best possible behaviors of all the other viable morphologies that exist [11]. Note that this notion of QD is not the same as finding the highest-fitness subset of all conceivable creatures because even the very best pogo stick may have significantly *lower* fitness than e.g. quadrupeds and bipeds. However, the point is that we still want to find that pogo stick and see how well it can do. The diversity components in QD also still differ from the separate objectives in multi-objective optimization because individual diversity components include no intrinsic ranking – for example, all morphologies in the space of creatures are equally of interest as long as they can walk at all.

To empower evolution to collect QD, a new breed of algorithms have appeared in recent years that augment algorithms like novelty search to push each unique variant towards its best possible performance, opening up new applications. For example, Lehman and Stanley [11] introduced the novelty search with local competition (NSLC) algorithm to evolve a wide diversity of successful ambulating creatures in a single run. Similarly, Szerlip and Stanley [27] collect a diversity of high-performing behaviors in a Sodarace-inspired two-dimensional creature domain. In an intriguing foreshadowing of future applications, Cully and Mouret [4] show that QD once collected can be aggregated into a useful *behavioral repertoire*, in this case a collection of diverse robot motion skills.

Cully et al. [5] later introduced an alternative algorithm for collecting QD called MAP-Elites, which showcased yet another intriguing application of behavioral diversity: a collection of ambulation strategies becomes a source of means to alter ambulation in the event of damage. Yet another application of QD is demonstrated by Nguyen et al. [20], who generate with MAP-Elites a diverse collection of high-quality spoof images that fool deep networks. This breadth of early applications of such QD algorithms suggests an important new research area with many applications yet to be realized.

The aim of this paper is to begin to understand the factors that contribute to successfully collecting QD under different conditions. A common component of all modern QD algorithms is the *behavior characterization* (BC), which formalizes the behavior of a candidate individual in the population and is used to determine its eligibility for selection [5, 11]. However, different approaches to QD treat the BC in different ways, and the consequences of these choices are currently poorly understood. For example, while novelty favors individuals with the most novel BC, MAP-Elites discretizes the behavior space into unique bins from which (when occupied) selection is equally probable. This paper focuses in particular on the trade-offs created by such differing treatments and begins to explore the possibility of hybridizations that may combine the benefits of different approaches.

3. EXPERIMENT

To effectively tease out the differences between competing quality diversity (QD) algorithms, a test domain is needed with both (1) a concrete measure of quality, and (2) a diversity of legitimate solutions. No standard such benchmark domain yet exists in the area of QD, and thus one of the contributions of this paper is to propose one suited specifically to the concerns of QD.

The first experiments with novelty search [12, 14] introduced a domain called *HardMaze* that has since become popular within the literature because of its explicit visual depiction of deception within a fitness landscape. The catch in HardMaze is that for a robot to navigate to the goal point of the maze it is necessary first to navigate *away* from the goal multiple times along the path. Additionally, there is an easily-reachable cul-de-sac that is close to the goal in terms of Euclidean distance but is actually farther away from the goal in terms of distance along the correct path. Importantly, searching for behavioral novelty alone (i.e. novelty search) in the HardMaze solves the maze much faster than a conventional objective-based search wherein fitness is the Euclidean distance to the goal point at the end of a trial (which, unlike novelty search, is easily drawn into the cul-de-sac). Thus, in HardMaze, Euclidean distance serves as a concrete measure of quality. However, HardMaze only contains *one* correct path through the maze (i.e. the diversity of legitimate solutions is limited), diminishing its utility for testing QD algorithms that seek many solutions.

Instead of HardMaze, in this paper, we augment the idea of a maze navigation domain that uses Euclidean distance as a concrete measure of quality to also encompass a diversity of possible solutions to the maze. This new domain, QD-Maze (figure 1), still contains several deceptive traps (albeit less difficult than those in HardMaze: all algorithms tend to find at least one solution) while also allowing many possible "correct paths" to the goal, thus allowing an explicit diversity of paths to the goal.

Aside from the change in map configuration, the setup for QD-Maze is identical to HardMaze. A robot agent is given a fixed time to move around the maze before the trial ends and the agent's *quality* is scored according to the Euclidean distance between its final position and the goal point (the score is maximum if the goal point is reached). Reaching the goal point prematurely ends the trial. Agents are equipped with a set of six rangefinders, five of which are equally spaced across the front-facing 180 degrees and the sixth facing the rear. Additionally, four pie slice sensors (front, right, rear, and left -facing) detect the direction of the goal by activating the pie slice facing the goal with maximal value. In all experiments in this paper, agents are driven by evolved neural networks.

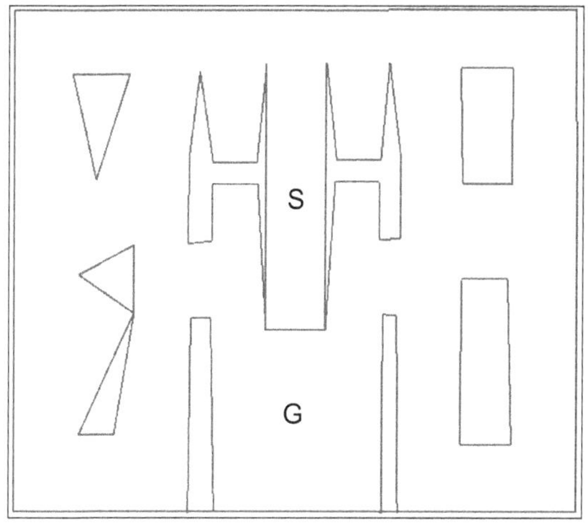

Figure 1: Quality diversity maze (QD-Maze). Individuals start at the point S and the highest quality solutions navigate to point G. While the maze is deceptive enough to challenge objective-based algorithms, it also contains a variety of solutions and thus serves as a benchmark for combining quality with diversity.

3.1 Behavior Characterizations (BCs)

The nature of the "diversity of solutions" available for discovery within the search depends heavily on how behaviors are characterized. In the original HardMaze experiments [12], agent behaviors are characterized according to their final position at the end of the trial (**EndpointBC**). This BC is notable for its strong alignment with the implicit objective of a maze. In other words, the neighborhood of behaviors around any particular trajectory endpoint generally share a similar level of quality, thereby aligning behavior with a notion of quality. Under the pressure of a strongly-aligned BC, searching for novelty *alone* may often be enough to find not only diversity, but also high-quality solutions to the domain, without even the need to explicitly optimize each behavioral neighborhood independently. To investigate the effect on different approaches to QD of varying the degree of the BC's alignment with the objective, three alternative BCs are also tested, each less aligned than the previous: FullTrajectoryBC, HalfTrajectoryBC, and DirectionBC.

Under **FullTrajectoryBC**, the agent's position is sampled at three points throughout its trial: one-third, two-thirds, and at the end of the trial, and all three (x, y) points are concatenated together to form the six-dimensional BC vector. This BC is less strongly aligned with the notion of quality than EndpointBC because only the final sampled point has a strong correlation to the final score within the domain. Even less aligned again is **HalfTrajectoryBC**, wherein the agent's position is sampled at three points throughout *only the first half* of its trial. The second half of the trial leaves sufficient time for an agent to reach the goal from any location within the maze, rendering HalfTrajectoryBC even less aligned with the objective than FullTrajectoryBC. Highlighting this point, in theory, every behavior under HalfTrajectoryBC can potentially achieve a maximum quality score (i.e. ultimately solving the maze).

The final and least-aligned BC, **DirectionBC**, samples the direction the robot is facing on each tick (north, east, south, or west) and divides the duration of the trial into five equal-length time slices. The BC then consists of five dimensions, each corresponding to the direction that the agent was facing most often during each of the five time slices (north = 0.125, east = 0.375, south = 0.625, west = 0.875). This characterization is almost completely agnostic to the notion of quality because the goal point of the maze can be approached from any direction and the agent is free to wander around the maze and face any direction at any time. Under DirectionBC, every possible behavior in the behavior space can potentially achieve a maximum score on the objective of reaching the goal and there is little to no correlation between quality and behavioral neighborhoods.

3.2 QD Algorithms

A variety of algorithms can collect QD in a given domain, some designed explicitly to do so and some more as a side effect. In this paper, we compare the performance of three existing algorithms (novelty search, novelty search with local competition, and MAP-Elites), the latter two designed explicitly for QD, and a new variant of MAP-Elites (MAP-Elites+Novelty). A conventional fitness-based search (which is not expected to excel at QD) also serves as a baseline for performance.

To normalize comparisons across the algorithms as much as possible, the SharpNEAT [10] distribution of the NEAT algorithm [24] serves as the underlying neuroevolution platform for all of them. Therefore, the neural networks are able to evolve increasing complexity, a central feature of NEAT. However, except in the pure fitness-driven baseline runs, to minimize potentially confounding factors, the conventional genetic diversity component of NEAT (also called *speciation*) is excluded. That way, the diversity facet of QD is exclusively focused on *behavior*, which is the focus of the majority of recent innovation in non-objective search algorithms and has exhibited significantly more impact on performance in such algorithms than genetic diversity [19]. Furthermore, because of preliminary experimental evidence that generational evolution can lead to instability or "jumping around the behavior space" in non-objective search populations, all algorithms are run in *steady state* mode, which means that a subset of the population (in this case 32 individuals evaluated in parallel) is replaced at a time instead of a whole generation (which is similar to the rtNEAT [26] variant of NEAT). In total five algorithms are compared:

The classic **novelty search (NS)** [12, 14] algorithm *only* searches for behavioral diversity with no notion of quality. It rewards behaviors that are maximally distant from previously discovered behaviors. However, if the BC is aligned with a notion of quality, then it is possible that NS without any special augmentation can itself collect QD effectively, a possibility thereby investigated in this experiment.

NS is augmented to explicitly seek QD in the **novelty search plus local competition (NSLC)** [11, 27] algorithm. In this variant, a multi-objective formulation implemented through NSGA-II [7] casts classic novelty as one objective and *local competition* (LC), which means a quality rank relative only to those with a *similar* BC, as another. The LC component encourages unique behaviors to improve in quality within their local behavioral neighborhoods, thereby aligning the search explicitly with the notion of QD. The LC approach contrasts with the idea of combining novelty with a *global competition* objective (NSGC), which has been previously shown less effective than NSLC for discovering a diversity of solutions within a search space [11] because global competition explicitly prunes out diversity, and is therefore not considered in this paper.

Unlike NS and NSLC, the recent **MAP-Elites (ME)** algorithm [5, 17, 20] divides the behavior space of the BC into discrete bins. Each bin then remembers the fittest (elite) genome ever to occupy it, and only one genome occupies any given bin at one time. Thus the elites within each bin capture the notion of quality and the whole set of bins capture the notion of diversity. In the classic formulation of ME, selection is very simple: the chance of producing an offspring is equal for each filled bin. Thus search effort tends to be spread uniformly across the known behavior space (rather than explicitly biased by novelty). One technical limitation of ME is that the BC must be constrained to a low number of dimensions because the total number of bins grows exponentially with BC dimensionality; for this reason and to keep the comparisons fair, none of the BCs in this paper includes more than six dimensions.

While the simplicity of selection in ME is appealing, its effect is that evolution is more likely to concentrate resources in regions of the behavior space already filled (i.e. because that is where most of the bins are occupied). This approach proved effective in ME applications so far, but it is easy to augment ME with pressure to concentrate effort on more novel regions by adding novelty pressure. In this **MAP-Elites+Novelty (ME-Nov)** variant tested for the first time here, the probability of selecting an occupied bin for reproduction is proportional to its novelty, creating a stronger pressure towards diversity than in the original ME. However, once all the bins are filled in ME-Nov, it collapses back to an approximation of regular ME. The question is whether the added initial pressure towards novelty might enhance ME's drive towards QD. Also, while ME has effectively filled most bins in experiments published so far [5, 20], in future domains in which some bins require very advanced solutions and therefore are unlikely all to be filled, the additional novelty pressure in ME-Nov could prove instrumental in covering as much of the space as possible.

Finally, a regular **fitness-based search (fitness)** (implemented as NEAT [24]) simply searches for objectively superior performance (though with NEAT's conventional genetic speciation fitness-sharing mechanism to give it at least some hope of maintaining diversity). This variant, which is susceptible to the trap of deception [14] and has no behavioral diversity mechanism, helps to highlight the need for specialized approaches to the problem of QD.

3.3 MAP-Elites as a QD assessment mechanism

To compare the ability of competing QD algorithms to collect quality diversity, a quantitative measure of quality diversity is needed. Interestingly, the MAP-Elites style of discretized behavior space can be collected for *all* variant algorithms, even those that are not MAP-Elites. As long as there are not too many dimensions in the BC (as is true in BCs in this paper), the best behavior found for every bin in the behavior space (regardless of through which method it was found) can simply be stored for later analysis.

For this purpose, for each BC, the behavior space is discretized into an appropriately small number of bins (i.e. small enough that MAP-Elites itself can be run efficiently and with a breeding pool of the same order of magnitude as the size of the breeding population in the NS, NSLC, and fitness-based algorithmic treatments): 900 bins for EndpointBC, 729 for FullTrajectoryBC and HalfTrajectoryBC, and 1,024 for DirectionBC. For each algorithmic treatment, all individuals are checked for eligibility in this MAP-Elites-style grid as they are evaluated. The performance (QD score) of each algorithm at any given point during the run is then measured as *the total fitness across all filled grid bins within the QD collection grid* (where higher fitness or quality means a final robot position closer to the goal). Throughout a run, algorithms therefore improve their QD score by either (1) discovering higher quality solutions for existing bins (increasing quality) or (2) discovering more bins (increasing diversity). To achieve the highest QD scores (which is possible in this domain), an algorithm must therefore excel with respect to both quality and diversity.

3.4 Experimental setup

Each of the methods (NS, NSLC, ME, ME-Nov, fitness) was combined with each of the behavior characterizations (EndpointBC, FullTrajectoryBC, HalfTrajectoryBC, DirectionBC) to comprehensively test the effects of both factors on QD. Except for the DirectionBC variants, each combination was evaluated over 20 runs capped at 250,000 evaluations. Because the DirectionBC variants converge to stable scores significantly more slowly (collecting QD across such a poorly-aligned BC is harder), they were capped at 750,000 evaluations. The population size was 500 for NS, NSLC, and fitness; NS and NSLC also keep an associated novelty archive of maximum size 2,500, after which the least novel is removed when a new entry is added. For MAP-Elites, as is standard the population at any given time was the size of the number of occupied bins. To enable parallel evaluation, steady state evolution is implemented in batches of 32 offspring at one time. Following the settings in the original novelty search experiments [14], the probabilities for mutating connections was 60%, for adding connections was 10%, and for adding neurons was 0.5%. Evolved networks are constrained to be strictly feedforward. All other settings follow standard SharpNEAT 1.0 defaults [10]. Source code for the entire experimental setup is available at http://eplex.cs.ucf.edu/uncategorised/software#QD

Performance for each method and BC combination was measured according to the total fitness across all filled grid bins (Section 3.3). Results were averaged across twenty runs for each of the 20 method-BC combinations (a total of 400 separate runs were performed). Additionally, pairwise comparisons were performed after every 160 evaluations to determine when exactly there are significant differences between methods. Tukey's test (with $p < 0.05$) was used to establish significance instead of the Student's t-test to account for the statistical problem of multiple pairwise comparisons.

4. RESULTS

Figures 2 through 5 show for each BC the total quality diversity (QD) discovered so far by each method over the course of 20 averaged runs for each method. Higher QD is better. Fitness runs, which are included only as a baseline, are unsurprisingly significantly below all other runs. Among the other four methods, a yellow bar at the top of each graph highlights the period during which significant differences are observed between the best and worst performing methods among those four. Note that in terms of both QD and significance testing, numerical comparisons are only meaningful between methods within the *same BC* because the total possible QD score depends on the BC. The main result is that the ranking of methods depends on the alignment of the BC with the notion of quality, suggesting that choosing a QD method for a particular problem can potentially become a principled decision in the future, though some methods are more generally robust across different BCs than others.

With the EndpointBC (figure 2), which is highly aligned with the notion of quality (i.e. closeness to the endpoint), the novelty search-based methods (NS and NSLC) significantly outperform all other methods for most of the run, with NS ending significantly (though only slightly) above NSLC. ME-Nov also significantly outperforms original ME, though is still significantly below NS and NSLC. (It is important to note that the differences between the methods

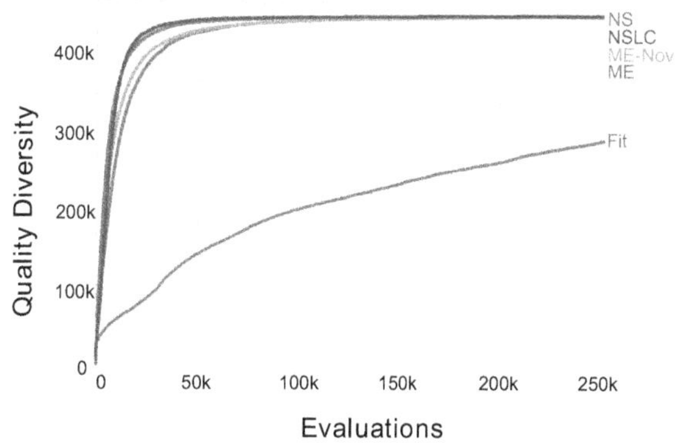

Figure 2: EndpointBC (very high alignment). In this performance comparison and others in this paper, the average QD (taken over 20 runs) for each variant method is shown across a run. The yellow strip at the top indicates the period during which there is a significant difference at least between the top and bottom method (exlcuding fitness, which is always significantly worse than all other methods). The method labels are color coded to match with their respective curves and are shown from top to bottom in the their rank order during the period of significance. Note that because of the large QD scale, sometimes significant differences exist even when not visually apparent. For EndpointBC, NS performs best, followed by NSLC.

as they converge near the end of the run can be difficult to perceive in the figures, but the QD scale is actually vast, so significant difference actually do persist in some cases where it is difficult to perceive visually.) The fact that novelty alone (NS) does so well highlights the fact that when the BC is aligned with fitness, additional sophisticated machinery designed to simultaneously reward quality and diversity is potentially unnecessary (perhaps depending on the difficulty of the domain), and in such situations novelty alone becomes a powerful force for QD.

However, as the alignment of the BC with quality reduces, the story changes. In the FullTrajectoryBC (figure 3), which is still fairly aligned with the notion of quality (i.e. because trajectories that lead to the goal are high quality), NS, NSLC, and ME-Nov are tied (i.e. not significantly different) throughout most of the run. For this BC, only ME performs significantly below the other methods. Thus NS retains its utility as a top choice, but no longer holds an advantage over NSLC or ME-Nov. ME is not well suited to BCs with high alignment because it is agnostic with respect to novelty, leading to a relative delay compared to novelty-driven approaches (including ME-Nov) in exploiting promising areas of behavior space.

The HalfTrajectoryBC (figure 4) aligns with quality even less, which leads to an interesting phenomenon seen only with this BC: After a very brief period at the start of the run, all methods effectively perform the same (although ME is still a bit below, the difference is not significant). In effect, HalfTrajectoryBC hits just the right level of misalignment that the advantages and disadvantages of respective methods become a wash. Surprisingly, even NS alone remains competitive, despite its lack of an explicit quality component.

Finally, DirectionBC (figure 5), which tracks facing di-

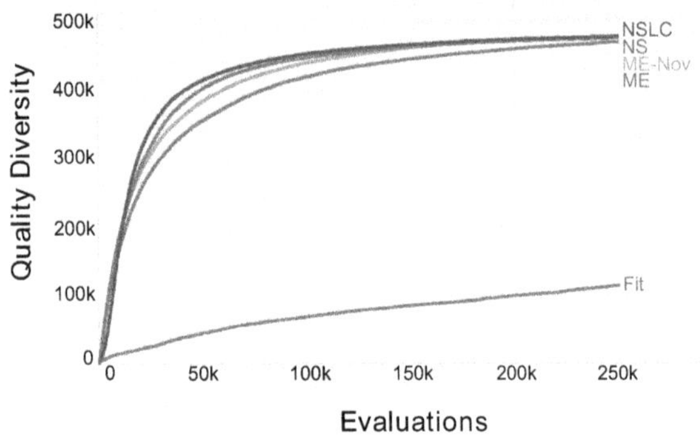

Figure 3: FullTrajectoryBC (high alignment). For this BC, which is slightly less aligned with quality than EndpointBC, NS, NSLC, and ME-Nov are effectively tied, with ME significantly behind.

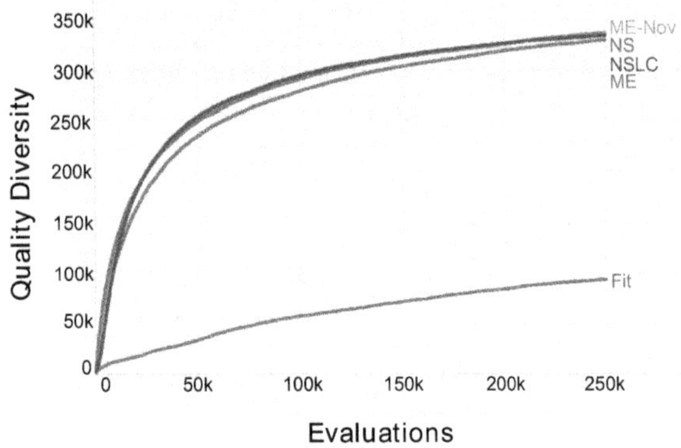

Figure 4: HalfTrajectoryBC (modest alignment). All the methods except fitness are tied for the vast majority of the run for this BC, which is even less aligned than FullTrajectoryBC.

rection only, aligns least with quality because it is largely detached from trajectory. For example, agents can arbitrarily spin around whenever they want without impacting their trajectory. Note that such low alignment is not unprecedented in serious applications. For example, an algorithm might search for diversity in terms of the height and mass of virtual creatures, which is hardly predictive of their quality as walkers [11]. The results with DirectionBC suggest that such a complete loss of alignment can significantly upend the utility of NS as a QD mechanism. In this scenario, NS drops to the bottom of the ranking, performing significantly below other approaches (each of which have quality-seeking components). Furthermore, while NSLC exceeds NS significantly (showing that the LC component of NSLC can indeed provide an advantage in QD), both ME and ME-Nov significantly outperform NSLC. In fact, ME alone effectively ties with ME-Nov, suggesting that in cases of high misalignment, the advantage of the novelty pressure is eclipsed by the advantage of a strong elitist mechanism that pushes towards higher quality.

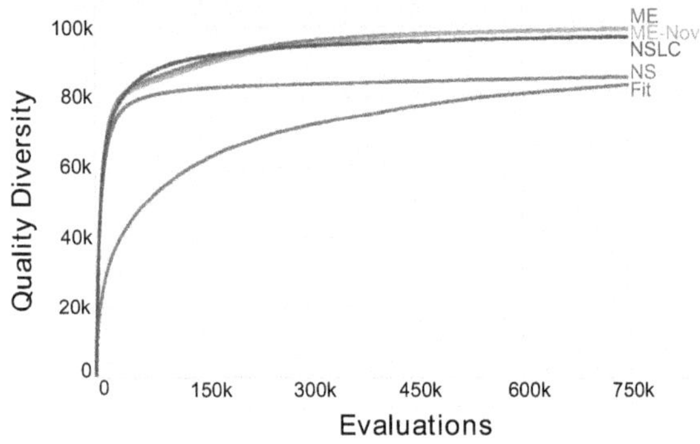

Figure 5: DirectionBC (low alignment). With an almost complete lack of alignment in this BC, ME and ME-Nov tie for first place, and NS trails far behind.

4.1 Visualizing Behavior Spaces

Recall that for all variant search algorithms, the highest-performing genomes are collected in a discretized behavior space "grid" (inspired by the MAP-Elites grid). Collecting elite behaviors in this way enables a convenient visualization of each algorithm's ability to collect QD within the domain. The visualization technique, proposed by Cully et al. [5], uses two dimensions to display an entire behavior space grid by nesting two-dimensional grids within other two-dimensional grids, each two-dimensional grid representing two dimensions of the behavior space. As an example, figures 6 through 8 depict the final state of the QD collection grid at the end of one typical run of Fitness, ME, and NS in the FullTrajectoryBC. These visualizations reveal that: (1) Fitness (figure 6) and MAP-Elites (figure 7) exhibit a diminished ability to fill the grid for this BC (corresponding to a diminished pressure towards diversity) while the highest performing algorithm (on FullTrajectoryBC), NS (figure 8), is able to fill the grid almost entirely after 250,000 evaluations. The visualizations also expose (2) the relatively strong alignment of the behavior space with the fitness measure through the smooth gradient in the outer two dimensions from low fitness at the top of the grid towards high fitness at the bottom-middle of the grid.

This paper is also accompanied by a website where sample interactive behavior space visualizations (including the ability to browse through the discovered behaviors within each bin) are available for all 20 method-BC combinations (including the three shown here):
http://eplex.cs.ucf.edu/QD/GECCO-15/compare.html

5. DISCUSSION

The main insight to emerge from the experiment concerns the two key forces operating in QD algorithms: the push for novelty and the push for quality. If the BC, which supplies the main push for novelty, is sufficiently aligned with a notion of quality, then novelty-based approaches are most effectively empowered. In contrast, if the BC is orthogonal to a notion of quality, a strong push for quality (as in the elitism of ME) becomes the more instrumental factor in QD performance. The apparent ability under some BCs for NS *alone* to succeed, even without any explicit push for quality, and ME *alone* in other BCs to succeed without any explicit

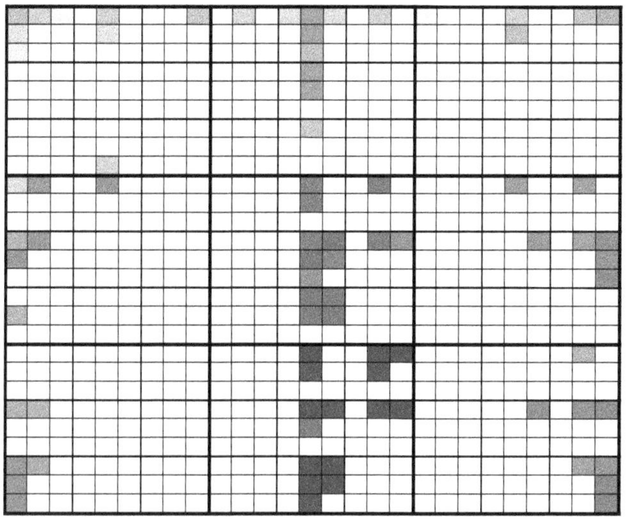

Figure 6: Fitness in the FullTrajectoryBC. In this example grid, the six-dimensional behavior space (FullTrajectoryBC) (discretized into three bins per dimension for a total of 729 bins) is visually depicted as a series of nested two-dimensional grids (each of which are 3×3). The color of each grid box corresponds to the quality of the solution found by the search algorithm after 250,000 evaluations: yellow corresponds to low quality, dark red to high quality, and white to unfilled bins. Fitness finds very few of the possible behaviors for this BC.

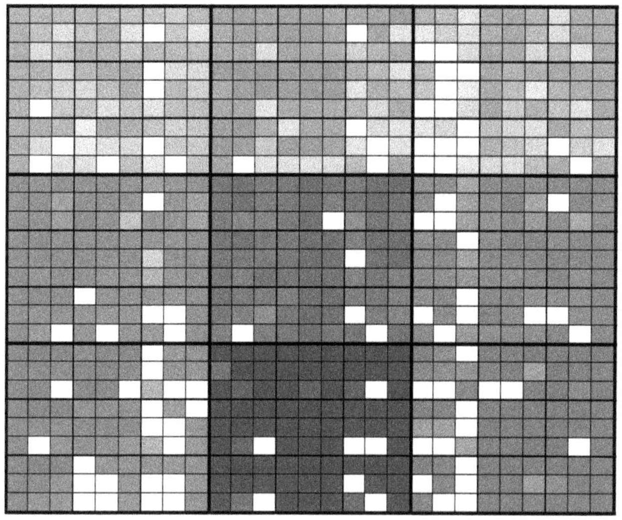

Figure 7: MAP-Elites in the FullTrajectoryBC. Compared to Fitness (figure 6), ME discovers far more QD under FullTrajectoryBC. Some bins remain unfilled (white), corresponding to the lack of pressure towards diversity within the ME algorithm.

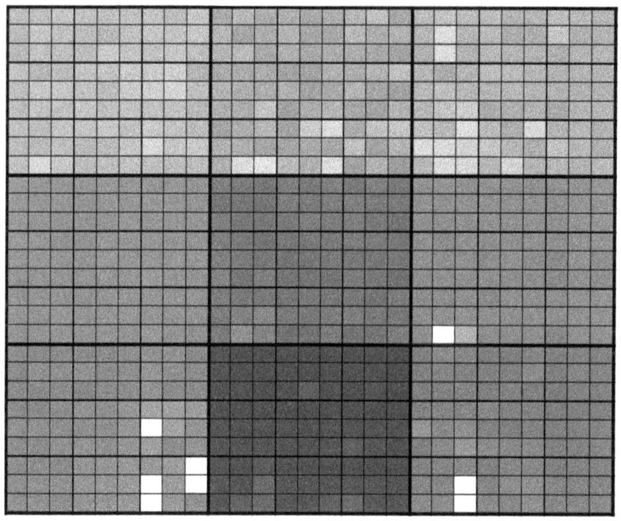

Figure 8: Novelty Search in the FullTrajectoryBC. Of the five compared algorithms, NS performs the best under the FullTrajectoryBC (featuring relatively high alignment between the BC and the objective) because it focuses exclusively on pursuing diversity. This conclusion is supported in the QD collection grid by almost all bins being filled (i.e. non-white).

push for novelty, highlights just how profoundly this apparent principle applies. Yet it also appears that augmenting these most simple methods with a component to cover what they lack, e.g. augmenting NS with LC and ME with novelty, carries generally little risk. In fact, in some cases it improves their results, especially when they are being applied in their respectively less ideal alignment circumstances, hinting that aiming for "best of both worlds" is not unrealistic and may even be attainable for future QD algorithms yet unrealized.

However, the results in this initial study should be qualified by the observation that the QD-Maze domain is relatively easy; all methods except for fitness eventually find diverse solutions. Because more ambitious applications of QD in the future are likely significantly more challenging (imagine e.g. much more challenging parallel mazes), a natural question is whether the results here will extend to future experiments. While of course further empirical research is necessary and this study is only a first step, there is still good reason to believe that the results reported here are at least somewhat general: First, even in much harder domains, as the length of runs approaches infinity, all methods are likely eventually to find most QD. The experiment here is simply shorter because the domain is less difficult. Yet the stratification of different methods observed during the course of these short runs can conceivably emerge similarly in more challenging domains, though simply over longer timescales. Second, the fact that the ranking of methods in QD-Mazes matches well our expectations for each method (i.e. that those more reliant on a separate measure of quality do better when the BC is poorly aligned with fitness) further supports the credibility of the results.

Of course, there are some other considerations outside QD performance alone that may arise in specific domains. For example, because it divides behavior space into discrete bins, ME (and ME-Nov) becomes increasingly difficult to apply to higher-dimensional BCs, an issue not present for NS or NSLC. Yet beyond its use as a *method*, the ME grid also turns out an excellent mechanism for collecting and measuring QD results, even for methods that are not ME. We anticipate that the results of future QD algorithms even unrelated to ME will ultimately often be visualized and quantified by placing them within in a classic ME grid.

6. CONCLUSION

The aim of this paper was to help to unify the emerging *quality diversity* (QD) research area by beginning to introduce benchmarks and principles for analyzing and contrasting methods in the area. For this purpose a new domain with many parallel solutions called the QD-Maze was introduced, and several QD methods (including a new variant called MAP-Elites+Novelty) were compared under different behavior characterizations in QD-Maze. The results begin to establish initial principles for understanding QD, namely that the alignment of the behavior characterization with the notion of quality significantly influences which QD methods will be most effective in a particular setup. This insight gives hope that an even broader understanding of QD can be reached in the future, thereby helping to expand the reach and impact of evolutionary computation.

Acknowledgments

This work was supported by the National Science Foundation under grant no. IIS-1421925. Any opinions, findings, and conclusions or recommendations expressed in this material are those of the authors and do not necessarily reflect the views of the National Science Foundation.

References

[1] C. M. Bishop. *Pattern Recognition and Machine Learning*, volume 1. Springer, New York, NY, 2006.

[2] A. Channon. Improving and still passing the alife test: Component-normalised activity statistics classify evolution in geb as unbounded. *Artificial Life*, 8: 173–181, 2003.

[3] C. Cortes and V. Vapnik. Support-vector networks. *Machine Learning*, 20(3):273–297, 1995.

[4] A. Cully and J.-B. Mouret. Behavioral repertoire learning in robotics. In *Proc. of the 15th Annual Conf. on Genetic and Evolutionary Computation (GECCO '13)*, pages 175–182, New York, NY, USA, 2013. ACM.

[5] A. Cully, D. Tarapore, J. Clune, and J.-B. Mouret. Robots that can adapt like natural animals. *arXiv preprint*, abs/1407.3501, 2014.

[6] K. A. De Jong. *Evolutionary Computation: A Unified Perspective.* MIT Press, Cambridge, MA, 2002.

[7] K. Deb, A. Pratap, S. Agarwal, and T. Meyarivan. A fast and elitist multiobjective genetic algorithm: NSGA-II. *IEEE Transactions on Evolutionary Computation*, 6(2):182–197, 2002.

[8] D. Floreano, P. Dürr, and C. Mattiussi. Neuroevolution: From architectures to learning. *Evolutionary Intelligence*, 1:47–62, 2008.

[9] J. Gomes and A. L. Christensen. Generic behaviour similarity measures for evolutionary swarm robotics. In *Proceedings of the Fifteenth Annual Conference on Genetic and Evolutionary Computation (GECCO '13)*, pages 199–206, New York, NY, USA, 2013. ACM.

[10] C. Green. SharpNEAT homepage, 2003–2006. URL http://sharpneat.sourceforge.net/.

[11] J. Lehman and K. O. Stanley. Evolving a diversity of virtual creatures through novelty search and local competition. In *Proc. of the Thirteenth Annual Conf. on Genetic and Evolutionary Computation (GECCO '11)*, pages 211–218, Dublin, Ireland, 2011. ACM.

[12] J. Lehman and K. O. Stanley. Exploiting open-endedness to solve problems through the search for novelty. In *Proc. of the 11th Intl. Conf. on Artificial Life (Alife XI)*, Cambridge, MA, 2008. MIT Press.

[13] J. Lehman and K. O. Stanley. Revising the evolutionary computation abstraction: Minimal criteria novelty search. In *Proc. of the 12th Annual Conf. on Genetic and Evolutionary Computation (GECCO '10)*, pages 103–110, New York, NY, USA, 2010. ACM.

[14] J. Lehman and K. O. Stanley. Abandoning objectives: Evolution through the search for novelty alone. *Evolutionary Computation*, 19(2):189–223, 2011.

[15] S. W. Mahfoud. *Niching Methods for Genetic Algorithms.* PhD thesis, University of Illinois at Urbana-Champaign, Urbana, IL, May 1995.

[16] T. M. Mitchell. *Machine Learning.* McGraw-Hill, New York, NY, 1997.

[17] J.-B. Mouret and J. Clune. Illuminating search spaces by mapping elites. *arXiv preprint*, 2015.

[18] J.-B. Mouret and S. Doncieux. Overcoming the bootstrap problem in evolutionary robotics using behavioral diversity. In *Proceedings of the IEEE Congress on Evolutionary Computation (CEC-2009)*, pages 1161–1168. IEEE, 2009.

[19] J.-B. Mouret and S. Doncieux. Encouraging behavioral diversity in evolutionary robotics: An empirical study. *Evolutionary Computation*, 20(1):91–133, 2012.

[20] A. Nguyen, J. Yosinski, and J. Clune. Deep neural networks are easily fooled: High confidence predictions for unrecognizable images. *arXiv preprint*, abs/1412.1897, 2014.

[21] C. Ofria and C. O. Wilke. Avida: A software platform for research in computational evolutionary biology. *Artificial Life*, 10(2):191–229, 2004.

[22] D. E. Rumelhart, G. E. Hinton, and R. J. Williams. Learning internal representations by error propagation. In *Parallel Distributed Processing, Volume 1*, pages 318–362. MIT Press, Cambridge, MA, 1986.

[23] L. Spector, J. Klein, and M. Feinstein. Division blocks and the open-ended evolution of development, form, and behavior. In *Proceedings of the Ninth Annual Conference on Genetic and Evolutionary Computation (GECCO '07)*, pages 316–323. ACM, 2007.

[24] K. O. Stanley and R. Miikkulainen. Evolving neural networks through augmenting topologies. *Evolutionary Computation*, 10:99–127, 2002.

[25] K. O. Stanley and R. Miikkulainen. A taxonomy for artificial embryogeny. *Artificial Life*, 9(2):93–130, 2003.

[26] K. O. Stanley, B. D. Bryant, and R. Miikkulainen. Real-time neuroevolution in the NERO video game. *IEEE Transactions on Evolutionary Computation Special Issue on Evolutionary Computation and Games*, 9(6):653–668, 2005.

[27] P. Szerlip and K. O. Stanley. Indirectly encoded sodarace for artificial life. In *Proceedings of the European Conference on Artificial Life (ECAL-2013)*, volume 12, pages 218–225, 2013.

[28] P. A. Szerlip, G. Morse, J. K. Pugh, and K. O. Stanley. Unsupervised feature learning through divergent discriminative feature accumulation. In *Proc. of the Twenty-Ninth AAAI Conference on Artificial Intelligence (AAAI-2015)*, Menlo Park, CA, 2015. AAAI Press.

Evolutionary Image Descriptor: A Dynamic Genetic Programming Representation for Feature Extraction

Harith Al-Sahaf[1] Mengjie Zhang[1] Mark Johnston[2]
[1]School of Engineering and Computer Science
[2]School of Mathematics, Statistics and Operations Research
Victoria University of Wellington, PO Box 600, Wellington 6140, New Zealand
{harith.al-sahaf, mengjie.zhang}@ecs.vuw.ac.nz, mark.johnston@msor.vuw.ac.nz

ABSTRACT

Texture classification aims at categorising instances that have a similar repetitive pattern. In computer vision, texture classification represents a fundamental element in a wide variety of applications, which can be performed by detecting texture primitives of the different classes. Using image descriptors to detect prominent features has been widely adopted in computer vision. Building an effective descriptor becomes more challenging when there are only a few labelled instances. This paper proposes a new Genetic Programming (GP) representation for evolving an image descriptor that operates directly on the raw pixel values and uses only two instances per class. The new method synthesises a set of mathematical formulas that are used to generate the feature vector, and the classification is then performed using a simple instance-based classifier. Determining the length of the feature vector is automatically handled by the new method. Two GP and nine well-known non-GP methods are compared on two texture image data sets for texture classification in order to test the effectiveness of the proposed method. The proposed method is also compared to three hand-crafted descriptors namely domain-independent features, local binary patterns, and Haralick texture features. The results show that the proposed method has superior performance over the competitive methods.

CCS Concepts

•**Computing methodologies → Genetic programming;** *Interest point and salient region detections; Matching;* Feature selection;

Keywords

Genetic Programming, Multiclass classification, Textures

1. INTRODUCTION

Texture analysis can be divided into at least four categories that each aim at investigating a specific task [25]. In *texture synthesis*, the aim is to build a model that can be used to construct the texture. *Texture segmentation* aims at dividing an image into a number of homogeneous regions based on their texture properties. In *texture classification*, the goal is to assign different class labels for instances of different classes. Finally, *shape extraction from texture* aims at exploiting texture information to construct a 3D surface projection from the 2D surface geometry.

A large number of methods for texture analysis have been proposed over the past few decades. Tuceryan and Jain [25] divided these methods into four approaches: (1) structural; (2) statistical; (3) transform; and (4) model-based. The methods in each of these four approaches perform texture analysis differently. For example, structural methods attempt to understand the underlying texture relying on well-known primitives and their arrangements; whereas statistical methods rely on the distribution of the gray levels to indirectly represent the texture using non-deterministic properties. More details can be found in [25].

Genetic Programming (GP) is a biologically inspired evolutionary computation technique that replicates the Darwinian principles of natural selection and survival of the fittest [10]. GP starts from a population of randomly generated programs, each of which represents a solution, then gradually evolves these solutions over a number of generations via using genetic operators to explore the solution space [20].

Over the past few decades, utilising GP for image related problems has attracted increasing interest [19, 1]. Two GP methods have been developed by Song et al. [21] for multiclass texture classification by utilising the *Static Range Selection* (SRS) [22, 30] and *Dynamic Range Selection* (DRS) [13] techniques. In [24] a GP methodology to detect interest points on images by synthesising low-level image operators has been described. In [18], Olague et al. extended the work of [24] by presenting an innovative GP method for evolving an interest points detector. Synthesising mathematical formulas using GP as a preprocessing step to improve the performance of the *Scale-invariant Feature Transform* (SIFT) descriptor [14] is proposed in [19]. On the contrary, Hindmarsh et al. [7] used GP as a postprocessing step to select a subset of the features detected by SIFT for object recognition. Recently, Albukhanajer et al. [1] adopted a multi-objective approach in conjunction with the *trace transform* to extract image features that are robust to noise and invariant to different geometric deformations.

Most of the aforementioned methods require either a large number of instances to evolve a model, and/or human inter-

GECCO '15, July 11 - 15, 2015, Madrid, Spain
© 2015 ACM. ISBN 978-1-4503-3472-3/15/07...$15.00
DOI: http://dx.doi.org/10.1145/2739480.2754661

vention (mostly domain experts) to design and extract a good set of features.

Conventionally, a program evolved by GP for *binary* classification produces a single value from the root node for each instance, which is then translated to a class label using the zero value to divide the real number line into two intervals [20]. Thus, the instance being evaluated is considered as belonging to one class (e.g. foreground) if the value resulting from the root node is negative; and belonging to the other class (e.g. background) if it is positive or zero.

Utilising GP for *multiclass* classification can be divided into at least four groups. Output translation is the first group, where the real number line is split into intervals each of which corresponds to one class, and the output of the evolved program is translated to a class label based on the interval it falls in [30]. Wrapper-based methods represent the second group, where a classifier is used with the program evolved by GP to predict the class label [29]. In the wrapper approach, the evolved program performs feature selection or extraction and those features are fed into the wrapped classifier to perform classification. Methods of the third group aim at producing multiple values from the evolved program, which require modifying the program representation [32]. In the fourth group, the problem of multiclass classification is decomposed into a number of binary classification tasks [13]. The second approach, i.e., wrapper, is adopted in this study where a simple instances-based classifier is used namely, *k-Nearest-Neighbour* (kNN) with k is set to 1 (1NN).

Goals

This paper aims at developing a new GP method for texture primitives detection. The new method performs two essential tasks. Firstly, automatically evolving a descriptor that is capable of detecting and extracting texture features. Secondly, performing multiclass texture classification using the features generated by the evolved descriptor and a simple classifier (1NN). Precisely, this paper aims at addressing the following research objectives:

- develop an appropriate individual representation and fitness function that allows GP to automatically detect and extract image features;
- investigate whether the proposed method is capable of outperforming other GP-based methods that are designed to operate on raw pixel values for multiclass texture classification; and
- investigate whether the evolved descriptor can compete with well-known descriptors that are designed by domain experts using nine widely used classifiers.

The rest of the paper is organised as follows. Three image feature extraction methods are briefly discussed in Section 2. Section 3 describes the proposed GP approach for evolving feature descriptors. The experimental setup, parameter settings, data sets, and baseline methods are presented in Section 4. Section 5 presents and discusses the results along with two evolved descriptors. Section 6 concludes this paper and highlights some future work directions.

2. RELATED WORK

This section describes two descriptors, namely *local binary patterns* [17] and *Haralick texture features* [6], and a domain-independent image feature extraction method [31].

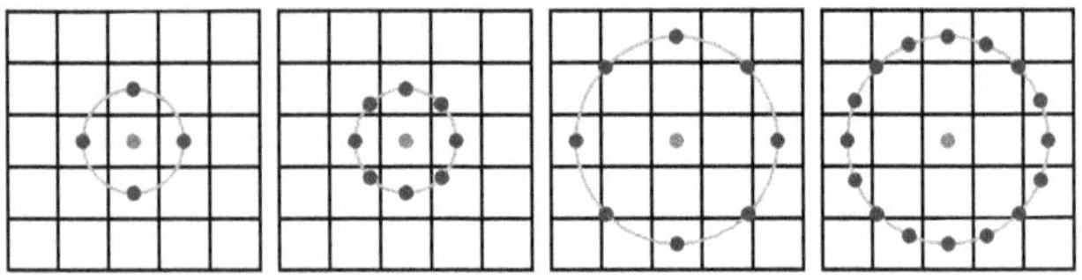

Figure 1: Examples demonstrate different settings of LBP by changing the value of n and r. From left to right, $LBP_{4,1}$, $LBP_{8,1}$, $LBP_{8,2}$, and $LBP_{16,2}$.

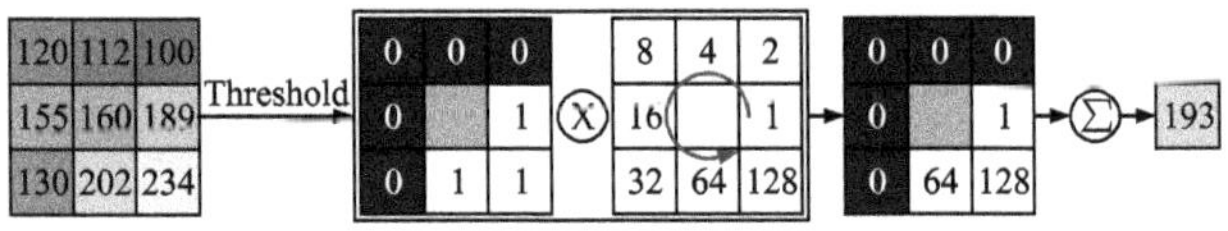

Figure 2: Example shows the required steps to generate a binary code, then convert the generated code to decimal value.

2.1 Local Binary Patterns

In 1994, Ojala et al. [17] proposed a new texture image descriptor called Local Binary Patterns (LBP). The main aim of LBP is to generate a binary code at each pixel relying on the values of the neighbouring pixels, and then use the generated codes to compute a histogram (i.e. feature vector). The process of computing the histogram consists of four steps. Firstly, a histogram of size 2^L bins is constructed and initialised, where L is the length of the binary code. The length of the binary code is defined based on two parameters: (1) the number of neighbouring pixels n; and (2) the distance between the central pixel and each of the neighbouring pixels, denoted as the radius r. LBP and these two parameters are denoted as $LBP_{n,r}$. Figure 1 shows different settings of n and r. Originally, LBP operated using a sliding window of size 3×3 pixels ($LBP_{8,1}$). Secondly, the image is scanned in a pixel-by-pixel fashion and each of the neighbouring pixels surrounding the current central pixel of the sliding window is set to 0 if its value is less than that of the central pixel; otherwise, it is set to 1 (as presented in Figure 2). Thirdly, these values are used to form a binary code, and then multiplied by powers of 2 in an anticlockwise direction to convert the binary code to a decimal value. Fourthly, the bin corresponding to the generated decimal value in the third step is incremented by 1.

2.2 Domain Independent Features (DIFs)

Zhang et al. [31] proposed three domain-independent terminal sets to extract image features: (1) rectilinear features; (2) circular features; and (3) pixel features. These methods use statistical properties, i.e., mean and standard deviation, of predefined image regions to extract the feature vector. Figure 3 highlights the regions of these three methods.

The rectilinear method is used in this study as a competitive method for feature extraction. A feature vector generated by the rectilinear method consists of 20 features that are extracted from 10 regions as listed in Table 1. This method combines both *global* (i.e. the entire image) and *local* (i.e. regions of the image) features, which has been shown to be more powerful than use only one of them [12].

2.3 Haralick Texture Features

Haralick Texture Features [6] is a statistical texture analysis method that uses the *Gray-Level Co-occurrence Matrix*

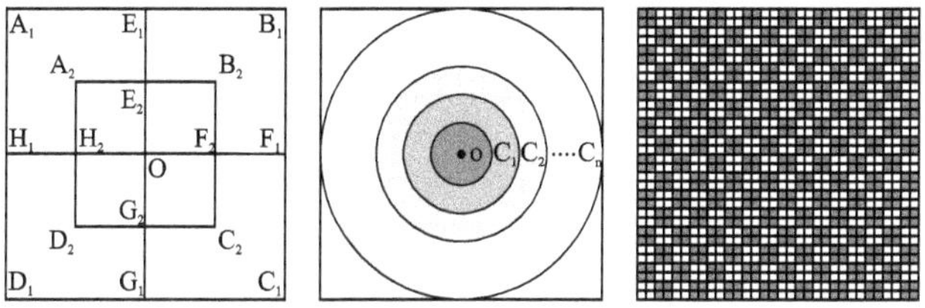

(a) (b) (c)

Figure 3: The regions of the (a) rectilinear, (b) circular, and (c) pixels features [31].

Table 1: Pixel statistics of the rectilinear method.

Features μ	σ	Regions of interest	Features μ	σ	Regions of interest
F_1	F_2	Square $A_1B_1C_1D_1$	F_{11}	F_{12}	Square $A_2B_2C_2D_2$
F_3	F_4	Quadrant $A_1E_1OH_1$	F_{13}	F_{14}	Horizontal line H_1F_1
F_5	F_6	Quadrant $E_1B_1F_1O$	F_{15}	F_{16}	Horizontal line H_2F_2
F_7	F_8	Quadrant $H_1OG_1D_1$	F_{17}	F_{18}	Vertical line E_1G_1
F_9	F_{10}	Quadrant $OF_1C_1G_1$	F_{19}	F_{20}	Vertical line E_2G_2

(GLCM) to extract texture features [25]. The process of extracting features from an image starts by generating a set of co-occurrence matrices each of which is generated by counting the number of adjacent pixels of a predefined offset and direction (i.e. angle). Then a number of features are calculated from each matrix to form the feature vector.

In this study, for each instance, four matrices are generated using a single pixel offset and the directions 0°, 45°, 90°, and 135°. The feature vector is then generated by calculating from each of the matrices the *Homogeneity* (inverse difference), *Dissimilarity* (absolute value), *Contrast* (inertia), *Energy* (angular second moment), *Entropy*, and *Correlation* that are formally defined as:

$$Homogeneity = \sum_{i=1}^{H}\sum_{j=1}^{W} \frac{p(i,j)}{1+|i-j|} \quad (1)$$

$$Dissimilarity = \sum_{i=1}^{H}\sum_{j=1}^{W} |i-j|\, p(i,j) \quad (2)$$

$$Contrast = \sum_{i=1}^{H}\sum_{j=1}^{W} (i-j)^2\, p(i,j) \quad (3)$$

$$Energy = \sum_{i=1}^{H}\sum_{j=1}^{W} p(i,j)^2 \quad (4)$$

$$Entropy = \sum_{i=1}^{H}\sum_{j=1}^{W} p(i,j)\left[-\log_2 p(i,j)\right] \quad (5)$$

$$Correlation = \sum_{i=1}^{H}\sum_{j=1}^{W} \frac{(i-\mu_i)(j-\mu_j)\, p(i,j)}{\sigma_i \sigma_j} \quad (6)$$

where H and W are, respectively, the height and width of the matrix, $p(i,j)$ is the value at the ith row and j^{th} column, and $|\cdot|$ returns the absolute value of the argument. The μ_i, μ_j, σ_i and σ_j are, respectively, the mean and standard deviation of the ith row and j^{th} column.

3. THE NEW METHOD

This section discusses the evaluation procedure, program representation, feature vector extraction, and fitness function of the proposed *Evolutionary Image Descriptor* (EID).

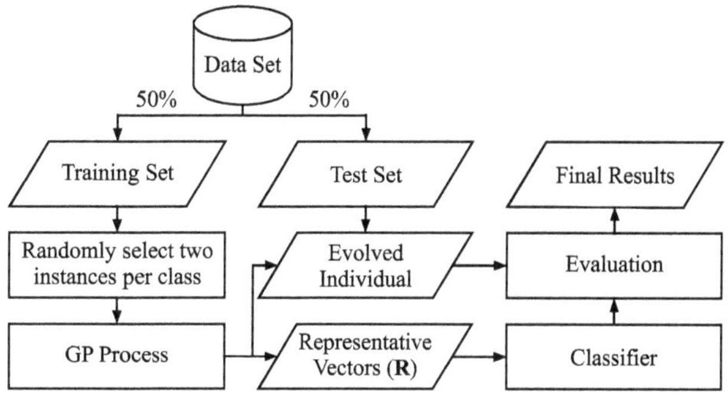

Figure 4: Flowchart shows the evaluation procedure.

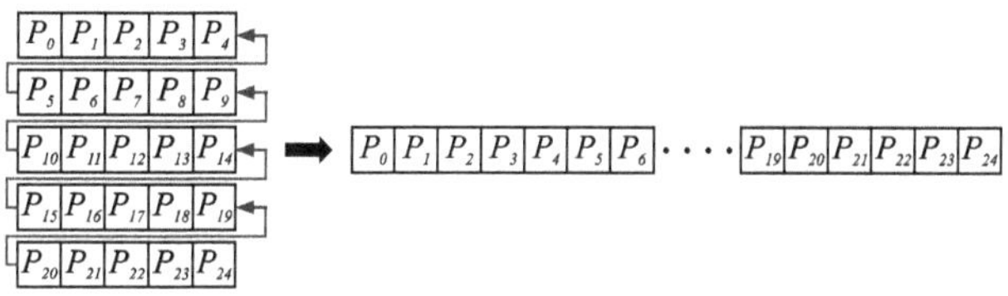

Figure 5: Converting a window of size 5×5 pixels to a 1D vector.

3.1 The Evaluation Procedure

The evaluation procedure of EID consists of the typical machine learning *training* and *testing* phases. As presented in Figure 4, the process starts by dividing the content of the data set equally between the training and test sets. The system randomly selects only two instances per class from the training set and feeds them to the GP process. The GP process runs until a stopping criterion is met. The results of the GP process are: (1) the best evolved program; and (2) a set of representative vectors denoted as **R**. The system then uses the evolved program to generate the feature vectors of the test set instances, and uses **R** as the knowledge base for a 1NN classifier to predict the class label of each instance. These steps are discussed more in the following subsections.

Only two instances of each class are randomly selected from the training set to evolve a program. Using different instances can give different results. Thus, the process depicted in Figure 4, apart from the step of dividing the data set into training and test sets, has been further repeated 30 times.

3.2 Program Representation

In this paper, the tree-based GP [10] program structure is used to represent an individual evolved by the proposed method. Moreover, *Strongly-typed GP* (STGP) is used to define constraints on the order of the different nodes in the program tree and to preserve the closure property [16].

The *terminal set* consists of the raw pixel values of a sliding window with a predefined size. In our experiment, the window size is set to 5×5 pixels. The pixels of each window are converted to a 1D vector as demonstrated in Figure 5. Thus, the terminal nodes are randomly selected from $\{P_0, P_1, \ldots, P_{24}\}$. The windows that exceed the boundaries of the instance being evaluated are discarded. The pixel with the coordinates $(0,0)$ represents the upper left corner of the image; whereas the pixel at the lower right corner of the image has the coordinates $(M-1, N-1)$ where M and N are, respectively, the width and height of the image.

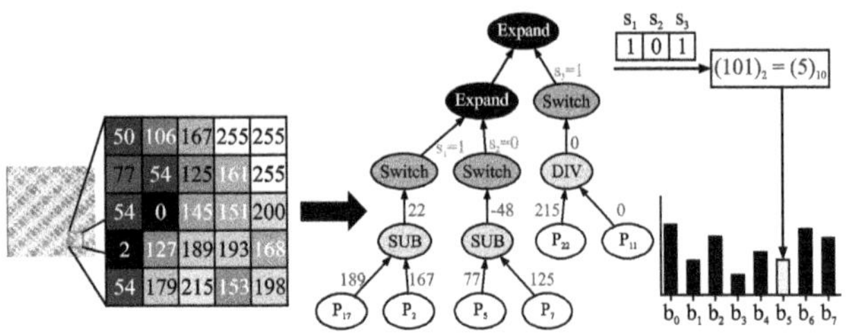

Figure 6: The steps required to generate the feature vector.

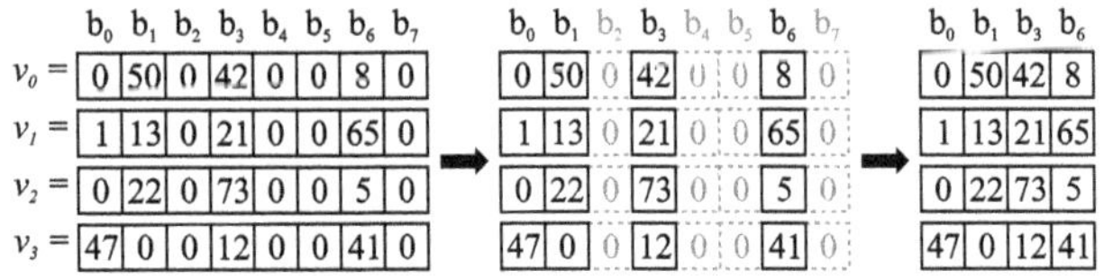

Figure 7: The steps to remove the unwanted bins from the extracted vectors v_0, v_1, v_2, and v_3.

The *function set* is made up of the four standard arithmetic operators +, −, ×, and ÷, in addition to the *Switch* and *Expand* nodes as shown in Figure 6. Each of the four mathematical operators has its regular meaning that applies the corresponding operation on two arguments and returns a single floating-point value. However, the ÷ operator returns 0 if the divisor is zero. The input and output of these four operators are of the same type; thus, they can be used to form a chain of operators. The *Switch* node takes only one argument and returns 0 if the input is negative, and 1 otherwise. Each *Switch* node represents a single bit of the code generated at each position of the sliding window (more details in the following subsection). Meanwhile, the *Expand* node takes two arguments, each of which can be *Switch* or *Expand* nodes; the *Expand* node is used to allow GP to evolve trees of different sizes.

3.3 Extracting the Feature Vector

The process of extracting the feature vector from an instance requires to iterate over the pixel values of the instance using a sliding window of a predefined size. The process starts by generating an empty vector of length 2^b, where b is the total number of *Switch* nodes in the tree. Then at each position of the sliding window, the system performs two steps as shown in Figure 6. Firstly, the system feeds the values of the current window to the terminal nodes, performs the arithmetic operations, and generates a binary code using the values returned by the *Switch* nodes. Secondly, the generated code is converted to decimal and the bin at the corresponding index of the vector is incremented by 1.

The resulting vectors can be too long due to having a large number of *Switch* nodes. Reserving large chunks of the machine memory can result in occupying the entire memory, which will lead to immediate termination. To prevent this situation, a simple analysis of the resulted vectors has been performed and show that many of these bins have zeros. Thus, these bins that have 0 across all vectors have been removed and reported as *unwanted* as shown in Figure 7.

3.4 Generating the Representative Vectors

The proposed method generates a single vector per class using the extracted feature vectors from the training set instances. The representative vector of a class is generated by averaging the values of each bin across all feature vectors of that class as presented in Figure 8. The generated representative vectors are stored in a set denoted as $\mathbf{R}$ that is used to perform two tasks, firstly, to help measure the fitness value (more details in the following subsection), and secondly, to serve as the knowledge base to classify the instances of the unseen data (i.e. test set). For each of the unseen instances, the system generates the feature vector, removes the previously indicated unwanted bins, calculates the distance between the instance being evaluated and every representative vector (Equation (10)), and returns the class label of the closest representative vector (1NN).

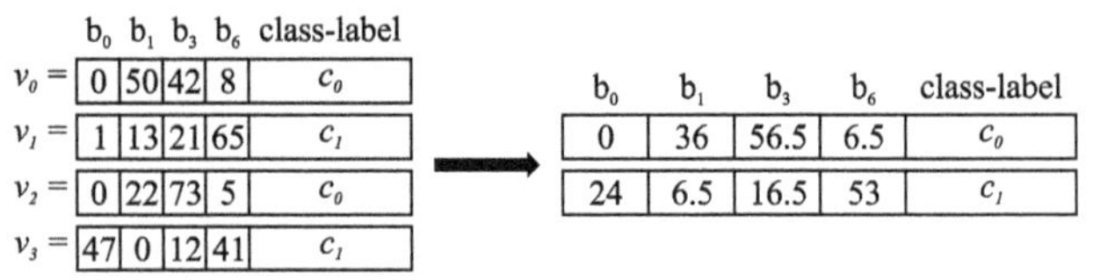

Figure 8: Generating the representative vectors of classes c_0 and c_1.

3.5 Fitness Function

Operating directly on the raw pixel values and using only two instances per class, are two essential components of EID. Thus, relying on the typical standard accuracy of the training set is inadequate due to having a large feature space and a few training instances. A compound fitness function is used in order to tackle both of these issues as shown in Equation (7).

$$Fitness = 1 - \left(\frac{Accuracy + Distance_{\mu}}{2}\right) \tag{7}$$

Here, *Accuracy* has its regular meaning, that is the proportion of correctly classified instances (N_{correct}) to the total number of instances (N_{total}) as in Equation (8).

$$Accuracy = \frac{N_{\text{correct}}}{N_{\text{total}}} \tag{8}$$

The accuracy measures the ability of the evolved program to correctly classify the instances of the training set. To calculate the accuracy, the system iterates over the instances of the training set and for each, the class label is predicted using the representative vectors as the knowledge base with 1NN. Then a `hit` is returned if the predicted label matches the actual label; otherwise, a `miss` is returned.

The proposed method also aims to generate a distinctive feature vector for instances in the same class compared to those instances of the other classes, which is handled by the second component of the fitness function, i.e., $Distance_{\mu}$. The $Distance_{\mu}$ component is the average distance between each representative vector of one class and the closest representative vector of other classes as presented in Equation (9).

$$Distance_{\mu} = \frac{1}{C} \sum_{\mathbf{v} \in \mathbf{R}} \underset{\{\mathbf{u} \in \mathbf{R} \setminus \mathbf{v}\}}{\operatorname{argmin}} D(\mathbf{v}, \mathbf{u}) \tag{9}$$

Here, C is the total number of classes, $\mathbf{R}$ is the set of representative vectors, and $\mathbf{v}$ and $\mathbf{u}$ are two vectors in $\mathbf{R}$. The $D(\cdot, \cdot)$ function measures the distance between two vectors, which is calculated using *Czekanowski Coefficient* [2] that is

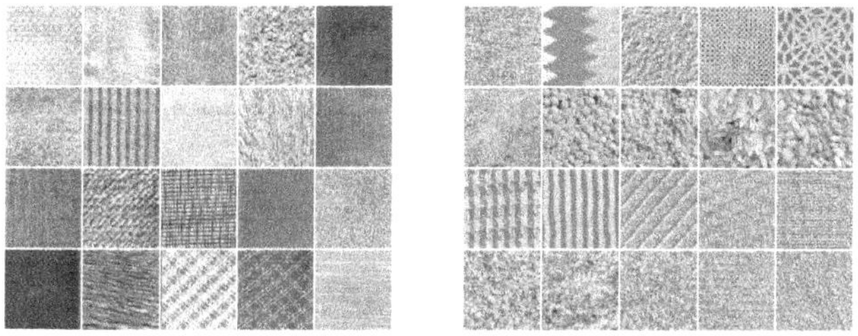

(a) (b)

Figure 9: Samples of (a) DS-Brodatz that are from left to right and top to bottom D1, D3, D4, D5, D6, D9, D11, D14, D15, D16, D17, D18, D20, D21, D24, D34, D37, D46, D47, and D49; and (b) DS-Kylberg that are from left to right and top to bottom blanket1, blanket2, ceiling1, ceiling2, floor1, floor2, lentils1, pearl-sugar1, rice1, rice2, scraf1, scarf2, screen1, seat1, seat2, stone1, stone2, stone3, stone-slab1, and wall1.

formally defined as:

$$D(\mathbf{v}, \mathbf{u}) = 1 - \left(\frac{2\left(\sum_{v\in\mathbf{v},u\in\mathbf{u}} \min(v, u)\right)}{\sum_{v\in\mathbf{v}} v + \sum_{u\in\mathbf{u}} u} \right) \quad (10)$$

where v and u are two corresponding elements in the vectors $\mathbf{v}$ and $\mathbf{u}$ respectively. Meanwhile, the $\min(\cdot,\cdot)$ function returns the minimum value of the two arguments.

4. EXPERIMENT SETUP

The data sets, instance preparation, baseline methods, and evolutionary parameters are outlined in this section.

4.1 Data Sets and Preparation

Two widely used, texture based, gray-scale data sets are used in this study to test the proposed method. The instances of the first data set are selected from the *Brodatz Texture* data set [3], and denoted as *DS-Brodatz* in this study. The original Brodatz data set consists of 112 classes, each consists of a single instance with size 640 × 640 pixels. Only 20 out of the 112 classes have been randomly drawn to form DS-Brodatz. Figure 9(a) shows samples and names of the selected classes.

The second data set (DS-Kylberg) is formed using 20 randomly selected classes of the *Kylberg Texture* data set [11] as shown in Figure 9(b). The Kylberg data set consists of 28 classes that each comes in *with* and *without* rotation. Only the latter type is considered in this study as extending the proposed method to handle the rotation variant will be investigated in the future. Each class of this group consists of 160 instances, each with size 576 × 576 pixels.

The instances of the DS-Kylberg data set have been resized to be of size 115 × 115 pixels each, in order to reduce the computation costs. Meanwhile, the single instance in each class of DS-Brodatz has been re-sampled by dividing the image into 100 sub-images with size 64 × 64 pixels each. The total number of instances has been equally split into training and test sets. Thus, each of the training and test sets of DS-Brodatz consists of 1,000 instances (50 instances × 20 classes); whereas each of the training and test sets of DS-Kylberg is made up of 1,600 instances (80 instances × 20 classes). Only two instances of each class are randomly selected to form the training set and the rest of the available pool is discarded; while the test set is kept identical in the entire experiment. The instances of both DS-Brodatz and DS-Kylberg have been standardised and normalised as preprocessing steps in order to eliminate or reduce the effect of illumination variation. Equation (11) is used for standardisation. The resulting instance after standardisation has zero mean and unit standard deviation. Then to normalise the standardised instance, Equation (12) is used. The pixel values after normalisation are in the interval $[0, 255]$.

$$x' = \frac{x - \bar{x}}{s} \quad (11)$$

$$x' = \left(\frac{x - x_{\min}}{x_{\max} - x_{\min}} \right) \times 255 \quad (12)$$

Here, x' and x are, respectively, the new and old pixel values. The mean and standard deviation are denoted by $\bar{x}$ and s, and $x_{\min}$ and $x_{\max}$ are the minimum and maximum values respectively.

4.2 Methods for Comparison

The proposed method is compared to 11 classifiers of different types. The competitive methods can be categorised into two groups: (1) GP-based; and (2) non-GP. The former group consists of the SRS and DRS methods, whilst the latter group consists of Naïve Bayes (NB), Support Vector Machines (SVM), Decision Trees (J48), hybridised Naïve Bayes/Decision Trees (NBTree), K* (KStar), Non-nested generalised (NNge), Adaptive Boosting M1 (ABM1), Multilayer Perceptron (MLP), and Random Forest (RF). We have reimplemented both of the SRS and DRS methods as in [21] using the platform provided by the *Evolutionary Computation Java-based* (ECJ) package [15]. Meanwhile, the implementation of the other methods have been taken from the *Waikato Environment for Knowledge Analysis* (WEKA) package [5] that is discussed in detail in [28].

4.3 Parameter Settings

The parameter settings of both GP and non-GP methods are highlighted here.

4.3.1 GP Evolutionary Parameters

The parameters of the three GP methods, i.e., SRS, DRS, and EID, are summarised in Table 2 and kept identical in the experiment to make fair comparisons. These parameters are based on previous work in the literature. The population of 200 individuals is generated using the ramped-half-and-half method [10]. The probabilities of the elitism, mutation, and crossover operators are, respectively, 0.01, 0.19, and 0.80. Selecting individuals to participate in generating the subsequent generation uses the tournament method with size 7. The minimum tree depth is set to 2, whereas the maximum depth is set to 10 to allow GP to evolve large trees, but not too large in order to avoid the *code bloating* problem [26]. The GP process is terminated after 50 generations if no *ideal* solution is found.

4.3.2 Non-GP Parameters

Some optimisation and parameter tuning have been applied to the non-GP methods. The number of neighbours in all instance-based methods such as NNge and KStar has been set to 1 due to having only two instances per class.

Table 2: The GP evolutionary parameters

Parameter	Value	Parameter	Value
Elitism Rate	0.01	Generations	50
Mutation Rate	0.19	Population Size	200
Crossover Rate	0.80	Selection Type	Tournament
Minimum Depth	2	Tournament size	7
Maximum Depth	10	Initial Population	Half-and-half

The structure of the MLP classification method has been set based on the guidelines proposed by Trenn [23], where the number of hidden neurons (N_{hidden}) is calculated as:

$$N_{\text{hidden}} = \left\lceil \frac{N_{\text{in}} + N_{\text{out}}}{2} \right\rceil \quad (13)$$

where N_{in} and N_{out} are, respectively, the number of neurons in the input and output layers.

A study by Keerthi and Lin [9] showed that SVM with a non-linear kernel has the potential to achieve comparable or better performance than that with a linear kernel. Therefore, SVM is used in this study with a Gaussian kernel instead of the default linear kernel of WEKA. Different classifiers have been tested with ABM1, and the best results have been achieved when LADTree [8] is used.

5. RESULTS AND DISCUSSIONS

The results obtained from the experiments are presented and discussed in this section.

5.1 Overall Results

The aim of the conducted experiments is to examine the performance of the proposed EID method. To this end, an experiment has been designed using the DS-Brodatz and DS-Kylberg data sets. The results of the experiment on each data set are presented in a table that vertically consists of two parts. The results of the three GP methods (SRS, DRS and EID) occupy the first (upper) part, whereas non-GP methods occupy the second (lower) part. Moreover, the second part horizontally is made up of three columns that each presents the performances of different classifiers using the features extracted by DIF, LBP, and GLCM. The *Wilcoxon signed-ranks* test [27, 4] with a significance level of 5% is used to identify whether the performance of EID is significantly different than that of the other methods, which is indicated using a "$*$" symbol.

Table 3 presents the results obtained on the DS-Brodatz data set. The proposed method has significantly outperformed both of the GP baseline methods. Compared to non-GP methods with three sets of hand-crafted features, EID has achieved significantly better performance.

The results on the DS-Kylberg data set are presented in Table 4. Similar to DS-Brodatz, the significance test shows that the gap between the performance of the proposed method and that of SRS and DRS is significant. Moreover, non-GP methods have performed significantly worse than the proposed method on this data set.

5.2 Further Discussion

In order to get better understanding of the structure of the program evolved by EID, one of the best programs evolved on each data set is selected for further discussion.

Figure 10 depicts the tree representation of a program evolved by EID on the DS-Brodatz data set. This program has achieved 95.80% accuracy on the unseen data. The program generates a feature vector of length 2^6 bins (assuming no unwanted bins need to be removed) due to having 6 *Switch* nodes. Thus, a binary code consists of 6 bits is generated for each position of the sliding window. Four out of those 6 bits are generated by simply subtracting the values of the arguments, whilst the other two require an additional operator to be applied. This reflects the simplicity and low-cost of the evolved program, and more importantly, it can be used for online applications. The use of the subtraction operator more than the other operators was expected due to the influence of this operator on flipping the sign of the resulting value (i.e. 0 to 1 and vice versa).

The tree representation of a program evolved by the proposed method on DS-Kylberg is depicted in Figure 11. On the unseen data, this program showed 96.94% accuracy. A closer inspection reveals that the feature vector generated for an instance by this program is of length 2^5 bins. Moreover, at most 4 operators are required to calculate the value of each bit of the binary code generated at each window position. Similarly, the subtraction operator appears more frequently than the other operators.

5.3 Discussion on Number of Instances

Another experiment is conducted in this study in order to investigate the effect of having a larger training set on the performance of the baseline methods. Thus, all the instances of the training set are used to train or evolve a model instead of selecting only two instances per class.

The results of the two GP baseline methods are presented in Table 5, which show that increasing the number of instances has improved the performance of SRS and DRS. However, these two methods still show very poor performances compared to that of EID using only two instances

Table 3: The accuracies (%) on the test set for DS-Brodatz ($\bar{x} \pm \sigma$).

	SRS	DRS	EID
	4.88 ± 0.14*	10.23 ± 0.61*	95.39 ± 0.90
	DIF	LBP	GLCM
NB	25.36 ± 5.86 *	67.22 ± 6.17 *	62.40 ± 8.18 *
SVM	39.58 ± 4.07 *	71.66 ± 4.93 *	75.94 ± 3.39 *
NBTree	42.77 ± 4.35 *	77.66 ± 4.38 *	64.33 ± 5.45 *
KStar	45.32 ± 3.19 *	79.26 ± 2.38 *	76.62 ± 4.97 *
NNge	41.60 ± 4.13 *	80.40 ± 3.48 *	78.71 ± 4.89 *
MLP	40.88 ± 2.73 *	84.10 ± 2.69 *	80.97 ± 4.59 *
ABM1	17.63 ± 4.64 *	56.00 ± 15.0 *	22.52 ± 6.27 *
J48	33.96 ± 5.09 *	32.41 ± 6.47 *	47.33 ± 8.11 *
RF	41.90 ± 3.00 *	63.99 ± 1.21 *	65.40 ± 3.80 *

Table 4: The accuracies (%) on the test set for DS-Kylberg ($\bar{x} \pm \sigma$).

	SRS	DRS	EID
	5.09 ± 0.18*	8.83 ± 0.53*	92.01 ± 1.02
	DIF	LBP	GLCM
NB	24.96 ± 4.76 *	76.22 ± 6.74 *	63.58 ± 5.61 *
SVM	27.54 ± 2.74 *	77.72 ± 4.51 *	79.80 ± 4.55 *
NBTree	30.14 ± 4.10 *	77.71 ± 5.93 *	65.96 ± 5.34 *
KStar	24.81 ± 2.17 *	87.09 ± 2.14 *	80.50 ± 5.39 *
NNge	34.40 ± 3.24 *	87.80 ± 2.54 *	80.32 ± 5.34 *
MLP	29.29 ± 2.83 *	85.83 ± 2.63 *	81.46 ± 4.55 *
ABM1	15.69 ± 4.24 *	54.91 ± 10.4 *	22.64 ± 5.32 *
J48	35.27 ± 4.41 *	35.89 ± 4.34 *	50.75 ± 5.22 *
RF	29.19 ± 1.81 *	68.48 ± 1.77 *	66.85 ± 3.89 *

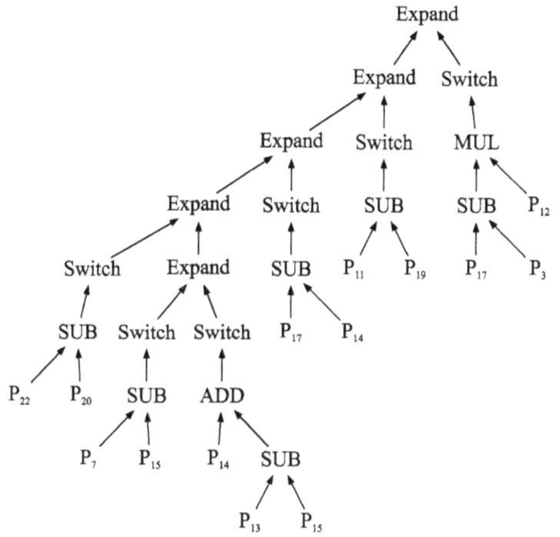

Figure 10: A program evolved on DS-Brodatz.

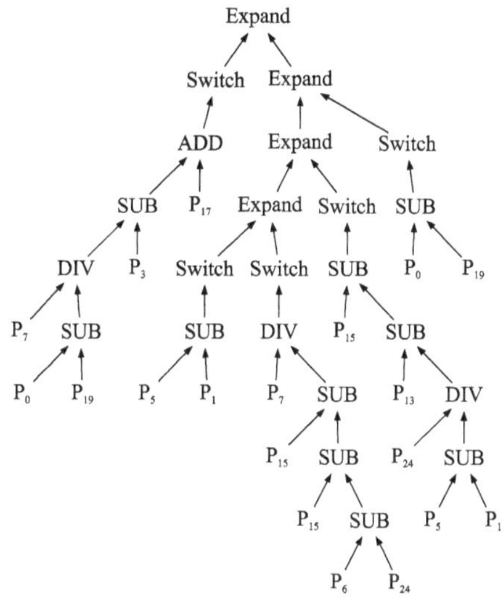

Figure 11: A program evolved on DS-Kylberg.

per class. Although SRS and DRS have been designed to tackle the multiclass classification problem and have been shown to achieve a high level of performance in [21], it requires further investigation to identify whether the number of classes or the size of those instances (e.g. Song et al. [21] used instances of size 16 × 16 pixels; whilst we are using instances with is 64 × 64 pixels) affects the performance.

Table 6 presents the results of all non-GP methods on the two data sets using the entire training set. The deterministic methods have been executed only one time and the achieved performance on the unseen data is reported in the table. Meanwhile, the average performance over 30 independent runs is reported for the non-deterministic methods (e.g. MLP). The obtained results show that increasing the number of training instances has the potential to improve the performances. Clearly, using all the instances in the training set increases the performances of all these commonly used machine learning methods over using only two instances per class. However, the new EID method using only two instances per class still achieved better (or comparable) results than most of these commonly used machine learning methods using a large number of instances in the training set. In the future, we will investigate why EID can perform so well using only two instances per class.

Table 5: The accuracies (%) of the GP baseline methods on the test set ($\bar{x} \pm \sigma$).

DS-Brodatz		DS-Kylberg	
SRS	DRS	SRS	DRS
6.73 ± 1.31	11.58 ± 1.21	7.35 ± 1.07	9.60 ± 0.74

Table 6: The accuracies (%) of the non-GP baseline methods on the test set.

	DS-Brodatz			DS-Kylberg		
	DIF	LBP	GLCM	DIF	LBP	GLCM
NB	72.20	92.70	88.40	70.75	95.63	91.00
SVM	50.00	67.00	77.20	38.81	76.63	85.13
NBTree	60.20	84.00	86.30	60.06	92.19	89.00
KStar	68.50	95.90	95.60	45.00	98.44	97.94
NNge	64.90	87.40	92.00	58.38	94.63	93.13
MLP	68.57	97.27	97.76	62.78	95.57	97.49
ABM1	41.80	92.80	33.10	44.69	53.63	63.69
J48	63.30	85.00	85.40	64.06	89.75	89.75
RF	68.65	94.25	91.28	65.55	95.77	94.38

6. CONCLUSIONS

The overall aim of this paper was to utilise GP for evolving a program that operates on the raw pixel values and capable of detecting texture primitives using only two instances per class. This goal has been successfully achieved as the program evolved by the proposed system generates the feature vector from the instance being evaluated using a sliding window, and predicts the class label relying on a knowledge base formed using the instances of the training set. Unlike hand-crafted image descriptors, the developed system automatically selects the length of the feature vector and the required formulas to generate this vector. To investigate the effectiveness of the proposed method, an experiment has been designed using two well-known and publicly available data sets namely, *Brodatz Texture* and *Kylberg Texture*. The experiment aims at investigating the ability of the developed system to discriminate between instances of different textures. The performance of the new method has been compared to two GP and nine non-GP widely used methods namely, NB, SVM, NBTree, KStar, NNge, MLP, ABM1, J48, and RF using three well-known hand-crafted feature extraction methods. The results suggest that the new method has significantly outperformed all comparative methods in terms of classification performance on both data sets and over the use of hand-crafted features.

The robustness of the proposed method to different distortions such as rotation, scale, and translation is an important direction that we will investigate in the future. Another direction is to analyse the complexity of the evolved descriptor and adopt a multi-objective approach to evolve a low-cost and high-performance descriptor. The effect of the features extracted by the proposed method on the performance of different classifiers will be investigated in the future.

7. REFERENCES

[1] W. Albukhanajer, J. Briffa, and Y. Jin. Evolutionary multiobjective image feature extraction in the presence of noise. *IEEE Transactions on Cybernetics*, pages 1–12, 2014.

[2] D. Androutsos, K. Plataniotis, and A. Venetsanopoulos. Distance measures for color

image retrieval. In *Proceedings of the International Conference on Image Processing*, volume 2, pages 770–774. IEEE, 1998.

[3] P. Brodatz. *Textures: A Photographic Album for Artists and Designers*. Dover Publications, 1999.

[4] J. Demšar. Statistical comparisons of classifiers over multiple data sets. *Journal of Machine Learning Research*, 7:1–30, 2006.

[5] M. Hall, E. Frank, G. Holmes, B. Pfahringer, P. Reutemann, and I. H. Witten. The WEKA data mining software: An update. *SIGKDD Explorations Newsletter*, 11(1):10–18, 2009.

[6] R. Haralick, K. Shanmugam, and I. Dinstein. Textural features for image classification. *IEEE Transactions on Systems, Man and Cybernetics*, SMC-3(6):610–621, 1973.

[7] S. Hindmarsh, P. Andreae, and M. Zhang. Genetic programming for improving image descriptors generated using the scale-invariant feature transform. In *Proceedings of the 27th International Conference on Image and Vision Computing New Zealand*, pages 85–90. ACM, 2012.

[8] G. Holmes, B. Pfahringer, R. Kirkby, E. Frank, and M. Hall. Multiclass alternating decision trees. In *Proceedings of the 13th European Conference on Machine Learning*, pages 161–172. Springer, 2002.

[9] S. Keerthi and C.-J. Lin. Asymptotic behaviors of support vector machines with gaussian kernel. *Neural Computation*, 15(7):1667–1689, 2003.

[10] J. R. Koza. *Genetic Programming: On the Programming of Computers by Means of Natural Selection*. MIT Press, 1992.

[11] G. Kylberg. The Kylberg texture dataset v. 1.0. External report (Blue series) 35, Centre for Image Analysis, Swedish University of Agricultural Sciences and Uppsala University, Uppsala, Sweden, 2011.

[12] K.-L. Lim and H. Galoogahi. Shape classification using local and global features. In *Proceedings of the 4th Pacific-Rim Symposium on Image and Video Technology*, pages 115–120. IEEE Computer Society, 2010.

[13] T. Loveard and V. Ciesielski. Representing classification problems in genetic programming. In *Proceedings of the IEEE Congress on Evolutionary Computation*, volume 2, pages 1070–1077. IEEE, 2001.

[14] D. G. Lowe. Object recognition from local scale-invariant features. In *Proceedings of the International Conference on Computer Vision*, pages 1150–1157. IEEE, 1999.

[15] S. Luke. *Essentials of Metaheuristics*. Lulu, second edition, 2013.

[16] D. J. Montana. Strongly typed genetic programming. *Evolutionary Computation*, 3(2):199–230, 1995.

[17] T. Ojala, M. Pietikäinen, and D. Harwood. Performance evaluation of texture measures with classification based on Kullback discrimination of distributions. In *Proceedings of the 12th International Conference on Pattern Recognition*, volume 1, pages 582–585. IEEE, 1994.

[18] G. Olague and L. Trujillo. Evolutionary-computer-assisted design of image operators that detect interest points using genetic programming. *Image and Vision Computing*, 29(7):484–498, 2011.

[19] C. B. Perez and G. Olague. Evolutionary learning of local descriptor operators for object recognition. In *Proceedings of the 11th Annual Conference on Genetic and Evolutionary Computation*, pages 1051–1058. ACM, 2009.

[20] W. Smart and M. Zhang. Using genetic programming for multiclass classification by simultaneously solving component binary classification problems. In *Proceedings of the 8th European Conference on Genetic Programming*, pages 227–239. Springer, 2005.

[21] A. Song, T. Loveard, and V. Ciesielski. Towards genetic programming for texture classification. In *Proceedings of the 14th Australian Joint Conference on Artificial Intelligence*, volume 2256 of *Lecture Notes in Computer Science*, pages 461–472. Springer, 2001.

[22] W. A. Tackett. Genetic programming for feature discovery and image discrimination. In *Proceedings of the 5th International Conference on Genetic Algorithms*, pages 303–311, 1993.

[23] S. Trenn. Multilayer perceptrons: Approximation order and necessary number of hidden units. *IEEE Transactions on Neural Networks*, 19(5):836–844, 2008.

[24] L. Trujillo and G. Olague. Automated design of image operators that detect interest points. *Evolutionary Computation*, 16(4):483–507, 2008.

[25] M. Tuceryan and A. K. Jain. Texture analysis. In C. H. Chen, L. F. Pau, and P. S. P. Wang, editors, *Handbook of Pattern Recognition & Computer Vision*, pages 235–276. World Scientific, 1993.

[26] P. Whigham and G. Dick. Implicitly controlling bloat in genetic programming. *IEEE Transactions on Evolutionary Computation*, 14(2):173–190, 2010.

[27] F. Wilcoxon. Individual comparisons by ranking methods. *Biometrics Bulletin*, 1(6):80–83, 1945.

[28] I. H. Witten and E. Frank. *Data Mining: Practical Machine Learning Tools and Techniques*. Morgan Kaufmann, second edition, 2005.

[29] L. Zhang, L. Jack, and A. Nandi. Extending genetic programming for multi-class classification by combining k-nearest neighbor. In *Proceedings of the IEEE International Conference on Acoustics, Speech, and Signal Processing*, volume 5, pages v/349–v/352, 2005.

[30] M. Zhang and V. Ciesielski. Genetic programming for multiple class object detection. In *Proceedings of the 12th Australian Joint Conference on Artificial Intelligence*, volume 1747 of *Lecture Notes in Computer Science*, pages 180–192. Springer, 1999.

[31] M. Zhang, V. Ciesielski, and P. Andreae. A domain-independent window approach to multiclass object detection using genetic programming. *EURASIP Journal on Advances in Signal Processing*, 2003(8):841–859, 2003.

[32] M. Zhang and M. Johnston. A variant program structure in tree-based genetic programming for multiclass object classification. In *Evolutionary Image Analysis and Signal Processing*, volume 213 of *Studies in Computational Intelligence*, pages 55–72. Springer, 2009.

Building Predictive Models via Feature Synthesis

Ignacio Arnaldo
Massachusetts Institute of Technology, CSAIL
Cambridge, MA
iarnaldo@mit.edu

Una-May O'Reilly
Massachusetts Institute of Technology, CSAIL
Cambridge, MA
unamay@csail.mit.edu

Kalyan Veeramachaneni
Massachusetts Institute of Technology, CSAIL
Cambridge, MA
kalyan@csail.mit.edu

ABSTRACT

We introduce Evolutionary Feature Synthesis[1] (EFS), a regression method that generates readable, nonlinear models of small to medium size datasets in seconds. EFS is, to the best of our knowledge, the fastest regression tool based on evolutionary computation reported to date. The *feature search* involved in the proposed method is composed of two main steps: *feature composition* and *feature subset selection*. EFS adopts a bottom-up feature composition strategy that eliminates the need for a symbolic representation of the features and exploits the variable selection process involved in pathwise regularized linear regression to perform the feature subset selection step. The result is a regression method that is competitive against neural networks, and outperforms both linear methods and Multiple Regression Genetic Programming, up to now the best regression tool based on evolutionary computation.

Categories and Subject Descriptors

I.2.2 [**Artificial intelligence**]: Automatic Programming

Keywords

Regression; Feature Synthesis; Feature Subset Selection

1. INTRODUCTION

Recent methods such as Multiple Regression Genetic Programming (MRGP) [2], Behavioral Genetic Programming (BGP) [13], and Kaizen Programming (KP) [4] explore the combination of Genetic Programming based symbolic regression with deterministic machine learning methods. Tree-based GP is used to form complex expressions and machine learning tools fine-tune the models (MRGP and KP), guide selection (KP and BGP), or determine appropriate crossover points (BGP). While these methods outperform state-of-the-art GP approaches, their running time remains a major drawback that arguably limits their adoption by the wider machine learning community.

Significant training time reduction can be achieved by adopting a search paradigm where the unit of selection is the *feature*, not the model itself, and where the goal is to evolve a small population of features that collectively allows a good model to be obtained. This method reduces bloat, population size, and number of evaluations, and introduces major conceptual changes in the evolutionary process [4]. For instance, with this approach, the *importance* of a given feature is relative to the other features present in the population. This represents a notable difference with typical evolutionary search processes, where the goal is to find individuals (features in this case) that perform well independently. In this paper, we introduce an efficient and robust feature subset selection method, i.e. a strategy for selecting a subset of *important features* from the population for use in model construction, that is critical for the success of the *feature synthesis* paradigm.

Although feature subset selection has been widely investigated (see [9] and therein), it remains a challenging problem. On the one hand, the quality of the subsets depends on the chosen model and learning algorithm. On the other, it can be computationally expensive to explore many subsets. To alleviate the computational burden, there are *stepwise* alternatives that start with an empty feature set and greedily add the feature that most improves performance. Another alternative for feature selection is the use of regularization methods. Regularization methods incorporate a penalty for complexity that results in sparse models, which in turn can be exploited for feature selection.

Evolutionary Feature Synthesis (EFS) is composed of two main steps: *feature composition* with variation operators and *feature subset selection*[2] via a pathwise regularization method [5]. Special focus is dedicated to 1) the development of a robust feature subset selection strategy, and 2) to motivate the design decisions that lead to an efficient feature search. The output of EFS is a readable model, expressed as a linear combination of the *evolved population of features*. Our approach provides fast learning times and yields competitive accuracy in the set of studied benchmarks when compared to neural networks, and outperforms both MRGP and linear methods. To the best of our knowledge, EFS is the first evolutionary method that learns competitive, yet readable models of small to medium sized datasets in seconds.

[1]Project website: http://flexgp.github.io/efs

[2]Not to be confused with the concept of training subset selection introduced by Gathercole and Ross in [8]

GECCO '15, July 11–15, 2015, Madrid, Spain

ISBN 978-1-4503-3472-3/15/07 . . . $15.00
DOI: http://dx.doi.org/10.1145/2739480.2754693

The paper is organized as follows. Section 2 introduces the machine learning methods at the core of EFS and Section 3 provides an overview of the method. In Section 4, we explain the feature composition step while in Section 5, we discuss feature subset selection techniques. Section 6 describes the experimental setup and we present the results in Section 7. Finally, Section 8 presents a review of related work and we conclude in Section 9.

2. BACKGROUND

We introduce the machine learning techniques at the core of our method, namely multiple linear regression, basis expansions, and pathwise LASSO regression (see [10]).

2.1 Multiple Linear Regression

Let us consider a dataset $(X^1, Y^1), \ldots, (X^n, Y^n)$ with univariate response variable Y and a $p-$dimensional vector of variables X. Multiple Linear Regression consists in finding the vector of coefficients $\hat{\beta}$ such that:

$$\hat{\beta} = \underset{\beta \in \mathbb{R}^p}{\operatorname{argmin}} ||Y - \sum_{i=1}^{p} \beta_i X_i||_2^2 \quad (1)$$

2.2 Basis Expansions

Linear Regression models can be extended with basis expansions to model nonlinear relations between the response variable Y and the variables X. We model a linear basis expansion in X as follows:

$$f(X) = \sum_{m=1}^{M} \beta_m h_m(X) \quad (2)$$

where $h_m(X) : \mathbb{R}^p \rightarrow \mathbb{R}$ is the mth transformation of X, $m = 1, \ldots, M$. In this context, the space determined by the basis functions $h_m, m = 1, \ldots, M$ is referred to as *feature space*, while the variables $X_j, j = 1, \ldots, p$ are referred to as *original variables*. The resulting regression problem is formulated as:

$$\hat{\beta} = \underset{\beta \in \mathbb{R}^m}{\operatorname{argmin}} ||Y - \sum_{m=1}^{M} \beta_m h_m(X)||_2^2 \quad (3)$$

Examples of simple transformations are $h(X) = cos(X_j)$, $h(X) = sin(X_j)$, $h(X) = log(X_j)$ [10]. One can also use functions involving several inputs, such as $h(X) = X_i \times X_j$. It is worth noting that the use of basis functions can make the dimensionality of the problem increase significantly. It is for this reason that the use of basis expansions is usually coupled with regularization methods.

2.3 Pathwise LASSO Regression

Least Absolute Shrinkage and Selection (LASSO) regression [18] is an extension of multiple linear regression where the regularization term $||\beta||_1$, the L1-norm of the weight vector, is added to the formulation of the problem, resulting:

$$\hat{\beta}^\lambda = \underset{\beta \in \mathbb{R}^m}{\operatorname{argmin}} ||Y - \sum_{m=1}^{M} \beta_m h_m(X)||_2^2 + \lambda \sum_{m=1}^{M} |\beta_m| \quad (4)$$

where $\lambda \in \mathbb{R}^+$ is the regularization coefficient. The LASSO penalty results in models with many coefficients close to zero, and a small subset larger and nonzero. Regularization is therefore helpful in problems where p is large, and is widely used for variable selection.

We resort to an efficient implementation of LASSO [6] based on the pathwise coordinate descent method introduced in [5]. This method computes the weights $\hat{\beta}$ for a decreasing sequence of regularization coefficients $\lambda \in \Gamma$. Note that the weights β^λ will vary for different values of λ.

3. METHOD OVERVIEW

EFS combines concepts of evolutionary computation with a state-of-the-art implementation of regularized linear regression. Our method relies on the assumption that the functions $h_m(X)$ introduced in Eq.(2) can be optimized by evolutionary computation. We design a population-based search where the unit of selection is *the feature*, as opposed to most related works where *models* are searched. In the following, we describe the steps involved in EFS (also depicted in Figure 1):

Initial Population The *population of features* is seeded with the functions $h_m(X) = X_m$, $m = 1, \ldots, p$, i.e. with the original variables of the problem.

Then, EFS executes an optimization loop composed of three steps: model generation, feature composition, and feature subset selection.

Model generation A first LASSO run obtains a linear combination of the features of the current population. The generated model is archived if it reduces the error of the best model found in previous iterations.

Feature composition In this step detailed in Section 4, variation operators augment the population with new features.

Feature subset selection We perform a second LASSO run on the augmented population of features and exploit the information generated during the regression process to estimate *feature importance*. The estimated *importance* is used to select the subset of the extended population that will be passed to the next generation. More details are provided in Section 5.

Stop criteria The process stops if the best model is not replaced in a preset number of iterations, or if a timeout is reached.

It is worth mentioning that, because the population of features is seeded with the original variables, our method guarantees an accuracy with respect to training data at least as good as that of the LASSO fit.

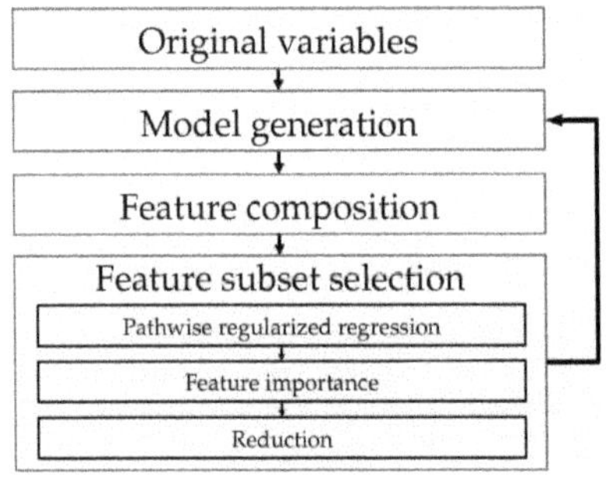

Figure 1: Steps involved in evolutionary feature synthesis.

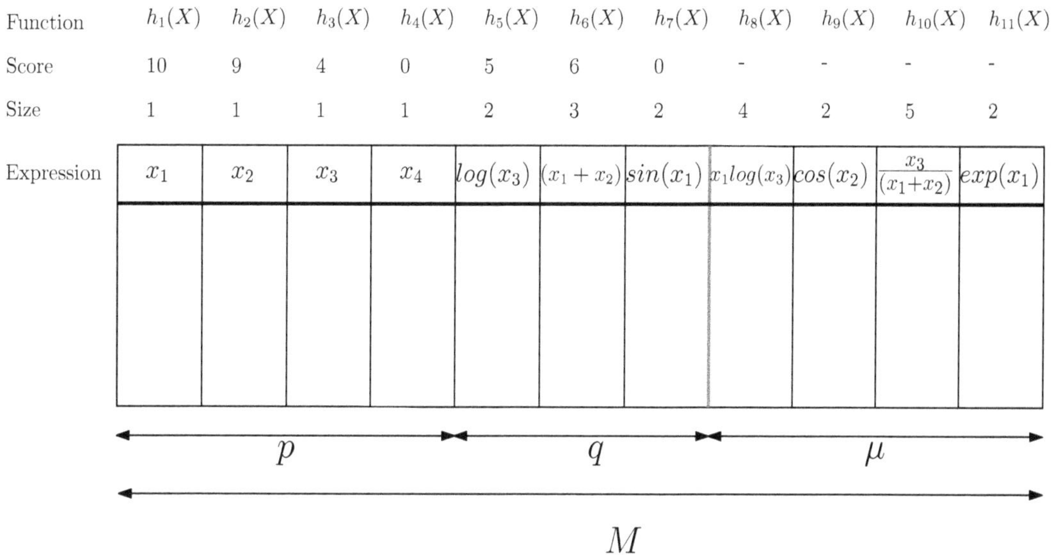

Figure 2: Feature Composition. Every generation, μ new features are composed by applying unary or binary operators to the current population of features. The size of the current population is given by $p+q$, where p is the dimensionality of the data and q is the number of composed features surviving from the previous generation.

4. FEATURE COMPOSITION

This step is inspired by the crossover and mutation steps performed in tree-based Genetic Programming and can be seen as generating new columns of the covariates matrix.

4.1 Bottom-up generation of new features

A set of μ features are composed by applying unary or binary mathematical operators to the existing features. The system admits the following set of operators:

$$O = \{+, -, *, /, exp, log, sqrt, square, cube, sin, cos\} \quad (5)$$

A tournament selection based on a precomputed *feature score* (see Section 5) is used to choose between $h_1, \ldots, h_{p+q}$, the features that will be combined to generate new features. We comment the example depicted in Figure 2. The values of the parameters are as follows:

- $p = 4$: the dimensionality of the problem,
- $q = 3$: the number of features added to the model,
- $\mu = 4$: the features composed in a given iteration,
- $M = p + q + \mu$: the population size.

We enumerate below the operations performed to the features $h_1, \ldots, h_7$ to generate the features $h_8, \ldots, h_{11}$:

- h_8: is a composition of h_1 and h_5 with the op. $*$,
- h_9: is a composition of h_2 with the op. cos,
- h_{10}: is a composition of h_3 and h_6 with the op. $/$,
- h_{11}: is a composition of h_1 with the op. exp.

4.2 Control for feature complexity

We set a maximum size for the generated features. We define the size of a feature as the count of *original variables* and *operators* appearing in the feature. For instance, the size of the features x_1, $log(x_1)$, and $\frac{x_3}{(x_1+x_2)}$ is respectively 1, 2, and 5. Newly generated features are discarded if their size is greater than the preset maximum. Let h_{p_1}, h_{p_2} be the features combined to generate a given feature h_i. Then, the size of h_i is given by:

$$size(h_i) = \begin{cases} size(h_{p_1}) + size(h_{p_2}) + 1, \text{ if binary } op \\ size(h_{p_1}) + 1, \text{ if unary } op \end{cases} \quad (6)$$

In this work, the maximum size is set to 5 in order to obtain readable features that can be interpreted by domain experts. This technique is also used to control model complexity in tree-based Genetic Programming. In fact, the proposed complexity measure can be seen as the size of the expression tree representing a given feature.

4.3 Differences with Genetic Programming

It is important to stress the following differences with respect to the crossover and mutation steps employed in tree-based Genetic Programming:

Vectorial operations vs. postponed evaluation: Given two existing features and an operator, the generation of a new feature is a vectorial (column-wise) operation. Vectorial operations are efficient and suitable for parallel execution. On the other hand, in tree-based Genetic Programming, crossover and mutation only modify the tree representation of the models. Later, in the evaluation step, each of the modified models needs to be traversed n times, where n is the number of exemplars in the dataset.

No symbolic representation: The values of a given feature are computed on the fly when the feature is first generated. Therefore, no symbolic representation is needed. Note that, however, a string representation of the generated feature is stored for logging purposes.

5. METHODS FOR FEATURE SELECTION

We introduce two strategies that run pathwise LASSO regression on the features of the population, and that exploit the generated information to guide feature selection.

5.1 Strategy 1: Flexible Model Size

Given a population of features P with size $|P| = M$, the goal is to select a subset $P' \subset P$ such that $|P'| \leq M$. As a first approach, we simply analyze the weights of the model obtained with LASSO on the augmented population and discard the features with zero weights. The steps involved in this first approach are described below:

Step 1: We run LASSO via pathwise coordinate descent (see [5]) on the extended population. As a result, we obtain the weight vectors β^{λ}, $\forall\lambda \in \Gamma$, i.e. for a set of decreasing regularization coefficients. Note that the coefficient of multiple correlation R^2 of each weight vector can be retrieved at no additional cost.

Step 2: We select the weights that maximize the coefficient of multiple correlation R^2. That is, we select the weights β^m such that $R^2_m \geq R^2_{\lambda}, \forall\lambda \in \Gamma$.

Step 3: We keep the original variables and the composed features with non-zero weights, and discard the rest. Note that the number of zero weights is not fixed beforehand, and thus the number of selected features will vary from an iteration to the other. The surviving features will be included in a new model and will be used to compose new features in the next generation.

This method presents one major drawback since, in the case where all the features have non-zero weights, no reduction occurs and the process stops prematurely.

As a preliminary test, we benchmark this approach with the heating energy efficiency (ENH) regression problem introduced in [19]. The characteristics of this dataset are summarized in Table 3. We explore three different population sizes $M = 2p = 16$, $M = 4p = 32$, and $M = 6p = 48$, where p is the number of original variables of the problem (in this case $p = 8$) and perform 20 runs for each of the three configurations.

Figure 3 shows the mean squared error (MSE) over time of the models obtained with the three population sizes. In the case where $M = 2p$ (Figure 3a), it can be seen that, although an average error of 5.866 is achieved, the method presents a great variance over the 20 runs. The variance is the consequence of premature stops of the search, observed when all the features of the population are assigned non-zero weights. In fact, all the 20 runs stopped in less than 0.44s and executed an average of only 13 generations. On the other hand, when $M = 4p$ or $M = 6p$ (Figure 3b), the average MSE is reduced over time, and achieves respectively 1.536 and 1.107 in less that 5 seconds. The variance seems to decrease for increasing population sizes since the case where $M = 6p$ presents the lowest variability between runs.

These results show that our method is capable of finding features leading to a better accuracy on the training set. However, this error reduction is achieved at the expense of an increased complexity of the final model. Next, we explore an extension of this approach that achieves simpler models.

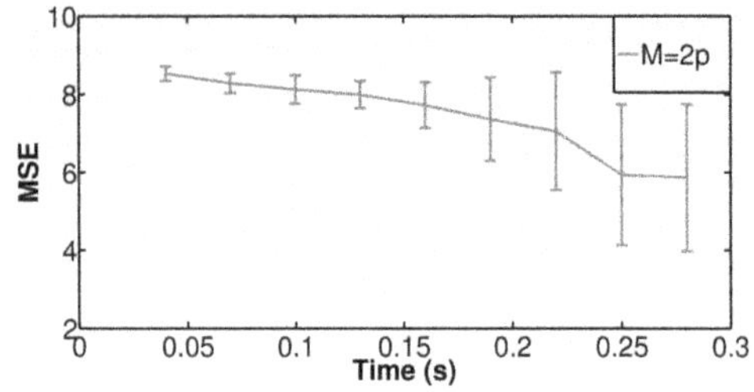

(a) Flexible model size: M=2p

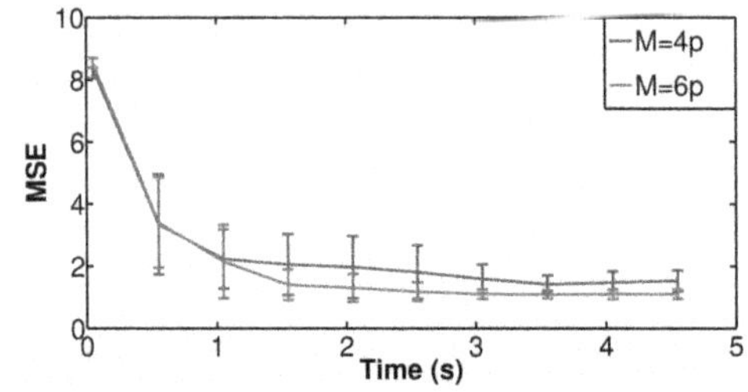

(b) Flexible model size: M=4p vs M=6p

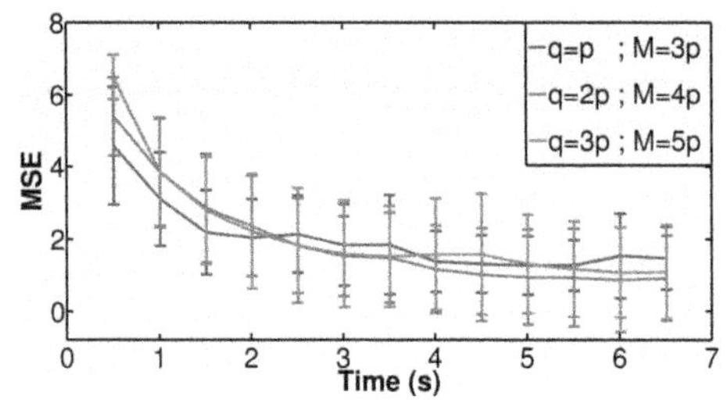

(c) Fixed model Size: (q=p;M=3p) vs (q=2p;M=4p) vs (q=3p;M=5p)

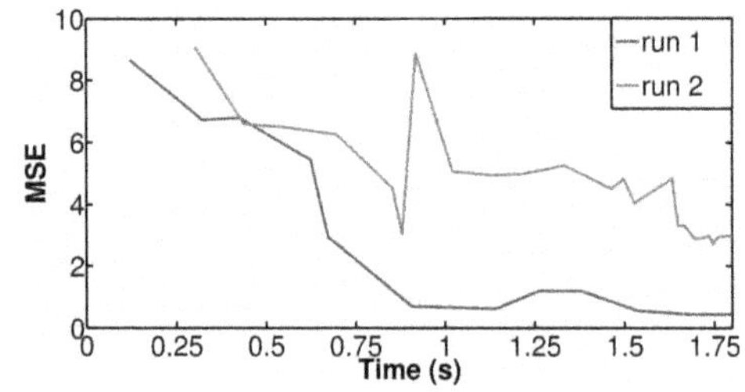

(d) Fixed model size: 2 example runs with (q = p; M=3p)

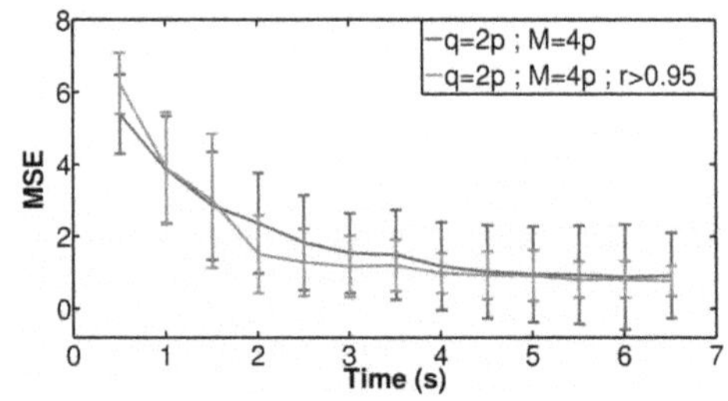

(e) Fixed model size: (q=2p;M=4p) vs correlation filtering with (q=2p;M=4p;r>0.95)

Figure 3: Mean Squared Error (MSE) on training data vs time (seconds) with the different studied subset selection strategies. The plots are obtained by averaging 20 runs on the heating energy efficiency dataset. The error bars show the standard deviation.

5.2 Strategy 2: Fixed Model Size

We set a maximum model size, that is, a maximum number of features included in the model. Note that, as in the previous strategy, we force the survival of the original variables of the problem.

Let P be a population of features with size $|P|=M$, then the goal is to select a subset of $P' \subset P$ such that $|P'|<M$ and $|P'|=p+q$, where p is the number of original variables of the problem and q is fixed and represents the number of composed features added to the model. This strategy results in a model including at most $p+q$ features and $\mu=M-(p+q)$ discarded features.

In this case, looking at non-zero weights is not enough, since the number of composed features with non-zero weights can be greater than the preset q. Instead, we perform a complete ranking of the M features of the population according to an estimation of their importance. The proposed *importance measure* captures the number of times a given feature appears in the model for different values of the regularization coefficient λ, as well as the accuracy of the models in which it appears:

Step 1: As in Strategy 1, we run LASSO via pathwise coordinate descent on the extended population.

Step 2: We estimate the *importance* of each feature h_j as:

$$importance(h_j) = \sum_{\lambda_i \in \Gamma} score(j, \beta^{\lambda_i}) \quad (7)$$

$$score(j, \beta^{\lambda_i}) = \begin{cases} R^2_{\lambda_i} \text{ if } \beta_j^{\lambda_i} \neq 0 \\ 0 \text{ otherwise} \end{cases} \quad (8)$$

where $R^2_{\lambda_i}$ and $\beta_j^{\lambda_i}$ are respectively the coefficient of multiple correlation and the weight of h_j obtained for λ_i.

Step 3: We rank the features according to the estimated *importance*. The p original variables and the top q composed features survive and will be used in the next generation to compose new features. The rest of the features are discarded.

We perform a preliminary test with the heating energy efficiency dataset also used to benchmark the previous selection strategy. Since the goal is to obtain simpler models, we explore the following configurations:

- $q=p; M=3p$: the model includes at most $2p$ features
- $q=2p; M=4p$: the model includes at most $3p$ features
- $q=3p; M=5p$: the model includes at most $4p$ features

Table 1 shows a model obtained with $q=2p$ and $M=4p$. Note that we verified that none of the 19 features of the presented model are constants, and that removing any of the features has an impact on the model's error.

Figure 3c shows the MSE over time of the models obtained with the three configurations. In all cases, the error is reduced over time. The first setup ($q=p; M=3p$) depicted in blue yields the highest MSE (1.278). The second configuration (green), minimizes the error of the resulting model (0.875) and also includes less features than the third (red) configuration (MSE= 1.081). Therefore, we fix the parameters $q=2p$ and $M=4p$ going forward.

The performed analysis reveals a great variance of the error over the different runs. This variance is due to the fact that model error is not systematically reduced after each selection step. Figure 3d shows two runs illustrating this issue. The first (run 1) is an example of appropriate behavior of the search where the MSE of the generated model decreases over time. On the other hand, in the second run there is a spike at 0.92s, corresponding to the 7th generation, where the MSE on the training set jumps from 3.064 to 8.878.

TRAIN SET MSE: 0.251		
-	40.763	
+	0.328	* X6
-	20.690	* X7
-	0.838	* X8
-	150.026	* (log(cos(cube(sin X4))))
+	2.528	* (sin(sin(sin(sin X2))))
-	0.434	* (sin(cube(* X5 X3)))
+	1.313	* (sin(cos(* X5 X3)))
+	1.280E-14	* (square(square(* X2 X5)))
-	0.066	* (sin(cos(+ X8 X5)))
+	12.014	* (sqrt(divide X5 (cos X7)))
+	8.156	* (exp(sqrt(* X1 X7)))
+	0.361	* (- (square(sin X8)) X6)
+	55.787	* (sqrt(divide(sqrt X8) X4))
-	12.661	* (cos(sin(divide X4 X1)))
-	0.487	* (sin X8)
-	3.417	* (sin(sin(divide X4 X1)))
+	8.834	* (sqrt(sqrt(square(cos X2))))
+	19.890	* (cos(square(square(cos X2))))
+	0.094	* (*(* X1 X7)X3)

Table 1: Model reached in 8.648 seconds for the ENH dataset with $q=2p; M=4p$. The maximum feature size is set to 5.

FEATURE	RANK	IMPORT.
(-(sin(cos X3))X5)	1st	87.3
(div(cube(cos X4))X1)	2nd	86.1
(* X3(* X7 X5))	3rd	83.8
(sqrt(sqrt(sqrt(sqrt X8))))	4th	67.1
(cos(cos(cube(sin X3))))	5th	64.4
(square X6)	6th	55.2
(sin(square X6))	7th	49.7
(cube(exp(sin X2)))	8th	49.7
----------------------------	----	----
(cos X2)	9th	43.7
(log(exp(sin X2)))	10th	42.3
(exp(cos X2))	11th	34.7
(div X1(square X6))	12th	30.9
(exp(sin X2))	13th	30.0
(cos X1)	14th	27.6
(exp X8)	15th	24.1

Table 2: Features present in the extended population and their rank and score. The two features in red (9th and 11th) are discarded because they are highly correlated ($r = 0.975$).

To understand the causes of such undesirable behavior, we report in Table 2 the ranking of the extended population of features at the end of the 7th generation. Note that, in this particular case, 8 features need to be selected. We highlight two features, $cosX2$ (9th) and $exp(cosX2)$ (11th), that are discarded although their estimated importance shows that they are relevant. These two features are highly correlated, with a Pearson correlation coefficient of 0.975. This shows that, because these two features are correlated, their importance is split between them and thus neither gets picked, while the desired behavior would be to pick one and discard the other. Next, we further improve our method to alleviate the issues caused by correlated variables.

5.3 Strategy 3: Correlation Filtering

A complete correlation analysis of the M features of the population is expensive since M^2 correlations need to be calculated, and each of the computations requires a pass over the data. To avoid the extra computational cost, we only check the Pearson correlation coefficient r of a given feature with its parent(s) (see Section 4): the feature in question is discarded if the correlation with any of its parents is higher than a given threshold t. We implement this filter during the feature composition step, updating the partial sums necessary for the computation of r as the values of the new feature are computed. This way, no extra passes over the data are required.

We set the correlation threshold to $t = 0.95$ and the parameters $q = 2p$ and $M = 4p$ and benchmark our method with the same heating energy dataset used previously. Figure 3e shows the MSE over time of the models obtained without correlation filtering and with the filter $r > 0.95$. The average MSE obtained with both approaches is almost identical. The variance over the 20 runs, however, is reduced when the filtering strategy is adopted. Therefore, the correlation check, done at a negligible cost, seems to improve the robustness of our method against correlated features.

With this final design, we turn to analyze whether EFS is competitive against state-of-the-art regression methods in terms of accuracy and running time, while generating readable symbolic models.

6. EXPERIMENTAL SETUP

In this section, we introduce the datasets and regression approaches used to benchmark EFS.

6.1 Datasets

We consider datasets where the variables correspond to physical measurements. Such benchmarks are suitable to analyze whether EFS is capable of finding higher-level features that result in a more accurate model. Table 3 summarizes the regression problems used in this study. The datasets ENH and ENC (energy efficiency of heating and cooling loads) come from simulations [19] while the NOx emissions dataset is a collection of real power plant data [20]. In both the red and white wine quality datasets, the original variables are physical measurements, but the dependent variable is a subjective grade, expressed on a scale from very bad (0) to excellent (10). Finally, the Million Song Dataset (MSD) year prediction challenge, introduced in [3], is a regression problem in which the goal is to predict the release year of a large set of songs. The size and dimensionality of the dataset are challenging, since it is composed of 515K songs, each described with 90 features and a year label.

6.2 Compared Approaches

We introduce the compared regression methods:

Multiple Linear Regression (MR): We obtain a linear model of the data using the least squares approach.

Dataset	p	Exemplars		
		Training	Test	Total
ENC	8	512	256	768
ENH	8	512	256	768
NOX	18	4017	1210	5227
WIR	11	1066	533	1559
WIW	11	3265	1633	4898
MSD	90	413124	102440	515564

Table 3: Benchmark datasets.

LASSO: The same implementation of LASSO embedded in EFS is used to perform L1-regularized linear regression.
Vowpal Wabbit (VW): Vowpal Wabbit [14] is a fast out-of-core online learning algorithm based on sparse gradient descent. VW generates linear models of large datasets (that might not fit in RAM) in minimal time.
Feed Forward Neural Networks (FFNN): We consider a configuration with one hidden layer of 10 neurons. We employ Matlab's Neural Network Toolbox [16] to train the FFNNs. The networks are trained via backpropagation with the Levenberg-Marquardt optimization.
Multiple Regression Genetic Programming (MRGP): MRGP is a hybrid method that combines tree-based Genetic Programming with LASSO [1, 2]. MRGP outperforms both multiple linear regression and traditional GP-based symbolic regression methods. We exploit MRGP's parallelism by executing it in a 4-threaded fashion.
EFS: We run EFS with the following parameters: $q = 2p$ and $M = 4p$ (see Section 5.2). Additionally, we adopt the correlation filtering strategy ($r > 0.95$) presented in Section 5.3.

7. RESULTS

We compare the mean squared error (MSE) and running time of the compared approaches. Note that we perform 20 runs of the algorithms that present a stochastic nature, that is, FFNN, MRGP, and EFS.

7.1 Comparison in terms of error

Table 4 reports the average test MSE achieved by the compared approaches for the different datasets and Figure 4 shows the boxplots generated with the 20 runs.

ENH: Nonlinear methods, i.e. FFNN, MRGP, and EFS clearly outperform the linear ones (MR, LASSO, and VW). In particular MRGP and EFS perform particularly well reaching an MSE of 0.314 and 0.317 respectively.
ENC: As in the previous case, FFNN, MRGP, and EFS significantly reduce the error of the linear methods. In this case, EFS presents the lowest MSE (2.548).
NOx: MRGP and EFS remain close to the linear methods in terms of accuracy. FFNN performs particularly well on this dataset, reaching an MSE of only 0.025.
WIR: This is the only dataset where the linear methods MR and LASSO, with an MSE of 0.400, outperform the rest of the methods. EFS remains close to the linear models with an MSE of 0.402.
WIW: Nonlinear methods improve the accuracy of MR or LASSO only marginally, reducing the MSE from 0.580 to 0.533 in the case of EFS.
MSD: MRGP obtains an MSE of 87.233, similar to that of the linear models. On the other hand, EFS obtains an error of 82.903 and FFNN further reduces it to 77.019.

Overall, FFNN and EFS present the lowest error, with an average rank of 2.333. They are followed by MRGP, LASSO, and MR with a rank of 3.167, 3.583, and 3.750 respectively. Finally, VW ranks 5.833 on average. It is worth mentioning that VW is sensitive to the parameters governing the learning process, and, according to our experience, it is possible to find a set of parameters that will achieve an accuracy close to that of MR.

	ENH		ENC		NOx		WIR		WIW		MSD		Rank	
	MSE	Time	MSE	Time	MSE	Time	MSE	Time	MSE	Time	MSE	Time	MSE	Time
MR	8.303	0.040	10.576	0.030	0.038	0.120	0.400	0.030	0.580	0.050	87.225	41.100	3.750	2.167
LASSO	8.282	0.142	10.584	0.154	0.038	0.319	0.400	0.162	0.580	0.224	87.217	17.409	3.583	2.833
VW	9.577	0.007	13.012	0.014	0.080	0.039	0.417	0.011	0.599	0.039	87.233	12.473	5.833	1.000
FFNN	0.400	1.036	2.649	1.042	0.025	3.186	0.414	0.622	0.542	1.415	77.019	2013.900	2.333	4.000
MRGP	0.314	60.000	2.703	60.000	0.037	60.000	0.407	60.000	0.548	60.000	87.313	3600.000	3.167	5.917
EFS	0.317	10.575	2.548	14.161	0.039	58.852	0.402	21.906	0.533	35.498	82.903	3600.000	2.333	5.083

Table 4: Testing set Mean Squared Error (MSE) and learning time in seconds of the compared regression techniques.

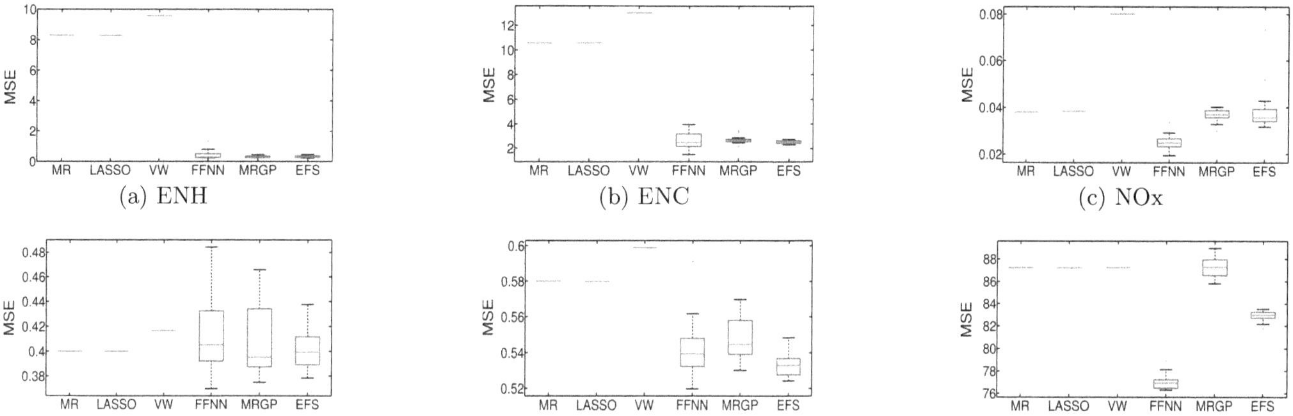

(a) ENH (b) ENC (c) NOx

(d) WIR (e) WIW (f) MSD

Figure 4: Testing set Mean Squared Error (MSE) of the compared regression techniques.

7.2 Comparison in terms of speed

As shown in Table 4, the studied methods are ranked by running time as follows.

VW: VW is the fastest method. It is worth mentioning that, in the case of the MSD dataset, it achieves an error close to that of MR in only 12.473 seconds.

MR and LASSO: The linear methods MR and LASSO rank second and third. The employed pathwise coordinate descent implementation is better suited for larger datasets. In fact, in the case of the largest dataset (MSD), MR runs for 41.100 seconds while LASSO needs 17.409 seconds to execute.

FFNN: FFNN are remarkably fast in the case of the ENH, ENC, NOx, WIR, and WIW datasets, taking between 0.622 and 3.186 seconds. The training time of FFNNs depends on the number of parameters that need to be learned. In the case of MSD, 910 parameters are learned, consuming an average of 2013.900 seconds.

EFS: Since we are interested in fast learning, we allowed EFS to run for one minute for the first five datasets, while the maximum running time for MSD was set to 60 minutes. EFS converged in 10.575 and 14.161 seconds for the ENH and ENC datasets respectively. In the case of the WIR (21.906s) and WIW (35.498s) datasets, it also finished before the established budget. On the other hand, the method did not converge in the established time for the NOx and MSD datasets.

MRGP: As for EFS, we allowed MRGP to run for 60 seconds for the ENH, ENC, NOx, WIR, and WIW datasets. For the larger MSD dataset, MRGP ran for one hour.

It is important to stress a key difference between MRGP and EFS and the rest of the approaches. The linear methods and FFNN focus the learning process on tuning the parameters of a model with a predefined structure. On the other hand, MRGP and EFS search for both the structure of the model and its parameters, resulting in longer training times which sometimes pay off with better accuracy while remaining acceptable in time cost.

7.3 A note on the complexity of the models

We comment the complexity of the retrieved models:

MR, LASSO, and VW: These linear methods obtain the simplest models. Given a dataset composed of p original variables, only $p+1$ weights need to be tuned during the learning process. In the case of LASSO and VW, the model is further simplified by means of a regularization penalty.

FFNN: The complexity of the FFNN is given by the structure of the network. In this case, although the designed network only counts one hidden layer of 10 neurons, the resulting model is hardly interpretable.

MRGP: MRGP models are expression trees coupled with a set of weights, each associated with one node of the tree. These models can be seen as highly complex basis expansion models (see Eq. (2)). Note that, in the case of a complete binary tree, the size of the resulting basis expansion model would be $2^h - 1$, where h denotes the height of the tree. The size of MRGP models can quickly explode for the standard maximum tree height $h=17$ used in tree-based GP.

EFS: EFS provides readable basis expansion models composed of the original variables and a set of composed features. We have determined that considering models of size p(original variables)+$2p$(additional features)= $3p$ provides appropriate performance in practice. In this work, we limited the size of the composed features to be at most 5 (5 elements between variables and operators). We consider that this setting results in readable models that can be analyzed and interpreted by domain experts.

8. RELATED WORK

A large corpus of research uses GP to generate features; examples are [15], [7] and [12]. The combination of GP with LASSO is also exploited by the MRGP method [2].

EFS shares the *feature synthesis paradigm* with Kaizen Programming [4]. The main difference between the two methods is the feature subset selection strategy. EFS exploits pathwise regularized linear regression to avoid search stagnation, thus eliminating the need of restarting the run with a larger population size. Additionally, EFS does not require a symbolic representation of the features, yet it still provides flexibility to model nonlinear data.

Basis expansions allow domain experts to include knowledge of the problem to model nonlinear data. FFX [17] is a non-evolutionary technique that exploits this idea: it generates *many* basis functions and uses regularized linear regression to combine them. Icke *et al.* expand the FFX approach by running GP-based symbolic regression on the augmented space of features [11]. In these two works, the set of augmented features is fixed beforehand and is not explored during the learning process. It is the realization that the feature space can be efficiently searched with evolutionary computation that led us to develop the EFS method.

9. SUMMARY AND FUTURE WORK

We have introduced Evolutionary Feature Synthesis (EFS). EFS generates readable, nonlinear models of small to medium size datasets in seconds. In terms of accuracy, it is competitive against neural networks and outperforms both linear methods and MRGP, up to now the best regression tool based on evolutionary computation.

In future work, we will exploit the variable selection procedures involved in other machine learning algorithms such as decision tree induction algorithms. Also, the exploration of the feature synthesis paradigm in combination with the link functions used in generalized linear models, such as the logistic function, opens an wide area for exploration.

10. ACKNOWLEDGMENTS

This work was supported by the Li Ka Shing Foundation.

11. REFERENCES

[1] Multiple regression genetic programming in Java. http://flexgp.github.io/gp-learners/, 2014.

[2] I. Arnaldo, K. Krawiec, and U.-M. O'Reilly. Multiple regression genetic programming. In *Proceedings of the 2014 Conference on Genetic and Evolutionary Computation*, GECCO '14, pages 879–886, New York, NY, USA, 2014. ACM.

[3] T. Bertin-Mahieux, D. Ellis, B. Whitman, and P. Lamere. The million song dataset. In *ISMIR 2011: Proceedings of the 12th International Society for Music Information Retrieval Conference, October 24-28, Miami, Florida*, pages 591–596, 2011.

[4] V. V. De Melo. Kaizen programming. In *Proceedings of the 2014 Conference on Genetic and Evolutionary Computation*, GECCO '14, pages 895–902, New York, NY, USA, 2014. ACM.

[5] J. H. Friedman, T. Hastie, and R. Tibshirani. Regularization paths for generalized linear models via coordinate descent. *Journal of Statistical Software*, 33(1):1–22, 2 2010.

[6] Y. Ganjisaffar. Lasso4j. https://code.google.com/p/lasso4j/, 2014.

[7] M. Garcia-Limon, H. J. Escalante, E. Morales, and A. Morales-Reyes. Simultaneous generation of prototypes and features through genetic programming. In *Proceedings of the 2014 Conference on Genetic and Evolutionary Computation*, GECCO '14, pages 517–524, New York, NY, USA, 2014. ACM.

[8] C. Gathercole and P. Ross. Dynamic training subset selection for supervised learning in genetic programming. In Y. Davidor, H.-P. Schwefel, and R. Manner, editors, *Parallel Problem Solving from Nature, PPSN III*, volume 866 of *Lecture Notes in Computer Science*, pages 312–321. Springer Berlin Heidelberg, 1994.

[9] I. Guyon and A. Elisseeff. An introduction to variable and feature selection. *Journal of Machine Learning Research*, 3:1157–1182, Mar. 2003.

[10] T. Hastie, R. Tibshirani, and J. Friedman. *The elements of statistical learning: data mining, inference and prediction.* Springer, 2nd edition, 2009.

[11] I. Icke and J. Bongard. Improving genetic programming based symbolic regression using deterministic machine learning. In *2013 IEEE Congress on Evolutionary Computation (CEC)*, pages 1763–1770, June 2013.

[12] U. Kamath, J. Lin, and K. De Jong. SAX-EFG: An evolutionary feature generation framework for time series classification. In *Proceedings of the 2014 Conference on Genetic and Evolutionary Computation*, GECCO '14, pages 533–540, New York, NY, USA, 2014. ACM.

[13] K. Krawiec and U.-M. O'Reilly. Behavioral programming: A broader and more detailed take on semantic GP. In *Proceedings of the 2014 Conference on Genetic and Evolutionary Computation*, GECCO '14, pages 935–942, New York, NY, USA, 2014. ACM.

[14] J. Langford, L. Li, and T. Zhang. Sparse online learning via truncated gradient. *Journal of Machine Learning Research*, 10:777–801, June 2009.

[15] Y. Lin and B. Bhanu. Evolutionary feature synthesis for object recognition. *IEEE Transactions on Systems, Man, and Cybernetics, Part C: Applications and Reviews*, 35(2):156–171, May 2005.

[16] MathWorks. Neural network toolbox, 2014.

[17] T. McConaghy. FFX: Fast, scalable, deterministic symbolic regression technology. In R. Riolo, E. Vladislavleva, and J. H. Moore, editors, *Genetic Programming Theory and Practice IX*, Genetic and Evolutionary Computation, pages 235–260. Springer New York, 2011.

[18] R. Tibshirani. Regression shrinkage and selection via the lasso. *Journal of the Royal Statistical Society, Series B*, 58:267–288, 1994.

[19] A. Tsanas and A. Xifara. Accurate quantitative estimation of energy performance of residential buildings using statistical machine learning tools. *Energy and Buildings*, 49(0):560–567, 2012.

[20] F. Xue, R. Subbu, and P. Bonissone. Locally weighted fusion of multiple predictive models. In *International Joint Conference on Neural Networks, 2006. IJCNN '06.*, pages 2137–2143, 2006.

An Efficient Structural Diversity Technique for Genetic Programming

Armand R. Burks
BEACON Center for the Study of Evolution in Action
Michigan State University, U.S.A.
burksarm@msu.edu

William F. Punch
BEACON Center for the Study of Evolution in Action
Michigan State University, U.S.A.
punch@msu.edu

ABSTRACT

Genetic diversity plays an important role in avoiding premature convergence, which is a phenomenon that stifles the search effectiveness of evolutionary algorithms. However, approaches that avoid premature convergence by maintaining genetic diversity can do so at the cost of efficiency, requiring more fitness evaluations to find high quality solutions. We introduce a simple and efficient genetic diversity technique that is capable of avoiding premature convergence while maintaining a high level of search quality in tree-based genetic programming. Our method finds solutions to a set of benchmark problems in significantly fewer fitness evaluations than the algorithms that we compared against.

Categories and Subject Descriptors

I.2.8 [**ARTIFICIAL INTELLIGENCE**]: Problem Solving, Control Methods, and Search

Keywords

genetic programming; diversity; premature convergence

1. INTRODUCTION

Premature convergence is one of the biggest problems that traditional evolutionary algorithms face. Premature convergence can be thought of as evolutionary stagnation, wherein the population reaches a point at which it is very difficult, or even impossible, to improve in fitness. As the population becomes more genetically similar, the traditional genetic operators such as crossover and mutation become less likely to escape local optima.

Evolutionary algorithms (EAs) have widely been applied to solve problems with enormous search spaces that usually contain an abundance of local optima. Therefore, the ability to effectively explore such spaces is critical to finding solutions. In many EAs, as the population converges genetically, the population also converges around a local peak in the fitness landscape. This has two notable impacts on the quality of the search process: (1) as individuals in the population become more genetically similar, the traditional crossover and mutation operators only produce offspring that highly resemble their parents and (2) the EA is reduced to a local search, incapable of effectively moving the population away from the local fitness peak in order to find global optima.

GECCO '15, July 11–15, 2015, Madrid, Spain
© 2015 ACM. ISBN 978-1-4503-3472-3/15/07...$15.00
DOI: http://dx.doi.org/10.1145/2739480.2754649

1.1 Genetic Programming

We consider the role of genetic diversity in avoiding premature convergence in genetic programming (GP). GP represents a class of heuristic techniques that extend from the traditional genetic algorithm. In classical tree-based GP, individuals are encoded with a tree structure, similar to an abstract syntax tree. As one of the main goals in GP is to evolve computer programs, this tree structure provides a generic way of representing such programs, and it allows the search through the space of possible programs with genetic operators such as crossover and mutation.

1.2 Premature Convergence in GP

The problem of premature convergence is perhaps even more puzzling for traditional tree-based GP because of the variable-size tree representation and the nature of the traditional genetic operators. Although it has been shown that GP populations do not converge the same way as in the classical binary-encoded genetic algorithm [10], premature convergence is still a problem for GP. Earlier analysis work showed that in classical tree-based GP using only subtree crossover, very few individuals from the initial population contribute *any* genetic material to the final population [12]. That work also showed that the entire population often inherits the rooted portion of their trees from a single ancestor, referred to as *Eve*, within just a few generations from the onset of the run. Additionally, over 70% of the population became completely identical to the *Eve* individual in the top four levels of their trees [12].

Other studies into the nature and effectiveness of the typical subtree crossover operator in GP have revealed some interesting properties that contribute to the major loss of genetic diversity [3, 13]. In the traditional subtree crossover, a node is uniformly randomly selected as the crossover point in each parent. The resulting subtrees rooted at each crossover point are exchanged between the parents to create two offspring. This directly contributes to the problem that trees tend to converge to the same structure near the top. Gathercole and Ross showed that nodes deeper in the tree are frequently selected for crossover, leaving upper portions of the trees untouched [3].

Due to the branching factors of the trees, there is a disproportionately large number of nodes in lower levels compared to those higher up in the trees. This means that uniformly randomly choosing a node is more likely to select a node at a lower level. Coupled with a depth limit, which is commonly used to avoid unrestricted tree growth, lower crossover points will result in failed crossover attempts, as they produce offspring that violate the depth limit. This has partly been addressed by simply adding a bias to probabilistically select function (internal) nodes more often than terminal (leaf) nodes. However, Poli and Langdon also showed that subtree crossover tends to exchange little genetic material, on average, producing offspring that are highly identical to one of the two parents [13].

2. EXISTING DIVERSITY TECHNIQUES

2.1 Genetic Diversity Metrics

Several metrics for measuring genetic diversity have been proposed [1]. Many of these metrics attempt to measure the degree to which two genotypes differ by taking into account some aspect of their tree structures. For example, one approach to calculating the the distance between trees considers the overlapping nodes when the two trees are overlaid [2]. After overlaying the trees, the distance is then calculated by taking the total number of differing nodes divided by the size of the smaller tree.

As Burke et al. discuss [1], the main intuition behind promoting diversity is that increased diversity gives the evolutionary process more opportunities to discover solutions. However, it is not always clear which type of diversity metric to employ, or how much diversity is sufficient. For many problem domains, although two genotypes are considered different by a genotypic distance metric, the two genotypes can encode the same (or very similar) behavior or phenotype, and ultimately yield the same fitness value.

With this issue in mind, other approaches have been proposed to explicitly maintain a diverse set of behaviors or phenotypes in the population [8, 11]. The fitness uniform selection scheme [8] attempts to maintain a spread of fitness values over the range of possible fitness values. On the other hand, the novelty search algorithm [11] completely ignores fitness and instead searches for unique behaviors during evolution to avoid the deceptive nature of fitness functions for certain problems. In its original implementation, the novelty search algorithm also benefits from a genetic diversity maintenance technique.

The Structure Fitness Sharing (SFS) algorithm [7] is another method that attempts to promote diversity based on tree structure. Motivated by the fitness sharing concept [4], SFS uses labels on tree structures to decrease the fitness of structures that are over-represented in the population. Instead of directly calculating and comparing genotypic distances, SFS labels each unique structure in the population and keeps track of the total individuals and best fitness for each structure.

2.2 Structured Populations

Instead of trying to enforce genetic diversity through an explicit diversity measure, alternative approaches impose a structure on the population to achieve the goal of avoiding premature convergence [5, 6]. One such approach is the Age-Layered Population Structure (ALPS) [5]. ALPS uses the concept of "genotypic age" to segregate the population into a hierarchy of several age layers, where genotypic age attempts to measure how long an individual's genetic material has been evolving.

The main idea behind ALPS is to localize competition by genotypic age so that younger, less-fit, individuals do not immediately become dominated by older more-fit individuals. This principle allows new randomly generated individuals to be regularly inserted into the population without immediately being outcompeted. This is a key feature of ALPS because the new random individuals could be located within a different region of the search space and contain valuable genetic material that can help the population escape local optima. Without the localized competition of the hierarchical structure, these new random individuals would likely be dominated by older individuals before having a chance to propagate useful genetic material throughout the population.

2.3 Multi-objective Optimization

Multi-objective approaches have also been proposed to optimize fitness while maintaining diversity. The FOCUS (find only and complete undominated sets) method transforms single objective problems into a three-dimensional search to simultaneously optimize fitness, diversity, and tree size [2]. The FOCUS method maintains genetic diversity by using the overlapping tree distance metric described in Section 2.1 to give preference to individuals with the least average squared distance to the entire population.

The Age-Fitness Pareto Optimization algorithm [14] is another multi-objective approach that attempts to maintain genetic diversity while optimizing fitness. Based on the genotypic age concept of ALPS, genotypic age is minimized in order to allow newer, younger solutions in different regions of the search space to direct search effort toward promising areas. This method allows a new random individual to be added to the population each generation without it being immediately dominated by older, more-fit individuals. This method avoids premature convergence without the need for an $O(n^2)$ distance calculation or a the extra overhead involved in maintaining a complicated hierarchical population structure. This method was demonstrated to outperform ALPS on a set of Symbolic Regression problems [14], and it is the basis upon which our approach is implemented.

3. METHOD

Inspired by the findings that GP populations tend to prematurely converge to an identical structure near the top of the trees [12], our approach uses *genetic markers* to actively avoid convergence to a particular rooted tree structure. This is achieved by maintaining a number of unique genetic markers in the population.

3.1 Genetic Markers

In order to place pressure on the population to explore different rooted tree structures, we developed *genetic markers* to gauge the genetic diversity among the top portions of the trees in the population. Figure 1 illustrates the process of generating a genetic marker by inspecting a partial tree. We perform a depth-first traversal, up to some depth, d, and the resulting Lisp-style partial expression becomes the genetic marker. This process is relatively inexpensive, and it can be done as the tree is parsed during the evaluation of

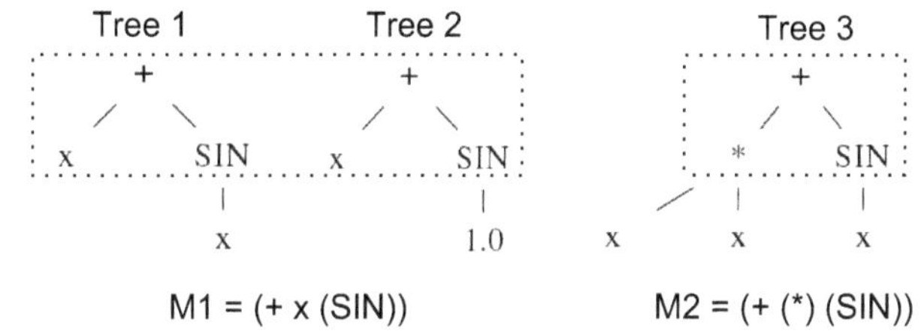

Figure 1: Performing a depth-first traversal from the root to depth 1 on three trees to create the two unique genetic markers $M1 =$ "(+ x (SIN))" and $M2 =$ "(+ (*) (SIN))".

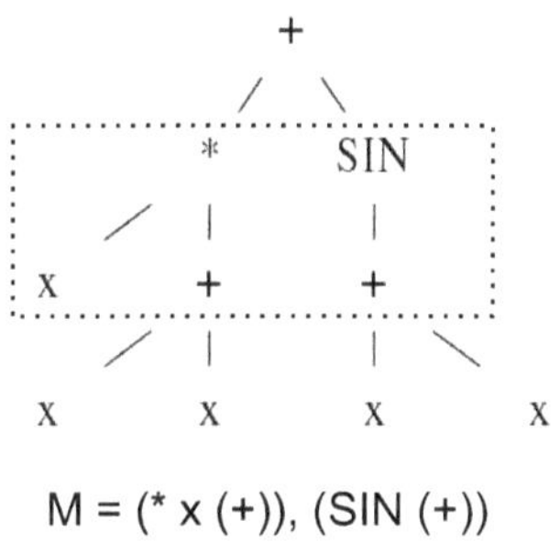

Figure 2: Performing a depth-first traversal starting at level 1 and stopping at level 2 to create the genetic marker $M =$ "(* x (+)), (SIN (+))".

an individual to save extra computational expense. It is important to note that the genetic marker need not contain a complete subtree. Also, the genetic marker can begin at an arbitrary level in the tree, in which case, the genetic marker will represent an ordered list of fragments as in Figure 2. Requiring that the list of fragments remain ordered (left to right) ensures that we capture the structure of the tree at that level, even though we do not need to preserve the root node.

3.2 Genetic Marker Density

Using genetic markers as described in Section 3.1, individuals can be grouped as in Figure 1 in order to determine the density of each unique genetic marker. This density measure allows us to determine how widely spread a particular genetic marker is in the population. The density, ρ_m, of a genetic marker, m, is the fraction of individuals in the population that contain the genetic marker, and it can be calculated as follows:

$$\rho_m = \frac{|P_m|}{|P|}, P_m = \{\forall p \in P \mid M(p) = m\} \tag{1}$$

where, P is the current population, P_m is the subset of individuals in the population that contain the genetic marker m, and $M(p)$ is a function that returns the genetic marker of individual p.

This density measure only requires $O(n)$ time to assign density values to the individuals in the population. Although it is well-known that the fitness evaluation is the most expensive part of the evolutionary process for large problems, the density calculation still introduces less overhead than the tree distance method that we discussed in Section 2.1. The tree distance method requires $O(n^2)$ comparisons because each individual must be compared to every other individual. Additionally, unlike the distance method which needs to examine the entire tree, our density measure only inspects partial trees. Even though we only consider a small portion of each tree, our density measure is able to capture useful dynamics of how genetic material propagates throughout the population, which we will discuss further in Section 5.1.

In addition to gauging how genetic markers propagate throughout the population, this measure of density can also be used to prevent a genetic marker from becoming too dense. This is the central idea of our approach to avoiding premature convergence. We now discuss how we use genetic marker density to promote and maintain genetic diversity.

3.3 Optimizing Density and Fitness

Our approach, which is an extension of the Age-Fitness Pareto Optimization algorithm [14], attempts to prevent the rooted portions of the trees in the population from becoming too structurally similar by maintaining a diverse set of genetic markers. Instead of using genotypic age, we focus on the density of genetic markers to promote genetic diversity. The main intuition behind this is that by maintaining more genetic markers, we can avoid converging to any one structure and therefore maintain a higher level of genetic diversity in the population. We calculate the density of each unique genetic marker in the population, and then minimize density while optimizing fitness in our multi-objective approach.

Each generation, the algorithm proceeds by probabilistically performing crossover, reproduction, and mutation on randomly selected parents to breed the next generation. The parent population as well as the new population are temporarily retained, doubling the population size from n to $2n$. We then use the Pareto tournament selection method [14] to remove dominated individuals in order to shrink the population down from $2n$ back to the target population size, n. This works by randomly selecting a tournament of individuals and then removing all dominated individuals from the population until the target size is reached or all remaining individuals in the population are non-dominated.

In order to determine domination, we calculate the density of each unique genetic marker in the population, and assign each individual a density value corresponding to that of its genetic marker. An individual A is said to dominate individual B only if A is at least equal to B on all objective values and A is strictly better than B in at least one objective value. In other words, A and B can be equal in either density or fitness, but A must either be more fit than B or A's density value must be smaller. In the case that individuals are equal on both objectives, we attempt to break ties by tree size, preferring the individual that contains fewer nodes. If individuals are equal on both objectives, and they are the same size, we simply choose one in order to prevent the population from becoming too large due to ties. As Schmidt and Lipson note [14], it is theoretically possible for the current set of non-dominated individuals to be larger than the target population size after performing Pareto tournament selection, but we did not observe this in any of our experiments.

Since selection still favors fitter individuals, there is still an incentive to improve fitness, which means that fitter individuals will still receive more breeding opportunities. However, since the density objective favors individuals that have less-represented genetic markers, highly-fit individuals are less likely to quickly sweep the population. This allows newer, perhaps less-fit, genotypes more of a chance to propagate valuable genetic material throughout the population. This also allows us to add a new randomly generated individual to the population at the end of each generation without it being immediately dominated in fitness alone.

One of the known reasons for premature convergence is that strong selection pressure causes an imbalanced sampling of genetic material because more fit individuals are constantly favored and selected [6]. The density objective actively avoids this issue by favoring less-represented genetic markers while still exploiting the fitter solutions. This is because individuals that contain denser genetic markers are required to be more fit in order to remain non-dominated.

Parameter	Value
Population size	500
Tournament size	2
Crossover probability	0.90
Reproduction probability	0.10
Max tree depth	17
Max tree size	300
Age layers (ALPS)	10
Age gap (ALPS)	20
Elites (ALPS)	2
Elites (standard GP)	50
Random initialization	ramped half & half
Maximum evaluations	10 million

Table 1: GP settings for all problems.

4. EXPERIMENTAL SETUP

In order to determine the effectiveness of our approach, we compared its performance to the original Age-Fitness Pareto Optimization algorithm as well as the Age-Layered Population Structure (ALPS). For the comparison experiments, we used standard GP as a control, where we consider standard GP as a generational tree-based GP system using fitness-based tournament selection and subtree crossover with 90% internal node bias. We implemented the ALPS and Age-Fitness Pareto Optimization algorithms, as described in [5] and [14] respectively, in our GP system.[1] We compared the algorithms on the following problems described below.

Boolean 11-Multiplexer (11-MUX) as in [10]: This problem requires a boolean function to correctly decode $k = 3$ address bits as a binary number in order to select as output one of the $2^k = 8$ data bits. The fitness cases are all combinations of 11-bit binary strings, and fitness is the proportion of correctly output instances. We used the terminal set $T = \{A_0 - A_2, D_0 - D_7\}$, where each A_i is an address bit, and each D_i is a data bit. The function set contained the standard boolean operators $F = \{AND, OR, NOT, IF\}$.

Even n-Parity [10]: This problem requires a boolean function to determine for each binary number of length n whether or not the number has an even number of bits set. Therefore, the fitness cases are all 2^n combinations of n-bit binary strings, and fitness is the proportion of correctly classified fitness cases. We used the following terminal set: $T = \{D_0, D_1, ..., D_{n-2}, D_{n-1}\}$, where each D_i represents the ith bit in the n-bit binary string. The function set $F = \{AND, OR, NAND, NOR\}$ contained standard boolean operators for this problem, with the exclusion of the XOR operator. It has previously been noted [9, 10] that this problem is more difficult without the XOR operator due to the complexity of the required structure of the solution, so this provides more of a challenge for the algorithms. We compared the algorithms using $n = 5$.

Modified Quartic Symbolic Regression as in [9]: GP tries to evolve the function $4x^4 + 3x^3 + 2x^2 + x$ instead of the more common $x^4 + x^3 + x^2 + x$. The addition of coefficients to the terms makes the required tree structure of the solution more complex because we do not include constants in the terminal set, so the coefficients must be manufactured arithmetically. We used the terminal set $T = \{x\}$ and the function set $F = \{+, -, *, \%, SIN, COS, EXP, RLOG\}$ where % is the protected division operator, and $RLOG$ is the protected natural logarithm operator as described in [10]. We used 20 randomly selected points between $[-1.0, 1.0]$, and fitness is based on the sum of absolute errors between an individual's output value and the target function value, if the difference is greater than 0.01. In the results reported in Section 5, fitness is normalized between $[0, 1.0]$ by using the following formula:

$$f = \frac{1}{(1+e)} \tag{2}$$

where e is the cumulative absolute error.

Table 1 lists the GP settings that we used for all algorithms for all problems. We did not use point mutation, as initial experiments showed that it had minimal impact on the results. In order to provide an accurate analysis of the performance of each algorithm, we conducted 100 independent trials for each problem. Each trial lasted until the optimal fitness (1.0 in each problem) was reached or 10 million fitness evaluations were used. All results represent the mean across the 100 trials unless stated otherwise.

For the density/fitness algorithm, genetic markers were generated using the first two levels in the tree, starting at the root for all problems, with the exception of the Symbolic Regression problem for which we used the first three levels. Initial experiments suggested that using the first three levels yields better performance for the Symbolic Regression problem. This is likely due to the larger function set with more differences in arity among the functions.

5. RESULTS

We first validate the genetic marker definition with an analysis of genetic marker propagation in a standard GP setup contrasted with that of our approach. Next, since we are interested in avoiding premature convergence while finding the solution as fast as possible, we compare the algorithms in terms of the mean number of fitness evaluations used until the optimal solution was found. From the set of all 100 independent replicate trials, we recorded the total number of fitness evaluations at the time that the optimal fitness was reached, for the trials in which the optimal fitness was reached. We then compare the algorithms in terms of search quality (fitness over time). In order to provide a fair comparison, we present the best fitness over time in fitness

[1] All source code and configuration files necessary for reproducing our results are available at https://github.com/burks-pub/gecco2015

evaluations, averaged over the 100 trials, because the algorithms consume a different number of fitness evaluations per generation. Finally, we test the scalability of our approach on the Even n-Parity problem. For space considerations, all tables and figures refer to standard GP as SGP, Age-Fitness Pareto Optimization as A/F, and Density/Fitness as D/F.

5.1 Genetic Marker Analysis

We analyzed the density of all genetic markers among the top 6 levels of the trees in the population for 1000 generations, otherwise using the same experimental settings detailed in Section 4. We use generations here because we are interested in how genetic markers change after each round of breeding. We simultaneously tracked the genetic markers from all levels in a top-down fashion, using two levels at a time. For each pair of levels, we recorded the genetic marker with the maximum density, using the density measure described in Section 3.2. For each level, i, in each tree in the population, genetic markers were generated as we described in Section 3.1, starting at level i and continuing through level j. For example, the genetic marker at levels $L_{0:1}$ will contain all the nodes of a tree from the root (level 0) through level 1. Except where noted, the results of this analysis were similar for all the benchmark problems, so we will only show results for the Symbolic Regression problem due to space considerations. The results shown represent the mean across 100 independent trials.

Figure 3 shows the mean maximum density of all genetic markers across the top 6 levels of the trees in the population in a standard GP setup. The population very quickly becomes nearly identical among the topmost portions of the trees, as a large percentage of the population shares the same genetic marker in the first few levels. By generation 200, nearly 60 percent of the population is identical across the top 6 levels in the trees. This confirms earlier findings that a large percentage of the population quickly converges to the same structure [12]. More importantly, this shows that our definition of genetic markers and the corresponding density measure captures useful dynamics of GP populations.

Figure 4 shows the effect that our approach has on genetic diversity, which highly contrasts with that of a standard GP setup as in Figure 3. This shows that our algorithm maintains a very diverse set of tree structures in the population while preventing a single structure from becoming too dense.

Interestingly, for the Symbolic Regression problem, the maximum density among all genetic markers in the topmost portion of the trees ($L_{0:1}$) still increases over time using our approach. However, this is not nearly as rapid as in the standard GP setup shown in Figure 3. As we discussed in Section 3.3, individuals with more dense genetic markers must have relatively high fitness in order to dominate individuals that have more unique genetic markers. This dynamic places a selective pressure on the population to improve in fitness while still exploring newer rooted tree structures. Figure 4 also shows that our approach maintains a very diverse set of genetic markers across the lower levels in the trees, even though we only explicitly minimize density at the topmost genetic marker level. This demonstrates that diversity among the upper portions of the trees has a major impact on the diversity at deeper levels in the trees.

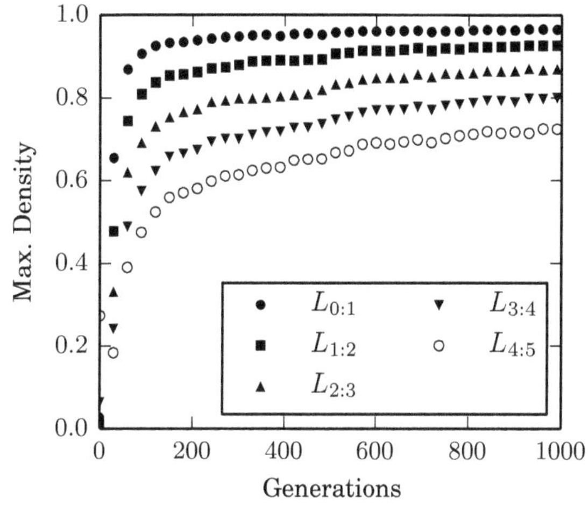

Figure 3: Mean maximum genetic marker density in the top 6 levels of the trees in the population using a standard GP setup on the Quartic Symbolic Regression benchmark problem.

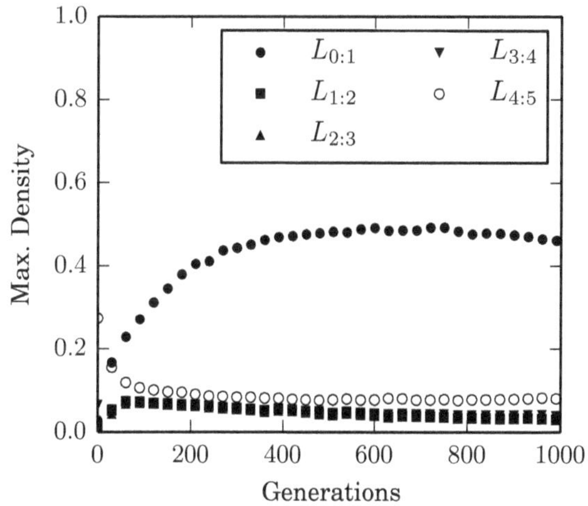

Figure 4: Mean maximum genetic marker density in the top 6 levels of the trees in the population using the density/fitness algorithm on the Quartic Symbolic Regression benchmark problem. Note that values for levels $L_{1:2}$, $L_{2:3}$, and $L_{3:4}$ are overlapping.

5.2 Performance

Figures 5, 6, and 7 show that our algorithm reaches the optimal fitness value in significantly fewer evaluations than the other algorithms in each benchmark problem (Mann-Whitney U test, $p < 0.001$). Table 2 shows that across all problems, D/F reaches optimal fitness at least twice as fast as the second fastest algorithm. Notably, D/F is 5 times faster than A/F on the Even 5-Parity problem, and over 15 times faster than ALPS on the 11 Multiplexer problem. These results show that although ALPS and A/F are successful at avoiding premature convergence, they can do so at the cost of requiring more fitness evaluations to find the optimal solution. However, our approach demonstrates that it

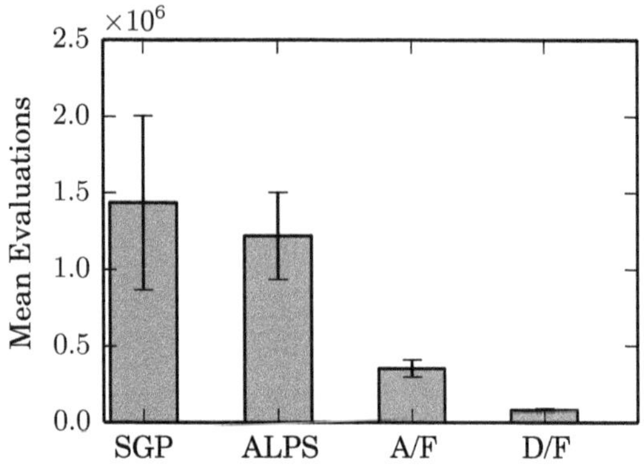

Figure 5: Mean number of evaluations (millions) until optimal fitness was reached on the Boolean 11-Multiplexer problem. Error bars represent the 95% confidence interval around the mean.

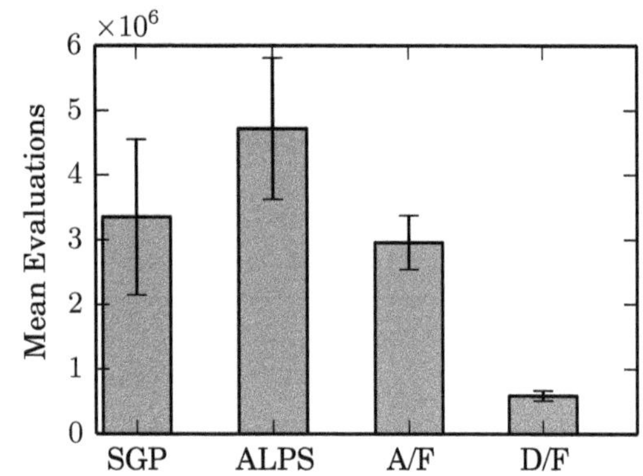

Figure 6: Mean number of evaluations (millions) until optimal fitness was reached on the Even 5-Parity problem. Error bars represent the 95% confidence interval around the mean.

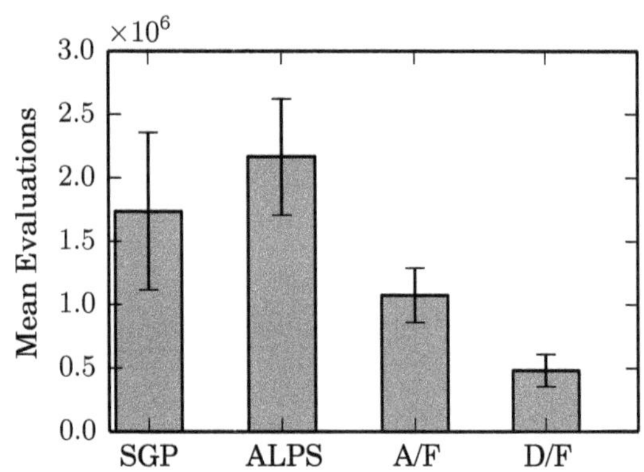

Figure 7: Mean number of evaluations (millions) until optimal fitness was reached on the modified Quartic Symbolic Regression problem. Error bars represent the 95% confidence interval around the mean.

	11-MUX	5-Parity	Regression
SGP	17.89	5.67	3.60
ALPS	15.18	7.98	4.49
A/F	4.40	5.00	2.23

Table 2: Performance factors compared to D/F mean evaluations required to find the solution for 11-MUX (80,304), 5-Parity (591,788) and Regression (481,249).

	11-MUX	5-Parity	Regression
SGP	57	23	56
ALPS	98	25	93
A/F	100	97	100
D/F	100	100	98

Table 3: Number of runs in which the optimal fitness was reached for each problem.

is possible to avoid premature convergence while still finding the solution in a relatively small number of fitness evaluations.

Table 3 shows that D/F found a solution in all of the trials for the 11 Multiplexer and Even 5-Parity problems, and in 98% of the runs for the Symbolic Regression problem. We conducted an additional 100 trials on the Symbolic Regression problem using genetic markers composed of only the first two levels in the trees as in the other problems. With this configuration, D/F found a solution in all of the runs. However, the mean number of evaluations required to find a solution was 1.9 times slower than when genetic markers were composed of the first three levels in the trees. This suggests that for some problems, there may be a trade-off between robustness and efficiency for our algorithm, depending on the composition of the genetic markers. This also suggests that the problem domain may influence the genetic marker dynamics.

5.3 Search Quality

Our second goal is to improve the general quality of search, so next we compare the algorithms in terms of the mean best fitness over time (fitness evaluations). Figures 8, 9, and 10 plot the mean best fitness value over time for each algorithm on each problem. Near the onset of the run, SGP and ALPS reach higher fitness values than both Pareto optimization approaches. This is because A/F and D/F are not only optimizing fitness, but also age and density, respectively. However, A/F and D/F surpass SGP and ALPS, reaching the higher fitness values much earlier in the run, on average. Figures 8 - 10 also show that D/F reaches the higher fitness values much earlier than A/F. This gives rise to the dramatic differences in the required number of evaluations to reach the optimal fitness, as reported in Figures 5 - 7.

5.4 Scalability

We performed an additional set of experiments in order to determine how well our algorithm scales on the n-Parity problem. We do not include results for SGP or ALPS for $n > 5$ because SGP only found a solution in one trial and ALPS only found a solution in two trials for $n = 6$ under these settings. Similarly, we do not report results for A/F beyond $n = 6$, because it only found one solution for $n = 7$. We

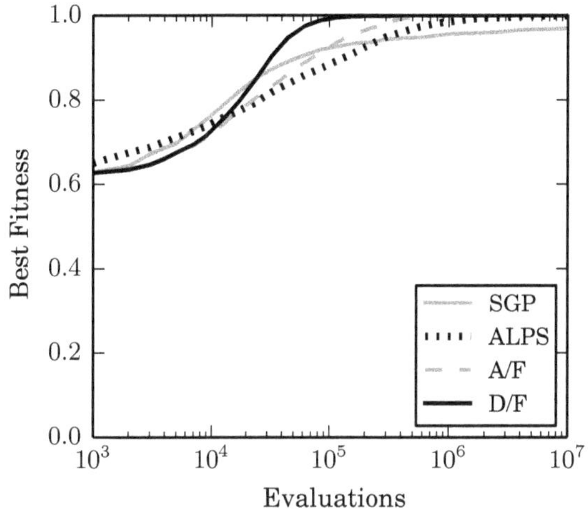

Figure 8: Mean best fitness over time (fitness evaluations) on the Boolean 11-Multiplexer problem. Error bars are omitted for clarity.

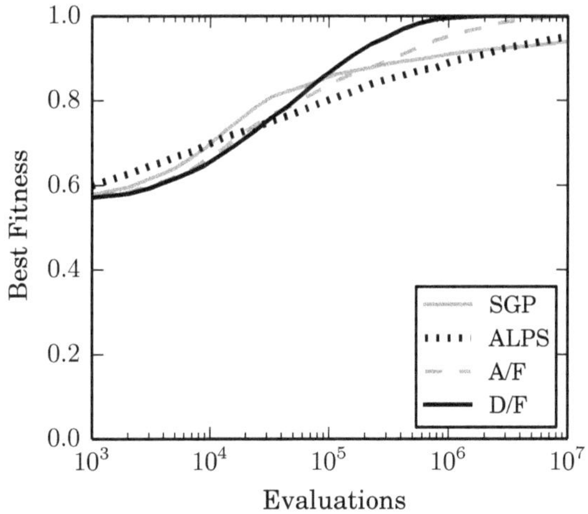

Figure 9: Mean best fitness over time (fitness evaluations) on the Even 5-Parity problem. Error bars are omitted for clarity.

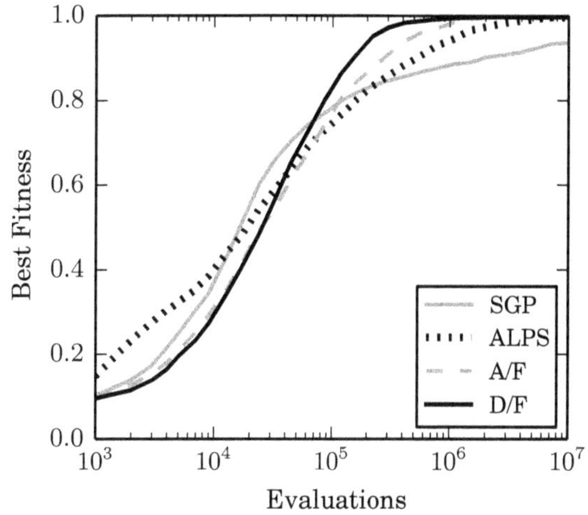

Figure 10: Mean best fitness over time (fitness evaluations) on the modified Quartic Symbolic Regression problem. Error bars are omitted for clarity.

	n = 5	n = 6	n = 7	n = 8
SGP	3.36 (23)	–	–	–
ALPS	4.72 (25)	–	–	–
A/F	2.96 (97)	6.56 (6)	–	–
D/F	0.59 (100)	3.08 (88)	4.48 (37)	5.73 (6)

Table 4: Mean number (in millions) of fitness evaluations required to reach the optimal fitness value for the Even n-Parity problem. Numbers in parentheses indicate the number of trials, out of 100 trials, in which a solution was found.

used the same function set as described in Section 4, so this problem becomes even more difficult as n increases because the required structure for the solution becomes increasingly complex without the XOR operator.

Table 4 shows the mean number of fitness evaluations, in millions, required for $n = 5, 6, 7, 8$, as well as the percentage of trials in which a solution was found. D/F is able to find a solution at a significantly higher rate than A/F in the Even 6-Parity problem. For $n = 6$, our approach finds a solution more than twice as fast as A/F. Additionally, our approach requires less evaluations for both $n = 7$ and $n = 8$ than A/F for $n = 6$. Of course, as n increases, in the absence of the XOR operator, the success rate of our algorithm decreases, and the required number of evaluations to find a solution increases. However, our approach still found a solution in 6 trials with $n = 8$ without the XOR operator, while the other algorithms did not find a solution in the majority of the trials with $n = 6$.

6. CONCLUSIONS

We have presented a new, efficient technique for avoiding premature convergence and improving search quality in tree-based genetic programming. By using tree fragments as genetic markers, the Density/Fitness algorithm prevents the population from converging to a single structure by incorporating genetic marker density into the optimization process. It has already been demonstrated that standard GP often experiences a rapid loss of genetic diversity, wherein the topmost portions of the trees in the population quickly converge to the same structure [12]. Our results show that by actively combating this phenomenon, we can significantly improve the performance, search quality, and scalability of GP, transforming the convergent nature of traditional GP into a more sustainable search algorithm.

In this study, we restricted the genetic markers to only contain the topmost portion of each tree in the population. This loose genotypic diversity measure, which does not consider the rest of the genotype (lower levels in the tree), significantly improved performance and search quality over standard GP as well as the other algorithms that we compared against. However, some questions that arise are how to effectively and efficiently incorporate more of the genotype into the algorithm, and whether or not this would yield further improvements.

One simple approach to this would be to increase the number of levels used in each genetic marker over time in order to focus on different levels in the trees in the population. However, the computational overhead increases with depth, as more of the tree needs to be traversed in order to create the genetic marker. An alternative approach could simply change the level at which we begin creating the genetic marker, as in Figure 2. Initial experiments with the latter approach did not show an improvement over the results we presented here, although further investigation into the rate at which the level changes, or different methods for changing the genetic markers may prove beneficial.

7. ACKNOWLEDGMENTS

This material is based in part upon work supported by the National Science Foundation under Cooperative Agreement No. DBI-0939454. Any opinions, findings, and conclusions or recommendations expressed in this material are those of the author(s) and do not necessarily reflect the views of the National Science Foundation.

This work was supported in part by Michigan State University through computational resources provided by the Institute for Cyber-Enabled Research.

8. REFERENCES

[1] E. Burke, S. Gustafson, and G. Kendall. Diversity in genetic programming: An analysis of measures and correlation with fitness. *Evolutionary Computation, IEEE Transactions on*, 8(1):47–62, 2004.

[2] E. de Jong, R. Watson, and J. Pollack. Reducing bloat and promoting diversity using multi-objective methods. In *Proceedings of the Genetic and Evolutionary Computation Conference*, GECCO 2001, pages 11–18. Morgan Kaufmann, 2001.

[3] C. Gathercole and P. Ross. An adverse interaction between crossover and restricted tree depth in genetic programming. In *Proceedings of the 1st Annual Conference on Genetic Programming*, pages 291–296, Cambridge, MA, USA, 1996. MIT Press.

[4] D. E. Goldberg. *Genetic Algorithms in Search, Optimization and Machine Learning.* Addison-Wesley Longman Publishing Co., Inc., Boston, MA, USA, 1st edition, 1989.

[5] G. S. Hornby. Alps: The age-layered population structure for reducing the problem of premature convergence. In *Proceedings of the 8th Annual Conference on Genetic and Evolutionary Computation*, GECCO '06, pages 815–822, New York, NY, USA, 2006. ACM.

[6] J. Hu, E. Goodman, K. Seo, Z. Fan, and R. Rosenberg. The hierarchical fair competition (hfc) framework for sustainable evolutionary algorithms. *Evol. Comput.*, 13(2):241–277, June 2005.

[7] J. Hu, K. Seo, S. Li, Z. Fan, R. C. Rosenberg, and E. D. Goodman. Structure fitness sharing (sfs) for evolutionary design by genetic programming. In *Proceedings of the Genetic and Evolutionary Computation Conference*, pages 780–787. Morgan Kaufmann Publishers, 2002.

[8] M. Hutter and S. Legg. Fitness uniform optimization. *Evolutionary Computation, IEEE Transactions on*, 10(5):568–589, 2006.

[9] D. Jackson. Mutation as a diversity enhancing mechanism in genetic programming. In *Proceedings of the 13th Annual Conference on Genetic and Evolutionary Computation*, GECCO '11, pages 1371–1378, New York, NY, USA, 2011. ACM.

[10] J. R. Koza. *Genetic Programming: On the Programming of Computers by Means of Natural Selection.* MIT Press, Cambridge, MA, USA, 1992.

[11] J. Lehman and K. O. Stanley. Abandoning objectives: Evolution through the search for novelty alone. *Evol. Comput.*, 19(2):189–223, June 2011.

[12] N. F. McPhee and N. J. Hopper. Analysis of genetic diversity through population history. In *Proceedings of the Genetic and Evolutionary Computation Conference*, pages 1112–1120. Morgan Kaufmann, 1999.

[13] R. Poli and W. Langdon. On the search properties of different crossover operators in genetic programming. In *Genetic Programming*, pages 293–301. Morgan Kaufmann, 1998.

[14] M. Schmidt and H. Lipson. Age-fitness pareto optimization. *Genetic Programming Theory and Practice VIII*, 8:129–146, 2011.

Geometric Semantic Genetic Programming with Local Search

Mauro Castelli
NOVA IMS, Universidade Nova de Lisboa
1070-312
Lisbon, Portugal
mcastelli@novaims.unl.pt

Leonardo Trujillo
Instituto Tecnológico de Tijuana
Tijuana, México
leonardo.trujillo@tectijuana.edu.mx

Leonardo Vanneschi
NOVA IMS, Universidade Nova de Lisboa
1070-312
Lisbon, Portugal
lvanneschi@novaims.unl.pt

Sara Silva
BioISI – Biosystems & Integrative Sciences Institute
Faculty of Sciences
University of Lisbon, Portugal
sara@fc.ul.pt

Emigdio Z-Flores
Instituto Tecnológico de Tijuana
Tijuana, México
emigdio.zflores@tree-lab.org

Pierrick Legrand
Université de Bordeaux
CQFD Team, INRIA Bordeaux Sud-Ouest
IMB, France
pierrick.legrand@u-bordeaux.fr

ABSTRACT

Since its introduction, Geometric Semantic Genetic Programming (GSGP) has aroused the interest of numerous researchers and several studies have demonstrated that GSGP is able to effectively optimize training data by means of small variation steps, that also have the effect of limiting overfitting. In order to speed up the search process, in this paper we propose a system that integrates a local search strategy into GSGP (called GSGP-LS). Furthermore, we present a hybrid approach, that combines GSGP and GSGP-LS, aimed at exploiting both the optimization speed of GSGP-LS and the ability to limit overfitting of GSGP. The experimental results we present, performed on a set of complex real-life applications, show that GSGP-LS achieves the best training fitness while converging very quickly, but severely overfits. On the other hand, GSGP converges slowly relative to the other methods, but is basically not affected by overfitting. The best overall results were achieved with the hybrid approach, allowing the search to converge quickly, while also exhibiting a noteworthy ability to limit overfitting. These results are encouraging, and suggest that future GSGP algorithms should focus on finding the correct balance between the greedy optimization of a local search strategy and the more robust geometric semantic operators.

1. INTRODUCTION

It is by now established that standard tree-based Genetic Programming (GP) [10] can be used as a powerful tool for automatic program induction, capable of solving problems from a wide range of domains. Nonetheless, recent works have proposed important new strategies that fundamentally change the manner in which the search for optimal computer programs or syntactic expressions is carried out. For instance, the Fast Function Extraction (FFX) algorithm [13] reformulates the symbolic regression problem as that of finding a linear combination of a subset of candidate basis functions. Another recent example is the Prioritized Grammar Enumeration (PGE) technique [24], that employs dynamic programming and eliminates the basic search operators of traditional GP. This paper focuses on Geometric Semantic GP (GSGP) [14], where the explicit search space for the GP algorithm is the space of all possible program outputs, also known as semantic space. This contrasts with the traditional GP approach, where the search process only considers program outputs indirectly through the fitness function, and instead performs the search by only focusing on syntax space. It has been shown that by explicitly exploiting semantic awareness, it is possible to construct a simple fitness landscape and search operators with strong evolvability [14], known as Geometric Semantic Operators (GSOs). GSGP has achieved strong results in several domains, particularly with regards to both training and testing performance, with almost no overfitting [20, 22, 4]. However, GSGP also suffers from several drawbacks, in particular it tends to converge rather slowly and it thus produces extremely large trees due to the accumulative effect of repeatedly applying GSOs [20, 22]. Moreover, since GSOs are basically linear combinations of GP trees, they require weight parameters to be set a priori, with no guarantees that such parameters are properly set for a particular fitness landscape. To overcome the above issues, in this paper GSOs are enhanced using a Local Search (LS) strategy, what is also known as a memetic algorithm in evolutionary computation literature [5]. In particular, LS is applied to the offspring produced by Geometric Semantic Mutation (GSM), something that is achieved directly using ordinary least squares regression. In this sense, this paper is part of a growing list of contributions that integrate LS into a GP search [25, 9], but it is also noteworthy given that it is the first of such approaches that is applied to GSGP.

The main objective of this work is to compare GSGP to our new version of GSGP integrated with LS (GSGP-LS from now on). The idea of this comparison is trying to understand if and how LS is useful to improve GSGP performance both on training and on unseen data. However, while doing this, it is appropriate to include in the comparison a hybrid GP system, joining GSGP and GSGP-LS in a single framework. In fact, while GSGP is well known for its ability to optimize training data by means of small variation steps,

GECCO '15, July 11 - 15, 2015, Madrid, Spain

DOI: http://dx.doi.org/10.1145/2739480.2754795

that also have the effect of limiting overfitting (as explained in [20, 22]), GSGP-LS may optimize training data much faster and overfit them. With the hybrid system we propose, we aim at catching, into a single framework, both the optimization speed of GSGP-LS and the ability of limiting overfitting of GSGP. Thus, this paper presents experiments on several benchmark real-world problems, comparing three different approaches: GSGP, GSGP-LS and a hybrid approach that combines GSGP and GSGP-LS.

The remainder of the paper is organized as follows. Section 2 provides an overview to GSGP and the original GSOs. Afterwards, Section 3 reviews previous work on integrations between GP and LS strategies and describes our proposal to integrate LS within GSGP. The experimental work and discussion of the results are presented in Section 4. Finally, concluding remarks are given in Section 5.

2. GEOMETRIC SEMANTIC OPERATORS

GSOs were originally introduced by Moraglio et al. [14] and are becoming more and more popular in the GP community [21] because of their property of inducing a unimodal fitness landscape on supervised learning problems, such as regression and classification.

To have an intuition of this property, let us consider a problem for Genetic Algorithms (GAs), in which the unique global optimum is known and the fitness of each individual (to be minimized) corresponds to its distance to the global optimum (our reasoning holds for any employed distance). In this problem, if we use, for instance, ball mutation[1] [11] (i.e. a variation operator that slightly perturbs some of the coordinates of a solution), then any possible individual different from the global optimum has at least one fitter neighbor (individual resulting from its mutation). So, there are no local optima. In other words, the fitness landscape is unimodal, and consequently the problem is characterized by a good evolvability.

Now, let us consider the typical GP problem of finding a function that maps input data into known target outputs (as we said, regression and classification are particular cases). The fitness of an individual for this problem is typically a distance between its predicted output values and the expected ones (error measure). GSOs simply define transformations on the syntax of the individuals that correspond to geometric crossover and ball mutation in the semantic space, thus allowing us to map the considered GP problem into the previously discussed GA problem.

In particular[2], *geometric semantic crossover* (GSC) generates the expression

$$T_{XO} = (T_1 \cdot T_R) + ((1 - T_R) \cdot T_2) \qquad (1)$$

as the unique offspring of parents $T_1, T_2 : \mathbb{R}^n \to \mathbb{R}$, where T_R is a random real function whose output values range in the interval $[0, 1]$. Analogously, *geometric semantic mutation* (GSM) returns the expression

$$T_M = T + ms \cdot (T_{R1} - T_{R2}) \qquad (2)$$

as the result of the mutation of an individual $T : \mathbb{R}^n \to \mathbb{R}$, where T_{R1} and T_{R2} are random real functions with codomain in $[0, 1]$ and ms is a parameter called mutation step.

Moraglio et al. [14] show that GSC corresponds to geometric crossover in the semantic space (i.e. the point representing the offspring stands on the segment joining the points representing the parents) and GSM corresponds to ball mutation in the semantic space (and thus induces a unimodal fitness landscape).

As Moraglio et al. point out, these operators create much larger offspring than their parents and the fast growth of the individuals in the population rapidly makes fitness evaluation unbearably slow. In [20, 3], a possible workaround to this problem was proposed, consisting in an implementation of Moraglio's operators that makes them not only usable in practice, but also very efficient. Basically, this implementation is based on the idea that, besides storing the initial trees, at every generation it is enough to maintain in memory, for each individual, its semantics and a reference to its parents. As shown in [20], the computational cost of evolving a population of n individuals for g generations is $O(ng)$, while the cost of evaluating a new, unseen, instance is $O(g)$.

However, GSO have a known limitation [21, 3] that is very important in practice: the reconstruction of the best individual at the end of a run can be hard (and sometimes even impossible), given its large size. This basically means that GSGP is a black-box system that generates highly uninterpretable solutions.

3. LOCAL SEARCH IN GENETIC PROGRAMMING

This section will first discuss previous approaches on applying a LS strategy during a GP run. All of them were developed for standard GP, and most of them focused on symbolic regression problems. Afterwards, the main contribution of this paper is presented, i.e. the first integration of a local searcher within GSGP.

Symbolic Regression with Genetic Programming.

In symbolic regression, the goal is to search for the symbolic expression $K^O : \mathbb{R}^p \to \mathbb{R}$ that best fits a particular training set $\mathbb{T} = \{(\mathbf{x}_1, y_1), \ldots, (\mathbf{x}_n, y_n)\}$ of n input/output pairs with $\mathbf{x}_i \in \mathbb{R}^p$ and $y_i \in \mathbb{R}$. The general symbolic regression problem can then be defined as

$$(K^O, \boldsymbol{\theta}^O) \leftarrow \underset{K \in \mathbb{G}; \boldsymbol{\theta} \in \mathbb{R}^m}{arg\ min}\ f(K(\mathbf{x}_i, \boldsymbol{\theta}), y_i)\ with\ i = 1, \ldots, p \qquad (3)$$

where $\mathbb{G}$ is the solution or syntactic space defined by the primitive set $\mathbb{P}$ (functions and terminals), f is the fitness function based on the distance between a program's output $K(\mathbf{x}_i, \boldsymbol{\theta})$ and the expected output y_i, like for instance the root mean square error (RMSE) as in this work, and $\boldsymbol{\theta}$ is a particular parametrization of the symbolic expression K, assuming m real-valued parameters.

In standard GP, parameter optimization is usually not performed explicitly, since GP search operators only focus on syntax. Therefore, the parameters are only implicitly considered. For instance, a GP individual might have the following syntax $K(x) = x + sin(x)$; in this case, we might propose the following parametrization: $\boldsymbol{\theta} = (\alpha_1, \alpha_2, \alpha_3)$, with $K(x) = \alpha_1 x + \alpha_2 sin(\alpha_3 x)$. In a traditional GP search, these parameters are usually all set to 1, which does not necessarily lead to the best possible performance for this particular syntax. Indeed, if the optimal solution is, for instance, $K^O(x) = 3.3x + 1.003sin(0.0001x)$, then individual K might be easily lost during the selection or survival processes. Some GP systems do include numerical terminals or random ephemeral constants. While these constants can act as coefficients in an evolved expression, they are usually not subject to optimization after they are introduced into the syntax of a particular individual. This seems to be a glaring weakness in the standard GP approach. While the syntactic-based search in GP has solved a variety of difficult problems, it is nonetheless very inefficient, leading to important practical limitations, such as search stagnation, bloat and uninterpretable

[1] Similar considerations hold for many types of crossover, including various kinds of geometric crossover [11].

[2] Here we report the definition of the geometric semantic operators as given by Moraglio et al. for real functions domains, since these are the operators we will use in the experimental phase. For applications that consider other types of data, the reader is referred to [14].

solutions [16]. In other words, GP performs a highly explorative search, since the search operators can produce large fitness changes with only modest syntactic modifications or vice-versa.

Local Search in Standard Genetic Programming.

Many works have studied how to combine an evolutionary algorithm with a local optimizer so far (also referred to as a refinement process). In general, such approaches are considered to be a simple type of memetic search [5]. The basic idea is straightforward: include within the optimization process an additional search operator that takes an individual (or several) as an initial point and searches for the local optima around it. Such a strategy can help ensure that the local region around each individual is fully exploited. However, there can be some negative consequences to such an approach. The most evident is computational overhead, while the cost of a single LS might be negligible, performing it on every individual might become inefficient. Second, LS can produce overfitted solutions, stagnating the search on local optima. These issues aside, these techniques have produced impressive results in a variety of scenarios, some of which are reviewed by Chen et al. [5].

A noteworthy aspect of this survey is an almost complete lack of papers that deal with GP. Of the more than two hundred papers covered by Chen et al., in fact, only a couple deal with memetic GP. This indicates that the GP community may have not addressed the topic adequately. Some examples are [23, 6], which present domain-specific memetic approaches, that are not intended for LS in symbolic regression with GP. In fact, LS in GP can be performed in two ways, in syntactic space or in parameter space as defined in Equation 3. Regarding the former, in [2] the authors proposed a syntactic LS operator that performs a greedy point mutation, with promising results on several benchmarks. For the latter approach, the complete optimization problem defined in Equation 3 has not received much attention.

In [19], gradient descent is used to optimize numerical constants within a GP tree, achieving good results on five symbolic regression problems. Similarly, in [26] and [7] a LS algorithm is used to optimize the value of constant terminal elements. In [26] gradient descent is used and tested on classification problems, while [7] uses resilient backpropagation and evaluates the proposal on a real-world problem, in both cases leading towards improved results. In [17], the authors include weight parameters for each function node, what the authors call inclusion factors; these weights modulate the importance that each node has within the tree. Indeed, the authors identify what we are here referring to as implicit program parameters, and optimize these values by applying gradient descent on all trees. The authors also propose a series of new search operators that explicitly consider the parametrization of each GP tree.

In a recent work [25], this problem was addressed by implementing a very simple parametrization of the tree, by constraining the number of internal parameters of each tree regardless of its size. Several different strategies were compared to determine when a local optimizer should be applied, showing that it is often best to apply it on either all the population or a subset of the best individuals. The LS used is called trust region optimization [18], and results showed substantial improvements in performance compared with standard GP search on several benchmark and real-world problems. A similar approach was developed by [9], with two noteworthy differences. First, parameters replace all constants present on a given tree, and each GP tree is enhanced by adding an artificial root tree that effectively adds a weight coefficient and a bias to the entire tree, then the Levenberg-Marquardt optimizer is used to find the optimal values for these parameters. Second, the authors apply constant optimization to the population using different probabilities, as well as a strict offspring selection variant for comparison.

Local Search in Geometric Semantic Operators.

The goal of this work is to integrate a LS strategy within GSGP. In particular, as an initial proposal, we include a local searcher within the GSM mutation operator, since previous works have shown that GSGP achieves its best performance using only mutation during the search [22]. In particular, the GSM with LS (GSM-LS) of a tree T generates an individual:

$$T_M = \alpha_0 + \alpha_1 \cdot T + \alpha_2 \cdot (T_{R1} - T_{R2}) \tag{4}$$

where $\alpha_i \in \mathbb{R}$; notice that α_2 replaces the mutation step parameter ms defined in Equation 2. This in fact defines a basic multivariate linear regression problem, which could be solved, for example, by Ordinary Least Square regression (OLS). However, in this case we have n linear equations, the number of fitness cases, and only three unknowns (the α_is). This gives an overdetermined multivariate linear fitting problem, which can be solved through SVD [3]. We argue that this should be seen as a LS operator, that attempts to determine the best linear combination of the parent tree and the random trees used to perturb it, local in the sense of the linear problem posed by the GSM operator. It should not be seen as a LS in the entire semantic space, since in that case the LS would necessarily converge to the optimal in this unimodal landscape.

This approach is similar to two previously proposed approaches. First, the linear fitting problem is reminiscent of the linear scaling procedure proposed in [8], which allows GP to fit the form of the desired output without necessarily optimizing the scale or bias. However, in that case the scaling process is only used to adjust the fitness value of each individual, while the search operators used are standard ones. Second, and more closely related, the non-isotropic Gaussian mutation proposed in [15], that is used to perform a runtime analysis of GSGP. However, the mutation proposed in that work considers a fixed set of basis functions instead of randomly generated GP trees, and perturbs the linear combination with Gaussian-noise instead of providing the best fit coefficients. Finally, the work presented by [12] also uses a multivariate linear regression approach to optimize evolved solutions, with several key differences. Particularly, the search is conducted by standard GP, not GSGP, and each tree is decomposed into a set of subtrees which are then linearly combined. The method is much more explorative then the one presented here.

Moreover, this approach contrasts with previous work [25], that relied on a non-linear local optimizer, since the linear assumption is mostly not satisfied by the expression evolved with standard GP and the corresponding parametrization. On the other hand, in this new approach, it is simple to apply a linear regression optimizer, given that the GSM operator defines a linear expression in the parameter space.

4. EXPERIMENTAL STUDY

Experimental Settings.

Three different GP variants are studied here: GSGP (as in [20]), GSGP-LS (GSGP using only GSM-LS) and a *hybrid* version [4].

[3]In this work, the GNU Scientific Library is used http://www.gnu.org/software/gsl/

[4]It is common to refer to memetic approaches that combine a global search method and a local searcher as hybrid. Here we do not follow this naming convention, and instead we refer to the hybrid algorithm as a combination of standard GSM and GSM-LS

The hybrid version is defined in a very simple way: it consists in using GSGP-LS from the beginning of the run until a given generation g, and GSGP from generation $g+1$ until the end of the run. The motivation for introducing this hybrid version is that we believe that GSGP-LS will have a great optimization power on training data, resulting in very small errors obtained in the first few generations. We are worried that this may imply an overfitting of the training set, with consequent poor performance on unseen data. GSGP has already shown a noteworthy generalization ability on many real-life applications, basically because of its ability of optimizing by means of very small mutation steps (a deeper motivation for the good generalization ability of GSGP can be found, for instance, in [20, 22]). For this reason, we believe that the qualities of GSGP-LS and GSGP may be integrated in a GP variant in which a fast optimization in the beginning of the run (given by GSGP-LS) is followed by a slower optimization in the second phase of the run (given by GSGP).

The parameters used in the presented experiments were as follows: all the GP runs used a population of 250 individuals, allowed to evolve for 500 generations. Trees initialization was performed with the Ramped Half-and-Half method [10] with a maximum initial depth equal to 6. Fitness was calculated as the root mean square error (RMSE) between target and calculated values. To create new individuals, only GSM was used, and for GSGP the mutation step was randomly generated with uniform distribution in the $[0, 1]$ at each mutation event, as suggested in [22]. Tournament selection was used, with a tournament size equal to 4. Survival from one generation to the other was always guaranteed to the best individual in the population (elitism). These values have been chosen after a preliminary tuning phase, in which several different combinations of parameter values have been tested. We finally selected the combination that returned the best results. In these very first experiments with the proposed hybrid version, the value of generation g where GSGP-LS is replaced by GSGP has arbitrarily been set to 10. Our current research is focused on a deep study of this parameter and on how it affects the performance of the system. A total of 30 runs were performed with each studied technique. In each run, a different partition between training and test data has been considered. In particular 70% of the instances have been used as training data, while the remaining have been used as test data.

Test Problems.

The first three considered test problems are real life applications in the field of pharmacokinetics. They have been chosen because they have been tackled in several previous studies, in particular using GP (see for instance [1]). They consist in predicting the value of three different pharmacokinetic parameters of a set of candidate drug compounds based on their molecular structure. The first pharmacokinetic parameter we consider is human oral bioavailability (represented as %F from now on), the second one is plasma protein binding level (or %PPB) and the third one is median lethal dose, also informally called toxicity (TOX). The datasets we have used are the same as in [1] (where they are also discussed in more details): the %F (respectively %PPB and TOX) dataset consists in a matrix composed by 260 (respectively 131 and 234) rows (instances) and 242 (respectively 627 and 627) columns (features). The remaining test problem we have used in our experiments consists in a regression problem over a dataset containing data relative to patients that have been diagnosed positive to Parkinson disease. Features represent clinic characteristics of the patients and the target value represents the seriousness of the disease assessed according to the Unified Parkinson's Disease Rating Scale. This dataset consists in a matrix composed by 5875 rows (instances) and 19 columns (features). For a deeper description of this problem, the reader is referred to [4]. All these datasets can be downloaded from: <Anonymized>

Experimental Results.

Figure 1 reports the obtained results. In particular, plot (a) (respectively (b)) reports the results on the training set (respectively test set) for the %F dataset; plot (c) (respectively (d)) reports the results on the training set (respectively test set) for the TOX dataset; Plot (e) (respectively (f)) reports the results on the training set (respectively test set) for the %PPB dataset; and finally plot (g) (respectively (h)) reports the results on the training set (respectively test set) for the Parkinson dataset. The experimental results are reported using curves of the fitness (RMSE) on the training and test sets and they were obtained in the following way. For each generation the training fitness of the best individual, as well as its fitness in the test set (that we call test fitness) were recorded. The curves in the plots report the median of these values for the 30 runs. The median was preferred over the mean because of its higher robustness to outliers.

Let us begin our analysis of the experimental results by discussing the behavior of GSGP-LS (black curves). As expected, GSGP-LS outperforms the other two studied methods on the training set: the unimodal fitness landscape induced by geometric semantic operators is navigated effectively and efficiently, thanks to the integration of a local search optimizer. At the same time, except for the case of the Parkinson dataset (in which GSGP-LS is able to outperform the other methods also on the test set), the behavior of GSGP-LS on the test set is not ideal: after a first phase (that usually lasts few generations) of fast improvement, the error starts rapidly growing on the test set. Furthermore, for the %F and the TOX datasets, the curve of GSGP-LS on the test set is not only rapidly growing, but it also looks irregular, with several jumps that induce us to think that GSGP-LS is overfitting training data. Nevertheless, we also point out that, for all the four studied problems, the point of minimum error of the GSGP-LS curve corresponds with the best test error found by any of the studied methods: if only we were able to interrupt the execution of the algorithm at that point, we would have an ideal performance both on the training set and on unseen data. If we now analyze the curves of GSGP (dotted and gray curves), we can see the expected behavior (already pointed out in [20, 22]): a slow and smooth improvement both on the training and on the test set (except for the particular case of the %PPB dataset, in which GSGP is able to outperform the other methods also on the test set). If we let the method run for many more generations (say 3000), GSGP is able to outperform the other studied methods both on the training and on the test set, but this is payed by a large amount of computational resources spent. The ability of GSGP of optimizing by means of small steps, which is probably one of the reasons for its ability to limit overfitting [20, 22], clearly also makes the process rather slow and many generations must be executed before being able to find good quality solutions. If we finally look at the curve of the hybrid method (dotted and black curves), we can see that by introducing this method we have been able to integrate the advantages of both GSGP and GSGP-LS: the hybrid method, in fact, outperforms GSGP on the training set (although it is outperformed by GSGP-LS) for all the studied problems, and at the same time, it does not show any sign of overfitting. On the other hand, the hybrid method is able to find solutions of a comparable quality than the ones of GSGP-LS approximately at the same generation (which is trivial given that the hybrid method is identical to GSGP-LS in the first generations), but, contrarily to GSGP-LS, it is able to keep these good quality solutions in the population until the end of the run and, in some case (like for instance for the Parkinson dataset) even to slightly improve them.

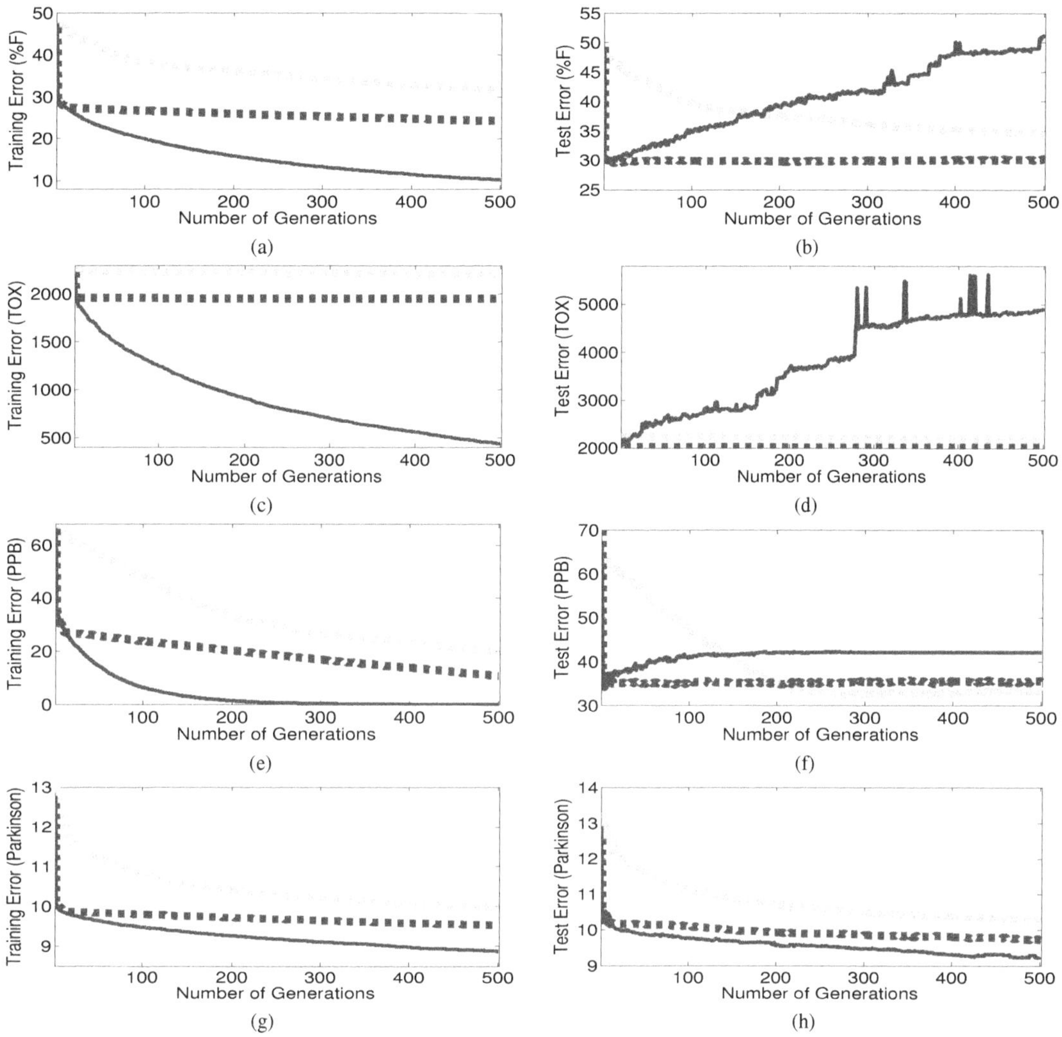

Figure 1: Each line of this figure reports the results obtained on a different dataset. On the first column we report the evolution of training error, and on the second column the evolution of test error. More in particular, plot (a) (respectively (b)) reports the results on the training set (respectively test set) for the $\%F$ dataset. Plot (c) (respectively (d)) reports the results on the training set (respectively test set) for the *TOX* dataset. Plot (e) (respectively (f)) reports the results on the training set (respectively test set) for the *%PPB* dataset. Plot (g) (respectively (h)) reports the results on the training set (respectively test set) for the *Parkinson* dataset. Medians over 30 independent runs are reported. The legend for all the plots is: GSGP — GSGP-LS ▪▪ HYBRID.

The statistical significance of all the results discussed so far has been studied. In particular, the Kolmogorov-Smirnov test has shown that the data are not normally distributed and hence a rank-based statistic has been used. The Wilcoxon rank-sum test for pairwise data comparison with Bonferroni correction has been used under the alternative hypothesis that the samples do not have equal medians. Two tails test was performed. The obtained p-values are shown in Table 1. Employing the usual significance level $\alpha = 0.05$, in the table we have reported in bold and underline font the results that are *not* statistically significant. As we can see, all the reported results are statistically significant except one: the difference between GSGP and the hybrid method on the TOX dataset.

One criticism that may be moved against the presented results is that the three studied methods are compared against generations, but GSGP-LS, which contains a local search optimizer, spends more computational resources than GSGP at each generation. To demonstrate that the presented comparison is fair, in Figure 2 we report the evolution of the median of the running time, expressed in seconds, of the same 30 experiments as in Figure 1. The experiments where performed on a PC with an Intel(R) Core(TM) 4750 GPU 2.00 GHz processor, with 16 GB RAM and a Windows 7, 64-bit operating system. As we can see, for the %F, TOX and %PPB datasets the plots of GSGP-LS (black curves) and the ones of GSGP (dotted and gray curves) are practically overlapping, indicating the fact that the running time of these two methods are practically the same. Indeed, both methods use the same implementation idea as in [3]. In other words, individuals are not stored in memory during the evolutionary process, but they are only represented by a set of memory pointers. Furthermore, in both GSGP and GSGP-LS the fitness calculation (that is the most computationally expensive step in traditional GP) is done without evaluating the trees, but only using the semantic vectors of the parents. Only for the Parkinson dataset, the difference between the GSGP-LS and the GSGP curves is visible, and GSGP-LS is slower. However, we can say that the difference is rather small: less than one minute, over a total running time approximately equal to 7 minutes, for completing the first 500

	%F			
	TRAINING		TEST	
	GSGP-LS	HYBRID	GSGP-LS	HYBRID
GSGG	3.02E-11	3.02E-11	3.16E-10	8.20E-07
GSGP-LS		3.02E-11		1.21E-10
	TOX			
	TRAINING		TEST	
	GSGP-LS	HYBRID	GSGP-LS	HYBRID
GSGG	3.02E-11	5.00E-09	4.50E-11	**0.0614**
GSGP-LS		3.02E-11		6.72E-10
	%PPB			
	TRAINING		TEST	
	GSGP-LS	HYBRID	GSGP-LS	HYBRID
GSGG	3.02E-11	3.02E-11	7.38E-10	3.97E-04
GSGP-LS		3.02E-11		2.48E-06
	PARKINSON			
	TRAINING		TEST	
	GSGP-LS	HYBRID	GSGP-LS	HYBRID
GSGG	3.01E-11	3.02E-11	3.33E-11	4.11E-07
GSGP-LS		3.01E-11		5.06E-10

Table 1: This table reports the p-values of the statistical tests that we have performed for the same experiments as in Figure 1. The test was the Mann-Witney test, with Bonferroni correction. Two tails test was performed.

generations. In conclusion, we can state that the overhead of time introduced by the execution of the local search method in GSGP-LS is either irrelevant (for the %F, TOX and %PPB datasets) or very small (for the Parkinson dataset).

5. CONCLUSIONS

Geometric Semantic Genetic Programming (GSGP) is one of the hot topics in the genetic programming community. In this paper, we have defined a new version of geometric semantic genetic programming (called GSGP-LS) able to navigate the unimodal fitness landscape induced by the geometric semantic operators faster than GSGP. GSGP-LS uses a local search method to optimize the parameters that characterize the individuals at each generation. Experimental results, presented on four complex real-life applications from the drug discovery and bio-medicine field, show that GSGP-LS outperforms GSGP on the training set, but overfits it. More precisely, GSGP-LS is able to find excellent solutions on the test set in the very first generations, but then these solutions are lost and the performance of GSGP-LS on the test set deteriorates along the run. On the other hand, GSGP, thanks to its small optimization steps, is slower on the training set, but does not overfit. Interestingly, in this paper we have also introduced an hybrid method, that corresponds with GSGP-LS in the very first generations, and is identical to GSGP in the subsequent generations. The hybrid method seems to join both advantages of GSGP and GSGP-LS, returning excellent results on the training set, without any corresponding overfitting.

Several future activities, related to the work presented here, are planned. For instance, different ways of integrating GSGP and GSGP-LS will be implemented and tested, including the definition of a dynamic threshold for switching between the two methods and a variant in which the two methods will be alternated according to various predefined patterns. Also, several local search strategies, different from the one used here, deserve investigation, with the objective of discovering if one of them may limit overfitting more than the others. Last but not least, one of the main tracks of our current research consists in the attempt to define new geometric semantic operators that do not cause code growth in the evolved problems.

Acknowledgments.

This work was partially supported by centre grant (to BioISI, Centre Reference: UID/MULTI/04046/2013) and by projects MaSSGP (PTDC/EEI-CTP/2975/2012), InteleGen (PTDC/DTP-FTO/1747/2012) and CancerSys (EXPL/EMS-SIS/1954/2013) from FCT/MCTES/PIDDAC, Portugal. Other funding for this work was provided by CONACYT Basic Science Research Project No. 178323, DGEST (México) Research Projects 5414.14-P and 5621.15-P, FP7-PEOPLE-2013-IRSES project ACOBSEC financed by the European Commission with contract No. 612689, and Emigdio Z-Flores was supported by CONACYT scholarship No. 294213.

6. REFERENCES

[1] Francesco Archetti, Stefano Lanzeni, Enza Messina, and Leonardo Vanneschi. Genetic programming for computational pharmacokinetics in drug discovery and development. *Genetic Programming and Evolvable Machines*, 8:413–432, 2007.

[2] Raja Muhammad Atif Azad and Conor Ryan. A simple approach to lifetime learning in genetic programming-based symbolic regression. *Evol. Comput.*, 22(2):287–317, 2014.

[3] Mauro Castelli, Sara Silva, and Leonardo Vanneschi. A C++ framework for geometric semantic genetic programming. *Genetic Programming and Evolvable Machines*, 16(1):73–81, 2015.

[4] Mauro Castelli, Leonardo Vanneschi, and Sara Silva. Prediction of the unified Parkinson's disease rating scale assessment using a genetic programming system with geometric semantic genetic operators. *Expert Systems with Applications*, 41(10):4608 – 4616, 2014.

[5] Xianshun Chen, Yew-Soon Ong, Meng-Hiot Lim, and Kay Chen Tan. A multi-facet survey on memetic computation. *Trans. Evol. Comp*, 15(5):591–607, 2011.

[6] Brent Eskridge and Dean Hougen. Imitating success: A memetic crossover operator for genetic programming. In

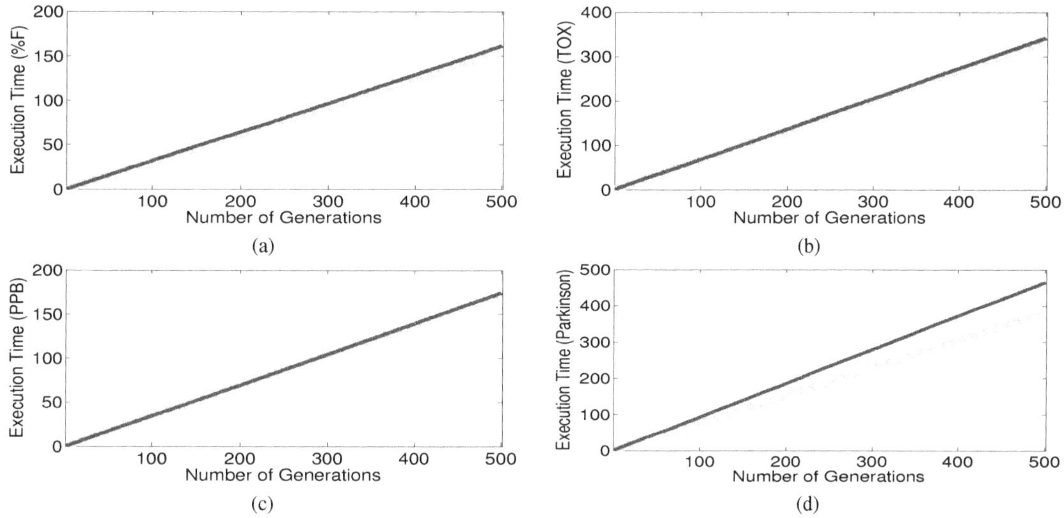

Figure 2: Median of the running time, expressed in seconds, for the same 30 independent runs as in Figure 1. Plot (a): %F dataset; plot (b): TOX dataset; plot (c): %PPB dataset; plot (d): Parkinson dataset. Black curve: GSGP-LS; gray and dotted curve: GSGP.

Proceedings of the 2004 IEEE Congress on Evolutionary Computation, pages 809–815, Portland, Oregon, 20-23 June 2004. IEEE Press.

[7] Mario Graff, Rafael PeĂČÂśa, and Aurelio Medina. Wind speed forecasting using genetic programming. In *IEEE Congress on Evolutionary Computation*, pages 408–415. IEEE, 2013.

[8] Maarten Keijzer. Improving symbolic regression with interval arithmetic and linear scaling. In *Proceedings of the 6th European Conference on Genetic Programming*, EuroGP'03, pages 70–82, Berlin, Heidelberg, 2003. Springer-Verlag.

[9] Michael Kommenda, Gabriel Kronberger, Stephan Winkler, Michael Affenzeller, and Stefan Wagner. Effects of constant optimization by nonlinear least squares minimization in symbolic regression. *Proceeding of the fifteenth annual conference companion on Genetic and evolutionary computation conference companion - GECCO '13 Companion*, pages 11–21, 2013.

[10] John R. Koza. *Genetic Programming: On the Programming of Computers by Means of Natural Selection*. MIT Press, Cambridge, MA, USA, 1992.

[11] Krzysztof Krawiec and Pawel Lichocki. Approximating geometric crossover in semantic space. In Guenther Raidl, Franz Rothlauf, Giovanni Squillero, Rolf Drechsler, Thomas Stuetzle, Mauro Birattari, Clare Bates Congdon, Martin Middendorf, Christian Blum, Carlos Cotta, Peter Bosman, Joern Grahl, Joshua Knowles, David Corne, Hans-Georg Beyer, Ken Stanley, Julian F. Miller, Jano van Hemert, Tom Lenaerts, Marc Ebner, Jaume Bacardit, Michael O'Neill, Massimiliano Di Penta, Benjamin Doerr, Thomas Jansen, Riccardo Poli, and Enrique Alba, editors, *GECCO '09*, pages 987–994. ACM, 8-12 July 2009.

[12] Krzysztof Krawiec and Una-May O'Reilly. Behavioral programming: A broader and more detailed take on semantic gp. In *Proceedings of the 2014 Conference on Genetic and Evolutionary Computation*, GECCO '14, pages 935–942, New York, NY, USA, 2014. ACM.

[13] Trent McConaghy. FFX: Fast, scalable, deterministic symbolic regression technology. In Rick Riolo, Ekaterina Vladislavleva, and Jason H. Moore, editors, *Genetic Programming Theory and Practice IX*, Genetic and Evolutionary Computation, chapter 13, pages 235–260. Springer, Ann Arbor, USA, 2011.

[14] Alberto Moraglio, Krzysztof Krawiec, and Colin G. Johnson. Geometric semantic genetic programming. In Carlos A. Coello Coello, Vincenzo Cutello, Kalyanmoy Deb, Stephanie Forrest, Giuseppe Nicosia, and Mario Pavone, editors, *Parallel Problem Solving from Nature*, volume 7491 of *LNCS*, pages 21–31. Springer, 2012.

[15] Alberto Moraglio and Andrea Mambrini. Runtime analysis of mutation-based geometric semantic genetic programming for basis functions regression. In *Proceedings of the 15th Annual Conference on Genetic and Evolutionary Computation*, GECCO '13, pages 989–996, New York, NY, USA, 2013. ACM.

[16] Sara Silva and Ernesto Costa. Dynamic limits for bloat control in genetic programming and a review of past and current bloat theories. *Genetic Programming and Evolvable Machines*, 10(2):141–179, 2009.

[17] Will Smart and Mengjie Zhang. Continuously evolving programs in genetic programming using gradient descent. In R I Mckay and Sung-Bae Cho, editors, *Proceedings of The Second Asian-Pacific Workshop on Genetic Programming*, page 16pp, Cairns, Australia, 2004.

[18] D. Sorensen. *Newton's Method with a Model Trust Region Modification*. Defense Technical Information Center, 1982.

[19] Alexander Topchy and William F. Punch. Faster genetic programming based on local gradient search of numeric leaf values. In Lee Spector, Erik D. Goodman, Annie Wu, W. B. Langdon, Hans-Michael Voigt, Mitsuo Gen, Sandip Sen, Marco Dorigo, Shahram Pezeshk, Max H. Garzon, and Edmund Burke, editors, *Proceedings of the Genetic and Evolutionary Computation Conference (GECCO-2001)*, pages 155–162. Morgan Kaufmann, 7-11 July 2001.

[20] Leonardo Vanneschi, Mauro Castelli, Luca Manzoni, and Sara Silva. A new implementation of geometric semantic GP and its application to problems in pharmacokinetics. In Krzysztof Krawiec, Alberto Moraglio, Ting Hu, A. Sima Uyar, and Bin Hu, editors, *Proceedings of EuroGP*, LNCS, pages 205–216. Springer, 2013.

[21] Leonardo Vanneschi, Mauro Castelli, and Sara Silva. A survey of semantic methods in genetic programming. *Genetic Programming and Evolvable Machines*, 15(2):195–214, 2014.

[22] Leonardo Vanneschi, Sara Silva, Mauro Castelli, and Luca Manzoni. Geometric semantic genetic programming for real life applications. In Rick Riolo, Katya Vladislavleva, and Jason Moore, editors, *Genetic Programming Theory and Practice XI*, Genetic and Evolutionary Computation. Springer US, Computer Science Collection, 2013. Invited article. To appear.

[23] Pu Wang, Ke Tang, Edward P. K. Tsang, and Xin Yao. A memetic genetic programming with decision tree-based local search for classification problems. In *IEEE Congress on Evolutionary Computation*, pages 917–924. IEEE, 2011.

[24] Tony Worm and Kenneth Chiu. Prioritized grammar enumeration: Symbolic regression by dynamic programming. In *Proceeding of the Fifteenth Annual Conference on Genetic and Evolutionary Computation Conference*, GECCO '13, pages 1021–1028, New York, NY, USA, 2013. ACM.

[25] Emigdio Z-Flores, Leonardo Trujillo, Oliver Schuetze, and Pierrick Legrand. Evaluating the effects of local search in genetic programming. In Alexandru-Adrian Tantar et al., editors, *EVOLVE - A Bridge between Probability, Set Oriented Numerics, and Evolutionary Computation V*, number 288 in Advances in Intelligent Systems and Computing, pages 213–228. Springer, 2014.

[26] Mengjie Zhang and Will Smart. Genetic programming with gradient descent search for multiclass object classification. In Maarten Keijzer, Una-May O'Reilly, Simon M. Lucas, Ernesto Costa, and Terence Soule, editors, *Genetic Programming 7th European Conference, EuroGP 2004, Proceedings*, volume 3003 of *LNCS*, pages 399–408, Coimbra, Portugal, 5-7 April 2004. Springer-Verlag.

Performance Optimization of Multi-Core Grammatical Evolution Generated Parallel Recursive Programs

Gopinath Chennupati
BDS Group
CSIS Department
University of Limerick, Ireland
gopinath.chennupati@ul.ie

R. Muhammad Atif Azad
BDS Group
CSIS Department
University of Limerick, Ireland
atif.azad@ul.ie

Conor Ryan
BDS Group
CSIS Department
University of Limerick, Ireland
conor.ryan@ul.ie

ABSTRACT

Although Evolutionary Computation (EC) has been used with considerable success to evolve computer programs, the majority of this work has targeted the production of serial code. Recent work with Grammatical Evolution (GE) produced *Multi-core Grammatical Evolution (MCGE-II)*, a system that *natively* produces parallel code, including the ability to execute recursive calls in parallel.

This paper extends this work by including practical constraints into the grammars and fitness functions, such as increased control over the level of parallelism for each individual. These changes execute the best-of-generation programs faster than the original MCGE-II with an average factor of 8.13 across a selection of hard problems from the literature.

We analyze the time complexity of these programs and identify avoiding *excessive parallelism* as a key for further performance scaling. We amend the grammars to evolve a mix of serial and parallel code, which spawns only as many threads as is efficient given the underlying OS and hardware; this speeds up execution by a factor of 9.97.

Categories and Subject Descriptors

I.2.8 [**Artificial Intelligence**]: Problem Solving, Control Methods, and Search - Heuristic methods

Keywords

Grammatical Evolution; Multi-cores; Symbolic Regression; OpenMP; Automatic Parallel Programming.

1. INTRODUCTION

Multi-core processors are shared memory multiprocessors integrated on a single chip and offer high processing power. However, some challenges remain in exploiting their potential, particularly because, as the number of cores increase (the so-called *death of scaling*[1]), the software needs to be designed explicitly to realize the true potential of these cores.

[1]http://www.gotw.ca/publications/concurrency-ddj.htm

GECCO '15, July 11 - 15, 2015, Madrid, Spain

 ISBN 978-1-4503-3472-3/15/07...$15.00

DOI: http://dx.doi.org/10.1145/2739480.2754746

OpenMP [13] is the *de facto* standard to write parallel programs on multi-cores in C/C++. Although a powerful tool, writing that is a non-trivial task, as sequential programmers still struggle with parallel design issues such as synchronization, locking and program decomposition.

To alleviate this difficulty, [6] introduced *MCGE-II* to generate *native* parallel code on multi-cores, proved it by parallelising recursive calls. MCGE-II adds OpenMP pragmas in GE grammars, and so solves the underlying problem such that the solution is a parallel program. Although successful, it made little attempt to optimize the efficiency, particularly in terms of the execution time and the ease of program evolution.

We re-design the MCGE-II grammars such that they now partition *data and task level parallelism* under different production rules making it convenient for evolution to select as appropriate. Furthermore, we modify the fitness function to explicitly take account of the execution time of the individuals. These changes combine to give an average speed-up factor of 8.13 across a range of hard recursive problems from the literature. Recursion is perfect for task level parallelism as each recursive call can be invoked in a separate thread.

However, one risk in evolving parallel recursion is *excessive* multi-threading that spawns a thread at every recursive call; thus, each thread does little useful work. This can degrade performance due to the overhead in first creating and then scheduling these threads. Scheduling can be especially expensive as a large number of threads compete to get a slice of CPU time. Therefore, we further tweak the grammars such that the evolved programs can control the creation of threads after a certain depth in their recursive trace. Thus, the lower level recursive calls run in serial by arresting thread creation, while the top level calls run in parallel, that results in an average speed-up of 9.97.

We also consider code growth in GE but find it surprisingly insignificant; therefore, code-growth does not affect program execution.

The rest of the paper is detailed as follows: section 2 introduces the existing literature of the paper; section 3 describes the proposed approach; section 4 presents the experiments; section 5 shows the results; section 6 discusses the factors that influence the performance, while section 7 enhances the performance; and finally, section 8 concludes.

2. BACKGROUND

Unlike MCGE-II, previous EC work has only treated evolving recursion and evolving parallel programs as separate challenges. Below we only briefly review these two topics.

2.1 Generation of Recursive Programs

Some of the earliest work on evolving recursion is from Koza [9, Chapter-18] which evolved a Fibonacci sequence; this work cached previously computed recursive calls for efficiency. Also, Brave [4] used *Automatically Defined Functions* (ADFs) to evolve recursive tree search. In this, recursion terminated upon reaching the tree depth. Then, [17] concluded that infinite recursions was a major obstacle to evolve recursive programs. However, [19] successfully used an adaptive grammar to evolve recursive programs; the grammar adjusted the production rule weights in evolving solutions.

Spector et al. [15] evolved recursive programs using PushGP by explicitly manipulating its execution stack. The evolved programs were of $O(n^2)$ complexity, which became $O(nlog(n))$ with an efficiency component in fitness evaluation.

Agapitos and Lucas [1, 2] evolved recursive quick sort with an Object Oriented Genetic Programming (OOGP) in Java. The evolved programs exhibited a time complexity of $O(nlog(n))$. Recently, Moraglio et al. [10] used a non-recursive scaffolding method to evolve recursive programs with a context free grammar based GP.

Next, we review automatic parallel programming with EC.

2.2 Automatic Evolution of Parallel Programs

This section describes research into the automatic generation of parallel programs irrespective of recursion. In general, automatic generation of parallel programs can be divided into two types: *auto-parallelization of serial code* and the *generation of native parallel code.*

Auto-parallelization requires an existing (serial) program. Using GP, [14, Chapter-5] proposed *Paragen* which had initial success, however, its reliance on the execution of candidate solutions ran into difficulties with complex and time consuming loops. Later, *Paragen-II* [14, Chapter-7] dealt the loop inter-dependencies, relying on a rough estimate of execution time. Then, [14] extended *Paragen-II* to merge independent tasks of different loops into one loop.

Similarly, genetic algorithms evolved *transformations*; [11] and [18] proposed *GAPS* (Genetic Algorithm Parallelization System) and, *Revolver* respectively. GAPS evolved sequence restructuring, while *Revolver* transformed the loops and programs, both optimized the execution time.

On the other hand, *native parallel code generation* produces a working program that is also parallel. With multi-tree GP, [16] concurrently executed autonomous agents for automatic design of controllers.

Recently, Chennupati et al., [5] evolved natively parallel regression programs. Then [6] introduced MCGE-II to evolve task parallel recursive programs. The minimal execution time of them was merely due to the presence of OpenMP pragmas which automatically map threads to cores. However, the use of a different OpenMP pragma alters the performance of the parallel program, and skilled parallel programmers carefully choose the pragmas when writing code. To that end, in this paper, we extend MCGE-II in two ways: we re-structure the grammars so task and data level parallelism is separate, and we explicitly penalize long executions.

3. MCGE-II

In this paper we extend MCGE-II [6] in two respects: first, through the design of the grammars (section 3.1), which are much richer and categorize rules better so as to accelerate

```
⟨program⟩     ::= ⟨condition⟩ ⟨parcode⟩

⟨omppragma⟩   ::= ⟨ompdata⟩ | ⟨omptask⟩

⟨ompdata⟩     ::= #pragma omp parallel
                | #pragma omp master
                | #pragma omp single
                | #pragma omp parallel for

⟨omptask⟩     ::= #pragma omp parallel sections
                | #pragma omp task

⟨shared⟩      ::= shared(⟨input⟩, temp, res) ⟨newline⟩ '{'

⟨private⟩     ::= private(a) | firstprivate(a) | lastprivate(a)

⟨condition⟩   ::= if(⟨input⟩ ⟨lop⟩ ⟨const⟩) '{' ⟨newline⟩
                  ⟨line1⟩; ⟨newline⟩ ⟨line2⟩; ⟨newline⟩'}'

⟨parcode⟩     ::= else '{' ⟨newline⟩ ⟨omppragma⟩
                  ⟨private⟩ ⟨shared⟩ ⟨blocks⟩ ⟨newline⟩
                  '}' ⟨newline⟩ '}' ⟨newline⟩ ⟨result⟩

⟨blocks⟩      ::= ⟨parblocks⟩ | ⟨blocks⟩ ⟨newline⟩ ⟨blocks⟩

⟨parblocks⟩   ::= ⟨secblocks⟩ | ⟨taskblocks⟩

⟨secblocks⟩   ::= #pragma omp section ⟨newline⟩ '{'
                  ⟨newline⟩ ⟨line1⟩; ⟨newline⟩ ⟨atomic⟩
                  ⟨newline⟩ ⟨line2⟩ ⟨bop⟩ a; ⟨newline⟩'}'

⟨taskblocks⟩  ::= #pragma omp task ⟨newline⟩ '{'
                  ⟨newline⟩ ⟨line1⟩; ⟨newline⟩ ⟨atomic⟩
                  ⟨line2⟩ ⟨bop⟩ a;⟨newline⟩'}'

⟨atomic⟩      ::= #pragma omp atomic

⟨line1⟩       ::= temp = ⟨expr⟩ | a = ⟨expr⟩;

⟨line2⟩       ::= res ⟨bop⟩= temp

⟨expr⟩        ::= ⟨input⟩ | ⟨stmt⟩ | ⟨stmt⟩ ⟨bop⟩ ⟨stmt⟩

⟨result⟩      ::= return res;

⟨stmt⟩        ::= fib(⟨input⟩ ⟨bop⟩ ⟨const⟩);

⟨input⟩       ::= n

⟨lop⟩         ::= '>=' | '<=' | '>' | '<' | '=='

⟨bop⟩         ::= + | - | * | /

⟨const⟩       ::= 0 | 1 | 2 | 3 | 4 | 5 | 6 | 7 | 8 | 9

⟨newline⟩     ::= \n
```

Figure 1: The design of MCGE-II grammar to generate natively parallel recursive Fibonacci programs.

evolution; and second, through a modified fitness function (section 3.2), which considers time in its evaluation. Both of them help optimize the performance (execution time) of the evolving parallel recursive programs.

3.1 Design of Grammars

The grammars in this paper are designed such that they offer clear separation among OpenMP pragmas, task and data parallel. This separation benefits the quick generation of candidate solutions because of grammatical bias [17]. Figure 1 shows the grammar that generates a natively parallel recursive *Fibonacci* program. The non-terminals `<omptask>` and `<ompdata>` represent the task and data parallel pragmas respectively, while `<omppragma>` selects one of the two options. Notice, the generation of the task level pragma shown in `<omptask>` forms the best fit individual as the goal is the automatic generation of task parallel recursion.

The programs take an integer (n) input (`<input>`), while the variable *res* returns the end result of the parallel program evaluation. Moreover, the two local variables (*temp, a*) store the intermediate results of recursive calls. The input and the two variables are shared among the threads with the clause (`<shared>`), while `a` is a thread private (`<private>`) variable. Evolution selects a private clause from the three OpenMP private (`<private>`) clauses.

Of the three private clauses: *private(a)* makes a variable thread specific, any changes on the variable are invisible after the parallel region; *firstprivate(a)* holds a value throughout the program despite the parallelization; *lastprivate(a)* keeps the changes of the last thread in the parallel region. Since the variable updates are thread specific, programs with *private(a)* are the best programs. Note, the other clauses degrade the fitness as they evolve incorrect solutions.

The non-terminal symbol `<stmt>` depicts the recursive call of the Fibonacci program. The non-terminal `<blocks>` generates a sequence of parallel blocks with each block containing an independent recursive call. To that end, section 7 presents a complete task parallel recursive program.

3.2 Performance Optimization

As the choice of OpenMP pragmas can significantly impact the performance of a program, we encourage the right degree of parallelism with its execution time in the fitness, which increases the pressure in choosing the best pragma.

Thus, the fitness function that we use in optimizing the performance is the product of two factors: execution time and the mean absolute error, both are normalized in the range $(0, 1)$ – a maximization function. The following equation represents the fitness of the evolved program (f_{pprog}):

$$f_{pprog} = \frac{1}{(1+t)} * \frac{1}{\left(1 + \frac{1}{N}\sum_{i=1}^{N}|y_i - \hat{y}_i|\right)} \quad (1)$$

where, t is the time taken by the evolved parallel program to evaluate across all the training cases (N); The terms y_i and, $\hat{y}_i$ represent the actual and, the evolved outputs respectively.

Since using an inapt pragma increases the time to execute the evolved program, the first term, *normalized execution time* in eq. 1 helps to select the correct pragma. Meanwhile, the second term, *normalized mean absolute error* (in eq. 1) enforces program correctness. Together, the two objectives push for a correct and efficient parallel program.

Table 1: The summary of the problems (in increasing order of difficulty) under investigation with the properties used in the experiments.

#	Problem	Type: Input	Type: Return	LV	Range
1	Sum-of-N	int	int	3	[1,1000]
2	Factorial	int	unsigned long long	3	[1,60]
3	Fibonacci	int	unsigned long long	3	[1,60]
4	Binary-Sum	int [ ], int, int	int	2	[1,1000]
5	Reverse	int [ ], int, int	void	2	[1,1000]
6	Quicksort	int [ ], int, int	void	3	[1,1000]

4. EXPERIMENTAL CONTEXT

We evaluate our approach on six recursive problems. Table 1 presents them with their properties: type of input and return values, the number of arguments, number of local variables (LV); the range of elements from which the input is considered. The output is the result of the conventional algorithm of the respective problem. The local variables (LV) are the auxiliary variables. The training set contains 30 data points. The first three (Sum-of-N, Factorial, Fibonacci) problems accept a single positive integer as input; for *Sum-of-N*, it is randomly generated from the range $[1, 1000]$ while, for *Factorial* and *Fibonacci* problems, it is in the range $[1, 60]$ due to the limitations in the data type range in C. While the remaining three problems (Binary-Sum, Reverse, Quicksort) accept an array of integers along with their start and end indices as input, for which, an array of 1000 elements are randomly generated from the range $[1, 1000]$. Note, the grammars are general enough except for a few minor changes with respect to the problem at hand.

Table 2 describes the algorithmic parameters along with the experimental environment used to evaluate our approach.

Table 2: Parameters and experimental environment.

GE parameter settings	
Parameter	**Value**
point mutation	0.1
one point crossover	0.9
selection	Roulette Wheel
replacement strategy	Steady state
initialization	Sensible
minimum depth	9
maximum depth	25
wrapping	disabled
population size	500
generations	100
runs	50
Experimental environment	
CPU	Intel (R) Xeon (R) E7-4820, 16 cores
OS	Debian Linux v 2.6.32, 64-bit
C++	GNU GCC v 4.4.5 libGE v 0.26
OpenMP	libgomp v 3.0
Timer utility	*omp_get_wtime*()

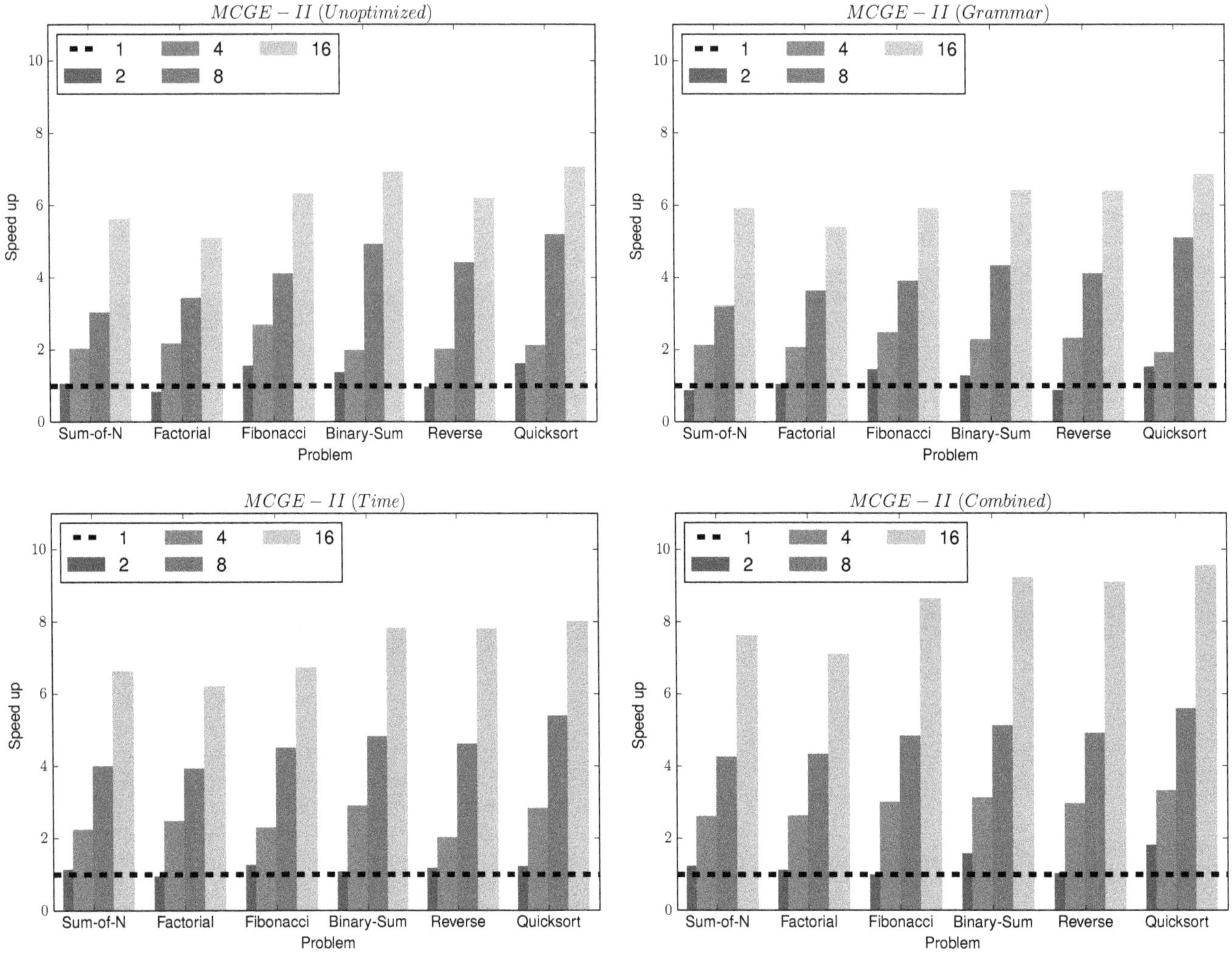

Figure 2: The speed-up of *MCGE-II (Unoptimized, Grammar, Time, Combined)* variants for all the six experimental problems. The number of cores vary as 2, 4, 8 and 16. The horizontal dashed line (–) represents the speed-up of 1 and acts as a reference for the remaining results.

Table 3: Friedman statistical tests with Hommel's post-hoc analysis on performance of all the four MCGE-II variants. The boldface shows the significance at $\alpha = 0.05$, while asterisk (*) shows the best variant.

Cores	MCGE-II variant	Average Rank	p value	p Hommel
4	Unoptimized	**3.25**	**0.0025**	**0.0167**
	Grammar	**3.1667**	**0.0036**	**0.025**
	Time	**2.5833**	**0.0331**	**0.05**
	Combined*	0.9999	-	-
8	Unoptimized	**3.1667**	**0.0036**	**0.025**
	Grammar	**3.6667**	**3.47E-4**	**0.0167**
	Time	2.1667	0.1175	0.1
	Combined*	1.0	-	-
16	Unoptimized	**3.4999**	**7.96E-4**	**0.0167**
	Grammar	**3.4999**	**7.96E-4**	**0.025**
	Time	1.9999	0.1797	0.05
	Combined*	1.0	-	-

Table 4: The mean best generation (mean $\pm$ [standard deviation]) of all the four MCGE-II variants (Unoptimized, Grammar, Time, Combined). The lowest value is in boldface.

#	MCGE-II			
	Unoptimized	Grammar	Time	Combined
	mean best generation	mean best generation	mean best generation	mean best generation
1	59.14 $\pm$ [4.96]	45.38 $\pm$ [2.81]	51.63 $\pm$ [6.19]	**43.27 $\pm$ [5.37]**
2	38.43 $\pm$ [2.85]	**31.19 $\pm$ [4.73]**	39.35 $\pm$ [3.19]	36.51 $\pm$ [3.67]
3	77.36 $\pm$ [5.58]	**44.73 $\pm$ [5.26]**	65.19 $\pm$ [6.43]	59.89 $\pm$[4.15]
4	71.83 $\pm$ [6.37]	**59.14 $\pm$ [5.34]**	68.88 $\pm$ [4.51]	61.43 $\pm$ [5.19]
5	56.68 $\pm$ [2.19]	47.53 $\pm$ [2.19]	51.09 $\pm$ [2.39]	**45.32 $\pm$ [4.92]**
6	49.25 $\pm$ [4.57]	**40.49 $\pm$ [5.23]**	52.49 $\pm$ [2.58]	47.28 $\pm$ [3.15]

Friedman tests with Hommel's post-hoc analysis. Boldface shows the significance at $\alpha = 0.05$, while asterisk (*) shows the best variant.

MCGE-II variant	Average Rank	p-value	p-Hommel
Unoptimized	**3.0**	**5.3205E-4**	**0.001596**
Grammar*	1.16666	-	-
Time	**2.33333**	**0.0321438**	**0.042**
Combined	**1.99999**	**0.0024787**	**0.02**

We compare the performance among four MCGE-II variants. The first variant, named as *MCGE-II (Unoptimized)* hereafter, does not separate task and data parallelism; instead, all the rules in `<omptask>` and `<ompdata>` are lumped together under `<omppragma>`. Thus, it is hard to omit data parallelism when it only requires task parallelism, while the fitness function is *only* the *normalized mean absolute error* (second term in eq. 1). The second variant (*MCGE-II (Grammar)*), uses the grammars shown in Figure 1, while the fitness function is the *normalized mean absolute error*. The third variant (*MCGE-II (Time)*), uses the same grammars as with the first variant (MCGE-II (Unoptimized)), but f_{pprog} (eq. 1) for fitness evaluation. The fourth variant, named as *MCGE-II (Combined)* hereafter, uses both the grammars as in Figure 1 and the fitness function f_{pprog}.

5. EXPERIMENTAL RESULTS

In this section we report the speed-up in terms of the *mean best execution time (MBT)*, that is, the average execution time of the best of generation programs in each of 50 runs. Now, the Speed-up $= \frac{T_{MBT-1-core}}{T_{MBT-n-cores}}$ where, $T_{MBT-1-core}$ is the *mean best execution time* on a single core, while $T_{MBT-n-cores}$ is that of n-cores of a processor.

Figure 2 presents the speed-up of all the four MCGE-II (*Unoptimized, Grammar, Time, Combined*) variants across all the six experimental problems. The speed-up is for varying the cores: 2, 4, 8, and 16, with respect to 1-core.

Table 3 shows the Friedman statistical tests with Hommel's post-hoc [8] analysis on the speed-up of the four MCGE-II variants for all the six problems at $\alpha = 0.05$. The first column indicates the number of cores under execution. The second column shows the MCGE-II variant, while the third column presents the average rank. The fourth and the fifth columns show the p-value and Hommel's critical value respectively. The lowest average rank shows the best (MCGE-II (Combined)) variant, and is marked with an asterisk (*). A variant is significantly different from the best variant if p-value is less than p-Hommel at $\alpha = 0.05$, is in boldface.

Although we do not show in Table 3, for 2 cores none of the variants is better than the others, which could be attributed to the multi-threading overhead offsetting the performance gains. However, we see differences with higher numbers of cores. For 4 cores, MCGE-II (Combined) significantly outperforms the remaining three variants (Unoptimized, Grammar, Time), while for 8 and 16 cores MCGE-II (Combined) significantly outperforms the two MCGE-II (Unoptimized, Grammar) variants, but the difference with MCGE-II (Time) is insignificant. We believe that this is due to the fact that both in MCGE-II (Time, Combined), include execution time in fitness evaluation.

We also investigate the effect of restructuring grammars in this study, on the ease of evolving the correct programs. To this end, we measure the mean number of generations required to converge to the best fitness, with a pre-condition that the program under consideration must be *correct*, averaged across 50 runs; we call it the *mean best generation*. Table 4 shows the mean best generation of all the four variants[2] along with significance tests. The lowest mean best generation is in boldface for the respective problem of an MCGE-II variant. The significance tests show that MCGE-II (Grammar) significantly outperforms MCGE-II (Unoptimized, Time, Combined) at $\alpha = 0.05$. That is MCGE-II (Grammar) requires less number of generations over the other variants in producing the best fit programs due to the grammatical bias [17] exerted through the changes (Figure 1) in the design of grammars.

However, the performance results (Table 3) indicate that, although MCGE-II (Grammar) quickly generates the parallel recursive programs, it has been outperformed by MCGE-II (Time, Combine) in terms of their efficiency. A pairwise comparison between MCGE-II (Time, Combined) at $\alpha = 0.05$ shows that MCGE-II (Combined) outperforms MCGE-II (Time) in terms of number of generations. That is, MCGE-II (Combined) quickly generates efficient parallel recursive programs than MCGE-II (Time) due to the grammatical bias. Hence, MCGE-II (Combined) is the best variant that reports an average (on all the problems) speed-up of 8.13 for 16 cores, a significant improvement of 23.86% over MCGE-II (Unoptimized) that reports 6.19 speed-up.

Although MCGE-II (Combined) boosts up the performance over the original system, it fails to fully utilize the power of multi-cores. That is, it reported a speed-up of 8.13 on 16 cores of processor, where the ideal case should be 16. Many factors contribute in obviating to achieve the ideal scale-up.

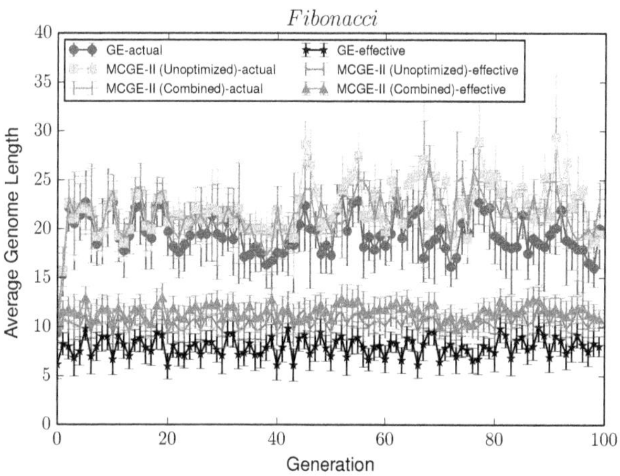

Figure 3: The lengths of GE, MCGE-II (Unoptimized, Combined) genotypes for *Fibonacci*. Space constraints do not allow reporting the graphs for all the problems but the trends are very similar.

6. DISCUSSION

The quality of parallel code is difficult to quantify as execution time often depends on the ability of OS to efficiently schedule the tasks. This job itself is complicated by other parallel threads (from other programs) running at the same time. OpenMP abstracts away much of these concerns from programmers, which makes it easier at the cost of some of fine control. In order to compensate this, it is often necessary to dig deeper by adapting to program to the hardware, which makes the programmer's job increasingly hard.

Hardware can cap the maximum number of threads; however, in the given grammars each recursive call spawns a new thread. Then, the OS-specific factors for the Linux ker-

[2]Note, the results are for 16 cores. They are similar for the remaining cores, but left out due to space constraints.

nels, which eventually fail to scale in scheduling the very high number of threads. Moreover, a parent thread spawns a child thread, it sleeps until all the child threads have finished. This process expensive, when a large number of threads are involved. Also, memory access restrictions over shared and private variables, as in section 3, can add to the complexity of the executing code.

Complexity in this instance comes from (at least) two key sources. Firstly, as with any evolved code, we run the risk of code growth, and, secondly, from the vagaries of scheduling what can be a very high number of threads. We first examine code growth.

6.1 Code Growth

We analyze the size of standard GE (without OpenMP pragmas; it evolves serial programs), and MCGE-II genotypes. GE genomes have two sizes [12]: actual and effective. Actual length is the total size of a genotype, while effective length is the part, used to generate the end program.

Figure 3 presents the actual and effective lengths of GE, MCGE-II (Unoptimized, Combined) averaged across 50 runs of 100 generations of *Fibonacci*. As expected, the actual and effective lengths vary significantly for the particular set-ups, with Wilcoxon Signed Rank Sum tests at $\alpha = 0.05$.

When we compare across approaches, surprisingly, the statistical tests show insignificant difference between the actual length of GE and MCGE-II (Unoptimized, Combined). In fact GE generates larger genotypes than required, thus, the MCGE-II grammars do not influence the actual length, as both use the same search engine. Instead, MCGE-II uses some of the actual size to map the OpenMP pragmas, hence, effective length increases. In GE, the actual lengths range from 25 to 47, while effective lengths range from 5 to 8 depending on the problem.

The **effective** lengths of MCGE-II (Unoptimized, Combined) are significantly larger than that of GE at $\alpha = 0.05$ due to the extra mapping steps. In MCGE-II, they range from 12 to 18, based on the problem. However, among the MCGE-II variants, the effective lengths do not vary significantly. It shows the fact that the changes in the design of MCGE-II grammars forfeit the overhead in code growth.

This slight increase in effective length may impact the performance of the programs only for 2 cores as is manifested in [7], hence, performance suffers (shown in section 5). However, for 4 cores and above, it has negligible implications, because now the impact of the extra cores is greater than that of the extra code. Also note, the code growth is independent of the number of cores under execution.

However, it is interesting to observe that GE does not bloat like GP, a phenomenon that was also noted in [3]. And, the reasons behind such observations remain unanswered, leaving a lot of scope for future work.

6.2 Computational Complexity

We also empirically analyze the computational complexity of MCGE-II (Combined) generated task parallel recursive programs. In this analysis, we consider the number of recursive calls of a program over the given input.

Although, space limitations do not permit reporting the details, the analysis shows that the problems *Sum-of-N*, *Factorial*, *Reverse* exhibit $O(n)$ (linear) complexity whereas, *Binary-Sum* and *Quick sort* exhibit $O(logn)$ and, $O(nlogn)$ complexity respectively, while *Fibonacci* shows $O(2^n)$ complexity. This demonstrates that the evolving programs are competitive with that of the conventional human written programs. It is to be noted that the use of parallel hardware can only reduce the computational load by dividing it among the existing processing elements, but not over the computational complexity. To that end in this paper, *Binary-Sum* exhibits the lowest complexity $(O(log(n)))$.

However, this analysis suggests that Fibonacci required an exponential number of recursive calls. In such cases the performance fails to scale-up due to *excessive parallelism*, because an exponential number of recursive calls create an exponential number of threads, where too many threads operate to perform too little individually. Clearly, this means that the degree of parallelism needs to be managed better. Hence, next we further optimize the performance.

$$\langle condition \rangle \quad ::= \text{if}(\langle input \rangle \langle lop \rangle \langle const \rangle)\text{‘\{’}\langle newline \rangle \langle line1 \rangle;\langle newline \rangle \langle line2 \rangle;\langle newline \rangle\text{‘\}’}$$

is altered to appear as

$$\langle condition \rangle \quad ::= \text{if}(\langle input \rangle \langle lop \rangle \langle const \rangle)\text{‘\{’}\langle newline \rangle \langle line1 \rangle;\langle newline \rangle \langle line2 \rangle;\langle newline \rangle\text{‘\}’} \langle newline \rangle \text{ else if } ((\langle input \rangle \langle lop \rangle \langle const \rangle \langle const \rangle) \text{ ‘\{’ } \langle newline \rangle \langle line1 \rangle; \langle newline \rangle \langle line2 \rangle; \langle newline \rangle\text{‘\}’}$$

Figure 4: The enhanced MCGE-II grammars to generate a program that is both serial and parallel.

```
if (n <= 2) { temp = n; res += temp; }
else if(n <= 39)
{ temp = fib(n-1)+fib(n-2); res += temp; }
else {
 #pragma omp parallel sections\
 private (a) shared(n, temp, res)
 { #pragma omp section
  { a = fib(n-1);
    #pragma omp atomic res += temp+a; }
   #pragma omp section
  { a = fib(n-2);
    #pragma omp atomic res += temp+a; }
} } return res;
```

Figure 5: Evolved program that combines both parallel and serial execution to increase the speed-up.

7. FURTHER PERFORMANCE SCALING

Armed with the knowledge from the previous section we seek to constrain the systems so as to reduce the chances of excessive parallelism. To do this, we combine parallel and serial implementations of the evolved programs, which, further improves the performance. This reduces the overhead caused due to excessive parallelism as the top level recursive calls distribute load across a number of threads, whereas the lower level recursive calls carry out appropriately sized chunks of work instead of merely invoking more threads. We leave it up to evolution to detect the appropriate *level* at which recursion switches from parallel to serial.

To replicate these changes, we enhance the MCGE-II grammars (in Figure 1) to appear as shown in Figure 4, termed

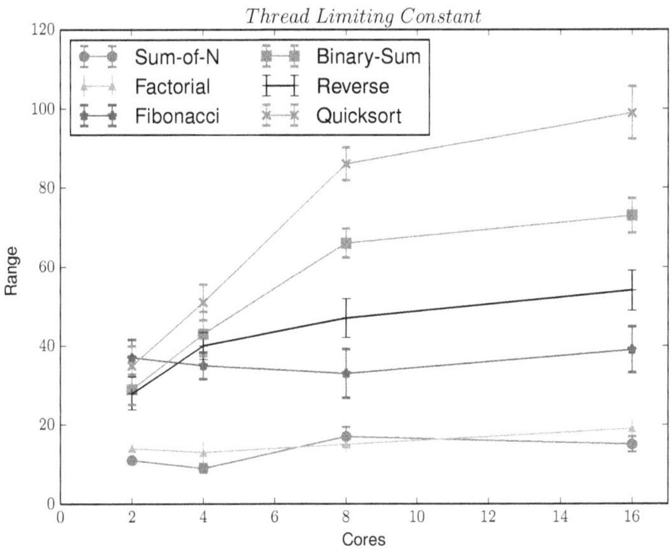

Figure 6: MCGE-II (Scaled) evolved thread limiting constants averaged across 50 runs.

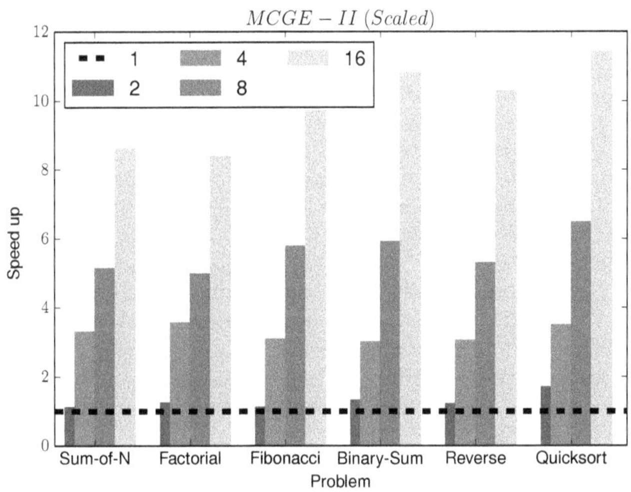

Figure 7: The performance of MCGE-II (Scaled).

Table 5: The mean best generation (mean ± [standard deviation]) of MCGE-II (Grammar, Combined, Scaled). The lowest value is in boldface.

#	MCGE-II Grammar mean best generation	MCGE-II Combined mean best generation	MCGE-II Scaled mean best generation
1	45.38 ± [2.81]	**43.27 ± [5.37]**	44.38 ± [2.81]
2	**31.19 ± [4.73]**	36.51 ± [3.67]	39.11 ± [4.73]
3	**44.73 ± [5.26]**	59.89 ±[4.15]	52.17 ± [4.45]
4	**59.14 ± [5.34]**	61.43 ± [5.19]	64.88 ± [3.51]
5	47.53 ± [2.19]	45.32 ± [4.92]	**44.53 ± [2.19]**
6	**40.49 ± [5.23]**	47.28 ± [3.15]	42.49 ± [5.23]

as *MCGE-II (Scaled)*, hereafter. We alter the non-terminal < *condition* > to generate nested *if-else* condition blocks. The changes generate a program that runs both in parallel as well as serial to reduce the execution time of the evolved programs. It also generates a two digit *thread limiting constant* automatically, at which, the serial execution is initiated.

Figure 5 shows the MCGE-II (Scaled) generated parallel recursive Fibonacci program. It adapts the thread limiting constant to the given problem and computational environment; this constant, arrests the further creation of threads and continues to execute serially. The intermediate result (*temp* in *else if*) is shared among the threads, thus, further optimizes the execution time, thereby, efficiently exploits the power of multi-cores.

The constant (39) in the *else if* (Figure 4) condition is the thread limiting constant for 16 cores. Figure 6 shows the thread limiting constants range (with standard deviation) with respect to the number of cores for all the six experimental problems. It evolves different limiting constants for each problem. Here, we evolve a two digit constant, which, for a large input (say, a 1000000 element array) may not be an optimal limitation, which might be a three or a four digit constant. This can be addressed with digit concatenation grammars [12, Chapter-5], a focus of the future research.

Figure 7 shows the speed-up of MCGE-II (Scaled) over all the six experimental problems. Overall, MCGE-II (Scaled) shows better performance over its counterparts.

Table 5 presents the *mean best generation* results of three MCGE-II variations. The results show that MCGE-II (Grammar) generates best programs faster than the two MCGE-II (Combined, Scaled) variants because of the grammatical bias, while the last two uses execution time in fitness evaluation, thus, makes the evolution slightly hard but generates the efficient task parallel recursive programs.

Table 6: Significance of *performance* and *mean best generation* of MCGE-II (Unoptimized, Grammar, Time, Combined, Scaled). Boldface shows the significance, while asterisk (*) shows the best variants.

MCGE-II variant	Average Rank	$p - value$	$p - Hommel$
Performance Optimization			
Unoptimized	**4.5**	**1.2604E-4**	**0.0125**
Grammar	**4.5**	**1.2604E-4**	**0.0166**
Time	**3.0**	**0.0284597**	**0.025**
Combined	**1.9998**	**0.0347332**	**0.05**
Scaled*	0.99999	-	-
Mean Best Generation			
Unoptimized	**4.333333**	**0.0019107**	**0.0125**
Grammar*	1.5	-	-
Time	**3.833333**	**0.0105871**	**0.01667**
Combined	**2.49998**	**0.0355132**	**0.05**
Scaled	**3.666667**	**0.0176221**	**0.025**

Table 6 shows the non-parametric Friedman tests with Hommel's post-hoc analysis on performance and mean best generation of MCGE-II (Unoptimized, Grammar, Time, Combined, Scaled). A variant with the lowest rank is the best among all of them, and is marked with an asterisk (*). Significantly different variants from the best variant at $\alpha = 0.05$

are in boldface, and is determined when the $p - value$ is less than p-Hommel. For *performance optimization*, MCGE-II (Scaled) outperforms the remaining four MCGE-II variants. Note, these results are for 16 cores of a processor, and are similar for the 8 cores, while they are insignificant with 4 cores and below. On average, for 16 cores, MCGE-II (Scaled) speeds up by a factor 9.97, which improves over MCGE-II (Combined) and MCGE-II (Unoptimized) by 17.45% and 37.91% respectively.

For *mean best generation*, the MCGE-II (Grammar) outperforms the remaining four MCGE-II variants. Note that these results are for 16 cores, while they are similar for 8 cores and below. Although MCGE-II (Scaled) requires slightly more number of generations over MCGE-II (Grammar, Combined), it is considered as the best variant as it generates efficient parallel programs.

However, a similar solution to avoid the inefficiency by the recursive calls is by keeping a table that records the result of a recursive call in its first evaluation. Then, we can refer the table for the repeated recursive calls, similar to Koza [9]. But this approach has often been criticized [10] in the EC community for not being an exact recursion.

8. CONCLUSION AND FUTURE WORK

In summary, we extended MCGE-II to automatically generate efficient task parallel recursive programs. This study offered a separation between the task and data parallelism in the design of the grammars along with the execution time in fitness evaluation. The modifications in the grammar favoured quick generation of programs, while the execution time helped in optimizing their performance.

We then analysed the effect of OpenMP thread scheduling and code growth on performance. Scheduling issues cause performance implications, while code growth (except for 2 cores) has negligible effect on performance of the evolving parallel programs. We also, analysed the computational complexity of the evolving programs, where excessive parallelism restricted the degree of parallelism in the evolving programs. We limited this behaviour with the evolution of programs that run both in serial (for lower level recursive calls) and parallel, thus, further optimized the performance.

Although the limiting constant that switches between parallel and serial modes of execution fails to generalize for large input because we limit it to two digits, it is easy to amend the grammar so that it can evolve a larger or smaller constant as the problem demands.

9. REFERENCES

[1] A. Agapitos and S. M. Lucas. Evolving efficient recursive sorting algorithms. In *IEEE Congress on Evolutionary Computation*, pages 2677–2684, 2006.

[2] A. Agapitos and S. M. Lucas. Evolving modular recursive sorting algorithms. In M. Ebner et.al., editor, *EuroGP 2007*, volume 4445 of *LNCS*, pages 301–310. Springer, Heidelberg, 2007.

[3] R. M. A. Azad and C. Ryan. The best things don't always come in small packages: Constant creation in grammatical evolution. In M. Nicolau et. al., editor, *EuroGP 2014*, volume 8599 of *LNCS*, pages 186–197. Springer, Heidelberg, 2014.

[4] S. Brave. Evolving recursive programs for tree search. In *Advances in Genetic Programming 2*, pages 203–220. MIT Press, 1996.

[5] G. Chennupati, R. M. A. Azad, and C. Ryan. Multi-core GE: automatic evolution of CPU based multi-core parallel programs. In *Proceedings of the Genetic and Evolutionary Computation Conference Companion*, pages 1041–1044. ACM, 2014.

[6] G. Chennupati, R. M. A. Azad, and C. Ryan. Automatic evolution of parallel recursive programs. In *EuroGP 2015*, volume 9025 of *LNCS*, pages 167–178. Springer, Heidelberg, 2015.

[7] G. Chennupati, J. Fitzgerald, and C. Ryan. On the efficiency of multi-core grammatical evolution (MCGE) evolving multi-core parallel programs. In *Proceedings of the 6th World Congress on Nature and Biologically Inspired Computing*, pages 238–243, 2014.

[8] S. García and F. Herrera. An extension on "statistical comparisons of classifiers over multiple data sets" for all pairwise comparisons. *Journal of Machine Learning Research*, 9:2677–2694, 2008.

[9] J. R. Koza. *Genetic Programming: On the Programming of Computers by Means of Natural Selection.* MIT Press, Cambridge, MA, USA, 1992.

[10] A. Moraglio, F. E. B. Otero, C. G. Johnson, S. Thompson, and A. A. Freitas. Evolving recursive programs using non-recursive scaffolding. In *IEEE CongressonEvolutionaryComputation*, pages 1–8, 2012.

[11] A. Nisbet. GAPS: A compiler framework for genetic algorithm (GA) optimised parallelisation. In P. Sloot et. al., editor, *High-Performance Computing and Networking*, volume 1401 of *LNCS*, pages 987–989. Springer, 1998.

[12] M. O'Neill and C. Ryan. *Grammatical Evolution: Evolutionary Automatic Programming in an Arbitrary Language.* Kluwer Academic Publishers, 2003.

[13] OpenMP Architecture Review Board. OpenMP application program interface version 3.0. http://www.openmp.org/mp-documents/spec30.pdf, May 2008.

[14] C. Ryan. *Automatic Re-engineering of Software Using Genetic Programming*, volume 2 of *Genetic Programming.* Springer, 1999.

[15] L. Spector, J. Klein, and M. Keijzer. The push3 execution stack and the evolution of control. In *Proceedings of Genetic and Evolutionary Computation Conference*, pages 1689–1696. ACM, 2005.

[16] A. Trenaman. Concurrent genetic programming, tartarus and dancing agents. In R. Poli et. al., editor, *EuroGP 1999*, volume 1598 of *LNCS*, pages 270–282. Springer, Heidelberg, 1999.

[17] P. A. Whigham and R. I. McKay. Genetic approaches to learning recursive relations. In X. Yao, editor, *Progess in Evolutionary Computation*, LNCS, pages 17–27. Springer, Heidelberg, 1995.

[18] K. P. Williams. *Evolutionary algorithms for automatic parallelization.* PhD thesis, University of Reading, 1998.

[19] M. L. Wong and T. Mun. Evolving recursive programs by using adaptive grammar based genetic programming. *GPEM*, 6:421–455, 2005.

A Re-Examination of the Use of Genetic Programming on the Oral Bioavailability Problem

Grant Dick, Aysha P. Rimoni, and Peter A. Whigham
Department of Information Science
University of Otago
Dunedin, New Zealand
grant.dick@otago.ac.nz, rimay025@student.otago.ac.nz, peter.whigham@otago.ac.nz

ABSTRACT

Difficult benchmark problems are in increasing demand in Genetic Programming (GP). One problem seeing increased usage is the oral bioavailability problem, which is often presented as a challenging problem to both GP and other machine learning methods. However, few properties of the bioavailability data set have been demonstrated, so attributes that make it a challenging problem are largely unknown. This work uncovers important properties of the bioavailability data set, and suggests that the perceived difficulty in this problem can be partially attributed to a lack of pre-processing, including features within the data set that contain no information, and contradictory relationships between the dependent and independent features of the data set. The paper then re-examines the performance of GP on this data set, and contextualises this performance relative to other regression methods. Results suggest that a large component of the observed performance differences on the bioavailability data set can be attributed to variance in the selection of training and testing data. Differences in performance between GP and other methods disappear when multiple training/testing splits are used within experimental work, with performance typically no better than a null modelling approach of reporting the mean of the training data.

Categories and Subject Descriptors

I.2.2 [**Automatic Programming**]; I.2.8 [**Problem Solving, Control Methods, and Search**]: *Heuristic methods*

Keywords

genetic programming; feature selection; bioavailability

GECCO '15, July 11 - 15, 2015, Madrid, Spain
© 2015 ACM. ISBN 978-1-4503-3472-3/15/07...$15.00
DOI: http://dx.doi.org/10.1145/2739480.2754771

1. INTRODUCTION

Recent work in genetic programming (GP) has argued the need for better benchmark problems from which to compare methods [14]. The human oral bioavailability problem was introduced into the GP community in 2006 by Archetti et al. [1]. Perhaps in response to the call for more challenging benchmarks, in addition to the paper introducing the problem being awarded best paper in its stream at GECCO, it has recently seen increased use to guide the development and evaluation of new methods and operators in GP. However, despite its increased use in GP, little work has been done to uncover the underlying properties of this problem. Other problems, such as the Boston housing problem, are typically selected for benchmarking use only after extensive analysis has been performed. The goal of this paper is to take the initial steps towards understanding this problem in greater detail, so that its usefulness as a benchmark problem can be properly understood. The initial findings of this work suggest that the problem contains a large number of redundant features, or features that present little or no information, that complicate the modelling process. Additionally, the performance differences observed in previous work, including the work of Archetti et al. [1], cannot be ruled out as just the consequences of the sampling process when building training and testing data.

The goal of this paper is not to examine new operators in GP, nor is it intended to demonstrate improved use of GP on the bioavailability problem: it is fundamentally about assessing data set properties. However, the bioavailability data set has seen little (if any) use outside the GP community, while seemingly taking on an increased importance within GP research. As such, the work here is relevant to GP researchers, even if the direct use of GP is somewhat limited.

The rest of this paper is structured as follows: §2 introduces the bioavailability problem, and brie y discusses examples of previous work using the data set; §3 presents an initial analysis of the key attributes of the bioavailability problem; §4 examines the usefulness of feature selection on the bioavailability data set, and examines the performance of occurrence-based metrics for feature selection in GP; §5 examines the degree to which sampling of training and testing sets interacts with the performance exhibited by models built on this data set; §6 revisits the performance of GP variants on the bioavailability problem relative to other machine learning methods; finally, §7 concludes the paper with a brief summary of its findings, and suggests areas of future work.

2. GENETIC PROGRAMMING AND BIOAVAILABILITY

The human oral bioavailability problem was first introduced into the GP research community in 2006 [1]. It is a straightforward regression problem, that attempts to characterise the relationship between a large number of molecular descriptors for a given compound, and the related percentage uptake of the molecule when it is ingested, in other words, how much of the molecule passes through into the circulatory system without being broken down during metabolism. Being able to predict such properties is desirable for pharmaceutical research, and it allows for faster, more economical screening of potential drugs. In addition to creating the data set, Archetti et al. reported that a variant of GP, augmented with linear scaling, provided the best overall prediction of bioavailability in comparison to a range of other machine learning methods. Moreover, it was claimed to achieve good performance without resorting to external feature selection methods; while other machine learning methods could eventually achieve comparable performance, they could only do so after the application of computationally-expensive feature selection methods.

Following the initial work of Archetti et al. [1]., the data set has been used to guide the development of bloat control methods [19, 18, 20, 21, 6], methods using structured population search [10], semantic methods [24, 5], and approaches that structure the training data into groups of varying complexity [9, 15]. The majority of work in GP involving the bioavailability data set has focused upon its use as a benchmark problem (for example, [25, 3]). There has been some work attempting to characterise the difficulty of the problem through the use of fitness clouds and negative slope coefficients [23]. However, beyond this, little work has been done to properly characterise the problem, in terms of its overall difficulty, and any properties that would make it suitable as a benchmark problem. Without this knowledge, comparisons using this data set resort to simple "A is better than B" comparisons, and do not provide useful insights into the search characteristics of a given method.

3. SUMMARY STATISTICS AND PRELIMINARY ANALYSIS

There are many sources for this data set, but it appears that the authoritative source of the data is: http://personal.disco.unimib.it/Vanneschi/bioavailability.txt, while descriptors for the features can be found at: http://personal.disco.unimib.it/Vanneschi/bioavailability_lookup.txt. In the original work of Archetti et al. [1], the data set was described as having 360 instances, however publicly available sources present 359 instances. Each instance represents the chemical and physical properties of a single molecule. The data set presents 241 features from which to build models to relate the response variable. All features are described as continuous, although many (e.g., feature 4, the number of atoms) appear to be discrete counts. The response variable, often referred to as %F in previous work, presents the known bioavailability of the molecule of the related instance.

Beyond the above described details, little is usually presented in previous work to describe the properties of this data set. However, rudimentary analysis of the data set raises some interesting points. Although the data set is described as containing 241 features, 47 of the features are empty, that is, they contain the same value (zero) across all instances. Therefore, they provide no useful information for modelling purposes. In addition, they may present challenges for several modelling techniques: for linear regression, they present singular values, and so make least squares optimisation of coefficients difficult; for genetic programming, including them in a parse tree at best does nothing (e.g., within addition or subtraction), or masks the behaviour of related sub-trees (e.g., during multiplication or division). In addition to the large number of empty features, the bioavailability data set contains a number of "sparse" features, which are features in which all but one instance contain a zero value. Ideally, these empty and sparse features should be identified and removed prior to modelling, reducing the data set to 172 features.

If the empty and sparse features are removed from the data set, then one further analysis that can take place is to identify linear dependencies in the data set. Some of the linearly-dependent features can be easily identified through the available feature descriptors: for example feature 4 describes the total number of atoms in the molecule, which is naturally the sum of the other features describing the number of atoms of different types (features 5 through 13). Others can be identified through singular value decomposition, which identifies a total of 12 linear dependencies in the data set. For example, singular value decomposition identifies that feature 178 is a linear composition of features 6 and 7. While linearly-dependent features should not present a major problem to GP, they can cause significant problems to modelling techniques built around linear least squares methods, and so should be managed as part of any modelling using such principles.

Finally, plotting the distance between instances in their feature space against their corresponding distance in the response space allows an assessment of the structural relationships in a data set. For a point of comparison, two other data sets are presented an artificial data set containing a trivial linear combination of two features, and the well-known Boston housing data set. The artificial data set is designed to show the characteristics of the distance relationship in the absence of noise or any confusion, while the Boston housing problem presents the characteristics that would be typical of a moderately difficult regression problem. The results of this comparison are shown in Figure 1. Essentially, each point in the plot compares an instance pair in terms of their (normalised) distance in the feature space on the horizontal axis, and the corresponding (normalised) distance in the response space on the vertical axis. The relationships shown in Figure 1 raise some interesting points; intuitively, we should expect that two instances that are "close" within the feature space should exhibit a corresponding closeness in the response space.[1] This manifests in the visualisation as an absence of points in the upper-left corner of the plot. Such a relationship is clearly evident in the trivial problem (shown in the right-most panel), and a reasonable signal can be seen in the Boston housing problem. However, the signal is not as strong in the bioavailability problem: there are a number of cases in which instances are close in the feature space, but this does not correspond to closeness in the response space. In its most extreme, the bioavailability problem presents in-

[1]Note that the opposite scenario does not need to be true it is easy to imagine cases where instances far apart in the feature space will be much closer in the response space.

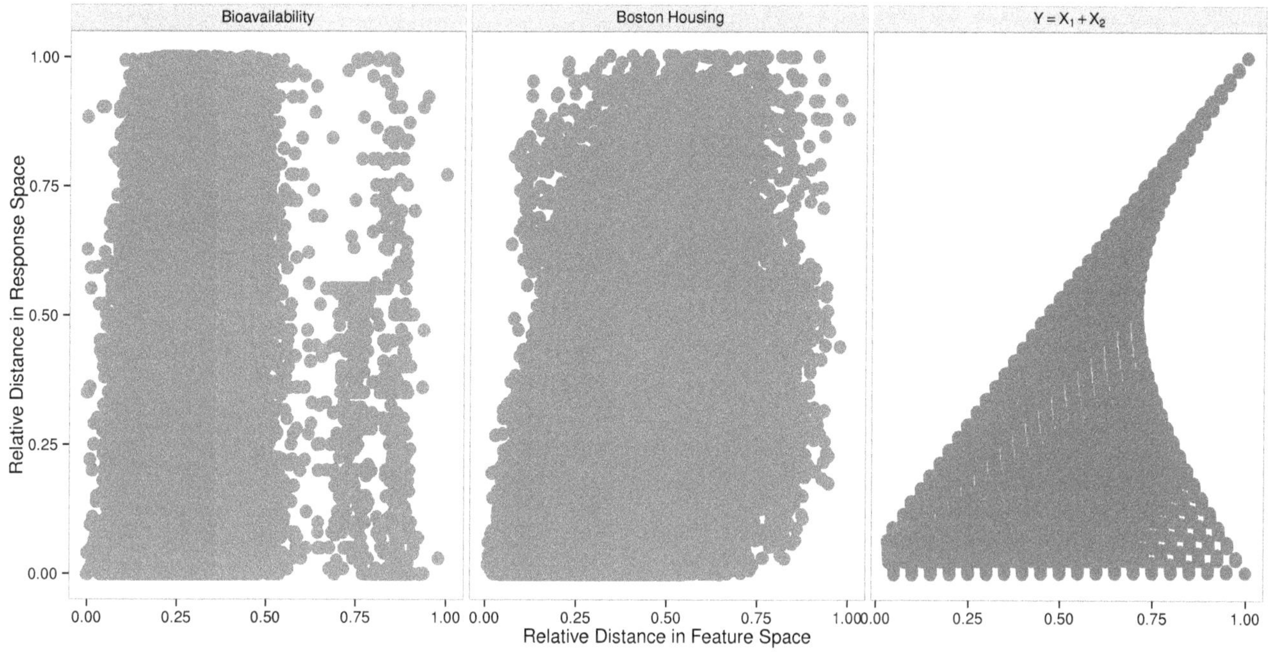

Figure 1: The distance relationship between instances in the feature and response spaces. Ideally, instances that are close in the feature space should be equally-close in the response space.

stances that are identical in the feature space (i.e., the distance between instances in terms of their features is zero), yet vary greatly in the response space. It is not clear if this is a true re ection of the problem, or an anomaly that was introduced during the construction of the data set. Given that there is no way to distinguish between these instances in terms of their features, there is little chance than any modelling approach will be able to provide accurate predictions for unseen cases similar to these instances.

4. FEATURE SELECTION

The initial work by Archetti et al. [1] argued that GP, due to constraints on tree sizes, performs strong feature selection within the evolutionary process. They presented the features selected by the best model evolved by their GP variant, which are reproduced here in Table 1. The feature selection method used by Archetti et al. was a simple occurrence model: if a feature appeared in the tree, it was considered important. However, it is interesting to note that eight of the 17 features selected by the best model appear in the list of 69 features outlined as empty or sparse in the previous section. This suggests that the post-hoc analysis of the presence of features in a single tree may not provide the required insights to perform effective feature selection.

4.1 Occurrence Counts vs. Sensitivity Analysis for Feature Selection in GP

Feature selection in GP has previously emphasised the use of occurrence counts of features in parse trees. The inclusion of a feature in a tree is assumed to indicate its importance in the problem. However, this does not consider that some features may enter into parse trees through means other than selection, for example as a consequence of bloat.

To test the effectiveness of occurrence counts as a metric we ran 30 instances of a typical GP implementation on the bioavailability data set. At the end of each run, we identified the features present in the best individual, and then tallied the number of runs in which a feature was present in the final model. The results of this analysis are presented in Figure 2. The result does not appear to provide concrete evidence towards strong feature selection: the strongest selected feature (213) appears in less than a third of all runs. Of the top ten features, in terms of their presence in the best models, three of them appear in the list of empty or sparse features discussed in §3. In fact, 59 of the empty or sparse features appeared at least once (and as many as six times) in the best model of a given run. Overall, there is not a clear signal towards any specific features, and the distribution over all features is arguably uniform.

The results presented in Figure 2 provide strong evidence that occurrence counts do not provide a useful metric for feature selection on the bioavailability data set. What is needed is a means by which the in uence that a given feature has on parse tree behaviour can be measured. One possible technique, inspired by the methods used in random forests to determine variable importance, can be defined as:

1. Split the data set into a training and testing portion (e.g., a 70-30 split, or a bootstrap resample).
2. Run GP on a training portion of the data set to determine the best evolved model.
3. Obtain the testing mean squared error of the best model.
4. For each feature, shu e the values within the testing data, and obtain the mean squared error of the best model on this configuration.

Table 1: Features selected by the best GP model presented in Archetti et al. [1]. Comments about the properties of these features within the data set appear in italics.

Feature #	Remark
5	Number of carbon atoms
9	Number of sulfur atoms
26	Number of aliphatic rings
34	atom-type E-state index for CH2 groups
69	atom-type E-state index for phosphinate (*contains no information*)
84	atom-type E-state index for Iodine groups (*all but one instance are zero*)
110	number of thiocarbonyl groups (*contains no information*)
126	number of nitrites groups (*contains no information*)
150	number of sulphate groups (*all but one instance are zero*)
188	Iso-thio-cyanate:1.0; thio-cyanate:0.5 (*contains no information*)
195	Compounds with OH groups attached to an aliphatic alcohol (*all but one instance are zero*)
206	Hydrocarbon compounds with at least one uorine groups (*contains no information*)
214	Number of hydrogen bond acceptors
218	Number of nitrogen based hydrogen bond acceptors
224	Sum of partial atomic charge on nitrogen based hydrogen bond acceptors
234	accumulative contribution of purely anionic species to fraction ionised at specific pH=7.4
240	Lone electron pair on NOSV divided by the number factor

5. Obtain the difference between the errors recorded in steps 3 and 4 as a measure of a feature's importance within the best model. A large difference indicates that the feature is important to prediction accuracy.

The above process was run 30 times on the data set, and the average importance for each feature was computed from these runs. The result of this is shown in Figure 3. In contrast to the results in Figure 2, the results show a much stronger focus upon specific features. The top ten selected features using this approach are (in descending order): 213, 29, 225, 143, 215, 219, 221, 27, 63, and 85. Interestingly, none of these features appear in the list of features in Table 1 that were identified by Archetti et al. [1].

To provide a point of comparison, we ran two other feature selection methods information gain [16], and random forest variable importance [4] on the data set. The results of this are shown in Figures 4 and 5, respectively. The results of information gain are surprising, with the analysis suggesting that only eight features contain any useful information: 219, 226, 213, 63, 225, 220, 221, and 85. Note the negative importance of features suggested by the random forest approach, which indicates that prediction error *reduces* when

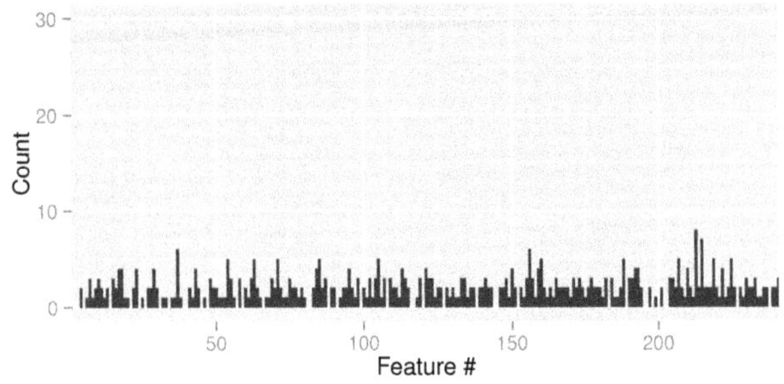

Figure 2: Results of GP-based feature selection using an occurrence count metric.

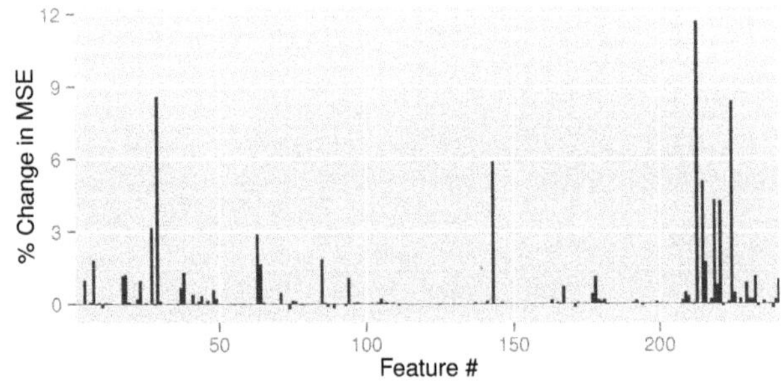

Figure 3: Results of GP-based feature selection using a metric that measures the change of out of sample mean squared error performance when feature values are shu ed.

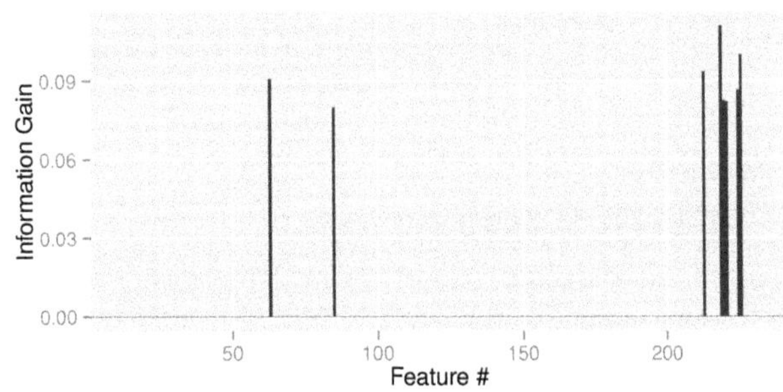

Figure 4: Result of feature ranking using information gain measures.

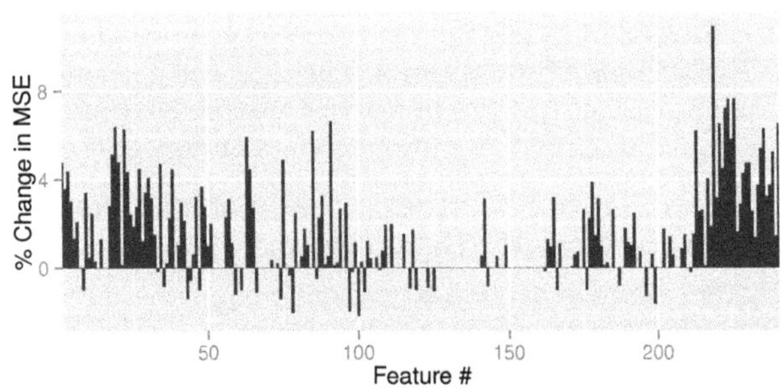

Figure 5: Ranking of variable importance using random forest out of sample analysis.

these features are perturbed. For the remaining features, the ten most important features identified by random forest (in descending order) are: 219, 226, 224, 223, 91, 241, 221, 19, 236, and 22.

A final remark about the feature selection process should be made here: the top features selected across all methods are inconsistent. There are only two features that are presented as important by all three methods (GP feature importance, information gain, and random forest): 219 and 221. These features relate to information about hydrogen bond acceptors and donors; given that hydrogen bond acceptors and donors are import components of "Lipinski's rule of five" [13], these would be reasonable features to select from the data set. However, it is interesting to note the inconsistency across feature selection methods on this data set in terms of the features identified as useful.

5. SAMPLING VARIANCE

The bioavailability problem has been used in previous work to demonstrate the superiority of newly developed methods and operators. In Archetti et al.'s original work, and also in some subsequent work exploring this data set, a single training and testing sample is drawn from the global data set. Then, due to the stochastic nature of GP, multiple runs are performed on this single training and testing split. Using a single training/testing split is not unusual in GP, and is a reasonable approach if the data set is well-behaved and the splits remain representative of the overall data set. However, this assumption of well-behaved distributions has never been examined in the bioavailability problem, so it is necessary to test this assumption.

In order to provide context for the results of previous work, it is necessary to demonstrate that the spread of the expected root mean squared errors resulting from a given model are outside that encountered through the use of a null model that predicts the mean of the training data.[2] If the distribution of errors of this null model encompasses that of the observed results, then we cannot rule out differences in behaviour being due to chance effects. We test this through the following framework:

1. Generate a bootstrapped resample of the data set to serve as our training data. Any instances not selected in our bootstrap sample will serve as our hold-out test set.

2. Compute the mean of the response variable from the training data.

3. Compute the residuals between the mean computed in the previous step, and the response values in the out-of-sample test data.

4. Compute the root mean square error of the residuals.

This process is performed 1000 times to provide a strong signal of the underlying distribution. The resulting distribution is shown in Figure 6. In addition, the mean and standard deviation of the results of the best and worse GP methods in Archetti et al. are included for reference as shaded and hatched regions, respectively.

[2]We could easily approximate this through the use of the standard deviation of the response data over the entire data set. However, for consistency's sake, we will build a true null model with a separation of training and testing data sets.

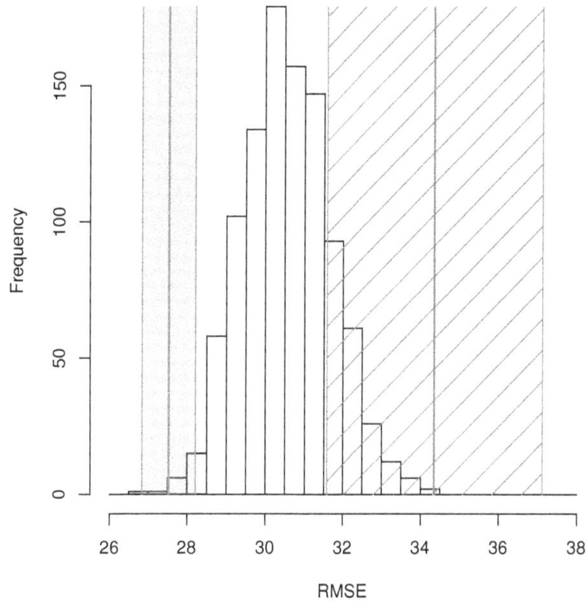

Figure 6: The underlying distribution of the bootstrapped root mean squared error of the response variable (equivalent to the bootstrap sample standard deviation) for the bioavailability data set. For comparison, the mean and standard deviation of the results of Archetti et al. [1] for standard GP (hatched) and LS2-C-GP (shaded) are included.

The distribution shown in Figure 6 paints an interesting picture. It can be seen that the standard GP approach from Archetti et al. has a mean performance that is far *worse* than that of the typical behaviour expected from a null model, while the best model falls on the other extreme, yet is still encompassed within the observed range of the null model. Certainly, there is considerable overlap between the results published by Archetti et al., and the performance of a null model. This makes it difficult to rule out the difference in performance being attributed to variance in the sampling of training and test data.

To further examine the impact that sampling has on performance, we created five random 70-30 training and testing splits from the global data set. Then on each split, we ran two variants of GP (standard GP, and LS2-C-GP from Archetti et al.), along with a penalised linear regression model (lasso). For each method on each split, 30 runs were performed. The results, in terms of testing root mean squared error performance, are shown in Figure 7. The results confirm that the sampling process has a large impact on the error performance of a given method, and can alter the relative ranking of the methods. For two of the splits, the GP variants appear to outperform the linear model, in the third split, all three methods are roughly equal (in terms of median performance), while in the final two splits, the linear model appears to work best. The implications for this are significant: if we had only taken one sample, any one of three possible outcomes could have been observed. This suggests that, in order to account for the variance in the sampling process for this data set, multiple samples must be drawn in addition to multiple runs being performed.

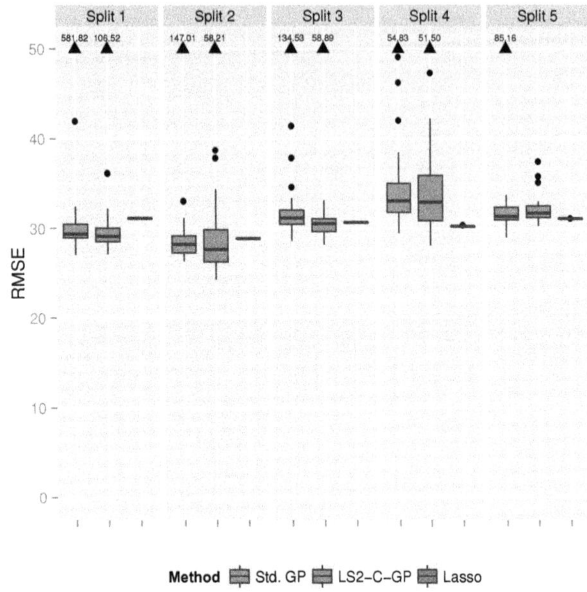

Figure 7: The result of sampling variance on root mean squared performance for GP and penalised linear regression. The ▲ symbol indicates the presence of outliers that fall outside the plotted region (the number following the symbol indicates the value of the largest outlier).

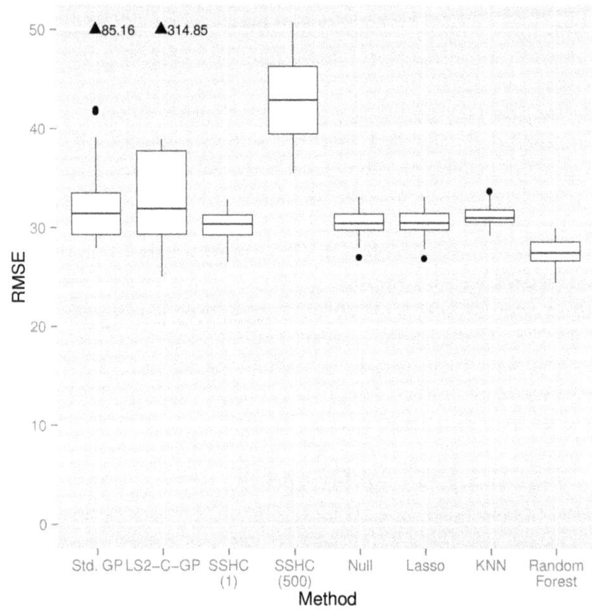

Figure 8: The root mean squared error performance of the compared methods over 30 independent runs. The ▲ symbol indicates the presence of outliers that fall outside the plotted region (the number following the symbol indicates the value of the largest outlier).

6. COMPARATIVE PERFORMANCE

In previous work, GP was shown to outperform other machine learning methods on the bioavailability problem. However, the results of the previous sections of this paper raise enough questions to warrant a re-examination of those results. In this section, we perform a robust comparison of GP against several traditional machine learning approaches. We also include a recently-presented method of geometric semantic GP as a representation of "state of the art" performance [8]. Additionally, we include a null regression model (that predicts the mean of the response of the training data) in the results; if a model is to be effective, then it should be expected to considerably outperform this null model. Finally, we use multiple resamplings of training and testing sets throughout the experiments to account for the biases observed in the previous section.

The chosen models are as follows:

Standard GP, as used in Archetti et al. [1].

LS2-C-GP, as used in Archetti et al. [1].

Stochastic Semantic Hill-climbing with Doubly Adaptive Bounded Mutation (SSHC) [8].

Penalised linear regression (the lasso), with regularisation parameter determined through 10-fold cross-validation of the training data [22, 7].

k-nearest neighbour (KNN) regression, with the neighbourhood size determined through leave-one-out cross-validation of the training data [17].

Random forest regression [4]. No attempt to tune parameters were made for this model, the default values from the R randomForest package were used [12].

For the two GP variants, all parameters were as outlined in Archetti et al.; for SSHC, the method was configured as in the original work (using 500 generations), as well as a "single step" approach as suggested by the authors (using a single generation) [8]. In total, 30 runs were performed; in each run, a new 70-30 training and testing split was identified, and then all methods were subsequently applied to that split. In each run, the testing root mean squared error was computed (in the case of GP models, the best model in the final generation was used as the representative model).

The testing root mean squared errors for the 30 runs for each method are shown in Figure 8. In contrast to earlier work, the relative performance of GP and the traditional machine learning methods has changed: the two GP variants present occasional outliers, and their median performance is slightly higher than the other methods, although not to a significant degree. The median error of SSHC when run for 500 generations (labelled 'SSHC (500)' in Figure 8) is slightly lower than that reported in previous work, while its single step performance (labelled 'SSHC (1)' in Figure 8) aligns with previously reported values [8]. The high RMSE error of SSHC (500) is likely due to over-fitting to the training data as a result of numerous applications of least-squares estimation of the model coefficients. Most interestingly, all the modelling approaches, with the exception of random forests and SSHC (500), perform at a level that is comparable to a null model of predicting the mean of the training data. Random forest is able to improve upon the null model, but the difference remains somewhat small.

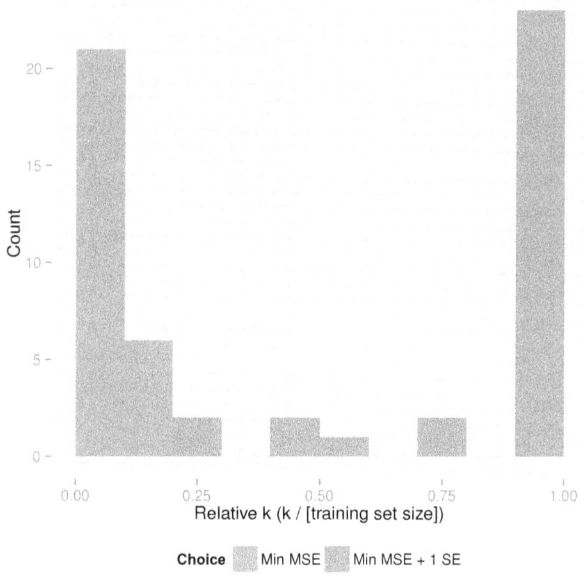

Figure 9: Histogram cross-validation selected sample size (k) for KNN regression, contrasted against the histogram of the selected k had "+ 1 standard error" criteria been adopted.

6.1 Further Properties

Both KNN and lasso regression performed at a similar level to a null model. Interestingly, the performance of the lasso method is almost identical to that of the null model. The lasso method regularises the coefficients of features in the model, so any feature with a coefficient set to zero is effectively eliminated from the model. Therefore, we can examine the degree to which the lasso method used the available feature information. At the end of each run, the number of non-zero coefficients (excluding the intercept term) identified by the lasso model was recorded. The tally of this analysis is shown in Table 2. Interestingly, in 22 of the 30 runs, the lasso method selected a model that eschewed any feature information, and instead relied upon a constant intercept term (i.e., degraded to a null model). When combined with the difficulty observed in §4 for selecting features, this suggests that the signal in the underlying data set that maps the features to the response variable is possibly overwhelmed by other sources of noise in the data.

Like the lasso model, the KNN approach also performed at a level comparable to that of a null model. Also like the lasso model, we can look at the properties of the training process (i.e., the leave-one-out process to select the neighbourhood size) to gain an insight into what is taking place. In this case, we can examine the neighbourhood size k selected during each run. The results for this are shown in Figure 9, where the number of neighbours k has been normalised by the size of the training set. In particular, two histograms are shown: the first shows the value of k that was selected to minimise the cross-validation error (this is labelled 'Min MSE'); the second histogram indicates that the largest k that could be selected for the same model without increasing the cross-validation error by more than one standard error (the so-called "one standard error" rule [11]). As can be seen, while the cross-validation process chose small neighbourhood sizes, it could have equally chosen very large neighbourhoods, encompassing the entire training set, without compromising performance greatly. Had such a large neighbourhood been chosen, then KNN would use all the available data, and would again degrade to the behaviour of a null model. Given that the difference between a very small neighbourhood, and using the entire data set, was less than one standard error, it is reasonable to again conclude that the underlying signal in the data source is, at best, weak.

Table 2: Tally of the number of times a certain number of features were incorporated in linear model developed through penalised (lasso) regression in 30 independent runs.

# of included. features				
0	**1**	**2**	**3**	**4**
22	1	2	4	1

7. CONCLUSION

GP needs better benchmarks. Increasingly, the bioavailability data set is being used in an attempt to address this need. However, this data set has not received the necessary attention to provide the context and understanding to make it a truly useful benchmark. The goal of this paper was to take the initial steps into increasing the GP community's understanding of this data set. In the process, it was found that the data set contains a large amount of redundant features, inconsistencies within the relationship between input features and response values, and does not respond well to the application of feature selection. The problem also presents challenges in selecting training and testing samples: this paper demonstrates that the natural deviation within the response values in the data set can plausibly explain the differences in performance exhibited in previous work. This means that many results in previous work cannot be ruled out as consequences of chance events. Additionally, when models are built from this data set, they will often resort to developing a null model that does not use information from the feature space and instead resorts to building models around the mean of the training data. Based upon this, the conclusions of this paper are that we cannot recommend the use of the bioavailability data set for benchmarking until these characteristics are properly understood and resolved.

7.1 Future Work

The work presented here raises several points for future research to explore. For the bioavailability data set, it is clear that more processing is required, including identifying transformations in the data, and constructing new features from the data. GP may be a useful component in the construction of these features, as well as more traditional methods.

There are several other data sets used in GP related to the bioavailability data set [2]: they too are seeing an increase in use, although not to the same extent as bioavailability. Future work should explore these problems in a similar manner to the analysis conducted here, in order to ensure that they are properly understood before further use as benchmarks.

Finally, it would be a useful exercise to revisit the Drug-

Bank and independently recreate the bioavailability data set: in the subsequent years since this data set was created, changes have been made to the ADMET Predictor software, and new molecules have been entered into the database. It is possible that incorporating these changes, along with the insights from this paper, into an updated data set may provide a useful and challenging problem for use in future research.

8. REFERENCES

[1] F. Archetti, S. Lanzeni, E. Messina, and L. Vanneschi. Genetic programming for human oral bioavailability of drugs. In *Proceedings of the 8th Annual Conference on Genetic and Evolutionary Computation*, GECCO '06, pages 255 262, New York, NY, USA, 2006. ACM.

[2] F. Archetti, S. Lanzeni, E. Messina, and L. Vanneschi. Genetic programming for computational pharmacokinetics in drug discovery and development. *Genetic Programming and Evolvable Machines*, 8(4):413 432, 2007.

[3] R. M. A. Azad and C. Ryan. A simple approach to lifetime learning in genetic programming-based symbolic regression. *Evolutionary computation*, 22(2):287 317, 2014.

[4] L. Breiman. Random forests. *Machine learning*, 45(1):5 32, 2001.

[5] M. Castelli, S. Silva, and L. Vanneschi. A C++ framework for geometric semantic genetic programming. *Genetic Programming and Evolvable Machines*, pages 1 9, 2014.

[6] G. Dick. Bloat and generalisation in symbolic regression. In G. Dick, W. Browne, P. Whigham, M. Zhang, L. Bui, H. Ishibuchi, Y. Jin, X. Li, Y. Shi, P. Singh, K. Tan, and K. Tang, editors, *Simulated Evolution and Learning*, volume 8886 of *Lecture Notes in Computer Science*, pages 491 502. Springer International Publishing, 2014.

[7] J. Friedman, T. Hastie, and R. Tibshirani. glmnet: Lasso and elastic-net regularized generalized linear models. *R package version*, 1, 2009.

[8] I. Goncalves, S. Silva, and C. M. Fonseca. On the generalization ability of geometric semantic genetic programming. In P. Machado, M. I. Heywood, J. McDermott, M. Castelli, P. Garc a-Sanchez, P. Burelli, S. Risi, and K. Sim, editors, *Genetic Programming*, volume 9025 of *Lecture Notes in Computer Science*, pages 41 52. Springer International Publishing, 2015.

[9] M. A. Haeri, M. M. Ebadzadeh, and G. Folino. Improving GP generalization: a variance-based layered learning approach. *Genetic Programming and Evolvable Machines*, 16(1):27 55, 2015.

[10] R. Harper. Spatial co-evolution: quicker, fitter and less bloated. In *Proceedings of the 14th Annual Conference on Genetic and Evolutionary Computation*, GECCO '12, pages 759 766. ACM, 2012.

[11] T. Hastie, R. Tibshirani, and J. Friedman. *The Elements of Statistical Learning*. Springer Series in Statistics. Springer New York Inc., second edition, 2009.

[12] A. Liaw and M. Wiener. Classification and regression by randomforest. *R News*, 2(3):18 22, 2002.

[13] C. A. Lipinski, F. Lombardo, B. W. Dominy, and P. J. Feeney. Experimental and computational approaches to estimate solubility and permeability in drug discovery and development settings. *Advanced Drug Delivery Reviews*, 23(1 3):3 25, 1997.

[14] J. McDermott, D. R. White, S. Luke, L. Manzoni, M. Castelli, L. Vanneschi, W. Jaskowski, K. Krawiec, R. Harper, K. De Jong, and U.-M. O'Reilly. Genetic programming needs better benchmarks. In *Proceedings of the 14th Annual Conference on Genetic and Evolutionary Computation*, GECCO '12, pages 791 798, New York, NY, USA, 2012. ACM.

[15] R. Muhammad Atif Azad, D. Medernach, and C. Ryan. Efficient approaches to interleaved sampling of training data for symbolic regression. In *The 6th World Congress on Nature and Biologically Inspired Computing (NaBIC)*, pages 176 183. IEEE, 2014.

[16] J. R. Quinlan. *C4.5: Programs for Machine Learning*. Morgan Kaufmann Publishers Inc., San Francisco, CA, USA, 1993.

[17] K. Schliep and K. Hechenbichler. *kknn: Weighted k-Nearest Neighbors*, 2014. R package version 1.2-5.

[18] S. Silva. Reassembling operator equalisation: a secret revealed. *ACM SIGEVOlution*, 5(3):10 22, 2011.

[19] S. Silva and L. Vanneschi. State-of-the-art genetic programming for predicting human oral bioavailability of drugs. In *Advances in Bioinformatics*, pages 165 173. Springer, 2010.

[20] S. Silva and L. Vanneschi. The importance of being at studying the program length distributions of operator equalisation. In *Genetic Programming Theory and Practice IX*, pages 211 233. Springer, 2011.

[21] S. Silva and L. Vanneschi. Bloat free genetic programming: Application to human oral bioavailability prediction. *International journal of data mining and bioinformatics*, 6(6):585 601, 2012.

[22] R. Tibshirani. Regression shrinkage and selection via the lasso. *Journal of the Royal Statistical Society. Series B (Methodological)*, pages 267 288, 1996.

[23] L. Vanneschi. Investigating problem hardness of real life applications. In *Genetic Programming Theory and Practice V*, pages 107 124. Springer, 2008.

[24] L. Vanneschi, M. Castelli, L. Manzoni, and S. Silva. A new implementation of geometric semantic gp and its application to problems in pharmacokinetics. In K. Krawiec, A. Moraglio, T. Hu, A. c. Etaner-Uyar, and B. Hu, editors, *Genetic Programming*, volume 7831 of *Lecture Notes in Computer Science*, pages 205 216. Springer Berlin Heidelberg, 2013.

[25] L. Vanneschi and S. Gustafson. Using crossover based similarity measure to improve genetic programming generalization ability. In *Proceedings of the 11th Annual conference on Genetic and Evolutionary Computation*, GECCO '09, pages 1139 1146. ACM,

Memetic Semantic Genetic Programming

Robyn Ffrancon
TAO, INRIA Saclay
Univ. Paris-Sud
Orsay, France
rffrancon@gmail.com

Marc Schoenauer
TAO, INRIA Saclay
Univ. Paris-Sud
Orsay, France
marc.schoenauer@inria.fr

ABSTRACT

Semantic Backpropagation (SB) was introduced in GP so as to take into account the semantics of a GP tree at all intermediate states of the program execution, i.e., at each node of the tree. The idea is to compute the optimal "should-be" values each subtree should return, whilst assuming that the rest of the tree is unchanged, so as to minimize the fitness of the tree. To this end, the Random Desired Output (RDO) mutation operator, proposed in [17], uses SB in choosing, from a given library, a tree whose semantics are preferred to the semantics of a randomly selected subtree from the parent tree. Pushing this idea one step further, this paper introduces the Local Tree Improvement (LTI) operator, which selects from the parent tree the overall best subtree for applying RDO, using a small randomly drawn static library. Used within a simple Iterated Local Search framework, LTI can find the exact solution of many popular Boolean benchmarks in reasonable time whilst keeping solution trees small, thus paving the road for truly memetic GP algorithms.

1. INTRODUCTION

Memetic Algorithms [9] have become increasingly popular recently (see e.g., [11]): the hybridization between evolutionary algorithms and non-evolutionary (generally local) search has resulted in highly efficient algorithms in practice, mainly in the field of combinatorial optimization.

There have been, however, very few works proposing memetic approaches in Genetic Programming (e.g., the term "GP" does not even appear in [11]). The main reason is certainly the lack of recognized efficient local optimization procedures in the usual GP search spaces (trees, linear-coded GP, Cartesian GP, ...).

However, from the EC point of view, a stochastic local search procedure in a given search space can be viewed as a specific mutation operator in which choices are biased, using domain-specific knowledge, toward improving the fitness of the parent individual. Clearly, the boundary between memetic and genetic operators is far from being crisp (a well-known example is the record-winning Evolutionary TSP solver [10]).

Historical Genetic Programming (GP) [5] evolves trees by manipulating subtrees in a syntactical way, blind to any possible bias toward fitness improvement, as is the rule in 'pure' Evolutionary Algorithms: Subtree crossover selects nodes at random from both parents and swaps them, along with their rooted subtrees. Similarly, point mutation randomly selects one subtree and replaces it with a randomly constructed other subtree. Subtrees are probabilistically (most often randomly) selected from the parents to which they belong, as opposed to their own usefulness as functions.

More recently, several works have addressed this issue, gradually building up the field that is now called *Semantic GP*. For a given set of values of the problem variables, the *semantics* of a subtree within a given tree is defined as the vector of values computed by this subtree for each set of input values in turn. In Semantic GP, as the name implies, the semantics of all subtrees are considered as well as the semantics of the context in which a subtree is inserted (i.e., the semantics of the its siblings), as first proposed and described in detail in [8] (see also [15] for a recent survey). Several variation operators have been proposed for use within the framework of Evolutionary Computation (EC) which take semantics into account when choosing and modifying subtrees.

One such semantically oriented framework is Behavioural Programming GP [6]. The framework facilitates the use of Machine Learning techniques in analyzing the internal semantics of individual trees so as to explicitly identify potentially useful subtrees. It constitutes a step towards archiving and reusing potentially useful subtrees based on the merits of their functionality rather than solely on the fitnesses of the full trees from which they derive. However, the usefulness of these subtrees is assessed globally, independent of the context to which they are to be inserted.

Semantic Backpropagation (SB) [17, 7, 12] addresses this issue: given a set of fitness cases, SB computes, for each subtree of a target tree, the desired outputs which they should return so as to minimize the fitness of the tree, assuming that the rest of the tree is unchanged. A small number of specialised operators have been proposed which exploit SB, the *Random Desired Output* (RDO) mutation operator is one example [17]. This operator firstly randomly picks a target node in the parent tree, then replaces this target node with a tree from a given *library* of trees whose outputs best match the desired values of the target node [17, 12]. Because it

GECCO '15, July 11 - 15, 2015, Madrid, Spain

ISBN 978-1-4503-3472-3/15/07...$15.00
DOI: http://dx.doi.org/10.1145/2739480.2754697

replaces, if possible, the tree rooted at the selected node of the parent tree with a tree that matches the local semantics of that node, RDO can also be viewed as a first step towards a memetic operator.

Building on RDO, the present work proposes *Local Tree Improvement* (LTI), a local search procedure in the space of GP trees which extends RDO with another bias toward a better fitness: Rather than selecting the target node in the parent tree at random, Local Tree Improvement selects the best possible semantic match between all possible nodes in the parent tree and all trees in the library. The resulting variation operator in the space of trees is then used within a standard Iterated Local Search procedure: LTI is repeatedly applied to one single tree with the hope of gradually improving the tree fitness – whereas a single application of LTI is not guaranteed to do so.

The prerequisites for the LTI procedure are those of Semantic Backpropagation[1]: i) a fitness defined by aggregation of some error on several fitness cases ii) a way to compute from the current context (as defined in [8]), at each node and for each fitness case, the optimal values which each node should return so that the the whole tree evaluates to the exact expected values. This is indeed possible in the case for Boolean, Categorical, and Symbolic Regression problems. However, only Boolean problems will be addressed in this work with Categorical and Regression problems left for future work (Section 7).

The rest of the paper firstly recalls (Section 2), in the interest of completeness, the general principles of Semantic Backpropagation, though instantiated in the Boolean context, and thus adopting a slightly different point of view (and notations) to [12]. Section 3 then details LTI, the main contribution of this work, and how it is used within the Iterated Local Search procedure ILTI. Experiments conducted with ILTI are presented in Section 4: The first goal of these experiments is to demonstrate the efficiency of ILTI as a stand-alone optimization procedure; the second goal is to study the sensitivity of the results with respect to the most important parameter of ILTI, the size of the library. Similarities and differences with previous works dealing with memetic GP are discussed in Sections 6, while links with previous Semantic Backpropagation works are highlighted and discussed in Section 7, together with related possible further research paths.

2. SEMANTIC BACKPROPAGATION

The powerful idea underlying Semantic Backpropagation is that, for a given tree, it is very often possible to calculate the optimal outputs of each node such that the final tree outputs are optimized. Each node (and rooted subtree) is analyzed under the assumption that the functionality of all the other tree nodes are optimal. In effect, for each node, the following question should be asked: What are the optimal outputs for this node (and rooted subtree) such that its combined use with the other tree nodes produce the optimal final tree outputs? Note that for any given node, its optimal outputs do not depend on its semantics (actual outputs). Instead, they depend on the final tree target outputs, and the actual output values (semantics) of the other nodes within the tree.

In utilizing the results of this analysis, it is possible to produce local fitness values for each node by comparing their actual outputs with their optimal outputs. Similarly, a fitness value can be calculated for any external subtree by comparing its actual outputs to the optimal outputs of the node which it might replace. If this fitness value indicates that the external subtree would perform better than the current one, then the replacement operation should improve the tree as a whole.

2.1 Hypotheses and notations

We suppose that the problem at hand comprises n fitness cases, were each case i is a pair (x_i, f_i). Given a loss function ℓ, the goal is to find the program (*tree*) that minimizes the global error

$$Err(tree) = \sum_{i=1}^{i=n} \ell(tree(x_i), f_i) \quad (1)$$

where $tree(x_i)$ is the output produced by the tree when fed with values x_i.

In the Boolean framework for instance, each input x_i is a vector of Boolean variables, and each output f_i is a Boolean value. A trivial loss function is the Hamming distance between Boolean values, and the global error of a tree is the number of errors of that tree.

In the following, we will be dealing with a *target tree* T and a *subtree library* $\mathcal{L}$. We will now describe how a subtree (node location) s is chosen in T **together with** a subtree s^* in $\mathcal{L}$ to try to improve the global fitness of T (aggregation of the error measures on all fitness cases) when replacing, in T, s with s^*.

2.2 Tree Analysis

For each node in T, the LTI algorithm maintains an *output vector* and an *optimal vector*. The ith component of the output vector is the actual output of the node when the tree is executed on the ith fitness case; the ith component of the optimal vector is the value that the node should take so that its propagation upward would lead T to produce the correct answer for this fitness case, all other nodes being unchanged.

The idea of storing the output values is one major component of BPGP [6], which is used in the form of a trace table. In their definition, the last column of the table contained target output values of the full tree – a feature which is not needed here as they are stored in the optimal vector of the root node.

Let us now detail how these vectors are computed. The output vector is simply filled during the execution of T on the fitness cases. The computation of the optimal vectors is done in a top-down manner. The optimal values for the top node (the root node of T) are the target values of the problem. Consider now a given fitness case, and a simple tree with top node A. Denote by a, b and c their output values, and by $\hat{a}$, $\hat{b}$ and $\hat{c}$ their optimal values (or set of optimal values, see below)[2]. Assuming now that we know $\hat{a}$, we want to compute $\hat{b}$ and $\hat{c}$ (top-down computation of optimal values).

[1]though the Approximate Geometric Crossover (AGX) can be defined in a more general context by artificially creating surrogate target semantics for the root node [7, 12].

[2]The same notation will be implicit in the rest of the paper, whatever the nodes A, B and C.

If node A represents operator F, then, by definition

$$a = F(b, c) \quad (2)$$

and we want $\hat{b}$ and $\hat{c}$ to satisfy

$$\hat{a} = F(\hat{b}, c) \text{ and } \hat{a} = F(b, \hat{c}) \quad (3)$$

i.e., to find the values such that A will take a value $\hat{a}$, assuming the actual value of the other child node is correct. This leads to

$$\hat{b} = F^{-1}(\hat{a}, c) \text{ and } \hat{c} = F^{-1}(\hat{a}, b) \quad (4)$$

where F^{-1} is the pseudo-inverse operator of F. In the Boolean case, however, this pseudo-inverse operator is ill-defined. For instance, for the AND operator, if $\hat{a} = 0$ and b=0, any value for $\hat{c}$ is a solution: this leads to set $\hat{c} = \#$, the "don't care" symbol, representing the set $\{0, 1\}$. On the other hand, if $\hat{a} = 1$ and b=0, no solution exists for $\hat{c}$. In this case, $\hat{c}$ is set to the value that does not propagate the impossibility (here for instance, $\hat{c} = 1$). Note that this is an important difference with the Invert function used in [12], where the backpropagation stops whenever either "don't care" or "impossible" are encountered. See the discussion in Section 7.

Function tables for the Boolean operators AND^{-1}, OR^{-1}, NAND^{-1}, and NOR^{-1} are given in Fig. 1. A "starred" value indicates that $\hat{a}$ is impossible to reach: in this case, the 'optimal' value is set for $\hat{c}$ as discussed above.

For each fitness case, we can compute the optimal vector for all nodes of T, starting from the root node and computing, for each node in turn, the optimal values for its two children as described above, until reaching the terminals.

2.3 Local Error

The local error of each node in T is defined as the discrepancy between its output vector and its optimal vector. The loss function ℓ that defines the global error from the different fitness cases (see Eq. 1) can be reused, provided that it is extended to handle sets of values. For instance, the Hamming distance can be easily extended to handle the "don't care" symbol # (for example: $\ell(0, \#) = \ell(1, \#) = 0$). We will denote the output and optimal values for node A on fitness case i as a_i and $\hat{a_i}$ respectively. The local error $Err(A)$ of node A is defined as

$$Err(A) = \sum_i \ell(a_i, \hat{a_i}) \quad (5)$$

2.4 Subtree Library

Given a node A in T that is candidate for replacement (see next Section 3.1 for possible strategies for choosing it), we need to select a subtree in the library $\mathcal{L}$ that would likely improve the global fitness of T if it were to replace A. Because the effect of a replacement on the global fitness are in general beyond this investigation, we have chosen to use the local error of A as a proxy. Therefore, we need to compute the *substitution error* $Err(B, A)$ of any node B in the library, i.e. the local error of node B if it were inserted in lieu of node A. Such error can obviously be written as

$$Err(B, A) = \sum_i \ell(b_i, \hat{a_i}) \quad (6)$$

Then, for a given node A in T, we can find $best(A)$, the set subtrees in $\mathcal{L}$ with minimal substitution error,

$$best(A) = \{B \in \mathcal{L}; Err(B, A) = min_{C \in \mathcal{L}}(Err(C, A)\}) \quad (7)$$

and then define the *Expected Local Improvement* $I(A)$ as

$$I(A) = Err(A) - Err(B, A) \text{ for some } B \in best(A) \quad (8)$$

If $I(A)$ is positive, then replacing A with any node in $best(A)$ will improve the local fitness of A. Note however that this does not imply that the global fitness of T will improve. Indeed, even though the local error will decrease, the cases in error might be different, and this could badly affect the whole tree. Furthermore, even if B is a perfect subtree, resulting in no more error at this level (i.e., $Err(B, A) = 0$), there could remain some impossible values in the tree (the "starred" values in Fig. 1 in the Boolean case) that would indeed give an error when propagated to the parent of A.

On the other hand, if $I(A)$ is negative, no subtree in $\mathcal{L}$ can improve the global fitness when inserted in lieu of A.

Furthermore, trees in $\mathcal{L}$ are unique in terms of semantics (output vectors). In the process of generating the library (whatever design procedure is used), if two candidate subtrees have exactly the same outputs, only the one with fewer nodes is kept. In this way, the most concise generating tree is stored for each output vector. Also, $\mathcal{L}$ is ordered based on tree size, from smallest to largest, hence so is $best(A)$.

3. TREE IMPROVEMENT PROCEDURES

3.1 Local Tree Improvement

Everything is now in place to describe the full LTI algorithm. Its pseudo-code can be found in Algorithm 1. The obvious approach is to choose the node S in T with the smallest error that can be improved, and to choose in $best(S)$ the smallest tree, to limit the bloat.

However, the selection process when no node can be improved is less obvious. Hence, the algorithm starts by ordering the nodes in T by increasing error (line 1). A secondary technical criterion is used here, the number of # (don't care) symbols in the optimal vector of the node, as nodes with many # symbols are more likely to be improved. The nodes are then processed one by one and selected using a rank-based selection from the order defined above. Note that all selections in the algorithm are done stochastically rather than deterministically, to avoid overly greedy behaviors [4].

Choosing the best improvement implies that if there exists a tree $B \in \mathcal{L}$ whose output vector perfectly matches the optimal vector of a given node $A \in \mathcal{T}$ (i.e., $Err(B, A) = 0$, Eq. 6), there is no need to look further in $\mathcal{L}$. Therefore, A is replaced with B and the algorithm returns (line 11). Otherwise, the algorithm proceeds by computing $best(A)$ for the node current A (lines 19-23). Importantly, the fact that there has been at least an improvement (resp. a decrease of local fitness) is recorded, line 14 (resp. 16). At the end of the loop over the library, if some improvement is possible for the node at hand (line 24), then a tree is selected in its best matches (rank-selection on the sizes, line 25), and the algorithm returns. Otherwise, the next node on the ordered list $\mathcal{L}$ is processed.

If no improvement whatsoever could be found, but some decrease of local fitness is possible (line 28), then a node should be chosen among the ones with smallest decrease. However, it turned out that this strategy could severely

$\hat{c}$ = AND$^{-1}(\hat{a}, b)$		
$\hat{a}$	b	$\hat{c}$
0	0	#
0	1	0
1	0	1*
1	1	1
#	0	#
#	1	#

$\hat{c}$ = OR$^{-1}(\hat{a}, b)$		
$\hat{a}$	b	$\hat{c}$
0	0	0
0	1	0*
1	0	1
1	1	#
#	0	#
#	1	#

$\hat{c}$ = NAND$^{-1}(\hat{a}, b)$		
$\hat{a}$	b	$\hat{c}$
0	0	1*
0	1	1
1	0	#
1	1	0
#	0	#
#	1	#

$\hat{c}$ = NOR$^{-1}(\hat{a}, b)$		
$\hat{a}$	b	$\hat{c}$
0	0	1
0	1	#
1	0	0
1	1	0*
#	0	#
#	1	#

Figure 1: Function tables for the AND^{-1}, OR^{-1}, NAND^{-1}, and NOR^{-1}.

Algorithm 1 Procedure LTI(Tree T, library $\mathcal{L}$)

```
Require: Err(A) (Eq. 5), Err(B, A) (Eq. 6), A ⊂ T, B ∈ 𝓛
 1: 𝒯 ← all T nodes ordered by Err↑, then number of #s↓
 2: Improvement ← False
 3: OneDecrease ← False
 4: for A ∈ 𝒯 do                        ▷ Loop over nodes in set 𝒯
 5:     Decrease(A) ← False
 6: while 𝒯 not empty do
 7:     A ← RankSelect(𝒯)                ▷ Select and remove from 𝒯
 8:     Best(A) ← ∅
 9:     minErr ← +∞
10:     for B ∈ 𝓛 do                     ▷ Loop over trees in library
11:         if Err(B, A) = 0 then        ▷ Perfect match
12:             Replace A with B
13:             return
14:         if Err(B, A) < Err(A) then
15:             Improvement ← True
16:         else if Err(B, A) > Err(A) then
17:             OneDecrease ← True
18:             Decrease(A) ← True
19:         if Err(B, A) < minErr then   ▷ Better best
20:             Best(A) = {B}
21:             minErr ← Err(B, A)
22:         if Err(B, A) = minErr then   ▷ Equally good
23:             Best(A) ← Best(A) + {B}
24:     if Improvement then
25:         B ← RankSelect(Best(A))      ▷ Order: size↑
26:         Replace A with B
27:         return
28: if OneDecrease then                  ▷ At least one decrease
29:     𝓜 ← {A ∈ T ; Decrease(A)}
30:     𝓜 ← top κ from 𝓜 ordered by depth↓
31:     A ← RankSelect(𝓜)                ▷ Order: Err↑
32:     B ← RankSelect(Best(A))          ▷ Order: size↑
33:     Replace A with B
34:     return
35: A ← uniformSelection(T)              ▷ Random move
36: B ← randomTree()
37: Replace A with B
38: return
```

damage the current tree (see Fig. 3 and the discussion in Section 5) when the replacement occurred high in the tree. This is why depth was chosen as the main criterion in this case: all nodes A with non-empty *best*(A) (the nodes with the same errors as A are discarded, to avoid possible loops in the algorithm) are ordered by increasing depth, and a rank-selection is made upon the top κ nodes of that list (line 31). The tree from the library is then chosen based on size (line 32). User-defined parameter κ tunes the relative weights of depth and error in the choice of target node, and was set to 3 in all experiments presented in Section 5 (i.e. depth is the main criterion). Finally, in the event that no improvement nor any decrease can be achieved, a random tree replaces a random node (line 37).

Complexity Suppose that the library $\mathcal{L}$ is of size o. The computation of the output vectors of all trees in $\mathcal{L}$ is done once and for all. Hence the overhead of one iteration of LTI is dominated, in the worst case, by the comparisons of the optimal vectors of all nodes in T with the output vectors of all trees in $\mathcal{L}$, with complexity $n \times m \times o$.

3.2 Iterated LTI

In the previous section, we have defined the LTI procedure that, given a target tree T and a library of subtrees $\mathcal{L}$, selects a node S in T and a subtree S^* in $\mathcal{L}$ to insert in lieu of node S so as to minimize some local error over a sequence of fitness cases. In this section we will address how T and $\mathcal{L}$ are chosen, and how one or several LTI iterations are used for global optimization.

LTI can be viewed as the basic step of some local search, and as such, it can be used within any Evolutionary Algorithm evolving trees (e.g., GP), either as a mutation operators, or as a local search that is applied on some individual in the population at every generation. Such use of local search is very general and common in Memetic Algorithm (see e.g., Chapter 4 in [11]). Because LTI involves a target tree and a library of subtrees, it could be used, too, to design an original crossover operator, in which one of the parents would be the target tree, and the library would be the set of subtrees of the other parents. However, because LTI is an original local search procedure that, to the best of our knowledge, has never been used before, a natural first step should be devoted to its analysis alone, without interference from any other mechanism.

This is why this work is devoted to the study of a (Local) Search procedure termed ILTI, that repeatedly applies LTI to the same tree, picking up subtrees from a fixed library, without any selection whatsoever. This procedure can also be viewed as a (1,1)-EA, or as a random walk with move operator LTI.

One advantage of starting simple is that ILTI does not have many parameters to tune, and will hopefully allow us to get some insights about how LTI actually works. The parameters of ILTI are the method used to create the initial tree (and its parameters, e.g., the depth), the method (and, again, its parameters) used to create the subtrees in the library, the parameter κ for node selection (see previous Section 3.1), and the size of the library. The end of the paper is devoted to some experimental validation of ILTI, and the study of the sensitivity of the results w.r.t. its most important parameter, the library size.

Table 1: **Results of the ILTI algorithm for Boolean benchmarks: 30 runs were conducted for each benchmark, always finding a perfect solution. A library size of 450 trees was used. BP columns are the results of the best performing algorithm (BP4A) of [6] (* indicates that not all runs found a perfect solution). The RDO column is taken from [17].**

	Run time [seconds]				Program size [nodes]					Number of iterations		
	max	**mean**	min	BP	max	**mean**	min	BP	RDO	max	**mean**	min
Cmp06	9.9	**8.6 ± 0.5**	7.8	15	77	**59.1 ± 7.2**	47	156	185	189	**63.9 ± 34.4**	19
Cmp08	54.8	**19.8 ± 7.8**	14.3	220	191	**140.1 ± 23.2**	81	242	538	2370	**459.1 ± 466.1**	95
Maj06	10.9	**9.5 ± 0.8**	8.4	36	87	**71.2 ± 10.1**	53	280	123	183	**89.1 ± 42.2**	27
Maj08	44.1	**26.7 ± 7.0**	18.2	2019*	303	**235.9 ± 29.8**	185	563*	-	2316	**938.6 ± 519.0**	307
Mux06	11.2	**9.4 ± 0.8**	8.5	10	79	**47.1 ± 11.2**	31	117	215	34	**20.0 ± 6.8**	11
Mux11	239.1	**100.2 ± 40.2**	59.0	9780	289	**152.9 ± 59.0**	75	303	3063	1124	**302.9 ± 216.4**	79
Par06	25.2	**16.7 ± 2.4**	12.5	233	513	**435.3 ± 33.2**	347	356	1601	2199	**814.8 ± 356.6**	326
Par08	854	**622 ± 113.6**	386	3792*	2115	**1972 ± 94**	1765	581*	-	22114	**12752 ± 3603**	6074
Par09	8682	**5850 ± 1250**	4104	-	4523	**4066 ± 186**	3621	-	-	142200	**54423 ± 24919**	31230

4. EXPERIMENTAL CONDITIONS

The benchmark problems used for these experiments are classical Boolean problems that have been widely studied, and are not exclusive to the GP community (see Section 6 also). We have chosen this particular benchmarks because they are used in [12, 6] (among other types of benchmarks). For the sake of completeness, we reiterate their definitions as stated in [6]: The solution to the *v-bit Comparator problem Cmp-v* must return *true* if the $\frac{v}{2}$ least significant input bits encode a number that is smaller than the number represented by the $\frac{v}{2}$ most significant bits. For the *Majority problem Maj-v*, *true* should be returned if more that half of the input variables are true. For the *Multiplexer problem Mul-v*, the state of the addressed input should be returned (6-bit multiplexer uses two inputs to address the remaining four inputs, 11-bit multiplexer uses three inputs to address the remaining eight inputs). In the *Parity problem Par-v*, *true* should be returned only for an odd number of true inputs.

All results have been obtained using an AMD Opteron(tm) Processor 6174 @ 2.2GHz. All of the code was written in Python[3].

In all experiments presented here, the library $\mathcal{L}$ was made of full trees of depth 2: there are hence a possible 64 × *#variables* different trees. Experiments regarding other initializations of $\mathcal{L}$ (e.g., other depths, or using the popular ramp-half-and-half method instead of building full trees) are left for further studies. Similarly, the target tree T was initialized as a full tree of depth 2. Several depths have been tested without any significant modification of the results. The only other parameter of LTI (and hence of ILTI) is parameter κ that balances the selection criterion of the target node for replacement in cases where no improvement could be found for any node (Section 3.1, line 30 of Algorithm 1). As mentioned, it was set to 3 here, and the study of its sensitivity is also left for further work.

After a few preliminary experiments, the runs were given strict run-time upper limits: 60s for all easy runs (xxx06), 100s for the more difficult Cmp08 and Maj08, 1000s for the much more difficult Mux11 and Par08, and 10800 (3 hours) for the very difficult Par09 (the only benchmark investigated in this paper that was not reported in [6]). If a run did not return a perfect solution within the time given, it was considered a failure.

[3]The entire code base is freely available at robynffrancon.com/LTI.html

5. EXPERIMENTAL RESULTS

Figure 2 plots standard boxplots of the actual run-time to solution of ILTI for library sizes in {50, 100, 200, 300, 400, 450, 500, 550} for all benchmarks. Note that the (red) numbers on top of some columns indicate the number of runs (out of 30) for library sizes which failed to find an exact solution.

On these plots, a general tendency clearly appears: the run-time increases with the size of the library for easy problems (Cmp06, Mux6, and Maj06, even though sizes 50 and 100 fail once out of 30 runs). Then, as the problem becomes more difficult (see Par06), the results of small library sizes start to degrade, while their variance increases, but all runs still find the perfect solution. For more difficult problems (Cmp08, Mux11, and Maj08) more and more runs fail, from small to medium sizes. Finally, for the very hard Par08 and Par09 problems, almost no run with size 50 or 100 can find the solution, while sizes 200 and 300 still have occasional difficulties to exactly solve the problem. These results strongly suggest that for each problem, there exists an optimal library size, which is highly problem dependent, with a clear tendency: the more difficult the problem the larger the optimal size. A method for determining the optimal size a priori, from some problem characteristics, is left for further work.

Regarding the tree sizes of the solutions, the results (not shown here) are, on the opposite, remarkably stable: all library sizes give approximately the same statistics on the tree sizes (when a solution is found) - hence similar to the results in Table 1, discussed next.

Based on the above, the comparative results of Table 1 use a library of size 450. They are compared with the Boolean benchmark results of the best performing Behavior Programming GP (BPGP) scheme, *BP4A* [6], and when possible with the results of RDO given in [17] or in [12].

We will first consider the success rates. All algorithms seem to solve all problems which they reported on. Note however that results for Par09 are not reported for BP, and results for Par08, Par09 and Maj08 are not reported for RDO. Furthermore, there are some small exceptions to this rule, the "*" in Table 1 for BP, and Par06 for RDO (success rate of 0.99 according to [17]).

Even though it is difficult to compare the run-times of ILTI and BPGP [6] because of the different computing environments, some comments can nevertheless be made regarding this part of Table 1: Firstly, both *BP4A* and ILTI have reported run-times of the same order of magnitude ... for the

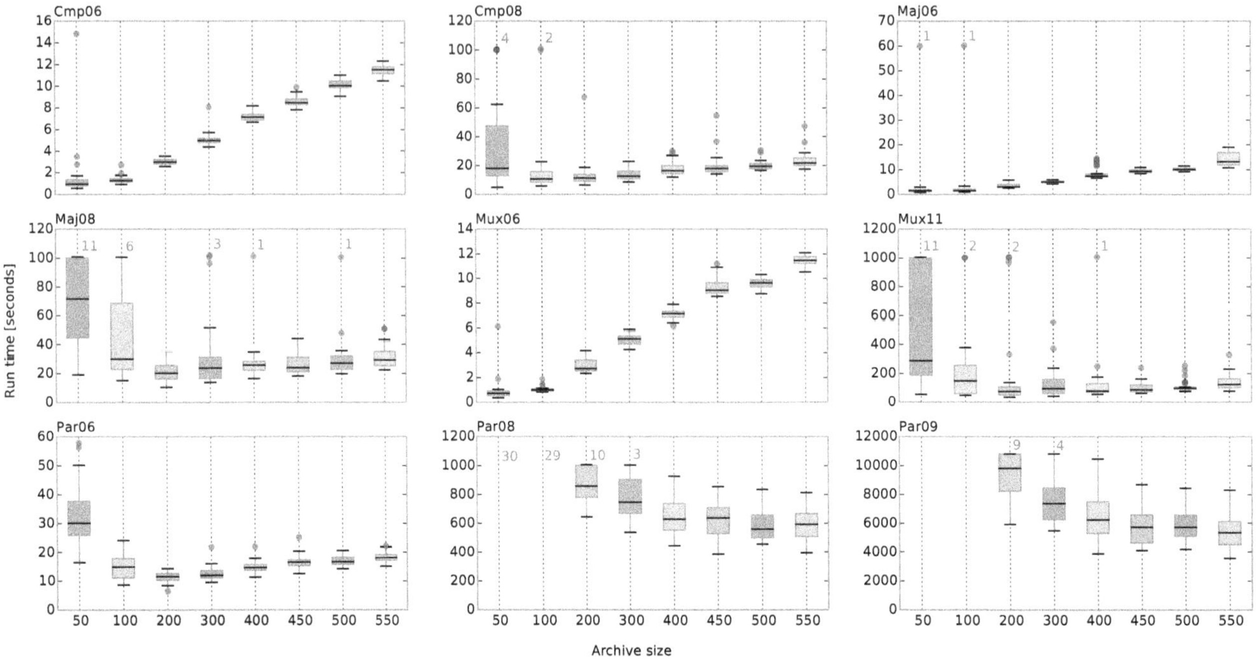

Figure 2: Comparative results: time to solution for different library sizes. The benchmark problems appear in the order of Table 1: Cmp06, Cmp08, Maj06; Maj08, Mux06, Mux11; Par06, Par08 and Par09.

easiest problems. But, when considering the results of more difficult problems, they also suggest that ILTI scales much more smoothly than *BP4A* with problem size/difficulty. ILTI clearly stands out when comparing the run-times of Cmp06 vs Cmp08, Maj06 vs Maj08, Mux06 vs Mux11 and, to a lesser extend, Par06 vs Par08. On the other hand, even though the runtimes were not directly available for the RDO results, the measure of "number of successes per hour" given in [17] suggests that obtaining the exact solution with RDO is one or two orders of magnitude faster than with ILTI or BP.

When considering the average tree size, ILTI seems more parsimonious than *BP4A* by a factor of around 2, with the exception of the parity problems. In particular, for Par08, the average size for *BP4A* is smaller than that of ILTI by a factor of 3. It is clear that the fine details of the parity problems deserve further investigations. On the other hand, RDO results [17] report much larger tree sizes, from twice to 20 times larger than those of ILTI.

Finally, Fig. 3 displays the evolution of the global error (of the whole tree T) during the 30 runs on the difficult problem Par08 for a library size of 450. It compares the behavior of ILTI using two different strategies for selecting the node to be replaced when no improvement could be found. On the left, the straightforward strategy, similar to the one adopted in case an improvement was found, which simply chooses the node with smallest error. On the right, the strategy actually described in Algorithm 1 which first favors depth, and then chooses among the deepest κ nodes based on their substitution error (lines 28-32 of Algorithm 1). As can be seen, the error-based strategy generates far more disastrous increases of the global error. A detailed analysis revealed

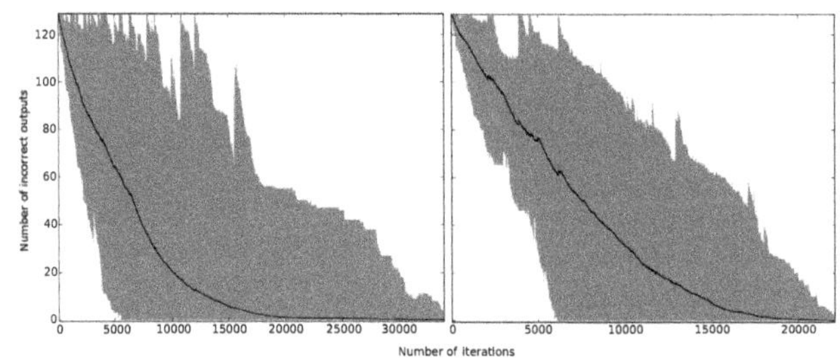

Figure 3: Evolution of the global error during 30 runs of ILTI on Par08 problem: average and range. Left: Node selection by error only; Right: node selection by depth first.

that this happens when nodes close to the root are chosen. Even if they have a small local error, the effect of modifying them might destroy many other good building blocks of the target tree. This was confirmed on the Par09 problem, for which the first strategy simply repeatedly failed – and this motivated the design of the depth-based strategy.

6. RELATED MEMETIC WORK

As mentioned in the introduction, there are very few works at the crossroad between GP and Memetic algorithms. Some papers claim to perform local search by doing offspring filtering, i.e., generating several offspring from the same parents and keeping only the best ones to include in the surviving pool [1]. Though this is indeed some sort of local search (the usual GP variation operators being used as elementary moves for the local search), it does not really involve any external search procedure with distinct search abilities from those of the underlying GP itself, and could in fact be presented as another parametrization of the GP algorithm. Furthermore, such procedure really makes sense only when the offspring can be approximately evaluated using some very fast proxy for the true fitness evaluation (see the 'informed operators' proposed in the context of surrogate modeling [13]).

Some real memetic search within GP has been proposed in the context of decision trees for classification [16]: the very specific representation of (Stochastic) Decision Trees is used, together with problem-specific local search procedures, that directly act on the subspaces defining the different classes of the classification. Though efficient in the proposed context, this procedure is by no way generic.

Probably the most similar work to LTI have been proposed in [3]: the authors introduce the so-called *memetic crossover*, that records the behavior of all trees during the execution of the programs represented by the trees (though the word 'semantic' is not present in that work), and choose the second parent after randomly choosing a crossover point in the first one, and selecting in the second parent a node that is complementary to the one of the first parent. However, this approach requires that the user manually has splitted the problem into several sub-problems, and has identified what are the positive and negative contributions to the different subproblems for a given node. This is a severe restriction to its generic use, and this approach can hence hardly be applied to other problems than the ones presented.

On the other hand, the generality of LTI has been shown here for the class of Boolean problems, and can be extended to regression problems very easily (on-going work). In particular, the high performances obtained on several very different hard benchmarks (like Maj08, Par09 and Mux11 demonstrate that this generality is not obtained by decreasing the performance. This needs to be confirmed on other domain (e.g., regression problems).

Regarding performances on Boolean problems, the very specific BDD (Binary Decision Diagrams) representation allowed some authors to obtain outstanding results using GP [18] and was first to solve the 20-multiplexer (Mux20); and 10 years later these results were consolidated on parity problems up to size 17 [2]. However, handling BDDs with GP implies to diverge from standard GP, in order to meet the constraints of BDDs during the search [14, 2], thus strictly limiting application domains to Boolean problems. It is hoped that the LTI-based approach is more general, and can be ported to other domains, like regression, as already suggested.

7. DISCUSSION AND FURTHER WORK

Let us finally discuss the main differences between LTI and previous work based on the idea of Semantic Backpropagation, namely RDO [17, 12], and some possible future research directions that naturally arise from this comparison.

The main difference lies in the choice of the target node for replacement in the parent tree: uniformly random for RDO, and biased toward local fitness improvement for LTI that looks for the best possible semantic match between the target node and the replacing tree. On the one hand, such exhaustive search explains that LTI seems much slower than the original RDO, though competitive with BP [6]. On the other hand, it is only possible for rather small libraries (see below). However, the computational costs seem to scale up more smoothly with the problem dimension for LTI than for RDO or BP (see e.g., problem Par09, that none of the other semantic-based methods was reported to solve. Nevertheless, the cost of this exhaustive search will become unbearable when addressing larger problems, and some trade-off between LTI exhaustive search and RDO random choice might be a way to overcome the curse of dimensionality (e.g., some tournament selection of the target node).

The other crucial difference is that the results of LTI have been obtained here by embedding it into a standard Iterated Local Search, i.e., outside any Evolutionary framework. In particular, ILTI evolves a single tree, without even any fitness-based selection, similar to a (1+10)-EA. However, though without any drive toward improving the fitness at the level of the whole tree itself, ILTI can reliably solve to optimality several classical Boolean problems that have been intensively used in the GP community (and beyond), resulting in solutions of reasonable size compared to other GP approaches. Hence it is clear that ILTI somehow achieves a good balance between exploitation and exploration. It would be interesting to discover how, and also to investigate whether this implicit trade-off could or should be more explicitly controlled. In particular, would some selection pressure at the tree level help the global search (i.e., replacing the current (1,1)-EA by some (1+1)-EA and varying the selection pressure)? Similar investigations should also be made at the level of LTI itself, which is the only component which drives a tree towards better fitness. Different node selection mechanisms could be investigated for the choice of a target node for replacement.

Finally, the way ILTI escapes local optima should also be investigated. Indeed, it was empirically demonstrated that even though it is necessary to allow LTI to decrease the global fitness of the tree by accepting some replacement that degrade the local performance (and hence the global fitness of the tree at hand), too much of that behaviour is detrimental on complex problems (though beneficial for easy ones) – see the discussion around Fig. 3 in Section 5.

Several other implementation differences should also be highlighted. First, regarding the library, LTI currently uses a small static library made of full trees of depth 2, whereas the libraries in [12] are either the (static) complete set of full trees up to a given depth (3 for Boolean problems, resulting in libraries from size 2524 for 6-bits problems to 38194 for Mux11), or the dynamic set of all subtrees gathered from the current population (of variable size, however reported to be larger than the static libraries of depth 3). Such large sizes probably explain why the perfect match with the semantics of the target node is found most of the time. On the other hand, it could be also be the case that having too many perfect matches is in fact detrimental in the framework of Iterated Local Search, making the algorithm too greedy. This is yet another possible parameter of the exploitation versus exploration trade-off that should be investigated.

Second, RDO implements a systematic test of the ephemeral constants that is chosen as replacement subtree if it improves over the best match found in the library. Such mechanism certainly decreases the bloat, and increases the diversity of replacing subtrees, and its effect within LTI should be investigated.

Also, LTI and RDO handle the "don't care" and "impossible" cases very differently ... maybe due to the fact that, at the moment, LTI has only been applied to Boolean problems. Indeed, as discussed in Section 2.2, the backpropagation procedure in RDO stops whenever an "impossible" value is encountered, whereas it continues in LTI, using the value that is least prone to impossibility as optimal value. But such strategy will not be possible anymore in the Symbolic Regression context: the extension of LTI to regression problems might not be as easy as to Categorical problems (such as the ones experimented with in [6]), which appears straightforward (on-going work).

Tackling continuous Symbolic Regression problems also raise the issue of generalization: How should we ensure that the learned model behaves well on the unseen fitness cases? Standard Machine Learning approaches will of course be required, i.e., using a training set, a test set, and a validation set. In order to avoid over-fitting the training set, the LTI procedure should not be run until it finds a perfect solution on the current training set, and several different training sets might be needed in turn. Interestingly, solving very large Boolean problems will raise similar issues, as it will rapidly become intractable to use all existing fitness cases together, for obvious memory requirement reasons.

Last but not least, further work should investigate the use of LTI within a standard GP evolutionary algorithm, and not as a standalone iterated procedure. All the differences highlighted above between LTI and RDO might impact the behavior of both RDO and AGX: Each implementation difference should be considered as a possible parameter of a more general procedure, and its sensitivity should be checked. Along the same line, LTI could also be used within the initialization procedure of any GP algorithm. However, again, a careful tuning of LTI will then be required, as it should probably not be applied at full strength. Finally, a reverse hybridization between LTI and GP should also be tested: when no improvement can be found in the library during a LTI iteration, a GP run could be launched with the goal of finding such an improving subtree, thus dynamically extending the library. However, beside the huge CPU cost this could induce, it is not clear that decreases of the local fitness are not the only way toward global successes, as discussed above.

Overall, we are convinced that there are many more potential uses of Semantic Backpropagation, and we hope to have contributed to opening some useful research directions with the present work[4].

8. REFERENCES

[1] A. Bhardwaj and A. Tiwari. A Novel GP Based Classifier Design Using a New Constructive Crossover Operator with a Local Search Technique. In D. Huang et al., editor, *Intelligent Computing Theories*, volume 7995 of *LNCS*, pages 86–95. Springer Verlag, 2013.

[2] R. M. Downing. Evolving Binary Decision Diagrams using Implicit Neutrality. In *Proc. IEEE CEC*, pages 2107–2113 Vol. 3, 2005.

[3] B. E. Eskridge and D. F. Hougen. Memetic Crossover for Genetic Programming: Evolution Through Imitation. In K. Deb, editor, *Proc. ACM-GECCO*, pages 459–470. LNCS 3103, Springer Verlag, 2004.

[4] D. E. Goldberg. Zen and the Art of Genetic Algorithms. In J. D. Schaffer, editor, *Proc. 3rd ICGA*, pages 80–85, 1989.

[5] John R Koza. *Genetic Programming: on the Programming of Computers by means of Natural Selection*, volume 1. MIT press, 1992.

[6] K. Krawiec and U.-M. O'Reilly. Behavioral Programming: A Broader and More Detailed Take on Semantic GP. In Dirk Arnold et al., editor, *Proc. GECCO*, pages 935–942. ACM Press, 2014.

[7] K. Krawiec and T. Pawlak. Approximating Geometric Crossover by Semantic Backpropagation. In Ch. Blum and E. Alba, editors, *Proc. 15th GECCO*, pages 941–948. ACM, 2013.

[8] N. F. McPhee, B. Ohs, and T. Hutchison. Semantic Building Blocks in Genetic Programming. In M. O'Neill et al., editor, *Proc. 11th EuroGP*, volume 4971 of *LNCS*, pages 134–145. Springer Verlag, 2008.

[9] P. Moscato. On Evolution, Search, Optimization, Genetic Algorithms and Martial Arts: Towards Memetic Algorithms. *Caltech concurrent computation program, C3P Report*, 826:1989, 1989.

[10] Y. Nagata. New EAX Crossover for Large TSP Instances. In Th. P. Runarsson et al., editor, *Proc. PPSN IX*, pages 372–381. LNCS 4193, Springer Verlag, 2006.

[11] F. Neri, C. Cotta, and P. Moscato, editors. *Handbook of Memetic Algorithms*. Number 379 in Studies in Computational Intelligence. Springer Verlag, 2012.

[12] T. Pawlak, B. Wieloch, and K. Krawiec. Semantic Backpropagation for Designing Search Operators in Genetic Programming. *Evolutionary Computation, IEEE Transactions on*, PP(99):1–1, 2014.

[13] K. Rasheed and H. Hirsh. Informed operators: Speeding up genetic-algorithm-based design optimization using reduced models. In D. Whitley et al., editor, *Proc. ACM-GECCO*, pages 628–635, 2000.

[14] H. Sakanashi, T. Higuchi, H. Iba, and Y. Kakazu. Evolution of Binary Decision Diagrams for Digital Circuit Design using Genetic Programming. In T. Higuchi, M. Iwata, and W. Liu, editors, *Evolvable Systems: From Biology to Hardware*, pages 470–481. LNCS 1259, Springer Verlag, 1997.

[15] L. Vanneschi, M. Castelli, and S. Silva. A Survey of Semantic Methods in GP. *Genetic Programming and Evolvable Machines*, 15(2):195–214, 2014.

[16] P. Wang, K. Tang, E.P.K. Tsang, and X. Yao. A Memetic Genetic Programming with Decision Tree-based Local Search for Classification Problems. In *Proc. IEEE-CEC*, pages 917–924, June 2011.

[17] B. Wieloch and K. Krawiec. Running Programs Backwards: Instruction Inversion for Effective Search in Semantic Spaces. In Ch. Blum and E. Alba, editors, *Proc. 15th GECCO*, pages 1013–1020. ACM, 2013.

[18] M. Yanagiya. Efficient Genetic Programming based on Binary Decision Diagrams. In *Proc. IEEE-CEC*, volume 1, pages 234–239, 1995.

[4]More recent results in the same research direction, including the handling of categorical context, will be presented during the SMGP workshop at the same GECCO 2015 conference (see Companion proceedings).

Strength Through Diversity: Disaggregation and Multi-Objectivisation Approaches for Genetic Programming

Jonathan E. Fieldsend
Computer Science
University of Exeter, UK
J.E.Fieldsend@exeter.ac.uk

Alberto Moraglio
Computer Science
University of Exeter, UK
A.Moraglio@exeter.ac.uk

ABSTRACT

An underlying problem in genetic programming (GP) is how to ensure sufficient useful diversity in the population during search. Having a wide range of diverse (sub)component structures available for recombination and/or mutation is important in preventing premature converge. We propose two new fitness disaggregation approaches that make explicit use of the information in the test cases (i.e., program semantics) to preserve diversity in the population. The first method preserves the best programs which pass each individual test case, the second preserves those which are non-dominated across test cases (multi-objectivisation). We use these in standard GP, and compare them to using standard fitness sharing, and using standard (aggregate) fitness in tournament selection. We also examine the effect of including a simple anti-bloat criterion in the selection mechanism. We find that the non-domination approach, employing anti-bloat, significantly speeds up convergence to the optimum on a range of standard Boolean test problems. Furthermore, its best performance occurs with a considerably smaller population size than typically employed in GP.

CCS Concepts

•**Computing methodologies** → **Genetic programming;** •**Applied computing** → **Multi-criterion optimization and decision-making;**

Keywords

Genetic programming, optimisation, multi-objectivisation, diversity

1. INTRODUCTION

Interest in semantic methods in Genetic Programming (GP) has increased over the last few years. In GP, a widely-adopted notion of semantics of a program is the vector of the program outputs for all (test) input combinations. The

GECCO '15, July 11 - 15, 2015, Madrid, Spain

ISBN 978-1-4503-3472-3/15/07...$15.00
DOI: http://dx.doi.org/10.1145/2739480.2754643

output vector can be also seen as the *disaggregation* of the fitness function in terms of its composite test cases. Recent results clearly indicate that use of semantics in GP considerably increases performance (e.g., [13]).

Several works have focused on using semantics to guide the design of novel mutation and crossover operators (e.g., [14, 10]). Other works have emphasized the importance of preserving semantic diversity in the population. McPhee et al. [12] analysed the impact of subtree crossover in Boolean problems in terms of semantic building blocks. They found that a major problem with this operator is that only 10% of crossover events result in a offspring semantically different from the parents. This may quickly lead to a loss of semantic diversity in the population, hence to stagnation. Beadle and Johnson [3] proposed a crossover operator that explicitly promotes semantic diversity during search obtaining improved performance. Jackson [7] also showed how another form of crossover that promotes semantic diversity results in better performance.

There are some works that use semantics in selection. A traditional work on this subject is fitness sharing in GP [11] which uses information from the individual test cases to determine a new fitness measure obtained by a linear combination of the contributions of the test cases each weighted by its relative frequency in the population. This is a commonly used diversity preservation approach in GP. Much more recent work [5] proposes to select parents for recombination such they are not only fit but also semantically different (in terms of semantic distance on output vectors). This therefore attempts to increase the probability of producing offspring semantically different from their parents.

Multi-objectivisation is the conversion of a uni-objective problem into a multi-objective version to improve search [8, 18]. Bi-objective formulations have regularly been used in GP where the second objective is to minimise bloat (program size) [15]. Recently, in [9], a multi-objectivisation of GP is proposed, based on features describing the intermediate behaviour of programs. Here we examine a multi-objectivisation of GP based on treating the entire output vector of a program (its semantics), i.e., its disaggregated fitness, as a vector of objectives. Disaggregation is appealing because it is a means to ensure that once an *individual* test case has been solved (i.e. passed) by a program in the population this capability is not subsequently lost. Furthermore, non-dominance naturally maintains rich semantic diversity in the population.

In this paper we look empirically at the Boolean domain, however we consider more general formulations at the end.

Algorithm 1 Simple Boolean GP algorithm.

```
Require: 𝒟          Assessment data, with n test cases
Require: s          Population size
Require: g          Number of generations
Require: k          Max. # of nodes permitted in a program
Require: c          Probability of crossover
Require: ρ          Probability of node being mutated
 1: X := initialise_population(s, k)
 2: for i := 1 to i := s do
 3:   Y_i := evaluate(X_i, 𝒟)
 4: end for
 5: for g generations do
 6:   for s repititions do
 7:     p := binary_tournament_selection(X)
 8:     if Uniform_draw() < c then
 9:       q := binary_tournament_selection(X \ {X_p})
10:       x := crossover(X_p, X_q, k)
11:     else
12:       x := mutate(X_p, ρ)
13:     end if
14:     y := evaluate(x, 𝒟)
15:     i := reverse_binary_tournament_selection(X,Y)
16:     X_i := x
17:     Y_i := y
18:   end for
19: end for
```

The paper proceeds as follows. In section 2 we describe the Boolean GP that is the foundation of the empirical work here, along with traditional fitness sharing in GP. In Section 3 we describe two disaggregation approaches, along with their properties, prior to the empirical comparison in Section 4. In Section 5 we discuss the results, their implications, and directions for future work.

2. THE BENCHMARK GP OPTIMISER

We employ a Boolean analogue of the symbolic regression TinyGP of [15] as the baseline algorithm, which is outlined in Algorithm 1. The low complexity of this algorithm enables us to focus on the effect of the disaggregation approaches without too many other interactions which may affect the results and therefore cloud the conclusions that may be reasonably drawn.

2.1 Basic algorithm

The algorithm maintains a population of fixed size, s. Each generation s offspring programs are created. These are either generated by crossover of two parents, each selected by binary tournament selection, or via mutation of a single parent selected by binary tournament selection. The quality measure used in the selection is the standard uni-objective aggregation – i.e. how many test cases have the two programs passed (all the test cases in $\mathcal{D}$ being processed). After the generation and evaluation of each child program (lines 6-13) a current population member is selected for replacement by the child. This is accomplished via reverse binary tournament selection. In the baseline algorithm all solutions, except the single best solution in the population, may be replaced in the reverse binary tournament selection, thus making the algorithm *elitest.* We denote the elite subset of the population by X_M and refer to its members as *marked solutions*, so for the benchmark optimiser $X_M = \{X_{best}\}$. By marking and protecting the best solution discovered so far, the best performing solution will improve monotonically.

We make available all 16 possible Boolean binary operators as the function set during the program initialisation (line 1), instead of limiting the set to e.g., AND, OR and NOT. In this fashion we do not bias the search domain in favour of gates that are known to be well-suited to the problems we will be experimenting with. The programs are denoted as trees, and represented internally as arrays of nodes. At initialisation, the root node is always chosen from the function set. All subsequent nodes in the tree have a 50/50 chance of being selected as a random member of the function set, or a random terminal (representing one of the input variables), as in [15]. The maximum permitted depth of the initialised program tree is 10 levels, so nodes at level 10 are always selected as terminals. There is no level constraint for child programs enforced by crossover or mutation. All trees also have the constraint that they must not contain in excess of k nodes in total. We use standard subtree crossover (line 10). If the resultant child contains more than k nodes, the crossover points are drawn again until a child is obtained within the k bound. We use standard point mutation (line 12), so if a terminal node is selected for mutation it is changed at random to a different terminal node; if a function set node is selected it is changed at random to another function set member. We denote this algorithm 'B' for benchmark.

All algorithms in our comparison are modifications of this baseline algorithm. They only differ in the reverse binary tournament selection (i.e. in the way they determine the population of programs that may be selected for replacement). To isolate the effect of the diversity in the population brought by the different replacement mechanisms, we do not change how parent programs are chosen during selection, or any other aspects of the baseline GP.

2.2 Fitness sharing

A standard approach to promote diversity in the population, which uses information from the test cases, is fitness sharing (see [11] for an early example of its use in GP). Here the raw aggregate fitness of a program is modified in light of how many other programs in the current population solve the same test cases from the set $\mathcal{D}$. In algorithm 'B', the aggregate fitness of the ith program in the population is:

$$f_{agg}(X_i, \mathcal{D}) = \sum_{d=1}^{n} f_d(X_i, \mathcal{D}_d) \tag{1}$$

Where $f_d(X_i, \mathcal{D}_d)$ returns 1 if the program is correct on the dth test case, and 0 otherwise. In fitness sharing f_{agg} is replaced by:

$$f_{share}(X_i, \mathcal{D}) = \sum_{d=1}^{n} \frac{f_d(X_i, \mathcal{D}_d)}{\max\left(1, \sum_{j=1}^{|X|} f_d(X_j, \mathcal{D}_d)\right)} \tag{2}$$

This fitness function down-weights the contribution of the test cases the ith program passes, in proportion to the number of programs in the population that also pass these test cases. The max function is used to ensure there are no divisions by zero.

We refer to Algorithm 1 employing fitness sharing in the reverse binary tournament selection subroutine (line 15) as variant 'F' for fitness sharing.

Population X

1	1	17	20				
2	2	1	17	18	19		
3	1	20	4	2	17	19	18
4	2	20	18				
5	7	5	20	18	17		

Test results Y

1	0	0	0	0
0	1	0	1	1
0	1	1	0	0
0	1	0	1	0
0	0	1	1	0

Population in tree representation

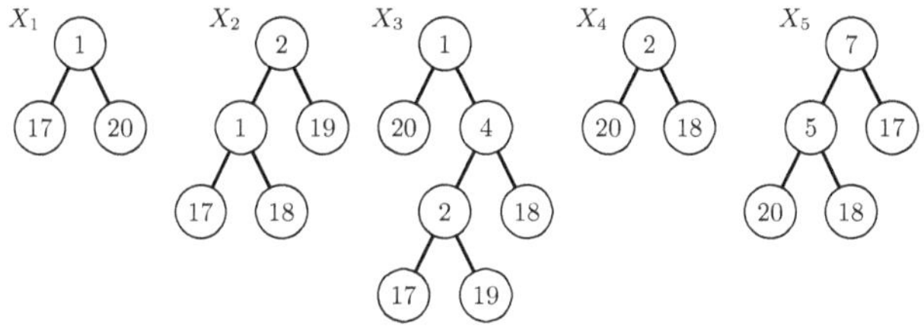

Figure 1: Illustration of the population, X, in array and tree notations, and corresponding test case results, Y. In X, the functional set elements are indicated with a value 1-16, and terminals with 17+. Each program has a corresponding row in Y, denoting the success, 1, or failure, 0, on the test cases. Due to space limitations, we display only five test cases.

3. DISAGGREGATION APPROACHES

A typical elitist approach is to ensure that the best solution in a population does not degrade in quality from one generation to the next. This is achieved by either marking the best solution in a population and ensuring it does not get selected for replacement, or equivalently, by ensuring the reverse binary tournament selection draws *without replacement* when drawing pairs.[1] In the illustration in Figure 1 this would mean X_2 is marked as it has an aggregation fitness of 3 (passing three out of five test cases), which is the highest in the population.

3.1 Preserving the best solver for each test case

In our first disaggregation approach, for each test case that has been passed (solved) by at least one member of the current population, we preserve one such program by marking it. In the worst case, this results in the marked subset of X, denoted X_M, consisting of n programs (one program for each of the n test cases). For instance, this maximum would occur if all programs only passed at most one test case, and all test cases have been passed by at least one population member. When there are many population members that have solved the same test case, the member of this subset which has solved the most test cases in total is the one marked as the best solver for the test concerned. Often the cardinality of the marked subset will be much smaller than n as the same solution may be selected to represent more than one test (as, if it solves many test cases, it is likely to have a high overall aggregate score, and therefore is likely to be ranked first for many of the test cases it solves). As long as X_M is a proper subset of X, the X_M solutions are not considered for replacement. For the test results in Figure 1 this would mean $X_M = \{X_1, X_2, X_3\}$ or $X_M = \{X_1, X_2, X_4\}$. X_1 is marked as it is the aggregate fittest (and only) solution that solves test 1. X_2 is marked as it is the aggregate fittest solver of tests 2, 4 and 5. Test 3 is solved by X_3 and X_5, which have equal aggregate fitness – in this case the program which was assessed first out of these two will be the marked program.

This approach has two attractive properties:

1. Weakly performing solutions that solve test cases that others do not are preserved, even if in aggregate they may be considered less fit (similar to fitness sharing).

2. The size of the marked set grows only linearly with the number of test cases – meaning with reasonably-sized populations it is unlikely that any of the X_M members will have to be discarded. To be certain of this, we could ensure $s \geq n$.

We denote this variant of Algorithm 1 by 'S' for best solvers.

3.2 Preserving the non-dominated members

Our second disaggregation approach treats passing each individual test as a separate *objective*, recasting the problem as a form of multi-objective optimisation. This means that each program is concerned with simultaneously maximising n objectives: $f_d(\mathbf{x})$, $d = 1, \ldots, n$. A program $\mathbf{x}$ is said to *dominate* another $\mathbf{x}'$ iff $f_d(\mathbf{x}) \geq f_d(\mathbf{x}') \quad \forall d = 1, \ldots, n$ and $\mathbf{f}(\mathbf{x}) \neq \mathbf{f}(\mathbf{x}')$. This is denoted as $\mathbf{x} \succ \mathbf{x}'$. To ensure diversity is maintained in this variant the non-dominated subset of the population is marked for preservation, meaning only dominated members are selected for replacement. In the illustration in Figure 1 this would mean $X_M = \{X_1, X_2, X_3, X_5\}$ as X_4 is the only dominated member of the population (being dominated by X_2).

Unfortunately, even for a simple toy problem like the 4-multiplexer, which has six Boolean inputs (four data signals and two selectors) and a single Boolean output, there are 64 different test cases and therefore effectively 64 different objectives. This results in what is commonly known as a *many*-objective problem in the multi-objective optimisation community [17, 6, 4] (i.e. one with four or more objectives). Traditional Pareto-dominance based approaches scale very badly on these types of problems, and the development of effective optimisers is still very much an open area of research.

However, in this situation *our underlying problem is uni-objective*, and the disaggregation into multiple competing objectives is for the purposes of diversity preservation (and subsequent exploitation). We will often deem a GP run which does not result in a solution satisfying *all* the test cases a failure – whereas it is usual in multi/many-objective optimisation to expect a set of solutions to be returned, from which the end-user will have to select one or more individuals to use. Furthermore, in Boolean problems the properties are rather different to those usually confronted in many-objective optimisation. In the Boolean GP situation the evaluation of each test case (objective) can result in one of only two values: correct or incorrect, rather than a wide range of values as would be the case if, for instance, a symbolic regression problem was being solved. Because of this we may determine, *a priori*, the maximum cardinality of the non-dominated set for any arbitrary Boolean problem (given we do not permit duplicates in quality), as a function

[1]Many implementations, including [15], draw with replacement, so, unless the elite member is not marked in some other fashion, there is no guarantee the best solution in the population will not degrade in quality from one generation to the next.

of the number of test problems, n, namely: $\binom{n}{\lfloor \frac{n}{2} \rfloor}$. In this worst case, the non-dominated set would consist entirely of solutions which solve exactly $\lfloor \frac{n}{2} \rfloor$ tests, with all possible permutations of the objective combinations present. Although this worst-case configuration is unlikely to occur regularly in practice, even approaching it will exceed the capacity of all but the most excessively large GP populations (e.g. $\binom{64}{32} > 10^{18}$).

If X_M (here the non-dominated members of X) is a proper subset of X then only the dominated members of X may be selected for replacement. If however $X_M = X$, then all members are available for replacement. In both cases it is the worst aggregated fitness (the uni-objective fitness) which is used to determine which of the two competing candidates is replaced by a new offspring program. This has the effect that programs with diverse combinations across test cases, which have good aggregated test performance, are preserved. We denote this algorithm variant 'D' for domination-based.

3.3 Preferring shorter equivalent programs

As well as the four algorithms detailed above, B, F, S and D, four variants are also compared here, which include a mechanism to encourage the evolution of smaller programs. Bias towards evolving programs that are much larger than the minimum possible to solve the problem at hand is a well-known issue for GP commonly referred to as program growth or bloat. As mentioned in the introduction, one way of confronting this is to cast the minimisation of the program size (e.g. number of nodes in the program tree) as an additional objective, other approaches to mitigate bloat include using penalty terms, and biasing how programs are evolved – a recent review of approaches is provided at the start of [16].

Here, rather than using program size as an explicit additional objective, or modifying the fitness calculation, or the search operators, we instead use program size as a differentiator in the reverse binary tournament selection when two solutions are otherwise characterised as equal. If the two are equal on their quality measure - the larger program is selected for replacement. Likewise, when offspring solutions are compared to currently marked solutions, if they are equal in quality to the currently marked solution, but shorter, then they will replace them in the marked set. Taking program length into consideration in this fashion ensures that the marked members of the population are the most parsimonious designs discovered so far for the quality performance they represent, and shorter programs are more likely to persist in the population. This means any differences in program structure are more likely to be related to differing performance on test cases. Furthermore, it is well-known (see e.g., [12]) that changes to the program structure by a genetic operator that are far from the root of the tree are likely not to have any effect on the semantics of the program, so producing offspring semantically equivalent to the parent. Preferring shorter individuals tend to lessen this problem, because in shorter individuals structural changes are necessarily closer to the root more often, hence more likely to have an effect on the semantics.

In the illustration in Figure 1, this would mean that in the parsimony preserving variant of the S algorithm, denoted S_P, X_5 would always be chosen over X_3 to be marked for test case 3, as although both programs solve test case 3, and have the same overall fitness, X_5 is the shorter of the two.

3.4 Algorithm differences

A subscript P (for parsimonious) denotes the variant of each algorithm which encourages smaller program sizes as described in Section 3.3. It is worth emphasising at this juncture that for all of the algorithms described above (B, B_P, F, F_P, S, S_P, D and D_P) the only difference between them is the tournament selection used for *replacing* population members (Algorithm 1, line 15). All other aspects of the algorithms are identical (though different storage costs may be incurred). We additionally implement a random optimiser, denoted R, which generates programs at random according to the initialisation approach used in the benchmark optimiser. This algorithm has no population as such, and merely records the aggregate best performing program it has generated so far in a run, until a perfect solver has been located or the limit on the number of function evaluations is reached.

4. EMPIRICAL COMPARISON

We employ a number of commonly used Boolean test problems [19] in the experiments here, specifically: the 6, 7 and 8 input versions of the Boolean even n-Parity problem and the Boolean majority problem (which have 2^n test cases each), the 2, 4 and 8-multiplexer problems[2], which have 2^3, 2^6 and 2^{11} test cases respectively and the 6, 8 and 10 input comparator problems. When a new offspring program is created it is assessed to check if the problem has been completely solved, in which case the algorithm records how many function evaluations were required in total.[3] A maximum of 10^6 function evaluations is permitted on each problem, if the problem remains unsolved after 10^6 evaluations the algorithm terminates.

Each algorithm was run 50 times, and the same 50 random seeds were used for each set of runs across the algorithms. Additionally four different population sizes were employed for each algorithm for each test problem: $s = \{10^1, 10^2, 10^3, 10^4\}$, which enables us to examine how different diversity preservation regimes perform in relation to the number of programs stored (as the population size would be expected to heavily affect the diversity). This results in a total of $8 \times 4 \times 12 \times 50 + 12 \times 50 = 19800$ algorithm runs in our experiments (representing the algorithm configurations across population sizes, problem types, and random seed plus the random optimiser for each problem and random seed). Other algorithm parameters are: crossover rate $c = 0.9$, point mutation probability $\rho = 0.05$, maximum number of nodes $k = 10^4$ (which match those used by the TinyGP of [15]).[4]

We now compare the algorithms based on their median performance on the problems (median evaluations required to find a program passing all test cases), their extreme performance (i.e. their rate of failure to find a zero-error program in 10^6 evaluations), examine the effect of using the parsimony preference, and investigate the dynamics of the marked subset of the population in the different approaches.

[2]These are sometimes referred to as 3, 6, and 11-multiplexer problems. This counts the total number of inputs as opposed to the number of data streams which is the standard naming convention in electronics (which we adhere to here).

[3]A single function evaluation here refers to the complete set of test cases being processed by a program.

[4]Java implementations of all the algorithms used here are available at https://github.com/fieldsend.

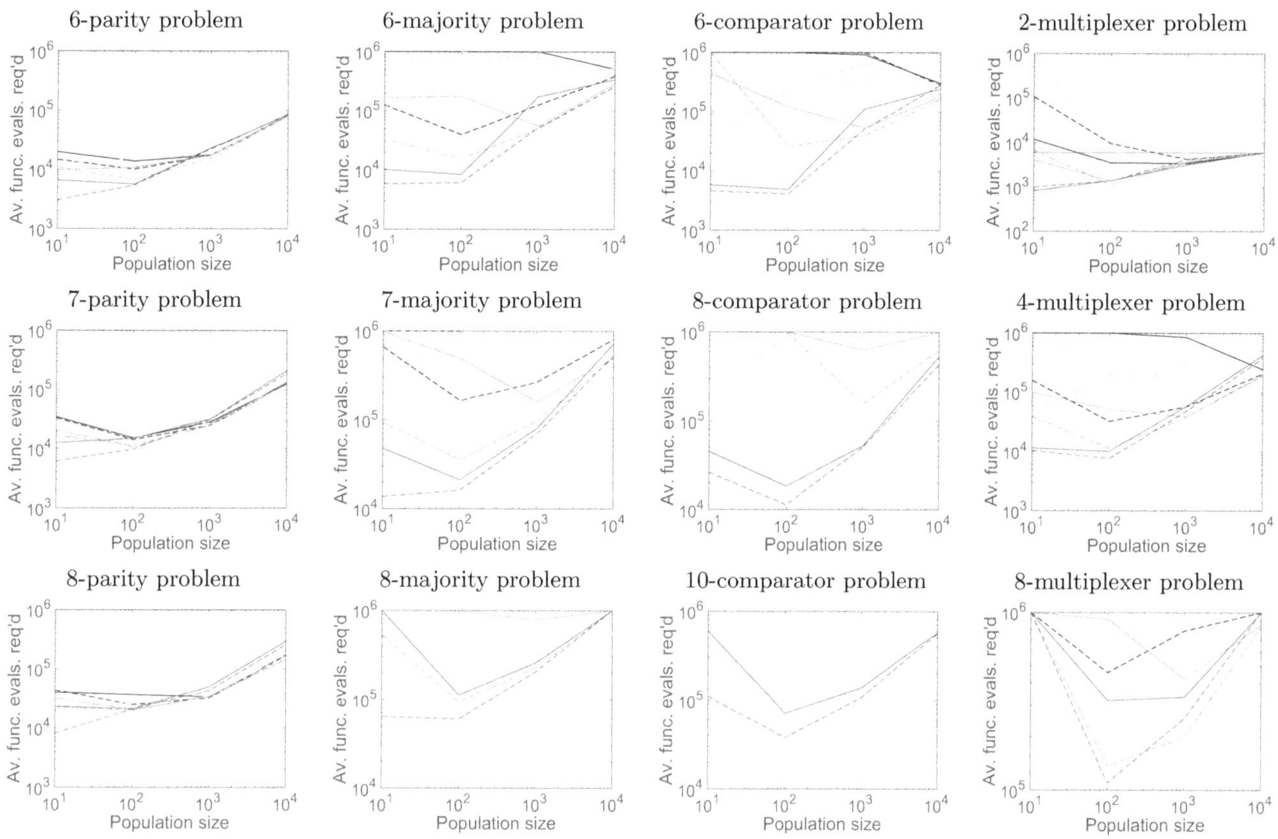

Figure 2: Average (median) number of function evaluations until problem solved, or 10^6 evaluations exhausted, for each population size. Algorithm B denoted with black line, F with a red line, S with green line and D with a blue line. B_P, F_P, S_P and D_P are denoted with the correspondingly coloured dashed lines. Axes are plotted on a log scale. The horizontal dotted line corresponds to random program generation (which does not depend on any population size). Only on the 2-multiplexer problem does the median random generator result solve the task within the 10^6 evaluation limit.

4.1 Perfomance comparison

Figure 2 shows the median performance of each of the algorithms on each test problem, for each of the population sizes. A number of interesting trends are immediately apparent. Algorithms D and D_P are able to solve many of the difficult problems not only with fewer function evaluations than the other approaches, but also with far smaller populations. Conversely maintaining the largest population size ($s = 10000$) is seen to cause relatively worse performance in D and D_P compared to the other algorithms. This is likely due to the preservation of proportionally more solutions that solve relatively few test cases, but are nevertheless non-dominated, meaning convergence to the perfect solution is delayed. This is because a sizeable amount of the search will be expended on spreading out the image of the non-dominated set in the n-dimensional test objective space, rather than pushing it forward. This does not affect the smaller population sizes to the same degree as the aggregate fitness is used to effectively strip weaker solutions from X whenever $X_M = X$.

As the number of test cases increases all algorithms converge more slowly, however B, B_P, S and S_P tend to degrade faster. All approaches tend to do better than random (for where this can be detected, i.e. where over half of the runs

Table 1: Best performing configuration(s) on each problem (written as: *alg-s*). The number of times the best is *significantly* better is given in parenthesis (maximum is 32). Assessed using the non-parametric Wilcoxon signed ranks test at the 5% level for all pairs of algorithms modified using Bonferroni correction - i.e. $\alpha = 0.05/33$.

Problem	# tests	Best alg(s)
6-parity	64	D_P-10 (30)
7-parity	128	D_P-10 (28)
8-parity	256	D_P-10 (32)
6-majority	64	D_P-100 (31)
7-majority	128	D_P-100 (30)
8-majority	256	D_P-100, D-100 (30)
6-comparator	64	D_P-100 (30)
8-comparator	256	D_P-100 (32)
10-comparator	1024	D_P-100 (32)
2-multiplexer	8	D-10 (27)
4-multiplexer	64	D_P-100 (30)
8-multiplexer	2048	D_P-100 (31)

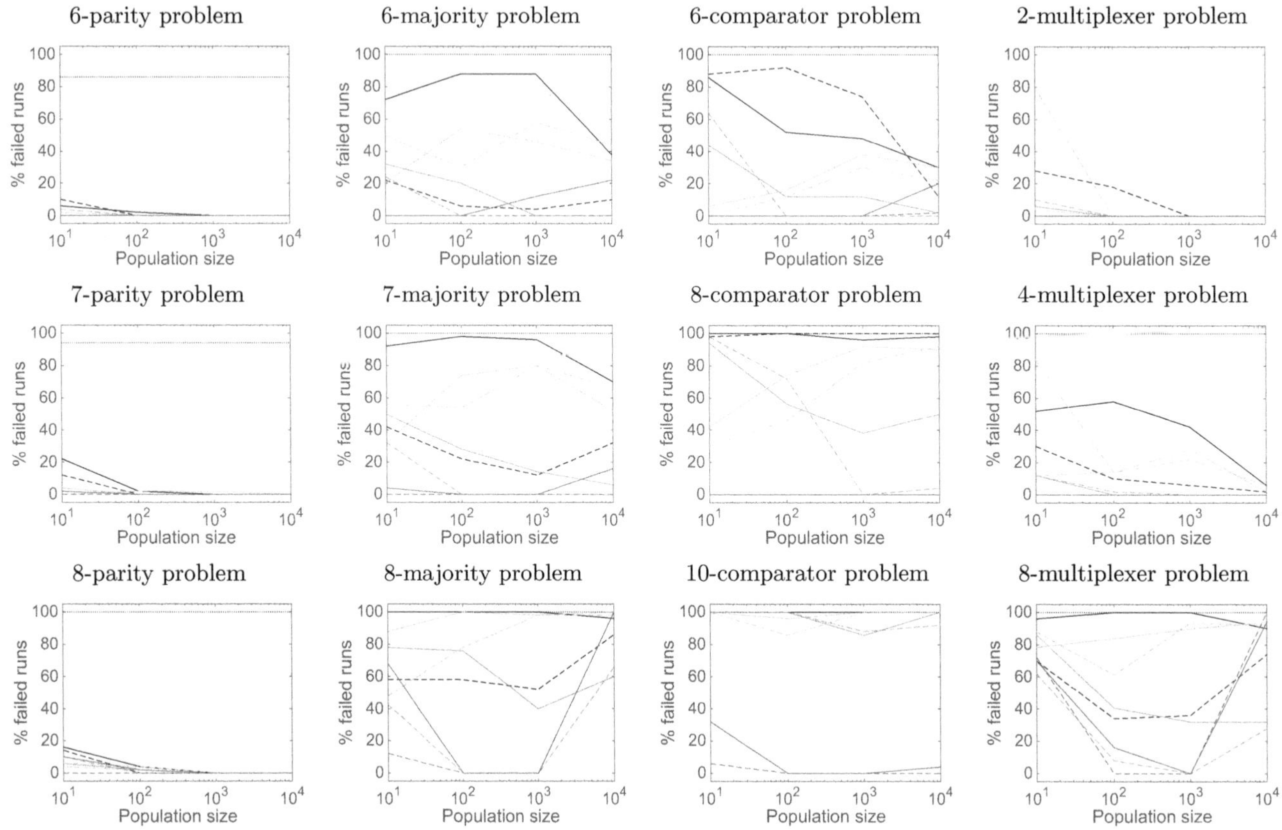

Figure 3: Percentage of runs where an algorithm failed to find a solution within 10^6 function evaluations, for each population size. Algorithm B denoted with black line, F with a red line, S with green line and D with a blue line. B_P, F_P, S_P and D_P are denoted with the correspondingly coloured dashed lines. Axes are plotted on a log scale. The dotted black line corresponds to random program generation (which does not depend on any population size).

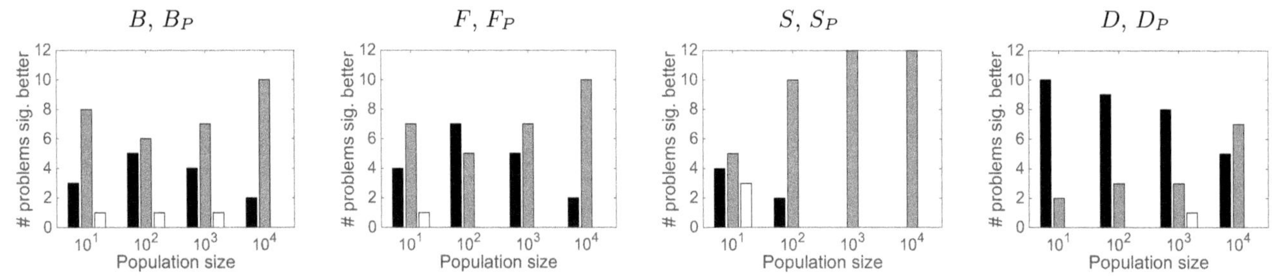

Figure 4: Number of problems where an anti-bloat variant was significantly better than its base algorithm (black bar), where there was no significant difference (grey bar) and where the base algorithm was significantly better than its anti-bloat variant (white bar), for each population size and optimiser.

find a solution within 10^6 function evaluations), except for on the 2-multiplexer problem. Here B, B_P, F_P and S_P when $s = 10$ and B_P when $s = 100$ all perform worse than the random optimiser. On inspection of the runs we find that the populations tend to rapidly fill with single node solutions containing terminals, meaning the population reaches a state where the optimum is no longer reachable given the search operators of TinyGP (as a member of the function set can only be introduced in a child program via recombination of parents which contain a function set member, or via mutation of a parent's existing function set node).

Table 1 presents the pairwise statistical comparison of convergence time of each optimiser with a particular population size, against all other algorithms and population sizes, and the random optimiser. The algorithm that significantly outperforms the most is recorded for each test problem. The D_P algorithm performs best (except on the 2-multiplexer), with the optimal population size being either 10 or 100.

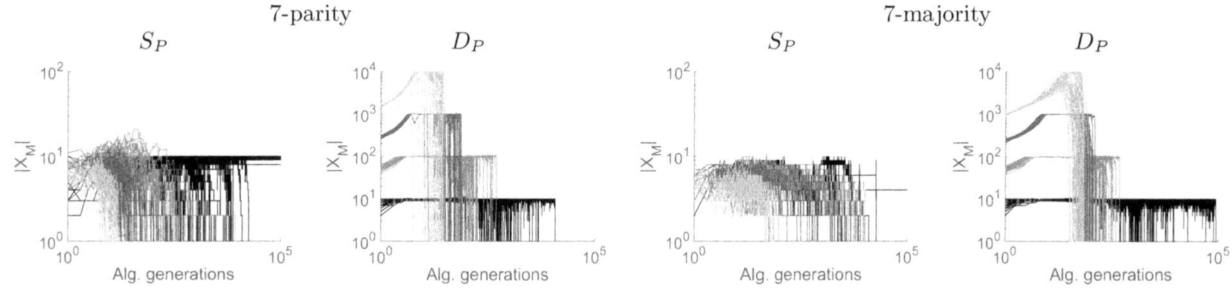

Figure 5: Marked subset sizes for algorithms S_P, and D_P as search progresses on each of the 50 runs for each population size on the Boolean even 7-parity and 7-majority problems. Green denotes $s = 10000$, blue $s = 1000$, red $s = 100$ and black $s = 10$ runs. Note that for D_P the marked set rapidly reaches the limit of $X = X_M$ and oscillates up to this bound until the problem is solved (causing X_M to collapse to a single solution). For S_P, although there are $n = 128$ test cases, $|X_M|$ is rarely above 10 on any of the runs (even those for which $|X|$ substantially exceeds this). Although the dimensionality of the problems is the same, we can see the non-dominated set in D_P takes longer to fill out for the 7-majority problem, highlighting the differences in search landscapes the two problems induce.

Figure 3 shows the percentage of runs where an algorithm failed to find a solution which passed all the test cases within 10^6 program evaluations, for each population size. D_P with both $s = 100$ and $s = 1000$ achieves convergence to a perfect solution within 10^6 function evaluations for *all* test problems for *every* run – this feat is not achieved by any other optimiser or configuration.

4.2 Anti-bloat effects

The use of the anti-bloat mechanism tends to improve the performance of all algorithms, or have no significant effect, as shown in Figure 4. Only for a handful of problems and algorithm configurations does it appear to make performance significantly degrade. Interestingly, approach D seems to benefit from this most. However, it should be highlighted that when the median results of evaluations of both the original algorithm, and its parsimony preserving variant, is 10^6 evaluations, then there will be insufficient evidence to support any significant difference in the distribution of results. As such, a high count of no significant difference comparisons is to be expected given the results shown in Figure 2 for many of the algorithms.

4.3 Marked subset dynamics

In algorithms B, B_P, F and F_P the marked subset only ever has a single member marked. For the disaggregation approaches the marked subset may vary in size throughout the run, though it is limited to $\texttt{min}(n, s)$ in the case of algorithm S and S_P and $\texttt{min}(\binom{n}{\lfloor \frac{n}{2} \rfloor}, s)$ in the case of algorithms D and D_P. Figure 5 illustrates the dynamics of $|X_M|$ for a couple of problems for S_P and D_P. $|X_M|$ in S_P is not greatly influenced by population size for either of these 128-test case problems. $|X_M|$ is however clearly limited by the population size in D_P variants, although the time to saturation does vary between problems.

Although the $|X_M|$ for the D_P algorithm appears to sit on the limit, on close inspection we find that the $|X_M|$ actually oscillates just below and up to the upper bound. This is because when $X_M = X$, then the weakest member of the population in terms of aggregate fitness is removed. Once this occurs there is one of three possibilities: (1) its replacement is itself mutually non-dominated with the remaining X_M, so it is inserted into X_M, which must again be truncated in the next iteration; (2) the child program is dominated, so $X_M \neq X$ and the dominated solution will be replaced in the next iteration; (3) the child dominates one or more members of the current X_M, resulting in X_M shrinking in size overall once the child program is entered. X_M therefore is forced to contain non-dominated solutions which are also in aggregate fit, the degree of aggregate fitness determined by $|X|$ – the larger the $|X|$ the less fit in aggregate a non-dominated solution needs to be in order to ensure its preservation. As such, there is an implicit balance between having a population size sufficient to contain solutions which cover all test cases, but not to such a degree where search is biased toward programs which only solve a small number of test cases (albeit in a combination not otherwise maintained). We can see from Figure 2 that for D_P a population in the range 100-1000 is sufficient for problems where $n = 2$ to $n = 2048$, at least for the range of problem types considered here. This is an encouraging result, as a wide population range covers a wide range of test sizes and types with good consistency.

5. CONCLUSION AND DISCUSSION

We have investigated the effect of a number of different diversity preservation approaches for deciding which population members to replace in GP, and also the effect within these of biasing the replacement of longer programs. Although disaggregating the problem and preserving programs which pass individual tests does not generally give better performance than fitness sharing, multi-objectivisation of the problem, preserving the non-dominated subset of programs and truncating when capacity is reached based on the aggregate fitness is seen consistently to give the best performance. This improvement is both in terms of median time to zero-error program discovery (sometimes over an order of magnitude faster), and in terms of consistency in finding zero-error solutions across repeated runs with different starting random seeds and starting population s.

Although we have undertaken nearly 20 000 separate runs across a range of problem types and sizes we have restricted our examination to Boolean problems here. Symbolic regression problems may also be approached using a similar multi-objectivisation approach to preserve diversity, however some additional considerations would need to be taken. Unlike in the Boolean case, it is impossible to derive a theoretical limit on the cardinality of X_M. Additionally it is not immediately obvious that the aggregate fitness will be the best differentiator when truncating non-dominated solutions when the X_M capacity is reached. For Boolean problems, selecting to reject based upon the aggregate fitness is equivalent to selection using the hypervolume, selection using the favour relation, and selection using the average rank. In general these quality measures are not equivalent, although they have all been proposed for use in many-objective optimisation (see e.g. the comparison in [4]), and it may be the case that some are better suited that others for the general multi-objectivisation of GP optimisation. The maintenance of a non-dominated set also has a cost: this part of our code took between 10^{-3} and 10^{-1}ms on average per update (on a 2.66GHz machine). However, the overall cost is marginal for the most effective $s = 100$ variant, taking 0.25–3.13% of the total run time (depending on the problem), and the use of specialised data structures can reduce this further [2].

Partially evaluating programs (only considering a random subset of tests) is often used in GP, giving an approximate fitness but with lower computational cost. Maintaining a non-dominated set for Boolean problems opens the possibility of leveraging such partial program evaluations in a systematic fashion, without introducing additional stochasticity. Given a current X_M, one can identify *a priori* the quality profiles that would be either accepted into X_M, or rejected. It would be possible therefore to undertake a partial evaluation and determine that, irrespective of the performance on the remaining tests, a program would be rejected (for instance if the aggregate will be lower than the least fit program currently in an X_M at capacity), rather than using a random selection of tests. Furthermore, as the overall quality of the X_M members improves, a fewer number of tests would need evaluating before poor solutions may be rejected. We intend to investigate empirically the speed up that might be attained in this fashion. Alternatively multi-objective algorithms for coping with delayed objectives could be exploited [1], as these employ techniques to cope with 'missing' objective values.

6. REFERENCES

[1] R. Allmendinger, J. Handl, and J. Knowles. Multiobjective optimization: When objectives exhibit non-uniform latencies. *European Journal of Operational Research*, 243(2):497–513, 2015.

[2] N. Altwaijry and M. Menai. Data structures in multi-objective evolutionary algorithms. *Journal of Computer Science and Technology*, 27(6):1197–1210, 2012.

[3] L. Beadle and C. Johnson. Semantically driven crossover in genetic programming. In *IEEE Congress on Evolutionary Computation*, pages 111–116, 2008.

[4] D. Corne and J. Knowles. Techniques for Highly Multiobjective Optimisation: Some Nondominated Points are Better than Others. In *Genetic and Evolutionary Computation Conference*, pages 773–780. ACM, 2007.

[5] E. Galvan-Lopez, B. Cody-Kenny, L. Trujillo, and A. Kattan. Using semantics in the selection mechanism in Genetic Programming: A simple method for promoting semantic diversity. In *IEEE Congress on Evolutionary Computation*, pages 2972 – 2979, 2013.

[6] E. J. Huges. Evolutionary many-objective optimisation: many once or one many? In *IEEE Congress on Evolutionary Computation*, volume 1, pages 222–227. IEEE, 2005.

[7] D. Jackson. Promoting phenotypic diversity in genetic programming. In *Parallel Problem Solving from Nature - PPSN XI*, volume 6239 of *Lecture Notes in Computer Science*, pages 472–481. Springer, 2010.

[8] J. Knowles, R. Watson, and D. Corne. Reducing local optima in single-objective problems by multi-objectivization. In *Evolutionary Multi-criterion Optimization, EMO'01*, pages 269–283. Springer, 2001.

[9] K. Krawiec and U.-M. O'Reilly. Behavioral programming: a broader and more detailed take on semantic GP. In *Genetic and Evolutionary Computation Conference*, 2014.

[10] K. Krawiec and T. Pawlak. Locally geometric semantic crossover: a study on the roles of Semantics and homology in recombination operators. *Genetic Programming and Evolvable Machines*, 14:31–63, 2013.

[11] R. I. McKay. Fitness sharing in genetic programming. In *Genetic and Evolutionary Computation Conference*, pages 435–442. Morgan Kaufmann, 2000.

[12] N. F. McPhee, B. Ohs, and T. Hutchison. Semantic building blocks in genetic programming. In *11th European conference on Genetic programming*, pages 134–145. Springer, 2008.

[13] A. Moraglio, K. Krawiec, and C. G. Johnson. Geometric semantic genetic programming. In *Parallel Problem Solving from Nature - PPSN XII*, volume 7491 of *Lecture Notes in Computer Science*, pages 21–31. Springer, 2012.

[14] Q. U. Nguyen, X. H. Nguyen, and M. O'Neill. Semantic aware crossover for genetic programming: The case for real-valued function regression. In *12th European Conference on Genetic Programming*, pages 292–302. Springer, 2009.

[15] R. Poli, W. B. Langdon, and N. McPhee. *A field guide to genetic programming*. Published via `http://lulu.com` and freely available at `http://www.gp-field-guide.org.uk`, 2008.

[16] R. Poli and N. McPhee. Parsimony Pressure Made Easy: Solving the Problem of Bloat in GP. In Y. Borenstein and A. Moraglio, editors, *Theory and Principled Methods for the Design of Metaheuristics*, Natural Computing Series, chapter 9, pages 181–204. Springer, 2014.

[17] R. C. Purshouse and P. Fleming. Evolutionary many-objective optimisation: An exploratory analysis. In *IEEE Congress on Evolutionary Computation*, volume 3, pages 2066–2073. IEEE, 2003.

[18] C. Segura, C. A. Coello Coello, G. Miranda, and C. León. Using multi-objective evolutionary algorithms for single-objective optimization. *4OR*, 11(3):201–228, 2013.

[19] D. White, J. McDermott, M. Castelli, L. Manzoni, B. Goldman, G. Kronberger, W. Jaśkowski, U.-M. O'Reilly, and S. Luke. Better GP benchmarks: community survey results and proposals. *Genetic Programming and Evolvable Machines*, 14:3–29, 2013.

General Program Synthesis Benchmark Suite

Thomas Helmuth
Computer Science
University of Massachusetts
Amherst, MA 01003
thelmuth@cs.umass.edu

Lee Spector
Cognitive Science
Hampshire College
Amherst, MA 01002
lspector@hampshire.edu

ABSTRACT

Recent interest in the development and use of non-trivial benchmark problems for genetic programming research has highlighted the scarcity of general program synthesis (also called "traditional programming") benchmark problems. We present a suite of 29 general program synthesis benchmark problems systematically selected from sources of introductory computer science programming problems. This suite is suitable for experiments with any program synthesis system driven by input/output examples. We present results from illustrative experiments using our reference implementation of the problems in the PushGP genetic programming system. The results show that the problems in the suite vary in difficulty and can be useful for assessing the capabilities of a program synthesis system.

Categories and Subject Descriptors

I.2.2 [**Artificial Intelligence**]: Automatic Programming—*Program synthesis*

Keywords

program synthesis; genetic programming; benchmarks

1. INTRODUCTION

Several genetic programming (GP) researchers have highlighted the need for better benchmark problems to guide research in the field [9, 17, 18]. While benchmarks have been proposed, few are for general programming problems (also called "traditional" or "algorithmic" programming problems) even though this category received the second highest level of interest in a recent community survey about the need for benchmarks [17].

Automating human programming has long been a goal of GP, as articulated for example in Koza's first book [7]. The purpose of a general program synthesis benchmark is to help researchers assess the ability of a system to automate human programming. Such problems should require a range of programming techniques including the use of control flow, modularity, and large, diverse instruction sets covering multiple data types and data structures. Also, minimal sizes for solution programs should cover a range beyond what could be found using brute-force search. This contrasts with most existing benchmark problems used in GP and other program synthesis fields [6], which prescribe small, domain-specific instruction sets and assess a system's abilities only on a narrow range of programming techniques.

In this paper we present a suite of 29 general program synthesis benchmark problems, systematically selected from sources of introductory computer science programming problems. We present each problem's specifications in the form of input/output examples, making them suitable to a wide range of program synthesis techniques, including GP. While the problems are not particularly challenging for skilled human programmers, they are reasonably challenging for beginners and many are arguably too difficult for existing program synthesis systems, including GP. As textbook problems, they are not likely representative of real general program synthesis applications, yet they should prove useful for assessing progress toward this goal.

2. BENCHMARK-BASED COMPARISONS

We designate the solution of a general program synthesis problem as a program that perfectly maps inputs to the correct outputs. While one might argue that human-written software is often useful even if it has known bugs, the goal here is to pass all input/output tests. Therefore, we are not interested in programs that are only approximately correct, as might be appropriate in the context of other problems for which GP is used, such as symbolic regression. We recommend measuring performance on the problems presented here primarily in terms of success rates, quantifying how often a stochastic algorithm finds a successful program across a set of runs[1]. A more thorough argument for assessment in terms of success rates can be found in [3]. Furthermore, in order to be considered successful, a program must not only achieve zero error on all of the example data used to train the program (the "training set"), but also on a set of withheld generalization data (the "test set").

When using this benchmark suite to compare different settings within one system, we recommend limiting computation with a budget based on the maximum number of program evaluations allowed in a run. This ensures that the

[1]For deterministic synthesis algorithms other measures must be used, such as whether a correct program is found within a set period of time.

GECCO '15, July 11 - 15, 2015, Madrid, Spain

DOI: http://dx.doi.org/10.1145/2739480.2754769

methods perform similar computational work. That said, it may nonetheless be difficult to justify fine-grained numerical comparisons among diverse techniques on these problems, as they may involve qualitatively different kinds of costs and each may be parameterized in radically different ways. In many cases, the most interesting question to ask vis-a-vis a particular system on a particular problem may just be whether the system can solve the problem at all, and if so, whether it can solve it reasonably reliably. Nevertheless, we aim here to describe specifications that will allow for as much cross-system comparability as possible.

3. PROBLEM SELECTION CRITERIA

In this section we describe the criteria we used when selecting problems for the benchmark suite. Several of our criteria overlap with those described in the GP benchmarks papers [9, 17], such as being varied, relevant, realistically difficult, representation-independent, and precisely defined.

This benchmark suite is designed for systems that use example inputs and their corresponding outputs as the specifications for desired programs. In the context of GP, we call the input/output pairs *test cases* for the problem. Thus, a problem must be defined on a range of inputs that have known correct outputs; it cannot simply specify the calculation of a single value. For example, a problem that requires the program to calculate the number of prime numbers less than 1000 would not qualify, since it only has one answer; but, a similar problem that requires the program to calculate the number of prime numbers less than an input integer n would meet this requirement, since we could then provide example inputs for n and their corresponding outputs. This requirement also ensures that test cases can be generated to fill the training and test set, as required to test generalization of successful programs.

Problems in the suite should present challenges typical of real programming tasks. This criterion leads us to choose problems that call for a range of programming constructs and data types. The problems should require a variety of sizes and shapes for solution programs, not just artificially small programs.

The benchmarks should not be biased toward a particular method of synthesis; it should be possible to attempt to solve them using various GP systems as well as analytic and search-based program synthesis systems. Since systems generate programs in a variety of languages, we avoid problems that require a specific language feature or non-standard data type (such as Java objects).

We take our problems from pre-existing sources of introductory programming problems. From each source, we include all problems that meet the criteria described above, aiming to avoid biasing the selection of problems. We rejected problems from other sources that did not meet our criteria, such as the inductive programming benchmark repository[2], other program synthesis and inductive programming papers, and programming competitions.

4. PROBLEM DESCRIPTIONS

We used two sources for problems: iJava [11], an interactive textbook for introductory computer science, and IntroClass [2, 1], a set of problems originally used as benchmarks for automatic program repair. Below we describe each of these sources in further detail and present our natural language description of each problem, summarized from the original source. All problems use functional arguments as inputs besides one that requires reading input from a file. Some problems require programs to return functional outputs, where others require the program to print results.

[2]http://www.inductive-programming.org/repository.html

4.1 iJava

iJava is an interactive introductory computer science textbook that contains a number of automatically graded programming problems [11]. Many of its problems are graded by testing programs against a range of inputs, making them easy to convert into benchmark problems.

Some sets of problems in iJava meet our criteria but test similar programming techniques; for these sets, we chose one representative problem from the group, ensuring a reasonable distribution of problem requirements. Along with each problem name and description, we provide the question or project number associated with the problem in iJava 3.1.

1. **Number IO (Q 3.5.1)** Given an integer and a float, print their sum.

2. **Small or Large (Q 4.6.3)** Given an integer n, print "small" if $n < 1000$ and "large" if $n \geq 2000$ (and nothing if $1000 \leq n < 2000$).

3. **For Loop Index (Q 4.11.7)** Given 3 integer inputs *start*, *end*, and *step*, print the integers in the sequence

$$n_0 = start$$
$$n_i = n_{i-1} + step$$

   for each $n_i < end$, each on their own line.

4. **Compare String Lengths (Q 4.11.13)** Given three strings $n1$, $n2$, and $n3$, return true if $length(n1) < length(n2) < length(n3)$, and false otherwise.

5. **Double Letters (P 4.1)** Given a string, print the string, doubling every letter character, and tripling every exclamation point. All other non-alphabetic and non-exclamation characters should be printed a single time each.

6. **Collatz Numbers (P 4.2)** Given an integer, find the number of terms in the Collatz (hailstone) sequence starting from that integer.

7. **Replace Space with Newline (P 4.3)** Given a string input, print the string, replacing spaces with newlines. Also, return the integer count of the non-whitespace characters. The input string will not have tabs or newlines.

8. **String Differences (P 4.4)** Given 2 strings (without whitespace) as input, find the indices at which the strings have different characters, stopping at the end of the shorter one. For each such index, print a line containing the index as well as the character in each string. For example, if the strings are "dealer" and "dollars", the program should print:

```
1 e o
2 a l
4 e a
```

9. **Even Squares (Q 5.4.1)** Given an integer n, print all of the positive even perfect squares less than n on separate lines.

10. **Wallis Pi (P 6.4))** John Wallis gave the following infinite product that converges to $\pi/4$:

$$\frac{2}{3} \times \frac{4}{3} \times \frac{4}{5} \times \frac{6}{5} \times \frac{6}{7} \times \frac{8}{7} \times \frac{8}{9} \times \frac{10}{9} \times ...$$

Given an integer input n, compute an approximation of this product out to n terms. Results are rounded to 5 decimal places.

11. **String Lengths Backwards (Q 7.2.5)** Given a vector of strings, print the length of each string in the vector starting with the last and ending with the first.

12. **Last Index of Zero (Q 7.7.8)** Given a vector of integers, at least one of which is 0, return the index of the last occurrence of 0 in the vector.

13. **Vector Average (Q 7.7.11)** Given a vector of floats, return the average of those floats. Results are rounded to 4 decimal places.

14. **Count Odds (Q 7.7.12)** Given a vector of integers, return the number of integers that are odd, without use of a specific `even` or `odd` instruction (but allowing instructions such as `mod` and `quotient`).

15. **Mirror Image (Q 7.7.15)** Given two vectors of integers, return `true` if one vector is the reverse of the other, and `false` otherwise.

16. **Super Anagrams (P 7.3)** Given strings x and y of lowercase letters, return true if y is a super anagram of x, which is the case if every character in x is in y. To be true, y may contain extra characters, but must have at least as many copies of each character as x does.

17. **Sum of Squares (Q 8.5.4)** Given integer n, return the sum of squaring each integer in the range $[1, n]$.

18. **Vectors Summed (Q 8.7.6)** Given two equal-sized vectors of integers, return a vector of integers that contains the sum of the input vectors at each index.

19. **X-Word Lines (P 8.1)** Given an integer X and a string that can contain spaces and newlines, print the string with exactly X words per line. The last line may have fewer than X words.

20. **Pig Latin (P 8.2)** Given a string containing lowercase words separated by single spaces, print the string with each word translated to pig Latin. Specifically, if a word starts with a vowel, it should have "ay" added to its end; otherwise, the first letter is moved to the end of the word, followed by "ay".

21. **Negative To Zero (Q 9.6.8)** Given a vector of integers, return the vector where all negative integers have been replaced by 0.

22. **Scrabble Score (P 10.1)** Given a string of visible ASCII characters, return the Scrabble score for that string. Each letter has a corresponding value according to normal Scrabble rules, and non-letter characters are worth zero.

23. **Word Stats (P 10.5)** Given a file, print the number of words containing n characters for n from 1 to the length of the longest word, in the format:

```
words of length 1:  12
words of length 2:  3
words of length 3:  0
words of length 4:  5
...
```

At the end of the output, print a line that gives the number of sentences and line that gives the average sentence length using the form:

```
number of sentences:  4
average sentence length:  7.452423455
```

A word is any string of consecutive non-whitespace characters (including sentence terminators). Every file will contain at least one sentence terminator (period, exclamation point, or question mark). The average sentence length is the number of words in the file divided by the number of sentence terminator characters.

4.2 IntroClass

The set of 6 problems in the IntroClass dataset [2, 1] was designed for the purpose of benchmarking automatic software defect repair systems. As such, the authors of this dataset provide a number of buggy programs written by students trying to solve each problem, taken from students in an introductory computer science class. For the purposes of general program synthesis from scratch, we will use the problems themselves but not the accompanying buggy programs.

24. **Checksum** Given a string, convert each character in the string into its integer ASCII value, sum them, take the sum modulo 64, add the integer value of the space character, and then convert that integer back into its corresponding character (the checksum character). The program must print `Check sum is X`, where X is replaced by the correct checksum character.

25. **Digits** Given an integer, print that integer's digits each on their own line starting with the least significant digit. A negative integer should have the negative sign printed before the most significant digit.

26. **Grade** Given 5 integers, the first four represent the lower numeric thresholds for achieving an A, B, C, and D, and will be distinct and in descending order. The fifth represents the student's numeric grade. The program must print `Student has a X grade.`, where X is A, B, C, D, or F depending on the thresholds and the numeric grade.

27. **Median** Given 3 integers, print their median.

28. **Smallest** Given 4 integers, print the smallest of them.

29. **Syllables** Given a string containing symbols, spaces, digits, and lowercase letters, count the number of occurrences of vowels (a, e, i, o, u, y) in the string and print that number as X in `The number of syllables is X`.

5. SYNTHESIS SPECIFICATIONS

The natural language descriptions of the problems in Section 4 do not provide all of the information needed to apply

Table 1: **For each problem, the types of the inputs and outputs, and the limits imposed on the inputs. Any printed outputs should be printed by the program to standard output. The columns Train and Test indicate the recommended sizes of the training set and test set respectively.**

Name	Inputs	Outputs	Train	Test
Number IO	integer in $[-100, 100]$, float in $[-100.0, 100.0]$	printed float	25	1000
Small Or Large	integer in $[-10000, 10000]$	printed string	100	1000
For Loop Index	integers `start` and `end` in $[-500, 500]$, `step` in $[1, 10]$	printed integers	100	1000
Compare String Lengths	3 strings of length $[0, 49]$	boolean	100	1000
Double Letters	string of length $[0, 20]$	printed string	100	1000
Collatz Numbers	integer in $[1, 10000]$	integer	200	2000
Replace Space with Newline	string of length $[0, 20]$	printed string, integer	100	1000
String Differences	2 strings of length $[0, 10]$	printed string	200	2000
Even Squares	integer in $[1, 9999]$	printed string	100	1000
Wallis Pi	integer in $[1, 200]$	float	150	50
String Lengths Backwards	vector of length $[0, 50]$ of strings of length $[0, 50]$	printed string	100	1000
Last Index of Zero	vector of integers of length $[1, 50]$ with each integer in $[-50, 50]$	integer	150	1000
Vector Average	vector of floats of length $[1, 50]$ with each float in $[-1000.0, 1000.0]$	float	100	1000
Count Odds	vector of integers of length $[0, 50]$ with each integer in $[-1000, 1000]$	integer	200	2000
Mirror Image	2 vectors of integers of length $[0, 50]$ with each integer in $[-1000, 1000]$	boolean	100	1000
Super Anagrams	2 strings of length $[0, 20]$	boolean	200	2000
Sum of Squares	integer in $[1, 100]$	integer	50	50
Vectors Summed	2 vectors of integers of length $[0, 50]$ with each integer in $[-1000, 1000]$	vector of integers	150	1500
X-Word Lines	integer in $[1, 10]$, string of length $[0, 100]$	printed string	150	2000
Pig Latin	string of length $[0, 50]$	printed string	200	1000
Negative To Zero	vector of integers of length $[0, 50]$ with each integer in $[-1000, 1000]$	vector of integers	200	2000
Scrabble Score	string of length $[0, 20]$	integer	200	1000
Word Stats	file containing $[1, 100]$ chars	printed string	100	1000
Checksum	string of length $[0, 50]$	printed string	100	1000
Digits	integer in $[-9999999999, 9999999999]$	printed integers	100	1000
Grade	5 integers in $[0, 100]$	printed string	200	2000
Median	3 integers in $[-100, 100]$	printed integer	100	1000
Smallest	4 integers in $[-100, 100]$	printed integer	100	1000
Syllables	string of length $[0, 20]$	printed string	100	1000

program synthesis systems to the problems. Here we provide the needed additional information, aiming to do so in a technique-independent and system-independent way.

Table 1 presents recommendations regarding training and test data for each problem. While these are merely guidelines, and there may be good reasons to diverge from them when using different techniques or systems, adhering to these guidelines will clarify comparisons among techniques and systems. The table describes the data types of the inputs and outputs and gives reasonable ranges for program inputs.

We also provide recommendations for numbers of cases to use in the training and test sets in Table 1. For most problems, we recommend between 100 and 200 training cases, depending on the difficulty of the problem as well as the dimensionality of the input space. A few problems use fewer, either because they have limited input spaces or are simple enough to solve with fewer cases. We usually recommend using a test set ten times as large as the training set; again, there are exceptions for problems with limited input spaces. The method of producing the training and test cases is system-specific; we recommend a combination of hand-chosen edge cases with randomly generated cases, and will describe our method in more detail in Section 6.

The question of which instructions to make available for a synthesis system to use for each problem is a complex one. It is important to not cherry pick a small set of instructions that are known to be sufficient to solve a problem; such a selection may be difficult for a real-world problem, where it might not be clear which instructions will be useful. On the other hand, using all available instructions for every problem expands the search space and may make problems more difficult than necessary. We recommend a compromise between these approaches in which one first determines which data types are likely to be useful for solving the problem and then uses all instructions that operate on those data types. For example, an instruction that compares the equality of two integers and returns a boolean would be included if the problem could potentially make use of integers and booleans. By specifying only the data type requirements for a problem, we can limit the number of instructions without cherry picking.

6. SYSTEM-SPECIFC PARAMETERS

Whereas Section 5 gave technique-independent recommendations for specifying the benchmark problems for a synthesis system, this section will give more detail about the system-specific parameters and decisions that must be made in order to implement these problems in a given program synthesis system. Here we will focus on our implementation in the PushGP genetic programming system, but we emphasize that this is just one possible approach and one possible implementation, and that the problems here could be used in any system that meets the requirements in Section 3.

PushGP evolves programs in Push, a stack-based programming language designed specifically for GP [16]. The reference implementation of our problems in PushGP can be found on GitHub[3]. In the rest of this section, we will describe some of the major decisions necessary for implementing these benchmark problems in this environment. As we do not have space to discuss every parameter and implementation choice, the technical report accompanying this paper supplements the information presented here [4].

When generating training and testing data, we use a combination of hand-picked edge cases that remain constant across runs and randomly generated inputs that vary across runs. For each problem, we specify one or more "data domains" [3], which consist of either a set of hard-coded inputs or a random input generator, as well as the number of training and test cases that should come from each domain. Details on using data domains can be found in [3], and our technical report gives our choices for data domains for each problem [4].

When using this benchmark suite with GP, we not only need the input/output cases, but also a method of measuring how well a particular program performs on each case—the *fitness function*. Many of the problems in this suite print results to standard output, and we generally treat these outputs as strings and use Levenshtein distance (a measure of string edit distance) as the fitness function. Other problems produce numeric outputs, either returned or printed; for these problems we use absolute error for fitness, parsing printed numbers when necessary and possible. Some problems produce boolean values, or are best measured by a simple binary right or wrong; here, we use a fitness of 0 for right and 1 for wrong. Finally, some problems require problem-tailored fitness functions, such as vector edit distance or string formatting requirements. We give the details of each fitness function in [4].

For some problems we found it appropriate to use multiple fitness functions per test case. For example, the Replace Space With Newline problem requires both a printed string and a returned integer. For problems like this, we produce multiple fitness values for a single case. Additionally, we find that PushGP performs better on some problems when we use more than one fitness value per case, even where not strictly necessary. For example, we found no solutions to the X-Word Lines problem when using Levenshtein distance as the only fitness function, but found solutions when adding additional fitness functions for the number of newline characters and summed errors of differences in number of words compared. When using multiple fitness values for a single training case, we treat each fitness value separately when the parent selection method requires it; in tournament selection, we simply sum all fitness values.

As discussed in Section 5, we have chosen to specify the data types relevant to each problem, and then include all instructions that use those data types in each problem's instruction set. Table 2 presents the Push data types we chose for each problem. The "exec" column signifies instructions that use Push's exec stack, which typically perform control flow manipulations such as conditionals, iteration, and subfunctions defined through tagging [15]. The "print" column includes instructions that print data to standard output, and "file input" includes a small set of file reading instructions.

Table 2 also gives the terminals used for each problem, which encompass constants and ephemeral random constants (ERCs). ERCs allow for the creation of random constants in randomly generated code during initialization and mutation. We used problem-specific ERC ranges, which can be found in the technical report [4].

We keep most of our PushGP system parameters constant across all problems, with specific details in [4]. The only significant parameters that we vary per problem are the maximum program size, the maximum number of instruction evaluations that a program may use per execution, and the maximum number of generations per run. We used a maximum of 300 generations for every problem besides Number IO, Median, and Smallest, for which we used 200 generations. Maximum program sizes varied from 200 to 1000 instructions depending on anticipated problem difficulty. We limited instruction executions to approximately 2 to 5 times the maximum program size, though for some problems that require many loops we increased this limit. By specifying the maximum generations, the population size (1000 for all of our runs), and the size of the training set (see Table 1), we also specify the program evaluation budget, which is the product of those values. In our implementation, this budget falls between 5 and 60 million program evaluations per run for every problem.

7. EXPERIMENTAL RESULTS

Whereas the relevance of a benchmark suite is determined by how well its problems reflect potential applications of the test systems, its utility is based on how well it differentiates between different approaches. We aim to include problems with a large range of difficulties, from those that can be solved reliably to those that extend beyond the abilities of current program synthesis systems. More importantly, we hope to include problems that are solved more often with some systems or settings than others, allowing us to compare their performances on these problems. In this section we present a simple experiment showing the utility of the benchmark suite presented here. This experiment compares three parent selection algorithms: tournament selection, implicit fitness sharing, and lexicase selection.

Implicit fitness sharing (IFS) is a modification of tournament selection designed to encourage diversity preservation in the population [10]. IFS selection greatly rewards individuals for solving training cases that are solved by a small

[3]http://thelmuth.github.io/GECCO_2015_Benchmarks_Materials/

Table 2: Instructions and data types used in our PushGP implementation of each problem. The column "# Instructions" reports the number of instructions, terminals, and ERCs used for each problem. The middle columns show which data types were used for each problem. For example, the Number IO problem used all instructions relevant to integers, floats, and printing. The last column lists the constants and ERCs used for the problem. Here, char constants are represented in the Clojure style, starting with a backslash, and strings are surrounded by double quotation marks. The "Problems" row simply counts how many problems use each data type. The "Instructions" row shows the number of Push instructions that primarily use each data type; some use multiple types but are only counted once.

Problem	# Instructions	exec	integer	float	boolean	char	string	vector of integers	vector of floats	vector of strings	print	file input	Terminals (besides inputs)
Number IO	50		x	x							x		integer ERC, float ERC
Small Or Large	103	x	x		x		x				x		"small", "large", integer ERC
For Loop Index	74	x	x		x						x		
Compare String Lengths	98	x	x		x		x						boolean ERC
Double Letters	132	x	x		x	x	x				x		\!
Collatz Numbers	102	x	x	x	x								0, 1, integer ERC
Replace Space with Newline	135	x	x		x	x	x				x		\space, \newline, string ERC, char ERC
String Differences	135	x	x		x	x	x				x		\space, \newline, integer ERC
Even Squares	72	x	x		x						x		
Wallis Pi	103	x	x	x	x								2 integer ERCs, 2 float ERCs
String Lengths Backwards	134	x	x		x		x			x	x		integer ERC
Last Index of Zero	101	x	x		x			x					0
Vector Average	88	x	x	x					x				
Count Odds	104	x	x		x			x					0, 1, 2, integer ERC
Mirror Image	102	x	x		x			x					boolean ERC
Super Anagrams	129	x	x		x	x	x						boolean ERC, char ERC, integer ERC
Sum of Squares	71	x	x		x								0, 1, integer ERC
Vectors Summed	68	x	x					x					[], integer ERC
X-Word Lines	134	x	x		x	x	x				x		\newline, \space
Pig Latin	141	x	x		x	x	x				x		"ay", \space, \a, \e, \i, \o, \u, "aeiou", string ERC, char ERC
Negative To Zero	102	x	x		x			x					0, []
Scrabble Score	158	x	x		x	x	x	x					vector containing Scrabble values (indexed by ASCII values)
Word Stats	281	x	x	x	x	x	x	x	x	x	x	x	\., \?, \!, \space, \tab, \newline, [], "words of length ", ": ", "number of sentences: ", "average sentence length: ", integer ERC
Checksum	136	x	x		x	x	x				x		"Check sum is ", \space, 64, integer ERC, char ERC
Digits	133	x	x		x	x	x				x		\newline, integer ERC [-10, 10]
Grade	112	x	x		x		x				x		"Student has a ", " grade.", "A", "B", "C", "D", "F", integer ERC
Median	75	x	x		x						x		integer ERC
Smallest	76	x	x		x						x		integer ERC
Syllables	141	x	x		x	x	x				x		"The number of syllables is ", "aeiouy", \a, \e, \i, \o, \u, \y, char ERC, string ERC
Problems		28	29	5	26	11	15	7	2	2	17	1	
Instructions		28	28	31	19	17	39	31	31	31	10	4	

Table 3: Number of successful runs out of 100 for each setting, where "Tourn" is size 7 tournament selection, "IFS" is implicit fitness sharing with size 7 tournaments, and "Lex" is lexicase selection. For each problem, underline indicates significant improvement over the other two selection methods at $p < 0.05$ based on a pairwise chi-square test with Holm correction [13], or a pairwise Fisher's exact test with Holm correction if any number of successes is below 5 [12]. The "Size" column indicates the smallest size of any simplified solution program.

Problem	Tourn	IFS	Lex	Size
Number IO	68	72	<u>98</u>	5
Small Or Large	3	3	5	27
For Loop Index	0	0	1	21
Compare String Lengths	3	6	7	11
Double Letters	0	0	6	20
Collatz Numbers	0	0	0	
Replace Space with Newline	8	16	<u>51</u>	9
String Differences	0	0	0	
Even Squares	0	0	2	37
Wallis Pi	0	0	0	
String Lengths Backwards	7	10	<u>66</u>	9
Last Index of Zero	8	4	<u>21</u>	5
Vector Average	14	13	16	7
Count Odds	0	0	<u>8</u>	7
Mirror Image	46	64	<u>78</u>	4
Super Anagrams	0	0	0	
Sum of Squares	2	0	6	7
Vectors Summed	0	0	1	11
X-Word Lines	0	0	<u>8</u>	15
Pig Latin	0	0	0	
Negative To Zero	10	8	<u>45</u>	8
Scrabble Score	0	0	2	14
Word Stats	0	0	0	
Checksum	0	0	0	
Digits	0	1	7	20
Grade	0	0	4	52
Median	7	43	45	10
Smallest	75	<u>98</u>	81	8
Syllables	1	7	18	14
Problems Solved	13	13	22	

fraction of the population, and gives less reward for solving cases that are solved by more of the population. Most of the problems here produce non-binary error values, for which we use the non-binary adaptation of IFS found in [8]. As required by this method, we normalize error values to $[0, 1]$ by dividing each error by a maximum allowed error value, which differs per problem based on the fitness function.

Lexicase selection [5], unlike tournament selection and IFS, does not base selection on a single fitness value. Instead, it uses a random ordering of the training set to select individuals that perform as well as possible on a subset of the cases even if they exhibit poor performance on other cases. Lexicase selection has been shown to improve the performance of a GP system on a variety of problems [5, 3].

Table 3 gives the results of our parent selection experiment. Over the 29 problems, PushGP with lexicase selection produced at least one successful run on nine more problems than either tournament selection or IFS. Additionally, there were 8 problems where lexicase selection achieved a significantly higher number of successful runs than the other two, where IFS showed significant improvement on just one problem and tournament selection none. These results strongly indicate the utility of lexicase selection for general program synthesis problems.

The data in Table 3 only reflect solutions that generalize by achieving zero error on the unseen test set. Some problems seem to lend themselves to generalization more than others; for example, PushGP using lexicase selection found 14 programs with zero error on the training set for the Super Anagrams problem, none of which generalized to the test set. For lexicase selection, five problems resulted in 20 or more runs that passed the training set that did not generalize (Small Or Large, Compare String Lengths, Last Index of Zero, Negative To Zero, and Median), and five problems had between 10 and 20 runs that did not generalize (String Lengths Backwards, Mirror Image, Digits, Smallest, and Super Anagrams). These 10 problems show an important area for future study: how to evolve programs that generalize to unseen data for general program synthesis problems. Among these problems are the only five in the suite that give a correct/incorrect binary error as fitness in our implementation: Compare String Lengths, Mirror Image, Super Anagrams, Median, and Smallest. This shows the difficulty of evolving general programs based entirely on correctness of output, and suggests that these problems might be better tackled if they can be transformed into problems with more informative error functions.

With regards to the problems themselves, this experiment illustrates the ability of this benchmark suite to provide useful comparisons between multiple systems or parameter settings. By looking at the number of problems solved by each technique, and how often each technique showed significant improvements over the others, we can clearly see that lexicase selection increases PushGP's ability to solve general program synthesis problems compared to tournament selection and IFS. The main goal of a benchmark suite is to support this type of experiment. Additionally, some problems in the suite were solved frequently by each system, whereas others were solved infrequently or not at all. This range of difficulties permits the suite to be useful for a variety of experiments, and allows it to remain relevant as program synthesis systems improve.

Of the seven problems on which PushGP found no generalizing solution, most are not surprising in that they involve extensive use of multiple programming constructs, the linking of many distinct steps, or a deceptive fitness space where fitness improvements do not lead toward perfect programs. We have written solutions to each of the unsolved problems by hand to ensure that each problem is solvable within the constraints we put on the system and instruction set.

The last column in Table 3 gives the size (in instructions) of the smallest simplified solution program. Here, we've used post-run simplification to automatically reduce the sizes of solution programs without changing their semantics on the training data [14]. While this hill-climbing simplification is not guaranteed to find the smallest semantically equivalent program, it reliably removes excess code, leaving the core functionality of the program [14]. The simplified program sizes present a reasonable proxy for the smallest solution program for each problem (using our instruction sets). While some problems can be solved with programs containing fewer than 10 instructions, none would likely be found using brute-force search over our instruction sets within the number of program evaluations allowed here. Searching over size 5 programs using the Number IO instruction set would require evaluating over 7 billion programs, much more than the 5 million we used in our GP runs. Other problems have smallest known solutions of over 20 instructions using instruction sets with more than 100 instructions, to our knowledge beyond the reach of all other program synthesis systems.

8. CONCLUSIONS

We have presented a suite of 29 general program synthesis benchmark problems, systematically selected from sources of introductory computer science programming problems. Through exposition and experimentation, we have demonstrated the potential utility of this suite to assess the capabilities of program synthesis systems. We expect that the application of this suite can help advance multiple fields of automatic program synthesis, including genetic programming, that have long employed simple benchmark problems not attuned to potential real-world applications.

9. ACKNOWLEDGMENTS

Thanks to the members of the Hampshire College Computational Intelligence Lab, Nicholas Freitag McPhee, Yuriy Brun, and David Jensen for discussions that helped to improve the work described in this paper, to Josiah Erikson for systems support, and to Hampshire College for support for the Hampshire College Institute for Computational Intelligence. This material is based upon work supported by the National Science Foundation under Grants No. 1017817, 1129139, and 1331283. Any opinions, findings, and conclusions or recommendations expressed in this publication are those of the authors and do not necessarily reflect the views of the National Science Foundation.

10. REFERENCES

[1] Y. Brun, E. Barr, M. Xiao, C. Le Goues, and P. Devanbu. Evolution vs. intelligent design in program patching. Technical Report https://escholarship.org/uc/item/3z8926ks, UC Davis: College of Engineering, 2013.

[2] C. L. Goues, N. Holtschulte, E. K. Smith, Y. Brun, P. Devanbu, S. Forrest, and W. Weimer. The ManyBugs and IntroClass benchmarks for automated program repair. *IEEE Transactions on Software Engineering*. Under Review.

[3] T. Helmuth and L. Spector. Word count as a traditional programming benchmark problem for genetic programming. In *GECCO '14: Proceedings of the 2014 conference on Genetic and evolutionary computation*, pages 919–926, Vancouver, BC, Canada, 12-16 July 2014. ACM.

[4] T. Helmuth and L. Spector. Detailed problem descriptions for general program synthesis benchmark suite. Technical Report UM-CS-2015-006, School of Computer Science, University of Massachusetts Amherst, 2015.

[5] T. Helmuth, L. Spector, and J. Matheson. Solving uncompromising problems with lexicase selection. *IEEE Transactions on Evolutionary Computation*, 2014.

[6] M. Hofmann, E. Kitzelmann, and U. Schmid. A unifying framework for analysis and evaluation of inductive programming systems. In *Proceedings of the Second Conference on Artificial General Intelligence*, pages 55–60. Citeseer, 2009.

[7] J. R. Koza. *Genetic Programming: On the Programming of Computers by Means of Natural Selection*. MIT Press, Cambridge, MA, USA, 1992.

[8] K. Krawiec and M. Nawrocki. Implicit fitness sharing for evolutionary synthesis of license plate detectors. In *Applications of Evolutionary Computing, EvoApplications 2012*, volume 7835 of *Lecture Notes in Computer Science*, pages 376–386, Vienna, Austria, 3-5 Apr. 2013. Springer.

[9] J. McDermott, D. R. White, S. Luke, L. Manzoni, M. Castelli, L. Vanneschi, W. Jaskowski, K. Krawiec, R. Harper, K. De Jong, and U.-M. O'Reilly. Genetic programming needs better benchmarks. In *GECCO '12: Proceedings of the Genetic and evolutionary computation conference*, pages 791–798, Philadelphia, Pennsylvania, USA, 7-11 July 2012. ACM.

[10] R. I. McKay. Fitness sharing in genetic programming. In *Proceedings of the Genetic and Evolutionary Computation Conference (GECCO-2000)*, pages 435–442, Las Vegas, Nevada, USA, 10-12 July 2000. Morgan Kaufmann.

[11] R. Moll. iJava. http://ijava.cs.umass.edu/index.html, 2014. Edition 3.1. Online; accessed September 2015.

[12] M. Nakazawa. *fmsb: Functions for medical statistics book with some demographic data*, 2014. R package.

[13] R Core Team. *R: A Language and Environment for Statistical Computing*. R Foundation for Statistical Computing, Vienna, Austria, 2012. ISBN 3-900051-07-0.

[14] L. Spector and T. Helmuth. Effective simplification of evolved Push programs using a simple, stochastic hill-climber. In *GECCO Companion '14*, pages 147–148, Vancouver, BC, Canada, 12-16 July 2014. ACM.

[15] L. Spector, B. Martin, K. Harrington, and T. Helmuth. Tag-based modules in genetic programming. In *GECCO '11: Proceedings of the 13th annual conference on Genetic and evolutionary computation*, pages 1419–1426, Dublin, Ireland, 12-16 July 2011. ACM.

[16] L. Spector and A. Robinson. Genetic programming and autoconstructive evolution with the push programming language. *Genetic Programming and Evolvable Machines*, 3(1):7–40, Mar. 2002.

[17] D. R. White, J. Mcdermott, M. Castelli, L. Manzoni, B. W. Goldman, G. Kronberger, W. Jaśkowski, U.-M. O'Reilly, and S. Luke. Better GP benchmarks: community survey results and proposals. *Genetic Programming and Evolvable Machines*, 14(1):3–29, Mar. 2013.

[18] J. Woodward, S. Martin, and J. Swan. Benchmarks that matter for genetic programming. In *GECCO 2014 4th workshop on evolutionary computation for the automated design of algorithms*, pages 1397–1404, Vancouver, BC, Canada, 12-16 July 2014. ACM.

A GP-based Video Game Player

Baozhu Jia, Marc Ebner, and Christian Schack
Institut für Mathematik und Informatik, Ernst Moritz Arndt Universität Greifswald
Walther-Rathenau-Straße 47, 17487 Greifswald, Germany
baozhuj@uni-greifswald.de, marc.ebner@uni-greifswald.de,
christian.schack@uni-greifswald.de

ABSTRACT

A general video game player is an an agent that can learn to play different video games with no specific domain knowledge. We are working towards developing a GP-based general video game player. Our system currently extracts game state features from screen grabs. This information is then passed on to the game player. Fitness is computed from data obtained directly from the internals of the game simulator. For this paper, we compare three different types of game state features. These features differ in how they describe the position to the nearest object surrounding the player. We have tested our genetic programming game player system on three games: Space Invaders, Frogger and Missile Command. Our results show that a playing strategy for each game can be found efficiently for all three representations.

Keywords

Genetic Programming; General Video Game Player; Game State Features

1. INTRODUCTION

The idea of general video game playing is to create a video game player that is able to learn to play different video games without domain-specific knowledge. When encountering a new game, the game player first needs to learn where the avatar is located, what is the goal of the game and what is the current game state. Most game state information can be obtained by image processing frame grabs of the game. Using this information, the game player is able to search for a good playing strategy by playing the game several times.

Playing video games is a challenging problem even for human game players. Each video game has a certain goal. Most video games give feedback to the player via a score which describes to what extent the player has achieved the this goal. Usually, we have one or more game agents that can be manipulated by the game player. For each game, a sequence of actions has to be found that for any given game state maximises the score that will eventually be achieved.

GECCO '15, July 11 - 15, 2015, Madrid, Spain
© 2015 ACM. ISBN 978-1-4503-3472-3/15/07... $15.00
DOI: http://dx.doi.org/10.1145/2739480.2754735

Hence, video games are excellent testbed for research in artificial intelligence or machine learning approaches.

Game state is extracted from frame grabs and conveyed to the learning algorithm. For this paper, we have used genetic programming [11, 12, 2] to evolve game playing strategies. The strategies are tested on three different video games: Space Invaders, Frogger and Missile Command. These games were implemented using the Python video game description language game engine developed by Tom Schaul [13]. The games are similar to old Atari 2600 games.

Three trees are used to determine the action of the player. Each tree computes a scalar value based on the current game state. The output of the first tree determines joystick movement in the horizontal direction, the second joystick movement in the vertical direction and the third tree determines whether a button is pressed or not. We have used ECJ [14] to evolve our individuals.

Section 2 summarises previous work on general video game playing. Section 3 introduces the image processing methods and algorithm for self detection which was implemented in this work. Section 4 describes the game state feature representations and also demonstrates how the game player is evolved through genetic programming. The result are discussed in section 5. The conclusion is given in the final section.

2. PREVIOUS WORK

Artificial intelligence research has achieved great progress in developing players for certain specific games, such as chess [15], Go [6] or Pac Man [1]. These game players are dedicated to playing their respective game but cannot be used to play another game.

The relatively new research area of general game playing focuses on developing general game players that are capable of playing arbitrary games. A competition on general game playing is annually held since the AAAI 2005 conference [7]. This competition, however, focuses on turn-taking board games. For general game playing, it is difficult to design an algorithm that can cope with a variety of games. Most successful participants of the general game playing competition use Monte Carlo Tree Search as their controlling algorithms [16, 17, 5].

The general video game AI Competition has been held since 2014 [4]. This competition aims to create a controller which can learn to play a variety of video games, without previously knowing which games are to be played. In this competition, there is no need to analyse screen grabs, because all game state information is accessible via encapsulated objects. Perez et al [21] describe a knowledge-based fast evolutionary Monte Carlo tree search approach for General Video Game Playing. A new score function is provided in this paper based on score change, knowledge change and distance change.

Naddaf [20] presented two approaches to play Atari 2600 console games without having any game-specific prior knowledge. The agent must analyse the screen grab to identify the game avatar as well as game state information. He used two methods to learn the game strategy: reinforcement learning based methods and search based methods. The reinforcement learning based methods use feature vectors extracted from the game screen to learn to play a given game. The search-based methods use the emulator to simulate the consequence of actions into the future, aiming to play as well as possible by only exploring a very small fraction of the state-space. Hausknecht et al. [9, 10] presented a HyperNEAT-based general game player. In this framework, a high level of game state representation can be extracted from game screen. It is said that such a method is capable of exploiting geometric regularities which is very important in game playing.

Mnih et al. [18, 19] first try to learn the vision features and control policies at the same time. A deep learning model, called DQN which had great achievement in playing some Atari games, has been presented. The model combines convolutional neural network and Q-Learning, which takes raw pixels as input and outputs a value function estimating future rewards.

Guo et al. [8] described another method which combines deep learning (DL) and MCTS planing. They collect training data from a UCT agent, where UCT is one of MCTS methods. Using these data, three convolutional neural network (CNN) are trained. They attempt to retain the Deep Learning advantage of not needing hand-crafted features and the online real-time play ability of the model-free Reinforcement Learning(RL) agents. They evaluated their model on seven Atari games and found that their model outperforms previous DQN models.

3. IMAGE PROCESSING AND SELF DETECTION

Before we are able to play a game, we need to acquire some knowledge about the game, i.e. Who am I? Where am I? What is the current game state and what is the game about? We only use screen grabs to find answers to these questions.

3.1 Visual Processing

Each game has several classes of objects. These objects may belong to the game agent, a goal position, enemies or food and so on. We need to locate these objects and determine the relationship between them. The objects can be identified using distinguishing features. The objects of the games used in this paper can be identified easily by their colour. Each object has a unique colour. Hence, we first compute a colour histogram. To do this, the image, originally an RGB image, is converted to a gray scale image by mapping each hue to a particular gray scale. This allows us to detect objects rapidly. A histogram is computed from the gray scale image (shown in Figure 1 for the game Frogger). From the histogram it is clear that there are six

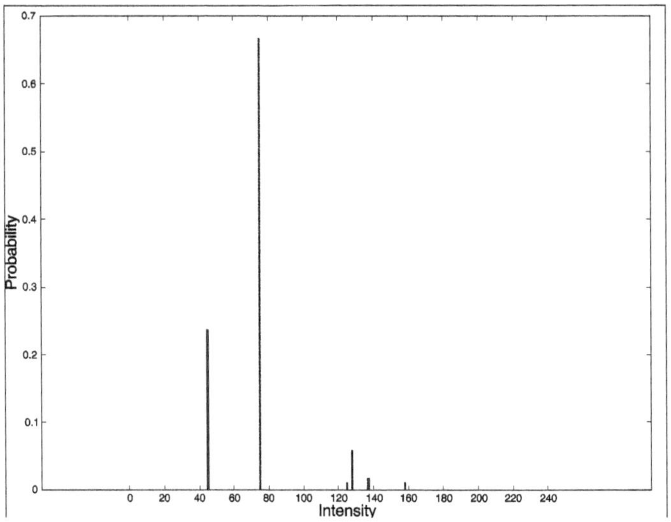

Figure 1: Histogram for Frogger.

object classes. Each peak in this histogram corresponds to one object class.

If each object is basically a blob of a unique colour, then its position can be determined easily by applying blur and then extracting local maxima. This would also work for games with more complex graphics by applying a convolution with a filter having the same graphics as the object to be extracted. To reduce the computation complexity, we first down sample the gray image using a blur filter to 1/16th of its original size. Next we apply a non-local maximum suppression filter on the down-sampled image. Each object in the game is then represented by one point. The position of these points are saved in a **feature list**. The list of features is used to detect the game agent and to acquire game state information. This will be explained in detail in the following sections. Figure 2 illustrates the image processing pipeline.

3.2 Avatar Identification

Avatar identification is another key task that has to be solved before the game can be played. We modify Hausknecht et al.'s method [9] to identify the avatar. The avatar is the entity, whose movement is affected most by actions of the game player. The movement of an object is represented by its velocity in the x direction v_x and its velocity in the y direction v_y. Two array lists are used to calculate the velocities of the objects. One array list List_c is used to record the position and the colour of feature points from the current frame. The second list List_p is used to record the position and the colour of feature points from the previous frame. For each element $a \in \text{List}_p$, we search List_c for objects which are located in a small neighbourhood around a to find the nearest object b which belongs to the same class as a. This object is assumed to be the same object as a. The difference between these two positions of objects b and a is the velocity (v_x, v_y) of object a. The velocity vector is mapped to a one-dimensional velocity with the range [-24, 24], as shown in Equation 1, where mod(x, y) is the modulo operation.

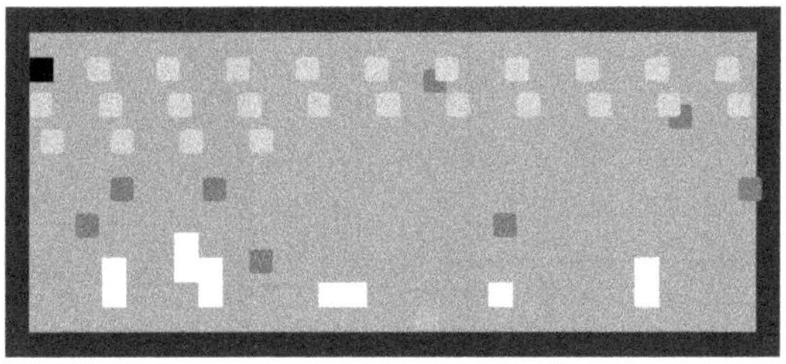

(a) RGB image

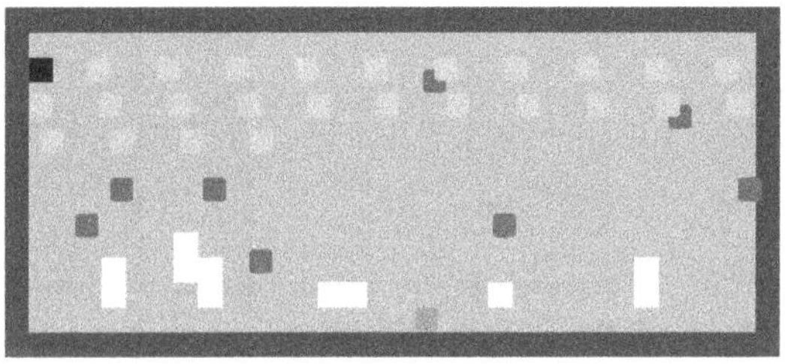

(b) Gray image

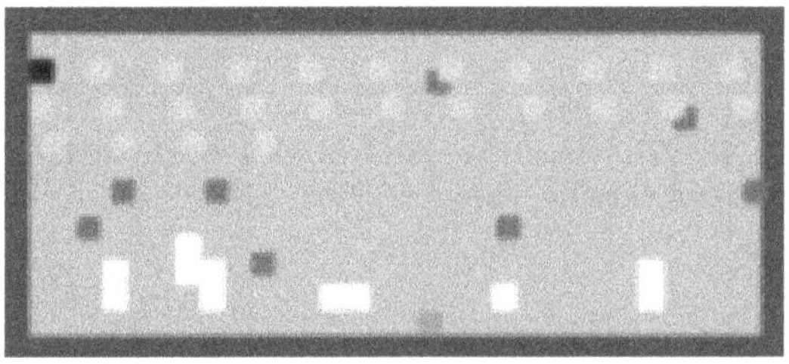

(c) Downsampled image

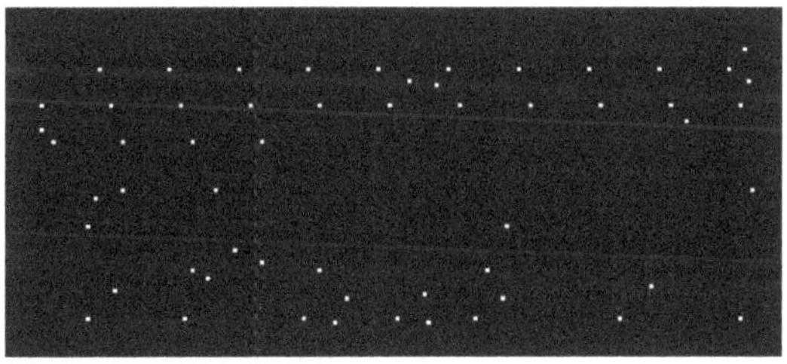

(d) Feature points

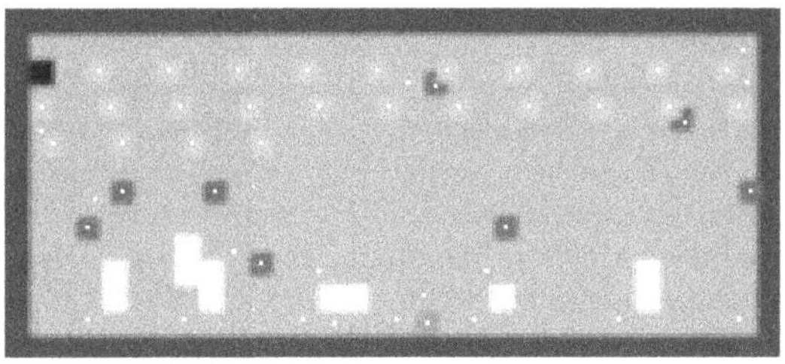

(e) Objects

Figure 2: Image processing for Space Invaders. (a) input RGB image. (b) gray scale image. (c) downsampled image. (d) feature points after using nonlocal maximum suppression. (e) feature points overlaid on RGB image.

Terminal Symbol	Description
X_i	x coordinate of the nearest object for class i relative to avatar
Y_i	y coordinate of the nearest object for class i relative to avatar
D_i	Euclidean distance between avatar and the nearest object for class i
A_i	Angle between vector pointing from self to the nearest object and the horizontal axis.

Table 1: Terminal symbols

Because we want to get an integer velocity here.

$$v = mod(max(min(v_x, 19), -19), 5) + mod(max(min(v_y, 19), -19), 5) * 7 \quad (1)$$

Naturally, there may be situations where the nearest object is actually some other object of the same class. In these cases, the velocity computation fails.

Hausknecht [9] proposed a method to identify the avatar using information gain which is the difference between one object's velocity entropy and the weighted sum of its selective entropy. Entropy is calculated using the formulation: $H(V) = \sum_{i=1}^{n} p(v_i) * ln(p(v_i))$. It uses the entire velocity history. Selective entropy is the entropy calculated by only implementing the velocities corresponding to one fixed action. The avatar's motion is affected by the actions of the game player. Hence, it should have the largest information gain. But it fails in some games in our work, because one object's information gain may be even larger than avatar's entropy. Then this object will be mistaken as avatar. A normalised information gain is used in our work, which is calculated using formulation:

$$I_r = I/H(o) \quad (2)$$

I is the information gain and H(o) is the entropy. There is an assumption that the movement of avatar is fixed when the same actions are taken. If the games do not obey this rule, this algorithm fails.

3.3 Game State Features

A game player needs to know what the current game state is before making a decision. A game player will be able to make a better decision the more information is known about the game. It would be ideal if our game agent had access to the position of all objects. If we would provide our game agent with the position of all objects, it would probably take a long time for the game agent to learn what objects are most useful in making the next step. We use a quite simplistic approach. We only provide information about the nearest object of each class to the game agent. The nearest object may be most dangerous to avatar if it is an enemy. It can also be the food the avatar is searching for.

The nearest object is the object which has the smallest Euclidean distance to the avatar. This feature is easy to compute and quite useful.

In this work, we present three representations for the game state to find solutions to each of these three games: Space Invaders, Frogger and Missile Command. They differ in the

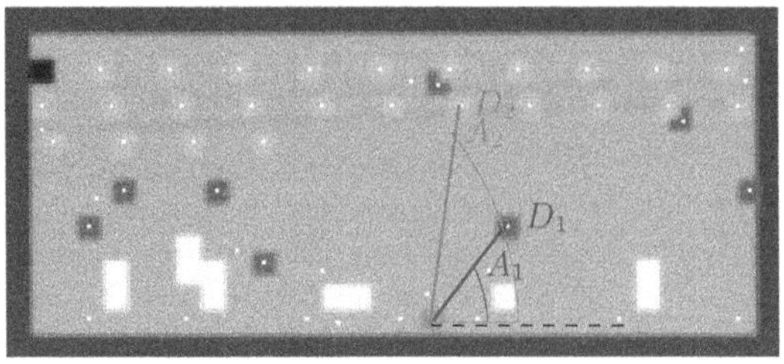

Figure 3: Computation of the angle and the Euclidean distance to the nearest object.

Function	Description
Add(arg1, arg2)	return arg1+arg2
Subtract(arg1,arg2)	return arg1-arg2
Divide(arg1,arg2)	return arg1/arg2 if arg2 != 0, otherwise return 100000
Multiply(arg1, arg2)	return arg1*arg2
Negate(arg1)	return -arg1
Sqrt(arg1)	return $\sqrt{arg1}$
Square(arg1)	return $arg1 * arg1$

Table 2: Set of elementary functions.

way how to represent the nearest object. The terminal symbols are shown in Table 1, where each terminal symbol is used for each $i \in \{1, ..., n\}$ where n is the number of different object classes. Representation A uses only terminal symbols X_i, Y_i, D_i. Representation B uses terminal symbols X_i, Y_i, D_i, A_i. Representation C uses only terminal symbols D_i, A_i. How the angle and the Euclidean distance to the nearest object is computed is shown in Figure 3 for a sample scene. The first representation is used to explore the importance of Cartesian coordinates. The third representation is used to explore the importance of Polar coordinates.

4. EVOLVING A GAME PLAYER USING GENETIC PROGRAMMING

We have used Sean Luke's ECJ System [14] to evolve our game agents. A modified version of Tom Schaul's py-vdgl game engine [13] was used to play the games. Both programs, the ECJ system which constructs the genetic programming individuals which need to be evaluated and the game engine are maintained as separate programs. They communicate with each other through the TCP/IP protocol. In each game step, ECJ system receives the game state feature vector from game engine, and then sends the calculated action back to it. The image processing program is carried out directly in the game engine.

The elementary functions that we use are shown in Table 2. This set consists of basic arithmetic functions. The terminal symbol which we have used for our representation have already been shown in Table 1.

Each individual consists of three trees. Figure 5 illustrates one example for the structure of each tree. The value of the first tree T_1 determines avatar's movement in the horizontal direction (left, right or no action). The value of the second tree T_2 determines the avatar's movement in vertical direction (up, down or no action). The value of the third

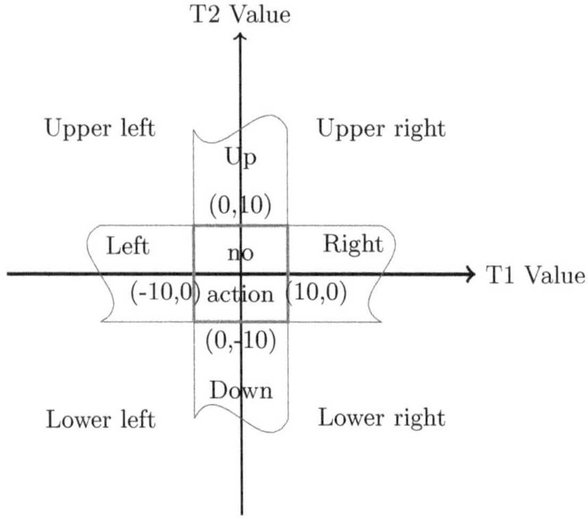

Figure 4: The moving direction of avatar depending on the value of Tree 1 and Tree 2.

Value of Tree 3	Actions
[0 , ∞)	Press_button
(-∞, 0)	No_action

Table 3: Whether the button will be pressed down depending on the value of Tree 3.

tree T_3 determines whether the button should be pressed or not. Figure 4 illustrates what motion will be chosen for the avatar depending on the values of the trees T_1 and T_2. Table 3 shows when the button will be pressed down depending on the value of T_3. One of a total of 18 different actions will be chosen depending on the value of these three trees.

5. EXPERIMENTS AND RESULTS

The parameters which we have used for our experiments are shown in Table 4. We have used a population of 200 individuals. Tournament selection is used to select individuals with a tournament size of 3. Evolution is carried out for 100 generations. As genetic operators we use crossover, mutation and reproduction. The probabilities with which these operators are applied are also shown in Table 4. Ephemeral random constants are mutated by adding a random value with a Gaussian distribution. The mutation operator tries to generate a subtree maximally twice before giving up if the mutated tree is not within the depth limit of 10. ECJ's halfBuilder is used to create individuals of the first generation.

In order to reduce noise, we evaluate each individual on several different game levels of a game. The levels differ in avatar's initial position and random seed which affects the behaviour of game sprites. The sum the game scores is used as the fitness of the individual.

Whenever an individual is evaluated, a new game is started. For each game step, the feature vector (with the terminal symbols as described above), is handed to the individual. The values for the three trees of this individual are calculated and then passed back to the game engine.

Parameter	Value
population size	200
tournament size	3
crossover probability	0.4
reproduction probability	0.4
mutation probability	0.1
ERC mutation probability	0.1
mutate.tries	2
builder	HalfBuilder

Table 4: Parameters for genetic programming.

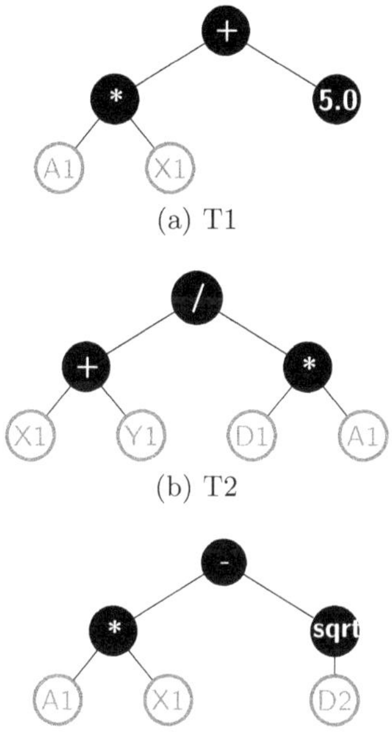

Figure 5: One example of the tree structure.

We use three different games to evaluate the representations: Space Invaders, Frogger and Missile Command. Space invaders is a classic arcade game. The goal is to protect the earth from the aliens coming in from above. The player has to shoot at the aliens with missiles. The player also needs to avoid bombs from aliens. Frogger is a game where a frog has to cross several roads to reach its home. The frog needs to move from the bottom of the screen to the goal position which is located at the top of screen. While finishing this task, the frog needs to be careful with cars on the roads. The agent will get some bonus when it moves up one step or reaches its home. Missile Command is a game where the player's cities are attacked by ballistic bombs. The player should intercept these bombs using missiles. The missile's moving direction is consistent with avatar's moving direction. These three games as implemented in Py-vdgl are illustrated in Figure 6.

For each representation, we carry out 10 runs with different random seeds. It usually takes 5 seconds to play a single game. In order to evaluate one individual, we need to play this game three times, as described above. It takes approximately two days to complete a run of 100 generations. Hence, we only carry out 10 runs for each representation.

The fitness of the best individual for every generation in each run and the average fitness over 10 runs are shown in Figure 7. As the figure shows, the fitness improves considerably after 100 generations. In over 90% of the runs for both representation A and B genetic programming is able to find a perfect strategy for all three games. Table 5 shows the average best fitness and standard deviation after 100 generations for each game. The results show that both representation A as well as representation B work well in finding a program which will play the respective game.

We use the Mann-Whitney U-test to compare the three game state representations. Both Repres.A and B perform significantly better than Repres.C ($p < 0.01$).

We also compare our method with three Monte Carlo tree search methods: Vanila MCTS, Fast-Evo MCTS, KB Fast-Evo MCTS [21], as shown in Table 5. These three methods all the game state from the emulator. Vanila MCTS is a normal Monte Carlo tree search method that estimates the average reward by iteratively sampling the actions and building a search tree. The game agent will take the action that is visited most often or provides the highest average reward. Fast-Evo MCTS embedded the roll-outs within evolution, dynamically adapting to the game features. KB Fast-Evo MCTS used both knowledge base and evolution to bias the roll-outs. For more details about these three algorithms, the reader is referred to [21]. Their results show that MCTS method outperforms previous approaches.

For Space Invaders, our genetic programming players perform slightly worse than MCTS and Fast-Evo MCTS. But for Frogger and Missile Command, our genetic programming players show a much better performance than the three MCTS-related methods. The latter three algorithms need game domain information. The game state information are obtained from the game simulator rather than from the screen grabs as presented in this paper. They also need to advance the game state [3] before making a decision. But for our method, once the same game is encountered again, the evolved playing strategy can be used directly.

In this paper, we only test our algorithm on three games because of the limitation of evolving time. In the future plan, we will add more games into our work.

6. CONCLUSION

In this paper, we present three simple representations for the game state. The results show that both Repres.A and B work better than Repres.C for these three games. But we lack evidence that the same results among these three representations will be obtained for other games. Genetic programming is used as the learning algorithm in our work. GP players achieved better performance than MCTS methods in finding the playing strategy for Frogger and Missile Command. The genetic programming method represents a first step towards a general video game player.

7. REFERENCES

[1] A.M.Alhejali and S. M. Lucas. Evolving diverse ms. pac-man playing agents using genetic programming. In *Workshop on Computer Intelligence*, pages 1–6, 2010.

[2] W Banzhaf, P Nordin, RE Keller, and FD Francone. *Genetic Programming - An Introduction: On the*

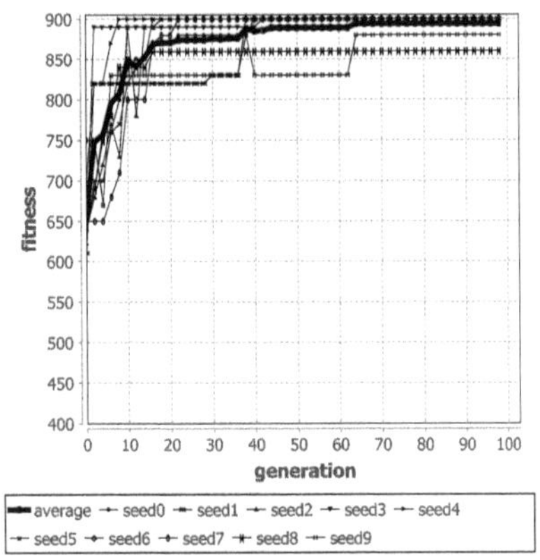

(a) Fitness of Space Invaders implementing Representation A

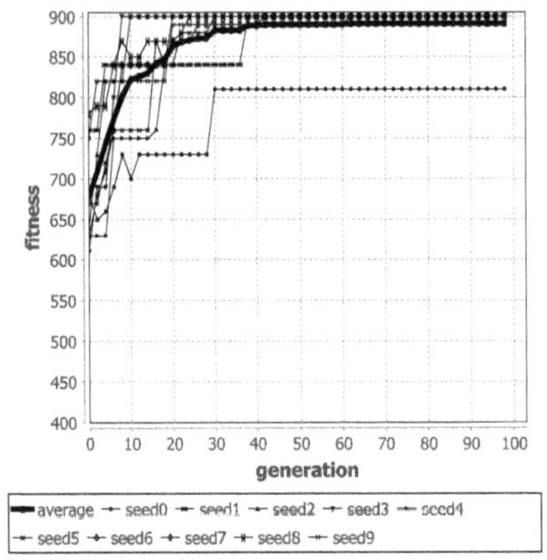

(b) Fitness of Space Invaders implementing Representation B

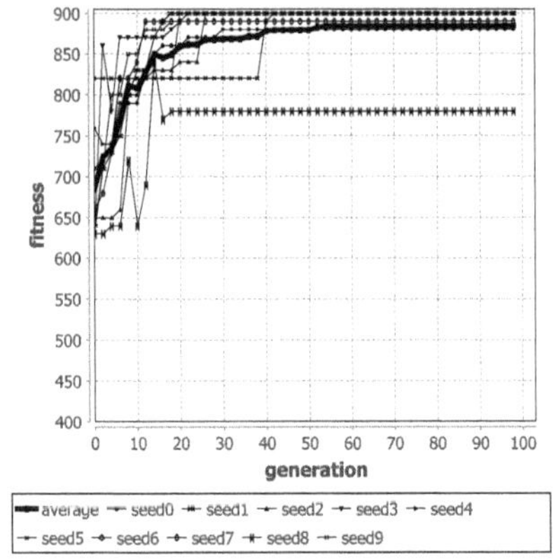

(c) Fitness of Space Invaders implementing Representation C

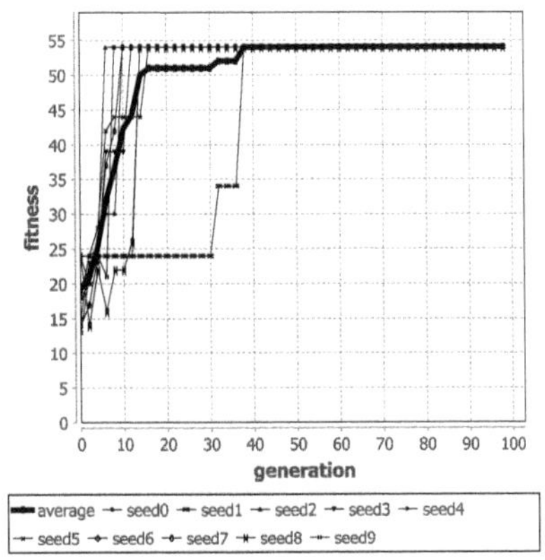

(d) Fitness of Frogger implementing Representation A

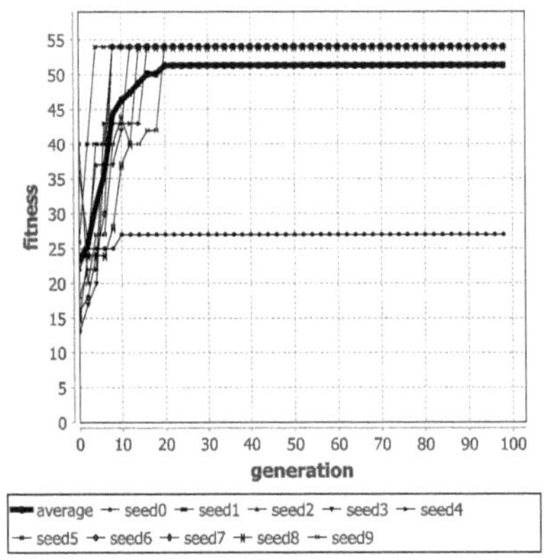

(e) Fitness of Frogger implementing Representation B

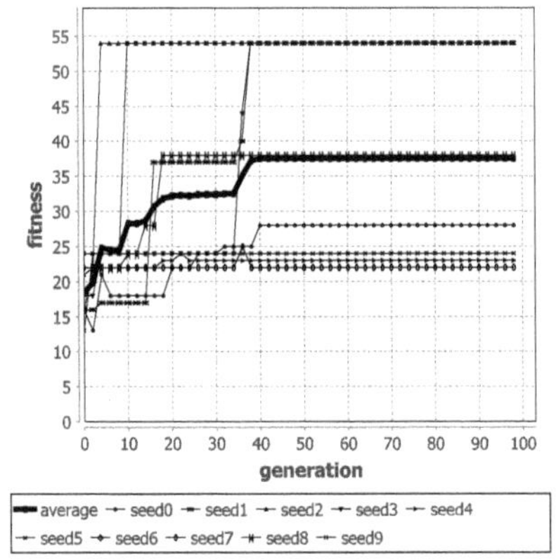

(f) Fitness of Frogger implementing Representation C

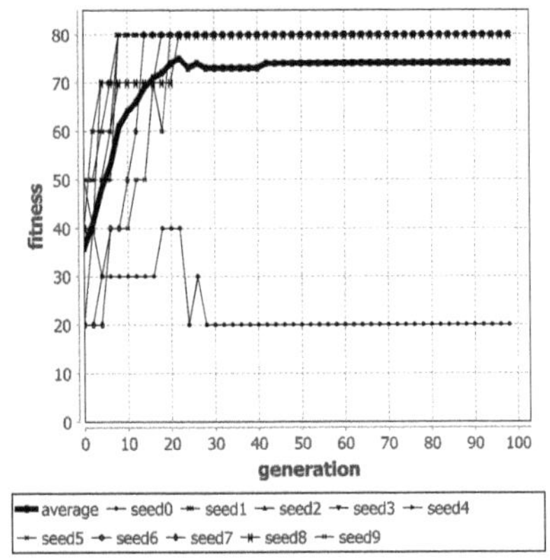

(g) Fitness of Missile Command implementing Representation A

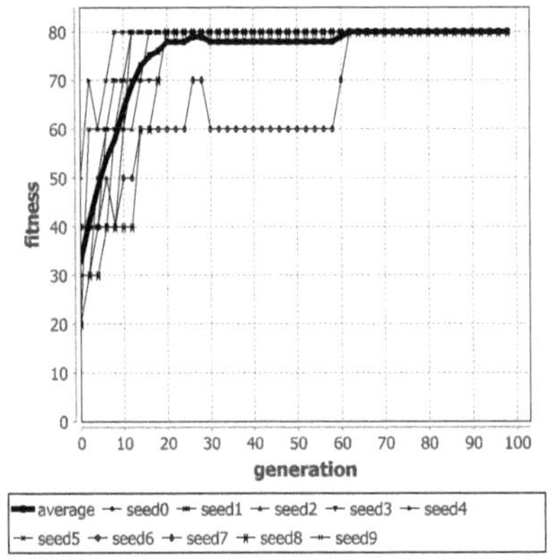

(h) Fitness of Missile Command implementing Representation B

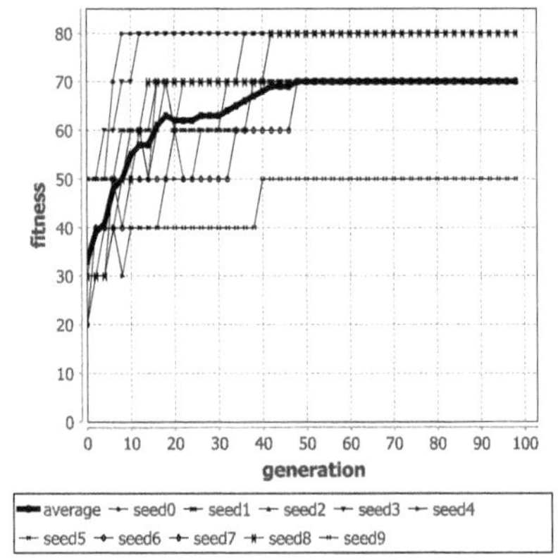

(i) Fitness of Missile Command implementing Representation C

Figure 7: Fitness of the best individual over 10 different runs for each game. The average fitness for each game is shown in the bold line.

	Average Score					
Game	GP+Repr.A	GP+Repr.B	GP+Repr.C	Vanila MCTS	Fast-Evo MCTS	KB Fast-Evo MCTS
Space Invaders	894 ±13.50	891±28.46	884±7.18	900 ±0	900 ±0	858±132.82
Frogger	54 ± 0	51.3±8.53	38.4±14.23	24.2±4.7563	25±3.16	37±10.59
Missile Command	77 ± 9.50	80 ±0	70 ±11.574	39±8.756	47.27±11.9	59±3.17

Table 5: Average scores over 10 runs obtained from the games: Space Invaders, Frogger, Missile Command. The maximum possible scores, Space Invaders:900, Frogger:54 and Missile Command:80.

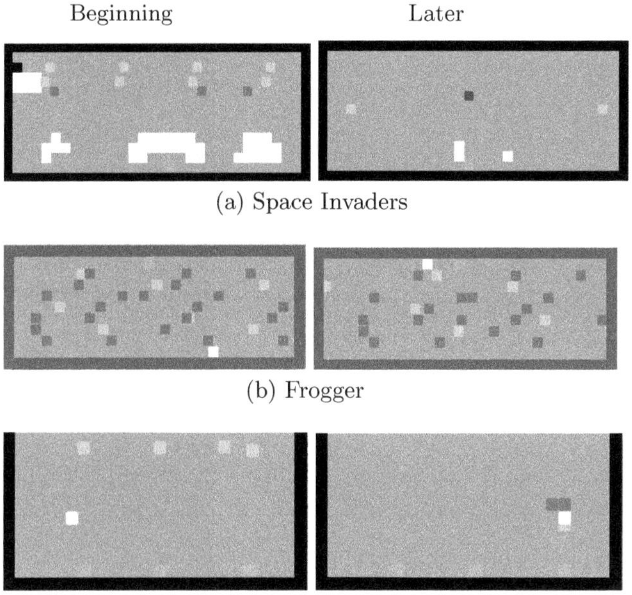

(a) Space Invaders

(b) Frogger

(c) Missile Command

Figure 6: For each py-vgdl game, two snapshots are shown. One from the beginning of the game and one well into the game.

Automatic Evolution of Computer Programs and Its Applications. dpunkt-Verlag and Morgan Kaufmann, 1998.

[3] E. Browne, C.B. andPowley, D. Whitehouse, S.M. Lucas, P.I. Cowling, P. Rohlfshagen, S. Tavener, D. Perez, S. Samothrakis, and S. Colton. A survey of monte carlo tree search methods. *IEEE Transactions on Computational Intelligence and AI in Games*, 4(2):1–43, 2012.

[4] D.Perez, S. Samothrakis, J. Togelius, T. Schaul, and S. Lucas. Gvg-ai competition. http://www.gvgai.net/index.php.

[5] H. Finnsson and Y. Bjornsson. Simulation-based approach to general game playing. In *Proceedings of the Twenty-Third AAAI Conference on Artificial Intelligence*, pages 259–264, 2008.

[6] S. Gelly and D.Silver. Monte carlo tree search and rapid action value estimation in computer go. *Artificial Intelligence*, 175:1856–1875, July 2011.

[7] M. Geneserech and N. Love. General game playing: Overview of the aaai competition. *AI Magazine*, 26:62–72, 2005.

[8] X. Guo, S. Singh, H. Lee, R. Lewis, and X. Wang. Deep learning for real-time atari game play using offline monte-carlo tree search planning. In *Advances in Neural Information Processing Systems 27*. 2014.

[9] M. Hausknecht, P. Khandelwal, R.Miikkulainen, and P. Stone. Hyperneat-ggp: A hyperneat-based atari general game player. In *Proceedings of Genetic and Evolutionary Computation Conference*, 2012.

[10] M. Hausknecht, J. Lehman, R. Miikkulainen, and P. Stone. A neuroevolution approach to general atrai game playing. *IEEE Transactions on Computational Intelligence and AI in Games*, 6:355–366, 2013.

[11] J. R. Koza. *Genetic Programming: On the Programming of Computers by Means of Natural Selection*. The MIT Press, 1992.

[12] J. R. Koza. *Genetic Programming II: Automatic Discovery of Reusable Programs*. The MIT Press, 1994.

[13] J. Levine, C. Bates Congdon, M. Ebner, G. Kendall, S. Lucas, R. Miikkulainen, T Schaul, and T. Thompson. General video game playing. In *Dagstuhl Follow-Ups*, volume 6, pages 77–83, 2013.

[14] Luke. *The ECJ Owner's Manual*, 22 edition, 2014.

[15] M.Campbell, A.Joseph Hoane Jr., and Feng-Hsiung Hsu. Deep blue. *Artificial Intelligence*, 134:57–83, 2002.

[16] J. Mehat and T. Cazenave. Monte-carlo tree search for general game playing. Technical report, LIASD, Dept. Informatique, Université Paris 8, 2008.

[17] J. Mehat and T. Cazenave. Combining uct and nested monte-carlo search for single-player general game playing. *IEEE Transactions on Computational Intelligence and AI in Games*, 2(4):225–228, 2010.

[18] V. Mnih, K. Kavukcuoglu, D. Silver, A. Graves, I. Antonoglou, D. Wierstra, and M.Riedmiller. Playing with deep reinforcement learning. In *Neural Information Processing Systems Workshop*, 2013.

[19] V. Mnih, K. Kavukcuoglu, D. Silver, A. Rusu, J. Veness, M. Bellemare, A. Graves, M. Riedmiller, A. Fidieland, G. Ostrovski, S. Petersen, C. Beattie, A. Sadik, I. Antonoglou, H. King, and D. Kumaran. Human-level control through deep reinforcement learning. *Nature*, 518:529–533, 2015.

[20] Y. Naddaf. Game-independent ai agents for playing atari 2600 console games. Master's thesis, University of Alberta, 2010.

[21] D. Perez, S. Samothrakis, and S. Lucas. Knowledge-based fast evolutionary mcts for general video game playing. In *Proceedings of IEEE Conference on Computational Intelligence and Games*, 2014.

Genetic Programming with Epigenetic Local Search

William La Cava*
Department of Mechanical and Industrial Engineering
University of Massachusetts
Amherst, MA 01003
wlacava@umass.edu

Thomas Helmuth
Department of Computer Science
University of Massachusetts
Amherst, MA 01003
thelmuth@umass.edu

Lee Spector
School of Cognitive Science
Hampshire College
Amherst, MA 01002
lspector@hampshire.edu

Kourosh Danai
Department of Mechanical and Industrial Engineering
University of Massachusetts
Amherst, MA 01003
danai@ecs.umass.edu

ABSTRACT

We focus on improving genetic programming through local search of the space of program structures using an inheritable epigenetic layer that specifies active and inactive genes. We explore several genetic programming implementations that represent the different properties that epigenetics can provide, such as passive structure, phenotypic plasticity, and inheritable gene regulation. We apply these implementations to several symbolic regression and program synthesis problems. For the symbolic regression problems, the results indicate that epigenetic local search consistently improves genetic programming by producing smaller solution programs with better fitness. Furthermore, we find that incorporating epigenetic modification as a mutation step in program synthesis problems can improve the ability of genetic programming to find exact solutions. By analyzing population homology we show that the epigenetic implementations maintain diversity in silenced portions of programs which may provide protection from premature convergence.

Categories and Subject Descriptors

I.2.2 [**Artificial Intelligence**]: Automatic Programming—*Program synthesis*; J.2 [**Computer Applications**]: Physical Science and Engineering—*Engineering*

Keywords

genetic programming; epigenetics; regression; program synthesis

*corresponding author

GECCO '15, July 11 - 15, 2015, Madrid, Spain

ISBN 978-1-4503-3472-3/15/07... $15.00
DOI: http://dx.doi.org/10.1145/2739480.2754763

1. INTRODUCTION

In genetic programming (GP), the role of epigenetics, that is, regulation of gene expression, is traditionally ignored (with some exceptions, e.g. [7]), despite the fact that the expression of biological genes is highly regulated. It has recently become clear that epigenetic processes can provide several evolutionary benefits. For example, they allow the underlying genotype to encode various expressions and allow neutral variation through crossover and mutation of noncoding segments. This neutrality may allow populations to avoid evolutionary bottlenecks or allow them to respond to changing evolutionary pressures [14]. In addition, they provide for phenotypic plasticity, i.e. the ability of gene expression to change in response to environmental pressure [5]. Furthermore, epigenetics allow adaptations to gene expression to be inherited in offspring without explicit changes to the genotype. Indeed, it is now accepted that the previously discredited ideas of Lamarck, i.e. the inheritability of lifetime adaptations, are possible through epigenetic processes [14, 12]. Hence epigenetic processes may provide evolutionary benefits by performing "local search" for survival. We investigate that hypothesis by designing an epigenetics-enabled GP system to perform experiments for analysis.

Local search methods have been developed and integrated into evolutionary algorithms [10, 35, 23, 9], especially in genetic algorithms (GAs), through prescribed changes to the genotype. In GP, especially within the field of symbolic regression, the role of structure optimization is typically left to the GP process while local search is constrained to constant optimization via stochastic hill-climbing [3], linear [13] or non-linear regression [30]. While this often improves symbolic regression performance, the methods are inherently limited to problem domains that require constant optimization and cannot be readily applied to other problems like software synthesis, nor can they improve program topology. Other more generic local search methods like tree snipping [3] focus on improving secondary metrics like size or legibility. In these cases the local search is conducted at the genome level.

Our study of the application of epigenetics to GP is motivated by two main hypotheses: first, that generalized local search methods can improve the performance of GP across problem domains; and second, that the benefits of epigenetic regulation observed in biology may confer analogous improvements on GP systems. Thus, we propose a new method for conducting topological optimization of genetic programs at level of gene expression via epigenetic local search. The contributions of this method are twofold: first, it introduces a generic method of topological search of the space of individual genotypes via modifications to gene expression. Second, unlike previous methods that focused on whether lifetime adaptations should be inheritable (the Lamarckian view) or only affect fitness (the Baldwinian view), epigenetic local search improves genetic programs without affecting the genotype *and* without discarding the acquired knowledge gained through the process. It does this by conducting local search on the epigenome rather than the genome and making these adaptations inheritable via evolutionary processes.

We begin by describing the method and its use in two stack-based GP environments. We then perform an experimental analysis of different epigenetic implementations on regression and program synthesis benchmarks. Finally we analyze population diversity to study how gene expression evolves for each implementation.

2. EPIGENETIC LINEAR GENETIC PROGRAMMING (ELGP)

We introduce epigenetic information into the GP representation by including an on/off condition on each element in an individual's genotype. Programs are encoded as postfix notation, linear genotypes with a corresponding set of on/off values, referred to as an epigenome. When evaluated together, the expressed program, i.e. phenotype, is produced by executing instructions that are on (active) and ignoring the instructions that are off (inactive). We refer to this general approach as epigenetic linear genetic programming (ELGP).

2.1 GP Representation

In order to accommodate the introduction of epigenetics, two stack-based GP systems are used. For the symbolic regression problems, a GP system known as ellenGP[1] is used. For the program synthesis problems, we implement an epigenetic extension to PushGP [28]. The stack-based GP systems used in our research are advantageous because the representation guarantees syntactic validity for arbitrary sequences of instructions. This allows instructions to be silenced or activated in a genotype without invalidating the program's ability to execute. This "syntax-free" property stands in contrast to tree-based representations that can become syntactically invalid due to changes to instructions and literals.

The syntactic robustness of the stack-based approach is achieved mainly by ignoring the execution of instructions that have an arity larger than the current size of the stack. For example, if a + operator attempts to execute and there is only one element on the stack, it instead does nothing. Furthermore, we base a program's behavior only on the top element(s) of the stack after execution which allows programs to contain unused arguments. The flexibility of this representation means that the genotypes of the following three programs $\mathbf{i_1}$, $\mathbf{i_2}$ and $\mathbf{i_3}$ all produce the identical phenotype $(x+y)$:

$$\begin{aligned} \mathbf{i_1} &= [\ x \quad y \quad +\ ] \Rightarrow (x+y) \\ \mathbf{i_2} &= [\ x \quad y \quad + \quad - \quad * \quad /\ ] \Rightarrow (x+y) \\ \mathbf{i_3} &= [\ z \quad + \quad x \quad / \quad x \quad y \quad +\ ] \Rightarrow (x+y) \end{aligned} \quad (1)$$

The executions of $-$, $*$ and $/$ in $\mathbf{i_2}$ are ignored due to insufficient stack size; in $\mathbf{i_3}$, the last element of the executed stack, $(x+y)$, is taken as the phenotype.

2.2 Epigenetic Learning and Evolution

The addition of epigenetic information makes it possible to alter the topology of and values expressed in the phenotype. For example, program $\mathbf{i_3}$ admits several phenotypes via epigenetic transformations, including,

$$\mathbf{i_3} \rightarrow \mathbf{i_3'} = \begin{bmatrix} 1 & 1 & 0 & 0 & 0 & 1 & 1 \\ z & + & x & / & x & y & + \end{bmatrix} \Rightarrow (z+y)$$

$$\mathbf{i_3} \rightarrow \mathbf{i_3''} = \begin{bmatrix} 1 & 1 & 1 & 1 & 0 & 0 & 0 \\ z & + & x & / & x & y & + \end{bmatrix} \Rightarrow (z/x)$$

$$\mathbf{i_3} \rightarrow \mathbf{i_3'''} = \begin{bmatrix} 1 & 0 & 1 & 1 & 0 & 1 & 1 \\ z & + & x & / & x & y & + \end{bmatrix} \Rightarrow (z/x+y)$$

Similarly, program $\mathbf{i_2}$ in Eq. 1 admits the phenotypes $(x+y)$, $(x-y)$, $(x*y)$, and (x/y) via epigenetic transformations. Thus the epigenetic layer introduces flexibility to the expression of a genotype by treating introns (i.e. unexpressed genes) as partial solutions to explore locally in the search space.

The components of ELGP are shown in Figure 1. The epigenetic markers are initialized randomly with a probability of being active (50% for the experimental studies in Section 4). The extent to which epigenetic information is learned and inherited is a research question we study by exploring different implementations. The simplest topological search method, **Ep1M**, mutates the epigenetic layer of each individual each generation; the hill climber in Figure 1 is skipped. Thus for **Ep1M**, epigenetic mutations face only evolutionary pressures. In contrast, the epigenetic hill climbing (EHC) cases **EHC1** and **EHC5** use the epigenetic information explicitly to improve individuals each generation (the EHC is described in Section 2.2.2). The two methods execute one and five iterations of EHC each generation, respectively. Two control methods, **Baseline** and **Ep0**, are used as comparison. In the **Baseline** case, individuals are represented as basic genotypes as in Eq. 1. The **Ep0** case acts like **Baseline** but with half of the genes in initial code permanently silenced. As such **Ep0** controls for the effect that passive introns might have. Neither **Baseline** or **Ep0** use the right half of the system in Figure 1 (i.e. the program never enters epigenetic mutation).

2.2.1 Epigenetic Mutation

Whitley et al. [35] introduced Lamarckian updating to GAs by conducting local search of the bit strings within 1 Hamming distance of the current bit string. In theory it would be possible to treat the epigenome as a bit string and proceed similarly. However the cost of GP fitness evaluations render this approach intractable. Instead, each generation, the epigenome is uniformly mutated with a probability of 10% at each gene. The mutation flips the binary value of the epigenome at the gene, thus activating or silencing that gene. The operation is uniform with respect to the number

[1] http://www.github.com/lacava/ellen

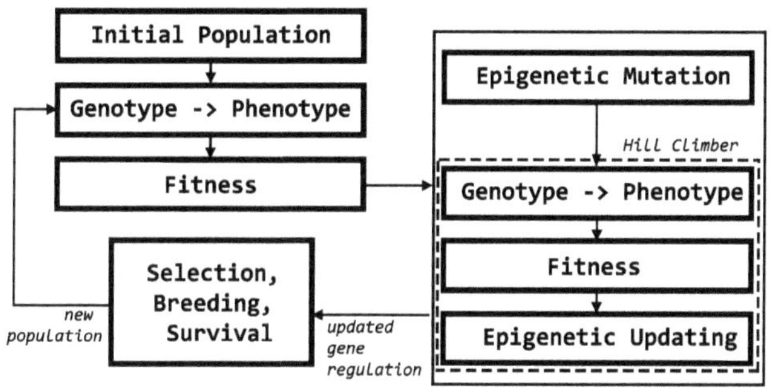

Figure 1: Block diagram of ELGP. After fitness evaluation and before selection, the population undergoes an iteration of epigenetic mutation, represented by the block on the right. For EHC1 and EHC5, the hill climbing step is then conducted.

of instructions. For the **EHC1** and **EHC5** implementations, the epigenetic mutation is followed by hill climbing, described next.

2.2.2 *Epigenetic Hill Climbing*

In order to mimic the acquisition of lifetime learning by epigenetic adaptation, the EHC implementations evaluate epigenetic changes $\mathbf{i} \rightarrow \mathbf{i}'$ to determine whether individuals should be updated. **EHC1** and **EHC5** undergo one and five iterations of epigenetic mutation, and at each iteration the epigenetic changes are tested for acceptance.

For the program synthesis problems, epigenetic changes to an individual are kept only if the fitness is improved or does not change, i.e. $f_{\mathbf{i}'} \leq f_{\mathbf{i}}$ (fitness f is being minimized). For the symbolic regression problems, we exploit the epigenetic layer's potential to reduce equation nonlinearity in order to break fitness ties. The complexity $C_{\mathbf{i}}$ of program $\mathbf{i}$ with active genotype $\mathbf{g_a} = [\ g_{a_1} \ \dots \ g_{a_\ell}\ ]$ is defined as $C_{\mathbf{i}} = \sum_{q=1}^{\ell} c(g_{a_q})$, where component function nonlinearities [26] are defined as

$$c(g_a) = \begin{cases} 4 & : \quad (g_a = \log) \vee (g_a = \exp) \\ 3 & : \quad (g_a = \sin) \vee (g_a = \cos) \\ 2 & : \quad (g_a = /) \\ 1 & : \quad \text{otherwise} \end{cases}$$

Lower-complexity programs with equivalent fitness are accepted, giving the condition

$$pass = (f_{\mathbf{i}'} < f_{\mathbf{i}}) \vee ((f_{\mathbf{i}'} = f_{\mathbf{i}}) \wedge (C_{\mathbf{i}'} < C_{\mathbf{i}})) \qquad (2)$$

If the epigenetically mutated individual $\mathbf{i}'$ does not pass Eq. 2, the changes are discarded and $\mathbf{i}$ is kept in the population. Otherwise $\mathbf{i}$ is replaced with $\mathbf{i}'$.

2.2.3 *Epigenetic Inheritance*

A key feature of ELGP is the inheritance of epigenetic values throughout the evolutionary process. During crossover the epigenetic values of the parent genes are kept intact such that the child receives the epigenetic states of the genes it has inherited. If a new gene is introduced via genetic mutation, that gene has the same probability of being active as the initial genes of the population (50% here).

3. RELATED WORK

There has been some work to incorporate epigenetic learning into GP, notably by Tanev [29]. In this case the focus was to model histone modification through a double cell representation and use it to solve a predator-prey problem. Unlike our approach, Tanev did not treat lifetime epigenetic modifications as inheritable, despite recent studies that support this idea in biology [31, 15, 6].

There have been a number of studies on the effects of non-coding segments in GP, some of which have found that the structural presence of introns can protect genotypes from destructive crossover operations (i.e. operations that produce children less fit than their parents) [21, 4]. Non-coding segments were found to be useful in evo-devo for evolution of arbitrary shapes as well [8]. In each of these studies, introns were either declared explicitly or measured during evolution, rather than actively manipulated by the system itself. Our preliminary study of epigenetic initialization found rates of beneficial crossover to be highest with the probability set to 50% [18].

Several GP systems use similar stack-based or linear genome representations such as Push-forth [17] and Gene Expression Programming [7] that could trivially implement the epigenetic layer suggested in this paper. In addition, there are methods that leverage neutrality (i.e. different genotypes with the same fitness) by creating a genotype - phenotype mapping, for example Cartesian GP [20] and Binary GP [2]. Rather than redefining the GP representation completely, our goal with ELGP is to explore whether local search of gene expression can be a viable, generic GP extension; hence its application to two different GP systems in this paper. As mentioned earlier, there are a plethora of studies on local search methods for improving GP by Lamarckian or Baldwinian means, yet very few that have considered these changes to occur at the epigenetic level rather than the genotype level. A notable exception is Multiple Regression GP [1], in which parameter values are implied at each node location and updated by linear regression. Still, the tangible improvements brought about by this and most other local search methods for symbolic regression are achieved by parametric, rather than topological, search.

4. EXPERIMENTAL ANALYSIS

4.1 Symbolic Regression with ellenGP

4.1.1 *Algorithm Settings*

In order to make our results relevant to state-of-the-art symbolic regression tools that often leverage Pareto optimization [26, 24], we use age-fitness Pareto survival [25], in which each individual is assigned an age equal to the number of generations since its oldest ancestor was created. Each generation, a new individual is introduced to the population as a means of random restart. Selection for breeding is random, and during breeding we create a number of children equal to the overall population size. At the end of each generation, we conduct culling tournaments of size 2 to reduce the set consisting of the current population and the newly created children down to the population size. In each tournament, we remove an individual from the population if their competitor Pareto-dominates them by the metrics of age (younger is better) and fitness. Culling continues until the population reaches its original size or until it conducts a

Table 1: Symbolic regression problem settings.

Setting	Value
Population size	1000
Crossover / Mutation	80/20%
Program length limits	[3, 50]
ERC range	[-10,10]
Termination criterion	max point evals or f < 1.0E-6
Trials	50 Tower & Keijzer-6, 100 rest

Problem	Terminal Set	Point Evals
Pagie-1	$\{x, y, +, -, *, /, 1.0\}$	2.5E+10
Nguyen-7	$\{x, +, -, *, /, \exp, \log, \text{ERC}\}$	2.5E+10
Uball5D	$\{x_1 \ldots x_5, +, -, *, /, \text{ERC}\}$	2.5E+10
Keijzer-6	$\{x, +, -, *, /, \exp, \log, \text{ERC}\}$	2.5E+10
Tower	$\{x_1 \ldots x_{25}, +, -, *, /, \sin, \cos, \exp, \log, \text{ERC}\}$	1.0E+11

maximum number of tournaments (10 times the population size in our implementation), at which point individuals with the worst fitness are removed.

The fitness metric is designed to minimize error and maximize correlation so that both mean absolute error (MAE) and the closeness of the output and target shapes, i.e. the coefficient of determination (R^2), can be compared in the results. For target $\mathbf{y}^*$ and output $\mathbf{y_i}$ $f_\mathbf{i}$ is defined as:

$$f_\mathbf{i} = \frac{1}{N}\sum_{q=1}^{N}|\mathbf{y}^*(k_q) - \mathbf{y_i}(k_q)|/R_\mathbf{i}^2 \tag{3}$$

$$R_\mathbf{i}^2 = \frac{(\text{cov}(\mathbf{y}^*, \mathbf{y_i}))^2}{\text{var}(\mathbf{y}^*)\text{var}(\mathbf{y_i})} \tag{4}$$

Run-time settings for the algorithm are shown in Table 1. A one-point crossover operator is used to produce two children from two parents. The mutation operator is applied uniformly to the chosen parent with a probability of 2.5% at each gene. If a constant gene is picked for mutation and ephemeral random constants (ERCs) are being used, the constant is perturbed by Gaussian noise with standard deviation equal to half the magnitude of the constant. Otherwise the instruction is mutated to a randomly chosen gene.

For problems utilizing ERCs, one iteration of parameter hill climbing is conducted each generation. The hill climber perturbs all constant values in the active genotype by Gaussian noise with a standard deviation equal to 10% of the value of the constant. These changes are kept if they result in a lower fitness for the individual.

Each trial was allocated a maximum number of point evaluations, i.e. gene executions, to normalize for the different program sizes among methods. A GP run will exit early if the fitness condition $f < 10^{-6}$ is achieved before the designated number of point evaluations has been reached. In practice, this fitness termination condition was sufficient to guarantee exact solutions for the problems studied.

4.1.2 *Optimizations*

The following optimizations are applied to the ellenGP system in order to reduce the number of point evaluations required to evaluate the fitness of an individual that has undergone epigenetic mutation. The majority of run-time in most GP systems (including ours) is spent in fitness evaluation, thus motivating the need for methods that can reduce the number of point evaluations required.

Fitness Escape.

EHC requires additional fitness evaluations in order to determine whether the prescribed epigenetic changes will be kept. Given that the fitness $f_\mathbf{i}$ of program $\mathbf{i}$ monotonically increases with the evaluation of more fitness cases $k_{1...n}$, evaluation of the epigenetically mutated individual $\mathbf{i}'$ can be halted if at any point the fitness $f_{\mathbf{i}'}(1...k_j) > f_\mathbf{i}(1...k_n)$ for $1 \leq j < n$. Since fitness is always equal to or larger than MAE (see Eq. 3), the halt condition can be defined conservatively using the mean absolute error (MAE) of $\mathbf{i}'$ and the fitness of $\mathbf{i}$ as

$$\frac{1}{N}\sum_{q=1}^{j}|\mathbf{y}^*(k_q) - \mathbf{y_{i'}}(k_q)| > f_\mathbf{i} \tag{5}$$

Stack Tracing.

In GP tree representations, typically the output of a node in the program is dependent only on the outputs of its child nodes (and those children's children and so forth). We can say conservatively with ellenGP representations that no instruction in the stack is dependent on an instruction to its right. Therefore, when a gene is silenced or activated, only the outputs of the genes to its right in the genotype are affected, hence only part of the program needs to be reevaluated. To avoid repeated instruction evaluations during epigenetic hill climbing, we save the intermediate program outputs of each gene and after epigenetic mutation reevaluate only those genes to the right of the left-most location of mutation. Saving the stack outputs is a trade-off between memory and time resources since it requires more memory to save the intermediate outputs but requires fewer point evaluations to evaluate epigenetically mutated individuals. The trade-off is favorable in our implementation because processor resources are much more limited than memory resources. Similar partial evaluation strategies have been proposed, e.g. in [19].

4.1.3 *Problems*

Five problems were chosen from the benchmark suite suggested by White et. al. [34]. The first four problems have the following forms[2]:

$$\text{Pagie-1 [22]} : \frac{1}{1+x^{-4}} + \frac{1}{1+y^{-4}} \tag{6}$$

$$\text{Nguyen-7 [32]} : \ln(x+1) + \ln(x^2+1) \tag{7}$$

$$\text{UBall5D [33]} : \frac{10}{5+\sum_{i=1}^{5}(x_i-3)^2} \tag{8}$$

$$\text{Keijzer-6 [16]} : \sum_{i}^{x}\frac{1}{i} \tag{9}$$

The settings for each problem are summarized in Table 1. Each of these problems use the training and validation sets provided in the original papers except for the Nguyen-7 validation set (not originally provided). We test validation on Nguyen-7 using 20 evenly spaced points from $x \in [2, 4]$. Keijzer-6 is unique here in that it does not admit an analytic solution, and can only be approximated. The final problem is an industrial data set known as the Tower problem[3] that uses data recorded from a chemical distillation tower. The

[2]UBall5D is also known as Vladislavleva-4.

[3]http://symbolicregression.com/?q=towerProblem

data is split into training and validation sets according the scaled extrapolation method used in [33]. The training set is comprised of data in the scaled range [0.02, 0.98] of input variables x_6, x_8, x_{11}, x_{17}, and x_{23}, and the validation set is comprised of data in $[0, 0.02) \cup (0.98, 1]$.

4.2 General Program Synthesis with PushGP

4.2.1 Algorithm settings

We conduct the program synthesis experiments in PushGP using standard tournament selection of size 7, a population size of 1000, and 100 trials for all problems. Table 2 shows the settings for each problem.

The new linear-genome PushGP allows us to use entirely uniform genetic operators. The crossover operator, which we use 20% of the time, alternates between parents, with a 1% chance of alternation at each instruction and an alignment deviation of 10, similar to ULTRA [27]. The mutation operator, which we use 20% of the time, gives a 1% chance of changing each instruction to a randomly selected one. The uniform close mutation operator, which we use 10% of the time, gives a 10% chance of adding or removing a closing parenthesis after each instruction. Finally, 50% of the time we perform a crossover followed by a mutation.

4.2.2 Problems

We perform tests on five program synthesis benchmark problems [11]. The problems used are:

- *Replace Space with Newline (RSWN)*: Given a string input, print the string, replacing spaces with newlines. The input string will not have tabs or newlines, but may have multiple spaces in a row. It will have maximum length of 20 characters. The program should also return the integer count of the non-whitespace characters.
- *String Lengths Backwards (SLB)*: Given a vector of strings with length ≤ 50, where each string has length ≤ 50, print the length of each string in the vector starting with the last and ending with the first.
- *Vector Average (VA)*: Given a vector of floats with length in [1,50], with each float in [-1000,1000], return the average of those floats.
- *Negative To Zero (N2Z)*: Given a vector of integers in [-1000,1000] with length ≤ 50, return the vector where all negative integers have been replaced by 0.
- *Syllables (Syl)*: Given a string (max length 20, containing symbols, spaces, digits, and lowercase letters), count the number of occurrences of vowels (a, e, i, o, u, y) in the string and print that number as X in "The number of syllables is X".

Instruction sets are determined by selecting potentially relevant data types for each problem, and then using all instructions that utilize those data types (shown in Table 2).

4.3 Results

We discuss the results of the symbolic regression and program synthesis experiments in the following two sections. In the third section, we look at population homologies for specific symbolic regression and program synthesis problems in order to shed light on the performance differences observed between methods.

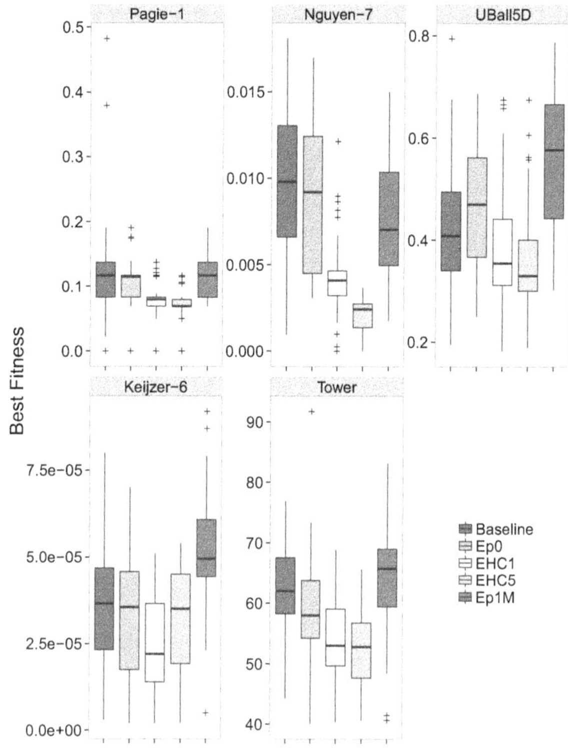

Figure 2: Boxplot comparison of best-of-run training fitnesses for the symbolic regression problems.

4.3.1 Symbolic Regression

The symbolic regression results are summarized in Table 3, and the best-of-run fitnesses are shown in Figure 2. We compare training performance in terms of exact solutions, mean best MAE, mean best R^2, and mean active program size (averaged from population averages recorded each generation for each trial). For the validation comparisons we report the percent of solutions that "generalize", defined as having a real-valued, finite output on validation data. We assign a poor fitness to non-generalizing solutions when calculating (non-parametric) statistics and report the median values of MAE and R^2 on the validation sets to account for outliers (i.e. non-generalizing models).

Overall, exact solutions are found only for the Pagie-1 and Nguyen-7 problems; for both cases, **EHC1** and **EHC5** find approximately 3 to 5 times more exact solutions than **Baseline** or **Ep0**. In all training cases, a significant improvement to MAE and R^2 is achieved by **EHC1** and/or **EHC5** except when all methods converge to mean best $R^2 = 1$ (Nguyen-7 and Keijzer-6). For the validation cases, **EHC1** and **EHC5** are significantly better on Pagie-1, Nguyen-7 and UBall5D, but on Keijzer-6 and Tower the results are not significant aside from **EHC1** R^2 on Keijzer-6 and **Ep1M** R^2 on Tower. Surprisingly, **Ep1M** significantly improves validation R^2 on Tower even though it has the poorest training fitness, perhaps due to the small program sizes produced by that method for that problem.

For all problems, **Ep1M** has the smallest average program sizes, followed by **Ep0**, **EHC1** and **EHC5**. All the epigenetic programs have significantly smaller programs than the

Table 2: PushGP settings for the program synthesis problems.

Problem	Replace Space with Newline	String Lengths Backwards	Vector Average	Negative To Zero	Syllables
Max Point Evals	3.0E+10	1.0E+10	1.0E+10	1.0E+10	1.0E+10
Max Program Size	800	300	400	500	800
Max Point Evals per Program Evaluation	1600	600	800	1500	1600
Instruction Set (all instructions in listed types)	:integer :boolean :string :char :exec :print	:string :vector_string :integer :boolean :exec :print	:vector_float :float :integer :exec	:integer :boolean :vector_integer :exec	:integer :boolean :string :char :exec :print
Terminal Set	input, '\n', ' ', visible char ERC, string ERC	input, integer ERC [-100, 100]	input	input, 0, []	input, "The number of syllables is ", "aeiouy", 'a', 'e', 'i', 'o', 'u', 'y', visible char ERC, string ERC
Error Function	printed string Levenshtein distance, integer absolute error	printed string Levenshtein distance	float absolute error	Levenshtein distance between vectors	printed string Levenshtein distance, printed integer absolute error

Baseline case. In general the symbolic regression problems seem to benefit from some level of epigenetic hill climbing, both in terms of fitness convergence and program size.

4.3.2 Program Synthesis

The results for the program synthesis problems are summarized in Table 4. Unlike symbolic regression problems, the goal is to generate a program that passes all tests, and so the results are compared only in terms of the number of exact solutions found. By this measure, the best performance case is always **Ep1M** or **EHC1**, although this performance boost is only significant for **Ep1M** on the RSWN and VA problems. Surprisingly, **Ep1M** outperforms **EHC1**, unlike in the symbolic regression case. We discuss reasons for why this might occur in the following section.

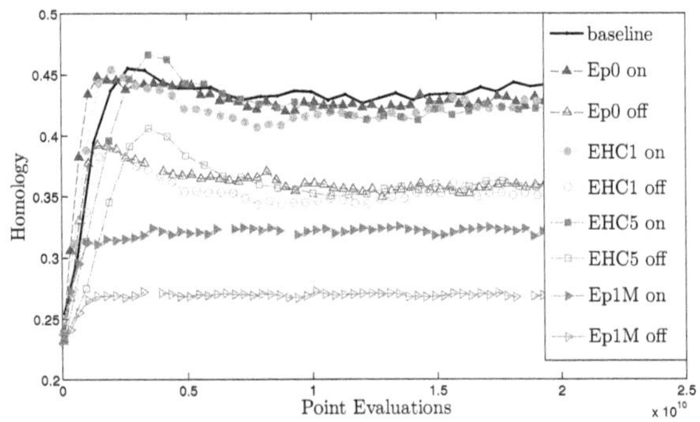

Figure 3: Active (on) and inactive (off) genotype homology for Uball5D problem, averaged over 100 trials.

4.3.3 Homology

We hypothesize that epigenetics provide protection from premature convergence in populations by preserving sections of the genome from fitness pressure and allowing them to drift genetically, thus providing an avenue for introduction of diversity and continued progress. We look at population homology in detail to determine whether this phenomenon of preserved diversity is evident. We define the homology H of a population using a Levenshtein distance comparison of P randomly sampled pairs of individuals $(|\mathbf{i}_j, \mathbf{i}_m|_L)$, normalized by the length, $|\cdot|$, of the longer individual:

$$H = 1 - \frac{1}{P}\sum_{n=1}^{P} \frac{|\mathbf{i}_j, \mathbf{i}_m|_L}{max(|\mathbf{i}_j|, |\mathbf{i}_m|)} \quad (10)$$

We sample homology separately for the active, inactive, and total (whole genome) portions of the genotypes with $P = 200$. In general we find that inactive genotypes have lower homology (i.e. higher diversity) than active genotypes for every epigenetic case. The homologies for the UBall5D problem are shown in Figure 3 as an example. The differences between active and inactive homologies are very significant in this example ($p < 10^{-14}$). The active gene homologies for **Ep0**, **EHC1**, and **EHC5** are slightly (yet significantly) lower than **Baseline** as well ($p < 10^{-13}$). This suggests the improvement in fitness convergence for the symbolic regression problems is linked to the extra diversity available during epigenetic local search. **Ep1M** displays much lower homology in both active and inactive genotypes, a trend also evident when comparing total genome homology for the VA problem in Figure 4. The program synthesis problems may therefore benefit mostly from increased genetic diversity over the total genome (afforded by **Ep1M**). We hypothesize that increased diversity in this context assures larger phenotypic coverage and hence a higher likelihood of finding exact solutions in non-convex fitness landscapes.

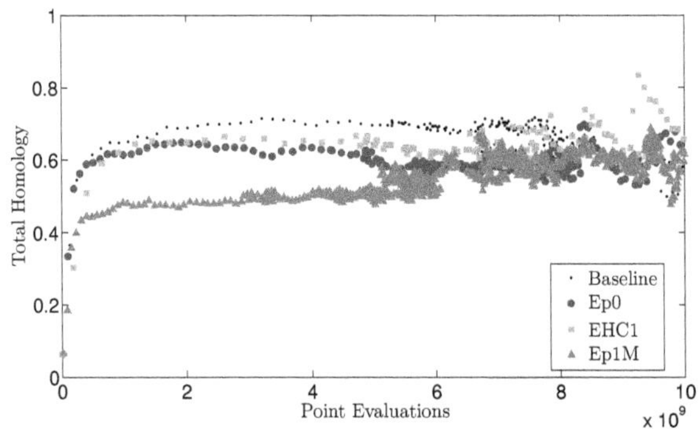

Figure 4: Total (whole genome) homology for the Vector Average problem.

Table 3: Comparison of best-of-run results for the symbolic regression benchmark problems. * and underline indicate significant ($p < 0.05$) improvement over Baseline and Ep0, respectively. Exact solution p-values are based on pairwise chi-squared tests with Holm correction. Fitness and size p-values are based on pairwise Wilcoxon rank-sum tests.

Problem	Exact Solutions (%)	Training			Validation		Mean Active
Method		Mean MAE	Mean R^2	Generalize (%)	Median MAE	Median R^2	Program Size
Pagie-1							
Baseline	1	0.114	0.930	100	0.116	0.960	31.7
Ep0	3	0.099	0.960	100	0.109	0.971	*19.21
EHC1	*12	*0.071	*0.968	100	*0.080	*0.972	*20.92
EHC5	*15	*0.065	*0.970	100	*0.078	*0.963	*21.35
Ep1M	0	0.104	0.962	100	0.111	*0.971	*18.3
Nguyen-7							
Baseline	10	5.04E-4	1	95	0.074	0.999	28.22
Ep0	10	7.08E-4	1	98	0.061	0.999	*17.77
EHC1	*27	4.34E-4	1	99	*0.024	0.999	*20.25
EHC5	*31	*3.46E-4	1	94	*0.019	*1.000	*21.20
Ep1M	11	1.10E-3	1	99	0.031	0.999	*15.41
UBall5D							
Baseline	0	0.130	0.325	100	0.165	0.124	33.20
Ep0	0	0.130	0.288	100	0.149	0.163	*18.70
EHC1	0	*0.122	0.334	100	*0.128	*0.287	*20.22
EHC5	0	*0.119	*0.352	100	*0.122	*0.293	*22.14
Ep1M	0	0.132	0.259	100	0.149	0.160	*17.77
Keijzer-6							
Baseline	n/a	3.65E-5	1	88	4.93E-5	1	25.84
Ep0	n/a	3.26E-5	1	90	4.31E-5	1	*16.62
EHC1	n/a	*2.42E-5	1	90	4.08E-5	*1	*19.44
EHC5	n/a	3.05E-5	1	94	4.53E-5	1	*20.23
Ep1M	n/a	5.10E-5	1	92	6.47E-5	1	*16.06
Tower							
Baseline	n/a	41.03	0.663	96	42.55	0.663	22.57
Ep0	n/a	40.08	0.682	98	42.99	0.667	*16.67
EHC1	n/a	*37.55	*0.706	100	38.56	0.705	*18.28
EHC5	n/a	*37.23	*0.715	98	40.64	0.697	*19.37
Ep1M	n/a	41.91	0.660	100	40.46	*0.752	*13.47

Table 4: Results of program synthesis runs. * and underline indicate significant ($p < 0.05$) improvement over Baseline and Ep0, respectively, according to chi-squared tests with Holm correction.

Problem	Solutions on training / validation set (%)			
	Baseline	Ep0	EHC1	Ep1M
RSWN	61/58	66/65	61/60	*85/83
SLB	14/14	11/10	23/23	15/14
VA	12/12	10/10	20/20	*43/43
N2Z	9/9	9/8	9/8	21/19
Syl	10/10	2/2	5/5	11/11

5. CONCLUSIONS

The results suggest that epigenetic local search can be a promising addition to GP. We have shown that the epigenetic layer is able to preserve diversity in the inactive sequences of genes and that, for the benchmark problems studied, epigenetic methods outperform a baseline implementation of GP in terms of fitness minimization, exact solutions, and program sizes. We have only considered epigenetic learning by mutation and hill climbing here, but we hope the results encourage further research into the use of epigenetic methods for structure optimization in GP.

6. ACKNOWLEDGMENTS

We thank Nicholas McPhee and anonymous reviewers for helping improve this paper. This work is partially supported by the NSF-sponsored IGERT: Offshore Wind Energy Engineering, Environmental Science, and Policy (Grant Number 1068864), as well as Grant No. 1017817, 1129139, and 1331283. Any opinions, findings, and conclusions or recommendations expressed in this publication are those of the authors and do not necessarily reflect the views of the National Science Foundation.

7. REFERENCES

[1] I. Arnaldo, K. Krawiec, and U.-M. O'Reilly. Multiple regression genetic programming. In *Proceedings of GECCO '14*, pages 879–886. ACM Press, 2014.

[2] W. Banzhaf. Genotype-phenotype-mapping and neutral variation - a case study in genetic programming. In *PPSN III*, pages 322–332. Springer, 1994.

[3] J. Bongard and H. Lipson. Automated reverse engineering of nonlinear dynamical systems. *PNAS*, 104(24):9943–9948, 2007.

[4] M. Brameier and W. Banzhaf. *Linear Genetic Programming*, volume 1. Springer, 1 edition, 2007.

[5] B. G. Dias and K. J. Ressler. PACAP and the PAC1 receptor in post-traumatic stress disorder. *Neuropsychopharmacology*, 38(1):245–246, Jan. 2013.

[6] B. G. Dias and K. J. Ressler. Parental olfactory experience influences behavior and neural structure in subsequent generations. *Nature Neuroscience*, 17(1):89–96, Jan. 2014.

[7] C. Ferreira. Gene expression programming: a new adaptive algorithm for solving problems. *arXiv:cs/0102027*, Feb. 2001. Complex Systems, 13(2) 87-129, 2001.

[8] A. Fontana. Epigenetic tracking: Biological implications. In *Advances in Artificial Life. Darwin Meets von Neumann*, number 5777 in Lecture Notes in Computer Science, pages 10–17. Springer Berlin Heidelberg, Jan. 2011.

[9] C. Giraud-Carrier. Unifying learning with evolution through baldwinian evolution and lamarckism. In *Advances in Computational Intelligence and Learning*, pages 159–168. Springer, 2002.

[10] F. Gruau and D. Whitley. Adding learning to the cellular development of neural networks: Evolution and the baldwin effect. *Evolutionary Computation*, 1(3):213–233, Sept. 1993.

[11] T. Helmuth and L. Spector. General program synthesi benchmark suite. In *Proceedings of GECCO '15*, 2015.

[12] R. Holliday. Epigenetics: a historical overview. *Epigenetics*, 1(2):76–80, 2006.

[13] H. Iba and T. Sato. Genetic programming with local hill-climbing. Technical Report ETL-TR-94-4, Electrotechnical Laboratory, 1-1-4 Umezono, Tsukuba-city, Ibaraki, 305, Japan, 1994.

[14] E. Jablonka and M. J. Lamb. The changing concept of epigenetics. *Annals of the New York Academy of Sciences*, 981(1):82–96, 2002.

[15] G. Kaati, L. O. Bygren, and S. Edvinsson. Cardiovascular and diabetes mortality determined by nutrition during parents' and grandparents' slow growth period. *European Journal of Human Genetics*, 10(11):682, Nov. 2002.

[16] M. Keijzer. Improving symbolic regression with interval arithmetic and linear scaling. In *Genetic Programming*, number 2610 in Lecture Notes in Computer Science, pages 70–82. Springer Berlin Heidelberg, Jan. 2003.

[17] M. Keijzer. Push-forth: A light-weight, strongly-typed, stack-based genetic programming language. In *Proceedings of GECCO '13 Companion*, GECCO '13 Companion, pages 1635–1640, New York, NY, USA, 2013. ACM.

[18] W. La Cava, L. Spector, K. Danai, and M. Lackner. Evolving differential equations with developmental linear genetic programming and epigenetic hill climbing. In *Companion proceedings of the 2014 conference on Genetic and evolutionary computation*, pages 141–142. ACM Press, 2014.

[19] W. B. Langdon. *Genetic Programming and Data Structures: Genetic Programming + Data Structures = Automatic Programming!*, volume 1 of *Genetic Programming*. Kluwer, Boston, 1998.

[20] J. F. Miller and P. Thomson. Cartesian genetic programming. In *Genetic Programming*, pages 121–132. Springer, 2000.

[21] P. Nordin, F. Francone, and W. Banzhaf. Explicitly defined introns and destructive crossover in genetic programming. In *Proceedings of the Workshop on Genetic Programming: From Theory to Real-World Applications*, pages 6–22, Tahoe City, California, USA, 1995.

[22] L. Pagie and P. Hogeweg. Evolutionary consequences of coevolving targets. *Evolutionary computation*, 5(4):401–418, 1997.

[23] B. J. Ross. A lamarckian evolution strategy for genetic algorithms. *Practical handbook of genetic algorithms: complex coding systems*, 3:1–16, 1999.

[24] M. Schmidt and H. Lipson. Distilling free-form natural laws from experimental data. *Science*, 324(5923):81–85, 2009.

[25] M. Schmidt and H. Lipson. Age-fitness pareto optimization. In *Genetic Programming Theory and Practice VIII*, pages 129–146. Springer, 2011.

[26] G. F. Smits and M. Kotanchek. Pareto-front exploitation in symbolic regression. In *Genetic Programming Theory and Practice II*, pages 283–299. Springer, 2005.

[27] L. Spector and T. Helmuth. Uniform linear transformation with repair and alternation in genetic programming. *Genetic Programming Theory and Practice XI*, 2013.

[28] L. Spector and A. Robinson. Genetic programming and autoconstructive evolution with the push programming language. *GPEM*, 3(1):7–40, 2002.

[29] I. Tanev and K. Yuta. Epigenetic programming: Genetic programming incorporating epigenetic learning through modification of histones. *Information Sciences*, 178(23):4469–4481, Dec. 2008.

[30] A. Topchy and W. F. Punch. Faster genetic programming based on local gradient search of numeric leaf values. In *Proceedings of GECCO '01*, pages 155–162, 2001.

[31] B. M. Turner. Histone acetylation and an epigenetic code. *Bioessays*, 22(9):836–845, 2000.

[32] N. Q. Uy, N. X. Hoai, M. O'Neill, R. I. McKay, and E. Galván-López. Semantically-based crossover in genetic programming: application to real-valued symbolic regression. *GPEM*, 12(2):91–119, 2011.

[33] E. Vladislavleva, G. Smits, and D. den Hertog. Order of nonlinearity as a complexity measure for models generated by symbolic regression via pareto genetic programming. *IEEE Transactions on Evolutionary Computation*, 13(2):333–349, 2009.

[34] D. R. White, J. McDermott, M. Castelli, L. Manzoni, B. W. Goldman, G. Kronberger, W. Jaśkowski, U.-M. O'Reilly, and S. Luke. Better GP benchmarks: community survey results and proposals. *GPEM*, 14(1):3–29, Dec. 2012.

[35] D. Whitley, V. S. Gordon, and K. Mathias. Lamarckian evolution, the baldwin effect and function optimization. In *PPSN III*, pages 5–15. Springer, 1994.

Improving CUDA DNA Analysis Software with Genetic Programming

William B. Langdon, Brian Yee Hong Lam, Justyna Petke, Mark Harman
Department of Computer Science, University College London Gower Street, WC1E 6BT, UK
University of Cambridge Metabolic Research Laboratories, Addenbrooke's Hospital, Cambridge CB2 0QQ
W.Langdon@cs.ucl.ac.uk, yhbl2@cam.ac.uk

ABSTRACT

We genetically improve BarraCUDA using a BNF grammar incorporating C scoping rules with GP. Barracuda maps next generation DNA sequences to the human genome using the Burrows-Wheeler algorithm (BWA) on nVidia Tesla parallel graphics hardware (GPUs). GI using phenotypic tabu search with manually grown code can graft new features giving more than 100 fold speed up on a performance critical kernel without loss of accuracy.

Categories and Subject Descriptor I.2.8 [search]: heuristic I.2.2 [Artificial Intelligence]: Automatic Programming D.2.8 [Software Engineering]: Metrics[complexity measures, performance measures]

Keywords SBSE; GPGPU; Bioinformatics; Genetic improvement

1. INTRODUCTION

Modern Biology is an increasingly data rich science. The central dogma of Biology states that the fundamental information for all forms of life is encoded in the DNA carried by every living cell. Next generation DNA sequencing machines were crucial to the decoding of the human genome in 2000 [5] and since have been used to decode the genomes of many other species and to map the variation of individual human genomes [1]. In a single run modern NextGen scanners can give hundreds of millions of short DNA sequences.

Typically before the (noisy) data are used their DNA sequence is located in a reference genome, such as the human genome. Since each can be compared to the reference genome independently, a common strategy is to run multiple instances of the DNA look up software in parallel. Barracuda [6] takes the approach of parallel running on GPU hardware. It is essentially a port of the well established BWA tool [17] written in nVidia's CUDA dialect of the C programming language. Before genetic improvement [8], on typical 100 base pair (bp) DNA data from The 1000 Genomes Project [1], with a top end Tesla K40 GPU, Barracuda processed on average 16 000 sequences per second. Figure 1 shows more than 100 fold speedup for a performance critical component of Barracuda during genetic improvement.

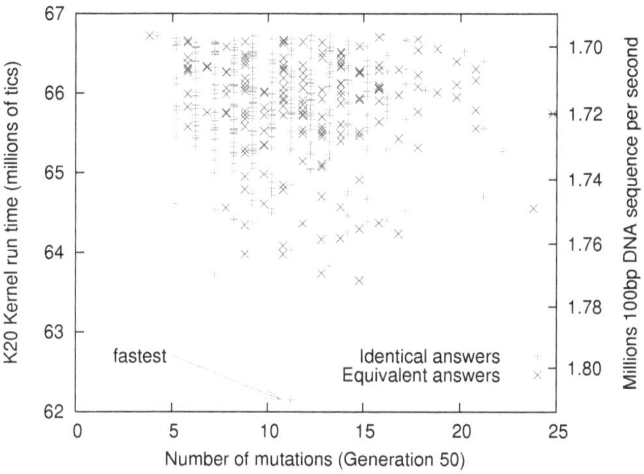

Figure 1: Distribution of speed and number of changes in top 500 correct Tesla K20 `cuda_find_exact_matches` kernels.

Barracuda, now including some of the genetic improvements described in Section 3.1, is available via Source Forge. (We evolved improvements to Barracuda release 0.7.0). Barracuda has been under development since 2009. It comprises 49 C source and include files containing more than 8000 lines of code, containing six CUDA kernels. (In [10] we evolved a complete kernel, whereas here GP [20] improves an existing kernel.) The code which aligns the sequences is largely implemented by the `cuda_split_inexact_match_caller` kernel, which makes heavy use of code in common with `cuda_find_exact_matches`. Typically 85% of NextGen DNA data generated by The 1000 Genomes Project matches the reference human genome exactly. Our approach is to concentrate upon these data and generate huge speed ups with the `cuda_find_exact_matches` code. DNA sequences which do not match exactly are passed to `cuda_split_inexact_match_caller` to be dealt with in the usual way. The complete GPU (device) alignment code is 696 lines of CUDA, whilst the GP works with 200 of these.

On a 2 496 processor Tesla K20 GPU, the original code could process on average 15 000 100bp sequences per second. (Bowtie2 typically processes more than 5000 such sequences per second per CPU core [9, Fig. 10].) The optimised `cuda_find_exact_matches` kernel processes well in

GECCO'15, July 11–15, 2015, Madrid.

ACM 978-1-4503-3472-3/15/07 $15.00.
DOI: http://dx.doi.org/10.1145/2739480.2754652 .

excess of a million such sequences per second. However, we must bear in mind that this speed up will be diluted by the rest of the code, nevertheless the lessons provided by GP on the exact code may possibly be applied to the whole program.

The next section describes our GP system, including the introduction of phenotypic tabu search, whilst Section 3 describes the results of applying it to Barracuda which include average speeds of 1.8–2.4 million 100bp DNA sequences per second (depending on hardware, i.e. K20 or K40). Section 4 includes discussion of our evolutionary process and the ultimate speedup we might get and Section 5 concludes.

2. GENETIC IMPROVEMENT SYSTEM

The manually produced CUDA code was automatically converted into a BNF grammar which describes each of its 200 lines, line by line [12, 19]. (Figure 2 contains fragments of the whole grammar.) The GP uses the grammar to control the mutations the GP can make. The grammar ensures that after each mutation the new code is still syntactically correct (but see Section 2.3).

2.1 Fixed Representation Parameters

The manually produced kernel has 15 configuration options which GP can selectively enable or disable by conditional compilation (see Table 2). This includes allowing evolution to set the number of threads used per DNA sequences query and the number of threads per block to all reasonable values. (Number of configuration options = $(2^{13} \times 7 \times 37 = 2\,121\,728.)$ The first part of each GP individual is of fixed length and codes each of these 15 options. (Figure 3 contains part of an example GP individual.) The second part describes each code mutation the GP individual makes via the grammar. Since the second part can contain any number of mutations: the search space of code changes is effectively unlimited. Notice unlike a traditional GA, our GP does not start at random but instead starts from the default (manually written) code. This is similar to seeding the initial population [14].

2.2 Variable Code: Grammar Types

Each line of the source code is represented by one or more rules in the BNF grammar. Evolution can change the contents of the kernel but is not permitted to change its structure. So it cannot remove any of the seven functions, their arguments (except as already permitted by manually written conditional compilation), declarations or return or other control flow statements. However, it can substantially change the code inside functions and between flow control statements including whether functions are called or not. Each variable rule belongs to one of nine types. Mutations only move code between rules of the same type.

43 of the variable rules are simple lines, almost all being assignments (e.g. <_Kkernel_bnf.cu_126> in Figures 2 and 3). Subject to the scoping rules, they can be exchanged with each other, or indeed inserted before other statements.

```
... cache_threads=4 ... <_Kkernel_bnf.cu_126>
```

Figure 3: Fragments of GP individual which sets the `cache_threads` configuration option to 4 (see Table 2). The code mutation `<_Kkernel_bnf.cu_126>` means that line 126 is deleted (see Section 2.6).

There are 24 IF rules. Mutation can delete these by simply setting the condition to always false or (subject to the scoping rules) it can replace the conditional part with the conditional part of another IF rule. There are also two ELSE rules.

There are 7 variable C `for` loops. `for` loop headers are split into their three components (by the ;). Subject to scooping rules, for1 type rules can be replaced by other for1 rules, for2 by for2 and for3 by for3. However in 4 cases the first part of the `for` loop includes a declaration (such as `for(int i = 0;...)` and so is not variable. We force loop termination via the grammar. The conditional part, `for2`, of every `for` loop includes testing that a local counter has not exceeded its maximum value. Evolution is not permitted to disrupt this in any way. The maximum value is set to twice the maximum number of iterations used in any loop in the manually written code. There is no special penalty on exceeding this limit, instead the fitness function will penalise kernels that calculate incorrect answers or run for a long time. The remaining three types are specials for CUDA.

The CUDA compiler allows the programmer to suggest (via a `#pragma`) that it unroll `for` loops. The grammar allows GP to use unroll pragma before every `for` loop and rely on the fitness function to see if the effect is beneficial. The default is not to use `#pragma`. Optionally each `#pragma unroll` statement takes an integer value from 1 to 11. Again evolution can chose to use this or not.

The compiler supports `__restrict__` on kernel and CUDA device functions. For nVidia GPUs since the K20, if all array arguments are marked `__restrict__`, the compiler may access read only arrays marked `const` via a small read-only cache. Actually this cache is shared with texture data. Since the texture cache may already be in use, it is not clear if reusing it as a read-only data cache will be beneficial. Instead the choice is left to evolution. To support this, the grammar has a single `<optrestrict` rule which evolution can enable or disable. The grammar links all array and pointer arguments so that they are all marked with `__restrict__` or not together. By default `__restrict__` is enabled.

The last CUDA special is the `<launchbounds` rules. These can appear immediately before the kernel is declared. The grammar allows evolution to choose to use it if it wants but ensures the `__launch_bounds__` syntax will be correct and relies on the fitness function to see if it has any benefit. The default is not to use `__launch_bounds`.

The 15 configuration options are implemented via a combination of C macros and conditional compilation. Evolution sets and clears these directly.

2.3 Scoping Rules

Earlier work with GP for bug fixing etc. [11, 13, 16] reported that the main reason why code does not compile is due to variables being moved out of scope. This is also true with the CUDA 6.0 C compiler. Therefore, the BNF grammar is automatically augmented with data indicating the scope limitation of every line of the grammar that can be changed.

A simple text file is used to hold, for each of the 113 variable rules, the locations the rule can be copied to. The locations are given as line numbers in the original source code. Typically these are within the function holding the line itself. Fifteen rules do not depend on any variable declared in a function and so they can be moved to any location, with a matching type, in the kernel. In all but 0.35% of cases the

Table 1: **GPU Hardware. Each GPU chip contains 13 or 15 identical independent multiprocessors (MP, column 4). Each MP contains 192 stream processors. (Total given in column 6). ECC enabled.**

GPU	Introduced	compute level	MP	total cores	Clock	L1 cache	L2 cache	Memory	Bandwidth
Tesla K20	2012	3.5		$13 \times 192 = 2496$	0.71 GHz	48KB	1.25 MB	5 GB	140 GB/s
Tesla K40	2013	3.5		$15 \times 192 = 2880$	0.88 GHz	48KB	1.50 MB	11 GB	180 GB/s

```
<Kkernel_bnf.cu_118>              ::= "unsigned int tmp = *data;\n"
                                       ...
<Kkernel_bnf.cu_119>              ::= " if" <IF_Kkernel_bnf.cu_119> " \n"
<IF_Kkernel_bnf.cu_119>           ::= "(*lastpos!=pos_shifted)"
                                       ...
<Kkernel_bnf.cu_126>              ::= "" <_Kkernel_bnf.cu_126> "\n"
<_Kkernel_bnf.cu_126>             ::= "*lastpos=pos_shifted;"
                                       ...
<okdeclaration_>                  ::= "#ifndef OKDEC\n" "OKDECLARATION\n" "#define OKDEC 1\n" "#endif
<okdeclaration_End>               ::= "#ifdef OKDEC\n" "#undef OKDEC\n" "#endif /*OKDEC*/\n"
<Kkernel_bnf.cu_415>              ::= <okdeclaration_> <pragma_Kkernel_bnf.cu_415> "for(" <for1_Kkernel_bnf.cu_415>
                                      ";" "OK()&&" <for2_Kkernel_bnf.cu_415> ";" <for3_Kkernel_bnf.cu_415> ")
                                      ((ldg_t*)mycache)[x/inc] = load(x);\n"
<pragma_Kkernel_bnf.cu_415>       ::= ""
<pragma_K0>                       ::= "#pragma unroll \n"
<pragma_K1>                       ::= "#pragma unroll 1\n"
                                       ...
<pragma_K11>                      ::= "#pragma unroll 11\n"
<for1_Kkernel_bnf.cu_415>         ::= ""
<for2_Kkernel_bnf.cu_415>         ::= "x<cache_loads"
<for3_Kkernel_bnf.cu_415>         ::= "x+=inc"
```

Figure 2: **Five fragments of the 200 rule BNF grammar describing the human coded kernel which is evolved by GI. <Kkernel_bnf.cu_118> is fixed and cannot be evolved. It simply describes line 118. The grammar can be thought of as having an implicit "start" rule for each line of source code. The conditional part of the `if` on line 119 is given by <IF_Kkernel_bnf.cu_119>. GI mutation can replace `"(*lastpos!=pos_shifted)"` with code taken from another IF. <_Kkernel_bnf.cu_126> is variable and can be deleted, replaced by another variable rule (starting with <_) or another variable rule can be inserted before it. <okdeclaration_> onwards are rules automatically generated to support the `for` loop on line 415. The OK() macro detects and aborts excessively long loops. Evolution can insert #pragmas. The three components of the `for` loop are described by <for1_Kkernel_bnf.cu_415> etc.**

scoping rules ensure mutated code compiles (see Figure 4). The only cases where mutants do not compile relate either to conditionally compiled code or to C macro definitions, which do not follow the normal nested scope rules.

2.4 Genotypic and Phenotypic Tabu Search

Initially, some mutations had absolutely no effect as they changed code which was then removed by conditional compilation. To avoid excessive silent mutations in hidden C code we introduced a two stage tabu search to GP.

The tabu list takes two forms: genetic and phenotypic. Nothing is removed from either, i.e. they grow with each generation. The genetic tabu list is simply every genotype that the GP has tried so far. Notice, even though we know there is some noise in the fitness function, we do not allow the GP to re-try complete solutions and its search is forced to diverge.

To prevent conditional compilation from hiding mutations, before GP individuals are compiled into object code the gcc -E C pre-processor is used to convert the GP modified source code into its "phenotype". We take a mutant's phenotype to be its code after conditional compilation and macro expansion. If a mutation changes only code excluded by

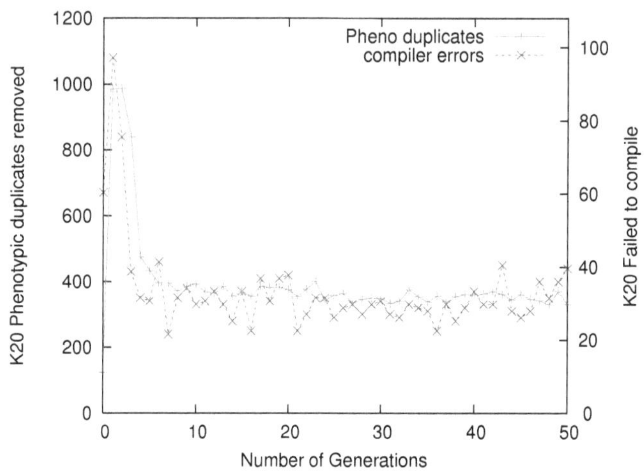

Figure 4: **In generation 1, 2 and 3, many phenotypic duplicates (+, Section 2.4) are created. However this quickly falls to about 300 per generation. Although the BNF grammar and scoping rules ensure most mutant kernels compile, typically about 30 of 1000 do not (×).**

Table 2: Fixed parameters for improving Barracuda. 3rd column is default. 4th column is number of lines of code directly affected in the default CUDA kernel.

BLOCK_W	int	64	all	threads per block. Must be a power of 2 (up to 32) or a multiple of 32 up to 1024.
cache_threads	"" int	""	44	number of threads used to load the human genome cache. Must be a power of 2 (up to 32) if used or "" if not used.
kl_par	binary	off	19	Calculate "k" and "l" in parallel. Doubles the number of threads per sequence.
occ_par	binary	off	76	Do bwt_cuda_occ1 loop in parallel (needs cache_threads)
many_blocks	binary	off	2	Allows number of blocks to exceed 65536 at the expense of more complex index calculations
direct_sequence	binary	on	63	Allows bwt_cuda_match_exact to read the next DNA base pair directly from global memory rather than using a local array to buffer the query sequence.
direct_index	binary	on	6	Calculates location of queries in global memory by requiring them all to be of the same size thus avoiding indirection via sequences_index_array
sequence_global	binary	on	16	read DNA queries directly from global memory rather than via a texture.
sequence_shift81	binary	on	30	Use >> rather than switch to unpack DNA base pairs (off no longer supported)
sequence_stride	binary	on	14	For efficiency DNA queries are blocked in 32 int (off no longer supported)
mycache4	binary	on	12	Read human reference genome via cache in 4 int (i.e. 16 bytes) units.
mycache2	binary	off	11	Read human reference genome in 2 int units. only active if mycache4 is disabled. If neither mycache4 nor mycache2 are active then the cache is loaded one int at a time.
direct_global_bwt	binary	off	2	read human reference genome from global memory directly. The default is to read it via __ldg().
cache_global_bwt	binary	on	65	Read human reference genome via cache.
scache_global_bwt	binary	off	35	Use up to 16 local scalars (rather than local array) to implement human reference genome cache. Ideally this means the reference genome cache is held in up to 16 registers rather than in half an L1 cache line.

conditional compilation, the post process code will be identical to the post process code of its parent and therefore it will be excluded by the tabu list. The phenotypic tabu list is simply implemented by keeping the post processed source code of every GP individual accepted into the population at each generation. At 340 MB, the tabu lists remains manageable even after 50 generations. (See also Figure 4.) Hashing these text files might be necessary with bigger populations or more long running GPs. If a mutation is discovered to have the same phenotype as another GP individual it is discarded and another is created.

The phenotypic tabu list is sufficient. However, the genotypic tabu list is also retained since it is easy to detect genetic duplicates and this avoids the overhead of generating source code and running the pre-processor.

We have treated the C source code after pre-processing as the individual's phenotype (rather than its run-time behaviour). This could be extended to later in the compiler tool chain. E.g. we could treat the assembler or even binary machine code as the phenotype. With simple compiler/assembler hierarchy this has been done [18]. However, the nVidia GPU tool stack includes both an optimising assembler and the possibility of just-in-time compilation at kernel load or launch time. The possible presence of version numbers, file names and time stamps embedded in binary files also complicates using differences later in the tool chain as proxies for difference in program behaviour.

2.5 Initial Population

The initial population of 1000 GP individuals is created using mutation. The genotypic and phenotypic tabu list are initialised with the empty (default) individual. This ensures each member of the initial population is unique.

2.6 Mutation and Crossover

Each member of the breeding pool, i.e. the top 500 individuals from the previous generation, is allocated two children. One child is created by mutating the parent. The second is created by crossover between it and another parent randomly selected from the breeding pool. If fewer than 500 individuals in the previous generation were selected, the missing children are created at random in the same way as the initial population was created (but subject to the now longer tabu lists).

Half the mutations are changes to the configuration and half are code mutations. With configuration changes, one of the fifteen parameters is chosen uniformly at random. There is a one in five chance it will be reset to its default value. For binary parameters, mutation simply flips their current value. If cache_threads is chosen and is currently undefined half the time it will be set to its default value (4), and half the time it will be set to one of its six legal numeric values. If it already has a numeric value half the time another value is chosen at random and half the time a neighbouring value is chosen. Mutating BLOCK_W follows the same strategy of making large jumps half the time and neighbouring moves the other half.

Our code mutations were inspired by those of Le Goues *et al.* [16] but act on the grammar at the level of lines of code rather than abstract syntax trees at the statement level. New code mutations are made by appending another code mutation onto the current mutation list. There are three types of code mutation: delete a line (e.g. right hand end of Figure 3), copy and replace the target line and copy and insert before the target line. E.g. <_Kkernel_bnf.cu_948><_Kkernel_bnf.cu_927> causes line 948 *l0 = 1; to be replaced with line 927 ((int*)k0)[1] = __shfl(((int*)&k)[1], 0, threads_per_sequence); Insert mutations are denoted by a + between the rule names. For example, `<_Kkernel_bnf.cu_852>+<_Kkernel_bnf.cu_922>`, which causes line 922 `*k0 = k;` to be inserted before line 852 `*k0 = 0;`

Crossover acts on the genetic representation. It creates a new child with the fixed parameters and a variable length list of code changes obtained from its two parents. The fixed part is obtained by performing uniform crossover [22] on the 15 compulsory parameters, whilst the list of code changes is given by two point crossover, like Koza's sub-tree crossover [7]. Notice crossover only selects genes from its two parents, it does not create new ones. If crossover is unable to create a new unique offspring after a small number of tries, the child is created by mutating the parent instead.

2.7 Fitness Function

It is well known that compiling the population in one go is typically more efficient than compiling each member of the population individually [4]. Therefore, all 1000 GP individuals are converted into a single file that is compiled and linked with the rest of Barracuda to give a single image that runs the 1000 kernels one at a time on about 16 megabytes of the same randomly chosen part of a randomly chosen example file downloaded from The 1000 Genomes Project's FTP site (see Section 3.3).

To allow even loading of the GPU, the number of DNA query sequences run in parallel is chosen to be a multiple of the number of stream processing cores in the GPU, see Table 1. Thus fitness testing on the K20 processes 159744 queries in parallel, while on the K40 161280 are used.

In order to be able to compare the genetically improved code with the original, the first kernel compiled and run is always a copy of the default (manually written) code. I.e. 1001 kernels are compiled and run. Running the compiler typically takes 71% of the total run time. (Mutation and crossover, including checking the tabu lists, takes about 9% and running the kernels and checking their answers takes about 18%. The rest is housekeeping such as monitoring device temperatures.)

We did not investigate parallel compilation, but given that the GPU's are hosted by powerful multicore cluster servers, it would be possible to split the population and compile it in a number of parallel streams [2].

Although our scoping rules (Section 2.3) eliminate almost all compilation errors, there are on average 51 errors per generation (see Figure 4). When a compilation fails, the kernels responsible are eliminated from the population and the new population is compiled. Typically only 1 or 2 attempts at compilation are needed. Notice that the compiler detects and reports errors in a fraction of the time it needs to generate optimised machine code, so running the first part of the compilation process multiple times is a small overhead.

2.7.1 Fitness testing: Burrows-Wheeler algorithm

There are two components to the fitness function: the quality of the answers returned and the speed at which the kernel executes. Quality is measured by comparing all of each kernel's answers one at a time with those given by the reference kernel. Thus each kernel is tested more than 100 000 times. Speed is measured using the GPU's own clocks.

The Burrows-Wheeler algorithm uses two pointers: "k" and "l", which not only indicate where the sequence occurs in the (compressed) human genome but also they indicate the range of possible locations it may match within the reference genome. Also the difference between them is the number of potential matches. k and l are initialised to span the whole of the human genome. As the search proceeds k and l should rapidly approach each other. If the query sequence is not present this is indicated by k exceeding l. If it occurs more than once then k and l will always be a certain distance a part. (This distance is actually the number of repeats.) Barracuda does not deal with ambiguous DNA base pairs in the query sequence, instead it stops the search immediately and reports this by setting k to zero. When the unmodified kernel is run, the k,l pairs it calculates for each query DNA sequence are stored. The fitness of each genetic variant is calculating by comparing the k,l pairs it calculates against those of the reference code. For each test case:

$k = 0$ (i.e. unknown base N in query sequence). Fitness penalty of 100 unless evolved kernel also sets its k to zero. (k' and l' refer to the k and l values calculated by the mutated kernel.) If the evolved kernel says the sequence does match (i.e. $k' \leq l'$) then also get another penalty of 100 (Notice otherwise l' is not checked.)

$k > l$ (i.e. query DNA sequence is not in human reference genome). if $k' \leq l'$ (provided $k' \neq 0$) then get a penalty of 100.

$k = l$ (i.e. exact unique match)

- $k' > l'$ or $k' = 0$ then penalty of 100
- $k' < l'$ then penalty is the number of matches the GP kernel predicts more than it should have, up to a maximum of 100.
- else (i.e. the GP also says they match) the penalty is the distance between k and k', up to a maximum of 10 and the same for the distance between l and l'.

$k < l$ (i.e. more than one match)

- $k' > l'$ or $k' = 0$ then the penalty is 100
- $k' \leq l'$ i.e. GP also says more than one match) The penalty is the difference between the number of matches calculated by the GP and the true number, subject to not exceeding 50.
- else (i.e. GP reports there is a unique match) the penalty is the distance between k and k', up to a maximum of 10 and the same for the distance between l and l'.

2.7.2 Elapse time measurement and variation

Generally, runtimes on GPUs are quite stable. Typically the measured standard deviation is only 0.2% of run time.

2.8 Selection

Like fitness, selection has two parts. Firstly, to be selected a GP individual must get no fitness penalties. Notice there are some cases (actually where the query sequence itself was ambiguous) where a program may get the right answer even though its answer differs in detail from that given by the manually written code. Secondly, it must be faster than the reference code. To allow for noise in the timing, by faster we

Table 3: GP to improve Barracuda

Representation:	Fix 15 discrete parameters (Table 2) plus a variable list of replacements, deletions and insertions into BNF grammar
Fitness:	Compile modified code. K20 run on 159744 (2496 × 64) (K40 161280 = 2880 × 56) 100bp sequences selected at random from recent NextGen DNA scans generated by The 1000 Genomes Project, Section 3.3. Compare its answers and run time with that of original kernel on the same hardware. See Sections 2.7 and 2.8.
Population:	Panmictic, non-elitist, generational. 1000 members.
Parameters:	Initial population of random single mutants. 50% truncation selection. 50% two point crossover, 50% mutation. No size limit. Stop after 50 generations.

mean the number of GPU ticks it took must be more than one million tics less than the human written code.

At the end of each generation the kernels whose answers attracted no fitness penalties and were faster than the human written code are sorted by their runtime and the first 500 are selected to be parents of the next generation.

3. RESULTS

The GP was run with a population of 1000 for fifty generations (see Table 3). Differences between the K20 and K40 are expected since they have different numbers of processors, clock speeds and memory bandwidths (see Table 1). Thus possibly evolution may find different trade offs between compute and memory operations in the two cases. Also evolution is open to stochastic variations, inherent in using real online timings (Section 2.7.2).

3.1 Choosing the Winner: Tesla K20

In one K20 run the final population contained 703 kernels better than the default starting program, 456 produced identical answers (see Figure 1).

The fastest correct program (11 mutations in Figure 1) contains three configuration changes and eight code changes (see Figure 5). The first configuration change (`scache_global_bwt`) switches from using a local memory array to using 4 `uint4` held in registers for the reference genome cache. The second (`cache_threads=2`) dedicates two threads per query. These are used for loading the reference human genome into this cache. The third (`BLOCK_W=128`) doubles the number of threads per block from 64 to 128.

The unroll pragma (see Section 2.2) is added to two `for` loops by changes 1 and 5. The first is in conditional code which is removed during pre-processing but, as we can see from Figure 5, the second (change 5) does indeed appear to help speed up the code. Changes 2 and 3 are both IF which have no effect. In the first, two conditions which are always true are swapped. Change 3 `<IF_Kkernel_bnf.cu_578>` disables the if statement `if(k == bwt_cuda.seq_len)`. Since k is always less than `bwt_cuda.seq_len` the condition could never be true so removing it does not cause the kernel to give wrong answers. Change 4 has no effect since the variable it changes, `l0`, is immediately updated by next line.

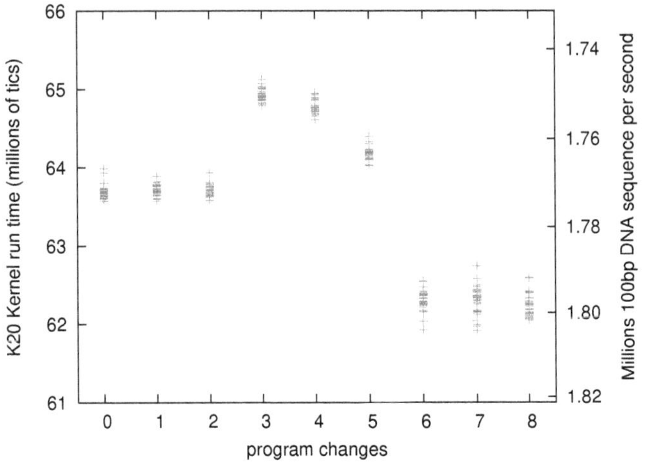

Figure 5: Performance of the fastest correct K20 kernel in last generation as more of its program changes are included.

Change 6, `<_Kkernel_bnf.cu_126>`, deletes line 126. Despite in-depth investigation, it is unclear why this is effective but it surely is. By deleting line 126, GP disables the small (8 base pair) cache used when reading DNA sequences from global memory. Ideally, CUDA will have ensured that these sequences are accessed via the GPU's read-only cache but even so, it would be expected that reading the cache 8 times instead of once would be more costly. Analysis of the CUDA compiler output and using performance tools reveals that deleting line 126 saves a single register but since the number of registers used does not appear to be near a critical number, it is not clear how this would increase performance. It may simply be that by reading the data more frequently they, and more particularly their neighbouring data, are kept in the hardware cache. Nevertheless, despite noise in the fitness function, GP has found this improvement, which is encouraging, since human programmers would be unlikely to discover it without the aid of GP.

Changes 7 and 8 also have no effect since they assign values to variables that are then immediately overwritten or they write a value to a variable which already has this value. In both cases we would expect the optimising compiler to be able to remove the inserted but non-harmful code.

3.2 Evolved Programs: Tesla K40

The fastest program in the last generation of a K40 run contains 9 changes. Although we shall describe the five coding changes in the next paragraph, they have little effect. We start by describing the four parameter changes: 1) instead of each thread processing one DNA sequence query, it uses four `cache_threads=4`. This allows the whole cache (16 words) to be loaded simultaneously. However, GP has not enabled other parallel processing options so each of the 4 threads remain synchronised and calculate the same answer four times. Nonetheless it appears that `cuda_find_exact_matches` is so I/O bound that effectively wasting three computational threads has little down side. 2) Correspondingly evolution increased the number of threads per block from 64 to 128 `BLOCK_W=128`. (This corresponds to 32 DNA queries per block.) 3) This parameter change also relates to the software cache. Setting `direct_global_bwt=1` means the human genome is read directly from global memory rather than via the hardware read only cache shared with the textures. 4) Again (see Section 3.1 above) `sequence_global` is disabled so that the query sequences are accessed via a texture.

There are five code changes. Two (`<_Kkernel_bnf.cu_948>` and `<_Kkernel_bnf.cu_947>`) delete lines 947 and 948 (`*k0 = k;` and `*l0 = 1;`) The GP has "spotted" that both k0 and l0 will have already been set to these values, so deleting these lines does not effect the kernel's answer and may speed it up. Another mutation sets the IF on line 446 to always false. This is fine as line 446 supports configuration `occ_par` which is disabled and so line 446 can never be executed. Disabling `occ_par` also means inserting `#pragma unroll 4` before the `for` loop on line 443 also has no effect. Mutation `<_Kkernel_bnf.cu_852>+<_Kkernel_bnf.cu_853>` has the effect of duplicating line 853, which does not have any harmful effects and the optimising compiler may be able to spot this and remove the duplication.

The speed up derives from using four threads to read data from the reference genome and grouping 128 threads together in a block. (Disabling `sequence_global` and `direct_global_bwt` have only a little effect on the K40). With just the thread changes the K40 processes 2.4 million short DNA sequences per second, a speed up of 54%.

On the K20, disabling `sequence_global` so that the DNA query sequences are read via a texture does have a noticeable effect. Together with `BLOCK_W=128` and `cache_threads=4`, it gives on the K20 a speed up of 28.8%, corresponding to processing 1.8 million DNA sequences per second.

3.3 Performance on Hold Out Data

The training and holdout data were randomly selected from recent popular nextGen DNA sequence data sets from The 1000 Genomes Project. (I.e. normal data, since 2 April 2012, paired-end, non-color space, 100 base-pair per end and not since withdrawn.) None of the hold out data had been used to train the GP. Over ten holdout sets the median speedup was 29.2% (49.1% on K40). The best evolved K40 program gave 53.4% (28.3% on K20) median speedup. This is on average 1 840 000 DNA sequences per second. (2 330 000 on K40) and the evolved K40 gives 2 410 000 (1 850 000 on K20). Remember `cuda_find_exact_matches` only completely deals with a fraction of the sequences. Nevertheless this is a substantial improvement over 15 000 (16 000 on K40) given by the original code averaged over all sequences.

4. DISCUSSION

4.1 Impact of Tabu Search

The impact of Tabu search is most noticeable in the initial random population and early generations (i.e. generations 1, 2 and 3) where almost as many programs are generated and discarded as are needed in the whole population (see Figure 4). As the population evolves the genetic operations find it easier to create phenotypically distinct programs. While in generation 1, only half of unique genotypes are also unique phenotypes, after generation 4, it is 82% on average.

4.2 Effectiveness of Grammar

The BNF grammar and new scoping rules have proved highly effective. The grammar ensures all offspring are syntactically correct CUDA kernel programs. After the first few generations, the population evolves with the scoping rules

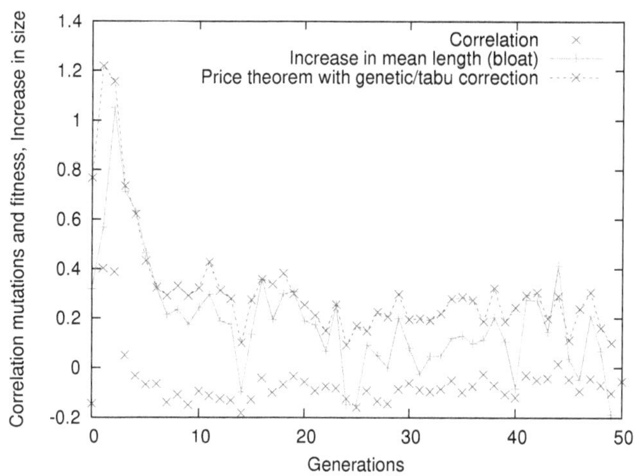

Figure 6: Actual bloat (solid line) v. Price's theorem plus mutation correction (dashed line).

to ensure on average 96.7% of new kernels compile. Enforce loop termination and array index bound protection ensures all launched GP kernels, run, terminate cleanly and can be assigned a fitness value. (0.06% of configurations were illegal, and so the kernel was not launched.)

4.3 Price's Theorem: Bloat Explained

Price's covariance theorem [21] applies to the average behaviour of populations and assumes mutation and crossover do not impose a bias on the population property of interest. The theorem says in large populations, the correlation in the current population between any property of interest (e.g. a gene) and the number of children will be equal to the change in the mean frequency of that gene between the current population and the next. Since in GP program size is inheritable, Price's theorem is readily applied to programs' lengths and so bloat is given by a positive correlation between length and fitness [15].

Notice half the time our mutation operator adds another mutation. I.e. it does not strictly follow Price's criterion. However, the dashed-$\times$ line in Figure 6 adds a correction for size changes directly caused by mutation and crossover and the tabu requirement to avoid programs which have already been tried. The actual increase is shown with the solid-$+$ line. In the initial generations the population is skewed by randomly introduced individuals. (Which are new and hence do not inherit from the previous generation). In later generations agreement is better.

4.4 Evolution of Fitness Diversity

Figure 7 shows that those kernels doing better than the manual implementation tend to have more mutations with time (bloat). (The median grows from 2 mutations in the initial random population to 11 by generation 50.) The number of kernels doing better than the manual implementation, and so eligible to be a parent, rises steadily from 136 in the initial population to on average 700 (over generations 10-50).

In the random population 46% of kernels compile and run but do not exceed the manual code. This falls to 11% (averaged over generations 10-50).

During evolution 96% of mutants compiled and 79% ran and returned all correct answers and 66% had no errors and were faster than the original code.

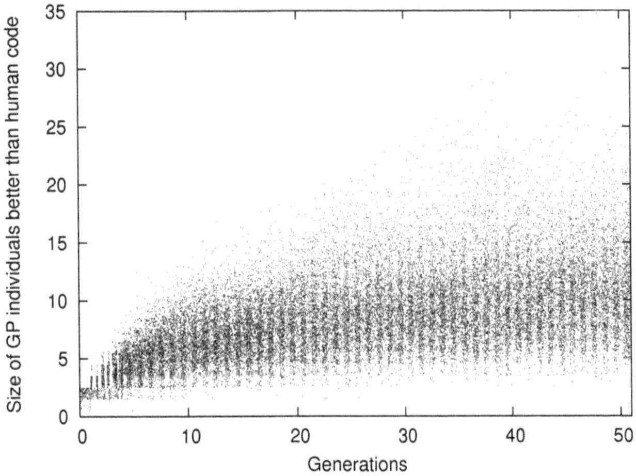

Figure 7: Evolution of number of changes in beneficial mutants (K20). Population size = 1000.

4.5 Performance Limits

The `cuda_find_exact_matches` kernel, indeed the Burrows-Wheeler algorithm itself, is fundamentally limited by the speed at which the human reference genome can be read. This is because modern GPU's have copious compute power for the BWA algorithm itself and the DNA query sequences are small and can easily be well structured for parallel operation. In contrast the BWA algorithm essentially requires random access to the reference genome for each k or l look up.

The genome data is structured so that all data for each k or l lie close together. In about 70% of cases genome data for k and l pairs are close to each other. (Both reasons make the cache of human reference genome data more effective.) Nonetheless for each base-pair in each query sequence approximately 10 integer values must be read. The software cache always reads 16 int, even if only 5 or 6 might be needed. With a K40 kernel processing 230 million base pairs per second (remember 100 base-pairs per query) it will be reading approximately 18GB per second. This is only 22% of the available bandwidth (cf. Table 1). Suggesting that a further factor of four is available.

5. CONCLUSIONS

Barracuda was developed from the widely used BWA tool (according to Google Scholar [17] has been cited more than 1000 times). Barracuda's authors [6] include both DNA sequencing and GPGPU experts. It has been under human development since 2009. Nevertheless genetic programming using phenotypic tabu search in combination with manually grown code can graft [3] speed up changes into the CUDA source. On large real world datasets, typical of current high-throughput DNA analysis, the improvement in a performance critical component is more than 100 times without loss of accuracy.

Over the complete mapping process (i.e. including all the non-CUDA code as well) on fourteen million pairs of DNA sequences with 76 bases each (note shorter sequences than the GP was trained on) barracuda_0.7.105 is 62% faster than Barracuda 0.6.2. Our version of BarraCUDA has been adopted into the core development (as barracuda_0.7.105). In the first month after it was made publicly available it was downloaded 146 times.

5.1 Acknowledgements

I am grateful for the assistance of njuffa, cbuchner1, CudaaduC, txbob, allanmac, Kevin Kang, and the many anonymous reviewers.

Tesla donated by nVidia. Funded by EPSRC grant EP/I033688/1.

GI code available via anonymous FTP and `http://www.cs.ucl.ac.uk/staff/W.Langdon/ftp/gp-code/barracuda_gp.tar.gz`

6. REFERENCES

[1] DURBIN, R. M., ET AL. A map of human genome variation from population-scale sequencing. *Nature 467*

[2] HARDING, S. L., ET AL. Distributed GP on GPUs using CUDA. In *Par. Arch. & Bioinspired Alg.*, 2009.

[3] HARMAN, M., JIA, Y., AND LANGDON, W. B. Babel pidgin: SBSE can grow and graft entirely new functionality into a real world system. In *SSBSE 2014, LNCS 8636*, pp. 247–252.

[4] HARRIS, C. *An investigation into the Application of Genetic Programming techniques to Signal Analysis and Feature Detection.* PhD thesis, UCL, 1997.

[5] Initial sequencing and analysis of the human genome. *Nature 409*, 6822, (15 Feb 2001), 860–921.

[6] KLUS, P., ET AL. BarraCUDA. *BMC Res. Notes 5*, 27

[7] KOZA, J. R. *Genetic Programming.* MIT press, 1992.

[8] LANGDON, W. B. Genetically improved software. In *Handbook of Genetic Programming Applications*, A. H. Gandomi et al., Eds. Springer.

[9] LANGDON, W. B. Mycoplasma contamination in the 1000 genomes project. *BioData Mining 7*, 3 (2014).

[10] LANGDON, W. B., AND HARMAN, M. Evolving a CUDA kernel from an nVidia template. In *WCCI 2010*

[11] LANGDON, W. B., AND HARMAN, M. Genetically improved CUDA C++ software. In *EuroGP 2014*.

[12] LANGDON, W. B., AND HARMAN, M. Optimising existing software with genetic programming. *IEEE Trans. on Evo. Comp. 19*, 1 (2015), 118–135.

[13] LANGDON, W. B., ET AL. Improving 3D medical image registration CUDA software with genetic programming. In *GECCO 2014*, ACM, pp. 951–958.

[14] LANGDON, W. B., AND NORDIN, J. P. Seeding GP populations. In *EuroGP'2000* pp. 304–315.

[15] LANGDON, W. B., AND POLI, R. Fitness causes bloat: Mutation. In *EuroGP 1998, LNCS 1391*, pp. 37–48.

[16] LE GOUES, C., ET AL. GenProg: A generic method for automatic software repair. *IEEE Transactions on Software Engineering 38*, 1 (2012), 54–72.

[17] LI, H., AND DURBIN, R. Fast and accurate long-read alignment with Burrows-Wheeler transform. *Bioinformatics 26*, 5 (2010), 589–595.

[18] PAPADAKIS, M., JIA, Y., HARMAN, M., AND LE TRAON, Y. Trivial compiler equivalence. In *ICSE 2015*

[19] PETKE, J., ET AL. Using genetic improvement and code transplants to specialise a C++ program to a problem class. In *EuroGP 2014*, pp. 137–149.

[20] POLI, R., ET AL.*A field guide to genetic programming.* `http://www.gp-field-guide.org.uk`, 2008.

[21] PRICE, G. R. Selection and covariance. *Nature 227* (1 August 1970), 520–521.

[22] SYSWERDA, G. Uniform crossover in genetic algorithms. In *FOGA 1989*, pp. 2–9.

Efficient Evolution of High Entropy RNGs Using Single Node Genetic Programming

Philip Leonard*
University of Cambridge
ppl22@cam.ac.uk

David Jackson
University of Liverpool
djackson@liverpool.ac.uk

ABSTRACT

Random Number Generators are an important aspect of many modern day software systems, cryptographic protocols and modelling techniques. To be more accurate, it is Pseudo Random Number Generators (PRNGs) that are more commonly used over their expensive, and less practical hardware based counterparts. Given that PRNGs rely on some deterministic algorithm (typically a Linear Congruential Generator) we can leverage Shannon's theory of information as our fitness function in order to generate these algorithms by evolutionary means. In this paper we compare traditional Genetic Programming (GP) against its graph based implementation, Single Node Genetic Programming (SNGP), for this task. We show that with SNGPs unique program structure and use of dynamic programming, it is possible to obtain smaller, higher entropy PRNGs, over six times faster and produced at a solution rate twice that achieved using Koza's standard GP model. We also show that the PRNGs obtained from evolutionary methods produce higher entropy outputs than other widely used PRNGs and Hardware RNGs (specifically recordings of atmospheric noise), as well as surpassing them in a variety of other statistical tests presented in the NIST RNG test suite.

Categories and Subject Descriptors

I.2.8 [**Artificial Intelligence**]: Problem Solving, Control Methods, and Search; I.2.2 [**Artificial Intelligence**]: Automatic Programming—*Program synthesis*; G.3 [**Probability and Statistics**]: Random Number Generation

Keywords

Single Node Genetic Programming, Pseudo Random Number Generator, True Random Number Generator, Information Entropy.

*This work was carried out while the author was at the University of Liverpool

GECCO '15, July 11 - 16, 2015, Madrid, Spain

ISBN 978-1-4503-3472-3/15/07...$15.00

DOI: http://dx.doi.org/10.1145/2739480.2754820

1. INTRODUCTION

Random Number Generators have many computational, scientific and societal applications. They are essential in cryptography, statistical sampling, Monte Carlo simulations, randomized algorithms, password generation, gambling and other applications where unpredictable behaviour must be modelled. There exists a wide variety of statistical [5, 14], psychological [1] and philosophical [4] interpretations of what constitutes a random sequence, but in reality, randomness has no strict mathematical definition. As far as statistics is concerned, there exists a plethora of tests at our disposal. These include the gap test, frequency test, runs test and information entropy test among others described in the NIST Test Suite for Random and Pseudo Random Number Generators for Cryptographic Applications [5]. There is no strict way to prove randomness; rather, it is a probabilistic property, meaning that a random sequence can be characterized and described in terms of probability. In this paper, our conception of randomness is illustrated through Shannon's test for information entropy [20], which is a measure of uncertainty in random variables of a sequence.

A Pseudo Random Number Generator (PRNG) is a deterministic algorithm that generates sequences of numbers that possess the characteristics of "truly"[1] random numbers. Mathematical operators are applied to some input in order to fabricate a "random" number or bit sequence. In practice, these PRNGs typically take the form of Linear Congruential Generators (LCGs), which require initial seeding[2], and which use the last random number generated as a component in a modulo function to generate the next. PRNGs differ from "True" Random Number Generators which employ specialist pieces of hardware to measure an unpredictable environmental occurrence such as atmospheric noise measured using a radio antenna [7], or recording quantum fluctuations in a vacuum state [21].

While the notion of a deterministic algorithm generating random numbers is somewhat counter intuitive, their efficiency and accessibility over their hardware counterparts make them more desirable for many real world applications. One benefit is that their generation rate is limited by the performance of a (commodity) computational device as opposed

[1] We use this term with caution throughout this paper to describe sequences of numbers generated by hardware RNGs. If God doesn't play dice then we could theoretically predict these readings. Quantum entanglement would disagree.

[2] A common seed value is the number of nanoseconds since the Unix epoch (00:00:00 (UTC), Thursday, 1 January 1970).

to the bandwidth of some expensive instrument. Evolving PRNGs is therefore an applicable problem instance for Genetic Programming, given that there is no known deterministic way of producing a RNG with high entropy. In this paper we show that it is possible to do this using both the GP and SNGP paradigms, and that SNGP proves a superior method of the two.

2. DEFINITION OF ENTROPY

In the work described here, we will apply our techniques to the same problem as that described by Koza [15], in which the goal is to genetically breed a RNG that randomises a sequence of consecutive integers J (from $1 \rightarrow 2^{14}$), and produces a vector of random binary digits of size J as its output. In practice the size of the sequence J is user defined, such that increasing this parameter will evolve RNGs to produce longer, higher entropy bit sequences. This is a clear trade-off between runtime and a solutions effectiveness over a bit stream size.

Again following Koza, we use the Shannon entropy equation from the field of Information Theory as our fitness function [6,20]. The entropy of a sequence of binary digits is the frequency distribution of a set of binary sub-sequences of length h in that sequence. The Shannon entropy equation for all possible 2^h binary sub-sequences of length h is:

$$E_h = -\sum_{j} P_{(hj)} \log_2 P_{(hj)}$$

Here j ranges over all possible sub-sequences of length h in the binary sequence (the RNG output in this case).

To calculate the entropy for the output of every RNG, we must evaluate it for more than one binary subsequence length. This is achieved by calculating the summation of the equation above for E_h, ranging over h from 1 to N_{max}:

$$E_{total} = \sum_{h=1}^{N_{max}} \left[-\sum_{j} P_{(hj)} \log_2 P_{(hj)} \right]$$

In order to achieve maximum entropy for E_h, the probabilities for all 2^h binary subsequences of length h must be equal to $\frac{1}{2^h}$.

For both our GP and SNGP implementations we follow Koza's implementation and define $N_{max} = 7$. This gives us the maximum entropy and therefore the maximum fitness of 28 (bits) for a single RNG:

$$E_{max} = \sum_{i=1}^{N_{max}} i = \frac{N_{max}(N_{max}+1)}{2} = 28$$

Again, in practice N_{max} is a user defined parameter. Increasing this parameter will evolve RNGs with higher entropies over the given sequence. This is a clear trade-off between runtime and the entropy of solutions.

Algorithm 1 contains the pseudo code for an efficient implementation of the Shannon entropy equation. At its core, the algorithm relies on the $O(m+n)$ Knuth-Morris-Pratt pattern matching algorithm [13], where m is the length of the pattern and n is the length of the string (equivalent to $O(j + |O|)$ in our implementation).

Algorithm 1 Shannon-Entropy(O, N_{max})

Input: RNG output vector O, and integer N_{max}
Output: Total entropy E_{total}, and scalar entropies $E_1, E_2, ..., E_{N_{max}}$

$E_{total} \leftarrow 0$
for $h \leftarrow 1$ to N_{max} **do**
  $F \leftarrow \emptyset$
  $tocc \leftarrow 0$

  $j \leftarrow 2^{h-1}$
  if $h == 1$ **then**
    $j \leftarrow 0$
  end if

  for j to $2^h - 1$ **do**
    $occ \leftarrow$KMP-Matching(j_2, O)
    $F \cup occ$
    $tocc \leftarrow tocc + occ$
  end for
  $E_h \leftarrow 0$
  for $\forall x \in F$ **do**
    $E_h \leftarrow E_h + (-1 * (\frac{x}{tocc} \log_2 \frac{x}{tocc}))$
  end for
  $E_{total} \leftarrow E_{total} + E_h$
end for
return $E_{total}, E_1, E_2, ..., E_{N_{max}}$

3. BACKGROUND ON SNGP

Single Node Genetic Programming is a distinct variation on the traditional GP methodology. In comparison with GP, SNGP is augmented around graphs and dynamic programming, giving rise to considerable efficiency and solution rate gains over GP [11].

Instead of a population of individual trees, SNGP is concerned with a population of individual nodes that form a single graph structure. As in GP, these nodes are selected from a set of functions and terminals, where leaf nodes are terminals and branches are functions. Crucially, each node in the graph represents the root of a tree in its own right.

Jackson [10] describes the SNGP model in the following way; A population is a set M of N members where:

$$M = \{m_0,\ m_1,\ ...,\ m_{N-1}\}$$

Each member m_i is a tuple of the form:

$$m_i = < u_i,\ r_i,\ S_i,\ P_i,\ O_i >$$

u_i	-	node $u_i \in \{T \cup F\}$
r_i	-	fitness of the node
S_i	-	set of successors of the node
P_i	-	set of predecessors of the node
O_i	-	output vector for this node

When the initial graph is generated, each member of the terminal set T is added exactly once, followed by $N - |T|$ randomly selected members of F.

SNGP makes use of dynamic programming, where solutions to subproblems are aggregated to form solutions to complete problems. As the nodes are added to the graph, the output for each node is calculated. When further nodes are added at a lower depth than the previous nodes, instead of evaluating the whole tree, the output for that node is calculated from the outputs of its successor nodes (picking successors at a lower depth also prevents looping in the graph).

SNGP makes use of only one evolutionary operator known as successor mutation (*smut*). This operation randomly selects a branch node in the graph, and randomly mutates one member of S_i to some other member of the graph (with a greater depth). It is therefore only necessary to recalculate the output vector for those nodes effected by this operation. Identifying nodes that have been effected involves recursively propagating up the graph, through the predecessor sets.

4. BREEDING A RNG USING GP

In order to replicate Koza's results [15], we must follow his defined GP implementation.

We begin by defining the terminal set T and the set of functions F:

$$T = \{J, \Re\}$$
$$F = \{+, -, *, /, \%\}$$

J, as discussed above, represents the value in the sequence 1 to 2^{14}, and $\Re$ represents a small random integer constant from the set $\{0, 1, 2, 3\}$. In our set F of functions, "/" denotes the protected integer quotient function and "%" denotes the protected modulus function, where both use the protected division function that returns 1 when attempting to divide by zero (otherwise returning the normal quotient). All terminals have an arity of 0, and all the functions have an arity of 2.

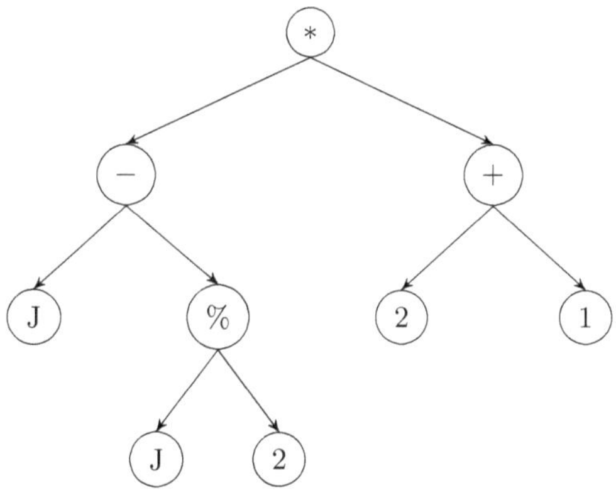

Figure 1: *Example RNG binary tree*

Recall that our fitness function has a maximum fitness of 28, given that $N_{max} = 7$. Koza suggests a termination fitness of 27.990 (99.96% entropy) and a run size of 51 generations (50 generations plus the initial population generation).

The first step is to create an initial population. As Koza suggests [18], we use a population size of 500 as a standard parameter[3]. In order to generate a wide and genetically diverse population, Koza also suggests the use of an even combination of both *grow* and *full* methods to generate program trees, known as the "ramped half and half method".

[3]Later we show the effect of altering this parameter

The *full* method ensures that trees are as large as they are permitted (by the max tree size parameter), and the *grow* method randomly decides when to terminate a branch on a tree, giving rise to trees of diverse shapes and sizes.

RNG trees are stored and evaluated as prefix expressions (the RNG in Figure 1 can be written as the prefix expression $* - J\%J2 + 21$). To calculate the output of each RNG tree, we must run through the sequence J from $i = 1$ to 2^{14}, substituting the occurrences of J with the value of i. The Least Significant Bit (LSB) of the output given $J = i$ corresponds to the value in the binary sequence at position i. The RNGs are therefore evolved on their ability to create a distribution of odd and even integers with high entropy (i.e. a binary stream). Once the randomised binary sequence O has been generated for each member of the population, it is then passed to the fitness function and the entropy/fitness for each RNG is calculated.

Koza defines that each new generation be produced using a 10% Fitness Proportionate Reproduction (FPR) to 90% crossover split of genetic operations. For crossover, one of the parents is selected based on fitness as opposed to both for FPR. We define this fitness selection mechanism in the following way, where p_i is the probability that i is selected:

$$p_i = \left(\frac{f_i}{\sum_{x=1}^{|P|} f_x} \right) \qquad \begin{array}{l} f_i \text{ - fitness value of } i \\ f_x \text{ - fitness value of } x \\ |P| \text{ - population size} \end{array}$$

The actual crossover mechanism takes two trees (as a result of the selection mechanism), and randomly selects a point in each tree based upon a 0.9 to 0.1 function to terminal selection probability. Two new offspring trees are generated by swapping the subtrees between the two selected crossover points in each original tree. This process is then repeated $\frac{|P|}{2}$ times, in order to generate a new population of offspring RNG trees. The entire process is then repeated until one or both of the termination criteria is satisfied.

5. BREEDING A RNG USING SNGP

For our SNGP implementation, the sets of functions and terminals are identical to those used in GP. We also use the same fitness function and the same approach to randomising a sequence J into a binary stream.

As discussed earlier, and as can be seen in Figures 2 and 3, the population is represented as a graph, where each node of the graph represents a member of the population and is the root of a RNG (program) tree in its own right, as well as a component of other RNGs.

For the SNGP implementation, we retain the termination entropy/fitness of 27.990 bits. We are also concerned with the number of successor mutation attempts rather than the number of generations. It is suggested [10] that 25,000 *smut* operations should be used as a termination value that matches the number of individuals generated in a GP run (population size of 500 * 50 generations). Later we will show that only a fraction is needed to produce high quality results, in order to conduct a trade-off for a reduction in computation time.

We now describe SNGPs evolution mechanism in the context of our problem. In the example in Figure 2, the graph represents the following population of prefix expressions (RNG trees) before mutation:

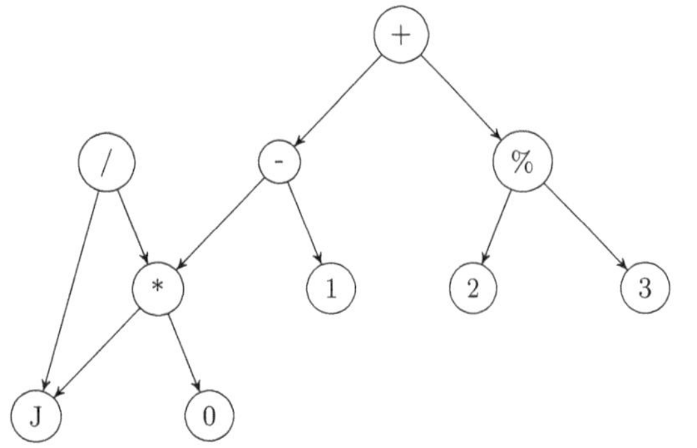

Figure 2: *Example population before successor mutation*

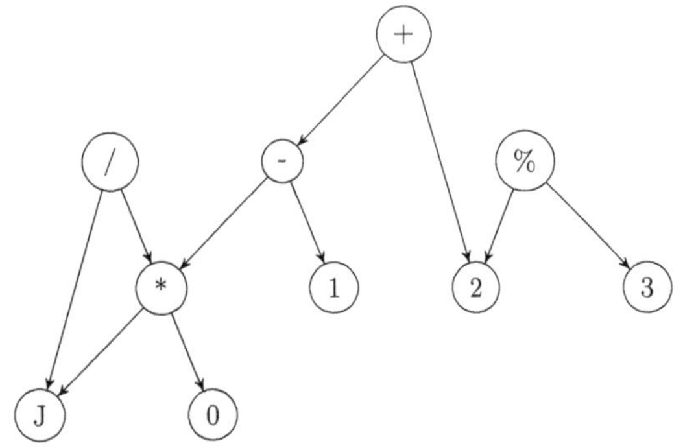

Figure 3: *Example population after sucessor mutation*

$$\{J\}, \{0\}, \{1\}, \{2\}, \{3\}, \{* \; J \; 0\}, \{/ \; J \; * \; J \; 0\},$$
$$\{- \; * \; J \; 0 \; 1\}, \{\% \; 2 \; 3\}, \{+ \; - \; * \; J \; 0 \; 1 \; \% \; 2 \; 3\}.$$

After the *smut* operation, the mutated graph in Figure 3 represents the following prefix expressions:

$$\{J\}, \{0\}, \{1\}, \{2\}, \{3\}, \{* \; J \; 0\}, \{/ \; J \; * \; J \; 0\},$$
$$\{- \; * \; J \; 0 \; 1\}, \{\% \; 2 \; 3\}, \{+ \; - \; * \; J \; 0 \; 1 \; 2\}$$

Mutations at deeper nodes in the graph have a greater effect on the shape and output of other, shallower members of the population.

Evolution is driven by a multi property hill climbing approach; where after successor mutation, the new graph is kept if either there is an increase in the fitness of the fittest node, or if the fitness sum of the population increases. Otherwise the effects of the *smut* operation are reversed (the new population is discarded).

We found this multi property hill climbing approach to be the most effective way of reducing average solution discovery time. While there is a possibility of fitness decay[4]; this mechanism proved to work better at keeping the population out of an evolutionary rut. Evolution is repeated until one or both of the termination criteria have been met.

6. COMPARING GP AND SNGP

In order to evaluate the performance of both GP and SNGP methodologies for evolving RNGs, we must state the characteristics which define the superior methodology for this problem. An ideal candidate will produce a higher rate of smaller solutions[5], with a higher average fitness and in a shorter space of time.

We conducted 50 runs of both the GP and SNGP implementations under the parameters described in sections 4 and 5. All of the following tests were carried out on a system with a 2.8GhZ AMD 5600+ processor, where our implementations were compiled as single threaded C programs in Microsoft Visual Studio, under identical load conditions.

After 50 runs of both implementations under standard parameters, the following average results in table 1 were achieved[6];

Table 1: *50 Run Average: GP vs SNGP*

	SNGP	GP
Avg Run Time	**606.9s**	4111.6s
Avg Sol Run Time	**483.2s**	2173.4s
Avg Non Sol Time	**1701.1s**	5403.8s
Solution Rate	**88%**	40%
Avg Sol Size	**27.9**	154.6
Avg Final Size	**30.1**	277.8
Avg Run Fitness	**27.88153318**	27.2570626
Best Sol Fitness	**27.995729**	27.995032
Avg Sol Fitness	27.9917378	**27.99195145**

SNGP comes out victorious in all but average solution fitness (which is only beaten by 0.00076% entropy). Over the 50 runs, SNGP finds over twice as many solutions, in under a quarter of the time. The solutions are also on average 5.5 times smaller given that branches in the trees are repeated (and can be calculated dynamically).

Table 2 shows the results of 10 SNGP runs where the number of *smut* operations is set to 25000. By doing so, we can achieve a desirable 100% solution rate. Comparing this with the 50 runs with a 2500 *smut* limit, reducing this parameter by one tenth does not reduce the solution rate by the same amount. It would appear that comparatively, most of the solutions are found in the first 2500 *smut* attempts.

Table 2: *10 Run Average: GP vs SNGP (25000 smut limit)*

	SNGP	GP
Avg Run Time	**1947.8s**	4111.6s
Avg Sol Time	**1947.8s**	2173.4s
Solution Rate	**100%**	40%
Avg Sol Size	**30.8**	154.6
Avg Final Size	**30.8**	277.8
Avg Run Fitness	**27.99154673**	27.2570626
Best Sol Fitness	**27.995936**	27.995032
Avg Sol Fitness	27.99154673	**27.99195145**

By increasing the number of *smut* attempts from 2500 to 25000 we obtain a 100% solution rate at the expense of an average solution run time close to that of GP.

[4]The fittest node fitness increases while the total fitness decreases, followed by the opposite happening in the next *smut* operation, resulting in both values being lower than they were originally

[5]Runs that terminate with a candidate with an fitness greater than or equal to 27.990

[6]In all of the following result tables, bold text indicates the winner for that specific criterion

Therefore we can also say that using 2 independent runs (which can be run in parallel) of our SNGP implementation given 2500 *smut* operations and a probability of success of $p_s = 0.88$, that the chance of success over those two runs is equal to $1 - (1 - 0.88)^2 = 0.9856$ or 98.56%. Therefore with a reduced *smut* operation parameter we can achieve a probability of success close to that of 100%[7] and benefit from a reduction in computation time.

Now we take a look at the performance implications when altering the population sizes of GP and SNGP implementations. In Figures 4 and 5 we can see the effect that a reduced population size has on the rate of solutions produced by both methodologies. For SNGP, we gathered data from 10 runs at each of the following 20% population size decrements (and a final 10% decrement) {100, 80, 60, 40, 20, 10}. We gathered the same data from the GP implementation for the population size decrements of {500, 400, 300, 200, 100, 50}. We obtained a 0% solution rate for a population size of 10 for SNGP and 50 for GP.

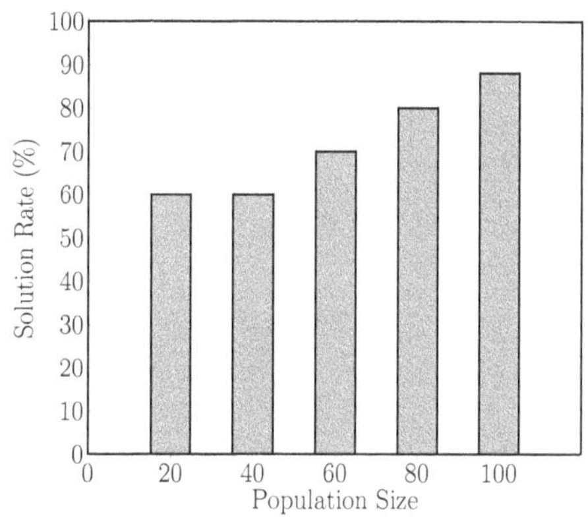

Figure 4: *Reduced pop size of SNGP*

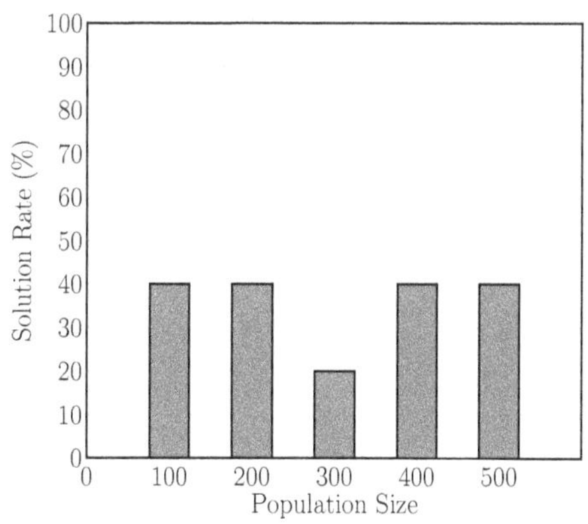

Figure 5: *Reduced pop size of GP*

From Figures 4 and 5, we see that both GP and SNGP are resilient to a reduction in population size, up until a size 10% that of the original. What is striking is that we still obtain a solution rate of 60% for a population size of 20 for SNGP. We also note that a reduction in population has a knock on effect to SNGPs solution sizes, and therefore a reduction in search space. As such, a reduction in population size for SNGP can be beneficial, whereas for GP its only effect is to reduce the size of the gene pool.

[7]Never 100% as $\lim_{x \to \infty} 1 - (1 - 0.88)^x = 1$

The surface plots in Figures 10 and 11 in the Appendix continue to illustrate SNGP superiority over GP concerning runtime, entropy and solution size. In Figure 11 we observe groupings of high entropy, succinct SNGP solutions, found far quicker than those produced by GP in figure 10.

During evaluation we gathered the prefix expressions of all of our solutions. The RNG tree in Figure 6 is a simplified version of our fittest SNGP solution, which achieved 27.996 bits of entropy.

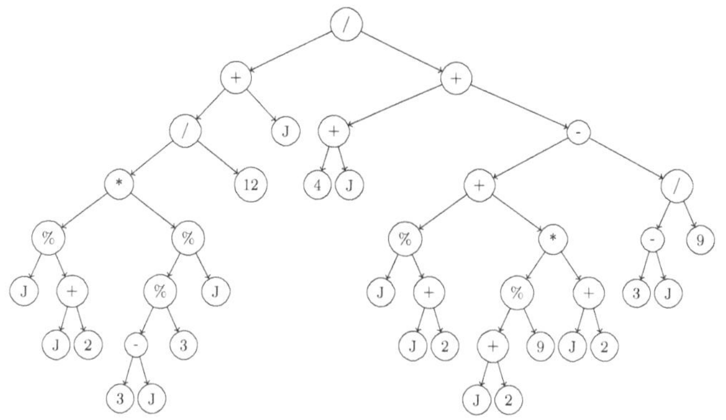

Figure 6: *Simplified RNG Tree*

This simplified tree can also be represented as the infix function $rand(J)$ below;

$$rand(J) = \frac{\left(\frac{(J \bmod (J+2)) \,*\, (((3-J) \bmod 3) \bmod J)}{12}\right)+J}{(4+J)+\left((J \bmod (J+2)+((J+2) \bmod 9)*(J+2))-(\frac{3-J}{9})\right)}$$

We were able to obtain a more succinct high entropy (27.995 bit) solution during our evaluation. It takes the form of the following infix function:

$$rand'(J) = \frac{(2-(2-J))}{J \mod (2-(\frac{J}{6}))}$$

We use $rand'(J)$ as our genetic RNG for the remainder of our evaluation. Such expressions may easily be incorporated into code and PRNG libraries.

7. COMPARING GENETIC AND CONVENTIONAL RNGS

We now take the RNGs obtained using the SNGP and GP paradigms and compare them against other conventional RNGs. We use a TRNG (specifically a device that collects atmospheric noise) provided by the random.org service [7]. This way we can compare our genetically bred randomisers to a source of non-deterministic random data (i.e. the random values are not the result of some deterministic algorithm or equation). We also use the C *rand*() function incorporated in the standard C programming language library as a comparable PRNG that (like our RNGs) produces numbers deterministically.

Unlike our RNGs which use a sequence of integers J, the C *rand*() function uses a Linear Congruential Generator (LCG) algorithm which bootstraps its calls. The output at call $n+1$ is calculated using the output of call n in some point in the equation. This LCG algorithm/equation is shown below:

$$X_{n+1} = (aX_n + c) \mod m$$

$m, 0 < m$	-	the modulo component
$a, 0 < a < m$	-	the multiplier
$c, 0 \leq c < m$	-	the increment
$X_0, 0 \leq X_0 < m$	-	the seed

LCGs are vulnerable to attack [8, 19]. The variable m in the equation above can be calculated given only 3 outputs since LCG outputs commonly fall into 3 dimensional planes. Using RNGs that are evolved genetically could have cryptographic advantages. Attackers wouldn't necessarily have knowledge of the the deterministic equation in the RNG, and the equation itself could be periodically updated, reducing the lifespan of cryptanalyst attacks.

We analyse the random data produced by these two methods in the same way as our fitness function in the genetically bred RNGs (seen in Algorithm 1). This way we can test all of our RNGs fairly under the same conditions, using the same metric.

We used the data from the 50 runs of our GP and SNGP implementations, and then ran the same number of tests on the conventional RNGs. The results can be seen in Table 3.

Table 3: *TRNG vs C PRNG vs SNGP vs GP*

	TRNG	C	SNGP	GP
Highest Entropy	27.9939	27.9919	**27.9957**	27.9950
Avg Entropy	27.9899	27.9898	27.9917	**27.9919**

From the results shown above, we can see that the RNGs produced by Genetic means outperform both the C *rand*() function and the TRNG in terms of entropy. SNGP produces the candidate with the highest fitness and GP produces the highest average fitness (slightly higher than that of SNGP which also beats the two conventional methods). Whilst the genetic RNGs only beat the conventional methods by a fraction, this small improvement can make all the difference when producing high entropy random sequences.

Although our genetic RNGs are evolved using entropy as a fitness metric, the NIST test suite [5] reveals that they also rank top when other statistical metrics are applied. This is illustrated in Table 4.

Table 4: *NIST test suite p-values*

	Genetic	TRNG	C
Block Freq	0.211219	0.351090	**0.823944**
Cusum (Fwd)	**0.985895**	0.275402	0.723854
Cusum (Rvs)	**0.831316**	0.305578	0.672568
FFT	0.000000	**0.807421**	0.000494
Frequency	**0.661749**	0.164339	0.511663
Lin Complex	**0.693358**	0.029617	0.642653
Longest Run	**0.916436**	0.407002	0.338103
Overlapping	0.343770	0.121702	**0.863446**
Rank	**0.633794**	0.313674	0.007379
Runs	**0.938917**	0.573378	0.460661
Serial	**0.856075**	0.467721	0.341481

Here the p-value of a test indicates the strength of the evidence against the null hypothesis. In terms of these tests, the p-value determines the probability that a perfect RNG would have produced a sequence less random for that test. Therefore a score of 1 indicates a perfect random sequence and a score of 0 indicates an non-random sequence in the domain of the test.

Random data can be interpreted through different media such as in audio, video and images. We can create 128x128 (i.e. $\sqrt{16384} \times \sqrt{16384}$) bitmaps for each of the methods by interpreting a single bit as a black pixel if it is equal to 1 or as a white pixel if it is equal to 0 from the sequence of 16834 bits.

The images in Figures 7, 8 and 9 were created from 3 runs chosen from each of the methods.

Figure 7: *Visualisation of C rand() output*

Figure 8: *Visualisation of TRNG output*

Figure 9: *Visualisation of rand′(J) output*

We can clearly see repetitions at uniform intervals in the C *rand*() function, giving rise to vertical patterns (the images are populated with pixels from top left to top right and then repeated down the image). This shows that certain sequences are repeated regularly at uniform intervals (giving rise to lower entropy compared to the other two methods). The data from random.org has no distinguishable patterns, however this does not necessarily correspond to a higher entropy, as numbers may still be repeated in a non-uniform fashion.

On close inspection, the data/image from the genetic RNG might show a subtle pattern to some viewers eyes. This is in fact what gives rise to its very high entropy; a uniformity in distribution and a lower repetition. As our genetic RNG has the highest entropy, in these 16384 bits/pixels every binary subsequence of length 1 to 7 needs to occur with (almost) equal probability. Therefore when GP and SNGP are engineering this through evolution, it causes the RNGs to produce some uniformity (causing it to fail the FFT test, which detects pattern repetition on a broader scale than our entropy metric).

8. RELATED WORK

Creating efficient and effective PRNGs is an important computational and statistical problem. One that has real world security implications [3,12] given that they are responsible for the production of large prime numbers in cryptographic key generation. This security demand, coupled with their various other applications, encourages statisticians and computer scientists alike to "manually" produce effective solutions to this problem [2, 17, 22].

Work on evolving PRNGs using GP and Evolutionary Computing (EC) methods is not an idea that has been left completely untouched since Koza's pioneering work in the field in the early 1990's. Work by Lamenca-Martinez et al. [16] takes a different approach to producing PRNGs through evolutionary means, using a mix of logical and bit-wise operators in the function set, and the χ^2 statistical test as a fitness function. They present Lamar as a single "holy grail" PRNG, that weighs in at 100 nodes and was found after 153 generations. The authors primary focus is around producing a single PRNG suitable for cryptographic application. In comparison, our focus has been on the EC means by which we can complete this task, and have presented SNGP as a more efficient method for generating PRNGs. As a result we obtain more succinct and efficient solutions to this problem.

Work by Julio Cesar et al. [9] is more akin to our work, with a focus on finding efficient solutions using the GP methodology. However the authors retain the use of the standard GP methodology, with a population size of 100 and a large generation target of 10000. We show that only a fraction of these parameters is required in order to gain a high solution rate using SNGP [8].

9. DISCUSSION

From our work we leave open further questions and avenues of research. A multi objective optimisation implementation for GP and SNGP using other statistical metrics [5], as well as Shannon entropy, might allow us to produce even more powerful RNGs (specifically for cryptographic purposes). Even though as we have seen, our Genetic RNGs perform comparably well in these tests, there is still space for improvement (especially with regards to the FFT test).

Further comparison of SNGP against GP and other EC techniques such as Genetic Algorithms, through new problem instances, will continue to push SNGP forward as a viable candidate for solving EC problems in the future.

Further mathematical and logical operators might also be added to the set of functions used in the GP and SNGP implementations. By taking x as the value of the left branch and y as the value of the right branch, we might employ any binary operation, be it mathematical or logical. This could include the exponent function (x^y) or the logarithmic function (i.e. $x \log_2 y$, or $\log_x y$). The xth root function might also be used in the form $\sqrt[x]{y}$ where again, x and y are the values of the two branches. It is hoped that we can identify a set of efficient and more effective operators.

An interesting future research approach might be to apply the work by Lamar [16], i.e. logical and bit-wise operators with a χ^2 fitness function, to our efficient SNGP model.

10. CONCLUSION

In this paper we have demonstrated that it is possible to breed high entropy RNGs using both the GP and SNGP paradigms. Taking Koza's research [15], we were able to replicate his implementation and expand it to the SNGP paradigm specified by Jackson [10].

We were then able to show that the SNGP paradigm produces better results for the application of evolving a RNG than standard GP, adding to the list of problems where this holds true [10]. For the means of evolving RNGs, SNGP produces solutions that are on average 5.5 times smaller, and at a rate of over twice that of GP. Not only this but these results are also produced close to 7 times quicker than GP (for solutions and non solutions combined).

Finally, we were then able to show that the RNGs produced by evolutionary means outperform two other common place RNGs, surpassing them in terms of entropy and, perhaps even more strikingly, a variety of other statistical tests presented in the NIST suite [5]. From our evaluation we were also able to obtain very succinct, high entropy PRNGs that appear to have been hiding in plain sight as possible alternatives to PRNGs used in programming languages and cryptographic protocols.

11. REFERENCES

[1] A. D. Baddeley. The capacity for generating information by randomization. *Quarterly Journal of Experimental Psychology*, 18(2):119–129, 1966. PMID: 5935121.

[2] Lenore Blum, Manuel Blum, and Mike Shub. A simple unpredictable pseudo-random number generator. *SIAM Journal on computing*, 15(2):364–383, 1986.

[3] Leo Dorrendorf, Zvi Gutterman, and Benny Pinkas. Cryptanalysis of the random number generator of the windows operating system. *ACM Transactions on Information and System Security (TISSEC)*, 13(1):10, 2009.

[4] Antony Eagle. Randomness is unpredictability. *The British Journal for the Philosophy of Science*, 56(4):749–790, 2005.

[8]Recall that we can achieve a 60% solution rate with a population size of 20 using 2500 *smut* operations. As a result processing only 20*2500=50000 individuals as opposed to Juilo Ceasar's 100*10000=1 million individuals (i.e. one twentieth)

[5] Andrew Rukhin et al. A statistical test suite for random and pseudorandom number generators for cryptographic applications, 2001.

[6] Robert M. Gray. *Entropy and Information Theory.* Springer-Verlag New York, Inc., New York, NY, USA, 1990.

[7] M Haahr. Random.org - true random number service. [online] random.org. *Available at: http://www.random.org [Accessed 27th March 2015].*

[8] Haldir[RET]. How to crack a linear congruential generator. *Reverse Engineering Team, Available at: http://www.reteam.org/papers/e59.pdf [Accessed 27th March 2015]*, 2004.

[9] J.C. Hernandez, A. Seznec, and P. Isasi. On the design of state-of-the-art pseudorandom number generators by means of genetic programming. In *Evolutionary Computation, 2004. CEC2004. Congress on*, volume 2, pages 1510–1516 Vol.2, June 2004.

[10] David Jackson. A new, node-focused model for genetic programming. In Alberto Moraglio, Sara Silva, Krzysztof Krawiec, Penousal Machado, and Carlos Cotta, editors, *Genetic Programming*, volume 7244 of *Lecture Notes in Computer Science*, pages 49–60. Springer Berlin Heidelberg, 2012.

[11] David Jackson. Single node genetic programming on problems with side effects. In *Parallel Problem Solving from Nature-PPSN XII*, pages 327–336. Springer, 2012.

[12] John Kelsey, Bruce Schneier, David Wagner, and Chris Hall. Cryptanalytic attacks on pseudorandom number generators. In *Fast Software Encryption*, pages 168–188. Springer, 1998.

[13] D. Knuth, J. Morris, Jr., and V. Pratt. Fast pattern matching in strings. *SIAM Journal on Computing*, 6(2):323–350, 1977.

[14] Donald Ervin Knuth. *The art of computer programming: sorting and searching*, volume 2, Seminumerical Algorithms. Pearson Education, 1998.

[15] John R. Koza. Evolving a computer program to generate random numbers using the genetic programming paradigm. In *ICGA*, pages 37–44. 1991.

[16] Carlos Lamenca-Martinez, Julio Cesar Hernandez-Castro, Juan M Estevez-Tapiador, and Arturo Ribagorda. Lamar: A new pseudorandom number generator evolved by means of genetic programming. In *Parallel Problem Solving from Nature-PPSN IX*, pages 850–859. Springer, 2006.

[17] Makoto Matsumoto and Takuji Nishimura. Mersenne twister: a 623-dimensionally equidistributed uniform pseudo-random number generator. *ACM Transactions on Modeling and Computer Simulation (TOMACS)*, 8(1):3–30, 1998.

[18] Riccardo Poli, William B. Langdon, and Nicholas Freitag McPhee. *A field guide to genetic programming.* Published via `http://lulu.com` and freely available at `http://www.gp-field-guide.org.uk`, 2008. (With contributions by J. R. Koza).

[19] James Reeds. Cracking a random number generator. *Cryptologia*, 1(1):20–26, 1977.

[20] C. E. Shannon. A mathematical theory of communication. *SIGMOBILE Mob. Comput. Commun. Rev.*, 5(1):3–55, January 2001.

[21] Thomas Symul, SM Assad, and Ping K Lam. Real time demonstration of high bitrate quantum random number generation with coherent laser light. *Applied Physics Letters*, 98(23):231103, 2011.

[22] Stephen Wolfram. Random sequence generation by cellular automata. *Advances in applied mathematics*, 7(2):123–169, 1986.

APPENDIX

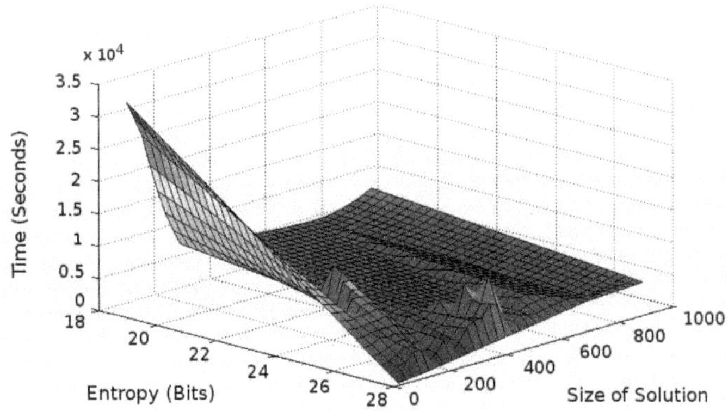

Figure 10: *GP 50 Run Performance Surface Plot*

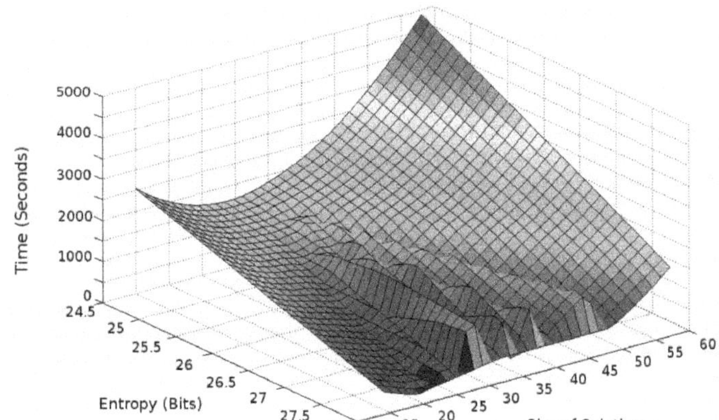

Figure 11: *SNGP 50 Run Performance Surface Plot*

In Figures 10 and 11 please note the reduced scale size for SNGP over GP on all 3 axes.

Impact of Crossover Bias in Genetic Programming

Nicholas Freitag McPhee
Div. of Science and Math
U of Minnesota, Morris
Morris, MN USA-56267

M. Kirbie Dramdahl
Div. of Science and Math
U of Minnesota, Morris
Morris, MN USA-56267

David Donatucci
Div. of Science and Math
U of Minnesota, Morris
Morris, MN USA-56267

ABSTRACT

In tree-based genetic programming (GP) with sub-tree crossover, the parent contributing the root portion of the tree (the *root parent*) often contributes more to the semantics of the resulting child than the *non-root parent*. Previous research demonstrated that when the root parent had greater fitness than the non-root parent, the fitness of the child tended to be better than if the reverse were true. Here we explore the significance of that asymmetry by introducing the notion of *crossover bias*, where we bias the system in favor of having the more fit parent as the root parent.

In this paper we apply crossover bias to several problems. In most cases we found that crossover bias either improved performance or had no impact. We also found that the effectiveness of crossover bias is dependent on the problem, and significantly dependent on other parameter choices.

While this work focuses specifically on sub-tree crossover in tree-based GP, artificial and biological evolutionary systems often have substantial asymmetries, many of which remain understudied. This work suggests that there is value in further exploration of the impacts of these asymmetries.

Categories and Subject Descriptors

I.2.2 [**Artificial Intelligence**]: Automatic Programming-Program transformation

Keywords

genetic programming; crossover bias; root parent; crossover asymmetry; sub-tree crossover

1. INTRODUCTION

As Figure 1 illustrates, the widely used sub-tree crossover operator in tree-based genetic programming (GP) [16] is an inherently asymmetric operation, with one parent contributing the root node and, in most cases, a substantially larger number of nodes than the other parent. This asymmetry has been noted before, e.g., [11] where they refer to the parent

GECCO '15, July 11 - 15, 2015, Madrid, Spain

ISBN 978-1-4503-3472-3/15/07...$15.00

DOI: http://dx.doi.org/10.1145/2739480.2754778

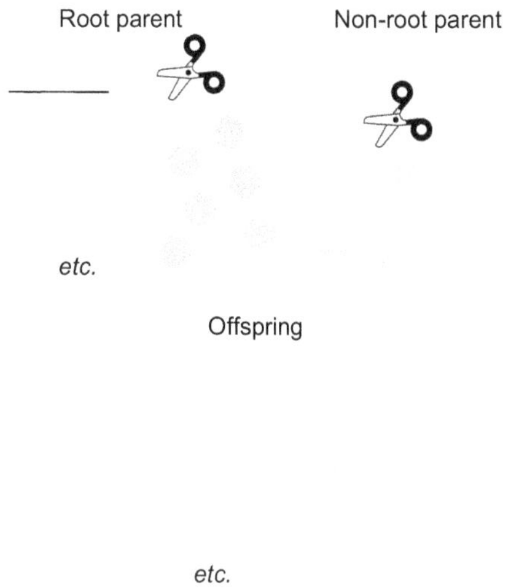

Figure 1: Sub-tree crossover, illustrating the asymmetric role of the *root* and *non-root* parents.

that contributes the root node as the *root parent* and the other parent as the *non-root parent*. It has also been previously observed [4, 10, 12] that the root parent often contributes more to the semantics of the resulting individual. This is in part because the root parent typically contributes more overall nodes, and because the nodes closest to the root of the tree frequently have a stronger impact on the result of evaluating the tree in question. While the specific impact of this asymmetry depends on the details of the function set and the particular trees chosen as parents, asymmetry has a substantial effect on the semantics of the offspring in many common GP settings.

An important impact of this asymmetry was recently noted in [10], where it was observed that the fitness of the offspring tended to improve when the root parent had better fitness than the non-root parent. To explore this further, we implemented what we refer to as *crossover bias*, which allowed us to probabilistically force the GP system to assign the individual with the greater fitness to be the root parent. After reviewing some related work (Section 2), we apply crossover bias (Section 3) to a variety of test problems (Section 4). The results (Section 5) make it clear that crossover bias can have a substantial impact on the performance of GP runs, but that the results are heavily param-

Algorithm 1 Crossover bias

Require: Two individuals are chosen as parents: RP (root parent) and NRP (non-root parent).
  if RANDOM(0, 1) $\leq$ XO_bias **then** ▷ Do we force bias?
    if FITNESS(RP) worse than FITNESS(NRP) **then**
      RP, NRP := NRP, RP ▷ Swap so RP is more fit
    end if
  end if

eter dependent and, to a lesser degree problem dependent. In general, however, we find (Section 6) that incorporating some crossover bias is, at least in these problems, usually either advantageous or neutral.

2. RELATED WORK

Several previous papers have deliberately created asymmetries between parents (e.g., [5, 19]) as a mechanism to increase diversity and (in the case of [19]) combat bloat.

There has also been a blossoming of work in the last few years based on the semantics of GP trees (e.g., [12, 13]). This includes a number of proposed mechanisms that encourage or force semantic differences (asymmetries) between parents and children [1, 21]. Some [22] also *limit* the differences between parents and offspring, in some sense reducing the impact of asymmetries between the parents, and smoothing out the fitness landscape as a result. These proposals typically focus on the semantic relationship between parents and children, however, and don't directly take into account any asymmetries between the parents.

3. CROSSOVER BIAS

To better understand parent asymmetries and the impact of bias in crossover, we implemented crossover bias with a parameter specifying the probability of forcing the more fit parent to be the root parent when performing crossover, as detailed in Algorithm 1. Every time a crossover event was to be performed, we would use this probability to decide whether to force the more fit parent to be the root parent. Note that when crossover bias isn't applied, there is still a 50% chance that the root parent is the more fit parent.

In this paper we focus on five levels of crossover bias:

- 0.00 bias - no crossover bias is applied, i.e., just standard sub-tree crossover; a 50% probability of the more fit parent being the root parent;
- 0.25 bias - system forced to use the more fit parent as the root parent in 25% of cases; a 62.5% total probability of the more fit parent being the root parent;
- 0.50 bias - system forced to use the more fit parent as the root parent in 50% of cases; a 75% total probability of the more fit parent being the root parent;
- 0.75 bias - system forced to use the more fit parent as the root parent in 75% of cases; a 87.5% total probability of the more fit parent being the root parent; and
- 1.00 bias - system forced to always use the more fit parent as the root parent, sometimes referred to as "with crossover bias".

We also experimented with *reverse bias*, where the weaker parent was always forced to be the root parent. In general, the results for reverse bias showed no statistically significant difference from standard crossover (no bias), so in the interest of simplification we've omitted reverse bias from the remainder of the paper.

4. EXPERIMENTAL SETUP

To better understand the impact of crossover bias on GP performance, we experimented with five problems: K Landscapes with $K = 6$ [23], ORDERTREE [8], U.S. Change, Sine regression [16], and Pagie-1 regression [15]. Three of these (K Landscapes, ORDERTREE, and Pagie-1 regression) are taken from recent benchmark suggestions [24]. The U.S. Change problem [26] has proven to be an interesting problem in evolutionary program synthesis [7], and sine regression is the example problem used in earlier work on the impact of root and non-root parents [10]. All experiments were run using a copy of ECJ 21[1] that we modified to support crossover bias.

The one problem not precisely described elsewhere in the literature is the U.S. Change problem. Here the task is to take as input an amount, and to return as output the minimum number of coins required to make that amount using (a subset of) standard U.S. coins with amounts 25, 10, 5, and 1. So, for example, given 118 as input, the result should be 9 since

$$\underline{4} \times 25 + \underline{1} \times 10 + \underline{1} \times 5 + \underline{3} \times 1 = 118,$$

and this set of 4+1+1+3 = 9 coins is the minimal set making a total of 118. Our function set for this problem was +, -, ×, %,[2] *mod*,[3] *min*, and *max*. The terminal set consisted of the input x, integer ephemeral random constants taken uniformly from the range $[-50, 50]$, and the set of constants $\{0, 1, 4, 5, 9, 10, 24, 25\}$. The test cases were all inputs in the range $[0, 150)$.

All our experiments used the previously published settings, function sets, fitness functions, etc., with the exception of the parameters listed in Table 1,[4] which are shared throughout these experiments. Our evolutionary system is generational, with all new individuals being generated via subtree crossover (i.e., no mutation or reproduction) unless there is a non-zero elitism percentage. Our primary goal was to better understand the impact of crossover bias, so we performed runs with a variety of crossover bias probabilities. In addition, we wanted to see how crossover bias might interact with some other commonly manipulated parameters as listed in Table 1. Unless otherwise noted, all plots, etc., in what follows will include results from all possible combinations of values in Table 1. Each box plot in Figure 3, for example, includes the results of 100 runs for

[1] http://cs.gmu.edu/~eclab/projects/ecj/

[2] Protected integer division (quotient), returning 1 if the denominator is 0.

[3] Also returns 1 if the denominator is 0.

[4] The function set for Pagie-1 specified in [15] is simply +, -, ×, and % (protected division). The function set given in [9] and implemented in ECJ is "koza2", which also includes various trigonometric and logarithmic functions. The performance of GP varies substantially between the two function sets; here we follow the original Pagie-1 paper and use the simpler function set.

Parameter	Values
Crossover bias	0, 0.25, 0.5, 0.75, and 1
Tournament size	2, 3, 5, and 7
Elitism %	0 and 1%
Population size	1,024 and 10,240
# of generations	100
# of runs per treatment	100

Table 1: Shared parameters

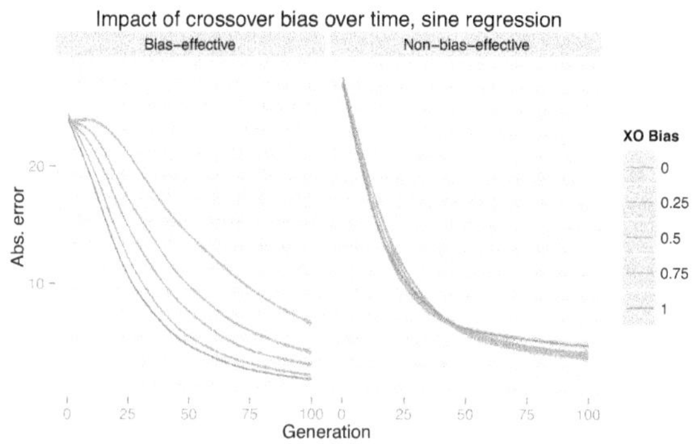

Figure 2: Impact of crossover bias over time on the sine symbolic regression problem with *bias-effective* and *non-bias-effective* parameter sets. In the left-hand panel (bias-effective settings), the curves stack in order (top to bottom) from crossover bias 0 to crossover bias 1.

each of the combinations of all four tournament sizes, both elitism proportions, and both population sizes.

In our experimentation we observed that there were quite substantial interactions between crossover bias and some of the other parameter settings. In particular, we found that there are parameter values where crossover bias appears to have a substantial and significant impact, and other parameter settings where crossover bias has almost no effect on the results. Based on these observed patterns, we found it useful to identify two specific subsets of the parameter settings listed in Table 1: "*bias-effective settings*" and "*non-bias-effective settings*". The bias-effective settings are binary tournaments, no elitism, and population size of 10,240; the non-bias-effective settings, conversely, are tournament size 7, non-zero elitism percentage, and population size 1,024. These terms will be used in the remainder of the paper, which will also include some discussion of why crossover bias might interact with these parameters in this way.

To illustrate the impact of these parameter settings, Figure 2 shows the fitness (absolute error) over time for the sine regression problem (see Section 5.3.2 for more on the sine regression results). The bias-effective settings (left-hand panel) show a clear difference in the performance as a function of crossover bias, where the non-bias-effective settings (right hand panel) show almost no difference as a function of the crossover bias probability.

5. RESULTS

All tests of differences in fitness or hits in this section are performed using pairwise Wilcoxon tests with Holm corrections. Tests of differences in the number of successes are performed using pairwise tests of proportions (chi-squared) with Holm corrections. All statistics calculations were performed with R [18] and all plots were generated using the ggplot2 package [25]. Statistical significance will require $p \leq 0.05$.

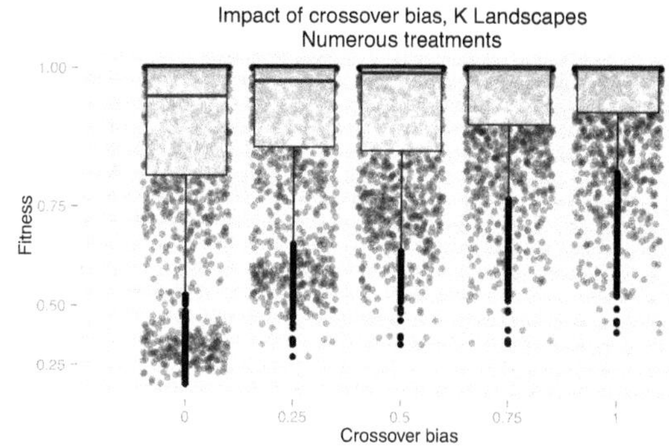

Figure 3: Impact of crossover bias on fitness for the K Landscapes problem, over all the combinations of parameters in Table 1.

5.1 Structural Problems

Most GP problems evaluate the evolved trees on a set of inputs, looking for some desired behavior or semantics. Structural problems (also referred to as constructed problems), however, have fitness functions that are entirely based on the overall structure of the evolved trees (e.g., size, shape, distribution of particular leaves) without any sort of "evaluation" being involved.

5.1.1 K Landscapes Problem

Fitnesses for the K Landscape problem are between 0 and 1, with a fitness of 1 being a perfect solution. Figure 3 shows the impact of crossover bias on this problem across all the combinations of parameter values in Table 1. Increasing the amount of crossover bias consistently improves the fitness of the results. All the differences are statistically significant ($p < 0.012$) except for the difference between bias probability 0.75 and 1.00.

Compare this to the results shown in Figure 4, which plots the same data separated out by tournament size. It is clear that for binary tournaments, increasing the crossover bias probability continues to improve the fitness – all the differences are strongly statistically significant ($p < 6 \times 10^{-08}$). This continues to be true for tournament size 3; all the differences are statistically significant except for those between bias 0.50 and 0.75, which was very close ($p = 0.056$). None of the differences for tournament size 5 are significant. For tournament size 7, however, it looks like the reverse is true, where increasing crossover bias actually hurts fitness. Almost none of the differences for tournament size 7 are statistically significant with the only exception being the difference between 0.25 and 1.00 ($p = 0.021$).

Figure 5 filters out only the data gathered using the bias-effective treatment, as defined in Section 4. It is clear that the impact of crossover bias is much stronger in this case than in the more general case shown in Figure 3. Here all the differences are strongly statistically significant ($p < 10^{-11}$). In addition to improvements in fitness, increasing the crossover bias also increases the number of "perfect"

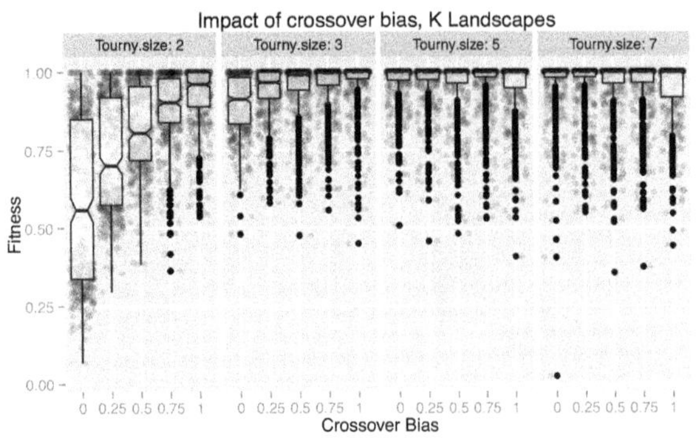

Figure 4: Impact of crossover bias on fitness for the K Landscapes problem, for various tournament sizes.

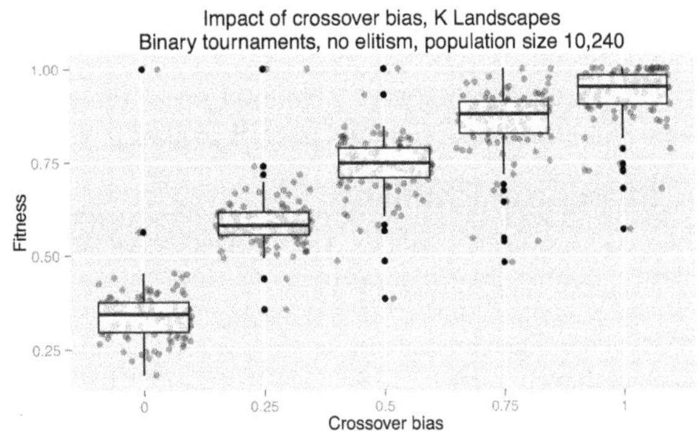

Figure 5: Impact of crossover bias on fitness for the K Landscapes problem, restricted to bias-effective parameter settings.

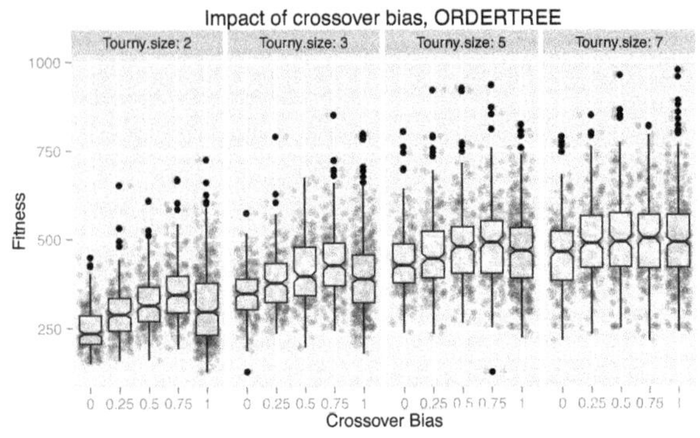

Figure 6: Impact of crossover bias on fitness for ORDERTREE problem for multiple tournament sizes.

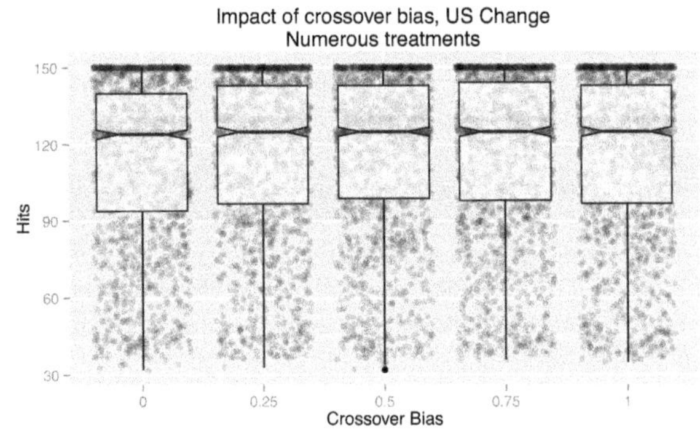

Figure 7: Impact of crossover bias on the number of hits for the U.S. Change problem for all the combinations of parameters in Table 1.

solutions discovered when using the bias effective settings. Out of 100 runs with a crossover bias setting of 1.00, 15 of these runs resulted in the discovery of a "perfect" solution. By comparison, only 1 or 2 runs out of 100 resulted in "perfect" solutions for each of the other crossover bias probabilities. These differences in the number of perfect solutions are statistically significant ($p \leq 0.03$).

5.1.2 ORDERTREE Problem

It should be noted that, for the ORDERTREE problem we used the full set of parameters outlined in Section 4, with one exception: the population size for the ORDERTREE runs was limited to 1,024. This was a consequence of the large trees generated for this problem, resulting in out of memory errors for the larger population size of 10,240.

ORDERTREE has a difficulty tuning parameter n; we used $n = 10$, which meant that the fitnesses ranged from 0 to 1,022 with larger values being better. The details for the ORDERTREE fitness computation are described in [8].

Figure 6 shows the impact of crossover bias across all parameter combinations. For binary tournaments, adding crossover bias leads to improved performance when compared to no crossover bias, but we observed a drop in fitness from bias 0.75 to bias 1.00, where the fitness for 1.00 is actually slightly below that for 0.50 as well. All the binary tournament differences are statistically significant ($p < 0.03$), with the exception of the difference between bias 0.25 and bias 1.00, so bias 0.75 is the clear winner in this scenario. This drop in fitness for bias 1.00 is consistent across the other three tournament sizes as well. However, it is also apparent from the figure that in general the impact of crossover bias lessens with the larger tournament sizes, both in the increase in fitness up to bias 0.75, and the drop from there to bias 1.00.

5.2 U.S. Change Problem

In contrast to the structural problems discussed in the previous section, which used fitness as the measure of success of a run, for the U.S. Change problem we measured success in "hits" (the number of test cases that are correctly solved). There are 150 test cases in our implementation, so an optimal program will have a score of 150 hits.

Figure 7 shows the impact of crossover bias on the number of hits for the U.S. Change problem across the full collection of parameter settings. This suggests that in general there is little consistent impact of crossover bias; while most of the differences in this plot are not statistically significant, two are: the differences between crossover bias 0.00 and crossover bias 0.50 and 0.75 are both statistically significant ($p \leq 0.015$), even if numerically small.

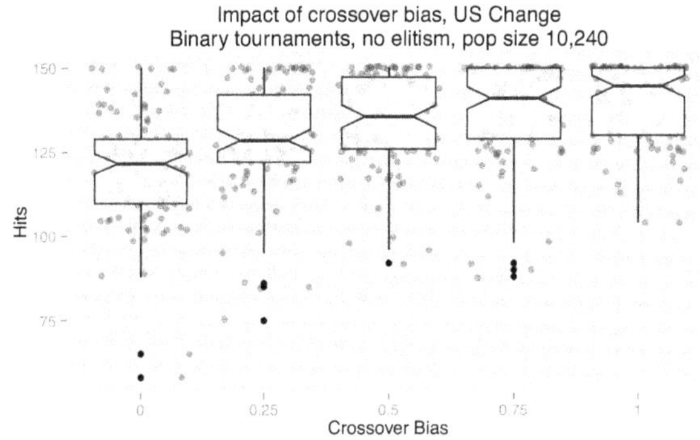

Figure 8: Impact of crossover bias on the number of hits for the U.S. Change problem, limited to bias-effective parameters.

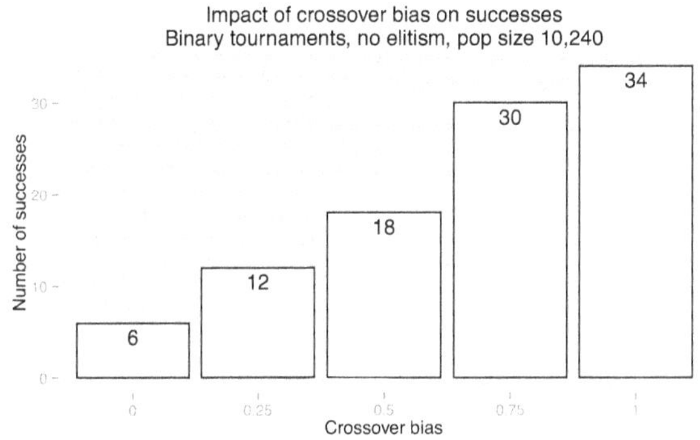

Figure 9: Impact of crossover bias on the number of successful runs for the U.S. Change problem when using bias-effective parameters.

However, if we limit our attention to the bias-effective parameter settings defined in Section 4, then we find that crossover bias has a substantial and statistically significant impact, as is seen in Figure 8. Here the bulk of these pairwise differences are statistically significant ($p < 0.0002$). The major exception is the difference between crossover bias 0.75 and 1.00 ($p = 0.43$). Two other adjacent pairs have p-values slightly above 0.05: crossover bias 0.25 *vs.* 0.50 ($p = 0.0504$), and 0.50 *vs.* 0.75 ($p = 0.0802$).

If complete success was considered vital (which might be the case if we were evolving software for use in a production system), then it would make sense to see if crossover bias has a significant impact on the success rate. Figure 9 shows the number of successes for the various crossover bias values when using the bias-effective parameter settings. None of the adjacent differences (for example, crossover bias 0.50 *vs.* 0.75) are statistically significant, while most of the non-adjacent differences (for example, crossover bias 0.25 *vs.* 0.75) are statistically significant, with the exceptions being crossover bias 0.00 *vs.* 0.50, and bias 0.50 *vs.* 1.00 ($p = 0.094$ in both cases).

5.3 Regression Problems

Regression problems attempt to evolve a function that is able to match a given set of input-output pairs. Success is

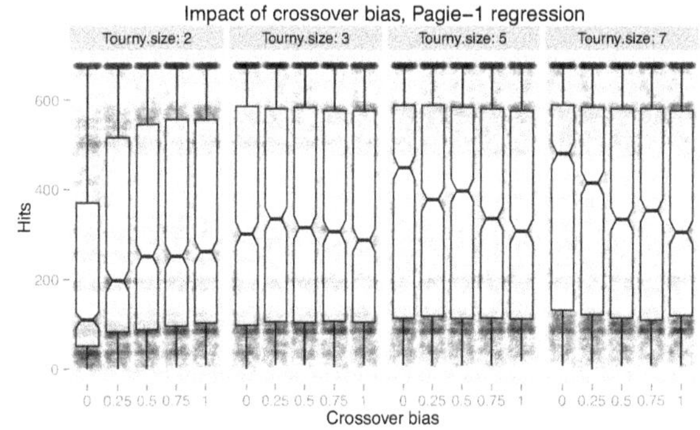

Figure 10: Impact of crossover bias on the number of hits for the Pagie-1 symbolic regression problem, broken out across the four different tournament sizes. The maximum number of possible hits is 676.

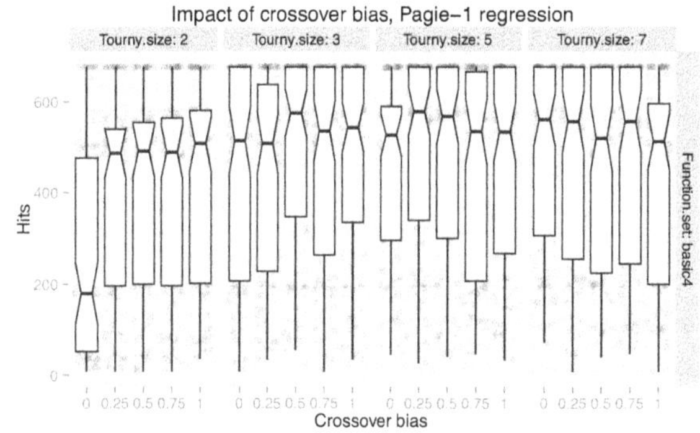

Figure 11: Impact of crossover bias on the number of hits for the Pagie-1 symbolic regression problem, broken out by tournament size, limited to bias-effective elitism (0) and population size (10,240).

here measured in hits, where a "hit" is awarded when the output of the evolved function is within 0.01 of the target value.

5.3.1 *Pagie-1 Problem*

Figure 10 shows the impact of crossover bias on the number of hits for the Pagie-1 regression problem, separated out by tournament size. Figure 11 is limited to population size 10,240 and no elitism.

Focusing on the binary tournament data in Figure 11, the differences between crossover bias 0.00 (standard subtree crossover) and all the other positive crossover bias values are statistically significant ($p < 0.0002$). None of the differences among 0.25, 0.50, 0.75, and 1.00 are statistically significant, however, and none of the differences for tournament sizes 3, 5, or 7 are statistically significant. This indicates that for binary tournaments, including crossover bias substantially and significantly improves the hit rate, although all bias rates above 0.25 are very similar. For larger tournament sizes, however, it appears that adding crossover bias doesn't have a significant effect and in some cases (e.g., tournament sizes 5 and 7 in Figure 10) may hurt performance.

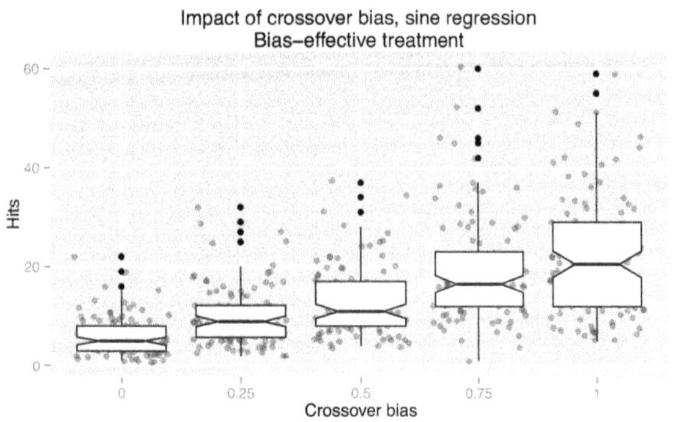

Figure 12: Impact of crossover bias on the sine symbolic regression problem with bias-effective settings.

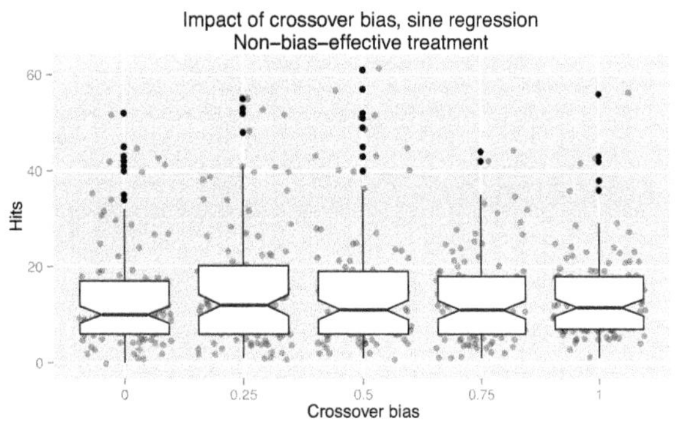

Figure 13: Impact of crossover bias on the sine symbolic regression problem with non-bias-effective settings.

5.3.2 Sine Problem

For the sine regression problem, we limited our runs to bias-effective and non-bias-effective settings as defined in Section 4.

Figure 12 shows the results for the number of hits for the sine regression problem using bias-effective settings. All these differences are statistically significant ($p < 10^{-5}$) except for the difference between the bias of 0.75 and 1.00. In Figure 2, the left panel illustrates the impact of crossover bias over time when using the bias-effective settings, demonstrating that the effects appear early in the run. Here, the fitnesses are consistently different throughout the time of the runs, with higher crossover bias settings arriving at fitter individuals earlier in the runs, although the differences are shrinking towards the end as many runs find fairly fit individuals.

Figure 13 shows the results for the sine regression problem using the non-bias-effective parameter settings; none of these differences are statistically significant. In Figure 2, the right panel illustrates the impact of crossover bias over time when using the non-bias-effective settings, demonstrating that with these settings the runs tend to be highly similar throughout the duration of the runs, regardless of crossover bias setting.

6. DISCUSSION

In general our results indicate that adding crossover bias improves performance, either generally (Figure 3) or when combined with certain other parameter choices (e.g., Figure 10). In some cases the improvements induced by crossover bias are quite substantial (e.g., Figures 5, 9, and 12), while in other situations the improvements were quite small in magnitude even when statistically significant (Figure 3). Not surprisingly, however, crossover bias is not universally helpful, and there are settings where some crossover bias improves performance more than when always applying crossover bias (Figure 6), and other settings where all tested crossover bias amounts were detrimental (tournament sizes 5 and 7 in Figure 10).

One general trend seems to be that crossover bias is more effective when using the *bias-effective* parameter settings, namely smaller tournaments (size 2 instead of 7), larger populations (10,240 instead of 1,024), and no elitism. One possible explanation for this pattern is that when using the *non-bias-effective* settings, the difference in fitness between the two parents is likely to be closer than when using bias-effective settings; this reduction in the difference between the fitness of the parents is thus likely to minimize the impact of crossover bias.

To test this hypothesis, we looked at the impact of tournament size on the relative difference in parent fitness for the K Landscapes problem and the sine regression problem. For each crossover event, we compute the relative difference in parent fitness as

$$|f_A - f_B|/(f_A + f_B)$$

where f_A and f_B are the fitnesses of the two chosen parents A and B. This has a minimum value of 0 when the two fitnesses are the same, and a maximum value approaching 1 for the case where one of the values is nearly 0.

Figure 14 shows the distribution of the relative differences in parent fitness for the K Landscapes problem both with (right-hand panel) and without (left-hand panel) crossover bias. For tournament size 7, the difference in fitness drops significantly as the run progresses; this, combined with the substantial improvements in fitness, suggests that both of the parents are highly fit. When using binary tournaments, the relative differences in parent fitness remains fairly stable and higher than for tournament size 7, which would suggest that crossover bias would continue to be effective throughout the run when using binary tournaments. We see similar results in the sine regression problem, as illustrated in Figure 15.

Our results also indicate that crossover bias may increase certain types of selection pressure, which could potentially increase the likelihood of premature convergence. There is a heightened focus on the better of the two parents which increases the chance of the more fit parent's semantics being carried across into the next generation. This might limit the diversity of the root structures causing premature convergence. Further research is needed to understand if this does in fact lead to premature convergence in some cases, but it's possible, for example, that this explains the fact that using some crossover bias (0.75) is better than always using crossover bias in the ORDERTREE problem (see, e.g., Figure 6).

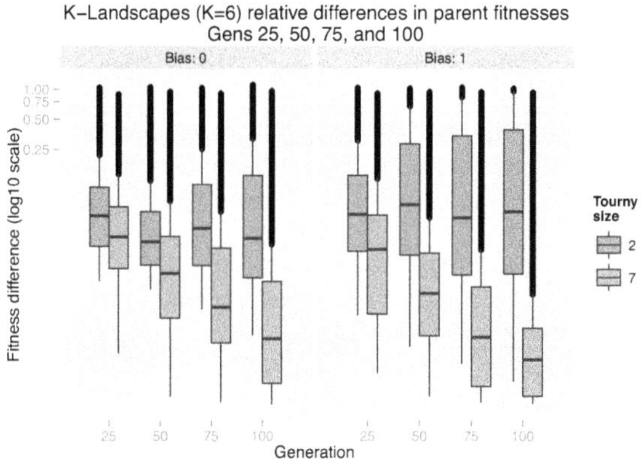

Figure 14: Plot of the normalized differences in parent fitnesses for the K Landscapes problem. The left-hand (and higher) boxplot in each pair of boxplots is for the binary tournament runs.

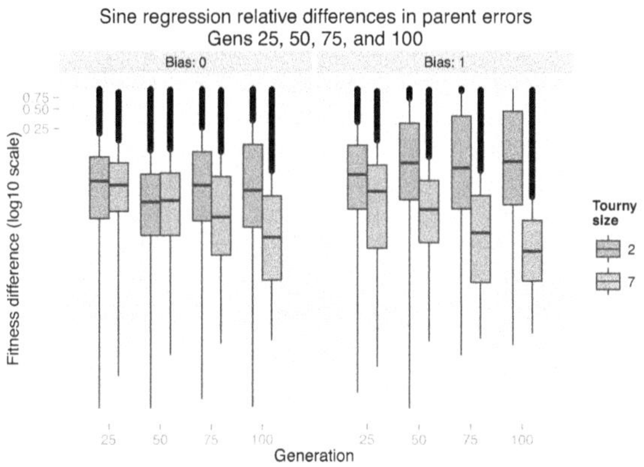

Figure 15: Plot of the normalized differences in parent errors for the sine symbolic regression problem. The left-hand (and higher) boxplot in each pair of boxplots is for the binary tournament runs.

7. CONCLUSIONS

Based on previous observations of interesting asymmetries in the behavior of sub-tree crossover (e.g., [10]), we introduced the idea of *crossover bias*, where we probabilistically force the more fit parent to be the *root parent* when performing crossover. We then applied this new bias to several different problems. In general, we found that adding crossover bias either helps or is neutral, although there were cases where its effect was detrimental.

Given these results, it seems worthwhile to at least try crossover bias, especially in settings where there are reasons to suspect that there are substantial differences between parental fitnesses. This is likely to be the case wherever selection pressure is weak (e.g., our use of binary tournaments), but could also happen when there are unavoidable steep changes in fitness, or in settings where the fitness function may vary over either time or as a function of some other variable such as location.

A question to consider based on these results is whether or not we should use larger tournaments instead of crossover bias, since in many cases the results with tournament size 7 without crossover bias was as good or better than those obtained with binary tournaments and crossover bias, e.g., Figure 4. According to Gustafson et al. [6], however, matings between similar parents are more likely to produce no change in fitness, whereas a more diverse crossover increases the chances of offspring improving fitness. Larger tournaments are more likely to select two parents that are similar, at least in fitness, as seen in Figures 14 and 15; an excellent illustration of this can be seen in Figure 2 in [2]. Another attempt to find a balance of diversity between parents is called sexual selection, proposed by Goh et al. [5]. Their sexual selection system mates individuals chosen at random (with no regard to fitness) with individuals chosen via tournament selection. This creates a strong asymmetry between the parents which appears to increase diversity in certain circumstances in ways that improve performance. Based on these examples, there may be circumstances where combining crossover bias with a weaker selection mechanism might be a reasonable alternative to using a larger tournament size.

Another outstanding question is how crossover bias affects generalization, especially since it's possible that crossover bias increases selection pressure and could consequently encourage overfitting. We didn't explore this question here, but it would be useful to expand the existing work to include validation to see what impact, if any, crossover bias has on how well evolved solutions generalize to unseen data.

While this paper focuses on asymmetry in the context of tree-based GP and sub-tree crossover, it's important to note that asymmetries like this are common in many evolutionary systems, both biological and artificial. Much eukaryote reproduction is sexual, and brings with it numerous sex-linked traits and related asymmetries; this may play an important role in speciation [17], arguably one of the most crucial of biological asymmetries. Many evolutionary computation systems other than tree-based GP also have significant asymmetries. Linear GP systems [3] and stack-based GP systems [20], for example, have asymmetries where the last instructions executed can have a disproportionate impact on the results. Similarly, changes near the front of grammatical evolution [14] strings will have a disproportionate impact by determining the important early choices in the grammar productions. Generally, these asymmetries weren't intentional, but were instead simple artifacts of other system design decisions. Hence, the potential impact of these asymmetries has been largely unstudied. The results presented here suggest that it may be important to more thoroughly explore the impact of such asymmetries, both to better understand the performance and behavior of existing systems, but also as an aid to the design and discovery of new tools like recombination operators that leverage these asymmetries.

Acknowledgements

Many thanks to the members of the Hampshire College Computational Intelligence Lab for suggestions and feedback as this work developed, with particular thanks to Thomas Helmuth, William La Cava, and Lee Spector. Thanks also to Thomas Helmuth for introducing us to the U.S. Change problem. Thanks to W. B. Langdon and our anonymous reviewers for valuable feedback and numerous suggestions.

David Donatucci's work was supported in part by a Morris Academic Partners grant from the Office for Academic Affairs and Dean at the University of Minnesota, Morris.

8. REFERENCES

[1] L. Beadle and C. G. Johnson. Semantically driven crossover in genetic programming. In *IEEE World Congress on Computational Intelligence*, pages 111–116, 2008.

[2] G. D. Boetticher and K. Kaminsky. The assessment and application of lineage information in genetic programs for producing better models. In *Information Reuse and Integration, 2006 IEEE International Conference on*, pages 141–146, Sept 2006.

[3] M. F. Brameier and W. Banzhaf. *Linear genetic programming*. Springer Science & Business Media, 2007.

[4] B. Burlacu, M. Affenzeller, M. Kommenda, S. Winkler, and G. Kronberger. Visualization of genetic lineages and inheritance information in genetic programming. In *Proceedings of the 15th annual conference companion on Genetic and evolutionary computation*, pages 1351–1358. ACM, 2013.

[5] K. Goh, A. Lim, and B. Rodrigues. Sexual selection for genetic algorithms. *Artificial Intelligence Review*, 19(2):123–152, 2003.

[6] S. Gustafson, E. Burke, and N. Krasnogor. On improving genetic programming for symbolic regression. In *Evolutionary Computation, 2005. The 2005 IEEE Congress on*, volume 1, pages 912–919 Vol.1, Sept 2005.

[7] T. Helmuth and L. Spector. General program synthesis benchmark suite. In *Proceedings of the 17th Annual Conference on Genetic and Evolutionary Computation*, GECCO '15, New York, NY, USA, 2015. ACM.

[8] T.-H. Hoang, N. X. Hoai, N. T. Hien, R. I. McKay, and D. Essam. ORDERTREE: a new test problem for genetic programming. In *Proceedings of the 8th annual conference on Genetic and evolutionary computation*, pages 807–814. ACM, 2006.

[9] J. McDermott, D. R. White, S. Luke, L. Manzoni, M. Castelli, L. Vanneschi, W. Jaskowski, K. Krawiec, R. Harper, K. De Jong, et al. Genetic programming needs better benchmarks. In *Proceedings of the 14th annual conference on Genetic and evolutionary computation*, pages 791–798. ACM, 2012.

[10] N. F. McPhee, D. Donatucci, and M. K. Dramdahl. Analysis of genetic programming ancestry using a graph database. In *Proceedings of Midwest Instruction and Computing Symposium*. MICS, 2014.

[11] N. F. McPhee and N. J. Hopper. Analysis of genetic diversity through population history. In *Proceedings of the Genetic and Evolutionary Computation Conference*, volume 2, pages 1112–1120. GECCO, 1999.

[12] N. F. McPhee, B. Ohs, and T. Hutchison. Semantic building blocks in genetic programming. In *Proceedings of the 11th European Conference on Genetic Programming*, EuroGP'08, pages 134–145, Berlin, Heidelberg, 2008. Springer-Verlag.

[13] A. Moraglio, K. Krawiec, and C. G. Johnson. Geometric semantic genetic programming. In *Parallel Problem Solving from Nature-PPSN XII*, pages 21–31. Springer, 2012.

[14] M. O'Neill and C. Ryan. *Grammatical evolution: evolutionary automatic programming in an arbitrary language*, volume 4. Springer Science & Business Media, 2003.

[15] L. Pagie and P. Hogeweg. Evolutionary consequences of coevolving targets. *Evolutionary computation*, 5(4):401–418, 1997.

[16] R. Poli, W. B. Langdon, and N. F. McPhee. *A Field Guide to Genetic Programming*. Published via `http://lulu.com` and freely available at `http://www.gp-field-guide.org.uk`, 2008. (With contributions by J. R. Koza).

[17] A. Qvarnström and R. I. Bailey. Speciation through evolution of sex-linked genes. *Heredity*, 102(1):4–15, 2009.

[18] R Core Team. *R: A Language and Environment for Statistical Computing*. R Foundation for Statistical Computing, Vienna, Austria, 2014.

[19] C. Ryan. Pygmies and civil servants. In *Advances in Genetic Programming*, pages 243–263. MIT Press, 1994.

[20] L. Spector and A. Robinson. Genetic programming and autoconstructive evolution with the push programming language. *Genetic Programming and Evolvable Machines*, 3(1):7–40, Mar. 2002.

[21] N. Q. Uy, N. X. Hoai, M. O'Neill, R. I. McKay, and E. Galván-López. Semantically-based crossover in genetic programming: application to real-valued symbolic regression. *Genetic Programming and Evolvable Machines*, 12(2):91–119, 2011.

[22] N. Q. Uy, N. X. Hoai, M. O'Neill, R. I. McKay, and D. N. Phong. On the roles of semantic locality of crossover in genetic programming. *Information Sciences*, 235:195–213, 2013.

[23] L. Vanneschi, M. Castelli, and L. Manzoni. The K landscapes: a tunably difficult benchmark for genetic programming. In *Proceedings of the 13th annual conference on Genetic and evolutionary computation*, pages 1467–1474. ACM, 2011.

[24] D. R. White, J. McDermott, M. Castelli, L. Manzoni, B. W. Goldman, G. Kronberger, W. Jaśkowski, U.-M. O'Reilly, and S. Luke. Better GP benchmarks: Community survey results and proposals. *Genetic Programming and Evolvable Machines*, 14:3–29, 2013.

[25] H. Wickham. *ggplot2: Elegant graphics for data analysis*. Springer New York, 2009.

[26] H. Zhan. A quantitative analysis of the simplification genetic operator. In *Proceedings of the 2014 conference companion on Genetic and evolutionary computation companion*, pages 1077–1080. ACM, 2014.

GEFPSO: A Framework for PSO Optimization based on Grammatical Evolution

Péricles B. C. Miranda
Universidade Federal Rural de Pernambuco
Recife, Brazil
pbcm@cin.ufpe.br

Ricardo B. C. Prudêncio
Universidade Federal de Pernambuco
Recife, Brazil
rbcp@cin.ufpe.br

ABSTRACT

In this work, we propose a framework to automatically generate effective PSO designs by adopting Grammatical Evolution (GE). In the proposed framework, GE searches for adequate structures and parameter values (e.g., acceleration constants, velocity equations and different particles' topology) in order to evolve the PSO design. For this, a high-level Backus–Naur Form (BNF) grammar was developed, representing the search space of possible PSO designs. In order to verify the performance of the proposed method, we performed experiments using 16 diverse continuous optimization problems, with different levels of difficulty. In the performed experiments, we identified the parameters and components that most affected the PSO performance, as well as identified designs that could be reused across different problems. We also demonstrated that the proposed method generates useful designs which achieved competitive solutions when compared to well succeeded algorithms from the literature.

Categories and Subject Descriptors

I.2.2 [**Artificial Intelligence**]: Automatic Programming

Keywords

Grammatical evolution; Particle Swarm Optimization

1. INTRODUCTION

Particle Swarm Optimization is a meta-heuristic technique developed in the 90's, inspired by the social behavior of flock when searching for food [6]. PSO has achieved an increasing interest over the years due to its flexibility as well as competitive results in different applications [1]. Besides, different developments were introduced to leverage the basic PSO algorithm. For instance, the inertia and constriction factors were proposed in order to improve the convergence and stability of the algorithm [2]. Also, different topologies were developed to define how the particles exchange information during the optimization process [1, 12]. Several of these developments have actually shown to be useful and improve PSO performance significantly.

As it occurs to other computational algorithms, the performance of PSO in a given problem may be strongly affected by the choice of its parameters [13]. For instance, the use of a global topology potentially favors the PSO for optimization problems with a low number of local minima, while a local topology would be more adequate for more complex landscapes. Such differences in performance can also be expected when other aspects of PSO are considered.

In this paper, we addressed the problem of *parameter design* for the PSO algorithm. Given an optimization problem, we aimed to generate a configuration of parameters (i.e., a *design*) for the PSO algorithm that is adequate in terms of optimization performance. We can identify in the literature previous works that performed empirical analysis on specific PSO parameters in isolation, which can be useful in practice [16, 17, 14, 4, 20]. However, few attempts have been made to generate more complete designs that could for instance be systematically reused across similar problems.

In this work, we propose a framework (GEFPSO) based on Grammatical Evolution (GE) [3] aiming to optimize the design (procedures and parameter values) of PSO. GE is a largely studied Genetic Programming algorithm (GP) which generates programs by using production rules in a Backus Naur form (BNF) grammar definition. GE overcomes certain problems which are present in traditional GP techniques, such as constructing syntactically incorrect programs [3, 4].

In the GEFPSO, a BNF grammar was defined to address the following aspects of PSO: population size, velocity equations, topologies and mutation operators. In the performed experiments, the GEFPSO was applied to optimize designs for 16 continuous optimization functions, associated to four categories of problems with different features and levels of difficulty: *Bowl-Shaped*, *Plate-Shaped*, *Valley-Shaped* and *Many Local Minima*. Different experiments were performed in order to investigate: (1) which are the best parameter values for each PSO design aspect considered and whether the generated designs can be reused across similar problems; and (2) whether the generated PSO designs were competitive compared to other promising algorithms in the literature (algorithms from the ICSI 14 competition [5]).

In the obtained results, we observed quite stable results concerning for instance the population size and the velocity equation. Higher values of population size can harm the convergence of the PSO and the constricted equation [13] for

GECCO '15, July 11–15, 2015, Madrid, Spain
© 2015 ACM. ISBN 978-1-4503-3472-3/15/07...$15.00
DOI: http://dx.doi.org/10.1145/2739480.2754819

updating the particles velocity was the most often observed option in the returned designs. Concerning the mutation, we observed that the use of such operators can be actually useful to improve the PSO performance. The results concerning the topology were more diverse. Simpler problems required simpler topologies, as the *Global* topology. In turn, the use of specific topologies, like *Von Neumann*, *Four Clusters* and *Clan* [1, 12], resulted in better results for intermediate and hard problems. In our experiments, we observed that generated designs presented certain regularities that favor the reuse to problems with similar features. Finally, the comparative experiments revealed that the designs generated by GEFPSO were comparable to the best algorithms evaluated, and in most cases, they resulted in solutions that were very close to the global minima.

This work is organized as follows. Section 2 presents the basic concepts of PSO and related work in PSO optimization. In Section 3, we described in detail the proposed framework. Section 4 brings the optimization functions considered in this work and the experimental methodology. In Section 5, the results are presented and discussed. Finally, in Section 6, the conclusions and possible future works are presented.

2. BACKGROUND

The PSO is an iterative algorithm. Initially, a predefined number of particles are initialized randomly in the search space. While a stopping criterion is not reached, the particles update their velocity and position. Each particle explores the search space guided by its velocity, which is a combination between the best position found by itself $\vec{p}(t)$ and by the best position found by its neighborhood $\vec{g}(t)$ (*gbest*) [6]. In the basic PSO algorithm, at each iteration, each particle updates its velocity by adopting the following equation:

$$\vec{v_i}(t+1) = \vec{v_i}(t) + c_1 r_1(\vec{p_i}(t) - \vec{x_i}(t)) + c_2 r_2(\vec{g_i}(t) - \vec{x_i}(t)), \quad (1)$$

where $i = 1, ..., N$, N is the number of particles; c_1 and c_2 are the cognitive and social acceleration coefficients; r_1 and r_2 are two random numbers between [0,1]. Once the particle updates its velocity, the equation 2 is used to update the particle's position:

$$\vec{x_i}(t+1) = \vec{x_i} + \vec{v_i}(t+1). \quad (2)$$

The PSO algorithm called the attention of researchers due to its simplicity and fast convergence. As said, different developments were proposed to the original PSO algorithm, bringing another problem which is how to define the best designs for the algorithm. For instance, an important issue of PSO is its social component, as good solutions found by a particle can be exchanged to their neighbors. What defines how the particles exchange information is the topology of communication. The particles can be connected in a simple global topology in which all particles communicate to each other. Nevertheless, other topologies were proposed to promote more diversity during the search process or to speedup convergence [1, 12].

Concerning the particles' velocity, new parameters were added to the original velocity updating equation in order to better control the particles' velocity [7, 8, 9]. Also, new velocity updating equations were created aiming to improve the balance between exploration and exploitation [10, 11]. Even the original parameters c_1 and c_2 can be important, depending on the problem [13]. The performance achieved by PSO strongly depends on adequate design choices and adjustment of parameters [13].

The task of deciding which is the best design to solve a particular problem is complicated due to the great number of possible variations and parameters to take into account [14]. Different previous work has dealt with the task of PSO design as another (meta)optimization problem. The search space in this case is the set of possible designs for the PSO on a problem. The objective function in turn is the same one adopted in the (base)optimization problem at hand. The use of optimization techniques to algorithm design is a systematic strategy adopted in the literature to avoid exhaustive or trial-and-error experiments on the candidate designs [14]. Parsopoulos et al. [15] investigated the automated fine-tuning of the inertia factor w, and c_1 and c_2 of PSO. In Liu [16], the authors applied a GA to optimize the parameters c_1, c_2 and the constriction factor χ of PSO. Such optimization techniques however are not adequate to evolve more complex designs and also to exploit different combinations of PSO components.

Genetic Programming (GP) is an evolutionary approach adequate to evolve computer programs. GP has potential advantages to algorithm design since it is flexible to represent and evolve more complex and flexible designs [4]. In the context of PSO design, GP has been applied in [17, 14] to create and optimize velocity equations for PSO, instead of simply adjusting parameters. In both works, each individual in the GP was a possible velocity equation for the PSO.

In our work we are focused on adopting Grammatical Evolution (GE), which is a GP approach based on context-free grammars. There are two reasons to combine GP with grammars [3]. First, the grammar can incorporate prior knowledge about the problem domain to help guide the GP search. Second, the production rules ensure syntactic correctness of the generated programs, differently from the traditional GP and GA.

Due to its flexibility in representing programs, GE is even more flexible than GP and GA to evolve algorithms and it was actually adopted for algorithm design in other contexts [18, 19]. In the context of PSO design, [20] adopted GE techniques to adjust the velocity equation, similarly to [17, 14]. However, the potential advantages of GE were not properly leveraged in [20], since it was also limited to evolve velocity updating equations. Other issues of PSO (e.g., the topology adopted) are important to convergence and quality of its solutions.

3. PROPOSAL

As it was motivated in the previous section, the application of GE in the PSO optimization has been little studied, and few parameters were considered. In this section, we introduce the GE algorithm and detail the proposed framework, GEFPSO.

3.1 Grammatical Evolution

GE is a GP algorithm which uses context-free grammar to evolve variable-length programs. The GE algorithm has three components: a search engine, a grammar and the mapping process. The search engine is an evolutionary algorithm that iteratively evolves the solutions represented as genotypes. These solutions are represented as variable-length binary strings (binary array), where each index of the array (codon) assumes numerical values of 8-bits. During the search engine execution, the fitness value of each genotype has to be computed. For this, the mapping process transforms each genotype (binary strings) to a corresponding phenotype (a program), and the fitness function is computed using the mapped program as input. The mapping process from genotype to phenotype uses a grammar in the Backus-Naur Form (BNF), which is domain-dependent [3] (i.e., specific to programs being evolved).

The BNF grammar is commonly represented as a tuple $< T, N, S, P >$ where T represents the terminal set, N is the non-terminal set, S is the start symbol, contained in N, and finally, P is the set of production rules. When there are more than one production rule in a particular N, the possible choices are separated by the symbol $|$.

The mapping process uses genotypes to map start symbols to terminal symbols. This happens through reading of the codon's value, which generates an integer value that indexes a specific rule in the BNF grammar:

$$\text{rule} = (\text{codon's value}) \\ \text{MOD} \\ (\text{number of rules of the current non terminal item}).$$

Consider the following rule for a terminal *op* that has four possible production rules:

$$\begin{aligned} < op > ::= &+ \quad (0) \\ | &- \quad (1) \\ | &/ \quad (2) \\ | &* \quad (3) \end{aligned}$$

Suppose that the genotype is represented by the binary string $(6, 203, 45, 51, 63)$, and the first codon (value 6) is the one associated to the terminal $< op >$. Since this terminal has 4 options and $6 \ MOD \ 4 = 2$, the third rule is mapped to the phenotype. The mapping process occurs in a circular way until there is no more possibility of expanding rules.

The output of this process is the phenotype or program. Once the phenotype was generated, it can be evaluated by the fitness function. We highlight that although the evaluation of a solution is in the phenotype format, the application of crossover and mutation operators occurs in the genotype format.

3.2 GEFPSO

In this work, we propose a framework based on GE which evolves the PSO design (components and parameter values) for a given optimization problem as input. The output of the GEFPSO is the best design of all generations. As the GEFPSO implements the GE, it also has a search engine, a BNF grammar and the mapping process. The search engine (GA) and the mapping process used in [3] were incorporated in the GEFPSO. The PSO algorithm with the parameters and procedures to be optimized is presented in Algorithm 1. The elements which are in the format of tag <> represent the parameters or procedures that can be replaced by values defined in the BNF grammar.

In our work, we defined a novel BNF grammar with different components and parameter values for PSO (see Figure 1). The grammar defines the possible options for a range of PSO components and parameters chosen due to their importance in the generation of good solutions [3]. In Section 2, we highlighted that the previous related work only optimized a limited amount of parameters (e.g., the velocity equation, c_1 and c_2, and χ). Below, we present the PSO components and parameters defined in the BNF grammar with optional values that are commonly used in literature [7]:

- Population size: the tag *<TAM>* expresses the size of the PSO population, which can affect the convergence and quality of the solutions returned by PSO;
- Velocity update: we adopted the two most known velocity updating equations for PSO [7]. The parameters of the velocity equations were set by the tags *<C1>*, *<C2>* and *<INERTIA>*;
- Topology: the tag *<GBEST>* represents the topology procedure that will be used to provide the neighborhood positions for the velocity equation. In this work, we considered seven well known topologies in literature [1, 12], which represent a variety of strategies for defining how particles interact during the search;
- Mutation: finally, the tag *<MUTATION>* represents possible mutation operators for the PSO. This tag can assume five mutation operators suggested by [23]. This tag also considers the possibility of using no mutation operator. The tag *<PROB-MUTATION>* defines the adopted values of mutation probability.

Algorithm .1: PSO algorithm to be optimized.

```
swarm = [random.rand()] * <TAM>
evaluate(swarm)
while stop criterion not reached do
    <UPDATE-VELOCITY>(individual)
    update_position(individual)
    <MUTATION>(individual)
    update_fitness(individual)
    update_pbest(individual)
    update_gbest(individual)
end
```

To illustrate the generation of PSO algorithms, it is considered the genotype $(220, 50, 34, 78, 95, 150, 27, 98)$. According to the mapping process presented in Section 3.1, the transcription from genotype to phenotype starts through the reading of the first codon 220 regarding to the tag *<TAM>*. As $220 \ MOD \ 3 = 1$, the second terminal value 50 is chosen. The next tag *<UPDATE-VELOCITY>* has two production rules. The operation $50 \ MOD \ 2 = 0$ results in choosing the first option for the velocity equation. As the last chosen rule has more four rules *<INERTIA>*, *<C1>*, *<GBEST>* and *<C2>*, the mapping process continues following the same steps performed here. According to the values of the genotype, the *<INERTIA>* is replaced by 0.5, $< C1 >$ assumes the value 2.5, *GBEST* adopts the *Hierarchical* topology and the $< C2 >$ replaced by 2.5. Once the tag *<UPDATE-VELOCITY>* is defined, the next to be chosen is *<MUTATION>*. This tag has six options to choose. The genotype has the value of 27 and as $27 \ MOD \ 6 = 3$, the fourth option is chosen in the phenotype. Finally, the last production rule *<PROB-MUTATION>* is mapped, and its value is 0.9.

$\langle$TAM$\rangle \models$ 30 | 50 | 70

$\langle$C1$\rangle \models$ 1 | 1.25 | 1.5 | 1.75... | 3

$\langle$C2$\rangle \models$ 1 | 1.25 | 1.5 | 1.75... | 3

$\langle$INERTIA$\rangle \models$ 0.1 | 0.2 | ... | 1.0

$\langle$PROB-MUTATION$\rangle \models$ 0.1 | 0.2 | ... | 1.0

$\langle$GBEST$\rangle \models$ Global
| Local
| Focal
| Von Neumann
| Hierarchical
| Four Clusters
| Clan

$\langle$UPDATE-VELOCITY$\rangle \models$
$(\langle\text{INERTIA}\rangle * v) + \langle\text{C1}\rangle * r_1 * (\langle\text{GBEST}\rangle - p) + \langle\text{C2}\rangle * r_2 * (pBest - p)$
| $\chi * (v + \langle\text{C1}\rangle * r_1 * (\langle\text{GBEST}\rangle - p) + \langle\text{C2}\rangle * r_2 * (pBest - p))$

$\langle$MUTATION$\rangle \models$ *Gaussian*($\langle$PROB-MUTATION$\rangle$)
| *Cauchy*($\langle$PROB-MUTATION$\rangle$)
| *Michalewicz*($\langle$PROB-MUTATION$\rangle$)
| *Levy*($\langle$PROB-MUTATION$\rangle$)
| *Random*($\langle$PROB-MUTATION$\rangle$)
| λ

Figure 1: Proposed BNF grammar for PSO optimization.

The generated design is one of the 2.041.200 million possible designs that can be generated from the proposed BNF grammar.

Figure 2 presents an overview of the general operation of GEFPSO. The first step is to define a BNF grammar. After that, a set of individuals or genotypes are generated randomly as the initial population of GA. Each individual in the population is mapped from genotype to phenotype through the mapping process. For each design, the PSO with the corresponding parameters is executed in the optimization problem at hand and the best fitness value is stored. These initial steps precede the iterative process of the framework. Once all individuals were evaluated, the best parents are selected and genetic operators are applied on them, and new individuals are generated. As the new individuals are in the genotype format, all of them are mapped to phenotype and their fitness values are stored. Only the best individuals have more chance to be selected to the next iteration. At the end of the iteration, whether the stop criterion was reached the algorithm is finished and the best PSO design is returned.

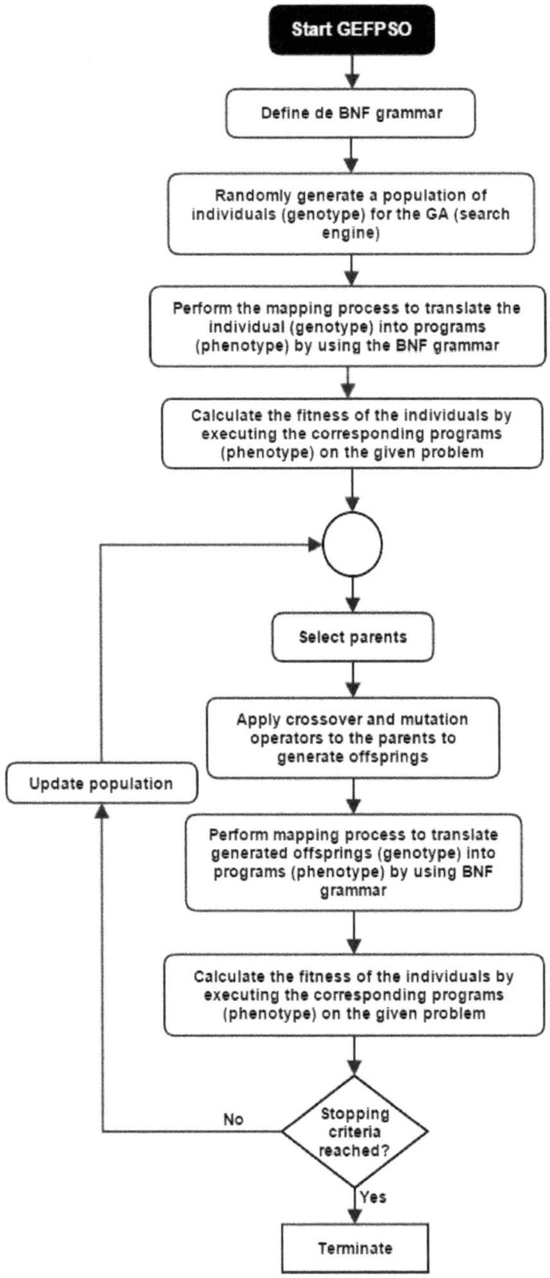

Figure 2: Overview of GEFPSO.

4. EXPERIMENTS

In this section, we present the benchmarks (optimization problems) adopted in our experiments and the methodology of experiments for two specific questions addressed in our work.

4.1 Problem domain

In our work, we adopted 16 continuous optimization functions without constraints with 30 dimensions as benchmarks for the experiments. These functions are associated to four categories: *Bowl-Shaped*, *Plate-Shaped*, *Valley-Shaped* and *Many Local Minima*, which enables us to evaluate the proposed approach for different levels of difficulty [22]. Four optimization functions were adopted in each category. All functions considered here are minimization problems whose global minimum is zero. In this work, the search space's bounds of all functions were limited to $(-100, 100)$.

We highlight that we have adopted a limited number of 16 optimization functions because they are related to specific categories of interest with distinguished features. In other words, our experiments are well controlled. In the future, we intend to perform experiments with more functions.

Functions of the *Bowl-Shaped* category present a convex fitness landscape and an unique global minimum solution. The functions in this category are: *Sphere* (f_1), *Powell Sum* (f_2), *Sum Squares* (f_3) and *Rotated Hyper-Ellipsoid* (f_4). All these functions are continuous, differentiable, separable, scalable and unimodal [21]. This set of characteristics makes them simpler to be optimized. An example of landscape associated to this category can be seen in Figure 3.

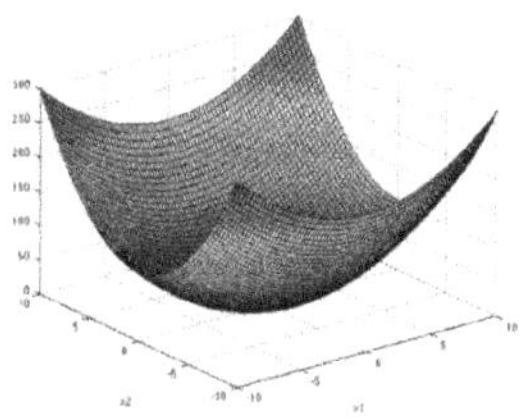

Figure 3: 3-D fitness landscape of 2-D functions in *Bowl-Shaped* category [22].

Functions of the *Plate-Shaped* have the global optimum located in an uniform plain (see Figure 4, as an example). Optimizers tend to find the plain easily, but, find the global minimum in the plain can be hard. The functions adopted in our work in this category are: *Zakharov* (f_5), *Bent Cigar* (f_6), *Elliptic* (f_7) and *Discus* (f_8). All these functions are continuous, differentiable, non-separable, scalable and unimodal [21]. The fact that these functions are non-separable makes them harder than the *Bowl-Shaped* functions.

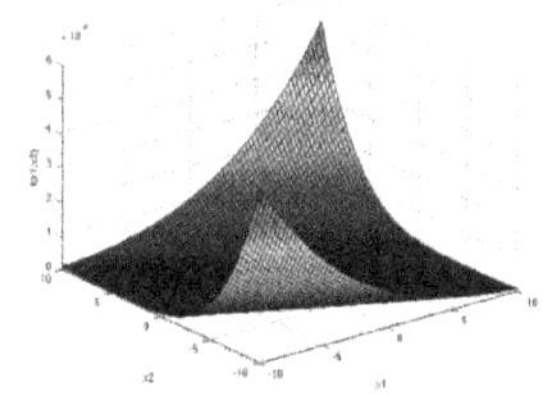

Figure 4: 3-D fitness landscape of 2-D functions in *Plate-Shaped* category [22].

The *Valley-Shaped* category is illustrated in Figure 5. Differently from the *Plate-Shaped* functions, the *Valley-Shaped* functions have a larger area of plain. As the global minimum is also located in the plain, the task of finding the global optimum is at least as hard as in the plate category. The functions adopted in this category are: *Rosenbrock* (f_9), *Shifted Rosenbrock* (f_{10}), *Shifted and rotated Rosenbrock* (f_{11}), and *Dixon-Price* (f_{12}). All these functions are continuous, differentiable, non-separable, scalable and unimodal [21].

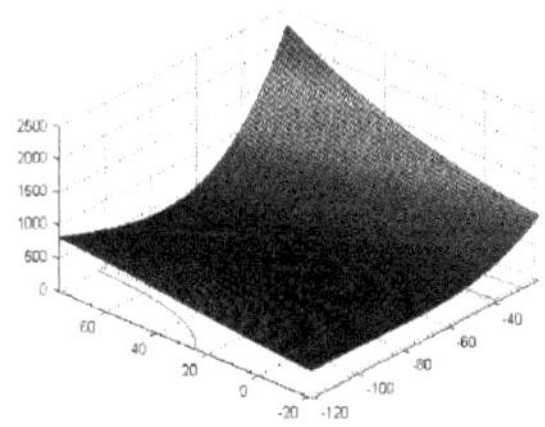

Figure 5: 3-D fitness landscape of 2-D functions in *Valley-Shaped* category [22].

The *Many Local Minima* category is composed by difficult optimization functions, due to the presence of local minima. This characteristic may turn the search more difficult because algorithms can be trapped in a local minimum. Figure 6 shows a fitness landscape with many local minima. The functions in this category are *Ackley* (f_{13}), *Griewank* (f_{14}), *Rastrigin* (f_{15}), and *Alpine* (f_{16}). All of them are continuous, scalable and multimodal. However, the first three functions are differentiable and non-separable, on the other hand, f_{16} is non-differentiable and separable [21].

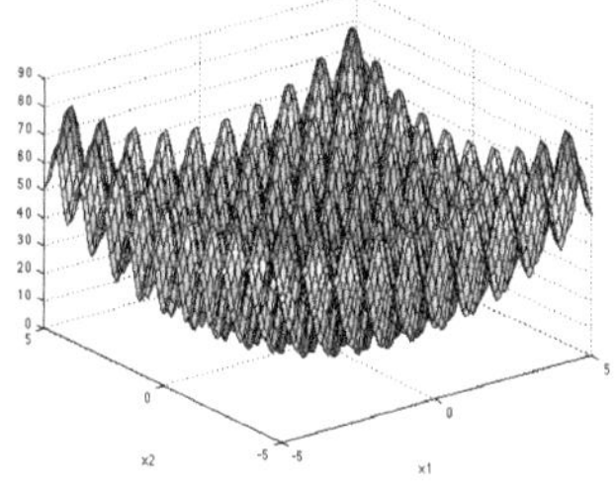

Figure 6: 3-D fitness landscape of a *Many Local Minima* 2-D function [22].

4.2 Methodology

For each problem, GEFPSO is executed by using the parameter values listed in Table 1. As it can be seen, all of them are related to the search engine (GA) of the framework. The choice of the parameter values was based on [19]. For each design generated by GEFPSO, the PSO uses a fixed execution time of 40 seconds as stop criterion. In this way, all designs would have the same amount of time to run and hence the obtained fitness values across designs can be fairly compared. Besides, the PSO is executed 20 times and the average objective function value is returned as the fitness of that design. After 20 generations, the best design found over all generations is returned as output. It is worth to mention that the experiments were performed on an Intel Core i7-5600U processor with 4M Cache, up to 3.20 GHz.

Table 1: GEFPSO settings

Parameter	Value
Population size	50
Number of generations	20
One point crossover probability	0.8
Point mutation probability	0.01
Cromossome length	8
Selection mechanism	Roulette Wheel
Generation model	Steady state

In our experiments, we evaluated the proposed framework addressing two distinct questions:

- Question (1) *What were the PSO designs generated by GEFPSO for each problem?*: We aim here to investigate which are the best components and parameter values for the PSO designs. Besides, we investigated how similar are these designs in order to verify if the GEFPSO generates generic designs that can be useful across problems;

- Question (2) *Does GEFPSO generate good PSO designs for the problems at hand?*: In order to answer this question, the fitness values obtained by the returned designs were compared to the results obtained by state-of-art algorithms in the same problems.

5. RESULTS

In this section, the obtained results are presented and analyzed considering the two issues raised in Section 4.2.

5.1 Question 1

In this battery of experiments, we stored for each problem the GEFPSO's output designs and identified the parameter values that were more often observed (across all runs and generations of the GE). Table 2 presents the obtained results for each problem. This table also shows the percentage of times that each parameter value was used in PSO designs during the simulations.

Considering the parameter *<TAM>*, the most often value in all designs for all problems was 30. As the number of individuals increases, the number of PSO evaluations also increases. As we adopted 40 seconds as stop criterion, higher values of population size harmed the convergence of the PSO. Regarding the velocity components the results were quite stable across problems. The resultant values of *<C1>* and *<C2>* are in the interval between 1.5 and 2.5. This result confirms the study performed in [13], which stated that a good balance between *exploration* and *exploitation* can be achieved when c_1 and c_2 assumes values in that interval. Considering the *<UPDATE-VELOCITY>*, we can see that the constricted velocity equation was better than the inertia equation and shown to be robust across different categories. As the inertia factor is not used in the constricted equation, it is not presented in Table 2. For the *<MUTATION>* parameter, the Gaussian operator was the most used operator across different categories. This shows that the use of mutation operators can be important for the PSO results.

Considering the *<GBEST>* parameter, it can be seen that the performance of PSO across categories strongly depended on the topology adopted, while the results observed for the other parameters were in general robust. Thus, we further investigated the frequencies of the other topologies for each problem (see Table 3).

Table 2 shows that the *Global* was the most used topology for problems in the *Bowl* category. As the problems in this category are simpler, they require topologies which favor *exploitation*. On the other hand, topologies with diversity mechanisms, e.g. *Four Clusters* and *Clan*, can waste time exploring the search space when, in fact, it is not necessary. Differently from *Bowl* category, problems in the *Plate* category need more exploratory topologies to avoid stagnation in the plain. For this reason, topologies like *Local*, *Hierarchical* and *Von Neumann* were more used. Although the topologies *Four Clusters* and *Clan* have exploratory mechanisms, they were used in at most 10% of the designs. The problems in *Valley* category are at least as hard as the problems with *Plate* shape and also resulted in the use of exploratory topologies. Although *Von Neumann* topology has been the most used here, it can be seen that more complex topologies, like *Four Clusters* and *Clan*, are also frequently observed.

Considering the *Many Local Minima* category, we can see a massive presence of more sophisticated topologies. The topologies *Four Clusters* and *Clan* were used in more than 60% of designs. Both topologies have mechanisms which provide a good balance between exploitation and exploration. In turn, topologies like the *Local* are not commonly used since it favors exploration in excess.

As it could be seen in Table 3, the designs adopted for problems in the same category are similar. In order to verify if the GEFPSO generates generic designs that can be useful in a determined category, which brings similar problems, we applied a leave-one-out procedure to generate a ranking of designs for each problem. Given a problem left-out (the test function), the design generated for that function is discarded and the other 15 designs, considered the best ones for the training problems, are tested in the problem left-out. A ranking of designs is generated for the test problem ordering them by the fitness achieved. The leave-one-out is repeated for each problem. We then can verify whether the PSO design associated to each function in a category is well placed in the rankings of designs for the problems in the same category. Table 4 presents the ranking of the three best designs for each problem. The generated design from the training phase (GEFPSO simulation) for each problem f_1 to f_{16} are named d_1 to d_{16}, respectively. For simplicity, only the top-3 ranked designs (from the 15 candidates for each problem) are shown in Table 4.

In Table 4 we can see that the best three designs of each category of problems were generated through problems of the same category. We can conclude that when a design is trained in a problem of a determined category, it can be reused in problems of the same category. Thus, although the training phase takes too much time, once the design is generated for a category of problems, it can be reused to another problem quite fast (in our case in 40 seconds, which corresponds to the stop criterion adopted in the GE grammar). Once we have designs generated by GEFPSO for problems with particular features of interest, we can recommend designs to similar problems. We highlight that we have in our experiments a priori knowledge about problems similarity since we adopted functions related to specific categories of interest with distinguished features. In other words, our experiments are well controlled. In general, however, it is not easy to identify how similar are two optimization problems. In the future, we intend to extend our work by investigating features of the fitness landscapes [24] to characterize optimization problems and thus, to recommend designs in practice based.

Table 4: Ranking of designs for each problem.

Category	Problems	Designs		
		1st	2nd	3rd
Bowl	f_1	d_3	d_4	d_2
	f_2	d_4	d_1	d_3
	f_3	d_1	d_2	d_4
	f_4	d_3	d_1	d_2
Plate	f_5	d_6	d_8	d_7
	f_6	d_7	d_8	d_5
	f_7	d_5	d_6	d_8
	f_8	d_7	d_6	d_5
Valley	f_9	d_{12}	d_{10}	d_{11}
	f_{10}	d_{12}	d_9	d_{11}
	f_{11}	d_{11}	d_{12}	d_9
	f_{12}	d_9	d_{11}	d_{10}
Many	f_{13}	d_{16}	d_{15}	d_{14}
	f_{14}	d_{13}	d_{15}	d_{16}
	f_{15}	d_{16}	d_{13}	d_{14}
	f_{16}	d_{15}	d_{14}	d_{13}

5.2 Question 2

In order to verify whether the GEFPSO generates competitive designs for PSO, the results obtained by the proposed framework were compared to the results of the algorithms from the ICSI 2014 competition [5]: HSDB (A_1), MPCPSO (A_2), MBO (A_3), dynFWA (A_4), DESP (A_5) and EFWA (A_6). We highlight that all algorithms from the competition used as stop criterion 40 seconds per simulation and executed 20 times in order to generate the mean of its fitness values. These setting values are the same adopted by

Table 2: Resultant designs for each problem.

Category	Problems	Parameters							
		TAM	C1	C2	UPDATE-VELOCITY	INERTIA	MUTATION	PROB-MUTATION	GBEST
Bowl	f_1	30 (78%)	2.0 (45%)	2.0 (42%)	*Constricted* (65%)	-	*Gauss.* (41%)	0.2 (49%)	*Global* (57%)
	f_2	30 (80%)	1.75 (47%)	2.0 (33%)	*Constricted* (75%)	-	*Gauss.* (39%)	0.2 (45%)	*Global* (60%)
	f_3	30 (75%)	1.75 (34%)	1.75 (31%)	*Constricted* (72%)	-	*Michal.* (33%)	0.3 (39%)	*Global* (58%)
	f_4	30 (72%)	1.5 (33.5%)	2.0 (31%)	*Constricted* (69%)	-	*Gauss.* (31%)	0.2 (39.5%)	*Global* (59%)
Plate	f_5	30 (69%)	2.5 (33%)	2.0 (33%)	*Constricted* (52%)	-	*Gauss.* (33%)	0.2 (34.5%)	*V.Neum.* (26%)
	f_6	30 (68%)	2.5 (31%)	2.5 (30%)	*Constricted* (55%)	-	*Gauss.* (33%)	0.3 (33%)	*V.Neum.* (33%)
	f_7	30 (68%)	2.5 (34%)	2.5 (31%)	*Constricted* (56%)	-	*Gauss.* (30%)	0.3 (35%)	*V.Neum.* (30%)
	f_8	30 (72%)	2.5 (35%)	2.5 (33%)	*Constricted* (56%)	-	*Gauss.* (32%)	0.3 (34%)	*V.Neum.* (29%)
Valley	f_9	30 (70%)	1.75 (31%)	2.5 (30%)	*Constricted* (66%)	-	*Gauss.* (31%)	0.2 (31.5%)	*V.Neum.* (30%)
	f_{10}	30 (70%)	2.0 (31%)	2.0 (32%)	*Constricted* (68%)	-	*Gauss.* (29%)	0.2 (32%)	*V.Neum.* (30%)
	f_{11}	30 (66%)	2.5 (30%)	2.0 (32%)	*Constricted* (66%)	-	*Gauss.* (29%)	0.2 (31%)	*V.Neum.* (28%)
	f_{12}	30 (71%)	2.0 (30%)	2.0 (32%)	*Constricted* (67%)	-	*Gauss.* (34%)	0.2 (31%)	*V.Neum.* (32%)
Many	f_{13}	30 (82%)	2.5 (38%)	2.5 (34%)	*Constricted* (67%)	-	*Gauss.* (34%)	0.4 (41%)	*Clan* (39%)
	f_{14}	30 (81%)	2.5 (40%)	2.5 (36%)	*Constricted* (70%)	-	*Gauss.* (40%)	0.4 (42%)	*Clan* (39%)
	f_{15}	30 (79%)	2.0 (34%)	2.0 (40%)	*Constricted* (75%)	-	*Gauss.* (43%)	0.4 (44%)	*Clan* (39%)
	f_{16}	30 (83%)	2.5 (42%)	2.5 (36%)	*Constricted* (69%)	-	*Gauss.* (42%)	0.4 (41%)	*Clan* (42%)

Table 3: <*GBEST*> values used during simulations.

Category	Problems	< *GBEST* >						
		Global	Local	Focal	V.Neumann	Hierar.	*Four-Clusters*	Clan
Bowl	f_1	**57%**	17%	5%	5%	3%	7%	5%
	f_2	**60%**	18%	4%	5%	3%	6%	4%
	f_3	**58%**	18%	3%	5%	3%	5%	6%
	f_4	**59%**	17%	4%	5%	3%	6%	4%
Plate	f_5	15%	14%	6%	**26%**	18%	10%	10%
	f_6	20%	15%	4%	**33%**	12%	9%	6%
	f_7	18%	15%	4%	**30%**	18%	8%	6%
	f_8	18%	15%	4%	**29%**	17%	10%	6%
Valley	f_9	7%	15%	4%	**30%**	10%	18%	16%
	f_{10}	8%	10%	4%	**30%**	12%	24%	12%
	f_{11}	10%	10%	4%	**28%**	9%	22%	16%
	f_{12}	8%	10%	7%	**32%**	8%	19%	15%
Many	f_{13}	5%	10%	2%	7%	6%	30%	**39%**
	f_{14}	8%	10%	7%	2%	6%	29%	**39%**
	f_{15}	6%	7%	3%	2%	6%	27%	**39%**
	f_{16}	6%	8%	3%	2%	6%	33%	**42%**

the PSO designs. We highlight that all algorithms from A_1 to A_6 used their default parameters used in the competition. Moreover, all benchmark optimization functions considered as search space's bounds $(-100, 100)$. This rule was defined in ICSI 2014.

We initially compared the average fitness value obtained by the recommended designs for each problem and the average fitness values obtained by the baselines adopted in our experiments. Table 5 presents the average ranks of algorithms across all problems (for each problem, rank $= 1$ is assigned to the best algorithm, rank $= 2$ is assigned to the second best, and so on). As it can be seen GEFPSO obtained the second best average rank from all algorithms. By applying the Wilcoxon signed-rank test with 95% of confidence, we verified that GEFPSO was statistically equivalent to A_2, A_5 and A_6 and statistically better than $A1$ and A_3.

Table 5: Ranking of algorithms across problems.

Algorithms						
A_1	A_2	A_3	A_4	A_5	A_6	GEFPSO
5.31250	2.15625	5.68750	4.25000	3.56250	3.62500	3.40625

Additionally, Table 6 presents the average fitness values achieved by the best competing algorithm and by GEFPSO for each problem. In almost all problems the designs generated by the GEFPSO resulted in fitness values that are close to 0 (the global optimum). By applying the Wilcoxon statistical test with 95% of confidence, the achieved fitness values were considered statistically identical '=' (see column *Result* in Table 6) to the results of the best algorithm. The PSO design generated by the GEFPSO achieved the best result for f_{12}.

Table 6: Mean of fitness values of the algorithms in each optimization problem.

Category	Problems	Algorithms		Result
		Best	GEFPSO	
Bowl	f_1	A_2: 4.95e-150	3.56e-138	=
	f_2	A_2: 4.35e-36	4.54e-24	=
	f_3	A_2: 2.87e-134	6.34e-119	=
	f_4	A_2: 1.87e-144	1.23e-133	=
Plate	f_5	A_2: 1.2e-2	0.009	=
	f_6	A_5: 3.02e-27	0.24e-26	=
	f_7	A_2: 2.33	2.36	=
	f_8	A_2: 2.15e-19	1.33e-15	=
Valley	f_9	A_4: 2.34	3.39	=
	f_{10}	A_4: 6.31	7.94	=
	f_{11}	A_4: 8.64	9.45	=
	f_{12}	-	0.49	=
Many	f_{13}	A_2: 2.78e-13	7.54e-5	=
	f_{14}	A_2: 0.0	0.0	=
	f_{15}	A_2: 1.19	3.07	=
	f_{16}	A_3: 1.29e-27	6.87e-19	=

It is important to highlight that the above experiments were performed to verify whether the PSO designs returned by GEFPSO were adequate. The comparative results to the other baselines should not be considered in an absolute sense since the baselines were applied directly using their default parameters, while PSO was optimized. In this sense, the comparison would be unfair. In this battery of experiments, our intention was only to verify if the GEFPSO generates PSO designs that result in good solutions to the optimization problems considered.

6. CONCLUSION

In this paper, the problem of *parameter design* for the PSO algorithm was addressed. Given an optimization problem, we aimed to generate a configuration of parameters for PSO that is adequate in terms of optimization performance. In this work, we proposed a framework based on grammatical evolution which optimizes iteratively the PSO design. For this, parameters that strongly influence the PSO convergence were taken into account, such as acceleration constants, topologies, mutation operators, velocity equations and population size.

In the experiments, we adopted 16 benchmark optimization functions, classified in four categories of hardness. The proposed framework was applied to all functions, generating as output an evolved PSO design for each problem. The results showed that the designs generated by the framework are capable to achieve competitive solutions when compared to state-of-art algorithms. Besides, the experiments revealed that the designs generated from problems within the same category are similar and thus can be reused.

As future work, we intend to develop a systematic way of categorizing optimization problems considering their fitness landscape features. Once a given problem is categorized, a suggestion of adequate designs would be performed based on designs that were previously evolved to similar problems.

Acknowledgment

The authors would like to thank CNPq, CAPES and FACEPE (Brazilian Agencies) for their financial support.

7. REFERENCES

[1] A. Engelbrecht. Computational Intelligence: An Introduction. 2 ed. Wiley, 2007. p. 628.

[2] A. E. Eiben, R. Hinterding, and Z. Michalewicz. Parameter control in evolutionary algorithms. In Trans. Evol. Comput., vol. 3(2), pp. 124–141, 1999.

[3] M. O'Neil and C. Ryan. Grammatical Evolution. In Trans. Evolut. Computation, v. 5(4), pp. 349–358, 2001.

[4] J. Woodward and J. Swan. Template method hyper-heuristics. In Comp. on Genetic and Evolut. Comput., pp. 1437-1438, 2014.

[5] Y. Tan, J. Li and Z. Zheng. Introduction and Ranking Results of the ICSI 2014 Competition on Single Objective Optimization. arXiv:1501.02128, 2015.

[6] J. Kennedy and R. Eberhart. Particle Swarm Optimization. In Int. Conf. on Neural Networks, p. 1942–1948, 1995.

[7] M. Clerc and J. Kennedy. The particle swarm—explosion, stability, and convergence in a multidimensional complex space. In Trans. on Evolut. Computation, v. 6(1), pp. 58–73, 2002.

[8] X. Yang, J. Yuan, H. Mao. A modified particle swarm optimizer with dynamic adaptation. In Appl. Math. Comput., v. 189, pp. 1205–1213, 2007.

[9] Y. Tang, Z.D. Wang, J.A. Fang. Feedback learning particle swarm optimization. In Appl. Soft Comput., v. 11, pp. 4713–4725, 2011.

[10] H. Yang. Particle swarm optimization with modified velocity strategy. In Energy Proced., v. 11, pp. 1074–1079, 2011.

[11] Gang Xu. An adaptive parameter tuning of particle swarm optimization algorithm,. In Appl. Math. and Comput., v. 219(9), pp. 4560-4569, 2013.

[12] J. Kennedy and R. Mendes. Population Structure and Particle Swarm Performance. In Conf. on Evolut. Comput., p.1671–1676, 2002.

[13] Y. Shi and R. Eberhart. Parameter selection in particle swarm optimization. In Evolut. Program. VII, pp. 591-600. Springer Berlin Heidelberg, 1998.

[14] R. Poli, C. Di Chio and W. Langdon. Exploring extended particle swarms: a genetic programming approach. In Conf. on Genetic and Evolut. Comput., pp. 169-176. ACM, 2005.

[15] K. Parsopoulos and M. Vrahatis. Recent approaches to global optimization problems through particle swarm optimization. In Natural Comput., v. 1, no. 2–3, pp. 235–306, 2002.

[16] J. Liu. Evolving Particle Swarm Optimization Implemented by a Genetic Algorithm. In Journal of Adv. Computat. Intell. and Intelligent Informatics, v.12(3), pp. 284-289, 2008.

[17] M. Rashid. Combining PSO Algorithm and Honey Bee Food Foraging Behavior for Solving Multimodal and Dynamic Optimization Problems. PhD diss., National University of Computer Emerging Sciences, 2010.

[18] E. Burke, M. Hyde and G. Kendall. Grammatical Evolution of Local Search Heuristics. In Trans. on Evolut. Comput., v. 16(3), pp. 406-417, 2012.

[19] N. Sabar, M. Ayob, G. Kendall and R. Qu. Grammatical Evolution Hyper-Heuristic for Combinatorial Optimization Problems. In Trans. on Evolut. Comput., v. 17(6), 2013.

[20] T. Si, A. De, A. Bhattacharjee. Grammatical Swarm Based-Adaptable Velocity Update Equations in Particle Swarm Optimizer. In Adv.in Intel. Systems and Computing, v. 247, pp. 197-206, 2014.

[21] M. Jamil and X. Yang. A literature survey of benchmark functions for global optimization problems. In Int. Journal of Math. Modelling and Num. Optimi., v. 4(2), pp. 150-194, 2013.

[22] S. Surjanovic and D. Bingham. Virtual Library of Simulation Experiments: Test Functions and Datasets. Retrieved January 30, 2015, from www.sfu.ca/ ssurjano.

[23] C. Li, S. Yang and I. Korejo. An adaptive mutation operator for particle swarm optimization. In UK Workshop on Comput. Intellig., pp. 165-170, 2008.

[24] K. Malan and A. Engelbrecht. Ruggedness, funnels and gradients in fitness landscapes and the effect on PSO performance. In Congress on Evolut. Comput., pp. 963-970, 2013.

Correlation Immunity of Boolean Functions: An Evolutionary Algorithms Perspective

Stjepan Picek
Faculty of Electrical Engineering and Computing
University of Zagreb, Croatia
stjepan@computer.org

Claude Carlet
LAGA, UMR 7539, CNRS
University of Paris XIII and University of Paris VIII, France
Claude.Carlet@univ-paris8.fr

Domagoj Jakobovic
Faculty of Electrical Engineering and Computing
University of Zagreb, Croatia
domagoj.jakobovic@fer.hr

Julian F. Miller
Department of Electronics
University of York, UK
julian.miller@york.ac.uk

Lejla Batina
Radboud University
Nijmegen, The Netherlands
lejla@cs.ru.nl *

ABSTRACT

Boolean functions are essential in many stream ciphers. When used in combiner generators, they need to have sufficiently high values of correlation immunity, alongside other properties. In addition, correlation immune functions with small Hamming weight reduce the cost of masking countermeasures against side-channel attacks. Various papers have examined the applicability of evolutionary algorithms for evolving cryptographic Boolean functions. However, even when authors considered correlation immunity, it was not given the highest priority. Here, we examine the effectiveness of three different EAs, namely, Genetic Algorithms, Genetic Programming (GP) and Cartesian GP for evolving correlation immune Boolean functions. Besides the properties of balancedness and correlation immunity, we consider several other relevant cryptographic properties while maintaining the optimal trade-offs among them. We show that evolving correlation immune Boolean functions is an even harder objective than maximizing nonlinearity.

Categories and Subject Descriptors

I.2.8 [**Computing Methodologies**]: Artificial Intelligence—*Problem Solving, Control Methods, and Search*

Keywords

Boolean Functions; Cryptography; Cartesian Genetic Programming; Genetic Programming

*This work was supported in part by the Technology Foundation STW (project 12624 - SIDES), The Netherlands Organization for Scientific Research NWO (project ProFIL 628.001.007) and the ICT COST action IC1204 TRUDEVICE.

GECCO '15, July 11 - 15, 2015, Madrid, Spain
© 2015 ACM. ISBN 978-1-4503-3472-3/15/07...$15.00
DOI: http://dx.doi.org/10.1145/2739480.2754764

1. INTRODUCTION

Evolutionary algorithms (EAs) found their place in many real-world applications where they offer a good balance between the ease of use and results. In particular, one area where EAs have shown good results is the generation of Boolean functions that are suitable for cryptography. However, since there are many possible design criteria for Boolean functions in cryptography, this domain is still wide open for research. In the rest of this paper, when we discuss Boolean functions suitable for cryptography, we primarily mean Boolean functions suitable to be used in combiner generators. In this paper, we are concentrating on the correlation immunity property of Boolean functions. To date, this property has not been the primary concern when evolving Boolean functions and although there exist papers considering this property, they are mainly concerned with other properties. Furthermore, correlation immunity is given a limited span of desired values (i.e. correlation immunity of first or second order) and only for balanced Boolean functions.

When discussing methods of generating Boolean functions with appropriate cryptographic properties, they can be divided into three groups: algebraic constructions, random generation and heuristics (and of course, different combinations between those methods). Among various heuristic approaches, EAs offer highly competitive results when generating Boolean functions for cryptography. This is discussed in Section 3. In this paper, we use EAs to experiment with two very different usages of Boolean functions, but where in both applications correlation immunity property has high importance.

The first application explores the evolution of Boolean functions appropriate for usage in combiner generators. The second deals with the correlation immune Boolean functions that have a small Hamming weight. Such functions have application in side-channel countermeasures [2]. Although we explore only those two applications, correlation immune functions have more utilizations. For instance, they are also directly related to those designs in mathematics called orthogonal arrays [4].

1.1 Our Contribution

Our first contribution is an extensive analysis of the difficulty of obtaining balanced Boolean functions suitable for cryptography that have various values of correlation immunity property. The second contribution is, as far as the authors know, the first application of EAs to find Boolean functions with minimal Hamming weight and different correlation immunity values. Both contributions have real-world applications.

The rest of this paper is organized as follows. In Section 2, we give necessary information about Boolean functions, their properties and trade-offs between some of those properties. Next, Section 3 enumerates some of the relevant work. In Section 4, we present experimental setup, Section 5 gives results, short discussion and some guidelines for the future work. Finally, Section 6 offers a summary of our work.

2. BACKGROUND AND MOTIVATION

Notation.

The inner product of two vectors $\vec{a}$ and $\vec{b}$ is denoted as $\vec{a} \cdot \vec{b}$ and equals $\vec{a} \cdot \vec{b} = \oplus_{i=1}^{n} a_i b_i$. Here, "$\oplus$" represents bitwise XOR. The set of all n-tuples of elements in the field $\mathbb{F}_2$ is denoted as $\mathbb{F}_2^n$ where $\mathbb{F}_2$ is the Galois field with 2 elements. An (n, m)-function (also called vectorial Boolean function) is any mapping F from $\mathbb{F}_2^n$ to $\mathbb{F}_2^m$. If m equals 1 then the function f is called a Boolean function. The Hamming weight (HW) of a vector $\vec{a}$, where $\vec{a} \in \mathbb{F}_2^n$, is the number of non-zero positions in the vector. The support *supp* of a Boolean function f is given by [5]:

$$supp(f) = x \in \mathbb{F}_2^n | f(x) = 1. \tag{1}$$

The Hamming weight of a Boolean function f on $\mathbb{F}_2^n$ is the size (cardinality) of its support.

Representations.

A Boolean function f on $\mathbb{F}_2^n$ can be uniquely represented by a truth table (TT), which is a vector (e.g. $f(\vec{0}), ..., f(\vec{1})$) that contains the function values of f, ordered lexicographically, i.e. $\vec{a} \leq \vec{b}$ [5].

A second unique representation of a Boolean function f is the Walsh transform W_f. It represents the correlation between $f(\vec{x})$ and the linear function $\vec{a} \cdot \vec{x}$ [5]. The Walsh transform of a Boolean function f equals:

$$W_f(\vec{a}) = \sum_{\vec{x} \in \mathbb{F}_2^n} (-1)^{f(\vec{x}) \oplus \vec{a} \cdot \vec{x}}. \tag{2}$$

A third unique representation of a Boolean function f on $\mathbb{F}_2^n$ is a polynomial in $\mathbb{F}_2 [x_0, ..., x_{n-1}] / (x_0^2 - x_0, ..., x_{n-1}^2 - x_{n-1})$. This form is called ANF and it is a multivariate polynomial P defined as [5]:

$$P(\vec{x}) = \oplus_{\vec{a} \in \mathbb{F}_2^n} h(\vec{a}) \vec{x}^{\vec{a}}, \tag{3}$$

where $h(\vec{a})$ is defined by the Möbius inversion principle [5].

The Properties.

A Boolean function is balanced if its Hamming weight (HW) is equal to 2^{n-1} [5]. Boolean functions need to be balanced; otherwise (for sufficiently large n) it would be possible to distinguish between the keystream output by the function and some random sequence when using filter and combiner generators [5].

The nonlinearity N_f of a Boolean function f can be expressed in terms of the Walsh coefficients as [5]:

$$N_f = 2^{n-1} - \frac{1}{2} max_{\vec{a} \in \mathbb{F}_2^n} |W_f(\vec{a})|. \tag{4}$$

A Boolean function needs to have high nonlinearity value in order to resist fast correlation attacks [5]. By high value we mean a value that is near the covering radius bound $2^{n-1} - 2^{\frac{n}{2}-1}$.

The algebraic degree *deg* of a Boolean function f is defined as the number of variables in the largest product term of the functions' ANF having a non zero coefficient. A Boolean function needs to have high enough value of algebraic degree to resist Berlekamp-Massey attack [5].

For a Boolean function f, we say it is correlation immune of order t (in brief, $CI(t)$) if the output of the function is statistically independent of the combination of any t of its inputs [5]. A characterization exists using the Walsh spectrum and it equals:

$$W_f(\vec{a}) = 0, \text{ for } 0 \leq HW(\vec{a}) \leq t. \tag{5}$$

A high value of correlation immunity property is necessary for resisting Siegenthaler correlation attack when Boolean functions are used in combiner generators [28].

A Boolean function f is t-resilient if it is balanced and with correlation immunity of degree t [5].

The algebraic immunity AI of a Boolean function f is the lowest degree of a nonzero function g from $\mathbb{F}_2^n$ into $\mathbb{F}_2$ for which $f \cdot g = \vec{0}$ or $(f \oplus \vec{1}) \cdot g = \vec{0}$ where f and g are Boolean functions [5]. Boolean functions need to have high values of algebraic immunity in order to resist algebraic attacks [15].

Bounds and Trade-offs.

Sarkar and Maitra showed that if a CI(t) Boolean function f has an even number of inputs n and $k \leq \frac{n}{2} - 1$ then its nonlinearity N_f is upper bounded as follows [27]:

$$N_f \leq 2^{n-1} - 2^{\frac{n}{2}-1} - 2^k, \tag{6}$$

where k equals $t+1$ if f is balanced or has Hamming weight divisible by 2^{t+1} and k equals t otherwise.

In the case when $k > \frac{n}{2} - 1$ then the nonlinearity is upper bounded with:

$$N_f \leq 2^{n-1} - 2^k. \tag{7}$$

The correlation immunity $CI(t)$ and the algebraic degree *deg* are conflicting properties and it is not possible to obtain a function with both properties optimal. For a resilient function where $t > 1$ and $t \neq n - 1$, the following Siegenthaler inequality holds [28]:

$$t \leq n - deg - 1. \tag{8}$$

Otherwise, the inequality is as follows:

$$t \leq n - deg. \tag{9}$$

The algebraic immunity is upper bounded by the number of input variables, more precisely [14]:

$$AI \leq \lceil \frac{n}{2} \rceil. \tag{10}$$

The next inequality shows a connection between the algebraic immunity and the algebraic degree properties:

$$AI \leq deg. \tag{11}$$

2.1 Motivation and Objectives

Symmetric key cryptography can be divided into block and stream ciphers [18]. In both categories, nonlinear elements play an important role by adding confusion to the algorithm. Informally speaking, without some nonlinear element, a cryptographic algorithm would be easy to break. Boolean functions are considered the best known nonlinear elements and they are used in stream ciphers, while vectorial Boolean functions (commonly known as Substitution boxes or S-boxes) are used in block ciphers.

Being more specific, many stream ciphers are realized as the combination by a Boolean function of some bits extracted from one or several Linear Feedback Shift Registers (LFSR), where LFSR is a linear construction used for generating a sequence of binary bits. Two often explored models that use an LFSR together with a nonlinear transformation are the so-called combiner and the filter generator models [5]. A combiner generator uses several LFSRs in parallel and then combines their output in a nonlinear way. In a filter generator, the output is obtained by a nonlinear function of some taps of one longer LFSR [5]. Both models are depicted in Figures 1a and 1b.

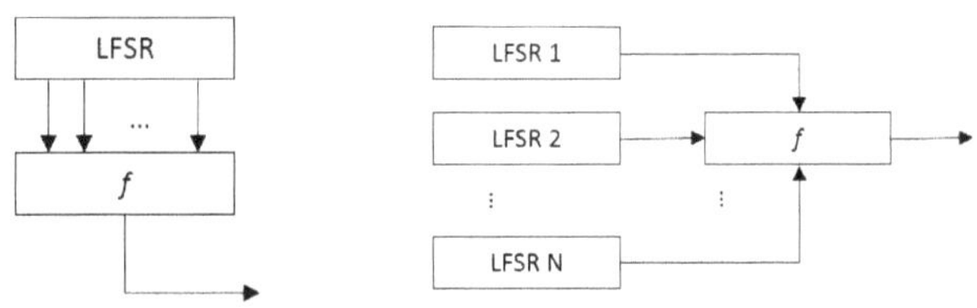

(a) Filter generator. (b) Combiner generator.

Figure 1: Principles of filter and combiner generators.

In general, for a Boolean function to be useful in such framework it needs to be balanced, with high nonlinearity, high algebraic immunity and a high algebraic degree. Moreover, to be used in a combiner generator it also needs to have a high value of correlation immunity [5, 23, 28]. However, if the correlation immunity is high, it is difficult to find high algebraic immunity, which has resulted in a decreased use of combiner generators.

For our **first** fitness objective, we are interested in Boolean functions that are appropriate for usage in combiner generators. Furthermore, we concentrate only on Boolean functions with eight inputs that have various values of correlation immunity property. As evident from the Section 3, EAs can be also used to evolve Boolean functions of larger size. However, we decided to experiment with only one input size in order to better answer the question of the difficulty of evolving Boolean functions with different correlation immunity values. Eight inputs is a relatively small size for Boolean functions for stream ciphers (it is commonly considered that 13 is a strict minimum for resisting algebraic attacks), but we still believe it presents an interesting case. Indeed, for instance ciphers RAKAPOSHI [12] and Achterbahn [17] use Boolean functions of that size.

In addition, we are interested in Boolean functions that can help resist side-channel attacks. Side-channel attacks do not rely on the security of the underlying algorithm, but rather on the implementation of the algorithm in a device. Implementations running on small devices often provide an adversary with unintentional output channels, often called side channels. On some occasions, these types of information leakages can be linked either to the types of operations that the cipher is performing, or to the data. This makes the leakages explorable by the adversary trying to extract the secret key as they are always looking for shortcuts in cryptanalysis [22]. One class of countermeasures against side-channel attacks are masking schemes. In masking schemes one randomizes the intermediate values that are processed by the cryptographic device. One obvious drawback of such an approach is the masking overhead which can be substantial in embedded devices or smart cards.

However, correlation immune Boolean functions can reduce the masking overhead in two ways [6, 9]. The first way is by applying leakage squeezing method [8, 9] and the other method uses Rotating S-box masking [6]. For the second case the key is to generate Boolean functions with as high as possible correlation immunity value and minimal Hamming weight of their support. In the first case, there is a constraint that f is the indicator of a permutation of $\mathbb{F}_2^{\frac{n}{2}}$.

In accordance to that, evolution of Boolean functions with minimal Hamming weight is the goal of our **second** objective. We note here that most of algebraic constructions are not a viable choice for this objective since they are designed to generate balanced Boolean functions. Since this is the first time EAs are to be used to evolve Boolean functions with such properties, we again work with eight input Boolean functions.

We conclude the case for our motivation with the citation from [5], page 97: "But designing constructions leading to large numbers of functions achieving good trade-offs between the nonlinearity, the algebraic degree and the resiliency order (if possible, on any numbers of variables) are still necessary for permitting to choose in applications cryptographic functions satisfying specific constraints."

3. RELATED WORK

In this section, we first briefly discuss applications of EAs to the evolution of Boolean functions where correlation immunity is a property of interest.

Millan et al. use GAs to evolve Boolean functions that have high nonlinearity [24]. In conjunction with the GA they use hill-climbing and a resetting step in order to find Boolean functions with even higher nonlinearity. They experiment with Boolean function sizes of up to 12 inputs and they find balanced eight input Boolean functions with nonlinearity 112 and correlation immunity equal to one.

Clark et al. use simulated annealing (SA) to generate Boolean functions with cryptographically relevant properties [13]. In their work they consider balanced function with high nonlinearity and with the correlation immunity less and equal to two.

Burnett et al. present two heuristic methods where the goal of the first method is generating balanced Boolean functions with high nonlinearity and low autocorrelation. The second method aims at generating resilient functions with high nonlinearity and algebraic degree that maximizes Siegenthaler inequality [3].

McLaughlin and Clark on the other hand use SA to generate Boolean functions that have optimal values of algebraic immunity, fast algebraic resistance and algebraic degree [23].

In their work they experiment with Boolean functions of size up to 16 inputs.

Picek et al. experiment with GA and GP to find Boolean functions that possess several optimal properties among which is correlation immunity [25]. As far as the authors know, this is the first application of GP when evolving cryptographically suitable Boolean functions.

When discussing algebraic constructions and bounds there exists a plethora of results on correlation immune Boolean functions. We give here only a subset of relevant works.

Tarannikov suggests a method to construct n-variable and t-resilient with maximal possible nonlinearity for $\frac{2n-7}{3} \leq m \leq n - \log_2 \frac{n-2}{3} - 2$ [29].

Carlet and Sarkar show the necessary condition on the ANF of correlation immune Boolean functions that reach maximal possible nonlinearity [10].

Maitra and Sarkar present constructions able to generate n-variable and t-resilient Boolean functions that maximize Siegenthaler inequality [21, 26].

Le Bars and Viola present a complete characterization of the first order correlation immune Boolean functions of up to seven inputs [20].

Carrasco et al. use the approach from [20] to develop a combinatorial method able to randomly generate first order correlation immune functions [11]. With that method they are able to generate eight input Boolean function with correlation immunity equal to one in slightly more than five seconds.

4. EXPERIMENTAL SETUP

In this section, we briefly discuss the algorithms we use and their parameters. We conduct a short two parameter sweep in order to investigate the best combination of parameters for each of the algorithms. Since there are more than two parameters for each algorithm, we try to consider only the most obvious choices for the tuning.

4.1 Representations and Common Parameters

The GA represents the individuals as strings of bits where values are truth tables of Boolean functions. GP uses a representation where individuals are trees of Boolean primitives which are then evaluated according to the truth table they produce. CGP solutions are directed graphs with Boolean primitives as nodes, that are also evaluated using the truth table they produce.

The following parameters of the experiments are common for every objective. The size of Boolean function is eight (the size of the corresponding truth table is 256) and the number of independent trials M for each experiment is 50 (the mean of best solutions from 50 runs is reported if not stated otherwise). Stopping criterion for all algorithms is 500 000 evaluations. Common parameters are also given in Table 1.

Table 1: Common parameters for EAs.

Parameter	Parameter value
Boolean function input size n	8
Number of experiments	50
Stopping criterion	500 000 evaluations

4.2 Genetic Programming

The function set for GP in all experiments is OR, XOR, AND, XNOR and AND with one input inverted. Terminals correspond to n Boolean variables. Boolean functions may be represented with only XOR and AND operators, but it is quite easy to transform it from one notation to the other. A small number of experiments were also conducted to select the appropriate operators, and based on that we used a simple tree crossover with 90% bias for functional nodes and a subtree mutation. We experiment with tree depth sizes of 5, 7, 8, 9 and 11 and population sizes of 100, 200, 500, 1 000 and 2 000.

4.3 Cartesian Genetic Programming

The function set n_f for the CGP is the same as for the GP. Setting the number of rows to be 1 and levels-back parameter to be equal to the number of columns is regarded as the best and most general choice [1]. We experiment with genotype sizes of 300, 700, 1 100, 1 500 and 1 900 and for mutation rates with values of 1%, 4%, 7%, 10% and 13%.

The number of input connections n_n for each node is two and the number of program output connections n_o is one. The population size for CGP equals five in all our experiments. For CGP individual selection we use a (1 + 4)-ES in which offspring are favored over parents when they have a fitness better than or equal to the fitness of the parent. The mutation operator is one-point mutation where the mutation point is chosen with a fixed probability. The number of genes mutated is defined as fixed percentage of the total number of genes. Note, the single output gene is not mutated and is taken from the last node in the genotype. The genes chosen for mutation might be a node representing an input connection or a function.

4.4 Genetic Algorithm

We use a simple GA with elimination tournament selection with size 3 [16]. A mutation is selected uniformly at random between a simple mutation, where a single bit is inverted, and a mixed mutation, which randomly shuffles the bits in a randomly selected subset. The crossover operators are one-point and uniform crossover, performed uniformly at random for each new offspring. For each of the fitness functions we experiment with population sizes of 50, 100, 200, 500 and 1 000 and mutation probabilities of 0.1, 0.3, 0.5, 0.7 and 0.9.

4.5 Fitness Functions

As discussed previously, we evolve Boolean functions for two different settings. In the first setting, we want to evolve balanced Boolean functions that have good correlation immunity values and that maximize the Siegenthaler inequality. First, we need to establish what are good values for correlation immunity of Boolean functions with eight inputs.

When a Boolean function is used in a filter generator, correlation immunity value of one is usually considered to be sufficient. To obtain this value, often it is possible to replace a Boolean function that has other good properties with a linearly equivalent function that has the correlation immunity equal to one [7].

However, when using Boolean functions in a combiner generator, high values for correlation immunity are necessary [28]. Therefore, in our experiments, we look for Boolean functions that have the correlation immunity *equal or larger than two* which we believe is sufficient for a Boolean function with eight inputs. We stop with a correlation immunity value of five in order to leave high enough value of the algebraic degree. Furthermore, such Boolean functions need to have the maximal nonlinearity value according to the Sarkar-Maitra divisibility bound. Therefore, for each of the target correlation immunity values t, we know what are the maximal values that the other properties can reach. In accordance to that, we can identify the global optimum for each target correlation immunity value.

We aim to *maximize* the following fitness function:

$$fitness_1 = BAL + t + \delta_{t,x}(N_f + AI + deg), \quad (12)$$

where $\delta_{t,x}$ is the Kronecker delta function that takes value one when $t = x$ and zero otherwise. Here, x is defined as the target correlation immunity value in the range $[2, 5]$.

The balancedness property (BAL) is calculated in the following way; if a function is balanced then we give it a value of zero, otherwise we give it a negative value that amounts to the absolute difference of the number of zeros and ones in the truth table. A two stage fitness is used here in which a fitness bonus equal to the sum of the nonlinearity, algebraic immunity AI and algebraic degree deg is awarded only to a solution that is t-resilient; otherwise, the fitness is only the sum of the balancedness penalty and the correlation immunity.

In the second setting, we look for *unbalanced* Boolean functions that have correlation immunity values t in the range $[1, 5]$ and minimal Hamming weight of their truth table representation (therefore, minimal cardinality of their support). These conditions are presented in the following equation where the goal is *maximization*:

$$fitness_2 = \begin{cases} t + \delta_{t,x}(2^n - HW(TT)), \text{if } t = x \\ (2^n - HW(TT) - 2^n \times abs(t - x), \text{otherwise.} \end{cases}$$

When the correlation immunity reaches some predefined value, then the fitness equals the sum of the correlation immunity and the difference between the maximal HW of a Boolean function's truth table and a current one. For solutions with incorrect correlation immunity values, we assign them a value that allows those solutions to be differentiated by their Hamming weight.

We do not apply multiobjective optimization since we regard different properties as constraints of a fixed target value, rather than independent objectives. This allows us to focus on the best fitness values we can obtain while the selected properties, such as balancedness, are held as constraints.

5. RESULTS AND DISCUSSION

5.1 The First Objective

When considering fitness function as given in Eq. (12), we know what are the optimal values for each of the properties we investigate. We give those values for each level of correlation immunity in Table 2. As explained in the previous section, it is obvious that the increase in the value of one property results in the decrease of the values of other properties. We can see that the particularly interesting case is when the correlation immunity equals two and three. For those values the nonlinearity and the algebraic immunity

Table 2: Optimal values of properties, $fitness_1$

t	N_f	AI	deg	Global optimum value
2	112	4	5	123
3	112	4	4	123
4	96	3	3	106
5	64	2	2	73

Table 3: Average fitness, $fitness_1$, CGP.

	Gen./mut.	1	4	7	10	13
	300	101.68	99.48	97.04	101.3	100.84
	700	105.08	114.38	106.26	110.36	112.7
t=2	1 100	110.32	116.56	114.68	116.16	115.84
	1 500	109.84	118.6	117.08	110.54	114.34
	1 900	111.72	116.12	117.42	116.92	115.28
	300	78.8	79.76	87.06	88.16	82.52
	700	93.86	95.04	95.66	99.52	97.52
t=3	1 100	90.94	103	103.56	101.9	100.6
	1 500	93.42	105.4	104.06	101.86	99.86
	1 900	95.3	103.38	100.5	101.12	101.76
	300	56.28	58.18	59.64	49.94	60.06
	700	60.28	81.18	71.76	77.82	79.8
t=4	1 100	75.68	79.88	84.62	90.68	75.78
	1 500	75.24	88.64	88.62	82.58	88.46
	1 900	73.04	82.56	85.3	87.26	89.92
	300	20.02	32.88	21.92	25.84	26.0
	700	34.16	32.78	35.56	34.34	39.28
t=5	1 100	36.98	39.58	41.04	38.62	43.64
	1 500	35.56	49.02	42.46	50.5	42.4
	1 900	30.44	50.42	54.12	40.9	38.62

properties have the same values. When reporting the obtained property values for a certain solution, we use the following notation: (N_f, t, deg, AI) and we only present balanced solutions. In Table 3, we present mean fitness values for CGP with the fitness function 1 for various target correlation immunity values.

We give the number of times that each CGP variant reached the global optimum in Table 4. When the target correlation immunity equals three, there were no successful runs and therefore we skip that case in the table. For all other correlation immunity values, CGP proves to be an efficient algorithm (when using fitness function as in Eq. (12)). The easiest case seems to be when the correlation immunity equals five, after that is the case when it is equal to four and then two. Finally, the most difficult case is when the target correlation immunity value equals three.

Next, we give average fitness values for GP and fitness function 1 in Table 5. In Table 6, we display the number of times that GP found the global optimum. As is the case with CGP, when the correlation immunity equals three, the algorithm could not find any global optimum solutions. Besides that, it is interesting to notice that the cases when the correlation immunity equals four and five are easier for GP than CGP. This is particularly apparent when correlation immunity equals five, since in that case GP has 100% successfulness in reaching the global optimum. However, when the correlation immunity equals two, then the performance of CGP is substantially better than that of GP.

When experimenting with GA and fitness function 1 we were unable to find any optimal solutions for any of the correlation immunity values and therefore we do not present similar tables with results for GA. We note that the maximal

Table 4: # of optimal solutions, $fitness_1$, CGP.

	Gen./mut.	1	4	7	10	13
t=2	300	0	2	2	4	6
	700	3	15	14	14	12
	1 100	7	17	21	16	14
	1 500	6	**25**	19	11	8
	1 900	12	20	22	20	15
t=4	300	6	11	13	7	16
	700	14	21	21	24	27
	1 100	21	25	30	**33**	27
	1 500	18	32	30	29	30
	1 900	21	29	23	32	28
t=5	300	11	20	12	15	15
	700	21	20	22	21	25
	1 100	23	25	26	24	28
	1 500	22	32	27	33	27
	1 900	18	33	**36**	26	24

Table 5: Average fitness, $fitness_1$, GP.

	Pop./depth	5	7	8	9	11
t=2	100	110.2	113.8	113.24	110.98	110.18
	200	109.94	112.46	113.7	111.16	110.6
	500	110.42	113.86	113.1	112.9	110.4
	1 000	112	112.3	111.54	113.24	110.48
	2 000	115.08	115.8	113.68	113.72	111.12
t=3	100	105.9	106	16.04	106.04	106.02
	200	105.9	106.02	106.02	106.06	106
	500	105.98	106.04	106	106.02	106.04
	1 000	106	106.08	106.02	106.02	106
	2 000	106.04	106	106.02	106.06	106
t=4	100	85.24	102.8	99.6	99.6	99.6
	200	89.8	96.36	98.92	99.58	94.44
	500	92.56	102.16	100.24	100.24	99.56
	1 000	97.04	101.52	97.66	102.16	97.66
	2 000	98.96	102.8	100.88	98.32	96.96
t=5	100	73	73	73	73	73
	200	73	73	73	73	73
	500	73	73	73	73	73
	1 000	73	73	73	73	73
	2 000	73	73	73	73	73

value of correlation immunity we were able to find with GA and bitstring encoding equals one.

When working with two-stage fitness function, there is always the possibility that the algorithm will not perform well since it cannot reach the second stage. This is obviously true for the GA case where most of the population at the end of each run still have negative fitness values which means that those solutions are unbalanced. In that case, solutions can drastically improve their fitness only by becoming balanced and with a correlation immunity value larger than zero. However, the results implicate there is not enough information (diversity) in the search pool to converge.

Therefore, we note that we could write the two-stage fitness function differently. Since we know what is the best possible nonlinearity value we can rewrite it as:

$$fitness_1 = BAL + N_f + \delta_{N_f,x}(t + AI + deg). \quad (13)$$

Next, we experiment with the Eq. (13) for cases when nonlinearity equals 112 (correlation immunity equal to two and three). We disregard the cases when correlation immunity equals four and five since those seems to be much easier problems. We do not present the results here, but

Table 6: # of optimal solutions, $fitness_1$, GP.

	Pop./depth	5	7	8	9	11
t=2	100	0	7	12	6	10
	200	2	11	13	8	7
	500	2	12	11	12	8
	1 000	1	8	7	15	5
	2 000	6	**19**	15	14	9
t=4	100	18	**45**	40	40	40
	200	25	35	39	40	32
	500	29	44	41	41	40
	1 000	36	43	37	44	37
	2 000	39	**45**	42	38	36
t=5	100	50	50	50	50	50
	200	50	50	50	50	50
	500	50	50	50	50	50
	1 000	50	50	50	50	50
	2 000	50	50	50	50	50

mention that again both CGP and GP reach the same value corresponding to the global optimum relatively easily. Furthermore, with this fitness function the GA also succeeds in reaching the same value as GP and CGP.

However, we observe that all algorithms, although reaching the global optimum value of the modified criteria, in this case do not find the Boolean functions we are originally looking for. Instead, in most of the cases solutions are either $(N_f, t, deg, AI) = (112, 0, 7, 4)$ or $(112, 1, 6, 4)$. All our experiments show that it is much easier to obtain a high algebraic degree value than the high correlation immunity value. In accordance to that, we need to further improve our fitness function and not allow the algebraic degree to go over a certain threshold value. Therefore, our new fitness function equals:

$$fitness_1 = BAL + N_f + \delta_{N_f,x}(t + AI + \delta_{deg,x}deg). \quad (14)$$

In this function, we look only for Boolean functions with nonlinearity 112 and algebraic degree less than a threshold value (here, we set it to four and five). When not allowing the algebraic degree to go over a value of five, we can reach the maximal correlation immunity of two. In this case, GP and CGP perform similarly as in fitness function given in Eq. (12). This means that the best solutions are of the form (112, 2, 5, 4).

However, when not allowing algebraic degree to be higher than four, we are able to find solutions that have correlation immunity equal to three. The caveat is that with this fitness function the nonlinearity does not go over the value 96. Therefore, the best solutions are of the form (96, 3, 4, 4).

Again, GA with this fitness function does not succeed in evolving solutions with correlation immunity equal to two or three. Actually, our results show that for the GA there is no statistical difference when using fitness function as in Eqs. (13) or (14).

When comparing the efficiency of all three algorithms we observe that GA is by far the worst. However, this might be the problem of fitness function although we experimented with several variations and never obtained a solution that has a correlation immunity higher than one. However, when trying to compare the efficiency of GP and CGP, the situation is much more fuzzy.

We have only two algorithms and four objectives (one fitness function, but four possible correlation immunity values)

Table 7: Results for $fitness_2$, GP and CGP.

	t=2	t=3	t=4	t=5
CGP, 500	197.73 (242)	175.8 (227)	132 (132)	88.33 (133)
CGP, 1500	206.27 (242)	169.93 (243)	134.13 (196)	131.67 (133)
GP, 500	178 (242)	171 (243)	138.4 (196)	133 (133)
GP, 5000	195.6 (242)	176.3 (243)	151.2 (196)	133 (133)

where one objective (correlation immunity equal to three) behaves the same for both algorithms. In the case when we use fitness function as in Eq. (12) then both algorithms cannot find any correct solution. In the case of fitness function as in Eq. (14), both algorithms always reach the same set of values (96, 3, 4, 4). Notice that in this case the maximal obtained nonlinearity value is the same as in the case when the correlation immunity equals four. Therefore, with regards to the nonlinearity property, these solutions are worse. Naturally, such solutions have slightly higher algebraic immunity which is a consequence of a trade-off between the algebraic degree and the algebraic immunity properties.

5.2 The Second Objective

In this phase, we do not perform a thorough parameter search; on the basis of the results from the previous phase, we select tree depth to be seven when using GP and mutation probability of 7% when using CGP.

To understand the difficulty of this problem, consider the function that has all ones in its truth table. Therefore, the cardinality of the support equals 256. In that case the correlation immunity equals eight. However, by randomly flipping a single bit, correlation immunity drops to zero (while algebraic degree increases). Therefore, it is to be expected that EAs will have problems to evolve such functions due to the extreme sensitivity of some of the properties.

In Table 7, we give average fitness values for two CGP and two GP variations when the correlation immunity ranges from two to five. Furthermore, in parentheses we give the maximal value that each algorithm reached. Recall that we aim for fitness values that equal the sum of correlation immunity and the number of zeros in truth table. Here, we write zeros since we aim to maximize the fitness function and we are looking for a minimal number of ones in the truth table.

We do not present results for the correlation immunity value equal to one since it appears to be a trivial case where both algorithms find the global optimum easily. We note that GA also succeeds in finding several minimal Hamming weights when the correlation immunity equals to one. However, for all other cases GA is unsuccessful.

When evaluating the quality of the obtained solutions, we refer to data from [2]. We see that when the correlation immunity equals two, the minimal value of the cardinality of support equals 12. However, the best solution we could find is 16. Next, for the correlation immunity value of three, the best cardinality equals 16 which is the same value as found in our experiments. Furthermore, for correlation immunity values of four and five the minimal cardinalities of support are 64 and 128, respectively. We observe that both CGP and GP reach those values.

Therefore, this scenario is in a sense similar to the first one, i.e. for fitness function 1. For one of the correlation immunity values EAs cannot find the optimal solutions, but for the other cases both CGP and GP are able to find the optimal values. This suggests that in general EAs are efficient enough for a problem of this size. However, we note that before giving the final verdict about the difficulty of these problems, one must find the missing solutions as well as conduct the analysis with more algorithms.

5.3 Future Work

As already mentioned, future work must encompass more experiments in an effort to reach all known optimal solutions for both fitness functions. There exists one simple improvement of fitness function 2 we could have added, but decided not to in order to assess the efficiency of our algorithms. Since we look for a Boolean function with a minimal weight, we could add a penalty to all solutions that have the correct correlation immunity value, but are balanced.

Furthermore, one natural research avenue is to investigate Boolean functions with more than eight inputs. It is said that for the bigger sizes (e.g. $n \geq 9$), EAs cannot compete with some combinations of algorithms (e.g. theory supplementing optimization methods) [19]. In [2], we can see that for the correlation immunity equal to four, five and six and Boolean functions of sizes 11, 12 and 13 there are no known minimal values for the cardinality of support. Finding those values would be an interesting goal not only from the EA perspective, but also from the cryptographic and mathematic perspectives, in design theory and even in statistics.

Finally, here we are interested only in Boolean functions that possess certain properties, while future research should include experiments where the goal is a Boolean function (a circuit) that is at the same time easy to implement [17].

6. CONCLUSION

This paper explores the performance of three evolutionary algorithms on finding Boolean functions for cryptographic applications with the focus on the correlation immunity property. In the first application scenario, the goal is to find balanced functions with varying correlation immunity, that allows their usage in combiner generators. The second objective considers Boolean functions with minimal Hamming weight, while attaining the desired correlation immunity. Although we encountered varying success for different algorithms, the results indicate that EAs are capable of obtaining optimal solutions for known function sizes, which supports their application in conditions where the optimum is not known in advance.

7. REFERENCES

[1] In J. F. Miller, editor, *Cartesian Genetic Programming*, Natural Computing Series. Springer Berlin Heidelberg, 2011.

[2] S. Bhasin, C. Carlet, and S. Guilley. Theory of masking with codewords in hardware: low-weight dth-order correlation-immune boolean functions. Cryptology ePrint Archive, Report 2013/303, 2013. http://eprint.iacr.org/.

[3] L. Burnett, W. Millan, E. Dawson, and A. Clark. Simpler methods for generating better Boolean

functions with good cryptographic properties. *Australasian Journal of Combinatorics*, 29:231–247, 2004.

[4] P. Camion and A. Canteaut. Correlation-immune and resilient functions over a finite alphabet and their applications in cryptography. *Des. Codes Cryptography*, 16(2):121–149, 1999.

[5] C. Carlet. Boolean Functions for Cryptography and Error Correcting Codes. In Y. Crama and P. L. Hammer, editors, *Boolean Models and Methods in Mathematics, Computer Science, and Engineering*, pages 257–397. Cambridge University Press, New York, NY, USA, 1st edition, 2010.

[6] C. Carlet, J.-L. Danger, S. Guilley, and H. Maghrebi. Leakage squeezing of order two. In S. Galbraith and M. Nandi, editors, *Progress in Cryptology - INDOCRYPT 2012*, volume 7668 of *Lecture Notes in Computer Science*, pages 120–139. Springer Berlin Heidelberg, 2012.

[7] C. Carlet and K. Feng. An Infinite Class of Balanced Functions with Optimal Algebraic Immunity, Good Immunity to Fast Algebraic Attacks and Good Nonlinearity. In J. Pieprzyk, editor, *Advances in Cryptology - ASIACRYPT 2008*, volume 5350 of *Lecture Notes in Computer Science*, pages 425–440. Springer Berlin Heidelberg, 2008.

[8] C. Carlet and S. Guilley. Side-channel indistinguishability. In *Proceedings of the 2Nd International Workshop on Hardware and Architectural Support for Security and Privacy*, HASP '13, pages 9:1–9:8, New York, NY, USA, 2013. ACM.

[9] C. Carlet and S. Guilley. Correlation-immune boolean functions for easing counter measures to side-channel attacks. In H. E. Niederreiter, O. E. Alina, and e. a. Daniel, Panario (Ed.), editors, *Algebraic Curves and Finite Fields. Cryptography and Other Applications.*, pages 41–70. Berlin, Boston: De Gruyter., 2014.

[10] C. Carlet and P. Sarkar. Spectral Domain Analysis of Correlation Immune and Resilient Boolean Functions. *Finite Fields Appl.*, 8(1):120–130, Jan. 2002.

[11] N. Carrasco, J.-M. L. Bars, and A. Viola. Enumerative encoding of correlation-immune boolean functions. *Theoretical Computer Science*, 487(0):23 – 36, 2013.

[12] C. Cid, S. Kiyomoto, and J. Kurihara. The RAKAPOSHI Stream Cipher. In S. Qing, C. Mitchell, and G. Wang, editors, *Information and Communications Security*, volume 5927 of *Lecture Notes in Computer Science*, pages 32–46. Springer Berlin Heidelberg, 2009.

[13] J. A. Clark, J. L. Jacob, S. Stepney, S. Maitra, and W. Millan. Evolving Boolean Functions Satisfying Multiple Criteria. In *Progress in Cryptology - INDOCRYPT 2002*, pages 246–259, 2002.

[14] N. Courtois. Fast Algebraic Attacks on Stream Ciphers with Linear Feedback. In D. Boneh, editor, *Advances in Cryptology - CRYPTO 2003*, volume 2729 of *Lecture Notes in Computer Science*, pages 176–194. Springer Berlin Heidelberg, 2003.

[15] N. Courtois and W. Meier. Algebraic Attacks on Stream Ciphers with Linear Feedback. In E. Biham, editor, *Advances in Cryptology - EUROCRYPT 2003*, volume 2656 of *Lecture Notes in Computer Science*, pages 345–359. Springer Berlin Heidelberg, 2003.

[16] A. E. Eiben and J. E. Smith. *Introduction to Evolutionary Computing*. Springer-Verlag, Berlin Heidelberg New York, USA, 2003.

[17] B. M. Gammel, R. Gottfert, and O. Kniffler. The Achterbahn Stream Cipher, 2005.

[18] J. Katz and Y. Lindell. *Introduction to Modern Cryptography*. Chapman and Hall/CRC, Boca Raton, 2008.

[19] S. Kavut, S. Maitra, and M. D. Yücel. There exist Boolean functions on n (odd) variables having nonlinearity $> 2^{n-1} - 2^{(n-1)/2}$ if and only if n > 7, 2006.

[20] J.-M. Le Bars and A. Viola. Equivalence classes of boolean functions for first-order correlation. In *Information Theory, 2007. ISIT 2007. IEEE International Symposium on*, pages 181–185, June 2007.

[21] S. Maitra and P. Sarkar. Highly Nonlinear Resilient Functions Optimizing Siegenthaler's Inequality. In M. Wiener, editor, *Advances in Cryptology - CRYPTO' 99*, volume 1666 of *Lecture Notes in Computer Science*, pages 198–215. Springer Berlin Heidelberg, 1999.

[22] S. Mangard, E. Oswald, and T. Popp. *Power Analysis Attacks: Revealing the Secrets of Smart Cards (Advances in Information Security)*. Springer-Verlag New York, Inc., Secaucus, NJ, USA, 2007.

[23] J. McLaughlin and J. A. Clark. Evolving balanced Boolean functions with optimal resistance to algebraic and fast algebraic attacks, maximal algebraic degree, and very high nonlinearity. Cryptology ePrint Archive, Report 2013/011, 2013. http://eprint.iacr.org/.

[24] W. Millan, A. Clark, and E. Dawson. Heuristic design of cryptographically strong balanced Boolean functions. In *Advances in Cryptology - EUROCRYPT '98*, pages 489–499, 1998.

[25] S. Picek, D. Jakobovic, and M. Golub. Evolving cryptographically sound boolean functions. In *Proceedings of the 15th Annual Conference Companion on Genetic and Evolutionary Computation*, GECCO '13 Companion, pages 191–192, New York, NY, USA, 2013. ACM.

[26] P. Sarkar and S. Maitra. Construction of nonlinear boolean functions with important cryptographic properties. In B. Preneel, editor, *EUROCRYPT*, volume 1807 of *Lecture Notes in Computer Science*, pages 485–506. Springer, 2000.

[27] P. Sarkar and S. Maitra. Nonlinearity bounds and constructions of resilient boolean functions. In M. Bellare, editor, *CRYPTO*, volume 1880 of *Lecture Notes in Computer Science*, pages 515–532. Springer, 2000.

[28] T. Siegenthaler. Correlation-immunity of nonlinear combining functions for cryptographic applications (corresp.). *IEEE Trans. Inf. Theor.*, 30(5):776–780, Sept. 2006.

[29] Y. Tarannikov. On Resilient Boolean Functions with Maximal Possible Nonlinearity. In *Proceedings of INDOCRYPT 2000, Lecture Notes in Computer Science*. Springer-Verlag, 2000.

On the Bias of Syntactic Geometric Recombination in Genetic Programming and Grammatical Evolution

Ann Thorhauer
Dept. of Information Systems and Business Administration
University of Mainz, Germany
thorhauer@uni-mainz.de

Franz Rothlauf
Dept. of Information Systems and Business Administration
University of Mainz, Germany
rothlauf@uni-mainz.de

ABSTRACT

For fixed-length binary representations as used in genetic algorithms, standard recombination operators (e.g., one-point crossover) are unbiased. Thus, the application of recombination only reshuffles the alleles and does not change the statistical properties in the population. Using a geometric view on recombination operators, most search operators for fixed-length strings are geometric, which means that the distances between offspring and their parents are less than, or equal to, the distance between their parents. In genetic programming (GP) and grammatical evolution (GE), the situation is different since the recombination operators are applied to variable-length structures. Thus, most recombination operators for GE and GP are not geometric. This paper focuses on the bias of recombination in GE and GP and studies whether the application of recombination alone produces specific types of solutions with a higher probability. We consider two different types of recombination operators: standard recombination and syntactic geometric recombination. In our experiments, we performed random walks through the binary tree search space and found that syntactic geometric recombination operators are biased and strongly reduce population diversity. In a performance comparison, we found that syntactic geometric recombination leads to large fitness improvements in the first generations, but that fitness converges after several generations and no further search is possible.

Categories and Subject Descriptors

I.2.8 [**Artificial Intelligence**]: Problem Solving,- Control Methods, and Search—*Heuristic methods*

Keywords

Genetic Programming; Grammatical Evolution; Bias; Geometric Recombination; Random Walk

GECCO '15, July 11 - 15, 2015, Madrid, Spain

ISBN 978-1-4503-3472-3/15/07... $15.00

DOI: http://dx.doi.org/10.1145/2739480.2754726

1. INTRODUCTION

For fixed-length binary representations as, e.g., used in genetic algorithms (GA), standard recombination operators like one-point crossover are unbiased. Unbiased means that the application of recombination alone only reshuffles the different alleles in the individuals of the population and does not change the statistical properties of the population. Instead, the recombination operator merely recombines the genetic material. Consequently, when applying no selection operator, the genetic diversity of individuals in a population is preserved over the following generations. In addition, the amount of genetic material that is available in a population of solutions of fixed length stays constant.

In genetic programming (GP) and grammatical evolution (GE), the situation is different. Standard GP [7] uses tree structures to represent individuals. Hence, by applying standard subtree crossover, the size and shape of the individuals changes during the search process. Daida [3] found that the use of tree structures to represent individuals has a bias towards certain structures. Although no genetic material is removed from the population and the genetic material therefore stays constant over the number of generations, the structures that can be produced by a random GP walk are limited [21]. Furthermore, the distribution of genetic material changes during random walks. Thus, the combination of search operators and representation is biased [21]. The same applies to GE. Instead of trees, GE [14] uses variable-length binary strings to encode the solutions and uses a grammar in Backus-Naur form (BNF) to map the binary genotypes to the tree phenotypes. As in GP, the size and shape of the solutions changes during the search process.

We distinguish between different types of recombination operators based on their "geometry". According to Moraglio [13], recombination operators are geometric if the distances between offspring and their parents are less than or equal to the distance between their parents [17]. Moraglio studied many different recombination operators and found that most reasonable recombination operators for fixed-length representations are geometric [10]. Interestingly, all these geometric recombination operators (such as uniform or n-point crossover) are also unbiased. The situation is different in GE and GP, where standard search operators are not geometric and, as discussed before, unbiased. Since a GE or GP solution encodes a program to solve a problem and not a single solution to a problem, there are two different types of geometry: syntactic and semantic geometry. The syntactic geometry concerns the syntactic distance between individuals (e.g., distances between tree structures), whereas the semantic geometry concerns the distances between fitness values or output vectors of solutions [11].

For GP, no successful examples of syntactic geometric recombination operators have been proposed. Instead, researchers suggest using semantic geometric operators. Indeed, research on theses operators reports that semantic operators perform better than syntactic operators [8, 11, 22]. Most authors argue that "small changes in syntax can lead to large changes in semantics" [24], which may mislead the search process. However, it is still currently unclear why syntactic geometric recombination works well for standard GA using fixed-length strings but fails for GE or GP. A possible answer may be that syntactic geometric recombination operators in GE and GP are biased, which would affect search performance and restrict the search process.

Consequently, in this paper we studied the bias of standard and syntactic geometric recombination in GE and GP. We followed two different approaches:

1. First, we removed the selective pressure from the search and performed random walks on the binary tree search space with GE and GP using standard recombination and syntactic geometric recombination. During the random walks, we measured how the structures represented by the population of solutions developed over time. Performing random walks is a standard approach to study the bias of search operators. The recombination operators are biased if the statistical properties in a population of solutions are changed over the number of random walk steps.

2. In the second experiment, we compared the performance of standard versus syntactic geometric recombination in GE and GP to study the implications of our random walk results. We defined random binary tree structures that served as target trees in our GE and GP experiments. The goal of GE and GP was to find these trees. Using this test problem, we studied whether the search performance depends on the bias of the different recombination operators.

We found that both standard and syntactic geometric recombination operators in GE and GP are biased. Furthermore, the bias of syntactic geometric recombination operators is stronger compared to the bias of standard recombination operators. In general, using syntactic geometric recombination strongly reduces the diversity of a population over the number of generations. In contrast, standard recombination loses less diversity since the non-geometry of the search operator randomizes the search. This makes it more difficult to focus the search on specific areas of the search space, but prohibits premature convergence.

In Sect. 2, we review the bias of search operators in GE and GP. In Sect. 3, we define the geometry of search operators. In Sect. 4, we review syntactic and semantic recombination operators in GE and GP. Experiments and results are presented in Sect. 5. The paper ends with some concluding remarks.

2. BIAS IN GP AND GE

A bias exists if some solutions or solution structures are visited more frequently than others during the run of a search procedure, or if certain actions are performed more frequently than others during the search. In general, all factors that influence the search process are referred to as bias [25]. The existence of a bias may be advantageous or disadvantageous for the search [18]. For example, a bias of search operators may be used to guide the search into a certain direction where promising solutions are presumed; this would be a desired bias. Unwanted bias occurs if there is an interaction between the used search operators and the chosen representation in such a way that the problem becomes deceptive [1].

In heuristic search methods like GE and GP, a desired bias comes from the selection process. By selecting highly-fit individuals for the next generation, selection pushes a population in the direction of fitter individuals. In addition, by using problem-specific recombination or mutation operators and suitable terminal and function sets, GP performance can be improved [25] [26].

Search bias can also be a result of redundant encodings [19]. Encodings are redundant if there are phenotypes that are encoded by more than one genotype. A redundant encoding is biased (non-uniformly redundant) if not all phenotypes are encoded by the same number of genotypes but some phenotypes are represented by a larger number. When using GE, there is a redundant representation since there is more than one genotype representing the same phenotype [15]. Non-uniform redundancy, where the phenotypes are non-uniformly represented by the genotypes, leads to a bias and causes structural difficulty since some solution structures are underrepresented.

Daida and Hilss [4] studied if there are any other mechanisms besides selection which influence GP search behavior. They were interested to know whether the search performance of GP is affected by the structure of the optimal solution. For binary trees, they found four different regions of structural difficulty in the search space. Depending on the structure of the optimal solution, problems can be 1) easy to solve (most problems), 2) more difficult to solve, 3) practically impossible to solve, or 4) the optimal solution can be inaccessible for binary trees. They concluded that not only the content of structures is responsible for the bias, but the structures themselves are responsible for it.

Inspired by the work of Daida [3], we found that a random walk with GE and GP using standard operators (GE: one-point crossover, duplication, mutation; GP: subtree crossover, reproduction) has a bias towards certain structures [21]. Although no genetic material is removed from the population during random walks, the structures that can be produced by GE or GP are limited. We observed differences in the bias between GE and GP, as GE has a stronger bias towards narrow tree structures than GP. In exchange, a random GP walk finds more dense tree structures.

3. GEOMETRY OF SEARCH OPERATORS

Each search space can be defined as a *topological space*, which describes similarities between solutions by defining the relationships between sets of solutions. Formally, a topological space is an ordered pair (X, T), where X is a set of solutions and T is a collection of subsets of X called open sets. We can define different topologies (search spaces) by combining X with different T. For example, *metric search spaces* are a specialized form of topological spaces where similarities between solutions are measured by a distance. In metric search spaces, there is a set X of solutions and a real-valued distance function (also called a metric) $d : X \times X \to \mathbb{R}$

that assigns a real-valued distance to any combination of two elements $x, y \in X$.

Both the locality of search operators [17] and the geometry of search operators [13] define search operators based on the metric of the search space. Thus, a recombination operator has high locality if the distances between offspring x^o and its parents are less than or equal to the distance between both parents x_1^p and x_2^p $(\max(d(x_1^p, x^o), d(x_2^p, x^o)) \leq d(x_1^p, x_2^p))$. Using the notion of geometry, a crossover is geometric if all offspring are in the space-specific segment between their parents [13]. "Showing that a given recombination operator is a geometric crossover requires finding a distance for which offspring are in the metric segment between parents" [10]. Since GE or GP solutions encode programs to solve a problem and not a single solution to a problem, we can distinguish between two different types of geometry such as syntactic geometry and semantic geometry. The syntactic geometry looks at the syntactic distances between individuals, whereas the semantic geometry concerns the distance between two fitness values or output vectors, respectively [11]. Therefore, semantic geometry takes into account the meaning of a solution.

This paper focuses on the bias of syntactic geometric recombination. Therefore, we do not consider the semantic distances (e.g., fitness values) between solutions, but rather focus on the syntactic distances between GE and GP solutions. Offspring that are produced by syntactic geometric recombination lie between parents. Consequently, the distance between both offspring and their parents has to be less than or equal to the distance between the parents. We define the distance between two solutions as the distance between their tree structures.

Moraglio [12] claims that "what is really important for an algorithm to perform better than random search is how problem and algorithm are connected via distance". Thus, a better understanding of syntactic recombination on variable-length structures will also helps us define better semantic recombination operators.

4. SYNTACTIC AND SEMANTIC SEARCH OPERATORS IN GP AND GE

4.1 Recombination in GP

Since standard GP uses tree structures to represent solutions, subtree crossover is used to recombine two parent solutions [7]. A subtree crossover randomly selects a subtree in each parent solution and exchanges these two subtrees between the parents. It is well known that this standard subtree crossover is not a geometric crossover since there is no distance for which all offspring lie in the metric segment between their parents [10].

A number of researchers have studied the impact of different syntactic and semantic crossover operators on the performance in GP [22, 23, 24]. Besides defining or using geometric recombination operators, researchers also suggest using other approaches for creating syntactically or semantically similar offspring. For example, Uy et al. [22] introduced a new implementation of a crossover operator in GP: the semantic similarity based crossover (SSC). They showed that GP performance can be increased due to semantic information. Subtrees that are exchanged during recombination have to be semantically similar for a set of random points. This leads to a crossover that creates offspring with lower fitness differences. The authors studied the performance and locality of the operator and compared the SSC with the standard subtree crossover as well as the semantic aware crossover (SAC). They found that SSC outperforms the other operators in almost all cases. In addition, the more complex the problem is, the better the new operator works. Uy et al. [23] also made a comparison between the syntactic similarity based crossover (SySC) and SSC in GP. The aim was to increase performance while increasing operator locality. To measure the syntactic differences between two subtrees, they used the Levenshtein tree distance. The general procedure of SySC is the same as that of SSC. The researchers found that SSC performance is higher than SySC performance in all cases and that SySC does not improve performance compared to standard crossover. Thus, they concluded that syntactic locality (similarity) is less important than semantic locality. McPhee et al. [9] studied the semantics of subtrees and contexts for Boolean functions. They found that about 75% "of crossover events are guaranteed to perform no immediately useful search in the semantic space" [9] and therefore do not change the semantic meaning of the program.

There are some recent papers which introduce new forms of GP [11] or new semantic forms of crossover operators [8]. Moraglio et al. [11] introduced a new form of GP: geometric semantic genetic programming (GSGP). They argued that "it is the meaning of programs that determines how successful search is at solving the problem" [11]. In their work, they showed how to implement geometric semantic operators. GSGP produces offspring which are in the semantic segment between parents (concerning distances between the output vectors of the solutions). As a result, the fitness landscape becomes a cone and is easy to search. In the experiments, GSGP showed very good performance for various test problems. Krawiec and Pawlak [8] proposed a new crossover operator based on semantics: the locally geometric semantic crossover (LGX). "LGX picks in [...][the parents] at random a structurally common (homologous) locus, calculates the semantics of subprograms located at that locus, finds a procedure that is semantically medial with respect to these subprograms, and replaces them with that procedure" [8]. In their experiments on symbolic regression problems, they showed that the performance of GP improves in comparison to other crossover operators.

Although the current trend in GP research focuses on developing semantic search operators, we decided to study syntactic geometric recombination. We wanted to understand why syntactic geometric recombination is not working. A better understanding of the problems of syntactic geometric recombination would help us to better understand GP search as well as to define better and superior recombination operators (including semantic ones) for GE and GP.

4.2 Recombination in GE

GE [14] is a variant of GP that can evolve complete programs in an arbitrary language using a variable-length binary string. In GE, phenotype expressions are created from binary genotypes by using a complex genotype-phenotype mapping. A genotype consists of groups of eight bits (denoted as codons) which encode an integer value that selects production rules from a grammar in BNF. These rules are used in the mapping process to create a phenotype. The

Table 1: GE parameters

pop size	500
initialization	random maximum 800 (100 codons)
crossover p_c	1.0
selection	tournament selection (size 3)
replacement	generational
generations	100

```
<expr>  ::= (<expr> + <expr>)
          | <var>
<var>   ::= X
```

Figure 1: Production rules in BNF

mapping process is deterministic since the same genotype always results in the same phenotype.

The standard GE one-point crossover [14] is similar to the cut and splice operator introduced in [6]. After selecting two parents, a crossover point is randomly selected for each parent. Then, the genetic material beyond these points is exchanged between the parents. As a result, rather than remaining constant, the length of the genotype changes during the search.

For GE, there are no studies that compare syntactic and semantic recombination. Castle and Johnson [2] studied the mutation and crossover points in GE and found "that events occurring at the first positions of a genotype are indeed more destructive, but also indicate that they may be the most constructive crossover and mutation points too"[2].

5. EXPERIMENTS AND RESULTS

This section studies the bias of standard versus syntactic geometric recombination operators in GE and GP. We performed two different types of experiments. First, we performed random walks on the binary tree search space and studied whether or not the structure and properties of the trees change over the number of generations (random walk steps), and what these changes are. In our analysis, we studied the following properties of tree structures: *density*, *depth*, *size* and *distance between parents* (d_{par}). Second, we solved a test problem, which was to find a random target tree structure using GE and GP and compared the resulting performances.

For both types of experiments, we used standard parameter settings for GE and GP. Details can be found in Tables 1 and 2. Of course, for the random walks, we consequently removed selective pressure for GE and GP. Since we were studying the bias of recombination operators, no other search operators were used. We defined the terminal and function set as $T = \{X\}$ and $F = \{+\}$, respectively. When using GE, a corresponding grammar in BNF had to be defined. Figure 1 shows the resulting production rules. In addition, a metric is required to measure distances between tree structures. In our case, we used the tree edit distance (TED) and the java implementation RTED from [16]. The TED "is defined as the minimum-cost sequence of node edit operations that transform one tree into another" [16]. The cost of a single edit operation (deletion, insertion and renaming) is one. Before calculating distances between two GE individuals, the derivation trees were transformed into syntax trees in order to be able to compare the results between GE and GP.

Table 2: GP parameters

pop size	500
initialization	ramped-half-and-half method (range 2-6)
crossover p_c	1.0 (with internal node-bias: 90% functions, 10% terminals)
selection	tournament selection (size 3)
replacement	generational
generations	100

5.1 Random Walks

We performed random walks on the binary tree search space with GE and GP. By performing a random walk without any selection operator, it is possible to observe if there are differences in the probabilities of visiting specific solutions. If all possible solutions are visited with equal probability, the representation/operator combination is unbiased; otherwise, the used combination of representation and search operator is biased.

Since we performed random walks on the binary tree search space, parents for recombination were selected randomly without replacement for GE and GP. Furthermore, we removed the constraint of a maximum allowable tree depth for GP and the wrapping-operator for GE, as we did not need it for the chosen grammar. We set the number of generations to 100. In total, we performed 100 independent random walks with GE and GP.

Throughout the random walks, we measured the properties *density*, *depth*, *size* and d_{par} of solutions for standard versus syntactic geometric recombination. The density r of a tree is defined as the ratio between the actual number of nodes ($nodes_{act}$) over the maximum possible number of nodes ($nodes_{max}$) for a given depth:

$$r = \frac{|nodes_{act}|}{|nodes_{max}|}$$

Since we normalized the density values for every tree structure between 0 and 1, we obtained the normalized density

$$r_{normalized} = \begin{cases} \frac{(r - r_{min})}{(r_{max} - r_{min})} & \text{if } r_{max} > r_{min}, \\ 1 & \text{otherwise.} \end{cases}$$

In the case where a GE solution had a smaller density than the minimum possible density of a valid binary tree at the same depth (mapping process does not terminate), the density was set to 0. The *size* of a solution is defined as the number of terminals plus the number of non-terminals (functions). The d_{par} is defined as the TED between the parent solutions. We calculated the values *size*, *depth*, and d_{par} for each solutions as usual, even if the mapping process of GE did not terminate.

We performed random walks with GE and GP using standard and syntactic recombination operators. We are aware that the standard subtree recombination operator in GP is not a geometric crossover because there is no such distance for which all offspring are in the metric segment between parents [10]. Thus, we made an adjustment to obtain a geometric variant of the standard subtree recombination operator. For the geometric variant, we used the standard subtree crossover operator for GP and measured the distance between the offspring and the parents. If both offspring were in the metric segment between their parents, we kept the offspring. If not, we discarded the children and performed recombination again until we found two offspring which were in the metric segment between parents. These "geometric" offspring were inserted into the new population. For GE, we followed the same approach. Using TED, we checked if the resulting offspring (tree structures) were in the metric segment between their parents.

We started our analysis with the results for GE using fixed-length genotypes (fixed size of 100 codons) and standard (GA-like) one-point crossover. In this case, the size of the genotypes is constant over the number of generations. Thus, the crossover points are identical in both parents. The situation is the same as in standard binary GA using one-point crossover, where crossover merely reshuffles the genetic material and has no bias. Column A of Fig. 2 presents the results for GE using fixed-length genotypes. We show the properties *density*, *depth*, *size* and d_{par} of the solutions over the number of generations visited during the random walks. For each property, we show the median (bold line) as well as the 25th and 75th percentile over the number of generations. The lower boundaries of the gray-colored areas show the 25th percentile, the upper boundaries show the 75th percentile, respectively. For a particular property the median means that 50% of the solutions have a larger value for this property and 50% have a lower value for this property. Reporting the development of the 25% and 75% percentiles allows us to study how the population diversity changes over time. As expected, we observe constant median and percentile values for all considered properties over the number of generations. This is a result of the GA-like "geometry" of the recombination operator at genotype level combined with the deterministic mapping-process of GE. Since the mapping process of GE is deterministic (the same genotype always results in the same phenotype) and the amount of genetic material does not change over the number of generations, the median and percentile values of all properties stay constant for standard fixed-length recombination in GE. Thus, standard recombination on fixed-length binary strings in GE is unbiased. Since the amount of genetic material stays constant over the number of generations, the amount of terminals and non-terminals in GE is fixed, too.

We then switched from fixed-length GE genotypes to variable-length genotypes as used in standard GE. The maximum initial codon size was set to 100. Columns B and C of Fig. 2 show the results of our random walk experiments. As before, we show the properties *density*, *depth*, *size*, and d_{par} of solutions over the number of generations.We differentiate the results for standard recombination (column B) from the results for syntactic geometric recombination (column C). The two plots in the first row show the development of *density* of solutions over the number of generations. Due to the GE grammar used, 50% the solutions have a size of 1 and therefore represent "full" tree structures. Therefore, the median of *density* is 1 for both types of recombination. There is no difference between the median curves for standard and syntactic geometric recombination. The two plots in the second row show the medians of the *depth* values of the solutions over the number of generations. Since no genetic material is removed/inserted into the population and the mapping-process of GE is deterministic, the median values of *depth* are almost identical throughout the generations for standard recombination (row two, column B). In contrast, the median values for syntactic geometric recombination slightly decrease over the first 10 generations, then stay constant at *depth* 0 (row two, column C). At the same time, the median values of *size* (row three, column C) of solutions decreases down to 1. This is a result of the situation that the random walk creates many solutions with a *size* of 1 and a *depth* of 0. Finally, the median values of d_{par} are constant over the number of generations for standard recombination (row four, column B), whereas the values for syntactic geometric recombination decrease throughout the generations (row four, column C). Thus, the solutions in the populations become more similar over time. Looking at the 25th and 75th percentile, a random walk with syntactic geometric recombination in GE strongly reduces the diversity in a population. During the random walk, the 75th percentile strongly decrease for *depth*, *size*, and d_{par}. For all properties, the regions between the 25th and 75th percentile are larger for standard recombination (column B). In addition, the median for *size*, *depth* and d_{par} are constant and higher for standard recombination. In summary, the results for standard recombination on variable-length genotypes are the same as for standard recombination on fixed-length genotypes. Both recombination operators are unbiased because the mapping-process from genotype to phenotype is deterministic. The situation is different for the geometric variant of the recombination operator, which has a strong bias towards short, less deep and denser structures. Of course, we should mention that this result depends on the chosen grammar. Different grammars prefer constructing different solutions. However, geometric recombination in GE strongly reduces the diversity in the population.

Columns D and E of Fig. 2 plot the results for standard recombination (subtree crossover) versus syntactic geometric recombination in GP. As before, the plots in the first row show the development of *density* of solutions over the number of generations. We find no large difference between both median curves. Due to the initialization method (half of the initial solutions are full tree structures), the initial median of the *density* is 1. Afterwards, both medians strongly decrease. After about 30 generations, the medians stay constant. Hence, the solutions become more sparse over the first 30 generations. As a result, both GP recombination operators are biased towards sparse tree structures. Both plots in row two show the *depth* of solutions over the number of generations. Since no genetic material is removed from the population (and the *density* decreases), the median values of *depth* increase. This means that the solutions are becoming more sparse and deep over time. The two plots in row three show the development of the median of *size*. The median and percentile values for standard recombination slightly increase over the first generations because the initial solutions have an upper size limit of $2^{6+1} - 1$ (a full individual of depth 6). After initialization, larger solutions can also be produced. After a few generations, the curves stay constant. The median and 25th percentile values for syntactic geometric recombination strongly increase until generation 20, indicating a loss of diversity in *size* (row three, column E). Both plots in the last row of columns D and E show the development of the d_{par}. The median values are larger for standard recombination (column D). The area between the 25th and 75th percentile for syntactic geometric recombination gets smaller over the number of generations (column E). This implies a strong loss of diversity

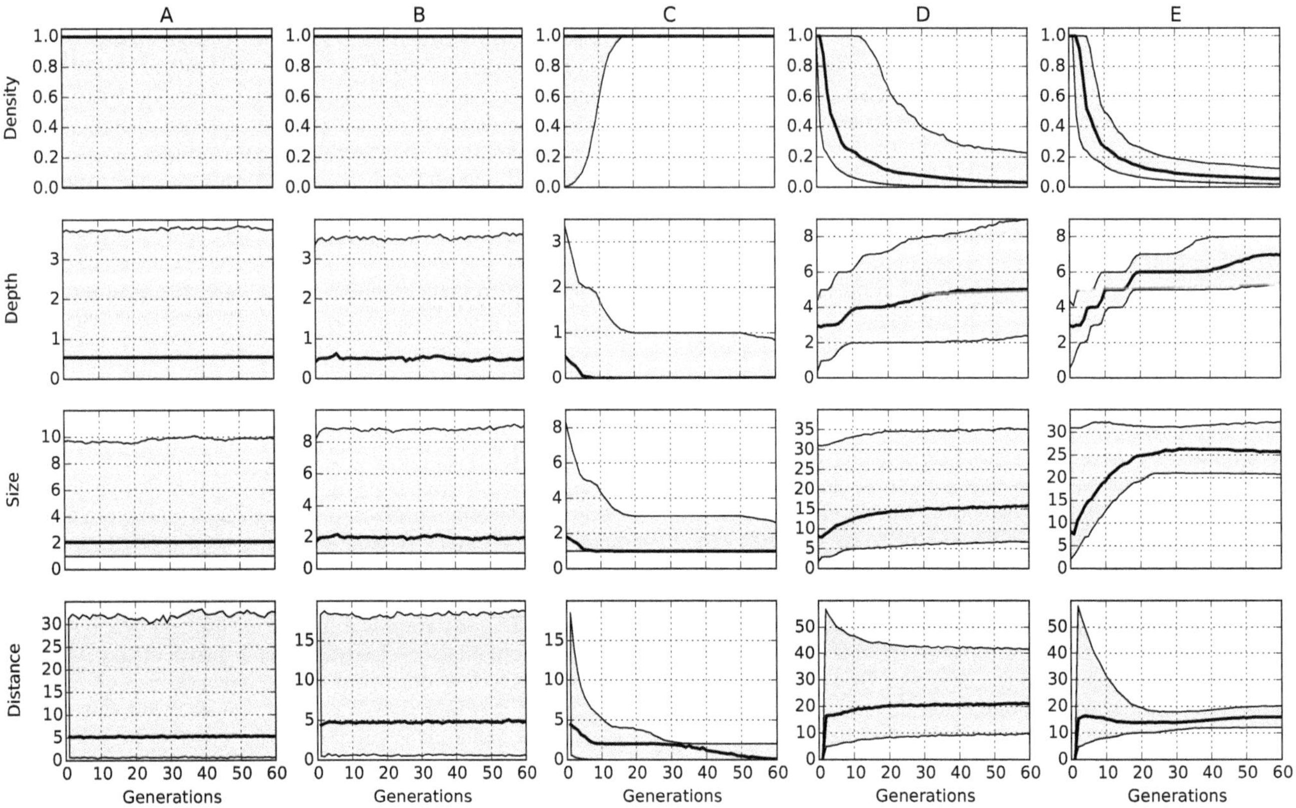

Figure 2: Properties of solutions visited during random walks. Column A: GE using standard one-point crossover on fixed length genotypes. Columns B and C: Standard recombination (B) versus syntactic geometric recombination (C) on variable-length genotypes in GE. Columns D and E: Standard recombination (D) versus syntactic geometric recombination (E) in GP.

since individuals in the later generations are very similar. The d_{par} for standard recombination remain relatively constant. Overall, we find that both recombination operators of GP are biased towards deep, sparse, and less dense solution structures. In addition, since the area between the 25th and 75th percentile is larger for standard geometric recombination in GP throughout all generations and for all considered properties, the non-geometric standard recombination operator produces more diverse tree structures than syntactic geometric recombination does. The solutions that are produced by syntactic geometric recombination become increasingly similar over the number of generations.

In summary, we observe that syntactic geometric recombination in GE and GP strongly reduces the diversity in a population of solutions. Furthermore, syntactic geometric recombination in GE and GP is biased. Hence, the effect of syntactic geometric recombination is different from GA with fixed-length binary representations. There are some differences between GE and GP. For GE, the regions between the 25th and 75th percentile are much smaller for the properties *size*, *depth* and d_{par}. This is partially explained by the less diversified initial population of GE where, due to the chosen grammar, 50% of the initial individuals have a size of 1. In addition, both search operators (standard and syntactic geometric recombination) in GP are biased. In GE, only syntactic geometric recombination is biased.

5.2 Performance of Syntactic Geometric Recombination in GE and GP

We compared the performance of standard versus syntactic geometric recombination in GE and GP. For this task, we had to define a problem where the syntactic structure of the optimal solution was relevant for the fitness of the solution. Daida et al. [5] introduced the Lid problem which searches for a binary tree of a pre-defined size and depth. Therefore, only the structure, and not the content of the structure, is relevant.

We used the idea of Daida and defined the target tree problem (TTP), where the goal is to find a randomly chosen tree structure (target tree) of a pre-defined shape and depth. The fitness of an individual is the number of edit operations that are necessary to transform its tree structure into the target tree. Consequently, a fitness value of 0 is optimal. We created 50 random binary target trees of depth 8, 10 and 12. Since there are differences in the probabilities of visiting certain structures between GE and GP [21], one half of the random target trees (25 individuals) was generated using GP and the grow method, the other half was generated using GE. We performed 10 independent GE and GP runs for every target tree and calculated the average best fitness value achieved in each generation. In addition, we averaged the best fitness values over all instances of the TTP of depth 8, 10 and 12.

We used the same parameter settings as in the random walk experiments (see Tables 1 and 2). Since we wanted to study the impact of different recombination operators on performance, again no other (e.g. mutation or duplication) search operators were used. First, we used GE and GP with standard recombination operators to solve the problem. For GP, we set the maximum allowable tree depth to 17. For GE, we discarded the wrapping operator, as we did not need it for the chosen grammar. Analogously, we used the syntactic geometric recombination operators for GE and GP. Here, we removed the constraint of a maximum allowable tree depth for GP.

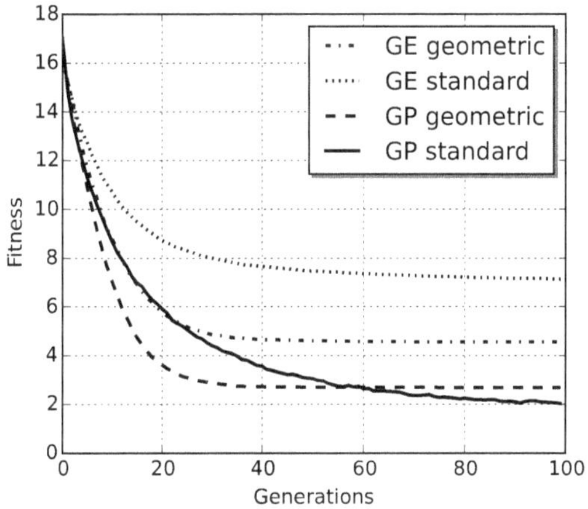

Figure 3: Performance of standard versus syntactic geometric recombination in GE and GP for TTP with depth 8.

Since we observed similar results for TTP of depth 8, 10 and 12, here we only present the results for TTP of depth 8. We want to emphasize that the fitness differences between GE and GP performance are of no interest to us, as we did not tune GE or GP for the problem. Instead, we wanted to study the effects of standard versus syntactic geometric recombination in GE and GP.

For TTP of depth 8, Fig. 3 compares the average best fitness of the population over the number of generations for standard versus syntactic geometric recombination in GE and GP. At the beginning of each run, we observe fast fitness improvements for GE and GP using syntactic geometric recombination. After several generations the improvement of the average best fitness stops and the fitness stays constant. No further improvement is possible. This is a result of the syntactic geometric recombination operators, which keeps the search focused but reduces the diversity of the population over time. This does not allow to explore new areas of the search space. After about 40 generations, the populations has converged and syntactic geometric recombination is not able to create new and diversified individuals. In contrast, the average best fitness of GE and GP with standard recombination operators improves much slower at the beginning of each run. Since standard recombination is not geometric, the diversity of the population is much higher, leading to a less focused search. However, this behavior allows GP with standard recombination to outperform GP with syntactic geometric recombination at later generations (after about 55 generations). These findings are in line with the results for the random walks, where the population diversity is higher for standard recombination operators in comparison to syntactic geometric recombination operators.

The results for the TTP reveal differences between GE and GP performance, depending on the used recombination operator. Syntactic geometric recombination in GP allows guided search since it generates more offspring similar to their parents. This allows a fast convergence towards high-quality solutions at the beginning of a run. However, after a few number of generations (around 40), the population has converged and no further improvements are possible. The situation is different for standard search operators, where offspring are not necessarily similar to their parents. This leads to a stronger randomization of search. Consequently, GP runs using standard recombination operators make less progress at the beginning of the search, since search is less focused. However, since standard recombination preserves the diversity in the population (see the results for random walks), the search process still makes some progress. As a result, search is slower, but on the long run – since the population does not converge due to recombination – standard recombination always outperforms the syntactic geometric recombination variants. The situation is different for GE. Here, the use of syntactic recombination shows a constantly better performance in comparison to standard recombination. This is probably caused by the partially random search behavior of GE. Changing one bit at genotype may change the whole phenotype [20]. Syntactic geometric recombination seems to prevent such occurrences, but similarly to GP, after some generations, no fitness improvements can be observed for syntactic geometric recombination.

6. CONCLUSIONS

This work studies the bias of standard as well as syntactic geometric recombination in GE and GP. We first performed random walks on the binary tree search space and then compared the performance of the different recombination operators. We found large differences between standard and syntactic geometric recombination operators in GE and GP. The results of our random walk experiments reveal that syntactic geometric recombination is biased and strongly reduces the diversity in a population of solutions. Thus, solutions become increasingly similar over the number of generations.

For a simple problem searching for random and pre-defined tree structures, syntactic geometric recombination outperforms standard recombination in GP over the first generations. This is due to the fact that geometric recombination allows a more guided search and offspring are more similar to their parents. However, on the long run, standard recombination in GP is more efficient since it stronger randomizes the search than syntactic geometric recombination and keeps the diversity of the population high. This allows GP search to make continuous progress. The situation is different for syntactic geometric recombination where the population converges after some generations and no further search is possible. The situation in GE is slightly different since GE with syntactic geometric recombination outperforms GE with standard recombination over all considered generations. Since our results hold for binary trees in combination with the chosen terminal and function set, future work will extend this study for non-binary trees, other problems and other distance metrics and recombination operators.

7. REFERENCES

[1] J. D. Caruana, Rich and Schaffer. Representation and Hidden Bias: Gray vs. Binary Coding for Genetic Algorithms. In *Proceedings of the Fifth International Workshop on Machine Learning*, 1988.

[2] T. Castle and C. G. Johnson. Positional effect of crossover and mutation in grammatical evolution. In *Genetic Programming*, volume 6021 LNCS, pages 26–37. Springer, 2010.

[3] J. M. Daida. Limits to expression in genetic programming: Lattice-aggregate modeling. In *Proceedings of the 2002 Congress on Evolutionary Computation, CEC 2002*, volume 1, pages 273–278. IEEE Press, 2002.

[4] J. M. Daida and A. M. Hilss. Identifying Structural Mechanisms in Standard Genetic Programming. In *Genetic and Evolutionary Computation – GECCO-2003*, volume 2724 LNCS, pages 1639–1651. Springer, 2003.

[5] J. M. Daida, H. Li, R. Tang, and A. M. Hilss. What Makes a Problem GP-Hard? Validating a Hypothesis of Structural Causes. In *Genetic and Evolutionary Computation – GECCO-2003*, volume 2724 LNCS, pages 1665–1677. Springer, 2003.

[6] D. Goldberg, B. Korb, and K. Deb. Messy Genetic Algorithms: Motivation, Analysis, and First Results. *Complex Systems*, 3:493–530, 1989.

[7] J. R. Koza. *Genetic Programming: On the Programming of Computers by Means of Natural Selection.* MIT Press, Cambridge, MA, 1992.

[8] K. Krawiec and T. Pawlak. Locally geometric semantic crossover: A study on the roles of semantics and homology in recombination operators. *Genetic Programming and Evolvable Machines*, 14(1):31–63, 2013.

[9] N. F. McPhee, B. Ohs, and T. Hutchison. Semantic Building Blocks in Genetic Programming. In *Proceedings of the 11th European Conference on Genetic Programming*, volume 4971 LNCS, pages 134–145, Naples, Italy, 2008. Springer.

[10] A. Moraglio. *Towards a geometric unification of evolutionary algorithms.* Phd, University of Essex, 2007.

[11] A. Moraglio, K. Krawiec, and C. G. Johnson. Geometric Semantic Genetic Programming. In *Parallel Problem Solving from Nature - PPSN XII*, volume 7491 LNCS, pages 21–31. Springer, 2012.

[12] A. Moraglio and R. Poli. Geometric landscape of homologous crossover for syntactic trees. In *Congress on Evolutionary Computation*, pages 427–434. IEEE, 2005.

[13] R. Moraglio, Alberto and Poli. Topological Interpretation of Crossover. In *Genetic and Evolutionary Computation – GECCO 2004*, volume 3102 LNCS, pages 1259–1271. Springer, 2004.

[14] M. O'Neill and C. Ryan. Grammatical Evolution. *IEEE Transactions on Evolutionary Computation*, 5(4):349–358, 2001.

[15] M. O'Neill, C. Ryan, M. Keijzer, and M. Cattolico. Crossover in Grammatical Evolution. *Genetic Programming and Evolvable Machines*, 4:67–93, 2003.

[16] M. Pawlik and N. Augsten. RTED: a robust algorithm for the tree edit distance. *Proceedings of the VLDB Endowment*, pages 334–345, 2011.

[17] F. Rothlauf. *Representations for genetic and evolutionary algorithms.* Springer, 2006.

[18] F. Rothlauf. *Design of Modern Heuristics.* Natural Computing Series. Springer, Berlin, Heidelberg, 2011.

[19] F. Rothlauf and D. E. Goldberg. Redundant Representations in Evolutionary Computation. *Evolutionary Computation*, 11:381–415, 2003.

[20] F. Rothlauf and M. Oetzel. On the Locality of Grammatical Evolution. In *Proceedings of the 9th European Conference on Genetic Programming*, volume 3905 LNCS, pages 320–330, Budapest, Hungary, 2006. Springer.

[21] A. Thorhauer and F. Rothlauf. Structural difficulty in grammatical evolution versus genetic programming. In *GECCO '13: Proceeding of the fifteenth annual conference on Genetic and evolutionary computation conference*, pages 997–1004. ACM, 2013.

[22] N. Uy, M. O'Neill, N. Hoai, B. Mckay, and E. Galván-López. Semantic Similarity Based Crossover in GP: The Case for Real-Valued Function Regression. In *Artifical Evolution*, volume 5975 LNCS, pages 170–181. Springer, 2010.

[23] N. Q. Uy, N. X. Hoai, M. O. Neill, and B. Mckay. The Role of Syntactic and Semantic Locality of Crossover in Genetic Programming. In *Parallel Problem Solving from Nature PPSN XI*, volume 6239 LNCS, pages 533–542. Springer, 2010.

[24] N. Q. Uy, N. X. Hoai, M. O'Neill, R. McKay, and D. N. Phong. On the roles of semantic locality of crossover in genetic programming. *Information Sciences*, 235:195–213, June 2013.

[25] P. A. Whigham. Grammatically-based Genetic Programming. In *Proceedings of the Workshop on Genetic Programming: From Theory to Real-World Applications*, pages 33–41. Morgan Kaufmann, 1995.

[26] P. A. Whigham. Search Bias, Language Bias, and Genetic Programming. In *Genetic Programming 1996: Proceedings of the First Annual Conference*, pages 230–237, 1996.

Examining the "Best of Both Worlds" of Grammatical Evolution

Peter A. Whigham
Department of Information Science
University of Otago
Dunedin, New Zealand
peter.whigham@otago.ac.nz

Grant Dick
Department of Information Science
University of Otago
Dunedin, New Zealand
grant.dick@otago.ac.nz

James Maclaurin
Department of Philosophy
University of Otago
Dunedin, New Zealand
james.maclaurin@otago.ac.nz

Caitlin A. Owen
Department of Information Science
University of Otago
Dunedin, New Zealand
oweca636@student.otago.ac.nz

ABSTRACT

Grammatical Evolution (GE) has a long history in evolutionary computation. Central to the behaviour of GE is the use of a linear representation and grammar to map individuals from search spaces into problem spaces. This genotype to phenotype mapping is often argued as a distinguishing property of GE relative to other techniques, such as context-free grammar genetic programming (CFG-GP). Since its initial description, GE research has attempted to incorporate information from the grammar into crossover, mutation, and individual initialisation, blurring the distinction between genotype and phenotype and creating GE variants closer to CFG-GP. This is argued to provide GE with the "best of both worlds", allowing degrees of grammatical bias to be introduced into operators to best suit the given problem. This paper examines the behaviour of three grammar-based search methods on several problems from previous GE research. It is shown that, unlike CFG-GP, the performance of "pure" GE on the examined problems closely resembles that of random search. The results suggest that further work is required to determine the cases where the "best of both worlds" of GE are required over a straight CFG-GP approach.

Categories and Subject Descriptors

I.2.2 [**Automatic Programming**]; I.2.8 [**Problem Solving, Control Methods, and Search**]: *Heuristic methods*

Keywords

grammar-based evolutionary search; grammatical evolution; genotype-to-phenotype mapping

GECCO '15, July 11 - 15, 2015, Madrid, Spain

DOI: http://dx.doi.org/10.1145/2739480.2754784

1. INTRODUCTION

The use of grammars for representing and controlling language and search bias within population-based stochastic search algorithms have been developed in a number of different frameworks [9]. These include extensions to genetic programming (GP) using context-free grammars (CFG-GP) [26], definite clause grammars and logic programs [29], probabilistic models [18] and developmental systems [3] . The reader is directed to the survey of grammar-based genetic programming by McKay et al. [9] for further details of the history and main themes in this field.

1.1 Grammar-based Genetic Programming

The earliest formal description of Genetic Programming [5] introduced the notion of closure, which defined a language without typing so that all functions and terminals could be mixed. Since a grammar explicitly allows typing constraints for a language, and therefore typed closure, there is a clear attraction for using a grammar to constrain the way in which components of a language can be integrated. This advantage was also argued by an explicit introduction of typing to GP [10]. As stated in [9], the incorporation of grammars into an evolutionary framework allow: the declaration of a language bias, therefore restricting the form of possible solutions; the introduction of explicit structure via the productions of a grammar; the introduction of semantic constraints, via homologous search operations, that ensure components of a solution that perform different roles are not mixed; and that extensions to GP (such as automatically-defined functions) can be incorporated merely through a change in the grammar specification.

1.2 GE Representation and Search

Grammatical Evolution (GE) evolves sentences in a language defined by a grammar. However, individuals do not explicitly represent a parse tree (as in GP) or derivation trees (as in traditional grammar-based GP systems). Rather, an individual's genome is represented by a variable-length binary string that is decoded as 8-bit integers (codons) and scanned from left-to-right, in conjunction with a grammar (G), to build a sentence in the language L(G). Commencing with a start symbol for the grammar, the current integer from the genome is used to select which production $A \rightarrow \alpha^*$, where $A \in N$ and $\alpha \in \{N \cup \Sigma\}$, is used to expand this non-terminal. Here N is the set of non-terminal symbols, while Σ is the set of terminal symbols. Since there are likely to be more than one production from the non-terminal A modulo arithmetic is used to select which production is used for the expansion. This expansion of the derivation tree is depth-first, left-most and continues until a sentence in the language has been produced. If the end of the binary-string (genome) is reached, the mapping process continues by recommencing from the start of the genome, in a process called "wrapping". The mapping process does not guarantee that an executable individual (i.e. where all nonterminals have been expanded to terminals) is produced and is therefore halted after a set number of wrappings. If an individual cannot be created it is assigned the lowest possible fitness. Previous work argued that wrapping is attractive as a form of intrinsic polymorphism, and that this may help the evolutionary process, or at worst do no harm [15].

The search operators for GE are applied to the linear genome. Crossover occurs between two parents by randomly selecting a cut point in each parent's bit-string and swapping the right-hand sides from the cut point, producing two children. Mutation is a point operator, randomly flipping a bit. Other aspects of GE, such as selection and population structure, are similar to standard evolutionary algorithms. Of particular note is the fact that the genotype is agnostic to the grammar. This was argued to be a useful feature since the same GE framework could be used with any form of grammar, and that it had an explicit genotype to phenotype mapping. The detailed arguments as to whether this mapping is desirable is beyond the scope of this work, however many of the extensions to GE described in Section 2 are a result of inadequacies resulting from this grammar-agnostic mapping. A detailed description of the original GE model is given in [16].

This paper will examine the historical development of GE in the context of representation and search, and argue that the introduction of grammar-based (derivation tree) concepts to GE has led to an evolutionary system that closely matches early work such as CFG-GP. Experimental evidence (Section 4) will show that the original GE system shows only marginal performance improvement over a random, grammar guided search and is often significantly worse than a derivation tree evolutionary system. We will show in Section 2 that the developments of GE have progressed to the point where the distinction between the strict separation of the genotype and phenotype have been blurred, resulting in effectively a derivation-tree based model. The current argument for GE being the "best of both worlds" is an acknowledgement that in current implementations of GE the user can choose between a strict GE with a genotype-phenotype mapping, or use a traditional derivation-tree based representation (albeit in a somewhat convoluted manner). However, this argument relies on the premise that the original GE model offers some benefits beyond the grammar-guided approaches that operate directly on derivation trees. This is the main assumption addressed in this work.

The remainder of this paper is structured as follows: Section 2 describes and explains the justification for the historical introduction of grammar-based concepts to GE. In Section 3 the experimental framework is presented, as well as a justification given for the selected problems. In Section 4 the results are described and discussed. Finally, Section 5 draws together the implications of this work and provides directions for future work.

2. RELATED WORK

This section will introduce the historical issues that led to the introduction of derivation-tree based concepts directly into the GE framework. It is worth noting that GE was initially completely agnostic to the grammar and therefore the search space of the genotype was disconnected from the phenotype. Although this was argued by GE proponents to possibly be an advantage, it is not clear from a theoretical perspective why this would be the case, although the subsequent use and success of GE would suggest that it did not matter.

Creating an initial population in GE can be difficult, often requiring repeated attempts to produce valid (executable) individuals. This is generally the case with grammars that are recursive and therefore not depth limited, however these are common forms of grammar since they do not explicitly restrict the size of an individual solution. In particular, recursive grammars are normal with problems such as symbolic regression, rule sets, combinatorial and heuristic models, finite-state machines, and so on [9]. Early work suggested that the initialisation of the GE population often produced over 70% invalid individuals [17]. The initialisation problem with GE was addressed by using the grammar G directly to produce the initial population [22]. This was similar to the approach first described in 1995 for grammar-based genetic programming (CFG-GP) [26], although extended to allow a ramped half-and-half population. However, once the grammar had been used to produce valid derivation-tree based representations of individuals they were mapped back to a linear representation, and the derivation tree information discarded. Although this solved the initialisation problem, once an individual genome was change due to crossover or mutation the standard GE mapping procedure could no longer guarantee valid individuals, resulting in a reduced search since many individuals were just copied [23]. Although GE has been extended to address this issue by methods such as repairing individuals and dynamic grammars, the solutions are rather ad-hoc and complex. It is worth noting that these issues do not, and cannot, occur with derivation-tree based approaches.

Although problems with initialisation can be easily solved using a derivation-tree approach, there are more significant issues relating to the search characteristics of GE. Since the genome is agnostic to G there are implications for the stability of individuals when considering small changes. At worst, a single mutation of a single bit in the first codon could produce a completely different sentence in L(G). This concept, referred to as locality [19] in the evolutionary computation field, has been previously examined for GE [21] where it was shown that for mutation-based operators GE leads to lower performance compared with standard GP. In general, GE has low locality when local search operators are required. This results in GE search being more akin to random search, resulting in a significantly longer time than other similar search methods to find a good solution [20]. It is interesting to note that, once a problem becomes sufficiently complex, subsequent increases in the complexity of G, may result in GE performing no better than a random search [27].

Point-based GE crossover (ripple crossover) is also clearly a disruptive operator to the tail of the representation of an individual due to the GE mapping process. Acknowledging the disruptive character of GE crossover an approach was developed that involved reading the binary GE genome in both directions [6]. This removed the tail bias associated with the original point crossover, however the issue of invalid individuals was not addressed. Other work that addressed mapping issues included the concept of evolving a position-independent mapping (πGE) between the genotype and phenotype [12]. Although this appeared to occasionally improve performance over some simple problems, the work did not consider addressing the more fundamental issues regarding the representation and mapping for complex grammars.

The most significant work associated with GE crossover was the structure preserving crossover (LHS) of Harper and Blair [4]. Here the genotype string was labelled with information from the grammar to ensure that crossover was always performed between the same non-terminals. Most significantly, the LHS replacement crossover used the grammar to "...constrain both the second point in the first parent and the first and second points in the second parent...", resulting in a crossover operator that was equivalent to crossover between derivation trees. Harper and Blair observed that this improved the performance of GE since "...more structural information is preserved with the LHS Replacement Crossover whilst maintaining the advantages of using a full BNF grammar." The paper concluded that it was this property that explained the improved performance of LHS compared with other crossover operators operating on the binary string representation.

The grammar-agnostic mapping in GE meant that point-based mutation was also potentially highly disruptive. An analysis of mutation behaviour in GE [2] described two different mutational effects on the phenotype, termed structural and nodal mutation. These properties could only be examined by considering the effect on the derivation tree and the associated grammar – a nodal mutation is one where a change in the genotype was related to a grammar production that led only to terminals, while a structural mutation changes the selection of a non-terminal expansion in a production. This concept, that relies on incorporating the derivation tree into the analysis of an individual, has been developed in GE as a context-sensitive mutation operator, to "...improve the sense of similarity between related individuals" [14]; i.e. to increase the locality properties of mutation. Incorporating information from the derivation tree was further emphasised by research that examined how the original grammar of GE could be modified based on a subset of fit population members [25, 24]. The authors concluded that "...ensuring that no information is disrupted during the grammar modification process, there are potential gains in performance." [24]. Of course, to ensure that no disruption occurred when a grammar was modified meant examining the grammar and carefully crafting new productions that would not affect the current individuals. It is worth noting that the difficulties arising from this model were due to the grammar-agnostic GE mapping, and that a previous grammar-modification model based on derivation trees did not suffer from the same complications [26].

In summary, the historical developments of GE have shown a gradual blurring of the separation between the genotype and phenotype, from the initial creation of the population through to the search operators, resulting in essentially two systems: a grammar-agnostic GE system, and a (convoluted) derivation-tree based approach. This has given rise to the idea of a "best of both worlds" approach in GE, where grammar-agnostic and grammar-aware operators can be interchanged to best suit any given problem. This, however, raises the question as to whether there are conditions under which the original GE operators present an advantage over operators more tightly coupled to the grammar.

3. EXPERIMENTAL FRAMEWORK

We assume that the "best of both worlds" in GE relates to the user being able to select operators at design-time to best suit their given problem. We argue that the best way to identify scenarios in which each representation is best suited is to examine them in isolation. Therefore an experimental framework is presented in which several problems from GE literature are examined using each set of search operators independently, and then relative performance differences measured.

A clean implementation code base was created for the experiments. This allowed the same code to be used for the evaluation and evolutionary operators, and therefore reduced the likelihood of different implementations introducing different biases in performance. In addition, the standard GEVA implementation was found to have a bug regarding the configuration file and the use of different operators, and there was no simple method for creating a random derivation-tree population from the grammar. The codebase used for all experiments in this paper is available for download from GitHub.[1] The GE implementation was based on the original GE model with no integration of the grammar into either the initialisation or search operators. The derivation-tree based model was based on the simple derivation-tree model CFG-GP [26], given this was an early grammar-based system and formed the basis for the later derivation-tree operators introduced into GE.

In addition to GE and CFG-GP, a random search model was included: this operated by repeatedly generating individuals using the random initialisation method from GE, and keeping the best individual found in all trials. To keep a consistent scale with the other two methods, this random process was broken into 51 groups of 1000 individuals for each run (equivalent to sampling 51 initial populations, each with 1000 individuals, and keeping the best individual found during the run). This was to match the fact that all experiments used a population size of 1000 and evolved over 50 generations. This model represents a baseline measure against which the effectiveness of the search operators of GE and CFG-GP, and the degree of difficulty for each problem, can be assessed.

The following problems were considered: Sante Fe artificial ant problem, 11-bit Boolean multiplexer, 5-bit even parity, quartic symbolic regression, Boston housing symbolic regression, and a hyper-heuristic bin packing problem [1]. The first four problems are acknowledged as poor benchmarks [28], however they are included for historical reasons as they have been used in the design and analysis of GE operators. The grammars, where possible, have been taken from the examples supplied in the GEVA package [13], or

[1]https://github.com/grantdick/libgges

```
<prog>    ::= <code>
<code>    ::= <line> | <code> <line>
<line>    ::= <condition> | <op>
<condition> ::=
  if(food_ahead()==1) {
    <opcode>
  } else {
    <opcode>
  }
<opcode> ::= <op> | <opcode> <op>
<op>      ::=  left(); | right(); | move();
```

(a) Artificial Ant

```
<prog> ::= <expr>
<expr> ::= <expr> <op> <expr>
         | ( <expr> <op> <expr> )
         | <pre-op> ( <expr> )
         | <protected-op> |<var>
<op> ::= + | * | -
<protected-op> ::= div( <expr>, <expr>)
<pre-op> ::= sin | cos | exp | inv | log
<var> ::= X | 1.0
```

(b) Symbolic Regression

```
<start>        ::=
  <choosebins> remove_pieces_from_bins <repack>
<choosebins> ::= <type> | <type> <choosebins>
<type>         ::=
  highest_filled <num> <ignore> <remove>
| lowest_filled <num> <ignore> <remove>
| random_bins <num> <ignore> <remove>
| gap_lessthan <num> <threshold> <ignore> <remove>
| num_of_pieces <num> <numpieces> <ignore> <remove>
<num>          ::= 2 | 5 | 10 | 20 | 50
<threshold>    ::= average | minimum | maximum
<numpieces>    ::= 1 | 2 | 3 | 4 | 5 | 6
<ignore>       ::= 0.995 | 0.997 | 0.999 | 1.0 | 1.1
<remove>       ::= ALL | ONE
<repack>       ::= best_fit_decreasing
                 | worst_fit_decreasing
                 | first_fit_decreasing
```

(c) Hyper-Heuristic Bin Packing

Figure 1: Examples of grammars used in this work.

from relevant previous work [1, 11] (the grammars used for the artificial ant, symbolic regression, and bin packing problems are shown in Figure 1). The Boston housing grammar extends the quartic grammar by including the additional explanatory variables used for predicting house price from the nonterminal **var**. For reasons of space the multiplexer and parity grammars are not shown, however they may be found in many previous published works of GE [11]. The common parameters for all experiments are shown in Table 1. Note that the settings have been selected from previous work and, although not tuned for particular problems, the results presented in Section 4 are similar to those presented in previous published work and therefore do not show a bias against the performance of GE.

All problems were defined in terms of minimising an error so that the results can be interpreted in the same way. The resulting figures are presented showing, for each generation,

Table 1: The parameters used for all experiments.

Parameter	Value GE	Value CFG-GP
Population Size	1000	
Generations	50	
Selection Method	Tournament	
Tournament Size	3	
Elitism Count	1	
Crossover Rate	0.9	
Reproduction Rate	0.1	
Mutation Rate	0.05	–
Crossover	Single-Point (variable length)	Subtree
Mutation	Pointwise (per-codon)	Subtree
Crossover Node Selection	Uniform	Koza-Style
Initialisation	Random	Ramped-Half & Half
Min. Initialisation Depth	–	2
Max. Initialisation Depth	–	6
Max. Tree Depth	–	17
Initial Codon Length	200	–
Wrapping	None	–

the mean of the best individual over 30 runs, with a 95% confidence interval about the mean. For the artificial ant problem the fitness was the number of pieces left over after the maximum number of steps, while for the multiplexer and parity problem it was the number of incorrect predictions. To create the 30 runs for the regression problem, we used 3 rounds of 10-fold cross-validation to determine the training and testing split for each run. At the end of each generation, the individual with the lowest training error was applied to the test set to establish its testing error. The fitness measure used was the root relative squared error (RRSE), which is zero for a perfect prediction. A 95% confidence interval was shown for all results to indicate statistical significance about the mean. The bin packing problem was more complex since each data set (Uniform 500, Uniform 1000, Scholl and Triples) had 10 instances per problem. Hence one instance was used for training and the remaining 9 instances used for testing. In addition, since the bin packing problem had to have a random ordering for the objects to be binned, each training example was run 10 times to get a reasonable estimate of fitness. This resulted in 90 runs per training/test cycle, which were repeated 30 times. Fitness was measured as the difference from a previously determined lower bound. The reader is referred to Burke et al. [1] for further details.

4. RESULTS

The Santa Fe Ant problem results are shown in Figure 2. The artificial ant problem is known to be hard when using the standard grammar, and the results support early work from GP that showed the performance is often only marginally better than random search [7]. The CFG-GP approach appears to be significantly better than random, although this is more difficult to justify for the GE model. Either way, no model performs very well. Note that here (as with all other experiments) the mean best fitness is shown for each generation. Previous work with the artificial ant problem often just states the number of times that a successful solution was discovered. This measure, however, effectively ignores those runs that perform poorly. Since we are interested in the overall pattern of behaviour the mean count of pieces remaining per generation was reported so that any extreme variation in performance would be observed. Note that the initial population fitness of CFG-GP performs worse than the random model, however after 10 generations the CFG-GP population has begun to be the best model (although not necessarily significantly better than GE).

The 11-bit multiplexer results are shown in Figure 3. Although GE is significantly better than the random model after 20 generations, the CFG-GP model clearly outperforms GE. Note that the GE model also shows only a very slow improvement after being very similar to the random model for the first 10 generations. In contrast, CFG-GP shows a rapid improvement over the first 30 generations and then starts to slow down, although there is still evidence of improvement.

The 5-bit even parity results are shown in Figure 4. Initially, and for the first 10 generations, all models have similar fitness and variance, however after this number of evaluations the CFG-GP model starts to show some improvement and is significantly better than the GE and random models. Note that although GE is significantly better than the random model after about 30 generations, the performance and rate of improvement is quite similar to random. In particular, both models have similar variance about the mean (i.e. the 95% confidence intervals are both narrow), while CFG-GP shows greater variance but significantly better average performance.

The training and test fitness results for the quartic regression problem are shown in Figure 5. This (and the subsequent problems) consider both the training and test results and therefore allow an analysis of the generalisation performance of the models. The training results for CFG-GP show a rapid decrease in the error and the population has largely converged by about 30 generations. Note that the error is close to zero, and that the variation in the population is gradually reducing. The training behaviour of GE is markedly different; for over 20 generations the fitness is no better than the random model, after which time there is a continual slow improvement. This type of slow improvement has been previously observed with GE, largely because it maintains a diverse population because of the agnostic mapping process with the grammar. This implies that GE is performing a slightly better search than the random model, but would certainly take many evaluations before it performed as well as CFG-GP. The test results (right panel) are the most relevant and interesting when building a predictive model. These clearly show that CFG-GP is significantly better than GE and shows good generalisation after 30 generations or so. Of more interest is the test performance of GE: here GE is only significantly better than the random model after about 40 generations, and is only marginally better after 50 generations. Although the random model appears to have converged by about 30 generations, this certainly suggests that GE is doing little better than a random search when it comes to finding general solutions to the quartic regression problem. The training and test results for the Boston Housing regression problem are shown in Figure 6. Note that for GE both the training and test results are slightly worse than the random model, while CFG-GP is clearly significantly better. In addition, both GE and random appear to show little improvement after about 40 generations. For GE this suggests that, even though there is diversity in the population, there is no overall maintenance of good partial solutions and therefore little ability to progress the evolutionary search. This is probably a result of the agnostic mapping from genotype tol phenotype, which means that the context of a good partial solution (think of building blocks for genetic algorithms) are not maintained and therefore cannot be guaranteed to produce the same concept in future generations for an individual.

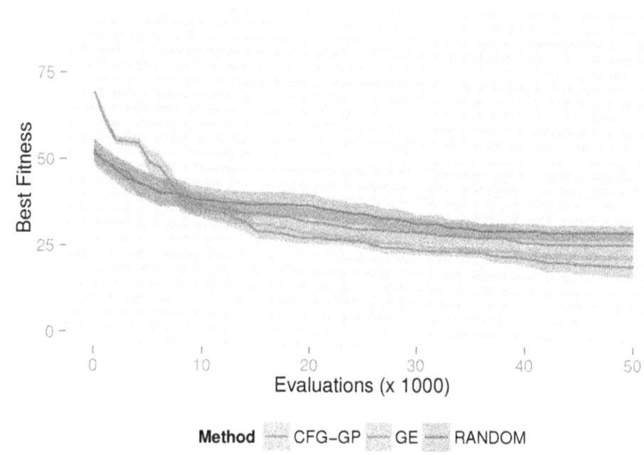

Figure 2: Evolution of best fitness on the Santa Fe ant trail problem.

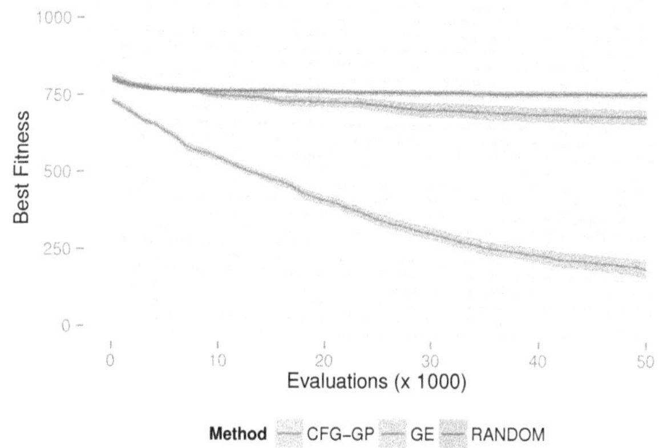

Figure 3: Evolution of best fitness on the 11-bit Boolean multiplexer problem.

The results for the four hyper-heuristic bin packing problems are shown in Figure 7. These results show little or no significant different between any of the models except for the Uniform 1000 problem, where both GE and CFG-GP outperform the random model. For all four problems there is little improvement of any model in either training or testing after the first 10 generations, suggesting that no progress can be made in searching for better combinations of heuristics. These result seem surprising but are completely consistent with the outcomes of the original study [1]. In this work the authors stated, "We considered the performance of the heuristics to be consistent, because the variation of their results on new problems is low", and that "...they obtained results which are mostly only one bin worse than the lower bound." This is exactly the results shown in Figure 7 for all three models. The conclusion of this work in terms of GE was that Burke et al. stated "This paper has shown that

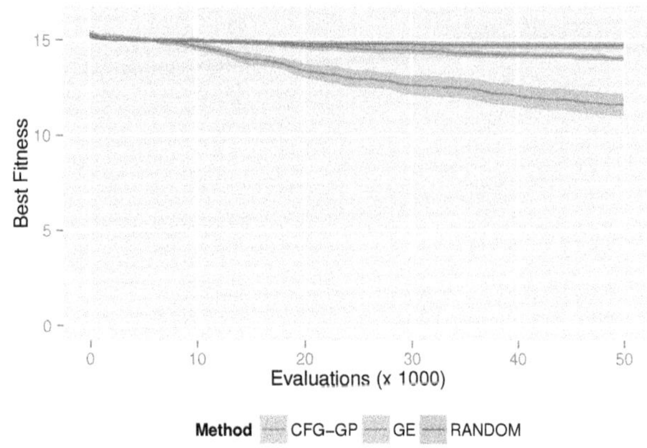

Figure 4: Evolution of best fitness on the 5-bit even parity problem.

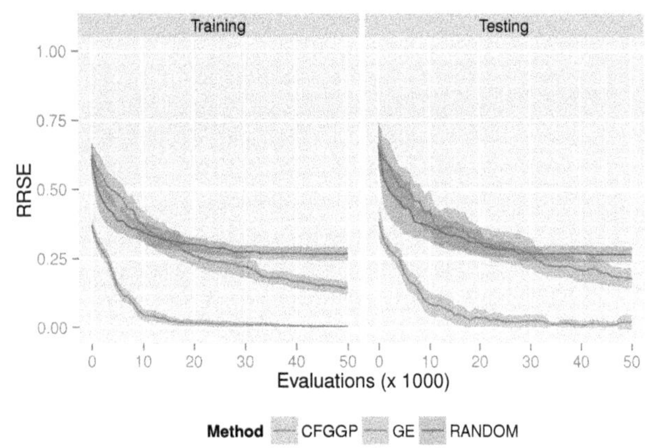

Figure 5: Evolution of training and testing fitness on the quartic symbolic regression problem.

it is possible to evolve efficient local search heuristics for bin packing, using grammatical evolution." However, if the authors had also used the grammar to generate random individuals they may well have concluded that the real work is being done by the bin selection (heuristic) methods and that probably a search for a small number of different combinations of heuristics would have performed as well as GE. This conclusion is supported by similar work on hyper-heuristic search using GE [8] for the capacitated vehicle routing problem. Here the authors found that heuristics with just a few operators proved to be as effective as those solutions that used many more heuristics, leading to the conclusion that "...increasing the number of operators in a sequence does not necessarily improve performance." [8]. This paper also briefly examined the influence of different types of crossover and mutation by mixing derivation tree and point-based operations in GE. The results showed that a derivation tree approach converged more rapidly than standard GE operators while also finding the best solution within approximately 10 generations. The GE operators maintained diversity in the population, but were much slower to find a good solution. These results are as much a comment on the structure of

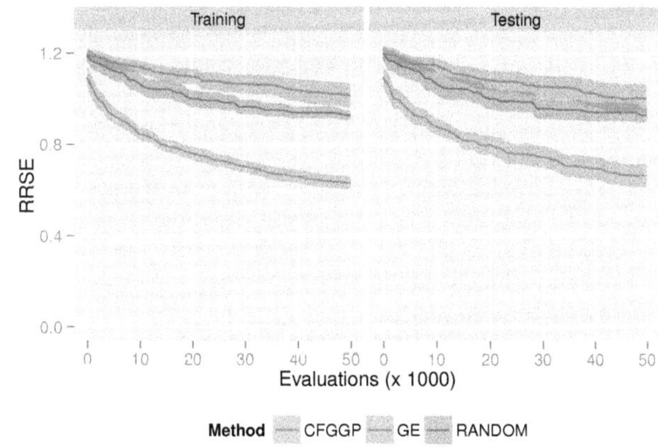

Figure 6: Evolution of training and testing fitness on the Boston Housing symbolic regression problem.

the routing problem and the heuristics used to construct a solution as they are a demonstration of the efficacy of evolutionary search – it is likely that a random model such as the one used here would perform as well as GE on the vehicle routing problem.

4.1 Discussion

The previous results cover a range of different problems, however in all cases there is no evidence that the original GE approach performs significantly better than a derivation-tree model. Although GE has been used for over fifteen years this alone does not mean that the model is the most appropriate framework for grammar-based GP. In fact, acknowledging the issues associated with the representation of GE has led to ongoing research to understand and improve the search behaviour of GE. We have argued that historically this has mainly been to address the problems with population initialisation and the effect of search operators on locality. The solution in most cases has been to introduce the structure of the grammar back into the population and therefore to be able to interpret the GE string representation in the context of a derivation tree. The subsequent development of derivation-tree crossover and mutation into GE has meant that a mixed model has been produced, which suggests that a "best of both worlds" is now offered by GE. But to argue that both models are required implies that the GE and CFG-GP models are both complementary and useful. To show that GE is a useful model, and that it should be maintained in conjunction with a derivation-based model, requires a demonstration that it can solve problems of real interest and complexity where CFG-GP consistently fails. Certainly the results from Section 4 demonstrate that the search characteristics of GE are different from CFG-GP, suggesting that there will be problems better suited to GE. However, since the search characteristics of GE appear to be more closely aligned with random search suggests that an equivalent behaviour could be created with CFG-GP by using a large mutation rate. In addition, the overheads required to produce a GE system that incorporates information from the grammar cannot be justified without proof that the original GE framework is an appropriate framework for general and effective grammar-guided evolutionary search.

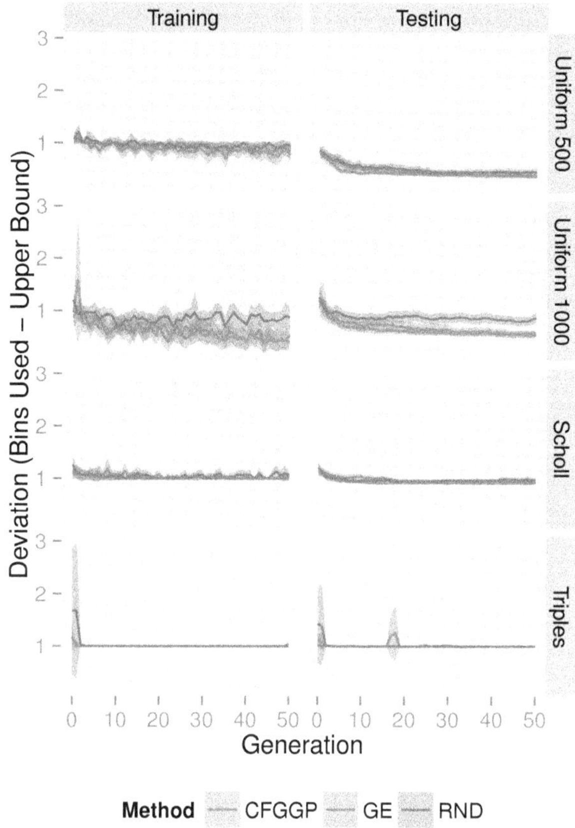

Figure 7: Evolution of training and test fitness on four hyper-heuristic bin packing problems.

5. CONCLUSION

This paper has considered the historical development of GE from a grammar-agnostic model to a hybrid model where information from the grammar and individual derivation-trees are incorporated in the search operators. We have argued that this is effectively just recreating the original grammar-based GP systems such as CFG-GP, and that the justification for integrating both approaches would require a demonstration that GE alone has properties that are useful and complementary to a derivation-tree model. The experiments show GE is often similar in characteristics to a random search model and does not perform any better (and often significantly worse) than a derivation-tree model. The argument that GE is now the "best of both worlds" cannot be supported given the current evidence – arguments of simplicity imply that a grammar-based model such as CFG-GP is sufficient for solving problems traditionally used with GE, and that the grammar-agnostic mapping of GE does not provide any advantage.

This conclusion will no doubt bring some strong criticism, and should therefore promote a range of future work. For example, understanding the characteristics of problems where GE may outperform CFG-GP would be a challenging and informative piece of work. This could involve considering what types of fitness landscape suit the search characteristics of GE, but are deceptive to a grammar-based model. From a theoretical perspective this may be too difficult, but even finding a specific problem where GE performs better than both CFG-GP and a random model, and showing what form of grammars (and language) create these results would be a useful starting point. In addition, creating freely available software platforms (in a range of programming languages) for CFG-GP style models would allow future researchers to compare GE and CFG-GP models, and therefore allow a large set of comparative evidence to be produced.

Finally, this paper has taken the view that the "best of both worlds" reflects design-time choices of operators to suit problem characteristics. An alternative view is that both types of operator could be integrated into a single system, and an adaptive or probabilistic approach to their use could be performed at run-time. The results presented here do not give much support to this approach, but there is a chance that such a configuration is able to outperform either representation when used in isolation. Therefore, future work could explore this idea.

6. REFERENCES

[1] E. K. Burke, M. R. Hyde, and G. Kendall. Grammatical evolution of local search heuristics. *IEEE Transactions on Evolutionary Computation*, 16(3):406–417, 2012.

[2] J. Byrne, M. O'Neill, J. McDermott, and A. Brabazon. An analysis of the behaviour of mutation in grammatical evolution. In A. I. Esparcia-Alcázar, A. Ekárt, S. Silva, S. Dignum, and A. S. Etaner-Uyar, editors, *Genetic Programming, Proceedings of EuroGP'2010*, volume 6021 of *Lecture Notes in Computer Science*, pages 14–25. Springer, 2010.

[3] W. Fontana. Algorithmic chemistry. In C. Langton, C. Taylor, J. Farmer, and S. Rasmussen, editors, *Artificial Life II*, volume 2, pages 159–209. Addison-Wesly, Reading, 1991.

[4] R. Harper and A. Blair. A structure preserving crossover in grammatical evolution. In *Proceedings of the 2005 IEEE Congress on Evolutionary Computation*, volume 3, pages 2537–2544. IEEE, 2005.

[5] J. R. Koza. *Genetic Programming: On the Programming of Computers by Means of Natural Selection*. MIT Press, Cambridge, MA, USA, 1992.

[6] J. Kubalik, J. Koutnik, and L. J. M. Rothkrantz. Grammatical evolution with bidirectional representation. In C. Ryan, T. Soule, M. Keijzer, E. Tsang, R. Poli, and E. Costa, editors, *Genetic Programming, Proceedings of EuroGP'2003*, volume 2610 of *LNCS*, pages 354–363, 2003.

[7] W. B. Langdon and R. Poli. Why ants are hard. In J. R. Koza, W. Banzhaf, K. Chellapilla, K. Deb, M. Dorigo, D. B. Fogel, M. H. Garzon, D. E. Goldberg, H. Iba, and R. Riolo, editors, *Genetic Programming 1998: Proceedings of the Third Annual Conference*, pages 193–201, University of Wisconsin, Madison, Wisconsin, USA, 22-25 July 1998. Morgan Kaufmann.

[8] R. Marshall, M. Johnston, and M. Zhang. Developing a hyper-heuristic using grammatical evolution and the capacitated vehicle routing problem. In G. Dick, W. Browne, P. Whigham, M. Zhang, L. Bui, H. Ishibuchi, Y. Jin, X. Li, Y. Shi, P. Singh, K. Tan,

and K. Tang, editors, *Simulated Evolution and Learning*, volume 8886 of *Lecture Notes in Computer Science*, pages 668–679. Springer International Publishing, 2014.

[9] R. I. McKay, N. X. Hoai, P. A. Whigham, Y. Shan, and M. O'Neill. Grammar-based genetic programming: a survey. *Genetic Programming and Evolvable Machines*, 11:365–396, 2010.

[10] D. J. Montana. Strongly typed genetic programming. *Evolutionary Computation*, 3(2):199–230, 1995.

[11] E. Murphy, M. O'Neill, E. G. López, and A. Brabazon. Tree-adjunct grammatical evolution. In *Proceedings of the 2010 IEEE Congress on Evolutionary Computation*, pages 1–8. IEEE, 2010.

[12] M. O'Neill, A. Brabazon, M. Nicolau, S. M. Garraghy, and P. Keenan. πgrammatical evolution. In K. Deb, R. Poli, W. Banzhaf, H.-G. Beyer, E. Burke, P. Darwen, D. Dasgupta, D. Floreano, J. Foster, M. Harman, O. Holland, P. L. Lanzi, L. Spector, A. Tettamanzi, D. Thierens, and A. Tyrrell, editors, *Genetic and Evolutionary Computation – GECCO-2004, Part II*, volume 3103 of *Lecture Notes in Computer Science*, pages 617–629. Springer-Verlag, 2004.

[13] M. O'Neill, E. Hemberg, C. Gilligan, E. Bartley, J. McDermott, and A. Brabazon. Geva: Grammatical evolution in java. *SIGEVOlution*, 3(2):17–22, July 2008.

[14] M. O'Neill, J. McDermott, J. M. Swafford, J. Byrne, E. Hemberg, A. Brabazon, E. Shotton, C. McNally, and M. Hemberg. Evolutionary design using grammatical evolution and shape grammars: Designing a shelter. *International Journal of Design Engineering*, 3(1):4–24, 2010.

[15] M. O'Neill and C. Ryan. Automatic generation of programs with grammatical evolution. In D. Bridge, R. Byrne, B. O'Sullivan, S. Prestwich, and H. Sorensen, editors, *Artificial Intelligence and Cognitive Science AICS 1999*, number 10 in , University College Cork, Ireland, 1-3 Sept. 1999.

[16] M. O'Neill and C. Ryan. Grammatical evolution. *IEEE Transactions on Evolutionary Computation*, 5(4):349–358, Aug. 2001.

[17] M. O'Neill and C. Ryan. *Grammatical Evolution: Evolutionary Automatic Programming in a Arbitrary Language*, volume 4 of *Genetic Programming*. Kluwer Academic Publishers, 2003.

[18] A. Ratle and M. Sebag. Avoiding the bloat with probabilistic grammar-guided genetic programming. In P. Collet, C. Fonlupt, J.-K. Hao, E. Lutton, and M. Schoenauer, editors, *Artificial Evolution 5th International Conference, Evolution Artificielle, EA 2001*, volume 2310 of *LNCS*, pages 255–266. Springer Verlag, 2001.

[19] F. Rothlauf. *Representations for genetic and evolutionary algorithms*. Springer, second edition, 2006.

[20] F. Rothlauf. *Design of Modern Heuristics*. Natural Computing Series. Springer, 2011.

[21] F. Rothlauf and M. Oetzel. On the locality of grammatical evolution. In P. Collet, M. Tomassini, M. Ebner, S. Gustafson, and A. Ekárt, editors, *Proceedings of the 9th European Conference on Genetic Programming*, volume 3905 of *Lecture Notes in Computer Science*, pages 320–330. Springer, 2006.

[22] C. Ryan and R. M. A. Azad. Sensible initialisation in grammatical evolution. In A. M. Barry, editor, *GECCO 2003: Proceedings of the Bird of a Feather Workshops, Genetic and Evolutionary Computation Conference*, pages 142–145. AAAI, 11 July 2003.

[23] C. Ryan and M. O'Neill. Grammatical evolution: A steady state approach. In J. R. Koza, editor, *Late Breaking Papers at the Genetic Programming 1998 Conference*, pages 180–185, University of Wisconsin, Madison, Wisconsin, USA, 22-25 July 1998. Stanford University Bookstore.

[24] J. M. Swafford, E. Hemberg, M. O'Neill, M. Nicolau, and A. Brabazon. A non-destructive grammar modification approach to modularity in grammatical evolution. In *Proceedings of the 13th Annual Conference on Genetic and Evolutionary Computation*, GECCO '11, pages 1411–1418, New York, NY, USA, 2011. ACM.

[25] J. M. Swafford, M. O'Neill, M. Nicolau, and A. Brabazon. Exploring grammatical modification with modules in grammatical evolution. In S. Silva, J. A. Foster, M. Nicolau, P. Machado, and M. Giacobini, editors, *Genetic Programming*, volume 6621 of *Lecture Notes in Computer Science*, pages 310–321. Springer Berlin Heidelberg, 2011.

[26] P. A. Whigham. Inductive bias and genetic programming. In A. M. S. Zalzala, editor, *First International Conference on Genetic Algorithms in Engineering Systems: Innovations and Applications, GALESIA*, volume 414, pages 461–466. IEE, 1995.

[27] B. C. White, J. C. Gilbert, D. M. Reif, and J. H. Moore. A statistical comparison of grammatical evolution strategies in the domain of human genetics. In D. Corne, Z. Michalewicz, M. Dorigo, G. Eiben, D. Fogel, C. Fonseca, G. Greenwood, T. K. Chen, G. Raidl, A. Zalzala, S. Lucas, B. Paechter, J. Willies, J. J. M. Guervos, E. Eberbach, B. McKay, A. Channon, A. Tiwari, L. G. Volkert, D. Ashlock, and M. Schoenauer, editors, *Proceedings of the 2005 IEEE Congress on Evolutionary Computation*, volume 1, pages 491–497, Edinburgh, UK, 2-5 Sept. 2005. IEEE Press.

[28] D. R. White, J. McDermott, M. Castelli, L. Manzoni, B. Goldman, G. Kronberger, W. Jaśkowski, U.-M. O'Reilly, and S. Luke. Better GP benchmarks: community survey results and proposals. *Genetic Programming and Evolvable Machines*, 14(1):3–29, 2013.

[29] M. L. Wong and K. S. Leung. Combining genetic programming and inductive logic programming using logic grammars. In *Proceedings of the 1995 IEEE Conference on Evolutionary Computation*, volume 2,

Using Model Checking Techniques For Evaluating the Effectiveness of Evolutionary Computing in Synthesis of Distributed Fault-Tolerant Programs

Ling Zhu
Department of Computer Science and Engineering
Michigan State University
East Lansing, Michigan 48824
zhuling@cse.msu.edu

Sandeep Kulkarni
Department of Computer Science and Engineering
Michigan State University
East Lansing, Michigan 48824
sandeep@cse.msu.edu

ABSTRACT

In most applications using genetic programming (GP), objective functions are obtained by a terminating calculation. However, the terminating calculation cannot evaluate distributed fault-tolerant programs accurately. A key distinction in synthesizing distributed fault-tolerant programs is that they are inherently non-deterministic, potentially having infinite computations and executing in an unpredictable environment. In this study, we apply a model checking technique - Binary Decision Diagrams (BDDs) - to GP, evaluating distributed programs by computing reachable states of the given program and identifying whether it satisfies its specification. We present scenario-based multi-objective approach that each program is evaluated under different scenarios which represent various environments. The computation of the programs are considered in two different semantics respectively: interleaving and maximum parallelism. In the end, we illustrate our approach with a Byzantine agreement problem, a token ring problem and a consensus protocol using failure detector S. For the first time, this work automatically synthesizes the consensus protocol with S. The results show the proposed method enhances the effectiveness of GP in all studied cases when using maximum parallelism semantic.

Categories and Subject Descriptors

I.2.2 [**Artificial Intelligence**]: Automatic Programming—*Program synthesis*; D.2.4 [**Software Engineering**]: Software/Program Verification—*Model checking*

Keywords

Fault-Tolerant; Program Synthesis; Genetic Programming; Model Checking; Binary Decision Diagrams; Multi-Scenario

1. INTRODUCTION

Traditionally, most applications of the genetic programming (GP) use test-based or simulation-based evaluation on generated programs to calculate objective functions. The generated programs are usually executed on a set of test cases, and the objective functions are typically an aggregation of these calculated executions. This evaluation process is considered as terminating calculation and in most cases it is used for sequential programs that do not have non-determinism. However, this method is not suitable for distributed programs. The evaluation of distributed programs is often complicated due to a large number of concurrent executions. Moreover, different race conditions that result in several possible runs make it difficult to analyze the correctness of distributed programs. The terminating calculation cannot evaluate distributed programs accurately because it cannot incorporate the specification entirely, and the program execution can be infinite. Hence in GP, using the traditional test-based method is not effective to evolve correct distributed programs.

This problem has been solved in practice using one of the formal methods techniques - model checking. In model checking, a program is deemed to be correct only if it satisfies the program specification. It statically checks the entire program state space to verify the program. In this study, we use model checking techniques to evaluate the generated distributed program. Model checking based execution is used to identify the effect of that program on all possible permitted initial states. This symbolic execution is then used to determine whether the specification is satisfied. In the event the specification is satisfied, the desired program is identified. Typical model checking has just two output values, correct or incorrect. However, this does not suffice in GP since not having enough number of objective values impedes the gradual improvements of GP search. To cope with this problem, we identify the number of possible states that result in violation of given properties and assign objective value accordingly. For implementation, we use a model checking technique, Binary Decision Diagrams (BDDs). Using BDD-based evaluation, not only are generated programs accurately evaluated, but also the objective has more possible values (the number of violated states). This method allows GP to search with better gradient.

Distributed program runs in an unpredictable environment where faults such as failures, crashes and malicious attacks could occur. We say a program is fault-tolerant if it masks or restores the expected behavior of a system following the occurrence of faults [10]. Most of the previous works on the addition of fault-tolerance focus on revising an existing program with the help of heuristics. These heuristics have limitations in automatically designing some difficult problems [5]. Alternatively, GP, as a more generic approach, can synthesize these problems. In this work, for the first

GECCO '15, July 11 - 15, 2015, Madrid, Spain

DOI: http://dx.doi.org/10.1145/2739480.2754779

time, we use GP to automatically synthesize the difficult fault-tolerant problem, consensus protocol using failure detector S.

We consider two types of typical faults - process crash failures and Byzantine faults. The correctness of fault tolerant programs is characterized by verification in various scenarios such as in the absence of faults, in the presence of one fault, and in the presence of multiple faults. To ensure the generated fault-tolerant programs are correct under these scenarios, we use scenario-based multiobjectivization (solving single objective problem using multi-objective principle), attempting to synthesize a program that works equally well in all scenarios. The program performance of each scenario is considered as an objective and NSGAII [8] is used to find optimal programs that maximize performance in all scenarios.

Due to several possible executions which may be possible from a given state, we need to consider a few possible executions to determine whether they satisfy the specification. In this paper, we consider the execution of distributed programs under two semantics: (1) interleaving semantics, and (2) maximum parallelism semantics. In interleaving semantics, one process is allowed to execute at a time, and in maximum parallelism semantics, all processes execute in one step. Thus, maximum parallelism semantics captures round-based execution where in each round processes communicate with each other and utilize the information they obtained in previous round to determine their next step.

Contributions of the paper

1. The BDD-based analysis improves the effectiveness of GP by accurately evaluating the programs, and also guarantees that evolved optimal programs satisfy the specification.
2. The BDD-based GP is more effective under maximum parallelism semantics than interleaving semantics.
3. GP automatically synthesize fault-tolerant programs such as Byzantine agreement, token ring and consensus problems, and this is the first successful approach to automated design of consensus protocol with failure detector S.

2. DISTRIBUTED PROGRAMS

2.1 Distributed programs structure

A distributed program consists of a set of variables and a set of actions. Each action is of the form $guard \longrightarrow st$ where $guard$ is a Boolean expression over program variables and st updates program variables. We say that an action is enabled if its guard is true in the current state. We consider execution of programs under two semantics:

Interleaving semantics. In interleaving semantics, in one step, we choose one enabled action to execute. If multiple actions are enabled, one of them is chosen non-deterministically. The new state of the system is obtained by executing the selected action. This process is repeated indefinitely or until we reach a state where no actions are enabled.

maximum parallelism semantics. In maximum parallelism semantics, in one step, we choose enabled actions of all processes to execute. All these actions utilize the current state to evaluate the guards and execute statements. (In other words, if two actions are chosen for execution together in maximum parallelism semantics, then their executions are not visible to each other.) The new state of the system is obtained by executing all actions. This process is repeated indefinitely until we reach a state where no actions are enabled.

Interleaving semantics is useful when we can serialize the actions of different processes. Examples of such systems have been discussed in [2, 3]. maximum parallelism semantics captures executions of round-based algorithms where in each round, each process communicates information with other processes and utilizes this information to decide its own successive state. It can also be utilized to define time-driven systems such as TTA [18]. A program designed in maximum parallelism semantics can be implemented in a distributed system by adding a round number to every message and requiring every process to act only on messages received in current round. Examples of such protocols include [7, 11, 12].

2.2 Program representation in GP

The goal of GP is to evolve the given set of programs. In this paper, we begin with a set of statements st_1, st_2, $\cdots$, st_n and focus on evolving the guards under which they can be executed. While these statements could be chosen arbitrarily, we select them automatically based on the two criteria: 1) For each variable v, create a statement that assigns v a value based on the specification of the given program; 2) For each variable v, create a statement that assigns v a value from domain of v. If the given program has multiple variables in a given process, the same process is repeated for each variable. However, to avoid explosion of possible number of statements, statements updating different variables are run in parallel. By running in parallel, we mean that that all conditions in the guard are evaluated based on the initial state, i.e., they do not consider the effect of updating one variable in updating other variables. Note that the parallel update of several variables prevents explosive growth in the number of conditions. For example, if we have two statements updating every variable then we would need to consider $2 * n$ possible conditions instead of 2^n possible conditions if the same condition was used to update all variables at once. Thus, the program structure containing variables x, y and z is as shown in Figure 1.

```
Actions for variable x
      if       (condition 1) statement 1 for updating x
      elseif   (condition 2) statement 2 for updating x
      ...
||Actions for variable y
      ...
||Actions for variable z
      ...
```

Figure 1: Program structure

We consider some alternative approaches in Section 5.3 to evaluate performance of GP with different representation.

2.3 Running example for byzantine agreement

As a case study we synthesize fault-tolerant programs for the Byzantine agreement problem. The Byzantine agreement problem consists of one general, g and three non-generals, j, k, and l. First, the general makes a decision and communicates the decision to the non-generals. After communication with the general and each other, the non-generals need to finalize their decisions. This communication could be subject to a Byzantine fault where the Byzantine participant (general or non-general) sends incorrect values to other participants. The Byzantine agreement problem requires following specification:

1. Validity: if the general is non-byzantine, then the final decision of a non-byzantine non-general must be the same as that of the general.
2. Agreement: the final decision of two non-Byzantine processes must be the same.
3. Termination: all non-Byzantine non-generals must eventually finalize their decisions.

Given the structure of the problem, each process maintains a decision variable d. We concatenate the process name to denote the variable of that process. Hence, $d.g$ denotes the decision of process g, and $d.j$ denotes the decision of process j, and so on. The decision of a non-general can be 1, 0, or $\perp$ (where $\perp$ denotes that the process has not yet received the decision from the general). Additionally, each process maintains a read-only variable b. Thus, $b.j$ denotes that process j is Byzantine. Finally, all non-generals maintain a variable f; $f.j$ denotes j has finalized its decision or whether the decision of j is temporary.

Consider variable $d.j$ from process j, the domain of $d.j$ is $0, 1, \perp$. Hence, by criterion 2, we need to consider the case where $d.j$ is assigned to either 0, 1 or $\perp$. Also, by criterion 1, we need to consider the case where $d.j$ is assigned to $d.g$ (due to validity requirement) or $d.j$ is assigned to $d.k$ or $d.l$ (due to agreement requirement), where k and l are other non-general processes. Of these, we do not include $d.j = \perp$ since $\perp$ is intended to be used as uninitialized value. Process j has another variable $f.j$. Based on the criteria above, we need to consider the case where $f.j$ assigned either 0 or 1. Based on the specification, i.e., once a process finalizes its decision, it cannot undo it, we only consider the case where f is set to 1. Thus, the modeling of Byzantine agreement is of the form:

```
Actions for variable d.j
    if        (condition 1) d.j = d.g
    elseif    (condition 2) d.j = d.k
    elseif    (condition 3) d.j = d.l
    elseif    (condition 4) d.j = 0
    elseif    (condition 5) d.j = 1
||Actions for variable f.j
    if        (condition 6) f.j = 1
```

Figure 2: Byzantine program structure

In our experiments, we find that while the statements $d.j = d.k$ and $d.j = d.l$ have less contribution for the GP search, the remaining four statements provide optimal performance. Hence, we focus on those four statements in most experiments. We evaluate the effect of other choices in Section 5.3.

3. GENETIC PROGRAMMING

The overall framework is as follows: User inputs program variables, their domains and desired fault-tolerance properties. We create the program structure based on the approach described in Section 2, and GP takes these inputs and generates the corresponding fault-tolerant program. To construct guarded commands of the distributed program, we consider linear representation[22], i.e., a linear sequence of statements, and implement evolution by stack-based GP [28, 23]. Stack-based GP represents a program as a list of functions that consume from its stacks. It is able to directly perform on the linear statements. For genome, we use a vector of integers which are decoded into elementary units of a statement. The decoded units comprise into conditional statements by a pair of stacks (an operator stack and an operand stack). These conditional statements are the conditions in Figure 1 which will be optimized by GP. To utilize above genetic approach, we need to identify how to construct the objective function, which will describe next.

3.1 Objective functions and scenario-based multiobjectivization

The objective function computes the extent to which the current program satisfies its specification. We consider two approaches to evaluate objective function.

Simulation-based objective function. In simulation-based objective function, we consider different possible runs of the given program to identify whether it satisfies the specification. For example, if a given objective consists of N properties, $Q_1, Q_2, \cdots, Q_N$, then the objective function of program P for run e is given by the following formula:

$$F(P)_e = \frac{1}{n}(f(P \models_e Q_1) + f(P \models_e Q_2) + ... + f(P \models_e Q_N)),$$

where $f(P \models_e Q_i) = 1$ if P satisfies Q_i in run e, and $f(P \models_e Q_i) = 0$ if P does not satisfy Q_i in run e. For the case where multiple runs are utilized (e.g., with different inputs), the objective function value is normalized by taking the average of them. Thus, in this approach the objective function is always between $[0 \cdots 1]$.

BDD-based objective function. In BDD-based objective function, instead of executing programs GP statically verifies programs using BDD. We obtain a BDD representation of the current program, then utilize reachability techniques to identify reachable states, say R, of the given program. We identify states in R where either safety or liveness requirement is violated. For safety requirement, we obtain $R \cap sv$, where sv identifies states that imply violation of the safety condition. For liveness requirement of the form p leads to q, we obtain (1) states in R that are reachable from p without reaching q and are deadlocked, and (2) states in R that are reachable from p and from where we could reach a cycle without reaching q. If the current program is correct then the obtained set is the empty set. If not, we identify the number of min-terms in the violation set. We note that BDD packages provide an efficient approach to count the min-terms without enumeration.

Scenario-based multiobjectivization A typical fault-tolerant program has several requirements that identify the desired behaviors in different scenarios: in the absence of faults, in the presence of a single fault, in the presence of multiple faults, etc. Our goal is to find programs that work equally well in all scenarios. In this work, we present scenario-based multiobjective method, which sets one objective function for each scenario, to evolve the optimal programs.

3.2 Running example for Byzantine agreement

Based on the description of the specification, we consider three scenarios for the agreement problem: (1) when no process is Byzantine, (2) when some non-general is Byzantine, and (3) when the general is Byzantine. The goal of GP is to evolve programs that work equally well in all these scenarios. The objective $F(P)$ consists of the following three objective functions.

$$F(P) = [F_{no\_byz}(P), F_{byz\_non\_general}(P), F_{byz\_general}(P)]$$

Simulation-based objective functions

Objective 1: Effectiveness when there is no Byzantine process: Objective function is calculated as the average of two distinct cases: the decision of the general $d.g$ is 0; $d.g$ is 1. For each case, the program is evaluated based on the nine properties as below.

- From validity: $Q_1 = (d.j == d.g), Q_2 = (d.k == d.g), Q_3 = (d.l == d.g)$
- From agreement: $Q_4 = (d.j == d.k), Q_5 = (d.k == d.l), Q_6 = (d.j == d.l)$
- From termination: $Q_7 = (f.j == 1), Q_8 = (f.k == 1), Q_9 = (f, l == 1)$

The objective function $F_{no\_byz}(P)$ is now calculated by counting the number of properties that are satisfied and normalizing to 1.

$$F_{no\_byz}(P) = \frac{1}{2}\sum_{d.g=1}^{2}\frac{1}{9}\sum_{i=1}^{9} f(P \models Q_i)$$

Objective 2: Effectiveness when one of the non-generals is Byzantine: Let l be the Byzantine process of a non-general. A byzantine process can send different decisions to different participants. If l is the Byzantine process, then only Q_1, Q_2, Q_4, Q_7 and Q_8 (denoted as $Q_{relevant_l}$) have to be satisfied. Since we have three non-generals, the objective function is defined as follows:

$$F_{byz\_non\_general}(P) = \frac{1}{2}\sum_{d.g=1}^{2}\frac{1}{3}\sum_{byz}^{j,k,l}\frac{1}{5}(f(P \models Q_{relevant_{byz}})$$

Objective 3: Effectiveness when the general is Byzantine: If the general is Byzantine, then only $Q_4 - Q_9$ need to be satisfied. This experiment is repeated t times (run t times to capture the randomness of Byzantine general) and the objective function, hence,

$$F_{byz\_general}(P) = \frac{1}{t}\sum_{m=1}^{t}\frac{1}{6}\sum_{i=4}^{9} f(P \models Q_i);$$

BDD-based objective functions

We use the same three objectives with BDDs as well. The only difference is the violation of these objectives would be determined based on the number of min-terms (states).

Reevaluation of objective functions

Running GP with the objective function results in the following possible outcomes: (1) we obtain a correct program, (2) we fail to obtain a program with optimum objective value, or (3) we find a program with an optimum objective function although it is incorrect (it only occurs in simulation-based approach, since simulation-based approach is only testing a subset of computations.) . For the third outcome, we create a new objective function based on the counter-example that demonstrates the violation of the specification and utilize it in running the program.

4. CASE STUDIES

In addition to the running example of Byzantine agreement, we investigate two additional case studies: token ring problem and consensus with failure detector S. Token ring circulation problem is subject to *restart* of a process, where a process fails and is restored to a fixed initial state. Solving consensus in the presence of the crash fault using failure detector S guarantees (1) there exists a non-failed process that is never suspected by any other process, and (2) if a process fails, then the process is eventually detected by all non-failed processes. This latter case study also illustrates how maximum parallelism semantics can assist in designing a protocol that can be subsequently implemented using round numbers in interleaving (and message passing) semantics.

4.1 Fault-tolerant token ring

This case study synthesizes a fault-tolerant binary token ring program. A token ring program can be used to implement mutual exclusion by requiring that a process enters critical section only if it has the token. The token ring program consists of $N+1$ processes $0, 1, ..., N$. The token circulates along the processes from 0 to N. Each process has one variable x with the domain of $\{0, 1, \perp\}$, where $\perp$ denotes that the x value has been corrupted by a detectable fault. Process j, $j \neq 0$, has the token if and only if processes j and $j-1$ are not corrupted and $x.j \neq x.(j-1)$. Process 0 has token if and only if $(x.0 == x.N)$ where processes 0 and N are not corrupted.

Modeling program statements and objective functions

The generated token ring program is expected to satisfy following specifications:

1. Safety Specification: There is one token in the ring at any time.
2. Liveness Specification: The token also should be circulated infinitely often.

Based on the specification and the two criteria for designing statements from the beginning of Section 2.2, we allow $x.j$ value of a process to be updated to either 0 or 1 or a value based on $x.(j-1)$. The values 0 and 1 are based on the domain of $x.j$ and value of $x.(j-1)$ is based on the definition of j having a token. Also, similar to the byzantine agreement program, we consider three scenarios: (1) in the absence of faults, (2) in the presence of one fault, and (3) in the presence of multiple faults. Thus, the objective function is:

$$F(P) = [F_{no\_fault}(P), F_{one\_fault}(P), F_{multiple\_faults}(P)]$$

These objective functions are computed using the approach similar to the Byzantine agreement problem. Due to space limitation, we omit the details.

4.2 Consensus with failure detector S

In this case study, we focus on the problem of consensus using failure detector S. In the consensus protocol, each process starts with a vote. The goal of the protocol is that all processes reach an unanimous decision based on the set of votes. The specification for consensus problem is as follows.

1. Termination: Every correct process eventually decides some value.
2. Uniform integrity: Every process decides at most once.
3. Agreement: No two correct processes decide differently.
4. Uniform validity: If a process decides a value v, then some process proposed v.

As the goal of this protocol is to share the votes of processes to obtain a uniform view, we include variable V_p (to denote knowledge about votes of process p) and the variable D_p (to denote the message sent by p to share votes). Each of these variables is an array and $V_p[q]$ denotes the knowledge that p has about q. Likewise, $D_p[q]$ denotes the message sent by $p$about its vote of q. Subsequently, we identify the statements by which V_p and D_p could be updated. Based on the semantics of V_p, $V_p[p]$ is initialized to 0 or 1 based on the vote of p. And, for $p \neq q$, $V_p[q]$ is initialized to $\perp$ denoting that p is not aware of the vote of q. Finally, $D_p[q]$ is initialized to $\perp$, since no process has received any messages before the first round.

Given the structure of the statements of programs from Section 2.2, we consider the case where $V_p[q]$ is assigned either 0, 1, $\perp$ or the message it received $D_p[q]$. Likewise, possible values for $D_p[q]$ are either 0, 1, $\perp$ or $V_p[q]$. Of these, we omitted the values 0 or 1 since process p should not unilaterally change vote of q, $p \neq q$. (This restriction is not absolutely necessary since those protocols where process p changes the vote of q will fail to satisfy safety property.) We use the following constraints to determine whether the specification is satisfied. Of these, constraint Q_1 captures that the set of votes collected is nonempty, which allows us to guarantee termination. Uniform integrity is guaranteed by the program structure since all processes finalize after the given number of rounds. Agreement is checked by constraint Q_2 by making sure that the votes collected by any two processes are identical. Uniform validity is guaranteed by constraint Q_3.

$Q_1 : \forall p, \exists q \text{ such that } (V_p[q] \neq \perp)$
$Q_2 : \forall p, \forall q : \forall j, (V_q[j] == V_p[j])$
$Q_3 : \forall p, \forall q, (V_p[q] \neq \perp) : (V_p[q] == V_q[q])$

For this case study, when we consider the program execution in maximum parallelism semantics, simulation-based GP is not able to synthesize the desired program in the first step. Based on the discussion about reevaluation of objective function from Section 3.2, we consider adding multiple programs for different rounds. In simulation-based approach, we could find the program when the number of programs was three. We consider three different scenarios in simulation-based approach described below. BDD-based approach only needs first two objectives.

Objective 1: Effectiveness when there is no message loss and failure: In this case, every process is correct and, hence, no messages are lost.

Objective 2: Effectiveness when there is one or more failures with different message loss models: This case simulates both message loss and process failures. In the simulation-based evaluation, to consider as many different situations as possible, we apply various message loss rates ranging from 20% to 80% combining with various number of failure processes. Programs are tested up to 20 times with the different loss rates in one simulation-based evaluation.

Objective 3: In simulation-based approach, with the use of these two objectives, we are able to obtain the programs that satisfy objective function, however, the programs do not satisfy the specification of consensus. Hence, we defined a objective function that captured the corresponding counterexample as Objective 3.

5. EXPERIMENTS

In this section, we describe the results of our analysis on the different case studies presented earlier. We perform experiments in maximum parallelism semantics and in interleaving semantics. We also perform experiments using simulations and BDD-based analysis.

In these experiments, we use the population size of 100 (for Byzantine agreement and token ring) and 500 (consensus with S) and each individual program in the population have three objective functions.

We use single point crossover with the probability of 0.95. For mutation, we randomly flip a bit in the gene with the probability ranging from of 0.05 to 0.1. We set the maximum number of generations to 500. All the experiments in this paper are based on Intel CORE-i7 (2.9 GHz) machine with 8 GB RAM.

We partition our experimental results based on the comparison of different semantics considered in the paper and based on the different approaches for evaluating objective functions. To show the comparison of objective value evolution we scale all objective values to the range of [0, 1] and convert to the maximization problem.

5.1 Simulation-based approach vs BDD-based approach

In this section, we compare the performance of GP using simulation and BDD-based analysis. We use all three case studies in maximum parallelism semantics.

Byzantine agreement. Recall that the program for Byzantine agreement is based on the structure in Figure 2. We consider one of the variations of this program which uses only conditions 1, 4 and 5. Figure 3 shows the variation of population-average objective value of each scenario with generation number. It is clear from the figure that all three objectives of BDD-based approach reach the maximum value quickly (before 15th generation), whereas simulation-based approach converges to optimal solution after running 40 generations.

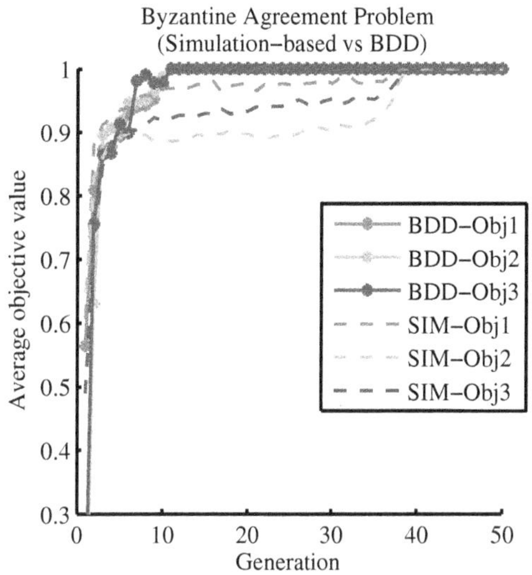

Figure 3: Variations of three objectives with generation is shown for the Byzantine agreement problem using BDD-based and simulation-based evaluation.

This is achieved partly due to the fact that a program may get *lucky* in simulation-based approach because the errors in the program are not discovered by the simulation. The states that indicate violation of the specification in BDD-based approach are significantly more fine-tuned than that of simulation-based approach.

Token ring. The results for token ring are as shown in Figure 4. A similar observation can be made here as well. Though the difference is not as much as Byzantine agreement problem (token ring problem is simpler than Byzantine agreement problem), the BDD-based approach still performs better.

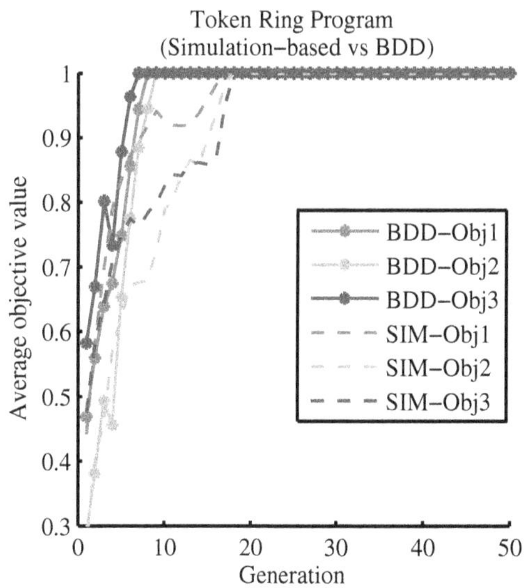

Figure 4: Variations of three objectives with generation is shown for the token ring program using BDD-based and simulation-based evaluation.

Consensus with failure detector S. The results for failure detector are as shown in Figure 5. The BDD-based approach shows better convergence, and equally emphasizes all three objectives. For simulation-based mehtod the first two objectives could reach the points near to the maximum quickly. However, the third objective fluctuates heavily throughout the evolution and does not converge to the optimal value. To summarize the outcome of these two

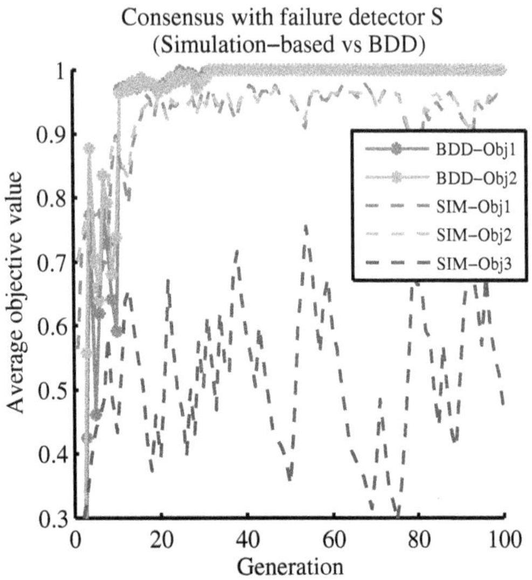

Figure 5: Variations of three objectives with generation is shown for the Consensus with failure detector S using BDD-based and simulation-based evaluation.

approaches, the performance metrics to obtain optimum programs are as shown in Table 1. We tabulate the number of successful runs (of up to 25 runs of GP) and best, median and worst number of generations required to arrive at the optimal solutions.

Table 1: Performance of simulation-based and BDD-based approach using maximum parallelism semantics

Optimization Problem	Evalutaion Method	Success Rate (%)	# of Gens to Converge Min	Median	Max
Byzantine	BDD	100	3	6	63
	Simulation	100	5	29	386
TokenRing	BDD	100	4	6	37
	Simulation	100	3	15	87
Consensus	BDD	80	7	33	404
	Simulation	72	8	179	479

The table shows that BDD-based approaches are quicker in the most of their runs, taking less number of generations to find the solution. Meanwhile, BDD-based reachability analysis is more effective. Also, we need to consider one symbolic run with BDDs as opposed to multiple runs (more than 20 time in consensus case study) with simulation-based approach. Besides, in consensus case study BDD-based one is even more successful. The simulation-based GP fails when we use objective 1 and objective 2. From the evolved programs of failed runs of GP, we derive counterexample and take it as third objective. The failure of GP at the first place is also expected as BDD-based approach provides higher graduation in objective value that allows better diversity, which is preferred in multi-objective optimization.

5.2 Comparison of maximum parallelism semantics and interleaving semantics

In this section, we compare the performance of GP under maximum parallelism semantics and interleaving semantics. The analysis performed in this section is based on BDD-based approach.

We use the same program format from Figure 2 for analysis of Byzantine agreement. The results are as mentioned in Figure 6. From this figure, we find that the GP works better with maximum parallelism semantics. The objective function converges faster in maximum parallelism semantics. This is due to the fact that for interleaving programs, processes are required to work well in all possible orders, which leads to smaller set of optimal solutions existing in the search space compared to maximum parallelism. In general, for the same program there are more reachable states in interleaving semantics than maximum parallelism semantics that increases the possibility of violated states.

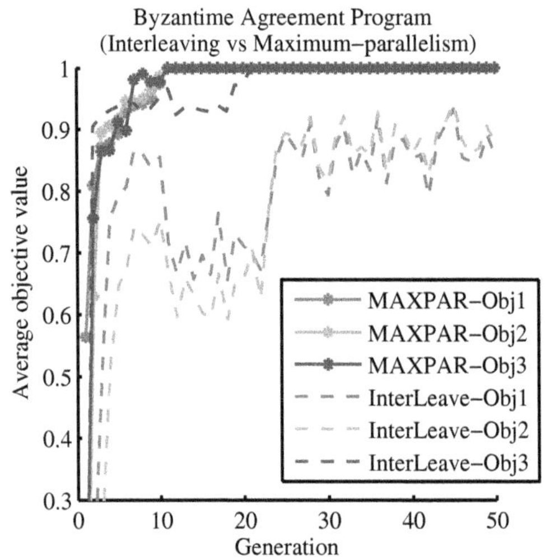

Figure 6: Variations of three objectives with generation is shown for the Byzantine agreement problem using maximum parallelism semantics and interleaving semantics.

For token ring shown in Figure 7, both approaches work equally well. We expect that this is due to simplicity of that program.

For the failure detector, we are unable to synthesize the required program in interleaving semantics. However, as mentioned earlier, the program in maximum parallelism semantics can be implemented in interleaving semantics with addition of round numbers.

Table 2 shows the performance metrics of maximum parallelism semantics and interleaving semantics. As mentioned above in the Byzantine agreement case study, the maximum parallelism outperforms in converging speed, and in this table it shows interleaving semantics are also less successful.

Table 2: Performance of maximum parallelism semantics and interleaving semantics using BDD evaluation

Optimization Problem	Semantics Format	Success Rate (%)	# of Gens to Converge Min	Median	Max
Byzantine	Max-Par	100	3	6	63
	Interleaving	24	189	309	443
TokenRing	Max-Par	100	4	6	37
	Interleaving	100	3	7	39

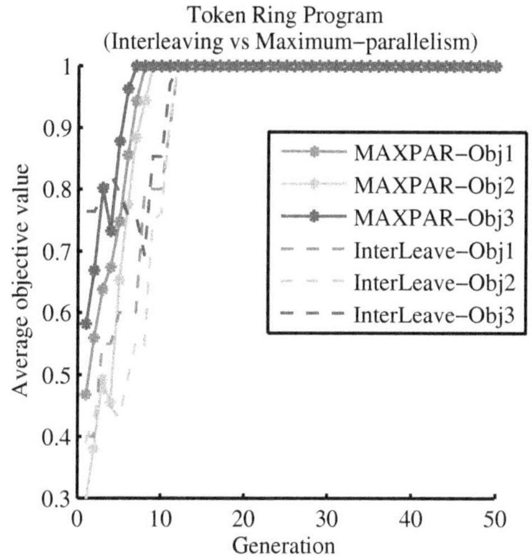

Figure 7: Variations of three objectives with generation is shown for the token ring program using maximum parallelism semantics and interleaving semantics.

5.3 Effect of choice of statements

We also consider the effect of using different statements in the synthesis. For example, Figure 2 identifies five possible statements for updating $d.j$ in Byzantine agreement program. We consider different subsets of these five statements to identify their effectiveness. In this experiment we test three different formats:
(1) *4-Statements-1* uses conditions 1, 4 and 5;
(2) *4-Statements-2* uses conditions 1, 2 and 3;
(3) *5-Statements* uses conditions 1, 4, 5 and compliment operation on $d.j$.
The results are presented in Table 3 . The table reveals an interesting fact that *4-Statements-2* has worst performance among all three variations of the program in both evaluation types, and the rest of two formats show the similar observation. This implies the program format influences the search process. We also observe that even in different program formats the BDD-based approach performs better overall.

Table 3: Performance of three different choices of statements solving Byzantine agreement problem in maximum parallelism semantics

Evaluation Type	Statements Format	Success Rate (%)	# of Gens to Converge Min	Median	Max
BDD	4-Statements-1	100	3	6	63
	4-Statements-2	96	4	18	222
	5-Statements	100	4	8	68
Sim	4-Statements-1	100	5	29	386
	4-Statements-2	88	6	68	111
	5-Statements	96	4	31	363

6. RELATED WORK

The related works for program synthesis can be categorized into several areas [13]: formal methods, machine learning based techniques (such as genetic programming), brute-force search and version space algebra, etc.

From the perspective of formal methods, some of the related works include program sketching [26], heuristic based addition of fault-tolerance [6, 14], controller synthesis [25] and Game-theoretic approaches [24]. In program sketching [26, 27], authors begin with a sketch of the program similar to ours and utilize tools such as SMT solvers to identify the conditions that are unspecified in the sketch. Literature on addition of fault-tolerance focuses on revising an existing program to add fault-tolerance with the help of heuristics. These heuristics attempt to manage the complexity of addition of fault-tolerance. However, if the heuristics fail, then addition of fault-tolerance fails. In contrast, GP uses evolutionary techniques to design the fault-tolerant program, hence, does not use heuristics. We expect that genetic approach will be more generic so it does not depend on pre-defined set of heuristics. Works on controller synthesis focus on adding a controller to an existing program (plant) so that it satisfies the desired specification. Game theoretic approaches for synthesizing controllers generally utilize the model of two-player games [29].

From the evolutionary perspective, GP automatically generates programs targeted toward a particular task. The GP can be used to search large problem spaces and find approximated solutions when it is allowed. GP could be an alternative method when other conventional techniques fail. It has a certain flexibility in aspect to enumerating complex programs and providing global perspective for the search. Due to the probabilistic feature of genetic operators GP has less chance of getting stuck. Most of the previous works focus on synthesizing the sequential program. In [1, 9], authors use GP to automatically repair software bugs. In [9], authors use tree-based program representation and employ test suite method to evaluate the candidate program by running on different test inputs. These work does not consider evloving distributed programs. In [31, 30], authors propose the approach of using rule-based GP to generate distributed programs. But their work does not consider fault-tolerant property and also does not apply model checking techniques. In [20], authors investigate the trading-off non-functional properties of a distributed program using genetic algorithm (GA) and PRISM. Several works [16, 15, 17] use model checking based fitness measurement for GP, however, these works does not consider the unpredictable environments.

One of the other search techniques for program synthesis is Brute-force and it is applied to find new programs in [4]. Compared to brute-force enumeration of programs, GP is a guided search process directed by given objectives. Version space algebra, introduced by [21], is a search technique which discovers a function that maps attributes to the binary sets from a set of hypotheses [21]. [19] uses version space algebra to synthesize repetitive robot programs and python programs.

7. CONCLUSION

In this paper, we focused on the use of genetic programming to synthesize fault-tolerant distributed programs. We evaluated their objective functions –either by simulation or by computing reachable states with the help of BDDs– based on the level to which they satisfy their specification. We adopted scenario-based multi-objectivization to consider program performance in different scenarios. We demonstrated effectiveness of BDD-based GP with a classic distributed problem - Byzantine agreement problem, token ring problem and consensus problem using failure detector S.

For the first time, we automatically synthesized consensus problem using failure detector S. Current pure heuristic methods failed to automatically synthesize this problem, because they have certain limitation on designing difficult distributed problems [5]. Evolutionary approach was more generic in that it did not depend on pre-defined set of heuristics but rather on the principle of evolution.

The experiments showed that analysis via BDDs improved effectiveness of GP by increasing the success rate and reducing the average number of generations before a solution can be found. This was achieved by effectively identifying all possible states from where specification is violated.

We also showed that synthesizing programs with maximum parallelism semantics was faster than that with interleaving semantics. Our analysis showed that GP was more effective under maximum parallelism semantics. This suggested that one way to make GP more effective in synthesizing distributed programs was to synthesize programs under maximum parallelism semantics and then transformed them into other models including interleaving semantics (via addition of round numbers) or more weaker formulations. Our case study in failure detector demonstrated the feasibility of this approach.

8. REFERENCES

[1] A. Arcuri and X. Yao. A novel co-evolutionary approach to automatic software bug fixing. In *Evolutionary Computation, 2008. IEEE World Congress on Computational Intelligence*, pages 162–168, 2008.

[2] A. Arora and M. Gouda. Closure and convergence: A foundation of fault-tolerant computing. *IEEE Trans. Software Engineering*, 19:1015–1027, 1993.

[3] A. Arora and M. G. Gouda. Distributed reset. *IEEE Trans. Computers*, 43(9):1026–1038, 1994.

[4] Y. Bar-David and G. Taubenfeld. Automatic discovery of mutual exclusion algorithms. In *Distributed Computing*, pages 136–150. Springer, 2003.

[5] B. Bonakdarpour, S. S. Kulkarni, and F. Abujarad. Symbolic synthesis of masking fault-tolerant distributed programs. *Distributed Computing*, 25(1):83–108, 2012.

[6] B. Bonakdarpour, S. S. Kulkarni, and F. Abujarad. Symbolic synthesis of masking fault-tolerant distributed programs. *Distributed Computing*, 25(1):83–108, 2012.

[7] T. D. Chandra and S. Toueg. Unreliable failure detectors for reliable distributed systems. *Journal of the ACM*, 43(2):225–267, Mar. 1996.

[8] K. Deb, A. Pratap, S. Agarwal, and T. Meyarivan. A fast and elitist multiobjective genetic algorithm: Nsga-ii. *IEEE Transactions on Evolutionary Computation*, 6(2):182–197, 2002.

[9] S. Forrest, T. Nguyen, W. Weimer, and C. L. Goues. A genetic programming approach to automated software repair. In *Proceedings of the 11th Annual conference on Genetic and evolutionary computation*, New York, NY, USA, 2009.

[10] S. Ghosh. *Distributed systems: an algorithmic approach.* CRC press, 2006.

[11] M. Gouda and F. Haddix. The linear alternator. *In Proceedings of the Third Workshop on Self-stabilizing Systems*, pages 31–47, 1997.

[12] M. Gouda and F. Haddix. The alternator. *In Proceedings of the Fourth Workshop on Self-stabilizing Systems*, pages 48–53, 1999.

[13] S. Gulwani. Dimensions in program synthesis. In *Proceedings of the 12th international ACM SIGPLAN symposium on Principles and practice of declarative programming*, pages 13–24. ACM, 2010.

[14] B. Jobstmann, A. Griesmayer, and R. Bloem. Program repair as a game. In *Computer Aided Verification*, pages 226–238, 2005.

[15] C. G. Johnson. Genetic programming with fitness based on model checking. In *Genetic Programming*, pages 114–124. Springer, 2007.

[16] G. Katz and D. Peled. Genetic programming and model checking: Synthesizing new mutual exclusion algorithms. In *Automated Technology for Verification and Analysis*, pages 33–47. Springer, 2008.

[17] G. Katz and D. Peled. Synthesizing, correcting and improving code, using model checking-based genetic programming. In *Hardware and Software: Verification and Testing*, pages 246–261. Springer, 2013.

[18] H. Kopetz and G. Bauer. The time-triggered architecture. *Proceedings of the IEEE*, 91(1):112–126, Jan 2003.

[19] T. Lau, P. Domingos, and D. S. Weld. Learning programs from traces using version space algebra. In *Proceedings of the 2Nd International Conference on Knowledge Capture*, K-CAP '03, pages 36–43, New York, NY, USA, 2003. ACM.

[20] A. Millard, D. White, and J. Clark. Searching for pareto-optimal randomised algorithms. In G. Fraser and J. Teixeira de Souza, editors, *Search Based Software Engineering*, volume 7515 of *Lecture Notes in Computer Science*, pages 183–197. Springer Berlin Heidelberg, 2012.

[21] T. M. Mitchell. Generalization as search. *Artificial Intelligence*, 18(2):203 - 226, 1982.

[22] M. Oltean, C. Grosan, L. Diosan, and C. Mihaila. Genetic programming with linear representation: a survey. *International Journal on Artificial Intelligence Tools*, 18(2):197–238, 2009.

[23] T. Perkis. Stack-based genetic programming. In *Evolutionary Computation, 1994. IEEE World Congress on Computational Intelligence., Proceedings of the First IEEE Conference on*, pages 148–153. IEEE, 1994.

[24] A. Pnueli and R. Rosner. On the synthesis of a reactive module. In *Principles of Programming Languages*, pages 179–190, 1989.

[25] P. J. Ramadge and W. M. Wonham. The control of discrete event systems. *Proceedings of the IEEE*, 77(1):81–98, 1989.

[26] A. Solar-Lezama. *Program Synthesis by Sketching*. PhD thesis, University of California, Berkeley, 2008.

[27] A. Solar-Lezama, R. Rabbah, R. Bodík, and K. Ebcioğlu. Programming by sketching for bit-streaming programs. In *ACM SIGPLAN Notices*, volume 40, pages 281–294. ACM, 2005.

[28] L. Spector and A. Robinson. Genetic programming and autoconstructive evolution with the push programming language. In *Genetic Programming and Evolvable Machines*, pages 7–40, 2002.

[29] W. Thomas. On the synthesis of strategies in infinite games. In *Theoretical Aspects of Computer Science*, pages 1–13, 1995.

[30] T. Weise and K. Tang. Evolving distributed algorithms with genetic programming. *IEEE Transactions on Evolutionary Computation*, 16(2):242–265, 2012.

[31] T. Weise, M. Zapf, and K. Geihs. Rule-based genetic programming. In *Bio-Inspired Models of Network, Information and Computing Systems, 2007. Bionetics 2007. 2nd*, pages 8–15, 2007.

Multiple Objective Vector-Based Genetic Programming Using Human-Derived Primitives

Jason Zutty, Daniel Long, Heyward Adams, and Gisele Bennett
Electro-Optical Systems Laboratory
Georgia Tech Research Institute
Atlanta, GA 30332
jason.zutty@gtri.gatech.edu,
daniel.long@gtri.gatech.edu,
heyward.adams@gtri.gatech.edu,
gisele.bennett@gtri.gatech.edu

Christina Baxter
Combating Terrorism Technical Support Office
Alexandria, VA 22350
christina.baxter@cttso.gov

ABSTRACT

Traditional genetic programming only supports the use of arithmetic and logical operators on scalar features. The GTMOEP (Georgia Tech Multiple Objective Evolutionary Programming) framework builds upon this by also handling feature vectors, allowing the use of signal processing and machine learning functions as primitives, in addition to the more conventional operators. GTMOEP is a novel method for automated, data-driven algorithm creation, capable of outperforming human derived solutions.

As an example, GTMOEP was applied to the problem of predicting how long an emergency responder can remain in a hazmat suit before the effects of heat stress cause the user to become unsafe. An existing third-party physics model was leveraged for predicting core temperature from various situational parameters. However, a sustained high heart rate also means that a user is unsafe. To improve performance, GTMOEP was evaluated to predict an expected pull time, computed from both thresholds during human trials.

GTMOEP produced dominant solutions in multiple objective space to the performance of predictions made by the physics model alone, resulting in a safer algorithm for emergency responders to determine operating times in harsh environments. The program generated by GTMOEP will be deployed to a mobile application for their use.

Categories and Subject Descriptors

• **Computing methodologies–Machine learning approaches** • **Computing methodologies–Genetic programming** • *Computing methodologies–Search methodologies* • Computing methodologies–Model development and analysis

GECCO '15, July 11 - 15, 2015, Madrid, Spain
Copyright 2015 ACM ISBN 978-1-4503-3472-3/15/07
DOI: http://dx.doi.org/10.1145/2739480.2754694 ...$15.00.

General Terms

Algorithms

Keywords

Genetic Programming; Evolutionary Programming; Machine Learning; Signal Processing

1. INTRODUCTION

Traditional genetic programming only supports the use of arithmetic and logical operators on scalar features. When approaching an optimization problem from this frame of reference, there are two apparent issues. First, any solutions created by genetic programming in this way must evolve up from the most basic of building blocks. This is a task that took nature billions of years to accomplish. Second, these low-level scalar features make it difficult to leverage the human-generated solutions that have already been discovered in many areas of application.

Adding support for higher-level features, such as vectors and matrices, enables the usage of more advanced primitives, such as signal processing and machine learning functions. Along with the standard set of primitives, we are able to evolve solutions in domains where genetic programming previously could not outperform even the most basic machine learning algorithms. We will show that when genetic programming can leverage the solutions we are trying to outperform, we can achieve dominant results.

There are many challenges that must be addressed in order to successfully work with high-level primitives in the way we have described. In order to support machine learners, training data and testing data must be passed through the program and the same operations that were performed on training data must be performed on testing data at any given step of the program. Strongly typed genetic programming enforces the rigidity required by the functional blocks we use, but the standard data types available are too limiting; they do not allow data to flow naturally from primitive to primitive. We require a custom type to contain our data and wrapper methods that allow our primitives to understand this type. This allows the output of any one block, whether it is a signal processor or a machine learner, to be an input to the next method.

The container type must also be understood by evaluation functions, since this formulation requires the object to be both the input to and output of the entire program.

Despite the use of more advanced basis functions, the fundamental attributes of genetic programming (mating, mutating, and selection) are still in place here, and this means evaluation of multitudes of individuals is still necessary. These individuals, however, are more expensive to evaluate than those in traditional genetic programming due to the cascading of machine learning functions and the use of larger amounts of data. Generating solutions in a reasonable amount of time requires access to a computer cluster that can support memory-intensive processes.

This is a natural evolution of previous work. Past attempts at combining genetic programming and machine learning have invoked a very rigid search space, focusing on either feature construction or the optimization of an existing learner or set of learners. There has been very little work performed which utilizes both of these approaches. When combined, there is much added benefit to be gained from the cascading of the results of these methods.

The GTMOEP (Georgia Tech Multiple Objective Evolutionary Programming) framework, introduced in this paper, builds on the standard set of primitives by handling feature vectors, in addition to scalar features. In this framework, we have wrapped many signal processing and machine learning functions as primitives, in addition to the more conventional operators. GTMOEP was used to produce an algorithm that predicts how long an emergency responder can remain in a hazmat suit before the effects of heat stress cause the user to become unsafe. This estimate is called the *downrange time.*

We supplement an externally created physics-based model for computing a user's core temperature under heat stress. This model is incomplete for our purposes because the downrange time depends on both the user's core temperature and heart rate. The results of this problem showcase many of GTMOEP's advanced capabilities, including support for human-derived algorithms as primitives, Monte Carlo evaluation of cross-folded data, multiple data sets, hypercube distance scaling, feature vectors, and seeding of the optimization using previously generated results.

2. BACKGROUND

While genetic programming has not been used to directly operate on both machine learning and signal processing algorithms simultaneously, it has been used in conjunction with existing machine learning and signal processing methods individually, often achieving significant performance gains over the base algorithms.

2.1 Feature Construction

Using genetic programming to perform feature construction or selection for machine learning is a well-researched field. There have been numerous approaches to allowing the evolution of optimal feature sets.

H. Guo et al. [5] used genetic programming from very basic operators to generate features for machine learning classifiers. The authors compared the results of an artificial neural network (ANN) and a support vector machine (SVM). For both types of classifiers, the features generated by genetic programming showed significant improvements over the standard signal processing techniques.

Holladay et al. [8] introduce a concept that we borrow heavily from, vector-based genetic programming. In this formulation of genetic programming, primitives act on vectors of inputs, rather than scalars. We combine this with a notion from Vera et al., [17] which uses genetic programming on vector-based time series data with the last value of the series representing the prediction. This provides us with a starting place from which to target combining both signal processing methods and machine learning functions with traditional primitives.

Streater [16] used genetic programming to evolve feature construction programs from basic primitives for inputs to machine learners and evolved parameters for the SVMs he used for classification. The results were scored for fitness based on the performance of several machine learning algorithms on the constructed feature set. Rather than working with scalar coefficients or derived features, the inputs to the genetic program were six matrices, each of which represents a different channel of an image. However, high-level primitives were not used in his instruction set and, rather than include the learners in the evolutionary tree, they were used solely for evaluation.

L. Guo et al. [6] applied genetic programming to the problem of feature extraction in electroencephalographic (EEG) signals. Their system consumes a feature vector, which is created by using a discrete wavelet transform (DWT), and evolves new features computed from the input set. The final set of features is sent to a k-Nearest Neighbors (kNN) classifier. It should be noted, however, that the genetic programming was only performed on scalar elements of the feature vector. While L. Guo et al. were able to show significant improvement over the kNN classification by itself, treating the DWT coefficients as scalars limited the traction they achieved.

Al-Sahaf et al. [1] developed a hybrid algorithm which uses a nearest neighbor classifier to map genetic programming output to a class label. This model was applied to a variety of health-related datasets from the UCI Machine Learning Repository [2]. While this approach showed improvements over naïve Bayes, SVM, and kNN applied directly to the data, the search space of evolved algorithms is limited by the small set of operators: addition, subtraction, multiplication, and division.

2.2 Classification and Prediction

Lee and Tong [10] showed the ability of genetic programming to combine with the autoregressive integrated moving average (ARIMA) filter to improve time series predictions. The hybrid methodology used the form $\hat{y}_t = \hat{L}_t + \hat{N}_t$, where the predicted signal $\hat{y}_t$ is the sum of the predictions of the ARIMA filter $\hat{L}_t$, which forecasts the linear component of the data, and the genetic programming $\hat{N}_t$, which forecast the non-linear residuals. For the non-linear portion, they found a lower dependence on the size of available data sets and were able to achieve higher quality results than other machine learning techniques, including SVM and ANN. While they did combine traditional machine learning techniques with genetic programming, they did so in a very limited fashion, applying it with a standard set of basic operators and only focusing on errors made by a linear model.

Ravisankar et al. [13] proposed a hybrid of genetic programming and machine learning in order to predict the failures of dotcom companies. The authors divided the problem into its two key pieces, feature selection and classification. A hybrid algorithm used a different machine learning technique for feature selection than for classification. However, the authors did not consider feature construction. Cascaded combinations of both selection and construction allow for more complicated solutions.

Zhang et al. [18] combined genetic programming with SVMs to produce credit scoring models, using a divide and conquer approach like Lee and Tong. Genetic programming was used to develop a set of classification rules for the data. Any residual data not assigned a class by genetic programming would be classified using an SVM. The authors were able to produce hybrid algorithms that had higher accuracies than any standalone machine learners. However, they enforce an unnecessary limitation on the type of machine learner used and limit genetic programming to only produce classification rules. Both of these human derived choices can themselves be open to optimization.

In Sherrah et al.'s work [15], the genetic program was allowed to not only create and select features but also choose from three different classifiers as well. When compared to standard machine learners, error was reduced in eight out of the nine tested data sets. However, once again the genetic program was limited by scalar features, basic primitives, and a rigid structure.

While it is clear that combining traditional machine learning techniques with genetic programming has been successfully accomplished in various areas of application, the current state of the art has not yet opened up the entire algorithm creation process to genetic programming. We enable the modification of features and cascade the results of machine learning operations by using genetic programming in order to create new solutions, thus addressing the limitations of the works presented in this section.

3. GTMOEP FRAMEWORK

The Georgia Tech Multiple Objective Evolutionary Programming (GTMOEP) framework is built on top of DEAP (Distributed Evolutionary Algorithms in Python) [4], an existing genetic programming framework. DEAP was selected for several reasons, including its active development, distributed evaluation, and plug and play design. Using this framework, we were able to drop in our own definitions of individuals, primitives, terminals, and genetic operators, allowing us to support a new data type that ties together training and testing data. GTMOEP combines signal processing and machine learning algorithms with boolean logic and arithmetic operators and other primitives in order to create high-level algorithms that are capable of outperforming human derived solutions.

3.1 Building Blocks

GTMOEP uses strongly typed genetic programming, which enforces a set of rules during the tree creation, mating, and mutation processes. In order to build complex classification and prediction algorithms, it was necessary to add the ability to pass data back and forth between signal processing functions and machine learning functions.

To handle these transactions, we created a Python class which stores various representations of the features and class information for each data set. These data objects were paired together in a new class which supports testing and training data. This allows the same signal processing methods to be applied to the testing and training data before and after going through the machine learning operations. GTMOEP also allows the truth data to be directly compared with the results of the test data at the end of the program.

Eighty-four functions from existing Python toolboxes such as Scikit [12] and Scipy [9] (as well as several hand coded methods) were wrapped so that they could be incorporated into a strongly typed tree structure using DEAP. Because this structure acts on pairs of training data and testing data, the wrapping function must be able to accept the input and produce the output in this format.

The machine learning methods that were wrapped include:

- Best Linear Unbiased Predictor (BLUP)
- Decision trees
- k-means clustering
- k-Nearest Neighbors (kNN)
- Naïve Bayes
- Orthogonal Matching Pursuit (OMP)
- Random forest
- Spectral clustering
- Support Vector Machines (SVM)

Feature construction and selection is handled mostly by signal processing functions, including:

- Autocorrelation
- Discrete Cosine Transform (DCT)
- Discrete Wavelet Transform (DWT)
- Fast Fourier Transform (FFT)
- Filters
- Principle Component Analysis (PCA)

Seven different terminal functions were needed to support the wrapped functions; generally, one to generate terminals of each input type: float, boolean, integer, and a few custom data specific types.

3.2 Mating and Mutation

GTMOEP supports multiple mating methods, including single point crossover, ephemeral-only crossover, headless chicken crossover, and headless chicken ephemeral crossover. Single point crossover is the traditional mating operator proposed by Koza and is leveraged directly from DEAP. Ephemeral-only crossover is a mating method we developed for the specialization of exchanging regeneratable terminals between individuals, rather than entire subtrees as in traditional crossover. This method of mating is our way of supporting tuning, making this technique closer in spirit to genetic algorithms than to genetic programming, as it is only transferring parameters. Headless chicken mating is single point crossover with a randomly generated tree. As one would expect, headless chicken ephemeral crossover is ephemeral-only crossover with a randomly generated tree.

The mutation methods we support are insertion, ephemeral, node replacement, uniform, and shrink. All five are implemented by DEAP. It is worth noting that in order for the shrink mutation (also known as the node removal operator) to function properly, an added objective is required: the depth of the tree. This is because an algorithm that performs as well as another should be considered to be dominant if it is smaller (less complex).

3.3 Selection

Selection was performed using the nondominated sorting genetic algorithm (NSGA-II) [3], a binary tournament in which dominance is given by

$$\begin{aligned} i \prec_n j \quad &\text{if} \quad (i_{\text{rank}} < j_{\text{rank}}) \quad \text{or} \\ &((i_{\text{rank}} = j_{\text{rank}}) \quad \text{and} \quad (i_{\text{distance}} > j_{\text{distance}})). \end{aligned} \tag{1}$$

Here, $i \prec_n j$ means that individual i dominates j, and this occurs if i_{rank}, the Pareto (nondomination) rank, is lower than j_{rank}, which means that i closer to the Pareto front. In the case of a tie in rank, $i \prec_n j$ if i_{distance}, the crowding distance of i, is greater than j_{distance}, indicating individual i falls in a less crowded region.

Crowding distances were modified prior to selection by applying the hypercube distance (HCD) scaling algorithm proposed by Rohling. [14] Two thresholds were determined for each of the objective functions: an "achievable" level and a "goal". GTMOEP iterates through each individual and modifies each crowding distance according to the formula

$$i_{\text{scaled distance}} = i_{\text{distance}} \times \frac{1+\alpha}{\alpha + \left(\sum_{k=0}^{K} HCD[k]\right)^{\frac{1}{p}}}, \tag{2}$$

where α and p are constant weight parameters (in our case chosen to be 0.5 and 2, respectively), K is the number of objectives, and $HCD[k]$ is

$$\begin{cases} 1, & f_k \geq \text{achievable}_k \\ 0, & f_k \leq \text{goal}_k \\ \left(\dfrac{f_k - \text{goal}_k}{\text{achievable}_k - \text{goal}_k}\right)^p, & \text{otherwise} \end{cases} \tag{3}$$

in a minimization scheme. In Equation 3, f_k represents the objective score, achievable_k is the threshold for an achievable result, and goal_k is a desired objective value. HCD scaling allows for the acceptance of an individual in a more crowded region if that region is more "interesting".

This procedure serves to steer the selection process towards regions of interest in objective space. The scaling factor in our usage is bounded to be between $\frac{3}{1+2\sqrt{K}}$ (occurring when the individual lies outside of the achievable region) and 3 (which occurs when the individual lies inside of the goal region).

In GTMOEP, an elite pool is maintained and used to create a gene pool in each generation by appending any evaluated offspring, performing selection, and recomputing the elite pool. Unlike the offspring selection process (which uses an NSGA-II scheme), a strength Pareto evolutionary algorithm (SPEA2) [19] truncation scheme is used to select the elite pool. A brief description of this process follows.

The fitness of each individual is computed as $F(i) = R(i) + D(i)$. Here, $R(i)$ is the raw fitness score of individual i and $D(i) = \frac{1}{\sigma_i^k + 2}$, where σ_i^k is the distance to the kth nearest data point to i. The gene pool is sorted in ascending order by fitness, since SPEA2 is a minimization scheme. After the SPEA2 sorting, the pool is truncated to the N_{elite} lowest (best) elements. These elements form the elite pool.

It is worth noting that the crowding distance in the elite pool calculation is not scaled using the HCD operator as it was for our modified NSGA-II. This can result in a wider coverage of the objective space in the elite pool than is desired by the thresholds set for each objective. The advantage, however, is slightly more genetic diversity being preserved from generation to generation.

4. APPLICATION

4.1 Problem Statement

Emergency responders are required to wear personal protective equipment when responding to a variety of threats, primarily chemical, nuclear, and biological agents. In addition to the dangers posed by these substances, the personnel also risk suffering the effects of heat stress from the microclimate inside their hazmat suits, the type of work being performed, and the external environment.

The effects of heat stress can be detected in changes in a user's core temperature or heart rate[1]. If a subject's heart rate is sustained[2] above $0.9 \times (220 - \text{Age})$ or the subject's core temperature exceeds 38.5 degrees Celsius, then the emergency responder is considered to be at risk. It is not recommended that an operator remain within a vapor-tight protective garment for greater than one hour. We have used this as an upper bound for our trials. The earliest time in the trial at which any of these constraints is violated is called the *expected pull time*.

GTMOEP was used to create algorithms which predict expected pull time, given characteristics of the user, the type of suit in question, and the environment under consideration.

4.2 Data Collection

Data was collected at two facilities by The Netherlands Organisation for Applied Scientific Research (TNO) in Delft, Netherlands and North Carolina State University (NCSU) in Raleigh, NC, USA. Subjects were asked to use a treadmill at varying intensities in different environments, wearing a selection of suits. The data collection matrix for the 163 trials that were performed is shown in Table 1. During the trials, numerous sensors recorded data, including one heart rate sensor, one core temperature sensor, five microclimate relative humidity sensors, five microclimate temperature sensors, and five different skin temperature sensors. Depending on the trial, data was sampled from each of the sensors at a rate of one sample every ten or fifteen seconds.

[1]Throughout this paper, heart rate is measured in beats per minute, temperature is measured in degrees Celsius, and age is measured in years.

[2]By sustained, we mean that the heart rate continuously stays above the threshold for at least a minute.

Table 1: Data Collection Matrix. Cells contain counts of trials.

Climate	Hot & Dry			Warm & Humid			Neutral			Total
Intensity	Low	Medium	High	Low	Medium	High	Low	Medium	High	
Suit A	0	8	0	0	8	0	6	6	6	34
Suit B	0	8	0	0	16	0	8	8	8	48
Suit C	0	0	0	0	8	0	0	9	0	17
Suit D	0	8	0	0	0	0	0	8	0	16
Suit E	0	0	0	0	8	0	8	8	8	32
Suit F	0	8	0	0	0	0	0	8	0	16
Total	0	32	0	0	40	0	22	47	22	163

4.3 Physics-Based Model

We received a first-principles physics-based model [11] from our sponsor. It was developed by physiologists for thermal analysis, and provides time series predictions for a subject's core temperature based on 331 parameters that describe the following:

- the clothing
- the activity being performed
- the environment
- physical attributes of the user

The model does not provide the ability to predict heart rate. Also, for accurate predictions, it requires information that will be unavailable to the user at time of use; most notably, an initial core temperature. The results of this model are used as one of our features, which are described in the next section.

4.4 Feature Space

Although GTMOEP has the capability to work with time-domain data frames, for this problem we concentrated on operating directly in feature space. We decided to frame the problem in this manner due to the unavailability of real-time heart rate and core temperature data from the subject during a trip downrange. All predictions will need to be constructed from actionable situational data: the physical description of the subject, the environmental parameters that can easily be measured in the field, and the parameters that make up the suit that the user will be wearing. The eight features we use to predict expected pull time are shown in Table 2. The physics model's predictions were all generated beforehand using the software package provided by TNO on each row in our dataset, in order to increase the efficiency of running the optimization. In the field, they will be generated on demand.

Out of the 163 trials performed, 120 were used for constructing the feature set. The trials in which the activity was terminated prior to the expected pull time were excluded because in these instances we do not have a truth value with which we can compare our predictions.[3]

[3]Actual pull time is the time at which the trial was actually concluded. This can be less than the expected pull time due to a measurement error or a subject voluntarily terminating his or her trial early. Both cases occurred.

Table 2: Input features used by GTMOEP to predict expected pull time.

Feature
Age (years)
Height (meters)
Weight (kg)
Intensity (discrete value, indicating 2.5, 4, or 5.5 km/hr)
Temperature (degrees Celsius)
Relative humidity (percent)
Suit (discrete value, meaning one of six hazmat suits)
Physics model prediction (seconds)

4.5 Evaluation

Individual algorithms were evaluated using five randomly generated folds of the data set. Care was taken to ensure that if a subject appeared in multiple trials, then all of that subject's trials would be in either the training or the testing set. For each fold, 80% of the subjects were placed in the training set and the remaining trials were used as testing data. The objective scores are calculated based on the algorithm's ability to successfully predict values for the test data, and each objective was averaged over the five folds of the data. GTMOEP stores the results of each evaluation in a hash table, where the keys are SHA-256 hashes of the parse tree representation of each individual. This allows GTMOEP to easily and efficiently recognize and retrieve already evaluated solutions, trading the expensive evaluation time for the inexpensive hash table look-up. Evaluations were limited in memory resources to ensure that the cluster of computers used to distribute this work remained healthy over the course of the optimization. Each evaluation spawns a separate process to monitor the memory usage during computation of the individual, and in this instance limited usage to 7.6 GB of memory per algorithm. This was rarely reached due to the relatively small number of rows in the data set.

Evaluation was performed on a cluster of eighteen computers running Red Hat Enterprise Linux (RHEL) 5. The individuals were distributed through DEAP's built-in integration with SCOOP (**S**calable **Co**ncurrent **O**perations in **P**ython) [7], which works in conjunction with our cluster's management software, Son of Grid Engine (SGE), to distribute the load across our nodes effectively. We used a parallel environment allocation rule in SGE to ensure that only three jobs were running on each machine. This yielded us fifty-three total evaluation slots and one root worker performing the evolutionary loop.

4.6 Evolutionary Parameters

For this problem, we used four mating operators with different rates of application: one-point crossover (50%), ephemeral-only crossover (50%), headless chicken crossover (10%), and headless chicken ephemeral crossover (10%). The mutation methods used and their rates of application were: insertion (5%), ephemeral (25%), node replacement (5%), uniform (5%), and shrink (5%).

The optimization began with a population of 512 individuals that were randomly created. The tree depth varied from one to five nodes. During the optimization depth was not fixed, however bloat was prevented by using depth as an objectve. The elite pool was chosen to be a fixed size of 512 individuals as well. Two hundred individuals were selected to be evaluated in each generation, meaning selection was generally performed from approximately 712 individuals, depending on the arrival of results.[4]

4.7 Objective Functions

Algorithms were produced by GTMOEP in two phases of optimization with two different sets of objectives.

If $\{y_j\}_{j=1}^N$ are the expected pull times (truth values) and $\{\hat{y}_j\}_{j=1}^N$ are the corresponding predictions (so that $\hat{y}_k$ is the predicted value of y_k for $k = 1, 2, \ldots, N$) and if $J = \{1, 2, \ldots, N\}$ is the set indexing the sequences, then $J_{\text{under}} = \{j \in J : \hat{y}_j < y_j\}$ is the set of indices where *under predictions* occurred and $J_{\text{over}} = \{j \in J : \hat{y}_j > y_j\}$ is the set of indices where *over predictions* occurred.

4.7.1 *First Set*

The first set of objective functions were chosen to minimize different types of errors in prediction. They were:

- Root Mean Squared (RMS) error, $\sqrt{\frac{1}{N}\sum_{k=1}^{N}(y_k - \hat{y}_k)^2}$
- mean over prediction, $f(J_{\text{over}})$
- mean under prediction, $f(J_{\text{under}})$
- percent error
- the depth of the algorithm's tree

where $f(K) = \frac{1}{|K|}\sum_{k \in K} |y_k - \hat{y}_k|$.

4.7.2 *Second Set*

For the second cycle, the Pareto front from the first cycle was used to seed the optimization. This set of objective functions was designed to explicitly reduce the variability in error in addition to the size of the error. They were:

- mean over prediction
- mean under prediction
- count of over predicted trials, $|J_{\text{over}}|$
- count of under predicted trials, $|J_{\text{under}}|$

[4]GTMOEP does not use generation synchronization, but rather creates a queue of solutions to evaluate. It spawns a new generation when the queue falls below a certain size (in this case, one hundred individuals).

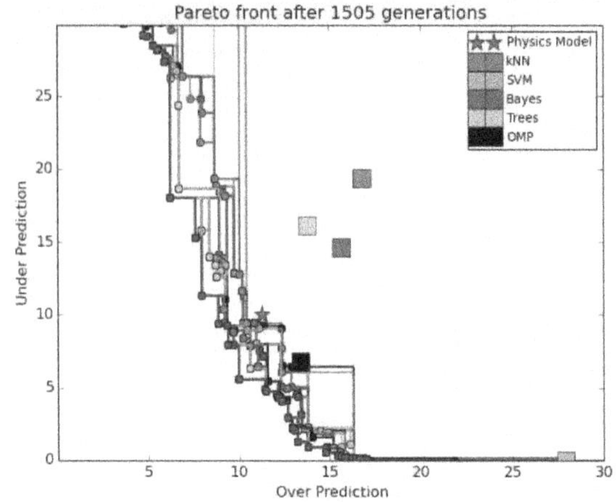

Figure 1: Pareto fronts generated by GTMOEP when projected from 5 dimensions to 2 dimensions: mean over and under prediction, displayed in minutes.

- standard deviation of over prediction, $g(J_{\text{over}})$
- standard deviation of under prediction, $g(J_{\text{under}})$
- maximum over prediction, $h(J_{\text{over}})$
- maximum under prediction, $h(J_{\text{under}})$
- the depth of the algorithm's tree

Here $g(K) = \sqrt{\frac{1}{|K|}\sum_{k \in K}(x_k - \bar{x})^2}$ is the standard deviation of $x_k = |y_k - \hat{y}_k|$ over the set K and $h(K) = \max_{k \in K} |y_k - \hat{y}_k|$.

5. RESULTS AND DISCUSSION

5.1 Baseline Results

Beginning our evolutionary process with a human-generated solution affords us a point in objective space against which we can compare our automatically generated algorithms. In this case, we used the physics-based model described in Section 4.3 by itself to predict a subject's core temperature over time. These predictions were used in turn to predict expected pull time, as described in Section 4.1. The results of evaluating the model against our objective functions from Section 4.7 can be seen in Table 3.

This table also shows the results of other human-derived primitives that were applied to the feature space and objective functions. As described in Section 3.1, these machine learning functions are used by GTMOEP as primitives. By itself, the physics-based model is dominant or codominant to all of these functions. When leveraged together, we were able to produce algorithms that are dominant to all of these single-element solutions.

5.2 First Cycle of GTMOEP: 5 Objectives

A graph of the Pareto fronts over time of two objectives from our five objective optimization is shown in Figure 1.

Table 3: 9 Objectives Machine Learner Performance. Errors are in minutes.

ID	Mean		Maximum		Standard Deviation		Depth of Tree
	Over	Under	Over	Under	Over	Under	
430	10.4	9.5	25.2	26.0	8.83	6.15	3
431	10.4	9.5	25.2	26.0	8.83	6.15	2
541	11.0	9.4	26.2	26.8	8.46	6.17	6
544	11.3	9.4	26.8	26.7	8.84	6.16	3
545	11.3	9.4	26.8	26.7	8.84	6.16	4
1359	10.9	8.0	28.1	22.9	8.68	6.01	3
1361	10.9	8.0	28.0	22.9	8.67	6.00	5
1451	11.3	9.0	28.3	24.2	8.21	6.15	4
1834	10.3	7.6	31.6	22.3	9.24	6.18	4
Physics Model	11.3	10.0	38.8	28.5	9.30	6.21	1
kNN	16.8	19.4	33.3	43.0	10.53	11.43	1
SVM	27.9	0.0	51.5	0.0	12.22	0.00	1
Bayes	15.7	14.6	38.1	24.1	11.09	7.37	1
Trees	13.8	16.1	40.7	28.9	11.62	9.65	1
Random Forest	16.9	13.3	42.9	29.8	12.15	9.47	1
k-means clustering	0.0	42.8	0.0	60.0	0.00	16.74	1
BLUP	1,099.0	764.7	5,885.3	2,348.5	1,575.09	722.45	1
OMP	13.4	6.8	29.1	22.6	8.99	5.48	1

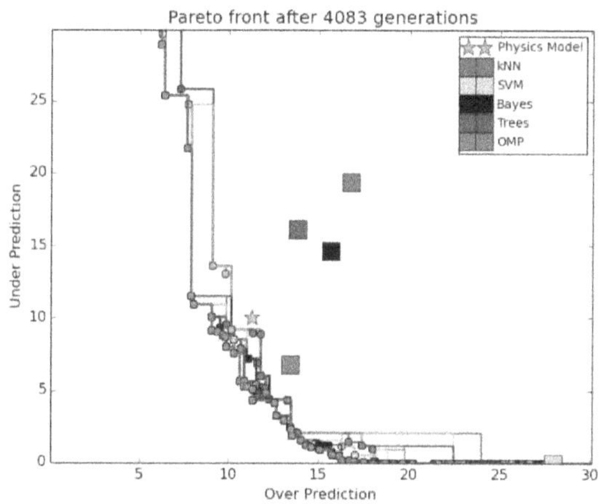

Figure 2: Pareto fronts generated by GTMOEP when projected from 9 dimensions to 2 dimensions: mean over and under prediction, displayed in minutes.

Because both objectives represent error metrics, they are both to be minimized. The inner-most (bottom left) line represents the final Pareto front computed in these two dimensions. Analysis of these scores illustrates the power of GTMOEP, which evolves starting with human-derived point solutions to reach Pareto-dominant solutions to human-generated algorithms. With a mean over prediction of 11.3 minutes, and a mean under prediction of 10.0 minutes for the physics-based model, there are numerous solutions on the final Pareto front to choose from. Each of the human-derived machine learners that are used as primitives in GTMOEP have been dominated by our solutions in the plotted objectives.

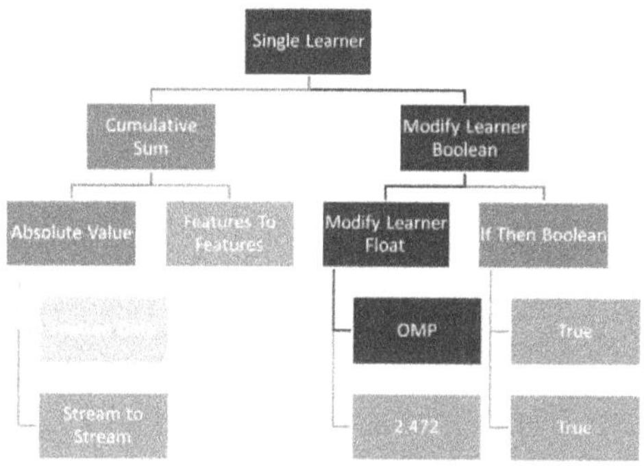

Figure 3: An algorithm which dominates the physics-based model. This result was chosen to be used in the field.

5.3 Second Cycle of GTMOEP: 9 Objectives

After presenting the results from Section 5.2 to our sponsor, they inquired about a further set of criteria, discussed in Section 4.7.2, which can be used to assess performance. A second optimization was performed using the Pareto front of the previous optimization as a set of seeds. The Pareto front over time for this cycle is shown in Figure 2. A selection of solutions which were dominant to the physics based model is shown in Table 3. [5] GTMOEP's dominance of the physics-based model and the basic machine learners holds in the two objectives of interest.

Table 3 shows the ten solutions in the nine objective space generated by GTMOEP that were dominant with respect to the physics-based model. There are also results not shown that are dominant in all objectives to the human-derived machine learners. The algorithm that was chosen for implementation corresponds to ID 1359 in the table and this

[5]Depth, count over, and count under do not factor into dominance. We seek to minimize these objectives, but they do not have negative effects on performance.

algorithm's tree is presented in Figure 3. This algorithm was selected over the other options because it offers similar performance in over prediction error, while significantly reducing under prediction error and maximum error in both the under and over predicted cases.

6. CONCLUSIONS

GTMOEP elevates the capabilities of standard genetic programming techniques to produce solutions that can outperform human generated algorithms. We have leveraged complex vector-based feature construction and machine learning functions as primitives to improve on the performance of predictions by a physics-based model, resulting in a safer algorithm for determining how long a first responder can spend in a hazmat suit. This algorithm will be distributed on mobile devices and deployed for use in pairing responders for tasks in hazardous environments.

7. FUTURE WORK

In solving the second set of objectives, we discovered quickly how problematic a Pareto front in nine dimensions becomes. While our results were successful, there is much to be gained from implementing *many objective* techniques in GTMOEP in order to better target productive search regions. We would also like to apply the capabilities of GTMOEP to a problem beginning from time-domain data, rather than feature data. Finally, we would like to do further work to compare performance to other cutting edge machine learning techniques, such as deep learning.

8. ACKNOWLEDGEMENTS

We would like to thank TNO and the U.S. Department of Defense's Combating Terrorism Technical Support Office (CTTSO) for sponsoring this effort. Financial support by CTTSO does not constitute an expressed or implied endorsement of the results or conclusions of the project by either CTTSO or the Department of Defense.

9. REFERENCES

[1] H. Al-Sahaf, A. Song, and M. Zhang. Hybridisation of genetic programming and nearest neighbour for classification. In *2013 IEEE Congress on Evolutionary Computation (CEC)*, pages 2650 – 2657. IEEE, June 2013.

[2] K. Bache and M. Lichman. University of california, irvine machine learning repository, 2013.

[3] K. Deb, A. Pratap, S. Agarwal, and T. Meyarivan. A fast and elitist multiobjective genetic algorithm: NSGA-II. *IEEE Transactions on Evolutionary Computation*, 6(2):182 – 197, 2002.

[4] F. Fortin, D. Rainville, M. G. Gardner, M. Parizeau, C. Gagné, et al. DEAP: Evolutionary algorithms made easy. *Journal of Machine Learning Research*, 13:2171 – 2175, July 2012.

[5] H. Guo, L. B. Jack, and A. K. Nandi. Feature generation using genetic programming with application to fault classification. *IEEE Transactions on Systems, Man, and Cybernetics, Part B: Cybernetics*, 35(1):89 – 99, February 2005.

[6] L. Guo, D. Rivero, J. Dorado, C. R. Munteanu, and A. Pazos. Automatic feature extraction using genetic programming: An application to epileptic eeg classification. *Expert Systems with Applications*, 38(8):10,425 – 10,436, August 2011.

[7] Y. Hold-Geoffroy, O. Gagnon, and M. Parizeau. Once you scoop, no need to fork. In *Proceedings of the 2014 Annual Conference on Extreme Science and Engineering Discovery Environment*, page 60. ACM, 2014.

[8] K. L. Holladay and K. A. Robbins. Evolution of signal processing algorithms using vector based genetic programming. In *15th International Conference on Digital Signal Processing*, pages 503 – 506. IEEE, 2007.

[9] E. Jones, T. Oliphant, P. Peterson, et al. SciPy: Open source scientific tools for Python, 2001–. [Online; accessed 2015-01-26].

[10] Y. Lee and L. Tong. Forecasting time series using a methodology based on autoregressive integrated moving average and genetic programming. *Knowledge-Based Systems*, 24(1):66 – 72, February 2011.

[11] A. J. K. Oudenhuijzen and J. D. J. Layden. From human operator to clothing parameters? 2011.

[12] F. Pedregosa, G. Varoquaux, A. Gramfort, V. Michel, B. Thirion, O. Grisel, M. Blondel, P. Prettenhofer, R. Weiss, V. Dubourg, J. Vanderplas, A. Passos, D. Cournapeau, M. Brucher, M. Perrot, and E. Duchesnay. Scikit-learn: Machine learning in Python. *Journal of Machine Learning Research*, 12:2825 – 2830, 2011.

[13] P. Ravisankar, V. Ravi, and I. Bose. Failure prediction of dotcom companies using neural network-genetic programming hybrids. *Information Sciences*, 180(8):1257 – 1267, April 2010.

[14] G. Rohling. *Multiple objective evolutionary algorithms for independent, computationally expensive objective evaluations.* PhD thesis, Georgia Institute of Technology, November 2004.

[15] J. R. Sherrah, R. E. Bogner, and A. Bouzerdoum. The evolutionary pre-processor: Automatic feature extraction for supervised classification using genetic programming. *Genetic Programming*, pages 304 – 312, 1997.

[16] J. Streater. Genetic programming for the automatic construction of features in skin-lesion image classification. Master's thesis, University of Edinburgh, 2010.

[17] C. D. Vera, E. Alfaro-cid, K. Sharman, and A. I. Esparcia-Alcázar. Genetic programming and serial processing for time series classification. *Evolutionary Computation*, 22(2):265 – 285, 2014.

[18] D. Zhang, M. Hifi, Q. Chen, and W. Ye. A hybrid credit scoring model based on genetic programming and support vector machines. volume 7, pages 8 – 12. IEEE, October 2008.

[19] E. Zitzler, M. Laumanns, and L. Thiele. Spea2: Improving the strength pareto evolutionary algorithm for multiobjective optimization. In *Evolutionary Methods for Design, Optimisation and Control with Application to Industrial Problems (EUROGEN 2001)*, pages 95 – 100. International Center for Numerical Methods in Engineering (CIMNE), 2002.

Evolving Strategies for Social Innovation Games

Erkin Bahçeci
Department of
Computer Science
University of Texas at Austin
Austin, TX, 78712, USA
erkin@cs.utexas.edu

Riitta Katila
Department of Management
Science & Engineering
Stanford University
Stanford, CA, 94305, USA
rkatila@stanford.edu

Risto Miikkulainen
Department of
Computer Science
University of Texas at Austin
Austin, TX, 78712, USA
risto@cs.utexas.edu

ABSTRACT

While evolutionary computation is well suited for automatic discovery in engineering, it can also be used to gain insight into how humans and organizations could perform more effectively in competitive problem-solving domains. This paper formalizes human creative problem solving as competitive multi-agent search, and advances the hypothesis that evolutionary computation can be used to discover effective strategies for it. In experiments in a social innovation game (similar to a fantasy sports league), neural networks were first trained to model individual human players. These networks were then used as opponents to evolve better game-play strategies with the NEAT neuroevolution method. Evolved strategies scored significantly higher than the human models by innovating, retaining, and retrieving less and by imitating more, thus providing insight into how performance could be improved in such domains. Evolutionary computation in competitive multi-agent search thus provides a possible framework for understanding and supporting various human creative activities in the future.

Categories and Subject Descriptors

I.2.1 [**Artificial Intelligence**]: Applications and Expert Systems—*Games*; I.2.6 [**Artificial Intelligence**]: Learning—*Connectionism and neural nets*

Keywords

Games; neural networks; empirical study; decision making; social science

1. INTRODUCTION

Many human creative activities can be described as competitive multi-agent search (CMAS; [1]), i.e. search where multiple agents search simultaneously for peaks in a common fitness landscape. The agents may observe each other, and the landscape may change as a result of their search. For example, companies in high-technology industries search for new products, such as smartphones, tablets, and smart watches, taking into account what they already have, what other companies have, and how well they are each doing. Similar search can be seen to take place in science, music, and art, where many people compete for discovering successful solutions in a common field.

Like other search problems such as single-agent search and cooperative multi-agent search, CMAS can be formulated mathematically and simulated computationally [1]. Evolutionary computation is then a possible way to discover effective strategies for it. For instance, simulations in abstract NK fitness landscapes showed that in order to maintain high fitness, the agent should hide some of its findings from the competitors (avoiding a "Twitter effect" where everyone follows the same leaders), and the agent should be quick to move to new and emerging areas (exploit the "wave-riding" effect) [1].

While abstract domains are useful in identifying such general principles of CMAS, it is also necessary to verify them in actual human domains. This task is undertaken in this paper, evaluating CMAS in a fantasy league game. Although this game was designed for a cognitive science laboratory study on social learning [9], it turns out appropriate for studying CMAS as well. Data from the laboratory study is used to generate a simulation domain where human search strategies can be characterized, compared, and evaluated wrt. strategies discovered automatically through evolution. More specifically, the first goal is to discover better strategies that people use in this domain, by building models of individual players. The second goal is to evaluate how well those strategies work, and whether it is possible to discover better strategies automatically using evolutionary optimization. For instance, do we need different strategies against opponents that imitate a lot vs. those that innovate more, in order to perform as well as possible? Are there strategies that would perform well in many different environments, or are the best strategies customized to each environment separately?

This paper aims to answer such questions using evolution as the method to optimize neural networks. Three experiments were conducted: First, in order to characterize environments and successful strategies, strategies were evolved against a uniform set of opponents of a certain type. Second, general strategies were evolved using multiple environments for fitness evaluation. Third, in order to show that better strategies can be discovered in complex real-world environments, strategies were evolved in the game groups of the human subject study. The results show that humans do follow a variety of general strategies, and it is possible to do better by opti-

GECCO '15, July 11 - 15, 2015, Madrid, Spain
 ISBN 978-1-4503-3472-3/15/07... $15.00
DOI: http://dx.doi.org/10.1145/2739480.2754790

mizing the strategy to the actual environment. Thus, these results demonstrate that CMAS is a productive formulation of a new area of human problem solving, making it amenable to analysis and optimization.

The paper is organized as follows: In Section 2, CMAS is first motivated from the real-world perspective of innovation search. A formalization of CMAS is given, and basic computational results on an abstract *NK* landscape reviewed. The social innovation game domain is described in Section 3, and how human subjects were modeled in this domain is described in Section 4. Section 5 describes how strategies were encoded and evolved in this domain, and presents a series of experiments comparing evolved strategies against human models.

2. BACKGROUND

The original motivation for CMAS comes from innovation search, which is part of organizational theory in management science. In this theory, search (i.e. organizational problem solving) is thought to take place in a *knowledge space*, conceptualized as a landscape. In particular in innovation search, firms generate, recombine, and manipulate knowledge within a pool of technological possibilities [3, 6]. The agents do not know the topography of the landscape but can sample it, i.e. search the landscape by generating and evaluating new points.

More formally, the search agent's knowledge $\mathcal{X}(t)$ of the landscape and its topography at time t consists of m points with fitness values z:

$$\mathcal{X}(t) = \{[\mathbf{x}_1, z(\mathbf{x}_1)], [\mathbf{x}_2, z(\mathbf{x}_2)], ...[\mathbf{x}_m, z(\mathbf{x}_m)]\}. \quad (1)$$

In the traditional *single-agent search*, the agent moves to the next (i.e. $(m+1)$th) point using a search strategy S based on what the agent already knows about the landscape, i.e. $\mathbf{x}_{m+1} = S[\mathcal{X}(t)]$. For instance, in order to find the best of a kind, the agent might search near the good points that it has already discovered (*exploit*), or if the existing points do not seem promising, avoid them, and make a long jump to an area far from them (*explore*). The search strategy S is stochastic, i.e. it contains an element of uncertainty due to bounded rationality. A good search strategy is a method for visiting new points such that high peaks are found as fast as possible.

In contrast, in *competitive multi-agent search* (CMAS; Figure 1), this formulation is extended in two ways: (1) The agent's knowledge of points $\mathcal{X}$ includes not only the points $\mathcal{X}_\text{h}$ it has discovered itself and keeps hidden from other agents, but also points $\mathcal{X}_\text{p}$ that the other agents have found and made public; (2) whenever new points are found in the neighborhood ρ of existing points, all their values are changed with a multiplicative factor α. These extensions model the knowledge that the agents have about their competitors' search, and the dynamic effects that the competitors' searches have on the landscape. Thus, a competitive search strategy consists of two components:

$$\mathbf{x}_{m+1} = S_1[\mathcal{X}_\text{h}(t), \mathcal{X}_\text{p}(t), \rho(t), \alpha(t)], \quad (2)$$

$$\begin{aligned}\mathcal{X}(t+1) &= \{\mathcal{X}_\text{h}(t+1), \mathcal{X}_\text{p}(t+1)\} \quad (3)\\ &= S_2[\mathcal{X}_\text{h}(t), \mathcal{X}_\text{p}(t), \mathbf{x}_{m+1}, z(\mathbf{x}_{m+1}), \rho(t), \alpha(t)],\end{aligned}$$

where S_1 generates a new point $\mathbf{x}_{m+1}$ given the knowledge about points and about the dynamic effects at time t, and S_2 updates this knowledge with the new point, i.e. generates the version of $\mathcal{X} = \{\mathcal{X}_\text{h}, \mathcal{X}_\text{p}\}$ for time $t+1$, where one of those

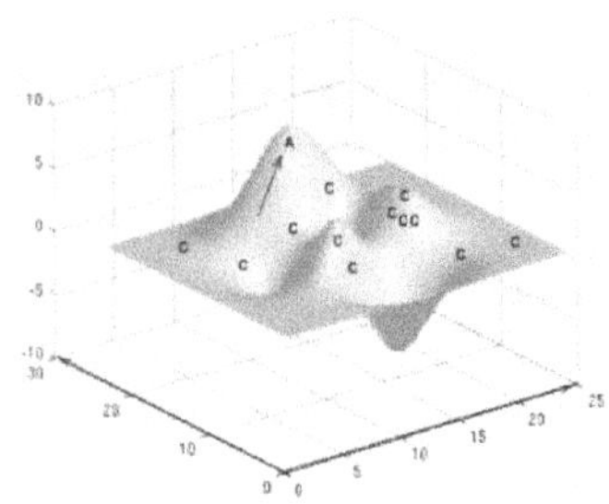

Figure 1: A conceptual illustration of CMAS search. Multiple agents search for fitness peaks in the same environment, modeling human creative problem solving.

knowledge bases includes the new point $\mathbf{x}_{m+1}$ and its fitness value $z(\mathbf{x}_{m+1})$.

This formulation of CMAS makes a new class of human problem-solving activity amenable to formal and computational analysis. The first step is to understand the general properties of CMAS problems. A good approach is to analyze CMAS in an abstract, mathematical domain that makes the conclusions clear. The binary *NK* landscape [4], where N is the dimensionality and K determines how complex the relationships between the dimensions are, serves as such a domain.

In a previous study of CMAS in an *NK* landscape [1], S_1 was represented as a vector of probabilities for taking an exploit and explore action from the best private and public point seen so far, based on the fitnesses of those points, and S_2 was represented as a vector of probabilities of placing the new point in private or public memory, based on the fitness of that point. Different search environments were established by creating opponent agents with different preferences for these actions. Such preferences determine how the agent searches (i.e. their strategy), which can be optimized through evolution. In prior work, specialized strategies were evolved for an agent for each different environment, and also a general strategy to perform well across multiple environments. These strategies turned out more effective and more complex than hand-designed strategies and a strategy based on traditional single-agent tree search. Using a novel spherical visualization of *NK* landscapes, insight was gained about how successful strategies work, including the Twitter and wave-riding effects mentioned in Section 1.

The next step, to be undertaken in this paper, is to evaluate these conclusions in a domain with actual human subjects. Such a domain will be described next.

3. THE SOCIAL INNOVATION GAME DOMAIN

To study competitive multi-agent search in a human domain, a dataset of human behavior in a competitive multi-agent search task was employed: a social innovation game created by Wisdom et al. [9]. The human dataset was collected under laboratory conditions at the Percepts and Concepts Laboratory of Robert L. Goldstone at Indiana University[1]. The task that human subjects performed was a multi-player problem-solving game similar to a fantasy sports league: The players tried to build a collection (or team) of icons that would score higher than the team of other players. The subjects, who were undergraduate students, were assigned to groups of size one through nine, in which they each played eight games.

A screenshot of the game's graphical user interface can be seen in Figure 2. During games that consisted of 24 rounds, each player built a team of five or six members (shown as *icons*

[1]http://cognitrn.psych.indiana.edu/

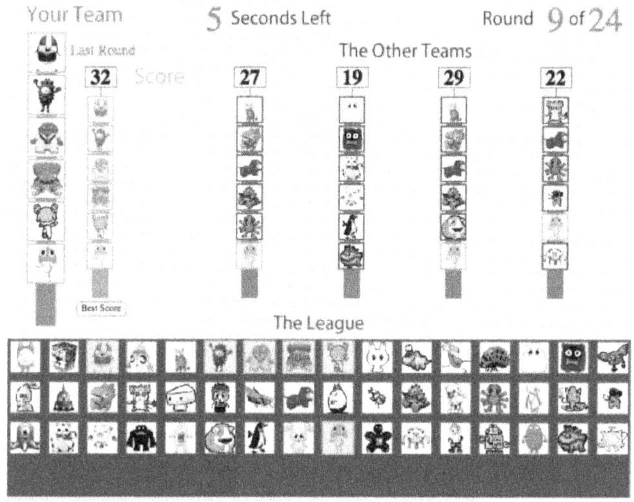

Figure 2: The graphical user interface for the social innovation game [9]. The player's current team is shown at the left hand side (labeled "Your Team") and the opponents teams at top right (labeled "The Other Teams"). The objective is to build a team of icons that has a better score than the other players' teams. The user interface also displays the current round and the total number of rounds at the top right corner, and the remaining time in the current round at the top center. (Used with permission from Robert L. Goldstone.)

on the interface) in each round. The players could add icons to their teams by dragging an icon from a source, and dropping it onto one of the player's own icons, replacing it. Icons could be copied in this manner from four sources: (1) player's last team (a *retaining* action), (2) player's best scoring team up until that point in the game (a *retrieval* action), (3) another player's last team (an *imitation* action), or (4) the league of all available icons (an *innovation* action). Depending on the game configuration, there were either 24 or 48 available icons in the league. The players could also copy any of the other teams in its entirety by dragging the score label above the team, and dropping onto their own current team. In each game, a fixed number of points was assigned to each icon in the league, and bonuses and penalties were assigned to a subset of distinct pairs of icons. These point assignments, which were not known by the human subjects, were determined by Wisdom et al. to make the game challenging by giving high bonuses to least valuable icons and high penalties to most valuable icons. At the end of each round, each player's score was calculated as the sum of points assigned to the individual icons in the player's team, as well as any bonuses or penalties for icon pairs. In each game, a fixed number of points in the range [1, 8] were assigned to each icon in the league, and penalties or bonuses in the range [-20, 20] were assigned to a subset of distinct pairs of icons. The range of possible scores was [-6, 60], and actual scores of human players were in the range [-2, 60].

The dynamics of this domain are simpler than those studied with abstract simulation on *NK* fitness landscapes [1] in that the fitness landscape does not change during the game. However, the domain is still a CMAS, and serves as a real-world example and application of competitive multi-agent search. Moreover, the human dataset allows modeling people's strategies in such domains, as well as determining if there are better strategies, through the use of evolutionary computation.

4. MODELING HUMAN SUBJECTS

Among other effects, Wisdom et al. identified effects of game round on the subjects' behavior in the aforementioned social innovation game [9]. The proportion of actions (i.e. icon sources) that the players employed changed with the round. As the game progressed, retention and retrieval increased slightly, while imitation and innovation decreased but overall the proportion of actions remained relatively stable. On average, subjects imitated 9.8%, innovated 13.7%, retained 73.9%, and retrieved 2.6% of the time. In sum, subjects were in general conservative in their gameplay, but became even more so over the course of 24 rounds.

Since those action ratios are known for human subjects, they can be used as distance measures comparing a model's behavior to that of a particular human subject. The smaller the difference between action ratios, the more useful a model is as a replacement for a human subject in a simulation. Thus, those action ratios, as well as the score of the players and the consistency of their icon choices, were used as distance objectives to evaluate models in this paper.

In order to simulate human subjects, gameplay data from each human subject was used to train a model for the subject in the form of two separate neural networks: one for high-level actions (i.e. copying a whole team) and another one for low-level actions (i.e. copying individual icons). Both types of neural network models chose actions probabilistically based on the relative activation of their output units, and were trained with backpropagation using 500 epochs, using a learning rate of 0.1, momentum of 0.1, and weight decay of 0.01.

The models with two separate neural networks were compared to the corresponding models created with two other modeling approaches based on human gameplay data, as well as a baseline model with uniform action choice. More specifically, four models were thus compared in Figure 3: (1) the baseline model where icon actions are picked based on fixed and uniform probabilities (i.e. 0.25 for each of the four icon actions), (2) another simplistic model with fixed probabilities, but with each action's probability set as the human subject's usage ratio for that action, calculated from the data, (3) a one-tiered neural network model that performs icon actions but not team actions, and (4) the two-tiered neural network model, which performs both team and icon actions.

While there was no significant difference between the two neural networks in innovation ratio, icon consistency, or the two score objectives, they did differ in three other distance objectives, including team and icon imitation ratio (i.e. first and second on the second row in Figure 3). The two-tiered models were significantly closer to human subjects along these objectives than the other model types (p-value $< 10^{-4}$). The main reason for the difference in team imitation ratio is that the other models did not perform any team actions, and therefore got the same result on team action ratio objectives (i.e. "team imitation ratio" and "team retrieval ratio"). However, unlike in the team imitation ratio, two-tiered models did not perform significantly better in the team retrieval ratio. A likely reason is that human subjects rarely performed that action: 27 out of 34 subjects did not do team retrieval at all, while the others did very rarely. The two-tiered models learned to rarely perform that action, which was not significantly different from not doing it at all. While the two-tiered models were

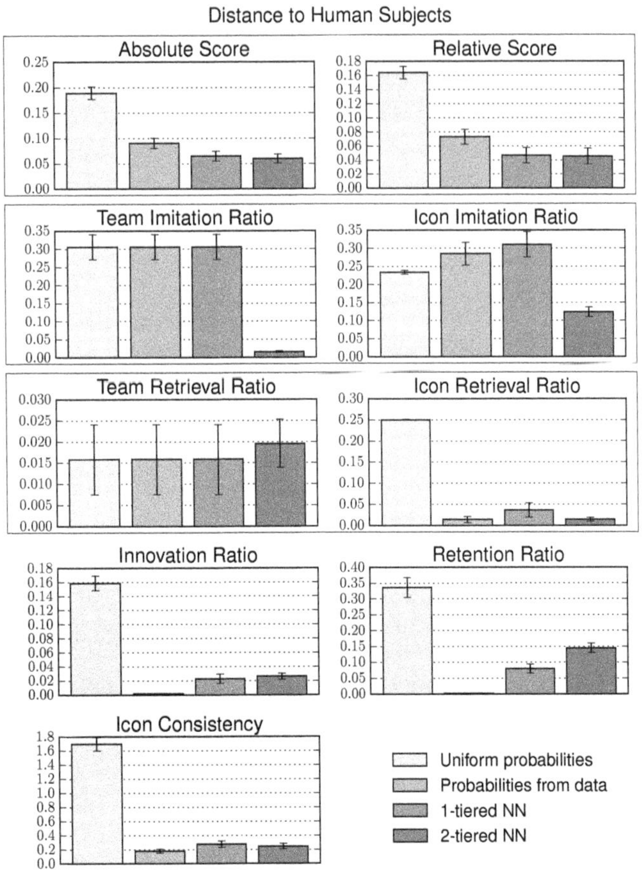

Figure 3: Different modeling approaches compared using several distance objectives. Values show average distance of the models to the corresponding human subject. Smaller values are better. Each distance objective is averaged across the human subjects. Error bars indicate one unit of standard error of the mean. Note that the y-axes have different scales. Related objectives are grouped in surrounding boxes. The two-tiered neural network models do significantly better than all others in team and icon imitation ratio objectives, whereas the difference with the one-tiered networks are not significant in other objectives. The reason why two-tiered network models do not do better in retrieval ratio objectives is that retrieval is done very rarely by humans, and therefore insufficient data for team and icon retrieval actions. The simpler models (i.e. second bar) that are based on probabilities from human gameplay data perform better in innovation and retention ratio objectives, but they cannot perform team and icon actions separately, unlike the two-tiered network models.

significantly worse in the retention ratio (p-value < 0.01), the advantage of two-tiered network models in the two imitation action ratio objectives and in their support for team actions make the two-tiered network models a better choice for modeling human subjects than the one-tiered ones.

The fact that these human models come close to human subjects in terms of their action ratios confirms that learning to imitate human players results in models that can be characterized like Wisdom et al. did as mentioned above. Besides characterizing human behavior, these models also allow simulating actual human players. It is much more practical to create hypothetical situations using models of human subjects than doing the same with the subjects themselves, which is important in optimizing strategies, as will be done in the next section.

5. OPTIMIZING SOCIAL INNOVATION

With models that mimic human players, one can create simulations of game environments that resemble those with human players. Such environments can then be used to discover strategies that perform well against human players, and ones that possibly perform even better than humans. An effective way to do so is through evolutionary computation. For instance, player strategies, encoded as neural networks, can be evolved by evaluating their fitness in game environments with human model opponents. A strategy encoding that is suitable for evolution will be described next.

5.1 Two-tiered Combined Neural Network

In Section 4, two separate neural networks were used to model human subjects. However, if such a model was used for evolving strategies, hidden network nodes that represent useful states would have to evolve separately twice (i.e. once per neural network). For instance, a hidden node may represent the state where the game is about to end and the relative score of the agent is lower than the player with the highest score, and the output of this hidden node may be useful for both high-level and low-level actions. Sharing such hidden nodes between the two network tiers would allow neural network representations to be evolved once and used for both high-level and low-level actions. Therefore, employing a combined neural network can reduce the search time for a neural network solution.

Thus, for the goal of optimizing strategies, a combined two-tiered neural network architecture was chosen to represent strategies. The neural network nodes had either a sigmoid or a Gaussian function as their activation function. As seen in Figure 4, high-level (i.e. team-level) actions and low-level (i.e. icon-level) actions were generated by separate outputs of the same neural network, as opposed to outputs of two separate neural networks as in Section 4. The next section details how these networks were optimized for the social innovation game domain.

5.2 Experimental Setup

The strategy for a single agent was optimized given an environment with a fixed set of opponents. As described in the previous section, a single neural network was used to represent a strategy, which made it straightforward to use neuroevolution methods to optimize it. Since NEAT [8] is a commonly used and effective neuroevolution method, it was used in this paper for evolving strategies.

Strategies were evolved in environments with eight opponents, each of which was the model of a human subject, created using supervised learning as described in Section 4. NEAT ran for 500 generations for each environment, with a population of size 100, and with 64 repetitions for each evolutionary setup.

The fitness of each evolved strategy was evaluated by running a simulation where the first agent used the evolved strategy and the opponents used a fixed strategy chosen to create a particular environment. The fitness was calculated as the normalized score of the first agent averaged across 200 games. As in human subjects' games, at the beginning of each game, each player had a team that was randomly selected from the

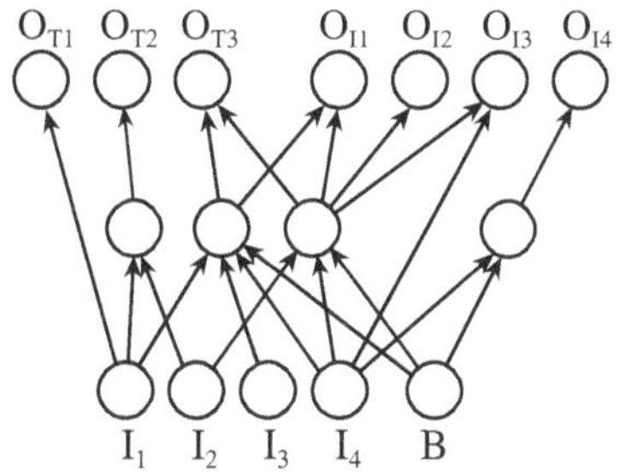

Figure 4: An example combined two-tiered neural network, with four inputs (i.e. current game round, player's score relative to the best opponent, icon's popularity, icon's age), three outputs for team actions (i.e. imitation, retrieval, and no action), and four outputs for icon actions (i.e. imitation, innovation, retrieval, and retention or no action). The outputs for icon actions are normalized and used as action probabilities for each icon of the player's team, while team action outputs are normalized separately and used as team action probabilities. In this design, the team and icon networks are combined, as opposed to the separate networks in Section 4. Hidden nodes representing game states that are useful for both team and icon actions are shared, and do not have to be evolved twice.

league. Moreover, as in human games, icon memorization was effectively prevented, since agents did not guess or keep scores for individual icons or pairs of icons.

With this setup, three experiments were conducted. In the first experiment, custom strategies are evolved for environments where all the opponents used the same strategy (Section 5.3). The second experiment investigates whether general strategies that would work across multiple such environments could be evolved (Section 5.4). These experiments demonstrate what is possible by evolving strategies for extremely different environments. The third experiment evaluates these questions in more realistic environments where the opponents use different strategies, modeling the actual games played in the laboratory study (Section 5.5).

5.3 Experiment 1: Evolving Specific Strategies

In order to see which strategies work well in different social innovation game environments, several evolutionary setups were created, each with a different set of opponent models. For each of the four icon actions (i.e. imitate, innovate, retain, and retrieve), the model for the subject that used that action the most was selected as the dominant model for that action, among the models for subjects who took part in games with at least five players. For each action, eight copies of the corresponding action-dominant model were used as the opponents in an environment, resulting in four homogeneous environments.

To make it easier to examine evolved strategies, the corresponding networks were used as CPPNs to generate patterns to fill state-action probability tables. The possible range of input values for the four CPPN inputs were discretized into three coarse values for the time input, and two for the remaining inputs: (1) beginning of game, mid-game, or end-game; (2) low or high score relative to the best opponent; (3) low or high icon popularity among players; and (4) old or new icon. Combinations of these input values correspond to 24 possible discrete game states for each icon. For each state, the agent had a choice of three team actions for the whole team, as well as four icon actions for each icon. As a result, from each evolved CPPN, a 24×7 state-action probability table was obtained.

To identify the differences between strategies evolved in different environments, action probabilities were compared using Student's t-test, separately for each action and for each of the 24 discrete states. This comparison resulted in 24 p-values for each pair of strategies median p-value was then used to determine whether strategies evolved in an environment had significantly higher or lower probabilities than those evolved in another environment.

Strategies evolved in the environment with imitate-dominant opponents do significantly more innovation (with median p-value $< 10^{-3}$) and less imitation (with median p-value for icon and team imitation 0.0134 and 0.0454, respectively), as well as more retrieval (with median p-value 0.0287). In such an environment, the source of imitation is always the highest-scoring player. Therefore, lower imitation and higher innovation and retrieval lead to higher diversity, which increases the chance of finding icons with higher score, beating the opponents.

On the other hand, strategies evolved with innovation-dominant opponents had significantly higher imitation at the team level (median p-value $= 0.022$) compared to strategies from other homogeneous environments, while there was no significant difference in icon imitation. A possible explanation is that when all other teams are innovating a lot (i.e. replacing their icons with random ones from the pool), team imitation is more reliable than icon imitation. Strategies evolved against retention-dominant opponents have increased team imitation as well, but it is not as significant (median p-value $= 0.066$).

With retrieve-dominant opponents, evolved strategies innovated significantly less (median p-value $< 10^{-4}$) than in other environments, and imitated somewhat more at the icon level (median p-value $= 0.094$). Innovation is getting a completely random icon, whereas icon imitation copies a random icon from the best-scoring opponent's team, which, in this environment, opponents are likely to have icons from the opponent's best team so far. Therefore, in this environment innovation is less likely to contribute positively to a player's score than imitation.

The 24×7 action probability tables were also used to examine the distribution of strategies. The probability tables of evolved strategies were treated as 168-dimensional vectors, and reduced to two-dimensional points via principal component analysis (PCA). The first two components captured 83% of the variance in the high-dimensional vectors, and therefore two-dimensional PCA plots were used to visualize the strategies. Table 1 shows the distribution of the best strategies from the 64 evolutionary runs for each environment.

The diagonal boundary line at the bottom left of the PCA plots represents maximum icon imitation (i.e. with probability 1.0), and the one at the bottom right corresponds to maximum team imitation; therefore there are no points below those two lines. The result that the strategies evolved against imitation-dominant opponents imitated less means that the points (i.e. strategies) are further away from the diagonals than in the other environments. The relatively high team imitation evolved against innovation- and retention-dominant opponents can also be observed in these plots: there is a strong cluster around the diagonal line at the right representing maximum team imitation in these environments. Similarly, for strategies evolved against retrieve-dominant opponents, rela-

Environment Id	Environment Opponents	PCA for Evolved Strategies
1	Imitate-dominant (8)	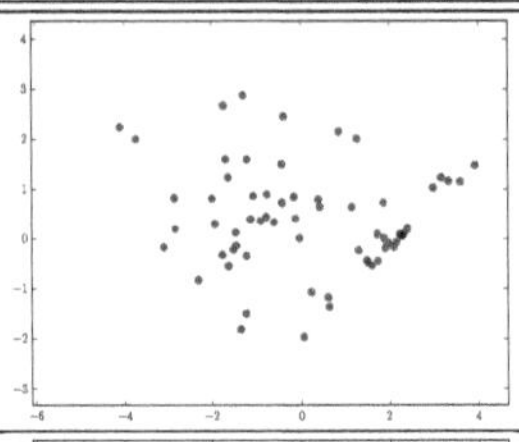
2	Innovate-dominant (8)	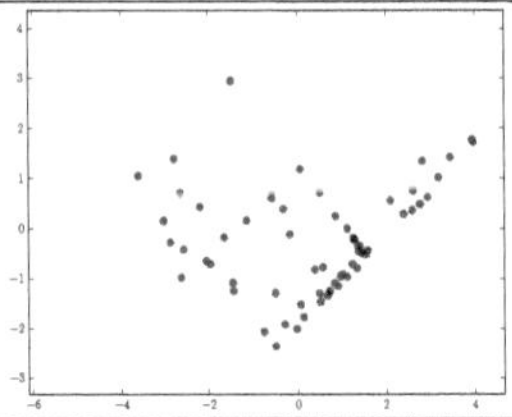
3	Retain-dominant (8)	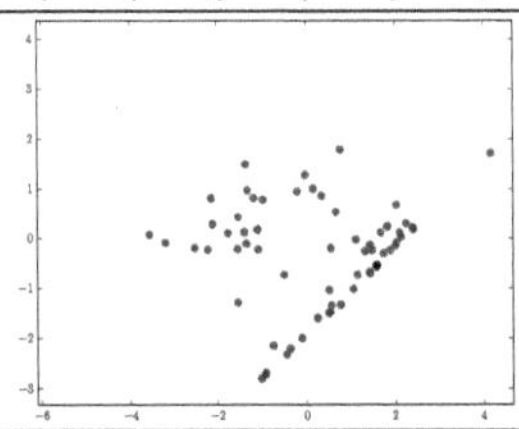
4	Retrieve-dominant (8)	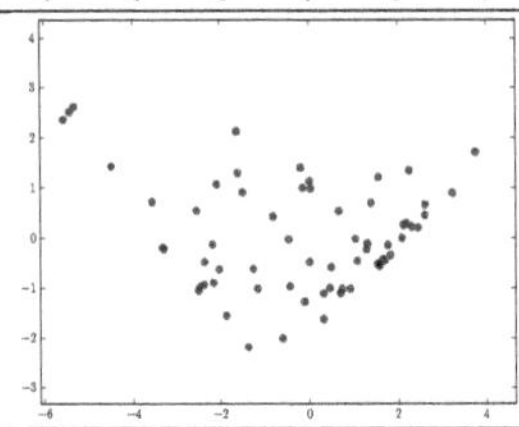
5	Heterogeneous (2 opponents from each of Environments 1-4 above)	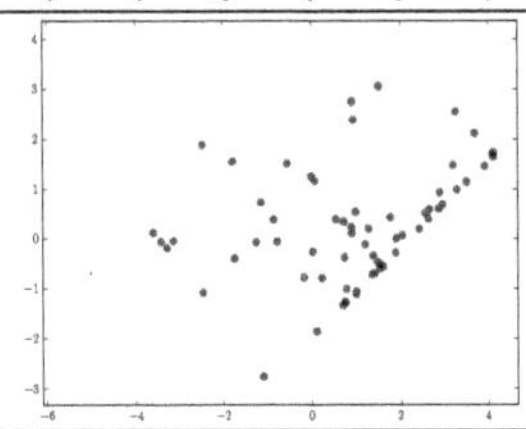
6	Multiple homogeneous (Fitness averaged over Environments 1-4 above)	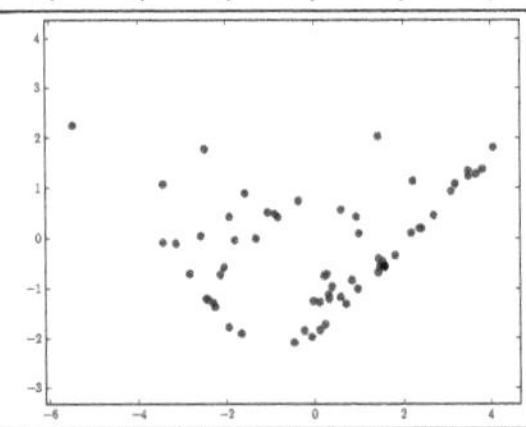

Table 1: Strategies evolved in homogenous and heterogeneous environments. Each PCA plot shows 64 evolved strategies. The PCA dimensions are shared across all evolved strategies. The diagonal boundary lines at the bottom left and bottom right (somewhat faint in this table but more clearly visible in Table 2) represent maximum icon imitation and maximum team imitation, respectively.

tively more numerous points can be seen near the diagonal at the left, which corresponds to higher icon imitation.

Performance of the evolved strategies across various environments is shown in Figure 5. For each homogeneous environment, the strategies evolved in the same particular environment significantly outperformed the ones evolved in other environments (p-value $< 10^{-19}$). This result shows that there is indeed value in optimizing the strategies for a particular en-

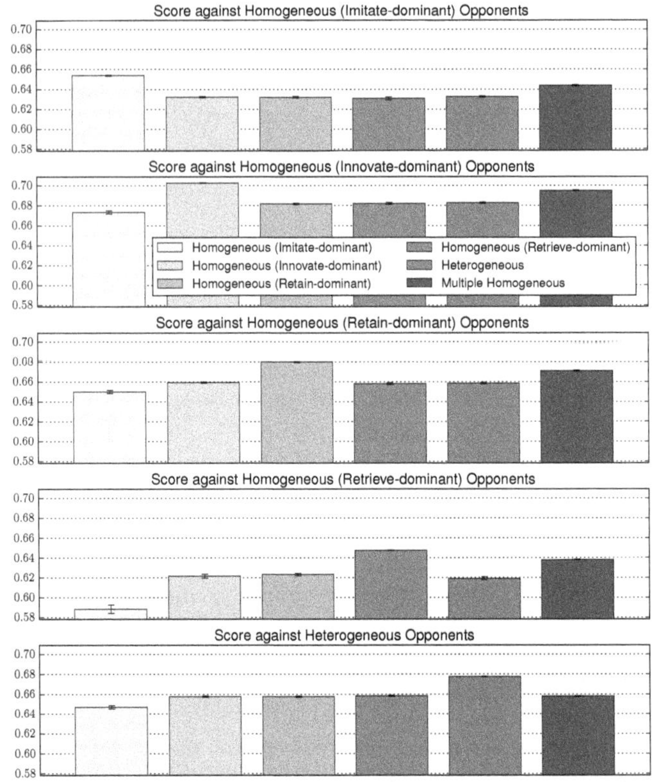

Figure 5: Performance comparison among strategies evolved in a single homogeneous, multiple homogeneous, and a heterogeneous environment. Each row shows the performance of strategies in one environment. Each column shows the average score of 64 strategies evolved in the environment indicated by the legend when they are evaluated in the environments that correspond to rows. Thus, the bars in the diagonal starting from top left show the performance of strategies that were evolved in the same environment as the one in which they are evaluated. Each group of evolved strategies on the diagonal perform significantly better than the other evolved strategies in the same row. Moreover, the strategies evolved in multiple homogeneous environments perform significantly better than others in all homogeneous environments (except the strategies evolved in the evaluation environment). Thus, evolution can produce customized strategies for given homogeneous and heterogenous environments, as well as general strategies that perform better than others in multiple environments.

vironment. Strategies deployed in foreign environments performed at similar levels with each other, except for the ones evolved against imitate-dominant opponents, which performed significantly worse than the others (p-value $< 10^{-4}$). A possible explanation is that the increased innovation is actually a handicap in those other environments.

While homogeneous environments are useful in evolving strategies to counter a specific type of opponent, a different approach is needed for evolving general-purpose strategies that can be used against different opponents, which will be the focus of the next section.

5.4 Experiment 2: Evolving General Strategies

In order to evolve general strategies, two more evolutionary setups were employed: (1) a setup where fitness of strategies are evaluated by averaging the score of the strategy across all four homogeneous environments, and (2) a setup with a heterogeneous environment where two copies of each of those four action-dominant models were used as opponents.

Figure 5 shows that strategies evolved in heterogeneous environments also performed better than other strategies in the heterogeneous environment itself, but did not show any benefit over other strategies in homogeneous environments. On the other hand, while strategies evolved in multiple homogeneous environments performed worse in each homogeneous environment than the ones evolved in that particular environment, they significantly outperformed the rest of the strategies (p-value $< 10^{-11}$). These results suggest that evolving strategies in a set of diverse homogeneous environments may be a useful approach to create strategies that generalize well.

So far, evolutionary environments consisted of an artificial combination of models, in order to understand how the different strategies interact. The next section looks at evolutionary results with sets of opponents that are determined in a more realistic way, taking into consideration the groups in the human subject experiment data.

5.5 Experiment 3: Evolving in Complex Environments

To see how strategies evolve in environments that are more realistic than the ones employed so far, evolutionary environments were created to simulate three groups of eight or nine players from the human experiment data. For each player in each group, the player was replaced with the evolving strategy and the opponents with the corresponding human subject's models that were created in Section 4, resulting in nine evolutionary environments for Group 1, and eight for Groups 2 and 3, with a total of 25 environments. Each pair of environments within each group shared all but one opponent, which makes them more similar compared to environments from the two other groups.

As in the previous experiments, 64 evolutionary runs were performed for each environment, and the best strategy at the end of each run was selected as the resulting evolved strategy from that run. Table 2 shows the distribution of those strategies, organized by originating human group. Since there are many more strategies displayed in the PCA plots, the two diagonal boundary lines mentioned above at the left and right are much more prominent in Table 2 than in Table 1.

Furthermore, a few more lines parallel to those two are visible about half-way and one-third of the way from the bottom convergence point to the left and right edges. Just like the left and right boundary diagonals correspond to maximum icon and team imitation, respectively, these lines correspond to 50% or 67% icon or team imitation. This result is likely an artifact of the employed configuration of NEAT, where each member of the initial evolution population is a minimal network, often having a zero value for all except one output of the network, which gets interpreted as a fractional action probability such as 0.5, 0.33, or 0.67. With more strategies in the PCA plots, it is also clearer that the corresponding points lie in a triangle (i.e. the bottom half of a rotated square), which means most of them have at least 50% of team or icon imitation.

The performance of the evolved strategies, grouped by originating human groups can be seen in Figure 6. As in Experiments 1 and 2, strategies evolved with similar opponents (i.e. within each group) performed significantly better in environments from the same group compared to strategies evolved in the other two groups' environments (p-value $< 10^{-32}$). The performance difference was smaller than in the first two experiments, which is to be expected because the environments are more similar in Experiment 3 than in Experiments 1 and 2. It is also more difficult to characterize the strategy difference upon which these performance improvements are based. They are subtle and numerous, and in combination, allow the strategy to beat its opponents.

Environment		PCA for Evolved Strategies
Id	**Opponents**	
1	Group 1 (8) ×9	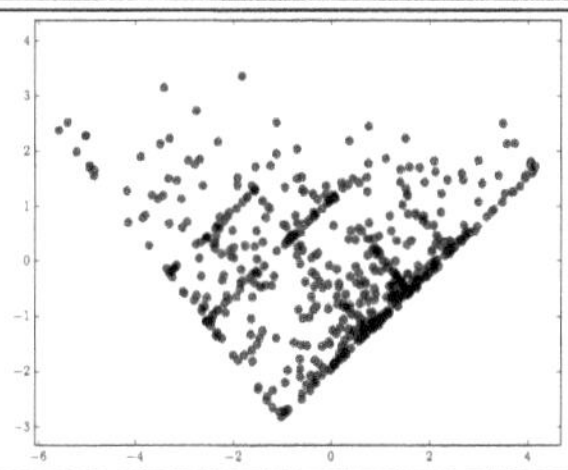
2	Group 2 (7) ×8	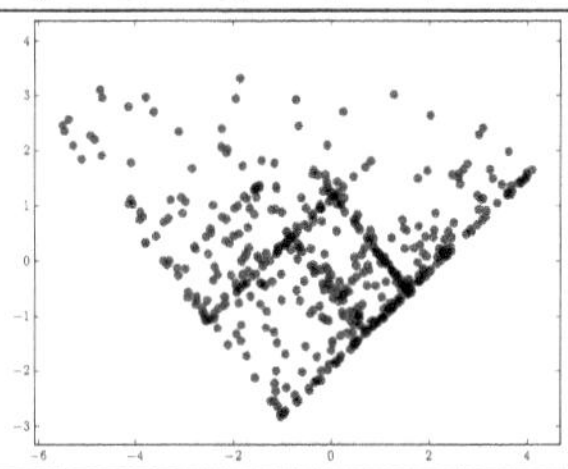
3	Group 3 (7) ×8	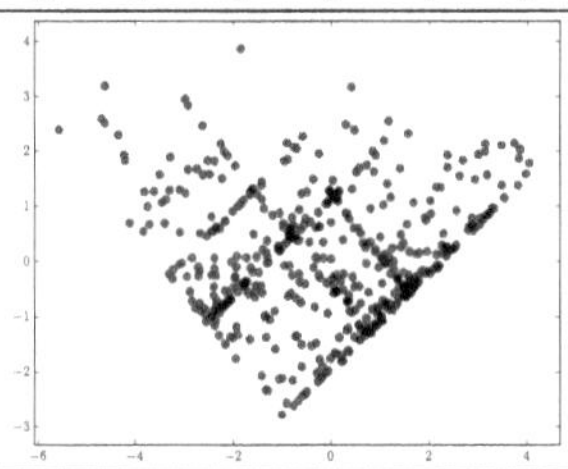

Table 2: Strategies evolved in environments with model groups that correspond to three human subject groups. For each group, the same number of environments were created as the number of players in the group, where in each environment, one model was replaced with the evolved strategy during fitness evaluation. The first PCA plot shows $64 \times 9 = 576$ evolved strategies since there are nine players in the first group, whereas the second and third plots show $64 \times 8 = 512$ strategies since those groups had eight players. The PCA dimensions are shared with the evolved strategies in Table 1. The diagonal boundary lines at the bottom left and bottom right represent maximum icon imitation and maximum team imitation, respectively, and they are more prominent than in Table 1 here due to the increased number of displayed strategies.

Most interestingly, the evolved strategies significantly outperformed the human subject models that they replaced during evolution by a difference of 0.1 normalized score (p-value $< 10^{-5}$). The score advantage of the evolved strategies can be explained by the difference in action ratios. Overall, the evolved strategies imitated 54% more than the human models, with 52% more team imitation (p-value $< 10^{-10}$). On the other hand, the evolved strategies retained their icons 41% less (p-value $< 10^{-8}$), retrieved icons 4.4% less (p-value $=$ 0.044), and innovated 4% less than the models (p-value $=$

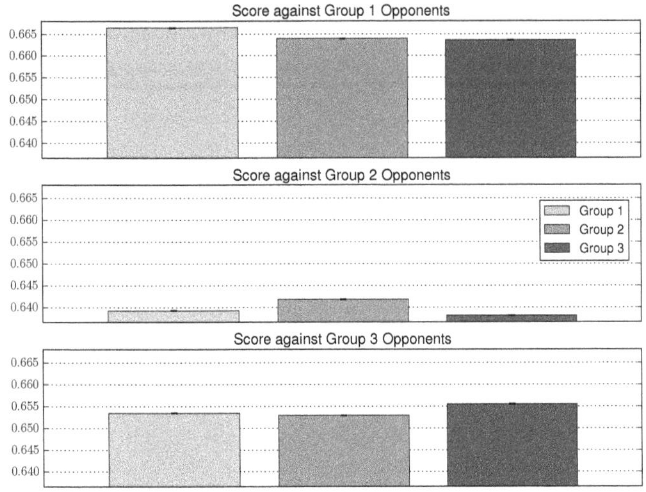

Figure 6: Performance comparison among strategies evolved in environments that correspond to three human subject groups, which are also compared with the average performance of models for human subjects in the group. The layout is similar to Figure 5. Again, the groups of strategies on the diagonal perform significantly better than the others shown in the same row (i.e. those evolved in other environments), though the difference is smaller than in Figure 5. The results demonstrate that evolution can produce customized strategies for given environments in this domain.

0.014). This result shows that it is indeed possible for evolution to discover and utilize opportunities in realistic human competitive multi-agent environments, and improve behavior over humans. Moreover, this result also provides insights into how human performance could be improved.

6. FUTURE WORK

The results in this paper suggest a possible application for CMAS: Creating competitive agents for social innovation games, such as fantasy sports leagues. Further, using the same approach, it should be possible to model and analyze other human problem solving activities like innovation search.

For general strategies like those evolved in Section 5.4 to scale up to even more diverse environments, it might be beneficial to allow multimodal behaviors, so that the same agent strategy can have distinct behaviors in different contexts [7]. A further step in this direction would be to coevolve all or a subset of the opponents as well. In this manner, the environment could present more diverse challenges, and more interesting and perhaps realistic general strategies could evolve.

A limitation of the experiment in Section 5.5 was that strategies were optimized against opponent models for only three groups of human subjects. More subject groups can be used as opponents; such an extension would make it possible to investigate the differences between strategies optimized against different sized groups. Because it is already known that group size affects ratios of utilized actions and the score, such a comparison might yield insights into what strategies work best against such diverse groups.

One downside of the evolutionary approach utilized in this paper is that it requires a large population and therefore a significant number of fitness evaluations. Thus, alternative evolutionary methods such as CMA-ES [2] and Estimation of Distribution Algorithms [5] may be considered. In those approaches, statistical models of the solutions and their fitness are maintained, making it possible to get by with fewer fitness evaluations in structured domains like CMAS.

7. CONCLUSION

This paper focused on optimization of strategies in the social innovation game domain. Three experiments explored strategies evolved in various environments with opponents that are models of subjects from the human study: (1) single homogeneous environments with opponents that dominantly perform one type of action, (2) multiple homogeneous environments and a single heterogeneous environment, and (3) environments with sets of opponents representing three diverse subject groups from the human study. The second experiment demonstrated that strategies that generalize across diverse sets of opponents can indeed be evolved. However, the first and third experiments both demonstrated that evolution was able to produce stronger strategies by tailoring them to the particular environment. The third experiment in particular showed that it is possible to discover and utilize subtle opportunities in realistic environments, and perform better than the human models by imitating more, and retaining, retrieving, and innovating less. These conclusions suggest that CMAS is a productive approach to understanding and perhaps even automating discovery in similar human creative problem solving domains.

8. ACKNOWLEDGMENTS

This research was supported in part by NSF grants DBI-0939454, IIS-0915038, and SBE-0914796, and by NIH grant R01-GM105042. The authors would like to thank Thomas N. Wisdom and Robert L. Goldstone at Indiana University for providing data and support for the game domain.

9. REFERENCES

[1] E. Bahceci. *Competitive Multi-Agent Search.* PhD thesis, The University of Texas at Austin, Austin, TX, 2014.

[2] N. Hansen, S. Müller, and P. Koumoutsakos. Reducing the time complexity of the derandomized evolution strategy with covariance matrix adaptation (CMA-ES). *Evolutionary Computation*, 11(1):1–18, 2003.

[3] R. Katila. New product search over time: Past ideas in their prime? *Academy of Management Journal*, 45(5):995–1010, 2002.

[4] S. A. Kauffman. *The Origins of Order.* Oxford University Press, New York, 1993.

[5] P. Larrañaga and J. A. Lozano. *Estimation of Distribution Algorithms: A New Tool for Evolutionary Computation*, volume 2. Springer, 2002.

[6] D. A. Levinthal and J. G. March. A model of adaptive organizational search. *Journal of Economic Behavior and Organization*, 2:307–333, 1981.

[7] J. Schrum and R. Miikkulainen. Evolving multimodal networks for multitask games. *IEEE Transactions on Computational Intelligence and AI in Games*, 4(2):94–111, June 2012.

[8] K. O. Stanley and R. Miikkulainen. Evolving neural networks through augmenting topologies. *Evolutionary Computation*, 10:99–127, 2002.

[9] T. N. Wisdom, X. Song, and R. L. Goldstone. Social learning strategies in networked groups. *Cognitive Science*, 37:1383–1425, 2013.

Knowledge Transfer from Keepaway Soccer to Half-field Offense through Program Symbiosis: Building Simple Programs for a Complex Task

Stephen Kelly
Dalhousie University,
Halifax, NS. Canada
skelly@cs.dal.ca

Malcolm I. Heywood
Dalhousie University,
Halifax, NS. Canada
mheywood@cs.dal.ca

ABSTRACT

Half-field Offense (HFO) is a sub-task of Robocup 2D Simulated Soccer. HFO is a challenging, multi-agent machine learning problem in which a team of offense players attempt to manoeuvre the ball past a defending team and around the goalie in order to score. The agent's sensors and actuators are noisy, making the problem highly stochastic and partially observable. These same real-world characteristics have made Keepaway soccer, which represents one sub-task of HFO, a popular testbed in the reinforcement learning and task-transfer literature in particular. We demonstrate how policies initially evolved for Keepaway can be reused within a symbiotic framework for coevolving policies in genetic programming (GP), with no additional training or transfer function, in order to improve learning in the HFO task. Moreover, the highly modular policies discovered by GP are shown to be significantly less complex than solutions based on traditional value-function optimization while achieving the same level of play in HFO.

CCS Concepts

•**Computing methodologies** → **Genetic programming;** *Transfer learning;*

Keywords

Coevolution; Multi-agent Systems; Task transfer; Games

1. INTRODUCTION

Task domains in which credit assignment is delayed imply that the learning agent is required to perform multiple interactions with the environment before feedback is received, or reinforcement learning (RL) [19]. Games potentially represent a generic example of a task with delayed feedback. The goal of the learning agent is to discover a policy to play the game at a suitably challenging level. However, when scaling RL to increasingly difficult task domains it is not always possible to directly solve the original task formulation. For example, the number of interactions with the task might be too costly to perform or there is complete disengagement between the learner and task, i.e. no 'learning gradient'.

One approach to deal with this issue is to first learn policies for some *source* task and then 'transfer' this to the required *target* task [21, 20]. In this work we are interested in a framework for task transfer under GP in which policies are constructed hierarchically, or a policy tree. First, lower level source / leaf policies are evolved for related but different source task(s). A second phase of evolution is conducted to learn how to reuse the source / leaf policies under the target task by evolving a higher level target policy.

We empirically test this 2-phase approach for hierarchical policy reuse under the challenging multi-agent soccer domain of Half-field Offense (HFO). In phase 1, policies are evolved under two independent *source tasks*: keepaway (which evolves policies for retaining possession of the ball) and shooting on the goal. Phase 2 evolves a policy for the *target task* of HFO by learning how to reuse a subset of the previously evolved behaviours. HFO is much closer to the full-scale Robocup soccer task and requires one team to defend their goal and the other team to score (the offense team has no goal or goalie). The objective, state, and action spaces are not the same for source and target tasks, a criteria for meaningful task transfer [21, 20]. We demonstrate that the final explicitly hierarchical policy (tree) achieves an equivalent level of performance as the current RL state-of-the-art, but at a fraction of the model complexity.

The architecture used to evolve policies is both highly modular and hierarchical. Specifically, a symbiotic bid-based (SBB) framework is used in which genetic algorithm (GA) and GP populations simultaneously coevolve to identify policies, i.e. programs are coevolved to collectively decompose the task and / or reuse previously evolved policies. Such a framework was applied to tasks that could be solved without task transfer [13, 4, 11]. Indeed, the SBB framework has been shown to be capable of strong performance under Keepaway [10], but appears to be comparatively poor at HFO. This work represents the first instance in which task transfer is used in combination with SBB to address a task in which SBB would otherwise fail to reach state-of-the-art levels of performance.

Section 2 details the nature of the source and target task domains. The formulation assumed for SBB is described in Section 3. The approach to combining SBB with task transfer is established in Section 4 and the experimental study detailed in Section 5. Section 6 concludes the paper.

GECCO '15, July 11 - 15, 2015, Madrid, Spain

ISBN 978-1-4503-3472-3/15/07...$15.00

DOI: http://dx.doi.org/10.1145/2739480.2754798

2. TASK CHARACTERIZATION

Robocup 2D Simulated Soccer is a widely-used environment for evaluating multi-agent machine learning systems. However, the full game of soccer is often too complex for a tabula rasa approach, i.e. learning agents try to master the entire task with a single monolithic policy and no prior task decomposition [17]. Thus, researchers have focused on sub-tasks of the full game [18, 16, 7, 14, 22, 8]. Keepaway and HFO soccer represent interesting reinforcement learning tasks in that they are: 1) multi-agent; 2) stochastic and non-Markovian; 3) utilize real-valued state variables; and 4) can be parameterized to represent a family of incrementally more difficult tasks. It is the latter property that has seen their recommendation as a benchmark for assessing the utility of reinforcement learning algorithms [7, 21].

2.1 Keepaway Task

Keepaway represents one sub-task of Robocup Soccer in which a team of K *keepers* tries to maintain possession of the ball while an opposing team of $K - 1$ *takers* attempt to gain possession [16]. The goal is for keepers to learn a policy that maximizes the length of play against the takers, which follow a pre-specified behaviour. The game ends if the ball is kicked out of bounds or captured by the takers. When a game ends, each keeper receives the game duration in milliseconds as a reward signal.

In this work we are specifically interested in a 4v3, or $K = 4$, version of the task. Our version of Keepaway is played on a 60×60 meter field, instead of the more common 25×25 meter bounding box, in order to increase the compatibility with the HFO task. The game is initialized with keepers in four corners of a 15×15 meter square at centre field, the ball placed near one keeper, and the takers in the centre. Keepers learn to deploy a set of domain-specific macro-actions $\{hold, getOpen, pass(k)\}$, at discrete timesteps of 100 milliseconds. Each macro-action may last more than one timestep, and control is returned to the player when the macro-action terminates. A keeper in possession of the ball has the option of either *hold* or $pass(k)$, where k indexes one of its $K-1$ teammates. Keepers not in possession of the ball automatically select the *getOpen* macro-action.

At each timestep, keepers receive state information in the form of 11 real-valued distance and angle sensor inputs that describe the location of other players on the field (Table 1). The sensors are noisy, thus players must cope with inaccurate state information. Furthermore, the players' actuators are unreliable, often resulting in inaccurate passes and fumbled attempts to hold the ball.

2.2 Half-field Offense Task

Half-field offense is another sub-task of Robocup Soccer with significantly more complexity than Keepaway [7]. In HFO, a team of offense players tries to manoeuvre the ball past a defending team and around the goalie in order to score. A game ends if the ball is kicked out of bounds, captured by an outfield defense player or the goalie, or a goal is scored. The defense team in HFO follow a pre-specified behaviour defined by the original task [7]. Each offense player receives one reward signal of either $\{0.8, 0.9, 2\}$ for end-game conditions {*captured by outfield defense* or *kicked out of bounds*, *caught by goalie*, *goal scored*}.

We are specifically interested in 4v4 HFO, in which the offense team has 4 players while the defense team is made up of 3 outfield defenders plus a goalie. HFO is played on one half of the full soccer field. All outfield players are initialized within a 15×15 meter square as in Keepaway, but in HFO the centre of the initialization box is stochastically placed somewhere on the field roughly 55 meters from the goal. Naturally, the goalie is initialized in the goal region.

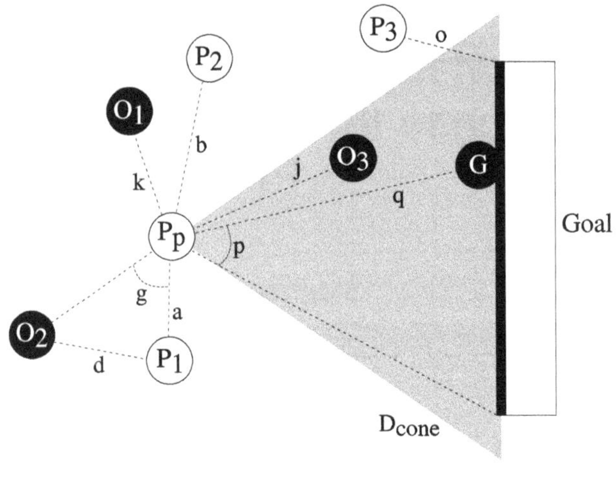

Figure 1: Sample sensor inputs for the 4v4 Half-field Offense task. See Table 1 for full description.

Offense players in HFO learn to deploy a slightly different set of macro-actions than in the Keepaway task. Their options at each timestep are $shoot, dribble, getOpen, pass(k)$. Thus, an offense player in possession of the ball has the option to either dribble towards the goal, pass to a teammate, or shoot. As per the Keepaway task, each macro-action may last more than one timestep and control is returned to the player when the macro-action terminates. In addition to the modified action space, the HFO task has 6 *additional* sensor inputs relative to the Keepaway task (Table 1). The additional sensors summarize distance to the goal for each offense player and the angle of the maximum scoring window for the player with the ball, i.e. how open the net is (Figure 1). As in Keepaway, all sensor inputs and actuators are unreliable. Readers are refereed to the original HFO paper for a complete definition of the task [7].

3. SYMBIOTIC BID-BASED GP

Symbiotic Bid-Based GP (SBB) is a hierarchical framework for symbiotically coevolving policies, or decomposing the task, over two distinct phases of evolution (Figure 2).[13, 4, 11, 10]. The first phase produces a library of diverse, specialist policies of limited capability. The second phase builds more general and robust policies by reusing a subset of policies from the first phase, essentially building generalist strategies from multiple specialists. Thus, diversity maintenance is critical during the first phase of evolution to ensure the identification of a wide range of specialist behaviours. See [10, 9] for an example of this within the context of the Keepaway task. Policies are represented by two distinct populations within the SBB algorithm: a host GA population defines group membership; and a symbiont population defines a pool of GP individuals that can potentially appear in a host group.

Table 1: Sensor inputs for the 4v3 Half-field Keepaway task and 4v4 Half-field Offense task. P_p is the player in possession of the ball. The rest of the players on P_p's team are numbered relative to their distance from P_p with P_1 being the closest. 'Opponent' refers to any taker in the Keepaway task and any 'defense' player in the HFO task. All sensor inputs are real-valued. Angle values range from $0°$ to $360°$ and distance values range from 0 to approximately 85 meters.

			Sensor Input	Description
Keepaway	Half-field Offense	a	$dist(P_p, P_1)$	Distance from P_p to closest teammate.
		b	$dist(P_p, P_2)$	Distance from P_p to second-closest teammate.
		c	$dist(P_p, P_3)$	Distance from P_p to third-closest teammate
		d	$dist(P_1, O_{min})$	Distance from P_1 to closest opponent.
		e	$dist(P_2, O_{min})$	Distance from P_2 to closest opponent.
		f	$dist(P_3, O_{min})$	Distance from P_3 to closest opponent.
		g	$min_{angle}(P_1, O_p, O_{min})$	Min. angle, with vertex at P_p, between P_1 and any opponent.
		h	$min_{angle}(P_2, O_p, O_{min})$	Min. angle, with vertex at P_p, between P_2 and any opponent.
		i	$min_{angle}(P_3, O_p, O_{min})$	Min. angle, with vertex at P_p, between P_3 and any opponent.
		j	$min_{dist}(P_p, O_{Dcone})$	Min. distance from P_p to any player in the dribble cone. The dribble cone is a cone with half angle $60°$ with its vertex at P_p and axis passing through the centre of the goal. D_{cone} is the set of defenders in the dribble cone.
		k	$dist(P_p, O_{min})$	Distance from P_p to closest opponent.
		l	$dist(P_p, GL)$	Distance from P_p to goal line.
		m	$dist(P_1, GL)$	Distance from P_1 to goal line.
		n	$dist(P_2, GL)$	Distance from P_2 to goal line.
		o	$dist(P_3, GL)$	Distance from P_3 to goal line.
		p	$max_{angle}(P_p, Goal)$	Max. angle with vertex at P_p, formed by rays connecting P_p and goalposts or opponents in the goal cone, which is the triangle formed by P_p and the two goalposts.
		q	$dist(P_p, Goalie)$	Distance from P_p to the goalie.

This section gives an overview of the components of SBB that are critical to understanding this work. Relative to previous instances of the SBB framework for reinforcement learning tasks ([13, 4, 11, 10]), this work adopts a more general approach to diversity maintenance as well as having to explicitly address the issue of knowledge transfer between different tasks.

3.1 Programs

The basic building blocks in SBB are linear genetic programs [1], or register machines, consisting of a sequence of instructions that operate on sensor inputs or internal registers. We refer to these programs as symbionts, because their role in the larger algorithm is inspired by biological symbiosis [12]. Each symbiont is associated with *one* domain-specific action, or **atomic action**, from the task domain.[1] For example $\{hold, getOpen, pass(k)\}$ in the Keepaway task (Section 2.1). Given all sensor inputs in the current timestep, the program outputs a single real valued 'bid', which expresses how confident this symbiont is about using its particular action, given the current state of the environment. Determining which of the available sensor inputs are actually used in the program, as well as the number of instructions and their operations, are both emergent properties of the evolutionary process. Variation operators modify symbionts by adding and/or removing instructions from the program, flipping a single bit in an instruction, or changing the symbiont's atomic action [12].

3.2 Policies

A single symbiont cannot represent a policy for any task because symbionts are only associated with a *single* action

[1]Section 3.4 generalizes this to previously evolved SBB individuals.

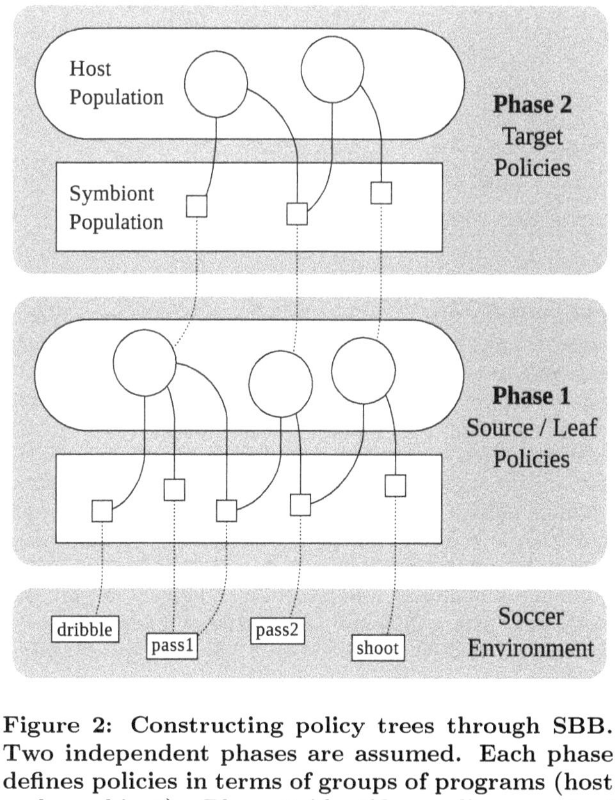

Figure 2: Constructing policy trees through SBB. Two independent phases are assumed. Each phase defines policies in terms of groups of programs (host and symbiont). Phase 1 identifies a diverse set of relatively simple 'source / leaf' policies. Phase 2 learns how to reuse phase 1 (source / leaf) policies for solving a different target task.

(Section 3.1). Therefore, a policy is constructed from a co-operative group of symbionts. These groups are defined by members of the host population, h_i, Figure 2. For a policy to make a decision at any point in time, each symbiont identified by the host ($sym \in h_i$) must observe the current sensor inputs and execute its program, resulting in a 'bid'. The policy will then deploy the action of the symbiont with the highest bid. Algorithm 1 summarizes this process under a generic Robocup soccer task. Note that policy h_i is deployed homogeneously across all learning agents.

Algorithm 1 Generic process for SBB to determine an action for the player in possession of the ball in Robocup Soccer, given a host policy h_i. *task* denotes the soccer simulator. The 'fail' condition may correspond, for example, to an opponent intercepting the ball or the ball exceeding the field boundary. Step 1f represents a reference to a previously evolved (source) policy, as encountered in phase 2.

1. DO
   (a) Present the state variables describing the current state for the player p in possession of the ball, or $\vec{s}_p(t_s)$ to host h_i;
   (b) $\forall sym \in h_i$, execute the symbiont programs to establish the corresponding symbiont bid, or $sym(bid(\vec{s}_p(t_s)))$;
   (c) Identify the 'winning' symbiont as that with the maximum bid from host h_i, $sym^* = \arg_{sym \in h_i} \max[sym(bid(\vec{s}_p(t_s)))]$;
   (d) IF ($sym^*(action) == atomic\ action$)
   (e) THEN Present the action from the winning symbiont to the soccer simulator, or $\vec{s}(t_s = t_s + 1) \leftarrow task \leftarrow sym^*(action)$
   (f) ELSE $h_i = sym^*(action)$ *Call* [Algorithm 1]
2. WHILE (!fail)

There is no reason why a host (policy) cannot contain two symbionts with the same action. This actually occurs frequently because a symbiont essentially learns a context, relative to sensor inputs, for deploying its action. This context is by definition specific to a particular region of the policy space, thus two symbionts may develop different contexts for the same atomic action. The bidding framework is the mechanism for facilitating task decomposition between symbionts in a host, and the nature of this decomposition defines the policy's behaviour in the environment.

The same symbiont may function effectively in multiple hosts, each with a different compliment of group members. Hosts are initialized with between 2 and 5 symbionts. Variation operators may remove symbionts from the host, add an existing symbiont from the symbiont population to the host, or create a new symbiont by cloning an existing host-member and applying the symbiont variation operators to ensure that it is unique [12]. Thus, the number of symbionts in a host varies over time subject to a minimum of 2 and maximum of ω. In each generation, the selection operator deletes the worst performing $Mgap$ hosts. Symbionts no longer associated with any host are assumed to be ineffective and are also deleted.

There is no concept of symbiont fitness, only the knowledge of whether or not it is useful in any host. In effect we are assuming multi-level selection in which a policy is only evaluated as a whole as opposed to the sum of its parts [15]. The host population size, $Msize$, remains fixed throughout evolution while the symbiont population size varies. In order to encourage the development of a variety of policies by the host population, special attention is given to diversity maintenance (Section 3.3). Previous research has established the significance of diversity maintenance under multiple RL tasks [14, 6, 4, 3, 10, 9].

3.3 Diversity Mechanisms

In Robocup Soccer, the fitness of a policy is the mean reward across all games played. Fitness is only assigned to the host under evaluation. However, in order to promote population diversity, each host's *novelty* must also factor into the selection process, where novelty refers to the degree of similarity between a host and all other members of the *same* population. Several methods to balance fitness and novelty exist, including fitness sharing, crowding, or multi-objective optimization. In this work we adopt a simple linear combination of fitness and novelty [2], thus each host's performance is defined prior to selection:

$$\mathcal{F}(h_i) = (1-p) \cdot \overline{Fit(h_i)} + p \cdot \overline{Nov(h_i)} \quad (1)$$

where $\overline{Fit}$ and $\overline{Nov}$ are the normalized fitness and novelty of host i, and p is a parameter to control the relative weight of novelty. The novelty component requires a method for measuring the 'distance' between each pair of hosts, discussed below. Moreover, rather than assuming a single measure of diversity, we switch between two different distance measures every $\tau = 10$ generations. Switching between dissimilar distance metrics avoids introducing yet another scalar weighting parameter, and has been shown to be as effective as explicitly multi-objective formulations [3].

3.3.1 Symbiont-utility Distance Metric

A symbiont-utility distance metric is used to characterize which symbionts are active within a host.[2] A symbiont is considered active if it has scored a winning bid, and thus suggested an action for the task domain, at least once during the life of the host. The distance between hosts is summarized as the ratio of active symbionts common to both hosts. Thus, the distance between hosts i and k is

$$dist(h_i, h_k) = 1 - \frac{Sym_{active}(h_i) \cap Sym_{active}(h_k)}{Sym_{active}(h_i) \cup Sym_{active}(h_k)} \quad (2)$$

where $Sym_{active}(h_x)$ represents the set of active symbionts in host x. $p = 0.2$ when using this diversity metric in Equation 1. Note that this diversity metric is task independent.

3.3.2 Behavioural Distance Metric

A behavioural distance metric characterizes a host by how it interacts with the environment. At each decision point in a game, the state (11 real-valued state variables in the case of 4v3 Keepaway) and subsequent action taken by the host are recorded. Each state variable is discretized to $[0, 1, 2]$, or

[2]The metric adopted is motivated by the approach taken in [14] for promoting diversity under a neuro-evolutionary setting.

low, medium, high. Thus, for each training game a *profile* vector is recorded, $\vec{p} = [\{a(t), s(t)\}, t \in T]$, where $a(t)$ is the atomic action taken, $s(t)$ is the discretized state observation, and T represents every decision point in the associated game. Note that this method of characterizing behaviour is also task-independent. Hosts maintain a historical record of the profile $\vec{p}$ for every game played. We define $\vec{P}$ to be the concatenation of all profile vectors $\vec{p}$ in a host's historical record. Behavioural distance between a pair of hosts can now be summarized as the Normalized Compression Distance [6] between their corresponding concatenated profile vectors: $dist(h_i, h_k) = ncd(\vec{P}_i, \vec{P}_k)$. $p = 0.4$ when using behavioural diversity in Equation 1.

3.4 Policy Trees

After a number of generations, the host population may not contain any suitable solutions [13, 4, 11, 10, 9]. However, diversity maintenance encourages a variety of *different* behaviours to be present (Section 3.3). These policies can be reused as building blocks within larger policy trees. Thus, a new phase of evolution begins with an entirely new SBB initialization (Figure 2 'Phase 2'). The only difference being that a symbiont in phase 2 references a policy previously evolved during phase 1 instead of an atomic action. Thus, symbionts at phase 2 are learning the appropriate context(s) in which to deploy previously evolved *source* policies which are selected and cached from the independent evolutionary cycle of 'phase 1'. The selection process is detailed in Section 4.1.2. At present only one level of the policy tree undergoes development at a time, thus policies identified during phase 1 are 'frozen' during phase 2.

When evaluating a policy in phase 2, Algorithm 1 is again called. However, this time the winning action at Step 1c is a reference to a previously evolved source / leaf policy from phase 1. Algorithm 1 is then recursively called at Step 1f in order to resolve which symbiont from the source / leaf policy is selected and therefore what atomic action is deployed (Step 1e).

Conceptually, policy trees learn to combine multiple, diverse *specialist* policies into a single *generalist* policy, a process which has been demonstrated in several previous works [13, 4, 11, 10]. The major contribution of this study is to show that policy trees can be used to transfer knowledge from a source task to a related, but more complex target task. Section 4 details how this is achieved with 3 sub-tasks of Robocup Soccer.

4. KNOWLEDGE TRANSFER IN SBB

Inter-task knowledge transfer refers to the ability of a learning algorithm to leverage experience gained by interacting with a *source* task environment in order to improve some aspect of learning in a *target* task [21, 20]. Keepaway soccer is clearly a sub-task of HFO. For example, from the stochastic start position in HFO (Section 2.2), offensive players essentially have to play Keepaway and dribble towards the goal before trying to score. It follows that knowledge gained while learning to play Keepaway should be useful in the context of HFO.

The problem of transfer from 4v3 Keepaway to HFO does not require an independent mapping interface between feature or action spaces. This is possible because most Keepaway inputs and actions have direct equivalents within the HFO task (Table 1). The one exception being the hold action in Keepaway, which is interpreted as a dribble-towards-goal action under HFO. It is therefore reasonable to deploy a policy trained in the 4v3 Keepaway task directly under HFO without modification. However, it will not represent a successful HFO policy on its own because in Keepaway there is no concept of goal scoring, or even a macro-action to support scoring goals. Furthermore, the ball-handling skills under HFO are different, requiring the players to maintain possession of the ball *and* move toward the goal region. Thus, additional capabilities are necessary in order to attempt HFO. Sections 4.1 and 4.2 describe how SBB policy trees can discover these policies over 2 phases of evolution.

4.1 Phase 1: Multiple Source Tasks

In addition to ball handling, which we aim to 'transfer' from Keepaway as a source task, the other basic component to HFO is scoring goals. In order to design an appropriate source task scenario to focus on goal scoring, we modify the HFO environment to restrict the initial position of players to within 15 meters of the goal. From this position, offense players no longer need to manoeuvre the ball down field and can therefore concentrate on scoring goals. During phase 1, multiple policies are evolved independently in each of the two *different* source tasks: Keepaway and Scoring. From these two groups, a subset of policies are selected to represent the *source task* policies, which will be combined in a policy tree for learning the target task, HFO. The sequence of events promoting this development takes the form of the following 3 steps.

4.1.1 Phase 1 Policy Development

First, we conduct $N = 10$ independent, single-phase runs of SBB in the Keepaway task. Each run is parameterized as per Table 2 with diversity maintenance (Section 3.3). After removing $Mgap$ policies at the final generation[3], each run produces 90 unique policies for a combined total over N runs of 900 Keepaway policies. The primary use for Keepaway policies will be to maintain possession of the ball. Successful transfer to the HFO task will generalize this to moving to the goal region. Likewise, $N = 10$ independent, single-phase runs of SBB are performed in the Scoring task, also returning a total of 900 candidate policies.

4.1.2 Pareto Ranking of Phase 1 Policies

Having established a pool of Keepaway and goal scoring behaviours (source tasks) we now adopt the following process to filter the number of policies before phase 2 of SBB (Figure 2). Each of the 900 *Keepaway* behaviours are deployed for 10 trial games in the full HFO environment. Information from two sensors are then used to characterize the utility of candidate Keepaway policies based on the following 2 objectives. **Distance to Goal** (Table 1 – mean of sensor input l): better policies should minimize the mean of this input over 10 games. **Distance to closest player in dribble cone** (Table 1 – mean of sensor input j): provides a sense of how congested the player in possession of the ball is, and how much space it has to dribble towards the goal without loosing possession. Hence, better policies should maximize this property.

[3]SBB is a breeder model where the worst $Mgap$ individuals are replaced at each generation [13, 4, 11, 10].

Given these two objectives, we find the set of Pareto non-dominated policies[4] from the pool of 900 candidates, which in this case returns a subset of 11 Keepaway policies.

In the case of *Scoring* behaviours, candidate Scoring policies are also deployed for 10 trial games in the HFO environment (modified for scoring-only as per Section 4.1) and ranked based on 3 objectives: 1) maximize sensor input j to reduce congestion (see above); 2) maximize sensor input p, which indicates the degree to which the goal is 'open'; and 3) maximize the main HFO objective, or number of goals scored. Given these 3 objectives, taking the set of Pareto non-dominated policies from the pool of 900 candidates returns a subset of 7 goal scoring policies.

4.1.3 Recombination of Source Task Policies

A pool of policies developed w.r.t. the source tasks have now been identified. These represent the 'actions' available during a second phase of evolution (Figure 2). SBB phase 2 constructs a 'root node' that learns to switch between source / leaf policies to solve the HFO task.

4.2 Phase 2: Target Task

In SBB phase 2, policy trees will be evolved for the HFO task, where each policy tree may combine any of the 18 source policies identified in phase 1 (Section 4.1). However, such a simplistic decomposition of HFO into two source tasks is just a starting point. Each source policy will have a unique specialization care of diversity maintenance (see Section 3.3) and the Pareto selection process of Section 4.1. The policy identified by SBB during phase 2 essentially evolves a root node in a policy tree. Such a root node identifies under what conditions to switch between two or more source policies (as previously evolved in phase 1). Thus, the potential exists to extend and recombine existing source policies into a new behaviour, or conversely associate a previous policy with a new action as in the case of learning to dribble the ball.

Phase 2 is conducted without diversity maintenance as the objective is strictly exploitative, i.e. $p = 0$ in Eqn. 1. Each run produces $Msize/2$ policy tree root nodes. A post-training validation phase is then conducted, in which each policy tree is evaluated over an additional 25 games. The policy with the highest average reward (Section 2.2) on validation is selected as champion of the run. Finally, due to the stochasticity of the task[5], 1000 post-training test games are required to provide an accurate measure of performance for the single champion policy from each run.

5. RESULTS

Three algorithms will be benchmarked: 1) **SBB-T**: Hierarchical SBB *with* transfer as per Section 4; 2) **SBB**: Hierarchical SBB *without* transfer or prior task decomposition. In this case the full HFO task is assumed during phase 1 and 2 of SBB solutions (Figure 2). The 3-objective Pareto ranking process, identical to that used for the Scoring source task, is used to filter phase 1 policies down to 14 source / leaf policies; and 3) **SarsaRBF**: The Sarsa Temporal Difference Method with Radial Basis Functions. SarsaRBF represents the current state-of-the-art in the HFO task [7].

[4]A solution a_i is said to dominate another solution a_j, if both of the following conditions are true: $a_i \succ a_j \leftrightarrow \forall k[f_k(a_i) \geq f_k(a_j)] \wedge \exists m[f_m(a_i) > f_m(a_j)]$.

[5]Sensor and actuator noise, as well as random start conditions for takers, keepers, and ball in each game.

Table 2: Parameterization of Host and Symbiont populations. p_{mx} denotes a mutation operator in which: $x \in \{d, a\}$ are the prob. of deleting or adding a symbiont respectively; $x \in \{m, n\}$ are the prob. of creating a new symbiont or changing the symbiont action respectively.

Host (GA) population			
Parameter	Value	Parameter	Value
t_{max} phase 1	250, 60	ω	30
t_{max} phase 2	125	t_{eval}	10
$Msize$	180	$Mgap$	50%
p_{md}	0.7	p_{ma}	0.7
p_{mm}	0.2	p_{mn}	0.1
Symbiont (GP) population			
$numRegisters$	8	$maxProgSize$	96
p_{delete}, p_{add}	0.5	p_{mutate}, p_{swap}	1.0

As per previous research, the Robocup Soccer Server[6] simulates the 2D soccer environment. Code from the designers of Keepaway[7] and HFO[8] provides full implementation of the tasks.

Table 2 summarizes the parameterization assumed for SBB-T. In the case of the number of generations (t_{max}), two limits appear at phase 1 on account of the goal scoring task being easier than Keepaway. Parameterizing SBB assumes the same parameterization as SBB-T *except* in the case of the phase 1 population size and generation limit. SBB-T evolves Keepaway and Scoring behaviours using independent populations of size 180 for 250 and 60 generations respectively. Thus, SBB evolves a single population of size $Msize = 2 \times 180$ for a total of $t_{max} = 250 + 60$ generations.

The fitness of each individual is determined following play against the predefined HFO defenders in at most t_{eval} stochastically initialized games. Such a constraint is enforced on account of the computational overhead in estimating fitness in this task domain. The total generations performed at *each* phase represent a computational cost of $\approx$ *24hrs*. During phase 2 a total of 20 runs are performed for each SBB experiment, of which results are reported on the top 10 as defined by validation performance post training (but before test). In short, the computational cost of the task precludes fitness evaluation over larger populations or more games per fitness evaluation. Other researchers have adopted similar schemes for identifying champion solutions for evaluating test performance [5]. Moreover, on the easier Keepaway task, neuro-evolutionary solutions have been limited to performing 5 runs alone, again on account of the computational cost of performing runs [14, 22].

5.1 Test Performance

Figure 3 reports test performance for the three approaches to learning the HFO task. It is apparent that both SarsaRBF and SBB-T reach similar levels of performance. Indeed, there is no statistical difference between their distributions (Mann-Whitney rank test, $P < 0.05$). SBB is unable to

[6]http://sourceforge.net/apps/mediawiki/sserver

[7]http://www.cs.utexas.edu/~AustinVilla/sim/keepaway

[8]http://www.cs.utexas.edu/~AustinVilla/sim/halffieldoffense

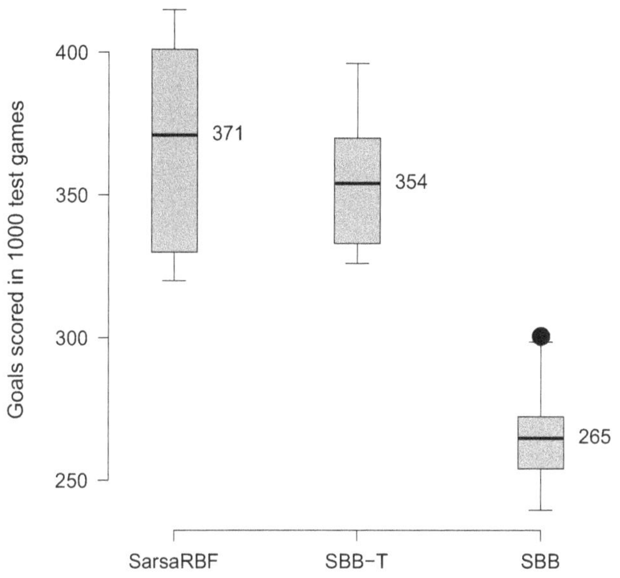

Figure 3: Post-training test results for each algorithm over 1000 games. Box plots summarize the quartile distribution over 10 independent runs. SarsaRBF represents a current state-of-the-art reinforcement learner for the HFO task; SBB-T is hierarchical SBB *with* task transfer; SBB is hierarchical SBB *without* task transfer.

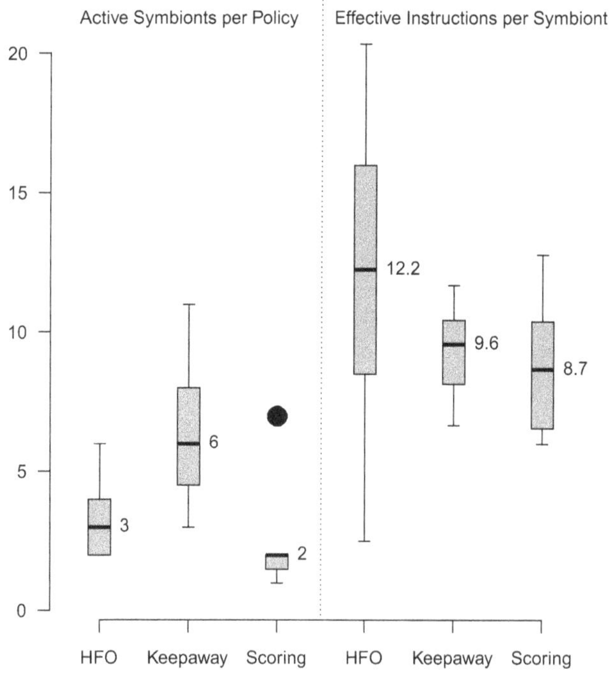

Figure 4: SBB-T solution complexity. Quartile statistics for number of symbionts (programs) per policy and instructions per program. 'HFO' denotes the SBB policy evolved against the target task (phase 2); 'Keepaway' and 'Scoring' denote the SBB policies evolved against source tasks (phase 1).

reach a competitive level, $P > 0.05$ relative to both SBB-T and SarsaRBF.

5.2 Complexity

All SBB policies are groups of symbionts working cooperatively (Section 3), and symbionts are essentially linear genetic programs. Thus, we can describe the complexity of a solution by counting the number of symbionts / instructions per symbiont referenced by a champion policy tree. Recall that two types of source task are employed during task transfer, denoted 'Keepaway' and 'Scoring' (Section 4.1). Figure 4 gives the distributions for the median number of symbionts and median number of instructions per symbiont, where both counts are post-intron removal [1], over all 10 runs of SBB-T.

For example, an HFO policy consisting of 3 symbionts, which each contain a median instruction count of ≈ 12.2, indexes three source / leaf policies. If two of these correspond to the more complex Keepaway leaf policy, each consisting of 6 programs with 9.6 instructions each, and the third is a Scoring leaf policy with 2 programs and 8.7 instructions each, then the total instruction count would be 169 instructions. This is in contrast to a SarsaRBF solution, which contains $16,320$ weight / RBF pairs that need to be calculated at each decision point. Note also that only one HFO solution ($3 \times 12.2 \approx 36$ instructions) and one Keepaway policy ($6 \times 9.6 \approx 58$ instructions) or Scoring policy ($2 \times 8.7 \approx 17$ instructions) require evaluation to produce a decision. In short, SBB policies are more efficient to implement post training. Empirically, the average CPU time required for SarsaRBF to make a decision over 1000 timesteps is 2.04 ms whereas SBB-T is an order of magnitude faster, requiring only 0.16 ms.

5.3 Solution Analysis

In order to understand the behaviour of policy trees in the HFO task, we can analyze a single champion tree from the SBB-T experiment. Figure 5 describes one tree that managed to score in 395 of 1000 test games. This policy tree has 4 active symbionts at the upper level, 3 of which index Keepaway source policies and 1 indexes a Scoring source policy. There are a total of 9 active symbionts across all source / leaf policies, covering the full scope of domain-specific atomic actions. To understand the strategy of this policy tree, we can trace the sequence of source / leaf policies deployed at each decision point during two HFO games that each ended with a goal for this policy. Game 1:[Start K_3 K_3 K_3 K_1 K_3 K_1 K_3 K_3 K_1 K_1 K_1 S S S S S S Goal]. Game 2: [Start K_1 K_2 K_3 K_1 K_1 K_1 K_1 K_1 S K_3 S Goal]. It is clear from these traces that the strategy is to interleave different Keepaway source policies while approaching the goal, then introduce the Scoring source policy shortly before achieving the winning shot. In the case of Game 1, multiple calls to the Scoring meta-action indicate that some passing occurred near the goal region before the winning kick on goal. Interestingly, the policy has made use of K_2, which is essentially a degenerate dribble policy, implying that it can be replaced with a dribble atomic action at the symbiont in the upper policy level.

6. CONCLUSION

The SBB framework for evolving policy trees has been refined to facilitate the utilization of task transfer. Task transfer represents a methodology for taking policies identi-

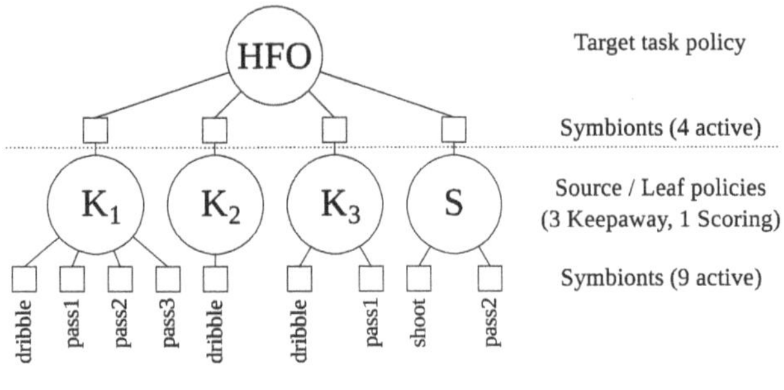

Figure 5: Example policy tree from the SBB-T experiment. Source / leaf policy 'K_2' is actually redundant, i.e. can be replaced by the 'dribble' atomic action.

fied under source tasks and learning how to extend or redeploy them to provide policies under a more difficult target task. In this case, the Half-field Offense sub-task of Robocup soccer is used as the target task, where HFO represents a benchmark known to be more difficult than the Keepaway task previously employed under task transfer. We show that SBB as originally formulated is not able to solve this task directly. In order to formulate task transfer for SBB we make the following recommendations: 1) use multiple source tasks; 2) evolve source task policies with diversity maintenance; and, 3) use Pareto dominance to refine the number of source task policies before attempting the target task.

The policy trees that were identified using task transfer achieved HFO performance competitive with the current state-of-the-art, and were significantly simpler. Conversely, it was not possible to evolve SBB policy trees with comparative performance without task transfer. Future work will continue to investigate mechanisms for making use of task transfer under SBB policy tree structures.

7. ACKNOWLEDGMENTS

The authors are grateful for support from the NSERC Discovery and CFI programs (Canada).

8. REFERENCES

[1] M. Brameier and W. Banzhaf. *Linear Genetic Programming.* Springer, 2007.

[2] G. Cuccu and F. Gomez. When novelty is not enough. In *EvoApp - Part I*, volume 6624 of *LNCS*, 2011.

[3] S. Doncieux and J.-B. Mouret. Behavioral diversity with multiple behavioral distances. In *IEEE Congress on Evolutionary Computation*, 2013.

[4] J. A. Doucette, P. Lichodzijewski, and M. I. Heywood. Hierarchical task decomposition through symbiosis in reinforcement learning. In *Proceedings of the ACM Genetic and Evolutionary Computation Conference*, 2012.

[5] C. Gagne, M. Schoenauer, M. Sebag, and M. Tomassini. Genetic programming for kernel-based learning with co-evolving subsets selection. In *PPSN*, volume 4193 of *LNCS*, 2006.

[6] F. Gomez. Sustaining diversity using behavioral information distance. In *ACM Conference on Genetic and Evolutionary Computation*, 2009.

[7] S. Kalyanakrishnan, Y. Liu, and P. Stone. Half field offense in robocup soccer: A multiagent reinforcement learning case study. In G. Lakemeyer, E. Sklar, D. Sorenti, and T. Takahashi, editors, *RoboCup-2006: Robot Soccer World Cup X*, volume 4434 of *Lecture Notes in Artificial Intelligence.* Springer, Berlin, 2007.

[8] S. Kalyanakrishnan and P. Stone. An empirical analysis of value function-based and policy search reinforcement learning. In *Proceedings of the International Conference on Autonomous Agents and Multiagent Systems*, 2009.

[9] S. Kelly and M. I. Heywood. Genotypic versus behavioural diversity for teams of programs under the 4-v-3 keepaway soccer task. In *Proceedings of the AAAI Conference on Artificial Intelligence*, 2014.

[10] S. Kelly and M. I. Heywood. On diversity, teaming, and hierarchical policies: Observations from the keepaway soccer task. In *European Conference on Genetic Programming*, volume 8599 of *LNCS.* Springer, 2014.

[11] S. Kelly, P. Lichodzijewski, and M. I. Heywood. On run time libraries and hierarchical symbiosis. In *IEEE Congress on Evolutionary Computation*, 2012.

[12] P. Lichodzijewski and M. I. Heywood. Symbiosis, complexification and simplicity under GP. In *Proceedings of the ACM Genetic and Evolutionary Computation Conference*, 2010.

[13] P. Lichodzijewski and M. I. Heywood. The Rubik cube and GP temporal sequence learning: an initial study. In *Genetic Programming Theory and Practice VIII*, chapter 3. Springer, 2011.

[14] J. H. Metzen, M. Edgington, Y. Kassahun, and F. Kirchner. Performance evaluation of EANT in the robocup keepaway benchmark. In *IEEE International Conference on Machine Learning and Applications*, 2007.

[15] S. Okasha. Multilevel selection and the major transitions in evolution. *Philosophy of Science*, 72:1013–1025, 2005.

[16] P. Stone, G. Kuhlmann, M. Taylor, and Y. Liu. Keepaway soccer: From machine learning testbed to benchmark. In *RoboCup 2005: Robot Soccer World Cup IX.* 2006.

[17] P. Stone and R. S. Sutton. Scaling reinforcement learning toward robocup soccer. In *The Eighteenth International Conference on Machine Learning*, 2001.

[18] P. Stone, R. S. Sutton, and G. Kuhlmann. Reinforcement learning for robocup-soccer keepaway. *Adaptive Behavior*, 13(3):165–188, 2005.

[19] R. R. Sutton and A. G. Barto. *Reinforcement Learning: An introduction.* MIT Press, 1998.

[20] M. E. Taylor and P. Stone. Transfer learning for reinforcement learning domains: A survey. *Journal of Machine Learning Research*, 10(1):1633–1685, 2009.

[21] M. E. Taylor and P. Stone. An introduction to inter-task transfer for reinforcement learning. *AI Magazine*, 32(1):15–34, 2011.

[22] S. Whiteson, M. E. Taylor, and P. Stone. Critical factors in the empirical performance of temporal difference and evolutionary methods for reinforcement learning. *Journal of Autonomous Agents and Multi-Agent Systems*, 21(1):1–27, 2009.

A Local Search Approach to Genetic Programming for Binary Classification

Emigdio Z-Flores[*], Leonardo Trujillo[†]
Instituto Tecnológico de Tijuana, México

Oliver Schütze[‡]
CINVESTAV-IPN, México

Pierrick Legrand[§]
Université of Bordeaux
CQFD Team, INRIA Bordeaux
IMB, France

ABSTRACT

In standard genetic programming (GP), a search is performed over a syntax space defined by the set of primitives, looking for the best expressions that minimize a cost function based on a training set. However, most GP systems lack a numerical optimization method to fine tune the implicit parameters of each candidate solution. Instead, GP relies on more exploratory search operators at the syntax level. This work proposes a memetic GP, tailored for binary classification problems. In the proposed method, each node in a GP tree is weighted by a real-valued parameter, which is then numerically optimized using a continuous transfer function and the Trust Region algorithm is used as a local search method. Experimental results show that potential classifiers produced by GP are improved by the local searcher, and hence the overall search is improved achieving significant performance gains, that are competitive with state-of-the-art methods on well-known benchmarks.

Categories and Subject Descriptors

I.2.2 [**Artificial Intelligence**]: Automatic Programming

Keywords

Genetic Programming; Local Search; Memetic Algorithms; Classification

1. INTRODUCTION

The general goal of the genetic programming (GP) paradigm is to evolve specialized syntactic expressions that can solve a user defined problem, mostly used in supervised learning tasks. In particular, GP is widely used to generate mathematical functions, or operators, that solve symbolic regression and classification problems, a task that can be stated as follows. The goal is to search for the symbolic expression $K^O : \mathbb{R}^p \rightarrow \mathbb{R}$ that best fits a particular training set $\mathbb{T} = \{(\boldsymbol{x}_1, y_1), \ldots, (\boldsymbol{x}_n, y_n)\}$ of n input/output pairs with $\boldsymbol{x}_i \in \mathbb{R}^p$ and $y_i \in \{0, 1\}$ for a binary classification problem, stated as

$$(K^O, \boldsymbol{\theta^O}) \leftarrow \underset{K \in \mathbb{G}; \boldsymbol{\theta} \in \mathbb{R}^m}{arg\ min}\ f(K(\boldsymbol{x}_i, \boldsymbol{\theta}), y_i)\ with\ i = 1, \ldots, p\ , \quad (1)$$

where $\mathbb{G}$ is the solution or syntactic space defined by the primitive set $\mathbb{P}$ of functions and terminals, f is the fitness function which is based on the difference between a program's output $K(\boldsymbol{x}_i, \boldsymbol{\theta})$ and the desired output y_i, and $\boldsymbol{\theta}$ is a particular parametrization of the symbolic expression K, assuming m real-valued parameters. This dual problem, of simultaneously optimizing syntax (structure) as well as its parametrization is also discussed in [21, 11]. The authors differentiate between two possible solution strategies. The first group is *hierarchical structure evolution* (HSE), when $\boldsymbol{\theta}$ has a strong influence on fitness, and thus a Local Search (LS) is required at each generation of the global (syntactic) search, configured as a nested process. The second group is called *simultaneous structure evolution* (SSE), when $\boldsymbol{\theta}$ has a marginal effect on fitness, in such cases a single evolutionary loop could simultaneously optimize both syntax and parameters. In general, it is reasonable to state that the standard GP approach falls in the SSE group. Here, standard GP refers to a GP system that uses a tree representation, subtree crossover and mutation, and tournament selection [18].

In GP, many researchers include constants as terminal elements within the primitive set, to allow the evolutionary process to explicitly include numerical values within the evolved expressions. However, mutation events are mostly rare compared to the use of subtree crossover, thus parameter optimization is usually not an integral part of the search process. On the contrary, GP performs a highly explorative search, since the search operators can produce large fitness changes with only modest syntactic modifications or vice-versa. Therefore, the inclusion of a LS method aimed at optimizing the (sometimes implicit) numerical parameters of the evolved expression could enhance search performance. This work proposes a methodology to parameterize GP trees, to employ a LS method to numerically tune them, and to implement this process for binary classification prob-

[*]emigdio.zflores@tree-lab.org
[†]Corresponding author: leonardo.trujillo@tectijuana.edu.mx
[‡]schuetze@cs.cinvestav.mx
[§]pierrick.legrand@u-bordeaux.fr

GECCO '15, July 11–15, 2015, Madrid, Spain
© 2015 ACM. ISBN 978-1-4503-3472-3/15/07...$15.00
DOI: http://dx.doi.org/10.1145/2739480.2754797

lems. Here, a domain specific fitness function is used, based on the Receiver Operating Characteristic (ROC) curve of each GP individual. Experimental results are encouraging in several problems, performance is significantly improved relative to a standard GP search, based both on fitness and solution size. Moreover, by using widely used real-world benchmarks, it is clear that our proposal compares favorably with other proposals from the GP and machine learning literature.

The remainder of this work is organized as follows. Section 2 reviews related work and highlights our main contributions. Then, Section 3 describes our approach and Section 4 presents the experimental work. Finally, concluding comments are given in Section 5.

2. PREVIOUS WORK

Many works have studied how to combine an evolutionary algorithm (EA) with a local optimizer, usually referred to as memetic algorithms, with impressive results in a variety of domains [5]. A useful taxonomy of memetic algorithms can be derived based on how inheritance is carried out during the evolutionary process [5]. Suppose that $(\mathbf{h}, \mathbf{h}^o) \in \mathbb{G}^2$, where $\mathbf{h}$ is an individual solution and $\mathbf{h}^o$ is the solution generated after a LS is applied on $\mathbf{h}$. Obviously, for a minimization problem, $f(\mathbf{h}^o) \leq f(\mathbf{h})$, where f is the objective function. Thus, $\mathbf{h} \neq \mathbf{h}^o$, unless $\mathbf{h}$ was in fact a local optima. Then, a memetic algorithm could proceed in two distinct ways with respect to inheritance. In a *Lamarckian* algorithm, the traits acquired during the local search, captured in $\mathbf{h}^o$, replace those of the original individual $\mathbf{h}$; i.e., the inheritance of acquired characteristics $(\mathbf{h}, f(\mathbf{h})) \rightarrow (\mathbf{h}^o, f(\mathbf{h}^o))$. On the other hand, in a *Baldwinian* algorithm, the local optimization process only modifies the fitness of an individual; $(\mathbf{h}, f(\mathbf{h})) \rightarrow (\mathbf{h}, f(\mathbf{h}^o))$; i,e., ontogenic evolution. In this work, we propose a Lamarckian approach for a GP system.

When applying a LS strategy to tree-based GP, there are basically two broad approaches to follow. (1) To apply a LS on the syntax of a tree or (2) to apply it numerically on the parameters of the tree, as described in Equation (1). Regarding the former, two recent works are noteworthy. In [2], the authors apply a greedy search on a randomly chosen GP node, attempting to determine the best function to use in that node among all the functions in the primitive set, constrained only by the arity of the initial function. Moreover, to reduce computational overhead the authors apply a heuristic decision rule to decide which trees are subject to local optimization, preferring smaller trees in the population. This heuristic has the positive effect that it biases the search towards smaller trees, so it is adopted in our current proposal. In [35], the authors propose a multiobjective GP algorithm to evolve decision tree classifiers, and use two specialized mutation operators that limit their resulting phenotypic variations within a local neighborhood of the parent classifier.

Regarding the optimization of numerical parameters within the tree, the following works are relevant. In [31], gradient descent is used to optimize numerical constants within a GP tree, achieving good results on symbolic regression problems. However, the work only optimizes the value of the terminal elements (tree leaves), and it does not consider parameters within internal nodes. Additionally, that work only considers training fitness, a highly deceptive measure of learning. Similarly, in [40] and [13] a LS algorithm is used to optimize the value of constant terminal elements. In [40], gradient descent is used and tested on classification problems, while [13] uses Resilient Backpropagation (RPROP) and evaluates the proposal on a real-world problem. In [40], the authors apply gradient descent on every individual of the evolving population, an obvious computational bottleneck, while [13] only applies RPROP on the best individual from each generation. However, it is not evident which strategy can offer the best results in new scenarios, particularly since both [40, 13] evaluate their approaches on specific problem instances.

Other recent works have completely changed the basic GP framework to include an explicit parametrization of syntactic expressions. The fast function extraction (FFX) algorithm [23], for instance, poses the symbolic regression problem as that of finding a linear combination of a subset of candidate basis functions. Thus, FFX builds linear in parameter models, and optimizes using a modified version of the elastic net regression technique, eliminating the evolutionary process altogether. In the prioritized grammar enumeration (PGE) technique [37], dynamic programming replaces the the basic search operators of traditional GP, and numerical parameters are optimized using the non-linear Levenberg-Marquardt algorithm.

In our previous work, [39], we proposed a very simple parametrization approach for GP trees, by constraining the number of internal parameters of each tree regardless of its size. That work evaluates several strategies to determine which individuals are subject to the LS process, concluding that it is often best to apply LS on the entire population or a subset of the best individuals. The LS method used is Trust Region optimization [29], and results showed substantial improvements on several symbolic regression problems relative to a standard GP. A similar approach was developed by [16], with some noteworthy differences; for instance, parameters are only used to replace constants terminals, and each tree is enhanced by adding a linear upper tree, that effectively adds a weight coefficient and a bias to the entire tree. Then, the Levenberg-Marquardt optimizer is used to find the optimal values for these parameters. Similarly, in [33], the authors propose a weighted GP by inserting coefficients in binary trees. In this work, weight optimization is done by means of GA, which requires parameter tuning itself to reach a global optimum. However, this study has some drawbacks, it lacks the study of the influence of optimized solutions in the evolutionary process, it is tested over an specific problematic and experimental reproducibility is not clear.

Finally, the work presented by [1] uses a multivariate linear regression approach to optimize evolved solutions for symbolic regression problems. Particularly, the search is conducted by standard GP, but the linear regression is used as a Baldwinian memetic algorithm, such that the tree is decomposed into a set of subtrees which are then linearly combined discarding the original tree structure, a much more explorative approach then the one presented here. Then, to control code growth a multiobjective approach us included to account for solution complexity.

Here, we propose a Lamarckian memetic algorithm, where the main goal is to combine the explorative capabilities of GP without changing its canonical implementation, and incorporate stronger exploitative features by means of numerical optimization.

3. INTEGRATING THE LOCAL SEARCH MECHANISM WITHIN GP

For binary classification, GP is used as a supervised learning problem, where a training set $\boldsymbol{x}$ of n-dimensional patterns with a known classification, are used to derive a mapping function $g(x): \mathbb{R}^n \rightarrow \{0,1\}$, with a threshold δ as classification decision. Afterwards, for convenience, we transform the classification problem into a regression one by inserting a continuous function in order to get gradient information, and to be able to use a numerical optimizer.

3.1 GP Tree Parameterization

First, we follow the strategy proposed in [16], where a small linear subtree is added on top of the root node of the original tree $K(\boldsymbol{x})$, such the new extended tree $K'(\boldsymbol{x})$ is given by

$$K'(\boldsymbol{x}) = \theta_2 + \theta_1(K(\boldsymbol{x})) \ , \tag{2}$$

where θ_1 and θ_2 are the first two parameters from $\boldsymbol{\theta}$, as shown in Figure 1. This subtree provides shifting and scaling properties, so the optimizer later on can have more freedom in its capabilities to find a better solution. This approach is closely related to the linear scaling technique [15], allowing the syntactic search operators to focus on evolving the desired shape of the evolved function without worrying about optimizing the scale or bias of the output.

Afterwards, for each node n_k in a given tree we add a weight coefficient $\theta_k \in \mathbb{R}$, such that each node is now defined by

$$n'_k = \theta_k n_k \ , \tag{3}$$

where n'_k is the new modified node, $k \in \{1,...,r\}$, $r = |Q|$ and Q is the tree representation. Notice that each node has an unique parameter that can be modified to help meet the overall optimization criteria of the non-linear expression.

At the beginning of the GP run, each parameter is initialized by $\theta_i = 1$, where $|\theta| = r$. During the GP syntax search, subtrees belonging to different individuals are swapped, added or removed (following the standard crossover/mutation rules) together with its corresponding parameters, without affecting their values; a memetic search process with Lamarckian inheritance.

3.2 A Continuous Transfer Function

In a binary classification problem, the desired output is either 0 or 1, a discrete output. Indeed, this discontinuity will have an homologous discontinuity in parameter space, and thus the LS algorithm can easily fail. To provide a continuous output, and provide gradient information to the LS method, a transfer function is added as a root node.

Here, a sigmoid function is used, producing the following non-linear tree

$$sig(K'(\boldsymbol{x},\boldsymbol{\theta})) = \frac{1}{1 + e^{\rho(K'(\boldsymbol{x},\boldsymbol{\theta})-\delta)}} \ , \tag{4}$$

where K' is the program output evaluated over the input vector $\boldsymbol{x}$, $\boldsymbol{\theta}$ is the parameter vector corresponding to the program K', ρ is the sigmoid slope parameter and δ is the classification threshold, where the function has a value of 0.5. The sigmoid function is normalized to the range [0,1]; therefore, if $sig(K'(\boldsymbol{x},\boldsymbol{\theta})) \leq 0.5$ then the class label is 0, and 1 otherwise. The proposed tree extensions and parameterizations are depicted in Figure 1.

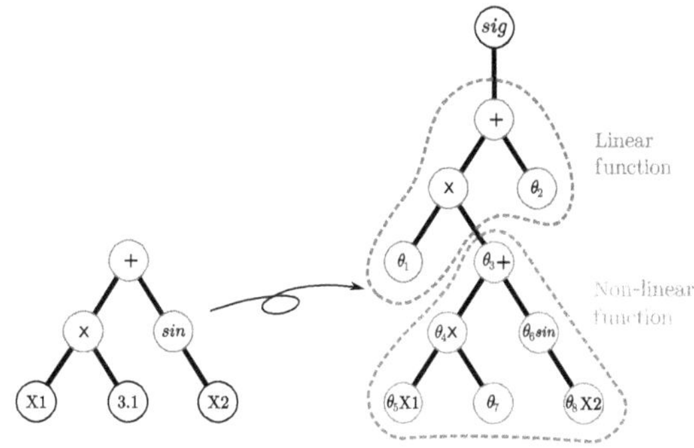

Figure 1: Example of tree transformation, product of parameterization and subtree addition.

3.3 The Local Search Mechanism

In this work we treat each tree as a non-linear expression. We also assume a non-discontinuity for the evaluated tree over the interval constrained by the input training data. The problem to be solved is an optimization one, where we want to best fit a non-linear function to an output vector containing either zero or one values (each class label). It can be formally defined as

$$\min_{\boldsymbol{\theta}} \|sig(K'(\boldsymbol{\theta},\boldsymbol{x})) - \boldsymbol{y}\|_2^2 = \min_{\boldsymbol{\theta}} \sum_i (sig(K'(\boldsymbol{\theta},x_i)) - y_i)^2 \ , \tag{5}$$

where $\boldsymbol{x}$ is the input data vector, $\boldsymbol{y} \in \{0,1\}$ is the known class label, sig is the sigmoid calculated over the program K', i is the index for the problem instances and $\boldsymbol{\theta}$ is the parameter vector.

The problem presented in (5) can be solved using different techniques [38, 19]. In this work, we prefer to use a well known algorithm, the Trust Region optimizer, belonging to the family of non-linear Gauss-Newton methods [29]. One example of this family is the recent approach to the Levenberg-Marquardt algorithm, which follows the Trust Region concept.

In the Trust Region algorithm, an iterative process is performed with the following goal

$$\min_{\boldsymbol{\theta} \in \mathbb{R}^m} \|sig(K'(\boldsymbol{\theta},\boldsymbol{x})) - \boldsymbol{y}\|_2^2, \ l_i \leq \theta_i \leq u_i \ \forall i \in \{1m\} \ , \tag{6}$$

where $l_i \in \{\mathbb{R} \cup \{-\infty\}\}$, $u_i \in \{\mathbb{R} \cup \{\infty\}\}$, and $K': \mathbb{R}^m \rightarrow \mathbb{R}$. Conceptually, a Trust Region approach replaces an m-dimensional unconstrained optimization problem by an m-dimensional constrained problem. This results in an approximate solution, since it does not needed to be solved with high accuracy. One of the appealing points of these methods is their strong convergence properties [6]. The idea behind a Trust Region method for $min_{\theta \in \mathbb{R}^m} K(\theta)$ is simple. The increment $s_j = x_{j+1} - x_j$ is an approximate solution to a quadratic subproblem with a bound on the step size

$$\min_{s \in \mathbb{R}^m} \left\{ \psi_j(s) \stackrel{def}{=} g_j^T s + \frac{1}{2} s^T B_j s : \|\overline{D}_j\| \leq \Delta_j \right\} \ , \tag{7}$$

where $g_j \stackrel{def}{=} \nabla f(x_j)$, B_j is a symmetric approximation to the Hessian matrix $\nabla^2 f(x_j)$, $\overline{D}_j$ is a scaling matrix, and Δ_j is a positive scalar representing the trusted region size. Solving (7) efficiently is not a trivial task, see [29, 25]; Figure 3 shows an illustration of the trust region method. Here, the method proposed in [7] is used, which does not require the solution of a general quadratic programming subproblem at

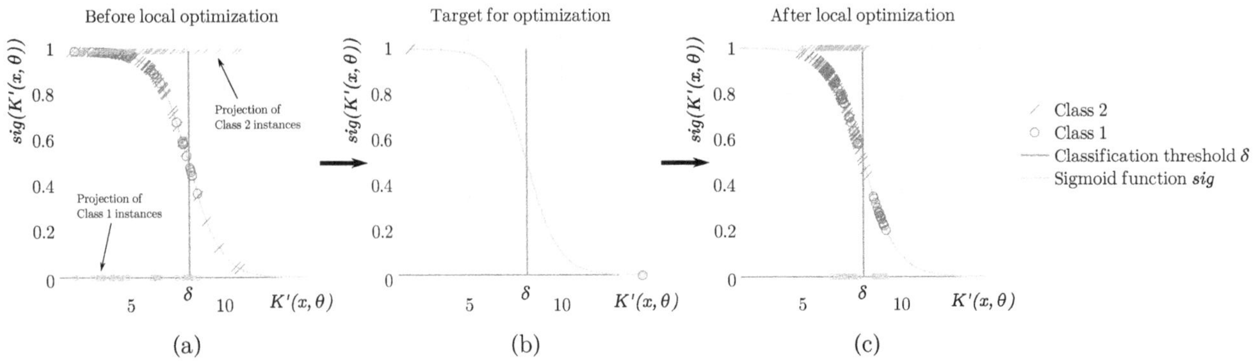

Figure 2: Example of the optimization effect over an actual individual for the Parkinsons problem [20]. Even though the solution was clearly a bad classifier, after optimization accuracy improved. Projection of both classes are shown for a clearer visualization on the position of instances relative to the classification threshold.

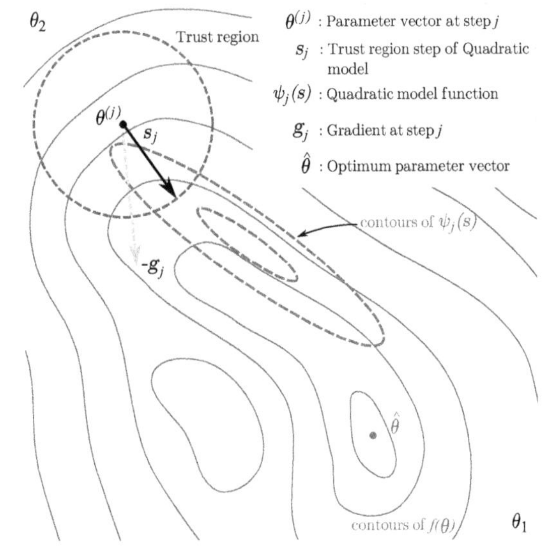

Figure 3: Visualization of the trust region algorithm showing the landscape of $f(\theta)$ as the objective function, equivalent to Equation 6, at iteration j.

each iteration. Figure 2 shows the effect of performing LS over a specific individual.

3.4 The Fitness Function

In the case of binary classification, a simple method is to consider only accuracy in the training stage [36, 9]. In this work we use the following fitness measure

$$fitness = 1 - Acc \ , \tag{8}$$

where *Acc* (accuracy; computed as the ratio of correctly classified instances among total number of cases) is calculated based on the best threshold found using the ROC curve. The ROC curve, which is commonly used by the machine learning community, can provide a robust measure of classifier performance even with an unbalanced dataset. Each operating point on a ROC curve represents the classification accuracy at a single threshold δ_i. The ROC curve is constructed by changing the classification threshold and evaluating its True Positives Rate (TPR) and False Positives Rate (FPR) values. These are calculated with TPR=TP/P and FPR=FP/N, respectively, where TP is the True Positive value, FP is the False Positive value, P is the total of positive instances and N the negative ones.

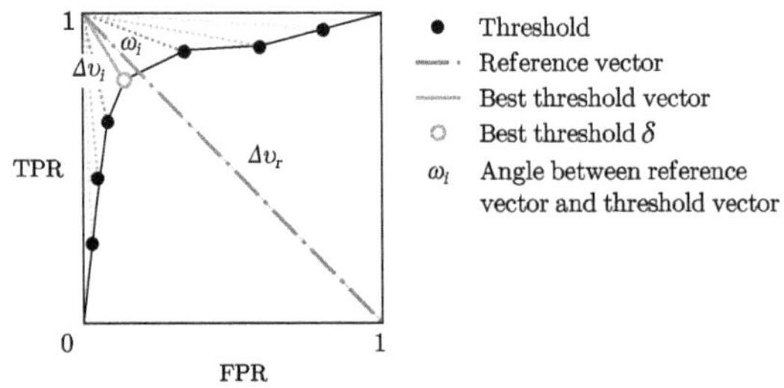

Figure 4: Example of a ROC curve and its best threshold. Note that each tree will generate a different ROC curve, thus presenting a different classification threshold.

In the implementation presented here, we used 10 uniformly spaced threshold values within $[min(K'(x,\theta)) - max(K'(x,\theta))]$, which is the range given by minimum and maximum output of the extended tree, over all fitness cases. This methodology is similar as the one presented in [4].

In the ROC curve, the top-left area represents the most accurate classification results. Ideally, a perfect classifier should have a TPR value of one with zero FPR. Based on this, we propose a simple method to choose the best threshold picked up from the ROC curve. A vector with 45 degree slope is traced with coordinates [0,1]-[1,0], in ROC space, which represent our reference vector v_r. We then build a numerical array $\overline{\omega}$ containing the angle differences between each threshold vector v_i, with coordinates [0,1]-[FPR$_i$,TPR$_i$,] and the reference vector, as seen in Figure 4. This is calculated by

$$\Delta v_i = v_i(y) - v_i(x), \Delta v_r = v_r(y) - v_r(x) \tag{9}$$

and

$$\omega_i = acos\left(\frac{(\Delta v_i \cdot \Delta v_r)|\Delta v_r|}{|\Delta v_i|}\right) \ , \tag{10}$$

where v_i is the vector corresponding to each threshold δ_i and ω_i is the difference angle expressed in radians. Consequently, the array $\overline{\omega} = [\omega_1, ..., \omega_k]$. The threshold corresponding to the minimum value in this array will represent our chosen threshold for the particular classifier, as seen in Figure 4.

3.5 Integrating LS into GP

Finally, we need to determine which individuals should be improved by the LS method. For instance, some researchers apply the LS to the best solution in the population, but [32]

Table 1: **Binary classification problems summary used to evaluate proposed algorithm in this work.**

Name	# of instances	# of features	Brief description
Parkinsons [20]	197	23	Biomedical voice measurements related to Parkinson's disease
Diabetes [3]	768	8	Diabetes present on Pima Indians patients
Wine [3]	178	13	Chemical analysis of wines
Sonar [3]	208	60	Sonar signals off metal cylinder at various angles and conditions
Wholesale [3]	440	8	Clients information of wholesale distributor
Banknote [3]	1372	5	Image information from genuine & forged banknote-like specimens
LSVT [34]	126	309	Signal data from speech rehabilitation treatment on Parkinson patients

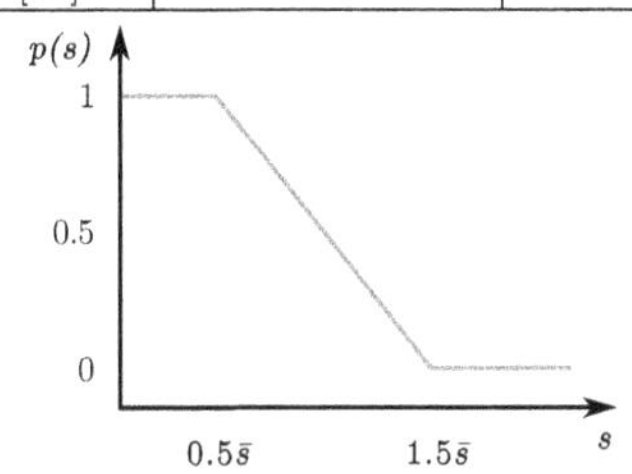

Figure 5: Transfer function for $p(s)$ corresponding to the heuristic method based on individuals tree sizes, selected for performing LS.

showed that better results are obtained when it is applied to all the population or a subset of the best solutions in each generation. However, in our case, the number of parameters grows proportionally with the size of the trees, providing incentive to limit the amount of times the LS is applied, especially for larger trees. Therefore, in this work we use the heuristic rule proposed by Muhammad and Ryan in [2], which they tested with a syntactic LS process. In [2], the LS method is applied stochastically for each tree, based on a probability $p(s)$ determined by the tree size s (number of nodes) and the average size of the population $\overline{s}$, based on

$$p(s) = \begin{cases} y = c - \frac{s}{\overline{s}} & \text{if } 0 \le y \le 1 \\ 1 & \text{if } y > 1 \\ 0 & \text{otherwise} \end{cases} . \quad (11)$$

Based on equation (11), shown in Figure 5, smaller trees are more likely to be optimized by the LS than larger trees; in particular, by setting $c = 1.5$ trees that are 50% larger than the population average are not subject to the LS process. This heuristic could provide two positive results. First, the LS method is mostly applied on small trees that have a relatively small number of parameters, simplifying the LS problem. Second, by focusing on improving smaller trees, this increases their chances for survival, increasing the chances of finding solutions that are not hampered by the bloat problem [28]. Hereafter, we call this method Local Search Heuristic by Size (LSHS).

4. EXPERIMENTATION

4.1 Experimental Setup

The algorithm LSHS was evaluated and compared with a canonical GP implementation as control method. The GP settings were the same between both variants, including the fitness function.

The LSHS algorithm was implemented using the GPLAB[1] Matlab toolbox [27]. The set of experiments covered a series of benchmark binary classification problems, taken from the UCI repository [3]; real problems with distinct complexity. Table 1 shows a summary of each evaluated problem. A couple of quality measurements were used to compare the results of the algorithm, the accuracy calculated over the test data and average population size, needed to assess the performance in terms of bloat and consumed resources. The evolution of these measure is analyzed with respect to the total number of fitness function evaluations instead of generations, to account for the LS iterations. The evaluations performed by the iterative Trust Region algorithm were also taken in account to provide a the fair comparison between standard GP and LSHS. The Trust Region algorithm performs a maximum of 500 iterations. The stopping criteria is a predefined number of function evaluations. The GP configuration used in this research is listed in Table 2.

[1] http://gplab.sourceforge.net/

Table 2: GP parameters

Parameter	Value
Runs	20
Population	200
Function evaluations	1'500,000
Training set	70% of complete data
Testing set	30% of complete data
Crossover operator	Standard subtree crossover, 0.8 prob.
Mutation operator	Mutation probability per node 0.15
Tree initialization	Ramped Half-and-Half, max. depth 6
Function set	+,-,×, sin,cos,log,sqrt,tan,tanh
Terminal set	Input features, constants
Selection for reproduction	Tournament selection of size 7
Elitism	Best individual survives
Maximum tree depth	15

4.2 Results

Figure 6 summarizes the results of the tested algorithm over several classification problems. The figure shows convergence plots for training and testing fitness with respect to the number of fitness function evaluations, showing the median over all runs. In each of the problems, the accuracy of LSHS testing data is either similar or better compared to standard GP. At least in four of them the improvement in the method is significant. Figures 6(a-c) show the results for the problems Parkinsons, Diabetes and Wine. In all of them we can see a superior solution quality evolved by the LSHS method. Notice that for the Wine problem, considered an easy classification problem, standard GP reaches almost zero error for testing data, yet the LSHS algorithm presents a perfect accuracy.

Figures 6(d-g) present the performance results for Sonar, Wholesale, Banknote and LSVT problems. For the Sonar problem the accuracy reached in the testing data is similar to the one obtained by standard GP. In the Banknote problem, the LSHS improvement is significant, where the classification error almost reaches zero.

Figure 7(a) discloses descriptive statistics from test fitness, at the end of each run, using notched box plots. The Wilcoxon rank sum test was calculated for the fitness test data, shown in first column of Table 3. The average population size is also presented in Figure 7(b), and its corre-

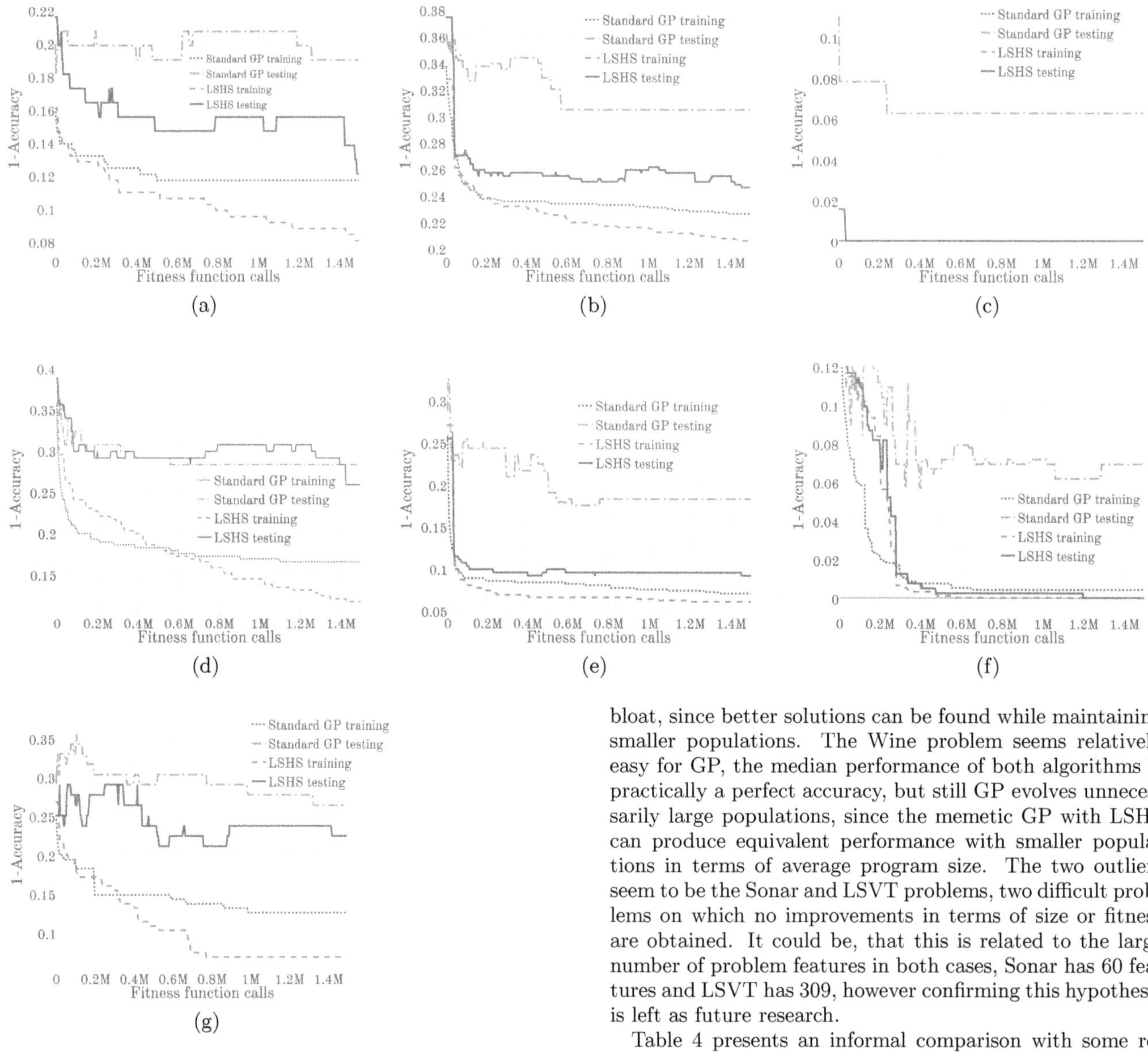

Figure 6: Results of fitness performance of problems Parkinsons (a), Diabetes (b), Wine (c), Sonar (d), Wholesale (e), Banknote (f) and LSVT (g). Fitness performance. Plots shows the median over 20 independent runs from the best-so-far solution.

sponding rank sum test is given in the second column of Table 3.

In both cases, the null hypothesis is that the underlying distributions in each pair of experiments have equal medians.

The statistical tests show that that the differences in performance exhibited by the standard GP and LSHS-GP are significant on four of the seven problems, particularly Parkinsons, Diabetes, Wholesale and Banknote, with $\alpha = 0.05$. Regarding size, statistical difference was detected on five problems, namely Parkinsons, Diabetes, Wine, Wholesale and Banknote. It is interesting to note, that on all four problems where performance improved, size was also reduced. Here we can state that for these problems, the increased average size in standard GP does indeed represent bloat, since better solutions can be found while maintaining smaller populations. The Wine problem seems relatively easy for GP, the median performance of both algorithms is practically a perfect accuracy, but still GP evolves unnecessarily large populations, since the memetic GP with LSHS can produce equivalent performance with smaller populations in terms of average program size. The two outliers seem to be the Sonar and LSVT problems, two difficult problems on which no improvements in terms of size or fitness are obtained. It could be, that this is related to the large number of problem features in both cases, Sonar has 60 features and LSVT has 309, however confirming this hypothesis is left as future research.

Table 4 presents an informal comparison with some recently published results for the seven problems tested here, using average classification accuracy. Thus providing a quick survey to contextualize the results presented above. The comparison is encouraging, the proposed LSHS method shows relatively strong performance on all problems, except on Parkinsons and LSVT. However, the best results on Parkinsons [22] uses a domain specific preprocessing stage, while other methods report similar results with our work. Similarly, [34] uses a state-of-the-art feature selection algorithm to reduce the dimensions of the problem given to the classifier, important for this dataset since it contains 309 features, while GP takes the entire feature vectors as input, a clear disadvantage.

5. CONCLUSION

In this study, a methodology to incorporate a LS method into GP was proposed, that tackles the challenges imposed by a supervised classification task. A tree parameterization is introduced where a candidate solution in GP is extended

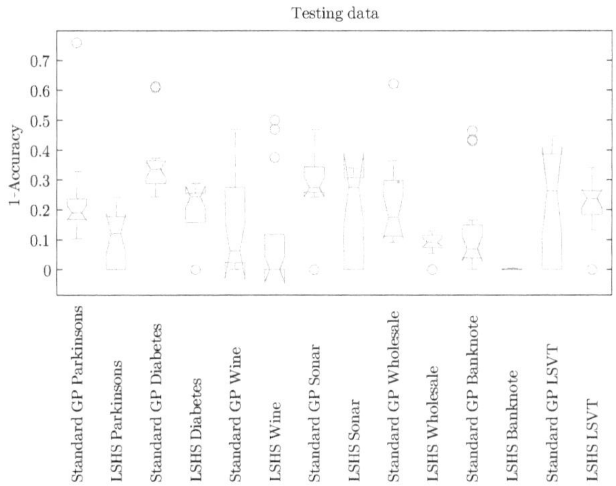

(a)

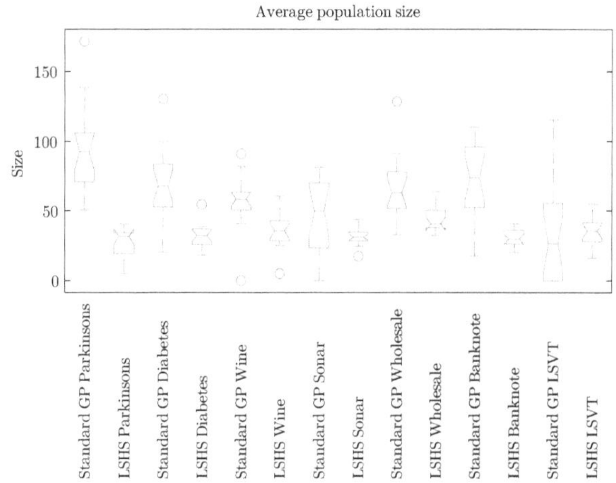

(b)

Figure 7: Notched box plots from 20 runs at the end of each run; where: (a) presents the test fitness of the best solution found during training; and (b) the average population size.

Table 3: Wilcoxon rank sum test, with $\alpha = 0.05$. Bold values are less than α.

	Fitness	Size
Problem	p-value	
Parkinsons	**0.0027**	**0.0000**
Diabetes	**0.0000**	**0.0000**
Wine	0.0630	**0.0001**
Sonar	0.0859	0.1212
Wholesale	**0.0001**	**0.0017**
Banknote	**0.0000**	**0.0000**
LSVT	0.2978	0.7043

by a simple mechanism where a weight is added to each node. Using a well known and robust non-linear optimizer the solution is improved targeting a better classification rate. A heuristic is used to determine which solutions are improved by the LS method, preferring smaller than average trees within the population.

The presented results illustrate the benefits of using a LS method during the GP search. Indeed, in most problems the improvements in terms of classification error was significant, and a survey of recently published results confirm the quality of the evolved solutions. Moreover, the evolution of program growth also provides interesting insights. In particular, GP+LS with LSHS was able to produce high quality solutions, in most cases significantly better than standard GP, while maintaining smaller individuals within the population in terms of average size. This suggests that code growth is not necessary to obtain improved performance if the search space is properly exploited, which the LS method allows us to do. Moreover, it is important to notice that the proposed LSHS-GP system should not increase the complexity, or more precisely reduce the interpretability of the evolved solutions relative to standard GP. In fact, it might help produce simpler trees (results at least show that they are smaller), since the LS process allows simple numerical tuning of the evolved programs to improve fitness; something that otherwise might require complex syntactical changes.

This contrast nicely with other recent approaches based on geometric semantic operators [24], that improve GP performance at the cost of lowering interpretability.

Future work will consider algorithmic improvements and rigorous comparisons with other methods. For instance, evaluating other transfer functions, utilizing gradient-free LS methods such as evolutionary strategies, and extending the method to multi-class problems, as well as comparing our proposal with a wider variety of classification methods.

6. ACKNOWLEDGMENTS

First author was supported by CONACYT (México) scholarship No. 294213. Funding for this work was provided by CONACYT Basic Science Research Project No. 178323, DGEST (México) Research Project 5414.14-P, and FP7-PEOPLE-2013-IRSES project ACOBSEC financed by the European Commission with contract No. 612689. Finally, the authors thank Ivan Campos, undergraduate student from Instituto Tecnológico de Tijuana, for assistance during the development of this research.

7. REFERENCES

[1] I. Arnaldo, K. Krawiec, and U.-M. O'Reilly. Multiple regression genetic programming. *Proceedings of the 2014 conference on Genetic and evolutionary computation - GECCO '14*, pages 879–886, 2014.

[2] R. Azad and C. Ryan. A Simple Approach to Lifetime Learning in Genetic Programming-Based Symbolic Regression. *Evolutionary computation*, 22(2):287–317, 2014.

[3] K. Bache and M. Lichman. UCI machine learning repository, 2013.

[4] U. Bhowan, M. Johnston, and M. Zhang. Developing new fitness functions in genetic programming for classification with unbalanced data. *IEEE Trans. on Systems, Man, and Cybernetics*, 42(2):406–21, Apr. 2012.

[5] X. Chen, Y.-S. Ong, M.-H. Lim, and K. C. Tan. A multi-facet survey on memetic computation. *Trans. Evol. Comp*, 15(5):591–607, 2011.

[6] T. F. Coleman and Y. Li. On the convergence of reflective Newton methods for large-scale nonlinear minimization subject to bounds, 1992.

[7] T. F. Coleman and Y. Li. An interior trust region approach for nonlinear minimization subject to bounds. Technical report, Ithaca, NY, USA, 1993.

[8] E. Dufourq and N. Pillay. A Comparison of Genetic Programming Representations for Binary Data Classification. In *Third World Congress on Information and Communication Technologies*, pages 134–140, 2013.

[9] J. Eggermont, A. Eiben, and J. van Hemert. Adapting the fitness function in GP for data mining. *Genetic Programming*, (2):193–202, 1999.

Table 4: **Classification accuracy comparison among several state-of-art methods, including from the GP community.**

Problem	Study	Accuracy (%)	Brief description of the study
Parkinsons	Ozcift and Gulten [26]	87.7 (5-fold CV)	Dirichlet process mixtures
	Ozcift and Gulten [26]	87.1 (10-fold CV)	CFS-RF
	Ma et al. [22]	**99.49** (10-fold CV)	SCFW-KELM with feature preprocessing
	Dufourq and Pillay [8]	86.7 (testing)	GP based (arithmetic, logical and decision trees)
	Koshiyama et al. [17]	89.33 (testing)	GP based (GPF-CLASS)
	Wang et al. [35]	86.96	GP based (MOGP maximizing ROCCH)
	This work	88.9 (testing)	GP + LS (LSHS)
Diabetes	Eggermont et al. [10]	74.1 (10-fold CV)	GP based (decision trees)
	This work	**75.5** (testing)	GP + LS (LSHS)
Wine	Tan and Dowe [30]	93.2 (90/10 training/testing)	Minimum message length Decision Trees
	This work	**100** (testing)	GP + LS (LSHS)
Sonar	Tan and Dowe [30]	76 (90/10 training/testing)	Minimum message length Decision Trees
	Koshiyama et al. [17]	**77** (testing)	GP based (GPF-CLASS)
	This work	74.2 (testing)	GP + LS (LSHS)
Wholesale	Jayadeva [14]	**92.72** (5-fold CV)	Minimal Complex Machine
	This work	91 (testing)	GP + LS (LSHS)
Banknote	Ghazvini et al. [12]	95.99 (10-fold CV)	MLP
	This work	**100** (testing)	GP + LS (LSHS)
LSVT	Tsanas et al. [34]	**90**	SVM with feature subset
	This work	78 (testing)	GP + LS (LSHS)

[10] J. Eggermont, J. N. Kok, and W. a. Kosters. Genetic Programming for Data Classification: Partitioning the Search Space. *SAC '04*, pages 1001–1005, 2004.

[11] M. Emmerich, M. Grötzner, and M. Schütz. Design of graph-based evolutionary algorithms: A case study for chemical process networks. *Evol. Comput.*, 9(3):329–354, 2001.

[12] A. Ghazvini, J. Awwalu, and A. A. Bakar. Comparative Analysis of Algorithms in Supervised Classification : A Case study of Bank Notes Dataset. *Computer Trends and Technology*, 17(1):39–43, 2014.

[13] M. Graff and R. Pe. Wind Speed Forecasting using Genetic Programming. *Evolutionary Computation*, pages 408–415, 2013.

[14] Jayadeva. Learning a hyperplane classifier by minimizing an exact bound on the VC dimension. *Neurocomputing*, 149:683–689, 2015.

[15] M. Keijzer. Improving symbolic regression with interval arithmetic and linear scaling. EuroGP'03, pages 70–82, Berlin, Heidelberg, 2003. Springer-Verlag.

[16] M. Kommenda, G. Kronberger, S. Winkler, M. Affenzeller, and S. Wagner. Effects of constant optimization by nonlinear least squares minimization in symbolic regression. *GECCO '13 Companion*, page 1121, 2013.

[17] A. Koshiyama, T. Escovedo, D. Dias, M. Vellasco, and R. Tanscheit. GPF-CLASS: A Genetic Fuzzy model for classification. *2013 IEEE Congress on Evolutionary Computation*, pages 3275–3282, June 2013.

[18] J. R. Koza. *Genetic programming: on the programming of computers by means of natural selection.* MIT Press, Cambridge, MA, USA, 1992.

[19] C. L. Lawson and R. J. Hanson. *Solving Least Squares Problems.* Society for Industrial and Applied Mathematics, 1995.

[20] M. Little, P. McSharry, S. Roberts, D. Costello, and I. Moroz. Exploiting nonlinear recurrence and fractal scaling properties for voice disorder detection. *BioMedical Engineering OnLine*, 6(1), 2007.

[21] R. Lohmann. Application of evolution strategy in parallel populations. In *Proceedings of the 1st Workshop on Parallel Problem Solving from Nature*, PPSN I, pages 198–208, London, UK, UK, 1991. Springer-Verlag.

[22] C. Ma, J. Ouyang, H.-l. Chen, and X.-h. Zhao. An Efficient Diagnosis System for Parkinson's Disease using Kernel-based Extre me Learning Machine with Subtractive Clustering Features Weighting Approach. 2014, 2014.

[23] T. Mcconaghy. FFX: Fast, Scalable, Deterministic Symbolic Regression Technology. In *Genetic Programming Theory and Practice IX*, chapter 13, pages 235–260. 2011.

[24] A. Moraglio, K. Krawiec, and C. G. Johnson. Geometric semantic genetic programming. *Lecture Notes in Computer Science (including subseries Lecture Notes in Artificial Intelligence and Lecture Notes in Bioinformatics)*, 7491 LNCS(PART 1):21–31, 2012.

[25] J. J. Moré and D. C. Sorensen. Computing a trust region step. *SIAM J. Scientific and Statistical Computing*, 4:553–572, 1983.

[26] A. Ozcift and A. Gulten. Classifier ensemble construction with rotation forest to improve medical diagnosis performance of machine learning algorithms. *Computer Methods and Programs in Biomedicine*, 104(3):443–451, 2011.

[27] S. Silva and J. Almeida. Gplab–a genetic programming toolbox for matlab. In L. Gregersen, editor, *Proceedings of the Nordic MATLAB conference*, pages 273–278, 2003.

[28] S. Silva and E. Costa. Dynamic limits for bloat control in genetic programming and a review of past and current bloat theories. *Genetic Programming and Evolvable Machines*, 10:141–179, 2009.

[29] D. Sorensen. *Newton's Method with a Model Trust Region Modification.* Defense Technical Information Center, 1982.

[30] P. J. Tan and D. L. Dowe. MML Inference of Oblique Decision Trees. *Proceedings of the 17th Australian Joint Conference on Artificial Intelligence*, pages 1082–1088, 2004.

[31] A. Topchy and W. F. Punch. Faster Genetic Programming based on Local Gradient Search of Numeric Leaf Values. *GECCO'01*, (1997):155–162, 2001.

[32] L. Trujillo, L. Muñoz, E. Naredo, and Y. Martínez. Neat, there's no bloat. In *Genetic Programming*, volume 8599 of *Lecture Notes in Computer Science*, pages 174–185. Springer Berlin Heidelberg, 2014.

[33] H. C. Tsai. Using weighted genetic programming to program squat wall strengths and tune associated formulas. *Engineering Applications of Artificial Intelligence*, 24(3):526–533, 2011.

[34] A. Tsanas, M. Little, C. Fox, and L. Ramig. Objective automatic assessment of rehabilitative speech treatment in parkinson's disease. *Neural Systems and Rehabilitation Engineering, IEEE Transactions on*, 22(1):181–190, Jan 2014.

[35] P. Wang, K. Tang, T. Weise, E. Tsang, and X. Yao. Multiobjective genetic programming for maximizing ROC performance. *Neurocomputing*, 125:102–118, Feb. 2014.

[36] S. Winkler, M. Affenzeller, and S. Wagner. Advanced Genetic Programming Based Machine Learning. *Journal of Mathematical Modelling and Algorithms*, 6(3):455–480, Mar. 2007.

[37] T. Worm and K. Chiu. Prioritized grammar enumeration: Symbolic regression by dynamic programming. *GECCO' 13*, pages 1021–1028, 2013.

[38] J. Y. Yuan. Numerical methods for generalized least squares problems. *Journal of Computational and Applied Mathematics*, 66(1):571 – 584, 1996.

[39] E. Z-Flores, L. Trujillo, O. Schütze, and P. Legrand. Evaluating the effects of local search in genetic programming. In *EVOLVE*, volume 288 of *Advances in Intelligent Systems and Computing*, pages 213–228. Springer International Publishing, 2014.

[40] M. Zhang and W. Smart. Genetic programming with gradient descent search for multiclass object classification. *Genetic Programming*, 2004.

Fast Knowledge Discovery in Time Series with GPGPU on Genetic Programming

Sungjoo Ha
School of Computer Science & Engineering
Seoul National University
1 Gwanak-ro, Gwanak-gu, Seoul, 151-744 Korea
shurain@soar.snu.ac.kr

Byung-Ro Moon
School of Computer Science & Engineering
Seoul National University
1 Gwanak-ro, Gwanak-gu, Seoul, 151-744 Korea
moon@snu.ac.kr

ABSTRACT

We tackle the problem of knowledge discovery in time series data using genetic programming and GPGPUs. Using genetic programming, various precursor patterns that have certain attractive qualities are evolved to predict the events of interest. Unfortunately, evolving a set of diverse patterns typically takes huge execution time, sometimes longer than one month for this case. In this paper, we address this problem by proposing a parallel GP framework using GPGPUs, particularly in the context of big financial data. By maximally exploiting the structure of the nVidia GPGPU platform on stock market time series data, we were able see more than 250-fold reduction in the running time.

Categories and Subject Descriptors

C.1.2 [**Processor architectures**]: Multiple Data Stream Architectures—*Interconnected architectures; Parallel processors; multiple-data-stream processors (SIMD)*; J.m. [**Computer Applications**]: Miscellaneous;

Keywords

patterns; technical patterns; GPU-based acceleration; multi-GPU systems; time series data; genetic programming; parallelization; speedup technique

1. INTRODUCTION

Processing and storing time series data has a long history. It is drawing ever stronger attention, particularly with the advent of big data. An increasing number of systems produce a massive amount of time series data. Traditional sources include stock markets and various scientific computing environments. More recent sources include monitoring metrics produced by millions of nodes in cloud computing infrastructures and various sensor devices. The vast amount of time series data gathered across various fields suggests that the importance of knowledge discovery in time series will be emphasized even further.

GECCO '15, July 11 - 16, 2015, Madrid, Spain

ISBN 978-1-4503-3472-3/15/07...$15.00

DOI: http://dx.doi.org/10.1145/2739480.2754669

Discovering knowledge in time series can be decomposed into two components. A discovery engine proposes a candidate pattern that is believed to possess some characteristics that can be interpreted as knowledge. A query engine takes this pattern and matches it against the time series database. Querying on a time series database has different aspects from querying on a database without the dimension of time. In traditional databases each record is independent of other records but in time series database, some of the attributes are related to one another by the time dimension.

There are a notable amount of research regarding the time series database (TSDB). Last *et al.* [12] described a general methodology for knowledge discovery in TSDB. Przymus and Kaczmarski [22] proposed query engine for time series data based on GPGPU and NoSQL databases. While such researches are promising, not enough mature implementations of GPGPUs are available. We exploit the problem-dependent structure with respect to GPGPU to further enhance the performance of such a system.

There are various instances of using evolutionary algorithms (EAs) for pattern mining [27][10]. Povinelli [21] proposed a genetic algorithm (GA) to find temporal patterns indicative of time series events. There are numerous researches in finding technical patterns in stock markets [20][14]. One such example is illustrated in Lee and Moon [13] where they applied genetic programming (GP) [8] for mining attractive technical patterns using a modular GP.

Extensive research has been done on parallelization of EA and local search algorithms [1][11][15][24][25][23]. The simplest form of parallelization is the master-slave model. In a master-slave model, a single population is maintained and fitness evaluation is distributed over multiple slaves; sometimes different genetic operators are assigned over them. This approach has the benefit of being simple and effective, especially when a memetic GA is used. Jaros and Tyrala [7] used a master-slave model to parallelize the evolution of communication schedules by offloading fitness evaluation to GPGPUs. Instead of offloading only the fitness function evaluation, Hidalgo *et al.* [5] parallelized the whole evolutionary process using GPGPUs. More careful design of EA to take advantage of GPU execution are also possible. Mussi *et al.* [18] organized a particle swarm optimization (PSO) algorithm that assigned a particle per block to get rid of explicit synchronization points. In a similar manner, Krömer *et al.* [9] suggested a many-threaded implementation of differential evolution where a candidate solution is assigned to each block and a vector coordinate is processed by each thread.

Another popular choice of parallelization scheme is the island model [19][16]. For an island model, multiple subpopulations are maintained; they are relatively independent from one another. Once in a while, these subpopulations exchange individuals by migration. Hrbacek and Sekanina [6] tried parallelization for Cartesian genetic programming in the domain of evolutionary circuit design under the island model.

There are also variants of GAs that employ a population that has a special topology whose spatial structure can be exploited to achieve parallelism [3]. Vidal and Alba [28] implemented a cellular genetic algorithm on multiple GPUs exploiting the toroidal structure of the population. Of course, there are approaches that combine multiple approaches together in order to further reduce the execution time [30].

The range of performance gain differs considerably depending on the domain. While some report more than a thousand-fold increase in the performance [19], most of the results fall somewhere between a few times to a few hundred times reduction in the execution time. In an application of parallel multi-swarm PSO to a task matching problem, Solomon *et al.* [26] achieved up to a 37-fold speedup over a sequential algorithm. Maitre *et al.* [17] tested coarse grain parallelization using the EASEA language [2] where they achieved a 105-fold speedup for the Weierstrass benchmark and a 60-fold reduction in the running time for the real world application of atomic model matching for chemical structures. Rocki and Suda [24] implemented the 2-opt and 3-opt local search method on GPUs to solve the traveling salesman problem (TSP). They limited the problem size and extensively used the shared memory to achieve over 500-fold reduction in running time against a sequential algorithm.

In this paper, we propose a parallel framework for GP using the CUDA platform on time series data. We describe the implementation details for this parallelization framework. We achieved a significant reduction of running time in finding interesting patterns from the time series data of Korean stock market.

The remainder of the paper is organized as follows. Section 2 formulates the problem. In Section 3 we explain the proposed parallelization framework in details. The evolution of precursor patterns using GP is described in Section 4. We present the experimental results in Section 5. Section 6 concludes the paper.

2. PROBLEM STATEMENT

A time series data set is a sequence of records each containing a set of attributes and a timestamp. Since we are dealing with time series data, it is natural to sort them on timestamps. Although the time step between two data points may not be discrete, there is always a finite number of points and we can assign an integer to refer to a single data point. If we need to work with the exact time differences between two data points, this value can be added into the record as an attribute. For example, in stock markets, we have various prices such as the opening price and the closing price being provided with a timestamp. Assuming the current record is indexed by an integer i, we can refer to the previous record with the index $i-1$. Time series data may be collected from multiple sources that share common characteristics. An example of such a case is where we have multiple companies in a given stock market. Each company stock may span a different range of time but they have the same attributes as other company stocks in the market.

Each attribute may contain categorical or real values but here we limit our discussion to real or Boolean valued attributes. We define a pattern as a conjunction of Boolean expressions. An expression is a combination of constants, comparison operators, arithmetic operators, logical operators, and attributes. Constants refer to real numbered values. Comparison operators, arithmetic operators, and logical operators may consist of operators such as $\{<,>,=,\leq,\geq\}$, $\{+,-,\times,/\}$, and $\{\wedge,\vee,\neg\}$, respectively. Depending on the domain of the time series data, we may choose to include whatever functions, in terms of the attributes, that seem appropriate. In the context of discovering attractive technical patterns for stock markets, a technical pattern may look something like "$1.1\times p_o(-1) < p_c(0) \wedge MA_{20}(0) > MA_{60}(0)$" which means that 1.1 times the opening price of the previous trading day is less than the closing price of today and the 20-day moving average of price is greater than that of 60-day moving average. The variables such as p_o, p_c, and MA are attributes or higher-level functions.

Knowledge discovery is a process of finding interesting patterns or structures from the given data. In time series data, we are interested in finding precursors to some events of interest.

Given a pattern, a time series index, and time series data, we say that an event occurred if a pattern matched at a given time series index returns *true*. Not every pattern will yield *true* all the time. Therefore there are inherent uncertainties associated with events. These uncertainties can be handled by taking the expectation of the events. This naturally extends to the case where we are interested in calculating some other values that are related to an event. For example, in a technical pattern analysis, we are interested in finding attractive technical patterns that are indicative of high profitability. We may calculate 10-day earning rates of the events associated with a technical pattern.

3. GPU ACCELERATION

3.1 CUDA Memory and Execution Model

In the CUDA platform, we define functions, called kernels, which are executed in parallel by multiple CUDA threads. Threads are organized into blocks which, in turn, are organized into grids. This is illustrated in Figure 1. The execution of threads is conducted in parallel with each unit of execution being a half warp. A warp consists of 32 threads that execute exactly the same instruction. If there are branches of instructions within a warp, the instructions are executed multiple times for different branches.

Threads within a block can cooperate with other threads within the same block using the shared memory. Thread blocks are required to execute independently which implies that they can be executed in any order. Such a design allows us to scale with the number of cores. But this also means that we cannot explicitly synchronize between blocks. For such a case where we need global synchronization, we adopt the divide-and-conquer strategy and decompose the problem into multiple kernels. A kernel launch serves as a global synchronization point.

A thread may access multiple memory spaces for data access and storage. Each thread has a private local memory space. A local memory space consists of thread local global

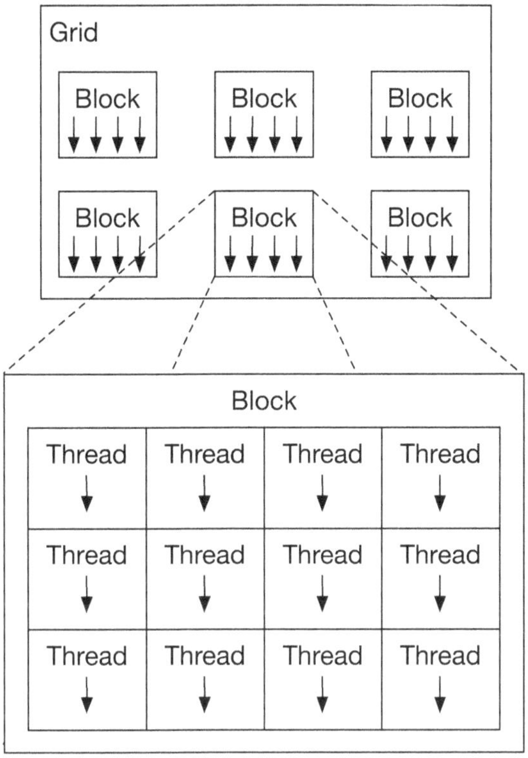

Figure 1: Grid of thread blocks

memory, which is often just called a local memory, and registers. While registers are very fast, they are scarce resources. If we allocate too many registers per thread, some of the data are spilled into the global memory which is called local memory in such a context. Each thread block has a shared memory that is shared and accessed by all the threads within the block. All threads in different blocks have access to the global memory. There are two additional read-only memory spaces: the constant memory and the texture memory. These two memory spaces are essentially a global memory optimized for different memory usages. The memory hierarchy is illustrated in Figure 2.

3.2 Parallelization Model

There are several ways to parallelize a GP program with GPGPUs. While it is possible to implement the whole GP framework on top of GPGPU, this approach has several downsides. The inherent complexity of programming on GPGPU discourages implementing the whole GP framework on GPGPU. For example, most EAs demand some form of randomness usually implemented by random number generation. There are multiple ways of providing random numbers and this imposes a design decision that has to be made. Although the current CUDA framework provides *Curand()* function for random number generation, this is not adequate for some problems [5]. Also, for hybrid GPs, overwhelming majority of the execution time is spent during the fitness evaluation of individuals. In Section 5 we show that this is the case for this work and more than 97% of the GP execution time is spent during the fitness evaluation. Therefore, a simpler approach is to only parallelize the fitness evaluation

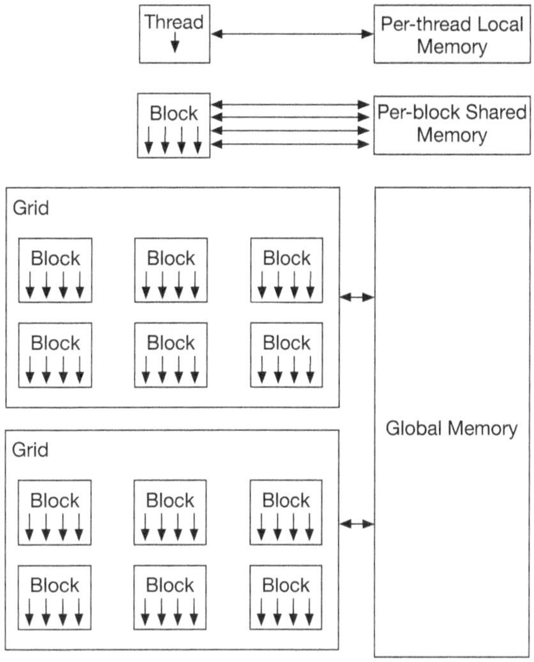

Figure 2: Memory hierarchy of CUDA framework

part. Not only is this approach much simpler, it also offers us the flexibility in the design of the GP framework.

3.3 Implementation Details

3.3.1 Structure of Parallel Framework

We divide the program into two parts: the evaluation part which evaluates the fitness of a given pattern and the rest of the genetic programming.

A pattern is expressed using a postfix notation and passed to the GPU in a form of an array. Such postfix trees can be easily evaluated with a stack. An obvious way to pass the pattern tree to GPU is through the constant memory. A pattern tree is small, relative to the whole data, and needs to be broadcasted to all the threads in exactly the same way which fits the memory access assumptions imposed on the constant memory.

We can extend the framework by using multiple GPUs. The time series data set is partitioned into different chunks and distributed over multiple GPUs. We can load the data once and perform asynchronous memory copy only for the newly created individuals and their partial aggregate results. A global synchronization barrier collects the partial evaluation results from GPU devices and aggregates the results as a whole in the host.

Since we are matching a pattern against the time series data and collecting the calculated aggregates, only a small amount of data is transferred between the host and the GPUs. This is desirable since the data transfer between the host and the GPUs is the top bottleneck candidate for the whole process. Partial aggregates from each kernel are passed to host using streams.

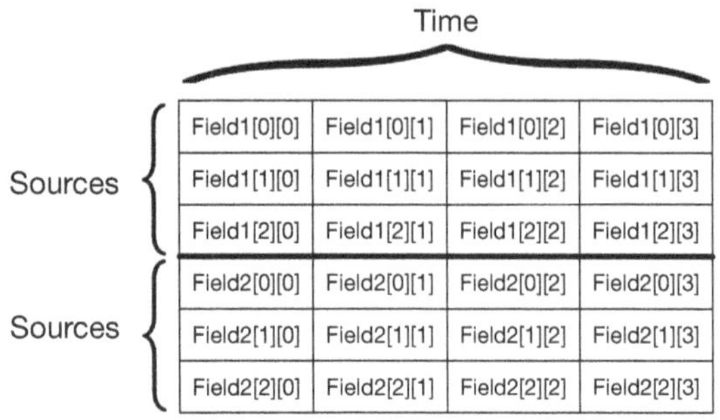

Figure 3: Layout of the time series data in the global memory. The whole data is divided into several chunks. Each chunk contains only a single attribute of the whole time series data. An attribute of a single input source is stored in a contiguous memory space. This spans multiple input sources to form a conceptual 2-dimensional array.

3.3.2 Memory Utilization

Each time series source and its related fields are arranged as a 1-dimensional array per field. This is illustrated in Figure 3. A warp accesses the same attribute of the same input source for different time indices. This suggests that we had better place these values in consecutive slots. When a single input source is processed, the warp jumps to the next input source and this behavior is naturally exploited by placing input sources consecutively.

We will match a pattern by moving along with time per source at a time; this leads to a better memory access pattern if we arrange the data correctly. Each source can span a different range of time, and in such cases we add dummy data to pad each source which reduces the complexity of the program. All of the time series data is stored in the global memory and passed to GPUs. When using multiple GPU devices, we can divide the data into an equal number of input sources and assign the divided data to multiple devices. A pattern is passed asynchronously to multiple devices using streams.

Each thread will accumulate the result of its calculation into the shared memory. This is later accumulated into a single number per block by parallel reduction. The partially accumulated values computed in blocks are returned to the host and a sequential reduction at the host is performed to compute the final result of the pattern match. If some calculation depends on multiple input sources, we accumulate the temporary values in the global memory and launch a different kernel for reduction. This does not cause a notable performance loss because hardware overhead of a kernel launch is negligible and software overhead is low [4].

The stack structure maintained by each thread is another aspect that needs deliberation. If we limit the size of the tree to a reasonable size, the stack part can position at the shared memory which is much faster than the global one. But the limitation on the size of the tree may be too much of a constraint for some domains. Not only that, in some cases, it is possible to achieve better performance by using a thread local global memory. Usually, the shared memory is much faster than the local memory but the actual performance may vary depending on the memory access pattern and the resource constraints imposed by the hardware. If the usage of the shared memory hinders the utilization of a large number of threads, it is better to use the local memory instead.

3.3.3 Single vs. Double Precision Floating Point

One decision to make is the choice between single and double precision for floating point numbers. While in CPU we don't suffer a notable speed loss by choosing double precision, in GPU it is not the case. When we experimented on our machine, we saw roughly 2-fold speed differences. Not only that, a double precision floating point number will use twice the number of registers compared to a single precision floating point. Therefore, it is reasonable to work with single precision floating point numbers unless it is absolutely necessary to have high precision. On CPU, accumulating many small numbers may lead to a significant numerical error. This happens because at the later stages of accumulation, we add large numbers with small numbers. On GPU this effect is somewhat mitigated because we perform parallel reduction and add numbers of comparable sizes.

4. EVOLUTION OF PATTERNS

A steady state genetic programming is used to evolve precursor patterns. A total of 500 individuals are evolved, where each individual represents a precursor pattern. Each individual is randomly initialized to a tree of depth 3.

The crossover operator chooses a random subtree of a parent and swaps it with a random subtree of the other parent to create a new offspring. For mutation, we choose a random subtree and replace it with a randomly created subtree.

Once an offspring is created, local optimization is applied until there is no improvement by corresponding local search operators. The local optimization traverses each node and changes the constants according to their types.

The fitness of an individual should reflect our notion of how interesting are the events associated with the precursor pattern. Here, we test with the problem of finding attractive technical patterns in a stock market. We assume that a technical pattern is attractive if it is profitable and statistically frequent.

The profitability of a technical pattern r is defined to be the expected earning rate of r after k trading days:

$$E_k[r] = \frac{1}{|R(r)|} \sum_{(i,j)\in R(r)} \frac{p_c(i, j+k)}{p_c(i,j)} \tag{1}$$

where $R(r) = \{(i,j)|r \text{ matches company } i \text{ on trading day } j\}$ and $p_c(i,j)$ is the closing price of company i at trading day j.

To account for the frequency of a given pattern, we define the attractiveness of a technical pattern as follows:

$$f(r) = \begin{cases} E_k[r] & \text{if } |R(r)| \geq k \\ 0 & \text{otherwise.} \end{cases} \tag{2}$$

The constant k is a predefined threshold value to determine whether the given pattern is frequent or not in a statistical point of view. The fitness of an individual is computed by Equation 2.

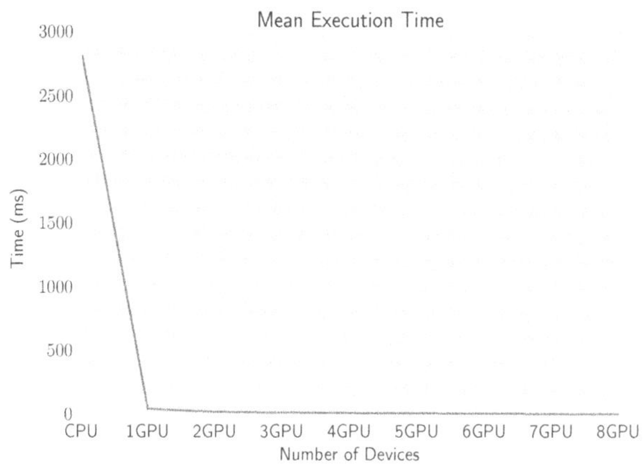

(a)

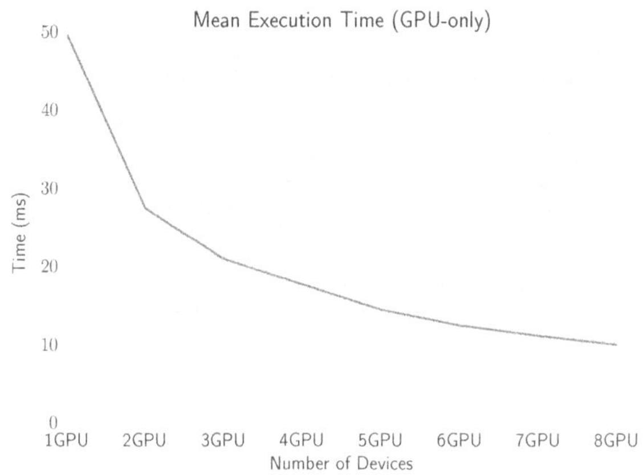

(b)

Figure 4: Mean execution time of a fitness evaluation function for different numbers of devices. (a) Comparison of the execution time among CPU and various number of GPU devices. (b) A close look at the difference over the numbers of GPU devices.

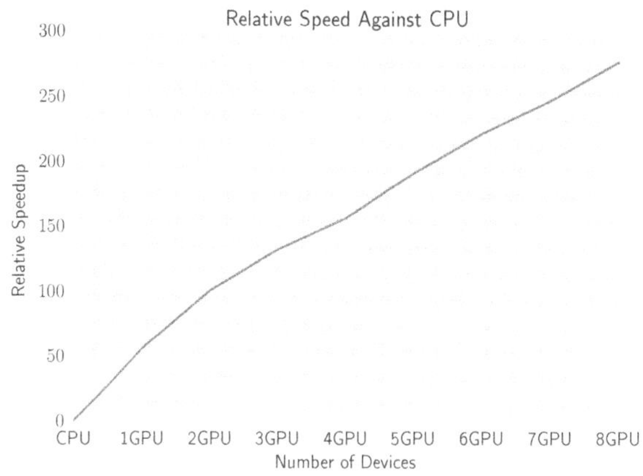

(a)

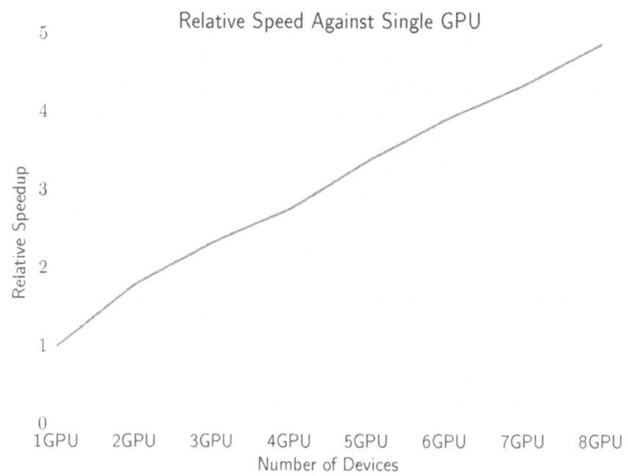

(b)

Figure 5: Relative speedup with different numbers of devices. (a) Relative speed against the CPU-only version. The speed of CPU is 1. (b) Comparison among multiple GPUs.

5. EXPERIMENTAL RESULTS

The experiment is conducted on the Korean stock market ranging from 2000 to 2014.

We run the sequential and CPU portion of the program on Intel(R) Core(TM) i7-3820 CPU @ 3.60GHz on Linux 3.2.0. For GPU parallelization, four GeForce GTX 690 cards, where each card has two devices leading to a total of eight GPU devices, were used. Programs were compiled using clang compiler and nvcc compiler.

A single GP generation, even though it is a steady-state GP, takes fairly long with the CPU version of the code. Therefore, we report the time it took to evaluate various pattern trees created during a typical GP run. We test a sequential version of the program implemented in CPU, a parallelized version of the program using a single GPU device, and one using multiple GPU devices.

A typical execution of GP for 50 generations (cut for this test) using 8 CUDA devices took around 120 $\sim$ 180 seconds to terminate. Roughly 17,000 to 21,000 fitness evaluations are performed during these 50 generations. Needless to say, the local optimization routine spent the majority of the execution time. For a typical GP run using 8 GPU devices, the local optimization took more than 97% of the time.

Appropriate thread/block/grid sizes are determined by cross validation. It is imperative that we choose these numbers carefully because they affect the occupancy of multiprocessors on GPUs. This, in turn, affects the performance of the whole system. It is not always better to allocate as many threads per block as possible due to the memory access pattern of the program and how instruction level parallelism is exploited. For this experiment, we used 512 threads per block and 256 blocks per grid. We only used a single grid.

5.1 Performance Comparison

We compare the execution time for evaluating a typical pattern tree and the relative speed over the numbers of GPU devices. Figure 4a compares the mean execution time of the fitness evaluation for a given tree. It is clear that parallelization using GPU leads to a dramatic performance gain. Switching from a sequential algorithm to a parallel version using a single GPU device resulted in 56-fold reduction of the execution time. The relative speeds against CPU with various numbers of GPU devices is shown in Figure 5a. We

# Devices	Relative Speed			
	Local		Shared	
	μ	σ	μ	σ
CPU	1.0	0	1.0	0
1 GPU	56.9	3.8	35.8	2.8
2 GPU	101.7	7.2	65.0	5.5
3 GPU	132.7	11.1	88.0	8.1
4 GPU	157.1	15.5	107.2	10.7
5 GPU	191.7	19.9	130.3	13.7
6 GPU	222.0	24.5	151.5	16.6
7 GPU	247.5	29.3	172.2	19.5
8 GPU	277.0	36.8	188.7	22.4

Table 1: Relative speeds against CPU with different numbers of GPU devices. Note that the thread local global memory is faster than the shared memory. The average relative speed is denoted by μ and σ represents its standard deviation.

see a strong linear relationship between the relative speed and the number of GPU devices. Fitness evaluation using 8 GPU devices was roughly 277 times faster than that of the CPU version of the program. Exact figures are provided in Table 1.

A close inspection of execution time shows a clearer picture of speed gains by additional introduction of GPU devices. Figure 4b shows that the execution time steadily decreases as GPU devices are increasingly added. The strong linear relationship shown in Figure 5b indicates that our parallelization framework scales well for this particular problem. While adding an additional device does not yield 100% performance gain possible, it roughly yields 80% gain per additional device. The strong scaling of the result suggests that there is room for additional performance gain by adding more GPUs.

5.2 Effect of Tree Sizes

We analyze the effect of the tree size on the execution time. The size of a pattern tree corresponds to the number of nodes in the tree. A large tree is relatively more costly to evaluate than a smaller one. This behavior is clearly shown in Figure 6a. As the number of nodes per tree increases from 31 to 55, the time for a single fitness evaluation nearly doubles with the CPU version of the code. In Figure 6b we see that using more devices leads to a slower increase of the execution time as the tree grows bigger. Thus, parallelization allows us to build increasingly complex trees. Exact figures are given in Table 2.

While a simpler tree is ideal for human interpretation, it might not be able to capture complex underlying behavior that can only be expressed by a complex tree. If we wish to explore such representations, we need to be able to evolve increasingly complex trees. The experiment result suggests that by adopting the parallel GP framework, we can expect additional performance gain from this.

5.3 Local vs. Shared Memory

While it is widely known that the shared memory is fast and the thread local global memory is slow, relatively, it may not be the case all the time. In the CUDA platform, the shared memory is allocated to blocks which are executed on a single multiprocessor on GPU devices. Allocating too much shared memory per block prevents multiple blocks to be executed on a single multiprocessor and reduces the occupancy. When a high occupancy of the multiprocessor is attained, the high latency of the global memory is hidden by switching to other warps being not stalled.

Since we have to maintain a stack per thread, a relatively large amount of shared memory has to be allocated. The performance penalty of storing a large array in the shared memory is shown in Table 1. Although the thread local global memory has high latency, this is effectively hidden by high occupancy. When a warp from one block is stalled by slow memory access, the multiprocessor simply processes some other warp that is not stalled. This led to roughly 1.5-fold speedup.

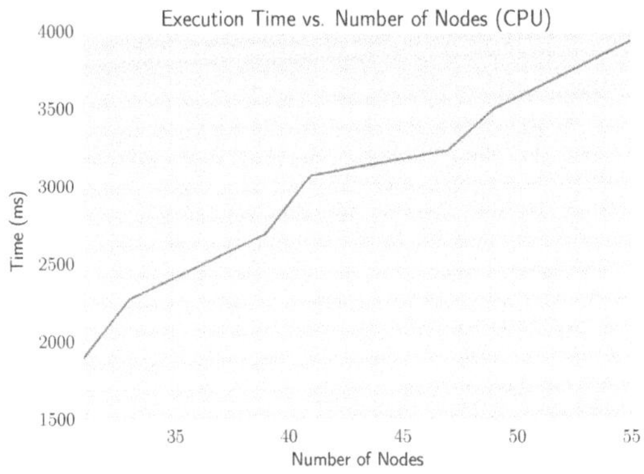

(a)

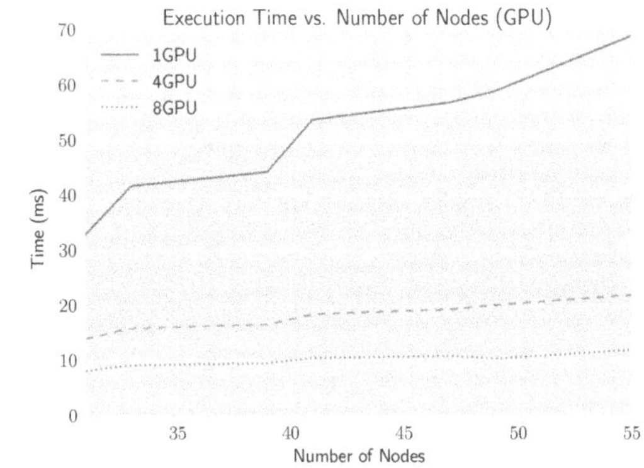

(b)

Figure 6: Execution time for different sizes of pattern trees. (a) The increase in execution time as the pattern tree grows. (b) Comparison for different numbers of GPU devices. Increasing the number of devices led to relatively slower increase of execution time with respect to the number of nodes.

6. CONCLUSIONS

We proposed a parallel framework for knowledge discovery in time series data using GP and GPGPU. We experimented on Korean stock market from 2000 to 2014 to find attractive technical patterns using the parallel GP framework. The experimental results show that this framework scales well and by using 8 GPU devices, we could reduce the execution time up to roughly 270 times that of a sequential version of the program.

Tree Size	CPU	1 Device	2 Devices	3 Devices	4 Devices	5 Devices	6 Devices	7 Devices	8 Devices
31	1904.1	33.0	19.4	15.9	14.0	11.6	10.1	9.3	8.2
33	2278.5	41.7	23.9	18.6	16.0	13.1	11.4	10.3	9.2
39	2696.9	44.2	24.9	19.4	16.7	13.6	11.8	10.7	9.6
41	3075.4	53.8	29.4	22.1	18.5	15.2	13.0	11.6	10.5
47	3236.8	56.9	31.1	23.3	19.4	15.9	13.7	12.2	10.9
55	3943.4	68.9	36.7	27.0	22.0	17.9	15.2	13.4	12.0

Table 2: Mean execution time (ms) for various tree sizes

Tree Size	CPU	1 Device	2 Devices	3 Devices	4 Devices	5 Devices	6 Devices	7 Devices	8 Devices
31	184.37	0.32	0.20	0.11	0.07	0.25	0.25	0.23	0.72
33	103.16	2.53	1.13	0.77	0.60	0.62	0.56	0.44	0.72
39	55.55	1.18	0.52	0.31	0.24	0.31	0.29	0.39	0.80
41	68.27	2.48	1.09	0.68	0.50	0.53	0.49	0.48	0.81
47	156.64	3.23	1.29	0.87	0.63	0.54	0.50	0.43	0.68
55	73.37	3.00	1.05	0.59	0.44	0.49	0.52	0.32	0.71

Table 3: Standard deviation of execution time (ms) for various tree sizes

We described how the framework was implemented by using multiple GPUs in CUDA platform. A careful choice of the structure of parallel framework and the memory utilization method, which led to excellent speedup, was discussed in details. Specifically, by choosing the local memory over the shared memory for the storage of stack structure led to more than 1.4-fold speed gain.

Note that the acceleration attained by using multiple GPGPUs does not influence the quality of the resulting GP solutions because we only parallelize the fitness evaluation and the rest of the evolutionary technique is left unmodified. The faster execution of the fitness evaluation naturally allows the evolutionary algorithm to search for better solutions given a restricted time budget. For knowledge discovery in time series data, we can leverage this fact and evolve more diverse yet interesting individuals.

Future work would include extending our framework to exploit the population level parallelism by using island model. Parallelism obtained by our framework can easily be extended by exploiting the parallelism on population level using multiple machines. The evolution of the population based on island model will lead to rich diversity of individuals which is desirable for knowledge discovery. While the current framework mainly focuses on the thread level parallelism, to reach the maximum performance gain, additional attention to the instruction level parallelism is required [29].

7. ACKNOWLEDGMENTS

This work is the result of a commercial project conducted at Optus Investment Inc. The work was also partly supported by the Engineering Research Center of Excellence Program of Korea Ministry of Science, ICT & Future Planning(MSIP) / National Research Foundation of Korea(NRF) (Grant NRF-2008-0062609). The ICT at Seoul National University provided some research facilities for this study.

References

[1] E. Cantú-Paz. A survey of parallel genetic algorithms. *Calculateurs Paralleles, Reseaux et Systems Repartis*, 10, 1998.

[2] P. Collet, E. Lutton, M. Schoenauer, and J. Louchet. Take it EASEA. *Parallel Problem Solving from Nature - PPSN VI*, volume 1917, pages 891–901, 2000.

[3] M. J. Gibson, E. Keedwell, and D. A. Savic. Understanding the efficient parallelisation of cellular automata on CPU and GPGPU hardware. *Genetic and Evolutionary Computation Conference*, pages 171–172, 2013.

[4] M. Harris. Optimizing parallel reduction in CUDA. Technical report, nVidia, 2008.

[5] J. I. Hidalgo, J. M. Colmenar, J. L. Risco-Martín, C. Sánchez-Lacruz, J. Lanchares, O. Garnica, and J. Díaz. Solving GA-hard problems with EMMRS and GPGPUs. *Genetic and Evolutionary Computation Conference*, pages 1007–1014, 2014.

[6] R. Hrbacek and L. Sekanina. Towards highly optimized cartesian genetic programming: From sequential via SIMD and thread to massive parallel implementation. *Genetic and Evolutionary Computation Conference*, pages 1015–1022, 2014.

[7] J. Jaros and R. Tyrala. GPU-accelerated evolutionary design of the complete exchange communication on wormhole networks. *Genetic and Evolutionary Computation Conference*, pages 1023–1030, 2014.

[8] J. R. Koza. *Genetic Programming: On the Programming of Computers by Means of Natural Selection*. MIT Press, 1992.

[9] P. Krömer, V. Snásel, J. Platos, and A. Abraham. Many-threaded implementation of differential evolution for the CUDA platform. *Genetic and Evolutionary Computation Conference*, pages 1595–1602, 2011.

[10] Y.-K. Kwon and B.-R. Moon. Personalized email marketing with a genetic programming circuit model. *Genetic and Evolutionary Computation Conference*, pages 1352–1358, 2001.

[11] W. B. Langdon. Graphics processing units and genetic programming: An overview. *Soft Computing*, 15(8): 1657–1669, 2011.

[12] M. Last, Y. Klein, A. Kandel, and A. K. Knowledge discovery in time series databases. *IEEE Transactions on Systems, Man, and Cybernetics*, 31:160–169, 2001.

[13] S.-K. Lee and B. R. Moon. A new modular genetic programming for finding attractive technical patterns in stock markets. *Genetic and Evolutionary Computation Conference*, pages 1219–1226, 2010.

[14] P. Lipinski. ECGA vs. BOA in discovering stock market trading experts. *Genetic and Evolutionary Computation Conference*, pages 531–538, 2007.

[15] T. V. Luong, N. Melab, and E.-G. Talbi. Parallel local search on GPU. Research Report RR-6915, 2009.

[16] T. V. Luong, N. Melab, and E.-G. Talbi. GPU-based island model for evolutionary algorithms. *Genetic and Evolutionary Computation Conference*, pages 1089–1096, 2010.

[17] O. Maitre, L. A. Baumes, N. Lachiche, A. Corma, and P. Collet. Coarse grain parallelization of evolutionary algorithms on GPGPU cards with EASEA. *Genetic and Evolutionary Computation Conference*, pages 1403–1410, 2009.

[18] L. Mussi, Y. S. Nashed, and S. Cagnoni. GPU-based asynchronous particle swarm optimization. *Genetic and Evolutionary Computation Conference*, pages 1555–1562, 12-16 July 2011.

[19] P. Pospichal, J. Jaros, and J. Schwarz. Parallel genetic algorithm on the CUDA architecture. *Applications of Evolutionary Computation*, pages 442–451, 2010.

[20] J.-Y. Potvin, P. Soriano, and M. Vallée. Generating trading rules on the stock markets with genetic programming. *Computers and Operations Research*, 31 (7):1033–1047, June 2004.

[21] R. J. Povinelli. Using genetic algorithms to find temporal patterns indicative of time series events. *GECCO 2000 Workshop: Data Mining with Evolutionary Algorithms*, pages 80–84, 2000.

[22] P. Przymus and K. Kaczmarski. Time series queries processing with GPU support. *17th East European Conference on Advances in Databases and Information Systems*, pages 53–60, 2013.

[23] A. K. Qin, F. Raimondo, F. Forbes, and Y.-S. Ong. An improved CUDA-based implementation of differential evolution on GPU. *Genetic and Evolutionary Computation Conference*, pages 991–998, 2012.

[24] K. Rocki and R. Suda. Accelerating 2-opt and 3-opt local search using GPU in the travelling salesman problem. *International Conference on High Performance Computing and Simulation*, pages 489–495, 2012.

[25] S. Shao, X. Liu, M. Zhou, J. Zhan, X. Liu, Y. Chu, and H. Chen. A GPU-based implementation of an enhanced GEP algorithm. T. Soule and J. H. Moore, editors, *Genetic and Evolutionary Computation Conference*, pages 999–1006, 2012.

[26] S. Solomon, P. Thulasiraman, and R. K. Thulasiram. Collaborative multi-swarm PSO for task matching using graphics processing units. *Genetic and Evolutionary Computation Conference*, pages 1563–1570, 2011.

[27] K. C. Tan, Q. Yu, and T. H. Lee. A distributed evolutionary classifier for knowledge discovery in data mining. *IEEE Transactions on Systems, Man, and Cybernetics, Part C*, 35(2):131–142, 2005.

[28] P. Vidal and E. Alba. A multi-GPU implementation of a cellular genetic algorithm. *IEEE Congress on Evolutionary Computation*, pages 1–7, 2010.

[29] V. Volkov. Better performance at lower occupancy. *GPU Technology Conference*, 2010.

[30] S. Zhang and Z. He. Implementation of parallel genetic algorithm based on CUDA. *Advances in Computation and Intelligence*, volume 5821 of *Lecture Notes in Computer Science*, pages 24–30, 2009.

Injection, Saturation and Feedback in Meta-Heuristic Interactions

Krzysztof Nowak
Advanced Concepts Team
European Space Agency (ESTEC)
Noordwijk, The Netherlands
Krzysztof.Nowak@esa.int

Dario Izzo
Advanced Concepts Team
European Space Agency (ESTEC)
Noordwijk, The Netherlands
Dario.Izzo@esa.int

Daniel Hennes
Advanced Concepts Team
European Space Agency (ESTEC)
Noordwijk, The Netherlands
Daniel.Hennes@esa.int

ABSTRACT

Meta-heuristics have proven to be an efficient method of handling difficult global optimization tasks. A recent trend in evolutionary computation is the use of several meta-heuristics at the same time, allowing for occasional information exchange among them in hope to take advantage from the best algorithmic properties of all. Such an approach is inherently parallel and, with some restrictions, has a straight forward implementation in a heterogeneous island model. We propose a methodology for characterizing the interplay between different algorithms, and we use it to discuss their performance on real-parameter single objective optimization benchmarks. We introduce the new concepts of *feedback*, *saturation* and *injection*, and show how they are powerful tools to describe the interplay between different algorithms and thus to improve our understanding of the internal mechanism at work in large parallel evolutionary set-ups.

Categories and Subject Descriptors

I.2.8 [**Artificial Intelligence**]: Problem Solving, Control Methods, and Search—*Heuristic methods*

Keywords

Global Optimization; Evolutionary Algorithms; Island Model; Parallel Computing; Differential Evolution; Particle Swarm Optimization; CMA-ES

1. INTRODUCTION

Search meta-heuristics have been growing in popularity over the years due to their performance in solving global optimization problems. Although meta-heuristics were shown to perform well across different problems, no single algorithm for global optimization is universal [1]. Established meta-heuristics, such as Differential Evolution (DE) [2], Particle Swarm Optimization (PSO) [3] or Covariance Matrix Adaptation Evolutionary Strategy (CMA-ES) [4, 5] are often used as building blocks for more sophisticated strategies that make use of hybridization [6], adaptiveness [7], multiple restarts [8] or more general: hyper-heuristics [9, 10]. The island model [11] using heterogeneous algorithms [12] is a natural and modular method to use different meta-heuristics to solve the same problem. In the heterogeneous island model, islands evolve populations using different meta-heuristics in parallel while information between islands is regulated by the migration topology. Although a heterogeneous setup in meta-heuristic parameters has been shown to be effective in [13, 14], heterogeneity in terms of distinct meta-heuristics has been only recently reported in [12, 15]. The beneficial effect of cooperation between different meta-heuristics has also been exploited in real world applications [16]. Thus, it seems that it is beneficial to deploy multiple meta-heuristics and use them in cooperation to find the optimal solution to the problem. To the best of our knowledge, there is no previous work that characterizes the mechanisms that give rise to or inhibit this cooperative behaviour.

In this paper we propose a framework to study and characterize the cooperation between different meta-heuristics and show its potential for improving the understanding of the internal mechanism at work in large parallel evolutionary set-ups. Furthermore, we discuss the taxonomy of possible algorithmic pairs interactions that give raise to cooperative or un–cooperative behaviours.

GECCO '15, July 11 - 15, 2015, Madrid, Spain

ISBN 978-1-4503-3472-3/15/07...$15.00

DOI: http://dx.doi.org/10.1145/2739480.2754729

2. MOTIVATION

The main motivation behind this research is the call for a better understanding of how migration affects the performance of different meta-heuristics. For example, the underlying reasons for certain algorithms preference to a specific type of topology [17] are not clear. We look at the problem from the perspective of a single meta-heuristic receiving and sending chromosomic material from and to an external unknown entity and we look at how the performances of the single meta-heuristic are modified by the incoming and outgoing individuals. To measure the algorithmic performance, we analyze the distribution of the function evaluations required until convergence to a known global minimum across different runs.

3. EXPERIMENTAL SETUP

The heterogeneous island-model used in this research unifies the already established concepts of *topology* and *migration frequency* [18] in a single parametrization of *migra-*

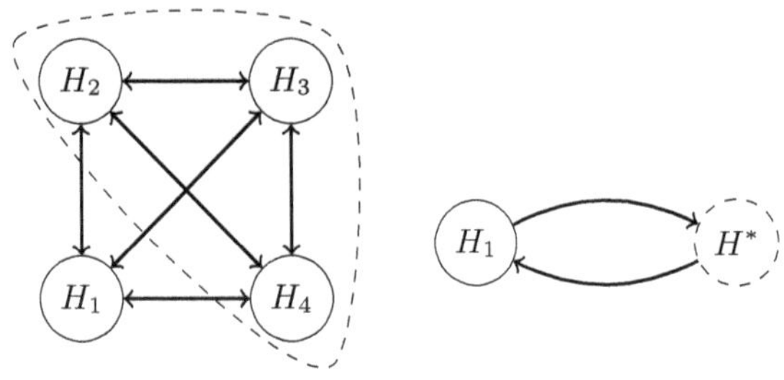

(a) (b)

Figure 1: a) Island model at the global scope. b) Reduction to the binary setup from the perspective of H_1.

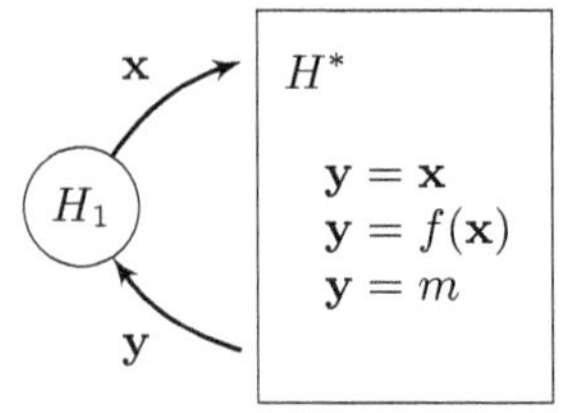

Figure 2: Set-up with an algorithm H_1 and an unknown optimization process H^*. We distinguish three different cases according to $\mathbf{y}$: *saturation*, *feedback* , *injection*

tion probabilities, modelled as weights of the directed acyclic graph of a fully connected topology. The *migration frequency* (f) and the *migration probability* (p), are two ways of parameterizing the same concept, i.e. the frequency of information exchange from one population to another. In this study we use the probabilistic representation, as it allows us to model wider range of effective migration frequencies, e.g., with $p = 0.8$ we can model migration every 1.25 migration step. Although this introduces extra stochasticity to the experimental setup, both methods converge to the same dynamics in the average case.

The archipelago presented in Figure 1(a), as seen from the perspective of island H_1, can be made equivalent to the reduced binary setup in Figure 1(b), as long as one aggregates all of the remaining islands H_2, H_3 and H_4 into a single evolutionary process. This perspective is especially convenient in meeting our goals of understanding the underlying mechanism behind migration, as the space of parameters is reduced substantially. Throughout this paper we will make extensive use of this perspective. The unobserved optimization process will be considered to be a given meta-heuristic serving the sole purpose of generating incoming individuals $\mathbf{y}$. Let us look at the migration from the perspective of a single solution migration occurring in a binary setup. Figure 2 presents a case where algorithm H_1 is migrating individuals to and from some unknown optimization process H^*. Individuals x are sent from H_1 to H^*, while the process H^* is sending back to H_1 individuals y. Let us consider the possible scenarios that can occur in-between this exchange:

1. $\mathbf{y} = \mathbf{x}$, the individual $\mathbf{x}$ is returned back without modification
2. $\mathbf{y} = f(\mathbf{x})$, algorithm H^* uses the individual $\mathbf{x}$ to produce a new solution, which is sent back to P_1.
3. $\mathbf{y} = m$, a new individual $\mathbf{y}$, not originating from $\mathbf{x}$, is injected into P_1.

In the first case, the individual $\mathbf{y}$ carries no additional *new* information to H_1 yet, as we show later, it may still entail benefits – we define the outcome of this behaviour as ***saturation***. The case where $\mathbf{x}$ is modified is of particularly high value, as it captures the notion of cooperation among meta-heuristics – if the individual $\mathbf{y}$ sent back to H_1 is beneficial, that means that the unknown evolutionary process H^* is doing something that H_1 could not do – we define this mechanism as ***feedback***. Finally, the case where $\mathbf{y} = m$ is defined as ***injection***. Being able to benefit from injection is a desirable property of meta-heuristics that is, contrary to common intuition, not always granted. For example, in a previous work by Hansen [19], a canonical version of CMA-ES is studied against external injections and found to be not able to benefit from them. In the same work a modification is proposed to the algorithm as to activate this property, we will show later that such a modification does not significantly improve the behaviour.

3.1 Methodology

In this chapter we describe the methodology used in our experiment. We will first start with describing our optimization procedure (see Algorithm 1).

In the description of Algorithm 1 we refer to the following:

1. f – optimized problem
2. P_1, P_2 – evolved populations
3. H_1, H_2 – meta-heuristics optimizing P_1 and P_2
4. p_1, p_2 – probability of migration from P_2 to P_1 and from P_1 to P_2 respectively

Two migration algorithms used in our experiments are based on the "best–replace–worst" strategy, i.e. the incoming solution, if better than the worst solution in the population, will replace it (see Algorithm 2). Since this strategy does not specify whether the incoming solution is new within the population, we provide an alternative to the original variant, which imposes a condition on the incoming migrant to be unique within the receiving population (see Algorithm 3)

We assign a fixed run budget of $B = 20,000$ function evaluations to the algorithm, and stop the evolution if any of the following conditions are met:

1. A solution within 10^{-8} from the global optimum is found
2. The function evaluation budget is exhausted
3. A population converges to a non-optimal point, i.e. the difference between the best and worst individual in the population is smaller than 10^{-12}

We repeat the experiment (run the optimization loop until stopping criteria) $1,000$ times, obtaining a pool of independent runs. Each of those runs could either be successful (condition 1 above) or unsuccessful (condition 2 or 3). We are interested in the expected run-time $\mathbb{E}(T)$ (ERT), which is defined as the expected number of function evaluations until the successful criterion is met by independent restarts of H_1 (and of the whole binary set-up). In order to estimate

Algorithm 1 Main optimization procedure

procedure OPTIMIZE($f, P_1, P_2, H_1, H_2, p_1, p_2, M$)
  $P_1, P_2 \leftarrow$ INITIALIZE(f) ▷ Initialize both populations
  do
    $P_1 \leftarrow$ EVOLVE(P_1, H_1, f)) ▷ Evolve P_1, using algorithm H_1, on a function f
    $P_2 \leftarrow$ EVOLVE(P_2, H_2, f))
    $q_1, q_2 \sim U(0,1)$ ▷ Sample q_1 and q_2 from uniform distribution
    if $q_1 < p_1$ **then**
      $P_2^* \leftarrow$ M(P_1, P_2) ▷ Migrate $P_1 \rightarrow P_2$ using migration algorithm M
    end if
    if $q_2 < p_2$ **then**
      $P_1^* \leftarrow$ M(P_2, P_1)
    end if
    $P_1, P_2 \leftarrow P_1^*, P_2^*$
  while not MEETSSTOPCRITERIA(P_1)
end procedure and **return** FEVALS(P_1), BEST(P_1)

Algorithm 2 Best-replace-worst migration

procedure $\mathrm{M}_1(P_1, P_2)$ ▷ Migrate from P_1 to P_2
  $P_2^* \leftarrow P_2$
  if BEST(P_1) < WORST(P_2) **then** ▷ Assuming minimization
    $P_2^* \leftarrow P_2 - \{\text{WORST}(P_2)\} + \{\text{BEST}(P_1)\}$
  end if
end procedure and **return** P_2^*

such a metric and other relevant statistics, we employ the formulas derived by Auger and Hansen in [20]:

$$\widehat{\mathbb{E}(T)} = \left(\frac{1-\widehat{p_s}}{\widehat{p_s}}\right) \widehat{\mathbb{E}(T^{us})} + \widehat{\mathbb{E}(T^s)}, \quad (1)$$

$$\widehat{\mathrm{Var}(T)} = \left(\frac{1-\widehat{p_s}}{\widehat{p_s^2}}\right) \widehat{\mathbb{E}(T^{us})}^2 + \widehat{\mathrm{Var}(T^s)}, \quad (2)$$

$$\widehat{\mathrm{STD}(T)} = \sqrt{\widehat{\mathrm{Var}(T)}} \quad (3)$$

where $\widehat{\mathbb{E}(T^s)}$ is the estimated number of function evaluations of successful runs, $\widehat{\mathbb{E}(T^{us})}$ is the estimated number of function evaluations of unsuccessful runs and $\widehat{p_s}$ is the estimated probability of a successful run.

3.2 Meta-heuristics

The focus of our study were three stochastic and population-based optimization meta-heuristics [1].In this section we briefly explain each of them.

3.2.1 Differential Evolution (DE)

The Differential Evolution algorithm proposed by Storn and Price [2] employs a simple, yet efficient iterative search process. The DE algorithm tries to replace $\mathbf{x}$ with a new individual created by selecting a triple $\vec{x}_1, \vec{x}_2$ and $\vec{x}_3$ at random without replacement from the current population P,

[1]Implementation of algorithms used in this research can be found at: https://github.com/esa/pagmo

Algorithm 3 Best-replace-worst without copies

procedure $\mathrm{M}_2(P_1, P_2)$ ▷ Migrate from P_1 to P_2 without copies
  $P_2^* \leftarrow P_2$
  if BEST(P_1) $\notin P_2$ **then**
    $P_2^* \leftarrow \mathrm{M}_1(P_1, P_2)$
  end if
end procedure and **return** P_2^*

and computing (rand/1/exp variant):

$$\vec{x}_{tmp} = \vec{x}_1 + F \cdot (\vec{x}_2 - \vec{x}_3),$$

where a scaling factor F is introduced. Crossover is then made with probability CR between $\vec{x}_{tmp}$ and $\vec{x}$ to produce a new individual x^*. The solution x^* replaces x if $f(x^*) < f(x)$ (assuming minimization). In our experiments we use a self-adaptive variant of DE called jDE [21] so that F and CR are adapted during each run.

3.2.2 Covariance Matrix Adaptation Evolutionary Strategy (CMA-ES)

The CMA-ES proposed by Hansen et al. [4, 5] optimizes the objective function by sampling λ solutions ($i = 1, \ldots, \lambda$) from the multivariate normal distribution:

$$x_i^{(t+1)} = \mathbf{m}^{(t)} + \sigma^{(t)} \cdot \mathcal{N}(0, \mathcal{C}^{(t)}),$$

where $\mathbf{m}^{(t)}$, $\mathcal{C}^{(t)}$ and $\sigma^{(t)}$ denote mean, covariance matrix and step-size of the distribution at time t. The covariance matrix and the mean are updated from the best λ solutions. We experiment with both the canonical version of CMA-ES with rank-μ update [5] and a variant recently proposed by Hansen which aims at allowing external injections to benefit from the evolutionary process [19].

3.2.3 Particle Swarm Optimization (PSO)

PSO is a bio-inspired stochastic search technique, which uses a swarm of particles in search of the best global solution. The velocity of each particle is dependent on the neighbourhood best (g_B) and local (p_B) best solution found so far, in accordance with equation:

$$x_i^{(t+1)} = x_i^{(t)} + v_i^{(t)},$$

where the velocity $v_i^{(t)}$ is updated as:

$$v_i^{(t+1)} = \omega\left(v_i^{(t)} + \eta_1 r_1 (p_B - x_i^{(t)}) + \eta_2 r_2 (g_B - x_i^{(t)})\right).$$

where r_1 and r_2 are two random numbers in $[0, 1]$, and $\omega = 0.5$, $\eta_1 = \eta_2 = 2.05$ are algorithmic parameters. We implement and use a canonical version of PSO with constriction factor [22], where particles are arranged on a ring and the neighbourhood is defined by the closest 4 particles.

3.3 Problems

We test each setup on selected problems from the CEC 2013 real–optimization benchmark suite (see Table 1). Since the main topic of our research in not focused at benchmarking over a multitude of problems and dimensions, but analyzing the behaviour of algorithms when subjected to migration in a qualitative fashion, we assume problem dimension D = 2, which in turn allows us to repeat each experimental

f	Properties	Name
f_1	U, S	Sphere
f_4	U, NS	Rotated Discus
f_6	M, NS	Rotated Rosenbrock's
f_7	M, NS	Rotated Schaffers F7
f_9	M, NS	Rotated Weierstrass
f_{12}	M, NS	Rotated Rastrigin
f_{13}	M, NS	Non-Continuous Rotated Rastrigin
f_{15}	M, NS	Rotated Schwefel's
f_{16}	M, NS	Rotated Katsuura

Table 1: A selection of CEC 2013 benchmark problems [23] used in this research. For each problem we note the modality (unimodal (U) or multimodal (M)) and separability (separable (S) or non-separable (NS)) with search range of $[-100, 100]^D$.

configuration multiple times and evaluate our results statistically. For each of the selected problems, 20,000 function evaluations is established as reasonable budget to converge to local minima (as proposed in the CEC 2013 benchmarks).

3.4 Binary meta-heuristics experiment

In this experiment we consider a two–island setup, where each population is evolved using one of the previously specified meta-heuristics (we denote the meta-heuristics of populations P_1 and P_2 as H_1 and H_2 respectively). We instantiate each population with 20 individuals, and migrate with some probability p on every generation, as the number of generations after which we migrate (gen) is directly related to p, e.g. $gen = 1$ and $p = 0.1$ is equivalent to $gen = 10$ and $p = 1.0$ in the average case. Migration between populations evolved by H_1 and H_2 occurs with probabilities p_1 (migration $P_1 \leftarrow P_2$) and p_2 (migration $P_1 \rightarrow P_2$). As stated previously, to get a deeper understanding of the effect of migration on individual algorithms, we do not observe the population P_2, but focus entirely on the population P_1, i.e. the stopping criteria and the number of function evaluations are considered and measured only "locally" for P_1. We run both algorithms synchronously to rule out the possibility of one algorithm evolving faster than another due to the operating system–specific factors, e.g. uneven load balancing across processes. To observe the effects of migration under changing magnitude, we gradually increase the parameter p_1 starting from 0.0 up to 1.0 by a step of 0.1, and consider two cases for the parameter p_2:

1. $p_2 = p_1$ – migration between P_1 and P_2 occurs with equal probability
2. $p_2 = 0.0$ – P_1 does not send any solutions to P_2

We run the experiments for all combination of pairs (H_1, H_2) of three evolutionary algorithms: DE, CMA-ES and PSO (see Figure 3), each migration algorithm: M_1, M_2, and across all of the problems mentioned in the previous section. We repeat the experiment 1,000 times with randomly instantiated populations, obtaining a pool of individual runs. We evaluate final performance of each configuration by computing the expected runtime and standard deviation over the pool of runs, using Equations 1 and 3 respectively.

The choice of the algorithms for our experiment was motivated by the difference in evolutionary operators, leading to

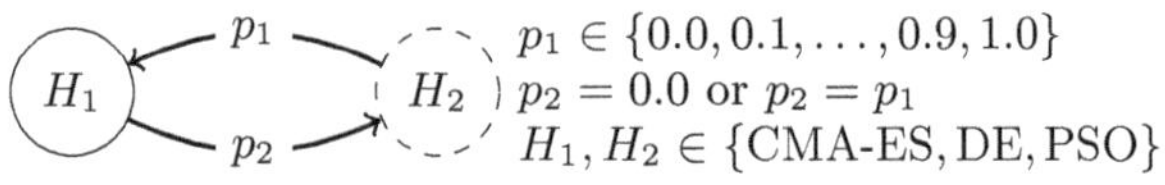

Figure 3: Two–island setup with both populations being evolved synchronously by H_1 and H_2 and migrating with probabilities p_1 and p_2. We observe only the results of H_1.

different performance levels on popular optimization problems. We aim at integrating the benefits of those differences by allowing for cooperative interplay of heterogeneous algorithms, hopefully resulting in an overall better performance than the homogeneous setups.

In the remainder of this section we will describe several previously defined migration effects emerging in our results, which can be later attributed to certain properties of each algorithm. We present those on examples by covering several specific cases for each phenomenon, and then provide a general overview of our findings.

3.4.1 Evidence for the distinctive migration effects

This section presents the empirical evidence for the previously defined migration effects: *injection*, *saturation* and *feedback*. Let us consider the following parameters: $H_1, H_2 =$ DE, DE, problem $f = f_7$, and parameters p_1 and p_2 varying as stated in the previous section. We compare our observation for two migration algorithms, M_1 and M_2, starting with the basic "best-replace-worst" migration M_1 (see Algorithm 2). Figure 4 presents the changing distribution of sequence of runs resampled until success (which simulates a restart strategy). The distributions above are approximated by a Gaussian kernel density estimation over varying parameters p_1 and p_2, with the expected runtime and standard deviation (error bars) below.

Two plots at the top of Figure 4 present the cases $p_2 = 0$ (left) and $p_1 = p_2$ (right). When describing the results we will always start by relating one–directional migration ($p_2 = 0, p_1 \geq 0.1$) to the no-migration ***baseline*** ($p_1 = 0, p_2 = 0$), and then to the two–directional migration ($p_2 = p_1 \geq 0.1$). Thus, looking at Figure 4, we first observe that for $p_1 = 0.3, p_2 = 0$, the ERT shifts from the baseline located at around 3,500 to 3,000 function evaluations, suggesting that the migration of solutions from P_2 improved the optimization process. Since there was no migration link from P_1 to P_2, the positive effect on the population P_1 can not be attributed to anything else besides the *injection* effect. The injection effects can easily be observed in our setup as soon as we observe that ERT for $p_1 \geq 0.1, p_2 = 0$ is much smaller than the baseline. Although one might take this effect for granted, not every meta-heuristic can benefit from it.

After the initial speedup, little change can be observed once $p_1 \geq 0.3$. As soon as we introduce the two–directional migration ($p_2 = p_1$), we notice an improvement in the distribution of the run-times and a gradual decrease in the ERT until $p_1 = p_2 = 0.7$. This particular behavior is especially interesting when we take into consideration that we observe the evolutionary process only from the perspective of a single (receiving) island. Intuitively, it must have been the already known "good" solutions from P_1, which were sent to P_2 that made the difference on the end performance of H_1. This suggests that migration in not a one–directional pro-

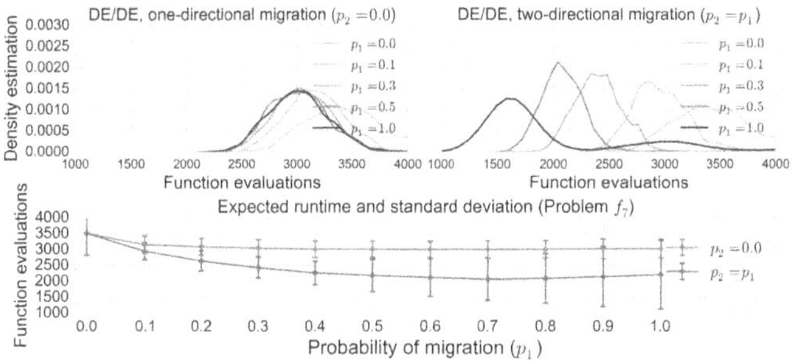

Figure 4: Runtime behaviour of homogeneous DE/DE setup on problem f_7 using migration algorithm M_1.

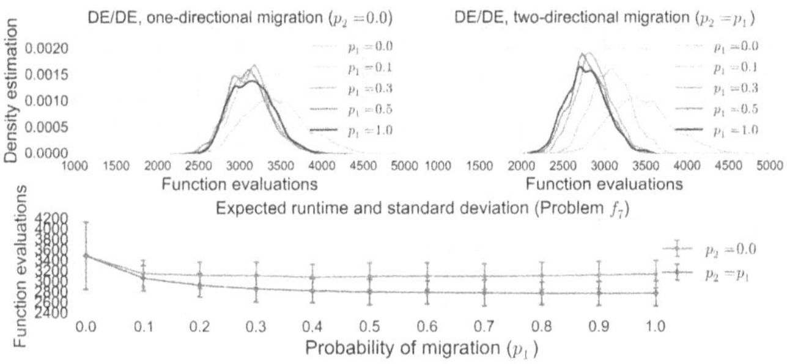

Figure 5: Runtime behaviour of DE/DE setup on problem f_7 and migration algorithm M_2.

cess and can be strongly reinforced by a mutual information exchange.

The only difference between the one–directional migration and two–directional migration was in the non-zero probability of sending solutions from P_1 to P_2. This single change made the difference in the expected run-time of over 1000 function evaluations (improvement by a factor of 2 over the one–directional migration). The well controlled environment of our setup leads us to conclusion that the solutions sent back by P_1 were further modified by the algorithm H_2, which in turn was able to send back superior solutions in the later migration steps. Such a conclusion would then attribute this effect to *feedback*. Another explanation could be the relaxed policy of migration algorithm M_1 towards the duplicated individuals, which indirectly guided the observed copy of DE towards a more exploitative search (*saturation*). To determine that, we repeat the same experiment with the migration policy M_2, which imposes the condition that the migrants must be unique within the receiving population. Figure 5 presents the result for the same experiment with migration algorithm M_2. Comparison of one–directional migration to the baseline for varying p_1 leads us to similar conclusions as before. However, when we consider the relative change of ERT for $p_2 = p_1$, we notice that the additional benefit of two–directional migration is still persisting, but to a lesser degree. In the best–case scenario for M_2 ($p_1 = p_2 = 1.0$), the reduction of ERT is of around 500 function evaluations (from 3200 to around 2700), compared to a difference of around 1000 in equivalent best–case of M_1.

Using the results of both experiments we can finally resolve our previous concern on whether the positive effect of mutual migration should be attributed to the feedback or saturation. Since the difference between two–directional

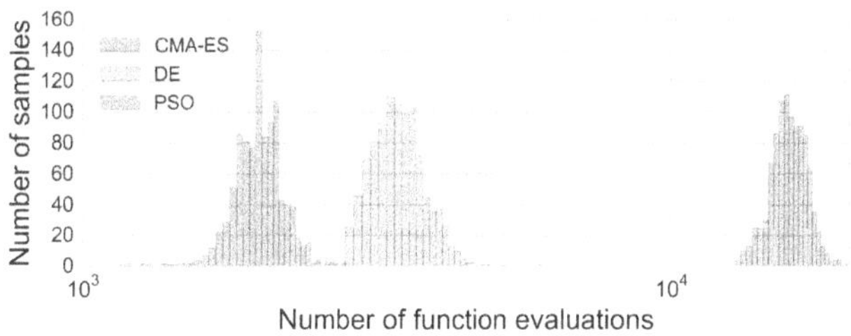

Figure 6: Distribution of individual runtimes for algorithms CMA-ES, DE and PSO on problem f_7.

cases of migration algorithms M_1 and M_2 is only in the rejection of the duplicated solutions, and the absolute ERT is higher for M_2 than for M_1, we can reason that some of the speed-up was obtained by the saturation effect. However, since in case of M_2 we do not accept the duplicates in P_1 anymore, and yet the difference between the one–directional and two–directional scenarios ($p_2 = 0$ vs $p_2 = p_1$) is observed, it must have been the migration of individuals from P_1 to P_2, which were used in producing superior solutions, which were then sent back to P_1 (feedback). This suggests that in the first experiment the decrease in ERT should be attributed to *saturation* and potentially also *feedback* (the latter cannot be determined with full certainty), while for the second experiment it was strictly the feedback effect which improved the ERT.

The type of reasoning demonstrated in this section, along with the observation of the differences in the behaviour of runtime distribution for varying parameters M_1, M_2, p_1 and p_2, are the core tools for pin-pointing the cause of the migration effects, and attribute those to either injection, saturation, feedback, or a combination of each. Throughout the remainder of this paper we will use those methods for demonstrating the existence of said effects for different problems and meta-heuristics.

3.4.2 Migration effects in heterogeneous meta-heuristic setups

In this section we extend our previous reasoning to the heterogeneous meta-heuristic setups, yet before we continue, let us first get a notion on the relative performances between the single instances of CMA-ES, DE and PSO optimizing the problem f_7 (see Figure 6). It is clear that on this particular problem DE is much faster than PSO, while CMA-ES is the fastest of the three.

Let us then consider a case where H_1=DE, H_2=PSO and $f = f_7$. The difference in ERT between the baseline and the one–directional migration is of around 100 function evaluations (see Figure 7). Since $p_2 = 0$, the only way P_1 can improve is by injection from P_2. This does not happen, as we can presume from Figure 6 that PSO has no strong candidate solutions to offer to DE. Here we uncover a property of the injection effect: slower algorithms have low chances to induce a positive injection effect in neighboring populations in a one–directional migration setting (we confirm this to be true for other problems). However, when $p_2 = p_1 \geq 0.1$, we can again observe an improving trend in ERT over the varying parameter p_1. Although this also happened in the previous heterogeneous case, it was not as surprising since the two algorithms were the same in terms of convergence speed. Here instead, we have an example of PSO, which is

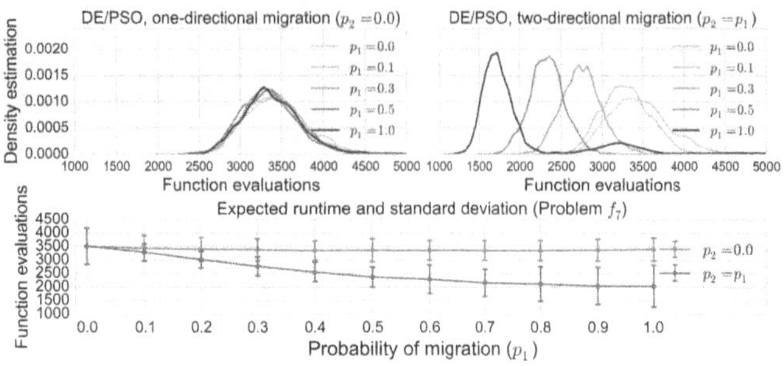

Figure 7: Runtime behaviour of DE/PSO setup on problem f_7 and migration algorithm M_1.

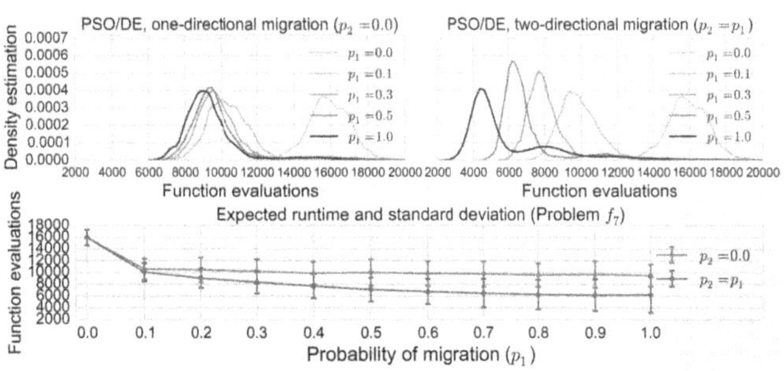

Figure 8: Runtime behaviour of PSO/DE setup on problem f_7 and migration algorithm M_1.

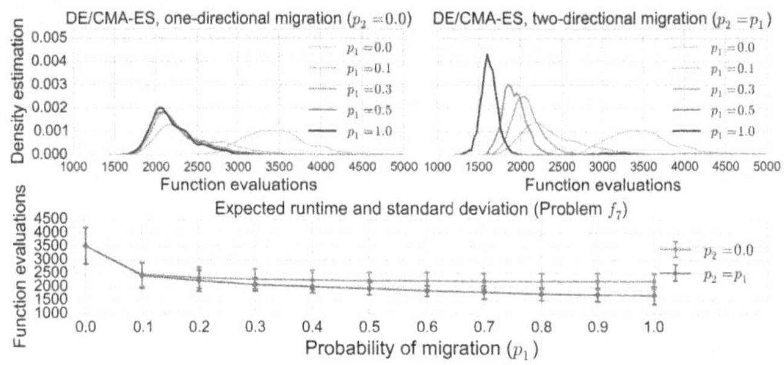

Figure 9: Runtime behaviour of DE/CMA-ES setup on problem f_7 and migration algorithm M_1.

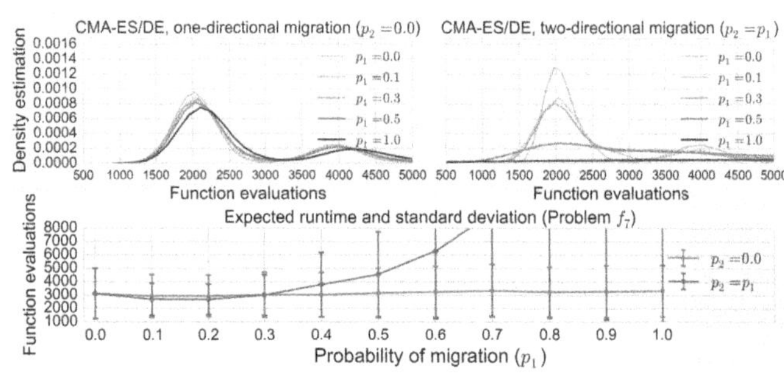

Figure 10: Runtime behaviour of CMA-ES/DE setup on problem f_7 and migration algorithm M_1.

much "slower" than DE on problem f_7, yet a two–directional migration is still beneficial for the "faster" DE. As we consider the case for M_2, we arrive at the same conclusions as for the DE/DE scenario: the benefits of migration for this heterogeneous case are attributed to a combination of saturation **and** feedback, meaning that the evolutionary operators of DE and PSO came into a *cooperative interplay*. Without that knowledge, a practitioner might be tempted to not include PSO when building a heterogeneous island setup, based solely on the observation that it is **individually** slower. Instead we show that relative difference between the individual run-times of algorithms starts to dissipate as the migration comes into play.

At this point we would like to introduce yet another behaviour which we would like to characterize: ***mutual cooperation***. We say that algorithms are in mutual cooperation when both respond well to migration from one another, i.e. when we notice a positive effect compared to the baseline in the distributions and expected run-times of H_2 and H_1 when $p_1 = p_2 > 0$. An example of mutually cooperative algorithms was already shown, yet not mentioned at the time: a pair of DE/DE, according to our definition, is in mutual cooperation. Although we only observe the run-time distribution of P_1 in a DE/DE setup, we can safely assume that the behaviour and distribution of P_2, evolved by another instance of DE, would be similar, as our methodology does not put H_2 at any disadvantage. We determine a mutual cooperation in homogeneous cases whenever we note a positive impact of two–directional migration in one observed binary setup (switching heuristics would not change the observation). To determine the mutual cooperation of DE and PSO, refer to the case opposite case of H_1=PSO,H_2=DE (Figure 8). Since we observe a positive impact of two–directional migration, we can determine that there exists a mutual cooperation between DE and PSO.

Let us now consider the case H_1=DE, H_2=CMA-ES, for problem f_7. Figure 9 shows the performance of the setup.

Comparison of one–directional migration with the baseline, suggests that DE improves by injection from CMA-ES, while the two–directional migration improves DE even further. By analyzing the H_2 case, we confirm that the reason for that is both feedback and saturation. When we swap the meta-heuristics, and consider the H_1=CMA-ES,H_2=DE case, we observe a deteriorating performance of CMA-ES as soon as $p_1 = p_2 \geq 0.3$ (see Figure 10). This concludes that the algorithms DE and CMA-ES are not in mutual cooperation, however, when we look at the best achieved ERT by all 4 setups of CMAES and DE, we can see that the heterogeneous pair of DE/CMA-ES achieves the best expected runtime of 1,600 function evaluations, compared to around 2,000 by DE/DE, 2,200 by CMA-ES/CMA-ES (not shown in a graph) and slightly below 3,000 by CMA-ES/DE. This suggests that the heterogeneity of operators, along with the previously presented effects of injection, saturation and feedback resulted in a cooperative behaviour. Analogously to previous reasoning, by comparing the results with non-copying migration M_2 we observe that the main effect of good performance of DE/CMA-ES is mainly due to initial injection from CMA-ES, and then from feedback and saturation by DE. Although the cooperation is not mutual since CMA-ES deteriorates by injections from DE, a practitioner should still consider the heterogeneous setup, as in a parallel computation setting, where both islands would be run in parallel, DE will on average find the solution faster than any homogeneous setup.

Poor performance of CMA-ES is related to its covariance

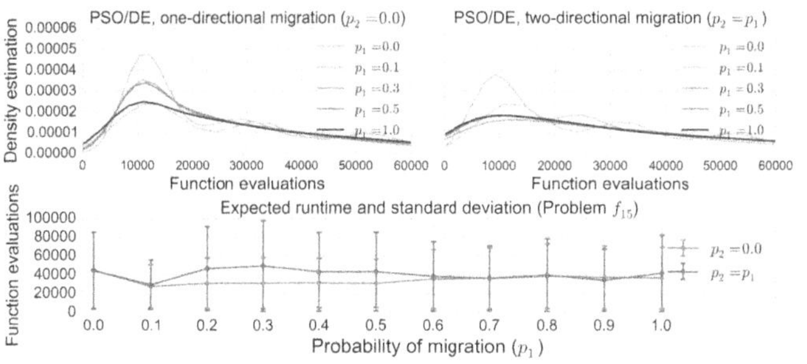

Figure 11: Runtime of PSO/DE for $f = f_{15}$ and $M = M_1$.

matrix adaptation scheme, which does not handle the injection of external solutions well. A variant of CMA-ES which aimed at solving this problem proposed by Hansen [19], updates the mean and the covariance matrix accordingly to the injected individual. Author reports improvement of CMA-ES when manually injecting a perturbed solution from the global minimum. In our case the migration in an island model is far more complex than that, as the injection can happen frequently from different locations of the search space, as well as originate from local minima. We have implemented and experimented with the proposed CMA-ES variation and found that it is still not able to handle injections from other meta-heuristics.

3.4.3 *Migration effects as leverage for exploration and exploitation*

In the previous section we have shown the empirical evidence for distinctive effects that occur during the migration between the meta-heuristics. In this section we just want to confirm the already known fact that those migration effects act as a tool for leveraging the long established notion of exploration–exploitation trade–off. Let us consider a "difficult" problem f_{15}, for which the heterogeneous evolutionary operators, combined with the previously presented migration effects, come into a more complex interplay.

For $f = f_{15}$, H_1=PSO,H_2=DE and migration algorithm $M = M_1$ we have the behaviour as presented in Figure 11. When we compare the baseline to one–directional migration, we see that for $p_1 = 0.1$ an improvement can be recorded (ERT decreases by around 20,000 function evaluations), however as soon as we continue increasing the probability of migration, the performance in terms of ERT and standard deviation degrades. Analogous case for M_2 exhibits a lesser, yet still existing, degrading effect, meaning that limiting saturation effect did not fix the problem, as the feedback was still in place. In the case of this problem, the migration achieves the best effect, when it is applied in moderation ($p_1 = 0.1$). This comes from the previously hinted notion that the effects of saturation a feedback magnify the exploitative behaviour, since they reduce the variety in the population.

3.4.4 *Migration effects across different problems*

To summarize our experimental results we provide the information on benefits of one–directional and two–directional migration across all of our tested problems in Tables [2,3,4]. Each table represents one of the three possible algorithms for H_1, while each column describe the combinations of H_2 and p_1. We determine each symbol as follows: for $p_2 = 0$, • stands for a case where migration improved the ERT over the baseline (determined within the margin of 5%) in all of the cases, ○ when ERT improved in only some cases, no symbol stands for no clear indication, while minus sign (-) stands for strict degradation of performance. Similarly for column $p_2 = p_1$, except in each of those cases we consider the relative performance to the $p_2 = 0$ case.

By analyzing those results, we get the outlook on meta-heuristic properties across problems, e.g., a good cooperative behaviour of DE and PSO (also in heterogeneous setups) and a less cooperative behaviour of CMA-ES with other algorithms, yet a strong effect of injection for migration CMA-ES→DE and CMA-ES→PSO.

4. CONCLUSIONS

We analyze in detail the migration effects occurring within the heterogeneous island model. We show how migration acts via three different and separate mechanisms defined by us as *saturation*, *feedback* and *injection*, which can considerably improve the performances of meta-heuristics as well as inhibit their internal mechanics. We show how saturation effects can, contrary to common intuition, be beneficial in exploitative behavior, while feedback is at the basis for cooperative behaviour among different meta-heuristics. We find the algorithms DE and PSO to exhibit cooperative behavior, while CMA-ES, in most cases, is unable to use the mentioned effects advantageously. We provide the reader with the tools for determining the collaboration properties of generic pairs of algorithms. We put our work forward as an important step in the direction of understanding the complex algorithmic interplay at work in large parallel setup using the heterogeneous island model or, in general, the hybridization of evolutionary operators.

$H_2 \rightarrow$	CMA-ES		DE		PSO	
$p_2 \rightarrow$	0	p_1	0	p_1	0	p_1
f_1	•	○	•	○		○
f_4	•	○	•	○		○
f_6	•	○	•	•	○	○
f_7	•	○	•	•	○	○
f_9	•	○	•	•	○	○
f_{12}	•	•	•	○	•	○
f_{13}	•	•	•	•	•	○
f_{15}	•	○	•	-	•	-
f_{16}	•	-	○	•	•	-

Table 2: Migration effects table for H_1=DE.

$H_2 \rightarrow$	CMA-ES		DE		PSO	
$p_2 \rightarrow$	0	p_1	0	p_1	0	p_1
f_1	•	○	•	○	•	○
f_4	•	-	•	○		
f_6	•	○	•	•	•	•
f_7	•	○	•	○	•	•
f_9	•	○	•	•	•	•
f_{12}	•	•	•	•	•	•
f_{13}	•	•	•	•	•	•
f_{15}	•	○	•	-	•	○
f_{16}	•	-		•	○	○

Table 3: Migration effects table for H_1=PSO.

$H_2 \rightarrow$	CMA-ES		DE		PSO	
$p_2 \rightarrow$	0	p_1	0	p_1	0	p_1
f_1		-	-	-		
f_4		-	-	-		-
f_6	○	-	-	-		-
f_7	•	-	○	○	-	○
f_9	-	-	-	-	-	○
f_{12}	○	○	○	○	•	○
f_{13}	•	○	○	•	•	•
f_{15}	○	○	-	○	○	○
f_{16}	-	-	-	○	-	○

Table 4: Migration effects table for H_1=CMA-ES.

5. REFERENCES

[1] David H. Wolpert and William G. Macready. No free lunch theorems for optimization. *Evolutionary Computation, IEEE Transactions on*, 1(1):67–82, 1997.

[2] Rainer Storn and Kenneth Price. Differential evolution–a simple and efficient heuristic for global optimization over continuous spaces. *Journal of global optimization*, 11(4):341–359, 1997.

[3] Kennedy James and Eberhart Russell. Particle swarm optimization. In *Proceedings of 1995 IEEE International Conference on Neural Networks*, pages 1942–1948, 1995.

[4] Nikolaus Hansen and Andreas Ostermeier. Completely derandomized self-adaptation in evolution strategies. *Evolutionary computation*, 9(2):159–195, 2001.

[5] Nikolaus Hansen, Sibylle D. Müller, and Petros Koumoutsakos. Reducing the time complexity of the derandomized evolution strategy with covariance matrix adaptation (CMA-ES). *Evolutionary Computation*, 11(1):1–18, 2003.

[6] Tianjun Liao and Thomas Stuetzle. Benchmark results for a simple hybrid algorithm on the CEC 2013 benchmark set for real-parameter optimization. In Luis Gerardo de la Fraga, editor, *2013 IEEE Conference on Evolutionary Computation*, volume 1, pages 1938–1944, Cancun, Mexico, June 20-23 2013.

[7] A. Kai Qin, Vicky Ling Huang, and Ponnuthurai N. Suganthan. Differential evolution algorithm with strategy adaptation for global numerical optimization. *Evolutionary Computation, IEEE Transactions on*, 13(2):398–417, 2009.

[8] Anne Auger and Nikolaus Hansen. A restart CMA evolution strategy with increasing population size. In *Evolutionary Computation, 2005. The 2005 IEEE Congress on*, volume 2, pages 1769–1776. IEEE, 2005.

[9] T. Vinkó, D. Izzo, and F. Pinna. Learning the best combination of solvers in a distributed global optimization environment. *Proceedings of Advances in Global Optimization: Methods and Applications (AGO), Mykonos, Greece*, pages 13–17, 2007.

[10] Edmund Burke, Graham Kendall, Jim Newall, Emma Hart, Peter Ross, and Sonia Schulenburg. Hyper-heuristics: An emerging direction in modern search technology. In *Handbook of metaheuristics*, pages 457–474. Springer, 2003.

[11] Erick Cantú-Paz. Topologies, migration rates, and multi-population parallel genetic algorithms. In *Proc. Genetic and Evolutionary Computation Conference (GECCO'99)*, volume 1, pages 91–98, 1999.

[12] Dario Izzo, Marek Ruciński, and Francesco Biscani. The generalized island model. In Francisco Fernández de Vega, José Ignacio Hidalgo Pérez, and Juan Lanchares, editors, *Parallel Architectures and Bioinspired Algorithms*, volume 415 of *Studies in Computational Intelligence*, pages 151–169. Springer Berlin Heidelberg, 2012.

[13] Mario García-Valdez, Leonardo Trujillo, Juan Julián Merelo-Guérvos, and Francisco Fernández de Vega. Randomized parameter settings for heterogeneous workers in a pool-based evolutionary algorithm. In Thomas Bartz-Beielstein, Jürgen Branke, Bogdan Filipič, and Jim Smith, editors, *Parallel Problem Solving from Nature – PPSN XIII*, volume 8672 of *Lecture Notes in Computer Science*, pages 702–710. Springer International Publishing, 2014.

[14] Y. Gong and A. Fukunaga. Distributed island-model genetic algorithms using heterogeneous parameter settings. In *Evolutionary Computation (CEC), 2011 IEEE Congress on*, pages 820–827, June 2011.

[15] Thiago T. Magalhães, Luis Henrique C. Nascimento, Eduardo Krempser, Douglas A. Augusto, and Helio J. C. Barbosa. Hybrid metaheuristics for optimization using a parallel islands model. In *Ibero-Latin American Congress on Computational Methods in Engineering*, November 2014.

[16] Matteo Rosa Sentinella and Lorenzo Casalino. Cooperative evolutionary algorithm for space trajectory optimization. *Celestial Mechanics and Dynamical Astronomy*, 105(1-3):211–227, 2009.

[17] M. Ruciński, D. Izzo, and F. Biscani. On the impact of the migration topology on the island model. *Parallel Comput.*, 36(10-11):555–571, October 2010.

[18] Erick Cantú-Paz. *Efficient and Accurate Parallel Genetic Algorithms*. Kluwer Academic Publishers, Norwell, MA, USA, 2000.

[19] Nikolaus Hansen. Injecting external solutions into CMA-ES. *CoRR*, abs/1110.4181, 2011.

[20] Nikolaus Hansen and Anne Auger. Performance evaluation of an advanced local search evolutionary algorithm. In *In Proceedings of the IEEE Congress on Evolutionary Computation*, pages 1777–1784. IEEE Press, 2005.

[21] Janez Brest, Viljem Zumer, and Mirjam Sepesy Maucec. Self-adaptive differential evolution algorithm in constrained real-parameter optimization. In *Evolutionary Computation, 2006. CEC 2006. IEEE Congress on*, pages 215–222. IEEE, 2006.

[22] Riccardo Poli, James Kennedy, and Tim Blackwell. Particle swarm optimization. *Swarm intelligence*, 1(1):33–57, 2007.

[23] J.J. Liang, B.Y. Qu, P.N. Suganthan, and Alfredo G. Hernández-Dıaz. Problem definitions and evaluation criteria for the CEC 2013 special session on real-parameter optimization. *Computational Intelligence Laboratory, Zhengzhou University, Zhengzhou, China and Nanyang Technological University, Singapore, Technical Report*, 201212, 2013.

A Model with Evolutionary Covariance-based Learning for High-Frequency Financial Forecasting

Ricardo de A. Araújo[1,2], Adriano L. I. Oliveira[2], Silvio Meira[2]
[1]Informatics Department, Federal Institute of Sertão Pernambucano, Ouricuri, PE, Brazil
[2]Informatics Center, Federal University of Pernambuco, Recife, PE, Brazil.
ricardo.araujo@ifsertao-pe.edu.br and {raa, alio, srlm}@cin.ufpe.br

ABSTRACT

Several approaches have been investigated to develop models able to solve forecasting problems. However, a limitation arises in the particular case of daily-frequency financial forecasting and is called the random walk dilemma (RWD). In this context, the concept of time phase adjustment can be included in forecasting models to overcome such a drawback. But the evolution of trading systems has increased the frequency for performing operations in the stock market for fractions of seconds, which requires the analysis of high-frequency financial time series. Thus, this work proposes a model, called the increasing decreasing linear neuron (IDLN), to forecast high-frequency financial time series from the Brazilian stock market. Furthermore, an evolutionary covariance-based method with automatic time phase adjustment is presented for the design of the proposed model, and the obtained results overcame those obtained by classical forecasting models in the literature.

Categories and Subject Descriptors

I.2.8 [**Artificial Intelligence**]: Problem Solving, Control Methods, and Search; G.3 [**Probability and Statistics**]: Time series analysis; I.6.5 [**Simulation and Modeling**]: Model Development

Keywords

Hybrid Model; Forecasting; Evolutionary Learning; High-Frequency Stock Market; Financial Time Series.

1. INTRODUCTION

A wide number of models have been presented in the literature to forecast time series. Among them, even with the limitation of its linearity, the autoregressive integrated moving average (ARIMA) [1] model has been commonly employed to forecast financial time series [2]. In the attempt to overcome this drawback, several nonlinear statistical models were proposed in the literature [2]. However, Clements *et al.* [2] argue that nonlinear statistical models have the same performance than linear statistical models, restricting its use in the practice.

In this way, artificial neural networks (ANNs) can be considered an alternative approach for financial forecasting [3–7]. It is worth mentioning that a particular class of ANNs presented in the literature to solve financial forecasting problems are the morphological neural networks (MNNs) [8–11]. In this context, hybrid forecasting models, composed of evolutionary algorithms (EAs) [12, 13] and ANNs [3–7] or MNNs [8–11] have been proposed in the literature to solve financial forecasting problems [14–18]. However, such approach uses a wide amount of computing resources to achieve accurate results [9, 19], restricting its practical use.

Even with sophisticated models presented in the literature, a drawback arises in the particular case of daily-frequency financial forecasting problems and is called the random walk dilemma (RWD). In this dilemma the forecasts have a one step ahead delay regarding real time series values [20]. Due to this behavior, Sitte and Sitte [20] argue that financial time series are generated by random processes and cannot be predicted. However, Sitte and Sitte [20] do not develop any conclusive proofs to support such a claim [9, 19].

In this context, Ferreira *et al.* [21] raised the assumption of a subdominant nonlinear component embedded in a dominant linear component in financial time series, and they proposed a procedure to overcome the RWD, called the phase adjustment procedure (PAP), for ANN models (multilayer perceptrons) built using a hybrid learning process composed by genetic algorithms (GAs) [12] and descending gradient-based techniques [22–25]. Through the introduction of the phase adjustment concept in financial time series, it is possible to find two studies investigating its use in ANN models [26–28].

The assumption presented by Ferreira *et al.* [21] was confirmed and formalized by Araújo [9, 19] through the lagplot analyzes of several daily-frequency financial time series, where nonlinear structures in high-order time lags could be identified, confirming the hypothesis of non-randomness of this particular kind of time series. Furthermore, Araújo [29] and Araújo and Sussner [30] have demonstrated that the nonlinear component of the generator phenomenon from financial time series sampled in daily-frequency can be approximated in terms of a nonlinear mapping with an increasing behavior. In this context, some works have been proposed in the literature investigating increasing models for daily-frequency financial forecasting [9, 19].

However, the high evolution of trading platforms has increased the frequency for performing operations on the stock market to fractions of seconds, and the growth of high-frequency operations suggests that the high-frequency stock market (HFSM) be a global trend, which requires the analysis of this kind of time series. Besides, it is also expected that the generator phenomenon of high-frequency financial time series has distinct behavior with respect to daily-frequency, which emphasizes the limitation of the work developed by Araújo [29] and Araújo and Sussner [30], since the increasing behavior found in daily-frequency financial time series cannot be generalized for any kind of financial time series.

In this context, this work presents a model for high-frequency fi-

GECCO '15, July 11 - 15, 2015, Madrid, Spain
 ISBN 978-1-4503-3472-3/15/07…$15.00
DOI: http://dx.doi.org/10.1145/2739480.2754815

nancial time series forecasting. Also, it is presented an evolutionary covariance-based method with automatic time phase adjustment to design the proposed model using the covariance matrix adaptation evolutionary strategy (CMA-ES) algorithm [13]. At the end, an experimental analysis is conduced using relevant high-frequency financial time series from the Brazilian stock market, where five relevant metrics and an evaluation function are used to assess the forecasting performance of the proposed model in the HFSM.

2. THE TIME SERIES FORECASTING PROBLEM

According to Box *et al.* [1], a time series is a sequence of observations, sampled in discrete or continuous space, about a phenomenon that evolves with time and formally defined by

$$\mathbf{x} = \{x_t \in \mathbb{R} \mid t = 1, 2, 3 \dots N\}, \quad (1)$$

where t is the temporal index and N is the number of observations. The term $\mathbf{x}$ is the set of all temporal observations equally spaced and temporally ordered by a chronological index t, which is called time and defines the granularity of observations of the temporal phenomenon.

In this way, the aim to forecast a time series $\mathbf{x}$ is to build a mapping able to estimate the future behavior of a temporal phenomenon, that is, to build a mechanism that allows, with certain accuracy, to estimate the future values of the time series, given by x_{t+h}, $h = 1, 2, \dots, H$, where h represents the prediction horizon of H steps ahead.

2.1 The Random Walk Dilemma in Financial Forecasting

Sitte and Sitte [20] have showed that the future observation (x_t) of a financial time series can be defined by

$$x_t = x_{t-1} + r_t, \quad (2)$$

where the term x_t is the current observation, the term x_{t-1} is the observation before x_t, and the term r_t is a Gaussian noise with zero mean and standard deviation σ ($r_t \approx N(0, \sigma)$), that is, a white noise.

According to Equation 2, it is possible to verify that the future of financial time series is unpredictable because x_{t-1} tends to x_t, that is, $E[\widehat{x_t}] \rightarrow E[x_{t-1}]$ [20]. This behavior occurs in financial forecasting problems and known as the random walk dilemma (RWD) or the random walk hypothesis (RWH) [20]. In this dilemma, the forecast of any model for financial time series has a one step ahead delay regarding the real time series value.

This problem is a hard task to be solved because the generator phenomenon of financial time series is very similar to random walk generator phenomenon, and any prediction model tends to be guided by this behavior [20]. However, according to Araújo [9, 19], an alternative procedure can be employed in forecasting models to overcome the RWD in the particular case of financial time series with daily-frequency, called the phase adjustment procedure (PAP) [21].

According to the Figure 1 the PAP has two steps: *i)* the input pattern $\{x_1, x_2, \dots, x_n\}$ (time lags) is presented to the prediction model to create an output (y_1), and *ii)* the input pattern is re-arranged including the output generated in the step *(i)*, given by $\{y_1, x_1, x_2, \dots, x_{n-1}\}$, and is presented to the same prediction model, where another output (y_2) is created. It is worth mentioning that y_2 represents the prediction with adjusted phase, that is, the prediction without the delay of one step ahead regarding real time series value.

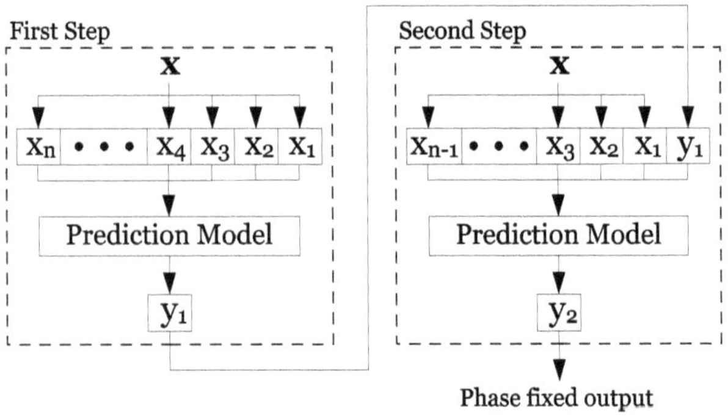

Figure 1: Time phase adjustment procedure.

3. HIGH-FREQUENCY FINANCIAL TIME SERIES

This section describes two high-frequency financial time series analyzed in this work: Banco do Brasil SA (BBAS3) and Brasil Foods SA (BRFS3). Both time series represent the opening value of the stock price, with frequency of one second, from the most important Brazilian stock market index, called the *Bolsa de Valores de São Paulo* (BOVESPA). The time series investigated in this work are composed by high-frequency observations of the stock prices at 2013/02/01, and they are illustrated in the Figure 2. The Figure 3 presents the lagplot graphic of these time series.

According to Figure 3, it can be verified the existence of a dominant linear relationship among time lags 1 and 25. However, in high order time lags (from 50 to 1000) it is possible to identify a subdominant nonlinear relationship embedded within linear relationship. Such fact confirms the hypothesis of high-frequency financial time series are not generated by random processes, but by a balanced combination of dominant linear relationship and a subdominant nonlinear relationship. Furthermore, through the analysis of Figure 2, it can be verified that this kind of time series has increasing and decreasing behavior, that is, the subdominant nonlinear component can be estimated using increasing and decreasing operators because in small, mid and long-term analysis of HFSM reveal a temporal phenomenon with increasing and decreasing components in its structure. Therefore, this work assumes that high-frequency financial time series are generated by $x_t = x_{t-1} + g(t) + r_t$, and composed by a dominant linear component and a subdominant nonlinear component with increasing and decreasing behavior.

4. THE PROPOSED MODEL

The proposed model, called the increasing decreasing linear neuron (IDLN), consists of a combination among increasing (dilation and erosion) and decreasing (anti-dilation and anti-erosion) morphological operators and a linear operator (linear perceptron), and it is defined as follows. It is worth mentioning that morphological operators are employed within the proposed model because according to [9] this kind of operators can efficiently estimate financial time series.

Let $\mathbf{x} = (x_1, x_2, \dots, x_n) \in \mathbb{R}^n$ be an input pattern, represented by the time lags, inside an i-th moving window and let y be the output (prediction) of the IDLN, which is defined by a hybrid morphological-linear operator whose transformation rule $\mathbf{x} \rightarrow y$ is given by

$$y = \lambda\alpha + (1 - \lambda)\beta, \qquad \lambda \in [0, 1], \quad (3)$$

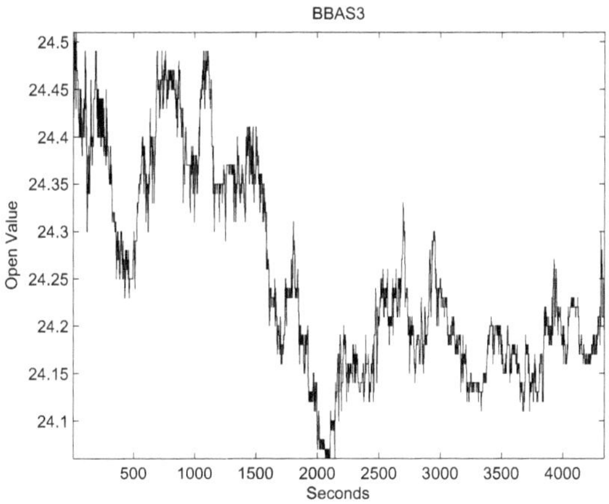

(a) BBAS3

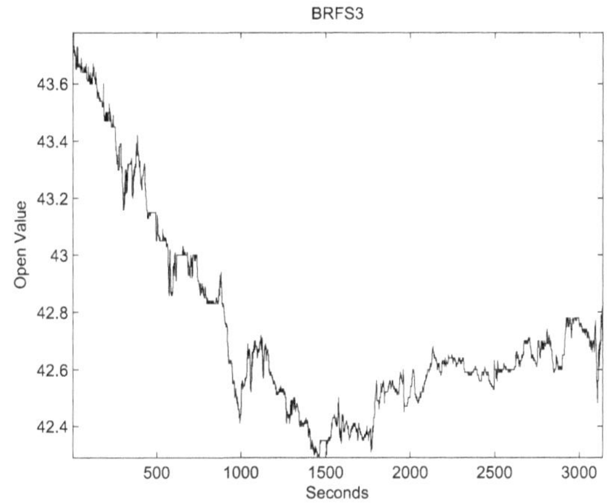

(b) BRFS3

Figure 2: Graphic of the time series.

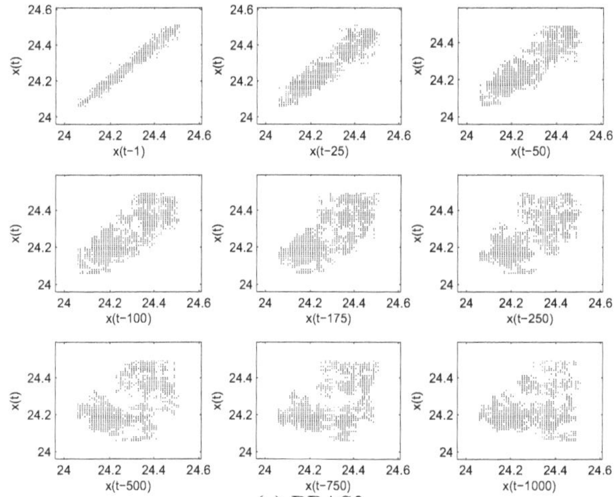

(a) BBAS3

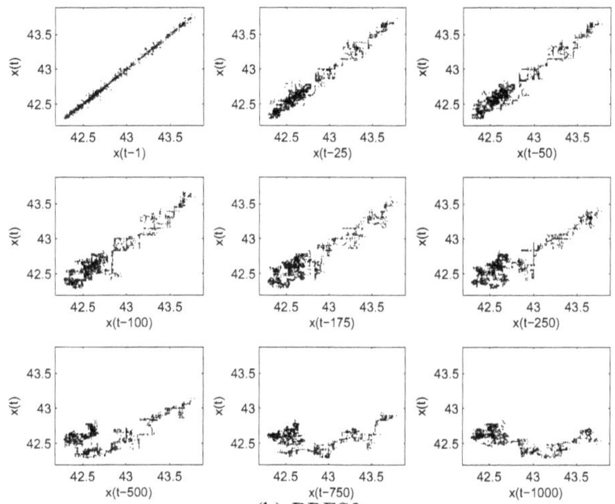

(b) BRFS3

Figure 3: Lagplot graphic of the time series.

where

$$\beta = \sum_{i=1}^{n} x_i p_i, \tag{4}$$

and

$$\alpha = \theta\tau + (1-\theta)\kappa, \qquad \theta \in [0,1], \tag{5}$$

in which

$$\tau = \varphi\delta + (1-\varphi)\varepsilon, \qquad \varphi \in [0,1], \tag{6}$$

and

$$\kappa = \omega\overline{\delta} + (1-\omega)\overline{\varepsilon}, \qquad \omega \in [0,1], \tag{7}$$

with

$$\delta = \delta_{\mathbf{a}}(\mathbf{x}) = \bigvee_{i=1}^{n}(x_i + a_i), \tag{8}$$

$$\varepsilon = \varepsilon_{\mathbf{b}}(\mathbf{x}) = \bigwedge_{i=1}^{n}(x_i +' b_i), \tag{9}$$

$$\overline{\delta} = \overline{\delta}_{\mathbf{c}}(\mathbf{x}) = \bigwedge_{i=1}^{n}(x_i^* +' c_i), \tag{10}$$

$$\overline{\varepsilon} = \overline{\varepsilon}_{\mathbf{d}}(\mathbf{x}) = \bigvee_{i=1}^{n}(x_i^* + d_i), \tag{11}$$

where term n represents the input pattern dimensionality, the terms $\lambda, \theta, \varphi, \omega \in \mathbb{R}$, and the terms $\mathbf{a}, \mathbf{b}, \mathbf{c}, \mathbf{d}, \mathbf{p} \in \mathbb{R}^n$. The term $\mathbf{p}$ represents the coefficients (weights) of the linear operator and term β represents the output of linear module. The term α represents the nonlinear module, given by a linear combination (the mixture term is given by θ) between an increasing nonlinear module (defined by τ) and a decreasing nonlinear module (defined by κ). Note that the term τ represents a linear combination (the mixture term is given by φ) between a dilation (δ) and an erosion (ε) morphological operators. In the same way, the term κ represents a linear combination (the mixture term is given by ω) between an anti-dilation ($\overline{\delta}$) and an anti-erosion ($\overline{\varepsilon}$) morphological operators. The vectors $\mathbf{a}$, $\mathbf{b}$, $\mathbf{c}$ and $\mathbf{d}$ represent the structuring elements (weights) of dilation ($\delta_{\mathbf{a}}(\mathbf{x})$) and erosion ($\varepsilon_{\mathbf{b}}(\mathbf{x})$) operators(employed within increasing nonlinear module) and of anti-dilation ($\overline{\delta}_{\mathbf{c}}(\mathbf{x})$) and anti-erosion ($\overline{\varepsilon}_{\mathbf{d}}(\mathbf{x})$) operators (employed within decreasing nonlinear module). At the end, the output y of the IDLN is given by a linear combination between linear and nonlinear modules (the mixture term is given by λ). Figure 4 describes the IDLN.

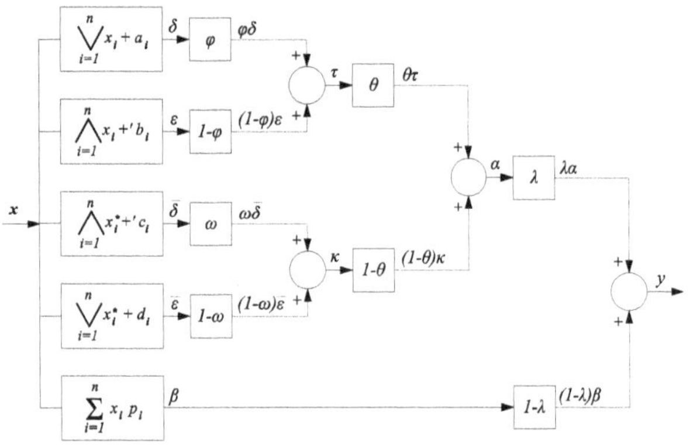

Figure 4: The proposed model.

According to Sussner [10, 11] the operation "$+'$" is given by

$$(-\infty) + (+\infty) = (+\infty) + (-\infty) = -\infty, \tag{12}$$

and

$$(-\infty) +' (+\infty) = (+\infty) +' (-\infty) = +\infty. \tag{13}$$

4.1 The Proposed Learning Process

After the definition of IDLN model, it can be verified that it requires the adjustment of the following parameters $\mathbf{a}, \mathbf{b}, \mathbf{c}, \mathbf{d}, \mathbf{p} \in \mathbb{R}^n$ and $\lambda, \theta, \varphi, \omega \in \mathbb{R}$. Therefore, the weight vector $\mathbf{w}$ (note that $\mathbf{w} \in \mathbb{R}^{5n+4}$) of the IDLN model is defined by

$$\mathbf{w} = (\mathbf{a}, \mathbf{b}, \mathbf{c}, \mathbf{d}, \mathbf{p}, \lambda, \theta, \varphi, \omega). \tag{14}$$

The proposed learning process employees a covariance matrix adaptation evolutionary strategy (CMAES) based on the work of Hansen [13], which uses the idea of covariance matrix adaptation from a multivariate normal distribution into the evolutionary process, to adjust the weights of the IDLN model according to an error criterion until convergence or until the end of CMAES generations. The reason for that is because the employed morphological operators are not differentiable of the classical way, which restricts the use of a gradient-based method to design the proposed model.

Each i-th individual from population represents a candidate weight vector (denoted by $\mathbf{w}_i^{(g)}$) for the IDLN model. The scheme to adjust the weight vector is initially to define a fitness function $fit(\mathbf{w}_i^{(g)})$, given by

$$fit(\mathbf{w}_i^{(g)}) = \frac{1}{M}\sum_{j=1}^{M} e^2(j), \tag{15}$$

where M is the number of input patterns and $e(j)$ is the instantaneous error, given by

$$e(j) = d(j) - y(j), \tag{16}$$

where $d(j)$ and $y(j)$ are the desired output signal and the actual model output for the training sample j, respectively.

The CMAES procedure starts with its parameters definition. There are eight initial parameters to be defined in the ($\varphi_{\mathbf{r}}$,γ)-CMAES [13]: i) γ is the population size, ii) φ is the parent individuals amount, that is, the search space points amount chosen into the population, iii) $\mathbf{r} = (r_1, r_2, \ldots, r_\varphi)$ is the recombination weight vector, iv) c_σ is a learning rate for the cumulation of step size control, v) e_σ is a damping parameter for step size update, vi) c_c is a learning rate for the cumulation of rank-one update of covariance matrix, vii) φ_{cov} is a weighting parameter between rank-one and rank-φ update, and viii) c_{cov} represents the learning rate for covariance matrix update. The standard values of these parameters presented by Hansen [13] are used in this paper.

Next, the evolution paths $\mathbf{p}_c^{(0)} = \mathbf{0}$ and $\mathbf{p}_\sigma^{(0)} = \mathbf{0}$, the covariance matrix $\mathbf{C}^{(0)} = \mathbf{I}$, the evolution path step size $\sigma^{(0)} \in \mathbb{R}_+$ and the mean of search distribution $\mathbf{m}^{(0)} \in \mathbb{R}^n$ are initiated. Note that the search space is initially restricted within a cube ($\mathbf{m}^{(0)} \pm 2\sigma^{(0)}\mathbf{1}$ with $\mathbf{1} = (1, \ldots, 1)^T$). Then, the CMAES starts a loop containing several steps to minimize the fitness function.

Into this loop, the first step is to build a set of candidate individuals, or search space points, denoted by $\mathbf{w}_i^{(g)} \in \mathbb{R}^{5n+4}$ with $i = 1, 2, \ldots, \gamma$ and $g = 1, 2, \ldots$, and sampled through a multivariate normal distribution. Then, the i-th population individual of the g-th CMAES generation is given by

$$\mathbf{w}_i^{(g)} \sim \mathcal{N}(\mathbf{m}^{(g)}, (\sigma^{(g)})^2\mathbf{C}^{(g)}), \tag{17}$$

where $\sim$ represents the equality among distributions. The term $\mathcal{N}(\mathbf{m}^{(g)}, (\sigma^{(g)})^2\mathbf{C}^{(g)}) \sim \mathbf{m}^{(g)} + \sigma^{(g)}\mathcal{N}(0, \mathbf{C}^{(g)}) \sim \mathbf{m}^{(g)} + \sigma^{(g)}\mathbf{B}^{(g)}\mathbf{D}^{(g)}\mathcal{N}(\mathbf{0}, \mathbf{I})$ represents a multi-variate normal distribution with mean $\mathbf{m}^{(g)}$ and covariance matrix $(\sigma^{(g)})^2\mathbf{C}^{(g)}$, in which $\mathbf{B}^{(g)} \in \mathbb{R}^{5n+4}$ is an orthogonal matrix of the eigenvectors from $\mathbf{C}^{(g)}$, $\mathbf{D}^{(g)} \in \mathbb{R}^{5n+4}$ is a diagonal matrix of the squared roots of the eigenvalues from $\mathbf{C}^{(g)}$, and $\mathcal{N}(\mathbf{0}, \mathbf{I})$ is a multi-variate normal distribution with zero mean and unitary covariance matrix.

The next steps definition is to update the parameters $\mathbf{m}^{(g)}$, $\mathbf{p}_\sigma^{(g)}$, $\sigma^{(g)}$, $\mathbf{p}_c^{(g)}$ and $\mathbf{C}^{(g)}$.

The mean of search distribution $\mathbf{m}^{(g)}$ can be updated by [13]

$$\mathbf{m}^{(g)} = \sum_{i=1}^{\varphi} r_i\, \mathbf{w}_{i:\gamma}^{(g)}, \tag{18}$$

with

$$\sum_{i=1}^{\varphi} r_i = 1,\ r_i > 0 \text{ for } i = 1, \ldots, \varphi, \tag{19}$$

where $\varphi \leq \gamma$, $r_{i=1,\ldots,\varphi} \in \mathbb{R}_+$ with $r_1 \geq r_2 \geq \cdots \geq r_\varphi$, and $\mathbf{w}_{i:\gamma}^{(g)}$ the i-th best individual. Note that the index $1:\gamma$ denotes the index of i-th individual and $f(\mathbf{w}_{1:\gamma}^{(g)}) \leq f(\mathbf{w}_{2:\gamma}^{(g)}) \leq \cdots \leq f(\mathbf{w}_{\gamma:\gamma}^{(g)})$.

The Equation 18 implements the recombination process using a weighted sum of φ individuals, as well as implements the selection operator choosing $\varphi < \gamma$ and setting distinct values of the recombination weights vector $\mathbf{r}$ [13].

The conjugate evolution path $\mathbf{p}_\sigma^{(g)} \in \mathbb{R}^{5n+4}$ can be updated by [13]

$$\mathbf{p}_\sigma^{(g)} = (1 - c_\sigma)\mathbf{p}_\sigma^{(g-1)} + \sqrt{c_\sigma(2 - c_\sigma)\varphi_{eff}}\,\mathbf{C}_\sigma^{(g-1)^{-\frac{1}{2}}}\frac{\mathbf{m}^{(g)} - \mathbf{m}^{(g-1)}}{\sigma^{(g-1)}}, \tag{20}$$

where $(1 - c_\sigma)$ is an adjustment factor, $\sqrt{c_\sigma(2 - c_\sigma)\varphi_{eff}}$ is a normalization constant, $\mathbf{C}_\sigma^{(g-1)^{-\frac{1}{2}}} \stackrel{def}{=} \mathbf{B}^{(g-1)}\mathbf{D}^{(g-1)^{-1}}\mathbf{B}^{(g-1)^T}$ with $\mathbf{C}_\sigma^{(g-1)} = \mathbf{B}^{(g-1)}(\mathbf{D}^{(g-1)})^2\mathbf{B}^{(g-1)^T}$ is an eigendecomposition from $\mathbf{C}_\sigma^{(g-1)}$, and $\mathbf{B}^{(g-1)}$ is an orthonormal basis of eigenvectors. The elements of diagonal matrix $\mathbf{D}^{(g-1)}$ are the squared roots of its correspondent positive eigenvalues.

The evolution path $\sigma^{(g)}$ can be updated by [13]

$$\sigma^{(g)} = \sigma^{(g-1)} \exp\left[\frac{c_\sigma}{e_\sigma}\left(\frac{\|p_\sigma^{(g)}\|}{E\|\mathcal{N}(\mathbf{0}, \mathbf{I})\|} - 1\right)\right], \tag{21}$$

in which

$$E\|\mathcal{N}(\mathbf{0}, \mathbf{I})\| = \frac{\sqrt{2}\Gamma(\frac{n+1}{2})}{\Gamma(\frac{n}{2})} \approx \sqrt{n}\left(1 - \frac{1}{4n} + \frac{1}{21n^2}\right). \tag{22}$$

Equations 20 and 21 implement the evolution step control [13].

The evolution path $\mathbf{p}_c^{(g)}$ can be updated by [13]

$$\mathbf{p}_c^{(g)} = (1-c_c)\mathbf{p}_c^{(g-1)} + \vartheta_\sigma^{(g)}\sqrt{c_c(2-c_c)\varphi_{eff}}\,\frac{\mathbf{m}^{(g)}-\mathbf{m}^{(g-1)}}{\sigma^{(g-1)}}, \tag{23}$$

in which

$$\vartheta_\sigma^{(g)} = \begin{cases} 1, & \text{if} \frac{\|\mathbf{p}_\sigma^{(g)}\|}{\sqrt{1-(1-c_\sigma)}} < \left(1.5 + \frac{1}{n-0.5}\right) E\|\mathcal{N}(\mathbf{0},\mathbf{I})\| \\ 0, & \text{otherwise} \end{cases} \tag{24}$$

At the end, the covariance matrix $\mathbf{C}^{(g)}$ can be updated by [13]

$$\mathbf{C}^{(g)} = (1-c_{cov})\mathbf{C}^{(g-1)} + \frac{c_{cov}}{\varphi_{cov}}\left[\mathbf{p}_c^{(g)}\mathbf{p}_c^{(g)^T} + \zeta(\vartheta_\sigma^{(g)})\mathbf{C}^{(g-1)}\right] + c_{cov}\left(1-\frac{1}{\varphi_{cov}}\right) r\varphi u, \tag{25}$$

in which

$$\zeta(\vartheta_\sigma^{(g)}) = (1-\vartheta_\sigma^{(g)})c_c(2-c_c). \tag{26}$$

and

$$r\varphi u = \sum_{i=1}^{\varphi}\left[r_i\left(\frac{\mathbf{w}_{i:\gamma}^{(g)}-\mathbf{m}^{(g-1)}}{\sigma^{(g-1)}}\right)\left(\frac{\mathbf{w}_{i:\gamma}^{(g)}-\mathbf{m}^{(g-1)}}{\sigma^{(g-1)}}\right)^T\right]. \tag{27}$$

Further details of CMAES can be found in [13]. Three stopping criteria are used in the proposed learning process [31]: i) The maximum generation number ($CMAES_{gen}$), ii) The decrease in the training error process training (Pt) of the fitness function, and iii) The increase in the generalization loss (Gl) of the fitness function. In order to automatically adjust time phase distortions that occur in the problem of high-frequency financial time series, it is included the phase fix procedure, defined in the Section 2.1, in the proposed learning process of the IDLN. The steps of the proposed learning process are illustrated in the Figure 5.

```
begin Learning Process
    Initialize CMAES parameters (γ, φ, r, c_σ, e_σ, c_c, φ_cov and c_cov)
    according to [13];
    Initialize the stop condition;
    g = 0;          // g: actual generation
    Initialize evolution paths (p_σ^(0) and p_c^(0)), and the covariance matrix
    (C^(0));
    Define the step size of evolution paths σ^(0) and the mean of search
    distribution m^(0);
    while not stop condition do
        g = g + 1;
        for i = 1 to γ do
            Create a candidate individual w_i^(g) using Equation (17);
            Initialize IDLN parameters with the values supplied by
            w_i^(g);
            Calculate y_1, y_2 and the instantaneous error for all input
            patterns;
            Evaluate the candidate individual f(w_i^(g)) using the
            Equation 15;
        end
        Update the mean of search distribution m^(g);
        Update the conjugate evolution path p_σ^(g);
        Update the step size of evolution paths σ^(g);
        Update the evolution path p_c^(g);
        Update the covariance matrix C^(g);
    end
end
```

Figure 5: The proposed learning process steps

5. EXPERIMENTAL RESULTS

Two high-frequency financial time series (BBAS3 and BRFS3) were used as a test bed for evaluation of the proposed model. These times series were normalized to lie within the range $[0, 1]$ and divided in three sets according to Prechelt [31]: i) training set (50% of the data), ii) validation set (25% of the data) and iii) test set (25% of the data). The training set is used to adjust the model parameters and the validation set is used with a criterium to stop the training process (according to the generalization loss of 5%). The most accurate prediction models according to [2, 9] from four approaches presented in the literature were elected to establish a performance study: i) ARIMA [1] (statistical model), ii) MLP [32, 33] (artificial neural network model), iii) IMP [9] (morphological neural network model), and iv) SHIF [26] (hybrid model). For the training process of each model investigated in this work we have used the same methodology described by authors in their works. It is worth mentioning that the phase adjustment procedure was applied to all forecasting models investigated in this work in order to ensure a fair comparison among them. The following metrics are used to evaluate prediction performance [9]: mean squared error (MSE), mean absolute percentage error (MAPE), theil statistics (THEIL), prediction of change in direction (POCID), average relative variance (ARV) and evaluation function (EF).

The choice of the time lags used in the proposed model was based on lagplot analysis presented in the Section 3, where the time lags from 2 to 1001 ($lags = 2-1001$) are fixed for all experiments. Note that the first time lag is not used because a random walk structure is necessary to use the phase adjustment procedure, since the key step of this procedure is the two step prediction to adjust time phase distortions. Three stop conditions are used in the evolutionary covariance-based learning process: i) $CMAES_{gen} = 10000$, ii) $Pt \leq 10^{-6}$, and iii) $Gl \leq 5\%$. For each model investigated in this work, ten experiments were performed, where the mean (MEAN), the standard deviation (SD), minimum (MIN) and maximum (MAX) statistics were calculated, as well as all confidence intervals (CI) with the assumption of normal distribution with 99% of certainty degree.

5.1 BBAS3 Series

The best configuration of the investigated models for the BBAS3 time series are: ARIMA(6; 5; 1), MLP(5; 10; 1), IMP(2–151; 25), SHIF(1, 3, 4, 5, 6, 9; MLP(6; 9; 1); levenberg marquardt) and IDLN(2–1001; 0.1; 0.005). The Table 1 presents the prediction performance of investigated models for the BBAS3 time series (test set). The Figure 6 presents a comparative graphic between real and predicted values generated by investigated models in this work for the BBAS3 time series (the last five points of the test set).

5.2 BRFS3 Series

The best configuration of the investigated models for the BRFS3 time series are: ARIMA(3; 2; 1), MLP(5; 10; 1), IMP(2–151; 10), SHIF(1, 7; MLP(2; 5; 1); levenberg marquardt) and IDLN(2–1001; 0.1; 0.005). The Table 2 presents the prediction performance of investigated models for the BRFS3 time series (test set). The Figure 7 presents a comparative graphic between real and predicted values generated by investigated models in this work for the last five points of the BRFS3 time series.

5.3 Considerations

The proposed model obtained better predictive performance than the best prediction models reported in the literature (under the same experimental conditions). Note that the proposed model overcame the random walk dilemma for high-frequency financial time series investigated in this work, since the THEIL value is closer to 0. In this way, the proposed model can be considered an accurate pre-

Table 1: Prediction performance for the BBAS3 time series (test set).

		Metric					
Model	Statistic	ARV	MAPE	MSE	POCID	THEIL	EF
ARIMA	MEAN	0.2714	0.0567	0.0002	82.64	2.9895	19.1391
	SD	0.0000	0.0000	0.0000	0.00	0.0000	0.0000
	MIN	0.2714	0.0567	0.0002	82.64	2.9895	19.1391
	MAX	0.2714	0.0567	0.0002	82.64	2.9895	19.1391
	CI	±0.0000	±0.0000	±0.0000	±0.00	±0.0000	±0.0000
MLP	MEAN	0.3999	0.0552	0.0004	85.04	4.4108	25.9414
	SD	0.55738	0.0399	0.0005	5.06	6.1475	12.5406
	MIN	0.0985	0.0267	0.0001	82.64	1.0860	4.2699
	MAX	1.7473	0.1436	0.0017	94.64	1.9273	37.3696
	CI	±0.4547	±0.0325	±0.0004	±4.13	±5.0155	±10.2315
IMP	MEAN	0.0950	0.0271	0.00009	82.64	1.0474	38.0888
	SD	0.00006	0.00003	0.00000006	0.00	0.0007	0.0148
	MIN	0.0949	0.0271	0.00009	82.64	1.0466	38.0628
	MAX	0.0951	0.0272	0.00009	82.64	1.0487	38.1055
	CI	±0.00005	±0.00003	±0.00000005	±0.00	±0.0006	±0.0121
SHIF	MEAN	0.0907	0.0243	0.00009	82.64	1.0003	39.0643
	SD	0.0001	0.0006	0.0000001	0.00	0.0021	0.0541
	MIN	0.0903	0.0226	0.00009	82.64	0.9957	39.0359
	MAX	0.0909	0.0245	0.00009	82.64	1.0015	39.1889
	CI	±0.0001	±0.0005	±0.0000001	±0.00	±0.0017	±0.0441
IDLN	MEAN	0.0001	0.0032	0.0000007	100.00	0.0017	99.4865
	SD	0.0001	0.0021	0.0000008	0.00	0.0018	0.4034
	MIN	0.000003	0.0004	0.00000001	100.00	0.00004	98.8479
	MAX	0.0004	0.0064	0.000002	100.00	0.0047	99.9521
	CI	±0.0001	±0.0017	±0.0000006	±0.00	±0.0014	±0.3291

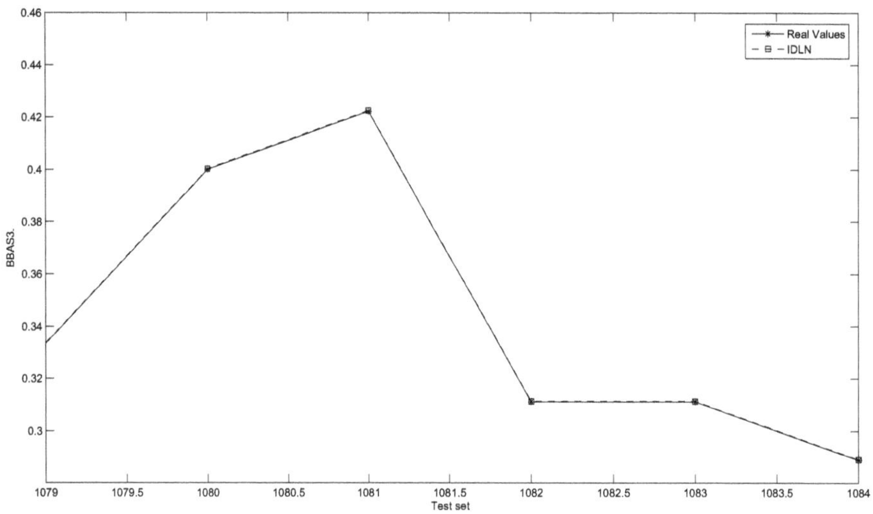

Figure 6: Prediction results of the BBAS3 time series (last five points of the test set).

diction model with high prediction performance. Besides, it is not possible to identify the presence of the one step ahead delay of the prediction with respect to the real time series value. It is important to note that ARIMA, MLP, IMP and SHIF models were not able to overcome the random walk dilemma for the investigated high-frequency financial time series, even with the use of the phase adjustment procedure, because the THEIL value is closer to 1.

Also, through the analysis of the parameters of the proposed model, it is possible to confirm the hypothesis that high-frequency financial time series are generated by a dominant linear component and a subdominant nonlinear component, since the IDLN has used ≈3% of nonlinear component and ≈97% of linear component. Also, it is possible to confirm the hypothesis that the nonlinear component has increasing and decreasing behavior, since the IDLN has used ≈50% of both increasing and decreasing modules.

6. CONCLUSION

A hybrid model was presented in this work to predict high-frequency financial time series. Also, it was presented an evolutionary covariance-based learning process with automatic time phase adjustment using ideas from the covariance matrix adaptation evolutionary strategy (CMAES) for the design of the proposed model.

The results were collected with two high-frequency financial time series from the Brazilian stock market. The experimental results demonstrated a consistent better performance of the proposed model when compared to the most common statistical, neural and hybrid prediction models. The reason for that is due to linear component and nonlinear component with increasing and decreasing behavior included within the proposed model, as well as by the inclusion of the time phase adjustment procedure within the proposed learning process.

Also, it is worth mentioning that all prediction models inves-

Table 2: Prediction performance for the BRFS3 time series (test set).

Model	Statistic	ARV	MAPE	MSE	POCID	THEIL	EF
ARIMA	MEAN	0.1689	0.0564	0.0007	87.74	3.8474	17.2936
	SD	0.0000	0.0000	0.0000	0.00	0.0000	0.0000
	MIN	0.1689	0.0564	0.0007	87.74	3.8474	17.2936
	MAX	0.1689	0.0564	0.0007	87.74	3.8474	17.2936
	CI	±0.0000	±0.0000	±0.0000	±0.00	±0.0000	±0.0000
MLP	MEAN	0.1312	0.0450	0.0006	87.74	2.9896	24.6767
	SD	0.0727	0.0183	0.0003	0.00	1.6557	10.0871
	MIN	0.0509	0.0222	0.0002	87.74	1.1624	11.7426
	MAX	0.2688	0.0774	0.0012	87.74	6.1243	39.2409
	CI	±0.0593	±0.0149	±0.0002	±0.00	±1.3508	±8.2297
IMP	MEAN	0.0438	0.0160	0.0002	87.74	1.0010	42.5686
	SD	0.000009	0.00006	0.00000004	0.00	0.0002	0.0059
	MIN	0.0438	0.0159	0.0002	87.74	1.0007	42.5605
	MAX	0.0439	0.0161	0.0002	87.74	1.0012	42.5765
	CI	±0.000007	±0.00005	±0.00000003	±0.00	±0.0001	±0.0048
SHIF	MEAN	0.0438	0.0161	0.0002	87.74	0.9997	42.5932
	SD	0.000008	0.00006	0.00000003	0.00	0.0001	0.0054
	MIN	0.0438	0.0160	0.0002	87.74	0.9993	42.5901
	MAX	0.0438	0.0161	0.0002	87.74	0.9998	42.6045
	CI	±0.000006	±0.00005	±0.00000003	±0.00	±0.0001	±0.0044
IDLN	MEAN	0.0001	0.0017	0.0000002	100.00	0.0026	99.5526
	SD	0.0001	0.0012	0.0000002	0.00	0.0027	0.4076
	MIN	0.000002	0.0002	0.000000006	100.00	0.000006	98.8868
	MAX	0.0003	0.0035	0.0000006	100.00	0.0073	99.9711
	CI	±0.00009	±0.0010	±0.0000002	±0.0000	±0.0022	±0.3325

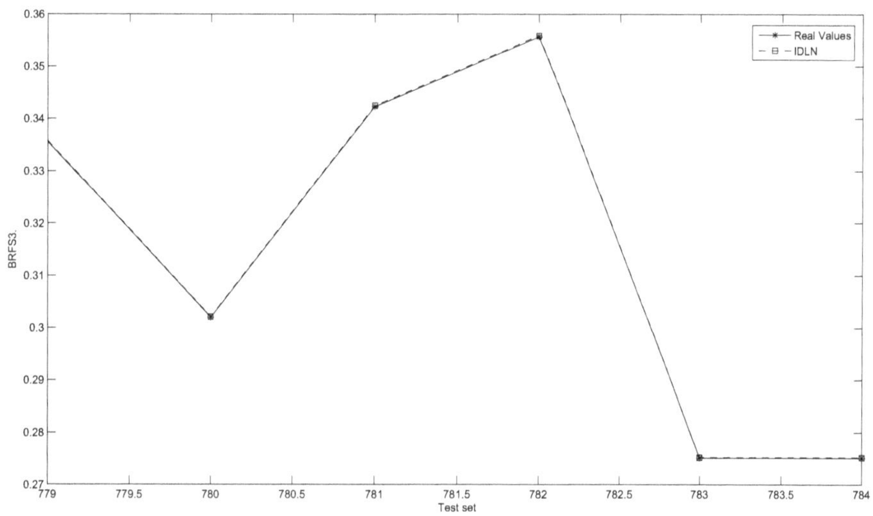

Figure 7: Prediction results of the BRFS3 time series (last five points of the test set).

tigated in this work were not able to overcome the random walk dilemma for high-frequency financial time series (THEIL $\approx$ 1). However, according to the obtained results with the proposed model, it can be verified that it was able to overcome the random walk dilemma in high-frequency financial time series (THEIL $\approx$ 0). A more detailed explanation of such behavior is that the proposed model was built with similar characteristics of high-frequency financial temporal phenomena, which implies in the minimization of the search space for the model design, as well as by the inclusion of the phase adjustment procedure within the learning process, which leads to a more precise time phase adjustment, since the relationship of high-frequency financial time series was directly mapped in the proposed model equations.

Besides, according to the analysis presented in the Section 3, it was possible to verify that the temporal phenomenon of this kind of time series can be represented by a balanced combination between a linear component and a nonlinear component. Note that this analysis revealed a subdominant nonlinear relationship embedded in a dominant linear relationship: i) there is a linear relationship within low order time lags, and ii) with the increase in the time lags degree, there is a nonlinear relationship. Also, considering the relationships of high-frequency financial generator phenomena, it could be supposed, through time series graphic, of the existence of an increasing and decreasing behavior within the nonlinear component in this kind of time series. Observe that both hypotheses could be confirmed analyzing the mixture terms (λ and θ) of the proposed model, which have used around 97% of the linear component and around 3% of nonlinear component, as well as used around 50% of both increasing and decreasing nonlinear modules.

As future works, an additional study must be developed to formalize and to explain the properties of the proposed model, as well as to determine its limitations with other kind of time series. Also, further studies, in terms of risk and financial return, must be developed in order to determine the additional economical benefits, for an investor, with the use of the proposed model in a trading system on high-frequency stock market.

7. REFERENCES

[1] G. E. P. Box, G. M. Jenkins, and G. C. Reinsel. *Time Series Analysis: Forecasting and Control*. Prentice Hall, New Jersey, third edition, 1994.

[2] M. P. Clements, P. H. Franses, and N. R. Swanson. Forecasting economic and financial time-series with non-linear models. *International Journal of Forecasting*, 20:169–183, 2004.

[3] A. K. Nassirtoussi, S. Aghabozorgi, T. Y. Wah, and D. C. L. Ngo. Text mining for market prediction: A systematic review. *Expert Systems with Applications*, 41(16):7653 – 7670, 2014.

[4] H. Park, N. Kim, and J. Lee. Parametric models and non-parametric machine learning models for predicting option prices: Empirical comparison study over {KOSPI} 200 index options. *Expert Systems with Applications*, 41(11):5227 – 5237, 2014.

[5] N. Kourentzes, D. K. Barrow, and S. F. Crone. Neural network ensemble operators for time series forecasting. *Expert Systems with Applications*, 41(9):4235 – 4244, 2014.

[6] W. Kristjanpoller, A. Fadic, and M. C. Minutolo. Volatility forecast using hybrid neural network models. *Expert Systems with Applications*, 41(5):2437 – 2442, 2014.

[7] Z. Ma, Q. Dai, and N. Liu. Several novel evaluation measures for rank-based ensemble pruning with applications to time series prediction. *Expert Systems with Applications*, 42(1):280 – 292, 2015.

[8] R. de A. Araújo, A. Oliveira, and S. Meira. A shift-invariant morphological system for software development cost estimation. *Expert Systems with Applications*, 38:4162–4168, 2011.

[9] R. de A. Araújo. A morphological perceptron with gradient-based learning for brazilian stock market forecasting. *Neural Networks*, 28:61–81, 2012.

[10] P. Sussner and E. L. Esmi. Morphological perceptrons with competitive learning: Lattice-theoretical framework and constructive learning algorithm. *Information Sciences*, 181(10):1929–1950, 2011.

[11] P. Sussner and E. L. Esmi. Morphological perceptrons with competitive learning: Lattice-theoretical framework and constructive learning algorithm. *Information Sciences*, 181(10):1929–1950, 2011.

[12] F. H. F. Leung, H. K. Lam, S. H. Ling, and P. K. S. Tam. Tuning of the structure and parameters of the neural network using an improved genetic algorithm. *IEEE Transactions on Neural Networks*, 14(1):79–88, January 2003.

[13] N. Hansen. The CMA evolution strategy: a comparing review. In J.A. Lozano, P. Larranaga, I. Inza, and E. Bengoetxea, editors, *Towards a new evolutionary computation. Advances on estimation of distribution algorithms*, pages 75–102. Springer, 2006.

[14] R. de A. Araújo and T. Ferreira. A morphological-rank-linear evolutionary method for stock market prediction. *Information Sciences*, 237:3–17, 2013.

[15] R. de A. Araújo. Evolutionary learning processes to design the dilation-erosion perceptron for weather forecasting. *Neural Processing Letters*, 37:303–333, 2013.

[16] J. Shahrabi, E. Hadavandi, and S. Asadi. Developing a hybrid intelligent model for forecasting problems: Case study of tourism demand time series. *Knowledge-Based Systems*, 43:112–122, 2013.

[17] M. Khashei and M. Bijari. Fuzzy artificial neural network (p, d, q) model for incomplete financial time series forecasting. *Journal of Intelligent and Fuzzy Systems*, 26(2):831–845, 2014.

[18] W. Du, S. Y. S. Leung, and C. K. Kwong. Time series forecasting by neural networks: A knee point-based multiobjective evolutionary algorithm approach. *Expert Systems with Applications*, 41(18):8049 – 8061, 2014.

[19] R. de A. Araújo. A class of hybrid morphological perceptrons with application in time series forecasting. *Knowledge-Based Systems*, 24:513–529, 2011.

[20] R. Sitte and J. Sitte. Neural networks approach to the random walk dilemma of financial time series. *Applied Intelligence*, 16(3):163–171, May 2002.

[21] T. A. E. Ferreira, G. C. Vasconcelos, and P. J. L. Adeodato. A new intelligent system methodology for time series forecasting with artificial neural networks. In *Neural Processing Letters*, volume 28, pages 113–129, 2008.

[22] M. Riedmiller and H. Braun. A direct adaptive method for faster backpropagation learning: The rprop algorithm. In *Proceedings of the IEEE Int. Conf. on Neural Networks (ICNN)*, pages 586–591, San Francisco, 1993.

[23] M. Hagan and M. Menhaj. Training feedforward networks with the marquardt algorithm. *IEEE Transactions on Neural Networks*, 5(6):989–993, November 1994.

[24] M. F. Moller. A scaled conjugate gradient algorithm for fast supervised learning. *Neural Networks*, 6:525–533, 1993.

[25] R. Battiti. One step secant conjugate gradient. *Neural Computation*, 4:141–166, 1992.

[26] R. de A. Araújo. Swarm-based hybrid intelligent forecasting method for financial time series prediction. *Learning and Nonlinear Models*, 5:137–154, 2007.

[27] R. de A. Araújo, A. Oliveira, and S. Soares. Overcoming the random walk dilemma using a covariance matrix adaptation evolutionary method. In *IEEE Conference on Systems, Man and Cybernetics*, 2010.

[28] P. Salgado, A. Lima, T. Ferreira, and G. Cavalcanti. An intelligent perturbative approach for the time series forecasting problem. In *International Joint Conference on Neural Networks*, 2010.

[29] R. de A. Araújo. Swarm-based translation-invariant morphological method for financial time series forecasting. *Information Sciences*, 180:4784–4805, 2010.

[30] R. de A. Araújo and P. Susner. An increasing hybrid morphological-linear perceptron with pseudo-gradient-based learning and phase adjustment for financial time series prediction. In *IEEE International Joint Conference on Neural Networks*, 2010.

[31] L. Prechelt. Proben1: A set of neural network benchmark problems and benchmarking rules. Technical Report 21/94, 1994.

[32] S. Haykin. *Neural networks: A comprehensive foundation*. Prentice Hall, New Jersey, 1998.

[33] S. Haykin. *Neural Networks and Learning Machines*. McMaster University, Canada, 2007.

Evolutionary Learning of Syntax Patterns for Genic Interaction Extraction

Alberto Bartoli
DIA - University of Trieste
Italy
bartoli.alberto@units.it

Andrea De Lorenzo
DIA - University of Trieste
Italy
andrea.delorenzo@units.it

Eric Medvet
DIA - University of Trieste
Italy
emedvet@units.it

Fabiano Tarlao
DIA - University of Trieste
Italy
fabiano.tarlao@phd.units.it

Marco Virgolin
DIA - University of Trieste
Italy
marco.virgolin@gmail.com

ABSTRACT

There is an increasing interest in the development of techniques for automatic relation extraction from unstructured text. The biomedical domain, in particular, is a sector that may greatly benefit from those techniques due to the huge and ever increasing amount of scientific publications describing observed phenomena of potential clinical interest.

In this paper, we consider the problem of automatically identifying sentences that contain interactions between genes and proteins, based solely on a dictionary of genes and proteins and a small set of sample sentences in natural language. We propose an evolutionary technique for learning a classifier that is capable of detecting the desired sentences within scientific publications with high accuracy. The key feature of our proposal, that is internally based on Genetic Programming, is the construction of a model of the relevant syntax patterns in terms of standard part-of-speech annotations. The model consists of a set of regular expressions that are learned automatically despite the large alphabet size involved.

We assess our approach on two realistic datasets and obtain 74% accuracy, a value sufficiently high to be of practical interest and that is in line with significant baseline methods.

Categories and Subject Descriptors

I.5.4 [**Pattern Recognition**]: Applications—*Text processing*; I.2.7 [**Artificial Intelligence**]: Natural Language Processing—*Text analysis*; J.3 [**Computer Applications**]: Life and Medical Science—*Biology and genetics*

Keywords

Regular Expressions; Genetic Programming; Programming by Example; Machine Learning

GECCO '15, July 11–15, 2015, Madrid, Spain

http://dx.doi.org/10.1145/2739480.2754706 .

1. INTRODUCTION

A huge amount of knowledge is expressed in natural language text and the recent years have seen an explosion of interest in automated techniques capable of extracting such knowledge effectively. Biomedical information extraction, in particular, is a vast and rapidly growing field facing many important challenges [32, 22, 33, 8, 34, 28, 18]. A problem that has captured much attention is the construction of a systematic and structured description of the observed interactions between entities of biomedical interest reported in the scientific literature [19, 17, 25].

In this paper, we investigate the feasibility of using *evolutionary computing* for attacking a challenging problem in this area: how to identify automatically, in scientific papers, sentences that contain interactions between genes and proteins, based on a dictionary of genes, proteins, interactors, and a small set of example sentences [8, 34, 28]. The problem is challenging because the mere occurrence of dictionary words in a sentence does not imply that the sentence is to be extracted (see Table 1). Evolutionary computing techniques have been applied to several problems in Natural Language Processing (NLP), including text summarization [26], sentence alignment for statistical machine translation [29], part-of-speech tagging [1], grammar induction from an annotated corpus [13, 31], word sense disambiguation [14]. A very good and broad review of evolutionary approaches to NLP is [2]. The *binary classification of sentences* that we consider here, though, has received very little attention so far and we are aware of only one evolutionary proposal in this area [7]. The cited work advocates the use of a probabilistic model called the hypernetwork classifier meant to capture the correlation between sets of words and the class in which a sentence containing those words belongs to. Actual values for the correlation between triplet of words and the output class in a learning corpus are computed by means of a stochastic procedure. The experimental evaluation considered 1 200 000 such triplets and executed some preprocessing operations on the text that were not fully described, including deletion of so-called redundant components and insignificant words, as well as conversion of string values into numerical values using a customized dictionary.

In our work we propose a different evolutionary technique based on *Genetic Programming* (GP). We learn a model of the *syntax patterns* that occur in the sentences of each class and classify sentences accordingly. Such patterns are expressed in terms of *regular expressions* over standard *part-of-speech* annotations. We solve the difficult problem of actually learning those regular expressions despite the *large alphabet size* involved, by leveraging on recent results in this area [4]. Working at the abstraction level of part-of-speech annotations has important practical advantages: one may build upon the existing state-of-the-art in NLP annotators, as well as switch to an annotator for a different language or incorporate any advances in annotation technology, without any changes in the framework.

We strove to design our framework without incorporating heuristic rules or findings from previous solutions to this problem. For example, part-of-speech patterns of interest are usually very short and include 2–4 words before and after entities of interest (i.e., genes or proteins) [19, 18]. Furthermore, one could refine a tentative pattern by carefully assigning different costs to each component of the pattern depending on its type—40 coefficients are proposed in [19] for weighing the contribution of 12 groups of part-of-speech tags depending on whether they are aligned correctly with a sample and, if not, depending on the nature of mismatch. We chose to not rely on any problem-specific heuristics because we were more interested in assessing the potential of evolutionary computation in this area than in squeezing accuracy figures. The opposite choice would have made it difficult to isolate the merit of evolutionary learning of syntax patterns from problem-specific heuristics—which of course deserve further investigation.

We remark that our evolutionary learning of syntax patterns is not aimed at grammar induction, a problem that has received much attention in the literature, both for natural text and for formal languages [12, 2]. Grammar induction aims at inferring a set of rules which describe the input data at differing granularity levels and, in the case of natural language, have a hierarchical structure [2, 15]. Usually, although not necessarily, the quality of a solution is assessed from a gold truth of rules [2]. Here we aim instead at *partitioning* text at the granularity level of full sentences, rules need not have any specific structure, no gold truth of rules exists and only the desired partitioning is specified. Of course, techniques for grammar induction could be useful in our scenario as well but it must be emphasized that grammar induction and binary classification of sentences are different problems.

A wealth of literature exist for building classifiers based on Genetic Programming [16], but natural text is outside of the scope of most proposals. Furthermore, classification of natural text is usually done at the level of full documents and such a granularity is excessively coarse in our context [20].

We assess our approach on a realistic dataset and compare the resulting accuracy to significant baseline methods. The results indicate that our GP-based proposal indeed learns syntax patterns from examples effectively, even in NLP scenarios of practical interest.

2. THE PROBLEM

We aim at generating a classifier C that takes a natural language sentence s in input and performs a binary classification based on whether s contains a genic-protein interaction.

We generate the classifier based on two *learning sets* S_L^+, S_L^-: sentences in S_L^+ contain a genic-protein interaction whereas sentences in S_L^- do not. Two dictionaries are also available of genes/proteins and interactors, as usually done in in applications of this sort [19, 17, 18].

In order to better appreciate nature and difficulty of the problem, it is useful to emphasize that sets S_L^+, S_L^-, are *not* labelled automatically based on some predefined pattern that is kept hidden to the classifier generation process. Instead, the labelling is done by domain experts which read and analyze the meaning of every single sentence as a whole. Domain experts do not choose the class for a sentence using a predefined pattern—a pattern suitable for classifying sentences as desired may not even exist.

3. OUR APPROACH

We aim at inferring a classifier capable of detecting *syntax patterns* of the sentences to be extracted, beyond the mere co-occurrence of relevant words. The classifier operates on sequences of Unicode characters which we call *ϕ-strings.* In a nutshell, we transform each sentence to a sequence of *Part-of-Speech (POS)* annotations, we group annotations of genes/proteins and interactors, and map each annotation to an arbitrarily chosen Unicode character. Full details of this procedure are provided in Section 3.1, an example is given in Figure 1.

The target classifier C consists of a set of *regular expressions* $\{r_1^\star, r_2^\star, \dots\}$. The output of C for an input ϕ-string x will be *positive* (i.e., C deems that the sentence corresponding to x contains a genic-protein interaction) if at least one $r_i^\star$ is matched by x or by a non-empty substring of x.

We attack the complex problem of actually generating $r_i^\star$ by means of a Genetic Programming (GP) procedure inspired by recent proposals for learning regular expressions from examples [3, 4]. The cited proposals are designed for solving text extraction problems at the level of short text snippets. We had to modify and tailor these proposals for a classification problem in a different domain—properties of text snippets and of POS sequences seem to be quite different. In particular, there are two significant differences between the two scenarios. First, regular expressions include constructs which enable generalization and compactness when applied on actual text but that are not very meaningful on sequences of POS annotations, i.e., character classes `\w` and `\d`. Second, the cited works assume that the examples consist of exactly the text snippets to be extracted, whereas in our context the examples consist of full sentences: the information to be captured by the target regular expression is much more noisy and diluted.

The number of regular expressions in the set C is not determined in advance and is instead discovered automatically. Specifically, we generate regular expressions one at a time by means of a *separate-and-conquer* procedure. Initially, we generate the first regular expression by using all the available data. Then, once a regular expression is found that provides adequate performance on a *subset* of the examples, we restart the evolutionary search from the scratch by using only the remaining examples that are not yet solved adequately. This procedure is also inspired by a recent proposal designed for extraction of short text snippets [5]: differently from the cited paper, here we focus on classification instead of extraction and allow the generation of regular expressions that do not exhibit perfect precision.

Sentences w/ genic-protein interaction	Sentences w/o genic-protein interaction
In this mutant, *expression* of the **spoIIG** gene, whose transcription depends on both **sigma(A)** and the phosphorylated **Spo0A** protein, **Spo0A-P**, a major transcription factor during early stages of sporulation, was greatly reduced at 43 degrees C.	From day 10, a significant increase in platelet count was observed in eight of the ten patients treated with heparin (p < 0.05), with return to the initial value after heparin cessation in six of the responders.
These results suggest that **YfhP** may act as a negative *regulator* for the transcription of **yfhQ**, **yfhR**, **sspE** and **yfhP**.	Two phosphopeptides, identified as **RS-[32P]SGASGLLTSEHHSR** and **S-[32P]SGASGLLTSEHHSR**, were obtained after stoichiometric *phosphorylation* and trypsinization of the peptide.
These results demonstrate that **sigmaK**-dependent transcription of **gerE** initiates a negative feedback loop in which GerE acts as a *repressor* to limit production of **sigmaK**.	Levels of **TSG-14** protein (also termed **PTX-3**) become elevated in the serum of mice and humans after injection with bacterial lipopolysaccharide, but in contrast to conventional acute phase proteins, the bulk of **TSG-14** *synthesis* in the intact organism occurs outside the liver.
In this study, we used footprinting and gel mobility retardation assays to reveal that bacterially sinthetized **Zta** fusion proteins *bound* directly to six **TGTGCAA**-like motifs within DSL.	No mutations were found in follicular adenomas.

Table 1: Eight sentences of the corpus used in our experimentation, 4 which include (left) and 4 which do not include (right) genic-protein interactions. For the sake or comprehension, we highlighted in bold those words belonging to the D_{genes} dictionary and in italic those belonging to the $D_{\text{interactors}}$ dictionary (see Section 3.1).

3.1 Sentence representation

Let D_{genes} and $D_{\text{interactors}}$ be the statically available dictionaries of words representing genes and interactors, respectively: Table 2 shows portions of the two dictionaries which we actually used in our experimentation. We transform each sentence s into a ϕ-string x, as follows. For ease of presentation, in the following we will always use the term "gene" to mean either a gene or a protein.

1. We split s into a sequence $\{t_1, \dots, t_n\}$ of tokens according to the Penn-Treebank procedure[1].

2. We execute a *Part-of-Speech* (POS) annotator over $\{t_1, \dots, t_n\}$ and obtain a sequence $\{a_1, \dots, a_n\}$ of annotations, with $a_i \in A$. The set A of possible annotations depends on the specific POS annotator being used; we assume that three disjoint subsets A_{verb}, A_{adj}, A_{noun} of A exist which correspond to verbs, adjectives, and nouns, respectively—A may include other elements not contained in $A_{\text{verb}} \cup A_{\text{adj}} \cup A_{\text{noun}}$. In our experiments we used the annotator developed by the Stanford Natural Language Processing Group[2]: Table 3 shows a partial list of the elements of the set A corresponding to this POS annotator.

3. We modify the sequence $\{a_1, \dots, a_n\}$ of annotations, as follows. We say that $t \in^* D$ if t is equal to or starts with an element of D—e.g., if $D = \{\texttt{sigmaB}, \texttt{katX}\}$, then `sigmaB-dependent` $\in^* D$ and `katX` $\in^* D$. For each i,

   - if $t_i \in^* D_{\text{genes}}$, we set $a_i :=$ GENEPTN;
   - if $t_i \in D_{\text{interactors}}$ and $a_i \in A_{\text{verb}}$, we set $a_i :=$ IVERB;
   - if $t_i \in D_{\text{interactors}}$ and $a_i \in A_{\text{adj}}$, we set $a_i :=$ IADJ;
   - Finally, if $t_i \in D_{\text{interactors}}$ and $a_i \in A_{\text{noun}}$, we set $a_i :=$ INOUN.

   We denote with $A' = A \cup \{\text{GENEPTN}, \text{IVERB}, \text{IADJ}, \text{INOUN}\}$ the set of possible annotations after this step.

[1] http://www.cis.upenn.edu/~treebank

[2] http://nlp.stanford.edu/software/tagger.shtml

D_{genes}	$D_{\text{interactors}}$
amyE	abrogation
bmrUR	activation
ComK	destabilization
DksA	expression
Esig29	repression
GerE	affect
katX	bind
KinC	destabilize
sigmaH	exhibit
SpoIIAB	regulate
others	*others*

Table 2: Portions of the two dictionaries of genes/proteins and interactors used in our experimentation.

4. Let U be the set of characters including digits, lowercase letters and uppercase letters and let $\phi : A' \to U$ be an injective function which maps annotations to characters (see rightmost column of Table 3). We obtain the ϕ-string x from $\{a_1, \dots, a_n\}$ by concatenating the characters resulting from the application of ϕ to each element of the sequence of annotations, i.e., we set $x = \phi(a_1) \dots \phi(a_n)$.

Figure 1 shows the intermediate and final outcomes of the procedure here described when applied to an example sentence.

3.2 Regular expression generation

We here describe our procedure based on GP for obtaining a regular expression $r^\star$ from two *training sets* X^+, X^- of ϕ-strings. The aim of this procedure is to generate a regular expression $r^\star$ such that: (i) for each ϕ-string x in X^+, x, or a non-empty substring of x, match $r^\star$; and (ii) for each ϕ-string x in X^-, x and all the substrings of x do not match $r^\star$. The relation between the training sets and the learning sets available for synthesizing the classifier (Section 2) will be clarified later.

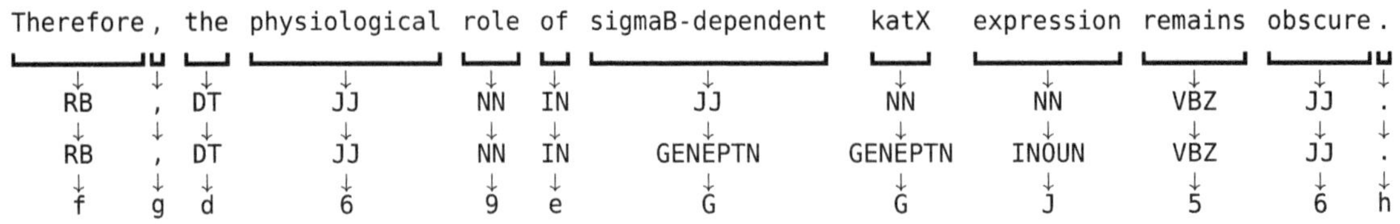

Figure 1: Example of sentence representation. The original textual sentence s (top) is transformed into a ϕ-string x (bottom) through two cascaded transformations: one producing a sequence of POS annotations and another where certain annotations are modified using the dictionaries (Section 3.1).

a	Meaning	Subset	$\phi(a)$
VB	verb, base form		0
VBD	verb, past tense		1
VBG	verb, pres. part. or gerund	A_{verb}	2
VBN	verb, past participle		3
VBP	verb, pres. tense, ¬3rd p. s.		4
VBZ	verb, pres. tense, 3rd p. s.		5
JJ	adjective or numeral, ordinal		6
JJR	adjective, comparative	A_{adj}	7
JJS	adjective, superlative		8
NN	noun, common, sing. or mass		9
NNP	noun, proper, singular	A_{noun}	a
NNPS	noun, proper, plural		b
NNS	noun, common, plural		c
CC	conjunction, coordinating		d
CD	numeral, cardinal		e
DT	determiner		f
	other annotations		
GENEPTN	gene or protein		G
IVERB	verb interactor	$A' \setminus A$	R
IADJ	adjective interactor		P
INOUN	noun interactor		J

Table 3: A partial list of the elements of A': for space constraints, only a subset of $A \setminus (A_{\text{verb}} \cup A_{\text{adj}} \cup A_{\text{noun}})$ is shown.

3.2.1 Solution representation and fitness definition

We represent a candidate solution, i.e., an *individual*, with a tree. Each tree represents a regular expression, as follows. The set of terminal nodes is composed of the wildcard character `.` and of each character in range(ϕ), i.e., each character in U which corresponds to an annotation in A'. The set of function nodes is composed of: the concatenator `⌑⌑`; the character class `[⌑]` and negated character class `[^⌑]`; the possessive quantifiers `⌑*+`, `⌑++`, `⌑?+` and `⌑{⌑,⌑}+`; and the non-capturing group `(?:⌑)`. A tree represents a regular expression by means of a depth-first visit in which each `⌑` symbol in a non-terminal node is replaced by the representation the corresponding child node.

The *fitness* of an individual r quantifies the behavior of the individual over the training sets. We define the fitness as a tuple $f(r) := (\text{FPR}(r, X^-) + \text{FNR}(r, X^+), \text{FPR}(r, X^-), \ell(r))$, where $\ell(r)$ is the length of the regular expression represented by r and $\text{FPR}(r, X^-)$ and $\text{FNR}(r, X^+)$ are the False Positive Rate and False Negative Rate, respectively, of r on the training sets. In more detail, $\text{FPR}(r, X^-)$ is the percentage of ϕ-strings $x \in X^-$ for which x, or a non-empty substring of x, match r; $\text{FPR}(r, X^+)$ is the percentage of ϕ-strings $x \in X^+$ for which x and all the substrings of x do not match r. For all the elements of the fitness tuple, the lower, the better. The first objective (i.e., $\text{FPR}(r, X^-) + \text{FNR}(r, X^+)$) is a proxy for the accuracy of classification of r on the examples in X^-, X^+. We chose not to use accuracy in order to accommodate possibly unbalanced learning sets (our experimental evaluation used balanced sets, though).

We *rank* individuals based on their fitness tuples according to Pareto-dominance and lexicographic order, as follows. First, individuals are sorted by their Pareto frontier: an individual belongs to the i-th frontier if and only if it is Pareto-dominated only by individuals, if any, belonging to j-th frontier, with $j < i$—an individual Pareto-dominates another individual if it is better on at least one fitness element and not worse on the other two elements. Second, a total ordering is established among individuals in the same Pareto frontier: individuals with lower FPR + FNR come first; in case of equal FPR + FNR individuals with lower FPR come first; in case of equal FPR + FNR and equal FPR individuals with lower ℓ come first.

As pointed out in the introduction, we purposefully avoided to include any problem-specific knowledge in the fitness definition—e.g., part-of-speech tags associated with either genes or interactors do not have any special status. We use a multiobjective approach aimed at maximizing accuracy while promoting compact solutions for preventing bloat [11]. We add a third objective beyond accuracy and length because, as detailed in Section 3.3, the classifier does not consist of a single regular expression and is instead composed of a set of regular expressions generated from progressively smaller training sets. A form of evolutionary pressure on the FPR of each member of the set turns out to be beneficial to the aggregate FPR of the full set.

3.2.2 Search procedure

We execute the GP search with a population of n_{pop} individuals. The initial population is composed of a portion of randomly generated individuals and a portion of individuals designed to match at least one ϕ-string in X^+. In detail, we build 3 individuals generated from each $x \in X^+$:

1. an individual r representing a regular expression which is equal to the ϕ-string x;

2. an individual r' obtained by replacing in r each leaf node not included in {ϕ(GENEPTN), ϕ(IVERB), ϕ(IADJ), ϕ(INOUN)} with a subtree corresponding to the regular expression [^ϕ(GENEPTN)ϕ(IVERB)ϕ(IADJ)ϕ(INOUN)], i.e., with the character class which excludes characters corresponding to genes and interactions;

3. an individual r'' obtained by replacing in r' consecutive repetitions of the character class which excludes genes and interactions with [^ϕ(GENEPTN)ϕ(IVERB)ϕ(IADJ),

ϕ(INOUN)]++, i.e., with the subtree corresponding to one or more repetitions of the character class.

If the number of individuals generated by this procedure is greater than n_{pop}, then we remove exceeding individuals chosen at random (this event does not occur in our experimental setting); otherwise, we generate missing individuals at random with a ramped half-and-half method.

We evolve the initial population by means of the following procedure. At each iteration (or *generation*), we generate n_{pop} new individuals: 80% of them by crossover between individuals in the current population; 10% of them by mutation of individuals in the current population; 10% of them at random with a ramped half-and-half method. We build the new current population by retaining only the n_{pop} individuals with best fitness from the resulting $2n_{\text{pop}}$ individuals (current population and new generated individuals). We select individuals for either crossover or mutation by means of a tournament selection of size 7. Whenever we generate an individual which represents a not valid regular expression, we discard that individual and generate a new one.

We enforce *genotypic diversity* among candidate solutions, i.e., whenever an individual r_1 is generated which represents the same regular expression represented by another individual r_2 in the current population, then r_1 is discarded and another individual is generated—a similar mechanism is used in [24] for preventing the creation of duplicated solutions. We chose to include this simple mechanism in the search—not present in [4]—because our earlier experiments clearly demonstrated its effectiveness in our scenario, the quality of generated solutions being substantially improved without any significant increase in processing time. Such an improvement is perhaps not surprising, because we do not start the search with a fully random population and because a multiobjective GP search may greatly benefit from an explicit mechanism for promoting forms of diversity among candidate solutions, either at the genotypic level or in the objective space or in their behavior [11, 9]. However, we remark that the mechanism that we have chosen is extremely easy to implement and, in particular, does not involve the problem of choosing how to *quantify* the amount of diversity between individuals. Furthermore, it does not involve the need of defining diversity as a *further objective* to be taken into account during the search, which might be difficult to achieve in our scenario since the resulting fitness would be composed of four indexes and thus more radical changes to the evolutionary strategy could be required [21]. A detailed analysis of the effectiveness of this mechanism, as well as of other possible diversity enforcement criteria (e.g., [11, 9]), is beyond the scope of this paper, though.

The search terminates when one of the following occurs: (i) a predefined number of n_{gen} iterations has been executed; or, (ii) the fitness tuple of the best individual has remained unchanged for n_{stop} consecutive iterations. The regular expression represented by the best individual of the final population is the outcome of the search procedure.

3.3 Classifier generation

We apply the procedure described in Section 3.1 and transform the *learning* sets S_L^+, S_L^- to sets of ϕ-strings X_L^+, X_L^-, respectively. Then, we randomly sample X_L^+, X_L^- to build the *training* sets X^+, X^-, respectively, ensuring that $\frac{|X^+|}{|X^-|} = \frac{|X_L^+|}{|X_L^-|}$.

We start from an initially empty set of regular expressions ($\mathcal{C} = \emptyset$) and repeat the following iterative procedure (τ_{FPR} is a predefined threshold): 1) execute a search on X^+, X^- and obtain $r^\star$; 2) if either $\text{FPR}(r^\star, X^-) \leq \tau_{\text{FPR}}$ or the search terminated after executing n_{gen} generations, then assign $\mathcal{C} := \mathcal{C} \cup \{r^\star\}$, otherwise terminate; 3) remove from X^+ the ϕ-strings x for which x, or a substring of x, match $r^\star$; 4) if X^+ is empty, then terminate, otherwise go to step 1. The outcome of this procedure is a classifier $\mathcal{C}$.

We perform n_{job} independent executions of the procedure, all starting with the same training sets X^+, X^- but with different random seeds. Thus, we obtain n_{job} (possibly) different classifiers and choose the one with lowest error rate on the learning sets X_L^+, X_L^-. In other words, we validate the n_{job} classifiers on data which was not available during the training in order to prevent overfitting the data.

In our experimentation, we set $\tau_{\text{FPR}} = 0.3$, $n_{\text{gen}} = 1000$, $n_{\text{stop}} = 200$, $n_{\text{pop}} = 1000$, and $n_{\text{job}} = 8$; we chose these values after preliminary experimentation and basing (in particular for n_{gen}, n_{pop}, and n_{job} parameters) on the abundant literature about GP.

4. EXPERIMENTAL EVALUATION

4.1 Datasets and baselines

We used a corpus of 456 sentences built by joining two corpora, both derived from genic-protein interactions extraction challenges of biomedical interest[3]. Each sentence was labelled by a domain expert. Table 1 shows some samples. It can be seen that the mere presence of words in the dictionaries D_{genes} and $D_{\text{interactors}}$ does not suffice to qualify a sentence as containing a genic-protein interaction.

In order to assess our results, we implemented several alternative classification techniques: a state-of-the-art evolutionary approach for inferring patterns from examples, two approaches that embed a large amount of problem-specific knowledge and two established methods for text classification.

4.1.1 DFA-based pattern evolutionary inference

We implemented a classifier based on the *Smart State Labelling Evolutionary Algorithm (SSLEA)* proposed in [27]. The cited work is a state-of-the-art algorithm for learning *deterministic finite automata (DFA)* from examples of the desired classification behavior. SSLEA was developed a few years after a competition that was highly influential in the grammar learning community and outperformed (optimized versions of) the winners of the competition, on the same class of problems [23, 10] and even in the presence of noisy data.

SSLEA represents a candidate solution (i.e., a DFA) by a pair composed of an output vector of size n and a transition matrix of size $n \times |\alpha|$, where n is the number of states in the target DFA and $|\alpha|$ is the number of symbols in the input alphabet: the former has one element for each DFA state and each element contains the label (accept or reject) for the corresponding state; the latter contains, for each state and transition, the corresponding destination state index. SSLEA implements a form of hill-climbing in which the fitness of a solution is the rate of examples classified correctly.

[3]http://genome.jouy.inra.fr/texte/LLLchallenge/#task1 and https://www2.informatik.hu-berlin.de/~hakenber/corpora/#bc

The search terminates when either a DFA with perfect fitness is found or a predefined number n_{it} of iterations have been executed. We refer the reader to the cited work for full details.

We implemented SSLEA and applied it to ϕ-strings. After some exploratory experimentation, we found that it delivers best results with $\alpha = \text{range}(\phi)$, $n = 7$ and $n_{\text{it}} = 5000$ and we used these values in our assessment. In particular, we verified experimentally that increasing the number n_{it} of available iterations, even by a large amount, did not lead to better accuracy on the testing data.

4.1.2 Problem-specific baselines

We implemented two classifiers that embed a substantial amount of problem-specific knowledge.

The classifier that we call *Annotations-Co-occurrence* classifies a sentence s positively if and only if s contains at least two genes/proteins and at least one interactor—i.e., it is tightly tailored to this specific problem.

The classifier that we call *Annotations-LLL05-patterns* is built on results from [19], which proposes a method for identifying syntax alignment-patterns that describe interactions between genes and proteins in scientific text. An alignment-pattern is described in terms of sequences of salient POS annotations which must occur in a sentence, but that does not specify any constraint on type and quantity of further annotations that might occur between those salient annotations. The method exploits a fair amount of domain-specific knowledge for tuning tens of coefficients used for weighting alignment-pattern errors related with specific POS annotations, as well as with genes and interactors. The cited work provides a list of the 10 most frequent alignment-patterns learned from the *whole* corpus used in that paper, which is much larger than ours ($\approx$ 1000 sentences). We built a classifier which classifies a sentence s positively if and only if s matches at least one of the 10 alignment-patterns in the aforementioned list. Our corpus is composed, for $\approx 90\%$ of the sentences, of a strict subset of that corpus.

4.1.3 Established methods for text classification

Finally, we implemented two well-established schemes for text classification [30], one based on Naive Bayes and the other based on Support Vector Machines (SVM).

We pre-process each sentence s as follows: (i) we replace each occurrence of a string contained in $D_{\text{interactors}}$ with `_interactor`; (ii) we replace each occurrence of a string contained in D_{genes} with `_geneptn`; (iii) we convert s to lowercase; (iv) we replace each non alphabetic (i.e., `[^a-zA-Z_]`) character with a space; (v) we perform stemming to each word (except of `_geneptn` and `_interactor`). We execute steps i and ii in order to exploit the knowledge embedded in the dictionaries, which would otherwise not available to the classifier.

In order to build the classifier:

1. We build a sorted set W of words composed of all words occurring at least once in the learning sets S_L^+, S_L^-.

2. We transform each sentence s into a vector $\mathbf{f}'$ in which the ith element corresponds to the number of occurrences in s of the word $w_i \in W$.

3. We execute a *feature selection* procedure (which is detailed below) for identifying the k elements of $\mathbf{f}'$ which best discriminate between sentences in S_L^+ or S_L^-. Let $\mathbf{f}$ be the vector obtained by keeping only those k elements from $\mathbf{f}'$—i.e., $\mathbf{f}$ contains only the occurrence counts of the words selected in the feature selection procedure.

4. Finally, we train a binary classifier using the vectors $\mathbf{f}$ corresponding to the sentences in the learning sets S_L^+, S_L^-.

Having built the classifier, to classify a previously unseen sentence s we: (i) pre-process s as described above; (ii) obtain the corresponding feature vector $\mathbf{f}$; and, finally, (iii) input $\mathbf{f}$ to the trained classifier.

The feature selection procedure is based on the vectors $\mathbf{f}'$. This procedure takes two numerical parameters k, k', with $k' \gg k$, and works in two steps, as follows. In the first step we compute, for each ith feature the relative difference δ_i between its mean value across sentences of the two sets:

$$\delta_i = \frac{\left| \frac{1}{|S_L^+|} \sum_{S_L^+} f'_i - \frac{1}{|S_L^-|} \sum_{S_L^-} f'_i \right|}{\max_{S_L^+ \cup S_L^-} f'_i}$$

We then select the k' features with the largest δ_i—among those for which $\max_{S_L^+ \cup S_L^-} f'_i > 0$. In the second step we compute, for each ith feature among the k' selected at the previous step, the mutual information I_i with the label—the label being a binary value which is positive for elements in S_L^+ and negative for elements in S_L^-. We then select the k features with the greatest I_i.

We built two binary classifiers with this scheme, which we call *Words-NaiveBayes* and *Words-SVM*, respectively. Concerning the feature selection parameters k' and k, we set $k' = 1000$ for both the classifiers and we chose the value of k for which each classifier obtained the best accuracy on the learning sets, i.e., $k = 25$ for *Words-NaiveBayes* and $k = 50$ for *Words-SVM*. Concerning SVM parameters, we used a Gaussian radial kernel with the cost parameter set to 1.

4.2 Results

We executed a 5-fold cross-validation, i.e., we generated 5 different problem instances from the corpus at random. For each instance we used $\approx 80\%$ of the data for learning and $\approx 20\%$ for testing, i.e., we built the learning sets S_L^+, S_L^- (with $|S_L^+| = |S_L^-| = 188$) and left two testing sets S_T^+, S_T^- aside for assessing the accuracy of the generated classifiers (with $|S_T^+| = |S_T^-| = 40$). We used the very same learning sets and testing sets for all the considered methods—our method and the baseline methods described in the previous section. For ϕ-SSLEA and our method, which are stochastic, we repeated the execution 10 times for each fold.

Table 4 shows the results obtained by the 6 methods. The results are expressed in accuracy, FPR and FNR, averaged across the 5 folds: for the two stochastic methods, we also report the accuracy standard deviation of the 10 executions averaged across the 5 folds.

It can be seen that our method and Words-SVM obtain the highest accuracies ($\approx$ 74%) among those 4 methods which learn a classifier only from examples and dictionaries—i.e., without any problem-specific knowledge. GP is indeed able to learn syntax patterns from examples effectively, even in NLP scenarios of practical interest. We believe this result is particularly relevant.

Classifier	Accuracy avg	Accuracy sd	FPR avg	FNR avg
Ann.-Co-occurrence	77.8		40.0	4.5
Ann.-LLL05-patterns	82.3		25.0	10.5
Words-NaiveBayes	51.3		25.0	95.0
Words-SVM	73.8		29.0	23.5
ϕ-SSLEA	59.8	3.8	44.0	33.5
Our method	73.7	1.7	23.5	22.5

Table 4: Results of our method and the 5 baselines.

$r_1 =$ `GENEPTN [ ^ RB ] [ ^ NNS VBN GENEPTN ] ++`
`GENEPTN [ ^ LRB DT NNS RRB ] [ ^ LRB NNS ]`
$r_2 =$ `. INOUN IN GENEPTN . [ ^ DT NN ]`

Figure 2: An example of a generated classifier composed of two regular expressions, shown using annotations, instead of symbols of U, for readability.

The accuracy of the two problem-specific classifiers is 82.3% and 77.8% for Annotations-LLL05-patterns and Annotations-Co-occurrence, respectively. We believe that the better accuracy exhibited by these methods is not surprising having considered that these methods build on a substantial amount of problem-specific knowledge, as clarified above. Indeed, the accuracy of Annotations-Co-occurrence is only slightly better than our method.

It is interesting to note that the accuracy obtained by ϕ-SSLEA is much worse than ours although the two approaches are based, broadly speaking, on similar tools—evolutionary learning of a DFA vs. evolutionary learning of sets of regular expressions. While this result might appear somewhat surprising—as pointed out above, ϕ-SSLEA exhibits state-of-the-art performance in DFA learning—we believe the reason is because benchmark problems in DFA learning consider short sequences of binary symbols, with training data drawn uniformly from the input space. Settings of this sort do not fit the needs of practical NLP applications, which have to cope with much longer sequences of symbols, from a much larger alphabet, not drawn uniformly from the space of all possible sequences. Our interpretation is corroborated by earlier claims from different authors: benchmark problems for DFA learning from examples are not inspired by any real world application [10] and the applicability of the corresponding learning algorithms to other application domains is still largely unexplored [6].

Figure 2 shows one of the classifiers obtained during our experimentation, composed of two regular expressions. For the sake of comprehension, expressions are shown using annotations (A') instead of symbols of U. It can be seen that the generated expressions include salient annotations (`GENEPTN` and `INOUN`) although those annotations were not given any special status. The two patterns are not easily readable, which is not surprising since we did not include any mechanism for favoring readable expressions. Indeed, readability could be a valuable objective to be pursued and we plan to investigate this respect in future work.

5. CONCLUDING REMARKS

We presented an evolutionary method for learning syntax patterns in natural text from examples. We applied this method to a sentence classification problem from the biomedical domain that is practically relevant and very challenging.

Our method is based on GP and builds on recent results for the automatic generation of regular expressions from examples of the desired behavior. We propose a technique for representing sentences as strings of symbols which can be manipulated by common regular expressions. Symbols correspond to POS annotations augmented with problem-specific dictionaries. Working at the abstraction level of POS annotations has many practical advantages, including modularity and the possibility of leveraging the steadily improving state-of-the-art in this area. The number of patterns to be learned from a set of example sentences is not known in advance, but is instead automatically determined by means of a separate-and-conquer procedure.

We assessed experimentally our method on a challenging corpus of 456 hand-labeled sentences and compared it against 5 significant baseline methods. We obtained good results which indicate that GP may indeed learn syntax patterns from examples effectively, even in NLP scenarios of practical interest.

6. REFERENCES

[1] L. Araujo. Symbiosis of evolutionary techniques and statistical natural language processing. *Trans. Evol. Comp*, 8(1):14–27, February 2004.

[2] Lourdes Araujo. How evolutionary algorithms are applied to statistical natural language processing. *Artif. Intell. Rev.*, 28(4):275–303, December 2007.

[3] Alberto Bartoli, Giorgio Davanzo, Andrea De Lorenzo, Marco Mauri, Eric Medvet, and Enrico Sorio. Automatic generation of regular expressions from examples with genetic programming. In *International Conference on Genetic and evolutionary computation (GECCO)*, pages 1477–1478. ACM, 2012.

[4] Alberto Bartoli, Giorgio Davanzo, Andrea De Lorenzo, Eric Medvet, and Enrico Sorio. Automatic synthesis of regular expressions from examples. *Computer*, 47:72–80, 2014.

[5] Alberto Bartoli, Andrea De Lorenzo, Eric Medvet, and Fabiano Tarlao. Learning text patterns using separate-and-conquer genetic programming. In *18-th European Conference on Genetic Programming (EuroGP)*, 2015.

[6] Josh Bongard and Hod Lipson. Active coevolutionary learning of deterministic finite automata. *The Journal of Machine Learning Research*, 6:1651–1678, 2005.

[7] Jakramate Bootkrajang, Sun Kim, and Byoung-Tak Zhang. Evolutionary hypernetwork classifiers for protein-proteininteraction sentence filtering. In *Proceedings of the 11th Annual Conference on Genetic and Evolutionary Computation*, GECCO '09, pages 185–192, New York, NY, USA, 2009. ACM.

[8] Markus Bundschus, Mathaeus Dejori, Martin Stetter, Volker Tresp, and Hans-Peter Kriegel. Extraction of semantic biomedical relations from text using conditional random fields. *BMC Bioinformatics*, 9(1):207, 2008.

[9] Edmund K Burke, Steven Gustafson, and Graham Kendall. Diversity in genetic programming: An analysis of measures and correlation with fitness. *Evolutionary Computation, IEEE Transactions on*, 8(1):47–62, 2004.
[10] Orlando Cicchello and Stefan C Kremer. Inducing grammars from sparse data sets: a survey of algorithms and results. *The Journal of Machine Learning Research*, 4:603–632, 2003.
[11] Edwin D De Jong and Jordan B Pollack. Multi-objective methods for tree size control. *Genetic Programming and Evolvable Machines*, 4(3):211–233, 2003.
[12] Colin De La Higuera. A bibliographical study of grammatical inference. *Pattern recognition*, 38(9):1332–1348, 2005.
[13] Guy De Pauw. Evolutionary computing as a tool for grammar development. In *Proceedings of the 2003 International Conference on Genetic and Evolutionary Computation: PartI*, GECCO'03, pages 549–560, Berlin, Heidelberg, 2003. Springer-Verlag.
[14] Bart Decadt, , Bart Decadt, Véronique Hoste, Walter Daelemans, and Antal Van Den Bosch. Gambl, genetic algorithm optimization of memory-based wsd. In *In Proceedings of ACL/SIGLEX Senseval-3*, pages 108–112, 2004.
[15] Arianna D'Ulizia, Fernando Ferri, and Patrizia Grifoni. A survey of grammatical inference methods for natural language learning. *Artificial Intelligence Review*, 36(1):1–27, 2011.
[16] Pedro G Espejo, Sebastián Ventura, and Francisco Herrera. A survey on the application of genetic programming to classification. *Systems, Man, and Cybernetics, Part C: Applications and Reviews, IEEE Transactions on*, 40(2):121–144, 2010.
[17] Katrin Fundel, Robert Küffner, and Ralf Zimmer. Relex—relation extraction using dependency parse trees. *Bioinformatics*, 23(3):365–371, 2007.
[18] Sonal Gupta, Diana L MacLean, Jeffrey Heer, and Christopher D Manning. Induced lexico-syntactic patterns improve information extraction from online medical forums. *Journal of the American Medical Informatics Association*, 21(5):902–909, 2014.
[19] Jörg Hakenberg, Conrad Plake, Ulf Leser, Harald Kirsch, and Dietrich Rebholz-Schuhmann. LLL'05 challenge: Genic interaction extraction-identification of language patterns based on alignment and finite state automata. In *Proceedings of the 4th Learning Language in Logic workshop (LLL05)*, pages 38–45, 2005.
[20] Laurence Hirsch, Robin Hirsch, and Masoud Saeedi. Evolving lucene search queries for text classification. In *Proceedings of the 9th annual conference on Genetic and evolutionary computation*, pages 1604–1611. ACM, 2007.
[21] Evan J Hughes. Evolutionary many-objective optimisation: many once or one many? In *Evolutionary Computation, 2005. The 2005 IEEE Congress on*, volume 1, pages 222–227. IEEE, 2005.
[22] Seth Kulick, Ann Bies, Mark Liberman, Mark Mandel, Ryan McDonald, Martha Palmer, Andrew Schein, Lyle Ungar, Scott Winters, and Pete White. Integrated annotation for biomedical information extraction. In *Proc. of HLT/NAACL*, pages 61–68, 2004.
[23] Kevin J. Lang, Barak A. Pearlmutter, and Rodney A. Price. Results of the abbadingo one DFA learning competition and a new evidence-driven state merging algorithm. In *Grammatical Inference*, page 1–12. Springer, 1998.
[24] W.B. Langdon and M. Harman. Optimizing existing software with genetic programming. *Evolutionary Computation, IEEE Transactions on*, 19(1):118–135, Feb 2015.
[25] Jiexun Li, Zhu Zhang, Xin Li, and Hsinchun Chen. Kernel-based learning for biomedical relation extraction. *Journal of the American Society for Information Science and Technology*, 59(5):756–769, 2008.
[26] Marina Litvak, Mark Last, and Menahem Friedman. A new approach to improving multilingual summarization using a genetic algorithm. In *Proceedings of the 48th Annual Meeting of the Association for Computational Linguistics*, ACL '10, pages 927–936, Stroudsburg, PA, USA, 2010. Association for Computational Linguistics.
[27] Simon M Lucas and T Jeff Reynolds. Learning deterministic finite automata with a smart state labeling evolutionary algorithm. *IEEE Transactions on Pattern Analysis and Machine Intelligence*, 27(7):1063–1074, 2005.
[28] Hoifung Poon, Chris Quirk, Charlie DeZiel, and David Heckerman. Literome: Pubmed-scale genomic knowledge base in the cloud. *Bioinformatics*, 2014.
[29] Luis Rodríguez, Ismael García-Varea, and José A. Gámez. On the application of different evolutionary algorithms to the alignment problem in statistical machine translation. *Neurocomput.*, 71(4-6):755–765, January 2008.
[30] Fabrizio Sebastiani. Machine learning in automated text categorization. *ACM computing surveys (CSUR)*, 34(1):1–47, 2002.
[31] J. Ignacio Serrano. Evolutionary algorithm for noun phrase detection in natural language processing. In *Proceedings of the 2005 IEEE Congress on Evolutionary Computing (IEEE Computer Society*, 2005.
[32] Martin Volk, Bärbel Ripplinger, Špela Vintar, Paul Buitelaar, Diana Raileanu, and Bogdan Sacaleanu. Semantic annotation for concept-based cross-language medical information retrieval. *International Journal of Medical Informatics*, 67(1):97–112, 2002.
[33] Akane Yakushiji, Yusuke Miyao, Tomoko Ohta, Yuka Tateisi, and Jun'ichi Tsujii. Automatic construction of predicate-argument structure patterns for biomedical information extraction. In *Proceedings of the 2006 Conference on Empirical Methods in Natural Language Processing*, pages 284–292. Association for Computational Linguistics, 2006.
[34] Lin Yao, Cheng-Jie Sun, Xiao-Long Wang, and Xuan Wang. Relationship extraction from biomedical literature using maximum entropy based on rich features. In *Machine Learning and Cybernetics (ICMLC), 2010 International Conference on*, volume 6, pages 3358–3361, July 2010.

A Closer Look At Differential Evolution For The Optimal Well Placement Problem

Grazieli L. C. Carosio*
Department of Mathematics and Statistics
Memorial University of Newfoundland
St. John's, Canada A1C 5S7
grazielilccdm@mun.ca

Thomas D. Humphries
Department of Mathematics
Oregon State University
Corvallis, USA 97331
humphrit@science.oregonstate.edu

Ronald D. Haynes
Department of Mathematics and Statistics
Memorial University of Newfoundland
St. John's, Canada A1C 5S7
rhaynes@mun.ca

Colin G. Farquharson
Department of Earth Sciences
Memorial University of Newfoundland
St. John's, Canada A1B 3X5
cgfarquh@mun.ca

ABSTRACT

Energy demand has increased considerably with the growth of world population, increasing the interest in the hydrocarbon reservoir management problem. Companies are concerned with maximizing oil recovery while minimizing capital investment and operational costs. A first step in solving this problem is to consider optimal well placement. In this work, we investigate the Differential Evolution (DE) optimization method, using distinct configurations with respect to population size, mutation factor, crossover probability, and mutation strategy, to solve the well placement problem. By assuming a bare control procedure, one optimizes the parameters representing positions of injection and production wells. The Tenth SPE Comparative Solution Project and MATLAB Reservoir Simulation Toolbox (MRST) are the benchmark dataset and simulator used, respectively. The goal is to evaluate the performance of DE in solving this important real-world problem. We show that DE can find high-quality solutions, when compared with a reference from the literature, and a preliminary analysis on the results of multiple experiments gives useful information on how DE configuration impacts its performance.

Categories and Subject Descriptors

G.1.6 [**Numerical Analysis**]: Optimization, global optimization, constrained optimization; G.1.10 [**Applications**]

*Corresponding author.

GECCO '15, July 11 - 15, 2015, Madrid, Spain
© 2015 ACM. ISBN 978-1-4503-3472-3/15/07...$15.00
DOI: http://dx.doi.org/10.1145/2739480.2754772

Keywords

Differential evolution; well placement; production optimization; combinatorial optimization; constrained optimization; derivative-free optimization

1. INTRODUCTION

Recently, energy demand has increased considerably with the growth of world population, inducing even more interest in the oil reservoir management problem. This involves effectively utilizing existing hydrocarbon resources by maximizing recovery and minimizing capital investment and operational costs. One approach to address this is to find optimal placement of wells. The parameters representing positions and orientations of injection and production wells are optimized, while a bare control procedure is assumed. In this work, we consider only vertical wells with (x, y)-coordinates representing a well's position.

The performance indicator or objective function of this optimization problem is usually either the Voidage Replacement Ratio (VRR) [9, 2] or the Net Present Value (NPV) [3, 16]. The VRR function corresponds to the ratio of the total volume of fluid injected (water injection) to the volume of fluid produced (water, oil and gas production). In turn, the NPV function involves the total amount of oil extracted, emphasizing an early oil production in the reservoir's life-time (due to the time value of money), and also typically includes the costs of water injection and disposal of any water produced. Since NPV is the primary objective function used in well placement optimization, we chose it for this study.

Since the reservoir model is represented as a discretized grid, the positions of injection and production wells are typically specified by integer co-ordinates, meaning that exact gradients of the objective function with respect to these parameters are not available. Thus, gradient-based methods have been used only after conversion of the discrete optimization problem into another optimization problem with continuous variables [30, 37]. Due mostly to the heterogeneous permeability field, the objective function is non-convex and may contain many local minima [28]. Moreover, gradient-based methods are typically local solvers. Here a global optimum is desired, hence the work presented herein uses a derivative-free (non-invasive, black-box) optimization method known as a meta-heuristic [32, 4].

Since gradients are not directly available, meta-heuristics are usually quite inefficient requiring several thousands of simulations and thus may have limited application to large-scale simulation models with many wells. However, whenever they are computationally feasible, meta-heuristics tend to provide high-quality solutions. Parallel programming can be used to obtain multiple independent runs simultaneously, or provide parallel function evaluations in a single run, thus the computational time may be decreased and the overall solution can be improved. Another important advantage of applying meta-heuristics is that the number of function evaluations is dependent on the size of the population and not the problem dimensionality [33]. Meta-heuristics that have been used to solve the well-placement problem include: genetic algorithms (GA) [35, 24, 21], simulated annealing (SA) [3], particle swarm optimization (PSO) [28, 17, 1, 16], covariance matrix adaptation evolutionary strategies (CMA-ES) [12, 5, 14], and differential evolution (DE) [27, 2].

DE is a meta-heuristic which has been successfully used to solve many global optimization problems [7], for example, problems in engineering design [11], electrical impedance tomography [19], the paper industry [34], and limited memory optimization [25]. Nevertheless, its application in well-placement is not common. Some researchers [27] indicate that DE is not appropriate for the well placement problem, suggesting its use only when hybridized with other stochastic methods. However, it is well-known that the choice of algorithmic parameters may have great influence on its behaviour. Therefore, in this paper we investigate DE to solve a well-placement problem on a widely studied real-world example, and present a preliminary analysis on its parameters. Our results may serve as reference for researchers intending to use DE to solve this kind of problem; allowing a more fair comparison by using a more appropriate DE configuration. Moreover, this study suggests a particular configuration that may make classical DE competitive with other methods to solve the well placement problem.

This paper is organized as follows: Section 2 presents the literature review; Section 3 presents the proposed methodology; Section 4 presents the results and discussions; Section 5 presents the conclusions.

2. LITERATURE REVIEW

The well placement problem involves determining the optimal location of one or more wells in order to obtain, for example, the maximum NPV of oil extracted with minimal operating costs, subject to different geological and economic constraints such as reservoir geology, well type, and physical properties of the fluid and rock. We focus this short review on DE, the optimization method investigated in this paper.

DE has been used in multi-objective approaches incorporating NPV and VRR to solve well placement optimization problems [15, 2]. A Pareto-based multi-objective approach to integrate NPV and VRR in a well placement optimization was presented by [15], obtaining several optimal solutions according to the Pareto front. The set of solutions in the Pareto optimal front are those that cannot be improved in any of the objectives without degrading at least one of the other objectives.

A similar study was presented by [2] using CMA-ES and DE to solve the multi-objective optimization problem by manually weighting NPV and VRR, resulting in a single-optimization problem. They concluded that CMA-ES outperformed DE for the majority of experiments, but that DE also obtained high-quality solutions.

A hybrid approach (HPSDE) was proposed by [27] combining the DE and PSO algorithms. The hybrid algorithm consistently outperformed both DE and PSO using NPV as performance measure in the three proposed example problems. The placement of one, two, and nine vertical wells were considered. They showed that the performance of DE and PSO, to an extent, depends on the 1) the total number of simulations, and 2) the population size, and that PSO was generally better than DE. However, the conclusion of that study was based on results obtained from a configuration that makes DE's convergence slow but able to avoid local optima. Therefore, more iterations would be necessary to show a competitive performance with that configuration. Their conclusions were based only 5 trials of each algorithm. We understand that an adequate statistical analysis of a stochastic algorithm requires a larger number of independent runs.

Given the above, our main contribution is to present a preliminary analysis using various DE configurations, including some suggested in the literature [31, 10], while solving a well placement problem. We show that DE can find high-quality solutions, contradicting the conclusions presented by [27], and indeed our DE obtained several results better than those from [16], which used a PSO with local-search (memetic PSO).

3. METHODOLOGY

In this section we present the well placement problem used as the case study, and introduce the Differential Evolution algorithm used to solve it.

3.1 Case Study

As in [16], we consider a small section of the reservoir block representing a subset of the Tenth SPE Comparative Solution Project [8] to run several instances of each DE configuration and to study the convergence behaviour. We adopt a $2D$ reservoir model consisting of 60×50 grid cells, each measuring 32×32 m^2 with a total field size of $1,600 \times 1,920$ m^2. A uniform saturation of 80:20, oil to water, is also assumed as in [16]. The physical parameters of the problem are shown in Table 1. Figures 1 and 2 show the porosity and permeability fields of the reservoir model, which are generated from the third layer of the SPE10 base case.

The objective function adopted is the NPV over the entire production period $[0, T]$. The NPV is computed as in [3]:

$$NPV(\mathbf{x}) = \int_0^T \sum_{n \in prod} c_o q_{n,o}^{-}(\mathbf{x}, t) - c_{w,disp} q_{n,w}^{-}(\mathbf{x}, t) - \sum_{n \in inj} c_{w,inj} q_{n,w}^{+}(\mathbf{x}, t)(1 + r)^t dt, \quad (1)$$

Table 1: **Physical parameters values as used in [16].**

Parameter	Value
Fluid viscosities μ_o and μ_w	2.4 and 1.0 cp
Fluid densities ρ_o and ρ_w	835 and $1,000$ kg/m^3
Initial reservoir pressure	260 bars
Injector BHP range	275 – 450 bars
Producer BHP range	100 – 250 bars
Production period	10 years
Control interval	2 years

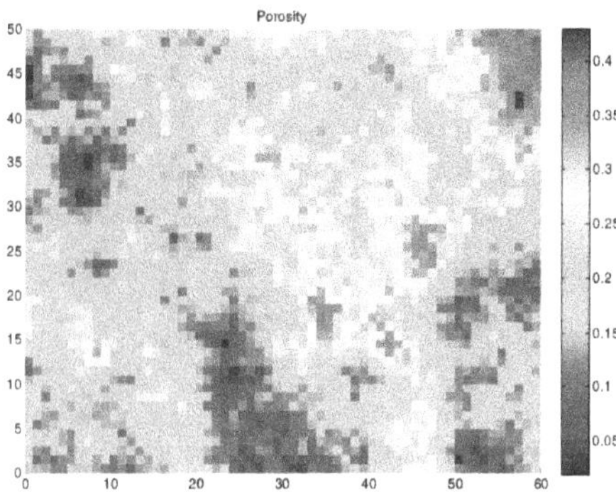

Figure 1: Porosity field.

where $\mathbf{x}$ is the solution vector encoding the spatial coordinates of each well, for instance, $\mathbf{x} = [x_1, x_2, ..., x_n]$, where (x_1, x_2) is the coordinate pair of the first well, (x_3, x_4) represents the coordinate pair of the second well, and so on. The parameters c_o, $c_{w,disp}$, and $c_{w,inj}$ represent, respectively, the value of each barrel of oil produced, the cost of disposing of each barrel of produced water, and the cost of injecting a barrel of water into the reservoir. The functions $q^-_{n,o}(\mathbf{x}, t)$ and $q^-_{n,w}(\mathbf{x}, t)$ are the oil and water production rates (barrels/day) at a producer, while $q^+_{n,w}(\mathbf{x}, t)$ is the daily water injection rate at an injector. Note that these rates are determined from a reservoir simulation according to the value of $\mathbf{x}$. The yearly interest rate is specified by r. The economic parameter values shown in Table 2 are the same as provided in [16] for all experiments.

Table 2: Economic parameters values as in [16].

Parameter	Value
c_o	80/bbl
$c_{w,disp}$	12/bbl
$c_{w,inj}$	8/bbl
r	10% or 0%
Threshold for water cut	78%

The experiments to calculate the NPV were completed using the Matlab Reservoir Simulation Toolbox (MRST) [20] which solves the flow and transport equations in alternating steps, in order to determine the phase pressures, flow rates and saturation at every time point. Modelling of simple vertical wells is provided using the Peaceman model [29].

The optimization problem consisted of the placement of two injectors and two producers in a reservoir model under conditions according to Table 1, constrained to a minimum distance between wells equal to 250m.

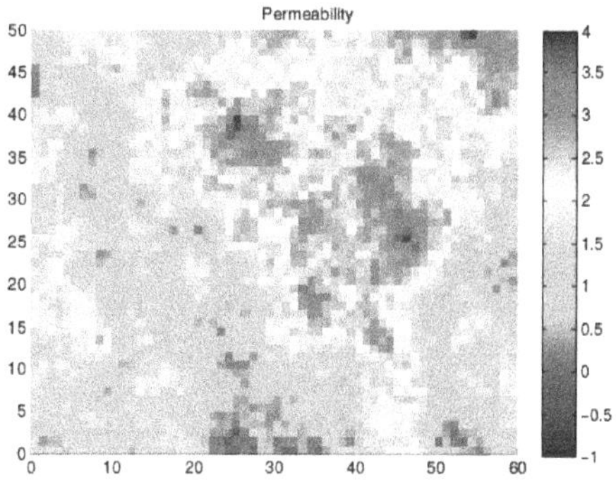

Figure 2: Permeability (mD) in logarithmic color scale.

We considered three optimization subproblems as in [16] in order to compare those results with the ones obtained in this paper:

- Case 1: no constraints regarding injection and production rates, and $r = 10\%$;
- Case 2: no constraints regarding injection and production rates, and $r = 0\%$;
- Case 3: maximum flow constraints regarding to injection and production rates equal to $1,000$ m^3/day, and $r = 10\%$.

The next section presents the meta-heuristic employed here to solve the well-placement problem.

3.2 Differential Evolution

DE [31] is a floating-point encoding populational meta-heuristic, working as an evolutionary algorithm, with only a few control parameters [10, 4]. Several papers have shown that the classical DE and its variants outperform many other optimization methods, in terms of both convergence speed and robustness, when applied to hard benchmark functions and real-world problems. These problems include unconstrained global optimization [39], constrained optimization [11], multi-objective optimization [23], large-scale optimization [6, 38], and optimization in dynamic and uncertain environments [22, 13].

The DE algorithm proceeds by randomly initializing (commonly using a uniform distribution) a population of D-dimensional vectors inside the problem bounds, and evaluating the objective/fitness function for all the vectors in the population. Then, until a stopping condition is satisfied, the algorithm performs an iterative evolutionary process of mutation, crossover, and selection operators.

For each vector $\mathbf{x}_i$ in a population of size N, the mutation operator uses the weighted difference of parent solutions to generate mutation vectors $\mathbf{v}_i$. The two well-known mutation strategies investigated in this work are **rand/1** and **current-to-best/1** [26], which are represented, respectively, by Eqs. 2 and 3:

$$\mathbf{v}_i = \mathbf{x}_{r1} + F.(\mathbf{x}_{r2} - \mathbf{x}_{r3}), \quad (2)$$

$$\mathbf{v}_i = \mathbf{x}_i + F.(\mathbf{x}_{best} - \mathbf{x}_i) + F.(\mathbf{x}_{r1} - \mathbf{x}_{r2}), \quad (3)$$

where $\mathbf{x}_{r1}$, $\mathbf{x}_{r2}$ and $\mathbf{x}_{r3}$ are three distinct and randomly chosen vectors from the population, $\mathbf{x}_{best}$ is the best vector from the population, $F \in [0, 2]$ is the mutation factor, and . denotes a scalar-vector product. In the *rand/1* strategy, the base vector to be perturbed is randomly selected from the population, and will move in the direction of the other two random vectors. Therefore, it is possible that only poor solutions are chosen to generate offspring. Obviously, the repetition of this could result in a poor search. Given that the best solution of the population is eventually chosen, the search tends to the best solution through the optimization process [18]. However, it is also clear that the bigger the population the lower the chance of selecting the current best solution.

On the other hand, the *current-to-best/1* strategy uses as a base vector each member of the population; thus all best solutions will always be chosen. Moreover, the best solution found so far is always used to calculate the difference vector, not only guiding the search towards the current best but also performing a localized search. In this case, smaller populations give faster convergence with lower exploratory capability and may result in the search getting trapped in low-quality optima [18].

The crossover operator is applied on $\mathbf{v}_i$ to generate the final offspring vector $\mathbf{u}_i$ whose j-th component is given as

$$\mathbf{u}_{i,j} = \begin{cases} \mathbf{v}_{i,j} & \text{if } U(0,1) \leq CR \text{ or } j = j_{rand}, \\ \mathbf{x}_{i,j} & \text{otherwise,} \end{cases} \quad (4)$$

where $U(0, 1)$ is a random floating-point number from a uniform distribution between 0 and 1 generated for each j, $CR \in [0, 1]$ is the crossover probability, and j_{rand} is a randomly chosen index from $[1, D]$.

Finally, the selection operator selects the best evaluated vector between $\mathbf{x}_i$ and $\mathbf{u}_i$. The offspring replaces the parent if its fitness value is better. Otherwise, the parent is maintained in the population.

As one may notice, DE has four parameters: N, F, CR, and the mutation strategy. Therefore, in this paper we experiment with several configurations to show that, when properly configured, DE can have a good performance in a well placement problem.

4. EXPERIMENTAL ANALYSIS

In this paper we investigate the performance of DE using eight distinct configurations to solve the three well-placement problems described in Section 3.1. The distinct configurations are specified in Table 3, and suggested by [36, 10]. The stopping criterion is 10,000 objective function evaluations (simulations using MRST) as in [16].

Table 3: DE configurations.

Configuration	N	CR	F	Mutation
1	100	0.5	0.9	rand/1
2	100	0.9	0.5	rand/1
3	200	0.5	0.9	rand/1
4	200	0.9	0.5	rand/1
5	100	0.5	0.9	current-to-best/1
6	100	0.9	0.5	current-to-best/1
7	200	0.5	0.9	current-to-best/1
8	200	0.9	0.5	current-to-best/1

As can be observed in Table 3, four parameters were modified. More extensive tests, using a larger number of configurations, could not be performed because the simulation is computationally expensive. Therefore, it is possible that an untested configuration leads to even better results than those in the current work. However, those eight configurations allow the identification of interesting behaviours.

Since meta-heuristics have stochastic components, it is necessary to perform multiple runs in order to assess the average performance. Thus, each configuration was independently run 30 times, with distinct seeds, to allow for a more accurate comparison.

A death penalty approach was adopted for constraint handling. That means 1) if DE generates a solution for well placement in which the minimum distance between wells is less than 250m, then the NPV for this solution is set to minus infinity; and 2) if the maximum flow of a well during the production time is above $1,000$ m^3/day, then the simulation is interrupted and the NPV is also set to minus infinity (only applied in Case 3).

4.1 Results

Tables 4-6 show the results for each DE configuration for each case described in Section 3.1 with respect to fitness value, i.e, NPV. The first column of the tables labels the methods (DE configurations and memetic PSO [16]). The second column gives the best NPV found during the optimization process, while the third shows the worst NPV obtained. The mean, standard deviation (SD), and median values of NPV are shown in the fourth, fifth, and sixth columns respectively. The last line of the tables presents the results from [16], which were obtained by decoupling the well placement and control problems. That approach can be described in three steps: 1) PSO was used to determine the optimal well positions under a fixed control procedure; 2) once optimal positions were found under the fixed control procedure, the controls and positions were optimized locally using general pattern search (GPS) with standard search directions. To generate our results with DE we used the optimal control strategy found in [16] and then determined optimal well placement.

Figures 3, 5, and 7 show bean plots of the NPV distribution (over 30 trials) for each DE configuration for Cases 1-3, and for memetic PSO [16]. The short horizontal lines are the NPVs for all trials. The median is represented by the thick horizontal black line. The average of all observations is presented as the dashed horizontal line.

Figures 4, 6, and 8 show the NPVs with respect to the number of function evaluations for each DE configuration for Cases 1-3. Each curve represents the mean performance of the 30 trials for each configuration.

Table 4: Results for Case 1 described in Section 3.1.

	NPV ($ \times 10^8$)				
Method	Best	Worst	Mean	SD	Median
Config. 1	5.99	5.50	5.67	0.13	5.63
Config. 2	6.21	5.56	5.83	0.18	5.82
Config. 3	5.82	5.33	5.57	0.12	5.56
Config. 4	5.88	5.36	5.64	0.16	5.60
Config. 5	6.24	5.61	5.95	0.16	5.96
Config. 6	6.51	5.34	5.98	0.29	6.03
Config. 7	6.06	5.43	5.79	0.15	5.77
Config. 8	6.49	5.40	6.11	0.27	6.18
memetic PSO [16]	6.30	5.97	6.15	-	-

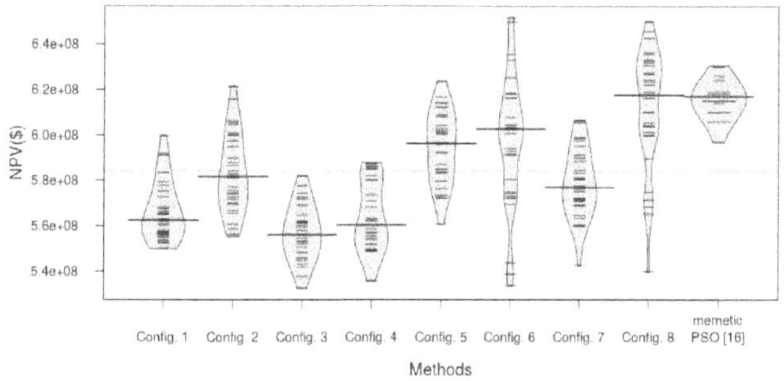

Figure 3: Bean plots of the NPV distribution for Case 1. The short horizontal lines are the NPVs for all trials. The median is represented by the thick horizontal black line. The average of all observations is presented as the dashed horizontal line.

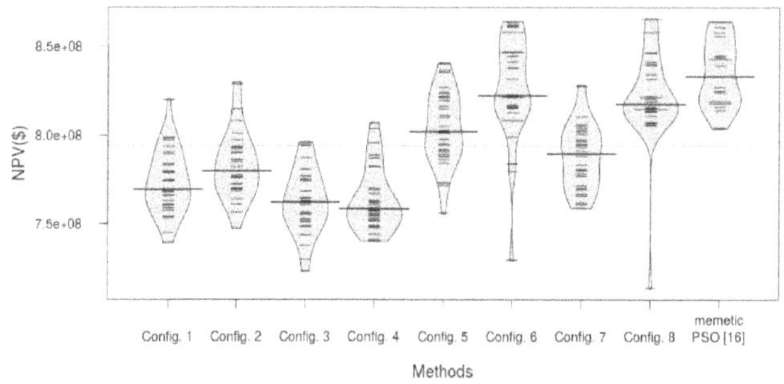

Figure 5: Bean plots of the NPV distribution for Case 2. The short horizontal lines are the NPVs for all trials. The median is represented by the thick horizontal black line. The average of all observations is presented as the dashed horizontal line.

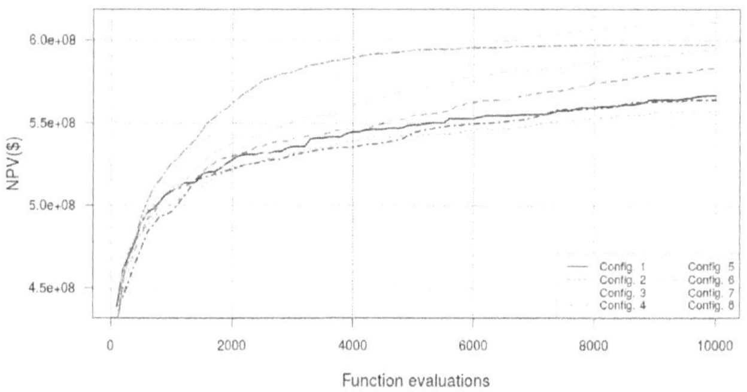

Figure 4: Convergence plots of the NPV versus the number of function evaluations for Case 1. Each curve represents the mean performance of the 30 trials for each DE configuration.

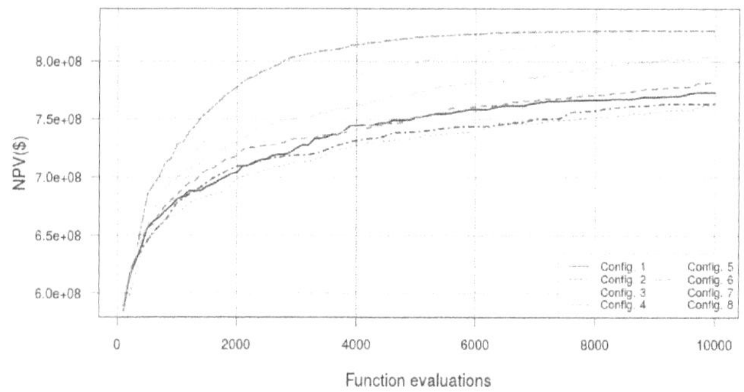

Figure 6: Convergence plots of the NPV versus the number of function evaluations for Case 2. Each curve represents the mean performance of the 30 trials for each DE configuration.

Table 5: Results for Case 2 described in Section 3.1.

	NPV ($\$ \times 10^8$)				
Method	Best	Worst	Mean	SD	Median
Config. 1	8.19	7.39	7.73	0.18	7.69
Config. 2	8.29	7.48	7.83	0.19	7.79
Config. 3	7.96	7.24	7.63	0.18	7.62
Config. 4	8.07	7.40	7.64	0.18	7.59
Config. 5	8.40	7.56	8.04	0.20	8.02
Config. 6	8.64	7.29	8.26	0.29	8.22
Config. 7	8.28	7.59	7.88	0.19	7.89
Config. 8	8.66	7.14	8.22	0.27	8.18
memetic PSO [16]	8.64	8.04	8.35	-	-

4.2 Discussions

Considering the experiments in this paper for Case 1, the best NPV, according to Table 4, was found by Config. 6, while the worst one was obtained by Config. 3. Configuration 8 presented the highest median NPV. In turn, Config. 6 showed the highest SD. DE was able to find better solutions than those found in [16] by the decoupled method, but the mean NPV was a little lower, and the worst solutions were lower than those from [16] because of the outliers. Given that we did not employ any local search method, the results of DE are very satisfactory. Moreover, one usually selects the best solution to solve a problem, not the mean solution.

As one can notice in Fig. 3, the distributions of the final NPVs for each DE configuration are clearly not Gaussian; thus the mean and SD are not adequate measures to describe the distributions. The average of all observations is presented as the dashed horizontal line right above 5.8×10^8.

Configs. 2, 4, 6, and 8, that used $CR = 0.9$ and $F = 0.5$, presented more variance in the distribution than the other configurations. However, the best results were obtained by Config. 6 and Config. 8. We noticed that Config. 8 gave the highest median, represented by the thick horizontal black line. Configuration 6 obtained the second best result, followed by Config. 5. The worst performance was presented by Config. 3. This information is also shown in Table 4, but the bean plot allows for the visualization of the concentration of solutions with similar values and the identification of outliers. For instance, Config. 6 and Config. 8 found the best solutions, but also some very poor ones. Configuration 8 had a high concentration of solutions close to 6.3×10^8 and 6.0×10^8. On the other hand, based on the plot one may say that the best solution found by Config. 6 was an outlier, since the high concentration was around 6.0×10^8.

Another pattern identified in Fig. 3 is that for *rand/1*, the bigger N, the worse the result (see Config. 1-4). For the *current-to-best/1* strategy, the increase in N considerably improved the solutions for Config. 8, but worsened the

Table 6: Results for Case 3 described in Section 3.1.

Method	NPV ($\$ \times 10^8$)				
	Best	Worst	Mean	SD	Median
Config. 1	5.60	5.02	5.35	0.14	5.35
Config. 2	5.78	5.07	5.46	0.18	5.42
Config. 3	5.56	4.98	5.22	0.15	5.20
Config. 4	5.73	5.11	5.34	0.16	5.31
Config. 5	5.94	5.31	5.59	0.16	5.58
Config. 6	6.18	5.19	5.81	0.28	5.87
Config. 7	5.75	5.26	5.46	0.12	5.45
Config. 8	6.17	5.25	5.81	0.24	5.82
memetic PSO [16]	6.05	5.63	5.89	-	-

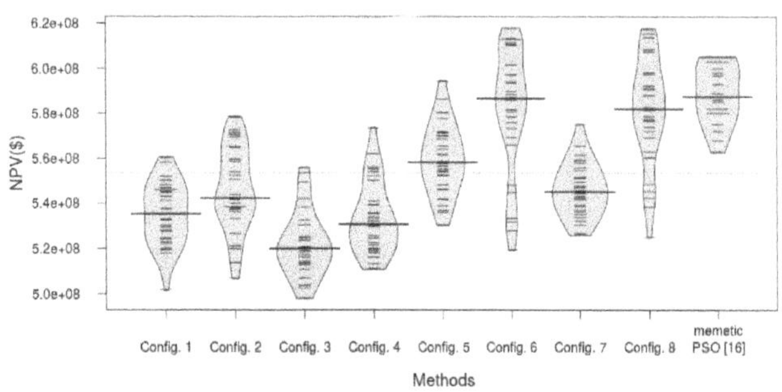

Figure 7: Bean plots of the NPV distribution for Case 3. The short horizontal lines are the NPVs for all trials. The median is represented by the thick horizontal black line. The average of all observations is presented as the dashed horizontal line.

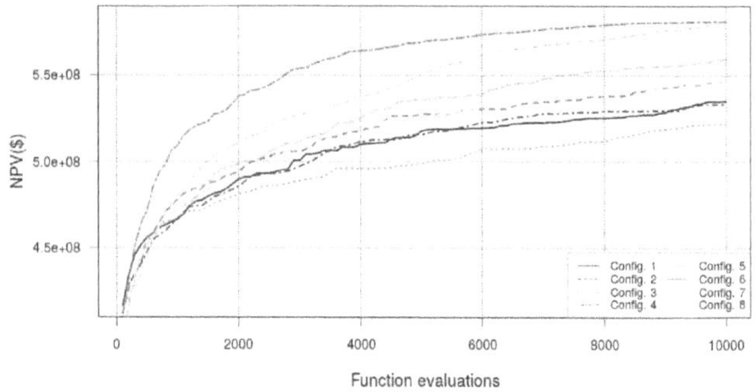

Figure 8: Convergence plots of the NPV versus the number of function evaluations for Case 3. Each curve represents the mean performance of the 30 trials for each DE configuration.

solutions for Config. 7. We believe that Config. 7 was worse than Config. 5 because when $CR = 0.5$, only 50% of the mutated vector will be incorporated into the trial solution. As N for Config. 7 is twice as in Config. 5, it is performing half the number of iterations. Therefore, it would need much more function evaluations to transfer useful information to the offspring.

Regarding the results from [16] shown in Fig. 3, one can notice that the distributions of the final NPVs seems Gaussian, and presents a high concentration of solutions around 6.17×10^8. In turn, Config. 8 obtained the highest median NPV and a greater concentration of solutions above the median compared to that from [16], even presenting more variance in the distribution. As shown in Table 4 and Fig. 3, Configs. 6 and 8 gave higher NPVs than the highest NPV found in [16]. Memetic PSO was more stable than DE for this case, giving smaller variance in the results. On the other hand, DE found several solutions considerably better than those of memetic PSO. Therefore, for Case 1 we conclude that even though the memetic PSO presents a higher mean NPV than DE, DE has a higher probability of finding better solutions than the memetic PSO.

In the convergence plots of Fig. 4, one may observe that Config. 6 was the fastest method to find high quality solutions; it presented the highest NPV using 6,000 function evaluations, but then stagnated. After 6,000 function evaluations, Config. 8 obtained the highest NPV. A possible explanation is that these configurations have 90% chance of considering the parent's information ($CR = 0.9$). Configuration 6 lost diversity faster than Config. 8, which kept improving because of a bigger N. Config. 5 shows a NPV close to Config. 6 in the end, and would probably outperform it if more iterations were allowed. The worst mean performance was presented by Config. 3. The other configurations showed an intermediate performance.

Regarding Case 2, one can see in Table 5 that the best solution was found by Config. 8, whereas both Config. 6 and memetic PSO [16] found the second-best solution. On the other hand, the mean value of the simulations in [16] is higher, as is the worst solution found. This means that DE got stuck in local optima more often than the memetic PSO in [16], or that DE could not properly refine the solutions. Nevertheless, it is reasonable to think that a DE with local search could be more competitive.

When evaluating the bean plots shown in Fig. 5, we can see that the worst values for Configs. 6 and 8 were outliers. Thus, the worst, mean, and SD from Table 5 must be carefully evaluated; they are descriptive statistics of the data, but do not tell the whole story.

Patterns observed in Case 1 bean plots for DE are also valid in Case 2. For instance, *current-to-best/1* was noticeably the best mutation strategy, even though it gave a higher variance. Choosing CR to be larger than F results in better median solutions, except for Config. 4. Also, for *rand/1* a larger N showed worse results than a smaller N. The main difference here is that Config. 6 was better than Config. 8, with more solutions near the best ones, i.e, with a high concentration of solutions close to 8.6×10^8, possibly due to a smaller N leading to faster convergence.

Another interesting fact is that the bean plot shapes of Config. 6 and [16] are similar, except for the tail of the bean plot for Config. 6 which is caused by the 4 poor solutions found. As in Case 1, memetic PSO presented a smaller variance in the results than DE. On the other hand, DE Config. 6 gave more solutions near the best overall even though it obtained a median NPV lower than that from [16].

In the convergence plots for Case 2 in Fig. 6, one can notice that, once again, Config. 6 gave a faster approximation to the best solution, followed by Config. 8. High-quality solutions were found by Config. 6 requiring less than 6,000 function evaluations, and the remaining function evaluations gave small adjustments in the solution. However, as the DE used in this work does not have a local-search mechanism, the refinement was insufficient to give dramatically better results in most runs.

For Case 3, one can observe in Table 6 that the best NPV was found by Config. 6, and Config. 8 found the second-best

NPV. Thus, two DE configurations were able to find better solutions than those found in [16]. However, as in Case 1, the mean performance of DE was a little lower and the worse solutions were lower than obtained in [16]. This confirms that a memetic DE could be more competitive, since DE got stuck in local optima more often than the memetic PSO used in [16].

Considering the bean plots of DE shown in Fig. 7 for Case 3, Config. 6 presented the highest median, followed by Config. 8. Analogous to Case 1, the worst performance was presented by Config. 3. This information can be seen in Table 6 and Fig. 8 as well. As in Cases 1 and 2, the patterns observed in Figs. 3 and 5 are also valid for Fig. 7 of Case 3. For example, worse NPVs are obtained with a large N. Better median NPVs are achieved when CR is larger than F. Even though presenting a higher variance, *current-to-best/1* was clearly the best mutation strategy. As in Case 2, Config. 6 presented more solutions near to the best ones, i.e, close to 6.18×10^8.

Analogous to Fig. 3, we can also see in Fig. 7 that Config. 6 and Config. 8 presented higher NPVs than the best NPV found by [16]. Although Config. 6 gave a higher variance in the results it obtained a median NPV close to that from [16].

According to Fig. 8, once again, Config. 6 presented the faster convergence, followed by Config. 8. As mentioned in Section 3.2, for the configurations that use *current-to-best/1* strategy, smaller N values give faster convergence. Also, Config. 3 showed the worst mean performance. As mentioned for Cases 1 and 2, we believe that all solutions could be better if a local-search was employed since the results from basic DE configurations were competitive with those from memetic PSO [16].

5. CONCLUSIONS AND FUTURE WORK

In this paper, we presented a study of the performance of eight DE configurations in solving a well placement problem. DE was tested with different values for N, CR, and F, and also two well-known distinct mutation strategies. The SPE10 base case was the benchmark dataset, and the simulator used was MRST. We solved three optimization problems with or without constraints, and with or without discounting rate. For each one, a bare control procedure was assumed with a control interval of 2 years, and the parameters representing spatial coordinates of vertical wells, injectors and producers, were optimized. Performance of DE in solving that problem was compared with results of the memetic PSO from [16].

According to the preliminary analysis performed in this paper, *current-to-best/1* was visibly the best mutation strategy, in spite of a higher variance in the NPV results. Choosing $CR = 0.9$ resulted in better median solutions than with $CR = 0.5$. Moreover, a larger N showed worse results. Thus, for the cases tested in this paper one should not expect good results using *rand/1* as mutation strategy or using $CR = 0.5$.

For all three optimization problems considered, DE found better NPVs than those found in [16]. On the other hand, the memetic PSO used in [16] was more stable with the highest mean NPV, and the poorest results found by memetic PSO were higher than the poorest results found by DE.

As future work we intend to use a DE algorithm capable of automatically adapting its parameters, and also add a local-search mechanism. Such a DE variant may not only be as stable as the memetic PSO, but also reach better median values for all problems.

Acknowledgments

The authors would like to thank the anonymous reviewers for their valuable comments and suggestions to improve the quality of the paper, and National Council for Scientific and Technological Development (CNPq), grant 248571/2013-3, and NSERC by support this research.

6. REFERENCES

[1] S. Afshari, M. R. Pishvaie, and B. Aminshahidy. Well placement optimization using a particle swarm optimization algorithm, a novel approach. *PETROL SCI TECHNOL*, 32(2):170–179, 2014.

[2] A. A. Awotunde and N. Sibaweihi. Consideration of voidage-replacement ratio in well-placement optimization. *SPE Economics & Management*, 6(1), 2014.

[3] W. Bangerth, H. Klie, M. Wheeler, P. Stoffa, and M. Sen. On optimization algorithms for the reservoir oil well placement problem. *COMPUTAT GEOSCI*, 10(3):303–319, 2006.

[4] I. Boussaïd, J. Lepagnot, and P. Siarry. A survey on optimization metaheuristics. *INFORM SCIENCES*, 237(0):82 – 117, 2013.

[5] Z. Bouzarkouna, D. Ding, and A. Auger. Well placement optimization with the covariance matrix adaptation evolution strategy and meta-models. *COMPUTAT GEOSCI*, 16(1):75–92, 2012.

[6] J. Brest, A. Zamuda, I. Fister, and M. Maučec. Large scale global optimization using self-adaptive differential evolution algorithm. In *IEEE C EVOL COMPUTAT*, pages 1–8, July 2010.

[7] U. K. Chakraborty. *Advances in Differential Evolution*. Springer, 2008.

[8] M. A. Christie and M. J. Blunt. Tenth spe comparative solution project: A comparison of upscaling techniques. In *SPE Reservoir Simulation Symposium*. SPE, Feb. 2001.

[9] R. A. Clark and B. Ludolph. Voidage replacement ratio calculations in retrograde condensate to volatile oil reservoirs undergoing eor processes. In *SPE Annual Technical Conference and Exhibition*. SPE, Oct. 2003.

[10] S. Das and P. N. Suganthan. Differential evolution: A survey of the state-of-the-art. *IEEE T EVOLUT COMPUT*, 15(1):4–31, 2011.

[11] V. V. de Melo and G. L. C. Carosio. Investigating multi-view differential evolution for solving constrained engineering design problems. *EXPERT SYST APPL*, 40(9):3370–3377, July 2013.

[12] Y. Ding. Optimization of well placement using evolutionary methods. In *Europec/EAGE Conference and Exhibition*. SPE, June 2008.

[13] M. du Plessis and A. Engelbrecht. Using competitive population evaluation in a differential evolution algorithm for dynamic environments. *EUR J OPER RES*, 218(1):7–20, 2012.

[14] R. Fonseca, O. Leeuwenburgh, P. Van den Hof, and J. Jansen. Improving the ensemble optimization method through covariance matrix adaptation (cma-enopt). In *Reservoir Simulation Symposium*. SPE, 2013.

[15] A. Hashim Ahmed, A. Awotunde, O. Mutrif Siddig, and M. Jamal. A pareto-based well placement optimization. In *76th EAGE Conference and Exhibition 2014*. EAGE, June 2014.

[16] T. D. Humphries, R. D. Haynes, and L. A. James. Simultaneous and sequential approaches to joint optimization of well placement and control. *COMPUTAT GEOSCI*, 18(3-4):433–448, 2014.

[17] O. J. Isebor, L. J. Durlofsky, and D. Echeverría Ciaurri. A derivative-free methodology with local and global search for the constrained joint optimization of well locations and controls. *COMPUTAT GEOSCI*, pages 1–20, 2013.

[18] S. Islam, S. Das, S. Ghosh, S. Roy, and P. Suganthan. An adaptive differential evolution algorithm with novel mutation and crossover strategies for global numerical optimization. *IEEE T SYST MAN CY B*, 42(2):482–500, Apr. 2012.

[19] J. Leskinen, F. Neri, and P. Neittaanmäki. Memetic variation local search vs. life-time learning in electrical impedance tomography. In M. Giacobini, A. Brabazon, S. Cagnoni, G. Di Caro, A. Ekárt, A. Esparcia-Alcázar, M. Farooq, A. Fink, and P. Machado, editors, *Applications of Evolutionary Computing*, volume 5484 of *LECT NOTES COMPUT SC*, pages 615–624. Springer, 2009.

[20] K. Lie, S. Krogstad, I. S. Ligaarden, J. R. Natvig, H. M. Nilsen, and B. Skaflestad. Open-source matlab implementation of consistent discretisations on complex grids. *COMPUTAT GEOSCI*, 16(2):297–322, 2012.

[21] J. Lyons and H. Nasrabadi. Well placement optimization under time-dependent uncertainty using an ensemble kalman filter and a genetic algorithm. *J PETROL SCI ENG*, 109(0):70 – 79, 2013.

[22] R. Mendes and A. S. Mohais. Dynde: a differential evolution for dynamic optimization problems. In *Congress on Evolutionary Computation*, pages 2808–2815, 2005.

[23] E. Mezura-Montes, M. Reyes-Sierra, and C. Coello. Multi-objective optimization using differential evolution: A survey of the state-of-the-art. In U. Chakraborty, editor, *Advances in Differential Evolution*, volume 143 of *STUD COMP INTELL*, pages 173–196. Springer, 2008.

[24] A. N. Morales, H. Nasrabadi, and D. Zhu. A modified genetic algorithm for horizontal well placement optimization in gas condensate reservoirs. In *SPE Annual Technical Conference and Exhibition*. SPE, Sept. 2010.

[25] F. Neri, G. Iacca, and E. Mininno. Disturbed exploitation compact differential evolution for limited memory optimization problems. *INFORM SCIENCES*, 181(12):2469 – 2487, 2011.

[26] F. Neri and V. Tirronen. Recent advances in differential evolution: a survey and experimental analysis. *ARTIF INTELL REV*, 33(1-2):61–106, 2010.

[27] E. Nwankwor, A. Nagar, and D. Reid. Hybrid differential evolution and particle swarm optimization for optimal well placement. *COMPUTAT GEOSCI*, 17(2):249–268, 2013.

[28] J. E. Onwunalu and L. J. Durlofsky. Application of a particle swarm optimization algorithm for determining optimum well location and type. *COMPUTAT GEOSCI*, 14(1):183–198, 2010.

[29] D. Peaceman. Interpretation of well-block pressures in numerical reservoir simulation. *SPE Journal*, 18(3):183–194, 1978.

[30] P. Sarma and W. H. Chen. Efficient well placement optimization with gradient-based algorithms and adjoint models. In *Reservoir Simulation Symposium*. SPE, Feb. 2008.

[31] R. Storn and K. Price. Differential Evolution - A Simple and Efficient Heuristic for Global Optimization over Continuous Spaces. *J GLOBAL OPTIM*, 11(4):341–359, Dec. 1997.

[32] E.-G. Talbi. *Metaheuristics - From Design to Implementation*. Wiley, 2009.

[33] C. Temizel, S. Purwar, K. Urrutia, A. Abdullayev, F. Md Adnan, A. Agarwal, A. Garcia, and S. E. Gorucu. Optimization of well placement in real-time production optimization of intelligent fields with use of local and global methods. In *SPE Annual Technical Conference and Exhibition*. SPE, Oct. 2014.

[34] V. Tirronen, F. Neri, T. Kärkkäinen, K. Majava, and T. Rossi. An enhanced memetic differential evolution in filter design for defect detection in paper production. *EVOL COMPUT*, 16(4):529–555, Dec. 2008.

[35] B. Yeten, L. J. Durlofsky, and K. Aziz. Optimization of nonconventional well type, location, and trajectory. *SPE Journal*, 8(3):200–210, 2003.

[36] J. Zhang and A. C. Sanderson. Jade: Adaptive differential evolution with optional external archive. *IEEE T EVOLUT COMPUT*, 13(5):945–958, 2009.

[37] K. Zhang, G. Li, A. C. Reynolds, J. Yao, and L. Zhang. Optimal well placement using an adjoint gradient. *J PETROL SCI ENG*, 73(3-4):220–226, 2010.

[38] X. Zhou, Z. Wu, and H. Wang. Elite opposition-based differential evolution for solving large-scale optimization problems and its implementation on gpu. In *Parallel and Distributed Computing, Applications and Technologies (PDCAT), 2012 13th International Conference on*, pages 727–732, Dec. 2012.

[39] D. Zou, J. Wu, L. Gao, and S. Li. A modified differential evolution algorithm for unconstrained optimization problems. *Neurocomputing*, 120(0):469 – 481, 2013. Image Feature Detection and Description.

An Integrated Approach to Stage 1 Breast Cancer Detection

Jeannie M. Fitzgerald
University of Limerick, Ireland
jeannie.fitzgerald@ul.ie

Conor Ryan
University of Limerick, Ireland
conor.ryan@ul.ie

David Medernach
University of Limerick, Ireland
david.medernach@ul.ie

Krzysztof Krawiec
Poznan University of Technology
krawiec@cs.put.poznan.pl

ABSTRACT

We present an automated, end-to-end approach for Stage 1 breast cancer detection. The first phase of our proposed work-flow takes individual digital mammograms as input and outputs several smaller sub-images from which the background has been removed. Next, we extract a set of features which capture textural information from the segmented images.

In the final phase, the most salient of these features are fed into a Multi-Objective Genetic Programming system which then evolves classifiers capable of identifying those segments which may have suspicious areas that require further investigation.

A key aspect of this work is the examination of several new experimental configurations which focus on textural asymmetry between breasts. The best evolved classifier using such a configuration can deliver results of 100% accuracy on true positives and a false positive per image rating of just 0.33, which is better than the current state of the art.

Categories and Subject Descriptors

1.2.2 [**Artificial Intelligence**]: ;Automatic Programming

Keywords

Mammography; Classification; Multi-Objective Genetic Programming

1. BACKGROUND

Routine mammographic screening, particularly at a national level, is by far the most effective tool for the early detection and subsequent successful treatment of breast cancer [30, 32]. It is essential to discover signs of cancer early, as survival is directly correlated with early detection [32].

GECCO '15, July 11 - 15, 2015, Madrid, Spain

ISBN 978-1-4503-3472-3/15/07...$15.00

DOI: http://dx.doi.org/10.1145/2739480.2754761

The introduction of breast screening programs has contributed to a significantly higher demand for radiologists, and a world wide shortage of qualified radiologists who specialize in mammography [3] has led to many radiologists being dangerously overworked [2]. This is likely to lead to (i) there being insufficient time for radiologists to interpret mammograms (which are notoriously difficult to read); (ii) an inability to provide redundant readings (second reader); and (iii) radiologists being overly conservative, which in turn is likely to increase the number of patient call backs, potentially resulting in unnecessary biopsies which may lead to patient anxiety and mistrust of the system.

Fortunately, the increased availability of digital mammography means that it is now much more feasible to use automated methods to assist with detection. A mammogram is performed by compressing the breast between two plates which are attached to a mammogram machine: an adjustable plate on top with a fixed x-ray plate underneath. An image is recorded using a digital detector located on the bottom plate. Two views of each breast are recorded: the craniocaudal (CC) view, which is a top down view, and the mediolateral oblique (MLO) view, which is a side view taken at an angle. Functional breast tissue is termed *parenchyma* and this appears as white areas on a mammogram, while the black areas are composed of adipose (non-functioning, fatty) tissue which is transparent under X-rays.

Various levels of automation exist in mammography, and these can generally be divided into Computer-Aided *Detection* (CAD) and Computer-Aided *Diagnosis* (CADx) [20]. In this work we concentrate exclusively on CAD. In particular, what is known as *Stage 1* detection.

A stage 1 detector examines mammograms and highlights *suspicious* areas that require further investigation. For this task, it is important to strike a balance: an overly conservative approach degenerates to marking every mammogram (or *segment* of) as suspicious, while missing a cancerous area can have disastrous consequences. Our objective is to develop a stage 1 detector that is highly accurate in terms of detecting suspicious areas (True Positives (TP)) with as few false alarms (False Positives (FP)) as possible. In the literature, it is relatively standard practice to convert FP to False Positives Per Image (FPPI).

The potential for CAD to improve screening mammography outcomes by increasing the cancer detection rate has been shown in several retrospective studies including that of Cupples et al. [5] who reported an overall increase of 16% in the cancer detection rates using CAD together with traditional detection methods. In that study, CAD increased the detection rate of small invasive cancers by 164%.

The remainder of this paper is organised as follows: In Section 2 we outline related work, then in Section 3 we provide a detailed description of our proposed workflow, next in Section 4 we further describe our experiments and report results and finally, in Section 5 we state our conclusions and propose avenues for future research.

2. RELATED WORK

Previous GP research effort such as that of Nandi et al. [14, 24] has successfully tackled both feature selection and the classification of previously identified abnormalities as either benign or malignant.

Other notable research using GP is that Ahmad et al. [1] who designed a Stage 2 cancer detector for the well known Wisconsin Breast Cancer dataset, in which they used the features extracted from a series of fine needle aspirations and an evolved neural network. Ludwig and Roos [19] used GP to estimate the prognosis of breast cancer patients from the same data set, using GP to reduce the number of features before evolving predictors. Langdon and Harrison [17] took a different approach, using biopsy gene chip data, but their system approached a similar level of automation.

More recent GP effort in mammography has been concerned with a combination of feature detection and classification. One such study by Ryan et al. [29] reports a best TP Rate of 100% with an FPPI of just 1.5%. In other work, the best reported seems to be that of Li et al [18] which reports a 97.3% TP rate and 14.81 FPPI. Similar work by Polakowski [27] had a lower TP rate (92%) but with a much lower FPPI rate (8.39).

The standard method of reporting results is to use a TP/FPPI breakdown, which is what we will present here. However, it is important to note that while TP rates may be directly comparable if the same volumes are used, FPPI may not be, as the metric depends to some extent on the number of mammographic regions examined and the detection objective of the system. See 3.1 for further explanation.

Regarding the various types of features that have been studied, those which capture aspects of shape [28], edge-sharpness [23] and texture [4] have been used for mass segmentation and detection. Nandi et al. [24] reported a classification accuracy of 98% using a combination of all three of these feature types.

The majority of existing GP systems operate only at the *classification stage* and rely upon previously extracted features, and with the exception of Ryan et al. [29], all of the previous work mentioned above, deals with a single breast in isolation. In this paper, we are influenced by the research of Tabar [33] which indicates that, in general, both breasts from the same patient have the same textural characteristics. Our hypothesis is that the existence of suspicious areas may be more likely if a patient's breasts are texturally different from each other.

Another strong argument in favour of considering textural aspects is the connection between breast density and breast cancer. Density of breast tissue is an important attribute of the parenchyma and it has been established that mammograms of dense breasts are more challenging for human experts. At the same time, repeated studies have demonstrated that women with dense tissue in greater than 75% of the breast are 4- to 6 times more likely to develop breast cancer compared with women with little to no breast density [22].

A complete review of the important relevant research is beyond the scope of this paper. The interested reader is directed to [26] for an evaluation of the recent state-of-the-art in computer-aided detection and diagnosis systems.

3. WORKFLOW

Given the importance of parenchymal density as a risk factor and the difficulty for human experts in identifying suspicious areas in this challenging environment, we believe that a stage 1 detector which focuses on *textural asymmetry* may have a strong decision support role to play in the identification of suspicious mammograms. GP is particularly suitable for this type of task as it is very flexible, is capable of automated feature selection and extraction, and most importantly in the medical domain – provides an explanation for classification decisions in the form of a human readable program.

With this in mind, we develop an automated stage 1 detection system with GP [15] at its centre, where parenchymal texture and textural asymmetry between both breasts of the same patient determines the choice of image features (feature detection) and the construction of input datasets which leverage this data. In doing so, we extend the work of [29] by considering a different set of features and a greater number of configurations.

Our work-flow begins with background suppression and image segmentation and then progresses to the generation of textural features. These are fed through the system, which performs feature reduction before passing the most salient ones to GP to evolve classifiers. The best resulting classifiers deliver results of 100% accuracy on true positives and a false positive per image rating of just 0.33, which is appreciably better than prior work.

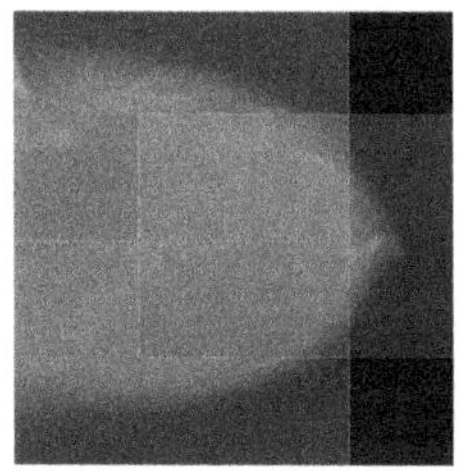

Figure 1: Image Segmentation

3.1 Background Suppression and Image Segmentation

The background of the mammographic image is never perfectly homogeneous, and it includes at least one tag letter indicating whether the image is either a right or left breast. This is often augmented by a string of characters indicating which view (CC or MLO) was taken. These backgrounds need to be replaced with homogeneous ones to correctly process the image in a later stage. We used the same approach as in [29] to suppress the image background.

We chose to divide each image into three segments, and to examine each segment separately. As there can be more than one suspicious area in an image, we return *true* for as many segments as the system finds suspicious, meaning that an image can have several positives returned. With Stage 1 detectors such as ours, this is described by the FPPI of an image. As the maximum FPPI is capped at the number of segments that the breast is divided into, using fewer segments means that the FPPI will be lower. On the other hand, accurate detection of the TPs is substantially more difficult as the area is larger.

Using the same algorithm as described in [29], we divided the breast images into three overlapping segments of roughly similar size as shown in figure 1: one segment captures the nipple area and one each for of the top and bottom of the remainder of the breast. The overlapping is designed to help reduce the possibility of a mass going undetected.

3.2 Feature Detection

Before attempting to classify mammograms as suspicious or not we must first extract *features* that GP can use to distinguish between classes. In this study, we have chosen to use Haralick's Texture Features [11]. Textural features are appropriate in this case because we are examining parenchymal patterns, and our hypothesis is that suspicious areas are likely to be texturally dissimilar to normal areas.

The seminal work of Haralick et al. [11] described a method of generating 14 measures which can be used to form textural features from a set of co-occurrence matrices or "grey tone spatial dependency matrices". When applied to pixel grey levels, the Grey Level Co-occurrence Matrix (GLCM) is defined to be the distribution of co-occurring values at a given offset. Using the co-occurrence matrix, different properties of the pixel distribution can be generating by applying various calculations to the matrix values.

To quantitatively describe the textural characteristics of breast tissue, we calculate a GLCM for each segment and for each breast. To keep the GLCM size manageable, we first reduce the number of gray levels to 256 (from 65535 in the original images). We independently calculate GLCMs for four orientations corresponding to two adjacent and two diagonal neighbours. Next, we calculate the Haralick features [11], which reflect (among others) contrast, entropy, variance, and correlation of pixel values. In this work we examine a neighbourhood of 1 and averaged the feature values for the four orientations. The down-sampling of gray levels, construction of GLCMs and extraction of Haralick features is achieved using Matlab [21].

Segments are rectangular and often extend beyond the breast, thus containing some background information. A GLCM calculated from such a segment in a conventional way would register very high values for black pixels and so distort the values of Haralick features. As many mammographic images contain sections of adipose tissue, which appears black in mammograms and, which is in its own right useful information, we should not ignore black pixels. Therefore, before calculating the GLCM, we increase by one the intensity of every pixel within the breast, using the information resulting from the segmentation stage. The pixels that already have the maximal value retain it (this causes certain information loss, albeit negligible one, as there are typically very few such pixels). Then, once the GLCM has been calculated, we simply "hoist" the GLCM up and to the left to remove the impact of the unmodified background pixels.

We conducted a preliminary analysis of the 13 computed Haralick features examining variance across and between both classes and then carried out a more formal analysis using several ranker methods [10] which ranked the attributes according to the concept of *information gain* [16]. In this context information gain can be thought of as a measure of the value of an attribute which describes how well that attribute separates the training examples according to their target class labels. These feature selection steps suggested that the most promising features in terms of discrimination were *contrast* and *difference entropy*. Accordingly, we discarded the other features and let GP focus on those two.

3.3 Dataset Construction

We use the University of South Florida Digital Database for Screening Mammography (DDSM) [13] which is a collection of 43 "volumes" of mammogram cases. A volume is a collection of mammogram cases and can be classified as either *normal*, *positive*, *benign* or *benign without callback*. All patients in a particular volume have the same classification. We use cases from the **cancer_02** and three of the **normal** volumes (volumes 1 to 3).

The incidence of positives within mammograms is roughly 5 in 1000 giving a massively imbalanced data set. To ensure that our training data maintains a realistic balance, we deliberately select only a single volume of positive cases. In constructing training and test data several images were discarded either because of image processing errors or because we were unable to confidently identify which segment/s were cancerous for a particular positive case. This initial processing resulted in a total of 294 usable cases 75 of which contain cancerous growths (which we call *positive* from now on). Each *case* initially consists of images for the left and right breasts and for the MLO and CC views of each breast. Once the segmentation step has been completed images are added for each of the three segments (nipple/top/bottom) for each view of each breast. Thus, there are a total of four images for each breast, for each view: one for the entire breast (A), and one for each of the three segments (A_t, A_b, A_n).

If we count the numbers of positives (P) and negatives (N) in terms of breasts rather than cases, which is reasonable, given that each is examined independently (i.e. most, but not all, patients with cancerous growths do not have them in both breasts), then the number of non-cancerous images increases significantly: giving two for each non-cancerous case and one for most cancerous growths. For the volumes studied, of the 75 usable positive cases, 3 have cancer in both breasts. Thus, considering full breast CC images only, we have 78 positive images and 510 (219 * 2 + 72) negative ones.

Turning our attention to segments (A_t, A_b, A_n) (excluding full breast images), and again considering only CC segments for the moment, for each non cancerous case we have 3 segments for each breast (left and right) together with 2 non cancerous segments for each cancerous breast which gives a total of 1686 non cancerous segments and 78 cancerous segments. Similarly, for the MLO view there are 1686 non cancerous segments and 78 cancerous ones.

Thus, we obtain three distributions: one for the non-segmented single views (CC or MLO) *full breast* images (78 positives (Ps), and 510 negatives, (Ns)); one for the *segmented* single views (78 Ps and 1686 Ns); and one for segmented combined CC MLO views (156 Ps and 3372 Ns). Each of these three distributions exhibit very significant class imbalance which, in and of itself, increases the level

Name	Ps	Ns	Breasts	Segs	Views	Description
B1S0V1	78	510	1	1	CC	Unsegmented (full breast image).
B1S1V1	78	1686	1	1	CC	Single segment.
B1S2V2	156	3372	1	2	CC + MLO	1 segment for each view.
B1S3V1	78	1686	1	3	CC	3 segments (A_t, A_b, A_n).
B2S0V1	78	510	2	2	CC	Unsegmented images from both breasts.
B2S2V1	78	1686	2	2	CC	1 segment from each breast.
B2S4+0V1	78	1686	2	4	CC	1 segment + unsegmented from each.
B2S3+0V1	78	1686	2	3	CC	1 segment from each + unsegmented from first.
B2S4V1	78	1686	2	4	CC	3 segments + one segment.
B2S6B1	78	1686	2	6	CC	3 segments + one segment + 2 unsegmented.

Table 1: Experimental Configurations. Each was generated from the *same* master data set.

of difficulty of the classification problem. The imbalance in the data was mitigated in all cases by using Proportional Individualised Random Sampling, as described in [8]

Based on this master dataset, we consider several setups representing different configurations of breasts, segments and views (see Table 1). The following terminology is used to describe the composition of *instances* for a given setup: $BXSYVZ$, where X is the number of breasts, Y the number of segments and Z the number of views *for a given instance*. In the cases where there is just one view (B1S1V1, B2S2V1, B1S3V1, B2S4V1) we use the CC views, while in the cases where the breast has been segmented, the system attempts to classify whether or not the *segment* has a suspicious area or not. In particular, the two breast (B2SYV1) special setups which investigate the use of asymmetry. These rely solely on the CC view: each instance is comprised of selected features from one breast CC segment/s together with the same features taken from the corresponding other breast CC segment/s for the same patient.

There are two setups which deviate slightly from the naming scheme above: B2S3+0V1 and B2S4+0V1. Here, +0 indicates that features for a non segmented image have been included.

We want to exploit any differences between a segment and the rest of the breast (i.e. between A and A_x) but also between a segment and the corresponding segment from the opposite breast, (say B and B_x), with the objective of evolving a classifier capable of *pinpointing a specific cancerous segment.* To facilitate this process, where we use more than one segment for a particular setup, features from the segment of interest are the first appearing data items in each instance for the dataset for that setup. Details of he specific setups used in the current study are as follows:

3.3.1 B1S0V1

This dataset configuration has an instance for the selected features of each full breast image. It uses the CC view only and has a separate instance for each breast for each patient.

3.3.2 B1S1V1

The BIS1V1 configuration also uses only the CC view, but this setup uses each of the three segments (A_t, A_b, A_n) separately, i.e each instance is comprised of the feature values for a single segment. Again there is an instance for each breast for each segment.

3.3.3 B1S2V2

Both views are used in the B2S2V2 setup. For each segment, excluding the full breast image, for each breast, each instance contains feature values for that segment and the corresponding segment for the other view (CC or MLO). So for a given segment, say A_t, there are instances for the following:

A_t LEFT_CC, A_t LEFT_MLO
A_t LEFT_MLO, A_t LEFT_CC
A_t RIGHT_CC, A_t RIGHT_MLO
A_t RIGHT_MLO, A_t RIGHT_CC

In this setup the *segments of interest* are A_t *LEFT_CC*, A_t *LEFT_MLO*, A_t *RIGHT_CC* and A_t *RIGHT_MLO* respectively, i.e the segment whose features occur *first.* This principle applies to all of the remaining setups, where more than one segment is used.

3.3.4 B1S3V1

This configuration uses three CC segments (A_t, A_b, A_n) for a single breast, where the first segment is alternated in successive instances For example, for a given single breast there are three training instances similar to:

A_t LEFT_CC, A_b LEFT_CC, A_n LEFT_CC
A_b LEFT_CC, A_n LEFT_CC, A_t LEFT_CC
A_n LEFT_CC A_t LEFT_CC, A_b LEFT_CC

Where the order of the remaining two segments does not matter.

3.3.5 B2S0V1

In the B2S0V1 we study a simple case of symmetry where each instance is comprises features for 2 segments: one for each full breast image, left and right, CC view only,

A LEFT_CC, A RIGHT_CC
A RIGHT_CC, A LEFT_CC

3.3.6 B2S2V1

In this configuration we investigate another case of symmetry: each entry consists of the feature values for a single CC segment from one breast combined with those of the corresponding CC segment from the other breast, for the same patient. In this case there are two entries for each segment: (A_x LEFT_CC, A_x RIGHT_CC) and (A_x RIGHT_CC, A_x LEFT_CC), where x represents a particular segment (A_t, A_b, A_n).

3.3.7 B2S3+0V1

Each instance in this setup is comprised of feature data from segmented and unsegmented images. It consists of information for a segment, the unsegmented image and the corresponding segment from the other breast. For example:

A_t LEFT_CC, A LEFT_CC,B_t LEFT_CC

3.3.8 B2S4+0V1

Similar to B2S3+0V1, each instance in this setup is again comprised of feature data from segmented and unsegmented images. It consists of information for a segment, the unsegmented image and the corresponding segment from the other breast together with the unsegmented image data for the other breast. For example:

A_t LEFT_CC, A LEFT_CC,B_t LEFT_CC,B LEFT_CC

3.3.9 B2S4V1

The B2S4V1 experimental setup is a combination of B1S3V1 and B2S2V1 where each training instance is comprised of the feature values for the three segments for a single breast (A) combined with the corresponding segment from the other breast (B) for the leftmost, first occurring segment of A. For example:

A_t LEFT_CC, A_b LEFT_CC, A_n LEFT_CC, B_t LEFT_CC

Where in this instance A_t LEFT_CC is the segment of interest.

3.3.10 B2S6V1

The final experimental setup is an extension of B2S4V1 where feature values for the full breast segment for the right and left breasts are added. For example:

A_t LEFT_CC, A_b LEFT_CC, A_n LEFT_CC,A LEFT_CC, B_t LEFT_CC, B LEFT_CC

Where in this instance A_t LEFT_CC is the segment of interest.

It is important to note here is that where more than one segment is used the segment of interest is the first occurring leftmost one. If that segment has been diagnosed as cancerous then the training / test instance in which it occurs is marked as positive, and if it has not been diagnosed as cancerous then the entire instance is marked as negative *regardless of the cancer status of any other segments used in that particular instance.* Thus, excluding the B1S0V1 setup, the objective is not simply to determine if a given breast is positive for cancer, but rather to *pinpoint which segments are positive.* If successful, this capability could pave the way for further diagnosis.

4. EXPERIMENTS AND RESULTS

All experiments used a population 200 individuals, running for 60 generations, with a crossover rate of 0.8 and mutation rate of 0.2. The minimum initial depth was 4, while the maximum depth was 17. The instruction set was small, consisting of just $+, -, *, \backslash$. The tree terminals (leaves) are selected from the available Haralick features, with two available per segment.

To transform a continuous output of a GP tree into a nominal decision (Positive, Negative), we binarize it using the method described in [7], which optimizes the binarization threshold individually for each GP classifier.

For our selection and replacement strategy we employed an NSGA-II [6] Multi Objective GP (MOGP) algorithm as described in [6] and updated in [9]. We chose to use the multi-objective algorithm due to the relationship between the main objectives for the mammography task. Preliminary experiments with various composite single objective fitness functions had not proved very successful and previous work [29] had demonstrated the effectiveness of the MOGP approach.

The NSGA-II algorithm was used to drive selection according to performance on three different objectives. When using this type of algorithm for problems which may necessitate trade-offs due to a natural tension between objectives, the system typically does not return a single best individual at the end of evolution, but rather a Pareto front, or range of individuals representing various levels of trade-off between the different objectives. However, for this particular task, we are not interested in the pareto front of individuals, after all, a model with a zero FPR and zero or very low TPR (every instance classified as N) is not of much practical use in this context. What we really care about is achieving the lowest possible FPR for the highest possible TPR. Thus, during evolution we maintained a single entry "hall of fame" (HOF) for each CV iteration, whereby as we evaluated each new individual on the training data, if it had a higher TPR or if it had an equal TPR but a lower FPR to the HOF incumbent for that CV iteration, the new individual replaced that HOF incumbent.

Using a population of 200, at each generation, 200 new offspring are generated, then parents and offspring are merged into one pool before running Pareto-based selection to select the best 200. During evolution, we aim to minimize **three** fitness objectives: FP Rate, $1-$TP Rate and $1-$AUC, where AUC is a the area under ROC, calculated using the Mann-Whitney [31] test.

We performed stratified five-fold cross-validation (CV, [12]) for all setups. However, we also retained 10% of the data as a "hold out" (HO) test set, where for each set of 5 cross-validated runs this HO test set data was separated from the CV data prior to the latter's allocation to folds for CV. The data partitioning was carried out using the sci-kit learn Machine Learning (ML) toolkit [25]. We conducted 50 cross-validated runs (each consisting of 5 runs) with identical random seeds for each configuration outlined in Table 1.

4.1 Results

In this section we present our experimental results firstly with regard to AUC measure on the training and test partitions of the CV phase, before we examine the TP and FP rates for this data. Finally we explore the results for each performance metric, this time taking the performance on hold-out data into consideration.

4.1.1 AUC

The plots in figure 2, show the evolution in population average AUC on the CV training data, development of the best population training AUC, change in population average AUC over the generations on the CV test data, and the evolution of the best population test AUC, where each of these represent metrics which are averaged over all cross-validated runs.

It seems that the best performing setups from the perspectives of both training and test CV data are those which leverage information from both breasts, the single breast configuration which uses all three segments or the single breast setup which uses features from the unsegmented image.

Clearly some of the worst AUC results are achieved with the configurations which use segments from a single breast,

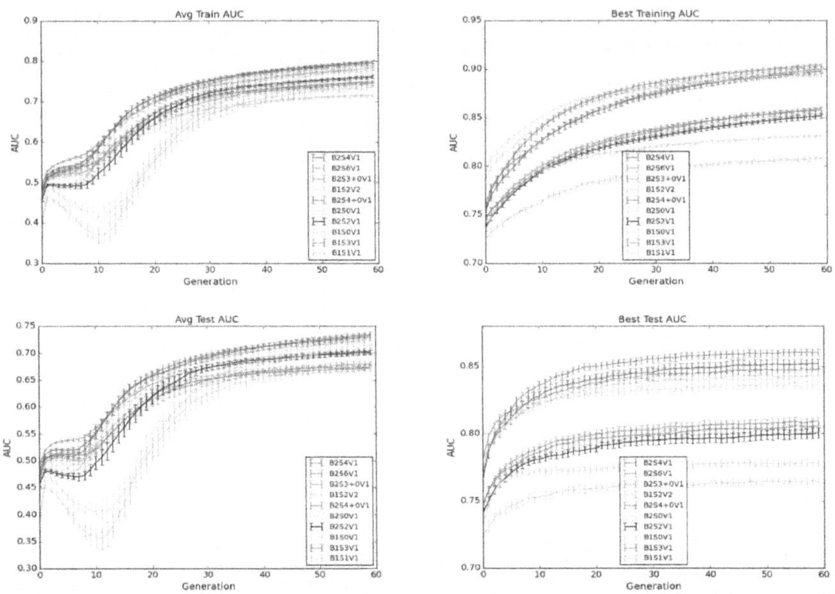

Figure 2:
Average and best population training and test AUC, averaged over all cross-validated runs.

particularly that which uses two views of the same breast. This is not very surprising as the features contain essentially the same information, and having features which are strongly correlated is known to be detrimental to accurate classification.

Overall, the results suggest that increasing the number of segments gives a significant boost to performance in terms of training fitness but that the strategy does not necessarily improve results on test data.

4.1.2 TP/FP Rates

Population average TP and FP rates for training data and the corresponding rates on test data can be seen in figure 3. The plots exemplify the tension which exists in the population between the two competing objectives of maximizing the True Positive Rate (TPR) while simultaneously trying to minimize the False Positive Rate (FPR). In general, a configuration which produces a higher than average TPR will also produce a correspondingly higher FPR. For any configuration, there will always be individuals within the population which classify all instances as either negative or positive. In order to accurately distinguish which configurations are likely to deliver a usable classification model it is better to examine the results of the *best performing* individuals in the population on the various metrics: TP rate, FP rate and AUC. We explore this aspect in section 4.1.3.

4.1.3 Model Selection

We report results on the training and test CV segments but the most important results are those for the HO test set, as these provide an indication of how the system might be expected to perform on new, unseen instances.

To compare with results from the literature we convert the FPR into FPPI which we report in table 3. Here, the results reported arise from the data shown in table 2 which represents the mean average results for the best trained individuals. Results for each HOF are firstly averaged for each run in a CV set and then averaged across the 50 cross-validated runs. These results refer to performance on the crucial hold HO data.

Clearly the best results are produced by the two breast non-segmented approach B2S2V1 with a TPR of 1 and an FPPI of 0.33. This is closely followed by its single breast counterpart B1S0V1 which again delivered a perfect TPR and an FPP1 of 0.41.

Of the segmented setups the two augmented configurations of B2S3+0V1 and B2S4+0V1 also produced good results with perfect TPR combined with good FPPIs of 1.11 and 1.08 respectively. Also the B2S4V1 method did very well with a TPR of 1 and FPP1 of 1.11.

Overall, several of our configurations proved capable of correctly classifying 100% of the cancerous cases while at the same time having a low FPPI, and the best results were delivered by individuals trained to view breast asymmetry.

5. CONCLUSIONS AND FUTURE WORK

TPR and FPPI produced by the most successful experimental configurations compare well with the results reported in section 2, and also reinforce the quality of previous results reported in [29] as different volumes have been used on this occasion. We hypothesise that the improvement in FPPI over the previous work is largely due to the addition of the Haralick contrast attribute.

The experimental set up with the lowest FPPI was the one that compared both entire breasts, showing that we successfully leveraged textural breast asymmetry as a potential indicator for abnormalities. Additionally, several of the segmented configurations also produced very good results, indicating that the system is capable of not only identifying with high accuracy which breasts are likely to have suspicious lesions but also which *segments* con<tain suspicious

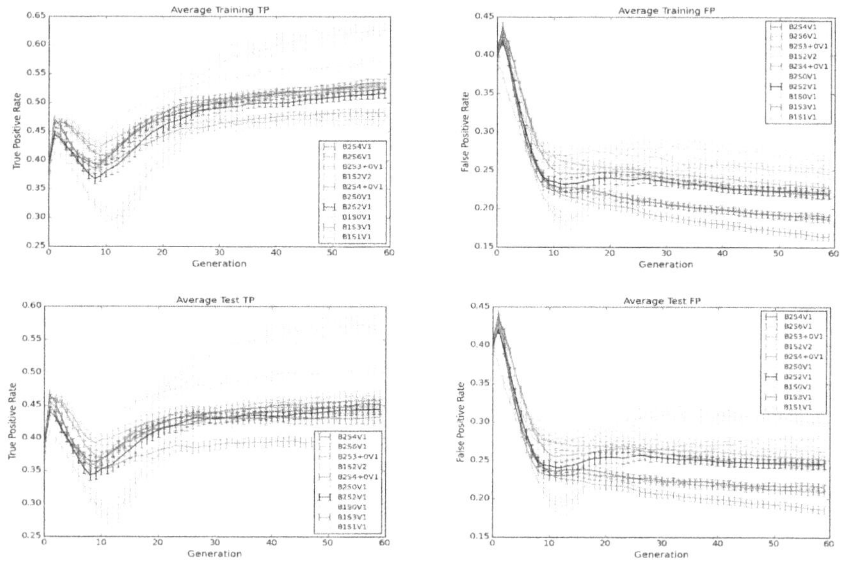

Figure 3:
Average and best population training and test TP and FP rates, averaged over all cross-validated runs

Method	Train TP	Train FP	Train AUC	Test TP	Test FP	Test AUC	HO TP	HO FP	HO AUC
B1S0V1	1	0.60	0.78	0.92	0.63	0.73	1	0.66	0.76
B1S1V1	1	0.62	0.74	0.94	0.65	0.69	1	0.65	0.80
B1S2V2	1	0.72	0.71	0.97	0.74	0.68	0.97	0.72	0.70
B1S3V1	1	0.48	0.82	0.93	0.50	0.77	0.96	0.51	0.76
B2S0V1	1	0.49	0.81	0.92	0.54	0.75	1	**0.51**	**0.83**
B2S2V1	1	0.55	0.77	0.96	0.58	0.74	1	0.57	0.82
B2S3+0V1	1	0.57	0.76	0.93	0.59	0.73	0.96	0.55	0.77
B2S4+0V1	1	0.54	0.76	0.92	0.57	0.71	0.96	0.52	0.78
B2S4V1	1	0.48	0.82	0.92	0.52	0.76	0.97	0.52	0.78
B2S6V1	1	0.40	0.84	0.92	0.45	0.77	0.86	0.46	0.73

Table 2: Mean average training, test and hold out TP, FP AUC of best trained individuals

Method	Avg TP	Avg FPPI	Best TP	Best FPP1
B1S0V1	1	0.61	1	0.41
B1S1V1	1	1.88	1	1.68
B1S2V2	0.97	2.03	0.95	1.86
B1S3V1	0.96	1.49	0.80	1.08
B2S0V1	1	0.45	1	0.33
B2S2V1	1	1.67	1	1.34
B2S3+0V1	0.96	1.57	1	1.11
B2S4+0V1	0.96	1.48	1	1.08
B2S4V1	0.97	1.52	1	1.11
B2S6V1	0.86	1.28	0.77	1.06

Table 3: Mean average TP and FPPI of best trained individuals, TP and FPPI of single best trained individual, on HO data.
Best trained individuals are selected according to the algorithm described in Section 4.

areas. The first of these capabilities could prove useful in providing second reader functionality to busy radiologists, whereas the second may provide inputs into an automated diagnostic system.

Future work will focus on further refining abnormality detection such that the specific location of suspicious areas within segments may be identified. We are also exploring the possibility of developing ensemble classifiers where each member may have been trained on a different type of X-Ray machine. This may be possible as digital mammograms are in a format which contains meta-data which includes details of the specific machine and location where the mammogram was taken.

6. ACKNOWLEDGEMENTS

K. Krawiec acknowledges support from the Ministry of Science and Higher Education grant 09/91/DSPB/0572. The remaining authors gratefully acknowledge the support of Science Foundation Ireland, grant number 10/IN.1/I3031.

References

[1] Arbab Masood Ahmad, Gul Muhammad Khan, Sahibzada Ali Mahmud, and Julian Francis Miller. Breast cancer detection using cartesian genetic programming evolved artificial neural networks. In Terry Soule et al., editors, *GECCO '12: Proceedings of the fourteenth international conference on Genetic and evolutionary computation conference*, pages 1031–1038, Philadelphia, Pennsylvania, USA, 7-11 July 2012. ACM.

[2] Leonard Berlin. Liability of interpreting too many radiographs. *American Journal of Roentgenology*, 175:17ÂŰ22, 2000.

[3] Mythreyi Bhargavan, Jonathan H. Sunshine, and Barbara Schepps. Too few radiologists? *American Journal of Roentgenology*, 178:1075–1082, 2002.

[4] Keir Bovis and Sameer Singh. Detection of masses in mammograms using texture features. In *Pattern Recognition, 2000. Proceedings. 15th International Conference on*, volume 2, pages 267–270. IEEE, 2000.

[5] Tommy E. Cupples, Joan E. Cunningham, and James C. Reynolds. Impact of computer-aided detection in a regional screening mammography program. *American Journal of Roentgenology*, 186:944–950, 2005.

[6] Kalyanmoy Deb, Amrit Pratap, Sameer Agarwal, and TAMT Meyarivan. A fast and elitist multiobjective genetic algorithm: Nsga-ii. *Evolutionary Computation, IEEE Transactions on*, 6(2):182–197, 2002.

[7] Jeannie Fitzgerald and Conor Ryan. Exploring boundaries: optimising individual class boundaries for binary classification problems. In *Proceedings of the 14th international conference on Genetic and evolutionary computation conference*, GECCO '12, pages 743–750, New York, NY, USA, 2012. ACM.

[8] Jeannie Fitzgerald and Conor Ryan. A hybrid approach to the problem of class imbalance. In *International Conference on Soft Computing*, Brno, Czech Republic, June 2013.

[9] Félix-Antoine Fortin and Marc Parizeau. Revisiting the nsga-ii crowding-distance computation. In *Proceedings of the 15th Annual Conference on Genetic and Evolutionary Computation*, GECCO '13, pages 623–630, New York, NY, USA, 2013. ACM.

[10] Mark Hall, Eibe Frank, Geoffrey Holmes, Bernhard Pfahringer, Peter Reutemann, and Ian H. Witten. The weka data mining software: an update. *SIGKDD Explor. Newsl.*, 11(1):10–18, November 2009.

[11] R. et al Haralick. Texture features for image classification. *IEEE Transactions on Systems, Man, and Cybernetics*, 3(6), 1973.

[12] Trevor Hastie, Robert Tibshirani and Jerome Friedman. *The elements of statistical learning*, volume 2. Springer, 2009.

[13] Michael Heath, Kevin Bowyer, Daniel Kopans, Richard Moore, and W. Philip Kegelmeyer. The digital database for screening mammography. In M.J. Yaffe, editor, *Proceedings of the Fifth International Workshop on Digital Mammography*, pages 212–218. Medical Physics Publishing, 2001.

[14] Rolando R Hernández-Cisneros, Hugo Terashima-Marín, and Santiago E Conant-Pablos. Comparison of class separability, forward sequential search and genetic algorithms for feature selection in the classification of individual and clustered microcalcifications in digital mammograms. In *Image Analysis and Recognition*, pages 911–922. Springer, 2007.

[15] J. Koza. Genetic programming: A paradigm for genetically breeding populations of computer programs to solve problems. Technical Report STAN-CS-90-1314, Dept. of Computer Science, Stanford University, June 1990.

[16] Solomon Kullback and Richard A Leibler. On information and sufficiency. *The Annals of Mathematical Statistics*, pages 79–86, 1951.

[17] W.B. Langdon and A.P. Harrison. Gp on spmd parallel graphics hardware for mega bioinformatics data mining. *Soft Computing*, 12(12):1169–1183, 2008.

[18] Huai Li, Yue Wang, KJ Ray Liu, S-CB Lo, and Matthew T Freedman. Computerized radiographic mass detection. i. lesion site selection by morphological enhancement and contextual segmentation. *Medical Imaging, IEEE Transactions on*, 20(4):289–301, 2001.

[19] Simone A. Ludwig and Stefanie Roos. Prognosis of breast cancer using genetic programming. In Rossitza Setchi et al., editors, *14th International Conference on Knowledge-Based and Intelligent Information and Engineering Systems (KES 2010), Part IV*, volume 6279 of *LNCS*, pages 536–545, Cardiff, UK, September 8-10 2010. Springer.

[20] M Markey M. Sampat and A Bovik. Computer-aided detection and diagnosis in mammography. In Alan C. Bovik, editor, *Handbook of Image and Video Processing*. Elsevier Academic Press, 2010.

[21] MATLAB. *version 8.2 (R2012a)*. MathWorks Inc., Natick, MA, 2013.

[22] Valerie A McCormack and Isabel dos Santos Silva. Breast density and parenchymal patterns as markers of breast cancer risk: a meta-analysis. *Cancer Epidemiology Biomarkers & Prevention*, 15(6):1159–1169, 2006.

[23] Naga R Mudigonda, Rangaraj M Rangayyan, and JE Leo Desautels. Gradient and texture analysis for the classification of mammographic masses. *Medical Imaging, IEEE Transactions on*, 19(10):1032–1043, 2000.

[24] R. J. Nandi, A. K. Nandi, R. Rangayyan, and D. Scutt. Genetic programming and feature selection for classification of breast masses in mammograms. In *28th Annual International Conference of the IEEE Engineering in Medicine and Biology Society, EMBS '06*, pages 3021–3024, New York, USA, August 2006. IEEE.

[25] F. Pedregosa et al. Scikit-learn: Machine learning in Python. *Journal of Machine Learning Research*, 12:2825–2830, 2011.

[26] Nicholas Petrick, Berkman Sahiner, Samuel G Armato III, Alberto Bert, Loredana Correale, Silvia Delsanto, Matthew T Freedman, David Fryd, David Gur, Lubomir Hadjiiski, et al. Evaluation of computer-aided detection and diagnosis systemsa). *Medical physics*, 40(8):087001, 2013.

[27] W. E. Polakowski, D. A. Cournoyer, and S. K. Rogers. Computer-aided breast cancer detection and diagnosis of masses using difference of gaussians and derivative-based feature saliency,. *IEEE Trans. Med. Imag.*, 16:811–819, 1997.

[28] Rangaraj M Rangayyan, Nema M El-Faramawy, JE Leo Desautels, and Onsy Abdel Alim. Measures of acutance and shape for classification of breast tumors. *Medical Imaging, IEEE Transactions on*, 16(6):799–810, 1997.

[29] Conor Ryan, Krzysztof Krawiec, Una-May O'Reilly, Jeannie Fitzgerald, and David Medernach. Building a stage 1 computer aided detector for breast cancer using genetic programming. In M. Nicolau et al., editors, *17th European Conference on Genetic Programming*, volume 8599 of *LNCS*, pages 162–173, Granada, Spain, 23-25 April 2014. Springer.

[30] Robert A Smith, Stephen W Duffy, and László Tabár. Breast cancer screening: the evolving evidence. *Oncology*, 26(5):471–475, 2012.

[31] Paul Stober and Shi-Tao Yeh. An explicit functional form specification approach to estimate the area under a receiver operating characteristic (roc) curve. *Available at, http://www2. sas. com/proceedings/sugi27/p226-227. pdf, Accessed March*, 7, 2007.

[32] Tabar, L. et al. A new era in the diagnosis of breast cancer. *Surgical oncology clinics of North America*, 9(2):233–77, April 2000.

[33] T. Tot, L. Tabar, and P. B. Dean. The pressing need for better histologic-mammographic correlation of the many variations in normal breast anatomy. *Virchows Archiv*, 437(4):338–344, October 2000.

Evolving Solutions to TSP Variants for Active Space Debris Removal

Dario Izzo
Advanced Concepts Team
European Space Agency
Noordwijk, The Netherlands
Dario.Izzo@esa.int

Ingmar Getzner
Advanced Concepts Team
European Space Agency
Noordwijk, The Netherlands
Ingmar.Getzner@esa.int

Daniel Hennes
Advanced Concepts Team
European Space Agency
Noordwijk, The Netherlands
Daniel.Hennes@esa.int

Luís F. Simões
VU University Amsterdam
Amsterdam, The Netherlands
luis.simoes@vu.nl

ABSTRACT

The space close to our planet is getting more and more polluted. Orbiting debris are posing an increasing threat to operational orbits and the cascading effect, known as Kessler syndrome, may result in a future where the risk of orbiting our planet at some altitudes will be unacceptable. Many argue that the debris density at the Low Earth Orbit (LEO) has already reached a level sufficient to trigger such a cascading effect. An obvious consequence is that we may soon have to actively clean space from debris. Such a space mission will involve a complex combinatorial decision as to choose which debris to remove and in what order. In this paper, we find that this part of the design of an active debris removal mission (ADR) can be mapped into increasingly complex variants to the classic Travelling Salesman Problem (TSP) and that they can be solved by the Inver-over algorithm improving the current state-of-the-art in ADR mission design. We define static and dynamic cases, according to whether we consider the debris orbits as fixed in time or subject to orbital perturbations. We are able, for the first time, to select optimally objects from debris clouds of considerable size: hundreds debris pieces considered while previous works stopped at tens.

Categories and Subject Descriptors

I.2.8 [**Artificial Intelligence**]: Problem Solving, Control Methods, and Search—*Heuristic methods*

Keywords

TSP; Space Debris; Clean Space; Inver-over; Vehicle Routing; Dynamic Travelling Salesman

GECCO '15, July 11 - 15, 2015, Madrid, Spain

ISBN 978-1-4503-3472-3/15/07...$15.00
DOI: http://dx.doi.org/10.1145/2739480.2754727

1. INTRODUCTION

Four years after the first artificial satellite was successfully launched in 1957 (Sputnik-1), a catastrophic explosion of an orbiting human-made object created more than 300 trackable pieces of orbital debris. Over the next decades, a steady increase in the use of artificial satellites resulted in more than 200 of these events and in a current population of roughly 10000 fragmentation debris. A major threat they pose is that of creating a cascading effect, first described by Kessler and Cour-Palais [1], that will eventually compromise the utilization of operational orbits. According to NASA scientists [2] the Low-Earth-Orbit region (LEO) has already reached such a critical state and its debris population will thus keep increasing even if no further launches will be made. Removing well chosen pieces of debris from a given contaminated orbital environment may then be the only option to continue exploiting near-Earth space. Previous works have considered, at a preliminary stage, the design of an Active space Debris Removal (ADR) mission. A spacecraft would be launched and rendezvous with the selected debris object to then de-orbit it by means of robotic manipulators, electrodynamic tethers, ion thrusters or some other technology. The same spacecraft would then move to the next piece of debris. Choosing the sequence of debris to be removed is a crucial part of the design for such missions. It has been already noted recently how the debris selection problem bears strong similarities to the Travelling Salesman Problem (TSP) [3, 4, 5]. One of the main differences is that "debris", unlike cities, are moving and the value of a visiting sequence thus depends on the visiting schedule (i.e. the exact epochs of rendezvous and departure from each debris). While for simple cases a brute force approach is viable to plan a debris removal tour [3], more complex cases have been approached applying simulated annealing [5], genetic algorithms [6] or the Series Method approach [4] (essentially a nearest neighbourhood search) but always on problems of moderate size (on the order of tens of debris) and, in any case, not exploiting the connection to the TSPs.

In this paper we introduce two new variants to the TSP classic formulation: the TSP city selection (TSP-CS) and the dynamic TSP city selection (TSP-DCS). We show how they relate to the design of ADR missions, and more generally to problems where the travelling salesman needs to select which cities to visit within a given budget and in a scenario where the cities are moving. We create a number of test-instances of these problems considering orbiting debris clouds created by past fragmentation events and we solve them applying an evolutionary technique (the inver-over algorithm [7]) and the Series Method approach [4]. We also formalize the very same problems as tree search problems and solve them using a breadth-first search (also known as "beam search") with fixed frontier, a popular approach in the context of interplanetary trajectory design (and yet never used for the design of ADR missions). Unlike previous work [4, 5, 3, 6] we consider large size debris collections.

The rest of the paper is organized as follows. In section 2 we discuss the used debris cloud data and their orbital characteristics. Section 3 explains the algorithms used. In section 4 we explain how the problem of finding a trajectory for an active debris removal mission can be modeled as a variation of the classic TSP. Further we test the performance of the algorithms described in section 3 on a spacial static case of the problem. In section 5 we consider the debris pieces as moving objects. We analyse this dynamic problem and again discuss the performance of our algorithms.

2. THE DEBRIS CLOUDS

In this section we introduce the orbital characteristics of three different debris clouds (i.e. sets of orbiting space debris originated from some past fragmentation event). We will be using these to create our test-instances. We consider the database of all orbiting objects visible to radar observations[1]. The orbital elements for each object in the database, in the two-line element (TLE) format, are periodically released by NORAD as to maintain a reasonable prediction capability on the position of all space objects. The released elements can then be used in a SGP4 orbital propagator [8] to predict the future position and velocity. In order to build some fictitious test scenarios we select three separated sets of orbiting objects deriving from distinct recent catastrophic collision events and containing the resulting fragmentation debris. We consider the 2009 Iridium 33-Cosmos 2251 collision and the 2007 Fengyun-1C event caused by a Chinese anti-satellite missile test. These fragmentation events created debris clouds that are a daily threat to all active satellites sharing the same orbital environment. In Table 1 we show the number of fragmentation debris belonging to each cloud at three different epochs: at breakup, as of 01/2015 and as of 01/2025 (decayed orbits were predicted using the SGP4 propagator). Due to the Earth's gravitational field and the effect of the residual atmospheric drag, the orbits of the debris change with time and some of them are naturally removed by decaying in the atmosphere. In Figure 2 we show, for the three debris clouds, the distribution of the orbital parameters (see Figure 1 for their definition) as of 01/2015. On the left column we show the Gabbard diagram, widely used to characterize fragmentation events [9] and showing the perigee and apogee of all fragments against their orbital period. On the right column we show the distribution of inclinations , i, versus the Right Ascension of the Ascending Node (RAAN), Ω. The importance of the Ω and i distributions derive from their importance in the computation of orbital transfers. A large contribution of such a cost derives from the relative orbital inclination which can be computed as:

$$\cos \Delta i = \cos i_1 \cos i_2 + \sin i_1 \sin i_2 \cos \Omega_1 \cos \Omega_2 + \\ + \sin i_1 \sin i_2 \sin \Omega_1 \sin \Omega_2 \quad (1)$$

It is the orbital transfer cost that is the equivalent of the city distance in classic TSPs: debris orbits having a large Δi are thus to be considered as distant, while debris orbits having a small Δi are to be considered as possibly close. Since we will eventually want to visit (and thus remove) the largest pieces of debris, we also show, in Figure 2, the dimension of each fragment of the debris cloud, as measured from radar observations and extracted from the SATCAT catalogue.

[1]The SATCAT catalogue can be downloaded from http://celestrak.com/pub/satcat.txt

	number of fragmentation debris (at breakup)	(1/2015)	(1/2025)
Iridium-33	598	368	191
Cosmos-2251	1603	1128	781
Fengyun	3312	2651	2363

Table 1: The cloud size slowly decreases as debris orbit naturally decay with time.

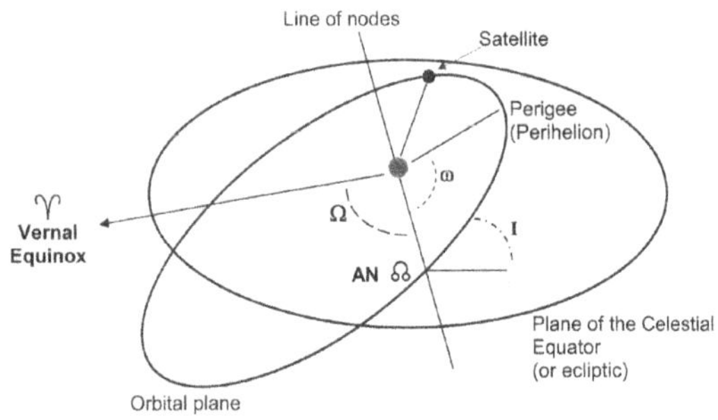

Figure 1: Orbital parameters for an Earth-bound orbit. The RAAN is denoted by Ω, the argument of perigee by ω and the orbital inclination by I, or i in the text.

3. METHODOLOGY

A classic TSP can be formulated as the problem of finding a minimum weight Hamiltonian path in a complete weighted graph $\mathcal{G} := \{\mathcal{V}, \mathbf{W}\}$, where $\mathcal{V}$ is the set containing the vertexes (cities) and $\mathbf{W} := \mathcal{V} \times \mathcal{V} \to \mathbb{R}^+$ is a map that associates to each ordered vertex pair a positive real number called edge weight and representing the distance between cities.

Here we define a TSP variant as an optimisation problem concerned to find the best possible Hamiltonian path in a graph, with respect to some predefined criteria. We indicate with n the cardinality of $\mathcal{V}$ (i.e. the number of cities), and we label each vertex in $\mathcal{V}$ with an increasing natural number, i.e. $1, 2, ..., n$. A Hamiltonian path is then to be encoded by a permutation of the set containing the first n natural numbers. Note that, in a classic TSP cycling a chosen permutation does not change the fitness function (i.e. the path length), but in the more complex variants introduced here this no longer needs to be the case. For example, [1,2,3] can have a different fitness with respect to, say, [3,1,2].

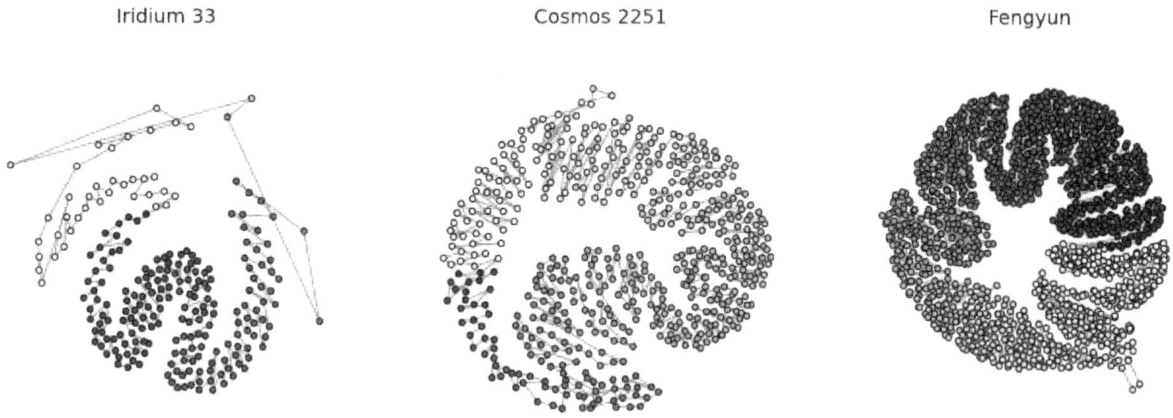

Figure 3: Best Hamiltonian tours found for the three debris clouds in the classic TSP variant. Each node represents an orbital debris. Node positioning given by a spring model (see text for details). As the problems are all non-metric, edges can cross. The color of each node is related to the RAAN of the debris it is representing.

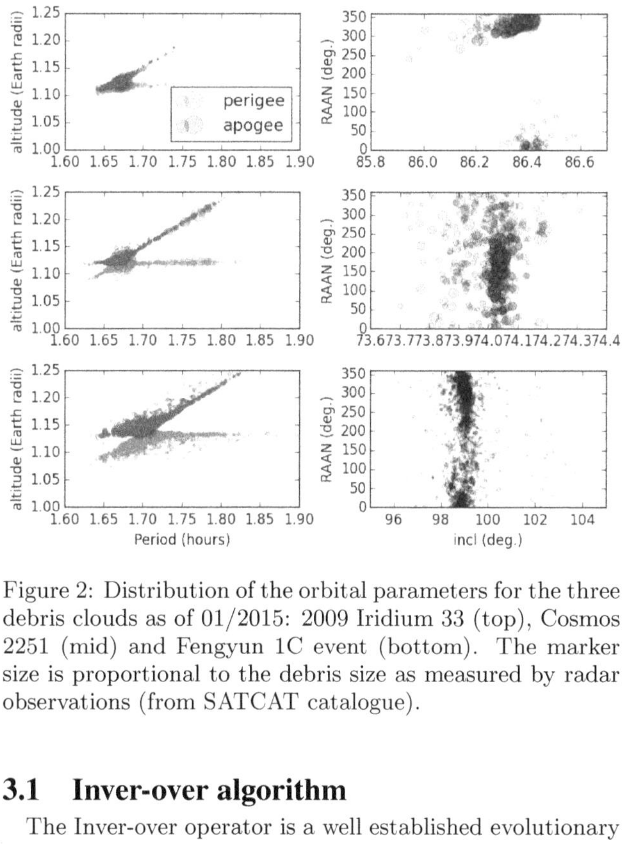

Figure 2: Distribution of the orbital parameters for the three debris clouds as of 01/2015: 2009 Iridium 33 (top), Cosmos 2251 (mid) and Fengyun 1C event (bottom). The marker size is proportional to the debris size as measured by radar observations (from SATCAT catalogue).

3.1 Inver-over algorithm

The Inver-over operator is a well established evolutionary technique that provides a powerful genetic operator for classic TSPs [7]. We used a slightly different version of the algorithm with respect to the originally proposed Inver-over. The version we implemented takes care of not making inversion of sections including the edge from the last city to the first one, a modification that improves considerably performances in the TSP variant that are not invariant to cycling. The algorithm's pseudo-code is sketched in Algorithm 1. The termination-condition could be a maximum amount of generations and ri denotes the chance of a random inversion and is thus called mutation probability. Note that without mutation the algorithm constructs an offspring by only using edges from the previous generation. Consider, as an example, the first iteration of the for loop given the following fictitious population of a five city problem:

$$S_1 = [1,5,2,3,6,4,7], \quad S_2 = [3,6,1,5,7,4,2],$$
$$S_3 = [2,5,4,7,6,3,1], \quad S_4 = [7,2,3,6,1,4,5],$$
$$S_5 = [4,1,3,2,7,6,5].$$

Since we look at the first iteration of the for-loop,

$$S_{tmp} = S_1 = [1,5,2,3,6,4,7].$$

We select randomly a city from S_{tmp}, lets say $c_1 = 5$. Next, assume our sampled uniformly distributed random number is larger than the mutation probability ri. Therefore we randomly select an individual, say $S_5 = [4,1,3,2,7,6,5]$ and look which city is following 5. In our case that would be $c_2 = 4$, since in the case of a closed TSP each individual is represented as a circular array. Since 5 is not an adjacent city of 4 in S_{tmp} we invert the segment from the city next to 5, namely 2, to city 4. We obtain

$$S_{tmp} = [1,5,4,6,3,2,7].$$

We proceed by setting c_1 to the city that followed $c_2 = 4$ in S_{tmp} before we inverted, namely 7 and by going back to the beginning of the repeat-loop. Assume that we again do not chose c_2 randomly. Therefore we select a random individual, say $S_3 = [2,5,4,7,6,3,1]$. The city following $c_1 = 7$ is 6. We set $c_2 = 6$ and observe that $c_2 = 6$ occurs before $c_1 = 7$ in S_{tmp}. In contrast to the previous repeat-loop iteration, where c_2 was in front of c_1 in S_{tmp}, we invert the section from c_2 to the city coming before c_1, namely 2. We get

$$S_{tmp} = [1,5,4,2,3,6,7].$$

For the following repeat-loop iteration we obtain $c_1 = 4$. That is the city that comes previous to 6 before the inversion. Assume our random generator returns a number larger than ri. We randomly select an individual from the population say $S_4 = [7,2,3,6,1,4,5]$ and check which city comes next to $c_1 = 4$. It is city 5. We set $c_2 = 5$ and after observing that c_2 is already next to c_1 in S_{tmp} we exit the repeat-loop

```
Initialization of the population P;
while termination-condition is not satisfied do
    for each individual S_i ∈ P do
        S_tmp = S_i;
        select randomly a city c_1 from S_tmp;
        repeat
            if rand() < ri then
                select randomly a city c_2 ≠ c_1 from S_tmp;
            else
                select randomly an individual S_ℓ ≠ S_i
                from P;
                select the city that follows c_1 in S_ℓ and
                name it c_2;
            end
            if c_2 is adjacent c_1 in S_tmp then
                exit from repeat loop;
            else
                if c_2 comes after c_1 in S_tmp then
                    invert section from the city that
                    comes after c_1 until c_2;
                    c_1 gets assigned the city that was
                    moved to the position of c_2 by the
                    previous inversion;
                else
                    invert section from c_2 until the city
                    that is previous to c_1;
                    c_1 gets assigned the city that comes
                    previous to c_2 before the inversion
                    was performed;
                end
            end
        until;
        if objfun(S_tmp) < objfun(S_ℓ) then
            S_ℓ = S_tmp;
        end
    end
end
```

Algorithm 1: Inver-over algorithm used.

and check if our newly generated S_{tmp} represents a better solution than S_1 with respect to our objective function. If so, we replace S_1 by S_{tmp}. The algorithm will proceed with a new iteration of the for-loop, this time trying to evolve S_2. In our experiments we use a population size of 100 and a mutation probability $ri = 0.05$. We stop the algorithm when no improvements are made to the objective function for more than 20000 iterations.

3.2 Nearest Neighbour Search

The nearest neighbour (NN) algorithm is well known in the context of classic TSPs. It returns solutions using small computational effort and that are quite close to the optimal solution, typically within some 20%. Interestingly, a substantially equivalent version of this algorithm is called Series Method and has been used for the design of ADR missions [4]. In trajectory design problems, the computation of the orbital transfer (i.e. the weights of the graph) can be quite demanding, thus methods that are able to return reasonable solutions computing a small number of these transfers are still of interest, which may justify its use in some special cases. The edge length, as commonly done in TSP studies, is used to define the nearest neighbour.

3.3 A Tree Search approach

The design of a mission for the removal of multiple orbiting debris is remarkably similar, from a trajectory design point of view, to the design of missions involving multiple asteroids rendezvous, or fly-bys. These missions have been the subject of extensive research in the past decade and, in particular, the design of their trajectories defined most of the problems released to the international community during the Global Trajectory Optimisation Competitions[2]. All of the solution methods of the most successful teams, in these competitions, were based on standard tree-searches (breadth-first with fixed frontier, depth-first with branch pruning, etc.). We thus implemented a simple breadth-first tree search with fixed frontier size FS (i.e. only the best FS solutions found at each depth are kept for further branching) to search for solutions to our TSP variants. While in the classic TSP case this algorithm is not likely to be comparable to known approaches, in the TSP variants introduced here, where not all cities are "scored", it actually may provide an efficient mechanism to select which cities to visit. A frontier size $FS = 10$ is considered for all tests performed.

4. STATIC CASE

How is an active debris removal (ADR) mission related to the TSP? In this section we formalize such a relation starting from the classic TSP and then introducing the City Selection TSP variant (TSP-CS). Given a set $\mathcal{V}$ of orbiting debris, any ADR mission will consist of one or more spacecraft that will have to visit all or part of the considered debris in order to de-orbit them. Such spacecraft will thus have to rendezvous and de-orbit each selected debris in a given order. When these orbits are considered as Keplerian, ignoring all perturbations acting upon them, we speak of a "static" case as the orbital parameters a, e, i, Ω, ω are considered as constants.

4.1 ADR as a classic TSP

We assume that we can model the propellant cost to transfer between orbits as a function $\mathbf{W} : \mathcal{V} \times \mathcal{V} \to R^+$. We consider one spacecraft with unlimited fuel budget (this very restrictive hypothesis will be discarded later when we will introduce variants to the classic TSP) and we ask ourselves what would the optimal visiting order be in order to minimize the cumulative transfer cost. Clearly, this creates a classic TSP where $\mathcal{G} := \{\mathcal{V}, \mathbf{W}\}$. The function $\mathbf{W}$ can be computed with the aid of basic spacecraft mechanics computations and with different degrees of approximations. Low-thrust transfers can be modelled using the Edelbaum approximation [10] or equivalents, while chemically propelled transfers can be modelled, at a preliminary mission design phase, using multiple impulse approximations. In this paper we use the widely used three impulse approximation (see [3] for example) where the first and last impulses are used to match the apogee and perigee of the orbits and the mid impulse is used to cancel the orbits' relative inclination (i.e. matching both i and Ω). Note, though, that our methodology can easily accommodate different choices. The classic TSP thus created is symmetric and non-metric. Let us consider three different instances: one for each of the selected debris clouds . Since the resulting problem dimensions are not exceedingly high[3], we are able to get convergence in all

[2]http://sophia.estec.esa.int/gtoc_portal/

[3]The full problem dimensions are 232, 533 and 1550 as we

	Total $\Delta V [km/sec]$		
	Inver-over tour	RAAN walk	Nearest Neighbourhood
Iridium-33	47.169	47.424	53.46
Cosmos-2251	63.19	65.63	89.21
Fengyun	155.29	186.9	199.39

Table 2: Summary of the results for the classic TSP case

algoritmic runs within a few minutes of CPU time[4]. In order to visualize the best tours found, we define on a 2-D plane the positions of the nodes representing the orbital debris as those defined by running a spring model on the fully connected graph $\mathcal{G}$ with spring constants inversely proportional to the edge weights. This ensures that orbiting debris having a small transfer cost will be occupying close-by positions. In Figure 3 we show the best tours found in the three cases. Each node of the graph, representing an orbital debris, was colored using the RAAN value. Surprisingly, we note how the optimal tour is such that the RAAN gradually increases (or decreases). We define a Hamiltonian path with a monotonously increasing Ω as "RAAN walk". In Table 2 we compare the total lengths (measuring the total mission ΔV [km/s]) of the tours found by inver-over to those defined by a RAAN walk and to those obtained running a nearest neighbourhood search. We find that the RAAN walk strategy is an extremely good guess on all three problems, significantly outperforming the nearest neighbourhood solution both in terms of quality and computational efficiency, requiring only one sorting. In Figure 4 we show, for the Fengyun-1C debris cloud, the RAAN along the three different tours. While the RAAN walk tour and the optimal tour are visually quite close, the nearest neighbour solution departs significantly from being monotonous. The ΔV values found are too high to be considered for any realistic space mission, but they are nevertheless useful to evaluate quantitatively the polluting effect of a given fragmentation event. With this metric, we can say that the Fengyun-1C fragmentation debris are roughly twice as hard to clean as those deriving from the Iridium 33 and Cosmos-2251 collision, which gives a quantitative measure of the impact of that fragmentation event.

4.2 ADR as a "City Selection" TSP

Consider the problem of a spacecraft with a limited ΔV capability, tasked to de-orbit multiple orbital debris chosen from a set $\mathcal{V}$ as to remove the maximum amount of collision risk from orbit. We consider the debris orbits as perfectly Keplerian and estimate the transfer cost via the three impulses approximation. Formally, this problem may be conveniently expressed as a problem in graph theory. We introduce a complete weighted graph $\mathcal{G} := \{\mathcal{V}, \mathbf{W}, \mathbf{p}\}$ and we assign to each vertex $V_i \in \mathcal{V}$ a corresponding value $p_i \in \mathbf{p}$. We search in $\mathcal{G}$ for the open walk having the maximum possible cumulative vertex value p, under the constraint that the cumulative edge weight is less than an assigned amount ℓ. We indicate with N the number of vertexes visited by the open walk. In TSP terminology, each city has a different value and the travelling salesman can only cover a

consider only debris orbits that do not decay within the next r weeks, where r is the debris cloud size as of 01/01/2015.

[4]All experiments in this paper were performed on a modern desktop machine equipped with i7 processors.

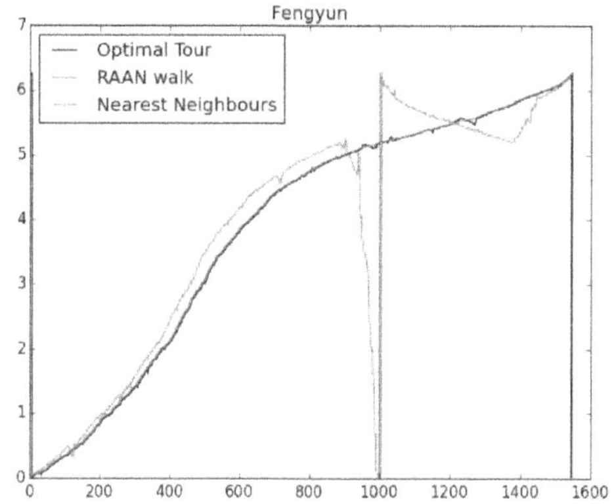

Figure 4: The RAAN walk strategy is very close to the optimal path

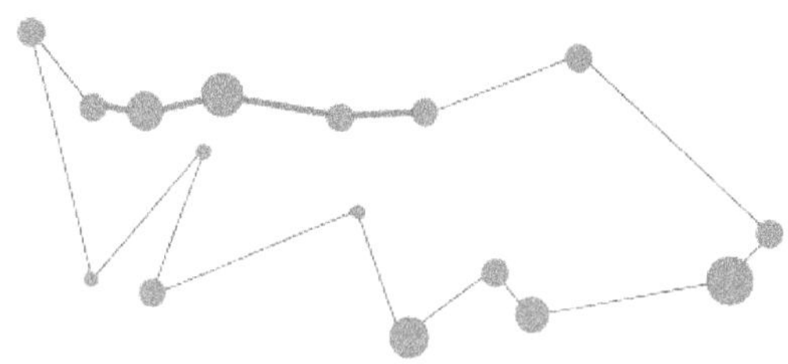

Figure 5: TSP-CS: Example of a maximal open walk (color red) embedded in a Hamiltonian path. Cities have different sizes to indicate their different value.

limited number of kilometers. He is then asked to select which cities to visit and in what order as to maximize the cumulative value of the cities visited in an open tour of limited length. We refer to this problem as to a city selection TSP (TSP-CS) problem. While it is not in the scope of this paper to rigorously analyze its complexity, we note that for each possible subset of cities, one still has to solve a classic TSP in order to find the best possible open walk. We also note that if we indicate with h the cumulative edge weight of the minimum weight Hamiltonian path in $\mathcal{G}$, then if $\ell \geq h$ a TSP-CS solution is the minimum weight Hamiltonian path (i.e. the problem becomes essentially a classic TSP). If we indicate with w_m the length of the shortest edge in $\mathcal{G}$, for $\ell < w_m$ the TSP-CS admits only the trivial solution $\emptyset$. This newly introduced TSP variant has, thus, a complexity that is related to the parameter ℓ. In the ADR application ℓ represents the spacecraft ΔV and the city values are the hazard risk they pose to the orbital environment, which is directly related to the cross-section area A [m^2].

4.2.1 *The maximal open walk*

In a TSP-CS we are looking for an open walk in a graph $\mathcal{G}$. To encode an open walk, we use the idea of having unexpressed genes in a chromosome of fixed length. We still encode the full Hamiltonian path (length h), but we only express, in it, the contiguous part having maximum cumulative vertex value p and cumulative weight $\hbar < \ell$. We will refer to it as to the maximal open walk embedded in a Hamiltonian path. In Figure 5 we visualize an example of a Hamiltonian path and its maximal open walk. While idea

Name	Debris Cloud	Size	ℓ [km/s]
ir33_100	Iridium-33	100	1
ir33_200	Iridium-33	200	1
ir33	Iridium-33	232	1
cos_100	Cosmos-2251	100	1
cos_200	Cosmos-2251	200	1
cos	Cosmos-2251	533	1
fen_100	Fengyun-1C	100	1
fen_200	Fengyun-1C	200	1
fen_400	Fengyun-1C	400	1
fen	Fengyun-1C	1550	1

Table 3: Problem instances considered.

of having hidden genes during the evolution of spacecraft trajectory encounters is not new as it was explored in [11, 12] for different missions, its use to decode a Hamiltonian path into an open walk is original with this work.

4.2.2 *An equivalent formulation*

Given the definitions above, we may restate the TSP-CS as the problem of maximizing the cumulative vertex value of the maximal open walk embedded in a Hamiltonian path of $\mathcal{G}$. In other words, we search for a Hamiltonian path, evaluating its value by computing its maximal open walk. This equivalent formulation of the problem allows us to apply the Inver-over algorithm also to this case. The only difference being that the fitness evaluation of a Hamiltonian path now requires us to find its embedded maximal open walk. During the evolutionary process, there will be offspring that have the very same maximal open walk, but still differ significantly in the unexpressed part of the chromosome. This suggests the idea to use the total length of the Hamiltonian path as a tie-breaker to accelerate evolution by biasing selection towards good unexpressed genes. This has an increasing importance for small values of ℓ, when one is choosing a few cities out of a large set and most of the chromosome is thus unexpressed.

4.2.3 *Experiments*

To instantiate a TSP-CS one needs to select $\mathcal{V}$, $\mathbf{W}$, $\mathbf{p}$ and ℓ. Similarly to what was done for the classic TSP case, we use the three debris clouds introduced (Iridium 33, Cosmos 2251 and Fengyun) to define $\mathcal{V}$ and the three impulse approximation to define $\mathbf{W}$. For $\mathbf{p}$ we use the radar cross-section area as reported in the SATCOM satellite catalogue. We consider several different problem instances of different complexity. In Table 3 we report some defining properties of the problem instances selected. The ir33, cos and fen instances were generated by downloading the TLE files from NORAD on January 2015 and removing all debris that do not decay within the next r weeks, where r is the debris cloud size as of 01/01/2015. The _XXX cases were generated considering only the largest XXX debris. The results are shown in Table 4. The best out of five runs is reported (only for inver-over, as the other approaches are deterministic). In all problem instances the inver-over outperforms or is equal to the other two approaches. The performance difference becomes more significant as the problem dimension increases.

	IO		NN		TS	
	A $[m^2]$	N	A $[m^2]$	N	A $[m^2]$	N
ir33_100	**3.0538**	20	**3.0538**	20	**3.0538**	20
ir33_200	**3.1103**	27	2.4942	23	3.0238	28
ir33	**3.1103**	27	2.3914	24	2.9862	22
cos_100	**2.5714**	12	2.3659	11	2.3659	11
cos_200	**2.6568**	15	2.4513	14	**2.6568**	15
cos	**2.6661**	16	2.2485	23	2.3224	18
fen_100	**1.8644**	8	**1.8644**	8	**1.8644**	8
fen_200	**1.9783**	10	1.9158	11	1.9158	11
fen_400	**2.2858**	19	2.1585	22	2.1585	22
fen	**2.2963**	28	1.5337	26	1.7675	30

Table 4: Performance of Inver-Over (IO), Nearest Neighbour (NN) and Tree Search (TS) in the City Selection TSP problem.

5. DYNAMIC CASE

The TSP-CS may have several applications to real world problems, but as far as ADR missions are concerned, the hypothesis of Keplerian orbits is to be considered as very restrictive. Removing this hypothesis increases the problem complexity considerably, but it is necessary if we want results to have a useful quantitative value for actual ADR missions. We must thus consider our cites as moving objects (dynamic TSP[5]) and select not only the city sequence to visit, but also the visiting epoch of each city. An A-B-C-D visit subsequence may then be very good or very bad depending on when A,B,C and D are visited and this is bound to make evolutionary operators developed for the static case less efficient. One option to formalize this type of dynamic TSP, pursued for example in [5], is to consider the orbital transfer cost as a function of the starting debris orbit, a starting epoch, the target debris orbit and an arrival epoch. The resulting problem is of great complexity and only small debris clouds could be analyzed in that work. We here follow a rather different approach as we assume that the transfer cost between orbiting debris only depends on the orbit geometry at the time of transfer (phase-less approximation) and not on the exact starting and arrival epochs. An ADR mission is infact unlikely to remove more than one piece of debris per week (already a rather optimistic number), while the duration of an orbital transfer between successive orbits is of a much shorter time-span (the period of debris in LEO is of a few hours). It is thus reasonable to assume that, within a week, a transfer opportunity will arise whose cost is very close to that evaluated by a phase-less approximation. Under this hypothesis, we only need to account for the changes in orbital parameters a, e, i, Ω, ω deriving from the orbital perturbation and we do not take care, at this level, for the positioning of the debris along the orbit.

5.1 ADR as a "Dynamic City Selection" TSP

The TSP variant that arises from our hypothesis will be called Dynamic City Selection TSP (TSP-DCS). It is similar to the TSP-CS variant, except that the city positions are computed at a time t_i, where i is the positional index of the city in the selected encoding representation. We keep

[5]A TSP variants called *dynamic* was already introduced in past work[13, 14], but referring to a quite different problem where all cities are to be visited at t and thus not applicable here.

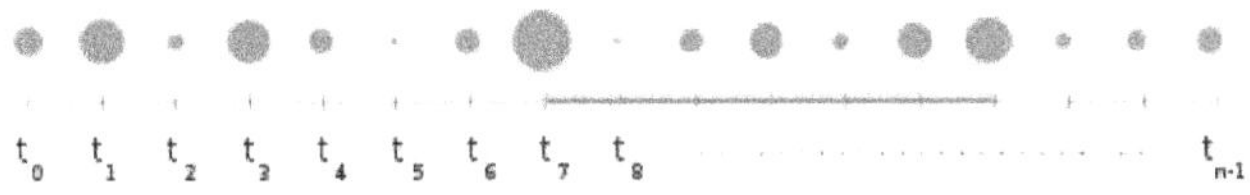

Figure 6: TSP-DCS: Example of a maximal open walk (color red) embedded in a Hamiltonian path. Cities have different sizes to indicate their different value.

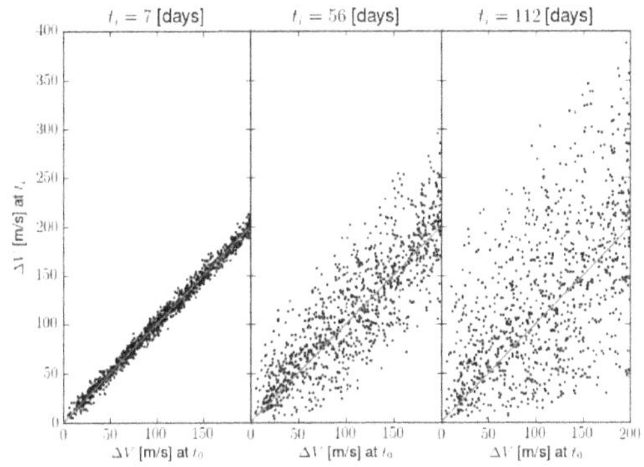

Figure 7: Transfer cost of all ir33 transfer pairs with $\Delta V \leq$ 200 m/s plotted at t_0 against $t_i \in \{7, 56, 112\}$.

the idea of the maximal open walk and are therefore able to search for Hamiltonian paths using a fixed length representation. In Figure 6 we visualize a maximal open walk embedded in a Hamiltonian path for the TSP-DCS problem. Formally, we introduce the ordered set of admissible epochs $\mathcal{T} := t_i, i = 0..n-1$ having the same cardinality as $\mathcal{V}$. Similarly to the static cases, we introduce a complete weighted graph $\mathcal{G} := \{\mathcal{V}, \overline{\mathbf{W}}, \mathbf{p}\}$, where $\overline{\mathbf{W}} : \mathcal{V} \times \mathcal{V} \times \mathcal{T} \rightarrow R^+$ represents the cost of transferring between two orbits when such a transfer is initiated at one of the admissible epochs.

5.1.1 Experiments

We follow the approach described for the static case to define a number of DCS-TSP problems (see Section 4.2.3). In order to define the transfer cost $\overline{\mathbf{W}}$, we compute the orbital elements of the departure and arrival debris at the relevant epoch using the SGP4 orbital propagator [8] and we then apply the three-impulses approximation to compute the ΔV required to perform the orbital transfer[6]. The results are shown in Table 5. Inver-over performs favourably in most cases, but the solution quality is impacted by an increase in problem complexity. In the static case we have seen an increase in area A for increasing problem dimension, e.g. from fen_100 to fen_200 trough fen (with 1550 debris pieces). This is to be expected, as including additional (yet smaller) debris pieces will always lead to an equal or better solution. In the dynamic case we see multiple instances where inver-over does not find a better or the same solution when allowing the complete debris set. Specifically, performance degrades from ir33_200 to ir33, from cos_200 to cos and from fen_400 to fen. As the increase in problem dimension did not constitute a problem in the static case we proceed with analysing the dynamic property of the problems and what causes the performance of the inver-over operate to degrade for larger debris sets.

[6]We thus assume that the relative orbits geometry do not vary significantly between t_i and t_{i+1}

	IO		NN		TS	
	A $[m^2]$	N	A $[m^2]$	N	A $[m^2]$	N
ir33_100	**3.0538**	20	3.0268	19	2.8928	18
ir33_200	**3.0820**	22	2.6155	22	2.9933	24
ir33	**3.0039**	22	2.5857	23	2.8823	23
cos_100	**2.5040**	11	2.3659	11	2.3827	11
cos_200	**2.6174**	14	2.4513	14	2.4681	14
cos	**2.5237**	8	2.4899	18	2.4578	14
fen_100	**1.8644**	8	**1.8644**	8	**1.8644**	8
fen_200	**2.0818**	12	**2.0818**	12	**2.0818**	12
fen_400	2.6603	15	2.5926	15	**2.7950**	21
fen	**2.4874**	12	2.4360	29	2.0015	31

Table 5: Performance of Inver-Over (IO), Nearest Neighbour (NN) and Tree Search (TS) in the Dynamic City Selection TSP problem.

5.1.2 How dynamic is our problem?

As debris orbits evolve over time the cost for transferring between two orbits changes as well. In order to quantify this dynamic property for various TSP-DCS problem instances, we use the following analysis. For each problem, we enumerate all possible pairs of debris. We evaluate the transfers at a reference epoch t_0 with the three-impulse approximation and select the transfers with a cost below $\Delta V_{\max} = 200$ m/s. Subsequently, each transfer pair gets re-evaluated at later epochs $t_i \forall i > 0$. Figure 7 shows the transfer cost of all 1014 transfer pairs with less than 200 m/s cost for the ir33 problem instance (i.e., 3.78% off all possible unique transfers). The ΔV of each pair at $t_0 = 5500$ [MJD2000] is plotted against the transfer cost one week, 8 weeks and 16 weeks later. All points above (below) the solid line represent transfers that are more (less) costly at t_i compared to t_0. Even after a relatively short time frame, some of the transfers incur costs that are twice as high compared to the reference epoch, thus showcasing how dynamic the problem really is.

For short time shifts (e.g. 7 days), there is a clear positive correlation between the cost of transfers. One might ask, up to which point this trend will persists and if it differs across problems. The operators of inver-over profit from any positive correlation between transfer cost at an earlier and later time, not necessarily a linear trend. We thus compute the Spearman's rank correlation coefficient ρ between the transfer cost for pairs at t_0 and t_i. The Spearman coefficient $\rho \in [-1, 1]$ is a measure of the dependence between two variables; if the relation between the two variables can be described by a monotonically increasing (decreasing) function the Spearman's correlation is at its extreme +1 (-1). Figure 8 shows the Spearman's rank correlation coefficient as a function of t_i for all three problems and dimensions. Smaller problems with dimension $100-200$ retain a correlation of $\rho = .9$ up to ≈ 50 days, while larger problems become more "dynamic" over the same time frame. The problem *cos* shows overall the steepest decline in correlation over $50-100$ days, which, assuming one visit per week, corresponds to a sequence of length ≈ 15.

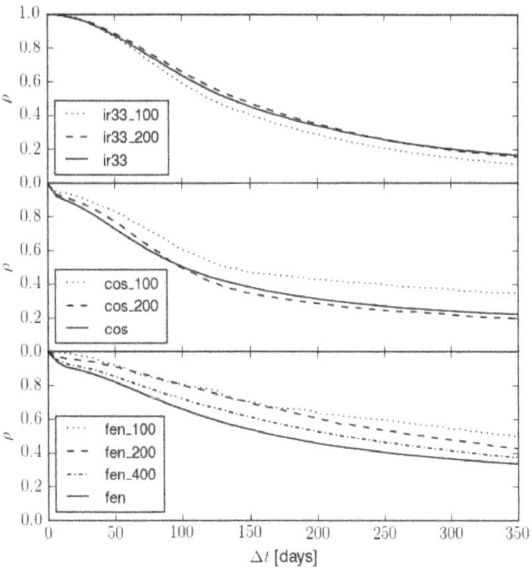

Figure 8: Spearman's rank correlation ρ as a function of time shift t_i for all three problems in various dimensions.

6. DISCUSSION

In previous works dealing with comparable ADR mission designs, brute force [3] or the Series Method approach (that is Nearest Neighbour) [4] were used to select and design the encounter sequence. In the scenario considered here, brute force would not be an option and NN reveals to be not a good approach as it performs consistently worse than our evolutionary approach or the fixed frontier tree search. Differences of up to 30% in the removed cross-section area were recorded. The approach of modelling the problem as a TSP-DCS and evolving its solution using the proposed inver-over algorithm seems overall very promising, while it reveals its limits as the evolutionary inver-over operator is tailored to static problems where edges retain their distances regardless of their position in the sequence. This calls for the design of better genetic operators for the dynamic case, likely to further improve performances and advance the TSP approach to ADR mission design to a point where it should be preferred, in all cases, to tree search methods. To facilitate this task, we made the problem instances available at the following address: http://www.esa.int/gsp/ACT/mad/projects/debris_removal.html

7. CONCLUSIONS

We have introduced a new methodology to design the debris removal sequence in an active debris removal mission. Our method is based on the formalization of the problem as a new variant to the Travelling Salesman Problem, which we call TSP-DCS (dynamic city selection), and on the use of a small modification to the inver-over evolutionary method. After instantiating a few test-cases we compare our approach to algorithms previously used to solve similar problems in the context of spacecraft mission design. We are able to select sequences of debris encounters choosing from large sets: we consider sets containing hundreds of debris while only tens could be considered in previous works on ADR mission design. Our results suggest that the use of evolutionary techniques on the proposed TSP variant is superior to current approaches, and call for the development of even better evolutionary operators, tailored for this domain.

8. REFERENCES

[1] Donald J Kessler and Burton G Cour-Palais. Collision frequency of artificial satellites: The creation of a debris belt. *Journal of Geophysical Research: Space Physics (1978–2012)*, 83(A6):2637–2646, 1978.

[2] J-C Liou and Nicholas L Johnson. Instability of the present leo satellite populations. *Advances in Space Research*, 41(7):1046–1053, 2008.

[3] Vitali Braun, A Lüpken, S Flegel, J Gelhaus, M Möckel, C Kebschull, C Wiedemann, and P Vörsmann. Active debris removal of multiple priority targets. *Advances in Space Research*, 51(9):1638–1648, 2013.

[4] Brent W Barbee, Salvatore Alfano, Elfego Pinon, Kenn Gold, and David Gaylor. Design of spacecraft missions to remove multiple orbital debris objects. In *Aerospace Conference, 2011 IEEE*, pages 1–14. IEEE, 2011.

[5] Max Cerf. Multiple Space Debris Collecting Mission-Debris Selection and Trajectory Optimization. *Journal of Optimization Theory and Applications*, 156(3):761–796, 2013.

[6] S. Hokamoto and J. Murakami. Genetic-algorithm-based randezvous trajectory design for multiple active debris removal. In *28th International Symposium on Space Technology and Science*, 2011.

[7] Guo Tao and Zbigniew Michalewicz. Inver-over operator for the tsp. In *Parallel Problem Solving from Nature-PPSN V*, pages 803–812. Springer, 1998.

[8] David A Vallado and Paul Crawford. SGP4 orbit determination. In *Proceedings of AIAA/AAS Astrodynamics Specialist Conference and Exhibit*, pages 18–21, 2008.

[9] Nicholas L Johnson, JR Gabbard, GT Devere, and EE Johnson. History of on-orbit satellite fragmentations. Technical report, NASA NTRS, ID:19840026390, 1984.

[10] Theodore N Edelbaum. Propulsion requirements for controllable satellites. *ARS Journal*, 31(8):1079–1089, 1961.

[11] Ahmed Gad and Ossama Abdelkhalik. Hidden genes genetic algorithm for multi-gravity-assist trajectories optimization. *Journal of Spacecraft and Rockets*, 48(4):629–641, 2011.

[12] Dario Izzo, Luís F Simões, Chit Hong Yam, Francesco Biscani, David Di Lorenzo, Bernardetta Addis, and Andrea Cassioli. GTOC5: Results from the European Space Agency and University of Florence. *Acta Futura*, 8:45–55, 2014.

[13] Aimin Zhou, Lishan Kang, and Zhenyu Yan. Solving dynamic tsp with evolutionary approach in real time. In *Evolutionary Computation, 2003. CEC'03. The 2003 Congress on*, volume 2, pages 951–957. IEEE, 2003.

[14] Changhe Li, Ming Yang, and Lishan Kang. A new approach to solving dynamic traveling salesman problems. In *Simulated Evolution and Learning*, pages 236–243. Springer, 2006.

Finding an Optimal LEGO® Brick Layout of Voxelized 3D Object Using a Genetic Algorithm

Sangyeop Lee
School of Computer Science & Engineering
Seoul National University
1 Gwanak-ro, Gwanak-gu
Seoul, 151-744 Korea
leesy714@soar.snu.ac.kr

Jinhyun Kim
School of Computer Science & Engineering
Seoul National University
1 Gwanak-ro, Gwanak-gu
Seoul, 151-744 Korea
jh@soar.snu.ac.kr

Jae Woo Kim
Computer Graphics Laboratory
Electronics and Telecommunications Research Institute (ETRI)
218 Gajeong-ro, Yuseong-gu
Daejeon, 305-700 Korea
jae_kim@etri.re.kr

Byung-Ro Moon
School of Computer Science & Engineering
Seoul National University
1 Gwanak-ro, Gwanak-gu
Seoul, 151-744 Korea
moon@snu.ac.kr

ABSTRACT

In this paper, we propose a genetic algorithm for a LEGO® brick layout problem. The task is to build a given 3D object with LEGO® bricks. A brick layout is modeled as a solution to a combinatorial optimization problem, through intermediate voxelization, which tries to maximize the connectivity and then minimize the number of used bricks. We attack the problem in the context of genetic search. The proposed randomized greedy algorithm produces initial solutions, and the solutions are effectively improved by an evolutionary process. New domain-specific methods are proposed as well, which include a random boundary mutation and a thickening approach. We tested our algorithm on various objects collected from the web. Experimental results showed that the algorithm produces efficient, and mostly optimal solutions for benchmark models. Unlike some previous works, our algorithm is not limited to assemble few specific objects, but it can deal with diverse kind of objects. To the best of our knowledge, this is the most extensive empirical study on the problem.

Categories and Subject Descriptors

I.2.8 [**Problem Solving, Control Methods, and Search**]: Heuristic methods

GECCO '15, July 11 - 15, 2015, Madrid, Spain

ACM ISBN 978-1-4503-3472-3/15/07...$15.00

DOI: http://dx.doi.org/10.1145/2739480.2754667

Keywords

Genetic algorithm; local search; LEGO®; brick layout problem; empirical study

1. INTRODUCTION

LEGO® is a line of brick-shaped toy manufactured by the LEGO® Group, and it consists of bricks with regular size and shape. Bricks can be attached on one another to assemble three dimensional objects. Since it can assemble various objects with regular bricks that are all reusable, LEGO® bricks are occasionally used in science and engineering fields for the purpose of prototyping [1, 4].

The problem of finding a way to assemble a 3D object with the LEGO® bricks seems to be started with the history of the toy. The LEGO® Group also openly presented this problem to academic fields [8, 13].

This problem can be divided into two steps. The first step is to transform the given three dimensional object into a voxelized model; this step is called voxelization. A voxel is an extended concept of a pixel from a two dimensional space and it is a unit cube in a three dimensional space. The goal of voxelization is to make the model as similar as possible to the original object [2, 12]. The second step is to assemble a voxelized object with real bricks. This is called the brick layout problem. Figure 1 shows an example of a 3D mesh object, a corresponding voxelized model, and a brick layout of the model.

Various methods have been proposed to deal with the brick layout problem. Most of the methods rely on evaluation schemes to measure the fitness of a brick layout, and various optimization techniques including heuristic approaches and a beam search were applied to maximize the fitness [3, 11]. Since there exists an exponential number of possible layouts, a naive search algorithm cannot cope with the problem properly. Most of the methods try to improve

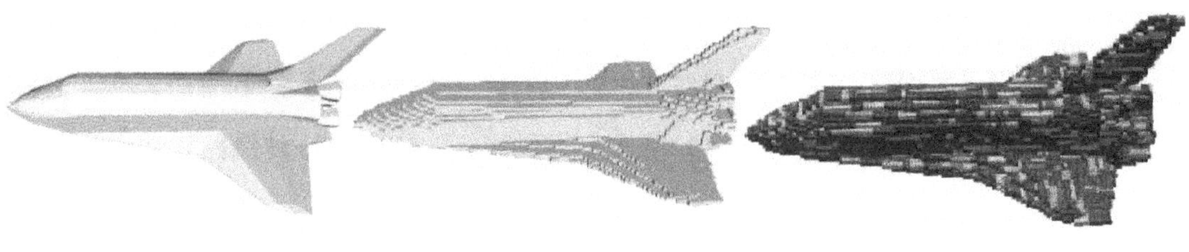

Figure 1: An example of brick layout problem for a *shuttle* model. The left picture shows the 3D mesh model, the center picture shows the voxelized model and the last picture shows the model assembled with bricks.

the initial solution found by a heuristic in an iterative way [3, 8, 11, 12].

To improve the solutions efficiently, it is the most important to keep good features of a layout unharmed and perturb only the critical points which determine the connectivity of the structure. A genetic algorithm, which evolves the solution by maintaining schemata inside the solution, is a good candidate for the brick layout problem. One of the proposed methods uses an evolutionary computation [8], but it was tested on only one 3D model. Due to the lack of experimental result, it is merely a suggestion of an algorithm.

In this paper, we propose a genetic algorithm to solve the brick layout problem. We first design a simple heuristics based on greedy algorithm, which is used as local optimization procedure later. We introduce a genetic algorithm framework to evolve solutions to better ones. Several problem-specific operators we designed are introduced as well, which give the algorithm more optimization power. We also present extensive experimental result with various voxelized models. The result proved that our genetic algorithm with local search can efficiently produce a brick layout which has high connectivity using less number of bricks.

2. RELATED WORKS

The brick layout problem appeared naturally along with the long history of LEGO® [11]. The problem has been studied at least since 1990s and several methods have been proposed so far. The LEGO® Group also have been paying attention to this problem, and they presented the problem in 1998 and 2001 to a study group and at an academic conference [8, 13].

Gower *et al.* [3] formulated the problem as a combinatorial optimization problem. When the object is given as a voxelized model, which is a 3D binary array, the problem is to find a layout of bricks that minimizes a penalty function. The goal was to connect the whole bricks as a single connected component, and a placement of a brick which diminishes the connectivity was penalized. They tried to reflect their prior knowledge on some good layouts to the penalty function, but the effect of their penalty function was neither properly analyzed nor tested.

Petrovic [8] improved the approach proposed by Gower *et al.* by using an evolutionary algorithm. Similarly to the penalty function, they used a fitness function which is represented by a weight sum of six score factors. The factors were designed to both minimize the number of used bricks and to increase the connectivity of the structure. One distinctive factor in their design was to minimize the number of isolated voxel. Starting from the population consisting of layouts generated by heuristics, the solutions were evolved for few thousands of generations. Experimental results showed that their algorithm successfully improved the initial layouts. However, the proposed algorithm has a limit since they tuned it on only one specific 3D object.

Smal [11] reviewed related previous methods and proposed some methods to improve a solution. They first obtain an initial layout with a heuristic, and used a beam search algorithm and a cellular automata to improve some part of the layout. Zijl and Smal [14] investigated some patterns of operations to improve a brick layout and used a cellular automata to imitate the patterns. They proposed a *merge* operation to combine some bricks into a single brick, and a *split* operation to divide a brick into voxel-sized bricks. An alternative and repeated use of the operations was effective in improving a single brick layout.

Testuz *et al.* [12] also proposed a merge and split based algorithm. They used a randomized greedy algorithm to find an initial solution. Then a graph algorithm was used to detect a part of the solution that has low connectivity, and if found, the split and merge operation was applied to that part. They also proposed hollowing operation on the voxelized model to reduce the number of used bricks. The algorithm was tested on 5 mesh models, but only few discussions followed.

Utilizing the brick layout in real world also has been studied. Peysakhov *et al.* [9, 10] used a messy genetic algorithm to evolve assemblies of the bricks in order to obtain complex and realistic electromechanical structures. Mueller *et al.* [6] used a 3D printer to print the bricks and used the layout in prototyping of an object. They showed that use of the bricks and its layout was fast and convenient. Zhang *et al.* [15] proposed an interactive system that transforms a 2D design into a 3D artwork by using the bricks.

3. BASIC ALGORITHM

3.1 Problem Formulation

We use the combinatorial optimization problem formulation which is widely used in literature. The input of the problem is represented as a 3D binary array, where each entry of 1 describes a voxel of the object, and entries of 0 mean emptiness. A solution of the problem corresponds to a brick layout, and the problem is to minimize the penalty function. We define the penalty function to be the number of connected components formed by the layout, and in case of tie, we compare the number of used bricks. This means that we first try to increase the connectivity and then try to increase the efficiency of the layout, as in some previous work [12].

Each brick in a layout is placed only in horizontal direction and it consists of the voxels from the same layer of the array. We only use the regular bricks of size $1 \times n$ and $2 \times n$, where

n is either 1, 2, 4, 6, or 8. The brick could be rotated but it should not be placed diagonally. We regard the layout as a graph to calculate the number of connected component. Each vertex represents a brick in a layout and two vertices are connected if corresponding bricks are attached to each other up-and-down.

3.2 Greedy Heuristics

We find a brick layout layer by layer by considering each layer in specific order, since each brick has to be placed in only one layer. For each layer, we first choose a voxel and place a bricks on that voxel in a greedy manner. All types of the bricks and all feasible arrangements are considered, and the one with the largest score is selected. We repeat it for every voxel in a layer, and repeat the whole process for each of the layer.

We adapted the ideas from previous works to compute the score of an arrangement [3, 8, 11]. The score is defined in a way that maximizing the score of the arrangements may lead to minimizing the penalty of the entire layout. Note that the score is defined on an arrangement of a brick, and the penalty is defined on the entire layout. The score is a weighted sum of three factors, and the factors used are as follows.

- **Cover factor** is used to increase the connectivity. Two bricks cover each other when they are placed in two consecutive layers and are connected up and down. Having more connection with the other bricks may increase the connectivity of the layout, and a perpendicular connection may provide more chance of connection to the others. We therefore count the number of covered bricks and use it as a cover factor, and the score is doubled when bricks are perpendicular.

- **Size factor** is used to increase the efficiency. The total number of bricks may decrease if larger bricks are used each time. Moreover, using a larger brick may provide more chance of connection to the bricks in the above and below layers. We therefore take the size of the brick into account and use it as a size factor.

- **Isolation factor** is to deal with a specific case that is vulnerable to loss of connectivity. If a single voxel has no connected voxel in the above and below layer, or if it has at most one adjacent voxel in the same layer, we define the voxel to be *isolated*. The isolated voxel must be a part of a brick with other voxels, otherwise it would easily form a disconnected component. We count the number of isolated voxels contained in a brick to be placed and use it as an isolation factor.

The order of the voxels and layers considered may affect the quality of the solution. We tried both a heuristic ordering and a randomized ordering. Since the heuristic ordering was not significantly better than the randomized ordering in the experiment, we choose the latter one. It was also reported that using randomness in the ordering may consistently produce a good solution [12].

After a significant number of experiments, we chose 10, 1, and 20 as the weights of the cover, size, and isolation factor, respectively.

4. GENETIC ALGORITHM

In this section, we propose a genetic algorithm to solve the brick layout problem by evolving the solutions.

4.1 Merge-Split Model

First, we need a method to change the solution slightly to improve it. Merging bricks into a larger one, or splitting a brick into smaller ones are used to modify the solutions in previous works [11, 14]. We adopt this idea to evolve the population of solutions in a genetic algorithm. The merge operation merges two or more bricks into one big brick if possible, and the split operation split a single brick into several 1×1 bricks. Given a brick layout, we can create several new solutions by splitting some bricks and merging them again with various orders and various combinations.

4.2 Basic Design

Algorithm 1 Genetic algorithm

```
Initialize population
repeat
    Select two parents parent1, parent2
    offspring ← Crossover(parent1, parent2)
    Mutation(offspring)
    Repair(offspring)
    Replace one chromosome with offspring
until Stop Condition
```

The basic framework of the GA is described in Algorithm 1. We implemented a 3000-generation steady-state GA with the following operators.

- **Representation** : We represent voxelized model directly as a three dimensional chromosome. Each gene points at the brick object which occupies that specific location. If there is a brick which is larger than 1×1, all of the genes covered by the brick point at that brick. It might seem inefficient to represent all 3 dimensional locations of the voxelized model. However, as the performance of merge-split method is affected not by the total size of the chromosome but by the number of bricks, a direct representation is quite intuitive and reasonable.

- **Population**: 128 chromosomes are generated. Each solution is a result of randomized heuristics in previous section.

- **Object Function**: We have two objectives to achieve; high connectivity and a less number of bricks. Connectivity is measured by the total number of connected components in the model. Our goal is to minimize both the number of connected components and the number of bricks. It is still more important to minimize the number of connected components than the number of bricks. We designed a function that scalarize two value into one number as follows:

$$f = (\#CCs) \times (D) \times (W) \times (H) + (\#Bricks),$$

where #CCs is the number of connected components, #Bricks is the number of bricks and D, W, H are the depth, the width and the height of the model, respectively. With this fitness, the number of blocks never exceeds the connectivity term because D×W×H is always larger than the number of bricks. By minimizing this function, we can minimize the number of connected components and the number of blocks if the number of components is the same.

- **Selection** : A rank based roulette-wheel-selection is used. The best solution is chosen with four times higher probability than the worst solution. We choose two different chromosomes with this operation.
- **Crossover** : We apply crossover operation on each layer separately. Two different crossover operators were used; one line crossover and RectCrossover. One-line crossover is an extension of the one-point crossover. Instead of using a straight line as a cutting line, this crossover cuts the layer with a line that starts at upper-left corner, repetitively move to right or down finally to lower-right corner. This is a variation of a multi-dimensional crossover suggested in [5]. A layer is divided into two area by this cutting line. Genes are copied from one parent in one side and from another parent in the other side. RectCrossover, which was used in several previous works, chooses random rectangular area, copy genes inside of the rectangle from one parent and copy other genes from the other parent [8, 11]. Blocks which cross the line or the boundary of rectangle are split into 1x1 bricks.
- **Mutation** : Several mutation operators are applied. A simple one is to choose some bricks with a specific rate and split them all, which is problem-blinded and inefficient. Therefore, we develop new mutation operator that is driven by the boundary between each connected components of the layout. Further explanation is in the next subsection.
- **Repair and Optimization** : Splitting bricks is not enough for generating decent and diverse solutions, though. After splitting some bricks, we run the randomized heuristic again to rebuild the solution. This procedure plays a role not only as repairing solutions but as a local optimization algorithm.
- **Replace** : The worst solution in the population is replaced by the new solution. By using this replacement policy, the genetic algorithm might converge earlier.

4.3 Boundary Split

The simplest mutation is to choose the bricks to mutate at a same rate, and then split the chosen ones. However, a promising schema in the chromosome could be destroyed during the mutation although sometimes it is helpful. Instead of splitting the bricks blindly, we may guide the operator to split only the bricks which require a modification.

One way is to split blocks near the boundary of the connected components. If a solution is not connected and there exists more than one connected component, we define the space that divides the bricks into multiple connected components to be the boundary of the components. To connect the divided parts, we have to merge adjacent bricks that are from the different components into a single brick. Since these set of bricks resides near the boundary, choosing the bricks to split from this area might be promising to improve connectivity

Algorithm 2 Largest boundary split

function LargestBoundarySplit(layer L, rate r)
    $B \leftarrow$ set of all pairs of different connected components in L
    $Bricks \leftarrow emptylist$
    for all (b_1, b_2) in B **do**
        $S \leftarrow$ Bricks adjacent to the boundary between b_1 and b_2
        Add the largest brick in S to *Bricks*
    end for
    Choose bricks in *Bricks* at rate r
    Split the chosen bricks
end function

With this idea, we developed four different mutation algorithms, namely largest boundary split(LB), random boundary split(RB), largest boundary with neighbor split(LBN), and random boundary with neighbor split(RBN). Algorithm 2 illustrates the mechanism of the largest boundary split. It gathers the largest bricks from the boundaries and split some of them with a given probability. Random boundary split works in a similar way but gathers random bricks from the the boundaries instead of the largest one.

It may not be enough to split just boundary bricks, for they may return to the previous state as there exists no proper bricks to merge with. To deal with this concern, with-neighbor operators split not only boundary bricks, but also the neighboring bricks of those. This may create flexibility on the merging algorithm thanks to small bricks nearby. Still, splitting neighbor bricks may destroy good schema of chromosomes as they split excessive number of bricks.

5. EXPERIMENTAL RESULTS

5.1 Dataset

The dataset consists of 17 different voxelized models. Five of them(*armadillo*, *bunny*, *dragon*, *happy*, and *lucy*) are from the Stanford 3D scanning repository[1] and the rest are from data files maintained by John Burkardt[2]. They are all 3-dimensional mesh object files. The `vtkImplicitModeller` class from the the visualization toolkit(VTK)[3] was used to voxelize most of the objects. However, since it could not handle the Stanford dataset properly, binvox[4] [7] was used to voxelize these objects. We did not fill the inner part of the models since filling this part uses much more bricks in total. The details of each model is presented in each of the website. We have conducted preliminary experiments and classified the models by difficulty. Some models, like *gourd*, *cube*, and *tetra*, are straightforward, so that even a simple heuristic finds the optimal layout with one single connected component. Some other models like *lamp*, *dragon*, and *lucy* are intermediate, and a simple heuristic may not find the optimal layout. There also exist very hard models as they have delicate voxels which must be covered cautiously to find an optimal layout. Although it is impossible to assemble those models with one connected component, we also conducted experiments on these models to see the perfor-

[1]http://graphics.stanford.edu/data/3Dscanrep/
[2]http://people.sc.fsu.edu/~jburkardt/data/obj/obj.html
[3]http://www.vtk.org/
[4]http://www.google.com/search?q=binvox

Model	No Xover	One line	RectXover
lamp	1.17	**1.00**	1.00
	1595.3	**1532.4**	1533.5
dragon	1.27	2.13	**1.07**
	1793.0	1836.1	**1733.7**
lucy	2.33	2.73	**1.27**
	844.1	880.9	**800.3**
airboat	154.47	**107.03**	107.26
	2485.9	**2530.8**	2517.1
shuttle	148.97	163.93	**102.27**
	2324.5	2405.3	**2322.8**

Table 1: The comparison of different crossover operators. The upper denotes the number of connected components and the lower denotes the number of the bricks. Values in bold denotes the best performance.

mance improvement achieved by our algorithm on varius kind of models. We will take a look at these models and find why these cannot be assembled into a single component and also study how to deal with them in next subsections of this paper.

For the experiments to compare the performance between the algorithms, we used *lamp*, *dragon*, and *lucy* as intermediate examples, *airboat* and *shuttle* as hard examples. We did not run our algorithm on easy examples, except for overall results as they made no differences with operator, parameter changes.

We used LEGO® Digital Designer tool[5] to visualize results of each models.

5.2 Effect of Crossover

We compared 3 kinds of GAs, one having the mutation operator only, one using the one-line crossover, and one using the RectCrossover. The result is presented on Table 1. In each cell, the upper shows the average number of connected components for GA with the corresponding crossover and the lower is the average number of bricks. Each instance was repeated 30 times.

One-line crossover showed slightly better result on the models *lamp* and *airboat*, but the differences were insignificant. On the other hand, RectCrossover showed much better performance on the models *dragon* and *shuttle*. One-line crossover was even worse than a GA with no crossover for the *shuttle* model.

This result reveals how the crossover operators work in the brick layout problem. Depending on the design of a crossover, it may play a more role on preservation than perturbation or vice versa. In the case of the brick layout problem, one-line crossover, which includes zigzag random walks, is good for perturbing a solution but it is vulnerable to loss of a schema. On the other hand, RectCrossover will preserve the solution compared to the one-line crossover, because it is less likely that straight lines of the rectangle cross huge bricks. The excellence of RectCrossover over one-line crossover reveals that it is much more important to preserve good schemata for problem space search, which in turn better leads creation of new attractive schemata.

[5]http://ldd.lego.com

Model	Rand	LB	RB	LBN	RBN
lamp	1.00	1.00	1.00	1.00	**1.00**
	1533.5	1516.7	1516.5	1523.8	**1513.9**
dragon	1.07	1.00	**1.00**	1.00	1.00
	1733.7	1741.8	**1726.3**	1737.7	1733.4
lucy	1.27	1.06	**1.00**	1.00	1.00
	800.3	802.2	**798.37**	818.4	810.0
airboat	**107.26**	123.27	118.73	152.77	150.13
	2517.1	2627.9	2584.8	2639.0	2623.4
shuttle	102.27	79.00	**51.30**	138.10	130.07
	2322.8	2413.6	**2336.7**	2422.0	2400.3

Table 2: The comparison of different mutations, fixing split rate at 0.7. The upper denotes the number of connected components and the lower denotes the number of bricks. Bold denotes the best performance.

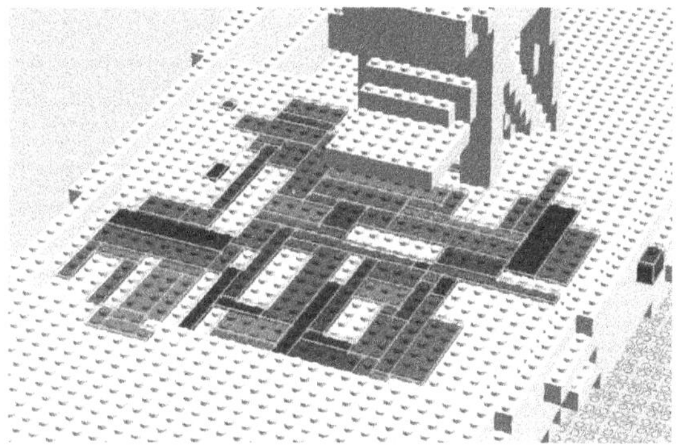

Figure 2: Isolated part of *airboat* model. Many isolated brick are adjacent to each other.

5.3 Analysis of Mutation Operators

We compared five types of mutations. One selects bricks to split randomly, and the others uses LB, RB, LBN and RBN mutation operators respectively. We choose 0.7 as a split rate after a significant number of experiments. Table 2 shows the result of experiments.

RandomBoundarySplit showed the best performance over other mutations. While being better than completely random mutations, LargestBoundarySplit was not better than RB. Since LB mutation operator chooses bricks to split in a deterministic policy, this operator tends to split similar bricks which in turn generates a solution similar to the parents. Thus, LB mutation operator may not generate diverse solutions compared to RB.

It is interesting that splitting the neighbors of boundary bricks did never improve the performance. Rather, it dropped the fitness even worse than the random mutation. This result points that it is enough to split only boundary bricks to connect the components. In fact, this result is consistent with the result of experiment on crossover operators. Splitting neighbors of boundary bricks will perturb the solution even more than LB or RB, end up with destroying much of good schema.

It was RBN who showed the best result for the *lamp* model, but the difference was insignificant. Moreover, for the *airboat* model, the random mutation operator showed significantly better result than RB mutation operator. To

Figure 3: Wing part of *shuttle* model. It is thin layers so that it is hard to assemble.

find the reason, we investigated the separated parts of the *airboat* model. Figure 2 shows the layout of the isolated parts. Colored bricks are parts of the *airboat* models which are not connected to the main connected component. Unlike other models like *shuttle*, the isolated parts of *airboat* are adjacent to each other. This creates a complicated boundaries between the bricks. Applying RB mutation operator leads to split these bricks and rebuild them in another form. It is changing the layout of the components which are already disconnected from a huge main part, and these parts remain isolated even when the mutation operator is applied. This does not improves the solution. The *airboat* model suggests an idea that we should evaluate each components not fairly but differently by their size.

5.4 Model Adjustment

Some models, like *airboat* and *shuttle*, have delicate structures which cannot be easily solved by the methods above. Figure 3 shows the unconnected parts of the *shuttle* model. Most of the disconnected components are located at the edge of two wings. Each wing of the *shuttle* model consists of only one or two layers which are attached to the body of the plane, and thus have little possibility to be connected to other components. The *airboat* model has a problem similar to the *shuttle* model as presented in the previous the section.

These problem can be solved in diverse ways. One approach is to fill the empty part inside the model with voxels. These kinds of models cannot be joined into a single connected component without adding more voxels, since most of the models are hollow, which means that the models are made of thin layers of voxels. Filling the inside of the models will make them thicker, which allows much stable layout. Although it offers a higher connectivity than unfilled model, this approach may need much more bricks compared to the original models.

We can compromise between the connectivity and the number of bricks. Without filling all of empty spaces inside, only adding voxels at locations adjacent to existing voxels may be sufficient to improve the performance. We define this as increasing the thickness. To increase the thickness, we first find the inner part of the model. This part is the space not reachable from the outside space due to the shell of voxels. Then, we find locations inside which are adjacent to existing voxels by a single unit and add a voxel on them.

We compared these three approaches on three models, *bunny*, *airboat*, and *shuttle*. Table 3 shows the result of the experiments. It is represented in a similar way used in previous tables.

Increasing thickness by one and filling inside both found optimal layouts at least once in 30 runs. The number of connected components drops dramatically for most of the models. Especially for the *airboat* model, it drops from 118 to 1. Note that the increasing the thickness uses much less number of bricks than filling inside. Fill-inside algorithm sometimes underperforms the increasing-thickness algorithm, even though they are more stable thanks to more number of bricks. This seems to caused by an exponential growth of the number of possible solutions after adding the voxels. It took more time for GA to converge.

Model	None	Thick+1	Fill
bunny	23.17	**1.00**	1.00
	2512.2	**2862.6**	4658.63
airboat	118.73	**1.00**	1.00
	2584.8	**2833.97**	3029.2
shuttle	51.30	**1.83**	2.17
	2336.7	**3055.8**	162610.8

Table 3: Model adjustment result. The upper denotes the number of connected components and the lower denotes the number of bricks. Bold denotes the best performance.

Figure 4: Isolated part of *sandal* model. Three voxels are completely separated from other voxels.

5.5 Overall Result

We have run out GA with the best operators, RectCrossover and RB mutation, and the best parameters for all models. Although RectCrossover and RB were slightly worse than other operators for some special cases, they were better than other operators by a wide margin in most of the models. All instances were repeated one hundred times, and we present the average and minimum number of components. We also calculated the mean brick size, which shows how efficiently the layout uses the space. More efficient layout will use bigger brick in average. The result is presented in Table 4.

The first three columns represent model name, model height-width-depth, and the number of voxels inside, repectively. The forth column is the average connected components as result of multi-start random heuristic for comparison. Multi-start random heuristic starts on 128 different instance and shows the best result. That is, the quality of initial solutions for the multi-start heuristic and the GA are the same. We repeat the algorithm 100 times to get the average of them. Other columns are the result of GA, the average and minimum numbers of connected components, average number of bricks, and mean brick size. We repeated the GA of 5000 generations 100 times and get the average and minimum of those. Mean brick size is the number of voxels divided by the number of bricks. We used this number to know how efficient the layout is.

The bold figures denote the instances our algorithm found a layout with single connected components at least once dur-

3D Models			avg. #CC(w/o GA)	Final #CC		#Bricks	Mean Brick Size
name	dimension	#voxels		average	min		
tetra	10 × 10 × 10	131	1.00	1.00	**1**	36.00	3.63
cube	10 × 10 × 10	296	1.00	1.00	**1**	32.00	9.25
gourd	14 × 31 × 19	723	1.00	1.00	**1**	215.15	3.36
icosahedron	17 × 17 × 17	968	1.00	1.00	**1**	231.44	4.18
lucy	50 × 50 × 50	3104	7.36	1.00	**1**	781.22	3.97
happy	50 × 50 × 50	4742	12.36	1.00	**1**	1261.44	3.75
al	23 × 58 × 54	5106	6.21	3.00	3	1189.34	4.29
lamp	48 × 116 × 43	5308	5.47	1.00	**1**	1469.35	3.61
armadillo	50 × 50 × 50	6093	9.04	1.00	**1**	1636.04	3.72
dragon	50 × 50 × 50	6257	7.88	1.00	**1**	1688.42	3.70
bunny	50 × 50 × 50	8697	51.53	17.27	12	2498.71	3.48
sandal	117 × 34 × 52	9346	204.74	118.59	97	1752.71	5.33
shuttle	146 × 55 × 93	13222	198.50	21.32	7	2300.49	5.74
airboat	56 × 47 × 162	15977	200.51	104.73	98	2518.20	6.34
humanoidtri	28 × 143 × 79	18052	104.98	35.53	**1**	2922.56	6.18
humanoidquad	28 × 143 × 79	18052	105.03	11.09	**1**	2881.49	6.26
slotmachine	103 × 211 × 140	101848	22.69	1.00	**1**	16738.48	6.08
bunny†	50 × 50 × 50	13007	1.54	1.00	**1**	2759.01	4.71
sandal†	117 × 34 × 52	11994	19.54	4.00	4	1872.55	6.40
shuttle†	146 × 55 × 93	18425	45.61	1.50	**1**	2940.90	6.26
airboat†	56 × 47 × 162	18789	29.84	1.00	**1**	2702.75	6.95
al_mod	22 × 58 × 54	5104	4.40	1.00	**1**	1181.17	4.32
sandal_mod†	117 × 34 × 52	9343	16.52	1.00	**1**	1872.60	6.40

† : thickened instance

Table 4: Overall result. Model *al_mod* and *sandal_mod* are modified models of *al* and *sandal* to be assembled into single components. Bold denote that the optimal solution was found at least one time.

Figure 5: Pattern which is impossible to assemble with one components

ing the 100 runs. For all of cases, GA outperforms the random heuristic algorithm remarkably. GA found optimal solutions for most of the models, while the heuristic could not find an optimal layout even for small models. It is interesting that the heuristic tends to find similar solutions mostly whether it is optimal or not. This implies that there exist some strong attractors in problem space so that the heuristic algorithm cannot easily get out of local optima. The GA did not show such a characteristic, meaning that it can search the problem space effectively.

We could never find an optimal solution for some models such as *al*, which has a specific pattern. See Figure 5. Since *al* includes two of that pattern, *al* cannot be assembled into less than three components: the big main component and the other two small components of the pattern. Therefore, 3 is the optimal number of connected components for this model. Unlike the hollow models introduced in the previous subsection, this model has to be adjusted in a different way to get a fully connected result.

The algorithm could not find an optimal solution with *bunny*, *sandal*, *airboat* and *shuttle* within given generations. These models are hollow inside as introduced in the previous subsection. If we increase their thickness by one, we could an the optimal solution for three of them, except for *sandal* model. Instances with '†' are these. We found the optimal solutions for all three instances.

The reason why our algorithm could not find the optimal solution for *sandal* seems because of the shape of some part in the model, like the model *al*. Figure 4 shows the isolated parts in one of the solutions for *sandal*. It is clear that these parts cannot be assembled into one component as they are separated from other voxels. Without this part, all the other voxels could be assembled in sone component.

For model *al* and *sandal*†, we need to repair the voxel model. We erased the isolated voxels. We erased 2 voxels for *al* and 3 for *sandal*, which did not affect the overall shapes of them at all. Instance *al_mod* and *sandal*†*_mod* is the result for these modified models. Our algorithm found the optimal layout for these modified models.

6. CONCLUSION

This paper dealt with the problem to assemble a given three dimensional object by using LEGO® bricks. First, to solve the problem as combinatorial optimization, we proposed a simple algorithm, which consists of evaluation of a layout, greedy-based heuristic, randomized method to get various solutions. Moreover, we used a genetic algorithm to improve the solutions. We also designed problem-specific mutation operators, LB and RB, to further improve the solutions. For some models which are hard to assemble, we adopted an algorithm that increase the thickness of the voxel structure. This algorithm assembles the hardest models into one component without using excessive number of bricks.

We implemented the algorithm and conducted experiment on 17 models which consist of 4 easy models, 6 intermediate models, 5 hard models, and two impossible models. Our algorithm found the optimal solutions for 10 of them; considering the modified version of the impossible models, we in fact found the optimal solutions for 11 models. Four models had some delicate structures, which is hard to assemble. Our algorithm applied a simple process increasing the thickness to improve faulty of structures without using too much bricks; we eventually found the optimal layout for all of them. In the end, our algorithm found the optimal solutions for all the benchmark models.

Unlike previous works, this paper actually dealt with real world applications of the brick layout problem. The models used in this paper are not artificially generated models but voxelized forms of tangible objects which were 3D scanned of real objects. Furthermore, our algorithm has found the optimal solutions for most of the models in the view point of connectivity. This suggests that given voxelized model, our work can be presented into a real brick-building guide with high reliability.

The proposed algorithm could be improved further. We used a thickness-increasing algorithm as a preprocessing on the models. Thus, it adds voxels not only where they are needed, but sometimes where they are unnecessary. Although it uses much less number of blocks than filling every empty inside part of the model, there is still room for improvement. If we make an algorithm which adds only few number of voxels only if they are needed, that will make a layout with a fewer number of bricks.

Our algorithm only considers the number of connected components and the number of bricks, but not voxelization algorithm and physical stability simulation. Designing a fitness function which considers these factors in an integrated way, it may be able to find a layout with higher physical stability.

LEGO® bricks are used in many fields, such as science, engineering, and art. With better algorithm to find stable and efficient brick layouts, we can better use the bricks to their full potential. s

7. ACKNOWLEDGMENTS

This research is supported by Ministry of Culture, Sports and Tourism (MCST) and Korea Creative Content Agency (KOCCA) in the Culture Technology (CT) Research & Development Program (Project ID: R2013040060). The work was also supported by the Engineering Research Center of Excellence Program of Korea Ministry of Science, ICT & Future Planning(MSIP) / National Research Foundation of Korea(NRF) (Grant NRF-2008-0062609). The ICT at Seoul National University provided research facilities for this study.

8. REFERENCES

[1] M. Ayers and R. Zeleznik. The LEGO interface toolkit. In *Proceedings of the 9th Annual ACM Symposium on User Interface Software and Technology*, pages 97–98, 1996.

[2] D. Cohen-Or and A. Kaufman. Fundamentals of surface voxelization. *Graphical models and image processing*, 57(6):453–461, 1995.

[3] R. Gower, A. Heydtmann, and H. Petersen. LEGO: Automated model construction. *32nd European Study Group with Industry - Final Report*, pages 81–94, 1998.

[4] L. Jensen, B. Kristensen, and Y. Demazeau. Flip: a platform to integrate embodied agent technology. In *Intelligent Agent Technology, 2003. IAT 2003. IEEE/WIC International Conference on*, pages 103–110, 2003.

[5] A. B. Kahng and B. R. Moon. Toward more powerful recombinations. In *Proceedings of the 6th International Conference on Genetic Algorithms*, pages 96–103, 1995.

[6] S. Mueller, T. Mohr, K. Guenther, J. Frohnhofen, and P. Baudisch. fabrickation: fast 3d printing of functional objects by integrating construction kit building blocks. In *Proceedings of the 32nd annual ACM conference on Human factors in computing systems*, pages 3827–3834, 2014.

[7] F. S. Nooruddin and G. Turk. Simplification and repair of polygonal models using volumetric techniques. *IEEE Transactions on Visualization and Computer Graphics*, 9(2):191–205, 2003.

[8] P. Petrovic. Solving LEGO brick layout problem using evolutionary algorithms. In *Proceedings to Norwegian Conference on Computer Science*, 2001.

[9] M. Peysakhov, V. Galinskaya, and W. C. Regli. Using graph grammars and genetic algorithms to represent and evolve LEGO assemblies. In D. Whitley, editor, *Late Breaking Papers at the 2000 Genetic and Evolutionary Computation Conference*, pages 269–276, 2000.

[10] M. Peysakhov and W. C. Regli. Using assembly representations to enable evolutionary design of LEGO structures. *Artificial Intelligence for Engineering Design, Analysis and Manufacturing*, 17(2):155–168, 2003.

[11] E. Smal. *Automated brick sculpture construction.* PhD thesis, Stellenbosch: Stellenbosch University, 2008.

[12] R. Testuz, Y. Schwartzburg, and M. Pauly. Automatic generation of constructable brick sculptures. In *Proc. Eurographics*, volume 13, 2013.

[13] O. Timcenko. LEGO: How to build with LEGO. *32nd European Study Group with Industry - Final Report*, pages xix–xxi, 1998.

[14] L. van Zijl and E. Smal. Cellular automata with cell clustering. In *Automata-2008: Theory and Applications of Cellular Automata*, pages 425–441, 2008.

[15] M. Zhang, J. Mitani, Y. Kanamori, and Y. Fukui. Blocklizer: Interactive design of stable mini block artwork. In *ACM SIGGRAPH 2014 Posters*, SIGGRAPH '14, pages 18:1–18:1, 2014.

On Evolutionary Approaches to Wind Turbine Placement with Geo-Constraints

Daniel Lückehe
Department of Geoinformation
Jade University of Applied Sciences
Oldenburg, Germany
daniel.lueckehe@uni-oldenburg.de

Markus Wagner
Optimisation and Logistics
University of Adelaide
Adelaide, Australia
markus.wagner@adelaide.edu.au

Oliver Kramer
Department of Computing Science
University of Oldenburg
Oldenburg, Germany
oliver.kramer@uni-oldenburg.de

ABSTRACT

Wind turbine placement, i.e., the geographical planning of wind turbine locations, is an important first step to an efficient integration of wind energy. The turbine placement problem becomes a difficult optimization problem due to varying wind distributions at different locations and due to the mutual interference in the wind field known as wake effect. Artificial and environmental geological constraints make the optimization problem even more difficult to solve. In our paper, we focus on the evolutionary turbine placement based on an enhanced wake effect model fed with real-world wind distributions. We model geo-constraints with real-world data from OpenStreetMap. Besides the realistic modeling of wakes and geo-constraints, the focus of the paper is on the comparison of various evolutionary optimization approaches. We propose four variants of evolution strategies with turbine-oriented mutation operators and compare to state-of-the-art optimizers like the CMA-ES in a detailed experimental analysis on three benchmark scenarios.

Categories and Subject Descriptors

G.1.6 [**Optimization**]: Constrained optimization; I.2.8 [**Artificial Intelligence**]: Problem Solving, Control Methods, and Search

Keywords

Wind Power, Wind Farm Layout, Evolutionary Optimization, Self-Adaptation, CMA-ES

1. INTRODUCTION

Renewable energy plays an increasing role in the energy supply world-wide. The integration of geo-information into planning processes becomes more and more important, resulting in a complex geo-planning problem with many constraints. In particular, the effective integration of wind energy is significantly influenced by the locations of wind turbines. Wind turbine placement optimization is the process of determining the placement of wind turbines within a specified land or offshore area, such that the output power of the wind farm is maximized. An optimized placement result allows wind farm installations to maximize their cost-effectiveness, thereby increasing their competitiveness in the energy market. However, the optimal placement of wind turbines considering geo-constraints is a complex optimization problem that is hard to solve by exact methods. The solution space is non-linear with respect to how sited turbines interact when considering wake loss and energy capture, in particular when facing constraints. In this paper, we employ evolutionary heuristics to solve the turbine placement problem.

Objective of this paper is to model a realistic wind turbine placement scenario by taking into account realistic wake effects, real-world wind data from a meteorological service, and geo-constraints from a topological map service. On the basis of this model, we define three benchmark scenarios and analyze turbine-oriented heuristics while comparing to state-of-the-art optimization algorithms like the covariance matrix adaptation evolution strategy (CMA-ES).

This paper is structured as follows. In Section 2, we present related work on turbine placement with evolutionary algorithms. Our enhanced wind model based on COSMO-DE data and Kusiak and Song's wake effects [10] is introduced in Section 3. In Section 4 we describe how OpenStreetMap data is modeled as geo-constraints. The evolutionary heuristics we employ for optimization are introduced in Section 5, followed by an experimental analysis on three benchmark scenarios in Section 6. Conclusions are drawn in Section 7.

2. RELATED WORK

For a very comprehensive overview on the single-objective wind farm layout problem, we refer the interested reader to the recent article by Herbert-Acero *et al.* [8]. For example, Wan et al. [19, 20] use cell-based approaches and compare different bio-inspired algorithms, each applied to the same set of wind farm models and parameters. An alternative to cell placement was explored in [10]: each turbine's location is a decision variable pair of real-valued, spatial (x, y) coordinates. In that paper, a simple evolution strategy (ES) [3] is used to optimize very small wind farms. In general, an ES is effective because it is easily parallelized and it self-

GECCO '15, July 11 - 15, 2015, Madrid, Spain

DOI: http://dx.doi.org/10.1145/2739480.2754690

adapts the extent to which it perturbs decision variables when generating a new potential solution. The more powerful CMA-ES has been used for the same problem in [18]. Despite being computationally expensive, it allows for the effective optimization of huge layouts for up to 1000 turbines. In [17] a random local search was presented that combines a problem-specific operator with an asymptotic speed-up of the computation time of the wake effects. Compared to the CMA-ES approach, the problem-specific local search produced higher quality placements in shorter time.

Many of the recent approaches make simplifying assumptions regarding the realism of the wake models. Even in some of the recent work, wakes are either completely ignored, and e.g., assumed to be constant or highly simplified. Nevertheless, we observe a trend towards the use of more realistic models, such as the Jensen [15] wake model. There, the wake effects decrease quadratically with the distance between the turbines. However, to make this model computationally viable, the model is simplified. For example, Kusiak and Song [10] suggest to discretize the wind directions. Not only are the resulting predictions less accurate, the model introduces many local optima which make the optimization an unnecessarily taxing task. To the best of our knowledge, this issue has not been reported in literature before, which is why we highlight and solve this later-on.

3. WIND MODEL

In this section, we introduce the employed wind model. For a given vector

$$\mathbf{x}_i = (x_1, x_2, \cdots, x_N) = (x_1^t, y_1^t, x_2^t, y_2^t, \cdots, x_{N/2}^t, y_{N/2}^t) \quad (1)$$

of $N/2$ turbine locations $\mathbf{t}_i = (x_i^t, y_i^t)$ with the length N, the model yields the power output of the corresponding setting with wind turbines. The model is based on the approach from Kusiak and Song [10] and our objective is to create a more realistic representation. For this purpose, we use power curves from a real wind turbine by Enercon and wind data from the German weather prediction model COSMO-DE by the German Weather Service.

3.1 Wind Power Calculation

In order to compute the power output E of a turbine i at position $\mathbf{t}_i = (x_i, y_i)$ for a given wind direction θ, the wind speed distribution $p_v(v, k(\mathbf{t}_i, \theta), c(\mathbf{t}_i, \theta))$ has to be multiplied with the turbine power curve $\beta_i(v)$, where v is the wind speed. The Weibull parameter $k(\cdot)$ and $c(\cdot)$ are functions depending on position and wind direction. For one wind direction it applies:

$$E_\theta(\mathbf{t}_i, \theta) = \int_0^\infty \beta_i(v) \cdot p_v(v, k(\mathbf{t}_i, \theta), c(\mathbf{t}_i, \theta))dv. \quad (2)$$

The output E for one turbine i considering all wind directions is:

$$E(\mathbf{t}_i) = \int_0^{360} p_\theta(\mathbf{t}_i, \theta) \cdot E_\theta(\mathbf{t}_i, \theta)d\theta \quad (3)$$

with the distribution $p_\theta(\cdot)$ of wind angles depending on position and wind direction. We solve these integrals like Kusiak and Song with a combination of an analytical solution and with the Riemann sum, because a purely analytical form is difficult to obtain [10]. This causes a discretization of the wind speed and the wind direction. Using the existing solution for this integral leads to a linear power curve $\beta_i(v)$ for the wind turbine:

$$\beta(v) = \begin{cases} 0 & v < v_{\text{cut-in}}, v_{\text{cut-out}} \leq v \\ \lambda \cdot v + \eta & v_{\text{cut-in}} \leq v < v_{\text{rated}} \\ P_{\text{rated}} & v_{\text{rated}} \leq v < v_{\text{cut-out}} \end{cases} \quad (4)$$

While $v_{\text{cut-in}}$ is the wind speed the turbine starts to produce power, v_{rated} denotes the minimal wind speed to get the maximum power from the turbine, and $v_{\text{cut-out}}$ is the speed when the turbine switches off for safety reasons. In our paper, we use the parameters of the Enercon E101 wind turbine, which we determined from the manufacturer's datasheet [5]: $\lambda = 277.0\,\text{kW}\cdot\text{s/m}$, $\eta = -551.6\,\text{kW}$, $P_{\text{rated}} = 3050\,\text{kW}$, $v_{\text{cut-in}} = 2\,\text{m/s}$, $v_{\text{rated}} = 13\,\text{m/s}$, $v_{\text{cut-out}} = 28\,\text{m/s}$.

3.2 Wind Analysis Data

We use the COSMO-DE analysis data from the German Weather Service [4] as the basis for the wind potential prediction for a position $\mathbf{t}_i$. This data provides a rotated latitude / longitude grid over Germany with $419_{\text{lat}} \cdot 459_{\text{lon}} = 192,321$ points. The distance between every grid point is approximately 2.8 km. Between the points, we will use a bilinear interpolation. For every data point, there are 50 different levels of height. As we use one turbine with the height of 135 m, we linearly interpolate from the model levels 46 and 47 with the height of approximately 180 m and 120 m – the levels in the COSMO-DE model are not at a fixed height.

In this work, we use the data of COSMO-DE 2012, which provides hourly wind vectors. We sort these vectors according to their wind direction θ and fit a Weibull distribution [21] for every wind direction θ. We employ the maximum likelihood estimation for fitting the distribution. The result is a Weibull function $p_v(v, k(\mathbf{t}_i, \theta), c(\mathbf{t}_i, \theta))$ representing the wind distribution for every position $\mathbf{t}_i$ and angle θ.

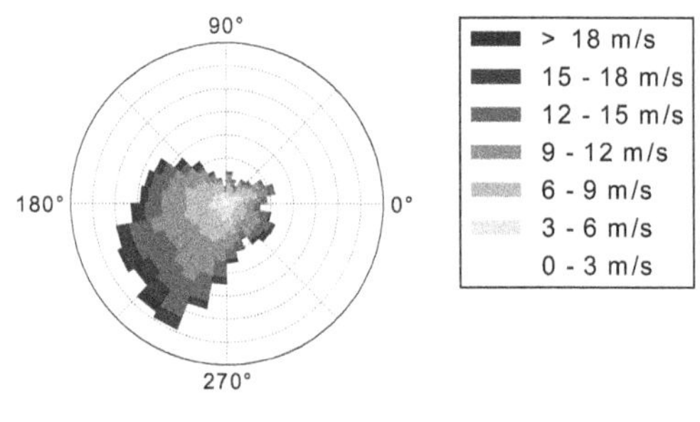

Figure 1: Example of a wind distribution at a location in Lower Saxony, Germany.

Figure 1 shows an exemplary wind rose that illustrates a wind distribution as an example based on the COSMO-DE data in decimal degrees at 53.410°, 8.074° and with height level 46 in Lower Saxony, Germany. The wind rose illustrates the distribution of wind directions (from where the wind comes at corresponding angle), and their frequency (represented by the length of the bars), and the corresponding wind speed (represented by color). The detailed wind data is employed for an accurate wake model that will be introduced in the following.

3.3 Wake Model

Like Kusiak and Song [10], we use the Jensen [15] wake model. Figure 2 shows the structure for one turbine.

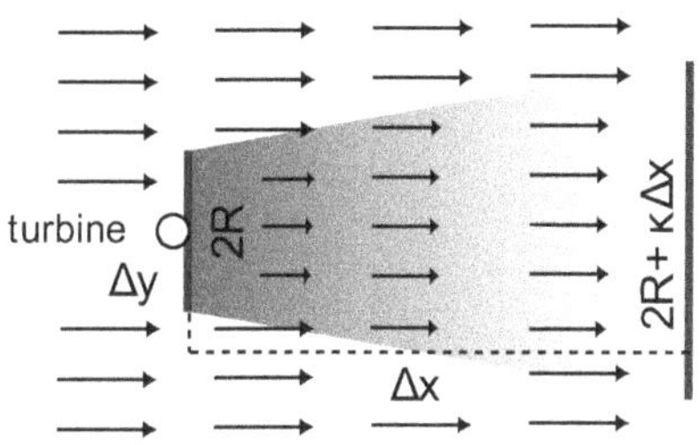

Figure 2: Structure of a single wake effect.

In the following, we describe the method to determine, if a turbine i at position $\mathbf{t}_i$ is affected by the wake effect of a turbine j, according to Kusiak and Song [10]. First, we need to compute the angle β_{ij} between the turbines:

$$\beta_{ij} = \cos^{-1}\frac{(x_i^t - x_j^t)\cdot\cos\theta + (y_i^t - y_j^t)\cdot\sin\theta + R/\kappa}{\sqrt{\left((x_i^t - x_j^t) + \frac{R}{\kappa}\cdot\cos\theta\right)^2 + \left((y_i^t - y_j^t) + \frac{R}{\kappa}\cdot\sin\theta\right)^2}} \quad (5)$$

where θ is the angle of the wind direction, R is the rotor radius of turbine j, κ is the wake spreading factor, and $x_i^t, x_j^t, y_i^t, y_j^t$ are the positions of the turbines i and j. Turbine i is affected by the wake effect of the turbine j when $0 \leq \beta_{ij} \leq \arctan(\kappa)$. A detailed description of this model can be found in [10]. We use a different specification by simply describing the three lines which limit the wake effect. By using the symmetry around the x-axis, we can simplify the description as follows. Turbine i at position $\mathbf{t}_i$ is affected by the wake effect of turbine j if:

$$\Delta x^t > 0 \wedge \left(\left|\Delta y^t\right| - R\right)/\Delta x^t < \kappa \quad (6)$$

with $\Delta x^t = \cos\theta\cdot(x_i^t - x_j^t) + \sin\theta\cdot(y_i^t - y_j^t)$ and $\Delta y^t = \cos\theta\cdot(y_i^t - y_j^t) - \sin\theta\cdot(x_i^t - x_j^t)$. The Equations 5 and 6 characterize the same behavior, but Equation 6 is computationally more efficient and can be modified more easily, what we show in the following. The velocity deficit through a wake effect is described in the Jensen model as follows:

$$\text{Vel\_def}_{ij} = \left(1 - \sqrt{1 - C_T}\right)/\left(1 + \kappa\cdot\Delta x^t/R\right) \quad (7)$$

and the summation of multiple wake effects of $N/2$ turbines with:

$$\text{Vel\_def}_i = \sqrt{\sum_{j=1, j\neq i}^{N/2} (\text{Vel\_def}_{ij})^2}. \quad (8)$$

Like in [10], we use $\kappa = 0.075$ and $C_T = 0.8$.

3.3.1 Local Optima Through Wind Discretization

The discretization of the wind direction, see Section 3.1, causes local optima in the solution space, which makes the optimization unnecessarily difficult. We will demonstrate and remove this issue in the following. Figure 3 shows the wake effects for one turbine with 32 wind directions that are equally distributed. In a real-world setting with equally distributed wind, we expect low wind potential next to the turbine and higher potential with increasing distance because the wake effects decrease. Although the wind is equally distributed, see Figure 3(a), there may occur multiple local optima on the potential map. Yellow stands for high potential, while blue represents low potential. This is due the fact that the wake effects are sampled for every direction, there is no smooth transition between the different directions.

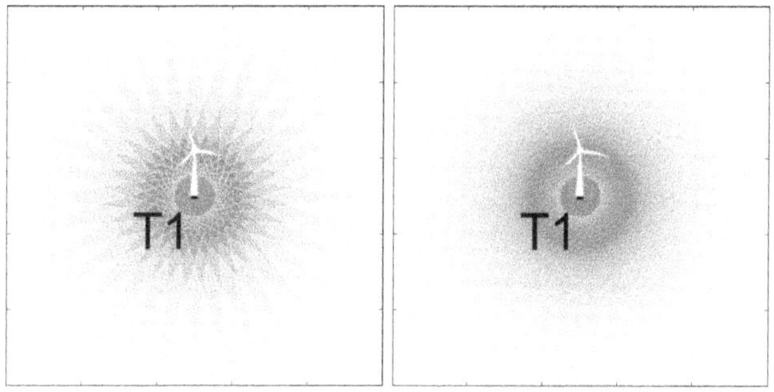

(a) before (b) after

Figure 3: Visualization of a wake effect: (a) the 15 degrees apart model as used by Kusiak and Song induces local optima, while (b) our approach leads to a smooth function.

We will add a smooth transition between the different directions into the model by modifing Equation 6 to:

$$\Delta x^t > 0 \wedge \left(\left|\Delta y^t\right| - R\right)/\Delta x^t < \kappa + \theta_{\text{inc}} \quad (9)$$

with $\theta_{\text{inc}} = \arctan\Delta\theta$ and $\Delta\theta$ is the angle increment between the wake effects. And we will change Equation 8 to:

$$\text{Vel\_def}_i = \sqrt{\sum_{j=1, j\neq i}^{N/2} (m\cdot\text{Vel\_def}_{ij})^2}. \quad (10)$$

with

$$m = \begin{cases} 1.0 & \text{if } \Delta x^t > 0 \wedge b \leq \kappa \\ 1.0 - (b - \kappa/\theta_{\text{inc}}) & \text{if } \Delta x^t > 0 \wedge b > \kappa \wedge b < \kappa + \theta_{\text{inc}} \\ 0.0 & \text{otherwise} \end{cases}$$

with $b = \left(\left|\Delta y^t\right| - R\right)/\Delta x^t$. Figure 3(b) shows the wake effects with the modification. Now there are no more local optima.

3.3.2 Rotor Size of the Affected Turbine

Our model is able to calculate how a point is affected by wake effects. For our optimization, however, we do not want to know the effect on a single point but for an entire turbine with a rotor dimension. We include this fact into the model by adding the rotor size of the affected turbine to the equations. Thus, Equation 9 changes to:

$$\Delta x^t > 0 \wedge \left(\left|\Delta y^t\right| - R_i - R_j\right)/\Delta x^t < \kappa + \theta_{\text{inc}} \quad (11)$$

where R_i is the rotor size of the affected turbine i and R_j is the rotor size of the turbine j, which is causing the wake effect. Also, we change b in Equation 3.3.1 to

$$b = \left(\left|\Delta y^t\right| - R_i - R_j\right)/\Delta x^t. \quad (12)$$

Figure 4 compares the result of two exemplary optimization runs (a) not considering the turbine rotor size, and (b) considering the rotor size. As we can see, T2's rotor is partially influenced by T1's and T3's wakes in 4(a), while this is not the case in 4(b) where we consider the rotor size.

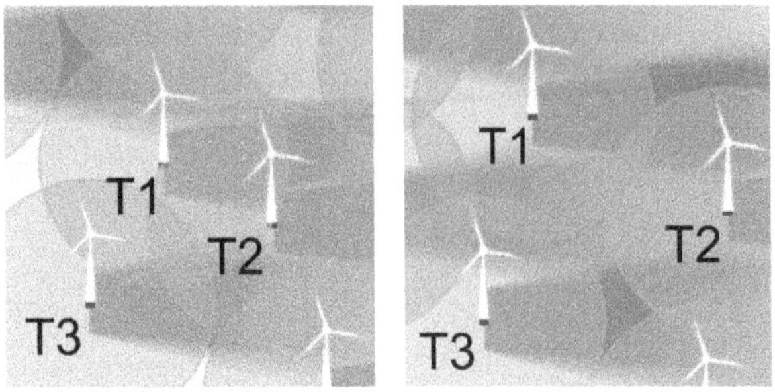

(a) Rotor size not considered (b) Rotor size considered

Figure 4: Two sectors of a larger map (a) without and (b) with consideration of the affected turbines' rotor size.

4. GEOGRAPHICAL DATA

Besides a detailed wind model, we consider data from OpenStreetMap [6] for a realistic geo-planning scenario. The geo-information adds constraints to our wind turbine placement optimization problem. In this section, we introduce OpenStreetMap and define three scenarios for the experiments.

4.1 OpenStreetMap

OpenStreetMap is a community-driven project, which was started in 2004 with the objective to create a license free world map. It contains geographical like positions of streets and buildings. Neis *et al.* [14] come to the conclusion that "[...] at least in countries, in which the OSM project is well developed, the data is becoming comparable in quality to other geodata from commercial providers [...]". The data is provided in easily processable XML files containing the geo-information. The overall amount of data is more than 400 GByte. For Germany 3.6 GByte geodata are available. In our simulation model, we dynamically load the relevant data for the corresponding sector and use the information to define constrained areas on the target. We model that the minimum distance between a turbine i and a street should be $1.5 \cdot h_i$ and 500 m to a building which is a good practice.

On the map plots in the remainder of this paper, yellow lines stands for streets, grey areas illustrate buildings and the constrainted areas around streets and buildings are visualized in red.

4.2 Scenarios

In this section, we introduce our scenarios to test the optimization algorithms. We focus on onshore wind farms. In Lower Saxony most wind farms consist of fewer than 30 turbines [16], and we define scenarios with this in mind. Even at this scale, a wind farm consisting of 20 Enercon E-101 wind turbines with 3000 kW and 60% of full load hours produces about 315 GWh/a. An output increase by 1% will increase the value of the produced energy on the basis of a price of 0.10 EUR/kWh by 315 000 EUR per year.

In the scenarios we define multiple constraints: (1) the OpenStreetMap data results in areas that are unavailable for the placement of turbines, and (2) we require like Manwell [12] a minimum safety distance depending on the rotor size r between every turbine i and j of $8 \cdot \max(r_i, r_j)$.

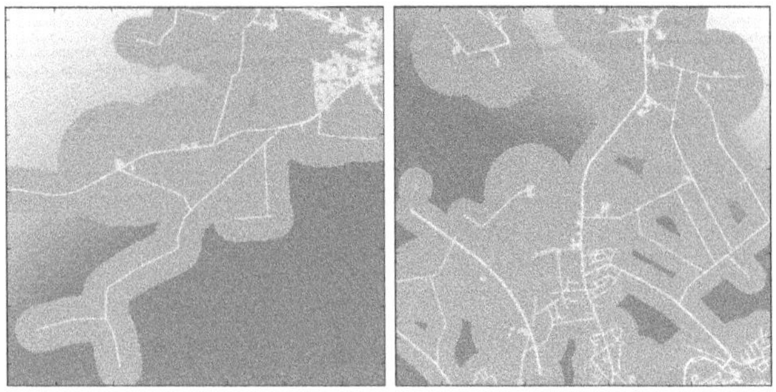

(a) Scenario 2 (b) Scenario 3

Figure 5: Illustration of benchmark Scenarios 2 and 3.

Scenario 1. In Scenario 1, the task is to place 25 turbines on an empty map of size $m_{\text{size}} = (3.0, 3.0)$ leading to an area of 9 km^2. The wind distribution is very similar to Figure 1. In addition, the potential in the right upper corner is slightly higher than on the rest of the map. A turbine will produce nearly 700 kW in mean per year at this position if it is not influenced by wake effects.

Scenario 2. In the upper right corner of Scenario 2 in Figure 5(a) Leerhafe, a part of the city Wittmund in Lower Saxony, can be seen. The scenario has the coordinates in decimal degrees $53.5015° - 53.5317°, 7.7346° - 7.7836°$, with size $m_{\text{size}} = (3.3, 3.3)$ leading to an area of 10.9 km^2. It contains 250 buildings and 64 streets consisting of 489 parts. All these elements lead to constraints. As the scenario is next to the position of the wind rose in Figure 1, the wind distribution is very similar to it.

Scenario 3. Scenario 3 on Figure 5(b) has many constrained areas. It lies at the position $53.4023° - 53.4433°, 8.0743° - 8.1412°$. It employs size $m_{\text{size}} = (4.5, 4.5)$ resulting in an area of 20.3 km^2 and contains 185 buildings and 229 streets consisting of 1493 parts. Its wind distribution can be seen in Figure 1.

5. EVOLUTIONARY STRATEGIES

The turbine placement problem is a continuous blackbox optimization problem $f : \mathbb{R}^N \to \mathbb{R}$ with constraints $g : \mathbb{R}^N \to \mathbb{B}$, i.e., a candidate solution $\mathbf{x} \in \mathbb{R}^N$ encodes the geo-positions of $N/2$ turbines that can be feasible ($g(\mathbf{x}) = 0$) w. r. t. geo-constraints or not ($g(\mathbf{x}) = 1$). In our implementation, a fitness function evaluation f first invokes a run of the geo-constraints module, and in case of feasibility a run of the wake model module determines the total power of the wind park. As fitness function f to maximize, we use the sum of the power output E of every turbine:

$$f(\mathbf{x}) = \sum_{i=1}^{N/2} E(\mathbf{t}_i). \tag{13}$$

where $\mathbf{t}_i$ is defined as in Equation 1. For optimization, we employ evolution strategies, as they are strong blackbox optimization heuristics in continuous solution spaces. In this section, we present the optimization variants we employ in the experimental section, and describe how solutions are initialized and how constraints are handled. We use six strategies that can be categorized into two groups. One group is formed by the strategies that optimize the solution vector $\mathbf{x}$ without any knowledge about which value represents which turbine. For this category we use the state for the art CMA-ES and an adaptive $(1+1)$-ES. In the other group the strategies modify individual turbines. These approaches use the knowledge which values represents which turbine and coordinate. For this category we use a replacing strategy, a deterministic $(1+1)$-ES, an adaptive $(1+1)$-ES and a new self-adaptive approach.

5.1 Constraint Handling

Infeasible solutions from the geo-constraints get a low fitness, i.e., if $g(\mathbf{x}) = 1$, we assign $f(\mathbf{x}) = 0$. This is a variant of death penalty that does not require a modification of the optimization algorithm with a feasibility control loop while generating offspring candidate solutions. This type of death penalty is similar the approach by Morales and Quezada [13].

5.2 Initialization

The initialization of the turbine locations can play an important part in the optimization. We experiment with chessboard and random initialization to create the initial solution $\mathbf{x}_0$. Chessboard initialization places the turbines equidistantly on a grid also taking into account the geo-constraints. If there is an infeasible area, the final chess pattern will look like a chessboard with missing fields. Random initialization places the turbines randomly on the map but only at valid positions taking into account the geo-constraints, if applicable.

5.3 Holistic Approaches

In the following, we introduce the optimization approach we employ in the following experiments. As stated before, our optimization approaches can be classified into holistic ones that treat the turbine placement task as N-dimensional optimization problem, and turbine-oriented approaches that use evolutionary operators oriented to the coordinates $\mathbf{t}_i$ of specific turbines that are randomly chosen.

5.3.1 *Adaptive* $(1+1)^N$*-ES*

The first holistic optimization approach is a simple $(1+1)$-ES [3] with Gaussian mutation

$$\mathbf{x}' = \mathbf{x} + \sigma \cdot \mathcal{N}(0,1) \quad (14)$$

and Rechenberg's step size control [3], which works as follows. The $(1+1)$-ES runs for a number G_r of generations. During this period, step size σ is kept constant and the number G_s of successful mutations is counted. From G_s, the success probability can be estimated as $P_s = G_s/G_r$. Step size σ is increased according to $\sigma' = \sigma \cdot \tau$, if $P_s > 1/5$, and decreased otherwise, with $\tau > 1$. We use $\tau = 1.1$, which turned out to be the best choice in preliminary experiments. The $(1+1)$-ES accepts the new candidate solution $\mathbf{x}'$, if its fitness is better than or equal to the fitness of $\mathbf{x}$, i.e., if $f(\mathbf{x}') \geq f(\mathbf{x})$. The ES terminates after G generations.

5.3.2 *CMA-ES*

Using a CMA-ES [7] for optimizing wind turbines on an empty map with various kinds of border shapes was already conducted by Wagner *et al.* [18]. Their experiments showed that the optimization results of the CMA-ES outperformed the optimization module of the industry tool OpenWind [1].

The CMA-ES starts with an initial solution $\mathbf{x}_0$. The initial standard deviation σ_0 is set to $\sigma_0 = 10.0$ corresponding to 10 m. A small standard deviation makes constraint violations less likely and prevents the CMA-ES to some extent from problems with infeasible mutations $\mathbf{x}'$ while adjusting its covariance matrix $\mathbf{C}$.

5.4 Turbine-oriented Approaches

The mutation operators of turbine-oriented approaches concentrate on the locations $\mathbf{t}_i$ of subsets of turbines $i \in \mathcal{T}$, in particular they concentrate on only one turbine for each mutation operator execution.

5.4.1 *Adaptive* $(1+1)^1$*-ES*

A special case of our turbine-oriented approaches is the adaptive $(1+1)^1$-ES that randomly selects one turbine i at location $\mathbf{t}_i$ from the set of turbines $\{1,\ldots,N/2\}$. From this turbine, only one coordinate (x_i or y_i) is randomly selected and subject to Gaussian mutation, see Equation 14. Like in case of the holistic adaptive $(1+1)^N$-ES, Rechenberg's step size control is employed.

5.4.2 *Replacing*

The replacing optimization is a simple optimization approach. In every step, the algorithms removes randomly one chosen turbine i at the position $\mathbf{t}_i$ from the solution $\mathbf{x}$ and replaces the turbine i at a randomly chosen new position $\mathbf{t}'_i$ to create a new solution $\mathbf{x}'$. If the fitness function value $f(\mathbf{x}')$ is greater than $f(\mathbf{x})$ the new solution is picked as basis for the next step. So it is a very basic $(1+1)$-ES but without any step size control.

5.4.3 *Deterministic* $(1+1)^{\mathbf{t}}$*-ES*

Lückehe *et al.* [11] proposed a turbine-oriented deterministic $(1+1)$-ES to place and optimize iteratively turbines on a map with constraints. We use the optimization part of this approach and combine it with the initial solutions $\mathbf{x}_0$. In this approach, the $(1+1)^{\mathbf{t}}$-ES picks in every generation one turbine i with the position $\mathbf{t}_i$, and mutates it by moving i to a new position $\mathbf{t}'_i$. It applies:

$$\mathbf{t}'_i = \mathbf{t}_i + \sigma(g) \cdot \mathbf{m}_{\text{size}} \cdot \mathcal{N}(0,1) \quad (15)$$

with the step size:

$$\sigma(g) = 1.0 - \left(\left(1.0 - \frac{1}{G}\right) \cdot \frac{g}{G}\right) \quad (16)$$

where g is the actual number of generation and G the total number of generations. After the mutation, the strategy evaluates the new solution and selects the solution with the highest fitness function value.

5.4.4 *Self-Adaptive* $(1+\lambda)$*-ES*

We want to improve the results by using a self-adaptive $(1+\lambda)$-ES. A self-adaptive step size $\sigma \in [0,1]$ should make it possible to react more flexibly to the scenarios. New positions are created like in Equation 15. We also want to extend the options for the strategy, and we do this as follows. First, we add the capability to move multiple turbines at the same time and not consecutively. How many turbines n shall be moved at the same time is controlled self-adaptively. The second new option for the strategy is to remove one turbine $\mathbf{t}_i$ from solution $\mathbf{x}$ and replace it at a new position $\mathbf{t}'_i$. The probability $p \in [0,1]$ that controls how often the strategy move or replace a turbine is also operated self-adaptively.

As step size σ and probability p are bound constrained, we employ the operator by Bäck and Schütz [2] for interval constrained self-adaptation:

$$\sigma' = \left(1 + \frac{1-p}{p} \cdot e^{\tau \cdot \mathcal{N}(0,1)}\right)^{-1}. \quad (17)$$

The parameter τ controls the magnitude of mutations. We choose the setting $\tau = 0.22$ like proposed in [2]. The number n of turbines to change in one step will be unchanged $n' = n$ with the probability 2/3 and increased or decreased by 1 with probability 1/6 with constraint $n \geq 1$. In initial tests, a population size of 50 showed a good performance.

6. EXPERIMENTAL RESULTS

In this section, we experimentally analyze the optimization variants introduced in the previous section on the three scenarios presented in Section 4.2.

6.1 Comparison of Evolutionary Algorithms

Table 1 shows the results of the two initialization variants combined with the six introduced optimization algorithms on benchmark Scenario 1, which does not have geo-constraints. The row *Init.* shows the fitness at initialization. The figures show the mean fitness with corresponding standard deviation and the best fitness achieved in 25 runs. Bold values show the best results achieved for Scenario 1, in which 25 turbines have to be placed ($N = 50$).

Init.	Chess		Random	
Algo.	Mean ± Std	Max	Mean ± Std	Max
Init.	14679.9 ± 0.0	14679.9	14136.4±207.2	14573.6
$(1+1)^N$	15169.1 ± 60.8	15281.6	14892.5±126.6	15083.3
CMA	15356.5 ± 48.6	15418.9	15359.5±110.9	15449.6
$(1+1)^1$	15408.8 ± 22.2	15446.6	15461.4 ± 32.6	15510.6
Rep.	15438.2 ± 25.1	15482.8	15443.8 ± 25.1	15505.5
$(1+1)^t$	**15532.1**±10.2	15552.0	**15527.5**±13.4	15551.0
$(1+\lambda)$	15525.6 ± 17.3	**15557.4**	15524.6 ± 18.9	**15556.4**

Table 1: Experimental results of Scenario 1. Selected corresponding statistical test can be found in Table 4.

We can observe that all optimization heuristics achieve a significant improvement in comparison to the initial solutions. The $(1+1)^t$-ES achieves the best results in average with a small standard deviation. The self-adaptive $(1+\lambda)$-ES achieves the second best mean result, but at the same time the best maximum of all strategies. The class of holistic optimizers is outperformed by all turbine-oriented methods, which is probably due to the fact that it treats the whole optimization problem in a *holistic* fashion, i.e., all N variables at once, although strong dependencies exist between the turbines. The $(1+1)^N$-ES achieves the worst results of all strategies and is outperformed by the CMA-ES, which has much stronger capabilities in adapting its Gaussian mutations. The replace strategy achieves higher wind potentials than the $(1+1)^1$-ES in the chessboard initialization case, and vice versa in the random intialization case. Both strategies are less specialized than the deterministic $(1+1)^t$-ES and the self-adaptive turbine-oriented $(1+\lambda)$-ES and perform worse, but still clearly outperform the holistic variants in mean and in the maximum achieved values. The statistical significance of the most important observations are confirmed with a Wilcoxon signed rank-sum test [9], see Table 4.

Init.	Chess		Random	
Algo.	Mean ± Std	Max	Mean ± Std	Max
Init.	10944.2 ± 0.0	10944.2	10626.5±145.2	10875.3
$(1+1)^N$	11221.3 ± 33.0	11287.3	11084.6±126.6	11280.2
CMA	11359.7 ± 12.5	11386.6	11348.4 ± 89.8	11475.2
$(1+1)^1$	11399.3 ± 17.5	11444.5	11437.8 ± 47.8	11502.5
Rep.	11484.0 ± 9.7	11505.0	11480.8 ± 12.1	11506.5
$(1+1)^t$	**11524.1** ± 8.4	**11538.2**	**11524.6** ± 6.6	11535.6
$(1+\lambda)$	11516.5 ± 11.7	11537.2	11519.9 ± 9.7	**11536.6**

Table 2: Experimental results of Scenario 2.

Table 2 shows the experimental comparison of all evolutionary approaches on benchmark Scenario 2. This benchmark problem is an $N = 36$-dimensional problem with 18 turbines. We observe a similar behavior of the algorithms in comparison to Scenario 1. Again, the deterministic $(1+1)^t$-ES and the self-adaptive $(1+\lambda)$-ES outperform the other approaches. Further, we can observe that the replace strategy is better than the $(1+1)^1$-ES for both initialization schemes, which is probably due to the highly constrained solution space.

Init.	Chess		Random	
Algo.	Mean ± Std	Max	Mean ± Std	Max
Init.	10537.7 ± 0.0	10537.7	10491.3±200.9	10815.4
$(1+1)^N$	10675.3 ± 32.7	10774.6	10814.4±144.4	11098.4
CMA	10831.0 ± 29.9	10859.1	11008.2±105.4	11187.8
$(1+1)^1$	10889.7 ± 51.5	11083.8	11083.6 ± 88.2	11234.1
Rep.	11261.5 ± 9.9	11286.9	11261.8 ± 11.9	11280.5
$(1+1)^t$	**11288.9** ± 8.0	11301.6	**11286.0** ± 6.9	**11300.7**
$(1+\lambda)$	11286.5 ± 9.8	**11302.7**	11283.8 ± 9.1	11295.8

Table 3: Experimental results of Scenario 3.

Last, we show the experimental results on Scenario 3 in Table 3. This problem employs the most constraints with 17 turbines resulting in an $N = 34$-dimensional problem. Again, $(1+1)^t$-ES and $(1+\lambda)$-ES perform best, i.e., with chessboard initialization, the $(1+1)^t$-ES achieves the best mean result, but the $(1+\lambda)$-ES reaches the highest fitness. With random initialization, the $(1+1)^t$-ES achieves the best mean and best overall fitness. Although the mean results are better, the $(1+1)^t$-ES does not perform significantly different than the $(1+\lambda)$-ES, see the Wilcoxon test in Table 4. Further, we can observe that the quality of the replace strategy is close to the two best turbine-oriented optimizers, probably because of the same argument like in Scenario 2, i.e., because of the highly constrained solution space.

	CMA	$(1+1)^t$	$(1+\lambda)$
CMA		+/+/+	+/+/+
$(1+1)^t$	+/+/+		−/+/−
$(1+\lambda)$	+/+/+	−/−/−	

Table 4: Statistical significance of comparison between selected experiments of Tables 1 to 3.

Table 4 shows an analysis of the statistical significance of selected experiments of Tables 1 to 3 employing the Wilcoxon signed rank-sum test. The runs of the CMA-ES, the $(1+1)^{\mathbf{t}}$-ES and the $(1+\lambda)$-ES are compared to each other on the three scenarios, corresponding to order of scenarios. If the p-value is lower than 0.05, the difference of the runs is statistically significant with a significance level of 5%, indicated by '+', otherwise indicated by '-'. The upper right triangle of the table shows the results for chessboard initialization, while the lower left part shows the corresponding results for random initialization.

In general, when comparing chessboard and random initialization, random tends to result in higher standard deviations. This is probably because of the varying starting conditions. Interestingly, there is no significant difference between chessboard and random initialization for the best optimization strategies $(1+1)^{\mathbf{t}}$-ES and $(1+\lambda)$-ES resulting in a p-value greater than 0.05. For the $(1+1)^{N}$-ES and the $(1+1)^{1}$-ES, the initialization makes a significant difference.

6.2 Evolutionary Runs

Now, we concentrate on the comparison of the evolutionary dynamics by analyzing the best evolutionary optimization runs of all experiments, see Figure 6.

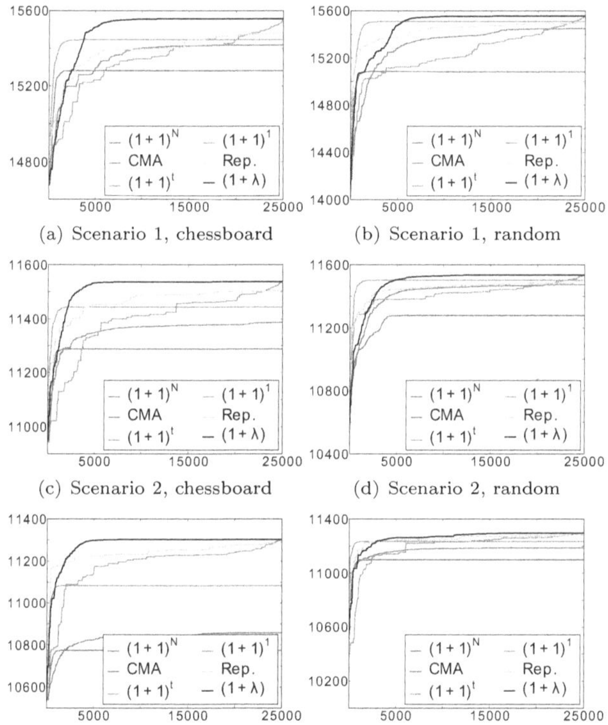

(a) Scenario 1, chessboard (b) Scenario 1, random

(c) Scenario 2, chessboard (d) Scenario 2, random

(e) Scenario 3, chessboard (f) Scenario 3, random

Figure 6: Development of best evolutionary runs when optimizing Scenarios 1, 2, and 3 with chessboard and random initialization. On the y-axis we show the energy output of the wind farm after x fitness evaluations.

We can observe that the $(1+1)^{1}$-ES shows the fastest process at the very beginning of the search, except for the chessboard initialization in Scenario 3 where the replacing strategy is the fastest one. After about 2000 to 5000 fitness function evaluations, depending on the initialization and scenario, both strategies are overtaken by the self-adaptive $(1+\lambda)$-ES. In later phases of the search, the $(1+\lambda)$-ES shows an excellent typically evolutionary convergence behavior. Interestingly, the deterministic $(1+1)^{\mathbf{t}}$-ES is optimizing comparatively slowly at the beginning of the search, but shows its strengths in later phases of the search. Although it shows phases of stagnation, the low mutation rates at the end of the search let the optimization progress accelerate in later generations. But at the end of the search, Equation 16 does not yield feasible mutation rates and in most cases the search ends before reaching the level of fitness achieved by $(1+\lambda)$-ES. We will analyze this behavior in the future and modify Equation 16 to allow a continued optimization without infeasible mutation rates.

6.3 Analysis of Operator Ratios

In the following, we analyze the operator frequencies applied during optimization with the $(1+\lambda)$-ES. Figure 7 shows the corresponding results of the best runs in Scenario 2 with (a) chessboard and (b) random initialization. At the beginning, the replacement operation (blue part) is applied in about one third of the generations, while two third are devoted to turbine shifting (red parts). In the following 25 generations, less turbines are replaced. At later phases of the search, the ratio of group shifting operations is increased while converging to the optimum.

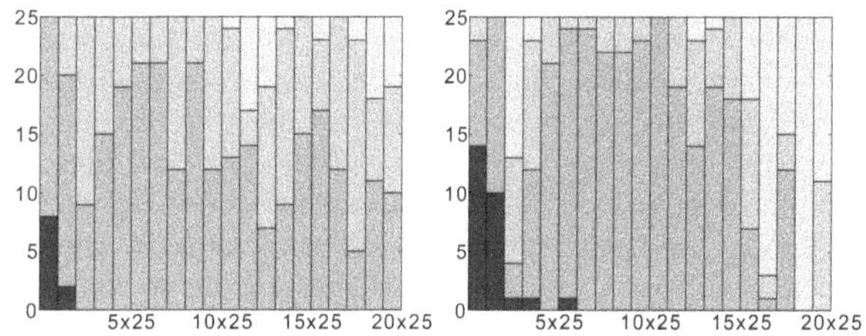

(a) Scenario 2 (chessboard) (b) Scenario 2 (random)

Figure 7: Exemplary development of operator frequencies applied every 25 generations during optimization with the $(1+\lambda)$-ES on Scenario 2 with (a) chessboard and (b) random initialization.

6.4 Optimal Placement Results

Last, we visualize the optimal turbine placements that are evolved by the $(1+1)^{\mathbf{t}}$-ES for Scenario 2 (see Table 2), and by the $(1+\lambda)$-ES for Scenario 3 (see Table 3) in Figure 8. We can observe that the majority of the turbines are placed at the borders of the map. In a few cases, small feasible islands between constrained areas are used in the middle of the map. It is obvious that the EA maximizes the distances between the turbines. Intuitively, this makes sense since the wake effects decrease with increasing distance. The horizontal inter-turbine distances are larger than vertical ones as the horizontal ratio of wind is comparatively large. The large free spaces stay free, as they are mostly influenced by wake effects, whose complex structures are clearly visible.

7. CONCLUSIONS

Turbine placement with a realistic wake effect model, real-world wind data, and also realistic geo-constraints results in a difficult optimization problem. In this work, we proposed four turbine-oriented optimization heuristics and performed a detailed experimental comparison on three benchmark scenarios in Lower Saxony. We compared our approaches to

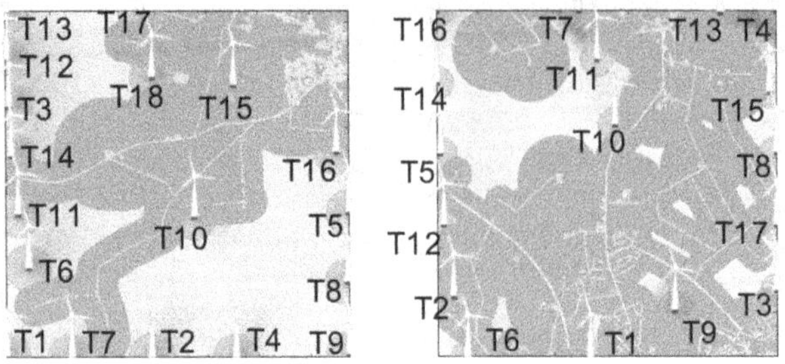

(a) Scenario 2 (b) Scenario 3

Figure 8: Final turbine placements after 25000 fitness function evaluations on (a) Scenario 2 evolved by the $(1+1)^{t}$-ES and (b) Scenario 3 optimized by the $(1+\lambda)$-ES.

a simple $(1+1)^{N}$-ES with adaptive step size control and to the CMA-ES, which belongs to the state-of-the-art approaches in continuous blackbox optimization and showed promising results in turbine placement tasks in the past. All turbine-oriented approaches outperformed the holistic strategies with statistically significance.

As future work, we plan to extend the experimental analysis to further scenarios, in particular concentrating on large-scale scenarios and also off-shore turbine placement with ground and ship route constraints. As constraints have an important part to play in realistic scenarios and the results have shown that the constraints make the optimization problems more difficult to solve, we will concentrate on more advanced constraint handling techniques in the future, ranging from penalty function to meta-modeling of the constraint boundary.

Acknowledgements

We thank the German Weather Service for providing the COSMO-DE data and the Ministry for Science and Culture of Lower Saxony for supporting this work with the PhD program *System Integration of Renewable Energy (SEE).*

References

[1] AWS Truepower. AWS Openwind, 2008. http://awsopenwind.org/.

[2] T. Bäck and M. Schütz. Intelligent mutation rate control in canonical genetic algorithms. In *Foundations of Intelligent Systems, 9th International Symposium, ISMIS '96, Zakopane, Poland, June 9-13, 1996, Proceedings*, pages 158–167, 1996.

[3] H. Beyer and H. Schwefel. Evolution strategies - A comprehensive introduction. *Natural Computing*, 1(1):3–52, 2002.

[4] Deutscher Wetterdienst. COSMO-DE: numerical weather prediction model for Germany, 2012. http://tinyurl.com/dwd-cosmo-de.

[5] ENERCON GmbH. Product Overview, 2015. http://tinyurl.com/enercon101.

[6] M. M. Haklay and P. Weber. Openstreetmap: User-generated street maps. *IEEE Pervasive Computing*, 7(4):12–18, Oct. 2008.

[7] N. Hansen. The CMA evolution strategy: a comparing review. In *Towards a new evolutionary computation. Advances in estimation of distribution algorithms*, pages 75–102. Springer, 2006.

[8] J. F. Herbert-Acero, O. Probst, P.-E. Rethore, G. C. Larsen, and K. K. Castillo-Villar. A review of methodological approaches for the design and optimization of wind farms. *Energies*, 7(11):6930–7016, 2014.

[9] G. Kanji. *100 Statistical Tests.* SAGE Publications, London, 1993.

[10] A. Kusiak and Z. Song. Design of wind farm layout for maximum wind energy capture. *Renewable Energy*, 35(3):685–694, 2010.

[11] D. Lückehe, O. Kramer, and M. Weisensee. An evolutionary approach to geo-planning of renewable energies. In *28th International Conference on Informatics for Environmental Protection: ICT for Energy Effieciency (EnviroInfo)*, pages 501–508, 2014.

[12] J. Manwell, J. McGowan, and A. Rogers. *Wind Energy Explained: Theory, Design and Application.* John Wiley and Sons Ltd, London, 2002.

[13] A. K. Morales and C. V. Quezada. C.v.: A universal eclectic genetic algorithm for constrained optimization. In *In: Proceedings 6th European Congress on Intelligent Techniques and Soft Computing (EUFIT*, pages 518–522. Verlag Mainz, 1998.

[14] P. Neis, D. Zielstra, and A. Zipf. The street network evolution of crowdsourced maps: Openstreetmap in germany 2007–2011. *Future Internet*, 4(1):1–21, 2011.

[15] H. Neustadter. Method for evaluating wind turbine wake effects on wind farm performance. *Journal of Solar Energy Engineering*, pages 107–240, 1985.

[16] The Wind Power. Wind farms in Lower Saxony, Germany, 2015. http://tinyurl.com/parks-lower-saxony.

[17] M. Wagner, J. Day, and F. Neumann. A fast and effective local search algorithm for optimizing the placement of wind turbines. *Renewable Energy*, 51(0):64–70, 2013.

[18] M. Wagner, K. Veeramachaneni, F. Neumann, and U.-M. O'Reilly. Optimizing the layout of 1000 wind turbines. In *European Wind Energy Association Annual Event*, 2011.

[19] C. Wan, J. Wang, G. Yang, X. Li, and X. Zhang. Optimal siting of wind turbines using real coded genetic algorithms. *European Wind Energy Association Conference and Exhibition*, 2009.

[20] C. Wan, J. Wang, G. Yang, and X. Zhang. Optimal micro-siting of wind farms by particle swarm optimization. In *Advances in Swarm Intelligence*, volume 6145 of *Lecture Notes in Computer Science*, pages 198–205. Springer, 2010.

[21] W. Weibull. A statistical distribution function of wide applicability. *Journal Applied Mechanics - Transactions of ASME*, 3(18):293–297, 1951.

Exploiting Linkage Information and Problem-Specific Knowledge in Evolutionary Distribution Network Expansion Planning

Ngoc Hoang Luong
Centrum Wiskunde & Informatica (CWI)
Amsterdam, The Netherlands
Hoang.Luong@cwi.nl

Han La Poutré
Centrum Wiskunde & Informatica (CWI)
Amsterdam, The Netherlands
Han.La.Poutre@cwi.nl

Peter A.N. Bosman
Centrum Wiskunde & Informatica (CWI)
Amsterdam, The Netherlands
Peter.Bosman@cwi.nl

ABSTRACT

This paper tackles the Distribution Network Expansion Planning (DNEP) problem that has to be solved by distribution network operators to decide which, where, and/or when enhancements to electricity networks should be introduced to satisfy the future power demands. We compare two evolutionary algorithms (EAs) for optimizing expansion plans: the classic genetic algorithm (GA) with uniform crossover and the Gene-pool Optimal Mixing Evolutionary Algorithm (GOMEA) that learns and exploits linkage information between problem variables. We study the impact of incorporating different levels of problem-specific knowledge in the variation operators as well as two constraint-handling techniques: constraint domination and repair mechanisms. Experiments show that the use of problem-specific variation operators is far more important for the classic GA to find high-quality solutions to the DNEP problem. GOMEA is found to have far more robust performance even when an out-of-box variant is used that doesn't exploit problem-specific knowledge. Based on experiments, we suggest that when selecting optimization algorithms for real-world applications like DNEP, EAs that have the ability to model and exploit problem structures, such as GOMEAs and estimation-of-distribution algorithms, should be given priority, especially when problem-specific knowledge is not straightforward to exploit, e.g. in the case of black-box optimization.

CCS Concepts

•Mathematics of computing → Evolutionary algorithms; •Hardware → Power networks;

Keywords

Power System, Capacity Planning, Linkage Learning, Variation Operators, Problem-Specific Knowledge

GECCO '15, July 11 - 15, 2015, Madrid, Spain

DOI: http://dx.doi.org/10.1145/2739480.2754682

1. INTRODUCTION

A typical power system consists of power plants that generate the electricity, transmission networks that carry the high-voltage (HV) electricity from far-off generating sites to substations near residential and industrial areas, and distribution networks that feed the medium-voltage (MV) and low-voltage (LV) electricity from the substations to homes and businesses. In this paper, the focus is on distribution networks, but the methodologies can also be extended to transmission networks. In order for distribution networks to work properly, distribution network operators (DNOs) have to ensure that the capacities of network cables are enough to handle the magnitude of the power flows that are carried through the cables to satisfy customers' power demands. Otherwise, bottlenecks can cause overload, which heats up the cable wires. This is detrimental to the normal operation and safety of the networks, and may cause blackouts or earlier cable replacements. Therefore, DNOs need to perform Distribution Network Expansion Planning (DNEP) to determine *what* kinds of network enhancements should be made and *where* these enhancements should be made. The dynamic DNEP formulation also involves the question *when* those reinforcement activities should be started during the planning horizon while in the static DNEP formulation this time-dependent decision making issue is omitted. The goal of DNEP is to find the most economical expansion plan, in terms of investment and operation costs, for which the network satisfies the power demand over the planning horizon.

DNEP is sometimes simplified to be scalably solved by classical mathematical programming methods, compromising the true non-linear nature of DNEP that is due to its complicated constraints, and thus leading to unsatisfactory representations of the real problem [9]. On the other hand, evolutionary algorithms (EAs) have been widely applied and achieved satisfying results in DNEP with more realistic formulations, see e.g. [1, 3, 9]. This is mostly due to the straightforward implementation and broad applicability of EAs. However, most DNEP researches in literature overlook several important issues. First, experiments are usually conducted by using only one, arbitrarily chosen, EA with a customized problem-specific variation operator (VO), omitting both questions why that specific EA should be chosen over other available EAs and what the advantages that VO has compared to other alternatives. Second, the comparison of how effective various constraint-handling mechanisms help the solvers traverse the search space is often disregarded. In this paper, while aiming to solve the DNEP problem, we also address these issues. We employ 2 EA solvers: the classic genetic algorithm (GA) and a Gene-pool Optimal Mixing Evolutionary Algorithm (GOMEA) [2, 10]. GA is arguably the most popular EA in DNEP literature, but it is rarely used out of the box in practice. Practitioners often have to customize GA's VOs (i.e. crossover and mutation) with expert and problem-specific knowledge (PSK) so that important problem structures are respected during variation, e.g. cables in the same feeder group in the network should be treated together when constructing new networks. Taking the perspective of black-box optimization, where such PSK is hardly available, GOMEA performs linkage learning (LL) to identify, during optimization, which variables are interdependent and considers them jointly when generating new solutions. Being a recently-developed LL EA, GOMEA has been shown to have superior performance and scalability on laboratory benchmarks and recently in power system optimization as well [6, 8]. The LL capability of GOMEA does not exclude the possibility of combining linkage knowledge with PSK if available. In this paper, we show how to combine the strength of LL with PSK exploitation.

Population sizes of EAs are often chosen arbitrarily or are customized to the specific problem instance at hand in DNEP literature [1, 3, 9]. This approach is difficult to generalize to applications elsewhere. Population size parameter settings have big impacts on how effective and how efficient problem instances are solved. Practitioners often need to manually try different population sizes to figure out a suitable population size for each problem instance, which is both time-consuming and difficult for comparing the performance of different EAs fairly. To get rid of this troublesome parameter, we adapt a population sizing-free scheme proposed in [7] and implement it into both GA and GOMEA.

The remainder of this paper is organized as follows. Section 2 formulates the DNEP problem. Section 3 outlines the two optimization algorithms GA and GOMEA together with the population sizing-free scheme. Section 4 introduces different variation operators and constraint-handling techniques for DNEP that can be incorporated into GA and GOMEA. Section 5 exhibits the experimental results. Section 6 concludes the paper.

2. DNEP FORMULATION

In this paper, we focus on optimizing expansion plans for medium voltage distribution (MV-D) networks. A typical MV-D network consists of cables branching out from HV/MV substations connecting MV nodes (MV/LV substations and MV customer substations) [6]. These cables form different feeder (cables) groups in ring-shaped or meshed structures. However, some cables are opened on one side, called normally open points (NOPs). Electricity cannot flow through those cables, so that every node is supplied its power demand through a single feed path. The whole network thus operates radially in normal situations. Figure 1 shows an example of a distribution network. We focus on expansion options for network cables as our main asset category. How the cables are connected and what types of cables are used, determine the capacity of the network. Increasing power demands in the future can create bottlenecks in some parts of the network, where the power flows have magnitudes that are greater than the nominal capacities of the cables. The goal of capacity planning is to find the best expansion op-

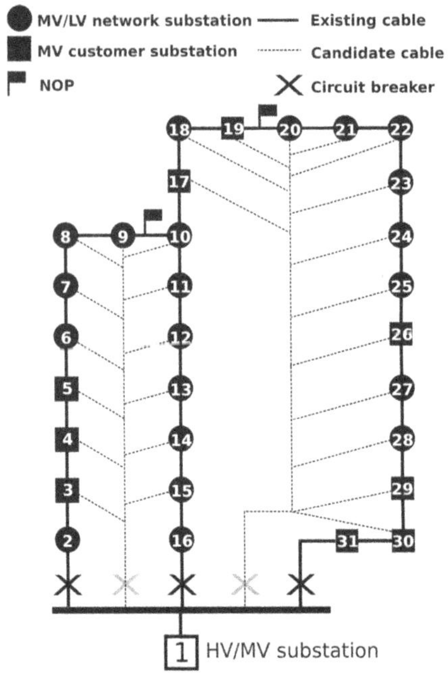

Figure 1: A distribution network example [6]

tions to solve these bottlenecks. Possible expansion options are: replacing existing cables with new cables of higher capacities or adding new cable connections and thus creating new feed paths to the network [6]. Adding new cables connections requires placements of new NOPs to satisfy the radiality constraint [6].

2.1 Decision Variables

We specify all the existing and potential cable connections (branches) that we want to consider for capacity planning. Let l denote the total number of branches. A distribution network can be represented as a vector of l integer elements:

$$\boldsymbol{x} = (x_1, x_2, \ldots, x_l), \quad |x_k| \in \Omega(x_k), \quad k \in \{1, 2, \ldots, l\} \quad (1)$$

where $\Omega(x_k)$ is the set of cable types that can be installed at the kth branch ($\Omega(x_k) \subseteq \mathbb{N}$). The value of x_k indicates the status and the type of cable installed:

- $x_k = ID > 0$: A cable of type $ID \in \Omega(x_k)$ is installed.
- $x_k = 0$: No cable is installed at the kth branch.
- $x_k = -ID < 0$: A cable of type $ID \in \Omega(x_k)$ is installed but is out of normal operation. This is an NOP.

2.2 Constraints

Given the forecast growth of the peak load at each node, the following constraints must be satisfied:

1. **Connectivity**: All nodes must be connected.
2. **Power flow constraint**: In normal operation, the voltage at each node stays within allowable limits and the magnitude of the power flow through each cable stays within the nominal capacity of that cable.
3. **Radiality constraint**: In normal operation, the power demand of each node is supplied by a single feed path.
4. **Reconfigurability constraint**: When an active cable ($x_k > 0$) fails, the part of the feeder group (from an HV/MV substation with circuit breaker to an NOP)

containing the failed cable is disconnected from the network. All customers connected to that feeder group are then out of service. The DNO has to bring the network back to operation by closing NOPs to temporarily re-route the power flow through other paths while the failed cable is being repaired. During this emergency situation, the radial operation constraint can be compromised and the network is allowed to endure a mild overload of 130% nominal capacity (as in [6]).

5. **Substation capacity constraint**: Each HV/MV substation has limited physical space to install new outgoing cables. We assume that maximum 3 new outgoing cables are allowed for each HV/MV substation (as [6]).

Alternating-current (AC) power flow calculations (PFCs [4]) are required to check constraints 2 and 4 for each solution plan. PFCs, which involve solving AC power flow models, are computationally expensive and dominate the computing time of the optimization process. Note that, due to the implementation, PFCs can only be performed for connected networks and the connectivity constraint is thus a crucial constraint that needs to be separately handled so that constraints 2 and 4 can be properly evaluated (see Section 4). Constraint evaluations are performed together with objective evaluations.

2.3 Objective Function

We employ the annuity method [11] to calculate the capital expenditures $CAPEX$ for new assets. The investment cost on a new asset is converted into a series of uniform annual payments, called annuities. We assume the length of this series to be equal to the (uniform) economic lifetime of the new asset t_{life}. The annuity AN_a of the asset a with a discount rate $i = 4.5\%$ (as in [6]) can be computed as:

$$AN_a = Price_a \cdot \frac{i}{1-(1+i)^{-t_{life}}} \tag{2}$$

$CAPEX$ for the asset a in a year t can be calculated as:

$$CAPEX_a(t) = \begin{cases} AN_a & \text{if } t_{inst_a} \leq t < t_{inst_a} + t_{life} \\ 0 & \text{else} \end{cases} \tag{3}$$

with t_{inst_a} is the time of installing the asset a. Let A denote the set of all new assets a's that will be installed in the planning period $[t_0, t_{horizon}]$. The total $CAPEX$ on the whole network in a year t is defined as:

$$CAPEX(t) = \sum_{a \in A} CAPEX_a(t) \tag{4}$$

The operational expenditure $OPEX$ can be calculated by capitalizing the energy loss. Energy loss of the network in a year t can be taken as in [6, 11]:

$$E_{loss}(t) = P_{peak\ loss}(t) \cdot T_{loss}(t) \tag{5}$$

where $P_{peak\ loss}(t)$ is the peak loss which can be obtained from the PFC regarding the peak loads in year t. $T_{loss}(t)$ is the service time of peak loss for year t, defined by the area of the yearly loss profile [6, 11]. Given the forecast electricity price in a year t, we can capitalize the energy loss and regard it as the $OPEX$ in year t.

$$OPEX(t) = E_{loss}(t) * Price_{electricity}(t) \tag{6}$$

2.3.1 *Total Cost Formulation*

We want to minimize the net present value (NPV) (i.e. at time t_0) of the total cost of both investment cost $CAPEX$ and operation cost $OPEX$ over a planning horizon of $t_{horizon}$ years with a discount rate i.

$$COST_{NPV} = \sum_{t=t_0}^{t_{horizon}} \frac{CAPEX(t) + OPEX(t)}{(1+i)^{t-t_0}} \tag{7}$$

2.3.2 *Static Planning*

The goal in static DNEP is to find the most economical solution plan that satisfies the peak load profile at the final year of the planning horizon. Static DNEP gives DNOs a general picture about what kinds of network reinforcements can be expected. However, the actual total cost objective function includes the important operation cost $OPEX$, which is the capitalized energy loss, that depends on the load profile and the specific network configuration at each year. We employ the following method, which has been proposed in [6], to estimate the $OPEX$ for a solution plan. Based on the (predicted) annual peak load growth rate R, we compute the peak load profile for each year from the beginning year t_0 until the final year $t_{horizon}$. We determine the year $t_{overload}$ when the first bottleneck happens in the network. We then assume that all expansion options in the solution plan are installed at the same time in the year $t_{overload}$, i.e. $t_{inst} = t_{overload}$ for all new assets. Therefore, to evaluate the total cost, from t_0 until $t_{overload}$, we use the current network topology, and from $t_{overload}$ until $t_{horizon}$ we switch to the new network topology at $t_{horizon}$.

2.3.3 *Dynamic Planning*

The question *when* each expansion options should be carried out is also an important issue that DNOs have to address. Dynamic DNEP formulations often contain time-dependent decision variables and complicated problem models that are much more difficult to solve than those of static DNEP. However, network cables (i.e. the main asset category in DNEP) generally have very long lifetimes (e.g. normally 30 years) while planning horizons of more than 30 years are regarded as impractical because it is difficult to properly predict power demand scenarios for a very distant future. These facts mean that $t_{inst}+t_{life} > t_{horizon}$, i.e. during a practical planning horizon, a network branch might require reinforcement only once (e.g. cable replacement or installation of a new cable connection). Situations such as installing a thin cable first and then upgrading with a different cable of higher capacity, or removing a previously-upgraded cable during the same planning horizon, are often regarded as impractical by DNOs. Thus, we propose a method to convert a static plan into a dynamic one, called the *decomposition heuristic*, as follows. Similarly to the static planning, we determine the year $t_{overload}$ when the first bottleneck occurs and assume that the whole solution plan is carried out in that year. We then loop through the list of all new assets in the solution plan in a random order and check if we can delay each expansion option by one year. If the postponement of an asset investment results in less total cost and all constraints are still satisfied, then we accept that postponement. Otherwise, that expansion option cannot be postponed further. We continue this postponement checking until no expansion option can be postponed any more. Finally, we obtain a solution plan with an investment time for each expansion option and the total cost objective value is evaluated accordingly. By employing this *decomposition heuristic*, we can bring the decision making about investment time into the static DNEP framework while still satisfying the requirements of DNOs in real-world practice.

3. OPTIMIZATION ALGORITHMS

Problem structures of DNEP are difficult for low-order local search (LS) to solve. For example an expansion option of adding a new cable connection requires the addition of a new NOP to make the network radial, which in turn requires relocations of other existing NOPs to obtain the topology with lowest energy loss. Such multivariate decision making cannot be found by a typical LS like bit-flip hillclimbing while higher-order LS would not be scalable. Global search meta-heuristics, like EAs, are more suitable for DNEP.

We will consider two EAs: the classic GA and a GOMEA variant, along with a population sizing-free scheme that can be integrated with any population-based optimization algorithm. Normally, EAs, like GA or GOMEA, start with randomly initialized populations. However, because DNEP is a highly-constrained engineering problem, randomly generated solutions are typically infeasible and violate many constraints. Therefore, we use a repair procedure that partially repairs infeasible solutions by comparing them with the current, i.e. starting, network situation. First, each decision variable x_k (i.e. a network branch) can only receive a random non-negative value (i.e. we do not place any NOPs yet) as long as it does not downgrade the currently existing cable. This also means that currently existing cables can only be left intact or replaced with cables of higher capacities. Existing connections are rarely removed because DNOs do not favor this. Solutions that are generated in this way satisfy the connectivity constraint because the current network is connected. Second, we go through HV/MV substations and check the number of cables branching out from each substation. If the number of outgoing cables is more than the allowable capacity of the substation (i.e. violating constraint 5), we randomly delete outgoing cables until constraint 5 is satisfied. Third, we go through all variables that have positive values (i.e. active cables) in a random order. For each positive-value decision variable, we try to place an NOP on that cable by negating its value. If the network is still connected, then the NOP can be placed; otherwise, undo the operation. This procedure returns a network of radial topology with random placements of NOPs (i.e. constraint 3 is satisfied). We do not repair the power flow and reconfigurability constraint (i.e. constraint 2 and 4) because they involve PFCs, which are computationally expensive.

3.1 Genetic Algorithm

We consider a typical implementation of the classic GA with uniform crossover and tournament selection. First, a population $\mathcal{P}$ of n candidate solutions is initialized following the initialization procedure mentioned above. Next, for every generation, we create an offspring population $\mathcal{O}$ of n new solutions from $\mathcal{P}$ by performing uniform crossover on every 2 randomly selected parent solutions, giving 2 offspring solutions. Then, we combine both the parent population $\mathcal{P}$ and the offspring population $\mathcal{O}$ into a selection pool $\mathcal{P}+\mathcal{O}$ of $2n$ solutions in total. We perform a tournament selection with tournament size 4 on this pool to select n survivor solutions, which form the new parent population $\mathcal{P}$ for the next generation, ensuring convergence by logistic growth of the optimal solutions [10]. Note that GAs in literature often have mutation operators, but we do not implement mutation here because mutation was not found to have positive impacts on the performance of GA solving our DNEP model.

3.2 Gene-pool Optimal Mixing EA

The performance of EAs depends on their ability to efficiently mix and preserve building blocks (BBs) (i.e. good partial solutions) in the population to create new solutions [10]. When just taken out of the box, classic EAs, like GA, are prone to disrupt these BBs due to their BB-blind variation operators (VOs). Practitioners then have to make them BB-aware by customizing them with problem-specific knowledge (PSK). If such valuable PSK is not available, BB information can be inferred from the working population of EAs by linkage learning (LL) procedures, in which problem variables having some degree of dependency are identified so that they can be jointly considered when generating new solutions. GOMEA [2, 10] is a recently developed LL EA that effectively exploits the learned linkage information.

We consider a popular variant of GOMEA that uses the Linkage Tree (LT) [2, 10] to model linkage. An LT is a set of linkage sets arranged in a hierarchical structure. Each linkage set contains variables having some degree of dependency. The lowest level (i.e. leaf nodes) contains singleton (univariate) sets of each variable separately. Other linkage sets at higher levels are multivariate sets that can be formed by merging pairs of lower sets until all sets are merged into a root node containing all variables. Thus, an LT can encode different levels of dependency, from the totally independent state (i.e. leaf nodes) to the all-dependent state (i.e. root node). The root node is removed from the LT because it assumes all variables should be jointly considered by VOs, which means no new solution is created. Note that while bit-flip hillclimbing is not generally useful for solving DNEP, the leaf nodes are still kept here because a solution plan might contain the expansion option of upgrading an existing cable, which is a univariate decision. An LT over a set of problem variables $\{1,2,3,4,5\}$ can be, for example, $\{\{1\},\{2\},\{3\},\{4\},\{5\},\{1,3\},\{2,5\},\{1,3,4\}\}$. Given a set of l variables and a population of n solutions, an LT can be constructed efficiently by the Unweighted Pair Grouping Method with Arithmetic-mean (UPGMA) in $\mathcal{O}(nl^2)$ time [5]

We also start GOMEA with a population $\mathcal{P}$ of n candidate solutions generated by the initialization procedure mentioned above. Every generation, we use tournament selection with tournament size 2 to select a set $\mathcal{S}$ of n solutions out of $\mathcal{P}$. The linkage model building procedure is then performed on $\mathcal{S}$ to build the LT. Using the obtained LT, we transform each existing parent solution $\boldsymbol{p} \in \mathcal{P}$ into a new offspring solution $\boldsymbol{o} \in \mathcal{O}$ whose fitness value is equal to or better than the fitness value of $\boldsymbol{p}$. The offspring population $\mathcal{O}$ completely replaces $\mathcal{P}$ and becomes the new parent population $\mathcal{P}$ for the next generation.

Instead of fully creating new solutions and then evaluating them like in GA, the VO of GOMEA, called Gene-pool Optimal Mixing (GOM [10]), uses the learned LT to evolve each existing parent $\boldsymbol{p}$ into a new offspring $\boldsymbol{o}$ in an iterative manner. First, $\boldsymbol{o}$ and a backup $\boldsymbol{b}$ are cloned directly from $\boldsymbol{p}$. Then, each linkage set in the LT is traversed iteratively. For each linkage set, a donor $\boldsymbol{d}$ is randomly selected from the current population $\mathcal{P}$. If the donor $\boldsymbol{d}$'s values for the variables indicated the linkage set differ from those in $\boldsymbol{o}$ in at least one position, these values are copied from $\boldsymbol{d}$ into $\boldsymbol{o}$. This partially-altered solution $\boldsymbol{o}$ is evaluated and compared against its backup $\boldsymbol{b}$. If $\boldsymbol{o}$ is equally good or better than $\boldsymbol{b}$ (i.e. $fitness[\boldsymbol{o}] \geq fitness[\boldsymbol{b}]$), the changes are accepted (i.e. the values copied from $\boldsymbol{d}$) and updated into $\boldsymbol{b}$ as well. Otherwise, the changes are undone and $\boldsymbol{o}$ reverts to its backup state $\boldsymbol{b}$. Note that the acceptance of solutions having equal fitness can be beneficial to move across a fitness plateau [2]. It can be seen that each linkage set corresponds with a mixing event, in which the current solution is recombined with a random donor solution and the variables in the same linkage set are treated together, preserving the BB structure. When we traverse the whole LT, an offspring $\boldsymbol{o}$ is then fully constructed, replacing the original parent $\boldsymbol{p}$ in the next generation.

It can happen that GOM cannot improve the current parent solution $\boldsymbol{p}$ into a new offspring or that, because of a significant plateau, GOM keeps transforming back and forth solutions of different genotypes but with the same fitness value. To overcome this, if GOM cannot yield a new offspring or when the number of subsequent generations that the best-found-so-far solution $\boldsymbol{x}^{best}$ does not change, i.e. the no-improvement stretch (NIS), exceeds a certain threshold, we invoke the Forced Improvement (FI [2]) procedure. In essence, FI is similar to GOM but we always use $\boldsymbol{x}^{best}$ as the only donor solution. FI only accepts the mixing event that results in a strict improvement (i.e. $fitness[\boldsymbol{o}] > fitness[\boldsymbol{b}]$) and FI stops as soon as such mixing event is found. Previous research [2] on GOMEA suggest a threshold for NIS of $1 + \lfloor \log_{10}(n) \rfloor$. If FI does not succeed in evolving $\boldsymbol{p}$, $\boldsymbol{x}^{best}$ is returned as the new offspring.

3.3 Population Sizing-free Scheme

Setting the population size parameter in real-world applications of EAs is hard because a suitable population size setting depends on the structure of the problem instance at hand and also on the specific EA being used. DNEP practitioners often need to experiment with different population sizes. Here, we adapt a population sizing-free scheme, proposed and tested on academic benchmarks in [7]. In essence, we run multiple instances of the EA in parallel. Each instance has a different population size but larger populations have a slower generational cycle. We start with the first population P_1 of some small size n_1. Then, by doubling the population size, the next population P_i is twice as large as the previous one, i.e. $n_i = 2n_{i-1}$ for $i > 1$. All the populations are scheduled with the principle that for every 2 generations of population P_i, 1 generation of population P_{i+1} is run (or initialized if it does not exist yet). A population is terminated when it converges, i.e., all solutions in that population have the same fitness value. Having no maximum population size, the EA runs and grows its populations until the computing time budget is used up.

4. VARIATION OPERATORS

Being popularly applied in black-box optimization, EAs require little problem-specific knowledge (PSK) and their variation operators (VOs) (i.e. procedures to generate new offspring solutions) can operate on a wide range of problem landscapes. However, in real-world applications like DNEP, the problems are often highly constrained such that it is difficult for general-purpose VOs to traverse the search space of feasible solutions efficiently. For industrial optimization, efficiency is of high importance because the evaluations of candidate solutions are typically computationally expensive. Full constraint evaluations of solution plans for DNEP involve the simulation and solving PFCs [4], which dominate the computing time of the optimization process. Thus, it is beneficial to incorporate PSK into VOs of EAs as efficiency enhancement methods. Local search heuristics can normally be used for efficiency enhancement, but typical operators like bit-flip hillclimbing was not found to be helpful in improving the efficiency of EAs solving our DNEP model because such local search often fails to reach expansion options of interdependent activities (e.g. adding new cables and NOPs and relocating existing NOPs).

Among the constraints of DNEP, the connectivity constraint needs to be handled separately because the PFC cannot be performed on unconnected networks and the power flow constraint and reconfigurability constraint cannot be checked without PFCs. Thus, in order to compare solution plans (e.g. when performing tournament selection), we need to quantify their disconnectivity and use that as the comparison criterion or we have to repair the connectivity so that other constraints can be evaluated. Here, we introduce different VOs for GA and GOMEA along with their corresponding connectivity constraint-handling techniques.

4.1 Disconnectivity Quantification

The VO presented here can be considered as the out-of-the-box VO of GA or GOMEA because it does not assume any connectivity knowledge when generating offspring solutions. If the network encoded in a solution plan is unconnected, we do not evaluate other constraints but we quantify its disconnectivity by comparing it with the topology of the existing network. Loop through all the decision variables and count the number of positions where the existing network has a positive value (i.e. an active branch) but the solution has a negative value (i.e. an NOP) or where the existing network has a non-positive value (i.e. no cable connection or an NOP) and the solution has a positive value. This number is considered as the disconnectivity value. Note that connected networks do not need this disconnectivity quantification and are assigned the disconnectivity value 0. Then, we can compare candidate networks as follows. If both networks are unconnected, the one with a smaller disconnectivity value is selected as the better one. If only one network is unconnected, then the connected network is the better solution. If both networks are connected, then they can be compared by using the other evaluated constraint values and their objective values. We call the VO used together with this connectivity-constraint domination mechanism DQ1.

However, even if we recombine two connected parent networks, it is still difficult for the uniform crossover operator of GA to generate connected offspring networks, especially for big networks with many cable connections. Thus, we also propose a different VO, in which we allow each recombination of two parent networks to retry uniform crossover to generate connected offspring networks. After 100 times, if the offspring networks are still unconnected, they will be evaluated for the disconnectivity value as above. For GOMEA, during the process of constructing an offspring, for each mixing event, if the partially-altered solution is an unconnected network, we allow it to select randomly a different donor maximum 100 times. We call this VO DQ100.

4.2 Connectivity Repair

For GA, this VO is much like DQ100, but after 100 trials, if the networks are still unconnected they will be reverted back to the parent solutions. Because all the candidate solutions in the initial population are connected networks, the use of this VO implies that only connected offspring are allowed to be evaluated and enter tournament selection. For GOMEA, in each mixing event, if the partially-altered solution becomes unconnected, this is because there exist some variables whose positive values are replaced by some non-positive values from the donor. We can simply revert these decision variables to their backup values. We call the VO that uses this connectivity repair scheme CRP (i.e. Connectivity Repair by Parent).

We also propose a different connectivity repair scheme that compares an unconnected network $\boldsymbol{x}$ with the (overall) best-found-so-far solution $\boldsymbol{x}^{best}$. For each decision variable k, if $x_k^{best} > 0$ and $x_k < 0$, then $x_k \leftarrow -x_k$; if $x_k^{best} > 0$ and $x_k = 0$, then $x_k \leftarrow x_k^{best}$. On the other hand, if $x_k^{best} < 0$ and $x_k > 0$, then $x_k \leftarrow -x_k$; if $x_k^{best} = 0$ and $x_k > 0$, then $x_k \leftarrow 0$. In other words, we try to transform the topology of the unconnected network to the best solution's topology. We call the VO that uses this connectivity repair scheme CRB (i.e. Connectivty Repair by the Best solution).

4.3 Branch Exchanging

This VO aims to directly generate connected offspring networks by following the principle that during the recombination of two connected networks $\boldsymbol{x}$ and $\boldsymbol{y}$, if we bring a cable connection from $\boldsymbol{x}$ to $\boldsymbol{y}$ (i.e. $x_i \leftrightarrow y_i, x_i > 0, y_i \leq 0$), we need to return a different cable connection from $\boldsymbol{y}$ to $\boldsymbol{x}$ (i.e. $x_j \leftrightarrow y_j, x_j \leq 0, y_j > 0$) and vice versa. For GA, when we recombine 2 parent solutions $\boldsymbol{x}$ and $\boldsymbol{y}$, for variables whose values are both positive (i.e. both are active cables) or both non-positive (i.e. no cable connections or NOPs), we can perform uniform crossover as normal since these positions have the same structure in both networks. For each variable i where $x_i > 0$ and $y_i \leq 0$ (or $x_i \leq 0$ and $y_i > 0$), if we perform crossover, we need to find a different variable j where $x_j \leq 0$ and $y_j > 0$ (or $x_j > 0$ and $y_j \leq 0$) such that exchanging values at variables i and j between 2 solutions $\boldsymbol{x}$ and $\boldsymbol{y}$ still maintains the connectivity of both networks. If we cannot find such a variable j then we do not perform crossover at the variable i. For GOMEA, in each mixing event, this procedure works similarly for the current solution $\boldsymbol{o}$ and a donor $\boldsymbol{d}$, but we only need to search for the variable j when $o_i > 0$ and $d_i \leq 0$ and the scope of searching for j is limited among the variables in the current linkage set. Also, we only need to maintain the connectivity of the current solution. This VO is problem-specific because it employs the connectivity knowledge of DNEP when generating new offspring. We call this VO BX (i.e. branch exchanging).

Originally, GOMEAs do not have mutation operators. We here experiment with DNEP-specific mutation. After every mixing event with a linkage set, but before the evaluation of the partially-altered solution, we go through every variable in the linkage set and perform a mutation with probability $1/l$ (l is the length of the solution). The mutated values must still maintain the connectivity of the network; otherwise the mutation is undone. In preliminary research, we also tried this mutation operator with GA but found that it did not have positive impact on GA. We call the branch exchanging VO with this mutation operator BX-M.

Table 1: Benchmark Network Size

ID	# Branches (Variables)	# Nodes	# HV/MV Substations	# Cable types
1	17	10	1	3
2	59	31	1	3
3	190	51	4	12

5. EXPERIMENTS

5.1 Benchmark Problems

We perform experiments on 3 benchmark networks of different sizes that are adapted from real distribution networks of a DNO. The sizes of benchmark networks are shown in Table 1. Details of network 1 and network 2 can be found in [8] and [6]. The maximum number of evaluations is 50000 for network 1, 100000 for network 2, and 200000 for network 3. The planning horizon is 30 years, and for each problem instance and each variation operator, GA and GOMEA are run 30 times. For computational reasons, for dynamic DNEP of network 3, the planning horizon is 10 years and each solver is run 10 times. The averaged convergence graphs showing the qualities of the obtained solutions during the optimization process from the beginning until termination are shown in Figures 2 and 3. Some graphs (especially in network 2) show a lot of fluctuation from the beginning until a certain point because we only consider feasible solutions, and it takes a different number of evaluations in each run before the first feasible solution is obtained.

5.2 Results

5.2.1 *Static DNEP*

Figure 2 shows the performance of GA and GOMEA integrated with different VOs solving the static DNEP. For networks 1 and 2, GAs and GOMEAs exhibit the same effectiveness in obtaining (near-)optimal solutions. After spending a certain number of evaluations (i.e. computing budget), all solvers have similar convergence until termination. For network 1, all GOMEA instances have a little better performance than their corresponding GA instances, reaching the same final network with slightly less evaluations. For network 2, GA-DQ100 and GA-CRP work slightly better than GOMEA-DQ100 and GOMEA-CRP. However, on small networks, these differences between GAs and GOMEAs, or between different VOs, can be seen as insignificant.

In contrast, when solving DNEP for a large network, the performance gap between GAs and GOMEAs and the impacts of different VOs are considerable. For network 3, the large DNEP instance, using the out-of-the-box VO, GA-DQ1 is unable to solve DNEP and hardly obtains any good solutions. Moreover, while also assuming no connectivity knowledge, given the same computing budget (i.e. number of evaluations), GOMEA-DQ1 clearly outperforms both GA-DQ1 and GA-DQ100, and obtains solution plans of much better quality. DQ100 gives GA multiple trials of recombination to generate new connected networks, and that indeed helps GA improve its performance a lot (but still worse than GOMEA-DQ1 in terms of the quality of obtained solutions at termination); but DQ100 can only slightly accelerate GOMEA. Similarly, while the connectivity repair VOs CRP and CRB clearly enhance the effectiveness and efficiency

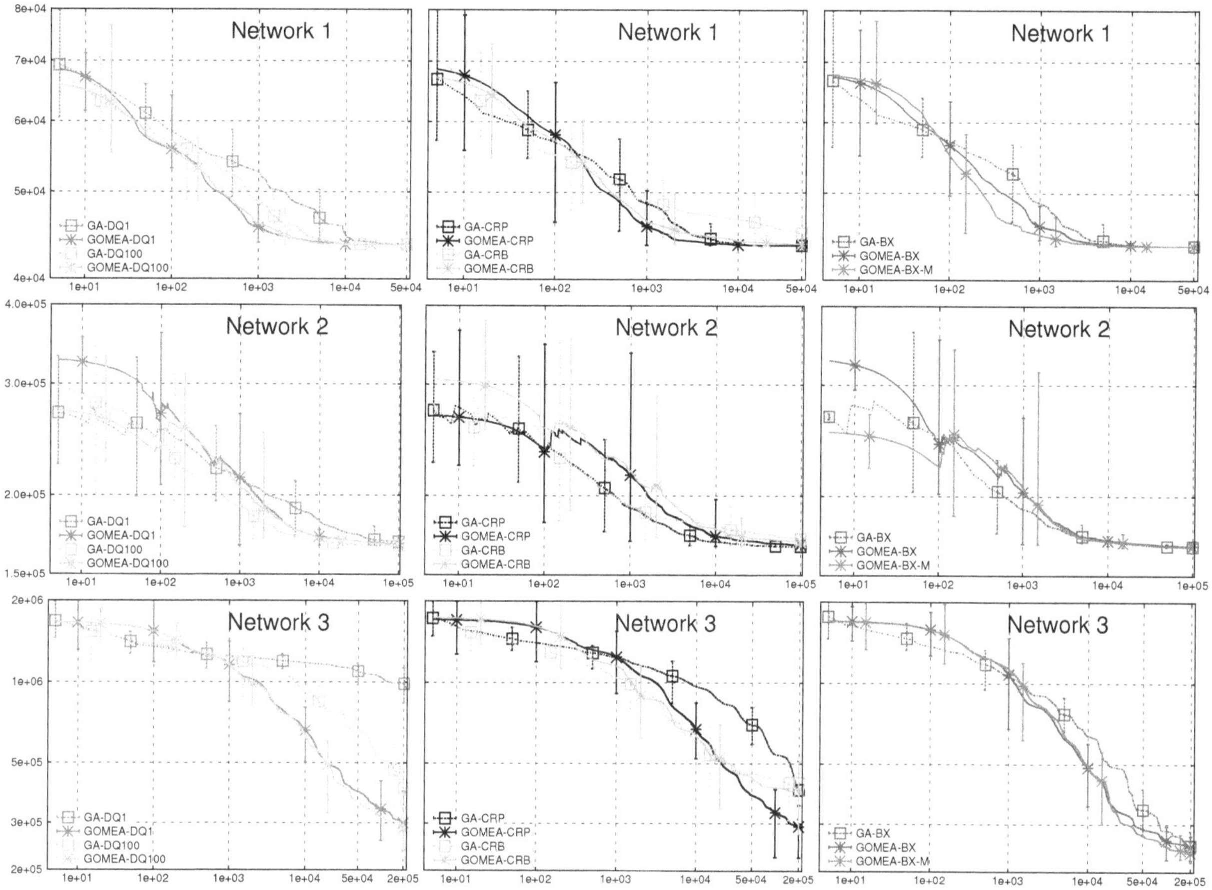

Figure 2: Static DNEP. Horizontal axis: number of evaluations. Vertical axis: NPV of total cost (EUR).

of GA, they does not show any significant improvement in speed over GOMEA-DQ1. Interestingly, repairing by parent solutions (CRP) appears to be better than repairing by the best solutions (CRB) for DNEP. This can be because it is difficult for general-purpose VOs to generate connected networks and keeping matching unconnected offspring networks with the slowly-changing best topology would reduce the beneficial diversity in the population, making the algorithm prone to premature convergence.

Solving the issue of maintaining connectivity, the customized VO branch exchanging (BX) brings out superior efficiency for EAs solving DNEP. GA-BX has excellent performance, similar to its corresponding GOMEA-BX in obtaining (near-)optimal solutions. BX also has positive impacts on GOMEA but the size of the effect is much less significant than on GA. The results here suggest 2 conclusions. First, problem-specific VOs are crucial for classic EAs, like GA, to efficiently solve (larger) real-world optimization problems. Second, EAs that can learn and exploit linkage structures, like GOMEA or estimation-of-distribution algorithms (EDAs), are indeed far more robust solvers, which can be used out-of-the-box and still obtain solutions of good quality close to those found by a customized EA with problem-dedicated VOs (i.e. comparing GOMEA-DQ1 in leftmost graphs with GA-BX and GOMEA-BX in rightmost graphs in Fig. 2). Besides, the mutation operator which we design for GOMEA here has a slight improvement over GOMEA-BX, making GOMEA-BX-M the best solver in this test case (i.e. the fastest solver given the upper bound on number of evaluations used in our experiments). While it might not be necessary for GOMEA solving many laboratory benchmarks, mutation can still be beneficial when tackling real-world problems.

5.2.2 *Dynamic DNEP*

Figure 3 exhibits the convergence performance of GAs and GOMEAs solving dynamic DNEP. The performances of GAs and GOMEAs are similar to those observed in static DNEP, suggesting that the use of the decomposition heuristic does not introduce addtional complexity to the optimization problem. GOMEAs are slightly better than their corresponding GAs in solving network 1, and GAs slightly outperform GOMEAs in solving network 2, but the these differences are insignificant. For network 3, GOMEAs have much better convergence than GAs even when the out-of-the-box variant GOMEA-DQ1 is used. The DNEP-specific branch exchanging (BX) VO is again shown to be able to greatly improve the efficiency of the classic GA while having a minor acceleration on GOMEA. GOMEA-BX-M is still the overall best solver.

6. CONCLUSIONS

This paper contributes guidelines and methodologies for the application of EAs in tackling the real-world optimization DNEP. First, we proposed a decomposition heuristic that can help available static planning solvers be able to solve the dynamic DNEP in a practical manner. Second, we suggested practitioners of DNEP to employ population sizing-free schemes to get rid of the notoriously-difficult-to-

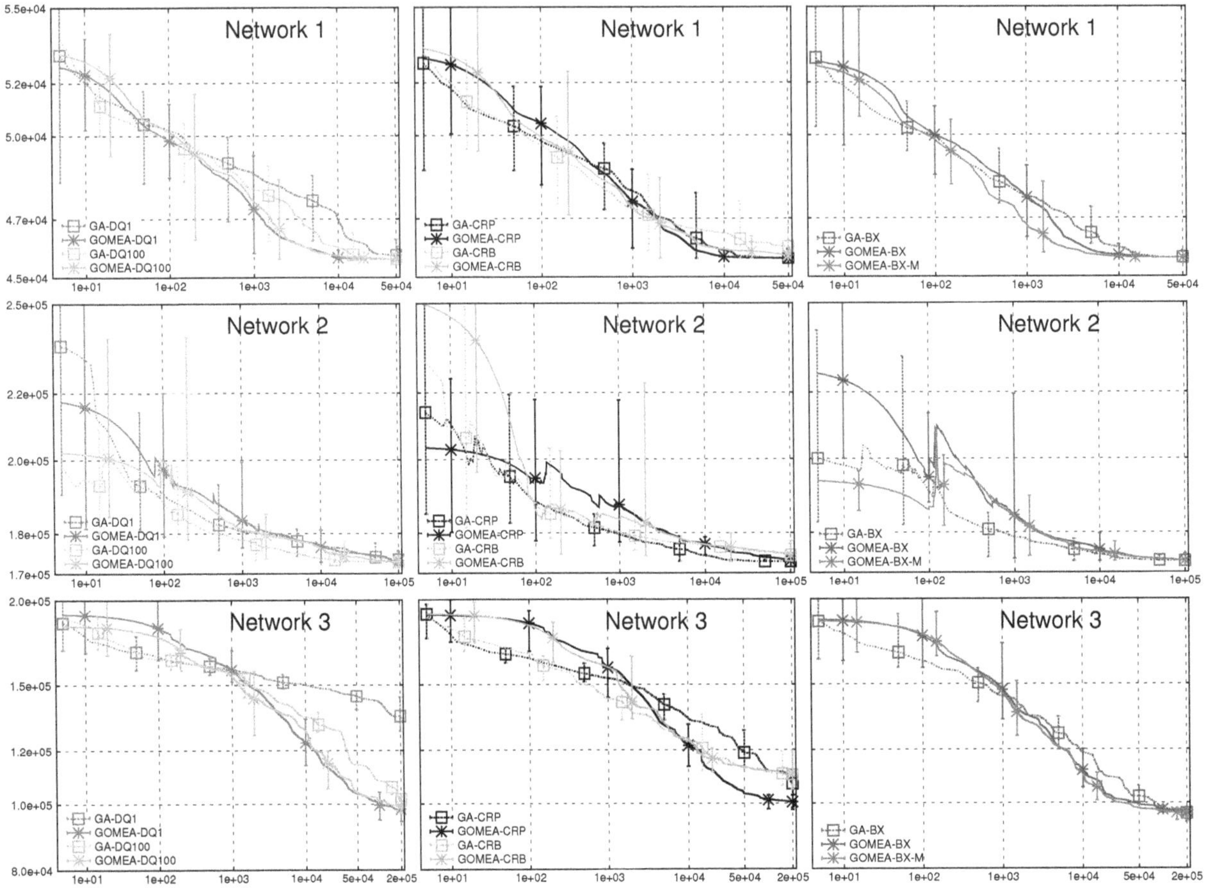

Figure 3: Dynamic DNEP. Horizontal axis: number of evaluations. Vertical axis: NPV of total cost (EUR).

set population size parameter. Third, we introduced multiple variation operators that can be employed by EAs solving DNEPs and showed their impacts on the performance of 2 typical EAs: the classic GA and the GOMEA, which is capable of linkage learning (LL) and exploiting linkage information. Due to LL, GOMEA is shown to be a far more robust solver for solving DNEP on our benchmark networks. Using the same number of solution evaluations like GA, GOMEA obtains better results even when assuming a minimal amount of problem-specific knowledge (PSK). Adding PSK to GOMEA improves performance results but the improvement gap, for a fixed budget of evaluations, is much less significant than that for classic GA, which again confirms the usefulness of LL in detecting problem structures. As problem size increases, LL is of great importance to the scalability of EAs. Lastly, based on the experiment results, we suggest that LL EAs, like GOMEA, should be given priority when selecting EAs for solving DNEP.

7. REFERENCES

[1] C. L. T. Borges and V. F. Martins. Multistage expansion planning for active distribution networks under demand and distributed generation uncertainties. *International Journal of Electrical Power & Energy Systems*, 36(1):107 – 116, 2012.

[2] P. A. N. Bosman and D. Thierens. More concise and robust linkage learning by filtering and combining linkage hierarchies. In *Proc. of the Genetic and Evolutionary Comp. Conf. - GECCO-2013*, pages 359–366. ACM, 2013.

[3] E. Diaz-Dorado, J. Cidras, and E. Miguez. Application of evolutionary algorithms for the planning of urban distribution networks of medium voltage. *IEEE Transactions on Power Systems*, 17(3):879–884, Aug 2002.

[4] J. J. Grainger and W. D. Stevenson. *Power System Analysis*. McGraw-Hill Education, 2003.

[5] I. Gronau and S. Moran. Optimal implementations of UPGMA and other common clustering algorithms. *Information Processing Letters*, 104(6):205 – 210, 2007.

[6] M. O. W. Grond, N. H. Luong, J. Morren, P. A. N. Bosman, J. G. Slootweg, and H. La Poutré. Practice-oriented optimization of distribution network planning using metaheuristic algorithms. In *18th Power Systems Computation Conference*, pages 1–8, 2014.

[7] G. R. Harik and F. G. Lobo. A parameter-less genetic algorithm. In *Proc. of the Genetic and Evolutionary Comp. Conf. (GECCO 1999)*, pages 258–265, 1999.

[8] H. N. Luong, M. O. W. Grond, P. A. N. Bosman, and H. La Poutré. Medium-voltage distribution network expansion planning with gene-pool optimal mixing evolutionary algorithms. In *Artificial Evolution - 11th International Conference, EA 2013*, pages 93–105, 2013.

[9] I. Ramirez-Rosado and J. Bernal-Agustin. Genetic algorithms applied to the design of large power distribution systems. *IEEE Transactions on Power Systems*, 13(2):696–703, May 1998.

[10] D. Thierens and P. A. N. Bosman. Optimal mixing evolutionary algorithms. In *Proceedings of the Genetic and Evolutionary Computation Conference - GECCO-2011*, pages 617–624. ACM, 2011.

[11] R. A. Verzijlbergh, M. O. W. Grond, Z. Lukszo, J. G. Slootweg, and M. D. Ilic. Network impacts and cost savings of controlled EV charging. *IEEE Transactions on Smart Grid*, 3(3):1203–1212, Sept 2012.

Selecting Best Investment Opportunities from Stock Portfolios Optimized by a Multiobjective Evolutionary Algorithm

Krzysztof Michalak
Department of Information Technologies
Institute of Business Informatics
Wroclaw University of Economics
Wroclaw, Poland
krzysztof.michalak@ue.wroc.pl

ABSTRACT

Multiobjective optimization of portfolios aims at finding sets of stocks which are expected to provide a possibly high return while retaining a moderate level of risk. The Pareto front of portfolios generated by the optimization algorithm represents attainable trade-offs between returns obtained by the portfolios and the level of risk involved in the investment. This paper studies the relationship between location of portfolios in the Pareto front and future returns of these portfolios. It is observed that the highest future returns can be obtained for the portfolios with the highest return and risk measures observed in the past but also for those with the lowest return and risk in the Pareto front. Neither constantly selecting portfolios with high return on historical data nor, conversely, those with low historical risk (but also low return) yields high future returns. Based on these observations a method is proposed for adaptively selecting the best portfolios for investment from solutions contained in the Pareto front. The proposed method selects high-return (but also high-risk) portfolios or low-risk (but also low-return) portfolios based on the behaviour of the stock marked index in the time period preceding the moment of investment. The proposed method outperforms both the strategy of always selecting the portfolios with the highest return from the past and the risk-averse strategy of selecting portfolios with low risk measure.

Keywords

stock portfolio optimization, multiobjective evolutionary optimization, average linkage method

1. INTRODUCTION

Evolutionary methods are frequently applied in finance to problems such as time series forecasting [10, 12, 19] and trading rules optimization [15, 21]. Portfolio optimization [4] is another problem to which evolutionary methods are often employed. In his seminal work Markowitz [16] proposed evaluating portfolios using the expected return and the variance as a measure of risk. This approach is often used to date, however, various risk measures are employed in addition to or as a replacement for the variance. Thus, the portfolio optimization problem is clearly a multiobjective one. In the literature, many approaches are used for optimizing portfolios such as mixed-integer programming [23], tabu search [1] and simulated annealing [6]. Evolutionary algorithms, however, are especially well suited for multiobjective optimization because they maintain an entire population of solutions to a given problem. These solutions can represent trade-offs between objectives and using properly designed algorithms it is possible to obtain an approximation of the Pareto front for a multiobjective optimization problem. Also, evolutionary algorithms can easily be used with various risk measures because, contrary to methods such as linear or quadratic programming, they do not rely heavily on specific properties of the evaluation function. Apart from optimization of portfolio parameters [11], evolutionary portfolio optimization has been used in the literature for other problems such as tracking a stock market index [2] or replicating the behaviour of an investment fund [17].

In this paper the NSGA-II [9] evolutionary algorithm is used for portfolio optimization. After the optimization step is completed, the relationship between location of portfolios in the Pareto front and future returns of these portfolios is studied. The investigation described in this paper has shown that quite often the best returns are obtained for portfolios that gave high returns in the past, but also high future returns are obtained for portfolios with the lowest value of the risk measure on historical data. Because of the properties of the Pareto front the latter portfolios are at the same time the portfolios with low returns obtained on historical data. In this paper an investment strategy is proposed which utilizes these observations for improving future returns.

Key elements of this paper are as follows:

1. A method is proposed for computing the expected daily returns and risk measures for portfolios using minute-granularity data. This approach makes it possible to effectively utilize minute-level data for a task of optimizing long term investments.

2. It is shown how historical performance of portfolios

GECCO '15, July 11 - 15, 2015, Madrid, Spain

ISBN 978-1-4503-3472-3/15/07...$15.00
DOI: http://dx.doi.org/10.1145/2739480.2754645

can be used for building portfolios with good future returns. The proposed method is compared to a strategy that selects portfolios with the highest return on historical data and to a risk-averse strategy that chooses portfolios with low risk measure obtained for historical data. The experiments have shown that it is possible to increase future profits by using a strategy which adaptively selects high-return or low-risk portfolios.

3. An evolutionary algorithm is used for finding a Pareto front of solutions so that it is possible to choose portfolios according to the proposed strategy. While the return-risk optimization problem can be solved using other approaches, population-based method are commonly used for multiobjective optimization and moreover for the method presented in this paper it is crucial to generate a large population of solutions to select from.

The rest of this paper is structured as follows. Section 2 presents the way in which portfolios are represented and in which the parameters of portfolios (return and risk) are evaluated. In Section 3 the details of the optimization procedure are given. The same section presents the clustering algorithm used for grouping similar portfolios in the Pareto front. Section 4 presents an experimental analysis of portfolio behaviour. Based on this analysis a simple portfolio selection strategy was formulated. This strategy is presented and tested in Section 5. Section 6 concludes the paper.

2. CONSTRUCTION AND EVALUATION OF PORTFOLIOS

For constructing portfolios we assume that a number N_s of stocks are available for investments. A portfolio is thus represented as a vector $w \in R^{N_s}$ in which each coordinate w_i is a "weight" of i-th stock. We require that:

$$\sum_{i=1}^{N_s} w_i = 1 \ , \tag{1}$$

so that w_i is the percentage of units of i-th stock per one unit of the portfolio. We calculate the quotation $p(t)$ of portfolio $w = [w_1, \dots, w_{N_s}]$ at time t as:

$$p(t) = \sum_{i=1}^{N_s} w_i q_i(t) \ , \tag{2}$$

where:
$q_i(t)$ - quotation of i-th stock at time t.

Denoting a matrix of quotations of all available stocks by Q (in which rows correspond to stocks and columns to time instants) we obtain an equation for a time series P of quotations of portfolio w:

$$P = w^T Q \ . \tag{3}$$

If Q contains daily quotations for stocks then daily quotations for portfolio w can be calculated using Eq. (3). Such an approach is, however, rather naive, because it assumes that the pricing for a given portfolio can be calculated exactly for a given day. It also neglects the possibility of evaluating the variability of portfolio prices on each day. In this paper we employ an approach which makes it possible to take into account fluctuations in the prices of the assets. In order to evaluate a portfolio using the expected return and a selected risk measure we use minute quotations of all the stocks. We assume that we want to buy the assets for the portfolio on a given day d_1 and subsequently sell them on some other day $d_2 > d_1$, but the exact moment at which we manage to buy or sell the assets in each of the days is not fixed. First, the average value $m_i(t)$ of each stock in each minute t is calculated based on the high $h_i(t)$ and low $l_i(t)$ values for this minute.

$$\forall i \in \{1, \dots, N_s\} \forall t : m_i(t) = \frac{h_i(t) + l_i(t)}{2} \ . \tag{4}$$

Then, a set R_{d_1,d_2} is built which contains all the possible returns that could be obtained if buying stocks in portfolio w on day d_1 and selling on day d_2:

$$R_{d_1,d_2} = \left\{ \frac{\sum_{i=1}^{N_s} w_i m_i(t_2)}{\sum_{i=1}^{N_s} w_i m_i(t_1)} : t_1 \in d_1 \wedge t_2 \in d_2 \right\} \ , \tag{5}$$

where:
$t_k \in d_j$ denotes a minute t_k in the day d_j.

The evaluation of the portfolio w in terms of the expected return E and the risk measure V is done using the values in the set R_{d_1,d_2}. The estimation of the expected return E is done by calculating the average return from the set R_{d_1,d_2}. The risk measures are also calculated using the values from this set. Therefore, the expected return and the risk measures are calculated with daily granularity based on minute stock quotations. It is important to note, that the evaluation scheme described above does not assume any method for determining the best moment for buying (during day d_1) and selling (during day d_2) the assets. This procedure is intended for estimating what return and risk measure value can be expected when buying on day d_1 and selling on day d_2, so we obtain daily estimates from minute quotations. Since portfolio optimization is usually performed for long time investments rather than for high frequency trading such granularity should be sufficient in most applications.

Because in finance various measures are used for expressing the investment risk, in this paper three different risk measures are used:

Variance calculated over the set R_{d_1,d_2}.

Semi-variance a variance calculated over these elements of the set R_{d_1,d_2} that are below the mean. Thus, only the variability of portfolio performance below the mean is treated as a risk-inducing factor. Fluctuations above the mean do not influence the semi-variance. This risk measure has the advantage over the variance in that it does not evaluate as risky those portfolios that give very high returns.

Sharpe ratio [3] introduced by Sharpe [22]. The Sharpe Ratio of a given asset is defined as:

$$S = \frac{E\left[R_a - R_b\right]}{\sqrt{\mathrm{var}\left[R_a - R_b\right]}} \ , \tag{6}$$

where:
$E[\cdot]$ - expected value operator,
var - the variance,
R_a - the return of the asset,
R_b - a risk-free return.

The risk-free return R_b used in the definition of the Sharpe ratio can be calculated on a basis of various assets. In this paper 2-year yields of the U.S. government bonds were used. The parameters of the U.S. government bonds obtained from [5] on 2014.01.10 were as follows: buy price $b_p = 99 - 23\frac{3}{4}$, coupon rate: $c_r = 0.25\%$. Traditionally, bond prices are given as a percentage of the face value with the number after a hyphen being the number of one-thirty-seconds. Thus, converted to decimal notation:

$$b_p = 99 + \frac{23\frac{3}{4}}{32}\% = 99.7421875 \ . \tag{7}$$

With 4 coupon payments (once every half a year) this yields an overall bond return of:

$$b_r = \frac{100 + 4 * c_r}{b_p} \approx 1.01261 \ . \tag{8}$$

This return has to be subsequently recalculated from 2 years to the return on the same period as the investment in the considered portfolio. Sharpe ratio is a measure of how well a given asset compensates the investor for higher risk by gaining higher returns. Since for this measure higher values are better whenever there is a need to minimize the risk measure we actually minimize $-S$.

3. OPTIMIZATION OF PORTFOLIOS

For the optimization of portfolios the NSGA-II algorithm [9] was chosen. This algorithm is, to this day, among the best-performing multiobjective optimization algorithms and is still used in many applications [13, 20]. Because NSGA-II uses the non-dominated sorting and the binary tournament selection [18] it works well with problems in which the objectives have disproportionate scales. Thus, it is well-suited for the discussed problem in which the values of the return and the risk measure usually have different magnitudes.

The genotype of each specimen represents a portfolio, thus it contains a vector of weights $w = [w_1, \ldots, w_{N_s}]$. Since the solved problem is real-valued the SBX crossover [7] and polynomial mutation [8, 14] are used. Because, as stated in Eq. (1), the weights in each portfolio sum to 1 a repair operator which normalizes the weights vector w is applied to new specimens and after application of the crossover and the mutation. This operator calculates the sum s of the weights in a portfolio and then divides all the weights by s. Thus, all zero weights remain zero and the sum of all weights after the normalization is equal to 1.

Optimization of the portfolios for the investment starting on the day d_0 is performed using the NSGA-II algorithm with two objective functions representing the return and the risk measure for a portfolio w on the period $[d_0 - h, d_0 - 1]$, where h is the length of historical data range used for optimizing portfolios. After portfolios are optimized on the interval $[d_0 - h, d_0 - 1]$, their future performance is evaluated by simulating investments starting on the day d_0 and lasting for a given period of f days. Starting days d_0 for investments are set every t_Δ days.

For each starting day d_0 the algorithm is allowed to run for N_{gen} generations using a population of N_{pop} specimens. The solutions found by the algorithm are subsequently grouped into N_c clusters using the Average Linkage Method (ALM) [24]. The clustering is done in the objective space, i.e. data points to be grouped represent the return and the risk measure calculated for each of the portfolios.

After the portfolios are clustered it is possible to compare historical and future performance of groups of similar portfolios. For the clusters produced by the Average Linkage Method two rankings are calculated: one according to the average return obtained by portfolios from each cluster on historical data $\overline{E(w, d_0 - h, d_0 - 1)}$ and the second according to the average return on future data $\overline{E(w, d_0, d_0 + f - 1)}$, where f and h are the lengths in days of the future and historical data intervals. After creating such rankings for $d_0 = d_{start}$, $d_0 = d_{start} + t_\Delta$, $d_0 = d_{start} + 2t_\Delta$, ... we can calculate a confusion matrix $C[r_h, r_f]_{N_c \times N_c}$ in which an element C_{ij} represents the number of times a cluster of portfolios was ranked at i-th position according to the return on historical data and at j-th position according to the future return. Of course, if there is a strong correspondence between the return on historical data and the future return the confusion matrix C should be approximately diagonal. If there is no relationship between historical and future returns the confusion matrix should be more or less equally filled.

4. EXPERIMENTAL ANALYSIS OF PORTFOLIO BEHAVIOUR

In the experiments 200 stocks from NYSE were used for building portfolios. Minute quotations for these stocks were taken from the interval from 2012.07.02 to 2014.10.17 which equals 120 weeks or $d_{all} = 578$ trading days. In this period 224,739 minute quotations were recorded for each stock.

Tests were performed for two different lengths of the investment period: $f = 30$ and 60 trading days. The length of the optimization period was set to six different values: $h =$ 30, 60, 90, 120, 150 and 180 trading days. The beginning of the first investment period was set on day $d_{start} = 181$ of the available data range for each optimization period length h in order to ensure that all the tests were performed on the same data range. Subsequent starting days were set every $t_\Delta = 5$ days from the first one. The number of investment periods was limited by the range of available data in which the testing period of f days had to fit. Therefore for $f = 30$ and 60 trading days in the testing period the number of investment periods was 74 and 68 respectively.

The parameters of the evolutionary algorithm were set as follows: the population size $N_{pop} = 500$ and the number of generations $N_{gen} = 50$ were used. The distribution index parameter was set to 20 for both the crossover and the mutation operators. The number of clusters was set to $N_c = 10$.

Due to limited space only the confusion matrices obtained for the investment period of $f = 30$ and the variance as the risk measure are presented in Fig. 1. For the investment period of $f = 60$ days and for the semi-variance and the Sharpe ratio as the risk measures similar confusion matrices were obtained, but with varying number of elements on the diagonals. Clearly, there is a strong relationship between the performance of portfolios on historical data and the performance of the same portfolios in the future, because the confusion matrices are not evenly filled by similar values. Some of the entries with high values are located on the diagonal D_1 between the bottom-left and upper-right corners. These entries represent situations in which the performance of portfolios from a certain cluster in the future is either equally poor as on historical data (bottom-left corner) or equally good (upper-right corner). Interestingly, there is a number of entries which are located on the other diagonal D_2, i.e. the one connecting the upper-left and bottom-right corners. These entries represent situations in which portfolios that were providing high returns in the past produce low returns in the future and vice versa. The portfolios are optimized by a multiobjective optimization algorithm which tries to find a trade-off between maximizing the return and minimizing the risk measure. Therefore, the entries on the diagonal D_2 represent situations in which the portfolios that provide the best return in the future come from among those for which the risk measure calculated on historical data was the lowest.

Two conclusions from this series of experiments are that:

1. Based on the confusion matrices it can be observed that choosing the portfolio with the highest return in the past may on some occasions provide high returns in the future, but also may lead to very poor results. At times, choosing a portfolio with the lowest observed risk level may be a better option.

2. Since the relationship between the past and future returns has two different characteristics within the same time interval one needs a way of telling which approach to choose when investing.

An investment strategy based on these observations is elaborated in the next section.

5. PORTFOLIO SELECTION STRATEGY

When selecting a portfolio of stocks for an investment we are interested, of course, in how well this portfolio will perform in the future, that is, what will the return be after we sell the stocks some days after we bought them. Unfortunately, we cannot see into the future and have to, therefore, optimize our portfolios based on their performance on historical data. Experiments summarized in the previous section have shown that on some occasions the portfolios behave in the future in more or less the same way as in the past and on some occasions quite to the opposite. These observations allow us to assume that high returns from portfolio investments could be obtained if we chose portfolios with high past returns in the first case and low past returns (but also low risk) in the second. In this section four simple portfolio selection strategies are studied in order to show how the observations made during the experiments could be used to improve investment payoffs.

All the tested strategies are based on the portfolio optimization procedure described in Section 3. When trying to find the best portfolio for an investment starting at day d_0 the portfolios are optimized on a time interval $[d_0 - h, d_0 - 1]$. Then, the resulting portfolios are grouped using the Average Linkage Method according to the parameters characterizing their performance i.e. the return and the risk measure. After the population of portfolios is prepared a single portfolio has to be chosen for an investment. The strategies studied in this section choose the portfolio for an investment in the following way:

- **C-RET** - The centroid is taken from the cluster in which the past returns are highest on average.

- **C-RISK** - The centroid is taken from the cluster in which the past risk measure is lowest on average.

- **IDX** - If the stock market index increased on historical data interval the centroid is taken from this cluster in which the past returns are highest on average. If the stock market index decreased on historical data interval the centroid is taken from this cluster in which the past risk measure is lowest on average. This strategy can be parameterized by the length g of the historical data interval on which the behaviour of the index is tested.

- **S-RET** - The portfolio which has shown the highest return on historical data interval is chosen. It cannot be guaranteed that historical returns are good predictors of future ones, but, based on the confusion matrices obtained in the experiments, it can be expected that portfolios which performed well in the past may frequently produce good returns in the future.

The presented strategies were evaluated by simulating investments in the following way. The investments began on the day $d_{start} = 181$, so at first $d_0 = d_{start} = 181$. A population of $N_{pop} = 500$ portfolios was optimized using the portfolio optimization procedure described in Section 3 for a chosen investment term of $f = 30$ or 60 trading days. Then, one portfolio was chosen using each of the four selection strategies. For the IDX selection strategy the quotations of the Dow Jones Industrial Average index were used with $g = 30$, 60, 90, 120, 150 and 180. The return obtained by selling the securities from each of the portfolios on the day $d_0 + f - 1$ was recorded. Each time a new investment was started right after the previous one by setting $d_0 \leftarrow d_0 + f$. These steps were repeated for the entire interval for which data were available. The accumulated return was calculated by multiplying the returns obtained in all the intervals. Therefore, it represents the return obtained when selecting the best portfolio for consecutive intervals of either $f = 30$ or 60 days. The procedure described above was repeated 10 times for each portfolio selection strategy and for each triple of values for f, g and h. The results from these 10 repetitions were averaged. Average cumulative returns obtained by the studied strategies are presented in Tables 1-6 along with standard deviations. In these tables the best result obtained for each optimization interval length of h is underlined. In Fig. 3 the total number of times each strategy produced the highest return (that is, produced the highest value in a column in one of the Tables 1-6) is presented.

For investment interval lengths of both $f = 30$ and 60 days the best strategy is clearly the IDX strategy that selects portfolios with the highest return or lowest risk measure depending on the behaviour of the index. The best length g of the historical data interval on which the index performance is evaluated seems to be $g = 30$ days. It is worth noticing that even though for $f = 30$ days, $h = 30$ days and the variance as the risk measure the IDX strategy with $g = 60$ days works best the same strategy with $g = 30$ days also outperforms C-RET, C-RISK and S-RET. Therefore $g = 30$ seems to be the best choice. In Table 7 a summary of the results is presented.

The investment interval length $f = 60$ trading days resulted in significantly higher returns than those obtained for $f = 30$ even though in both cases the investments were made on the entire available data range from $d_{start} = 181$ onwards. For all three risk measures a similar return of about 20% was obtained. In five out of six cases the best

Table 1: Average cumulative returns (and standard deviations) obtained for the investment period length of $f = 30$ days with the variance used as the risk measure.

	$h = 30$	$h = 60$	$h = 90$	$h = 120$	$h = 150$	$h = 180$
C-RET	1.0944 (0.0079)	1.0821 (0.0149)	1.0919 (0.0170)	1.0797 (0.0130)	1.0750 (0.0151)	1.0911 (0.0125)
C-RISK	1.0753 (0.0115)	1.1005 (0.0091)	1.1091 (0.0053)	1.0917 (0.0075)	1.0887 (0.0121)	1.0949 (0.0081)
IDX (g=30)	1.0969 (0.0113)	1.1041 (0.0080)	1.1139 (0.0159)	1.1069 (0.0105)	1.0922 (0.0127)	1.1078 (0.0091)
IDX (g=60)	1.0989 (0.0095)	1.0897 (0.0139)	1.0992 (0.0148)	1.0750 (0.0136)	1.0726 (0.0132)	1.0872 (0.0130)
IDX (g=90)	1.0944 (0.0079)	1.0821 (0.0149)	1.0919 (0.0170)	1.0797 (0.0130)	1.0750 (0.0151)	1.0911 (0.0125)
IDX (g=120)	1.0944 (0.0079)	1.0821 (0.0149)	1.0919 (0.0170)	1.0797 (0.0130)	1.0750 (0.0151)	1.0911 (0.0125)
IDX (g=150)	1.0944 (0.0079)	1.0821 (0.0149)	1.0919 (0.0170)	1.0797 (0.0130)	1.0750 (0.0151)	1.0911 (0.0125)
IDX (g=180)	1.0944 (0.0079)	1.0821 (0.0149)	1.0919 (0.0170)	1.0797 (0.0130)	1.0750 (0.0151)	1.0911 (0.0125)
S-RET	1.0896 (0.0093)	1.0815 (0.0101)	1.0929 (0.0061)	1.0830 (0.0087)	1.0708 (0.0067)	1.0878 (0.0135)

Table 2: Average cumulative returns (and standard deviations) obtained for the investment period length of $f = 60$ days with the variance used as the risk measure.

	$h = 30$	$h = 60$	$h = 90$	$h = 120$	$h = 150$	$h = 180$
C-RET	1.1628 (0.0080)	1.1931 (0.0098)	1.1994 (0.0091)	1.2016 (0.0090)	1.1892 (0.0103)	1.1959 (0.0130)
C-RISK	1.1380 (0.0061)	1.1967 (0.0117)	1.1742 (0.0101)	1.1924 (0.0067)	1.1678 (0.0068)	1.1833 (0.0086)
IDX (g=30)	1.1639 (0.0060)	1.2131 (0.0095)	1.2067 (0.0109)	1.2150 (0.0129)	1.1861 (0.0113)	1.2023 (0.0094)
IDX (g=60)	1.1628 (0.0080)	1.1931 (0.0098)	1.1994 (0.0091)	1.2016 (0.0090)	1.1892 (0.0103)	1.1959 (0.0131)
IDX (g=90)	1.1628 (0.0080)	1.1931 (0.0098)	1.1994 (0.0091)	1.2016 (0.0090)	1.1892 (0.0103)	1.1959 (0.0131)
IDX (g=120)	1.1628 (0.0080)	1.1931 (0.0098)	1.1994 (0.0091)	1.2016 (0.0090)	1.1892 (0.0103)	1.1959 (0.0131)
IDX (g=150)	1.1628 (0.0080)	1.1931 (0.0098)	1.1994 (0.0091)	1.2016 (0.0090)	1.1892 (0.0103)	1.1959 (0.0131)
IDX (g=180)	1.1628 (0.0080)	1.1931 (0.0098)	1.1994 (0.0091)	1.2016 (0.0090)	1.1892 (0.0103)	1.1959 (0.0131)
S-RET	1.1599 (0.0112)	1.2006 (0.0099)	1.2037 (0.0127)	1.2028 (0.0076)	1.1867 (0.0065)	1.1919 (0.0111)

Table 3: Average cumulative returns (and standard deviations) obtained for the investment period length of $f = 30$ days with the semi-variance used as the risk measure.

	$h = 30$	$h = 60$	$h = 90$	$h = 120$	$h = 150$	$h = 180$
C-RET	1.0922 (0.0068)	1.0885 (0.0087)	1.0975 (0.0086)	1.0720 (0.0101)	1.0926 (0.0093)	1.0916 (0.0054)
C-RISK	1.0842 (0.0111)	1.1078 (0.0062)	1.1271 (0.0060)	1.0948 (0.0103)	1.1051 (0.0144)	1.1160 (0.0075)
IDX (g=30)	1.1006 (0.0101)	1.1130 (0.0052)	1.1176 (0.0077)	1.0987 (0.0119)	1.1120 (0.0114)	1.1171 (0.0088)
IDX (g=60)	1.0962 (0.0089)	1.0935 (0.0089)	1.1064 (0.0095)	1.0698 (0.0108)	1.0889 (0.0098)	1.0896 (0.0068)
IDX (g=90)	1.0922 (0.0068)	1.0885 (0.0087)	1.0975 (0.0086)	1.0720 (0.0101)	1.0926 (0.0093)	1.0916 (0.0054)
IDX (g=120)	1.0922 (0.0068)	1.0885 (0.0087)	1.0975 (0.0086)	1.0720 (0.0101)	1.0926 (0.0093)	1.0916 (0.0054)
IDX (g=150)	1.0922 (0.0068)	1.0885 (0.0087)	1.0975 (0.0086)	1.0720 (0.0101)	1.0926 (0.0093)	1.0916 (0.0054)
IDX (g=180)	1.0922 (0.0068)	1.0885 (0.0087)	1.0975 (0.0086)	1.0720 (0.0101)	1.0926 (0.0093)	1.0916 (0.0054)
S-RET	1.0961 (0.0105)	1.0858 (0.0068)	1.1009 (0.0117)	1.0721 (0.0067)	1.0906 (0.0086)	1.0928 (0.0074)

Table 4: Average cumulative returns (and standard deviations) obtained for the investment period length of $f = 60$ days with the semi-variance used as the risk measure.

	$h = 30$	$h = 60$	$h = 90$	$h = 120$	$h = 150$	$h = 180$
C-RET	1.1578 (0.0124)	1.2047 (0.0132)	1.1927 (0.0107)	1.1932 (0.0144)	1.1889 (0.0059)	1.1970 (0.0118)
C-RISK	1.1378 (0.0109)	1.1957 (0.0117)	1.1819 (0.0094)	1.1893 (0.0113)	1.1720 (0.0050)	1.1932 (0.0106)
IDX (g=30)	1.1569 (0.0108)	1.2241 (0.0104)	1.2007 (0.0104)	1.2058 (0.0145)	1.1860 (0.0054)	1.2078 (0.0108)
IDX (g=60)	1.1578 (0.0124)	1.2047 (0.0132)	1.1927 (0.0107)	1.1932 (0.0144)	1.1889 (0.0059)	1.1970 (0.0118)
IDX (g=90)	1.1578 (0.0124)	1.2047 (0.0132)	1.1927 (0.0107)	1.1932 (0.0144)	1.1889 (0.0059)	1.1970 (0.0118)
IDX (g=120)	1.1578 (0.0124)	1.2047 (0.0132)	1.1927 (0.0107)	1.1932 (0.0144)	1.1889 (0.0059)	1.1970 (0.0118)
IDX (g=150)	1.1578 (0.0124)	1.2047 (0.0132)	1.1927 (0.0107)	1.1932 (0.0144)	1.1889 (0.0059)	1.1970 (0.0118)
IDX (g=180)	1.1578 (0.0124)	1.2047 (0.0132)	1.1927 (0.0107)	1.1932 (0.0144)	1.1889 (0.0059)	1.1970 (0.0118)
S-RET	1.1599 (0.0090)	1.2079 (0.0109)	1.1940 (0.0151)	1.1996 (0.0083)	1.1878 (0.0065)	1.1964 (0.0120)

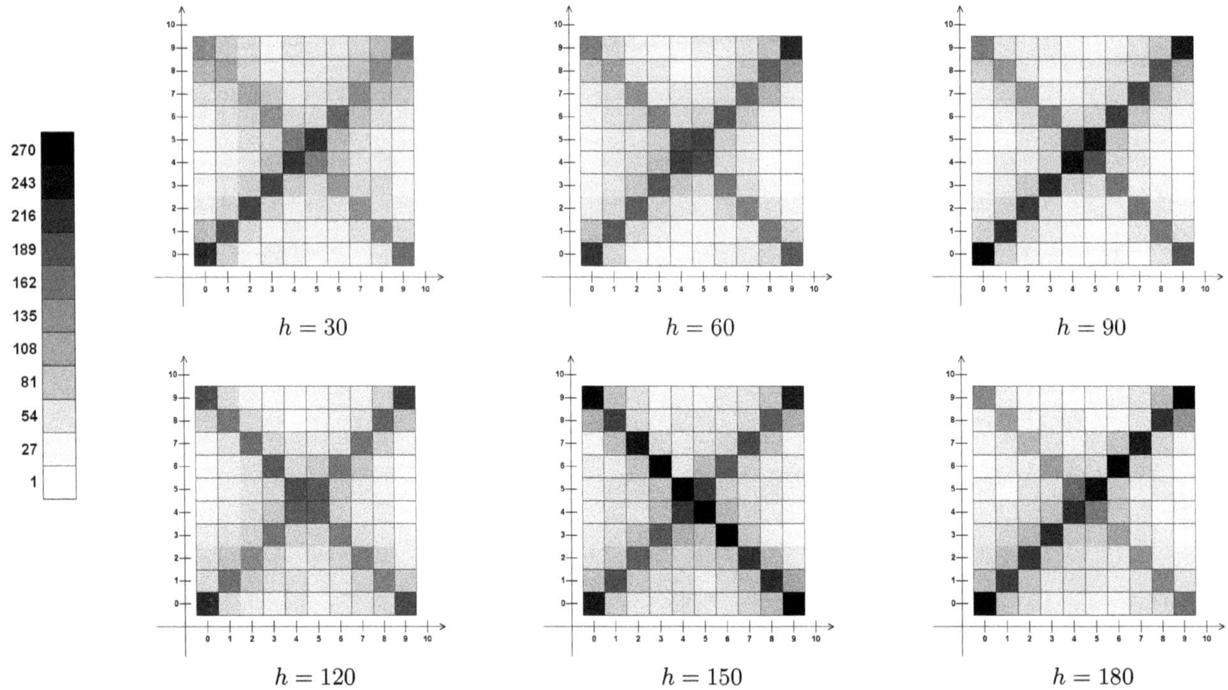

Figure 1: Confusion matrices obtained in the experiments for the investment interval length $f = 30$ with the variance used as the risk measure.

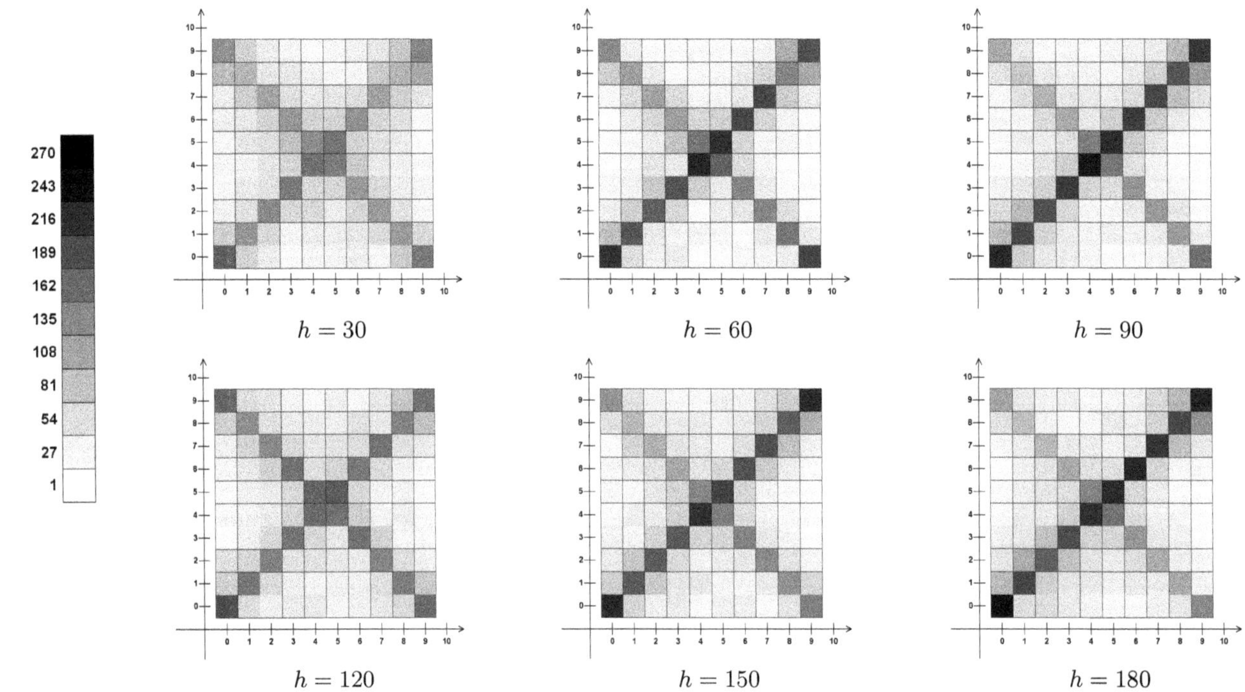

Figure 2: Confusion matrices obtained in the experiments for the investment interval length $f = 60$ with the variance used as the risk measure.

Table 5: **Average cumulative returns (and standard deviations) obtained for the investment period length of $f = 30$ days with the Sharpe ratio used as the risk measure.**

	$h = 30$	$h = 60$	$h = 90$	$h = 120$	$h = 150$	$h = 180$
C-RET	1.1047 (0.0112)	1.0702 (0.0109)	1.0763 (0.0103)	1.0699 (0.0089)	1.0806 (0.0119)	1.0875 (0.0080)
C-RISK	1.1008 (0.0107)	1.0726 (0.0069)	1.0784 (0.0073)	1.0829 (0.0103)	1.0770 (0.0104)	1.0927 (0.0106)
IDX (g=30)	1.1082 (0.0091)	1.0727 (0.0129)	1.0828 (0.0090)	1.0814 (0.0081)	1.0799 (0.0120)	1.0932 (0.0047)
IDX (g=60)	1.1054 (0.0111)	1.0725 (0.0098)	1.0760 (0.0108)	1.0702 (0.0088)	1.0802 (0.0116)	1.0883 (0.0092)
IDX (g=90)	1.1047 (0.0111)	1.0702 (0.0109)	1.0763 (0.0103)	1.0699 (0.0089)	1.0806 (0.0119)	1.0875 (0.0080)
IDX (g=120)	1.1047 (0.0111)	1.0702 (0.0109)	1.0763 (0.0103)	1.0699 (0.0089)	1.0806 (0.0119)	1.0875 (0.0080)
IDX (g=150)	1.1047 (0.0111)	1.0702 (0.0109)	1.0763 (0.0103)	1.0699 (0.0089)	1.0806 (0.0119)	1.0875 (0.0080)
IDX (g=180)	1.1047 (0.0111)	1.0702 (0.0109)	1.0763 (0.0103)	1.0699 (0.0089)	1.0806 (0.0119)	1.0875 (0.0080)
S-RET	1.1009 (0.0082)	1.0650 (0.0072)	1.0713 (0.0130)	1.0741 (0.0108)	1.0802 (0.0099)	1.0827 (0.0084)

Table 6: **Average cumulative returns (and standard deviations) obtained for the investment period length of $f = 60$ days with the Sharpe ratio used as the risk measure.**

	$h = 30$	$h = 60$	$h = 90$	$h = 120$	$h = 150$	$h = 180$
C-RET	1.1740 (0.0135)	1.2037 (0.0075)	1.2028 (0.0068)	1.1995 (0.0065)	1.1934 (0.0190)	1.1929 (0.0192)
C-RISK	1.1695 (0.0076)	1.2043 (0.0073)	1.2053 (0.0096)	1.2024 (0.0093)	1.1877 (0.0169)	1.1767 (0.0194)
IDX (g=30)	1.1766 (0.0110)	1.2106 (0.0124)	1.2063 (0.0072)	1.2080 (0.0059)	1.1959 (0.0184)	1.1933 (0.0208)
IDX (g=60)	1.1740 (0.0135)	1.2037 (0.0075)	1.2028 (0.0068)	1.1995 (0.0065)	1.1934 (0.0190)	1.1929 (0.0192)
IDX (g=90)	1.1740 (0.0135)	1.2037 (0.0075)	1.2028 (0.0068)	1.1995 (0.0065)	1.1934 (0.0190)	1.1929 (0.0192)
IDX (g=120)	1.1740 (0.0135)	1.2037 (0.0075)	1.2028 (0.0068)	1.1995 (0.0065)	1.1934 (0.0190)	1.1929 (0.0192)
IDX (g=150)	1.1740 (0.0135)	1.2037 (0.0075)	1.2028 (0.0068)	1.1995 (0.0065)	1.1934 (0.0190)	1.1929 (0.0192)
IDX (g=180)	1.1740 (0.0135)	1.2037 (0.0075)	1.2028 (0.0068)	1.1995 (0.0065)	1.1934 (0.0190)	1.1929 (0.0192)
S-RET	1.1729 (0.0095)	1.2019 (0.0079)	1.1994 (0.0094)	1.1979 (0.0076)	1.1965 (0.0168)	1.1876 (0.0246)

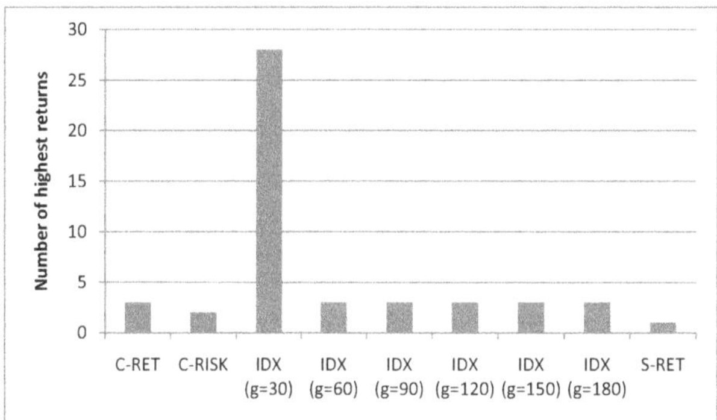

Figure 3: The total number of times each strategy produced the highest return.

Table 7: **The best returns obtained for the tested risk measures and for investment interval length of $f = 30$ and 60 trading days.**

Risk measure	Return	Strategy	h
$f = 30$			
Variance	1.1139	IDX ($g = 30$)	90
Semi-variance	1.1271	C-RISK	90
Sharpe ratio	1.1082	IDX ($g = 30$)	30
$f = 60$			
Variance	1.2150	IDX ($g = 30$)	120
Semi-variance	1.2241	IDX ($g = 30$)	60
Sharpe ratio	1.2106	IDX ($g = 30$)	60

result was achieved by the IDX strategy which made investment decision based on the index behaviour on a range of $g = 30$ days. When investments were made for $f = 60$ days intervals the IDX strategy with $g = 30$ days produced the best results for all risk measures.

When optimizing portfolios for future investment not only the portfolio selection strategy has to be chosen, but the length h of the historical data period for optimization as well. For investment interval of $f = 30$ days the best result was obtained using the IDX portfolio selection strategy with $g = 30$ days and for $h = 90$ days. When the investment interval was set to $f = 60$ days the best result was also obtained using the IDX strategy with $g = 30$ days but for $h = 60$ days. It can be concluded that extending the period on which the portfolios are evaluated during optimization above 90 days can be expected to provide little to none improvement for the performance of the portfolios in the future.

6. CONCLUSION

This paper studies the relationship between the performance of portfolios optimized using a multiobjective evolutionary algorithm on historical data and in future investments. When the behaviour of portfolios located in various parts of the Pareto front is analyzed two distinct patterns can be found. The first one is a situation in which those portfolios that worked well in the past work well in the future. Apart from this pattern, however, another type of behaviour can be found. In some situations the portfolios that give the highest future returns are those that achieved the lowest risk on historical data.

Based on the observations concerning the behaviour of the

portfolios located in various parts of the Pareto front a strategy was developed for selecting the best portfolios for future investments. The proposed strategy selects portfolios either from those that produced the highest return on historical data or from those that achieved the lowest risk. The decision which portfolios to choose from is made on the basis of the behaviour of the stock marked index in the time period preceding the moment of investment.

The proposed strategy was compared with other portfolio selection strategies for investments made for $f = 30$ and 60 trading days. The new strategy was found to outperform the competitive approaches.

Future work may include using other risk measures or developing adaptive strategies for deciding from which cluster to select a portfolio for future investments.

7. REFERENCES

[1] M. M. Aldaihani and T. M. Aldeehani. Portfolio optimization models and a tabu search algorithm for the kuwait stock exchange. *Investment Management and Financial Innovations*, 5(2):30–39, 2008.

[2] K. Andriosopoulos, M. Doumpos, N. C. Papapostolou, and P. K. Pouliasis. Portfolio optimization and index tracking for the shipping stock and freight markets using evolutionary algorithms. *Transportation Research Part E: Logistics and Transportation Review*, 52:16–34, 2013.

[3] B. R. Auer and F. Schuhmacher. Performance hypothesis testing with the sharpe ratio: The case of hedge funds. *Finance Research Letters*, 10(4):196–208, 2013.

[4] M. J. Best. *Portfolio Optimization.* Chapman&Hall/CRC, 2010.

[5] Bloomberg Markets. United states government bonds. http://www.bloomberg.com/markets/rates-bonds/government-bonds/us/, 2014. Online: accessed 2014.01.10.

[6] Y. Crama and M. Schyns. Simulated annealing for complex portfolio selection problems. *European Journal of Operational Research*, 150(3):546–571, 2003.

[7] K. Deb and R. Agarwal. Simulated binary crossover for continuous search space. *Complex Systems*, 9(2):115–148, 1995.

[8] K. Deb and M. Goyal. A combined genetic adaptive search (GeneAS) for engineering design. *Computer Science and Informatics*, 26:30–45, 1996.

[9] K. Deb, A. Pratap, S. Agarwal, and T. Meyarivan. A fast and elitist multiobjective genetic algorithm: NSGA-II. *IEEE Transactions on Evolutionary Computation*, 6:182–197, 2002.

[10] J. P. Donate, P. Cortez, G. G. Sanchez, and A. S. de Miguel. Time series forecasting using a weighted cross-validation evolutionary artificial neural network ensemble. *Neurocomputing*, 109:27–32, 2013.

[11] F. C. Duran, C. Cotta, and A. J. Fernández. Evolutionary optimization for multiobjective portfolio selection under markowitz's model with application to the caracas stock exchange. In R. Chiong, editor, *Nature-Inspired Algorithms for Optimisation*, volume 193 of *Studies in Computational Intelligence*, pages 489–509. Springer Berlin Heidelberg, 2009.

[12] W. Froelich and J. L. Salmeron. Evolutionary learning of fuzzy grey cognitive maps for the forecasting of multivariate, interval-valued time series. *Int. J. Approx. Reason.*, 55(6):1319–1335, 2014.

[13] A. Haghighi and A. Z. Asl. Uncertainty analysis of water supply networks using the fuzzy set theory and NSGA-II. *Engineering Applications of Artificial Intelligence*, 32:270–282, 2014.

[14] M. Hamdan. On the disruption level of polynomial mutation for evolutionary multi-objective optimisation algorithms. *Computing and Informatics*, 29:783–800, 2010.

[15] Y. Hu, B. Feng, X. Zhang, E. Ngai, and M. Liu. Stock trading rule discovery with an evolutionary trend following model. *Expert Systems with Applications*, 42(1):212–222, 2015.

[16] H. Markowitz. Portfolio selection. *The Journal of Finance*, 7(1):77–91, 1952.

[17] K. Michalak, P. Filipiak, and P. Lipinski. Evolutionary approach to multiobjective optimization of portfolios that reflect the behaviour of investment funds. In A. Ramsay and G. Agre, editors, *Artificial Intelligence: Methodology, Systems, and Applications*, volume 7557 of *Lecture Notes in Computer Science*, pages 202–211. Springer Berlin Heidelberg, 2012.

[18] B. L. Miller and D. E. Goldberg. Genetic algorithms, tournament selection, and the effects of noise. *Complex Systems*, 9:193–212, 1995.

[19] R. Mohammadi, S. F. Ghomi, and F. Zeinali. A new hybrid evolutionary based RBF networks method for forecasting time series: A case study of forecasting emergency supply demand time series. *Engineering Applications of Artificial Intelligence*, 36:204–214, 2014.

[20] J. Sadeghi, S. Sadeghi, and S. T. A. Niaki. A hybrid vendor managed inventory and redundancy allocation optimization problem in supply chain management: An NSGA-II with tuned parameters. *Computers & Operations Research*, 41:53–64, 2014.

[21] U. Sahin and A. M. Ozbayoglu. TN-RSI: Trend-normalized RSI indicator for stock trading systems with evolutionary computation. *Procedia Computer Science*, 36:240–245, 2014.

[22] W. F. Sharpe. Mutual fund performance. *The Journal of Business*, 39(1):119–138, 1966.

[23] P. Xidonas, G. Mavrotas, and J. Psarras. Portfolio construction on the athens stock exchange: a multiobjective optimization approach. *Optimization*, 59(8):1211–1229, 2010.

[24] E. Zitzler, M. Laumanns, and L. Thiele. SPEA2: Improving the Strength Pareto Evolutionary Algorithm for Multiobjective Optimization. In K. Giannakoglou et al., editors, *Evolutionary Methods for Design, Optimisation and Control with Application to Industrial Problems (EUROGEN 2001)*, pages 95–100. International Center for Numerical Methods in Engineering (CIMNE), 2002.

Diversity Guided Evolutionary Mining of Hierarchical Process Models

Thomas Molka
HANA Cloud Computing,
Systems Engineering, SAP
Belfast, UK
thomasmolka@gmail.com

David Redlich
HANA Cloud Computing,
Systems Engineering, SAP
Belfast, UK
d.redlich@gmx.de

Marc Drobek
HANA Cloud Computing,
Systems Engineering, SAP
Belfast, UK
marcdrobek@gmx.de

Xiao-Jun Zeng
The University of Manchester
Manchester, UK
x.zeng@manchester.ac.uk

Wasif Gilani
HANA Cloud Computing,
Systems Engineering, SAP
Belfast, UK
wasif.gilani@sap.com

ABSTRACT

Easy-to-understand and up-to-date models of business processes are important for enterprises, as they aim to describe how work is executed in reality and provide a starting point for process analysis and optimization. With an increasing amount of event data logged by information systems today, the automatic discovery of process models from process logs has become possible. Whereas most existing techniques focus on the discovery of well-formalized models (e.g. Petri nets) which are popular among researchers, business analysts prefer business domain-specific models (such as Business Process Model Notation, BPMN) which are not well formally specified. We present and evaluate an approach for discovering the latter type of process models by formally specifying a hierarchical view on business process models and applying an evolution strategy on it. The evolution strategy efficiently finds process models which best represent a given event log by using fast methods for process model conformance checking, and is partly guided by the diversity of the process model population. The approach contributes to the field of evolutionary algorithms by showing that they can be successfully applied in the real-world use case of process discovery, and contributes to the process discovery domain by providing a promising alternative to existing methods.

Keywords

business process management; process mining; evolutionary algorithms; population diversity

1. INTRODUCTION

In today's enterprises, the work carried out is organized in business processes. These processes define a collection of tasks along with their order of execution needed to achieve a certain business goal. Documentation on these processes in the shape of process models is essential to analyzing and optimizing the process, as well as for process stakeholders to make informed decisions. In most cases, however, there are no such models available. Often, the available models are created manually and become outdated when the underlying process is adapted or optimized, or simply do not reflect the process as executed in reality.

At the same time, processes are increasingly supported by information systems which, as a by-product, create event logs documenting the execution of the tasks along with additional information such as the time of execution or the resources involved. These event logs can be used to mine (i.e. automatically extract) process models, models describing the interaction of resources, or even simulation models used for process performance predictions [13, 14]. While most process mining techniques focus on the extraction of well-formalized models such as Petri nets, these models tend to get complex and difficult to understand, especially in case of larger processes [12]. Business process stakeholders prefer less formal models from the business process domain, such as BPMN [10], which are typically used to document processes when drawn manually by business process analysts.

We propose an approach which uses an evolution strategy to mine business process domain models that allow the consumer to abstract from complex behaviour by viewing the process at a desired level of detail. The approach can deal with noise in event logs and allows the user to configure the set of business process constructs permitted in the mined models.

In the remainder of this paper we formally define the model we use for representing business processes (Section 2), define a set of operations for modifying these kind of models (Section 3), and explain the evolution strategy used to mine them (Section 4). We conclude by evaluating the approach (Section 5), setting it into the context of related work (Section 6), and summarizing our results (Section 7).

2. PROCESS MODEL

Our genotype for the optimization problem is constituted by two representations of business process. Firstly, we use a process model which consists of basic business process control-flow elements as described in Section 2.1. For the implementation of this model we take a definition provided in [11] which fulfils our requirements regarding well-structuredness of process models, and for which process conformance measures are already defined (measures for determining how well a process model reflects the real execution of

GECCO '15, July 11 - 15, 2015, Madrid, Spain

ISBN 978-1-4503-3472-3/15/07 ... $15.00

DOI: http://dx.doi.org/10.1145/2739480.2754765

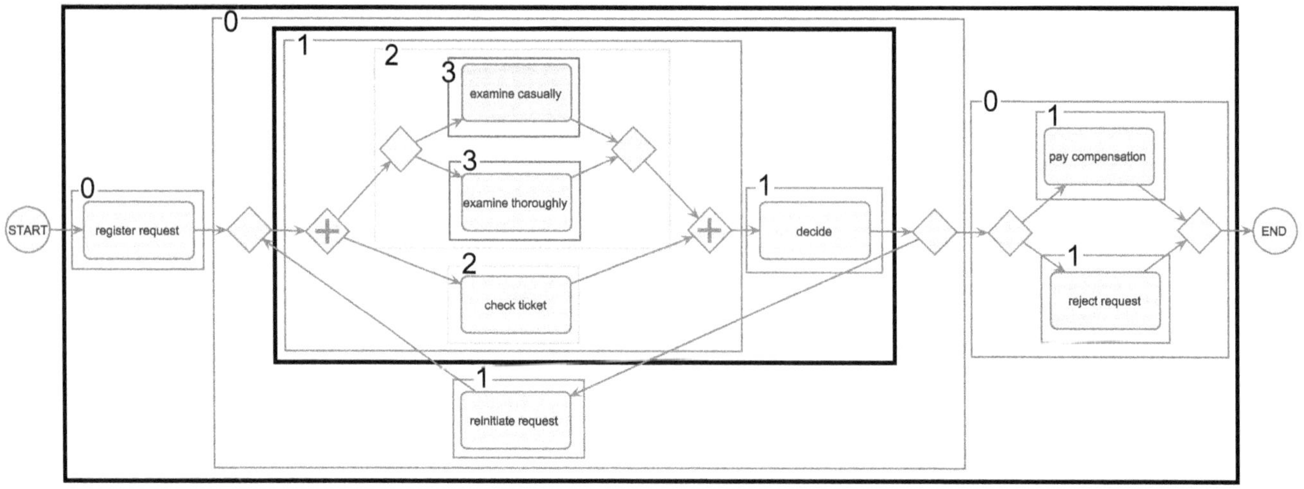

Figure 1: Example of a business process model and its hierarchical view.

the process as documented in an event log). Secondly, the genotype is expressed as a hierarchical view which we define as an abstraction layer on top of the control-flow (Section 2.2). This hierarchical view provides the user with easy-to-understand models and allows the evolution strategy to perform efficient operations.

2.1 Control-Flow

The set of business process elements used in our models (also supported by the most common business process modelling languages BPMN and EPC) consists of: event nodes marking the *start* and *end* of the process, *activities* which represent process steps in which work is carried out, *decisions* representing a split of a branch into exclusive choice branches, *merges* to connect exclusive branches again, *forks* for splitting a branch into parallel branches, and *joins* to synchronize parallel branches.

In the following, we use a definition given in [11] as formal description of the control-flow model. There, a business process model is defined as a tuple $BP = (B, C)$ containing a set of business process elements $B = B_A \cup B_D \cup B_M \cup B_F \cup B_J \cup \{s\} \cup \{e\}$, and a connection relation $C \subseteq B \times B$. The set of business process elements consists of activities B_A, decisions B_D, merges B_M, forks B_F, joins B_J, exactly one start event s, and exactly one end event e. The connection relation C describes which business process element follows another process element (being one of its "targets") or is followed by another process element (being one of its "sources") [11]:

- $C \subseteq \{(a,b) \in B \times B \mid a \neq b \wedge a \neq e \wedge b \neq s\}$ (an element can't be its own source or target, the end element has no target, and the start element has no source),
- $\forall a \in B_A \cup B_M \cup B_J \cup \{s\} : |\{(a,b) \in C \mid b \in B\}| = 1$ (activities, merges, joins, and the start element have exactly one target),
- $\forall a \in B_A \cup B_D \cup B_F \cup \{e\} : |\{(b,a) \in C \mid b \in B\}| = 1$ (activities, decisions, forks, and the end element have exactly one source),
- $\forall a \in B_M \cup B_J : |\{(b,a) \in C \mid b \in B\}| \geq 1$ (merges and joins have at least one source element),
- $\forall a \in B_D \cup B_F : |\{(a,b) \in C \mid b \in B\}| \geq 1$ (decisions and forks have at least one target element), and
- $\forall a \in B : \exists (s,a) \in C^+ \wedge \exists (a,e) \in C^+$ (all elements in B of the process (B,C) are on a path from s to e (C^+ being the transitive closure of C))

2.2 Hierarchical Model

In order to provide a better structure for operations on the genotype, i.e. the process model, carried out by the evolutionary algorithm, we create a hierarchical view on process models, consisting of two types of elements: *atomic graphs* $\mathfrak{A}$ and *sequences of atomic graphs* $\mathfrak{S}$. Atomic graphs are constructs representing a part of the control-flow model. This part can either be a single activity, or a block structure (exclusive, parallel, or loop) which consists of two branches (branches are sequences of atomic graphs). Figure 1 shows an example of the control-flow model of a process and a hierarchical view on it (marked by additional frames around parts of the control-flow). The control-flow contains activities in the shape of rounded rectangles, gateways in the shape of diamonds (empty diamonds denote decisions and merges, diamonds with a "+" denote forks and joins), and the start and end node (circles). The black rectangles with thick stroke indicate sequences of atomic graphs with a length of two or more. All other rectangles frame atomic graphs. The number on the top left of each rectangle represents the hierarchy level of the atomic graph. The main process sequence contains three atomic graphs (on hierarchy level 0): a simple activity, a loop construct, and an exclusive choice construct. The loop construct has a parallel construct in one of its branches, which in turn contains an exclusive construct, extending the hierarchy level to 3.

In the following we provide the formal definition for hierarchical views. Let $B = B_A \cup B_D \cup B_M \cup B_F \cup B_J \cup \{s\} \cup \{e\}$ be a set of business process control flow elements (cf. Section 2.1). Then a hierarchical view $\mathfrak{h} = (\mathfrak{A}, \mathfrak{S}, B)$ on them is defined by:

- $\mathfrak{A} = \mathfrak{A}_A \cup \mathfrak{A}_E \cup \mathfrak{A}_P \cup \mathfrak{A}_L$ (atomic graphs can be atomic activities, exclusive constructs, parallel constructs, or loops)
- $\mathfrak{S} = \mathfrak{S}_B \cup \{\mathfrak{s}_p\}$ (the set of sequences consists of branch sequences and one "root" process sequence $\mathfrak{s}_p$)
- $\forall \mathfrak{s} \in \mathfrak{S}\ \exists n \in \mathbb{N}\ \exists A \subseteq \mathfrak{A} : \mathfrak{s} \in \{0...n\} \to A$ (sequences are functions assigning each index an atomic graph)
- $\forall (f, l, \mathfrak{s}_1, \mathfrak{s}_2) \in \mathfrak{A} : f, l \in B \wedge \mathfrak{s}_1, \mathfrak{s}_2 \in \mathfrak{S}_B \cup \{\$\}$ (all atomic graphs have a first and a last control flow element, and two branch sequences)
- $\forall (a, a, \$, \$) \in \mathfrak{A}_A : a \in B_A$ (atomic activities contain only one activity and no branch sequences, the $ sign shall express the lack of a branch)

- $\forall \mathfrak{e} \in \mathfrak{A}_E \; \exists d \in B_D \; \exists m \in B_M \; \exists \mathfrak{s}_1, \mathfrak{s}_2 \in \mathfrak{S} : \mathfrak{e} = (d, m, \mathfrak{s}_1, \mathfrak{s}_2)$ (exclusive constructs have a decision as first element, a merge as last element, and two branch sequences)
- $\forall \mathfrak{l} \in \mathfrak{A}_L \; \exists d \in B_D \; \exists m \in B_M \; \exists \mathfrak{s}_1, \mathfrak{s}_2 \in \mathfrak{S} : \mathfrak{l} = (m, d, \mathfrak{s}_1, \mathfrak{s}_2)$ (loop constructs have a merge as first element, a decision as last element, and two branch sequences)
- $\forall \mathfrak{p} \in \mathfrak{A}_P \; \exists f \in B_F \; \exists j \in B_J \; \exists \mathfrak{s}_1, \mathfrak{s}_2 \in \mathfrak{S} : \mathfrak{p} = (f, j, \mathfrak{s}_1, \mathfrak{s}_2)$ (parallel constructs have a fork as first element, a join as last element, and two branch sequences)
- $\forall \mathfrak{a} \in \mathfrak{A} \; \exists_{=1} \mathfrak{s} \in \mathfrak{S} \; \exists_{=1} n < |\mathfrak{s}| : (n, \mathfrak{a}) \in \mathfrak{s}$ (every atomic graph occurs exactly once in exactly one sequence of atomic graphs, i.e. every atomic graph is unique)
- $\forall \mathfrak{s} \in \mathfrak{S}_B \; \exists_{=1} (f, l, \mathfrak{s}_1, \mathfrak{s}_2) \in \mathfrak{A} : \mathfrak{s} = \mathfrak{s}_1 \vee \mathfrak{s} = \mathfrak{s}_2$ (every branch sequence is a branch of exactly one atomic graph, i.e. every branch sequence is contained in exactly one atomic graph)

3. PROCESS MODEL OPERATORS

In this section we define a set of operators for modifying a hierarchical model. These operators are used by the evolutionary algorithm described in Section 4. The operators we use are *move* ($\rightsquigarrow$) for moving parts of the process model to a different position in the model; *complexify* ($\oplus$, $\otimes$, $\circlearrowright$) for introducing complex constructs such as parallel, exclusive or loop constructs; and *simplify* ($\bigcirc$) for resolving complex constructs into a sequential shape. As we know all activities that are to be part of the model (by pre-processing the event log) we do not need to remove or insert activities in the model, but only the three above-mentioned operators for changing the structure of how the activities are connected.

The $\rightsquigarrow$ operator is used to move a subsequence of atomic graphs to a different part of the model (i.e. into another sequence of atomic graphs, or into a different position within the same sequence). The destinations of each move are limited to sequences which are no children of any of the graphs that are being moved (informally: an atomic graph cannot be moved into itself). Formally, in a hierarchical model $(\mathfrak{A}, \mathfrak{S}, B)$, the set of sequences $S \subseteq \mathfrak{S}$ a set of atomic graphs $A \subseteq \mathfrak{A}$ can be moved to, is defined as:

$$S = \mathfrak{S} \setminus \{\mathfrak{s} \mid (a, \mathfrak{s}) \in P^+ \wedge a \in A \wedge \mathfrak{s} \in \mathfrak{S}_B\}$$

where P^+ is the transitive closure of the combined parent relationship between atomic graphs and sequences:

$$P = \{(a,b) \mid (a = parentOfSequence(b) \vee a = parentOfGraph(b)\}$$

where the function returning the parent atomic graph for a sequence of atomic graphs is defined as

$$\begin{aligned} parentOfSequence &: \mathfrak{S}_B \to \mathfrak{A} \\ \mathfrak{s} &\mapsto (f, l, \mathfrak{s}_1, \mathfrak{s}_2) \mid \mathfrak{s} = \mathfrak{s}_1 \vee \mathfrak{s} = \mathfrak{s}_2 \end{aligned}$$

and the function returning the parent sequence for an atomic graph is defined as

$$\begin{aligned} parentOfGraph &: \mathfrak{A} \to \mathfrak{S} \\ \mathfrak{a} &\mapsto \mathfrak{s} \mid \exists (i, \mathfrak{a}) \in \mathfrak{s} \end{aligned}$$

Note that P contains only direct parent relations between atomic graphs and their parent sequence, and between branch sequences and their parent atomic graph, i.e. $P \subseteq (\mathfrak{A} \times \mathfrak{S}) \cup (\mathfrak{S} \times \mathfrak{A})$. In contrast, P^+ additionally contains the indirect (transitive) relations on the set of atomic graphs and sequences, i.e. $P^+ \subseteq (\mathfrak{A} \cup \mathfrak{S}) \times (\mathfrak{A} \cup \mathfrak{S})$.

In order to shorten the definition of the $\rightsquigarrow$ operator, we first define two functions on sequences of atomic graphs. The "remove" function $rmv(\mathfrak{s}, k, l)$ returns a sequence of atomic graphs representing sequence $\mathfrak{s}$ without the atomic graphs at indices k to l (the atomic graph at index $l+1$ is then at index k etc.):

$$\begin{aligned} rmv &: (\mathfrak{S}, \mathbb{N}, \mathbb{N}) \to \mathfrak{S} \\ rmv(\mathfrak{s}, k, l) &= (\mathfrak{s} \setminus \{(i, \mathfrak{a}) \in \mathfrak{s} \mid i \geq k\}) \\ &\quad \cup \{(i + k - l - 1, \mathfrak{a}) \mid (i, \mathfrak{a}) \in \mathfrak{s} \wedge i > l\} \end{aligned}$$

The "insert" function $ins(\mathfrak{s}_1, k, l, \mathfrak{s}_2, m)$ returns a sequence containing all the atomic graphs of sequence $\mathfrak{s}_2$ with some additional atomic graphs from sequence $\mathfrak{s}_1$ (the ones at indices k to l in $\mathfrak{s}_1$) inserted at index m (the atomic graphs after index m being moved back by $l - k + 1$):

$$\begin{aligned} ins &: (\mathfrak{S}, \mathbb{N}, \mathbb{N}, \mathfrak{S}, \mathbb{N}) \to \mathfrak{S} \\ ins(\mathfrak{s}_1, k, l, \mathfrak{s}_2, m) &= (\mathfrak{s}_2 \setminus \{(i, \mathfrak{a}) \in \mathfrak{s}_2 \mid i \geq m\}) \\ &\quad \cup \{(i + l - k + 1, \mathfrak{a}) \mid (i, \mathfrak{a}) \in \mathfrak{s}_2 \wedge i \geq m\} \\ &\quad \cup \{(i + k, \mathfrak{a}) \mid (i + k, \mathfrak{a}) \in \mathfrak{s}_1 \wedge i \leq l - k\} \end{aligned}$$

For instance, $ins(\mathfrak{s}_1, 0, \infty, \mathfrak{s}_2, 4)$ would return a sequence where all atomic graphs of $\mathfrak{s}_1$ are inserted at index 4 in $\mathfrak{s}_2$.
Using the two functions rmv and ins, we define the move operation as follows ($\mathfrak{H}$ being the domain of hierarchical models):

$$\begin{aligned} \rightsquigarrow &: (\mathfrak{H}, \mathfrak{S}, \mathbb{N}, \mathbb{N}, \mathfrak{S}, \mathbb{N}) \to \mathfrak{H} \\ \rightsquigarrow ((\mathfrak{A}, \mathfrak{S}, B), \mathfrak{s}_1, k, l, \mathfrak{s}_2, m) &= (\mathfrak{A}, \mathfrak{S}', B) \end{aligned}$$

where $\mathfrak{S}' = (\mathfrak{S} \setminus \{\mathfrak{s}_1, \mathfrak{s}_2\}) \cup \{rmv(\mathfrak{s}_1, k, l), ins(\mathfrak{s}_1, k, l, \mathfrak{s}_2, m)\}$.

When the operators $\oplus$, $\otimes$, or $\circlearrowright$ are applied on a part of a sequence of atomic graphs, this part is made more complex as it is used to create a parallel, exclusive or loop construct. This part of the sequence is split into two subparts, each of which will constitute a branch in the newly created construct. These operations modify the set $\mathfrak{A}$ by adding a new atomic graph, modify the set $\mathfrak{S}$ by adding two new sequences (and modifying the original sequence which contained the part), and add two new gateways to the set of control-flow elements B:

$$\begin{aligned} com &: (\mathfrak{H}, \mathfrak{S}, \mathbb{N}, \mathbb{N}, \mathbb{N}) \to \mathfrak{H} \\ com((\mathfrak{A}, \mathfrak{S}, B), \mathfrak{s}_1, k, l, m) &= (\mathfrak{A} \cup \{\mathfrak{a}\}, (\mathfrak{S} \setminus \{\mathfrak{s}_1\}) \cup \{\mathfrak{s}'_1, \mathfrak{s}_2, \mathfrak{s}_3\}, \\ &\qquad B \cup \{a, b\}) \end{aligned}$$

where

$$\begin{aligned} \mathfrak{a} &= (a, b, \mathfrak{s}_2, \mathfrak{s}_3) \wedge \\ \mathfrak{s}_2 &= \{(i, \mathfrak{b}) \mid k \leq i \leq l\} \wedge \\ \mathfrak{s}_3 &= \{(i, \mathfrak{b}) \mid l < i \leq m\} \wedge \\ \mathfrak{s}'_1 &= ins(\{(0, \mathfrak{a})\}, 0, 0, rmv(\mathfrak{s}_1, k, m), k) \end{aligned}$$

The types of the two business process control-flow elements a and b introduced into the model depend on the specific operation which is applied. In case of $\oplus$ a fork and join are created so that $a \in B_F$ and $b \in B_J$. When $\otimes$ is applied a decision and a merge are created so that $a \in B_D$ and $b \in B_M$, and in case of the loop operator $\circlearrowright$ a decision and a merge are created so that $a \in B_M$ and $b \in B_D$.

We use the simplify operator $\bigcirc$ in order to reduce model complexity by resolving complex constructs into a sequential shape. This means that an atomic graph in shape of a parallel, exclusive, or a loop construct is removed from the set $\mathfrak{A}$, its two branches are removed from the set $\mathfrak{S}$ and their contents are inserted into the parent sequence of the atomic graph (at the position the atomic graph

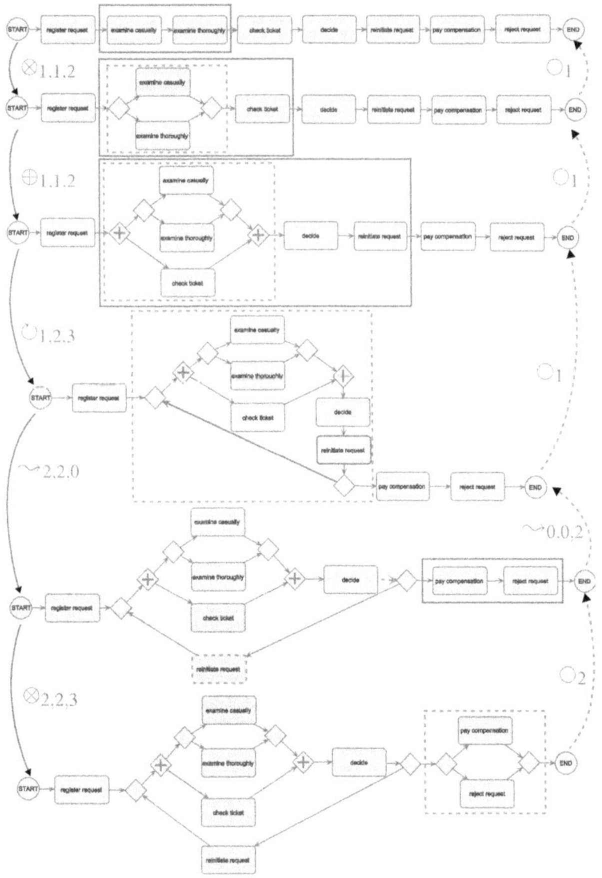

Figure 2: Examples of Operators on a Hierarchical Model

was at). Also, the set B is modified by removing the two gateways belonging to the atomic graph to be simplified:

$$\ominus : (\mathfrak{H}, \mathfrak{A}) \rightarrow \mathfrak{H}$$

$$\ominus((\mathfrak{A}, \mathfrak{S}, B), \mathfrak{a}) = (\mathfrak{A} \setminus \{\mathfrak{a}\},\ (\mathfrak{S} \setminus \{\mathfrak{s}_1, \mathfrak{s}_2, \mathfrak{s}_3\}) \cup \{\mathfrak{s}_3'\},\ B \setminus \{f, l\})$$

where

$$\begin{aligned} \mathfrak{a} &= (f, l, \mathfrak{s}_1, \mathfrak{s}_2) \wedge \\ \exists i &\in \mathbb{N} \mid (i, \mathfrak{a}) \in \mathfrak{s}_3 \wedge \\ \mathfrak{s}_3' &= ins(\mathfrak{s}_1, 0, \infty, ins(\mathfrak{s}_2, 0, \infty, rmv(\mathfrak{s}_3, i, i), i), i) \end{aligned}$$

i.e. the atomic graph $\mathfrak{a}$ to be simplified is located at index i in its parent sequence $\mathfrak{s}_3$.

Figure 2 shows an example of a business process model and the operators applied on it. The left side of the figure shows three complexify operations, one move operation, and another complexify operation being applied on an initially strictly sequential model, evolving it into a more complex model from the top of the figure to the bottom. The right side of the figure shows the inverse operations being applied on the model from bottom to top (one simplify, followed by one move and another three simplify operations). The complexify operator symbols on the left side of the picture have three indices which specify the parameters k, l, m, i.e. the indices in a sequence of atomic graphs denoting the part of the sequence to be complexified. For instance, the operation $\oplus_{1,1,2}$ performed on the main process sequence creates a graph at index 1 with two parallel branches, the first branch containing the graphs from index 1 (inclusive) to index 1 (inclusive) and the second containning the graphs from index 1 (exclusive) to index 2 (inclusive). The simplify operator symbols have one index which denotes the position of the atomic graph in a sequence to be simplified, e.g. $\ominus_1$ simplifies the atomic graph at index 1 in a specified sequence of atomic graphs. Similarly, the indices at the move operator specify the part of a sequence to be moved and the destination. For instance, $\rightsquigarrow_{2,2,0}$ moves the range of atomic graphs from index 2 (inclusive) to index 2 (inclusive) of a specified source sequence to index 0 in a specified destination sequence. For visual purposes, the parameters specifying the affected sequences are not shown in Figure 2. Instead, the parts affected by the operations on the left side are highlighted in the picture (red, thick), as well as the parts affected by the inverse operations on the right side (green, dashed). Using a sequence of the above described operations, any process model conforming to the definition of the hierarchical perspective can be transformed to any other model conforming to the same definition.

Algorithm 1: Evolution Strategy

Data: *log*
Result: *bestModel*
begin
  initialModel ← `createSequentialModel`(*log*);
  pop ← (*initialModel*);
  for *i=2* **to** μ **do** *pop* ← *pop* ∘ `mutate`(*initialModel*);
  while *not terminated* **do**
    newPop ← *pop*;
    for *i=1* **to** λ **do**
      parentModel ← `selectUniform`(*pop*);
      newPop ← *newPop* ∘ `mutate`(*parentModel*);
    end
    `sortDescending`(*newPop*);
    $pop \leftarrow newPop_0 \ldots newPop_{\mu-1}$;
    $bestModel \leftarrow pop_0$;
  end
end

4. EVOLUTION STRATEGY

For mining process models from a given event log we use a $(\mu+\lambda)$-ES (Algorithm 1), where the individuals are process models represented by their control-flow model (used for determining fitness, i.e. a process model is fit if it conforms well to the given event log) and their hierarchical view (for performing operations on the model). We start the evolution strategy by creating a sequential model that contains all distinct activities occurring in the event log (ordered by their first appearance), and mutating that model to create an initial population of μ process models. Throughout the optimization, we use a uniform random selection for selecting parents and a best selection as survivor selection. For the experiments carried out in this paper, we use a population size of $\mu = 1000$ individuals and generate $\lambda = 5000$ child models in each generation.

4.1 Mutation

In order to create a mutation of a process model we copy it and modify this copy by randomly applying some of the operators *move*, *complexify* and *simplify*. With a finite concatenation of these three operators any valid hierarchical model can be reached from any other valid hierarchical model, thus permitting the algorithm to find the best fitting model. The parameters for each operation are also randomized within boundaries ensuring model validity (e.g. which atomic graphs are moved to which sequence by $\rightsquigarrow$, the possible destination sequences being limited to ones described in Section 3). In addition to avoiding the creation of invalid models the algorithm to some degree anticipates operations which have no effect on the model behaviour. For instance, in cases where the model is strictly sequential, we remove ○ from the set of possible operators. When moving parts of the model we ensure they are moved to a different position, and after moving the last atomic graph from a complex construct with a ⤳ operation, the construct is automatically removed (simplified).

While there is no self-adaptation of the step-size or mutation strength in our implementation, we perform a random concatenation of multiple of the above mentioned operators in one mutation (to allow for a sufficient amount of change in process model behaviour to be introduced).

4.2 Diversity

In evolutionary algorithms, a balance of exploration and convergence is important for overcoming local optima and refining solution candidates' fitness. A diverse population is desired to ensure good coverage of the search space, thus reducing the likelihood of missing the part of the search space in which the global optimum resides. If there is no individual near the global optimum, but the whole population has converged to a local optimum, the benefits of population-based optimization are eliminated. Therefore, a diversity measure – indicating how similar the individuals of a population are – can be used to monitor the optimization and take countermeasures if the optimization has converged prematurely.

One option to measure population diversity for individuals with a binary fixed-length genotype is to compute the sum of hamming distances between all individuals in a population (pair-wise). Since this computation has a quadratic runtime-complexity (with regards to the population size) it is not suitable for large populations, such as ≥ 1000 individuals). We therefore measure diversity by computing the sum of absolute distances from each individual to the "mean individual" of the population. We consider a population p to be a vector of individuals, and each individual p_i as a vector of zeroes and ones, i.e. its genotype in shape of a bit string (in our context of process discovery, an individual is a process model and its bit string representation reflects a direct-neighbour relationship between activities in the process model). The mean individual $\bar{p}$ of a population with n individuals is defined as:

$$\bar{p} = \frac{\sum_{i=1}^{n} p_i}{n}$$

Note that the contents of the mean genotype $\bar{p}$ are real-valued, between 0 and 1. We then define the population diversity as the sum of Manhattan distances from each individual to the mean individual:

$$div = \sum_{i=1}^{n} \|p_i - \bar{p}\|_1$$

In order to draw conclusions from a diversity value, it is useful to know the boundaries for diversity. While the minimum diversity of 0 is reached if all individuals are equal, the maximum diversity depends on the length of the genotype and the size of the population. Maximum diversity across the whole length of the genotype is reached when the diversity is maximal for every single bit of the genotype (if the bits are independent). The population diversity in a single bit j is defined as:

$$div_j = \sum_{i=1}^{n} |p_{ij} - \bar{p}_j|$$

Let $\#1_j$ denote the number of individuals in population p which have a 1 in bit j. The number of individuals with a 0 in bit j is then $\#0_j = n - \#1_j$. The value of the mean individual at index j is $\bar{p}_j = \frac{\#1_j}{n}$. The diversity in bit j can then be expressed as a function of the number of ones in bit j:

$$\begin{aligned} div_j(\#1_j) &= \#0_j * \bar{p}_j + \#1_j * (1 - \bar{p}_j) \\ &= (n - \#1_j) * \frac{\#1_j}{n} + \#1_j * (1 - \frac{\#1_j}{n}) \\ &= 2 * \#1_j - 2 * \frac{\#1_j^2}{n} \end{aligned}$$

The first derivative is then:

$$\frac{\Delta div_j(\#1_j)}{\Delta \#1_j} = 2 - 4 * \frac{\#1_j}{n}$$

with its root at

$$\begin{aligned} 0 &= 2 - 4 * \frac{\#1_j}{n} \\ \#1_j &= \frac{n}{2} \end{aligned}$$

The second derivative test yields $-\frac{4}{n} < 0$ indicating a maximum in the diversity of

$$\begin{aligned} maxdiv_j &= div_j(\frac{n}{2}) \\ &= 2 * \frac{n}{2} - 2 * \frac{(\frac{n}{2})^2}{n} \\ &= \frac{n}{2} \end{aligned}$$

This means the diversity in bit j reaches its maximum of $\frac{n}{2}$ if half of the population has a 1 in bit j and the other half has a 0 in bit j. For a population where every one of the n individuals has a genotype of length g, the maximum diversity is:

$$maxdiv = \frac{n}{2} * g$$

4.3 Fitness

The goal of process discovery is to find a process model that best represents a given event log. Hence, we evaluate the fitness of process models by comparing the behaviour they reflect to the behaviour that is evident in the event log. The evolution strategy tries to maximize the coherence of log and model behaviour, i.e. models that better represent the event log are considered fitter. An event log is split into *traces*, where each trace is a sequence of events logged during a single process instance, i.e. the execution of the business process from the start node to the end node. Each logged event represents the execution of a single activity. Consider the event log $L = \{(a,b)^2, (b,a)^2 (b,a,c)^4, (a,b,c,c,c)^3\}$ which consists of 11 traces, of which 4 are unique (i.e. the process has been executed in 4 different variants). A process model reflecting this event log should contain the three activities a, b, and c. They should be organized in such a way that the process starts with a parallel construct with a in one branch and b in the other (since the event logs shows that a and b maybe be executed in an interchangeable order). After that parallel construct, a loop construct should follow which allows for executing activity c multiple times (or not at all). The starting point for comparing log and model behaviour is the *directly-follows footprint*, a relation between activities that indicates whether they may directly follow each other in the execution of the process. This relation is extracted from the process model by applying graph traversal algorithms, and is also extracted from the log by analyzing its traces. For instance, in the above mentioned log L, activity a may be followed by b or c or no activity (in one of the traces a is the last activity to be executed, i.e. not followed by another event). Activity b may be followed by *a* or *c* or no activity. Activity *c* can be followed by either itself or no activity. Once we have extracted the directly-follows footprint of the model and the directly-follows footprint of the log, we compare them in two directions: *recall* indicates how much of the behaviour evident in the log is also found in the model (i.e. how many tuples in the log directly-follows relation are also found in the model directly-follows relation), and *precision* indicates how much of the behaviour exhibited by the model is supported by the event log. In addition to this footprint conformance measure which only compares how events / activities directly follow each other, we measure replay conformance, i.e. how capable the model is of replaying whole traces of the event log. We then define the overall conformance between model m and log l as the average of these two conformance measures (described in more detail in [11]:

$$\texttt{conf}(m,l) = \frac{\texttt{conf}_{rp}(m,l) + \texttt{conf}_{fp}(m,l)}{2}$$

Both footprint and replay conformance measures, and thus also the overall conformance measure, yield values in $[0,1]$. To avoid large models with overly complex branching behaviour we define a fitness function $\texttt{fit}_1$ that is based on the conformance of model and log, and penalizes models with many loops, exclusive or parallel constructs:

$$\texttt{fit}_1(m,l) = \texttt{conf}(m,l) * 0.99^{\#\texttt{cs}(m)}$$

Here, $\#\texttt{cs}(m)$ is the number of exclusive, parallel or loop constructs in the model m. The factor initially reduces the fitness of a model by around 1% for every such construct, with a decreasing penalty in case of complex models.

When performing experiments using this fitness function, however, the population often prematurely converges to local optima. Therefore, we improve the fitness function to avoid early convergence by making it dependent on two more factors: the size of the problem (i.e. the number of activities present in an event log) and the population diversity:

$$\texttt{fit}_2(m,l) = \texttt{conf}(m,l) - \frac{div}{maxdiv} * \frac{\#\texttt{cs}(m)}{(\#\texttt{act}(l)+1)^2}$$

where $\#\texttt{act}$ represents the number of distinct activities occurring in a given event log. Here, the penalty for complex models consists of the number of constructs divided by the size of the directly-follows footprint matrix (a matrix which stores for each combination of two activities whether one follows the other or not, including the relation to "no activity", i.e. the start/end of the process, hence $\#\texttt{act}(l)+1$). The factor $\frac{div}{maxdiv}$ describes how diverse the current population is relative to the maximum obtainable diversity. It is calculated according to the equations in Section 4.2, when considering the directly-follows footprint matrix of a process model as its genotype. This aims to allow for more complex models when population diversity is low, therefore encouraging exploration, while enforcing simplification when population diversity is very high (the rationale is that allowing for higher complexity extends the accessible search space, thus permitting populations with a higher diversity). In experiments with multiple event logs we have found that this dynamic fitness function is less prone to getting stuck in local optima.

5. EVALUATION

We evaluate the performance of our approach by using eight event logs to mine process models. The resulting models are compared to the results of three other state of the art / related process mining algorithms applied on the same event logs. Since the approaches have a different representation of the resulting models, all models are transformed into Petri nets to allow for their comparison. To evaluate the quality of the mined process models we use existing measures defined on Petri nets [15]: *trace fitness* (a measure of recall) and *precision*. The plugin *PNetReplayer* in the toolkit ProM [16] is used to determine these two measures. Furthermore, we determine model simplicity by counting the number of elements (places, transitions, and arcs) in the resulting Petri nets. A low number of elements indicates a simpler, easier to understand, model.

Table 1: Conformance results of the different discovery algorithms

Log	Trace Fitness				Precision				Simplicity			
	HM	IM	DGEM	GM	HM	IM	DGEM	GM	HM	IM	DGEM	GM
L_1	0.679	0.863	**1.000**	0.868	0.532	0.529	**0.550**	0.497	86	91	**78**	94
EX5	0.985	0.935	**1.000**	**1.000**	0.495	0.560	**0.681**	0.480	155	102	**81**	262
REP	**1.000**	**1.000**	**1.000**	**1.000**	0.905	**0.955**	**0.955**	0.943	72	**46**	49	70
BE1	0.991	**1.000**	**1.000**	0.721	**0.838**	0.814	0.821	0.707	192	132	**130**	167
BE2	0.924	0.981	**1.000**	0.882	**0.737**	0.594	0.684	0.635	196	156	**115**	203
BE3	0.822	0.983	**1.000**	0.981	**0.891**	0.443	0.808	0.732	178	149	**114**	222
DF	**1.000**	0.911	**1.000**	0.906	0.563	0.559	**0.588**	0.276	177	136	**133**	176
FL_A	0.974	**1.000**	**1.000**	**1.000**	0.920	0.695	0.953	**0.965**	98	**62**	77	193
AVG	0.922	0.959	**1.000**	0.920	0.735	0.644	**0.755**	0.654	144.3	109.3	**97.1**	173.4

The first of eight event logs used for evaluating the process mining algorithms is defined as $L_1 = \{\ (b,a)^4,\ (a,b,d,e)^5,\ (b,a,e,d)^4,\ (b,a,c,a,b,c,b,a,d,e,e,d)^6,\ (g,g)^2,\ (f,h)^3,\ (f,f,h,f,g,h,g,f,h)^8,\ (g,h,f)^2\}$. It contains 34 traces of which eight are unique, and eight activities. EX5 and REP are example event logs that come with the toolkit ProM (exercise5 which contains 14 activities, and repairExample which contains 8 activities). The three logs BE1, BE2, and BE3 have been generated by us, using simulation on randomly created complex models with 20 activities (the models were created by performing a sequence of the operators described in Section 3 on initially sequential models with 20 activities). Log DF is extracted from an eHealth process which contains 18 activities [7], and FL_A a is an excerpt of a loan application process log with ten activities used in the Business Process Intelligence Challenge 2012 (process "A").

The three state of the art mining algorithms used for comparison are the heuristic miner (HM) [1], inductive miner (IM) [9] and genetic miner (GM) [2]. HM uses heuristic nets as process representation, and is considered as one of the best process mining algorithms [5]. GM also mines heuristic nets, using a genetic algorithm. IM mines process trees, which are a block-structured representation, similar to the hierarchical model we use. Both HM and IM are deterministic algorithms which require little time to execute, even for big event logs. For GM and our approach (called DGEM) we provide a maximum of two hours optimization time per event log and take the best model obtained after this time.

The performance of the four algorithms on the eight event logs is presented in Table 1. The bottom row shows for each algorithm and conformance metric the average score over all event logs. The best result for each event log and metric is marked bold and green while the worst result is marked with red colour. Our approach (DGEM, using fitness function $\texttt{fit}_2$) performs well across all event logs, achieving highest scores in recall (trace fitness) while maintaining best or second best scores in precision and simplicity. Due to the use of well structured models both IM and DGEM score much better in simplicity than HM and GM. For the log FL_A algorithm GM found a model with superior recall and precision. This model is, however, roughly three times as big as the one found by DGEM. On average, HM scores very well in precision, where it outperforms DGEM in the three event logs which have been generated by simulating complex models.

In Figure 3 the results of the different mining algorithms, when mining a model from log EX5, are shown in the shape of Petri nets.

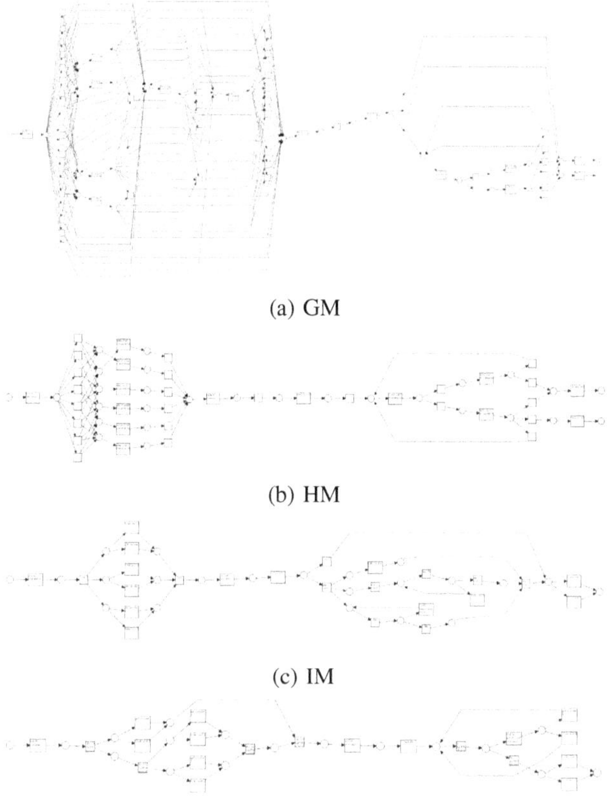

(a) GM

(b) HM

(c) IM

(d) DGEM

Figure 3: Models mined by the different algorithms for log EX5, a log pertaining to a scientific publication review process

The pictures reflect the conclusions drawn from the previous evaluation regarding the simplicity of process models: IM and DGEM tend to produce results which are much easier to read. Note that in this case, however, the model mined by IM only reflects 93.5% of the behaviour in log EX5 whereas the other algorithms' results have a trace fitness close or equal to a 100%.

Figure 4 shows the results of a performance comparison between GM (thin lines) and DGEM (thick lines) carried out using the event log DF. The chart shows how trace fitness, precision, and simplicity change over the course of the optimization. Note that DGEM relatively quickly finds a model with good trace fitness (reaches perfect trace fitness of 1.0 after 12 seconds) at the cost of precision and simplicity. Only after no more improvements in trace fitness can be made, the algorithm improves precision and simplicity. This is likely due to the higher emphasis of recall in the fitness function (replay and footprint) of DGEM. After one minute of optimization, no more improvements are found. In contrast, the genetic miner takes 30 minutes to find a model with close to perfect trace fitness, while simplicity and precision – although slightly improving over time – do not reach the results of DGEM, even after 2 hours of optimization.

Figure 5 shows the progress of two runs of our evolution strategy on the event log DF, each with a different fitness function of the ones defined in Section 4.3 ($\texttt{fit}_1$ on the left, and the diversity-influenced fitness function $\texttt{fit}_2$ on the right). In the pictures, the fitness (best, average, and worst individual) and the population diversity are plotted over the number of generations. In Figure 5, the fitness is monotonically increasing over the course of the optimization while the diversity is the fluctuating line, being high in the

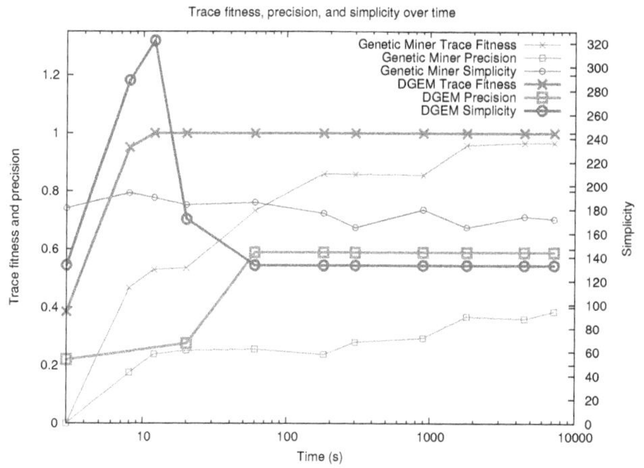

Figure 4: Performance of DGEM and GM

beginning and converging to zero once the optimum is reached. As can be seen, the run with the normal fitness function on the left side shows several plateaus in the fitness value, e.g. from generation 200 to 550 there has been no fitness improvement. One can also see that the fitness improvements around generation 550 are preceded by a build-up of population diversity (starting around generation 430). Here, the optimum is reached after 700 generations. In contrast, when using the diversity-dependent fitness function (the picture on the right side), the diversity does not flatten out at zero until the optimum is reached. Also, the progress of the fitness is different: there is a steady increase to the optimum, which is already reached at generation 180. While the results are hard to compare (since different fitness functions are used in both figures), the resulting process models were the same in both cases. We observed this kind of pattern repeatedly throughout the set of eight event logs we used for evaluation. In the more complex cases (BE1-3), the results of the optimizations runs with diversity-dependent fitness function consistently outscored the results obtained using the standard fitness function (within a time frame of 2h).

6. RELATED WORK

Several techniques have been developed for the discovery of Petri nets from event logs [3]. An approach that also uses computational intelligence and similar notions of conformance for evaluating process models is presented in [2], where the authors use a genetic algorithm to mine Petri nets (without any further structure than given by the basic Petri net elements). In [17] a two step approach mines first a state transition system and then transforms it into Petri nets. The approach does not consider noise, but as in our approach it allows for user guided discovery, by letting the user choose from different abstractions to balance underfitting and overfitting.

A type of model that is structured in a way similar to the hierarchical model presented in Section 2 is defined by process structure trees [6]. Whereas process structure trees are model representations of business processes themselves which can be transformed into other representations such as Petri nets or business process models, our hierarchical model is a view on top of an existing business process model. In [4] an approach for mining process structure trees is presented that uses genetic algorithms. Compared to the operators defined in Section 3 the mutation operators used in [4] are of a lower level nature. For instance, the $\rightsquigarrow$ operator we use to move a part of a sequence of atomic graphs would be expressed by several remove and add operations in [4]. In contrast to our approach the authors allow for duplicate activities which can lead to unrealistic, overfitting models (e.g. a big model consisting of a single

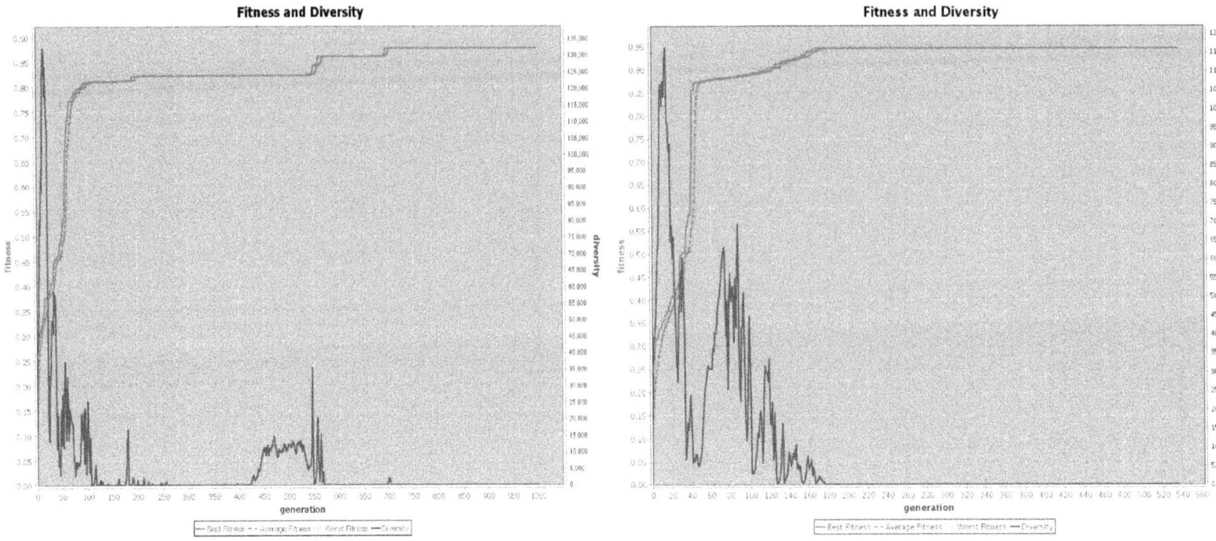

(a) standard fitness function (b) diversity-dependent fitness function

Figure 5: Comparison of evolution progress when using different fitness functions

exclusive choice between many branches, each representing a trace in the log). As in our approach, fitness is evaluated as a weighted average of several conformance measures, with the weights being defined by the user to allow for guided process discovery. However the precision measure used in [4] does not detect underfitting very well (one of the mined examples with a perfect precision score exhibits loop behaviour which is not present in the original model used to produce the log, thus allowing for more behaviour than in the log).

In [8] an approach for diversity guided evolutionary algorithms is proposed which also uses the distance to the "average" individual for measuring diversity. This approach controls the optimization by switching between two discrete modes (exploitation, i.e. recombination, and exploration, i.e. mutation), based on the absolute population diversity exceeding some pre-defined thresholds. Our approach, in contrast, continuously adapts the fitness function by determining how far the current diversity is from the maximum obtainable diversity.

7. CONCLUSION

We have presented an evolutionary computation based approach to mine BPMN based hierarchically structured process models from business process event logs. Our approach is able to find process models which are small and easy-to-understand when compared to the results of existing process mining approaches, and yet maintain a high accuracy in reflecting the behaviour of the event log. By defining a diversity-adapted fitness function, the optimization avoids early convergence to local optima.

Our approach may be further improved by examining which sequences of operators ($\leadsto$, $\oplus$, $\otimes$, ↻, ○) lead to successful individuals, and using this information to create self-adaptive mutations. Furthermore, an extensive evaluation of all parameters such as population size, number of mutations, methods for parent and survivor selection, etc. is expected to provide a set-up which yields better results.

Whether the concept of using relative diversity to guide the optimization may be applied in other use cases of evolutionary computation is subject to further research. For instance, in fitness-proportionate selection, relative diversity could be used for scaling fitness values (e.g. as alternative to sigma-scaling).

8. REFERENCES

[1] A. J. M. M. Weijters and J. T. S. Ribeiro, *Flexible Heuristics Miner (FHM)*. IEEE Symposium on Computational Intelligence and Data Mining. 2011.

[2] A. K. Alves De Medeiros , A. J. M. M. Weijters, and W.M.P. van der Aalst, *Genetic process mining: an experimental evaluation*. Data Mining and Knowledge Discovery. 14(2): 245-304, 2007.

[3] B. F. Dongen, A. K. Alves de Medeiros, and L. Wen, *Process Mining: Overview and Outlook of Petri Net Discovery Algorithms*. Transactions on Petri Nets and Other Models of Concurrency II: 225-242, 2009.

[4] J. C. A. M. Buijs, B. F. Van Dongen, and W. M. P. van der Aalst, *A Genetic Algorithm for Discovering Process Trees*. 2012 IEEE Congress on Evolutionary Computation, 2012.

[5] J. De Weerdt, M. De Backer, J. Vanthienen, B. Baesens. *A multi-dimensional quality assessment of state-of-the-art process discovery algorithms using real-life event logs*. Information Systems 37(7): 654-676, 2012.

[6] J. Vanhatalo, H. Voelzer, J. Koehler. *The Refined Process Structure Tree*. BPM 2008 Proceedings of the 6th International Conference on Business Process Management, 2008.

[7] M. Galushka, W. Gilani, *DrugFusion - Retrieval Knowledge Management for Prediction of Adverse Drug Events*. 17th International Conference on Business Information Systems, 2014.

[8] R. K. Ursem, *Diversity-Guided Evolutionary Algorithms*. Parallel Problem Solving from Nature - PPSN VII, 2002.

[9] S. J. J. Leemans, D. Fahland, W. M. P. van der Aalst. *Discovering Block-Structured Process Models from Event Logs Containing Infrequent Behaviour*. Business Process Management Workshops, 2013.

[10] T. Allweyer. *BPMN 2.0 – Introduction to the Standard for Business Process Modeling*. BoD, 2010.

[11] T. Molka, D. Redlich, M. Drobek, A. Caetano, X.-J. Zeng, and W. Gilani, *Conformance Checking for BPMN-Based Process Models*. Proceedings of the 29th Annual ACM Symposium on Applied Computing, 2014.

[12] W. M. P. van der Aalst. *Process mining: discovering and improving Spaghetti and Lasagna processes*. In Proceedings of the IEEE Symposium on Computational Intelligence and Data Mining (editors: N. Chawla, I. King and A. Sperduti): 13-20, 2011.

[13] W. M. P. van der Aalst, *Process Mining: Discovery, Conformance and Enhancement of Business Processes*. Springer, 2011.

[14] W. M. P. van der Aalst et al, *Process Mining Manifesto*. BPM 2011 International Workshops, 2011.

[15] W. M. P. van der Aalst, A. Adriansyah, B. F. van Dongen, *Replaying History on Process Models for Conformance Checking and Performance Analysis*. WIREs Data Mining and Knowledge Discovery, 2(2): 182-192, 2012.

[16] W. M. P. van der Aalst, B. F. van Dongen, *ProM : The Process Mining Toolkit*. Industrial Engineering, 489: 1-4, 2009.

[17] W. M. P. van der Aalst, V. Rubin, H. M. W. Verbeek, B. F. van Dongen, E. Kindler, C. W. Günther. *Process mining: a two-step approach to balance between underfitting and overfitting*. Software and System Modeling, 9: 87-111, 2010.

Diversifying Multi-Objective Gradient Techniques and their Role in Hybrid Multi-Objective Evolutionary Algorithms for Deformable Medical Image Registration

Kleopatra Pirpinia
Netherlands Cancer Institute
k.pirpinia@nki.nl

Tanja Alderliesten
Academic Medical Center
t.alderliesten@amc.uva.nl

Jan-Jakob Sonke
Netherlands Cancer Institute
j.sonke@nki.nl

Marcel van Herk
Netherlands Cancer Institute
m.v.herk@nki.nl

Peter A.N. Bosman
Centrum Wiskunde & Informatica
Peter.Bosman@cwi.nl

ABSTRACT

Gradient methods and their value in single-objective, real-valued optimization are well-established. As such, they play a key role in tackling real-world, hard optimization problems such as deformable image registration (DIR). A key question is to which extent gradient techniques can also play a role in a multi-objective approach to DIR. We therefore aim to exploit gradient information within an evolutionary-algorithm-based multi-objective optimization framework for DIR. Although an analytical description of the multi-objective gradient (the set of all Pareto-optimal improving directions) is available, it is nontrivial how to best choose the most appropriate direction per solution because these directions are not necessarily uniformly distributed in objective space. To address this, we employ a Monte-Carlo method to obtain a discrete, spatially-uniformly distributed approximation of the set of Pareto-optimal improving directions. We then apply a diversification technique in which each solution is associated with a unique direction from this set based on its multi- as well as single-objective rank. To assess its utility, we compare a state-of-the-art multi-objective evolutionary algorithm with three different hybrid versions thereof on several benchmark problems and two medical DIR problems. Results show that the diversification strategy successfully leads to unbiased improvement, helping an adaptive hybrid scheme solve all problems, but the evolutionary algorithm remains the most powerful optimization method, providing the best balance between proximity and diversity.

CCS Concepts

•Mathematics of computing → Evolutionary algorithms; •Applied computing → Multi-criterion optimization and decision-making;

GECCO '15, July 11 - 15, 2015, Madrid, Spain

DOI: http://dx.doi.org/10.1145/2739480.2754719

Keywords

Evolutionary algorithms; Multi-objective Optimization; Gradients; Memetic Algorithms; Deformable Image Registration

1. INTRODUCTION

Local search algorithms that employ the gradient (i.e., the direction of greatest increase) of a function to iteratively arrive at a (locally) optimal solution have been studied for a long time in single-objective continuous optimization. In such approaches, gradient-based methods constitute a very powerful mathematical tool and are an efficient and practical way of finding (local) optima, especially when the function f to be optimized possesses desirable properties such as differentiability. As a consequence, their use is widespread in solving real-world optimization problems.

In contrast to local search algorithms, population-based algorithms such as evolutionary algorithms (EAs) seek to exploit the global properties of the search space. The synergy of EAs with local search has been investigated and has resulted in the so-called memetic algorithms or genetic local search [8], which are frequently successfully applied in single-objective- and multi-objective optimization.

Multi-objective optimization problems arise frequently in real-world situations, where it is often the case that optimal decisions need to be taken in the presence of two or more conflicting objectives. In a multi-objective approach, there are sets of optimal solutions to the problem, which represent the most efficient trade-offs that can be considered to be equally good [5].

One of the real-world problems that could benefit from such an approach is deformable image registration (DIR). DIR is a medical image processing task that can be of great value for healthcare. Its clinical implementation is still limited and presents many challenges [9]. Currently, a registration outcome is computed based on a single combination of different objectives, using predominantly single-objective gradient methods. However, there is currently no insightful way of finding the singular optimal combination of the objectives beforehand, thus making clinical implementation of such algorithms difficult. Different combinations lead to different outcomes, which can ultimately only be judged in quality by experts. For this reason, multi-objective optimization where multiple optimal outcomes with efficient trade-offs are computed and presented simultaneously could be the key in obtaining wider clinical use. In this framework, studying the design and use of gradient-based methods for DIR becomes also of interest, as their efficient use could help achieve improved results.

However, as a consequence of the existence of these numerous (possibly infinite) trade-offs between objectives, the notion of improvement also becomes different. This makes the use of gradient information in multi-objective optimization less straightforward than in the single-objective case. For this reason, many different strategies have been proposed for its exploitation in such settings. In some cases, gradient information is not used explicitly [10]. Other multi-objective methods make explicit use of the gradient after having reduced the multi-objective problem to a single-objective one by constructing one function via weighted aggregation (see e.g., [11]) which is then optimized. Therefore, there is no guarantee that all objectives improve simultaneously. In another approach, the direction of greatest simultaneous improvement has been derived analytically [7], and applied in a hybrid algorithm [4]. Such approaches however can lead to a bias, if the objectives have different ranges, towards the objective with the largest range. Moreover, there are still infinitely many directions, that cannot be compared to each other; each one of them improves one objective more than the others. A complete analytic description of the best improving directions has been derived and has subsequently been utilized as a part of a multi-objective gradient search method [2]. Even then, a non-uniform spatial distribution of directions can lead to a bias due to differences in range or difficulty of the objectives. Therefore, to ensure gradient exploitation leads to a well-spread set of optimal solutions, it is essential to determine a strategy in which the multi-objective gradient is exploited such that it results in a balanced improvement of all objectives.

In this paper, we propose a diversification technique to exploit in such an unbiased way this multi-objective gradient information. We assess its utility by comparing a state-of-the-art multi-objective evolutionary algorithm to three different hybrid versions thereof on several benchmark problems, which gives us insight into the performance of the proposed approach when it comes to problems with great variation in difficulty and scale. Additionally, we test the best performing hybridization scheme on two DIR problems. Considering that the objectives of our DIR problem have a large difference in difficulty, we aim to assess whether the new technique results in a clearer advantage of the hybrid algorithm compared to the EA.

The remainder of the paper is organized as follows. In Section 2 we present some definitions for multi-objective optimization. In Section 3 we discuss the selected benchmark problems with an emphasis on those which exhibit the aforementioned behavior. In Section 4 we discuss in more detail the initial multi-objective gradient technique and the new diversification technique. Further, we present results of their comparison. In Section 5 we discuss the hybridization schemes, and the DIR problems we will test them on. In Section 6 we compare the performance of the schemes on all problems and in Section 7 we discuss our findings and conclusions.

2. DEFINITIONS

2.1 Multi-objective optimization

We assume to have m objective functions $f_i(\boldsymbol{x})$, $i \in \{0, 1, \ldots, m\}$ and, without loss of generality, we assume that the goal is to *minimize* all objectives. A solution $\boldsymbol{x}^1$ is said to (Pareto) dominate a solution $\boldsymbol{x}^2$ (denoted $\boldsymbol{x}^1 \succ \boldsymbol{x}^2$) if and only if $f_i(\boldsymbol{x}^1) \leq f_i(\boldsymbol{x}^2)$ holds for all $i \in \{0, 1, \ldots, m\}$ and $f_i(\boldsymbol{x}^1) < f_i(\boldsymbol{x}^2)$ holds for at least one $i \in \{0, 1, \ldots, m\}$. A *Pareto set* (denoted $\mathcal{P}_S$) of size n is a set of solutions $\boldsymbol{x}^j$, $j \in \{0, 1, \ldots, n\}$ for which no solution dominates any other solution, i.e., there are no $j, k \in \{0, 1, \ldots, n\}$ such that $\boldsymbol{x}^j \succ \boldsymbol{x}^k$ holds. A *Pareto front* (denoted $\mathcal{P}_F$) corresponding to a Pareto set is the set of all m-dimensional objective function values corresponding to the solutions, i.e., the set of all $\boldsymbol{f}(\boldsymbol{x}^j)$, $j \in \{0, 1, \ldots, n\}$. A solution $\boldsymbol{x}^1$ is said to be *Pareto optimal* if and only if there is no other $\boldsymbol{x}^2$ such that $\boldsymbol{x}^2 \succ \boldsymbol{x}^1$ holds. Further, the *optimal Pareto set* is the set of all Pareto-optimal solutions and the *optimal Pareto front* is the Pareto front that corresponds to the optimal Pareto set.

2.2 Multi-objective gradient

For any real-valued function $f(\boldsymbol{x})$, $\boldsymbol{x} = (x_0, x_1, \ldots, x_{l-1})$, the gradient of f is defined as:

$$\nabla f(\boldsymbol{x}) = \left(\frac{\partial f(\boldsymbol{x})}{\partial x_0}, \ldots, \frac{\partial f(\boldsymbol{x})}{\partial x_{l-1}} \right).$$

The directional derivative then is a function that gives the rate of change of f in direction $\hat{\boldsymbol{u}}$ at any $\boldsymbol{y}$:

$$\nabla_u f(\boldsymbol{x})(\boldsymbol{y}) = (\nabla f(\boldsymbol{x})(\boldsymbol{y}))^T \hat{\boldsymbol{u}}. \quad (1)$$

Therefore, to find the direction of greatest decrease the following single-objective optimization problem must be solved:

$$\min_{\hat{u}} \{\nabla_u f(\boldsymbol{x})(\boldsymbol{y})\}.$$

It is easy to see that the directional derivative at a point is minimal when the direction points to the direction of the negative gradient, i.e., the solution to this problem is naturally $-\nabla f(\boldsymbol{x})(\boldsymbol{y})$.

If we extend the notion of gradient and directional derivatives to a multi-objective setting, we must now solve the optimization problem

$$\min_{\hat{u}} \{\nabla_u \boldsymbol{f}(\boldsymbol{x})(\boldsymbol{y})\},$$

where $\boldsymbol{f} = (f_0, f_1, \ldots, f_{m-1})$. The directional derivative of $\boldsymbol{f}$ is now also a vector whose i-th component is the directional derivative in the i-th objective, i.e., $(\nabla_u \boldsymbol{f}(\boldsymbol{x}))_i = \nabla_u f_i(\boldsymbol{x})$ and therefore (1) for the multi-objective case is formulated as

$$\nabla_u \boldsymbol{f}(\boldsymbol{x}) = \boldsymbol{G}\hat{\boldsymbol{u}},$$

where $\boldsymbol{G} = (\nabla f_0(\boldsymbol{x}), \ldots, f_{m-1}(\boldsymbol{x}))^T$. Now, similar to the single-objective case we are ultimately interested in the direction that maximizes the improvement (i.e., the negative gradient). However, now this is a multi-objective optimization problem. Hence, no single direction of greatest increase of $\boldsymbol{f}$ starting from $\boldsymbol{y}$ exists, but a set of directions that correspond to the optimal Pareto front of all improving directions. A parametric description of these Pareto-optimal directions is available [2], and a method called Combined-Objectives-Repeated-Line search (CORL), that will be explained in more detail in Section 4, exploits them by choosing a random direction from this parametrically described set. However, choosing a direction at random can lead to a bias, in particular when the objectives to be optimized vary a lot in difficulty. To investigate this, we have specifically chosen some problems in our multi-objective optimization test suite that exhibit this bias.

3. BENCHMARK PROBLEMS

We have selected a set of well-known benchmark problems in multi-objective evolutionary optimization, see Table 1. We first considered the well-known problems ZDT_i, $i \in \{1, 2, 3, 6\}$. The initialization ranges (IRs) of the ZDT_i problems are also constraints. For more details, see [12].

We also considered two problems with smooth properties. These are the most simple ones, and they are a generalization of the MED (Multiple Euclidean Distances) problems, which we will refer to as GenMED. There are two cases, one where the optimal Pareto front is concave and one where it is convex, but both cases are smooth functions with equally scaled objectives and without any local Pareto fronts.

Lastly, we have selected two more problems, which are characterized by a strong difference in difficulty between their objectives. Both of these problems, labeled BD_i, $i = 1, 2$, make use of the Rosenbrock function in one of their objectives. The real-world problems we are interested in share this difference in difficulty.

Name	Objectives	IR
ZDT_1	$f_0 = x_0, \quad f_1 = \gamma\left(1 - \sqrt{f_0/\gamma}\right)$ $\gamma = 1 + 9\left(\sum_{i=1}^{l-1} x_i/(l-1)\right)$	$[0;1]^{30}$ $(l = 30)$
ZDT_2	$f_0 = x_0, \quad f_1 = \gamma\left(1 - (f_0/\gamma)^2\right)$ $\gamma = 1 + 9\left(\sum_{i=1}^{l-1} x_i/(l-1)\right)$	$[0;1]^{30}$ $(l = 30)$
ZDT_3	$f_0 = x_0, \quad f_1 = \gamma\left(1 - \sqrt{f_0/\gamma} - (f_0/\gamma)\sin(10\pi f_0)\right)$ $\gamma = 1 + 9\left(\sum_{i=1}^{l-1} x_i/(l-1)\right)$	$[0;1]^{30}$ $(l = 30)$
ZDT_6	$f_0 = 1 - e^{-4x_0}\sin^6(6\pi x_0), \quad f_1 = \gamma\left(1 - (f_0/\gamma)^2\right)$ $\gamma = 1 + 9\left(\sum_{i=1}^{l-1} x_i/(l-1)\right)^{0.25}$	$[0;1]^{10}$ $(l = 10)$
BD_1	$f_0 = x_0, \quad f_1 = 1 - x_0 + \gamma$ $\gamma = \sum_{i=1}^{l-2}\left(100(x_{i+1} - x_i^2)^2 + (1 - x_i)^2\right)$	$[0;1] \times$ $[-5.12; 5.12]^9$ $(l = 10)$
BD_2^s	$f_0 = \frac{1}{l}\sum_{i=0}^{l-1} x_i^2$ $f_1 = \frac{1}{l-1}\sum_{i=0}^{l-2}\left(100(x_{i+1} - x_i^2)^2 + (1 - x_i)^2\right)$	$[-5.12; 5.12]^{10}$ $(l = 10)$
$\text{GenMED}_{1,2}$	$f_0 = \lVert\frac{1}{2}(\boldsymbol{x} - \boldsymbol{c}^0)\rVert^d$ $f_1 = \lVert\frac{1}{2}(\boldsymbol{x} - \boldsymbol{c}^1)\rVert^d$ $\boldsymbol{c}^0 = (1, 0, 0, \dots) \quad \boldsymbol{c}^1 = (0, 1, 0, 0, \dots) \quad d = 1, \frac{1}{2}$	$[-1;1]^{10}$ $(l = 10)$

Table 1: The MO problem test suite.

4. EXPLOITING MULTI-OBJECTIVE GRADIENT INFORMATION

4.1 Combined Objectives Repeated Line-search (CORL)

In this multi-objective version of gradient descent, the set of all Pareto-optimal improving directions for a vector function $\boldsymbol{f}$ is initially calculated [2]. To do so, every direction $\hat{\boldsymbol{u}}$ is mapped to its directional derivative $\nabla_{\hat{\boldsymbol{u}}}\boldsymbol{f}$ from a unit l-dimensional hypersphere (where l is the problem dimensionality) to the surface and interior of an m-dimensional hyperellipsoid, where m is the number of objectives. The directions that are of interest, i.e., that lead to maximum improvement of all objectives, correspond to the negative non-dominated directional derivatives which lie in the intersection of the surface of the hyperellipsoid with $(-\infty, 0]^m$ (Figure 1). This set of directions can be described and sampled.

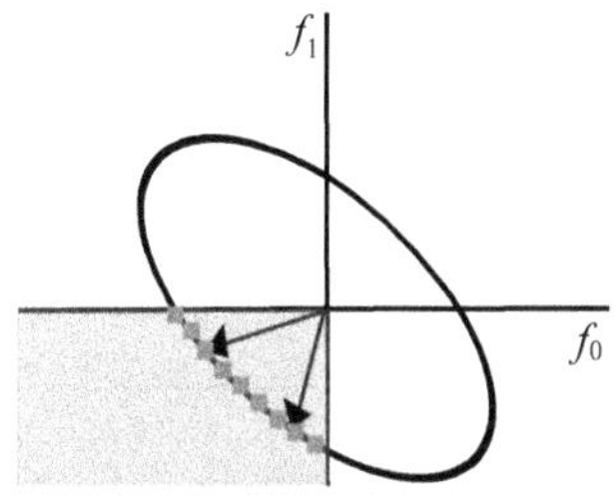

Figure 1: Part of the ellipsoid (in red) that includes the non-dominated improving directions.

One of these promising directions is chosen randomly and a multi-objective line search is performed along that direction. Typically, in a single-objective line search scheme, it is decided how far the algorithm should move in the chosen search direction to reach a local minimum along that direction, which maximizes the objective value difference between the starting point and the point where the line search ends. The multi-objective version of line-search is a natural generalization of that scheme, where the negative scaled Euclidean distance in objective space between the starting point $\boldsymbol{x}$ and the local minimum is used instead. The further $\boldsymbol{x} + \alpha\hat{\boldsymbol{u}}$ travels in objective space along the chosen direction $\hat{\boldsymbol{u}}$ while improving upon the starting point, the better. When the line search terminates, a new promising direction is sampled and a line search is repeated. This technique is called Combined Objectives Repeated Line-search (CORL).

To understand why a uniform distribution of directions is not necessarily preserved, one needs to look at the mapping of a direction $\hat{\boldsymbol{u}}$ from the parameter space to its directional derivative in the objective space. When one chooses a direction $\hat{\boldsymbol{u}}$, this direction is taken from the unit l-dimensional hypersphere. This direction is then collapsed onto the surface of the m-dimensional hyperellipsoid via a sequence of rotations, translations, and a projection. Therefore, the uniform distribution of the directions in the hypersphere is not necessarily preserved in the distribution of the directional derivatives on the hyperellipsoid, which depends on the orientation of the hyperellipsoid as well as its scale.

The lack of a spatially uniform distribution is possibly one of the reasons why in problems where the objectives have a large difference in difficulty, powerful single-objective methods such as conjugate gradients applied randomly or alternatingly to the different objectives perform better than CORL.

4.2 Rank-Based Combined Objectives Repeated Line-search (RB-CORL)

In this technique, we change the way directions are chosen for each member of the population. The multi-objective line search remains the same as in CORL.

4.2.1 *A rank-based scheme*

Aiming to exploit the analytically described set of Pareto-optimal improving directions in a truly uniform manner, we employ a diversification scheme, where as a first step the solutions are classified according to their multi-objective rank, which is calculated using the well-known domination-ranking scheme [6]. Consequently, the non-dominated solutions are of rank 0, the second best ones rank 1, and so on.

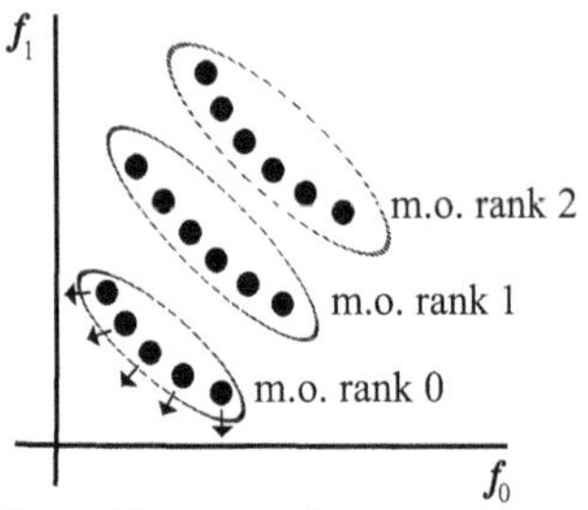

Figure 2: Directions assigned according to their multi-objective (m.o.) as well as their single-objective rank (within each multi-objective rank separately).

Subsequently, in each set of solutions that belong to the same rank, the solutions get a direction that depends on their ranks with respect to the individual objectives. In other words, the better a solution ranks in one objective compared to the other solutions that belong in the same multi-objective rank, the more favorable the direction for that objective (Figure 2). Each direction is associated with a solution in objective space that expresses this relation. Therefore, if we have k grouped solutions for one multi-objective rank, and r_0 is the rank of a solution s according to f_0, r_1 the rank of s according to f_1, r_{m-1} the rank of s according to f_{m-1}, the corresponding vector

$$\left(\frac{k-1-r_0}{k}, \frac{k-1-r_1}{k}, \ldots, \frac{k-1-r_{m-1}}{k}\right)$$

will be used to find a direction via sampling.

4.2.2 *Monte-Carlo sampling*

A uniform spatial distribution of the directional derivatives is what we need in order to assign the directions according to our rank-based scheme. We aim to partition uniformly the set of directional derivatives in objective space. The set of directional derivatives is parametrically described (see [2]) and therefore it can be sampled. This set can be easily visualized for $m = 2$ objectives, as in Figure 1. We initially normalize the directions to the observed ranges of solutions in the population, to ensure that the outcome is independent of the scaling of the objectives. To obtain a discrete uniformly distributed approximation, we employ Monte-Carlo sampling of this set of directions. Subsequently, each direction (which is an m-dimensional vector) is mapped via spherical coordinates to $m-1$ angles. For instance, if $m = 2$, each direction gets associated with one angle. We partition our objective space into equisized bins, each represented by an angle, and consequently by the direction associated with that angle.

Finally, we can map the direction we want from the rank-based scheme (by also converting it to spherical coordinates) to its closest available one from our obtained discrete set.

4.3 CORL versus RB-CORL

We first tested the new technique alone in a random-restart fashion, i.e., we applied it iteratively to 10000 randomly generated starting points. We are mostly interested in its behavior on problems with great difference in difficulty between objectives, such as BD_1 and BD_2.

We see that for BD_1, applying the multi-objective gradient method and choosing a random improving direction does not lead to a uniformly distributed improvement (Figure 3). CORL pushes all the members of the population to the vertical axis, as a result of the difficult landscape of the objective on the vertical axis, that uses the Rosenbrock function. The different level of difficulty as well as scale between the objectives translates into uneven spatial distribution of the directional derivatives in objective space. It demonstrates furthermore the need for a spatial uniformization of the choice of directions. The new technique is able to arrive much closer to the Pareto front of the problem, while achieving a much better spread of the population, as is the case also for BD_2. Moreover, it performs equally well on the GenMED problems (Figure 3). For BD_1 neither of the two techniques alone are able to actually find points on the optimal Pareto front, and therefore the hybridization of the new technique with an EA is considered necessary.

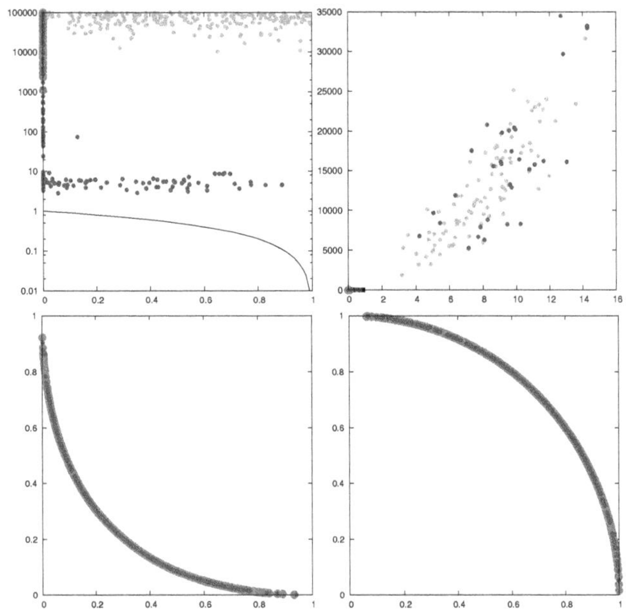

Figure 3: Distributions of optimized solutions using CORL and RB-CORL on BD_1 (upper left), BD_2 (upper right), convex (lower left) and concave (lower right) GenMED.

5. EXPERIMENT SETUP

5.1 Hybridization

5.1.1 iMAMaLGaM

Here we describe briefly the multi-objective EA we use for our hybridization schemes. We use an Estimation-of-Distribution Algorithm (EDA). EDAs are model-building EAs that aim to exploit structural features of the problem landscape. EDAs do so by estimating a probability distribution from selected solutions and sampling the estimated distribution to generate offspring.

The EDA we use is called iMAMaLGaM - incremental Multi-objective Adapted Maximum-Likelihood Gaussian Model. iMAMaLGaM, in contrast to well-known algorithms such as NSGA-II [6], is specifically designed for real-valued, multi-objective optimization. It should be noted that the variation operators of iMAMaLGaM could be easily used within NSGA-II as well and would approximately give the same results. In iMAMaLGaM, the selected solutions are grouped into clusters in objective space. For each cluster a multivariate Gaussian distribution is estimated using maximum-likelihood estimates, which are subsequently potentially adapted to prevent premature convergence. iMAMaLGaM samples then the Gaussian distributions to generate new solutions. An elitist archive of non-dominated solutions is also maintained. iMAMaLGaM has been shown to perform excellently in various benchmark as well as real-world problems [3].

5.1.2 Three hybridization schemes

In a multi-objective setting, it is not clear what is the most efficient way of integrating local search. For this reason, we consider different integration schemes. We compare these hybrid variants of iMAMaLGaM to iMAMaLGaM alone as well as to an adaptive hybridization scheme that was considered before for CORL [2]. The first two hybridization schemes are common in evolutionary optimization and local search [8].

Genetic Local Search 1 (GLS1): Given the large improvement obtained in initial stages of optimization using gradient techniques, in this hybridization scheme RB-CORL is applied only during initialization to all randomly generated solutions.

Genetic Local Search 2 (GLS2): In this scheme, RB-CORL is additionally called at the end of every evolutionary cycle to all members of the population.

Adaptive Genetic Local Search (AGLS): In this method RB-CORL is integrated in an adaptive hybridization scheme taken from literature [2], which exploits gradient information in three different ways. In this scheme, for maximum efficiency, the scheme decides during the run which exploitation method to use at the end of each evolutionary cycle, based on the number of improved solutions found by that method compared to the total number of evaluations used. The first exploitation method is called Random Objective Conjugate Gradients (ROCG); here, every time the method is called, one objective is chosen randomly and the conjugate gradients technique is performed for that objective only. The second exploitation method is called Alternating Objectives Repeated Line search (AORL). AORL performs a line search in the direction of the negative gradient of an alternatingly chosen objective. The third method of this hybrid scheme is CORL. We call this scheme *old AGLS*.

We made some changes to obtain a *new AGLS* version. Considering that both ROCG and AORL play approximately the same role during optimization - that is, they are able to find extreme points on the Pareto front, in this paper for the adaptive scheme we choose to only consider a variant of ROCG. Moreover, instead of applying conjugate gradients to a randomly chosen objective for a solution, we apply the method to only members of the population following again a rank-based scheme. More specifically, conjugate gradients is applied to (maximum) two solutions of each multi-objective rank that rank best at each objective individually. Therefore, conjugate gradients is applied to the solution that ranks best in one objective to further improve it. Finally, we replaced the old CORL with RB-CORL.

5.2 Benchmark problems

The problems we use to test the performance of iMAMaLGaM and our hybridization schemes are described in Table 1.

5.2.1 Measuring performance

To measure performance we consider the set of the non-dominated solutions of the final population of the EDA, which we denote by S. To measure how well S approximates the optimal Pareto set $\mathcal{P}_S$ of each problem, we use a well-known indicator in multi-objective optimization which takes into account proximity to $\mathcal{P}_S$ as well as the spread along $\mathcal{P}_S$. This indicator, called Inverted Generational Distance (IGD) does so by computing the average distance to the closest solution in an approximation set S over all solutions in $\mathcal{P}_S$. The lower the value of the IGD, the better the overall approximation is, and IGD is 0 if and only if the approximation set and $\mathcal{P}_S$ are identical. IGD is denoted by $D_{P_f \to S}$, and formulated as follows:

$$D_{P_f \to S}(S) = \frac{1}{|\mathcal{P}_S|} \sum_{\boldsymbol{x}^1 \in \mathcal{P}_S} \min_{\boldsymbol{x}^0 \in S} \{d(\boldsymbol{x}^0, \boldsymbol{x}^1)\},$$

where $d(\boldsymbol{x}^0, \boldsymbol{x}^1)$ is the Euclidean distance between the objective values $f(\boldsymbol{x}^0)$, $f(\boldsymbol{x}^1)$. For the problems in our test suite, given the ranges of the objectives for the optimal Pareto front configurations, a value of 0.01 for the $D_{P_f \to S}$ indicator corresponds to fronts that are quite close to the optimal Pareto front.

5.2.2 Algorithmic setup

We experimentally investigate the performance of RB-CORL as part of hybridization with iMAMaLGaM on the benchmark problems taken from literature shown in Table 1. We gave each algorithm a budget of 1,000,000 evaluations (per objective). The number of clusters was set to 20, since it was shown previously to yield good results. The cluster size for problems of dimension 10 was 11 and for problems of dimension 30 was 19. The selection percentile was set to $\tau = 0.35$, and the elitist archive target size was set to 1000. The evaluations for the computation of the gradient were not counted, considering that for our real-world application where we would like to use our hybrid version the gradient can be computed analytically.

5.3 Deformable image registration

5.3.1 *Definition*

Deformable image registration, i.e., finding the optimal transformation to align two images, is of great value in medical imaging. Healthcare specialists use it to combine images of different imaging modalities, as well as images taken at different time points. This allows them to get a clearer and more complete picture of the situation at hand as well as see how the anatomy of a patient changes over time. This is very important for example for radiation treatment planning, for diagnostic as well as for follow-up purposes.

In image registration, one image is referred to as the source image, whereas the other image is referred to as the target image. In the case of affine transformations (e.g. rotations or translations), the registration is called rigid. If non-affine transformations are needed to transform one image to the other (in the case of large anatomical differences, e.g., due to different positioning of the patient in image acquisitions) the registration is called deformable.

In this work, DIR is approached from a multi-objective optimization perspective [1]. This approach removes the need for pre-determining a singular combination of objectives, which is difficult to determine but necessary in existing registration methods. Moreover, since multiple outcomes are produced, this approach gives more options to the expert to choose the best outcome for the case at hand.

An image registration algorithm can be decomposed in three parts: the transformation model (the representation of all possible transformations from one image to the other image), the objective(s) to be optimized, and the optimization method.

5.3.2 *Transformation model*

We use a dual-dynamic transformation model based on B-splines that allows us to formulate differentiable objectives and calculate the gradient analytically.

B-splines (cubic polynomial functions used to model deformable objects) are widely used in image registration because they provide flexibility, transformation smoothness, and computational efficiency. In such transformation models, the source image is deformed by manipulating an underlying grid of control points that govern, via interpolation, the deformation and thereby the transformation of the image. In our dual-dynamic transformation model we have two grids associated with source- and target image, respectively, allowing us to handle large deformations. The correspondence between these two grids is established via a mapping from a 'virtual' fixed grid to the other two (Figure 4). More specifically, we loop over the virtual grid and we map the points to a location in the source- and a location in the target image. These locations are derived via the B-spline transformations T_s, T_t(which depend on the control points). Finally, the grey value at the obtained location is derived via pixel grey value interpolation. The sets of control points ϕ_s, ϕ_t that correspond to the source- and target- image are the parameters to be optimized.

5.3.3 *Objectives*

There are at least two objectives that are of interest in DIR and have to be minimized simultaneously. The first objective is quality of fit, i.e., the degree of similarity between the two images. The second objective is related to the smoothness of the transformation and aims to prevent implausible deformations.

The similarity measure we use is the sum of squared differences in pixel grey values between the source- and the target image:

$$Similarity = \sum_{x,y} \left[I_s(T_s(x,y;\phi)) - I_t(T_t(x,y;\phi))\right]^2,$$

where I_s, I_t are the grey values at a point (x, y) on the source- and target image, respectively, and T_s, T_t are the B-spline transformation functions that determine the deformation of the source- and target- image. I_s, I_t are interpolated functions constructed again via B-splines which make them differentiable.

The second objective is introduced to measure smoothness, using the sum of squared second order derivatives of each B-spline transformation $\left(\frac{\partial^2 T}{\partial x^2}\right)^2$, $\left(\frac{\partial^2 T}{\partial y^2}\right)^2$. We formulate the smoothness objective as the sum of the squared differences of the smoothing terms evaluated at pairs of points in the source- and target image. This objective is easier to optimize than the similarity objective, as no displacement of control points is already (close to) an optimum.

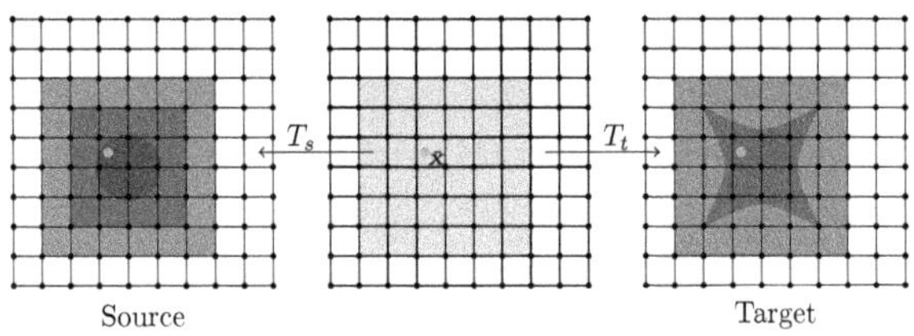

Figure 4: Dual-dynamic transformation model.

5.3.4 *Optimization method*

We apply three optimization methods to the DIR problems: iMAMaLGaM alone, the old AGLS scheme and and the new AGLS scheme. We use settings for the EDA which were shown to yield good results [3].

5.3.5 *Algorithmic setup*

We considered two test cases; the first one is a large-deformation registration case: prone-supine breast MRI registration. All MRI scans were acquired from a healthy volunteer. First, the two MRI scans were rigidly registered on the bony anatomy. Subsequently, one central pair of 2D slices was selected. The second case concerns MRI bladder registration, where there is also a large deformation of the bladder between image acquisitions, with an empty bladder in one image and a full bladder in the other. For both cases, we performed registration using two 8×8 grids of control points, which resulted in 256 parameters to be optimized. These settings are not necessarily sufficient to obtain the best possible registration result, but certainly sufficient to demonstrate the capabilities of the approach, and the impact of choosing different multi-objective optimizers.

6. RESULTS

6.1 Results on the benchmark problems

Results show that the use of gradient-based local search every generation, i.e., in the traditional GLS sense, is very

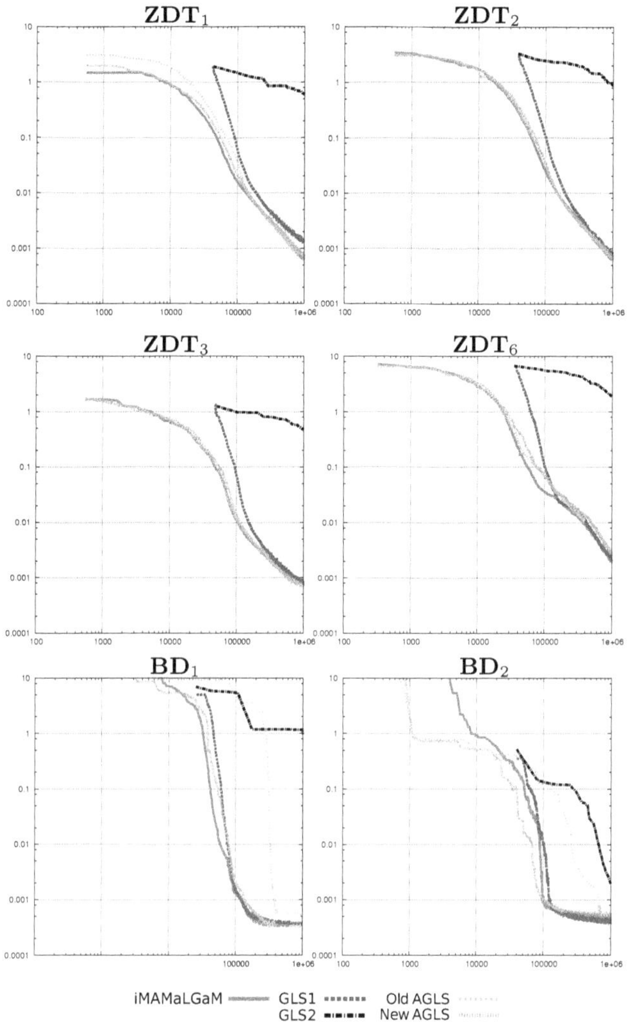

Figure 5: Convergence of all algorithms on 6 benchmark problems, averaged over 10 runs. Horizontal axis: number of evaluations (both objectives per evaluation). Vertical axis: $D_{\mathcal{P}_F \rightarrow \mathcal{S}}$.

computationally expensive (Figure 5). Note that evaluations required to approximate gradients are not even counted here as we are interested in the real-world application case where we have analytical expressions for the gradients of the objectives. iMAMaLGaM is capable of making many improvements all along the Pareto front at a much smaller budget of evaluations, which results in overall superior performance. This is in line with the common conception that EAs are well-suited and among the state-of-the-art for multi-objective optimization. Only by making use of the adaptive scheme for gradient integration that only uses gradient exploitation methods more often if they are really capable of making improvements more frequently than the EA, results can be obtained that come close to the performance of iMAMaLGaM. However, for problems BD_1 and BD_2, which exhibit most strongly the difference in objective complexity that we are interested in and that we redesigned AGLS for, the performance of the new version of AGLS is equal or even better than iMAMaLGaM. Moreover, the new AGLS clearly outperforms the old version of AGLS on these problems, which was one of our main objectives.

6.2 Results on the registration problems

For the breast MRI problem, iMAMaLGaM finds the most interesting solutions (i.e., solutions with a low value for the similarity measure, resulting in highly similar images). Compared to the old AGLS, we see that the new AGLS finds solutions which are slightly better in the interesting region, and it is closer to the final Pareto front of iMAMaLGaM (Figure 6). For the bladder MRI case, we can see a large difference between the old and the new AGLS; the new AGLS is able to obtain much better solutions regarding both objectives compared to the old AGLS. Also here, the EA is the most successful at finding solutions in the interesting region (Figure 6).

Although iMAMaLGaM finds the best solutions in a strict sense, the registration results of all algorithms on the breast MRI case are visually comparably good (Figure 7). For the bladder MRI case (Figure 8), the registration outcomes are overall not as good, however iMAMaLGaM and the new AGLS are able to obtain much better registration results compared to the old AGLS. It is worth noting that both the bladder and the breast MRI cases are difficult tasks, since there can be structures between these image acquisitions that move in the non-visible third plane, making it impossible to find a perfect match. Furthermore, many small structures do remain visible but are difficult to match using a low complexity deformation model of 8×8 control points. Therefore, it is possible that a larger number of control points is necessary to improve the registration results, especially in the bladder case. Additional guidance information such as contours could also be of great help.

Nonetheless, the above test cases demonstrate the capability of producing promising registration results using a multi-objective optimization approach to DIR. Moreover, the ability of RB-CORL to improve in an unbiased way all objectives, as shown in problems such as BD_1 and BD_2, can have a potentially large effect when it is part of a hybridization scheme: on hard, DIR problems like the bladder MRI case, the new AGLS is capable of obtaining results as good as of iMAMaLGaM. Lastly, its use could become more favourable in a hybridization scheme where not only the number of improvements are taken into account, but also the length of each improvement.

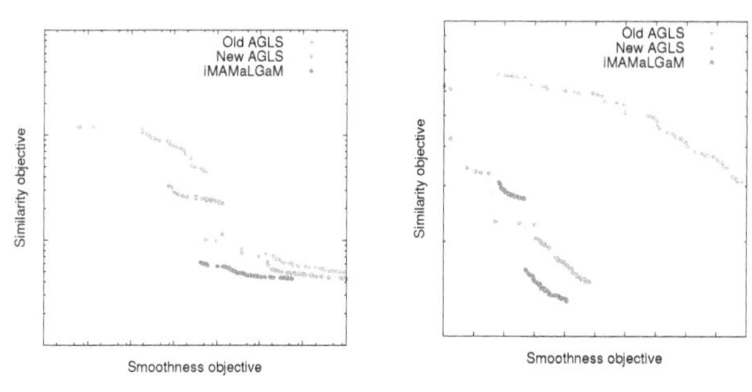

Figure 6: Final Pareto fronts for the breast MRI case (left) and the bladder MRI case (right).

7. DISCUSSION AND CONCLUSIONS

In this work, we developed and studied a new diversification technique for the exploitation of multi-objective gradient information, based on an analytically described set of Pareto-optimal improving directions. We assessed whether

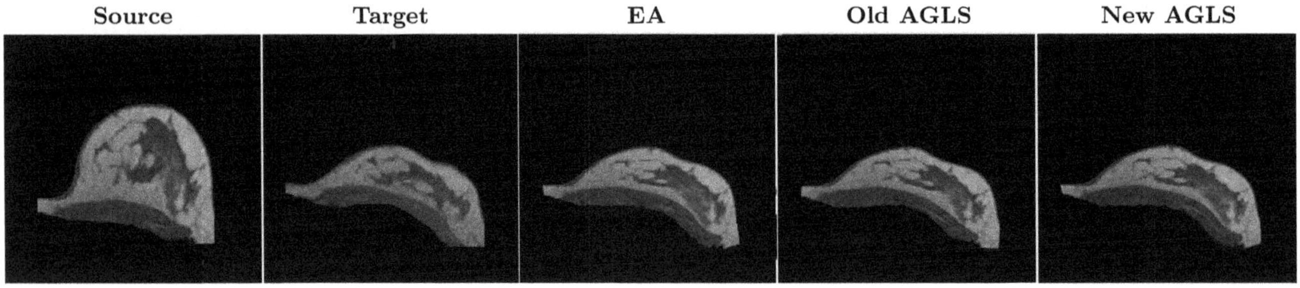

Figure 7: Selected DIR results on the breast MRI problem instance.

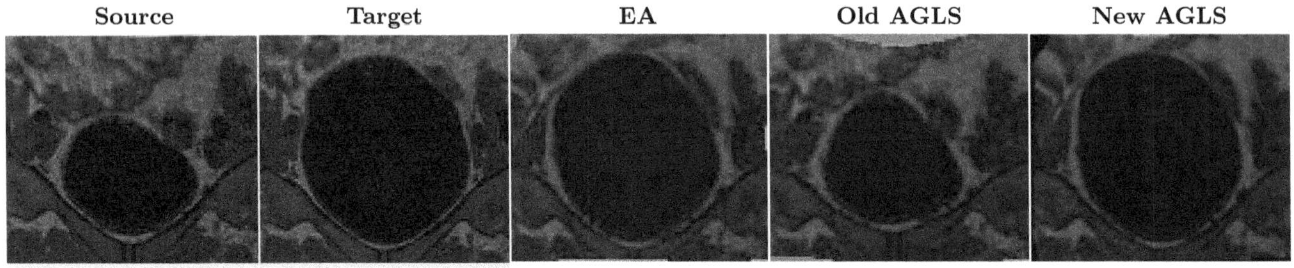

Figure 8: Selected DIR results on the bladder MRI problem instance.

this new technique can be combined efficiently with a multi-objective evolutionary algorithm, by considering three different hybridization schemes. Results showed improvement over existing adaptive hybridization schemes, especially for the problems we are particularly interested in: when there is a large difference in difficulty and/or scale between the objectives to be optimized, as is the case for the deformable image registration problem. The unbiased improvement of all objectives in a multi-objective gradient technique as part of a hybridization scheme was indeed successful at solving the tested hard DIR cases, as opposed to a previously introduced adaptive hybridization scheme. Nonetheless, the EA is still the most robust and powerful optimization algorithm, having the best balance between proximity and diversity. This is testimony again to the power of state-of-the-art EAs for multi-objective optimization, even for medical image processing applications, that have predominantly been solved using other types of algorithms, albeit from a single-objective optimization perspective.

For problems such as DIR, where a particular region of the Pareto front is of interest, it would also be interesting to investigate methods that are able to discover individual solutions on only part of the Pareto front, using linear/Chebyshev combinations of objectives.

8. ACKNOWLEDGMENTS

This work was funded by the Dutch Cancer Society (Grant No. KWF 2012-5716).

9. REFERENCES

[1] T. Alderliesten, J.-J. Sonke, and P. A. N. Bosman. Multi-objective optimization for deformable image registration: proof of concept. In *Proceedings of SPIE Medical Imaging*, pages 831420–831420, 2012.

[2] P. A. N. Bosman. On gradients and hybrid evolutionary algorithms for real-valued multiobjective optimization. *IEEE Transactions on Evolutionary Computation*, 16(1):51–69, 2012.

[3] P. A. N. Bosman and T. Alderliesten. Incremental Gaussian model-building in multi-objective edas with an application to deformable image registration. In *Proceedings of Genetic and Evolutionary Computation - GECCO-2012*, pages 241–248. ACM, 2012.

[4] M. Brown and R. E. Smith. Effective use of directional information in multi-objective evolutionary computation. In *Proceedings of Genetic and Evolutionary Computation - GECCO 2003*, pages 778–789. Springer, 2003.

[5] C. A. C. Coello, D. A. Van Veldhuizen, and G. B. Lamont. *Evolutionary algorithms for solving multi-objective problems*, volume 242. Springer, 2002.

[6] K. Deb, A. Pratap, S. Agarwal, and T. Meyarivan. A fast and elitist multiobjective genetic algorithm: NSGA-II. *IEEE Transactions on Evolutionary Computation*, 6(2):182–197, 2002.

[7] J. Fliege and B. F. Svaiter. Steepest descent methods for multicriteria optimization. *Mathematical Methods of Operations Research*, 51(3):479–494, 2000.

[8] A. Jaszkiewicz. On the performance of multiple-objective genetic local search on the 0/1 knapsack problem-a comparative experiment. *IEEE Transactions on Evolutionary Computation*, 6(4):402–412, 2002.

[9] M. R. Kaus and K. K. Brock. Deformable image registration for radiation therapy planning: algorithms and applications. In C. T. Leondes, editor, *Biomechanical systems technology: computational methods*, pages 1–28. World Scientific Publishing Company, Incorporated, 2007.

[10] J. D. Knowles and D. W. Corne. M-PAES: A memetic algorithm for multiobjective optimization. In *Proceedings of Congress on Evolutionary Computation - CEC 2000*, volume 1, pages 325–332. IEEE, 2000.

[11] M. Lahanas, D. Baltas, and S. Giannouli. Global convergence analysis of fast multiobjective gradient-based dose optimization algorithms for high-dose-rate brachytherapy. *Physics in Medicine and Biology*, 48(5):599, 2003.

[12] E. Zitzler, K. Deb, and L. Thiele. Comparison of multiobjective evolutionary algorithms: Empirical results. *Evolutionary Computation*, 8(2):173–195, 2000.

Efficient Sampling of PI Controllers in Evolutionary Multiobjective Optimization

Gilberto Reynoso-Meza
Industrial and Systems Engineering Graduate Program (PPGEPS)
Pontifical Catholic University of Parana (PUCPR)
Curitiba, PR, Brazil
g.reynosomeza@pucpr.br

Leandro d.Santos Coelho
Industrial and Systems Engineering Graduate Program (PPGEPS)
Pontifical Catholic University of Parana (PUCPR)
Curitiba, PR, Brazil
leandro.coelho@pucpr.br

Roberto Z. Freire
Industrial and Systems Engineering Graduate Program (PPGEPS)
Pontifical Catholic University of Parana (PUCPR)
Curitiba, PR, Brazil
roberto.freire@pucpr.br

ABSTRACT

Proportional-Integral (PI) controllers remain as a practical and reliable solution for multivariable control for several industrial applications. Efforts to develop new tuning techniques fulfilling several performance indicators and guaranteeing robustness are worthwhile. Evolutionary multiobjective optimization (EMO) has been used for multivariable PI controller tuning, due to their flexibility and its advantages to depict the trade off among conflicting objectives. It is a regular practice bounding the search space as a hyperbox; nevertheless, the shape of the feasible space of PI parameters which are internally stable for a given control loop is irregular. Therefore, such hyperbox could enclose feasible and unfeasible solutions or contain a subset of the feasible set. In the former case, convergence capabilities of an algorithm could be compromised; in the latter case, search space is not fully explored. In this work, a coding mechanism is proposed in order to explore more efficiently the PI parameters feasible set (that is, all feasible solutions and only feasible solutions) in EMO. With the example provided, the advantages to approximate a Pareto front for 2, 3 and 5 objectives are shown, validating the mechanism as useful for EMO in multivariable PI controller tuning.

Categories and Subject Descriptors

-.- [**Applied computing Decision analysis**]: Applied computing Multi-criterion optimization and decision-making

Keywords

Multivariable PI controllers; evolutionary algorithms.

1. INTRODUCTION

Proportional - Integral (PI) controllers remain as reliable and practical control solutions for several industrial processes [2, 15]. Owing to this, research for new tuning techniques is an ongoing research topic [4]. Current research points to guarantee reasonable stability margins as well as a good overall performance for a wide variety of processes. One of the main advantages of PI controllers is their ease of implementation as well as their tuning, giving a good tradeoff between simplicity and cost to implement [23, 22].

New tuning techniques are being focused on the fulfilment of several objectives and requirements, sometimes in conflict among them [1, 11]. Some tuning procedures are based on optimization statements [8, 24, 3, 15] and some cases they are solved by means of evolutionary algorithms [17]. As noticed in [20], evolutionary multiobjective optimization (EMO) could be a valuable tool for multivariable controller tuning, since it enables the designer to have a different embedment into the tradeoff analysis. Nevertheless, in the case of PI controller tuning, the search process has to be carefully performed; besides the (and often uncommented) preliminary step of defining the boundaries in the search process, not all parameter combinations in a PI guarantees closed loop stability given a nominal process.

It is a regular practice bounding the search space for a multivariable PI controller as a hyperbox; nevertheless, the shape of the feasible space of PI parameters which are internally stable for a given control loop is irregular [21]. Therefore, such hyperbox could enclose feasible and unfeasible solutions or contain a subset of the feasible set. In the former case, convergence capabilities of an algorithm could be compromised; in the latter case, search space is not fully explored. Therefore, providing mechanisms for an active seek of preferable solutions (in the EMO sense) in the entire feasible set (and only the feasible set) are worthwhile to develop.

In this work, a coding mechanism is proposed in order to explore more efficiently the PI parameters feasible set (that is, all feasible solutions and only feasible solutions) in EMO. It focus on multivariable processes where each of their sub-processes can be modelled as a first order plus dead time (FOPDT) process. The remainder of this work is as follows: in section 2, a brief background on multivariable PI controller tuning, multiobjective optimization and the shape of the feasible parameters for a PI controller are given; in section 3 the coding and sampling procedure is presented, whilst in section 4 its usefulness is validated with 3 different test cases. Finally, some concluding remarks are given.

GECCO '15, July 11 - 15, 2015, Madrid, Spain

DOI: http://dx.doi.org/10.1145/2739480.2754807

2. BACKGROUND

Basic background on multivariable control tuning and multiobjective optimization are presented below. At the end of this section, a brief discussion on the search space for those PI parameters is provided.

2.1 Background on multivariable PI controller tuning

A basic control loop is depicted in Figure 1. It comprises transfer functions $P(s)$ and $C(s)$ of a process and a controller respectively. The objective of this control loop is to keep the desired output $Y(s)$ of the process $P(s)$ in the desired reference $R(s)$.

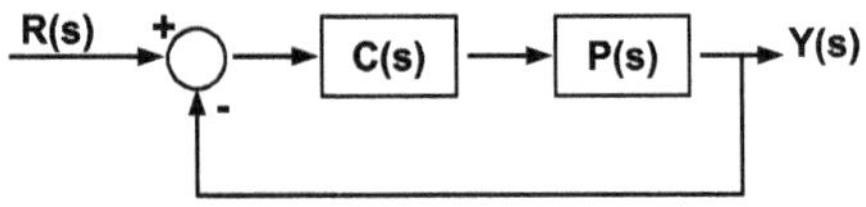

Figure 1: Basic control loop.

For a NxN MIMO (multiple-input, multiple-output) process, $P(s)$ is composed of several sub-processes P_{ij} with $i, j \in \{1, \ldots, N\}$ and it has the following structure:

$$P(s) = \begin{bmatrix} P_{11}(s) & \ldots & P_{1N}(s) \\ \vdots & \ddots & \vdots \\ P_{N1}(s) & \ldots & P_{NN}(s) \end{bmatrix} \quad (1)$$

The complexity of a process like this is mainly due to its coupling effects between inputs and outputs. There are several alternatives to control a MIMO system, and the selection of one technique over another depends on the desired balance between complexity and tradeoff between design specifications. PI controllers are simple but successful solutions, and their performance can be improved with complementary techniques [4]; because of this, they are used in this work. The decoupled PI controller $C(s)$ has N SISO (single-input, single-output) PI controllers:

$$C(s) = \begin{bmatrix} C_1(s) & \ldots & 0 \\ \vdots & \ddots & \vdots \\ 0 & \ldots & C_N(s) \end{bmatrix} \quad (2)$$

Equation (3) shows the transfer function of the selected structure of the PI controller:

$$C_j(s) = k_{p_j}\left(1 + \frac{1}{T_{i_j}s}\right)E(s) \quad (3)$$

where $j \in \{1, \ldots, N\}$, k_{p_j} is the proportional gain, T_{i_j} the integral time (s), and $E(s) = R(s) - Y(s)$ the error signal.

The control problem consists in selecting values for proportional gain k_p and integral gain $k_{i_j} = \frac{k_{pj}}{T_{i_j}}$ for each one of the PI controllers $C_j(s)$. The control engineer will select certain values for those controllers in order to achieve a desirable performance of the overall process $P(s)$ as well as *fair* robust stability margins. This is an important issue, since the control engineer must consider uncertainties in the process modelling. This control problem is well known and it has been addressed with several techniques. Given the coupling effects among sub-processes $P_{ij}(s)$, conflictive objectives may appear, at least related with the performance of each individual control loop. For this reason, EMO techniques have been used for PI controller tuning.

2.2 Multi-objective optimisation statement

As referred in [14], a multi-objective problem (MOP) with m objectives[1], can be stated as follows:

$$\min_{\boldsymbol{\theta}} \boldsymbol{J}(\boldsymbol{\theta}) = [J_1(\boldsymbol{\theta}), \ldots, J_m(\boldsymbol{\theta})] \quad (4)$$

subject to:

$$\boldsymbol{K}(\boldsymbol{\theta}) \leq 0 \quad (5)$$
$$\boldsymbol{L}(\boldsymbol{\theta}) = 0 \quad (6)$$
$$\underline{\theta_i} \leq \theta_i \leq \overline{\theta_i}, i = [1, \ldots, n] \quad (7)$$

where $\boldsymbol{\theta} = [\theta_1, \theta_2, \ldots, \theta_n]$ is defined as the decision vector with $\dim(\boldsymbol{\theta}) = n$; $\boldsymbol{J}(\boldsymbol{\theta})$ as the objective vector and $\boldsymbol{K}(\boldsymbol{\theta})$, $\boldsymbol{L}(\boldsymbol{\theta})$ as the inequality and equality constraint vectors respectively; $\underline{\theta_i}, \overline{\theta_i}$ are the lower and the upper bounds in the decision space.

It has been noticed that there is not a single solution in MOPs, because there is not generally a better solution in all the objectives. Therefore, a set of solutions, the Pareto set, is defined. Each solution in the Pareto set defines an objective vector in the Pareto front. All the solutions in the Pareto front are a set of Pareto optimal and non-dominated solutions (See Figure 2):

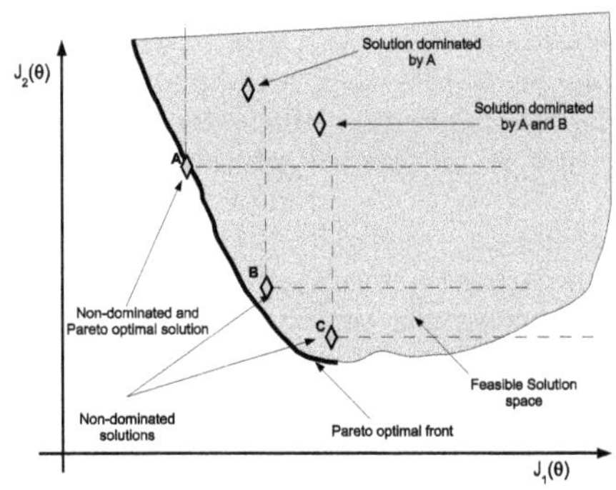

Figure 2: Pareto optimality and dominance concepts.

- Pareto optimality [14]: An objective vector $\boldsymbol{J}(\boldsymbol{\theta}^1)$ is Pareto optimal if there does not exist another objective vector $\boldsymbol{J}(\boldsymbol{\theta}^2)$ such that $J_i(\boldsymbol{\theta}^2) \leq J_i(\boldsymbol{\theta}^1)$ for all $i \in [1, 2, \ldots, m]$ and $J_j(\boldsymbol{\theta}^2) < J_j(\boldsymbol{\theta}^1)$ for at least one j, $j \in [1, 2, \ldots, m]$.
- Dominance [7]: An objective vector $\boldsymbol{J}(\boldsymbol{\theta}^1)$ is dominated by another objective vector $\boldsymbol{J}(\boldsymbol{\theta}^2)$ iff $J_i(\boldsymbol{\theta}^2) \leq J_i(\boldsymbol{\theta}^1)$ for all $i \in [1, 2, \ldots, m]$ and $J_j(\boldsymbol{\theta}^2) < J_j(\boldsymbol{\theta}^1)$ for

[1] A maximisation problem can be converted to a minimisation problem. For each of the objectives that have to be maximised, the transformation: $\max J_i(\boldsymbol{\theta}) = -min(-J_i(\boldsymbol{\theta}))$ could be applied.

at least one j, $j \in [1, 2, \ldots, m]$. This is denoted as $\boldsymbol{J}(\boldsymbol{\theta_2}) \preceq \boldsymbol{J}(\boldsymbol{\theta_1})$.

Within the context of the decoupled PI controller $C(s)$ of equation 2 for a multivariable process $P(s)$ (equation 1), the decision space is defined as $\boldsymbol{\theta} = [k_{p_1}, T_{i_1}, \ldots, k_{p_N}, T_{i_N}]$.

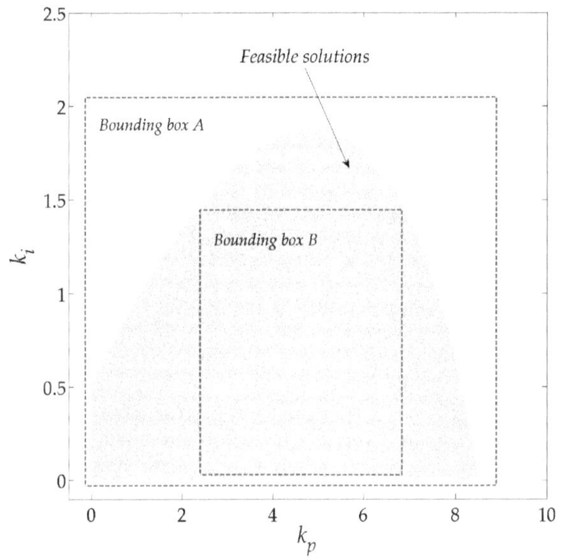

(a) PI controller

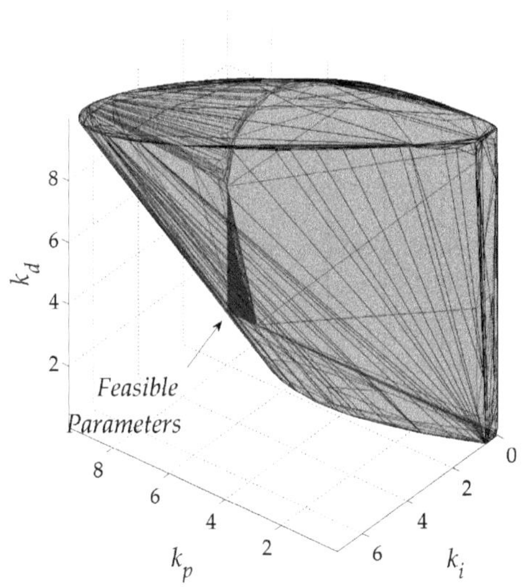

(b) PID controller

Figure 3: Stabilizing PI - PID parameters for a given process.

2.3 Stabilizing PI parameters

In [17, 20] it was noticed that evolutionary techniques has been useful for finding appropriate tuning parameters for PI or PID (a PI controller with derivative action) controllers. Nevertheless, in spite of the efforts for defining useful and meaningful cost functions, bounding the search space has devoted less attention.

In Figures 3, the stabilizing parameters k_p, k_i, k_d (proportional, integral and derivative gains) for a PI and a PID controllers are depicted respectively. As it can be noticed, the shape in both cases is irregular. Usually, for the optimisation statement, the search space is bounded using an hyperbox enclosing this feasible space (Bounding Box A in Figure 3a) or one inside (Bounding Box B in Figure 3b). In the former case, non feasible parameters are included in the search space; on the latter, the feasible search space is not fully considered. Therefore, a mechanism which enables sampling only the feasible space and (potentially) any feasible parameter combination could be valuable for the optimisation stage.

It is worthwhile noticing that such feasible set will be *reshaped* if coupling effect among several controllers are considered. That is, when several PI-like controllers are used for a multivariable process. This will be taken into consideration for the coding proposal.

3. DEVELOPMENT

Firstly, it will be briefly explained how is characterized the subset of stabilizing PID controllers $\mathbb{C}$ and afterwards, it will be explained how to sample controller from such subset.

3.1 Computation of $\mathbb{C}$

We will consider in this work FOPDT transfer function $P(s)$ and the PID controller $C(s)$. Both are described by the equations:

$$P(s) = \frac{k}{Ts+1}e^{-Ls} \tag{8}$$

$$C(s) = k_p + \frac{k_i}{s} + k_d s \tag{9}$$

where $k > 0$ is the process proportional gain, T the time constant and L the lag of the system; k_p, k_i, k_d the proportional, integral and derivative gains of the controller. According to [21], the set $\mathbb{C} \subset \Re^3$ of stabilizing controllers given the $P(s)$ process is given by subsets $\mathbf{T}$, $\boldsymbol{\Delta}$ and $\mathbf{Q}$ (Figure 4).

The range of k_p values for which $P(s)$ is stable is given by:

$$-\frac{1}{k} < k_p < k_u \tag{10}$$

where k_u is usually known as the ultimate gain

$$k_u = \frac{1}{k}\left[\frac{T}{L}\alpha_1 \sin(\alpha_1) - \cos(\alpha_1)\right] \tag{11}$$

and α_1 is the solution of the equation

$$\tan(\alpha) = -\frac{T}{T+L}\alpha, \alpha \in [0, \pi] \tag{12}$$

The complete stabilization region is given by:

1. For each $k_p \in [-\frac{1}{k}, \frac{1}{k})$, the corresponding region in (k_i, k_d) space is the quadrilateral $\boldsymbol{Q}$ of Figure 4.
2. For $k_p = \frac{1}{k}$, the corresponding region in (k_i, k_d) space is the triangle $\boldsymbol{\Delta}$ of Figure 4.

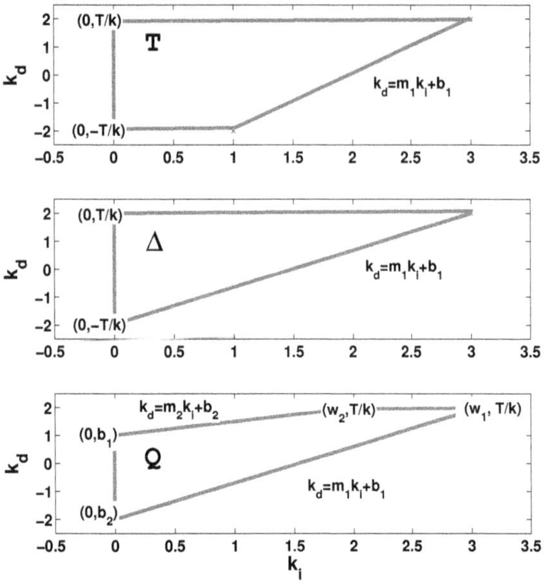

Figure 4: PID stable regions.

3. For each $k_p \in [\frac{1}{k}, k_u)$, the corresponding region in (k_i, k_d) space is the trapezoid $\boldsymbol{T}$ of Figure 4, where $k_u = \frac{1}{k}\left[\frac{T}{L}\alpha_1 \sin(\alpha_1) - \cos(\alpha_1)\right]$.

Where relevant variables m_j, b_j, w_j, $j = [1, 2]$ are calculated as follows:

$$m_j = \frac{L^2}{z_j^2} \tag{13}$$

$$b_j = -\frac{L}{k \cdot z_j}\left[\sin(z_j) + \frac{T}{L} z_j \cos(z_j)\right] \tag{14}$$

$$w_j = \frac{z_j}{kL}\frac{(1 + kk_p)[1 + \cos(z_j)]}{\sin(z_j)} \tag{15}$$

with z_1, z_2 being the roots of

$$k \cdot k_p + \cos(z) - \frac{T}{L} z \sin(z) = 0 \tag{16}$$

Therefore, set $\mathbb{C}$ is composed by subsets $\mathbf{T}$ (for $k_p \in [-\frac{1}{k}, \frac{1}{k})$), $\boldsymbol{\Delta}$ (for $k_p = \frac{1}{k}$) and $\bigcup \mathbf{Q}$ (for $k_p \in [\frac{1}{k}, k_u)$).

$$\mathbb{C} = \mathbf{T} \bigcup \boldsymbol{\Delta} \bigcup \mathbf{Q} \tag{17}$$

3.2 Sampling on $\mathbb{C}$

It is stated that, given a subset $\mathbb{S} \in \Re^3$ and a process $P(s)$, two important features for PID $C(s)$ parameter sampling from $\mathbb{S}$ should be fulfilled:

1. Any sampled controller $C(s)$ from $\mathbb{S}$ must stabilize the closed loop.

2. Any stabilizing controller $C(s)$ of the process $P(s)$ must be contained in $\mathbb{S}$.

A common approach for feature 1 is to define bounds on the parameter which avoid all non-stable but also some stable PID parameters; therefore, feature 2 is not fulfilled. A second alternative, is to bound the search space with all stable PID parameters, but including non-stable parameters, which are verified whilst the algorithm is running. This obviously does not fulfill feature 1, and could misspent computational resources.

It is necessary sampling controllers from $\mathbb{C}$ in order to fulfill both features. It will be assumed that controllers matching $k_p > 0$, $ki > 0$, $k_d > 0$ are the only accepted by the designer to stabilize $P(s)$. According to this, an injective function $\Re^3 \rightarrow \Re^3$ to map from the unitary cube to $\mathbb{C}$ is defined:

$$F(a, b, c) = [k_p, k_i, k_d] \tag{18}$$

$$\{a, b, c\} \in [0, 1] \tag{19}$$

where:

$$k_p = a \cdot k_u \tag{20}$$

$$k_d = c \cdot \frac{T}{K} \tag{21}$$

$$k_i = \begin{cases} b \cdot \frac{k_d - b_1}{m_1} & if \quad k_p \leq 1/k \\ \frac{k_d - b_2}{m_2} + b \cdot \left[\frac{k_d - b_1}{m_1} - \frac{k_d - b_2}{m_2}\right] & if \quad 1/k < k_p \end{cases} \tag{22}$$

Therefore the algorithm to generate stabilizing controllers, for a single FOPDT process, is:

	Algorithm I: *PID.Sampling*
1 :	Read values k, T, L
2 :	Calculate k_u (equation 11)
3 :	Read values a, b, c
4 :	Calculate k_p (equation 20)
5 :	Calculate k_d (equation 21)
6 :	Determine roots $z_j, j = [1, 2]$ (equation 16)
7 :	Determine values $m_j, b_j, j = [1, 2]$ (equations 13,14)
8 :	Determine k_i (equation 22)
9 :	Return k_p, k_i, k_d
10:	Return $T_i = k_p/k_i$ $T_d = k_d/k_p$

Simple analytic solutions using Newton-Raphson optimization method could be employed. Line 1 and 2 could be calculated *off-line* if a fixed FOPDT is under consideration. If not required, line 10 could be omitted. Since this guarantees feasible controllers for each individual loop (a given pair controller and sub-process), overall stability should be verified.

The last sampling procedure, while useful for single objective optimization instances [19], could be also useful for EMO; nevertheless, such usability still needs to be evaluated. This will be addressed in the following section.

4. EVALUATION

In order to show the applicability of the sampling approach for multivariable PI tuning, the well-known distillation column model defined by Wood and Berry will be used [5, 25]. It represents the control of the composition of two products (a mixture of methanol and water for this specific case), where the manipulated variables are the reflux and steam flows:

$$P(s) = \begin{bmatrix} P_{11}(s) & P_{12}(s) \\ P_{21}(s) & P_{22}(s) \end{bmatrix} = \begin{bmatrix} \frac{12.8e^{-s}}{16.7s+1} & \frac{-18.9e^{-3s}}{21s+1} \\ \frac{6.6e^{-7s}}{10.9s+1} & \frac{-19.4e^{-3s}}{14.4s+1} \end{bmatrix} \tag{23}$$

This process has been widely used to compare evolutionary algorithms [9, 10, 13, 13] as well as evolutionary multi-objective optimisation performance [18]. The process $P(s)$ (Equation (23)) will be controlled with a decentralized PI controller structure $C(s)$ (Equation (24)). The designer is interested in improving the performance of the initial solution $\boldsymbol{\theta}_0$ (stated by the BLT [12] methodology).

$$C(s) = \begin{bmatrix} k_{p1}\left(1+\frac{1}{T_{i1}s}\right) & 0 \\ 0 & k_{p2}\left(1+\frac{1}{T_{i2}s}\right) \end{bmatrix} \tag{24}$$

The following design objectives are considered:

- Integral gain

$$J_{k_i}(k_p, T_i) = -\frac{k_p}{T_i} \tag{25}$$

- Biggest log modulus

$$J_{L_{cm}}(\boldsymbol{\theta}) = 20\log\left|\frac{W(s)}{1+W(s)}\right| \leq L_{cm}^{max} \tag{26}$$

- Maximum value of the sensitivity function

$$J_{M_s}(k_p, T_i) = \left\|(1+P(s)C(s))^{-1}\right\|_{\infty} \tag{27}$$

Design objective $J_{k_i}(k_p, T_i)$ is a classical performance index, used to evaluate the performance of a PI controller in the control loop. It measures the capacity of dealing with a disturbance in order to keep the desired reference value; design objective $J_{L_{cm}}(\boldsymbol{\theta})$, $\boldsymbol{\theta} = [k_{p1}, T_{i1}, k_{p2}, T_{i2}]$ is a robustness measure: the lower $J_{L_{cm}}(\boldsymbol{\theta})$, the better the control loop to deal efficiently with un-modelled dynamics or differences between the overall nominal model (used to adjust the PI parameters) and the real model (real process implementation); finally, design objective $J_{M_s}(k_p, T_i)$ is also a robustness measure but for an individual loop.

Three different optimization statements (Equations 29, 30 and 31) are defined:

$$\begin{aligned} \min \boldsymbol{J}(\boldsymbol{\theta}) &= [J_{k_{i1}}(k_{p1}, T_{i1}), J_{k_{i2}}(k_{p2}, T_{i2})] \\ &s.t. \\ J_{L_{cm}}(\boldsymbol{\theta}) &\leq 4 \\ Re[\lambda] &< 0 \end{aligned} \tag{28}$$

$$\begin{aligned} \min \boldsymbol{J}(\boldsymbol{\theta}) &= [J_{k_{i1}}(k_{p1}, T_{i1}), \\ & \quad J_{k_{i2}}(k_{p2}, T_{i2}), \\ & \quad J_{L_{cm}}(\boldsymbol{\theta})] \\ &s.t. \\ J_{L_{cm}}(\boldsymbol{\theta}) &\leq 4 \\ Re[\lambda] &< 0 \end{aligned} \tag{29}$$

$$\begin{aligned} \min \boldsymbol{J}(\boldsymbol{\theta}) &= [J_{k_{i1}}(k_{p1}, T_{i1}), \\ & \quad J_{k_{i2}}(k_{p2}, T_{i2}), \\ & \quad J_{L_{cm}}(\boldsymbol{\theta}), \\ & \quad J_{M_{s1}}(k_{p1}, T_{i1}), \\ & \quad J_{M_{s2}}(k_{p2}, T_{i2})] \\ &s.t. \\ J_{L_{cm}}(\boldsymbol{\theta}) &\leq 4 \\ J_{M_{s1}}(k_{p1}, T_{i1}) &\leq 2.0 \\ J_{M_{s2}}(k_{p2}, T_{i2}) &\leq 2.0 \\ Re[\lambda] &< 0 \end{aligned} \tag{30}$$

Constraints on $J_{L_{cm}}(\boldsymbol{\theta})$, $J_{M_{s1}}(k_{p1}, T_{i1})$ and $J_{M_{s2}}(k_{p2}, T_{i2})$ are usually stated in order to guarantee reasonable robustness margins for practical applications. Constraint on the eigenvaluaes $Re[\lambda]$ is required to guarantee overall internal stability (since internal stability of individual loops does not guarantee the internal stability of the overall loop).

The aim of this test design is to validate the hypothesis H_0 that the proposed sampling approach will improve an algorithm performance to calculate Pareto optimal PI parameters. For this paper (and due to limitation of space) only one algorithm will be evaluated; in this case, it is selected the multiobjective optimization algorithm provided by Matlab©, *gamultiobj* (with default parameters). It will be executed twice, in order to test the sampling proposal:

1. An execution using the stochastic sampling previously explained (H_0); therefore, for each decision variable upper and lower limit are bounded by $[0, 1]$.
2. An execution using standard bounds on $k_{p1,p2} \in [0, 5]$, $T_{i1,i2} \in [0, 100]$ (H_1).

For such purpose, a total of 100 generations have been used and 51 independent runs are carried out; A standard desktop [2] is used to calculate the Pareto front approximations. To met the imposed constraints, a basic penalty function [18] is used to identify feasible from non-feasible solutions. Performance of the approximated Pareto fronts will be evaluated using the hypervolume indicator, using as reference points the vectors $[0, 0]$, $[0, 0, 4]$ and $[0, 0, 4, 2, 2]$ respectively.

Numerical results are shown in Table 1 and graphically depicted with box-plots and violin-plots for each case in Figure 5. In the case of optimization statements of Equations 29 and 30, there are statistical differences according to the Wilcoxon test at 95%, while in the case of the optimization statement of equation 31 there is not (due to the success rate for both algorithms). In all cases, a better median for the attained hypervolume is achieved.

Finally, attainment surfaces at 50% are depicted in Figures 6 and 7. Visualization of attainment surfaces is helpful to evaluate the performance of the approximated Pareto fronts, since a bigger hypervolume indicator does not imply a dominance relation between approaches. In Figure 6, standards 2D and 3D visualizations are enough to show the Pareto front approximations for 2 and 3 design objectives, while in the case of 5 design objectives a Level Diagrams [6]

[2] Windows 8 system, processor Intel Core i7-4790, 3.60 GHz with 32.00 GB RAM.

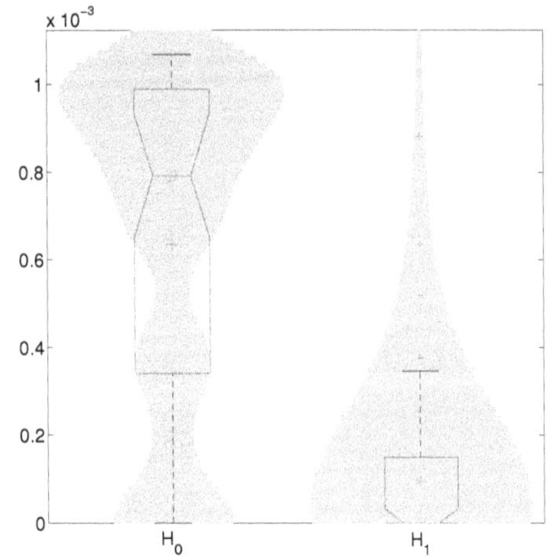

(a) 2 design objectives

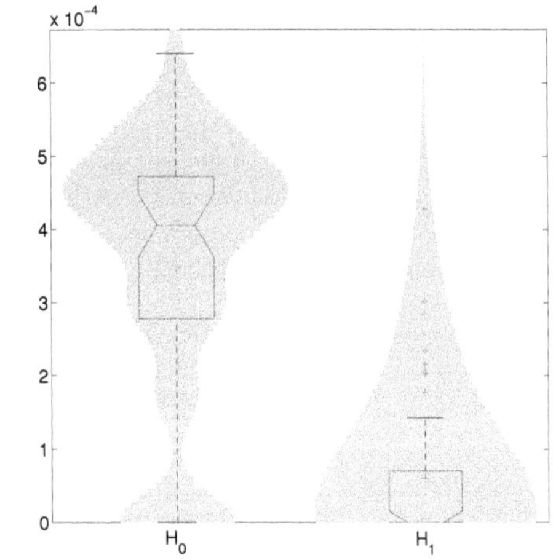

(b) 3 design objectives

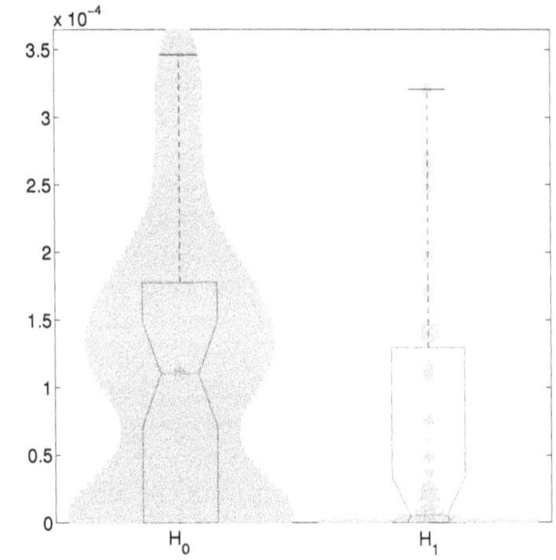

(c) 5 design objectives

Figure 5: Boxplots and violin plots for hypervolume indicator

visualization is used. Although it is possible to appreciate the dominance relation between Pareto front approximations for 2 and 3 design objectives, it is not easy for 5 design objectives. Therefore, a complementary visualization using Level Diagrams for design concepts comparison (different Pareto front approximations) as explained in [16] is used; in such visualization, a portion of the attainment surface above 1 is dominated by a portion of the other attainment surface, which is below 1. With this complementary information, it is possible to appreciate easily that Pareto front approximations (using the 50% attained surface) for 3 and 5 design objectives using the proposed sampling approach dominate the other approximation.

5. CONCLUSIONS AND FUTURE WORK

In this work, it has been presented a simple coding to sample internal stable PID controllers given a FOPDT process and its usefulness to approximate a Pareto front for multivariable processes. This coding could be potentially used by any multiobjective evolutionary algorithm, to improve their efficiency in the global search procedure. In summary, the main advantages of this proposal are:

- Function evaluations are used more efficiently, since the offspring is always in the feasible space, where all controllers stabilize each individual loop.
- All stabilizing controllers are contained in the set for a given loop; therefore, *a priori*, the algorithm could evolve a solution to any feasible tuning configuration.
- No guesses or hints are made about the decision search space for the evolutionary algorithm; the search space is straightforward bounded.

Whilst a simple example has been shown in this paper (due to limitation of space), the approach is suitable to face more demanding optimizations statements by including constraints. Limitations and future work are:

- In spite of its usefulness, the code is presented just for FOPDT processes. Future work should focus on extend the sampling properly to multivariable processes.
- Only PI-like controllers can be tuning with this procedure; it should be extended to more complex PI-like control configurations.
- Obviously, this procedure was evaluated with a single multiobjective optimization algorithm. More tests with different algorithms should be performed, to evaluate the usefulness of this mechanism.

6. ACKNOWLEDGMENTS

We are grateful to anonymous reviewers for their constructive comments which contributed to improve this paper. First author gratefully acknowledges the support provided by the post-doctoral fellowship BJT-304804/2014-2 from the National Council of Scientific and Technologic Development of Brazil (CNPq) for the development of this work.

Table 1: Hypervolume indicator in performance test for 2,3 and 5 design objectives. Success means the number of executions were it was possible to find a Pareto front approximation fulfilling the imposed constraints.

	2 design objectives		3 design objectives		5 design objectives	
	H0	H1	H0	H1	H0	H1
minimum	0.0000	0.0000	0.0000	0.0000	0.0000	0.0000
median	**7.9185e-4**	0.0000e-4	**4.0545e-4**	0.0000e-4	**1.1011e-4**	0.0538e-4
maximum	1.06813-3	0.8815e-3	6.4030e-4	4.2761e-4	3.4628e-4	3.2050e-4
mean	6.3536e-4	0.9539e-4	3.4904e-4	0.5997e-4	1.1226e-4	0.6138e-4
variance	1.4694e-7	0.3485e-7	3.3297e-8	1.1277e-8	1.0180e-8	0.8278e-8
success	**42**	22	**44**	19	**37**	29

7. REFERENCES

[1] K. H. Ang, G. Chong, and Y. Li. PID control system analysis, design, and technology. *IEEE Transactions on Control Systems Technology*, 13(4):559 – 576, 2005.

[2] K. Åström and T. Hägglund. The future of PID control. *Control Engineering Practice*, 9(11):1163 – 1175, 2001.

[3] K. Åström, H. Panagopoulos, and T. Hägglund. Design of PI controllers based on non-convex optimization. *Automatica*, 34(5):585 – 601, 1998.

[4] K. J. Åström and T. Hägglund. *Advanced PID Control*. ISA - The Instrumentation, Systems, and Automation Society, Research Triangle Park, NC 27709, 2005.

[5] M. W. Berry. Terminal composition control of a binary distillation column. Master's thesis, Deptartment of Chemical and Petroleum Engineering, University of Alberta., Edmonton, Alberta, 1973.

[6] X. Blasco, J. Herrero, J. Sanchis, and M. Martínez. A new graphical visualization of n-dimensional Pareto front for decision-making in multiobjective optimization. *Information Sciences*, 178(20):3908 – 3924, 2008.

[7] C. A. C. Coello and G. B. Lamont. *Applications of Multi-Objective evolutionary algorithms*. World scientific publishing, advances in natural computation vol. 1 edition, 2004.

[8] M. Ge, M.-S. Chiu, and Q.-G. Wang. Robust PID controller design via LMI approach. *Journal of process control*, (12):3 – 13, 2002.

[9] M. W. Iruthayarajan and S. Baskar. Evolutionary algorithms based design of multivariable PID controller. *Expert Systems with Applications*, 36(5):9159 – 9167, 2009.

[10] M. W. Iruthayarajan and S. Baskar. Covariance matrix adaptation evolution strategy based design of centralized PID controller. *Expert Systems with Applications*, 37(8):5775 – 5781, 2010.

[11] Y. Li, K. H. Ang, and G. Chong. PID control system analysis and design. *IEEE Control Systems*, 2006.

[12] W. L. Luyben. Simple method for tuning SISO controllers in multivariable systems. *Industrial and Engineering Chemistry Process Design*, (25):654 – 660, 1986.

[13] M. I. Menhas, L. Wang, M. Fei, and H. Pan. Comparative performance analysis of various binary coded PSO algorithms in multivariable PID controller design. *Expert Systems with Applications*, 39(4):4390 – 4401, 2012.

[14] K. M. Miettinen. *Nonlinear multiobjective optimization*. Kluwer Academic Publishers, 1998.

[15] H. Panagopoulos, K. Åström, and T. Hägglund. Design of PID controllers based on constrained optimisation. *Control Theory and Applications, IEE Proceedings -*, 149(1):32 – 40, 2002.

[16] G. Reynoso-Meza, X. Blasco, J. Sanchis, and J. M. Herrero. Comparison of design concepts in multi-criteria decision-making using level diagrams. *Information Sciences*, 221:124 – 141, 2013.

[17] G. Reynoso-Meza, X. Blasco, J. Sanchis, and M. Martínez. Evolutionary algorithms for PID controller tuning: Current trends and perspectives (in spanish). *Revista Iberoamericana de Automática e Informática Industrial*, 10(3):251 – 268, 2013.

[18] G. Reynoso-Meza, J. Sanchis, X. Blasco, and J. M. Herrero. Multiobjective evolutionary algortihms for multivariable PI controller tuning. *Expert Systems with Applications*, 39:7895 – 7907, 2012.

[19] G. Reynoso-Meza, J. Sanchis, X. Blasco, and J. M. Herrero. A stabilizing PID controller sampling procedure for stochastic optimizers. In *Memories of the 19th World Congress IFAC 2014*. August 2014.

[20] G. Reynoso-Meza, J. Sanchis, X. Blasco, and M. Martínez. Controller tuning using evolutionary multi-objective optimisation: current trends and applications. *Control Engineering Practice*, 1:58 – 73, 2014.

[21] G. Silva, A. Datta, and S. Bhattacharyya. New results on the synthesis of PID controllers. *Automatic Control, IEEE Transactions on*, 47(2):241–252, 2002.

[22] G. Stewart and T. Samad. Cross-application perspectives: Application and market requirements. In T. Samad and A. Annaswamy, editors, *The Impact of Control Technology*, pages 95 – 100. IEEE Control Systems Society, 2011.

[23] W. Tan, J. Liu, F. Fang, and Y. Chen. Tuning of PID controllers for boiler-turbine units. *ISA Transactions*, 43(4):571 – 583, 2004.

[24] R. Toscano. A simple robust PI/PID controller design via numerical optimization approach. *Journal of process control*, (15):81 – 88, 2005.

[25] R. K. Wood and M. W. Berry. Terminal composition control of a binary distillation column. *Chemical Engineering Science*, 28(9):1707 – 1717, 1973.

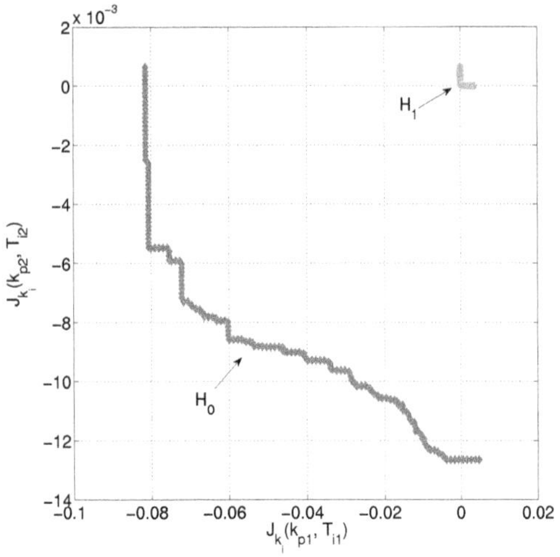

(a) 2 design objectives

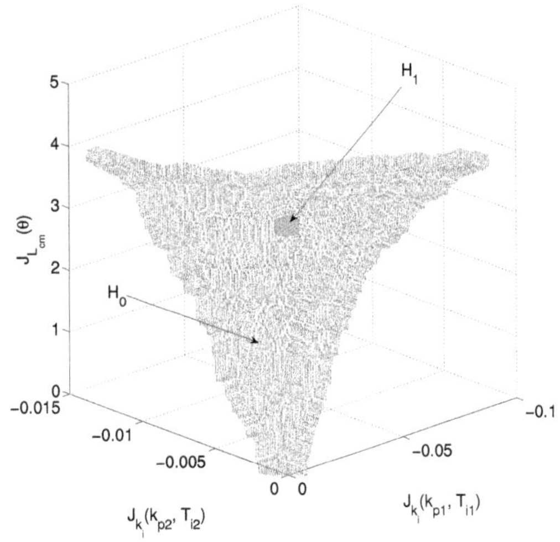

(b) 3 design objectives

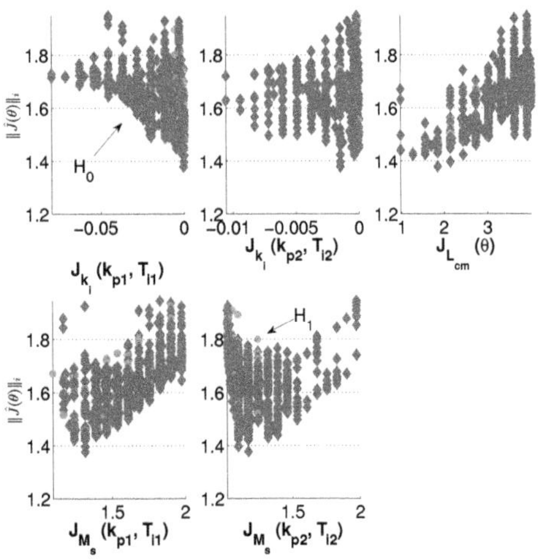

(c) 5 design objectives

Figure 6: Attainment surfaces at 50%

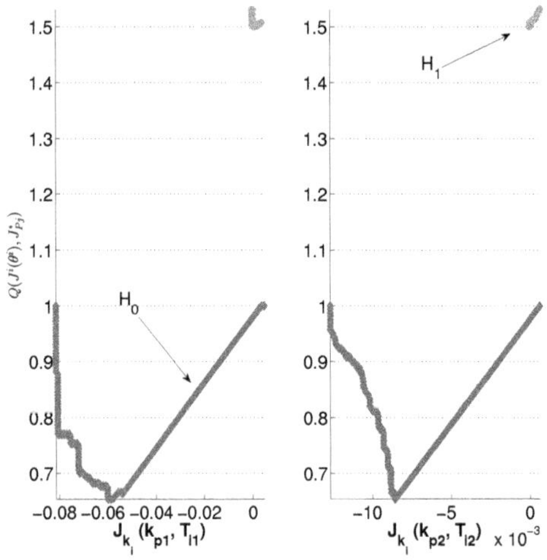

(a) 2 design objectives

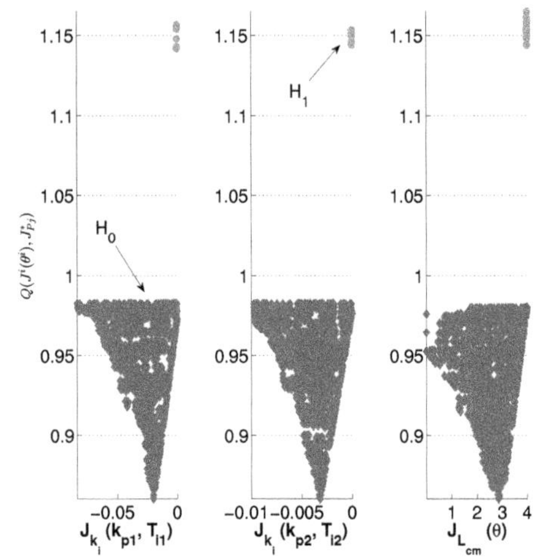

(b) 3 design objectives

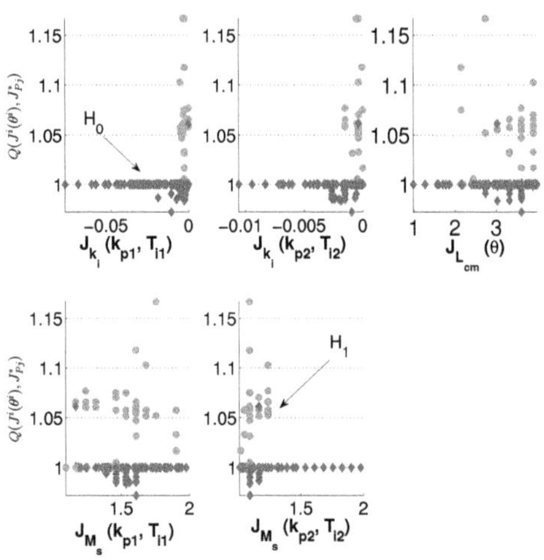

(c) 5 design objectives

Figure 7: Design cncepts comparison using Level Diagrams for H_0 and H_1.

Using Multi-Objective Artificial Immune Systems to Find Core Collections Based on Molecular Markers

Shana Schlottfeldt
Dept of Computer Science
University of Brasilia
Brasilia, DF, Brazil
shanass@unb.br

Maria Emilia M. T. Walter
Dept of Computer Science
University of Brasilia
Brasilia, DF, Brazil
mia@cic.unb.br

Jon Timmis
Dept of Electronics
University of York
York, United Kingdom
jon.timmis@york.ac.uk

André C.P.L.F. Carvalho
Dept of Computer Science
University of Sao Paulo
São Carlos, SP, Brazil
andre@icmc.usp.br

Mariana P.C. Telles
Institute of Biological Sciences
Federal University of Goias
Goiania, GO, Brazil
tellesmpc@gmail.com

José Alexandre F. Diniz-Filho
Institute of Biological Sciences
Federal University of Goias
Goiania, GO, Brazil
diniz@ufg.br

ABSTRACT

Germplasm collections are an important strategy for conservation of diversity, a challenge in ecoinformatics. It is common to select a core to represent the genetic diversity of a germplasm collection, aiming to minimize the costs of conservation, while ensuring the maximization of genetic variation. For the problem of finding a core for a germplasm collection, we proposed the use of a constrained multi-objective artificial immune algorithm (MAIS), based on principles of systematic conservation planning (SCP), and incorporating heterozygosity information. Therefore, optimization takes genotypic diversity and variability patterns into account. As a case study, we used *Dipteryx alata* molecular marker information. We were able to identify within several accessions, the exact entries that should be chosen to preserve species diversity. MAIS presented better performance measure results when compared to NSGA-II. The proposed approach can be used to help construct cores with maximal genetic richness, and also be extended to *in situ* conservation. As far as we know, this is the first time that an AIS algorithm is applied to the problem of finding a core for a germplasm collection using heterozygosity information as well.

CCS Concepts

•Applied computing → Environmental sciences; •Mathematics of computing → *Evolutionary algorithms;* **•Computing methodologies →** *Discrete space search;*

GECCO '15, July 11 - 15, 2015, Madrid, Spain
© 2015 ACM. ISBN 978-1-4503-3472-3/15/07. . . $15.00
DOI: http://dx.doi.org/10.1145/2739480.2754653

Keywords

multi-objective optimization; artificial immune systems; systematic conservation planning; germplasm; core collection; genetic variability; biodiversity

1. INTRODUCTION

Nowadays, biodiversity, sustainability, and climate change represent strategic research issues, compelling researchers to deal with integration of data within and among distinct disciplines, and rapid conversion of those data into information required by decision-makers [16].

In this context, ecoinformatics plays an important role as an emerging multidisciplinary field that develops methods and tools for the understanding, generation, processing, and dissemination of ecological data [22]. While the components of this field are not new [16], there is a novel emphasis on the integrated treatment of the area, associated with the increasing social awareness of ecological and environmental issues and their social, economic, and political impacts [20, 27]. As a consequence, ecoinformatics is experiencing a fast growing, similarly to the one seen in bioinformatics, some decades ago.

A focal research challenge in ecoinformatics is related to plant germplasm maintenance. *Plant germplasm* is a living tissue from which new plants can be grown. There are several ways to store germplasm, e.g., as seed collections, pollen storage, in a nursery (field), *in vitro* [13], comprising what is called *germplasm collection.* Germplasm collections are an important strategy for conservation and maintenance of genetic resources since they preserve the genetic diversity of plants [9], which, therefore, is made available for further study or for habitat restoration projects.

The maintenance of a germplasm collection is expensive and its costs are related to storage space, controlled temperature, relative humidity, and amount of equipment [15]. These factors depend mainly on the quantities of germplasm to be stored. This leads us to the concept of *core collection,* a subset from a larger collection of a particular species that represents, with a minimum level of repetitiveness, the genetic diversity of that species [3, 14]. A core collection is not a surrogate of the whole collection, but it captures the complete diversity of the entire collection it is derived from; thus, it is a useful tool for organizing and analyzing representative sets of genotypes in a germplasm collection.

We use the term *accession* to refer to any sample in the whole collection, and *entry* to refer to any accession selected for inclusion in the core [3].

Methodologically, efforts to create germplasm core collections commonly use complex but primitive tools based on statistical and clustering methods [2, 28, 29].

In the development of a core collection, we look for minimizing the overall cost of conservation while maximizing the genetic diversity. This problem can be mapped to the systematic conservation planning (SCP), a widely accepted biodiversity-focused approach to determine the most cost effective way of investing in conservation actions. In short, SCP is the problem of finding a minimum set of elements (in this case, entries for the core collection) with the maximal representation of some feature (here the genetic diversity) [19]. Evidently, there are at least two conflicting objectives, which makes the problem a perfect candidate for multi-objective optimization (MOO). SCP can be modeled by the well known NP-hard minimum set covering problem [6].

SCP has been generally applied at species level (or hierarchically higher), but has also been used in conservation genetics, aiming to maximize molecular variation within populations [12]. In this study, this is attained by using molecular markers. The use of molecular markers to achieve the representativeness of a core collection is important chiefly because population persistence and resilience to environmental changes are consistently correlated with genetic diversity.

Previously, our group successfully applied MOO to a problem of *in situ* conservation (i.e., preserving plant species in their natural habitat) [24]. At that time, the well known NSGA-II [11] was employed.

Here we propose a more sophisticated MOO approach using a constraint-handling multi-objective algorithm inspired by the immune system (i.e., an artificial immune system – AIS) and based on individual molecular variability aiming to guide sampling to find germplasm core collections. We represented the known alleles, but incorporated individual *heterozygosity* information[1]. Thus, optimization also takes genotypic diversity and variability patterns into account. By including these characteristics, accessions can better represent the genetic diversity, allowing to identify sets with a higher probability of persistence throughout time.

As far as we know, this is the first time that an AIS multi-objective algorithm is applied to a SCP problem, in particular to the problem of finding a germplasm core collection using heterozygosity information as well.

The remainder of the paper is structured as follows. Section 2 describes the material and methods adopted in this study, in special, briefly presents the used constrained multi-objective AIS algorithm. In Section 3, we discuss the results obtained so far. Conclusions and future work are presented in Section 4.

[1]Heterozygosity is the state of being heterozygous, i.e., having two different alleles of the same gene; it is positively correlated with genetic variation and evolutionary potential.

2. MATERIAL AND METHODS

2.1 Data

As a case study for our method, we used a *Dipteryx alata* data set composed of 642 individual trees sampled in 25 local populations throughout *D. alata*'s geographic range (Fig. 1) (see [26] for sampling methodological details). This data set will be hereafter referred as our germplasm collection, and each sample as an accession.

The *D. alata* samples were genotyped for nine microsatellite *loci*, finding a total of 55 distinct alleles. These microsatellites (also known as simple sequence repeats – SSRs) are our molecular markers.

Figure 1: Samples of *Dipteryx alata*, also known as baru, a widely distributed tree species in Cerrado biome, Central Brazil. It is used as lumber, for charcoal production, shade in pasture, and it is source of raw material for handcraft, cosmetics, and food industries, playing an important role in local economy [7]. Most of the *D. alata* diversity is found only in nature, and many such populations are increasingly threatened by habitat reduction. Additionally, individual trees are often geographically wide ranging, making it costly to collect representative samples.

Based on these data, we produced an allele-by-accession presence-absence matrix $A_{k \times m}$, where $k = 642$ (accessions corresponding to the sampled individual trees) and $m = 55$ (alleles), a_{ij} represents the occurrence of allele j in accession i. In this matrix, alleles in homozygosity received value 1, and alleles in heterozygosity, value 2; by doing this, we benefited solutions with higher content of heterozygosity.

2.2 Problem Formalization

The overall problem is to maximize the number of alleles while minimizing the number of entries required to represent these alleles, maximizing, at the same time, the heterozygosity.

A candidate solution for the problem is a vector $\overrightarrow{x} = \{x_1, ..., x_k\}$, where k is the number of accessions (sampled individual trees), $x_i \in \{0, 1\}$, such that $x_i = 1$, if the accession i is selected to compose the solution; or 0, otherwise. Each site i have a cost c_i, and each feature j a desired representation level r_j. The aim is to obtain:

$$min \left(\sum_{i=1}^{k} c_i x_i \right) \tag{1}$$

Subject to:

$$\forall j \in \{1, 2, ..., m\}, \sum_{i=1}^{k} a_{ij} x_i \geq r_j \tag{2}$$

Where m = total number of alleles (i.e., m = 55), and $r_j = 1$.

As fitness functions, we have as many representations of Eq. 1 as objectives to be optimized, varying c_i according to the objective under consideration. This allowed us to simultaneously optimize distinct objectives instead of aggregating them into one single function. So, regarding the MOO approach, we optimized three objectives:

1. Minimize the number of selected accessions (i.e., the number of entries for the core);

$$min(f_1(\overrightarrow{x})) = min(selected\_accessions(\overrightarrow{x})) \tag{3}$$

2. Maximize the representation of alleles;

$$\begin{aligned} max(f_2'(\overrightarrow{x})) &= max(alleles(\overrightarrow{x})) \Leftrightarrow \\ min(f_2(\overrightarrow{x})) &= min(lacking\_alleles(\overrightarrow{x})) \\ &= min(m - alleles(\overrightarrow{x})) \end{aligned} \tag{4}$$

3. Maximize the heterozygosity.

$$\begin{aligned} max(f_3'(\overrightarrow{x})) &= max(heterozygosity(\overrightarrow{x})) \Leftrightarrow \\ min(f_3(\overrightarrow{x})) &= min(-heterozygosity(\overrightarrow{x})) \end{aligned} \tag{5}$$

We worked with minimization, henceforth, based on the duality principle, w.l.o.g., we converted all objectives to their equivalent minimization representation (e.g., for Eq. 4, optimization consisted in minimizing the number of lacking alleles, which is the same as maximizing the number of alleles).

According to the literature, the core chosen to represent as much as possible of the collection diversity is composed of about 10% of the total collection [3]. Hence, we defined $\approx$ 10% of lacking alleles, and $\approx$ 15% from the number of accessions as constraints to delimit our objective space. Corroborated this decision, the experts (biologists) information that solutions with more than 5 lacking alleles and 107 entries would not be acceptable in practice. As a result, constraints were defined as penalties based on the objective functions as follow:

$$c_1(\overrightarrow{x}) = \begin{cases} f_1(\overrightarrow{x}) - 107, & \text{if } f_1(\overrightarrow{x}) > 107; \\ 0, & \text{otherwise.} \end{cases} \tag{6}$$

$$c_2(\overrightarrow{x}) = \begin{cases} f_2(\overrightarrow{x}) - 5, & \text{if } f_2(\overrightarrow{x}) > 5; \\ 0, & \text{otherwise.} \end{cases} \tag{7}$$

In this context, a solution that violates any constraint is said to be *infeasible*, otherwise, it is *feasible*.

Henceforth, we used the concept of *constrained-dominance* [11], where a solution i is said to constrained-dominate a solution j ($i \preceq_{cd} j$) if any of the following conditions is true:

1. Solution i is feasible and solution j is not;
2. Solution i and j are both infeasible, but solution i has smaller overall constraint violation;
3. Solutions i and j are feasible and solution i dominates solution j.

2.3 MAIS: the Constrained Multi-Objective AIS Algorithm

The constrained multi-objective AIS algorithm (MAIS), proposed here, is based on the clonal selection principle [4, 10] and consider two entities: *antigens (Ag)* and *antibodies (Ab)*. The input is the antigen-problem, and the output is composed of antibodies-solutions that recognize-solve Ag.

Algorithm 1 MAIS

```
1: P ← generateNewAb()
2: Pm ← ∅
3: while not(stopCondition()) do
4:     evaluate(P)
5:     Psel ← select(P)
6:     Pm ← updateMemory(Pm, Psel)
7:     Pc ← clone(Psel)
8:     Phyp ← hypermutate(Pc)
9:     Pmut ← mutate(P \ Psel)
10:    P ← P ∪ Phyp ∪ Pmut
11:    if (#OfGenerations mod X) = 0 then
12:        Pnew ← generateNewAb()
13:        P ← P ∪ Pnew
14:    end if
15:    return2OriginalSize(P)
16: end while
17: Pm ← updateMemory(Pm, P)
18: return Pm
```

We used a secondary population (memory – Pm), which keeps the best Ab's found (the *known Pareto front* – PF_{known}), and an *adaptive grid* (see [18]), to maintain the spread of solutions in the memory.

MAIS steps are as follow (Algorithm 1): randomly generate an initial population (P) (line 1) – at this moment, the memory (Pm) is empty (line 2). Evaluate P based on constrained-dominance (line 4). At the end of this step, P is sorted according to the following hierarchy of solutions:

1. Feasible non-dominated;
2. Feasible dominated;
3. Infeasible non-dominated;
4. Infeasible dominated.

Dominated solutions are sorted in ascending order, according to the number of solutions that dominates them. Infeasible solutions are sorted in ascending order as well, but according to the amount of constraint violations. Select the best Ab's (i.e., all feasible non-dominated Ab; if the number of feasible non-dominated individuals is less than 10% of the population size, then select Ab's following the constrained-dominance hierarchy until reaching a number of individuals equal to the 10% of the population size) to be cloned (line 5). Copy the best Ab's obtained in the previous step into Pm (line 6). Entrance into memory is regulated using the adaptive grid. For each Ab selected in line 5, the constrained-dominance is verified against those that are already in memory:

1. If the selected Ab is dominated by any Ab already present in the memory, the new Ab is discarded;
2. All the Ab's belonging to the memory that are dominated by the new Ab are removed. Then, the possibility of the new Ab composing the memory is verified:
   (a) If the memory is not full, the Ab is allowed to enter;
   (b) Otherwise, if the new Ab belongs to the most populated region, it is not allowed to enter;

(c) Otherwise, it enters the memory, but an individual from the most populated cell is removed leaving space for the new Ab (the memory size is maintained).

For Ab's selected in line 5, clone them proportionally to their distance to the k-nearest neighbor, obtaining Pc (line 7). Hypermutate Pc inversely proportional to the hierarchy defined by constrained-dominance – feasible non-dominated Ab's suffer less mutation than hierarchically worse solutions, e.g., infeasible dominated ones (line 8). In line 9, a uniform mutation is applied to Ab's that were not selected in line 5 (we empirically verified that this step improved the overall final solution). At each set of X generations (here, $X = 25$), a number of new Ab's is generated and added to the main population (as a way of generating diversity, explore the objective space, and rescue the search from local maxima) (lines 10-14). Return the population P to its original size (select as many individuals as the original population size using the criterion of hierarchies taken by the constrained-dominance) (line 15). Repeat the process from line 3 until a stop criterion is achieved (here, number of evaluation = $500,000$). At the end of execution, return Pm, the set of the best Ab's found.

2.4 Experiments

The objective of this study is two fold: (1) to present a new approach to deal with the problem of finding a core to a germplasm collection; and (2) to assess the performance of MAIS by comparing it to a state-of-the-art MOO algorithm (e.g., NSGA-II).

We addressed the problem of defining a core collection by identifying, within our germplasm collection, the minimal set of accessions needed to represent all the genetic variability exhibited by the germplasm collection; therefore, we considered the heterozygosity. Our aim was to find out if the proposed MOO approach is viable, and also if the optimization of heterozygosity as an additional objective would result in some advantage when selecting accessions to compose the core, hence, improving the overall quality of results. We optimized the three objectives stated in Eqs. 3 to 5, subject to constraints expressed in Eqs. 6 and 7.

2.5 Experimental Setup

Algorithms. We used MAIS, and, as baseline, NSGA-II in its constrained version [11]. For each run, a population of initial solutions was randomly generated. These solutions were then evolved using MAIS and NSGA-II. Both algorithms were implemented in Matlab®.

Aleatory Uncertainties. To determine the number of runs required to mitigate aleatory uncertainty inherent to the stochastic algorithms, we used Spartan (Simulation Parameter Analysis R Toolkit Application) [1]. Following Spartan protocol, we analyzed 20 subsets sample sizes of 1, 5, 10, 50, 100, and 300 runs each, requiring, therefore, 9,320 individual runs (for each algorithm, MAIS and NSGA-II). For both algorithms, it was found that 300 runs were sufficient to reduce the effect magnitude of aleatory uncertainty on results to less than "small" (the desired level) (Fig. 2).

Parameter Settings. Before running the experiments, we used a sample set to estimate, empirically, the most suitable parameter values, which for MAIS were set to: pop.[2] size = 500; secondary pop. size = 500; clone rate = proportionally to k-nearest neighbor; hypermutation rate = inversely proportional to the hierarchy of constrained-dominance; uniform mutation = 1/L (where L is the number of accessions); number of new Ab's created at each 25 generations=20% of pop. size. NSGA-II parameter values were set to: pop. size = 500; crossover probability = 0.90; mutation probability = 0.5; mutation rate = 1/L. Besides, we used: crossover operator = single point crossover (SPX); selection by binary tournament.

[2]population.

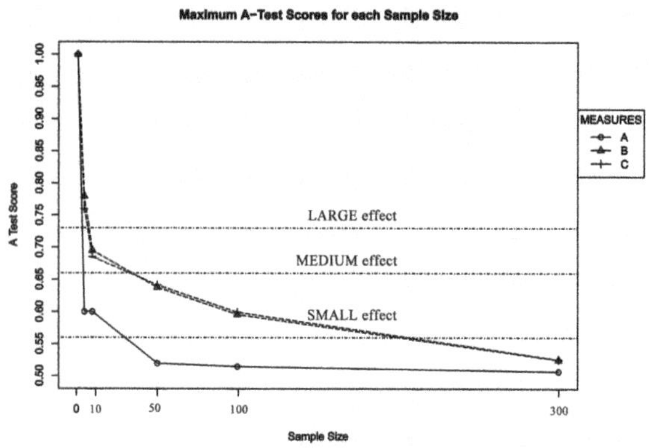

Figure 2: Spartan's Technique 1 applied to MAIS. This technique identifies which simulation results can be attributed to the dynamics of the modeled system, rather than artifacts of uncertainty or parametrization, or simulation stochasticity. At 300 runs, stochasticity over objectives A (lacking alleles), B (number of selected accessions), and C (heterozygosity) attains a small effect. Due to space limitation we present only MAIS results, but NSGA-II results were similar.

To grant an adequate comparison, we adopted the criteria suggested by Coello et al [5]: all algorithms executed the same number of fitness evaluations (500,000) ensuring a very nearly equivalent computational effort; pop. sizes and parameter values (whenever it was possible) were the same as well.

Computer Infrastructure The experiments were performed on a computer cluster consisting of 49 computers equipped with Intel(R) Core(TM) i5-2500 CPU 3.30GHz, 8GB RAM; and 9 computers with Intel(R) Core(TM) Duo CPU E7500 2.93GHz, 2GB RAM.

2.6 Performance Measures (Metrics)

According to Zitzler et al. [30], an optimization should:

1. Minimize the distance of the non-dominated set to the Pareto-optimal front;
2. Obtain a good spread of solutions;
3. Maximize the extent of the obtained non-dominated front (i.e., for each objective, a wide range of values should be covered by the non-dominated solutions).

In this study, these targets were assessed by the following performance measures:

Function C [30]. Let $\vec{x}'$ and $\vec{x}''$ be two sets of decision vectors. The function C maps the ordered pair ($\vec{x}'$, $\vec{x}''$) to the interval [0,1]:

$$C(\vec{x}', \vec{x}'') = \frac{|\{x' \in \vec{x}'; \exists x'' \in \vec{x}'' : x' \preceq_{cd} x''\}|}{|\vec{x}''|} \quad (8)$$

Using the function C, it can be seen if the outcomes of an algorithm dominate the outcomes of the other (i.e., a pair of non-dominated sets is compared by calculating the fraction of each set that is covered by the other). $C(\overrightarrow{x}', \overrightarrow{x}'') = 1$ implies that all solutions in $\overrightarrow{x}''$ are constrained-dominated by solutions in $\overrightarrow{x}'$, while $C(\overrightarrow{x}', \overrightarrow{x}'') = 0$, indicate that none of the solutions in $\overrightarrow{x}''$ is covered by the set $\overrightarrow{x}'$. Both $C(\overrightarrow{x}', \overrightarrow{x}'')$ and $C(\overrightarrow{x}'', \overrightarrow{x}')$ should be considered, since $C(\overrightarrow{x}', \overrightarrow{x}'')$ is not necessarily equal to $1 - C(\overrightarrow{x}'', \overrightarrow{x}')$.

Empirical attainment function (*EAF*) [5, 8]. EAF is a quality indicator used for stochastic algorithmic evaluation. It is computed from the combined collection of approximation sets. Let $b_1(z)...b_n(z)$ be n runs of the optimizer, then the EAF is defined as $EAF : \mathbb{R}^d \longmapsto [0, 1]$ with

$$EAF = \frac{1}{n}\sum_{i=1}^{n} b_i(z) \tag{9}$$

It offers a useful description of the solution distribution location. Differences in the frequency with which certain goals are met by the respective algorithms are represented graphically. The intensity of the shading corresponds to the frequency of the solution.

Hypervolume (*H*) [18]. For the set X of non-dominated vectors $\overrightarrow{x_i}$, and a reference vector $\overrightarrow{x}^{ref}$, which is dominated by all members of X and whose components are the maximum value on each objective (i.e., $\overrightarrow{x}^{ref} = \{max(f_1(\overrightarrow{x})), max(f_2(\overrightarrow{x})), max(f_3(\overrightarrow{x}))\} = \{642, 55, 0\}$), the *hypervolume* is the summation of all rectangular areas bounded by X and $\overrightarrow{x}^{ref}$ according to:

$$H(X, \overrightarrow{x}^{ref}) \triangleq \bigcup_{i \in 1..|X|} H(\overrightarrow{x_i}, \overrightarrow{x}^{ref}) \tag{10}$$

Higher values of H correspond to better solutions.

Spacing S [25]. This metric is used to numerically assess the spread of vectors in PF_{known}. It measures the distance variance between each solution and its nearest neighbor according to:

$$S = \sqrt{\frac{1}{n-1}\sum_{i=1}^{n}(\bar{d} - d_i)^2} \tag{11}$$

Where $d_i = min_j ||f(\overrightarrow{i}) - f(\overrightarrow{j})||$, i.e., the norm/distance to the nearest neighbor of i; $i, j = 1, ..., n$; $\bar{d}$ is the mean of all d_i; f is an objective function (Eqs. 3 to 5); n is the number of vectors in PF_{known}. If $S = 0$, the algorithm has found the ideal distribution of non-dominated vectors (all vectors are uniformly spaced).

Extent E [30]. Let X be a set of objective vectors. E uses the maximum extent of decision vectors $\overrightarrow{a}, \overrightarrow{b} \in X$ in each dimension m to estimate the range to which the front spreads out:

$$E = \sqrt{\sum_{i=1}^{m} max||a_i - b_i||} \tag{12}$$

Where $||\cdot||$ is the norm/distance between two points. Concerning the value of E, the bigger the better.

Function C, EAF, and H metrics assess optimization target 1; S metric, target 2; and E metric, target 3.

3. RESULTS AND DISCUSSION

3.1 MAIS to find a Core Collection

The objective of the optimization was to select the smallest set of sites capable of representing the most amount of alleles (preferably all alleles), but at the same time optimizing heterozygosity, an additional objective.

We found that from the 642 accessions composing our germplasm collection, it is possible to preserve the allele diversity (55 alleles) by keeping a core of 16 selected accessions (only 2,5% of the germplasm collection). Even if the aim is to obtain a minimum set, our method identifies a portfolio of solutions, indicating sets with individuals that fulfill the objectives, providing decision-makers with additional alternatives for achieving their conservation targets. It is worth noting that there is no hierarchy among results, i.e., all of the solutions are equally good in the considered context and in the absence of additional preferences. As mentioned before, there is a flexibility on the core size, that is generally composed of about 10% of the total collection. The proposed method is important to define strategies to provide a set of genetically diverse material while selecting the most representative accessions. By maximizing genetic diversity in germplasm collections (throughout maximization of heterozygosity), resources available for conservation of biodiversity can be allocated more efficiently.

The output of 6,000 individual runs were unified[3], and we calculated the frequency for each accession in the union set. This frequency indicates the relative importance of an accession in order to fulfill the optimization objectives. This frequency can be taken as an estimator for accession *irreplaceability*[4] [21], e.g., the rarest alleles (there are three) appear in only one accession each, if one of them is not selected, the conservation goal of representing all the alleles is not achieved. These accessions are #145, #474, and #477, not surprisingly, they are among the most frequently selected in solutions. The used approach also privileged accessions with greater diversity of alleles, e.g., accessions #99 and #441, both with 16 different alleles[5] and 17 other accessions, with 15 different alleles each (Fig. 3).

We verified that there was a significant improvement in the retention of alleles in the selected accessions, suggesting that this approach is adequate to define a core collection.

The proposed approach is straightforward. Once the matrix based on the molecular markers is generated, there is no need of expertise to proceed the selection of accessions. Furthermore, it is simpler than the statistical and clustering methods, traditionally used.

The use of constraints allowed us to concentrate the exploration of the objective space in a more rational and efficient way, privileging feasible solutions over non-dominated ones, since the former are more valuable to decision-makers.

[3]since we already had 20 folders of 300 individual runs ($20 \times 300 = 6,000$) as a result of Spartan analysis, we used these data.

[4]a measure that indicates the proportion that an accession contributes to the overall solution, e.g., accessions with irreplaceability converging to 1 tend to be irreplaceable, i.e., if they are lost, the conservation goal may not be accomplished.

[5]*D. alata* germplasm collection was genotyped for 9 *loci*, since it is an diploid species, each accession has $9 \times 2 = 18$ possibly distinct alleles.

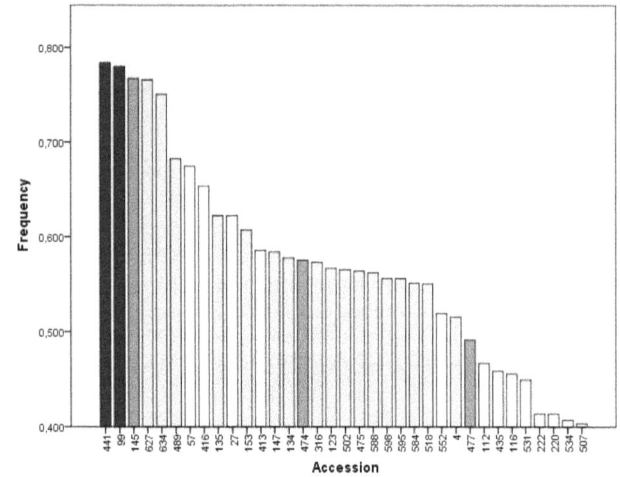

Figure 3: Solutions' accession frequency. Frequency scales from 0 to 1. Only accessions with frequency higher than 0.4 were plotted. It is possible to identify accessions: (1) with greater diversity (with 16 different alleles, in dark gray – #99 and #441 –, and with 15 different alleles, in light gray); (2) with the rarest alleles (in medium gray – #145, #474, and #477).

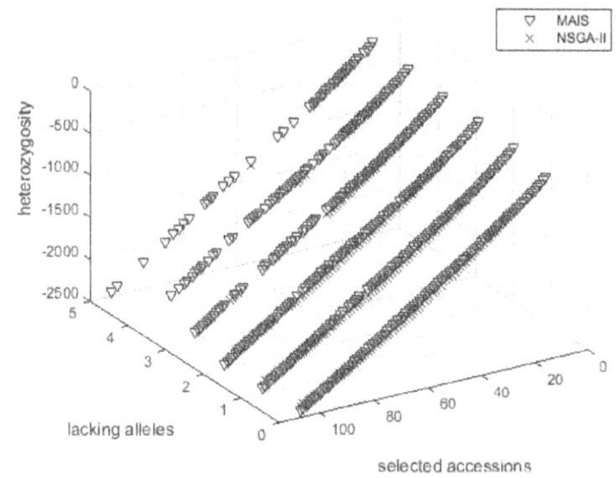

Figure 4: Non-dominate fronts achieved by MAIS and NSGA-II.

To the biologists, one of the most important contributions of this work is to identify, in the context of SCP, within a population of several individuals, the exact samples that should be chosen in order to preserve the species diversity.

This approach can be extended to the *in situ* conservation (selection of individual species to be preserved in their own habitat). Previous approaches [12] generally indicate a population to be preserved; the proposed method indicates exactly which individuals within the population should be sampled/kept. Indeed, this approach may be extended to any problem that can be mapped into the minimum set covering problem.

In Eq. 2, experts defined $r_j = 1$, $j \in \{1, ..., 55\}$, i.e., all of the alleles should be represented at least once. Nevertheless, it could be settled a different desired representation level $r_j \geq n > 1$, where n is the minimum number of times an allele should be present in solution. By doing so, allele representation in the core collection is heightened, benefiting persistence throughout time.

3.2 Comparison between MAIS and NSGA-II

To assess the performance of MAIS we compared it to NSGA-II. Firstly, per algorithm, the outcome of the 6,000 runs were unified, and then the dominated solutions were removed from the union set [30]. The remaining points were plotted (Fig. 4). It can be seen that MAIS is more effective in exploring the objective space, has better extent, was able to find smaller core collections, and has a better spread of solutions.

Additionally to the graphical presentation, the algorithms were assessed by using the performance measures defined in Subsection 2.6.

We calculated the function C using the previously described non-dominated front as input. We found *C(MAIS, NSGA-II)= 0.515217* and *C(NSGA-II,MAIS) = 0.5032*, meaning that, although slightly, solutions found by MAIS covered NSGA-II, i.e., there were more MAIS solutions that constrained-dominated NSGA-II solutions than the opposite. This support the hypothesis that MAIS was able to find a better approximation to the true Pareto front (PF_{true}) – even though in this real-world problem PF_{true} is unknown.

The remaining metrics were computed for 6,000 independent runs of each algorithm[6].

By analyzing the EAF surfaces (Fig. 5), it can be seen that MAIS was able to obtain smaller core collections, and closer to the origin axis (i.e., likely closer to PF_{true}). Furthermore, MAIS has solutions more regular and smoothly distributed on the objective space delimited by the constraints, being able to better explore it.

Table 1 shows H, S, and E values for MAIS and NSGA-II.

In all individual runs of MAIS, H values where higher than the ones found for NSGA-II. The graphical analyses of Fig. 4 and EAF surfaces (Fig. 5), associated with the values for function C and H metric (Table 1 and Fig. 6a) corroborates the assumption that MAIS was able to find solutions closer to the PF_{true}.

Moreover, MAIS was able to find core collections more regularly spread throughout the PF_{known}, as can be seen in the S metric (Table 1 and Fig. 6b).

The E metric (Table 1 and Fig. 6c) shows that MAIS was more effective in extent the non-dominated front, exploring a wider range of the objective space.

Given these points, it can be said that in the problem of finding a core collection, MAIS presented better performance measure results when compared to NSGA-II, being able to find smaller and better distributed core collections, and to explore a larger extent of the objective space.

4. CONCLUSIONS AND FUTURE WORK

The problem of finding a core for a germplasm collection is NP-hard, nevertheless, decision-makers still need a solution for it. This is a relevant problem in ecology with real impact on resources availability (whether financial or genetic), and on biodiversity conservation. This work is inserted in the context of the emerging field of ecoinformatics.

As far as we know, this paper is pioneer in showing how principles of SCP and the use of a constrained multi-objective AIS algorithm (MAIS) associated to molecular marker information can be applied to successfully help construct core col-

[6]the same observation made at footnote 3 applies here.

Table 1: Performance measures for MAIS and NSGA-II calculated for 6,000 independent runs. Best results are indicated in bold.

	Hypervolume (H)		Spacing (S)		Extent (E)	
	MAIS	NSGA-II	MAIS	NSGA-II	MAIS	NSGA-II
Mean	$\mathbf{7.75}\times10^7$	7.12×10^7	**2.1996**	2.2498	**46.966**	36.834
(Std.dev.)	($\mathbf{0.35}\times10^4$)	(1.64×10^4)	(**0.0029**)	(0.0079)	(**0.399**)	1.624
Best	$\mathbf{7.88}\times10^7$	7.55×10^7	1.4430	**0.9904**	**48,166**	42,273
Worst	$\mathbf{7.58}\times10^7$	6.35×10^7	**3.0489**	6.2388	**44.944**	30.364

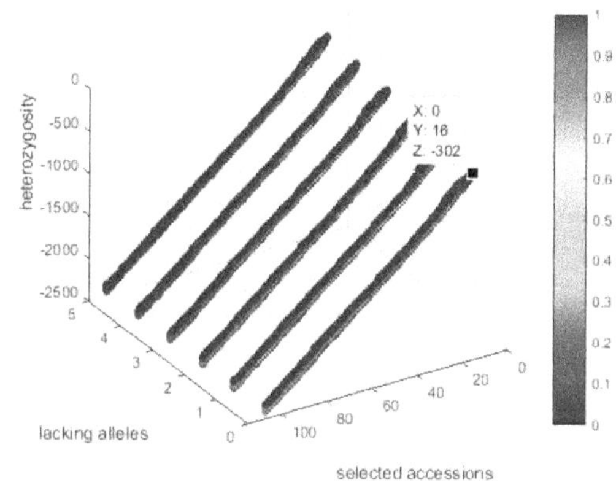

(a) MAIS

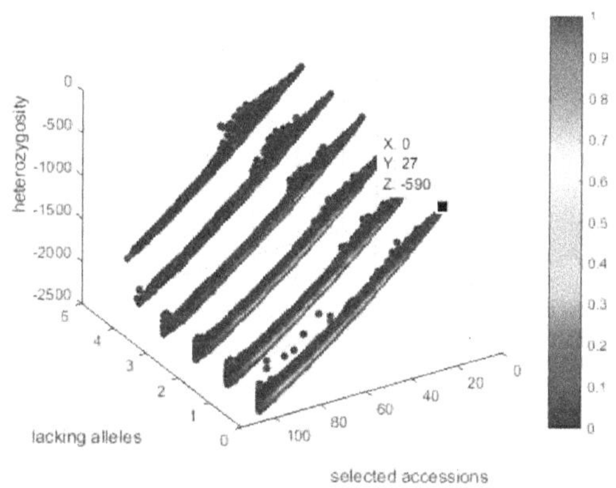

(b) NSGA-II

Figure 5: EAF surfaces showing the probabilities of attaining goals with (a) MAIS, and (b) NSGA-II. Results obtained after 6,000 independent runs. MAIS was able to find not only smaller cores when compared to NSGA-II, but also more regular and smoothly distributed solutions on the constrained objective space. X = lacking alleles; Y = selected accessions; Z = heterozygosity.

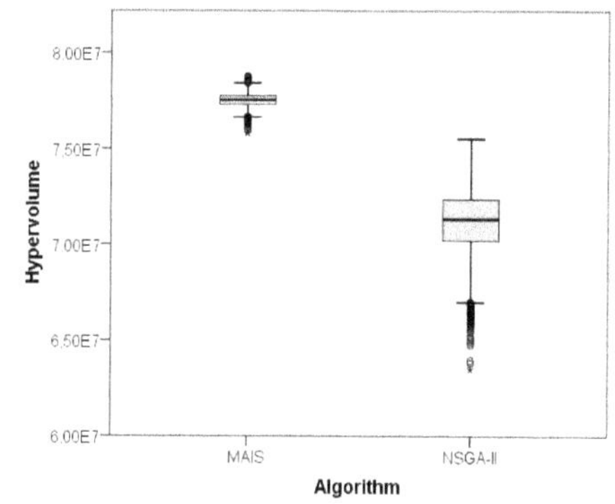

(a) Hypervolume (higher values are better)

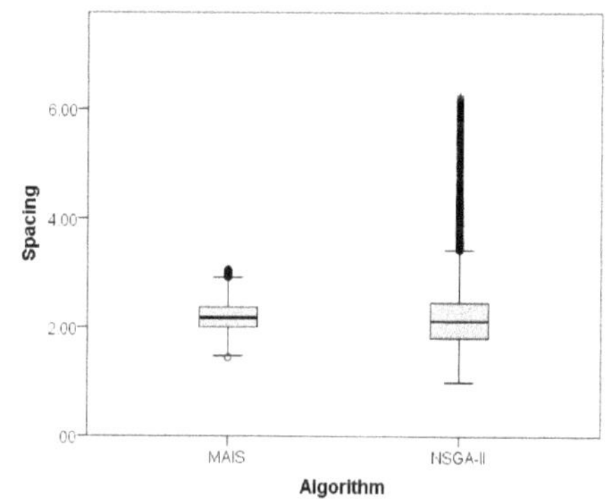

(b) Spacing (lower values are better)

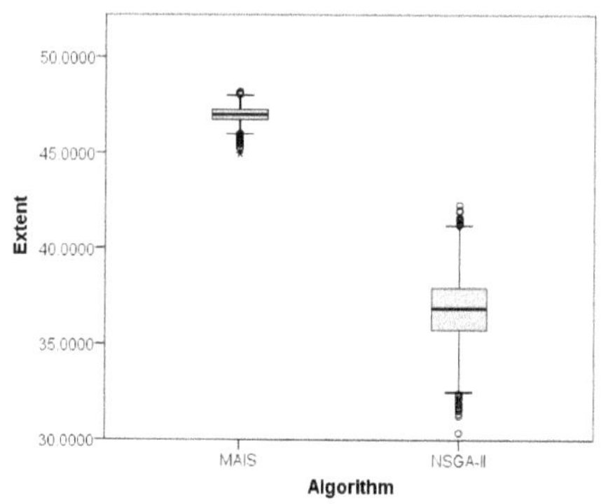

(c) Extent (higher values are better)

Figure 6: Boxplot of performance measures for MAIS and NSGA-II: (a) Hypervolume (H), (b) Spacing (S), and (c) Extent (E).

lections with maximum allelic richness and minimum number of accessions.

We performed comparisons of MAIS with NSGA-II and found that MAIS surpassed NSGA-II in all tested performance measures, being able to find better solutions, i.e., closer to PF_{true}, more evenly spread and exploring a larger extent of the objective space.

Moreover, using the proposed approach, it is possible to include additional optimization objectives to the problem, e.g., the distance from the germplasm collection facility to *in situ* individual trees; thus, reducing displacement costs associated with collection of samples for complementing the germplasm collection.

Having established that the proposed approach is viable, a future work is to apply it to other kinds of molecular markers (e.g., single nucleotide polymorphism – SNP, and diversity arrays technology – DArT) in order to verify its feasibility for this kind of data.

We did not use domain information in MAIS, so there is still room for improvement. MAIS uses standard operators for hypermutation and cloning. Our future work will focus on the use of more complex operators (e.g., contiguous hypermutation, aging), which have shown interesting results in the literature [17, 23].

5. ACKNOWLEDGMENTS

SS wishes to thank the University of York and Prof. Jon Timmis for the PhD stay, and the support from CNPq throughout a Science without Borders scholarship. GENPAC has been supported by CNPq/MCT/CAPES. Work by MEMTW, ACPLFC, MPCT, RDL and JAFDF have been continuously supported by productivity fellowships from CNPq. Jon Timmis is part funded by The Royal Society and The Royal Academy of Engineering.

6. REFERENCES

[1] K. Alden et al. Spartan: A Comprehensive Tool for Understanding Uncertainty in Simulations of Biological Systems. *PLoS Comput Biol*, 9(2):e1002916+, Feb. 2013.

[2] A. Belaj et al. Developing a Core Collection of Olive (Olea europaea L.) Based on Molecular Markers (DArTs, SSRs, SNPs) and Agronomic Traits. *Tree Genet Genomes*, 8(2):365–378, Apr. 2012.

[3] A. Brown. Core Collections: a Practical Approach to Genetic Resources Management. *Genome*, 31(2):818–824, 1989.

[4] C. A. Coello Coello and N. C. Cortés. Solving Multiobjective Optimization Problems Using an Artificial Immune System. *Genet Program Evol M*, 6(2):163–190, 2005.

[5] C. A. Coello Coello, G. B. Lamont, and D. A. Van Veldhuizen. *Evolutionary Algorithms for Solving Multi-Objective Problems*. Springer-Verlag, New York, second edition, Sept. 2007. ISBN 978-0-387-33254-3.

[6] T. H. Cormen et al. *Introduction to Algorithms*. The MIT Press, 2 edition, 2001.

[7] G. C. Correa et al. Physical Determinations in Fruit and Seeds of Baru (*Dipteryx alata* Vog.), Cajuzinho (*Anacardium othonianum* Rizz.) and Pequi (*Caryocar brasiliense* Camb.), Aiming Genetic Breeding. *Biosci J*, 24(4):42–47, 2008.

[8] V. G. da Fonseca et al. Inferential Performance Assessment of Stochastic Optimisers and the Attainment Function. In E. Zitzler et al., editors, *EMO'2001*, volume 1993 of *Lect Notes Comput Sc*, pages 213–225. Springer-Verlag, 2001.

[9] I. Dawson and J. Were. Collecting Germplasm from Trees – Some Guidelines. *Agroforestry Today*, 9(2):6–9, 1997.

[10] L. N. de Castro and J. Timmis. *Artificial Immune Systems: A New Computational Intelligence Approach*. Springer-Verlag New York, Inc., NJ, USA, 2002.

[11] K. Deb et al. A Fast Elitist Non-Dominated Sorting Genetic Algorithm for Multi-Objective Optimization: NSGA-II. In *Proceedings of the PPSN'2000*, pages 849–858, London, UK, UK, 2000. Springer-Verlag.

[12] J. A. F. Diniz-Filho et al. Planning for Optimal Conservation Geographical Genetic Variability within Species. *Conserv Genet*, 13:1085–1093, 2012.

[13] J. Engels, L. Visser, and International Plant Genetic Resources Institute. *A Guide to Effective Management of Germplasm Collections*. IPGRI Handbooks for Genebanks. International Plant Genetic Resources Institute, 2003.

[14] O. H. Frankel. *Genetic Manipulation: Impact on Man and Society*, chapter Genetic perspectives of germplasm conservation, pages 161–170. Cambridge University Press, 1984.

[15] A. Gupta et al. Cost of Conservation of Agrobiodiversity. Technical Report WP2002-05-03, Indian Institute of Management Ahmedabad, Research and Publication Department, 2002.

[16] J. Helly et al. Technical report, National Center for Ecological Analysis and Synthesis, Santa Barbara, California, 1995. Available at http://www.nceas.ucsb.edu/papers/compecol/compecol.pdf.

[17] T. Jansen and C. Zarges. Analyzing Different Variants of Immune Inspired Somatic Contiguous Hypermutations. *Theor Comput Sci*, 412:517–533, 2011.

[18] J. D. Knowles and D. W. Corne. Properties of an Adaptive Archiving Algorithm for Storing Nondominated Vectors. *IEEE T Evolut Comput*, 7(2):100–116, 2003.

[19] C. R. Margules and R. L. Pressey. Systematic Conservation Planning. *Nature*, 405(6783):243–253, 2000.

[20] D. P. McCarthy et al. Financial Costs of Meeting Global Biodiversity Conservation Targets: Current Spending and Unmet Needs. *Science*, 338(6109):946–949, Nov. 2012.

[21] E. Meir, S. Andelman, and H. P. Possingham. Does Conservation Planning Matter in a Dynamic and Uncertain World? *Ecol Lett*, 7(8):615–622, 2004.

[22] W. K. Michener et al. Ecological informatics: A long-term Ecological Research Perspective. *Japanese Journal of Ecology (Otsu)*, 51(3):291–303, 2001.

[23] P. S. Oliveto and D. Sudholt. On the Runtime Analysis of Stochastic Ageing Mechanisms. In *Proceedings of the 2014 Conference on Genetic and Evolutionary Computation*, GECCO '14, pages 113–120, New York, NY, USA, 2014. ACM.

[24] S. Schlottfeldt et al. A Multi-Objective Optimization Approach Associated to Climate Change Analysis to Improve Systematic Conservation Planning. In A. Gaspar-Cunha et al., editors, *EMO'2015*, volume 9019 of *Lect Notes Compt Sc*, pages 458–472. Springer International Publishing, 2015.

[25] J. R. Schott. Fault Tolerant Design Using Single and Multicriteria Genetic Algorithm Optimization. Master's thesis, Department of Aeronautics and Astronautics, Massachusetts Institute of Technology, Cambridge, Massachusetts, May 1995.

[26] T. N. Soares et al. Development of Microsatellite Markers for the Neotropical Tree Species *Dipteryx alata* (Fabaceae). *Am J Bot*, 99:e72–e73, 2012.

[27] A. Waldron et al. Targeting global conservation funding to limit immediate biodiversity declines. *Proceedings of the National Academy of Sciences*, 110(29):12144–12148, 2013.

[28] Y. Wang et al. Construction and Evaluation of a Primary Core Collection of Apricot Germplasm in China. *Sci Hort*, 128:311–319, 2011.

[29] P. Zhang et al. Population Structure and Genetic Diversity in a Rice Core Collection (*Oryza sativa* L.) Investigated with SSR Markers. *PLoS One*, 6(12):e27565+, Dec. 2011.

[30] E. Zitzler, K. Deb, and L. Thiele. Comparison of Multiobjective Evolutionary Algorithms: Empirical Results. *Evol Comput*, 8(2):173–195, 2000.

Genetic Programming for Estimation of Heat Flux between the Atmosphere and Sea Ice in Polar Regions

Karolina Stanislawska
Finnish Meteorological Institute
00560 Helsinki, Finland
karolina.stanislawska@fmi.fi

Krzysztof Krawiec
Poznan Univ. of Technology
60965 Poznań, Poland
krawiec@cs.put.poznan.pl

Timo Vihma
Finnish Meteorological Institute
00560 Helsinki, Finland
timo.vihma@fmi.fi

ABSTRACT

The Earth surface and atmosphere exchange heat via turbulent fluxes. An accurate description of the heat exchange is essential in modelling the weather and climate. In these models the heat fluxes are described applying the Monin-Obukhov similarity theory, where the flux depends on the air-surface temperature difference and wind speed. The theory makes idealized assumptions and the resulting estimates often have large errors. This is the case particularly in conditions when the air is warmer than the Earth surface, i.e., the atmospheric boundary layer is stably stratified, and turbulence is therefore weak. This is a common situation over snow and ice in the Arctic and Antarctic. In this paper, we present alternative models for heat flux estimation evolved by means of genetic programming (GP). To this aim, we utilize the best heat flux data collected in the Arctic and Antarctic sea ice zones. We obtain GP models that are more accurate, robust, and conceptually novel from the viewpoint of meteorology. Contrary to the Monin-Obukhov theory, the GP equations are not solely based on the air-surface temperature difference and wind speed, but include also radiative fluxes that improve the performance of the method. These results open the door to a new class of approaches to heat flux prediction with potential applications in weather and climate models.

Categories and Subject Descriptors

I.2.6 [**Artificial Intelligence**]: Learning—*Induction*; I.6.3 [**Simulation and Modeling**]: Applications

Keywords

Modeling; genetic programming; symbolic regression; meteorology

GECCO '15, July 11 - 15, 2015, Madrid, Spain

ACM ISBN 978-1-4503-3472-3/15/07...$15.00

DOI: http://dx.doi.org/10.1145/2739480.2754675

1. INTRODUCTION

The net heat flux (NF) at the Earth surface is of critical importance for the energetic balance of our planet and consist of the following components:

$$NF = (1-\alpha)SWR_{\downarrow} + LWR + H + LE + C, \qquad (1)$$

where $SWR_{\downarrow}$ is the downward solar shortwave radiation, and α is the fraction of it that is reflected from the surface (called as the surface albedo). LWR is the difference of the downward thermal longwave radiation from the atmosphere ($LWR_{\downarrow}$) and the upward longwave radiation emitted by the Earth surface ($LWR_{\uparrow}$). H and LE are the turbulent fluxes of *sensible heat* and *latent heat*, respectively. The latent heat flux is the flux of water vapour, due to evaporation or condensation, multiplied by the latent heat of evaporation. The last term, C, is the heat flux to/from the layers below the Earth surface. All fluxes are defined positive towards the surface. $SWR_{\downarrow}$ depends above all on the solar zenith angle and clouds, and α mostly depends on the physical properties of the surface. The downward longwave radiation depends on the temperature and emissivity profiles of the atmosphere, clouds being the most important factor affecting the latter, and the longwave radiation emitted by the Earth surface depends on the surface temperature and emissivity. On solid surface types, C is due to heat conduction. The turbulent fluxes H and LE are driven by the surface-air differences in temperature and specific humidity, respectively.

As a global annual average, the heat budget of the Earth surface is closed so that the the main heat input is $SWR_{\downarrow}$, balanced by heat loss via LWR, H, and LE. C is typically a small term being positive during night/winter and negative during day/summer. During night or winter in polar regions, however, there is no solar radiation, and the main heat input to the Earth surface is via H and C, balanced by heat loss via LWR. The heat fluxes control the evolution of the Earth surface temperature: a positive NF results in warming and a negative one in cooling. The surface temperature is, however, not affected if the positive NF is entirely used to melt ice or snow, or a negative NF causes freezing of water surfaces. One of the most striking signals of the recent climate warming has been the extensive reduction of the Arctic sea ice [3] and Arctic and mid-latitude terrestrial snow cover [5]. The larger heat input from the atmosphere to snow and ice have had a dominating role in the snow and ice melt [6].

To successfully model the evolution of weather and climate, the terms in (1) need to be accurately described.

The problem is that the heat fluxes are generated by small-scale physical processes (radiation, turbulence, molecular heat conduction) but weather and climate models have to cover large geographical areas, and therefore have a coarse resolution. A typical horizontal grid spacing in numerical weather prediction (NWP) models, which form the basis of short-term weather forecasts, is of the order of 10 km and for climate models of the order of 100 km. The vertical grid spacing is smallest in the lowest layers of the atmosphere, so that the lowest atmospheric model level is typically 10-50 m above the Earth surface, which itself forms another level of the model. Hence, the heat fluxes need to be described as functions of the variables that are resolved by the model grid, i.e., via so-called *subgrid-scale parameterization*. The resolved variables include wind speed and direction, air temperature and humidity, as well as cloud water/ice content. Likewise, at the Earth surface, the model calculates the temperature and humidity.

Particularly in polar regions, the parameterization of all terms in (1) includes challenges [17]. In the case of radiative fluxes these are mostly related to cloud physics, and in the case of the conductive heat flux to the snow and ice properties. Handling the turbulent fluxes, H and LE, is most challenging when the air is warmer than the snow/ice surface, i.e. the lowermost atmosphere is statically stably stratified. Then the turbulent fluxes are small and liable to parameterization errors. As there are not many accurate observations available on the latent heat flux, in this paper we focus on the parameterization of sensible heat flux over Arctic and Antarctic sea ice. We review the main problems in conventionally applied parameterization methods (Section 2), discuss the factors that affect H and argue about the suitability of using genetic programing for flux modeling (Section 3), and describe two high-quality data sets that capture the dynamics of the sensible heat flux in the polar regions (Section 4). The original contributions of this study start with Section 5, where we present a novel approach to heat flux modeling based on genetic programming. Section 6 presents and discusses the evolved models, which we then compare to the conventional parameterization in Section 7, to conclude the paper with Section 8.

2. LIMITATIONS OF CONVENTIONAL MODELS OF FLUX PREDICTION

In climate and NWP models, the parameterization of the turbulent flux of sensible heat H is based on the classical Monin-Obukhov theory [11]. According to the theory, H depends on the vertical profile of potential temperature, the momentum flux, and a parameter describing the static stability. This yields a practical equation for H, the so-called *bulk formula*:

$$H = \rho c_p C_H(\theta_s - \theta_a)V, \tag{2}$$

where ρ is the air density, c_p is the specific heat, C_H is the turbulent heat exchange coefficient, θ_s is the surface potential temperature, θ_a is the air potential temperature, and V is the wind speed. The C_H is calculated on the basis of the stability parameter and two parameters characterizing the surface roughness from the point of view of turbulent mixing. The Monin-Obukhov theory includes, however, idealized assumptions: horizontal homogeneity, semi-stationarity, and that the turbulent flux is constant in the vertical from the Earth surface up to the lowest atmospheric model level. In conditions of stable stratification, when turbulence only exists in a shallow layer close to the Earth surface, the last assumption is highly idealized. Further, the effect of the static stability of C_H can only be determined experimentally, and in conditions of stable stratification there is a lot of scatter between various experimental formulae for C_H. Observations indicate that when the stratification is very stable, the magnitude of H may decrease although the air-surface potential temperature difference, $\theta_s - \theta_a$, increases [10]. This is due to the dominating effect of decreasing C_H, but the sensitive interaction is very difficult to reproduce in models.

We note that the results for H based on (2) depend on how the surface roughness effects and stability dependence of C_H are parameterized. In this study, we calculate H according to (2) using the roughness and stability parameterization as in the operational NWP model of the European Centre for Medium-Range Weather Forecasts (ECMWF)[1]. Hereafter, the ECMWF method of calculating H is referred as *conventional model.*

Hence, NWP and climate models typically have their largest errors in surface and near-surface air temperature under stable stratification in high latitudes. Even in short-term forecasts by NWP models the errors of estimation of 2-m air temperature may reach 10K [2]. In experiments involving six regional climate models for the Arctic sea ice zone, the observed and modelled H did not correlate [16]. In general, in conditions of stable stratification, models tend to overestimate H [15]. These problems urgently call for new approaches for parameterization of H.

3. GENETIC PROGRAMMING FOR DETERMINING HEAT FLUX

Given the difficult nature of the turbulent flux of the sensible heat and the unsatisfactory performance of the conventional models, in this paper we resort to genetic programming (GP) as a means for synthesizing a heat flux model from experimental data. In doing so, we anticipate obtaining models that (i) at least tie with the conventional models with respect to error on experimental data, (ii) are to some extent transparent/interpretable, and by this token (iii) possibly cast new light on the nature of the complex phenomenon of heat flux.

Genetic programming is a heuristic, stochastic approach to program synthesis. GP synthesizes a program in a given domain-specific language by maintaining a working population of programs (candidate solutions) and manipulating them by means of search operators. This iterative search process is driven by a domain-specific fitness function, which evaluates the quality of candidate solutions and so imposes certain selection pressure; this in turn causes some programs to be appointed as parents and so give rise to the subsequent generation of models. Given an appropriately designed domain-specific language, GP can be also used to induce functional models of dependencies between multiple observables, i.e., independent input variables that form program input and a dependent output variable that is to be predicted by a program. Applying GP in this mode is also known as *symbolic regression.*

[1]Details of the ECMWF scheme can be found at http://old.ecmwf.int/research/ifsdocs/CY40r1/IFSPart4.pdf (Section 3.2).

In our search for alternative parameterizations of the turbulent flux of sensible heat H, we not only rely on the non-orthodox method of model synthesis (GP), but consider also all potentially relevant variables, including those absent in the traditional parameterization (2). One approach is to regard $SWR_{\downarrow}$ and $LWR_{\downarrow}$ as external drivers for the atmosphere-surface heat exchange and H, LE, C, and $LWR_{\uparrow}$ as fluxes that respond to the external drivers, all depending on the surface temperature. This approach could yield parameterization schemes based on $SWR_{\downarrow}$ and $LWR_{\downarrow}$ (or on the factors controlling these radiative fluxes, such as the solar zenith angle and cloud cover). Another approach would be to keep the potential temperature difference $(\theta_s - \theta_a)$, as in (2), but abandon the highly idealized Monin-Obukhov similarity theory. The dependence of H on $(\theta_s - \theta_a)$ and various other meteorological variables could be tested experimentally. It is also possible to combine the above-mentioned approaches, and parameterize H on the basis of both radiative fluxes and the variables used in (2).

In this paper, we delegate the choice of relevant variables almost entirely to GP, providing only three compound inputs for the models (differences of temperature and radiation). The choice of the variables is to an extent dependent also on the availability and quality of experimental data, which we cover in the next section.

4. EXPERIMENTAL DATA ON HEAT FLUX

To drive the GP evolution we use the best and temporally most extensive meteorological datasets ever collected from the Arctic and Antarctic sea ice zones. These originate from projects Ice Station Weddell (ISW) in 1992 and the Surface Heat Budget of the Arctic Ocean (SHEBA) in 1997-1998. Since then the data from these field campaigns have been widely used by polar scientists, as there have not been other as comprehensive long-term measurement campaigns over polar sea ice since ISW and SHEBA.

ISW was a joint US-Russian project to investigate the atmosphere, sea ice, and ocean in the Weddell Sea, Antarctic [1]. The station was located on a sea-ice flow drifting northwards from 72°S up to 66°S from February to June 1992. The station location deep in the Antarctic sea ice zone and its operation period in austral autumn and early winter gave an excellent opportunity to make observations on the stable boundary layer. In total, over 2,000 hours of nearly continuous data on radiation, temperature, sensible and latent heat, wind speed and other variables were collected.

SHEBA was a year-round campaign to take comprehensive measurements that would help understanding processes that drive the surface energy budget in the Arctic [12]. The experiments spanned from October 1997 to September 1998 and were performed on an ice floe drifting in the Beaufort and Chukchi Seas in the Arctic, between 74°N and 81°N.

The SHEBA and ISW datasets contain respectively 6,004 and 1,024 hourly resolved observations with valid measurements of all variables. To monitor the extent of overfitting in our GP experiments, we split these datasets into training and test parts: approximately 50 percent of randomly selected observations form the former, and the remaining ones the latter. By relying on random partitioning rather than splitting the timeline into two continuous time intervals, we hope to avoid the risk of biasing the training process towards a particular time interval. This preprocessing resulted in the SHEBA dataset being partitioned into 3,004 training observations and 3,000 testing observations, and ISW partitioned into, respectively, 515 and 509 observations. The dataset variables are listed in the top part of Table 1.

Table 1: The terminal nodes (leaves of expression trees) used in the evolved models.

Original inputs (the variables present in the datasets)	
ShortIn	incoming (downward) shortwave radiation
ShortOut	outgoing (upward) shortwave radiation
LongIn	incoming (downward) longwave radiation
LongOut	outgoing (upward) longwave radiation
SurfTemp	surface temperature
AirTemp	air temperature
WindSpeed	wind speed
SpecHum	specific humidity
Derived inputs (compounds of original variables)	
NetShort	incoming minus outgoing shortwave radiat.
NetLong	incoming minus outgoing longwave radiat.
TempDiff	air minus surface temperature
Constants	
CKarman	von Karman constant = 0.405
CSpecHeat	specific heat of air = 1004
ERC	constant drawn uniformly from [-100,100]

Note that although heat flux is naturally a temporal phenomenon, and each observation is associated with a specific timestamp, it is widely agreed in meteorology that H should be parameterized *diagnostically*, i.e., using the simultaneous values of other variables (rather than *prognostically*, i.e., to predict the future values of H). We adhere to that convention in this study. The models we discuss in the subsequent sections are thus time-free in the sense that they express the momentary dependency of the output variable on the input variables. In other words, we pose the problem as a conventional regression problem in terms of statistics and machine learning.

5. EXPERIMENTAL SETUP

We rely on the tree-based GP [7], the genre of GP that is arguably the most natural for handling functional (side effect-free) expressions. A single model is an expression tree that fetches the values of input variables (independent variables) and returns the predicted value of the dependent variable. The terminals (tree leaves), presented in Table 1, include the input variables provided in the SHEBA and ISW datasets (Section 4), simple compounds of them (radiation and temperature differences), and constants (random and domain-specific). The set of instructions (inner nodes of expression trees) comprises arithmetic operators (+, -, *, /), inversion, negation, and selected transcendental functions (*sqr*, *sqrt*, *log*, x^y). Where needed, the functions are protected against invalid arguments. We anticipate that inclusion of the transcendental functions may be essential, given the prevalence of various forms of nonlinearity in physical phenomena governing the turbulent heat flux.

All GP configurations considered in this paper implement generational evolutionary workflow with fairly conventional settings. Parent models are appointed via tournament of size 7. A new model is built from them via subtree-swapping crossover (with probability 0.5), subtree-replacing mutation (0.1), ERC constant mutation (0.3) or cloning (0.1). The

Table 2: Mean absolute error (MAE) of the best-of-run models obtained with particular approaches (for GP, averaged over 30 evolutionary runs and accompanied by 0.95 confidence intervals). All results in W/m^2.

	SHEBA dataset (Arctic)				*ISW dataset (Antarctic)*			
Configuration	*Training MAE*		*Test MAE*		*Training MAE*		*Test MAE*	
Conventional model	3.7568		3.7186		12.6011		11.9325	
LR	4.6465		4.5882		6.0205		6.5886	
GP-MAE	3.3690	[3.286, 3.452]	3.3213	[3.239, 3.404]	5.4819	[5.341, 5.623]	6.0480	[5.837, 6.259]
GP-COR	3.0764	[3.037, 3.115]	3.0213	[2.980, 3.063]	5.2207	[5.179, 5.262]	5.9091	[5.796, 6.022]
GP-MAE+COR	3.1712	[3.130, 3.212]	3.1032	[3.062, 3.145]	5.0804	[5.033, 5.127]	5.7368	[5.640, 5.834]
GP-MAE+COR+LR	3.1377	[3.094, 3.181]	3.0702	[3.027, 3.114]	5.0950	[5.054, 5.136]	5.7474	[5.679, 5.816]

remaining parameters are set to the defaults of ECJ package that our software implementation is built upon [9].

Our goal is to synthesize a model with possibly low Mean Absolute Error (MAE), i.e.,

$$f_{MAE} = \frac{1}{|I|}\sum_{i\in I}|\hat{y}_i - y_i|,$$

where y_i is the actual (observed) value of the heat flux, $\hat{y}_i$ is the output of a model, and I is the set of indices of samples (observations) of interest. f_{MAE} is thus our *objective performance measure*, and we use it for reporting throughout this paper. However, as we argued elsewhere [8], in general there is no rationale to claim that an objective performance is necessarily the best *search driver*, i.e., the best means to navigate the search process. The experimental evidence we gathered in the cited work actually suggests the opposite: in many cases, an alternative search driver may prove more effective at guiding an evolutionary search process (program/model synthesis in particular) towards the well-performing solutions.

There is a multitude of alternative search drivers that might be used for the heat flux problem. In our earlier studies, we compared a range of them when modeling the global temperature anomaly [14]. The overall conclusion was the superior efficiency of the Pearson correlation coefficient $\phi(\hat{y}, y)$. Following that past work, we define the (minimized) fitness as

$$f_{COR} = 1 - |\phi(\hat{y}, y)|.$$

f_{COR}, when applied as a fitness function in GP runs, was in most cases able to find models that were better (in terms of MAE) than the models evolved by GP driven by f_{MAE}. We attribute this interesting result to the fact that f_{COR} 'seeks' *any* linear dependency between the variables in question, and will for instance reward a model that captures the temporal dynamics of the dependent variable but diverges in amplitude (or in offset) from the desired values. A linear transformation of the output of such a model may form a very good predictor. $\phi(\hat{y}, y)$ implicitly performs such a transformation by standardizing the variables in question, i.e., subtracting the average and dividing by standard deviation. By this token, for any $\hat{y}$ and y and any $\alpha, \beta \in \mathbb{R}$, $\alpha \neq 0$ it holds $\phi(\hat{y}, y) = \phi(\alpha\hat{y} + \beta, y)$. f_{MAE}, to the contrary, puts an emphasis on the absolute differences between the actual and predicted values, and may overlook such linearly-related models.

Given a symbolic regression problem, GP can usually quickly find a model that coarsely captures the dependencies between the variables. However, further progress may be difficult, because significant improvement may require fundamental overhaul of a model, which may be hard to achieve, especially with a single application of a search operator. This in turn may lead to premature convergence, symptomized by a population becoming dominated by very similar or even identical models. To mitigate this problem, several population diversification methods have been proposed in the past. Here, we turn the original model synthesis process from a single-objective into a multi-objective one. Technically, we evaluate each model with respect to f_{MAE} *and* f_{COR}, and treat these two measures as search objectives to be used in parallel. To exploit the multi-aspect characteristic captured in these objectives without naively aggregating them into one scalar value, we employ the Non-domination Sorting Genetic Algorithm (NSGA-II [4]), a state-of-the art technique of multiobjective selection. To select the most promising candidate solutions (here: models), NSGA-II builds a Pareto-ranking of the combined current population and an *archive*, and uses tournament selection on Pareto ranks to select the parents solutions that give rise to the next generation of candidate solutions. Ties on Pareto ranks are resolved using a *sparsity* measure, which promotes the solutions that feature unique characteristics in terms of criteria. See [4] for the detailed coverage of NSGA-II.

6. THE EVOLVED MODELS

In this section, we report the aggregated statistics on particular approaches. Following the arguments made in the previous section, we designed four GP configurations:

1. GP-MAE: single-objective GP driven by f_{MAE},
2. GP-COR: single-objective GP driven by f_{COR},
3. GP-MAE+COR: two-objective GP driven by f_{MAE} and f_{COR},
4. GP-MAE+COR+LR: two-objective GP driven by f_{MAE} and f_{COR}, with modified selection of the best-of-run model.

Each GP variant works with a population of 5000 models (individuals, candidate solutions) and lasts for 50 generations. When a GP run terminates, we select from its final population the *best-of-run* model. For GP-MAE and GP-MAE+COR it is the model with the smallest f_{MAE}. For GP-COR, it is the model with the smallest f_{COR}. GP-MAE+COR+LR runs proceed exactly as GP-MAE+COR and diverge from it only in the way the best-of-run model is appointed. For each model in the Pareto front of the final population, we perform linear regression of the output of that model $\hat{y}$ onto the output variable y *for the training data*. Then we calculate f_{MAE} of the resulting compound model, i.e., of $\alpha\hat{y}+\beta$, with α and β, also on the training set. The model with the smallest f_{MAE} calculated in this way is the best-of-run individual.

For each configuration, 30 independent evolutionary runs were performed. Table 2 presents the MAE of the best-of-run models averaged over the runs, accompanied with 0.95-confidence intervals. In the same table, we report also two baselines: the performance of the conventional model (2) and of multiple linear regression (LR).

The outcomes for particular datasets are substantially different, so in the following we discuss them separately. The interesting feature of all SHEBA-trained models is that they do not seem to overfit: the performance on the training and test part is very similar. In terms of averages, the test error is actually smaller than the training one for all methods. As this relationship holds also for the conventional model, which does not involve any training, we hypothesize that this is more due to the particular random division of the SHEBA dataset into the training and test part, rather than due to the merits of particular methods (note that overfitting does take place for the ISW dataset).

In terms of average error, LR fares the worst, indicating that the underlying phenomenon cannot be captured using linear dependencies. The nonlinear conventional model achieves a notably better performance. Nevertheless, the models synthesized by all variants of GP improve upon this result even further. As their upper confidence intervals are far from the performance of the conventional model, we may deem this difference statistically significant. The GP-COR method seems to perform the best on this dataset, reducing the prediction error by almost 20 percent on average, when compared to the conventional model. Nevertheless, the proximity of its confidence intervals to those of the other methods does not allow us find the differences between the GP variants statistically significant.

All GP-based methods offer a remarkably low variance of MAE. The leader in this respect is again GP-COR: its 0.083-wide confidence interval is less than 3 percent of the average. This suggest that GP can, despite inherent stochasticity, serve as a robust technique for modeling heat flux.

The results for the Antarctic ISW dataset present a less coherent picture. All models perform here much worse than on SHEBA, which is in part due to much larger variance of the observed heat flux for the ISW dataset ($\sigma_H = 11.83$, compared to 8.68 for SHEBA). Another factor is the smaller size of the ISW dataset (515 training observations vs. 3,004 for SHEBA). The conventional model commits the greatest error overall (we discuss this surprising underperformance in Section 7). LR fares better, but still worse than on SHEBA, which suggests that the ISW dataset is inherently more difficult to model. Despite this, GP is still capable to make better predictions.

For both datasets, using f_{COR} as a search driver is beneficial when compared to GP-MAE. This is confirmed also in terms of the overall-best models: the SHEBA model with the lowest training MAE (of all 30 evolutionary runs) of 2.843 has been found by GP-COR; for ISW, the overall-best model with f_{MAE}= 4.914 evolved in GP-MAE+COR. The use of linear regression in GP-MAE+COR+LR also reduces the error in comparison to GP-MAE+COR, albeit only slightly.

The disparity of MAE between the SHEBA and ISW datasets is also reflected in the sizes of the evolved models, which we report in Table 3. The models evolved for ISW are systematically more complex than those evolved for SHEBA. Apparently, in order to attain evolutionary advantage, the consecutive generations of good models in ISW runs needed to get more and more complex, and do so at a greater rate than for SHEBA (the GP runs for both datasets start from identical initial populations). This might have to some extent contributed to the overfitting on MAE (cf. Table 2). More importantly however, the models evolved using the bi-objective approach (GP-MAE+COR, GP-MAE+COR+LR) tend to produce, for both datasets, smaller models than those evolved by the single-objective GP-COR. The models in question are not smaller than those produced by GP-MAE, but GP-MAE is the least attractive configuration in terms of error. The GP-MAE+COR configuration offers a compromise between accuracy and complexity.

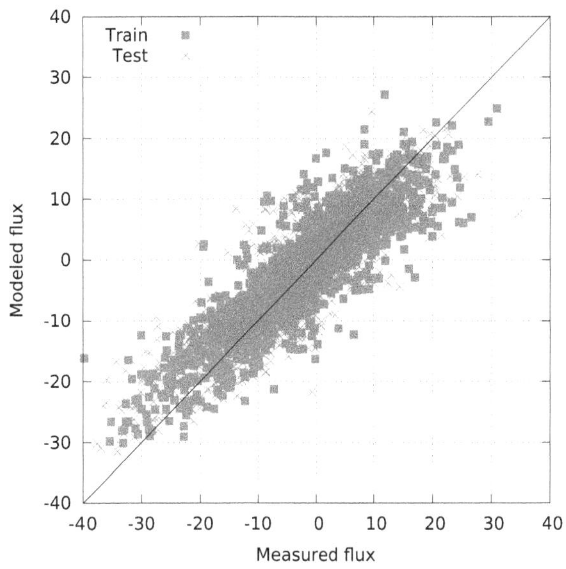

Figure 1: Best SHEBA model vs. measurements.

The models may seem large in absolute terms, but can be usually simplified. In Fig. 4, we present the simplified version of the overall smallest model, which happened to be evolved by GP-COR for the SHEBA dataset. The MAE of this model on the training and test set amounts to, respectively, 3.168 and 3.104.

7. COMPARISON WITH OBSERVATIONS AND CONVENTIONAL MODEL

In this section, we take a closer look at the characteristics of the evolved models and discuss them also from the meteorological perspective.

We first consider the model with the lowest MAE on the training set for the SHEBA dataset. This model comprises 188 nodes and commits MAE of 2.844 and 2.813 on the training and test set, respectively. In Fig. 1, we confront the observed heat flux (horizontal axis) with the predicted one (vertical axis), for both the training and the test part of this dataset. The plot reveals strong correlation of model's predictions with the observed data. The outliers are few and far between, so the model may be considered robust.

In Fig. 2, we present an analogous graph for the smallest SHEBA model, comprising 47 nodes and committing MAE of 3.168 and 3.104 on the training and test set, respectively.

Table 3: Complexity of the evolved best-of-run models, expressed as the number of nodes in expression trees, averaged over 30 evolutionary runs (with 0.95 confidence intervals).

	SHEBA dataset (Arctic)		*ISW dataset (Antarctic)*	
GP-MAE	97.27	[81.52, 113.02]	103.03	[89.35, 116.72]
GP-COR	137.77	[121.8, 153.74]	183.47	[160.59, 206.34]
GP-MAE+COR	101.37	[86.75, 115.98]	140.27	[122.55, 157.99]
GP-MAE+COR+LR	107.07	[94.56, 119.57]	144.83	[129.56, 160.11]

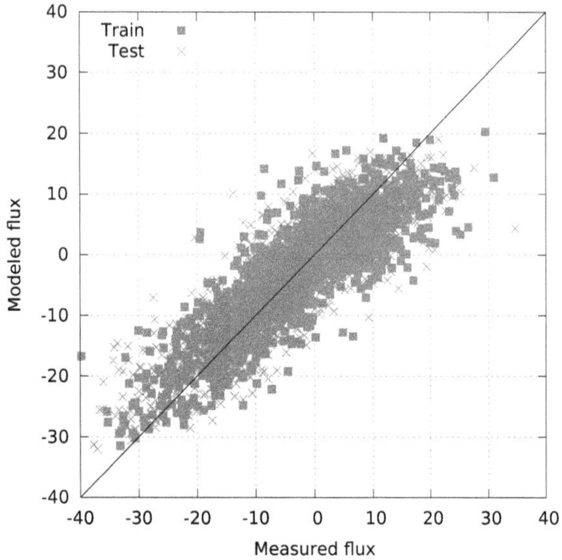

Figure 2: Smallest SHEBA model vs. measurements.

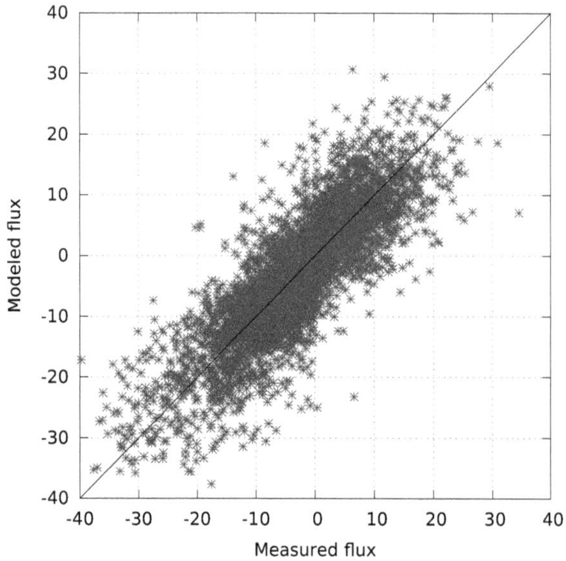

Figure 3: Conventional model vs. measurements (SHEBA).

The datapoints are more dispersed than in Fig. 1, but overall this model's behavior is also predictable.

For reference, Fig. 3 shows the same type of graph of the conventional model. Expectedly, the datapoints are even more dispersed than in Fig. 2, which reflects the overall worse MAE of this model.

A closer inspection of these graphs reveals an interesting difference between the GP models and the conventional model: the former tend to better at predicting negative flux, while the latter does not seem to show a significant preference in this respect.

Figures 6-8 present the analogous graphs for the ISW dataset: the lowest-MAE model (Fig. 6, MAE of 4.914 on training and of 5.840 on testing set), the smallest model (Fig. 7, MAE of 5.477 on training and of 6.016 on testing set), and the conventional model (Fig. 8). As expected, the points are more dispersed due to larger overall MAE. Interestingly, the tendency of producing better predictions for negative fluxes observed for SHEBA seems to occur here as well for the evolved models. The conventional model in Fig. 8 strongly underestimates the flux and occasionally exhibits tendency for predicting zero flux (notice the prominent horizontal agglomeration of observations). Both these phenomena can be explained by the context in which the ISW dataset was collected, which is however beyond the scope of this paper.

We attempt now to interpret the causality revealed by the smallest models evolved for both datasets. The smallest model for the SHEBA dataset, shown in Fig. 4, comprises 36 nodes after simplification. The dominant effect of the air-surface temperature difference (*TempDiff*) seems to be that surface warmer than the air favors an upward heat flux, in accordance with the conventional model in (2). However, the temperature difference appears in several places of the model, suggesting that the relationship between the heat flux and temperature difference is fairly complex. Both in (2) and this model, a strong wind (*WindSpeed*) favors a large heat flux, which is relevant as the wind shear is the primary source of turbulence in conditions when the surface is not strongly heated (which is always the case over sea ice). Net shortwave radiation (*NetShort*) tends to reduce the heat flux. The direct causal effect should be opposite, as net shortwave radiation heats the snow/ice surface favoring a heat flux from snow/ice to air. However, in SHEBA clouds warmed the snow/ice surface all the year except July and August, and their effect in increasing downward longwave radiation dominated over their effect in decreasing downward shortwave radiation [13]. Hence, under clear skies, with a lot of net shortwave radiation, the snow/ice surface was typically colder than under cloudy skies with less net shortwave radiation. Finally, a large specific humidity (*SpecHum*) is associated with a large heat flux. This is related to the above-mentioned cloud effects, as cloudy skies are associated with a large specific humidity and a warm snow/ice surface, favoring an upward heat flux.

The smallest model evolved for the ISW dataset is shown in Fig. 5 and comprises 44 nodes (60 nodes before simplification). In this model, the air-surface temperature difference and wind speed are both major factors, as in the conventional model in (2), but the complexity of their combined effect may suggest that (2) is too simplistic (we note that the temperature difference and wind speed also affect the static stability that affects C_H in (2)). The role of net shortwave radiation is opposite to that in SHEBA. This is probably related to the fact that ISW drifted at lower latitudes, and therefore the surface temperature under clear skies, with a lot of solar radiation, is not necessarily lower than under cloudy skies.

It is noteworthy that, contrary to the conventional model, the discussed SHEBA and ISW models were not solely based on the air-surface temperature difference and wind speed, but also on the radiative fluxes, which might have helped reducing their errors.

8. DISCUSSION AND CONCLUSIONS

In this study, we demonstrated the feasibility of using GP to synthesize viable models of turbulent heat flux of sensible heat from experimental data. Many evolved models we produced here outperformed the method applied in the ECMWF operational weather forecasting model, which is considered the world's best numerical weather prediction model (see e.g. the forecast score statistics calculated by the World Meteorological Organization[2]). The best model commits MAE of 2.813 on the test part of the SHEBA dataset, i.e., 24 percent smaller than the error of the conventional model. The best model evolved for the ISW dataset has test-set MAE of 5.840, 51 percent smaller than the conventional model.

When it comes to GP-related aspects of this study, we brought substantial evidence that using an alternative 'search driver' (here: f_{COR}) as a fitness function in place of the objective that is normally employed to assess the models in a domain (f_{MAE}) can have essential positive impact on the outcome. This observation holds also for the multiobjective evolutionary approaches, which, though not necessarily outperform the single-objective methods on error, may improve the models with respect to other, 'non-functional' properties like complexity.

There are several directions in which this research can be taken further. This study abstracts from the temporal nature of the heat flux phenomenon; as a consequence, the models we evolved here are inherently incapable of capturing the cumulative characteristics of the underlying physics. A natural next step could be thus to extend the repertoire of input variables (which now reflect the state of the system at a given time instant) with extra variables that capture the history of the process.

Employing a model evolved by GP in a numerical weather prediction or climate model would open the door to many interesting possibilities. A more accurate parameterization for the surface heat flux should directly improve the accuracy of the simulated surface heat budget (1), surface temperature, and near-surface air temperature. Further, it should also indirectly improve the simulations of near-surface wind speed, air humidity, occurrence of fog, melt of snow and ice, and growth of sea and lake ice. These are essential issues in both numerical weather prediction and climate research, and particularly actual now when a dramatic loss of sea ice and terrestrial snow is going on in the Arctic.

Acknowledgments. The work of KS and TV was supported by the Academy of Finland through the CACSI project (contract 259537). KK acknowledges support from project 09/91/DSPB/0572.

[2]http://apps.ecmwf.int/wmolcdnv/scores/mean/850_t

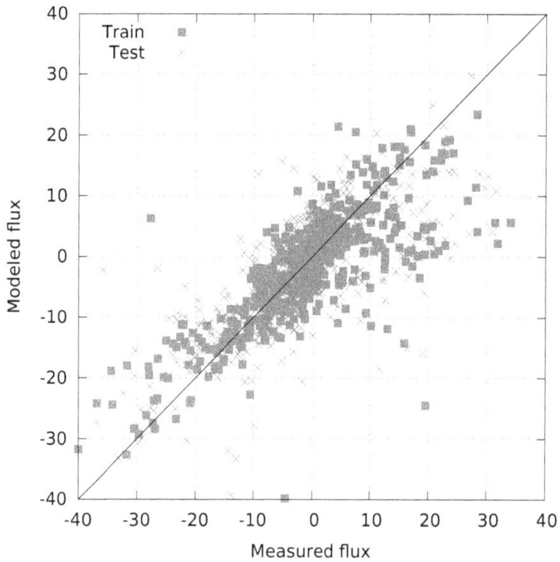

Figure 6: Best ISW model vs. measurements.

9. REFERENCES

[1] E. L. Andreas, R. E. Jordan, and A. P. Makshtas. Parameterizing turbulent exchange over sea ice: The Ice Station Weddell results. *Boundary-Layer Meteorology*, 114:439–460, 2005.

[2] Evgeny Atlaskin and Timo Vihma. Evaluation of NWP results for wintertime nocturnal boundary-layer temperatures over Europe and Finland. *Quarterly Journal of the Royal Meteorological Society*, 138(667):1440–1451, 2012.

[3] D. J. Cavalieri and C. L. Parkinson. Arctic sea ice variability and trends, 1979–2010. *The Cryosphere*, 6(4):881–889, 2012.

[4] K. Deb, A. Pratap, S. Agarwal, and T. Meyarivan. A fast and elitist multiobjective genetic algorithm: NSGA-II. *Evolutionary Computation, IEEE Transactions on*, 6(2):182 –197, apr 2002.

[5] C. Derksen and R. Brown. Spring snow cover extent reductions in the 2008–2012 period exceeding climate model projections. *Geophysical Research Letters*, 39(19), 2012.

[6] R. Döscher, T. Vihma, and E. Maksimovich. Recent advances in understanding the Arctic climate system state and change from a sea ice perspective: a review. *Atmospheric Chemistry and Physics*, 14(24):13571–13600, 2014.

[7] John R. Koza. *Genetic Programming: On the Programming of Computers by Means of Natural Selection*. MIT Press, Cambridge, MA, USA, 1992.

[8] Krzysztof Krawiec and Una-May O'Reilly. Behavioral programming: A broader and more detailed take on semantic GP. In *Proceeding of the sixteenth annual conference on Genetic and evolutionary computation conference*, GECCO '14, New York, NY, USA, 2014. ACM.

[9] Sean Luke. ECJ evolutionary computation system, 2002. (http://cs.gmu.edu/ eclab/projects/ecj/).

[10] L. Mahrt. Stably stratified boundary layer. In J. P. Holton, J. A. Curry, and J. Pyle, editors, *Encyclopedia*

$$-TempDiff * 0.893^{TempDiff} * [\frac{WindSpeed}{0.798^{TempDiff}} - TempDiff + 0.0126 * (SpecHum - NetShort + 0.405) * (TempDiff - 0.0146 * NetLong * 0.636^{TempDiff})] * 1.953 + 0.39$$

Figure 4: The smallest best-of-run heat flux model evolved for the SHEBA dataset (originally composed of 47 nodes, manually simplified to 36 nodes). This model attains MAE of 3.168 on the training set and 3.104 on the test set.

$$[2 * (WindSpeed + TempDiff - WindSpeed * TempDiff) + 10^{-6} * LongOut^2 * WindSpeed * (NetShort + NetLong) + \sqrt{\frac{WindSpeed}{ShortOut+87.45}} * (NetLong + 0.001 * LongOut * WindSpeed * (NetShort + NetLong))] * 0.405 + WindSpeed$$

Figure 5: The smallest best-of-run heat flux model evolved for the ISW dataset (originally composed of 60 nodes, manually simplified to 44 nodes). This model attains MAE of 5.476 on the training set and 6.016 on the test set.

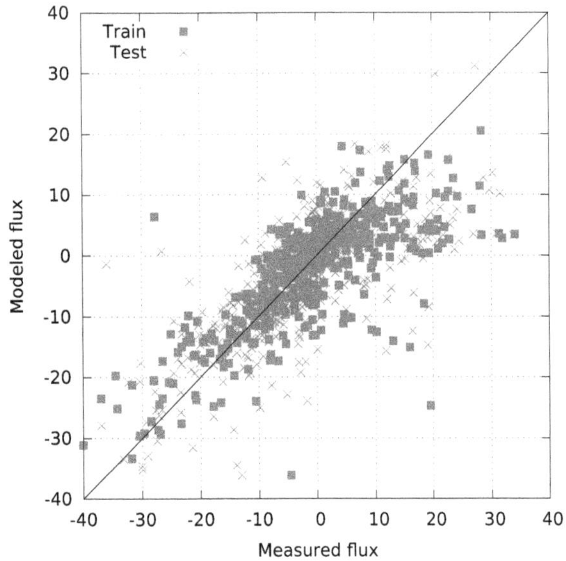

Figure 7: Smallest ISW model vs. measurements.

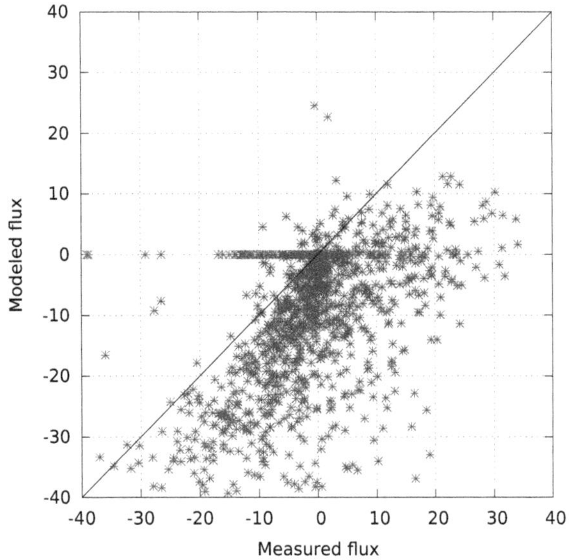

Figure 8: Conventional model vs. measurements (ISW).

of *Atmospheric Sciences*, pages 298–305. Academic Press, London, 2002.

[11] A. S. Monin and A. M. Obukhov. Basic laws of turbulent mixing in the surface layer of the atmosphere (in Russian). *Tr. Akad. Nauk SSSR Geofiz. Inst.*, 24:163–187, 1954.

[12] P. Ola G. Persson, Christopher W. Fairall, Edgar L. Andreas, Peter S. Guest, and Donald K. Perovich. Measurements near the Atmospheric Surface Flux Group tower at SHEBA: Near-surface conditions and surface energy budget. *Journal of Geophysical Research: Oceans*, 107(C10):SHE 21-1–SHE 21-35, 2002.

[13] M. D. Shupe and J. M. Intrieri. Cloud radiative forcing of the Arctic surface: the influence of cloud properties, surface albedo, and solar zenith angle. *Journal of Climate*, 17:616–628, 2004.

[14] Karolina Stanislawska, Krzysztof Krawiec, and Zbigniew W. Kundzewicz. Modelling global temperature changes with genetic programming. *Computer & Mathematics with Applications*, 64(12):3717–3728, 2012.

[15] G. Svensson, A.A.M. Holtslag, V. Kumar, T. Mauritsen, G.J. Steeneveld, W.M. Angevine, E. Bazile, A. Beljaars, E.I.F. de Bruijn, A. Cheng, L. Conangla, J. Cuxart, M. Ek, M.J. Falk, F. Freedman, H. Kitagawa, V.E. Larson, A. Lock, J. Mailhot, V. Masson, S. Park, J. Pleim, S. Söderberg, W. Weng, and M. Zampieri. Evaluation of the diurnal cycle in the atmospheric boundary layer over land as represented by a variety of single-column models: the second GABLS experiment. *Boundary-Layer Meteorology*, 140(2):177–206, 2011.

[16] M. Tjernström, M. Zagar, G. Svensson, J.J. Cassano, S. Pfeifer, A. Rinke, K. Wyser, K. Dethloff, C. Jones, T. Semmler, and M. Shaw. Modelling the Arctic boundary layer: an evaluation of six ARCMIP regional-scale models using data from the SHEBA project. *Boundary-Layer Meteorology*, 117:337–381, 2005.

[17] T. Vihma, R. Pirazzini, I. Fer, I. A. Renfrew, J. Sedlar, M. Tjernström, C. Lüpkes, T. Nygård, D. Notz, J. Weiss, D. Marsan, B. Cheng, G. Birnbaum, S. Gerland, D. Chechin, and J. C. Gascard. Advances in understanding and parameterization of small-scale physical processes in the marine Arctic climate system: a review. *Atmospheric Chemistry and Physics*, 14(17):9403–9450, 2014.

Smart Mobility Policies with Evolutionary Algorithms: The Adapting Info Panel Case

Daniel H. Stolfi
LCC, University of Malaga
ETSI Informática, Campus de Teatinos
29071, Málaga, Spain
dhstolfi@lcc.uma.es

Enrique Alba
LCC, University of Malaga
ETSI Informática, Campus de Teatinos
29071, Málaga, Spain
eat@lcc.uma.es

ABSTRACT

In this article we propose the Yellow Swarm architecture for reducing travel times, greenhouse gas emissions and fuel consumption of road traffic by using several LED panels to suggest changes in the direction of vehicles (detours) for different time slots. These time intervals are calculated using an evolutionary algorithm, specifically designed for our proposal, which evaluates many working scenarios based on real cities, imported from OpenStreetMap into the SUMO traffic simulator. Our results show an improvement in average travel times, emissions, and fuel consumption even when only a small percentage of drivers follow the indications provided by our panels.

Categories and Subject Descriptors

I.6.3 [**Simulation and Modeling**]: Applications

Keywords

Application; evolutionary algorithm; road traffic; smart city; smart mobility; LED Panels

1. INTRODUCTION

Year after year cities grow in number of inhabitants, many of whom are arriving at the city for the first time [9]. However, urban infrastructures do not scale properly where they are needed. This implies a notable increase in the number of trips citizens have to take nowadays and their duration [15]. These journeys are usually to commute or take children to school, which usually occurs at the same time of day.

Evidence of the problems described above can be seen in the number of traffic jams [14] which have increased in frequency over the last decade. They occur not only in the main streets of the city but also near to schools, hospitals, shopping centers, etc. As a consequence, traveling by car is becoming slower than it used to be and it is a common source of delays, economic loss, and stress because of the effect traffic congestion has on peoples' leisure time and work.

GECCO '15, July 11–15, 2015, Madrid, Spain

DOI: http://dx.doi.org/10.1145/2739480.2754742

Another consequence, which is usually ignored as it is not immediately noticed by citizens, is the amount of greenhouse gases emitted to the atmosphere. The more people driving at low speeds or even stuck in a traffic jam, the greater the emissions from the vehicles' motor. These emissions are Carbon Monoxide (CO), Carbon Dioxide (CO_2), Hydrocarbons (HC), Particulate Matter (PM), and Nitrogen Oxides (NO), which not only contribute to global warming, but also jeopardize people's health via different respiratory and cardiovascular diseases as well as lung cancer [4, 7].

It also has an economic impact, reducing productivity through the loss of working days. In 2011, congestion caused urban Americans to travel 5.5 billion hours more and to purchase an extra 2.9 billion gallons of fuel at a congestion cost of $121 billion [11]. Moreover, air pollution can also damage buildings and it has a clear impact on the climate, since some air pollutants behave as greenhouse gases [2].

Our proposal, called Yellow Swarm, is an architecture for redirecting road traffic by using LED (Light-Emitting Diode) panels, placed at strategic points of the city, to suggest possible changes in the direction drivers can take (continue straight on, turn left, turn right, etc.). By using Yellow Swarm we are able to evenly spread the traffic throughout the city (without interfering too much with the drivers' itineraries), prevent traffic jams, and reduce travel times, greenhouse gas emissions and fuel consumption.

The rest of this paper is organized as follows. In the next section we review several publications related to our proposal. In Section 3 we describe the Yellow Swarm architecture and present the characteristics of the different geographical areas we have optimized. Section 4 focuses on the studies done and discusses the results. And finally, in Section 5, conclusions and future work are presented.

2. RELATED WORK

The following articles present solutions to different problems related to smart mobility such as reducing travel times and emissions in urban areas.

A method to reduce travel times is presented in [8]. It consists of an algorithm capable of controlling traffic signals that relies on traffic observations made by available sensor devices and local communication between traffic lights. To evaluate the system developed, a realistic traffic model was made using information supplied by the City of Ottawa, Canada. The results presented show an increase of the average speed of vehicles by 6.58% with respect to static traffic light plans. The advantages presented by the authors are failure tolerance, dynamic response, and the fact that the

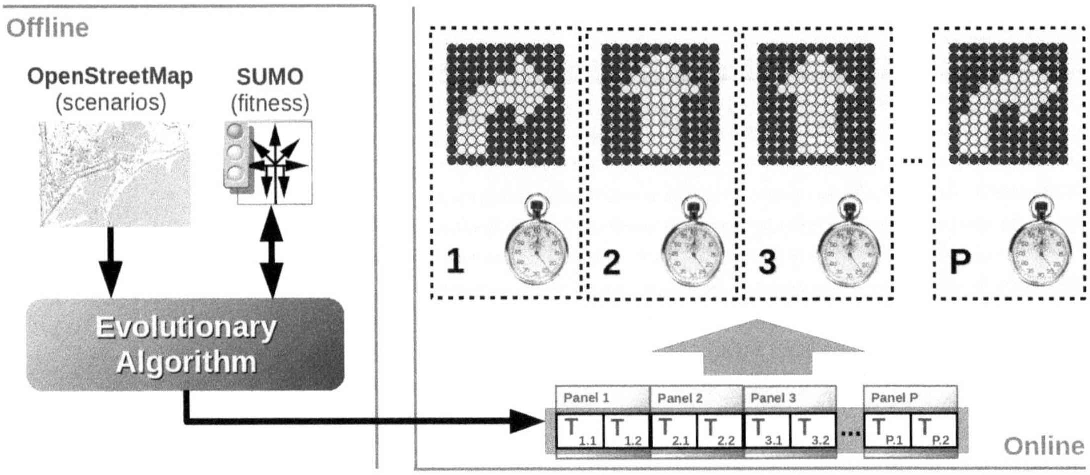

Figure 1: The Yellow Swarm architecture: In the *Offline* stage, it defines city scenarios and analyzes them with the EA, and in the *Online* stage, the previously calculated configuration is applied to the LED panels in order to suggest changes in the direction of the vehicles.

simulations used to validate this approach are based on historical data. However, as the authors themselves admit, the algorithm cannot adaptively generate green waves and, due to the limitations of the traffic information available, the model of traffic used is composed of just a small number of single intersection snapshots.

In [6] the authors propose an Adaptive Traffic Light Control (ATLC) using Vehicular Ad-Hoc Networks (VANET), which takes into account the vehicle density as well as the relative position of vehicles with respect to junctions. They present a case study based on a specific intersection in the city of Moncton, Canada. The proposed system is validated with real traffic data by dynamically adjusting the periods of green lights. The results of the simulation show that the algorithm proposed improves traffic flows and the current configuration of the city just as well as some other algorithms in the literature. Although the scenario chosen is intended to be a realist one by using historical traffic data and the results are promising, the study is limited to just one intersection. As a result, the utility of the system when considering a larger scenario needs to be evaluated.

In [13] a new architecture to reduce vehicles' travel times as well as greenhouse gas emissions and fuel consumption, is presented. In the article, the authors use a series of spots distributed throughout the city, normally installed in traffic lights, to suggest alternative routes to drivers by using WiFi communications. Having tested their proposal in different cities of Europe, the authors show improvements in most of the scenarios tested after completing an optimization process. Compared to our work in the present paper, this article differs in that the driver has to use on-board devices or smartphones as well as specific installed software, in order to receive the new routes. In our approach, not only can we dispense with such devices, but also it is not necessary to look at anything but the road to follow a proposed detour. This is a valuable characteristic because it improves safety by avoiding distractions.

In [10] a system to prevent traffic jams and reduce congestion by assigning new routes to vehicles is proposed. The route assignation, which excludes heavy load streets, is done during each vehicle's journey of each vehicle so that the driver is able to react to unexpected situations such as accidents, etc. To do this, the authors also use on-board systems such as tablets on which the position of each vehicle as well as the new route calculated are shown. They have experimented with the road network of the island of Manhattan in New York imported from OpenStreetMap, and reduced travel times by to 33%. Again, this work is different from ours in that each driver needs a wireless device with GPS, Internet connectivity, and a screen to be able to use it.

Another method for optimizing urban traffic is presented in [1]. It consists of the analysis of each junction topology by using basic heuristics and computationally efficient simulations in order to understand the outcomes they present with different traffic patterns and intensity. Then, the minimum delay route is calculated for the whole city by using the knowledge acquired. The results show remarkable improvements in waiting times and vehicle flows for the strategies used for the load balance and shortest path. The reduced number of maps used in the experiment impedes validating the results presented.

To sum up, we can find several approaches that have case studies that are limited in size or even unrealistic, with the additional requirement of using some type of intelligent device in order to take advantage of the systems described. Within our proposal, we analyze case studies that are based on real geographical areas of the cities of Malaga and Madrid which encompass about $10Km^2$ each. Additionally, our system does not require that users need to have any device with connectivity and GPS to use it, as it uses LED panels to inform of possible changes in direction throughout the city. This reinforces the road safety and makes the system cheaper and easier to implement, develop and use.

3. THE YELLOW SWARM

The Yellow Swarm architecture, presented in Figure 1, has two stages: The *Offline* stage in which the system is configured, and the *Online* stage in which drivers are informed about the suggested detours. If we carry out the two contiguous stages with a given frequency we can improve the dynamics of the proposal and better fit changing scenarios in the city.

In the *Offline* stage, our Evolutionary Algorithm (EA) analyzes different scenarios (traffic distributions) of our case studies, using the SUMO traffic simulator [5] which is controlled by the TraCI module [16], in order to implement the decisions that drivers made during their journey. The urban maps used to build the case studies have been imported from OpenStreetMap so that we can test our system in realistic city districts including traffic lights, roundabouts, etc. The training carried out in this phase results in the configuration of the LED panels to be used in the next stage.

In the *Online* stage, the LED panels show the different detour options to drivers depending on the time slots calculated in the previous stage. The possible signs are: go straight on, turn left, and turn right. However, their availability depends on the type of junction the vehicles are approaching, i.e. the possible detour options, and the street where the panel is placed. The first sign is visible during its previously calculated fixed time interval, after that the next sign in the sequence will be presented to the drivers. Once the cycle has finished (in this study all cycles are of two signs: go straight on and turn) it again starts with the first of the sequence. By using this strategy, Yellow Swarm is able to prevent possible traffic jams in the city as well as improve the use of most of the secondary streets of the city.

3.1 Case Studies

In this approach we have analyzed two central areas each of which belong to one of two important cities of Spain, Malaga and Madrid, both of which suffer from traffic congestion at peak hours.

After importing the maps into SUMO from OpenStreetMap we solved several issues observed, such as those junctions, roundabouts, and traffic lights which tended to form traffic jams. Our objective was to build more robust scenarios, more difficult to optimize as they consist of a greater number of vehicles. Furthermore, we have defined two case studies for each city. One of them corresponds to the case in which the vehicles use various streets in the city to arrive at their destination, and the other (TT subscript) in which only faster routes are used (TT stands for travel time). All these flows were generated by the DUAROUTER utility included in SUMO which uses different streets' weights such as travel time, emissions, and fuel consumption to build the routes. Consequently, we have named these scenarios as the experts' solution from SUMO in this article. By changing the seed of a scenario we have modified the order and pace that vehicles enter an area in order to define multiple scenarios of the same case study.

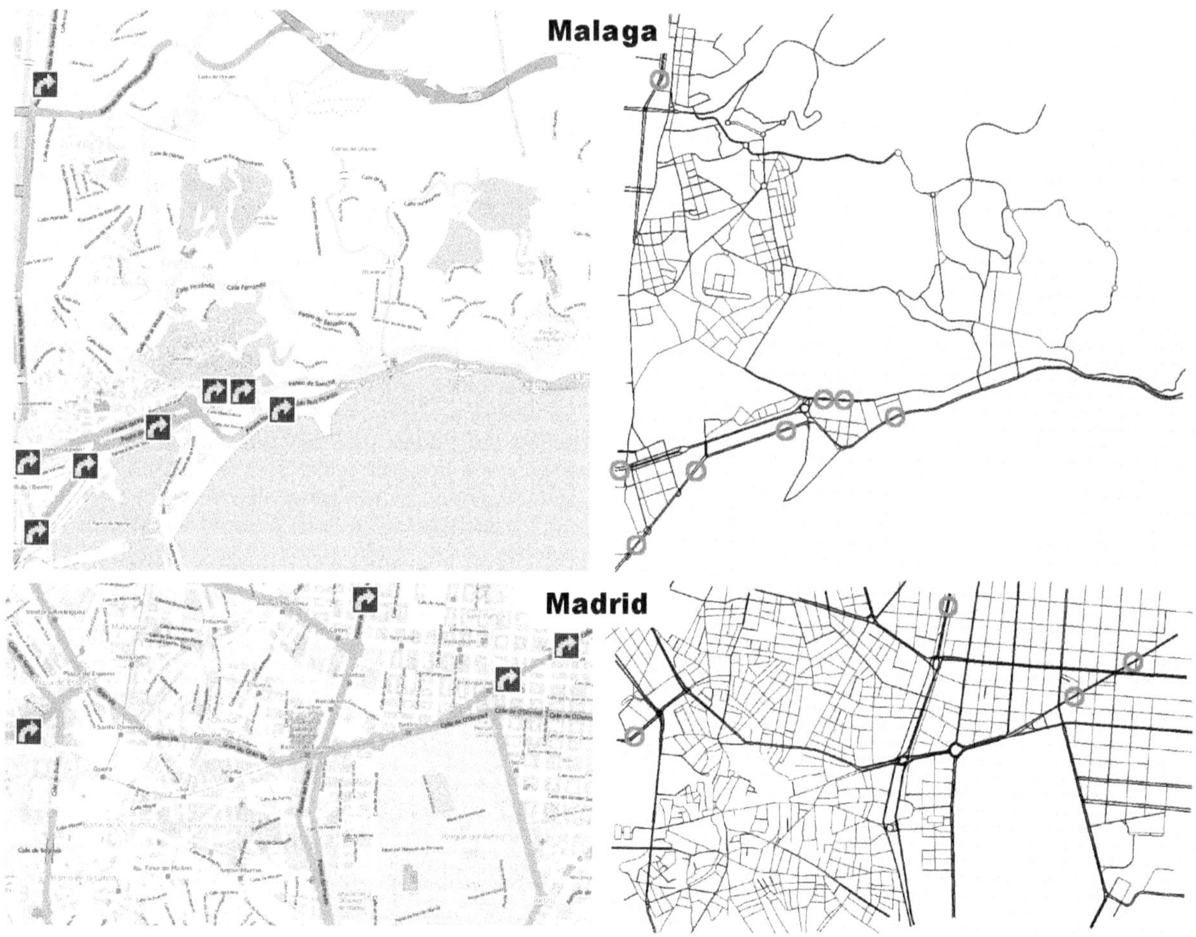

Figure 2: Case studies: *Malaga* (upper row) and *Madrid* (lower row). Exported from OpenStreetMap (left) to SUMO (right).

Table 1: **Type and characteristics of vehicles.**

Type	Arrival prob.	MaxSpd. (Km/h)	Accel. (m/s^2)	Decel. (m/s^2)	Length (m)	Emission class
truck	0.10	40	0.6	3.5	6.0	HDV_3_3
wagon	0.15	50	0.7	4.0	4.3	P_14_12
van	0.25	100	0.8	4.5	4.2	P_14_8
sedan	0.50	160	0.9	5.0	3.8	P_7_7

Table 2: Characteristics of the four case studies.

Case study	*Malaga*	$Malaga_{TT}$	*Madrid*	$Madrid_{TT}$
Analysis time (s)	7200	7200	7200	7200
# Vehicles	4500	4500	4840	4840
# Traffic lights	515	515	942	942
# LED panels	8	8	4	4
# Vehicle types	4	4	4	4
# Source streets	18	18	14	14
# Destinations	8	8	25	25
# Vehicle routes	365	134	1641	574

In order to make our study more realistic, we have defined four different vehicle types: sedan, van, wagon, and truck. Each one has its own characteristics according to the class they belong to, e.g. trucks are longer, slower and more pollutant than sedans, etc. The rest of characteristics are the probability of arriving, maximum speed, acceleration, deceleration, length, and the emission class from the HBEFA database [3]. In Table 1 the type of vehicles and their characteristics are listed.

We have analyzed the behavior of 4500 vehicles in *Malaga* and 4840 in *Madrid* for 7200 seconds. In *Malaga* we placed eight LED panels but in *Madrid* only four were effective, especially due to the geographic characteristics of this capital city, e.g. wide avenues, huge roundabouts, lots of parallel streets. The localizations of the panels were mainly chosen by taking into account several hot spots in the cities where traffic jams were more likely to happen. Due to the streets distribution of *Madrid*, we have up to 1641 different routes in this case study, compared with 365 in *Malaga*. Additionally, the rest of the characteristics of the case studies are shown in Table 2.

The geographical area analyzed in the city of Malaga includes the following areas: *Centro Histórico*, *Olletas*, *Ciudad Jardín*, and *El Limonar*, which together encompass an area of about $10.7Km^2$. The case study *Madrid* includes the areas *Barrio de la Latina*, *Parque del Retiro*, *Salamanca*, *Chueca*, *Plaza de España*, and *Malasaña*. The total area analyzed from Madrid is about $10.3Km^2$.

In Figure 2 both geographical areas are depicted, the maps from OpenStreetMap are in the left-hand column, and in the right-hand one, the corresponding models imported into SUMO. Additionally, the locations of the LED panels are also represented in this figure.

3.2 Evolutionary Algorithm (EA)

We have designed a (10+2)-EA (an elitist steady state EA with a population of ten individuals generating two new individuals at each step) in order to obtain the periods of time that each sign is presented to drivers. We have used Binary Tournament as the selection operator, Uniform Crossover as the recombination operator, and elitism as the replacement policy. The mutation operator was designed especially for our problem as described later in Section 3.2.3.

3.2.1 *Problem Representation*

In Figure 3 we can see the status vector containing time values for each sign to be shown to drivers. In this study each pair of values corresponds to the configuration of one single panel as there are only two possible signs on each one. The total number of panels (P) will depend on the characteristics of the streets in which they are placed.

The status vector for the case study *Malaga* consists of 16 integers which can take values between 30 and 300 as the number of seconds the corresponding sign is active. For *Madrid* we placed four LED panels consisting of two signs each (eight integers).

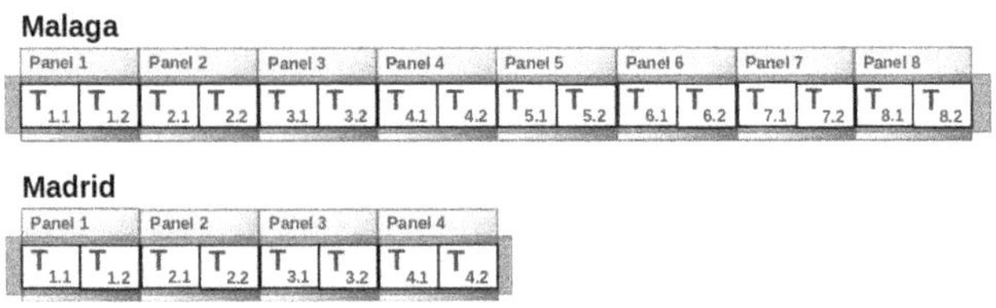

Figure 3: Status vectors of ***Malaga*** **and** ***Madrid*****.**

3.2.2 *Evaluation Function*

We want to reduce the average travel times of vehicles and observe how this optimization affects the emissions and fuel consumption. To achieve our objective, we propose the evaluation function presented in Equation 1 which is used to calculate the fitness of each individual.

There, N is the total number of vehicles entering the city, n is the number of vehicles leaving the city during the period of time analyzed, and $travel\ time_i$ is the travel time spent by the vehicle i for its journey.

$$F = \alpha_1(N - n) + \alpha_2^{-1}\frac{1}{n}\sum_{i=1}^{n} travel\ time_i \quad (1)$$

Moreover, α_1 and α_2 are the weights of each term calculated in order to normalize the fitness value calculated by the function. Note that the first term of the function penalizes individuals with one unit for each vehicle ($\alpha_1 = 1$) when there are still vehicles in the city at the end of the analysis period. Only when all vehicles end their journeys can we include the metrics from all of them in the fitness function computation, thereby the penalization term is not present ($N = n$). Additionally, we have calculated α_2 as described in Equation 2, so that the fitness of the experts' solution is equal to 1. There, λ is equal to four as we are evaluating four scenarios and averaging their fitness values during the optimization process in order to achieve more robust configurations to test in several unseen scenarios.

$$\alpha_2 = \frac{1}{\lambda}\sum_{i=1}^{\lambda}\frac{1}{n_i}\sum_{j=1}^{n_i} travel\ time_{ij} \quad (2)$$

Note that α_2 will be different for *Malaga* and *Madrid* as the average travel time of vehicles is different as well. It takes about one minute to calculate each fitness value as we need to test the configuration of the training scenarios using SUMO. As we are minimizing these variables of the problem, the lower the fitness value, the better.

3.2.3 Operators

As we stated before, we have used Binary Tournament, Uniform Crossover, and elitism as the replacement policy. The specific mutation operator is described in Algorithm 1.

Algorithm 1 Mutation Operator

```
procedure MUTATE(individual)
    panelConfigs ← getPanels(individual)
    for all p ∈ panelConfigs do
        if random() < P_m then
            signs ← getAllSigns(p)
            s ← selectOneSignRND(signs)
            for all ss ∈ signs do
                if ss == s then
                    incrementTime(ss, τ1)
                else
                    decrementTime(ss, τ2)
                end if
            end for
        end if
    end for
    return individual
end procedure
```

First, all panels from the individual are obtained. Second, some panel configurations are selected to be changed depending on the mutation probability (P_m). Third, all signs (all the different detours) from the panel selected are obtained and one of them is randomly chosen to have its time value incremented in τ_1. The rest of the signs on the panel (just one here as we have two detours on each panel) have their time value decremented in τ_2 Note that the time values are kept in the range of 30 – 300 so that the values can be truncated if necessary. Finally, when the main loop ends, the modified individual is returned.

In Figure 4 an example of the mutation of an individual is depicted. We can see that the third panel has been selected for mutation and its time values have been changed from (61, 274) to (56, 279).

Additionally, we have experimentally found the values of the crossover probability ($P_c = 0.6$), the mutation probability ($P_m = 1/L, L = \textit{status vector length}$), and $\tau_1 = \tau_2 = 5$.

4. EXPERIMENTS AND RESULTS

In the following sections we address the optimization of the case studies *Malaga* and *Madrid*. Second, we test the best solution from each algorithm in 200 different scenarios

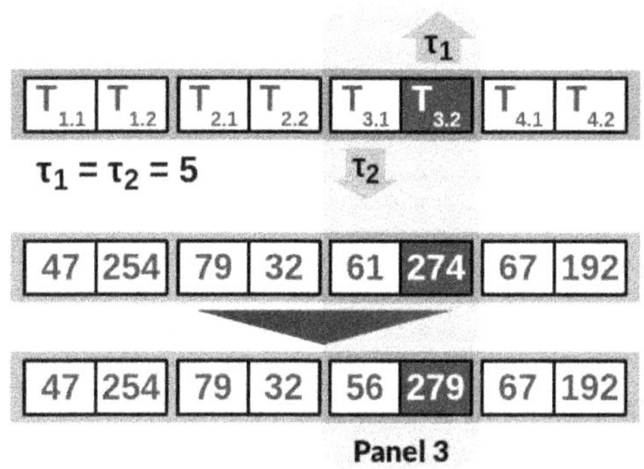

Figure 4: Example of the mutation operator applied to an individual. Note that $T_{3.2}$ is incremented in $\tau_1 = 5$ and $T_{3.1}$ in decremented in $\tau_2 = 5$.

(*Malaga*, $Malaga_{TT}$, *Madrid*, and $Madrid_{TT}$) in order to discover how robust and scalable the solutions are. Finally, we carry out a deep analysis of data and how Yellow Swarm behaves when the use rate is lower than 100%.

4.1 Training

We optimized four different scenarios of the case study *Malaga* (in total, 18000 vehicles) as well as four of *Madrid* (19360 vehicles) in order to achieve a robust configuration for the Yellow Swarm, using the EA. In previous similar approaches [12] this strategy has been used to achieve more robust solutions as it is better than using just only one. We completed 30 independent runs on each case study (the same four scenarios) and achieved the results presented in Table 3.

We can observe the mean values of not only travel times but also emissions, fuel consumption, and distances, as well as the standard deviation. We present the mean and standard deviation of the metrics from the experts' solution versus Yellow Swarm in both case studies, *Malaga* and *Madrid*, as well as the improvement achieved and the Wilcoxon p-value. The best improvements are observed in travel time values as this is the metric we are optimizing. However, we have also achieved a reduction of emissions and fuel consumption. Distances traveled are slightly longer when vehicles take the detours suggested (0.2% maximum). However, this was to be expected as they are driving through alternatives streets which are not part of the shortest path in order to achieve the global improvements discussed. Note that we have assumed, in this training, that drivers always follow the detours shown in the panels.

Table 3: Results of the optimization process of both case studies when optimizing four scenarios. Note that the improvements achieved are in bold.

	Malaga						*Madrid*					
Metrics	Experts' solution		Yellow Swarm		Impr.	Wilcoxon	Experts' solution		Yellow Swarm		Impr.	Wilcoxon
	Mean	StdDev	Mean	StdDev		p-value	Mean	StdDev	Mean	StdDev		p-value
Travel Time (s)	1903.2	2.3%	1562.1	2.5%	**17,9%**	0,00	1374.7	1.3%	1318.5	2.9%	**4.1%**	0,00
CO (mg)	15744.6	3.4%	13829.2	2.5%	**12.1%**	0,00	12144.2	2.0%	11705.8	2.7%	**3.6%**	0,04
CO_2 (mg)	1418052.7	1.5%	1332355.0	1.7%	**6.0%**	0,00	1165631.8	1.0%	1148906.4	1.8%	**1.4%**	0,00
HC (mg)	2360.3	3.2%	2103.4	3.4%	**10.9%**	0,00	1828.7	1.5%	1779.4	2.3%	**2.7%**	0,01
PM (mg)	224.9	6.2%	207.7	6.1%	**7.6%**	0,00	172.4	3.1%	171.4	2.6%	**0.6%**	0,15
NO (mg)	8904.6	5.2%	8483.0	5.5%	**4.7%**	0,00	7188.5	2.2%	7158.3	2.2%	**0.4%**	0,11
Fuel (ml)	562.6	1.4%	529.0	1.7%	**6.0%**	0,00	463.1	1.0%	456.5	1.7%	**1.4%**	0,00
Distance (m)	3451.3	0.7%	3457.2	0.3%	-0.2%	0,00	3096.3	0.2%	3099.8	0.2%	-0.1%	0.18

Table 4: **Configuration of panels obtained by the EA.**

Malaga															
Panel 1		Panel 2		Panel 3		Panel 4		Panel 5		Panel 6		Panel 7		Panel 8	
$T_{1.1}$	$T_{1.2}$	$T_{2.1}$	$T_{2.2}$	$T_{3.1}$	$T_{3.2}$	$T_{4.1}$	$T_{4.2}$	$T_{5.1}$	$T_{5.2}$	$T_{6.1}$	$T_{6.2}$	$T_{7.1}$	$T_{7.2}$	$T_{8.1}$	$T_{8.2}$
38	172	260	280	141	80	89	238	290	66	90	257	300	30	43	286

Madrid							
Panel 1		Panel 2		Panel 3		Panel 4	
$T_{1.1}$	$T_{1.2}$	$T_{2.1}$	$T_{2.2}$	$T_{3.1}$	$T_{3.2}$	$T_{4.1}$	$T_{4.2}$
194	30	215	294	30	228	46	286

Furthermore, we have calculated the Wilcoxon p-value to be sure that the improvements reported on each metric are statistically significant. We can see that in *Malaga* all the results of the optimization have a confidence level of greater than 99%. However, in *Madrid* only *Travel Time*, CO_2, HC, and *Fuel* have that confidence level, which as we are mainly optimizing travel times, is satisfactory in spite of the lower confidence level of the other metrics (96% in CO, 85% in PM, 89% in NO, and 82% in *Distance*).

Table 4 shows the values obtained as the configuration of Yellow Swarm for each case study. We can see that Panels 7 and 8 in *Malaga* and Panels 3 and 4 in *Madrid* present a highly asymmetric configuration (91%, 88%, 87%, and 86%, respectively). That is, the traffic which arrives at these panels is mainly being directed towards just one detour. It denotes that the other detours have almost been discarded by the EA because they produce worser traffic flows. Nevertheless, other time slots are more balanced, e.g. Panel 2 (48%) in *Malaga*, and Panel 2 (42%) in *Madrid*.

4.2 Test of 50 Scenarios

We have tested our Yellow Swarm on 50 new different scenarios of each case study (*Malaga* and *Madrid*) and a further 100 scenarios where vehicles only use the fastest routes (50 scenarios of $Malaga_{TT}$ and 50 of $Madrid_{TT}$) which results in a total of 200 different scenarios.

Table 5 shows the average improvements obtained in the four case studies when we compare the experts' solution to Yellow Swam. In addition, the best scenario and the percentage of scenarios improved are shown.

In the case study *Malaga*, we can observe an average improvement of: 13.4% (18.4% max.) in travel times, 10.3% (12.9% max.) in CO emissions, 5% (7.4% max.) in CO_2 emissions, 9.5% (11.8% max.) in HC, 7.6% (10.6% max.) in PM, 4.9% (7,2% max.) in NO, and 4.9% (7.4% max.) in fuel consumption. Furthermore, the distance traveled by vehicles is 0.9% longer on average as we are suggesting detours that are not part of the shortest path. This, however, is negligible, especially when compared to the improvement achieved in travel times. Yellow Swarm was able to improve upon the experts' solution in all 50 scenarios tested (100%) in both travel times and emissions.

In $Malaga_{TT}$ we achieved even better results (vehicles' travel times are up to 32.3% shorter on average) as its routes involve only the fastest ones. Consequently, as traffic jams are more likely to happen in that situation, Yellow Swarm has turned out to be more efficient preventing them.

When we decided to include *Madrid* in this study, we wanted to compare two cities with different topologies. While the geographical area of *Malaga* consists of narrow streets and very few avenues and roundabouts, *Madrid* boasts wide avenues with up to ten lanes, huge roundabouts, and square blocks. Although it allowed us to include more vehicles in the study of *Madrid*, it also made it more difficult to optimize. Regardless, our results show travel times of 2.1% shorter on average (8.1% max.) and reductions in the gases emitted between 0.7% and 1.5% (10.1% max.). Moreover, we were able to improve travel times in 72% of the 50 scenarios as well as emissions in more than 60% of them.

Finally, in the case study $Madrid_{TT}$ the results are better than in *Madrid* for the same reasons explained when comparing *Malaga* to $Malaga_{TT}$, i.e. vehicles are taking only faster routes.

Table 5: Improvement achieved in the average vehicles' travel times, gas emissions, fuel consumption, and distance traveled in the four case studies.

		Travel Time	CO	CO_2	HC	PM	NO	*Fuel*	*Distance*
Malaga	Average 50 Scenarios	13.4%	10.3%	5.0%	9.5%	7.6%	4.9%	4.9%	-0.9%
	Best Scenario	18.4%	12.9%	7.4%	11.8%	10.6%	7.2%	7.4%	-0.6%
	% Scenarios Improved	100.0%	100.0%	100.0%	100.0%	100.0%	100.0%	100.0%	8.0%
$Malaga_{TT}$	Average 50 Scenarios	22.2%	17.9%	9.8%	16.2%	13.1%	9.0%	9.6%	-2.6%
	Best Scenario	32.3%	25.3%	16.5%	23.3%	22.9%	16.6%	16.4%	-1.1%
	% Scenarios Improved	100.0%	100.0%	100.0%	100.0%	100.0%	100.0%	100.0%	2.0%
Madrid	Average 50 Scenarios	2.1%	1.5%	0.8%	1.3%	1.1%	0.7%	0.8%	-0.5%
	Best Scenario	8.1%	10.1%	3.2%	8.9%	3.7%	2.5%	3.2%	0.5%
	% Scenarios Improved	72.0%	66.0%	68.0%	68.0%	60.0%	62.0%	68.0%	34.0%
$Madrid_{TT}$	Average 50 Scenarios	2.3%	1.7%	0.8%	1.6%	1.4%	0.8%	0.8%	-0.4%
	Best Scenario	9.1%	7.5%	3.8%	6.4%	3.9%	2.9%	3.8%	-0.2%
	% Scenarios Improved	74.0%	70.0%	64.0%	70.0%	68.0%	68.0%	64.0%	16.0%

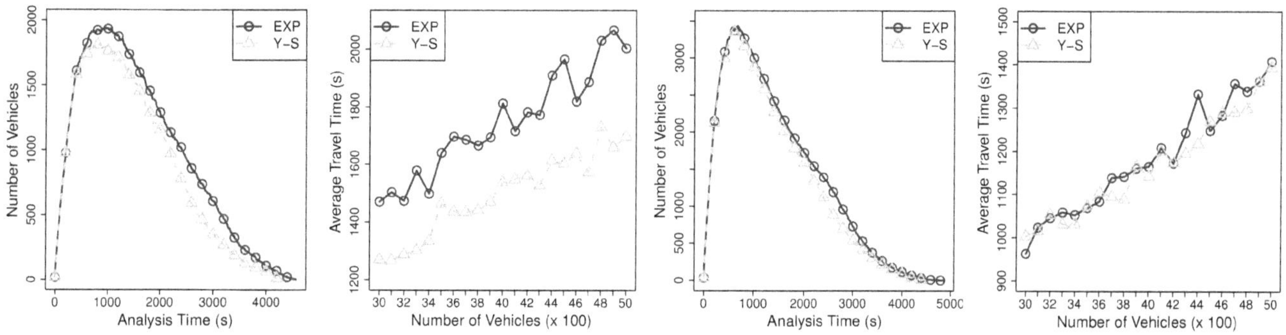

(a) *Malaga* (b) *Malaga* (c) *Madrid* (d) *Madrid*

Figure 5: Traffic density and travel time vs. number of vehicles in *Malaga* and *Madrid*. We compare the values from the experts' solution to the Yellow Swarm ones.

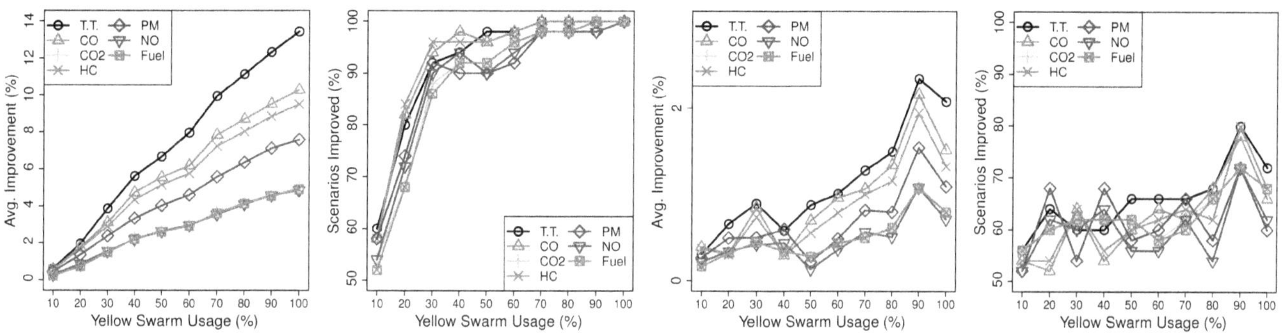

(a) *Malaga* (b) *Malaga* (c) *Madrid* (d) *Madrid*

Figure 6: Average improvement and scenarios improved vs. panel use when a only percentage of the drivers decide to follow the detours. The grater the acceptation of drivers, the greater the sustainability of the city.

4.3 Further analysis

Our next step in our experimentation focused on analyzing the data collected even further. We have studied the traffic density and the number of vehicles in the city when vehicles follow the routes of the experts' solution and when they follow the detours proposed by Yellow Swarm. In Figure 5 we show plots on traffic density and number of vehicles in the city. Figure 5(a) shows how vehicles behave during the analysis in *Malaga* where we can see that Yellow Swarm keeps the number of vehicles to lower than the experts' solution and also how it ensures the last vehicle leaves the city earlier. Figure 5(b) shows how the system scales with respect to the number of vehicles in the city. We can see that the average travel time is always shorter when drivers follow the detours suggested by Yellow Swarm as it does not depend on the number of vehicles. Figures 5(c) and 5(d) present the same study for *Madrid*. In this case the curves are not so different although the behavior is still better when vehicles follow the signs from the Yellow Swarm.

Our final step consists of testing Yellow Swarm when it is used by just a few vehicles. This situation makes common sense, as the directions are just suggestions and we cannot expect all drivers to follow them (confusions, lack of trust or information, etc.) We have tested it on 50 scenarios from a use rate of 10% to 90% (100% has been studied previously in this article). All in all, it adds up to 450 scenarios of *Malaga* and 450 of *Madrid* which have been used to produce the graphs presented in Figure 6. The average improvement in *Malaga* as well as the percentage of scenarios improved are depicted in Figures 6(a) and 6(b) respectively. As can be seen, Yellow Swarm always reduces the average travel times and levels of gas emitted in each case study, even at low penetration rates. This confirms our optimization strategy as well as the correct placing of the panels. Nevertheless, the number of scenarios improved when not all vehicles are following the detours decreases: fewer users, lower the improvement, as one could expect.

However, the behavior of Yellow Swarm in *Madrid* has turned out to be different from *Malaga*. In spite of the fact that the metrics are always improved for all the usage rates, figures 6(c) and 6(d) show a behavior that is not as neat as in *Malaga*, especially due to the reasons we have discussed before. However, it is clear that there is an improvement in each metric when we use Yellow Swarm, even for penetration rates as low as 10%.

5. CONCLUSIONS

In this article we have presented the reduction of travel times, greenhouse gas emissions, and fuel consumption of road traffic in two cities of Spain: Malaga and Madrid.

We have designed an evolutionary algorithm to optimize the training scenarios by using a series of LED panels to propose detours to vehicles, and found solutions that improve upon the experts' ones during the optimization process with statistical significance.

We have achieved average reductions of 13.4% in travel times, 10.3% in CO, 9.5% in HC, 7.6% in PM, and about 5% in the rest of the emissions and fuel consumption. We have observed an increase in route lengths (2.6% max.) which is a consequence of detouring vehicles via alternative streets which are not included in the shortest path.

Our results, after generalizing our solution to 200 different scenarios, show that Yellow Swarm has worked in all of them and reduced travel times in 87% of them, while emissions were shorter in at least 60% of these scenarios.

As we have considered different cities (topologies, avenues, roundabouts, intersections) we have observed several variations in the results. However, we have improved all the metrics, even when only 10% of vehicles are obeying the instructions of Yellow Swarm.

As a matter for future work, we are testing different strategies to optimally place LED panels throughout the city. We are also looking at possible complex operators for the EA which take into account deeper relationships existing between the panels. Moreover, we want to improve upon our results, especially in the harder scenarios, extend our study to the entire city (slower evaluations as SUMO needs more time and the search space is bigger), and include actual traffic distributions at different times of the day obtained from data published by city councils in order to adapt our system to the many possible variations

6. ACKNOWLEDGMENTS

This research is partially funded by project number 8.06/5.47.4142 in collaboration with the VSB-Technical University of Ostrava, project number 8.06/5.47.4356, and UMA/FEDER FC14-TIC36. Daniel H. Stolfi is supported by a FPU grant (FPU13/00954) from the Spanish Ministry of Education, Culture and Sports. University of Malaga. International Campus of Excellence Andalucia TECH.

7. REFERENCES

[1] F. Angius, M. Reineri, C. Chiasserini, M. Gerla, and G. Pau. Towards a realistic optimization of urban traffic flows. In *Intelligent Transportation Systems (ITSC), 2012 15th International IEEE Conference on*, pages 1661–1668, Sept. 2012.

[2] C. Guerreiro, F. de Leeuw, and V. Foltescu. Air quality in Europe - 2013 report. Technical report, European Environment Agency, 2013.

[3] S. Hausberger, M. Rexeis, M. Zallinger, and R. Luz. Emission Factors from the Model PHEM for the HBEFA Version 3. Technical Report I, 2009.

[4] O. Hertel, S. S. Jensen, M. Hvidberg, M. Ketzel, R. Berkowicz, F. Palmgren, P. Wåhlin, M. Glasius, S. Loft, P. Vinzents, O. Raaschou-Nielsen, M. Sø rensen, and H. Bak. Assessing the Impacts of Traffic Air Pollution on Human Exposure and Health. In *Road Pricing, the Economy and the Environment*, Advances in Spatial Science, pages 277–299. Springer Berlin Heidelberg, 2008.

[5] D. Krajzewicz, J. Erdmann, M. Behrisch, and L. Bieker. Recent Development and Applications of SUMO – Simulation of Urban MObility. *International Journal On Advances in Systems and Measurements*, 5(3):128–138, 2012.

[6] S. Kwatirayo, J. Almhana, and Z. Liu. Adaptive Traffic Light Control using VANET: A case study. In *Wireless Communications and Mobile Computing Conference (IWCMC), 2013 9th International*, pages 752–757, July 2013.

[7] D. Loomis, Y. Grosse, B. Lauby-Secretan, F. El Ghissassi, V. Bouvard, L. Benbrahim-Tallaa, N. Guha, R. Baan, H. Mattock, and K. Straif. The carcinogenicity of outdoor air pollution. *The Lancet Oncology*, 14(13):1262–1263, 2013.

[8] D. Mckenney and T. White. Distributed and Adaptive Traffic Signal Control Within a Realistic Traffic Simulation. *Eng. Appl. Artif. Intell.*, 26(1):574–583, Jan. 2013.

[9] U. Nations. World Urbanization Prospects The 2011 Revision. Technical report, 2011.

[10] T. Saber, A. Ventresque, and J. Murphy. ROThAr: Real-Time On-Line Traffic Assignment with Load Estimation. In *Proceedings of the 2013 IEEE/ACM 17th International Symposium on Distributed Simulation and Real Time Applications*, DS-RT '13, pages 79–86, Washington, DC, USA, 2013. IEEE Computer Society.

[11] D. Schrank, B. Eisele, and T. Lomax. TTI's 2012 Urban Mobility Report. Technical report, Texas A&M Transportation Institute, 2012.

[12] D. H. Stolfi and E. Alba. Eco-friendly Reduction of Travel Times in European Smart Cities. In *Proceedings of the 2014 Conference on Genetic and Evolutionary Computation*, GECCO '14, pages 1207–1214, New York, NY, USA, 2014. ACM.

[13] D. H. Stolfi and E. Alba. Red Swarm: Reducing travel times in smart cities by using bio-inspired algorithms. *Applied Soft Computing*, 24(0):181–195, Nov. 2014.

[14] Y. Sugiyama, M. Fukui, M. Kikuchi, K. Hasebe, A. Nakayama, K. Nishinari, S.-i. Tadaki, and S. Yukawa. Traffic jams without bottlenecks: experimental evidence for the physical mechanism of the formation of a jam. *New Journal of Physics*, 10(3), Mar. 2008.

[15] TNS Opinion & Social. Attitudes of Europeans towards urban mobility. Technical Report June, 2013.

[16] A. Wegener and M. Piórkowski. TraCI: An Interface for Coupling Road Traffic and Network Simulators. In *Proceedings of the 11th Communications and Networking Simulation Symposium*, CNS '08, pages 155–163, New York, NY, USA, 2008. ACM.

A Genetic Programming Approach to Cost-Sensitive Control in Resource Constrained Sensor Systems

Afsoon Yousefi Zowj
Dept. of Computer Science
University of Vermont
ayousef1@uvm.edu

Josh C Bongard
Dept. of Computer Science
University of Vermont
jbongard@uvm.edu

Christian Skalka
Dept. of Computer Science
University of Vermont
skalka@cs.uvm.edu

ABSTRACT

Resource constrained sensor systems are an increasingly attractive option in a variety of environmental monitoring domains, due to continued improvements in sensor technology. However, sensors for the same measurement application can differ in terms of cost and accuracy, while fluctuations in environmental conditions can impact both application requirements and available energy. This raises the problem of automatically controlling heterogeneous sensor suites in resource constrained sensor system applications, in a manner that balances cost and accuracy of available sensors. We present a method that employs a hierarchy of model ensembles trained by genetic programming (GP): if model ensembles that poll low-cost sensors exhibit too much prediction uncertainty, they automatically transfer the burden of prediction to other GP-trained model ensembles that poll more expensive and accurate sensors. We show that, for increasingly challenging datasets, this hierarchical approach makes predictions with equivalent accuracy yet lower cost than a similar yet non-hierarchical method in which a single GP-generated model determines which sensors to poll at any given time. Our results thus show that a hierarchy of GP-trained ensembles can serve as a control algorithm for heterogeneous sensor suites in resource constrained sensor system applications that balances cost and accuracy.

Categories and Subject Descriptors

I.2 [**Computing Methodologies**]: Artificial Intelligence

Keywords

Genetic Programming, Resource Constrained Sensor Systems, Cost-Sensitive Control, Sensor Fusion

1. INTRODUCTION

Resource constrained sensor systems (RCSS) such as Wireless Sensor Networks have revolutionized environmental monitoring by combining low cost with flexibility in sensor capabilities [29]. They have been used in diverse environmental monitoring applications and continue to be adapted in new fields. Because RCSS are often, even typically, deployed in remote locations, and thus rely on combinations of battery power and energy harvesting, a major challenge in RCSS design is to minimize system power consumption.

Minimizing power consumption can be accomplished in a variety of ways, in particular by adapting sensor control strategies that optimize the balance between measurement accuracy and the cost of powering sensors [28]. In this paper, we propose new sensor control algorithms for RCSS with heterogeneous sensor suites that balance cost and accuracy, obtained using genetic programming (GP) techniques.

By "heterogeneous sensor suite", we mean RCSS equipped with multiple types of sensors for prediction of the same phenomena. Each of these sensors is characterized by its accuracy in relation to the phenomena, and a cost of use which is often measured by its power consumption. Such systems support multi-modal sensor fusion, a well-studied technique where data from multiple sensor modalities (types) is combined to predict a single variable [28]. The contribution of our work is a consideration of cost in multi-modal sensor fusion, and the development and testing of associated control algorithms. These algorithms will call upon particular sensors only when needed, and otherwise rely on the cheapest available sensors at any given time. Our problem is distinguished from adaptive sampling [28], in that the latter is concerned with optimally modulating sampling frequency of a given sensor, not choosing between a suite of possible sensors.

While various multi-modal sensor fusion applications exist, we are especially interested in the Snowcloud system which combines snow density telemetry with snow depth and air temperature sensors to predict areal snow water equivalent (SWE) [22]. We envision extending Snowcloud to incorporate ground based light detection and ranging (LIDAR) scanning [4] to be used for SWE estimation as part of its sensor suite. However, while LIDAR yields more accurate data than existing Snowcloud telemetry, it does so at significant additional power cost. Thus, the challenge is to commit these resources only at optimal times. It is also a refinement of multi-modal sensor fusion, since we are mainly interested in settings where available data gathering techniques differ in accuracy, with less accurate sensors being cheaper than more accurate ones.

A fundamental component of our approach is the use of prediction *uncertainty* to drive sensor usage. We propose a scheme whereby predictions are attempted using lower-cost sensors at first. If uncertainty is below an acceptable threshold, then the prediction is used. Otherwise we switch to higher-cost sensors, make a new prediction based on those inputs, evaluate uncertainty again, and continue to move the burden of prediction to more accurate and costly sensors as needed. This scheme is discussed in detail in Section 3.4 and described graphically in Figure 2. Note that while the Snowcloud system is an intended application of this scheme, it

GECCO '15, July 11 - 15, 2015, Madrid, Spain
© 2015 ACM. ISBN 978-1-4503-3472-3/15/07...$15.00
DOI: http://dx.doi.org/10.1145/2739480.2754751

can be generalized to any RCSS application using heterogeneous sensor suites comprising sensors with varying cost and accuracy.

To quantify uncertainty we are aided by machine learning ensemble methods– we use entropy in ensemble predictions as a proxy for uncertainty [21]. To obtain predictive models themselves, in this work we use genetic programming (GP). This is largely due to characteristics of our intended application space. Previous work has demonstrated that the relationships between snow cover and the topographic and meteorological factors that influence it include nonlinearities [24], while the spatial distribution of SWE is nonlinear because it is influenced simultaneously by various forcing effects [25]. Nonlinear predictors are therefore desirable. Furthermore, recent results [6] show that GP has advantages over other approaches (such as C4.5) due to associated techniques for preventing overfitting, e.g. treating model size minimization as an objective [11]. Although C4.5 only supports classification, sufficiently fine classification granularity can achieve competitive performance on regression problems, and this approach is popular in the environmental science community [6]. Finally, GP is appealing due to its white-box nature: it can potentially provide physical insights into modeled phenomena.

An alternative approach to our problem is to not rely on external measures of entropy to switch between sensors, but to treat cost as an additional objective in a multi-objective optimization problem. We explore this option in our work, in direct comparison to the hierarchical approach. However, due to the "curse of dimensionality", adding another optimization dimension may have deleterious effects on prediction performance, especially since selection for size to avoid overfitting already imposes a multi-objective optimization regime [5]. We therefore hypothesize that a hierarchical approach will outperform a non-hierarchical approach in settings where multiple sensors with differing predictive abilities, and we explore this comparison in our experiments.

2. RELATED WORK

Previous work on adaptive sampling [28] has aimed to reduce sampling rates in RCSS applications to balance sensor cost and accuracy. In particular, Alippi *et al.* [3] have tried to find the optimal adaptive frequency of sampling for avalanche monitoring. It has further been claimed that compressed sensing — sending aggregated data instead of raw data — performs better in conjunction with reducing sampling rates, rather than just reducing the sampling rate alone [15]. A variety of methods for compressed sensing [8] have been proposed. Although these methods have achieved cost reduction in monitoring, they are not applicable to our problem since we intend not to change the rate of sampling one sensor type, but rather to reduce sampling cost by switching between available sensors of different type and accuracy.

Another line of work focuses on finding the optimal location for sensors in distributed deployments, in order to maximize accuracy while minimizing deployment densities. Krause *et al.* [13] have used a probabilistic method to predict the communication cost for a given deployment topology. Papadimitriou *et al.* [17] have employed GP and a Bayesian statistical method to minimize entropy over a set of sensor locations. In contrast, our work is concerned with reducing the cost of sampling from an available set of sensors at any given time, not with reducing the densities of sensor topologies.

In work on so-called multi-modal sensor fusion, data from multiple sensors in a potentially heterogeneous suite are aggregated to monitor a specific measurement application [26, 9]. This method has been widely used, for example in visual monitoring [16, 18] and target tracking [19, 23]. Data-fusion focuses on sensor applications that need to compute the correlation between multiple sensor modules and cannot be measured by a single sensor. However, these works do not consider the cost of using different sensors, or minimizing cost.

Cost sensitive multi-modal sensor fusion methods have been developed to balance cost against accuracy, with an eye towards providing fault tolerance [12]. However, we are not concerned with fault tolerance, but strictly between selecting sensors from heterogeneous suites. Willett *et al.* [28] use a small number of sensors to send their readings to a fusion center, and based on the correlation among the sensed data, the fusion center decides which additional sensors should be activated. The same concept has also been tried in a distributed fashion [14]. However, sensing costs in these cases are a function of the number of sensors sampled, not their type.

Perhaps most related to our work is that of Wang *et al.* [27]. They propose a method to find the optimal set of sensors to be polled, using a hybrid tree, where non-leaf nodes act as a decision tree and leaves are standard regression models using a subset of sensors. However, these trees support decision making based on external constraints, i.e. which sensors to use depending on an organization's goals and resources. In contrast, our models are intended to support sensor control in RCSS during deployments.

Outside of the adaptive sampling and sensor fusion fields, multi-objective optimization has been used for cost-sensitive modeling. For example Kim [11] set error as one objective and tree size as another, as we do here. Zhao [30] sets the false negative rate and false positive rate as the two objectives. However, these works do not consider the hierarchical approach that we do.

3. METHODS

This section provides a formalization of the problem, how genetic programming is applied to solve it, and the two variants of genetic programming that we compare in this work. All of the material for replicating the work described here is available online [1].

3.1 Problem Formalization

Let us assume that t values of some environmental phenomenon $\mathbf{g}$ (the ground truth) are known at time steps $1, \ldots t$. These values are stored in $\mathbf{g} = g_1, \ldots g_t$. Let us further assume there are k sensors $s_1, \ldots s_k$ available that can be used to predict $\mathbf{g}$. Let $r_i^{(t)}$ denote the reading of sensor i taken at time t. Moreover, let $s^{(t)}$ and $r^{(t)}$ denote a subset of sensors, and readings taken from them, at time t. We denote the amount of variance of $\mathbf{g}$ explained by sensor i as $v_{r_i}^{(\mathbf{g})}$. This value is determined by linearly regressing only r_i against g. Finally, let $e_i = 100(1 - v_{r_i}^{(\mathbf{g})})$ and c_i represent the prediction error and cost of using sensor i respectively. Using this formulation, e_i represents the percentage of prediction error incurred by just using sensor i to predict $\mathbf{g}$.

The cost of a sensor c_i is usually inversely proportional to its error e_i, so for the work reported below, we set $c_i = v_{\mathbf{r}_i}^{(\mathbf{g})}$ for each sensor. In certain sensor deployments there may be other factors that affect c_i such as power consumption, market price, effort required to collect a sensor's reading, proprietary issues, and so on.

We suppose that an ordering of sensors exists such that s_1 is the least expensive sensor with the highest error and s_k is the most expensive sensor with the lowest error. Formally,

$$\forall i, j \,.\, 1 \leq i < j \leq k \rightarrow e_i > e_j \wedge c_i < c_j .$$

Let us denote the prediction of a model using a subset of sensors at time t by $p^{(t)}$, i.e., $p^{(t)}$ is a function on $\mathbf{r}^{(t)}$. Then, the error of each sampling $e^{(t)}$ would be

$$e^{(t)} \triangleq |p^{(t)} - g^{(t)}|.$$

The cost of each sampling, $c^{(t)}$ is the cumulated cost of all sensors $s_i \in \mathbf{s}^{(t)}$ that were polled for that sampling:

$$c^{(t)} \triangleq \sum_{j \in \{i | s_i \in \mathbf{s}^{(t)}\}} c_j.$$

It is desired that each sampling $\mathbf{s}^{(t)}$ entails low error and cost. That is, the following equality is desirable:

$$\underset{\mathbf{s}^{(t)}}{\operatorname{argmin}}\, e^{(t)} = \underset{\mathbf{s}^{(t)}}{\operatorname{argmin}}\, c^{(t)}.$$

Our goal is to design models which combine and transform sensor readings to accurately predict the outcome measure, but can also intelligently determine which sensors to poll when cheap, less accurate sensors exhibit uncertainty about the current prediction.

3.2 General Genetic Programming approach

Genetic programming has widely been employed for regression tasks in which the functional form of the equations relating inputs to outputs is unknown. Here, inputs are sensor values and output is a prediction for a given outcome measurement.

Although many recent improvements have been proposed for GP, here we have kept the genetic programming algorithm simple and instead focused on comparing GP-generated hierarchical and non-hierarchical models. Thus, GP is restricted to the four simple algebraic operators, and each evolutionary trial is initialized with a fixed-sized population of randomly-generated solutions containing three nodes. Maximum tree depth is not set since the tree size is considered as an objective in multi-objective optimization. The crossover rate is set to 0.2 and no fitness stall is considered. If the number of non-dominated solutions reaches 50% of the population size, the training restarts. At the conclusion of each generation, four values are computed for each solution: (1) *error* on training data as defined below, (2) the combined *cost* of the sensors used to make the prediction, (3) the *size* of the solution, and (4) the *age* of the solution. We now discuss each in turn.

Error: Let n be the population size and j range over $\{1, \cdots, n\}$. Let t_j be some solution tree. We represent the error of sampling at time t using solution t_j with $e^{(t)}_{t_j}$. Moreover, d^{train} and d^{test} denote the training dataset and testing dataset, respectively. Then, we define the error on training data using solution t_j by $e^{\text{train}}_{t_j}$ and as the average of $e^{(t)}_{t_j}$ on all samples in d^{train}, i.e.,

$$e^{\text{train}}_{t_j} \triangleq \sum_{g^{(t)} \in d^{\text{train}}} \frac{e^{(t)}_{t_j}}{|d^{\text{train}}|}.$$

Each solution t_j was allowed to use a subset (possibly empty) of available sensors. The cost of each solution depends on the sensors that are employed and the sampling.

Cost: As described in the following sub-sections, the current readings of the sensors may trigger readings from additional sensors. Thus, different $r^{(t)}_i$ may cause t_j to need different $\mathbf{s}^{(t)}$. The average cost of a tree on training data $c^{\text{train}}_{t_j}$ is thus defined as the cost of all of the sensors that have been used to predict the outcome for each training instance, averaged over all instances in the training data set:

$$c^{\text{train}}_{t_j} \triangleq \sum_{\mathbf{r}^{(t)} \in d^{\text{train}}} \sum_{l \in \{i | s_i \in \mathbf{s}^{(t)}\}} \frac{c_l}{|d^{\text{train}}|}.$$

If a solution uses a sensor more than once, no extra cost is incurred: because the sensor has already been polled, its output is already available and can thus be re-used as often as required.

Size: To avoid bloat, solution size was incorporated into the fitness objectives during the optimization process [7].

Age: We employed the Age-Fitness Pareto Optimization (AFPO) method [20], which injects a new randomly-generated solution into the population at each generation and compares the solutions with same age in an effort to guard against convergence. Each solution's age is defined as the number of generations since its oldest ancestor was injected into the population. A new solution produced by mutating an existing solution inherits the same age as its parent. If two existing parents are crossed to produce two new offspring, the offspring inherit the age of the older of the two parents. AFPO is an multiobjective optimization method as solution age is used as an additional fitness objective during optimization.

Optimization. At the end of each generation, the Pareto front is computed according to the objectives used, and the dominated solutions are discarded. Multi-objective optimization with all four objectives described above could easily lead to population collapse in the sense that all members of the population could become non-dominated. To guard against this eventuality, one possibility is to restart the evolutionary run with new solutions if no dominated solutions are detected in the population at the end of a given generation. Alternatively, a very large population size can be employed. However, both of these solutions greatly increase the computational effort required to obtain satisfactory solutions to the given problem. To avoid this situation, different multi-objective optimization approaches has been proposed. One of the simplest non-parametric approaches is to reduce the number of objectives by multiplying objectives together and using the result in the optimization process [10]. In this experiment, since error is the most important outcome, error is used for the primary objective and the second objective is the result of multiplying cost, size and age together.

Once the dominated solutions are deleted, the empty slots in the population are then filled by mutating and crossing copies of the non-dominated solutions. Tournament selection is used to select parents from the front for these operations. After the last generation, age is discarded when computing members of the Pareto front, since the goal is to use only small, accurate and cost-effective solutions for prediction, regardless of their age.

3.3 Non-hierarchical GP

A naive approach to cost-sensitive modeling using GP would be to evolve individual trees that add conditional and comparative operators to the base set of operators, and allow the tree to poll the values of all sensors if desired, as shown in Figure 1.A. In this way, different parts of the solution tree will be visited depending on the current values of the sensors. Successful solutions may evolve which only visit nodes containing references to expensive sensors—which are then polled—if less expensive sensors report certain combinations of values that signal these sensors are unlikely to predict well given the current circumstances. $e^{\text{train}}_{t_j}$ and $c^{\text{train}}_{t_j} * \text{age} * \text{size}$ are employed as the two main objectives in the optimization process.

Figure 1.B shows an hypothetical example of a GP solution t_j that has evolved to encode a useful conditional. In this example, an inexpensive sensor s_1 is first polled. If its reported value $r^{(t)}_1$ is below some threshold, the reading of a more expensive sensor s_2 is going to be used. It is assumed here that s_1 tends to make poor predictions of the outcome if its reading is below 1.43. If this threshold is exceeded, $r^{(t)}_1$ is then used to predict the outcome.

Conditional operators should, indirectly, encode the differential effects on the available sensors, and the relative costs of those sen-

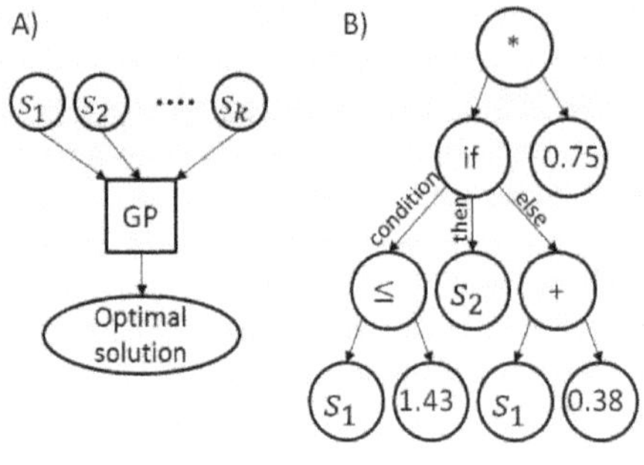

Figure 1:A)Non-hierarchical framework.B)A non-hierarchical sample solution.

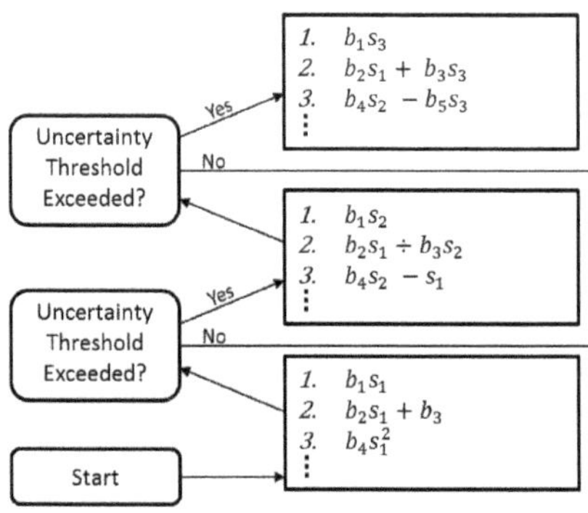

Figure 2: Hierarchical framework.

sors. Note that this is possible even if GP does not have direct access to these differential effects and costs, as they are indirectly reflected in the errors and costs incurred when each solution is evaluated. This issue is worth mentioning in that these effects are complex, non-linear and noisy, and even field experts cannot define them precisely.

3.4 Hierarchical GP

An alternative approach to reconciling prediction error and prediction cost is to build a hierarchy of models: models in the lower layers only have access to inexpensive sensors, while models in the upper layers have access to a greater subset of the sensors, including more expensive ones. When deployed, the overall model returns a prediction from a lower layer if the inexpensive sensors are confident of their combined prediction. If they are not, predictions are drawn from a higher layer.

Briefly, constructing such a model proceeds in two phases:

1. First, build a set of k layers, one for each sensor modality. For each layer i, run GP to find a set of accurate and low-cost solutions that use one or more sensors from the set $s_1, s_2, \ldots s_i$.
2. Define conditions which determine which layer should be allowed to provide the prediction, given the current environmental conditions.

Figure 2 illustrates what such a hierarchical model looks like. At the outset of attempting to provide a prediction for the current environmental conditions, the models stored in the lowest layer are evaluated, which only have access to the least expensive sensor s_1. If the certainty of their combined predictions is acceptable, return the combined prediction of these models. Otherwise, evaluate the models at the next layer, which have access to s_1 and the next least expensive sensor s_2. If these models are acceptably confident in the prediction, return their combined prediction; otherwise, evaluate the solutions at the next layer, and so on. If the top layer is reached, the combined predictions of the models found there are returned as the overall prediction, regardless of their level of certainty. The incremental construction of these models is described next.

Starting with the least expensive sensor s_1, GP is used to find the best models for converting $r_1^{(t)}$ to $g^{(t)}$. When GP terminates, the final non-dominated solutions are then organized as a group named layer L_1. The same process is repeated for s_2, except for the fact that since s_1 is already polled in L_1, it may be incorporated into models during evolution without incurring an extra cost for the solution tree that makes use of it. Similarly, for each sensor s_i, a separate GP run is performed with sensors s_1 to s_i available as input to construct layer L_i. These layers are then organized in a hierarchical fashion. The order of layers is based on the cost of the most expensive sensor they are representing, from L_1 to L_k. Suppose each layer L_i consists of n_i solutions and the jth solution t_j in L_i is denoted as $t_{i,j}$. Let $p_{t_{i,j}}^{(t)}$ denote the prediction of $g^{(t)}$ that $t_{i,j}$ provides. Then, the final prediction of layer L_i for $g^{(t)}$ is

$$p_{L_i}^{(t)} \triangleq \sum_{j=1}^{n_i} \frac{p_{t_{i,j}}^{(t)}}{n_i}.$$

The error that corresponds to $p_{L_i}^{(t)}$ is

$$e_{L_i}^{(t)} \triangleq |p_{L_i}^{(t)} - g^{(t)}|.$$

In the second phase, a conditional must be formulated to determine whether the current layer should return its prediction, or whether the burden of prediction should be passed up to the next layer. One common method for measuring how confident an ensemble of models is, is to compute the variance in their predictions [21]: if variance is low, and those models are sufficiently independent of one another, there is a greater likelihood that their combined predictions can be trusted. If variance is high, this is likely the result of differing assumptions encoded in the models, which cannot all be true reflections of the hidden relationship being modeled. Note the assumption here that the models are relatively independent: a set of identical models will never exhibit a variance in their predictions, regardless of how accurate the individual models are. We can be somewhat confident of the independence of our models, as they are produced by the AFPO algorithm: models with differing ages are likely to arrive on the final Pareto front used to build each layer, and such differently-aged genomes are likely to be somewhat independent because of their different genetic origins.

Formally: Let $p_{L_i}^{\text{train(t)}}$ and $e_{L_i}^{\text{train(t)}}$ denote $p_{L_i}^{(t)}$ and $e_{L_i}^{(t)}$ using $\mathbf{r}^{(t)}$ on d^{train}, respectively. Similarly, $p_{L_i}^{\text{test(t)}}$ and $e_{L_i}^{\text{test(t)}}$ respectively denote $p_{L_i}^{(t)}$ and $e_{L_i}^{(t)}$ using $\mathbf{r}^{(t)}$ on d^{test}. Moreover, assume $v_i^{\text{train(t)}}$ and $v_i^{\text{test(t)}}$ are the variances of all $p_{t_{i,j}}^{(t)}$s on d^{train} and d^{test}. Also, v_i^{train} denotes $v_i^{\text{train(t)}}$ averaged over all the samplings in d^{train}.

To determine whether the burden of prediction should remain with the current layer or passed off to a higher layer, we measure the difference in prediction variance between the models when presented with the training data (v_i^{train}) or with the testing data, i.e. the current environmental conditions ($v_i^{\text{test(t)}}$). When $v_i^{\text{test(t)}}$ is almost the same as v_i^{train}, there is a high probability that $e_{L_i}^{\text{test(t)}}$ is an approximation of $e_{L_i}^{\text{train(t)}}$, and we can be relatively confident that these

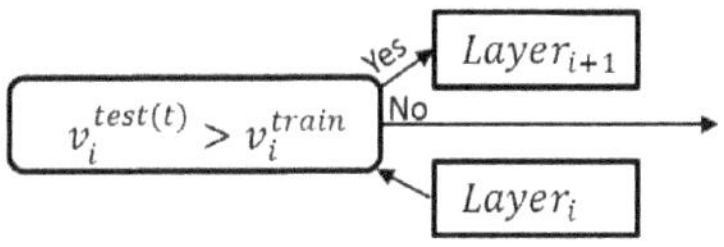

Figure 3: Using the difference between training data prediction variance and test data prediction variance as the condition for switching between model layers.

models will yield a good collective prediction of $g^{(t)}$. When the variance of test data prediction is significantly higher than prediction on the training data, this signals that the solutions in that layer are exhibiting increased disagreement regarding the current environmental conditions. This could be due to the fact that a specific sensor is not physically able to predict under the current conditions, or the solutions have not been trained for the current situation. In such an eventuality it would be advantageous to switch to the next layer, in the hope that its models will exhibit more confidence in their ability to predict the current conditions. In this paper, the variance is considered as a proxy for entropy, but any other entropy related metric could be used instead. Figure 3 illustrates how this intuition is encoded into the switching condition in the hierarchy of layers.

By considering the amount of difference between prediction variance on training and testing data, we can dynamically tune how conservative or liberal the overall hierarchical model is: if little difference is tolerated, the burden of prediction will often be passed to higher layers, resulting in expensive yet accurate predictions; if much difference is tolerated, lower levels will tend to predict, resulting in less expensive and less accurate predictions. The advantage of this approach is that the amount of tolerance could be dynamically tuned based on the current available budget for sensing.

For example, for larger budgets, more cost could be expended in order to obtain more accurate results. In this regard, the tolerance of the difference between variances could be decreased, transferring the burden of prediction to higher layers. Similarly for small budgets, the tolerance would be increased. Through this adjustment, more disagreement would be tolerated and less accurate predictions would be obtained for lower cost. To implement this dynamic tuning given a fluctuating budget, a tolerance parameter $\tau \in [0, 1]$ is defined, reflecting the tolerance of disagreement between the solutions of a given layer. Equation (1) demonstrates how this parameter is used to determine which level should be activated for prediction.

$$p^{(t)} = \begin{cases} p^{(t)}_{L_i} & \text{if } v_i^{\text{train}} < |1-\tau| \cdot v_i^{\text{test}(t)} \\ p^{(t)}_{L_{i+1}} & \text{otherwise} \end{cases} \quad (1)$$

It should be noted that in the present work, the same value for τ is used at the interstices between each pair of layers. However, different values for τ could be employed between different layers to enable the model to respond better to changes in the overall available budget. The extreme cases occur when $\tau = 0$ or $\tau = 1$. The former ensures that the conditional is only true when the prediction variance on the testing data is greater than the prediction variance on the training data which has a high probability of occurring. Thus, the method tends to extract the predictions from the solutions on the uppermost layer. The latter ensures that the conditional is only true whenever the variance on the testing data is finite, which is always true. In this case, the first layer always provides the prediction. Values greater than $\tau = 1$ are not investigated in this work, but are possible. Greater τ value increases the probability of the conditional to be true. $\tau = \infty$ causes the conditional to always be true, thus the method always collects predictions from the last layer.

Table 1: Available sensors and their features.

Name	Equation Template of $r_i^{(t)}$	Cost
s_3	$g^{(t)}$	3
s_2	$b_{2,1}g^{(t)} + b_{2,2}$	2
s_1	$b_{1,1}(g^{(t)})^2 + b_{1,2}g^{(t)} + b_{1,3}$	1

4. RESULTS

The proposed methods are evaluated over two set of experiments, using a synthesized dataset and ten actual datasets. This section summarizes these datasets, experimental setups, and quantitative results.

4.1 Synthesized Data

In these experiment, the proposed methods have been evaluated on a synthetic system monitored by three different sensors. Table 1 shows these three sensors, their readings in relation to $g^{(t)}$, and their cost.

To create the training and testing datasets, at first coefficients in the equations of the sensor relations, i.e., $b_{i,j}$s, were randomly selected in the range $[0, 1]$. Then, random numbers were generated for $g^{(t)}$, and used to calculate the sensor readings based on the given template and selected coefficients. The training and testing dataset sizes were 150 and 50, respectively, and each experiment were repeated 40 times.

Non-hierarchical setup. The population size is 100 and is trained for 300 generations. The optimization process during the last generation does not consider *age* as an objective and Pareto front is selected using *error* and *cost* × *size* as two separate objectives. After training, the knee of the non-dominated solutions is selected and tested using the testing dataset.

Hierarchical setup. The population size for each layer is 100 and each layer was trained for 100 generations, for the sake of fairness in comparisons. Similarly to the non-hierarchical setup, during the last generation, *age* is not considered in the Pareto optimization process, and non-dominated solutions are selected based on *error* and *cost* × *size* as two separate objectives. After training, for each layer L_i, the variance of the solutions output on training data v_i^{train} is computed and stored as the threshold of switching to the next layer L_{i+1}. This variance is not computed for the layer corresponding to the most expensive sensor, i.e., L_3, since there are no more sensors to be called. The experiment was repeated 40 times for each of the different tolerance parameters $\tau = 0.0, 0.1, 0.2, 0.4, 0.6, 0.8$.

4.1.1 Results on Synthesized Data

Average error. The average error of the non-hierarchical method is $e^{\text{test}}_{t_j}$, where t_j is the final selected solution. The average error of the hierarchical method is the average of $e^{\text{test}}_{L_i}$, where L_i is the last layer reached in the hierarchy, during the sampling. As can be seen in Figure 4, the largest difference in error occurs at maximum tolerance i.e. $\tau = 0.8$ where the error of the hierarchical method is 1.34% higher than the non-hierarchical method. The hierarchical method tends to achieve lower average error when the tolerance parameter is $\tau < 0.4$. P-values obtained for different tolerance

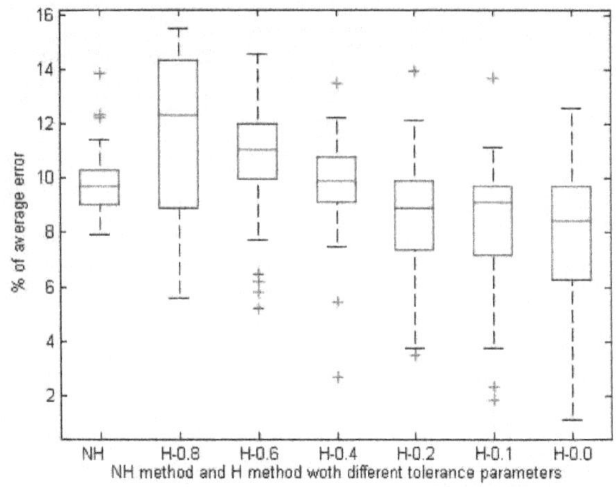

Figure 4:Average error on the test data for the non-hierarchical and the hierarchical methods with different tolerance parameters. Statistical significance of these results are represented in Table 2.A)

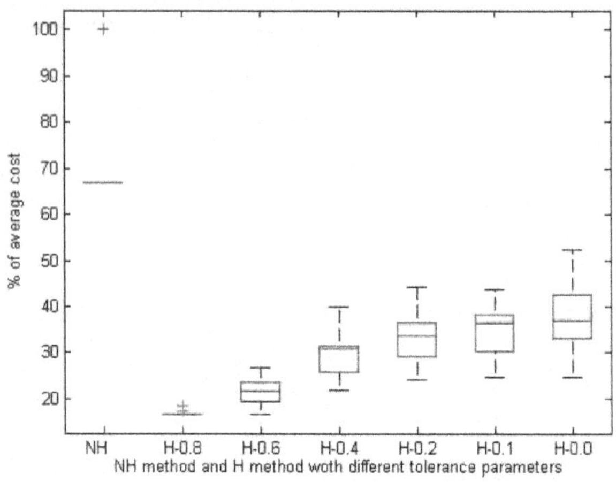

Figure 5:The average cost on the test data for the non-hierarchical and the hierarchical methods with different tolerance parameters. Statistical significance of these results are represented in Table 2.B)

Table 2: A) P-values considering error of the non-hierarchical and the hierarchical methods with different tolerance parameters. B) P-values considering cost of the non-hierarchical and the hierarchical methods with different tolerance parameters.

A	P-values	B	P-values
$\tau = 0.8$	0.013414	$\tau = 0.8$	$\ll 0.001$
$\tau = 0.6$	0.046626	$\tau = 0.6$	$\ll 0.001$
$\tau = 0.4$	0.635566	$\tau = 0.4$	$\ll 0.001$
$\tau = 0.2$	0.001309	$\tau = 0.2$	$\ll 0.001$
$\tau = 0.1$	$\ll 0.001$	$\tau = 0.1$	$\ll 0.001$
$\tau = 0.0$	$\ll 0.001$	$\tau = 0.0$	$\ll 0.001$

parameters are represented in Table 2.A) and show that $\tau = 0.4$ is the boundary where the hierarchical method begins to outperform the non-hierarchical method.

Average cost. By considering t_j as the final selected solution in the non-hierarchical method, the average cost is $c_{t_j}^{\text{test}}$. The average cost of the hierarchical method is the average of $c_{L_i}^{\text{test}}$, when the last layer reached during the sampling is L_i. In order to compare both methods and understand how much of the potential cost each method uses, the cost of each method is represented as the percentage of cost of using all available sensors. Figure 5 shows that the average cost of the hierarchical method is significantly lower than the non-hierarchical method (at most 54.88% and at least 33.81% lower cost). Table 2.B) summarizes the p-values to show how significantly the cost of the hierarchical method is lower than the non-hierarchical method.

4.2 Actual Data

In this experiment, ten datasets are selected from the UCI database repository [2] based on the number of instances and features from the regression section. Table 3 summarizes these datasets and their features. For these datasets, we treat the individual features as individual sensors. Each experiment in this section were repeated 30 times.

In order to determine the accuracy of each sensor s_i in predicting $g^{(t)}$, the value of $v_{\mathbf{r}_i}^{(\mathbf{g})}$ is calculated for each available sensor of each dataset, using linear regression. The greater $v_{\mathbf{r}_i}^{(\mathbf{g})}$ is, the better that sensor can predict $g^{(t)}$.Table 4 summarizes the values of $v_{\mathbf{r}_i}^{(\mathbf{g})}$ for all of the sensors of the Auto MPG dataset, as an exampl. We define the cost of each sensor in these datasets as $v_{\mathbf{r}_i}^{(\mathbf{g})}$.

Table 3: Used UCI datasets.

DS No.	DS Name	No. of Instances	No. of sensors	$g^{(t)}$ Average
DS_1	Auto MPG	398	7	23.51457
DS_2	Housing	506	13	22.53281
DS_3	Forest Fires	517	12	0.031663
DS_4	Energy Efficiency	768	8	22.3072
DS_5	Concrete Compressive Strength	1030	8	35.81796
DS_6	Solar Flare	1389	9	0.300188
DS_7	Airfoil Self-Noise	1503	5	124.8359
DS_8	SkilCraft1 Master Table Dataset	3395	19	4.184094
DS_9	Wine Quality	4898	11	5.877909
DS_{10}	Parkinson's Telemonitoring	5875	17	29.01894

Table 4: Value of $v_{\mathbf{r}_i}^{(\mathbf{g})}$ for all the sensors of Auto MPG dataset.

DS No.	s_1	s_2	s_3	s_4	s_5	s_6	s_7
Auto MPG	0.1766	0.3175	0.3356	0.5951	0.6012	0.6467	0.6918

Table 5: Minimum and maximum amount of variance a sensor accounts for, in each dataset.

DS No.	min $v_{\mathbf{r}_i}^{(\mathbf{g})}$	max $v_{\mathbf{r}_i}^{(\mathbf{g})}$
DS_1	0.1766	0.6918
DS_2	0.0307	0.5441
DS_3	0.0002	0.2578
DS_4	0.0076	0.7911
DS_5	0.0112	0.2478
DS_6	0.000	0.096
DS_7	0.0157	0.1527
DS_8	0.0005	0.4542
DS_9	0.0001	0.1897
DS_{10}	0.0037	0.0263

Table 6: Average error percentages and the corresponding P-values for the hierarchical and the non-hierarchical methods.

DS No.	NH: error %	H: error %	P-value
DS_1	20.85	25.81	$\ll 0.001$
DS_2	25.90	28.93	$\ll 0.001$
DS_3	126.49	202.12	0.565
DS_4	29.19	36.70	$\ll 0.001$
DS_5	35.29	39.68	0.393
DS_6	110.63	111.08	0.223
DS_7	0.00	0.00	0.082
DS_8	37.59	28.65	0.194
DS_9	10.79	10.67	0.197
DS_{10}	32.11	29.88	0.423

Table 7: Average cost percentages and the corresponding P-values for the hierarchical and the non-hierarchical methods.

DS No.	NH: cost %	H: cost %	P-value
DS_1	38.89	12.33	0.022
DS_2	23.18	1.26	$\ll 0.001$
DS_3	6.83	15.81	$\ll 0.001$
DS_4	32.90	4.18	$\ll 0.001$
DS_5	53.63	28.63	0.004
DS_6	0.00	0.98	0.040
DS_7	11.58	7.35	0.005
DS_8	2.55	0.00	$\ll 0.001$
DS_9	0.02	0.00	$\ll 0.001$
DS_{10}	20.62	3.88	0.009

Non-hierarchical setup. The population size is 200 and for each dataset with k features, it is trained for $200 * k$ generations.

Hierarchical setup. The population size for each layer is 200. Similar to synthesized data experiments, In order to equalize search effort in both methods, each layer was trained for 200 generation. After training, a subset of the non-dominated solutions with least error are selected and organized in the corresponding layer. The cardinality of this subset is 2% of the population size. This experiment was conductedof for tolerance parameter $\tau = 0.1$. This value is selected based on the results in 4.1 and will be discussed in more detail in Section 5.1.

4.2.1 Results on Actual Data

Average error. The average error for the non-hierarchical and the hierarchical methods are $e^{\text{test}}_{t_j}$ and $e^{\text{test}}_{L_i}$ respectively, where t_j is the final selected solution in the non-hierarchical method and L_i is the last layer reached during the sampling in the hierarchical method. Table 6 summarizes the average error of both methods on all the datasets as a percentage of error. It can be seen that for some datasets, the average error of the hierarchical method is higher than the average error of the non-hierarchical method. However, the P-value for the two-tailed t-test shows that generally, this difference is not significant. There are three cases where the difference is significant i.e., DS_1, DS_2 and DS_4.

Average cost. Similar to 4.1.1, the average cost is represented as the percentage of the maximum possible cost. Table 7 summarizes the percentage of the average cost each method uses for prediction. The cost of the hierarchical method is significantly lower in all cases except for DS_3 and DS_6.

5. DISCUSSION

Our results in all experiments suggest that the hierarchical method is better at balancing cost and accuracy than the non-hierarchical approach. We believe this is because meaningful sensor control conditions for managing cost are complex and require considerable computational effort to be discovered. Using hand-tuned prediction uncertainty to drive sensor control is more effective. Furthermore, our results show that the latter approach better supports dynamic adaptation to changes in available energy, through modulation of tolerance. The non-hierarchical approach cannot adapt to such changes without retraining from scratch, or aggressive online learning. As mentioned in Section 3.2, in these experiments a basic genetic programming approach was deployed. We anticipate that if we were to use a more powerful underlying GP approach, the error of both hierarchical and non-hierarchical models would be reduced.

In the remainder of this Section we discuss results as they pertain specifically to experiments with synthesized and actual data.

5.1 Synthesized Data

Average error. As can be seen in Figure 4, the hierarchical method achieved significantly better accuracy than the non-hierarchical method for $\tau < 0.4$. In general, results show that higher tolerance allows the algorithm to accept more uncertainty in the prediction and rely on less expensive sensors which are less accurate. This avoids the use of more expensive sensors, but causes average error to rise. A tolerance of $\tau < 0.4$ is apparently the threshold where average error in the hierarchical method exceeds that of the non-hierarchical method.

Average cost. Results reported in Figure 5 show that the hierarchical method significantly outperforms the non-hierarchical method with regard to cost on this dataset, even when tolerance is low. This suggests that the use of variance in ensemble predictions to serve as a proxy for prediction uncertainty is not easy to learn, and serves as a good mechanism for control. Results in Figures 4 and 5 suggest that $\tau = 0.1$ is a "sweet spot" for balancing cost and accuracy, though the value could be increased or decreased if greater frugality or accuracy were needed, respectively.

5.2 Actual Data

For testing on actual data, we fixed $\tau = 0.1$ due to results on synthetic data demonstrating a nice balance between cost and accuracy with this tolerance level.

Average error. Table 6 shows that the average error of the hierarchical and the non-hierarchical methods were not significantly different, except for datasets DS_1, DS_2 and DS_4 where the latter method achieves better prediction accuracy. This is probably due to the characteristics of these datasets, where the difference between the least prediction variances $v^{(\mathbf{g})}_{\mathbf{r}_i}$s and the greatest ones is large. The majority of sensors in these datasets are not informative but have low costs and the remaining sensors are informative enough but come with very higher costs. Thus, lower levels of the hierarchy "struggle" compared to upper ones in terms of accuracy. Nevertheless, accuracy rate with the hierarchical method is still competitive even in these cases, and cost reduction is significant. Also, it can be seen that as the size of the datasets grows, the difference between the error rate of the non-hierarchical and the hierarchical methods decreases, and in the three largest datasets the hierarchical method also achieves lower error rates.

Average cost. The hierarchical method achieved significantly lower cost than the non-hierarchical method on all the real world datasets, as shown in Table 7, except for DS_3 and DS_6. As represented in Table 5, in these two datasets, just a small subset of sensors are relatively informative. Since the tolerance parameter for the hierarchical method is low, the hierarchical method employs more informative sensors. Taken together, results shown in Tables

6 and 7 clearly indicate an advantage of the hierarchical method for balancing cost and accuracy.

6. CONCLUSION AND FUTURE WORK

All resource constrained sensor systems have to face a trade-off between measurement accuracy and the cost of sensor sampling. In networks supporting multiple sensor types, it is therefore desirable to develop cost-sensitive control algorithms that sample more expensive sensors only when necessary. In this paper, a hierarchical method is proposed where GP solutions are sorted in a hierarchy of layers based on the cost of the sensors they use. Switching to the next more expensive layer takes place only if the prediction variance indicates uncertainty at lower layers. We compare this method to a non-hierarchical GP method where cost is treated as an additional optimization objective in fitness selection. In experiments using a synthesized dataset and ten real datasets, the hierarchical method is shown to have significantly lower prediction costs than the non-hierarchical method. As the datasets grow bigger and more complex, competitive and sometimes lower error rates are achieved by the hierarchical method. Future work includes consideration of how to dynamically tune the balance of cost and accuracy based on available energy and budget. Other directions for future work include methods for online learning to support adaptation of control algorithms to particular deployments, and application of hierarchical control algorithms in real resource constrained sensor system deployments.

Acknowledgements

This work was supported in part by the NSF awards PECASE-0953837 and INSPIRE-1344227.

7. REFERENCES

[1] github code public repository. http://git.io/vfmGB. Accessed: 2015-04-18.

[2] UCI machine learning repository. http://archive.ics.uci.edu/ml/datasets.html. Accessed: 2015-02-03.

[3] C. Alippi, G. Anastasi, C. Galperti, F. Mancini, and M. Roveri. Adaptive sampling for energy conservation in wireless sensor networks for snow monitoring applications. In *IEEE 4th International Conference on Mobile Adhoc and Sensor Systems, MASS 2007, 8-11 October 2007, Pisa, Italy*, pages 1–6, 2007.

[4] E. H. Bair, R. E. Davis, D. C. Finnegan, A. L. LeWinter, E. Guttmann, and J. Dozier. Can we estimate precipitation rate during snowfall using a scanning terrestrial lidar? In *International Snow Science Workshop*, pages 923–929, Anchorage, AK, 2012.

[5] Brockhoff, Dimo, Zitzler, and Eckart. Are all objectives necessary? On dimensionality reduction in evolutionary multiobjective optimization. In *Parallel Problem Solving from Nature-PPSN IX*, pages 533–542. Springer, 2006.

[6] D. Buckingham, C. Skalka, and J. Bongard. Inductive learning of snowpack distribution models for improved estimation of areal snow water equivalent. *Journal of Hydrology*, 2015. Accepted for Publication.

[7] E. D. de Jong and J. B. Pollack. Multi-objective methods for tree size control. *Genetic Programming and Evolvable Machines*, 4(3):211–233, 2003.

[8] D. L. Donoho. Compressed sensing. *IEEE Transactions on Information Theory*, 52(4):1289–1306, 2006.

[9] D. Hall and J. Llinas. *Multisensor data fusion*. CRC press, 2001.

[10] G. Hornby. ALPS: the age-layered population structure for reducing the problem of premature convergence. In *Genetic and Evolutionary Computation Conference, GECCO 2006, Proceedings, Seattle, Washington, USA, July 8-12, 2006*, pages 815–822, 2006.

[11] D. Kim. Structural risk minimization on decision trees using an evolutionary multiobjective optimization. In *Genetic Programming*, pages 338–348. Springer, 2004.

[12] F. Koushanfar, S. Slijepcevic, M. Potkonjak, and A. Sangiovanni-Vincentelli. Error-tolerant multimodal sensor fusion. In *IEEE CAS Workshop on Wireless Communication and Networking*, pages 5–6, 2002.

[13] A. Krause, C. Guestrin, A. Gupta, and J. Kleinberg. Near-optimal sensor placements: Maximizing information while minimizing communication cost. In *Proceedings of the 5th international conference on Information processing in sensor networks*, pages 2–10. ACM, 2006.

[14] S. Maleki, A. Pandharipande, and G. Leus. Two-stage spectrum sensing for cognitive radios. In *Proceedings of the IEEE International Conference on Acoustics, Speech, and Signal Processing, ICASSP 2010, 14-19 March 2010, Sheraton Dallas Hotel, Dallas, Texas, USA*, pages 2946–2949, 2010.

[15] M. L. Malloy and R. D. Nowak. Near-optimal adaptive compressed sensing. *IEEE Transactions on Information Theory*, 60(7):4001–4012, 2014.

[16] A. Martinelli. Vision and IMU data fusion: Closed-form solutions for attitude, speed, absolute scale, and bias determination. *IEEE Transactions on Robotics*, 28(1):44–60, 2012.

[17] C. Papadimitriou, J. L. Beck, and S.-K. Au. Entropy-based optimal sensor location for structural model updating. *Journal of Vibration and Control*, 6(5):781–800, 2000.

[18] C. Pohl and J. V. Genderen. Review article multisensor image fusion in remote sensing: concepts, methods and applications. *International Journal of Remote Sensing*, 19(5):823–854, 1998.

[19] H. Ren, D. Rank, M. Merdes, J. Stallkamp, and P. Kazanzides. Multisensor data fusion in an integrated tracking system for endoscopic surgery. *IEEE Transactions on Information Technology in Biomedicine*, 16(1):106–111, 2012.

[20] M. Schmidt and H. Lipson. Age-fitness pareto optimization. In R. Riolo, T. McConaghy, and E. Vladislavleva, editors, *Genetic Programming Theory and Practice VIII*, volume 8 of *Genetic and Evolutionary Computation*, pages 129–146. Springer New York, 2011.

[21] H. S. Seung, M. Opper, and H. Sompolinsky. Query by committee. In *Proceedings of the Fifth Annual Workshop on Computational Learning Theory*, COLT '92, pages 287–294, New York, NY, USA, 1992. ACM.

[22] C. Skalka and J. Frolik. Snowcloud: A complete data gathering system for snow hydrology research. In *Real-World Wireless Sensor Networks*, pages 3–14. Springer, 2014.

[23] D. Smith and S. Singh. Approaches to multisensor data fusion in target tracking: A survey. *IEEE Trans. Knowl. Data Eng.*, 18(12):1696–1710, 2006.

[24] H. Tabari, S. Marofi, H. Z. Abyaneh, and M. R. Sharifi. Comparison of artificial neural network and combined models in estimating spatial distribution of snow depth and snow water equivalent in Samsami basin of Iran. *Neural Comput. Appl.*, 19(4):625–635, 2010.

[25] U. Tappeiner, G. Tappeiner, J. Aschenwald, E. Tasser, and B. Ostendorf. GIS-based modelling of spatial pattern of snow cover duration in an alpine area. *Ecol. Model.*, 138:265–275, 2001.

[26] E. L. Waltz and D. M. Buede. Data fusion and decision support for command and control. *IEEE Transactions on Systems, Man, and Cybernetics*, 16(6):865–879, 1986.

[27] D. Wang, H. Ahmadi, T. F. Abdelzaher, H. Chenji, R. Stoleru, and C. C. Aggarwal. Optimizing quality-of-information in cost-sensitive sensor data fusion. In *Distributed Computing in Sensor Systems, 7th IEEE International Conference and Workshops, DCOSS 2011, Barcelona, Spain, 27-29 June, 2011, Proceedings*, pages 1–8, 2011.

[28] R. Willett, A. Martin, and R. Nowak. Backcasting: adaptive sampling for sensor networks. In *Proceedings of the Third International Symposium on Information Processing in Sensor Networks, IPSN 2004, Berkeley, California, USA, April 26-27, 2004*, pages 124–133, 2004.

[29] J. Yick, B. Mukherjee, and D. Ghosal. Wireless sensor network survey. *Comput. Netw.*, 52(12):2292–2330, 2008.

[30] H. Zhao. A multi-objective genetic programming approach to developing pareto optimal decision trees. *Decision Support Systems*, 43(3):809–826, 2007.

Extracting Variability-Safe Feature Models from Source Code Dependencies in System Variants

Wesley K. G. Assunção[1,2], Roberto E. Lopez-Herrejon[3], Lukas Linsbauer[3], Silvia R. Vergilio[1], Alexander Egyed[3]
[1]DINF - Federal University of Paraná, CP: 19081, 81531-980, Curitiba, Brazil
[2]COINF - Technological Federal University of Paraná, 85902-490, Toledo, Brazil
[3]ISSE - Johannes Kepler University Linz, 4040 Linz, Austria
{wesleyk, silvia}@inf.ufpr.br, {roberto.lopez, lukas.linsbauer, alexander.egyed}@jku.at

ABSTRACT

To effectively cope with increasing customization demands, companies that have developed variants of software systems are faced with the challenge of consolidating all the variants into a Software Product Line, a proven development paradigm capable of handling such demands. A crucial step in this challenge is to reverse engineer feature models that capture all the required feature combinations of each system variant. Current research has explored this task using propositional logic, natural language, and search-based techniques. However, using knowledge from the implementation artifacts for the reverse engineering task has not been studied. We propose a multi-objective approach that not only uses standard precision and recall metrics for the combinations of features but that also considers variability-safety, i.e. the property that, based on structural dependencies among elements of implementation artifacts, asserts whether all feature combinations of a feature model are in fact well-formed software systems. We evaluate our approach with five case studies and highlight its benefits for the software engineer.

Categories and Subject Descriptors

I.2.8 [**Artificial Intelligence**]: Problem Solving, Control Methods, and Search—*Heuristic Methods*

Keywords

Reverse Engineering; Feature Models; Multi-Objective Evolutionary Algorithms

1. INTRODUCTION

Software Product Lines (SPLs) are families of related software systems where each product has a different combination of features [3]. SPL practices have extensive and proven technological and economical advantages [19]. However, the effective adoption of SPLs poses several challenges. Salient among them is the reverse engineering of SPLs from existing software system variants, the most prevalent scenario in industry. A first requirement to tackle this challenge is extracting *feature models* that effectively describe the combinations of features present in the existing system variants. Current approaches rely on configuration scripts [17], propositional logic expressions [5, 18], natural language [20], ad hoc algorithms [1, 8, 9], and even search-based algorithms [12, 13, 14]. However, to the best of our knowledge, none of them exploit information on how the system variants are actually implemented or take a multi-objective perspective whereby different quality aspects of the reverse engineering task are simultaneously considered.

The driving motivation of our work is to extract feature models that are *variability-safe*, which means that, based on a concrete set of implementation artifacts, *all* the feature combinations of the variants denoted by a feature model are structurally well-formed, e.g. they do not have unresolved references to undefined elements. In this paper, we take a multi-objective perspective for reverse engineering feature models where the objective functions not only consider the recall and precision of the feature combinations of the obtained feature models, but also if they are variability-safe. The latter is computed from dependency information among elements of the source code artifacts that implement the system variants. The multi-objective approach that we propose gives software engineers the capacity to detect inconsistencies between the desired feature combinations and the implementation artifacts (e.g. infeasible products), and to analyze different trade-offs among the three objectives (e.g. offering more well-formed products than currently existing variants). We evaluated our approach with five case studies of different domains and dimensions. The results clearly illustrate the advantage as well as the feasibility of a multi-objective perspective for this vital reverse-engineering task.

GECCO '15, July 11 - 15, 2015, Madrid, Spain

DOI: http://dx.doi.org/10.1145/2739480.2754720

2. BACKGROUND

In this section we briefly present the basic background knowledge on feature models and introduce our running example which we use to illustrate the source code dependencies we consider in our reverse engineering approach.

2.1 Features Models

Feature Models (FMs) are a de facto standard for modelling the different combinations of features desired in an SPL [10]. Features are depicted as labelled boxes connected by lines to other features they relate with, all collectively forming a tree-like structure.

A feature can either be *mandatory*, which is selected in a system whenever its parent feature is also selected, or *optional*, which may or may not be selected whenever its parent feature is selected. They are respectively represented with filled and empty circles at the end of the feature relation as shown in Figure 1(a) and Figure 1(b).

Features can be grouped into *alternative groups* where if the parent feature of the group is selected then *exactly* one feature from the group must be selected, or into *or groups* where if the parent feature of the group is selected then *one or more* features from the group can be selected. Feature groups are depicted with lines connecting the parent feature (`P`) with the group features (`C1`, `C2`, and `C3`), crossed by an empty arc for *alternative* groups and by a filled arch for *or* groups as illustrated in Figure 1(c) and Figure 1(d).

Besides the hierarchical relations among features, features can also relate across different branches of the feature model with *Cross-Tree Constraints (CTCs)* [4]. The most common types are *requires* relation whereby if a feature `A` is selected a feature `B` must also be selected, and *excludes* relation whereby if a feature `A` is selected then feature `B` *must not* be selected, and vice versa. These relations are commonly depicted, respectively, with a single and double-arrow dashed line as illustrated in Figure 1(e).

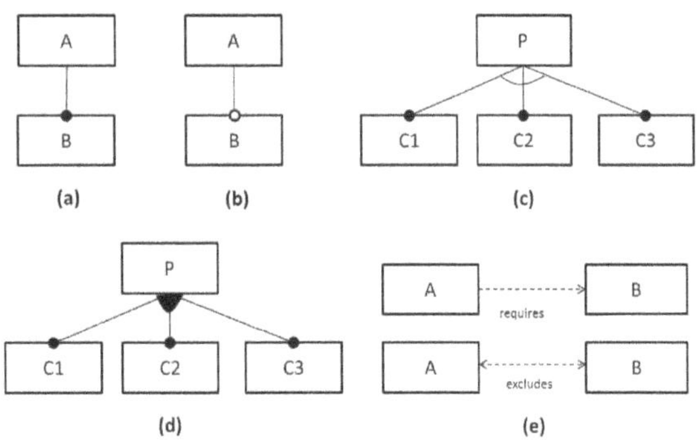

Figure 1: Feature Models Graphical Notation

2.2 Running Example

As our running example, let us consider a group of system variants of drawing applications which we would like to consolidate into a product line called *Draw Product Line (DPL)*. Each variant contains different combinations of the following features: the ability to handle a drawing area (`BASE`), draw lines (`LINE`), draw rectangles (`RECT`), select a color to draw with (`COLOR`), draw filled rectangles (`FILL`), and clean the drawing area (`WIPE`). Table 1 lists the 16 variants of DPL where the selected features are denoted with ✓, while the unselected features are left empty. We formally refer to each feature combination as a *feature set* defined as follows [12]:

DEFINITION 1. ***Feature Set.*** *A feature set is a 2-tuple [*$\texttt{sel}, \overline{\texttt{sel}}$*] where* $\texttt{sel}$ *and* $\overline{\texttt{sel}}$ *are respectively the set of selected and not-selected features of a system variant. Let FL be the list of features of a feature model, such that* $\texttt{sel}, \overline{\texttt{sel}} \subseteq FL$, $\texttt{sel} \cap \overline{\texttt{sel}} = \emptyset$, *and* $\texttt{sel} \cup \overline{\texttt{sel}} = FL$.

Table 1: Feature Sets for DPL

Products	BASE	LINE	RECT	COLOR	FILL	WIPE
ProductX_1	✓	✓				✓
ProductX_2	✓	✓		✓		
ProductX_3	✓	✓	✓	✓		
ProductX_4	✓	✓	✓	✓	✓	
ProductX_5	✓	✓	✓			✓
ProductX_6	✓	✓				
ProductX_7	✓	✓		✓		✓
ProductX_8	✓	✓	✓			
ProductX_9	✓		✓			
ProductX_{10}	✓		✓			✓
ProductX_{11}	✓		✓	✓		
ProductX_{12}	✓		✓	✓	✓	
ProductX_{13}	✓		✓	✓		✓
ProductX_{14}	✓		✓	✓	✓	✓
ProductX_{15}	✓	✓	✓	✓		✓
ProductX_{16}	✓	✓	✓	✓	✓	✓

2.3 Source Code Dependency Graphs

Variability safety is the property of feature models that guarantees that *all* the variants that a feature model describes are structurally well-formed with respect to a set of concrete implementation artifacts, for example that they do not have unresolved references to undefined variables.

In this paper, we describe how information regarding dependencies among the code artifacts that implement the existing software variants can be exploited to reverse engineer variability-safe feature models. For this purpose, we rely on the terminology and tool support presented by Linsbauer et al. [7, 11]. Their work distinguishes two kinds of *modules* in the system variants:

DEFINITION 2. ***Base Module.*** *A* base *module implements a feature regardless of the presence or absence of any other features and is denoted with the feature's name written in lowercase.*

DEFINITION 3. ***Derivative Module.*** *A* derivative *module* $m = \delta^{\texttt{n}}(\texttt{c}_0, \texttt{c}_1, ..., \texttt{c}_\texttt{n})$ *implements feature interactions, where* c_i *is* `F` *(if feature* `F` *is selected) or* $\neg$`F` *(if not selected), and n is the order of the derivative.*

Linsbauer et al.'s extraction algorithm automatically produces a set of traces between both types of modules and the implementation artifacts (e.g. source code fragments) that implement them [11]. These code fragments can be of any granularity level, from entire classes down to individual statements. Let us consider the examples shown in Figure 2. This figure shows as comments some of the traces computed by our algorithm. Line 5 defines a field that traces to the base module of feature `Color`, which is defined in class `Canvas` regardless of the presence of other feature combinations in any product variant. As another example, consider method with signature $mousePressedLine(MouseEvent)$ in Line 7. The method header and most of its body trace to base module `Line`, meaning that these statements will be included in class `Canvas` whenever feature `Line` is included regardless of any other selected feature combination. Notice now that Line 10 traces to derivative module $\delta^1(Color, Line)$, which means this assignment statement will be part of its containing method whenever both features `Color` and `Line` are present in a system variant.

DEFINITION 4. ***Module Expression.*** *A module expression is the propositional logic representation of modules. For*

```
1 public class Canvas ... {
2   List<Shape> shapes = new LinkedList<Shape>();
3   Point start;
4   Line newLine = null; // Line
5   Color color = Color.BLACK; // Color
6   ...
7   void mousePressedLine(MouseEvent e) { // Line
8    if (newLine == null) {
9       start = new Point(e.getX(), e.getY());
10      newLine=new Line(color,start);//δ¹(Color, Line)
11      shapes.add(newLine);
12   }
13  }
14 }
```

Figure 2: Source Code Snippet for DPL Example

a base module b, the module expression is its own literal b. For a derivative module $m = \delta^n(\mathtt{c_0}, \mathtt{c_1}, ..., \mathtt{c_n})$ *its module expression corresponds to* $c_0 \wedge c_1 \wedge ... \wedge c_n$.

For example, the module expression of base module `Line` is *Line*. As another example, consider module δ^1(`Color`, `Line`), which expresses the interaction of features `Color` and `Line`, and is represented by the module expression $Color \wedge Line$.

Based on the output of Linsbauer et al.'s algorithm, our work uses dependencies between code fragments, such as method calls and field references, as described next.

DEFINITION 5. ***Dependency.*** *A dependency establishes a requirement relationship between two sets of modules and it is denoted with a three-tuple* (*from*, *to*, *weight*)*, where from and to each are a set of modules (or module expressions) of the related modules, and weight expresses the strength of the dependency, i.e. the number of dependencies of structural elements in modules from on structural elements in modules to. We use the dot (.) operator to reference elements of a tuple, e.g. the weight of a dependency* `dep` *is denoted by* `dep.weight`*. A dependency's propositional logic representation is defined as:*

$$\bigvee_{mfrom \in dep.from} mfrom \Rightarrow \bigwedge_{mto \in dep.to} mto$$

DEFINITION 6. ***Dependency Graph.*** *A dependency graph is simply defined as a set of dependencies, where each node in the graph corresponds to a set of modules (or module expressions), and every edge in the graph corresponds to a dependency as defined above. Edges are annotated with natural numbers that represent the dependencies' weights.*

Figure 3 shows the dependency graph of our running example DPL considering all its variants. The nodes are labelled with the corresponding trace's lowest order modules as they are the most important ones, higher order modules are not depicted to avoid clutter. Also for readability self-dependencies are not shown. Base modules are depicted with solid border while derivative modules are depicted with dashed border. It is worth noting that edges with the highest values tend to be those that go to base modules (e.g. `Fill` to `Rect`, or `Line` to `Base`), and that the core feature `Base` has the highest incoming values.

Let us now illustrate the propositional logic representation of dependencies using code snippet in Figure 2. As a first example, consider the dependency between module $\delta^1(Color, Line)$ and module *Color* that comes from the fact that `newLine = new Line(color,start);` in Line 10 which belongs to module $\delta^1(Color, Line)$ accesses the field `color` (Line 5) which belongs to module *Color*. The corresponding propositional logic expression that must hold for this dependency is $(Color \wedge Line) \Rightarrow Color$.

Another example, consider module $\delta^1(Color, Line)$ which depends on module *Line* because the same statement in Line 10 is contained in the method `public void mousePressedLine(MouseEvent e)` (Line 7) which belongs to module *Line*. The statement requires the method to be present, because otherwise the statement could not exist in isolation. The propositional logic representation is then $(Color \wedge Line) \Rightarrow Line$.

The dependency graph of the DPL can also be represented as a dependency matrix as shown in Table 2. Every row in the matrix represents a dependency, where the first column of the matrix is its ID number. The second and third columns are respectively the modules that depend on each other, i.e. the modules in column *from* require (i.e. depend on) the modules in column *to*. The weight of each dependency is presented in the fourth column. The fifth column presents the normalized weight values. The weights of the edges are normalized so that the sum of all weights in the dependency graph is 1. We use these normalized values in our multi-objective approach as described in the next section.

Notice that some of the propositional logic constraints derived from the dependencies (e.g. the 2 examples above) are tautologies that will always hold, like $(Color \wedge Line \Rightarrow Line) \Leftrightarrow TRUE$. This is not a mistake, but merely an indication that the implementation is consistent with the variability represented in the feature model.

Table 2: Dependency Matrix for DPL

ID	From	To	Weight	Normalized
1	Line	Base	21	0.1304
2	Wipe	Base	10	0.0621
3	Color	Base	19	0.1180
4	Rect	Base	20	0.1242
5	Fill	Base	17	0.1056
6	Fill	Rect	23	0.1429
7	Fill	Color	3	0.0186
8	Fill	δ^1(Rect, Color)	1	0.0062
9	δ^1(Rect, ¬Color)	Rect	12	0.0745
10	δ^1(Rect, Color)	Rect	3	0.0186
11	δ^1(¬Color, Line)	Line	8	0.0497
12	δ^1(Color, Line)	Color	1	0.0062
13	δ^1(Color, Line)	Line	10	0.0621
14	δ^2(Rect, Color, ¬Fill)	δ^1(Rect, Color)	1	0.0062
15	δ^2(Rect, Color, ¬Fill)	Rect	11	0.0683
16	δ^2(Rect, Color, ¬Fill)	Color	1	0.0062
		Total:	161	1.0000

3. A MULTI-OBJECTIVE PERSPECTIVE

In this section we describe and illustrate the objective functions that our approach employs which rely on information retrieval measures and that also exploit the information provided in the dependency graphs.

3.1 Objective Functions Definitions

We start by defining some auxiliary functions. In the following definitions, let $\mathcal{FM}$ denote the universe of feature models, $\mathcal{SFS}$ the universe of sets of feature sets, and sfs the initial set of feature sets defined by the software engineer (e.g. as shown in Table 1 for our DPL running example).

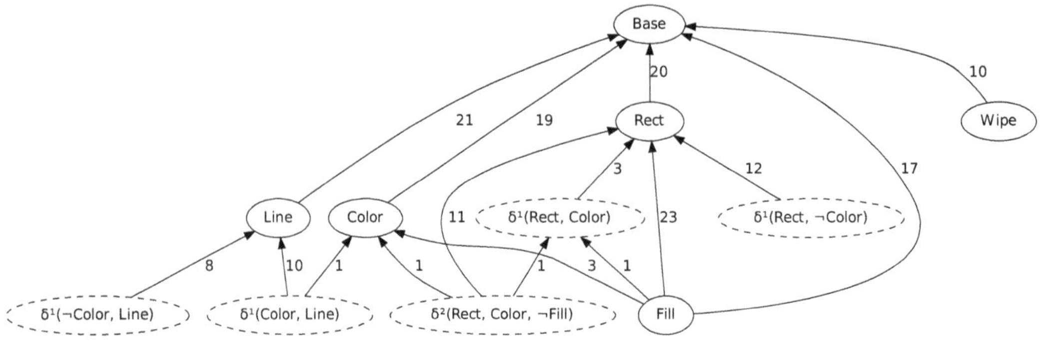

Figure 3: Dependency Graph for DPL

DEFINITION 7. ***featureSets***. *Function featureSets returns the sets of feature sets denoted by a feature model.*

$$featureSets : \mathcal{FM} \rightarrow \mathcal{SFS}$$

The dependencies of a dependency graph must hold in order to guarantee variability safety of system variants. A system variant that violates at least one of the dependencies will not be well-formed because at least one of the source code dependencies is not fulfilled for at least one feature set.

DEFINITION 8. ***holds***. *Function holds(dep, fs) returns* 1 *if dependency dep holds on the feature set (of a system variant) fs and* 0 *otherwise. A dependency dep holds for a feature set fs if:*

$$\left(\bigwedge_{f \in fs.sel} f \wedge \bigwedge_{g \in fs.\overline{sel}} \neg g\right) \Rightarrow (dep.from \Rightarrow dep.to)$$

For example, consider dependency $Fill \Rightarrow Rect$, and the system with features `Base` and `Line` selected, i.e. with feature set $[\{Base, Line\}, \{Fill, Rect, Wipe, Color\}]$. Function `holds` returns 1 because the following propositional logic formula evaluates to true: $(Base \wedge Line \wedge \neg Fill \wedge \neg Rect \wedge \neg Wipe \wedge \neg Color) \Rightarrow (Fill \Rightarrow Rect)$.

Now we define the three objective functions that our work considers. The first two are based on information retrieval metrics (see [15]), and the third captures variability safety based on the source code dependencies.

DEFINITION 9. ***Precision (P)***. *Precision expresses how many of the feature sets denoted by a reverse-engineered feature model fm are among the desired feature sets sfs.*

$$precision(sfs, fm) = \frac{|sfs \cap featureSets(fm)|}{|featureSets(fm)|}$$

DEFINITION 10. ***Recall (R)***. *Recall expresses how many of the desired feature sets are denoted by the reverse-engineered feature model fm.*

$$recall(sfs, fm) = \frac{|sfs \cap featureSets(fm)|}{|sfs|}$$

DEFINITION 11. ***Variability Safety (VS)***. *We express the degree to which a reverse-engineered feature model fm is* variability-safe *with respect to a dependency graph dg as follows:*

$$variabilitySafety(fm, dg) =$$

$$\sum_{dep \in dg} dep.weight \times \left(\frac{\sum_{fs \in featureSets(fm)} holds(dep, fs)}{|featureSets(fm)|} \right)$$

$VS = 0$ means every product variant in fm violates every dependency constraint in dg, and $VS = 1$ means every product variant in fm satisfies every dependency constraint in dg. Next we illustrate our three objective functions.

3.2 Objective Functions Illustration

In this section we illustrate our three objective functions, based on the feature sets of sfs in Table 1, the dependency graph dg from Figure 3, and the normalized weight values for dg from Table 2. Consider the three examples of extracted feature models shown in Figure 4 along with their respective values of precision, recall and variability safety.

The feature model FM1, Figure 4(a), is an example of an ideal feature model for the feature sets sfs we are considering. It has $|featureSets(FM1)| = |sfs| = 16$ valid configurations, and exactly the same as shown in Table 1. Hence, the values for both precision and recall are 1.000. In addition, the variability safety value is also 1.000, which means that the features sets of FM1 satisfied all the dependencies. Take for example the system with feature set $[\{Base, Rect, Color\}, \{Wipe, Line, Fill\}]$ and the dependency with ID 14 in Table 2, expressed as $\delta^2(Rect, Color, \neg Fill) \Rightarrow \delta^1(Rect, Color)$. The evaluation of function *holds* returns 1, meaning that this dependency is satisfied by the example feature set.

Let us now consider the feature model FM2, Figure 4(b), which has $|featureSets(FM2)| = 12$ feature sets of which $|sfs \cap featureSets(FM2)| = 10$ are contained in the input feature sets sfs. Hence the value for precision is 0.833 and for recall is 0.625. For this feature model, some of its denoted feature sets do not satisfy all dependencies. For instance, for the feature set $[\{Base, Line, Rect, Fill\}, \{Wipe, Color\}]$, the dependencies ID 7 ($\texttt{Fill} \Rightarrow \texttt{Color}$) and ID 8 ($\texttt{Fill} \Rightarrow \delta^1(\texttt{Rect}, \texttt{Color})$) are not satisfied. According to dependency ID 7, when the feature `Fill` is included in a feature set, feature `Color` must also be included. Similarly for dependency ID 8, when feature `Fill` appears, features `Rect` and `Color` must also be included. This feature set hence breaks these two dependency constraints. In other words, FM2 is not fully variability-safe with final value of VS of 0.996.

For feature model FM3, Figure 4(c), there are 6 configurations possible, and all are contained in the input feature sets sfs, in other words, $|featureSets(FM3)| = 6$ and $|sfs \cap featureSets(FM3)| = 6$. Hence, the value of precision is 1.000 and the value of recall is 0.375. Now let us consider the variability safety objective that has a value of 1.000. As mentioned before for FM1, this value indicates

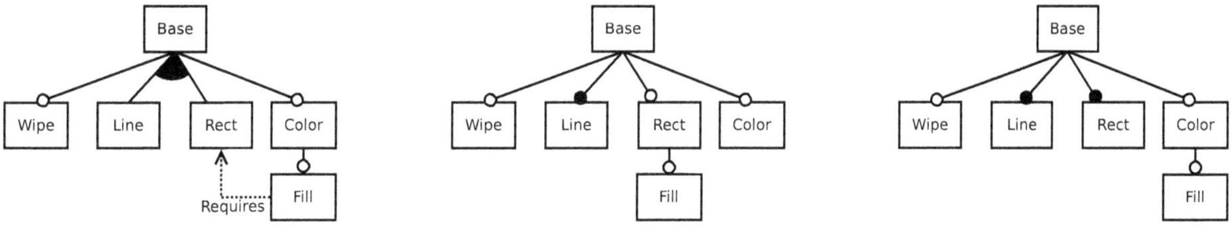

(a) FM1

Precision = 16/16 = 1.000
Recall = 16/16 = 1.000
VS = 1.000

(b) FM2

Precision = 10/12 = 0.833
Recall = 10/16 = 0.625
VS = 0.996

(c) FM3

Precision = 6/6 = 1.000
Recall = 6/16 = 0.375
VS = 1.000

Figure 4: Examples of Extracted Feature Models for DPL

that for all denoted feature sets, no dependency constraint is broken. For example, let us consider the feature set: $[\{Base, Line, Rect, Color, Fill\}, \{Wipe\}]$. For this feature set the dependencies with IDs {1, 3, 4, 5, 6, 7, 8, 10, 12, 13} in Table 2 are satisfied because both the depending modules (*from* column) as well as the modules they depend on (*to* column) are contained. For instance, according to dependency with ID 1, when feature `Line` is selected in a feature set, feature `Base` must also be in the feature set, which is the case because `Base` is the root feature and `Line` is its mandatory child. Furthermore, the dependencies with IDs {2, 9, 11, 14, 15, 16} are also satisfied because the depending modules (*from* column) are not contained. For instance, dependency with ID 2 states that when feature `Wipe` is selected, feature `Base` must also be selected, but since in our feature set example feature `Wipe` is not selected, it is not required that feature `Base` be selected.

Considering the three feature models presented in Figure 4 it is also possible to observe trade-offs among the objectives. It is clear that FM1 is the optimal solution for the given input, but this ideal solution is not known in the beginning of the evolutionary process. If we consider FM2 and FM3, it is not simple to decide which one is better. They have different values for the three objectives. FM2 has a better value for recall than FM3, but on the other hand, FM3 has better values for precision and variability safety than FM2. These types of trade-offs give the software engineer the flexibility to decide which solution(s) work(s) best for his/her concrete reverse engineering task.

4. EVALUATION

In this section we provide details of the case studies used in our evaluation, our experimental set up, the results obtained with their corresponding analysis, and the threats to validity we identified. The implementation and data are available online for replication[1].

4.1 Case Studies

Table 3 presents the systems used in the evaluation of the proposed approach. Draw Product Line (DPL), briefly presented in our running example, is a simple drawing application. Video On Demand (VOD) implements video-on-demand streaming. ArgoUML is an open source UML modelling application. ZipMe is a system for files compression. Game Of Life (GOF) is a customizable game.

[1]http://isse.jku.at/tools/gecco15

Table 3: Case Studies Overview

System	#F	#P	LoC	#Nodes	#Edges
DPL	6	16	282 - 473	12	27
VOD	11	32	4.7K - 5.2K	7	11
ArgoUML	11	256	264K - 344K	49	114
ZipMe	7	32	5K - 6.2K	29	60
GOL	15	65	874 - 1.9K	12	24

#F: Number of Features, #P: Number of Products, LoC: Lines of Code, #Nodes: Number of Nodes in the Dependency Graph, #Edges: Number of Edges, i.e. Dependencies, in the Dependency Graph

4.2 Experimental Setup

As explained before, we used three objective functions precision, recall, and variability safety and normalized their values in the interval between 0 and 1. The goal is to maximize the values of all objective functions. Hence, the best solution is *precision*=1.0, *recall*=1.0, and *variability safety*=1.0.

For our implementation, we relied on the same genetic programming representation and evolutionary operators proposed by Linsbauer et al. [12], whose parameter settings are replicated in Table 4. In contrast with their single-objective work, we not only use recall and precision but also add variability-safety as objective function and use the *Non-Dominated Sorting Genetic Algorithm (NSGA-II)* [6], implemented in the ECJ Framework[2]. We performed 30 independent runs of our algorithm for each case study. The runs were performed on a machine with an Intel® Core^{TM} i7-4900MQ CPU with 2.80 GHz, 16 GB of memory running a Linux platform.

Table 4: Algorithm's Parameters based on [12].

Parameter	Value
Number of Generations	1000
Population Size	100
Crossover	0.7
Feature Tree Mutation	0.5
CTCs Mutation	0.5
Number of Elites	1
Selection Method	Tournament
Tournament Size	6
Maximium CTC Percentage for Builder*	0.1
Maximium CTC Percentage for Mutator*	0.5

* relative to number of features

[2]http://cs.gmu.edu/~eclab/projects/ecj/

4.3 Results and Analysis

For the analysis we composed the approximated *Pareto Front (PF)* by merging all the solutions of each run and leaving only the non-dominated solutions. The PF for each case study is presented in Table 5. The average runtime of the algorithm NSGA-II in each run for the case studies were: ArgoUML = 7m 16s 337ms, DPL = 9s 854ms, GOL = 45s 036ms, VOD = 574ms, and ZipMe = 40s 263ms.

Table 5: Non-Dominated Solutions

System		Precision	Recall	Variability Safety
ArgoUML		1.0	1.0	0.9999630
		1.0	0.9375	0.9999654
		1.0	0.875	0.9999683
		1.0	0.75	1.0
DPL		1.0	1.0	1.0
GOL		1.0	0.5538462	1.0
		0.8333333	0.6153846	1.0
		0.8000000	0.7384616	1.0
		0.4851485	0.7538462	1.0
		0.4827586	0.8615385	1.0
		0.4571429	0.9846154	1.0
		0.2826087	1.0	1.0
VOD		1.0	1.0	1.0
ZipMe	(A)	1.0	0.75	1.0
	(B)	1.0	0.875	0.9999600
	(C)	0.9696970	1.0	0.9999548
	(D)	1.0	1.0	0.9999534

For the case studies DPL and VOD the PF is composed by only one solution. This single solution has the best values for the three objectives, therefore it dominates any other existing solution. The reverse-engineered feature model denotes all the feature sets used as input (recall=1.0), the feature sets denoted are exactly those used as input (precision=1.0) and none of the feature sets break any of the dependency constraints (variability safety=1.0). During the analysis of the reason why these systems have only one solution, we figured out that their features are mainly connected by optional and mandatory relationships, the depth of the feature model tree has only two levels, and the input feature sets could be achieved by different FMs. These characteristics allow the values of precision and recall to reach 1.0 in the same solution. Furthermore, these two systems have few dependencies (see Table 3), making it easier to reach 1.0 for variability safety. In other words, these two systems impose less constraints on the search space which makes finding a solution easier.

For the systems ArgoUML, GOL and ZipMe the approximated PF has four, seven and four solutions, respectively. This indicates that there are some conflicts to optimize the three measures simultaneously. This is an important benefit of using a multi-objective approach, since no single solution is the best one, but a set of acceptable solutions exists and their respective trade-offs can be considered by the software engineer. We now illustrate in more detail the decision making support that our approach can provide to software engineers. We use the ZipMe case study because it has a good trade-off among the solutions and because of its size, only seven features, which allows us to depict some of the feature models that were reverse-engineered.

Figure 5 shows the solutions of ZipMe for each combination of two dimensions in the search space. The solutions are labelled with letters for easy reference, see Table 5 last row. Figure 5(a) presents the measures of precision and recall. In an initial analysis, considering only these two objectives, solution *D* is the best one, with value 1.0 for precision and recall. However, these solutions have different values of variability safety, as depicted in the other graphs. In Figure 5(b), it can be seen that solution *D* has the worst value for variability safety with the value 0.9999534. This value indicates that some dependencies are broken for some feature sets, in particular one dependency is broken by eight feature sets. Solution *A* has the best value for variability safety, i.e. 1.0, which indicates that there are no feature sets that break any dependency. In this same solution, the value of precision is still excellent (precision=1.0), but the value of recall of this solution is the worst (recall=0.75), as presented in Figure 5(c). In this figure, we can also observe that the value of recall increases while the value of variability safety decreases. The solutions *C* and *D* have the best value of recall (recall=1.0) and a slight difference of variability safety with values of 0.9999548 and 0.9999534 respectively. Solution *C* has better value of variability safety than solution *D*, but on the other hand has the worst value of precision (Figure 5(b)). Solution *B* has the best value of precision, as well as solutions *A* and *D*, has a slightly better value of variability safety than solutions *C* and *D*, but on the other hand has a worse value of recall than solutions *C* and *D*.

Let us now analyze the meaning of the values for each objective function using the solutions of ZipMe shown in Figure 6. It is important to point out that we identified the dependency from feature `GZip` to feature `CRC` as the only broken dependency in solutions *B*, *C*, and *D*. In the FM of solution *A*, shown in Figure 6(a), we observe that all dependencies are satisfied (variability safety = 1.0). The dependency broken in the other FMs is not possible here because feature `GZip` is child of `CRC`. But this feature model does not denote the same feature sets used as input, for example, those with feature `GZip` and without feature `CRC`. From the 32 feature sets used as input only 24 are denoted, hence the value of recall decreases to 0.75. The FM of solution *B*, shown in Figure 6(b), denotes 28 feature sets belonging to the input (recall=0.875). The feature sets missing are because of the *or group* that forces the selection of at least one of the features `CRC`, `ArchiveCheck` and `Extract`. From these 28 feature sets, six break the dependency between features `GZip` and `CRC`, i.e. variability safety = 0.9999600. The FM of the solution *C*, shown in Figure 6(c), denotes all the 32 input feature sets (recall=1.0). However, one more additional feature set is also denoted, namely, a feature set with only the feature `Base`. This surplus decreases the value of precision to 0.9696970. Out of these 33 feature sets, the dependency between `GZip` and `CRC` is broken in eight of them. The FM in solution *D*, Figure 6(d), denotes all the 32 feature sets used as input (recall=1.0), there are no additional feature sets (precision=1.0), and eight feature sets break the dependency between `GZip` and `CRC`. Even though the number of broken dependencies is the same as in solution *C*, the value of variability safety of solution *D* (i.e. 0.9999534) is worse because solution *C* (i.e. 0.9999548) has more feature sets.

In summary, based on the obtained solutions, the software engineer can decide which combinations of objective functions and trade-offs are more relevant to his/her task.

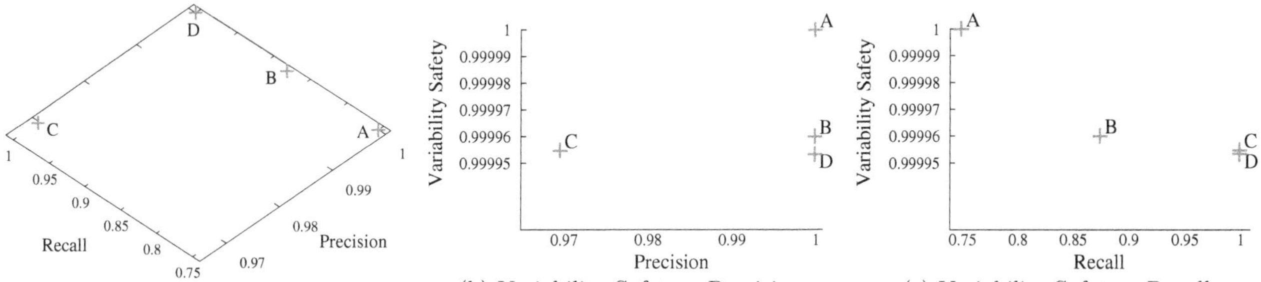

(a) Precision x Recall (b) Variability Safety x Precision (c) Variability Safety x Recall

Figure 5: ZipMe Non-Dominated Solutions

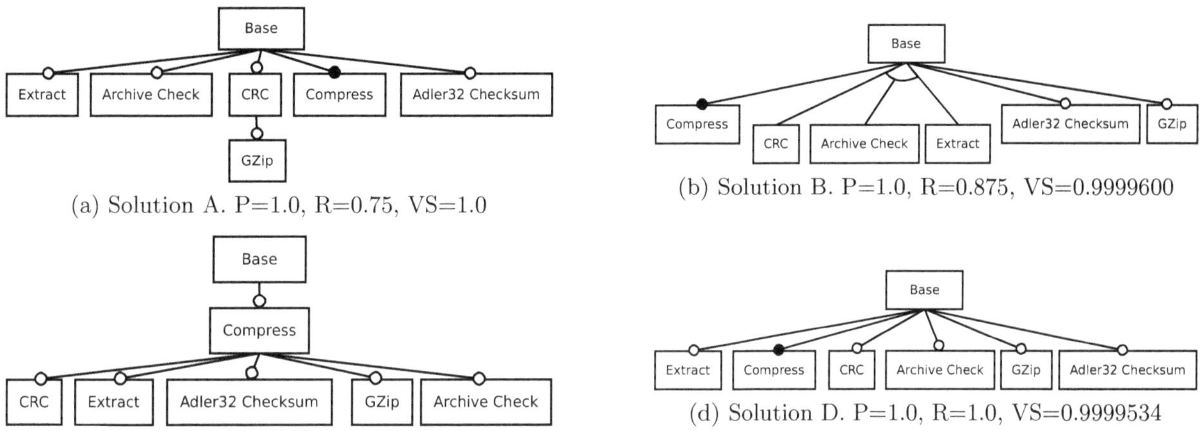

(a) Solution A. P=1.0, R=0.75, VS=1.0

(b) Solution B. P=1.0, R=0.875, VS=0.9999600

(c) Solution C. P=0.9696970, R=1.0, VS=0.9999548

(d) Solution D. P=1.0, R=1.0, VS=0.9999534

Figure 6: ZipMe Feature Models

For instance, if the recall is more important, solutions *C* and *D* are the best options. If he/she has precedence for variability safety, solution *A* is the best. On the other hand, if the goal is a solution with good trade-off considering all objectives, solution *D* can be a better option. Regarding the practical use of the variability safety, if the software engineer chooses a solution with variability safety less than 1.0 (e.g. solution B), he/she must resolve the broken dependencies (e.g. applying refactorings) so that the affected systems can be actually realized if so desired.

In contrast with ZipMe, the case studies ArgoUML and GOL only exhibit trade-offs between two objective functions, see Table 5. Regarding ArgoUML, the values of precision for all solutions are the best (precision=1.0), so the software engineer should decide among recall or variability safety values. For GOL, the value of variability safety is the best for all solutions (variability safety=1.0), with diversity of values for precision and recall to choose from.

4.4 Threats to Validity

The first threat to validity that we identified was the selection of parameter settings for our algorithm. To address this threat, we relied on the standard values employed by Linsbauer et al. [12]. Certainly, other parameter values could yield different results. A detailed analysis is outside of the scope of this paper and part of our future work. The second threat concerns the selection of case studies. To address this threat, we selected five case studies from different application domains and dimensions. These case studies have been substantially used for SPL research for multiple purposes [2]. Based on this we argue that they are representative of the reverse engineering scenario targeted by our approach. A third threat regards the comparison against related work. We should remark that, to the best of our knowledge, our work is the first to propose a multi-objective perspective and include information from artifacts such as dependency graphs for reverse engineering feature models. Therefore a comparison against such approaches is not adequate.

5. RELATED WORK

There is increasing literature in reverse engineering feature models. In this section, we summarize those pieces of work closest to ours. The closest related work is Linsbauer et al. [12], on which we based our feature model representation and evolutionary operators. In contrast with our work, they propose a single-objective algorithm for F1 — a measure that considers recall and precision with equal preference — and do not consider any information from implementation artifacts for their reverse engineering of feature models.

Work by Haslinger et al. proposes an ad hoc algorithm to reverse engineer feature models from feature sets that works by identifying occurrence patterns in the selected and not selected features that are mapped to parent-child relations of feature models [8]. This work has been extended to consider requires and excludes CTCs [9]; however, it does not support more general types of CTCs. In contrast with our work, they do not consider any domain knowledge information, just the input feature sets, for the reverse engineering task.

Work by Czarnecki and Wasowski reverse engineers feature models from sets of propositional logic formulas by means of an ad hoc algorithm that can potentially extract from a single propositional logic formula multiple feature models while trying to preserve the original formulas and reduce redundancies [5]. A recent extension of this work provides improved algorithms based on CNF and DNF constraints [18]. In contrast with our work, their starting point are configuration files, documentation files, and constraints expressed in propositional logic.

Acher et al. also tackle the reverse engineering of feature models from feature sets by mapping each feature set into a feature model which are later merged into a single feature model [1]. Besides this difference, they do not consider any other domain knowledge information. Sannier et al. perfomed an analysis of matrices for product comparison available at Wikipedia [16]. Their product matrices can contain other values, rather than selected or not selected, as in our case. Based on these matrices, their work identifies variability patterns in the values of the cells, and portrays the challenges and potential benefits of exploiting that information, among other things, to extract models such as feature models. However, to the best of our knowledge, at present there is no algorithm, let alone tool support, that capitalizes on this information to aid the reverse engineering effort.

6. CONCLUSIONS AND FUTURE WORK

This paper presented a multi-objective approach to reverse engineering FMs. We introduced a measure to evaluate variability safety in addition to recall and precision. For computing variability safety we considered dependency graphs representing the source code dependencies. Our evaluation showed that a multi-objective approach can indeed offer a set of solutions with good trade-offs. From this set of solutions the software engineer has the power to select which objective function to favour based on his/her needs.

Note that variability safety is not restricted to dependencies of source code. A similar objective function can be computed on other types of implementation artifacts. Furthermore this type of objective function expresses a conformance of a candidate FM to a set of constraints, which can also include for instance those given by domain experts based on their knowledge of the legacy system variants. Along these lines, in our future work we plan to extract and use dependency information from other sources besides code. In addition, we plan to apply and study other multi-objective algorithms, analyze parameter settings, and use our approach on more case studies.

Acknowledgments

This work was supported by Brazilian Agencies CAPES and CNPQ and the Austrian Science Fund (FWF): P 25289-N15.

7. REFERENCES

[1] M. Acher, A. Cleve, G. Perrouin, P. Heymans, C. Vanbeneden, P. Collet, and P. Lahire. On extracting feature models from product descriptions. In *VaMoS*, pages 45–54, 2012.

[2] W. K. G. Assunção, R. E. Lopez-Herrejon, L. Linsbauer, S. R. Vergilio, and A. Egyed. A systematic mapping study on migrating software systems to software product lines. 2015. submitted.

[3] D. S. Batory, J. N. Sarvela, and A. Rauschmayer. Scaling step-wise refinement. *IEEE Trans. Software Eng.*, 30(6):355–371, 2004.

[4] D. Benavides, S. Segura, and A. R. Cortés. Automated analysis of feature models 20 years later: A literature review. *Inf. Syst.*, 35(6):615–636, 2010.

[5] K. Czarnecki and A. Wasowski. Feature diagrams and logics: There and back again. In *SPLC*, pages 23–34. IEEE Computer Society, 2007.

[6] K. Deb, A. Pratap, S. Agarwal, and T. Meyarivan. A fast and elitist multiobjective genetic algorithm: NSGA-II. *Trans. on Evol. Comp.*, 6(2):182–197, 2002.

[7] S. Fischer, L. Linsbauer, R. E. Lopez-Herrejon, and A. Egyed. Enhancing clone-and-own with systematic reuse for developing software variants. In *ICSME*, 2014.

[8] E. N. Haslinger, R. E. Lopez-Herrejon, and A. Egyed. Reverse engineering feature models from programs' feature sets. In *WCRE*, pages 308–312, 2011.

[9] E. N. Haslinger, R. E. Lopez-Herrejon, and A. Egyed. On extracting feature models from sets of valid feature combinations. In *FASE*, pages 53–67, 2013.

[10] K. Kang, S. Cohen, J. Hess, W. Novak, and A. Peterson. Feature-Oriented Domain Analysis (FODA) Feasibility Study. Technical Report CMU/SEI-90-TR-21, SEI, CMU, 1990.

[11] L. Linsbauer, R. E. Lopez-Herrejon, and A. Egyed. Recovering traceability between features and code in product variants. In *SPLC*, pages 131–140, 2013.

[12] L. Linsbauer, R. E. Lopez-Herrejon, and A. Egyed. Feature model synthesis with genetic programming. In *SSBSE*, pages 153–167, 2014.

[13] R. E. Lopez-Herrejon, J. A. Galindo, D. Benavides, S. Segura, and A. Egyed. Reverse engineering feature models with evolutionary algorithms: An exploratory study. In *SSBSE*, pages 168–182, 2012.

[14] R. E. Lopez-Herrejon, L. Linsbauer, J. A. Galindo, J. A. Parejo, D. Benavides, S. Segura, and A. Egyed. An assessment of search-based techniques for reverse engineering feature models. *Journal of Systems and Software*, 103(0):353 – 369, 2015.

[15] C. D. Manning, P. Raghavan, and H. Schütze. *Introduction to information retrieval.* CUP, 2008.

[16] N. Sannier, M. Acher, and B. Baudry. From comparison matrix to variability model: The wikipedia case study. In *ASE*, pages 580–585. IEEE, 2013.

[17] S. She, R. Lotufo, T. Berger, A. Wasowski, and K. Czarnecki. Reverse engineering feature models. In *ICSE*, pages 461–470. ACM, 2011.

[18] S. She, U. Ryssel, N. Andersen, A. Wasowski, and K. Czarnecki. Efficient synthesis of feature models. *Inf. & Softw. Techn.*, 56(9):1122–1143, 2014.

[19] F. J. van d. Linden, K. Schmid, and E. Rommes. *Software Product Lines in Action: The Best Industrial Practice in Product Line Engineering.* Springer, 2007.

[20] N. Weston, R. Chitchyan, and A. Rashid. A framework for constructing semantically composable feature models from natural language requirements. In *SPLC*, pages 211–220, 2009.

Operator Selection using Improved Dynamic Multi-Armed Bandit

Jany Belluz
Grenoble INP - Ensimag
681, rue de la passerelle - Domaine universitaire - BP 72
Saint Martin d'Hères, France
jany.belluz@ensimag.fr

Marco Gaudesi, Giovanni Squillero
DAUIN, Politecnico di Torino
Corso Duca degli Abruzzi, 129
Torino, Italy
{marco.gaudesi, giovanni.squillero}@polito.it

Alberto Tonda
UMR 782 GMPA, INRA
1 av. Lucien Brétignères
78850, Thiverval-Grignon, France
alberto.tonda@grignon.inra.fr

ABSTRACT

Evolutionary algorithms greatly benefit from an optimal application of the different genetic operators during the optimization process: thus, it is not surprising that several research lines in literature deal with the self-adapting of activation probabilities for operators. The current state of the art revolves around the use of the Multi-Armed Bandit (MAB) and Dynamic Multi-Armed bandit (D-MAB) paradigms, that modify the selection mechanism based on the rewards of the different operators. Such methodologies, however, update the probabilities after each operator's application, creating possible issues with positive feedbacks and impairing parallel evaluations, one of the strongest advantages of evolutionary computation in an industrial perspective. Moreover, D-MAB techniques often rely upon measurements of population diversity, that might not be applicable to all real-world scenarios. In this paper, we propose a generalization of the D-MAB approach, paired with a simple mechanism for operator management, that aims at removing several limitations of other D-MAB strategies, allowing for parallel evaluations and self-adaptive parameter tuning. Experimental results show that the approach is particularly effective with frameworks containing many different operators, even when some of them are ill-suited for the problem at hand, or are sporadically failing, as it commonly happens in the real world.

Categories and Subject Descriptors

I.2.8 [**Computing Methodologies**]: Artificial Intelligence—*Problem Solving, Control Methods, and Search*

Keywords

Adaptivity; Operator selection; Multi-Armed Bandit; Self-adapting

GECCO '15 July 11–15, 2015, Madrid, Spain

ISBN 978-1-4503-3472-3/15/07... $15.00
DOI: http://dx.doi.org/10.1145/2739480.2754712

1. INTRODUCTION

With each passing year, evolutionary algorithms (EAs) are more and more adopted in industries as optimization techniques, thanks to their ability of efficiently navigating the search space of NP-hard problems, thus delivering acceptable solutions in a reasonable amount of time [17]. Nevertheless, their wide-spread adoption is slowed down by the expert knowledge needed to fine-tune parameters such as population size, type of individual selection, and – more importantly – activation probabilities for the genetic operators. It is no coincidence if the EAs most popular outside the evolutionary community require little to no parameter tuning at all [19, 9, 6].

Several research lines focus on self-adapting EAs' parameters during the optimization, in order to free the users from the burden of finding the optimal settings for their specific application. A considerable number of articles in literature deal with the self-adaptation of the activation probabilities of the genetic operators. Regardless the strategy, that may range from encoding probabilities directly into the genome, to inserting heuristic triggers in the algorithm, an optimal choice of the best operators can significantly enhance the optimization process. However, properly tweaking the probabilities of application for a certain operator over the different phases of the process is quite challenging, especially when an evolutionary framework includes several specialized mutations, and different kinds of crossovers.

In order to deal with such complexity, the scientific community traditionally resorted to the Multi-Armed Bandit (MAB) paradigm: initially developed by game theorists [11, 1], this framework tries to balance the exploration for better operators with the exploitation of the best ones. Since the optimal operator to apply during the evolution is likely to change during the evolutionary process, the problem has been re-stated to be solved as a Dynamic Multi-Armed Bandit (D-MAB) approach.

The most successful MAB-based operator selection frameworks share a common requirement: new individuals should be evaluated between each operator application [4, 12, 7]. However, industrial use cases for EA optimization usually feature computationally intensive evaluation functions, that may run complex simulations [3] or even test a candidate solution on a physical device [8]. Such problems make it mandatory to parallelize the evaluation process, which is clearly incompatible with the current limitations of MAB-based operator selection schemes. Finally, in use cases where the structure of a solution is extremely complex and several operators are available, even an operator that produces good solutions can fail sporadically, and such a possibility should be acknowledged and correctly handled as part of the operator selection strategy, whereas failing operators are often completely removed from previous D-MAB approaches.

In this paper, we propose a generalization of the D-MAB approach, aimed at removing the requirements for sequential evaluations. The proposed approach makes more sensible choices during the period in which we must select λ operators in a row without receiving any new information. Indeed, our strategy improves over naïvely selecting λ times the same operator by maintaining a part of exploration during the same period. The new mechanism is tuned to be fully exploitable in μGP, an industrial-grade generic evolutionary toolkit [16].

The rest of the paper is organized as follows. Section 2 briefly presents the necessary concepts to introduce the scope of this work. Section 3 illustrates the proposed approach, while Section 4 shows the experimental results on a set of test cases. Finally, Section 5 summarizes the conclusions drawn from the experience.

2. BACKGROUND

This section briefly introduces the necessary notions related to the scope of this work. First, the D-MAB framework is described; then, an overview of previous operator-selection framework is presented.

2.1 The Multi-Armed Bandit Framework

The "Exploration vs. Exploitation" dilemma has been intensively studied in game theory [2], especially in the context of the MAB framework [11, 1]. Let's consider an hypothetical slot machine with N arms (the bandit); at time t_k, the i-th arm, when selected, gets a reward 1 with probability p_i, and 0 otherwise. A solution to the MAB problem is a decision making algorithm that selects an arm at every time step, with the goal of maximizing the cumulative reward gathered during the process.

Generalizing the widely-studied Upper Confidence Bound (UCB) algorithm [1], that shows how to maximize the cumulative reward with optimal convergence rate on simple 0-1 arms, the player should select at each time step t the arm i that maximizes the following quantity:

$$\hat{p}_{i,t} + C \cdot \sqrt{\frac{\log \sum_k n_{k,t}}{n_{i,t}}} \tag{1}$$

where $n_{i,t}$ is the number of times the i-th arm has been activated from the beginning of the process to time t; while $\hat{p}_{i,t}$ denotes the average empirical reward received from arm i. C is a (critical) scaling factor not present in the original UCB definition, where normalization was not necessary, and it controls the trade-off between exploration, favored by the right term of the equation; and exploitation, favored by the left part of the equation, that pushes for the option with the best average empirical reward.

2.2 DMAB and Operators Selection in EA

The MAB problem can be intuitively applied to operator selection in EAs: every arm of the bandit can be mapped to one operator. Using the UCB metric, the algorithm keeps exploring all arms, while favoring good operators. However, contrary to the theoretical bandit, an evolutionary run is a dynamic environment, in which the standard MAB algorithm would require a considerable amount of time to detect that the best operator has changed. To solve this issue, [4] proposed to use a statistical change detection test, creating the Dynamic MAB (D-MAB) algorithm. Specifically, the Page-Hinkley test [10] is used to detect whether the empirical rewards collected for the best current operator undergo an abrupt change. In the D-MAB, if the PH test is triggered, suggesting that the current best operator is no longer the best one, the MAB algorithm is restarted.

An overview of the most successful D-MAB based mechanisms can be found in [7]. Further works build on the D-MAB algorithm most notably by comparing various credit assignment mechanisms and measuring how well they complement the D-MAB selection scheme. In [12], for example, the authors propose to combine the D-MAB with a credit assignment scheme called *Compass*, that evaluates the performance of operators by considering not only the fitness improvements from parent to offspring, but also the way they modify the diversity of the population, and their execution time.

3. PROPOSED APPROACH

We propose a D-MAB selection strategy that not only allows operators to sporadically fail without being completely removed from the process, but is also able to consecutively apply several operators without needing a performance feedback after each application. For our approach, we consider the following EA structure:

```
operators ← {available operators and their MAB state};
policy.init(operators);
parents ← {some random individuals};
until reached a stop condition do
    offspring ← [];
    applications ← [];
    policy.before_selections(operators);
    until λ successful operator applications do
        op ← policy.select(operators);
        children ← op.apply(parents);
        if children = ∅ then
            policy.failure(op);
        else
            policy.success(op);
            applications.append((op, children));
            offspring.append(children);
    evaluate(offspring);
    policy.reward(parents, offspring, applications);
    parents ← selection(parents, offspring);
```

Algorithm 1: Outline of our target EA

This general structure is shared by different EAs, such as the μGP toolkit [16], that will be our case study. In this type of architecture the evaluation phase can be easily parallelized, and operators can occasionally fail without being removed from the selection process. We adopt the general term "operators" to denote both mutation and crossover operators, as one operator in μGP is not bound to operate on a specific number of parents nor to produce a given offspring size.

During the current generation, the only information that the policy can gather is whether the selected operator actually produced children, through the functions `policy.success()` and `policy.failure()`. After the evaluation phase, the policy can access more information: the fitness of the newly produced offspring makes tournaments possible.

3.1 Notations

Each operator is considered as an arm of a MAB and is associated to several counters. First, *op.pending* keeps track of the number of successful applications awaiting a reward in each generation. Then, the *op.enabled* and *op.tokens* counters account for this operator's applicability. An operator is said to be *enabled* when it can produce new offspring and has already proved so at least once. Furthermore, an enabled operator can be selected only if it has a positive number of *tokens*. We use these tokens to limit the computation time spent in unadapted operators. Finally, we maintain a short history of the last obtained rewards in *op.window* and the classical D-MAB statistics, in *op.n*, *op.*$\hat{p}$, *op.m* and *op.n* [12]. Algorithm 2 covers the initialization of these variables. The initial number of tokens assigned to operators is set to a small number, such as $\kappa = 3$.

```
function policy.init(operators) is
    foreach op in operators do
        // Intra generational call count
        op.pending ← 0;
        // Failure handling statistics
        op.enabled ← False;
        op.tokens ← κ;
        // Compass-like window
        op.window ← queue of size τ;
        // D-MAB statistics
        op.n ← 0;
        op.p̂ ← 0;
        op.m ← 0;
        op.M ← 0;
```

Algorithm 2: Initialization of the operator statistics

3.2 Operator failures

We define a "failure" as the application of an operator that does not result in any new usable solution. This can happen for three reasons: the operator always produces an invalid individual (e.g., it removes or adds an element when the problem solution is a fixed-length list); the operator is never applicable (e.g., it performs a Gaussian mutation, but the genome is a bit string); its execution can sporadically fail based on the structure of the selected parents or other details (e.g., it concatenates two genomes and creates an individual too long to be valid). Such a notion, adopted in μGP and not quite common in classic combinatorial optimization, is essential to alleviate the burden of selecting the perfect set of operators [13].

In μGP, λ genetic operators are used in each generation. There is no distinctions between mutations and recombinations. As *failures* are not included in the count, more than λ operators could be selected and activated in order to reach the desired number. It is necessary to distinguish operators that always fail because inapplicable to the current problem, from operators that do not provide good solutions in the specific phase of the optimization process, or sporadically fail.

We adaptively handle inapplicable operators by considering all operators *disabled* until they prove their usefulness building one valid solution. All operators are called periodically to check whether some emergent characteristic of the population enables them to work in a later stage of evolution. As a consequence, when an unforeseen edge case is encountered during its execution, an operator can just fail without any penalty: this also makes it easier to add new operators to a framework, as foreseeing their effect on all possible genomes is not necessary.

Performance problems can arise if an operator is computationally intensive, builds very good solutions, but fails most of the time. Such an operator might get called repeatedly and use a considerable amount of CPU time for the production of few viable children. To avoid this situation, we use the idea of *failure tokens*, that is, a maximum number of failed calls allowed per generation. In this case, we set that a disabled operator will be tested again once every 10 generations. Once enabled, an operator will have a budget of λ authorized failures per generation, as shown by the first function of Algorihtm 3. The rest of our failure handling mechanism is implemented in the second function as a "filter" before the real selection strategy. Finally, the last two functions account for the consumption of tokens and the enabling of operators.

3.3 Credit assignment

A well-known approach to aggregate the different goals of exploration and exploitation is the Compass method [14, 12]. Compass associates the application of an operator with the variation of two characteristics of the population on which it operates: ΔD (mean diversity) and ΔQ (mean fitness). Its execution time T is also stored. These three values, averaged over a window of the last τ applications of the operator, are used to compute a reward. The meta-parameter Θ defines a compromise between the two first criteria ΔD and ΔQ: according to the authors, it affects the *Exploration vs. Exploitation* (EvE) orientation of the algorithm, and this compromise value is divided by the execution time of the operator to produce its reward.

This technique cannot be translated directly into all EAs, and, specifically, it requires several adjustment to be applied in μGP. Despite the several characteristics that needed to be left out, its underlying ideas proved to be extremely useful. First of all, μGP does not use the Θ angle: the tool already features a self-adapted σ parameter that controls how much the offspring diverges from the parent in mutation operators, and effectively regulates the amount of exploration [16].

As for diversity preservation and promotion, μGP provides different mechanisms such as fitness sharing, fitness scaling, delta entropy, and fitness holes, which encapsulate the *diversity vs. quality* problem into the comparison of individuals, either during selection of parents (fitness hole) or selection of survivors (scaled fitness) [15, 5, 16].

Moreover, even the ΔQ criteria is thus not available in μGP: the toolkit does not make any assumption about the fitness function. As in many industrial problems, candidate solutions can only be ranked, but their relative goodness cannot be evaluated on any absolute scale.

We therefore replace the $(\Delta Q, \Delta D, \Theta)$ triple with a single measure: we organize a soccer-style tournament between

```
function policy.before_selections(operators) is
    foreach op ∈ operators do
        op.pending ← 0;
        if op.enabled then
            op.tokens ← λ;
        else
            if current generation mod 10 = 0 then
                op.tokens ← 1;

function policy.select(operators) is
    foreach op in operators where ¬ op.enabled do
        if op.tokens > 0 then
            return op;
    enabled ← {op ∈ operators | op.enabled};
    if enabled = ∅ then
        redistribute κ tokens to all operators;
        return any operator;
    selectable ← {op ∈ enabled | op.tokens > 0};
    if selectable = ∅ then
        redistribute λ tokens to all enabled operators;
        selectable ← enabled;
    if ∃o ∈ selectable | o.n = 0 then
        return argmin_{o∈selectable} o.n + o.pending;
    return policy.real_select(selectable);

function policy.failure(operator) is
    operator.tokens ← operator.tokens − 1;

function policy.success(operator) is
    operator.pending ← operator.pending + 1;
    if ¬operator.enabled then
        operator.enabled ← True;
        operator.tokens ← λ;
```

Algorithm 3: Execute at least once all operators before using DMAB and limit failure rate

all the parents and all the freshly evaluated offspring, and reward the offspring proportionally to their final rank. This procedure provides a comparison of the new offspring with respect to their parents.

We choose not to consider the execution time T: μGP has been designed to target industrial-scale problems where the evaluation cost is usually predominant over the time spent in the evolutionary loop [18]. Moreover, the architecture has been designed to impose the lowest possible coupling between the evaluator and the evolutionary algorithm, and may not be meaningful or correlated with the generating operator.

One feature of interest remains from Compass: the time window of the last τ values of $(\Delta Q, \Delta D, \Theta)$. Our selection scheme will indeed use a window of past fitness improvements to distribute rewards. However, the original version of Compass[14] and the more recent work to pair it with D-MAB [12] differ: while the former computes a mean, the latter argues that using extreme values (i.e. the max) yields better results, borrowing the idea from Whitacre et al. [21]. We choose to compromise between the two options by computing a weighted sum of the values, assigning exponentially decreasing weights ($w = \vartheta^i = \frac{1}{2^i}$) to the sorted values. Whenever required, the compromise could be further tuned adjusting the discount $\vartheta \in [0, 1]$: a value of $\vartheta = 0$ gives the maximum, a value of $\vartheta = 1$ the mean.

This leads us to Algorithm 4 for reward distribution.

```
function policy.reward(parents, offspring, applications) is
    tournament ← parents ∪ offspring;
    sort tournament by increasing fitness;
    foreach (op, children) in applications do
        improvement ← max_{children} tournament.rank(child) / tournament.size();
        op.window.append(improvement);
        W ← sorted op.window in decreasing order;
        r ← (Σ_{i=0}^{W.size()} W_i 2^{-i}) / (Σ_{i=0}^{W.size()} 2^{-i});
        // D-MAB algorithm from DaCosta
        op.p̂ ← 1/(op.n+1) (op.n op.p̂ + r);
        op.n ← op.n + 1;
        op.m ← op.m + (op.p̂ − r + δ);
        op.M ← max(op.M, op.m);
        if op.M − op.m > γ then
            reset all MAB statistics of all operators;
```

Algorithm 4: Credit assignment

3.4 Operator selection

The limitation we found to the D-MAB selection scheme lies in the exclusive dependence of an operator's selection on its obtained rewards: in our case it means that, during one generation, D-MAB will select the same operator λ times. Experimental results will show that this strategy is suboptimal with higher values of λ, because when the D-MAB takes the decision to exploit an operator it does so λ times in a row without any exploration, and conversely, when exploration is needed for an operator, it is called λ times even if it's the worst available.

We propose to mitigate this "all or nothing" intragenerational effect in the following way: we consider that operator applications during the generation receive immediately a fake reward equal to their current estimated reward. I.e., given an operator *op*, we simply increment the number of successful executions *op.n* for each successful application while maintaining the three other MAB statistics (*op.r̂*, *op.m*, *op.M*) to their original values.

This makes the DMAB scores vary enough during the generation to allow exploration to happen. After the evaluation of all candidates, the other D-MAB statistics are updated as usual using the actual rewards. We call this strategy PDMAB (Parallelized D-MAB).

```
function policy.real_select(operators) is
    total_n ← Σ_{o∈operators} o.n + o.pending;
    return argmax_{o∈operators} o.p̂ + C sqrt( log total_n / (o.n+o.pending) )
```

Algorithm 5: PDMAB strategy

4. EXPERIMENTAL RESULTS

4.1 Reference strategies

We compare our custom strategy with both the original DMAB and a completely random selection, used as a baseline soundness check. We use the following values for the meta-parameters: $\gamma = 1$, $C = \sqrt{2}$, $\delta = 0.15$. Since all the considered strategies are DMAB-based and share the same parameters, the comparison requires no off-line parameter tuning.

The simulations and actual tests have been carried with various values of $\lambda = 1, 20, 50, 100$. The steady case ($\lambda = 1$) is not interesting in our comparison, but we ran it to make sure that our PDMAB strategy is actually equivalent to standard DMAB. The other extreme, $\lambda = 100$, will not be discussed either because we found that intermediary values of λ already illustrate our point well enough.

4.2 Simulated behavior

We begin by implementing the strategies in a reduced environment that simulates operator application and individual evaluation by directly drawing a reward from selected statistical distributions. This allows us to compute the cumulative regret of the different strategies and make empiric predictions about their asymptotic behavior, with the strong hypothesis of a "perfect" credit assignment strategy, which would provide an exact representation of the quality of operators.

We use several "operator reward landscapes": a simple case with one constantly good operator and ten bad ones, a dynamic version of this test where the role of the good operator changes smoothly several times during the evolution, and finally an environment with several mediocre operators and an occasionally very good one. All these situations are tested with and without an added white noise.

These simulations show that the accumulated regret of the pure D-MAB strategy augments as λ grows, as shown by figure 1. On the first graph, which represents the static situation, we see that the DMAB accumulates more regret than PDMAB during the learning phase, at the beginning. Indeed, when the DMAB selects a bad operator for exploration, it is applied 50 times in a row, while the PDMAB distributes the exploration over time more smoothly. Even if on this static case the difference between the two approaches is progressively reduced as PDMAB catches up on exploration, in a dynamic setting the first part is repeated after each reset, which means the DMAB accumulates a lot of regret after each change in the environment. This is shown by the second and third graphs.

The second graph of figure 1 showcases the situation that is most representative of a real evolutionary run: at each stage of the evolution one operator is more than the others (left). While the D-MAB is the best strategy for a steady-state algorithm (equivalent to PDMAB for $\lambda = 1$, not shown), it starts accumulating more regret than PDMAB for $\lambda = 20$ (middle) and becomes clearly suboptimal for $\lambda \geq 50$ (right). On the third graph, we explain the advantage of PDMAB by the fact that its continuous exploration allows it to reset faster than the classic DMAB when the intermittent operator changes its state.

4.3 Full-stack benchmark

We ran two full tests, using μGP as the evolutionary engine. First, a specially crafted variation on OneMax is used to validate our simulated results on a simple and well known problem. Then, the newer Lamps benchmark demonstrates the applicability of the proposed strategies to Group Evolution [20].

Our version of One Max consists in maximizing the number of ones in an initially null string of 10,000 bits, using two groups of mutation operators: *static* and *dynamic*. The chances of creating an individual fitter than the parent is constant in the former group, while it depends on the current phase of the optimization process for the latter group. In more detail, static operators are: *RandomFlip* (randomly change the value of a bit), *Set*, and *Reset* (assign a given value to the bit). Dynamic operators are: *LocalMajoritySet*, consider a bit's immediate neighbors in the string and, if both are of the same value, set it to the same value; *GlobalMajoritySet*, considers the whole string and assign the bit the most common value. In an analogous way, we define the *Local-* and *GlobalMinorityReset* operators. Obviously with such definitions, when the individual fitness reaches the middle value of 5,000, the performance of the global operators will be brutally inverted, while the quality of the local version will slowly change during the whole evolution.

In order to stress the failure handling mechanism, all these operators have been defined very lazily: for example, if the "set one bit" operator randomly selects a 1, it will fail instead of trying again. In addition to that, we threw in all the available μGP operators, however irrelevant they might be. Most of them will fail constantly and stay disabled, the others will at most reset the whole bit string and be scorned by the D-MAB.

The experimental results show that the OneMax benchmark perfectly reproduces the simulated behavior, as shown by figure 2. The dominance of PDMAB over DMAB is statistically significant with a p-value of 0 using the Kolmogorov-Smirnov two-sample test, for both value of λ.

The results on Lamps with $\lambda = 20, 50$ are not statistically significant, with p-values of 0.13 and 0.5. We therefore conclude that our approach is at least as good as the standard DMAB on group evolution problems, and we propose to improve these results in a later work through an in-depth study of credit assignment and operator selection in the context of group evolution.

5. CONCLUSIONS

In this paper, we presented an extension to the Dynamic Multi-Armed Bandit approach for operator selection for evolutionary algorithms. Our approach brings the performance benefits of the DMAB strategy to industrial-grade generational algorithms such as μGP, with the added benefit of simplifying its usage, removing the need to select operators beforehand, and relaxing the constraints on operator definitions, as operators can fail sporadically.

Our simulation and experimental results on two benchmarks demonstrate that the extension indeed yields in all setups a performance at least equal to the DMAB approach for specific problems and clearly better in other cases.

Further works will focus on the validation of this selection scheme on more complex problems, and will conduct a more precise study of the proposed credit assignment.

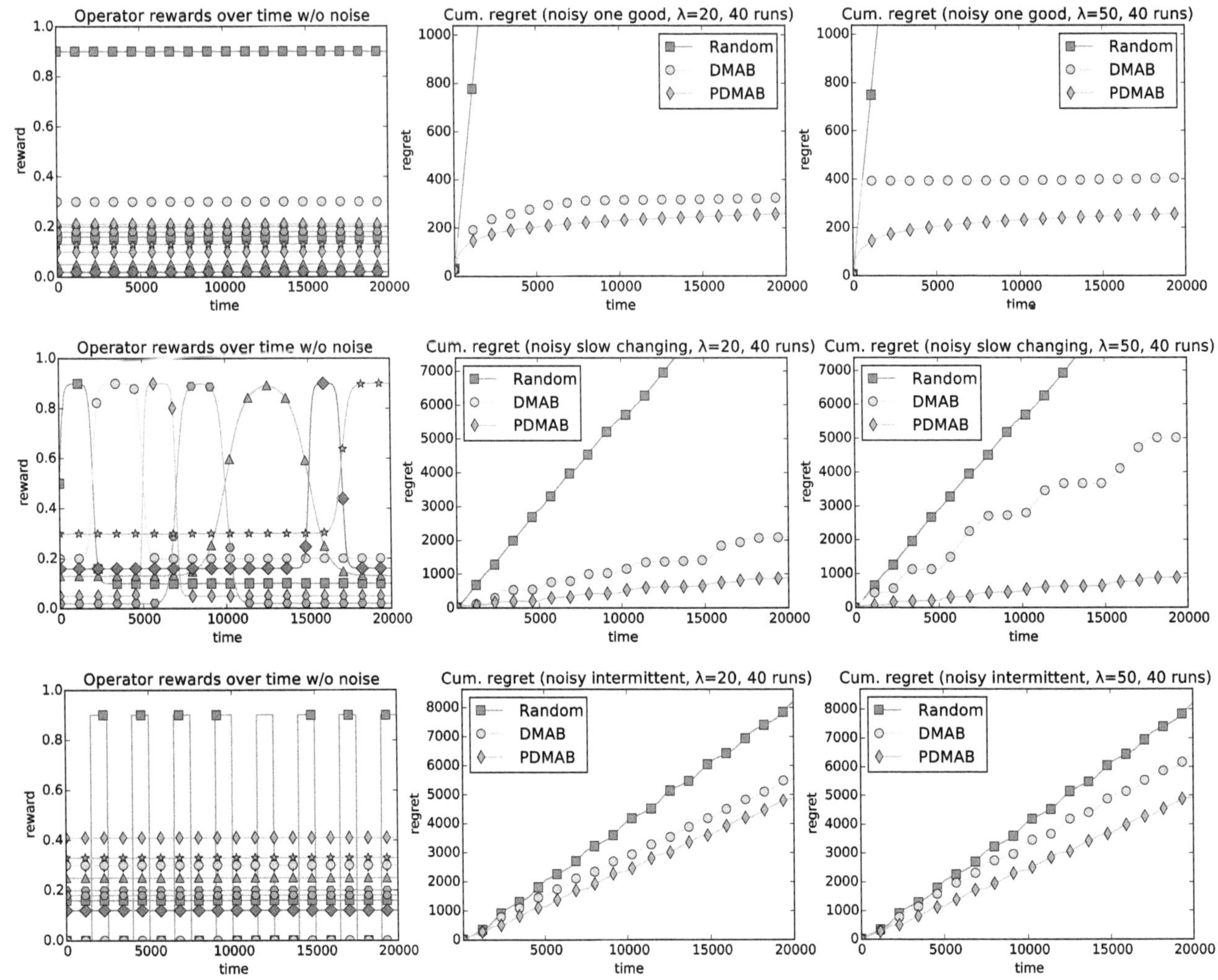

Figure 1: Simulation results for the three strategies (baseline Random, reference DMAB and modified PDMAB), over the three operator setups, for $\lambda = 20, 50$. Lower regret is better.

6. REFERENCES

[1] P. Auer, N. Cesa-Bianchi, and P. Fischer. Finite-time analysis of the multiarmed bandit problem. *Machine learning*, 47(2-3):235–256, 2002.

[2] N. Cesa-Bianchi and G. Lugosi. *Prediction, learning, and games*. Cambridge University Press, 2006.

[3] F. Corno, E. Sánchez, and G. Squillero. Evolving assembly programs: how games help microprocessor validation. *Evolutionary Computation, IEEE Transactions on*, 9(6):695–706, 2005.

[4] L. DaCosta, A. Fialho, M. Schoenauer, and M. Sebag. Adaptive operator selection with dynamic multi-armed bandits. In *Proceedings of the 10th annual conference on Genetic and evolutionary computation*, pages 913–920. ACM, 2008.

[5] K. Deb and D. E. Goldberg. An investigation of niche and species formation in genetic function optimization. In *Proceedings of the 3rd International Conference on Genetic Algorithms*, pages 42–50. Morgan Kaufmann Publishers Inc., 1989.

[6] K. Deb, A. Pratap, S. Agarwal, and T. Meyarivan. A fast and elitist multiobjective genetic algorithm: Nsga-ii. *Evolutionary Computation, IEEE Transactions on*, 6(2):182–197, 2002.

[7] Á. Fialho, L. Da Costa, M. Schoenauer, and M. Sebag. Analyzing bandit-based adaptive operator selection mechanisms. *Annals of Mathematics and Artificial Intelligence*, 60(1-2):25–64, 2010.

[8] S. Gandini, W. Ruzzarin, E. Sanchez, G. Squillero, and A. Tonda. A framework for automated detection of power-related software errors in industrial verification processes. *Journal of Electronic Testing*, 26(6):689–697, 2010.

[9] N. Hansen and A. Ostermeier. Completely derandomized self-adaptation in evolution strategies. *Evolutionary computation*, 9(2):159–195, 2001.

[10] D. V. Hinkley. Inference about the change-point from cumulative sum tests. *Biometrika*, 58(3):509–523, 1971.

[11] T. L. Lai and H. Robbins. Asymptotically efficient adaptive allocation rules. *Advances in applied mathematics*, 6(1):4–22, 1985.

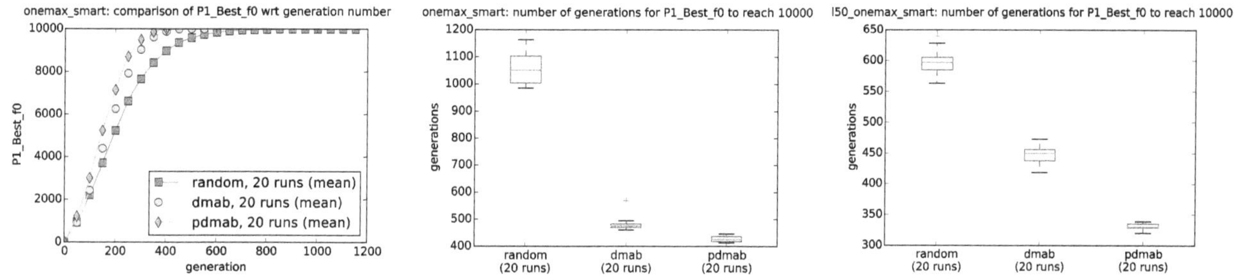

Figure 2: Experimental results for OneMax: fitness over time for $\lambda = 20$, number of generations before convergence for $\lambda = 20, 50$. Fewer generations is better.

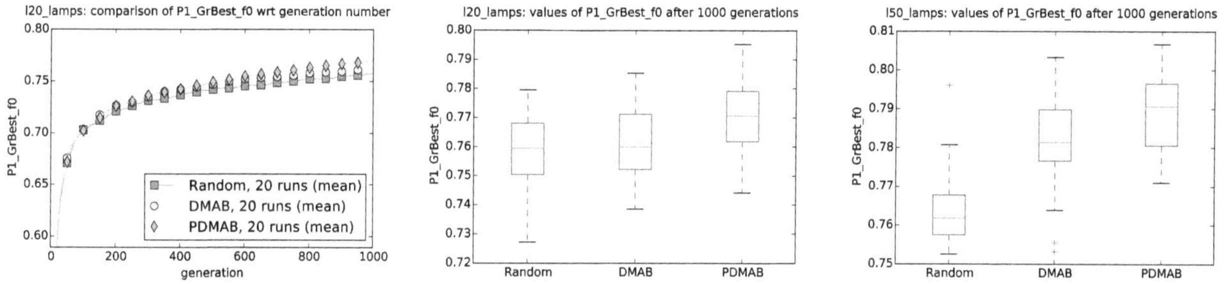

Figure 3: Experimental results for Lamps: fitness over time for $\lambda = 20$, maximum group fitness after 1000 generations for $\lambda = 20, 50$. Higher fitness is better.

[12] J. Maturana, Á. Fialho, F. Saubion, M. Schoenauer, and M. Sebag. Extreme compass and dynamic multi-armed bandits for adaptive operator selection. In *Evolutionary Computation, 2009. CEC'09. IEEE Congress on*, pages 365–372. IEEE, 2009.

[13] J. Maturana, F. Lardeux, and F. Saubion. Autonomous operator management for evolutionary algorithms. *Journal of Heuristics*, 16(6):881–909, 2010.

[14] J. Maturana and F. Saubion. A compass to guide genetic algorithms. In *Parallel Problem Solving from Nature–PPSN X*, pages 256–265. Springer, 2008.

[15] R. Poli. A simple but theoretically-motivated method to control bloat in genetic programming. In *Genetic Programming*, pages 204–217. Springer, 2003.

[16] E. Sanchez, M. Schillaci, and G. Squillero. *Evolutionary Optimization: the μGP toolkit*. Springer, 2011.

[17] E. Sanchez, G. Squillero, and A. Tonda. *Industrial applications of evolutionary algorithms*, volume 34. Springer, 2012.

[18] E. Sanchez, G. Squillero, and A. Tonda. *Industrial applications of evolutionary algorithms*, volume 34. Springer, 2012.

[19] M. Schmidt and H. Lipson. Distilling free-form natural laws from experimental data. *science*, 324(5923):81–85, 2009.

[20] A. Tonda, E. Lutton, and G. Squillero. Lamps: A test problem for cooperative coevolution. In *Nature Inspired Cooperative Strategies for Optimization (NICSO 2011)*, pages 101–120. Springer, 2011.

[21] J. M. Whitacre, T. Q. Pham, and R. A. Sarker. Use of statistical outlier detection method in adaptive evolutionary algorithms. In *Proceedings of the 8th annual conference on Genetic and evolutionary computation*, pages 1345–1352. ACM, 2006.

Learning Feature-Parameter Mappings for Parameter Tuning via the Profile Expected Improvement

Jakob Bossek
University of Münster, Germany
bossek@wi.uni-muenster.de

Bernd Bischl
TU Dortmund, Germany
bischl@statistik.tu-dortmund.de

Tobias Wagner
TU Dortmund, Germany
wagner@isf.de

Günter Rudolph
TU Dortmund, Germany
guenter.rudolph@tu-dortmund.de

ABSTRACT

The majority of algorithms can be controlled or adjusted by parameters. Their values can substantially affect the algorithms' performance. Since the manual exploration of the parameter space is tedious – even for few parameters – several automatic procedures for *parameter tuning* have been proposed. Recent approaches also take into account some characteristic properties of the problem instances, frequently termed *instance features*.

Our contribution is the proposal of a novel concept for feature-based algorithm parameter tuning, which applies an approximating surrogate model for learning the continuous feature-parameter mapping. To accomplish this, we learn a joint model of the algorithm performance based on both the algorithm parameters and the instance features. The required data is gathered using a recently proposed acquisition function for model refinement in surrogate-based optimization: the *profile expected improvement*. This function provides an avenue for maximizing the information required for the *feature-parameter mapping*, i.e., the mapping from instance features to the corresponding optimal algorithm parameters. The approach is validated by applying the tuner to exemplary evolutionary algorithms and problems, for which theoretically grounded or heuristically determined feature-parameter mappings are available.

Categories and Subject Descriptors

I.2.6 [**Artificial Intelligence**]: Learning—*Parameter learning*

Keywords

Model-based Optimization; Parameter Tuning; Evolutionary Algorithms

GECCO '15, July 11 - 15, 2015, Madrid, Spain

ISBN 978-1-4503-3472-3/15/07... $15.00
DOI: http://dx.doi.org/10.1145/2739480.2754673

1. INTRODUCTION

In recent years, the systematic use of optimization approaches for tuning the parameters of evolutionary computation methods – and other computational algorithms in general – has attained increasing attention [7]. Many researchers have documented the superiority of automatic tuning approaches over manual trial-and-error procedures, e.g., see [2, 13, 15]. In particular, employing surrogate models in the tuning process is known to usually speed-up the discovery of good parameter settings while also providing information w.r.t. the parameters' effects and interactions [2, 5, 13].

As evolutionary computation methods are often considered to be general-purpose approaches, they have to cope with a wide variety of application problems. In many cases, however, a single parameter set cannot achieve suitable results for all problems in a domain of interest, and hence, setting algorithm parameters w.r.t. instance features that describe the characteristics of the problem at hand might be beneficial. For continuous black-box optimization, e.g., exploratory landscape analysis provides a large set of features for problem instances [17, 18] that have already been used for the related problem of algorithm selection [4].

The feature-dependent configuration problem is tackled in, e.g., ISAC [15] and HYDRA [20]. While the former employs a clustering in feature space and configures the algorithm on each cluster, the latter uses the instance features for algorithm selection based on a pre-constructed set of complementary algorithm configurations. Hence, both algorithm do not provide a continuous mapping from features to parameters, as either fixed instance clusters or algorithm configurations are pre-constructed. Surrogate models could efficiently learn the joint relation between instance features and algorithm parameters to algorithm performance. But to the best of our knowledge, no sequential model-based optimization technique for parameter tuning actually defines a point acquisition function that takes instance features into account during the sequential planning of experiments. The popular sequential model-based SMAC algorithm [13] does use instance features, but only to stabilize its search process for a single configuration which works well on all instances.

Motivated by applications in reliability engineering, Ginsbourger et al. [9] recently proposed a criterion for sequential experiments with regard to the estimation of profile optima. The authors are considering scenarios where the variable space is partitioned into a group of controllable decision variables and a second group of uncontrollable nuisance parameters. They now would like to estimate a worst-case scenario. i.e., for each control paramater the worst response w.r.t. to all nuisance settings must be estimated. They applied kriging models, also popular in model-based parameter tuning [1,16]. While their perspective and motivation is quite different to ours, the mapping from instance features to optimal algorithm parameters can also be considered as a profile optimum and we can rather directly transfer their acquisition function to the scenario of parameter tuning.

Our contribution is the adoption of the approach by [9] to the field of model-based optimization for automatic parameter tuning. Note that the method neither directly optimizes parameters for a single instance nor (on average) for a set of instances, but instead defines a new sequential design-of-experiments procedure to learn a mapping from instance features to algorithm parameters. The resulting model provides the basis for a tuner that explicitly uses features of problem instances to predict the corresponding parameters.

We evaluate the approach on synthetic test problems and exemplary parameter tuning tasks. In this first concept study, we restrict ourselves to the simple case of a single feature and algorithm parameter, as it allows the visualization of the feature-parameter mappings and their development in the sequential planning process.

2. METHODOLOGY

In this section, the methodological foundations of our feature-based parameter tuning approach are presented. After a brief review of the general procedure of Sequential Model-Based Optimization (SMBO), we describe its extension utilizing the Profile Expected Improvement for learning the joint surrogate model.

2.1 Sequential Model-Based Optimization

Let $f : \Theta \to \mathbb{R}$ be a black-box function we would like to minimize over our search space Θ. In case of SMBO, we usually assume that f is expensive to evaluate, so we can only spend a severely restricted budget of function evaluations.

Algorithm 1: Generic SMBO approach.

Data: Expensive function f, Parameter space Θ.
Result: Estimated minimum $\boldsymbol{\theta}^*$.
begin
- $\mathcal{X} \leftarrow$ generateDesign(Θ)
- Evaluate $\boldsymbol{y} \leftarrow f(\mathcal{X})$
- **while** *Termination condition not satisfied* **do**
  - $\hat{m} \leftarrow$ fitModel($\mathcal{X}, \boldsymbol{y}$)
  - $y_{\min} \leftarrow \min(y)$
  - $\boldsymbol{\theta}_{new} \leftarrow$ optimizeInfillCrit($\Theta, \hat{m}, y_{\min}$)
  - Evaluate $y_{new} \leftarrow f(\boldsymbol{\theta}_{new})$
  - append($\mathcal{X}, \boldsymbol{\theta}_{new}$), append($\boldsymbol{y}, y_{new}$)
- **return** *Estim. minimum* $\boldsymbol{\theta}^*$ *from design* $\mathcal{X}$.

The general outline of SMBO is given in Algorithm 1. In each iteration, we approximate f based on all available evaluations via a surrogate model, optimize an infill criterion (or acquisition function) which balances exploration of the search space and exploitation of promising areas, evaluate the proposed point and update our model.

Kriging models [14] are frequently used in the context of SMBO due to their flexibility with regard to possible response surfaces and the possibility to estimate the model uncertainty. The latter is necessary for the Expected Improvement (EI) acquisition function which provides the foundation of the Efficient Global Optimization (EGO) algorithm by Jones et al. [14]. In the following, we discuss how to transfer SMBO approaches like EGO to parameter tuning.

2.2 SMBO for Parameter Tuning

Let us assume a configurable algorithm $\mathcal{A}$ with parameter space Θ which has to solve problem instances $I \in \mathcal{I}$ drawn i.i.d. from distribution $P_{\mathcal{I}}$. Hence, $P_{\mathcal{I}}$ reflects the probability with which instances $I \in \mathcal{I}$ will be presented to $\mathcal{A}$. A cost function $c(I, \boldsymbol{\theta})$ assigns a cost or performance value to $\mathcal{A}$ with configuration $\boldsymbol{\theta}$ on instance $I \in \mathcal{I}$.

We can configure $\mathcal{A}$ either on a single instance I by solving[1]

$$\boldsymbol{\theta}^* = \arg\min_{\boldsymbol{\theta}\in\Theta} f(\boldsymbol{\theta}) = \arg\min_{\boldsymbol{\theta}\in\Theta} c(I, \boldsymbol{\theta})$$

or with regard to the expectation over all instances

$$\boldsymbol{\theta}^* = \arg\min_{\boldsymbol{\theta}\in\Theta} f(\boldsymbol{\theta}) = \arg\min_{\boldsymbol{\theta}\in\Theta} \int_{I\in\mathcal{I}} c(I, \boldsymbol{\theta}) dP_{\mathcal{I}},$$

usually by approximating the integral via summing over a given, finite set of representative instances $\mathcal{J} \subset \mathcal{I}$

$$\boldsymbol{\theta}^* = \arg\min_{\boldsymbol{\theta}\in\Theta} f(\boldsymbol{\theta}) = \arg\min \sum_{I\in\mathcal{J}} c(I, \boldsymbol{\theta}).$$

One obvious problem of the latter formulation is that we only try to find a configuration which behaves well on average for all instances in $\mathcal{J}$ and do not exploit any specific knowledge we might have about the instances and their properties. This drawback is addressed in the following.

2.3 Feature Parameter Mapping

Now, we will assume a feature mapping $\delta : \mathcal{I} \to \Delta$, assigning instance I the describing feature vector $\delta(I)$. In general, these features are continuous, such that$\Delta \subseteq \mathbb{R}^p$. The feature mapping should reflect the properties of I and should not be too expensive to calculate. In this case, it should help us to determine a reasonable parameter setting $\boldsymbol{\theta}$ for $\mathcal{A}$ on I. Formally, we would like to obtain a feature parameter mapping (FPM)

$$m : \boldsymbol{\delta} \in \Delta \to \boldsymbol{\theta}^*_{\boldsymbol{\delta}} \in \Theta \tag{1}$$

where $\boldsymbol{\theta}^*_{\boldsymbol{\delta}}$ minimizes our cost when we integrate out over all instances I which map to $\boldsymbol{\delta}$:

$$\boldsymbol{\theta}^*_{\boldsymbol{\delta}} = \arg\min_{\boldsymbol{\theta}\in\Theta} \int_{\delta(I)=\boldsymbol{\delta}} c(I, \boldsymbol{\theta}) dP_{\mathcal{I}}$$

With a slight abuse of notation we will now extend the function c from the space $\mathcal{I} \times \Theta$ to the space$\Delta \times \Theta$ by setting $c(\boldsymbol{\delta}, \boldsymbol{\theta}) = \int_{\delta(I)=\boldsymbol{\delta}} c(I, \boldsymbol{\theta}) dP_{\mathcal{I}}$

Our task now is to learn this profile, i.e. the whole set of all $\boldsymbol{\theta}^*_{\boldsymbol{\delta}}$ elements, as good as possible during an offline training phase. Given some prior experiments $(\boldsymbol{\delta}_i, \boldsymbol{\theta}_i, c_i)_{i=1...,n}$, where $\mathcal{A}$ was run on instance I_i with feature vector $\boldsymbol{\delta}_i = \delta(I_i)$ and produced numerical costs $c_i = c(I_i, \boldsymbol{\theta}_i)$, we would

[1]To simplify notation, we have assumed here that the algorithm is deterministic, otherwise replace $c(I, \boldsymbol{\theta})$ by $E_{\boldsymbol{\theta}}(I, \boldsymbol{\theta})$.

like to learn a joint model $\hat{c}$ on$\Delta \times \Theta$ that predicts the costs of a configuration $\boldsymbol{\theta}$ when run on an instance with features $\boldsymbol{\delta}_i$. We have to stress in this context that the use of the features allows the instances to be reasonably located in the respective space Δ, but that, depending on the mapping δ, we may observe different instances $I \in \mathcal{I}$ which are mapped to the same feature vector $\boldsymbol{\delta}$. As a consequence, we may only obtain a single sample of a distribution of results based on a single experiment.

This leads to the following approximation of the FPM. Given a new instance I, we calculate its feature vector $\delta(I)$ and optimize the joint model in the subspace while fixing its first argument to $\delta(I)$:

$$\boldsymbol{\theta}^* = \arg\min_{\boldsymbol{\theta}\in\Theta} \hat{c}(\delta(I), \boldsymbol{\theta})$$

to obtain the configuration $\boldsymbol{\theta}^*$ we would use to run $\mathcal{A}$ on I. Hence, assuming we could learn a perfect model $\hat{c}$ for c, we could predict accurately for a given instance I, how well $\mathcal{A}$ would perform on average on all instances with the same features as I.

To learn this joint model, we again employ a regression approach as in SMBO, now defined on$\Delta \times \Theta$ and with the aim of estimating the profile with minimal costs. The main problem is to find an efficient sampling procedure to iteratively plan our configuration experiments. For this, we cannot use the EI, as the aim is no longer to only estimate the global optimum, but to approximate the whole profile of $\boldsymbol{\theta}^*_{\boldsymbol{\delta}}$ for all $I \in \mathcal{I}$.

2.4 Profile Expected Improvement

As potential solution, Ginsbourger et al. have introduced the Profile-EI (PEI) [9]. With regard to their work, the *Profile-Improvement* PI($\boldsymbol{\delta}$, $\boldsymbol{\theta}$) of a potential $(i+1)$-th experiment $(\boldsymbol{\delta} = \delta(I), \boldsymbol{\theta})$ on an instance I is defined by

$$PI(\boldsymbol{\delta}, \boldsymbol{\theta}) = \max\left\{0, C_{\boldsymbol{\delta},\boldsymbol{\theta}} - \max\{c_{\min}, \hat{c}(\boldsymbol{\delta}, \hat{\boldsymbol{\theta}^*_{\boldsymbol{\delta}}})\}\right\},$$

where $\hat{c}(\boldsymbol{\delta}, \hat{\boldsymbol{\theta}^*_{\boldsymbol{\delta}}})$ are the estimated costs for the estimated best configuration on the given feature vector $\boldsymbol{\delta}$ depending on the current approximation of the FPM, $c_{\min} = \min_{i=1,\dots,n} c_i$ is the minimum observed cost value over all experiments, and $C_{\boldsymbol{\delta},\boldsymbol{\theta}}$ is the corresponding random variable from the posterior distribution defined by the current surrogate model $\hat{c}$.

In case of a Gaussian process model, $C_{\boldsymbol{\delta},\boldsymbol{\theta}}$ is normally distributed as $N(\hat{c}(\boldsymbol{\delta}, \boldsymbol{\theta}), \hat{s}(\boldsymbol{\delta}, \boldsymbol{\theta})^2)$, with the mean prediction $\hat{c}(\boldsymbol{\delta}, \boldsymbol{\theta})$ and the local uncertainty $\hat{s}(\boldsymbol{\delta}, \boldsymbol{\theta})$. This corresponds to the definition of the EI in EGO. In contrast to EGO, where we would only use $c_{\min}$ for the approximation of the current optimum, the potentially infinite number of instances $I \in \mathcal{I}$ requires a more specific definition.

Ginsbourger et al. recommend to use the predicted costs $\hat{c}(\boldsymbol{\delta}, \hat{\boldsymbol{\theta}^*_{\boldsymbol{\delta}}})$ of the approximated model optimum

$$\hat{\boldsymbol{\theta}^*_{\boldsymbol{\delta}}} = \arg\min_{\boldsymbol{\theta}\in\Theta} \hat{c}(\boldsymbol{\delta}, \boldsymbol{\theta})$$

for the fixed feature vector $\boldsymbol{\delta}$. The capping by means of the overall observed optimum cost value $c_{\min}$ is recommended to ensure global exploration, even in cases $\hat{c}(\boldsymbol{\delta}, \boldsymbol{\theta})$ locally overshoots the actual cost function [9].

With these definitions, the *Profile-Expected-Improvement* is then computed as $PEI(\boldsymbol{\delta}, \boldsymbol{\theta}) = E\left(PI(\boldsymbol{\delta}, \boldsymbol{\theta})\right)$ in a similar fashion as the EI. After plugging in the respective proxies, we obtain the following closed-form definition:

$$PEI(\boldsymbol{\delta}, \boldsymbol{\theta}) = \begin{cases} \hat{s}(\boldsymbol{\delta}, \boldsymbol{\theta})\left[g(\boldsymbol{\delta}, \boldsymbol{\theta})\Phi(g(\boldsymbol{\delta}, \boldsymbol{\theta})) \right. & \\ \quad \left. +\phi(g(\boldsymbol{\delta}, \boldsymbol{\theta}))\right], & \text{if } \hat{s}(\boldsymbol{\delta}, \boldsymbol{\theta}) \neq 0 \\ 0, & \text{otherwise} \end{cases}$$

where ϕ and Φ are the probability density and cumulative density function of the standard normal distribution, respectively, and $g(\boldsymbol{\delta}, \boldsymbol{\theta}) = (c^{\boldsymbol{\delta}}_{\min} - \hat{c}(\boldsymbol{\delta}, \boldsymbol{\theta}))/\hat{s}(\boldsymbol{\delta}, \boldsymbol{\theta})$.

Algorithm 2: FBSMBO-Training

Data: Training instances $\mathcal{J}$, parameter space Θ, feature mapping δ, algorithm $\mathcal{A}$, cost function $c(I, \boldsymbol{\theta})$.
Result: Mapping $\hat{m} : \Delta \to \Theta$.

```
begin
    X ← generateDesign(J, δ, Θ)
    X now consists of tuples (I, δ, θ)
    y ← Evaluate each element of X with c(I, θ)
    while Termination condition not satisfied do
        ĉ ← fitModel(X, y)
        c_min ← min(y)
        for I_j ∈ J do
            δ ← δ(I_j)
            c^δ_min ← optMeanOnInstance(ĉ, I_j, c_min)
            PEI[j], θ[j] ← optPEIOnInstance(ĉ, I_j, c^δ_min)
        Set I_new, θ_new by taking the max of PEI[·]
        Run A(I_new, θ_new), i.e. y_new ← c(I_new, θ_new);
        append (X, [I_new, δ(I_new), θ_new])
        append (y, y_new)
    return m̂ : Δ → Θ
```

2.5 Feature-Based SMBO

Our Feature-Based SMBO (FBSMBO) configurator works in a similar fashion as the standard SMBO algorithm. We start by generating an initial design $\mathcal{X} = \{\mathbf{x}_1, \dots, \mathbf{x}_n\}$ with $\mathbf{x}_i = [\boldsymbol{\delta}_i, \boldsymbol{\theta}_i] \in \Delta \times \Theta$, which is evaluated by running the associated experiments. Hence, in addition to SMBO an instance I_i is connected to each design point, since algorithm $\mathcal{A}$ needs the instance for the evaluation of the design point and the respective feature vector $\delta(I_i)$ is used as additional input for the model fitting. This data is then used to fit the machine learning model $\hat{c}$ of the cost landscape.

The evaluation of the parameter/feature-vector pair will result in a noisy response for two reasons. First, most evolutionary computation methods are stochastic in nature which may lead to different outcomes of the same parameterization on the same instance. Second, the feature mapping, such as the input dimension of a respective instance, may result in the same feature-vector $\boldsymbol{\delta}$ for different problem instances. If experiments with the same algorithm parameters $\boldsymbol{\theta}$ are performed on all these instances, the performance values $\boldsymbol{y}$ will likely differ. As the surrogate model $\hat{c}$ maps from $\boldsymbol{\theta} \times \boldsymbol{\delta}$ to $\boldsymbol{y}$, a high variation within the response of a single input vector can occur. Hence, the *fitModel* is implemented by utilizing the reinterpolation procedure proposed by Forrester et al. in [8] for noisy computer experiments. In this procedure, first a regressing kriging model is fitted. Then, the predictions of this model are used as proxies for the expected response values of the design points, to which another interpolating model is fitted. The resulting model is then used for determining further design points in an SMBO manner. By these means, the variations in the responses are smoothed while allowing the variance of the model still to be used for ensuring a global search [8].

Within the FBSMBO loop (see Algorithm 2), FBSMBO iterates over all instances $I \in \mathcal{I}$ to compute (a) the respective minimum cost value proxies $c^{\delta}_{\min}$ for the PEI formula (optMeanOnInstance) and (b) the optimal configuration and PEI value on the subspace of algorithm parameters given the fixed instance features $\boldsymbol{\delta} = \delta(I)$: $\max_{\boldsymbol{\theta} \in \Theta} PEI(\boldsymbol{\delta}, \boldsymbol{\theta})$. Here the feature vector is fixed and optimization takes place on the subset of algorithm parameters.

The instance I with maximal $PEI(\boldsymbol{\delta}, \boldsymbol{\theta}^*_{\boldsymbol{\delta}})$ and corresponding estimated optimal parameter vector is selected to be considered for the next experiment. This process is repeated until a stopping condition is met. The offline phase returns an FPM $\hat{m} : \Delta \to \Theta$, which is constructed from the joint model $\hat{c}(\boldsymbol{\delta}, \boldsymbol{\theta})$ by optimizing over the subspace of algorithm parameters given a fixed feature vector $\boldsymbol{\delta}$. The FPM can be applied to determine parameters for previously unseen instances I as part of the online (application) phase, as shown in section 2.3.

3. EVALUATION

In this section, we empirically evaluate the proposed FBSMBO approach for parameter tuning. We start by analyzing the behavior of the configurator on synthetic examples, before we apply it to some practical parameter tuning scenarios. All of our experiments were performed in R by using the BatchJobs and BatchExperiments packages [3].

3.1 Synthetic functions

For the first set of experiments, we consider an artificial two-dimensional scenario. The first dimension will be regarded as the "instance feature" $\boldsymbol{\delta}$, while the second dimension represents the "algorithm parameter" $\boldsymbol{\theta}$. We hence model a two-dimensional cost function $c : \Delta \times \Theta \to \mathbb{R}$, which we assume to follow a deterministic test function. This allows quick test runs and a visual check of the results to be performed in a known scenario. For the preliminary experiments, we selected the well-known black-box optimization functions Branin, Himmelblau, and Goldstein-Price [11,14]. Moreover, we defined a simple Double-Sum to obtain profile curves $\boldsymbol{\theta}^*_{\boldsymbol{\delta}}$ of different complexity and shape.

For the active learning of the FPM, we ran both the PEI infill strategy and – for comparison – a random sampling (RANDOM) on each test function. The latter selects the instances and algorithm parameters $(\boldsymbol{\delta}, \boldsymbol{\theta})$ evaluated for fitting the model completely at random. Each strategy was started from the same initial design of 10 points and was allowed a budget of 30 subsequent evaluations. This experiment was replicated 30 times, resulting in 30 models $\hat{m}$ for the FPM of each strategy. To quantify the approximation quality of each FPM $\hat{m}^S$ based on infill strategy S, we computed the mean absolute difference between the algorithm performance based on the proposed and the known optimum parameters over an equidistant grid of features $\boldsymbol{\delta}_1, \ldots, \boldsymbol{\delta}_k \in \Delta$. More specific, if m is the true FPM based on the original test function, the performance measure is computed by the formula

$$PERF(S) = \frac{1}{k} \sum_{i=1}^{k} |c(\boldsymbol{\delta}_i, \hat{m}(\boldsymbol{\delta}_i)) - c(\boldsymbol{\delta}_i, m(\boldsymbol{\delta}_i))| .$$

We compare the infill strategies by means of this quality measure, whereby lower PERF values are favorable.

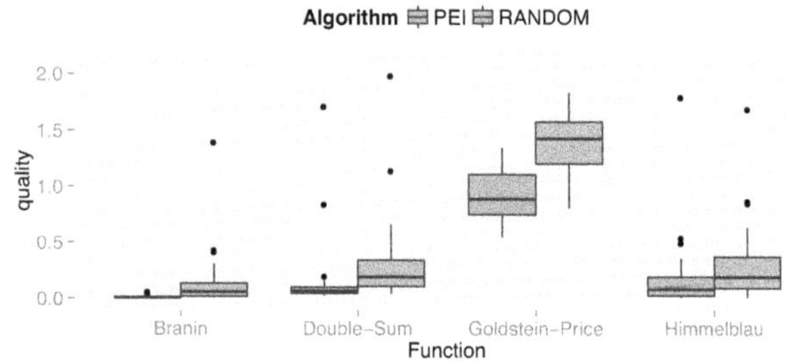

Figure 1: Boxplots of the distributions of the performance values reached in the experiments separated by test function and infill strategy used.

Figure 1 shows the distribution of performance values for each infill strategy used. Obviously, the quality of the model learned with the PEI is notably better. For Branin, Double-Sum and Goldstein-Price the upper quartile of PEI coincides with the lower quartile of random sampling. In case of the Himmelblau function, the upper quartile at least coincides with the respective median.

Function	Min.	Median	Mean	Max.	p-value
Branin	-1.38	**-0.05**	**-0.13**	0.01	**0.01**
Double-Sum	-3.95	**-0.11**	**-0.30**	1.43	**0.04**
Goldstein-Price	-1.03	**-0.54**	**-0.46**	0.37	**0.00**
Himmelblau	-1.55	**-0.07**	**-0.13**	1.72	0.09

Table 1: Statistics based on the paired differences of the performance values of both strategies per run and *p*-values of the respective *t*-test for the synthetic functions.

In addition, Table 1 summarizes measures of central tendency and the p-values of the paired t-test checking the one-sided null hypothesis of a zero mean of the paired differences per experiment. For significance level $\alpha = 0.05$, all functions but Himmelblau result in significant improvements. This result is strong, since the test functions are known to be predicted well with only about half of the design points used in our experiments [14]. Nevertheless, we see notable statistical evidence for the superiority of the PEI approach as compared with the naive sampling of random infill points for profile curve reconstruction.

3.2 Mutation rate of the (1+1)-GA

In this section, we analyze whether FBSMBO is capable of learning the optimum parameter configurations for the (1+1) Genetic Algorithm (GA) on the `OneMax` test function. The (1+1)-GA operates on binary representations of dimension n, maintains a population of only a single individual and makes solely use of a simple bit-flip mutation operator with mutation rate $p_m \in (0, 1)$. For linear functions of type $y(\mathbf{x}) = \tau + \sum_{i=1}^{n} w_i x_i$, $\tau \in \mathbb{R}$ and non-negative weights $w_i, i = 1, \ldots, n$, the expected runtime of the (1+1)-GA is in $\Theta(n \log n)$ [6]. This result, however, is only valid if $p_m = c/n$ for some constant c. Setting $c = 1$, this requirement resulted in the common recommendation for the mutation rate widely used in the field of evolutionary computation. It defines a *reference FPM*, as it defines the mutation rate p_m as a function of the problem feature decision space dimension n.

We applied FBSMBO to approximate a similar FPM based on experiments with the (1+1)-GA on the OneMax function

$$\texttt{OneMax} : \{0,1\}^n \to \mathbb{N}, \texttt{OneMax}(\mathbf{x}) = \sum_{i=1}^{n} \mathbf{x}_i.$$

The main research question is whether FBSMBO is capable of finding parameter configurations, which are competitive with the theoretical reference parameters with regard to the actual average runtime.

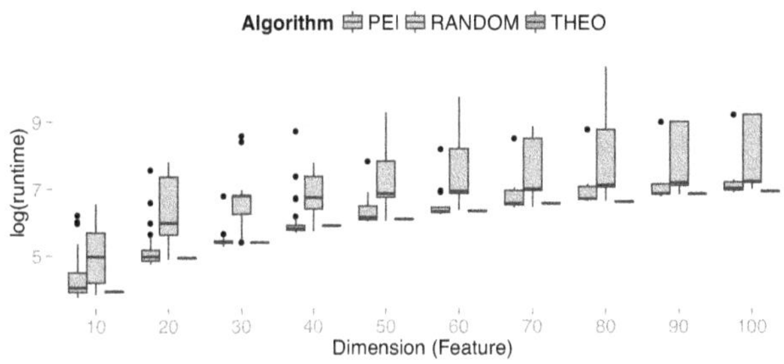

Figure 2: Boxplots of the ERT of the (1+1)-GA with mutation rates p_m set according to the FPMs obtained by FBSMBO with Profile-EI (PEI), random sampling (RANDOM), or the theoretical recommendation (THEO).

To answer this question, we ran 30 experiments with PEI and random sampling. In each experiment, we started with an initial design of size 20 and performed 100 sequential optimization steps to learn the optimal feature parameter mapping. The training set consists of all n-dimensional OneMax problems with $n \in \{10, \ldots, 100\}$, as preliminary experiments indicated, that for $n < 10$ the effect of the initialization resulted in a too high relative variance. During the training phase, the number of evaluations used by the GA until finding the optimum solution was used as cost function c. For the a-posteriori evaluation of the resulting FPMs, the (1+1)-GA with the respective mutation probability performed 10 runs with at most n^2 function evaluations at each design point to estimate the *expected running time* (ERT) [11]. This resulted in 30 runtime estimates for each infill strategy. As a reference performance, we used the ERT of the (1+1)-GA with the theoretically recommended value $p_m = \frac{1}{n}$.

Figure 2 shows boxplots of the distributions of the log-transformed ERTs partitioned by problem dimension with only a part of the considered dimensions being shown for reasons of visual clarity. The superiority of the FPMs learned using the PEI infill strategy opposed to ones of random sampling can clearly be observed. The recommended parameters outperform the latter for all values of the feature parameter. The Wilcoxon test[2] for paired samples rejects the null hypothesis of equal runtimes in all cases.

Moreover, Figure 2 reveals that there is a low variance in the PEI recommendations. This indicates that the corresponding configurator determined similar FPMs in all experiments. In comparison, the FPMs learned with RANDOM show a high variance. Hence, the PEI-based training phase provides more robust FPMs.

This observation is supported by the visualization of the FPMs in Figure 3. Except for the experiments 2, 3, 10, 11, 14, 15, and 24, the PEI profile curves mimic the theoretical profile curves. In contrast, the profile curves obtained by a RANDOM sampling of the training data have a very high variance with no recurring pattern. In some cases, the theoretical trend of decreasing p_m with increasing n is even inverted. Whereas the focused sampling around the estimated FPM stabilizes model prodiction, RANDOM sampling may lead to penalized, nonconverging algorithm runs. These runs lead to a higher variation in the model landscape and thus to a deterioration of the prediction quality.

The restriction to one problem feature and one algorithm parameter makes it possible to visually analyze this issue over the sequential training process. Figure 4 shows a typical FPM based on the kriging model after the initial design, and its evolution after 50 respectively 100 sequential infill experiments. It is hard for the model to predict the FPM using only the initial design (Figures 4a and 4b).

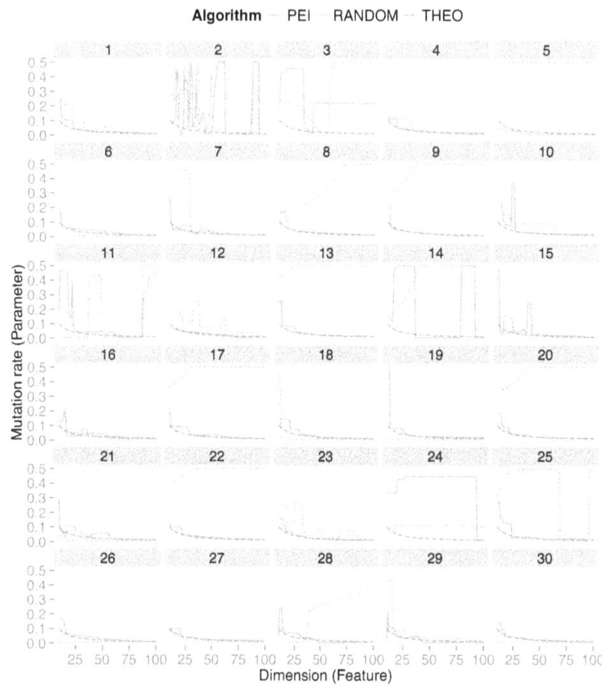

Figure 3: FPMs obtained from theory (THEO) or the model based on the training data obtained by the respective sampling strategy (PEI or RANDOM) in run 1 to 30.

However, after 50 iterations, the PEI-based FPM can predict the general trend of the reference profile curve $p_m = \frac{1}{n}$ (see Figure 4c). The increased sample density of the sequential points (blue) in the vicinity of the FPM is clearly visible. In contrast, the RANDOM-based FPM shows an oscillating behavior (see Figure 4d) indicating an instable model. Even if the oscillations can be reduced with 100 sequential samples, the approximation of PEI-based FPM remains better.

[2]We used the Wilcoxon test in this case, because the normality assumptions of the t-test were violated.

FBSMBO with a PEI-based infill strategy produces FPMs, which are 1) almost similar regarding runtime and 2) mimic the theoretically known FPMs. We can thus confirm its suitability based on this study.

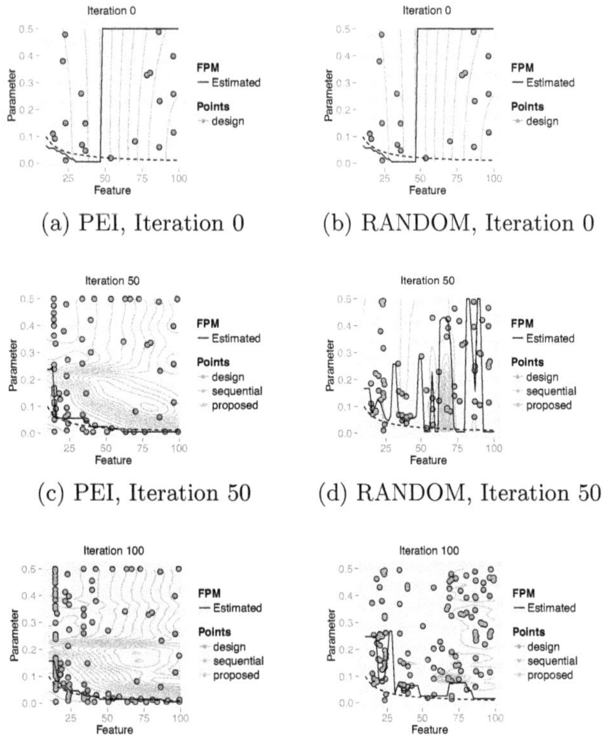

(a) PEI, Iteration 0 (b) RANDOM, Iteration 0

(c) PEI, Iteration 50 (d) RANDOM, Iteration 50

(e) PEI, Iteration 100 (f) RANDOM, Iteration 100

Figure 4: Typical sampling during the training phase of FBSMBO for the configuration of the (1+1)-GA. Model landscape, proposed FPM (solid black) and reference FPM (dashed black) after 0, 50 and 100 sequential experiments according to the PEI (left column) or random sampling (right column) infill strategy.

3.3 Population size for the CMA-ES

In our second practical example, we consider the tuning of the well-known *Covariance-Matrix-Adaption Evolutionary Strategy* (CMA-ES) [10], which is one of the state-of-the-art optimizers for numerical black-box optimization. Specifically, we consider the offspring size λ, as the official CMA-ES implementation by Nikolaus Hansen proposes a default setting $\lambda = 4 + \lfloor 3\log(n) \rfloor$ which can be considered as *reference FPM*. We term this setting the λ-rule in the following. Again n denotes the number of decision space dimensions and is considered as the only problem feature. In contrast to the former GA experiment, the λ-rule comes with no theoretical guarantees and is of heuristic nature. For instance, Hansen et al. showed by empirical means that for highly multimodal functions $\lambda \gg n$ can be beneficial [12]. This result indicates that the FPM should be adapted for different kinds of test problems.

Our experiments aim at learning an FPM from the problem dimension n to the offspring size λ by applying FBSMBO to the CMA-ES on different subsets of the well-

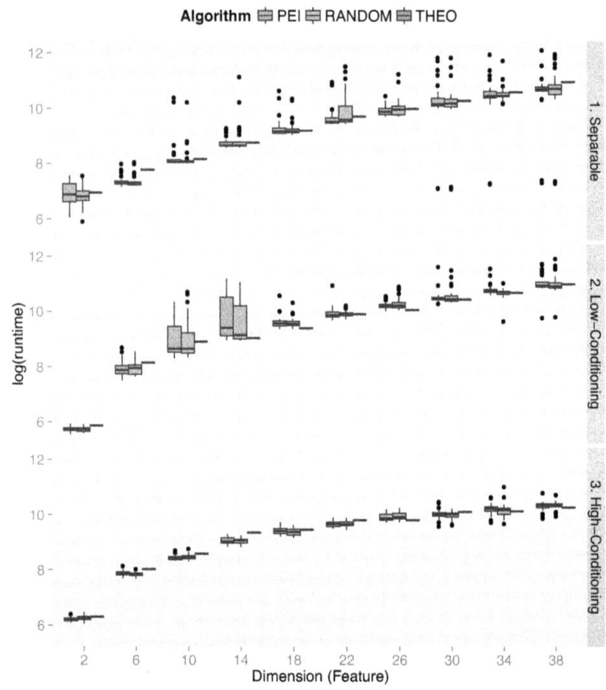

Figure 5: Boxplots of the ERT of the CMA-ES with offspring size λ set according to the FPMs obtained by FBSMBO with Profile-EI (PEI), random sampling (RANDOM), or the heuristic λ-rule (THEO).

known noiseless testbed of the BBOB2009 benchmarking functions. More specific, we investigated the first three BBOB2009 groups of functions: the separable ones, the ones with low or moderate condition, and the high or ill-conditioned ones [11]. For each, models $\hat{m}$ for estimating the FPM are learned. The experimental setup is similar to the one described in the previous section, but we needed to reduce the number of experiments due to an increased computational effort of a single experiment. Concretely, after the initial design of size 10 we reduced the budget to 40 sequential experiments based on PEI and RANDOM sampling strategy. Again 30 independent experiments with different initial designs were performed on each BBOB group.

The instance training set consists of all functions from the respective BBOB group with dimensions $n \in \{2, \dots, 40\}$ that have a BBOB instance ID $i \in \{1, 2, 3\}$, where i denotes the specific variant of the test function. To estimate the ERT [11] of the CMA-ES, we ran it five times on each design point with a captime of 200,000 function evaluations. If the global optimum was not approximated up to a tolerance of 0.03 within the given time budget in any of the five runs[3], the execution was penalized by a value of $3 \cdot 200,000$.

In Figure 5, boxplots of the resulting ERT distributions are shown in groups according to exemplary problem dimensions and the distinct BBOB groups. All strategies are capa-

[3]The tolerance was set in order to have a sufficiently high number of successful (unpenalized) experiments within the maximum budget (cf. Table 2). Higher budgets were not feasible due to restrictions with regard to the computational time required for the experiments.

ble of identifying the increase of λ with increasing dimension. In general, no significant differences between the λ-rule and the FPMs obtained by PEI and RANDOM can be observed with respect to the median performance. Nevertheless, the results of the sampling strategies are not satisfying due to the high variation in the ERTs – in particular on the second BBOB group.

Group	function	success	failure
group 1	Büche-Rastrigin	3 (0.9)	320 (99.1)
	Ellipsoidal	288 (95.7)	13 (4.3)
	Linear Slope	249 (84.1)	47 (15.9)
	Rastrigin	27 (9.9)	246 (90.1)
	Sphere	307 (100.0)	0 (0.0)
group 2	Attractive Sector	372 (100.0)	0 (0.0)
	Rosenbrock (original)	372 (95.6)	17 (4.4)
	Rosenbrock (rotated)	350 (95.6)	16 (4.4)
	Step Ellipsoidal	87 (23.3)	286 (76.7)
group 3	Bent Cigar	299 (100.0)	0 (0.0)
	Different Powers	315 (100.0)	0 (0.0)
	Discus	303 (100.0)	0 (0.0)
	Ellipsoidal	272 (94.1)	17 (5.9)
	Sharp Ridge	197 (67.0)	97 (33.0)

Table 2: Absolute and relative (percentage) number of successes (finding the global minimum in at least one of the five runs) and failures (running until the captime in all five runs) for the functions of the considered BBOB groups.

For further analyzing this variation, Table 2 shows an overview of the successful and failed runs separated by BBOB group and test function. In the table, "failed" means that the global minimum was not reached up to the desired tolerance within the captime in any of the five repetitions. Each group – groups one and two in particular – contains at least one function which is rarely minimized successfully. In addition, the ERTs of the CMA-ES on the distinct functions vary in orders of magnitude. Hence, it is possible that identical design points show extremely distinct ERT values. The feature vector $\boldsymbol{\delta}$ and the BBOB classification do not provide sufficient information about the characteristics of each instance. The intra-group heterogeneity is high. For instance, the first group of separable functions consists of the unimodal Sphere function as well as the highly multimodal Rastrigin and Büche-Rastrigin functions with approximately 11^n local optima. The noise level of the cost function to be learned by the model is thus extremely high. In addition, the penalization forces discontinuities within the response surface. The underlying Gaussian process model of FBSMBO, hence, has to cope with a high noise variance and irregular response values. Both aspects deteriorate the prediction quality of the model. As the latter issue could be addressed by using log- or rank-transformation of the performance values before model fitting [19], the former aspect requires the use of more powerful instance features [4]. We will investigate this in near future.

For improving the model quality, we reduced the set of training instances considerably and tried to learn FPMs for the Sphere function only. As a consequence, inhomogeneities within the training instances no longer exist. The observed ERTs for this setup are shown in Figure 6. It can be observed that the ERTs of the CMA-ES can be improved in comparison to the λ-rule for almost all problem dimensions. This observation holds for the FPMs obtained by both infill strategies. The PEI-based FPMs, however, still improve the ERTs by a statistically significant amount for all problem dimensions.

The reasons for these improvements are shown in Figure 7. The computed FPMs differ considerably from the general λ-rule, while still showing a monotonically increasing trend with higher problem dimensions. Whereas the FPM recommends offspring sizes around $\lambda = 5$ for $n = 10$ and between $\lambda = 6$ and $\lambda = 9$ for $n = 38$, the λ-rule would recommend $\lambda = 6$ for $n = 10$ and $\lambda = 15$ for $n = 38$. Again, the FPMs obtained by the PEI-based training data show a more consistent trend than the ones with random sampling. They also maintain monotonicity in almost all cases.

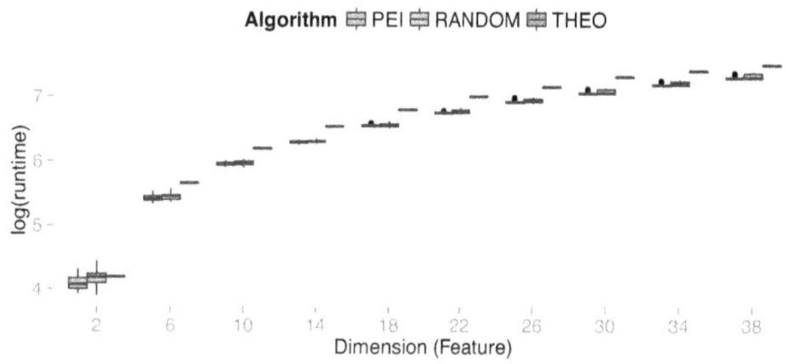

Figure 6: Boxplots of the ERT of the CMA-ES with offspring size λ set according to the FPMs obtained by FBSMBO with Profile-EI (PEI), random sampling (RANDOM), or the heuristic λ-rule (THEO) on the sphere functions.

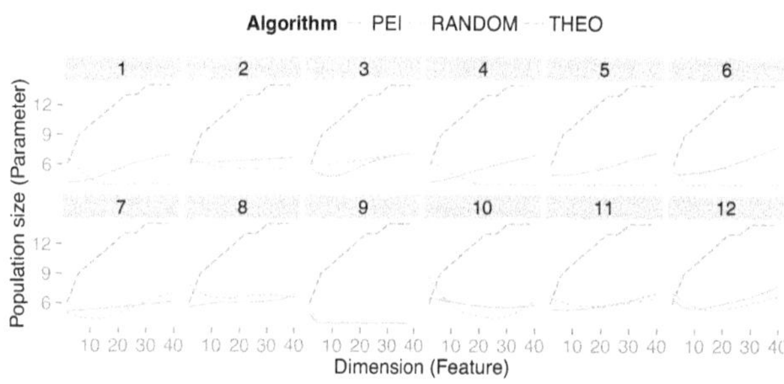

Figure 7: FPMs obtained from theory (THEO) or the model based on the training data obtained by the respective sampling strategy (PEI or RANDOM) in run 1 to 12 of the CMA-ES on the sphere function.

4. CONCLUSIONS

In this paper, we proposed how to use a surrogate model to learn a mapping from features describing the characteristics of problem instances to the respective optimum control parameters of the optimization algorithm. Our experiments revealed that the concept of profile expected improvement is capable to guide the sequential sampling process for refining the joint surrogate model. The feature parameter mapping obtained from the so-trained model can significantly increase the quality of the resulting configurator. In addition, practical experiments with the CMA-ES highlighted the requirement to find features that are meaningful with regard to the algorithm's performance. In this context, ELA features [17] might be a good starting point.

In the presented case studies, we only learned mappings from a single feature to a single continuous parameter. In the future, we plan further experiments to confirm the suitability and the potential of our approach for the general case of multiple features and algorithm parameters. Clearly, using more than just a single feature for the mapping should have beneficial effects. Further options for improving the configurator are transformations of the performance values prior to the modeling step.

In contrast to the tuning of continuous algorithm parameters, so-called algorithm configuration is more complicated. For instance, categorical and dependent parameters have to be considered. It should be noted that our ideas, as they mainly deal with the definition of an appropriate acquisition function, can in principle be applied to more complex parameter spaces. Forthcoming work will investigate the FBSMBO approach to configure algorithms including more complex parameters by exchanging the currently used continuous kriging model with a better suited model for mixed spaces (e.g. random forests).

5. REFERENCES

[1] T. Bartz-Beielstein, C. Lasarczyk, and M. Preuss. Sequential parameter optimization. In *Proceedings of the IEEE Congress on Evolutionary Computation, CEC 2005, 2-4 September 2005, Edinburgh, UK*, pages 773–780, 2005.

[2] M. Birattari. *Tuning Metaheuristics: A Machine Learning Perspective*. Springer, 1st ed. 2005. 2nd printing edition, 2009.

[3] B. Bischl, M. Lang, O. Mersmann, J. Rahnenführer, and C. Weihs. BatchJobs and BatchExperiments: Abstraction mechanisms for using R in batch environments. *Journal of Statistical Software*, 64(11), 3 2015.

[4] B. Bischl, O. Mersmann, H. Trautmann, and M. Preuss. Algorithm selection based on exploratory landscape analysis and cost-sensitive learning. In *Proc. of the 14th GECCO conference*, pages 313–320, 2012.

[5] S. P. Coy, B. L. Golden, G. C. Runger, and E. A. Wasil. Using experimental design to find effective parameter settings for heuristics. *Journal of Heuristics*, 7(1):77–97, 2001.

[6] S. Droste, T. Jansen, and I. Wegener. On the analysis of the (1+1) evolutionary algorithm. *Theoretical Computer Science*, 276(1–2):51–81, 2002.

[7] A. E. Eiben and S. K. Smit. Evolutionary algorithm parameters and methods to tune them. In Y. Hamadi, E. Monfroy, and F. Saubion, editors, *Autonomous search*, pages 15—36. Springer, Berlin Heidelberg, 2012.

[8] A. I. J. Forrester, A. J. Keane, and N. W. Bressloff. Design and analysis of 'noisy' computer experiments. *AIAA Journal*, 44(10):2331–2339, 2006.

[9] D. Ginsbourger, J. Baccou, C. Chevalier, F. Perales, N. Gerland, and Y. Monerie. Bayesian adaptive reconstruction of profile optima and optimizers. *SIAM/ASA Journal on Uncertainty Quantification*, 2(1):490–510, 2014.

[10] N. Hansen. The CMA evolution strategy: a comparing review. In J. A. Lozano, P. Larranaga, I. Inza, and E. Bengoetxea, editors, *Towards a new evolutionary computation. Advances on estimation of distribution algorithms*, pages 75–102. Springer, Berlin, Heidelberg, 2006.

[11] N. Hansen, S. Finck, R. Ros, and A. Auger. Real-parameter black-box optimization benchmarking 2009: Noiseless functions definitions. Technical Report RR-6829, INRIA, 2009.

[12] N. Hansen and S. Kern. Evaluating the CMA evolution strategy on multimodal test functions. In X. Yao et al., editors, *Proc. of PPSN VIII*, volume 3242 of *LNCS*, pages 282–291, 2004.

[13] F. Hutter, H. H. Hoos, and K. Leyton-Brown. Sequential model-based optimization for general algorithm configuration. In C. A. Coello Coello, editor, *Proc. of LION-5, Rome*, pages 507–523. Springer, 2011.

[14] D. R. Jones, M. Schonlau, and W. J. Welch. Efficient global optimization of expensive black-box functions. *Journal of Global Optimization*, 13(13):455–492, 1998.

[15] S. Kadioglu, Y. Malitsky, M. Sellmann, and K. Tierney. ISAC – instance–specific algorithm configuration. In H. Coelho, R. Studer, and M. Wooldridge, editors, *Proc. 19th European Conference on Artificial Intelligence*, pages 751–756. IOS Press, 2010.

[16] P. Koch, B. Bischl, O. Flasch, T. Bartz-Beielstein, C. Weihs, and W. Konen. Tuning and evolution of support vector kernels. *Evolutionary Intelligence*, 5(3):153–170, 2012.

[17] O. Mersmann, B. Bischl, H. Trautmann, M. Preuss, C. Weihs, and G. Rudolph. Exploratory landscape analysis. In *Proc. of the 13th GECCO conference*, pages 829–836, New York, NY, USA, 2011. ACM.

[18] O. Mersmann, M. Preuss, and H. Trautmann. Benchmarking evolutionary algorithms: Towards exploratory landscape analysis. In R. Schaefer, C. Cotta, J. Kolodziej, and G. Rudolph, editors, *Proc. of PPSN XI*, volume 6238 of *Lecture Notes in Computer Science*, pages 73–82. Springer, 2010.

[19] T. Wagner and S. Wessing. On the effect of response transformations in sequential parameter optimization. *Evolutionary Computation*, 20(2):229–248, 2012.

[20] L. Xu, H. Hoos, and K. Leyton-Brown. Hydra: Automatically configuring algorithms for portfolio-based selection. In *Proceedings of the Twenty-Fourth AAAI Conference on Artificial Intelligence, AAAI 2010, Atlanta, Georgia, USA, July 11-15, 2010*, 2010.

Reducing Energy Consumption Using Genetic Improvement

Bobby R. Bruce
University College London
London
United Kingdom
r.bruce@cs.ucl.ac.uk

Justyna Petke
University College London
London
United Kingdom
j.petke@ucl.ac.uk

Mark Harman
University College London
London
United Kingdom
mark.harman@ucl.ac.uk

ABSTRACT

Genetic Improvement (GI) is an area of Search Based Software Engineering which seeks to improve software's non-functional properties by treating program code as if it were genetic material which is then evolved to produce more optimal solutions. Hitherto, the majority of focus has been on optimising program's execution time which, though important, is only one of many non-functional targets. The growth in mobile computing, cloud computing infrastructure, and ecological concerns are forcing developers to focus on the energy their software consumes. We report on investigations into using GI to automatically find more energy efficient versions of the MiniSAT Boolean satisfiability solver when specialising for three downstream applications. Our results find that GI can successfully be used to reduce energy consumption by up to 25%.

Categories and Subject Descriptors

D.2 [**Software**]: Software Engineering

Keywords

Search based software engineering, SBSE, genetic improvement, GI, optimisation, energy optimisation, energy efficiency, energy consumption, Boolean satisfiability

1. INTRODUCTION

Less than a decade ago the quality of software (outside of end-user design preferences) could broadly be described as the extent to which software met its specification while minimising the prevalence of bugs and usage of traditional computer resources such as CPU time and memory allocation. The growth in two new technologies, mobile computing devices and cloud services, has led to a new environment for software engineers where they must now consider the energy an application consumes; the quality of software is now measured in Joules, as well as bug counts, seconds, and megabytes. At present there are more smartphones in the world than personal computers [22], each containing a limited store of energy between charges that must be used efficiently. The energy required to run large server clusters has grown considerably in the last decade, estimated to be between 1.1% to 1.5% of global electricity consumption in 2010 [26], putting strain on energy suppliers and the budgets of those responsible for purchasing this energy [7]. The total ICT infrastructure generated 1.9% of global CO_2 emissions in 2011 [5] (larger than the entire United Kingdom estimated at 1.47% for the 2010-2014 period [42]) indicating that computer science has a role to play in mitigating climate change.

Thus we believe it important that software engineers find ways of programming computers with energy efficiency in mind to appease the demands from consumers for longer battery life, from companies to reduce their energy bills, and from society's desire to minimise humanity's impact on the environment.

One of the largest hurdles in producing energy-efficient software is the developer's disconnect between the source code they write and the energy that will be consumed from the compiled product they deliver [33]. Without a deep understanding of how a particular compiler works, along with an equally deep understanding of how much energy a given instruction will consume, the problem remains difficult for many developers. It has been found that metrics previously believed to guide developers to more energy efficient solutions are, in reality, poor at doing so [38]. Subtle changes, such as introducing inline methods [41], swapping API implementations [33], and constructing semantically equivalent (but structurally inequivalent) algorithms [8] have all been shown to influence energy consumption. However this influence is difficult to determine outside of the ad hoc and inefficient process of trial-and-error. Tools have been developed to guide users to energy-inefficient areas of their software [2, 11, 30, 19] though the developer retains responsibility for rectifying these inefficiencies.

We suggest that the most under explored method of decreasing software's energy consumption lies in automated processes. Such processes would allow developers to focus solely on meeting the specification requirements with worries about non-functional attributes like energy consumption left to an algorithm capable of refactoring software to a more optimal state.

Genetic Improvement (GI) [20, 25, 27, 28, 29, 36, 37, 45, 44] is a Search Based Software Engineering (SBSE) technique [21] which treats program code as if it were genetic material that can then be evolved to produce optimised solutions. GI has previously been found effective at optimis-

GECCO '15, July 11 - 16, 2015, Madrid, Spain
© 2015 ACM. ISBN 978-1-4503-3472-3/15/07... $15.00
DOI: http://dx.doi.org/10.1145/2739480.2754752

ing software's execution time [20, 28, 37, 44] and similar genetic techniques have been shown effective at reducing energy consumption, albeit as a post-compilation process [40]. We therefore seek to investigate whether GI can be used at the source-code level to minimise energy consumption in a widely-used piece of software.

In 2014 Petke et al. [37] demonstrated that MiniSAT[1], a popular Boolean satisfiability solver (SAT Solver), can be optimised for execution time, producing a solver 17% faster than any human-written equivalent for the Combinatorial Interaction Testing (CIT) domain. SAT solvers are crucial components in many applications [4, Part 2], from AI planning [24] through to package management [43] and predicting crosstalk in integrated circuits [9]. Due to this inherent flexibility [32] and previous success in improving its non-functional attributes, we shall attempt to improve MiniSAT's energy consumption using GI techniques.

We set out to answer the following research questions:

RQ1 To what extent can MiniSAT's energy consumption be reduced using Genetic Improvement?

RQ2 Do different downstream MiniSAT applications require different optimisations?

RQ3 Does reduction in energy consumption correlate to reduction in execution time when GI is applied?

2. OPTIMISING ENERGY CONSUMPTION WITH GENETIC IMPROVEMENT

We build on an approach to GI first outlined by Langdon and Harman in 2013 [28] and later modified by Petke et al. in 2013 [36] and again in 2014 [37] for their MiniSAT experiments. We apply modifications to the fitness function, taking into account energy estimates made by the Intel Power Gadget (see Section 2.4) instead of the number of lines executed (a metric previously used to optimise for execution time). We also modify the selection and mutation procedure in an attempt to tackle the phenomenon of bloat. As in Petke et al.'s work [36, 37], all modification occurs in MiniSAT's `Solver.C` class which contains the main solving algorithm.

2.1 Program and Genotype Representation

Modification to the software is made at the source code level. The source code is converted into a customised template format, captured using BNF notation. The BNF notation allows lines to be tagged with discrete markers that indicate whether a line can be modified or not. Methods, opening and closing brackets, and initialisation lines are declared unmodifiable in order to reduce the percentage of solutions developed which are uncompilable. Figure 1 shows an example of the tagging format used in our experiments.

A genotype represents a list of modifications made to this format that is then translated to its phenotype by applying these modifications to the original source code. The three modifications permitted are to DELETE, REPLACE or COPY a line of source code. A DELETE operation removes a line, a REPLACE operation replaces one line with another and a COPY operation copies a line to another location. All genetic material used is contained within the

[1]Available at http://minisat.se/MiniSat.html.

```
<Solver_235>       ::=    " if"<IF_Solver_235> " \n"
<IF_Solver_235>    ::=    "(order_heap.empty())"
<Solver_236>       ::=    "{\n"
<Solver_237>       ::=    "" <_Solver_237> "\n"
<_Solver_237>      ::=    "next = (-1);"
<Solver_238>       ::=    " break;\n"
<Solver_239>       ::=    "}\n"
```

Figure 1: A Solver.C snippet converted to our GI format. Lines starting with "<Solver" are unmodifiable.

original source code. This development is based on the observation that source code is redundant [14, 28] to the extent that genetic material necessary to produce an improved result is likely to be contained within the source code itself. Special cases exist for conditional statements so that predicate expressions can only be replaced or deleted with predicates found in the same type of conditional statement (the DELETE operation replaces a predicate expression with '0' to avoid compilation issues). For example, a while loop (e.g., x>5) can only be replaced with the condition of another while loop (e.g., y==2) and can never be replaced with a random line found elsewhere in the software (e.g., z=z*2;). Figure 2 shows how these modifications are represented inside a population of solutions.

```
 #DELETE line 205
<_Solver_205>

 #REPLACE if condition in line 154 with if
 #condition in line 307
<IF_Solver_154><IF_Solver_307>

#COPY line 299 and insert above line 325
<_Solver_325>+<_Solver_299>

#REMOVE line 56 and REPLACE line 78 with
#line 145
<_Solver_56> <_Solver_78><_Solver_145>
```

Figure 2: An example population of four solutions.

2.2 Fitness Function, Selection, Crossover and Mutation

The fitness of a candidate solution is determined by measuring the total energy consumed (see Section 2.4) across all tests selected from the training set (see Section 2.3) when using the original unmodified software divided by the energy consumed by the phenotype across the selected tests. Thus a fitness greater than 1 indicates a solution that consumes less energy while a fitness less than 1 indicates a solution that consumes more energy.

Each selected test case can either be passed or failed. A test is deemed to have passed when the modified version categorises a test as satisfiable or unsatisfiable with that categorisation equal to the categorisation produced by the original MiniSAT. We thereby use the original code as an oracle [3] to guide the GI to functionally correct solutions. When a test is found to have failed, the energy consumption for that test case is not included in the fitness evaluation and, instead, an appropriate penalty is applied.

To be selected for the next generation, a solution must have a fitness of above 0.95, have passed an appropriate number of the selected test cases, and be in the top 50% of the population. Crossover is carried out by selecting one parent based on fitness and another chosen randomly from the selected individuals. Due to the simplicity of the genotype representation, crossover consists of appending one genotype to another; producing a new individual. Crossover is carried out until the population size, after selection, has doubled.

After crossover, mutations are applied to the selected genotypes. Prior investigations have shown GI frameworks such as this can lead to bloat [28, 37], resulting in effective solutions being encumbered with ineffective mutations. For this reason elitism has been implemented so that the top 5 solutions in each generation move forward to the next without mutation. The remaining selected individuals have a 50% chance of having a mutation applied. Mutations consist of adding a random DELETE, REPLACE, or COPY modification to the genotype. If the population after crossover has not met the preset population size, then single, random mutations are added as entirely new genotypes until the population size is met. The initial generation is seeded in this manner; a population consisting entirely of single, randomly chosen, modifications.

2.3 Training Set

For each MiniSAT downstream application a training and test set are constructed, representative of that application's use. Within each generation only a small subset of tests are selected from the training set to evaluate the solutions. A subset is chosen both to avoid over-fitting and to reduce execution time. The number of tests is dependent on the MiniSAT application: four for CIT (see Section 3.1) and five for Ensemble and AProVE (see Sections 3.2 and 3.3). To ensure this selection is representative of the entire training set, a binning system is introduced (originally presented by Langdon and Harman in 2013 [28]) which decomposes training set tests into bins based on complexity and type. A random test from each bin is selected in each generation. For our experiments we form bins based on execution time and satisfiability. Bins 1 and 3 contain satisfiable solutions while bins 2 and 4 contain unsatisfiable solutions. Bins 1 and 2 are examples of tests with small execution times while bins 3 and 4 are tests with larger execution times. If a 5th bin is present, then it contains both satisfiable and unsatisfiable solutions that have a larger execution time than those in bins 3 and 4. This test case selection process guarantees that fitness evaluation is always carried out against both satisfiable and unsatisfiable tests of varying difficulty.

2.4 Estimating Energy Consumption

We estimate the energy consumed in computing these tests using the Intel Power Gadget API for Mac OS X[2] which estimates the energy consumption of 2nd Generation and higher Intel Core processors. Given MiniSAT's singled-threaded, CPU-bound nature we believe this method of estimation is suitable for our requirements, however it should be noted that Intel Power Gadget estimations do not include energy consumed in main memory nor that consumed during I/O tasks.

Intel Power Gadget uses drivers and libraries to read the processor's special energy model-specific registers (MSRs) over a specified time period. These register readings are then used to calculate the total energy consumed.

We have built this API into a C++ application that takes a terminal command as input, estimates the CPU's energy usage during command execution, and returns the amount of energy consumed over this time in Joules. Running MiniSAT against a test case using this program gives us the energy consumption of MiniSAT for that test case.

When carrying out our experiments we were careful to avoid running processes that may have caused large variations in energy estimations. All unnecessary background processes were terminated while experiments were running. Running the original MiniSAT on a typical test case for 200 iterations, taking energy readings each time, we found a standard deviation of 5.23% in estimates; a variance within the limits we deem acceptable for our experiments.

[2]Available at software.intel.com/en-us/articles/intel-power-gadget/.

3. EXPERIMENT SETUP

We modify the main solving algorithm in MiniSAT2-070721 (hereinafter simply referred to as "MiniSAT"). In each experiment the GI framework is run for 20 generations with a population of 100. Once complete each solution that has achieved a fitness greater than 1.05 is run against all tests within the training set to give an overall ranking of the best solutions based on the total energy consumed. This step has been included as it was found that many solutions with a high fitness only performed well on the tests selected for that generation. The step can be considered a method of determining the "true fitness" of the best solutions, as opposed to the fitness value given by the GI framework. The top solution is chosen from this "true fitness" list and declared the "champion" solution.

The champion solution is then run against the test set 20 times with the energy readings averaged to give a value which is then compared to the original MiniSAT's performance against that test set (run 20 times then averaged) to obtain an overall percentage improvement.

We run three experiments, each specialising MiniSAT for a different downstream application (see Sections 3.1, 3.2, and 3.3). In practice each experiment simply requires that we use a different training set (and test set for the final results).

To answer **RQ1** (*To what extent can MiniSAT's energy consumption be reduced using Genetic Improvement?*) we observe the energy improvements between the original, unmodified MiniSAT and the champion for each downstream application. As the champion solution and the original MiniSAT are run 20 times on the test set we are able to determine how statistically significant these results are.

RQ2 (*Do different downstream MiniSAT applications require different optimisations?*) is answered by running the champion solution for each downstream application against the test sets of the other applications. If a comparable energy reduction is observed when using other test sets then the modifications applied are general (in the sense they are improvements across all the downstream applications tested), however if the energy reductions are significantly smaller, crashes occur, or timeout events are triggered then the modifications must be specialised in some manner. We also analyse the modifications made to the software to produce the champion solutions in an attempt to determine whether any similarities can be found. Where solutions are found to be specialised, we investigate why modifications applied to one champion are less effective (or ineffective) when used on another MiniSAT downstream application.

In order to answer **RQ3** (*Does reduction in energy consumption correlate to reduction in execution time when GI is applied?*), we take each experiment champion and measure the total time required to compute all tests within their respective test set. These times are then compared to the execution time of the original, unmodified software when computing the test set to give a percentage improvement of execution time. This can then be compared to the energy percentage improvement. If the energy improvements are comparable to improvements in execution time we can add weight to the argument the two are related, if not we can claim this relationship is not valid in all cases. To obtain a deeper understanding of the time-energy relationship we also sample random solutions from each experiment (20 from each experiment, 60 in total) and measure their execution times and energy consumption estimates on their respective test sets. Analysing the data we are able to determine how correlated these readings are.

The following subsections describe the MiniSAT downstream applications we specialise for. We have carefully selected three applications areas we believe are suitably diverse in real-world or academic usage. For each we describe the purpose of the downstream application and give a description of the training and test set provided.

3.1 Specialising for CIT

Combinatorial Interaction Testing (CIT) is a black box test sampling technique used to test highly configurable software [34]. With highly configurable software, such as database management systems and architectures like software product lines, testing all configuration combinations is impossible though it remains important to ensure no combination of configuration variables exist that results in the software failing. CIT's role is to produce a test suite which sufficiently covers the configurations while minimising the execution time of such tests. CIT has been successfully translated and run as a Boolean satisfiability problem [1, 34], though running these SAT problems is a computationally intensive task. In 2014 Petke et al. [37] optimised MiniSAT to reduce the computation time for this domain, we aim to reduce the energy consumption.

The CIT training set contains 58 tests, 23 of which are satisfiable, spread evenly over 4 bins. The mean execution time for bins 1 and 2 is 3.33s, the mean execution time for bins 3 and 4 is 10.68s. The test set contains 20 tests, 11 of which are satisfiable with an average execution time of 13.07s.

3.2 Specialising for Ensemble Computation

Ensemble Computation is the study of an NP-complete variant of the Boolean circuit problem where one must find the smallest circuit that satisfies a set of Boolean functions simultaneously [23]. This problem can be translated into a satisfiability problem, which MiniSAT can then seek to solve.

The Ensemble training set contains 25 tests, 12 of which are satisfiable, spread evenly over 5 bins. The mean execution time for bins 1 and 2 is 4.21s, the mean execution time for bins 3 and 4 is 9.89s. The average execution time for Bin 5 is 28.87s. The test set contains 14 tests contain, 4 of which are satisfiable with an average execution time of 14.23s.

3.3 Specialising for AProVE

AProVE, Automated Program Verification Environment[3] [16, 17, 18], is a system for the generation of automated termination proofs of term rewrite systems. AProVE uses a Boolean satisfiability solver to determine which paths can or cannot be reached. Proving termination is a much discussed area in computer science [6, 12, 15, 31] with SAT solvers frequently used to aid analysis [10, 13, 39]. In this example the SAT solver is a component in a much larger application. This distinguishes it from the two other applications we optimise (where SAT solvers take a central role in problem solving). It serves as a reminder that GI need not be applied to an entire application but individual components within an application. Any component, when receiving the correct training data, can be optimised. Improving the parts that, in-turn, improve the whole.

The AProVE training set contains 24 tests, 13 of which are satisfiable, spread evenly over 5 bins. The mean execution time for bins 1 and 2 is 6.27s while the mean execution time for bins 3 and 4 is 19.04. The average execution time for Bin 5 is 25.33s. The test set contains 11 tests, 5 of which are satisfiable, with an average execution time of 17.83s.

4. RESULTS AND DISCUSSION

In this section we report the results obtained from carrying out the experiments described in Section 3. All three experimental runs, each optimising a different MiniSAT downstream application, completed successfully.

4.1 RQ1: Energy Reduction

Application	Original(J)	Champ(J)	Reduction(%)
CIT	3111	2969	4.58
Ensemble	2232	1665	25.39
AProVE	3145	2973	5.44

Table 1: The original MiniSAT's total Energy consumption across all test-set tests compared to the Champion solutions' energy consumption.

All three experiments produced champion solutions which out-performed the original MiniSAT, in terms of energy efficiency, for their respective test sets. Table 1 shows the improvements. The CIT and AProVE champions achieve modest energy consumption reductions of approximately 5% while the Ensemble champion achieves 25.39%. Further analysis of the results has shown that these energy estimations are statistically significant ($p <= 0.01$) using the Wilcoxon signed rank test (we found CIT, AProVE, and Ensemble to have the equal p-values of 3.716×10^{-12}).

We carried out the Vargha-Delaney-A statistic on all three experiments and found each to have a score of 1. This score shows that the energy efficiency of the champion solutions are entirely superior to the original MiniSAT for their respective application domains. Figure 3 shows box-plots that visually demonstrate this significant effect size.

[3] Available at http://aprove.informatik.rwth-aachen.de/

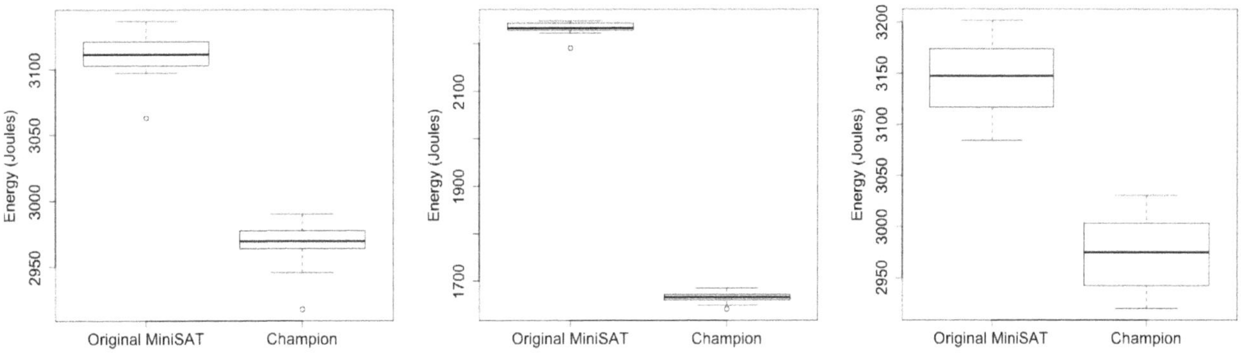

(a) CIT (b) Ensemble (c) AProVE

Figure 3: Boxplots of the Champion solutions' Energy Consumption compared to that of the original MiniSAT

When taking into account that MiniSAT is a relatively small program and that it is already considered to be quite efficient (at least in terms of execution time), it is encouraging that a reduction in energy consumption of 25% has been achieved.

4.2 RQ2: Specialisation differences

-	On CIT	On Ensemble	On AProVE
CIT	-	X	X
Ensemble	X	-	X
AProVE	3.56%	3.86%	-

Table 2: The best solutions' energy consumption when computing other test-sets. An X indicates a timeout event when running the test set.

When the champion solution for each application was run against the test sets for the other two (see Table 2) we found that both the CIT and Ensemble champions timeout when attempting to run on the other two test sets (this timeout is set at 5 minutes per test case, no test set used here exceeds 90 seconds when run on the original MiniSAT). This indicates that these champions are "specialised" in such a way that they cannot be generalised as optimisations for all SAT problem sets. The AProVE champion functions correctly on the other test sets but does not achieve the same performance improvement as seen when run in AProVE domain. It appears that this may be a general improvement to MiniSAT unlike the other two solutions.

The AProVE champion solution, already shown to be a general MiniSAT improvement, is found to be the removal of an assert statement. Removing assert statements has previously been shown to produce good results for execution time when optimising MiniSAT [37]. Our experiments show that the same is true for optimising energy consumption. It is also easy to understand why such a modification does not result in specialisation as it will not produce a version of MiniSAT that is functionally different to the original, unmodified version.

The more interesting results come from the specialisation cases (CIT and Ensemble). In the CIT solution we find a mutation that results in a `if` statement being disabled (the predicate replaced with a zero through a DELETE operation) in MiniSAT's `pickBranch` function. The statement is used for picking a random variable for assignment and is called 2% of the time. The condition within the `if` statement itself involves running a random number generator which may be an unnecessary cost for such an under-used piece of code. It is currently unknown why this modification results in the solutions performing so poorly on the AProVE and Ensemble test sets. It is perhaps the case that this rarely entered `if` statement does result in significant impacts on performance for Ensemble and AProVE, to the extent that it is of benefit for them, but not for CIT.

For the Ensemble application, the application with the largest reduction in energy, we found the specialisation made a single modification to a `switch` statement. A modification equivalent in outcome to changing MiniSAT's polarity mode from `polarity_false` to `polarity_true`. This causes the solver to try an assignment of True instead of False to each variable that has been picked for branching. It seems that this polarity mode is of benefit in Ensemble Computation , however, as previously stated, why these changes produce measurable gains in performance is not fully understood.

One of the more unexpected, but nonetheless interesting, observations is that the champion in each experiment has always been a genotype containing only one modification. We reject the idea that single modifications are truly optimal. Not only does this run counter to optimal solutions found in similar experiments [28, 37], the champion solution found within the AProVE experiment is a general optimisation which could easily be crossed-over with the champions found for CIT and Ensemble to produce better results for each. Though mutation, and to a lesser extent crossover, always carries a high risk of producing poor solutions, it may be the case that our policy of elitism and employing only a 50% mutation rate to reduce this risk, make it more difficult to produce longer, fitter genotypes. Further research is needed to investigate these possibilities. However we believe that the results reported here are encouraging and thereby justify further study.

4.3 RQ3: Energy-Time Relationship

Table 3 shows the reduction in execution time for each specialisation. When compared to the energy reduction re-

Application	Unmodified(s)	Champion(s)	Reduction
CIT	268	261	2.58%
Ensemble	219	162	25.89%
AProVE	280	261	6.69%

Table 3: The original MiniSAT's execution time across all test-set tests compared to the champion solutions' execution times.

sults in Table 1 it can be seen that the values appear to correlate to the execution time.

To investigate the correlation further we sampled 20 functionally correct solutions from each experiment, and ran each solution against the entire test set with both energy estimated and time measured for each test. Figure 4 shows the data produced from this analysis with each test case's energy and time costs plotted. Visually the relationship between energy and time is stark, Table 4 gives the Pearson Correlation Coefficient for each experiment showing each to have a very strong energy-time correlation.

Application	N	Correlation	p
CIT	1160	0.988	$< 2.2 \times 10^{-16}$
Ensemble	457	0.995	$< 2.2 \times 10^{-16}$
AProVE	481	0.989	$< 2.2 \times 10^{-16}$

Table 4: The number of Data-Points, the Pearson Correlation Coefficient and p-value for the Energy-Time relationship in each experiment.

These findings show that for CPU-bound processes, such as MiniSAT, optimising execution time exclusively has the side effect of producing more energy-efficient solutions (and vice-versa). This provides further incentive to investigate using execution time as a metric for reducing energy consumption for CPU-bound, single-threaded applications. If energy consumption and execution time can be bundled into a single metric, developers may find it easier to reduce energy as methods to reduce program execution time are already well understood.

Although this result is somewhat expected and unsurprising, the effect has not been demonstrated empirically in the context of SBSE. We are therefore pleased this work may aid future research in providing evidence to their claims about Energy-Time relationships in CPU-bound, single-threaded applications.

5. THREATS TO VALIDITY

It is worthwhile mentioning there exists some threats to validity for the results produced and the conclusions drawn within this investigation. The first is the relatively small area of code optimised (478 lines). Working on such a small example is essentially reducing the search-space of the application, making it easier to navigate and optimise for. Techniques have been introduced for GI to optimise larger applications [28] but they have only been demonstrated for execution time optimisation. It is currently unknown how well these techniques would translate over to optimising for Energy Consumption.

The Intel Power Gadget has been chosen as a power estimation API for this investigation as it produced estimation with low variance, is easy to implement, and is supplied by a reputable hardware manufacturer though questions still remain over how accurate this API is. The true relationship between this estimation and the true energy consumption is unknown. Intel provide no formal documentation on this API, nor has there been any research into its validity meaning this research has been undertaken on the assumption the Intel Power Gadget functions within an acceptable degree of accuracy. Furthermore, the gadget is limited to CPU activity exclusively, therefore results presented here ignore any potential energy increases occurring elsewhere and limits the findings of this paper to CPU-bound applications.

6. FUTURE WORK

Our results show that optimisation is possible though there are still questions that must be answered to allow GI for energy optimisation to move from academia to real-world developers.

The first and foremost of these questions is how energy can be measured to capture usage outside of the CPU. This is of particular importance for mobile applications which are more likely to use components understood to consume relatively large quantities of energy such as GPS or WiFi [35]. Though there has been work in this area [19, 30, 35, 46] it is unknown how effectively these can be integrated into a the GI framework and therefore further research is required.

We highlighted in Section 5 that using GI to improve energy efficiency has yet to be applied to larger applications. Thus we believe future investigations should focus on optimising larger applications for energy consumption in order to better understand how the techniques presented can be scaled.

We also believe more work into Genetic Improvement is required. The genotypes produced in our experiments are smaller than we believe to be truly optimal. New techniques require development and testing to ensure the best results are delivered to the user.

7. CONCLUSION

We evolved MiniSAT, a popular Boolean satisfiability solver, to reduce its energy consumption on three applications. We found that energy efficiency can be improved by as much as 25%, though this varies greatly depending on the downstream application being optimised. We also discovered GI is able to find solutions to reduce energy consumption that would be difficult for human developers to find.

Two of the three champion solutions were found to be specialised to their respective downstream applications in a manner that they were no longer applicable to other MiniSAT downstream applications. This finding adds to the arguments presented in previous research that GI can be used to specialise solutions for specific environments [27, 37].

Our further investigations into the results produced in our experiments found that the energy savings corresponded to decreases in execution time most likely due to the CPU-bound nature of the application optimised. The very strong correlations found provides evidence that for applications with similar characteristics to MiniSAT (that is CPU bound, singled threaded, and with limited I/O activity) execution time and energy consumption may be considered interchangeable metrics.

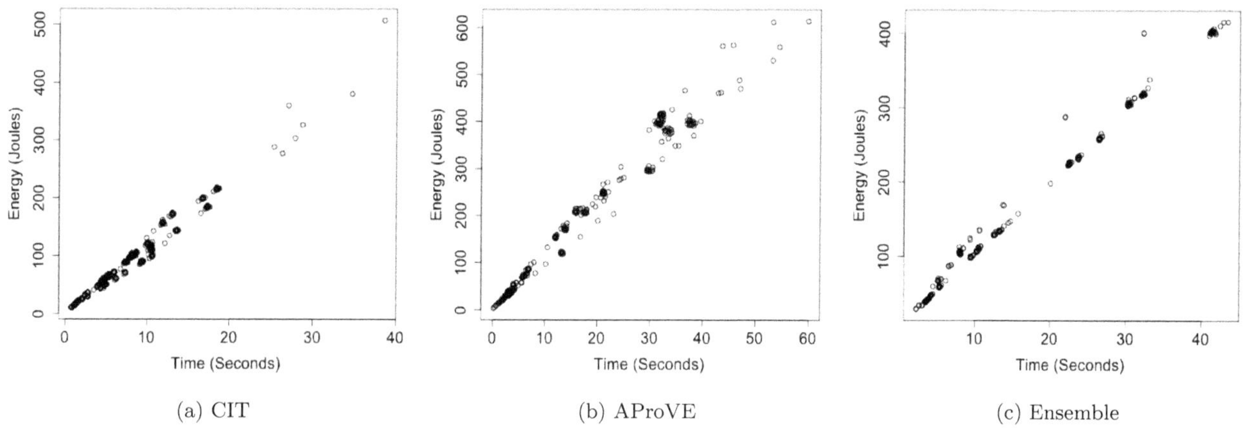

Figure 4: Scatterplot of the Energy-Time relationship within the three experiments

8. REFERENCES

[1] M. Banbara, H. Matsunaka, N. Tamura, and K. Inoue. Generating combinatorial test cases by efficient SAT encodings suitable for CDCL SAT solvers. In *Logic for Programming, Artificial Intelligence, and Reasoning*, pages 112–126. Springer, 2010.

[2] A. Banerjee, L. K. Chong, S. Chattopadhyay, and A. Roychoudhury. Detecting energy bugs and hotspots in mobile apps. In *Proceedings of the 22nd ACM SIGSOFT International Symposium on Foundations of Software Engineering - FSE 2014*, pages 588–598, New York, New York, USA, Nov. 2014. ACM Press.

[3] E. T. Barr, M. Harman, P. McMinn, M. Shahbaz, and S. Yoo. The oracle problem in software testing: A survey. *IEEE Transactions on Software Engineering*, 2015.

[4] A. Biere, M. Heule, and H. van Maaren. *Handbook of satisfiability*, volume 185. IOS press, 2009.

[5] Boston Consulting Group. GeSI SMARTer2020: The role of ICT in driving a sustainable future. http://gesi.org/SMARTer2020, 2012. [Online; accessed 10-January-2015].

[6] A. R. Bradley, Z. Manna, and H. B. Sipma. Termination analysis of integer linear loops. In *CONCUR 2005–Concurrency Theory*, pages 488–502. Springer, 2005.

[7] D. J. Brown and C. Reams. Toward energy-efficient computing. *Communications of the ACM*, 53(3):50–58, 2010.

[8] C. Bunse, H. Höpfner, S. Roychoudhury, and E. Mansour. Choosing the" best" sorting algorithm for optimal energy consumption. *ICSOFT*, 2009.

[9] P. Chen and K. Keutzer. Towards true crosstalk noise analysis. In *Proceedings of the 1999 IEEE/ACM international conference on Computer-aided design*, pages 132–138. IEEE Press, 1999.

[10] M. Codish, I. Gonopolskiy, A. M. Ben-Amram, C. Fuhs, and J. Giesl. SAT-based termination analysis using monotonicity constraints over the integers. *Theory and Practice of Logic Programming*, 11(4-5):503–520, 2011.

[11] H. David, E. Gorbatov, U. R. Hanebutte, R. Khanna, and C. Le. RAPL: Memory power estimation and capping. In *Low-Power Electronics and Design (ISLPED), 2010 ACM/IEEE International Symposium on*, pages 189–194, 2010.

[12] N. Dershowitz, N. Lindenstrauss, Y. Sagiv, and A. Serebrenik. A general framework for automatic termination analysis of logic programs. *Applicable Algebra in Engineering, Communication and Computing*, 12(1-2):117–156, 2001.

[13] C. Fuhs, J. Giesl, A. Middeldorp, P. Schneider-Kamp, R. Thiemann, and H. Zankl. *SAT solving for termination analysis with polynomial interpretations.* Springer, 2007.

[14] M. Gabel and Z. Su. A study of the uniqueness of source code. In *Proceedings of the eighteenth ACM SIGSOFT international symposium on Foundations of software engineering - FSE '10*, pages 147–156, New York, New York, USA, Nov. 2010. ACM Press.

[15] J. Giesl. Termination analysis for functional programs using term orderings. In *Static Analysis*, pages 154–171. Springer, 1995.

[16] J. Giesl, M. Brockschmidt, F. Emmes, F. Frohn, C. Fuhs, C. Otto, M. Plücker, P. Schneider-Kamp, T. Ströder, S. Swiderski, et al. Proving termination of programs automatically with AProVE. In *IJCAR*, volume 14, 2014.

[17] J. Giesl, P. Schneider-Kamp, and R. Thiemann. AProVE 1.2: Automatic termination proofs in the dependency pair framework. In *Automated Reasoning*, pages 281–286. Springer, 2006.

[18] J. Giesl, R. Thiemann, P. Schneider-Kamp, and S. Falke. Automated termination proofs with AProVE. In *Rewriting Techniques and Applications*, pages 210–220. Springer, 2004.

[19] S. Hao, D. Li, W. G. J. Halfond, and R. Govindan. Estimating mobile application energy consumption using program analysis. In *2013 35th International Conference on Software Engineering (ICSE)*, pages 92–101. IEEE, May 2013.

[20] M. Harman, W. B. Langdon, Y. Jia, D. R. White, A. Arcuri, and J. A. Clark. The GISMOE challenge:

constructing the pareto program surface using genetic programming to find better programs. In *Proceedings of the 27th IEEE/ACM International Conference on Automated Software Engineering - ASE 2012*, pages 1–14, New York, New York, USA, Sept. 2012. ACM.

[21] M. Harman, P. McMinn, J. T. De Souza, and S. Yoo. Search based software engineering: Techniques, taxonomy, tutorial. In *Empirical software engineering and verification*, pages 1–59. Springer, 2012.

[22] J. Heggestuen. Business Insider: One In Every 5 People IN The World Own A Smartphone, One in Every 17 Own A Tablet. http://www.businessinsider.com/smartphone-and-tablet-penetration-2013-10, 2013. [Online; accessed 9-January-2015].

[23] M. Järvisalo, P. Kaski, M. Koivisto, and J. H. Korhonen. Finding efficient circuits for ensemble computation. In *Theory and Applications of Satisfiability Testing–SAT 2012*, pages 369–382. Springer, 2012.

[24] H. Kautz and B. Selman. Planning as satisfiability. In *Proceedings of the 10th European Conference on Artificial Intelligence (ECAI 92)*, pages 359–363, Vienna, Austria, 1992.

[25] Z. Kocsis, G. Neumann, J. Swan, M. Epitropakis, A. E. Brownlee, S. O. Haraldsson, and E. Bowles. Repairing and optimizing Hadoop hashCode implementations. *Search-Based Software Engineering*, pages 259–264, 2014.

[26] J. Koomey. Growth in data center electricity use from 2005 to 2010, Aug. 2011.

[27] W. B. Langdon and M. Harman. Evolving a CUDA kernel from an nVidia template. In *IEEE Congress on Evolutionary Computation*, pages 1–8. IEEE, July 2010.

[28] W. B. Langdon and M. Harman. Optimising existing software with genetic programming. *IEEE Transactions on Evolutionary Computation*, 2013.

[29] C. Le Goues, S. Forrest, and W. Weimer. Current challenges in automatic software repair. *Software Quality Journal*, 21(3):421–443, 2013.

[30] D. Li, S. Hao, W. G. J. Halfond, and R. Govindan. Calculating source line level energy information for android applications. In *Proceedings of the 2013 International Symposium on Software Testing and Analysis - ISSTA 2013*, pages 78 – 89, New York, New York, USA, July 2013. ACM Press.

[31] N. Lindenstrauss and Y. Sagiv. Automatic termination analysis of logic systems. In *Logic Programming: Proceedings of the Fourteenth International Conference on Logic Programming*, page 63. MIT Press, 1997.

[32] S. Malik and L. Zhang. Boolean satisfiability: from theoretical hardness to practical success. *Communications of the ACM*, 52(8):76–82, 2009.

[33] I. Manotas, L. Pollock, and J. Clause. SEEDS: a software engineer's energy-optimization decision support framework. In *Proceedings of the 36th International Conference on Software Engineering - ICSE 2014*, pages 503–514, New York, New York, USA, May 2014. ACM Press.

[34] C. Nie and H. Leung. A survey of combinatorial testing. *ACM Computing Surveys (CSUR)*, 43(2):11, 2011.

[35] A. Pathak, Y. C. Hu, and M. Zhang. Where is the energy spent inside my app?: fine grained energy accounting on smartphones with eprof. In *Proceedings of the 7th ACM european conference on Computer Systems - EuroSys '12*, pages 29–42, New York, New York, USA, Apr. 2012. ACM Press.

[36] J. Petke, W. B. Langdon, and M. Harman. Applying genetic improvement to MiniSAT. In *Search Based Software Engineering*, pages 257–262. Springer, 2013.

[37] J. Petke, W. B. Langdon, M. Harman, and W. Weimer. Using genetic improvement & code transplants to specialise a C++ program to a problem class. In M. Nicolau, K. Krawiec, and M. Heywood, editors, *Proceedings of the 17th European Conference on Genetic Programming (EuroGP)*, Granada, Spain, 2014.

[38] C. Sahin, L. Pollock, and J. Clause. How do code refactorings affect energy usage? In *Proceedings of the 8th ACM/IEEE International Symposium on Empirical Software Engineering and Measurement*, page 36. ACM, 2014.

[39] P. Schneider-Kamp, R. Thiemann, E. Annov, M. Codish, and J. Giesl. Proving termination using recursive path orders and SAT solving. In *Frontiers of Combining Systems*, pages 267–282. Springer, 2007.

[40] E. Schulte, J. Dorn, S. Harding, S. Forrest, and W. Weimer. Post-compiler software optimization for reducing energy. *Proceedings of the 19th international conference on Architectural support for programming languages and operating systems - ASPLOS '14*, pages 639–652, 2014.

[41] W. G. P. Silva, L. Brisolara, U. B. Corrêa, and L. Carro. Evaluation of the impact of code refactoring on embedded software efficiency. In *Proceedings of the 1st Workshop de Sistemas Embarcados*, pages 145–150, 2010.

[42] The World Bank. http://data.worldbank.org/indicator/EN.ATM.CO2E.KT/countries. [Online; accessed 10-January-2015].

[43] C. Tucker, D. Shuffelton, R. Jhala, and S. Lerner. Opium: Optimal package install/uninstall manager. In *Software Engineering, 2007. ICSE 2007. 29th International Conference on*, pages 178–188. IEEE, 2007.

[44] D. R. White, A. Arcuri, and J. A. Clark. Evolutionary improvement of programs. *IEEE Transactions on Evolutionary Computation*, 15(4):515–538, Aug. 2011.

[45] D. R. White, J. Clark, J. Jacob, and S. M. Poulding. Searching for resource-efficient programs: Low-power pseudorandom number generators. In *Proceedings of the 10th annual conference on Genetic and evolutionary computation*, pages 1775–1782. ACM, 2008.

[46] L. Zhang, B. Tiwana, Z. Qian, Z. Wang, R. P. Dick, Z. M. Mao, and L. Yang. Accurate online power estimation and automatic battery behavior based power model generation for smartphones. In *Proceedings of the eighth IEEE/ACM/IFIP international conference on Hardware/software codesign and system synthesis - CODES/ISSS '10*, page 105, New York, New York, USA, Oct. 2010. ACM Press.

Optimal Parameter Choices Through Self-Adjustment: Applying the 1/5-th Rule in Discrete Settings

Benjamin Doerr
École Polytechnique
Univ. Paris-Saclay, France

Carola Doerr
CNRS & Univ. Pierre et Marie Curie
Paris, France

ABSTRACT

While evolutionary algorithms are known to be very successful for a broad range of applications, the algorithm designer is often left with many algorithmic choices, for example, the size of the population, the mutation rates, and the crossover rates of the algorithm. These parameters are known to have a crucial influence on the optimization time, and thus need to be chosen carefully, a task that often requires substantial efforts. Moreover, the optimal parameters can change during the optimization process. It is therefore of great interest to design mechanisms that dynamically choose best-possible parameters. An example for such an update mechanism is the one-fifth success rule for step-size adaption in evolutionary strategies. While in continuous domains this principle is well understood also from a mathematical point of view, no comparable theory is available for problems in discrete domains.

In this work we show that the one-fifth success rule can be effective also in discrete settings. We regard the $(1+(\lambda,\lambda))$ GA proposed in [Doerr/Doerr/Ebel: From black-box complexity to designing new genetic algorithms, TCS 2015]. We prove that if its population size is chosen according to the one-fifth success rule then the expected optimization time on OneMax is linear. This is better than what *any* static population size λ can achieve and is asymptotically optimal also among all adaptive parameter choices.

Categories and Subject Descriptors

F.2.2 [**Theory of Computation**]: Analysis of Algorithms and Problem Complexity—*Nonnumerical Algorithms and Problems*

Keywords

Theory; Runtime Analysis; Genetic Algorithms; Adaptive Parameter Choice; Parameter Control

GECCO '15, July 11 - 16, 2015, Madrid, Spain

ISBN 978-1-4503-3472-3/15/07... $15.00
DOI: http://dx.doi.org/10.1145/2739480.2754684

1. INTRODUCTION

It is widely acknowledged that setting the parameters of evolutionary algorithms (EA) is one of the key difficulties in evolutionary optimization. Eiben, Hinterding, and Michalewicz [14] call this challenge "one of the most important and promising areas of research in evolutionary computation". This statement retains its topicality 15 years after the original publication of [14] as many talks at evolutionary computation conferences certify. We also understand today that even small changes in the parameters can yield to exponential performance gaps of the regarded algorithms [11,12].

Substantial research efforts have been undertaken to find good parameter settings for general EAs, see for example [4]. Around the same time it has been discovered that it may be sub-optimal to use a fixed set of parameters throughout the whole optimization process. It was suggested instead to change the parameters of the algorithms by some dynamic update rules, often using some sort of feedback of the fitness landscape that the algorithm is facing. For example, it can be beneficial in earlier parts of the process to invest in *exploration* of the fitness landscape, while the algorithm should become more stable and focus on one or few areas of attraction in the later *exploitation* phase(s).

Interestingly, while in continuous domains parameter control[1] is analyzed also theoretically [2,16,18], adaptive parameter choices play only a marginal role in theoretical investigations of EAs for discrete search spaces, the few exceptions showing an advantage of adaptive parameter settings being the fitness-dependent mutation rates for the (1+1) evolutionary algorithm on LeadingOnes analyzed in [3] and the fitness-dependent choice of the population size in [10] for the $(1+(\lambda,\lambda))$ GA on OneMax, respectively. Both these adaption schemes, however, require a very solid understanding of the problem at hand and are thus likely to be of limited practical relevance. Another example from the discrete EA literature are reductions of the parallel runtime (but not the total optimization time) for several test functions when doubling the number of parallel instances in a parallel EA after each unsuccessful iteration [20].

With this work we provide a first example for a discrete optimization problem where a self-adjusting (i.e., adaptive, but not fitness-dependent) parameter choice yields an expected optimization time that is better by more than a constant factor than any static parameter choice. The parameter update rule is extremely simple and does not require

[1]We use here and in the following a slightly adapted version of the terminology for parameter setting suggested in [14]. This terminology is summarized in Section 3.1 and Figure 1.

any problem-specific insights. More precisely, we analyze the runtime of the already mentioned $(1+(\lambda,\lambda))$ GA with population sizes chosen according to the one-fifth success rule on the generalized OneMax problem. We also show that the one-fifth success update scheme is optimal in this setting, that is, no alternative update mechanism can yield a significantly smaller runtime. In fact, we show that, throughout the whole optimization process, the one-fifth success rule suggests parameter settings that closely follow the theoretically best possible choices.

1.1 The One-Fifth Rule

One of the earliest adaptive update rules suggested in the evolutionary computation literature is the *one-fifth success rule*. It was independently discovered in [5,22,23] and constitutes today one of the best known and most widely applied techniques in parameter control. Several empirical results (cf. [15] and references therein) suggest that EAs using the one-fifth rule for adaptive parameter control are quite capable of finding optimal or close to optimal parameter settings. Since the parameters are updated without the intervention of the user, such update mechanisms are a very convenient way to minimize parameter tuning efforts. Furthermore, the one-fifth success rule does not require any problem-specific knowledge and is thus widely applicable.

Originally, the one-fifth rule was designed to control the step size of evolution strategies. In intuitive terms, it suggests that if the probability to create an offspring of better than current-best fitness is greater than 1/5, then the step size should be increased, while it should be decreased if the probability is lower than 1/5. Today, this rule has found applications much beyond the adaptation of the step size. Here in this work we use it for adjusting the offspring population size of a genetic algorithm.

Without going into details, we note that many other adaptive update rules have been experimented with in the evolutionary computation literature, cf. [14], [15, Chapter 8], and [19] for excellent surveys.

1.2 The $(1+(\lambda,\lambda))$ GA

We regard the $(1+(\lambda,\lambda))$ GA, which has been proposed in [10] as a first example of an evolutionary algorithm optimizing the generalized OneMax problem using $o(n\log n)$ function evaluations. For the theory of evolutionary algorithms, this is a big success as it shows for the first time that even for such simple problems the usage of crossover can be beneficial (all previously known evolutionary algorithms need $\Omega(n\log n)$ function evaluations in expectation to optimize the generalized OneMax problem).

An important parameter of the $(1+(\lambda,\lambda))$ GA is λ, the number of offspring generated in the mutation phase and the subsequent crossover phase of the algorithm. In the original paper [10] it is shown that for $\lambda = O(\sqrt{\log n})$ the expected optimization time of the $(1+(\lambda,\lambda))$ GA on OneMax is $O(n\sqrt{\log n})$. In [8] we improve the runtime bound to $\Theta(\max\{n\log(n)/\lambda, n\lambda\log\log(\lambda)/\log(\lambda)\})$. This expression is minimized for $\lambda = \Theta(\sqrt{\log(n)\log\log(n)/\log\log\log(n)})$, giving an optimization time of $\Theta(n\sqrt{\log(n)\log\log\log(n)/\log\log(n)})$. While this exact expression is irrelevant for the purposes of the present paper, it is important to note that this tight bound is super-linear for every possible choice of λ.

It was also observed in [10] that the $(1+(\lambda,\lambda))$ GA has only linear expected optimization time on OneMax when the population size λ is chosen adaptively depending on the fitness of the current-best individual. While theoretically appealing, this result has limited practical implications since the proposed fitness-dependent parameter choice crucially requires a very good understanding of the optimization process and thus, of the problem at hand. This is testified by the optimal relation of the population size to the current fitness-distance d to the optimum, which is $\Theta(\sqrt{n/d})$. Guessing such a functional relationship for real-world optimization problems is typically not doable with reasonable efforts.

Interestingly, an alternative approach based on the one-fifth success rule was suggested in [10]. In a series of experimental evaluations it was shown that if the population size λ is chosen according to this rule, the performance of the resulting $(1+(\lambda,\lambda))$ GA is among the best ones for a series of test problems. In that algorithm the population size is increased if no improvement has happened in the last iteration, while it is decreased otherwise. More precisely, for a suitable constant $F>1$, the population size parameter λ is multiplied by $F^{1/4}$ after each iteration in which the fitness of the current-best individual could not be improved, and it is divided by F otherwise, i.e., if the fitness of the current-best search point increased in that iteration.

1.3 Our Results

While the observations made in [10] are purely empirical, we provide with this work a theoretical analysis of the suggested self-adjusting $(1+(\lambda,\lambda))$ GA. We prove that the suggested implementation of the one-fifth success rule yields a linear expected optimization time of the $(1+(\lambda,\lambda))$ GA on the generalized OneMax problem. As noted above this is better than what any static parameter choice can achieve and is also best possible among all comparison-based algorithms as we shall comment in Section 4. In particular, our bound shows that the one-fifth success rule suggests population sizes that are asymptotically optimal among all possible (static and dynamic) choices.

To the best of our knowledge, this is the first time that in a discrete search environment a self-adjusting parameter choice is shown to be superior to any static choice. Indeed the $(1+(\lambda,\lambda))$ GA is the first proven example in discrete evolutionary algorithmics where a non-fitness-dependent parameter choice reduces the optimization time by more than a constant factor. The results that come closest to this are the mentioned results from [3,20], which are either constant factor reductions of the expected runtime (in case of [3]) or reductions of the parallel expected runtime but not the total number of function evaluations (in case of [20]).

Our proof gives some general insights in the working principles of adaptive parameter choices in discrete domains, which hopefully lead to future applications of this approach in discrete search.

Our paper is organized as follows. We first introduce the $(1+(\lambda,\lambda))$ GA with static population sizes, give background on the generalized OneMax problem, and recall known bounds for the expected optimization time of the $(1+(\lambda,\lambda))$ GA on OneMax functions in Section 2. In Section 3 we present the $(1+(\lambda,\lambda))$ GA with self-adjusting parameter choices along with a brief summary of the mentioned (slightly adapted) classification scheme of Eiben, Hinterding, and Michalewicz [14] for parameter settings. We also present in Section 3 the runtime analysis of the self-adjusting $(1+(\lambda,\lambda))$ GA (see Section 3.3), followed by a discussion of the general insights obtained through that analysis (Section 3.4). Finally, we show in Section 4 that the one-fifth success rule suggests optimal or close to optimal parameter settings.

Disclaimer: For reasons of space we cannot give all details of the rather technical runtime analysis. We illustrate instead the main proof ideas. The complete proofs can be found the full version [7].

2. THE $(1+(\lambda,\lambda))$ GA WITH STATIC POPULATION SIZE

Adopting the conventions and notation from [10], we regard here in this work only search spaces with bit string representations, we write $x = x_1 \dots x_n$, $[k] := \{1, 2, \dots, k\}$, and $[0..k] := [k] \cup \{0\}$ for any bit string $x \in \{0,1\}^n$ and any non-negative integer k. By $\mathcal{B}(n,p)$ we denote the binomial distribution with n trials and success probability p; i.e., $\mathcal{B}(n,p)(\ell) = \binom{n}{\ell} p^\ell (1-p)^{n-\ell}$ for any $\ell \in [0..n]$.

The $(1+(\lambda,\lambda))$ GA is given in Algorithm 1. It uses the following two variation operators.

- The unary mutation operator $\text{mut}_\ell(\cdot)$ which, given some $x \in \{0,1\}^n$, creates from x a new bit string y by flipping exactly ℓ bit entries in it.
- The binary crossover operator $\text{cross}_c(\cdot,\cdot)$ with crossover probability c, which, given two bit strings x and x', chooses $y := \text{cross}_c(x, x')$ by choosing for each $i \in [n]$ $y_i := x'_i$ with probability c and choosing $y_i = x_i$ otherwise.

Thus, after a random initialization of the algorithm, in each iteration the following steps are performed.

- In the *mutation phase*, λ offspring are sampled from the current-best solution x by applying λ times independently the mutation operator $\text{mut}_\ell(\cdot)$ to x, where the step size ℓ is chosen at random from $\mathcal{B}(n,p)$ before the generation of the first offspring.
- In the *crossover phase*, λ offspring are created from x and (one of) the best of the λ offspring from the mutation phase, x', by sampling independently from $\text{cross}_c(x, x')$.
- *Elitist selection*: The best of the individuals of the crossover phase replaces x if its fitness is at least as large as the fitness of x. If there are several offspring with best fitness, we disregard those that are equal to x and choose one of the remaining ones uniformly at random.

Throughout this paper we shall use $p = \lambda/n$ and $c = 1/\lambda$, choices which are well justified in [10, Sections 2 and 3]. Only in Section 4 we regard arbitrary choices of the parameters λ, p, and c.

As performance measure we regard the expected *running time* of the $(1+(\lambda,\lambda))$ GA, that is, the expected number of function evaluations that the algorithm performs until it evaluates for the first time an optimal search point $x \in \arg\max f$. This is the common measure in runtime analysis and is sometimes referred to as the expected *optimization time*. Note that for algorithms performing more than one fitness evaluation per iteration, such as the $(1+(\lambda,\lambda))$ GA, the expected runtime can be much different from the expected number of *iterations* (generations).

Algorithm 1: The $(1+(\lambda,\lambda))$ GA with offspring population size λ, mutation probability p, and crossover probability c.

Initialization: Sample $x \in \{0,1\}^n$ uniformly at random and query $f(x)$;
Optimization: **for** $t = 1, 2, 3, \dots$ **do**
    Mutation phase:
        Sample ℓ from $\mathcal{B}(n,p)$;
        for $i = 1, \dots, \lambda$ **do**
            Sample $x^{(i)} \leftarrow \text{mut}_\ell(x)$ and query $f(x^{(i)})$;
        Choose $x' \in \{x^{(1)}, \dots, x^{(\lambda)}\}$ with $f(x') = \max\{f(x^{(1)}), \dots, f(x^{(\lambda)})\}$ u.a.r.;
    Crossover phase:
        for $i = 1, \dots, \lambda$ **do**
            Sample $y^{(i)} \leftarrow \text{cross}_c(x, x')$ and query $f(y^{(i)})$;
        If exists, choose $y \in \{y^{(1)}, \dots, y^{(\lambda)}\} \setminus \{x\}$ with $f(y) = \max\{f(y^{(1)}), \dots, f(y^{(\lambda)})\}$ u.a.r.; otherwise, set $y := x$;
    Selection step: **if** $f(y) \geq f(x)$ **then** $x \leftarrow y$;

2.1 The Generalized OneMax Problem

In [10, Section 4] the $(1+(\lambda,\lambda))$ GA is analyzed by experimental means. The results show that it performs well on OneMax functions, linear functions with random weights, and royal road functions. A theoretical investigation, an improved bound of which is stated below in Theorem 1, however, is currently available only for the generalized OneMax problem. As this problem is also the focus of our present work, we give a short introduction here.

The classical OneMax function counts the number of ones in a bit string. Optimizing it therefore corresponds to finding the all-ones bit string. Of course, we want the performance of an evolutionary algorithm to be independent of the problem encoding. More specifically, the algorithms that we typically regard have exactly the same optimization behavior on any *generalized* OneMax *function*

$$\text{Om}_z : \{0,1\}^n \to \mathbb{R}; x \mapsto |\{i \in \{1, \dots, n\} \mid x_i = z_i\}|,$$

which counts the number of positions in which the bit strings x agrees with the *target string* z. It is easy to see that z is the unique (global and local) optimum of Om_z. Note also that the classic OneMax function counting the number of ones in a bit string is the function Om_z with $z = (1, \dots, 1)$. It is therefore justified to call the set $\{\text{Om}_z \mid z \in \{0,1\}^n\}$ the *generalized* OneMax *problem.* For convenience we often drop the word "generalized" in the following. All statements made below hold for arbitrary OneMax functions.

The expected runtime of most search heuristics on OneMax is $\Omega(n \log n)$, due to a phenomenon called coupon collector's problem (see, e.g., [6, Section 1.5] or [21]). In intuitive terms, the argument is as follows. When the initial bit string is taken uniformly at random from $\{0,1\}^n$ then each bit has a probability of $1/2$ of being in the wrong initial configuration, i.e., it has to be touched with probability $1/2$. The coupon collector's problem states that if we touch one random bit at a time, then it takes $\Omega(n \log n)$ iterations until we have touched each bit at least once. Since many evolutionary algorithms (including, for example, $(1+1)$ EA and Randomized Local Search) change on average one bit per iteration, this implies the $\Omega(n \log n)$ bound. It was a long-standing open question whether genetic algorithms can perform better on OneMax than this lower bound. Sudholt [24] gave a first example of a crossover-based genetic algorithm outperforming the $(1+1)$ EA on OneMax. But while his (2+1) GA (for a suitably chosen mutation rate) is better by a constant factor than the $(1+1)$ EA, it does not improve upon RLS. The $(1+(\lambda,\lambda))$ GA thus gave a first positive answer to this question, as we recall in the next section.

2.2 Runtimes for Static and Fitness-Dependent Population Sizes

The following statement, proven in [8], provides a tight bound for the expected runtime of the $(1+(\lambda,\lambda))$ GA on OneMax.

Theorem 1 ([8]). *The expected optimization time of the $(1+(\lambda,\lambda))$ GA with $p = \lambda/n$ and $c = 1/\lambda$ on every generalized* OneMax *function is*

$$\Theta\left(\max\left\{\frac{n\log(n)}{\lambda}, \frac{n\lambda\log\log(\lambda)}{\log(\lambda)}\right\}\right).$$

Consequently, $\lambda = \Theta(\sqrt{\log(n)\log\log(n)/\log\log\log(n)})$ is the optimal choice for the parameter λ and this yields an expected optimization time of $\Theta(n\sqrt{\log(n)\log\log\log(n)/\log\log(n)})$.

It is also known [10] that a fitness-dependent (and thus, inherently non-static) choice of the population size can decrease the runtime even further.

Theorem 2 (Theorem 8 in [10]). *The expected runtime of the $(1+(\lambda,\lambda))$ GA with $p = \lambda/n$, $c = 1/\lambda$, and fitness-dependent choice of $\lambda := \lceil\sqrt{n/(n-f(x))}\rceil$ on every generalized* OneMax *function is linear in n.*

We will use the latter bound in our analysis of the self-adjusting $(1+(\lambda,\lambda))$ GA. More precisely, we show that the population sizes suggested by the one-fifth success rule typically do not deviate much from the fitness-dependent choice analyzed in Theorem 2. This observation has also been made experimentally in [10], see Figure 5 there for a graph showing the close relationship between the self-adjusting population sizes and the optimal fitness-dependent ones. That graph plots this comparison for a typical run of the $(1+(\lambda,\lambda))$ GA on OneMax.

Two milestones in the analysis of the $(1+(\lambda,\lambda))$ GA in [10] are the success probabilities of the mutation and the selection phase, respectively. Since we shall make use of these two bounds, we briefly repeat them below.

Note for Lemma 3 that for an offspring x' of x with OM_z-value greater than $\text{OM}_z(x) - \ell$ there exists at least one position i such that $x'_i = z_i$ while $x_i \neq z_i$. It is therefore possible to extract in the crossover phase this entry from x' and thus increasing the overall fitness of the current best search point. This is why we call the mutation phase successful if $\text{OM}_z(x') > \text{OM}_z(x) - \ell$ holds.

Lemma 3 (Lemma 5 in [10]). *In the notation of Algorithm 1, for all ℓ and x, the probability that in the mutation phase a search point x' is created with $\text{OM}_z(x') > \text{OM}_z(x) - \ell$ is at least $1 - \left(\frac{\text{OM}_z(x)}{n}\right)^{\lambda\ell}$.*

Lemma 4 (Lemma 6 in [10]). *In the notation of Algorithm 1, consider fixed outcomes of ℓ, x, and x'. Then the random outcome y of the crossover phase satisfies*

$$Pr[\text{OM}_z(y) > \text{OM}_z(x) \mid \text{OM}_z(x') > \text{OM}_z(x) - \ell] \geq 1 - \left(1 - c(1-c)^{\ell-1}\right)^{\lambda}.$$

3. THE $(1+(\lambda,\lambda))$ GA WITH SELF-ADJUSTING POPULATION SIZES

Being the first provable super-constant speed-up via a fitness-dependent parameter choice, the linear optimization time obtained in [10] is a big success in the theory of evolutionary algorithms. From the practical point of view, though, the question remains how in an actual application the user of the $(1+(\lambda,\lambda))$ GA would guess the fitness-dependent optimal choice of λ. In this section, we show that this is not needed. A self-adjusting choice inspired by the classic one-fifth rule can give the same (optimal, as the result in Section 4 shows) linear optimization time. To the best of our knowledge, this is the first result proving a reduced optimization time via parameter self-adjustment in discrete search spaces. We are optimistic that our approach can be applied to other discrete problems. At the end of this section, we give some general hints that might be useful for such purposes.

3.1 Terminology for Parameter Settings

Since the literature is unanimous with respect to the terminology for parameter settings, we have adopted and slightly extended in this work the taxonomy of Eiben, Hinterding, and Michalewicz [14]. Figure 1, an adapted version of Figure 1 in [14], illustrates this classification, which we briefly summarize below.

The efforts of choosing the right parameters in an evolutionary algorithm is called *parameter setting.* The first difference is between *static* and *dynamic* parameter settings. In the former the parameters are set before the actual run of the algorithm and they are not changed during the optimization process. In typical applications, a *parameter tuning* step precedes the application of the EA. In this phase, suitable parameter choices are sought through initial experimental investigations, either for all parameters simultaneously, or in an iterative process.

Optimizing dynamic parameter choices is called *parameter control* in [14]. Three principals are discussed: deterministic, adaptive, and self-adaptive parameter control. A dynamic parameter choice is called *deterministic* if it does not depend on the fitness landscape encountered by the algorithm. That is, there is no feedback between the fitness values and the dynamic parameters.[2] *Adaptive* parameter choices are those dynamic rules where the update rule depends on the optimization process. Within this class (and this is different from the classification scheme proposed in [14]) we distinguish between *functionally-dependent* parameter choices (where the parameters depend only on the current state of the algorithm, i.e., the current population)

[2] As noted in [14] this does not exclude randomized update schemes.

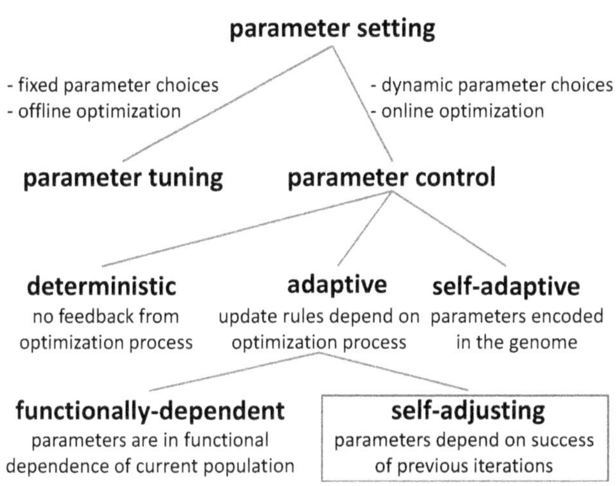

Figure 1: An extended version of the classification scheme from [14]. We regard in this work self-adjusting parameter choices.

and *self-adjusting* adaptive choices, where the parameters depend on the success of (all) previous iterations. It is easy to see that the one-fifth success rule considered in this paper classifies as a self-adjusting parameter setting, while the fitness-dependent parameter choice considered in Theorem 2 is an example for a functionally-dependent parameter choice. Finally, *self-adaptive* parameter choices are encoded themselves in the genome of the search points and are subject to variation operators. The hope is that the better parameter choices yield better offspring and thus survive the evolutionary process.

3.2 The Algorithm

Recall that the one-fifth success rule in evolution strategies is used to change the step-size in a self-adjusting manner. When the empirical success probability is large, the step-size is increased to hopefully speed-up the exploration. When is it low, it is reduced to hopefully increase the chance of a success. This is done in a way that an average success probability of one fifth leads to no change of the step-size on average.

In discrete search spaces, naturally, things are very different. However, we can still come up with a natural variant of the one-fifth success rule. Note that in our $(1+(\lambda,\lambda))$ GA (with the suggested choices $p=\lambda/n$ and $c=1/\lambda$ for the mutation rate and the crossover rate, respectively), increasing λ will increase the success probability of one iteration, however, at the price of an increased number of function evaluations, that is, higher runtime. Consequently, it makes sense to increase λ when the empirical success probability is low (to speed up the process of finding an improvement), but to reduce it when the success probability is large (to hopefully save computational effort).

Taking Auger's [1] implementation of the one-fifth success rule as example, we design the following self-adjusting version of the $(1+(\lambda,\lambda))$ GA, see also Algorithm 2. After an iteration that led to an increase of the fitness of x ("success"), indicating an easy success, we reduce λ by a constant factor $F>1$ (of course, not letting λ drop below 1). If an iteration

Algorithm 2: The self-adjusting $(1+(\lambda,\lambda))$ GA with mutation probability p, crossover probability c, and update strength F.

1 **Initialization:** Sample $x \in \{0,1\}^n$ uniformly at random and query $f(x)$;
2 Initialize $\lambda \leftarrow 1$;
3 **Optimization: for** $t = 1,2,3,\dots$ **do**
4   Mutation phase:
5   Sample ℓ from $\mathcal{B}(n,p)$;
6   **for** $i=1,\dots,\lambda$ **do**
7   Sample $x^{(i)} \leftarrow \text{mut}_\ell(x)$ and query $f(x^{(i)})$;
8   Choose $x' \in \{x^{(1)},\dots,x^{(\lambda)}\}$ with $f(x') = \max\{f(x^{(1)}),\dots,f(x^{(\lambda)})\}$ u.a.r.;
9   Crossover phase:
10   **for** $i=1,\dots,\lambda$ **do**
11   Sample $y^{(i)} \leftarrow \text{cross}_c(x,x')$ and query $f(y^{(i)})$;
12   If exists, choose $y \in \{y^{(1)},\dots,y^{(\lambda)}\} \setminus \{x\}$ with $f(y) = \max\{f(y^{(1)}),\dots,f(y^{(\lambda)})\}$ u.a.r.; otherwise, set $y := x$;
13   Selection and update step:
14   **if** $f(y) > f(x)$ **then** $x \leftarrow y$; $\lambda \leftarrow \max\{\lambda/F, 1\}$;
15   **if** $f(y) = f(x)$ **then** $x \leftarrow y$; $\lambda \leftarrow \min\{\lambda F^{1/4}, n\}$;
16   **if** $f(y) < f(x)$ **then** $\lambda \leftarrow \min\{\lambda F^{1/4}, n\}$;

was not successful, we increase λ by a factor of $F^{1/4}$ (since we analyze the algorithm for mutation probability $p=\lambda/n$ we do not let λ exceed n). Consequently, after a series of iterations with an average success rate of 1/5, we end up with the initial value of λ (unless the lower barrier of 1 was hit).

As a technical remark we note that where an integer is required in Algorithm 2 (e.g., lines 6 and 10) we round λ to its closest integer, i.e., instead of λ we regard $\lfloor\lambda\rfloor = \lambda - \{\lambda\}$ if the fractional part $\{\lambda\}$ of λ is less then 1/2 and we regard $\lceil\lambda\rceil := \lfloor\lambda\rfloor + 1$ otherwise.

3.3 Runtime Analysis

We show that the self-adjusting $(1+(\lambda,\lambda))$ GA (with standard parameters $p=\lambda/n$ and $c=1/\lambda$) solves the generalized OneMax problem in linear time when the self-adjusting speed factor F is not too large.

The proof of this result is rather technical. For this reason, we are only able to show a linear optimization time when F is smaller than a certain constant F^*, but we do not make this F^* precise. In general, making implicit constants precise is a difficult task in runtime analysis, and for many much simpler problems the implicit constants are not known. In the experiments conducted in [9], see in particular Figure 4 there, all values $F \in [1,2]$ worked well (recall that in Auger's implementation [1] $F=1.5$ was used). At the end of this section, we give some indication why F-values larger than 2.25, however, may lead to an exponential expected optimization time.

Our main result is the following.

THEOREM 5. *The optimization time of the self-adjusting $(1+(\lambda,\lambda))$ GA with parameters $p=\lambda/n$ and $c=1/\lambda$ on every generalized* OneMax *function is $O(n)$ for any sufficiently small update strength $F>1$.*

To prove Theorem 5, roughly speaking, we show that the population sizes λ suggested by the one-fifth success rule are usually not very far from the fitness-dependent choice $\lambda^* = \lceil\sqrt{n/(n-f(x))}\rceil$ analyzed in [10, Theorem 8] (which is restated above as Theorem 2). Intuitively, if λ happens to be much larger than λ^*, the success probability of the $(1+(\lambda,\lambda))$ GA is so large that with reasonably large probability one of the next iterations is successful and, as a consequence, the value of λ is then adjusted to its previous value divided by F, thus approaching again λ^*. A key argument in this proof is the following lemma, which shows that for large values of λ the success probability of the $(1+(\lambda,\lambda))$ GA is indeed reasonably large. This lemma can be seen as a generalization of Lemma 7 in [10].

LEMMA 6. *Let $x \in \{0,1\}^n$. Let $\lambda \geq C_0\lceil\sqrt{n/(n-f(x))}\rceil$. Let $q = q(\lambda)$ be the probability that one iteration of Algorithm 1 (with parameters $p = \lambda/n$ and $c = 1/\lambda$) starting in x is successful. There exists a constant C such that for all $C_0 > C$ we have $q > 1/5$.*

While the proof of Lemma 6 is rather straightforward, the proof of the main theorem, i.e., Theorem 5, is much more involved. Let us denote again by $\lambda^* := \lceil\sqrt{n/(n-f(x))}\rceil$ the fitness-dependent parameter choice of Theorem 2.

We partition the optimization process into phases. The first phase starts with the first fitness evaluation. A phase ends with an iteration at whose end we have increased the fitness of x and $\lambda \leq C_0\lambda^*$ holds, for a sufficiently large constant C_0 that we do not compute explicitly. (C_0 is determined by Lemma 6.)

We show that each phase has an expected cost of $O(\lambda^*)$ fitness evaluations. From this is it not difficult to conclude the proof by the same arguments used in the proof of Theorem 2. Intuitively, if the cost of each iteration of the self-adjusting $(1+(\lambda,\lambda))$ GA is almost the same as the one for the fitness-dependent choice, then the overall expected runtimes should be similar as well.

Unfortunately, the runtime analysis for the phases is rather technical. We make a case distinction with respect to *"short"* phases, in which $\lambda < C_0\lambda^*$ holds throughout, and *"long"* phases, in which $\lambda \geq C_0\lambda^*$ for at least one iteration. Analyzing short phases is significantly easier than analyzing long phases. Indeed, in the short phases, there is exactly one iteration in which the fitness of x is increased. That is, the value of λ has first been multiplied $t-1$ times by $F^{1/4}$ until there was a fitness increase and the λ-value has been shrunk as a consequence of the fitness increase. Using this, it is not difficult to derive the overall number of function evaluations in such a short phase.

For the analysis of the long phases we subdivide the phase again into an *opening phase*, which ends with the last iteration in which $\lambda < C_0\lambda^*$ holds, and a *main phase*. Let T denote the number of fitness evaluations during the phase and let I denote the number of iterations in the main (!) phase. As in the analysis of the short phase it will be easy to see that $E[T \mid I = t] = D\lambda^* F^{t/4}$ for all t and some fix constant D. The most technical part of this proof is to bound the probability that the main phase of a long phase requires t iterations; i.e., $\Pr[I = t]$ given that we are in a long phase. We show that this probability is at most $\exp(-ct)$ for some positive constant c. It is well known that the geometric series $(\sum_{\ell=1}^{t} F^{t/4}\exp(-ct))_{\ell\in\mathbb{Z}_{>0}}$ converges if $F^{1/4} < \exp(c)$. The overall expected number of fitness evaluations during a long phase is thus $\sum_{t=1}^{\infty} E[T \mid I = t]\Pr[I = t] \leq D\lambda^* \sum_{t=1}^{\infty} F^{t/4}\exp(-ct)$, which is $O(\lambda^*)$ as desired.

3.4 General Insights from the Runtime Analysis

The analysis above reveals the following facts, which might be helpful in general when trying to use a one-fifth success rule or a related self-adjusting rule in discrete search spaces.

The adjustment rule must fit to the limiting success probability. In the proof above, it was crucial that the success probability shown in Lemma 6 was a constant larger than 1/5. It is easy to see that if the success probability was uniformly bounded from above by a constant $\sigma < 1/5$, then $\log_F(\lambda)$ in expectation would increase by a positive constant in each round. Consequently, λ would show an exponential growth, quickly leading to wastefully large values. This can partially be overcome by imposing an upper barrier for λ (we have such a barrier, namely $\lambda \leq n$, to ensure that the mutation probability $p = \lambda/n$ is at most 1), however, this would still lead to the algorithm mostly working with this maximal value of λ instead of a value close to the ideal λ^*.

In general, there is no reason for not trying success rules with other ratios $1/r$ than one-fifth, that is, increasing λ by $F^{1/(r-1)}$ instead of $F^{1/4}$ in case of non-success. In general, a larger value of r will slightly decrease the speed of adjustment, but is more likely to overcome the problem described in the previous paragraph. Note that for our problem, when $\lambda = \omega(1)$, the success probability is uniformly bounded from above by $(1+o(1))e^{-1/e} \approx 0.31$. Consequently, the one-fifth rule avoids the exponential growth of λ, whereas a one-third rule or a one-half rule (e.g., doubling or halving the parameter as in [20]) would not.

The constant F matters. Even when the combination of update rule and success probability avoids an expected exponential growth of λ, things can still go wrong when the update strength F is too large. Here is an example (where, to ease the presentation, we assume that we have no upper barrier on λ; with an upper barrier, as above, the problem remains, though possibly to a smaller extent): Imagine that we start with some value λ_0. Above, we saw that the success probability of an iteration is bounded from above by 0.31. Consequently, the probability of having exactly m consecutive non-successes is at least $0.31 \cdot 0.69^m$. The optimization time of the last iteration alone is $\lambda_0 F^{m/4}$. Consequently, the expected effort of finding one improvement is at least $0.31\lambda_0 \sum_{m=0}^{\infty}(0.69F^{1/4})^m$. When $0.69F^{1/4} > 1$, this series does not converge, i.e., the expected effort for one improvement is infinite. In our case, this happens (at least) when $F > 4.41$. Note that this was a rough estimate aimed at quickly demonstrating that large F-values can be dangerous. Better values can be achieved with more effort. E.g., the probability that among $6m$ iterations, we have at most m successes, is more than $(0.755+o(1))^m$; this can be seem from approximating the binomial distribution with a normal distribution. Since this event also increases the initial λ value by $F^{m/4}$, the corresponding series already diverges for $F \geq 3.08$. Optimizing the ratio of successes and non-successes, we see that the probability of having γ successes among $1+5\gamma$ trials is more than $(0.8167+o(1))^m$, showing that any $F \geq 2.25$ leads to an exponential expected optimization time. We do not know to what extent this argument can be improved. For this reason, we would rather suggest to choose a small value of F, clearly below 2, and trade in the possibly faster adjustment to the ideal parameter value for a reduced risk of an expected infinite optimization time.

4. A LINEAR LOWER BOUND FOR ALL POSSIBLE PARAMETER CHOICES

In the previous section we have seen that the self-adjusting $(1 + (\lambda, \lambda))$ GA is faster on average than with any static population size. We next show that it is asymptotically best possible also among all dynamic parameter choices. That is, regardless of how the parameters are updated in each iteration, the $(1+(\lambda, \lambda))$ GA always has an expected runtime on OneMax that is at least linear in n.

Theorem 7. *For every (possibly dynamic) choice of the mutation probability p, the crossover probability c, and the population size λ, the $(1 + (\lambda, \lambda))$ GA performs at least linearly many function evaluations on average before it evaluates for the first time the unique global optimum. That is, regardless of the parameter update scheme, the expected runtime of the $(1 + (\lambda, \lambda))$ GA on* OneMax *is $\Omega(n)$.*

For parameter choices that do not depend on absolute fitness values, Theorem 7 follows from an elegant technique in black-box complexity. Since we believe this intuitive argument to be of general interest to the Self-* research community, we present it in the following section. It can be seen as a nice, yet powerful tool for analyzing the limitations of evolutionary and other black-box optimization algorithms.

For fitness-dependent parameter choices, Theorem 7 also holds, but needs a different argument as we shall comment in Section 4.2.

4.1 Lower Bound for Self-Adjusting Parameter Choices

We start the exposition of the lower bound by introducing the concept of *comparison-based algorithms.*

Definition 8. *A comparison-based black-box algorithm does not make use of absolute fitness values. Instead, it bases all decisions solely on the comparison of search points.*

To see that the self-adjusting $(1 + (\lambda, \lambda))$ GA is a comparison-based algorithm, we reformulate the algorithm slightly, see Algorithm 3. This alternative presentation shows that indeed all decisions of the $(1 + (\lambda, \lambda))$ GA are entirely based on comparisons between at most two search points. A lower bound that holds for *all* comparison-based algorithms thus immediately implies a lower bound for the $(1 + (\lambda, \lambda))$ GA. We therefore expand our view and regard the whole class of comparison-based algorithms. Theorem 7 for non-fitness-dependent parameter choices follows from the following statement, which is folklore knowledge in black-box complexity and has been formally stated (in much more general form) in [25, Corollary 2].

Theorem 9. *Every comparison-based algorithm needs at least $\Omega(n)$ comparisons on average to optimize a generalized* OneMax *function.*

The intuitive argument for Theorem 9 is pretty simple. In order to optimize a OneMax function OM_z we need to identify z. That is, we need to *learn* the n bits of z. Roughly speaking, with each query we learn at most one bit of information about z, namely in the mutation phase we learn whether $\text{OM}_z(x^{(i)}) \geq \text{OM}_z(x')$ or not, and in the crossover phase we learn the bit whether or not $\text{OM}_z(y^{(i)}) \geq \text{OM}_z(y)$. Finally, we learn the one bit of information whether or not $\text{OM}_z(y) \geq \text{OM}_z(x)$. Thus one iteration with λ offspring in the mutation and the crossover phase each gives us a total of $2(\lambda - 1) + 1$ bits of information. Thus, amortized over the 2λ offspring that were created, this is a bit less than one bit of information per query. Since we need to learn all n bits of z, this shows (intuitively) that we need to sample and compare at least n search points in total. This implies the lower bound.

It is not too difficult to make this intuitive argument formal. To this end, one employs Yao's Minimax Principle [26], a powerful tool in black-box complexity. The interested reader can find a quite accessible exposition of Yao's Principle along with some easy to follow examples from evolutionary computation in [13].

Algorithm 3: A reformulation of the $(1 + (\lambda, \lambda))$ GA with possibly adaptive (but not fitness-dependent) parameters p, c, and λ.

Initialization: Sample $x \in \{0, 1\}^n$ uniformly at random;
Optimization: for $t = 1, 2, 3, \ldots$ **do**
  Depending on x (but not $f(x)$) choose $\lambda \in [n]$, $p \in [0, 1]$, and $c \in [0, 1]$;
  <u>Mutation phase:</u>
    Sample ℓ from $\mathcal{B}(n, p)$ and $x' := x^{(1)} \leftarrow \text{mut}_\ell(x)$;
    for $i = 2, \ldots, \lambda$ **do**
      Sample $x^{(i)} \leftarrow \text{mut}_\ell(x)$;
      if $f(x^{(i)}) \geq f(x')$ **then** $x' \leftarrow x^{(i)}$;
  <u>Crossover phase:</u>
    Initialize $y := y^{(1)} \leftarrow \text{cross}_c(x, x')$;
    for $i = 2, \ldots, \lambda$ **do**
      Sample $y^{(i)} \leftarrow \text{cross}_c(x, x')$;
      if ($y^{(i)} \neq x$ and $f(y^{(i)}) \geq f(y)$) **then** $y \leftarrow y^{(i)}$;
  <u>Selection and update step:</u>
    if $f(y) \geq f(x)$ **then** $x \leftarrow y$;

4.2 Lower Bound for Fitness-Dependent Parameter Choices

The proof given in Section 4.1 does not work for parameter choices that possibly depend on the absolute fitness of intermediate search points. Intuitively, the problem here is that $\text{OM}_z(x) \in [0..n]$ and knowing (or, rather, using knowledge about) the absolute fitness value of x provides $\log_2(n+1)$ bits of information. This would only yield a lower bound of order $n/\log n$. Still the statement, i.e., Theorem 7, holds also for fitness-dependent parameter choices, as we shall briefly comment in this section. Note that this bound also implies the optimality of the fitness-dependent choice suggested in [10].

In the analysis of [8] it is shown (for the recommended parameter choices $p = \lambda/n$ and $c = 1/\lambda$) that the expected fitness gain in one iteration of the $(1+(\lambda, \lambda))$ GA with population size λ is of order at most $\log \lambda / \log \log \lambda$ (see the proof of the upper and lower bounds of Theorem 2 in [8]). That is, for "investing" 2λ function evaluations we obtain a fitness gain of order at most $\log \lambda / \log\log \lambda$. This shows that the average fitness gain per function evaluation cannot be more than constant, thus implying the linear lower bound. To make this formal, one can use the additive drift theorem [17].

To show Theorem 7 in full generality, one has to redo the analysis from [8] for general p and c, a tedious but straightforward work that we omit here for reasons of space.

5. CONCLUSIONS

We have analyzed the $(1 + (\lambda, \lambda))$ GA with self-adjusting population sizes. We have shown that it optimizes any generalized OneMax function in linear time. This is best possible for any (static or dynamic) parameter choice and is better by a $\Theta(\sqrt{\log(n) \log\log\log(n) / \log\log(n)})$ factor than any $(1 + (\lambda, \lambda))$ GA with static population size. Our result thus shows for the first time that self-adjusting parameter choices can be provably beneficial in discrete optimization problems.

We hope that our work inspires more work on the running time of evolutionary algorithms with self-adjusting parameter choices. We have provided some general insights that should be regarded when implementing a one-fifth success rule in discrete search spaces.

While our work focuses on an adjustment of the population size, we are confident that also for other parameters of evolutionary algorithms, e.g., the mutation or crossover rates, self-adjusting choices can be analyzed theoretically.

Acknowledgments

The authors would like to thank Anne Auger and Nikolaus Hansen for valuable discussions on various aspect of this project.

6. REFERENCES

[1] A. Auger. Benchmarking the (1+1) evolution strategy with one-fifth success rule on the BBOB-2009 function testbed. In *Proc. of GECCO'09 (Companion)*, pages 2447–2452. ACM, 2009.

[2] A. Auger and N. Hansen. Linear convergence on positively homogeneous functions of a comparison based step-size adaptive randomized search: the (1+1) ES with generalized one-fifth success rule. *CoRR*, abs/1310.8397, 2013.

[3] S. Böttcher, B. Doerr, and F. Neumann. Optimal fixed and adaptive mutation rates for the leadingones problem. In *Proc. of PPSN'10*, volume 6238 of *LNCS*, pages 1–10. Springer, 2010.

[4] K. A. De Jong. *An Analysis of the Behavior of a Class of Genetic Adaptive Systems.* PhD thesis, 1975.

[5] L. Devroye. *The compound random search.* PhD thesis, 1972.

[6] B. Doerr. Analyzing randomized search heuristics: Tools from probability theory. In A. Auger and B. Doerr, editors, *Theory of Randomized Search Heuristics*, pages 1–20. World Scientific Publishing, 2011.

[7] B. Doerr and C. Doerr. Optimal parameter choices through self-adjustment: Applying the 1/5-th rule in discrete settings. *CoRR*, abs/1504.03212, 2015.

[8] B. Doerr and C. Doerr. A tight bound for the runtime of the $(1 + (\lambda, \lambda))$ genetic algorithm on onemax. In *Proc. of GECCO'15.* ACM, 2015.

[9] B. Doerr, C. Doerr, and F. Ebel. Lessons from the black-box: Fast crossover-based genetic algorithms. In *Proc. of GECCO'13*, pages 781–788. ACM, 2013.

[10] B. Doerr, C. Doerr, and F. Ebel. From black-box complexity to designing new genetic algorithms. *Theoretical Computer Science*, 567:87–104, 2015.

[11] B. Doerr, T. Jansen, D. Sudholt, C. Winzen, and C. Zarges. Mutation rate matters even when optimizing monotonic functions. *Evolutionary Computation*, 21:1–27, 2013.

[12] S. Droste, T. Jansen, and I. Wegener. On the analysis of the (1+1) evolutionary algorithm. *Theoretical Computer Science*, 276:51–81, 2002.

[13] S. Droste, T. Jansen, and I. Wegener. Upper and lower bounds for randomized search heuristics in black-box optimization. *Theory of Computing Systems*, 39:525–544, 2006.

[14] A. E. Eiben, R. Hinterding, and Z. Michalewicz. Parameter control in evolutionary algorithms. *IEEE Transactions on Evolutionary Computation*, 3:124–141, 1999.

[15] A. E. Eiben and J. E. Smith. *Introduction to Evolutionary Computing.* Springer Verlag, 2003.

[16] N. Hansen, A. Gawelczyk, and A. Ostermeier. Sizing the population with respect to the local progress in (1,λ)-evolution strategies - a theoretical analysis. In *Proc. of CEC'95*, pages 80–85. IEEE, 1995.

[17] J. He and X. Yao. Drift analysis and average time complexity of evolutionary algorithms. *Artificial Intelligence*, 127:57–85, 2001.

[18] J. Jägersküpper. Rigorous runtime analysis of the (1+1) ES: 1/5-rule and ellipsoidal fitness landscapes. In *Proc. of FOGA'05*, volume 3469 of *LNCS*, pages 260–281. Springer, 2005.

[19] G. Karafotias, M. Hoogendoorn, and A. Eiben. Parameter control in evolutionary algorithms: Trends and challenges. *IEEE Transactions on Evolutionary Computation*, 19:167–187, 2015.

[20] J. Lässig and D. Sudholt. Adaptive population models for offspring populations and parallel evolutionary algorithms. In *Proc. of FOGA'11*, pages 181–192. ACM, 2011.

[21] R. Motwani and P. Raghavan. *Randomized Algorithms.* Cambridge University Press, 1995.

[22] I. Rechenberg. *Evolutionsstrategie.* Friedrich Fromman Verlag (Günther Holzboog KG), 1973.

[23] M. Schumer and K. Steiglitz. Adaptive step size random search. *IEEE Transactions on Automatic Control*, 13(3):270–276, 1968.

[24] D. Sudholt. Crossover speeds up building-block assembly. In *Proc. of GECCO'12*, pages 689–702. ACM, 2012.

[25] O. Teytaud and S. Gelly. General lower bounds for evolutionary algorithms. In *Proc. of PPSN'06*, volume 4193 of *LNCS*, pages 21–31. Springer, 2006.

[26] A. C.-C. Yao. Probabilistic computations: Toward a unified measure of complexity. In *Proc. of FOCS'77*, pages 222–227. IEEE, 1977.

A Hyper-Heuristic for the Multi-Objective Integration and Test Order Problem

Giovani Guizzo, Gian M. Fritsche, Silvia R. Vergilio and Aurora T. R. Pozo
Computer Science Department
Federal University of Paraná
Curitiba, Paraná, Brazil
{gguizzo, gmfritsche, silvia, aurora}@inf.ufpr.br

ABSTRACT

Multi-objective evolutionary algorithms (MOEAs) have been efficiently applied to Search-Based Software Engineering (SBSE) problems. However, skilled software engineers waste significant effort designing such algorithms for a particular problem, adapting them, selecting operators and configuring parameters. Hyper-heuristics can help in these tasks by dynamically selecting or creating heuristics. Despite of such advantages, we observe a lack of works regarding this subject in the SBSE field. Considering this fact, this work introduces HITO, a *Hyper-heuristic for the Integration and Test Order Problem*. It includes a set of well-defined steps and is based on two selection functions (Choice Function and Multi-armed Bandit) to select the best low-level heuristic (combination of mutation and crossover operators) in each mating. To perform the selection, a quality measure is proposed to assess the performance of low-level heuristics throughout the evolutionary process. HITO was implemented using NSGA-II and evaluated to solve the integration and test order problem in seven systems. The introduced hyper-heuristic obtained the best results for all systems, when compared to a traditional algorithm.

Categories and Subject Descriptors

I.2.8 [**Artificial Intelligence**]: Problem Solving, Control Methods, and Search; D.2.5 [**Software Engineering**]: Testing and Debugging

Keywords

Hyper-heuristic, multi-objective algorithm, search-based software engineering

1. INTRODUCTION

Multi-objective algorithms have been successfully applied in the Search Based Software Engineering (SBSE) field to solve a large variety of software engineering problems. Among them, the evolutionary ones (Multi-objective Evolutionary Algorithms – MOEAs) are the most popular and used [13]. However, the solutions proposed are sometimes problem dependent, and generally designed and evaluated for a particular problem. Many times, the use of a search based approach demands highly skilled software engineers, who waste significant time adapting implementation details, configuring parameters (e.g. crossover and mutation rates), manually selecting evolutionary operators, and so on.

To avoid such problems and to design flexible approaches, the hyper-heuristic concept has emerged. A hyper-heuristic can be defined as a methodology to automate the design and tuning of heuristic methods to solve hard computational search problems [5]. Hyper-heuristics are called "heuristics to choose heuristics", because they are designed to select or create heuristics while the algorithms are being executed [5]. A distinctive characteristic of hyper-heuristics is that they operate on the search space of heuristics, rather than on the search space of solutions.

To deal with an optimization problem, a high-level algorithm coordinates a number of low-level heuristics (e.g. operators and metaheuristics) by combining them to obtain the solutions. The motivation to use hyper-heuristics is mainly because there are a lot of possibilities to solve a problem, but there is no guide about how to choose the right algorithm and configuration. The application of a set of heuristics can yield better results than using each one alone. Hyper-heuristics help in the selection and generation of heuristics, and contribute to develop more generic algorithms.

Due to these advantages, hyper-heuristics have recently raised interest in the SBSE community. Harman et al [12] advocate that a hyper-heuristic could contribute to reach a holistic and generic SBSE. To this end, the development of hyper-heuristics for the SBSE field is fundamental. We found in the literature some initiatives with this goal. In [3] the authors applied hyper-heuristic to evolve an algorithm for the generation of effort-prediction decision trees. Their hyper-heuristic uses existing heuristic blocks in order to create new top-down decision tree algorithms. The algorithm created by their hyper-heuristic obtained better results than some state-of-the-art algorithms. In [15] the authors proposed an algorithm called *Fast Multi-objective Hyper-heuristic Genetic Algorithm* (MHypGA) to solve the multi-objective module clustering problem. Their hyper-heuristic selects low-level heuristics composed by selection, mutation and crossover operators, while the genetic algorithm is being executed. In [14] the authors proposed an online hyper-heuristic algorithm to intelligently learn and apply combinatorial interaction testing strategies. Their hyper-heuristic

GECCO '15, July 11 - 15, 2015, Madrid, Spain
© 2015 ACM. ISBN 978-1-4503-3472-3/15/07...$15.00
DOI: http://dx.doi.org/10.1145/2739480.2754725

performed well on constrained and unconstrained problems in several instances.

We can observe that hyper-heuristic SBSE has not been enough investigated. To contribute to this research topic and considering the importance of MOEAs in SBSE, this paper proposes HITO, a *Hyper-heuristic for the Integration and test Order Problem.* HITO is designed to select recombination operators (low-level heuristics), while MOEAs are being executed, in order to improve the quality and diversity of solutions. We adapted and implemented two selection functions in HITO: Choice Function (CF) [17] and Multi-armed Bandit (MAB) [11].

HITO has some main characteristics that includes: i) a set of steps to be used with MOEAs; ii) a set of low-level heuristics, composed by evolutionary operators applied in a population usually adopted in permutation problems; iii) CF and MAB based selection functions, where the selection considers a quality measure that takes into account the dominance concept and the number of matings of the algorithm; and iv) the low-level heuristic selection is done for each recombination in the evolutionary process, in contrast with other works [15, 17], which select and update the low-level heuristics for each generation. Another distinctive characteristic of HITO when compared to other works is that, the assessment of the low-level heuristic quality uses only both parents and both children, rather than a quality indicator such as hypervolume [20], which uses a whole population. We acknowledge that these low-level heuristic selection functions and this quality reward strategy can yield good results.

The integration and testing order problem has been investigated in the search-based literature by many works [19] and has some characteristics that make it suitable for the application of hyper-heuristics. This problem is multi-objective, impacted by many factors, and allows the use of different evolutionary operators. The use of a hyper-heuristic, like HITO, can be very advantageous, since this problem is found in different contexts, such as object, aspect and component oriented software testing. In this way, depending on the context, it can be necessary to test different kind of configurations and operators. The use of a hyper-heuristics eases the work of the software engineer, and increases the applicability of the search based approach to solve the problem in different contexts.

Experiments were conducted with 7 systems, and HITO was compared to *Non-dominated Sorting Genetic Algorithm-II* (NSGA-II [7]). The results were evaluated using the hypervolume indicator [20] on thirty independent runs and statistically analyzed. The hyper-heuristic found the best results for all systems. Moreover, CF and MAB selection functions were compared.

This work is organized as follows: Section 2 reviews basic concepts and related work on hyper-heuristics. Section 3 introduces HITO. Section 4 presents the empirical evaluation conducted, its results and analysis. Finally, Section 5 concludes this work and discusses future works.

2. HYPER-HEURISTICS

This section presents some hyper-heuristics concepts. An in-depth review can be found in [5].

Hyper-heuristics are often defined as "heuristics to choose heuristics". Burke et al [5] introduced a classification, generally used in the heuristic optimization field, which includes two categories: hyper-heuristics for selection and generation of heuristics. In the first category, the idea is to select, from a pool of low-level heuristics, a heuristic to be used by the algorithm. In the second one, the idea is to build heuristics from a pool of existing components (or operators). The hyper-heuristics can also be classified as on-line and off-line [5]. In the first category, the learning process occurs during the optimization of the problem. In the second one, a set of benchmark instances is used for the learning process. The output is an algorithm that potentially best solves any instance of the problem.

Selection hyper-heuristics generally work with a division line, named domain barrier, separating problem details from the hyper-heuristic technique. This barrier tries to ensure that a hyper-heuristic is not coupled to the problem and avoids the usage of the problem domain information on the heuristic selection, in order to allow the same hyper-heuristic strategy to be used for any problem, by only changing the implemented low-level heuristics.

This work is related to hyper-heuristics for dynamic (on-line) selection of evolutionary operators to be applied during the execution of a MOEA. In this study, a low-level heuristic is a combination of crossover and mutation. HITO is based on two recent works [11, 17] and on two kind of selection functions: Choice Function (CF) and Multi-armed Bandit (MAB). They were chosen because they address the Exploration versus Exploitation (EvE) dilemma. Briefly, it is important to apply more often the operators with a better performance (exploitation), but also it is important to apply poor operators in order to obtain a better population diversity (exploration). These functions are presented next.

2.1 Choice Function

The original Choice Function [6] is given by:

$$f(h_i) = \alpha f_1(h_i) + \beta f_2(h_j, h_i) + \delta f_3(h_i) \tag{1}$$

where h_i is a low-level heuristic being evaluated; f_1 is the individual performance of a low-level heuristic; f_2 is the performance of pairs of low-level heuristics (h_i and h_j); and f_3 is the elapsed CPU time since h_i has been executed. Both f_1 and f_2 are responsible for intensification (exploitation) and f_3 for diversification (exploration). The parameters α, β and δ are weights for f_1, f_2 and f_3 respectively.

Equation 2 shows a simplified version of CF used in [17]. This version contains only two components from the original function: f_1 and f_3. The parameters α and β are used to balance exploration and exploitation.

$$CF(h) = \alpha f_1(h) + \beta f_3(h) \tag{2}$$

2.2 Multi-armed Bandit

The Multi-armed Bandit (MAB) function has been studied to solve the EvE dilemma and to properly select low-level heuristics in a deterministic way. In fact, MAB is an optimization problem that for a set of arms (the operators), aims to select the most suitable to be used.

Generally the MAB function works in the following way. First a low-level heuristic is selected and applied, using information about their previous applications. After, the quality of the applied low-level heuristic is calculated, based on its performance (Credit Assignment). In the selection, the function simply selects the solution with the highest credit assignment value. The credit assignment value is calculated according to the MAB strategy used and takes into account both exploration and exploitation factors. This calculation is presented next.

Each operator i has an empirical reward q_i and a confidence interval n_i based on the number of times that the operator i has been executed. For each step, the MAB algorithm selects the operator that maximizes the selection rule, given by Equation 3.

$$q_i + C \times \sqrt{\frac{2 \log \sum_k n_{k,it}}{n_{i,it}}} \quad (3)$$

The scaling factor (C) is used to balance the algorithm between exploitation (to select the operator with the best empirical reward) *versus* exploration (to select an operator executed just a few times). If exploration is preferable, then C must be increased. On the other hand, if exploitation must be focused C is decreased. However, the selection rule may present some struggle in the adaptive operator selection environment. The environment is dynamic and the operator quality changes along the search process. The default MAB algorithm would take a long time to realize that a new operator became the best one [11]. To deal with this problem, in [11] the authors proposed the Sliding Multi-Armed Bandit (SlMAB) algorithm. This function updates the empirical reward using a sliding time window, in order to evaluate the operators for the current stage of the search process as shown in Equations 4 and 5.

$$q_{i,it+1} = q_{i,it} \times \frac{W}{W + (t)} + r_{i,it} \times \frac{1}{n_{i,it} + 1} \quad (4)$$

$$n_{i,it+1} = n_{i,it} \times \left(\frac{W}{W + (t)} + \frac{1}{n_{i,it} + 1} \right) \quad (5)$$

where it is the current iteration; t is the elapsed time since the low-level heuristic was executed; W is the size of the sliding window; and r is the reward obtained by the low-level heuristic – it can be the reward of the last time applied, or the best or average of the last W iteration depending on the implementation. In this work we use the best reward obtained by the low-level heuristic on the last W iterations, since it is the best strategy [11]. If a low-level heuristic is almost always applied, its n_i rapidly increases to W and stops, while its q_i shows exactly its current quality. If a low-level heuristic is not executed in the last W times, its quality is not updated, but its n_i value is slowly increased along with its chance of being executed. In other words, the SlMAB algorithm stores the performance of a low-level heuristic in a time interval W, and performs several calculations to assess its real quality and chance of being executed next.

The advantage of the MAB function is its capability in learning about the operators during the search process. It stores the low-level heuristic performances and constantly uses this information to select the best one in a time window. It can provide a more accurate evaluation of the operators, since an operator can generate a bad result and even then be the best in the moment because of its previous applications. We used MAB in this work due to its promising functionality and good results in other works of the literature [5, 11].

2.3 Discussion

Hyper-heuristics have been applied recently to mono-objective problems and, few works address the multi-objective ones. When faced to multi-objective problems a first issue that must be addressed is how to measure the performance of the low-level heuristics. In [17], a multi-objective problem is solved by using three MOEAs as low-level heuristics and CF was used to dynamically choose which MOEA must be executed at next. Hence, the performance information used by the authors measured the quality of the Pareto front produced by the MOEAs. In [16], a MAB function is used inside of the multiobjective evolutionary algorithm based on decomposition (MOEA/D) to select the most appropriate operator to be applied. MOEA/D decomposes a multiobjective optimization problem into a number of scalar optimization sub problems and optimizes them simultaneously. Thus, the performance could be measured as in mono-objective problems. In the study presented here, however, we propose to use a measure based on the Pareto dominance concept. This measure and the HITO approach are presented next.

3. HITO

HITO (*Hyper-heuristic for the Integration and Test Order Problem*) is a hyper-heuristic for selection of low-level heuristics composed of mutation and crossover operators used by evolutionary algorithms. HITO includes: i) a set of steps to be used with MOEAs; ii) a set of low-level heuristics; iii) CF and MAB based functions, where the selection considers a quality measure that takes into account dominance concepts, and the elapsed number of low-level heuristic applications; and iv) the recombination context in which the low-level heuristics are evaluated. These matters are better explained next.

The steps to apply HITO follow the flow presented in Figure 1. In the first step, named Initial Configuration, some information is provided, related to the population representation and objectives (fitness). In this step an algorithm and a selection function are chosen, as well as their parameters.

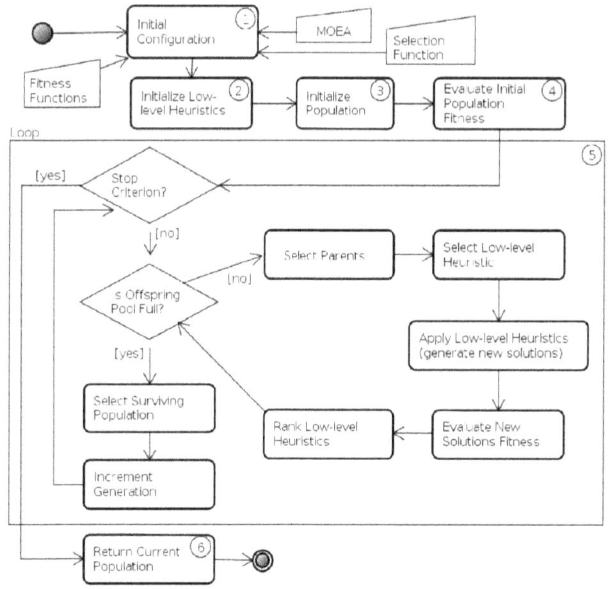

Figure 1: HITO flow

We can observe that different evolutionary algorithms and selection functions can be used. In our evaluation, we use

NSGA-II. Similarly to other Genetic Algorithms (GAs), it uses a crossover and mutation operators to, respectively, recombine parents solutions in order to generate children solutions, and mutate these children solutions in order to increase the diversity of the population. These are the operators that compose low-level heuristics, which in turn are dynamically selected by HITO. In this work, a low-level heuristic is a combination of one crossover operator and one mutation operator, and the ones used by HITO are presented in Section 3.1.

The second step of HITO is the low-level heuristics initialization. Each low-level heuristic has a quality measure in the range [0, 1], denoted as r, and an elapsed time factor, denoted as t. These measures are initialized with 0. The higher the r value of a low-level heuristic, the better its results. On the other hand, the time factor t counts the number of applications of any operator, since the last usage of the corresponding low-level heuristic.

The third step is the initial population generation, and the fourth is the fitness evaluation of each individual, according to the objectives given by the user.

After the fourth step, a loop starts and continues until the stop criterion is reached. At each generation, an offspring pool (or offspring population) is first created. The size of this pool can vary for each MOEA, but usually it is equal to the population size. Nevertheless, to generate the children individuals it is necessary to first select the parents. This is also done by the MOEA being executed. For instance, NSGA-II does a binary tournament between some parents and selects the best two to recombine.

After that, the selection function, chosen by the user, selects a low-level heuristic, and then applies its corresponding crossover and mutation operators in order to generate the children. If the new solutions violate any constraint, then a correction algorithm can be applied. These children are then evaluated by the fitness functions and added to the offspring pool. At the end of the iteration, the low-level heuristic has its r and t values updated. For that update we propose a procedure, presented in Section 3.2.

After these values updates, if the offspring pool is not yet full, then more recombinations are necessary. However, if it is full, then the MOEA being executed selects the surviving population and increments the generation. When the stop criterion is achieved, the current population is returned as result, and the execution ends. Only the non-dominated solutions are returned.

The following sections present: the low-level heuristics; the procedure to update the values r and t associated to each low-level heuristic; and the CF and MAB based selection functions used in this work.

3.1 Low-level Heuristics

HITO low-level heuristics are suitable for permutation problems and evolutionary algorithms. To establish the low-level heuristic set, we used combinations of three crossover operators and two mutation operators, according to Table 1: i) Two Points Crossover, PMX Crossover and Uniform Crossover; and ii) Swap Mutation and Simple Insertion Mutation [10]. Each cell in the middle represents a low-level heuristic, i.e., a combination of the crossover operator (line) and the mutation operator (column). Each low-level heuristic is composed either by one crossover operator and one mutation operator (h2, h3, h5, h6, h8 and h9), or only by a crossover operator (h1, h4 and h7), since crossover is a distinguishing feature of evolutionary and genetic algorithms [18].

Table 1: Low-level heuristics composition

	Mutation		
Crossover	–	Swap	Simple Insertion
Two Points	h1	h2	h3
Uniform	h4	h5	h6
PMX	h7	h8	h9

3.2 Updating r and t

The r update takes into account both parents and the children (generally two). The update of r associated to a low-level heuristic is given by the following equation:

$$r = 0.125 * \sum_{c \in C} \sum_{p \in P} \begin{cases} 2 & \text{if } c \prec p \\ 0 & \text{if } p \prec c \\ 1 & \text{otherwise} \end{cases} \tag{6}$$

where, c is a child; C is the set of generated children at the current mating; p is a parent; and P is the set of parents used in this mating. The measure r always is in the range [0, 1], 0 being the worst value and 1 being the best value. For example, in a scenario where two children were generated by a low-level heuristic with the mating of two parents, the value of r for this low-level heuristic would be 1 if both children dominate ($\prec$) both parents. Another situation is when both parents dominate both children, which is a bad performance for the low-level heuristic, thus giving its r a value of 0. If a low-level heuristic generates two non-dominated children in relation to their parents, then its r would be 0.5.

The r quality measure and its updating equation are originally proposed in this work. As far as we are aware, there are no measures in the literature that take into account the Pareto dominance explicitly. An advantage of this measure is its fast and relatively simple calculation. It only uses both parents and both generated children (not a whole population), and is calculated using a single equation that has a summation of constant values.

The time factor t counts how many matings have passed since the last time the low-level heuristic has been used. At each mating, all the low-level heuristics that were not executed have their t value incremented by 1, and the executed low-level heuristic has its t set to 0. We think that the way t is calculated better captures exploration than the CPU time used in other works.

It is important to note that, at the first generation, all low-level heuristics are applied to receive an initial value for r and t. This initial value will then be used in the next generation to select the best low-level heuristic. By executing all low-level heuristics at the beginning, we give a fair start for each one of them.

3.3 Selection Functions

The selection function provided by the user is applied in the *Rank Low-Level Heuristics* activity (Figure 1). We propose two functions based on CF [17] and MAB [11], implementing some adaptations as described next.

For CF we adjusted the equation by not using all the ranking schemes proposed in [17], but rather considering the measures r and t directly. Therefore, the CF value of a low-level heuristic is given by the following equation:

$$CF(h) = \alpha r_h + \beta t_h \tag{7}$$

where h is the low-level heuristic being evaluated; r_h and t_h are the measures of h; α is the weight of r_h; and β is the weight of t_h. In this work, the weights α and β are decimal values between 0 and 1. If the user wants to give preference to the quality measure, then he/she needs to increase α. If the time factor is preferable, then β must be increased. It is important to balance both measures, such that the low-level heuristics can be applied even when they have been generating bad results (in order to increase exploration), but not too much to preserve a good exploitation.

For MAB we adapted the Sliding Multi-Armed Bandit (SlMAB) proposed in [11]. In our implementation the $r_{i,it}$ measure of a low-level heuristic h is the best r value of h on the sliding window, that means, the best reward r obtained by the low-level heuristic on the last W iterations, where r is calculated using Equation 6. Whereas t measures the difference between the current mating and the last mating in which h has been applied.

If CF is the function being used, then the low-level heuristics are ranked by their CF value after they are evaluated by this function. If MAB is being used, then the low-level heuristics are ranked by their respective MAB value computed in Equation 3. Nevertheless, in the next mating, the low-level heuristic with the highest CF or MAB value is selected to be applied. If there is a tie, then a random tied low-level heuristic is selected.

4. EMPIRICAL EVALUATION

Experiments were conducted to empirically evaluate the HITO applicability. This evaluation was guided by the following research questions.

RQ1: How is the HITO performance for the integration and test order problem? This question investigates if the use of HITO contributes to improve the results of an algorithm to solve the integration and test order problem (briefly described in Section 4.1). In this case the problem should be properly solved by MOEAs, and in addition to this, the set of low-level heuristics proposed should be applicable.

RQ2: How is the performance of both proposed selection functions? This question investigates if the adaptations proposed can produce good results and if there is difference between the performance of CF and MAB based functions.

To answer these questions we implemented HITO and both functions (CF and MAB), and used 7 real world systems in the experimentation. The results were compared using the hypervolume indicator [20].

4.1 The problem

During the integration test of systems it is necessary to determine a sequence to integrate and test the units. This problem has been addressed by many works in the literature. For a brief review on this subject see [19]. Most works consider that this sequence should be associated to a minimal cost, given by the cost for stubs construction, which is impacted by many factors. Hence, most promising solutions are search-based and use multi-objective algorithms, mainly the evolutionary ones. Such works use a graph to represent the dependences between the units. This graph is named Object Relation Diagram (ORD) [4]. In the context of object-oriented systems the units are classes, but the graph was also extended for other contexts, such as component-based, aspect and product line oriented systems [2]. In this graph, the vertices represent the units, and the edges represent the relations between them.

To evaluate the cost, different measures (objectives) are used. In this paper we use two objectives, generally used by related work [4]: number of attributes (A) and number of methods (O); both to be emulated in the stub if the dependencies between two modules were broken.

This problem was chosen in our evaluation due to its main characteristics, which make the application of hyper-heuristics very suitable: i) it is properly solved by multi-objective algorithms [1]; ii) the representation of the population used is analogous to that one adopted to a permutation problem, and allows the use of several operators in the evolutionary process; iii) the problem is found in different domains such as the test of object, aspect, and component oriented software, which can impact the performance of the algorithms and low-level heuristics. In the literature we did not find any work that use hyper-heuristic in the solution of this problem. Other similar problems such as selection and prioritization of test cases are suitable too, and should be explored in future works.

We used 7 systems implemented in Java and AspectJ. They vary in size (lines of code (LOC)), and number of dependencies between the units (described in Table 2). The greater the number of dependencies the greater the number of solutions to the problem.

Table 2: Systems used in the study

Name	Units	Dependencies	LOC
MyBatis	331	1271	23535
AJHSQLDB	301	1338	68550
AJHotDraw	321	1592	18586
BCEL	45	289	2999
JHotDraw	197	809	20273
HealthWatcher	117	399	5479
JBoss	150	367	8434

4.2 Implementation and configuration aspects

To solve the integration and test order, we adopted the same representation for the population, constraints and fitness evaluation adopted in [2]. We implemented the NSGA-II algorithm and HITO by using jMetal [9], an object-oriented framework developed in Java and used in multi-objective optimization with metaheuristics. NSGA-II receives the system ORD as input, as well matrices, which represent dependencies between the units and cost for the construction of a stub, related to the metrics: number of attributes (A) and number of methods/operations (O). These metrics are used in the fitness calculation. The individual in the population is represented by a list of units ID (genes) that must be integrated and tested in order. The size of this list is the number of units in the system. If a client unit is positioned before one of its supplier unit in the list, then the client unit will be integrated and tested before the supplier unit, implying in the need of a stub for this supplier unit.

In order to answer the RQs above, we designed three experiments named: i) MOEA; ii) HITO-CF; and iii) HITO-MAB. The first experiment encompasses only the usage of NSGA-II. The second and third experiments encompass the usage of HITO with, respectively, the Choice Function and Multi-armed Bandit adaptations of this work. We used NSGA-II as MOEA algorithm for the optimization. We did not use other MOEAs because the objective of this work is to discuss the results of the hyper-heuristic implemented in HITO, not the results of different MOEAs.

Each experiment was executed 30 times for each system. The NSGA-II parameters were set equally as the ones described in the related work [2]. Also, some other parameters were fixed for CF and MAB functions according to [17] and [16] respectively. The parameters not described in these two works were defined manually after an empirical tuning. The fixed NSGA-II, CF and MAB parameters for this study are presented in Table 3.

Table 3: Parameters

NSGA-II	CF	MAB
Population Size: 300	α: 1.0	w: 150
Max Generations: 200	β: 0.00005	c: 5

In addition, for the experiments MOEA, HITO-CF and HITO-MAB we used different mutation and crossover probabilities. For the MOEA experiment we used 95% for crossover and 2% for mutation probabilities such as in [2]. For HITO-CF and HITO-MAB we used 100% for crossover and mutation probabilities. This was defined because of the deterministic characteristic of both selection functions (CF and MAB). If other values were used, the low-level heuristics could be evaluated by the selection functions without being executed if the probability was not achieved. By setting the probabilities to 100%, we ensure that the low-level heuristics are executed and evaluated by their recent performance. One may think that 100% for mutation probability is too high, however, the selection functions determine when the mutation should or should not be used and respectively select a low-level heuristic with one of the mutation operators or a low-level heuristic containing only a crossover operator. This is an advantage of using hyper-heuristics.

In this evaluation the true Pareto fronts (PF_{true}) are unknown. Due to this, each PF_{true} is composed by all non-dominated solutions of the known Pareto fronts (PF_{known}) for the system. A PF_{known} is composed by all non-dominated solutions found in the 30 executions of an experiment. Therefore, each experiment obtains a PF_{known} for each system and the best solutions found by all experiments are used to compose the PF_{true} of that system.

4.3 Results and Discussion

Table 4 shows the mean hypervolume found for the 7 systems (standard deviation in parenthesis) and obtained from the 30 executions of the three experiments. Values in bold are the best ones or statistically equivalent to the best values. The statistical test used is the Kruskal-Wallis test [8] at 95% of significance.

Table 4: Hypervolume averages

System	MOEA	HITO-CF	HITO-MAB
MyBatis	7.25E-1 (4.60E-2)	**7.64E-1 (3.14E-2)**	**7.45E-1 (3.56E-2)**
AJHSQLDB	5.51E-1 (1.42E-1)	**6.74E-1 (8.78E-2)**	**6.19E-1 (1.35E-1)**
AJHotDraw	5.73E-1 (1.17E-1)	**8.07E-1 (8.80E-2)**	**8.01E-1 (9.51E-2)**
BCEL	2.87E-1 (5.15E-3)	**7.87E-1 (8.01E-3)**	**7.81E-1 (3.51E-2)**
JHotDraw	4.38E-1 (2.82E-1)	**8.41E-1 (1.35E-1)**	**9.12E-1 (8.08E-2)**
HealthWatcher	**2.20E-1 (4.16E-2)**	**2.65E-1 (1.17E-1)**	**3.35E-1 (2.10E-1)**
JBoss	9.80E-5 (0.00E0)	**8.50E-1 (2.32E-1)**	**9.14E-1 (1.65E-1)**

As seen in Table 4, for all systems, using either MAB or CF as selection functions in HITO (experiments HITO-CF and HITO-MAB) resulted in the same best results when compared to the simple NSGA-II (experiment MOEA). Only for one system the results of the three experiments are statistically equivalent, but yet the hypervolume averages are higher for HITO-CF and HITO-MAB. In 3 of the 7 systems the experiment HITO-MAB got the highest values, but the Kruskal-Wallis test showed no difference when compared with the hypervolume results of HITO-CF. HITO-CF however got the best values for 4 systems (the 4 biggest systems), but Kruskal-Wallis test also showed no difference when compared to the HITO-MAB results.

Table 5 presents the hypervolume of the PF_{known} fronts found for each system. The first column presents the systems, and the second, third and fourth columns present respectively the hypervolume of the PF_{known} fronts found by the experiments in each system.

Table 5: Hypervolume of the PF_{known} fronts found

System	MOEA	HITO-CF	HITO-MAB
MyBatis	7.55E-1	**7.72E-1**	7.56E-1
AJHSQLDB	8.17E-1	**8.97E-1**	8.03E-1
AJHotDraw	5.44E-1	8.47E-1	**9.05E-1**
BCEL	2.53E-1	8.02E-1	**8.09E-1**
JHotDraw	1.73E-2	**2.65E-1**	**2.65E-1**
HealthWatcher	9.80E-5	5.05E-1	**1.00E0**
JBoss	9.80E-5	**1.00E0**	**1.00E0**

Table 5 shows that HITO can find the best PF_{known} fronts for all systems. In 5, out of 7 systems, the experiment HITO-MAB found the best solutions, while in 4 of them HITO-CF was the best. In two systems HITO-CF and HITO-MAB found the same fronts because of the small size of these systems. When compared to MOEA, HITO-CF and HITO-MAB always found better fronts.

Briefly, when using hypervolume to compare the results, HITO-CF and HITO-MAB yielded the best results, considering both the average hypervolume and the best PF_{known} fronts. Comparing both, HITO-CF found better hypervolume averages and HITO-MAB found better PF_{known} fronts.

Table 6: Average number of low-level heuristic applications by HITO-CF

System	h1	h2	h3	h4	h5	h6	h7	h8	h9
MyBatis	**13232.8**	4004.93	5856.63	1218.6	1010.5	1092.87	998.5	1115.13	1320.03
AJHSQLDB	**13367.43**	3758.87	5879	843.13	736.17	755.43	2376.57	970.3	1163.1
AJHotDraw	**11661.43**	3024.07	4437	1093.6	1055.3	1077.2	4378.4	1459	1664
BCEL	1117.57	843.57	950.07	808.8	729.1	764.9	**23098.63**	750.9	786.47
JHotDraw	**9121.9**	2894.53	4082.23	1468.57	1392.9	1424.4	5928.93	1672.63	1863.9
HealthWatcher	**10798.9**	3124.5	4317.1	1932.17	1675.1	1743.57	2559.93	1760.03	1938.7
JBoss	4690.1	2991.07	3473.83	2282.07	2242.1	2264.83	**7029**	2402.9	2474.1

Table 7: Average number of low-level heuristic applications by HITO-MAB

System	h1	h2	h3	h4	h5	h6	h7	h8	h9
MyBatis	**8868.23**	4456.4	5954.93	1419.27	1219.13	1289.4	2111.9	2057.13	2473.6
AJHSQLDB	**9954.8**	4264.73	6180.57	1020.93	1026.57	991.97	2837.63	1509.27	2063.53
AJHotDraw	**9593.33**	2900.47	4297.03	1209.2	1166.7	1223.13	5632.07	1623.57	2204.5
BCEL	2882.47	1571.43	1956.6	1445.13	1424.57	1508.8	**15418.27**	1537.17	2105.57
JHotDraw	7366.13	2713.3	4373.1	1266.03	1288.07	1402.93	**7414.67**	1653.63	2372.13
HealthWatcher	**6254.83**	4129.4	5435.83	1697.9	1515.8	1542.07	4241.17	2154.77	2878.23
JBoss	3318.23	1887.2	2582.37	1163.93	1244.33	1206.47	**14779.07**	1509.13	2159.27

We also analyzed the number of times that each low-level heuristic was applied in each experiment for HITO to yield these good results. Tables 6 and 7 present respectively the average number of times each low-level heuristic was applied in each of the 30 executions of HITO-CF and HITO-MAB.

We found out that for all systems in all scenarios, the low-level heuristics that use only crossover operators (*h1*, *h4* and *h7*) are the most applied ones. The most applied low-level heuristic is *h1* (Two Points Crossover) and the second most applied is *h7* (PMX Crossover). In fact, *h7* always had a higher number of applications for BCEL and JBoss, and for JHotDraw by HITO-MAB.

In all the other scenarios *h1* was the most applied low-level heuristic. These numbers point out that, regardless of which selection function is being used, the PMX Crossover operator is the most suitable crossover for BCEL and JHotDraw, and the Two Points Crossover operator is the most suitable for the other systems. In addition to this, we observed that in the majority of the cases, the low-level heuristics using Simple Insertion Mutation were applied a greater number of times than the low-level heuristics with the same crossover operator and Swap Mutation. It shows that Simple Insertion Mutation is the best mutation operator for this problem.

We can state that the use of only crossover generates better children throughout the search process for this kind of problem, and that the usage of mutation operators can degrade the quality of the solutions in some cases. This can also be evidenced by the most applied mutation operator (Simple Insertion Mutation), which changes the position of only one gene of the chromosome, whereas the other one changes two genes. Furthermore, the crossover operators Two Points Crossover and PMX Crossover were chosen more often because they generated better solutions by changing less the order of the genes. Therefore, changing too much the order of the units can result in worse solutions.

4.4 Answering the Research Questions

RQ1: How is the HITO performance for the integration and test order problem? In this study, HITO was able to obtain better results than the simple NSGA-II, used for comparison. For all systems HITO found the best hypervolumes values, and in six of them (out of 7) with statistical difference. In addition, the best PF_{known} sets were also found by HITO for all systems. This evidences and supports the capability of hyper-heuristics (specially HITO) in yielding better results than the use of only simple algorithms.

RQ2: How is the performance of both selection functions proposed? This question investigates if the adaptations proposed can produce good results and if there is difference between the performance of CF and MAB based functions. According to the experiments, CF obtained the best hypervolume averages for 4 of the 7 systems, while MAB obtained the best averages for 3. However, the Kruskal-Wallis test showed no difference between their hypervolume values for all cases. Regarding the PF_{known} fronts found, CF was able to obtain better fronts than MAB in two systems, but MAB obtained better fronts in 3 systems. Both functions obtained very similar results, but CF was able to find the best or equivalent results in every system regarding hypervolume, and the best PF_{known} for the biggest problems. We expected MAB to yield statistically better results than CF [5], but the quality measure used in this work may have been more compatible with CF. As future works we intend to increase the measure accuracy by changing its equation to obtain better results.

5. CONCLUDING REMARKS

MOEAs have being successfully used to solve software engineering problems. However, skilled software engineers waste significant amount of time configuring them and even designing and/or selecting recombination operators. To reduce efforts and ease the application of an approach in different contexts, this paper introduced HITO.

HITO dynamically selects low-level heuristics (combination of crossover and mutation operators) while a given algorithm is being executed. HITO has a set of steps and uses two selection functions (CF and MAB) to select the best low-level heuristic in each mating. To address this issue, we proposed a new and simpler measure that uses only both parents and children in the calculation, while using the elapsed number of applications as exploration factor. This led to the implementation of CF and MAB adaptations in HITO that use this performance assessment. We designed HITO to explore these new characteristics and also to solve the integration and test order problem.

HITO was empirically evaluated using 7 systems and two objectives. We compared the results of HITO to the results of NSGA-II. The results show that HITO is able to obtain better solutions than NSGA-II for all systems. CF yielded competitive results when compared to MAB, but performed slightly better according to the hypervolume indicator.

It is important to note that HITO is independent of the MOEA being used, and potentially can be used for any software engineering problem. Other similar problems, such as test case selection and prioritization can be explored in the future, as well as other evolutionary algorithms to assess these possibilities. Future studies include the investigation of new quality measures in order to increase the selection accuracy, allowing a fine-grained evaluation of low-level heuristic quality by graduating how much it improves the solutions fitness in each mating. Moreover, HITO should be evaluated using other operators and selection functions. Furthermore, we will investigate the possibility of using other hyper-heuristic techniques, such as on-line parameter tuning, acceptance functions and algorithm selection. Finally, there are several other fields in software engineering that can benefit from hyper-heuristics and future works should also consider them.

6. REFERENCES

[1] W. K. G. Assunção, T. E. Colanzi, A. Pozo, and S. R. Vergilio. Establishing integration test orders of classes with several coupling measures. In *13th Genetic and Evolutionary Computation Conference (GECCO'2011)*, pages 1867–1874, 2011.

[2] W. K. G. Assunção, T. E. Colanzi, S. R. Vergilio, and A. Pozo. A multi-objective optimization approach for the integration and test order problem. *Information Sciences*, 267(0):119 – 139, 2014.

[3] M. P. Basgalupp, R. C. Barros, T. S. da Silva, and A. C. P. L. F. Carvalho. Software Effort Prediction: A Hyper-heuristic Decision-tree Based Approach. In *Proceedings of the 28th SAC*, pages 1109–1116. ACM, 2013.

[4] L. C. Briand, J. Feng, and Y. Labiche. Using genetic algorithms and coupling measures to devise optimal integration test orders. In *Proceedings of the 14th SEKE*, pages 43–50. ACM, 2002.

[5] E. K. Burke, M. Hyde, G. Kendall, G. Ochoa, E. Ozcan, and R. Qu. A survey of hyper-heuristics. Technical report, School of Computer Science and Information Technology, University of Nottingham, 2009.

[6] P. Cowling, G. Kendall, and E. Soubeiga. A Hyperheuristic Approach to Scheduling a Sales Summit. In E. Burke and W. Erben, editors, *Practice and Theory of Automated Timetabling III*, volume 2079 of *Lecture Notes in Computer Science*, pages 176–190. Springer Berlin Heidelberg, 2001.

[7] K. Deb, A. Pratap, S. Agarwal, and T. Meyarivan. A fast and elitist multiobjective genetic algorithm: NSGA-II. *IEEE Transactions on Evolutionary Computation*, 6(2):182–197, Apr. 2002.

[8] J. Derrac, S. García, D. Molina, and F. Herrera. A practical tutorial on the use of nonparametric statistical tests as a methodology for comparing evolutionary and swarm intelligence algorithms. *Swarm and Evolutionary Computation*, 1(1):3 – 18, 2011.

[9] J. J. Durillo and A. J. Nebro. jMetal: A Java framework for multi-objective optimization. *Advances in Engineering Software*, 42:760–771, 2011.

[10] A. E. Eiben and J. E. Smith. *Introduction to evolutionary computing.* Springer Science & Business Media, 2003.

[11] A. Fialho, L. Da Costa, M. Schoenauer, and M. Sebag. Analyzing bandit-based adaptive operator selection mechanisms. *Annals of Mathematics and Artificial Intelligence*, 60(1-2):25–64, 2010.

[12] M. Harman, E. Burke, J. Clarke, and X. Yao. Dynamic adaptive search based software engineering. In *Proceedings of the 6th ESEM*, Laud, Sweden, 2012. ACM.

[13] M. Harman, S. A. Mansouri, and Y. Zhang. Search-based Software Engineering: Trends, Techniques and Applications. *ACM Computing Surveys*, 45(1):11–61, 2012.

[14] Y. Jia, M. Cohen, M. Harman, and J. Petke. Learning combinatorial interaction test generation strategies using hyperheuristic search. In *Proceedings of the 37th International Conference on Software Engineering (ICSE'15)*, May 2015. To appear.

[15] A. C. Kumari, K. Srinivas, and M. P. Gupta. Software module clustering using a hyper-heuristic based multi-objective genetic algorithm. In *Proceedings of the 3rd IACC*, pages 813–818, Feb. 2013.

[16] K. Li, A. Fialho, S. Kwong, and Q. Zhang. Adaptive operator selection with bandits for a multiobjective evolutionary algorithm based on decomposition. *IEEE Transactions on Evolutionary Computation*, 18(1):114–130, Feb 2014.

[17] M. Maashi, E. Özcan, and G. Kendall. A multi-objective hyper-heuristic based on choice function. *Expert Systems with Applications*, 41(9):4475–4493, 2014.

[18] M. Mitchell. *An Introduction to Genetic Algorithms.* MIT Press, Cambridge, MA, USA, 1996.

[19] Z. Wang, B. Li, L. Wang, and Q. Li. A brief survey on automatic integration test order generation. In *Proceedings of the 23rd SEKE*, pages 254–257, 2011.

[20] E. Zitzler and L. Thiele. Multiobjective evolutionary algorithms: a comparative case study and the strength Pareto approach. *IEEE Transactions on Evolutionary Computation*, 3(4):257–271, 1999.

Web Service Antipatterns Detection Using Genetic Programming

Ali Ouni[1], Raula Gaikovina Kula[1], Marouane Kessentini[2], Katsuro Inoue[1]

[1]Graduate School of Information Science and Technology, Osaka University, Japan
{ali, raula-k, inoue}@ist.osaka-u.ac.jp

[2]Department of Computer and Information Science, University of Michigan, USA
marouane@umich.edu

ABSTRACT

Service-Oriented Architecture (SOA) is an emerging paradigm that has radically changed the way software applications are architected, designed and implemented. SOA allows developers to structure their systems as a set of ready-made, reusable and compostable services. The leading technology used today for implementing SOA is Web Services. Indeed, like all software, Web services are prone to change constantly to add new user requirements or to adapt to environment changes. Poorly planned changes may risk introducing antipatterns into the system. Consequently, this may ultimately leads to a degradation of software quality, evident by poor quality of service (QoS). In this paper, we introduce an automated approach to detect Web service antipatterns using genetic programming. Our approach consists of using knowledge from real-world examples of Web service antipatterns to generate detection rules based on combinations of metrics and threshold values. We evaluate our approach on a benchmark of 310 Web services and a variety of five types of Web service antipatterns. The statistical analysis of the obtained results provides evidence that our approach is efficient to detect most of the existing antipatterns with a score of 85% of precision and 87% of recall.

Categories and Subject Descriptors

D.2.7 **[Distribution, Maintenance, and Enhancement]:** *Restructuring, reverse engineering, and reengineering*

Keywords

Web services; antipatterns; search-based software engineering.

1. INTRODUCTION

Service Oriented Architecture (SOA) has emerged as the next generation of software systems. As part of the service-oriented computing paradigm, SOA revolutionizes the process of developing and deploying distributed software applications as a set of reusable composable services [1]. SOA provides many architectural benefits including reusability, flexibility, adaptability, and maintainability [1]. This architectural style can be implemented utilizing a variety of SOA technologies, such as Web Services, OSGi, SCA, and REST. Today, Service-Based Systems (SBS) have become prevalent and omnipresent in our everyday life such as Facebook, Dropbox, Google Maps, PayPal, FedEx, and so on.

GECCO '15 July 11 - 15, 2015, Madrid, Spain.
 ISBN 978-1-4503-3472-3/15/07. . . $15.00.
http://dx.doi.org/10.1145/2739480.2754724

Web services must be carefully designed and implemented to adequately fit in the required system's design with high QoS [2]. Indeed, there is no generalized recipe for proper service design. A set of guiding quality principles for service-oriented design exist such as service flexibility, operability, composability, and loose coupling principles [1]. However, the design of services is influenced mostly on context and usage [3]. Even though the programmers are familiar with these principles, business factors such as deadline pressures may lead to violations of quality principles. The presence of programming patterns associated with bad design and bad programming practices, known as "antipatterns", are an indication of such violations [4] [5].

Common Web service antipatterns include the nanoservice, and multiservice. Nanoservice is an antipattern where a service is too fine-grained characterized with few low cohesive operations, and whose overhead (communications, maintenance, and so on) outweighs its utility [3]. In contrast, the multiservice antipattern describes about the other extreme, i.e., the largest service. Multiservice corresponds to a god service that contains a large number of very low cohesive operations related to different business logics. Nanoservice and multiservice antipatterns can cause many maintenance and evolution problems such as poor performance, fragmented logic, overhead, client breakages and unavailability.

Consequently, there is a high need for efficient techniques that both Web service users and providers can use to detect and prevent antipatterns in their SBSs. Although there are several tools and techniques to detect antipatterns and code-smells in object-oriented (OO) systems [6] [7] [8], Web service antipatterns detection is not mature enough to provide efficient detection techniques [9] [10]. Indeed, despite the importance and extensive usage of Web services in last years, no automated approach for the detection of such antipatterns in Web services has been proposed.

In this paper, we introduce a novel automated approach for detecting Web service antipatterns. We propose a search-based approach to automatically infer antipattern detection rules from a base of real-world examples of Web service antipatterns. The problem is to find, from a large list of Web service metrics, the best combination of metrics and their appropriate threshold values, for each antipattern type. We thus express antipatterns detection as an optimization problem, using genetic programming (GP) to generate detection rules. A candidate detection rule is expressed as a combination of metrics and their appropriate threshold values; and should detect as much as possible the number of antipatterns from the base of examples. We present an empirical study to evaluate our approach on a benchmark composed of 310 Web services from six different application domains including 136 antipattern instances. We compare our approach to two other popular algorithms and random search. The statistical results reveal that our approach was significantly better than particle swarm optimization, simulated

Table 1. Web service antipattern definitions.

Antipattern	Definition
Multiservice	Also called god object Web service, represents a service implementing a multitude of methods related to different business and technical abstractions. This service aggregates too many methods into a single service, and it is not easily reusable because of the low cohesion of its methods and is often unavailable to end-users because it is overloaded [16].
Nanoservice	is a too fine-grained service whose overhead (communications, maintenance, and so on) outweighs its utility. This antipattern refers to a small Web service with few operations implementing only a part of an abstraction. It often requires several coupled Web services to complete an abstraction, resulting in higher development complexity, reduced usability [16]
Chatty Service	represents an antipattern where a high number of operations, typically attribute-level setters or getters, are required to complete one abstraction. This antipattern may have many fine-grained operations, which degrades the overall performance with higher response time [9].
Data service	an antipattern that contains typically accessor operations, i.e., getters and setters. In a distributed environment, some Web services may only perform some simple information retrieval or data access operations. A Data Web Service usually deals with very small messages of primitive types and may have high data cohesion [10].
Ambiguous Service	is an antipattern where developers use ambiguous or meaningless names for denoting the main elements of interface elements (e.g., port-types, operations, and messages). Ambiguous names are not semantically and syntactically sound and affect the discoverability and the reusability of a Web service [17].

annealing as well as random search with more than 85% of precision and 87% of recall.

The remainder of this paper is organized as follows. Section 2 describes the background and motivation challenges. Section 3 introduces our search-based approach. In section 4, we present and discuss the validation results. Section 5 discusses the different threats to validity. Section 6 surveys the existing work. Finally, we conclude and outline our future research directions in section 7.

2. BACKGROUND

In this section, we provide a brief overview of SOA, Web services and Web service antipatterns. Then, we outline the different problems and challenges that motivate our approach.

2.1 Definitions

SOA is a logical way for designing complex distributed software systems using functionality implemented by third-party providers. In a SOA, the service requester satisfies its specific needs by using services offered by service providers, through published and discoverable interfaces.

Web services is nowadays the fittest and popular technology to implement SOA [11]. According to the W3C (World Wide Web Consortium), a Web Service is defined as "a software application identified by a URI, whose interfaces and bindings are capable of being defined, described, and discovered as XML artefacts" [12]. Its interface is described as a WSDL (Web service Description Language) document that contains structured information about the Web service's location, its offered operations and the input/output parameters, and so on. The aim of the Web services platform is to provide the required level of interoperability among different applications using predefined web standards.

Antipatterns are symptoms of poor design and implementation practices that describe a bad solution to a recurring design problem. They often lead to negative effects on software quality for which maintenance and evolution become harder [13]. Software engineers often introduce antipatterns unintentionally during the initial design or during software development due to bad design decisions, ignorance or time pressure. Therefore, antipatterns should be detected and removed from the software design as early as possible. Table 1 summaries the common Web service antipatterns including multiservice, nanoservice, chatty service, data service, and ambiguous service. In this paper, We focus mainly on these five antipattern types in our experiments as they are the most frequently occurring ones in SBSs based on recent studies [10] [14] [15].

2.2 Web service antipatterns detection challenges

The most challenging issues when detecting Web service antipatterns is how to find the best metrics that characterize such antipattern, how to find the appropriate threshold values for these metrics; and most importantly how to find the best combination of these metrics. Indeed, most of the existing works are limited to provide definitions to Web service antipatterns and/or characterize their common symptoms towards an antipattern catalog. However, automating the detection of such antipatterns is still a very challenging task.

In recent approaches [10] [18] [19], Web service antipatterns detection relies on declarative rule specification using domain-specific language (DSL). In these settings, rules are manually defined to identify the key symptoms that characterize a Web service antipattern using combinations of mainly quantitative (metrics), structural, and/or lexical information. However, in an exhaustive scenario, the number of possible antipatterns to manually characterize and formulate with rules can be very large. Unfortunately, it is very difficult to find a consensus to characterize and formulate such symptoms. Moreover, even when consensus is met, the same symptom could be associated to many antipattern types, which may compromise the precise identification of antipattern instances. Indeed, translating antipattern definitions from the natural language to metrics is still mainly a subjective task. That is, different antipatterns are characterized by the same metrics.

Another inherent problem is related to the definition of threshold values when dealing with quantitative information. Indeed, there is no general agreement on extreme manifestations of Web service antipatterns [16]. That is, for each antipattern, rules that are expressed in terms of metrics need substantial calibration efforts to find the right threshold value for each metric, above which an antipattern is said to be detected. Since there is no consensus in defining SOA antipatterns, different threshold values should be tested to find the best one. For instance, the multiservice detection involves information such as service size, number of operations, number of port types, and cohesion. Although we can measure the number of operations of a service, an appropriate threshold value is not trivial to define. A service considered large in a given context could be considered as normal in another.

Furthermore, detecting Web service antipatterns is more complicated than OO ones. That is, Web service source code is located in the provider side, and clients could only access and invoke services through their interfaces described in WSDL documents. This makes the situation more difficult to assess, detect, and prevent badly designed Web service, i. e., antipatterns.

2.3 Motivating examples

The WSDL fragment below illustrates the salient aspects of a multiservice antipattern, in the form of a service interface. The core identifying aspect of a multiservice antipattern is that it implements multiple core business and/or technical abstractions with low operations cohesion. This is manifested at the service interface as different public methods that involve different entities or abstractions. In this example, it can be seen that there are methods that operate on different core functionalities. For instance, the bookFlight() method used to book a flight trip, while the reserveHotel() method attempts to reserve the specified hotel room. Overall, this multiservice supports the functionalities flight, car and hotel booking, payment, invoice services, and so on. Each of these is a significant core business abstraction, and typically will have many associated methods. Therefore, while this example is simplified and is merely illustrative, in reality, a typical multiservice will include many methods related to each abstraction, resulting in a service with huge number of methods.

On the other extreme, i. e., nanoservice, we consider the example of a Calculator service taken from real-world Web service provided by Apache Geronimo[1]. A basic calculator service would not be complicated; it supports several simple operations such as add, subtract, multiply, divide and other operations. The example of Apache Geronimo shows the WSDL file from the Apache Calculator service, which performs addition of two integers. This is a very fine-grained service as all it can do is accept two numbers and return the sum. However, there is a lot of code (and overhead) for this simple operation. As services are consumed over network (Internet, LAN), they might be bound by the limitations and costs incurred by communications over those networks (e.g., the time needed to send/receive messages) [3]. The problem becomes more disturbing when considering this level of granularity in other more complicated real-life services.

For non-expert clients the line between nanoservices, multiservices and appropriately sized services is not obvious. In addition, even for service providers, service logics may look

```
<wsdl:definitions>
    <wsdl:types>
     ...
    </wsdl:types>
    ...
    <wsdl:portType name="FlightPortType">
        <wsdl:operation name="bookFlight">
           ...
        </wsdl:operation>
        <wsdl:operation name="reserveFlight">
           ...
        </wsdl:operation>
        <wsdl:operation name="cancelFlight">
         ...
        </wsdl:operation>
   </wsdl:portType>
   <wsdl:portType name="OtherServicePortType">
        <wsdl:operation name="reserveCar">
           ...
        </wsdl:operation>
        <wsdl:operation name="cancelCar">
           ...
        </wsdl:operation>
        <wsdl:operation name="reserveHotel">
           ...
        </wsdl:operation>
        <wsdl:operation name="checkDates">
           ...
        </wsdl:operation>
        <wsdl:operation name="modifyBooking">
           ...
        </wsdl:operation>
        <wsdl:operation name="acceptPayment">
           ...
        </wsdl:operation>
        <wsdl:operation name="validateCredit">
           ...
        </wsdl:operation>
        <wsdl:operation name="generateInvoice">
           ...
        </wsdl:operation>
            ...
    </wsdl:portType>
        ...
</wsdl:definitions>
```

[1]https://cwiki.apache.org/confluence/display/GMOxDOC21/jaxws-calculator+-+Simple+Web+Service+with+JAX-WS

Table 2. List of used metrics.

Metric	Description
NPT	Number of port-types
NOD	Number of operations declared
NOPT	Average number of operations in port-types
NPO	Average number of parameters in operations
NCT	Number of complex types
NAOD	Number of accessor operations declared
NCTP	Number of complex type parameters
COUP	Coupling
COH	Cohesion
NOM	Number of messages
NST	Number of primitive types
ALOS	Average length of operations signature
ALPS	Average length of port-types signature
ALMS	Average length of message signature
RPT	Ratio of primitive types over all defined types
RAOD	Ratio of accessor operations declared
ANIPO	Average number of input parameters in operations
ANOPO	Average number of output parameters in operations
NPM	Average number of parts per message
AMTO	Average number of meaningful terms in operation names
AMTM	Average number of meaningful terms in message names
AMTP	Average number of meaningful terms in port-type names

promising at design level, but can prove to be antipatterns when they are implemented. To make the situation worst, a comprehensive service contract does not guarantee that a service is not an antipattern. Thus, it is very important to provide efficient techniques to support both Web service clients and providers.

To address or circumvent the above mentioned issues and challenges, we introduce a search-based approach to automatically derive Web service antipattern detection rules.

3. APPROACH

In this section, we describe our approach for Web service antipatterns detection. The key idea is to see the detection problem as a search based combinatorial optimization problem to find the sought detection rules from a large list of possible metrics and thresholds.

3.1 Approach overview

Figure 1 provides a high-level overview of the approach proposed in this paper. Our approach uses knowledge from a base of examples that contains real instances of Web service antipatterns. These examples will serve to generate new Web service antipattern detection rules based on combinations of Web service metrics and threshold values. The detection rules are automatically derived by an optimization process that learns from the available examples.

As shows in Figure 1, our approach takes as inputs a base (*i.e.*, a set) of Web service antipattern examples and a set of Web service metrics. As output, our approach derives a set of detection rules. Using GP [20], our rules' derivation process generates randomly, from a given list of metrics, a combination of metric/threshold for each antipattern type. Thus, the generation process can be viewed as a search-based combinatorial optimization to find the suitable combination of metrics/thresholds that best detect the antipattern instances in the base of examples. In other words, the best set of rules is the one that detects the maximum number of antipatterns in terms of precision and recall.

The base of examples contains different Web service antipatterns from different application domains (e.g., weather, finance, shipping, etc.) that can be collected from different Web service search engines, such as eil.cs.txstate.edu/ServiceXplorer, and programmableweb.com, etc. These antipatterns were manually

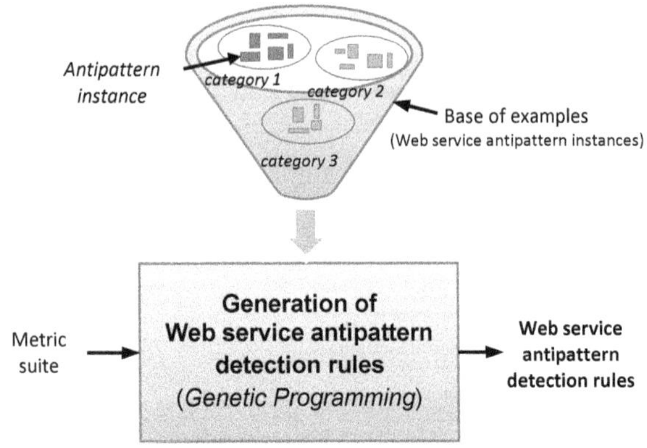

Figure 1. Approach overview

inspected and validated based on existing guidelines from the literature [3] [16]. During a training stage, these antipatterns are iteratively evaluated using rules generated by GP [20]. The process is driven by a fitness function that calculates the quality of each candidate solution (detection rule) by comparing the list of detected antipatterns with the expected ones from the base of examples.

Our metric suite is based on a set of Web service metrics. Table 1 summarizes the used metrics. The first fourteen metrics (NPT-ALMS) are defined in the literature [5] [10] [21] [19]. We also adapted and defined eight other metrics (RPT-AMTP). The last three metrics, AMTO, AMTM, and AMTP, are implemented based on WordNet[2], a widely used lexical database. Each operation, port-type and message identifier is tokenized based on camel case splitter. Then, we assume that the more the extracted tokens exist in WordNet database, the more the identifier is meaningful, i.e., semantically and syntactically sound.

As many metrics combinations are possible, the detection rules generation process is, by nature, a combinatorial optimization problem. The number of possible solutions quickly becomes huge as the number of metrics and possible threshold values increases. A deterministic search is not practical in such cases, and the use of heuristic search is warranted. The dimensions of the solution space are set by the metrics, their threshold values, and logical operations between them: union (metric1 OR metric2) and intersection (metric1 AND metric2). A solution is determined by assigning a threshold value to each metric. The search is guided by the quality of the solution according to the number of detected antipatterns in comparison to the expected ones form the base of examples.

3.2 SBSE formulation

Complex decision problems with multiple variables and large search spaces such as this are well-matched to search based software engineering (SBSE), which has proven good performance in providing decision support in several software engineering problems [22]. Our approach uses SBSE [22] [23], as it provides best practice to define a heuristic search algorithm, solution representation, fitness function, change operators, and so on [23]. In this section we describe our SBSE approach.

3.2.1 Search algorithm

As a search method, we employed a widely used computational search technique, GP [20], which have shown good performance in solving many software engineering problems [22]. GP takes as input a set of SOAP metrics and a set of Web service antipattern examples, and finds as output the optimal solution that corresponds to a set of rules that should detect the antipattern instances in the base of examples. For more details about GP, interested readers can refer to [20]. In the following, we need to define problem-specific solution encoding, genetic operators and fitness function to ensure best performance.

3.2.2 Solution representation

Candidate solutions to the problem are antipattern detection rules. A solution is represented as a set of IF – THEN rules. A detection rule has the following structure:

IF "Combination of metrics with their threshold values" **THEN** "antipattern type"

The IF clause describes the conditions or situations under which an antipattern type is detected. These conditions correspond to logical expressions that combine some metrics and their threshold values using logic operators (AND, OR). If some of these conditions are satisfied by a Web service, then it is detected as the antipattern type figuring in the THEN clause of the rule. We will have as many rules as types of antipatterns to be detected. In our case, mainly for illustrative reasons, and without loss of generality, we focus on the detection of five common types, namely multiservice, nanoservice, dataservice, chatty service, and ambiguous service (cf. Table 1). For instance, let us consider the following detection rules, in the iteration i, and its interpretation:

R1:	**IF** (NOD(s)≥17 AND COH(s)≤0.43 AND NOPT(s)≥7.8) OR (NOD(s)≥24 AND COH(s)≤0.39 AND NPT(s)≥2 AND NST(s)≥41 OR NCT(s)≥32) **THEN** MultiService(s)
R2:	**IF** (NCT(s)≤5 OR NST(s)≤8 AND NPT(s)≤2 AND NOD(s)≤5 AND COH(s)≥0.42) OR (NOPT(s)≤4.2 AND COUP(s)≥0.36 AND COH(s)≥0.39 AND NOD(s)≤6 OR NPT(s)≤2) **THEN** NanoService(s)
R3:	**IF** ((ANIPO(s)≥4 OR ANOPO(s)≥4) AND (NCT(s)≥31 OR NOM(s)>=79) AND COH(s)≥0.31 AND NAOD(s)>=13) **THEN** DataService(s)
R4:	**IF** (NPT(s)≤3 AND NOD(s)≥10 AND RAOD(s)≥0.38 AND (NCT(s)≥15 OR ANOPO(s)≥8.1) AND (NOM(s)>=38 OR NPM(s)>=2.2) AND COH(s)≤0.42) **THEN** ChattyService(s)
R5:	**IF** (ALOS(s)≤1.6 OR ALOS(s)≥4.9 AND AMTO(s)≤0.6 AND NIOP(s)≥4 OR AMTM(s)≤0.52) **THEN** AmbiguousService(s)

We encoded a solution as tree where each subtree represents a detection rules for a particular antipattern type. Figure 2 represents the correspondent tree for the multiservice antipattern, i.e., R1.

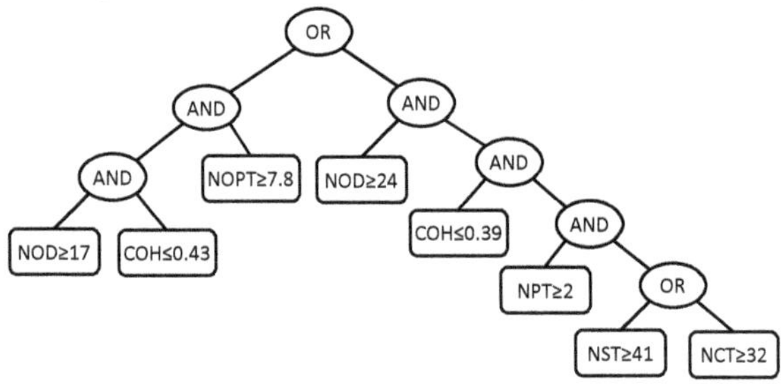

Figure 2. Solution encoding for the multiservice antipattern.

The initial population, composed by n solutions, was randomly obtained by assigning to each subtree m metrics ranging from 1 to nbMetrics (the number of considered metrics). For each metric we randomly assign a threshold value as defined in Section 3.1.

3.2.3 Fitness function

To evaluate the fitness of each solution we employed a fitness function that maximizes the number of detected antipatterns in comparison to the expected ones in the base of examples. In this

[2] wordnet.princeton.edu

Table 3. Web services used in the empirical study.

Category	# services	# antipatterns	Average # of operations	Average # of messages	Average # of complex types
Financial	94	67	29.52	57.31	19.01
Science	34	3	8.47	17.14	96.73
Search	37	13	8.35	18.94	26.13
Shipping	38	10	13.36	27.76	20.21
Travel	65	28	16.09	33.13	121.13
Weather	42	15	8.54	17.16	9.14
All	310	136	17.08	34.2	48.6

Table 4. Algorithms parameters.

Algorithm	Parameters	Values
GP	Population size	100
	Crossover probability	0.9
	Mutation probability	0.1
	Number of crossing points	1
	Selection	Roulette-wheel selection
SA	Initial temperature	100
	Final temperature	0.0232
	Cooling coefficient	0.99
	Number of iterations	30
PSO	Number of particles in a swarm	200
	Acceleration coefficient c_1	2
	Acceleration coefficient c_2	2

context, we define the fitness function of a candidate solution, as the average of both precision and recall as follows:

$$fitness = \frac{\frac{\sum_{i=1}^{p} a_i}{t} + \frac{\sum_{i=1}^{p} a_i}{p}}{2} \in [0,1]$$

where t is the number of antipatterns in the base of examples, p is the number of detected antipatterns, and a_i has value 1 if the ith detected service exists in the base of examples with the same antipattern type, i.e., true positive, and value 0 otherwise.

3.2.4 Genetic operators

Crossover: We use a random, single point crossover operator. Two parent solutions are selected, and a sub tree is picked on each one. Then, the crossover operator swaps the nodes and their relative sub trees from one parent to the other. The crossover operator can be applied only on parents having the same type of antipattern. Each child thus combines information from both parents.

Mutation: The mutation operator can be applied either to a function node or a terminal node. This operator can modify one or many nodes. For a selected individual, the mutation operator first randomly selects a node in the tree. Then, if the selected node is a terminal (quality metric), it is replaced by another terminal (metric or another threshold value); if the selected node is a function (AND-OR operators), it is replaced by a new function (e.g., AND becomes OR). If a tree mutation is to be carried out, the node and its subtree are replaced by a new randomly generated subtree.

4. VALIDATION

This section explains the design of our empirical study; the research questions we set out to answer, the methods and statistical tests we used to answer these questions. The experimental material is available for replication purposes[3].

4.1 Research questions

We designed our experiments to answer the following research questions:

RQ1 (SBSE Validation): How does the proposed GP-based approach performs compared to random search and other existing search-based algorithms?

RQ2 (Efficiency): To which extent can the proposed approach detect Web service antipatterns?

RQ3 (Sensitivity): What types of Web service antipatterns does it detect correctly?

4.2 Experimental setting

4.2.1 Analysis method

To answer RQ1, we compared our GP formulation with random search (RS) [24] to make sure that there is a need for an intelligent method to explore the search space. In addition, to justify the adoption of GP, we compared our approach to two other popular search algorithms namely particle swarm optimization (PSO) [25] and simulated annealing (SA) [26]. RQ1 is a standard 'baseline' question asked in any attempt at an SBSE formulation [23]. To evaluate the efficiency of each algorithm in detecting Web service antipatterns in comparison to RS, PSO and SA, we use precision and recall metrics, which are defined as follows:

$$Recal = \frac{true\ positives}{total\ number\ of\ antipatterns\ in\ the\ base\ of\ examples}$$

$$Precision = \frac{true\ positives}{number\ of\ detected\ antipatterns}$$

To answer RQ2, we also use both recall and precision criteria to evaluate the efficiency of our approach in identifying antipatterns. We considered five common Web service antipattern types, namely multiservice, nanoservice, chatty service, data service, and ambiguous service (see Section 2.1).

To answer RQ3, we investigated the antipattern types that were detected to find out whether there is a bias towards the detection of specific antipattern types.

4.2.2 Web services used in the empirical study

Unlike OO open-source systems, Web service providers do not make their source code publicly available; instead, they only provide Web service interface described as a WSDL document. We collected different Web services using different search engines including eil.cs.txstate.edu/ServiceXplorer, biocatalogue.org, webservices.seekda.com, taverna.org.uk, programmableweb.com, and myexperiment.org. Furthermore, to not bias our empirical study, we used different Web services from different application domains. Table 3 and Figure 4 summarize the collected services ranging from a variety of six categories, i.e., application domains, including financial, science, search, shipping, travel and weather. All services were manually inspected and validated to identify antipatterns based on guidelines from the literature [3] [16].

In our study, we used a 6-fold cross validation procedure. We split our data into training data and evaluation data. For each fold, one category of services is evaluated by using the remaining five categories as a base of examples. For instance, weather services are analyzed using antipattern instances from travel, shipping, search, science and financial services. Hence, precision and recall scores are calculated automatically by comparing the detected antipatterns with the expected ones.

4.2.3 Inferential statistical test methods used

Due to the stochastic nature of the used algorithms, they may produce slightly different results when applied to the same problem instance over different runs. To cope with this stochastic nature, the use of a rigorous statistical testing is essential to provide support to the conclusions derived from analyzing such data. Thus, we used

[3]http://sel.ist.osaka-u.ac.jp/~ali/WebServiceAntipatterns

the Wilcoxon rank sum test in a pairwise fashion [27] in order to detect significant performance differences between the algorithms under comparison. We set the confidence limit, α, at 0.05. In these settings, each experiment is repeated 31 times, for each algorithm and for each category. The obtained results are subsequently statistically analyzed with the aim to compare our GP approach to PSO, SA, as well as RS. The results reported in this paper are the median values of the 31 runs.

The Wilcoxon rank sum test allows verifying whether the results are statistically different or not. However, it does not give any idea about the difference magnitude. To assess the effect size, we use the Cohen's *d* statistic [27]. The effect size is considered: (1) small if $0.2 \leq d < 0.5$, (2) medium if $0.5 \leq d < 0.8$, or (3) high if $d \geq 0.8$.

4.2.4 Parameter Tuning and Setting

An important aspect for metaheuristic search algorithms lies in the parameters tuning and selection, which is necessary to ensure not only fair comparison, but also for potential replication. To this end, we report in Table 4 our algorithmic parameter tuning and selection used to facilitate the replication of our findings. The initial population/solution of GP, PSO, SA, and RS are completely random. The stopping criterion is when the maximum number of fitness evaluations, set to 25000, is reached. The max depth of the tree is fixed to 10. After several trial runs of the simulation, the parameter values of the four algorithms are fixed. There are no general rules to determine these parameters, and thus, we set the combination of parameter values by trial-and-error method, which is commonly used in the SBSE community [28].

4.3 Results and discussions

This section presents the experimental results obtained for our three research questions.

Results for RQ1. Table 5 and Figure 3 report the statistical results for RQ1. As presented in Table 5 and Figure 3, over 31 runs, the RS did not perform well in terms of precision and recall (only 30% and 42% respectively) due to the huge search-space of possible combinations of metrics and threshold values to explore. Indeed, in any attempt at an SBSE formulation of a problem, if the proposed formulation does not allow an intelligent computational search technique to outperform random search convincingly, then there is clearly something wrong with the formulation [23].

On the other hand, for the different categories, the statistical analysis provide evidence that our GP-based approach performs better (with a 95% confidence level) than two other metaheuristic search algorithms (PSO and SA). GP provides better performance than SA in all the six categories with high Cohen effect size. The median recall and precision scores of GP for all studied services (union of the six categories) are 87% and 85% respectively, whereas SA provide only 70% of both recall and precision. Similarly, according to Figure 3 and Table 5, GP provides better performance than PSO in four out of six cases with high effect size. Only in science and travel Web services, GP and PSO provide similar results with small effect size in terms of recall, but still with better performance for GP in terms of precision manifested by high Cohen effect size. Overall, the median recall and precision scores of GP for all studied services were better than PSO that provides only 82% of recall and 76% of precision.

Based on these results, we can conjecture that GP performs much better in comparison with PSO and SA. Moreover, we notice that SA turns out to be the worst algorithm in comparison with GP and PSO. Thus, it seems that population-based metaheuristic algorithms tend to be more efficient than local search

Table 5. Precision and recall median values of GP, PSO, SA, and RS over 31 independent simulation runs.

Category	GP		PSO		SA		RS	
	Precision (%)	*Recall* (%)	*Precision* (%)	*Recall* (%)	*Precision* (%)	*Recall* (%)	*Precision* (%)	*Recall* (%)
Financial	88 (o-++)	85 (o+++)	79 (-o++)	78 (+o++)	75 (++o+)	75 (++o+)	42 (+++o)	45 (+++o)
Science	75 (o+++)	100 (o+++)	50 (+o-+)	100 (+o-+)	43 (+-o+)	100 (-+o+)	17 (+++o)	67 (+++o)
Search	85 (o+++)	85 (o+++)	79 (+o++)	85 (+o++)	63 (++o+)	77 (++o+)	26 (+++o)	46 (+++o)
Shipping	90 (o+++)	90 (o+++)	53 (+o-+)	80 (+o-+)	57 (+-o+)	80 (+-o+)	19 (+++o)	40 (+++o)
Travel	80 (o+++)	86 (o-++)	89 (+o++)	86 (-o++)	81 (++o+)	79 (++o+)	27 (+++o)	36 (+++o)
Weather	76 (o+++)	87 (o-++)	72 (+o++)	87 (-o++)	61 (++o+)	73 (++o+)	20 (+++o)	33 (+++o)
All	85 (o+++)	87 (o+++)	76 (+o++)	82 (+o++)	70 (++o+)	76 (++o+)	30 (+++o)	42 (+++o)

A "+" symbol at the ith position means that the algorithm precision median value is statistically different from the ith algorithm one; while a "-" symbol at the ith position means the opposite. A "o" symbol refer to the current position of the algorithm. For instance, for financial services, GP precision is not statistically different from PSO one, however, it is statistically different from SA and RS ones).

metaheuristics for this problem especially that we use tree representation.

Results for RQ2. To answer RQ2, we focus only on the results of our GP presented in Table 5 and Figure 3. Overall, as shown in Table 5, we were able to detect antipatterns on the different service categories with a precision score of 85 percent. For science and weather services, the precision is lower than the other categories with respectively 75 and 76 percent. This can be explained by the fact that these services are medium-sized and often contain too much data and accessor operations to these data which might be relatively confusing between multiservice, data service and chatty service. For financial and shipping services, the precision score is higher (88 and 100 percent), i.e., most of the detected antipatterns are true positives. In terms of recall, the obtained results are higher than precision. According to Table 5, the median GP recall score on all services is 87 percent. We found that, science and shipping services have the highest recall scores with 100% and 90% respectively. We also had a good trade-off between both recall and precision. Therefore, we can conclude that our approach provides good performance to detect most of the existing antipatterns, which could be very helpful to provide advice to both service clients and providers on the quality of their Web services.

Results for RQ3. Based on the results of Figure 5, we noticed that our technique does not have a bias towards the detection of specific antipattern types. Figure 5 shows that we had, in all categories, a relatively equitable detection results in terms of both precision and recall for each antipattern type. For some categories such as weather and search, the distribution of antipatterns detection is not as balanced (cf. Figure 4). This is principally due to the number of actual antipattern types in these categories (none dataservice instance exists in weather and search category). Consequently, any single false positive will lead to 0% of precision score.

Overall, all the five antipattern types are detected with good precision and recall scores (85% and 87% respectively). Most of detected antipatterns are true positives and we do not miss any existing antipattern type. This ability to identify different types of antipatterns underlines a key strength to our approach. Most other existing approaches [10] rely heavily on the notion of size to specify antipatterns. This is reasonable considering that some antipatterns like the multiservice are associated with a notion of size. For antipatterns like data service and ambiguous service, however, the notion of size is less important and this makes this type of antipatterns hard to detect using structural information. The obtained results provides evidence that such difficulty does not

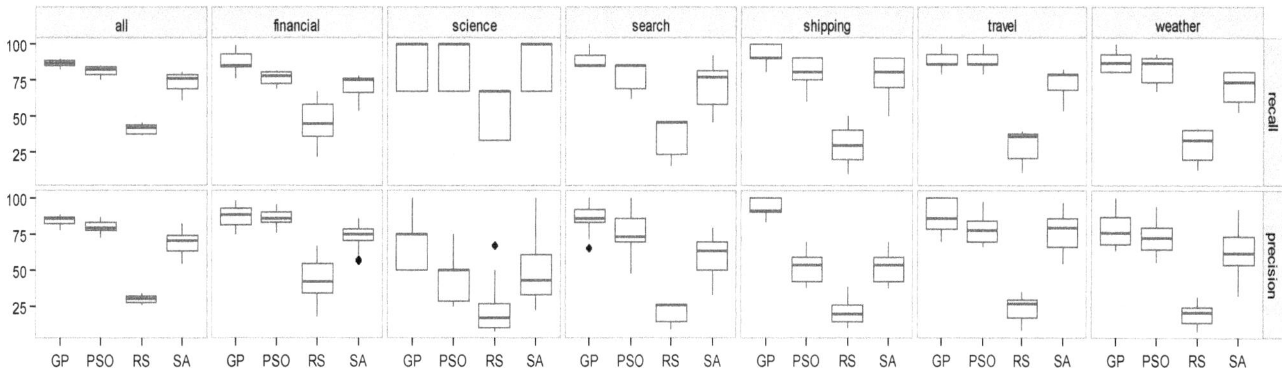

Figure 3. Boxplots for the obtained detection results in terms of recall and precision, for each Web service category, and for each search algorithm GP, PSO, SA and RA.

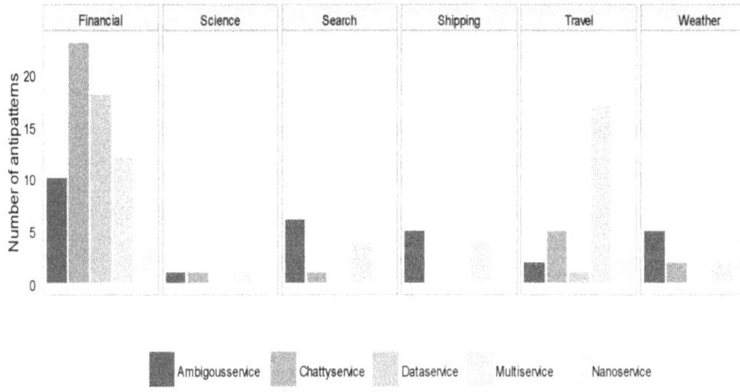

Figure 4. Antipatterns distribution for each category.

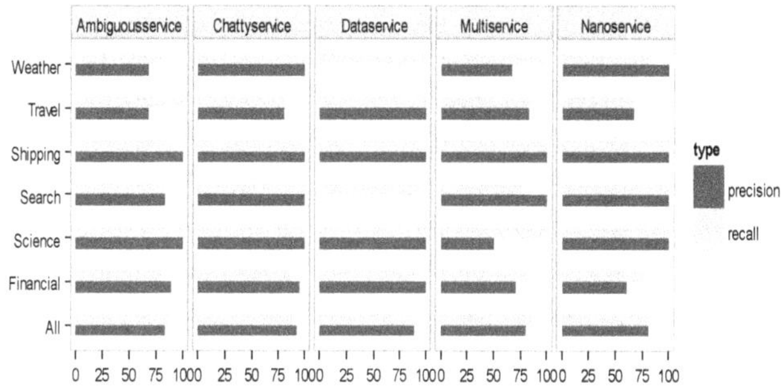

Figure 5. Detection results for each antipattern type.

limits the performance of our approach in well detecting these types of antipatterns. Thus, we can conclude that our GP-based approach detects well all types of the considered antipatterns (RQ3).

Furthermore, it is important to evaluate the scalability of the performance of our approach, as scalability is widely considered as one of the key issues for software engineering research and development. To evaluate scalability of our approach for services of increasing size, we executed our approach on the six categories of services. Figure 6 illustrates the evolution of precision, recall and CPU time with respect to the increase of service size (in terms of number of operations). We see from this figure that the precision and recall values are relatively stable (between [75, 90]) even if the services size increases. The same observation could be seen for CPU time which is between [224, 241] seconds. We can say that our approach is scalable with respect to service size since it gives high precision and recall values, and acceptable execution time.

5. THREATS TO VALIDITY

In our study, external threat to validity may arise because, although we considered five types of Web service antipatterns, we did not evaluate the detection of other antipattern types. In addition, we validated our approach on SOAP Web services; and we cannot generalize our results to other technologies such as REST. In future work, we plan to evaluate the performance of our approach to detect other types of antipatterns, and other SOA technologies.

Construct threats to validity can be related to the set of used metrics, and the corpus of antipattern examples as developers may not all agree if a candidate Web services is an antipattern or not according to their level of expertise on antipatterns. Since we are the first to address this problem for automating the detection of web service antipatterns, there is no currently established state of the art in terms of automated detection. We also found few literature to guide us on what we should consider to inspect Web service antipatterns [9] [16] [10]. In future work, we will consider more static and dynamic Web service metrics, and ask some new experts to extend the existing corpus and provide additional feedback.

6. RELATED WORK

Detecting and specifying antipatterns in SOA and Web service is relatively a new field. Only few works have addressed the problem of SOA antipatterns. The first book in the literature was written by Dudney et al. [16] where a set of Web service antipatterns have been informally defined. Recently, a new book [3] have been written to describe the symptoms of some other SOA antipatterns. Furthermore, Král et al. [14] listed seven "popular" SOA antipatterns that violate SOA principles. In addition, some few research works have addressed the detection of such antipatterns. Recently, Palma et al. [10] have proposed an approach to detect Web service antipatterns. The proposed approach relies on declarative rule specification using domain-specific language (DSL) to specify/identify the key symptoms that characterize an antipattern. Similarly, Moha et al. [19] have proposed a rule-based approach called SODA for SCA systems (Service Component Architecture). However, unlike our approach, in an exhaustive scenario, the number of possible antipatterns to manually characterize with rules can be very large; and rules that are expressed in terms of metric combinations need substantial calibration efforts to find the right threshold value for each metric. In another study, Rodriguez et al. [2] [9] [17] provided a set of guidelines for service providers to avoid bad practices while writing WSDLs. Based on some heuristics, the authors detected eight bad practices in the writing of WSDL for Web services.

Unlike service-oriented systems, there is an extensive research effort on detecting object oriented antipatterns and code-smells [6] [29] [7] [8]. For instance, Marinescu el al. [29] have proposed a mechanism called "detection strategy" OO code-smells by formulating metric-based rules that capture deviations from good

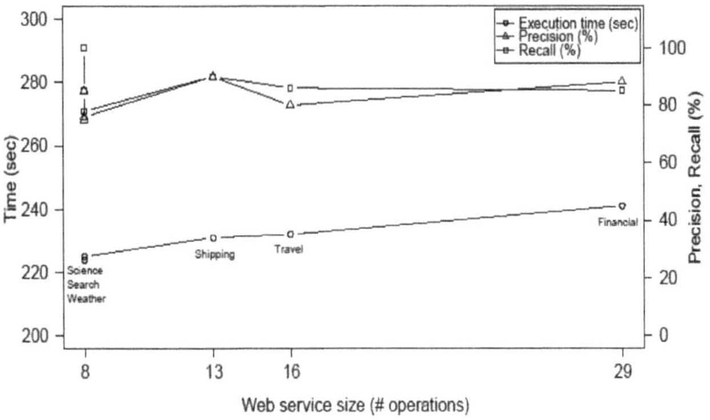

Figure 6. Scalability with respect to Web service size.

design principles and heuristics. Ouni et al. [7] proposed a search-based approach to detect code-smells in OO software systems. However, OO antipatterns detection techniques are not applicable in the context of Web services as we deal with different level of granularity (service vs class levels), and different metrics. Furthermore, unlike OO systems, Web service source code is not publicly available; that is only WSDL interfaces are available for clients. This makes the detection of such antipatterns harder.

7. CONCLUSIONS AND FUTURE WORK

In this paper, we introduced a new search-based approach for Web service antipatterns detection. In our GP adaptation, detection rules are represented as a combination of metrics and threshold values that should detect as much as possible the number of antipatterns from a base of examples. The statistical analysis of the obtained results provides compelling evidence that GP outperforms particle swarm optimization, simulated annealing as well as random search based on a benchmark of 310 Web services including 136 real-world antipattern instances. As future work, we plan to validate our approach with additional antipattern types, and SOAP static and dynamic metrics in order to conclude about the general applicability of our methodology. Another research direction worth to explore is to consider both bad and good Web service instances to deduce antipattern detection rules, i.e., good detection rules should maximize the distance with well-designed Web services while minimizing the distance with badly-designed ones. Furthermore, in this paper, as we mainly focus on the detection of Web service antipatterns, we are planning to extend the approach by automating their correction using SBSE.

Acknowledgments. This work is supported by Japan Society for the Promotion of Science, Grant-in-Aid for Scientific Research (S) (No.25220003), and also by Osaka University Program for Promoting International Joint Research.

8. REFERENCES

[1] M. P. Singh and M. N. Huhns, *Service-oriented computing - semantics, processes, agents*: Wiley, 2005.

[2] J. Rodriguez, M. Crasso, C. Mateos, A. Zunino, "Best practices for des-cribing, consuming, and discovering web services: a comprehensive to-olset," *Software: Practice and Experience,* vol. 43, pp. 613-639, 2013.

[3] A. Rotem-Gal-Oz, *SOA Patterns*: Manning Publications, 2012.

[4] J. Král M. Žemlička, "Crucial Service-Oriented Antipatterns," *Int. Journal On Advances in Software,* vol. 2, pp. 160-171, 2009.

[5] J. L. O. Coscia, M. Crasso, C. Mateos, and A. Zunino, "Estimating Web Service interface quality through conventional object-oriented metrics," *CLEI Electron. J.,* vol. 16, 2013.

[6] N. Moha, G. Yann-Gaël, L. Duchien, A. Le Meur, "DECOR: A Method for the Specification and Detection of Code and Design Smells," *Software Engineering, IEEE Transactions on,* vol. 36, 2010.

[7] A. Ouni, M. Kessentini, H. Sahraoui, and M. Boukadoum, "Maintainability defects detection and correction: a multi-objective approach," *Automated Software Engineering,* vol. 20, pp. 47-79, 2013.

[8] W. Kessentini, M. Kessentini, H. Sahraoui, S. Bechikh, and A. Ouni, "A Cooperative Parallel Search-Based Software Engineering Approach for Code-Smells Detection," *Software Engineering, IEEE Transactions on,* vol. 40, pp. 841-861, 2014.

[9] C. Mateos, M. Crasso, A. Zunino, J. L. O. Coscia, "Avoiding WSDL Bad Practices in Code-First Web Services," *SADIO Electronic Journal of Informatics and Operational Research,* vol. 11, pp. 31-48, 2012.

[10] F. Palma, N. Moha, G. Tremblay, and Y.-G. Guéhéneuc, "Specification and Detection of SOA Antipatterns in Web Services," in *Software Architecture*. vol. 8627, P. Avgeriou and U. Zdun, Eds., ed: Springer International Publishing, pp. 58-73, 2014.

[11] M. zur Muehlen, J. V. Nickerson, and K. D. Swenson, "Developing web services choreography standards - the case of REST vs. SOAP," *Decision Support Systems,* vol. 40, pp. 9-29, 2005.

[12] R. Chinnici, J.-J. Moreau, A. Ryman, and S. Weerawarana, "Web services description language (wsdl) version 2.0 part 1: Core language," *W3C recommendation,* vol. 26, p. 19, 2007.

[13] M. Mäntylä and C. Lassenius, "Subjective evaluation of software evolvability using code smells: An empirical study," *Empirical Software Engineering,* vol. 11, pp. 395-431, 2006.

[14] J. Král M. Zemlicka, "Popular SOA Antipatterns," in *Future Computi-ng, Service Computation, Cognitive, Adaptive, Content, Patterns.. Computation World:,* 2009, pp. 271-276.

[15] J. Krai and M. Zemlicka, "The Most Important Service-Oriented Antipatterns," in *Software Engineering Advances, 2007. ICSEA 2007. International Conference on,* 2007.

[16] B. Dudney, J. Krozak, K. Wittkopf, S. Asbury, and D. Osborne, *J2EE Antipatterns*: John Wiley; Sons, Inc., 2003.

[17] J. M. Rodriguez, M. Crasso, A. Zunino, and M. Campo, "Automatically detecting opportunities for web service descriptions improvement," in *Software Services for e-World,* ed: Springer, pp. 139-150, 2010.

[18] M. Nayrolles, F. Palma, N. Moha, and Y.-G. Guéhéneuc, "Soda: A Tool Support for the Detection of SOA Antipatterns," in *Service-Oriented Computing - ICSOC 2012 Workshops*. vol. 7759, A. Ghose, H. Zhu, Q. Yu, A. Delis, Q. Sheng, O. Perrin, *et al.*, Eds., ed: Springer Berlin Heidelberg, pp. 451-455, 2013.

[19] N. Moha, F. Palma, M. Nayrolles, B. Conseil, Y.-G. Guéhéneuc, B. Baudry, "Specification and Detection of SOA Antipatterns," in *Service-Oriented Computing*. vol. 7636, C. Liu, H. Ludwig, F. Toumani, and Q. Yu, Eds.,Springer Berlin Heidelberg, pp. 1-16, 2012.

[20] J. R. Koza, *Genetic programming: on the programming of computers by means of natural selection*: MIT Press, 1992.

[21] P. Mikhail, R. Caspar, and T. Zahir, "The Impact of Service Cohesion on the Analyzability of Service-Oriented Software," *IEEE Transactions on Services Computing,* vol. 3, pp. 89-103, 2010.

[22] M. Harman, P. McMinn, J. de Souza, and S. Yoo, "Search Based Software Engineering: Techniques, Taxonomy, Tutorial," in *Empirical Software Engineering and Verification*. vol. 7007, B. Meyer and M. Nordio, Eds., ed: Springer Berlin Heidelberg, , 2012.

[23] M. Harman and B. F. Jones, "Search-based software engineering," *Information and Software Technology,* vol. 43, pp. 833-839, 2001.

[24] D. C. Karnopp, "Random search techniques for optimization problems," *Automatica,* vol. 1, pp. 111-121, 1963.

[25] J. Kennedy and R. Eberhart, "Particle swarm optimization," in *Neural Networks, 1995. Proceedings., IEEE International Conference on,* , pp. 1942-1948, vol.4, 1995.

[26] S. Kirkpatrick, C. D. Gelatt, and M. P. Vecchi, "Optimization by Simulated Annealing," *Science,* vol. 220, pp. 671-680, 1983.

[27] J. Cohen, *Statistical power analysis for the behavioral sciences*, 2nd ed.: Lawrence Erlbaum Associates, Inc, 1988.

[28] A. E. Eiben and S. K. Smit, "Parameter tuning for configuring and analyzing evolutionary algorithms," *Swarm and Evolutionary Computation,* vol. 1, pp. 19-31, 2011.

[29] R. Marinescu, "Detection strategies: metrics-based rules for detecting design flaws," in *Software Maintenance, 2004. Proceedings. 20th IEEE International Conference on,* , pp. 350-359, 2004.

Heuristic Model Checking using a Monte-Carlo Tree Search Algorithm

Simon Poulding
Software Engineering Research Laboratory
Blekinge Institute of Technology
SE-371 79 Karlskrona, Sweden
simon.poulding@bth.se

Robert Feldt
Software Engineering Research Laboratory
Blekinge Institute of Technology
SE-371 79 Karlskrona, Sweden
robert.feldt@bth.se

ABSTRACT

Monte-Carlo Tree Search algorithms have proven extremely effective at playing games that were once thought to be difficult for AI techniques owing to the very large number of possible game states. The key feature of these algorithms is that rather than exhaustively searching game states, the algorithm navigates the tree using information returned from a relatively small number of random game simulations. A practical limitation of software model checking is the very large number of states that a model can take. Motivated by an analogy between exploring game states and checking model states, we propose that Monte-Carlo Tree Search algorithms might also be applied in this domain to efficiently navigate the model state space with the objective of finding counterexamples which correspond to potential software faults. We describe such an approach based on Nested Monte-Carlo Search—a tree search algorithm applicable to single player games—and compare its efficiency to traditional heuristic search algorithms when using Java PathFinder to locate deadlocks in 12 Java programs.

Categories and Subject Descriptors

D.2.5 [**Software Engineering**]: Model Checking; G.1.6 [**Numerical Analysis**]: Optimization; E.1 [**Data**]: Data Structures; I.6.8 [**Simulation and Modelling**]: Monte-Carlo

Keywords

Model Checking; Monte-Carlo Tree Search; Search-Based Software Engineering

1. INTRODUCTION

Model checking represents software as an abstract model, and explores the states of this model to verify properties of the software [4]. However there may be too many states, particularly in concurrent software, to feasibly check all of the states; a more realistic objective may be to efficiently locate counterexamples—states within the model at which desirable properties are violated—using a heuristic to guide the search.

In this paper we propose the use of a Monte-Carlo Tree Search (MCTS) algorithm called Nested Monte-Carlo Search (NMCS) [3] as a heuristic search method for model checking. Our motivation is that MCTS algorithms have shown great success in playing games, such as Go, which are thought to be particularly difficult problems for AI techniques to solve [2]. Our objective is to improve the time efficiency of heuristic search in model checking, i.e. the time required to find a counterexample state.

We propose an extension to the NMCS algorithm when it used for heuristic model checking: a parameter controlling the length of the random simulations it uses to choose which state to move to next. Our rationale is that the path to a terminal state in the model may be so long that performing simulation until such a state is reached could lead to a computationally inefficient algorithm. The effect of the parameter is investigated by locating deadlocks in 12 Java programs from the Software-artifact Infrastructure Repository, and comparing the time and space efficiency of NMCS to the out-of-box heuristic search algorithms that ship with Java PathFinder (JPF). The results provide compelling evidence of the potentially superior efficiency of NMCS when the length of the random simulation is set appropriately.

Section 2 provides an overview of model checking using heuristic search and describes the standard NMCS algorithm. In Section 3, we propose how NMCS could be used for model checking and identify the need for the parameter controlling the length of random simulations. The proposed algorithm is investigated empirically in Section 4. We relate this paper to existing work in Section 5, and summarise our conclusions in Section 6.

2. BACKGROUND

2.1 Model Checking

Model checking is a technique for verifying properties of the software. Often it is a static technique that builds an abstract model of the software, although Java PathFinder (JPF), the model checker used in the empirical investigation of this paper, builds the model by dynamically executing the software. The model is typically a directed graph, where each node represents a state of the software and edges represent possible transitions between the states.

A state is characterised by the current point of execution and the values of the program's data. When the software is

GECCO '15, July 11 - 15, 2015, Madrid, Spain
© 2015 ACM. ISBN 978-1-4503-3472-3/15/07...$15.00
DOI: http://dx.doi.org/10.1145/2739480.2754767

concurrent, the state is additionally characterised by which thread is currently active. One of the particular advantages of model checking as a verification technique for concurrent software is that it can consider all possible interleaving of threads in contrast to dynamic testing during which there may be no method to control thread interleavings.

Model checking can be used to verify that desirable properties hold for every state of the software; for example, the absence of deadlocks and race conditions in concurrent software. However the number of states in the model may be so large that such an exhaustive check of each state is infeasible. Instead the approach taken may instead be to efficiently locate counterexamples: states at which the desirable property is violated.

2.2 Heuristic Search

One approach for finding counterexamples efficiently, i.e. by visiting as few states as possible, is to use a suitable heuristic to guide the exploration of states in the model [7]. A heuristic in this context is a function that maps a state to a numeric value that quantifies how close a state is to violating the desired property and so being a counterexample. This has obvious similarities to the fitness function used in metaheuristic techniques and, indeed, in this paper, we interpret the exploration of a model for counterexamples as sharing many characteristics with metaheuristic search on a fitness landscape.

Best-first search is an example of heuristic search. Starting from a root state, each of the state's children is considered and the heuristic calculated for each. These child states are added to a queue. The state with the best heuristic value is then retrieved from the queue and similarly explored: each of its child states are considered and the heuristic is calculated. The search proceeds in this manner until a counterexample is found or no more states can be reached.

2.3 Nested Monte-Carlo Search

Monte-Carlo Tree Search (MCTS) methods are machine learning algorithms that derive a path through a tree, where each node represents a decision to be made. They have demonstrated significant success in the domain of automated game playing, and in this context, the tree is a game tree in which nodes represent game states, and the decision to be made is which action to take at each turn in order to improve the computer's ability to win the game. Browne et al. provide a detailed survey of the current state-of-the-art in MCTS and, in particular, the application of these methods to game playing [2].

The key feature of MCTS methods are that at each node in the tree, the possible decisions are assessed by making a small number of random simulations of future game play from the current state to a state at which the game ends. The premise is that although a small sample of random simulation will provide a noisy signal as to which move to take, there is nonetheless sufficient signal that over a series of moves the computer's game play is effective, and the use of a small set of simulations is much more efficient than an exhaustive exploration of the game tree.

In this work we propose the use of Nested Monte-Carlo Search (NMCS), a variant of MCTS described by Cazenave for the purpose of playing single-player games [3]. To decide which move to take at the current game state, NMCS makes one simulation for each of the possible moves. The simulation starts by making that move and then proceeds by random moves until the simulated game comes to an end, at which point the end state is assessed by a reward function. The simulation that returns the best reward determines the move that is taken, or, if no simulation is better than the simulation that led to the current game state, the move is determined by that earlier simulation.

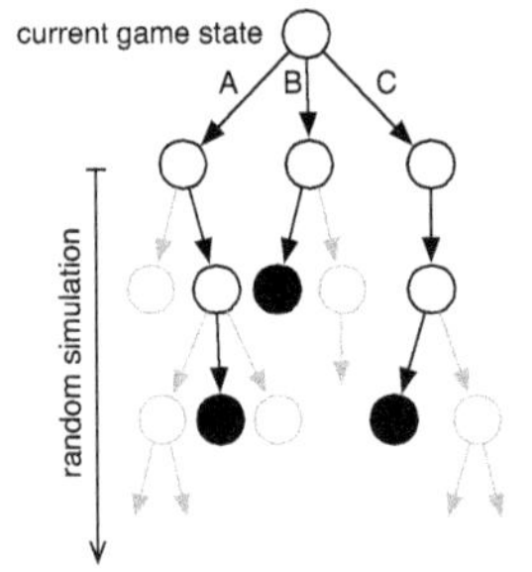

Figure 1: NMCS applied to a game tree

Figure 1 illustrates the algorithm for a game state with three possible moves, A, B, and C. A random simulation (represented by the black arrows) is run from each of the moves until an end state (indicated by a filled node) is reached where no further moves are possible. The reward function is measured at the end states, and whichever of A, B, and C leads to the end state with the best reward (say, C) is the move that is taken. The algorithm is then applied again at the new node reached when the move C is taken.

Instead of random simulation, the algorithm may instead use NMCS itself to determine the moves to make during simulation. This is the nested aspect of the algorithm, and a parameter—the nesting level taking integer settings of 1 or greater—controls the degree of nesting.

3. PROPOSED ALGORITHM

Our proposal is to apply a form of NMCS as heuristic search method in model checking. Our hypothesis is that we may realise, for model checking, the same efficacy and efficiency of Monte-Carlo Tree Search methods that is exhibited in the context of automated game play.

The transfer of NMCS to the domain of model checking is, for the most part, straightforward: states in the model are equivalent to states in the game tree, and the model-checking heuristic function is equivalent to the game-playing reward function. However, a complication arises with the stopping criterion for the simulations. In game playing, the simulation continues until no further moves are possible (one of the players has won, or a stalemate has been reached). In model checking, following a path of model states until an end node is reached may not be practical. Not only can the model be extremely large, but is often a graph rather than a tree: many cycles in the graph may require an extremely long path if an end state is to be reached.

For this reason, we introduce a new parameter to the form of NMCS used in this work: the *simulation depth*. This parameter limits the length of the path that is followed during a simulation. The heuristic is measured at the state when this limit is reached (or at an end state if one is reached before the limit). Figure 2 describes the proposed NMCS algorithm using pseudo-code.

```
function nmcs(state, nestingLevel, simDepth,
                currentLevel:=nestingLevel)
  chosenPath := empty sequence
  bestValue := -infinity
  bestPath := empty sequence
  depth = 0
  while state is not terminal and
    (currentLevel == nestingLevel or depth < simDepth)
    for each move possible from state
      state' := apply move to state
      if currentLevel == 1
        (value, path) := simulate(state', simDepth)
      else
        (value, path) := nmcs(state', nestingLevel,
                              simDepth, currentLevel-1)
      end
    end
    highValue := highest value of the moves from state
    if highValue > bestValue
      bestValue := highValue
      chosenMove := move associated with highValue
      bestPath := path associated with highValue
    else
      chosenMove := first move in bestPath
      bestPath := remove first move from bestPath
    end
    state := apply chosenMove to state
    depth := depth + 1
    chosenPath := append chosenMove to chosenPath
  end
  return (bestValue, chosenPath)

function simulate(state, simDepth)
  chosenPath := empty sequence
  depth = 0
  while state is not terminal and depth < simDepth
    pick chosenMove from state at random
    state := apply chosenMove to state
    depth := depth + 1
    chosenPath := append chosenMove to chosenPath
  end
  value := heuristic(state)
  return (value, chosenPath)
```

Figure 2: The Nested Monte-Carlo Search algorithm, adapted from [3], and extended with a limit on simulation depth

4. EMPIRICAL INVESTIGATION

4.1 Research Questions

The objective of the empirical investigation is to assess the efficiency of our proposed NMCS algorithm for model checking in comparison to the other heuristic algorithms. We use Java PathFinder (JPF) as the model checker for these experiments, and for this reason the comparison are against the best-first search and beam search algorithms supplied with JPF.

We consider three aspects of efficiency. Firstly, the proportion of algorithm trials—the success rate—during which a counterexample state is found. Secondly, the time taken to find a counterexample. The time is measured in two ways: (a) the number of states visited by the algorithm, and, (b) the elapsed wall-clock time. The difference between the two is that the number of visited states is independent of the performance of algorithm's implementation. Thirdly, the space required by an algorithm trial, measured as the maximum memory consumption reported by JPF.

The research questions we seek to answer are:

RQ1 To what extent does the efficiency of NMCS depend on the setting of the simulation depth parameter?

RQ2 How does efficiency of NMCS compare to JPF's best-first and beam search algorithms?

4.2 Java PathFinder

Java PathFinder (JPF) differs from most model checking tools in that it dynamically executes Java bytecode rather than an abstract model of the software [12]. JPF is, in essence, a Java virtual machine (itself written in Java) and this enables JPF to control and measure many aspects of software's execution. In particular, it can enumerate and control the choices made at non-deterministic points in the program, such as the generation of pseudo-random numbers and—most importantly for the experiments here—the interleaving of separate threads in concurrent program. The degree control of JPF exerts over the interleaving of threads is not available when using a standard Java virtual machine, and thus JPF is particularly useful in finding potential faults in concurrent programs.

JPF ships with a number of search algorithms, such as depth-first search, breadth-first search, and heuristic search. The default heuristic search algoritm, implemented as the `SimplePriorityHeuristic` class, is a form of breadth-first search of the type described above in Section 2.2. A priority queue (which, by default, has a maximum size of 1024 entries) is maintained of all the states visited so far, and the state with the best heuristic is explored next by calculating the heuristic value at each of its child state. These states are added to the priority queue, and then again the state with the best heuristic is explored; this need not be one of the children of the state just explored. The exploration process continues until there are no further states to explore.

This search can be modified, using the parameter setting `search.heuristic.beam_search=true`, to a form of beam search. The effect of this setting is to clear the priority queue each time a new state is chosen to explore, and this guarantees that the next state explored *is* one of the children of the state just explored. The exploration process continues until the current state has no children, which indicates either the end of program, or a deadlock condition.

JPF is highly extensible through mechanisms such as class inheritance and specifying call-back listeners when specific event occurs during the execution of the program. It is the former mechanism we use to implement Nested-Monte Carlo Search in the form of a new class `NMCSSearch` that inherits from the base `Search` class.

4.3 Software-Under-Test

In the following experiments the counterexample that is sought is a deadlock, i.e. a state in which no thread is able to proceed since it is waiting on one or more other threads.

The SUTs are taken from the Software-artifact Infrastructure Repository at the University of Nebraska-Lincoln [5]. The repository includes a number of Java SUTs with seeded concurrency faults and that may be run using JPF. For the experiments we select those SUTs from the repository where the only seeded concurrency fault is a deadlock.

We exclude one of the SUTs, `pool5`, since it raises a `NoSuchElementException` exception rather than a deadlock in our execution environment. We exclude a further SUT, piper, because it consistently exhausts the memory when using best-first search, and so would limit the quantitative comparisons that would be possible against the remaining algorithms. This leaves 12 SUTs, the names of which are listed in the first column of table 2. All the SUTs were executed with the input arguments used in the JPF scripts provided by the repository.

4.4 Heuristic

The 'most blocked' heuristic is used to guide the search for deadlocks, and is calculated as:

$$h_{\text{mostblocked}} = N_{\text{alive}} - N_{\text{runnable}} \tag{1}$$

where N_{alive} and N_{runnable} are the numbers of threads that have not finished ('alive') and that are currently available to execute ('runnable'), respectively. The higher the value of $h_{\text{mostblocked}}$, the more threads are prevented from executing ('blocked'), and thus the closer the state is to being a deadlock.

We choose this heuristic since it is used commonly in model checking for this purpose, and because JPF includes it as an example heuristic. For NMCS we utilise the same code to calculate this heuristic as does the 'out-of-the-box' JPF implementation in the class `MostBlocked`.

4.5 Method

The search algorithms evaluated in the experiment are:

- The JPF implementation of best-first search. This algorothm is labelled 'B-F' in the results below.
- The JPF implementation described as beam search. This algorithm is labelled 'Beam' in the results.
- Our proposed NMCS algorithm. Since this algorithm has two parameters—the nesting level and simulation depth—we considered 10 different parameter combination. All had the nesting level set to 1, and the simulation depth set to powers of 2 between 1 and 512. (We have experimented with different nesting levels, but for clarity and brevity, we report here only the experiments at nesting level 1 as algorithm with this parameter setting typically demonstrated the best efficiency.) These ten algorithm variants are labelled 'N1,*d*', where *d* is the simulation depth, in the results.

For each combination of SUT and search algorithm, 30 trials of the algorithm were run. Since all the search algorithms considered here are stochastic, each trial used a different sequence of pseudo-random numbers by means of the JPF parameter setting `cg.randomize_choices=VAR_SEED`. These 30 trials will therefore provide a more accurate estimate of each algorithm's *average* efficiency.

For each trial, the following responses were recorded from statistics provided by JPF:

- Whether or not a deadlock state was found.
- The number of states visited. We calculate this as the sum of the JPF counts of 'new', 'visited', and 'end' states. Therefore it is not necessarily the number of unique states visited, but instead is the number of transitions to new states made by JPF that require a decision by the search process. This value is used as a metric because it is indicative of how much of the search space that algorithm has had to explore to find a counterexample, and in JPF transitioning to states is a computationally expensive action.
- The elapsed (wall-clock) time taken (JPF records this to the nearest second).
- the maximum amount of memory consumed by JPF.

The experiments were run on a mid-2013 MacBook Air 13" which had a 1.3GHz Intel Core i5 CPU, and 8 GB of 1600 MHz DDR3 memory. The operating system was OS X 10.10.2. Java PathFinder was version 7.0 (rev 1225), and the JRE was Oracle Java 1.7.0_40.

4.6 Results and Analysis

4.6.1 Success Rate

We define success rate as the proportion of the JPF trials that found a deadlock state. In table 1, we present this result for each combination of algorithm and SUT: the figure is therefore the proportion of the 30 trials for each algorithm / SUT combination that was successful (rounded to 3 significant figures).

The final row, labelled 'Average (Arith. Mean)', is average success rate of each algorithm considered over all 12 SUTs, and is calculated using the arithmetic mean.

These results are consistent with the nature of the algorithms. Best-first search is an exhaustive algorithm: each state is explored until a deadlock is found or there are no more states to explore. Thus for these SUTs which have seeded deadlocks, all trials would be expected to be successful. In contrast, both Beam Search and NMCS take a single path to an end state, the choice of nodes on the path being informed by the heuristic. The end state need not be a deadlock—it might also be the end of the program—and thus there is not reason to expect a success rate of 1 for these two algorithms.

We make no further comment here on these results since the success rate is not an efficiency metric that we consider in isolation. Instead we use it to adjust the time efficiency metrics so that we can compare the algorithms in a consistent manner; this process is described in the following section.

4.6.2 Time Efficiency

In practice, a tester would run repeated trials of the algorithm until a deadlock were found. In order to compare algorithms in terms of the time efficiency, we therefore calculate the average *total* time required to a deadlock, i.e. across the multiple trials of the algorithm that the tester may need to perform. We calculate this total time by combining the raw time data with the success rates shown in table 1 as follows.

If the success rate is ρ, then the average *total* time taken, i.e. over multiple failed and one successful trial, to find the deadlock, $\bar{t}_*$, is:

$$\bar{t}_* = \frac{(1-\rho)}{\rho}\bar{t}_- + \bar{t}_+ \tag{2}$$

where $\bar{t}_+$ and $\bar{t}_-$ are the average times of failed and successful trials respectively. The factor $1 - \rho/\rho$ arises since this process is a sequence of independent Bernoulli trials and so the number of failed trials until a success has a Geometric distribution with its mean given by this factor.

The average time of a successful trial, $\bar{t}_+$ is calculated as:

$$\bar{t}_+ = \frac{1}{\rho M} \sum_{i \in I_+} t_i \tag{3}$$

where t_i are times observed for the M trials—both failed and successful—and I_+ is the set of indices, i, for successful trials. The denominator is ρM since, from the definition of ρ this must be the number of successful trial and thus the size of the set I_+. (Here, $M = 30$ for each algorithm / SUT combination.)

Similarly, $\bar{t}_-$ is calculated as:

$$\bar{t}_- = \frac{1}{(1-\rho)M} \sum_{i \in I_-} t_i \tag{4}$$

Substituting for $\bar{t}_+$ and $\bar{t}_-$ in (2) gives:

$$\begin{aligned}\bar{t}_* &= \frac{(1-\rho)}{\rho} \cdot \frac{1}{(1-\rho)M} \sum_{i \in I_-} t_i + \frac{1}{\rho M} \sum_{i \in I_+} t_i \\ &= \frac{1}{\rho M} \left(\sum_{i \in I_-} t_i + \sum_{i \in I_+} t_i \right) \\ &= \frac{1}{M} \sum_i \frac{t_i}{\rho} \end{aligned} \tag{5}$$

This final equation shows if we *adjust* all observed times for an algorithm / SUT combination by dividing by the success rate of that combination, then the arithmetic mean of these adjusted times will be the average *total* time taken, $\bar{t}_*$, which is our desired metric.

We perform this adjustment for both the number of visited states reported in Table 2, and for the elapsed time reported in Table 3 [1]. In both tables, lower values—fewer states visited or shorter elapsed times—are indicative of better time efficiency. If no adjustment is possible because none of the 30 trials were successful (i.e., $\rho = 0$), we set the number visited states and elapsed time to arbitrarily high values of 10^7 states and 1000 seconds, respectively.

In these tables, the row labelled 'Average (Geom. Mean)' is a measure of the average time efficiency of the algorithm across all 12 SUTs. Since the values vary by orders of magnitude between SUTs, we calculate this average by the following process using the geometric mean. For each i, where i is the index of a trial in a SUT / algorithm combination ranging from 1 to 30, the geometric mean is calculated of the ith time responses across all 12 SUTs. The geometric mean of K values, $x_1, x_2, ..., x_K$, is:

$$\left(\prod_{j=1}^{K} x_j \right)^{\frac{1}{K}} \tag{6}$$

and thus, in contrast to the arithmetic mean, it considers multiplicative changes in the values: a change by any of the values by the same factor results the same changes in the geometric mean regardless of the magnitude of that value. Having calculated 30 geometric means in this way (one for each value of i) for the algorithm, the value reported for the algorithm in the row 'Average (Geom. Mean)' is the arithmetic mean of these 30 values.

[1] A dataset of the raw observations, including the unadjusted time data, is available from www.simonpoulding.net.

The sample of 30 geometric means for each algorithm is also the data summarised in the boxplots of Figures 3 and 4. One boxplot is shown for each of the algorithms, and summarises the distribution of the average performance of the algorithm across the 12 SUTs.

We discuss these results in section 4.7 below.

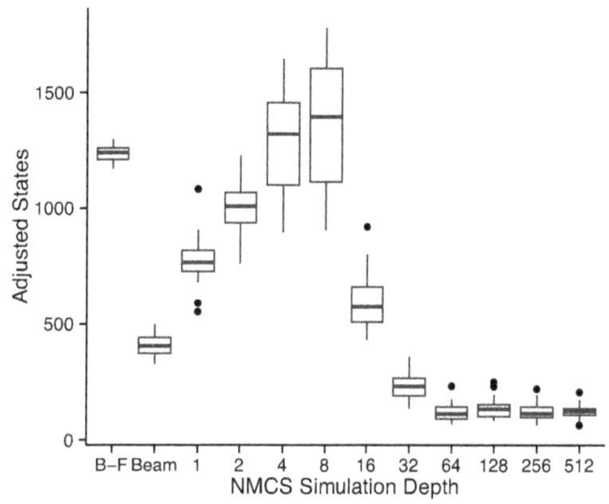

Figure 3: Boxplots of number of states visited (adjusted for success rate) for each algorithm, averaged across all SUTs

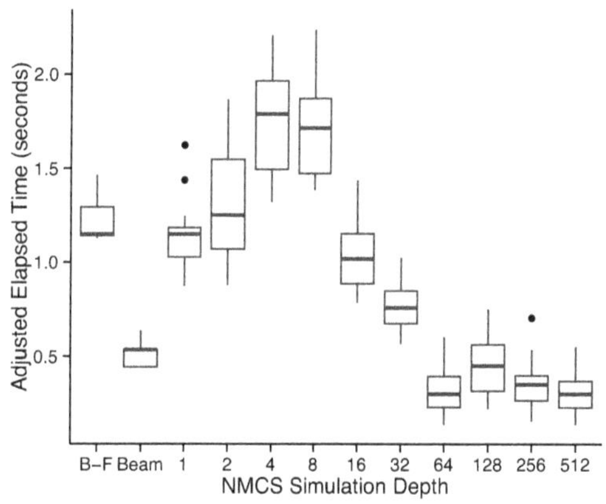

Figure 4: Boxplots of elapsed time in seconds (adjusted for success rate) for each algorithm, averaged across all SUTs

4.6.3 Space Efficiency

The space efficiency metric is the maximum memory consumed during a JPF trial. In table 4, the maximum value across the 30 trials in a SUT / algorithm combination is reported: lower values are better. The row 'Average (Geom. Mean)' summarises average memory usage of an algorithm across all 12 SUTs. It is calculated by forming a sample of 30 geometric means as for the time efficiency metrics, and then taking the maximum value. Figure 5 summarises the distribution of the average memory efficiency of each algorithm across the 12 SUTs.

SUT	B-F	Beam	N1,1	N1,2	N1,4	N1,8	N1,16	N1,32	N1,64	N1,128	N1,256	N1,512
boundedbuffer	1	1	1	1	1	1	1	1	1	1	1	1
clean	1	0.0667	0.1	0.1	0.367	0.5	0.467	0.7	0.7	0.6	0.633	0.533
deadlock	1	0.5	0.633	0.667	0.833	0.967	1	1	1	1	1	1
diningPhilosophers	1	1	1	1	1	1	1	1	1	1	1	1
groovy	1	0.333	0.533	0.467	0.567	0.5	0.9	1	1	1	1	1
log4j1	1	0.933	1	0.967	1	1	1	1	1	1	1	1
loseNotify	1	1	1	1	1	1	1	1	1	1	1	1
nestedmonitor	1	0.667	1	1	1	1	1	1	1	1	1	1
pool4	1	0.3	0.633	0.433	0.4	0.4	0.5	1	0.867	0.9	0.967	0.8
pool6	1	0.0333	0	0	0	0	0.0667	0.133	0.4	0.133	0.267	0.4
replicatedworkers	1	0	0.0667	0.133	0.0333	0.0667	0.1	0.2	1	1	1	1
sleepingBarber	1	1	1	1	1	1	1	1	1	1	1	1
Arithmetic Mean	1	0.569	0.664	0.647	0.683	0.703	0.753	0.836	0.914	0.886	0.906	0.894

Table 1: Mean success rate

SUT	B-F	Beam	N1,1	N1,2	N1,4	N1,8	N1,16	N1,32	N1,64	N1,128	N1,256	N1,512
boundedbuffer	235000	187	1240	1050	1600	3100	3540	3530	156	158	127	153
clean	79.8	4460	5580	8720	2850	3040	6360	4530	15600	25000	21600	31600
deadlock	262	62.9	94.8	125	140	123	35.8	40.7	49.3	38.7	37.7	34.8
diningPhilosoph'rs	969	95.5	177	229	356	466	407	100	51.1	61.8	59.5	62.7
groovy	243	236	155	263	336	581	282	45.6	50.6	43.5	39.8	50
log4j1	485	55.4	106	153	215	306	384	43.1	34.5	34.3	32.6	32.8
loseNotify	75.4	26.8	50.5	66.7	72.5	53.3	14.3	14.8	14.2	14.5	14	14.7
nestedmonitor	68.6	45.8	64.5	81.3	117	54.9	39.2	54.5	78.2	110	151	48
pool4	1020	390	182	436	769	1140	1020	106	588	410	160	750
pool6	13900	1470	1e+07	1e+07	1e+07	1e+07	11700	7870	1430	4220	2460	1410
replicatedwork'rs	545000	1e+07	56700	41900	278000	250000	308000	290000	3410	2760	2490	2970
sleepingBarber	590	72.5	140	201	289	409	346	29.5	27.6	27.8	28.1	28.1
Geometric Mean	1240	408	772	1010	1290	1350	601	231	119	136	119	124

Table 2: Mean number of states visited (adjusted for success rate)

SUT	B-F	Beam	N1,1	N1,2	N1,4	N1,8	N1,16	N1,32	N1,64	N1,128	N1,256	N1,512
boundedbuffer	23.7	0	0.667	0.833	0.967	1.13	1.43	1.83	0.0667	0.0333	0	0
clean	0	0	1.67	4.33	1.55	1	1.36	0.81	2.29	3.56	3.53	4.62
deadlock	0	0	0	0	0	0	0	0	0	0	0	0
diningPhilosophers	0.267	0	0	0	0	0.0333	0	0	0	0	0	0
groovy	0.0667	0	0	0.0714	0.176	0.0667	0	0	0	0	0	0
log4j1	1	0.536	0.833	1	1	1	1	0.433	0.433	0.867	0.233	0.0333
loseNotify	0	0	0	0	0	0	0	0	0	0	0	0
nestedmonitor	0.0333	0	0	0	0.0333	0	0	0	0.0667	0.1	0.167	0
pool4	1	0	0.0526	0.0769	0.583	1.08	1	0	0.231	0.148	0.0345	0.375
pool6	4	0	1000	1000	1000	1000	15	7.25	2	7	3.5	2.08
replicatedworkers	66.4	1000	43.5	25.5	129	78	69.3	54.3	6.2	5.27	4.93	5.5
sleepingBarber	1	0.333	0.133	0.233	1	1.43	0.967	1.23	0.1	0.1	0	0
Geometric Mean	1.2	0.521	1.17	1.29	1.76	1.72	1.05	0.768	0.322	0.45	0.341	0.307

Table 3: Mean elapsed time in seconds (adjusted for success rate)

SUT	B-F	Beam	N1,1	N1,2	N1,4	N1,8	N1,16	N1,32	N1,64	N1,128	N1,256	N1,512
boundedbuffer	603	123	370	156	156	225	226	156	156	123	123	123
clean	123	123	123	156	156	156	225	357	416	422	407	429
deadlock	123	123	123	123	123	123	123	123	123	123	123	123
diningPhilosophers	123	123	123	123	123	123	123	123	123	123	123	123
groovy	123	123	123	123	123	123	123	123	123	123	123	123
log4j1	156	123	123	123	123	123	123	123	123	123	123	123
loseNotify	123	123	123	123	123	123	123	123	123	123	123	123
nestedmonitor	123	123	123	123	123	123	123	123	123	442	304	123
pool4	156	123	123	123	123	123	123	123	156	156	123	156
pool6	370	123	123	123	123	123	123	123	123	123	123	123
replicatedworkers	967	123	457	481	466	476	533	544	889	910	864	910
sleepingBarber	123	123	123	123	123	123	123	123	123	123	123	123
Geometric Mean	189	123	150	140	143	147	152	153	163	161	169	161

Table 4: Maximum memory used in MB

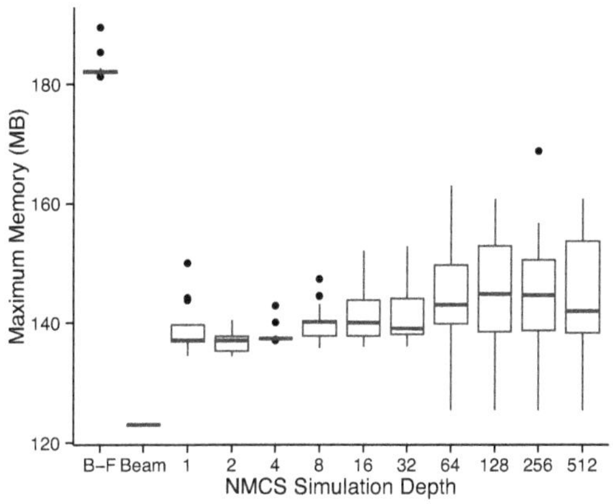

Figure 5: Boxplots of maximum memory used in MB for each algorithm, averaged across all SUTs

4.7 Discussion

4.7.1 RQ1: effect of simulation depth parameter

We first consider the NMCS algorithm time efficiencies, averaged across the SUTs. The number of visited states (Figure 3) shows a surprising pattern: as the NMCS simulation depth increases from 1 to 8, the number of states increases and therefore time efficiency become worse, but then rapidly improves as the simulation depth increases to 64. There is relatively little difference in the time efficiency using simulation depths of 64, 128, 256 and 512. A similar pattern for the elapsed time (Figure 4), showing that the pattern is not an artefact of our decision of how to calculate the number of visited states.

The implementation of beam search provided out-of-the-box by JPF might be thought of as NMCS with a simulation depth 0: the heuristic is calculated at the children of the state currently being explored with no simulation. We note, with interest, that with this interpretation of JPF's beam search, its time efficiency is consistent with the pattern seen for NMCS with simulation depth from 1 to 8.

Figure 3 and 4 demonstrate clearly that the simulation depth parameter has a very significant effect on the time efficiency. (For completeness: Kruskall-Wallis tests with the null hypothesis that the depth parameter has no effect on time efficiency gives p-values much less than 10^{-4} for both the number of visited states and the elapsed time.)

Table 4 shows that a similar pattern exists for each SUT individually. For some SUTs—such as `diningPhilosophers` and `loseNotify`—the deadlock can be found by visiting only a few tens of states, and therefore are often found during the first simulation by NMCS. The difference in time efficiency between, say, simulation depths of 8 and 64 is relatively small for these SUTs, but is still evident. However for SUTs for which the deadlock is much harder to find, the effect size is much greater. As an example, the deadlock in `replicatedworkers` is found by visiting approximately 73 times more states when the NMCS simulation depth is 8 than when it is 64.

Considering now the space efficiency in terms of the memory used by JPF, there is much less difference in the boxplots of Figure 5 for NMCS: the average memory used increases only slightly as the simulation depth increases, although at higher depth the spread of values of the distribution is larger. (A Kruskal-Wallis test here also gives a p-value much less than 10^{-4}.)

We conclude that the average time efficiency of NMCS depends on the simulation depth in a complex way: the best efficiency across these SUTs is achieved when the simulation depth is 64 or more. There is a much smaller effect of the simulation depth on space efficiency.

These experiments do not, by themselves, provide an explanation for the relationship between time efficiency and the NMCS simulation depth. The results in table 2 show that one contributing effect is that increasing the simulation depth increases the success rate, and so the total time required to find a deadlock—equation (2)—is reduced, but this is a trade-off since more states are visited when each simulation goes deeper.

For simpler SUTs such as `log4j1` and `losenotify`, it is apparent that the efficiency of NMCS at larger simulation depths is because deadlocks can be found easily once a certain depth is reached in the model. At these depths, the average number of states visited for these SUTs is less than the simulation depth and this suggests that a deadlock is typically found on the first random simulation to an appropriate depth. But this is not a general explanation. We performed an additional experiment using `replicatedworkers`—a more complex SUT where NMCS shows significant efficiency gains when the simulation depth increases to 64—that explored 10,000 random paths to depth 64. On none of these paths was a deadlock found, and so the efficiency of NMCS in this case is not because deadlocks are more easy to find at this depth.

4.7.2 RQ2: comparison to best-first & beam search

For RQ2, we compare the efficiency of NMCS with JPF's implementation of best-first search and beam search. To simplify the discussion, we make this comparison using the NMCS variant with a simulation depth of 64 as this gives close the best time efficiency across the 12 SUTs.

Figure 3 and Table 2 show that NMCS is significantly better than best-first search for most SUTs: the difference on average is a factor of approximately of 10.4 in terms of the number of visited states. (This difference is statistically significant: a Wilcoxon rank sum test gives a p-value of less than 10^{-4}.) We note that this difference is not true of all SUTs: for the SUT `clean`, best-first search is better than all variants of NMCS. Figure 4 and Table 3 show a qualitatively similar pattern in terms of elapsed time, although the pattern is more difficult to discern because JPF records elapsed time only to the nearest second and many trials finish in less than one second.

In general, JPF's beam search is much more time efficient than best-first search, but NMCS (again using simulation depth of 64 for this comparison) is still more time efficient by a factor of approximately 3.4 in terms of the number of visited states. (The difference is statistically significant according to a Wilcoxon rank sum test: the p-value is less than 10^{-4}.) A qualitatively similar pattern is seen in terms of elapsed time, but here NMCS is better by a factor of only approximately 1.6 (although again this figure may be unreliable owing to the reporting of elapsed time by JPF to only the nearest second).

Figure 5 and Table 4 shows that NMCS uses, on average, 25MB less memory than best-first search, but 40MB more memory than beam search, for the SUTs considered in these experiments. However, these differences have little practical impact given that JPF in this environment always used at least 123MB.

We conclude that, at the best settings of simulation depth, NMCS is more time efficient than both best-first search and beam search. It is less space efficient than beam search, but this difference has little practical difference.

5. RELATED WORK

We believe this work to be first application of Monte-Carlo Tree Search methods in model checking. However it is not the first application to software testing: Poulding and Feldt have recently used Nested Monte-Carlo Search to generate test data [9]. We note that in their application, it was not necessary to limit the depth of simulation: instead a limit was placed on the number of child states considered.

A number of researchers have applied metaheuristic search to the detection of concurrency bugs using model checking. For example, Godefroid and Khurshid [6], Alba et al. [1], and Shousha et al. [10] use evolutionary algorithms to construct a path that is then applied in the model in order to assess its fitness using the heuristic. In contrast, Staunton and Clark [11] use an Estimation of Distribution Algorithm to guide the selection of paths within the model itself; it is this work that is therefore closest to the approach taken in this paper.

6. CONCLUSION

In this paper we proposed the application of a Monte-Carlo Tree Search method, the Nested Monte-Carlo Search (NMCS) algorithm, as a heuristic search algorithm for model checking. We identified the need for an additional parameter to the standard NMCS algorithm to limit the length of the random simulations. We implemented the NMCS algorithm in Java PathFinder (JPF), and compared the time and space efficiency of the algorithm to JPF's best-first and beam search algorithms on 12 Java programs. The result showed that, on average, NMCS had superior time efficiency when the simulation depth was set to 64 or greater.

These results suggest a number of opportunities for further research.

Firstly, many of the SUTs used in the empirical work appear to be relatively simple: deadlocks could be found using most heuristic search algorithms in a few seconds. We wish to understand whether NMCS continues to demonstrate superior time efficiency for much larger models. The result provide some evidence that this might be case: the SUT `replicatedworkers` appears to be the most difficult for all of the algorithms, and for this SUT NMCS demonstrated a particularly large speed-up: approximately 160 times fewer states were visited by NMCS than by best-first search, and beam search never found a deadlock for this SUT.

Secondly, the best time efficiency for NMCS was achieved when the simulation depth parameter was 64 or greater. We intend to investigate whether the same limit is effective for a wider range of SUTs. One aspect of this investigation would be to investigate characteristics of the fitness landscape induced by the heuristic in the model, and whether the 'scale' of this landscape is related to the simulation depth.

Finally, we will investigate other model-checking heuristics. Although we have no reason to suspect that the NMCS algorithm is particularly suited to the 'most blocked' heuristics, we wish to replicate the results using other concurrency heuristics as well as structural metrics of type used by Groce and Visser in [8].

Acknowledgments

This work was funded by The Knowledge Foundation (KKS) through the project 20130085, Testing of Critical System Characteristics (TOCSYC).

7. REFERENCES

[1] E. Alba, F. Chicano, M. Ferreira, and J. Gomez-Pulido. Finding deadlocks in large concurrent Java programs using genetic algorithms. In *Proc. 10th Annual Conference on Genetic and Evolutionary Computation*, pages 1735–1742, 2008.

[2] C. Browne, E. Powley, D. Whitehouse, S. Lucas, P. Cowling, P. Rohlfshagen, S. Tavener, D. Perez, S. Samothrakis, and S. Colton. A survey of Monte Carlo tree search methods. *IEEE Trans. Computational Intelligence and AI in Games*, 4(1):1–43, 2012.

[3] T. Cazenave. Nested Monte-Carlo search. In *Proc. 21st Int'l Joint Conf. Artificial Intelligence (IJCAI)*, pages 456–461, 2009.

[4] E. M. Clarke, O. Grumberg, and D. Peled. *Model checking*. MIT press, 1999.

[5] H. Do, S. Elbaum, and G. Rothermel. Supporting controlled experimentation with testing techniques: An infrastructure and its potential impact. *Empirical Software Engineering*, 10(4):405–435, 2005.

[6] P. Godefroid and S. Khurshid. Exploring very large state spaces using genetic algorithms. In *Tools and Algorithms for the Construction and Analysis of Systems*, pages 266–280. Springer, 2002.

[7] A. Groce and W. Visser. Heuristic model checking for java programs. In *Model Checking Software*, pages 242–245. Springer, 2002.

[8] A. Groce and W. Visser. Model checking java programs using structural heuristics. In *ACM SIGSOFT Software Engineering Notes*, volume 27, pages 12–21. ACM, 2002.

[9] S. Poulding and R. Feldt. Generating structured test data with specific properties using Nested Monte-Carlo Search. In *Proceedings of the Genetic and Evolutionary Computation Conference (GECCO 2014)*, pages 1279–1286, 2014.

[10] M. Shousha, L. C. Briand, and Y. Labiche. A UML/MARTE model analysis method for uncovering scenarios leading to starvation and deadlocks in concurrent systems. *IEEE Transactions on Software Engineering*, 38(2):354–374, 2012.

[11] J. Staunton and J. A. Clark. Searching for safety violations using estimation of distribution algorithms. In *Proc. 3rd International Workshop on Search-Based Software Testing*, pages 212–221, 2010.

[12] W. Visser, C. S. Păsăreanu, and S. Khurshid. Test input generation with java pathfinder. *ACM SIGSOFT Software Engineering Notes*, 29(4):97–107, 2004.

Random or Genetic Algorithm Search for Object-Oriented Test Suite Generation?

Sina Shamshiri, José Miguel Rojas, Gordon Fraser, Phil McMinn
Department of Computer Science, University of Sheffield
Regent Court, 211 Portobello, Sheffield, UK, S1 4DP

ABSTRACT

Achieving high structural coverage is an important aim in software testing. Several search-based techniques have proved successful at automatically generating tests that achieve high coverage. However, despite the well-established arguments behind using evolutionary search algorithms (e.g., genetic algorithms) in preference to random search, it remains an open question whether the benefits can actually be observed in practice when generating unit test suites for object-oriented classes. In this paper, we report an empirical study on the effects of using a genetic algorithm (GA) to generate test suites over generating test suites incrementally with random search, by applying the EvoSuite unit test suite generator to 1,000 classes randomly selected from the SF110 corpus of open source projects. Surprisingly, the results show little difference between the coverage achieved by test suites generated with evolutionary search compared to those generated using random search. A detailed analysis reveals that the genetic algorithm covers more branches of the type where standard fitness functions provide guidance. In practice, however, we observed that the vast majority of branches in the analyzed projects provide no such guidance.

Categories and Subject Descriptors. D.2.5 [Software Engineering]: Testing and Debugging – *Testing Tools*;

Keywords. Automated Unit Test Generation; Random Testing; Genetic Algorithms; Search-Based Testing

1. INTRODUCTION

Automatically generating software test cases is an important task with the objective of improving software quality. Many different algorithms and techniques for different types of software testing problems have been proposed. One particular application area where search-based techniques have been successfully applied is the unit testing of object-oriented programs, where test cases are sequences of object constructor and method calls. There are various search-based tools available for languages such as Java and .NET, ranging from tools based on random search such as Randoop [21], JCrasher [5], JTExpert [23], NightHawk [2], T3 [22], or Yeti-Test [20], to tools based on evolutionary search such as EvoSuite [7], eToc [25] or Testful [4].

Although the tools based on evolutionary search techniques are commonly thought to be superior, it is unclear whether this is actually the case in practice. It could be that differences in performance across tools may be accounted for by the differences in the programming language that they target, or in the way they have been engineered, as opposed to any specific benefits of the particular search algorithm that they apply. In order to shed more light on these questions, in this paper we report on experiments to contrast the use of a genetic algorithm (GA) to optimize unit test suites for code coverage with an algorithm that optimizes code coverage by adding random tests to a test suite. Specifically, we make the following contributions in this study:

1. We report on the effectiveness of using a GA compared to an algorithm based on random search for the purpose of generating test suites with high branch coverage for object-oriented programs.
2. We investigate the influence of certain types of branches within the classes under test on the performance of each technique.
3. Finally, in order to better understand the effect of the search budget on the performance of each technique, we study the techniques' effectiveness at each time step during the search process.

To allow for a fair comparison, we use the GA and a common version of random test generation implemented in the same tool – EvoSuite, which generates branch covering test suites for Java classes. We run experiments on a random sample of 1,000 classes from the SF110 corpus of open source projects [11] and evaluate both techniques in terms of the achieved code coverage. Our results suggest that, in practice, there is little difference between the use of the GA and random search. While the two approaches have different performance profiles over time, the main reason for this finding is actually because of the types of branches that are prevalent in object-oriented programs. Fitness-guided searches like GAs work well when trying to cover branches that result in a smooth gradient of fitness values, which the search can "follow" to the required test case. These branches are typically characterized by numerical comparisons. However, our study found that in practice such "gradient branches" are relatively few in number; allowing random search to generate test cases without much relative disadvantage, and with a similar level of effectiveness.

GECCO '15, July 11 - 15, 2015, Madrid, Spain

ISBN 978-1-4503-3472-3/15/07... $15.00
DOI: http://dx.doi.org/10.1145/2739480.2754696

2. SEARCH-BASED TEST GENERATION

In this paper, we study the application of both random and GA search to automatic test suite generation, as implemented in the EvoSuite tool. EvoSuite aims to generate unit test suites that cover as many branches of a Java class as possible, while also executing all methods that are devoid of branches, referred to as "branchless" methods.

2.1 Random Search for Tests

One strategy for finding branch-covering test cases is simply to generate sequences of statements to the class under test at random, coupled with randomly-generated inputs. If a randomly-generated test case covers new branches that have not been executed before, it is added to a test suite for the class, else it can be discarded. One disadvantage of this approach is the size of the resulting test suite, which can be very large and therefore carry a high execution cost.

A further problem is finding inputs that need to be certain "magic" values required to execute certain branches, such as constant values, specific strings etc. that are unlikely to be generated fortuitously. One way of circumventing this problem is to enhance the algorithm through *seeding*.

2.1.1 *Seeding*

The process of *seeding* involves biasing the search process towards certain input values that are likely to improve the chances of executing more coverage goals [1,8,19]. EvoSuite obtains seeds both statically and dynamically (as documented by Fraser and Arcuri [8]). The static approach takes place before test generation: EvoSuite collects all literal primitive and string values that appear in the bytecode of the class of the test. Then, while tests are being generated, literals that are encountered at runtime may also be dynamically added to the pool of seeds. Some of these seeds are specially computed, according to a set of predefined rules. For instance, if the test case includes the statement "`foo.startsWith(bar)`", involving the strings `foo` and `bar`, the concatenation `bar + foo` will be added to the seed pool. During the search process, EvoSuite will then choose to use a seed from the pool instead of generating a fresh value, according to some probability.

We study random search with and without seeding enabled in this paper. We refer to the enhanced version of random search incorporating seeding as *Random+*, and the basic implementation without seeding as *Pure Random*.

2.2 Genetic Algorithm Search for Test Suites

While random search relies on encountering solutions by chance, guided searches aim to find solutions more directly by using a problem-specific "fitness function". A fitness function scores better potential solutions to the problem with better fitness values. A good fitness function will provide a gradient of fitness values so that the search can follow a "path" to increasingly better solutions that are increasingly fit for purpose. With a good fitness function, guided search-based approaches are capable of finding suitable solutions in extremely large or infinite search spaces (such as the space of possible test cases for a class as considered in this paper).

Genetic Algorithms (GAs) are one example of a directed search technique that uses simulated natural evolution as a search strategy. GAs evolve solutions to a problem based on their fitness. GAs evolve several candidate solutions at once in a "population". The initial population of candidate solutions is generated randomly. Each iteration of the algorithm seeks to adapt these solutions to ones with an increased fitness: "Crossover" works to splice two solutions to form new "offspring" while "mutation" randomly changes a component of a solution. The new solutions generated are taken forward to the next iteration depending on their fitness.

With EvoSuite's GA, a "solution" is a whole test suite, consisting of a series of test cases [10]. Whenever a new test case is generated at random (as with the construction of the initial population), it is done so as described in the last section, with seeding enabled. Crossover involves recombining test cases across two test suites while mutation works at two levels: at test case level and the test suite level. At the test case level, the mutation operator either randomly adds new statements, removes existing ones, or modifies them and their parameters. At the test suite level, it adds a fresh, randomly-generated test case to an existing test suite.

To guide the search towards achieving a high coverage test suite, the fitness value can be calculated based on the number of covered goals. However, a fitness function based solely on the number of *covered* goals provides no guidance to goals that remain *uncovered*. As with previous works in search-based test generation [18], EvoSuite incorporates branch distance metrics, which indicate how "far" a branch is from being executed. For example, if a conditional "`if (a == b)`" is to be executed as true, the "raw" distance can be computed as "$|\mathtt{a} - \mathtt{b}|$". In this way, the closer the values of `a` and `b` are to one another, the lower the branch distance is, and the closer the search is to covering the goal.

Since EvoSuite aims to evolve test suites where each test case covers as many branches as possible, the fitness function involves adding the distance value $d(b, T)$ for each branch b within a test suite T, computed as follows [10]:

$$d(b,T) = \begin{cases} 0 & \text{if the branch has been covered,} \\ \nu(d_{min}(b,T)) & \text{if the predicate has been executed at least twice,} \\ 1 & \text{otherwise.} \end{cases}$$

where $d_{min}(b, T)$ is the minimum raw distance value for the b for T, and ν is a function that normalizes a distance value between 0 and 1. Since the test suite must cover both the true and false outcomes of each individual branch, a distance value is not computed until the conditional is executed twice by the test suite. This is so that the initial execution of the predicate, with some specific true/false evaluation, is not lost in the process of pursuing the alternative outcome.

As longer test suites require more memory and execution time, controlling the length of the test suite can improve search performance [9]. Therefore, when deciding which test suites should proceed into the population for the next iteration of the search, EvoSuite prefers shorter test suites to test suites with the same fitness but whose test cases of composed of cumulatively higher number of statements.

Java programs are compiled to bytecode in order to be executed by the Java Virtual Machine (JVM), and it is at the level of the bytecode at which EvoSuite works – branch distances are computed by instrumenting and monitoring bytecode instructions. Different types of bytecode instruction can therefore give rise to different types of fitness landscape that may or may not be useful in guiding the search, as we discuss in the next section.

(a) Int-Int Branch

```
void m(int a) {
  if (a == 1) {
    // uncovered branch
  }
}
```

(a-i) Source code

```
void m(int);
  0: iload_1
  1: iconst_1
  2: if_icmpne 7
     [uncovered branch]
  7: return
```

(a-ii) Bytecode

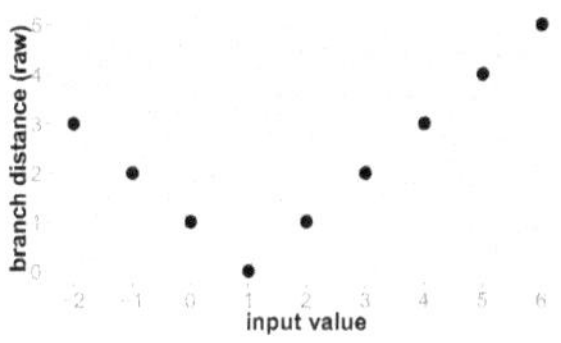

(a-iii) Raw branch distance

(b) Int-Zero Branch

```
void m(int a) {
  boolean x = false;
  if (a == 1) x = true;
  if (x) {
    // uncovered branch
  }
}
```

(b-i) Source code

```
void m(int);
   0: iconst_0
   1: istore_2
   ...
   9: iload_2
  10: ifeq 15
      [uncovered branch]
  15: return
```

(b-ii) Bytecode

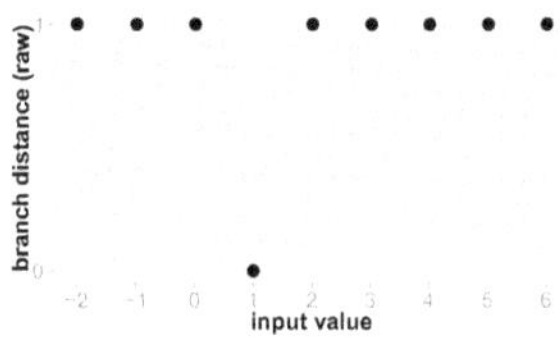

(b-iii) Raw branch distance

(c) Ref-Ref Branch

```
void m(int a) {
  Object x = null;
  if (a == 1) x = this;
  if (this == x) {
    // uncovered branch
  }
}
```

(c-i) Source code

```
void m(int);
   0: aconst_null
   1: astore_2
   ...
   9: aload_0
  10: aload_2
  11: if_acmpne 16
      [uncovered branch]
  16: return
```

(c-ii) Bytecode

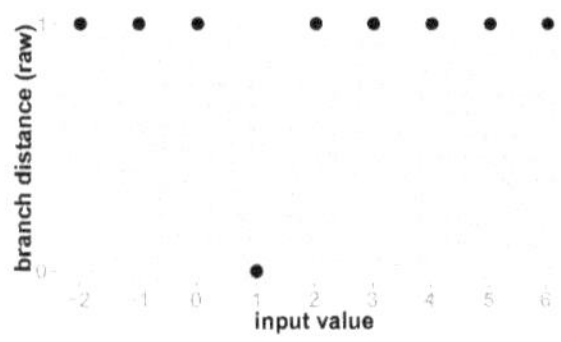

(c-iii) Raw branch distance

(d) Ref-Null Branch

```
void m(int a) {
  Object x = null;
  if (a != 1) x = new Object();
  if (x == null) {
    // uncovered branch
  }
}
```

(d-i) Source code

```
void m(int);
   0: aconst_null
   1: astore_2
   ...
  15: aload_2
  16: ifnonnull 21
      [uncovered branch]
  21: return
```

(d-ii) Bytecode

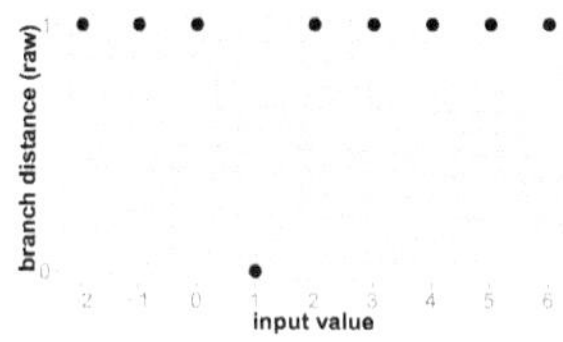

(d-iii) Raw branch distance

Figure 1: Examples of different branch types (denoted "uncovered branch") and their effect on the respective fitness landscape for the GA through raw (unnormalized) branch distance values. We show both the original Java source and the compiled bytecode, as processed by EvoSuite. Note that the target true/false evaluation of the branches is inverted by the Java compiler. The first column gives an example of a "gradient" branch, providing true guidance to the search. Conversely, the remaining examples do not provide good guidance, with the majority of inputs to the method resulting in the same distance value, and consequently a fitness landscape that is flat other than for the value required to execute the branch of concern.

3. BRANCH TYPES IN JAVA BYTECODE

Given that the fitness function is one of the key differences between the GA and random search, and that a major component of the fitness function is the calculation of distances for the branches in the class under test, we now classify the types of branches that occur in the bytecode of Java programs, and discuss the level of guidance they can potentially afford the GA search in EvoSuite.

This is important because it has been long known that not all branch predicates give "good" guidance, the archetypal example being that involving the boolean flag [3, 14]. Boolean conditions in branch predicates can only ever evaluate to true or false, offering one of only two distance values. Since one of these values corresponds to execution of the branch, no guidance is given to the search. Nevertheless, several branch predicates do indeed provide guidance, and result in a smooth "gradient" in the fitness landscape that a guided search can use to easily find test inputs.

3.1 "Integer-Integer" Branches

"Integer-Integer" branches involve the comparison of two integer values. The range of values possible for this comparison can potentially create a gradient for the search. Figure 1a shows an example of such a comparison, in which a method receives an integer parameter "a", and has a conditional statement on the parameter ("`a == 1`") (part a-i of the figure). The bytecode (part a-ii) shows this is compiled to a "`if_icmpne`" instruction, which compares the last two integers pushed to the stack, performing a jump to some other instruction in the bytecode if those two integers are not equal. Part a-iii of the figure shows how the distance value decreases as the chosen input value gets closer to the value that would execute the uncovered branch.

Of course, "Integer-Integer" branches may not always result in a gradient: it depends on the underlying program. One example of this is where two boolean values are compared, since boolean values are represented as the integer values 0 and 1 in Java bytecode. Therefore, source code comparisons involving two boolean values are compiled to an integer comparison involving the usage of the `if_icmpne` instruction. However, and as already discussed, boolean conditions do not induce any useful landscape gradient.

Furthermore, EvoSuite's special handling of `switch` statements falls into the "Integer-Integer" category. Java `switch` statements are compiled to either a `tableswitch` or `lookupswitch` bytecode instruction. These instructions pop the top of the stack to look up a "jump" target instruction in a map data structure, for which the keys are the values originally used in each `case` of the `switch`. For ease of fitness computation, EvoSuite simply instruments the bytecode by adding an explicit `if_icmpeq` for each case before the original `tableswitch` or `lookupswitch` instruction, comparing the top of the stack to each `case` value.

3.2 "Integer-Zero" Branches

"Integer-Zero" branches involve the comparison of an integer value with zero. One type of "Integer-Zero" branch occurs when boolean predicates are evaluated[1], for example as shown by Figure 1b. Here the branch involves the evaluation of the boolean value `x` (part b-i of the figure).

[1]Note that boolean predicate evaluations in branches differ in bytecode from comparing two boolean values – the latter type of branch falls into the "Integer-Integer" category.

```
void m(double a) {
  if (a == 1.0) {
    // uncovered branch
  }
}
```

(i) Source code

```
void m(double);
  0: dload_1
  1: dconst_1
  2: dcmpl
  3: ifne 10
  [uncovered branch]
  10: return
```

(ii) Bytecode

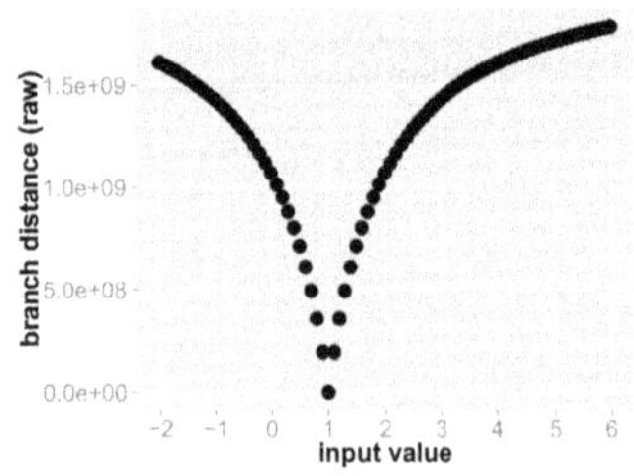

(iii) Raw branch distance

Figure 2: An example of handling a **double** comparison, showing the source code (i) and the bytecode (ii). Although these branches fall into the "Int-Zero" category, EvoSuite instruments the bytecode so that distances are recovered, resulting in a gradient landscape (iii).

The corresponding bytecode evaluates x, pushing the result (an integer, 0 or 1) to the stack. The **ifeq** bytecode instruction then pops this value, performing a jump if it is zero. Such a condition can only be either true or false, and as such can only have one of two distance values, which, as shown by Figure 1b-iii, are not useful to guiding the GA to covering the branch. The "right" input must therefore be discovered purely by chance.

A further type of "Integer-Zero" branch occurs as result of comparisons involving values of **float**, **double** and **long** primitive Java types. Figure 2 shows an example of a double comparison. The original source (part i of the figure) performs the comparison in the branch predicate. This is decomposed into a sequence of bytecode instructions shown by part ii of the figure. The comparison is performed by the **dcmpl** in relation to the top two double values pushed to the stack. The **dcmpl** instruction pushes an integer to the stack: **-1** if the first value is greater than the second, **1** if the first is less than the second, else 0 if they are equal. The **ifne** then performs a jump if the top of the stack is not 0.

Since the original numerical comparison in the source code is transformed to a boolean comparison in the bytecode, a significant amount of useful distance information is "lost" in the compilation process that would have been useful in guiding the search. EvoSuite therefore instruments the bytecode so that distance information can be recovered. The branch distance plot for the example, shown by Figure 2, therefore restores a gradient that can be used to optimize input values towards execution of the uncovered branch.

3.3 "Reference-Reference" branches

"Reference-Reference" branches are where two object references are compared for equality. Since references are not ordinal types, no meaningful distance metric can be applied, and the situation is similar to boolean flags – either the references are the same or they are not. Figure 1c shows an example of this. The original source code conditional is "**if (this == x)**" (part c-i of the figure), which Java compiles to the bytecode instructions 9–11 in part c-ii of the figure. Instructions 9 and 10 push the references onto the stack. Instruction 11 is the branching point in the bytecode, with "**if_acmpne**" popping the top two stack references and performing a jump if they are not equal. The resulting plot of branch distances (part c-iii) shows the resulting plateau, providing no guidance to the required input that makes the references equal and executes the uncovered branch.

3.4 "Reference-Null" branches

"Reference-Null" branches are similar to "Reference-Reference" branches, except one side of the comparison is **null**. Again, no meaningful distance metric can be applied. Figure 1d shows an example. The source code compares **x** with **null**. In the bytecode, **x** is pushed onto the stack by instruction 15. Instruction 16 is the branching point, where the **ifnonnull** instruction performing the jump if the element popped off the top of the stack is not **null**.

3.5 Summary

We have summarized and classified the different types of branches that can occur in Java bytecode. Some of these instructions will potentially give rise to a "gradient" in the fitness landscape, while others will not. We now study the prevalence of these types of branches in real-world code, whether they potentially involve a gradient, and their potential impact on the relative performance of random search and fitness-guided GA search.

4. EXPERIMENTAL SETUP

We designed an empirical study to test the relative effectiveness of test case generation using random and GA search, with the aim of answering the following research questions:

RQ1: Is the use of GA search more effective at generating unit tests than random search?

RQ2: How do the results of the comparison depend on the types of branches found in the code under test?

RQ3: How do the results of the comparison depend on the time allowed for the search?

To answer the research questions, we performed experiments on an initial sample of classes from SourceForge.

4.1 Subjects

In order to compare and contrast the relative effectiveness and performance of random and GA search, we selected a sample of classes from the SF110 corpus of open source projects [11]. The SF110 corpus is made up of 110 open source projects from the SourceForge open source repository (http://sourceforge.net), where 10 of the projects were the most popular by download at the time at which the corpus was constructed (June 2014) and the remaining 100 projects selected at random. Due to the large variation in the number of classes available in each project, we stratified our random sampling over the 110 projects, such that our sample involved at least one class from each of the 110 projects in the corpus, and comprised 1000 classes in total. However, 22 classes were removed from the sample for reasons such as not having any testable methods (e.g., they consisted purely of enumerated types, or did not have any public methods) or test suites could not be generated for some other reason that would allow us to sensibly compare the techniques (e.g., the class contained a bug or other issue that meant it could not be loaded independently without causing an exception).

The final number of classes in the study therefore totaled 978, comprising small classes with just a single coverage goal to larger classes with over 1,000 coverage goals, as shown by Table 1. In this table, *Branchless Methods* indicates the number of methods without conditional statements that can be covered by simply calling the method concerned.

Table 1: Statistics for the sample of 978 classes.

	Min	Avg	Max	SD
Total Branches	0	26.91	1,020	79.2
Branchless Methods	0	7.2	155	11.4
Total Goals	1	34.1	1,030	84.0

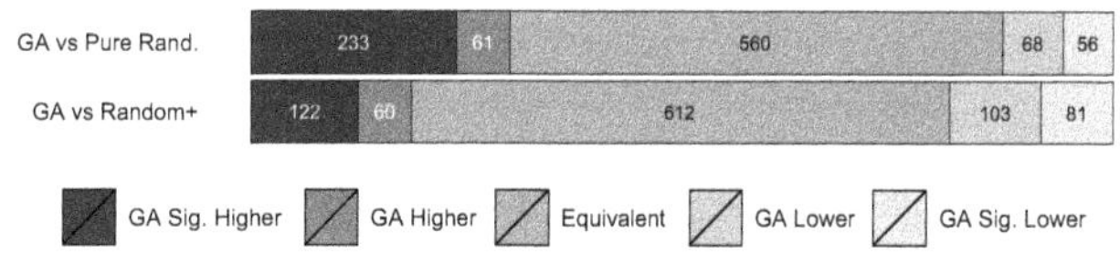

Figure 3: Comparing *GA* performance with *Pure Random* and *Random+* over the 978 SourceForge classes.
("GA Sig. Higher" is the number of classes for which *GA* obtained significantly higher coverage than *Random+* over the 50 runs of the experiment; "GA Higher" - the number of class where a higher average coverage was obtained (but not significantly); "Equivalent", the number of classes where the average coverage level was the same, etc.)

4.2 Collation of Branch Type Statistics

So that we could answer RQ2, we collated a series of statistics on the types of branches in the bytecode of each class.

Firstly, we simply collected the numbers of branches that fall into each of the categories detailed in Section 3 (i.e., "Integer-Integer" etc.) by simply analyzing the bytecode of each class in turn.

Secondly, we attempted to classify each branch as either *potentially* having a gradient distance landscape ("Gradient Branches"'), or, a plateau landscape ("Plateau Branches"). We programmed EvoSuite so that during test suite generation it would monitor the distance value of the predicate leading to the branch. If in any of the searches in the experiments, a value other than 0 or 1 is observed, we assume a wider range of distance values is available for fitness computation and label the branch as a "Gradient Branch". Otherwise the search is labelled as a "Plateau Branch". Clearly, this analysis is only indicative (but helps in understanding our results, as we will show in the answer to RQ2). This is because a range of values does not necessarily imply a gradient that will be useful for guiding the search. Nor does only finding the distances 0 and 1 for a branch mean that there are not further distance values that could be encountered. For instance, given a branch predicate $x > 5$, if for the whole duration of the search only the values $x \in \{4, 5, 6\}$ are used, then this will result in the distance values of 1, 0, and 1 respectively; and the branch will be incorrectly classified as a plateau branch. However, it is quite unlikely that the branch would only be attempted with these values over the course of several searches.

4.3 Experimental Procedure

We applied EvoSuite to conduct our experiments, with implementations of the *GA*, *Random+* and *Pure Random* as described in Section 2. We used *Pure Random* in RQ1 only, in order to analyze for possible effects with *Random+* due to its seeding mechanism.

For RQ1 we applied each technique with a search time of two minutes (which has been shown to be a suitable stopping condition in previous work [11]). To answer RQ2, we investigated the influence of the type of conditional predicates on the outcome of each technique. To do so, we used the statistics on branch types, collected as we described in the last section. To better understand the influence of the search budget over the outcome of the techniques for RQ3, we executed EvoSuite using the *GA* and *Random+* configurations with an increased search time of ten minutes and measured the level of coverage at one minute intervals.

We conducted the University of Sheffield's HPC Cluster (http://www.shef.ac.uk/wrgrid/iceberg). Each node has a Sandy-bridge Intel Xeon processor with 3GB real and 6GB virtual memory. We used EvoSuite's default configuration and ran it under Oracle's JDK 7u55.

4.4 Threats to Validity

Threats to the *internal validity* of our study include its usage of only one test generation tool (EvoSuite). While this was deliberate to facilitate a more controlled, fair comparison, it is plausible that specific implementation choices made in EvoSuite may limit the extent to which our results generalize (an associated external threat). The size of the test suites, for example, may influence the comparison; whereas *Random+* has no constraint in the test suite size, the GA evolves test suites with limited size (100 test cases by default) which imposes boundaries in the search space.

Another threat to internal validity stems from the branch-classification analysis described in Section 4.2, which can miscategorize branches in certain cases. While we acknowledge the results of this analysis may only be approximate, however during testing the analysis categorized all branches correctly. Furthermore, chance can affect the results of randomized search algorithms. To mitigate this threat, we repeated all experiments 50 times.

Threats to *external validity* affect the generalization of our results. While we used a randomly selected sample of Java classes as subjects, our results may not generalize beyond the SourceForge project repository or to other programming languages/paradigms. Furthermore, we also used branch coverage as a proxy measure of the quality of the resulting test suites: results may vary for other test suite properties (e.g., size, length or fault detection ability).

5. RESULTS

RQ1: Coverage Effectiveness. On average, *GA* attains 67.84% branch coverage, *Random+* achieves 67.94%, while *Pure Random* obtains 65.22%. Figure 3 summarizes the number of classes for which *GA* achieved a significantly higher or lower level of coverage than *Pure Random* and *Random+* over the 50 repetitions of the experiments. We computed significance using the Mann-Whitney U test at a level of $\alpha = 0.05$. While there are 122 classes for which the *GA* achieves significantly higher coverage, there are also 81 classes on which *Random+* attains significantly higher coverage than *GA*. Figure 4a plots the p-values for the significant cases for the *GA* and *Random+* comparison showing that the majority of cases are highly significant (particularly in the *GA* case) and thus unlikely to represent type-I errors.

We observe further similarities in the coverage achieved by *GA* and *Random+* with Figure 4b, which shows effect sizes computed with Vargha-Delaney's $\hat{A}_{12}$ statistic [26]. Here, the effect size estimates the probability that a run of *GA* achieves higher coverage than *Random+*. A value of $\hat{A}_{12} = 0.5$ indicates that both search strategies perform equally, $\hat{A}_{12} = 1$ indicates that all runs of *GA* will achieve higher coverage than *Random+*, and vice versa for $\hat{A}_{12} = 0$. The overall average effect size amounts to 0.51, which indicates that *GA* is only very marginally more effective.

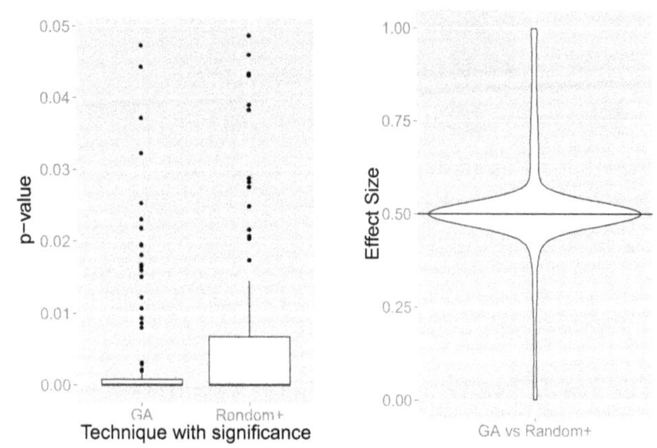

(a) Box Plot (b) Violin Plot

Figure 4: Comparing *GA* performance with *Random+*. (a) Box plot of *p*-values for classes where a significantly higher level of coverage was achieved with either the *GA* or *Random+*. (b) Violin plot of the effect sizes obtained using Vargha-Delaney's $\hat{A}_{12}$ statistic, here computing the proportion of the 50 repetitions for which the *GA* scores a higher level of coverage than *Random+* for each class; thereby reflecting its relative effectiveness.

For 612 classes *GA* and *Random+* achieve identical coverage. To a large extent, this can likely be attributed to the simplicity of these classes: *GA* achieves 100% coverage on 456 classes, and *Random+* on 440 classes. Classes with lower but identical coverage are possibly due to problems that EvoSuite cannot overcome regardless of search algorithm (e.g., due to environmental factors such as classes depending on databases or web services that were not available during the experiments).

The comparison between *GA* and *Pure Random* shows larger differences, with 233 classes where *GA* achieves significantly higher coverage. This indicates that optimizations such as constant and dynamic seeding which are used in *Random+* are effective and help covering non-trivial classes.

RQ1. Our experiments showed no significant difference between *GA* and *Random+* in 78% of the classes, and only slightly more classes with increase for *GA* over *Random+* than classes with a decrease.

RQ2: Influence of Branch Types. Although the comparison between *GA* and *Random+* showed 612 classes with no difference in coverage, there were also 203 classes with significant differences. RQ2 aims to shed light on this by studying the influence of different types of branches in a class on the effectiveness of the search algorithms.

Figure 5a shows the distribution of different branch types as taken from the bytecode of the classes. In total, there are 11,677 branches in the 987 classes. "Reference-Reference" branches are rare: this is not surprising as in most cases in Java a comparison is performed using the `equals` method on the objects, rather than comparing references. "Reference-Null" comparisons are more common accounting for approximately one quarter of the branches. Almost half of the branches (5,741) are "Integer-Zero" branches, from which only 303 involve `double`, `float` or `long` comparisons. Only these 303 branches, along with the 3,346 "Integer-Integer" branches have the potential to provide gradients.

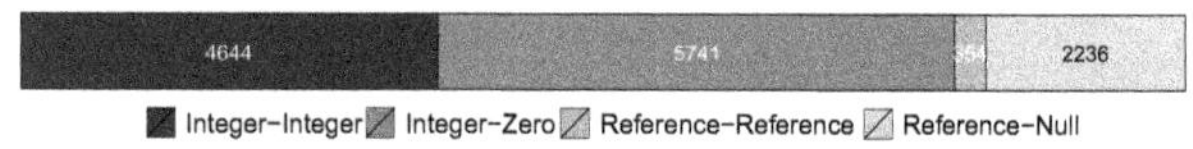

(a) Numbers of Branches Classified by Bytecode Branch Type

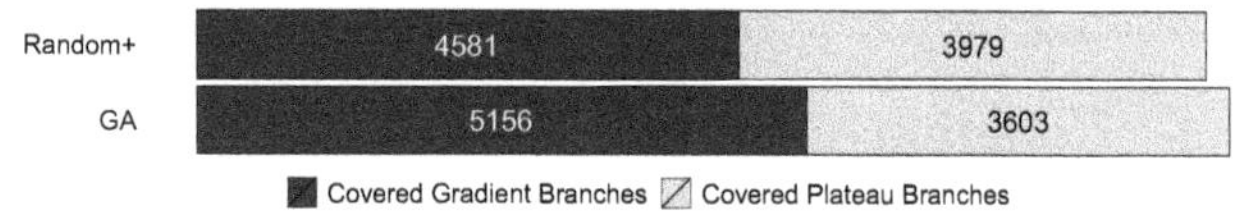

(b) Numbers of Branches Classified as "Gradient" or "Plateau"

Figure 5: Numbers of different branch types in the classes under test.

Effectiveness on Gradient Branches. Intuitively, one would expect that the *GA* should achieve higher coverage on gradient branches, as the branch distance values will influence the search operators and guide the search towards covering additional branches. Figure 6a compares *GA* and *Random+* in terms of the coverage achieved when only considering gradient branches; that is, the coverage is only calculated for classes that have at least one gradient branch, and the coverage values exclude non-gradient branches. There are 105 classes where *GA* achieves significantly higher coverage of the gradient branches, with only eight classes where the coverage is significantly lower. Figure 5b shows that overall the *GA* covered 5,156 gradient branches, whereas *Random+* covered only 4,581. This confirms that the *GA* benefits from the branch distances provided by the gradient branches.

The eight cases where *Random+* has significantly higher coverage can be explained by their large number of branches (69 total goals and 18 gradient branches on average): The fitness function that guides the *GA* considers all branches at the same time; this means that a test suite that is close to covering many gradient branches may have a better fitness value than a test suite that fully covers fewer branches. In these cases, the *GA* would simply require more time to eventually fully cover all these branches.

Effectiveness on Plateau Branches. Figure 6b compares *GA* and *Random+* when only considering the coverage of plateau branches. There are 158 classes in which the *GA* has significantly lower coverage compared to *Random+*, and 70 classes with significantly higher coverage. Figure 5b shows that overall the *GA* covered 3,603 plateau branches, whereas *Random+* covered 3,979; that is, even though the *GA* covered more branches overall, it covered fewer plateau branches. Since the branch distance for these branches only has two values there is no guidance that the *GA* could exploit – a plateau branch is either covered or it is not covered. The lower coverage of the *GA* can be attributed to a loss of diversity: Over time, the *GA* in EvoSuite prefers smaller test suites and gets rid of random "noise", focusing the search operators on the exploitation of achieved coverage and mutating existing objects. On the other hand, *Random+* is not biased by the search and continuously creates independent new objects and call sequences.

Effectiveness on Branchless Methods. Branchless methods represent a special case similar to plateau branches, and intuitively they are simple to cover – they just require test cases to call the method. Figure 6c compares *GA* and *Random+* with respect to the coverage of methods. Although *GA* achieves significantly higher cover than *Random+* in 18 cases, there are 75 classes where the *GA* results in lower coverage, which is similar in proportions to the plateau

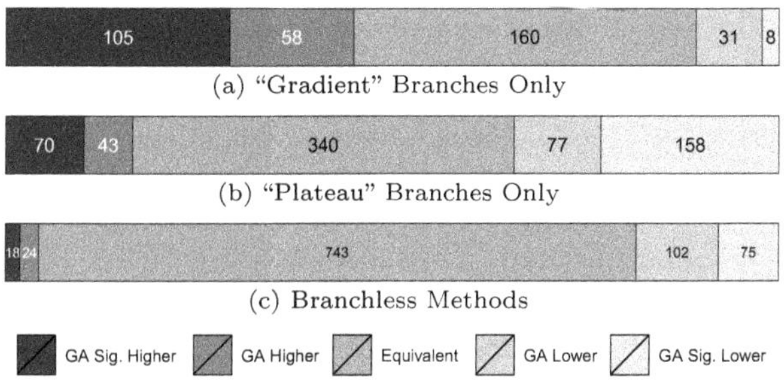

(a) "Gradient" Branches Only

(b) "Plateau" Branches Only

(c) Branchless Methods

Figure 6: Comparing *GA* performance with *Random+* for different types of branch and with branchless methods. ("GA Sig. Higher" is the number of classes for which *GA* obtained significantly higher coverage than *Random+* over the 50 runs of the experiment; "GA Higher" – the number of class where a higher average coverage was obtained (but not significantly); "Equivalent", the number of classes where the average coverage level was the same, etc.)

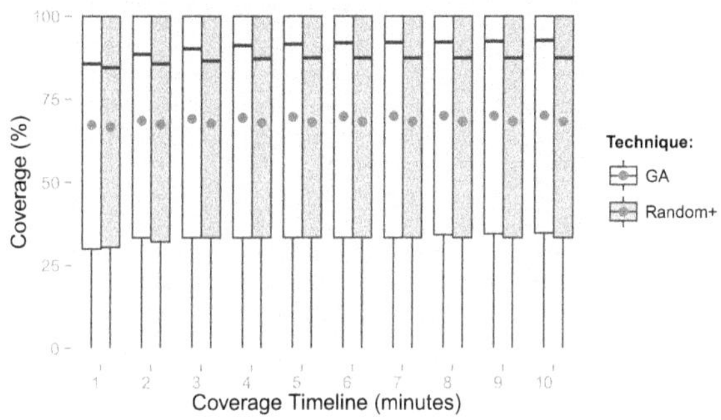

Figure 7: Branch coverage comparison between *GA* vs. *Random+* over 10 minutes with one minute intervals. Dots represent mean averages.

branches. It is maybe surprising that there can be difference in so simple coverage goals in the first place. Our conjecture is that this is because *Random+* has a higher probability of inserting new method calls: The *GA* only mutates a test suite with a certain probability, and then each test in turn is only mutated with a certain probability, and finally insertion of new statements again does not always happen. In contrast, *Random+* generates tests by repeatedly adding new statements. Again it would only be a matter of time for the *GA* to fully cover all branchless methods, although possibly more time than for *Random+*. Interestingly, classes on which the *GA* achieved more than 90% coverage have a median proportion of 100% branchless methods out of all coverage goals, providing further evidence that many classes in practice are trivial.

> **RQ2.** Our experiments show that *GA* achieves higher coverage of gradient branches compared to *Random+*, but lower coverage of plateau branches, which constitute the majority of branches.

RQ3: Effect of the Time Allowed For the Search. The results so far have shown that *GA* and *Random+* perform similarly for the majority of classes after two minutes of search, with some differences in performance on plateau and gradient branches. This raises the question whether the results are influenced by the allocated search budget – given more time, do the results change?

To analyze the impact of the search budget, we repeated the experiments with *GA* and *Random+* using a search budget of 10 minutes, and measured the coverage values at one minute intervals. Figure 7 compares the average coverage per class for each interval: There is a slight increase of coverage for both *GA* and *Random+* over time, and after 10 minutes *GA* achieves an overall average of 70% branch coverage, while *Random+* achieves 68.3%.

Figure 8: Branch coverage comparison between *GA* and *Random+* using a search budget of 10 minutes. (Legend is as for Figure 6.)

Given more time, *GA* will catch up on branchless methods and plateau branches covered compared to *Random+*. Figure 8 compares *GA* with *Random+* after 10 minutes, and shows that the *GA* has significantly lower coverage on only 41 classes after 10 minutes, compared to 81 after two minutes (Note that the number of classes with coverage data after 10 minutes is only 955, as there were 32 additional classes for which EvoSuite did not produce any data after 10 minutes). The *GA* will also continue to optimize gradient branches; however, the dynamic seeding used in EvoSuite will also help *Random+* in many cases to cover gradient branches. Figure 8 shows that there are 127 classes where *GA* has higher coverage after 10 minutes, compared to 122 after two minutes. For 699 classes the coverage is identical, which is likely because the maximum achievable level of coverage has been reached by both algorithms.

> **RQ3.** Our experiments show a slightly higher increase of coverage over time for *GA* compared to *Random+*, but equivalent coverage in the majority of cases.

6. DISCUSSION

Our results indicate that, while the techniques have a similar outcome for the majority of classes, there are differences that influence the effectiveness. However, the fact that *Random+* can outperform the *GA* in a number of subjects raises the question of why this happens in practice. In this section we look at some of the factors in the search algorithms that may be the cause of these surprising results.

Although *GA* and *Random+* were applied with the same time limit in our experiments, *Random+* executed 1.3 times as many statements as the *GA* in the same time. This can be attributed to the search operators of the *GA*, and the resulting frequent copy operations on test cases and cached execution traces as implemented in EvoSuite. Without such an overhead, *Random+* can spend more time executing tests and exploring the search landscape. Nevertheless, as shown in Figure 7 even increasing the *GA*'s budget by 30% to match the number of executed statements can only result in small improvements, and does not affect the overall findings.

The analysis of RQ2 also suggests that the search operators of the *GA* have an effect on the diversity: The *GA* has a lower probability of generating new tests, and may thus be slower at covering plateau branches or branchless methods (cf. Figure 6, part b and c).

A further influencing factor is that a test suite produced by the *GA* may not cover all branches that were covered throughout the search. This is because the fitness function aims to maximize coverage: For instance, given a test suite T_1 that covers goals $\{A, B\}$, and another test suite T_2 that covers goals $\{B, C, D\}$, assuming T_2 has a better fitness value it will be selected as the best solution. As a result, although goal A was covered by T_1, it remains uncovered in the resulting test suite. In contrast, *Random+* generates a new test case on each iteration, and if the new test covers any new goals, it is added to the test suite. This suggests that creating an archive of solutions that cover new coverage goals would be important for the *GA*.

The large number of plateau branches could potentially be reduced by introducing testability transformation [15]; although EvoSuite implements certain transformations (e.g., on floating point numbers or string comparisons) it does not apply a transformation of boolean flags.

7. RELATED WORK

There have been several papers that have compared GAs with random search in the procedural domain (e.g. [16], [27]). This work has found guided search to always outperform random. In general, procedural code tends to consist of larger functions than methods in OO code, and each function tends to involve more parameters. While random search typically covers a large percentage of the branches involved, the GA covers significantly more.

Sharma et al. [24] showed on 13 examples that random testing of OO container classes achieves the same coverage as shape abstraction, a systematic technique specific for container classes. The results of our experiments suggest that in practice, many OO classes are, similarly to container classes, simple in nature and thus well suited for random testing.

Earlier experiments with EvoSuite on the SF100 corpus [11] showed that a large number of classes are either trivially covered, or uncoverable without providing the test generator with additional features (e.g. to handle environmental inputs such as web services or databases). This finding is in line with our results; however, a comparison with Randoop [21] in the same study suggested a large improvement of *GA* over random testing. The results of our experiments suggest that this improvement is largely due to the engineering of the tool rather than the search algorithm; for example, Randoop does not use seeding.

Eler et al. [6] analyzed the SF100 corpus from the point of view of test data generation using dynamic symbolic execution. They also reported the large number of reference comparisons and the challenges of handling those in a constraint solver. They further reported the relatively low number of branches involving integer comparisons, which result in constraints that DSE is typically strong at handling.

8. CONCLUSIONS

In this paper, we presented an empirical study comparing the effectiveness of a GA and a random search-based algorithm for generating branch coverage test suites for real-world Java classes. One might expect the GA to be more suitable than random search for this task, but surprisingly we observed that both algorithms behaved similarly on the majority of classes, in particular when applying optimisations such as seeding. Although a GA can exploit the guidance provided by certain types of branches, in practice there are many more branches that provide no such guidance, and on some classes with many such branches the GA resulted in lower coverage than random search – even when a large search budget was used.

There certainly is some room for improving the GA for the task, as for example suggested by different optimisations not included in our experiments [12,13,17]. However, if the objective is to quickly achieve a decent level of branch coverage on object-oriented classes, then using random search with seeding may be sufficient.

Acknowledgments. This work is supported by the EPSRC project "EXOGEN" (EP/K030353/1). The authors would like to thank Chris Wright for help with R.

9. REFERENCES

[1] Alshahwan, N., Harman, M.: Automated web application testing using search based software engineering. In: ASE. IEEE (2011)
[2] Andrews, J.H., Li, F.C., Menzies, T.: Nighthawk: A two-level genetic-random unit test data generator. In: ASE. ACM (2007)
[3] Baresel, A., Sthamer, H.: Evolutionary testing of flag conditions. In: GECCO. Springer (2003)
[4] Baresi, L., Lanzi, P.L., Miraz, M.: Testful: an evolutionary test approach for Java. In: ICST. IEEE (2010)
[5] Csallner, C., Smaragdakis, Y.: JCrasher: an automatic robustness tester for Java. Softw. Pract. Exper. 34(11) (2004)
[6] Eler, M., Endo, A., Durelli, V.: Quantifying the characteristics of Java programs that may influence symbolic execution from a test data generation perspective. In: COMPSAC. IEEE (2014)
[7] Fraser, G., Arcuri, A.: EvoSuite: automatic test suite generation for object-oriented software. In: FSE. ACM (2011)
[8] Fraser, G., Arcuri, A.: The seed is strong: Seeding strategies in search-based software testing. In: ICST. IEEE (2012)
[9] Fraser, G., Arcuri, A.: Handling test length bloat. Softw. Test., Verif. Reliab. 23(7) (2013)
[10] Fraser, G., Arcuri, A.: Whole test suite generation. IEEE Trans. on Software Engineering 39(2) (2013)
[11] Fraser, G., Arcuri, A.: A large-scale evaluation of automated unit test generation using EvoSuite. ACM TOSEM 24(2) (2014)
[12] Fraser, G., Arcuri, A., McMinn, P.: A memetic algorithm for whole test suite generation. J. Syst. Software 103(0) (2014)
[13] Galeotti, J.P., Fraser, G., Arcuri, A.: Improving search-based test suite generation with dynamic symbolic execution. In: ISSRE. IEEE (2013)
[14] Harman, M., Hu, L., Hierons, R., Baresel, A., Sthamer, H.: Improving evolutionary testing by flag removal. In: GECCO. MK Pub. (2002)
[15] Harman, M., Hu, L., Hierons, R., Wegener, J., Sthamer, H., Baresel, A., Roper, M.: Testability transformation. IEEE Trans. on Software Engineering 30(1) (2004)
[16] Harman, M., McMinn, P.: A theoretical and empirical study of search-based testing: Local, global, and hybrid search. IEEE Trans. on Software Engineering 36(2) (2010)
[17] Li, Y., Fraser, G.: Bytecode testability transformation. In: SSBSE, pp. 237–251. Springer (2011)
[18] McMinn, P.: Search-based software test data generation: a survey. Softw. Test., Verif. Reliab. 14(2) (2004)
[19] McMinn, P., Shahbaz, M., Stevenson, M.: Search-based test input generation for string data types using the results of web queries. In: ICST. IEEE (2012)
[20] Oriol, M., Tassis, S.: Testing .NET code with YETI. In: ICECCS. IEEE (2010)
[21] Pacheco, C., Ernst, M.D.: Randoop: feedback-directed random testing for Java. In: OOPSLA. ACM (2007)
[22] Prasetya, I.W.B.: T3, a combinator-based random testing tool for Java: benchmarking. In: FITTEST'13. Springer (2014)
[23] Sakti, A., Pesant, G., Gueheneuc, Y.G.: Instance generator and problem representation to improve object oriented code coverage. IEEE Trans. on Software Engineering 41(3) (2015)
[24] Sharma, R., Gligoric, M., Arcuri, A., Fraser, G., Marinov, D.: Testing container classes: Random or systematic? In: FASE. Springer (2011)
[25] Tonella, P.: Evolutionary testing of classes. ACM SIGSOFT Softw. Eng. Notes 29(4) (2004)
[26] Vargha, A., Delaney, H.D.: A critique and improvement of the "CL" Common Language Effect Size Statistics of McGraw and Wong. Educational and Behavioral Statistics 25(2) (2000)
[27] Wegener, J., Baresel, A., Sthamer, H.: Evolutionary test environment for automatic structural testing. Information and Software Technology 43(14) (2001)

Deep Parameter Optimisation

Fan Wu
CREST, UCL
London, UK
fan.wu.12@ucl.ac.uk

Westley Weimer
University of Virginia
Virginia, USA
weimer@cs.virginia.edu

Mark Harman,
Yue Jia, Jens Krinke
CREST, UCL
London, UK
{mark.harman, yue.jia,
j.krinke}@ucl.ac.uk

ABSTRACT

We introduce a mutation-based approach to automatically discover and expose 'deep' (previously unavailable) parameters that affect a program's runtime costs. These discovered parameters, together with existing ('shallow') parameters, form a search space that we tune using search-based optimisation in a bi-objective formulation that optimises both time and memory consumption. We implemented our approach and evaluated it on four real-world programs. The results show that we can improve execution time by 12% or achieve a 21% memory consumption reduction in the best cases. In three subjects, our deep parameter tuning results in a significant improvement over the baseline of shallow parameter tuning, demonstrating the potential value of our deep parameter extraction approach.

Keywords

Parameter tuning; parameter exposure; memory allocation

1. INTRODUCTION

Many software systems can reap significant performance benefits from workload- or runtime-specific configurations or optimisations. Software developers often expose a set of parameters for users to re-configure such software systems adaptively. However, manual parameter tuning is a demanding challenge because users are usually required not only to have extensive knowledge about the system and the workload, but also to balance many competing objectives, such as memory consumption and execution time.

Many studies have reported on the challenges of automated parameter tuning [1, 6, 15, 17, 20, 29, 30]. Early work focused on finding optimal values with mathmatical approaches [6, 20, 29, 30], while search-based software engineering (SBSE) [10] has been used in more recent research [1, 15, 17] on this problem. Although these approaches can automatically re-configure a system, their improvements are limited to changes to existing, explicit parameters.

Many software systems contain undocumented internal variables or expressions that also affect the performance of the systems. Thus, these elements could also be good candidates for automated parameter tuning. However, many of these elements are 'private', undocumented, or otherwise unexposed. Moreover, some internal values may not even be stored in variables, private or otherwise, but may merely exist as fleeting sub-expression evaluation outcomes. Identifying these variables and expressions is very difficult for general users, as it requires a deep understanding of the source code of the system.

In this paper, we propose an automatic technique to discover internal variables and expressions that normally cannot be accessed directly, but impact non-functional properties of interest. Our goal is to expose new parameters that can directly influence the values of these internal variables and expressions. To distinguish from parameters exposed by software designers (which we call 'shallow parameters'), we call these exposed parameters 'deep parameters' [13]. Modifying shallow parameter values does not necessarily change the internal code elements represented by deep parameters. Therefore, deep parameters provide additional opportunities for subsequent automated parameter tuning.

In previous work, there has been an attempt to automate the exposure of a limited form of 'deep' parameters with the Software Tuning panel for Autonomic Control (STAC) [4]. However, it requires initial human effort to characterise shallow parameters and can only find a subset of deep parameters. Hutter et al. [16], on the other hand, exposed almost all potential deep parameters and required much more computation effort. To overcome these limitations, we apply a mutation-based sensitivity analysis to fully automate the process of locating influencial deep parameters and subsequently apply NSGA-II [7] to search for optimal values for these parameters to balance non-functional properties of interest.

In this paper, we focused on two non-functional properties, memory consumption and execution time, because they are important objectives for many applications and because they are often naturally conflicting, thereby yielding an interesting and rewarding multi-objective solution space. We illustrate the approach by re-configuring a general purpose memory allocator, *dlmalloc*. We choose memory allocators because they are critical to the memory consumption of many programs and can account for up to 60% of the total execution time in some scenarios [33]. As a result, memory optimisation is a widely-studied topic [25, 26]. We evaluate our approach using four specimen systems drawn from benchmarks for *dlmalloc* and real world applications. Our approach neither touches the source code of the application itself nor requires any knowledge about the application under optimisation, instead only tuning the parameters for *dlmalloc* library, making it applicable to other C applications with little effort.

The paper presents evidence that deep parameter optimisation targeting *dlmalloc* is an effective approach for improving program's non-functional properties. The experimental results

GECCO '15, July 11 - 15, 2015, Madrid, Spain

ISBN 978-1-4503-3472-3/15/07...$15.00
DOI: http://dx.doi.org/10.1145/2739480.2754648

suggest that deep parameter optimisation competes favourably with both shallow optimisation and default configurations. For four subjects, deep parameter optimisation reduces memory consumption by 21% or execution time by 12% in the best cases. The contributions of the paper are summarised as follows:

1. We introduce an automated approach to discover and expose deep parameters. The discovery of these parameters enhances search-based parameter tuning.
2. We report the results of an empirical study comparing the traditional shallow parameter tuning approach with our approach. On four applications totaling over 70,000 lines of code and guarded by over 700 tests, the results show that our approach can reduce memory usage by 21% and execution time by 12%, whereas shallow tuning alone achieves only a 16% and 10% corresponding reduction.
3. Furthermore, we evaluate the offline optimisation-time cost of our approach. For example, in our experiments, deep parameter tuning can improve memory savings by 14%, at the cost of 13% longer offline optimisation time. When deep parameter tuning is not helpful, this extra optimisation-time cost reduces to a mere 0.7%, compared to shallow parameter tuning.

2. MOTIVATING EXAMPLE

We illustrate the idea of deep parameters with an example found by our approach for *dlmalloc* (version 2.8.6) [22].

```
1 static void* sys_alloc(mstate m,size_t nb) {
2 ...
3   if (ss == 0){ //check if first time through
4     char* base = (char*)CALL_MORECORE(0);
5   ...
6 }
```

Figure 1: sys_alloc function in *dlmalloc*

Figure 1 shows a part of the sys_alloc function in *dlmalloc*. We explain its internal operation here to give the reader a feeling for the opportunities for optimisation. Of course, our parameter exposing and search-based tuning are general purpose techniques that have no knowledge of how *dlmalloc* operates. *Dlmalloc* maintains an internal structure to organize the heap for memory reuse. Only when *dlmalloc* cannot find a suitable chunk of memory for a memory request does it call sys_alloc() to extend the current heap.

Our approach begins with a form of mutation analysis that evaluates subexpressions in the program to determine their utility as candidate deep parameters. A subexpression is evaluated by mutating it, running the resulting program variant against a test suite, and evaluating the results in terms of functional and non-functional properties. A subexpression that can be profitably mutated to optimise a non-functional property while retaining functional correctness can serve as a deep parameter.

In this example, the mutation analysis finds that mutants generated from mutating Line 4 have a notable affect on the memory consumption and the execution time of *dlmalloc.* We take a close took at Line 4. It calls the CALL_MORECORE() function, which takes an integer as input. CALL_MORECORE() is a macro wrapping the system call that extends or shrinks the current heap and returns the beginning address of the newly allocated region of heap. Specifically, CALL_MORECORE(0) neither extends nor shrinks the heap but simply returns the current address of the heap, which is the original purpose of Line 4 mentioned above.

Changing the input value for CALL_MORECORE() in Line 4 allows us to control the amount of memory pre-allocated. However, although *dlmalloc* provides several tuneable parameters to programmers, allowing them to adjust behaviours (see Section 5 for details), none of these shallow parameters can affect the CALL_MORECORE() function directly. Our algorithm exposes this as a new deep parameter by transforming Line 4 into the code below, where D is the deep parameter exposed that controls the pre-allocated heap.

```
char * base = (char*)CALL_MORECORE(0 + D);
```

The optimal size of pre-allocated memory depends on the specific program using this tunable memory allocator. Too much pre-allocation may result in waste. On the other hand, too little means that later requests must call CALL_MORECORE() again to extend the heap, increasing runtime. By tuning the deep parameter D, an SBSE approach can balance time and space consumption. This is just one example of a potential deep parameter. In our mutation analysis experiments, our tool 'discovers' that by changing the value of this deep parameter, it can achieve a modest (2.5%) time reduction without increasing heap space in one of our subjects.

3. DEEP PARAMETER OPTIMISATION

Figure 2 shows the work flow of our deep parameter optimisation. The approach takes the source code of the program, a set of test data and a set of non-functional properties of interest. It first applies mutation analysis and a non-dominated rank algorithm to discover potential locations for deep parameters, as explained in Section 3.1. It then exposes deep parameters based on the type of expressions found at the locations (Section 3.2). Finally, to tune the program, a multi-objective search algorithm is used to search for optimised values for both shallow and deep parameters (Section 3.3).

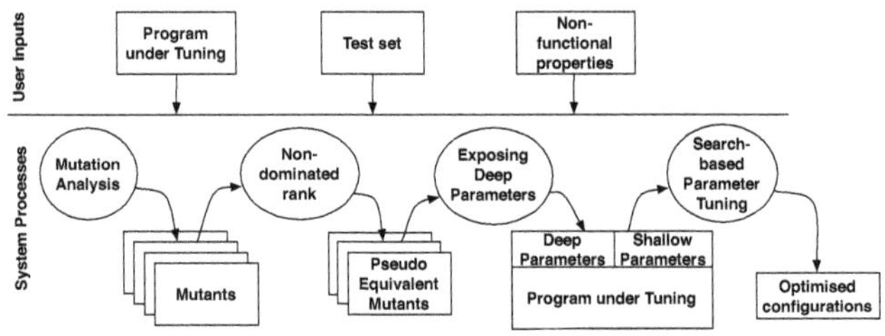

Figure 2: Deep parameter optimisation workflow. Given a program, test suite and non-functional properties, our approach applies mutation analysis, exposes deep parameters, and optimises them.

3.1 Discovering Locations for Deep Parameters

The first step is to identify potential locations at which we could expose deep parameters. In our approach, we represent the input program as an Abstract Syntax Tree (AST) and a potential location L is an expression node of the AST. We want to find a set of locations L_D such that, when we tune the value of the expression at L_D, some non-functional properties of the program could be improved while the program retains identical functional behaviour. We use a suite of regression test data to validate the correctness from the optimisation, following other established Genetic Improvement approaches [11, 21, 24]. We assume the presence of a test suite with each target application.

We use mutation analysis to automate the process of searching for locations L_D. Mutation analysis deliberately makes simple syntactic changes to the input program, to create a set of various versions of a program called mutants, each containing a different syntactic change [19]. A transformation rule that generates a mutant from the input program is known as a mutation operator.

Table 1: Selected mutation operators

Mutation Operators	Changes Between
CRCR – Constant replacement	constants, 0, 1, −1
OAAN – Arithmetic operator	+, -, *, /, %
OAAA – Arithmetic assignment	+=, -=, *=, /=, %=
OCNG – Logical context negation	*expr*, ! *expr*
OIDO – Increment/decrement	++x, --x, x++, x--
OLLN – Logical operator	&&, ||
OLNG – Logical negation	x op y, x op !y, !x op y, !(x op y)
ORRN – Relational operator	>, >=, <, <=, ==
OBBA – Bitwise assignment	&=, |=
OBBN – Bitwise operator	&, |

By carefully choosing mutation operators, we can use mutants to simulate the effect of making changes at those locations Ls from which a potential deep parameter may be exposed. Table 1 lists the operators we used to generate mutants, covering locations of constants, relational, logical and arithmetic expressions. These so-called 'selective' mutation operators have been widely used in mutation analysis experiments [19].

To assess the quality of a mutant, we test each mutant against the input test set and record the values of the non-functional properties. If the functional result of running a mutant is different from the result of running the original program for any test data in the input test set, then the mutant is said to be 'killed', otherwise it is said to have 'survived'. After all mutants are executed, we first filter out the killed mutants which fail to retain the functional behaviour. A mutant is called **pseudo equivalent** with respect to a given test suite T iff it passes the regression test of T. Thus we only select pseudo equivalent mutants which preserve the functional behaviour of the original program while potentially changing non-functional behaviour.

In practice, there is a large number of pseudo equivalent mutants [23, 28, 31] generated. We desire a subset from them that represents the locations that could have the greatest impact on the non-functional properties of interest while also maintaining a diversity of choices. We achieve this by ranking the mutants based on their non-functional properties using the non-dominated sorting approach of the NSGA-II algorithm [7]. Each mutant is assigned a Pareto Level value and a Crowd Distance value, where Pareto Level n means a mutant will be on the Pareto Front after all the mutants with Pareto Level less than n are removed, while Crowd Distance indicates how close a mutant is to its neighbours on the same Pareto Level. For example, a mutant with Pareto Level 1 is on the Pareto Front among all the mutants and has the priority to be considered first. A mutant is better than another in terms of non-dominated sorting if its Pareto Level is smaller or if their Pareto Levels are the same but the former is less crowded (larger Crowd Distance) than the latter. After sorting all the mutants in terms of their non-functional properties, we apply a greedy algorithm to pick the first k locations that could best influence the non-functional properties of the original, where k is the desired number of deep parameters one wants to expose.

3.2 Exposing Deep Parameters

The second step is to expose deep parameters that allow users to modify the value of the expression at selected locations. Based on the type of mutation, we first classify the selected mutants into two sets. Set 1 contains mutants generated from CRCR, OAAN, OAAA and OIDO operators, which simulate locations with non-logical expressions. Set 2 contains mutants generated from the OCNG, OLLN, OLNG and ORRN operators, which simulate locations with logical expressions (Table 1). Given a location L, E_L is the expression at the location L, we use the following transformation rules to rewrite E_L with a new parameter v_L.

$$E_L \rightarrow \begin{cases} (E_L + v_L) & \text{if } L \in \text{Set 1} \\ (E_L)\ xor\ v_L & \text{if } L \in \text{Set 2} \end{cases} \quad (1)$$

We use addition to affect the value of non-logical expression and `exclusive or` to affect the logical ones. Finally we expose v_L as a 'public' parameter so that users can assign a value to v_L through parameter passing or APIs.

3.3 Search-based Parameter Tuning

Although the exposed deep parameters can provide additional 'knobs' [15] to tune the program, a set of k deep parameters need not necessarily subsume the existing shallow parameters of the program. Thus, in this work, we propose to use both shallow parameters and deep parameters and tune them together using SBSE [10]. Because we are interested in multiple conflicting properties, we consider this as a multi-objective optimisation problem, thus a multi-objective Genetic Algorithm, NSGA-II [7], is applied to search for optimal values for both shallow and deep parameters.

We use an integer vector to represent the tuning parameters. Each integer stores a solution value for one parameter. At each generation, our NSGA-II implementation first applies tournament selection, followed by a uniform crossover and a uniform mutation operation. In our experiments our fitness functions are designed to capture two non-functional properties: execution time and memory consumption, while preserving the functionality by assigning the worst value to both non-functional properties. To measure execution time, *Glibc*'s `wait4` system call is used to calculate the CPU time (mean of 10 evaluations). For memory consumption, we instrumented the program to record the high-water mark of the virtual memory consumption. We chose this instrumentation approach because the physical memory reported by the OS is not always deterministic but depends on the workload and the OS, and because the virtual memory requirement is an upper bound of the physical memory actually needed. For a subject program with configuration c, we measure the execution time $t_i(c)$ and the high-water-mark of memory consumption $m_i(c)$ of each test case i. Then the fitness functions for the configuration c regarding execution time and memory consumption can be formulated as:

$$f_t(c) = \sum_i t_i(c) \qquad f_m(c) = \sum_i m_i(c).$$

After fitness evaluation, a standard NSGA-II non-dominated selection creates the next generation. Finally, all non-dominating solutions in the final population are returned.

4. EXPERIMENTS

To assess the improvement of our Deep Parameter Tuning approach, we compared it with Shallow Parameter Tuning:

RQ1 How much performance improvement, with respect to the unmodified program, can be obtained by Shallow Parameter Turning using random search or NSGA-II?

We consider RQ1 to provide a baseline result against which we compare the results from Deep Parameter Tuning. We used NSGA-II algorithm (described in Section 3.3) and Random algorithm to search for better values for the shallow parameters in *dlmalloc*, then compare the performance with *dlmalloc*'s default configuration.

RQ2 How much additional improvement can be achieved by our Deep Parameter Tuning algorithm compared with Shallow Parameter Tuning alone?

We ask RQ2 to evaluate how useful our approach is at finding better configurations for the given non-functional properties. In these experiments, our Deep Parameter Tuning approach uses a custom mutation analysis to identify the most sensitive parts of the program, followed by an application of NSGA-II to optimise both explicit and implicit parameters for *dlmalloc*.

RQ3 What are the optimisation-time costs for these approaches to find their solutions?

Since our Deep Parameter Tuning approach exposes additional parameters which are then optimised in conjunction with the baseline shallow parameters, it may require extra resources at optimisation time. We thus measure the baseline cost of Shallow Parameter Tuning, as well as the extra computation required by our Deep Parameter Tuning. The user may use this gain/cost ratio to decide whether to employ Shallow or Deep Parameter Tuning.

4.1 Experiment Target

Many memory allocation strategies and managers have been proposed and studied by many researchers to efficiently manage dynamic memory. Among them, Doug Lea's malloc (*dlmalloc*) is "among the fastest, most space-conserving, tunable, and portable general purpose allocators" [22]. A study by Berger et al. [3] shows that many other custom memory allocators do not perform significantly better than *dlmalloc*, and are sometimes worse. We focus on *dlmalloc* as an indicative starting point and optimise its configuration to each of the subject applications.

Dlmalloc is a general memory allocator for C programs. Although it provides a number of configuration parameters, it is usually used with its default values. We call these configurable parameters provided by the original author shallow parameters. In these experiments we consider the nine shallow parameters that are more relevant to the tradeoff between runtime and memory high-water-mark. Table 2 briefly describes these shallow parameters.

4.2 Experiment Setup

For our evaluation, we selected four applications: *espresso*, *gawk*, *flex* and *sed*. *Espresso* is a fast application for simplifying complex digital electronic gate circuits. We use the *espresso* benchmark source code and test cases from the *DieHard* project [2]. *Gawk* is the GNU *awk* implementation for string processing. We collect Version 4.1.0 of this application, as well as its test suite, from the GNU archives. *flex* is a tool for generating scanners, programs which recognizes lexical patterns in text, and *sed* is an editor that automatically modifies files given a set of rules. We obtain these last two programs and corresponding test suites from the SIR repository [8]. Summary data for these subject programs is listed in Table 3.

4.3 Experiment Procedures

We first used the shallow parameters only and applied the NSGA-II algorithm with a population of 50 for 300 generations, using 5000 randomly generated chromosomes as seeds. These standard values were chosen after a few trial experiments to have the best performance and ensure convergent result for the algorithms. A random search was also applied with the same computation budget in optimising the shallow parameters.

Table 3: Subject applications

Name	Loc	# Tests	Description
espresso	13256	19	Digital circuit simplification
gawk	45241	334	String processing
flex	9597	62	Fast lexical analyzer generator
sed	5720	362	Special file editor

We used the open source C mutation testing tool MILU [12, 18] to automatically generate mutants from the selective operators shown in Table 1. This mutation based pre-analysis finds the equivalent mutants that are sensitive to the non-functional properties under optimisation. These equivalent mutants are transformed and exposed into 9 deep parameters (the same number as the provided shallow parameters for a fairer comparison) for each subject program separately, as described in Section 3. Combining shallow and deep parameters, we again applied NSGA-II and random search with other identical experimental settings. All experiments were repeated for 20 runs to admit statistical analyses.

All experiments were carried out on desktop machines with a quad-core CPU and 7.7 GB memory runing 64-bit Ubuntu 14.04. We used *dlmalloc* version 2.8.6, which was compiled with gcc 4.8.1 with -O3 option. To capture the execution time and memory consumption precisely, we developed our own performance tool to measure the CPU time and the high-water-mark vitural memory consumption (see Section 3.3). The tool is publicly available at https://github.com/FanWuUCL/memory.

5. RESULTS

We formalise the metrics we use to compare multi-objective optimisation approaches in this section. The results are presented in Section 5.2, and are used to answer the **RQ**s.

5.1 Metrics

To investigate RQ1 and RQ2, we collect the non-dominated set of solutions from each algorithm for 20 runs, and report it in an attainment surface as introduced by Fonseca [9]. To quantitatively compare the quality of each algorithm, we calculate Hypervolume and Contribution indicators to assess the multi-objective Pareto Front.

Hypervolume: The Hypervolume indicator [32] measures the space dominated by the solutions. It is defined as the hypervolume of the union of hypercubes dominated by each solution on the Front. The bigger the Hypervolume is, the larger the area dominated by the Pareto Front in the objective space is, and thus the better the performance is.

Contribution: Since there is no way to know the true Pareto Front, we use the non-dominated set of joint solutions from all experiments to approximate the true Pareto Front, forming a 'reference' front. The Contribution indicator represents the ratio of solutions on the reference front that are found by a given algorithm. A higher ratio indicates a more successful search.

To allow comparison across subject programs, objectives are normalised to the original performance of each subject.

5.2 Answers to RQs

For brevity we use *Sha* to refer to shallow parameters and *All* to refer to all parameters including shallow and deep parameters, followed by *Rand* or *NSGA* to indicate the search method used

Table 2: *dlmalloc* selective shallow parameters made available by the developers and used in our experiments

Name	Default	Range	Type	Description
MALLOC_ALIGNMENT	2∗*sizeof(void∗)*	(1 – 16)∗*sizeof(void∗)*	2^n∗*sizeof(void∗)*	Alignment unit
FOOTERS	*false*	*true* or *false*	boolean	Additional information of each chunk
INSECURE	*false*	*true* or *false*	boolean	Secure check
NO_SEGMENT_TRAVERSAL	*false*	*true* or *false*	boolean	Traversal of chunks before coalescing
MORECORE_CONTIGUOUS	*true*	*true* or *false*	boolean	Contiguous heap extension support
DEFAULT_GRANULARITY	0	4 KB – 512 KB or 0	2^n KB or 0	Unit of heap extension
DEFAULT_TRIM_THRESHOLD	2048 KB	64 KB – 16 MB	2^n KB	Threshold of trimming
DEFAULT_MMAP_THRESHOLD	256 KB	16 KB – 2 MB	integer	Threshold of direct memory mapping
MAX_RELEASE_CHECK_RATE	4095	1000 – 10000	integer	Frequency of coalescing

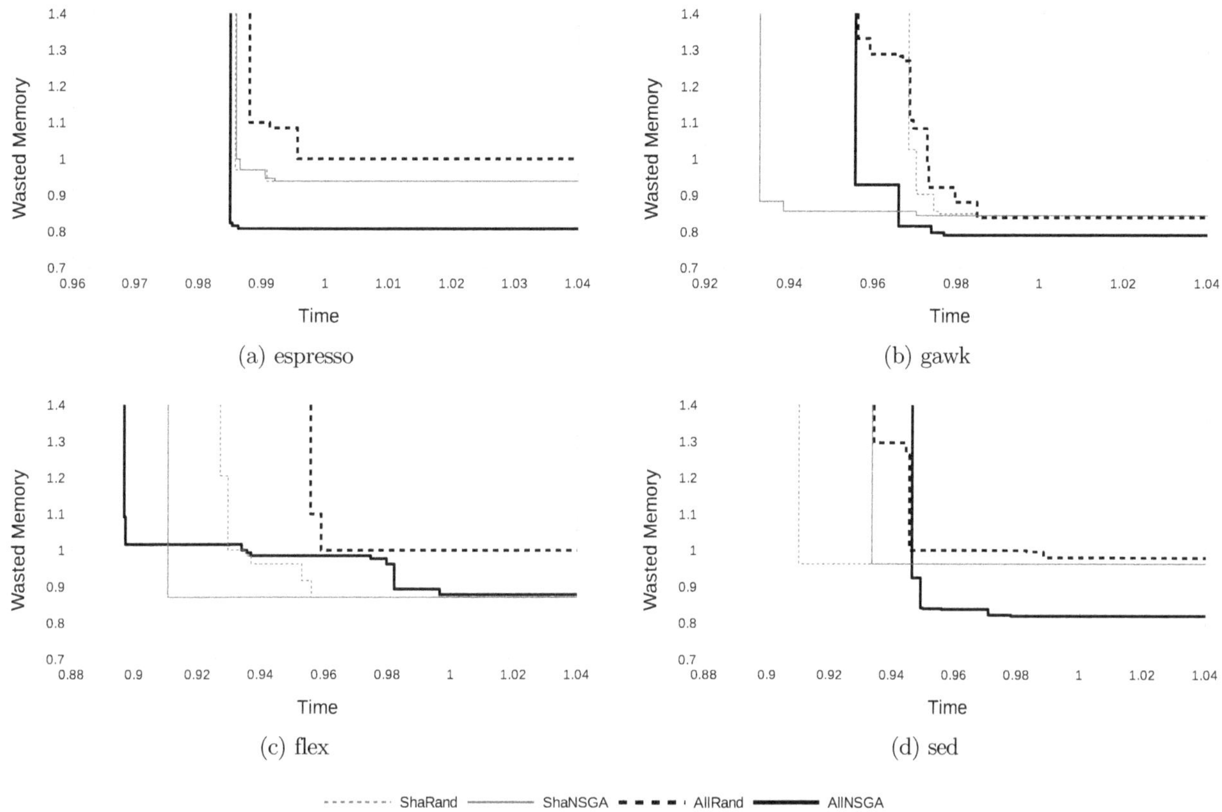

Figure 3: Combined best solutions from the results of *ShaRand*, *ShaNSGA*, *AllRand*, *AllNSGA* over 20 runs for each application. Lower and lefthand solutions dominate high and righthand solutions. 'Wasted' memory is memory that is used but not needed.

(random search or NSGA-II). For example, *ShaNSGA* refers to using NSGA-II to search for better values for shallow parameters.

To answer RQ1 and RQ2, we first report the 0%-attainment surfaces (the 'reference front' that combines best solutions over all runs) of the results of *ShaRand*, *ShaNSGA*, *AllRand* and *AllNSGA* on all subjects in Figure 3. The solutions are plotted according to their execution time and memory usage (at the 'high-water-mark') compared to the original performance. Specially, the original always lies at (1, 1) and is pinpointed by light grey dashed lines. The high-water-mark is our primary target since the remaining non-wasted memory is needed and thus cannot be reduced. The figure shows that all algorithms can reduce time or memory consumption without reducing the other objective, implying that the default configuration of *dlmalloc* is not optimal for any application considered. This finding motivates the use of SBSE for tuning memory allocators. In three subjects (*espresso*, *gawk* and *sed*), *AllNSGA* outperforms the other three on memory objective. In terms of time, no algorithm is strictly better and each has its own strengths on different subjects.

We calculated the Hypervolume and Contribution indicator of each algorithm on every subject, and report them in Figure 4 and 5 respectively for all 20 runs. In Figure 4, all the values are normalised to the hypervolume of the 0% attainment reference front, and the closer the value to 1 is, the better the result is. It is clear that *AllNSGA* outperforms the others on subject *espresso* and *sed* while it performs poorly on subject *flex*, and on subject *gawk* the best value reached by *AllNSGA* is better than that of the others. In terms of Contribution, the performance of all algorithms is similar to that of Hypervolume. In general *AllNSGA* is no worse than other algorithms on all subjects but *flex*, where *ShaNSGA* has the highest Contribution value.

Since *AllNSGA* is good at finding better performance on memory consumption, we report the most memory-saving performance found by each algorithm of each of 20 runs in Figure 6. On subject *espresso* and *sed*, *AllNSGA* finds more memory

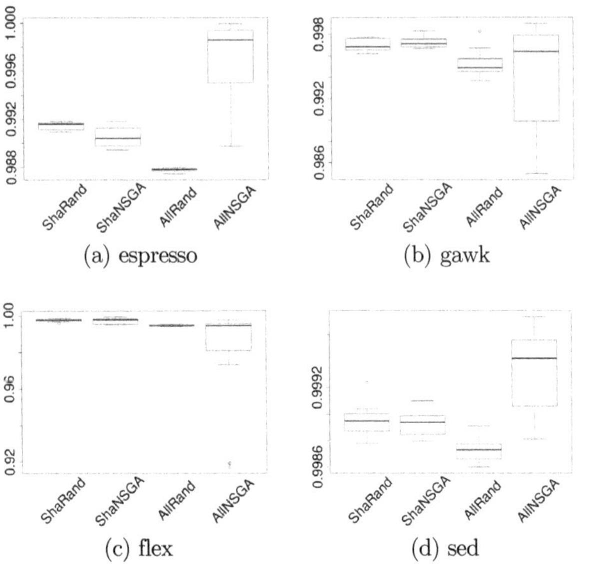

Figure 4: Hypervolume indicator of *ShaRand*, *ShaNSGA*, *AllRand*, *AllNSGA* on all subjects. Larger values are better.

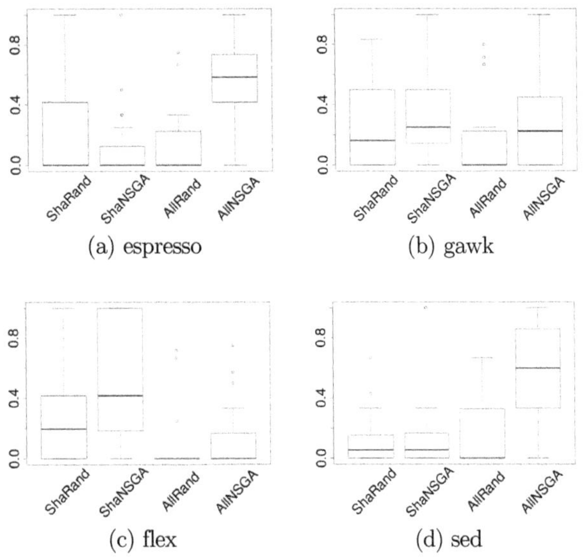

Figure 5: Contribution indicator of *ShaRand*, *ShaNSGA*, *AllRand*, *AllNSGA* on all subjects. Larger values are better.

reduction than the other approaches. On *gawk*, it does not perform as consistently, but can also find more memory reduction than other approaches in the best case.

Inferential statistical tests were applied to the Hypervolume, Contribution and Best-Memory-Reduction results over all subjects. We used the Mann-Whitney-Wilcoxon U-test since we make no assumptions about results distributions and apply a Bonferroni Correction (catering for 16 total statistical tests) to draw conservative conclusions with no risk of Type 1 error. For those p-values less than $0.05/16 = 0.003125$, we apply the Vargha-Delaney ($\hat{A}_{12}$) effect size measure (see Table 4). The effect sizes are all large (either above 0.79 or below 0.21).

In all experiments involving *All** we generated and evaluated invalid configurations (i.e., those that that cause the program to crash). However, this issue is not specific to our deep-parameter

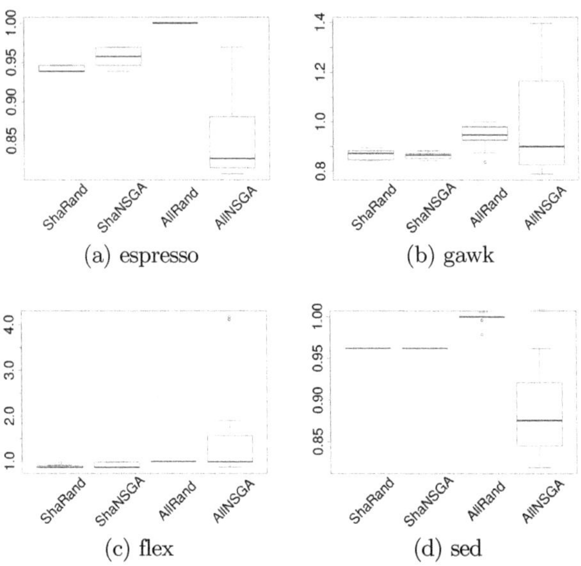

Figure 6: The least memory consumption found by each algorithm. Smaller numbers are better.

approach: surprisingly, even by just tuning the programmer-specified shallow parameters (*ShaRand* and *ShaNSGA* optimisations) we *also* encounter (and discard) some configurations that crash the program. This suggests that SBSE memory allocator tuning can be used as a search based testing technique [14]. Without any guidance, *AllRand* finds valid configurations less often than *ShaRand*, and thus requires more optimisation time than *ShaRand*. Holding the searches to the same budget means that *AllNSGA*, which must explore a higher search space, will exhibit a higher variance. Despite this more challenging search space, exposing and optimising deep parameters still allows *AllNSGA* to find better configurations than *ShaNSGA*.

To enable a more quantitative look at maximal time and memory savings, we examine the extreme performance observed in our experiments. We report those that have the best performance on one objective, even at the cost of reducing performance on the other objective, found by each algorithm on each subject and summarise them in Table 5. Some of these results are significant departures from the original and are thus not plotted in Figure 3.

To answer RQ3, we provide the average optimisation computation time for each of the apporaches in Table 6. Recall that *AllRand* generates and evaluates numerous invalid configurations. However, since crashing or incorrect mutants can be discarded immediately, the computation time of *AllRand* is the lowest among all approaches (given a fixed budget in terms of mutants considered). Similarly, *AllNSGA* generates invalid configurations more often than *ShaNSGA*, so it costs less computation time than *ShaNSGA*. Taking the deep parameter discovery time into account, *AllNSGA* requires slightly more time than *ShaNSGA* does, and the percentage of the extra computation time is reported in the last column of Table 6. Ultimately, *AllNSGA* requires at most 18% more computation time than *ShaNSGA* (on *espresso*), but requires only 0.7% more computation time on *flex*, on which *AllNSGA* does not perform as well as *ShaNSGA*. Overall, since this optimisation step is a compile-time rather than run-time cost and can be done before deployment, we view the benefits of deep parameter optimisation as significantly outweighing their slight additional optimisation time cost.

Table 4: Vargha-Delaney effect sizes of Hypervolume, Contribution and Best Memory Reduction for any two of the approaches on all subjects. Only the effect sizes of tests with p-value less than $5\%/16 = 0.3125\%$ are reported.

Comparing Approachs		Hypervolume				Contribution				Best Memory Reduction			
		espresso	*gawk*	*flex*	*sed*	*espresso*	*gawk*	*flex*	*sed*	*espresso*	*gawk*	*flex*	*sed*
AllNSGA	*AllRand*	1.000	–	–	0.975	0.859	–	–	0.835	0.000	–	–	0.000
	ShaNSGA	0.935	–	0.105	0.808	0.868	–	0.191	0.868	0.063	–	0.950	0.050
	ShaRand	0.900	–	0.035	0.785	0.814	–	–	0.875	0.100	–	0.979	0.050
AllRand	*ShaNSGA*	0.000	0.053	0.038	0.045	–	–	0.144	–	1.000	0.940	1.000	1.000
	ShaRand	0.000	0.070	0.000	0.040	–	–	–	–	1.000	0.928	1.000	1.000
ShaNSGA	*ShaRand*	0.198	–	–	–	–	–	–	–	0.800	–	–	–

Table 5: Best reduction of time or memory (separately) found by each algorithm

Subject	Time Original (s)	Time Reduction (%)				Memory Original (Peak/Wasted KB)	Wasted Memory Reduction (%)			
		ShaRand	*ShaNSGA*	*AllRand*	*AllNSGA*		*ShaRand*	*ShaNSGA*	*AllRand*	*AllNSGA*
espresso	7.24	1.4	1.4	1.5	1.5	3500/521	6.1	6.1	0	19.2
gawk	3.43	3.2	6.7	4.4	4.4	29680/3552	15.6	15.6	16.2	20.9
flex	0.13	7.9	10.0	6.2	11.6	10816/525	13.0	13.0	0	12.2
sed	0.25	9.4	7.0	7.0	5.4	7048/948	3.8	3.8	2.1	17.9

Table 6: Computation Cost in Time

Subject	Optimisation Time (h)				Exposing Time (h)	Extra Time Needed for *NSGA (%)
	ShaRand	*ShaNSGA*	*AllRand*	*AllNSGA*		
espresso	39.7	46.4	9.0	39.3	12.5	18.5
gawk	22.7	18.4	13.9	16.4	5.4	11.7
flex	7.7	6.3	5.3	5.0	1.3	0.7
sed	9.4	7.6	5.9	6.6	1.9	12.6

5.3 Threats to Validity

Internal Validity When exposing deep parameters, we used a mutation-based sensitivity analysis because of its advantages in terms of efficiency and automation. Whether it is the best way to expose deep parameters remains to be proven. In addition, we have not formally investigated the relative merits of the Mutation Operators used. Intuitively, our Mutation Operators change a constant or an operator in an expression, and thus are likely to change the values of expressions to different degrees, allowing us to capture the sensitivity of that program's non-functional behaviour to the value of that expression. Any lack of efficacy of these Mutation Operators at capturing sensitivity information introduces a threat to the effectiveness of our approach. A formal evaluation of mutation operators for deep parameter tuning remains as future work.

Another threat to the internal validity is that the execution time measured may depend on the workload of the machine. We mitigate this threat by averaging the execution time of 10 trials on an otherwise-unloaded machine.

External Validity Our choice of benchmark programs and their associated test suites influences the generality of our results. Even a good test suite that achieves high branch coverage, for example, could still differ from real world inputs, in which case the optimised configuration over this test suite may neither achieve the best performance nor retain required functionality. We attempt to mitigate this threat by including two subjects (*flex* and *sed*) from the SIR repository [8]. These subjects come with sets of high quality test suites, which achieve multiple adequacy testing criteria.

Another aspect of generality is whether these results hold on other applications. We attempt to mitigate this threat by selecting subject applications from different fields, but our results may not generalize beyond these benchmarks.

6. RELATED WORK

State-of-the-art dynamic memory managers usually combine several different allocation strategies to serve memory requests with different sizes. Risco-Martín et al. [27, 5] search for the best allocation strategy for different sizes as well searching for the best range of sizes on which each strategy should be applied. Their work requires human effort to implement the allocation strategies. In our approach, changing the parameters not only (indirectly) changes the separators of size ranges and allocation strategy applied on each range, but also influences strategy behaviour.

ParamILS [17] is an automatic framework proposed by Hutter et al., which automatically configures an algorithm's parameters to optimise performance on a given test suite. While targeting parameter tuning as well, our approach focuses on standard library code, based on the assumption that the general-purpose memory allocators may not be optimal for each specific application. In addition, *ParamILS* can only optimise existing (shallow) parameters, while our approach exposes additional parameters and adjusts their values to gain more improvement.

Hoffmann et al. [15] proposed *PowerDial*, a system which dynamically adjusts an application's behaviour to make it adaptable to fluctuating workloads. Whenever *PowerDial* detects a resource shortage it sacrifices output quality by changing the values of variables, allowing the application to 'survive the crisis'. One limitation of this work is that the search space of configuration variables must be small enough to admit an exhaustive search. In our work the search space is too large to use such an exhaustive search, and thus we applied search-based techniques. *PowerDial* only operates on existing (shallow) parameters.

Hutter et al. [16] have tuned the parameters of a SAT solver, SPEAR, by adjusting not only the explicit parameters but also many implicit parameters. They expose almost all possibly tunable variables and thereby a much larger search space than we do. To reduce the computation effort by limiting the search space, we use a mutation-based technique to find the most influential parts of the code and focus the search on just them. This sensitivity analysis effectively reduces the space, admitting practical searches.

In previous work, the Software Tuning panel for Autonomic Control (STAC) [4] automated the expsoure of a limited form of 'deep' parameters. Although STAC can discover some deep parameters effectively, it suffers from two limitations. First, STAC requires initial human effort to characterise shallow parameters. Second, STAC can only find a subset of deep parameters, those that have similar data transition patterns to the known shallow parameters. To overcome these limitations, we apply a mutation-based sensitivity analysis to fully automate the process of locating potential deep parameters and subsequently apply NSGA-II to search for optimal values for these parameters to balance non-functional properties of interest.

7. CONCLUSIONS

In this paper we propose an automatic algorithm for discovering and optimising deep parameters to tune programs with respect to non-functional properties. In particular, we focus on tuning *dlmalloc*, a memory allocator, to reduce the time and memory high-water-mark requirements of off-the-shelf programs. Our approach combines mutation analysis to discover sensitive deep parameters as well as an SBSE approach which subsequently optimises these parameters, while retaining the functionality expressed in a test suite. In a series of experiments involving over 70,000 lines of code and 700 test cases we found that our deep parameter approach outperformed baseline optimisations (which use only the programmer-provided shallow parameters), ultimately improving execution time by 12% and memory consumption by 21% in the best cases. In addition, despite the larger search space considered, the additional optimisation time cost of our approach is acceptably low. Overall, we feel that deep parameter tuning approaches show much promise for the automated improvement of software with respect to non-functional properties.

8. REFERENCES

[1] A. Arcuri and G. Fraser. On parameter tuning in search based software engineering. In *Search Based Software Engineering*. 2011.

[2] E. D. Berger and B. G. Zorn. Diehard: Probabilistic memory safety for unsafe languages. In *Programming Language Design and Implementation*, PLDI '06, 2006.

[3] E. D. Berger, B. G. Zorn, and K. S. McKinley. Reconsidering custom memory allocation. In *Object-oriented Programming, Systems, Languages, and Applications*, OOPSLA '02, 2002.

[4] N. Brake, J. R. Cordy, E. Dan Y, M. Litoiu, and V. Popes U. Automating discovery of software tuning parameters. In *Workshop on Software Engineering for Adaptive and Self-managing Systems*, SEAMS '08, 2008.

[5] J. M. Colmenar, J. L. Risco-Martín, D. Atienza, and J. I. Hidalgo. Multi-objective optimization of dynamic memory managers using grammatical evolution. In *Conference on Genetic and Evolutionary Computation*, GECCO '11, 2011.

[6] C. Ţăpuş, I.-H. Chung, and J. K. Hollingsworth. Active harmony: Towards automated performance tuning. In *Conference on Supercomputing*, Supercomputing '02, 2002.

[7] K. Deb, A. Pratap, S. Agarwal, and T. Meyarivan. A fast and elitist multiobjective genetic algorithm: NSGA-II. *Evolutionary Computation, IEEE Transactions on*, 6(2), 2002.

[8] H. Do, S. Elbaum, and G. Rothermel. Supporting controlled experimentation with testing techniques: An infrastructure and its potential impact. *Empirical Software Engineering*, 10(4), 2005.

[9] C. Fonseca and P. Fleming. On the performance assessment and comparison of stochastic multiobjective optimizers. In *PPSN*. Springer Berlin Heidelberg, 1996.

[10] M. Harman. The current state and future of search based software engineering. In *2007 Future of Software Engineering*, FOSE '07, 2007.

[11] M. Harman, Y. Jia, and W. Langdon. Babel pidgin: Sbse can grow and graft entirely new functionality into a real world system. In *Search-Based Software Engineering*, volume 8636 of *Lecture Notes in Computer Science*, pages 247–252. Springer International Publishing, 2014.

[12] M. Harman, Y. Jia, and W. B. Langdon. Strong higher order mutation-based test data generation. In *Proceedings of the 19th ACM SIGSOFT Symposium and the 13th European Conference on Foundations of Software Engineering*, ESEC/FSE '11, pages 212–222, 2011.

[13] M. Harman, Y. Jia, W. B. Langdon, J. Petke, I. H. Moghadam, S. Yoo, and F. Wu. Genetic improvement for adaptive software engineering (keynote). In *Symposium on Software Engineering for Adaptive and Self-Managing Systems*, SEAMS, 2014.

[14] M. Harman, Y. Jia, and Y. Zhang. Achievements, open problems and challenges for search based software testing (keynote). In 8th *IEEE International Conference on Software Testing, Verification and Validation (ICST 2014)*, Graz, Austria, April 2015.

[15] H. Hoffmann, S. Sidiroglou, M. Carbin, S. Misailovic, A. Agarwal, and M. Rinard. Dynamic knobs for responsive power-aware computing. In *Architectural Support for Programming Languages and Operating Systems*, 2011.

[16] F. Hutter, D. Babic, H. H. Hoos, and A. Hu. Boosting verification by automatic tuning of decision procedures. In *Formal Methods in Computer Aided Design, 2007. FMCAD '07*, Nov 2007.

[17] F. Hutter, H. H. Hoos, K. Leyton-Brown, and T. Stützle. ParamILS: an automatic algorithm configuration framework. *Journal of Artificial Intelligence Research*, 36(1), 2009.

[18] Y. Jia and M. Harman. MILU: A Customizable, Runtime-Optimized Higher Order Mutation Testing Tool for the Full C Language. In *Proceedings of the TAIC PART'08*, pages 94–98, Windsor, UK, 29-31 August 2008.

[19] Y. Jia and M. Harman. An analysis and survey of the development of mutation testing. *Software Engineering, IEEE Transactions on*, 37(5), 2011.

[20] T. Katagiri, K. Kise, H. Honda, and T. Yuba. Fiber: A generalized framework for auto-tuning software. In *High Performance Computing*. 2003.

[21] W. B. Langdon, M. Modat, J. Petke, and M. Harman. Improving 3d medical image registration cuda software with genetic programming. In *Conference on Genetic and Evolutionary Computation*, GECCO '14, 2014.

[22] D. Lea and W. Gloger. A memory allocator, 2000. http://g.oswego.edu/dl/html/malloc.html.

[23] M. Papadakis, Y. Jia, M. Harman, and Y. L. Traon. Trivial Compiler Equivalence: A Large Scale Empirical Study of a Simple Fast and Effective Equivalent Mutant Detection Technique. In *Proceedings of the 37th International Conference on Software Engineering*, 15. To appear.

[24] J. Petke, M. Harman, W. Langdon, and W. Weimer. Using genetic improvement and code transplants to specialise a c++ program to a problem class. In *Genetic Programming*. 2014.

[25] J. L. Risco-Martín, D. Atienza, J. M. Colmenar, and O. Garnica. A parallel evolutionary algorithm to optimize dynamic memory managers in embedded systems. *Parallel Computing*, 36(10 - 11), 2010. Parallel Architectures and Bioinspired Algorithms.

[26] J. L. Risco-Martín, D. Atienza, R. Gonzalo, and J. I. Hidalgo. Optimization of dynamic memory managers for embedded systems using grammatical evolution. In *Conference on Genetic and Evolutionary Computation*, GECCO '09, 2009.

[27] J. L. Risco-Martín, J. M. Colmenar, J. I. Hidalgo, J. Lanchares, and J. Díaz. A methodology to automatically optimize dynamic memory managers applying grammatical evolution. *Journal of Systems and Software*, 91(0), 2014.

[28] E. Schulte, Z. Fry, E. Fast, W. Weimer, and S. Forrest. Software mutational robustness. *Genetic Programming and Evolvable Machines*, 15(3), 2014.

[29] R. Vuduc, J. W. Demmel, and J. Bilmes. Statistical models for automatic performance tuning. In *International Conference on Computational Science (ICCS)*, 2001.

[30] R. C. Whaley and J. J. Dongarra. Automatically tuned linear algebra software. In *Conference on Supercomputing*, Supercomputing '98, 1998.

[31] X. Yao, M. Harman, and Y. Jia. A study of equivalent and stubborn mutation operators using human analysis of equivalence. In *Proceedings of the 36th International Conference on Software Engineering*, ICSE 2014, pages 919–930, 2014.

[32] E. Zitzler and L. Thiele. Multiobjective evolutionary algorithms: a comparative case study and the strength pareto approach. *IEEE Transactions on Evolutionary Computation*, 3(4), Nov 1999.

[33] B. Zorn and D. Grunwald. Empirical measurements of six allocation-intensive C programs. *SIGPLAN Not.*, 27(12), Dec. 1992.

SPRINT Multi-Objective Model Racing

Tiantian Zhang
University of Central Florida
4000 Central Florida Blvd.
Orlando, FL, USA, 32816
zhangtt@knights.ucf.edu

Michael Georgiopoulos
University of Central Florida
4000 Central Florida Blvd.
Orlando, FL, USA, 32816
michaelg@ucf.edu

Georgios C. Anagnostopoulos
Florida Institute of Technology
150 W. University Blvd
Melbourne, FL, USA, 32901
georgio@fit.edu

ABSTRACT

Multi-objective model selection, which is an important aspect of Machine Learning, refers to the problem of identifying a set of Pareto optimal models from a given ensemble of models. This paper proposes SPRINT-Race, a multi-objective racing algorithm based on the Sequential Probability Ratio Test with an Indifference Zone. In SPRINT-Race, a non-parametric ternary-decision sequential analogue of the sign test is adopted to identify pair-wise dominance and non-dominance relationship. In addition, a Bonferroni approach is employed to control the overall probability of any erroneous decisions. In the fixed confidence setting, SPRINT-Race tries to minimize the computational effort needed to achieve a predefined confidence about the quality of the returned models. The efficiency of SPRINT-Race is analyzed on artificially-constructed multi-objective model selection problems with known ground-truth. Moreover, SPRINT-Race is applied to identifying the Pareto optimal parameter settings of Ant Colony Optimization algorithms in the context of solving Traveling Salesman Problems. The experimental results confirm the advantages of SPRINT-Race for multi-objective model selection.

CCS Concepts

•Mathematics of computing → Hypothesis testing and confidence interval computation; •Computing methodologies → Sequential decision making; •Applied computing → Multi-criterion optimization and decision-making;

Keywords

Racing Algorithm; Model Selection; Multi-objective Optimization; Sequential Probability Ratio Test

1. INTRODUCTION

Given an ensemble of models, the task of Model Selection (MS) is to identify a subset of models that are optimal in terms of certain optimization criteria. There are a variety of MS problems, including feature selection, algorithm and learning strategy selection, hyper-parameter selection, etc.

The problem of Single-Objective Model Selection (SOMS), in which only one optimization criterion is considered, has received much attention in the literature of stochastic Multi-Armed Bandit (MAB) as *best arm(s) identification* problem [8, 5]. Among them, Racing Algorithms (RAs) are regarded as an elimination-type MAB, which tries to minimize the computational effort needed to achieve a predefined confidence about the quality of the returned models (fixed confidence setting). A RA is an iterative procedure that starts off with an initial ensemble of candidate models (*candidate pool*). The candidate models are evaluated by solving randomly sampled problem instances in a sequential manner and their performances are measured according to a single task-specific criterion of model optimality (e.g. prediction accuracy, convergence speed, etc). Under-performing models are eliminated as soon as sufficient statistical evidence is amassed. Consequently, a RA saves (unnecessary) computational cost spent on trying to exploit poor-performing models. In other words, a RA trades off some computational effort with the likelihood that the model(s) returned by the racing procedure is (are) indeed the optimal one(s).

Ever since the first RA was developed, RAs have been widely used in parameter tuning and configuration [2, 16], algorithm design [11], and some industrial applications [1]. Several leading RAs for SOMS have been proposed in the literature: Hoeffding Racing (HR) [17], BRACE [20], Bernstein Racing (BR) [19, 15], and F-Race [3].

However, in real-world Machine Learning (ML) applications, model selection is often multi-objective in nature [12]. In Multi-Task Learning, for instance, all task objectives should be optimized simultaneously. Moreover, in the context of evolutionary computation, computational cost is always considered as an additional selection criterion besides the quality of the best solution obtained. Model selection in terms of multiple conflicting optimization criteria is referred to as Multi-objective Model Selection (MOMS). A straightforward way of solving a MOMS problem is to convert it to a SOMS problem, either by considering the conic linear combination or the Chebyshev scalarization of all the objectives, or by adopting other unary quality indicators [14] (e.g. hypervolume, epsilon indicator). However, Pareto optimality plays an important role in MOMS. Optimizing any single optimization objective does not provide any insight into the trade-offs among multiple conflicting objectives. The first Multi-objective Racing Algorithm (MORA), namely S-

GECCO '15, July 11 - 15, 2015, Madrid, Spain

ISBN 978-1-4503-3472-3/15/07 . . . $15.00

DOI: http://dx.doi.org/10.1145/2739480.2754791

Race, which addresses the problem of MOMS in the sense of Pareto optimality was put forward by the seminal paper of Zhang et al. [25]. In S-Race, the probabilistic dominance relationship between two models is statistically inferred by the non-parametric sign test based on the observed performance vectors. Moreover, the total probability of not making any Type I errors (falsely rejecting the null hypothesis and inferring pair-wise dominance) is strictly controlled by Holm's step-down procedure, which is accomplished by adjusting the significance level of each individual hypothesis in multiple comparisons. In the same paper, S-Race was applied to selecting Support Vector Machines for binary-/ternary-classification. The obtained experimental results demonstrated that S-Race is an efficient and effective algorithm for automatic model selection.

Nevertheless, S-Race has certain limitations. First of all, in S-Race, unlike the total probability of not committing any Type I errors, the probability of making any Type II errors (falsely inferring the absence of dominance) is not strictly controlled. Moreover, the sign test adopted in S-Race can only identify dominance relationships, *i.e.*, whether model A dominates model B or the opposite. When two non-dominated models are compared and no dominance relation is discerned, the comparison continues until the available problem instances are exhausted. In other words, S-Race spends unnecessary computational cost on comparing non-dominated models. Most important of all, the sign test employed in S-Race is not an optimum test procedure, as explained in Section 2.2. If establishing dominance based on the sign test is good in terms of error probability, replacing it by the optimal test procedure should yield a MORA with improved overall sample complexity. Note that the sample complexity of a test comparing two models refers to the expectation of the final size of the sample required to reach a decision.

To overcome these limitations of S-Race, here we introduce SPRINT-Race, a MORA based on the Sequential Probability Ratio Test (SPRT) with an Indifference Zone. SPRINT-Race hinges on a ternary-decision, sequential analogue of the sign test. The comparison between two models terminates, when either dominance or non-dominance is established with certain confidence. As a result, SPRINT-Race is able to stop automatically, when no more sampling is needed for further comparisons. In addition, both Type I and Type II errors are strictly controlled via the SPRT. Therefore, SPRINT-Race is capable of strictly confining the error probability of returning dominated models and, simultaneously, abandoning non-dominated models at a predefined level. Moreover, the concept of an indifference zone is introduced in SPRINT-Race to aid in reducing the possibility of miscategorizing Pareto optimal models by chance.

SPRINT-Race infers dominance or lack thereof between a pair of models based on a ternary-decision SPRT procedure, namely dual-SPRT, which consists of two component SPRTs. Section 2 provides some necessary background on the SPRT and introduces the proposed SPRINT-Race procedure. Furthermore, the analysis of the overall error probability of SPRINT-Race, *i.e.*, the total probability of any false discoveries, is discussed in Section 2.4. The efficiency and effectiveness of SPRINT-Race for MOMS are evaluated via a series of experiments described in Section 3. First, the performance of SPRINT-Race is evaluated on artificially-constructed MOMS problems with known ground-truth solutions. Additionally, SPRINT-Race is applied to selecting Pareto optimal parameter settings of Ant Colony Optimization (ACO) algorithms in the context of Traveling Salesman Problems (TSPs). Overall, the experimental results confirm the potential advantages of SPRINT-Race for addressing MOMS problems. Finally, key findings are summarized in Section 4.

2. SPRINT-RACE DESCRIPTION

SPRINT-Race addresses the problem of MOMS in the sense of Pareto optimality. The (non-)dominance relationship between a pair of models is determined via a ternary-decision SPRT procedure dubbed dual-SPRT. Moreover, the error probability of SPRINT-Race, meaning the total probability of falsely retaining any dominated model or removing any non-dominated model during the SPRINT-Race, is strictly controlled at a user-specified level.

2.1 Problem Formulation

SPRINT-Race assumes the following setting: the decision maker is in possession of an ensemble of M models $\{C_1, C_2, \cdots, C_M\}$, which are to be compared according to D optimization objectives $\{f_i(C)\}_{i=1,\cdots,D}$. Without loss of generality, we will assume that all the objectives are to be maximized. Let $\mathbf{f}(C) \triangleq [f_1(C), f_2(C), \cdots, f_D(C)]$ be the performance vector of a model C. Following traditional conventions [6], $\mathbf{f}(C) \succ \mathbf{f}(C')$ is defined as follows

$$\begin{aligned} &f_i(C) \geqslant f_i(C') \quad \forall\, i \in \{1, 2, \cdots, D\} \\ &\text{and } \exists\, j \in \{1, 2, \cdots, D\} \mid f_j(C) > f_j(C') \end{aligned} \tag{1}$$

There are three possible outcomes of a pairwise comparison between model C and C', namely C dominates C', C' dominates C, and non-dominance. They are denoted as $C \succ C'$, $C \prec C'$ and $C \sim C'$, respectively. Given a model C, it is generally assumed that the objective value $f_i(C)$ is stochastic in nature. This assumption reflects the models' search process randomness or noisy performance measurements. Therefore, SPRINT-Race decides that $C \succ C'$ if $Pr\{\mathbf{f}(C) \succ \mathbf{f}(C')\} > \frac{1}{2}$; $C \prec C'$ if $Pr\{\mathbf{f}(C) \succ \mathbf{f}(C')\} < \frac{1}{2}$; and $C \sim C'$ otherwise. If there is no model that dominates model C, model C is defined as Pareto optimal. In the context of MOMS, in principle, one is interested in identifying the entire set of Pareto front models. However, if desired or if mandated by practicalities, additional subjective criteria might be employed by a decision maker to sub-sample the Pareto front and, potentially, identify a single model that reflects her/his particular preference.

2.2 Sequential Probability Ratio Test

For any testing procedure, let us denote the probability of a Type I error by $\alpha \in [0, 1]$ and the probability of a Type II error by $\beta \in [0, 1]$. Given α and β, the hypothesis test which minimizes the expected number of required samples, over the entire parameter space, is called the uniformly most efficient test of the given hypothesis test problem. It was shown that SPRT can be regarded as a locally most efficient test [23] in the sense that its expected sample complexity is minimized for some proper subset of the parameter space, for all practical purposes. Therefore, given a predefined maximum error probability, adopting SPRT for dominance inference in a MORA should result in a superior algorithm that only necessitates a near-minimum sample complexity.

Assume $\{x_1, x_2, \cdots, x_N\}$ is a sequence of independent and identically distributed observations sampled from an unknown distribution. Let $g_\theta(x_i)$ be the density of the ith sample parametrized by a parameter θ. In a traditional fixed-sample test with two simple hypotheses, one of two possible decisions is made based on the observed random samples: accept the null hypothesis $H_0 : \theta = \theta_0$, or accept the alternative hypothesis $H_1 : \theta = \theta_1$. For a fixed-sample test, α is typically predetermined, but β, which is a function of α, is unknown and left uncontrolled. Therefore, given the sample size N and α, the test procedure that minimizes β is preferred; such a test is referred to as the uniformly most powerful test for the given hypothesis test problem and parameter space. The Neyman-Pearson lemma [10, p.52] implies that the likelihood ratio test yields the most powerful test for testing two simple hypotheses. To be more specific, the test statistic is computed as the ratio of the likelihood of the data under H_1 to their likelihood under H_0.

$$\lambda_N = \prod_{i=1}^{N} \frac{g(x_i|\theta_1)}{g(x_i|\theta_0)} \tag{2}$$

Distinct from fixed-sample testing, there is a third possible action in sequential testing: neither accept H_0 nor accept H_1 but continue sampling with the hope that gathering additional evidence may allow one to decide between the two hypotheses. The sample size of a sequential test is not predetermined and the samples are collected sequentially until either H_0 or H_1 is accepted. SPRT [23] is the first sequential testing procedure proposed in the literature and it proceeds as follows: assume λ_t is the test statistic at step t. Then, if $\lambda_t \leq B$, H_0 is accepted; if $\lambda_t \geq A$, H_1 is accepted; if $B \leq \lambda_t \leq A$, no decision is made and sampling resumes. As suggested in [23], by choosing $A = \frac{1-\beta}{\alpha}$ and $B = \frac{\beta}{1-\alpha}$, the probabilities of Type I and Type II errors does not exceed α and β respectively.

2.3 Dominance/Non-Dominance Inference

Due to the stochastic nature of the performance vectors, the dominance and non-dominance relationship between a pair of models can only be established via a formal test of hypothesis. A pair-wise and non-parametric test procedure is preferred due to its robustness. In a pair-wise test, each sample consists of paired observations, which effectively reduces the variability caused by external factors (e.g. differences between problem instances). Moreover, non-parametric tests have the advantage of being free of distributional assumptions. Therefore, a sequential analogue of the pair-wise non-parametric sign test [18] is adopted in SPRINT-Race to establish dominance and non-dominance between a pair of candidate models. Its motivation is straightforward: if a racing based on the sign test is good in terms of error probabilities, replacing it by the local optimal SPRT should improve it even further in terms of reducing the overall sample complexity.

Assume that a pair of candidate models C_i and C_j is compared, whose performances have been evaluated on a series of problem instances. Let N_{ij} (a random variable) denote the number of times that C_i dominates C_j and let n_{ij} be its observed value. Moreover, let $S \triangleq N_{ij} + N_{ij}$ and let its observed value be $s \triangleq n_{ij} + n_{ij}$. If $p \triangleq Pr\{N_{ij} = 1 | S = 1\}$, then, obviously, $N_{ij} | \{S = s\} \sim \text{Binomial}(s, p)$. Therefore, the relationship between C_i and C_j is established in the following manner: if $p < \frac{1}{2}$, C_i is dominated by C_j; if $p = \frac{1}{2}$, C_i and C_j are non-dominated to each other; and if $p > \frac{1}{2}$, C_i dominates C_j. In other words, the problem of inferring dominance and non-dominance between a pair of models translates to making a decision among three mutually exclusive and exhaustive hypotheses

$$H_0 : p < 1/2 \quad H_1 : p = 1/2 \quad H_2 : p > 1/2 \tag{3}$$

Subsequently, if H_0 is accepted, model C_i will be eliminated from racing; if H_2 is accepted, model C_j will eliminated; if H_1 is accepted, both C_i and C_j will be retained by the racing procedure.

Moreover, the concept of indifference zone is introduced for practical considerations: i) in real world applications, a thorough investigation is usually uneconomical and one is willing to take near-optimal decisions; and ii) it mitigates the possibility of omitting Pareto optimal models due to inaccurate performance measurements (e.g. noise). More specifically, in SPRINT-Race, the following three hypotheses are considered:

$$H_0 : p \leq 1/2 - \delta \quad H_1 : p = 1/2 \quad H_2 : p \geq 1/2 + \delta \tag{4}$$

where $\delta \in (0, 1/2)$ is chosen by the decision maker. The intervals $(1/2 - \delta, 1/2)$ and $(1/2, 1/2 + \delta)$ will be referred to as indifference zones. When $p \in (1/2 - \delta, 1/2)$, we assume that we have no strong preference between H_0 and H_1, but the rejection of H_2 is strongly preferred. Similarly when $p \in (1/2, 1/2 + \delta)$, no error is committed if either H_1 or H_2 is considered. Note that the selection of δ is not a statistical problem, but should be made based on practical concerns.

The previously described ternary-decision test, referred to as dual-SPRT, is constructed by combining two component binary-hypothesis SPRT [22] as shown in Equation (5). The decision procedure of the dual-SPRT is summarized in Table 1.

$$\begin{array}{lll} \textbf{SPRT}^1 & H_0^1 : p \leq \frac{1}{2} - \delta & H_1^1 : p \geq \frac{1}{2} \\ \textbf{SPRT}^2 & H_0^2 : p \leq \frac{1}{2} & H_1^2 : p \geq \frac{1}{2} + \delta \end{array} \tag{5}$$

Table 1: Testing procedure of dual-SPRT

$SPRT^1$ accepts	$SPRT^2$ accepts	dual-SPRT accepts
$H_0^1 : p \leq \frac{1}{2} - \delta$	$H_0^2 : p \leq \frac{1}{2}$	$H_0 : p \leq \frac{1}{2} - \delta$
$H_1^1 : p \geq \frac{1}{2}$	$H_0^2 : p \leq \frac{1}{2}$	$H_1 : p = \frac{1}{2}$
$H_1^1 : p \geq \frac{1}{2}$	$H_1^2 : p \geq \frac{1}{2} + \delta$	$H_2 : p \geq \frac{1}{2} + \delta$

Due to the monotonic likelihood ratio property of the binomial distribution, the component SPRTs described in Equation (5) are equivalent to the following tests

$$\begin{array}{lll} \textbf{SPRT}^1 & H_0^1 : p = \frac{1}{2} - \delta & H_1^1 : p = \frac{1}{2} \\ \textbf{SPRT}^2 & H_0^2 : p = \frac{1}{2} & H_1^2 : p = \frac{1}{2} + \delta \end{array} \tag{6}$$

Assume that, at the tth step, there are n_{ij}^t times that C_i dominates C_j and n_{ji}^t times that C_j dominates C_i. In each component SPRT with $H_0 : p = p_0$ and $H_1 : p = p_1$, the test statistic is calculated as follows:

$$\lambda_t = \frac{p_1^{n_{ij}^t} (1 - p_1)^{n_{ji}^t}}{p_0^{n_{ij}^t} (1 - p_0)^{n_{ji}^t}} \tag{7}$$

which leads to the following simple rules

$$\begin{cases} \textbf{if } n_{ij}^t \leq \frac{\log B}{r - \bar{r}} - (n_{ij}^t + n_{ji}^t)\frac{\bar{r}}{r - \bar{r}}, \textbf{ accept } H_0 \\ \textbf{if } n_{ij}^t \geq \frac{\log A}{r - \bar{r}} - (n_{ij}^t + n_{ji}^t)\frac{\bar{r}}{r - \bar{r}}, \textbf{ accept } H_1 \\ \quad \textbf{otherwise, continue sampling} \end{cases} \tag{8}$$

where $A \triangleq \frac{1-\beta}{\alpha}$, $B \triangleq \frac{\beta}{1-\alpha}$, $r \triangleq \log \frac{p_1}{p_0}$, and $\bar{r} \triangleq \log \frac{1-p_1}{1-p_0}$. Note that SPRINT-Race's two component SPRTs utilizes common α and β values in order to reduce the number of parameters that need to be specified.

2.4 SPRINT-Race and its Analysis

The whole SPRINT-Race procedure is illustrated in Algorithm 1. Initially, a dual-SPRT is established for each pair of models, which means that a total of $\binom{M}{2}$ dual-SPRTs are initialized at the beginning of the race for M candidate models. During a single step of the race, a problem instance is randomly chosen from the problem's sampling space. The performances of the two models involved in each active dual-SPRT are evaluated on the selected problem instance, and the resulting performance vectors are utilized to generate a new sample for the corresponding dual-SPRT. The test statistics are computed and, hence, decisions are made according to Equation (8). If H_0 is accepted, C_i is identified as being dominated by C_j and, thus, will be eliminated from the race. Consequently, all the dual-SPRTs involving C_i are stopped. On the other hand, if H_2 is accepted, C_i is identified as dominating C_j and, therefore, C_j is removed from the race. As a result, all the dual-SPRTs containing C_j are stopped. If H_1 is accepted, C_i and C_j are regarded as neither dominating the other. The current dual-SPRT will be terminated since no more comparisons are needed to verify the dominance relation between C_i and C_j. Otherwise, if no decision is made, the relevant dual-SPRT will be reapplied in the next step. When all the dual-SPRTs are terminated, the race concludes.

Algorithm 1 SPRINT-Race Pseudo-code

Initialize $Pool \leftarrow \{C_1, C_2, \cdots, C_m\}\ (m \geq 2)$
Initialize $t = 1$
repeat
  Randomly sample a problem instance from the problem pool
  for each model $C_i \in Pool$ **do**
    for each model $C_j \in Pool\ \ s.t.\ i < j$ **do**
      if the corresponding dual-SPRT continues **then**
        Evaluate C_i and C_j on the selected instance
        Update n_{ij}^t and n_{ji}^t
        if H_0 is accepted **then**
          $Pool \leftarrow Pool \setminus \{C_i\}$
          Stop all dual-SPRTs involving C_i
        else if H_2 is accepted **then**
          $Pool \leftarrow Pool \setminus \{C_j\}$
          Stop all dual-SPRTs involving C_j
        else if H_1 is accepted **then**
          Stop the dual-SPRT involving C_i and C_j
        end if
      end if
    end for
  end for
  $t = t + 1$
until All dual-SPRTs are terminated
return *Pool*

For SPRINT-Race, being a fixed confidence model selection algorithm, the total probability of making any erroneous discovery needs to be strictly controlled. In a ternary-decision dual-SPRT, there are multiple erroneous decisions that can be made. Hence, a more careful analysis is warranted, when compared to the case of a traditional binary-decision SPRT, which gives rise only to Type I and Type II errors. Similar to the analysis in [4, 22], the probability of any incorrect decision of the dual-SPRT procedure, denoted by $\gamma(p)$, is provided in Table 2.

Table 2: Error probability analysis of dual-SPRT

Interval	Wrong Decisions	$\gamma(p)$
$p \leq \frac{1}{2} - \delta$	accept H_1 or H_2	$\gamma(p) \leq \alpha$
$\frac{1}{2} - \delta < p < \frac{1}{2}$	accept H_2	$\gamma(p) < \alpha$
$p = \frac{1}{2}$	accept H_0 or H_2	$\gamma(p) \approx \alpha + \beta$
$\frac{1}{2} < p < \frac{1}{2} + \delta$	accept H_0	$\gamma(p) < \beta$
$p \geq \frac{1}{2} + \delta$	accept H_0 or H_1	$\gamma(p) \leq \beta$

The maximum $\gamma(p)$ over the interval $[0, 1]$, denoted by γ^*, is called the true level of significance of the dual-SPRT. According to Table 2, it follows that $\gamma^* \triangleq \max_{p \in [0,1]} \gamma(p) = \max\{\alpha, \alpha + \beta, \beta\} = \alpha + \beta$.

We define the error probability Γ of SPRINT-Race to be the overall probability of falsely removing any Pareto optimal model or failing to eliminate any dominated model. Obviously, Γ is dependent on the true significance levels of a total of $\binom{M}{2}$ dual-SPRTs, where M is the size of the initial candidate pool. Using the Bonferroni inequality, we have

$$\Gamma \leq \sum_{i=1}^{\binom{M}{2}} \gamma_i^* = \sum_{i=1}^{\binom{M}{2}} (\alpha_i + \beta_i) \tag{9}$$

where α_i and β_i refers to the α and β values assigned for the ith dual-SPRT in SPRINT-Race. To further reduce the number of parameters involved in SPRINT-Race, we set $\alpha_i = \beta_i = \epsilon$ for all $i = 1, 2, \cdots, \binom{M}{2}$. Then, Equation (9) reduces to

$$\Gamma \leq 2\binom{M}{2}\epsilon = M(M-1)\epsilon \tag{10}$$

Equation (10) suggests a way of strongly controlling the error probability of SPRINT-Race by properly assigning the ϵ value. Let Γ_{max} denote the maximum error probability allowed for SPRINT-Race. From Equation (10), we have

$$\epsilon = \frac{\Gamma_{max}}{M(M-1)}. \tag{11}$$

Obviously, the smaller Γ_{max} is, the smaller the ϵ value will be. Consequently, more samples are required to reach a decision in each component SPRT. On the contrary, larger Γ_{max} allows for less computational effort, but also more error. Therefore, the selection of the desired Γ_{max} value represents a trade-off between the probability of returning a final ensemble of models that matches as close as possible to the true Pareto front and the computational effort exerted by SPRINT-Race.

3. EXPERIMENTS

In this section, the performance of SPRINT-Race [1] is first investigated by selecting the Pareto optimal models based on artificially-generated data. To further demonstrate its performance, SPRINT-Race was applied to selecting the Pareto

[1]MATLAB® code of SPRINT-Race is available at https://github.com/watera427/SPRINT-Race_v1. If you have any queries, please contact the primary author via email.

optimal parameter settings of ACO algorithm for solving TSPs. Note that SPRINT-Race and S-Race are incomparable because (i) the concept of indifference zone of SPRINT-Race is not employed in S-Race, (ii) the maximum number of steps is known in S-Race but unknown in SPRINT-Race, and (iii) the probability of making any Type II errors is not strictly controlled by S-Race. Therefore, it is meaningless to compare SPRINT-Race and S-Race in neither the fixed confidence setting nor the fixed sample complexity setting.

3.1 Performance Metrics

Two performance metrics were considered to measure the quality of SPRINT-Race, *retention* R and *excess* E [25], which are defined as follows:

$$R \triangleq \frac{|\mathcal{P}_R \cap \mathcal{P}_{PF}|}{|\mathcal{P}_{PF}|} \tag{12}$$

$$E \triangleq \frac{|\mathcal{P}_R \setminus \mathcal{P}_{PF}|}{|\mathcal{P}_R|} = 1 - \frac{|\mathcal{P}_R \cap \mathcal{P}_{PF}|}{|\mathcal{P}_R|} \tag{13}$$

where $\mathcal{P}_R$ is the set of models returned by SPRINT-Race, and $\mathcal{P}_{PF}$ is the ensemble of models constituting the true Pareto front.

Just as their names imply, R measures SPRINT-Race's ability of retaining Pareto optimal models. Meanwhile, E measures its ability of identifying and eliminating dominated models that do not belong to $\mathcal{P}_{PF}$. Ideally, we would like to have $R = 1$ and $E = 0$, which means SPRINT-Race is able to return exactly the ensemble of Pareto front models. However, in practice, a SPRINT-Race yielding high R and low E values is acceptable, when contrasted to the savings in computational cost. As discussed in Section 2.4, the R and E values are dependent on Γ_{max}, the predefined maximum error probability of SPRINT-Race.

R and E focus on the quality of the final ensemble identified by SPRINT-Race. Aside from these quantities, the sample complexity T, which is measured as the total number of samples used, is also considered as a performance measurement of SPRINT-Race. Note that the number of samples used by a dual-SPRT in SPRINT-Race equals the total number of times the candidate models are evaluated. Regarding the computational complexity of SPRINT-Race, it is easy to show that SPRINT-Race takes $O(D\,\overline{V}\,\overline{M}^2)$ pair-wise comparisons for D-objectives model selection, where $\overline{M}$ is the average number of models competing throughout the entire race, and $\overline{V}$ is the average sample complexity of a dual-SPRT. In reality since pair-wise comparisons between models will be terminated once sufficient statistical evidence is collected, it is expected that $\overline{M} \ll M$ and $\overline{V} \ll V$, where V is the sample complexity of a corresponding ternary-decision fixed-sample test for dominance and non-dominance relationship inference.

3.2 Artificially Constructed MOMS Problems

We consider a few simple experiments here to illustrate the efficiency of SPRINT-Race. Assume that there are M initial models for each experiment of D objectives, represented by M randomly generated D-dimensional vectors. Subsequently, $\binom{M}{2}$ Bernoulli distributions are constructed and all relevant p values are stored in a matrix P. $P_{i,j} (j > i)$ is drawn from a uniform distribution on the open interval (0.5,1), if the ith D-dimensional vector dominates the jth D-dimensional vector. If neither dominates the other, $P_{i,j}$ is set to 0.5. Otherwise, $P_{i,j}$ is selected from $(0, 0.5)$, where $P_{i,j} = 1 - P_{i,j}$. Finally, $P_{i,j}$ is set to 0.5, if $i = j$. This way, $\mathcal{P}_{PF}$, the Pareto front models, are known in advance. After P is constructed, SPRINT-Race commences and, whenever a new sample is needed to be used for a dual-SPRT, the new sample is randomly generated from a Bernoulli distribution with the corresponding $P_{i,j}$ entry of P.

3.2.1 *Impact of Number of Objectives*

In this set of experiments, we fixed M at 100, δ at 0.05 and $\Gamma_{max} = 0.1$, but varied the number of objectives D from 2 to 14. Each experiment was repeated for 30 runs. The average R and E values for SPRINT-Race are presented in Table 3. Moreover, the average sample complexity T and the average Pareto front size $|\mathcal{P}_{PF}|$ are presented as well.

Table 3: Average retention R, excess E, sample complexity T and the size of the Pareto front $|\mathcal{P}_{PF}|$ for varying D values over 30 runs

D	R	E	T	$\lvert\mathcal{P}_{PF}\rvert$
2	1.000	0.075	1.65e4	5.4
3	1.000	0.061	3.13e4	15.1
4	1.000	0.053	5.25e4	29.05
5	1.000	0.040	7.47e4	44.05
6	1.000	0.027	1.00e5	60.85
7	1.000	0.019	1.18e5	71.55
8	0.999	0.010	1.31e5	81.75
9	0.999	0.010	1.44e5	90.00
10	0.998	0.008	1.46e5	92.55
11	0.999	0.003	1.52e5	96.25
12	1.000	0.002	1.52e5	97.45
13	0.999	0.001	1.55e5	99.00
14	1.000	0.001	1.55e5	99.55

The corresponding R values are all close to 1, which means that all Pareto optimal models are kept and returned by the racing procedure. From Table 3, we also observe that the E values are all smaller than 0.1, indicating that SPRINT-Race is able to successfully identify and eliminate almost all dominated models based on the predefined confidence level. Hence, SPRINT-Race returns almost exactly the problem's true Pareto front. As defined in Section 3.1, $1 - R$ measures the probability of falsely removing any non-dominated models in SPRINT-Race, while E measures the probability of mistakenly retaining any dominated models in SPRINT-Race. Therefore, as we discussed before, the desired significant level Γ_{max} of SPRINT-Race, which was set to be 0.1 in this experiment, implicitly controls $1 - R + E$. It is observed that the sum of $1 - R$ and E is strictly below 0.1 as expected. However, most of them are far less than 0.1, implying that SPRINT-Race may be too conservative.

From Table 3, we also notice that when the number of objectives increases, more models are deemed Pareto optimal, as indicated by $|\mathcal{P}_{PF}|$. When $D = 14$, almost all the models are on the Pareto front; this explains why E values decrease in this case. Also, T increases monotonically with growing D. Generally, in SPRINT-Race, it takes longer to identify non-dominated models than dominated ones. When most of the models are non-dominated, it is expected that SPRINT-Race will require more samples to discover non-dominant ones. However, the growth rate of T as a function of D is not dramatic, since, once sufficient statistical evidence is collected indicating a non-dominance relation, no more sampling is needed. In Figure 1, the sample complexity of each step in several runs of SPRINT-Race with $D = 2$ is depicted. As generally observed, the sample complexity falls rapidly between the 100th step and the 190th step. After about 200 steps, only less than 10% of the initial models are still racing for a fine comparison.

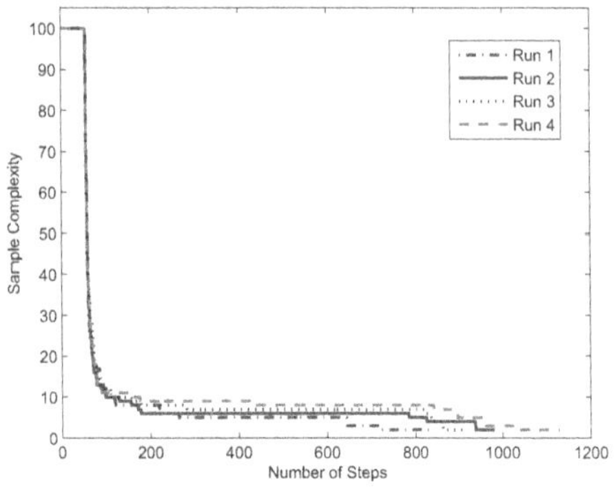

Figure 1: The number of samples needed at each step in several runs of SPRINT-Race with binary-objective

3.2.2 *Impact of δ Values*

The value of δ determines the size of the indifference zone of each ternary-decision SPRT in SPRINT-Race. In this set of experiments, we aim at understanding how δ influences the performance of SPRINT-Race. The parameter settings were $M = 10$, $\Gamma_{max} = 0.1$, $\delta \in \{0.01, 0.02, \ldots, 0.1\}$ and $D \in \{2, 3\}$ since binary-objective and ternary-objective MS are common in real world problem settings. Note that each experiment was repeated for 30 runs.

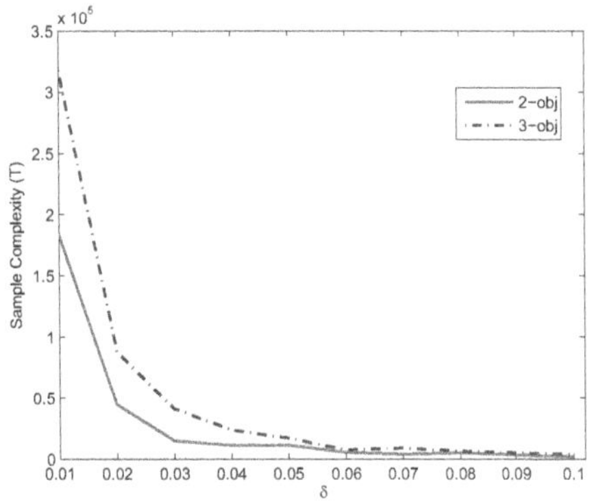

Figure 2: Changes of sample complexity T with varying δ

It is observed that δ has a significant impact on the sample complexity T (see Figure 2). In Figure 2, the average values of T over 30 runs are depicted for the 2-objective and 3-objective MS problem. The sample complexity of SPRINT-Race decreases with increasing δ. Such trend is expected because larger values of δ result in wider indifference zone and, when the indifference zone is broad, it is easier for the test procedure to reach a decision. As noticed in Figure 3, the error of SPRINT-Race, measured by $1 - R + E$, grows slightly with increasing δ. Because when δ grows, more dominated models will be regarded as Pareto optimal. As a result, the distinction between $\mathcal{P}_R$ of SPRINT-Race and $\mathcal{P}_{PF}$ becomes more significant.

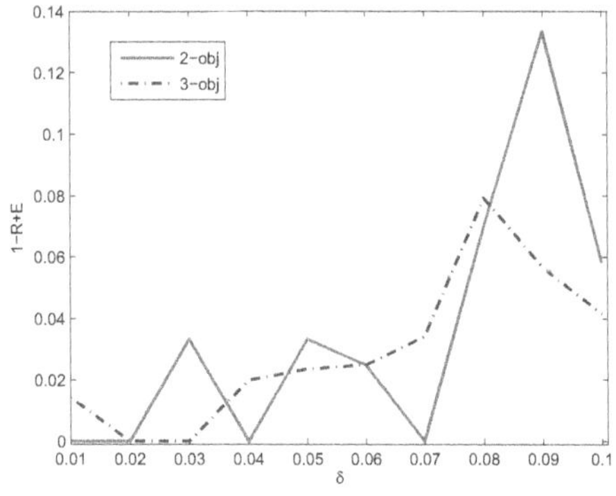

Figure 3: Changes of $1 - R + E$ with varying δ

3.2.3 *Impact of Γ_{max} Values*

In this set of experiments, the impact of the Γ_{max} value to the performance of SPRINT-Race was studied. The parameter settings were $M = 10$, $\Gamma_{max} \in \{0.01, 0.05, 0.1, 0.15, 0.2\}$, $D \in \{2, 3\}$ and $\delta = 0.01$. As the experimental results demonstrate, decreasing Γ_{max} will definitely increase the computational cost of SPRINT-Race, since more samples are required to infer any pair-wise model dominance or lack thereof. However, the R and E values only slightly varied within a reasonable range, which reflects SPRINT-Race's conservativeness.

In conclusion, the selection of δ and Γ_{max}, which are the only parameters of SPRINT-Race, results in a trade-off between the probability of returning a final ensemble of models that matches the true Pareto front and the computational effort exerted by SPRINT-Race. There is no generally-accepted "optimal" setting of the two aforementioned parameters; the determination of the exact δ and Γ_{max} values is totally depended on the user's preference pertaining to this trade-off.

3.3 ACO Selection for TSPs

In this section, we experimentally evaluated the performance of SPRINT-Race in terms of selecting the Pareto optimal parameter settings of ACO as TSP solvers. The ACO system [7] was first introduced in 1992 and is one of the most popular swarm intelligence algorithms. Ever since its inception, ACO and its variations have been widely used in a variety of combinatorial optimization problems, including scheduling problems, vehicle routing problems, assignment problems and set cover problems. Just like other swarm intelligence algorithms, the performance of ACO depends largely on its parameter settings, and, consequently, the effect of its parameters has been studied extensively in the literature of ACO [9, 21]. However, the parameter tuning process of ACO is time-consuming, when considering ever larger ensembles of parameter settings assessed on ever larger problem sets. RAs play an important role in ACO selection [2, 3] to maintain a certain level of confidence in retaining the optimal ACOs, while mitigating the computational burden. On the other hand, the TSP is one of the most famous NP-hard combinatorial optimization problems, it has been extensively studied in the literature and often serves as a standard benchmark problem. In this work, a bi-objective ACO parameter selection problem was considered. In specific, the task in question is to identify Pareto optimal ACOs, which serve as TSP solvers. An ACO parameter setting is deemed optimal, if it minimizes both the TSP tour length and the actual computation time to find this tour.

In this experiment, the `ACOTSPJava` [24] software was used, in which several ACO algorithms are implemented for solving TSPs. Prior to the race, a pool of 125 candidate models were initialized with diverse configurations in terms of different combinations of three parameters as shown in Table 4: i) α_{ACO}, the influence of pheromone trials; ii) β_{ACO}, the influence of heuristic information; and iii) ρ_{ACO}, the pheromone trail evaporation rate. The other parameters were set to the default values used in `ACOTSPJava`. Moreover, the TSP instances were all generated by the DIMACS TSP instance generator [13]. At each step, a random TSP instance was generated and the performance of each remaining models was evaluated by solving the generated TSP problem. Correspondingly, a new performance vector of each remaining model was collected, containing the length of the best tour found and the time spent of finding the best tour. SPRINT-Race was applied at each step, aiming at removing dominated models and stopping unnecessary comparison of a pair of Pareto optimal models as early as possible. 30 races were performed using $\Gamma_{max} = 0.01$ and $\delta = 0.05$.

Table 4: ACO Parameter Description

parameter	values
α_{ACO}	$\{0.01, 1.01, 2.01, 3.01, 4.01\}$
β_{ACO}	$\{0.1, 2.1, 4.1, 6.1, 8.1\}$
ρ_{ACO}	$\{0.1, 0.3, 0.5, 0.7, 0.9\}$

The resulting average R, E, T and $|\mathcal{P}_R|$ values over 30 runs were 1.000, 0.001, 4.46e5 and 17.933, respectively. It is observed that the R value is about 1 and the E value is close to 0, which illustrates that SPRINT-Race is able to retain exactly the ensemble of Pareto front models. Note that in this experiment the true $\mathcal{P}_{PF}$ is unknown. So the probability of dominance between pairs of models was estimated based on the collected performance vectors and the resulting ensemble of non-dominated models were regarded as $\mathcal{P}_{PF}$. To illustrate the accuracy of SPRINT-Race, we depicted the minimum probability of dominance of each model in Figure 4 of one run. For each model C_i, the minimum probability of dominance is calculated as $\min_{i \neq j} Pr\{C_i \succ C_j\}$. Considering $\delta = 0.05$, the minimum probability of dominance of any non-dominated models returned by SPRINT-Race should be no smaller than 0.45. Moreover, all the models with the minimum probability of dominance larger than 0.5 are expected to be returned by SPRINT-Race as Pareto optimal models. In Figure 4, a blue circle ($\circ$) represents a dominated model and a red bullet ($\bullet$) stands for a non-dominated model returned by SPRINT-Race. As shown in Figure 4, SPRINT-Race performs well and returns all the Pareto optimal models as expected without erroneously including any dominated model. Furthermore, we compared the performance of the Pareto optimal models selected by SPRINT-Race and the rest of models, which were identified as dominated models on a test set containing 2500 randomly generated TSP instances. The average normalized values of their performance vectors are displayed in Figure 5. It is

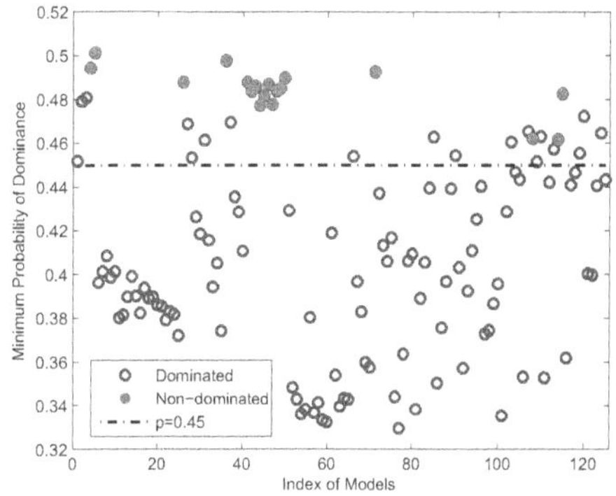

Figure 4: Models' Minimum Probability of Dominance

observed that the Pareto optimal models are concentrated at the bottom left and right corners, where either the first objective or the second objective is minimized. In other words, the experimental results demonstrate that the Pareto optimal models selected based on the validation set of TSP instances are also Pareto optimal for the unseen set of TSP instances.

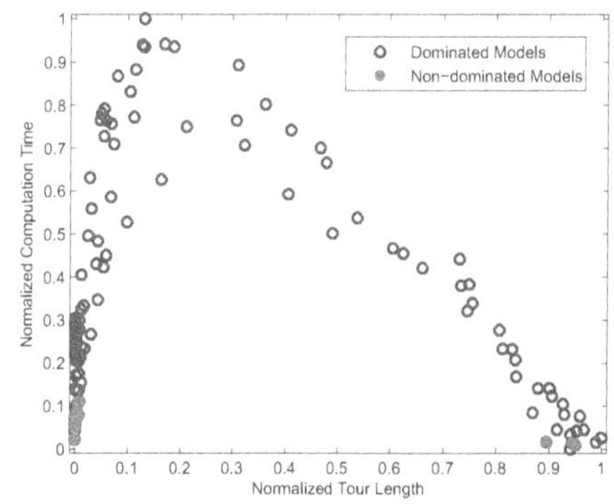

Figure 5: Performance comparison of dominated and non-dominated models returned by SPRINT-Race on a test set

4. CONCLUSIONS

In this paper, a new Multi-objective Racing Algorithm (MORA) for Multi-objective Model Selection (MOMS), named SPRINT-Race, was proffered. SPRINT-Race addresses the problem of MOMS in the proper sense of Pareto optimality by employing probabilistic dominance. Identifying dominated and non-dominated models is accomplished via a ternary-decision process, that is the sequential analogue of the non-parametric sign test. Moreover, in the fixed confidence setting of SPRINT-Race, the total probability of falsely retaining any dominated model and removing any non-dominated model is strictly controlled at a user-specified level. The racing procedure automatically stops, when sufficient statistical evidence is collected to make decisions. A key characteristic of SPRINT-Race is that it is able to balance the need for retaining all Pareto optimal models with high probability and computational cost limitations.

Experimental results were provided to illustrate the efficiency and effectiveness of SPRINT-Race. These results show that SPRINT-Race is able to return almost exactly the true Pareto front but at a reduced cost. The impact of SPRINT-Race's parameter values on its performance was analyzed on model selection problems, whose Pareto optimal solution was known beforehand. It was observed that the selection of δ and Γ_{max} results in a trade-off between the probability of returning a final ensemble of models that matches the true Pareto front and the computational effort exerted by SPRINT-Race. In addition, SPRINT-Race was applied to selecting the Pareto optimal parameter settings of Ant Colony Optimization (ACO) algorithms for solving Traveling Salesman Problems (TSPs). SPRINT-Race performs well and retains all the Pareto optimal models as expected with little error probability of including any dominated model. Overall, the experimental results confirm the potential of SPRINT-Race in MOMS.

It is worth pointing out that, while our work was singularly focused on MOMS problems, SPRINT-Race is readily applicable to optimal model initialization and configuration problems along the lines investigated in [3]; it is our intention to examine this possibility in one of our future works.

5. ACKNOWLEDGMENTS

T. Zhang acknowledges partial support from National Science Foundation (NSF) grants No.1200566 and No.0525429. Moreover, M. Georgiopoulos acknowledges partial support from NSF grants No.0525429, No.0963146, No.1200566 and No.1161228. Additionally, G. C. Anagnostopoulos acknowledges partial support from NSF grant No.1263011. Any opinions, findings, and conclusions or recommendations expressed in this material are those of the authors and do not necessarily reflect the views of the NSF.

6. REFERENCES

[1] S. Becker, J. Gottlieb, and T. Stützle. Applications of racing algorithms: An industrial perspective. In *Artificial Evolution*, volume 3871, chapter Artificial Evolution, pages 271–283. Springer, 2005.

[2] M. Birattari, Z. Yuan, P. Balaprakash, and T. Stützle. Automated algorithm tuning using F-races: Recent developments. In *Proc. of the 8th Metaheuristics Int. Conf.*, 2009.

[3] M. Birattari, Z. Yuan, P. Balaprakash, and T. Stützle. F-race and iterated F-race: An overview. Technical report, IRIDIA, 2011.

[4] J. D. Boer. Sequential test with three possible decisions for testing an unknown probability. *Appl. Sci. Res., Sect. B*, 3:249 – 259, 1954.

[5] S. Bubeck, T. Wang, and N. Viswanathan. Multiple identifications in multi-armed bandits. In *Proc. of the 25th Int. Conf. on Mach. Learn.*, 2013.

[6] K. Deb. *Multi-Objective Optimization Using Evolutionary Algorithms*. John Wiley & Sons, 2009.

[7] M. Dorigo. *Optimization, Learning and Natural Algorithm*. PhD thesis, Politecnico di Milano, 1992.

[8] V. Gabillon, M. Ghavamzadeh, and A. Lazaric. Best arm identification: A unified approach to fixed budget and fixed confidence. In *Adv. Neural. Inf. Process. Syst. 25*, pages 3221 – 3229, 2012.

[9] D. Gaertner and K. Clark. On optimal parameters for ant colony optimization algorithms. In *Proc. of the Int. Conf. on Artif. Intell.*, 2005.

[10] B. K. Ghosh. *Sequential Tests of Statistical Hypotheses*. Addison-Wesley Publishing Company, Inc., 1970.

[11] V. Heidrich-Meisner and C. Igel. Hoeffding and bernstein races for selecting policies in evolutionary direct policy search. In *Proc. of the 26th Annual Int. Conf. on Mach. Learn.*, pages 401–408, 2009.

[12] Y. Jin and B. Sendhoff. Pareto-based multi-objective machine learning: An overview and case studies. *IEEE Trans. Syst., Man, Cybern. C, Appl. Rev.*, 38:397 – 415, 2008.

[13] D. S. Johnson, L. A. McGeoch, C. Rego, and F. Glover. 8th DIMACS Implementation Challenge: The Traveling Salesman Problem. http://dimacs.rutgers.edu/Challenges/TSP/, 2001. Accessed: Fri 8th May, 2015.

[14] J. D. Knowles, L. Thiele, and E. Zitzler. A tutorial on the performance assessment of stochastic multiobjective optimizers. Technical report, CENL, ETH Zurich, 2006.

[15] P.-L. Loh and S. Nowozin. Faster hoeffding racing: Bernstein races via jackknife estimates. In *Proc. 24th Int. Conf. on Algorithm Learn.*, pages 203–217, 2013.

[16] M. Lopez-Ibanez and T. Stützle. Automatic configuration of multi-objective ACO algorithms. In *Swarm Intelligence*, pages 95–106, 2010.

[17] O. Maron and A. Moore. Hoeffding races: Accelerating model selection search for classification and function approximation. *Adv. Neural Inf. Process. Syst.*, 6:59–66, 1994.

[18] W. Mendenhall, D. D. Wackerly, and R. L. Scheaffer. Nonparametric statistics. *Math. Stat. with App.*, pages 674–679, 1989.

[19] V. Mnih and C. Szepesvari. Empirical bernstein stopping. In *Proc. of the 25th Int. Conf. on Mach. Learn.*, 2008.

[20] A. W. Moore. Efficient algorithms for minimizing cross validation error. In *Proc. of the 11th Int. Conf. on Mach. Learn.*, pages 190–198, 1994.

[21] P. Shunmugapriya, S. Kanmani, S. Devipriya, J. Archana, and J. Pushpa. Investigation on the effects of ACO parameters for feature selection and classification. *Adv. in Comm., Netw., and Comput.*, 108:136–145, 2012.

[22] M. Sobel and A. Wald. A sequential decision procedure for choosing one of three hypotheses concerning the unknown mean of a normal distribution. *The Ann. of Math. Stat.*, 20:502–522, 1949.

[23] A. Wald. *Sequential Analysis*. Dover, 1948.

[24] A. Wilke. ACOTSPJava. http://adibaba.github.io/ACOTSPJava/. Accessed: Fri 8th May, 2015.

[25] T. Zhang, M. Georgiopoulos, and G. C. Anagnostopoulos. S-Race: A multi-objective racing algorithm. In *Proc. of the Genet. and Evol. Comput. Conf.*, pages 1565–1572, 2013.

An Evolutionary Game Theoretic Analysis of Difference Evaluation Functions

Mitchell Colby
Oregon State University
colbym@engr.orst.edu

Kagan Tumer
Oregon State University
kagan.tumer@oregonstate.edu

ABSTRACT

One of the key difficulties in cooperative coevolutionary algorithms is solving the credit assignment problem. Given the performance of a team of agents, it is difficult to determine the effectiveness of each agent in the system. One solution to solving the credit assignment problem is the difference evaluation function, which has produced excellent results in many multiagent coordination domains, and exhibits the desirable theoretical properties of alignment and sensitivity. However, to date, there has been no prescriptive theoretical analysis deriving conditions under which difference evaluations improve the probability of selecting optimal actions. In this paper, we derive such conditions. Further, we prove that difference evaluations do not alter the Nash equilibria locations or the relative ordering of fitness values for each action, meaning that difference evaluations do not typically harm converged system performance in cases where the conditions are not met. We then demonstrate the theoretical findings using an empirical basins of attraction analysis.

Categories and Subject Descriptors

I.2.11 [**Computing Methodologies**]: Artificial Intelligence —Distributed Artificial Intelligence —*Multiagent systems*

1. INTRODUCTION

Coordinating multiple agents to achieve a system objective is a key step in addressing many real world problems including distributed sensor network and distributed mobile robot control [4]. One approach to developing policies for multiagent systems is the use of Cooperative Coevolutionary Algorithms (CCEAs), where multiple populations evolve in parallel, with each population evolving a policy for a particular agent or set of agents. One of the key difficulties of CCEAs is the credit assignment problem: given the performance of a team of agents, how does one assign fitness values reflecting each agent's individual performance?

GECCO '15, July 11 - 15, 2015, Madrid, Spain
 ISBN 978-1-4503-3472-3/15/07...$15.00
DOI: http://dx.doi.org/10.1145/2739480.2754770

In a CCEA, fitness assignment is context dependent and subjective, because the fitness of an agent is not only a function of the agent's policy, but also the selection and policies of its collaborating agents. In multiagent settings, this leads to the promotion of agents which perform well with a wide variety of collaborators, rather than agents which perform optimally with a particular set of collaborators. Thus, the credit assignment problem changes the problem subtly, and often leads to robust, rather than optimal, solutions [8].

In order to promote good system performance while using CCEAs, the credit assignment problem is addressed through fitness function shaping. One approach to assigning fitness is the difference evaluation function, which approximates each agent's individual contribution to the overall system performance [1]. Difference evaluation functions have provided tangible benefits in a variety of domains [1, 4].

However, to date, there has been no prescriptive theoretical analysis deriving conditions under which difference evaluations are expected to improve the probability of selecting optimal actions, limiting their applicability. This paper conducts a theoretical analysis of difference evaluations as fitness assignment operators in CCEAs, using an evolutionary game theoretic framework. The specific contributions of this paper are to:

1. Prove difference evaluations improve the probability of selecting best response actions when the expected payoffs of those actions are relatively low (Section 5.1).
2. Prove that difference evaluations do not alter the Nash equilibria locations in the system (Section 5.2).
3. Prove that difference evaluations do not alter the ordering of expected payoffs for each action (Section 5.2).
4. Provide an empirical basins of attraction analysis which showcases the results of the theorems (Section 7).

Although there have been multiple studies involving the performance benefits of difference evaluation functions, this paper provides the first prescriptive theoretical analysis of difference evaluation functions, proving conditions under which they improve the probabilities of each agent to select its best response action. The rest of this paper is organized as follows. Section 2 provides details on background information and related work, Section 3 demonstrates how difference evaluations are incorporated into an evolutionary game theoretic model, Section 4 derives normalized fitness values for the evolutionary game theoretic model, Section 5 contains the proofs of our theorems, Section 6 provides an empirical demonstration of the implications of the theorems, Section 7 provides an empirical basins of attraction analysis of the proved theorems, and Section 8 concludes the paper.

2. BACKGROUND

The following sections introduce cooperative coevolutionary algorithms, difference evaluation functions, and the evolutionary game theoretic model for cooperative coevolution.

2.1 Cooperative Coevolutionary Algorithms

Evolutionary algorithms (EAs) are a class of stochastic search algorithms, which have been shown to work well in complex domains where gradient information is not readily available. EAs typically contain two basic mechanisms: mutation and selection [12]. These mechanisms act on an initial set of candidate solutions in order to generate new solutions and to retain solutions which show improvement as evolutionary time progresses. Coevolutionary algorithms are an extension of EAs in which multiple populations evolve in parallel, and are well suited for multiagent domains [5, 15]. In a coevolutionary algorithm, the fitness of an agent depends on the interactions it has with other agents. Thus, assessing the fitness of each agent is context-sensitive and subjective [8]. We focus on *Cooperative* Coevolutionary Algorithms (CCEAs), where a group of agents succeed or fail as a team.

One key issue with CCEAs is that they tend to favor stable, rather than optimal, solutions [2, 8]. As agents are paired with multiple different sets of collaborators in CCEAs during different evolutionary time steps, agents which learn to coordinate with a wide variety of teammates tend to receive higher fitness values than agents which learn to coordinate optimally with a specific set of collaborators [8]. For example, if an optimal agent only performs well with a specific set of collaborators, then that agent will likely receive a low fitness value during evolution, and be removed from the population. The difference evaluation function aims to address the subjective nature of fitness assignments associated with CCEAs, by determining agent-specific fitness values based on the value of a particular agent's policy.

2.2 Difference Evaluation Functions

The agent-specific difference evaluation function $D_i(z)$ is defined as [1]:

$$D_i(z) = G(z) - G(z_{-i} + c_i) \tag{1}$$

where $G(z)$ is the global evaluation function, and $G(z_{-i}+c_i)$ is the global evaluation function without the effects of agent i. The term c_i is the *counterfactual*, which is used to replace agent i, and must not depend on the actions of agent i. In general, the counterfactual term is chosen to either remove the agent from the system or to replace the agent with an "average" agent. We demonstrate how a counterfactual may be chosen in Section 3. Intuitively, the difference evaluation function gives the impact of agent i on the global evaluation function, because the second term removes the portions of the global evaluation function not dependent on agent i.

Difference evaluations have two key theoretical properties which allow for improved system performance. First, any action which increases $D_i(z)$ also increases $G(z)$. This property is termed *alignment* [1]. Second, as the second term in the difference evaluation removes the effects of all agents other than agent i, the difference evaluation provides a feedback signal with much less noise than $G(z)$. This property is termed *sensitivity* [1].

Although difference evaluations have produced excellent empirical results and exhibit the desirable theoretical properties of alignment and sensitivity, the theoretical advantages of difference evaluations have not been well developed. To date, there has been no prescriptive theoretical analysis which determines under what conditions difference evaluations are expected to improve system performance. This paper addresses these theoretical questions by analyzing difference evaluations using an evolutionary game theoretic framework.

2.3 EGT Model for Cooperative Coevolution

This section introduces the Evolutionary Game Theoretic (EGT) model we use for our analysis. EGT is well suited as a model of cooperative coevolutionary algorithms, and thus provides a theoretical framework in which we can analyze the effects of different fitness assignment operators [6, 9, 10, 11, 13, 14]. This analysis is restricted to cooperative coevolutionary algorithms with two agents learning in stateless domains, and each agent having a finite number of actions. The model assumes that the populations are infinite, and that the proportions of individuals in the populations are computed at each time step during evolution. If the first agent has a finite number of n distinct actions it can take, then its population at each generation is an element of the unit simplex $\Delta^n = \{x \in [0,1]^n | \sum_{i=1}^n x_i = 1\}$. A higher value x_i corresponds to a higher probability that the agent selects action i. If the second agent has m actions to choose from, then its population at each generation is an element of the unit simplex $\Delta^m = \{y \in [0,1]^m | \sum_{j=1}^n y_j = 1\}$. The EGT model for CCEAs we use is the discrete time replicator dynamics with fitness proportional selection, defined as in [8, 13]:

$$u_i^{(t),c} = \sum_{j=1}^{m} c_{ij} y_j^{(t)} \tag{2}$$

$$w_j^{(t),c} = \sum_{i=1}^{n} c_{ij} x_i^{(t)} \tag{3}$$

$$x_i^{(t+1),c} = \left(\frac{u_i^{(t),c}}{\sum_{k=1}^{n} x_k^{(t)} u_k^{(t),c}} \right) x_i^{(t)} \tag{4}$$

$$y_j^{(t+1),c} = \left(\frac{w_j^{(t),c}}{\sum_{k=1}^{m} y_k^{(t)} w_k^{(t),c}} \right) y_j^{(t)} \tag{5}$$

Where:

- $u_i^{(t),c}$ is the fitness of agent 1 taking action i at time t, while using the global payoff matrix.
- $w_j^{(t),c}$ is the fitness of agent 2 taking action j at time t, while using the global payoff matrix.
- $x_i^{(t)}$ is the probability agent 1 takes action i at time t.
- $y_j^{(t)}$ is the probability agent 2 takes action j at time t.
- $x_i^{(t+1),c}$ is the updated probability agent 1 takes action i at time $t+1$, when the update is completed using the global payoff matrix.
- $y_j^{(t+1),c}$ is the updated probability agent 2 takes action j at time $t+1$, when the update is completed using the global payoff matrix.

Note that the fitness values of each action are simply the expected payoffs of taking each action, given the collaborating agent's probability distribution for action selection. For this analysis, we make the following assumptions:

A1) All elements of the payoff matrix are non-negative. If there are negative terms in a payoff matrix, a positive constant is added to each element to ensure each element is non-negative.

A2) There are at least two distinct elements in the payoff matrix (not all elements have the same value).

Assumption A1 is a common assumption in evolutionary game theory; non-negative payoff matrix elements ensure that the system remains invariant in the simplex [7, 14]. Assumption A2 is needed in the proofs, but it is worth noting that if this assumption does not hold, then we have a trivial payoff matrix where every element has equal value.

3. DIFFERENCE PAYOFF MATRICES

We now demonstrate how difference evaluation functions are incorporated into the EGT model. Suppose that each agent is given agent-specific feedback rather than global feedback. We can directly apply the difference evaluation function from Equation 1 to the global payoff matrix C, creating the agent-specific *difference payoff matrices* D^1 and D^2, which are defined as:

$$d^1_{ij} = c_{ij} - \frac{1}{n}\sum_{k=1}^{n} c_{kj} + c_{max} \tag{6}$$

$$d^2_{ij} = c_{ij} - \frac{1}{m}\sum_{k=1}^{m} c_{ik} + c_{max} \tag{7}$$

Note that to compute the counterfactual term, we calculate the average payoff for an agent across all of its potential actions, given the action of the collaborating agent. In general, it is desirable to choose a counterfactual which effectively removes an agent from the system. However, in a game-theoretic setting, agents cannot be removed, because each agent must select an action to find a joint payoff. So, rather than removing the agent from the system, the counterfactual term in the difference payoff matrices replace the agent with an average agent with a uniform random policy. The term c_{max} is added to ensure that all elements of the difference payoff matrix are non-negative, where:

$$c_{max} = max_{ij}\{|c_{ij}|\}$$

The fitness assignment operators from the EGT model (Equations 2 and 3) are altered by directly incorporating the difference payoff matrices from Equations 6 and 7. The EGT model for CCEAs with difference evaluations is thus:

$$u_i^{(t),d} = \sum_{j=1}^{m} d^1_{ij} y_j^{(t)} \tag{8}$$

$$w_j^{(t),d} = \sum_{i=1}^{n} d^2_{ij} x_i^{(t)} \tag{9}$$

$$x_i^{(t+1),d} = \left(\frac{u_i^{(t),d}}{\sum_{k=1}^{n} x_k^{(t)} u_k^{(t),d}}\right) x_i^{(t)} \tag{10}$$

$$y_j^{(t+1),d} = \left(\frac{w_j^{(t),d}}{\sum_{k=1}^{m} y_k^{(t)} w_k^{(t),d}}\right) y_j^{(t)} \tag{11}$$

Where:

- $u_i^{(t),d}$ is the fitness of agent 1 taking action i at time t, while using the difference payoff matrix.
- $w_j^{(t),d}$ is the fitness of agent 2 taking action j at time t, while using the difference payoff matrix.
- $x_i^{(t+1),d}$ is the updated probability agent 1 takes action i at time $t+1$, when the update is completed using the difference payoff matrix.
- $y_j^{(t+1),d}$ is the updated probability agent 2 takes action j at time $t+1$, when the update is completed using the difference payoff matrix.

Note that the only difference between the traditional EGT model and the EGT model incorporating difference evaluations occurs in the fitness assignment stage. Rather than using the global payoff matrix to assign fitness, we use the difference payoff matrices.

4. NORMALIZED FITNESS VALUES

As the difference evaluation function alters the elements of the payoff matrix, we must normalize fitness values in order to compare performance when using difference payoff matrices versus the global payoff matrix. In the following sections we derive normalized fitness values for agents using both global and difference evaluation functions.

4.1 Global Evaluation Function

Fitness values for each agent using the global payoff matrix are defined in Equations 2 and 3. We normalize these fitness values such that $\sum_{i=1}^{n} \bar{u}_i^{(t),c} = 1$ and $\sum_{j=1}^{m} \bar{w}_j^{(t),c} = 1$. The normalized expected payoff for the first agent taking action i and using the global evaluation function at time t is:

$$\bar{u}_i^{(t),c} = \frac{u_i^{(t),c}}{\sum_{k=1}^{n} u_k^{(t),c}} \tag{12}$$

$$= \frac{\sum_{j=1}^{m} c_{ij} y_j^{(t)}}{\sum_{k=1}^{n}\sum_{j=1}^{m} c_{kj} y_j^{(t)}} \tag{13}$$

A similar derivation for the second agent yields:

$$\bar{w}_j^{(t),c} = \frac{\sum_{i=1}^{n} c_{ij} x_i^{(t)}}{\sum_{i=1}^{n}\sum_{k=1}^{m} c_{ik} x_i^{(t)}} \tag{14}$$

4.2 Difference Evaluation Function

We now define the fitness for an agent using the difference payoff matrices in terms of the global payoff matrix. The fitness for the first agent taking the action i while using the difference evaluation function at time t is:

$$u_i^{(t),d} = \sum_{j=1}^{m} d^1_{ij} y_j^{(t)} \tag{15}$$

$$= \sum_{j=1}^{m}\left(c_{ij} - \frac{1}{n}\sum_{k=1}^{n} c_{kj} + c_{max}\right) y_j^{(t)} \tag{16}$$

$$= u_i^{(t),c} - \frac{1}{n}\sum_{k=1}^{n}\sum_{j=1}^{m} c_{kj} y_j^{(t)} + c_{max} \tag{17}$$

The normalized fitness for the first agent taking action i

while using the difference evaluation at time t is:

$$\bar{u}_i^{(t),d} = \frac{u_i^{(t),d}}{\sum_{k=1}^n u_i^{(t),d}} \tag{18}$$

$$= \frac{u_i^{(t),c} - \frac{1}{n}\sum_{k=1}^n \sum_{j=1}^m c_{kj} y_j^{(t)} + c_{max}}{\sum_{l=1}^n \left(u_l^{(t),c} - \frac{1}{n}\sum_{k=1}^n \sum_{j=1}^m c_{kj} y_j^{(t)} + c_{max}\right)} \tag{19}$$

$$= \frac{u_i^{(t),c} - \frac{1}{n}\sum_{k=1}^n \sum_{j=1}^m c_{kj} y_j^{(t)} + c_{max}}{\sum_{l=1}^n u_l^{(t),c} - \sum_{k=1}^n \sum_{j=1}^m c_{kj} y_j^{(t)} + n \cdot c_{max}} \tag{20}$$

$$= \frac{u_i^{(t),c} - \frac{1}{n}\sum_{k=1}^n u_k^{(t),c} + c_{max}}{\sum_{l=1}^n u_l^{(t),c} - \sum_{k=1}^n u_k^{(t),c} + n \cdot c_{max}} \tag{21}$$

$$= \frac{u_i^{(t),c} - \frac{1}{n}\sum_{k=1}^n u_k^{(t),c} + c_{max}}{n \cdot c_{max}} \tag{22}$$

A similar derivation yields the normalized fitness for the second agent taking action j and using the difference evaluation at time t:

$$\bar{w}_j^{(t),d} = \frac{w_j^{(t),c} - \frac{1}{m}\sum_{k=1}^m w_k^{(t),c} + c_{max}}{m \cdot c_{max}} \tag{23}$$

5. DIFFERENCE EVALUATIONS THEORY

In the following sections, we derive the conditions under which difference evaluations improve the probability of selecting best response actions. We then prove that in cases where these conditions are not met, difference evaluations do not negatively affect the game.

5.1 Optimal Payoff Theory

We define the joint expected system payoff at time t as:

$$E_{tot}^{(t)}[C] = \sum_{i=1}^n \sum_{j=1}^m c_{ij} x_i^{(t)} y_j^{(t)} \tag{24}$$

We now prove that in cases where the optimal action (corresponding to the optimal Nash equilibrium) has a relatively low expected payoff, difference evaluations result in higher probabilities of selecting best response actions compared to the global evaluation.

THEOREM 1. *If the fitness values for the best response actions i^* and j^* are less than the joint expected system payoff, then difference evaluations result in higher probabilities of selecting the best response actions as compared to the global evaluation function.*

$$E_{tot}^{(t)}[C] > u_{i*}^{(t),c} \Rightarrow x_{i*}^{(t+1),d} > x_{i*}^{(t+1),c} \tag{25}$$

PROOF. Starting with Equation 25, we have that:

$$E_{tot}^{(t)}[C] > u_{i*}^{(t),c}$$

$$\sum_{i=1}^n \sum_{j=1}^m c_{ij} x_i^{(t)} y_j^{(t)} > u_{i*}^{(t),c}$$

Noting that $u_i^{(t),c} = \sum_{j=1}^m c_{ij} y_j^{(t)}$, we have that:

$$\sum_{i=1}^n u_i^{(t),c} x_i^{(t)} > u_{i*}^{(t),c}$$

We now multiply both sides of the inequality by a positive constant A:

$$A \sum_{i=1}^n u_i^{(t),c} x_i^{(t)} > A u_{i*}^{(t),c}$$

Noting that $\sum_{i=1}^n A x_i^{(t)} = A$, we have that:

$$A \sum_{i=1}^n u_i^{(t),c} x_i^{(t)} > u_{i*}^{(t),c} \sum_{i=1}^n A x_i^{(t)}$$

We add $u_{i*}^{(t),c} \sum_{i=1}^n u_i^{(t),c} x_i^{(t)} - u_{i*}^{(t),c} \sum_{i=1}^n u_i^{(t),c} x_i^{(t)} = 0$ to the right hand side of the inequality in order to allow factoring of terms, yielding:

$$A \sum_{i=1}^n u_i^{(t),c} x_i^{(t)} > u_{i*}^{(t),c} \left[\sum_{i=1}^n u_i^{(t),c} x_i^{(t)} + \sum_{i=1}^n A x_i^{(t)} - \sum_{i=1}^n u_i^{(t),c} x_i^{(t)}\right]$$

$$\Rightarrow A \sum_{i=1}^n u_i^{(t),c} x_i^{(t)} > u_{i*}^{(t),c} \left[\sum_{i=1}^n \left(u_i^{(t),c} + A\right) x_i^{(t)} - \sum_{i=1}^n u_i^{(t),c} x_i^{(t)}\right]$$

$$\Rightarrow A \sum_{i=1}^n u_i^{(t),c} x_i^{(t)} + u_{i*}^{(t),c} \sum_{i=1}^n u_i^{(t),c} x_i^{(t)} > u_{i*}^{(t),c} \sum_{i=1}^n \left(u_i^{(t),c} + A\right) x_i^{(t)}$$

$$\Rightarrow \left(u_{i*}^{(t),c} + A\right) \sum_{i=1}^n u_i^{(t),c} x_i^{(t)} > u_{i*}^{(t),c} \sum_{i=1}^n \left(u_i^{(t),c} + A\right) x_i^{(t)} \tag{26}$$

We now focus on the term A from Equation 26. Recall that:

$$u_i^{(t),d} = \sum_{j=1}^m \left(c_{ij} - \frac{1}{n}\sum_{k=1}^n c_{kj} + c_{max}\right) y_j^{(t)}$$

$$= \sum_{j=1}^m c_{ij} y_j^{(t)} - \frac{1}{n}\sum_{k=1}^n \sum_{j=1}^m c_{kj} y_j^{(t)} + \sum_{j=1}^m c_{max} y_j^{(t)}$$

$$= u_i^{(t),c} - \frac{1}{n}\sum_{k=1}^n \sum_{j=1}^m c_{kj} y_j^{(t)} + c_{max}$$

We thus define A as:

$$A = -\frac{1}{n}\sum_{k=1}^n \sum_{j=1}^m c_{kj} y_j^{(t)} + c_{max}$$

Note that A is strictly positive by assumptions A1 and A2 from Section 2.3. With this definition of A, we have that:

$$u_i^{(d),t} = u_i^{(c),t} + A \tag{27}$$

Combining Equations 26 and 27 yields:

$$u_{i*}^{(t),d} \sum_{i=1}^n u_i^{(t),c} x_i^{(t)} > u_{i*}^{(t),c} \sum_{i=1}^n u_i^{(t),d} x_i^{(t)}$$

$$\Rightarrow \frac{u_{i*}^{(t),d}}{\sum_{i=1}^n u_i^{(t),d} x_i^{(t)}} > \frac{u_{i*}^{(t),c}}{\sum_{i=1}^n u_i^{(t),c} x_i^{(t)}} \tag{28}$$

Note that the terms in the inequality from Equation 28 are equivalent to the coefficients in the population update rules from Equations 4 and 10. We thus have:

$$x_{i*}^{(t+1),d} > x_{i*}^{(t+1),c} \tag{29}$$

A similar derivation for the second agent yields:

$$E_{tot}^{(t)}[C] > w_{j*}^{(t),c} \Rightarrow y_{j*}^{(t+1),d} > y_{j*}^{(t+1),c} \tag{30}$$

□

Thus, if the fitness values for the optimal actions i^* and j^* are less than the joint expected system payoff (i.e. the expected payoff of the optimal actions is relatively low), then difference evaluations result in higher probabilities of selecting the optimal actions than the global evaluation function does. Equations 25 and 30 prescribe conditions under which difference evaluations will result in better system performance than the global evaluation function. For clarity, Section 6 provides a numerical example demonstrating the results of this theorem.

5.2 Game Characteristics Theory

In Section 5.1, we proved that in cases where the expected payoffs of the optimal actions are relatively low, difference evaluations increase the probability of selecting the optimal actions compared to global evaluations. However, this also means that agents using difference evaluations have lower probabilities of selecting optimal actions in cases where the expected payoff of the optimal actions are relatively high. Even though this is the case, difference evaluations typically do not harm converged system performance when the prescribed condition from Theorem 1 does not hold. We now provide two theorems which give the intuition for why this is the case.

We first prove that all Nash equilibria in the game when using the global payoff matrix remain Nash equilibria when using difference payoff matrices. This theorem demonstrates that attractor points in the population space are not altered when applying difference evaluation functions.

THEOREM 2. *All Nash equilibria remain Nash equilibria when agents use difference payoff matrices for feedback.*

PROOF. A Nash equilibrium (i^*, j^*) in a symmetric game with a payoff matrix C is defined as:

$$c_{i^*j^*} > c_{ij^*} \ \forall\, i \neq i^* \tag{31}$$

$$c_{i^*j^*} > c_{i^*j} \ \forall\, j \neq j^* \tag{32}$$

When agents are using difference evaluations, the game is not symmetric, so a Nash equilibrium (i^*, j^*) is defined as:

$$d^1_{i^*j^*} > d^1_{ij^*} \ \forall\, i \neq i^* \tag{33}$$

$$d^2_{i^*j^*} > d^2_{i^*j} \ \forall\, j \neq j^* \tag{34}$$

Suppose we have a Nash equilibrium (i^*, j^*) that satisfies Equations 31 and 32. We now demonstrate that this implies that Equations 33 and 34 are also satisfied. We begin with Equation 31, and add $-\frac{1}{n}\sum_{k=1}^{n} c_{kj^*} + c_{max}$ to both sides of the inequality:

$$c_{i^*j^*} > c_{ij^*} \ \forall\, i \neq i^*$$

$$c_{i^*j^*} - \frac{1}{n}\sum_{k=1}^{n} c_{kj^*} + c_{max} > c_{ij^*} - \frac{1}{n}\sum_{k=1}^{n} c_{kj^*} + c_{max} \ \forall i \neq i^*$$

Noting that $d^1_{ij} = c_{ij} - \frac{1}{n}\sum_{k=1}^{n} c_{kj} + c_{max}$, we have that:

$$d^1_{i^*j^*} > d^1_{ij^*} \ \forall i \neq i^*$$

We can similarly start from Equation 32 and derive that:

$$d^2_{i^*j^*} > d^2_{i^*j} \ \forall j \neq j^*$$

□

So, difference evaluations do not alter the location of Nash equilibria from the original game using global evaluations. Thus, difference evaluations do not alter the location of attractor points in the population space.

We now prove that the relative ordering of fitness values is identical whether difference or global evaluations are used.

THEOREM 3. *If:*

$$u_a^{(t),c} > u_{a'}^{(t),c} \tag{35}$$

Then:

$$u_a^{(t),d} > u_{a'}^{(t),d}$$

PROOF. We start with Equation 35:

$$u_a^{(t),c} > u_{a'}^{(t),c}$$

$$\Rightarrow \sum_{j=1}^{m} c_{aj} y_j > \sum_{j=1}^{m} c_{a'j} y_j$$

Adding $-\frac{1}{n}\sum_{k=1}^{n}\sum_{j=1}^{m} c_{kj} y_j + \sum_{j=1}^{m} c_{max} y_j$ to both sides of the inequality yields:

$$\sum_{j=1}^{m} c_{aj} y_j - \frac{1}{n}\sum_{k=1}^{n}\sum_{j=1}^{m} c_{kj} y_j + \sum_{j=1}^{m} c_{max} y_j > \sum_{j=1}^{m} c_{a'j} y_j - \frac{1}{n}\sum_{k=1}^{n}\sum_{j=1}^{m} c_{kj} y_j + \sum_{j=1}^{m} c_{max} y_j$$

$$\Rightarrow \sum_{j=1}^{m}\left(c_{aj} - \frac{1}{n}\sum_{k=1}^{m} c_{kj} + c_{max}\right) y_j > \sum_{j=1}^{m}\left(c_{a'j} - \frac{1}{n}\sum_{k=1}^{m} c_{kj} + c_{max}\right) y_j$$

Noting that $d^1_{ij} = c_{ij} - \frac{1}{n}\sum_{k=1}^{n} c_{kj} + c_{max}$, we have that:

$$\sum_{j=1}^{m} d^1_{aj} y_j > \sum_{j=1}^{m} d^1_{a'j} y_j$$

$$\Rightarrow u_a^{(t),d} > u_{a'}^{(t),d}$$

We can conduct a similar proof for the second agent, yielding:

$$w_a^{(t),c} > w_{a'}^{(t),c} \Rightarrow w_a^{(t),d} > w_{a'}^{(t),d}$$

□

Thus, if an action a has a higher fitness than action a' when using the global evaluation, then a also has a higher fitness than a' when using the difference evaluation.

From Theorem 1, we know that in cases where the optimal action has a low expected payoff, then difference evaluations improve system performance. When the conditions from Theorem 1 are not satisfied (i.e. the optimal actions have relatively high payoffs), Theorems 2 and 3 imply that difference evaluations will not alter the location of the optimal Nash equilibrium, and that the optimal actions will still have relatively high payoffs when using difference evaluations. Thus, in cases where the conditions from Theorem 1 do not hold, then difference evaluations should not negatively impact system performance.

6. PAYOFF MATRIX ANALYSIS

In Section 5.1, we proved that difference evaluations increase the probability of selecting the optimal action if the expected payoff of the optimal action is lower than the joint expected system payoff. To illustrate the effects of the difference evaluation on the dynamics of a coordination game, we will analyze how difference evaluations impact the *penalty game*, a game with a variable parameter which can alter the risk associated with the optimal Nash equilibria [3, 8]. The penalty game is defined by the joint payoff matrix:

$$C = \begin{pmatrix} 10 & 0 & p \\ 0 & 2 & 0 \\ p & 0 & 10 \end{pmatrix} \quad (36)$$

where $p \in (-\infty, 10)$. The penalty game has three Nash equilibria: $(1,1)$, $(2,2)$, and $(3,3)$. The $(2,2)$ Nash equilibrium is suboptimal, but may be less risky depending on the value of the penalty term p. For example, if $p = -10$, then the $(2,2)$ Nash equilibrium is more forgiving if one agent deviates from its strategy. As p becomes smaller, the risk associated with the optimal Nash equilibria increases. Conversely, as p approaches 10, the risk associated with the optimal Nash equilibrium is minimized.

We can vary the value of p to alter whether or not the prescriptive conditions from Theorem 1 hold, as low values of p result in low expected payoffs for the optimal actions. We assume the agents have just started to learn and have no knowledge about the payoff matrix. As such, we assume the agents initially select their actions by sampling from a uniform random distribution. Further, we assume that the penalty term p is defined as $p = -10$. Thus, the fitness values for each action the first agent may take are:

$$u_{a_1}^{(t),c} = \frac{10 + 0 - 10 + 30}{3} = 10.0 \quad (37)$$

$$u_{a_2}^{(t),c} = \frac{0 + 2 + 0 + 30}{3} = 10.67 \quad (38)$$

$$u_{a_3}^{(t),c} = \frac{-10 + 0 + 10 + 30}{3} = 10.0 \quad (39)$$

Note that 10 is added to each element of the payoff matrix to ensure all values are non-negative. This ensures that under fitness proportional selection, the populations will remain invariant in the unit simplex. We now find the joint expected system payoff using the fitness values (expected payoffs for each action) found above:

$$\begin{aligned} E_{tot}^{(t)} &= \sum_{i=1}^{3}\sum_{j=1}^{3} c_{ij} x_i y_j \\ &= \sum_{i=1}^{3} \frac{10.0 + 10.67 + 10.0}{3} \\ &= 10.22 \end{aligned}$$

We see that $u_{a_1}^{(t),c} < E_{tot}^{(t)}$, so from Theorem 1, we know that difference evaluations will lead to a higher probability of selecting the optimal action than global evaluations will. The optimal action has a relatively low fitness, because as $y_1 = y_3$ we have the optimal Nash equilibrium payoff and penalty term canceling each other out when computing the expected payoff of the optimal action. In cases such as this where the optimal action has a low expected payoff, we know that difference evaluations increase the probability of selecting the optimal action. The normalized fitness values for the first agent taking each action are:

$$\bar{u}_{a_1}^{(t),c} = \frac{10.0}{10.0 + 10.67 + 10.0} = 0.326 \quad (40)$$

$$\bar{u}_{a_2}^{(t),c} = \frac{10.67}{10.0 + 10.67 + 10.0} = 0.348 \quad (41)$$

$$\bar{u}_{a_3}^{(t),c} = \frac{10.0}{10.0 + 10.67 + 10.0} = 0.326 \quad (42)$$

The difference payoff matrix for the first agent playing the penalty game is found by applying Equation 6 to the penalty game payoff matrix:

$$D_1 = \begin{pmatrix} 30 & 19.33 & 10 \\ 20 & 21.33 & 20 \\ 10 & 19.33 & 30 \end{pmatrix} \quad (43)$$

Retaining the assumption that each agent plays a uniform random strategy, the fitness values for each action that may be taken by the first agent are:

$$u_{a_1}^{(t),d} = \frac{30 + 19.33 + 10}{3} = 19.78 \quad (44)$$

$$u_{a_2}^{(t),d} = \frac{20 + 21.33 + 20}{3} = 20.44 \quad (45)$$

$$u_{a_3}^{(t),d} = \frac{10 + 19.33 + 30}{3} = 19.78 \quad (46)$$

In this case, the normalized fitness values for the first agent taking each action are:

$$\bar{u}_{a_1}^{(t),d} = \frac{19.78}{19.78 + 20.44 + 19.78} = 0.330 \quad (47)$$

$$\bar{u}_{a_2}^{(t),d} = \frac{20.44}{19.78 + 20.44 + 19.78} = 0.340 \quad (48)$$

$$\bar{u}_{a_3}^{(t),d} = \frac{19.78}{19.78 + 20.44 + 19.78} = 0.330 \quad (49)$$

From Theorem 1, we know that in the above example, difference evaluations result in a higher probability of selecting optimal actions. Comparing Equations 40-42 and 47-49, we see that the fitness values for the optimal actions are higher when the agent uses difference evaluation functions. Although the difference between these values is relatively small, it is of note that these differences occur after only one iteration of the EGT model. As seen in the next Section, these differences in fitness do lead to difference evaluations resulting in better performance than global evaluations.

7. EMPIRICAL RESULTS

In this section, we analyze the basins of attraction created by difference and global evaluations in the penalty game with varying values of p. We simulate the EGT model for global evaluations using Equations 2-5, and the EGT model for difference evaluations using Equations 8-11. We run 5000 simulations, using different initial population vectors (uniformly distributed across joint population space) for each simulation. Simulations are run for either 5000 generations or until the probability of selecting an action exceeds 0.995. As fitness proportional selection requires individuals to have non-negative fitness values, we add a constant term in the payoff matrix C to ensure all payoffs are non-negative.

We use the technique developed in [9] to visualize the basins of attraction. The simplex for each population is projected onto a one dimensional line segment. The line contains six regions, where all points in a given region have the same ordering of genotype proportion (1s are more common than 2s, which are more common than 3s, for example). Combining all six of these regions provides a one dimensional representation of the unit simplex. A cartesian product of two of these simplex projections provides a two dimensional representation of a two agent population space, as shown in Figure 1. Within this two dimensional space, we can visualize the basins of attraction for agents using either difference or global evaluation functions. For clarity, we have labeled

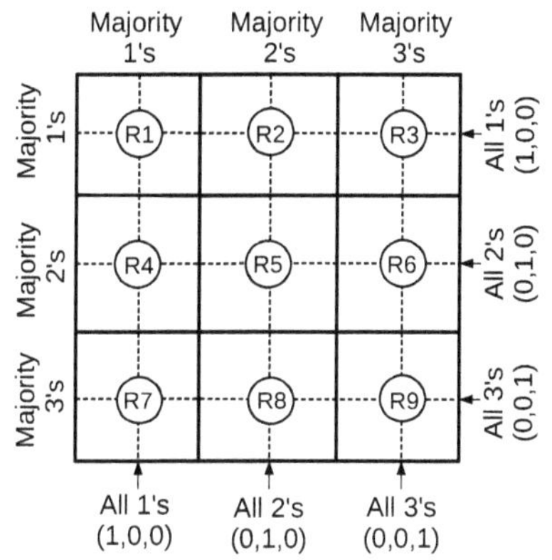

Figure 1: Visualization of the cartesian product of two simplexes, for visualing basins of attraction.

each region of the space from regions $R1$ to $R9$. See [9] for more details on the visualization process.

We analyze the basins of attraction for the penalty game when $p = -50$ and when $p = 0$. When $p = -50$, the risk associated with the optimal Nash equilibria is very high, which makes reaching the optimal Nash equilibria difficult, because both agents must consistently coordinate in order to avoid the large penalty. When $p = 0$, the optimal Nash equilibria are not difficult to reach, because there is no risk associated with the optimal actions. The values of $p = -50$ and $p = 0$ were chosen because they demonstrate three distinct cases in which difference evaluations improve system performance in the penalty game. Figure 2 shows the basins of attraction when agents use either global or difference evaluation functions and $p = -50$. Figure 3 shows the basins of attraction when agents use either global or difference evaluation functions and $p = 0$.

In Figures 2 and 3, gray areas indicate the basins of attraction around the optimal Nash equilibria for agents using either global or difference evaluation functions. Black areas indicate the regions where agents using difference evaluations converge to optimal Nash equilibria, while agents using global evaluations converge to the suboptimal Nash equilibrium. The white area indicates the basin of attraction for the suboptimal Nash equilibria $(2, 2)$ for agents using either difference or global evaluations.

As seen in Figures 2 and 3, difference evaluations improve system performance by expanding the basins of attraction around optimal Nash equilibria in three types of situations. The first case is seen in regions $R2$, $R4$, $R6$, and $R8$ of Figure 2. In this case, one agent is likely to select the suboptimal action (action 2), while the collaborating agent is likely to select an optimal action (action 1 or 3). When one agent selects the optimal action, the other agent is unlikely to do so, resulting in a poor expected payoff for the optimal action. This first case exists when $p = -50$, but not when $p = 0$. When $p = 0$, there is no penalty for an agent deviating from the optimal Nash equilibrium, meaning that the expected payoff of the optimal action is not significantly decreased.

The second case where difference evaluations are beneficial is seen in regions $R3$ and $R7$ of Figure 2. Here, one agent is likely to select an optimal action, while the collaborating agent is likely to select the mismatched optimal action. In this case, the expected payoff of the optimal action is low,

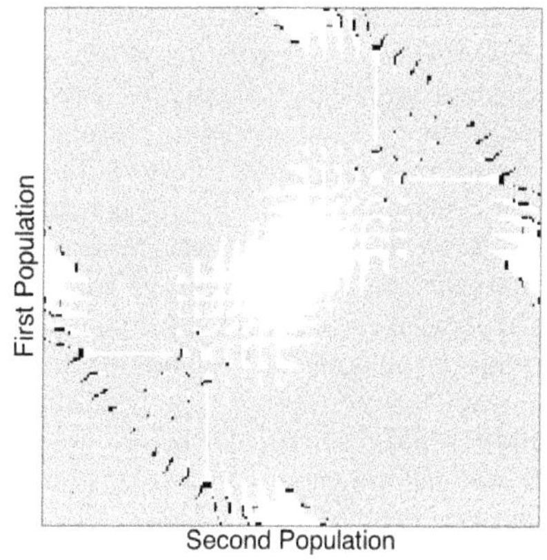

Figure 2: Basins of attraction for penalty game when $p = -50$. Gray areas: both difference and global evaluations lead to optimal Nash equilibria. Black areas: difference evaluations lead to optimal Nash equilibria, but global evaluations do not. White areas: neither difference or global evaluations lead to optimal Nash equilibra

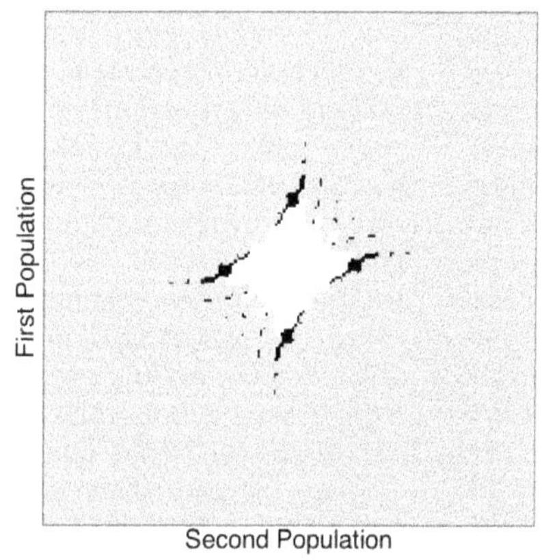

Figure 3: Basins of attraction for penalty game when $p = 0$. Gray, black, and white areas are defined as in Figure 2.

because the expected payoff of the optimal action is dominated by the penalty term. As in the first case, this case only appears when $p = -50$, not when $p = 0$. This is because when $p = 0$, the penalty term for deviating from the optimal Nash equilibria is no worse than the penalty for deviating from the suboptimal Nash equilibrium, so the penalty does not push agents towards suboptimal solutions.

The third case where difference evaluations are beneficial is seen in region $R5$ of Figure 3. In this case, both agents are likely to select the suboptimal action 2. Here, the expected payoffs of the optimal actions are low, because they are dominated by the 0 terms in the payoff matrix. This improvement is not seen when $p = -50$, because the large penalty dramatically increases the risk associated with leaving the $(2, 2)$ suboptimal Nash equilibrium.

In all three cases where difference evaluations improve system performance by expanding the basins of attraction around the optimal Nash equilibria, we see that the fitness (expected payoff) associated with the optimal action is low, which is consistent with Theorem 1. We also see that in cases where the expected payoff of the optimal action is not relatively low, both difference and global evaluation functions lead to converging to the optimal Nash equilibria, which is consistent with Theorems 2 and 3. These results demonstrate that in cases where the optimal Nash equilibrium is deceptive, difference evaluations improve the probability of selecting optimal actions, allowing agents using difference evaluations to reach the optimal Nash equilibria while agents using global evaluations converge to a suboptimal Nash equilibrium. In cases where the optimal Nash equilibria are not deceptive, agents will converge to optimal policies whether they use difference evaluations or global evaluations. We see that in some cases difference evaluations improve system performance, but they never harm system performance.

8. DISCUSSION AND CONCLUSION

Difference evaluations are effective fitness assignment operators in cooperative coevolutionary algorithms, as they provide agent-specific feedback related to the agent's impact on the overall system performance. Difference evaluations have been shown to provide superior results in a variety of multiagent coordination domains. However, to date, there has been no prescriptive theoretical analysis which derives conditions under which difference evaluations are expected to improve the probability of selecting optimal actions.

In this paper, we prove that if the fitness of the optimal action is lower than the joint expected system payoff, then difference evaluations improve the probability of selecting optimal actions. Thus, in cases where the optimal Nash equilibrium is deceptive, then difference evaluations improve system performance. Next, we proved that in cases where this condition is not met, difference evaluations do not negatively impact system performance, because they do not alter the locations of the Nash equilibria, or the relative ordering of the fitness values for each action. This means that in games where the optimal Nash equilibrium is not deceptive, then both difference and global evaluations resulting in high fitnesses for optimal actions, meaning that both fitness assignment operators promote the optimal action.

We simulated the evolutionary game theoretic model in the penalty game, and showed that the basins of attraction around optimal Nash equilibria are expanded when the conditions from Theorem 1 hold, and that difference evaluations do not negatively affect converged performance when the conditions from Theorem 1 do not hold. We find that in cases where the optimal Nash equilibria are deceptive, difference evaluations are helpful; in cases where the optimal Nash equilibria are not deceptive, difference evaluations do not harm system performance.

Future work involves extending this theory to more than two agents. The EGT framework easily extends to these cases, and early analysis shows Theorems 1-3 hold for three or more agents. We also plan on performing a theoretical analysis for multiagent reinforcement learning systems, as well as investigating different sets of replicator dynamics.

Acknowledgements

We would like to thank Dr. Karl Tuyls and Dr. Daniel Hennes for their valuable feedback on this research. This work was partially supported under NETL DE-FE0012302.

9. REFERENCES

[1] A. Agogino and K. Tumer. Analyzing and Visualizing Multiagent Rewards in Dynamic and Stochastic Environments. *Journal of Autonomous Agents and Multi-Agent Systems*, 17(2):320–338, 2008.

[2] A. Bucci and J. Pollack. Thoughts on Solution Concepts. In *Proceedings of the 9th annual conference on Genetic and evolutionary computation*, GECCO '07, pages 434–439, New York, NY, USA, 2007. ACM.

[3] C. Claus and C. Boutilier. The dynamics of reinforcement learning in cooperative multiagent systems. In *In Proceedings of National Conference on Artificial Intelligence (AAAI-98*, pages 746–752, 1998.

[4] M. Colby and K. Tumer. Shaping Fitness Functions for Coevolving Cooperative Multiagent Systems. In *Proceedings of the 11th International Joint Conference on Autonomous Agents and Multiagent Systems*, pages 425–432, Valencia, Spain, 2012.

[5] S. Ficici, O. Melnik, and J. Pollack. A Game-Theoretic and Dynamical-Systems Analysis of Selection Methods in Coevolution. *Evolutionary Computation, IEEE Transactions on*, 9(6):580 – 602, Dec 2005.

[6] D. Hennes, D. Bloembergen, M. Kaisers, K. Tuyls, and S. Parsons. Evolutionary advantage of foresight in markets. In *Proceedings of the 14th Annual Conference on Genetic and Evolutionary Computation*, GECCO '12, pages 943–950, New York, NY, USA, 2012. ACM.

[7] J. Hofbauer and K. Sigmund. *Evolutionary Games and Population Dynamics.* Cambridge University Press, 1998.

[8] L. Panait, K. Tuyls, and S. Luke. Theoretical Advantages of Lenient Learners: An Evolutionary Game Theoretic Perspective. *J. Mach. Learn. Res.*, 9:423–457, June 2008.

[9] L. Panait, R. Wiegand, and S. Luke. A visual demonstration of convergence properties of cooperative coevolution. In *Parallel Problem Solving from Nature (PPSN 04)*, pages 892–901, 2004.

[10] K. Tuyls, A. Nowe, T. Lenaerts, and B. Manderick. An evolutionary game theoretic perspective on learning in multi-agent systems. *Synthese*, 139(2):pp. 297–330, 2004.

[11] K. Tuyls and S. Parsons. What evolutionary game theory tells us about multiagent learning. *Artificial Intelligence*, 171(7):406 – 416, 2007. Foundations of Multi-Agent Learning.

[12] D. Whitley. An Overview of Evolutionary Algorithms: Practical Issues and Common Pitfalls. *Information and Software Technology*, 43(14):817 – 831, 2001.

[13] R. Wiegand. *An Analysis of Cooperative Coevolutionary Algorithms.* PhD thesis, George Mason University, 2004.

[14] R. P. Wiegand, W. C. Liles, and K. A. De Jong. Analyzing cooperative coevolution with evolutionary game theory. In *Proceedings of the Congress on Evolutionary Computation on 2002.*, CEC '02, pages 1600–1605, Washington, DC, USA, 2002. IEEE Computer Society.

[15] C. Yong and R. Miikkulainen. Cooperative Coevolution Of Multi-Agent Systems. Technical Report AI07-338, Department of Computer Sciences, The University of Texas at Austin, 2001.

On Easiest Functions for Somatic Contiguous Hypermutations And Standard Bit Mutations

Dogan Corus
School of Computer Science
University of Nottingham
Nottingham, NG8 1BB, UK
dqc@cs.nott.ac.uk

Jun He
Dep. of Computer Science
Aberystwyth University
Aberystwyth, SY23 3DB, UK
jqh@aber.ac.uk

Thomas Jansen
Dep. of Computer Science
Aberystwyth University
Aberystwyth, SY23 3DB, UK
t.jansen@aber.ac.uk

Pietro S. Oliveto
Dep. of Computer Science
University of Sheffield
Sheffield S1 4DP, UK
p.oliveto@sheffield.ac.uk

Dirk Sudholt
Dep. of Computer Science
University of Sheffield
Sheffield S1 4DP, UK
d.sudholt@sheffield.ac.uk

Christine Zarges
School of Computer Science
University of Birmingham
Birmingham B15 2TT, UK
c.zarges@bham.ac.uk

ABSTRACT

Understanding which function classes are easy and which are hard for a given algorithm is a fundamental question for the analysis and design of bio-inspired search heuristics. A natural starting point is to consider the easiest and hardest functions for an algorithm. For the (1+1) EA using standard bit mutation it is well known that OneMax is an easiest function with unique optimum while Trap is a hardest.

In this paper we extend the analysis of easiest function classes to the contiguous somatic hypermutation (CHM) operator used in artificial immune systems. We define a function MinBlocks and prove that it is an easiest function for the (1+1) EA using CHM, presenting both a runtime and a fixed budget analysis. Since MinBlocks is, up to a factor of 2, a hardest function for standard bit mutations, we consider the effects of combining both operators into a hybrid algorithm. We show that an easiest function for the hybrid algorithm is not just a trivial weighted combination of the respective easiest functions for each operator. Nevertheless, by combining the advantages of both operators, the hybrid algorithm has optimal asymptotic performance on both OneMax and MinBlocks.

Categories and Subject Descriptors

F.2.2 [**Analysis of Algorithms and Problem Complexity**]: Nonnumerical Algorithms and Problems

Keywords

Running time analysis, Theory, Hybridisation, Evolutionary Algorithms, Artificial Immune Systems

1. INTRODUCTION

GECCO '15, July 11 - 15, 2015, Madrid, Spain

ISBN 978-1-4503-3472-3/15/07 . . . $15.00

DOI: http://dx.doi.org/10.1145/2739480.2754799

Over the past years many bio-inspired search heuristics such as evolutionary algorithms, swarm intelligence algorithms, or artificial immune systems, have been developed and successfully applied to various optimisation problems. These heuristics have different strengths and weaknesses in coping with different fitness landscapes. Determining which heuristic is the best choice for a given problem is a fundamental and important question.

We use rigorous theoretical analyses to contribute to a better understanding of bio-inspired algorithms. A natural step is to investigate which functions are easy and which are hard for a given algorithm (assuming all functions have the same global optima) as this yields fundamental insights into their working principles, particularly with respect to their strengths and weaknesses.

Knowing how well an algorithm performs on its easiest and hardest functions, with regards to the expected optimisation time, provides general insights, as the expected optimisation time of *every* function will be no less than that of an easiest function and no more than that of a hardest function. With respect to applications, such research may also provide guidelines for the design of benchmarks for experimental studies [6].

For a simple elitist (1+1) evolutionary algorithm using only standard bit mutations (SBM) it is well-known that OneMax, a function simply counting the number of ones in a bit string, is the easiest problem among all functions with a single global optimum [4, 6]. On the other hand the highly deceptive function Trap is the hardest function for this algorithm [6].

In this work we consider typical mutation operators in artificial immune systems where no such results are available. Mutation operators in artificial immune systems [3] usually come with much larger mutation rates than mutation operators in evolutionary algorithms. One such example is the somatic contiguous hypermutation (CHM) operator from the B-cell algorithm (BCA) [15], where large contiguous blocks of a bit string are flipped simultaneously. Previous theoretical work on comparing SBM and CHM has contributed to the understanding of their benefits and drawbacks in the context of its runtime on different problems [8, 10, 11], the expected solution quality after a pre-defined number of steps [14] and in dynamic environments [12]. It is easy to see that hardest functions for CHM with respect to expected optimisation times are those where the algorithm gets trapped with positive probability such that the optimisation time is not finite, e. g., if there exists a second best search point for which all direct mutations to the optimum involve non-contiguous bits [10]. However, it is an open problem and next step forward to determine what kind of functions are easiest for this type of mutation operator.

The BCA uses standard bit mutations alongside CHM and thus can be considered as a hybrid algorithm combining two mutation operators. The interplay between these two operators has been investigated for the vertex cover problem [8].

Hybridisations such as hyper-heuristics [19] and memetic algorithms [18] have grown very popular over recent years. But despite their practical success their theoretical analysis is still in its infancy, noteworthy examples being the work in [1, 16, 21, 22]. However, nothing is known about easiest or hardest functions for such algorithms.

The goals of this paper are twofold. We first want to understand what functions are easy for CHM and investigate the performance of CHM and SBM on these functions. Afterwards we consider an hybridisation of SBM and CHM and easiest functions for such algorithms. We first use the method by He, Chen, and Yao [6], explained in Section 3, to derive an easiest function for CHM which we call MinBlocks. In Section 4 we present an analysis for the optimisation time as well as a fixed budget analysis for CHM on MinBlocks. We then show that SBM alone is not able to optimise the constructed function and that an hybridisation of SBM and CHM can have significant advantages (Section 5.1). Finally, we investigate properties of easiest functions for such hybrid algorithms (Section 5.2).

2. PRELIMINARIES

We are interested in all strictly elitist (1+1) algorithms with time independent variation operators. This generalised algorithmic scheme keeps a single solution x as a population and creates a single offspring at every generation. The new offspring is accepted if it is strictly fitter than the parent. Apart from the explicit requirement of time independence, the variation operator is implicitly restricted to the domain of unary variation operators since the population size is one. For a maximisation problem, it is formally defined as Algorithm 1.

Algorithm 1 (1+1) A

```
1: input: fitness function f;
2: generate a solution x;
3: while the maximum value of f is not found do
4:     y ← is mutated from parent x;
5:     if f(y) > f(x) then
6:         let x ← y;
7:     end if
8: end while
9: output: the maximal value of f.
```

We will use two different mutation operators for line 4 of Algorithm 1. The first is the most common unary variation operator, standard bit mutation, and the resulting algorithm is called (1+1) EA. This variation operator independently flips each bit with probability $1/n$.

Algorithm 2 Standard Bit Mutation (SBM)

```
for i := 0 to n − 1 do
    With probability 1/n set x[i] := 1 − x[i].
end for
```

The other variation operator of interest is the contiguous hypermutation operator (CHM) which mutates a bitstring by picking a bit position and flipping a random number of bits that follow it (in a wrapping around fashion). For an input $x \in \{0,1\}^n$ CHM works as follows.

Algorithm 3 Somatic Contiguous Hypermutation (CHM)

```
Select p ∈ {0, 1, ..., n − 1} uniformly at random.
Select l ∈ {0, 1, ..., n} uniformly at random.
for i := 0 to l − 1 do
    With probability r set x[(p + i) mod n] := 1 −
    x[(p + i) mod n] .
end for
```

As done in previous work (see, e. g., [10]) we only consider the extreme case here and set $r = 1$. We will refer to the (1+1) A that uses a CHM operator as (1+1) CHM.

3. EASIEST AND HARDEST FUNCTIONS

Our work is based on previous work by He, Chen, and Yao [6]. We consider the problem of maximising a class of fitness functions with the same optima. An instance of the problem is to maximise a fitness function f:

$$\max\{f(x); x \in S\}, \tag{1}$$

where S is a finite set.

Let $T(A, f, x)$ denote the expected number of generations for (1+1) A to find an optimal solution for the first time when starting at x (*expected hitting time*). In the following we only consider algorithms and functions that lead to a finite expected hitting time.

Definition 1. *[6, Definition 1] Given a (1+1) A for maximising a class of fitness functions with the same optima (denoted by $\mathcal{F}$), a function f in the class is said to be the* easiest *function for the (1+1) A if $T(A, f, x) \le T(A, g, x)$ for every $g \in \mathcal{F}$ and every $x \in S$. A function f in the class is said to be the* hardest *function for the (1+1) A if $T(A, f, x) \ge T(A, g, x)$ for every $g \in \mathcal{F}$ and every $x \in S$.*

The above definition of the easiest and hardest functions is based on a point-by-point comparison of the runtime of the EA on two fitness functions. Being *the* easiest function is used according to the Definition 1 throughout the paper and being *an* easiest function is used from time to time with the same meaning.

The following criterion for determining whether a fitness function is the easiest function for a (1+1) A is given in [6].

Lemma 2. *[6, Theorem 1] Given a (1+1) A, and a class of fitness functions with the same optima, if the following* monotonically decreasing condition *holds,*

- *for any two points x and y, if $T(A, f, x) < T(A, f, y)$, then $f(x) > f(y)$,*

then f is the easiest in the fitness function class.

In a similar way, we have the following criterion of determining whether a fitness function is the hardest function for a (1+1) A, assuming that all expected optimisation times are finite[1]. The monotonically decreasing condition in the above lemma is replaced by the monotonically increasing condition.

LEMMA 3. *[6, Theorem 2] Given a (1+1) A, and a class of fitness functions with the same optima, if the following* monotonically increasing condition *holds,*

- *for any two non-optimal points x and y, if $T(A, f, x) < T(A, f, y)$, then it holds $f(x) < f(y)$,*

then f is the hardest in the class.

However the conditions in the above lemmas need a change if we consider (1+1) A without strict selection (that is, the parent x is replaced by the child y if $f(y) \geq f(x)$). The modified criteria of determining the easiest and hardest functions are given as follows.

LEMMA 4. *Given a (1+1) A without strict selection, and a class of fitness functions with the same optima, if the following* strictly monotonically decreasing condition *holds,*

- *for any two points x and y, $T(A, f, x) < T(A, f, y)$ if and only if $f(x) > f(y)$,*

then f is the easiest in the fitness function class.

LEMMA 5. *Given a (1+1) A without strict selection, and a class of fitness functions with the same optima, if the following* strictly monotonically increasing condition *holds,*

- *for any two non-optimal points x and y, $T(A, f, x) < T(A, f, y)$ if and only if $f(x) < f(y)$,*

then f is the hardest in the class.

Their proofs are the same as those of Theorems 1 and 2 in [6]. For any pair of two points x and y such that $T(A, f, x) = T(A, f, y)$ and $f(x) = f(y)$, we may regard them as an identical point, thus the proofs in [6] do not need any change.

4. CONTIGUOUS HYPERMUTATIONS ON AN EASIEST FUNCTION WITH UNIQUE GLOBAL OPTIMUM

We are now ready to derive an easiest function with unique global optimum for contiguous hypermutations and analyse the performance of the (1+1) CHM on this function.

4.1 Notation and Definition

We use $x = x[0]x[1]\cdots x[n-1] \in \{0,1\}^n$ as notation for bit strings of length n. For $a, b \in \{0, 1, \ldots, n-1\}$ we denote by $x[a..b]$ the concatenation of $x[a]$, $x[(a+1) \bmod n]$, $x[(a+2) \bmod n]$, $\ldots$, $x[(a+i) \bmod n]$ where i is the smallest number from $\{0, 1, \ldots, n-1\}$ with $(a+i) \bmod n = b$. We denote by $|x[a..b]|$ the number of bits in $x[a..b]$, i.e., its length. We say that $x \in \{0,1\}^n$ contains a 1-block from a to b if $x[a..b] = 1^{|x[a..b]|}$ and $x[(a-1) \bmod n] = x[(b+1) \bmod n] = 0$ hold. Analogously we may speak of a 0-block from a to b. Note that bit strings need to contain at least one 0-bit and at least one 1-bit to contain a 0-block or a 1-block. It is easy to see that each $x \in \{0,1\}^n \setminus \{0^n, 1^n\}$ contains an equal number of 0-blocks and 1-blocks.

[1]Hardest functions are formally only defined for functions and algorithms with finite expected optimisation times. However, we regard functions leading to infinite expected times as being harder than those with finite expected times.

DEFINITION 6. *We define an easiest function with unique global optimum for contiguous hypermutations by defining a partition $L_0 \dot\cup L_1 \dot\cup L_2 \dot\cup \cdots \dot\cup L_l = \{0,1\}^n$ and assigning fitness values accordingly. We call the function* MINBLOCKS *and define* MINBLOCKS$(x) = l - i$ *for $x \in L_i$. We define $l = \lfloor n/2 \rfloor + 1$ and level sets $L_0 = \{1^n\}$, $L_1 = \{0^n\}$ and $L_i = \{x \in \{0,1\}^n \mid x$ contains $i-1$ different 1-blocks$\}$ for each $i \in \{2, 3, \ldots, l\}$.*

The function has a unique global optimum 1^n with function value $l = \lfloor n/2 \rfloor + 1$. The second best bit string is 0^n with function value $l - 1$. All other bit strings contain an equal number of 0-blocks and 1-blocks. Their function value equals $l - i$ where i denotes the number of 1-blocks.

We defer the proof that MINBLOCKS is indeed an easiest function for (1+1) CHM to the next section (Corollary 8) in order to make use of arguments from the analysis of the expected optimisation time performed there.

4.2 Expected Optimisation Time

We analyse the expected optimisation time of the (1+1) CHM on MINBLOCKS, i.e., the expected number of function evaluations executed until the global optimum is reached [7]. To facilitate our analysis, we start with an analysis of the expected optimisation time starting from a bit string from a particular level set which will in turn allow us to prove that MINBLOCKS is the easiest function for (1+1) CHM. We will then continue with the overall upper and lower bounds for the optimisation time.

LEMMA 7. *We consider contiguous hypermutations on* MINBLOCKS *as defined in Definition 6. For $i \in \{0, 1, \ldots, l\}$ (where $l+1$ is the number of sets in the partition from Definition 6) let T_i denote the random number of steps needed to reach the unique global optimum 1^n when started in a bit string from L_i. The expected numbers of steps are* $\mathrm{E}(T_0) = 0$, $\mathrm{E}(T_1) = n + 1$, $\mathrm{E}(T_2) = (n+1)^2/2$ *and*

$$\mathrm{E}(T_i) = \frac{n(n+1)}{(2i-2)(2i-3)} + \mathrm{E}(T_{i-1})$$

for all $i \in \{2, 3, \ldots, l\}$.

PROOF. The statement about $\mathrm{E}(T_0)$ is trivial. For $\mathrm{E}(T_1)$ it suffices to observe that any hypermutation which chooses as mutation length n leads from 0^n to the unique global optimum 1^n. Such a mutation has probability $1/(n+1)$ which implies $\mathrm{E}(T_1) = n + 1$. For $\mathrm{E}(T_2)$ we observe that for each $x \in L_2$ there are two mutations which lead to $L_0 \cup L_1$, one leading to L_0 and the other leading to L_1. Since L_0 and L_1 are reached with equal probability 1/2 we have $\mathrm{E}(T_2) = n(n+1)/2 + \mathrm{E}(T_1)/2 = (n+1)^2/2$. For $\mathrm{E}(T_i)$ with $i > 2$ we observe that only mutations that reduce the number of 1-blocks can lead to some L_j with $j < i$. It is easy to see that the number of 1-blocks can only be reduced by 1 in one contiguous hypermutation. In order to achieve that a mutation must start at the first bit of a block (either a 0-block or a 1-block) and end at the last bit of a block (either a 0-block or a 1-block) but this block cannot be the one just before the block containing the first flipped bit (otherwise the length of the mutation is n, the bit string is inverted and the number of 1-blocks remains unchanged). Thus, if there are j blocks in the bit string the number of such mutations equals $j(j-1)$. For $x \in L_i$ the number of 1-blocks equals $i-1$ and therefore the number of blocks equals $2i-2$ so that there are $(2i-2)(2i-3)$ such mutations. Thus, the expected time to leave L_i equals $n(n+1)/((2i-2)(2i-3))$ and $\mathrm{E}(T_i) = n(n+1)/((2i-2)(2i-3)) + \mathrm{E}(T_{i-1})$ follows. □

In order to get a result which is valid for both the proposed algorithm (1+1) CHM and the identical algorithm without strict replacement policy, we prove that MINBLOCKS is the easiest function for the (1+1) CHM as a corollary to Lemma 4.

COROLLARY 8. *MINBLOCKS is an easiest function for the (1+1) CHM among all functions with unique optimum 1^n.*

PROOF. For $f :=$ MINBLOCKS,

$$f(x) > f(y) \Leftrightarrow x \in L_i \wedge y \in L_j \wedge i < j.$$

According to Lemma 7 for $A := (1+1)\ CHM$,

$$T(A, f, x) = \mathrm{E}(T_i) > \mathrm{E}(T_j) = T(A, f, y).$$

Therefore, MINBLOCKS is an easiest function for the algorithm $(1+1)\ CHM$ since it satisfies the criterion $f(x) > f(y) \Leftrightarrow T(A, f, x) < T(A, f, y)$ from Lemma 4 . □

We continue our analysis of the expected optimisation time. Note that the following bound asymptotically matches the lower bound of $\Omega(n^2)$ for contiguous hypermutations proven by Jansen and Zarges [10].

THEOREM 9. *Let T denote the expected optimisation time of the (1+1) CHM on MINBLOCKS. $\mathrm{E}(T) = \ln(2)n^2 \pm O(n)$ holds.*

PROOF. Consider $x \in \{0,1\}^n$ selected uniformly at random. For each $i \in \{0, 1, \ldots, n-1\}$ we have that a block ends at $x[i]$ if $x[i] \neq x[(i+1) \bmod n]$ holds. Thus, $x[i]$ is the end of a block with probability 1/2 and we see that the expected number of blocks equals $n/2$. Let I denote the number of blocks. An application of Chernoff bounds yields that for any constant ε with $0 < \varepsilon < 1$ we have $\Pr(I \geq (1-\varepsilon)n/2) = 1 - e^{-\Omega(n)}$.

We know that $\mathrm{E}(T \mid I = 2(i-1)) = \mathrm{E}(T_i)$ holds and have

$$\begin{aligned}
\mathrm{E}(T_i) &= \frac{n(n+1)}{(2i-2)(2i-3)} + \mathrm{E}(T_{i-1}) \\
&= \frac{n(n+1)}{(2i-2)(2i-3)} + \frac{n(n+1)}{(2(i-1)-2)(2(i-1)-3)} + \mathrm{E}(T_{i-2}) \\
&= \cdots = \mathrm{E}(T_2) + n(n+1) \sum_{j=0}^{i-3} \frac{1}{(2(i-j)-2)(2(i-j)-3)} \\
&= \mathrm{E}(T_2) + n(n+1) \sum_{j=0}^{i-3} \frac{1}{2j+3} + \frac{1}{2j+4} - \frac{1}{j+2} \\
&= \mathrm{E}(T_2) + n(n+1) \left(\left(\sum_{j=3}^{2i-2} \frac{1}{j} \right) - \left(\sum_{j=2}^{i-1} \frac{1}{j} \right) \right) \\
&= \mathrm{E}(T_2) + n(n+1) \left(H_{2i-2} - H_{i-1} - \frac{1}{2} \right)
\end{aligned}$$

where H_j denotes the jth Harmonic numbers. Using $H_j = \ln(j) + \gamma + 1/(2j) - o(1/j)$ we obtain

$$\begin{aligned}
&\mathrm{E}(T \mid I = 2(i-1)) \\
&= \frac{(n+1)^2}{2} + n(n+1) \left(\ln(2) - \frac{1}{2} \right) - O(n^2/i) \\
&= \ln(2)n^2 + O(n) - O(n^2/i).
\end{aligned}$$

For the lower bound on $\mathrm{E}(T)$ we use $i = n/4$ (and have $\Pr(I \geq n/4) = 1 - e^{-\Omega(n)}$, of course) and obtain

$$\begin{aligned}
\mathrm{E}(T) - \left(1 - e^{-\Omega(n)}\right) \cdot \left(\ln(2)n^2 + O(n) - O(n)\right) \\
= \ln(2)n^2 \pm O(n)
\end{aligned}$$

as claimed.

For the upper bound on $\mathrm{E}(T)$ we have

$$\mathrm{E}(T) \leq \mathrm{E}(T_{n/2}) = \ln(2)n^2 + O(n) - O(n) = \ln(2)n^2 \pm O(n)$$

as claimed. □

4.3 Fixed Budget Analysis

It has been pointed out that the notion of optimisation time does not always capture the nature of how randomised search heuristics are applied in practice. As a result, fixed budget analysis has been introduced as an alternative theoretical perspective [13]. Let x_t denote the current population after t rounds of contiguous hypermutation and selection. In fixed budget analysis we want to analyse $\mathrm{E}(f(x_t))$ for all $t \leq \mathrm{E}(T)$ where $\mathrm{E}(T)$ is the expected optimisation time. We do this here for MINBLOCKS to give a more complete picture about the performance of the (1+1) CHM. Note that a comparison of the (1+1) EA and the (1+1) CHM under the fixed budget perspective has previously been performed for some example functions [14].

We begin with a statement about the expected initial function value and prove that it is roughly $(n-2)/4 \pm 1/2$.

THEOREM 10. *Let $x \in \{0,1\}^n$ be selected uniformly at random and $f :=$ MINBLOCKS from Definition 6.*
For the initial function value

$$\begin{aligned}
\frac{2\lfloor n/2 \rfloor + 1}{2^n} + \left(1 - 2^{-n+1}\right)\left(\left\lfloor \frac{n}{2} \right\rfloor - \frac{n}{4} - 1\right) \\
\leq \mathrm{E}(f(x_0)) \leq \\
\frac{2\lfloor n/2 \rfloor + 1}{2^n} + \left(1 - 2^{-n+1}\right)\left(\left\lfloor \frac{n}{2} \right\rfloor - \frac{n}{4}\right)
\end{aligned}$$

holds.

PROOF. Let $l = \lfloor n/2 \rfloor + 1$ (the value defined in Definition 6). We know that either $x_0 \in \{0^n, 1^n\}$ or x_0 contains at least one 1-block. We have $f(1^n) = l$ and $f(0^n) = l - 1$. This yields $\mathrm{E}(f(x_0)) = (l/2^n) + (l-1)/2^n + (1 - 2^{-n+1}) \cdot \mathrm{E}(f(x_0) \mid x_0 \notin \{0^n, 1^n\})$.

If $x_0 \notin \{0^n, 1^n\}$ then x_0 contains a positive random number z of 0-blocks and $f(x_0) = l - z - 1$ holds. From the analysis of the expected optimisation time in Subsection 4.2 we know that the expected number of blocks in x_0 equals $n/2$. This expectation is unconditional and, consequently, is a lower bound on the expected number of blocks under the condition that x_0 contains at least one 0-block. We know that $n/2$ blocks translate into $n/4$ 0-blocks and we conclude that $l - (n/4) - 1$ is an upper bound on $\mathrm{E}(f(x_0) \mid x_0 \notin \{0^n, 1^n\})$. We conclude that

$$\mathrm{E}(f(x_0)) \leq \frac{2l-1}{2^n} + \left(1 - 2^{-n+1}\right)\left(l - \frac{n}{4} - 1\right)$$

holds.

For a lower bound we need an upper bound on the expected number of blocks in x_0 given that it contains at least 1 block. Remembering that blocks always appear in pairs of one 0-block and one 1-block we see that $(n/2) + 2$ is an upper bound on the conditional expected number of blocks. This translates in $(n/4) + 1$ 0-blocks and we obtain

$$\mathrm{E}(f(x_0)) \geq \frac{2l-1}{2^n} + \left(1 - 2^{-n+1}\right)\left(l - \frac{n}{4} - 2\right).$$

With $l = \lfloor n/2 \rfloor + 1$ this yields the claimed bound. □

We now give upper and lower bounds on the expected function value after t iterations of the (1+1) CHM.

THEOREM 11. *Let $x_t \in \{0,1\}^n$ denote the current search point after random initialisation and t rounds of contiguous hypermutation and selection on $f :=$ MINBLOCKS.*

$$\mathrm{E}(f(x_0)) + (\lfloor n/2 \rfloor + 1 - \mathrm{E}(f(x_0)))\left(1 - \left(1 - \frac{2}{n(n+1)}\right)^t\right)$$
$$\leq \lfloor n/2 \rfloor + 1 - (\lfloor n/2 \rfloor + 1 - \mathrm{E}(f(x_0))) \cdot (1 - 3/(n(n+1)))^t$$
$$\leq \mathrm{E}(f(x_t)) \leq$$
$$\left(\sum_{z=1}^{n/2} \binom{n/2}{z} 2^{-n/2} \cdot \left(((n/2) - z) + 1 - \left(1 - \frac{1}{n+1}\right)^t \right.\right.$$
$$\left.\left. + \sum_{d=2}^{z+1} 1 - \left(1 - \frac{(2d-2)(2d-3)}{n(n+1)}\right)^t\right)\right) + n \cdot 2^{-n+1}$$

holds.

PROOF. The function value can increase at most $\lfloor n/2 \rfloor + 1 - z$ times if the initial function value is z since the maximal function value is $\lfloor n/2 \rfloor + 1$. For an upper bound we consider the actual probabilities for increasing the function value which equal $(2d-2)(2d-3)/(n(n+1))$ if the current number of 0-blocks is d and $1/(n+1)$ for 0^n. For each of these events we add the expected contribution after t steps. This contribution equals the probability to have at least one such increasing step in t steps which equals $1 - (1-p)^t$ if p denotes the probability for an increasing step. Adding these yields an upper bound since it pretends that for each level t steps are available to create an increasing step whereas in reality decreasing the number of 0-blocks from d to $d-1$ is only possible after it has been decreased to d from $d+1$ before. Since initialisation in 0^n or 1^n has probability 2^{-n+1} the contribution of these cases is $O(n/2^n)$. Let Z denote the random number of 0-blocks in the initial bit string. We obtain

$$\mathrm{E}(f(x_t)) \leq \left(\sum_{z=1}^{n/2} \Pr(Z = z) \cdot \left((l - (z+1))\right.\right.$$
$$\left.\left. +1 - \left(1 - \frac{1}{n+1}\right)^t + \sum_{d=2}^{z+1} 1 - \left(1 - \frac{(2d-2)(2d-3)}{n(n+1)}\right)^t\right)\right)$$
$$+ l \cdot 2^{-n+1}$$

using the law of total probability. We obtain an upper bound by noting that Z is binomially distributed with parameters $n/2$ and $1/2$, and by remembering that $l = \lfloor n/2 \rfloor + 1$ holds.

For the smaller of the two lower bounds we replace the actual probabilities by the smallest probability for an increase in function value which equals $2/(n(n+1))$. We can improve on this weak lower bound slightly by using a technique called multiplicative fixed budget drift as recently introduced by Lengler and Spooner [17]. For a lower bound we need a lower bound on the expected change in function value in one generation given the current function value. If the current bit string contains i bits we know that the expected change equals $(2i-2)(3i-2)/(n(n+1)) > 3i^2/(n(n+1)) > 3i/(n(n+1))$ where the last inequality is made because Theorem 1 in [17] requires a statement about this drift that is linear. Using this we obtain $\lfloor n/2 \rfloor + 1 - (\lfloor n/2 \rfloor + 1 - \mathrm{E}(f(x_0))) \cdot (1 - 3/(n(n+1)))^t$ as lower bound on the expected function value after t steps. □

To obtain actual lower and upper bounds we use the lower and upper bounds for the initial expected function value from Theorem 10. While the bounds from Theorem 11 are not simple and in particular the upper bound is not even a closed form we can easily evaluate them numerically for reasonable values of n. In Figure 1 we display them for $n = 100$ together with the maximal function value 51 and empirical results averaged over 100 runs. We see that while the upper bound yields reasonable results both lower bounds are rather weak.

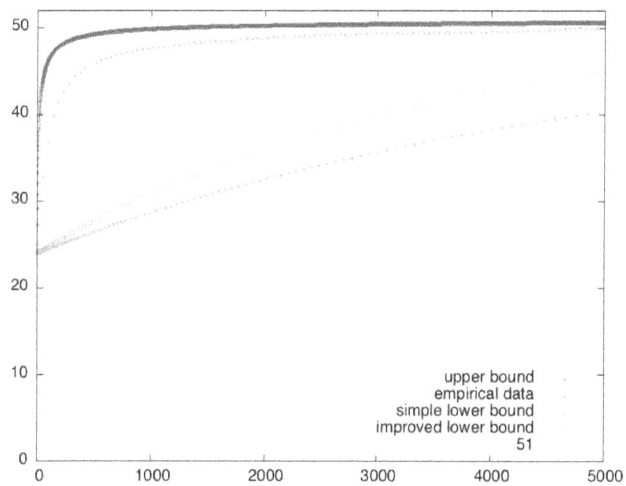

Figure 1: Average function values of CHM on an easiest function for CHM with unique global optimum for $n = 100$ after a given number of function evaluations, averaged over 100 runs, together with the theoretical bounds from Theorem 11. The number of function evaluations are on the x-axis, the function values on the y-axis.

5. HYBRIDISING OPERATORS

A popular approach in areas such as memetic algorithms or hyper-heuristics is to combine several operators in one algorithm. There are many ways of hybridising algorithms – here, we consider hybrids that execute one of two operators.

Given two (1+1) As, A_1 and A_0, a hybrid (1+1) A, A_p, is given as follows:

Algorithm 4 (1+1) Hybrid (A_p)

1: **input**: fitness function f;
2: generate a solution x;
3: **while** the maximum value of f is not found **do**
4: with probability p, apply one iteration (mutation + selection) of A_1 to update x;
5: or with probability $1-p$, apply one iteration (mutation +selection) of A_0 to update x
6: **end while**
7: **output**: the maximal value of f.

The B-cell algorithm (BCA) [15] is an example of an algorithm that uses both SBM and CHM considered in this paper. However, the BCA uses both operators in each iteration. Jansen, Oliveto and Zarges [8] proposed a variant of the BCA that only uses CHM with constant probability $0 < p < 1$ and were able to show significantly improved upper bounds on the optimisation time for this algorithm on the vertex cover problem. The (1+1) Hybrid framework with $0 < p < 1$ constant considered here is a possible implementation of this proposed variant.

In the following subsection we will first consider the general hybrid algorithmic framework and then specialise the results to the combination of the CHM and SBM.

5.1 The Advantage of Hybridisation

The easiest functions for SBM and CHM are OneMax and MinBlocks, respectively. Before analysing hybrid algorithms using both operators, it is natural to consider the effect of one operator on the easiest function for the other operator. It is well known that the (1+1) CHM needs $\Theta(n^2 \log n)$ expected time on OneMax [10, 14].

Here we consider the expected optimisation time of the (1+1) EA on MinBlocks and show that it is very inefficient.

Theorem 12. *The expected optimisation time of the (1+1) EA on* MinBlocks *is at least $n^n/2$.*

Proof. The function MinBlocks has the following property: for all search points except for 0^n and 1^n, the number of 0-blocks equals the number of 1-blocks. Notice that inverting all bits in a bit string turns all 0-blocks into 1-blocks and vice versa. Hence for all $x \notin \{0^n, 1^n\}$ we have $\text{MinBlocks}(x) = \text{MinBlocks}(\overline{x})$.

Let $x_0, x_1, \ldots$ be the trajectory of the (1+1) EA and $T \in \mathbb{N}_0$ be the first hitting time of a search point in $\{0^n, 1^n\}$. Since $x_0, x_1, \ldots, x_T$ has the same probability as $\overline{x_0}, \overline{x_1}, \ldots, \overline{x_T}$ and $x_T \in \{0^n, 1^n\}$, we have $\Pr(x_T = 0^n) = 1/2$. In this case the only accepted search point is the global optimum 1^n, for which all bits have to be flipped in one mutation. This has probability n^{-n} and expected waiting time n^n. Combined with the probability of reaching this state, the expected optimisation time is at least $T + n^n/2 \geq n^n/2$. □

Note that the expected optimisation time of the (1+1) EA on MinBlocks is only by a factor of at most 2 smaller than the expected optimisation time of the (1+1) EA on its hardest function, Trap, which is almost n^n [5].

Using multiple operators, the hope is that the advantages of each operator are combined. However, this is not always true: new operators can make a hybrid algorithm follow an entirely different search trajectory and lead to drastically increased optimisation times. This behaviour was demonstrated for memetic algorithms [20] as well as for standard bit mutations cycling between different mutation rates [9].

We show that such effects cannot occur when dealing with easiest functions. If f is an easiest function for A which is a (1+1) A, then the following theorem allows to transfer an upper bound on the expected optimisation time of A to A_p.

Theorem 13. *If A_1, A_0 are (1+1) A, and f is an easiest function for A_1, then the expected hitting time of A_p on f is bounded by*

$$T(A_p, f, x) \leq \frac{1}{p} \cdot T(A_1, f, x).$$

Proof. We follow the analysis in [6, Section III] and choose the runtime $T(A_1, f, x)$ as the drift function:

$$d(x) = T(A_1, f, x).$$

For algorithm A_1 we then apply Lemma 3 in [6]. For any non-optimal point x, let y be its child, then the drift of algorithm A_1 satisfies

$$\Delta_{A_1}(x) = E(d(x) - d(y)) = 1. \tag{2}$$

Now we estimate the drift of algorithm A_p, which is

$$\Delta_{A_p}(x) = p\Delta_{A_1}(x) + (1-p)\Delta_{A_0}(x).$$

First we investigate the negative drift of algorithm A_p. Given any two non-optimal points x and y such that $d(x) < d(y)$, according to the monotonically decreasing condition, $f(x) > f(y)$. Since both algorithms A_1 and A_0 adopt elitist selection, the transition probability from x to y is 0. Denote the negative drift $\Delta^- = \mathrm{E}(d(x) - d(y) : d(x) < d(y))$. Then the negative drift of algorithms A_1 and A_0 satisfies

$$\Delta^-_{A_1} = \Delta^-_{A_0} = 0.$$

Thus the drift of A_p satisfies:

$$\Delta^-_{A_p} = 0.$$

Next we investigate the positive drift of algorithm A_p. We have $\Delta^+_{A_0} \geq 0$ as whenever A_0 accepts a transition from x to y, we have $f(y) > f(x)$ and $T(A_1, f, y) \leq T(A_1, f, x)$, as the contrary would contradict f being an easiest function for A_1. Denote the positive drift $\Delta^+ = \mathrm{E}(d(x) - d(y) : d(x) > d(y))$, then

$$\Delta^+_{A_p} = p\Delta^+_{A_1} + (1-p)\Delta^+_{A_0} \geq p\Delta^+_{A_1}(x).$$

The drift of algorithm A_p satisfies

$$\Delta_{A_p} \geq p\Delta^+_{A_1} + (1-p)\Delta^+_{A_0} \geq p\Delta_{A_1}(x) = p.$$

According to Lemma 1 in [6], we know that the expected hitting time of A_p on f is $\frac{d(x)}{p}$. Then we come to the required conclusion. □

Using Theorem 13 as well as Theorem 9, we get the following corollary concerning the SBM and CHM operators.

Corollary 14. *Consider the algorithm A_p that executes one standard bit mutation with probability p and a contiguous somatic hypermutation otherwise. If $0 < p < 1$ is constant, the expected optimisation time of A_p on* OneMax *is $O(n \log n)$ and its expected optimisation time on* MinBlocks *is $O(n^2)$.*

The hybrid algorithm is hence able to combine the advantages of both operators on the two easiest functions for its two operators.

5.2 On the Easiest Function for Hybrid Algorithms

He, Chen and Yao [6] explain how an easiest function can be computed. We construct EASIESTHYBRID$_p$, an easiest fitness function for the hybrid algorithm A_p from Corollary 14 by implementing their construction procedure and performing the necessary computations numerically. Clearly, this is computationally feasible only for small values of n. Using the unique global optimum as a starting point and level L_0 we can compute the next level of search points with next best and equal fitness by computing for each search point which does not yet have a level the expected time needed to reach L_0 either directly or via a mutation to a search point that already has a level. Search points with minimal time in this round make up the next level. Note that this is actually Dijkstra's algorithm for computing shortest paths (see, e. g., [2]). Note that the numerical computation of the actual expected waiting times is easy since the exact transition probabilities for mutations leading from one bit string to another are all known and waiting times are all simply geometrically distributed.

The easiest function for the (1+1) CHM is composed of $n/2 + 1$ different fitness levels, $L_0, \ldots, L_{n/2}$, defined by a number of 1-blocks (i. e., $L_0 = \{1^n\}$, $L_1 = \{0^n\}$, $L_i = \{x \in \{0,1\}^n \mid x \text{ contains } i-1 \text{ different 1-blocks}\}$ for each $i \in \{2, \ldots, n/2+1\}$). On the other hand, the fitness level set of the easiest function for the (1+1) EA (i. e., ONEMAX) has $n + 1$ different levels defined by a number of 1-bits (i. e., $L_i = \{x \in \{0,1\}^n \mid x \text{ contains } n-i \text{ 1-bits}\}$ for each $i \in \{0, \ldots, n\}$). If EASIESTHYBRID$_p$ was a mere weighted combination of ONEMAX and MINBLOCKS, its fitness levels would be defined by a combination of a number of 1-blocks and a number of 1-bits. Also, the product between the number of levels of the easiest functions for each operator, $(n/2 + 1) \cdot (n + 1)$, would be an upper bound on the number of levels for EASIESTHYBRID$_p$. In the following we show that neither of these two considerations are true and that the fitness levels of the easiest function for the hybrid algorithm are more complicated. In particular, bitstrings having in common the same number of 1-blocks and the same number of 1-bits can belong to different fitness levels of EASIESTHYBRID$_p$. Rather, the *length of the blocks* comes into play to define the fitness levels even though such a feature does not define the levels of either ONEMAX or MINBLOCKS.

We consider Algorithm $A_{1/2}$ which at each step executes either a SBM or a CHM with probability $p = 1/2$ and report in Table 1 the different fitness levels $L_0, \ldots, L_{12}$ of EASIESTHYBRID$_{1/2}$ when $n = 6$. From the table it can be noticed that both levels L_7 and L_8 contain bitstrings with two 1-blocks and four 1-bits. However, the lengths of the two 1-blocks are different (i. e., three and one for L_7 and two and two for L_8). The reason why levels L_7 and L_8 are distinct is highlighted in the last two columns of Table 1, which report the probabilities of reaching levels of higher fitness, respectively from levels L_7 and L_8. For any point of the search space belonging to level L_7 there are three different CHMs leading to points in L_2 and L_3 while there are only two CHMs from points in L_8. These extra CHMs lead to higher transition probabilities, hence lower runtimes, to reach levels L_2 and L_3 from L_7, compared to L_8. Also the probability of reaching level L_6 is higher from L_7, mainly because the level may be reached by flipping only one bit while at least three bits need to be flipped for bitstrings in L_8. Since the transition probabilities to the remaining levels of higher fitness are the same, the expected runtime from L_7 is lower than that from L_8, explaining why the two levels are distinct (recall that, by construction, the levels are ordered according to increasing expected runtimes).

Concerning the number of different fitness levels, these increase as the problem size n increases. Already for $n = 10$ EASIESTHYBRID$_{1/2}$ has 78 different levels, more than the product of the number of ONEMAX and MINBLOCKS levels for $n = 10$ (i. e. 66). It is indeed the increase in number of fitness levels as n grows that makes it hard to give a precise definition of the EASIESTHYBRID$_{1/2}$ function. We leave this as an open problem for future work.

6. CONCLUSIONS

We have extended the analysis of easiest function classes from standard bit mutations to the contiguous somatic hypermutation (CHM) operator used in artificial immune systems. With the runtime and fixed budget analysis of the (1+1) CHM on MINBLOCKS, the corresponding easiest function, we established a lower bound on the (1+1) CHM's performance on any function. We also showed that MINBLOCKS is exponentially hard for the standard (1+1) EA, complementing the known result that the (1+1) CHM performs asymptotically worse by a factor of $\Theta(n)$ than the (1+1) EA on ONEMAX. A simple hybrid algorithm combining the (1+1) CHM and the (1+1) EA solves both MINBLOCKS and ONEMAX only a constant factor slower than the pure algorithms. Finally, we elaborated on the basic intuition that a combination of the easiest functions for two algorithms will be the easiest function for the hybrid algorithm. For small instance sizes, we provided the exact fitness landscape of the easiest function for the hybrid algorithm, EASIESTHYBRID$_{1/2}$, and observed that its structure is more complex than a simple weighted combination of ONEMAX and MINBLOCKS. We leave constructing and analysing easiest functions for other operators that fit the (1+1) A scheme for future work. Similarly, the question about the easiest functions for different schemes of hybridisation remains open.

Acknowledgment: The research leading to these results has received funding from the European Union Seventh Framework Programme (FP7/2007-2013) under grant agreement no 618091 (SAGE).

7. REFERENCES

[1] F. Alanazi and P. K. Lehre. Runtime analysis of selection hyper-heuristics with classical learning mechanisms. In *Proc. of CEC*, pages 2515–2523. IEEE, 2014.

[2] T. H. Cormen, C. E. Leiserson, R. L. Rivest, and C. Stein. *Introduction to Algorithms.* MIT Press, 2001.

[3] L. N. de Castro and J. Timmis. *Artificial Immune Systems: A New Computational Intelligence Approach.* Springer, 2002.

Table 1: Fitness level landscape of the EasiestHybrid$_{1/2}$ function for $n = 6$. Columns P_{L_7} and P_{L_8} report the probabilities of reaching levels of higher fitness respectively from levels L_7 and L_8. Values are only reported when $P_{L_7,L_i} \neq P_{L_8,L_i}$ for $i \in \{0, \dots 6\}$. $P_{CHM} = 1/(6 \cdot 7)$ is the probability of one specific CHM and $P_{SBM_i} = (1/6)^i \cdot (5/6)^{6-i}$ is the probability of a specific SBM flipping i bits.

Level	Definition	Size	Example	P_{L_7}	P_{L_8}
L_0	|1-blocks|=0, $x = \{1^n\}$	1	111111	=	=
L_1	|1-blocks|=0, $x = \{0^n\}$	1	000000	=	=
L_2	|1-blocks|=1; length={5}	6	111110	$1/2 \cdot (3P_{CHM} + 2P_{SBM_1} + 4P_{SBM_3})$	$1/2 \cdot (2P_{CHM} + 2P_{SBM_1} + 4P_{SBM_3})$
L_3	|0-blocks|=1; length={5}	6	000001	$1/2 \cdot (3P_{CHM} + 4P_{SBM_3} + 2P_{SBM_5})$	$1/2 \cdot (2P_{CHM} + 4P_{SBM_3} + 2P_{SBM_5})$
L_4	|1-blocks|=1; length={4}	6	111100	=	=
L_5	|0-blocks|=1; length={4}	6	000011	=	=
L_6	|1-blocks|=1; length={3}	6	111000	$1/2 \cdot (2P_{CHM} + 1P_{SBM_1} + 1P_{SBM_3} + 1P_{SBM_5})$	$1/2 \cdot (4P_{CHM} + 6P_{SBM_3})$
L_7	|1-blocks|=2; length={3,1}	6	111010		
L_8	|1-blocks|=2; length={2,2}	3	110110		
L_9	|0-blocks|=2; length={3,1}	6	000101		
L_{10}	|1-blocks|=2; length={2,1}	12	110100		
L_{11}	|0-blocks|=2; length={2,2}	3	001001		
L_{12}	|1-blocks|=3; length={1,1,1}	2	101010		

[4] B. Doerr, D. Johannsen, and C. Winzen. Drift analysis and linear functions revisited. In *IEEE Congress on Evolutionary Computation (CEC '10)*, pages 1967–1974, 2010.

[5] S. Droste, T. Jansen, and I. Wegener. On the analysis of the (1+1) evolutionary algorithm. *Theoretical Computer Science*, 276:51–81, 2002.

[6] J. He, T. Chen, and X. Yao. On the easiest and hardest fitness functions. *IEEE Trans. Evolut. Comput.*, 19(2):295–305, 2015.

[7] T. Jansen. *Analyzing Evolutionary Algorithms. The Computer Science Perspective.* Springer, 2013.

[8] T. Jansen, P. S. Oliveto, and C. Zarges. On the analysis of the immune-inspired B-cell algorithm for the vertex cover problem. In *Proc. of ICARIS*, pages 117–131. Springer, 2011.

[9] T. Jansen and I. Wegener. On the choice of the mutation probability for the (1+1) EA. In *Proc. of PPSN*, pages 89–98. Springer, 2000.

[10] T. Jansen and C. Zarges. Analyzing different variants of immune inspired somatic contiguous hypermutations. *Theor. Comput. Sci.*, 412(6):517–533, 2011.

[11] T. Jansen and C. Zarges. Computing longest common subsequences with the B-cell algorithm. In *Proc. of ICARIS*, pages 111–124. Springer, 2012.

[12] T. Jansen and C. Zarges. Evolutionary algorithms and artificial immune systems on a bi-stable dynamic optimisation problem. In *Proc. of GECCO*, pages 975–982. ACM, 2014.

[13] T. Jansen and C. Zarges. Performance analysis of randomised search heuristics operating with a fixed budget. *Theor. Comput. Sci.*, 545:39–58, 2014.

[14] T. Jansen and C. Zarges. Reevaluating immune-inspired hypermutations using the fixed budget perspective. *IEEE Trans. Evolut. Comput.*, 18(5):674–688, 2014.

[15] J. Kelsey and J. Timmis. Immune inspired somatic contiguous hypermutations for function optimisation. In *Proc. of GECCO*, pages 207–218. Springer, 2003.

[16] P. K. Lehre and E. Özcan. A runtime analysis of simple hyper-heuristics: to mix or not to mix operators. In *Proc. of FOGA*, pages 97–104. ACM, 2013.

[17] J. Lengler and N. Spooner. Fixed budget performance of the (1+1) EA on linear functions. In *Proc. of FOGA*, pages 52–61, 2015.

[18] F. Neri, C. Cotta, and P. Moscato, editors. *Handbook of Memetic Algorithms.* Springer, 2013.

[19] P. Ross. Hyper-heuristics. In E. K. Burke and G. Kendall, editors, *Search Methodologies*, pages 611–638. Springer, 2014.

[20] D. Sudholt. The impact of parametrization in memetic evolutionary algorithms. *Theor. Comput. Sci.*, 410(26):2511–2528, 2009.

[21] D. Sudholt. Hybridizing evolutionary algorithms with variable-depth search to overcome local optima. *Algorithmica*, 59(3):343–368, 2011.

[22] D. Sudholt and C. Zarges. Analysis of an iterated local search algorithm for vertex coloring. In *Proc. of ISAAC*, pages 340–352. Springer, 2010.

Populations can be Essential in Dynamic Optimisation

Duc-Cuong Dang
ASAP Research Group
School of Computer Science
University of Nottingham
duc-cuong.dang
@nottingham.ac.uk

Thomas Jansen
Dept. of Computer Science
Aberystwyth University
t.jansen@aber.ac.uk

Per Kristian Lehre
ASAP Research Group
School of Computer Science
University of Nottingham
perkristian.lehre
@nottingham.ac.uk

ABSTRACT

Real-world optimisation problems are often dynamic. Previously good solutions must be updated or replaced due to changes in objectives and constraints. It is often claimed that evolutionary algorithms are particularly suitable for dynamic optimisation because a large population can contain different solutions that may be useful in the future. However, rigorous, theoretical demonstrations for how populations in dynamic optimisation can be essential are sparse and restricted to special cases.

This paper provides theoretical explanations of how populations can be essential in evolutionary dynamic optimisation. The ability of evolutionary algorithms to track optimal solutions is investigated by considering a Hamming ball of optimal points that moves randomly through the search space. It is shown that algorithms based on a single individual are likely to be unable to track the optimum while non-elitist population-based evolutionary algorithms can be able to do so with overwhelmingly high probability. It is shown that this holds for a range of the most commonly used selection mechanisms even without diversity enhancing mechanisms. Appropriate parameter settings to achieve this behaviour are derived for these selection mechanisms.

Categories and Subject Descriptors

F.2 [**Theory of Computation**]: Analysis of Algorithms and Problem Complexity

Keywords

Runtime Analysis, Population-based Algorithm, Dynamic Optimization

1. INTRODUCTION

In a classical optimisation setting, so-called *static optimisation*, the focus is usually directed to finding an optimal or a high quality solution as fast as possible. In real-world optimisation, problem specific data may change over time, thus previously good solutions can lose their quality and must be updated or replaced. Automatic optimal control is a typical illustration of these situations, e. g. parameters of a machine can be set optimally under ideal conditions of a factory but those need to be adapted to changes in a new environment upon deployment. *Dynamic optimisation* is an area of research that is concerned with such optimisation problems that change over time. A specific characteristic is that it does not only focus on locating an optimal solution but also on tracking a moving optimum (see [4] for a rigorous definition).

It is often suggested that Evolutionary Algorithms (EAs), especially population-based approaches, are suitable for dynamic optimisation because a large population can contain different solutions which could be useful in the future [20]. However, rigorous, theoretical demonstrations for how populations in dynamic optimisation can be essential are sparse and restricted to special cases. The ability of a very simple EA without a population, the $(1+1)$ EA, to track a target bitstring in a OneMax-like function is analysed in [3, 18]. The analysis has recently been extended from bitstrings to larger alphabets [8]. The influence of magnitude and frequency of changes on the efficiency of the $(1+1)$ EA in optimising a specifically designed function was investigated in [17], showing that some dynamic optimisation problems become easier with higher frequency of change. The analysis of the $(1+\lambda)$ EA that uses a larger offspring population but still not a real population on a simple lattice problem is presented in [6]. The efficiencies of specific diversity mechanisms when using an actual population were compared in [16]. This was done for a specific example function (introduced by [17]) and considering low frequency of changes. It was shown in [9] that a Min-Max Ant System (MMAS) can beat the $(1+1)$ EA in a deterministic dynamic environment. The comparison was later extended to general alphabets and to the $(\mu+1)$ EA that preserves genotype diversity [11]. With that particular setting of the $(\mu+1)$ EA, the size of the alphabets defines a threshold on μ so that the algorithm is able to track and reach the optimal solution in polynomial time. The result was also extended the single-destination Shortest Path Problem by [12]. Comparisons were also made between EAs and Artificial Immune System (AIS) in [7] on a OneMax-like problem with the dynamic being periodic.

Considering the above analyses we can in summary note two shortcomings that leave the impression that important fundamental questions about dynamic optimisation are still not answered satisfactorily. One shortcoming is the concen-

GECCO '15, July 11 – 15, 2015, Madrid, Spain

ISBN 978-1-4503-3472-3/15/07... $15.00
DOI: http://dx.doi.org/10.1145/2739480.2754808

tration on simple evolutionary algorithms and other search heuristics that do not make use of an actual population. Clearly, the advantages of a population-based approach cannot be explored and explained this way. The other is that many studies consider very complex dynamic environments that make it hard to see the principal and fundamental issues. Therefore, the fundamental question why a simple population can be helpful in dynamic environments requires more attention. Motivated by this fact, we will show using a simple argument on a very general class of functions that a population is essential to keep track of the optimal region. In our function class, the so-called *Moving Hamming Ball*, we only make a distinction between *good* and *bad* solutions, which typically is associated with an automatic optimal control. The goal here is that after the intuition is explained, we will show that rigorous proofs can be easily established.

The remainder of the paper is organised as follows. In the next section, the function class is described, of which it will be very clear to the reader why a single-solution approach will fail independently on the magnitude or frequency of changes. Next, the performance analysis of the $(1+1)$ EA and RLS on the function class is detailed. The argument on the efficiency of population-based algorithms is then explained with rigorous proofs. Here we use the setting of non-elitist populations and show that with a sufficient selective pressure, the ability of the populations to track the moving optima is overwhelmingly high with respect to the population size. On the other hand, as a consequence of a fair comparison to a single-individual approach, the population must not be too big in order to capture the frequency of changes. Finally some conclusions are drawn.

1.1 Preliminaries

The paper uses the following notation and terminology. For any positive integer n, define $[n] := \{1, 2, \ldots, n\}$. The natural logarithm is denoted by $\ln(\cdot)$, and the logarithm to the base 2 is denoted by $\log(\cdot)$. The Hamming distance is denoted by $\mathrm{H}(\cdot, \cdot)$ and the Iverson bracket is denoted by $[\cdot]$. For a given bitstring $x \in \{0,1\}^n$, the Hamming ball around x with radius r is denoted by $\mathrm{B}_r(x) := \{y \in \{0,1\}^n \mid \mathrm{H}(x,y) \leq r\}$. An event is said to occur with overwhelmingly high probability (w.o.p.) with respect to a parameter n, if the probability of the event is bounded from below by $1 - e^{-\Omega(n)}$.

2. THE FUNCTION CLASS

The *static version* of the function studied in this paper has the following form.

DEFINITION 1. *The Hamming Ball function around a target bitstring x^* and a radius r is defined as,*

$$\mathrm{HB}^{r,x^*}(x) = \begin{cases} 1 & \text{if } x \in \mathrm{B}_r(x^*), \\ 0 & \text{otherwise.} \end{cases}$$

The function is general in the sense that it divides the search space into two regions: the optimal one of $\sum_{i=0}^{r} \binom{n}{i}$ solutions and the non-optimal one containing the other points of the search space. By changing x^* in sequential steps the location of the optimal region can be moved around.

The choice of only two fitness values is simplistic, in reality there could be some ruggedness within each region. Different function values in the non-optimal region could also either guide the algorithm towards the optimal region (making the problem easier) or lure it away from the optimal region (making it potentially harder). Nevertheless, the idea here is that we only make the distinction between *good enough* solutions that we want to track and the rest, e. g. by applying a threshold during solution evaluations. This keeps the problem definition as simple as possible and allows us to concentrate solely on the aspect we are most interested in, the tracking abilities of a population-based search heuristic.

Intuitively, the function is easy to optimise when $r \geq n/2$, so we are only interested in $r = cn$ for some $c \in (0, 1/2)$. In that setting, if the $(1+1)$ EA starts with a non-optimal solution, e. g. outside of the Hamming ball, then it will be asymptotically unlikely that the algorithm will find an optimal solution in reasonable time (see Theorem 5 in [15]). Indeed, we are not interested in locating an optimum from scratch in the present paper, but rather the ability of an algorithm to track the optima when the objective function changes. So we always assume that all algorithms start with solutions within the Hamming ball.

With the above starting condition, the $(1+1)$ EA will still be drifting toward search points with $n/2$ 1-bits due to the neutrality of the optimal region. The algorithm will then hit the border between the two regions, but eventually stay on it since the strict selection hinders the algorithm to leave the optimal region. Now, for any dynamic setting applied to the function, the $(1+1)$ EA will end up outside of the optimal region and the only hope for it to recover is via a lucky mutation, of which the probability is generally small since it is more likely to move away from the optimal region than to move back into it. To improve, the algorithm needs a population. In this paper we only focus on a non-trivial setting for populations, the *non-elitist* one.

For a convenient comparison between the two approaches, single-individual versus non-elitist population, we use the following dynamic setting for the function. The next points in time that the target x^* will be changed are determined by random variables drawn from a Poisson distribution.

DEFINITION 2. *Let $(X_i)_{i \geq 0}$ be a sequence of random variables independently sampled from a Poisson distribution with parameter θ, $X_i \sim \mathrm{Pois}(\theta)$, k be some integer in $[n]$, x^* be some starting target bitstring, and $(x_i^*)_{i \geq 0}$ be a sequence of bitstrings generated by*

$$x_i^* = \begin{cases} x^* & \text{if } i = 0, \\ \sim \mathrm{Unif}(\{y \mid \mathrm{H}(x_{i-1}^*, y) = k\}) & \text{otherwise.} \end{cases}$$

The Moving Hamming Ball function with parameters r, k, θ and x^* is defined as

$$\mathrm{MHB}_t^{r,k,\theta,x^*}(x) = \mathrm{HB}^{r,x^*(t)}(x)$$
$$\text{where } x^*(t) = x^*_{\max\{j \mid \sum_{i=1}^{j} X_i \leq t\}}.$$

Informally, the function starts with some target x^* at time $t = 0$ and it generates a Poisson random variable telling the next point in time that the target will be moved to a new point with an exact Hamming distance of k. The process is then repeated at that next point in time. The frequency of changes is parametrised by θ and the magnitude of changes is indicated by the parameter k in this setting. Note that the reason for the moving distance being fixed to a deterministic k is to simplify the writing and to have a specific magnitude of change. The results presented in this paper indeed still hold for that distance being randomly chosen (not necessarily uniformly at random) in $[k]$.

The class of functions we define is extremely simple and resembles to some extent the well known needle in the haystack problem. This simple function is sufficient to study the aspect we are interested in: the question how well evolutionary algorithms are able to track an optimal solution in dynamic optimization. When studying how well evolutionary algorithms can find an optimum of a dynamic problem the properties of the function outside optimal solution become very important and it is no longer sufficient to study a single class of functions. Such considerations are outside the scope of this paper.

We remark that we do not make any assumption about the changes of the function and the speed of the algorithm. Clearly, the speed of the execution platform where the algorithm runs and the speed of change of the function are independent in general and the speed of the execution platform has significant influence on the ability of the algorithm to cope with the changing functions. Jansen and Zarges [7] discuss this in some detail. Many researchers who study the performance of evolutionary algorithms on dynamic functions naively assume that the function cannot change within one generation (see [7] for references and note that the same assumption is made explicitly there). We do not make this assumption here and explicitly allow for the function to change within one generation. To the best of our knowledge the only other theoretical study where this was done is due to Branke and Wang [1] who analyse a (1, 2) EA.

The first algorithm which will be analysed in this paper is the single-individual approach described in Algorithm 1. Here we allow the algorithm to make a *static copy* of the dynamic function at any time, so that solutions are evaluated on the same referenced function. This approach corresponds to an implementation where the necessary data to evaluate the optimisation function is collected before calling a bundle of evaluations. Meanwhile the true function may have changed more or less depending on the number of evaluations of the bundle, e. g. only 2 for Algorithm 1.

We consider two standard mutation operators $p_{\mathrm{mut}}^{\mathrm{EA}}$ and $p_{\mathrm{mut}}^{\mathrm{RLS}}$ which correspond to the $(1+1)$ EA and random local search (RLS), respectively. For the $(1+1)$ EA we parameterise the mutation probability using a parameter $\chi > 0$. Formally, let $x \in \{0,1\}^n$, then $x' = p_{\mathrm{mut}}^{\mathrm{EA}}(x)$ where

$$x'(i) = \begin{cases} 1 - x(i) & \text{with prob. } \chi/n, \\ x(i) & \text{with prob. } 1 - \chi/n, \end{cases}$$

and $x' = p_{\mathrm{mut}}^{\mathrm{RLS}}(x)$ where

$$x'(i) = \begin{cases} 1 - x(i) & \text{if } i = l, \\ x(i) & \text{otherwise} \end{cases} \quad \text{with } l \sim \mathrm{Unif}([n]).$$

We are mostly interested in the influence of the population size, designated by the parameter λ, on the ability of an EA to track the moving optimal region. We concentrate on non-elitist EAs as described in Algorithm 2. This algorithm uses standard bitwise mutation (here denoted by $p_{\mathrm{mut}}^{\mathrm{EA}}$), no crossover operator, and an unspecified selection mechanism p_{sel}. The selection mechanism is any random operator p_{sel} that given a population P and access to the fitness function, returns one of the individuals in P. By specifying the selection mechanism p_{sel}, Algorithm 2 can instantiate a large number of evolutionary algorithms, including the (μ, λ) EA.

Algorithm 1 Single-individual Algorithm (Dyn. Opt.)

Require: initial solution x_0 at the optimum x^*.
for $\tau = 0, 1, 2, \ldots$ until termination condition met **do**
  $x' = p_{\mathrm{mut}}(x_\tau)$.
  $v_1 = f_{2\tau}(x')$.
  $v_2 = f_{2\tau}(x_\tau)$.
  if $v_1 \geq v_2$ **then**
    $x_{\tau+1} = x'$.
  else
    $x_{\tau+1} = x_\tau$.
  end if
end for

The algorithm maintains a population P_τ of λ individuals which during one generation (steps 2–6) is replaced by a newly created population $P_{\tau+1}$ of the same size. As for the (1+1) EA, we assume that the initial population P_0 consists of λ copies of the target string x^*. Each individual in the next population $P_{\tau+1}$ is created by making a copy x of one parent individual which is selected from the current population (step 4, selection), and flipping each bit in the selected individual independently with probability χ/n (step 5, mutation).

When selecting individuals, the algorithm must take into account that multiple changes to the fitness function can occur during one generation. Here, we assume that the algorithm makes a static copy of the fitness function $f_{\tau\lambda}$ at the beginning of each generation, i.e. at time $\tau\lambda$. The selection mechanism p_{sel} compares all individuals in a generation using the static copy. Note that if the population size λ is too large with respect to the problem parameter θ (which controls the frequency of change of the dynamic function), then the optimal region may change several times between two consecutive generations. Hence, the population size should not be too large. However, we will show in the next section that a sufficiently large population is also essential to keep the population within the optimal region.

Algorithm 2 Non-elitist EAs (Dyn. Opt.)

Require: initial population $P_0 = \{x^*\}^\lambda$ in optimum x^*.
1: **for** $\tau = 0, 1, 2, \ldots$ until termination condition met **do**
2:   evaluate solutions of P_τ with $f_{\tau\lambda}(\cdot)$.
3:   **for** $i = 1, 2, \ldots, \lambda$ **do**
4:     $x = p_{\mathrm{sel}}(P_\tau)$.
5:     $P_{\tau+1}(i) = p_{\mathrm{mut}}^{\mathrm{EA}}(x)$.
6:   **end for**
7: **end for**

3. PERFORMANCE ANALYSIS

To measure the ability of an algorithm $\mathcal{A}$ to track the moving optima of $\mathrm{MHB}^{r,k,\theta,x^*}$, we consider the probability that $\mathcal{A}$ is able to keep a constant fraction of the population in the optimal region in each generation, given that in the previous generation it has some (or all) solutions within the optimal region. In our setting, the optimality is considered with respect to the static copy of the function at any generation τ, e. g. the recognition is consistent with saved data.

DEFINITION 3. *The ability of an algorithm $\mathcal{A}$, which makes use of populations $(P_\tau)_{\tau\in\mathbb{N}}$ with $|P_\tau| = \lambda$, to track the moving optima of* $\mathrm{MHB}^{r,k,\theta,x^*}$ *is defined as the smallest probability*

$$\Pr\left(|P_{\tau+1} \cap \mathrm{B}_r(x^*((\tau+1)\lambda))| \geq \lceil \gamma\lambda \rceil\right)$$

given that $|P_\tau \cap \mathrm{B}_r(x^*(\tau\lambda))| \geq \lceil\gamma\lambda\rceil$ *for all generation τ and some constant $\gamma \in (0,1)$.*

The above definition is useful in the sense that if the defined probability is overwhelmingly high, then algorithm $\mathcal{A}$ will remain within the optimal region for a very long period of time. On the other hand, if the probability is small enough, i. e. upper bound by a constant, and if the algorithm frequently hits the border between the two regions, it is clear that $\mathcal{A}$ cannot stay within the optimal region for long.

3.1 Inefficiency of a single individual

In Algorithm 1, λ is 1. Because the newly generated solution has to be compared with the current solution on the same static copy, two evaluations are required per generation, or $t = 2\tau$. Overall, the algorithm has the advantage of frequently updating the dynamic function, e. g. there are not many changes to the function between generations. However, when there is a change to the function and in the worst case the current solution is exactly on the border of the Hamming ball, there is no more than a constant probability that the next generation remains within the optimal region.

Since RLS only flips one bit at a time, it is clear that the algorithm cannot recover from any $\mathrm{MHB}^{r,k,\theta,x^*}$ with $k > 1$. For $k = 1$, the following result holds.

THEOREM 4. *The ability of RLS to track the moving optima of* $\mathrm{MHB}^{r,1,\theta,x^*}$ *where $r = cn$ and with arbitrary θ is at most $c + o(1)$.*

PROOF. Since the smallest probability should cover all cases, we consider the case that $\mathrm{H}(x_\tau, x^*(2\tau)) = r$, then the target bitstring moves so that $\mathrm{H}(x_\tau, x^*(2(\tau+1))) = r+1$. In order to recover the optimal region $\mathrm{H}(x', x^*(2(\tau+1)))$ must be r again, and this requires RLS to flip one of the $r+1$ mismatched bit positions. The probability in that case is $(r+1)/n = c + 1/n = c + o(1)$. □

THEOREM 5. *The ability of the (1+1) EA with standard mutation rate $1/n$ to track the moving optima of* $\mathrm{MHB}^{r,1,\theta,x^*}$ *with arbitrary θ is at most $1 - 1/e + o(1)$.*

PROOF. We consider the same case as in the proof of Theorem 4. However, for the (1+1) EA, x' is an identical copy of x_τ with probability at least $(1-1/n)^n = \Omega(1)$. In that case $x_{\tau+1}$ cannot recover the optimal region, and therefore

$$\begin{aligned}\Pr\left(x' \in \mathrm{B}_r(x^*(2(\tau+1)))\right) &\leq 1 - \left(1 - \frac{1}{n}\right)^n \\ &= 1 - \left[\left(1-\frac{1}{n}\right)^{n-1}\right]^{(1+1/(n-1))} \\ &\leq 1 - e^{-1} + o(1) \quad \square\end{aligned}$$

For a general setting of $\mathrm{MHB}^{r,k,\theta,x^*}$ and bitwise mutation with mutation rate χ/n, we have the following results for the $(1+1)$ EA using a simple argument of the moment generating function.

THEOREM 6. *The ability of the $(1+1)$ EA with mutation rate χ/n to track the moving optima of* $\mathrm{MHB}^{r,k,\theta,x^*}$ *with arbitrary θ is no more than*

$$\exp\left(-\frac{\chi+k}{2} + \frac{3\chi(r+k)}{2n-\chi}\right).$$

PROOF. Again we consider the case that x_τ has $n-(r+k)$ correctly set bits and $r+k$ mismatched bits and we want to recover at least k bits of the mismatching ones with the mutation operator. Let X be the number of mismatched bits being flipped by the mutation, so $X \sim \mathrm{Bin}(r+k, \frac{\chi}{n})$, and Y be the number of matched bits being flipped, so $Y \sim \mathrm{Bin}(n-(r+k), \frac{\chi}{n})$.

For any $\eta > 0$, by Markov's inequality and the independence of X and Y, we have

$$\begin{aligned}&\Pr\left(x' \in \mathrm{B}_r(x^*(2(\tau+1)))\right) \\ &= \Pr\left(n-(r+k)+X-Y \geq n-r\right) \\ &= \Pr\left(X-Y \geq k\right) = \Pr\left(e^{\eta(X-Y)} \geq e^{\eta k}\right) \\ &\leq \frac{\mathbf{E}\left[e^{\eta(X-Y)}\right]}{e^{\eta k}} = \frac{\mathbf{E}\left[e^{\eta X}\right]\mathbf{E}\left[e^{-\eta Y}\right]}{e^{\eta k}} \\ &= \left(1 - \frac{\chi}{n} + \frac{e^{\eta}\chi}{n}\right)^{r+k}\left(1 - \frac{\chi}{n} + \frac{e^{-\eta}\chi}{n}\right)^{n-(r+k)}\left(\frac{1}{e^{\eta k}}\right)\end{aligned}$$

By setting $\eta = \ln 2$, we get

$$\begin{aligned}&\Pr\left(x' \in \mathrm{B}_r(x^*(2(\tau+1)))\right) \\ &\leq \left(1+\frac{\chi}{n}\right)^{r+k}\left(1-\frac{\chi}{2n}\right)^{n-(r+k)}\left(\frac{1}{2^k}\right) \\ &= \left(1-\frac{\chi}{2n}\right)^{n}\left(1+\frac{3\chi}{2n-\chi}\right)^{r+k}\left(\frac{1}{2^k}\right) \\ &= \left(1-\frac{\chi}{2n}\right)^{\left(\frac{2n}{\chi}\cdot\frac{\chi}{2}\right)}\left(1+\frac{3\chi}{2n-\chi}\right)^{\left(\frac{2n-\chi}{3\chi}\right)\cdot\frac{3\chi(r+k)}{2n-\chi}}\left(\frac{1}{2^k}\right) \\ &< \exp\left(-\frac{\chi}{2}\right)\exp\left(\frac{3\chi(r+k)}{2n-\chi}\right)\exp\left(-\frac{k}{2}\right) \\ &= \exp\left(-\frac{\chi+k}{2} + \frac{3\chi(r+k)}{2n-\chi}\right). \quad \square\end{aligned}$$

We have the following corollary.

COROLLARY 7. *The ability of the $(1+1)$ EA with any mutation rate to track the moving optima of* $\mathrm{MHB}^{r,k,\theta,x^*}$ *with $r+k \leq n/6$ and arbitrary θ is no more than $1/\sqrt{e}$.*

PROOF. Given that $r+k \leq n/6$, we get

$$\frac{\chi}{2} - \frac{3\chi(r+k)}{2n-\chi} \geq \frac{\chi}{2} - \frac{3\chi(n/6)}{2n-n} \geq 0$$

Then it follows from Theorem 6 that

$$\begin{aligned}&\Pr\left(x' \in \mathrm{B}_r(x^*(2(\tau+1)))\right) \\ &< \exp\left(-\frac{k}{2} - \left(\frac{\chi}{2} - \frac{3\chi(r+k)}{2n-\chi}\right)\right) \\ &\leq \exp\left(-\frac{k}{2}\right) \leq \exp\left(-\frac{1}{2}\right). \quad \square\end{aligned}$$

Note that when both k and r are large, the dynamic function can be easy, e. g. if $k = n$ over time there are only 2 optimal regions in the search space. The corollary implies that when r is too small, e. g. less than some constant function of n, and k is fixed as a constant, the (1 + 1) EA can lose track of the optimal region with a constant probability. Therefore, to keep track of the dynamic the important point is to have a sufficiently large population.

3.2 Population size for non-elitist EAs

Any given selection mechanism p_{sel} can be used by Algorithm 2, and typically we are looking for the setting of p_{sel} so that the tracking ability is efficient. Formally, p_{sel} is a function $p_{\text{sel}}: \mathcal{X} \times \mathcal{X}^\lambda \to [0,1]$, where $p_{\text{sel}}(y \mid P)$ represents the probability of selecting a specific individual y from the population P. Sometimes, we write $t = p_{\text{sel}}(P)$ to express that x is sampled from the distribution over P given by $p_{\text{sel}}(\cdot, P)$. We use $x_{(i)}$ to denote the ith best individual of P, or the so-called (i/λ)-ranked individual. Similar to [2, 10], we characterise p_{sel} by the cumulative selection probability.

Definition 8 ([10]). *Given a fitness function $f: \mathcal{X} \to \mathbb{R}$, the* cumulative selection probability *β associated with selection mechanism p_{sel} is defined on f for all $\gamma \in (0,1]$ and $P \in \mathcal{X}^\lambda$ by*

$$\beta(\gamma, P) := \sum_{y \in P} p_{\text{sel}}(y \mid P) \cdot [f(y) \geq f(x_{(\lceil \gamma\lambda \rceil)})]$$

Informally, $\beta(\gamma, P)$ is the probability of selecting an individual with fitness at least as good as that of the γ-ranked individual, assuming that P is sorted according to fitness values. We are interested in a lower bound function of $\beta(\gamma, P)$. Most often this lower bound is independent of P, and in that case we write the cumulative selection probability as function just of γ, i. e. as $\beta(\gamma)$.

For uniform selection, we have that $\beta(\gamma) \geq \gamma$, i. e. a straight line from the origin with slope 1, and the algorithm makes a random walk through the search space (which makes it an inefficient algorithm). For all other selection mechanisms that pick solutions with better fitnesses more often, we expect $\beta(\gamma)$ to be strictly above the line. Therefore, for all γ smaller than some γ_0, the function can be lower bounded by another line with slope $1 + \delta$ for some $\delta \in (0, 1)$. Figure 1 illustrates an example of $(1+\delta)\gamma$ line for a selection mechanism where $\beta(\gamma) \geq 1 - (1-\gamma)^2$ (e. g. see tournament selection of size 2 later on).

Many popular selection mechanisms can be set so that the lower bound holds for any given constant δ.

- In *k-tournament selection*, k individuals are sampled uniformly at random with replacement from the population, and the fittest of these individuals is returned.
- In *(μ, λ)-selection*, parents are sampled uniformly at random among the fittest μ individuals in the population.
- A function $\alpha: \mathbb{R} \to \mathbb{R}$ is a ranking function [5] if $\alpha(x) \geq 0$ for all $x \in [0, 1]$, and $\int_0^1 \alpha(x)\,\mathrm{d}x = 1$. In ranking selection with ranking function α, the probability of selecting individuals ranked γ or better is $\int_0^\gamma \alpha(x)\,\mathrm{d}x$. $\eta \in (1, 2]$. *Exponential ranking* selection uses $\alpha(x) := \eta e^{\eta(1-x)}/(e^\eta - 1)$ for some $\eta > 0$.

Lemma 9. *For any $\delta > 0$, there exists a $\gamma_0 \in (0,1)$ such that the cumulative selection probability satisfies $\beta(\gamma) \geq (1+\delta)\gamma$ for all $\gamma \leq \gamma_0$ and for*

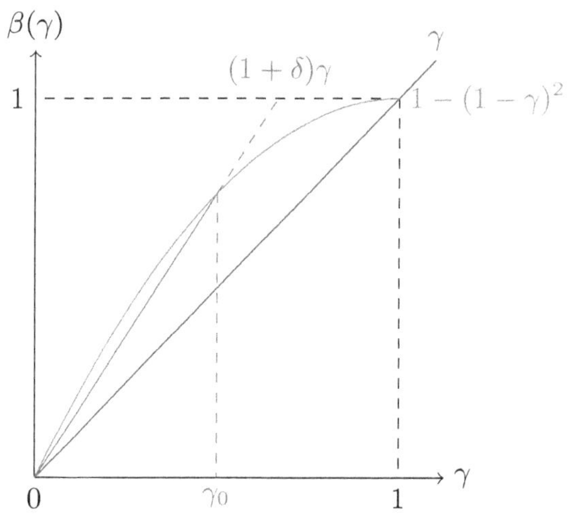

Figure 1: Example of bounding $\beta(\gamma) \geq 1-(1-\gamma)^2$ (in red) further by some $(1+\delta)\gamma$ function (in green).

- *k-tournament selection with $k \geq 2(1+\delta)$,*
- *(μ, λ)-selection with $\lambda/\mu \geq (1+\delta)$,*
- *exponential ranking selection with $\eta \geq 2(1+\delta)$.*

Proof. In k-tournament selection with $k \geq 2(1+\delta)$ and $\gamma_0 := (1/2)(1/(1+\delta))$, we have that for all $\gamma \leq \gamma_0$

$$\begin{aligned}\beta(\gamma) &\geq 1-(1-\gamma)^k \geq 1 - \frac{1}{e^{k\gamma}} \geq 1 - \frac{1}{1+k\gamma}\\ &\geq 1 - \frac{1}{1+2(1+\delta)\gamma} = \frac{2(1+\delta)\gamma}{1+2(1+\delta)\gamma}\\ &\geq \frac{2(1+\delta)\gamma}{1+2(1+\delta)(1/2)(1/(1+\delta))} = (1+\delta)\gamma.\end{aligned}$$

In (μ, λ)-selection, we have that $\beta(\gamma) = \lambda\gamma/\mu$ for all $\gamma \in (0, \mu/\lambda]$. So, with $\lambda/\mu \geq (1+\delta)$ and $\gamma_0 := \mu/\lambda$,

$$\beta(\gamma) \geq \frac{\lambda\gamma}{\mu} \geq (1+\delta)\gamma$$

In exponential ranking selection, we have

$$\begin{aligned}\beta(\gamma) &\geq \int_0^\gamma \frac{\eta e^{\eta(1-x)}\,\mathrm{d}x}{e^\eta - 1} = \left(\frac{e^\eta}{e^\eta - 1}\right)\left(1 - \frac{1}{e^{\eta\gamma}}\right)\\ &\geq 1 - \frac{1}{1+\eta\gamma}\end{aligned}$$

The rest of the proof is similar to tournament selection with η in place of k, e. g. based on the input condition on η it suffices to pick $\gamma_0 := (1/2)(1/(1+\delta))$. □

The following theorem gives general conditions so that Algorithm 2 can recover the optimal region of $\text{MHB}^{r,k,\theta,x^*}$ with a probability that is overwhelmingly close to 1 in each generation.

Theorem 10. *Let γ_0 be a constant in $(0,1)$ and $r = cn$, k, θ, $\delta \in (0,1)$ and $z > 1$ be parameters such that Algorithm 2 with bitwise mutation rate χ/n for a constant $\chi > 0$, satisfies*

(C1) $\dfrac{1+z\delta}{1+\delta} > \left(\dfrac{k}{c\chi}\right)^k e^\chi,$

(C2) $\forall \gamma \in (0, \gamma_0) \quad \beta(\gamma) \geq (1 + z\delta)\gamma,$

(C3) $\exists d > 0 \quad \lambda = \theta/(1+d),$

then if $|P_\tau \cap \mathrm{B}_r(x^*(\tau\lambda))| \geq \lceil \gamma_0 \lambda \rceil$, *we have*

$$\begin{aligned}\Pr\left(|P_{\tau+1} \cap \mathrm{B}_r(x^*((\tau+1)\lambda))| \geq \lceil \gamma_0\lambda \rceil\right) \\ \geq 1 - 2\exp\left(-\frac{\lambda}{2}\min\left\{\frac{d^2}{1+d}, \frac{\delta^2\gamma_0}{1+\delta}\right\}\right).\end{aligned}$$

Conditions (C1) and (C2) put a requirement on a sufficiently strong selective pressure of the selection mechanism while condition (C3) tells the algorithmic setting for the population size and the mutation rate. When all conditions are satisfied, we have the stated result on the ability of the algorithm to keep track of the optimal region of $\mathrm{MHB}^{r,k,\theta,x^*}$.

With respect to the population size, we want $\lambda \leq \theta$ so that it is uncommon to have many changes between two generations. However, the stability of the algorithm to stay within the optimal region is also depending on λ asymptotically. The application of the theorem for the case of $k = 1$ is discussed in Corollaries 11 and 12, which further imply the long-term behaviour of the algorithm under the right setting (e.g. see Corollary 13).

The outline of the proof of the theorem is the following. We first use the property of the Poisson distribution to show that the probability of having more than 1 change per generation is exponentially small with respect to λ. Otherwise, we assume that the 1 change eventually occurs during the generation then show that the probability of creating at least $\gamma_0\lambda$ new individuals inside the new Hamming ball is overwhelmingly high due to the strong selective pressure and a sufficient number of samplings. The final result is obtained by combining the two arguments using an union bound.

PROOF. We define X to be the random variable indicating the number of time steps (or evaluations) until the next change of the target bitstring. Note that there is more than 1 change if and only if $X \leq \lambda$. It then follows from Theorem 15 and (C3) that

$$\begin{aligned}\Pr(X \leq \lambda) &\leq e^{-\theta}\left(\frac{e\theta}{\lambda}\right)^{\lambda} = e^{-(1+d)\lambda}\left((1+d)e\right)^{\lambda} \\ &= e^{-d\lambda}(1+d)^{\lambda} \leq e^{-d\lambda}e^{\lambda\cdot\frac{d}{2}\cdot\frac{d+2}{d+1}} \\ &= \exp\left(-\frac{\lambda}{2}\left(\frac{d^2}{d+1}\right)\right)\end{aligned}$$

The last inequality is due to Lemma 17. Assuming that the event $\{X \leq \lambda\}$ does not happen or there is at most 1 change to the function. In the worst case, that particular change happens and all solutions of the population are no longer optimal for the next generation. That is to say $|P_\tau \cap \mathrm{B}_r(x^*(\tau\lambda))| \geq \lceil\gamma_0\lambda\rceil$ and for each $x \in P_\tau \cap \mathrm{B}_r(x^*(\tau\lambda)))$, we only have $\mathrm{H}(x, x^*((\tau+1)\lambda)) = r + k'$ for some $k' \in [k]$. Particularly, we wish to recover those solutions by mutation. By (C2), for any arbitrarily small constant $\varepsilon > 0$ the probability of such an event is

$$\begin{aligned}&\Pr\left(P_{\tau+1}(i) \in \mathrm{B}_r(x^*((\tau+1)\lambda))\right) \\ &\geq \beta(\gamma_0)\binom{r+k'}{k'}\left(\frac{\chi}{n}\right)^{k'}\left(1-\frac{\chi}{n}\right)^{n-k'} \\ &\geq (1+z\delta)\gamma_0\left(\frac{r+k'}{k'}\right)^{k'}\left(\frac{\chi}{n}\right)^{k'}\left(1-\frac{\chi}{n}\right)^{\left(\frac{n}{\chi}-1\right)\chi\left(1+\frac{\chi}{n-\chi}\right)} \\ &\geq (1+z\delta)\gamma_0\left(\left(\frac{r}{k'}+1\right)\frac{\chi}{r/c}\right)^{k'} e^{-(1+\varepsilon)\chi} \\ &> (1+z\delta)\gamma_0\left(\frac{c\chi}{k'}\right)^{k'} e^{-(1+\varepsilon)\chi}\end{aligned}$$

It follows from (C1) that

$$\frac{1+z\delta}{1+\delta} \geq \left(\frac{k}{c\chi}\right)^{k} e^{(1+\varepsilon)\chi} \geq \left(\frac{k'}{c\chi}\right)^{k'} e^{(1+\varepsilon)\chi} \quad \forall k' \in [k]$$

This is equivalent to $(1+z\delta)\left(\frac{c\chi}{k'}\right)^{k'} e^{-(1+\varepsilon)\chi} \geq (1+\delta)$, and we have $\Pr\left(P_{\tau+1}(i) \in \mathrm{B}_r(x^*((\tau+1)\lambda))\right) \geq (1+\delta)\gamma_0$.

Let Y be the random variable counting the number of solutions within the next optimal region conditioned on $X > \lambda$, $Y = \{|P_{\tau+1}(i) \cap \mathrm{B}_r(x^*((\tau+1)\lambda))| \mid X > \lambda\}$, then $Y \sim \mathrm{Bin}(\lambda, p \geq (1+\delta)\gamma_0)$ and in expectation $\mathbf{E}[Y] \geq (1+\delta)\gamma_0\lambda$. By Theorem 14, we get

$$\begin{aligned}\Pr(Y < \lceil\gamma_0\lambda\rceil) &\leq \Pr(Y \leq \gamma_0\lambda) \\ &= \Pr\left(Y \leq \left(1 - \frac{\delta}{1+\delta}\right)(1+\delta)\gamma_0\lambda\right) \\ &\leq \Pr\left(Y \leq \left(1 - \frac{\delta}{1+\delta}\right)\mathbf{E}[Y]\right) \\ &\leq \exp\left(-\frac{\delta^2\mathbf{E}[Y]}{2(1+\delta)^2}\right) \leq \exp\left(-\frac{\delta^2\gamma_0\lambda}{2(1+\delta)}\right)\end{aligned}$$

When both events $X > \lambda$ and $Y \geq \lceil\gamma_0\lambda\rceil$ happen, the recovery of the optimal region is guaranteed. The result is obtained by a union bound,

$$\begin{aligned}&\Pr\left(|P_{\tau+1}(i) \cap \mathrm{B}_r(x^*((\tau+1)\lambda))| \geq \lceil\gamma_0\lambda\rceil\right) \\ &\geq 1 - \exp\left(-\frac{\lambda}{2}\left(\frac{d^2}{d+1}\right)\right) - \exp\left(-\frac{\delta^2\gamma_0}{1+\delta}\cdot\frac{\lambda}{2}\right) \\ &\geq 1 - 2\exp\left(-\frac{\lambda}{2}\min\left\{\frac{d^2}{d+1}, \frac{\delta^2\gamma_0}{(1+\delta)}\right\}\right). \quad \square\end{aligned}$$

The following corollaries are direct consequences of the theorem.

COROLLARY 11. *The ability of Algorithm 2 with* $\lambda = (2/3)\theta$, *the standard mutation rate of* $1/n$ *and*

- *tournament selection of size* $l \geq 9/c$, *or*
- (μ, λ)*-selection with* $\lambda/\mu \geq 9/(2c)$, *or*
- *exponential ranking selection with* $\eta \geq 9/c$,

to track the moving optima of $\mathrm{MHB}^{cn,1,\theta,x^*}$ *with any constant* $c \in (0, 1/2)$ *is at least* $1 - e^{-\Omega(\theta)}$.

PROOF. In this particular setting, we have $\lambda = \theta/(1+1/2)$ or $d = 1/2$, $\chi = 1$ and $k = 1$. We first pick arbitrarily $\delta = 1/2$, then find a value for z that satisfies (C1). This implies solving the equation $\frac{1+z/2}{1+1/2} > \frac{e}{c}$. and requires $z > 3e/c - 2$.

Therefore, the choice of $z = 9/c - 2$ and $\delta = 1/2$ satisfies (C1) of Theorem 10.

In addition, we have that $1+z\delta = 1+(9/c-2)/2 = 9/(2c)$. It then follows from Lemma 9 that (C2) is satisfied for the particular choices of the parameters and for some constant $\gamma_0 \in (0,1)$.

Condition (C3) holds for $d = 1/2$ and $\chi = 1$. The result then follows from the theorem, the ability of Algorithm 2 to track the moving optima is at least

$$1 - 2\exp\left(-\frac{\lambda}{2}\min\left\{\frac{1/4}{3/2}, \frac{1/4\gamma_0}{3/2}\right\}\right)$$
$$= 1 - 2\exp\left(-\frac{\theta}{3}\cdot\frac{\gamma_0}{6}\right) = 1 - e^{-\Omega(\theta)}. \quad \square$$

Note that the result of the corollary should hold for any constant $d > 0$ because the choice of d (and eventually γ_0) will only influence the leading factor of $e^{-\Omega(\theta)}$. In addition, despite k being fixed to 1, larger k only imply a stronger requirement on the selective pressure induced by conditions (C1) and (C2), e. g. increasing the fraction λ/μ in a (μ, λ)-selection and consequently having a smaller constant γ_0. On the other hand, if the dynamic of the function is slow enough, e. g. $\theta = O(\ln n)$, Algorithm 2 can keep track of the optimal solutions with high probability.

COROLLARY 12. *The ability of Algorithm 2 being set as in Corollary 11 to track the moving optima of* $\text{MHB}^{cn,1,\theta,x^*}$ *with any constant* $c \in (0, 1/2)$ *is at least* $1 - o(1)$ *for* $\theta = \Omega(\ln n)$*, and* $1 - e^{-\Omega(n)}$ *for* $\theta = \Omega(n)$.

In the previous section when only a single solution is available to the algorithm in each generation and for c small enough (approximately 1/6), we have shown that with a constant probability, the algorithm risks losing track of the optimal region. Those results are independent of θ, e. g. it still holds for a low frequency of change. Corollary 12 now shows that any constant $c \in (0, 1/2)$ that probability can be reduced to either $o(1)$ with a sufficiently large population if the frequency of changes is not too high, i. e. $\theta = \Omega(\ln n)$. Particularly for $\lambda = \theta = \Omega(n)$ and the right settings for the selection mechanism, the population will stay within the optimal region for an exponential number of iterations with a probability that is overwhelmingly close to 1.

COROLLARY 13. *Consider Algorithm 2 configured as in Corollary 11 and applied to fitness function* $\text{MHB}^{cn,1,\theta,x^*}$ *for any constant* $c \in (0, 1/2)$ *and* $\theta = \Omega(n)$. *Then there exists a constant* $b > 0$ *such that with probability* $1 - e^{-bn/2}$, *there is an individual in the optimal region during each of* $e^{bn/2}$ *consecutive generations.*

PROOF. Let $\mathcal{E}_\tau$ be the event that at least $\gamma_0\lambda$ individuals of the populations are optimal to $f_{\tau\lambda}$. It follows from Corollary 12 that $\Pr(\mathcal{E}_\tau \mid \mathcal{E}_{\tau-1}) \geq 1 - e^{-bn}$ for some constant b and all τ. By induction we have

$$\begin{aligned}\Pr(\mathcal{E}_\tau \mid \mathcal{E}_0) &\geq \Pr(\mathcal{E}_\tau \mid \mathcal{E}_{\tau-1})\Pr(\mathcal{E}_{\tau-1} \mid \mathcal{E}_0)\\ &= (1 - e^{-bn})\Pr(\mathcal{E}_{\tau-1} \mid \mathcal{E}_0)\\ &\geq \cdots \geq (1 - e^{-bn})^\tau \Pr(\mathcal{E}_0)\\ &\geq 1 - \tau e^{-bn}\end{aligned}$$

The last inequality is due to Theorem 16 and the assumption $\Pr(\mathcal{E}_0) = 1$. The result then follows by taking $\tau = e^{bn/2}$. $\square$

4. CONCLUSION

This paper describes an extremely simple class of dynamic fitness functions where population-based EAs perform much better than single individual EAs.

We have proved that for this function class, single-individual approaches, such as the (1+1) EA and RLS, have a constant risk of losing the optimal solution region at any given time. Moreover, these single-individual algorithms not only lose the optimal region with constant probability, but are also likely to drift away from the optimal region subsequently.

On the other hand, assuming a not too high frequency of change, we describe sufficient conditions such that a non-elitist population-based evolutionary algorithm will remain within the optimal region with overwhelmingly high probability. Our analysis cover a range of the most commonly used selection mechanisms, and we provide appropriate parameter settings for each of them. Furthermore, the success of the population-based EA does not rely on an explicit diversity mechanism. Our analysis gives further explanations, using only a very simple example, of how and why populations can be essential in dynamic optimisation.

As future work, we would like to investigate further the influence of population settings within this class of dynamic functions, such as elitist populations, the necessary condition for the population size with respect to the frequency and magnitude of changes and how a population could rebuild itself after losing a few optimal solutions.

Acknowledgments

The research leading to these results has received funding from the European Union Seventh Framework Programme (FP7/2007-2013) under grant agreement no 618091 (SAGE).

5. REFERENCES

[1] J. Branke and W. Wang. Theoretical analysis of simple evolution strategies in quickly changing environments. In *Proceedings of the 5th Annual Conference on Genetic and Evolutionary Computation*, GECCO'03, pages 537–548, 2003.

[2] D.-C. Dang and P. K. Lehre. Refined upper bounds on the expected runtime of non-elitist populations from fitness-levels. In *Proceedings of the 16th Annual Conference on Genetic and Evolutionary Computation Conference*, GECCO'14, pages 1367–1374, New York, NY, USA, 2014. ACM.

[3] S. Droste. Analysis of the (1+1) EA for a dynamically bitwise changing OneMax. In *Proceedings of the 2003 International Conference on Genetic and Evolutionary Computation*, GECCO'03, pages 909–921. Springer-Verlag, 2003.

[4] H. Fu, P. R. Lewis, B. Sendhoff, K. Tang, and X. Yao. What are dynamic optimization problems? In *Proceedings of the IEEE Congress on Evolutionary Computation, 2014*, pages 1550–1557, 2014.

[5] D. E. Goldberg and K. Deb. A comparative analysis of selection schemes used in genetic algorithms. In *Foundations of Genetic Algorithms*, FOGA 1991, pages 69–93. Morgan Kaufmann, 1991.

[6] T. Jansen and U. Schellbach. Theoretical analysis of a mutation-based evolutionary algorithm for a tracking problem in the lattice. In *Proceedings of the 7th*

Annual Conference on Genetic and Evolutionary Computation, GECCO'05, pages 841–848. ACM, 2005.
[7] T. Jansen and C. Zarges. Evolutionary algorithms and artificial immune systems on a bi-stable dynamic optimisation problem. In *Proceedings of the 2014 Conference on Genetic and Evolutionary Computation*, GECCO'14, pages 975–982. ACM, 2014.
[8] T. Kötzing, A. Lissovoi, and C. Witt. (1+1) EA on generalized dynamic onemax. In *Proceedings of the 13th ACM SIGEVO Workshop on Foundations of Genetic Algorithms*, FOGA 2015, 2015. To Appear.
[9] T. Kötzing and H. Molter. ACO beats EA on a dynamic pseudo-boolean function. In *Proceedings of the 12th International Conference on Parallel Problem Solving from Nature - Volume Part I*, PPSN'12, pages 113–122. Springer-Verlag, 2012.
[10] P. K. Lehre. Fitness-levels for non-elitist populations. In *Proceedings of the 13th Annual Conference on Genetic and Evolutionary Computation*, GECCO'11, pages 2075–2082, New York, NY, USA, 2011. ACM.
[11] A. Lissovoi and C. Witt. MMAS vs. population-based EA on a family of dynamic fitness functions. In *Proceedings of the 2014 Conference on Genetic and Evolutionary Computation*, GECCO'14, pages 1399–1406. ACM, 2014.
[12] A. Lissovoi and C. Witt. Runtime analysis of ant colony optimization on dynamic shortest path problems. *Theor. Comput. Sci.*, 561:73–85, 2015.
[13] D. S. Mitrinović. *Elementary Inequalities*. P. Noordhoff Ltd, Groningen, 1964.
[14] M. Mitzenmacher and E. Upfal. *Probability and Computing: Randomized Algorithms and Probabilistic Analysis*. Cambridge University Press, New York, NY, USA, 2005.
[15] P. S. Oliveto and C. Witt. Simplified drift analysis for proving lower bounds in evolutionary computation. *Algorithmica*, 59(3):369–386, 2011.
[16] P. S. Oliveto and C. Zarges. Analysis of diversity mechanisms for optimisation in dynamic environments with low frequencies of change. *Theoretical Computer Science*, 561:37–67, 2015.
[17] P. Rohlfshagen, P. K. Lehre, and X. Yao. Dynamic evolutionary optimisation: An analysis of frequency and magnitude of change. In *Proceedings of the 11th Annual Conference on Genetic and Evolutionary Computation*, GECCO'09, pages 1713–1720. ACM, 2009.
[18] S. A. Stanhope and J. Daida. (1+1) genetic algorithm fitness dynamics in a changing environment. In *Proceedings of Congress in Evolutionary Computation*, IEEE CEC'99, pages 1851–185, 1999.
[19] F. Topsøe. Some bounds for the logarithmic function. In Y. J. Cho, J. K. Kim, and S. S. Dragomir, editors, *Inequality Theory and Applications*, volume 4, pages 137–151. Nova Science Publishers, Incorporated, 2007.
[20] S. Yang and X. Yao, editors. *Evolutionary Computation for Dynamic Optimization Problems*, volume 490 of *Studies in Computational Intelligence*. Springer, 2013.

APPENDIX

THEOREM 14 (CHERNOFF BOUND). *If $X = \sum_{i=1}^{m} X_i$, where $X_i \in \{0,1\}, i \in [m]$ are independent random variables, then for any $\varepsilon \in [0,1]$ it holds that*

$$\Pr(X \le (1-\varepsilon)\mathbf{E}[X]) \le \exp\left(-\frac{\varepsilon^2 \mathbf{E}[X]}{2}\right).$$

THEOREM 15 (THEOREM 5.4 IN [14]). *Let $X \sim \mathrm{Pois}(\theta)$, then for all $\theta > x > 0$*

$$\Pr(X \le x) \le e^{-\theta}\left(\frac{e\theta}{x}\right)^x.$$

THEOREM 16 (BERNOULLI'S INEQUALITY [13]).

$$\forall x \ge -1 \quad (1+x)^n \ge 1 + nx.$$

LEMMA 17 (INEQUALITY (3) IN [19]).

$$\forall x \ge 0 \quad 1 + x \le \exp\left(\frac{x}{2} \cdot \frac{x+2}{x+1}\right).$$

Improved Runtime Bounds for the (1+1) EA on Random 3-CNF Formulas Based on Fitness-Distance Correlation

Benjamin Doerr
École Polytechnique
Université Paris-Saclay
Palaiseau, France

Frank Neumann
School of Computer Science
University of Adelaide
Adelaide, Australia

Andrew M. Sutton
Hasso-Plattner-Institut
Universität Potsdam
Potsdam, Germany

ABSTRACT

With this paper, we contribute to the theoretical understanding of randomized search heuristics by investigating their behavior on random 3-SAT instances. We improve the results for the (1+1) EA obtained by Sutton and Neumann [PPSN 2014, 942–951] in three ways. First, we reduce the upper bound by a linear factor and prove that the (1+1) EA obtains optimal solutions in time $O(n \log n)$ with high probability on asymptotically almost all high-density satisfiable 3-CNF formulas. Second, we extend the range of densities for which this bound holds to satisfiable formulas of at least logarithmic density. Finally, we complement these mathematical results with numerical experiments that summarize the behavior of the (1+1) EA on formulas along the density spectrum, and suggest that the implicit constants hidden in our bounds are low.

Our proofs are based on analyzing the run of the algorithm by establishing a fitness-distance correlation. This approach might be of independent interest and we are optimistic that it is useful for the analysis of randomized search heuristics in various other settings. To our knowledge, this is the first time that fitness-distance correlation is explicitly used to rigorously prove a performance statement for an evolutionary algorithm.

Categories and Subject Descriptors

F.2 [**Theory of Computation**]: Analysis of Algorithms and Problem Complexity

Keywords

Runtime analysis; satisfiability; fitness-distance correlation

1. INTRODUCTION

The analysis of randomized search heuristics has made tremendous progress over the past fifteen years. A wide range of randomized search heuristics such as randomized local search, evolutionary algorithms, and ant colony optimization has been analyzed for specific fitness functions as well as problems from combinatorial optimization. We refer the reader to the timely books [19, 5, 12] for a comprehensive presentation.

Tail bounds on the runtime of the (1+1) EA on randomly generated high-density satisfiable 3-CNF formulas were derived in [23] where a bound of $O(n^2 \log n)$ was shown to hold with probability $1 - o(1)$. The main results of our paper is to improve this bound to $O(n \log n)$ and establish results for lower density formulas. We obtain this result by determining a fitness-distance correlation that allows a partitioning of the set of search points into different layers that correlate with the Hamming distance to an optimal solution.

The notion of fitness distance correlation (FDC) [13] has been widely used in the area of evolutionary computation to explain the difficulty of solving certain problems. All randomized search heuristics are guided by their fitness function and FDC is frequently used to determine the hardness of a problem by considering how the distance of search points to the optimum relates to their fitness values. The intuition is that problems are easy to solve if the fitness improves with decreasing distance to the optimum and hard to solve if the fitness is pointing in the opposite direction. While the intuition sounds sensible, it does not always translate directly into an accurate prediction of algorithm performance. Usually, the FDC is established by sampling search points on relatively small instances and calculating the empirical correlation between fitness and the distance to a known optimum. Different counterexamples have been presented in the literature that show FDC is not always a good predictor of algorithm performance (see e.g. [4, 11, 20]).

A strong FDC is only a reliable predictor if a randomized search heuristic does not encounter any deviations from the assumed usual behavior. In the case that a deviation from the predicted behavior becomes very unlikely, a strong FDC can potentially be used to accurately predict the runtime of randomized search heuristics. This property is explored in this paper, and we show that there is a strong FDC for highly dense 3-CNF formulas. Usually, FDC is determined empirically on a finite sample of points in the search space. In order to make it useful for upper bounds on the runtime of randomized search heuristics, we must be able to make rigorous statements about the properties of the relationship between fitness and distance and show that those properties hold with high probability. Furthermore, we require such statements to explicitly depend on the input size, where usual experimental investigations deal with problems

GECCO '15, July 11 - 15, 2015, Madrid, Spain

ISBN 978-1-4503-3472-3/15/07...$15.00

DOI: http://dx.doi.org/10.1145/2739480.2754659

of relatively small fixed size. We prove rigorous bounds on the FDC for high-density 3-CNF formulas in dependence of the input size n and use it to derive tail bounds on the runtime of the (1+1) EA for this class of problems. We show that the probability that the optimization time exceeds $O(n \log n)$ vanishes with increasing problem size for this problem class. This matches the lower bound on the expected runtime for asymptotically almost all high-density satisfiable 3-CNF formulas as described in [23].

We specifically study the *planted* model of random 3-CNF distributions and extend our results to the *filtered* model using a correspondence due to Ben-Sasson et al. [6]. Planted distributions for the maximum clique problem in graphs have also been studied by Storch [22] in the context of randomized search heuristics. In propositional satisfiability, the planted distribution of 3-CNF formulas is known to be easy to solve for classical algorithms [15], and our objective is to advance the theoretical analysis of evolutionary algorithms on random satisfiability models.

The outline of the paper is a follows. We introduce the model and algorithm under investigation in Section 2. We start our analysis by investigating formulas of high (linear) density in Section 3 and prove the $O(n \log n)$ bound. We then extend this analysis to formulas of logarithmic density. Finally, we give a short proof in Section 4 that the runtime of the (1+1) EA is faster than exponential for very low constant densities. Our theoretical results are complemented by experimental investigations in Section 5. We conclude the paper in Section 6.

2. PRELIMINARIES

A k-CNF formula F is constructed from a set of n Boolean variables $\{x_1, x_2, \ldots, x_n\}$ by forming a logical conjunction of exactly m clauses $F = C_1 \wedge C_2 \wedge \ldots \wedge C_m$. Each clause is the logical disjunction of exactly k literals, $C_i = \ell_{i_1} \vee \cdots \vee \ell_{i_k}$ and each literal ℓ_{i_j} is either an occurrence of a variable x or its negation $\neg x$. A k-CNF formula F is *satisfiable* if and only if there is an assignment of variables to truth values so that every clause contains at least one true literal.

The set of all assignments to a set of n Boolean variables is isomorphic to $\{0,1\}^n$ by interpreting the bit at each position i of the string as the state of exactly one Boolean variable x_i. For a length-m formula F on n variables, we define the fitness function $f = f_F \colon \{0,1\}^n \to \{0, \ldots, m\} := x \mapsto |\{C \in F : C \text{ is satisfied by } x\}|$. If F is satisfiable, the task of finding a satisfying assignment reduces to the task of maximizing f.

The standard (1+1) EA, illustrated in Algorithm 1, is a basic evolutionary algorithm that maintains a size-one population and produces a single offspring in each step. It can be characterized as a stochastic hill-climbing search that uses the standard bit-wise uniform mutation operator. Given a length-m formula F on n variables we seek an asymptotic bound on the runtime of the (1+1) EA searching for a satisfying assignment to F by optimizing the corresponding pseudo-Boolean function $f = f_F$. We study the infinite stochastic process $\{x^{(t)} : t \in \mathbb{N}_0\}$ on $\{0,1\}^n$ where $x^{(t)}$ is the assignment generated in iteration t of Algorithm 1. The runtime of the (1+1) EA is the random variable $T = \inf\{t \in \mathbb{N}_0 : f(x^{(t)}) = m\}$.

In order to bound the runtime of the (1+1) EA, we will consider the sequence $(x^{(0)}, x^{(1)}, \ldots)$ of assignments generated by the (1+1) EA and study the drift of corresponding stochastic processes that measure fitness values and distance values along this sequence. To make precise statements about the runtime, we rely heavily on the following drift theorem.

Algorithm 1: The (1+1) EA.

```
choose x ∈ {0,1}^n uniformly at random;
repeat forever
    y ← x;
    flip each bit of y independently with prob. 1/n;
    if f(y) ≥ f(x) then x ← y;
```

Theorem 1 (Multiplicative Drift [8, 9]). *Let $\{X_t : t \in \mathbb{N}_0\}$ be a sequence of random variables over $\mathbb{R}_{\geq 0}$. Let T be the random variable that denotes the earliest point in time $t \geq 0$ such that $X_t < 1$. If there exists $\delta > 0$ such that, for all a,*

$$\mathrm{E}(X_t - X_{t+1} \mid T > t, X_t = a) \geq \delta\, a,$$

then, for all a,

$$\mathrm{E}(T \mid X_0 = a) \leq \frac{1 + \ln(a)}{\delta},$$

and

$$\Pr\left(T > \frac{\lambda + \ln(a)}{\delta} \;\middle|\; X_0 = a\right) \leq e^{-\lambda} \text{ for all } \lambda > 0.$$

2.1 Random 3-CNF distributions

We consider distributions of 3-CNF formulas consisting of m clauses of length $k = 3$ over n variables. We also impose the assumption that each clause consists of distinct variables. This assumption is quite natural for 3-CNF formulas since any length-3 clause that contains repeating variables can be immediately reduced to an equivalent length-2 clause (if there are repeating variables with the same polarity) or a tautology (if there are repeating variables with opposite polarity). However, we do allow repeated clauses in F.

Definition 1. *Let $\Omega_{n,m}$ be the finite set of all 3-CNF formulas over n variables and m clauses.*

We associate random 3-CNF distributions with categorical distributions over the sample space $\Omega_{n,m}$. In particular, the well-known uniform distribution $\mathcal{U}_{n,m}$ is defined by

$$\Pr(F \mid F \sim \mathcal{U}_{n,m}) = |\Omega_{n,m}|^{-1}.$$

The filtered distribution is the uniform distribution conditioned on satisfiability.

$$\Pr(F \mid F \sim \mathcal{U}^{\mathrm{SAT}}_{n,m}) = |\{F \in \Omega_{n,m} : F \text{ is satisfiable}\}|^{-1}.$$

The planted distribution $\mathcal{P}_{n,m}$ is the uniform distribution conditioned on satisfiability by a planted assignment $x^\star$.

$$\Pr(F \mid F \sim \mathcal{P}_{n,m}) = |\{F \in \Omega_{n,m} : F \text{ is satisfied by } x^\star\}|^{-1}.$$

When considering a formula F constructed from $\mathcal{P}_{n,m}$, without loss of generality we will hereafter assume that the planted solution $x^\star = (1, 1, \ldots, 1)$ since the behavior of the (1+1) EA is invariant to negation operations on literals of F. We define the function $d \colon \{0,1\}^n \to \{0, \ldots, n\} := x \mapsto |\{i : x_i = 0\}|$ that measures the Hamming distance to the planted solution.

Definition 2. *Fix a constant $\epsilon > 0$. We define $\mathcal{H} = \mathcal{H}_\epsilon \subseteq \{0,1\}^n \times \{0,1\}^n$ such that $(x, y) \in \mathcal{H}$ if and only if*

1. $|\{i : x_i \neq y_i\}| = 1$,
2. $d(y) = d(x) - 1$, *and*
3. $d(x) \leq (1/2 + \epsilon)n$

The following lemma introduces a two-sided bound on the expected difference in fitness between pairs in $\mathcal{H}$, provided that F is drawn from the $\mathcal{P}_{n,m}$ distribution.

Lemma 1. *Let $(x, y) \in \mathcal{H}$, then*

$$\frac{3m}{7n}(1 - \gamma(n)) \leq \mathrm{E}(f(y) - f(x) \mid F \sim \mathcal{P}_{n,m}) \leq \frac{3m}{7n}$$

where $\gamma(n) = (1 + o(1))(3/4 + \epsilon - \epsilon^2)$.

Proof. Let A be the set of all 3-CNF clauses on n variables with at least one positive literal that are not satisfied by x but are satisfied by y. Similarly, let B be the set of all 3-CNF clauses on n variables with at least one positive literal that are satisfied by x but not satisfied by y. Let $C \supset A \cup B$ be the set of all 3-CNF clauses on n variables with at least one positive literal.

Suppose $F \sim \mathcal{P}_{n,m}$. Let Z_A be the random variable that counts the occurrences of clauses from A in F and Z_B be the random variable that counts the occurrences of clauses from B in F. Since F contains exactly m clauses chosen from C independently with replacement, $E(Z_A) = m|A|/|C|$, and $E(Z_B) = m|B|/|C|$. Hence,

$$\mathrm{E}(f(y) - f(x)) = \mathrm{E}(Z_A - Z_B) = m\left(\frac{|A| - |B|}{|C|}\right),$$

and the bounds follow from the fact that $|C| = 7\binom{n}{3}$ and Lemma 1 of [23], which states $|A| = \binom{n-1}{2}$ and $0 \leq |B| \leq \gamma(n)\binom{n-1}{2}$, where $\gamma(n)$ is as claimed. □

Taking the random variable $Z := Z_A - Z_B$ as the sum of m independent random variables, the following lemma follows from 1 by Chernoff bounds on Z.

Lemma 2. *For n sufficiently large, let $(x, y) \in \mathcal{H}$ be chosen arbitrarily. Then*

$$\Pr\left(\frac{c_1 m}{n} < f(y) - f(x) < \frac{c_2 m}{n} \;\middle|\; F \sim \mathcal{P}_{n,m}\right) = 1 - e^{-\Omega(m/n)}$$

for specific constants $c_1 < 1 - \gamma(n) < c_2$.

2.2 Constraint density

The *constraint density* of a formula is the ratio of clauses to variables m/n. The constraint density quantifies the average number of constraints that are imposed on a variable. Boolean formulas with low constraint density are expected to be easy to satisfy, since each variable has, on average, few constraints. On the other hand, formulas with high constraint density are, on average, easy to refute because backtracking search algorithms can quickly derive a contradiction. The study of a threshold phenomenon in the uniform random 3-CNF distribution $\mathcal{U}_{n,m}$ has been the focus of intense study in the last two decades. The *satisfiability threshold conjecture* [2] asserts that for all $k \geq 3$ if is a formula drawn uniformly at random from the set of all k-CNF formulas with n variables and m clauses, there exists a real number r_k such that

$$\lim_{n\to\infty} \Pr\{F \text{ is satisfiable}\} = \begin{cases} 1 & m/n < r_k; \\ 0 & m/n > r_k. \end{cases}$$

Experimental studies on 3-CNF formulas suggest a threshold around $r_3 \approx 4.26$. There are currently no exact results for the location of this threshold (if it exists), and only upper and lower bounds are known. For a more detailed treatment of random satisfiability along with an exposition of recent developments, see the chapter by Achlioptas [1].

3. HIGH-DENSITY REGIME

We now study the runtime of the (1+1) EA on high-density planted formulas. We begin with linear densities in Section 3.1, namely, length-m formulas on n variables where $m/n \geq cn$ for a specific constant c. In this regime we prove that for asymptotically almost all formulas, the (1+1) EA finds a satisfying assignment in $O(n \log n)$ time with high probability. This improves by a linear factor the previous known tail bounds for the (1+1) EA at these densities [23].

In Section 3.2, we consider sparser formulas where $m/n \geq c \log n$ for a particular c. We treat these densities separately because the randomness of both the algorithm and the formula sampling process must be handled more carefully.

3.1 Linear density

Definition 3. *We say a formula F has* strong FDC *if the following two properties hold.*

Property A. $\forall (x, y) \in \mathcal{H}$, $c_1 m/n < f(y) - f(x) < c_2 m/n$,

Property B. $\forall x, y \in \{0,1\}^n$ *with* $n/2 + \epsilon n \geq d(x) \geq n/2 + 3\epsilon n/4$ *and* $y \leq n/2 + \epsilon n/2$, $f(x) < f(y)$.

Here $c_1 < c_2$ are the constants introduced in Lemma 2.

Lemma 3. *Let $F \sim \mathcal{P}_{n,m}$ where $m/n \geq cn$ for a sufficiently large positive constant c. The probability (taken on $\Omega_{n,m}$) that F has strong FDC is at least $1 - e^{-\Omega(n)}$.*

Proof. By Lemma 2 together with a union bound over the elements of $\mathcal{H}$, Property A of Definition 3 holds with probability $1 - e^{-\Omega(n)}$. For Property B, let $z, z' \in \{0,1\}^n$ such that $d(z) = d(z') = i$. Note that $E_i = \mathrm{E}(f(z)) = \mathrm{E}(f(z'))$ is independent of z, where we take the expectation over $\mathcal{P}_{n,m}$. Let $u, v \in \{0,1\}^n$ where $n/2 + \epsilon n \geq d(u) \geq n/2 + 3\epsilon n/4$ and $d(v) \leq n/2 + \epsilon n/2$. Denote $a := d(u)$ and $b := d(v)$. Note that u can be transformed to v by changing $a - b \geq \epsilon n/4$ zeros to ones. We argue that $E_b \geq E_a + \Theta(m)$. By the above stated independence, $\mathrm{E}(f(v) - f(u)) = E_b - E_a$. Furthermore, by a repeated application of Lemma 1, we have $E_b \geq E_a + (3/7)(1 - \gamma(n))(m/n)(\epsilon n/4) = E_a + \Theta(m)$.

Let $q := (E_a + E_b)/2$ and let y be any search point with $d(y) = b$. Note that $f(y)$ is a random variable that can be written as sum of m independent 0/1 random variables. Consequently, the additive Chernoff bound shows that

$$\Pr(f(y) \leq q) = \Pr(f(y) \leq E_b - (E_b - E_a)/2) \leq e^{-\Theta(m)}.$$

The same argument shows that any x with $d(x) = a$ has a fitness greater than q with probability $e^{-\Theta(m)}$ only. Applying a union bound over the applicable pairs $x, y \in \{0,1\}^n$, we conclude that Property B of Definition 3 holds with probability at least $1 - e^{-\Omega(n)}$. A final union bound over both properties concludes the proof. □

Theorem 2. *Let $m/n \geq cn$ for a sufficiently large positive constant c. The runtime of the (1+1) EA is bounded by $O(n \log n)$ with probability $1 - o(1)$ on every planted formula with n variables and m clauses except for a set of measure tending to zero exponentially fast with n.*

PROOF. By Lemma 3, every planted formula at density at least cn has strong FDC except for an $e^{-\Omega(n)}$-fraction, so we will assume for the remainder of the proof that we are working with a formula that has the strong FDC property.

If F has strong FDC, then for states that are not too far away from the planted assignment, the fitness and distance are tightly correlated in the following sense. $\forall (x,y) \in \mathcal{H}$,

$$f(x) + c_2 d(x)m/n \geq m, \text{ and } f(x) + c_1 d(x) m/n \leq m \quad (1)$$

since each step on a path of length $d(x)$ to 1^n increases the fitness by at least (respectively at most) a constant number multiplied by m/n and $f(1^n) = m$.

We consider the drift of the stochastic process $\{X_t : t \in \mathbb{N}_0\}$ where $X_t = m - f(x^{(t)})$. Assume at iteration t that $0 < d(x^{(t)}) \leq (1/2 + \epsilon)n$ (we will later show this holds with high probability over the run). There must be a set $S \subsetneq \{0,1\}^n$ consisting of $d(x^{(t)})$ elements such that for each $y \in S$, $(x^{(t)}, y) \in \mathcal{H}$. For each such y, since $f(y) > f(x^{(t)}) + c_1 m/n > f(x^{(t)})$, a mutation from $x^{(t)}$ to y is clearly accepted by selection. Furthermore, selection does not accept mutation to lower fitness values so $X_t - X_{t+1} \geq 0$. Let $\mathcal{E}$ denote the event that mutation produces some $y \in S$ from $x^{(t)}$. By the law of total expectation,

$$\begin{aligned} \mathrm{E}(X_t - X_{t+1} \mid X_t) &\geq \mathrm{E}(X_t - X_{t+1} \mid X_t, \mathcal{E}) \Pr(\mathcal{E}) \\ &\geq \mathrm{E}(X_t - X_{t+1} \mid X_t, \mathcal{E}) \frac{d(x^{(t)})}{en}. \end{aligned}$$

By the inequality in (1),

$$\frac{m - f(x^{(t)})}{c_2 m/n} = \frac{X_t}{c_2 m/n} \leq d(x^{(t)})$$

so we can bound the drift as

$$\begin{aligned} \mathrm{E}(X_t - X_{t+1} \mid X_t) &\geq \mathrm{E}(X_t - X_{t+1} \mid X_t, \mathcal{E}) \frac{X_t}{en(c_2 m/n)} \\ &= (f(y) - f(x^{(t)})) \frac{X_t}{en(c_2 m/n)}, \end{aligned}$$

and, since F has strong FDC and $(x^{(t)}, y) \in \mathcal{H}$,

$$\geq X_t \frac{c_1 m/n}{en(c_2 m/n)} = X_t \frac{c_1/c_2}{en}. \quad (2)$$

We only need to show that with high probability, the process never leaves $\mathcal{H}$. Using the multiplicative Chernoff bound, the initial search point generated uniformly at random has $d(x^{(0)}) \leq n/2 + \epsilon n/2$ with high probability. In this case, by Property B of Definition 3, the EA can never reach a search point with distance b or worse in $\mathcal{H}$. Since $\mathcal{H}$ by definition contains points at distance at most $(1/2 + \epsilon)n$, in order for the process to leave $\mathcal{H}$, it must jump over the gap between $n/2 + 3\epsilon n/4$ and $n/2 + \epsilon n$. This can only occur after mutating at least $\epsilon n/4$ bits: an event that occurs with probability at most $e^{-\Omega(n \log n)}$ under uniform mutation.

We thus assume that the process does not leave $\mathcal{H}$, and so the inequality of (2) is valid for all times t. Finally, we apply Theorem 1 using inequality (2) by setting $\delta = c_1/(c_2 en)$ and $\lambda = \log n$ to obtain the tail bound. □

Let F^* be any formula on n variables and m clauses with exactly one satisfying assignment. Ben-Sasson et al. [6] proved that for densities above $m/n > c \ln n$ for a particular constant c, the probability of generating F^* from $\mathcal{P}_{n,m}$ is asymptotically equal to the probability of generating F^* from the filtered distribution $\mathcal{U}^{\mathrm{SAT}}_{n,m}$. They also prove that with high probability in this regime, a formula from either distribution has a unique satisfying assignment. Thus we can extend our result to the uniform distribution conditioned on satisfiability to obtain the following corollary that covers all satisfiable formulas in the high-density regime.

Corollary 1. *Let $m/n > cn$ for a sufficiently large positive constant c. The runtime of the (1+1) EA is bounded by $O(n \log n)$ with probability $1 - o(1)$ on all satisfiable 3-CNF formulas on n variables and m clauses except for a set of measure tending to zero exponentially fast with n.*

We conclude the typical runtime of the (1+1) EA very rarely deviates above $O(n \log n)$ for asymptotically almost all satisfiable formulas of sufficiently high linear density. This complements the $\Omega(n \log n)$ lower bound on the *expected* runtime derived for the same class of formulas in [23, Theorem 6]. A corresponding upper bound on the expected runtime is trickier since there is still a very low probability that the (1+1) EA can escape $\mathcal{H}$ and become trapped for a long time at a local optimum. Our results yield a simple solution to such a heavy-tailed runtime: perform sufficiently frequent restarts and apply Theorem 2 or Corollary 1 to obtain a matching upper bound on the expectation.

3.2 Logarithmic density

For smaller densities we can also obtain a similar tail bound on the runtime, but we have to take a slightly different approach. At high densities, Theorem 2 makes a statement about the runtime over all but a vanishing fraction of formulas. At densities asymptotically lower, we can make a statement about the likelihood of a runtime of $O(n \log n)$, but the probability is taken over both the dynamics of the (1+1) EA process and the sampling of the random formula.

For any $x \in \{0,1\}^n$ with $d(x) = k$ we define $P(x) := (x = x_1, x_2, \ldots, x_k = 1^n)$ to be the unique path where x_{i+1} is constructed from x_i by flipping the leftmost zero bit of x.

Lemma 4. *Let c be a sufficiently large positive constant and let $F \sim \mathcal{P}_{n,m}$ with $m/n > c \ln n$. If $d(x) \leq (1/2 + \epsilon)n$, then for every $x_i, x_{i+1} \in P(x)$, $c_1 m/n \leq f(x_{i+1}) - f(x_i) \leq c_2 m/n$ with probability at least $1 - n^{-3}$.*

PROOF. Define the indicator random variable $\chi \colon \{0,1\}^n \times \{0,1\}^n \times \Omega_{n,m} \to \{0,1\}$ where

$$\chi(x, y; F) = \begin{cases} 1 & \text{if } \frac{c_1 m}{n} < f(y) - f(x) < \frac{c_2 m}{n}, \\ 0 & \text{otherwise.} \end{cases}$$

For all $x_i, x_{i+1} \in P(x)$, by the union bound

$$\begin{aligned} &\Pr\left(\bigcup_{x_i, x_{i+1} \in P(x^{(t)})} \chi(x_i, x_{i+1}; F) = 0 \;\middle|\; F \sim \mathcal{P}_{n,m} \right) \\ &\leq \sum_{x_i, x_{i+1} \in P(x^{(t)})} \Pr\left(\chi(x_i, x_{i+1}; F) = 0 \mid F \sim \mathcal{P}_{n,m}\right) \\ &\leq n e^{-\Omega(m/n)} \leq n^{-3}, \end{aligned}$$

where we have applied Lemma 2 and used the fact that $m > cn \ln n$, c sufficiently large. □

Lemma 4 bounds the probability that the fitness and distance are sufficiently correlated along a path to the planted solution on a random formula of density at least $c \ln n$ for a specific constant c. We now apply this result to derive a bound on the runtime of the (1+1) EA over such a formula.

Theorem 3. *Let $F \sim \mathcal{P}_{n,m}$, $m/n > c \ln n$ for a sufficiently large positive constant c. The runtime of the (1+1) EA is bounded by $O(n \log n)$ with probability polynomially close to one, where the probability is taken over both the random sampling of the formula and the random optimization time.*

PROOF. Let r be a sufficiently large constant. We consider the first $rn \ln n$ steps of the (1+1) EA on a formula F drawn from $\mathcal{P}_{n,m}$ uniformly at random and show that, with probability polynomially close to one, the (1+1) EA has found a satisfying assignment.

We say a bitstring $x \in \{0,1\}^n$ has an *FDC path* if the following two properties hold at x.

Property A′. $\forall x_i, x_{i+1} \in P(x)$, $c_1 m/n \leq f(x_{i+1}) - f(x_i) \leq c_2 m/n$.

Property B′. $d(x) \leq n/2 + 3\epsilon n/4$,

We say the process has *failed* at time t if there is any $0 \leq s \leq t$ such that $x^{(s)}$ does not have an FDC path. We argue by induction that the probability that the process fails at time t conditioned on the event that it has not failed at time $t-1$ is sufficiently high. Specifically, in each step we show that if process has not yet failed, Property B′ holds with probability $1 - e^{-\Omega(n)}$, and the probability of Property A′ conditioned on B′ is polynomially close to one.

For the initial point, we assume a slightly stronger condition than Property B′: that $d(x^{(0)}) \leq n/2 + \epsilon n/2$, which by Chernoff bounds holds with probability exponentially close to one. Let $h = f(x^{(0)})$. If $t > 0$ and the process has not yet failed at time $t-1$, then Property B′ can be violated only if the (1+1) EA accepts a point sufficiently further away from the planted solution. Let y be the offspring generated in iteration t of the (1+1) EA. We make a case distinction on three disjoint events occurring in the mutation step.

Case $d(y) > n/2 + \epsilon n$. This event occurs only with probability $e^{-\Omega(n \log n)}$ since Property B′ holds at $x^{(t-1)}$, and so $\epsilon n/4$ bits must change during mutation to produce y.

Case $n/2 + \epsilon n \geq d(y) > n/2 + 3\epsilon n/4$. By an argument similar to the one in the proof of Lemma 3 that Property B of Definition 3 holds at high densities, we have $f(y) \geq h$ only with $e^{-\Theta(m)}$ probability. Since the fitness of points can only monotonically increase during a run of the (1+1) EA, under this event $f(y) < h \leq f(x^{(t-1)})$ and so $x^{(t)} = x^{(t-1)}$ since y would not be accepted.

Case $d(y) \leq n/2 + 3\epsilon n/4$. In this case, Property B′ will also not be violated by $x^{(t)}$ because, $x^{(t)} = y$ or $x^{(t)} = x^{(t-1)}$, both of which satisfy Property B′.

Since the first two events occur with exponentially small probability (and the events partition the probability space), we can conclude that, as long as the process has not failed by iteration $t-1$, then with probability $1 - e^{-\Omega(n)}$, Property B′ holds at $x^{(t)}$.

Assuming Property B′ holds at $x^{(t)}$, we can apply Lemma 4 and conclude the conditional probability that Property A′ also holds at $x^{(t)}$ is at least $1 - n^{-3}$. The joint probability that both properties hold is therefore at least $1 - O(n^{-3})$.

Now by induction on t, the process does not fail for $rn \ln n$ steps with probability at least $1 - O(n^{-1})$. Conditioning on the event that the process has not failed for a phase of $rn \ln n$ steps, the bound on the drift during this phase is the same as with inequality (2). We can again apply Theorem 1 with $\lambda = \log n$ to obtain the tail bound. □

4. LOW-DENSITY REGIME

On the uniform distribution, 3-CNF formulas that seem to be difficult for complete search algorithms lie near the proposed critical threshold $r_3 \approx 4.26$. However, at very low densities, random formulas become easy to solve again, even by very simple backtracking-free heuristics. The *pure literal heuristic* operates by iteratively finding a *pure literal* in the formula (i.e., one whose negation does not appear), setting it to true, and then removing all clauses that contains it. This approach succeeds with high probability for uniform random formulas at constraint densities $m/n < 1.637$ [17, 18]. A similar backtracking-free heuristic called the *generalized unit clause heuristic* succeeds with asymptotically positive probability on uniform random formulas with $m/n < 3.003$ [10]. Alekhnovich and Ben-Sasson [3] discovered a deep connection between constraint-directed random walk (iteratively flipping a random variable in a random unsatisfied clause) and the pure literal heuristic. They proved that the random walk finds a satisfying assignment with high probability in linear time for constraint densities at most 1.637.

In the interest of a more complete picture, we would also like to understand the behavior of the (1+1) EA at very sparse densities. Such formulas are likely easy to solve because most assignments to a random formula are already satisfying, and we conjecture that the (1+1) EA also runs in polynomial time at these densities. This conjecture is strongly supported by empirical evidence in Section 5, however proving the conjecture is likely to require different techniques than the ones that are useful for high density formulas. In this section, we show that if the density is low enough, the structure of constraints is so sparse that the formula breaks up into small components that the (1+1) EA can solve separately. From this we easily derive a $2^{o(n)}$ subexponential time bound and at least conclude that the runtime for the (1+1) EA is faster than any exponential function at low densities.

Lemma 5. *Let $H = H_d(n,m)$ denote a random d-uniform hypergraph with n vertices and exactly m hyperedges selected uniformly at random with replacement from the family of $\binom{n}{d}$ possible d-sets.*

Let $\alpha = dm/n$ denote the average degree *of H. If $\alpha < (d-1)^{-1}$, then with high probability, the number of vertices in the largest connected component of H is $O(\log n)$.*

PROOF. We consider m rounds of selecting edges uniformly at random with replacement. Let $X_1, X_2, \ldots, X_m$ denote the sequence of random variables where X_i corresponds to the size of the largest connected component in round i. Moreover, let $\widehat{X}_1, \widehat{X}_2, \ldots, \widehat{X}_m$ be the same sequence corresponding to the process of selecting edges uniformly at random *without* replacement. Note that for all $1 \leq i < m$, $\Pr(X_{i+1} > X_i \mid X_i) \leq \Pr(\widehat{X}_{i+1} > \widehat{X}_i \mid \widehat{X}_i)$ since if we use replacement sampling, there are only more chances to add a pre-existing edge, which has no effect on the size of any component. Therefore X_m is stochastically dominated by $\widehat{X}_m$ and so for every $k \in \mathbb{N}$, $\Pr(X_m < k) \geq \Pr(\widehat{X}_m < k)$. Finally the result that $\Pr(\widehat{X}_m = O(\log n)) = 1 - o(1)$ is due to Schmidt-Pruzan and Shamir [21]. □

The *constraint hypergraph* of a formula is a hypergraph $H = (X, E)$ where X corresponds to the set of variables in F and E is a sequence of m nonempty subsets of X constructed as follows. Each clause C of F corresponds to a unique $S \in E$ that contains exactly the variables that appear as literals in C. Thus every 3-CNF formula on n variables with m clauses has a unique 3-regular constraint hypergraph with m hyperedges (parallel hyperedges are allowed). It is easy to see that at very low constant densities, the constraint structure of Boolean formulas breaks up into small components that the (1+1) EA can solve separately. This is captured by the following theorem.

Theorem 4. *Let F be a 3-CNF formula drawn from $\mathcal{U}_{n,m}$ with density $m/n < 1/6$. Then with high probability the (1+1) EA finds a satisfying assignment for F in subexponential time.*

PROOF. We consider the average degree α of the constraint hypergraph H of F. Since F is sampled uniformly at random from $\Omega_{n,m}$, its constraint hypergraph is a random 3-uniform hypergraph with n vertices and m edges sampled uniformly at random with replacement since each of the 2^3 distinct clauses associated with each unique 3-set is also selected uniformly at random. Since $\alpha = 3m/n < 1/2$, by Lemma 5, with high probability the largest connected component in H contains $O(\log n)$ vertices.

In this case, let q be the number of connected components in H. We partition the clause set $\{S_1, S_2, \ldots, S_q\}$ where S_i is the set of clauses that contain only variables from the i-th connected component of H. The fitness function f can be expressed as $f(x) = \sum_{i=1}^{q} f_i(x)$ where $f_i(x)$ counts the number of clauses in S_i that are satisfied by x. Since each f_i depends on at most $O(\log n)$ bits of x, f is decomposable into linearly separable subfunctions of bounded size.

The proof is then completed by a simple fitness levels argument [24]. In particular, let $(A_0, \ldots, A_m)$ be a partition of $\{0,1\}^n$ such that for all $x \in A_j$, $f(x) = j$. Let t be an arbitrary iteration in the execution of the (1+1) EA and set $k := f(x^{(t)})$. As long as there is an unsolved subfunction f_i with respect to the assignment corresponding to $x^{(t)}$, the (1+1) EA can generate a strictly improving offspring by solving f_i and flipping no other bit outside of S_i. The resulting offspring must lie in some A_ℓ with $\ell > k$. The probability of this event is at least $(1 - 1/n)^{n-|S_i|}(1/n)^{|S_i|} \geq n^{-|S_i|}/e$, and the waiting time to increase the fitness level by at least one is bounded by $en^{|S_i|}$. Since there are at most $m = O(n)$ suboptimal fitness levels, the expected time until F is solved is bounded by $n^{O(\log n)} = 2^{o(n)}$. □

5. EXPERIMENTS

In this section we report numerical experiments that investigate the constants in the asymptotic bounds proved in this paper, and to explore the runtime character of the (1+1) EA at lower densities. In Figure 1(a) we investigate the runtime divided by $n \ln n$ as a function of $n = 10, 20, \ldots, 1000$ for the $\mathcal{P}_{n,m}$ model with $m/n = n$. For each value if n we generate 100 random 3-CNF formulas, and conduct 100 runs of the (1+1) EA, measuring the first iteration in which it finds a satisfying assignment. We then calculate the quartiles of the number of iterations to solve the formula at each value of n as a robust statistic for the runtime as a function of n. The plot is converging to a constant near e, providing empirical evidence that the runtime bound proved in this paper is tight, and suggests that the true runtime is concentrated around $en \ln n \pm O(n)$. We repeat this experiment for asymptotically lower densities and plot the results in Figure 1(b). In this case, we set $m/n = c \ln n$ for each random formula corresponding to the statement of Theorem 3. We determined $c = 4$ to be a sufficiently high constant, meaning that the (1+1) EA would not always converge to a solution on densities for $c < 4$. On the other hand, convergence was always observed for densities above $4 \ln n$. The behavior in 1(b) is very similar to the linear density case, and the true runtime appears to be concentrated around $en \ln n \pm O(n)$ for formulas of logarithmic densities.

5.1 Phase transition behavior

As discussed in Section 4, we conjecture that the (1+1) EA can also easily solve 3-CNF formulas at very low densities. To more precisely understand the behavior of the (1+1) EA on random planted 3-CNF formulas across the density spectrum, we performed numerical experiments and measured the time until a satisfying assignment was found at different densities for some distinct values of n.

On the $\mathcal{P}_{n,m}$ model, for three distinct values of n, i.e., $n \in \{100, 300, 1000\}$, we generate formulas using 100 equidistant values of m such that the constraint density ranges from 1 to 10. For each distinct density value, we generate 100 formulas from the random $\mathcal{P}_{n,m}$ model and run the (1+1) EA 100 times on each formula. Runs that do not complete in at most 10^7 iterations are halted and removed from consideration. Of the runs that do not fail, the median runtime as a function of constraint density for these trials is plotted in Figure 2(a). We also plot the percentage of runs that failed as a function of constraint density in Figure 2(b).

In these results, we also observe the classical easy-hard-easy pattern similar to the one that occurs for complete DPLL solvers on the uniform random model [16, 7]. This corresponds to the so-called *phase transition* phenomenon in random satisfiability where formulas near the sat/unsat transition have high decision complexity [14].

Remarkably, our experiments suggest that there is also a critical density in the *planted* model $\mathcal{P}_{n,m}$ for the (1+1) EA at which formulas are on average more difficult to optimize. We also observe that the hardness peak for the (1+1) EA occurs close to density values of $m/n \approx 4.26$, which is the critical density for DPLL solvers on the uniform model $\mathcal{U}_{n,m}$. This corresponds to the conjectured satisfiability threshold r_3 for random unfiltered, unplanted formulas.

Below the hardness peak, the (1+1) EA finds a satisfying assignment quickly, and we conjecture that there exists a constant $c < 4.26$ such that the (1+1) EA runs in polynomial time with high probability on random satisfiable formulas with density at most c. As density increases beyond the critical point, the empirical running time in Figure 2(a) appears to converge again toward $en \ln n$ for each n value. Theorem 3 establishes an asymptotic bound on the density at which most formulas become easy again. An interesting open problem is the location of the critical density below which formulas become difficult on average for the (1+1) EA.

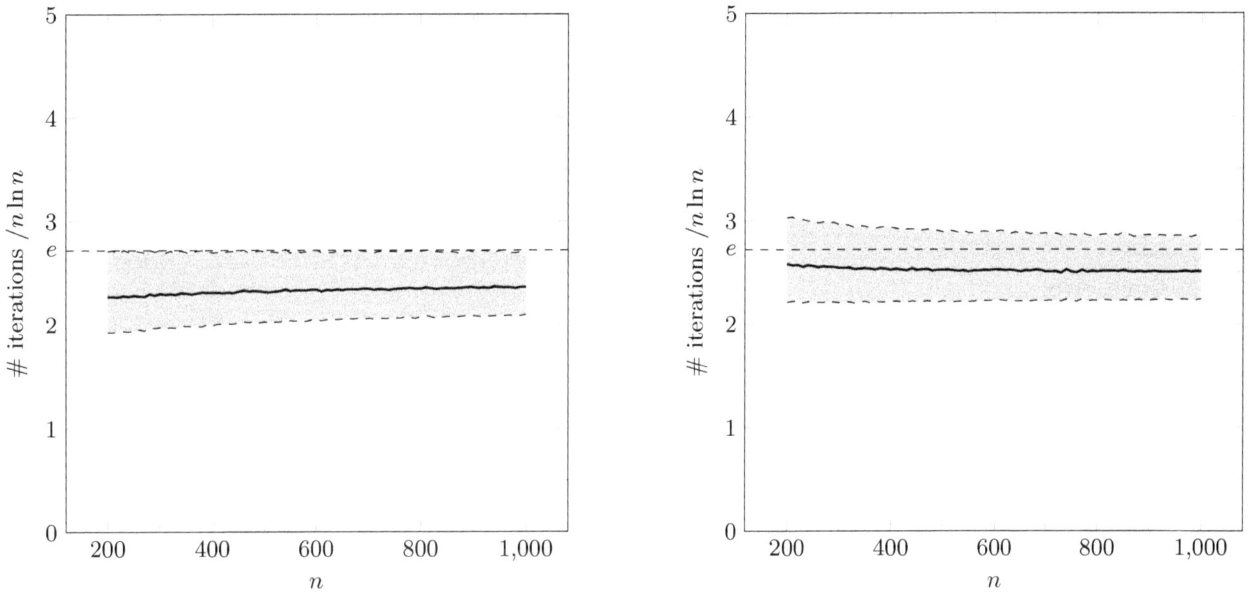

(a) $m = n^2$ (constraint density is $\Theta(n)$).

(b) $m = 4n \ln n$ (constraint density is $\Theta(\log n)$).

Figure 1: Median runtime of the (1+1) EA divided by $n \ln n$ as a function of n for the $\mathcal{P}_{n,m}$. The shaded region denotes the interquartile range. The statistics are taken from 100 runs each on 100 random formulas generated for each value of n.

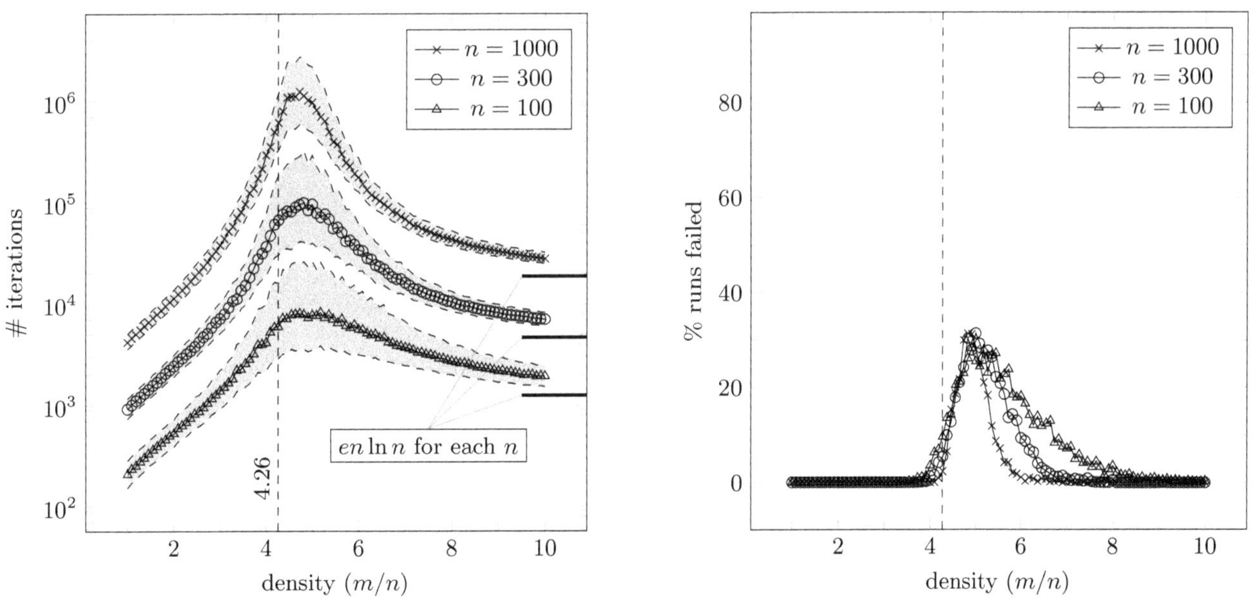

(a) Runtime statistics. The marked lines denote the median runtime. The shaded regions denote the interquartile range.

(b) Percentage of runs (out of 10000) requiring $\geq 10^7$ iterations at each density value.

Figure 2: Results for the (1+1) EA on the $\mathcal{P}_{n,m}$ model controlling m for constraint density. The statistics are taken from 100 runs each on 100 random formulas generated for each value of m/n.

6. CONCLUSIONS

We have presented an improved runtime analysis of the (1+1) EA for randomly constructed 3-CNF formulas. Investigating the fitness distance correlation for high density formulas, we have shown an improved bound of $O(n \log n)$ on the (1+1) EA. In extension to the investigations in [23] , the $O(n \log n)$ bound holds for formulas of logarithmic density with probability $1 - o(1)$. Our complementary experimental investigations imply the leading constants in our asymptotic bounds are low, and extend the investigations to other density ratios.

Acknowledgements

The research leading to these results has received funding from the Australian Research Council (ARC) under grant agreement DP140103400 and from the European Union Seventh Framework Programme (FP7/2007-2013) under grant agreement no 618091 (SAGE).

7. REFERENCES

[1] Dimitris Achlioptas. Random satisfiability. In Armin Biere, Marijn Heule, Hans van Maaren, and Toby Walsh, editors, *Handbook of Satisfiability*, volume 185 of *Frontiers in Artificial Intelligence and Applications*, pages 245–270. IOS Press, 2009.

[2] Dimitris Achlioptas, Amin Coja-Oghlan, and Federico Ricci-Tersenghi. On the solution-space geometry of random constraint satisfaction problems. *Random Structures and Algorithms*, 38(3):251–268, 2011.

[3] Mikhail Alekhnovich and Eli Ben-Sasson. Linear upper bounds for random walk on small density random 3-CNFs. *SIAM Journal on Computing*, 36(5):1248–1263, 2007.

[4] Lee Altenberg. Fitness distance correlation analysis: An instructive counterexample. In Thomas Bäck, editor, *Proceedings of the Seventh International Conference on Genetic Algorithms*, pages 57–64. Morgan Kaufmann, 1997.

[5] Anne Auger and Benjamin Doerr. *Theory of Randomized Search Heuristics: Foundations and Recent Developments.* World Scientific Publishing Co., Inc., 2011.

[6] Eli Ben-Sasson, Yonatan Bilu, and Danny Gutfreund. Finding a randomly planted assignment in a random 3-CNF. Manuscript, 2002.

[7] James M Crawford and Larry D Auton. Experimental results on the crossover point in satisfiability problems. In *Proceedings of the Eleventh National Conference on Artificial Intelligence (AAAI-93)*, pages 21–27, 1993.

[8] Benjamin Doerr and Leslie Ann Goldberg. Adaptive drift analysis. *Algorithmica*, 65(1):224–250, 2013.

[9] Benjamin Doerr, Daniel Johannsen, and Carola Winzen. Multiplicative drift analysis. *Algorithmica*, 64(4):673–697, 2012.

[10] Alan Frieze and Stephen Suen. Analysis of two simple heuristics on a random instance of k-SAT. *Journal of Algorithms*, 20(2):312–355, 1996.

[11] Thomas Jansen. On classifications of fitness functions. In Leila Kallel, Bart Naudts, and Alex Rogers, editors, *Theoretical Aspects of Evolutionary Computing*, Natural Computing Series, pages 371–385. Springer Berlin Heidelberg, 2001.

[12] Thomas Jansen. *Analyzing Evolutionary Algorithms - The Computer Science Perspective.* Natural Computing Series. Springer, 2013.

[13] Terry Jones and Stephanie Forrest. Fitness distance correlation as a measure of problem difficulty for genetic algorithms. In Larry J. Eshelman, editor, *Proceedings of the Sixth International Conference on Genetic Algorithms*, pages 184–192. Morgan Kaufmann, 1995.

[14] Scott Kirkpatrick and Bart Selman. Critical behavior in the satisfiability of random Boolean expressions. *Science*, 264(5163):1297–1301, 1994.

[15] Michael Krivelevich and Dan Vilenchik. Solving random satisfiable 3CNF formulas in expected polynomial time. In *Proceedings of the Seventeenth Symposium on Discrete Algorithms (SODA'06)*, pages 454–463, 2006.

[16] David Mitchell, Bart Selman, and Hector Levesque. Hard and easy distributions of SAT problems. In *Proceedings of the Tenth National Conference on Artificial Intelligence (AAAI-92)*, pages 459–465, 1992.

[17] Michael Mitzenmacher. Tight thresholds for the pure literal rule. Technical Report 1997-011, Digital SRC, 1997.

[18] Michael Molloy. Cores in random hypergraphs and Boolean formulas. *Random Structures and Algorithms*, 27(1):124–135, 2005.

[19] Frank Neumann and Carsten Witt. *Bioinspired Computation in Combinatorial Optimization: Algorithms and Their Computational Complexity.* Springer, 2010.

[20] R. J. Quick, Victor J. Rayward-Smith, and G. D. Smith. Fitness distance correlation and ridge functions. In A. E. Eiben, Thomas Bäck, Marc Schoenauer, and Hans-Paul Schwefel, editors, *Proceedings of the Fifth International Conference on Parallel Problem Solving from Nature (PPSN V)*, volume 1498 of *Lecture Notes in Computer Science*, pages 77–86. Springer, 1998.

[21] Jeanette Schmidt-Pruzan and Eli Shamir. Component structure in the evolution of random hypergraphs. *Combinatorica*, 5(1):81–94, 1985.

[22] Tobias Storch. Finding large cliques in sparse semi-random graphcs by simple randomized search heuristics. *Theoretical Computer Science*, 386:114–131, 2007.

[23] Andrew M. Sutton and Frank Neumann. Runtime analysis of evolutionary algorithms on randomly constructed high-density satisfiable 3-CNF formulas. In Thomas Bartz-Beielstein, Jürgen Branke, Bogdan Filipic, and Jim Smith, editors, *Proceedings of the Thirteenth International Conference on Parallel Problem Solving from Nature (PPSN XIII)*, volume 8672 of *Lecture Notes in Computer Science*, pages 942–951. Springer, 2014.

[24] Carsten Witt. Fitness levels with tail bounds for the analysis of randomized search heuristics. *Information Processing Letters*, 114(1–2):38 – 41, 2014.

A Tight Runtime Analysis of the $(1+(\lambda,\lambda))$ Genetic Algorithm on OneMax

Benjamin Doerr
École Polytechnique
Univ. Paris-Saclay, France

Carola Doerr
CNRS & Univ. Pierre et Marie Curie
Paris, France

ABSTRACT

Understanding how crossover works is still one of the big challenges in evolutionary computation research, and making our understanding precise and proven by mathematical means might be an even bigger one. As one of few examples where crossover provably is useful, the $(1+(\lambda,\lambda))$ Genetic Algorithm (GA) was proposed recently in [Doerr, Doerr, Ebel. Lessons From the Black-Box: Fast Crossover-Based Genetic Algorithms. TCS 2015]. Using the fitness level method, the expected optimization time on general ONEMAX functions was analyzed and a $O(\max\{n\log(n)/\lambda, \lambda n\})$ bound was proven for any offspring population size $\lambda \in [1..n]$.

We improve this work in several ways, leading to sharper bounds and a better understanding of how the use of crossover speeds up the runtime in this algorithm. We first improve the upper bound on the runtime to $O(\max\{n\log(n)/\lambda, n\lambda\log\log(\lambda)/\log(\lambda)\})$. This improvement is made possible from observing that in the parallel generation of λ offspring via crossover (but not mutation), the best of these often is better than the expected value, and hence several fitness levels can be gained in one iteration.

We then present the first lower bound for this problem. It matches our upper bound for all values of λ. This allows to determine the asymptotically optimal value for the population size. It is $\lambda = \Theta(\sqrt{\log(n)\log\log(n)/\log\log\log(n)})$, which gives an optimization time of $\Theta(n\sqrt{\log(n)\log\log\log(n)/\log\log(n)})$. Hence the improved runtime analysis both gives a runtime guarantee improved by a super-constant factor and yields a better actual runtime (faster by more than a constant factor) by suggesting a better value for the parameter λ.

We finally give a tail bound for the upper tail of the runtime distribution, which shows that the actual runtime exceeds our runtime guarantee by a factor of $(1+\delta)$ with probability $O((n/\lambda^2)^{-\delta})$ only.

Categories and Subject Descriptors

F.2.2 [**Theory of Computation**]: Analysis of Algorithms and Problem Complexity—*Nonnumerical Algorithms and Problems*

Keywords

Theory; Runtime Analysis; Genetic Algorithms

1. INTRODUCTION

The role of crossover in evolutionary computation is still not very well understood. On the one hand, it is used intensively in practice, on the other hand, few rigorous theoretical or experimental investigations support clearly the usefulness of crossover. The difficulties both in experimentally supporting early explanation models like the building block hypothesis [17] or in constructing artificial example functions (e.g. [14]) such that simple evolutionary algorithms perform better with crossover than without (note that this would still only be a very weak support for the concept of crossover) rather suggest that crossover is not that easily employed with success. In the meantime, a few less artificial examples were found where crossover provably leads to a runtime having a smaller asymptotic order of magnitude, namely a simplified variant of the Ising model on rings [9]) and on trees [20] as well as a series of works on the all-pairs shortest path problem ([4], [7], and [5]).

In this work, we build on the latest algorithm where crossover was proven to be useful, the $(1+(\lambda,\lambda))$ GA proposed in [3]. Unlike most previous works, here crossover has a super-constant speed-up even for very simple functions like the ONEMAX test function. However, experiments show that the algorithm performs well also on linear functions, royal road functions, and maximum satisfiability instances [10] (in fact, the latter work shows that the $(1+(\lambda,\lambda))$ GA outperforms hill climbers for several problems, for MaxSat it also outperforms the Linkage Tree Genetic Algorithm). The $(1+(\lambda,\lambda))$ GA uses crossover in a different way than the previous works. Instead of trying to combine particularly fit solution parts, here a biased uniform crossover is used as a repair mechanism. Having such a crossover-based repair mechanism, we can use mutation with a higher rate, leading to a faster exploration of the search space.

Given this different working-principle not seen before in discrete evolutionary optimization, there is a strong motivation to gain a deeper understanding of the $(1+(\lambda,\lambda))$ GA and its working principles. While in the first analysis of the $(1+(\lambda,\lambda))$ GA on the ONE-

GECCO '15, July 11 - 16, 2015, Madrid, Spain

ISBN 978-1-4503-3472-3/15/07 ... $15.00
DOI: http://dx.doi.org/10.1145/2739480.2754683

MAX test function OM : $\{0,1\}^n \to \{0,1,\ldots,n\}; x \mapsto \sum_{i=1}^n x_i$ only an upper bound of $O(\max\{n\log(n)/\lambda, \lambda n\})$ for the expected number of fitness evaluations was shown, we now determine the precise expected runtime to be $\Theta(\max\{n\log(n)/\lambda, n\lambda \log\log(\lambda)/\log(\lambda)\})$ for all values of $\lambda \in [1..n]$. We thus both improve the upper bound and give the first lower bound, which in addition matches the upper bound.

We further prove a strong concentration result for the runtime, showing that deviations above the expectation are unlikely: For all $\delta > 0$, the probability that the actual runtime exceeds a bound as above by a factor of $(1+\delta)$ is at most $O((n/\lambda^2)^{-\delta})$.

Our result on the expected runtime has two implications beyond showing that the $(1+(\lambda,\lambda))$ GA is slightly (but still by a super-constant factor) faster than what the previous work guaranteed. (i) The previous upper bound gave the best runtime guarantee for $\lambda = \Theta(\sqrt{\log n})$, namely $O(n\sqrt{\log n})$ with the old bound (and $\Theta(n\sqrt{\log n})$ with our new bound). From our new and sharp runtime estimate, however, we derive a better value for λ (together with the guarantee that it is asymptotically optimal), namely $\lambda = \Theta(\sqrt{\log(n)\log\log(n)/\log\log\log(n)})$. This gives an optimization time of $\Theta(n\sqrt{\log(n)\log\log\log(n)/\log\log(n)})$. Hence we also improve the performance by determining a better value for the parameter λ. (ii) Our analysis leading to these results also gives the desired additional insights in the working principles of this crossover operator and its interplay with mutation. The improved runtime guarantee is based on the observation that when generating λ offspring in parallel, some have a fitness significantly better than expected. We exploit this to show that sufficiently often we gain sufficiently many fitness levels in one generation. Interestingly, the good runtimes shown for the $(1+(\lambda,\lambda))$ GA only stem from better-than-expected individuals in the crossover phase, but not in the mutation phase.

With the few runtime results on crossover-based EAs and, also, still the majority of the runtime results for EA in general being for evolutionary algorithms having trivial population sizes, we feel that our work also advances the state of the art in terms of analysis methods. Our argument that one out of λ offspring can have a significantly better fitness than the expected fitness of one offspring resembles a similar one made by Jansen, De Jong, and Wegener [13], who used multiple fitness level gains to prove that for the $(1+\lambda)$ EA optimizing ONEMAX a linear speed-up (compared to $\lambda = 1$) exists if and only if $\lambda = O(\log(n)\log\log(n)/\log\log\log(n))$. Note that this result is different from ours in two respects, namely in that it does not show a positive influence of λ on the optimization time (number of fitness evaluation), but only on the number of generations, and in that there the better-than-expected offspring is generated by mutation, whereas by crossover in our setting. A second difference is that the random experiment producing the new generation for the $(1+(\lambda,\lambda))$ GA has stochastic dependencies that are not present in the $(1+\lambda)$ EA, which require different arguments (e.g., a balls-into-bins argument).

2. THE $(1+(\lambda,\lambda))$ GA

The $(1+(\lambda,\lambda))$ GA is a simple evolutionary algorithm using crossover. Following [2, 3] we present it here for the

Algorithm 1: The $(1+(\lambda,\lambda))$ GA from [2] with offspring population size λ, mutation probability p, and crossover bias c. The standard choices for the latter two parameters are $p = \lambda/n$ and $c = 1/\lambda$. The mutation operator mut_ℓ generates an offspring from one parent by flipping exactly ℓ random bits (without replacement). The crossover operator cross_c performs a biased uniform crossover, taking bits independently with probability c from the second argument and with probability $1-c$ from the first parent.

Initialization: Choose $x \in \{0,1\}^n$ uniformly at random and evaluate $f(x)$;
Optimization: for $t = 1, 2, 3, \ldots$ **do**
  Mutation phase: Sample ℓ from $\mathcal{B}(n,p)$;
  for $i = 1, \ldots, \lambda$ **do**
    $x^{(i)} \leftarrow \text{mut}_\ell(x)$ and evaluate $f(x^{(i)})$;
  Choose $x' \in \{x^{(1)}, \ldots, x^{(\lambda)}\}$ with $f(x') = \max\{f(x^{(1)}), \ldots, f(x^{(\lambda)})\}$ u.a.r.;
  Crossover phase: for $i = 1, \ldots, \lambda$ **do**
    $y^{(i)} \leftarrow \text{cross}_c(x, x')$ and evaluate $f(y^{(i)})$;
  Choose $y \in \{y^{(1)}, \ldots, y^{(\lambda)}\}$ with $f(y) = \max\{f(y^{(1)}), \ldots, f(y^{(\lambda)})\}$ u.a.r.;
  Selection step: if $f(y) \geq f(x)$ **then** $x \leftarrow y$;

maximization of pseudo-Boolean functions $f : \{0,1\}^n \to \mathbb{R}$. Its pseudo-code is given in Algorithm 1.

The $(1+(\lambda,\lambda))$ GA is initialized with a solution candidate drawn uniformly at random from $\{0,1\}^n$. It then proceeds in iterations (rounds) consisting of a mutation, a crossover, and a selection phase. In an important contrast to many other genetic algorithms, the mutation phase *precedes* the crossover phase. This allows to use crossover as a repair mechanism, as we shall discuss in more detail below.

In the *mutation phase* of the $(1+(\lambda,\lambda))$ GA, we create λ offspring from the current-best solution x by applying to it the mutation operator $\text{mut}_\ell(\cdot)$, which samples ℓ (different) positions uniformly at random and generates a new bit string from the input by flipping the bits in these ℓ positions. That is, $\text{mut}_\ell(x)$ is a bit string in which for ℓ random positions i the entry $x_i \in \{0,1\}$ is replaced by $1 - x_i$. The *step size* ℓ is chosen randomly according to a binomial distribution $\mathcal{B}(n,p)$ with n trials and success probability p; in our analyses we follow the suggestion in [3] and use $p = \lambda/n$. The expected distance of a random offspring to x is thus λ. To ensure that all mutants have the same distance from the father x, the same ℓ is used for all λ offspring. The fitness of the λ offspring is computed and the best one of them, x', is selected to take part in the crossover phase. If there are several offspring having maximal fitness, we pick one of them uniformly at random (u.a.r.).

When x is already close to an optimal solution, the offspring created in the mutation phase are typically all of much worse fitness than x. Our hope is though that they have discovered some parts of the optimum solution that is not yet reflected in x. In order to preserve these parts while at the same time not destroying the good parts of x, the $(1+(\lambda,\lambda))$ GA creates in the *crossover phase* λ offspring from x and x'. Each one of these offspring is sampled from a uniform crossover with bias c to take an entry from x'. That is, each of the offspring $\text{cross}_c(x, x')$ is created by taking independently for each position i the entry x'_i with probability c and taking the entry from x_i otherwise. Again we follow the suggestion from [3] and use $c = 1/\lambda$. With this choice, we try to ensure that the new individual y is close to x even then the mutation rate is high. Note that $\text{cross}_c(x, \text{mut}_\lambda(x))$ is just the outcome of applying to x standard-bit mutation with mutation probability $1/n$. Of course, due to the intermediate selection of x', our new individual y follows a more complicated distribution (which is the reason for the performance of our algorithm). Again we evaluate the fitness of the λ new offspring and select the best one of them, which we denote by y. If there are several offspring of maximal fitness, we simply take one of them uniformly at random.[1]

Finally, in the *selection step* the current-best solution x is replaced by its offspring y if and only if the fitness of y is at least as good as the one of x.

As common in the runtime analysis community, we do not specify a termination criterion. The simple reason is that we study as a theoretical performance measure the expected number of function evaluations that the $(1+(\lambda,\lambda))$ GA performs until it evaluates for the first time a search point of maximal fitness (the so-called optimization time). Of course, for an application to a real problem a termination criterion has to be specified.

3. RUNTIME ANALYSIS

Runtime analysis is one of the most successful theoretical tools to understand the performance of evolutionary algorithms. The *runtime* or *optimization time* of an algorithm (e.g., our $(1 + (\lambda, \lambda))$ GA) on a problem instance (e.g., the OneMax function) is the number of fitness evaluations that are performed until for the first time an optimal solution is evaluated.

If the algorithm is randomized (like our $(1 + (\lambda, \lambda))$ GA), this is a random variable T, and we usually make statements on the expected value $E[T]$ or give bounds that hold with some high probability, e.g., $1-1/n$. When regarding a problem with more than one instance (e.g., traveling salesman instance on n cities), we take a worst-case view. This is, we regard the maximum expected runtime over all instances, or we make statements like that the runtime satisfies a certain bound for all instances.

In this work, the optimization problem we regard is the classic OneMax test problem consisting of the single instance $\text{Om} : \{0,1\}^n \to \{0, 1, \ldots, n\}; x \mapsto \sum_{i=1}^n x_i$, that is, maximizing the number of ones in a bit-string. Despite the simplicity of the OneMax problem, analyzing randomized search heuristics on this function has spurred much of the progress in the theory of evolutionary computation in the last 20 years, as is documented, e.g., in the recent textbook [12].

Of course, when regarding the performance on a single test instance, then we should ensure that the algorithm does not exploit the fact that there is only one instance. A counter-example would be the algorithm that simply evaluates and outputs $x^* = (1, ..., 1)$, giving a perfect runtime of 1. One way of ensuring this is that we restrict ourselves to unbiased algorithms (see [16]) which treat bit-positions and bit-values in a symmetric fashion. Consequently, an unbiased algorithm for the OneMax problem has the same performance on all problems with isomorphic fitness landscape, in particular, on all (generalized) OneMax functions $\text{Om}_z : \{0,1\}^n \to \{0, 1, \ldots, n\}; x \mapsto \text{eq}(x, z)$ for $z \in \{0,1\}^n$, where $\text{eq}(x, z)$ denotes the number of bit-positions in which x and z agree. It is easy to see that the $(1 + (\lambda, \lambda))$ GA is unbiased (for all parameter settings). We will henceforth not stress this fact anymore. Any other algorithms we will discuss are also all unbiased.

The result we build on is this work is the runtime analysis of the $(1 + (\lambda, \lambda))$ GA for various parameter settings on the OneMax problem in [3]. This analysis suggested, in particular, certain settings for the parameters to which we will restrict ourselves in the following. For these settings, the following upper bound for the expected runtime was proven (Theorem 4 in [3] for $\lambda = k$, note that the case $\lambda = 1$ excluded there is trivial for $\lambda = k$ since in this case, the $(1 + (\lambda, \lambda))$ GA imitates the $(1 + 1)$ EA).

Theorem 1 ([3]). *Let $\lambda \in [1..n]$, possibly depending on n. The expected optimization time of the $(1+(\lambda,\lambda))$ GA with mutation probability $p = \lambda/n$ and crossover bias $c = 1/\lambda$ on OneMax is*

$$O\left(\max\left\{\frac{n \log n}{\lambda}, \lambda n\right\}\right).$$

In particular, for $\lambda = \Theta(\sqrt{\log n})$, the expected optimization time is of order at most $n\sqrt{\log n}$.

The main result of this work is the following improvement and strengthening of the previous result.

Theorem 2 (our main result). *Let $\lambda \in [1..n]$. The expected optimization time of the $(1+(\lambda,\lambda))$ GA with mutation probability $p = \lambda/n$ and crossover bias $c = 1/\lambda$ on the OneMax test function is*

$$\Theta\left(\max\left\{\frac{n \log(n)}{\lambda}, \frac{n\lambda \log\log(\lambda)}{\log(\lambda)}\right\}\right).$$

For all $\delta > 0$, the probability that the actual runtime exceeds a bound of this magnitude by a factor of more than $(1 + \delta)$ is at most $O((n/\lambda^2)^{-\delta})$.

The expected runtime is minimized by the parameter choice $\lambda = \Theta(\sqrt{\log(n) \log\log(n)/ \log\log\log(n)})$. This yields an expected optimization time of

$$\Theta(n\sqrt{\log(n) \log\log\log(n)/ \log\log(n)}).$$

4. NOTATION AND TECHNICAL TOOLS

In this section, besides fixing some very elementary notation, we collect the main technical tools we shall use. Mostly, these are large deviations bounds of various types. For the convenience of the reader, we first state the known ones. We then prove a tail bound for sums of geometric random variables with expectations bounded from above by the reciprocals of the first positive integers. We finally state the well-known additive drift theorem.

[1]In [2, Section 4.4] and [3] a different selection rule is suggested for the crossover phase, which is more suitable for functions with large plateaus of the same fitness value. Since we consider in this work only the OneMax function, for which both algorithms are identical by symmetry reasons, we refrain from stating in Algorithm 1 the slightly more complicated version proposed there, which selects the parent solution x only if there is no offspring $\neq x$ of fitness value at least as good as the one of x.

4.1 Notation

As the reader has experienced already, we write $[a..b]$ to denote the set $\{z \in \mathbb{Z} \mid a \leq z \leq b\}$ of integers between a and b. We also use the short-hand $[a] := [1..a]$. We write $\log(n)$ to denote the binary logarithm of n and $\ln(n)$ to denote the natural logarithm of n. However, to avoid unnecessary case distinctions, we define $\log(n) := 1$ for all $n \leq 2$ and $\ln(n) := 1$ for all $n \leq e$.

4.2 Known Chernoff Bounds

The following large deviation bounds are well-known and can be found, e.g., in [1]. We call all these bounds Chernoff bounds (CB) despite the fact that it is now known that some have been found earlier by other researchers.

THEOREM 3 (CLASSIC CHERNOFF BOUNDS). *Let $X_1, \ldots, X_n$ be independent random variables taking values in $[0,1]$. Let $X = \sum_{i=1}^n X_i$.*

(a). Let $\delta \geq 0$. Then
$\Pr[X \geq (1+\delta)E[X]] \leq (\frac{e^\delta}{(1+\delta)^{1+\delta}})^{E[X]}$.

(b). Let $\delta \in [0,1]$. Then
$\Pr[X \geq (1+\delta)E[X]] \leq \exp(-\delta^2 E[X]/3)$.

(c). Let $\delta \in [0,1]$. Then
$\Pr[X \leq (1-\delta)E[X]] \leq \exp(-\delta^2 E[X]/2)$.

Binary random variables $X_1, \ldots, X_n$ are called *negatively correlated*, if for all $I \subseteq [1..n]$ we have $\Pr[\forall i \in I : X_i = 0] \leq \prod_{i \in I} \Pr[X_i = 0]$ and $\Pr[\forall i \in I : X_i = 1] \leq \prod_{i \in I} \Pr[X_i = 1]$.

THEOREM 4 (CB, NEGATIVE CORRELATION). *Let $X_1, \ldots, X_n$ be negatively correlated binary random variables. Let $a_1, \ldots, a_n \in [0,1]$ and $X = \sum_{i=1}^n a_i X_i$. Then X satisfies the Chernoff bounds given in Theorem 3 (b) and (c).*

Chernoff bounds also hold for *hypergeometric* distributions. Let A be any set of n elements. Let B be a subset of A having m elements. If Y is a random subset of A of N elements (chosen uniformly at random from all N-element subsets of A, then $X := |Y \cap B|$ has a hypergeometric distribution with parameters (n, N, m).

THEOREM 5 (CB, HYPERGEOMETRIC DISTRIBUTIONS). *If X has a hypergeometric distribution with parameters (n, N, m), then $E[X] = Nm/n$ and X satisfies the Chernoff bounds given in Theorem 3.*

4.3 A Chernoff Bound for Geometric Random Variables

To prove the concentration statement in Theorem 2, we need a tail bound for the upper tail of a sum of a sequence of independent geometric random variables having expectations that are upper-bounded by a multiple of the harmonic series. While generally Chernoff bounds for geometric random variables are less understood than for bounded random variables, Witt [23] proves such a bound. Witt's bound is sufficient for our purposes. For two reasons, we prove the following alternative result below. (i) Our proof is a simple reduction to the well-understood coupon collector process, and thus much simpler than Witt's. (ii) At the same time, our proof gives a stronger bound (for our setting, Witt's bound on the failure probability is roughly the fourth root of ours). Since scenarios as treated here are quite common in runtime analysis (for example, they appear whenever the fitness level method is employed in a situation where the probability of a progress is inversely proportional to the fitness distance from the optimum), we feel that presenting our result is justified here.

We say that X has a geometric distribution with success probability p if for each positive integer k we have $\Pr[X = k] = (1-p)^{k-1}p$. For all $n \in \mathbb{N}$, let $H_n := \sum_{i=1}^n (1/i)$ denote the nth Harmonic number.

LEMMA 6. *Let $X_1, \ldots, X_n$ be independent geometric random variables with success probabilities p_i. Assume that there is a number $C \leq 1$ such that $p_i \geq Ci/n$ for all $i \in [n]$. Let $X = \sum_{i=1}^n X_i$. Then $E[X] \leq (1/C)nH_n \leq (1/C)n(\ln(n)+1)$ and $\Pr[X \geq (1+\delta)(1/C)n\ln(n)] \leq n^{-\delta}$ for all $\delta > 0$.*

Proof. For $i \in [n]$, let X_i' be a geometric random variable with success probability exactly $Ci/n =: p_i'$. Let the X_i' be independent. Then X_i' dominates X_i for all $i \in [n]$, and consequently, $X' := \sum_{i=1}^n X_i'$ dominates X. Recall that a random variable Y' dominates a random variable Y if for all $r \in \mathbb{R}$, $\Pr[Y \geq r] \leq \Pr[Y' \geq r]$. Note that this implies that $E[Y] \leq E[Y']$ and that all upper tail bounds for Y' immediately take over to Y. Consequently, we can conveniently argue for X' instead of X.

For the statement on the expectation, we recall that the expectation of a geometric random variable with success probability p is $1/p$. Consequently, by linearity of expectation, we have $E[X'] = \sum_{i=1}^n E[X_i'] = \sum_{i=1}^n (1/p_i') = (n/C)\sum_{i=1}^n (1/i) = (n/C)H_n$.

For the tail bound, consider the following coupon collector process. There are n different types of coupons. In each round (independently), with probability C we obtain a coupon having a type chosen uniformly at random and with probability $1-C$ we obtain nothing. We are interested in the number T of rounds until we have each type of coupon at least once. For $i \in [n]$, let T_i denote the number of rounds needed to get a coupon of a type not yet in our possession given that we have already $n-i$ different types. In other words, T_i is the time we need to go from "i types missing" down to "$i-1$ types missing". We observe that T_i has the same distribution as X_i and that $T = \sum_{i=1}^n T_i$. Consequently, T and X are equally distributed.

The advantage of this reformulation is that it allows us a different view on $X' \sim T$: The probability that after t rounds of the coupon collector process we do not have a fixed type is exactly $(1-C/n)^t$. Using a union bound, we see that the probability that after t rounds some coupon is missing, is at most $n(1-C/n)^t$. For $t = (1+\delta)(1/C)n\ln(n)$, this is at most $n(1-C/n)^t \leq n\exp(-Ct/n) = n\exp(-(1+\delta)\ln(n)) = n^{-\delta}$. □

Note that in the proof of Lemma 6, once we have defined the coupon collector process (but not before), we could have also used multiplicative drift. This would, however, not have given better bound, nor a shorter proof.

4.4 Additive Drift

Drift analysis comprises a couple of methods to derive from information about the expected progress (e.g., in terms of the fitness distance) a result about the time needed to achieve a goal (e.g., finding an optimal solution). We shall several times use the following additive drift theorem from [11] (see also Theorem 2.7 in [18]).

THEOREM 7 (ADDITIVE DRIFT THEOREM). *Let $X_0, X_1, \ldots$ be a Markov process over a finite state space S. Let $g : S \to \mathbb{R}_{\geq 0}$. Let $T := \min\{t \geq 0 \mid X_t = 0\}$. Let $\delta > 0$.*

(i) If for all t, we have $E[X_t - X_{t+1} | X_t > 0] \geq \delta$, then $E[T|X_0] \leq g(X_0)/\delta$.

(ii) If for all t, we have $E[X_t - X_{t+1} | X_t > 0] \leq \delta$, then $E[T|X_0] \geq g(X_0)/\delta$.

5. PROOF OF THE UPPER BOUND

In this section, we prove the upper bound statement of Theorem 2, that is, that the $(1 + (\lambda, \lambda))$ GA with standard parameter settings optimizes every ONEMAX function using a number of $O\left(\max\left\{\frac{n \log(n)}{\lambda}, \frac{n\lambda \log\log(\lambda)}{\log(\lambda)}\right\}\right)$ fitness evaluations both in expectation and with probability $1 - n^{-c}$, where c is an arbitrary positive constant.

The proof of the previous upper bound (Theorem 1) was based on the fitness level method (first used in [21] in the proof of Theorem 1, more explicit in [22], see also [18]). In its classic version, this method pessimistically estimates the runtime via the sum of the times needed to leave each fitness level. It thus does not profit from the fact that a typical run of the algorithm might not visit every fitness level. By a more careful analysis of the mutation phase (Lemma 8) and the crossover phase (Lemma 9), we shall show that this indeed happens. For all values of λ, we obtain that when starting an iteration with a search point x having *fitness distance* $d(x) := n - \text{OM}(x)$ at least $n \log\log(\lambda)/\log(\lambda)$, then the average fitness improvement is $\Omega(\log(\lambda)/\log\log(\lambda))$. Consequently, additive drift analysis (Theorem 7) tells us that only $O(n \log\log(\lambda)/\log(\lambda))$ iterations are needed to find a search point with fitness distance at most $n \log\log(\lambda)/\log(\lambda)$. Note that the fitness range from the typical initial fitness distance of $n/2$ to a fitness distance of $n \log\log(\lambda)/\log(\lambda)$ contains $\Omega(n)$ fitness levels. Hence the previous analysis would have given only a bound of $O(n)$ rounds.

There is an intuitive explanation for these numbers based on the balls-into-bins paradigm. When our current search point x is in distance n/D from the optimum, then already $x^{(1)}$ has an expected number of at least λ/D "good bits", i.e., bit positions that are zero in x and one in $x^{(1)}$. The same is true for x'. Each of these good bits is copied in each of the $y^{(j)}$ generated in the crossover phase with probability $1/\lambda$. The total number of copies of good bits in $y^{(1)}, \ldots, y^{(\lambda)}$ thus is around λ/D again. Since they are uniformly spread over the $y^{(j)}$, we are in a situation closely resembling the *balls-into-bins* scenario, in which λ/D balls are uniformly thrown into λ bins. By a result of Raab and Steger [19], we know that when D is at most polylogarithmic in λ, then the most-loaded bin will contain $\Theta(\log(\lambda)/\log\log(\lambda))$ balls. For our setting, this means that we expect one of the $y^{(j)}$ to inherit $\Omega(\log(\lambda)/\log\log(\lambda))$ good bits. Unfortunately, since we do not distribute the good bits completely independently, we cannot transform this intuitive argument into a rigorous proof, but need to argue differently.

We start by analyzing the mutation phase. Since we aim at understanding those iterations where we gain more than a constant number of fitness levels, we restrict ourselves to the case that $\lambda = \omega(1)$, which eases the calculations.

LEMMA 8. *Let $\varepsilon > 0$. Assume that $\lambda = \omega(1)$. Let $x \in \{0,1\}^n$. Let D be such that $d := d(x) = n/D$. Assume that $D = o(\lambda)$. Consider one run of the mutation phase of Algorithm 1. As in the description of the algorithm, denote by ℓ the actual mutation strength and by x' the winner individual. Let $B' := \{i \in [n] \mid x_i = 0 \wedge x'_i = 1\}$ the set of 1-bits that x' has gained over x.*

Then with probability $1 - o(1)$, we have both $|\ell - \lambda| \leq \varepsilon\lambda$ and $|B'| \geq (1-\varepsilon)\lambda/D$.

We omit the proof for reasons of space. It follows easily from Theorem 3 and 5.

We next analyze a run of the crossover phase. While in the previous lemma we only exploited that an individual generated in the mutation phase has roughly as many good bits as expected, we shall now exploit that the best of the λ individuals generated in the crossover phase is much better than the average one.

LEMMA 9. *Let $x, x' \in \{0,1\}^n$ such that their Hamming distance $\ell := H(x, x')$ satisfies $\ell \leq 2\lambda - 2$. Let D' be such that $B' := \{i \in [n] \mid x_i = 0 \wedge x'_i = 1\}$ satisfies $|B'| \geq \lambda/D'$. Consider a run of the crossover phase starting with these variable values and computing an offspring $y \in \{0,1\}^n$.*

Then with probability at least $1 - 1/e$, we have $\text{OM}(y) - \text{OM}(x) \geq \lfloor \min\{(\frac{1}{2}\ln(\lambda) - 1)/(\ln\ln(\lambda) + \ln(D')), \lambda/D'\}\rfloor$.

Proof. Let $\gamma \leq \lambda/D'$ be a positive integer. Consider the outcome $y^{(j)}$ of a single crossover operation for some $j \in [\lambda]$ in Algorithm 1. Let A_j be the event that $\text{OM}(y^{(j)}) \geq \text{OM}(x) + \gamma$. This event in particular occurs when the crossover operation selects γ "good bits" (those with index in B') from x' and none of the "bad bits" (those, in which x and x' differ, but that are not in B'). Consequently,

$$\begin{aligned}
\Pr[A_j] &\geq \binom{|B'|}{\gamma}(1/\lambda)^{\gamma}(1-1/\lambda)^{\ell-\gamma} \qquad (1)\\
&\geq \left(|B'|/\gamma\right)^{\gamma}(1/\lambda)^{\gamma}(1-1/\lambda)^{2(\lambda-1)}\\
&\geq (\lambda/(D'\gamma))^{\gamma}(1/\lambda)^{\gamma}(1/e^2)\\
&= \exp(-2 - \gamma\ln\gamma - \gamma\ln D').
\end{aligned}$$

For $\gamma = \lfloor \min\{(\frac{1}{2}\ln(\lambda) - 1)/(\ln\ln(\lambda) + \ln(D')), \lambda/D'\}\rfloor$ we have $\Pr[A_j] \geq 1/\lambda$. Consequently, the probability that at least one of the A_j holds, is at least $1 - (1 - 1/\lambda)^{\lambda} \geq 1 - 1/e$. □

We note that the argument up to (1) is very similar to the reasoning in the proof of Theorem 5 in [13], where it is shown that the $(1 + \lambda)$ EA optimizing ONEMAX performs superconstant improvements in the early part of the optimization process. The choice of our γ, however, is different due to the different relation of λ and n. Interestingly, in the analysis of the mutation phase, such arguments do not seem to give significant additional improvement (recall that there we only used the expected gain from a fixed single offspring).

Above, we showed that in the early part of the optimization process, we regularly gain more than one fitness level in one iteration. For the remainder, we re-use the fitness level type argument of [3], which is summarized in the following lemma (Lemma 7 of [2] in the special case that $k = \lambda$).

LEMMA 10. *Assume $\lambda \geq 2$. In the notation of the $(1 + (\lambda, \lambda))$ GA, the probability that one iteration produces a* *search point y that is strictly better than the parent x, is at least*

$$p_{d(x)} := C\left(1-\left(\frac{n-d(x)}{n}\right)^{\lambda^2/2}\right),$$

where C is an absolute constant.

We are now ready to prove the main result of this section.

Proof of the upper bound in Theorem 2. We regard the different regimes of the optimization process separately, since they need very different arguments. If $\lambda = \omega(1)$, then let $d_0 := n \ln\ln(\lambda)/\ln(\lambda)$, else let $d_0 = n$ (and there is no first phase).

First phase: From the random starting point to a solution x with $d(x) \leq d_0 := n\ln\ln(\lambda)/\ln(\lambda)$ in $O(n\log\log(\lambda)/\log(\lambda))$ iterations. Let $\bar{D} = \ln(\lambda)/\ln\ln(\lambda)$. Let $x \in \{0,1\}^n$ be any search point with $d(x) > d_0 = n/\bar{D}$. By Lemma 8 and 9, we see that with probability $p = 1-(1/e)-o(1)$, one iteration of the main loop of Algorithm 1 produces a solution y with $\text{OM}(y) \geq \text{OM}(x) + \Delta$, where Δ is some number satisfying $\Delta = \Omega(\log(\lambda)/\log\log(\lambda))$. This seems to call for an application of additive drift (Theorem 7), but in particular for the derivation of the large deviation claim, the following hand-made solution seems to be easier (despite several tail bounds for additive drift existing, see, e.g., [15] and the references therein).

For $t = 1, 2, \ldots$ lets us define the following binary random variable X_t. If at the start of iteration t we have $d(x) > d_0$, then $X_t = 1$ if and only if $\text{OM}(y) \geq \text{OM}(x) + \Delta$. If $d(x) \leq d_0$, let $X_t = 1$ with probability p independent from all other random decisions. For all $T > 0$, we observe that $X_T := \sum_{i=1}^{T} X_t \geq n/\Delta$ implies that $T_0 \leq T$, that is, our $(1+(\lambda,\lambda))$ GA needed at most T iterations to find a search point x with $d(x) \leq d_0$. We have $E[X_T] = Tp$ and $\Pr[X_T \leq (1/2)E[X_T]] \leq \exp(-E[X_T]/8)$. In particular, for $T = 2n/(\Delta p)$, we have $E[X_T] = 2n/\Delta$ and $\Pr[X_T \leq n/\Delta] \leq \exp(-E[X_T]/8) = \exp(-n/(4\Delta)) = \exp(-n^{1-o(1)})$.

Second phase: From a solution with d-value at most d_0 to one with d-value at most $d_1 := \lfloor n/(2\lambda^2)\rfloor$ in $O(n\log\log(\lambda)/\log(\lambda))$ iterations. Once we have a solution of fitness distance at most d_0, we use the fitness level argument analogous to the proof of Theorem 1. We reformulate the proof slightly to allow proving a large deviation bound for the optimization time. By Lemma 10, the remaining number of iterations is dominated by a sum of geometric random variables $X_{d_0}, \ldots, X_1$ where $\Pr[X_d = m] = (1-p_d)^{m-1}p_d$ for all $m = 1, 2, \ldots$ and $p_d = C\,(1-(\frac{n-d(x)}{n})^{\lambda^2/2})$ is as in Lemma 10.

Note that for $d \geq d_1$, $p_d = C'$ for some absolute constant C'. Hence the expected number T_1 of iterations to reduce the fitness distance to d_1 is at most $E[T_1] = E[X_{d_0} + \cdots + X_{d_1-1}] \leq (1/C')(d_0 - d_1) \leq (1/C')d_0 = O(n\log\log(\lambda)/\log(\lambda))$ by linearity of expectation. Since each iteration with $d(x) \geq d_1$, independent of what happened in the previous iterations, has a success chance of at least C', we observe that the probability to have fewer than $(d_0 - d_1)$ successes in $2(1/C')(d_0-d_1)$ iterations is at most $\exp(-(d_0-d_1)/(4C')) = \exp(-\Theta(d_0)) = \exp(-n^{1-o(1)})$. Note that to apply the (multiplicative) Chernoff bound, here we used the "moderate independence" argument of Lemma 1.18 of [1].

Third phase: From a solution with fitness distance at most d_1 to an optimal solution in $O(n\log(n)/\lambda^2)$ iterations. We continue to use the fitness level method as in the previous section of the proof, but note that for $d \leq d_1$, we have $p_d = C(1-(1-d/n)^{\lambda^2/2}) \geq C(1-\exp(d\lambda^2/(2n))) \geq Cd\lambda^2/(4n)$, where we used the estimate $e^{-x} \leq 1 - x/2$ valid for all $x \in [0,1]$. We thus see that the remaining time T_2 to get to the optimal solution is dominated by $X = X_{d_1} + \cdots + X_1$, which is a sum of independent geometric random variables with harmonic expectations. Hence by Lemma 6, we have $E[T_2] \leq E[X] \leq \frac{4n(\ln(d_1)+1)}{C\lambda^2} = O(n\log(n)/\lambda^2)$ and $\Pr[T_2 \geq (1+\delta)\frac{4n\ln(d_1)}{C\lambda^2}] \leq d_1^{-\delta}$ for any $\delta > 0$.

In total, we see that the number $T = T_0 + T_1 + T_2$ of iterations until the optimum is found has an expectation of at most $E[T] = E[T_0] + E[T_1] + E[T_2] = O(\max\{n\log(n)/\lambda^2, n\log\log(\lambda)/\log(\lambda)\})$ and the probability that this upper bound is exceeded by a constant factor of $(1+\delta)$ is only $O((n/\lambda^2)^{-\delta})$.

Since in each iteration the fitness of $O(\lambda)$ search points is computed, we proved the claimed upper bound of $O(\max\{n\log(n)/\lambda, n\lambda\log\log(\lambda)/\log(\lambda)\})$ for the expected optimization time, and again, exceeding this expectation by a factor of $1+\delta$ has a probability of only $O((n/\lambda^2)^{-\delta})$. □

6. A MATCHING LOWER BOUND

In this section, we prove the first lower bound for the runtime of the $(1+(\lambda,\lambda))$ GA. It matches the new upper bound proven in the previous section, so the two bound determine the asymptotic runtime of the $(1+(\lambda,\lambda))$ GA for all $\lambda \in [1..n]$. This sharp runtime result immediately gives the optimal value for the population size λ.

THEOREM 11. *For all $\lambda \leq n$ the $(1+(\lambda,\lambda))$ GA with the standard parameter setting $p = \lambda/n$ and $c = 1/\lambda$ needs an expected number of*

$$\Omega\left(\max\left\{\frac{n\log(n)}{\lambda}, \frac{n\lambda\log\log(\lambda)}{\log(\lambda)}\right\}\right)$$

fitness evaluations to find the optimum of any ONEMAX *function.*

To prove the theorem, we show that the expected optimization time is both $\Omega(\frac{n\log(n)}{\lambda})$ and $\Omega(\frac{n\lambda\log\log(\lambda)}{\log(\lambda)})$ (at least for sufficient ranges of λ). We do this separately in the following two subsections. The proof of Theorem 11 then is an immediate consequence of Lemmas 12 and 13.

We remark without proof that also the lower tail of the runtime distribution admits tail bounds. Since such bounds are less relevant for the use of algorithms, we do not give further details.

6.1 First Lower Bound

To prove that $\Omega(n\log(n)/\lambda)$ is a lower bound, we use the standard argument that in order to find the optimum at least each bit that was not initially set to one has to be touched at least once by a mutation operator. This argument has been used, e.g., in the classic proof for the lower bound of the runtime of the $(1+1)$ EA in [8]. We have to be slightly more careful though, because our random experiment has two types of dependencies: (i) Each individual in the mutation phase is not generated by standard bit mutation (flipping each bit independently), but by flipping a fixed number ℓ of bits. (ii) This ℓ is chosen randomly, but all λ individuals generated in one mutation phase are generated using the same value of ℓ.

LEMMA 12. *Let λ be an integral function of n with $1 \leq \lambda \leq n/4$. The probability that the $(1+(\lambda,\lambda))$ GA with standard parameters $p = \lambda/n$ and $c = 1/\lambda$ has found the optimum within $T = \lfloor n\log(n)/(8\lambda^2)\rfloor$ iterations (equivalent to $2\lambda T$ fitness evaluations) is $\exp(-\Omega(\min\{\lambda T, \sqrt{n}\}))$. In particular, the expected optimization time is $\Omega(n\log(n)/\lambda)$.*

Proof. Using the Chernoff bound of Theorem 3 (c), we see that with probability $1-\exp(-\Omega(n))$, the initial search point has at least $n/3$ bits valued zero ("missing bits"). Let us consider what happens in the first $T = \lfloor n\log(n)/(8\lambda^2)\rfloor$ iterations. Denote by $\ell_1,\ldots,\ell_T$ the values of ℓ chosen by the algorithm in these iterations. Again, with probability $1-\exp(-\Omega(n))$, all ℓ_i are at most $n/2$ (Chernoff bound of Theorem 3 (a) and union bound, note that a binomially distributed random variable is a sum of independent $0,1$ random variables). Using these arguments a second time as well as the fact that the ℓ_i are independent, we obtain that with probability $1-\exp(-\Omega(\lambda T))$, we have $\sum_{i=1}^T \ell_i \leq 2\lambda T$. Conditional on none of these exceptional event occurring, the probability that a particular one of the missing bits is never flipped in the mutation phases of the first T iterations is

$$\prod_{i=1}^{T}(1-\ell_i/n)^\lambda \geq \prod_{i=1}^{T}\exp(-2\ell_i/n)^\lambda = \exp\Big(-2\lambda\sum_{i=1}^{T}\ell_i/n\Big)$$
$$\geq \exp(-4\lambda^2 T/n) \geq n^{-1/2},$$

where we have used in the first step that $1-c \geq e^{-2c}$ for $0<c<1/2$.

The events that a bit was never flipped in a certain time interval are not independent, since also in a single application of the mutation operator the bits are not treated independently. However, since we always flip a fixed number of bits (not necessarily the same in each iteration), these events are negatively correlated. We omit this proof, because it is technical and lengthy, but neither difficult and nor insightful. From this, we conclude that the probability that there is a missing bit that was never flipped up to iteration T is at least $1-(1-n^{-1/2})^{n/3} \geq 1-\exp(-n^{-1/2})^{n/3} = 1-\exp(-n^{1/2}/3)$, this time using the estimate $1+x \leq e^x$ valid for all $x \in \mathbb{R}$.

Consequently, with probability at least $1-\exp(-\Omega(n)) - \exp(-\Omega(\lambda T)) - \exp(-n^{1/2}/3)$, the $(1+(\lambda,\lambda))$ GA needs more than T iterations to find the optimum. This immediately implies the claimed bound on the expected optimization time. □

6.2 Second Lower Bound

We prove the second lower bound via drift analysis. We show that the expected fitness increase in each round is $O(\log(\lambda)/\log\log(\lambda))$. Then the additive drift theorem yields the lower bound on the expected optimization time. While our arguments are valid also for constant λ, in particular the asymptotic notation becomes easier when assuming $\lambda = \omega(1)$. We can make this assumption freely, since for constant λ the first lower bound is stronger anyway.

LEMMA 13. *Let $\lambda = \omega(1)$. Then the expected optimization time of the $(1+(\lambda,\lambda))$ GA with parameters $p = \lambda/n$ and $c = 1/\lambda$ is at least $\Omega(n\lambda\log\log(\lambda)/\log(\lambda))$.*

Proof. Let x be any search point different from the optimum. We first analyze what happens in a typical iteration of the main loop of the $(1+(\lambda,\lambda))$ GA and later treat the exceptional cases. Let ℓ, x', and $y^{(1)},\ldots,y^{(\lambda)}$ be as in the pseudo-code of Algorithm 1.

With probability $1-\exp(-\Theta(\lambda))$, we have $\ell \leq 2\lambda$ (Chernoff bound of Theorem 3 (b)). Hence, trivially, $B := \{i \in [n] \mid x_i = 0 \wedge x'_i = 1\}$ has cardinality at most 2λ. Let $Y_j := \{i \in B \mid y_i^{(j)} = 1\}$ the set of new 1-bits that made it into $y^{(j)}$. We aim at showing that $|Y_j|$ is not very large. We have $E[|Y_j|] = |B|/\lambda \leq 2$. There is nothing to show if $E[|Y_j|] = 0$, hence let us assume that $E[|Y_j|] > 0$. Let $r := (2e\ln(\lambda)/\ln\ln(\lambda))/E[|Y_j|]$ and note that $r \geq e\ln(\lambda)/\ln\ln(\lambda) =: r'$. Then the strong version of the Chernoff bound (Theorem 3 (a)) yields

$$\begin{aligned}
&\Pr[|Y_j| \geq 2e\ln(\lambda)/\ln\ln(\lambda)] = \Pr[|Y_j| \geq rE[|Y_j|]] \\
&\leq (\tfrac{e^{r-1}}{r^r})^{E[|Y_j|]} \leq (e/r)^{rE[|Y_j|]} = (e/r)^{2r'} \leq (e/r')^{2r'} \\
&= \exp(\ln((e/r')^{2r'})) = \exp(-2e\ln(\lambda)(1-o(1)) \\
&= \lambda^{-2e+o(1)}.
\end{aligned}$$

Hence, with probability at least $1-\lambda^{-2e+1+o(1)}$, none of the $|Y_j|$ is larger than $2r'$, which implies that $\textsc{Om}(y) \leq \textsc{Om}(x) + 2r'$.

It remains to treat the exceptional cases. If $\ell > 2\lambda$, which happens with probability at most $\exp(-\Theta(\lambda))$, the expected value of ℓ is still only $E[\ell|\ell > 2\lambda] < 3\lambda+1$, and thus $E[\textsc{Om}(y)] \leq \textsc{Om}(x) + 3\lambda + 1$. The second exceptional case occurs when $\ell \leq 2\lambda$, but (with a probability of at most $\lambda^{-2e+1+o(1)}$) we have $\textsc{Om}(y) > \textsc{Om}(x) + 2r'$. In this case, however, we still have $\textsc{Om}(y) \leq \textsc{Om}(x) + \ell \leq \textsc{Om}(x) + 2\lambda$.

From all this, we see that

$$\begin{aligned}
&E[\textsc{Om}(y) - \textsc{Om}(x)] \\
&\leq (1-\exp(-\Theta(\lambda))) \\
&\quad \Big((1-\lambda^{-2e+1+o(1)})(2e\log(\lambda)/\log\log(\lambda)) + \lambda^{-2e+1+o(1)}2\lambda\Big) \\
&\quad + \exp(-\Theta(\lambda))(3\lambda+1) \\
&\leq O(\log(\lambda)/\log\log(\lambda)).
\end{aligned}$$

We now apply the classic additive drift theorem (Theorem 7) and obtain an expected number of rounds of $\Omega(n\log\log(\lambda)/\log(\lambda))$, equivalent to an optimization time of $\Omega(n\lambda\log\log(\lambda)/\log(\lambda))$. □

7. CONCLUSION

We conducted a tight runtime analysis for the $(1+(\lambda,\lambda))$ GA on OneMax giving an improved upper bound for the expected optimization time, the first lower bound (which matches the upper bound for all values of λ), and a tail bound for the upper tail of the runtime distribution. This analysis both shows that the $(1+(\lambda,\lambda))$ GA is faster than what could be shown in [3], and it gives the asymptotically optimal value for the off-spring population size λ, again leading to a super-constant factor speed-up over the runtime stemming from the value giving the best bound in the previous work.

Our sharp bounds also give more insight in the working principles of this algorithm. In particular, we observe that in its crossover phase generating λ offspring in parallel often produces at least one offspring that is significantly better that the expected outcome of a crossover application. This allows to gain several (including regularly a super-constant number in the early time of the optimization process) fitness levels in one iteration. This advantage of larger offspring population sizes seems to have been rarely analyzed rigorously (with the analyses of the $(1+\lambda)$ EA in [6, 13] being the only exceptions known to us). The more common use of larger offspring population sizes in the literature seems to be that an offspring population size of λ reduces the waiting time for a fitness level gain by approximately a factor of λ (given that this waiting time is large enough). This latter argument, naturally, does not reduce the (total) optimization time (number of fitness evaluations), but only the parallel one (number of generations).

With the proof methods developed in this work, which include a number of clever combinations of drift and Chernoff bounds we are optimistic that it is now possible to analyze the $(1+(\lambda,\lambda))$ GA also on more complicated optimization problems. The first experimental results for several standard test functions [3] and combinatorial optimization problems [10] suggest that this is a fruitful direction of research.

Acknowledgments

We thank an unknown reviewer for very detailed comments and pointing us to the work Witt [23].

8. REFERENCES

[1] B. Doerr. Analyzing randomized search heuristics: Tools from probability theory. In A. Auger and B. Doerr, editors, *Theory of Randomized Search Heuristics*, pages 1–20. World Scientific Publishing, 2011. Available at http://www.worldscientific.com/doi/suppl/10.1142/7438/suppl_file/7438_chap01.pdf.

[2] B. Doerr, C. Doerr, and F. Ebel. Lessons from the black-box: Fast crossover-based genetic algorithms. In *Proceedings of the Annual Genetic and Evolutionary Computation Conference (GECCO'13)*, pages 781–788. ACM, 2013.

[3] B. Doerr, C. Doerr, and F. Ebel. From black-box complexity to designing new genetic algorithms. *Theoretical Computer Science*, 567:87–104, 2015.

[4] B. Doerr, E. Happ, and C. Klein. Crossover can provably be useful in evolutionary computation. *Theoretical Computer Science*, 425:17–33, 2012.

[5] B. Doerr, D. Johannsen, T. Kötzing, F. Neumann, and M. Theile. More effective crossover operators for the all-pairs shortest path problem. *Theoretical Computer Science*, 471:12–26, 2013.

[6] B. Doerr and M. Künnemann. Optimizing linear functions with the (1+λ) evolutionary algorithm—different asymptotic runtimes for different instances. *Theoretical Computer Science*, 561:3–23, 2015.

[7] B. Doerr and M. Theile. Improved analysis methods for crossover-based algorithms. In *Proceedings of the Annual Genetic and Evolutionary Computation Conference (GECCO'09)*, pages 247–254. ACM, 2009.

[8] S. Droste, T. Jansen, and I. Wegener. On the analysis of the (1+1) evolutionary algorithm. *Theoretical Computer Science*, 276:51–81, 2002.

[9] S. Fischer and I. Wegener. The Ising model on the ring: Mutation versus recombination. In *Proceedings of the Annual Genetic and Evolutionary Computation Conference (GECCO'04)*, volume 3102 of *Lecture Notes in Computer Science*, pages 1113–1124. Springer, 2004.

[10] B. W. Goldman and W. F. Punch. Parameter-less population pyramid. In *Proceedings of the Annual Genetic and Evolutionary Computation Conference (GECCO'14)*, pages 785–792. ACM, 2014.

[11] J. He and X. Yao. Drift analysis and average time complexity of evolutionary algorithms. *Artificial Intelligence*, 127:57–85, 2001.

[12] T. Jansen. *Analyzing Evolutionary Algorithms—The Computer Science Perspective*. Springer, 2013.

[13] T. Jansen, K. A. De Jong, and I. Wegener. On the choice of the offspring population size in evolutionary algorithms. *Evolutionary Computation*, 13:413–440, 2005.

[14] T. Jansen and I. Wegener. The analysis of evolutionary algorithms – a proof that crossover really can help. *Algorithmica*, 34:47–66, 2002.

[15] T. Kötzing. Concentration of first hitting times under additive drift. In *Proceedings of the Annual Genetic and Evolutionary Computation Conference (GECCO'14)*, pages 1391–1398. ACM, 2014.

[16] P. K. Lehre and C. Witt. Black-box search by unbiased variation. *Algorithmica*, 64:623–642, 2012.

[17] M. Mitchell, J. H. Holland, and S. Forrest. When will a genetic algorithm outperform hill climbing? In *Proceeding of the 7th Neural Information Processing Systems Conference (NIPS)*, volume 6 of *Advances in Neural Information Processing Systems*, pages 51–58. Morgan Kaufmann, 1993.

[18] P. S. Oliveto and X. Yao. Runtime analysis of evolutionary algorithms for discrete optimization. In A. Auger and B. Doerr, editors, *Theory of Randomized Search Heuristics*, pages 21–52. World Scientific Publishing, Singapore, 2011.

[19] M. Raab and A. Steger. "Balls into bins" – a simple and tight analysis. In *Proceedings Randomization and Approximation Techniques in Computer Science (RANDOM'98)*, volume 1518 of *Lecture Notes in Computer Science*, pages 159–170. Springer, 1998.

[20] D. Sudholt. Crossover is provably essential for the Ising model on trees. In *Proceedings of the Annual Genetic and Evolutionary Computation Conference (GECCO'05)*, pages 1161–1167. ACM Press, 2005.

[21] I. Wegener. Theoretical aspects of evolutionary algorithms. In F. Orejas, P. G. Spirakis, and J. van Leeuwen, editors, *Proc. of the 28th International Colloquium on Automata, Languages and Programming (ICALP'01)*, volume 2076 of *Lecture Notes in Computer Science*, pages 64–78. Springer, 2001.

[22] I. Wegener. Methods for the analysis of evolutionary algorithms on pseudo-Boolean functions. In R. Sarker, M. Mohammadian, and X. Yao, editors, *Evolutionary Optimization*, pages 349–369. Kluwer, 2002.

[23] C. Witt. Fitness levels with tail bounds for the analysis of randomized search heuristics. *Information Processing Letters*, 114:38–41, 2014.

OneMax in Black-Box Models with Several Restrictions

Carola Doerr
CNRS & Univ. Pierre et Marie Curie
Paris, France

Johannes Lengler
ETH Zürich
Zürich, Switzerland

ABSTRACT

As in classical runtime analysis the ONEMAX problem is the most prominent test problem also in black-box complexity theory. It is known that the unrestricted, the memory-restricted, and the ranking-based black-box complexities of this problem are all of order $n/\log n$, where n denotes the length of the bit strings. The combined memory-restricted ranking-based black-box complexity of ONEMAX, however, was not known. We show in this work that it is $\Theta(n)$ for the smallest possible size bound, that is, for (1+1) black-box algorithms.

We extend this result by showing that even if elitist selection is enforced, there exists a linear time algorithm optimizing ONEMAX with failure probability $o(1)$. This is quite surprising given that all previously regarded algorithms with $o(n \log n)$ runtime on ONEMAX, in particular the quite natural $(1 + (\lambda, \lambda))$ GA, heavily exploit information encoded in search points of fitness much smaller than the current best-so-far solution.

Also for other settings of μ and λ we show that the $(\mu+\lambda)$ *elitist memory-restricted ranking-based black-box complexity* of ONEMAX is as small as (an advanced version of) the information-theoretic lower bound.

Our result enlivens the quest for natural evolutionary algorithms optimizing ONEMAX in $o(n \log n)$ iterations.

Categories and Subject Descriptors

F.2.2 [**Theory of Computation**]: Analysis of Algorithms and Problem Complexity—*Nonnumerical Algorithms and Problems*

Keywords

Theory; Runtime Analysis; Black-Box Complexity; Memory-Restricted; Ranking-Based; Comparison-Based; Elitist Selection

GECCO '15, July 11 - 16, 2015, Madrid, Spain

ISBN 978-1-4503-3472-3/15/07...$15.00

DOI: http://dx.doi.org/10.1145/2739480.2754678

1. INTRODUCTION

Black-box complexity aims at analyzing the influence of algorithmic choices such as the population size, the variation operators in use, or the selection principles on the running time of evolutionary algorithms (EAs). Lower bounds from black-box complexity theory provide information about the limits of certain classes of evolutionary algorithms (e.g., memory-restricted, ranking-based, or unbiased EAs), while upper bounds can serve as an inspiration for the development of new EAs.

One of the first test problems that is typically regarded when introducing a new black-box model is the well-known ONEMAX function (or, more precisely, the class of all functions isomorphic to ONEMAX). Indeed, it is known that the black-box complexity of the class of ONEMAX functions is very low for most black-box models. For example, its unrestricted black-box complexity is of order only $n/\log n$ [1, 10], which is much lower than the typical $\Omega(n \log n)$ expected runtime that most EAs exhibit on this problem. Restricting the memory of the regarded algorithms, a method suggested in [9], does not significantly increase this complexity. Instead, even for the smallest possible size bound, in which algorithms may store only one previous search point and its fitness, an $O(n/\log n)$ algorithm exists [5]. Similarly, in the ranking-based model, in which the algorithms learn only the ranking of the fitnesses, but not their absolute values, the generalized ONEMAX problem can still be solved in an expected number of $O(n/\log n)$ function evaluations [6]. Only in the unary unbiased model it is known that ONEMAX cannot be solved on average in less than $Cn \log n$ steps (for some constant C) [13].

While previous work focused on single restrictions of the algorithms, we regard in this work *combinations* of algorithmic constraints. In a first step, we study the combined memory-restricted ranking-based model, i.e., we study the black-box complexity of ONEMAX with respect to $(\mu + \lambda)$ memory-restricted ranking-based algorithms. For the (1+1) case, such algorithms are easily seen to be *comparison-based*, i.e., they learn with each query only whether the offspring has better, equal, or worse fitness than its parent. Therefore, by a simple information-theoretic argument (cf., e.g., [9, Theorem 2]), their expected runtimes on ONEMAX are at least linear in n. This already shows that the combined (1+1) memory-restricted ranking-based black-box complexity of ONEMAX is asymptotically higher than either the purely ranking-based or the purely memory-restricted complexity. However, this is not the end of the story. In this work we show lower bounds for the combined (1+1) model that are by a constant factor stronger than the best known bounds for comparison-based algorithms. Thus they are stronger than any bound obtained by reducing the combined model to an existing black-box model with a single restriction. On the other hand, we show that the mentioned linear lower bound is asymptotically tight. That is, we provide a linear time algorithm solving OneMax in a (1+1) scheme and using only relative fitness information. Also for many other combinations of μ and λ we show that the information-theoretic lower bound is matched by a $(\mu + \lambda)$ memory-restricted ranking-based algorithm.

In a next step, we combine the memory-restricted ranking-based model with yet another restriction, namely with the recently introduced $(\mu+\lambda)$ elitist black-box model [8]. That is, we additionally require that the algorithm selects the μ *fittest* individuals out of the $\mu + \lambda$ parents and offspring (where it may break ties arbitrarily).[1] Notably, the asymptotic runtime stays the same, though in a slightly different sense as we shall discuss below. This is rather surprising, as all previous black-box optimal algorithms make substantial use of non-elitist selection.

While at a first glance the linear upper bounds may seem to be a shortcoming of the model (most EAs need $\Omega(n \log n)$ steps to optimize OneMax-functions), it does not have to be. In light of [3], where a simple and natural EA has been designed that optimizes OneMax in $o(n \log n)$ time, it is well possible that such a result can be extended further (of particular interest is an extension to (1+1)-type algorithms). As we know from [3], black-box complexity results like our mentioned OneMax bound can give an inspiration for developing such algorithms.

Our upper bounds nicely combine previous techniques from the black-box complexity literature with some new tools that we develop for the most restrictive model, the (1+1) memory-restricted ranking-based elitist black-box model. We believe that the insights from these tools will be useful in future research in evolutionary computation, both in algorithm analysis and in algorithm design.

For the lower bounds, a technical difficulty that we face in the proofs is a putative non-applicability of Yao's Principle. More precisely, there may be randomized algorithms that even in the worst case perform much better than any deterministic algorithm on a random problem instance, cf. Section 4 and [8]. We overcome these problems by expanding the class of algorithms regarded. This needs some care as we do not want to decrease the complexity too much by this expansion.

Our paper is structured as follows. Since most of our proofs work directly in the elitist black box model, we start with a formal introduction of the models in Section 2, followed by a brief discussion on the difference between Las Vegas and Monte Carlo complexities, which can be crucially different in the regarded models. In a nutshell, the *Las Vegas* complexity measures the expected time until an optimal search point is hit, while the *p-Monte Carlo complexity* asks for the time needed until an optimum is hit with probability at least $1 - p$. These bounds can be exponentially far apart as shown in [8] and thus need to be regarded separately.

In Section 3 we formally introduce the generalized OneMax functions and recapitulate the known bounds on its complexity in different black box models. In Section 4 we provide the mentioned lower bounds for the $(\mu+\lambda)$ memory-restricted ranking-based black-box complexity of OneMax for a wide range of μ and λ.

The remainder of the paper is devoted to the proofs of the upper bounds in the elitist model, which imply the same upper bounds for the memory-restricted ranking-based model. We first give a simple linear upper bound for the (2+1) (Las Vegas and Monte Carlo) elitist black-box complexity of OneMax (Section 5). At the heart of this paper is Section 6, where we show the linear upper bound for the (1+1) Monte Carlo elitist black-box complexity of OneMax. In Sections 7 and 8, we consider more generally $(1 + \lambda)$ and $(\mu + 1)$ elitist black-box algorithms. Finally, in Section 9 we give some remarks on the (μ, λ) elitist black-box complexities of OneMax and point out some important differences from the $(\mu + \lambda)$ complexities.

Table 1, taken from [2] and extended to cover the results of the present paper, summarizes known lower and upper bounds of the complexity of OneMax in the different black-box models. Bounds given without reference follow trivially from identical bounds in stronger models, e.g., the $\Omega(n/\log n)$ lower bound for the memory-restricted black-box complexity follows directly from the same bound the unrestricted model.

Disclaimer: We do not consider in this work $(\mu + \lambda)$ elitist algorithms for μ and λ both being strictly greater than one. We feel that the required tools are given in the $(1+\lambda)$ and $(\mu+1)$ settings, so that analyzing the additional settings would not give sufficiently many new insights.

Proofs omitted in this abstract can be found in the full version, which is available online at http://arxiv.org/abs/1504.02644.

2. THE ELITIST BLACK-BOX MODEL

We are primarily interested in analyzing the memory-restricted ranking-based black-box complexities of OneMax. An important difference to purely memory-restricted algorithms is that the available memory is strictly smaller in this combined memory-restricted and ranking-based model. If we regard, for example, the (1+1) case, then in the pure memory-restricted model, the algorithm does not only have access to the current search point, but also to its fitness value. It thus has strictly more than n bits of information when sampling the offspring. If, on the other hand, the algorithm is in addition also ranking-based, then it may not access the fitness; thus its available information is restricted to exactly n bits. So the fitness-based variant has effectively a larger available memory than the ranking-based one (but of course both are not completely free in how to use the memory).

Quite surprisingly, it turns out that instead of working in the memory-restricted ranking-based models, we can also enforce elitist selection decisions without increasing the black-box complexity of OneMax by more than a constant factor. We therefore directly work in the recently proposed *elitist black-box model* [8], which in particular requires the algorithms to be memory-restricted and ranking-based. That is, we regard in this work black-box complex-

[1]As mentioned in [8] we remark that the usage of "elitist selection" is not standardized in the EA literature. Some subcommunities would therefore rather call our elitist black-box model a *black-box model with truncation selection.*

Model	Lower Bound		Upper Bound	
unrestricted	$\Omega(n/\log n)$	info.-theo.	$O(n/\log n)$	[1, 10]
unbiased, arity 1	$\Omega(n \log n)$	[13]	$O(n \log n)$	
unbiased, arity $2 \le k \le \log n$	$\Omega(n/\log n)$		$O(n/k)$	[3, 7]
r.b. unrestricted	$\Omega(n/\log n)$		$O(n/\log n)$	[6]
r.b. unbiased, arity 1	$\Omega(n \log n)$		$O(n \log n)$	
r.b. unbiased, arity $2 \le k \le n$	$\Omega(n/\log n)$		$O(n/\log k)$	[6]
(1+1) comparison-based	$\Omega(n)$	info.-theo.	$O(n)$	
(1+1) memory-restricted	$\Omega(n/\log n)$		$O(n/\log n)$	[5]
(1+1) elitist Las Vegas	$\Omega(n)$	Thm. 4	$O(n \log n)$	
(1+1) elitist $\log n/n$-Monte Carlo	$\Omega(n)$	Thm. 4	$O(n)$	Thm. 6
(2+1) elitist Monte Carlo/Las Vegas	$\Omega(n)$	Thm. 4	$O(n)$	Thm. 5
(1+λ) elitist Monte Carlo (# generations)	$\Omega(n/\log \lambda)$	Thm. 4	$O(n/\log \lambda)$	Thm. 10
(μ+1) elitist Monte Carlo	$\Omega(n/\log \mu)$	Thm. 4	$O(n/\log \mu)$	Thm. 11
(1, λ) elitist Monte Carlo/Las Vegas (# generations)	$\Omega(n/\log \lambda)$	cf. Section 9	$O(n/\log \lambda)$	Thm. 12

Table 1: The black-box complexities of OneMax in the different models. r.b. abbreviates ranking-based; info-theo. the information-theoretic bound [15], cf. also [9]; for $(1 + \lambda)$ and $(1, \lambda)$ we assume $1 < \lambda < 2^{n^{1-\varepsilon}}$ for some $\varepsilon > 0$, and for $(\mu + 1)$ we assume that $\mu = \omega(\log^2 n/\log\log n)$ and $\mu \le n$.

ities with respect to algorithms that follow the structure of Algorithm 1.[2]

Algorithm 1: The $(\mu + \lambda)$ elitist black-box algorithm for maximizing an unknown function $f : \{0,1\}^n \to \mathbb{R}$

```
1 Initialization:
2   X ← ∅;
3   for i = 1, ..., μ do
4     Depending only on the multiset X and the
      ranking ρ(X, f) of X induced by f, choose a
      probability distribution p^(i) over {0,1}^n and
      sample x^(i) according to p^(i);
5     X ← X ∪ {x^(i)};
6 Optimization: for t = 1, 2, 3, ... do
7   Depending only on the multiset X and the ranking
    ρ(X, f) of X induced by f choose a probability
    distribution p^(t) on ({0,1}^n)^λ_{i=1} and sample
    (y^(1), ..., y^(λ)) according to p^(t);
8   Set X ← X ∪ {y^(1), ..., y^(λ)};
9   for i = 1, ..., λ do Select x ∈ arg min X and
    update X ← X \ {x};
```

Note that the only difference to the $(\mu + \lambda)$ memory-restricted ranking-based black-box model is the enforced elitist selection in line 9, which in the former model can be replaced by

for $i = 1, \ldots, \lambda$ **do** Select $x \in X$ and update $X \leftarrow X \setminus \{x\}$;

Since the elitist model is more restrictive than the combined memory-restricted ranking-based one, every upper bound on the $(\mu+\lambda)$ elitist black-box complexity also holds for the $(\mu+\lambda)$ memory-restricted ranking-based black-box complexity.

2.1 Las Vegas vs. Monte Carlo Complexities

Elitist black-box algorithms cannot do simple restarts. Regarding expected runtimes can therefore be significantly different from regarding algorithms with allowed positive failure probability. In fact, it is not difficult to see that these two notions can be exponentially far apart [8, Theorem 3]. One may argue that this is a rather artificial problem since in practice there is no reason why one would not want to allow restarts. Also almost all algorithms used to show upper bounds in the previous black-box models have small complexity thanks only to the possibility of doing random restarts. One convenient way around this problem is to allow for small probabilities of failure. Such (high) probability statements are actually often found in the evolutionary computation literature. The following definition captures its spirit.

Let us regard for a black-box algorithm A the smallest number T of function evaluations that is needed such that for any problem instance $f \in \mathcal{F}$ the optimum of f is found with probability at least $1-p$. We call $T = T(A, \mathcal{F})$ the p-Monte Carlo black-box complexity of A on $\mathcal{F}$. The *p-Monte Carlo black-box complexity* of $\mathcal{F}$ with respect to a class $\mathcal{A}$ of algorithms is $\min_{A\in\mathcal{A}} T(A, \mathcal{F})$. If we make a statement about the Monte Carlo complexity without specifying p, then we mean that for *every constant* $p > 0$ the statement holds for the p-Monte Carlo complexity.

The standard black-box complexity (which regards the maximal *expected* time that an algorithm A needs to optimize any $f \in \mathcal{F}$) is called *Las Vegas black-box complexity* in [8]. We adopt this notation.

We recall from [8] that, by Markov's inequality, every Las Vegas algorithm is also (up to a factor of $1/p$ in the runtime) a p-Monte Carlo algorithm. We also repeat the following convenient tool to bound p-Monte Carlo complexities.

REMARK 1 (REMARK 1 IN [8]). *Let $p \in (0, 1)$. Assume that there is an event $\mathcal{E}$ of probability $p_\mathcal{E} < p$ such that conditioned on $\neg\mathcal{E}$ the algorithm A finds the optimum after* expected *time at most T. Then the p-Monte Carlo complexity of A on f is at most $(p - p_\mathcal{E})^{-1}T$. In particular, if $p - p_\mathcal{E} = \Omega(1)$ then the p-Monte Carlo complexity is $O(T)$.*

3. BACKGROUND ON ONEMAX COMPLEXITIES AND OVERVIEW OF RESULTS

One of the most prominent problems in the theory of randomized search heuristics is the running time of evolutionary algorithms and other heuristics on the ONEMAX problem.

[2]As discussed in [8], several variants of the elitist model exist. With the exception of the (μ, λ) strategies regarded in Section 9, we regard in this work only the version defined via Algorithm 1.

OneMax is the function that counts the number of ones in a bitstring. Maximizing OneMax thus corresponds to finding the all-ones string.

Search heuristics are typically invariant with respect to the problem encoding, and as such they have the same runtime for any function from the generalized OneMax function class

$$\text{OneMax} := \{\text{OM}_z \mid z \in \{0,1\}^n\},$$

where OM_z is the function

$$\text{OM}_z : \{0,1\}^n \to \mathbb{R}, x \mapsto n - \sum_{i=1}^{n} (x_i \oplus z_i), \qquad (1)$$

assigning to x the number of positions in which x and z agree. We call z, the unique global optimum of function OM_z, the *target string* of OM_z. Whenever we speak of the OneMax problem or a OneMax function we mean the whole class of OneMax functions or an unknown member of it, respectively.

The OneMax problem is by far the most intensively studied problem in the runtime analysis of EAs and, due to its close relation to the classic board game *Mastermind* [5], to cryptographic applications, and to coin-weighing problems, it is also studied in other areas of theoretical computer science. Also for black-box complexities it is the most commonly found test problem. Without going too much into detail, we recall that the unrestricted black-box complexity of OneMax is $\Theta(n/\log n)$ [1, 9, 10]. While the lower bound is a simple application of Yao's Principle (cf. Section 4), the upper bound is achieved by an extremely simple, yet elegant algorithm: sampling $O(n/\log n)$ random search points and regarding their fitness values, with high probability, reveals the target string z. We shall make use of (variants of) this strategy in some of our proofs of upper bounds.

Another important bound for the OneMax problem is the simple $\Theta(n)$ bound for comparison-based algorithms as introduced in [14].[3] Since (1+1) memory-restricted ranking-based algorithms are comparison-based, this gives a linear lower bound for their complexity on OneMax.

Remark 2. *The (1+1) memory-restricted ranking-based black-box complexity of* OneMax *is $\Omega(n)$, thus implying a linear lower bound for the (1+1) elitist Las Vegas and Monte Carlo black-box complexity of* OneMax.

If we consider the leading constants hidden in the Ω-notation, then the lower bounds coming from the comparison-based complexity are not optimal. In Theorem 4 we will prove lower bounds for memory-restricted ranking-based algorithms that are by a non-trivial constant factor larger than the best known bounds for comparison-based algorithms.

A very simple heuristic optimizing OneMax in $\Theta(n \log n)$ steps is *Randomized Local Search* (RLS). Since this heuristic will be important in later parts of this paper, we state it here for the sake of completeness. RLS is initialized with a uniform sample x. In each iteration one bit position $j \in \{1, 2, \ldots, n\}$ is chosen uniformly at random. The j-th bit of x is flipped and the fitness of the resulting search point y is evaluated. The better of the two search points x and y is kept for future iterations (favoring the newly created individual in case of ties). As is easily verified, RLS is a unary unbiased (in the sense of [13]) (1+1) elitist black-box algorithm.

[3]The lower bound is again a simple application of Yao's Principle, while the upper bound is attained, for example, by the algorithm which checks one bit at a time, going through the bitstring from one end to the other. Alternatively, the upper bound is also verified by the $(1+(\lambda, \lambda))$ GA of [3], thus showing that it can also be achieved by unbiased algorithms of arity two.

In the following sections we essentially show that there are elitist black-box optimization algorithms optimizing OneMax much more efficiently than typical heuristics like RLS or evolutionary algorithms. In particular we show that the (1+1) elitist Monte Carlo black-box complexity is at most linear (which is best possible by Theorem 4). Our results are summarized in the lower part of Table 1. Note that the upper bounds for elitist algorithms immediately imply upper bounds for the (Monte Carlo and Las Vegas) black-box complexity of OneMax in the respective memory-restricted ranking-based models. The lower bounds also carry over in asymptotic terms (i.e., up to constant factors), cf. Theorem 4. Since the memory-restricted ranking-based bounds were the original motivation for our work, we collect them in the following statement.

Corollary 3. *The (1+1) memory-restricted ranking-based (Las Vegas) black-box complexity of* OneMax *is $\Theta(n)$. For $1 < \lambda < 2^{n^{1-\varepsilon}}$, $\varepsilon > 0$ being an arbitrary constant, its $(1+\lambda)$ memory-restricted ranking-based black-box complexity is $\Theta(n/\log \lambda)$ (in terms of generations), while for $\mu = \omega(\log^2(n)/\log\log n)$, $\mu \leq n$, its $(\mu+1)$ memory-restricted ranking-based black-box complexity is $\Theta(n/\log \mu)$.*

4. LOWER BOUNDS

In this section we show that the $(1+1)$ memory-restricted ranking-based black-box complexity of OneMax is at least $\Omega(n)$. In fact, we show this bound for a large range of function classes. We also show (mostly tight, as the algorithms in subsequent sections will show) lower bounds for general $(\mu + \lambda)$ elitist black-box algorithms.

We use Yao's Principle [15], which in some cases implies that the runtime T of a best-possible *deterministic* algorithm on a *random* input is a lower bound to the best-possible performance of a *random* algorithm on an *arbitrary* input. However, as outlined in [8], Yao's Principle is not directly applicable to memory-restricted or elitist black-box algorithms. For example, every deterministic $(1+1)$ memory-restricted ranking-based algorithm that ever rejects a search point (i.e., stays with the old search point) will be caught in an infinite loop on OneMax with positive probability if the input is chosen uniformly at random. Hence, such an algorithm will have infinite expected runtime. On the other hand, if the algorithm does not reject any search point, then it is easy to see that its expected runtime on OneMax is $\Omega(2^n)$. However, there are certainly $(1+1)$ memory-restricted ranking-based randomized algorithms (e.g., RLS) that optimize OneMax in expected time $O(n \log n)$. To solve this putative non-applicability of Yao's Principle, we apply it to a suitable superset of algorithms, yielding the following bounds. (See [8] for a more detailed discussion; in particular, Yao's principle applies to every set of algorithms that have access to their whole search histories.)

Theorem 4. *Let $\mathcal{F}$ be a class of functions such that for every $z \in \{0,1\}^n$ there is a function $f_z \in \mathcal{F}$ with unique optimum z. Then the (1+1) memory-restricted ranking-based* *black-box complexity of $\mathcal{F}$ (and thus, also the elitist (1+1) Las Vegas black-box complexity) is at least $n-1$. Moreover, for every $p>0$ the p-Monte Carlo black-box complexity of $\mathcal{F}$ is at least $n+\lceil\log(1-p)\rceil$.*

In general, for every $\mu \geq 1$ and $\lambda \geq 1$, the following statements are true for the memory-restricted ranking-based black box complexity, for the elitist Las Vegas black box complexity, and for the elitist p-Monte Carlo black box complexity for every constant $p>0$.

- *The $(1+\lambda)$ black-box complexity of $\mathcal{F}$ is at least $n/\log(\lambda+1)-O(1)$.*
- *The $(\mu+1)$ black-box complexity of $\mathcal{F}$ is at least $n/\log(2\mu+1)-O(1)$.*
- *The $(\mu+\lambda)$ black-box complexity of $\mathcal{F}$ is at least $n/(b+o(1))$, where $b=\log(\binom{\mu+\lambda}{\mu})+\mu(\log\mu-1-\log\ln 2)-1$.*

PROOF. For simplicity, we only give the proof for the elitist case. The memory-restricted ranking-based case is similar, but more technical.[4]

We first give the argument for the (1+1) case to elucidate the line of reasoning. We use Yao's principle on the set $\mathcal{A}'$ of all algorithms A satisfying the following restrictions. A is a comparison-based (1+1) black-box algorithm that has access to the whole search history. The algorithm learns about f by oracle queries of the following form. It may choose a search point x that it has queried before (in the first round, it simply chooses a search point without querying), and a search point y. Then A may choose between the two queries "$f(x)<f(y)$?" and "$f(x) \leq f(y)$?", and the oracle will return *yes* or *no* as answer to the chosen query.

Let $\mathcal{A}$ be the set of all (1+1) elitist black-box algorithms. We need to show that $\mathcal{A} \subseteq \mathcal{A}'$, so let $A \in \mathcal{A}$. When the current search point of A is x, the algorithm may first decide on a new search point y (i.e., it assigns to each search point y a probability p_y to be queried). If the oracle (of the elitist model $\mathcal{A}$) tells the algorithm "$f(x)>f(y)$" or "$f(x)<f(y)$" then the algorithm is forced to stay in x or to go to y, respectively. If the oracle returns "$f(x)=f(y)$" then A may choose to stay in x with some probability p and to go to y with probability $1-p$. We may simulate A in the model $\mathcal{A}'$ by choosing the query "$f(x)<f(y)$?" with probability $p_y(1-p)$, and the query "$f(x) \leq f(y)$?" with probability $p_y p$. If the answer to our query is *yes* then we go to y, and if the answer is *no* then we stay in x. By an easy case distinction on whether $f(x)$ is less, equal, or larger than $f(y)$, we find that in all cases the probability of going to y (conditioned on choosing y for the query) is the same as for the algorithm A. Thus we can simulate A in the model $\mathcal{A}'$.

It remains to prove a lower bound on the $\mathcal{A}'$-complexity of $\mathcal{F}$. By Yao's Principle, it suffices to prove such a bound for the expected runtime of every deterministic algorithm $A \in \mathcal{A}'$ on a randomly chosen function. We regard a distribution on $\mathcal{F}$ where for each $z \in \{0,1\}^n$ exactly one function with optimum z has probability 2^{-n} to be drawn, and all other functions in $\mathcal{F}$ have zero probability. Note that the $\mathcal{A}'$-oracle gives only two possible answers (one bit of information) to each query. By a standard information-theoretic argument [9] the probability that the i-th query of A is the optimum is at most 2^{-n+i-1}. By the union bound the probability that the optimum is among the first i queries is at most $\sum_{j=1}^{i} 2^{-n+i-1} < 2^{i-n}$. This immediately implies the statement on the (1+1) Monte Carlo complexity. For the Las Vegas complexity, the claim follows by estimating the number T of queries of find the optimum by

$$\begin{aligned} \mathrm{E}[T] &\geq \sum_{i=0}^{n-1} \Pr[T>i] \geq \sum_{i=0}^{n-1}(1-2^{i-n}) \\ &= n-2^{-n}\sum_{i=0}^{n-1} 2^i = n-(1-2^{-n}) \geq n-1. \end{aligned}$$

For the $(1+\lambda)$-case with $\lambda \geq 1$ we require the algorithm to use queries of the form "Which of the $\lambda+1$ search points is the largest with ties broken according to the rules R", where R runs through all the (finitely many) deterministic tie breaking rules between the $\lambda+1$ search points. In this way, the algorithm learns only $\log(\lambda+1)$ bits per query. Similarly as before, the probability that the i-th query of a deterministic algorithm is the optimum is at most $(\lambda+1)^{i-1}2^{-n}$, and a similar calculation as before shows that $\Pr[T \leq i] \leq (\lambda+1)^i 2^{-n}$ and $\mathrm{E}[T] \geq n/\log(\lambda+1)-O(1)$.

For $\mu>1$ and $\lambda=1$ we learn the position of the new search point among the μ previous search points. There are at most $2\mu+1$ positions for the new search point (its fitness can equal the fitness of one of the other search points, or lie in between them). Thus we only learn at most $\log(2\mu+1)$ bits of information per query, and we can derive the complexities in the same manner as before.

If both μ and λ are larger than 1, then there are at most $\binom{\mu+\lambda}{\mu}$ ways to select μ out of $\mu+\lambda$ search points, and there are $B_\mu=(1+o(1))\mu!(\ln 2)^{-\mu}/2$ weak orderings on these μ elements (i.e., orderings with potentially equal elements), where B_μ is the μ-th ordered Bell number [11]. Hence, the algorithm can learn at most $b:=\log((1+o(1))\binom{\mu+\lambda}{\mu}\mu!(\ln 2)^{-\mu}/2)$ bits per query. Since $b=\log(\binom{\mu+\lambda}{\mu})+\mu(\log\mu-1-\log\ln 2)-1+o(1)$, this implies the claim in the same way as before. □

Note that the lower bounds given by Theorem 4 are by a constant factor stronger than the lower bounds for general comparison-based algorithms (that are not memory-restricted) that learn all comparisons among the $\mu+\lambda$ current search points. For example, in the classical case where we may compare exactly two search points (corresponding to the (1+1) case), we only get a lower bound of $n/\log(3)-O(1)$ instead of $n-1$. Intuitively speaking, the reason is that a comparison-based algorithm may use the three possible outcomes "larger", "less", or "equal" of a comparison, while memory-restricted comparison-based algorithms only get two outcomes "stay at x" or "go to y".

We remark that the analysis for $\mu>1$ can be tightened in several ways. Firstly, for the elitist $(\mu+1)$ black-box complexity, we only have 2μ cases instead of $2\mu+1$ since we can – sloppily speaking – not distinguish between the case that the new search point is discarded because it has worse fitness than the worst of the μ old ones, or whether it is discarded because it has equal fitness to the worst of the μ old search points. Moreover, for all black-box models under consideration we learn $\log(2\mu+1)$ bits of information in the i-th round only if all previous search points have different fitnesses; otherwise, we get less information. However, if the

[4]A full proof can be found in the complete version attached to this paper.

new search point has fitness equal to one of the old fitnesses, then with the next query we get less information. Also for the case ($\mu > 1$ *and* $\lambda > 1$) the bound in Theorem 4 can be tightened at the cost of a more technical argument.

5. THE (2+1) ELITIST BLACK-BOX COMPLEXITY OF ONEMAX

For the $(2+1)$ elitist black-box complexity, a simple algorithm turns out to have complexity at most $n+1$. The algorithm is deterministic, so it provides an upper bound to both the Monte Carlo and the Las Vegas complexity.

THEOREM 5. *The (Monte Carlo and Las Vegas) (2+1) elitist black-box complexity of* ONEMAX *is at most* $n+1$.

PROOF. Throughout the algorithm, we maintain the invariant that in the i-th step we have two strings x_i and x'_i that are both optimal in the first i bits, that are both zero on bits $i+2, \dots, n$ and that differ on bit $i+1$ (one of them is 0, the other is 1).

We thus start with the all-zero string $x_0 = (0, \dots, 0)$ and the string $x'_0 = (1, 0, \dots, 0)$. Given x_i and x'_i, take the string with the smaller fitness (say x'_i), and flip both the i-th and the $(i+1)$-st bit in it, giving a string x'_{i+1}. (The index i is determined by x_i and x'_i.) Since the i-th bit in x'_i was incorrect, the fitness of x'_{i+1} is at least as high as the fitness of x'_i and we may thus replace x'_i by x'_{i+1}. The invariant is maintained with $x_{i+1} = x_i$, since both x_{i+1} and x'_{i+1} are optimal on the i-th bit (and on all previous bits by induction). In this way, the n-th generation will contain an optimal search string, and at most $n+1$ fitness evaluations are needed in these n generations. □

6. THE (1+1) ELITIST BLACK-BOX COMPLEXITY OF ONEMAX

While the algorithm and the analysis in Section 5 are rather straightforward, the analysis for the (1+1) situation is considerably more difficult. In fact, we do not know the Las Vegas black-box complexity of ONEMAX for (1+1) elitist algorithms. As we shall discuss below, if we only had one additional bit that we could manipulate in an arbitrary way, we could show that it is of linear order, but we do not know how to create such a bit. Still, the general ideas for that algorithm show a linear Monte Carlo black-box complexity. According to the lower bound (Theorem 4), this is best possible.

THEOREM 6. *The* $\log n/n$*-Monte Carlo (1+1) elitist black-box complexity of* ONEMAX *is* $\Theta(n)$.

The proof of the linear upper bound is rather involved. We can thus only give a high level overview here, together with a sketch of some of the key subroutines. As in previous works on black-box complexities for ONEMAX, in particular the memory-restricted algorithm from [5], we will use some parts of the bit string for storing information about the search history.

The main idea of the algorithm is similar to the one of the previous section. That is, we aim at optimizing one bit at a time. Since we cannot anymore encode the current iteration in a second member of the population, we implement instead a counter which tells us which bit is to be tested next. The main difficulty is in *(i)* designing a counter that does not affect the fitness of the bit string, and *(ii)* optimizing a bit with certainty in constant time. As we shall see in Lemma 8, a counter can be implemented reserving $O(\log n)$ bits of the string exclusively for this counter, solving *(i)*. Point *(ii)* can be solved if we may access a small pool of non-optimal bits (which we call *trading bits*). The key idea is that throughout the algorithm in expectation we gain more trading bits than we spend, so we never run out of trading bits.

The main steps of the algorithm verifying Theorem 6, all of which can fail with some small probability, are thus as follows.

1. Create a neutral counter for counting numbers from 1 to n.
2. Create a pool of $\omega(\log n)$ trading bits, all of which are non-optimal.
3. Using the trading bits, optimize the remaining string (the part unaffected by the counter) by testing one bit after the other. Use the counter to indicate which bit to test next. At the same time, try to recover trading bits if possible.
4. Using RLS, optimize the part which had been used as a counter. We use bit b_0 as a flag bit to indicate that we are in Step 4.
5. Optimize b_0.

The technically most challenging parts are Step 1 and Step 3. But, interestingly enough, the key problem in turning the Monte Carlo algorithm into a Las Vegas one lies in separating Step 5 from Step 4: we need to test every once in a while during the fourth phase whether or not bit b_0 is optimal. If we test too early, that is, before Step 4 is finished, it may happen that we have to accept this offspring and thus misleadingly assume that we are in one of the first three steps, yielding the algorithm to fail. Note though that this problem could be completely ignored if we had just one bit that we could manipulate as we want (i.e., without having to use elitist operations). This would already lead to a (1+1) Las Vegas elitist black-box complexity. Unfortunately, it is unclear how to achieve a linear expectation without an additional bit of memory.

The key ingredients for the proof are the following lemmas. The first lemma allows us to write arbitrary information into small substrings with high probability.

LEMMA 7. *Assume we have a set B of b known bit positions, of which at least $b_0 = \beta b$ bits are non-optimal, for some $\beta > 0$, and the position of the non-optimal bits are uniformly at random in B. Assume further that we have two sets C, C' of bit positions such that $|C| = |C'| = o(b_0)$, and that B, C, C' are pairwise disjoint.*

Then there is a (1+1) elitist black-box strategy that for every $c > 0$ copies the bits from C into C' in $c \cdot |C| \cdot \log(n)/\beta$ iterations with probability $1 - n^{-\Omega(c)}$. The same strategy can be used to overwrite C' with a fixed string (e.g., $(1, \dots, 1)$). After the copy operation, B may be used for further copy operations.

To prove the lemma, we flip in each step one bit in C and B simultaneously and accept the offspring if and only if its fitness is at least as good as that of its parent.

Lemma 7 is a key step to prove the existence of a neutral counter.

Lemma 8 (Neutral Counter). *For every $0 < p < 1/2$, $p = e^{-o(n)}$, there is $\ell = O(\log(1/p))$ such that the following holds. Let x be a bit string in $\{0,1\}^n$ such that $x_1 = x_2 = \ldots = x_{\ell+2} = 0$ and $(x_{\ell+3}, \ldots, x_n)$ is uniformly distributed in $\{0,1\}^{n-\ell+3}$.*

Then there exists a (1+1) elitist black-box strategy that with probability at least $1-p$ implements in x a counter which can be used during future iterations without changing the OneMax value of the string. For counting up to $j = O(n)$, the counter requires a total number of $O(\log j)$ bits that are blocked in all iterations in which the counter is active. The setup of the counter requires $O(\ell \log j \log\log j)$ function evaluations.

The basic idea for the counter is to use the fact that all substrings with exactly $k/2$ correct bits of a k-bit-string have the same fitness. So we optimize a string C of k bits, where $\binom{k}{k/2} \geq j$. Then we copy the optimized C into another string C', and invert half of the bits in C (both times using Lemma 7). Then by going through all strings in C with $k/2$ optimal bits we can count up to $\binom{k}{k/2}$. The $\ell+2$ zero bits are used to estimate the time spend for the optimization of C.

The following lemma allows us to optimize a large part of the string in linear time, provided that we have some small area B' with "trading bits", i.e., with bits that are non-optimal.

Lemma 9. *Let $0 < \alpha, \alpha' < 1$ be constants. Assume we have two counters C, C' that can count up to n and a flag bit b that is set to 0. Assume further that we have two blocks B, B', with $|B|, |B'| = \omega(\log n)$ such that all bits in B' are non-optimal, and that at least an α fraction of the bits in B is non-optimal, their positions distributed uniformly at random. Then there is a (1+1) elitist black-box algorithm that optimizes B and B' in linear time with probability at least $1 - 1/n$.*

The i-th round of the algorithm in Lemma 9 is as follows. The counter C and C' track i and the number i' of trading bits, respectively. In each step we flip a coin. If it turns head (with probability $1-p$ for a suitable $p > 0$), then we flip the $i+1$-st bit in B, increase C, flip the (optimal) i'-th bit of B' and decrease C'. If the offspring has equal fitness, we accept it. Note that the fitness is equal if and only if the bit in B was non-optimal, and that we recover one of the non-optimal trading bits in B' in this case. On the other hand, if the bit in B was optimal in the original string then the fitness of the new search point is strictly smaller than the previous one so that the offspring is immediately discarded. So we only accept an increase in C if the i-th of B is correct in the new string. If the coin flip was tail (with probability p) then we just flip the $i+1$-st bit in B, flip the $i'+1$-st bit in B', and increase C' (but do not touch C). Note that we may (and will) accept the offspring in any case.

Analyzing this algorithm, we find that the number of trading bits that are spent (i.e., optimized) is a random variable with negative drift. Therefore we do not run out of trading bits with high probability if $|B'| = \omega(\log n)$. Moreover, we only need an expected constant number of steps to optimize each bit, yielding a linear time bound with high probability.

Combining the previous three lemmas with the proof outline given on page yields Theorem 6.

7. THE $(1+\lambda)$ ELITIST BLACK-BOX COMPLEXITIES OF ONEMAX

We have already seen in Section 5 that a slight increase of the population size of the elitist black-box model can significantly simplify the OneMax problem. In the (2+1) model considered in Section 5 we were in the comfortable situation that we could use the two strings of the memory to encode an iteration counter. In this section we regard the $(1+\lambda)$ elitist black-box model. Intuitively, this model is less powerful than the $(\lambda+1)$ model since we have to base our sampling strategies solely on the one search point in the memory. Still the model allows to check and compare several alternatives at the same time, so it should be considerably easier than the (1+1) situation.

Theorem 10. *Let $\varepsilon, C > 0$, and let $1 < \lambda < 2^{n^{1-\varepsilon}}$. For suitable $p = O(\log^2 n \log\log n \log \lambda / n)$ there exists a $(1+\lambda)$ p-Monte Carlo elitist black-box algorithm that needs at most $O(n/\log \lambda)$ generations on* OneMax.

We emphasize that the bound in Theorem 10 is in number of generations, not in terms of function evaluations. We feel that this is the more useful measure, in particular when the λ offspring can be generated in parallel. Note that an algorithm optimizing for the number of function evaluations can be substantially different from the ones minimizing the number of generations.

Proof Sketch. We optimize most bits by splitting the string into blocks of length at most $\lfloor \log_2 \lambda \rfloor$. In the i-th step we do exhaustive search for one block, i.e., we test all $2^{\lfloor \log_2 \lambda \rfloor} \leq \lambda$ possible inputs for this block. The best offspring will have optimized the i-th block. We use counters as for the $(1+1)$ EA to keep track of our current position, and optimize the counters in the very end by random local search. □

8. THE $(\mu+1)$ ELITIST BLACK-BOX COMPLEXITIES OF ONEMAX FOR $\mu > 2$

For the $(\mu+1)$ model we implement a variant of the *random sampling* optimization strategy of Erdős and Rényi [10] (see Section 3). The main technical difficulty is in making this approach satisfy the ranking-basedness condition, the memory-restriction, and the elitist selection requirement. Luckily, the first two problems have been solved in previous works, though not for both restrictions simultaneously (see our comment in the introduction).

Following previous work (see for example [7] for a description of this method invented in [4]), we can split the string into smaller blocks of size m each such that $t(m) \leq \mu$ random queries are sufficient to determine the optimal entries for one such block. We optimize these $n/t(m)$ blocks iteratively. Note that this is different from the strategy in Section 7, where all 2^t possible entries for a block of size t are sampled. Some care is needed to obtain an elitist algorithm, but this can be done using some of the tools developed for the (1+1) case.

Theorem 11. *For constant μ, the $(\mu+1)$ (Monte Carlo and Las Vegas) elitist black-box complexity of* OneMax *is $\Theta(n)$.*

For $\mu = \omega(\log^2 n / \log\log n) \cap O(n/\log n)$, for any constant $p > 0$ the $(\mu+1)$ p-Monte Carlo elitist black-box complexity of OneMax *is $\Theta(n/\log \mu)$.*

There exists a constant $C > 1$ such that for $\mu \geq Cn/\log n$, the $(\mu + 1)$ (p-Monte Carlo and Las Vegas) elitist black-box complexity is $\Theta(n/\log n)$.

9. REMARK ON (μ, λ) ELITIST BLACK-BOX COMPLEXITIES

It is interesting to note that it can be significantly easier in the elitist black-box model to optimize a function when allowed to use so-called *comma* strategies instead of the *plus* strategies described by Algorithm 1. To make things formal, we call an algorithm that follows the scheme of Algorithm 1 with Line 8 replaced by

$$\text{Set } X \leftarrow \{y^{(1)}, \ldots, y^{(\lambda)}\}$$

and Line 9 running only to $\lambda - \mu$ a (μ, λ) elitist algorithm. That is, a (μ, λ) elitist algorithm has to keep in each iteration the μ best sampled offspring, but it is allowed (and forced) to ignore the parent solutions (which, consequently, can be of better fitness). If the algorithm wants to maintain parts of the parental population, it can simply resample those individuals that should be kept.

Note in particular that (μ, λ) elitist algorithms can do restarts. Therefore, as discussed in Section 2.1, to bound the Las Vegas complexity of (μ, λ) elitist algorithms, it suffices to bound its Monte Carlo complexity. Note further that for all λ' with $\mu + \lambda' \leq \lambda$ we can imitate every $(\mu + \lambda')$ elitist black-box algorithm by a (μ, λ) elitist black-box algorithm. Thus, Theorems 6 and 10 immediately imply that there are $(1, \lambda)$ (Las Vegas and Monte Carlo) elitist black-box algorithm needing $O(n/\log \lambda)$ generations on OneMax for $2 \leq \lambda \leq 2^{n^{1-\varepsilon}}$. This bound is asymptotically tight since matching lower bounds follow from the same information-theoretic arguments as used in Theorem 4. By applying similar techniques as for the $(1 + \lambda)$ case we can easily improve the bounds as follows.

Theorem 12. *The (1,2) Las Vegas elitist black-box complexity of* OneMax *is at most $2n + 1$, and the correspnding algorithm needs at most $n + 1$ generations.*

For any $\lambda \geq 2$ there are $(1, \lambda)$ Las Vegas and Monte Carlo elitist black-box algorithms that need at most $\lceil n/\lfloor \log_2 \lambda \rfloor \rceil$ generations on OneMax.

For completeness, we note that the (1,1) (Las Vegas or Monte Carlo) complexity of OneMax is $\Theta(2^n)$. The Las Vegas upper bound is given by random sampling, and it implies the Monte Carlo upper bound as discussed in Section 2.1. For the lower bound, it is easy to see that the problem is at least as hard as the needle-in-haystack problem Needle where all search point except the optimum have the same fitness.

10. CONCLUSIONS

We have analyzed black-box complexities of OneMax with respect to $(\mu + \lambda)$ memory-restricted ranking-based algorithms. Moreover, we have shown that the complexity does not change if we also require the algorithms to be elitist, provided that we regard Monte-Carlo complexities. For different settings of μ and λ we have seen that such algorithms can be fairly efficient and attain the information-theoretic lower bounds.

An interesting open question arising from our work is a tight bound for the Las Vegas complexity of OneMax in the (1+1) elitist black-box model. We have sketched in Section 6 the main difficulties in turning our Monte Carlo algorithm into a Las Vegas heuristic. The possible discrepancy between these two notions also raises the question which problems can be optimized substantially more efficiently with restarts than without, an aspect for which some initial findings can be found in the literature, e.g., [12], but for which no strong characterization exists.

Acknowledgments

This research benefited from the support of the "FMJH Program Gaspard Monge in optimization and operation research", and from the support to this program from EDF.

11. REFERENCES

[1] G. Anil and R. P. Wiegand. Black-box search by elimination of fitness functions. In *FOGA'09*, pages 67–78. ACM, 2009.

[2] B. Doerr and C. Doerr. Black-box complexity: from complexity theory to playing Mastermind. In *GECCO'14, Companion Material*, pages 623–646. ACM, 2014. Tutorial slides.

[3] B. Doerr, C. Doerr, and F. Ebel. From black-box complexity to designing new genetic algorithms. *Theoretical Computer Science*, 567:87–104, 2015.

[4] B. Doerr, D. Johannsen, T. Kötzing, P. K. Lehre, M. Wagner, and C. Winzen. Faster black-box algorithms through higher arity operators. In *FOGA'11*, pages 163–172. ACM, 2011.

[5] B. Doerr and C. Winzen. Playing Mastermind with constant-size memory. *Theory of Computing Systems*, 55:658–684, 2014.

[6] B. Doerr and C. Winzen. Ranking-based black-box complexity. *Algorithmica*, 68:571–609, 2014.

[7] B. Doerr and C. Winzen. Reducing the arity in unbiased black-box complexity. *Theoretical Computer Science*, 545:108–121, 2014.

[8] C. Doerr and J. Lengler. Elitist black-box models: Analyzing the impact of elitist selection on the performance of evolutionary algorithms. In *GECCO'15*. ACM, 2015.

[9] S. Droste, T. Jansen, and I. Wegener. Upper and lower bounds for randomized search heuristics in black-box optimization. *Theory of Computing Systems*, 39:525–544, 2006.

[10] P. Erdős and A. Rényi. On two problems of information theory. *Magyar Tudományos Akadémia Matematikai Kutató Intézet Közleményei*, 8:229–243, 1963.

[11] O. A. Gross. Preferential arrangements. *The American Mathematical Monthly*, 69(1):pp. 4–8, 1962.

[12] T. Jansen. On the analysis of dynamic restart strategies for evolutionary algorithms. In *PPSN'02*, volume 2439 of *LNCS*, pages 33–43. Springer, 2002.

[13] P. K. Lehre and C. Witt. Black-box search by unbiased variation. *Algorithmica*, 64:623–642, 2012.

[14] O. Teytaud and S. Gelly. General lower bounds for evolutionary algorithms. In *PPSN'06*, volume 4193 of *LNCS*, pages 21–31. Springer, 2006.

[15] A. C.-C. Yao. Probabilistic computations: Toward a unified measure of complexity. In *FOCS'77*, pages 222–227. IEEE, 1977.

Population Size vs. Mutation Strength for the (1+λ) EA on OneMax

Christian Gießen
DTU Compute
Technical University of Denmark

Carsten Witt
DTU Compute
Technical University of Denmark

ABSTRACT

The (1+λ) EA with mutation probability c/n, where $c > 0$ is an arbitrary constant, is studied for the classical ONEMAX function. Its expected optimization time is analyzed exactly (up to lower order terms) as a function of c and λ. It turns out that $1/n$ is the only optimal mutation probability if $\lambda = o(\ln n \ln\ln n/\ln\ln\ln n)$, which is the cut-off point for linear speed-up. However, if λ is above this cut-off point then the standard mutation probability $1/n$ is no longer the only optimal choice. Instead, the expected number of generations is (up to lower order terms) independent of c, irrespectively of it being less than 1 or greater.

The results are obtained by a careful study of order statistics of the binomial distribution and variable drift theorems for upper and lower bounds.

Categories and Subject Descriptors

F.2 [**Theory of Computation**]: Analysis of Algorithms and Problem Complexity

Keywords

Runtime Analysis; Populations; Mutation

1. INTRODUCTION

The runtime analysis of evolutionary algorithms (EAs) is a research area that emerged from the analysis of classical randomized algorithms, where the aim is to prove rigorous statements on the expected runtime and approximation quality of the algorithm depending on the problem size. Since the late 1990s, a number of results on the runtime of simple and moderately complex evolutionary algorithms as well as of other nature-inspired algorithms have emerged [1, 10, 15]. Both simple benchmark functions such as ONEMAX and more complex combinatorial optimization problems were considered. The vast majority of these results are asymptotic, i. e., use O-notation. While such a result in O-notation tells how the runtime in the worst case scales with the problem size, it does not allow a direct comparison of different algorithms or parameter settings in a specific algorithm. For instance, the O-expression omits an implicit constant factor in front of the expression, which might be astronomically large. Hence, an $O(n^3)$-algorithm indeed might be more efficient for practical problem sizes than another $O(n \ln n)$-algorithm. This incomparability even persists if the upper bounds are supplemented by asymptotic lower bounds, e. g., $\Omega(n^3)$. Moreover, if a change of a parameter value such as mutation probability accounts only for a non-asymptotic change of the runtime, this will not become visible in the bound. As a consequence, the optimal setting of the parameter, which minimizes the runtime, is hard to determine.

In recent years, there has been increasing interest in non-asymptotic, tight analyses of EAs. Such analyses are more exact than asymptotic ones and therefore typically harder to derive. For instance, while the expected runtime of the simple (1+1) EA on ONEMAX had been known to be $\Theta(n \ln n)$ since the early days of the research area, the first tight lower bound of the kind $(1 - o(1))en \ln n$ was not proven until 2010 [3, 18]. For the more general case of linear functions, a long series of research result was published (e. g., [6, 9]) until Witt [19] finally proved that the expected runtime of the (1+1) EA equals $(1 \pm o(1))en \ln n$ for any linear function with non-zero weights.

Result like Witt's reveal the leading term in the representation of the expected runtime as a polynomial of n exactly and show that the underlying leading coefficient is in fact small (here $e = 2.71\dots$). This could not be read off from the classical $\Theta(n \ln n)$ result. However, there is greater potential in such a non-asymptotic analysis. It had for a long time been a rule of thumb to set the mutation probability of the (1+1) EA to $1/n$, i. e., to flip each bit independently with probability $1/n$; however, there was limited theoretical evidence for this. Doerr and Goldberg [5] were the first to prove that the $\Theta(n \ln n)$ bound for the (1+1) EA on linear functions also holds if the mutation probability is changed to c/n for an arbitrary positive constant c. Hence, changing the mutation probability to, say, $1/(10n)$ or $10/n$ does not change the asymptotic runtime behavior. Witt's study [19] proves the more general, tight (up to lower order terms) bound $(1 \pm o(1))\frac{e^c}{c} n \ln n$, which exhibits an interesting dependency on the factor $c > 0$ from the mutation probability. Since the factor $\frac{e^c}{c}$ is minimized for $c = 1$, this proves that the most often recommended mutation probability of $1/n$ is optimal for all linear functions.

GECCO '15, July 11–15, 2015, Madrid, Spain

ISBN 978-1-4503-3472-3/15/07...$15.00

DOI: http://dx.doi.org/10.1145/2739480.2754738

However, it is by no means clear that $1/n$ is the best choice under all circumstances. For instance, Böttcher, Doerr and Neumann [2] determined the expected optimization time of the (1+1) EA depending on the mutation probability p exactly for the LEADINGONES function. It turned out that the standard choice $p = 1/n$ is not optimal here, but a value of roughly $1.59/n$ minimizes the expected time. A similar result is represented by Sudholt's [17] analysis of a simple crossover-based EA on ONEMAX, where the optimal mutation probability turns out as $1.618/n$. Note that in both cases a more aggressive mutation than the standard choice is beneficial.

Our study continues this line of research on tight analyses; however, in addition to the mutation probability, we consider a second parameter, namely the population size of the underlying evolutionary algorithm. More precisely, we analyze the (1+λ) EA with mutation probability c/n, where c is an arbitrary positive constant, on the classical ONEMAX function. Our aim is to describe the expected runtime as a function of both the parameter λ (the population size) and the parameter c, in a non-asymptotically tight (up to lower order terms) manner. One aim is to determine the best parameter setting of c, depending on λ. We also pick up the so far quite limited line of work on the (1+λ) EA [7,8,11], which has been restricted to the standard mutation probability $1/n$, and where ONEMAX was analyzed before. From this line of work, the bound $\Theta(\frac{n \ln n}{\lambda} + n\frac{\ln\ln\lambda}{\ln\lambda})$ on the expected number of generations has been known; the computational effort in terms of the number of function evaluations is by a factor of λ bigger. A remarkable insight drawn from this bound is that the number of generations enjoys a linear speed-up with respect to λ as long as $\lambda = o(\ln n \ln\ln n/\ln\ln\ln n)$. If λ is above this threshold (the so-called *cut-off* point), the second term from the time bound becomes relevant and the linear speed-up ceases to exist. Another insight is that $\lambda = 1$ is at least asymptotically the best choice to minimize the expected number of f-evaluations; with respect to the standard mutation probability, this has actually been proven to be the absolute truth without asymptotics [11]: increasing λ never decreases the expected number of f-evaluations. Therefore, we are primarily interested in optimizing the mutation probability c depending on λ, assuming a sufficiently large parallel architecture allowing the λ offspring evaluations to be done in parallel.

In this paper, we prove that the expected runtime (i. e., number of generations) of the (1+λ) EA with mutation probability c/n on ONEMAX equals

$$(1 \pm o(1))\left(\frac{e^c}{c} \cdot \frac{n \ln n}{\lambda} + \frac{1}{2} \cdot \frac{n \ln\ln\lambda}{\ln\lambda}\right),$$

which greatly generalizes the previous $\Theta(\frac{n \ln n}{\lambda} + n\frac{\ln\ln\lambda}{\ln\lambda})$ bound. Hence, as long as λ is below the cut-off point, more precisely, if $\lambda = o(\ln n \ln\ln n/\ln\ln\ln n)$, the leading term of the expected runtime is the same as for linear functions with the (1+1) EA, and setting $c = 1$ minimizes the expected runtime. However, when λ is above the cut-off, more precisely, if $\lambda = \omega(\ln n \ln\ln n/\ln\ln\ln n)$, such that the second term becomes the leading term, one may choose c as an arbitrarily small or large constant without changing the expected runtime (up to lower order terms). So somewhat counter-intuitively, mutations are also allowed to occur less frequently than in a (1+1) EA. These exact results follow from a careful study of order statistics of the binomial distribution and are obtained by variable drift theorems for upper and lower bounds.

Altogether, our study gives advice on the choice of the mutation probability and also determines the cut-off point for speed-up for different mutation probabilities. To the best of our knowledge, this represents the first tight (upper to lower order terms) runtime analysis of a population-based EA, and it seems also be novel in developing such a tight expression for the runtime depending on two parameters. We remark that our analyses build on the insights by Doerr and Künnemann [8], who also give asymptotic results holding for arbitrary linear functions.

This paper is structured as follows. Section 2 introduces the framework, and presents drift theorems as well as properties of order statistics used for the analysis. Section 3 proves our main result and discusses its implications. We finish with some conclusions.

2. PRELIMINARIES

2.1 Algorithm

We consider the (1+λ) EA for the minimization of pseudo-boolean functions $f\colon \{0,1\}^n \to \mathbb{R}$, defined as Algorithm 1. The case of $c = 1$ in the mutation probability was considered in [7,8,11]. If both $\lambda = 1$ and $c = 1$, the algorithm simplifies to the classical (1+1) EA [1]. Throughout the paper, c is assumed to be constant, i. e., it may not depend on n.

Algorithm 1 (1+λ) EA

```
Select x* uniformly at random from {0,1}^n.
for t ← 1, 2, ... do
    for i ← 1, ..., λ do
        Create x_i by flipping each bit of x* independently
          with probability c/n.
    x_m ← arg min_{x_i} f(x_i) (breaking ties randomly)
    if f(x_m) ≤ f(x*) then
        x* ← x_m
```

The *runtime*, also called the *optimization time*, of the (1+λ) EA is the smallest t such that an individual of minimum f-value has been found. Note that t corresponds to a number of iterations (also called generations), where each generation creates λ offspring. Since each of these offspring has to be evaluated, the number of function evaluations, which is a classical cost measure, is by a factor of λ larger than the runtime as defined here. However, assuming a massively parallel architecture that allows for parallel evaluation of the offspring, counting the number of generations seems also a valid cost measure. In particular, a speed-up on the function ONEMAX$(x_1, \dots, x_n) := x_1 + \dots + x_n$ by increasing λ can only be observed in terms of the number of generations. As proven by Jansen, De Jong and Wegener [11], the (1+1) EA performs on ONEMAX stochastically at most the same number of function evaluations as any (1+λ) EA for $\lambda > 1$ and $c = 1$. For arbitrary c and even more general population-based algorithms, a corresponding statement is proven in [19]. Note that for reasons of symmetry, it makes no difference whether ONEMAX is minimized (as in the present paper) or maximized (as in several previous research papers).

Throughout the paper, all O-notation (mostly of the kind "$o(1)$") will be with respect to the problem size n.

2.2 Drift Theorems

Our results are obtained by variable drift analysis, which is also used in the asymptotic analysis of the (1+λ) EA on OneMax and other linear functions [8]. The first theorems stating upper bounds on the hitting time using variable drift go back to [12, 14]. These theorems were subsequently generalized in [16] and [13]. We use the latter version.

Theorem 1 (Variable Drift, Upper Bound; [13]). *Let $(X_t)_{t\geq 0}$, be a stochastic process adapted to a filtration $\mathcal{F}_t$ over some state space $S \subseteq \{0\} \cup [x_{\min}, x_{\max}]$, where $x_{\min} > 0$. Let $h(x)\colon [x_{\min}, x_{\max}] \to \mathbb{R}^+$ be a monotone increasing function such that $1/h(x)$ is integrable on $[x_{\min}, x_{\max}]$ and $E(X_t - X_{t+1} \mid \mathcal{F}_t) \geq h(X_t)$ if $X_t \geq x_{\min}$. Then it holds for the first hitting time $T := \min\{t \mid X_t = 0\}$ that*

$$E(T \mid X_0) \leq \frac{x_{\min}}{h(x_{\min})} + \int_{x_{\min}}^{X_0} \frac{1}{h(x)}\,\mathrm{d}x \ .$$

To prove lower bounds on the hitting time by variable drift, we need additional assumptions like the one in the following lemma, a special case of which was first proposed in [4].

Theorem 2 (Variable Drift, Lower Bound; [13]). *Let $(X_t)_{t\geq 0}$, be a stochastic process adapted to a filtration $\mathcal{F}_t$ over state space $S \subseteq \{0\}\cup[x_{\min}, x_{\max}]$, where $x_{\min} > 0$. Suppose there exists two functions $\xi, h\colon [x_{\min}, x_{\max}] \to \mathbb{R}^+$ such that $h(x)$ is monotone increasing and $1/h(x)$ integrable on $[x_{\min}, x_{\max}]$, and for all $t \geq 0$,*

(i) $X_{t+1} \leq X_t$,

(ii) $X_{t+1} \geq \xi(X_t)$ for $X_t \geq x_{\min}$,

(iii) $E(X_t - X_{t+1} \mid \mathcal{F}_t) \leq h(\xi(X_t))$ for $X_t \geq x_{\min}$.

Then it holds for the first hitting time $T := \min\{t \mid X_t = 0\}$ that

$$E(T \mid X_0) \geq \frac{x_{\min}}{h(x_{\min})} + \int_{x_{\min}}^{X_0} \frac{1}{h(x)}\,\mathrm{d}x \ .$$

2.3 Tight Bounds on Order Statistics

When the (1+λ) EA optimizes OneMax, it samples λ offspring and takes the so-called winner individual from the offspring having minimum OneMax-value, breaking ties arbitrarily. This problem is strongly related to analyzing how many one-bits are flipped in the offspring that flips most one-bits (however, this is not necessarily the winner individual). The number of flipping one-bits per offspring follows a binomial distribution, which is why the following lemma on order statistics of the binomial distribution is crucial.

Lemma 1. *Let X_i, where $i \in \{1, \dots, \lambda\}$, independent random variables being identically distributed as $X_i \sim \mathrm{Bin}(k, c/n)$ for some $k \leq n$ and constant $c > 0$. Let $X^* := \max\{X_1, \dots, X_\lambda\}$ be the maximum order statistic of the X_i. Then*

1. *If $\lambda ck/n = o(1)$ then $E(X^*) = (1 - o(1))\lambda E(X_1) = (1 - o(1))\lambda ck/n$.*
2. *If $\lambda ck/n \geq \alpha$ for $\alpha > 0$ then $E(X^*) \geq \alpha/(1 + \alpha)$.*
3. *If $\lambda = \omega(1)$ and $k = n/(\ln^\alpha \lambda)$, where $\alpha \geq 0$ and $\alpha = O(1)$, then $E(X^*) = \frac{(1\pm o(1))}{1+\alpha}\frac{\ln\lambda}{\ln\ln\lambda}$.*

Proof. We start with the first item. Note that for $j \geq 0$,

$$\Pr(X^* = j) \geq \binom{\lambda}{1} \Pr(X_1 = j)\,(\Pr(X_1 < j))^{\lambda-1} \ ,$$

since the maximum equals j if exactly one of the variables takes this value and the remaining ones are less; to denote a single of the identically distributed random variables, we always refer to X_1.

The last bound is

$$\lambda\Pr(X_1 = j)\,(1 - \Pr(X_1 \geq j))^{\lambda-1} \geq \lambda\Pr(X_1 = j)\,(1 - \lambda\Pr(X_1 \geq j))$$

according to Bernoulli's inequality. If $j \geq 1$ then

$$\Pr(X_1 \geq j) \leq E(X_1)/j \leq E(X_1)$$

by Markov's inequality. Altogether,

$$\begin{aligned}\Pr(X^* = j) &\geq \lambda\Pr(X_1 = j)(1 - \lambda E(X_1)) \\ &= (1 - o(1))\lambda\Pr(X_1 = j)\end{aligned}$$

by our assumption that $\lambda E(X_1) = \lambda ck/n = o(1)$. The item now follows since

$$\begin{aligned}E(X^*) &= \sum_{j=1}^{n} j \cdot \Pr(X^* = j) \\ &\geq \sum_{j=1}^{n} j(1 - o(1))\lambda\Pr(X_1 = j) \\ &= (1 - o(1))\lambda E(X_1)\end{aligned}$$

along with the trivial upper bound $E(X^*) \leq \lambda E(X_1)$.

To show the second item, we note that

$$\begin{aligned}E(X^*) &= \sum_{\ell\geq 1} \Pr(X^* \geq \ell) \\ &\geq \Pr(X^* \geq 1) \\ &= 1 - (\Pr(X_1 = 0))^\lambda \ ,\end{aligned}$$

since the maximum is at least 1 if it does not happen that all λ random variables evaluate to 0. Hence, using $e^x \geq 1 + x$ and $e^{-x} \leq 1/(1 + x)$ for $x \in \mathbb{R}$, we have

$$\begin{aligned}E(X^*) &\geq 1 - \left(\left(1 - \frac{c}{n}\right)^k\right)^\lambda \\ &\geq 1 - \left(\left(1 - \frac{c}{n}\right)^{\frac{\alpha n}{c\lambda}}\right)^\lambda \\ &\geq 1 - \left(e^{-\frac{\alpha}{\lambda}}\right)^\lambda \\ &= 1 - e^{-\alpha} \\ &\geq 1 - \left(\frac{1}{1+\alpha}\right) \\ &= \frac{\alpha}{1+\alpha} \ .\end{aligned}$$

To prove the third item, we will first show $E(X^*) \leq (1 + o(1))\frac{\ln\lambda}{(1+\alpha)\ln\ln\lambda}$ and then $E(X^*) \geq (1-o(1))\frac{\ln\lambda}{(1+\alpha)\ln\ln\lambda}$. We use that

$$\begin{aligned}\Pr(X^* \geq j) &= 1 - (\Pr(X_1 < j))^\lambda \\ &= 1 - (1 - \Pr(X_1 \geq j))^\lambda \ .\end{aligned}$$

Furthermore,

$$\Pr(X_1 \geq j) \leq \binom{n/(\ln^\alpha \lambda)}{j}\left(\frac{c}{n}\right)^j$$
$$\leq \left(\frac{c}{\ln^\alpha \lambda}\right)^j \frac{1}{j!}$$
$$\leq \left(\frac{ce}{j\ln^\alpha \lambda}\right)^j ,$$

where the last inequality uses $j! \geq (j/e)^j$. Plugging this in our expression for $\Pr(X^* \geq j)$, we have

$$\Pr(X^* \geq j) \leq 1 - \left(1 - \left(\frac{ce}{j\ln^\alpha \lambda}\right)^j\right)^\lambda .$$

The aim now is to inspect the last bound for $j = \frac{\ln\lambda}{(1+\alpha)\ln\ln\lambda} + \beta$, where $\beta \geq \delta(\lambda) := 4\frac{\ln\lambda(\ln\ln\ln\lambda+1+\ln c+\ln(1+\alpha))}{(\ln\ln\lambda)^2}$ (the choice of $\delta = \delta(\lambda)$ is to some extent arbitrary). We will estimate the inner term $(ce/(j\ln^\alpha\lambda))^j = e^{-j(\ln(j/(ce))+\alpha\ln\ln\lambda)}$ from above. We start with the first term in the last exponent and compute

$$\begin{aligned}
&j(\ln(j/(ce)))\\
&= \left(\frac{\ln\lambda}{(1+\alpha)\ln\ln\lambda}+\beta\right)\ln\left(\frac{\ln\lambda}{(1+\alpha)ce\ln\ln\lambda}+\frac{\beta}{ce}\right)\\
&\geq \left(\frac{\ln\lambda}{(1+\alpha)\ln\ln\lambda}+\beta\right)(\ln\ln\lambda-\ln\ln\ln\lambda-\ln(ce(1+\alpha)))\\
&\geq \frac{\ln\lambda}{1+\alpha}+\frac{\beta(\ln\ln\lambda)^2/2-\ln\lambda(\ln\ln\ln\lambda+\ln(ce(1+\alpha))}{\ln\ln\lambda} ,
\end{aligned}$$

where the last inequality assumes $\ln\ln\lambda - \ln\ln\ln\lambda - \ln(ce(1+\alpha)) \geq (\ln\ln\lambda)/2$, which holds for large enough λ, and uses $1+\alpha \geq 1$.

By definition of δ, we have $\beta(\ln\ln\lambda)^2/2 - \ln\lambda(\ln\ln\ln\lambda + 1 + \ln c + \ln(1+\alpha)) \geq \beta(\ln\ln\lambda)^2/4$, and therefore

$$j\ln(j/(ce)) \geq \frac{\ln\lambda}{1+\alpha} + \frac{\beta}{4}(\ln\ln\lambda) .$$

Therefore, the whole exponent is bounded from below according to

$$\begin{aligned}
j(\ln(j/(ce)) + (\alpha\ln\ln\lambda)) &\geq \frac{\ln\lambda}{1+\alpha}+\frac{\beta}{4}(\ln\ln\lambda)\\
&\quad + \alpha\ln\ln\lambda\left(\frac{\ln\lambda}{(1+\alpha)\ln\ln\lambda}+\beta\right)\\
&\geq \ln\lambda + \frac{\beta}{4}(\ln\ln\lambda) .
\end{aligned}$$

Plugging this in our expression for $\Pr(X^* \geq j)$, we have for $\beta' := \beta/4$

$$\begin{aligned}
\Pr(X^* \geq j) &\leq 1 - \left(1 - e^{-\ln\lambda - \beta'(\ln\ln\lambda)}\right)^\lambda\\
&\leq 1 - \left(1 - \frac{1}{\lambda}e^{-\beta'(\ln\ln\lambda)}\right)^{\frac{\lambda e^{\beta'(\ln\ln\lambda)}}{2}\cdot\frac{2}{e^{\beta'(\ln\ln\lambda)}}}\\
&\leq 1 - e^{-2e^{-\beta'(\ln\ln\lambda)}}\\
&\leq 1 - (1 - 2e^{-\beta'(\ln\ln\lambda)}) = 2e^{-\beta'(\ln\ln\lambda)} ,
\end{aligned}$$

using first $(1-1/x)^{x/2} \geq e^{-1}$ for $x \geq 2$ and then $e^{-x} \geq 1-x$ for $x \in \mathbb{R}$.

Now,

$$\begin{aligned}
E(X^*) &= \sum_{j\geq 1}\Pr(X^* \geq j)\\
&\leq \frac{\ln\lambda}{(1+\alpha)\ln\ln\lambda} + \delta + \sum_{j\geq \frac{\ln\lambda}{(1+\alpha)\ln\ln\lambda}+\delta}\Pr(X^* \geq j) .
\end{aligned}$$

The last sum is now split in sub-sums consisting of δ terms each, where still $\delta = 4\frac{\ln\lambda(\ln\ln\ln\lambda+1+\ln c+\ln(1+\alpha))}{(\ln\ln\lambda)^2}$. We get

$$\begin{aligned}
&\sum_{j>\frac{\ln\lambda}{(1+\alpha)\ln\ln\lambda}+\delta}\Pr(X^* \geq j)\\
&\leq \sum_{i=1}^{\infty}\delta\cdot\Pr\left(X^* \geq \frac{\ln\lambda}{(1+\alpha)\ln\ln\lambda}+i\delta\right)\\
&\leq \sum_{i=1}^{\infty}2\delta e^{-i(\delta/4)(\ln\ln\lambda)} = o(1)
\end{aligned}$$

according to our bound on $\Pr(X^* \geq j)$ and the geometric series. Altogether,

$$E(X^*) \leq \frac{\ln\lambda}{(1+\alpha)\ln\ln\lambda} + \delta + o(1) = \frac{1+o(1)}{1+\alpha}\frac{\ln\lambda}{\ln\ln\lambda} ,$$

which proves the upper bound on $E(X^*)$ from the third item.

We are left with the lower bound. Note that for $j \geq 1$,

$$\begin{aligned}
\Pr(X_1 \geq j) &\geq \binom{n/\ln^\alpha\lambda}{j}\left(\frac{c}{n}\right)^j\left(1-\frac{c}{n}\right)^{n-j}\\
&\geq \left(\frac{n}{j\ln^\alpha\lambda}\right)^j\left(\frac{c}{n}\right)^j e^{-2c}\\
&= e^{-2c}\left(\frac{c}{j\ln^\alpha\lambda}\right)^j .
\end{aligned}$$

Thus, we get

$$\Pr(X^* < j) \leq \left(1 - e^{-2c}\left(\frac{c}{j\ln^\alpha\lambda}\right)^j\right)^\lambda .$$

Similarly to the upper bound, we consider the last bound for $j = \frac{\ln\lambda}{(1+\alpha)\ln\ln\lambda} - \beta$, where $\beta = 2\frac{\ln\lambda\ln(c(1+\alpha)\ln\ln\lambda)}{(\ln\ln\lambda)^2}$. Using the equality $(c/(j\ln^\alpha\lambda))^j = e^{-j(\ln(j/c)+\alpha\ln\ln\lambda)}$, we get that

$$j\ln(j/c) \leq \frac{\ln\lambda}{1+\alpha} - \beta\ln\ln\lambda .$$

Since $j\ln(j/c) + j\alpha\ln\ln\lambda \leq \ln\lambda - \beta\ln\ln\lambda$ we have in total

$$\begin{aligned}
\Pr(X^* < j) &\leq \left(1 - e^{-2c}\left(\frac{c}{j\ln^\alpha\lambda}\right)^j\right)^\lambda\\
&\leq \left(1 - e^{-\ln\lambda - 2c + \beta\ln\ln\lambda}\right)^\lambda\\
&\leq \left(1 - \frac{1}{\lambda e^{2c-\beta\ln\ln\lambda}}\right)^{\lambda e^{2c-\beta\ln\ln\lambda}\cdot\frac{1}{e^{2c-\beta\ln\ln\lambda}}}\\
&\leq e^{-e^{-2c+\beta\ln\ln\lambda}} ,
\end{aligned}$$

which is $o(1)$. By the law of total probability we have that for all j

$$\begin{aligned}
E(X^*) &\geq \Pr(X^* \geq j)E(X^* \mid X^* \geq j)\\
&\geq j(1 - \Pr(X^* < j)) ,
\end{aligned}$$

Plugging in $j = \frac{\ln \lambda}{(1+\alpha)\ln\ln\lambda} - \beta$ immediately gives the desired bound

$$E(X^*) \geq \left(\frac{\ln \lambda}{(1+\alpha)\ln\ln\lambda} - \beta\right)(1-o(1)) = \frac{1-o(1)}{1+\alpha}\frac{\ln\lambda}{\ln\ln\lambda} \ . \quad \square$$

The parameter k used in Lemma 1 above will correspond to the number of one-bits in the current individual (recall that the aim is to create an individual with all zeros since we are minimizing). Hence, the progress can be as big as X^*, the maximum number of flipping one-bits in the λ trials creating offspring. However, it is not guaranteed that the offspring flipping most one-bits is accepted. For instance, it could flip even more zero-bits. Therefore, the following lemma will be used to estimate the probability of accepting the individual related to the number X^*.

LEMMA 2. *Assume that an individual with k one-bits is mutated by flipping each bit independently with probability c/n, where $c > 0$ is a constant. The probability that no zero-bit flips in this mutation is at least*

$$(1-o(1))e^{-c+\frac{kc}{n}} \ .$$

Moreover, the probability that the mutation creates an individual with at most k one-bits (i. e., at most the same ONEMAX*-value) is at most*

$$(1+o(1))e^{-c+\frac{k(c+c^2)}{n}} \ .$$

PROOF. We start with the first claim. The probability of not flipping a zero-bit equals

$$\left(1-\frac{c}{n}\right)^{n-k} = \left(1-\frac{c}{n}\right)^{n}\left(1-\frac{c}{n}\right)^{-k} \geq (1-o(1))e^{-c}e^{kc/n} \ ,$$

where we have used that c is a constant.

To create an individual with at most k one-bits, it is necessary that at least the same number of one-bits as zero-bits flips. The probability of flipping at least j one-bits is bounded from above $\binom{k}{j}\left(\frac{c}{n}\right)^j$ and the probability of flipping exactly j zero-bits equals $\binom{n-k}{j}\left(\frac{c}{n}\right)^j\left(1-\frac{c}{n}\right)^{n-k-j}$. Hence, the probability of obtaining at most k one-bits is at most

$$\sum_{j=0}^{\max\{k,n-k\}} \binom{k}{j}\binom{n-k}{j}\left(\frac{c}{n}\right)^{2j}\left(1-\frac{c}{n}\right)^{n-k-j}$$
$$\leq \left(1-\frac{c}{n}\right)^{n-k}\left(\sum_{j=0}^{\ln n}\binom{k}{j}\binom{n-k}{j}\left(\frac{c}{n}\right)^{2j}\left(1-\frac{c}{n}\right)^{-\ln n} + e^{-\Omega(\ln n \ln\ln n)}\right) \ ,$$

where we have used that the probability of flipping at least $\ln n$ bits is $e^{-\Omega(\ln n \ln \ln n)}$ for any mutation probability c/n. Using $\binom{a}{b} \leq \frac{a^b}{b!}$ and subsuming lower order terms into a $o(1)$-term, our bound is at most

$$(1+o(1))e^{-c+kc/n}\left(\sum_{j=0}^{\ln n}\frac{k^j(n-k)^j}{j!\cdot j!}\left(\frac{c^2}{n^2}\right)^j\right)$$
$$\leq (1+o(1))e^{-c+kc/n}\left(\sum_{j=0}^{\infty}\frac{(c^2(k/n)((n-k)/n))^j}{j!}\right)$$
$$\leq (1+o(1))e^{-c+kc/n}e^{c^2\frac{k}{n}\frac{n-k}{n}} \leq (1+o(1))e^{-c+\frac{k}{n}(c+c^2)} \ ,$$

where the last inequality used $(n-k)/n \leq 1$. $\square$

Finally, to a similar purpose as described before Lemma 2, we will need the following lemma to correct the progress made by the individual flipping most one-bits by the number of flipping zero-bits. The statement is given in a general framework without appealing to a particular distribution; the notation $\succ$ denotes stochastic dominance.

LEMMA 3. *Let $X_1, \dots, X_\lambda$ and $Y_1, \dots, Y_\lambda$ be two sequences of independent, identically distributed random variables. Let $Z_i := X_i - Y_i$ for $i \in \{1, \dots, \lambda\}$ and $Z^* := \max\{Z_i \mid i \in \{1, \dots, \lambda\}\}$. Then*

$$Z^* \succ \max\{X_i \mid i \in \{1, \dots, \lambda\}\} - Y_1 \ ,$$

where the index 1 without loss of generality refers to any of the Y_i.

PROOF. We show the lemma only for $\lambda = 2$; the general case follows in the same way. We abbreviate $\tilde{Z}^* := \max\{X_i \mid i \in \{1, \dots, \lambda\}\} - Y_1$ and note that we have to show

$$\Pr(Z^* \geq x) \geq \Pr\left(\tilde{Z}^* \geq x\right)$$

for all $x \in \mathbb{R}$. By definition and using independence

$$\Pr(Z^* \geq x) = 1 - (\Pr(X_1 - Y_1 < x) \cdot \Pr(X_2 - Y_2 < x))$$

and due to dependence

$$\Pr\left(\tilde{Z}^* \geq x\right) = 1 - (\Pr(X_1 - Y_1 < x) \cdot \Pr(X_2 - Y_1 < x \mid X_1 - Y_1 < x)) \ .$$

The lemma follows if we can show that $\Pr(X_2 - Y_2 < x) \leq \Pr(X_2 - Y_1 < x \mid X_1 - Y_1 < x)$. To see this, note that $Y_1 \sim Y_2$ without any conditioning. The condition is $Y_1 > X_1 - x$, so given this lower bound the probability of also $Y_1 > X_2 - x$ happening only becomes larger. $\square$

3. ANALYSIS OF (1+λ) EA ON ONEMAX

The following theorem is our main result.

THEOREM 3. *Suppose $\lambda \leq n^r$ for some natural number r and let T denote the optimization time (i. e., number of generations) of the (1+λ) EA with mutation probability c/n, where $c > 0$ is a constant, on* ONEMAX*. Then*

$$E(T) = (1 \pm o(1))\left(\frac{e^c}{c}\cdot\frac{n\ln n}{\lambda} + \frac{1}{2}\cdot\frac{n\ln\ln\lambda}{\ln\lambda}\right).$$

Before we prove the theorem, we discuss its implications. If $\lambda = o(\ln n \ln\ln n/\ln\ln\ln n)$, the first term is asymptotically largest and we observe the linear speed-up by a factor of λ. Since $\frac{e^c}{c}$ is minimized for $c = 1$, the optimal mutation probability (minimizing the expected optimization time) is $1/n$. Neither mutation probabilities that are by a constant factor larger or by a constant factor smaller are optimal.

If $\lambda = \omega(\ln n \ln\ln n/\ln\ln\ln n)$, i.e., is above the cut-off point for speed-up, the second term from the bound becomes the leading term and it turns out that choosing c arbitrarily small or large (but constant) is no worse than the standard choice $c = 1$. A large population makes the algorithm more robust with respect to the choice of the mutation probability.

PROOF OF THEOREM 3. Let X_t denote the number of one-bits of the current search point of the (1+λ) EA at generation t and $\Delta_t := X_t - X_{t+1}$. Recall that the aim is to reach an X_t-value of 0.

In order to show the upper bound we will for some regions only consider steps of the process where progress towards the optimum occurs from one-bits only, i. e., for some regions we condition the process on the event that no zero-bit flips in the offspring with largest number of flipping one-bits. According to Lemma 2, this probability is at least $(1-o(1))e^{-c+cX_t/n} \geq (1-o(1))e^{-c}$. Conditioning on this event, which considers the mutation of the zero-bits and is independent of the mutation of the one-bits, we can estimate the drift for different regimes w. r. t. X_t.

We first consider the case of $\lambda = \omega(1)$. We have that $E(\Delta_t \mid X_t) \geq h(X_t)$, where

$$h(X_t) := \begin{cases} (1-o(1))\frac{\ln\lambda}{\ln\ln\lambda} & \text{if } X_t \geq \frac{n}{(\ln\lambda)^{\frac{1}{\ln\ln\ln\lambda}}} \\ (1/2-o(1))e^{-c}\frac{\ln\lambda}{\ln\ln\lambda} & \text{if } X_t \geq \frac{n}{\ln\lambda} \\ (1-o(1))e^{-c}\min\{c,1\}/2 & \text{if } X_t \geq \frac{n}{\lambda} \\ (1-o(1))e^{-c}\frac{c}{\sqrt{\ln n}} & \text{if } X_t \geq \frac{n}{\lambda\sqrt{\ln n}} \\ (1-o(1))ce^{-c}\lambda X_t/n & \text{if } X_t < \frac{n}{\lambda\sqrt{\ln n}} \end{cases} .$$

The bound on the drift for the first regime can be obtained from $E(\Delta_t \mid X_t) \geq (1-o(1))E(X^*)$, where X^* denotes the maximum number of flipping ones over λ offspring at generation t which can be shown as follows. Let Y_i, where $1 \leq i \leq \lambda$, denote the progress of an offspring of a parent of fitness k in one step (after selection). Then, $Y_i \sim \max\{0, Y_i^1 - Y_i^0\}$, where $Y_i^0 \sim \text{Bin}(n-k, c/n)$ and $Y_i^1 \sim \text{Bin}(k, c/n)$ denote the random number of zeros and ones flipped by mutation, respectively. Clearly, $Y_i \succ Y_i^1 - Y_i^0$ and $\max\{Y_i \mid 1 \leq i \leq \lambda\} \succ \max\{Y_i^1 - Y_i^0 \mid 1 \leq i \leq \lambda\}$. From Lemma 3 it follows that

$$\Delta_t = \max\{Y_i \mid 1 \leq i \leq \lambda\} \succ \max\{Y_i^1 \mid 1 \leq i \leq \lambda\} - Y_1^0,$$

where the index 1 is without loss of generality and refers to an arbitrary of the λ offspring. Since $\max\{Y_i^1 \mid 1 \leq i \leq \lambda\} = X^*$, by linearity of expectation this yields $E(\Delta_t \mid X_t) \geq E(X^*) - c = (1-o(1))E(X^*)$ if $E(X^*) = \omega(1)$. Applying the third statement of Lemma 1 with $\alpha = (\ln\ln\ln\lambda)^{-1}$ recalling that $\lambda = \omega(1)$ provides us with the desired bound. Note this argument is specific for the first regime. For all the other regimes, we instead condition on the event that the offspring flipping most one-bits does not flip zero-bits, introducing the aforementioned factor of $(1-o(1))e^{-c}$ for each bound.

The second bound on the drift is obtained by applying the third statement of Lemma 1 with $\alpha = 1$.

The third bound on the drift stems from the second statement of Lemma 1 with $\alpha = \min\{c, 1\}$.

The fourth regime's bound on the drift stems from the second statement of Lemma 1 with $\alpha = c/\sqrt{\ln n}$. Finally, the last bound stems from the first statement of Lemma 1. Note also that h is monotone increasing w. r. t. X_t (choosing the smallest $1-o(1)$ function from the five regimes and using $\lambda = \omega(1)$) and that its reciprocal is integrable on $\mathbb{R}^+$.

Now that we have established bounds on the drift we can apply Theorem 1 with minimal distance $x_{\min} = 1$ and get

$$E(T \mid X_0) \leq \frac{1}{h(1)} + \int_1^{X_0} \frac{1}{h(x)}\,\mathrm{d}x .$$

The first term is

$$\frac{1}{h(1)} = \frac{1}{(1-o(1))\lambda c e^{-c}\frac{1}{n}} = (1+o(1))\frac{e^c n}{\lambda c} ,$$

which is a lower order term in the total expected optimization time as we will see in the following.

We will now examine each regime's contribution to the expected optimization time by splitting up the integral at the corresponding bounds. Due to our definition of h the first four regimes' contribution can be easily computed since they do not depend on X_t.

For the first regime, we first determine X_0. Using a Chernoff bound, the probability that the initial individual is created within $[n/2 - n^{2/3}, n/2 + n^{2/3}]$ is at least $1 - 2e^{-\frac{2n^{1/3}}{3}}$, so we will condition on this in the following, introducing a small error probability absorbed by the $o(1)$-term of the theorem.

The first regime contributes a term of at most

$$\int_{\frac{n}{(\ln\lambda)^{\frac{1}{\ln\ln\ln\lambda}}}}^{\frac{n}{2}+n^{\frac{2}{3}}} \frac{\mathrm{d}x}{(1-o(1))\frac{\ln\lambda}{\ln\ln\lambda}} \leq (1+o(1))\frac{\left(\frac{n}{2}+n^{\frac{2}{3}}\right)\ln\ln\lambda}{\ln\lambda} \leq (1+o(1))\frac{1}{2}\frac{n\ln\ln\lambda}{\ln\lambda} .$$

The second regime contributes a term of at most

$$\int_{\frac{n}{\ln\lambda}}^{\frac{n}{(\ln\lambda)^{\frac{1}{\ln\ln\ln\lambda}}}} \frac{\mathrm{d}x}{(\frac{1}{2}-o(1))e^{-c}\frac{\ln\lambda}{\ln\ln\lambda}} \leq (2+o(1))\frac{e^c n\ln\ln\lambda}{(\ln\lambda)^{1+\frac{1}{\ln\ln\ln\lambda}}} .$$

This term is clearly asymptotically smaller than the first, due to the denominator's exponent.

The third regime contributes a term of at most

$$\int_{\frac{n}{\lambda}}^{\frac{n}{\ln\lambda}} \frac{\mathrm{d}x}{(1-o(1))e^{-c}\min\{c/2, 1/2\}} \leq \frac{(1+o(1))\,2e^c n}{\min\{c,1\}\ln\lambda} ,$$

and is thus asymptotically smaller than the first term as well.

The fourth regime contributes a term of at most

$$\int_{\frac{n}{\lambda\sqrt{\ln n}}}^{\frac{n}{\lambda}} \frac{\mathrm{d}x}{(1-o(1))e^{-c}\frac{c}{\sqrt{\ln n}}} \leq (1+o(1))\frac{e^c n\sqrt{\ln n}}{c\lambda} ,$$

which is dominated by the following term.

The fifth regime contributes a term of at most

$$\int_1^{\frac{n}{\lambda\sqrt{\ln n}}} \frac{e^c n}{(1-o(1))\lambda c x}\,\mathrm{d}x \leq (1+o(1))\frac{e^c n\ln n}{c\lambda} .$$

Summing up the individual contributions we end up with

$$E(T) \leq (1+o(1))\left(\frac{e^c}{c}\cdot\frac{n\ln n}{\lambda} + \frac{1}{2}\cdot\frac{n\ln\ln\lambda}{\ln\lambda}\right) ,$$

since the unconditional error introduced by the conditioning on the initialization is of lower order. Note that this holds for the case of $\lambda = \omega(1)$.

In case of $\lambda = O(1)$ the first four regimes can be subsumed; using the same arguments as in the previous case we have $E(\Delta_t \mid X_t) \geq \hat{h}(X_t)$, where

$$\hat{h}(X_t) := \begin{cases} (1-o(1))e^{-c}\frac{c}{\sqrt{\ln n}} & \text{if } X_t \geq \frac{n}{\lambda\sqrt{\ln n}} \\ (1-o(1))ce^{-c}\lambda X_t/n & \text{if } X_t < \frac{n}{\lambda\sqrt{\ln n}} \end{cases} .$$

The first regime contributes a term of at most

$$\int_{\frac{n}{\lambda\sqrt{\ln n}}}^{\frac{n}{2}+n^{\frac{2}{3}}} \frac{\mathrm{d}x}{(1-o(1))e^{-c}\frac{c}{\sqrt{\ln n}}} \leq \left(\frac{1}{2}+o(1)\right)\frac{e^c n\sqrt{\ln n}}{c} ,$$

which is clearly dominated by the second regime's contribution which is the same as in the previous case by reusing the same arguments. Hence, for $\lambda = O(1)$, we have $E(T) \leq (1+o(1))\left((e^c/c) n \ln n\right)$.

Combining both cases, i. e. for all $\lambda \leq n^r$, we end up with the desired bound of

$$E(T) \leq (1+o(1))\left(\frac{e^c}{c}\cdot\frac{n\ln n}{\lambda} + \frac{1}{2}\cdot\frac{n\ln\ln\lambda}{\ln\lambda}\right) .$$

Using Theorem 2, we will now show the matching lower bound. Theorem 2 requires a monotone process and a function ξ bounding the progress towards the optimum. We define $\xi : \mathbb{R}^+ \to \mathbb{R}^+, x \mapsto x - \log_2 x - 1$.

Note that $\Pr(X_t < \xi(X_t)) \leq \Pr(X_t \leq \xi(X_t))$. Due to our assumption that $\lambda \leq n^r$ we have

$$\begin{aligned}\Pr(X_{t+1} \leq \xi(X_t)) &\leq \lambda\binom{X_t}{\log_2 X_t + 1}\left(\frac{1}{n}\right)^{\log_2(X_t)+1} \\ &\leq n^r\left(\frac{eX_t}{n\log_2(X_t)+n}\right)^{\log_2(X_t)+1} .\end{aligned}$$

Setting $x_{\min} := 2^r$, the last term assumes its maximum at $X_t = x_{\min}$ within $[x_{\min}, \ldots, n]$ for sufficiently large n and takes the value r'/n^{r+1}, where $r' = ((ex_{\min})/(r+1))^{r+1}$. We condition on the event that $X_{t+1} \geq \xi(X_t)$ holds for the at most $O(n \ln n)$ generations we consider; by a union bound this introduces an error of $o(1)$. Note also that this condition only decreases the drift.

We first deal with the case of $\lambda < \ln^2 n$. We have that $E(\Delta_t \mid X_t) \leq h^*(X_t)$, where

$$h^*(X_t) := \begin{cases}(1+o(1))\frac{\ln\lambda}{\ln\ln\lambda} & \text{if } X_t \geq \frac{n}{\lambda\sqrt{\ln n}} \\ (1+o(1))ce^{-c}\lambda X_t/n & \text{if } X_t < \frac{n}{\lambda\sqrt{\ln n}}\end{cases} ,$$

where the bounds on the drift follow from the fourth statement with $\alpha = 0$ and the first statement of Lemma 1, respectively. In the first region, we estimate the drift from above by the number of flipping one-bits. We may introduce the factor $(1+o(1))e^{-c}$ for the last region since by Markov's inequality the probability that more than one offspring flips at least one one-bit is $o(1)$ and also the probability that more than one one-bit is flipped in the winner individual is $o(1)$. We work under the condition that $\lambda - 1$ offspring do not flip one-bits and one of them at most one one-bit. This conditioning introduces only a lower order term. Now, the probability that the only individual flipping one-bits can make progress is at most $(1+o(1))e^{-c}$ by the second statement of Lemma 2.

Note that h^* is increasing. Note also that ξ^{-1} exists and that it is increasing as well. We can define $\tilde{h} := h^* \circ \xi^{-1}$. By applying Theorem 2 we obtain

$$\begin{aligned}E(T \mid X_0) &\geq \frac{x_{\min}}{\tilde{h}(x_{\min})} + \int_{x_{\min}}^{X_0} \frac{1}{\tilde{h}(u)}\,\mathrm{d}u \\ &= \frac{x_{\min}}{h^*(\xi^{-1}(x_{\min}))} + \int_{\xi^{-1}(x_{\min})}^{\xi^{-1}(X_0)} \frac{\left(1-\frac{1}{x}\right)}{h^*(x)}\,\mathrm{d}x .\end{aligned}$$

The last equality is due to integration by substitution and due to $(\xi^{-1})' = (\xi')^{-1}$ which holds for ξ on the considered domain. Hereinafter, we abbreviate $h^{**}(x) := h^*(x)/\left(1-\frac{1}{x}\right)$.

Due to the definition of $x_{\min}$ the first term is

$$\frac{2^r}{\tilde{h}(2^r)} = \frac{2^r}{(1+o(1))\lambda ce^{-c\frac{2\cdot 2^r}{n}}} = (1-o(1))\frac{e^c n}{2\lambda c} ,$$

where we used $\xi^{-1}(x) \leq 2x$ for $x \geq 4$ which is easy to see. This is a lower order term as we will see in the following.

Regarding the integral, we again split the integral into the regimes that we bounded the drift on, in order to analyze those individually. We get

$$\int_{\xi^{-1}(x_{\min})}^{\xi^{-1}(X_0)} \frac{\mathrm{d}x}{h^{**}(x)} = \int_{\xi^{-1}(x_{\min})}^{\frac{n}{\lambda\sqrt{\ln n}}} \frac{\mathrm{d}x}{h^{**}(x)} + \int_{\frac{n}{\lambda\sqrt{\ln n}}}^{\xi^{-1}(X_0)} \frac{\mathrm{d}x}{h^{**}(x)} .$$

We start with the first integral. We have

$$\begin{aligned}\int_{\xi^{-1}(x_{\min})}^{\frac{n}{\lambda\sqrt{\ln n}}} \frac{1}{h^{**}(x)}\,\mathrm{d}x &\geq \int_{2x_{\min}}^{\frac{n}{\lambda\sqrt{\ln n}}} \frac{n\left(1-\frac{1}{x}\right)}{(1+o(1))ce^{-c}\lambda x}\,\mathrm{d}x \\ &= \frac{e^c n}{(1+o(1))c\lambda}\int_{2x_{\min}}^{\frac{n}{\lambda\sqrt{\ln n}}}\left(\frac{1}{x}-\frac{1}{x^2}\right)\mathrm{d}x \\ &= \frac{e^c n}{(1+o(1))c\lambda}\Bigg(\ln n - \ln\lambda - \frac{\ln\ln n}{2} \\ &\qquad - \ln(2x_{\min}) + \frac{\lambda\sqrt{\ln n}}{n} - \frac{1}{2x_{\min}}\Bigg) \\ &\geq (1-o(1))\frac{e^c n\ln n}{c\lambda}\end{aligned}$$

since $\lambda < \ln^2 n$.

Similar to the proof of the upper bound, we have that the algorithm initializes with high probability in $[n/2 - n^{2/3}, n/2 + n^{2/3}]$ by using a Chernoff bound, i. e., $X_0 \geq n/2 - n^{2/3}$. In the following we condition on this event, introducing only a small error absorbed by the $o(1)$-term.

Now, for the second integral it holds that

$$\begin{aligned}\int_{\frac{n}{\lambda\sqrt{\ln n}}}^{\xi^{-1}(X_0)} \frac{1}{h^{**}(x)}\,\mathrm{d}x &\geq \int_{\frac{n}{\lambda\sqrt{\ln n}}}^{X_0} \frac{\ln\ln\lambda\left(1-\frac{1}{x}\right)}{(1+o(1))\ln\lambda}\,\mathrm{d}x \\ &\geq \frac{\ln\ln\lambda}{(1+o(1))\ln\lambda}\left(\frac{n}{2} - n^{\frac{2}{3}} - \frac{n}{\lambda\sqrt{\ln n}}\right) \\ &\quad - \frac{\ln\ln\lambda}{(1+o(1))\ln\lambda}\left(\ln\left(\frac{\frac{n}{2}-n^{\frac{2}{3}}}{\frac{n}{\lambda\sqrt{\ln n}}}\right)\right) \\ &\geq \frac{\ln\ln\lambda}{(1+o(1))\ln\lambda}\left(\frac{(1-o(1))n}{2}\right) \\ &\geq (1-o(1))\frac{1}{2}\frac{n\ln\ln\lambda}{\ln\lambda} ,\end{aligned}$$

where the first inequality follows from $\xi^{-1}(x) \geq x$ and the third inequality is due to the subtracted summand being a lower order term.

If $\lambda \geq \ln^2 n$, we have that $E(\Delta_t \mid X_t) \leq \tilde{h}^*(X_t)$, where

$$\tilde{h}^*(X_t) := (1+o(1))\frac{\ln\lambda}{\ln\ln\lambda}$$

for all $X_t \geq 0$. Reusing the analysis of the contribution of the first region in $h^*(X_t)$ above, we get the lower bound

$$(1-o(1))\frac{1}{2}\frac{n\ln\ln\lambda}{\ln\lambda}$$

in this case, which is the leading term in the bound from the theorem since λ is above the cut-off point.

Now we can give a bound on the expected runtime for all $\lambda \leq n^r$. Summing up the individual contributions, we end up with

$$E(T) \geq (1 - o(1)) \left(\frac{e^c}{c} \cdot \frac{n \ln n}{\lambda} + \frac{1}{2} \cdot \frac{n \ln \ln \lambda}{\ln \lambda} \right) ,$$

since the unconditional error introduced by the conditioning is of lower order. □

Conclusions

We have presented the first tight runtime analysis of a population-based EA, depending on population size and mutation probability. More precisely, we have analyzed the well-known (1+λ) EA with mutation probability c/n, where $c > 0$ is a constant, on the classical ONEMAX function. Our results show that $1/n$ is the only optimal mutation probability if $\lambda = o(\ln n \ln \ln n / \ln \ln \ln n)$, which is the cut-off point for linear speed-up. However, if λ is above this cut-off point then the standard mutation probability $1/n$ is no longer the only optimal choice and the algorithm is more robust with respect to this choice. In fact, the expected number of generations is independent of c then (up to lower order terms), irrespectively of c being less than 1 or greater.

Our results shed light on the interplay of population size and mutation probability in evolutionary algorithms. At the same time, we have extended our reservoir of methods for the analysis. We are optimistic that our study paves the ground for tight analyses of more complex population-based EAs on also more complex function classes.

Acknowledgements

This work was supported by the Danish Council for Independent Research (DFF), grant no. 4002–00542.

4. REFERENCES

[1] Anne Auger and Benjamin Doerr, editors. *Theory of Randomized Search Heuristics: Foundations and Recent Developments.* World Scientific Publishing, 2011.

[2] Süntje Böttcher, Benjamin Doerr, and Frank Neumann. Optimal fixed and adaptive mutation rates for the leadingones problem. In *Proc. of Parallel Problem Solving from Nature (PPSN 2010)*, volume 6238, pages 1–10. Springer, 2010.

[3] Benjamin Doerr, Mahmoud Fouz, and Carsten Witt. Quasirandom evolutionary algorithms. In *Proc. of the Genetic and Evolutionary Computation Conference (GECCO 2010)*, page 1457–1464. ACM Press, 2010.

[4] Benjamin Doerr, Mahmoud Fouz, and Carsten Witt. Sharp bounds by probability-generating functions and variable drift. In *Proc. of the Genetic and Evolutionary Computation Conference (GECCO 2011)*, pages 2083–2090. ACM Press, 2011.

[5] Benjamin Doerr and Leslie Ann Goldberg. Adaptive drift analysis. *Algorithmica*, 65(1):224–250, 2013.

[6] Benjamin Doerr, Daniel Johannsen, and Carola Winzen. Multiplicative drift analysis. *Algorithmica*, 64(4):673–697, 2012.

[7] Benjamin Doerr and Marvin Künnemann. Royal road functions and the (1+λ) evolutionary algorithm: Almost no speed-up from larger offspring populations. In *Proc. of the IEEE Congress on Evolutionary Computation (CEC 2013)*, pages 424–431. IEEE Press, 2013.

[8] Benjamin Doerr and Marvin Künnemann. Optimizing linear functions with the (1+λ) evolutionary algorithm – different asymptotic runtimes for different instances. *Theoretical Computer Science*, 561:3–23, 2015.

[9] Jens Jägersküpper. Combining markov-chain analysis and drift analysis – the (1+1) evolutionary algorithm on linear functions reloaded. *Algorithmica*, 59(3):409–424, 2011. Preliminary version in Proc. of PPSN '08.

[10] Thomas Jansen. *Analyzing Evolutionary Algorithms - The Computer Science Perspective.* Natural Computing Series. Springer, 2013.

[11] Thomas Jansen, Kenneth A. De Jong, and Ingo Wegener. On the choice of the offspring population size in evolutionary algorithms. *Evolutionary Computation*, 13(4):413–440, 2005.

[12] Daniel Johannsen. *Random combinatorial structures and randomized search heuristics.* PhD thesis, Universität des Saarlandes, Germany, 2010.

[13] Per Kristian Lehre and Carsten Witt. Concentrated hitting times of randomized search heuristics with variable drift. In *Proc. of ISAAC '14*, volume 8889 of *Lecture Notes in Computer Science*, pages 686–697. Springer, 2014. Full technical report at http://arxiv.org/abs/1307.2559.

[14] Boris Mitavskiy, Jonathan E. Rowe, and Chris Cannings. Theoretical analysis of local search strategies to optimize network communication subject to preserving the total number of links. *International Journal of Intelligent Computing and Cybernetics*, 2(2):243–284, 2009.

[15] Frank Neumann and Carsten Witt. *Bioinspired Computation in Combinatorial Optimization – Algorithms and Their Computational Complexity.* Natural Computing Series. Springer, 2010.

[16] Jonathan E. Rowe and Dirk Sudholt. The choice of the offspring population size in the (1, λ) evolutionary algorithm. *Theoretical Computer Science*, 545:20–38, 2014. Preliminary version in Proc. of GECCO 2012.

[17] Dirk Sudholt. Crossover speeds up building-block assembly. In *Proc. of the Genetic and Evolutionary Computation Conference (GECCO 2012)*, pages 689–702. ACM Press, 2012.

[18] Dirk Sudholt. A new method for lower bounds on the running time of evolutionary algorithms. *IEEE Transactions on Evolutionary Computation*, 17(3):418–435, 2013. Preliminary version in Proc. of PPSN '10.

[19] Carsten Witt. Tight bounds on the optimization time of a randomized search heuristic on linear functions. *Combinatorics, Probability & Computing*, 22(2):294–318, 2013. Preliminary version in Proc. of STACS '12.

On the Utility of Island Models in Dynamic Optimization

Andrei Lissovoi
DTU Compute, Technical University of Denmark
Kongens Lyngby, Denmark

Carsten Witt
DTU Compute, Technical University of Denmark
Kongens Lyngby, Denmark

ABSTRACT

A simple island model with λ islands and migration occurring after every τ iterations is studied on the dynamic fitness function MAZE. This model is equivalent to a (1+λ) EA if $\tau = 1$, i. e., migration occurs during every iteration. It is proved that even for an increased offspring population size up to $\lambda = O(n^{1-\epsilon})$, the (1+$\lambda$) EA is still not able to track the optimum of MAZE. If the migration interval is increased, the algorithm is able to track the optimum even for logarithmic λ. Finally, the relationship of τ, λ, and the ability of the island model to track the optimum is investigated more closely.

Categories and Subject Descriptors

F.2 [**Theory of Computation**]: Analysis of Algorithms and Problem Complexity

Keywords

Evolutionary Algorithms; Island Models; Dynamic Problems; Populations; Runtime Analysis

1. INTRODUCTION

Evolutionary algorithms (EAs) are a class of nature-inspired algorithms which can be applied to solve a wide variety of optimization problems. Rigorous runtime analysis of nature-inspired algorithms, building on mathematical methods from the analysis of classical algorithms, has advanced considerably in recent years [3, 15]. While most of these studies focus on so-called static optimization problems, whose set of optima is fixed, there has been increasing interest in the analysis of evolutionary and other nature-inspired algorithms on so-called dynamic problems. Many real-world optimization problems are subject to dynamics in that the optimal solution may change as the problem conditions change over time, and the algorithms therefore need to be able to not only find or approximate the optimum at some point of time, but also to *track* the optimal solution over time as the problem changes.

Application of EAs to dynamic optimization problems is the subject of study in the Evolutionary Dynamic Optimization field, which in recent years has attracted much activity. Many applications of evolutionary algorithms on dynamic problems are considered in the literature [2, 16], and there are already a number of runtime analyses of evolutionary algorithms for dynamic problems [6–8, 10, 17].

Despite the increasing interest in the area, it has not been well understood what mechanisms allow EAs or related nature-inspired algorithms to efficiently track the optimum of a dynamic problem. In [11], Kötzing and Molter introduced a dynamic pseudo-Boolean function called MAZE that separates simple evolutionary algorithms and ant colony optimization. More precisely, the paper shows that while a Max-Min Ant System (MMAS) is able to track the changes occurring in the MAZE fitness function and finds the optimum within polynomial time, a (1+1) EA loses track of the optimum and requires with high probability an exponential amount of time to find the optimum. Very recently, Lissovoi and Witt [13] have built upon this study and shown that introducing a parent population makes the evolutionary algorithm efficient in tracking the MAZE again. Moreover, they present a generalization of the MAZE function that allows for a hierarchy result. More precisely, a family of functions parameterized by μ is defined such that a parent population size of μ allows efficient tracking of the optimum, while population size $\mu - 1$ makes the algorithm lose track of the optimum with high probability. Moreover, a simple MMAS is proved insensitive with respect to the parameter as it is able to track the optimum without any modifications for a wide range of values for μ.

In this work, we consider a different mechanism and analyze its benefit in tracking the optimum of the MAZE benchmark function. More precisely, we focus on parallel nature-inspired algorithms, which are heavily employed in practice due the rapid development of parallel computer architectures. The survey by Alba, Luque and Nesmachnow [1] describes important applications and theoretical studies in this area. In particular, it refers to experiments with parallel nature-inspired algorithms in dynamic optimization, including a study of a parallel swarm algorithm for dynamic vehicle routing problems [9]. It is therefore interesting to determine the theoretical properties of parallel nature-inspired algorithms that allow them to track the optimum of a dynamic problem. Both the number of so-called islands (independent subpopulations) and the communication between them

GECCO '15 July 11–15, 2015, Madrid, Spain

ISBN 978-1-4503-3472-3/15/07...$15.00
DOI: http://dx.doi.org/10.1145/2739480.2754734

seem influential. From a more general perspective, [16] emphasizes the usefulness of memory and diversity-maintaining operators in EAs for dynamic optimization.

Our contribution is represented by a runtime analysis of a parallel EA for the dynamic MAZE problem. We define a simple parallel EA using an island model with communication occurring within regular intervals, the so-called migration intervals, in the style of Lässig and Sudholt [12], who pioneered the runtime analysis of parallel EAs. The impact of two parameters is studied, namely the number of islands λ and length of the migration intervals τ. In the extreme case that $\tau = 1$, i. e., migration occurs in every generation, the model boils down to a (1+λ) EA. It is shown that offspring population sizes, i. e., number of islands, of up to $\lambda = O(n^{1-\epsilon})$, where n is the problem size and ϵ an arbitrarily small positive constant, do not allow this algorithm to track the MAZE efficiently. In contrast, if τ is chosen appropriately, ensuring that migration does not occur too frequently, already $\lambda = \Omega(\log n)$ islands allow efficient tracking of the optimum of the MAZE. Moreover, more general conditions on the choice of τ are worked out, resulting in either efficient tracking or losing track of the optimum. To the best of our knowledge, our contribution represents the first runtime analysis of parallel EAs in dynamic optimization. The results indicate that carefully choosing the migration policy and thereby the communication strategy of an island model can be more advantageous than a mere increase of offspring population size.

This paper is structured as follows. In Section 2, we introduce the parallel EA and the dynamic optimization problem MAZE studied throughout the paper. Moreover, important tools for the analysis are defined. Section 3 is concerned with the negative result for the parallel EA with $\tau = 1$, i. e., the (1+λ) EA. The case of appropriately chosen τ, leading to efficient tracking with a small number of islands, is analyzed in Section 4. Moreover, the section elaborates on the impact of the choice of τ on efficient tracking in a more general sense. We finish with some conclusions.

2. PRELIMINARIES

The MAZE fitness function, proposed in [11], and defined formally below, consists of $n+1$ phases of $t_0 = kn^3 \log n$ iterations each. This phase length was used in [11] to allow the Max-Min Ant System (MMAS) algorithm time to adjust the pheromone values during each phase, and is preserved here for mostly historical reasons. For convenience, we will assume that k is chosen such that t_0 is a multiple of 3.

During the first phase of the MAZE, which we will for convenience refer to as phase 0, the function is equivalent to ONEMAX: the fitness of an n-bit string is equal to the number of 1-bits in the string. During phase p, where $1 \le p \le n$, higher fitness values $n+1$ and $n+2$ are assigned to two individuals determined by the phase in an oscillating pattern: every two iterations out of three, the OPT_p individual is assigned the fitness value $n+2$ while the ALT_p individual is assigned the fitness value $n+1$, and during every third iteration, these assignments are reversed; all other individuals retain their ONEMAX values. Past the last oscillating phase ("phase n"), MAZE behaves in a fashion similar to TRAP: all individuals except 0^n are assigned ONEMAX values, while 0^n is the global optimum, being assigned the highest fitness value. [11] proves that a (1+1) EA loses track of the optimum of this MAZE function, reverting to optimizing ONEMAX, and is therefore not able to construct the final $\text{OPT}_n = 0^n$ optimum in a polynomial number of iterations.

$$\text{MAZE}(x,t) = \begin{cases} n+2 & \text{if } t > (n+1)\cdot t_0 \wedge x = 0^n \\ n+2 & \text{if } t > t_0 \wedge x = \text{OPT}(t) \\ n+1 & \text{if } t > t_0 \wedge x = \text{ALT}(t) \\ \text{ONEMAX}(x) & \text{otherwise} \end{cases}$$

$$\text{OPT}(t) = \begin{cases} \text{OPT}_{\lfloor t/t_0 \rfloor} & \text{if } t \neq 0 \mod 3 \\ \text{ALT}_{\lfloor t/t_0 \rfloor} & \text{otherwise} \end{cases}$$

$$\text{ALT}(t) = \begin{cases} \text{ALT}_{\lfloor t/t_0 \rfloor} & \text{if } t \neq 0 \mod 3 \\ \text{OPT}_{\lfloor t/t_0 \rfloor} & \text{otherwise} \end{cases}$$

$$\text{OPT}_p = 0^p 1^{n-p} \qquad \text{for } p \le n$$

$$\text{ALT}_p = 0^{p-1} 1^{n-p+1} \qquad \text{for } p \le n$$

$$\text{ALL}_p = \{\text{ALT}_p, \text{OPT}_p\}$$

We note that the clock t is considered external to the MAZE function, allowing the fitness value of multiple solutions to be evaluated in each clock value t. For the (1+λ) EA, and the λ island model, this corresponds to having hardware available to evaluate many solutions in parallel, or having the problem changes occur at fixed intervals regardless of the number of parallel evaluations.

We consider the behavior of the (1+λ) EA, shown as Algorithm 1, and that of a simple island model running λ (1+1) EAs in parallel, using a complete migration topology (i. e. during migration, all islands communicate with all other islands), with various choices for the frequency of migration, shown as Algorithm 2, on the MAZE function. Both algorithms use the standard bit mutation operator, formalized in Definition 1.

Notably, the (1+λ) EA is a special case of the island model where migration occurs during every iteration.

Algorithm 1 (1+λ) EA

```
Select x* uniformly at random from {0,1}^n.
for t ← 1,2,... do
    for i ← 1,...,λ do
        x_i ← mutate(x*)
    x_m ← arg max_{x_i} f(x_i, t)
    if f(x_m, t) ≥ f(x*, t) then
        x* ← x_m
```

Algorithm 2 Island model with λ islands running (1+1) EAs in parallel.

```
for i ← 1,...,λ do
    Select x_i* uniformly at random from {0,1}^n.
for t ← 1,2,... do
    if migration occurs during iteration t then
        Let x_m = arg max_{x_i*} f(x_i*, t)
        x_i* ← x_m for all i ∈ {1,...,λ}
    for i ← 1,...,λ in parallel do
        x_i ← mutate(x_i*)
        if f(x_i, t) ≥ f(x_i*, t) then
            x_i* ← x_i
```

DEFINITION 1 (STANDARD BIT MUTATION). *The mutation operator* mutate(x) *creates an image* $y \in \{0,1\}^n$ *from*

$x \in \{0,1\}^n$ *by independently replacing each bit* x_i *of* x $(1 \leq i \leq n)$ *with* $1 - x_i$ *with probability* $1/n$.

In the analysis of the (1+λ) EA and the simple island model, we make use of Markov chain mixing times to bound the probability that the algorithm is in a particular state (i. e. has a particular best-so-far individual) after a certain number of iterations. This has been applied to ant colony optimization in [18] and to analyze the $(\mu+1)$ EA on MAZE in [13]; for completeness, we repeat the definitions of mixing and coupling times below.

DEFINITION 2 (MIXING TIME). *Consider an ergodic Markov chain over a state space* Ω *with stationary distribution* π. *Let* $p_x^{(t)}$ *denote the distribution of the Markov chain* t *iterations after starting in state* x, *and let*

$$t(\varepsilon) := \max_{x\in\Omega} \min\left\{t : \frac{1}{2}\sum_{y\in\Omega} p_x^{(t)}(y) - \pi(y) \leq \varepsilon\right\}.$$

The mixing time t_{mix} *of the Markov chain is then defined as* $t_{mix} = t(1/(2e))$.

DEFINITION 3 (COUPLING TIME). *Consider a pair process* $(X^{(t)}, Y^{(t)})$, *where both* $X^{(t)}$ *and* $Y^{(t)}$, *viewed in isolation, are instances of the same Markov chain. Coupling time* T_{xy} *is the random time until the two processes, initialized in different states* x *and* y, *are in the same state for the first time:*

$$T_{xy} = \min\{t : X^{(t)} = Y^{(t)} \mid X^{(0)} = x,\, Y^{(0)} = y\}.$$

As shown in [18], coupling time can be used as an upper-bound on mixing time:

LEMMA 4. *The worst-case coupling time of a Markov chain over a state space* Ω *is an upper bound on its mixing time:*

$$t(\varepsilon) \leq \min\left\{t : \max_{x,y\in\Omega} P(T_{xy} > t) \leq \varepsilon\right\}.$$

Additionally, the following drift theorem, adapted from [4, 5], is useful when considering longer migration intervals.

THEOREM 5 (MULTIPLICATIVE DRIFT). *Let* $S \subseteq \mathbb{R}$ *be a finite set of positive numbers with minimum* $s_{\min} > 0$. *Let* $\{X^{(t)}\}_{t\geq 0}$ *be a sequence of random variables over* $S \cup \{0\}$. *Let* T *be the random first point in time* $t \geq 0$ *for which* $X^{(t)} = 0$.

Suppose there exists a $\delta > 0$ *such that*

$$E(X^{(t)} - X^{(t+1)} \mid X^{(t)} = s) \geq \delta s$$

for all $s \in S$ *with* $P(X^{(t)} = s) > 0$. *Then for all* $s_0 \in S$ *with* $P(X^{(0)} = s_0) > 0$,

$$E(T \mid X^{(0)} = s_0) \leq \frac{\ln(s_0/s_{\min}) + 1}{\delta}$$

Moreover, it holds that $P(T > (\ln(s_0/s_{\min}) + r)/\delta) \leq e^{-r}$ *for any* $r > 0$.

Several lemmas throughout this paper state that "a specific event occurs with high probability." Definition 6 provides a more formal definition of this concept.

DEFINITION 6. *An event* E *is said to occur* with high probability *if, for every constant* $c > 0$, $P(E) = 1 - O(n^{-c})$.

In general, we say that an algorithm is able to track the optimum of the MAZE when it is able to construct the OPT_n individual in polynomial time (with high probability). Typically, this would correspond to maintaining at most a constant Hamming distance to the OPT_p intermediate optima during the oscillating phases.

3. (1+λ) EA ON MAZE

In this section, we analyze the behavior of the (1+λ) EA on MAZE. As long as λ is not too large (trivializing the problem by exploring the entire neighborhood of hamming distance 1 during every iteration), the EA is not able to track the optimum of the MAZE, and reverts to optimizing ONEMAX. This is formalized in the following theorem, whose proof is inspired by the strategy taken in [13].

THEOREM 7. *The (1+λ) EA with* $\lambda \in O(n^{1-\epsilon})$, *for any constant* $\epsilon > 0$, *will with high probability lose track of the optimum of* MAZE, *i. e. with high probability it will require an exponential number of iterations to construct* OPT_n.

We first note that the EA is able to find the $\text{OPT}_0 = 1^n$ optimum easily during the initial phase. For the subsequent n oscillating phases, we will show that the EA has at most a constant probability of ending each phase with $x^* = \text{OPT}_p$. Additionally, if an oscillating phase $p > n/2+3$ begins with $x^* \notin \text{ALL}_p$ (i. e. $x^* \neq \text{OPT}_{p-1}$), there is at least a constant probability that it will end with $x^* = 1^n$, and if this occurs, the (1+λ) EA will with high probability not be able to construct the 0^n optimum at the end of the MAZE.

LEMMA 8. *The (1+λ) EA constructs* $OPT_0 = 1^n$ *with high probability after* $O(n \log n)$ *iterations during the initial phase.*

PROOF. The initial phase consists of optimizing ONEMAX, which a (1+1) EA accomplishes in $O(n \log n)$ iterations with high probability. Increasing the size of the offspring population λ can only decrease time required; and we note that t_0 is asymptotically greater than $O(n \log n)$.

To prove this for both (1+1) EA and (1+λ) EA, Theorem 5 can be applied. Let $X^{(t)}$ be the number of zero-bits in the bit string x^* during iteration t:

$$E(X^{(t)} - X^{(t+1)} \mid X^{(t)} = x) \geq \frac{x(1-1/n)^{n-1}}{n} \geq \frac{1}{ne}x,$$

noting that for the (1+λ) EA, this is a coarse lower bound stemming from the assumption that only the first offspring in each iteration may have a higher ONEMAX value than x^*. As $X^{(0)} \leq n$,

$$E(T) \leq \frac{\ln(n)+1}{1/(ne)} = ne\ln(n) + ne.$$

Applying the tail-bound with $r = c_1 \ln n$ yields an upper bound on the probability of exceeding the expected number of iterations to reach $X^{(t)} = 0$ (i. e. to find the 1^n optimum) by more than $c_2 n \ln n$ additional iterations, where both c_1, c_2 are constants:

$$e^{-c_1 \ln n} = n^{-c_1}$$

i. e. 1^n is constructed by the EA in $ne\ln(n) + ne + c_2 n \ln n = O(n \log n)$ iterations with probability $1 - n^{-c_1}$. □

LEMMA 9. *The probability that the (1+λ) EA with* $\lambda = O(n^{1-\epsilon})$ *ends phase p with* OPT_p *as the best-so-far individual, given that* $x^* \in ALL_p$ *at least* $c\lambda/n$ *iterations before the end of phase p, where c is a sufficiently large constant, is at least* $\Omega(1)$ *and at most* $1 - \Omega(1)$.

PROOF. Once an ALL_p individual is constructed, all future best-so-far individuals within a phase will either be OPT_p or ALT_p, with single-bit mutations at specific iterations of the oscillation allowing the EA to switch between the two.

Let p_1 be the probability that a mutation flipping only one particular bit of x^* occurs in a single iteration of the (1+λ) EA, i.e. the probability OPT_p is constructed from ALT_p (or vice versa) as at least one of the λ offspring individuals:

$$p_1 = 1 - \left(1 - (1 - 1/n)^{n-1}/n\right)^{\lambda}$$

which can be bounded by assuming $n \geq 2$, and using $1-x \leq e^{-x}$ and $e^{-x} \leq 1 - x/2$ (for $x \leq 1$) for the upper and lower bounds respectively:

$$1 - (1 - 1/(en))^{\lambda} \leq p_1 \leq 1 - (1 - 1/(2n))^{\lambda}$$
$$\lambda/(2en) \leq 1 - e^{-\lambda/(en)} \leq p_1 \leq \lambda/(2n).$$

Consider the phase as a series of oscillations, each consisting of three iterations. During the first two iterations of an oscillation, OPT_n has a higher fitness value than ALT_n (and vice versa during the third and final iteration). We then consider the probabilities p_A and p_O of the best-so-far individual switching to ALT_p from OPT_p, and to OPT_p from ALT_p, respectively, over a single oscillation. For p_A, a specific one-bit mutation has to occur during the final iteration of the oscillation, while for p_O, a specific one-bit mutation has to occur during either the first or the second iteration of the oscillation, and a specific one-bit mutation must not occur during the third iteration:

$$\begin{aligned} p_A &= p_1 \\ p_O &= (p_1 + (1 - p_1)p_1)(1 - p_1) \\ &= 2p_1 - 3{p_1}^2 + {p_1}^3 \\ &= p_1(2 - 3p_1 + {p_1}^2) \end{aligned}$$

The identity of the best-so-far individual x^* of the (1+λ) EA, observed at the end of each OPT-OPT-ALT oscillation can be modeled using a two-state Markov chain, with one state corresponding to $x^* = \text{OPT}_p$, the other to $x^* = \text{ALT}_p$, and transition probabilities between the states as above.

Let π_O and $\pi_A = 1 - \pi_O$ be the steady-state probabilities of $x^* = \text{OPT}_p$ and $x^* = \text{ALT}_p$ respectively; as the Markov chain only contains two states, the following holds for the steady-state:

$$\begin{aligned} \pi_O p_A &= \pi_A p_O \\ \pi_O p_1 &= (1 - \pi_O)p_1(2 - 3p_1 + {p_1}^2) \\ \pi_O &= \frac{2 - 3p_1 + {p_1}^2}{3 - 3p_1 + {p_1}^2} \end{aligned}$$

i.e. π_O approaches a constant; we note that $\pi_O \leq 2/3$, and as $\lambda \in o(n)$ and hence $p_1 \leq \lambda/(2n) \leq 0.5$, $\pi_O \geq 3/7$.

Over time, the probability of OPT_p being the best-so-far individual at the end of an oscillation will approach the steady-state probability π_O. By applying Lemma 4, coupling time can be used as a bound on the Markov chain mixing time, and hence on the number of oscillations required until this probability is within a sufficiently small ϵ of π_O.

For our two-state Markov chain, the pair processes used to determine the worst-case coupling time are initialized in opposite states (i.e. one with $x^* = \text{OPT}_p$ and the other with $x^* = \text{ALT}_p$). During each step, the probability that coupling does not occur is the sum of probabilities that neither, or both, of the processes changed state:

$$\begin{aligned} \max P(T_{xy} > t) &= (p_A p_O + (1 - p_A)(1 - p_O))^t \\ &= (1 + 2p_A p_O - p_A - p_O)^t \\ &= (1 - p_1(3 - 7p_1 + 7{p_1}^2 - 2{p_1}^3))^t \\ &\leq \left(1 - \frac{\lambda}{2en}\left(3 - \frac{7\lambda}{2n} + \frac{7\lambda^2}{4e^2n^2} - \frac{2\lambda^3}{8n^3}\right)\right)^t \\ &< \left(1 - \frac{\lambda}{2en}\right)^t \end{aligned}$$

by recalling that $\lambda = o(n)$, and observing that the expression in the inner parentheses is greater than 1 when $\lambda/n \leq 0.5$. Then, an upper bound on the coupling time is:

$$t(\varepsilon) \leq \min\left\{t : (1 - \lambda/(2en))^t \leq \varepsilon\right\}$$

After at most $t(0.01) < 9.22en/\lambda$ steps of the Markov chain, or at most $76n/\lambda$ iterations of the (1+λ) EA, the probability that $x^* = \text{OPT}_p$ is therefore within $[\pi_O - 0.01, \pi_O + 0.01]$, which, as $3/7 \leq \pi_O \leq 2/3$, proves the lemma. □

LEMMA 10. *If a phase* $p > n/2+3$ *begins with* $x^* \notin ALL_p$ *satisfying* $f(x^*) > n - p + 1$, *the (1+λ) EA with offspring population size* $\lambda = O(n^{1-\epsilon})$, *for any constant* $\epsilon > 0$, *ends the phase with* $x^* = 1^n$ *with at least constant probability.*

PROOF. At the start of phase p, x^* contains strictly more 1-bits than any individual in ALL_p, and the Hamming distance between x^* and the closest ALL_p individual is at least 1. Let $p_R \leq p_1$ be the probability that an ALL_p individual is constructed during an iteration (where p_1 is the probability of at least one of the λ offspring being constructed via a specific single-bit mutation, as used in the proof of Lemma 9).

We want to consider the probability that the number of 1-bits in x^* exceeds that in any ALL_p individual by at least 3 (i.e. is at least $n+4-p \leq n/2$) before an ALL_p individual is constructed. An individual with a greater ONEMAX value is constructed via a single-bit mutation with probability at least p_L:

$$\begin{aligned} p_L &\geq 1 - (1 - n/2 \cdot (1 - 1/n)^{n-1}/n)^{\lambda} \\ &\geq 1 - 0.75^{\lambda} \geq 1/4 \end{aligned}$$

as there are at least $n/2$ 0-bits that can be flipped to increase ONEMAX value. We note that after at most 2 ONEMAX-improvements, constructing the closest ALL_p individual requires at least 3 1-bits to be flipped simultaneously.

Consider the probability that two ONEMAX improvements occur before an ALL_p individual is constructed. Let L be the event that a ONEMAX-improving single-bit mutation occurs, and R be the event that an ALL_p individual is constructed:

$$P(R \mid R \vee L) \leq \frac{p_R}{p_R + p_L} \leq \frac{\lambda}{2n\left(\frac{\lambda}{2en} + 1/4\right)}$$
$$= \frac{2e\lambda}{en + 2\lambda} \in O(\lambda/n)$$

assuming, as before, $\lambda \in O(n^{1-\epsilon})$, where $\epsilon > 0$.

Let D be the event that $f(x^*) \geq n + 4 - p$, i.e. either $x \in \text{ALL}_p$, or x^* has at least three more 1-bits than any individual in ALL_p:

$$P(x \notin \text{ALL}_p \mid D) \geq (1 - P(R \mid R \vee L))^2 \in \Omega(1),$$

by pessimistically requiring that at least two separate improvements to the OneMax value occurred (L) without an ALL_p individual being constructed (R).

Let T_D be the number of iterations between the start of the phase and the first time D occurs. We can upper-bound $E(T_D)$ considering the time required for two one-bit mutations that increase OneMax value of x^* occur; noting that there are $\Omega(n)$ 0-bits in x^* at the start of the phase, the probability that a one-bit mutation improving the OneMax value occurs during an iteration is at least a constant, and hence $E(T_D) \leq c$ for some constant c. Applying Markov's inequality, $P(T_D > 2c) \leq 1/2$, and hence the probability that D occurs within $c' \cdot cn = O(n)$ iterations is at least $1 - 2^{-c'n} = 1 - 2^{-\Omega(n)}$.

Once D occurs and $x^* \notin \text{ALL}_p$, and if no ALL_p individuals are constructed in subsequent iterations, we can consider the fitness function equivalent to OneMax, and per Lemma 8, 1^n is found with high probability in $O(n \log n)$ iterations. As constructing an ALL_p individual after D has occurred requires at least 3 specific bits to be mutated simultaneously (which occurs with probability at most $1/n^3$ during each mutation), the probability that an ALL_p individual is constructed within the $O(n \log n)$ iterations before $x^* = 1^n$ is at most $O(\lambda n \log n/n^3) = o(1)$, i.e. with at least constant probability, this will not occur, and $x^* = 1^n$ will be found as in Lemma 8. Once $x^* = 1^n$, constructing an ALL_p individual requires at least $n/2$ specific bits to mutate simultaneously, which with high probability will not occur in a polynomial number of iterations.

Thus, the (1+λ) EA has at least a constant probability of ending the phase with $x^* = 1^n$. □

These lemmas can then be combined to prove Theorem 7.

Proof of Theorem 7. With high probability, $\text{OPT}_0 = 1^n$ is found during phase 0 per Lemma 8. At the start of each subsequent phase p, $f(x^*) > n - p$, as only individuals in the ALL sets of the preceding phases can be accepted while decreasing the number of 1-bits in x^*, and the minimum OneMax value of any individual in sets $\text{ALL}_0, \ldots, \text{ALL}_{p-1}$ is $n - p + 1$. Furthermore, if $x^* \notin \text{ALL}_p$, $f(x^*) > n - p + 1$, as this excludes $x^* = \text{OPT}_{p-1}$, which had the lowest fitness value of all individuals in the union of the previous ALL sets.

If $x^* \neq 1^n$ at the start of phase $p \geq n/2 + 3$, the phase has at least a constant probability of ending with $x^* \neq \text{OPT}_p$ per Lemma 9, and hence $x^* \notin \text{ALL}_{p+1}$.

If phase $p + 1$ begins with $x^* \notin \text{ALL}_{p+1}$, it has at least a constant probability of ending with $x^* = 1^n$ per Lemma 10.

Thus, at least a constant fraction of $\Omega(n)$ phases beyond $n/2 + 3$ have at least a constant probability of ending with $x^* = 1^n$; i.e. with high probability, at least one of those phases will end with $x^* = 1^n$. Constructing an ALL_p individual from 1^n in future phases requires at least $\Omega(n)$ bits to be flipped simultaneously, which with high probability does not occur in polynomial time. □

We note that the proof of Theorem 7 relies on $\lambda = o(n)$ primarily in Lemma 9's bounds on p_1, although, if λ is increased a little further to $\Omega(n \log n)$, the behavior described by Lemma 10 would also no longer occur, allowing the (1+λ) EA to recover from any phase which ends with an ALT_p with high probability.

Theorem 11. *The (1+λ) EA with offspring population size $\lambda \geq c_1 n \log n$, where $c_1 > 0$ is a sufficiently large constant, is able to track the optimum of the* Maze *function, constructing OPT_n at the end of the* Maze *with high probability.*

Proof. We pessimistically assume that all of the n oscillating Maze phases which start with, or discover an ALL_p individual, end with $x^* = \text{ALT}_p$ rather than $x^* = \text{OPT}_p$. Notably, the initial phase ends with $x^* = 1^n$ with high probability per Lemma 8, so the first oscillating phase starts with an ALL_1 individual.

Consider the probability p_r that an oscillating phase p which begins with $x^* = \text{ALT}_{p-1}$ recovers immediately – i.e. constructs (and hence also accepts) an ALL_p individual in its first iteration. This probability can be lower-bounded by the probability that ALT_p is constructed from ALT_{p-1}, i.e. a specific one-bit mutation occurs:

$$p_r = 1 - (1 - (1 - 1/n)^{n-1}/n)^{c_1 n \log n}$$
$$\geq 1 - (1 - 1/(ne))^{c_1 n \log n}$$
$$\geq 1 - e^{-c_2 \log n} = 1 - n^{-c_2},$$

where $c_2 > 0$ is a constant absorbing c_1 and e.

As there are only n oscillating phases, at most n such recoveries are necessary to allow the last phase to end with $x^* \in \text{ALL}_p$. We can then lower-bound the probability p_R that all phases that begin with $x^* = \text{ALT}_{p-1}$ construct an ALL_p individual in their first iteration, and hence also that all phases end with an ALL_p individual conditioned on the initial phase finding $x^* = 1^n$:

$$p_R \geq 1 - n \cdot n^{-c_2} \geq 1 - n^{1-c_2}.$$

Thus, by choosing a sufficiently large constant c_1 in $\lambda = c_1 n \log n$, we can ensure that the (1+λ) EA ends the first iteration following a phase transition with $x^* \in \text{ALL}_p$ with high probability, and is therefore able to track the optimum of the Maze. □

4. A SIMPLE ISLAND MODEL

Splitting the λ offspring onto λ islands, which only compare the fitness values of their x^* individuals periodically (for instance, every τ iterations, where $\tau > 0$ is the migration interval), allows the resulting island model to track Maze even with a modest λ. In this section, we consider the effect of various migration schedules on how the island model is able to track the Maze.

To begin with, consider an island model where migration occurs on the first iteration of every phase, i.e. every $\tau = t_0$ iterations of the Maze. This ensures that an ALL_p individual migrates to all islands if any of the islands end the preceding phase with $x^* = \text{OPT}_{p-1}$.

THEOREM 12. *An island model with $\lambda = c \log n$ islands, where c is a sufficiently large constant, each island running a (1+1) EA, and migration occurring during the first iteration of every phase (i. e. with migration interval $\tau = t_0$) is able to find the OPT_n optimum of the* MAZE *with phase length $t_0 = kn^3 \log n$ in polynomial time with high probability.*

PROOF. We note that individually, the islands behave exactly like a (1+1) EA on MAZE, and the effects of synchronization are limited to selecting the best-so-far individual at the start of each phase, and propagating it to all islands. Thus, as long as any island ends phase p with $x^* = \text{OPT}_p$, all islands will begin phase $p + 1$ with $x^* \in \text{ALL}_{p+1}$.

The initial ONEMAX optimum, OPT_0, is found during phase 0 on each island with high probability. Lemma 9, applied with $\lambda = 1$, states that the probability that an island that begins phase p with $x^* \in \text{ALL}_p$ ends the phase with $x^* = \text{OPT}_p$ with at least constant probability; let $p_s = \Omega(1)$ be a lower bound on this probability, and p_f an upper bound on the probability that all λ islands end the phase with $x^* \neq \text{OPT}_p$. As long as the latter event does not occur, all islands will begin the next phase with an ALL_{p+1} individual due to migration, allowing the argument to be repeated inductively. A union bound can then be used to upper-bound the probability of failing in any of the n phases:

$$p_f \leq (1 - p_s)^\lambda$$
$$np_f \leq n(1 - p_s)^\lambda \leq nc_1^{c_2 \log n} \leq n^{1+c_2 \log c_1}$$

noting that for any constant $c > 0$, choosing $c_2 \geq -(1 + c)/\log c_1$ (recall that $c_1 \leq p_f < 1$, so $\log(c_1)$ is negative) results in $p_f \leq n^{-c}$.

Thus, with $\lambda = c_2 \log n$ islands, where c_2 is a sufficiently large constant, at least one island ends each phase with $x^* = \text{OPT}_p$ with high probability; this individual is propagated to all other islands at the start of the next phase, allowing OPT_n to be constructed and propagated to all islands at the end of the last phase. □

4.1 Shorter migration intervals

It is also possible to track MAZE with shorter migration intervals $\tau < t_0$. We first consider the case where migration may occur multiple times during a phase, as long as the final migration occurs at least $\Omega(n)$ iterations before the end of the phase, allowing the islands time to reconstruct OPT_p if migration propagated ALT_p to all islands.

THEOREM 13. *With the migration interval $\tau \leq t_0$, $\lambda = c_1 \log n$ islands are sufficient to track the optimum of the* MAZE *as long as no migration occurs during $c_2 n$ iterations preceding any phase transition, where c_1 and c_2 are sufficiently large constants, and migration occurs at least once during each phase.*

PROOF. We follow the proof of Theorem 12, and pessimistically assume that the last synchronization during each phase occurs $c_2 n$ iterations before the end of the phase, where $c_2 > 0$ is a sufficiently large constant, during an ALT-favoring iteration, and propagates the ALT individual to all islands.

Lemma 9 can then be applied: on each island, the probability of ending phase p with $x^* = \text{OPT}_p$ is then at least a constant greater than 0, as $x^* = \text{ALT}_p \in \text{ALL}_p$ has been propagated to the island at least $c_2 n$ iterations before the end of the phase. Thus, the situation at the end of the phase returns to that considered in Theorem 12: each of $\lambda = \Omega(\log n)$ islands has at least a constant probability of ending phase p with $x^* = \text{OPT}_p$.

With a large-enough λ, we can with high probability conclude that during each phase p, migration ensures that all islands have an ALL_p individual as the best-so-far solution at least $c_2 n$ iterations before the end of the phase, and therefore each phase will with at least one island having $x^* = \text{OPT}_p$. That island will therefore have an ALL_{p+1} individual during the next phase, which will migrate to the any islands which lose track of the MAZE during the next phase, allowing the argument to be repeated inductively for each of n phases. □

Additionally, if migration is only allowed to occur during iterations assigning the OPT individual the greatest fitness value, ALT_p individuals can never migrate to islands where $x^* = \text{OPT}_p$; in this case, migration can occur close to the end of each phase without negative consequences.

THEOREM 14. *When migration occurs only during iterations when $f(ALT_p) < f(OPT_p)$, and occurs for the first time at least $c_1 n$ iterations before the end of each phase, $\lambda = c_2 \log n$ islands, where c_1 and c_2 are sufficiently large constants, are sufficient to track the optimum of the* MAZE.

PROOF. The initial ONEMAX phase still succeeds with high probability, as synchronization cannot decrease the fitness of x^* on each island, and will instead only increase the fitness of the islands lagging behind the current global best-so-far.

During the subsequent MAZE phases, synchronization only occurs when OPT individuals have the highest fitness value, and therefore cannot replace an OPT best-so-far individual on an island with an ALT individual; thus, it can only increase the probability that $x^* = \text{OPT}_p$ on an island at any given time in comparison with the situation considered in Theorem 12.

Thus, the argument from the proof of Theorem 12 applies: by selecting a sufficiently-large constant for $\lambda = c \log n$, the probability that all islands end phase p with $x^* \neq \text{OPT}_p$ can be made small enough to ensure that this event does not occur with high probability during the n phases of MAZE: then, as long as at least one island ends each phase with $x^* = \text{OPT}_p$, that island's $x^* \in \text{ALL}_{p+1}$ will be propagated to the other islands, and per Lemma 9, $c_1 n$ iterations later, every island will once again have at least a constant probability of having $x^* = \text{OPT}_{p+1}$. □

Thus, we have shown that $\lambda = c_2 \log n$ islands running a (1+1) EA are sufficient to track the optimum of the MAZE with varying migration intervals, as long as migration occurs at least $c_1 n$ iterations before a phase transition, and any migration occurring within $c_1 n$ iterations prior to a phase transition occurs only while the OPT individual has a higher fitness value than the ALT individual. Both theorems rely on a mixing time argument to ensure that at least a constant fraction of the $\Omega(\log n)$ islands end the phase with $x^* = \text{OPT}_p$, and migration is used to repopulate any islands that lose track of the MAZE prior to the next phase transition.

4.2 Longer migration intervals

A straightforward consequence of Theorem 12 is that migration phases longer than the MAZE phase length are also viable: there is no need to repopulate all islands after *every* phase transition, and choosing e.g. $\tau = c\,t_0$ where $c > 1$ is a constant is also viable with $\Omega(\log n)$ islands. However, the migration interval cannot be increased much further than that: we will show that if $\tau \geq c\,t_0 \log \lambda$, $\lambda = O(\log n)$ islands are no longer sufficient to track the MAZE.

THEOREM 15. *For $\tau = c_1\, t_0 \log \lambda$, where $c_1 > 0$ is a sufficiently large constant, $\lambda = O(\log n)$ islands are not sufficient to track the optimum of the* MAZE.

PROOF. Consider an interval of $c\,t_0 \log \lambda$ iterations during which no migration will occur, where $c_1 \geq c > 0$ is a sufficiently large constant, starting at the beginning of some phase p, such that $n/2 + 3 < p < n - \log \lambda$. Pessimistically assume that before the start of phase p, none of the $\lambda = c \log n$ islands lost track of the MAZE, and thus all islands begin phase p with at least a constant probability of having an ALL_p individual per Lemma 9.

Considering each island individually, each of the $\log \lambda$ phases in the interval has at least a constant probability of ending with $x^* \neq \mathrm{OPT}_p$, causing the next phase to have at least a constant probability of ending with $x^* = 1^n$; let $p_L > 0$ be a constant lower bound on the probability of each phase ending with $x^* = 1^n$. Let $X^{(t)}$ be the number of islands with $x^* \neq 1^n$ at the start of phase $p+t$ (and $X^{(0)} = \lambda$); it then holds that:

$$E(X^{(t)} - X^{(t+1)} \mid X^{(t)}) \geq p_L X^{(t)}.$$

Applying Theorem 5, the expected number of phase transitions $T = \min_t\{X^{(t)} = 0\}$ until all islands have lost track of the MAZE (i.e. have $x^* = 1^n$) is:

$$E(T \mid X^{(0)}) \leq \frac{\ln(X^{(0)}) + 1}{1 - p_L} = O(\ln \lambda).$$

By applying Markov's inequality, we can bound $P(T \geq 2E(T \mid X^0)) \leq 1/2$, and hence, by choosing a sufficiently large constant c such that $\tau = c \log \lambda \geq 2E(T \mid X^0)$, lower-bound the probability of all islands ending the interval with $x^* = 1^n$ by at least $1/2$. As there are $\Omega(n/(\log \lambda)) = \Omega(n/(\log \log n))$ such intervals following phase $p > n/2 + 3$, the probability that the island model does lose track of the MAZE in at least one of these intervals is at least $1 - 2^{-\Omega(n/\log \log n)}$. □

5. CONCLUSIONS

We have presented a first runtime analysis of parallel EAs in dynamic optimization. A simple island model with λ islands and length of the migration interval τ was studied on the dynamic benchmark function MAZE. In the case of extreme communication, i.e., $\tau = 1$, even a large number of islands does not allow efficient tracking of the optimum. However, with a carefully chosen value for τ, already a logarithmic number of islands was proven to be sufficient for efficient tracking. Finally, the relationship of τ, λ, and the ability of the island model to track the optimum was investigated more closely. Our results indicate that the careful choice of the migration policy, and more generally, the communication in parallel EAs, can be significantly more advantageous than a large population.

In future work, we would like to study parallel EAs on different dynamic optimization problems in order to understand the interplay of migration intervals and number of islands more thoroughly. As our positive results are crucially dependent on a proper choice of τ, it may also be worth studying adaptive or even self-adaptive choices of the migration interval in order to automatically determine a good value for τ. Here the adaptive model suggested in [14] could be interesting.

6. REFERENCES

[1] Enrique Alba, Gabriel Luque, and Sergio Nesmachnow. Parallel metaheuristics: recent advances and new trends. *International Transactions in Operational Research*, 20(1):1–48, 2013.

[2] Enrique Alba, Amir Nakib, and Patrick Siarry. *Metaheuristics for Dynamic Optimization*. Studies in Computational Intelligence. Springer, 2013.

[3] Anne Auger and Benjamin Doerr, editors. *Theory of Randomized Search Heuristics: Foundations and Recent Developments*. World Scientific Publishing, 2011.

[4] Benjamin Doerr and Leslie Ann Goldberg. Adaptive drift analysis. *Algorithmica*, 65(1):224–250, 2013.

[5] Benjamin Doerr, Daniel Johannsen, and Carola Winzen. Multiplicative drift analysis. *Algorithmica*, 64(4):673–697, 2012.

[6] Stefan Droste. Analysis of the (1+1) EA for a dynamically bitwise changing OneMax. In *Proceedings of the Genetic and Evolutionary Computation Conference (GECCO 2003)*, pages 909–921. Springer, 2003.

[7] Thomas Jansen and Ulf Schellbach. Theoretical analysis of a mutation-based evolutionary algorithm for a tracking problem in the lattice. In *Proceedings of the Genetic and Evolutionary Computation Conference (GECCO 2005)*, pages 841–848. ACM Press, 2005.

[8] Thomas Jansen and Christine Zarges. Evolutionary algorithms and artificial immune systems on a bi-stable dynamic optimisation problem. In *Proceedings of the Genetic and Evolutionary Computation Conference (GECCO 2014)*, pages 975–982. ACM Press, 2014.

[9] Mostepha Redouane Khouadjia, Briseida Sarasola, Enrique Alba, Laetitia Jourdan, and El-Ghazali Talbi. Multi-environmental cooperative parallel metaheuristics for solving dynamic optimization problems. In *Proceedings of 2011 IEEE International Parallel & Distributed Processing Symposium*, pages 395–403. IEEE Press, 2011.

[10] Timo Kötzing, Andrei Lissovoi, and Carsten Witt. (1+1) EA on generalized dynamic OneMax. In *Proceedings of Foundations of Genetic Algorithms Workshop (FOGA 2015)*. ACM Press, 2015. To appear.

[11] Timo Kötzing and Hendrik Molter. ACO beats EA on a dynamic pseudo-boolean function. In *Proceedings of Parallel Problem Solving from Nature XII (PPSN '12)*, pages 113–122. Springer, 2012.

[12] Jörg Lässig and Dirk Sudholt. General upper bounds on the runtime of parallel evolutionary algorithms. *Evolutionary Computation*, 22(3):405–437, 2014.

[13] Andrei Lissovoi and Carsten Witt. MMAS versus population-based EA on a family of dynamic fitness functions. *Algorithmica*, 2015. In press, DOI

http://dx.doi.org/10.1007/s00453-015-9975-z, preliminary version in GECCO 2014.

[14] Andrea Mambrini and Dirk Sudholt. Design and analysis of adaptive migration intervals in parallel evolutionary algorithms. In *Proceedings of the Genetic and Evolutionary Computation Conference (GECCO 2014)*, pages 1047–1054. ACM Press, 2014.

[15] Frank Neumann and Carsten Witt. *Bioinspired Computation in Combinatorial Optimization – Algorithms and Their Computational Complexity.* Natural Computing Series. Springer, 2010.

[16] Trung Thanh Nguyen, Shengxiang Yang, and Jürgen Branke. Evolutionary dynamic optimization: A survey of the state of the art. *Swarm and Evolutionary Computation*, 6:1–24, 2012.

[17] Philipp Rohlfshagen, Per Kristian Lehre, and Xin Yao. Dynamic evolutionary optimisation: An analysis of frequency and magnitude of change. In *Proceedings of the Genetic and Evolutionary Computation Conference (GECCO 2009)*, pages 1713–1720. ACM Press, 2009.

[18] Dirk Sudholt. Using markov-chain mixing time estimates for the analysis of ant colony optimization. In *Proceedings of Foundations of Genetic Algorithms Workshop (FOGA 2011)*, pages 139–150. ACM Press, 2011.

First Steps Towards a Runtime Comparison of Natural and Artificial Evolution

Tiago Paixão
IST Austria
Am Campus 1, 3400
Klosterneuburg, Austria

Jorge Pérez Heredia
University of Sheffield
Sheffield, S1 4DP, United Kingdom

Dirk Sudholt
University of Sheffield
Sheffield, S1 4DP, United Kingdom

Barbora Trubenová
IST Austria
Am Campus 1, 3400
Klosterneuburg, Austria

ABSTRACT

Evolutionary algorithms (EAs) form a popular optimisation paradigm inspired by natural evolution. In recent years the field of evolutionary computation has developed a rigorous analytical theory to analyse their runtime on many illustrative problems. Here we apply this theory to a simple model of natural evolution. In the Strong Selection Weak Mutation (SSWM) evolutionary regime the time between occurrence of new mutations is much longer than the time it takes for a new beneficial mutation to take over the population. In this situation, the population only contains copies of one genotype and evolution can be modelled as a (1+1)-type process where the probability of accepting a new genotype (improvements or worsenings) depends on the change in fitness.

We present an initial runtime analysis of SSWM, quantifying its performance for various parameters and investigating differences to the (1+1) EA. We show that SSWM can have a moderate advantage over the (1+1) EA at crossing fitness valleys and study an example where SSWM outperforms the (1+1) EA by taking advantage of information on the fitness gradient.

Categories and Subject Descriptors

F.2.2 [**Analysis of Algorithms and Problem Complexity**]: Nonnumerical Algorithms and Problems

Keywords

Runtime analysis, natural evolution, population genetics, theory, strong selection weak mutation regime

1. INTRODUCTION

GECCO '15, July 11 - 15, 2015, Madrid, Spain

ISBN 978-1-4503-3472-3/15/07 ... $15.00

DOI: http://dx.doi.org/10.1145/2739480.2754758

In the last 20 years evolutionary computation has developed a number of algorithmic techniques for the analysis of evolutionary and genetic algorithms. These methods typically focus on runtime, and allow for rigorous bounds on the time required to reach a global optimum, or other well-specified high-fitness solutions. The runtime analysis of evolutionary algorithms has become one of the dominant concepts in evolutionary computation, leading to a plethora of results for evolutionary algorithms [1, 8, 14] as well as novel optimisation paradigms such as swarm intelligence [14] and artificial immune systems [9].

Interestingly, although evolutionary algorithms are heavily inspired by natural evolution, these methods have seldom been applied to natural evolution as studied in mathematical population genetics. This is a missed opportunity: the time it takes for a natural population to reach a fitness peak is an important question for the study of natural evolution. The kinds of results obtained from runtime analysis, namely how the runtime scales with genome size and mutation rate, are of general interest to population genetics. Moreover, recently there has been a renewed interest in applying computer science methods to problems in evolutionary biology with contributions from unlikely fields such as game theory [2], machine learning [22] and Markov chain theory [3]. Here, we present a first attempt at applying runtime analysis to the so-called Strong Selection Weak Mutation regime of natural populations.

The Strong Selection Weak Mutation model applies when the population size, mutation rate, and selection strength are such that the time between occurrence of new mutations is long compared to the time a new genotype takes to replace the parent genotype [6]. Under these conditions, only one genotype is present in the population most of the time, and evolution occurs through "jumps" between different genotypes, corresponding to a new mutation replacing the resident genotype in the population. The relevant dynamics can then be characterized by a (1+1)-type stochastic process. This model is obtained as a limit of many other models, such as the Wright-Fisher model. One important aspect of this model is that new solutions are accepted with a probability $\frac{1-e^{-2\beta\Delta f}}{1-e^{-2N\beta\Delta f}}$ that depends on the fitness difference Δf between the new mutation and the resident genotype. Here

N reflects the size of the underlying population, and β represents the selection strength. One can think of f as defining a phenotype that is under selection to be maximized; β quantifies how strongly a unit change in f is favoured. This probability was first derived by Kimura [12] for a population of N individuals that are sampled binomially in proportion to their fitness.

This choice of acceptance function introduces two main differences to the (1+1) EA: First, solutions of lower fitness (worsenings) may be accepted with some positive probability. This is reminiscent of the Metropolis algorithm (Simulated Annealing with constant temperature) which can also accept worsenings (see, e. g. [10]). Second, solutions of higher fitness can be rejected, since they are accepted with a probability that is roughly proportional to the relative advantage they have over the current solution.

We cast this model of natural evolution in a (1+1)-type algorithm referred to as SSWM, using common mutation operators from evolutionary algorithms. We then present first runtime analyses of this process. Our aims are manifold:

- to explore the performance of natural evolution in the context of runtime, comparing it against simple evolutionary algorithms like the (1+1) EA,
- to investigate the non-elitistic selection mechanism implicit to SSWM and its usefulness in the context of evolutionary algorithms, and
- to show that techniques for the analysis of evolutionary algorithms can be applied to simple models of natural evolution, aiming to open up a new research field at the intersection of evolutionary computation and population genetics.

Our results are summarised as follows. For the simple function OneMax we show in Section 3 that with suitably large population sizes, when $N\beta \geq \frac{1}{2}\ln(11n)$, SSWM is an effective hill climber as it optimises OneMax in expected time $O((n \log n)/\beta)$. However, when the population size is by any constant factor smaller than this threshold, we encounter a phase transition and SSWM requires exponential time even on OneMax.

We then illustrate the particular features of the selection rule. In Section 4 we consider a function Cliff_d where a fitness valley of Hamming distance d needs to be crossed. For $d = \omega(\log n)$ the (1+1) EA needs time $\Theta(n^d)$, but SSWM is faster by a factor of $e^{\Omega(d)}$ because of its ability to accept worse solutions. Finally, in Section 5 we illustrate on the function Balance [19] that SSWM can drastically outperform the (1+1) EA because the fitness-dependent selection drives it to follow the steepest gradient. While the (1+1) EA needs exponential time in expectation, SSWM with overwhelming probability finds an optimum in polynomial time.

The main technical difficulties are that in contrast to the simple (1+1) EA, SSWM is a non-elitist algorithm, hence fitness-level arguments based on elitism are not applicable. Level-based theorems for non-elitist populations [4] are not applicable either because they require population sizes larger than 1. Moreover, while for the (1+1) EA transition probabilities to better solutions are solely determined by probabilities for flipping bits during mutation, for SSWM these additionally depend on the probability of fixation and hence the absolute fitness difference. The analysis of SSWM is more challenging than the analysis of the (1+1) EA, and requires tailored proof techniques. We hope that these techniques will be helpful for analysing other evolutionary algorithms with fitness-based selection schemes.

Some proofs were shortened or omitted due to space restrictions; we refer to a full version of this work [18].

2. PRELIMINARIES

We define the optimisation time of SSWM as the first generation where the optimum is accepted as new individual.

The model resembles the (1+1) EA in that it only maintains one genotype that may be replaced by mutated versions of it. Mutants are accepted with probability

$$p_{\text{fix}}(\Delta f) = \frac{1 - e^{-2\beta\Delta f}}{1 - e^{-2N\beta\Delta f}} \tag{1}$$

where $\Delta f \neq 0$ is the fitness difference to the current solution and $N \geq 1$ is the size of the underlying population. For $\Delta f = 0$ we define $p_{\text{fix}}(0) := \lim_{\Delta f \to 0} p_{\text{fix}}(\Delta f) = \frac{1}{N}$, so that p_{fix} is continuous and well defined for all Δf. If $N = 1$, we get $p_{\text{fix}}(s) = 1$, meaning that any offspring will be accepted, and if $N \to \infty$, it will only accept solution for which $\Delta f > 0$. This expression was first derived by Kimura [12] and represents the *probability of fixation*, that is, the probability that a gene that is initially present in one copy in a population of N individuals is eventually present in all individuals.

Since the acceptance function in this algorithm depends on the absolute difference in fitness between genotypes, we include a parameter $\beta \in (0, 1]$ that effectively scales the fitness function and that in population genetics models the strength of selection on a phenotype. By incorporating β as a parameter of this function (and hence of the algorithm) we avoid having to explicitly rescale the fitness functions we analyse, while allowing us to explore the performance of this algorithm on a family of functions. This function has a sigmoid shape (strictly increasing—see [18, Lemma 15]) with limits $\lim_{\Delta f \to -\infty} p_{\text{fix}}(\Delta f) = 0$ and $\lim_{\Delta f \to \infty} p_{\text{fix}}(\Delta f) = 1$. As such, for large $|\beta \Delta f|$ this probability of acceptance is close to the one in the (1+1) EA, as long as $N > 1$, defeating the purpose of the comparison. By bounding β to 1, we avoid artefactual results obtained by inflating the fitness differences between genotypes.

We can then cast the SSWM regime as Algorithm 1, where the function mutate(x) can be either standard bit mutation (mutate all bits independently with probability $p_m = 1/n$, called *global mutations*) or flipping a single bit chosen uniformly at random (called *local mutations*). SSWM is valid when the expected number of new mutants in the population is much less than one, which implies that local mutations are a better approximation for this regime. However, we also consider global mutations in order to facilitate a comparison with evolutionary algorithms such as the (1+1) EA (Algorithm 2), which uses global mutations.

Next, we derive upper and lower bounds for $p_{\text{fix}}(\Delta f)$ that will be useful throughout the manuscript.

Lemma 1. *For every $\beta \in \mathbb{R}^+$ and $N \in \mathbb{N}^+$ the following inequalities hold. If $\Delta f \geq 0$ then*

$$\frac{2\beta\Delta f}{1 + 2\beta\Delta f} \leq p_{\text{fix}}(\Delta f) \leq \frac{2\beta\Delta f}{1 - e^{-2N\beta\Delta f}}.$$

If $\Delta f \leq 0$ then

$$\frac{-2\beta\Delta f}{e^{-2N\beta\Delta f}} \leq p_{\text{fix}}(\Delta f) \leq \frac{e^{-2\beta\Delta f}}{e^{-2N\beta\Delta f} - 1}.$$

Algorithm 1 SSWM

Choose $x \in \{0,1\}^n$ uniformly at random
repeat
  $y \leftarrow \text{mutate}(x)$
  $\Delta f = f(y) - f(x)$
  Choose $r \in [0,1]$ uniformly at random
  if $r < p_{\text{fix}}(\Delta f)$ **then**
    $x \leftarrow y$
  end if
until stop

Algorithm 2 (1+1) EA

Choose $x \in \{0,1\}^n$ uniformly at random
repeat
  $y \leftarrow \text{mutate}(x)$
  if $f(y) \geq f(x)$ **then**
    $x \leftarrow y$
  end if
until stop

3. SSWM ON ONEMAX

The function $\textsc{OneMax}(x) := \sum_{i=1}^{n} x_i$ has been studied extensively in natural computation because of its simplicity. It represents an easy hill climbing task, and it is the easiest function with a unique optimum for all evolutionary algorithms that only use standard bit mutation for variation [21]. Showing that SSWM can optimise ONEMAX efficiently serves as proof of concept that SSWM is a reasonable optimiser. It further sheds light on how to set algorithmic parameters such as the selection strength β and the population size N. To this effect, we first show a polynomial upper bound for the runtime of SSWM on ONEMAX. We then show that SSWM exhibits a phase transition on its runtime as a function of $N\beta$; changing this parameter by a constant factor leads to exponential runtimes on ONEMAX.

Another reason why studying ONEMAX for SSWM makes sense is because not all evolutionary algorithms that use a fitness-dependent selection perform well on ONEMAX. Oliveto and Witt [17] showed that the Simple Genetic Algorithm, which uses fitness-proportional selection, fails badly on ONEMAX even within exponential time, with a very high probability.

3.1 Upper Bound for SSWM on OneMax

We first show the following simple lemma, which gives an upper bound on the probability of increasing or decreasing the number of ones in a search point by k in one mutation.

LEMMA 2. *For any positive integer $k > 0$, let $\text{mut}(i, i \pm k)$ for $0 \leq i \leq n$ be the probability that a global mutation of a search point with i ones creates an offspring with $i \pm k$ ones. Then*

$$\text{mut}(i, i+k) \leq \left(\frac{n-i}{n}\right)^k \left(1 - \frac{1}{n}\right)^{n-k} \cdot \frac{1.14}{k!}$$
$$\text{mut}(i, i-k) \leq \left(\frac{i}{n}\right)^k \left(1 - \frac{1}{n}\right)^{n-k} \cdot \frac{1.14}{k!}.$$

The proof is omitted (see [18, Appendix]); it uses arguments from the proof of Lemma 2 in [21]. The second inequality follows immediately from the first one due to the symmetry $\text{mut}(i, i-k) = \text{mut}(n-i, n-i+k)$.

Now we introduce the concept of drift and find some bounds for its forward and backward expression.

DEFINITION 1. *Let X_t be the number of ones in the current search point, for all $1 \leq i \leq n$ the forward and backward drifts are*

$$\Delta^+(i) = E[X_{t+1} - i \mid X_t = i, X_{t+1} > i] \cdot P(X_{t+1} > i \mid X_t = i)$$
$$\Delta^-(i) = E[X_{t+1} - i \mid X_t = i, X_{t+1} < i] \cdot P(X_{t+1} < i \mid X_t = i)$$

and the net drift is the expected increase in the number of ones

$$\Delta(i) = \Delta^+(i) + \Delta^-(i).$$

LEMMA 3. *Consider SSWM on ONEMAX and mutation probability $p_m = \frac{1}{n}$. Then for global mutations, the forward and backward drifts can be bounded by*

$$\Delta^+(i) \geq \frac{n-i}{n} \left(1 - \frac{1}{n}\right)^{n-1} p_{\text{fix}}(1)$$
$$|\Delta^-(i)| \leq 1.14 \left(1 - \frac{1}{n}\right)^{n-1} \cdot (p_{\text{fix}}(-1) + e \cdot p_{\text{fix}}(-2)).$$

For local mutations the relations are as follows

$$\Delta^+(i) = \frac{n-i}{n} \cdot p_{\text{fix}}(1)$$
$$|\Delta^-(i)| \leq p_{\text{fix}}(-1).$$

Proof. For global mutations firstly we compute the lower bound for the forward drift,

$$\Delta^+(i) = \sum_{j=1}^{n-i} \text{mut}(i, i+j) \cdot j \cdot p_{\text{fix}}(j)$$

where $\text{mut}(i, i+j)$ is the probability of mutation increasing the ONEMAX value by j and i is the number of ones of the current search point.

$$\Delta^+(i) \geq \text{mut}(i, i+1) \cdot p_{\text{fix}}(1)$$
$$\geq \frac{n-i}{n} \left(1 - \frac{1}{n}\right)^{n-1} p_{\text{fix}}(1).$$

Secondly we calculate the upper bound for the backward drift

$$|\Delta^-(i)| = \sum_{j=1}^{i} \text{mut}(i, i-j) \cdot j \cdot p_{\text{fix}}(-j)$$

where j is now the number of new zeros. We can upper bound $\text{mut}(i, i-j)$ for the probability of flipping any j bits, which from Lemma 2 yields

$$\leq \sum_{j=1}^{i} \frac{1.14}{j!} \cdot \left(1 - \frac{1}{n}\right)^{n-1} \cdot j \cdot p_{\text{fix}}(-j).$$

Separating the case $j = 1$ and bounding the remaining fixation probabilities by $p_{\text{fix}}(-2)$

$$\leq 1.14\left(1-\frac{1}{n}\right)^{n-1} p_{\text{fix}}(-1)$$
$$+ 1.14\left(1-\frac{1}{n}\right)^{n-1} \cdot \sum_{j=2}^{i} \frac{1}{(j-1)!} \cdot p_{\text{fix}}(-2)$$
$$\leq 1.14\left(1-\frac{1}{n}\right)^{n-1} (p_{\text{fix}}(-1) + e \cdot p_{\text{fix}}(-2)).$$

Finally, the case for local mutations is straightforward since the probability of a local mutation increasing the number of ones is $\frac{n-i}{n}$ and that of decreasing it is at most 1. □

The following theorem shows that SSWM is efficient on OneMax for $N\beta \geq \frac{1}{2}\ln(11n)$, since then $p_{\text{fix}}(1)$ starts being greater than $n \cdot p_{\text{fix}}(-1)$ allowing for a positive drift even on the hardest fitness level ($n-1$ ones). The upper bound increases with $1/\beta$; this makes sense as for small values of β we have $p_{\text{fix}}(1) \approx 2\beta$ (cf. Lemma 1). In this regime absolute fitness differences are small and improvements are only accepted with a small probability.

Theorem 4. *If $N\beta \geq \frac{1}{2}\ln(11n)$ and $\beta \in (0,1]$ then the expected optimisation time of SSWM on OneMax with local or global mutations is $O\left(\frac{n\log n}{\beta}\right)$ for every initial search point.*

Proof. Introducing $N\beta \geq \frac{1}{2}\ln(11n)$ in the fixation probabilities, we get

$$p_{\text{fix}}(1) = \frac{1-e^{-2\beta}}{1-e^{-2N\beta}} \geq \frac{1-e^{-2\beta}}{1-(11n)^{-1}} = \frac{11(1-e^{-2\beta})}{11-\frac{1}{n}}$$
$$p_{\text{fix}}(-1) = \frac{e^{2\beta}-1}{e^{2N\beta}-1} \leq \frac{e^{2\beta}-1}{11n-1} \qquad (2)$$
$$p_{\text{fix}}(-2) = \frac{e^{4\beta}-1}{e^{4N\beta}-1} \leq \frac{e^{4\beta}-1}{(11n)^2-1} = O(n^{-2}).$$

Plugging these bounds into the results of Lemma 3

$$\Delta(i) \geq \frac{1}{e}\left[(n-i)\cdot\frac{11(1-e^{-2\beta})}{11n-1} - 1.14\frac{e^{2\beta}-1}{11n-1} - O(n^{-2})\right]$$

since we need a positive net drift even in the last step ($n-i=1$) we lower bound the function $\frac{11(1-e^{-2\beta})-1.14\cdot(e^{2\beta}+1)}{11n-1}$, which is concave for $\beta \in (0,1]$, with a straight line going through the points $\beta = 0$ and 1. Using $\frac{1}{5n}$ as a lower bound for the height of this second point we obtain

$$\geq \frac{1}{e}\cdot\left(\frac{n-i}{n}\cdot\frac{\beta}{5}\right) - O(n^{-2}) \geq \frac{\beta}{14}\cdot\frac{n-i}{n} \qquad (3)$$

for sufficiently large values of n.

Now we apply Johannsen's variable drift theorem [11] to the number of zeros. Using $h(z) := E(X_t - X_{t+1} \mid X_t = z)$ then

$$E(T \mid X_0) \leq \frac{z_{\min}}{h(z_{\min})} + \int_{z_{\min}}^{X_0} \frac{1}{h(z)}dz$$

where z is the number of zeros, X_t the current state and T the optimisation time. Introducing $z_{\min} = 1$, $X_0 = n$ and

$$\Delta(i) \geq \frac{z\beta}{14n} = h(z)$$

we obtain an upper bound for the runtime

$$E(T \mid X_0) \leq \frac{1}{h(1)} + \int_1^n \frac{1}{h(z)}dz \leq \frac{14n}{\beta} + \int_1^n \frac{14n}{\beta z}dz$$
$$= \frac{14n}{\beta}(1+\log n) = O\left(\frac{n\log n}{\beta}\right).$$ □

3.2 A Critical Threshold for SSWM on OneMax

The upper bound from Theorem 4 required $N\beta \geq \frac{1}{2}\ln(11n) = \frac{1}{2}\ln(n) + O(1)$. This condition is vital since if $N\beta$ is chosen too small, the runtime of SSWM on OneMax is exponential with very high probability, as we show next.

If $N\beta$ is by a factor of $1-\varepsilon$, for some constant $\varepsilon > 0$, smaller than $\frac{1}{2}\ln n$, the optimisation time is exponential in n, with overwhelming probability. SSWM therefore exhibits a phase transition behaviour: changing $N\beta$ by a constant factor makes a difference between polynomial and exponential expected optimisation times on OneMax.

Theorem 5. *If $1 \leq N\beta \leq \frac{1-\varepsilon}{2}\ln n$ for some $0 < \varepsilon < 1$, then the optimisation time of SSWM with local or global mutations on OneMax is at least $2^{cn^{\varepsilon/2}}$ with probability $1-2^{-\Omega(n^{\varepsilon/2})}$, for some constant $c > 0$.*

The idea behind the proof of Theorem 5 is to show that for all search points with at least $n - n^{\varepsilon/2}$ ones, there is a negative drift for the number of ones. This is because for small $N\beta$ the selection pressure is too weak, and worsenings in fitness are more likely than steps where mutation leads the algorithm closer to the optimum.

We then use the negative drift theorem with self-loops presented in Rowe and Sudholt [20] (an extension of the negative drift theorem [16] to stochastic processes with large self-loop probabilities). The proof of Theorem 5 applies this theorem with respect to the number of zeros on an interval of $[0, n^{\varepsilon/2}]$. A full proof can be found in [18].

4. ON TRAVERSING FITNESS VALLEYS

We have shown that with the right parameters, SSWM is an efficient hill climber. On the other hand, in contrast to the (1+1) EA, SSWM can accept worse solutions with a probability that depends on the magnitude of the fitness decrease. This is reminiscent of the Metropolis algorithm—although the latter accepts every improvement with probability 1, whereas SSWM may reject improvements.

Jansen and Wegener [10] compared the ability of the (1+1) EA and a Metropolis algorithm in crossing fitness valleys and found that both showed similar performance on *smooth integer* functions: functions where two Hamming neighbours have a fitness difference of at most 1 [10, Section 6].

We consider a similar function, generalising a construction by Jägersküpper and Storch [7]: the function Cliff_d is defined such that non-elitist algorithms have a chance to jump down a "cliff" of height roughly d and to traverse a fitness valley of Hamming distance d to the optimum (see Figure 1).

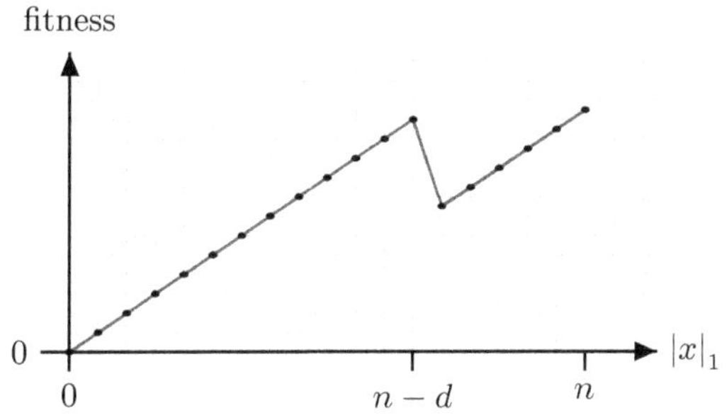

Figure 1: Sketch of the function CLIFF_d**.**

DEFINITION 2 (CLIFF).

$$\text{CLIFF}_d(x) = \begin{cases} |x|_1 & \text{if } |x|_1 \le n-d \\ |x|_1 - d + \frac{1}{2} & \text{otherwise} \end{cases}$$

where $|x|_1 = \sum_{i=1}^{n} x_i$ *counts the number of ones.*

The (1+1) EA typically optimises CLIFF_d through a direct jump from the top of the cliff to the optimum, which takes expected time $\Theta(n^d)$.

THEOREM 6. *The expected optimisation time of the (1+1) EA on* CLIFF_d*, for* $2 \le d \le n/2$*, is* $\Theta(n^d)$.

In order to prove Theorem 6, the following lemma will be useful for showing that the top of the cliff is reached with good probability. More generally, it shows that the conditional probability of increasing the number of ones in a search point to j, given it is increased to some value of j or higher, is at least 1/2.

LEMMA 7. *For all* $0 \le i < j \le n$*,*

$$\frac{\text{mut}(i,j)}{\sum_{k=j}^{n} \text{mut}(i,k)} \ge \frac{1}{2}.$$

The proof of this lemma is presented in [18].

Proof of Theorem 6. From any search point with $i < n-d$ ones, the probability of reaching a search point with higher fitness is at least $\frac{n-i}{en}$. The expected time for accepting a search point with at least $n-d$ ones is at most $\sum_{i=0}^{n-d-1} \frac{en}{n-i} = O(n \log n)$. Note that this is $O(n^d)$ since $d \ge 2$.

We claim that with probability $\Omega(1)$, the first such search point has $n-d$ ones: with probability at least 1/2 the initial search point will have at most $n-d$ ones. Invoking Lemma 7 with $j := n-d$, with probability at least 1/2 the top of the cliff is reached before any other search point with at least $n-d$ ones.

Once on the top of the cliff the algorithm has to jump directly to the optimum to overcome it. The probability of such a jump is $\frac{1}{n^d}(1-\frac{1}{n})^{n-d}$ and therefore the expected time to make this jump is $\Theta(n^d)$. □

SSWM with global mutations also has an opportunity to make a direct jump to the optimum. However, compared to the (1+1) EA its performance slightly improves when considering shorter jumps and accepting a search point of inferior fitness. The following theorem shows that for large enough cliffs, $d = \omega(\log n)$, the expected optimisation time is by a factor of $e^{\Omega(d)}$ smaller than that of the (1+1) EA. Although both algorithms need a long time for large d, the speedup of SSWM is significant for large d.

THEOREM 8. *The expected optimisation time of SSWM with global mutations and* $\beta = 1, N = \frac{1}{2}\ln(11n)$ *on* CLIFF_d *with* $d = \omega(\log n)$ *is at most* $n^d/e^{\Omega(d)}$.

Proof sketch for Theorem 8. We define R as the expected time for reaching a search point with either $n-d$ or n ones, when starting with a worst possible non-optimal search point. Let T_{peak} be the random optimisation time when starting with any search point of $n-d$ ones, hereinafter called a *peak*. Then the expected optimisation time from any initial point is at most $R + \text{E}(T_{\text{peak}})$. Let p_{success} be the probability of SSWM starting in a peak will reach the optimum before reaching a peak again. We call such a time period a *trial*. After the end of a trial, taking at most R expected generations, with probability $1 - p_{\text{success}}$ SSWM returns to a peak again, so

$$\text{E}(T_{\text{peak}}) \le R + (1 - p_{\text{success}}) \cdot \text{E}(T_{\text{peak}})$$
$$\Leftrightarrow \text{E}(T_{\text{peak}}) \le \frac{R}{p_{\text{success}}}. \quad (4)$$

We first bound the worst-case time to return to a peak or a global optimum as $R = O(n \log n)$. Let S_1 be the set of all search points with at most $n-d$ ones and $S_2 := \{0,1\}^n \setminus S_1$. As long as the current search point remains within S_2, SSWM essentially behaves like on ONEMAX. Repeating arguments from the proof of Theorem 4, in expected time $O((n \log n)/\beta) = O(n \log n)$ (as here $\beta = 1$) SSWM either finds a global optimum or a search point in S_1. Likewise, as long as the current search point remains within S_1, SSWM essentially behaves like on ONEMAX and within expected time $O(n \log n)$ either a peak or a search point in S_2 is found.

SSWM can switch indefinitely between S_1 and S_2 within one trial, as long as no optimum or peak is reached. The conditional probability of creating a peak—when from a search point with $i < n-d$ ones either a peak or a non-optimal search point in S_2 is reached—is

$$\frac{\text{mut}(i, n-d) \cdot p_{\text{fix}}(n-d-i)}{\sum_{k=n-d}^{n-1} \text{mut}(i,k) \cdot p_{\text{fix}}(k-i-d+1/2)} \ge \frac{\text{mut}(i,j)}{\sum_{k=j}^{n} \text{mut}(i,k)}$$

as $p_{\text{fix}}(n-d-i) \ge p_{\text{fix}}(k-i-d+1/2)$ for all $n-d < k < n$. By Lemma 7, the above fraction is at least 1/2. Hence SSWM in expectation only makes $O(1)$ transitions from S_1 to S_2, and the overall expected time spent in S_1 and S_2 is at most $R = O(1) \cdot O(n \log n)$.

The remainder of the proof now shows a lower bound on p_{success}, the probability of a trial being successful. A sufficient condition for a successful trial is that the next mutation creates a search point with $n-d+k$ ones, for some integer $1 \le k \le d$, that this point is accepted, and that from there the global optimum is reached before returning to a peak.

We estimate the probabilities for these events separately in order to get an overall lower bound on the probability of a trial being successful.

From any peak there are $\binom{d}{k}$ search points at Hamming distance k that have $n-d+k$ ones. Considering only such mutations, the probability of a mutation increasing the number of ones from $n-d$ by k is at least

$$\text{mut}(n-d, n-d+k) \ge \frac{1}{n^k} \cdot \left(1 - \frac{1}{n}\right)^{n-1} \cdot \binom{d}{k}$$
$$\ge \frac{1}{en^k} \cdot \left(\frac{d}{k}\right)^k.$$

The probability of accepting such a move is

$$p_{\mathrm{fix}}(k-d+1/2) = \frac{e^{2\beta(d-k-1/2)}-1}{e^{2N\beta(d-k-1/2)}-1} \geq \frac{e^{2(d-k-1/2)}-1}{(11n)^{(d-k-1/2)}}.$$

We now fix $k := \lfloor d/e \rfloor$ and estimate the probability of making and accepting a jump of length k:

$$\begin{aligned}
&\mathrm{mut}(n-d, n-d+k) \cdot p_{\mathrm{fix}}(k-d+1/2)\\
&\geq \frac{1}{en^k} \cdot \left(\frac{d}{k}\right)^k \cdot \frac{e^{2(d-k-1/2)}-1}{(11n)^{(d-k-1/2)}}\\
&= \Omega\left(n^{-d+1/2} \cdot \left(\frac{d}{k}\right)^k \cdot \left(\frac{e^2}{11}\right)^{d-k}\right)\\
&= \Omega\left(n^{-d+1/2} \cdot \left(e^{1/e} \cdot \left(\frac{e^2}{11}\right)^{1-1/e}\right)^d\right)\\
&= \Omega\left(n^{-d+1/2} \cdot \left(\frac{10}{9}\right)^d\right).
\end{aligned}$$

Finally, we show that, if SSWM does make this accepted jump, with probability $1 - n^{-\omega(1)}$ it climbs up to the global optimum before returning to a search point in S_1. To this end we apply the negative drift theorem with self-loops [20] to the number of ones in the interval $[a := \lceil n-d+k/2 \rceil, b := n-d+k]$ and show that, since we start in state b, a state a or less is unlikely to be reached in polynomial time. Details of this application are given in [18].

This implies that following a length-k jump, a trial is successful with probability $1 - n^{-\omega(1)}$. This establishes $p_{\mathrm{success}} := \Omega\left(n^{-d+1/2} \cdot \left(\frac{10}{9}\right)^d\right)$. Plugging this into (4), adding time R for the time to reach the peak initially, and using that $O(n^{1/2} \log n) \cdot (9/10)^d = e^{-\Omega(d)}$ for $d = \omega(\log n)$ yields the claimed bound. □

5. SSWM OUTPERFORMS (1+1) EA ON BALANCE

Finally, we investigate a feature that distinguishes SSWM from the (1+1) EA as well as the Metropolis algorithm: the fact that larger improvements are more likely to be accepted than smaller improvements.

To this end, we consider the function BALANCE, originally introduced by Rohlfshagen, Lehre, and Yao [19] as an example where rapid dynamic changes in dynamic optimisation can be beneficial. The function has also been studied in the context of stochastic ageing by Oliveto and Sudholt [15].

In its static (non-dynamic) form, BALANCE can be illustrated by a two-dimensional plane, whose coordinates are determined by the number of leading ones (LO) in the first half of the bit string, and the number of ones in the second half, respectively. The former has a steeper gradient than the latter, as the leading ones part is weighted by a factor of n in the fitness (see Figure 2).

DEFINITION 3 (BALANCE [19]). *Let $a, b \in \{0,1\}^{n/2}$ and $x = ab \in \{0,1\}^n$. Then,* $\mathrm{BALANCE}(x) =$

$$\begin{cases} n^3 & \text{if } \mathrm{LO}(a) = n/2\text{, else}\\ |b|_1 + n \cdot \mathrm{LO}(a) & \text{if } n/16 < |b|_1 < 7n/16\text{, else}\\ n^2 \cdot \mathrm{LO}(a) & \text{if } |a|_0 > \sqrt{n}\text{, else}\\ 0 & \text{otherwise.} \end{cases}$$

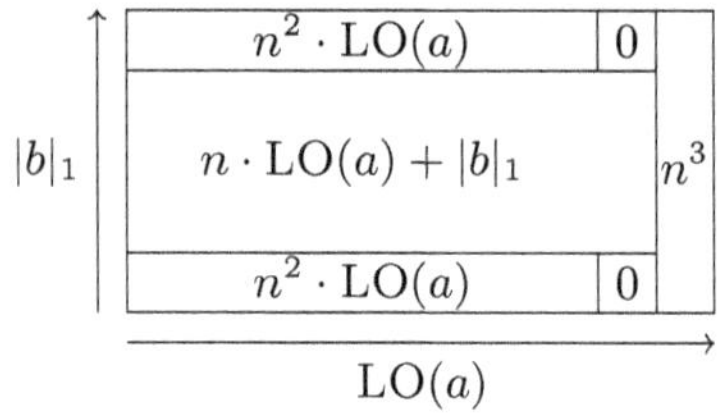

Figure 2: Visualisation of BALANCE [19].

where $|x|_1 = \sum_{i=1}^{n/2} x_i$, $|x|_0$ is a number of zeros and $\mathrm{LO}(x) := \sum_{i=1}^{n/2} \prod_{j=1}^{i} x_j$ counts the number of leading ones.

The function is constructed in such a way that all points with a maximum number of leading ones are global optima, whereas increasing the number of ones in the second half beyond a threshold of $7n/16$ (or decreasing it below a symmetric threshold of $n/16$) leads to a trap, a region of local optima that is hard to escape from.

Rohlfshagen, Lehre, and Yao [19, Theorem 3] showed the following lower bound for the (1+1) EA, specialised to non-dynamic optimisation:

THEOREM 9 ([19]). *The expected optimisation time of the (1+1) EA on* BALANCE *is $n^{\Omega(n^{1/2})}$.*

We next show that SSWM with high probability finds an optimum in polynomial time. For appropriately small β we have sufficiently many successes on the LO-part such that we find an optimum before the ONEMAX-part reaches the region of local optima. This is because for small β the probability of accepting small improvements is small. The fact that SSWM is slower than the (1+1) EA on ONEMAX by a factor of $O(1/\beta)$ turns into an advantage over the (1+1) EA on BALANCE.

The following lemma shows that SSWM effectively uses elitist selection on the LO-part of the function in a sense that every decrease is rejected, with overwhelming probability.

LEMMA 10. *For every $x = ab$ with $n/16 < |b|_1 < 7n/16$ and $\beta = n^{-3/2}$ and $N\beta = \ln n$, the probability of SSWM with local or global mutations accepting a mutant $x' = a'b'$ with $\mathrm{LO}(a') < \mathrm{LO}(a)$ and $n/16 < |b'|_1 < 7n/16$ is $O(n^{-n})$.*

Proof. The loss in fitness is at least $n - (|b'|_1 - |b|_1) \geq n/2$. The probability of SSWM accepting such a loss is at most

$$p_{\mathrm{fix}}(-n/2) \leq \frac{1 - e^{-2\beta(-n/2)}}{1 - e^{-2N\beta(-n/2)}} \leq \frac{e^{2\beta(n/2)}}{e^{2N\beta(n/2)} - 1}.$$

Assuming $\beta = n^{-3/2}$ and $N\beta = \ln n$, this is at most

$$\frac{e^{\frac{\sqrt{n}}{n}}}{n^n - 1} \leq \frac{e}{n^n - 1} = O(n^{-n}). \quad \square$$

The following lemma establishes the optimisation time of the SSWM algorithm on either the ONEMAX or the LO-part of BALANCE.

For global mutations we restrict our considerations to *relevant steps*, defined as steps where no leading ones in the first half of the bit string is flipped. The probability of a relevant step is always at least $(1 - 1/n)^{n/2} \approx e^{-1/2}$. When using local mutations, all steps are defined as relevant.

LEMMA 11. *Let $\beta = n^{-3/2}$ and $N\beta = \ln n$. With probability $1 - e^{-\Omega(n^{1/2})}$, SSWM with either local or global mutations either optimises the LO part or reaches the trap (all search points with fitness $n^2 \cdot \mathrm{LO}(a)$) within*

$$T := \frac{n^2}{4} \cdot \frac{1}{p_{\text{fix}}(n - \sqrt{n})} \cdot \left(1 + n^{-1/4}\right)$$

relevant steps.

Proof. Consider a relevant step, implying that global mutations will leave all leading ones intact. With probability $1/n$ a local or global mutation will flip the first 0-bit. This increases the fitness by $k \cdot n - \Delta_{\mathrm{OM}}$, where Δ_{OM} is the difference in the ONEMAX-value of b caused by this mutation and k is the number of consecutive 1-bits following this bit position after mutation. The latter bits are called *free riders* and it is well known (see [13, Lemma 1 and proof of Theorem 2]) that the number of free riders follows a geometric distribution with parameter $1/2$, only capped by the number of bits to the end of the bit string a.

The probability of flipping at least $\sqrt{n}$ bits in one global mutation is at most $1/(\sqrt{n})! = e^{-\Omega(\sqrt{n})}$ and the probability that this happens at least once in T relevant steps is still of the same order (using that $T = \mathrm{poly}(n)$ as $p_{\text{fix}}(n - \sqrt{n}) \geq 1/N \geq 1/\mathrm{poly}(n)$). We assume in the following that this does not happen, which allows us to assume $\Delta_{\mathrm{OM}} \leq \sqrt{n}$. We also assume that the number of leading ones is never decreased during non-relevant steps as the probability of accepting such a fitness decrease is $O(n^{-n})$ by Lemma 10 and the expected number of non-relevant steps before T relevant steps have occurred is $O(T)$.

We now have that the number of leading ones can never decrease and any increase by mutation is accepted with probability at least $p_{\text{fix}}(n - \sqrt{n})$. In a relevant step, the probability of increasing the number of leading ones is hence at least $1/n \cdot p_{\text{fix}}(n - \sqrt{n})$ and the expected number of such improvements in

$$T := \frac{n^2}{4} \cdot \frac{1}{p_{\text{fix}}(n - \sqrt{n})} \cdot (1 + n^{-1/4})$$

relevant steps is at least $n/4 + n^{3/4}/4$. By Chernoff bounds [5], the probability that less than $n/4 + n^{3/4}/8$ improvements happen is $e^{-\Omega(n^{1/2})}$. Also the probability that during this number of improvements less than $n/4 - n^{3/4}/8$ free riders occur is $e^{-\Omega(n^{1/2})}$. If these two rare events do not happen, a LO-value of $n/2$ is reached before time T. Taking the union bound over all rare failure probabilities proves the claim. □

We now show that the ONEMAX part is not optimized before the LO part.

LEMMA 12. *Let $\beta = n^{-3/2}$, $N\beta = \ln n$, and T be as in Lemma 11. The probability that SSWM starting with $a_0 b_0$ such that $n/4 \leq |b_0|_1 \leq n/4 + n^{3/4}$ creates a search point ab with $|b|_1 \leq n/16$ or $|b|_1 \geq 7n/16$ in T relevant steps is $e^{-\Omega(n^{1/2})}$.*

It will become obvious that in T relevant steps SSWM typically makes a progress of $O(n)$ on the ONEMAX part. The proof of Lemma 12 requires a careful and delicate analysis to show that the constant factors are small enough such that the stated thresholds for $|b|_1$ are not surpassed.

Proof sketch for Lemma 12. We only prove that a search point with $|b|_1 \geq 7n/16$ is unlikely to be reached with the claimed probability. The probability for reaching a search point with $|b|_1 \leq n/16$ is clearly no larger, and a union bound for these two events leads to a factor of 2 absorbed in the asymptotic notation.

Note that for $\beta = n^{-3/2}$ we have

$$p_{\text{fix}}(n - \sqrt{n}) \geq \frac{2\beta(n - \sqrt{n})}{1 + 2\beta(n - \sqrt{n})} \geq 2\beta n \cdot (1 - O(n^{-1/2})).$$

Hence

$$T \leq \frac{n^2}{4} \cdot \frac{1}{2\beta n} \cdot \left(1 + O(n^{-1/2})\right) = \frac{n}{8\beta} \cdot \left(1 + O(n^{-1/2})\right).$$

We call a relevant step *improving* if the number of ones in b increases and the step is accepted.

We first consider only steps where the number of leading ones stays the same. Then the probability that the ONEMAX value increases from k by j, adapting Lemma 2 to a string of length $n/2$, is at most

$$p_j \leq \left(\frac{n/2 - k}{n}\right)^j \cdot \frac{1.14}{j!} \cdot p_{\text{fix}}(j)$$

using $n/2 - k \leq n/4$

$$\leq \frac{1.14 \cdot 4^{-j}}{j!} \cdot p_{\text{fix}}(j) \leq \frac{1.14 \cdot 4^{-j}}{j!} \cdot \frac{2\beta j}{1 - e^{-2N\beta j}}$$
$$\leq 2.28\beta \cdot 4^{-j} \cdot \frac{1}{1 - e^{-2N\beta j}} =: p_j.$$

In the following, we work with pessimistic transition probabilities p_j. Note that for all $j \geq 1$

$$\frac{p_j}{p_1} = 4^{-(j-1)} \cdot \frac{1 - e^{-2N\beta}}{1 - e^{-2N\beta j}} \leq 4^{-(j-1)}.$$

Let p^+ denote (a lower bound on) the probability of an improving step, then

$$p^+ \leq \sum_{j=1}^{\infty} p_j \leq p_1 \cdot \sum_{j=1}^{\infty} 4^{-(j-1)} = p_1 \cdot \frac{4}{3}.$$

The conditional probability of advancing by j, given an improving step, is then

$$\frac{p_j}{p^+} \leq 4^{-(j-1)} \cdot \frac{p_1}{p^+} = \left(1 - \frac{3}{4}\right)^{j-1} \cdot \frac{3}{4},$$

which corresponds to a geometric distribution with parameter $3/4$.

Now, by Chernoff bounds, the probability of having more than $S := (1 + n^{-1/4}) \cdot p^+ \cdot T$ improving steps in T relevant steps is $e^{-\Omega(n^{1/2})}$. Using a Chernoff bound for geometric random variables [5, Theorem 1.14], the probability of S improving steps yielding a total progress of at least $(1 + n^{-1/4}) \cdot 4/3 \cdot S$ is $e^{-\Omega(n^{1/2})}$.

If none of these rare events happen, the progress is at most

$$(1 + O(n^{-1/4})) \cdot \frac{4}{3} \cdot p^+ \cdot T$$
$$= (1 + O(n^{-1/4})) \cdot \frac{16}{9} \cdot p_1 \cdot T$$
$$\leq (1 + O(n^{-1/4})) \cdot \frac{1.14}{9} \cdot n.$$

We also have at most $n/2$ steps where the number of leading ones increases. If the number of leading ones increases by $d \geq 1$, the fitness increase is $dn + |b'|_1 - |b|_1$. Hence the above estimations of jump lengths are not applicable. We call these *special* steps; they are unorthodox as the large fitness increase makes it likely that any mutation on the OneMax part is accepted. Note that this applies to mutations increasing $|b|_1$ as well as to those decreasing it. By similar arguments as used before, in at most $n/2$ special steps, the net gain in the number of ones is at most $O(n^{3/4})$ with probability $1 - e^{-\Omega(n^{1/2})}$. For details we refer to [18].

Together with all regular steps, the progress on the OneMax part is at most $1.14n/9 + O(n^{3/4})$, which for large enough n is less than the distance $7n/16 - (n/4 + n^{3/4})$ to reach a point with $|b|_1 \geq 7n/16$ from initialisation. This proves the claim. □

Finally, we put the previous lemmas together into our main theorem that establishes that SSWM can optimise Balance in polynomial time.

Theorem 13. *With probability* $1 - e^{-\Omega(n^{1/2})}$ *SSWM with* $\beta = n^{-3/2}$ *and* $N\beta = \ln n$ *optimises* Balance *in time* $O(n/\beta) = O(n^{5/2})$.

Proof. By Chernoff bounds, the probability that for the initial solution $x_0 = a_0 b_0$ we have $n/4 - n^{3/4} \leq |b_0|_1 \leq n/4 + n^{3/4}$ is $1 - e^{-\Omega(n^{1/2})}$. We assume pessimistically that $n/4 \leq |b_0|_1 \leq n/4 + n^{3/4}$. Then Lemma 12 is in force, and with probability $1 - e^{-\Omega(n^{1/2})}$ within T relevant steps, T as defined in Lemma 11, SSWM does not reach a trap or a search point with fitness 0. Lemma 11 then implies that with probability $1 - e^{-\Omega(n^{1/2})}$ an optimal solution with $n/2$ leading ones is found.

The time bound follows from $T = O(n/\beta)$ and that, again by Chernoff bounds, we have at least T relevant steps in $3T$ iterations of SSWM, with probability $1 - e^{-\Omega(n^{1/2})}$. □

6. CONCLUSIONS

The field of evolutionary computation has matured to the point where techniques can be applied to models of natural evolution. Our analyses have demonstrated that runtime analysis of evolutionary algorithms can be used to analyse a simple model of natural evolution, and uncovered constraints on biologically relevant parameters such as population size and strength of selection, imposing fundamental limits to what is possible by natural selection.

From a computational perspective, we have shown that SSWM can overcome obstacles such as posed by Cliff_d and Balance in different ways to the (1+1) EA, due to its non-elitistic selection mechanism. We have seen how the probability of accepting a mutant can be tuned to enable hill climbing, where fitness-proportional selection fails, as well as tunnelling through fitness valleys, where elitist selection fails. For Balance we showed that SSWM can take advantage of information about the steepest gradient. The selection rule in SSWM hence seems to be a versatile and useful mechanism. Future work could investigate its usefulness in the context of population-based evolutionary algorithms.

Acknowledgments: The research leading to these results has received funding from the European Union Seventh Framework Programme (FP7/2007-2013) under grant agreement no 618091 (SAGE). The authors thank the anonymous GECCO reviewers for their many constructive comments.

7. REFERENCES

[1] A. Auger and B. Doerr, editors. *Theory of Randomized Search Heuristics – Foundations and Recent Developments.* Number 1 in Series on Theoretical Computer Science. World Scientific, 2011.

[2] E. Chastain, A. Livnat, C. Papadimitriou, and U. Vazirani. Algorithms, games, and evolution. *Proceedings of the National Academy of Sciences*, 111(29):10620–10623, July 2014.

[3] K. Chatterjee, A. Pavlogiannis, B. Adlam, and M. A. Nowak. The time scale of evolutionary innovation. *PLoS Computational Biology*, 10(9), Sept. 2014.

[4] D. Corus, D.-C. Dang, A. V. Eremeev, and P. K. Lehre. Level-based analysis of genetic algorithms and other search processes. In *PPSN 2014*, pages 912–921. Springer, 2014.

[5] B. Doerr. Analyzing randomized search heuristics: Tools from probability theory. In *[1]*, pages 1–20. World Scientific, 2011.

[6] J. H. Gillespie. Molecular evolution over the mutational landscape. *Evolution*, 38(5):1116–1129, 1984.

[7] J. Jägersküpper and T. Storch. When the plus strategy outperforms the comma strategy and when not. In *Proc. of IEEE FOCI 2007*, pages 25–32. IEEE, 2007.

[8] T. Jansen. *Analyzing Evolutionary Algorithms. The Computer Science Perspective.* Springer, 2013.

[9] T. Jansen, P. S. Oliveto, and C. Zarges. On the analysis of the immune-inspired B-Cell algorithm for the Vertex Cover problem. In *Proc. of ICARIS 2011*, pages 117–131. Springer, 2011.

[10] T. Jansen and I. Wegener. A comparison of simulated annealing with a simple evolutionary algorithm on pseudo-Boolean functions of unitation. *Theoretical Computer Science*, 386(1-2):73–93, 2007.

[11] D. Johannsen. *Random Combinatorial Structures and Randomized Search Heuristics.* PhD thesis, Universität des Saarlandes, Saarbrücken, Germany and the Max-Planck-Institut für Informatik, 2010.

[12] M. Kimura. On the probability of fixation of mutant genes in a population. *Genetics*, 47(6):713–719, 1962.

[13] P. K. Lehre and C. Witt. Black-box search by unbiased variation. *Algorithmica*, 64(4):623–642, 2012.

[14] F. Neumann and C. Witt. *Bioinspired Computation in Combinatorial Optimization – Algorithms and Their Computational Complexity.* Springer, 2010.

[15] P. S. Oliveto and D. Sudholt. On the runtime analysis of stochastic ageing mechanisms. In *Proc. of GECCO 2014*, pages 113–120. ACM Press, 2014.

[16] P. S. Oliveto and C. Witt. Simplified drift analysis for proving lower bounds in evolutionary computation. *Algorithmica*, 59(3):369–386, 2011.

[17] P. S. Oliveto and C. Witt. On the runtime analysis of the simple genetic algorithm. *Theoretical Computer Science*, 545:2–19, 2014.

[18] T. Paixão, J. Pérez Heredia, D. Sudholt, and B. Trubenová. First steps towards a runtime comparison of natural and artificial evolution. *ArXiv e-prints*, 2015. Available from http://arxiv.org/abs/1504.06260.

[19] P. Rohlfshagen, P. K. Lehre, and X. Yao. Dynamic evolutionary optimisation: an analysis of frequency and magnitude of change. In *Proc. of GECCO '09*, pages 1713–1720. ACM Press, 2009.

[20] J. E. Rowe and D. Sudholt. The choice of the offspring population size in the (1,λ) evolutionary algorithm. *Theoretical Computer Science*, 545:20–38, 2014.

[21] D. Sudholt. A new method for lower bounds on the running time of evolutionary algorithms. *IEEE Transactions on Evolutionary Computation*, 17(3):418–435, 2013.

[22] L. G. Valiant. Evolvability. *J. ACM*, 56(1):3:1–3:21, 2009.

Author Index

www.ingramcontent.com/pod-product-compliance
Ingram Content Group UK Ltd.
Pitfield, Milton Keynes, MK11 3LW, UK
UKHW051419290926
15471UKWH00009B/1682